# The American Psychiatric Publishing
# Textbook of Neuropsychiatry and Clinical Neurosciences

## Fourth Edition

# Editorial Board

# The American Psychiatric Publishing
# Textbook of Neuropsychiatry and Clinical Neurosciences

## Fourth Edition

*Edited by*

## Stuart C. Yudofsky, M.D.
## Robert E. Hales, M.D.

American **Psychiatric** Publishing, Inc.

Washington, DC
London, England

Books published by American Psychiatric Publishing, Inc., represent the views and opinions of the individual authors and do not necessarily represent the policies and opinions of APPI or the American Psychiatric Association.

Diagnostic criteria included in this textbook are reprinted, with permission, from the *Diagnostic and Statistical Manual of Mental Disorders*, 4th Edition, Text Revision. Copyright 2000, American Psychiatric Association.

06  05  04  03  02    5  4  3  2  1
Fourth Edition


American Psychiatric Publishing, Inc.
1400 K Street, N.W.
Washington, DC 20005
www.appi.org

**Library of Congress Cataloging-in-Publication Data**
The American Psychiatric Publishing textbook of neuropsychiatry and clinical neurosciences / edited by Stuart C. Yudofsky, Robert E. Hales.—4th ed.
    p. ; cm.
  Rev. ed. of The American Psychiatric Press textbook of neuropsychiatry. 3rd ed. c1997.
  Includes bibliographical references and index.
  ISBN 1-58562-004-1 (alk. paper)
   1. Neuropsychiatry. I. Title: Textbook of neuropsychiatry and clinical neurosciences.
II. Title: Neuropsychiatry and clinical neurosciences. III. Yudofsky, Stuart C. IV. Hales, Robert E. V. American Psychiatric Publishing. VI. American Psychiatric Press textbook of neuropsychiatry.
  [DNLM: 1. Delirium, Dementia, Amnestic, Cognitive Disorders. 2. Nervous System Diseases. 3. Neuropsychology. WM 140 A51277 2002]
  RC341.A44 2002
  616.8—dc21

                                                              2001045100

**British Library Cataloguing in Publication Data**
A CIP record is available from the British Library.

In honor of Nancy Andreasen, M.D., Ph.D., and Gary Tucker, M.D.,
with appreciation, admiration, and affection
for two pioneers of the modern reemergence of neuropsychiatry,
and two wonderful mentors, colleagues, and friends.

"And gladly wolde he lerne, and gladly teche."

The Clerk of Oxenford
*Canterbury Tales*
Geoffrey Chaucer

# Contents

**Contributors** . . . . . . . . . . . . . . . . . . . . . . . . . . . . . . . . . . . . . . . . . . . . . . . . . . . . . . . . . . . **xiii**

**Preface** . . . . . . . . . . . . . . . . . . . . . . . . . . . . . . . . . . . . . . . . . . . . . . . . . . . . . . . . . . . . . . . **xix**

## PART I

## Basic Principles of Neuroscience

**1 Cellular and Molecular Biology of the Neuron** . . . . . . . . . . . . . . . . . . . . . . . . . . . . . . .3

A. Kimberley McAllister, Ph.D.
W. Martin Usrey, Ph.D.
Arnold R. Kriegstein, M.D., Ph.D.
Stephen Rayport, M.D., Ph.D.

**2 Human Electrophysiology and Basic Sleep Mechanisms** . . . . . . . . . . . . . . . . . . . . .43

Robert W. McCarley, M.D.

**3 Functional Neuroanatomy: Neuropsychological
Correlates of Cortical and Subcortical Damage** . . . . . . . . . . . . . . . . . . . . . . . . . . . .71

Daniel Tranel, Ph.D.

**4 Nervous, Endocrine, and Immune System Interactions in Psychiatry** . . . . . . . . . .115

Jane F. Gumnick, M.D.
Dwight L. Evans, M.D.
Andrew H. Miller, M.D.

## PART II

# Neuropsychiatric Assessment

**5** **Bedside Neuropsychiatry: Eliciting the Clinical Phenomena of Neuropsychiatric Illness** . . . . . . . . . . . . . . . . . .153

Fred Ovsiew, M.D.

**6** **Electrodiagnostic Techniques in Neuropsychiatry** . . . . . . . . . . . . . . . . . . . . . .199

Thomas C. Neylan, M.D.
Charles F. Reynolds III, M.D.
David J. Kupfer, M.D.

**7** **The Neuropsychological Evaluation** . . . . . . . . . . . . . . . . . . . . . . . . . . . . .217

Diane B. Howieson, Ph.D.
Muriel D. Lezak, Ph.D.

**8** **Clinical Imaging in Neuropsychiatry** . . . . . . . . . . . . . . . . . . . . . . . . . . . . .245

Robin A. Hurley, M.D.
L. Anne Hayman, M.D.
Katherine H. Taber, Ph.D.

**9** **Functional Neuroimaging in Psychiatry** . . . . . . . . . . . . . . . . . . . . . . . . . . .285

James C. Patterson II, M.D., Ph.D.
Kathryn J. Kotrla, M.D.

**10** **Epidemiologic and Genetic Aspects of Neuropsychiatric Disorders** . . . . . . . . . .323

Dolores Malaspina, M.D., M.S.P.H.
Cheryl Corcoran, M.D.
Steven P. Hamilton, M.D., Ph.D.

## PART III

# Neuropsychiatric Symptomatologies

**11** **Neuropsychiatric Aspects of Pain Management** . . . . . . . . . . . . . . . . . . . . . . .419

William G. Brose, M.D.
Raymond Gaeta, M.D.
David Spiegel, M.D.

**12** **Neuropsychiatric Aspects of Primary Headache Disorders.** . . . . . . . . . . . . . . . . . .**451**

Stephen D. Silberstein, M.D., F.A.C.P.
Richard B. Lipton, M.D.
Naomi Breslau, Ph.D.

**13** **Neuropsychiatric Aspects of Disorders of Attention** . . . . . . . . . . . . . . . . . . . . . .**489**

Ronald A. Cohen, Ph.D.
Stephen Salloway, M.D.
Tricia Zawacki, Ph.D.

**14** **Neuropsychiatric Aspects of Delirium.** . . . . . . . . . . . . . . . . . . . . . . . . . . . . . . . . .**525**

Paula T. Trzepacz, M.D.
David J. Meagher, M.D., M.R.C.Psych., M.Sc. (Neuroscience)
Michael G. Wise, M.D.

**15** **Neuropsychiatric Aspects of Aphasia and Related Disorders** . . . . . . . . . . . . . . .**565**

Mario F. Mendez, M.D., Ph.D.
Jeffrey L. Cummings, M.D.

**16** **Neuropsychiatric Aspects of Aggression and Impulse Control Disorders.** . . . . . .**579**

Eric Hollander, M.D.
Nicole Posner, M.D.
Scott Cherkasky, M.D.

**17** **Neuropsychiatric Aspects of Memory and Amnesia** . . . . . . . . . . . . . . . . . . . . . . .**597**

Yaakov Stern, Ph.D.
Harold A. Sackeim, Ph.D.

# PART IV

## Neuropsychiatric Disorders

**18** **Neuropsychiatric Aspects of Traumatic Brain Injury** . . . . . . . . . . . . . . . . . . . . . .**625**

Jonathan M. Silver, M.D.
Robert E. Hales, M.D., M.B.A.
Stuart C. Yudofsky, M.D.

**19** **Neuropsychiatric Aspects of Seizure Disorders** . . . . . . . . . . . . . . . . . . . . . . . . . .**673**

Gary J. Tucker, M.D.

**20** **Neuropsychiatric Aspects of Sleep and Sleep Disorders** . . . . . . . . . . . . . . . . . . . . . .697

Max Hirshkowitz, Ph.D., A.B.S.M.

**21** **Neuropsychiatric Aspects of Cerebrovascular Disorders** . . . . . . . . . . . . . . . . . . . .723

Robert G. Robinson, M.D.
Sergio E. Starkstein, M.D., Ph.D.

**22** **Neuropsychiatric Aspects of Brain Tumors** . . . . . . . . . . . . . . . . . . . . . . . . . . . . .753

Trevor R.P. Price, M.D.
Kenneth L. Goetz, M.D.
Mark R. Lovell, Ph.D.

**23** **Neuropsychiatric Aspects of Human Immunodeficiency**
**Virus Infection of the Central Nervous System** . . . . . . . . . . . . . . . . . . . . . . . . . .783

Francisco Fernandez, M.D.
George M. Ringholz, M.D., Ph.D.
Joel K. Levy, Ph.D.

**24** **Neuropsychiatric Aspects of Rheumatic Disease.** . . . . . . . . . . . . . . . . . . . . . . . . .813

Fred Ovsiew, M.D.
Tammy Utset, M.D., M.P.H.

**25** **Neuropsychiatric Aspects of Endocrine Disorders.** . . . . . . . . . . . . . . . . . . . . . . . .851

Elizabeth B. Boswell, M.D.
Theodore J. Anfinson, M.D.
Charles B. Nemeroff, M.D., Ph.D.

**26** **Neuropsychiatric Aspects of Poisons and Toxins** . . . . . . . . . . . . . . . . . . . . . . . . .877

Shreenath V. Doctor, M.D., Ph.D.

**27** **Neuropsychiatric Aspects of Ethanol and Other Chemical Dependencies** . . . . . .899

Eric J. Nestler, M.D., Ph.D.
David W. Self, Ph.D.

**28** **Neuropsychiatric Aspects of Dementias Associated With Motor Dysfunction** . . .923

Alan J. Lerner, M.D.
Peter J. Whitehouse, M.D., Ph.D.

**29** **Neuropsychiatric Aspects of Alzheimer's Disease and**
**Other Dementing Illnesses.** . . . . . . . . . . . . . . . . . . . . . . . . . . . . . . . . . . . . . . . . .953

Sylvia Askin-Edgar, M.D., Ph.D.
Katherine E. White, M.D.
Jeffrey L. Cummings, M.D.

**30** **Neuropsychiatric Aspects of Schizophrenia** . . . . . . . . . . . . . . . . . . . . . . . . . . . . . . . . **989**

Carol A. Tamminga, M.D.
Gunvant K. Thaker, M.D.
Deborah R. Medoff, Ph.D.

**31** **Neuropsychiatric Aspects of Mood and Affective Disorders** . . . . . . . . . . . . . . . **1021**

Helen S. Mayberg, M.D.
Michelle Keightley, M.A.
Roderick K. Mahurin, Ph.D.
Stephen K. Brannan, M.D.

**32** **Neuropsychiatric Aspects of Anxiety Disorders** . . . . . . . . . . . . . . . . . . . . . . . . . . . **1049**

Dan J. Stein, M.D., Ph.D.
Frans J. Hugo, M.B.Ch.B., M.Med.(Psych.)

**33** **Neuropsychiatric Disorders of Childhood and Adolescence** . . . . . . . . . . . . . . . . **1069**

Martin H. Teicher, M.D., Ph.D.
Susan L. Andersen, Ph.D.
Carryl P. Navalta, Ph.D.
Ann Polcari, Ph.D., R.N.
Dennis Kim, M.D.

# PART V

# Neuropsychiatric Treatments

**34** **Intracellular and Intercellular Principles of Pharmacotherapy for Neuropsychiatric Disorders** . . . . . . . . . . . . . . . . . . . . . . . **1123**

W. Dale Horst, Ph.D.
Michael J. Burke, M.D., Ph.D.

**35** **Psychopharmacologic Treatments for Patients With Neuropsychiatric Disorders** . . . . . . . . . . . . . . . . . . . . . . . . . . . . . . . . . . . . . . **1151**

Peter P. Roy-Byrne, M.D.
Mahendra Upadhyaya, M.D.

**36** **Psychotherapy for Patients With Neuropsychiatric Disorders** . . . . . . . . . . . . . . . **1199**

David V. Forrest, M.D.

**37** **Cognitive Rehabilitation and Behavior Therapy for Patients With Neuropsychiatric Disorders** . . . . . . . . . . . . . . . . . . . . . . . . . . . . . . . . .1237

Michael D. Franzen, Ph.D.
Mark R. Lovell, Ph.D.

## PART VI

## Special Topics

**38** **Ethical and Legal Issues in Neuropsychiatry** . . . . . . . . . . . . . . . . . . . . . .1257

Robert I. Simon, M.D.

**39** **Educational and Certification Issues in Neuropsychiatry** . . . . . . . . . . . . . . .1289

Sheldon Benjamin, M.D.
Linda Mah, M.D.

**Index** . . . . . . . . . . . . . . . . . . . . . . . . . . . . . . . . . . . . . . . . . . . . . . . . .1311

# Contributors

**Susan L. Andersen, Ph.D.**
Assistant Professor, Department of Psychiatry, Harvard Medical School, Developmental Biopsychiatry Research Program and Laboratory of Developmental Psychopharmacology, McLean Hospital, Belmont, Massachusetts

**Theodore J. Anfinson, M.D.**
Assistant Professor of Psychiatry, Department of Psychiatry and Behavioral Sciences, Emory University School of Medicine, Atlanta, Georgia

**Sylvia Askin-Edgar, M.D., Ph.D.**
Instructor, Department of Neurology, University of California at Los Angeles School of Medicine, Los Angeles, California

**Sheldon Benjamin, M.D.**
Associate Professor of Psychiatry and Neurology, Director of Psychiatric Education and Training, Director of Neuropsychiatry, University of Massachusetts Medical School, Worcester, Massachusetts

**Elizabeth B. Boswell, M.D.**
Assistant Professor of Psychiatry, Department of Psychiatry and Behavioral Sciences, Emory University School of Medicine, Atlanta, Georgia

**Stephen K. Brannan, M.D.**
Clinical Research Physician, U.S. Medical Division, Lilly Technology Center, Indianapolis, Indiana

**Naomi Breslau, Ph.D.**
Professor, Department of Psychiatry, Case Western University School of Medicine, Cleveland, Ohio; Clinical Professor, Department of Psychiatry, University of Michigan School of Medicine, Ann Arbor, Michigan; Director of Research, Department of Psychiatry, Henry Ford Health System, Detroit, Michigan

**William G. Brose, M.D.**
Clinical Associate Professor, Department of Anesthesia, Stanford University School of Medicine, Stanford, California

**Michael J. Burke, M.D., Ph.D.**
Associate Professor, Department of Psychiatry and Behavioral Sciences, The University of Kansas School of Medicine, Wichita, Kansas

**Scott Cherkasky, M.D.**
Psychiatry Research Fellow, Department of Psychiatry, Mount Sinai School of Medicine, New York, New York

**Ronald A. Cohen, Ph.D.**
Associate Professor, Department of Psychiatry and Human Behavior, Brown Medical School; Director of Neuropsychology, The Miriam Hospital, Providence, Rhode Island

**Cheryl Corcoran, M.D.**
Research Fellow, Columbia University, College of Physicians and Surgeons, Schizophrenia Research Unit, New York State Psychiatric Institute, New York, New York

**Jeffrey L. Cummings, M.D.**
Professor, Departments of Neurology and Psychiatry and Biobehavioral Sciences; Director, UCLA Alzheimer's Disease Center, University of California at Los Angeles School of Medicine, Los Angeles, California

**Shreenath V. Doctor, M.D., Ph.D.**
Voluntary Clinical Faculty, Baylor College of Medicine, Houston, Texas

**Dwight L. Evans, M.D.**
Ruth Maltzer Professor and Chair, Department of Psychiatry, University of Pennsylvania School of Medicine, Philadelphia, Pennsylvania

**Francisco Fernandez, M.D.**
Professor and Chairperson, Department of Psychiatry & Behavioral Sciences, Loyola University Chicago Stritch School of Medicine, Maywood, Illinois

**David V. Forrest, M.D.**
Clinical Professor of Psychiatry, Consultation-Liaison Psychiatrist in Neurology; Faculty, Columbia Psychoanalytic Center, Columbia University College of Physicians and Surgeons, New York, New York

**Michael D. Franzen, Ph.D.**
Associate Professor of Psychiatry (Psychology), Medical College of Pennsylvania Hahnemann University; Chief, Section of Psychology and Neuropsychology, Allegheny General Hospital, Pittsburgh, Pennsylvania

**Raymond Gaeta, M.D.**
Associate Professor of Anesthesia, Director, Pain Clinic, Stanford Medical Center, Stanford, California

**Kenneth L. Goetz, M.D.**
Associate Professor of Psychiatry, Department of Psychiatry, Medical College of Pennsylvania Hahnemann University, Philadelphia, Pennsylvania

**Jane F. Gumnick, M.D.**
Postdoctoral Fellow, Department of Psychiatry and Behavioral Sciences, Emory University School of Medicine, Atlanta, Georgia

**Robert E. Hales, M.D., M.B.A.**
Professor and Chair, Department of Psychiatry, University of California, Davis School of Medicine; Director, Behavioral Health Center, UC Davis Health System; Medical Director, Sacramento County Mental Health Services, Sacramento, California

**Steven P. Hamilton, M.D., Ph.D.**
Research Fellow, Columbia University, College of Physicians and Surgeons, Schizophrenia Research Unit, New York State Psychiatric Institute, New York, New York

**L. Anne Hayman, M.D.**
Professor, Department of Psychiatry and Behavioral Sciences; Professor, Department of Radiology; Professor, Herbert J. Frensley Center for Imaging Research, Baylor College of Medicine, Houston, Texas

**Max Hirshkowitz, Ph.D., A.B.S.M.**
Associate Professor, Department of Psychiatry and Department of Medicine, Baylor College of Medicine; Director, Houston VAMC Sleep Research Center, Houston, Texas

**Eric Hollander, M.D.**
Professor, Department of Psychiatry, Mount Sinai School of Medicine, New York, New York

**W. Dale Horst, Ph.D.**
Research Professor, Department of Psychiatry; Director, The Psychiatric Research Institute, The University of Kansas School of Medicine, Wichita, Kansas

**Diane B. Howieson, Ph.D.**
Associate Professor of Neurology and Psychiatry, Oregon Health & Science University, Portland, Oregon

**Frans J. Hugo, M.B.Ch.B., M.Med.(Psych.)**
Neuropsychiatry Unit, Department of Psychiatry, University of Stellenbosch, Cape Town, South Africa

**Robin A. Hurley, M.D.**
Assistant Professor, Department of Psychiatry and Behavioral Sciences; Assistant Professor, Department of Radiology; Assistant Professor, Herbert J. Frensley Center for Imaging Research, Baylor College of Medicine; Medical Director, Integrated Mental Health Program, Mental Health Care Line, Houston Veterans Affairs Medical Center, Houston, Texas

**Michelle Keightley, M.A.**
Ph.D. candidate, Department of Psychology, University of Toronto, Toronto, Ontario, Canada

**Dennis Kim, M.D.**
Instructor, Department of Psychiatry, Harvard Medical School, Developmental Biopsychiatry Research Program and Bipolar and Psychotic Disorders Outpatient Program, McLean Hospital, Belmont, Massachusetts

**Kathryn J. Kotrla, M.D.**
Assistant Professor, Department of Psychiatry and Behavioral Sciences, Baylor College of Medicine; Chief, Psychiatry Service, Ben Taub General Hospital, Houston, Texas

**Arnold R. Kriegstein, M.D., Ph.D.**
Professor, Departments of Neurology and Pathology and the Center for Neurobiology and Behavior, Columbia University, New York, New York

**David J. Kupfer, M.D.**
Thomas Detre Professor and Chairman, Department of Psychiatry, University of Pittsburgh School of Medicine, Pittsburgh, Pennsylvania

**Alan J. Lerner, M.D.**
Associate Professor of Neurology, Case Western Reserve University School of Medicine, Cleveland, Ohio

**Joel K. Levy, Ph.D.**
Assistant Professor, Department of Neurology, Baylor College of Medicine, Houston, Texas

**Muriel D. Lezak, Ph.D.**
Professor of Neurology and Psychiatry, Oregon Health & Science University, Portland, Oregon

**Richard B. Lipton, M.D.**
Professor of Neurology, Professor of Psychiatry, Epidemiology and Social Medicine, Albert Einstein College of Medicine, Bronx, New York

**Mark R. Lovell, Ph.D.**
Assistant Professor of Orthopedics and Director, UPMC Sports Medicine Concussion Program, University of Pittsburgh School of Medicine, Pittsburgh, Pennsylvania

**Linda Mah, M.D.**
Clinical Fellow, Cognitive Neuroscience Section, National Institute of Neurological Disorders and Stroke (NINDS), National Institutes of Health, Bethesda, Maryland

**Roderick K. Mahurin, Ph.D.**
Clinical Associate Professor, Department of Psychiatry and Behavioral Sciences; Research Scientist, Department of Neurology, University of Washington, Seattle, Washington

**Dolores Malaspina, M.D., M.S.P.H.**
Assistant Professor of Clinical Psychiatry, Columbia University, College of Physicians and Surgeons; Unit Chief, Schizophrenia Research Unit, New York State Psychiatric Institute, New York, New York

**Helen S. Mayberg, M.D.**
Professor of Psychiatry and Medicine (Neurology), Sandra Rotman Chair in Neuropsychiatry, Rotman Research Institute, University of Toronto, Toronto, Ontario, Canada

**A. Kimberley McAllister, Ph.D.**
Assistant Professor, Center for Neuroscience and Department of Neurology, University of California, Davis, Davis, California

**Robert W. McCarley, M.D.**
Professor and Director, Neuroscience Laboratory; Chair, Department of Psychiatry, Harvard Medical School, VA Boston Healthcare System, Brockton Campus, Brockton, Massachusetts

**David J. Meagher, M.D., M.R.C.Psych., M.Sc. (Neuroscience)**
Consultant Psychiatrist, Midwestern Regional Hospital, Limerick, Ireland

**Deborah R. Medoff, Ph.D.**
Assistant Professor, Schizophrenia-Related Disorders Program, Maryland Psychiatric Research Center, University of Maryland School of Medicine, Baltimore, Maryland

**Mario F. Mendez, M.D., Ph.D.**
Professor of Neurology and Psychiatry and Biobehavioral Sciences, University of California at Los Angeles School of Medicine; Director, Neurobehavior Unit, West Los Angeles Veterans Affairs Medical Center, Los Angeles, California

**Andrew H. Miller, M.D.**
Professor, Department of Psychiatry and Behavioral Sciences, Emory University School of Medicine, Atlanta, Georgia

**Carryl P. Navalta, Ph.D.**
Instructor, Department of Psychiatry, Harvard Medical School, Developmental Biopsychiatry Research Program and Child Outpatient Services, McLean Hospital, Belmont, Massachusetts

**Charles B. Nemeroff, M.D., Ph.D.**
Reunette W. Harris Professor and Chairman, Department of Psychiatry and Behavioral Sciences, Emory University School of Medicine, Atlanta, Georgia

**Eric J. Nestler, M.D., Ph.D.**
Lou and Ellen McGinley Distinguished Professor and Chair, Department of Psychiatry, The University of Texas Southwestern Medical Center, Dallas, Texas

**Thomas C. Neylan, M.D.**
Assistant Professor in Residence, Department of Psychiatry, University of California, San Francisco; Medical Director, Posttraumatic Stress Disorders Program, Veterans Affairs Medical Center, San Francisco, California

**Fred Ovsiew, M.D.**
Associate Professor of Clinical Psychiatry and Chief, Clinical Neuropsychiatry, University of Chicago Hospitals, Chicago, Illinois

**James C. Patterson II, M.D., Ph.D.**
Assistant Professor, Department of Psychiatry; Director, PET Neuroimaging Research, Biomedical Research Institute PET Imaging Center, Louisiana State University Health Sciences Center, Shreveport, Louisiana

**Ann Polcari, Ph.D., R.N.**
Research Associate, Developmental Biopsychiatry Research Program, McLean Hospital, Belmont, Massachusetts

**Nicole Posner, M.D.**
Resident in Psychiatry, Mount Sinai School of Medicine, New York, New York

**Trevor R.P. Price, M.D.**
Professor of Psychiatry and Medicine and Chair, Department of Psychiatry, Medical College of Pennsylvania Hahnemann University, Philadelphia, Pennsylvania

**Stephen Rayport, M.D., Ph.D.**
Associate Professor, Departments of Psychiatry, Anatomy, and Cell Biology and the Center for Neurobiology and Behavior, Columbia University, New York, New York

**Charles F. Reynolds III, M.D.**
Professor of Psychiatry and Neurology, Director, MHCRC for Late-Life Mood Disorders, Department of Psychiatry, University of Pittsburgh School of Medicine, Pittsburgh, Pennsylvania

**George M. Ringholz, M.D., Ph.D.**
Assistant Professor and Chief, Department of Neurology, Section of Behavioral Neurology and Neuropsychology, Baylor College of Medicine, Houston, Texas

**Robert G. Robinson, M.D.**
Professor and Head, Department of Psychiatry, University of Iowa College of Medicine, Iowa City, Iowa

**Peter P. Roy-Byrne, M.D.**
Professor and Vice Chair, Department of Psychiatry and Behavioral Sciences, University of Washington; Chief of Psychiatry, Harborview Medical Center, Seattle, Washington

**Stephen Salloway, M.D.**
Associate Professor, Departments of Clinical Neurosciences and Psychiatry and Human Behavior, Brown Medical School; Director of Neurology, Butler Hospital, Providence, Rhode Island

**David W. Self, Ph.D.**
Lydia Bryant Test Associate Professor, Department of Psychiatry, The University of Texas Southwestern Medical Center, Dallas, Texas

**Stephen D. Silberstein, M.D., F.A.C.P.**
Professor of Neurology, Thomas Jefferson University School of Medicine; Director, Jefferson Headache Center, Thomas Jefferson University Hospital, Philadelphia, Pennsylvania

**Jonathan M. Silver, M.D.**
Clinical Professor of Psychiatry, New York University of School Medicine; Assistant Director for Clinical Services and Research, Department of Psychiatry, Lenox Hill Hospital, New York, New York

**Robert I. Simon, M.D.**
Clinical Professor of Psychiatry, and Director, Program in Psychiatry and Law, Georgetown University School of Medicine, Washington, D.C.

**David Spiegel, M.D.**
Professor, Department of Psychiatry and Behavioral Services, Director, Center on Stress and Health, Stanford University School of Medicine, Stanford, California

**Sergio E. Starkstein, M.D., Ph.D.**
Director, Buenos Aires Neuropsychiatric Center, Buenos Aires, Argentina

**Dan J. Stein, M.D., Ph.D.**
Director, Medical Research Council Unit on Anxiety Disorders, Department of Psychiatry, University of Stellenbosch, Cape Town, South Africa, and University of Florida, Gainesville, Florida

**Yaakov Stern, Ph.D.**
Professor of Clinical Neuropsychology in Neurology, Psychiatry, and Sergievsky Center, College of Physicians and Surgeons of Columbia University; Director of Neuropsychology, Memory Disorders Clinic, Department of Biological Psychiatry, New York State Psychiatric Institute, New York, New York

**Katherine H. Taber, Ph.D.**
Assistant Professor, Department of Psychiatry and Behavioral Sciences; Assistant Professor, Department of Radiology; Assistant Professor, Herbert J. Frensley Center for Imaging Research, Baylor College of Medicine, Houston, Texas

**Carol A. Tamminga, M.D.**
Professor of Psychiatry and Pharmacology, University of Maryland School of Medicine; Chief, Inpatient Program, Maryland Psychiatric Research Center, Baltimore, Maryland

**Martin H. Teicher, M.D., Ph.D.**
Associate Professor, Department of Psychiatry, Harvard Medical School, Developmental Biopsychiatry Research Program and Laboratory of Developmental Psychopharmacology, McLean Hospital, Belmont, Massachusetts

**Gunvant K. Thaker, M.D.**
Professor of Psychiatry, University of Maryland School of Medicine; Chief, Functional Neuroimaging Laboratory, Maryland Psychiatric Research Center, Baltimore, Maryland

**Daniel Tranel, Ph.D.**
Professor, Department of Neurology, Division of Cognitive Neuroscience, University of Iowa College of Medicine, Iowa City, Iowa

**Paula T. Trzepacz, M.D.**
Clinical Professor of Psychiatry and Neurology, University of Mississippi Medical School, Jackson, Mississippi; Adjunct Professor of Psychiatry, Tufts University Medical School, Boston, Massachusets; and Lilly Research Laboratories, Indianapolis, Indiana

**Gary J. Tucker, M.D.**
Professor Emeritus, Department of Psychiatry and Behavioral Sciences, University of Washington, Seattle, Washington

**Mahendra Upadhyaya, M.D.**
Director of Geriatric Psychiatry Services, Covenant Medical Group, Lubbock, Texas

**W. Martin Usrey, Ph.D.**
Assistant Professor, Center for Neuroscience and Department of Neurobiology, Physiology, and Behavior, University of California, Davis, Davis, California

**Tammy Utset, M.D., M.P.H.**

Assistant Professor of Clinical Medicine, Department of Medicine, Section of Rheumatology, University of Chicago, Chicago, Illinois

**Katherine E. White, M.D.**

Assistant Clinical Professor, Departments of Neurology and Psychiatry and Biobehavioral Sciences, University of California at Los Angeles School of Medicine, Los Angeles, California

**Peter J. Whitehouse, M.D., Ph.D.**

Professor of Neurology, Psychiatry, Neuroscience, Psychology, Nursing, Organizational Behavior, and Biomedical Ethics, Case Western Reserve University, Cleveland, Ohio

**Michael G. Wise, M.D.**

Clinical Professor of Psychiatry, University of California, Davis; Adjunct Professor of Psychiatry, Uniformed Services University of the Health Sciences, F. Edward Hebert School of Medicine, Bethesda, Maryland

**Stuart C. Yudofsky, M.D.**

D.C. and Irene Ellwood Professor and Chairman, Department of Psychiatry and Behavioral Sciences, Baylor College of Medicine; Chief, Psychiatry Service, The Methodist Hospital, Houston, Texas

**Tricia Zawacki, Ph.D.**

Postdoctoral Fellow in Neuropsychology, Instructor in Psychiatry and Human Behavior, Brown Medical School, Providence, Rhode Island

# Preface

It has been 15 years since the publication of the first edition of the *Textbook of Neuropsychiatry*, which, at that time, was the only multi-authored, comprehensive textbook devoted to this subject. In the preface to the first edition, we stated that we were "convinced that the data base, complexity, and relevance of the field have expanded to the point that a new format, utilizing many individual investigators and clinicians with specialized knowledge of critical areas of neuropsychiatry, would have value and usefulness." We acknowledged, at that time, outstanding, single-authored European contributions to the scholarship in neuropsychiatry and behavioral neurology such as Lishman's classic book, *Organic Psychiatry: The Psychological Consequences of Cerebral Disorders*. We also set forth what we considered to be the "new turf" of the *Textbook:* if the previous, grand European texts could be considered an elegant Rolls Royce, we wished to offer a book that could be likened to a hard-working, dependable American Jeep. Specifically, we strove to craft a comprehensive text that would be also clinically relevant and practical to use by medical students, residents of a broad range of medical specialties, psychiatrists, neurologists, psychologists and neuropsychologists, and a broad range of professionals who work in a wide range of clinical settings. Thus, it was our intention that the *Textbook* would be useful to students and clinicians who treat patients in the general hospital setting, in physical medicine/rehabilitation hospitals, in psychiatric institutes and community mental health centers, in alcohol and chemical dependency programs, and in outpatient services and doctors' offices.

For the fourth edition, we have labored to maintain the original goals of the *Textbook*. Additionally, in light of the great advances in the basic and clinical sciences that comprise the scholarly underpinnings and foundations, the focus on the neurosciences has been expanded in this edition. Great strides have been made over the past decade in the clinical neurosciences, which include, but are not limited to, structural and functional brain imaging, electrophysiology and electrodiagnosis, cell and molecular biology, genetics, and neuropsychopharmacology. Reflecting this intensification, the title of the *Textbook* has been changed and now includes *Clinical Neurosciences*. This title change reflects an increased emphasis in the *Textbook* on the neurosciences in which translational research has already taken place or where it soon will occur. We have worked to effect this transition over the third and fourth editions in ways that these inclusions complement the clinical utility and practicality of the *Textbook*. Thus we still hope that our product is a dependable American sport utility vehicle, but with more useful accessories and options than were available for the 1987 model. A prototypic example is Dr. Malaspina and colleagues' chapter on epidemiologic and genetic aspects of neuropsychiatric disorders. Although an extensive consideration in the previous edition at 59 pages, the chapter now comprises 93 pages. This 60% increase reflects the dramatic growth of knowledge in this realm over the past 5 years.

Over the past 15 years since the publication of the first edition of the *Textbook of Neuropsychiatry*, the subspecialty considerations of neuropsychiatry and behavioral neurology have become more mainstream in their respective clinical specialty disciplines. Even the most casual perusal of the current volumes of leading journals of psychiatry, such as *The American Journal of Psychiatry*, gives evidence to this change. The American Neuropsychiatric Association (ANPA), a professional organization comprising psychiatrists, neurologists, and neurologists who specialize in neuropsychiatry, has grown steadily over the past decade. In addition to providing a vibrant and supportive home for students, clinicians, and researchers who are drawn to neuropsychiatry, the ANPA has taken on the mission of defining the requisite knowledge base and educational experience for the discipline. Because so many students and professionals have written to us requesting information about the requirements for subspecialization in neuropsychiatry, we have included in this edition of the *Textbook* a new chapter reviewing this timely consideration, "Educational and Certification Issues in Neuropsychiatry," by Sheldon Benjamin, M.D., and Linda Mah, M.D. We commend this chapter to all readers considering subspecialization in neuropsychiatry. Over the previous three editions, we have also learned from readers' comments that very few people read the *Textbook* from cover to cover. Most read only a portion of a chapter or a single chapter during any particular period. Consequently, we have endeavored to ensure that each chapter will be complete in itself. As a result, there is some intentional overlap among certain chapters, for we have judged that this is necessary from an information retrieval standpoint to prevent readers from having to jump from section to section. We also believe that neuropsychiatry is inherently interesting, and we wish for students and clinicians to enjoy reading each chapter as an intact entity.

This book would not have been possible without the help and support of many people. First, we wish to thank our chapter authors who have labored diligently toward fashioning contributions that we consider to be scholarly and enjoyable to read. We have endeavored to select chapter authors who are not only recognized as leaders in their fields but who are also good writers. In every instance, the chapter authors exceeded our requests and expectations. Nonetheless, many chapters were edited and rewritten to enhance the content, the clarity of exposition, to emphasize the clinical relevance to practitioners, and to minimize overlap. Those chapter authors exhibited good humor, restraint, and good sportsmanship in the compulsive and sometimes painful process of editing and revising. At this time, we especially extend our gratitude to David V. Forrest, M.D., Michael D. Franzen, Ph.D., Mark R. Lovell, Ph.D., Robert G. Robinson, M.D., and Jonathan M. Silver, M.D., who have been chapter authors throughout all four editions of the *Textbook*. Considering that this edition features 88 authors and coauthors, the fact that only 6 authors from the first edition continue to contribute to the current edition reflects the consistent evolution of the book.

Second, we wish to thank the officers and members of the American Neuropsychiatric Association. As are we, many of our authors are members of this association that provides inspiration, leadership, and service through its multifarious educational and public service activities. Almost every chapter author has been a peer reviewer for, and author of, original research articles in the *Journal of Neuropsychiatry and Clinical Neurosciences*, the official journal of the American Neuropsychiatric Association. We believe that the *Journal*, now flourishing in its 14th year, is a fine complement to this textbook, in that the scientific and clinical information presented here will be systematically updated and expanded by articles that appear in the *Journal*. We encourage readers of the *Textbook of Neuropsychiatry and Clinical Neurosciences* to consider joining the American Neuropsychiatric Association. For information regarding application for membership to the association please consult the website at www.neuropsychiatry.com, or e-mail requests to anpa@postbox.acs.ohio-state.edu. For information regarding subscriptions to the *Journal of Neuropsychiatry and Clinical Neurosciences* please consult the American Psychiatric Publishing, Inc.'s (APPI) web site at www.appi.org, or e-mail questions to us at appi@psych.org.

Third, we wish to acknowledge the perennial support of Carol C. Nadelson, M.D., who recently ended her long term as President and Chief Executive Officer of APPI. In addition to being a close friend and supportive colleague, Carol has been a visionary and inspiration with regard to the publication of each edition of this textbook. Claire Reinburg, Editorial Director of APPI, is a treasure. Over the past three editions of this textbook, Claire has worked closely with us on each detail of its conceptualization, editing, and ultimate publication. Our every interaction with Claire has been a pleasure; and we are truly blessed to have her as a friend and partner in the complex enterprise inherent in publishing a book of this genre and size. Since its inception over 15 years ago, Ronald E. McMillen, Chief Executive Officer of APPI, has participated actively in, and contributed substantively to, each publishing element of each edition of this textbook. We cherish and value our long and productive publishing partnership—and friendship—with Ron. Martin Lynds has been Project Editor for this edition of the *Textbook*. This was our first major collaboration with Martin, whom we discovered to be hard working, responsive, and an innovative problem solver. There are seemingly endless details required to put together a textbook of this size—such as the securing of legal permission for the publication of tables and figures that have appeared in journals and other textbooks—and Martin has stayed on top of each of these. Finally, we express our deep appreciation to Mrs. Paula Medlin, executive assistant to Dr. Yudofsky at Baylor College of Medicine. Paula worked tirelessly and effectively to help coordinate the entire project. Always persistent, but pleasant, Paula was an invaluable liaison among the chapter authors, the Editors, and the staff at APPI. No question from authors or editors was left unanswered, and each of their communications was afforded a response. From inception of the book's fourth edition to its completion, no detail was overlooked by Mrs. Medlin.

We thank our wives, Beth Yudofsky, M.D., and Dianne Hales, M.A., for their encouragement, advice, and editorial assistance concerning many aspects of this book. In addition, because the large portion of our work was accomplished on weekends, evenings, and holidays, they also deserve special credit and appreciation for assuming increased familial responsibilities to permit us to spend so much of our free time on this project.

Finally, and most importantly, we thank the many people who purchased the previous three editions of the *Textbook*. We are grateful for the many letters, calls, e-mails, and face-to-face communications from psychiatrists, neurologists, neuropsychologists, and other health care professionals and trainees who gave us suggestions and told us what they found useful for their practices, teaching duties, and personal edification in the previous editions. They also informed us about what they believed was omitted or should have been omitted in the past editions. We have listened and tried to respond accordingly in the fourth edition. We hope that our efforts and those of our dedicated chapter authors and the staff of APPI will be manifested in a useful book for professionals who care deeply about understanding and helping the many people among us who suffer from neuropsychiatric disorders.

*Stuart C. Yudofsky, M.D.*

*Robert E. Hales, M.D., M.B.A.*

## About the Front Cover Image

The brain image on the front cover is from the SPL/NSL Brain Browser, a project developed by members of the Surgical Planning Laboratory (SPL), MRI Division, Department of Radiology, Brigham and Women's Hospital, Harvard Medical School; by members of the Clinical Neuroscience Division, Laboratory of Neuroscience, Department of Psychiatry, VAMC-Brockton, Harvard Medical School; and by collaborators from the Artificial Intelligence Laboratory of MIT. The Brain Browser and the expanded Anatomy Browser allow highly detailed, hierarchical representations of human anatomy to be viewed on ordinary computers. More information about the SPL/NSL Anatomy Browser can be found at http://www.spl.harvard.edu:8000/pages/papers/Anatomy Browser/current/index.html.

The work was supported in part by grants from the National Institutes of Health and National Institute of Mental Health to M.E. Shenton, R.W. McCarley, R. Kikinis, and F.A. Jolesz. The image is used with permission from Harvard University.

Special thanks to Katherine Taber, Ph.D., and Robin A. Hurley, M.D., for their help selecting the image.

# Basic Principles of Neuroscience

# CHAPTER 1

# Cellular and Molecular Biology of the Neuron

A. Kimberley McAllister, Ph.D.

W. Martin Usrey, Ph.D.

Arnold R. Kriegstein, M.D., Ph.D.

Stephen Rayport, M.D., Ph.D.

Many neuropsychiatric disorders can be traced to aberrations in neurodevelopmental mechanisms. In the initial stages of brain development, cell-cell interactions are the dominant force in the assembly of the brain. As circuits form, individual neurons and connections are pruned on an activity-dependent basis, driven by intrinsic activity and competition for trophic factors. With further maturation, experience becomes the dominant force in shaping neuronal connections and regulating their efficacy. In the mature brain, these neurodevelopmental mechanisms are harnessed in muted form and mediate most plastic processes (Black 1995; Kandel and O'Dell 1992). Neuropsychiatric disorders arising from problems in early brain development are more likely to be intrinsically or genetically based, whereas those arising during later stages are more likely to be experience based. In senescence, neurodegenerative processes may unravel neural circuits by erroneously engaging neurodevelopmental mechanisms.

Experience is so pivotal in fine-tuning neural connectivity that aberrant experience—particularly during critical periods in development—may give rise to or exacerbate neuropsychiatric disorders. For example, monocular occlusion or strabismus in young animals results in permanent pathologic connectivity of the visual system (Hubel et al. 1977). In humans, failure to achieve conjugate gaze in childhood results in permanent visual loss. Similar but subtler changes occur in adulthood during learning. From work on the simple nervous systems of organisms such as the marine snail *Aplysia* (Kandel 1989), it is known that changes in synaptic connections encode memories. Here, too, abnormal experiences may permanently alter patterns of neuronal connectivity. In the human brain, imaging studies have begun to reveal changes in regional brain activity that occur after learning and are suggestive of changes in the strength of neuronal connections (Pantev et al. 1998; Sadato et al. 1996). Some functional neuropsychiatric disorders have now been shown to have a direct impact on brain structure; for example, posttraumatic stress disorder has been associated with alterations in hippocampal size (Bremner et al. 1995).

In this chapter, we first focus on the cellular function of neurons and then on how they develop. The pace of recent advances makes us confident that, in the not-too-distant future, it may be possible to intervene either during early development to correct aberrant neuronal growth and differentiation, or later to correct neuronal signaling, and thus achieve revolutionary treatments for neuropsychiatric disorders.

## Cellular Function of Neurons

Individual neurons in the brain receive signals from thousands of neurons and, in turn, send information to thousands of others. Whereas activity in peripheral sensory neurons may represent particular bits of information, activity of networks of neurons in the central nervous system (CNS) represents integrated sensory and associational information. CNS neurons may be seen as part of dynamic cellular ensembles that shift their participation from one network to another as information is used in varied tasks. The sophistication of these networks depends on both the properties of the neurons themselves and the patterns and strength of their connections.

## Cellular Composition of the Brain

Brain cells comprise two principal types: neurons and glia. Neurons are the substrate for most information processing, whereas glia are classically believed to play a supporting role. Neurons are highly differentiated cells that show considerable heterogeneity in shape and size; in fact, there are more types of neurons than types of cells in any other part of the body. Some are among the largest cells in the body, as in the case of the upper motor neurons that project to the lumbar spinal cord and have axons that are a meter or more in length; others are among the smallest cells in the body, as in the case of the granule cells of the cerebellum. Neurons are quite numerous, and their interconnections, called synapses, are still more numerous. The human brain contains between $10^{12}$ and $10^{13}$ neurons. If each neuron forms an average of $10^3$ connections, which is a minimal estimate, then the brain has at least $10^{15}$–$10^{16}$ synapses.

Glial cells can be divided into three classes: 1) astrocytes, 2) oligodendrocytes, and 3) microglia. Astrocytes have three traditional functions: they provide the scaffolding of the brain, form the blood-brain barrier, and guide neuronal migration during development. Evidence is accumulating, however, that astroglial cells are more dynamic than was previously suspected and are capable of cell-cell signaling over long distances (Dani et al. 1992; Murphy et al. 1993). Moreover, they can influence neuronal activity, enhance neuronal connectivity, and play critical roles in regulating neuronal excitability during normal processes as well as in disease states (Araque et al. 1999; Mennerick and Zorumski 1994; Nedergaard 1994; Pfrieger and Barres 1997). Oligodendrocytes produce the myelin sheath that speeds conduction of the action potential along axons. Thus, in patients with multiple sclerosis, which results from an immune attack on the principal protein of the myelin sheath (myelin basic protein), there is a failure in action potential conduction. Microglia are the macrophages of the brain; as a rule they are quiescent until activated by neuronal injury.

## Neuronal Shape

Neurons share a common organization dictated by their function—which is to receive, process, and transmit information. The great Spanish neuroanatomist Santiago Ramón y Cajal called this dynamic polarization (Craig and Banker 1994). Although neurons show a wide diversity of sizes and shapes, they generally have four well-defined regions (Figure 1–1): 1) dendrites, 2) cell body, 3) axon, and 4) synaptic specializations. Each region has distinct functions. Dendrites receive signals from other neurons, process and modify this information, and then convey these signals to the cell body. As in all cells, the cell body contains the genetic information resident in the nucleus that codes for the fabrication of the necessary elements of cellular function, as well as sites for their manufacture, processing, and transport. The axon conveys information over long distances, and then branches to form synapses. Synaptic specializations are distinguished by highly specific connections with postsynaptic dendrites; the key elements are the presynaptic active zone, where neurotransmitter is released, and the postsynaptic density, where neurotransmitter receptors are concentrated in the membrane of the postsynaptic dendrite.

A neuron's shape is determined by its cytoskeleton. The essential building blocks of the cytoskeleton are three filamentous proteins: 1) microtubules, 2) actin, and 3) neurofilaments (Schwartz and Westbrook 2000). Microtubules, which are composed of tubulin subunits, form bundles that extend throughout the major processes of the neuron; they are stabilized by microtubule-associated proteins. Microtubules are the principal component of the dendritic cytoskeleton, whereas neurofilaments are the principal component of the axonal cytoskeleton. Neurofilaments are much more stable than microtubules. Neurofilaments pathologically aggregate in Alzheimer's disease to form neurofibrillary tangles. Actin filaments, together with several actin-binding proteins, form a dense network concentrated just under the cell membrane that provides the motive force for plasticity of axonal and dendritic structure. Beyond its essential structural role, the cytoskeleton mediates the intracellular trafficking of proteins and organelles to the axon and dendrites (Burack et al. 2000). Thus, cytoskeletal defects cause devastating neuronal damage; impairing axonal and dendritic transport not only interferes with neuronal signaling but often results in cell death.

## Neuronal Excitability

Neurons are capable of transmitting information because they are electrically and chemically excitable. This excitability is conferred by several ion channel families that

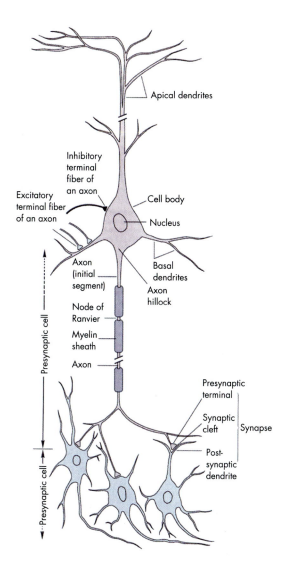

Apical dendrites

Inhibitory terminal fiber of an axon

Excitatory terminal fiber of an axon

Cell body

Nucleus

Axon (initial segment)

Basal dendrites

Axon hillock

Node of Ranvier

Myelin sheath

Axon

Presynaptic terminal

Synaptic cleft

Synapse

Postsynaptic dendrite

Presynaptic cell

Presynaptic cell

**FIGURE 1–1.** Functional organization of the neuron. Neurons have distinct cellular regions subserving the input, integration, conduction, and output of information: the dendrites, cell body, axon, and synaptic specializations, respectively. Excitatory and inhibitory neurotransmitters released by other neurons induce depolarizing or hyperpolarizing current flow in dendrites. These currents converge in the cell body; if the resulting polarization is sufficient to bring the initial segment of the axon to threshold, an action potential is initiated. The action potential travels down the axon, speeded by myelination, to reach the synaptic terminals. Axon terminals form synapses with other neurons or effector cells, renewing the cycle of information flow in postsynaptic cells. As in all cells, the cell body (or perikaryon) is also the repository of the neuron's genetic information (in the nucleus) and the principal site of macromolecular synthesis.

*Source.* Reprinted from Kandel ER, Schwartz JHS, Jessell TM: *Principles of Neural Science*, 3rd Edition. Stamford, CT, Appleton & Lange, 1991. Used with permission.

are selectively permeable to specific ions and that are regulated by voltage (voltage-gated channels), by neurotransmitter binding (ligand-gated channels), or by pressure or stretching (mechanically gated channels) (Hille 1992). In general, neuronal ion channels conduct ions across the plasma membrane at extremely rapid rates—100 million ions may pass through a single channel in a second. This large flow of current causes rapid changes in membrane potential and is the basis for the action potential, the biophysical mechanism for information transfer *within* neurons, and for fast synaptic responses, the substrate for information transfer *between* neurons. As might be expected, diverse and devastating diseases result from defects in ion channels. For example, in hyperkalemic periodic paralysis, muscle stiffness and weakness following exercise are caused by a point mutation in voltage-gated $Na^+$ channels; episodic ataxia results from several point mutations in a delayed-rectifier voltage-gated $K^+$ channel, and myasthenia gravis results from an immune attack on nicotinic acetylcholine receptors (Koester and Siegelbaum 2000). Ligand-gated channels are often targets for psychiatric drugs and anesthetics, as well as neurotoxins.

Neurotransmitters released by one neuron (the presynaptic cell) at a synapse activate receptors (ligand-gated channels) on dendrites of another neuron (the postsynaptic cell) and induce ion flux across the membrane. The resulting electrical signals spread passively over some distance, often reaching the cell body in this way. In addition to passive conductances, localized regenerative mechanisms similar to those that give rise to the action potential (discussed later in this section) amplify dendritic input signals, boosting them so that they reach the cell body (Eilers and Konnerth 1997; Yuste and Tank 1996). In the cell body, these synaptic inputs combine and, if they are sufficient, depolarize the initial segment of the axon, or axon hillock, which is the part of the axon closest to the cell body and that has the lowest threshold for activation. When a threshold level of depolarization is reached, the action potential is initiated. The action potential, or spike, is an electrical wave that propagates down the axon. In the axon terminals, this wave triggers an influx of calcium ($Ca^{2+}$), which leads to exocytosis of neurotransmitters from synaptic vesicles at specialized areas of the synapse called active zones. The released neurotransmitter crosses the synaptic cleft and activates receptors in the postsynaptic density on the postsynaptic cell's dendrites. Ultimately, this information flow reaches effector cells, principally motor fibers that mediate movement and thus generate behavior.

The ability of neurons to generate an action potential derives from the presence of strong ionic gradients across the membrane; sodium (Na$^+$) and chloride (Cl$^-$) are highly concentrated outside the membrane, whereas potassium (K$^+$) is highly concentrated inside. These gradients are generated by the continuous action of membrane pumps energized by the hydrolysis of adenosine triphosphate (ATP). Also in the membrane are voltage-gated ion channels that regulate the flow of Na$^+$, K$^+$, and Ca$^{2+}$ ions across the membrane. At rest, K$^+$ and Cl$^-$ channels are open so that K$^+$ and Cl$^-$ gradients determine the membrane potential, causing the cell to be negative inside by about –50 to –75 mV. However, if the membrane is depolarized past the threshold potential for generating an action potential, voltage-gated Na$^+$ channels open rapidly. Because inflow of Na$^+$ depolarizes the membrane, this confers a regenerative property—once a threshold potential is reached, increased Na$^+$ influx leads to depolarization, which opens more Na$^+$ channels, further enhancing Na$^+$ influx, and so on. Thus, once threshold is reached, the membrane potential switches to +50 mV quite rapidly. The membrane potential stays depolarized for only about a millisecond, because Na$^+$ channels then show a time-dependent inactivation (Figure 1–2). Simultaneously, voltage-dependent K$^+$ channels, which are also activated by depolarization but at a slower rate, increase their permeability (Figure 1–2). Because K$^+$ flows along its concentration gradient out of the cell, this, together with reduction in Na$^+$ current, leads to the repolarization of the membrane. Thus, the membrane potential peaks at a depolarized level determined by the Na$^+$ gradient and then rapidly returns to the resting potential, determined by the K$^+$ gradient. Once repolarized, Na$^+$ inactivation wears off (the time this takes accounts for the refractory period of the neuron—a brief period when the threshold for firing an action potential is elevated), and the cell can fire again.

The regenerative property of the action potential not only serves to amplify threshold potentials (its principal function in dendrites) but also confers long-distance signaling capabilities to the axon (Figure 1–3). When the membrane potential peaks under the control of the increase in Na$^+$ permeability, adjacent regions of the axon become sufficiently depolarized so that they are, in turn, brought to threshold and generate an action potential. As successive axonal segments are depolarized, the action potential conducts at great speed down the axon. This is further enhanced by myelination that increases the rate of conduction several-fold by restricting the current flow required for action potential conduction to the gaps between myelin segments, the nodes of Ranvier (Figure 1–3). Because of its all-or-none characteristics and ability to conduct over long distances, the action potential provides a high-quality digital signaling mechanism in the neuron.

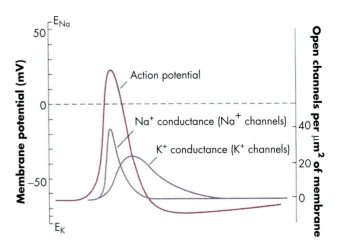

**FIGURE 1–2.** Opening of ion channels gives rise to the action potential. The action potential is composed primarily of two currents, the sodium (Na$^+$) and potassium (K$^+$) currents. Once a neuron reaches the threshold potential for firing an action potential, voltage-activated sodium channels open, giving rise to a rapid inward Na$^+$ current and to the rapid rising phase of the action potential. Subsequently, Na$^+$ channels rapidly inactivate at depolarized potentials, curtailing the duration of the Na$^+$ current and thereby contributing to the falling phase of the action potential. The outward K$^+$ current also contributes to the falling phase of the action potential, as K$^+$ channels are slow to open but stay open for much longer than Na$^+$ channels. Abbreviations: E$_{Na}$ and E$_k$=the reversal potentials for Na$^+$ and K$^+$, respectively.

*Source.* Reprinted from Kandel ER, Schwartz JH, Jessell TM: *Principles of Neural Science*, 4th Edition. New York, McGraw-Hill, 2000, p. 158. Used with permission.

Although the information that a neuron integrates comes from synaptic input, how the neuron processes that information depends on its intrinsic properties (Llinás 1988). Many CNS neurons have the ability to generate their own patterns of activity in the absence of synaptic input, firing either at a regular rate (pacemaker firing) or in clusters of spikes (burst firing) (McCormick and Bal 1997). This endogenous activity is driven by specialized ion channels with their own voltage and time dependence that periodically bring the initial segment of the axon to threshold. These channels can be modulated by the membrane potential of the cell or by second-messenger systems. Furthermore, CNS neurons may profoundly change how they respond to a given synaptic input as a function of slight changes in resting potential (Llinás and Jahnsen 1982; Sherman 1996) (Figure 1–4). For example, a thalamic neuron fires as a pacemaker when stimulated from slightly depolarized levels, whereas it fires in bursts of action potentials when stim-

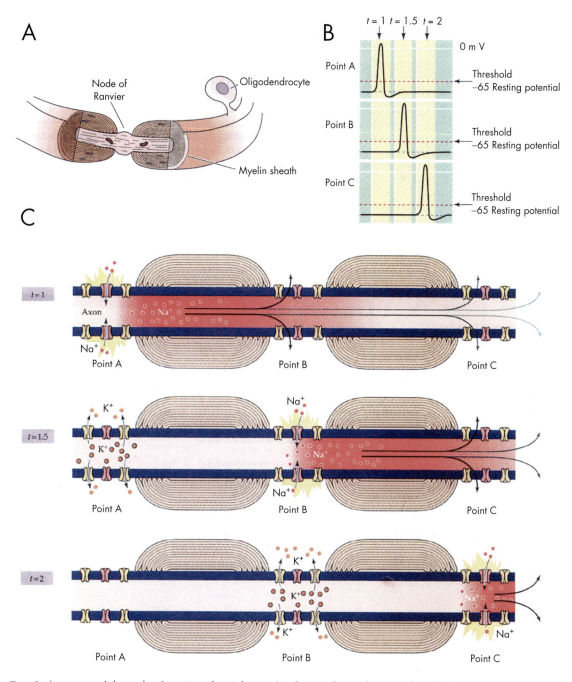

**FIGURE 1–3.** Action potential conduction. *Panel A.* Schematic of a myelinated axon. Oligodendrocytes produce the myelin sheath that surrounds axons. Myelin prevents current leakage between nodes of Ranvier, where Na$^+$ channels are concentrated, and thus enhances the conduction velocity of the action potential. *Panel B.* Because sodium channels are activated by membrane depolarization and also cause depolarization, they have regenerative properties. Not only does this underlie the "all-or-nothing" properties of the action potential, it also explains the rapid spread of the action potential down the axon. The action potential is an electrical wave, as shown in this panel. As each segment of the axon is depolarized, it in turn depolarizes the subsequent one, leading to changes in local current produced by action potential initiation at particular sites, as depicted in Panel C. *Panel C.* The Na$^+$ ion flow underlying the action potential is shown in three successive images at 0.5-millisecond (ms) intervals and corresponds to the current traces in Panel B. As the action potential travels to the right, Na$^+$ channels go from closed to open to inactivated to closed. In this way, an action potential initiated at the initial segment of the axon conducts reliably to the axon terminals. Because of both Na$^+$ channel inactivation and K$^+$ channel activation, there is a refractory period after the action potential; thus, conduction proceeds in just one direction.
*Source.* Reprinted from Purves D, Augustine GJ, Fitzpatrick D, et al. (eds): *Neuroscience.* Sunderland, MA, Sinauer Associates, 1997, p. 67. Used with permission.

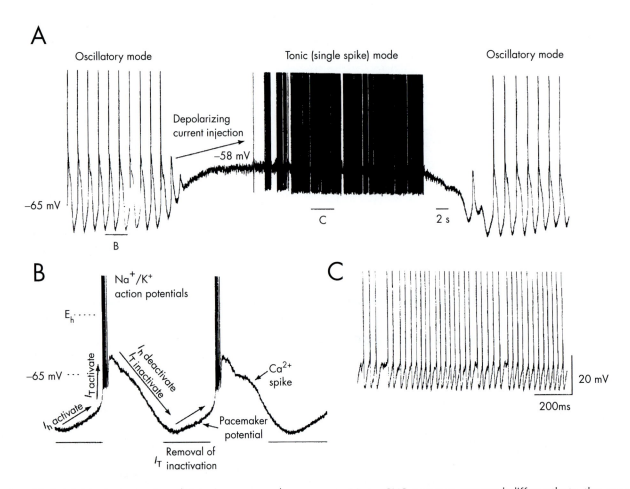

**FIGURE 1–4.** Intrinsic properties determine neuronal responses. Many CNS neurons respond differently to the same inputs, depending on their level of depolarization. *Panel A.* Thalamic neurons spontaneously generate bursts of action potentials, resulting from interactions between an inward pacemaker current and a $Ca^{2+}$ current. Depolarization of these neurons changes their firing to a tonic mode. *Panel B.* Action potential bursts at higher time resolution from trace in Panel A. *Panel C.* Higher time resolution of currents in the tonic mode from Panel A. Abbreviations: $I_h$ and $I_T$=the currents through a hyperpolarization-activated channel and a T-type calcium channel respectively.

*Source.* Reprinted from McCormick DA: "Membrane Potential and Action Potential," in *Fundamental Neuroscience.* Edited by Zigmond MJ, Bloom FE, Landis SC, et al. San Diego, CA, Academic Press, 1999, p. 150. Used with permission.

ulated from somewhat hyperpolarized levels. Changes in second-messenger levels may also profoundly affect the activity or response properties of neurons, lending still a greater repertoire to the functioning of individual neurons. Therefore, synaptic inputs may not only evoke a response in a postsynaptic neuron but may also shape intrinsic firing patterns, cause a cell to shift from one mode of activity to another, or modulate responses to other synaptic inputs.

## Signaling Between Neurons

Neurons communicate with one another at specialized sites of close membrane apposition called synapses. The prototypic axodendritic synapse connects a presynaptic axon terminal with a postsynaptic dendrite. This arrange-

ment is typical for projection neurons that convey information from one region of the brain to another. In contrast, local circuit interneurons interact with neighboring neurons. Whereas interneurons may make axodendritic and axosomatic connections, they can also form several other kinds of synaptic contacts that greatly increase their functional sophistication (Figure 1–5). In some cases, dendrites may synapse with dendrites (dendrodendritic connections) or cell bodies with cell bodies (somatosomatic connections), forming local neural circuits that convey information without action potential firing. Axons may synapse onto the axon terminals of other axons (axoaxonic connections) and modulate transmitter release by presynaptic inhibition or facilitation. Some neurons may function both as interneurons and projection neurons, the most prominent example being the

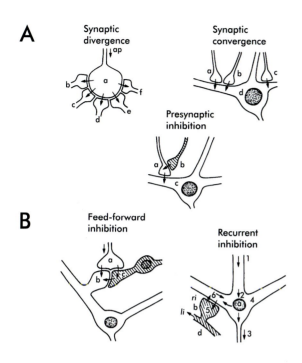

**FIGURE 1–5.** Modes of interneuronal communication. *Panel A.* Different connection patterns dictate how information flows between neurons. In synaptic divergence, one neuron (*a*) may disseminate information to several postsynaptic cells (*b–f*) simultaneously. Alternatively, in the case of synaptic convergence, a single neuron (*d*) may receive input from an array of presynaptic neurons (*a–c*). In presynaptic inhibition, one neuron (*b*) can modulate information flowing between two other neurons (from *a* to *c*) by influencing neurotransmitter release from the presynaptic neuron's terminals; this can be inhibitory (as shown) or facilitatory. *Panel B.* Neurons may modulate their own actions. In feed-forward inhibition, the presynaptic cell (*a*) may directly activate a postsynaptic cell (*b*) and at the same time modulate its effects through also activating an inhibitory cell (*c*), which in turn inhibits cell (*b*). In recurrent inhibition (information flow is shown by arrows), a presynaptic cell (*a*) activates an inhibitory cell (*b*) that synapses back onto it, limiting the duration of its activity. Abbreviations: ap=action potential; *li*=lateral inhibition; *ri*=recurrent inhibition.

*Source.* Adapted from Shepherd GM, Koch C: "Introduction to Synaptic Circuits," in *The Synaptic Organization of the Brain.* Edited by Shepherd GM. New York, Oxford University Press, 1990, pp. 3–31. Used with permission.

medium spiny γ-aminobutyric acid (GABA) neurons of the striatum, which constitute about 95% of the neurons in the region (A.D. Smith and Bolam 1990).

A minority of local connections are mediated by electrical synapses that do not require chemical neurotransmitters at all. Electrical synapses are formed by multisubunit channels, called gap junctions, that link the cytoplasm of adjacent cells (Bennett et al. 1991), allowing both small molecules and ions carrying electrical signals to flow directly from one cell to another. Electrical synapses couple dendrites or cell bodies of adjoining cells of the same kind, typically dendrite to dendrite or cell body to cell body. The ability to pass small molecules between cells, including second messengers, is important during embryonic development to set up morphogenic gradients (Dealy et al. 1994) and, during early brain development, to regulate cell proliferation and establish patterns of connectivity (Kandler and Katz 1995). In the mature CNS, electrical synapses act to synchronize the electrical activity of groups of neurons and mediate high-frequency transmission of signals (Bennett 1977; Brivanlou et al. 1998; Tamas et al. 2000). Glial cells are also connected by gap junctions that link these cells into large syncytia and provide avenues for intercellular propagation of chemical signals mediated by small molecules and ions, such as $Ca^{2+}$ (S.J. Smith 1994). The importance of gap junctions for glial cell function is underscored by the fact that the X-linked form of Charcot-Marie-Tooth disease is caused by a single mutation in a connexin gene required for the formation of gap junctions between Schwann cells (reviewed in Schenone and Mancardi 1999).

Most CNS synaptic connections are mediated by chemical neurotransmitters. Although chemical synapses are slower than electrical ones, they allow for signal amplification, may be inhibitory as well as excitatory, are susceptible to a wide range of modulation, and can modulate the activities of other cells through the release of transmitters activating second-messenger cascades. There are two primary classes of neurotransmitters in the nervous system: small molecule transmitters and neuropeptides. In general, small molecule transmitters mediate fast synaptic transmission, are stored in small, clear synaptic vesicles, and include glutamate, GABA, glycine, acetylcholine, serotonin, dopamine, norepinephrine, epinephrine, and histamine. The cellular and molecular mechanisms of release of these synaptic vesicles are described below. In contrast, the neuropeptides are a very large family of neurotransmitters that modulate synaptic transmission, are stored in large dense-core vesicles, and include somatostatin, the hypothalamic-releasing hormones, endorphins, enkephalins, and the opioids. Interestingly, small molecule transmitters and neuropeptides are often released from the same neuron and can act in concert on the same target (Hökfelt et al. 1984).

Small neurotransmitter molecules are stored in clear, small, membrane-bound granules called synaptic vesicles (Figure 1–6). Each synaptic vesicle contains several thou-

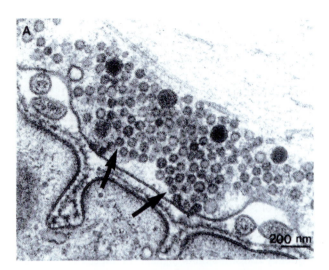

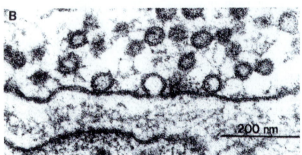

**FIGURE 1–6.** Electron micrographs of chemical synapses. Neuromuscular junctions from frog sartorius muscle were flash-frozen milliseconds after high potassium treatment to increase synaptic transmission. *Panel A.* Synaptic vesicles are clustered at two active zones (*arrows*), which are sites where vesicles can fuse with the plasma membrane and release their neurotransmitter. *Panel B.* After stimulation, omega profiles of vesicles in the process of releasing their neurotransmitter are visible.

*Source.* Reprinted from Zucker RS, Kullmann DM, Bennett M: "Release of Neurotransmitters," in *Fundamental Neuroscience.* Edited by Zigmond MJ, Bloom FE, Landis SC, et al. San Diego, CA, Academic Press, 1999, p. 156. Used with permission.

sand neurotransmitter molecules. When a presynaptic action potential invades the terminal region, it activates voltage-dependent $Ca^{2+}$ channels (Figures 1–6 and 1–7). The subsequent $Ca^{2+}$ influx causes a very high increase in $Ca^{2+}$ concentration near the active zone that promotes synaptic vesicle fusion and neurotransmitter release, termed exocytosis. The neurotransmitter then diffuses a short distance across the synaptic cleft and binds to postsynaptic receptors. The dynamics and modulation of synaptic transmission are fundamental to alterations in synaptic connections that underlie both normal and pathologic learning and memory. The molecular machinery (Figure 1–8) of synaptic transmission has now been worked out (Scheller 1995; Sudhof 1995). Interestingly,

several potent neurotoxins act directly on this machinery (see following). Synaptic transmission comprises a complex sequence of presynaptic and postsynaptic events. Six major events are involved in the synaptic vesicle cycle (see Figure 1–7):

1. Vesicles dock at active zones before exocytotic release.
2. Priming occurs, whereby vesicles become ready to respond to increases in intracellular $Ca^{2+}$ (the potent neurotoxins botulinum and tetanus toxin block synaptic transmission by proteolysis of key molecules involved in priming).
3. Triggered by an influx in $Ca^{2+}$, fusion/exocytosis then occurs in less than a millisecond, releasing the neurotransmitter into the synaptic cleft.
4. Endocytosis recovers the synaptic vesicle membrane.
5. Synaptic vesicles are refilled with neurotransmitter, driven by an intravesicular acidic or voltage gradient.
6. The filled synaptic vesicles are transported back to the active zone, completing the cycle.

Neurotransmitter activity is typically limited in duration by several mechanisms that rapidly remove released neurotransmitter from the synaptic cleft. First, all neurotransmitters to some extent diffuse out of the cleft. Second, neurotransmitters may be enzymatically degraded; for example, acetylcholine is hydrolyzed by acetylcholinesterase bound to the postsynaptic membrane adjacent to the receptors. Finally, although the monoamine and amino acid neurotransmitters are also subject to enzymatic degradation, they are principally removed from the synaptic cleft by rapid reuptake mechanisms and are subsequently repackaged in synaptic vesicles or metabolized (Amara and Kuhar 1993).

Monoamine neurotransmitter transporters (Figure 1–9), which mediate this rapid reuptake process, are the sites of action of a number of drugs and neurotoxins. Prominent among these are the tricyclic antidepressants, the selective serotonin reuptake inhibitors (SSRIs), the psychostimulants, and the neurotoxin 1-methyl-4-phenyl-1,2,3,6-tetrahydropyridine (MPTP) (Giros and Caron 1993; Jaber et al. 1997). The tricyclics block serotonin and norepinephrine reuptake, while the SSRIs, as their name suggests, block serotonin reuptake selectively. Other newer antidepressants block feedback inhibition of release, thereby increasing synaptic serotonin levels. Cocaine prevents dopamine and serotonin reuptake, whereas amphetamine both slows reuptake of dopamine and serotonin and induces dopamine release (Ramamoorthy and Blakely 1999; Saunders et al. 2000). Molecular studies have also suggested that cocaine binding and

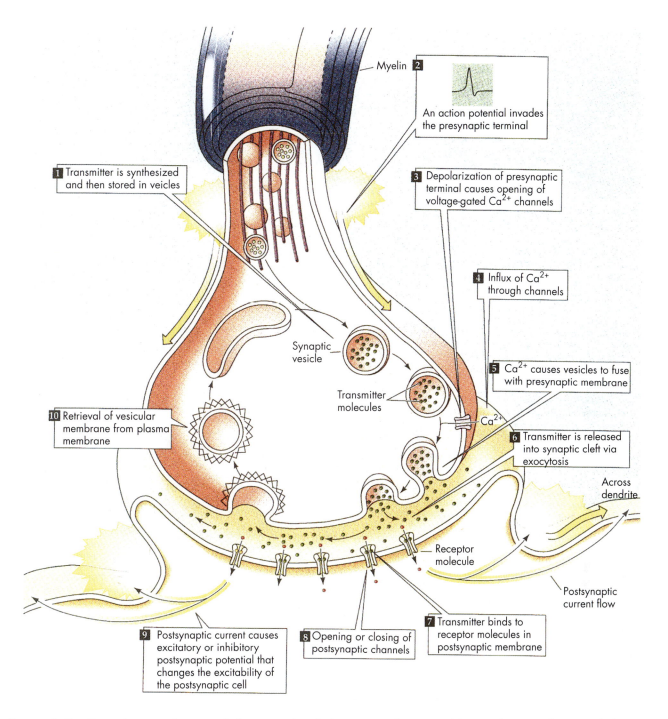

**Myelin** 2

An action potential invades the presynaptic terminal

1 Transmitter is synthesized and then stored in veicles

3 Depolarization of presynaptic terminal causes opening of voltage-gated $Ca^{2+}$ channels

4 Influx of $Ca^{2+}$ through channels

Synaptic vesicle

5 $Ca^{2+}$ causes vesicles to fuse with presynaptic membrane

Transmitter molecules

$Ca^{2+}$

10 Retrieval of vesicular membrane from plasma membrane

6 Transmitter is released into synaptic cleft via exocytosis

Across dendrite

Receptor molecule

Postsynaptic current flow

9 Postsynaptic current causes excitatory or inhibitory postsynaptic potential that changes the excitability of the postsynaptic cell

8 Opening or closing of postsynaptic channels

7 Transmitter binds to receptor molecules in postsynaptic membrane

**FIGURE 1–7.** Steps in synaptic transmission at a chemical synapse. The essential steps in synaptic transmission are numbered.

*Source.* Reprinted from Purves D, Augustine GJ, Fitzpatrick D, et al. (eds): *Neuroscience.* Sunderland, MA, Sinauer Associates, 1997, p. 88. Used with permission.

dopamine reuptake occur at separate sites on the transporter, suggesting the possibility that cocaine action could be successfully blocked without impeding normal reuptake (Kitayama et al. 1992). Mice lacking the dopamine transporter show a profound persistence of synaptic dopamine, so they *appear* as if they are permanently on psychostimulants; psychostimulants have no effect on these animals, confirming that the dopamine transporter is critical to the action of these drugs (Giros et al. 1996). MPTP is taken up by the dopamine transporter selectively (Javitch and Snyder 1984) and then causes increased oxidative stress, leading to the demise of dopaminergic neurons and to drug-induced Parkinson's disease (Przedborski and Jackson-Lewis 1998).

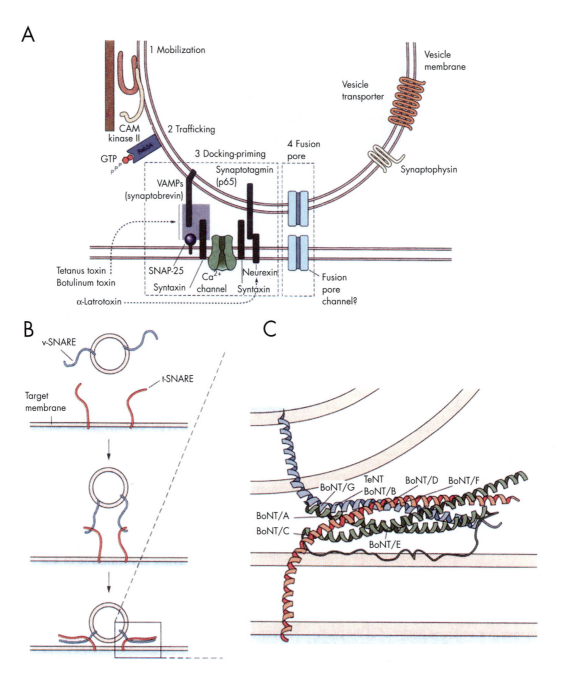

**FIGURE 1–8.** Molecular events in synaptic vesicle docking and fusion. A coordinated set of proteins are involved in the positioning of vesicles at the presynaptic membrane and in controlling release by membrane fusion. *Panel A.* Many of the synaptic vesicle proteins that have recently been cloned are integral to this process. Some of these proteins interact with the cytoskeleton to position the vesicles at the terminal, while other proteins are integral to the fusion process. In addition, several of these synaptic vesicle proteins are targets for neurotoxins that function by influencing neurotransmitter release. *Panel B.* The current theory for how synaptic vesicles fuse with the membrane and release neurotransmitter is called the SNARE hypothesis. Both the synaptic vesicles and the plasma membrane express specific proteins that mediate docking and fusion: v-SNAREs (synaptic vesicles) and t-SNAREs (plasma membrane). Vesicles are brought close to the membrane through interactions between VAMP (synaptobrevin), syntaxin, and SNAP-25. *N*-ethylmaleimide-sensitive fusion protein (NSF) then binds to the complex to facilitate fusion. Calcium influx is required to stimulate fusion, but the precise binding partner for calcium and the exact events leading to fusion remain obscure. *Panel C.* The crystal structure of the fusion complex, as shown here, is consistent with the SNARE hypothesis. Abbreviations: BoNT=botulinum; TeNT=tetanus toxin.
*Source.* Adapted from Kandel ER, Schwartz JH, Jessell TM: *Principles of Neural Science*, 4th Edition. New York, McGraw-Hill, 2000, pp. 271–273. Used with permission.

## A Vesicle transporters

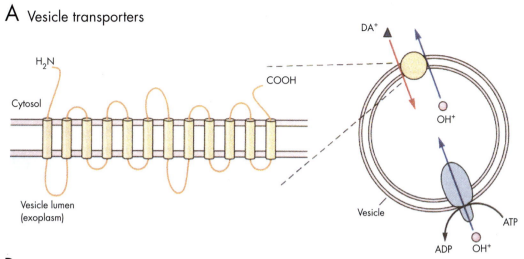

## B Glutamate uptake

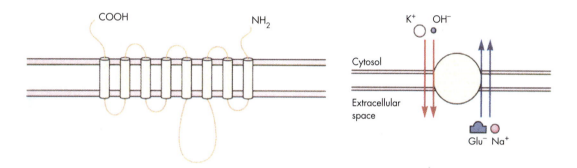

## C Uptake of other transmitters

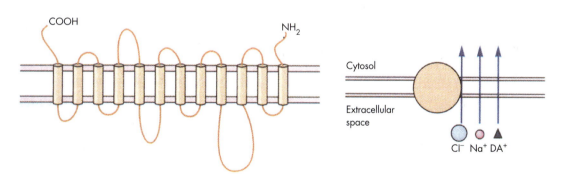

**FIGURE 1–9.** Neurotransmitter transporters. Synaptic transmission in the CNS is terminated for the most part by reuptake of neurotransmitter by specific transporters with shared molecular motifs. These transporters carry neurotransmitters across membranes against concentration gradients, and thus require metabolic energy. Most often, this energy is provided by cotransport of an ion down its concentration gradient. *Panel A.* One family of transporters in synaptic vesicles serves to load neurotransmitter or transmitter precursors into synaptic vesicles. *Panel B.* A second family of transporters in the plasma membrane with eight transmembrane domains handles amino acid neurotransmitters, such as glutamate and GABA. *Panel C.* A third family of transporters in the plasma membrane with twelve transmembrane domains handles the monoamines dopamine, norepinephrine, and serotonin.

*Source.* Reprinted from Kandel ER, Schwartz JH, Jessell TM: *Principles of Neural Science,* 4th Edition. New York, McGraw-Hill, 2000, p. 287. Used with permission.

# Rapid Postsynaptic Responses

The action of a neurotransmitter depends on the properties of the postsynaptic receptors to which it binds. Postsynaptic receptors activated by neurotransmitter fall into two classes: ionotropic and metabotropic receptors (discussed in the following section). Ionotropic receptors are directly linked to an ion channel; these receptors undergo a conformational change upon neurotransmitter binding that opens the channel. This results in either depolarization, giving rise to an excitatory postsynaptic potential, or hyperpolarization, giving rise to an inhibitory postsynaptic potential. The neuromuscular junction is the prototypic excitatory synapse; simultaneous binding of two acetylcholine molecules opens a channel in the receptor that is permeable to both $Na^+$ and $K^+$ (Karlin and Akabas 1995). This results in a strong depolarization of the postsynaptic membrane mediated by $Na^+$ influx (and moderated by $K^+$ efflux), leading to an action potential in the motor fiber that evokes contraction. Ligand-gated channels are found at synapses such as the neuromuscular junction, where rapid and reliable activation of the postsynaptic cell is required. At the neuromuscular junction, the postsynaptic response is sufficiently strong so that there is a one-to-one translation of motor neuron spikes into muscle fiber spikes, thus ensuring reliable muscle contraction.

Unlike the neuromuscular junction, CNS neurons function in dynamic networks so that generally no individual cell has so strong a synaptic connection with another cell that it alone brings it to threshold. Rather, groups of neurons—active in concert—converge on a postsynaptic neuron to generate multiple postsynaptic potentials. These potentials may summate within regions of the postsynaptic neuron (spatial summation) if they occur sufficiently close together in time to cause the postsynaptic neuron to fire. As a rule, fast ligand-gated channels mediate the flow of information representing patterns of sensory input and associations between sensory modalities, underlying central representations that ultimately give rise to motor outputs. In the CNS, glutamate receptors mediate most fast excitatory transmission; GABA and glycine are the most common inhibitory neurotransmitters.

## Glutamate Receptors

Glutamate receptors are broadly divided into three general types: N-methyl-D-aspartate (NMDA) receptors, non-NMDA ionotropic receptors, and metabotropic glutamate receptors (Dingledine et al. 1999; Hollmann and Heinemann 1994). The glutamate receptors are all multimeric proteins, usually composed of four subunits. NMDA receptors are formed from combinations of NR1 and NR2 subunits; the NR1 subunit is universally expressed in neurons, whereas the NR2, which comes in several subtypes, is heterogeneously expressed both during development and among different neurons, giving rise to different response properties (Schoepfer et al. 1994). NMDA receptors depolarize cells by opening channels that principally allow $Ca^{2+}$ to enter the cell (MacDermott et al. 1986). The most striking property of NMDA receptors is that the ion channel is usually blocked by $Mg^{2+}$ at membrane potentials more negative than about $-40$ mV (Mayer et al. 1984). As a result, at the resting potential of most neurons, the NMDA receptor channel is occluded. For current to flow through NMDA channels, glutamate must bind to the receptor and the membrane must be depolarized simultaneously to displace the $Mg^{2+}$. This dual requirement underlies the unique role of NMDA receptors in processes as varied as synaptogenesis, learning and memory, and even cell death. NMDA receptors are also likely to be critical for proper psychiatric functioning; transgenic mice with reduced NMDA receptor expression display behaviors similar to those seen in patients with schizophrenia (Mohn et al. 1999).

The non-NMDA glutamate receptors are further divided into α-amino-3-hydroxy-5-methylisoxazole-4-propionic acid (AMPA) receptors and kainate receptors on the basis of their affinities for these glutamate analogs. AMPA receptors are formed from combinations of subunits GluR1 to GluR4, and kainate receptors are formed from combinations of GluR5 to GluR7 plus KA1 and KA2. The complexity in the types of possible glutamate receptors is even further increased by the existence of flip and flop conformations of GluR1 to GluR4 subunits and posttranslational editing of glutamate receptor mRNA (Puchalski et al. 1994; Seeburg 1996; Sommer et al. 1990). Non-NMDA receptors generally gate channels that allow $Na^+$ but not $Ca^{2+}$ to cross the membrane. The GluR2 subunit of the AMPA receptor channel is responsible for blocking $Ca^{2+}$ passage. Recently, neurons have been identified that express AMPA receptors that lack the GluR2 subunit and therefore allow $Ca^{2+}$ as well as $Na^+$ to cross the channel (Geiger et al. 1995). Neurons that express such $Ca^{2+}$-permeable AMPA receptors may be particularly vulnerable to excitotoxic cell death in certain disease states.

## GABA Receptors

Inhibitory postsynaptic potentials in the brain are mediated primarily by GABA receptors. Several classes of GABA receptors have been identified. $GABA_A$ receptors are ionotropic receptors and form Cl⁻-selective channels that mediate fast synaptic inhibition in the brain. GABA$_B$ receptors are metabotropic receptors, tend to be slower acting, and play a modulatory role; they are often found on presynaptic terminals, where they inhibit transmitter release. GABA$_A$ receptors are members of the nicotinic acetylcholine receptor superfamily (DeLorey and Olsen 1992; Schofield et al. 1990). The GABA$_A$ receptor-channel complex is composed of a mixture of five subunits from $\alpha$, $\beta$, $\gamma$, and $\rho$ families. This gives rise to receptors with varying properties, depending on the specific receptor subunit composition. Because most of the subunit families have multiple subtypes, some of which can undergo RNA splicing, there is a potential for an extraordinary diversity of GABA$_A$ receptor function.

The mRNA sequences for individual or multiple receptor subunits can be injected into oocytes or cultured mammalian cells, and the properties of the subsequently expressed receptor subunit combinations can be defined. This approach has shown how the properties of a particular GABA$_A$ receptor depend on the subunit composition as well as on interactions among the subunits. Site-directed mutagenesis has been applied to localize binding sites of specific ligands on receptor subunits. The $\alpha$ subunit, for example, has a binding site for benzodiazepines (Pritchett et al. 1989). The clinical actions of benzodiazepines, along with two other classes of CNS-depressant drugs, barbiturates and anesthetic steroids, seem to be related to their ability to bind to GABA$_A$ receptors and to enhance GABA$_A$ receptor currents (Callachan et al. 1987; Choi et al. 1981; MacDonald and Barker 1978; Majewska et al. 1986). Individual GABA$_A$ channels do not open continuously in the presence of GABA but rather flicker open and closed, often in bursts. Benzodiazepines increase GABA current by increasing the frequency of channel openings without altering open time or conductance (Study and Barker 1981). Barbiturates prolong the channel open time without altering opening frequency or conductance (MacDonald et al. 1989; Mathers and Barker 1981). Steroids such as androsterone and pregnenolone increase the open time and the frequency of bursts (Twyman and MacDonald 1992). Despite the different mechanisms of action, each drug enhances GABAergic transmission, accounting for their shared properties as anticonvulsants. In fact, they may directly counteract a GABA deficit due to a reduction in GABA transporter numbers in epileptogenic cortex that may be etiologic in epilepsy (During et al. 1995). Most recently, general anesthetics, as well as alcohol, have been shown to act via binding to GABA$_A$ (and also to glycine receptors) (Mascia et al. 2000; Mihic et al. 1997).

## Metabotropic Receptors

Longer-term modulatory effects are generally mediated by metabotropic receptors. These non-channel-linked receptors regulate cell function via activation of G proteins that couple to second-messenger cascades. Although other non-channel-linked receptors may also be catalytic, in the CNS only G protein–linked receptors are found. In fact, the majority of neurotransmitters and neuromodulators exert their effects through binding to G protein receptors. G protein–linked receptors are so named because they couple to intracellular guanosine triphosphate (GTP)-binding regulatory proteins. G proteins are formed from a complex of three membrane-bound proteins ($G_{\alpha\beta\gamma}$); when the receptor is activated, the $\alpha$ subunit ($G_\alpha$) binds GTP and dissociates from a complex of the $\beta$ and $\gamma$ subunits ($G_{\beta\gamma}$). Both $G_\alpha$ and $G_{\beta\gamma}$ may go on to trigger subsequent events. Activated G proteins have a life span of seconds to minutes; $G_\alpha$ autoinactivates by hydrolyzing its bound GTP, after which it reaggregates with $G_{\beta\gamma}$, returning to the resting state. Continued transmitter binding to the receptor may reinitiate the cycle.

G proteins are the first link in signaling cascades that either directly activate protein kinases—enzymes that phosphorylate cellular proteins (Walaas and Greengard 1991)—or raise intracellular $Ca^{2+}$ and indirectly activate kinases (Figure 1–10) (Ghosh and Greenberg 1995). Proteins undergo conformational changes when they are phosphorylated that may lead to either their activation or inactivation. Proteins affected may include membrane channels, cytoskeletal elements, and transcriptional regulators of gene expression. In this way, modulatory actions mediated by second messengers control most cellular processes. The potential for amplification, combined with divergence and convergence of signals, provides the requisite mechanisms for enduring changes in neuronal function, especially for mechanisms essential for learning and memory and for development. The three major second-messenger cascades involving G proteins and their interaction with $Ca^{2+}$ are schematized in Figure 1–10.

As these G protein receptors are the targets of many therapeutic and abused drugs, understanding their regulation is of paramount clinical importance. Recently, major advances have been made in defining the mechanisms mediating downregulation of G protein–coupled receptors (Tsao and Von Zastrow 2000). Receptor downregulation is generally induced by prolonged activation of receptors, leading to receptor internalization. For example, prolonged activation of D$_1$ dopamine receptors in striatal neurons by agonist injection in vivo causes rapid internalization of dopamine receptors (Dumartin et al.

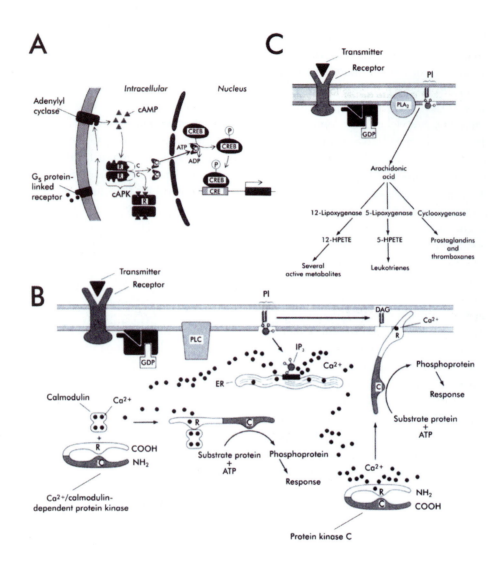

**FIGURE 1–10.**  Major intracellular signaling pathways in neurons. Ligand binding to receptors activates three major signaling pathways via G proteins. *Panel A.* In the cyclic adenosine monophosphate (cAMP) system, a G protein link couples ligand binding to activation of adenylyl cyclase. This in turn generates cAMP, which binds to the regulatory units (R) of cAMP-dependent protein kinase (cAPK), releasing the catalytic subunits (C). These in turn activate cAMP response element binding proteins (CREB), which bind to cAMP response elements (CRE) and regulate gene expression after being phosphorylated (P). *Panel B.* In the inositol phospholipid system, G proteins activate phospholipase C (PLC), which hydrolyzes membrane phospholipids to produce two second messengers, diacylglycerol (DAG) and inositol triphosphate (IP$_3$). IP$_3$ triggers the release of Ca$^{2+}$ from the endoplasmic reticulum (ER). Ca$^{2+}$, in turn, triggers the translocation of protein kinase C (PKC) to the cell membrane, where it is activated by DAG. Because it becomes membrane bound with activation, PKC may be especially important in the modulation of membrane channels. Also shown is another action of Ca$^{2+}$, which is on Ca$^{2+}$/calmodulin-dependent protein kinase; when activated, other sets of proteins are phosphorylated. Ca$^{2+}$ released from intracellular stores may act similarly to Ca$^{2+}$ that enters from outside the cell (not shown); however, because cells regulate Ca$^{2+}$ levels very tightly, Ca$^{2+}$ increases are generally highly localized. *Panel C.* In the arachidonic acid system, G proteins may couple to phospholipase A$_2$ (PLA$_2$), forming arachidonic acid by hydrolysis of membrane phospholipids. Arachidonic acid is either a second messenger in its own right or a precursor of the lipoxygenase pathway giving rise to a family of membrane-permeant second messengers. The cyclooxygenase pathway is principally important outside the brain in prostaglandin production. Abbreviations: ATP=adenosine triphosphate; HPETE=hydroperoxyeicosatetraenoic acid; PI=phosphatidylinositol.

*Source.*   Panel A reprinted from Lodish H, Berk A, Zipursky L, et al.: *Molecular Cell Biology*, 3rd Edition. New York, Scientific American Books, 1995; Panels B and C adapted from Kandel ER, Schwartz JH, Jessell TM: *Principles of Neural Science*, 4th Edition. New York, McGraw-Hill, 2000. Used with permission.

1998). This receptor internalization is mediated by highly specific dynamin-dependent and dynamin-independent mechanisms (Vickery and von Zastrow 1999). Determining the mechanisms of G protein receptor downregulation may identify targets for the development of new classes of drugs useful for the therapeutic manipulation of G protein receptor signaling. For instance, mutant mice lacking β-arrestin 2 show no tolerance to opioids (Bohn et al. 1999).

The slower actions of metabotropic receptors are responsible for altering neuronal excitability and the strength of synaptic connections, often reinforcing neural pathways involved in learning (Bailey et al. 2000). Activation of these receptors generally does not change the membrane potential at all. Rather, receptor binding activates second-messenger cascades that can dramatically alter the response properties of other receptors. In the retina, for example, dopamine appears to mediate light adaptation (Djamgoz and Wagner 1992; Dowling 1987). Dopamine released by interplexiform cells acts on horizontal cells via dopamine $D_1$ receptors that in turn activate adenylyl cyclase and raise cyclic adenosine monophosphate (cAMP) levels. This cAMP has two effects: 1) it increases the sensitivity of the horizontal cells to cone inputs and 2) it decreases electrical coupling among horizontal cells, reducing receptive field size and thereby increasing acuity. These two effects thus switch the retina from scotopic to photopic color vision. In the CNS, several modulatory actions have been ascribed to dopaminergic projections. Most profoundly, second messengers may translocate to the nucleus, where they may control gene expression, exerting longer-term changes in cell function (Lodish et al. 1995) via the activation of genes in a temporal sequence (Charney et al. 1999).

## Organization of Postsynaptic Receptors at Synapses

Most neurotransmitter receptors are clustered at postsynaptic sites closely apposed to the presynaptic terminal. Recently, several laboratories have made remarkable progress in identifying the molecular components of the postsynaptic scaffold that holds synaptic receptors in place (Figure 1–11) (S. H. Lee and Sheng 2000; Kim and Huganir 1999). One of the most abundant proteins in the postsynaptic density is PSD-95 (a postsynaptic density protein of 95 kd). PSD-95 is a cytoplasmic protein that contains three domains important for protein binding, called PDZ domains. These domains of PSD-95 bind to the NMDA receptor, to the Shaker $K^+$ channel, and to

cell adhesion proteins called neuroligins. In contrast, AMPA receptors bind a distinct PDZ domain protein called GRIP, and metabotropic glutamate receptors interact with HOMER. These PDZ proteins are believed to cluster neurotransmitter receptors and other important components of the synapse at the postsynaptic density and to mediate rapid insertion or removal of receptors from the synapse, as may occur during synaptic plasticity (Kim and Huganir 1999).

### Gases as Transcellular Modulators

Surprisingly, nitric oxide (NO), a gas, has been shown to mediate interneuronal signaling, functioning as a second messenger with neurotransmitter properties (Brenman and Bredt 1997; Dawson and Snyder 1994; Schulman 1997). NO is extremely short lived and is rapidly synthesized on demand from arginine by the enzyme nitric oxide synthase (NOS). NOS is activated by increases in intracellular $Ca^{2+}$ concentration. Unlike conventional intracellular messengers that are localized to the postsynaptic cell, where they have their effects, NO diffuses across membranes to adjacent presynaptic or postsynaptic cells and activates guanylyl cyclase, raising levels of cyclic guanosine 3´,5´-monophosphate (cGMP) and in turn triggering the production of other intracellular messengers. NO, as well as carbon monoxide (CO) and arachidonic acid, which have similar roles, may coordinate presynaptic and postsynaptic changes in synaptic plasticity (O'Dell et al. 1994). Excitotoxicity due to excessive activation of the NMDA class of glutamate receptors appears to be mediated in part by NO (Dawson et al. 1993).

## Synaptic Modulation in Learning and Memory

Second messengers profoundly increase the range of responses a neuron may show to synaptic input. They activate kinases that both amplify and prolong signals by phosphorylating other proteins. Phosphorylated proteins remain active—often for a much longer period than agonist remains bound to receptor—until they are dephosphorylated by protein phosphatases. Because second messengers trigger numerous cellular functions, activation of a single receptor may trigger a coordinated cellular response involving several systems. This may include activity-dependent modulation of genomic transcription, leading to enduring changes in cellular function. Learning and memory require both short- and long-term changes at individual synapses between neurons.

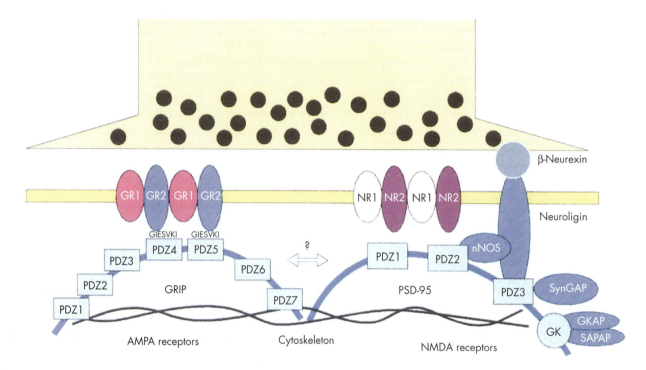

**FIGURE 1–11.** Some of the molecular components of a typical CNS glutamatergic synapse. α-Amino-3-hydroxy-5-methylisoxazole-4-propionic acid (AMPA) receptor subunits are tethered to GRIP through PDZ domain interactions, and the *N*-methyl-D-aspartate (NMDA) receptor subunits are bound to PSD-95. Both GRIP and PSD-95 also interact with the cytoskeleton, providing a protein scaffold for glutamate receptors in the postsynaptic density. This scaffold may regulate the dynamic, activity-dependent insertion or removal of glutamate receptors from CNS synapses. Abbreviations: GIESVKI=the amino acids critical for binding GR2 to PDZ4 and PDZ5; nNOS=neuronal nitric oxide synthase.

*Source.* O'Brien RJ, Lau L-F, Huganir RL: "Molecular Mechanisms of Glutamate Receptor Clustering at Excitatory Synapses." *Current Opinion in Neurobiology* 8:364–369, 1998. Used with permission.

## Simple Learning in *Aplysia*

Investigations using the marine mollusk *Aplysia californica* have been fundamental to current understanding of the cellular mechanisms of learning and memory. The 2000 Nobel Prize in Physiology or Medicine was awarded to Eric Kandel for this work. Because its nervous system is composed of relatively few neurons that are identifiable from animal to animal, changes in *Aplysia* behavior can be traced to alterations in individual synaptic connections (Kandel and Hawkins 1992). *Aplysia* exhibits a simple defensive behavior, the gill-withdrawal reflex, that shows several elementary forms of learning. Mild stimulation to the siphon skin overlying the gill leads to its reflex withdrawal. If a shock is delivered to the tail, the reflex shows sensitization; subsequent siphon stimulation elicits a more brisk reflex. If siphon stimulation is paired with tail shock, the animal shows associative learning manifested in an increased reflex response to the mild siphon stimulation. In effect, *Aplysia* learns that mild siphon stimulation predicts tail shock.

Sensitizing stimuli to the tail activate serotonergic facilitator neurons that synapse on sensory neuron terminals. The serotonin released produces presynaptic facilitation by activating adenylyl cyclase via a G protein link; cAMP binds to the regulatory subunits of cAMP-dependent protein kinase, releasing the catalytic subunits, which phosphorylate a class of voltage-dependent K$^+$ channels (S-K$^+$ channels) and inactivate them. Because less K$^+$ current is evoked, the membrane remains depolarized a bit longer with a given action potential, there is more Ca$^{2+}$ influx, and thus more transmitter is released. Associative learning appears to be due to facilitator neuron activation closely following sensory neuron activation. The spike-triggered Ca$^{2+}$ influx in the sensory neuron terminal and serotonin-activated second-messenger systems, when activated together, produce enhanced C kinase activity (Braha et al. 1990). This is termed activity-dependent enhancement of presynaptic facilitation, and it provides the coincidence detection inherent in associative learning (Figure 1–12). In all of these short-term forms of learning, the mechanisms involve covalent modification of existing proteins, principally by phosphorylation.

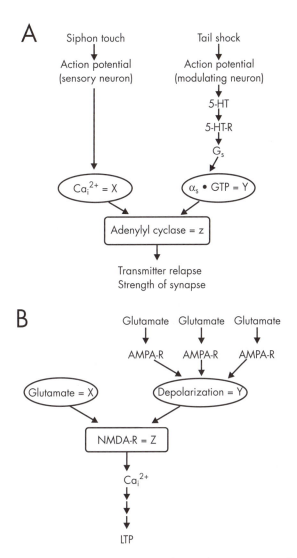

**FIGURE 1–12.** Molecular coincidence detectors. *Panel A.* In the *Aplysia* gill withdrawal reflex, siphon touch, which leads to $Ca^{2+}$ influx, and tail shock, which leads to stimulation of adenylyl cyclase, can together induce a greater activation of adenylyl cyclase and greater transmitter release, leading to enhanced synaptic efficacy. *Panel B.* In the hippocampus, long-term potentiation results from the coincident activation of *N*-methyl-D-aspartate (NMDA) receptors (NMDA-R) and postsynaptic depolarization. Abbreviations: AMPA-R=α-amino-3-hydroxy-5-methylisoxazole-4-propionic acid receptor; GTP=guanosine triphosphate; 5-HT= 5-hydroxytryptamine; 5-HT-R=5-HT receptor; LTP=long-term potentiation; $Ca_i^{2+}$=internal calcium; $G_s$=G protein; $\alpha_s$=alpha subunit.

*Source.* Reprinted from Bourne HR, Nicoll R: "Molecular Machines Integrate Coincident Synaptic Signals." *Neuron* 10 (suppl):65–75, 1993. Used with permission.

In contrast, long-term memory requires changes in gene transcription. The same mechanisms that mediate short-term sensitization also initiate long-term memory formation. In long-term as in short-term sensitization, the memory is encoded by a strengthening of sensorimotor synapses. There is increased transmitter release, and S-$K^+$ channels are closed, leading to increased $Ca^{2+}$ influx. Serotonin and cAMP are the first and second messengers, and a characteristic set of proteins are phosphorylated (Sweatt and Kandel 1989). For long-term memory, however, there is an absolute requirement for gene transcription and the synthesis of new proteins. cAMP affects gene transcription by binding to the cAMP-response element binding protein (CREB), which then binds to regulatory sites on DNA known as the cAMP-response element. Thus, injection of exogenous CREB blocks long-term but not short-term sensitization (Dash et al. 1990). CREB in turn induces ubiquitin transcription, which leads to the cleavage of the regulatory subunit of cAMP-dependent protein kinase and an enduring upregulation of the kinase (Hegde et al. 1993). Ultimately, the changes triggered by repeated tail stimulation, activation of facilitatory interneurons, serotonin application, or cAMP injection lead to specific structural changes (Glanzman et al. 1990) involving the growth of new processes and increased numbers and size of synapses. These morphological changes are mediated in part by cell adhesion molecules, akin to ones that play crucial roles in the assembly of the nervous system (Bailey et al. 1992). Thus, short-term changes in synaptic strength translate into enduring structural changes orchestrated by interactions among second-messenger systems in turn inducing gene transcription.

## Long-Term Potentiation in the Mammalian CNS

In the mammalian CNS, a similar increase in synaptic strength occurs in the hippocampus when certain synapses are stimulated briefly at high frequency; this increase lasts for days to weeks in the intact animal (Bliss and Lomo 1973). Because this long-term potentiation (LTP) occurs in brain regions critical to the encoding of memory—the hippocampus and cerebral cortex—LTP is thought to be a crucial synaptic process for memory formation. The three major synaptic circuits in the hippocampus show LTP, each with distinct but shared mechanisms. At the most studied synapse between CA3 and CA1 pyramidal neurons (Figure 1–13), LTP is initiated by $Ca^{2+}$ influx into the postsynaptic neuron (Figures 1–12B, 1–13). Glutamate released by CA3 neurons acts on NMDA and non-NMDA receptors. However, only high-frequency firing (that triggers LTP) activates sufficient numbers of AMPA receptors to cause a significant postsynaptic depolarization and to relieve the voltage-dependent $Mg^{2+}$ block of the NMDA receptors. NMDA receptors then facilitate $Ca^{2+}$ influx into the postsynaptic dendritic spine (Murphy et al. 1994; Petrozzino et al.

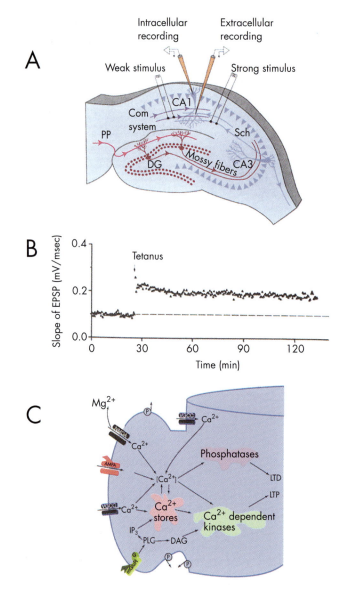

**FIGURE 1–13.** Long-term potentiation (LTP) in the hippocampus. *Panel A.* Typical recording paradigm for LTP at the CA3-CA1 synapse in the hippocampus. Transverse slices are used from rodent hippocampus. Two nonoverlapping inputs to pyramidal neurons in CA1 are stimulated with extracellular stimulating electrodes—one pathway is stimulated with high intensity and the other with lower intensity. Postsynaptic responses are recorded either intracellularly from CA1 pyramidal neurons or extracellularly from the CA1 region. *Panel B.* After high-frequency stimulation (tetanus) of inputs to CA1, or coincident presynaptic stimulation and postsynaptic depolarization, long-term enhancement of responses in CA1 neurons is recorded. This panel shows the slope of the excitatory postsynaptic potential before and after stimulation. The postsynaptic response is dramatically increased after tetanus in response to the same magnitude stimulus. *Panel C.* A schematic illustrating the molecular events required for LTP and long-term depression (LTD). This diagram shows the effects of increased calcium in a postsynaptic dendritic spine in response to LTP or LTD-inducing stimuli. After depolarization removes the $Mg^{2+}$ block, *N*-methyl-D-aspartate (NMDA) channels open to allow $Ca^{2+}$ influx. Calcium also enters from voltage-gated calcium channels (VGCCs) and some α-amino-3-hydroxy-5-methylisoxazole-4-propionic acid (AMPA) receptors. Activation of metabotropic glutamate receptors also contributes to an increase in intracellular $Ca^{2+}$ through $Ca^{2+}$ release from intracellular stores stimulated by phospholipase C (PLC) activation and a subsequent increase in inositol triphosphate ($IP_3$). Activation of particular kinases facilitates the induction and expression of LTP, whereas activation of phosphatases predisposes the cell to express LTD. Abbreviations: DAG=diacylglycerol; EPSP=excitatory postsynaptic potential; G=G protein; mGluR=metabotropic glutamate receptor.

*Source.* Reprinted from Beggs JM, Brown TH, Byrne JH, et al.: "Learning and Memory: Basic Mechanisms," in *Fundamental Neuroscience.* Edited by Zigmond MJ et al. San Diego, CA, Academic Press, 1999, pp. 1439, 1444. Used with permission.

1995), which initiates an enhancement in synaptic strength. Because $Ca^{2+}$ does not flow through the NMDA receptor channel unless neurotransmitter is bound and the postsynaptic membrane is simultaneously depolarized, the NMDA receptor acts as a coincidence detector (Figure 1–12).

The cellular mechanisms that underlie the expression of LTP have been the focus of intense investigation—they appear to involve increased neurotransmitter release and/or an increase in the number and/or sensitivity of postsynaptic receptors (Malenka and Nicoll 1999). Although there is increasingly compelling support for a postsynaptic locus for LTP expression (described below), there is also compelling evidence that LTP involves increased release of neurotransmitter from presynaptic terminals (Stevens and Sullivan 1998; Stevens and Wang 1995). In the latter case, the question arises, how could postsynaptic events triggered by NMDA receptor activation lead to changes in presynaptic neurotransmitter release? A retrograde second messenger that could diffuse across the synapse and act on the presynaptic terminal seems to be required (O'Dell et al. 1994; Schuman and Madison 1991; Zhuo et al. 1993). Several experiments indicate that NO or CO may convey such a retrograde signal, diffusing from postsynaptic to nearby presynaptic sites, and activate guanylyl cyclase to induce an elevation in cGMP in the presynaptic terminal. Such an LTP-dependent increase in synaptic transmission has been visualized directly (Malgaroli et al. 1995). This enhancement in transmitter release is also $Ca^{2+}$ dependent, implying a presynaptic coincidence detector (Zhuo et al. 1994). In addition to diffusible gases, a family of growth factors called the neurotrophins has been shown recently to act as retrograde signals to facilitate long-term synaptic strengthening, including LTP (McAllister et al. 1999).

Over the last few years, the evidence supporting a postsynaptic locus for LTP expression has become overwhelming (Malinow et al. 2000). There are currently two favored mechanisms for increasing synaptic efficacy postsynaptically: 1) changing the sensitivity of exsisting glutamate receptors, and 2) adding AMPA receptors to functionally silent synapses. The elevation in postsynaptic $Ca^{2+}$ levels due to high-frequency synaptic transmission activates several kinases that are crucial for LTP and memory: $Ca^{2+}$/calmodulin-dependent kinase II (CamKII), protein kinase C (PKC), and protein kinase A. These kinases phosphorylate GluR1, an AMPA receptor subunit, increasing the sensitivity of these receptors, as blocking this phosphorylation blocks expression of LTP (H.K. Lee et al. 2000). Consistent with a critical role for kinases in LTP, mice deficient in CamKII show reduced LTP as well as deficits in spatial learning (Bach et al. 1995). Gene-knockout approaches, in which mutant animals are generated with defects in a targeted gene and then bred to homozygosity to fully eliminate the given protein, show that other kinases are required for LTP (Mayford and Kandel 1999). For instance, Fyn kinase knockout mice are deficient in LTP in CA1. Probing the substrates for Fyn kinase shows that there is a deficiency in the phosphorylation of focal adhesion tyrosine kinase (Grant et al. 1995). This finding suggests that cell adhesion processes of the sort that are important in development are required for the consolidation of this memory process.

Recently, several laboratories have shown that *silent synapses*—synapses that contain only NMDA receptors before induction of LTP—may be activated by stimulation-dependent insertion of new AMPA receptors, providing a novel mechanism for LTP (Malinow et al. 2000). Increases in AMPA-receptor function at previously silent synapses after LTP-inducing stimuli have been observed by many laboratories. Most importantly, this process has been visualized directly by imaging the insertion of AMPA receptors, tagged with the green fluorescent protein, into silent synapses after LTP induction (Shi et al. 1999). Research in this field is now focusing on the intracellular mechanisms of AMPA receptor trafficking and promises soon to yield a comprehensive understanding of the molecular mechanisms underlying postsynaptic modifications in LTP.

LTP is composed of at least two phases: early LTP and late LTP. Early LTP lasts for the first 3 hours after induction and does not require protein synthesis. In contrast, late LTP lasts for several hours and does require both new transcription and translation. As described above for long-term synaptic enhancement in *Aplysia*, late LTP involves activation of CamKII, production of cAMP, and activation of gene transcription through a CREB-dependent process. Recent evidence indicates that LTP can also stimulate the growth of new synaptic connections, which could mediate more permanent synaptic alterations underlying learning and memory (Engert and Bonhoeffer 1999; Toni et al. 1999).

How is the strengthening of synapses by LTP kept in check? Hippocampal synapses also show long-term depression (LTD), which involves a similar array of mechanisms activated by low-frequency synaptic activation (Linden and Connor 1995). LTD results in a decrease in synaptic strength and may be mediated by a decrease in neurotransmitter release and/or a decrease in postsynaptic responsiveness from lowered numbers or sensitivity of glutamate receptors. Thus, through a dynamic balance between LTP and LTD (Zhuo et al.

1994), memories of irrelevant information may be eliminated and lasting memories fine-tuned. The regulation of synaptic strength can also be tied to the predominant theta rhythm in the hippocampus. Stimulation at the theta frequency produces LTP, whereas slower stimulation associated with more moderate $Ca^{2+}$ increases leads to LTD. The theta frequency appears to be under cholinergic control, suggesting a mechanism by which acetylcholine may modulate memory (Huerta and Lisman 1993). More generally, Llinás and colleagues argue that the theta rhythm mediates thalamocortical integration, the disruption of which is associated with impaired mentation in a range of neuropsychiatric disorders (Llinás et al. 1999).

## Development of Neurons

How neurons are able to modify the strength of their connections with experience reflects only a fraction of the mechanisms harnessed during CNS development (Figure 1–14). If synaptic modification in the adult resembles or utilizes developmental mechanisms, other forms of plasticity may exist in the adult that are vestiges of developmental processes. For example, during development certain neurons undergo genetically programmed cell death, known as apoptosis, which is apparently triggered by a process of competition for one or more survival factors. Neuropsychiatric disorders may result from aberrant activation of such mechanisms (Nijhawan et al. 2000). In acquired or genetically based neurodegenerative diseases, a cell death program could be inappropriately activated in a specific cell population. In diseases as varied as Alzheimer's disease, Huntington's disease, amyotrophic lateral sclerosis, epilepsy, and stroke, specific neurons are selectively vulnerable to apoptosis, thereby echoing a mechanism normally utilized during brain development. Other disorders, such as autism, may be explained by a failure of programmed cell death during development (Piven et al. 1995). Several developmental disorders result from aberrant growth or migration of neurons or defective synapse formation. For example, schizophrenia may result from the failure of mesocortical dopaminergic neurons to make appropriate connections with frontal cortical neurons (Weinberger and Lipska 1995) or from the aberrant migration of cortical neurons (Akbarian et al. 1993). These two defects may be related by the observations that dopamine plays a role in both neuronal migration and differentiation (Todd 1992). Consequently, insight into developmental mechanisms is likely to be fundamental to gaining insight into the etiology of neuropsychiatric disorders.

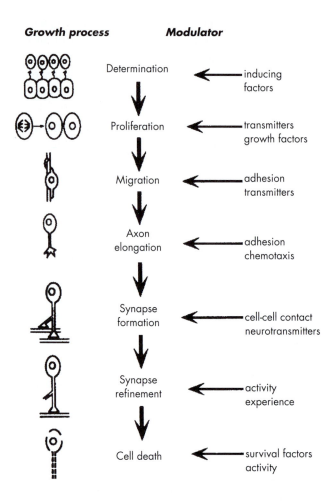

**FIGURE 1–14.** Stages of neuronal development and their modulation. At each stage, neurodevelopment is regulated by local environmental factors and at later stages also by activity. This form of assembly provides the plasticity to accommodate individual variation, both intrinsic and experiential. Because of the interplay between intrinsic factors and experience, there are multiple points at which pathologic alterations in intrinsic factors or experience may alter the outcome in subtle or dramatic ways.
*Source.* Rayport S, Kriegstein AR: "Cellular and Molecular Biology of the Neuron," in *The American Psychiatric Press Textbook of Neuropsychiatry*, 3rd Edition. Edited by Yudofsky SC, Hales RE. Washington, DC, American Psychiatric Press, 1997, p. 19. Used with permission.

## Birth and Migration

Neurons and glia arise in proliferative zones lining the embryonic neural tube at the stage of folding of the head segments and expansion of the ventricular cavities. Superficially, the proliferative neuroepithelial cells in these zones appear quite similar, but as development proceeds they generate the most diverse number of phenotypically, chemically, and molecularly distinct cell types of any organ in the adult animal, all organized into the most complex structure found in living things. The precise position and connectivity of each of the myriad cell types is critical to the functioning of the whole organism.

How neurons arrive at their appropriate locations and form appropriate connections is incompletely understood. Theoretically, the specific fate of each cell could be intrinsically determined solely by its lineage history, as appears to be the case in certain invertebrates such as the worm *Caenorhabditis elegans* (Kenyon 1986). Lineage studies in vertebrates, however, demonstrate that local environmental factors significantly influence the ultimate phenotype, location, and connectivity of individual neurons (Lumsden and Krumlauf 1996; Rubenstein et al. 1998). The molecular signals that influence cell fate are diverse and developmentally regulated and include diffusible factors and cell surface recognition molecules.

## Determination

The early stages of development of the CNS involve a series of inductive steps in which diffusible factors produced by neighboring tissues trigger specific patterns of gene expression in neural tissue. The process of CNS development begins with induction of the neural ectoderm during gastrulation, triggered by the release of an inducing factor from the adjacent mesoderm (Hamburger 1969). Once the neural plate is formed, a pattern of regional differences emerges under the control of diffusible or contact-mediated inducing factors produced by surrounding tissues. For example, in chicken embryos, the notochord induces development of the floor plate by a cell contact–dependent signal and subsequently triggers the production of motor neurons by release of a diffusible factor (Placzek et al. 1993; Yamada et al. 1993). The proper patterning of the neural plate likely involves the interaction of multiple inducing factors from several sources to establish regional differences along the anteroposterior, mediolateral, and dorsoventral axes (Ruiz i Altaba 1994).

Early in brain development, the neuraxis becomes partitioned into compartments. Segmentation is an ancient and ubiquitous principle of organization expressed in all embryos and evident in the body plan of many invertebrates. Recently, genes have been identified that govern the development of specific body segments. For example, the identity of segments in the insect body plan, and in the mammalian hindbrain, is controlled by the expression of a family of segment identity genes, known collectively as homeobox or Hox genes (Maconochie et al. 1996). The Hox genes encode transcription factors that in turn regulate other genes that determine the unique development of each segment. The Hox genes can alter the identity of the corresponding

segments in both insects and vertebrates and induce the development of supernumerary segments when artificially inserted into embryos (Rijli et al. 1993). In a remarkable instance of evolutionary conservation, homologues of insect Hox genes have been found in all vertebrates, including humans (McGinnis and Krumlauf 1992); it has even been possible to successfully replace a fruit fly segment-polarity gene with the homologous gene, known as sonic hedgehog, found in zebra fish (Krauss et al. 1993). As development proceeds, new compartments arise as segments become progressively subdivided. Segmentation in the vertebrate nervous system is clearly visible in the spinal cord and also in the segmental pattern of rhombomeres in the developing hindbrain (Lumsden and Krumlauf 1996; Tanabe and Jessell 1996). At first glance, the forebrain lacks the segmental appearance of more caudal CNS regions, but the forebrain is also segmentally organized, and at least 30 Hox genes have now been identified that are regionally expressed in the mouse forebrain (Rubenstein et al. 1998). These studies demonstrate that the embryonic neural axis is divided into a precise pattern of segments with boundaries that restrict intersegmental mixing of neuroepithelial cells and commit their descendants to a particular segmental fate.

## Proliferation

As neurogenesis proceeds, neuroepithelial precursor cells in the proliferative zones lining the cerebral ventricles divide to produce cortical neurons. Within a region of cortex, neurons sharing the same birthday generally follow the same pattern of differentiation and populate the same layer of cortex. Nonetheless, multiple epigenetic influences are involved in determining the ultimate fate of each individual neuron. Lineage studies with replication-incompetent retroviruses have been used to map the fates of the descendants of individual cortical precursor cells. Labeled clonal descendants sometimes include widely dispersed cells that populate different brain regions and occupy multiple cortical layers (Grove et al. 1993; Mione et al. 1994; C. Walsh and Cepko 1993). Similarly, results of experiments with chimeric mice argue against strict lineage-dependent mechanisms for regional or laminar specification (Crandall and Herrup 1990; Fishell et al. 1990; Goldowitz 1989). However, cortical cells do become committed to a laminar fate at the time of their final cell division, before they migrate out of the proliferative zone. In heterochronic transplant experiments, McConnell (1988) transplanted ventricular-zone cells from an embryo where cells destined for deep layers were being generated into older host brains where cells destined for superficial layers were being generated and challenged them to change their laminar fate. Cells could adopt a host-appropriate laminar fate if transplanted before, but not after, the final round of cell division.

Neuroepithelial cells can alter their proliferative activity in response to local signaling factors, including amino acid neurotransmitters. During early stages of cerebral cortical development, progenitor cells in the ventricular zone already express specific receptor subtypes for the transmitters GABA and glutamate (LoTurco et al. 1991, 1995). During later stages of corticogenesis, activation of these receptors by endogenously released neurotransmitter inhibits DNA synthesis and decreases the number of precursor cells entering the DNA synthesis phase of the cell cycle (LoTurco et al. 1995). Some evidence also suggests that certain growth factors may regulate neurogenesis. For example, basic fibroblast growth factor receptors are expressed on embryonic neuroepithelial cells (Reid et al. 1990), and basic fibroblast growth factor stimulates neuronal precursor cell division (Gensburger et al. 1987). The neuronal circuits that regulate the activity of precursor cell populations in the CNS are just beginning to be explored.

## Migration

Having completed their final cell divisions, neurons migrate to their definitive locations, guided by physical and chemical signals (Figure 1–15). In cortex, for example, during development a temporary scaffolding of radial glial cells is established that appears to be fundamental to the later columnar organization of the cortex (Rakic 1988). When cells complete their final division, they attach to these glial guides via cell adhesion molecules, such as astrotactin (Hatten 1993), and move from the ventricular and subventricular zones to the superficial surface of the cortex (Figure 1–15). The movement of neurons along glial fibers appears to be regulated by diffusible signals, such as glutamate acting at NMDA receptors on the surface of migrating neurons (Komuro and Rakic 1993). In addition to radial migration of neurons from ventricular zones to the pial surface, neurons can also migrate tangentially in parallel to the pial surface. In the cerebral cortex, pyramidal neurons migrate radially from the ventricular zone to their specific layer within the cortical plate (Rakic 1978). In contrast, a large fraction of GABAergic neurons are born in the subcortical ganglionic eminence of the telencephalon and migrate tangentially into the cortical plate (Anderson et al. 1997).

Embryonic cortical development occurs in two stages (Marin-Padilla 1992). The earliest-generated neu-

rons are a transitory cell population. They form the first cortical layer, called the primordial plexiform layer, or preplate. The second stage of cortical development begins when cortical neurons born in the periventricular germinal zone migrate into the preplate, effectively splitting this layer into two parts. Later-arriving neurons bypass earlier arrivals so that the cortical layers develop in an inside-out pattern (Rakic 1974). As the cortex grows in thickness, early neurons continue to form the boundary layers above and below the developing cortical plate, known as the marginal zone and the subplate, respectively. The largest cells of the embryonic marginal zone are the Cajal-Retzius cells. Like many other cell types of the marginal and subplate zones, the Cajal-Retzius cells appear to undergo programmed cell death in early postnatal stages after cortical lamination has been established (Mienville 1999).

Several recent findings support the importance of the marginal zone and subplate cells in helping to organize corticogenesis. The first synapses to form during cortical development are located in the marginal zone and subplate. In the visual cortex, subplate cells send the first axons from cortex to the lateral geniculate nucleus of the thalamus. They, in turn, receive synaptic contacts from lateral geniculate nucleus axons before these axons reach their cortical targets in layer 4 (Allendoerfer and Shatz 1994). Because ablating the subplate cells early prevents lateral geniculate nucleus axons from entering the cortex (Ghosh et al. 1990), and ablating them later prevents ocular dominance columns from forming (Ghosh and Shatz 1992), these cells appear to be critical for patterning thalamocortical connections.

An important clue concerning the importance of marginal zone cells in regulating migration in laminar brain structures has been provided by studies of the mutant mouse *reeler*. In *reeler* mice, an error in the molecular mechanisms governing migration results in abnormal cortical layering (Caviness 1982). The first stage of corticogenesis proceeds normally, and a normal-appearing preplate is formed. However, when migrating neurons reach the cortical plate, they fail to bypass earlier arrivals, and the cortex develops in an outside-in or inverted pattern. The wild-type gene at the *reeler* locus has now been identified. The gene encodes a protein, reelin (D'Arcangelo et al. 1995), that has no transmembrane domains and is thus likely to be an extracellular protein; histologic studies have localized reelin to the external surfaces of Cajal-Retzius cells (Ogawa et al. 1995). These findings underscore the importance of the transient cells of the primordial plexiform layer in establishing cortical lamination.

In addition to *reelin*, a number of other genes have

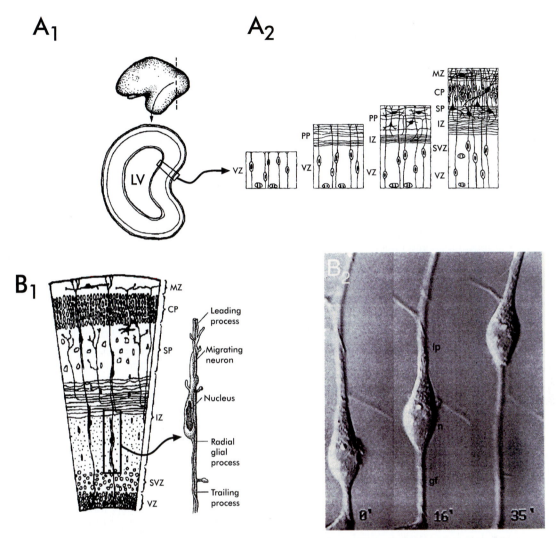

**FIGURE 1–15.**   Neuronal migration and cortical development. *Panel A₁.* A cross-section of the developing cerebral cortex illustrating the ventricular zone (VZ) lining the ventricle (LV) where all cortical neurons are born. *Panel A₂.* As development proceeds (from left to right), the earliest-born neurons migrate from the VZ to form the preplate (PP). Later-born neurons, destined to form the cortical plate (CP), migrate from the ventricular zone through the intermediate zone (IZ) and split the preplate into the marginal zone (MZ) and subplate (SP). The cortical plate will ultimately develop multiple layers as new neurons are added. The subventricular zone (SVZ) is the chief source of glial cells in cortex. *Panel B₁.* Most newborn neurons migrate along radial glial fibers. The migratory neuron is characterized by a leading process with filopodia, a trailing process, and a nucleus pushed back toward the trailing end of the cell body. Neurons generated from a single precursor cell can sometimes be dispersed tangentially in the cortex, suggesting that nonradial neuronal migration also occurs during cortical development. *Panel B₂.* Developing neurons and glia recombined in culture show migration profiles. Successive frames at about 15-minute intervals are shown of a migrating hippocampal neuron. The neuron (n) moves in a stop-and-go fashion along the radial glial fiber (gf). A leading process (lp) extending above the cell has numerous highly active filopodial extensions. Both a trailing process and a posteriorly displaced nucleus are also evident. Neurons will migrate on glia from different brains, suggesting that there is a shared molecular recognition system throughout the brain used in guiding migration.

*Source.*   Panel A₁ and left side of Panel B₁ reprinted with permission from Rakic P: "Radial Unit Hypothesis of Cerebral Cortical Evolution." *Experimental Brain Research* 21 (suppl):25–43, 1991; Panel A₂ reprinted from Uylings HBM, Van Eden CG, Parnavelas JG, et al.: "The Prenatal and Postnatal Development of the Rat Cerebral Cortex," in *The Cerebral Cortex of the Rat.* Edited by Kolb B, Tees RC. Cambridge, MA, MIT Press, 1990, pp. 35–76; right side of Panel B₁ reprinted from Rakic P: "Mode of Cell Migration to the Superficial Layers of Fetal Monkey Neocortex." *Journal of Comparative Neurology* 145:61–83, 1972, copyright John Wiley and Sons; Panel B₂ reprinted from Hatten ME: "Riding the Glial Monorail: A Common Mechanism for Glial-Guided Neuronal Migration in Different Regions of the Developing Mammalian Brain." *Trends in Neurosciences* 13:179–184, 1990. Used with permission.

recently been implicated in neuronal migration, including the mouse disabled gene (*mdab1*), the VLDL and ApoE2 receptors, cyclin-dependent kinase-5 (cdk5), p35, astrotactin, β1 integrin, α3 integrin, and neuregulin (reviewed in C.A. Walsh 2000). Deletion of some of these genes is associated with mild to devastating neurodevelopmental disorders in humans (C.A. Walsh 2000; C.A. Walsh and Goffinet 2000). Mutations in the gene encoding filamin cause human X-linked periventricular heterotopia, resulting in the formation of islands of ectopic neurons near the ventricles, and mild cognitive impairment. Filamin is an actin cross-linking phosphoprotein and is required for locomotion of many cell types. Mutation of LIS1 is associated with type 1 lissencephaly in humans and causes cortical, hippocampal, and olfactory bulb disorganization in mice (C.A. Walsh and Goffinet 2000) with severe cognitive consequences. These disorders highlight the neuronal migration process as the prime pathological substrate for cortical developmental disorders.

## Neuronal Differentiation

Having migrated to their definitive locations, neurons begin to elaborate processes. During several days to weeks, each neuron elaborates a characteristic dendritic arbor and a highly specific axonal projection pattern. Neuronal differentiation is critical for proper brain functioning, as the structure of the neuron determines the number and types of inputs the cell receives as well as the number and types of cells it contacts. Neurite outgrowth is mediated by specialized structures called growth cones, which form at the tips of extending processes. Growth cones control the insertion of new membrane elements into the cell membrane, release proteolytic enzymes to open pathways through the extracellular matrix, and extend finer processes (filopodia) that guide the growing process to its proper target (Purves and Lichtman 1985; Suter and Forscher 2000). Axonal growth cones may move as much as 1 mm per day. As they advance, a cytoskeleton of microtubules and neurofilaments forms in the elongating process. In addition to maintaining the structure of the growing process, these cytoskeletal elements also convey necessary membrane and structural proteins from synthetic sites in the cell body to the newly generating process and convey trophic substances back to the cell body.

Axon guidance is controlled by a large number of signals that fall primarily into four categories: chemoattraction or chemorepulsion and contact attraction or repulsion (Figure 1–16). Initially, growth cones depend on the intrinsic adhesiveness of neighboring cells. Later, they are

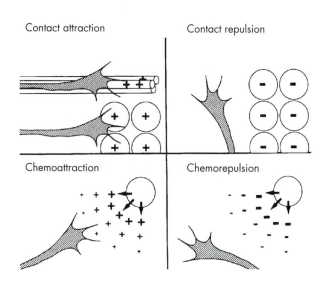

**FIGURE 1–16.** Forces involved in axon guidance. Proper guidance of axons to their targets involves the coordinate action of four types of guidance cues: contact attraction, contact repulsion, chemoattraction, and chemorepulsion. There are both short-range (contact) and long-range (chemo) cues that can act to either inhibit/repel or attract axonal growth cones.

*Source.* Goodman CS, Tessier-Lavigne M: "Molecular Mechanisms of Axon Guidance and Target Recognition," in *Molecular and Cellular Approaches to Neural Development.* Edited by Cowan WM, Jessell TM, Zipursky SL. New York, Oxford University Press, 1997, p 114. Used with permission.

guided by their targets or by intermediate guidepost cells. Appropriate targets may express adhesion molecules or release diffusible chemoattractant factors, whereas inappropriate targets may provide contact-mediated or diffusible repulsive signals. The target ultimately validates correctly connected cells by providing trophic substances that support the survival of the innervating neurons. Cells that fail to make the appropriate connections undergo apoptosis (i.e., programmed cell death) for lack of such substances.

The formation of specific connections has been extensively studied in sensory neurons of grasshopper limbs. These cells are born in the periphery and subsequently send axons into the developing CNS (Goodman and Shatz 1993). The first neurons to send out processes form the pioneer fibers. Later-developing neurons are guided by adhesive interactions with pioneer fibers. Particular cells in the epithelium, called guidepost cells, serve as intermediate targets. The growth cones of pioneer fibers extend filopodia that transiently make gap junctional contacts with the guidepost cells, probably exchanging small molecules that act as intracellular regulators. If these filopodia are disrupted pharmacologically, growth continues, but in an undirected fashion (Bentley and Toroian-Raymond 1986). The pioneer fibers proceed from guidepost cell to guidepost cell until they reach their ultimate targets. Later, guidepost cells themselves develop into neurons, which send their own processes into the CNS, following the pioneer fibers they guided.

Recent work has shown that similar developmental mechanisms operate in the formation of the mammalian CNS. In developing spinal cord, commissural neurons in the dorsolateral spinal cord orient chemotactically to the floor plate in the ventral cord. On reaching the floor plate, the processes use it as a guidepost, changing direction and growing into the contralateral spinothalamic tract. Chemoattractant molecules, such as the netrins (Cook et al. 1998; Kennedy et al. 1994; Tear 1999), control this process. Similarly, in the developing brain stem after corticospinal pioneer fibers have extended into the spinal cord, secondary processes arise that innervate the pons under the control of a diffusible pons-derived chemoattractant (Sato et al. 1994).

As growth cones navigate through the brain, they rely on differential adhesion to the axons they contact for guidance. Several families of such neuronal cell adhesion molecules have been discovered, along with a diverse family of receptors for extracellular matrix molecules (Reichardt and Tomaselli 1991; F.S. Walsh and Doherty 1997). Particular forms of adhesion molecules are expressed by subsets of developing axons that fasciculate with each other to form bundles of axon fibers. Remarkably, neurons may selectively express adhesion molecules and receptors in certain regions of the axon and can turn their expression on and off at appropriate times. For example, in the developing spinal cord, commissural axons express certain glycoproteins on their processes as they grow toward and across the midline. These axons then switch to expressing different glycoproteins as they turn and follow longitudinal tracts on the contralateral side (Dodd et al. 1988; Tear 1999).

Developing neurons may rely on repulsive as well as attractive signals to reach their targets. Recently, an increasingly large number of these molecules have been characterized (Goodman 1996). For example, in the ventral floor plate of the developing neural tube in vertebrates and in the optic chiasm of mammals with binocular vision, those axons destined to cross the midline do so. Those not destined to cross behave as though they have encountered a repulsive signal; the leading growth cones collapse on reaching the midline and then turn away (Godement et al. 1990; Sretavan 1990). One attractive candidate for such a signal is the ephrin family of axon guidance molecules (Flanagan and Vanderhaeghen 1998; Nakagawa et al. 2000). Another family of repulsive factors is the semaphorins (Raper 2000); ingrowing sensory axons of the dorsal root ganglion are directed by repulsive signals mediated by the semaphorins (Messersmith et al. 1995). In addition, in the developing fruit fly, some axons of interneurons in each neuromere reach the midline and cross, whereas others turn away and remain uncrossed; these midline interactions appear to be mediated by interactions between the proteins encoded by the *robo* and *slit* gene families (Brose and Tessier-Lavigne 2000; Seeger 1994). To add even more complexity, it has recently been demonstrated that a single axon guidance molecule can act to attract or repel the same axon, depending on the local intracellular concentration of cAMP or cGMP in the growth cone (Song and Poo 1999).

## Synapse Formation

When the axonal growth cone reaches a target cell, a complex series of interactions commences, ultimately resulting in the formation of a synapse. Although there is still much to be learned about the formation of synapses in the CNS, the basic process of synaptogenesis at the neuromuscular junction (the synapse between a motor neuron and a muscle cell) has been well described (Figure 1–17). Both the motor neuron and the muscle fiber have the necessary molecular machinery prefabricated before synapse formation (J.R. Sanes and Lichtman 1999). The motor neuron growth cone functions like a protosynapse, showing activity-dependent neurotransmitter release, and noninnervated postsynaptic cells have transmitter receptors distributed over much of their surface. Within minutes of initial contact, a rudimentary form of synaptic transmission begins. Over subsequent days, connections become stronger and stabilize as the growth cone matures into a presynaptic terminal, gathering the cellular elements necessary for focused release of neurotransmitter at active zones. In parallel, the postsynaptic cell concentrates receptors at the site of contact, removing them from other regions, and, over the course of days, develops postsynaptic specializations (J.R. Sanes and Lichtman 1999).

Although this basic series of events is likely to model synapse formation between CNS neurons, there will certainly be dramatic differences because of the great diversity of CNS synapses. For CNS synapses to form, the major components of the synapse must be recruited to sites of physical contact between axons and dendrites. For instance, both presynaptic and postsynaptic hippocampal neurons contain some synaptic machinery before synapse formation. AMPA and NMDA receptors are present in dendrites and synaptic vesicle proteins are present in distal axons before contact (Craig et al. 1993;

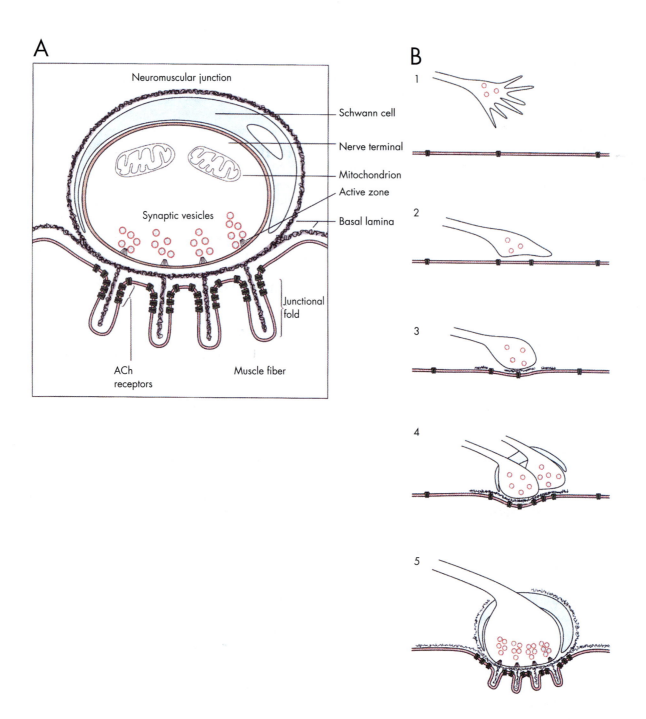

**FIGURE 1–17.** Synapse formation of the neuromuscular junction (NMJ). *Panel A.* Schematic view of the molecular components of a typical neuromuscular junction. At a mature NMJ, the presynaptic terminal is separated from the postsynaptic muscle cell by the synaptic cleft. Synaptic vesicles filled with acetylcholine are clustered at active zones, where they can fuse with the plasma membrane upon depolarization to release their transmitter into the synaptic cleft. Acetylcholine receptors are found postsynaptically, and glial cells called Schwann cells surround the synaptic terminal. *Panel B.* Stages in the formation of the NMJ. (1) An isolated growth cone from a motor neuron is guided to the muscle by axon guidance cues. (2) The first contact is an unspecialized physical contact. (3) However, synaptic vesicles rapidly cluster in the axon terminal, acetylcholine receptors start to cluster under the forming synapse, and a basal lamina is deposited in the synaptic cleft. (4) As development proceeds, multiple motor neurons innervate each muscle. (5) Over time, however, all of the axons except one are eliminated through an activity-dependent process, and the remaining terminal further differentiates.
*Source.* Reprinted from Kandel ER, Schwartz JH, Jessell TM: *Principles of Neural Science,* 4th Edition. New York, McGraw-Hill, 2000, p. 1088. Used with permission.

Fletcher et al. 1991; Kraszewski et al. 1995). Contact between presynaptic and postsynaptic neurons is followed by recruitment of synaptic vesicles to new synapses within hours of contact (Ahmari et al. 2000). Through unknown mechanisms, contact between axon and dendrite results in clustering of glutamate receptors at synaptic sites on the postsynaptic cell (Craig et al. 1993). In low-density cultures of hippocampal neurons, NMDA receptors, AMPA receptors, and postsynaptic scaffolding proteins accumulate in synapses with distinct time courses, implying that they are targeted to synapses by different mechanisms (Friedman et al. 2000; Rao et al. 1998). Several independent groups have demonstrated that NMDA receptors are expressed before AMPA receptors at newly formed hippocampal synapses and that, as development proceeds, AMPA receptors accumulate gradually in these synapses (Isaac et al. 1997; Liao et al. 1999; Petralia et al. 1999; Wu et al. 1996). However, other investigators have separately shown the opposite result—that AMPA receptors are the first to cluster at hippocampal synapses, followed by NMDA receptors and scaffolding proteins (Friedman et al. 2000; Rao et al. 1998). The precise timing of insertion of AMPA and NMDA receptors has significant implications for mechanisms of synaptic strengthening during cortical development, as the two receptor types mediate quite different forms of synaptic plasticity (Kim and Huganir 1999).

## Neuronal Maturation and Survival

Maturation of the postsynaptic cell requires de novo protein synthesis, as do learning-dependent, long-term changes in the adult CNS. Immediate–early response genes (IEGs) (Morgan and Curran 1989) are among the first genes activated by postsynaptic depolarization, stimulated by elevations in $Ca^{2+}$, cAMP, cGMP, inositol triphosphate ($IP_3$), or diacylglycerol (DAG). The prototype of this family of proto-oncogenes is *c-fos*. Transcription of IEGs leads to the synthesis of proteins (e.g., fos) that modulate or induce transcription of other genes that directly or indirectly induce structural changes in the cell. For instance, nerve growth factor (NGF) synthesis may be controlled by *c-fos* transcription; lesions of the sciatic nerve lead to a rapid increase in levels of fos, which binds to the transcription initiation site for NGF and causes NGF production (Hengerer et al. 1990). Long-term sensitization in *Aplysia* (Barzilai et al. 1989), hippocampal LTP (Cole et al. 1989; Wisden et al. 1990), and structural plasticity of dendrites (Lyford et al. 1995) are associated with the specific activation of IEGs.

Interactions between presynaptic and postsynaptic neurons can act to enhance and modulate their differen-

tiation. For example, secretion of trophic factors by postsynaptic cells can determine whether innervating presynaptic neurons survive or undergo apoptosis. More subtle regulation of presynaptic cell differentiation occurs as well. In the developing sympathetic nervous system, young neurons are exclusively noradrenergic before synapse formation. Depending on the target tissue, they may be induced to become cholinergic, retaining only traces of the noradrenergic phenotype (Landis 1990). This target-dependent effect is mediated by the release of a soluble cholinergic differentiation factor by the postsynaptic cells. Once synaptic contact is established, cholinergic activation of the postsynaptic cell by presynaptic spikes suppresses the release of cholinergic differentiation factor. Thus, synapse formation may trigger far-reaching changes, both presynaptically and postsynaptically, extending to the choice of neurotransmitter by a presynaptic neuron.

In many areas of the vertebrate nervous system, neurons are initially produced in excess. To survive, many neurons must receive an adequate supply of one or more trophic factors produced by their target neurons. Competition for limited supplies of these factors ensures that surviving neurons will be correctly connected and that the number of neurons will be matched to the size of the target. In general, cells deprived of neurotrophic factors undergo apoptosis, a genetically programmed form of cell death characterized by cytoplasmic shrinkage, chromatin condensation, and degradation of DNA into oligonucleosomal fragments (Edwards et al. 1991). Unlike necrosis, this process does not stimulate an inflammatory response. Apoptosis is an active process that requires RNA and protein synthesis (Oppenheim et al. 1991; Scott and Davies 1990). Data are accumulating to support the remarkable hypothesis that apoptosis is the default program for most cells and that widespread cell suicide is prevented only by the continual presence of survival signals that suppress the intrinsic cell death program (Raff 1992). The best-studied neuronal example is the dependence of sympathetic and sensory neurons on NGF, which is produced by the target tissue. Although approximately half of the sympathetic neurons normally undergo apoptosis, exogenously applied NGF prevents most of the cells from dying; in contrast, neutralizing antibodies to NGF produce widespread sympathetic cell death (Raff et al. 1993).

Several families of growth factors and their receptors have been identified (Figure 1–18), including the neurotrophins that bind to members of the Trk family of receptor tyrosine kinases (Bothwell 1991; Chao 1992; Glass and Yancopoulos 1993). These include NGF, brain-derived neurotrophic factor, and neurotrophins 3,

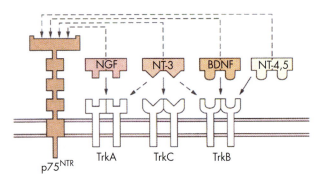

**FIGURE 1–18.** Neurotrophins exert their effects through binding to two types of receptors: the low-affinity nerve growth factor receptor, also called p75, and the high-affinity tyrosine kinase receptors, the Trk receptors. Nerve growth factor (NGF) binds primarily to TrkA, and brain-derived neurotrophic factor (BDNF) and neurotrophin-4 (NT-4) bind primarily to TrkB. The specificity of neurotrophin-3 (NT-3) is less precise. Although it mostly binds to TrkC, it can also bind TrkA and TrkB under some cellular contexts. In addition, all of the neurotrophins bind to p75.

*Source.* Adapted from Kandel ER, Schwartz JH, Jessell TM: *Principles of Neural Science,* 4th Edition. New York, McGraw-Hill, 2000, p. 1057. Used with permission.

4/5, and 6. Another family includes ciliary neurotrophic factor, growth-promoting activity, and leukemia inhibitory factor. Additional neurotrophic factors include basic fibroblast growth factor and glia cell line–derived neurotrophic factor. Transgenic mice with targeted null mutations in neurotrophic genes or their receptors have been produced and have abnormalities in selected populations of neurons (Davies 1994). Neuronal survival factors are not exclusively target derived, and sources also include innervating neurons, glial cells, and circulating hormones. Recently, the ability of trophic factors to promote neuronal survival has been attributed to the phosphatidylinositide 3′-OH kinase/c-Akt kinase cascade acting through at least two components of the intracellular cell death pathway, BAD and caspase-9, and the transcription factor NF-κB (Datta et al. 1999).

The cellular mechanisms of apoptosis appear to involve a complex interplay of several signaling cascades (Sastry and Rao 2000). In the worm C. *elegans, ced-3* and *ced-4* are required for apoptosis (Ellis et al. 1991). The gene product of *ced-3* is a cysteine protease and has a mammalian homologue called interleukin-1β converting enzyme (ICE). A large number of cysteine proteases have recently been discovered in many species that play diverse roles in cell death; these proteins are classified as members of the large caspase (for *c*ysteine-requiring *asp*artate prote*ase*) family of proteins (D.H. Sanes et al. 2000). Some of the caspases are considered the final effector proteins in the cell death cascade. In contrast to the cell death genes *ced-3* and *ced-4, ced-9* acts to prevent apoptosis in normally surviving C. *elegans* cells. A mutation in *ced-9* leads to widespread apoptosis and death of the embryo (Hengartner et al. 1992). The *ced-9* gene found in worms is homologous to the human oncogene *Bcl-2,* which is overexpressed in human B cell lymphomas (Tsujimoto et al. 1984). The human gene can block cell death in a variety of in vivo and in vitro systems and has been transferred to C. *elegans,* where, remarkably, it can substitute for *ced-9* and prevent apoptosis of C. *elegans* cells. In recent years, the family of Bcl-2-like proteins has grown dramatically. Although some of these proteins inhibit cell death, others can promote apoptosis. In general, results to date suggest that there may be several apoptotic pathways that may depend on the cell type and the inducing agent; however, most of these pathways appear to converge at the ICE/caspase step (D.H. Sanes et al. 2000). Although the precise steps in the cell death pathway remain unclear, the molecular mechanisms of apoptosis clearly have been conserved evolutionarily.

The molecular events that underlie apoptosis in neuronal and nonneuronal cells are likely to include an array of initiators, mediators, and inhibitors, but several common features are emerging. There is evidence that reactive oxygen species can trigger apoptosis in neurons (Greenlund et al. 1995), and *Bcl-2* may prevent apoptosis by suppressing production of free radicals (Hockenbery et al. 1993; Kane et al. 1993). This hypothesis has led to attempts to use antioxidants and inhibitors of free-radical production as therapeutic agents in several neurodegenerative diseases, trauma, and stroke. For example, superoxide dismutase (a free-radical scavenger) protects neurons from ischemic injury. Transgenic mice that overexpress superoxide dismutase have smaller infarcts after arterial occlusion (Kinouchi et al. 1991). Mutations in the Cu/Zn superoxide dismutase gene are associated with certain forms of familial amyotrophic lateral sclerosis, suggesting that oxygen radicals may be responsible for motor neuron degeneration in patients with this disease (Rosen et al. 1993).

## Experience-Dependent Synaptic Refinement

Normal sensory experience is essential to the maturation of neural connections in both the peripheral and central nervous systems. Sensory experience shapes the development of many diverse brain regions during a specific time window during development, called the critical period. The process of synaptic refinement assumes clinical significance as it continues to be important throughout the life span, providing mechanisms for activity-dependent modification of neuronal structure and connectivity. The integral role of sensory activity in brain development, and the ability of experience to alter perception, has been most extensively documented in the visual system. In the visual system, overlapping visual input from the two eyes must be combined in an orderly way to maximize acuity and stereopsis (Figure 1–19). In animals with binocular vision—such as humans, cats, and monkeys—visual stimuli from a specific region of visual space activate neurons in the contralateral visual cortex. Neurons in the left hemiretinas of right and left eyes both convey signals to the left cortex, and similarly, neurons in the right hemiretinas convey signals to the right cortex (Figure 1–19A). Thus, visual information emanating from the same external source is temporarily separated into right- and left-eye–specific pathways and then reunited in the same cortical hemisphere.

How is this visual information recombined? The eye-specific segregation of inputs from each retina is maintained in the visual thalamus, or lateral geniculate nucleus (LGN), and in the projection layers of the visual cortex, but then eventually converges in other layers of the primary visual cortex (V1). In geniculate-recipient layers of V1 in the adult, inputs from the two eyes project to separate columns of cells. The ocular dominance (OD) columns thus formed are arranged adjacent to each other in alternate stripes dominated by one eye or the other (Figure 1–19) (Hubel and Wiesel 1977). The pattern of stripes formed on the surface of the cortex resembles those of a zebra (Figure 1–19B, D). Output neurons in the ocular dominance columns project to other cortical layers, where the visual information derived from inputs to both eyes is recombined and stereopsis clues are extracted. How separate signals from each eye are handled in parallel, recombined, and separated again is representative of a more general pattern in the processing of visual information (Livingstone and Hubel 1988).

During development, the OD columns arise through activity-dependent processes (Hubel et al. 1977). Initially, geniculate axons carrying information from both eyes overlap. However, as development proceeds, these axons slowly begin to segregate into OD columns (Figure 1–19B,C). During this period, the pattern of distinct stripes, evenly divided between the two eyes, depends on normal visual activity. If vision in one eye is impaired or there is strabismus, input from the normal or dominant eye comes to control most of the visual cortex, and the other eye becomes functionally blind (Figure 1–19E). In the cortex, the ocular dominance columns of the normal or dominant eye expand at the expense of those of the impaired eye. The segregation of the optic fibers into columns is activity dependent (Constantine-Paton et al. 1990; Shatz and Stryker 1988). It depends on discordant inputs from the two eyes; segregation fails if all visual input to the cortex is blocked (with tetrodotoxin) or artificially synchronized in both eyes (by simultaneous electrical stimulation) (Shatz 1990).

Different patterns of electrical activity in each optic radiation, as occurs normally, mediate OD segregation. Segregation also requires the activity of postsynaptic cortical cells; infusion of the inhibitory drug muscimol (a $GABA_A$ agonist) causes a reversal of ocular dominance so that, paradoxically, the weak rather than the strong eye gains the larger cortical influence (Reiter and Stryker 1988). Thus, appropriate segregation of cortical inputs requires the coordination of both normal presynaptic activity and postsynaptic responses. Similar activity dependence is also found in retinal axons impinging on LGN cells (Goodman and Shatz 1993). Indeed, activity-dependent segregation of sensory inputs into functional columns appears to be an inherent property of topographic projections in sensory systems. In frogs, which have neither binocular vision nor ocular dominance columns, when an extra eye is transplanted into a tadpole, the optic fibers from the third eye compete with the other eye innervating that side of the brain and produce ocular dominance columns (Constantine-Paton and Law 1978).

The cellular and molecular mechanisms underlying activity-dependent synaptic refinement are just beginning to be elucidated. Many of these mechanisms are remarkably similar to the cellular mechanisms that underlie learning and memory in the adult brain. In the visual system, geniculate afferents are believed to undergo segregation into OD columns based on a hebbian learning rule (Hebb 1949), whereby neurons that fire together are strengthened selectively. This rule predicts that neurons that fire synchronously will strengthen their synapses, whereas asynchronous firing will weaken synapses. LTP and LTD are attractive candidates for mediating the process of OD column formation (Bear and Rittenhouse 1999). In addition to activity, other factors may also act to selectively strengthen coincidentally active synapses. One of the most attractive candidates for such a role is the neurotrophins family of growth factors. The neurotrophins are produced in limiting amounts by cortical neurons, their expression is increased by activity, and they can increase synaptic strength as well as alter dendritic and axonal arborizations of cortical neurons (McAllister et al. 1999). Consistent with this hypothesis, either infusion of excess neurotrophins or blockade of the neurotrophins prevents the formation of OD columns (Cabelli et al. 1995, 1997). Thus, the neurotrophins are

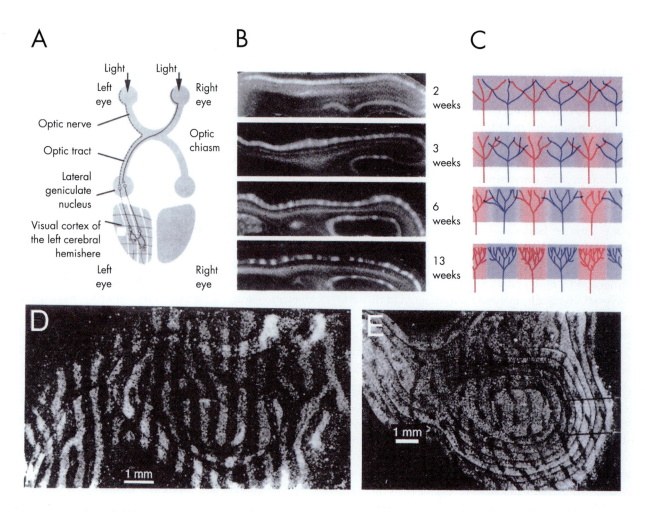

**FIGURE 1–19.** Ocular dominance columns in visual cortex. *Panel A.* In the human visual pathway, optic fibers from each eye split at the optic chiasm, half going to each side of the brain. In this schematic drawing, fibers conveying visual information from the left sides of each retina are shown projecting to the left lateral geniculate nucleus (LGN). LGN neurons (in different layers) in turn project to ipsilateral visual cortex (principally to layer 4c). In the geniculate-recipient layers of the mature visual cortex, inputs from the eyes segregate into ocular dominance (OD) columns. *Panel B.* Radioactive proline injections into one eye of a two-week-old kitten uniformly label layer 4 in coronal sections of visual cortex, indicating that afferents from that eye are evenly distributed in cortex at this age. However, over the next few weeks, similar injections show a segregation of geniculate afferents into OD columns. *Panel C.* Schematic diagram of the formation of OD columns within layer 4 of cortex during normal development. *Panel D.* One eye of a normal monkey was injected with a radioactive tracer that was transported transsynaptically along the visual pathways. Cortical areas receiving inputs from the injected eye are labeled white, revealing an alternating pattern of evenly spaced stripes (section cut tangentially through layer 4c). *Panel E.* Monocular deprivation alters the development of OD columns. Here the tracer was injected into the nondeprived eye, revealing broader stripes and thus an expansion of the area innervated by the nondeprived eye. Thus, normal experience is a prerequisite to the correct wiring of the cortex.

*Source.*   Panel A reprinted from Kandel ER, Schwartz JH, Jessell TM: *Principles of Neural Science*, 3rd Edition. Stamford, CT, Appleton & Lange, 1991; Panels B and C reprinted from Purves D, Augustine GJ, Fitzpatrick D, et al. (eds): *Neuroscience.* Sunderland, MA, Sinauer Associates, 1997, p. 427; Panels D and E reprinted from Hubel DH, Wiesel TN, LeVay S: "Plasticity of Ocular Dominance Columns in Monkey Striate Cortex." *Philosophical Transactions of the Royal Society of London,* Series B: Biological Sciences 278:377–409, 1977. Used with permission.

in a prime position to mediate experience-dependent synaptic refinement during development. In addition, because of their role in modulating synaptic strength, the neurotrophins have also been hypothesized to be involved in neurodegenerative diseases.

## Neurotrophic and Neurotoxic Actions of Neurotransmitters

Neurotransmitters themselves may have trophic or toxic roles in the shaping of neurons and their interconnections

(Lipton and Kater 1989). The progress of growth cones is regulated by local intracellular levels of $Ca^{2+}$, which act within a narrow window. When levels are low, growth cones are quiescent; when levels rise, growth cones begin to move. Above a certain level, however, further elevations of $Ca^{2+}$ arrest growth and cause retraction or destruction of neuronal processes (al-Mohanna et al. 1992). Glutamate can regulate the growth of neuronal processes through the control of $Ca^{2+}$ influx. This can be countered by inhibitory neurotransmitters as well as by provision of increased amounts of trophic factors (Mattson and Kater 1989; Mattson et al. 1989). Dopamine acting at $D_1$ receptors can inhibit growth cone motility by activating adenylyl cyclase and raising intracellular concentrations of cAMP (Lankford et al. 1988); acting at $D_2$ receptors, it can induce neurite outgrowth (Todd 1992).

Higher levels of glutamate produce excitotoxicity, perhaps reflecting the pathologic functioning of these developmental signaling systems (Kater et al. 1989). Alternatively, excitotoxicity may have a normal function in regulating cell numbers and connectivity. Excitotoxicity appears to be mediated acutely by the entry of $Na^+$ through AMPA channels. This leads to neuronal swelling (resulting in brain edema). Sustained $Ca^{2+}$ entry through NMDA receptor channels causes a delayed mode of excitotoxicity that kills neurons, probably by activation of intracellular proteases and/or generation of free radicals, including NO (Choi 1994; Dawson et al. 1994). In addition to mediating $Na^+$ influx and swelling, AMPA receptors may be coupled to the $IP_3$/DAG pathway, leading also to increases in intracellular $Ca^{2+}$ and C kinase activation.

Excitotoxicity probably underlies neuronal loss in strokes, status epilepticus, hypoglycemia, and head trauma (Choi and Rothman 1990). These brain insults are linked in that all lead to neuronal depolarization, which results in excessive electrical activity, evoking excessive increases in glutamate release. In each case, elevated levels of extracellular glutamate are present in experimental models, and their cytopathology can be mimicked by intracerebral injections of excitatory amino acids. The same neurons spared in these disease states are also less affected in the experimental models, probably because they have fewer excitatory amino acid receptors. Injured neurons show increased intracellular levels of $Ca^{2+}$, and excitatory amino acid antagonists, especially those blocking NMDA receptors or channels, prevent or dramatically reduce neuronal loss in these conditions.

Evidence supporting a role for excitatory amino acid toxicity in neurodegenerative disorders is less complete (Choi 1988; Meldrum and Garthwaite 1990). One rare neurologic disease that is uniformly fatal in childhood appears to be due to a deficiency in sulfite oxidase, resulting in elevations of the excitatory amino acid l-sulfocysteine. Also, a recessive form of olivopontocerebellar degeneration that is fatal in adult life is associated with glutamate dehydrogenase deficiency. Finally, two geographically localized neurodegenerative disorders have been tied to the ingestion of excitotoxins. Guam amyotrophic lateral sclerosis/parkinsonism-dementia complex results from ingestion of the excitatory amino acid β-n-methylamino-l-alanine, which is found in the cycad plant. Lathyrism, found in regions of Africa fraught with famine, is causally related to ingestion of the chickpea excitotoxin β-n-oxalylamino-l-alanine.

Similarities between other neuropsychiatric disorders and idiopathic neurodegenerative disorders suggest a pervasive role for excitotoxic mechanisms. Intriguingly, a growing body of findings implicate excitotoxic mechanisms in the pathology of Huntington's disease. The neuropathology of Huntington's disease is mimicked by the injection of excitatory amino acids, and certain classes of striatal neurons are spared in both cases (Wexler et al. 1991). In addition, measures of striatal NMDA receptors in patients dying of Huntington's disease reveal a selective loss of cells bearing these receptors, supporting the role of NMDA-mediated excitotoxicity in the pathogenesis of the disorder (Young et al. 1988).

## Perspectives

Brain development is not determined merely by cell-autonomous genetic programs but is instead highly interactive, depending on complex hierarchies of signaling factors operating to progressively restrict cell fate. Once cells have achieved a specific phenotype and have arrived at an appropriate location, competition for survival factors provides another opportunity for environmental influence over developmental outcome. The cellular development of the brain is therefore not strictly lineage dependent, but rather involves a remarkable degree of interactive signaling. In many brain areas, pruning of exuberant synaptic contacts on an activity-dependent basis is yet another example of a mechanism by which experience can refine structural aspects of brain development. One consequence of these developmental mechanisms is that no two outcomes will be exactly the same, even in a case of twins with identical genetic makeup. Another consequence is the potential for pathologic disruption of normal development by physical, chemical, or infectious agents in the fetal or neonatal period.

It is becoming increasingly clear that the adult brain retains a significant degree of plasticity throughout life and that changes in cortical organization can be induced by behaviorally important, temporally coincident sensory inputs (Buonomano and Merzenich 1998). Behavioral training of adult owl monkeys in discrimination of the temporal features of a tactile stimulus can alter the spatial and temporal response properties of cortical neurons (Recanzone et al. 1992b). When adult owl monkeys are rewarded for responding to a 30-Hz tactile stimulation of a single digit on one hand, there is an increase in the number of cortical locations and in the area of somatosensory cortex over which neurons show appropriate frequency-following responses after training (Recanzone et al. 1992a). In a related series of experiments, the cortical representation of the nipple-bearing skin increases almost twofold in lactating rats in comparison to virgin control rats or matched postpartum nonlactating rats (Xerri et al. 1994). Nursing behavior in female rats constitutes a naturally occurring change in regionally localized, behaviorally significant sensory input that is associated with a reorganization of primary sensory cortex.

The kinds of changes in the organization of somatosensory cortex also occur in primary auditory cortex. Owl monkeys trained for several weeks to discriminate small differences in the frequency of sequentially presented tones demonstrate progressive improvement in performance with training. At the end of the training period, the amount of cortex responding to behaviorally relevant frequencies is increased (Recanzone et al. 1993). In control studies with equivalent stimulation procedures in which stimuli are unattended, no significant representational changes were recorded (Recanzone et al. 1992b, 1993). Thus, attended, rewarded behaviors can induce changes in the organization of primary sensory cortex that are correlated with an improvement in perceptual acuity (Merzenich and Sameshima 1993). These experiments begin to suggest ways in which life experiences—including psychotherapy—can potentially modify cortical function and alter perception or behavior.

These plastic changes appear to share a common molecular language first expressed during development involving activity-dependent mechanisms. Neural activity is essential to activity-dependent synaptic refinement, LTP, LTD, and excitotoxicity (Brown et al. 1990; Choi and Rothman 1990; Constantine-Paton et al. 1990; Hawkins and Kandel 1984; Lipton and Kater 1989). The key player is the NMDA receptor, which requires both agonist binding and depolarization for activation. This appears to be the essential requirement for pairing specificity, a mode of synaptic plasticity initially postulated by Hebb (1949), whereby simultaneous activation of presynaptic and postsynaptic elements strengthens connections. Simultaneously, correlation of presynaptic activity with postsynaptic inhibition may selectively weaken connections (Reiter and Stryker 1988). The $Ca^{2+}$ influx mediated by the NMDA receptor may trigger changes in the strength of synapses, in time leading to more permanent structural changes in synapse numbers. At higher levels, $Ca^{2+}$ may arrest the growth of neurites, cause their retraction, or selectively lesion the susceptible cell.

Many neuropsychiatric disorders no doubt play out in this context. To consider a few examples, most of which we have already mentioned, striatal degeneration in Huntington's disease appears to be due to the overproduction of a synaptic vesicle–associated protein (DiFiglia et al. 1995; Sharp et al. 1995) that may translate into NMDA receptor–mediated excitotoxicity (Wexler et al. 1991). In Parkinson's disease, a selective loss of dopaminergic neurons in the substantia nigra may be the delayed result of a viral process, lesioning by dopaminergic neurotoxins exemplified by MPTP, or a deficiency in the neurotrophic factors brain-derived neurotrophic factor or glia cell line–derived neurotrophic factor, which may be essential for the survival of dopaminergic neurons. In Alzheimer's disease, the loss of cholinergic neurons may result from a deficiency or perhaps aberrant handling of NGF once it is taken up by neurons in the basal forebrain. Clearly, elucidation of the cellular and molecular events that occur during normal brain development, maturation, and aging, as well as those that underlie neuropsychiatric disorders, will greatly enhance approaches to their treatment and prevention.

Perhaps the most exciting and revolutionary possible intervention to treat neuropsychiatric diseases is the potential use of stem cells to repair the damaged brain (S.H. Lee et al. 2000). Despite tremendous efforts by the neuroscience community during the last century, there are currently no feasible therapies for repairing the damaged adult human brain. Clearly, treatment of many neuropsychiatric diseases would be greatly enhanced if new neurons could be added to a particular damaged brain region and stimulated to differentiate into the appropriate neuronal type and form appropriate connections. There are currently two approaches to achieving this goal. First, pluripotent stem cells are being used, with increasing success, to repopulate damaged brain regions. For example, adult rats with symptoms similar to Parkinson's disease can regain function after implantation of dopaminergic neurons created in vitro from fetal rat neuronal precursors (Studer et al. 1998). Second, newly discovered intrinsic repair mechanisms in the adult brain are being studied for their therapeutic potential. Recently, neurogenesis has been discovered in several regions of the adult brain, including the dentate gyrus of the hippocampal formation. These neurons migrate into the brain, differentiate, and form functional connections. Moreover, experience, learning, and physical exercise enhance neuronal proliferation in the adult (Fuchs and Gould 2000). The discovery of neurogenesis in the adult brain suggests that the adult brain may have intrinsic mechanisms for repair that could be manipulated to treat neurodegenerative disease (Fuchs and Gould 2000). As the mechanisms of neuropsychiatric disorders are resolved at the cellular and molecular levels, and the tremendous potential of stem cell research is harnessed, it is likely that revolutionary treatments for many neuropsychiatric diseases will be forthcoming.

# References

Ahmari SE, Buchanan J, Smith SJ: Assembly of presynaptic active zones from cytoplasmic transport packets. Nat Neurosci 3:445–451, 2000

Akbarian S, Bunney WE Jr, Potkin SG, et al: Altered distribution of nicotinamide-adenine dinucleotide phosphate-diaphorase cells in frontal lobe of schizophrenics implies disturbances of cortical development. Arch Gen Psychiatry 50:169–177, 1993

Allendoerfer KL, Shatz CJ: The subplate, a transient neocortical structure: its role in the development of connections between thalamus and cortex. Annu Rev Neurosci 17:185–218, 1994

al-Mohanna FA, Cave J, Bolsover SR: A narrow window of intracellular calcium concentration is optimal for neurite outgrowth in rat sensory neurones. Brain Res Dev Brain Res 70:287–290, 1992

Amara SG, Kuhar MJ: Neurotransmitter transporters: recent progress. Annu Rev Neurosci 16:73–93, 1993

Anderson SA, Eisenstat DD, Shi L, et al: Interneuron migration from basal forebrain to neocortex: dependence on Dlx genes. Science 278:474–476, 1997

Araque A, Parpura V, Sanzgiri RP, et al: Tripartite synapses: glia, the unacknowledged partner. Trends Neurosci 22:208–215, 1999

Bach ME, Hawkins RD, Osman M, et al: Impairment of spatial but not contextual memory in CaMKII mutant mice with a selective loss of hippocampal LTP in the range of the theta frequency. Cell 81:905–915, 1995

Bailey CH, Chen M, Keller F, et al: Serotonin-mediated endocytosis of apCAM: an early step of learning-related synaptic growth in *Aplysia*. Science 256:645–649, 1992

Bailey CH, Giustetto M, Huang YY, et al: Is heterosynaptic modulation essential for stabilizing Hebbian plasticity and memory? Nat Rev Neurosci 1:11–20, 2000

Barzilai A, Kennedy TE, Sweatt JD, et al: 5-HT modulates protein synthesis and the expression of specific proteins during long-term facilitation in *Aplysia* sensory neurons. Neuron 2:1577–1586, 1989

Bear MF, Rittenhouse CD: Molecular basis for induction of ocular dominance plasticity. J Neurobiol 41:83–91, 1999

Bennett MVL: Electrical transmission: a functional analysis and comparison to chemical transmission, in Handbook of Physiology, Vol 1: The Nervous System. Edited by Kandel ER. Bethesda, MD, American Physiological Society, 1977, pp 357–416

Bennett MVL, Barrio LC, Bargiello TA, et al: Gap junctions: new tools, new answers, new questions. Neuron 6:305–320, 1991

Bentley D, Toroian-Raymond A: Disoriented pathfinding by pioneer neurone growth cones deprived of filopodia by cytochalasin treatment. Nature 323:712–715, 1986

Black IB: Trophic interactions and brain plasticity, in The Cognitive Neurosciences. Edited by Gazzaniga MS. Cambridge, MA, MIT Press, 1995, pp 9–17

Bliss TV, Lomo TJ: Long-lasting potentiation of synaptic transmission in the dentate area of the anaesthetized rabbit following stimulation of the perforant path. J Physiol 23:331–56, 1973

Bohn LM, Lefkowitz RJ, Gainetdinov RR, et al: Enhanced morphine analgesia in mice lacking beta-arrestin 2. Science 286:2495–2498, 1999

Bothwell M: Keeping track of neurotrophin receptors. Cell 65:915–918, 1991

Braha O, Dale N, Hochner B, et al: Second messengers involved in the two processes of presynaptic facilitation that contribute to sensitization and dishabituation in *Aplysia* sensory neurons. Proc Natl Acad Sci U S A 87:2040–2044, 1990

Bremner JD, Randall P, Scott TM, et al: MRI-based measurement of hippocampal volume in patients with combat-related posttraumatic stress disorder. Am J Psychiatry 152:973–981, 1995

Brenman JE, Bredt DS: Synaptic signaling by nitric oxide. Curr Opin Neurobiol 7:374–378, 1997

Brivanlou IH, Warland DK, Meister M: Mechanisms of concerted firing among retinal ganglion cells. Neuron 20:527–539, 1998

Brose K, Tessier-Lavigne M: Slit proteins: key regulators of axon guidance, axonal branching, and cell migration. Curr Opin Neurobiol 10:95–102, 2000

Brown TH, Kairiss EW, Keenan CL: Hebbian synapses: biophysical mechanisms and algorithms. Annu Rev Neurosci 13:475–511, 1990

Buonomano DV, Merzenich MM: Cortical plasticity: from synapses to maps. Annu Rev Neurosci 21:149–186, 1998

Burack MA, Silverman MA, Banker G: The role of selective transport in neuronal protein sorting. Neuron 26:465–472, 2000

Cabelli RJ, Hohn A, Shatz CJ: Inhibition of ocular dominance column formation by infusion of NT4/5 or BDNF. Science 267:1662–1666, 1995

Cabelli RJ, Shelton DL, Segal RA, et al: Blockade of endogenous ligands of trkB inhibits formation of ocular dominance columns. Neuron 19:63–76, 1997

Callachan H, Cottrell GA, Hather NY, et al: Modulation of the GABA$_A$ receptor by progesterone metabolites. Proc R Soc Lond B Biol Sci 231:359–369, 1987

Caviness VS: Neocortical histogenesis in normal and reeler mice: a developmental study based on [$^3$H] thymidine autoradiography. Brain Res Dev Brain Res 4:293–302, 1982

Chao MV: Neurotrophin receptors: a window into neuronal differentiation. Neuron 9:583–593, 1992

Charney DS, Nestler EJ, Bunnery BS: Neurobiology of Mental Illness. New York: Oxford University Press, 1999

Choi DW: Glutamate neurotoxicity and diseases of the nervous system. Neuron 1:623–634, 1988

Choi DW: Calcium and excitotoxic neuronal injury. Ann N Y Acad Sci 747:162–171, 1994

Choi DW, Rothman SM: The role of glutamate neurotoxicity in hypoxic-ischemic neuronal death. Annu Rev Neurosci 13:171–182, 1990

Choi DW, Farb DH, Fischbach GD: Chlordiazepoxide selectively potentiates GABA conductance of spinal cord and sensory neurons in cell culture. J Neurophysiol 45:621–631, 1981

Cole AJ, Saffen DW, Baraban JM, et al: Rapid increase of an immediate early gene messenger RNA in hippocampal neurons by synaptic NMDA receptor activation. Nature 340:474–476, 1989

Constantine-Paton M, Law MI: Eye-specific termination bands in tecta of three-eyed frogs. Science 202:639–641, 1978

Constantine-Paton M, Cline HT, Debski E: Patterned activity, synaptic convergence, and the NMDA receptor in developing visual pathways. Annu Rev Neurosci 13:129–154, 1990

Cook G, Tannahill D, Keynes R: Axon guidance to and from choice points. Curr Opin Neurobiol 8:64–72, 1998

Craig AM, Banker G: Neuronal polarity. Annu Rev Neurosci 17:267–310, 1994

Craig AM, Blackstone CD, Huganir RL, et al: The distribution of glutamate receptors in cultured rat hippocampal neurons: postsynaptic clustering of AMPA-selective subunits. Neuron 10:1055–1068, 1993

Crandall JE, Herrup K: Patterns of cell lineage in the cerebral cortex reveal evidence for developmental boundaries. Exp Neurol 109:131–139, 1990

Dani JW, Chernjavsky A, Smith SJ: Neuronal activity triggers calcium waves in hippocampal astrocyte networks. Neuron 8:429–440, 1992

D'Arcangelo G, Miao GG, Chen SC, et al: A protein related to extracellular matrix proteins deleted in the mouse mutant reeler. Nature 374:719–723, 1995

Dash PK, Hochner B, Kandel ER: Injection of the cAMP-responsive element into the nucleus of *Aplysia* sensory neurons blocks long-term facilitation. Nature 345:718–721, 1990

Datta SR, Brunet A, Greenberg ME: Cellular survival: a play in three Akts. Genes Dev 13:2905–2927, 1999

Davies AM: The role of neurotrophins in the developing nervous system. J Neurobiol 25:1334–1348, 1994

Dawson TM, Snyder SH: Gases as biological messengers: nitric oxide and carbon monoxide in the brain. J Neurosci 14:5147–5159, 1994

Dawson TM, Dawson VL, Snyder SH: Nitric oxide as a mediator of neurotoxicity. NIDA Res Monogr 136:258–271, 1993

Dawson TM, Zhang J, Dawson VL, et al: Nitric oxide: cellular regulation and neuronal injury. Prog Brain Res 103:365–369, 1994

Dealy CN, Beyer EC, Kosher RA: Expression patterns of mRNAs for the gap junction proteins connexin43 and connexin42 suggest their involvement in chick limb morphogenesis and specification of the arterial vasculature. Dev Dyn 199:156–167, 1994

DeLorey TM, Olsen RW: Gamma-aminobutyric acidA receptor structure and function (review). J Biol Chem 267:16747–16750, 1992

DiFiglia M, Sapp E, Chase K, et al: Huntingtin is a cytoplasmic protein associated with vesicles in human and rat brain neurons. Neuron 14:1075–1081, 1995

Dingledine R, Borges K, Bowie D, et al: The glutamate receptor ion channels. Pharmacol Rev 51:7–61, 1999

Djamgoz MB, Wagner HJ: Localization and function of dopamine in the adult vertebrate retina. Neurochem Int 20:139–191, 1992

Dodd J, Morton SB, Karagogeos D, et al: Spatial regulation of axonal glycoprotein expression on subsets of embryonic spinal neurons. Neuron 1:105–116, 1988

Dowling JE: The Retina: An Approachable Part of the Brain. Cambridge, MA, Harvard University Press, 1987

Dumartin B, Caille I, Gonon F, et al: Internalization of D1 dopamine receptor in striatal neurons in vivo as evidence of activation by dopamine agonists. J Neurosci 18:1650–1661, 1998

During MJ, Ryder KM, Spencer DD: Hippocampal GABA transporter function in temporal-lobe epilepsy. Nature 376:174–177, 1995

Edwards SN, Buckmaster AE, Tolkovsky AM: The death programme in cultured sympathetic neurones can be suppressed at the posttranslational level by nerve growth factor, cyclic AMP, and depolarization. J Neurochem 57:2140–2143, 1991

Eilers J, Konnerth A: Dendritic signal integration. Curr Opin Neurobiol 7:385–390, 1997

Ellis RE, Yuan JY, Horvitz HR: Mechanisms and functions of cell death. Annual Review of Cell Biology 7:663–698, 1991

Engert F, Bonhoeffer T: Dendritic spine changes associated with hippocampal long-term synaptic plasticity. Nature 399:66–70, 1999

Fishell G, Rossant J, van der Kooy D: Neuronal lineages in chimeric mouse forebrain are segregated between compartments and in the rostrocaudal and radial planes. Dev Biol 141:70–83, 1990

Flanagan JG, Vanderhaeghen P: The ephrins and Eph receptors in neural development. Annu Rev Neurosci 21:309–345, 1998

Fletcher TL, Cameron P, De Camilli P, et al: The distribution of synapsin 1 and synaptophysin in hippocampal neurons developing in culture. J Neurosci 11:1617–1626, 1991

Friedman HV, Bresler T, Garner CC, et al: Assembly of new individual excitatory synapses: time course and temporal order of synaptic molecule recruitment. Neuron 27:57–69, 2000

Fuchs E, Gould E: In vivo neurogenesis in the adult brain: regulation and functional implications. Eur J Neurosci 12:2211–2214, 2000

Geiger JRP, Melcher T, Koh D-S, et al: Relative abundance of subunit mRNAs determines gating and $Ca^{2+}$ permeability of AMPA receptors in principal neurons and interneurons in rat CNS. Neuron 15:193–204, 1995

Gensburger C, Labourdette G, Sensenbrenner M: Brain basic fibroblast growth factor stimulates the proliferation of rat neuronal precursor cells in vitro. FEBS Lett 217:1–5, 1987

Ghosh A, Greenberg ME: Calcium signaling in neurons: molecular mechanisms and cellular consequences. Science 268:239–247, 1995

Ghosh A, Shatz CJ: Involvement of subplate neurons in the formation of ocular dominance columns. Science 255:1441–1443, 1992

Ghosh A, Antonini A, McConnell SK, et al: Requirement for subplate neurons in the formation of thalamocortical connections. Nature 347:179–181, 1990

Giros B, Caron MG: Molecular characterization of the dopamine transporter. Trends Pharmacol Sci 14:43–49, 1993

Giros B, Jaber M, Jones SR, et al: Hyperlocomotion and indifference to cocaine and amphetamine in mice lacking the dopamine transporter. Nature 379:606–612, 1996

Glanzman DL, Kandel ER, Schacher S: Target-dependent structural changes accompanying long-term synaptic facilitation in Aplysia neurons. Science 249:799–802, 1990

Glass DJ, Yancopoulos GD: The neurotrophins and their receptors. Trends Cell Biol 3:262–268, 1993

Godement P, Salaun J, Mason CA: Retinal axon pathfinding in the optic chiasm: divergence of crossed and uncrossed fibers. Neuron 5:173–186, 1990

Goldowitz D: The weaver granuloprival phenotype is due to intrinsic action of the mutant locus in granule cells: evidence from homozygous weaver chimeras. Neuron 2:1565–1575, 1989

Goodman CS: Mechanisms and molecules that control growth cone guidance. Annu Rev Neurosci 19:341–377, 1996

Goodman CS, Shatz CJ: Developmental mechanisms that generate precise patterns of neuronal connectivity. Cell 72 (suppl):77–98, 1993

Grant SGN, Karl KA, Kiebler MA, et al: Focal adhesion kinase in the brain: novel subcellular localization and specific regulation by Fyn tyrosine kinase in mutant mice. Genes Dev 9:1909–1921, 1995

Greenlund LJ, Deckwerth TL, Johnson E Jr: Superoxide dismutase delays neuronal apoptosis: a role for reactive oxygen species in programmed neuronal death. Neuron 14:303–315, 1995

Grove EA, Williams BP, Li DQ, et al: Multiple restricted lineages in the embryonic rat cerebral cortex. Development 117:553–561, 1993

Hamburger V: Hans Spemann and the organizer concept. Experientia 25:1121–1125, 1969

Hatten ME: The role of migration in central nervous system neuronal development. Curr Opin Neurobiol 3:38–44, 1993

Hawkins RD, Kandel ER: Is there a cell-biological alphabet for simple forms of learning? Psychol Rev 91:375–391, 1984

Hebb DO: The Organization of Behavior: A Neuropsychological Theory. New York, Wiley, 1949

Hegde AN, Goldberg AL, Schwartz JH: Regulatory subunits of cAMP-dependent protein kinases are degraded after conjugation to ubiquitin: a molecular mechanism underlying long-term synaptic plasticity. Proc Natl Acad Sci U S A 90:7436–7440, 1993

Hengartner MO, Ellis RE, Horvitz HR: Caenorhabditis elegans gene ced-9 protects cells from programmed cell death. Nature 356:494–499, 1992

Hengerer B, Lindholm D, Heumann R, et al: Lesion-induced increase in nerve growth factor mRNA is mediated by c-fos. Proc Natl Acad Sci U S A 87:3899–3903, 1990

Hille B: Ionic Channels of Excitable Membranes, 2nd Edition. Sunderland, MA, Sinauer Associates, 1992, pp 59–83

Hockenbery DM, Oltvai ZN, Yin XM, et al: Bcl-2 functions in an antioxidant pathway to prevent apoptosis. Cell 75:241–251, 1993

Hökfelt T, Johansson O, Goldstein M: Chemical anatomy of the brain. Science 225:1326–1334, 1984

Hollmann M, Heinemann S: Cloned glutamate receptors. Annu Rev Neurosci 17:31–108, 1994

Hubel DH, Wiesel TN: Ferrier lecture: functional architecture of macaque monkey visual cortex. Proc R Soc Lond B Biol Sci 198:1–59, 1977

Hubel DH, Wiesel TN, LeVay S: Plasticity of ocular dominance columns in monkey striate cortex. Philos Trans R Soc Lond B Biol Sci 278:377–409, 1977

Huerta PT, Lisman JE: Heightened synaptic plasticity of hippocampal CA1 neurons during a cholinergically induced rhythmic state. Nature 364:723–725, 1993

Isaac JT, Crair MC, Nicoll RA, et al: Silent synapses during development of thalamocortical inputs. Neuron 18:269–280, 1997

Jaber M, Jones S, Giros B, et al: The dopamine transporter: a crucial component regulating dopamine transmission. Mov Disord 12:629–633, 1997

Javitch JA, Snyder SH: Uptake of MPP(+) by dopamine neurons explains selectivity of parkinsonism-inducing neurotoxin, MPTP. Eur J Pharmacol 106:455–456, 1984

Kandel ER: Genes, nerve cells, and the remembrance of things past. J Neuropsychiatry Clin Neurosci 1:103–125, 1989

Kandel ER, Hawkins RD: The biological basis of learning and individuality. Sci Am 267:78–86, 1992

Kandel ER, O'Dell TJ: Are adult learning mechanisms also used for development? Science 258:243–245, 1992

Kandler K, Katz LC: Neuronal coupling and uncoupling in the developing nervous system. Curr Opin Neurobiol 5:98–105, 1995

Kane DJ, Sarafian TA, Anton R, et al: Bcl-2 inhibition of neural death: decreased generation of reactive oxygen species. Science 262:1274–1277, 1993

Karlin A, Akabas MH: Toward a structural basis for the function of nicotinic acetylcholine receptors and their cousins. Neuron 15:1231–1244, 1995

Kater SB, Mattson MP, Guthrie PB: Calcium-induced neuronal degeneration: a normal growth cone regulating signal gone awry (?). Ann N Y Acad Sci 568:252–261, 1989

Kennedy TE, Serafini T, de la Torre JR, et al: Netrins are diffusible chemotropic factors for commissural axons in the embryonic spinal cord. Cell 78:425–435, 1994

Kenyon C: A gene involved in the development of the posterior body region of C. *elegans*. Cell 46:477–487, 1986

Kim JH, Huganir RL: Organization and regulation of proteins at synapses. Curr Opin Cell Biol 11:248–254, 1999

Kinouchi H, Epstein CJ, Mizui T, et al: Attenuation of focal cerebral ischemic injury in transgenic mice overexpressing CuZn superoxide dismutase. Proc Natl Acad Sci U S A 88:11158–11162, 1991

Kitayama S, Shimada S, Xu H, et al: Dopamine transporter site-directed mutations differentially alter substrate transport and cocaine binding. Proc Natl Acad Sci U S A 89:7782–7785, 1992

Koester J, Siegelbaum SA: Propagated signaling: the action potential, in Principles of Neuroscience, 4th Edition. New York, McGraw-Hill, 2000, pp 167–169

Komuro H, Rakic P: Modulation of neuronal migration by NMDA receptors. Science 260:95–97, 1993

Kraszewski K, Mundigl O, Daniell L, et al: Synaptic vesicle dynamics in living cultured hippocampal neurons visualized with CY3-conjugated antibodies directed against the lumenal domain of synaptotagmin. J Neurosci 15:4328–4342, 1995

Krauss S, Concordet JP, Ingham PW: A functionally conserved homolog of the *Drosophila* segment polarity gene hh is expressed in tissues with polarizing activity in zebrafish embryos. Cell 75:1431–1444, 1993

Landis SC: Target regulation of neurotransmitter phenotype. Trends Neurosci 13:344–350, 1990

Lankford KL, DeMello FG, Klein WL: D1-type dopamine receptors inhibit growth cone motility in cultured retina neurons: evidence that neurotransmitters act as morphogenic growth regulators in the developing central nervous system. Proc Natl Acad Sci U S A 85:4567–4571, 1988

Lee HK, Barbarosie M, Kameyama K, et al: Regulation of distinct AMPA receptor phosphorylation sites during bi-directional synaptic plasticity. Nature 405:955–959, 2000

Lee SH, Sheng M: Development of neuron-neuron synapses. Curr Opin Neurobiol 10:125–131, 2000

Lee SH, Lumelsky N, Studer L, et al: Efficient generation of midbrain and hindbrain neurons from mouse embryonic stem cells. Nat Biotechnol 18:675–679, 2000

Liao D, Zhang X, O'Brien R, et al: Regulation of morphological postsynaptic silent synapses in developing hippocampal neurons. Nat Neurosci 2:37–43, 1999

Linden DJ, Connor JA: Long-term synaptic depression. Annu Rev Neurosci 18:319–357, 1995

Lipton SA, Kater SB: Neurotransmitter regulation of neuronal outgrowth, plasticity and survival. Trends Neurosci 12:265–270, 1989

Livingstone M, Hubel D: Segregation of form, color, movement, and depth: anatomy, physiology, and perception. Science 240:740–749, 1988

Llinás R: The intrinsic electrophysiological properties of mammalian neurons: insights into central nervous system function. Science 242:1654–1664, 1988

Llinás R, Jahnsen H: Electrophysiology of mammalian thalamic neurones in vitro. Nature 297:406–408, 1982

Llinás RR, Ribary U, Jeanmonod D, et al: Thalamocortical dysrhythmia: a neurological and neuropsychiatric syndrome characterized by magnetoencephalography. Proc Natl Acad Sci U S A 96:15222–15227, 1999

Lodish H, Baltimore D, Berk A, et al: Molecular Cell Biology, 3rd Edition. New York, Scientific American Books, 1995

LoTurco JJ, Blanton MG, Kriegstein AR: Initial expression and endogenous activation of NMDA channels in early neocortical development. J Neurosci 11:792–799, 1991

LoTurco JJ, Owens DF, Heath MJS, et al: GABA and glutamate depolarize cortical progenitor cells and inhibit DNA synthesis. Neuron 15:1287–1298, 1995

Lumsden A, Krumlauf R: Patterning the vertebrate neuraxis. Science 274:1109–1115, 1996

Lyford GL, Yamagata K, Kaufmann WE, et al: Arc, a growth factor and activity-regulated gene, encodes a novel cytoskeleton-associated protein that is enriched in neuronal dendrites. Neuron 14:433–445, 1995

MacDermott AB, Mayer ML, Westbrook GL, et al: NMDA-receptor activation increases cytoplasmic calcium concentration in cultured spinal cord neurones. Nature 321:519–522, 1986

MacDonald R, Barker JL: Benzodiazepines specifically modulate GABA-mediated postsynaptic inhibition in cultured mammalian neurones. Nature 271:563–564, 1978

MacDonald RL, Rogers CJ, Twyman RE: Kinetic properties of the GABA$_A$ receptor main conductance state of mouse spinal cord neurones in culture. J Physiol 410:479–499, 1989

Maconochie M, Nonchev S, Morrison A, et al: Paralogous Hox genes: function and regulation. Annu Rev Genet 30:529–556, 1996

Majewska MD, Harrison NL, Schwartz RD, et al: Steroid hormone metabolites are barbiturate-like modulators of the GABA receptor. Science 232:1004–1007, 1986

Malenka RC, Nicoll RA: Long-term potentiation—a decade of progress? Science 285:1870–1874, 1999

Malgaroli A, Ting AE, Wendland B, et al: Presynaptic component of long-term potentiation visualized at individual hippocampal synapses. Science 268:1624–1628, 1995

Malinow R, Mainen ZF, Hayashi Y: LTP mechanisms: from silence to four-way traffic. Curr Opin Neurobiol 10:352–357, 2000

Marin-Padilla M: Ontogenesis of the pyramidal cell of the mammalian neocortex and developmental cytoarchitectonics: a unifying theory. J Comp Neurol 321:223–240, 1992

Mascia MP, Trudell JR, Harris RA: Specific binding sites for alcohols and anesthetics on ligand-gated ion channels. Proc Natl Acad Sci U S A 97:9305–9310, 2000

Mathers DA, Barker JL: GABA- and glycine-induced Cl⁻ channels in cultured mouse spinal neurons require the same energy to close. Brain Res 224:441–445, 1981

Mattson MP, Kater SB: Excitatory and inhibitory neurotransmitters in the generation and degeneration of hippocampal neuroarchitecture. Brain Res 478:337–348, 1989

Mattson MP, Guthrie PB, Kater SB: Intrinsic factors in the selective vulnerability of hippocampal pyramidal neurons. Prog Clin Biol Res 317:333–351, 1989

Mayer ML, Westbrook GL, Guthrie PB: Voltage-dependent block by Mg²⁺ of NMDA responses in spinal cord neurones. Nature 309:261–263, 1984

Mayford M, Kandel ER: Genetic approaches to memory storage. Trends Genet 15:463–470, 1999

McAllister AK, Katz LC, Lo DC: Neurotrophins and synaptic plasticity. Annu Rev Neurosci 22:295–318, 1999

McConnell SK: Fates of visual cortical neurons in the ferret after isochronic and heterochronic transplantation. J Neurosci 8:945–974, 1988

McCormick DA, Bal T: Sleep and arousal: thalamocortical mechanisms. Annu Rev Neurosci 20:185–215, 1997

McGinnis W, Krumlauf R: Homeobox genes and axial patterning. Cell 68:283–302, 1992

Meldrum B, Garthwaite J: Excitatory amino acid neurotoxicity and neurodegenerative disease. Trends Pharmacol Sci 11:379–387, 1990

Mennerick S, Zorumski CF: Glial contributions to excitatory neurotransmission in cultured hippocampal cells. Nature 368:59–62, 1994

Merzenich MM, Sameshima K: Cortical plasticity and memory. Curr Opin Neurobiol 3:187–196, 1993

Messersmith EK, Leonardo ED, Shatz CJ, et al: Semaphorin III can function as a selective chemorepellent to pattern sensory projections in the spinal cord. Neuron 14:949–959, 1995

Mienville JM: Cajal-Retzius cell physiology: just in time to bridge the 20th century. Cereb Cortex 9:776–782, 1999

Mihic SJ, Ye Q, Wick MJ, et al: Sites of alcohol and volatile anaesthetic action on GABA(A) and glycine receptors. Nature 389:385–389, 1997

Mione MC, Danevic C, Boardman P, et al: Lineage analysis reveals neurotransmitter (GABA or glutamate) but not calcium-binding protein homogeneity in clonally related cortical neurons. J Neurosci 14:107–123, 1994

Mohn AR, Gainetdinov RR, Caron MG, et al: Mice with reduced NMDA receptor expression display behaviors related to schizophrenia. Cell 98:427–436, 1999

Morgan JI, Curran T: Stimulus-transcription coupling in neurons: role of cellular immediate-early genes. Trends Neurosci 12:459–462, 1989

Murphy TH, Blatter LA, Wier WG, et al: Rapid communication between neurons and astrocytes in primary cortical cultures. J Neurosci 13:2672–2679, 1993

Murphy TH, Baraban JM, Wier WG, et al: Visualization of quantal synaptic transmission by dendritic calcium imaging. Science 263:529–532, 1994

Nakagawa S, Brennnan C, Johnson KG, et al: Ephrin-B regulates the ipsilateral routing of retinal axons at the optic chiasm. Neuron 25:599–610, 2000

Nedergaard M: Direct signaling from astrocytes to neurons in cultures of mammalian brain cells. Science 263:1768–1771, 1994

Nijhawan D, Honarpour N, Wang X: Apoptosis in neural development and disease. Annu Rev Neurosci 23:73–87, 2000

O'Dell TJ, Huang PL, Dawson TM, et al: Endothelial NOS and the blockade of LTP by NOS inhibitors in mice lacking neuronal NOS. Science 265:542–546, 1994

Ogawa M, Miyata T, Nakajima K, et al: The reeler gene-associated antigen on Cajal-Retzius neurons is a crucial molecule for laminar organization of cortical neurons. Neuron 14:899–912, 1995

Oppenheim A, Altuvia S, Kornitzer D, et al: Translation control of gene expression. J Basic Clin Physiol Pharmacol 2:223–231, 1991

Pantev C, Oostenveld R, Engelien A, et al: Increased auditory cortical representation in musicians. Nature 392:811–814, 1998

Petralia RS, Esteban JA, Wang Y-X, et al: Selective acquisition of AMPA receptors over postnatal development suggests a molecular basis for silent synapses. Nat Neurosci 2:31–36, 1999

Petrozzino JJ, Pozzo-Miller LD, Connor JA: Micromolar Ca²⁺ transients in dendritic spines of hippocampal pyramidal neurons in brain slice. Neuron 14:1223–1231, 1995

Pfrieger FW, Barres BA: Synaptic efficacy enhanced by glial cells in vitro. Science 277:1684–1687, 1997

Piven J, Arndt S, Bailey J, et al: An MRI study of brain size in autism. Am J Psychiatry 152:1145–1149, 1995

Placzek M, Jessell TM, Dodd J: Induction of floor plate differentiation by contact-dependent, homeogenetic signals. Development 117:205–218, 1993

Pritchett DB, Sontheimer H, Shivers BD, et al: Importance of a novel GABA$_A$ receptor subunit for benzodiazepine pharmacology. Nature 338:582–585, 1989

Przedborski S, Jackson-Lewis V: Mechanisms of MPTP toxicity. Mov Disord 13:35–38, 1998

Puchalski RB, Louis JC, Brose N, et al: Selective RNA editing and subunit assembly of native glutamate receptors. Neuron 13:131–147, 1994

Purves D, Lichtman JW: Principles of Neural Development. Sunderland, MA, Sinauer, 1985

Raff MC: Social controls on cell survival and cell death. Nature 356:397–400, 1992

Raff MC, Barres BA, Burne JF, et al: Programmed cell death and the control of cell survival: lessons from the nervous system. Science 262:695–700, 1993

Rakic P: Neurons in rhesus monkey visual cortex: systematic relation between time of origin and eventual disposition. Science 183:425–427, 1974

Rakic P: Neuronal migration and contact guidance in primate telencephalon. Postgrad Med J 54:25–40, 1978

Rakic P: Specification of cerebral cortical areas. Science 241:170–176, 1988

Ramamoorthy S, Blakely RD: Phosphorylation and sequestration of serotonin transporters differentially modulated by psychostimulants. Science 285:763–766, 1999

Rao A, Kim E, Sheng M, et al: Heterogeneity in the molecular composition of excitatory postsynaptic sites during development of hippocampal neurons in culture. J Neurosci 18:1217–1229, 1998

Raper JA: Semaphorins and their receptors in vertebrates and invertebrates. Curr Opin Neurobiol 10:88–94, 2000

Recanzone GH, Jenkins WM, Hradek GT, et al: Progressive improvement in discriminative abilities in adult owl monkeys performing a tactile frequency discrimination task. J Neurophysiol 67:1015–1030, 1992a

Recanzone GH, Merzenich MM, Schreiner CE: Changes in the distributed temporal response properties of SI cortical neurons reflect improvements in performance on a temporally based tactile discrimination task. J Neurophysiol 67:1071–1091, 1992b

Recanzone GH, Schreiner CE, Merzenich MM: Plasticity in the frequency representation of primary auditory cortex following discrimination training in adult owl monkeys. J Neurosci 13:87–103, 1993

Reichardt LF, Tomaselli KJ: Extracellular matrix molecules and their receptors: functions in neural development. Annu Rev Neurosci 14:531–570, 1991

Reid HH, Wilks AF, Bernard O: Two forms of the basic fibroblast growth factor receptor-like mRNA are expressed in the developing mouse brain. Proc Natl Acad Sci U S A 87:1596–1600, 1990

Reiter HO, Stryker MP: Neural plasticity without postsynaptic action potentials: less-active inputs become dominant when kitten visual cortical cells are pharmacologically inhibited. Proc Natl Acad Sci U S A 85:3623–3627, 1988

Rijli FM, Mark M, Lakkaraju S, et al: A homeotic transformation is generated in the rostral branchial region of the head by disruption of Hoxa-2, which acts as a selector gene. Cell 75:1333–1349, 1993

Rosen DR, Siddique T, Patterson D, et al: Mutations in Cu/Zn superoxide dismutase gene are associated with familial amyotrophic lateral sclerosis. Nature 362:59–62, 1993

Rubenstein JL, Shimamura K, Martinez S, et al: Regionalization of the prosencephalic neural plate. Annu Rev Neurosci 21:445–77, 1998

Ruiz i Altaba A: Pattern formation in the vertebrate neural plate. Trends Neurosci 17:233–243, 1994

Sadato N, Pascual-Leone A, Grafman J, et al: Activation of the primary visual cortex by Braille reading in blind subjects. Nature 380:526–528, 1996

Sanes DH, Reh TA, Harris WA: Development of the Nervous System. San Diego, CA, Academic Press, 2000, pp 277–279

Sanes JR, Lichtman JW: Development of the vertebrate neuromuscular junction. Annu Rev Neurosci 22:389–442, 1999

Sastry PS, Rao KS: Apoptosis and the nervous system. J Neurochem 74:1–20, 2000

Sato M, Lopez-Mascaraque L, Heffner CD, et al: Action of a diffusible target-derived chemoattractant on cortical axon branch induction and directed growth. Neuron 13:791–803, 1994

Saunders C, Ferrer JV, Shi L, et al: Amphetamine-induced loss of human dopamine transporter activity: an internalization-dependent and cocaine-sensitive mechanism. Proc Natl Acad Sci U S A 97:6850–6855, 2000

Scheller RH: Membrane trafficking in the presynaptic nerve terminal. Neuron 14:893–897, 1995

Schenone A, Mancardi GL: Molecular basis of inherited neuropathies. Curr Opin Neurol 12:603–616, 1999

Schoepfer R, Monyer H, Sommer B, et al: Molecular biology of glutamate receptors. Prog Neurobiol 42:353–357, 1994

Schofield PR, Shivers BD, Seeburg PH: The role of receptor subtype diversity in the CNS. Trends Neurosci 13:8–11, 1990

Schulman H: Nitric oxide: a spatial second messenger. Mol Psychiatry 2:296–299, 1997

Schuman EM, Madison DV: A requirement for the intercellular messenger nitric oxide in long-term potentiation. Science 254:1503–1506, 1991

Schwartz JH, Westbrook GL: The cytology of neurons, in Principles of Neuroscience, 4th Edition. New York, McGraw-Hill, 2000, pp 67–87

Scott SA, Davies AM: Inhibition of protein synthesis prevents cell death in sensory and parasympathetic neurons deprived of neurotrophic factor in vitro. J Neurobiol 21:630–638, 1990

Seeburg PH: The role of RNA editing in controlling glutamate receptor channel properties. J Neurochem 66:1–5, 1996

Seeger MA: Genetic and molecular dissection of axon pathfinding in the Drosophila nervous system. Curr Opin Neurobiol 4:56–62, 1994

Sharp AH, Loev SJ, Schilling G, et al: Widespread expression of Huntington's disease gene (IT15) protein product. Neuron 14:1065–1074, 1995

Shatz CJ: Impulse activity and the patterning of connections during CNS development. Neuron 5:745–756, 1990

Shatz CJ, Stryker MP: Prenatal tetrodotoxin infusion blocks segregation of retinogeniculate afferents. Science 242:87–89, 1988

Sherman SM: Dual response modes in lateral geniculate neurons: mechanisms and functions. Vis Neurosci 13:205–213, 1996

Shi SH, Hayashi Y, Petralia R, et al: Rapid spine delivery and redistribution of AMPA receptors after synaptic NMDA receptor activation. Science 284:1811–1816, 1999

Smith AD, Bolam JP: The neural network of the basal ganglia as revealed by the study of synaptic connections of identified neurones. Trends Neurosci 13:259–265, 1990

Smith SJ: Neural signalling. Neuromodulatory astrocytes. Curr Biol 4:807–810, 1994

Sommer B, Keinaenen K, Verdoorn TA, et al: Flip and flop: a cell-specific functional switch in glutamate-operated channels of the CNS. Science 249:1580–1585, 1990

Song HJ, Poo MM: Signal transduction underlying growth cone guidance by diffusible factors. Curr Opin Neurobiol 9:355–363, 1999

Sretavan DW: Specific routing of retinal ganglion cell axons at the mammalian optic chiasm during embryonic development. J Neurosci 10:1995–2007, 1990

Stevens CF, Sullivan JM: Regulation of the readily releasable vesicle pool by protein kinase C. Neuron 21:885–893, 1998

Stevens CF, Wang Y: Facilitation and depression at single central synapses. Neuron 14:795–805, 1995

Studer L, Tabar V, McKay RD: Transplantation of expanded mesencephalic precursors leads to recovery in parkinsonian rats. Nat Neurosci 1:290–5, 1998

Study RE, Barker JL: Diazepam and (–)-pentobarbital: fluctuation analysis reveals different mechanisms for potentiation of gamma-aminobutyric acid responses in cultured central neurons. Proc Natl Acad Sci U S A 78:7180–7184, 1981

Sudhof TC: The synaptic vesicle cycle: a cascade of protein-protein interactions. Nature 375:645–653, 1995

Suter DM, Forscher P: Substrate-cytoskeletal coupling as a mechanism for the regulation of growth cone motility and guidance. J Neurobiol 44:97–113, 2000

Sweatt JD, Kandel ER: Persistent and transcriptionally dependent increase in protein phosphorylation in long-term facilitation of Aplysia sensory neurons. Nature 339:51–54, 1989

Tamas G, Buhl EH, Lorincz A, et al: Proximally targeted GABAergic synapses and gap junctions synchronize cortical interneurons. Nat Neurosci 3:366–371, 2000

Tanabe Y, Jessell TM: Diversity and pattern in the developing spinal cord. Science 274:1115–1123, 1996

Tear G: Axon guidance at the central nervous system midline. Cell Mol Life Sci 55:1365–1376, 1999

Todd RD: Neural development is regulated by classical neurotransmitters: dopamine D2 receptor stimulation enhances neurite outgrowth. Biol Psychiatry 31:794–807, 1992

Toni N, Buchs PA, Nikonenko I, et al: LTP promotes formation of multiple spine synapses between a single axon terminal and a dendrite. Nature 402:421–425, 1999

Tsao P, von Zastrow M: Downregulation of G protein-coupled receptors. Curr Opin Neurobiol 10:365–369, 2000

Tsujimoto Y, Yunis J, Onorato-Showe L, et al: Molecular cloning of the chromosomal breakpoint of B-cell lymphomas and leukemias with the t(11;14) chromosome translocation. Science 224:1403–1406, 1984

Twyman RE, MacDonald RL: Neurosteroid regulation of GABA$_A$ receptor single-channel kinetic properties of mouse spinal cord neurons in culture. J Physiol (Lond) 456:215–245, 1992

Vickery RG, von Zastrow: Distinct dynamin-dependent and -independent mechanisms target structurally homologous dopamine receptors to different endocytic membranes. J Cell Biol 144:31–43, 1999

Walaas SI, Greengard P: Protein phosphorylation and neuronal function. Pharmacol Rev 43:299–349, 1991

Walsh CA: Genetics of neuronal migration in the cerebral cortex. Mental Retard Dev Disabil Res Rev 6:34–40, 2000

Walsh CA, Cepko CL: Clonal dispersion in proliferative layers of developing cerebral cortex. Nature 362:632–635, 1993

Walsh CA, Goffinet AM: Potential mechanisms of mutations that affect neuronal migration in man and mouse. Curr Opin Genet Dev 10:270–274, 2000

Walsh FS, Doherty P: Neural cell adhesion molecules of the immunoglobulin super family: role in axon growth and guidance. Annu Rev Cell Dev Biol 13:425–456, 1997

Weinberger DR, Lipska BK: Cortical maldevelopment, antipsychotic drugs, and schizophrenia: a search for common ground. Schizophr Res 16:87–110, 1995

Wexler NS, Rose EA, Housman DE: Molecular approaches to hereditary diseases of the nervous system: Huntington's disease as a paradigm. Annu Rev Neurosci 14:503–529, 1991

Wisden W, Errington ML, Williams S, et al: Differential expression of immediate early genes in the hippocampus and spinal cord. Neuron 4:603–614, 1990

Wu G, Malinow R, Cline HT: Maturation of a central glutamatergic synapse. Science 274:972–976, 1996

Xerri C, Stern JM, Merzenich MM: Alterations of the cortical representation of the rat ventrum induced by nursing behavior. J Neurosci 14:1710–1721, 1994

Yamada T, Pfaff SL, Edlund T, et al: Control of cell pattern in the neural tube: motor neuron induction by diffusible factors from notochord and floor plate. Cell 73:673–686, 1993

Young AB, Greenamyre JT, Hollingsworth Z, et al: NMDA receptor losses in putamen from patients with Huntington's disease. Science 241:981–983, 1988

Yuste R, Tank DW: Dendritic integration in mammalian neurons, a century after Cajal. Neuron 16:701–716, 1996

Zhuo M, Small SA, Kandel ER, et al: Nitric oxide and carbon monoxide produce activity-dependent long-term synaptic enhancement in hippocampus. Science 260:1946–1950, 1993

Zhuo M, Kandel ER, Hawkins RD: Nitric oxide and cGMP can produce either synaptic depression or potentiation depending on the frequency of presynaptic stimulation in the hippocampus. Neuroreport 5:1033–1036, 1994

# Human Electrophysiology and Basic Sleep Mechanisms

Robert W. McCarley, M.D.

The first part of this chapter consists of a brief note on evoked potential and electroencephalogram (EEG) analysis. This section was primarily written for the reader with some knowledge of cellular neurophysiology (even in the far distant past) who wishes a brief review of fundamental concepts. The second part is a survey of current concepts in the regulation of sleep and wakefulness, an area of recent advances in understanding fundamental mechanisms relevant to behavior and to pathology. The two parts may be read independently of each other.

Since the publication of the last edition of this book, basic sleep research has made major advances. The discovery of orexins, new knowledge about the role of adenosine as a sleep factor, and the growing role of molecular biological techniques are examples covered in this chapter.

Some of the references cited in this chapter can be consulted for general information. The book by Regan (1989) is a standard text on evoked potentials that emphasizes short-latency potentials. For basic sleep neurobiology, the book by Borbély et al. (2000) is a state-of-the-art reference (and is available for free download from the Human Frontier Science Program at http://www.hfsp.org/scientific_activities/scientific_activities_workshop8.htm). For sleep disorders and also a survey of basic topics, the books by Chokroverty (1999) and Kryger et al. (2000) are good sources.

## Basics of Evoked Potentials and the Electroencephalogram

Chapter 1 in this volume details the basics of cellular electrophysiology and cellular communication. Obviously, recording of individual neurons can be done in humans only under very special circumstances, and much of our knowledge of human systems electrophysiology comes through recordings of evoked potentials (EPs) and the electroencephalogram (EEG). These techniques use large electrodes and do not record the activity of individual neurons but rather the summed activity of many neural elements. I here briefly outline the essential concepts relevant to EP/EEG generation, taking the EP first. Evoked potentials may be thought of as summations of the voltage alterations generated by populations of neural elements in response to a stimulus, typically an external sensory stimulus.

Most of the components of the evoked potential arise from postsynaptic potentials (PSPs) and not from action potentials, which generally are too brief and too asynchronous to summate and produce an EP. (Some of the very short-latency [<10 ms] brainstem auditory evoked potential components are derived from synchronous volleys of action potentials and are an important exception to this rule.)

Work supported by awards from the Department of Veterans Affairs, Medical Research Service, and the National Institute of Mental Health (R37 MH39,683, R01 MH62522, and R01 MH40,799). Portions of this chapter were adapted with permission from McCarley RW, Greene RW, Rainnie D, et al.: Brain Stem Neuromodulation and REM Sleep. *Seminars in the Neurosciences* 7:341–354, 1995.

Figure 2–1 illustrates a depolarizing PSP in the soma; this PSP is generated by the influx of positive ions. The influx of positive ions defines the soma as a current "sink" in this case, since by convention current is composed of positive ion flow. The apical dendrites, in contrast, act as a "source" of current flow. This current flow pattern defines a *dipole*, literally a "two pole" with the positive pole in the dendrites and the negative in the soma. In the case of a hyperpolarizing PSP in the soma the dipole polarity would be reversed, with source (positive pole) in the soma and sink in the dendrites; it will be recalled that membrane hyperpolarization arises as the consequence of a net efflux of positive ions. In cerebral structures with a regular laminar structure such as the cortex and hippocampus, such a simple dipole model repeated over many constituent neurons provides a reasonable first approximation of how evoked potentials are generated. Many investigators are currently exploring the utility of modeling "equivalent dipoles" as a representation of the average amplitude and polarity within a cerebral region, such as the sensory receiving areas of the cortex.

Practical constraints to localizing the source of evoked potentials include the use of scalp recordings and the consequent "smearing" of current flow as the boundaries between zones of different conductivities are traversed; for example, the brain and its extracellular fluid are much better conductors than the scalp. Studies by Cuffin et al. (1991) have applied an experimental approach to the question of the accuracy of source localization possible with electrical signals. Using patients who had deep electrodes implanted to locate the seizure source before surgery, these investigators passed a low-level signal through two deep electrodes (a true dipole source!) and then examined how closely the signal source within the brain could be localized from scalp electrode recordings. Brain localization was found to be surprisingly good, being correct on the average within about 1 cm.

Finally, it is important to emphasize that the biological evoked potential signals recorded from the scalp are quite low level, often a few microvolts; thus signal averaging is typically used for recording of evoked potentials to extract the signal from the ongoing EEG and from noise sources such as muscle activity.

The EEG can be understood as the record of spontaneous voltage fluctuations, as "endogenously generated evoked potentials," although the brain source of the recorded fluctuations is often difficult to pinpoint, with the important exceptions of large-amplitude changes due to pathological synchronization of neural elements such as the case of spikes from seizure discharge. The EEG serves a very useful purpose in pinpointing changes in alertness and sleep stages by changes in its frequency con-

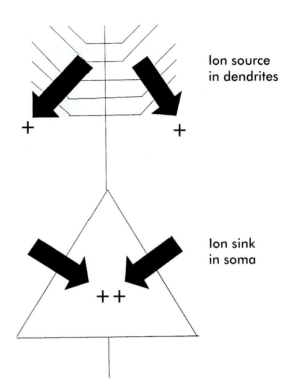

Ion source in dendrites

Ion sink in soma

**FIGURE 2–1.** Dipole generated by soma depolarization in a pyramidal neuron. See text for discussion.

**TABLE 2–1.** EEG frequency bands

| Name | Frequency range (Hz) |
|------|----------------------|
| Delta | 0.5–4 |
| Theta | 4–8 |
| Alpha | 8–14 |
| Beta | 14–32 |
| Gamma (see text) | 20–60+ |

tent, a topic discussed in the next part of this chapter.

The EEG is perhaps most useful in its roles in detecting the presence of seizure activity (discussed elsewhere in this volume), in pinpointing changes in alertness and sleep stages (a major topic of this chapter), and in analysis of gamma band activity (in which there is a growing interest). The EEG is described in terms of the amplitude of its waves and their frequency. As shown in Table 2–1, EEG frequencies are grouped into bands that range from the very low frequencies (delta, 0.5–4 Hz) to the very high frequencies (beta, 14–32 Hz, and gamma, discussed in the next section). As a general rule, the delta EEG frequencies are associated with states of consciousness with little complex processing, such as non–rapid eye movement (REM) sleep, whereas those with higher frequencies are associated with more complex processing, such as occurs in wakefulness and REM sleep (dream sleep).

**TABLE 2–2.** Polysomnographic definitions of wakefulness, non-REM sleep, and REM sleep

| State | EEG amplitude and main frequencies | Rapid eye movement (EOG) | Muscle tone (EMG) |
|---|---|---|---|
| Waking | Low-voltage, fast | + | + |
| Non-REM sleep | High-voltage, slow | − | − |
| REM sleep | Low-voltage, fast | + | − |

The alpha rhythm has a frequency range of 8–14 Hz and is best recorded over the occipital scalp region. It occurs during wakefulness, often appearing on eye closure and disappearing with eye opening. Depth recordings in animals indicate alpha rhythm frequencies may also be present in visual thalamus (lateral geniculate body, pulvinar), and the cortical component appears to be generated in relatively small cortical areas, which act as epicenters. Unfortunately, there are as yet no definitive studies of the genesis of this rhythm, although interaction of corticocortical and thalamocortical neurons has been postulated. Origins of the delta waves are discussed below, in the sleep section.

## Control of Sleep and Wakefulness

### Sleep Architecture

One-third of our lives is spent in sleep. No other single behavior occupies so much of our time, yet few other behaviors have been so mysterious. We are now beginning to unravel at least some of these mysteries, and, although much work remains, the fairly substantial revisions to this chapter from the previous edition index this progress.

Sleep is divided into two phases. REM sleep is associated with vivid dreaming and a high level of brain activity. The other phase of sleep, called non-REM sleep or slow-wave sleep (SWS), is associated with reduced neuronal activity; unlike dreaming, thought content during this state in humans is usually nonvisual and ruminative. A typical study of sleep includes recordings of the EEG, of eye movements (the electro-oculogram, or EOG), and of muscle tone (the electromyogram, or EMG). This ensemble of records is known as a polysomnogram and the recording process is called polysomnography. These key records enable us to describe the main stages of sleep. As sleep onset approaches, the low-amplitude, high-frequency EEG of alert wakefulness, often with alpha present (Figure 2–2A), yields to Stage I sleep, a brief transitional phase between wakefulness and "true" sleep. This stage is often called descending Stage I because it is a prelude to deeper sleep stages and is char-

acterized by low-voltage (amplitude), relatively high-frequency EEG patterns and slow, rolling eye movements. During Stage II sleep, there are episodic bursts of rhythmic, 14- to 16-Hz waveforms in the EEG, known as sleep spindles, interspersed with occasional short-duration, high-amplitude K complexes, so named because of their morphologic resemblance to this letter. During stage II the EEG slows still further. Stages III and IV are defined, respectively, by lesser and greater occurrence of high-amplitude, slow (0.5–4 Hz) waveforms, called delta waves. The low-voltage, fast EEG pattern of REM sleep is in marked contrast to delta sleep and resembles the non-alpha EEG pattern of active wakefulness and Stage I descending. REM sleep is further characterized by the presence of bursts of rapid eye movements (hence the name) and by loss of muscle tone in certain major muscle groups of the limbs, trunk, and neck. Often the non-REM sleep stages are lumped together and simply termed non-REM sleep. (Researchers working with animals often use the term *slow-wave sleep* for non-REM sleep, and this term sometimes appears in the literature on human sleep, although, properly speaking, Stages I and II do not have slow waves.) Table 2–2 summarizes the chief differences between waking, non-REM sleep, and REM sleep in a polysomnographic recording.

There is a rather predictable pattern of shifting between one sleep state and another during a typical night's sleep (Figure 2–2B). As the night begins, there is a stepwise descent from wakefulness to Stage I through to Stage IV sleep, followed by a more abrupt ascent back toward Stage I. However, in place of Stage I, the first REM sleep episode usually occurs at this transition point, about 70–90 minutes after sleep onset. The first REM sleep episode in humans is short. After the first REM sleep episode, the sleep cycle repeats itself with the appearance of non-REM sleep and then, about 90 minutes after the start of the first REM period, another REM sleep episode. This rhythmic cycling persists throughout the night. The cycle length of REM sleep is 90 minutes in humans, and the duration of each REM sleep episode after the first is approximately 30 minutes. During the course of the night, delta wave activity tends to diminish, and non-REM sleep has waves of higher frequencies and

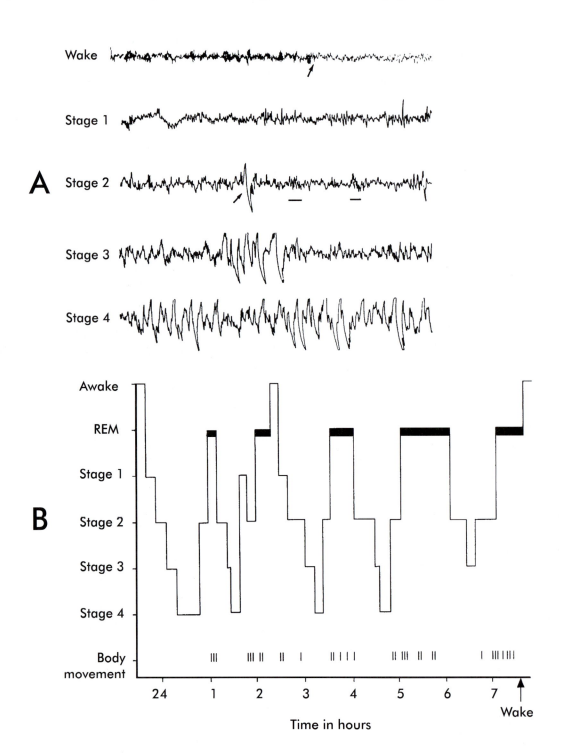

**FIGURE 2–2.** The EEG patterns associated with wakefulness and the stages of sleep (*Panel A*) and the time course of sleep stages during a night's sleep in a healthy young man (*Panel B*). During wakefulness there is a low-voltage, fast EEG pattern, often with alpha waves, as shown at the top of Panel A. At the arrow there is a transition to Stage I sleep, with loss of the alpha rhythm and the presence of a low-voltage, fast EEG. As sleep deepens, the EEG frequency slows more and more. Stage II is characterized by the presence of K complexes (arrow) and sleep spindles (underlined). During Stage III, delta waves (0.5–4 Hz) appear, and in Stage IV they are present more than 50% of the time. During REM sleep (dark bars in Panel B) the EEG pattern returns to a low-voltage fast pattern. The percentage of time spent in REM sleep increases with successive sleep cycles, while the percentage of time in Stages III and IV decreases. (EEG segments were recorded from C3, except the waking segment, which was recorded from O2 to show the alpha rhythm most clearly.)
*Source.* Adapted from Carskadon and Dement 1989.

lower amplitude. As Figure 2–2B makes clear, body movements during sleep tend to cluster just before and during REM sleep. In general, the ease of arousal from sleep parallels the ordering of the sleep stages, with REM and Stage I being the easiest for arousal and Stage IV the most difficult.

## Sleep Ontogeny and Phylogeny

Periods of immobility and "rest" are present in many lower animals, including insects and lizards. Because of the absence of a cortical brain structure like that of humans, it is difficult to say whether the absence of slow waves in these animals means they are not having the equivalent of human non-REM sleep or whether this is present but expressed in a different form, one not detectable with EEG recordings. Recent work in molecular biology suggests that evaluation of changes in gene expression in activity periods versus rest periods, as well as adenosine pharmacology (see discussion of adenosine below) may help evaluate similarities and differences in lower and higher animals during quiescence and non-REM sleep (Hendricks et al. 2000). REM sleep is present in all mammals, with the exception of egg-laying mammals (monotremes), such as the echidna (spiny anteater). Birds have very brief bouts of REM sleep. REM sleep cycles vary in duration according to the size of the animal, with elephants having the longest cycle and smaller animals having shorter cycles. For example, the cat has a sleep cycle of approximately 22 minutes, whereas the sleep cycle in the rat is about 12 minutes.

In utero, mammals spend a large percentage of time in REM sleep, ranging from 50% to 80% of a 24-hour day. At birth, animals born with immature nervous systems have a much higher percentage of REM sleep than do the adults of the same species. For example, in the human newborn, sleep occupies two-thirds of the time, with REM sleep occupying one-half of the total sleep time, or about one-third of an entire 24-hour period. The percentage of REM sleep declines rapidly in early childhood so that by approximately age 10 the adult percentage of REM sleep is reached, 20% of total sleep time. Obviously, the predominance of REM sleep in the young suggests an important function in promoting nervous system growth and development (see Function(s) of Non-REM and REM Sleep, later in this chapter).

Delta sleep (non-REM sleep stages III and IV) is minimally present in the newborn but increases during the first years of life, reaching a maximum about age 10 and declining thereafter. Feinberg and colleagues (1990) noted that the first three decades of this time course can be fit by a gamma distribution and that approximately

the same time course obtains for synaptic density and positron-emission tomography measurements of metabolic rate in human frontal cortex. These authors speculate that the reduction in these three variables may reflect a pruning of redundant cortical synapses that is a key factor in cognitive maturation, allowing greater specialization and sustained problem solving.

Physicians are frequently asked how much sleep is needed. As discussed above, the answer partly depends on the age of the individual. A good general rule is that enough sleep is needed to prevent daytime drowsiness. Each individual seems have a particular "set-point" of need. In adults, the modal value of sleep need appears to be close to the traditional 8 hours, but there is considerable individual variation. If someone functions and feels well with less sleep, there is little need for concern.

## Circadian Time of Day and Prior Wakefulness as Factors in Sleepiness

### Circadian Factors

In adult humans, the period of maximal sleepiness occurs at the time of the circadian low point of the temperature rhythm (Figure 2–3). (*Circadian* means about a day—*circa*, about; *dies*, day—and the circadian rhythm of man can be thought of as a sine-wave function with a minimum that occurs between 4:00 and 7:00 A.M. in subjects with a normal daytime activity schedule.) It is no accident that accidents are most frequent at the time near circadian temperature minima, since this is the time of maximal sleepiness. Per vehicle mile, the risk for truck accidents is greatest at this time, and the nuclear reactor incidents at both Chernobyl and Three Mile Island also occurred in the early morning hours. There is a secondary peak of sleepiness that occurs about 3:00 P.M. (Figure 2–3), corresponding to a favored time for naps. Human newborns do not have a strong circadian modulation of sleep, and some species, such as the cat, do not have much circadian modulation even as adults.

### Extent of Prior Wakefulness

Mathematical models of sleep propensity have been developed by Kronauer and colleagues (1982), who emphasize circadian control, and by Borbély (1982), who emphasizes the extent of prior wakefulness. Borbély's model postulates that the intensity and amplitude of delta-wave activity (as measured by power spectral analysis) indexes the level of sleep factor(s) and SWS drive. In this model the time course of delta activity during the night, a declining exponential, reflects the dissipation of the sleep factor(s). These workers have not specified the

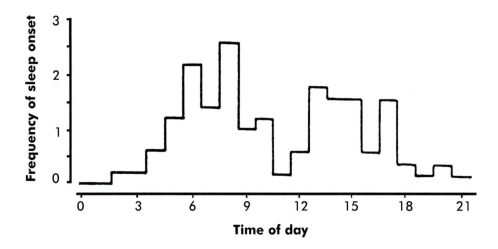

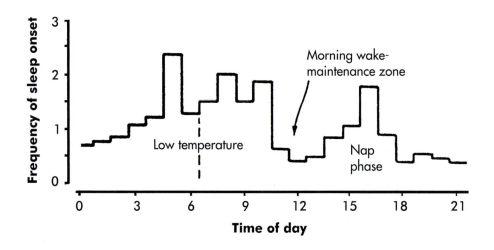

**FIGURE 2–3.** Circadian control of sleepiness and sleep onset. *Top panel.* Sleepiness at various clock times for subjects on a constant routine. Sleepiness was measured by Carskadon (see Carskadon and Dement 1989) as frequency of unintended microsleeps in subjects instructed to stay awake, with a frequency of 1 indicating the average across all measurements. Note the major peak about 6:00 A.M., at the presumptive time of temperature minimum, and a secondary peak about 3:00 P.M., a favored time for a nap. *Bottom panel.* Sleep propensity measured as the number of self-selected bedtimes/sleep onsets in subjects in whom temperature was continuously monitored. Note that, as in the top panel, the maximum number of sleep onsets occur near temperature minimum, and a secondary peak occurs at a circadian phase corresponding to about 3:00 P.M.. These subjects were maintained without circadian cues and showed decoupling of the activity and the temperature rhythms ("internal desynchronization") that are otherwise synchronized by external circadian cues, such as dawn and dusk. The sleep onsets were converted to approximate times of day by assuming a temperature minimum at 6:30 A.M.

*Source.* Adapted from Strogatz 1986.

nature of the underlying sleep factor(s), but candidates are discussed below.

The main functional consequence of deprivation of sleep seems to be the presence of "microsleeps"; that is, very brief episodes of sleep during which sensory input from the outside is diminished and cognitive function is markedly altered (Dinges et al. 1997). Furthermore, there are also long-duration effects of sleep deprivation on performance and physiology, termed *sleep debt*, that persist even after a night of recovery sleep. Deprivation-induced transcriptional changes may underlie the presence of sleep debt (see further discussion below in the context of adenosine as a sleep factor).

# EEG Phenomena of Wakefulness and Non-REM Sleep

## EEG Synchronization and Desynchronization: Neural Substrates

The high-voltage, slow-wave activity in cortex during non-REM sleep—termed *EEG synchronization*—contrasts sharply with the low-voltage, fast pattern—often termed *activated*—that is characteristic of both waking and REM sleep and that consists of frequencies in the beta range and higher. A term often used to describe the EEG of wakefulness and REM sleep is *desynchronized*, meaning that the slow waves of non-REM sleep are not visible.

## Gamma Activity

It should be noted, however, that recent work indicates that high-frequency (gamma) synchronized waves may be present in waking and in REM sleep, although these are of low amplitude. As the term is currently used, gamma frequencies are centered about 40 Hz and range from about 20 to 60 Hz, and even higher. (Table 2–1 shows an overlap between gamma and beta frequencies. This arose because the beta frequency band was originally designated in a largely arbitrary, ad hoc manner, whereas the current concept of gamma frequency activity is based on considerable basic and clinical neuroscience work. Thus, the term *gamma frequency* has come to supplant the term *beta activity*.) Gamma activity may index synchronous activity of cortical cell columns involved in neural processing, and recent work in cognitive neuroscience suggests that fast EEG activity in the gamma band (20–60 Hz) increases during—and may be involved in—the formation of percepts and memory, linguistic processing, and other behavioral and perceptual functions, including associative learning (see, for example, Miltner et al. 1999). Furthermore, recent work from our laboratory

(Kwon et al. 1999) indicates gamma activity may be deficient in schizophrenia; this paper and the associated commentary offer a short review of this area of intense current work.

One of the major advances during the late 1980s and early 1990s was the establishment of the importance of a cholinergic activating system in EEG activation. This is likely a major component of the so-called ascending reticular activating system (ARAS), a concept that arose before methods were available for labeling of neurons utilizing specific neurotransmitters. We now know that a group of neurons in the brainstem cholinergic nuclei near the pons-midbrain junction has high discharge rates in waking and REM sleep and low discharge rates in SWS. Figures 2–4 and 2–5 indicate the location of the cholinergic laterodorsal and pedunculopontine tegmental nuclei (LDT/PPT). There is also extensive anatomical evidence that these brainstem cholinergic neurons project to thalamic nuclei important in EEG desynchronization and synchronization. Both in vitro and in vivo neurophysiological studies have indicated that the target neurons in the thalamus respond to cholinergic agonists in a way consistent with EEG activation, as detailed below.

Cholinergic systems are not the exclusive substrate of EEG activation; brainstem reticular neuronal projections to thalamus, likely utilizing excitatory amino acid neurotransmission, and also noradrenergic projections from locus coeruleus and serotoninergic projections from the dorsal raphe nucleus (DRN) (for waking, since locus coeruleus and DRN monoaminergic neurons are silent in REM sleep) may also play important roles.

In addition to brainstem cholinergic systems, cholinergic and noncholinergic input to cortex and to thalamus from the basal forebrain cholinergic nucleus basalis of Meynert also plays an important role in EEG activation. Work since the previous edition has now strongly implicated the neurochemical adenosine in the regulation of wakefulness by this basal forebrain region (see below).

## Sleep Spindles

Spindles occur during Stage II of human sleep and in the light SWS phase of animals. They are composed of waves of approximately 10–12 Hz in frequency; the wave amplitude waxes and then wanes over the spindle duration of 1–2 seconds. Wave frequency varies between species and is higher in primates. Spindles are relatively well understood at the cellular level. Studies by Steriade and colleagues (reviewed in Steriade and McCarley 1990) indicate that spindle waves arise as the result of interactions between spindle pacemaker GABAergic thalamic nucleus reticularis (RE) neurons and thalamocortical neurons. Spindle waves are blocked by cholinergic brain-

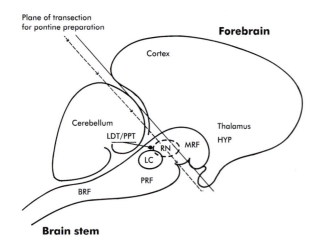

**FIGURE 2–4.** Schematic of a sagittal section of a mammalian brain (cat) showing the plane of transection that preserves REM sleep signs caudal to the transection but abolishes them rostral to the transection. Abbreviations: BRF, PRF, and MRF=bulbar, pontine, and mesencephalic reticular formations; LDT/PPT=laterodorsal and pedunculopontine tegmental nuclei, the principal site of cholinergic (acetylcholine-containing) neurons important for REM sleep and EEG desynchronization; LC=locus coeruleus, where most norepinephrine-containing neurons are located; RN=dorsal raphe nucleus, the site of many serotonin-containing neurons; HYP=hypothalamus. The basal forebrain cholinergic region lies just anterior (rostral) to the hypothalamus.
*Source.* Adapted from McCarley 1989.

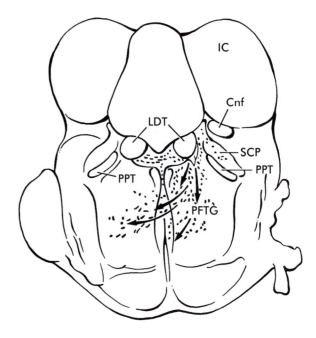

**FIGURE 2–5.** Frontal (coronal) section of the brainstem at the pons-midbrain junction showing the location of the acetylcholine-containing neurons most important for REM sleep in the laterodorsal tegmental nucleus/pedunculopontine tegmental nucleus (LDT/PPT) and a schematic of projections of LDT to pontine reticular formation. (PFTG is an abbreviation of one component of the pontine reticular formation). Abbreviations: IC=inferior colliculus; Cnf= cuneiform nucleus; SCP=superior cerebellar peduncle.
*Source.* Adapted from Mitani et al. 1988.

stem-thalamus projections, which act to hyperpolarize the RE neurons. The forebrain nucleus basalis also provides cholinergic and hyperpolarizing GABAergic input to RE that assists brainstem input in disrupting the spindles.

## Delta EEG Activity

The cellular basis of delta waves (0.5–4 Hz) is now fairly well understood. Figure 2–6 is a schematic of mechanisms proposed for the generation of delta waves by thalamocortical neurons. This sketch portrays intracellularly recorded events in a thalamocortical neuron during delta-wave generation and is based on both in vitro recordings by McCormick (1989,1990) and McCormick and Pape (1990a, 1990b) and also on in vivo work by Steriade and colleagues (1990, 1991; reviewed in Steriade and McCarley 1990). The basic concept is that a hyperpolarized membrane potential permits the occurrence of delta waves in thalamocortical circuits. Any factors depolarizing the membrane will block delta waves. During waking, input from the cholinergic forebrain nucleus basalis is

important for suppression of slow-wave activity, as shown by lesion studies (Buzsaki et al. 1988). Also, brainstem norepinephrinergic and serotoninergic projections may disrupt delta activity in waking, although they are inactive during REM sleep. During REM sleep, cholinergic input from brainstem is a major factor producing membrane depolarization, with reticular formation input— likely utilizing excitatory amino acid neurotransmission—also playing an important role. This membrane depolarization leads to suppression of delta wave activity. Thus, delta waves during sleep may be seen to represent thalamocortical oscillations occurring in the absence of activating inputs. From the standpoint of the cellular physiologist, the relative intensity of cortical desynchronization correlates well with the intensity of cholinergic input to thalamus; conversely, the relative intensity of cortical synchronization, including delta waves, correlates well with the relative absence of cholinergic activity. The identification of desynchronizing processes in sleep with ascending brainstem cholinergic and reticular activation means that the increasing intensity of EEG desynchronization preceding REM sleep is related to the

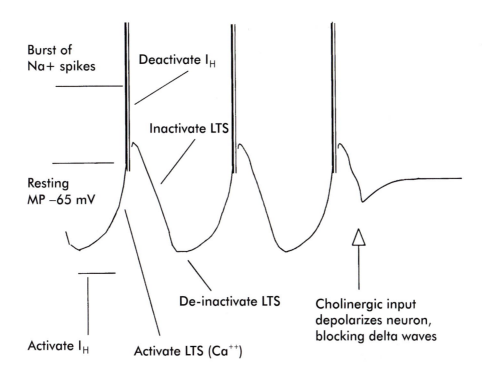

**FIGURE 2–6.** The mechanisms proposed for generation of delta waves by thalamocortical neurons. Without exogenous input, these neurons show a spontaneous oscillation of membrane potential and action potential production thaat is in the delta frequency range and likely drives the cortical delta rhythm. Oscillation occurs because of the interplay of intrinsic membrane currents. When the membrane potential is hyperpolarized (−80 mV), a particular cation current, called $I_H$ (I=current, h=hyperpolarized), is activated. This inward flow of positive ions from $I_H$ depolarizes the membrane and thereby activates a calcium current called the low-threshold spike (LTS). The inrush of calcium ions further depolarizes the neuron to the firing threshold of the sodium action potential, and a burst of action potentials is produced. Ih is turned off or deactivated at depolarized potentials. The LTS current is automatically turned off by another process called inactivation. The membrane then returns to its previous hyperpolarized level, which removes the LTS current inactivation and renders it ready for activation. The cycle then repeats itself. Delta oscillations are halted by exogenous, depolarizing input, such as the illustrated brainstem cholinergic input.

*Source.* This figure and the mechanisms described are based on the in vitro data of McCormick and Pape (1990a, 1990b) and the in vivo data of Steriade and colleagues (1990, 1991).

increasing level of activity of REM-related cholinergic and reticular activity that precedes this state (see discussion in next section).

## The "Burst Mode" of Thalamic Relay Cell Discharge and Failure of Information Transmission

Extracellular recordings by McCarley and Benoit (reviewed in Steriade and McCarley 1990) demonstrated that dorsolateral geniculate relay neurons discharged in stereotyped bursts during non-REM sleep but not during waking or REM sleep. Subsequent in vivo (by Steriade and colleagues) and in vitro investigations (by McCormick and colleagues) indicate that the bursting in thalamocortical neurons occurs when the sleep membrane is

hyperpolarized, as illustrated in Figure 2–6, in association with the delta EEG rhythm (McCormick 1989, 1990; Steriade et al. 1990, 1991). This hyperpolarization removes the inactivation of particular $Ca^{2+}$ channels and enables the production of a *calcium spike* (i.e., an inrush of depolarizing calcium ions) when a small depolarization occurs. This depolarizing calcium spike is termed a *low-threshold spike* (LTS) to distinguish it from other calcium currents with different triggering thresholds. The LTS depolarizes the neuron sufficiently to reach the threshold for fast sodium action potentials, and a burst of these action potentials rides on the LTS. However, the production of an LTS limits the following frequency of relay neurons and hence blocks rapid information transmission, as illustrated in Figure 2–7.

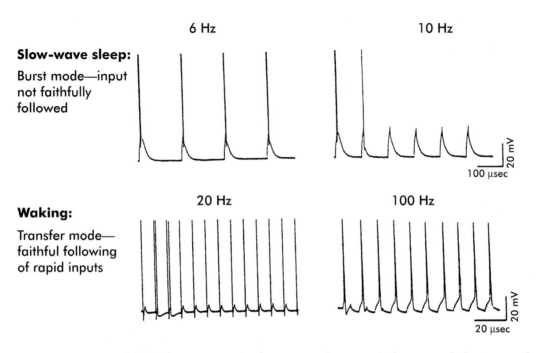

**FIGURE 2–7.**   Visual system transmission in lateral geniculate relay neurons is blocked during non-REM sleep when the neurons are in the burst mode. See text for discussion. Abbreviations: LGN=lateral geniculate nucleus; NE=norepinephrine; 5-HT=5-hydroxytryptamine (serotonin); $I_H$=hyperpolarization current; ACh=acetylcholine; GABA=γ-aminobutyric acid.

## Sleep Factors

### Humoral Sleep Factors

Several humoral factors have been proposed to account for non-REM sleep—alternatively termed SWS by us and by the literature, although, properly speaking, Stage II has few slow waves.

Pappenheimer, Karnovsky, and Krueger (reviewed in Krueger 1990) demonstrated that muramyl peptides were concentrated in the cerebrospinal fluid and urine of sleep-deprived animals. These muramyl peptides have the capability of reliably inducing SWS when injected into the lateral ventricles or into the basal part of the forebrain. The compounds also induce hyperthermia. They are derived from bacterial cell walls, and it has been theorized they might act like "vitamins" for the production of sleep. Another sleep factor is interleukin-1. Interleukin-1 is a cytokine that is produced in response to infections (and also by injections of components of bacterial cell walls such as muramyl peptides). It increases SWS and also produces hyperthermia. Hyperthermia

itself may increase SWS, but blocking the hyperthermic effects of interleukin-1 does not block the non-REM sleep–inducing effects (Krueger 1990). The argument that interleukin-1 is important in the hypersomnia associated with infections is therefore strong. There is also evidence supporting a role for interleukin-1, tumor necrosis factor, and growth hormone releasing hormone as part of the humoral mechanisms regulating physiological sleep (see review by Krueger et al. 1999). Their injection enhances non-REM sleep, whereas their inhibition reduces spontaneous sleep and sleep rebound after sleep deprivation. Changes in their mRNA levels and changes in their protein levels in the brain are consistent within their proposed role in sleep regulation, as are results from transgenic and mutant animals. They appear to be involved in the regulation of the propensity to sleep over longer time periods than the actions of adenosine, discussed below.

Hayaishi (1988, 1997) and colleagues reported that injections of prostaglandin $D_2$ into the third ventricle and the ependymal surface of the ventral forebrain reliably produce SWS. They have proposed that it is a natural sleep regulatory factor. Interestingly, these researchers have found that at least some of the sleep-inducing effects of prostaglandin could be mediated by changes in extracellular adenosine, and Krueger and Fang (1997) have suggested a model in which some of the effects of interleukin-1 might be mediated by adenosine. The possibility exists, then, that adenosine might be a "final common factor" for some other sleep factors. The recent reviews by Hayaishi (2000) and Krueger (2000) should be consulted for further details of this rapidly developing story.

## Adenosine: A Mediator of the Sleep-Inducing Effects of Prolonged Wakefulness

A growing body of evidence supports the role of the purine nucleoside adenosine as a mediator of the sleepiness following prolonged wakefulness, a role in which its inhibitory actions on the basal forebrain wakefulness-promoting neurons may be especially important (This topic is reviewed in detail by McCarley et al. [2000] and by Strecker et al. [2000], who also provide detailed literature citations). Commonsense evidence that adenosine has a role in sleepiness comes from the nearly universal use of coffee and tea to increase alertness, since these beverages contain the adenosine receptor antagonists caffeine and theophylline. We have advanced the hypothesis that, during prolonged wakefulness, adenosine accumulates selectively in the basal forebrain and promotes the transition from wakefulness to SWS by inhibiting, via the adenosine A1 receptor, cholinergic and noncholinergic wakefulness-promoting basal forebrain neurons. Regulation of the extracellular concentration of adenosine depends first on metabolism. Increased metabolism leads to reduced high-energy phosphate stores and increased adenosine, which, via an equilibrative transporter, leads to increases in extracellular adenosine (Figure 2–8A), which acts to inhibit the basal forebrain neurons that are important in the promotion of wakefulness and cortical activation (Figure 2–8B). Extracellular adenosine may also be increased by the release of adenosine triphosphate (ATP) as a cotransmitter and its breakdown, by 5′-ectonucleotidases, to adenosine. (And, as described above, adenosine may play a role in the action of other sleep factors.) Support for an adenosine-metabolism link hypothesis comes from the fact that EEG arousal is known to diminish as a function of the duration of prior wakefulness and also with brain hyperthermia, both associated with increased brain metabolism.

Earlier sections of this chapter describe how a subpopulation of cholinergic neurons in LDT/PPT and the cholinergic neurons in the basal forebrain are active during both REM sleep and waking and may contribute to the production of electroencephalographic arousal. Using an in vitro rat brainstem slice preparation, Rainnie and colleagues (1994) demonstrated that mesopontine cholinergic neurons are under the tonic inhibitory control of endogenous adenosine. Whole-cell and extracellular recordings of identified cholinergic neurons showed an adenosine inhibitory tone that was mediated postsynaptically by an inwardly rectifying potassium conductance and by an inhibition of a hyperpolarization-activated current ($I_H$). Similar inhibition of discharges mediated by the adenosine A1 receptor occurred in basal forebrain cholinergic and noncholinergic neurons. Moreover, Benington et al. (1995), using systemic and intracerebroventricular injections, showed that A1 receptor stimulation mimicked the electroencephalographic effects of sleep deprivation.

In vivo work in animals by Portas and colleagues (1997) demonstrated that microdialysis perfusion of adenosine in the basal forebrain or LDT/PPT (brainstem) zones of cholinergic neurons produced a strong reduction in wakefulness and in the activated EEG. This pointed to this region as a specifically important site of adenosine action. Key evidence that adenosine fulfilled the criteria for being a factor mediating sleep after prolonged wakefulness was the finding that, in the basal forebrain, extracellular adenosine progressively accumulated with each succeeding hour of wakefulness (Porkka-Heiskanen et al. 1997). Moreover, use of a nucleoside transport blocker to increase the basal forebrain adenosine concentration to approximately the level found during sleep deprivation mimicked the effect of sleep deprivation on both the EEG power spectrum and behavioral state distribution: wakefulness was decreased, and there were increases in SWS and REM sleep. As predicted, microdialysis application of the specific A1 receptor antagonist cyclopentyltheophylline in the basal forebrain produced the opposite effects on behavioral state, increasing wakefulness and decreasing SWS and REM sleep. Data from combined unit recording and microdialysis studies have shown that basal forebrain neurons selectively active in wakefulness, compared with SWS, have discharge activity suppressed by both adenosine and the A1-specific agonist cyclohexyladenosine, whereas discharge activity is increased by the A1 receptor antagonist cyclopentyltheophylline.

Does adenosine exert its effects in the brain locally, that is, in specific regions, or globally? Measurements in multiple brain areas showed that sustained adenosine accumulation during prolonged wakefulness (6 hours) occurred only in the cat basal forebrain, and to a lesser extent in cerebral cortex (Porkka-Heiskanen et al. 2000). Somewhat to the surprise of these investigators, adenosine concentrations did not increase elsewhere during

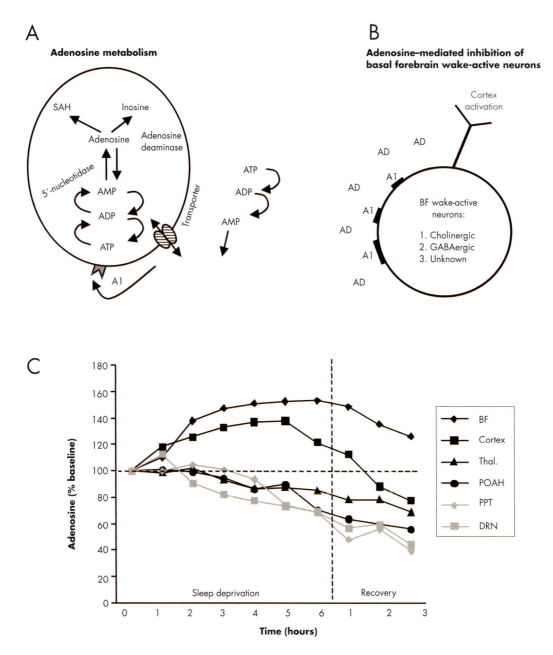

**FIGURE 2–8.** *Panel A.* Schematic of main intracellular and extracellular metabolic pathways of adenosine. The intracellular pathway from adenosine 5′-triphosphate (ATP) to adenosine diphosphate (ADP) to adenosine monophosphate (AMP) to adenosine is respectively regulated by the enzymes ATPase, ADPase, and 5′-nucleotidase and extracellularly by the respective ectoenzymes. Adenosine kinase converts adenosine to AMP, whereas adenosine deaminase converts adenosine to inosine. The third enzyme to metabolize adenosine is S-adenosylhomocysteine hydrolase, which converts adenosine to *S*-adenosylhomocysteine (SAH). Adenosine concentration between the intracellular and extracellular spaces is equilibrated by nucleoside transporters. *Panel B.* Schematic of the effects of adenosine on cells in the basal forebrain (BF). Extracellular adenosine (AD) acts on the A1 adenosine receptor subtype to inhibit neurons promoting EEG activation and wakefulness. *Panel C.* Adenosine concentrations in six different brain areas during sleep deprivation and recovery sleep. Note that in basal forebrain (BF, top line) adenosine levels increase progressively during the 6 hours of sleep deprivation, then decline slowly in recovery sleep. Visual cortex most closely resembles BF, but adenosine levels decrease during the last hour and fall precipitously during recovery. Other brain areas show no sustained rise in adenosine levels with deprivation. This pattern and other data (see text) suggest that basal forebrain is likely a key site of action for adenosine as a mediator of the sleepiness following prolonged wakefulness.

*Source.* Panels A and B adapted from Figure 8, and Panel C from Figure 6, in Porkka-Heiskanen et al. 2000.

prolonged wakefulness even in regions important in behavioral state control, such as the preoptic-anterior hypothalamus region, DRN, and nor did it increase in the ventrolateral/ventroanterior thalamic nuclei (Figure 2–8C). These data suggest the presence of brain region–specific differences in adenosine transporters and/or degradation that become evident with prolonged wakefulness, even though adenosine concentrations were higher in all brain sites sampled during the naturally occurring (and shorter-duration) episodes of wakefulness compared with sleep episodes in the freely moving and behaving animals.

## Adenosine and Sleep Debt

Recent data indicate that sleep deprivation may alter transcriptional activity in the basal forebrain via the induction of the transcription factor nuclear factor kappa B (NF-κB); in vitro experiments show that induction of NF-κB is mimicked by adenosine (Basheer et al. 2001b). It is possible that the production of NF-κB and other transcriptional factors may lead to the long-term changes in alertness and cognitive performance that occur with sleep deprivation, often termed *sleep debt*. The recent finding that sleep deprivation causes an increase in mRNA for the adenosine $A_1$ receptor (Basheer et al. 2001b) and the fact that NF-κB is a transcription factor for the $A_1$ receptor suggest that some of the sleep debt changes may be caused by increased $A_1$ receptor availability and hence increased sensitivity to adenosine.

## Active Non-REM Sleep–Promoting Mechanisms

Electrophysiological recordings of basal forebrain and anterior hypothalamic neurons indicate that some are selectively active during non-REM sleep and might represent an active sleep-promoting mechanism (see review by Szymusiak [1995]). Work by Sherin and colleagues (1996) used the immediate early gene protein product c-fos to detect neurons in the ventrolateral preoptic area that were selectively active during non-REM sleep; immunohistochemistry suggested that these neurons were GABAergic, whereas anatomical studies indicated projections to wakefulness-promoting histaminergic neurons in posterior hypothalamus and to brainstem nuclei important in EEG arousal. Much current work is investigating the interaction of these neurons with other systems important in sleep.

# REM Sleep Physiology and Relevant Brain Anatomy

The brain physiology and neurotransmitters important for the generation of REM sleep are, in general, better understood than those for SWS, although many important questions about REM sleep mechanisms and especially about the function of REM sleep remain unanswered.

## Neural Machinery of the REM Sleep Rhythm

Transection studies show that the brainstem contains the neural machinery of the REM sleep rhythm. As illustrated in Figure 2–4, a transection made just above the junction of the pons and midbrain produces a state in which the periodic occurrence of REM sleep can be found in recordings made in the isolated brainstem, whereas, in contrast, recordings in the isolated forebrain show no sign of REM sleep. These lesion studies by Jouvet and colleagues in France (reviewed in Jouvet 1979) established the importance of the brainstem in REM sleep.

## Reticular Formation Neurons

Brainstem reticular formation neurons are important as effectors in the production of the physiological events of REM sleep. As in humans, the cardinal signs of REM sleep in lower animals are muscle atonia, EEG desynchronization (low-voltage, fast pattern), and rapid eye movements. PGO (for pons, geniculate, and occipital) waves are also an important component of REM sleep found in recordings from deep brain structures in many animals. (They are visible in the cat recordings of Figure 2–9.) There is suggestive evidence that PGO waves are present in humans, but the depth recordings necessary to establish their existence have not been done. Their features have been extensively described in animals. PGO waves are spiky EEG waves that arise in the pons and are transmitted to the thalamic lateral geniculate nucleus (a visual system nucleus) and to the visual occipital cortex, hence the name PGO waves. PGO waves represent an important mode of brainstem activation of the forebrain during REM sleep and are also present in nonvisual thalamic nuclei.

Most of the physiological events of REM sleep have effector neurons located in the brainstem reticular formation, with important neurons especially concentrated in the pontine reticular formation (PRF). Thus PRF neuronal recordings are of special interest for information on mechanisms of production of these events. Intracellular recordings of PRF neurons (Figure 2–9) show that these neurons have relatively hyperpolarized membrane potentials and generate almost no action potentials during non-REM sleep. As illustrated in Figure 2–9, PRF neurons begin to depolarize even before the occurrence of the first EEG sign of the approach of REM sleep, the PGO

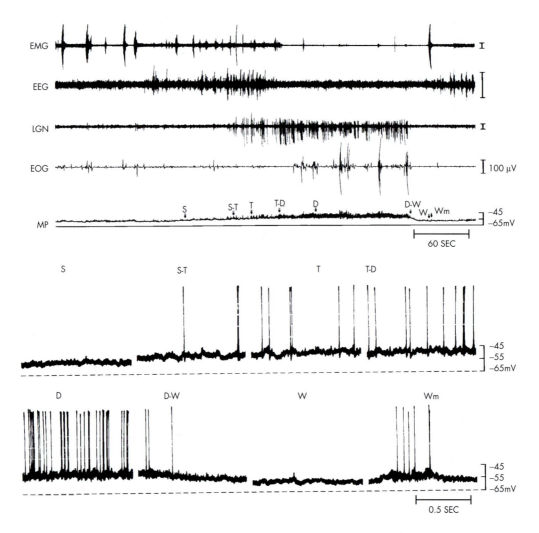

**FIGURE 2–9.** Changes in action-potential frequency and membrane potential alteration of an intracellularly recorded medial pontine reticular formation neuron in a cat during a sleep-wake cycle. The top panel shows the inkwriter record defining state and the record of membrane potential (MP) with action potentials filtered out; the lower panel shows cathode ray oscilloscope photographs taken at the indicated points in the inkwriter record. The record begins in waking (W): note there is eye movement activity in the EOG record; a low-voltage, fast electroencephalogram (EEG); and activity in the EMG record, indicating somatic movement. During waking, the membrane potential was about –60 mV and remained at approximately the same level with the onset of sleep (S) (note the EEG slow-wave activity). Postsynaptic potential (PSP) activity in sleep was low. Even before the onset of the first PGO wave in the lateral geniculate nucleus (LGN) record, the MP showed a gradual onset of MP depolarization. By the time of the first LGN PGO wave (labeled S-T), the PSP activity had increased and there was one action potential. With the advent of more PGO waves (segment T, transition period) and the onset of REM sleep (indicated by the letter D—for desynchronized sleep, another name for REM sleep) there was further MP depolarization and an accompanying increase in action potentials and PSPs (bottom panel, T and T-D); the increase in PSPs is visible as the thickening of the inkwriter MP trace. With the onset of full REM sleep (D) and during runs of the phasic activity of PGO waves and REMs, there were storms of depolarizing PSP activity and corresponding action potentials (segment D). The MP remained tonically depolarized about –50 mV throughout REM sleep, with further phasic depolarizations. With the end of REM sleep and the onset of waking (D-W), there was a membrane repolarization to about the same tonic –57 mV level seen in the initial waking episode. At the point marked Wm, there was a somatic movement that was accompanied by increased PSPs, a transient (phasic) membrane depolarization, and a burst of action potentials, before the MP returned to its baseline waking polarization level. Abbreviations: EMG=nuchal electromyogram; EEG=sensorimotor cortex electroencephalogram; LGN=EEG record from lateral geniculate nucleus; EOG=electro-oculogram.

*Source.* Adapted from Steriade and McCarley 1990.

waves that occur 30–60 seconds before the onset of the rest of the electroencephalographic signs of REM sleep. As PRF neuronal depolarization proceeds and the threshold for action potential production is reached, these neurons begin to discharge (generate action potentials). Their discharge rate increases as REM sleep is approached, and the high level of discharge is maintained throughout REM sleep due to the maintenance of a membrane depolarization.

Throughout the entire REM sleep episode almost the entire population of PRF neurons remains depolarized. The resultant increased action potential activity leads to the production of the REM sleep physiological signs that have their physiological bases in PRF neurons. REM sleep can be viewed as the state arising from increases in activity of the various populations of reticular formation neurons that are important as effectors of REM sleep phenomena. PRF neurons are important for the rapid eye movements (the generator for saccades is in the PRF) and the PGO waves (a different group of neurons), and a group of dorsolateral PRF neurons controls the muscle atonia of REM sleep (these neurons become active just before the onset of muscle atonia). Neurons in the midbrain reticular formation (MRF) (see Figure 2–4) are especially important for EEG desynchronization for the low-voltage, fast EEG pattern. As mentioned earlier, these neurons were originally described as making up the ARAS, the set of neurons responsible for EEG desynchronization. Subsequent work has enlarged this original ARAS concept to include cholinergic neurons.

## Cholinergic Mechanisms

The neurotransmitter acetylcholine has been shown to be of great importance for REM sleep. The essential data supporting this conclusion are outlined below (for more detailed reviews, see Greene and McCarley 1990, McCarley et al. 1995, and Steriade and McCarley 1990).

1. *Injection of compounds that are acetylcholine agonists into the PRF produces a REM-like state that very closely mimics natural REM sleep.* The latency to onset and duration are dose dependent. Muscarinic receptors appear to be especially critical, with nicotinic receptors of lesser importance.
2. *There are naturally occurring cholinergic projections to reticular formation neurons.* These arise in the two nuclei at the pons-midbrain junction (Figures 2–4 and 2–5): the LDT and the PPT (see Mitani et al. 1988).
3. *In vitro studies show that a majority (80%) of reticular formation neurons are excited by cholinergic agonists,* *with muscarinic effects being especially pronounced.* In vitro studies in the PRF slice preparation show that the increased excitability and membrane depolarization produced by cholinergic agonists is a direct effect, since it persists when synaptic input has been abolished by the addition of tetrodotoxin.
4. (a) *Experiments involving lesions of the LDT/PPT nuclei confirm their importance in producing REM sleep phenomena.* Destruction of the cell bodies of LDT/PPT neurons by local injections of excitatory amino acids leads to a marked reduction of REM sleep. (b) *Electrical stimulation of the LDT increases REM sleep.*
5. *A group of LDT/PPT neurons discharges selectively in REM sleep, and the onset of activity begins before the onset of REM sleep.* This LDT/PPT discharge pattern and the presence of excitatory projections to the PRF suggest that these cholinergic neurons may be important in producing the depolarization of reticular effector neurons for REM sleep events. The group of LDT/PPT and reticular formation neurons that become active in REM sleep are often referred to as *REM-on neurons.*
6. *Cholinergic neurons are important in the production of the low-voltage, fast (LVF) EEG pattern (representing "cortical activation") in both REM sleep and waking.* A different group of cholinergic neurons in the LDT/PPT is active during this LVF pattern in both REM sleep and waking. As described, this cholinergic system is especially important in generating the LVF EEG pattern, often called the *activated EEG;* also playing a role in forebrain activation are projections from midbrain reticular neurons and aminergic neurons, especially those in locus coeruleus. Together these neuronal groups form the ARAS. Evidence that multiple systems are involved in EEG desynchronization comes from the inability of lesions of any single one of these systems to disrupt EEG desynchronization on a permanent basis.

*Peptides.* The reader should be aware of the many peptides that are co-localized with the neurotransmitter acetylcholine in LDT/PPT neurons; this co-localization likely also means that they have synaptic co-release with acetylcholine. The peptide substance P is found in about 40% of LDT/PPT neurons, and overall, more than 15 different co-localized peptides have been described. The role of these peptides in modulating acetylcholine activity relevant to wakefulness and sleep remains to be elucidated. Noncholinergic neurons in the LDT/PPT contain the peptide vasoactive intestinal peptide, and several different investigators have

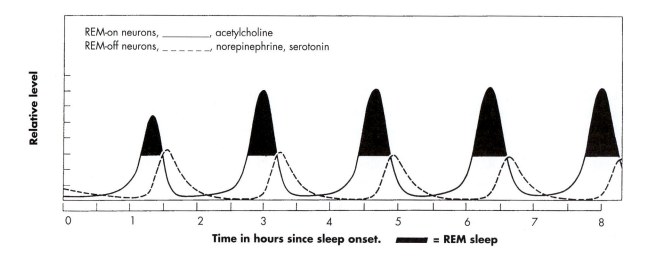

**FIGURE 2–10.**　Schematic of a night's course of REM sleep in humans showing the occurrence and intensity of REM sleep as dependent on the activity of populations of "REM-on" (i.e., REM-promoting) neurons, indicated by the solid line. As the REM-promoting neuronal activity reaches a certain threshold, the full set of REM signs occurs (black areas under curve indicate REM sleep). Note, however, that, unlike the steplike EEG diagnosis of stages seen in Figure 2–2, the underlying neuronal activity is a continuous function. The neurotransmitter acetylcholine is thought to be important in REM sleep production, acting to excite populations of brainstem reticular formation neurons to produce the set of REM signs. Other neuronal populations utilizing the monoamine neurotransmitters serotonin and norepinephrine are likely REM-suppressive; the time course of their activity is sketched by the dashed line. (These curves mimic actual time courses of neuronal activity, as recorded in animals, and were generated by a mathematical model of REM sleep, the limit cycle reciprocal interaction model of McCarley and Massaquoi 1986).

reported its ability to enhance REM sleep percentages when it is injected intraventricularly.

*REM-on neurons* are neurons that become active in REM sleep (compared with SWS and waking) and presumably have a protagonist role in the production of REM sleep phenomena. Figure 2–10 illustrates the time course of these neurons and also of those neurons with an opposite discharge time course that become inactive in REM sleep, called *REM-off neurons*. REM-off neurons are most active in waking, have discharge activity that declines in SWS, and are virtually silent in REM sleep until they resume discharge toward the later portion of the REM sleep episode. This inverse pattern of activity to REM-on neurons and to REM sleep phenomena such as PGO waves has led to the hypothesis that these neurons may be REM-suppressive and interact with REM-on neurons in control of the REM sleep cycle. As noted in Figure 2–10, norepinephrine- and serotonin-containing neurons are REM-off and are discussed in the next section. *Histamine-containing neurons* are located in the posterior hypothalamus and are REM-off. This system has been conceptualized as one of the wakefulness-promoting systems, in agreement with drowsiness as a common side effect of antihistamin-

ics. Transection studies indicate, however, that the histaminergic neurons are not essential for the REM sleep oscillation.

## Suppression of REM Sleep Phenomena by REM-Off Neurons

**Inhibitory modulation of cholinergic neurons by serotonin and norepinephrine.**　Thus far, we have described how reticular effector neurons are modulated by cholinergic and other neurotransmitter activity. But what controls the cholinergic neurons, and how does this influence REM sleep? Early extracellular recordings of neurons in the locus coeruleus and in the DRN documented that these neurons were maximally active in waking, had diminished activity during non-REM sleep, and virtually ceased discharge as REM sleep was approached and entered. As this discharge time course was often described as a "REM-off" pattern, these neurons are referred to as *REM-off neurons* (see review in McCarley et al. 1995). *Norepinephrine-containing neurons* are principally located in the locus coeruleus, called the "blue spot" because of its appearance in unstained brain. *Serotonin-containing neurons* are located in the *raphe system* of the brainstem, the midline collection of neurons that extends from the bulb to the midbrain, with higher concentrations of serotonin-containing neurons in the more rostral raphe nuclei. The finding of REM-off neurons led to a structural and mathematical model of REM sleep by McCarley and Hobson (1975) (the reciprocal interaction model), that had as one of its postulates that the REM-off neurons inhibited the REM-promoting, REM-on neurons. For many years this was regarded as a highly controversial postulate. Work during the last 5 years, however, has supported this hypothesis.

There is anatomical evidence indicating that the DRN sends serotoninergic projections and that the locus coeruleus sends norepinephrinergic projections to both LDT and PPT (see citations and review of data in this paragraph in McCarley et al. 1995). In vitro experiments in a number of laboratories have now shown that serotonin inhibits cholinergic neurons of the LDT and PPT. For example, Luebke et al. (1992) showed that about two-thirds of histologically identified cholinergic neurons recorded in the rat in vitro preparation responded to the application of serotonin with a membrane hyperpolarization and decrease in input resistance. Whole-cell patch clamp recordings revealed that the hyperpolarizing response was mediated by an inwardly rectifying potassium current. Pharmacologic studies have shown that the serotonin (5-HT) effect was mimicked by application of the selective 5-HT$_{1A}$ receptor agonist 8-hydroxy-2-(di-n-propylamino) tetralin (8-OH DPAT), suggesting that a 5-HT$_{1A}$ receptor was involved. The same results were obtained with tetrodotoxin present in the bathing medium, indicating that the serotonin effects were direct.

Williams and Reiner (1993) obtained very similar inhibitory results with norepinephrine. Ninety-two percent of histologically identified cholinergic LDT neurons in the rat in vitro preparation were hyperpolarized in response to norepinephrine, whereas noncholinergic neurons exhibited mixed responses. A direct effect of norepinephrine was indicated by the persistence of hyperpolarizing effects in low-$Ca^{2+}$, high-$Mg^{2+}$ solutions. This hyperpolarization was mimicked by the $\alpha_2$ adrenoceptor agonist UK-14,304 and was blocked by the $\alpha_2$ adrenoceptor antagonist idazoxan, which suggests an $\alpha_2$ receptor–mediated response. Interestingly, the norepinephrine response in the cholinergic LDT neurons was mediated by an inwardly rectifying potassium current similar to that activated by serotonin.

**In vivo modulation of REM sleep by decreasing serotoninergic activity of the dorsal raphe nucleus.** The in vitro data are quite clear about the strong inhibitory effect of serotonin on cholinergic LDT neurons. However, the systems neurophysiology question remains as

to the strength of this input. We have mentioned that DRN neurons (presumptively serotoninergic) slow and virtually cease discharge with the approach and onset of REM sleep. Could this withdrawal of inhibitory input be sufficiently strong as to disinhibit the cholinergic neurons and permit the occurrence of a REM sleep episode? The capability to use microdialysis techniques in the DRN of freely moving cats offered an opportunity for a direct test of the hypothesis of serotoninergic inhibition of REM sleep. Portas and McCarley (1994) inserted microdialysis probes into the DRN; using high-performance liquid chromatography and electrochemical detection techniques, they demonstrated a capability of detecting changes of a few femtomoles in serotonin concentrations. In samples collected over spontaneously occurring sleep cycles, the serotonin concentrations in the DRN had the same ordering as did presumptively serotoninergic unit discharge rates: waking followed by non-REM sleep (SWS), followed by REM sleep. This presumptively reflected the detection of serotonin released by DRN recurrent collaterals (and this ordering of concentrations matched that found in forebrain recordings, as reviewed in McCarley et al. 1995). These investigators reasoned that if one were able to inhibit the DRN, the degree of subsequent enhancement of REM sleep would provide an index of the strength of DRN inhibitory control. For inhibition of the DRN, the specific 5-HT$_{1A}$ agonist 8-OH DPAT was selected, since it is known to exert powerful inhibitory effects via soma-dendritic 5-HT$_{1A}$ receptors. The experimental protocol (Portas et al. 1996) involved measurement of behavioral state percentages and serotonin concentrations during a control period, and then addition of 8-OH DPAT in 10-$\mu$M concentrations to the incoming artificial cerebrospinal fluid in the dialysis probe. As illustrated in Figure 2–11, the effects during the period of perfusion with 8-OH DPAT were clear: 1) there was a strong reduction in extracellular concentration of 5-HT, indicating inhibition of DRN activity, and 2) there was a 300% increase in the percentage of REM sleep, presumptively reflecting the disinhibition of brainstem LDT/PPT cholinergic neurons.

Using in vivo microdialysis of the selective agonist for 5-HT$_{1A}$ receptors, 8-OH DPAT, combined with single-unit recording, Thakkar et al. (1998) demonstrated that the discharge of REM-on neurons was almost completely suppressed by 8-OH DPAT (Figure 2–12A). Unlike the REM-on neurons, the wake/REM-on neurons were not inhibited by microdialysis of 8-OH DPAT (Figure 2–12B), and there was no overlap between the two populations (Figure 2–12C).

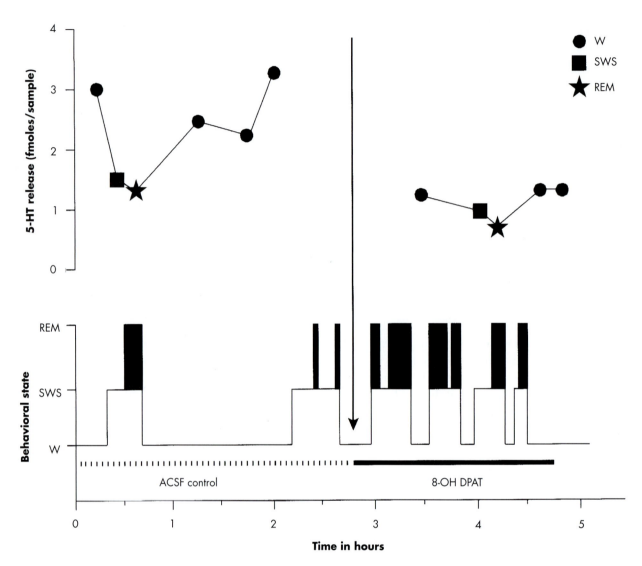

**FIGURE 2–11.** Time course of serotonin (5-HT) levels (top portion of figure) and behavioral state (bottom portion of figure) before and microdialysis perfusion of the 5-HT$_{1A}$ receptor agonist 8-hydroxy-2-(di-n-propylamino) tetralin (8-OH DPAT) in the dorsal raphe nucleus during a typical experiment in a spontaneously behaving animal. Note that, in the control perfusion of artificial cerebrospinal fluid (ACSF) (interrupted horizontal line), waking DRN 5-HT levels (circles) are higher than those in slow-wave sleep (SWS) (squares) and REM sleep (stars). Each 5-HT value is expressed as femtomoles per 7.5-μL sample and was obtained during an uninterrupted 5-minute sequence of the behavioral state. On the onset of perfusion of 10 μM of 8-OH DPAT (arrow), the 5-HT level dropped quickly to levels as low as those normally present in SWS or REM sleep, because of the inhibitory action of 8-OH DPAT on the 5-HT$_{1A}$ somatodendritic receptors on serotonin-ergic neurons. Behaviorally, 8-OH DPAT administration markedly increased REM sleep (black bars in the hypnogram) by more than 300%. These data support the hypothesis of a REM inhibitory effect of serotoninergic dorsal raphe neurons.
*Source.* Adapted from Portas et al. 1996.

## Mathematical and Structural Model of the Occurrence of REM Sleep Based on the Interaction of REM-Off and REM-On Neurons

The reciprocal interaction model, originally proposed by Hobson and McCarley (McCarley and Hobson 1975), rather accurately predicts the timing and percentage of REM sleep during a night of human sleep and its variation

with the circadian temperature rhythm. The results of McCarley and Massaquoi's (1986) revised limit cycle mathematical formulation are presented in Figure 2–10 and are sufficiently faithful to the actual human sleep data to furnish a good schematic. Figure 2–13 depicts the interaction of groups of neurons proposed to generate REM sleep. The area of most intense current investigation is examining why raphe nucleus and locus coeruleus

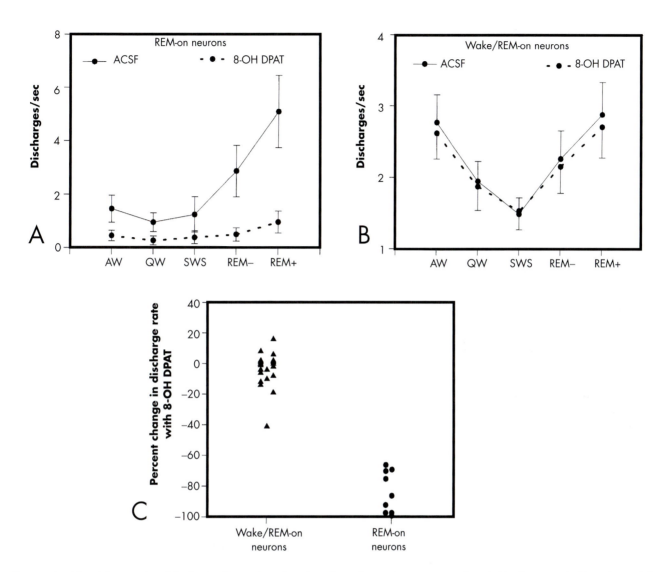

**FIGURE 2–12.** Neuronal activity in the laterodorsal and pedunculopontine tegmental nuclei brainstem cholinergic nuclei. *Panel A.* REM-on units mean (+SEM) of discharge rate in each behavioral state before (solid line, ACSF) and after (dotted line) 10 μM 8-hydroxy-2-(di-n-propylamino) tetralin (8-OH DPAT) was added to the perfusate. Note the suppression of activity (highly statistically significant). *Panel B.* Wake/REM-on units mean (+SEM) discharge rate before (solid line, ACSF) and after (dotted line) 10 μM 8-OH DPAT was added to the perfusate. Note no significant effect of 8-OH DPAT. *Panel C.* Scattergram showing, for each wake/REM-on unit and each REM-on unit, the mean percentage change (across all behavioral states) in the discharge rate during 8-OH DPAT perfusion. Note that the wake/REM-on and REM-on populations of neurons do not overlap. These data support the hypothesis of a suppressive effect of serotonin on REM-on neurons. Abbreviations: AW=active wakefulness; QW=quiet wakefulness; SWS=slow-wave sleep; REM+, REM–=REM sleep discharge rate during the presence of, and in the absence of, eye movements and PGO waves.

activity declines during the sleep cycle and becomes nearly absent in REM sleep. One explanation is that the discharge activity of locus coeruleus and DRN neurons diminishes as a result of feedback inhibition from the recurrent inhibitory collaterals that are present in both locus coeruleus and DRN neurons (illustrated as 3 in Figure 2–13). This recurrent inhibition acts at $5\text{-HT}_{1A}$ receptors in the DRN and at $\alpha_2$ receptors in the locus coeruleus. However, although the evidence for recurrent inhibition is strong, there is currently no direct evidence for second-messenger-mediated inhibitory effects, needed because of the long duration of the inhibition. Another (nonexclusive) possibility, illustrated as 4 in Figure 2–13, is that GABAergic input, active during REM sleep, inhibits DRN and locus coeruleus neurons. Reports from Nitz and Siegel (1997a, 1997b) indicate that GABA levels, as measured with in vivo microdialysis, are significantly increased in REM sleep compared with waking at

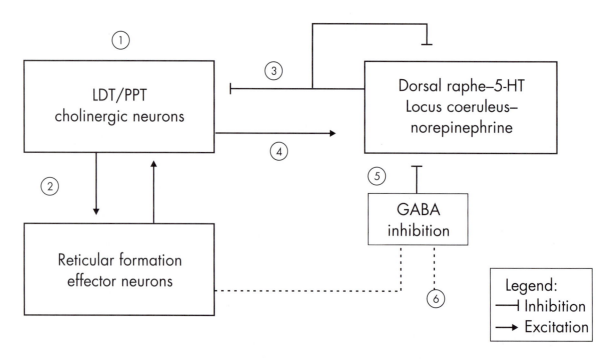

**FIGURE 2–13.** Structural model of REM sleep control (reciprocal interaction model). (1) Cholinergic neurons activate (2) reticular formation neurons in a positive-feedback interaction to produce the onset of REM sleep. REM sleep is terminated by the inhibitory activity of (3) REM-off monoaminergic neurons (top right box), which become active at the end of a REM sleep period due to their recruitment by REM-on activity (4). REM-off neuronal activity decreases in slow-wave sleep and becomes minimal at the onset of REM sleep, possibly due to self-inhibitory feedback and/or GABAergic inhibitory input (5), which may arise from a subset of reticular formation neurons which are GABAergic and/or other sources (6), such as periaqueductal gray (PAG) or ventrolateral preoptic area (VLPOA) (the dashed line indicates the current uncertainty about this mechanism). This decreased REM-off activity disinhibits REM-on neurons and allows the onset of a REM sleep episode. The cycle then repeats itself.

both DRN and locus coeruleus sites. The interrupted line in Figure 2–13 from reticular formation to the GABAergic neurons indicates the uncertainty about the exact source of increased GABA in the DRN and locus coeruleus. Recent data suggest that this might come from GABAergic neurons outside these nuclei. Gervasoni et al. (2000) found that microiontophoresis of the GABA$_A$ antagonist bicuculline restores tonic DRN discharge during REM sleep and that retrograde labeling showed that GABAergic (GAD-positive) neurons from widely dispersed areas project to the DRN. These areas include the hypothalamus (most dense projection), the substantia nigra reticular part, the ventral tegmental area, the ventral pontine periaqueductal gray substance, and the rostral oral pontine reticular nucleus and other brainstem regions, including the parabrachial region and prepositus hypoglossi. However, unit recordings in these areas have yet to identify neurons with the proper time course of activity to produce, through inhibition, the observed state-related decrease in DRN activity in non-REM sleep and the virtual silence in REM sleep.

## Orexin, Narcolepsy, and the Control of Sleep and Wakefulness

An exciting recent development is the discovery of the important role of lateral hypothalamic neurons containing the neuropeptide orexin (alternatively known as hypocretin) in behavioral state regulation and narcolepsy/cataplexy. Narcolepsy is a chronic sleep disorder that is characterized by excessive daytime sleepiness, fragmented sleep, and other symptoms that are indicative of abnormal REM sleep expression; these latter symptoms include cataplexy, hypnagogic hallucinations, sleep-onset REM periods, and sleep paralysis (Aldrich 1998; Sinton and McCarley 2000a, in press). An abnormality in the gene for the orexin type II receptor has been found to be the basis of canine inherited narcolepsy (Lin et al. 1999), whereas orexin knockout mice (−/−) have increased REM sleep, sleep-onset REM periods, and also cataplexy-like episodes entered directly from states of active movement (Chemelli et al. 1999; see Figure 2–14). Cataplexy in canines and rodents consists of attacks

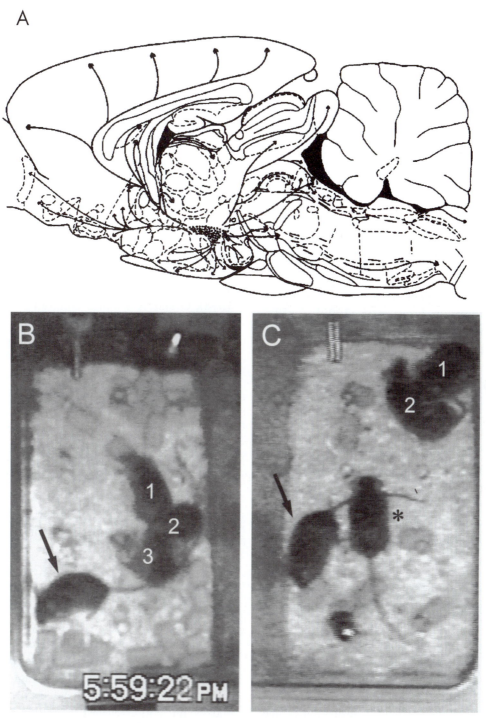

**FIGURE 2–14.** *Panel A.* Schematic sagittal section drawing of the location of orexin-containing neurons (dots in hypothalamus) and their widely distributed projection pathways in the rat brain. *Panel B.* Digitally captured infrared video image of orexin knockout mice at age 4 weeks. Note that one mouse (arrow) has completely fallen onto his side in a cataplexy episode (confirmed in other mice by EEG). The film shows the fuzziness (motion artifact) associated with body movement in behaving, active littermates, designated 1 to 3. *Panel C.* Digitally captured infrared video image of orexin knockout mice at age 4 weeks. Note that one mouse has fallen completely onto his side (arrow), while the another has collapsed onto his ventral surface (asterisk). Littermates designated 1 and 2 are quietly sleeping in their usual corner of the cage. In both B and C, the onset of the dark (active) phase was at 5:30 P.M., and Panel C was recorded at 8:26 P.M.

*Source.* Panel A modified from Figure 14 in Peyron et al. 1998. Panels B and C reproduced with permission from Figure 3 in Chemelli et al. 1999; a video of these episodes is available at http://www.cell.com/cgi/content/full/98/4/437/DC1.

of sudden bilateral atonia in antigravity muscles, with consequent collapse; these episodes last from a few seconds to a few minutes and are often provoked by emotion or excitement, such as food presentation to dogs (Chemelli et al. 1999; Mignot 1998). Recent confirmation in humans of the importance of orexin has been provided by Nishino et al. (2000), who reported that narcoleptic humans often have undetectable levels of orexin in CSF. In addition to the control of wakefulness and sleep, orexins may have a neuromodulatory role in several neuroendocrine and homeostatic functions such as food intake, body temperature regulation, and blood pressure regulation, (Chemelli et al. 1999; de Lecea et al. 1998; Peyron et al. 1998; van den Pol 1999).

## The Orexin System

In late 1997, orexin/hypocretin was identified by two independent groups. de Lecea et al. (1998) identified two related peptides, hypocretin-1 and hypocretin-2, using a direct-tag polymerase chain reaction subtraction technique to isolate mRNA from hypothalamic tissue. Shortly thereafter, and using a different approach, Sakurai et al. (1998) identified these same two peptides, which they termed orexin-A (hypocretin-1) and orexin-B (hypocretin-2). Sakurai et al. (1998) used a systematic biochemical search to find endogenous peptide ligands that would bind to G protein–coupled cell surface receptors that had no previously known ligand (orphan receptors). These first two reports indicated that neurons containing the orexins are found exclusively in the dorsal and lateral hypothalamic areas (de Lecea et al. 1998; Sakurai et al. 1998) and that the orexins may function as neurotransmitters, since they were localized in synaptic vesicles and had neuroexcitatory effects on hypothalamic neurons (de Lecea et al. 1998). Orexin-A and orexin-B are neuropeptides of 33 and 28 amino acids, respectively; they are derived from a single precursor protein.

As shown in Figure 2–14, immunohistochemical studies reveal a distribution of orexin projections that is remarkable for the targeting of a number of distinct brain regions known to be involved in the regulation of sleep and wakefulness, including both brainstem and forebrain systems (Date et al. 1999; Elias et al. 1998; Horvath et al. 1999a; Nambu et al. 1999; Peyron et al. 1998). Orexin projections to forebrain include the cholinergic basal forebrain (in the rat this includes the horizontal limb of the diagonal band of Broca, the magnocellular preoptic nucleus, and the substantia innominata) and the histaminergic tuberomamillary nucleus. Brainstem targets include the pontine and medullary brainstem reticular formation, the cholinergic mesopontine tegmental nuclei (including the LDT), the locus coeruleus, and the DRN (see brainstem schematic in Figure 2–4).

Orexin-A has been shown to excite the noradrenergic neurons of the locus coeruleus, providing at least one documented mechanism by which orexin can promote wakefulness (Hagan et al. 1999; Horvath et al. 1999b) and suppress REM sleep. However, orexin is not always excitatory, and the work by van den Pol et al. (1998) reveals the variety and complexity of orexinergic effects at the cellular level, both presynaptic and postsynaptic. The net effect of these actions on a particular brain circuit system physiology and consequent behavioral effects needs to be determined at the systems level for each brain region.

## Orexin Receptors and Their Distribution

Two orexin receptors have been identified (Sakurai et al. 1998). Orexin-A is a high-affinity ligand for the orexin receptor type I, whose affinity for orexin-B is one to two orders of magnitude lower. The orexin receptor type II exhibits equally high affinity for both peptides. Currently there are no ligands sufficiently specific for orexin type I and II receptors to define their distribution. In situ hybridization studies of orexin receptor mRNAs (Chemelli et al. 1999, citing their own unpublished data; Trivedi et al. 1998) have shown a diffuse pattern, consistent with the widespread nature of orexin projections, although there was a marked differential distribution of the orexin type I and II mRNAs. Of the brain regions involved in state control, only the DRN and the locus coeruleus appear to show a predominance of mRNA for type I receptors.

## Orexin and the Control of REM-Related Phenomena

The knockout and canine narcolepsy data suggested that an absence of orexin or a defective orexin type II receptor would produce cataplexy. Where might this be mediated? In the absence of an effective antagonist to orexin receptors, our laboratory decided to use antisense oligodeoxynucleotides against the mRNA for orexin type II receptors (Thakkar et al. 1999), thereby producing a "reversible knockout" of the type II orexin receptor. Spatial specificity was obtained by microdialysis perfusion of orexin type II receptor antisense in the rat PRF just ventral to the locus coeruleus (but presumably not affecting the locus coeruleus, which has predominantly type I receptors). This treatment, as predicted, increased REM sleep two- to threefold during both the light period (quiescent phase) and the dark period (active phase). Furthermore, this manipulation produced increases in behavioral cataplexy, suggesting that the REM sleep and narcolepsy-related role of orexin is mediated via the action of orexin in the brainstem nuclei that control the expression of REM sleep signs.

## Orexin and the Control of Wakefulness

Chemelli et al. (1999), as well as others (David Rye, personal communication, November 1999), have noted a heavy concentration of orexin-containing fibers around the somata of cholinergic neurons of the basal forebrain. This suggested that orexin might act not only on REM-related phenomena but also on wakefulness control. Our laboratory has recently found that microdialysis perfusion of orexin into the cholinergic basal forebrain of the rat produced a dose-dependent enhancement of wakefulness, with the highest dose producing more than a five-fold increase in wakefulness (Thakkar et al. 2001).

## Orexin Release: Linked to Circadian Cycle and/or to Behavioral State?

Remarkably, very little is known about whether orexin release is a function of the circadian cycle and/or a function of behavioral state. This is an important theoretical question, since simulations based on the McCarley-Massequoi-Hobson model described above showed that circadian effects on the REM cycle could be faithfully mimicked by postulating an excitatory drive on locus coeruleus and DRN neurons during times of circadian activity, with withdrawal of the drive during times of circadian inactivity leading to sleep. Taheri et al. (2000) have described diurnal variation in orexin-A immunoreactivity and prepro-orexin mRNA expression in the rat, findings that suggest a circadian fluctuation in orexin release, as do very preliminary ELISA orexin assays in our laboratory (unpublished data).

At the time of writing, the field of orexin research is one of intense activity. Orexin is particularly interesting to sleep researchers and clinicians because it affects both REM sleep and wakefulness and is likely closely linked to the human sleep disorder narcolepsy.

## Molecular Biology of Sleep

An early round of studies focused on immediate early genes (IEGs), such as *c-fos*, and found that, in a number of species, the expression of IEGs is very low or absent during non-REM sleep but, as a rule, is very high when the animal is spontaneously awake or sleep deprived (see review in Tononi et al. 2000). To be noted as an exception is c-fos expression in the ventrolateral preoptic area, where some cells express c-fos as a function of time

asleep (see previous discussion of the Sherin et al. 1996 findings). Recently, other techniques have been used to obtain more specific indicators of which genes might be differentially expressed, including differential display and cDNA microarray technology. Interestingly Tononi et al. (2000) report that only a small subset (<0.01%) of genes have expression altered during the sleep cycle, and an even smaller subset are affected by long-term sleep deprivation. Wakefulness expression of IEGs seems to be under the control of the locus coeruleus. The mRNA transcripts of genes affected by wakefulness and sleep fall into three main groups: 1) genes resident in mitochondria, probably reflecting changes in energy demand during wakefulness and relatively short-term (3 hours in the rat) sleep deprivation; 2) IEGs and genes for transcription factors, perhaps related to plasticity; and 3) a heterogeneous group of other genes, including growth factors brain-derived neurotropic factor and bone morphogenetic protein 2. This latter group showed more expression after long-term sleep deprivation (8 hours in the rat), a pattern not seen in the first two groups. There is increasing interest in rest-activity cycles in lower animals, such as *Drosophila*, where an analysis of genetic expression is simpler than in higher organisms (see the description of changes in the adenosine section of this chapter). Obviously, the knowledge of the molecular biology of sleep is in a phase of rapid advancement, and its integration with the considerable body of knowledge concerning sleep mechanisms appears to be an important future pathway for progress.

## The Form of Dreams and the Biology of REM Sleep

REM sleep is strongly associated with dreaming, with about 80% of awakenings during the REM state producing a dream report. In experiments involving awakenings at random intervals throughout the night, 80% of all such randomly elicited dream reports have been found to occur during REM sleep. Dreams that do occur in non-REM sleep have been found to be less vivid and intense than REM sleep dreams, suggesting that they may represent a pre-REM state during which brainstem neuronal activity is approximating that of REM sleep but the EEG has not yet changed.

Dreams have a long history of interest both in popular culture and in psychiatry. Sigmund Freud, writing before the presence of the biological state of REM sleep was known, suggested that dreams represented a symbolic disguise of an unacceptable unconscious wish (e.g., sexual or aggressive wishes); the purpose of the disguise was to prevent the disruption of sleep that would occur with consciousness of the undisguised wish. Today the activation of the neural systems responsible for REM sleep would seem to be a more accurate and simple explanation for the instigation of the dream state that is linked to the cyclic appearance of REM sleep. There remains the question, however, of why dreams have their own distinctive characteristics and are different from waking consciousness (a review of this topic is in McCarley 1993).

The *activation-synthesis hypothesis* proposed by Hobson and McCarley (1977) suggests that many of the characteristic formal features of dreams are isomorphic (i.e., parallel) with distinctive features of the physiology of REM sleep. By formal features is meant universal aspects of dreams, distinct from the dream content particular to an individual (McCarley and Hoffman 1981). As an example of a formal feature of a dream, consider the presence of motor activity in dreams. At the physiological level, it is known that motor systems, both at the motor cortex and at the brainstem level, are activated during REM sleep episodes. Paralleling motor system activation at the physiological level is the finding that movement in dreams is extremely common, with almost one-third of all verbs in dreams indicating movement and 80% of dreams having some occurrence of leg movement (a movement that was easily and reliably scored in dream reports).

Similarly, there is activation of sensory systems during REM sleep. The visual system is intensely activated in REM sleep, and all dreams have visual experiences (and indeed these are one of the defining features of a dream). An important source of visual system activation during REM sleep is from the PGO waves. The activation-synthesis theory suggests that this intense activation of visual and other sensory systems is the substrate for dream sensory experiences. Supporting this theory is the rather frequent occurrence—about 9% of all REM sleep dreams—of dreams with intense "vestibular sensations," that is, dreams of flying, floating, falling, soaring, tumbling, and so on, easily relatable to the vestibular system functions of sensing position of the body in space and changes of position. The presence of dreams with vestibular sensations was highly atypical of the daytime sensory experience of the subjects whose dream reports were examined and is thus incompatible with any dream theory linked to a simple "recall" of previous experiences. Rather, the dream experience may reflect the intense vestibular system activation of REM sleep, followed by its elaboration and synthesis into dream content. The final product, the dream, thus represents the synthesis of both the brainstem-induced motor and sensory activation with the par-

ticular memories and personality characteristics of the dreamer.

Lesion-induced release of REM sleep motor activity supports 1) the presence of neural commands for patterned motor activity in REM sleep and 2) a direct correspondence of the motor system commands and the subjective content of the dream. Activation of motor systems in REM sleep can be observed in cats with a lesion of the muscle atonia zone of the PRF and a consequent *REM sleep without atonia*, a state in which motor activity is released but all of the other signs of REM sleep are present. The failure of muscle atonia is also observed in a human disorder called *REM sleep behavior disorder.* In individuals with this disorder, the muscle activity observed has been found always to parallel the dreamed activity. This close linkage between the physiology and psychology of REM sleep and dreams supports the activation-synthesis hypothesis.

When the activation-synthesis hypothesis was first proposed, it aroused considerable controversy, perhaps because it seemed to threaten psychological interpretation of dreams. Although this theory clearly places instigation of the dream state as a concomitant of a basic biological rhythm, there appears, at least to this author, to be more than ample room for the addition of personal characteristics in the process of synthesis of brainstem-instigated activation. For example, interpretations of the Rorschach cards are rich sources of information on personality, although the images on the cards themselves were certainly not generated by psychologically meaningful mechanisms.

Finally, it should be noted that as more is learned about forebrain processing during REM sleep, a more complete and complex theory will emerge. Recent neuroimaging studies in both humans and cats have indicated activation of the limbic system, with little activation of the prefrontal cortex (reviewed in Maquet 2000). These data suggest a biological basis of activation of memories and emotions in REM sleep and also, perhaps, a mechanism of their linkage, as well as the absence of prefrontal activation being reflected in the absence of a sense of control over one's activities in the dream. Also, as described in the next section on REM sleep function, many current theories postulate a role for this state in memory processing, and dreams may come by their unusual character as a result of the complex associations that are culled from memory during the REM sleep state.

## Function(s) of Non-REM and REM Sleep

In contrast to the previous edition, in which it was suggested that "there are many theories but relatively few solid data on the function of sleep," work in the past several years has begun to bear fruit in unraveling the deep mystery of the functions of sleep, although much remains to be learned. Space limitations restrict me to a brief summary.

## Non-REM Sleep

**Behavioral immobilization or "out of harm's way."** The theory of behavioral immobilization suggests that sleep evolved as a way of arresting behavior at a time when it might not be advantageous, such as night activity in animals with poor night vision and vulnerability to predators.

**Rest theory.** Neuronal recordings and brain metabolic studies indicate the presence of rest on the neural level as well as the behavioral level during non-REM sleep. This naturally raises the question of what is rested or restored, and where in the brain this might occur. The new data on adenosine (see above) are highly compatible with a restoration of high-energy phosphates during non-REM sleep, especially in the wakefulness-related centers highly active during this state. However, direct experimental demonstration of reduced high-energy phosphates in wakefulness still awaits demonstration, although there is evidence for repletion of glycogen stores during non-REM sleep (J.D. Geiger, personal communication, June 2001).

**Memory processing.** Buzsaki and colleagues (Nadasdy et al. 1999) have presented data supporting the theory that, during non-REM sleep in the rat, neuronal spike sequences observed during waking wheel running were "replayed" at a faster time scale during single sharp-wave bursts of slow-wave sleep. The hypothesis is that the endogenously expressed spike sequences during sleep reflect reactivation of the circuitry modified by previous experience, which may serve to consolidate information in neocortex.

## REM Sleep

The following theories are not mutually exclusive. Indeed, it seems a cogent argument that a complex behavioral state such as REM sleep may have multiple functions and, as for wakefulness, it may not be meaningful to speak of "the" function of REM sleep.

**Promotion of growth and development of the nervous system.** The abundance of this metabolically and neurally active state in the young argues for the hypothesis that REM sleep promotes the growth and development of the nervous system. The French scientist Jouvet has suggested that the stereotyped motor command patterns of REM sleep are useful in promoting epigenetic development of these circuits (reviewed in Jouvet 1979) and that during the periodic PGO bursts of REM sleep during each episode of REM sleep, an endogenous programming is activated that integrates genetic and cortical information and underpins psychological individuation (Jouvet 2000).

**A "circuit exercise/maintenance function" in the adult.** It is postulated that maintenance of neural circuits requires use, and that with increasing diversity of behaviors possible in more advanced animals, REM sleep serves as a "fail-safe" mode for ensuring the activation and consequent maintenance of sensorimotor circuits. Crick and Mitchison (1983) have proposed that REM sleep is a state in which unwanted processing modes are eliminated; chief among these are cortical "parasitic oscillations," a kind of neural analog to obsessive thoughts. In this theory, the PGO wave activity acts to reset and redirect the unwanted neural loops. The authors themselves note that a full test of this theory will have to be postponed until our ability to monitor complex neural processing has greatly increased.

**Memory processing.** Memories may be consolidated and/or processed during sleep. Hippocampal neurons that encode spatial location and that are activated during wakefulness are preferentially activated in subsequent REM periods compared with the non-wake-activated neurons; the inference is that "memories" are being related to other brain information (summarized in Winson 1990). Winson suggests that a general function of REM sleep is "off-line" processing of information acquired during the day by comparison with other information acquired throughout the individual's lifetime. These data are compatible with recent work by Poe et al. (2000), who found that hippocampal cells active in familiar places during waking exhibited a reversal of firing phase relative to local theta oscillations in REM sleep. Because firing phase can influence whether synapses are strengthened or weakened, this experience-dependent phase shift, which developed progressively over multiple sessions in the environment, was consistent with the hypothesis that circuits may be restructured during REM sleep by selectively strengthening recently acquired memories and weakening older ones (this paper also provides a good review of recent work in this area). It is of note that some visuospatial perceptual learning has been demonstrated to be dependent on REM sleep (Karni et al. 1994).

## Prospects for the Future

As is detailed in a subsequent chapter of this volume, investigation of the sleep alterations associated with psychiatric disorders has proved to be one of the richer fields of clinical research. The vistas for future clinical applications appear even more promising as we come to know the basic neurobiology of both the REM and the non-REM phases of sleep. It will become increasingly important for clinical researchers to know about these neurobiological advances to be able to pose the most relevant questions in their studies of disordered human sleep. The ultimate prospect is for a clinical science of psychiatry that is firmly rooted in basic neurobiology.

## References

Aldrich MS: Diagnostic aspects of narcolepsy. Neurology 50:S2–S7, 1998

Basheer R, Halldner L, Lauri A, et al: Opposite changes in adenosine A1 and A2A receptor mRNA in the rat following sleep deprivation. Neuroreport 12:1577–1580, 2001a

Basheer R, Rainnie DG, Porkka-Heiskanen T, et al: Adenosine, prolonged wakefulness, and A1-activated NF-κB DNA binding in the basal forebrain of the rat. Neuroscience 104:731–739, 2001b

Benington JH, Kodali SK, Heller HC: Stimulation of A1 adenosine receptors mimics the electroencephalographic effects of sleep deprivation. Brain Res 692:79–85, 1995

Borbély AA: A two process model of sleep regulation. Human Neurobiology 1:195–204, 1982

Borbély AA, Hayaishi O, Sejnowski TJ, et al: The Regulation of Sleep. Strasbourg, France, Human Frontier Science Program, 2000

Buzsaki G, Bickford RG, Ponomareff G, et al: Nucleus basalis and thalamic control of neocortical activity in the freely moving rat. J Neurosci 8:4007–4026, 1988

Carskadon MA, Dement WA: Normal human sleep: an overview, in Principles and Practices of Sleep Medicine. Edited by Kryger MH, Roth T, Dement WC. New York, WB Saunders, 1989, pp 3–13

Chemelli RM, Willie JT, Sinton CM, et al: Narcolepsy in orexin knockout mice: molecular genetics of sleep regulation. Cell 98:437–451, 1999

Chokroverty S (ed): Sleep Disorders Medicine, 2nd Edition. Boston, MA: Butterworth-Heinemann, 1999, pp 21–50

Crick F, Mitchison G: The function of dream sleep. Nature 304:111–114, 1983

Cuffin BN, Cohen D, Yunokuchi K, et al: Tests of EEG localization accuracy using implanted sources in the human brain. Ann Neurol 29:132–138, 1991

Date Y, Ueta Y, Yamashita H: Orexins, orexigenic hypothalamic peptides, interact with autonomic, neuroendocrine and neuroregulatory systems. Proc Natl Acad Sci U S A 96:748–753, 1999

de Lecea L, Kilduff TS, Peyron C, et al: The hypocretins: hypothalamus-specific peptides with neuroexcitatory activity. Proc Natl Acad Sci U S A 95:322–327, 1998

Dinges DF, Pack F, Williams K, et al: Cumulative sleepiness, mood disturbances and psychomotor vigilance performance decrements during a week of sleep restricted to 4–5 hours per night. Sleep 20:267, 1997

Elias CF, Saper CB, Maratos-Flier E, et al: Chemically defined projections linking the mediobasal hypothalamus and the lateral hypothalamic area. J Comp Neurol 402:442–459, 1998

Feinberg I, Thode HC, Chugani HT, et al: Gamma function describes maturational curves for delta wave amplitude, cortical metabolic rate and synaptic density. J Theor Biol 142:149–161, 1990

Gervasoni D, Peyron C, Rampon C, et al: Role and origin of the GABAergic innervation of dorsal raphe serotonergic neurons. J Neurosci 20:4217–4225, 2000

Greene RW, McCarley RW: Cholinergic neurotransmission in the brainstem: implications for behavioral state control, in Brain Cholinergic Systems. Edited by Steriade M, Biesold D. Oxford, UK, Oxford University Press, 1990, pp 224–235

Hagan JJ, Leslie RA, Patel S, et al: Orexin A activates locus coeruleus cell firing and increases arousal in the rat. Proc Natl Acad Sci U S A 96:10911–10916, 1999

Hayaishi O: Sleep-wake regulation by prostaglandins $D_2$ and $E_2$. J Biol Chem 263:14593–14596, 1988

Hayaishi O: Prostaglandin D2 and sleep, in Sleep and Sleep Disorders: From Molecule to Behavior. Edited by Hayaishi O, Inoue S. Tokyo, Academic Press/Harcourt Brace, 1997, pp 3–10

Hayaishi O: Regulation of sleep by prostaglandin D2 and adenosine, in The Regulation of Sleep. Edited by Borbély AA, Hayaishi O, Sejnowski TJ, et al. Strasbourg, France, Human Frontier Science Program, 2000, pp 97–102

Hendricks JC, Finn SM, Panckeri KA, et al: Rest in Drosophila is a sleep-like state. Neuron 25:129–138, 2000

Hobson JA, McCarley RW: The brain as a dream state generator: an activation-synthesis hypothesis of the dream process. Am J Psychiatry 134:1335–1348, 1977

Horvath TL, Diano S, van den Pol AN: Synaptic interaction between hypocretin (orexin) and neuropeptide Y cells in the rodent and primate hypothalamus: a novel circuit implicated in metabolic and endocrine regulations. J Neurosci 19:1072–1087, 1999a

Horvath TL, Peyron C, Diano S, et al: Hypocretin (orexin) activation and synaptic innervation of the locus coeruleus noradrenergic system. J Comp Neurol 415:145–159, 1999b

Jouvet M: What does a cat dream about? Trends Neurosci 2:15–16, 1979

Jouvet M: REM sleep as a genetic programming system for psychological individuation, in The Regulation of Sleep. Edited by Borbély AA, Hayaishi O, Sejnowski TJ, et al. Strasbourg, France, Human Frontier Science Program, 2000, pp 171–178

Karni A, Tanne D, Rubenstein BS, et al: Dependence on REM sleep of overnight improvement of a perceptual skill. Science 265:679–682, 1994

Kronauer RE, Czeisler CA, Pilato SF, et al: Mathematical model of the human circadian system with two interacting oscillators. Am J Physiol Regul Integr Comp Physiol 242(11): R3–R17, 1982

Krueger JM: Somnogenic activity of immune response modifiers. Trends Pharmacol Sci 11:122–126, 1990

Krueger JM: Cytokines and growth factors in sleep regulation, in The Regulation of Sleep. Edited by Borbély AA, Hayaishi O, Sejnowski TJ, et al. Strasbourg, France, Human Frontier Science Program, 2000, pp 122–130

Krueger JM, Fang J: Cytokines in sleep regulation, in Sleep and Sleep Disorders: From Molecule to Behavior. Edited by Hayaishi O, Inoue S. Tokyo, Academic Press/Harcourt Brace, 1997, pp 261–277

Krueger JM, Obal F, Fang J: Humoral regulation of physiological sleep: cytokines and GHRH. J Sleep Res 8 (suppl 1):53–59, 1999

Kryger MH, Roth T, Dement WC: Principles and Practices of Sleep Medicine, 3rd Edition. New York: WB Saunders, 2000

Kwon JS, O'Donnell BF, Wallenstein GV, et al: Gamma frequency range abnormalities to auditory stimulation in schizophrenia. Arch Gen Psychiatry 56:1001–1005, 1999

Lin L, Faraco J, Li R, et al: The sleep disorder canine narcolepsy is caused by a mutation in the hypocretin (orexin) receptor 2 gene. Cell 98:365–376, 1999

Luebke JI, Greene RW, Semba K, et al: Serotonin hyperpolarizes cholinergic low threshold burst neurons in the rat laterodorsal tegmental nucleus in vitro. Proc Natl Acad Sci U S A 89:743–747, 1992

Maquet PAA: Functional neuroanatomy of normal human sleep, in The Regulation of Sleep. Edited by Borbély AA, Hayaishi O, Sejnowski TJ, et al. Strasbourg, France, Human Frontier Science Program, 2000, pp 86–93

McCarley RW: The biology of dreaming sleep, in Principles and Practices of Sleep Medicine. Edited by Kryger MH, Roth T, Dement WC. New York, WB Saunders, 1989, pp 173–183

McCarley RW: Dreams and the biology of sleep, in Principles and Practices of Sleep Medicine, 2nd Edition. Edited by Kryger MH, Roth T, Dement WC. New York, WB Saunders, 1993, pp 373–383

McCarley RW, Hobson JA: Neuronal excitability modulation over the sleep cycle: a structural and mathematical model. Science 189:58–60, 1975

McCarley RW, Hoffman EA: REM sleep dreams and the activation-synthesis hypothesis. Am J Psychiatry 138:904–912, 1981

McCarley RW, Massaquoi SG: A limit cycle mathematical model of the REM sleep oscillator system. Am J Physiol 251:R1011–R1029, 1986

McCarley RW, Greene RW, Rainnie D, et al: Brain stem neuromodulation and REM sleep. Seminars in the Neurosciences 7:341–354, 1995

McCarley RW, Strecker RE, Thakkar MM, et al: Adenosine and 5-HT as regulators of behavioural state, in The Regulation of Sleep. Edited by Borbély AA, Hayaishi O, Sejnowski TJ, et al. Strasbourg, France, Human Frontier Science Program, 2000, pp 103–112

McCormick DA: Cholinergic and noradrenergic modulation of thalamocortical processing. Trends Neurosci 12:215–221, 1989

McCormick DA: Cellular mechanisms of cholinergic control of neocortical and thalamic neuronal excitability, in Brain Cholinergic Systems. Edited by Steriade M, Biesold D. Oxford, UK, Oxford University Press, pp 236–264, 1990

McCormick DA, Pape HC: Noradrenergic and serotonergic modulation of a hyperpolarization-activated cation current in thalamic relay neurons. J Physiol (Lond) 431:319–342, 1990a

McCormick DA, Pape HC: Properties of a hyperpolarization-activated cation current and its role in rhythmic oscillation in thalamic relay neurons. J Physiol (Lond) 431:291–318, 1990b

Mignot E: Genetic and familial aspects of narcolepsy. Neurology 50 (suppl 1):S16–S22, 1998

Miltner WHR, Braun C, Arnold M, et al: Coherence of gamma-band EEG activity as a basis for associative learning. Nature 397:434–436, 1999

Mitani A, Ito K, Hallanger AH, et al: Cholinergic projections from the laterodorsal and pedunculopontine tegmental nuclei to the pontine gigantocellular tegmental field in the cat. Brain Res 451:397–402, 1988

Nadasdy Z, Hirase H, Czurko A, et al: Replay and time compression of recurring spike sequences in the hippocampus. J Neurosci 19:9497–9507, 1999

Nambu T, Sakurai T, Mizukami K, et al: Distribution of orexin neurons in the adult rat brain. Brain Res 827:243–260, 1999

Nishino S, Ripley B, Overeem S, et al: Hypocretin (orexin) deficiency in human narcolepsy. Lancet 355:39–40, 2000

Nitz D, Siegel JM: GABA release in the dorsal raphe nucleus: role in the control of REM sleep. Am J Physiol Regul Integr Comp Physiol 273:R451–R455, 1997a

Nitz D, Siegel JM: GABA release in the locus coeruleus as a function of sleep/wake state. Neuroscience 78:795–801, 1997b

Peyron C, Tighe D, van den Pol A, et al: Neurons containing hypocretin (orexin) project to multiple neuronal systems. J Neurosci 18:9996–10015, 1998

Poe GR, Nitz DA, McNaughton BL, et al: Experience-dependent phase-reversal of hippocampal neuron firing during REM sleep. Brain Res 855(1):176–180, 2000

Porkka-Heiskanen T, Strecker RE, Thakkar MM, et al: Adenosine: a mediator of the sleep-inducing effects of prolonged wakefulness. Science 276:1265–1268, 1997

Porkka-Heiskanen T, Strecker RE, McCarley RW: Brain site-specificity of extracellular adenosine concentration changes during sleep deprivation and spontaneous sleep: an in vivo microdialysis study. Neuroscience 99(3):507–517, 2000

Portas CM, McCarley RW: Behavioral state-related changes of extracellular serotonin concentration in the dorsal raphe nucleus: a microdialysis study in the freely moving cat. Brain Res 648:306–312, 1994

Portas CM, Thakkar M, Rainnie D, et al: Microdialysis perfusion of 8-OH-DPAT in the dorsal raphe nucleus decreases serotonin release and increases REM sleep in the freely moving cat. J Neurosci 16:2820–2828, 1996

Portas CM, Thakkar M, Rainnie DG, et al: Role of adenosine in behavioral state modulation: a microdialysis study in the freely moving cat. Neuroscience 79:225–235, 1997

Rainnie DG, Grunze HCR, McCarley RW, et al: Adenosine inhibits mesopontine cholinergic neurons: implications for EEG arousal. Science 263:689–692, 1994

Regan D: Human Brain Electrophysiology. New York, Elsevier, 1989

Sakurai T, Amemiya A, Ishii M, et al: Orexins and orexin receptors: a family of hypothalamic neuropeptides and G protein-coupled receptors that regulate feeding behavior. Cell 92:1, 1998

Sherin JE, Shiromani PJ, McCarley RW, et al: Activation of ventrolateral preoptic neurons during sleep. Science 271:216–219, 1996

Sinton CM, McCarley RW: Neuroanatomical and neurophysiological aspects of sleep: basic science and clinical relevance. Semin Clin Neuropsychiatry 5(1):6–19, 2000a

Sinton CM, McCarley RW: Sleep Disorders. Encyclopedia of Life Sciences, Macmillan Reference Ltd. (in press)

Steriade M, McCarley RW: Brainstem Control of Wakefulness and Sleep. New York, Plenum, 1990

Steriade M, Gloor P, Llinás RR, et al: Basic mechanisms of cerebral rhythmic activities. Electroencephalogr Clin Neurophysiol 76:481–508, 1990

Steriade M, Curró Dossi R, Nuñez A: Network modulation of a slow intrinsic oscillation of cat thalamocortical neurons

implicated in sleep delta waves: cortically induced synchronization and brainstem cholinergic suppression. J Neurosci 11:3200–3217, 1991

Strecker RE, Morairty S, Thakkar MM, et al: Adenosinergic modulation of basal forebrain and preoptic/anterior hypothalamic neuronal activity in the control of behavioral state. Behav Brain Res 115(2):183–204, 2000

Strogatz SH: The Mathematical Structure of the Human Sleep-Wake Cycle. New York, Springer-Verlag New York, 1986

Szymusiak R: Magnocellular nuclei of the basal forebrain: substrates of sleep and arousal regulation. Sleep 18:478–500, 1995

Taheri S, Sunter D, Dakin C, et al: Diurnal variation in orexin A immunoreactivity and prepro-orexin mRNA in the rat central nervous system. Neurosci Lett 279(2):109–112, 2000

Thakkar MM, Strecker RE, McCarley RW: Behavioral state control through differential serotonergic inhibition in the mesopontine cholinergic nuclei: a simultaneous unit recording and microdialysis study. J Neurosci 18:5490–5497, 1998

Thakkar MM, Ramesh V, Cape EG, et al: REM sleep enhancement and behavioral cataplexy following orexin (hypocretin) II receptor antisense perfusion in the pontine reticular formation. Sleep Res Online 2:113–120, 1999

Thakkar MM, Ramesh V, Strecker RE, et al: Microdialysis perfusion of orexin-A in the basal forebrain increases wakefulness in freely behaving rats. Arch Ital Biol 139:313–328, 2001

Tononi G, Cirelli C, Shaw PJ: Molecular correlates of sleep, the awake state and sleep deprivation, in The Regulation of Sleep. Edited by Borbély AA, Hayaishi O, Sejnowski TJ, et al. Strasbourg, France, Human Frontier Science Program, 2000

Trivedi P, Yu H, MacNeil DJ, et al: Distribution of orexin receptor mRNA in the rat brain. FEBS Lett 438:71–75, 1998

van den Pol AN: Hypothalamic hypocretin (orexin): robust innervation of the spinal cord. J Neurosci 19:3171–3182, 1999

van den Pol AN, Gao XB, Obrietan K, et al: Presynaptic and postsynaptic actions and modulation of neuroendocrine neurons by a new hypothalamic peptide, hypocretin/orexin. J Neurosci 18:7962–7971, 1998

Williams JA, Reiner PB: Noradrenaline hyperpolarizes identified rat mesopontine cholinergic neurons in vitro. J Neurosci 13:3878–3883, 1993

Winson J: The meaning of dreams. Sci Am 263:86–96, 1990

# CHAPTER 3

# Functional Neuroanatomy

*Neuropsychological Correlates of Cortical and Subcortical Damage*

Daniel Tranel, Ph.D.

Nearly a century and a half ago, investigators began to note that damage to discrete brain regions could lead to highly selective deficits in behavior (for a historical review, see Feinberg and Farah 1997). For example, in the 1860s the surgeon and physical anthropologist Paul Broca made the observation that damage to the anterior part of the left side of the brain led to a deficit in the production of speech, while sparing speech comprehension (Broca 1863, 1865). A complementary observation was reported some 10 years later by the neuropsychiatrist Carl Wernicke, who noted that damage to the posterior part of the left hemisphere led to a disturbance in the comprehension of speech, while sparing speech production (Wernicke 1874). These observations eventually led to the notion that humans speak and process language with the left side of the brain. In fact, these early writings became the cornerstones on which the fields of neuropsychology, neuropsychiatry, and cognitive neuroscience were established. By now, many consistent relationships between brain and behavior have been established, and a wide range of cognitive and behavioral capacities associated with particular brain regions can be highlighted. In this chapter, a variety of brain-behavior relationships are described, with a focus on the correlations between brain and behavior that are scientifically most robust and clinically most important.

Much of the work described in this chapter was done with the lesion method approach in humans. In this method, the demonstration of reliable relationships between particular cognitive defects and damage to particular neural structures is taken as evidence that those neural structures are related to those cognitive functions in the normal human brain. This level of analysis focuses on neural systems, that is, macroscopic neural structures and their interconnections, and on higher-order cognitive and behavioral capacities such as memory, language, decision making, and moral reasoning. This is to be distinguished from other levels of analysis regarding the central nervous system (e.g., single-cell recording, analysis of molecular and cellular mechanisms) which, while very much valid in their own right, do not figure as prominently in current understanding of higher-order brain-behavior relationships. The lesion method is grounded in the notion that dysfunction in varied neuroanatomical systems in the human brain leads to predictable and reliable cognitive and behavioral manifestations, which may include, depending on the area of neural damage, changes in intellect, memory, language, perception, judgment and decision making, or personality. The method has benefited enormously from recent advances in neuroanatomical analysis, which were fueled in turn by the development of modern neuroimaging techniques—computed

I have been fortunate to have Antonio and Hanna Damasio as my teachers. I thank them for their loyal mentorship, and for their unwavering support of my acquisition of knowledge about mind facts and brain facts. Supported by NINDS Grant P01 NS19632.

tomography (CT) in the 1970s and magnetic resonance (MR) scanning in the early 1980s (H. Damasio 1995; H. Damasio and Damasio 1997; H. Damasio and Frank 1992; Frank et al. 1997). Dating back to the innovative formulations of Geschwind (1965), there has been a resurgence of interest in the lesion method. The aforementioned increased precision and reliability of neuroimaging definition, together with advances in neuropsychological measurement and cognitive experimentation (Benton 1988, 1994; Lezak 1995; Tranel 1996), have allowed more powerful analyses of brain-behavior relationships and more elaborate theoretical specification (cf. A.R. Damasio 1989a, 1989b; A.R. Damasio and Damasio 1993, 1994; Kosslyn and Koenig 1995). Such advances have enhanced the viability of the lesion method as a technique for scientific inquiry and have helped overcome the limitations of small subject groups and single case studies. Our understanding of brain-behavior relationships has reached a level only hinted at in the work of two or three decades past.

The discussion makes several important background assumptions that warrant brief comment. Unless otherwise indicated, it is assumed that the human brain under consideration is endowed with conventional hemispheric dominance, whereby speech and language functions are lateralized to the left hemisphere and nonverbal, visuospatial functions are lateralized to the right hemisphere (e.g., Levy 1990). The discussion also assumes normal acquisition and development of cognitive capacities; thus, the principles outlined here may not apply to persons with developmental learning disabilities, long-standing psychiatric disease, or inadequate educational opportunity. Finally, as mentioned earlier, many of the findings reviewed here were derived from research focusing on cognitive experimentation in adult humans with focal brain lesions. In general, such lesions are caused by cerebrovascular disease, surgical ablation of nonmalignant cerebral tumors, some viral infections of the central nervous system (especially herpes simplex encephalitis), and traumatic brain injury and degenerative diseases.

Other approaches to the investigation of brain-behavior relationships include techniques referred to under the rubric of functional imaging (for an excellent review of these, see Raichle 1997); these techniques have witnessed an explosion in popularity over the past decade and have come to occupy a prominent position in the exploration of brain-behavior relationships (for a comprehensive review, see Cabeza and Nyberg 2000). Positron emission tomography (PET) involves the measurement of brain cell activity such as glucose metabolism and local blood flow. In PET, it is possible to study which brain regions are "active" during particular cognitive tasks, allowing inferences about how certain neural units are related to certain mental functions (Grabowski et al. 1995; G. McCarthy 1995; Posner et al. 1988; Raichle 1990, 1997; Roland 1993). Another powerful new technique is functional magnetic resonance imaging (fMRI). Similar to PET, fMRI can be used to measure activity levels in various brain regions during cognitive tasks, permitting inferences about how neural units relate to mental activity. Magnetoencephalography (e.g., Poolos 1995), event-related potentials (e.g., Fabiani et al. 2000), and transcranial magnetic stimulation (e.g., Hallett 2000) are other methods used to investigate brain-behavior relationships.

It is worth mentioning that despite the proliferation of functional imaging studies in the last several years, the importance of the lesion method in the investigation of brain-behavior relationships has by no means been diminished. A careful examination of the contributions of functional imaging to the understanding of the neural bases of higher-order cognitive and behavioral functions reveals that thus far, the vast majority of these studies have served to confirm notions that were already established or at least hinted at in previous lesion-based work (cf. Cabeza and Nyberg 2000). Lesion probes continue to provide a powerful tool by which to uncover new insights into brain-behavior relationships, and they continue to fuel many of the most exciting, novel, and testable hypotheses regarding how different brain sectors mediate different cognitive and behavioral functions.

## Brain-Behavior Relationships

The discussion begins with several principles regarding brain-behavior relationships, including lateral and longitudinal brain specialization.

## Lateral Specialization: Left Versus Right

As hinted at in the early observations of Broca and Wernicke, there are several fundamental differences between the left and right hemispheres of the human brain that constitute some of the most robust principles of neuropsychology. In the vast majority of adults, the left side of the brain is specialized for language and for processing verbally coded information. This is true of nearly all (about 98%) right-handed individuals (who constitute roughly 90% of the adult population), and the majority (about 70%) of left-handed persons. This principle applies irrespective of the mode of input. Thus, verbal information apprehended through either the auditory (e.g., speech) or visual (e.g., written text) channel is processed preferentially by the left hemisphere. The principle also applies to both the input and output aspects of language—not only do we understand language with our left hemisphere, we also produce language (spoken and written) with our left hemisphere. Moreover, there is now compelling evidence that this applies not only to languages that are auditory based, but also to languages that are based on visuogestural signals (e.g., American Sign Language) (Bellugi et al. 1989; Hickok et al. 1996; Poizner et al. 1987). Figure 3–1 illustrates the typical arrangement of language in the left hemisphere.

The right hemisphere has a very different type of specialization. It processes nonverbal information such as complex visual patterns (e.g., faces) or auditory signals (e.g., music) that are not coded in verbal form. Structures in the right temporal and occipital regions are critical for learning and navigating geographical routes (Barrash et al. 2000). The right side of the brain is also dedicated to the mapping of "feeling states," that is, patterns of bodily sensations linked to emotions such as anger and fear. A related right-hemisphere capacity concerns the perception of our bodies in space, in both intrapersonal and extrapersonal terms. For example, an understanding of where our limbs are in relationship to our trunk, and where our body is in relationship to the space around us, is under the purview of the right hemisphere. Figure 3–2 depicts some of the fundamental capacities of the right hemisphere.

In early conceptualizations of the left and right hemispheres, a prevailing notion was that the left hemisphere was major, or dominant, while the right hemisphere was minor, or nondominant. This attitude reflected an emphasis on language in human cognition and behavior. As a highly observable capacity, language received the most scientific and clinical attention and was considered the quintessential and most important human faculty. In fact, for many decades the right hemisphere was believed to contribute little to higher-level cognitive functioning. Since lesions to the right hemisphere typically did not produce language disturbances, it was often concluded that a patient had lost little in the way of higher-order function after right-sided brain injury.

As the field evolved, and it became clear that each hemisphere was dedicated to specific—albeit different— cognitive capacities, the notion of dominance gave way to the idea of specialization. Each hemisphere was "dominant" for certain cognitive functions. Early work had already established the role of the left hemisphere in language. Other studies documented the role of the right hemisphere in visuospatial capacities. Many of the breakthroughs came from studies of split-brain patients, a line

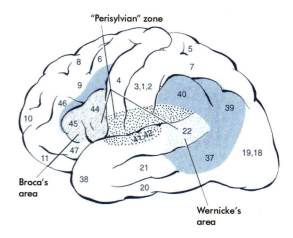

**FIGURE 3–1.** Lateral view of left hemisphere. The principal language-related regions are highlighted, including Broca's area (yellow) and Wernicke's area (green). The "perisylvian" zone includes Broca's and Wernicke's areas and the zone marked in pink. Broca's area is dedicated to speech output, that is, language expression, whereas Wernicke's area is responsible for language comprehension. Other language-related regions are highlighted in blue; included are the supramarginal gyrus (area 40), the angular gyrus (area 39), part of area 37, and the region immediately above and anterior to Broca's area. Not pictured are left-sided subcortical structures (basal ganglia, thalamus) that also participate in speech and language functions.
*Source.* Reprinted with permission from Tranel D: "Higher Brain Function," in *Neuroscience in Medicine.* Edited by Conn PM. Philadelphia, PA, JB Lippincott, 1995a, pp. 555–580.

of work led by the late psychologist Roger Sperry (e.g., Sperry 1968). To prevent partial seizures from spreading from one side of the brain to the other, patients underwent an operation in which the corpus callosum was cut. The left and right hemispheres were no longer in communication. Careful investigations of these patients revealed that each side of the brain had its own "consciousness," with the left side operating in a verbal mode and the right in a nonverbal mode. Sperry's work and that of others (e.g., Bogen 1993; Gazzaniga 1987; see Trevarthen 1990 for reviews) led to several fundamental distinctions between the cognitive functions for which the left and right hemispheres are specialized (Table 3–1).

## Longitudinal Specialization: Anterior Versus Posterior

Another useful organizational principle for understanding brain-behavior relationships is an anterior-posterior distinction. The major demarcation points are the rolandic sulcus, the major fissure separating the frontal lobes from the parietal lobes, and the sylvian fissure, the boundary

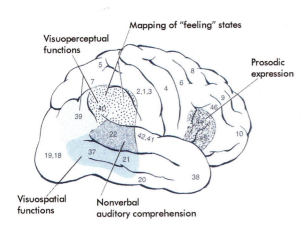

**FIGURE 3–2.** Lateral view of right hemisphere, depicting several primary regions with a label corresponding to their functional correlates. Orange=prosodic expression; pink + brown=mapping of "feeling" states; green + brown= visuoperceptual functions; blue=visuospatial functions; yellow=nonverbal auditory comprehension. Many of these functions overlap both psychologically and anatomically, and the areas depicted in the figure should be considered approximate.

*Source.* Reprinted with permission from Tranel D: "Higher Brain Function," in *Neuroscience in Medicine.* Edited by Conn PM. Philadelphia, PA, JB Lippincott, 1995a, pp. 555–580.

**TABLE 3–1.** Functional dichotomies of left and right hemispheric dominance

| Left | Right |
| --- | --- |
| Verbal | Nonverbal |
| Serial | Parallel |
| Analytic | Holistic |
| Controlled | Creative |
| Logical | Pictorial |
| Propositional | Appositional |
| Rational | Intuitive |
| Social | Physical |

*Source.* Adapted from Benton 1991.

between the temporal lobes and the frontal/parietal lobes (Figure 3–3).

In general, the posterior regions of the brain are dedicated to sensation and perception. The primary sensory cortices for vision, audition, and somatosensory perception are located in the posterior sectors of the brain in occipital, temporal, and parietal regions, respectively. Thus, apprehension of sensory data from the world outside is mediated by posterior brain structures. Note that the "world outside" is actually two distinct domains: 1) the world that is outside the body and brain, and 2) the world outside the brain but inside the body. The latter, the soma, comprises the smooth muscle, the viscera, and other bodily structures innervated by the central nervous system.

Anterior brain regions, by contrast, generally comprise effector systems, specialized for the execution of behavior. For example, the primary motor cortices are located immediately anterior to the rolandic sulcus. The motor area for speech, known as Broca's area, is located in the left frontal operculum. The right-hemisphere counterpart of Broca's area, in the right frontal operculum, is important for executing stresses and intonations that infuse speech with emotional meaning (prosody). Perhaps most importantly, a variety of "executive functions" such as judgment, decision making, and the capacity to construct and implement various plans of action are associated with structures in the frontal lobes.

In what follows, I review a variety of brain-behavior relationships. I have used as an organizing principle gross anatomical subdivisions, for example, different lobes of the brain and various sectors within each lobe, and for each, I discuss the most well-established cognitive and behavioral correlates. I hasten to point out, though, that the neuroanatomical arrangement is partly one of efficiency and economy—in a number of places, I have taken the liberty of including topics because they fit best within the overall context of the discussion, and not because they necessarily belong to the anatomical division under consideration (e.g., the basal forebrain is discussed in the section on the frontal lobes; the posterior superior temporal gyrus is discussed as part of the temporoparietal junction).

## The Temporal Lobes

Several major subdivisions can be designated within the temporal lobe: 1) The mesial temporal lobe, including the hippocampus, amygdala, entorhinal and perirhinal cortices, and an additional portion of the anterior parahippocampal gyrus; 2) The remaining nonmesial portion of the temporal lobe, which includes the temporal pole (TP), the inferotemporal region (IT), and, for purposes of the present discussion, the region of transition between the posterior temporal lobe and the inferior occipital lobe (the occipitotemporal junction); 3) The posterior portion of the superior temporal gyrus (area 22), which, on the left side, forms the heart of what is traditionally known as Wernicke's area (Figure 3–4). Neuropsychological correlates of the mesial, TP, and IT subdivisions are summarized in Table 3–2. Correlates of

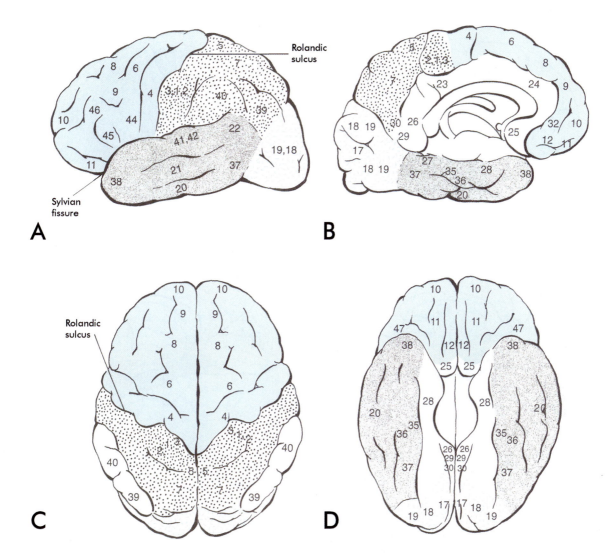

**FIGURE 3–3.** Lateral (*A*), mesial (*B*), superior (*C*), and inferior (*D*) views of the brain, depicting major demarcation points, including the rolandic sulcus and the sylvian fissure. The four main lobes are shown in different colors: frontal=blue; parietal=pink; occipital=green; temporal=yellow. [Only the left hemisphere is depicted in the lateral and mesial views (*A* and *B*), but the mapping would be the same on the right hemisphere.] The unmarked zone—including the cingulate gyrus (areas 24 and 23) and areas 25, 26, 27, and 28—corresponds to a region commonly referred to as the limbic lobe (the reader is referred to A.R. Damasio and Van Hoesen [1983] for a more extensive discussion of the anatomy and functional correlates of the limbic lobe). In the superior perspective (*C*), the left hemisphere is on the left, and the right hemisphere is on the right; the sides are reversed in the inferior perspective (*D*).

*Source.*   Reprinted with permission from Tranel D: "Higher Brain Function," in *Neuroscience in Medicine*. Edited by Conn PM. Philadelphia, PA, JB Lippincott, 1995a, pp. 555–580.

the posterior superior temporal region are considered in a later section.

## Mesial Temporal Region

The mesial temporal lobe comprises the hippocampus, amygdala, entorhinal and perirhinal cortices, and the anterior portion of parahippocampal gyrus not occupied by the entorhinal cortex (Figure 3–4). Many of these structures play a crucial role in memory.

## Hippocampal Complex

The hippocampus and the adjacent entorhinal and perirhinal cortices can be referred to as the hippocampal complex. The components of the hippocampal complex are highly interconnected by means of recurrent neuroanatomical circuits. In turn, the hippocampal complex is extensively interconnected with higher-order association cortices located in the temporal lobe. Those cortices receive signals from the association cortices of all sensory modalities and

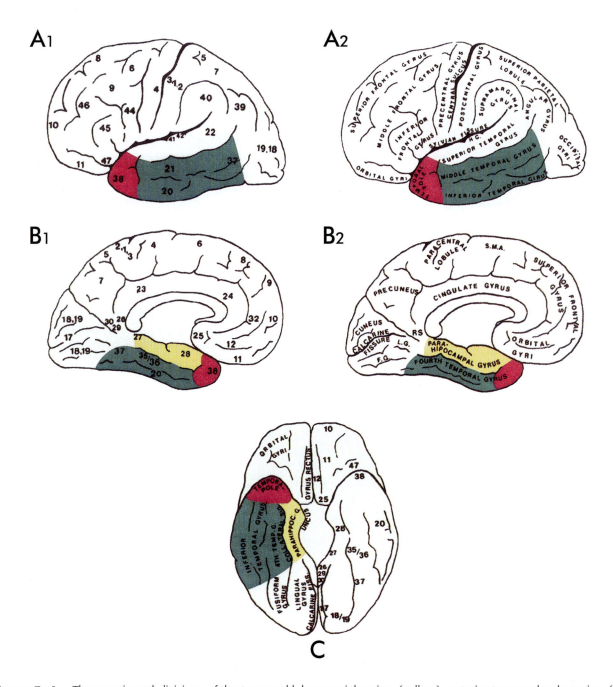

**FIGURE 3–4.** Three major subdivisions of the temporal lobe: mesial region (yellow), anterior temporal pole region (red), and inferotemporal region (green). Numbers corresponding to Brodmann's cytoarchitectonic areas are depicted in *Panels A₁* and *B₁* and the right side (left hemisphere) of *Panel C*, and standard gyrus names are shown in the corresponding *Panels A₂* and *B₂* and the left side (right hemisphere) of *Panel C*. Lateral (*Panels A₁* and *A₂*), mesial (*Panels B₁* and *B₂*), and inferior (*Panel C*) views are represented.

also receive feedback projections from the hippocampus (Hyman et al. 1988; Van Hoesen 1982). Hence, structures in the hippocampal complex have access to, and influence over, signals from virtually the entire brain. The system is thus in a position to create integrated records of various aspects of memory experiences, including visual, auditory, and somatosensory information.

In a general sense, it is reasonable to describe the principal function of the hippocampal complex as the acquisition of new factual knowledge. The system is essential for acquiring records of interactions between the organism and the world outside, as well as thought processes such as those engaged in planning. The precise computational operations performed by the hippocam-

**TABLE 3–2.** Neuropsychological manifestations of temporal lobe lesions

| | Hemispheric side of lesion | | |
| | Left | Right | Bilateral |
| --- | --- | --- | --- |
| Mesial | Anterograde amnesia for verbal material | Anterograde amnesia for nonverbal material | Severe anterograde amnesia for verbal and nonverbal material |
| Temporal pole | Impaired retrieval of proper nouns | Impaired retrieval of concepts for unique entities; impaired memory for episodic, declarative knowledge | Impaired retrieval of concepts and names for unique entities; impaired episodic memory |
| Inferotemporal | Impaired retrieval of common nouns | Impaired retrieval of concepts for some nonunique entities | Impaired retrieval of concepts and names for some nonunique entities |
| Occipitotemporal junction | "Deep" prosopagnosia; impaired retrieval of concepts for some nonunique entities | Transient or mild prosopagnosia; impaired retrieval of concepts for some nonunique entities | Severe, permanent prosopagnosia; visual object agnosia |

pus, however, have not been fully clarified (cf. Mishkin 1978; Squire 1992). There are two hippocampal complexes, one in the left hemisphere and one in the right. Anatomically, the two are roughly equivalent, but there are major differences in their functional roles. Specifically, the two hippocampal complexes are specialized for different types of material in a manner that parallels the overall functional arrangement of the brain: the left has verbal specialization and the right, nonverbal.

The landmark report by Scoville and Milner (1957) on patient HM, who became severely amnesic after undergoing bilateral mesial temporal lobe resection for control of intractable seizures, established the mesial aspect of the temporal lobes—and the hippocampus in particular—as being unequivocally linked to memory, specifically, to the acquisition of new information (i.e., anterograde memory). More than three decades of research on HM (summarized in Corkin [1984]; see also Gabrieli et al. [1988] and Corkin et al. [1997]) and studies in similar patients have confirmed this relationship. Patient RB of Zola-Morgan and colleagues (Zola-Morgan et al. 1986), who had pathologically confirmed bilateral lesions limited to the CA1 sector of the hippocampus, is another important example of the marked anterograde amnesia that can occur after circumscribed bilateral hippocampal lesions; this finding was replicated and extended in another study in which postmortem pathological confirmation was available (Rempel-Clower et al. 1996). It has been established that more extensive mesial temporal damage, involving the perirhinal cortex and parahippocampal gyrus in addition to the hippocampal region and entorhinal cortex, tends to produce a proportionate increase in the severity of amnesia (Squire and Zola 1996). Another source of evidence comes from patient Boswell, who has bilateral damage to the entire

mesial sector of the temporal lobes (hippocampus, amygdala, entorhinal cortex) and also nonmesial temporal damage (Figure 3–5). In the anterograde compartment, Boswell's profile is similar to the patterns reported for HM and RB; however, unlike HM and RB, Boswell also has a severe impairment on the retrograde side (A.R. Damasio et al. 1985a, 1989a; Tranel et al. 2000b). Studies with functional imaging have also confirmed the role of the mesial temporal lobe in memory (Nyberg et al. 1996).

With respect to the nature of the amnesia associated with hippocampal damage, several relationships have been firmly established. First, there is a consistent relationship between the side of the lesion and the type of learning impairment. Specifically, damage to the left hippocampal system produces an amnesic syndrome that affects verbal material (e.g., spoken words, written material) but spares nonverbal material; conversely, damage to the right hippocampal system affects nonverbal material (e.g., complex visual and auditory patterns) but spares verbal material (e.g., Frisk and Milner 1990; Milner 1968, 1972; M.L. Smith and Milner 1989). For example, after damage to the left hippocampus, a patient may lose the ability to learn new names but remain capable of learning new faces and spatial arrangements (e.g., Tranel 1991a). By contrast, damage to the right hippocampal system frequently impairs the ability to learn new geographical routes (Barrash et al. 2000).

A second point is that the hippocampal system does not appear to play a role in the learning of perceptuomotor skills and other knowledge that has been referred to as nondeclarative memory (e.g., Squire 1992). Patient HM, for example, can learn skills such as mirror drawing and mirror reading (Corkin 1965, 1968; Gabrieli et al. 1993), even though he has no recall of the situation in

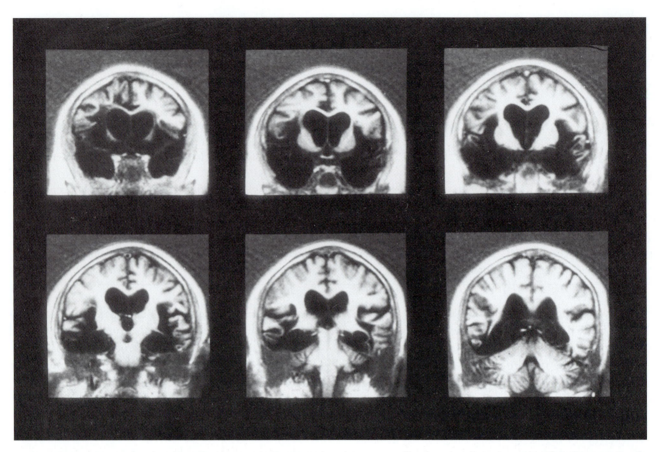

**FIGURE 3–5.** T1-weighted magnetic resonance images of patient Boswell, who developed severe global amnesia after having herpes simplex encephalitis. In these coronal sectional images, the left hemisphere is on the right, and the most anterior image is in the upper left corner of the figure. The lesions, which show as black areas, include the anterior temporal regions (amygdala, hippocampus, parahippocampal gyrus, and temporal pole [area 38]) and the anterior portion of the inferior, middle, and superior temporal gyri (areas 20, 21, and anterior 22).

which the learning of those skills took place. Similar findings have been reported in patient Boswell and other patients with bilateral mesial temporal lobe damage (Tranel et al. 1994b, 2000b). In fact, not only can Boswell acquire perceptuomotor skills such as rotor pursuit and mirror tracing at a normal level, but he retains those skills for many years after the initial learning, despite the fact that he cannot recall any shred of knowledge regarding the circumstances of the learning situations. Thus, the role of the hippocampus in memory is principally for acquiring declarative knowledge—that is, facts, faces, names, and other information that can be "declared" and brought into the mind's eye.

Another source of evidence comes from patients with Alzheimer's disease (AD). In the early and middle stages of the disease, AD patients develop a marked impairment of anterograde memory, which, as in patients HM and Boswell, spares the learning of nondeclarative information such as new perceptuomotor skills (Eslinger and Damasio 1986; Gabrieli et al. 1993). The neural hall-

mark in AD patients is damage to the hippocampal system (Hyman et al. 1984; Van Hoesen and Damasio 1987; Van Hoesen et al. 1986). The cerebellum and neostriatum, which are intact in the various patients cited above, have been implicated as crucial structures underlying acquisition of motor skills (Eslinger and Damasio 1986; Fiez et al. 1992; Gao et al. 1996; Grafman et al. 1992; Heindel et al. 1993; McCormick and Thompson 1984; Saint-Cyr et al. 1988; Schmahmann 1991; Thompson 1986).

A final comment pertains to the role of the hippocampus in the retrieval of old (sometimes referred to as "remote") information (retrograde memory). Milner (1972) argued that the hippocampus is not needed for the retrieval of remote memories, and findings in HM and RB, neither of whom had defects in the retrograde compartment, support this contention. Patient Boswell is also consistent with this notion, inasmuch as his severe defects in the retrograde compartment are attributable to his extensive nonmesial, anterior temporal lobe damage (A.R. Damasio et al. 1985a; Tranel et al. 2000b). The weight of the evidence points to the conclusion that the hippocampal system is not the principal repository for old memories. The role of mesial temporal structures in retrograde memory has also been explored in nonhuman primates (e.g., Horel 1978; Murray 1990; Zola-Morgan and Squire 1986).

## Amygdala

The role of the amygdala in memory has been a source of controversy. Studies in nonhuman primates have yielded conflicting results, with some laboratories reporting that the amygdala is critical for normal learning (e.g., Mishkin 1978; Murray 1990; Murray and Mishkin 1985, 1986) and others maintaining that the amygdala does not play a crucial role (e.g., Zola-Morgan et al. 1989). Results in the few human cases available are also equivocal (Lee et al. 1988; Nahm et al. 1993; Tranel and Hyman 1990). Recently, however, studies have begun to clarify this issue, and it now appears that the amygdala is important for the acquisition and expression of emotional memory, but perhaps not for neutral memory. Specifically, the amygdala contributes critically to the potentiation of memory traces for emotional stimuli during their acquisition and consolidation into long-term declarative memory (Adolphs et al. 2000; Cahill et al. 1995; Phelps et al. 1998). This conclusion is also supported by functional imaging studies (Cahill et al. 1996; Hamann et al. 1999). These findings are in accord with other evidence indicating that the amygdala is important for the recognition of emotion, especially fear, in facial expressions (Adolphs et al. 1994, 1995; Young et al. 1995) and in the processing of other information that has emotional significance (Markowitsch et al. 1994). Also, it has been shown that the amygdala is important for classical conditioning of autonomic responses. Bechara et al. (1995) found that a patient with circumscribed bilateral amygdala damage was able to acquire declarative knowledge normally but was impaired in acquiring conditioned autonomic responses; a patient with circumscribed bilateral hippocampal damage (but with intact amygdala) showed the opposite pattern. These findings have led to the idea that the amygdala is important for processing stimuli that communicate emotional significance in social situations; specifically, the amygdala may orchestrate patterns of neural activation in disparate sectors of the brain that would encode both the intrinsic physical features of stimuli (e.g., shape, position in space) and the value that certain stimuli have to the organism, especially emotional significance (Adolphs and Tranel 2000).

# Anterior, Lateral, and Inferior Temporal Regions

## Retrograde Memory

The anterior and nonmesial sectors of the temporal lobes play important roles in retrograde memory, specifically, the retrieval of knowledge that was acquired before the onset of a brain injury (e.g., Hunkin et al. 1995; for reviews, see Kapur 1993; Kopelman 1992; Markowitsch et al. 1993). In a case reported by Kapur et al. (1994), the patient had damage to anterior lateral and ventral temporal structures but not to mesial structures, forming a pattern the authors described as a "mirror-image" lesion to that of HM. The patient's amnesia profile was the inverse of HM's, with severe disruption of retrograde memory and relative sparing of anterograde memory. Other case studies of retrograde amnesia have been reported (e.g., Cermak and O'Connor 1983; De Renzi and Lucchelli 1993; O'Connor et al. 1992; Tulving et al. 1988), and in cases for which anatomical information is available, the findings appear to be consistent with the notion that retrograde memory is related to nonmesial, anterior and lateral temporal regions and not to the hippocampal complex.

We recently reported a case in which serial neuropsychological assessments and serial structural and functional neuroimaging studies provided further support for the notion that the retrieval of old, factual, concrete knowledge (retrograde memory) and learning of new, factual, concrete knowledge (anterograde memory) depend on distinct systems in the temporal lobe (Jones et al. 1998). A 70-year-old, right-handed woman with limbic encephalitis attributed to thymoma was evaluated 4 months after diagnosis. Severe multimodal anterograde and retrograde memory defects were found. A fluorodeoxyglucose (FDG) 18 F resting PET scan showed diffuse cortical—but especially right anterolateral—temporal hypometabolism. Two years later, there was marked resolution of the retrograde memory defect, with persistent anterograde amnesia. A follow-up FDG resting PET scan showed improved metabolism in the anterolateral temporal cortex and in other cortical regions. Metabolism in both mesial temporal regions declined markedly. Striking recovery of retrograde memory occurred in conjunction with the improvement in anterolateral temporal metabolism and despite reduction in mesial temporal metabolism. These findings provide further support for the hypotheses that 1) mesial temporal structures are not the repository of retrograde factual knowledge, and 2) anterolateral temporal lobe structures, especially on the right, may be critical for retrieval of retrograde factual knowledge.

## Lexical Retrieval

Structures in the anterior and inferolateral left temporal lobe play a key role in lexical retrieval, or what is commonly known as naming. For example, when a familiar person or object is encountered, the word that denotes that person or object is normally recalled. This process occurs virtually automatically, although it may be encumbered by factors such as fatigue, distraction, or aging (Burke et al. 1991). Recent evidence has shown that neural structures in different parts of the left temporal lobe are important for the naming of objects from different conceptual categories.

The neural regions under consideration here include the TP and the IT region (Figure 3–6A). These regions are mostly outside the classic language areas in the left hemisphere. Preliminary studies in neurological patients hinted that these regions might have an important role in lexical retrieval (A.R. Damasio et al. 1990a; Goodglass et al. 1986; Graff-Radford et al. 1990a; Hart et al. 1985; Heilman et al. 1972; Semenza and Zettin 1989; Stafiniak et al. 1990; Warrington and McCarthy 1983). In several large-scale studies of patients with focal brain lesions, we have confirmed and extended these observations (H. Damasio et al. 1996; Tranel et al. 1997b; 1998).

Our lesion studies, which have been corroborated by a companion study using PET (H. Damasio et al. 1996), demonstrated that there are separable neural sectors in the left temporal lobe that are relatively specialized for naming entities from different conceptual categories. Specifically, naming of unique persons (e.g., John Wayne, Joe Montana) was associated with the left TP. Naming of nonunique animals (e.g., skunk, zebra) was associated with the anterior aspect of IT, in a region immediately posterior to the TP. Naming of nonunique tools (e.g., hammer, wrench) was associated with the posterior aspect of IT, and an adjacent area in the temporo-occipitoparietal junction (Figure 3–6). Our findings are consistent with evidence from electrophysiological (Nobre et al. 1994; Ojemann 1991) and other functional imaging studies (Mazoyer et al. 1993; Petersen et al. 1988). It is important to note that lesions in these regions do not typically cause permanent defects in other aspects of language operation; in particular, grammar, syntax, phonetic implementation, and repetition are normal. The defect is confined to lexical access, and the findings have been interpreted as supporting the idea that these neural structures play an intermediary or mediational role in lexical retrieval. For example, when the concept of a given tool is evoked (based on the activation of several regions that support pertinent conceptual knowledge and promote its explicit representation in sensorimotor terms), an intermediary region becomes active and promotes (in the appropriate sensorimotor structures) the explicit representation of phonemic knowledge pertaining to the word form that denotes the given tool. When a concept from another category is evoked, say, that of a particular person, a different intermediary region is engaged. The process can operate in reverse to link word form information to conceptual knowledge; for example, hearing the word *buffalo* would activate an intermediary region that would in turn allow us to conjure up the image of a buffalo and other pertinent semantic knowledge that defines our concept of buffalo (for a detailed discussion of this model, see Tranel et al., in press).

Neuropsychological correlates of damage to the right anterolateral temporal region remain poorly understood, but there are several intriguing findings available thus far. In two cases with this type of lesion, the patients had a selective defect in naming facial expressions (e.g., happiness, fear) (Rapcsak et al. 1989, 1993). The patients did not have difficulty naming other entities, such as objects and actions, and there was no defect in proper naming (famous faces, buildings). Also, the patients did not have impaired recognition, even with regard to emotional facial expressions not named correctly. For example, the patients could match facial expressions to emotional prosody, and to emotional scenes, at a normal level.

Structures in the right anterolateral temporal region appear to play an important role in the recognition of unique entities (e.g., familiar persons and landmarks). For example, it has been shown that lesions in the right temporal pole produce impairments in the retrieval of conceptual knowledge for familiar persons (Tranel et al. 1997a). This finding has been corroborated by a PET study, which demonstrated activation of this region when subjects were identifying familiar persons and landmarks (Grabowski et al. 2000). These results are also consistent with the discussion earlier, which emphasized the importance of anterior and lateral aspects of the right temporal lobe in the retrieval of retrograde memories. Together with interconnected right prefrontal cortices, the right anterolateral temporal region is probably of critical importance for the retrieval of unique factual memories (Tranel et al. 2000b).

## Visual Recognition

Disorders of visual recognition are associated with damage to the posterior part of the IT region, along with the inferior portion of Brodmann's areas 18 and 19 in the occipital region, a transition area known as the occipito-temporal junction. Lesions to the occipitotemporal junction, especially when they are bilateral, produce unimo-

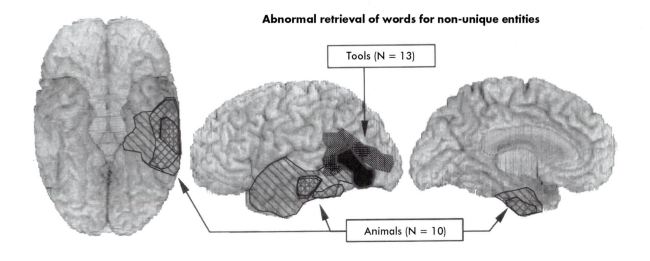

**Abnormal retrieval of words for non-unique entities**

Tools (N = 13)

Animals (N = 10)

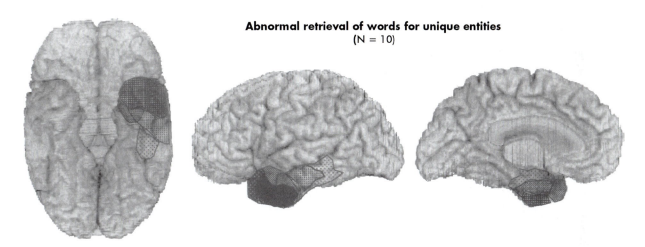

**Abnormal retrieval of words for unique entities**
**(N = 10)**

**FIGURE 3–6.** Regions in the left temporal lobe that are important for lexical retrieval, including the left temporal pole (TP) and the inferotemporal (IT) region. Results of analysis based on magnetic resonance (or computed tomographic) scans processed for three-dimensional reconstruction in each subject with Brainvox (H. Damasio and Frank 1992). The top section depicts defective retrieval of words for animals or tools; the bottom section depicts defective retrieval of words for persons. Abnormal retrieval of words for persons correlated with damage clustered in the left TP. Abnormal retrieval of words for animals correlated with damage in the left IT; maximal overlap occurred in lateral and inferior IT regions. Abnormal retrieval of words for tools correlated with damage in the posterolateral IT, along with the junction of lateral temporo-occipitoparietal cortices (posterior IT+).

dal, visually based disorders of recognition. Patients lose the ability to recognize visual stimuli at the level of unique identity. They cannot recognize familiar faces or familiar landmarks. Usually, basic visual perception is largely unaltered, and the presentation thus conforms to the classic notion of associative agnosia, that is, a "normal percept stripped of its meaning" (Teuber 1968). The disturbance can affect any number of visual stimuli that normally require recognition at a unique level (e.g., faces, buildings, landmarks), but the best studied manifestation is agnosia for faces, known as prosopagnosia (for review, see Kanwisher and Moscovitch 2000). Prosopagnosia is hallmarked by an inability to recognize the identities of previously known faces and an inability to learn new ones. The defect can be severe, as patients may lose the ability to recognize faces of family members, close friends, and even themselves in a mirror, but it is confined to the visual channel, and exposure to the voice that belongs to the unrecognized face will elicit prompt and accurate recognition. In most individuals with prosopagnosia, the ability to recognize facial expressions, and to judge gender and estimate age from face information, is well preserved (Bruyer et al. 1983; Davidoff and Landis 1990; Tranel et al. 1988). Also, many prosopagnostic patients remain capable of recognizing identity based on visual but nonfacial information, such as characteristics of gait or posture (A.R. Damasio et al. 1982b, 1989b, 1990a, 1990b). Some prosopagnostic patients have impaired perception of texture (Newcombe 1979), and defects in color perception are common (A.R. Damasio et al. 1980; Meadows 1974b). Finally, there is intriguing evidence that many patients with severe prosopagnosia are capable of generating discriminatory autonomic responses to familiar faces, indicating that there is some preservation of face recognition at a nonconscious level (Bauer 1984; Tranel 2000; Tranel and Damasio 1985; Tranel et al. 1995).

Associative prosopagnosia (Figure 3–7) is nearly always associated with bilateral lesions to the occipitotemporal junction (Benton 1990; A.R. Damasio et al. 1982b, 1990b; Meadows 1974a). Prosopagnosia resulting from unilateral right-sided lesions nearly always has a substantial perceptual component, thus constituting a more apperceptive form of the condition (see Apperceptive Visual Agnosia, below, in this chapter). Unilateral occipitotemporal lesions usually do not cause severe and lasting prosopagnosia, although such lesions may cause significant disturbances in face recognition. On the left, such lesions can produce a partial recognition defect that has been termed *deep prosopagnosia* (A.R. Damasio et al. 1988), in which target faces are misidentified as someone who is very similar to the correct person in terms of gender, age, activity, etc. (e.g., recognizing Betty Grable as Marilyn Monroe, or recognizing Magic Johnson as Michael Jordan). Right-sided occipitotemporal lesions may cause slow and erratic face recognition, but again, pervasive prosopagnosia is uncommon (A.R. Damasio et al. 1990b). Also, as noted earlier, right temporal polar lesions frequently produce impaired recognition of familiar faces, albeit not in the pervasive manner that is characteristic of the classic conceptualization of prosopagnosia.

In addition to disturbances of recognition of unique visual stimuli, lesions in the vicinity of the occipitotemporal junction may cause impairments in the visual recognition of nonunique stimuli from various categories, such as animals or tools. For example, when confronted with a picture of a fox, the patient may indicate that it is an animal but may not be able to come up with the specific type. Shown a screwdriver, the patient may respond "some kind of tool; I can't think of which one." This impairment affects recognition at the level of basic objects. In general, the patients can still recognize the superordinate category to which the entity belongs but not the subordinate, basic object level.

An especially intriguing discovery is that an impairment of visual recognition may not affect all types of entities equally but instead may be restricted to one or a few conceptual categories. A number of investigators have reported patients who demonstrated category-related impairments in visual recognition of entities such as animals, fruits and vegetables, or tools and utensils. For example, patients have been described in whom recognition of animals was impaired but recognition of objects from other categories was normal; conversely, some patients have shown impaired recognition of tools and utensils but normal recognition of animals (for reviews, see Caramazza 2000; Forde and Humphreys 1999; Gainotti et al. 1995). In a large-scale lesion-based study of this phenomenon, we found a double dissociation relative to recognition profile and lesion site (Tranel et al. 1997a). Specifically, one group of patients had defects in the recognition of animals, but recognition of tools was normal; another group had defective recognition of tools but normal recognition of animals. Defective recognition of animals was associated with lesions in the right mesial occipital/ventral temporal region and also in the left mesial occipital region, whereas defective recognition of tools was associated with lesions in the occipital-temporal-parietal junction in the left hemisphere. These findings, which have been supported by functional imaging studies (for review, see Martin et al. 2000), support the idea that recording and retrieving knowledge for different conceptual categories depends on partially segregated neural systems.

## The Occipital Lobes

The neuroanatomical arrangement of structures in and near the occipital lobes is depicted in Figure 3–8. On the lateral aspect of the hemispheres, the occipital lobes comprise the visual association cortices in Brodmann's areas 18 and 19. These areas continue in the mesial aspect. The mesial sector also includes the primary visual cortices (area 17), which are formed by the cortex immediately above and below the calcarine fissure. For purposes of establishing neuropsychological correlates of the occipital lobes, the region can be subdivided in the vertical plane at the level of the calcarine fissure, so that dorsal (superior) and ventral (inferior) components can be designated (Figure 3–8). Neuropsychological correlates of occipital lobe lesions are summarized in Table 3–3.

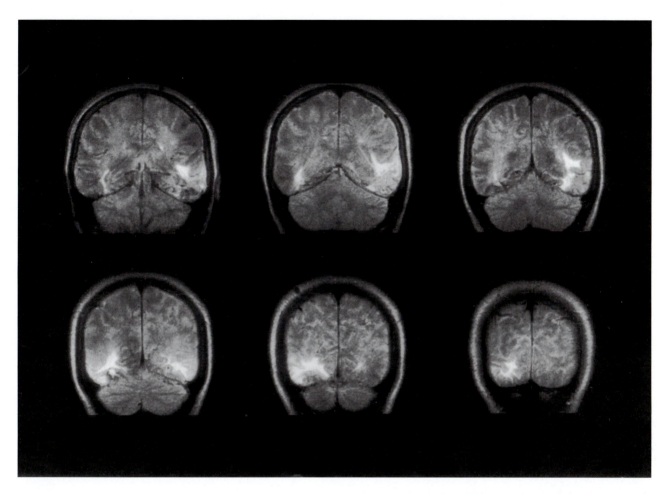

**FIGURE 3–7.** T2-weighted magnetic resonance image of a 67-year-old, right-handed woman, which shows bilateral occipitotemporal lesions (showing as white, or "bright" signal). In these coronal sections, the left hemisphere is on the right, and the most anterior image is in the upper left corner of the figure. The woman developed severe, permanent prosopagnosia after sustaining these lesions.

**TABLE 3–3.** Neuropsychological manifestations of occipital lobe lesions

| | Hemispheric side of lesion | | |
| --- | --- | --- | --- |
| | **Left** | **Right** | **Bilateral** |
| Dorsal | Partial or mild Balint's syndrome | Partial or mild Balint's syndrome | Balint's syndrome (visual disorientation, ocular apraxia, optic ataxia); defective motion perception; astereopsis |
| Ventral | Right hemiachromatopsia; "pure" alexia; impaired mental imagery | Left hemiachromatopsia; apperceptive visual agnosia; defective facial imagery | Full-field achromatopsia; visual object agnosia; impaired mental imagery; prosopagnosia |

## Dorsal Component

The dorsal component of the occipital lobes comprises the primary visual cortex superior to the calcarine fissure (area 17) and the superior portion of the visual association cortices (areas 18 and 19). This region will be considered in combination with the anteriorly adjacent parietal areas, including the posterior part of the superior parietal lobule (area 7) and the posterior part of the angular gyrus (area 39). When situated in the primary visual cortex of area 17 and/or its connections, lesions to the dorsal sector of the occipital region lead to a loss of form

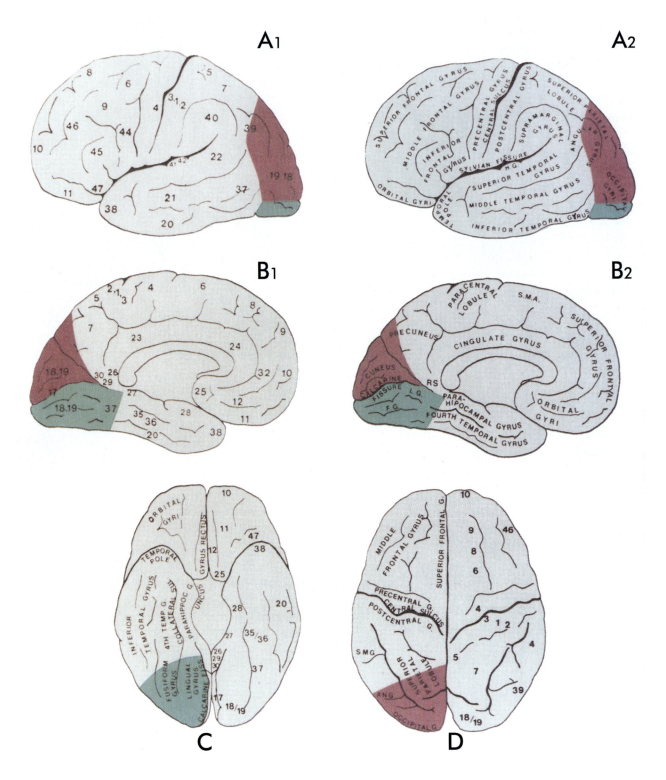

**FIGURE 3–8.**  Two major subdivisions of the occipital lobe: dorsal (superior) component (shown in red), and ventral (inferior) component (shown in green). Numbers corresponding to Brodmann's cytoarchitectonic areas are depicted in *Panels A₁* and *B₁* and the right side (left hemisphere) of *Panels C* and *D*; standard gyrus names are shown on corresponding *Panels A₂* and *B₂* and the left side (right hemisphere) of *Panels C* and *D*. Lateral (*Panels A₁* and *A₂*), mesial (*Panels B₁* and *B₂*), inferior (*Panel C*), and superior (*Panel D*) views are represented.

vision (i.e., blindness) in the inferior visual field contralateral to the lesion, and bilateral lesions of this type will produce an inferior altitudinal hemianopia. An intriguing presentation occurs when the lesions spare the primary visual cortex and involve the association cortices of areas 18 and 19. When such lesions encroach into the adjacent parietal region comprising areas 39 and 7, patients commonly develop a constellation of defects known as Balint's syndrome. An example of a CT of a patient with this type of presentation is shown in Figure 3–9. Balint's syndrome is based on the presence of three components: 1) visual disorientation (also known as simultanagnosia), 2) ocular apraxia (also known as psychic gaze paralysis), and 3) optic ataxia. The key constituent in the syndrome is visual disorientation, and there is considerable variability in the emphasis that is placed on the other components (A.R. Damasio 1985; Newcombe and Ratcliff 1989; see also Rizzo 1993; Rizzo and Nawrot 1993).

## Visual Disorientation

Visual disorientation (simultanagnosia) can be conceptualized as an inability to attend to more than a very limited sector of the visual field at any given moment. Patients report that they can see clearly in only a small part of the field, the rest being "out of focus" and in a sort of "fog." The sector of clear vision is unstable and may shift without warning in any direction, so that patients experience a literal "jumping about" of their visual perception. Such patients are incapable of constructing a spatially coherent visual field, and they cannot follow trajectories of stimuli or place stimuli in their proper locations in space. Perception of motion is often impaired, and such patients fail to notice when objects have moved about in their visual field, or fail to recognize the meaning of movements they have otherwise perceived correctly. For example, patients may fail to recognize a familiar gait or stride or fail to understand pantomime (A.R. Damasio et al. 1989b; 1990b). Isolated disturbances of motion detection, however, are quite rare; one of the few such cases was described by Zihl et al. (1983). Patients with visual disorientation can perceive color and shape normally, if the objects are appreciated within a clear sector of the visual field.

## Ocular Apraxia

Ocular apraxia (psychic gaze paralysis) is a deficit of visual scanning. It consists of an inability to direct the gaze voluntarily toward a stimulus located in the peripheral vision to bring it into central vision. Thus, patients fail to direct saccades toward stimuli that have appeared in the panorama of their visual fields, or they produce saccades that are inaccurate and miss the target. Ocular apraxia is not necessary for the development of visual disorientation (Newcombe and Ratcliff 1989; Rizzo and Hurtig 1987), although it always occurs together with either visual disorientation or optic ataxia (A.R. Damasio et al. 2000).

## Optic Ataxia

Optic ataxia is a disturbance of visually guided reaching behavior. Patients are not able to point accurately at a target, under visual guidance. They cannot point precisely to the examiner's fingertip or to items such as a cup or coin. Interestingly, pointing to targets on their own body does not pose a problem, as this can be accomplished on the basis of somatosensory information. Also, the patients have no difficulty pointing to sound sources (A.R. Damasio and Benton 1979). Optic ataxia can occur in isolation, particularly when lesions are at the border of the occipital and parietal regions or in the parietal region exclusively.

The full Balint's syndrome is generally associated with bilateral occipitoparietal lesions, although a unilateral lesion, especially on the right, can also produce the syndrome. When lesions are confined to the superior occipital cortices without extension into the parietal region, visual disorientation is likely to occur without associated ocular apraxia or optic ataxia. The defects in motion perception that occur frequently in patients with Balint's syndrome are probably related to damage in the lower parietal/lateral occipital region. (In fact, there is a growing body of evidence, especially from functional imaging studies, that structures in the vicinity of the temporal-occipital-parietal junction may play an important role in retrieving knowledge about the typical motion patterns of objects [Kourtzi and Kanwisher 2000; Martin et al. 2000; Tootell et al. 1995]). Many patients with Balint's syndrome have an impairment of stereopsis, that is, the process of depth perception from visual information dependent on binocular visual interaction, although complete astereopsis is seen only in the setting of bilateral lesions (Rizzo 1989; Rizzo and Hurtig 1987).

As noted earlier, bilateral damage to the ventral occipitotemporal sector has been linked to prosopagnosia, whereas damage to the dorsal occipitoparietal sector has been linked to simultanagnosia. It was also mentioned that some prosopagnosic patients produce discriminatory autonomic responses (skin conductance responses) to familiar faces despite the fact that the faces are not recognized consciously. Such a finding has never been reported in connection with dysfunction of the dorsal

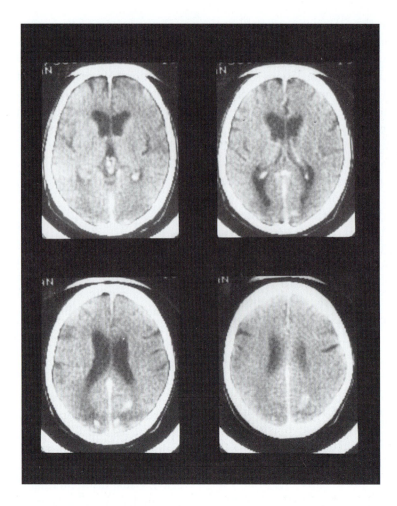

**FIGURE 3–9.** Contrast-enhanced computed tomographic scan of a 74-year-old, right-handed man, showing bilateral lesions (areas of increased density) in the superior occipital region corresponding to the supracalcarine visual association cortices. The man developed a complex visual disturbance (Balint's syndrome) in connection with these lesions.

visual system, but we recently encountered just such a case (Denburg et al. 2000). LA is a 50-year-old woman diagnosed with a rare visual variant of Alzheimer's disease, with associated Balint's syndrome, including simultanagnosia. MR and PET studies confirmed focal damage to and dysfunction in the occipitoparietal cortices bilaterally. Neuropsychological testing revealed preservation of anterograde memory, language, and executive functions, in the context of severely defective complex visual skills. Neuro-ophthalmologic studies demonstrated normal visual fields and acuity. We conducted an experiment in which the patient's skin conductance responses were measured during presentation of each of 20 neutrally and 20 negatively valenced visual stimuli. The patient consistently showed large-amplitude skin conductance responses to negative stimuli, even though her conscious report demonstrated that those stimuli were severely misperceived and rated as neutral in valence. In contrast, neutral stimuli that were accurately perceived and rated as neutral in valence evoked significantly smaller skin

conductance responses. This case demonstrates nonconscious recognition of affective valence in a patient with simultanagnosia and dorsal visual system dysfunction.

## Ventral Component

The ventral component of the occipital lobes comprises the primary visual cortex immediately below the calcarine fissure (area 17) and the inferior portion of the visual association cortices (areas 18 and 19). The latter component corresponds to the lingual and fusiform gyri (Figure 3–8C). This region will be considered together with the posterior part of area 37, that is, the occipitotemporal junction. Damage to primary visual cortex and/or its connections in the inferior bank of the calcarine fissure will produce a form vision defect (blindness) in the contralateral superior visual field. Damage to nearby structures may spare vision for form, either partially or entirely, while producing a number of other higher-order visual impairments. Several examples are elaborated below, including acquired achromatopsia, apperceptive visual agnosia, and acquired alexia.

## Acquired (Central) Achromatopsia

Acquired (central) achromatopsia is a disorder of color perception involving all or part of the visual field, with preservation of form vision, caused by damage to the inferior visual association cortex and/or its subjacent white matter (A.R. Damasio et al. 1980, 2000; Meadows 1974b; Paulson et al. 1994; Rizzo et al. 1993; for review see Tranel 2001). Patients lose color vision in a quadrant, a hemifield, or the entire visual field. The loss may be partial, in which case patients complain that colors appear "washed out" or "dirty," or may be complete, in which case everything is seen in shades of black and white. Perception of form is unaltered, and depth and motion perception are also normal. It is important to note that the disorder is acquired. It is not a hereditary (retinal) disorder of color vision, such as the red-green color blindness that is fairly common in men, hence the designation *central* achromatopsia. Also, the inability to name colors is not part of the disorder. The latter type of patient has, instead, *color anomia*, and it can be demonstrated that this patient is capable of passing color perception tests such as the Ishihara Color Plate Test and the Farnsworth-Munsell 100-Hue Test. Nor is achromatopsia a disturbance of color association (a disorder known as *color agnosia*); achromatopsic patients can correctly answer prompts such as "the color of grass is _____" or "the color of blood is _____" (see Tranel 2001, for further discussion of these distinctions).

The purest form of central achromatopsia is left hemiachromatopsia associated with a unilateral right occipitotemporal lesion, unaccompanied by other neuropsychological defects. A comparable lesion on the left will produce right hemiachromatopsia, but most of those patients will typically also have alexia. An example of a CT from the latter type of patient is shown in Figure 3–10. As the case illustrates, an upper-quadrant form vision defect is generally encountered in the colorless hemifield. This is because the occipitotemporal lesion generally disrupts optic radiations or encroaches into primary visual cortex on the inferior bank of the calcarine fissure. Bilateral occipitotemporal lesions may cause full-field achromatopsia, and such patients will frequently also manifest associative visual agnosia (especially prosopagnosia).

The most precise anatomical studies based on the lesion method have indicated that the middle third of the lingual gyrus is the most common site of damage in patients with central achromatopsia (Rizzo et al. 1993), followed by damage to the white matter immediately behind the posterior tip of the lateral ventricle. In our experience, lesions confined to the fusiform gyrus or to the white matter beneath the ventricle do not produce achromatopsia. Studies using functional neuroimaging techniques have corroborated and extended the lesion-based work. It has been shown that when subjects are given tasks requiring inspection or searching for colored stimuli, there are areas of activation in the region of the lingual and fusiform gyri, or putative human area V4, essentially the same area implicated by lesion work (Chao and Martin 1999; Clark et al. 1997; Corbetta et al. 1990; Lueck et al. 1989; Zeki et al. 1991). The functional imaging and lesion studies are also consistent with neurophysiology work in animals (Hubel and Livingstone 1987; Livingstone and Hubel 1988; for review, see Zeki 1990) and with studies using event-related potentials (Rosler et al. 1995). The work in nonhuman primates has indicated that separate cellular channels within area 17 are differently dedicated to the processing of color, form, and motion (Hubel and Livingstone 1987; Livingstone and Hubel 1988) and that some visual association cortices have an important specialization for color processing (Van Essen and Maunsell 1983; Zeki 1973).

A disorder closely related to achromatopsia involves defective color imagery, that is, the inability to imagine objects in color. In fact, it has been argued that defective color perception invariably results in defective color imagery (Beauvois and Saillant 1985; Farah 1989). This conclusion is supported by recent functional imaging studies, which have shown that imagining and naming the colors associated with various entities activates a region in the fusiform gyrus bilaterally, but more strongly on the left (Martin et al. 1995). Disorders of color recognition (color agnosia) tend to be associated with unilateral left or bilateral lesions to the occipitotemporal junction, although the neural correlates of color agnosia are very poorly understood (Luzzatti and Davidoff 1994; Schnider et al. 1992; Tranel 2001).

## Apperceptive Visual Agnosia

Apperceptive agnosia was originally attributed to the disturbed integration of otherwise normally perceived components of a stimulus (Lissauer 1890), and in general, the concept has persisted as a useful designation for recognition defects in which there is a substantial perceptual component (Bauer 1993; Tranel and Damasio 1996). Like associative agnosia described earlier, apperceptive agnosia involves the defective recognition of familiar stimuli. Perception and recognition, rather than being discrete processes, operate on a physiological continuum;

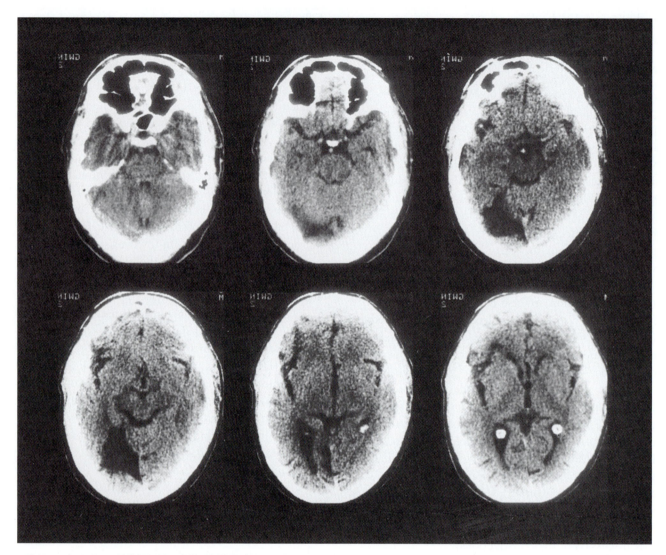

**FIGURE 3–10.** Computed tomographic scan of a 67-year-old, right-handed man, showing a lesion (area of decreased density) in the left infracalcarine visual association cortices. The man had a right superior quadrantanopia. In the lower right field, form vision was normal, but the patient was unable to see color (achromatopsia). He also had acquired ("pure") alexia.

thus, the distinction between apperceptive and associative agnosia can be somewhat arbitrary. The term agnosia should not be applied to patients in whom recognition defects develop in connection with major disturbances of basic perception (Tranel and Damasio 1996).

A common form of apperceptive agnosia occurs in the visual modality in connection with right-sided lesions involving both the inferior and superior sectors of the posterior visual association cortices. Such a lesion in a patient of this type is illustrated in Figure 3–11. A number of authors have described cases of prosopagnosia following this type of lesion (A.R. Damasio et al. 1989b, 1990b; De Renzi 1986; Landis et al. 1986; Michel et al. 1986; Sergent and Villemure 1989). Patients with apperceptive visual agnosia have difficulty perceiving all parts

of a visual array simultaneously and in generating the image of a whole entity when given a part. When shown a part of a house or a car, for example, the patient will be unable to imagine the whole object to which the part belongs and will fail to recognize the stimulus. A related defect is the inability to assemble parts of a model into a meaningful ensemble. For instance, the patient will be unable to assemble various face parts to form a spatially correct whole. This type of defect has been described in connection with faces and other objects (e.g., A.R. Damasio et al. 1990b). Many such patients also report an inability to image faces (Farah 1989; Kosslyn 1988). Unlike those with associative prosopagnosia, persons with apperceptive agnosia will fail many standard neuropsychological tests of visual perception, such as matching

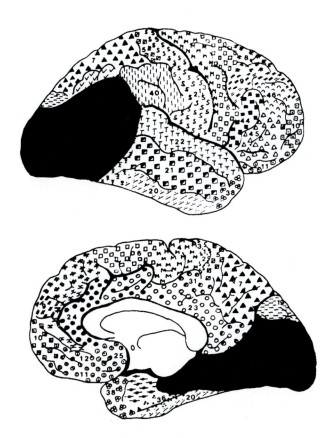

**FIGURE 3–11.** Depiction of the lesion of a 68-year-old, right-handed man who suffered an infarction that destroyed the right posterior parietal and occipital cortices. Note that the lesion (marked in black) includes visual association cortices both above and below the calcarine fissure. The man had apperceptive prosopagnosia.

differently lit photographs of faces and mentally assembling puzzle pieces to form a whole object.

## Acquired (Pure) Alexia

Lesions that disconnect both right- and left-sided visual association cortices from the dominant, language-related temporoparietal cortices can produce a complete or partial impairment in reading, a condition known as acquired (pure) alexia. Pure alexia can be caused by a single lesion strategically placed in the region behind, beneath, and under the occipital horn of the left lateral ventricle, by damaging pathways from the corpus callosum and from the left visual association cortex (A.R. Damasio and Damasio 1983). Another setting is the combination of a lesion in the corpus callosum, which disconnects right-to-left visual information transfer, and a lesion in the left occipital lobe, which disconnects the left visual association cortex from the left language cortex (Geschwind 1965; Greenblatt 1983). Such lesions are likely to produce right hemianopia, and this sign is a frequent,

although not invariable (Greenblatt 1973), accompaniment of pure alexia. Another neuropsychological correlate of pure alexia is color anomia (Davidoff and De Bleser 1994). The "purity" of the condition stems from the fact that patients with these lesions do not develop disturbances in writing or in other aspects of speech and linguistic functioning, separating this type of alexia from the types of reading defects that are common in aphasic patients (Benson et al. 1971). In this sense, pure alexia can be construed as a disturbance of visual pattern recognition. Pure alexia is also known as alexia without agraphia, or pure word blindness.

Patients with pure alexia are unable to read most words and sentences, and in severe cases, even reading of single letters is impaired. The problem is not one of visual acuity. The fact that the patient can see the sentences, words, and letters that cannot be read can be readily demonstrated by having the patient copy those stimuli, a task that will be executed normally (Tranel 1994b). Thus, most patients with pure alexia have normal visual acuity (although a quadrantanopia or hemianopia may be present), and most have normal recognition of nonverbal visual stimuli such as objects and faces.

## The Parietal Lobes

On the lateral aspect of the cerebral hemispheres, the parietal lobes comprise a large expanse of cortex bounded by the central sulcus anteriorly, the sylvian fissure inferiorly, and the occipital cortices posteriorly (Figure 3–12). It is important to maintain a clear distinction between the right and left hemispheres, as many cognitive and behavioral correlates of the parietal region are highly lateralized. The parietal lobes will be considered together with several anatomically and functionally related neighboring regions. Principal neuropsychological correlates of lesions in these regions are summarized in Table 3–4.

## Temporoparietal Junction

In the left hemisphere, an area of cortex formed by the posterior part of the superior temporal gyrus (posterior area 22) constitutes the core of a region known as Wernicke's area. The posterior part of the inferior parietal lobule (including parts of the supramarginal and angular gyri) is usually included as part of greater Wernicke's area. This region subserves a set of core speech and language functions whose disruption constitutes the syndrome known as Wernicke's aphasia (Benson 1989; H. Damasio 1998; Tranel and Anderson

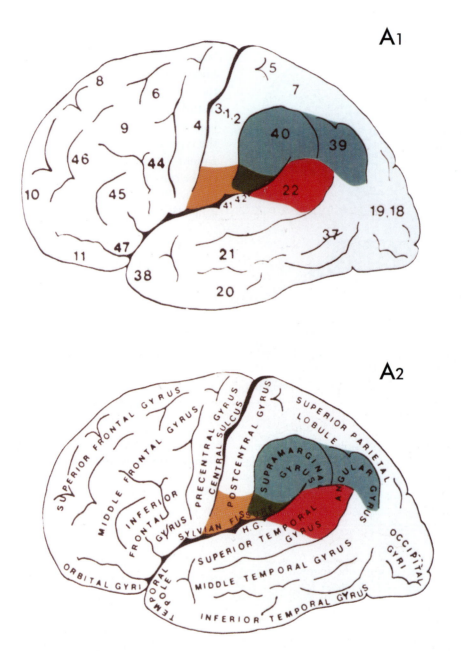

**FIGURE 3–12.** Subdivisions of the parietal lobe and nearby regions. The temporoparietal junction, formed by the posterior part of the superior temporal gyrus (area 22), is shown in red. The inferior parietal lobule, depicted in green, is formed by the angular (area 39) and supramarginal (area 40) gyri. The parietal operculum is formed by the inferior aspect of the postcentral gyrus (shown in yellow) and a bit of the anteroinferior aspect of the supramarginal gyrus (shown in overlapping yellow and green). Numbers corresponding to Brodmann's cytoarchitectonic areas are depicted in *Panel A₁*, and standard gyrus names are shown on the corresponding *Panel A₂*. The panels depict a lateral view.

1999). Wernicke's aphasia is hallmarked by fluent, paraphasic speech, impaired repetition, and defective aural comprehension. Patients produce speech without hesitation, and the phrase length and melodic contour of utterances are normal; however, there are frequent errors in the choice of individual words used to express an idea (paraphasias). Phonemic (also known as literal) (e.g., substituting *sephalot* for *elephant*) and semantic

(also known as verbal) (e.g., substituting *superintendent* for *president*) paraphasias are common. Repetition of sentences is impaired and may be limited to single words. Repetition of digits is usually impaired as well. The comprehension defect can be quite severe and frequently involves both aural and written forms of language. The typical lesion associated with Wernicke's aphasia is depicted in Figure 3–13.

**TABLE 3–4.** Neuropsychological manifestations of parietal lobe lesions

| | Hemispheric side of lesion | | |
| --- | --- | --- | --- |
| | **Left** | **Right** | **Bilateral** |
| Temporoparietal junction (including posterior part of superior temporal gyrus) | Wernicke's aphasia | Amusia; defective music recognition; "phonagnosia" | Auditory agnosia |
| Inferior parietal lobule | Conduction aphasia; tactile object agnosia; acalculia | Neglect; anosognosia; anosodiaphoria; tactile object agnosia | Body schema disturbances; anosognosia; anosodiaphoria |

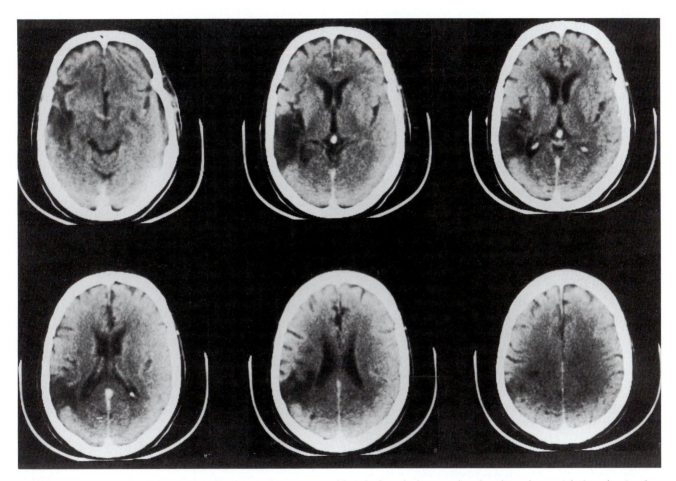

**FIGURE 3–13.** Computed tomographic scan of a 56-year-old, right-handed man who developed Wernicke's aphasia after sustaining a left middle cerebral artery infarction. The lesion (area of low density) is centered squarely in Wernicke's area, including the posterior superior temporal gyrus (top row) and part of the inferior parietal lobule (bottom row).

In the right hemisphere, lesions in the region of the temporoparietal junction do not cause disturbances of propositional speech but instead may impair the processing of music and spectral auditory information. A patient of this type was reported by A.R. Damasio et al. (1990d; for a further description of this case, see Tranel 2000). After sustaining a lesion to the right temporoparietal region, the patient developed a severe defect in music recognition. The case was of particular interest because the patient was a trained musician and singer, and the loss of the ability to identify specific singing voices and musical arrangements was especially striking.

Another intriguing neuropsychological correlate of this region is the ability to recognize familiar voices. Van Lancker and her associates reported that lesions to the right parietal cortices disrupt this function, even though auditory acuity is fundamentally unaltered, a condition the authors termed phonagnosia (Van Lancker and Kreiman 1988; Van Lancker et al. 1988). More inferior lesions, confined to the temporal cortices, tend to disrupt perception of auditory spectral information (Robin et al. 1990) but may not disrupt voice recognition (Van Lancker et al. 1989).

Bilateral lesions to the posterior part of the superior temporal gyrus lead to the syndrome of auditory agnosia, in which the patient is unable to recognize both speech and nonspeech sounds (Vignolo 1982; for reviews, see Bauer 1993; Tranel and Damasio 1996). Almost always caused by stroke, the condition involves the sudden and complete inability to identify the meaning of verbal and nonverbal auditory signals, including spoken words and familiar environmental sounds such as a telephone ringing or a knock on the door. Full-blown auditory agnosia is rare. In most cases there is a good deal of perceptual impairment together with a recognition defect, and the term *agnosia* should be applied with qualification.

## Inferior Parietal Lobule

The inferior parietal lobule comprises the supramarginal and angular gyri. On the left side, lesions to the supramarginal gyrus and the neighboring parietal operculum (the area of cortex formed by the inferiormost portion of the postcentral gyrus) or the underlying white matter, or both, cause a speech and language disturbance known as conduction aphasia (e.g., Benson 1993). An example of a CT scan from such a patient is shown in Figure 3–14. The core feature of this aphasia is a marked defect in verbatim repetition, which is disproportionately severe compared with other speech and language defects. Speech production is fluent but is dominated by phonemic paraphasias. Comprehension is only mildly compromised. Naming is defective and is dominated by phonemic errors, such as substitution of incorrect phonemes into target naming responses. Reading aloud is impaired, but reading comprehension may be normal. Another distinctive feature of conduction aphasia is that patients cannot write to dictation; however, they can write normally or nearly normally when writing spontaneously or when copying a written example.

Conduction aphasia has also been reported with lesions that damage the primary auditory cortex (areas 41 and 42) and extend into the insular cortex and underlying white matter (H. Damasio and Damasio 1980). Another interesting example is a case described by Hyman and Tranel (1989), in which conduction aphasia occurred together with a complete right hemianesthesia. The lesion in this patient was in the white matter subjacent to the inferior parietal and posterior temporal cortices, with extension into the posterior part of the insula.

Left-sided lesions to the parietal region, especially in the inferior parietal lobule, have also been associated with an acquired disturbance in mathematical abilities, a condition known as acalculia (for review, see Denburg and Tranel, in press). Patients lose the ability to perform various calculations—such as adding, subtracting, multiplying, and dividing—and may even be impaired in the simple reading and/or writing of numbers. A careful review of the literature indicates that the neural correlates of acalculia are not well understood; moreover, the condition is frequently accompanied by disturbances of language (e.g., aphasia) or visuospatial processing that confound its interpretation. Nonetheless, it has been suggested that the left parietal region constitutes the "mathematical brain" in humans, and this idea has attracted a reasonable amount of scientific support (Butterworth 1999).

On the right side, the most consistent and striking neuropsychological correlates of lesions to the inferior parietal lobule are neglect and anosognosia. Neglect, associated especially with temporoparietal lesions that include areas 39 and 40 (e.g., Heilman et al. 1983; 1993; see Robertson and Marshall 1993 for review), refers to a condition whereby the patient fails to attend to stimuli in the contralateral hemispace. In the visual modality, for example, the patient will not attend to the left hemifield and will fail to report stimuli from that side even when it can be demonstrated that there is no impairment of form vision (hemianopia). In principle, neglect can occur in relationship to any sensory modality, but in practice the visual and auditory varieties are most common. Some investigators have attributed neglect to an impairment of the attentional mechanisms necessary for normal perception (e.g., Heilman et al. 1985, 1993; Weintraub and Mesulam 1989). Figure 3–15 shows a typical example of a patient with a large right hemisphere lesion that includes the inferior parietal lobule. The patient had severe neglect, anosognosia, and visuospatial impairments.

Neglect can involve intrapersonal as well as extrapersonal space. For example, patients may fail to use, or even deny the existence of, the contralateral arm and leg, even when there is no motor impairment (e.g., Tranel 1995b). Representations conjured up in recall can also be affected. When asked to imagine or draw an object, the patient may omit the left half as though it did not exist. Asked to describe well-known scenes from memory, patients may report only the elements from the right side of the representation. The omissions, however, are specific to the patient's perspective, and it can be demonstrated that the patient does have the capacity to access the full array of information. Bisiach and Luzzatti (1978), for example, asked patients to describe a well-known scene from a particular perspective, and then rotated the

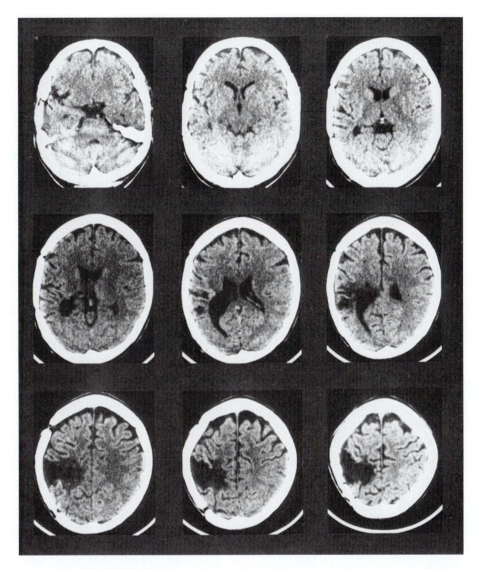

**FIGURE 3–14.** Computed tomographic scan of a 35-year-old, right-handed woman, showing a lesion (area of low density) in the left supramarginal gyrus (area 40). Note that the lesion spares the primary auditory cortex and the main part of Wernicke's area (posterior area 22). The woman had conduction aphasia.

perspective by 180 degrees, and asked the patients again to describe the scene. In the first description, patients reported information only from the right side of the scene. In the second condition, the patients again reported information only from the right side of the scene, but since the perspective had been rotated, this was precisely the same information that had been neglected in the first description.

Anosognosia is another frequent correlate of damage to the right inferior parietal lobule. The term was originally applied to patients who denied that a paretic limb was in fact paretic, or that it even belonged to them (Babinski 1914). Denial of sensory loss (e.g., a visual field defect) and cognitive disturbance have also been included under the concept of anosognosia (Anderson

and Tranel 1989). In a strict sense, anosognosia denotes a true recognition defect in which the patient is unaware of acquired motor, sensory, or cognitive deficits. This can be distinguished from denial of illness, which refers to the adaptive psychological condition that allows patients under severe stress to adapt to the calamitous consequences of disease. Anosognosia can be operationally defined as a significant discrepancy between the patients' reporting of their disabilities and the objective evidence regarding their level of functioning. A related term is *anosodiaphoria*, which refers to the condition in which patients appear unconcerned with or minimize the significance of neurological and neuropsychological deficits. It is common for patients to manifest anosognosia early in the course of illness and then for this to evolve gradually

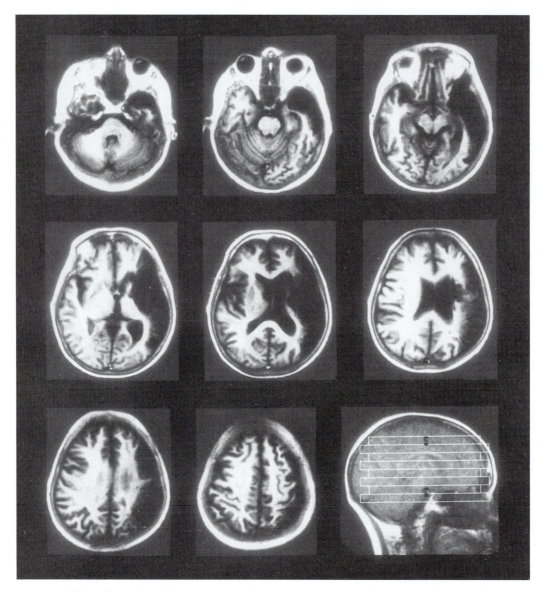

**FIGURE 3–15.** T1-weighted magnetic resonance imaging of a 34-year-old, right-handed woman, showing a large right middle cerebral artery infarction. The lesion (showing as a black region) includes a significant portion of the inferior parietal lobule (areas 39 and 40). The woman had severe left-sided neglect, anosognosia, and visuospatial deficits.

into anosodiaphoria. In both conditions, common neuropsychological correlates are defects in visuospatial and visuoconstructional abilities and left hemispatial neglect (Benton 1985; Benton and Tranel 1993).

One other intriguing condition that has been described in connection with lesions to the inferior parietal lobule and nearby posterior/superior temporal cortices on either the right or left side is tactile object agnosia (Caselli 1991, 1993; Reed and Caselli 1994). Patients lose the ability to recognize objects presented via the tactile modality, even when basic aspects of somatosensory function are normal or near normal. The condition is different from prosopagnosia in that it involves a disruption of recognition at the basic object level rather than at the level of unique identity (Tranel 1991b).

Thus, patients with tactile agnosia cannot recognize stimuli such as keys, pencils, and eating utensils when those items are presented in the somatosensory modality. The condition is far less disabling than a disorder such as prosopagnosia, and many patients with tactile object agnosia will not even complain of a defect. In fact, the impairment may only be demonstrable under careful laboratory testing conditions.

## The Frontal Lobes

The frontal lobes constitute about half of the entire cerebral mantle, and there are numerous functional correlates of this portion of the brain. For reviews of functional correlates of the frontal lobes, the reader is referred to Boller and Spinnler (1994), A.R. Damasio and Anderson (1993), Fuster (1989), and Levin et al. (1991). To consider cognitive and behavioral correlates, it is helpful to divide the frontal lobes into several distinct anatomical sectors (Figure 3–16). The specific neuropsychological correlates of these different sectors are summarized in Table 3–5.

## Frontal Operculum

The frontal operculum is formed by areas 44, 45, and 47 (Figure 3–13). On the left side, the heart of this region (areas 44 and 45) is known as Broca's area. The region is dedicated to a set of speech and language functions whose disruption produces a distinctive pattern of aphasia termed *Broca's aphasia*. Patients with Broca's aphasia have nonfluent speech, characterized by short utterances, long response latencies, and flat melodic contour. There is a marked decrease in the density of words per unit time, and the speech production has long gaps in which the patient is struggling unsuccessfully to produce sounds. A severe disturbance of grammar is also characteristic of Broca's aphasia. Paraphasias are common, usually involving omission of phonemes or addition of incorrect phonemes (phonemic paraphasias). In severe cases, speech may be virtually unintelligible. A defect in repetition is invariably present, and most individuals with Broca's aphasia have defective naming and impaired writing. By contrast, language comprehension is relatively preserved. Persons with Broca's aphasia can comprehend simple conversations, and they generally comprehend and execute two- and even three-step commands. Reading comprehension may also be relatively preserved. An example of a CT scan from a typical patient with Broca's aphasia is shown in Figure 3–17.

When lesions are confined to Broca's area, speech and language recovery can be fairly extensive (Mohr et al. 1978). If the damage involves other frontal fields in the dorsolateral sector in addition to Broca's area or if it cuts deeper into frontal white matter, a poorer pattern of recovery is observed (Mohr et al. 1978). When lesions involve the lower motor or premotor cortices or the subjacent white matter, aphemia rather than aphasia results (Schiff et al. 1983). Patients develop articulatory defects and hesitant speech, but a true linguistic impairment is not present. Lesions in structures anterior, superior, and deep to Broca's area, but sparing most or all of areas 44 and 45, will commonly produce transcortical motor aphasia (e.g., Rubens 1976), which resembles Broca's aphasia except that there is no repetition defect.

Recent studies have revealed an intriguing pattern of naming impairment associated with lesions in the premotor/prefrontal region, in and near the left frontal operculum. Patients with such lesions demonstrate a disproportionate impairment in the ability to name actions (with verbs) and, by contrast, have normal naming of concrete entities (with nouns) (A.R. Damasio and Tranel 1993; Tranel et al., in press). In other words, defective verb retrieval is associated with lesions in the left premotor/prefrontal region. The findings are consistent with other studies that have demonstrated a higher incidence of verb retrieval impairment in patients with agrammatic aphasia, many of whom presumably had lesions involving the left frontal operculum (Daniele et al. 1994; Goodglass et al. 1994; Hillis and Caramazza 1995; Miceli et al. 1988; Miozzo et al. 1994). An example of a CT scan from a patient with this type of naming pattern is shown in Figure 3–18. The patient had normal retrieval of common and proper nouns (naming of concrete entities) but defective retrieval of verbs (naming of actions). It is intriguing to note that this is the opposite pattern of the one associated with left temporal lobe lesions (see Lexical Retrieval, above, in this chapter); those patients have defective retrieval of words for concrete entities (nouns) but normal retrieval of words for actions (verbs). These findings thus constitute a double dissociation with regard to both word type (nouns versus verbs) and site of lesion (left temporal versus left premotor/prefrontal).

In the right hemisphere, lesions to the frontal operculum have been linked to defects in paralinguistic communication, but propositional speech and language are not affected (Ross 1981). Specifically, patients may lose the ability to implement normal patterns of prosody and gesturing. Communication is characterized by flat, monotone speech, loss of spontaneous gesturing, and impaired ability to repeat affective contours (e.g., to implement emotional tones in speech, such as happiness, sadness, etc.).

## Superior Mesial Region

The superior mesial aspect of the frontal lobes comprises a set of structures that are critical for the initiation of movement and emotional expression. The supplementary motor area (the mesial aspect of area 6) and the anterior cingulate gyrus (area 24) are especially important (Figure 3–16). Lesions in this region produce a syndrome known as akinetic mutism (A.R. Damasio and Van Hoesen 1983), in which the patient makes no effort to communicate, either verbally or by gesture, and maintains an empty, noncommunicative facial expression. Movements are limited to tracking of moving targets with the eyes and performing body and arm movements

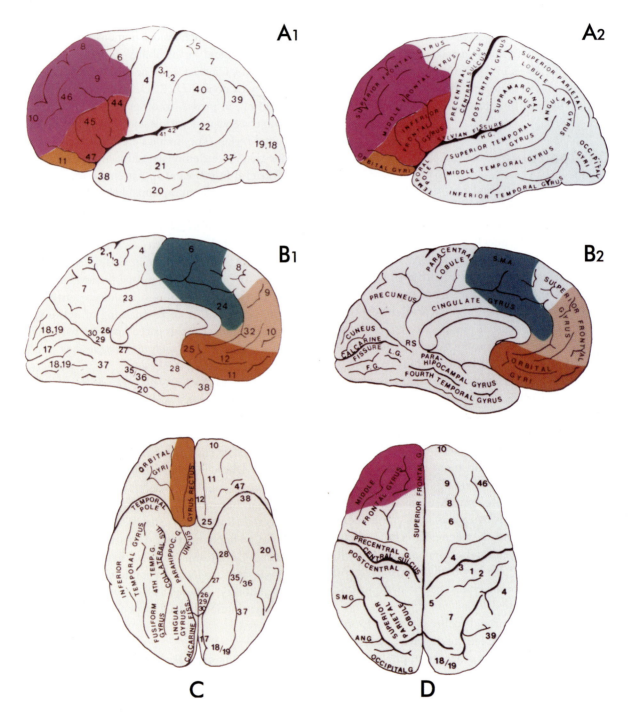

**FIGURE 3–16.** Major subdivisions of the frontal lobe: the frontal operculum, formed by areas 44, 45, and 47, shown in red; the superior mesial region, formed by the mesial aspect of area 6 and the anterior part of the cingulate gyrus (area 24), shown in green; the inferior mesial region, formed by the orbital cortices (areas 11, 12, and 25), shown in dark yellow (the basal forebrain is immediately posterior to this region); and the lateral prefrontal region, formed by the lateral aspects of areas 8, 9, 46, and 10, shown in purple. The ventromedial frontal lobe comprises the orbital and the lower mesial (area 32 and the mesial aspect of areas 10 and 9) cortices (dark yellow and light yellow, respectively). Numbers corresponding to Brodmann's cytoarchitectonic areas are depicted in *Panels A₁* and *B₁* and the right side (left hemisphere) of *Panels C* and *D*, and standard gyrus names are shown in the corresponding *Panels A₂* and *B₂* and the left side (right hemisphere) of *Panels C* and *D*. Lateral (*Panels A₁* and *A₂*), mesial (*Panels B₁* and *B₂*), inferior (*Panel C*), and superior (*Panel D*) views are represented.

**TABLE 3–5.** Neuropsychological manifestations of frontal lobe lesions

| | Hemispheric side of lesion | |
|---|---|---|
| | **Left** | **Right** |
| **Frontal operculum** | Broca's aphasia; defective retrieval of words for actions (verbs) | "Expressive" aprosody |
| **Superior mesial region** | Akinetic mutism[a] | Akinetic mutism[a] |
| **Inferior mesial region** | | |
| Basal forebrain[b] | Anterograde and retrograde amnesia with confabulation; worse for verbal stimuli | Anterograde and retrograde amnesia with confabulation; worse for nonverbal stimuli |
| Orbital | Defective social conduct; "acquired" sociopathy[a]; prospective memory defects | Defective social conduct; "acquired" sociopathy[a]; prospective memory defects |
| **Dorsolateral prefrontal region** | Impaired working memory for verbal material; impaired verbal intellect; defective recency and frequency judgments for verbal material; defective verbal fluency; impaired "executive functions" | Impaired working memory for nonverbal spatial material; impaired nonverbal intellect; defective recency and frequency judgments for nonverbal material; defective design fluency; impaired "executive functions" |

[a]Condition is similar for left-sided and right-sided lesions; bilateral lesions produce a more severe version of the same condition.
[b]The basal forebrain is not part of the frontal lobes proper; it is included here for ease of exposition. See text for additional details.

connected with daily necessities such as eating, pulling up bedclothing, and going to the bathroom. Otherwise, the patient does not move or speak. The mutism can be distinguished from aphasia by the fact that, in the latter condition, patients will invariably exhibit an intent to communicate. They will show frustration at their inability to speak and will seek compensatory strategies, such as gesturing or writing. By contrast, patients with akinetic mutism appear content to lie motionless and silent, and they do not respond to reasonable queries from the examiner or to other prompts. An example of the lesion in a patient with akinetic mutism is illustrated in Figure 3–19.

There does not appear to be a significant difference in the profile of akinetic mutism as a function of the side of the lesion; left- and right-sided lesions lead to more or less equivalent defects. However, the defects are more severe, and persist longer, with bilateral lesions. Patients with unilateral lesions may recover very quickly, sometimes within a few weeks.

## Inferior Mesial Region

Inferiorly, the mesial aspect of the frontal lobes is composed of the orbital region, which includes areas 11 and 12. The basal forebrain (not part of the frontal lobes proper) is situated immediately behind the posterior-most extension of the inferior mesial region (Figure 3–16).

### Basal Forebrain

The basal forebrain is composed of a set of bilateral paramidline gray nuclei that include the septal nuclei, the diagonal band of Broca, the nucleus accumbens, and the substantia innominata. Lesions to this area, commonly caused by the rupture of aneurysms located in the anterior communicating artery or in the anterior cerebral artery, cause a distinctive neuropsychological syndrome in which memory defects figure most prominently (A.R. Damasio et al. 1985b, 1989a; Tranel et al. 2000b; Volpe and Hirst 1983). An example of this type of presentation is shown in Figure 3–20. The amnesic profile of patients with basal forebrain lesions has several intriguing features. It is characterized by an impairment in the integration of different aspects of stimuli, wherein patients are able to learn and recall separate component features of entities and events but cannot associate those components into an integrated memory. For example, the patient may learn the name of a person, that person's face, and the person's personality traits. When attempting to recall the target individual, the patient will not bring this information together but will assign the individual the wrong name or the wrong personality traits. This modal mismatching defect affects the retrograde compartment as well.

Another frequent manifestation in patients with basal forebrain lesions is a proclivity for confabulation. The fabrications have a dreamlike quality and occur spontaneously. They are not prompted by the need to fill gaps of missing information in attempting to respond to an examiner's questions. In some instances, the internal experience of the patient may even include fantasies that are not recognized as such. The patient will not be capable of distinguishing reality from nonreality in his or her own recall (A.R. Damasio et al. 1985b, 1989a; Tranel et al. 2000b). The memory defects of patients with basal

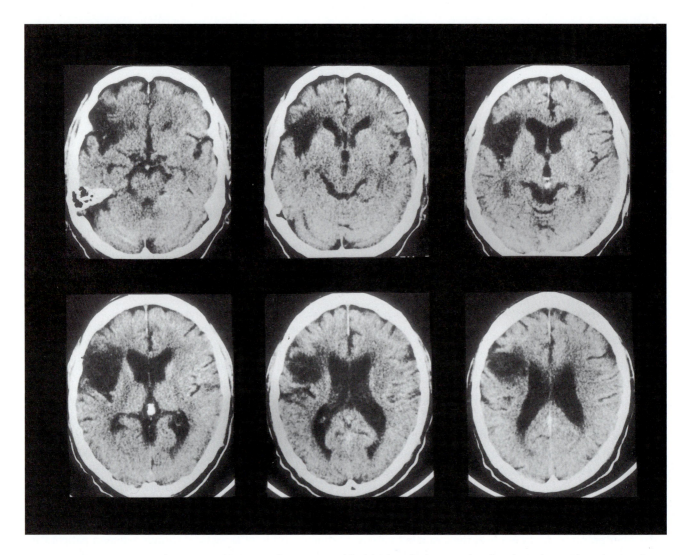

**FIGURE 3–17.** Computed tomographic scan of a 76-year-old, right-handed man who developed Broca's aphasia after a left frontal infarction. The lesion, showing as a well-defined area of low density, is squarely in the heart of Broca's area, that is, the frontal opercular region formed by areas 44 and 45.

forebrain lesions can persist well into the chronic phase of recovery; even after many years, patients continue to manifest learning and recall deficits and a tendency to confabulate. In the chronic phase, however, patients usually gain some insight into their difficulties. They learn to mistrust their own recall and to cross-check their own memories against an external source.

## Ventromedial Region

The orbital and lower mesial frontal cortices (including Brodmann's areas 11, 12, 25, and 32 and the mesial aspect of 10 and 9; see Figure 3–16) constitute the ventromedial frontal lobe, and a number of important neuropsychological correlates have been established for this region. Patients with ventromedial frontal lobe damage develop a severe disruption of social conduct, including defects in planning, judgment, and decision making

(Bechara et al. 1994; 1996; A.R. Damasio 1994; Tranel 1994a; Tranel et al. 2000a), a condition that has been termed *acquired sociopathy* (Barrash et al. 2000; A.R. Damasio et al. 1990c, 1991). Provided that the lesion does not extend into the basal forebrain, such patients do not generally develop memory disturbances; in fact, such patients are remarkably free of conventional neuropsychological defects (A.R. Damasio and Anderson 1993; Stuss and Benson 1986; Tranel et al. 1994a). Patient EVR, initially described by Eslinger and Damasio (1985), is prototypical (Figure 3–21).

Throughout the history of neuropsychology, investigators have called attention to the seemingly bizarre development of abnormal social behavior following frontal brain injury, especially damage to the ventromedial sector (e.g., Ackerly and Benton 1948; Brickner 1934, 1936; Harlow 1868; Hebb and Penfield 1940). The

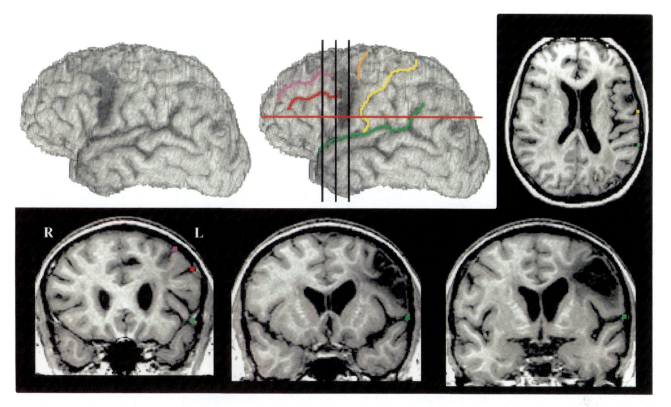

**FIGURE 3–18.** Three-dimensional reconstruction of the brain of a patient with a lesion in the left premotor/prefrontal region. The patient had impaired retrieval of words for actions (verbs) but normal retrieval of words for concrete entities (nouns). This patient, and a number of others of this type that we have studied, had a recovered nonfluent aphasia.

patients have a number of features in common (see A.R. Damasio and Anderson 1993), including the inability to organize future activity and hold gainful employment; diminished capacity to respond to punishment; a tendency to present an unrealistically favorable view of themselves; stereotyped but correct manners; a tendency to display inappropriate emotional reactions; and normal intelligence. It is crucial to keep in mind that in all cases, this personality and behavioral profile developed after the onset of frontal lobe damage in individuals with previously normal personalities and socialization.

Other investigators have called attention to similar characteristics in patients with ventromedial frontal lobe damage. For example, Blumer and Benson (1975) noted a personality type that characterized patients with orbital damage (which the authors termed pseudo-psychopathic), in which salient features were puerility, a jocular attitude, sexually disinhibited humor, inappropriate and nearly total self-indulgence, and complete lack of concern for others. Stuss and Benson (1984, 1986) emphasized that such patients demonstrate a remarkable lack of empathy and a general lack of concern about others. The patients tend to show callous unconcern, boastfulness, and unrestrained and tactless behavior. Other descriptors

include impulsiveness, facetiousness, and diminished anxiety and concern for the future. Mesulam (1986) emphasized the following personality features of patients with frontal lobe damage: puerile, profane, facetious, irresponsible, grandiose, irascible; erosion of foresight, judgment, and insight; loss of ability to delay gratification; loss of capacity for remorse; tendency to jump to premature conclusions; loss of capacity to grasp the context and gist of a complex situation; poor inhibition of immediate but inappropriate response tendencies; sustained shallowness and impulsivity of thought and affect.

A.R. Damasio (1994, 1995) has articulated a theory of emotion and feeling, which can be used to account for the somewhat enigmatic neuropsychological profiles of patients with a damaged ventromedial region. The theory posits that the response selection impairment in patients with ventromedial damage and acquired sociopathy is due to a defect in the activation of somatic markers that must accompany the internal and automatic processing of possible response options. The patients are deprived of a somatic marker that normally assists, both consciously and covertly, with response selection, reducing their chances of responding in the most advantageous manner and increasing their chances of generating responses that

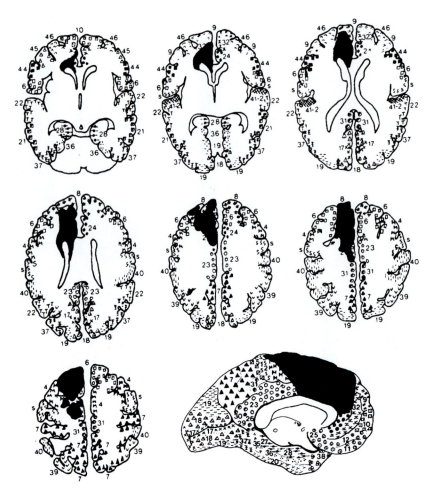

**FIGURE 3–19.** Depiction of the lesion in a 40-year-old, right-handed man, marked in black on transverse templates and on the mesial brain. The lesion is in the left hemisphere and involves the mesial aspect of area 6 and the anterior part of the cingulate gyrus (area 24). Initially, the man had severe akinetic mutism, but, by 3 months after onset, he demonstrated excellent recovery.

will lead to negative consequences.

According to the theory, a somatic marker provides the individual with a conscious "gut feeling" on the merits of a given response. It would also force attention on the positive or negative nature of various response options based on their foreseeable consequences. Another effect, which would be covert, would be the modification of neural systems that propitiate appetitive or aversive behaviors, for instance, the dopamine and serotonin nonspecific systems that can alter processing in the cerebral cortex. This effect, activated by the somatic marker, would increase or decrease the chances of immediate response. For example, a negative somatic state would inhibit appetitive behaviors, while a positive somatic state would facilitate appetitive behaviors. This would occur even if the somatic state itself was not conscious.

In normal individuals, the ventromedial frontal corti-

ces receive signals from a large range of neural structures engaged by perception, including external information from vision, audition, and olfaction, and internal somatic information from skeletal and visceral states. The signals arrive in the orbital region via projections from higher-order association cortices in temporal, parietal, and insular regions. In addition, the ventromedial cortices are a known source of projections from frontal regions toward central autonomic control structures; also, the ventromedial cortices receive and reciprocate projections from the hippocampus and amygdala (see A.R. Damasio et al. 1990c, 1991). Thus, the ventromedial cortices are in a position to form conjunctive records of concurrent signals hailing from external and internal stimuli, within neuron ensembles of the type that have been termed *convergence zones* (A.R. Damasio 1989a, 1989b). These cortices can also activate somatic effectors. A.R. Damasio (1994, 1995) has elaborated how this explanation can

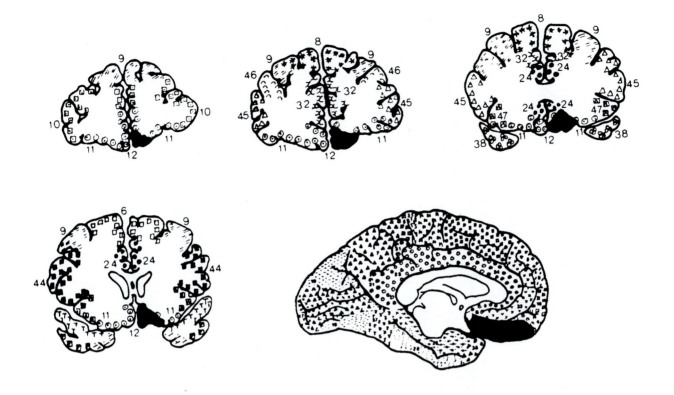

**FIGURE 3–20.** Depiction of the lesion in a 32-year-old, right-handed man, who experienced rupture of an anterior communicating artery aneurysm. The lesion, shown in black on coronal sections (left hemisphere on the right) and on the mesial aspect of the hemisphere, involves the left gyrus rectus and the left basal forebrain. The man had a distinctive amnesic syndrome with confabulation and both anterograde and retrograde deficits.

account for various facets of acquired sociopathy and other related conditions.

The ventromedial frontal region may also play a role in prospective memory, the capacity of "remembering in the future" (Wilkins and Baddeley 1978). Take as an example the following scenario. You are supposed to remember to call your spouse around midday to arrange plans for picking up the children from school. You can appose a "somatic marker" to this stimulus configuration so that when noontime arrives, you are "reminded" by your brain via a signal from the ventromedial frontal region—which may come as the feeling that "something needs to be done"—to call your spouse.

## Dorsolateral Prefrontal Region

The dorsolateral aspect of the frontal lobes comprises a vast expanse of cortex that occupies Brodmann's areas 8, 9, 46, and 10 (Figure 3–16). The functions of the lateral prefrontal region (exclusive of the frontal operculum and other language-related structures discussed previously) in humans are not well understood. Some of the better established correlates are reviewed below.

One function to which the dorsolateral prefrontal region has been linked is working memory. Working memory refers to a relatively short (on the order of minutes) window of mental processing, during which information is held "on-line," and operations are performed on it. For example, the demands of the Digit Span backwards test from the Wechsler Adult Intelligence Scale—Revised, or of the "serial 7s" test, are examples of working memory. In essence, working memory is a temporary storage and processing system used for problem solving and other cognitive operations that take place over a limited time frame (Baddeley 1992). Working memory is used to bridge temporal gaps, that is, to hold representations in a mental workspace long enough so that we can make appropriate responses to stimulus configurations or contingencies in which some, or even all, of the basic ingredients are no longer extant in perceptual space. The prefrontal cortex has been implicated in the mediation of working memory (Alivisatos and Milner 1989; Fuster 1989; Goldman-Rakic 1987; Jonides et al. 1993; G. McCarthy et al. 1994; Milner et al. 1985; Petrides et al. 1993; E. E. Smith et al. 1995; Wilson et al. 1993), and Goldman-Rakic has suggested that this is the exclusive

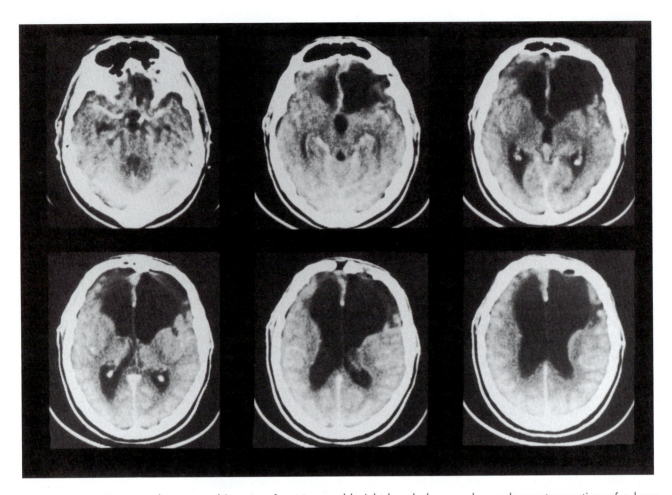

**FIGURE 3–21.**   Computed tomographic scan of a 44-year-old, right-handed man who underwent resection of a large orbitofrontal meningioma. The lesion, showing as an area of low density, encompasses bilateral destruction of the orbital and lower mesial frontal cortices. The basal forebrain is spared. The man developed severe changes in personality but did not manifest defects in conventional neuropsychological procedures.

memory function of the entire prefrontal cortex, each region being connected with a particular domain of operations. There is evidence for left- and right-sided specialization of the prefrontal regions with regard to working memory, following the typical left-verbal/right-spatial arrangement (E.E. Smith et al. 1996).

Our work has yielded findings consistent with this notion. For example, we found that patients with damage to the dorsolateral prefrontal cortex had severe impairments in working memory tasks involving delayed responding, but relatively preserved performance on decision-making tasks (Bechara et al. 1998). The reverse outcome—impaired decision making and normal working memory—was obtained in patients with ventromedial prefrontal damage, suggesting that different sectors of the frontal lobe are specialized for these two cognitive operations.

The dorsolateral prefrontal region also appears to be involved in higher-order integrative and executive control functions, and damage to this sector has been linked to intellectual deficits (see Stuss and Benson 1986). Another manifestation noted by several investigators is a memory impairment that affects judgments of recency and frequency of events but not the content of the events. Patients fail to remember how often, or how recently, they have experienced a certain stimulus, but they do recognize the stimulus as familiar (Milner and Petrides 1984; Milner et al. 1985; M.L. Smith and Milner 1988). The reverse dissociation—impaired recognition of content but preserved recency and frequency discrimination—was reported in connection with a lesion involving the mesial temporal lobes bilaterally, but sparing the dorsolateral prefrontal cortices (Sagar et al. 1990).

The dorsolateral frontal cortices have been linked to the verbal regulation of behavior (Luria 1969), and verbal fluency, as measured by the ability to generate word lists under certain stimulus constraints, is notably impaired in many patients with dorsolateral lesions, especially when those lesions are bilateral or on the left (Benton 1968). Unilateral right dorsolateral lesions may impair fluency in the nonverbal domain. For instance, patients may lose the capacity to produce designs in a fluent manner (Jones-Gotman and Milner 1977). Finally, deficits on laboratory tests of executive function, which test the ability to form, maintain, and change cognitive sets, as well as the tendency to perseverate (the Wisconsin Card Sorting Test is a paradigmatic example), can be fairly pronounced in patients with dorsolateral lesions, although they are by no means specific (Anderson et al. 1991; Milner 1963; Tranel et al. 1994a).

## Subcortical Structures

Two sets of subcortical structures are considered——the basal ganglia and the thalamus. A summary of some neuropsychological correlates of damage to these structures is presented in Table 3–6.

**TABLE 3–6.** Neuropsychological manifestations of subcortical lesions

| | |
|---|---|
| **Basal ganglia** | Atypical aphasia (left-sided lesions); dysarthria; aprosody; impaired nondeclarative memory; defective motor skill learning |
| **Thalamus** | Thalamic aphasia (left-sided lesions); anterograde amnesia with confabulation; retrograde amnesia with temporal gradient; impairments in "executive functions"; attention/concentration defects |

## Basal Ganglia

The basal ganglia are a set of deep gray nuclear structures, the caudate nucleus and the lenticular nucleus, with the latter being divided into the putamen and the globus pallidus. On the left side, lesions to these structures produce a speech and language disturbance that involves a mixture of manifestations that cannot be easily classified according to standard aphasia nomenclature; hence, the pattern has come to be known as *atypical aphasia* (Alexander 1989; A.R. Damasio et al. 1982a; Naeser et al. 1982). Because damage in this region will almost invariably include the anterior limb of the internal capsule, right hemiparesis is a common accompanying manifestation. The aphasia is characterized by speech that is usually fluent but is paraphasic and dysarthric; (typically) poor auditory comprehension; and, in some cases,

impaired repetition. An example of MR imagery from a patient with a basal ganglia lesion and atypical aphasia is shown in Figure 3–22.

It has been noted that patients with basal ganglia lesions and atypical aphasia nearly always have lesions that involve the head of the caudate nucleus, together with the putamen and anterior limb of the internal capsule (H. Damasio 1989). Lesions confined to the putamen, or to laterally adjacent structures such as the anterior insula and subjacent white matter, do not produce an aphasic disturbance, although defects in articulation and prosody may be noted. Other authors, however, have pointed out that in the key reports of aphasia-producing lesions to the basal ganglia (Cappa et al. 1983; A.R. Damasio et al. 1982a; Naeser et al. 1982), the patients all had significant damage to white matter structures in addition to basal ganglia involvement (Alexander 1989). One additional note of importance is that patients with basal ganglia lesions and aphasia tend to show very good recovery (H. Damasio et al. 1984).

As alluded to earlier (see Mesial Temporal Region above, in this chapter), the basal ganglia have also been linked to various forms of nondeclarative memory, including learning of motor skills and other capacities that do not require any conscious mental inspection of the contents of memory. The caudate nucleus, which together with the putamen forms the striatal component of the basal ganglia, may have nondeclarative memory functions that have to do with the development of habits and other nonconscious response tendencies. The tendencies we develop to respond to certain situations in certain ways, behaviors such as following the same route home each day or repeatedly seeking out a particular person for moral support and encouragement, are examples of habits and response tendencies that we engage on a fairly automatic basis with little or no conscious deliberation. These types of "memory" behavior have been linked to the striatum and, in particular, the caudate nucleus.

To illustrate this effect, consider a study we completed in patient Boswell (Tranel and Damasio 1993). We showed that Boswell, who has severe anterograde amnesia covering all aspects of declarative memory, could demonstrate the acquisition of new knowledge, covertly, if this knowledge was associated with positive or negative affective valence during the time of acquisition. During the course of several days, Boswell was exposed to three different stimulus persons: 1) a "Good Guy," who treated Boswell very kindly and granted requests for treats and rewards; 2) a "Bad Guy," who never gave Boswell treats and who was always responsible for having Boswell perform tedious neuropsychological experi-

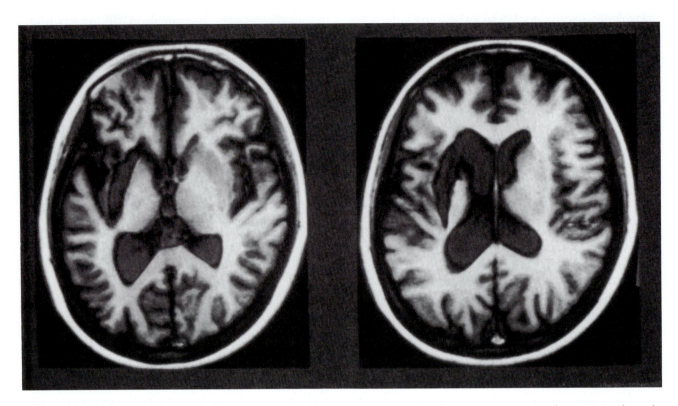

**FIGURE 3–22.** T1-weighted magnetic resonance imaging of a 35-year-old, right-handed woman who sustained a subcortical hemorrhage. The lesion, showing as an area of black on these transverse sectional images, involves the left basal ganglia, including the head and body of the caudate nucleus, and part of the putamen. The woman had a characteristic basal ganglia type of aphasia, with marked dysarthria and mixed linguistic impairments.

ments; 3) a "Neutral Guy," who approached Boswell in a completely neutral fashion. At the end of a week of exposure, Boswell was tested for declarative knowledge of the three persons, of which he had none. However, in a forced choice paradigm in which he was asked, "Choose the person you would go to for a reward," Boswell systematically selected the Good Guy over unfamiliar foils and systematically selected against the Bad Guy. Since Boswell's lesions guarantee that the entorhinal and perirhinal cortices, hippocampus, amygdala, and higher-order neocortices in the anterior temporal region are not required to support this form of covert learning and retrieval, we suggested that such learning might depend on neural circuits involving the basal ganglia, including the caudate nucleus.

## Thalamus

Disturbances of speech and language have been linked to damage in the dominant thalamus (e.g., Mohr et al. 1975). The language disorder tends to be primarily a deficit at the semantic level, with prominent word-finding impairment, defective confrontation naming, and semantic paraphasias. This pattern has a number of resem-

blances to the transcortical aphasias, and it has been linked in particular to damage in anterior thalamic nuclei (e.g., Graff-Radford and Damasio 1984; Graff-Radford et al. 1985).

Another well-studied neuropsychological correlate of thalamic lesions is memory impairment. In the setting of chronic alcoholism and the development of Korsakoff's syndrome, such lesions typically involve the dorsomedial nucleus of the thalamus along with other diencephalic structures such as the mamillary bodies. The amnesic profile associated with such lesions has been extensively investigated (Butters 1984; Butters and Stuss 1989; Victor et al. 1989). In general, such patients develop a severe anterograde amnesia that covers all forms of declarative knowledge. However, similar to patients such as HM and Boswell, nondeclarative learning, such as the acquisition of new perceptuomotor skills, is spared. A distinctive feature of Korsakoff's syndrome patients is their tendency to confabulate when asked direct questions regarding recent memory (Victor et al. 1989).

Individuals with diencephalic amnesia generally show some defect in the retrograde compartment. The impairment typically shows a temporal gradient, so that recall and recognition improve steadily with increasing distance between the present and the time of initial learning. Remote memories are retrieved more successfully (e.g., Cohen and Squire 1981). Also relatively common in patients with diencephalic amnesia is a disturbance of problem solving, along with other characteristics reminiscent of frontal lobe defects (Butters and Stuss 1989).

Thalamic lesions occurring as a consequence of stroke can also produce significant amnesia (Graff-Radford et al. 1985). Recent observations have indicated that the memory impairment is most severe when the lesions are anterior and bilateral (Graff-Radford et al. 1990b). Such lesions, which may interfere with hippocampus-related neural systems such as the mamillothalamic tract and with amygdala-related systems such as the ventroamygdalofugal pathway, produce an amnesic profile characterized by severe anterograde amnesia that spares nondeclarative learning, and a retrograde defect that is temporally graded. Posterior thalamic lesions, even when bilateral, were not associated with significant or lasting amnesia (Graff-Radford et al. 1990b).

The diencephalon gives rise to a number of important neurochemical systems that innervate widespread regions of cerebral cortex. Thus, structures such as the mamillary bodies and certain thalamic nuclei may provide to the cortex important neurotransmitters that are needed for normal memory function. It follows that damage to the diencephalon may not only disrupt important neuroanatomical connections between limbic regions (including the hippocampal complex) and the neocortex, but it might also interfere with memory-related neurochemical influences on the cortex.

## Conclusions

Understanding the principal neuropsychological correlates of variously placed cerebral lesions is of obvious importance for the accurate diagnosis and effective management of patients who experience brain injury. Another consideration, of no less importance, is the relevance of such understanding for the development of theoretical formulations regarding brain-behavior relationships (e.g., A.R. Damasio 1989b). As our understanding advances, it becomes increasingly important to appreciate the significance of both sides of the brain-behavior equation.

I have focused here on the neuropsychological manifestations of focal brain damage and have not considered to any length various psychiatric features, the latter of

which are taken up elsewhere in this textbook. It should be mentioned that there are close interrelationships between cognitive and psychiatric disabilities in patients with brain injuries. A patient who has had a stroke, for example, may be as handicapped by severe depression as by aphasia, perhaps even more so (e.g., Robinson et al. 1988). Psychiatric manifestations in patients with head injury are common and may constitute the major source of morbidity (see reviews in Rizzo and Tranel 1996). Understanding the types of cognitive defects that commonly arise in connection with damage to particular brain areas can facilitate the diagnosis and management of psychiatric manifestations and help avoid situations in which patients are mistakenly or carelessly labeled as "functional" or "organic."

## References

Ackerly SS, Benton AL: Report of a case of bilateral frontal lobe defect. Research Publications—Association for Research in Nervous and Mental Disease 27:479–504, 1948

Adolphs R, Tranel D: The amygdala and processing of facial emotional expressions, in The Amygdala, 2nd Edition. Edited by Aggleton J. New York, Wiley-Liss 587–630, 2000

Adolphs R, Tranel D, Damasio H, et al: Impaired recognition of emotion in facial expressions following bilateral damage to the human amygdala. Nature 372:669–672, 1994

Adolphs R, Tranel D, Damasio H, et al: Fear and the human amygdala. J Neurosci 15:5879–5891, 1995

Adolphs R, Tranel D, Denburg N: Impaired emotional declarative memory following unilateral amygdala damage. Learning and Memory 7:180–186, 2000

Alexander MP: Clinical-anatomical correlations of aphasia following predominantly subcortical lesions, in Handbook of Neuropsychology, Vol 2. Edited by Boller F, Grafman J. Amsterdam, Elsevier, 1989, pp 47–66

Alivisatos B, Milner B: Effects of frontal or temporal lobectomy on the use of advance information in a choice reaction time task. Neuropsychologia 27:495–503, 1989

Anderson SW, Tranel D: Awareness of disease states following cerebral infarction, dementia, and head trauma: standardized assessment. Clin Neuropsychol 3:327–339, 1989

Anderson SW, Damasio H, Jones RD, et al: Wisconsin Card Sorting Test performance as a measure of frontal lobe damage. J Clin Exp Neuropsychol 13:909–922, 1991

Babinski J: Contribution a l'etude des troubles mentaux dans l'hemiplegie organique cerebrale (agnosognosie). Rev Neurol 27:845–847, 1914

Baddeley AD: Working memory. Science 255:566–569, 1992

Barrash J, Damasio H, Adolphs R, et al: The neuroanatomical correlates of route learning impairment. Neuropsychologia 38:820–836, 2000

Barrash J, Tranel D, Anderson SW: Acquired personality changes associated with bilateral damage to the ventromedial prefrontal region. Dev Neuropsychol 18:355–381, 2000

Bauer RM: Autonomic recognition of names and faces in prosopagnosia: a neurophysiological application of the Guilty Knowledge Test. Neuropsychologia 22:457–469, 1984

Bauer RM: Agnosia, in Clinical Neuropsychology, 3rd Edition. Edited by Heilman KM, Valenstein E. New York, Oxford University Press, 1993, pp 215–278

Beauvois MF, Saillant B: Optic aphasia for colours and colour agnosia: a distinction between visual and visuo-verbal impairments in the processing of colours. Cognitive Neuropsychology 2:1–48, 1985

Bechara A, Damasio AR, Damasio H, et al: Insensitivity to future consequences following damage to prefrontal cortex. Cognition 50:7–12, 1994

Bechara A, Tranel D, Damasio H, et al: Double dissociation of conditioning and declarative knowledge relative to the amygdala and hippocampus in humans. Science 269:1115–1118, 1995

Bechara A, Tranel D, Damasio H, et al: Failure to respond autonomically to anticipated future outcomes following damage to prefrontal cortex. Cereb Cortex 6:215–225, 1996

Bechara A, Damasio H, Tranel D, et al: Dissociation of working memory from decision making within the human prefrontal cortex. J Neurosci 18:428–437, 1998

Bellugi U, Poizner H, Klima E: Language, modality and the brain, in Brain Development and Cognition. Edited by Johnson MH. Cambridge, MA, Blackwell Publishers, 1989, pp 403–423

Benson DF: Classical syndromes of aphasia, in Handbook of Neuropsychology, Vol 1. Edited by Boller F, Grafman J. Amsterdam, Elsevier, 1989, pp 267–280

Benson DF: Aphasia, in Clinical Neuropsychology, 3rd Edition. Edited by Heilman KM, Valenstein E. New York, Oxford University Press, 1993, pp 17–36

Benson DF, Brown J, Tomlinson EB: Varieties of alexia. Neurology 21:951–957, 1971

Benton AL: Differential behavioral effects in frontal lobe disease. Neuropsychologia 6:53–60, 1968

Benton AL: Visuoperceptual, visuospatial, and visuoconstructive disorders, in Clinical Neuropsychology, 2nd Edition. Edited by Heilman KM, Valenstein E. New York, Oxford University Press, 1985, pp 151–186

Benton AL: Neuropsychology: past, present, and future, in Handbook of Neuropsychology, Vol 1. Edited by Boller F, Grafman J. Amsterdam, The Netherlands, Elsevier, 1988, pp 1–27

Benton AL: Facial recognition 1990. Cortex 26:491–499, 1990

Benton AL: The Hecaen-Zangwill legacy: hemispheric dominance examined. Neuropsychol Rev 2:267–280, 1991

Benton AL: Neuropsychological assessment. Annu Rev Psychol 45:1–23, 1994

Benton AL, Tranel D: Visuoperceptual, visuospatial, and visuoconstructional disorders, in Clinical Neuropsychology, 3rd Edition. Edited by Heilman KM, Valenstein E. New York, Oxford University Press, 1993, pp 165–214

Bisiach E, Luzzatti C: Unilateral neglect of representation space. Cortex 14:129–133, 1978

Blumer D, Benson DF: Personality changes with frontal and temporal lobe lesions, in Psychiatric Aspects of Neurologic Disease. Edited by Benson DF, Blumer D. New York, Grune & Stratton, 1975, pp 151–169

Bogen J: The callosal syndromes, in Clinical Neuropsychology, 3rd Edition. Edited by Heilman KM, Valenstein E. New York, Oxford University Press, 1993, pp 337–407

Boller F, Spinnler H (eds): The frontal lobes, in Handbook of Neuropsychology, Vol 9. Edited by Boller F, Grafman J. Amsterdam, The Netherlands, Elsevier, 1994, pp 3–255

Brickner RM: An interpretation of frontal lobe function based upon the study of a case of partial bilateral frontal lobectomy. Research Publications—Association for Research in Nervous and Mental Disease 13:259–351, 1934

Brickner RM: The Intellectual Functions of the Frontal Lobes: Study Based upon Observation of a Man after Partial Bilateral Frontal Lobectomy. New York, Macmillan, 1936

Broca P: Localisation des fonctions cerebrales: siege du langage articule. Bulletin for the Society of Anthropology 4:200–204, 1863

Broca P: Sur la faculte du langage articule. Bulletin for the Society of Anthropology 6:337–393, 1865

Bruyer R, Laterre C, Seron X, et al: A case of prosopagnosia with some preserved covert remembrance of familiar faces. Brain Cogn 2:257–284, 1983

Burke DM, MacKay DG, Worthley JS, et al: On the tip of the tongue: what causes word finding failures in young and older adults? Journal of Memory and Language 30:542–579, 1991

Butters N: Alcoholic Korsakoff's syndrome: an update. Semin Neurol 4:226–244, 1984

Butters N, Stuss DT: Diencephalic amnesia, in Handbook of Neuropsychology, Vol 3. Edited by Boller F, Grafman J. Amsterdam, The Netherlands, Elsevier, 1989, pp 107–148

Butterworth B: What counts: how every brain is hardwired for math. New York, Free Press, 1999

Cabeza R, Nyberg L: Imaging cognition II: an empirical review of 275 PET and fMRI studies. J Cogn Neurosci 12:1–47, 2000

Cahill L, Babinsky R, Markowitsch HJ, et al: The amygdala and emotional memory. Nature 377:295–296, 1995

Cahill L, Haier RJ, Fallon J, et al: Amygdala activity at encoding correlated with long-term, free recall of emotional information. Proc Natl Acad Sci U S A 93:8016–8021, 1996

Cappa SF, Cavalotti G, Guidotti M, et al: Subcortical aphasia: two clinical-CT scan correlation studies. Cortex 19:227–241, 1983

Caramazza A: The organization of conceptual knowledge in the brain, in The New Cognitive Neurosciences, 2nd Edition. Edited by Gazzaniga MS. Cambridge, MA, MIT Press, 2000, pp 1037–1046

Caselli RJ: Rediscovering tactile agnosia. Mayo Clin Proc 66:129–241, 1991

Caselli RJ: Ventrolateral and dorsomedial somatosensory association cortex damage produces distinct somesthetic syndromes in humans. Neurology 43:762–771, 1993

Cermak LS, O'Connor M: The anterograde and retrograde retrieval ability of a patient with amnesia due to encephalitis. Neuropsychologia 21:213–234, 1983

Chao LL, Martin A: Cortical regions associated with perceiving, naming, and knowing about colors. J Cogn Neurosci 11:25–35, 1999

Clark VP, Parasuraman R, Keil K, et al: Selective attention to face identity and color studied with fMRI. Hum Brain Mapp 5:293–297, 1997

Cohen NJ, Squire LR: Retrograde amnesia and remote memory impairment. Neuropsychologia 19:337–356, 1981

Corbetta M, Miezin FM, Dobmeyer S, et al: Attentional modulation of neural processing of shape, color, and velocity in humans. Science 248:1556–1559, 1990

Corkin S: Tactually guided maze learning in man: effects of unilateral cortical excisions and bilateral hippocampal lesions. Neuropsychologia 3:339–351, 1965

Corkin S: Acquisition of motor skill after bilateral medial temporal-lobe excision. Neuropsychologia 6:255–264, 1968

Corkin S: Lasting consequences of bilateral medial temporal lobectomy: clinical course and experimental findings in HM. Semin Neurol 4:249–259, 1984

Corkin S, Amaral DG, Johnson KA, et al: HM's MRI scan shows sparing of the posterior half of the hippocampus and parahippocampal gyrus. J Neurosci 17:3964–3979, 1997

Damasio AR: Disorders of complex visual processing: agnosias, achromatopsia, Balint's syndrome, and related difficulties of orientation and construction, in Principles of Behavioral Neurology. Edited by Mesulam M-M. Philadelphia, PA, FA Davis, 1985, pp 259–288

Damasio AR: The brain binds entities and events by multiregional activation from convergence zones. Neural Comput 1:123–132, 1989a

Damasio AR: Time-locked multiregional retroactivation: a systems-level proposal for the neural substrates of recall and recognition. Cognition 33:25–62, 1989b

Damasio AR: Descartes' Error: Emotion, Reason, and the Human Brain. New York, Grossett/Putnam, 1994

Damasio AR: Toward a neurobiology of emotion and feeling: operational concepts and hypotheses. The Neuroscientist 1:19–25, 1995

Damasio AR, Anderson SW: The frontal lobes, in Clinical Neuropsychology, 3rd Edition. Edited by Heilman KM, Valenstein E. New York, Oxford University Press, 1993, pp 409–460

Damasio AR, Benton AL: Impairment of hand movements under visual guidance. Neurology 29:170–174, 1979

Damasio AR, Damasio H: Anatomical basis of pure alexia. Neurology 33:1473–1583, 1983

Damasio AR, Damasio H: Cortical systems underlying knowledge retrieval: evidence from human lesion studies, in Exploring Brain Functions: Models in Neuroscience. New York, Wiley, 1993, pp 233–248

Damasio AR, Damasio H: Cortical systems for retrieval of concrete knowledge: the convergence zone framework, in Large-scale Neuronal Theories of the Brain. Edited by Koch C. Cambridge, MA, MIT Press, 1994, pp 61–74

Damasio AR, Tranel D: Nouns and verbs are retrieved with differently distributed neural systems. Proc Natl Acad Sci U S A 90:4957–4960, 1993

Damasio AR, Van Hoesen GW: Emotional disturbances associated with focal lesions of the limbic frontal lobe, in Neuropsychology of Human Emotion. Edited by Heilman KM, Satz P. New York, Guilford Press, 1983, 85–110

Damasio AR, Yamada T, Damasio H, et al: Central achromatopsia: behavioral, anatomical and physiologic aspects. Neurology 30:1064–1071, 1980

Damasio AR, Damasio H, Rizzo M, et al: Aphasia with lesions in the basal ganglia and internal capsule. Arch Neurol 39:15–20, 1982a

Damasio AR, Damasio H, Van Hoesen GW: Prosopagnosia: anatomic basis and behavioral mechanisms. Neurology 32:331–341, 1982b

Damasio AR, Eslinger P, Damasio H, et al: Multimodal amnesic syndrome following bilateral temporal and basal forebrain damage. Arch Neurol 42:252–259, 1985a

Damasio AR, Graff-Radford NR, Eslinger PG, et al: Amnesia following basal forebrain lesions. Arch Neurol 42:263–271, 1985b

Damasio AR, Tranel D, Damasio H: "Deep" prosopagnosia: a new form of acquired face recognition defect caused by left hemisphere damage. Neurology 38 (suppl 1):172, 1988

Damasio AR, Tranel D, Damasio H: Amnesia caused by herpes simplex encephalitis, infarctions in basal forebrain, Alzheimer's disease, and anoxia, in Handbook of Neuropsychology, Vol 3. Edited by Boller F, Grafman J. Amsterdam, Elsevier, 1989a, pp 149–166

Damasio AR, Tranel D, Damasio H: Disorders of visual recognition, in Handbook of Neuropsychology, Vol 2. Edited by Boller F, Grafman J. Amsterdam, Elsevier, 1989b, pp 317–332

Damasio AR, Damasio H, Tranel D, et al: Neural regionalization of knowledge access: preliminary evidence. Cold Spring Harb Symp Quant Biol 55:1039–1047, 1990a

Damasio AR, Tranel D, Damasio H: Face agnosia and the neural substrates of memory. Annu Rev Neurosci 13:89–109, 1990b

Damasio AR, Tranel D, Damasio H: Individuals with sociopathic behavior caused by frontal damage fail to respond autonomically to social stimuli. Behav Brain Res 41:81–94, 1990c

Damasio AR, Tranel D, Damasio H: Music and the Brain. Miami, FL, American Academy of Neurology, 1990d

Damasio AR, Tranel D, Damasio H: Somatic markers and the guidance of behavior: theory and preliminary testing, in Frontal Lobe Function and Dysfunction. Edited by Levin HS, Eisenberg HM, Benton AL. New York, Oxford University Press, 1991, pp 217–229

Damasio AR, Tranel D, Rizzo M: Disorders of complex visual processing, in Principles of Behavioral and Cognitive Neurology, 2nd Edition. Edited by Mesulam MM. New York, Oxford University Press, 2000, pp 332–372

Damasio H: Neuroimaging contributions to the understanding of aphasia, in Handbook of Neuropsychology, Vol 2. Edited by Boller F, Grafman J. Amsterdam, The Netherlands, Elsevier, 1989, pp 3–46

Damasio H: Human Brain Anatomy in Computerized Images. New York, Oxford University Press, 1995

Damasio H: Neuroanatomical correlates of the aphasias, in Acquired Aphasia, 3rd Edition. Edited by Sarno MT. New York, Academic Press, 1998, pp 43–70

Damasio H, Damasio AR: The anatomical basis of conduction aphasia. Brain 103:337–350, 1980

Damasio H, Damasio AR: The lesion method in behavioral neurology and neuropsychology, in Behavioral Neurology and Neuropsychology. Edited by Feinberg TE, Farah MJ. New York, McGraw-Hill, 1997, pp 69–82

Damasio H, Frank RJ: Three-dimensional in vivo mapping of brain lesions in humans. Arch Neurol 49:137–143, 1992

Damasio H, Eslinger P, Adams HP: Aphasia following basal ganglia lesions: new evidence. Semin Neurol 4:151–161, 1984

Damasio H, Grabowski TJ, Tranel D, et al: A neural basis for lexical retrieval. Nature 380:499–505, 1996

Daniele A, Giustolisi L, Silveri MC, et al: Evidence for a possible neuroanatomical basis for lexical processing of nouns and verbs. Neuropsychologia 32:1325–1341, 1994

Davidoff JB, De Bleser R: Impaired picture recognition with preserved object naming and reading. Brain Cogn 24:1–23, 1994

Davidoff J, Landis T: Recognition of unfamiliar faces in prosopagnosia. Neuropsychologia 28:1143–1161, 1990

Denburg NL, Tranel D: Body schema and acalculia, in Clinical Neuropsychology, 4th Edition. Edited by Heilman KM, Valenstein E. New York, Oxford University Press (in press)

Denburg NL, Jones RD, Adolphs R, et al: Recognition without awareness in a patient with simultanagnosia. Journal of the International Neuropsychological Society 6:115, 2000

De Renzi E: Prosopagnosia in two patients with CT scan evidence of damage confined to the right hemisphere. Neuropsychologia 24:385–389, 1986

De Renzi E, Lucchelli F: Dense retrograde amnesia, intact learning capability and abnormal forgetting rate: a consolidation deficit? Cortex 29:449–466, 1993

Eslinger PJ, Damasio AR: Severe disturbance of higher cognition after bilateral frontal lobe ablation: patient EVR. Neurology 35:1731–1741, 1985

Eslinger PJ, Damasio AR: Preserved motor learning in Alzheimer's disease: implications for anatomy and behavior. J Neurosci 6:3006–3009, 1986

Fabiani M, Gratton G, Coles MGH: Event-related brain potentials: methods, theory, and applications, in Handbook of Psychophysiology, 2nd Edition. Edited by Cacioppo JT, Tassinary LG, Berntson CG. Cambridge, UK, Cambridge University Press, 2000, pp 53–84

Farah MJ: The neuropsychology of mental imagery, in Handbook of Neuropsychology, Vol 2. Edited by Boller F, Grafman J. Amsterdam, The Netherlands, Elsevier, 1989, pp 395–413

Feinberg TE, Farah MJ: The development of modern behavioral neurology and neuropsychology, in Behavioral Neurology and Neuropsychology. Edited by Feinberg TE, Farah MJ. New York, McGraw-Hill, 1997, pp 3–23

Fiez JA, Petersen SE, Cheney MK, et al: Impaired non-motor learning and error detection associated with cerebellar damage. Brain 115:155–178, 1992

Forde EME, Humphreys GW: Category-specific recognition impairments: a review of important case studies and influential theories. Aphasiology 13:169–193, 1999

Frank RJ, Damasio H, Grabowski TJ: Brainvox: an interactive, multimodal, visualization and analysis system for neuroanatomical imaging. NeuroImage 5:13–30, 1997

Frisk V, Milner B: The relationship of working memory to the immediate recall of stories following unilateral temporal or frontal lobectomy. Neuropsychologia 28:121–135, 1990

Fuster JM: The Prefrontal Cortex: Anatomy, Physiology, and Neuropsychology of the Frontal Lobes. New York, Raven Press, 1989

Gabrieli JDE, Cohen NJ, Corkin S: The impaired learning of semantic knowledge following bilateral medial temporal-lobe resection. Brain Cogn 7:157–177, 1988

Gabrieli JDE, Corkin S, Mickel SF, et al: Intact acquisition and long-term retention of mirror-tracing skill in Alzheimer's disease and in global amnesia. Behav Neurosci 107:899–910, 1993

Gainotti G, Silveri MC, Daniele A, et al: Neuroanatomical correlates of category-specific semantic disorders: a critical survey. Memory 3:247–264, 1995

Gao J-H, Parsons LM, Bower JM, et al: Cerebellum implicated in sensory acquisition and discrimination rather than motor control. Science 272:545–547, 1996

Gazzaniga MS: Perceptual and attentional processes following callosal section in human. Neuropsychologia 25:119–133, 1987

Geschwind N: Disconnexion syndromes in animals and man. Brain 88:237–294, 585–644, 1965

Goldman-Rakic PS: Circuitry of primate prefrontal cortex and regulation of behavior by representational memory, in Handbook of Physiology: The Nervous System. Edited by

Plum F. Bethesda, MD, American Physiological Society, 1987, pp 373–417

Goodglass H, Wingfield A, Hyde MR, et al: Category specific dissociations in naming and recognition by aphasic patients. Cortex 22:87–102, 1986

Goodglass H, Christiansen JA, Gallagher RE: Syntactic constructions used by agrammatic speakers: comparison with conduction aphasics and normals. Neuropsychology 8:598–613, 1994

Grabowski TJ, Damasio H, Frank RJ, et al: Neuroanatomical analysis of functional brain images: validation with retinotopic mapping. Hum Brain Mapp 2:134–148, 1995

Grabowski TJ, Damasio H, Tranel D: Physiologic correlates of retrieving names for unique entities. Neurology 54 (suppl 3):A397–A398, 2000

Graff-Radford NR, Damasio H: Disturbances of speech and language associated with thalamic dysfunction. Semin Neurol 4:162–168, 1984

Graff-Radford NR, Damasio H, Yamada T, et al: Nonhemorrhagic thalamic infarctions: clinical, neurophysiological and electrophysiological findings in four anatomical groups defined by CT. Brain 108:485–516, 1985

Graff-Radford NR, Damasio AR, Hyman BT, et al: Progressive aphasia in a patient with Pick's disease: a neuropsychological, radiologic, and anatomic study. Neurology 40:620–626, 1990a

Graff-Radford NR, Tranel D, Van Hoesen GW, et al: Diencephalic amnesia. Brain 113:1–25, 1990b

Grafman J, Litvan I, Massaquoi S, et al: Cognitive planning deficit in patients with cerebellar atrophy. Neurology 42:1493–1496, 1992

Greenblatt SH: Alexia without agraphia or hemianopia: anatomical analysis of an autopsied case. Brain 96:307–316, 1973

Greenblatt SH: Localization of lesions in alexia, in Localization in Neuropsychology. Edited by Kertesz A. New York, Academic Press, 1983, pp 323–356

Hallett M: Transcranial magnetic stimulation and the human brain. Nature 406:147–150, 2000

Hamann SB, Ely TD, Grafton ST, et al: Amygdala activity related to enhanced memory for pleasant and aversive stimuli. Nat Neurosci 2:289–293, 1999

Harlow JM: Recovery from the passage of an iron bar through the head. Publications of the Massachusetts Medical Society 2:327–347, 1868

Hart J, Berndt RS, Caramazza A: Category-specific naming deficit following cerebral infarction. Nature 316:439–440, 1985

Hebb DO, Penfield W: Human behavior after extensive bilateral removals from the frontal lobes. Archives of Neurology and Psychiatry 44:421–438, 1940

Heilman KM, Wilder BJ, Malzone WF: Anomic aphasia following anterior temporal lobectomy. Transactions of the American Neurological Association 97:291–293, 1972

Heilman KM, Valenstein E, Watson RT: Localization of neglect, in Localization in Neuropsychology. Edited by Kertesz A. New York, Academic Press, 1983, pp 471–492

Heilman KM, Watson RT, Valenstein E: Neglect and related disorders, in Clinical Neuropsychology, 2nd Edition. Edited by Heilman KM, Valenstein E. New York, Oxford University Press, 1985, pp 243–293

Heilman KM, Watson RT, Valenstein E: Neglect and related disorders, in Clinical Neuropsychology, 3rd Edition. Edited by Heilman KM, Valenstein E. New York, Oxford University Press, 1993, pp 279–336

Heindel WC, Salmon DP, Butters N: Cognitive approaches to the memory disorders of demented patients, in Comprehensive Handbook of Psychopathology, 2nd Edition. Edited by Sutker PB, Adams HE. New York, Plenum, 1993, 735–761

Hickok G, Bellugi U, Klima E: The neurobiology of sign language and its implications for the neural basis of language. Nature 381:699–702, 1996

Hillis AE, Caramazza A: Representations of grammatical categories of words in the brain. J Cogn Neurosci 7:396–407, 1995

Horel JA: The neuroanatomy of amnesia: a critique of the hippocampal memory hypothesis. Brain 101:403–445, 1978

Hubel DH, Livingstone MS: Segregation of form, color, and stereopsis in primate area 18. J Neurosci 7:3378–3415, 1987

Hunkin NM, Parkin AJ, Bradley VA, et al: Focal retrograde amnesia following closed head injury: a case study and theoretical account. Neuropsychologia 33:509–523, 1995

Hyman BT, Tranel D: Hemianesthesia and aphasia: an anatomical and behavioral study. Arch Neurol 46:816–819, 1989

Hyman BT, Damasio AR, Van Hoesen GW, et al: Alzheimer's disease: cell specific pathology isolates the hippocampal formation. Science 225:1168–1170, 1984

Hyman BT, Kromer LJ, Van Hoesen GW: A direct demonstration of the perforant pathway terminal zone in Alzheimer's disease using the monoclonal antibody Alz-50. Brain Res 450:392–397, 1988

Jones RD, Grabowski TG, Tranel D: The neural basis of retrograde memory: evidence from positron emission tomography for the role of non-mesial temporal lobe structures. NeuroCase 4:471–479, 1998

Jones-Gotman M, Milner B: Design fluency: the invention of nonsense drawings after focal cortical lesions. Neuropsychologia 15:653–674, 1977

Jonides J, Smith EE, Koeppe RA, et al: Spatial working memory in humans as revealed by PET. Nature 363:623–625, 1993

Kanwisher N, Moscovitch M: The cognitive neuroscience of face processing: an introduction. Cognitive Neuropsychology 17:1–11, 2000

Kapur N: Focal retrograde amnesia in neurological disease: a critical review. Cortex 29:217–234, 1993

Kapur N, Ellison D, Parkin AJ, et al: Bilateral temporal lobe pathology with sparing of medial temporal lobe structures:

lesion profile and pattern of memory disorder. Neuropsychologia 32:23–38, 1994

Kopelman MD: The neuropsychology of remote memory, in Handbook of Neuropsychology, Vol 8. Edited by Boller F, Grafman J. Amsterdam, The Netherlands, Elsevier, 1992, pp 215–238

Kosslyn SM: Aspects of a cognitive neuroscience of mental imagery. Science 240:1621–1626, 1988

Kosslyn SM, Koenig O: Wet Mind: The New Cognitive Neuroscience. New York, Free Press, 1995

Kourtzi Z, Kanwisher N: Activation in human MT/MST by static images with implied motion. J Cogn Neurosci 12:48–55, 2000

Landis T, Cummings JL, Christen L, et al: Are unilateral right posterior cerebral lesions sufficient to cause prosopagnosia? Clinical and radiological findings in six additional patients. Cortex 22:243–252, 1986

Lee GP, Meador KJ, Smith JR, et al: Clinical case report: preserved crossmodal association following bilateral amygdalotomy in man. Int J Neurosci 40:47–55, 1988

Levin HS, Eisenberg HM, Benton AL (eds): Frontal Lobe Function and Dysfunction. New York, Oxford University Press, 1991

Levy J: Regulation and generation of perception in the asymmetric brain, in Brain Circuits and Functions of The Mind. Edited by Trevarthen C. Cambridge, UK, Cambridge University Press, 1990, pp 231–246

Lezak MD: Neuropsychological Assessment, 3rd Edition. New York, Oxford University Press, 1995

Lissauer H: Ein fall von Seelenblindheit nebst einem Beitrag zur theorie derselben. Archiv für Psychiatrie und Nervenkrankheiten 21:22–70, 1890

Livingstone MS, Hubel DH: Segregation of form, color, movement, and depth: anatomy, physiology, and perception. Science 240:740–749, 1988

Lueck CJ, Zeki S, Friston KJ, et al: The color centre in the cerebral cortex of man. Nature 340:386–389, 1989

Luria AR: Frontal lobe syndromes, in Handbook of Clinical Neurology, Vol 2. Edited by Vinken PG, Bruyn GW. Amsterdam, The Netherlands, North Holland, 1969, pp 725–757

Luzzatti C, Davidoff J: Impaired retrieval of object-colour knowledge with preserved colour naming. Neuropsychologia 32:933–950, 1994

Markowitsch HJ, Calabrese P, Haupts M, et al: Searching for the anatomical basis of retrograde amnesia. J Clin Exp Neuropsychol 15:947–967, 1993

Markowitsch HJ, Calabrese P, Wuerker M, et al: The amygdala's contribution to memory: a study on two patients with Urbach-Wiethe disease. Neuroreport 5:1349–1352, 1994

Martin A, Haxby JV, Lalonde FM, et al: Discrete cortical regions associated with knowledge of color and knowledge of action. Science 270:102–105, 1995

Martin A, Ungerleider LG, Haxby JV: Category specificity and the brain: the sensory/motor model of semantic representations of objects, in The New Cognitive Neurosciences, 2nd Edition. Edited by Gazzaniga MS. Cambridge, MA, MIT Press, 2000, pp 1023–1036

Mazoyer BM, Tzourio N, Frak V, et al: J Cogn Neurosci 5:467–479, 1993

McCarthy G: Functional neuroimaging of memory. The Neuroscientist 1:155–163, 1995

McCarthy G, Blamire AM, Puce A, et al: Functional magnetic resonance imaging of human prefrontal cortex activation during a spatial working memory task. Proc Natl Acad Sci U S A 91:8690–8694, 1994

McCormick DA, Thompson RF: Cerebellum: essential involvement in the classically conditioned eyelid response. Science 223:296–299, 1984

Meadows JC: The anatomical basis of prosopagnosia. J Neurol Neurosurg Psychiatry 37:489–501, 1974a

Meadows JC: Disturbed perception of colors associated with localized cerebral lesions. Brain 97:615–632, 1974b

Mesulam MM: Frontal cortex and behavior. Ann Neurol 19:320–325, 1986

Miceli G, Silveri MC, Nocentini U, et al: Patterns of dissociation in comprehension and production of nouns and verbs. Aphasiology 2:351–358, 1988

Michel F, Perenin MT, Sieroff E: Prosopagnosie sans hemianopsie apres lesion unilaterale occipito-temporale droite. Revue Neurologique 142:545–549, 1986

Milner B: Effects of different brain lesions on card sorting: the role of the frontal lobes. Arch Neurol 9:90–100, 1963

Milner B: Visual recognition and recall after right temporal-lobe excision in man. Neuropsychologia 6:191–209, 1968

Milner B: Disorders of learning and memory after temporal lobe lesions in man. Clin Neurosurg 19:421–446, 1972

Milner B, Petrides M: Behavioural effects of frontal-lobe lesions in man. Trends Neurosci 7:403–407, 1984

Milner B, Petrides M, Smith ML: Frontal lobes and the temporal organization of memory. Human Neurobiology 4:137–142, 1985

Miozzo A, Soardi S, Cappa SF: Pure anomia with spared action naming due to a left temporal lesion. Neuropsychologia 32:1101–1109, 1994

Mishkin M: Memory in monkeys severely impaired by combined but not separate removal of amygdala and hippocampus. Nature 273:297–298, 1978

Mohr JP, Watters WC, Duncan GW: Thalamic hemorrhage and aphasia. Brain Lang 2:3–17, 1975

Mohr JP, Pessin MS, Finkelstein S, et al: Broca aphasia: pathologic and clinical aspects. Neurology 28:311–324, 1978

Murray EA: Representational memory in nonhuman primates, in Neurobiology of Comparative Cognition. Edited by Kesner RP, Olton DS. Hillsdale, NJ, Erlbaum, 1990, pp 127–155

Murray EA, Mishkin M: Amygdalectomy impairs crossmodal association in monkeys. Science 228:604–606, 1985

Murray EA, Mishkin M: Visual recognition in monkeys following rhinal cortical ablations combined with either amygdalectomy or hippocampectomy. J Neurosci 6:1991–2003, 1986

Naeser MA, Alexander MP, Helm-Estabrooks N, et al: Aphasia with predominantly subcortical lesion sites. Arch Neurol 39:2–14, 1982

Nahm FKD, Tranel D, Damasio H, et al: Cross-modal associations and the human amygdala. Neuropsychologia 31:727–744, 1993

Newcombe F: The processing of visual information in prosopagnosia and acquired dyslexia: functional versus physiological interpretation, in Research in Psychology and Medicine. Edited by Osborne DJ, Bruneberg MM, Eiser JR. London, Academic Press, 1979, pp 315–322

Newcombe F, Ratcliff G: Disorders of visuospatial analysis, in Handbook of Neuropsychology, Vol 2. Edited by Boller F, Grafman J. Amsterdam, The Netherlands, Elsevier, 1989, pp 333–356

Nobre AC, Allison T, McCarthy G: Word recognition in the human inferior temporal lobe. Nature 372:260–263, 1994

Nyberg L, McIntosh AR, Houle S, et al: Activation of medial temporal structures during episodic memory retrieval. Nature 380:715–717, 1996

O'Connor M, Butters N, Miliotis P, et al: The dissociation of anterograde and retrograde amnesia in a patient with herpes encephalitis. J Clin Exp Neuropsychol 14:159–178, 1992

Ojemann GA: Cortical organization of language. J Neurosci 11:2281–2287, 1991

Paulson HL, Galetta SL, Grossman M, et al: Hemiachromatopsia of unilateral occipitotemporal infarcts. Am J Ophthalmol 118:518–523, 1994

Petersen SE, Fox PT, Posner MI, et al: Positron emission tomographic studies of the cortical anatomy of single-word processing. Nature 331:585–589, 1988

Petrides M, Alivisatos B, Evans AC, et al: Dissociation of human mid-dorsolateral from posterior dorsolateral frontal cortex in memory processing. Proc Natl Acad Sci U S A 90:873–877, 1993

Phelps EA, LaBar K, Anderson AK, et al: Specifying the contributions of the human amygdala to emotional memory: a case study. Neurocase 4:527–540, 1998

Poizner H, Klima ES, Bellugi U: What the Hands Reveal about the Brain. Cambridge, MA, Harvard University Press, 1987

Poolos NP: Magnetoencephalography as a noninvasive probe of brain activity: the state of the art. The Neuroscientist 1:127–129, 1995

Posner MI, Petersen SE, Fox PT, et al: Localization of cognitive operations in the human brain. Science 240:1627–1631, 1988

Raichle ME: Exploring the mind with dynamic imaging. Seminars in Neurosciences 2:307–315, 1990

Raichle ME: Functional imaging in behavioral neurology and neuropsychology, in Behavioral Neurology and Neuropsychology. Edited by Feinberg TE, Farah MJ. New York, McGraw-Hill, 1997, pp 83–100

Rapcsak SZ, Kaszniak AW, Rubens AB: Anomia for facial expressions: evidence for a category specific visual-verbal disconnection syndrome. Neuropsychologia 27:1031–1041, 1989

Rapcsak SZ, Comer JF, Rubens AB: Anomia for facial expressions: neuropsychological mechanisms and anatomical correlates. Brain Lang 45:233–252, 1993

Reed CL, Caselli RJ: The nature of tactile agnosia: a case study. Neuropsychologia 32:527–539, 1994

Rempel-Clower NL, Zola-Morgan SM, Squire LR, et al: Three cases of enduring memory impairment after bilateral damage limited to the hippocampal formation. J Neurosci 16:5233–5255, 1996

Rizzo M: Astereopsis, in Handbook of Neuropsychology, Vol 2. Edited by Boller F, Grafman J. Amsterdam, The Netherlands, Elsevier, 1989, pp 415–427

Rizzo M: "Balint's syndrome" and associated visuospatial disorders, in Bailliere's International Practice and Research. Edited by Kennard C. London, WB Saunders, 1993, pp 415–437

Rizzo M, Hurtig R: Looking but not seeing: attention, perception, and eye movements in simultanagnosia. Neurology 37:1642–1648, 1987

Rizzo M, Nawrot M: Human visual cortex and its disorders. Current Opinion in Ophthalmology 4:38–47, 1993

Rizzo M, Tranel D (eds): Head injury and postconcussive syndrome. New York, Churchill Livingstone, 1996

Rizzo M, Smith V, Pokorny J, et al: Color perception profiles in central achromatopsia. Neurology 43:995–1001, 1993

Robertson IH, Marshall JC (eds): Unilateral Neglect: Clinical and Experimental Studies, Hillsdale NJ, Erlbaum, 1993

Robin DA, Tranel D, Damasio H: Auditory perception of temporal and spectral events in patients with focal left and right cerebral lesions. Brain Lang 39:539–555, 1990

Robinson RG, Boston JD, Starkstein SE, et al: Comparison of mania with depression following brain injury: causal factors. Am J Psychiatry 145:172, 1988

Roland PE: Brain Activation. New York, Wiley-Liss, 1993

Rosler F, Heil M, Henninghausen E: Distinct cortical activation patterns during long-term memory retrieval of verbal, spatial, and color information. J Cogn Neurosci 7:51–65, 1995

Ross ED: The aprosodias: functional-anatomic organization of the affective components of language in the right hemisphere. Arch Neurol 38:561–569, 1981

Rubens AB: Transcortical motor aphasia, in Studies in Neurolinguistics, Vol 1. Edited by Whitaker H, Whitaker HA. New York, Academic Press, 1976, pp 293–303

Sagar HJ, Gabrieli JDE, Sullivan EV, et al: Recency and frequency discrimination in the amnesic patient HM. Brain 113:581–602, 1990

Saint-Cyr JA, Taylor AE, Lang AE: Procedural learning and neostriatal dysfunction in man. Brain 111:941–959, 1988

Schiff HB, Alexander MP, Naeser MA, et al: Aphemia: clinic-anatomic correlations. Arch Neurol 40:720–727, 1983

Schmahmann JD: An emerging concept: the cerebellar contribution to higher function. Arch Neurol 48:1178–1187, 1991

Schnider A, Landis T, Regard M, et al: Dissociation of color from object in amnesia. Arch Neurol 49:982–985, 1992

Scoville WB, Milner B: Loss of recent memory after bilateral hippocampal lesions. J Neurol Neurosurg Psychiatry 20:11–21, 1957

Semenza C, Zettin M: Evidence from aphasia for the role of proper names as pure referring expressions. Nature 342:678–679, 1989

Sergent J, Villemure J-G: Prosopagnosia in a right hemispherectomized patient. Brain 112:975–995, 1989

Smith EE, Jonides J, Koeppe RA, et al: Spatial versus object working memory: PET investigations. J Cogn Neurosci 7:337–356, 1995

Smith EE, Jonides J, Koeppe RA: Dissociating verbal and spatial working memory using PET. Cereb Cortex 6:11–20, 1996

Smith ML, Milner B: Estimation of frequency of occurrence of abstract designs after frontal or temporal lobectomy. Neuropsychologia 26:297–306, 1988

Smith ML, Milner B: Right hippocampal impairment in the recall of spatial location: encoding deficit or rapid forgetting? Neuropsychologia 27:71–81, 1989

Sperry RW: The great cerebral commissure. Sci Am 210:42–52, 1968

Squire LR: Memory and hippocampus: a synthesis from findings with rats, monkeys, and humans. Psychol Rev 99:195–231, 1992

Squire LR, Zola SM: Ischemic brain damage and memory impairment: a commentary. Hippocampus 6:546–552, 1996

Stafiniak P, Saykin AJ, Sperling MR, et al: Acute naming deficits following dominant temporal lobectomy: prediction by age at 1st risk for seizures. Neurology 40:1509–1512, 1990

Stuss DT, Benson DF: Neuropsychological studies of the frontal lobes. Psychol Bull 95:3–28, 1984

Stuss DT, Benson DF: The Frontal Lobes. New York, Raven Press, 1986

Teuber H-L: Alteration of perception and memory in man: reflections on methods, in Analysis of Behavioral Change. Edited by Weiskrantz L. New York, Harper & Row, 1968, pp 274–328

Thompson RFL: The neurobiology of learning and memory. Science 233:941–947, 1986

Tootell RBH, Reppas JB, Kwong KK, et al: Functional analysis of human MT and related visual cortical areas using functional magnetic resonance imaging. J Neurosci 15:3215–3230, 1995

Tranel D: Dissociated verbal and nonverbal retrieval and learning following left anterior temporal damage. Brain Cogn 15:187–200, 1991a

Tranel D: What has been rediscovered in "Rediscovering tactile agnosia"? Mayo Clin Proc 66:210–214, 1991b

Tranel D: "Acquired sociopathy": the development of sociopathic behavior following focal brain damage, in Progress in Experimental Personality and Psychopathology Research, Vol 17. Edited by Fowles DC, Sutker P, Goodman SH. New York, Springer, 1994a, pp 285–311

Tranel D: Assessment of higher-order visual function. Current Opinion in Ophthalmology 5:29–37, 1994b

Tranel D: Higher brain function, in Neuroscience in Medicine. Edited by Conn PM. Philadelphia, PA, JB Lippincott, 1995a, pp 555–580

Tranel D: Where did my arm go? Contemporary Psychology 40:885–887, 1995b

Tranel D: The Iowa-Benton school of neuropsychological assessment, in Neuropsychological Assessment of Neuropsychiatric Disorders, 2nd Edition. Edited by Grant I, Adams KM. New York, Oxford University Press, 1996, pp 81–101

Tranel D: Non-conscious brain processing indexed by psychophysiological measures, in Progress in Brain Research: The Biological Basis for Mind Body Interactions, Vol 122. Edited by Mayer EA, Saper C. Amsterdam, The Netherlands, Elsevier Science, 2000, pp 315–330

Tranel D: Central color processing and its disorders, in Handbook of Neuropsychology, 2nd Edition, Vol 4. Edited by Boller F, Grafman J. Amsterdam, The Netherlands, 2001, pp 1–14

Tranel D, Anderson, SW: Syndromes of aphasia, in Concise Encyclopedia of Language Pathology. Edited by Fabbro F. Amsterdam, The Netherlands, Elsevier, 1999, pp 305–319

Tranel D, Damasio AR: Knowledge without awareness: an autonomic index of facial recognition by prosopagnosics. Science 228:1453–1454, 1985

Tranel D, Damasio AR: The covert learning of affective valence does not require structures in hippocampal system or amygdala. J Cogn Neurosci 5:79–88, 1993

Tranel D, Damasio AR: The agnosias and apraxias, in Neurology in Clinical Practice, 2nd Edition. Edited by Bradley WG, Daroff RB, Fenichel GM, Marsden CD. Stoneham, MA, Butterworth, 1996, pp 119–129

Tranel D, Hyman BT: Neuropsychological correlates of bilateral amygdala damage. Arch Neurol 47:349–355, 1990

Tranel D, Damasio AR, Damasio H: Intact recognition of facial expression, gender, and age in patients with impaired recognition of face identity. Neurology 38:690–696, 1988

Tranel D, Anderson SW, Benton AL: Development of the concept of "executive function" and its relationship to the frontal lobes, in Handbook of Neuropsychology, Vol 9. Edited by Boller F, Grafman J. Amsterdam, The Netherlands, Elsevier, 1994a, pp 125–148

Tranel D, Damasio AR, Damasio H, et al: Sensorimotor skill learning in amnesia: additional evidence for the neural basis of nondeclarative memory. Learning and Memory 1:165–179, 1994b

Tranel D, Damasio H, Damasio AR: Double dissociation between overt and covert face recognition. J Cogn Neurosci 7:425–432, 1995

Tranel D, Damasio H, Damasio AR: A neural basis for the retrieval of conceptual knowledge. Neuropsychologia 35:1319–1327, 1997a

Tranel D, Damasio H, Damasio AR: On the neurology of naming, in Anomia: Neuroanatomical and Cognitive Correlates. Edited by Goodglass H, Wingfield A. New York, Academic Press, 1997b, pp 65–90

Tranel D, Damasio H, Damasio AR: The neural basis of lexical retrieval, in Fundamentals of Neural Network Modeling: Neuropsychology and Cognitive Neuroscience. Edited by Parks RW, Levine DS, Long DL. Cambridge, MA, MIT Press, 1998, pp 271–296

Tranel D, Bechara A, Damasio AR: Decision making and the somatic marker hypothesis, in The New Cognitive Neurosciences. Edited by Gazzaniga MS. Cambridge, MA, MIT Press, 2000a, pp 1047–1061

Tranel D, Damasio AR, Damasio H: Amnesia caused by herpes simplex encephalitis, infarctions in basal forebrain, and anoxia/ischemia, in Handbook of Neuropsychology, 2nd Edition, Vol 1. Edited by Boller F, Grafman J. Amsterdam, The Netherlands, Elsevier Science, 2000b, pp 37–62

Tranel D, Adolphs R, Damasio H, et al: A neural basis for the retrieval of words for actions. Cognitive Neuropsychology (in press)

Trevarthen C (ed): Brain Circuits and Functions of the Mind: Essays in Honor of R.W. Sperry. Cambridge, MA, Cambridge University Press, 1990

Tulving E, Schacter DL, McLachlan DR, et al: Priming of semantic autobiographical knowledge: a case study of retrograde amnesia. Brain Cogn 8:3–20, 1988

Van Essen CD, Maunsell JHR: Hierarchical organization and functional streams in the visual cortex. Trends Neurosci 6:370–375, 1983

Van Hoesen GW: The parahippocampal gyrus. Trends Neurosci 5:345–350, 1982

Van Hoesen GW, Damasio AR: Neural correlates of cognitive impairment in Alzheimer's disease, in Handbook of Physiology: Higher Functions of the Nervous System. Edited by Mountcastle V, Plum F. Bethesda, MD, American Physiological Society, 1987, pp 871–898

Van Hoesen GW, Hyman BT, Damasio AR: Cell-specific pathology in neural systems of the temporal lobe in Alzheimer's disease, in Progress in Brain Research. Edited by Swaab D. Amsterdam, The Netherlands, Elsevier, 1986, pp 361–375

Van Lancker D, Kreiman J: Unfamiliar voice discrimination and familiar voice recognition are independent and unordered abilities. Neuropsychologia 25:829–834, 1988

Van Lancker D, Cummings J, Kreiman J, et al: Phonagnosia: a dissociation between familiar and unfamiliar voices. Cortex 24:195–209, 1988

Van Lancker D, Kreiman J, Cummings J: Voice perception deficits: neuroanatomical correlates of phonagnosia. J Clin Exp Neuropsychol 11:665–674, 1989

Victor M, Adams RD, Collins GH: The Wernicke-Korsakoff Syndrome and Related Neurologic Disorders Due to Alcoholism and Malnutrition, 2nd Edition. Philadelphia, PA, FA Davis, 1989.

Vignolo LA: Auditory agnosia. Philos Trans R Soc Lond B Biol Sci 298:49–57, 1982

Volpe BT, Hirst W: Amnesia following the rupture and repair of an anterior communicating artery aneurysm. J Neurol Neurosurg Psychiatry 46:704–709, 1983

Warrington EK, McCarthy RA: Category-specific access dysphasia. Brain 106:859–878, 1983

Weintraub S, Mesulam M-M: Neglect: hemispheric specialization, behavioral components and anatomical correlates, in Handbook of Neuropsychology, Vol 2. Edited by Boller F, Grafman J. Amsterdam, The Netherlands, Elsevier, 1989, pp 357–374

Wernicke C: Der aphasische Symptomencomplex. Breslau, Cohn und Weigert, 1874

Wilkins A, Baddeley A: Remembering to recall in everyday life: an approach to absentmindedness, in Practical Aspects of Memory. Edited by Gruneberg MM, Morris PE, Sykes RN. New York, Academic Press, 1978, pp 27–34

Wilson FAW, O'Scalaidhe SP, Goldman-Rakic PS: Dissociation of object and spatial processing domains in primate prefrontal cortex. Science 260:1955–1958, 1993

Young AW, Aggleton JP, Hellawell DJ, et al: Face processing impairments after amygdalotomy. Brain 118:15–24, 1995

Zeki SM: Colour coding in Rhesus monkey prestriate cortex. Brain Res 53:422–427, 1973

Zeki SM: A century of cerebral achromatopsia. Brain 113:1727–1777, 1990

Zeki SM, Watson JDG, Lueck CJ, et al: A direct demonstration of functional specialization in human visual cortex. J Neurosci 11:641–649, 1991

Zihl J, Von Cramon Z, Mai N: Selective disturbances of movement vision after bilateral brain damage. Brain 106:313–340, 1983

Zola-Morgan S, Squire LR: Memory impairment in monkeys following lesions of hippocampus. Behav Neurosci 100:165–170, 1986

Zola-Morgan S, Squire LR, Amaral DG: Human amnesia and the medial temporal region: enduring memory impairment following a bilateral lesions limited to field CA1 of the hippocampus. J Neurosci 6:2950–2967, 1986

Zola-Morgan S, Squire LR, Amaral DG, et al: Lesions of perirhinal and parahippocampal cortex that spare the amygdala and hippocampal formation produce severe memory impairment. J Neurosci 9:4355–4370, 1989

# Nervous, Endocrine, and Immune System Interactions in Psychiatry

Jane F. Gumnick, M.D.

Dwight L. Evans, M.D.

Andrew H. Miller, M.D.

During the past several decades, great strides have been made toward understanding the pathways by which the central nervous system and the immune system interact. Data indicate that immune cells and tissues have the capacity to receive signals from the brain and endocrine system, and immune-derived molecules (cytokines) have potent effects on nervous system function. In addition to elucidating the details of these communication pathways at a biochemical and molecular biological level, a major challenge has been to place interactions among the nervous, endocrine, and immune systems into a clinical context. Investigators have examined the relevant impact of neuropsychiatric conditions and stress on immune responses and immune-related disorders as well as the role of the immune system in neuropsychiatric disease. This chapter provides an overview of the results of these investigations along with information on the mechanisms involved.

## Overview of the Immune System

Before considering the relationship among the nervous, endocrine, and immune systems, it is important to review the general purpose and internal organization of the immune response.

The immune system is a group of cells and tissues that protect the body from invading pathogens and malig-

nantly transformed cells. It also helps clear the body of damaged and dead cells and mobilizes subsequent repair pathways. It thus protects the organism from invading external threats such as bacteria, viruses, fungi, and parasites and from internal threats such as neoplasms and tissue damage and destruction. The immune system must be able to distinguish healthy "self" cells from "nonself" cells, and intricate mechanisms are in place for accomplishing this task. (Here *self* and *nonself* are used for the sake of simplicity; in actuality, *nonself* is also meant to include malignantly transformed or virally infected cells targeted by the immune system.) The immune system must also be able to balance destructive responses to invading pathogens so that the body is not destroyed in the process of eliminating pathogens.

The immune system is made up of solid tissues, including bone marrow, thymus, lymph nodes, and spleen, and mobile leukocytes (Abbas et al. 2000; Roitt et al. 1996). Areas of high exposure to external pathogens—such as the digestive tract, the pulmonary tract, and the skin—also contain specialized lymphoid tissues. All immune cells originate from hematopoietic stem cells in the bone marrow. Their differentiation proceeds along paths of myeloid or lymphoid differentiation, depending on the body's needs at a given time. Signaling molecules such as cytokines and hormones create the chemical environment in the bone marrow that determines along which path the precursor cells develop. Cytokines called colony-stimulating factors are one such type of signaling molecule. The myeloid cell line includes monocytes and granulocytes such as neutrophils, basophils, and eosinophils. Monocytes and basophils differentiate further into macrophages and mast cells, respectively, and take up residence in tissues throughout the body. The lymphoid cell line includes B cells, T cells, and natural killer (NK) cells.

After production in the bone marrow, the cells that will become B lymphocytes mature in the bone marrow, whereas T lymphocytes travel to the thymus, where they will mature (Delves and Roitt 2000a). The bone marrow and thymus are for this reason termed primary immune tissues. Because immune cells are constantly being produced with random recognition sites for an enormous variety of antigens, an important part of the maturational process for both types of lymphocytes is the elimination of cells that would react with self antigens. This essential and complex step occurs in the primary immune tissues. After maturation, cells circulate and take up residence in the secondary immune tissues (such as the spleen and lymph nodes) that provide sites for interaction with circulating pathogens.

Regulation of the immune system depends on many mediators, including soluble immune signaling factors called cytokines. The word *cytokine* (*cyto*, cell; *kinesis*, movement) derives from the original identification of these factors as important regulators of cell movement. However, these molecules have been found to have local and systemic effects on a wide range of body functions not limited to the immune system. Cytokines are produced by a number of cells, including activated leukocytes, astrocytes, endothelial cells, fibroblasts, and adipocytes. A variety of cytokines have been identified, and their regulatory effects on the immune, nervous, and endocrine systems are being actively studied. Different cytokines have overlapping functions, and a cytokine can exert different effects on different target cells. A cytokine can act on the cell producing it, cells nearby, or distant cells (autocrine, paracrine, and endocrine activity, respectively). Cytokines participate in the processes of innate immunity, acquired immunity, and cell growth and differentiation (Table 4–1). Cytokines are broadly classed by category, depending on their currently known functions. One group, the so-called proinflammatory cytokines, is produced early in the process of infection or inflammation primarily by monocytes and macrophages. This group includes interleukin-1 (IL-1), interleukin-6 (IL-6), and tumor necrosis factor-alpha (TNF-α). These cytokines, along with chemokines (which attract other cell types to the site of inflammation/infection) are involved in a cascade of immune responses that magnifies

early innate immune responses. In conjunction with IL-1 and TNF, IL-6 induces the production of acute phase proteins by the liver, thus constituting the acute phase response (see below). The type I interferons, interferon (IFN)-α and IFN-β, are another class of cytokine released early during the immune response. Type I IFNs have antiviral activity and other immunostimulatory effects, as well as antiproliferative effects. Given these activities, IFN-α is used therapeutically for treatment of viral infections (e.g., hepatitis C) and malignant disorders (e.g., malignant melanoma). Cytokines have multiple effects on activity and differentiation of immune cells. Interleukin-12, for example, stimulates both production of interferon-γ (IFN-γ) and differentiation of IFN-γ–producing cells. Some cytokines have inhibitory effects; for example, interleukin-10 (IL-10) inhibits the production of IFN-γ and TNF by macrophages.

## Natural Immunity

For simplicity, the immune system may be divided into two functional arms: natural (or innate) immunity and specific (or acquired) immunity. Features of these functional arms are summarized in Table 4–2. Natural immunity is the body's first line of defense and does not require previous exposure to antigen. Acquired immunity is more specialized, depends on previous exposure to antigen, and typically is magnified on the body's reexposure to antigen. Despite the pedantic distinction between innate and acquired immune functions, these two parts of the immune system constantly fine-tune the immune response by mutual cellular interactions and soluble factors such as cytokines and hormones.

Innate immunity is mediated in large part by phagocytes (e.g., monocytes and neutrophils) and NK cells. These cells detect microorganisms through pattern recognition receptors and engulf or lyse invading pathogens (Delves and Roitt 2000a). In addition, these cells when activated release proinflammatory cytokines that in turn induce the expression of various adhesion molecules and chemokines. Together, these factors attract other inflammatory cells to the site of invasion, stimulate a response by the liver called the acute phase response, and signal systemic neural and hormonal feedback mechanisms in the brain (see Figure 4–1). TNF and IL-1 induce fever by activating prostaglandin pathways that stimulate hypothalamic cells involved in the regulation of body temperature. These cytokines also have effects on other hypothalamic functions, including the regulation of sleep, appetite, and sexual drive (described below).

The acute phase response, induced by the proinflammatory cytokines, occurs when the liver produces pro-

**TABLE 4–1.** Cytokines

| Cytokine | Made by | Activities |
|---|---|---|
| Interleukin-1 | Activated macrophages, B cells, neutrophils, astrocytes, epithelial and endothelial cells | Activates B cells, helper T cells, endothelial cells<br>Stimulates acute phase protein production<br>Promotes inflammation and hematopoiesis<br>Centrally induces fever, somnolence, anorexia |
| Interleukin-2 | Antigen-activated Th1 cells | Promotes growth and differentiation of T and B lymphocytes<br>Promotes NK cell proliferation |
| Interleukin-4 | Th2 cells, mast cells, basophils, eosinophils | Promotes B cell growth and differentiation<br>Promotes production of immunoglobulin E |
| Interleukin-5 | Th2 cells, mast cells, eosinophils | Promotes B cell growth and differentiation<br>Promotes eosinophil differentiation |
| Interleukin-6 | Th2 cells, macrophages, fibroblasts, epithelium, adipocytes | Promotes B cell growth and differentiation<br>Promotes antibody secretion<br>Stimulates hepatocytes to produce acute phase proteins |
| Interleukin-8 | T cells, macrophages, epithelium | Promotes activation and chemotaxis of neutrophils, basophils, T cells |
| Interleukin-10 | Th2 cells, macrophages, epithelium, monocytes | Suppresses Th1-produced cytokines (interleukin-1, tumor necrosis factor-α, interleukin-2). |
| Interleukin-12 | B cells, macrophages | Stimulates production of interferon-γ by helper T and NK cells<br>Promotes induction of helper T cells |
| Tumor necrosis factor-α | Macrophages, NK cells, T cells, B cells, mast cells | Promotes inflammation<br>Activates monocytes and neutrophils<br>Induces fever |
| Tumor necrosis factor-β | Th1 cells, B cells | Promotes angiogenesis<br>Promotes inflammation |
| Transforming growth factor β | Macrophages, T cells, B cells, mast cells | Promotes immunosuppression |
| Granulocyte-macrophage colony-stimulating factor | T cells, macrophages, NK cells, B cells | Promotes granulocyte and monocyte growth |
| Interferon-α | Macrophages, fibroblasts, lymphoblastoid cells, virally infected cells, epithelial cells | Increases expression of major histocompatibility molecules<br>Induces fever, reduces appetite<br>Induces resistance to virus<br>Stimulates NK cell activity |
| Interferon-β | Fibroblasts, endothelial cells, virally infected cells | Stimulates NK cell activity<br>Induces resistance to virus |
| Interferon-γ | Activated Th1 cells, NK cells, B cells, macrophages | Activates macrophages<br>Inhibits Th2 cells<br>Blocks interleukin-4 effects on B cells<br>Prevents class switching |

*Note.* Th1 = T helper 1; Th2 = T helper 2; NK = natural killer.

teins called *acute phase reactants* that help isolate and destroy invading pathogens, control damage to self tissues and stimulate repair pathways (Baumann and Gauldie 1994). These proteins include C-reactive protein, macroglobulin, fibrinogen, and antiproteases. C-reactive protein coats bacteria for phagocytosis, whereas fibrinogen aids in clotting. Elevated fibrinogen contributes in part to the elevated sedimentation rate in inflammatory disorders by enhancing rouleaux formation (stacking/ clustering of red blood cells). Antiproteases control tissue destruction by inactivating destructive proteases produced by immune cells. The activation of the acute phase response is a good example of the regulation and counterregulation that occurs both to stimulate and to control the immune response; immune cells produce proinflammatory cytokines and proteases, stimulating production of acute phase proteins by the liver, which in turn control immune-induced tissue destruction. Feedback of this

**TABLE 4–2.** Features of innate and acquired immunity

|  | Innate (natural) immunity | Acquired immunity |
|---|---|---|
| Circulating molecules | Complement<br>Acute phase proteins | Antibodies |
| Cell types | Phagocytes (macrophages, neutrophils)<br>Natural killer cells | T and B lymphocytes |
| Soluble mediators | Type I interferons (α, β)<br>Tumor necrosis factor, IL-1, IL-6 | Interferon-γ<br>IL-2, IL-4, IL-10 |
| Other | Surface barriers, cilia, lysozyme, secretions (tears,<br>mucus, saliva), pH, normal flora |  |

Note.   IL = interleukin.

kind occurs at many levels of immune function and is discussed in greater detail below.

The system of complement proteins is another important component of innate, or nonspecific, immunity. These proteins are produced by the liver and interact in a sequential "cascade," which can amplify the immune response at the site of injury (Abbas et al. 2000; Delves and Roitt 2000b). Complement proteins have effects on cell lysis and opsonization and can attract other immune cells and stimulate their activity. They can also help neutralize antigen-antibody complexes. The NK cells, phagocytes, cytokines, and complement proteins all make up the branch of innate immunity that produces the body's first-line, nonspecific response to threat.

## Acquired Immunity

Acquired, or specific, immunity is provided by a complex set of cells and signaling molecules that enable the body to discriminate between foreign antigens and "remember" them so that a more robust response is mobilized on reexposure to stimulus. Several features of the acquired immune response are illustrated in Figure 4–2. B and T lymphocytes are the primary cells responsible for the acquired immune response. Acquired immunity occurs in four conceptually distinct phases: an induction phase, in which an infectious agent or antigen is detected; an activation phase, in which immune cells proliferate and mobilize; an effector phase, in which the agent or antigen is neutralized and eliminated; and a memory phase, in which immune cells capable of responding to reexposure to antigen are maintained in the circulation. Although both B and T lymphocytes have surface receptors that are genetically programmed to recognize foreign antigens, the mechanisms of activation and the function of each cell type are quite different. The synthesis of a B or T cell receptor depends on the random rearrangement of multiple gene products that allow for the potential to recognize $10^8$ distinct antigens. Because this rearrangement is random, this process allows for production of receptors that might react with self antigens. As mentioned before, elimination of these autoimmune cells is an important step in lymphocyte maturation in the primary immune tissues.

## B cells

Acquired immunity mediated by B cells has been termed *humoral immunity*, because this immunity can be transferred by transfusion of cell-free blood products such as plasma. The B cell first recognizes a foreign antigen when that antigen binds to the B cell surface receptor that specifically matches that antigen. The B cell receptor is surface immunoglobulin (Ig), which has two identical binding sites, each of which can recognize the tertiary structure of a foreign antigen. In addition to binding the antigen, the B cell also requires a signal (generally a cytokine) from a helper T cell in order to become fully activated (Delves and Roitt 2000b). The activated B cell then proliferates into clonally identical cells that differentiate further into plasma cells that produce soluble antibodies of the same binding specificity as the surface receptor (Figure 4–2A). Although antibodies produced by a specific B cell or its clone are identical in structure at the antigen binding site, other portions of the antibody can vary depending on the antibody's class. Different classes of antibody (e.g., IgM, IgA, IgG, and IgD) have specific class-dependent functions. For example, IgM, a large immunoglobulin, has five identical antigen binding sites and is capable of activating the complement system. In a similar way, other classes of antibodies have their own class-specific functions.

## T cells

The activation of T cells is more complex, and the immunity conferred by T cell–dependent processes is termed *cell-mediated*, because it depends on cellular functions rather than antibody production and can be transferred

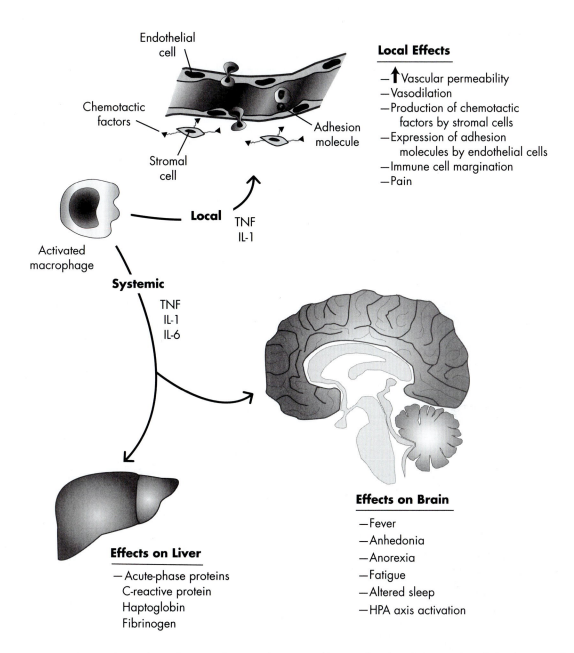

**FIGURE 4–1.** Innate immunity. Activated macrophages release cytokines at the site of tissue injury/infection. Locally, these cytokines act on endothelial and tissue stromal cells. Tissue stromal cells produce chemotactic factors, recruiting other immune cells to the site of injury. The endothelial cells produce adhesion molecules, enhancing immune cell margination and diapedesis. In the brain, proinflammatory cytokines—including interleukin (IL)-1, IL-6, and tumor necrosis factor-alpha (TNF-α)—activate the hypothalamic-pituitary-adrenal (HPA) axis and induce sickness behavior and fever. The proinflammatory cytokines also induce the liver to produce acute phase proteins.

from one individual to the next only through cells. The T cell receptor has only one binding site for antigen and cannot bind freely circulating, whole antigen. The T cell receptor must "see" antigen in a specific context on another cell to bind to the antigen and become activated. One type of T cell, the helper T cell, is so named because of its role in producing mediators that activate other immune cells. It is also termed a CD4+ cell because of

the presence on its surface of a particular cell surface protein. Helper T cells require the assistance of phagocytic cells that must first ingest and digest foreign material. The phagocytic cell then "presents" the digested fragments on its surface in association with a particular set of self surface molecules called major histocompatability complex (MHC) molecules. The CD4+ T cell, on binding to the antigen-MHC complex on a phagocytic cell,

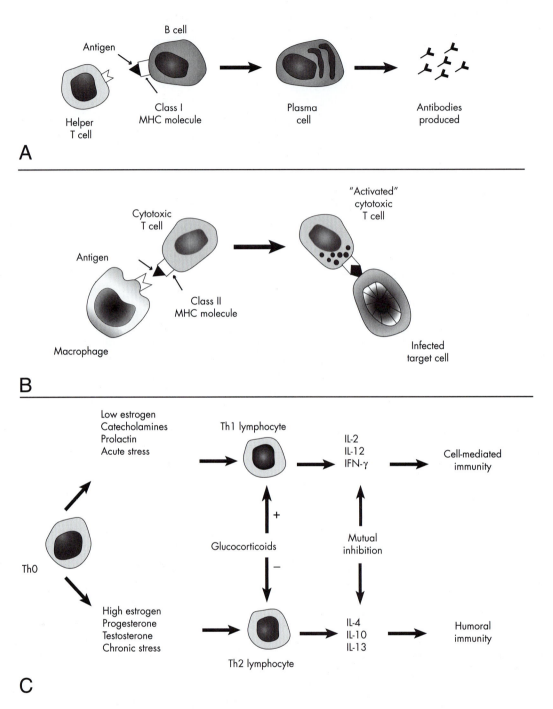

**FIGURE 4–2.** Processes of acquired immunity. *Panel A.* B cell activation. The B cell presents antigen to a helper T cell, which then secretes cytokines that stimulate development of the B cell into an antibody-producing plasma cell. The helper T cell recognizes antigen in association with a major histocompatibility complex (MHC) molecule. *Panel B.* Cell killing by cytotoxic T cell. A cytotoxic T cell becomes activated by an encounter with an antigen-presenting cell (such as a macrophage) in the presence of stimulating cytokines. The activated cytotoxic T cell produces toxic granules. When the cytotoxic T cell binds to the target cell, the granules are released, killing the target cell. *Panel C.* T helper (Th) lymphocytes develop along Th1 and Th2 pathways. Naïve helper T lymphocytes (Th0) develop along Th1 or Th2 pathways under the influence of stimulating factors such as hormones and catecholamines. Th1 and Th2 cells produce characteristic cytokine profiles with specific immune system effects. Th1 cells generally stimulate forms of cell-mediated immunity such as the delayed-type hypersensitivity (DTH) response and natural killer (NK) cell activity, whereas Th2 cells stimulate humoral immunity. Glucocorticoids inhibit the Th1 response and stimulate the Th2 response. The Th1 and Th2 pathways mutually inhibit each other.

then becomes activated and produces cytokines, such as IL-2 and IL-4, which in turn promote growth and activation of other immune cells. CD4+ cells may also become memory cells that remain latent and help the body respond rapidly and efficiently when reexposed to the same stimulus. The presence of circulating soluble CD4 and CD8 molecules represents immune activation. Other markers of immune activation are indirect and represent negative feedback, that is, the body's attempt to control the immune response. Interleukin-10 (IL-10) and transforming growth factor β (TGF-β) are two cytokines that are involved in modulating immunity. Interleukin-1-receptor antagonist (IL-1Ra) is another circulating mediator that binds to the IL-1 receptor, thus limiting the effects of the cytokine IL-1.

Cell-mediated immunity also provides mechanisms for fighting viral infection and malignancy. Cells of the body, when virally infected or malignantly transformed, may present antigen such as virus particles on their surface, in association with a different class of MHC molecules. When the cytotoxic T lymphocyte detects this antigen–MHC molecule complex on a cell, the cytotoxic cell releases enzymes that kill the affected cell (see Figure 4–2B). The cytotoxic T lymphocyte is also called a CD8+ cell because it has a cell surface protein called CD8, analogous to the CD4 protein on helper T lymphocytes. CD8 cells play a critical role in the clearance of viruses like human immunodeficiency virus (HIV). Cell-mediated immunity thus depends on a complex set of cellular and molecular interactions. The surface MHC molecules play a key role. They are genetically coded, and how effective one's MHC molecules are in binding and presenting antigen depends on one's genetic endowment. Their effectiveness at the process of binding and presenting antigen in turn affects one's ability to develop immunity to foreign and self antigens. The particular set of MHC genes an individual carries will thus play a key role in determining resistance to disease and susceptibility to autoimmune disorder. This important issue is addressed in more detail later.

Recently acquired data indicate that T helper cell subclasses, identified as Th1 and Th2 cells, exhibit distinct patterns of immune activation within cell-mediated immunity (see Figure 4–2C). Th1 cells secrete IFN-γ and IL-2, are involved in cell-mediated immunity, and assist with cytotoxic T lymphocyte activation. Th2 cells secrete IL-4, IL-6, and IL-10 and are involved in antibody formation and allergic responses. These subclasses thus have different functional patterns. They also appear to have different responses to neuroendocrine control (see below).

## Tests of Immunity

Several laboratory tests have commonly been used in studying the relationship between immune function and stress or psychiatric illness. They can be divided into enumerative and functional tests. Enumerative studies count circulating immune cells of various types and subtypes, for example, neutrophils or CD4+ lymphocytes. Cells can be identified by morphologic characteristics (as is determined in a complete blood cell count and differential) or by expression of unique cell surface molecules (referred to as clusters of differentiation or CD markers). Cell surface molecules are determined using flow cytometry. Functional studies examine different in vivo and in vitro measures of immune function. For example, white blood cells taken from patients diagnosed with illness have been tested in vitro for their ability to proliferate/divide or produce cytokines in response to various mitogens. Mitogens are plant lectins that have the capacity to crosslink receptors on various immune cell types (including T cells, B cells, and macrophages), thereby activating cellular function (Abbas et al. 2000). NK cell activity is another type of in vitro functional immune assay in which isolated NK cells are incubated with radiolabeled tumor cells, and the amount of tumor cell killing is measured by the amount of radioactivity released. In vivo functional tests of immunity include measures of cytokines or acute phase proteins in the blood or cerebrospinal fluid (CSF), response to antigens such as in the delayed-type hypersensitivity (DTH) reaction, or antibody production against vaccines or latent viruses.

## Immunity and Disease

Diseases of immune dysfunction help to illustrate how finely tuned the system is and how essential the immune system's role is in maintaining health. Disorders of immunity can be broadly grouped into immune deficiencies, allergic diseases, and autoimmune disorders. In diseases of immune deficiency, the body is unable either to identify or to fight pathogens or malignancies. An example of this is the syndrome of severe combined immunodeficiency (SCID), in which both B and T cell functions are grossly impaired. Usually congenital, this disorder of both humoral and cell-mediated immunity prevents the body from fighting off infections of all sorts. Without treatment, affected individuals typically succumb rapidly to bacterial, viral, or fungal infection (or a combination of these). Other immune deficiencies are more specific. For example, certain cancer chemotherapy regimens that preferentially cause neutropenia make patients especially vulnerable to infection by extracellular bacteria.

The acquired immune deficiency syndrome (AIDS), associated with infection with HIV, demonstrates how deficiency in one component of the immune system can cause widespread pathology. The virus binds to the CD4+ protein on the surface of the helper T lymphocyte, enters the cell, and interferes with the cell's functioning in a variety of ways. Since the helper T lymphocyte plays such a pivotal role in immunity, loss of helper T cell function predisposes affected individuals to a variety of immune-related disorders. Patients are susceptible to opportunistic infections with organisms such as *Cryptococcus*, *Mycobacterium* species, and *Toxoplasma*. Reactivation or severe infection with cytomegalovirus or herpes viruses can occur. Patients with HIV infection are also at risk for cancers such as Kaposi's sarcoma and central nervous system (CNS) lymphoma. The syndrome of HIV/AIDS demonstrates how dysfunction of one immune cell type reverberates throughout a number of immune processes.

Disorders of immunity also include those of excessive immunity. These fall into two types: allergic diseases, in which the immune system responds excessively to nonpathogenic environmental antigens, or autoimmune diseases, in which the system fails to prevent reaction to self antigens. These processes have multiple pathologic consequences. They can waste body energy resources, injure self tissues, and keep the immune system from functioning at an efficient level against external pathogens. Allergic reactions are typically mediated by the immunoglobulin IgE. Contact with the antigen causes the release of histamine by mast cells, increased capillary permeability, and smooth muscle contraction. The most severe form of allergy is the anaphylactic reaction, occurring when exposure to an antigen induces bronchospasm or a hypotensive reaction.

Autoimmune diseases occur when the system misidentifies self cells as foreign, and the cascade of immune events results in damage of self tissue. These multifactorial illnesses arise from a combination of events, including individual genetic predisposition, exposure to an antigen, and hormonal patterns. Several mechanisms may permit this. Lymphocytes that should be eliminated for binding too robustly to self antigens may survive to maturity. Viral infections or other stimuli may cause surface changes of self cells, which cause immune cells to identify these cells as foreign and attack them. By these mechanisms, direct tissue damage can occur. Secondary effects can also occur, as in systemic lupus erythematosus (SLE), when circulating antigen-antibody complexes are deposited in and damage renal tissue. These examples of immune deficiency states and autoimmune disorders reflect the variety and severity of diseases that can occur

when immune regulation is impaired.

Although immunologists have elucidated many of the intricacies of internal regulation of the immune response, a growing database has led to an increasing appreciation that factors and pathways external to the immune system, including those involving the nervous and endocrine systems, are intimately involved in immune regulation. The foundation for this expanded consideration of immune regulation derives from multiple studies demonstrating meaningful communication among the nervous, endocrine, and immune systems. Relevant areas of research include 1) the impact of stress and psychiatric disease on immune function and immune-related disorders, 2) the influence of the immune system and immune-related disorders on the brain and neuropsychiatric disorders, and 3) shared pathways of communication among nervous, endocrine, and immune systems, including nervous innervation of lymphoid tissue and shared expression of receptors for multiple transmitters.

## Stress and Immunity

One of the most well-studied areas of the relationship among the nervous, endocrine, and immune systems is the impact of stress on immune function. Stress may be defined most simply as a stimulus that challenges an organism to reach new homeostasis (Chrousos and Gold 1992). The stimulus may be physical—such as injury, hunger, or cold—and/or psychological—such as bereavement, exposure to a predator, or social isolation. Although the earliest studies on laboratory animals suggested that stress inhibits immune function, subsequent animal and human research has presented a more complicated picture. Instead of a stressor turning the immune system "up" or "down," a better description might be that a stressor sets off a cascade of physiological and molecular biological events, beginning with detection by the immune or nervous system and ending with a new homeostasis. Most studies are only able to examine a cross section of this process, looking at limited aspects of the entire physiological and molecular biological response at selected time points.

## Stress and Immunity in Laboratory Animals

Early investigators exposed laboratory animals to various stressors and measured susceptibility to disease induced by infection or inoculation with tumor cells. Rasmussen and colleagues performed some of the first of these experiments in the 1950s and 1960s (Rasmussen et al. 1957). For example, mice exposed to stressors such as shock, restraint, and loud noise were found to exhibit increased susceptibility to a number of viral infections if the stressor was applied after virus exposure. Ader and Friedman demonstrated that handling and mild electric shock administered during the first few weeks of life also modified the rates of tumor development and survival in rats injected with Walker 256 sarcoma cells as adults (Ader and Friedman 1965). These investigations confirmed an association between stress and disease susceptibility, leading researchers to examine what specific changes in immune system parameters might be involved.

One of the first studies documenting the impact of stress on the immune system was conducted by Keller and colleagues (1981), who exposed adult rats to 19 hours of tail shock. The animals exhibited profound reductions in the proliferation of peripheral blood T cells in response to in vitro stimulation by the nonspecific T cell mitogen phytohemagglutinin. Subsequent studies have shown that a wide variety of stressors—including handling, foot shock, restraint, rotation, crowding, noise, forced exercise, light-dark cycle inversion, and exposure to a predator—are capable of altering a similarly wide variety of immune parameters, including decreases in peripheral blood lymphocytes, lymphocyte proliferation, cytokine production, NK cell activity, phagocytic function, and antibody formation (Weiss and Sundar 1992). In most of this research, the stressors have been acute and have led to immune findings that suggest immune suppression. Nevertheless, the data have in large part derived from immune compartments of the blood and spleen, which represent a fraction of the immune processes occurring in the body at any particular time. Table 4–3 summarizes immune changes in laboratory animals in response to stress.

Immune suppression in the context of acute stress does not appear to be adaptive from an evolutionary standpoint, especially given that survival might be enhanced by mobilization of the immune response in the context of impending injury or infection, such as during a challenge from a predator. Moreover, the finding of immune suppression during stress does not explain the clinical observation of stress-induced exacerbation of autoimmune and inflammatory disorders (see below). Addressing these issues is the work of Dhabhar and colleagues (1995), who have found that acute stress causes a redistribution of lymphocytes from blood and spleen (where immunosuppression is typically observed) to areas such as lymph nodes, skin, and bone marrow. This

**TABLE 4–3.** Stress-induced changes in immune function: studies in laboratory animals

**Immune responses to acute stress**

Decreased number of circulating lymphocytes

Decreased lymphocyte proliferative responses to mitogens

Decreased phagocyte function

Decreased/increased natural killer cell activity

Increased antibody production

Increased cutaneous delayed-type hypersensitivity

Increased acute phase proteins ($\alpha_1$-antitrypsin, C-reactive protein, haptoglobin)

Increased proinflammatory cytokines (interleukin-1, interleukin-6, tumor necrosis factor-alpha)

**Immune responses to chronic stress**

Decreased numbers of circulating lymphocytes and monocytes

Decreased lymphocyte proliferative response to mitogens

Decreased natural killer cell activity

Increased susceptibility to viral infection

Increased rate of tumor development

Decreased antibody production

Decreased delayed-type hypersensitivity

margination appears to represent a state of increased immune surveillance in these tissues. Examining the skin as a target organ for reallocation of immune resources, these researchers found that skin exhibits increased immune activity as manifested by increased DTH after exposure to acute stress (Dhabhar and McEwen 1996). This increased immune activity in skin has been shown to impart resistance to certain local infections. In contrast, chronic stress was associated with suppression of the DTH response in skin and increased vulnerability to infectious challenge. Recently published work by this group has found that IFN-$\gamma$ appears to play a key role in mediating acute stress–induced enhancement of skin DTH responses (Dhabhar et al. 2000). In addition to increases in DTH responses, a number of groups have observed increases in acute phase proteins and proinflammatory cytokines during acute stress in animals and humans. Increases in circulating levels of acute phase proteins such as $\alpha_1$-antitrypsin, C-reactive protein, and haptoglobin have been reported, along with increases in the proinflammatory cytokines IL-6, IL-1, and TNF-$\alpha$. Increased cytokine expression has been apparent both in the periphery and in the brain. Thus, increases in innate immunity may accompany decreases in cell-mediated immunity (especially in the blood and spleen) during acute stress (LeMay et al. 1990; Zhou et al. 1993), whereas chronic (and severe) stress may be most likely accompanied by immune suppression.

## Stress and Immunity in Humans: Naturalistic Stressors

Researchers have examined a variety of immune parameters in apparently healthy humans undergoing naturalistic or laboratory stressors. Table 4–4 summarizes immune findings in humans in acute and chronic stress. Naturalistic stressors such as caregiving for patients with Alzheimer's disease and undergoing academic examinations have been studied extensively. Elderly caregivers of spouses with Alzheimer's disease, presumably experiencing chronic stress, have been found to exhibit a variety of immune abnormalities, including decreased lymphocyte proliferation and IL-2 production, decreased ratio of T helper to T suppressor cells (Pariante et al. 1997), and decreased NK cell activity (Esterling et al. 1996). Medical students during examination stress show a similar pattern of altered immune responses. A large meta-analysis by Herbert and Cohen (1993) examined studies of stress effects on human immune parameters. Immunologic effects observed across studies of long-term naturalistic stressors include increased white blood cells, decreased peripheral blood lymphocytes, decreased cytotoxic/suppressor T cells, decreased lymphocyte responses to phytohemagglutinin and concanavalin A, and increased antibody titers to herpes simplex virus type 1 and Epstein-Barr virus. Increased viral antibody titers presumably reflect virus reactivation secondary to altered cell-mediated (acquired) immune function. The type of stressor seems to play a role also, with social (interpersonal) stressors having more profound effects than nonsocial ones.

Data suggest that the immunologic changes associated with stress may have implications for health and disease. A study of spousal caregivers of dementia patients found impaired wound healing compared with age-matched control subjects (Kiecolt-Glaser et al. 1995). Investigations of healthy subjects also have demonstrated that stress increases the likelihood of both infection and symptom development after standardized inoculation with several rhinoviruses (S. Cohen et al. 1991). Finally, decreased antibody responses to hepatitis B and influenza vaccines, respectively, have been found in medical students experiencing acute examination stress (Glaser et al. 1992) and spousal caregivers of Alzheimer's disease patients (Kiecolt-Glaser et al. 1996). Overall, these data indicate that humans undergoing naturalistic stressors exhibit evidence of immune dysfunction, generally consistent with decreased immune system responsiveness, increased susceptibility to infection, and impaired wound healing.

**TABLE 4–4.** Stress-induced changes in immune function: human studies

**Immune responses to acute stress**
 Increased white blood cell count
 Increased natural killer cell number
 Decreased number of T lymphocytes
 Decreased proliferative responses to mitogens
 Increased natural killer cell activity
 Increased antibody titers to viruses
 Decreased antibody response to vaccine

**Immune responses to chronic stress**
 Increased white blood cell count
 Decreased number of lymphocytes
 Decreased T helper:T suppressor ratio
 Decreased lymphocyte proliferative responses to mitogens
 Decreased lymphocyte production of interleukin-2 by stimulated lymphocytes
 Decreased natural killer cell activity
 Increased antibody titers to viruses
 Decreased antibody response to vaccine
 Delayed wound healing

## Stress and Immunity in Humans: Laboratory Stressors

Laboratory stressors are generally mild, acute stressors, including cognitive tasks such as public speaking or mental arithmetic. Although some alterations in immune parameters are similar between studies of naturalistic and experimentally induced stressors, other immune changes following stress in the laboratory are distinct. Laboratory stressors have been associated with decreased lymphocyte proliferative responses to mitogen stimulation, similar to changes found with chronic life stress. However, in contrast to naturalistic stressors, laboratory stressors have been associated with increased NK cell number and in vitro NK cell activity. These NK cell findings are transient and have been correlated with increased cardiovascular reactivity (Benschop et al. 1995, 1996; Herbert et al. 1994).

Work by Pike and colleagues (1997) evaluated immune responses to acute psychological stress (mental arithmetic) in individuals who were or were not undergoing chronic life stress. Although the subjects exhibited no baseline differences in NK cell number or activity, when subjects were exposed to an acute stressor, individuals experiencing chronic stress in daily life had neuroendocrine and immune responses different from those under low stress. Chronically stressed individuals exhibited increased peak epinephrine responses and blunted peak levels of β-endorphin in response to the task. Both groups responded to the acute stressor with increased NK cell number, but the NK activity per cell was decreased in the subjects under chronic stress. Chronic stress thus appears to cause changes in the immune system that alter the individual's responses to acute stress. These findings may be especially relevant to the role of stress in the chronically mentally or medically ill.

Some work exists addressing issues of how psychological or dispositional attitudes and controllability of a stressor interact to affect the immune response to laboratory stressors (G.E. Miller et al. 1999a, 1999b). Peters and colleagues (1999) recently reported experiments in humans in which effort and controllability were separated experimentally. The amount of effort expended in performing a task was associated with transient increases in CD8 and CD16 cell numbers and NK cell activity, whereas uncontrollability was associated with increased serum cortisol and decreased production of IL-6 by stimulated lymphocytes. Similarly, the expectation of success (optimism) in law students was found to be associated with increased CD4 cell number and increased NK cell activity during students' first semester of law school (Segerstrom et al. 1998). These findings suggest an interaction among psychological characteristics, stress, and immune function.

## Stress, Depression, and Immunity: Impact on Disease

Physicians have long been interested in the effects of stress, depression, and other psychological factors on the onset and course of illnesses related to the immune system, including cancer, infectious diseases, and autoimmune disorders.

## Cancer

Anecdotal reports have suggested an association between the development of cancer and preceding stressful life events. Findings have included an increase in stressful life events before the development of colorectal cancer (Courtney et al. 1993) but no such association between stressful life events and the development of breast cancer (Roberts et al. 1996). In general, studies of this type have been retrospective and examine only patients with one type of cancer. Retrospective investigations are confounded by the fact that the diagnosis of cancer itself can alter the patient's recall of events preceding diagnosis.

Because of the small number of new cases and the long period over which many diseases develop, prospective epidemiologic studies with large numbers of subjects

and lengthy follow-up periods must be performed before an association between stress (or depression) and the incidence of disease can be demonstrated. A recent survey of more than 11,000 parents of children diagnosed with cancer was conducted on Danish national health registries to examine the impact of the severe stressor—the diagnosis of cancer in one's child—on the development of disease. This survey found no association between the diagnosis of cancer in one's child and an increased odds ratio for the development of cancer, allergies, or autoimmune disease during a period ranging from 7 to 49 years after the child's cancer diagnosis (Johansen and Olsen 1997). Few studies of this sort are available that provide such strong data about the association between stress and the development of disease.

Regarding the impact of depression on the development of cancer, the data have been underwhelming. In a meta-analysis of prospective studies by McGee and colleagues (1994), a small but statistically significantly increased risk of cancer in patients with depression was revealed. In a more recent review of more than 50 studies on mortality and depression by Wulsin and colleagues (1999), the authors concluded that although depression seems to increase the risk of death by cardiovascular disease, especially in men, depression does not seem to increase the risk of death by cancer. Both reviews comment on the lack of high-quality studies controlling for potential mediating variables. Of note are studies finding an increased incidence of cancer in depressed smokers (Linkins and Comstock 1990), an increased incidence of lung cancer in depressed men (Knekt et al. 1996), and an increased incidence of cancer in men with high levels of hopelessness (Everson et al. 1996). Taken together, the data suggest that depression may not in itself put individuals at substantially higher risk but may increase the risk of cancer in individuals with other risk factors, especially smoking.

Although the impact of stress and/or depression on the development of cancer may be relatively small, data support the notion that psychological factors may have a greater effect once cancer is diagnosed. Mounting evidence suggests that susceptibility to immune-related diseases, including cancer, is related to genetic factors. Therefore, if stress, depression, and other psychological factors are associated with altered immune function, then the impact of these factors may be the greatest on patients with immune-related disorders and genetic predisposition to immune dysfunction. Ramirez and colleagues (1989) reported that severe life events and difficulties are associated with increased risk of breast cancer relapse. In addition, depression is relatively common in cancer patients (Evans et al. 1986), and depressive symptoms have been associated with decreased survival in patients with lung cancer (Buccheri 1998; Faller et al. 1999). Hopelessness has also been found to be associated with decreased survival in women with early-stage breast cancer (Watson et al. 1999). In a study by Walker and colleagues (1999), scores of depression and anxiety were independent predictors of therapeutic outcome in patients with newly diagnosed breast cancer.

Because stress or psychiatric symptoms may predispose to worse outcomes in patients with cancer, clinicians have wondered whether psychosocial interventions that address these factors might alter disease outcome. To test these notions, Spiegel et al. (1989) and Fawzy et al. (1993) treated patients with cancer with group psychotherapy under controlled conditions and found improved outcomes in the intervention group compared with those receiving standard therapy. These outcomes included lengthened survival in patients with metastatic breast cancer and decreased recurrence in patients with malignant melanoma. Not all studies have reproduced these findings. Two studies, using cognitive behavior therapy in patients with metastatic breast cancer, found no improved survival in the intervention group (A.J. Cunningham et al. 1998; Edelman et al. 1999). A problem with the few studies in this area is that all patients have been included, not simply those who might be psychiatrically vulnerable to stress-related immune alterations. It remains to be determined whether more powerful treatment effects would be observed if studies targeted patients with psychosocial risk factors, including depressive symptoms, reduced social support, or impaired coping strategies.

## Infection: AIDS

Infection with HIV is a worldwide epidemic and, because of increasing availability of antiretroviral medications in developed countries, large numbers of patients are living longer with the illness. Of particular interest has been the neuropsychiatric aspects of HIV infection, including the relationship among psychosocial factors in infected individuals, their immune functioning, and their clinical status (Evans et al., in press). Although some studies have found no differences in immune variables in patients with HIV infection who are experiencing increased life stress (Rabkin et al. 1991), other research has found altered immune parameters in HIV-infected, stressed individuals (Evans et al. 1995; Leserman et al. 1997; Perry et al. 1992; Petitto et al. 2000). A meta-analysis by Zorrilla and colleagues (1996) concluded that there is a significant association between an increase in stressful life events and decreased NK cell number and

activity. More recently, Leserman and colleagues reported an association between faster progression from HIV disease to AIDS in association with stressful life events and higher serum cortisol levels (Leserman et al. 2000). Investigators have also reported that life event stress including bereavement leads to more rapid early HIV disease progression as well as progression to AIDS (Evans et al. 1997; Leserman et al. 1997, 1999). Moreover, bereavement combined with negative expectation about one's future health status has been found to predict shorter survival in men with AIDS and increased likelihood of the development of HIV-related symptoms in men with HIV infection (Cole and Kemeny 2001; Reed et al. 1999).

In contrast to life stress, the relationship between depressive symptoms and HIV disease has been somewhat elusive. Some researchers have found an association between depressive symptoms and HIV disease progression without increased mortality (Burack et al. 1993; Lyketsos et al. 1993; Page-Schafer et al. 1996), and others have reported both disease progression and increased mortality (Mayne et al. 1996). Other work has reported no association between depression and disease progression (Lyketsos et al. 1996; Perry et al. 1992; Rabkin et al. 1991). A meta-analysis by Zorrilla and colleagues (1996) reported an association between depressive symptoms and symptoms of HIV infection but not lymphocyte subsets. More recently, Leserman and colleagues (1997) reported that stress and depressive symptoms, particularly when they occur jointly, are associated with decreased cytotoxic T lymphocyte subsets. Data from up to 7.5 years of a prospective study of HIV-infected men provide evidence that stress, social support, coping style, and depression can affect disease progression (Leserman et al. 1999, 2000). Interestingly, hopelessness as an individual variable has been shown to affect disease progression, at least by CD4 count measures (Perry et al. 1992). Overall, it appears that life event stress, particularly bereavement, can affect disease progression, although the relationship between depression and disease progression is less clear and warrants further study.

## Other Viral Infections

Several viral infections of humans, such as herpes simplex and herpes zoster viruses, cause initial infection and then enter into a state of latency, becoming reactivated at later times. The reactivation of these viruses is known to be associated with immune compromise, such as occurs during chemotherapy or in AIDS. However, the data are mixed regarding how psychological factors—including stress, depression, and coping style—affect the body's interaction with these viruses. Elevated titers of antibodies against herpes viruses have been reported in stressed individuals, and, although some clinicians suggest that this indicates decreased containment of latent viruses by the immune system, the clinical relevance remains unclear. A large meta-analytic review by Zorilla and colleagues (1996) concluded that depressive symptoms were related to increased risk of recurrence of herpes simplex virus, whereas stress was not. In contrast, a recent prospective study (F. Cohen et al. 1999) of women with genital herpes found that persistent stress was associated with increased risk of recurrence, whereas short-term stress or depressed mood showed no such association. Irwin and colleagues (1998) recently reported that patients with major depression demonstrated a decreased number of varicella-zoster virus responder cells compared with controls. Interestingly, this pattern resembles the immunity pattern found in older patients (over age 60 years). These findings of changes in viral activity provide further evidence for the clinical significance of the altered immune parameters found during stress and depression.

## Autoimmune Diseases

Autoimmune diseases are thought to result from a process of self antigens being misidentified as nonself, with subsequent proliferation of immune responses against self tissues. The mechanisms by which this occurs are unknown, but a combination of genetic predisposition, environmental stimuli such as physical stressors and viral exposures, and psychological factors are believed to be involved. Work in the last decade has identified particular patterns of immune activation associated with the various systemic autoimmune illnesses. For example, rheumatoid arthritis is characterized by increased cellular, or Th1, immunity, whereas excessive humoral, or Th2, immunity is associated with SLE (see Figure 4–2C for a summary of Th1 and Th2 immune processes). The interactions among an individual's HLA makeup, environmental exposures to antigens, and hormonal pathways seem to be crucial to initiating and maintaining these illnesses. One's HLA type helps determine the capacity of the immune system to respond to particular antigens. Important hormonal pathways involved in autoimmune disorders include the adrenal and gonadal steroids; in particular, the immunoregulatory activity of estrogen is thought to contribute to the high prevalence of autoimmune disease in women (see Figure 4–2C). Because both immune suppression and immune activation can occur in response to various stressors, the interactions among psychological factors and the clinical course of these diseases are complex. This section presents evidence for how stress and depression affect the onset and course of autoimmune diseases, including multiple sclerosis, SLE, rheumatoid arthritis, and Graves' disease.

### Multiple Sclerosis

Multiple sclerosis (MS) is a relapsing and remitting neurologic disease characterized by focal areas of central nervous system demyelination. Although the precise etiology of MS is unknown, autoimmunity against myelin and probably other central nervous system antigens appears to be involved. The course of MS typically waxes as new lesions (accompanied by inflammation) appear and wanes as the inflammation resolves. In general, though, the disease is progressive as new areas of demyelination continue to appear and neurologic impairment increases. Clinicians have long debated how psychological factors affect the course of MS and have speculated that stress, negative life events, or psychological factors might be associated with clinical exacerbations of the illness. Results of studies have been mixed. Some studies have reported an association between stressors and the onset or exacerbation of MS, whereas others have found no such association. A particularly well-constructed study by Grant and colleagues (1989) found that patients with MS reported more life difficulties in the year preceding the onset of MS or within several months before exacerbations of the illness. In this study, only patients who were recently diagnosed or did not yet have a confirmed diagnosis of MS were included, and thus the subjects had only limited symptomatology at the time of study. In addition, structured interviews of adverse life events were complemented by a consensus rating of the severity of the stressor, thus avoiding inclusion of trivial events. Mohr and colleagues (2000) recently reported results of a prospective, two-year study examining the relationship between life stress, conflict, or psychological distress and new MS lesions on magnetic resonance images. They found that an increase in conflict and disruption of life routine (but not psychological distress) were associated with new lesions found on magnetic resonance images four and eight weeks later, but conflict, disruption of routine, and psychological distress were not related to clinical exacerbation of symptoms. These data suggest that certain psychological factors are associated with pathophysiological changes of MS, although not necessarily with clinical findings. An interesting prospective study by Nisipeanu and Korczyn (1993) evaluated 32 patients with MS exposed to the threat of missile attacks during the Persian Gulf War. The researchers reported a decrease in the number of relapses in these patients during this period of extremely high stress. Therefore, it is possible that very high levels of stress are associated with marked increases in cortisol that inhibit disease activity. Further suggestion of a role for the hypothalamic-pituitary-adrenal (HPA) axis in MS patients was recently provided by Then Bergh and colleagues (1999), who found that MS patients exhibited glucocorticoid resistance as manifested by an altered dexamethasone/corticotropin-releasing hormone challenge.

## Rheumatoid Arthritis

Rheumatoid arthritis (RA) is an inflammatory disease manifested by chronic and disabling destruction of the joints. As with other autoimmune diseases, the disease is more common in women, and hormonal mechanisms appear to be important to the development and progression of the disease. RA is accompanied by an excess of Th1 cell activation. A variety of psychosocial factors also appear to be related to the disease course, including acute and chronic stressors, individual personality variables, and social support. Some evidence suggests that major life events are associated with the onset of RA in predisposed individuals. One serologic marker for RA is the presence of "rheumatoid factors" (RFs). Stewart and colleagues (1994) evaluated RA patients who were either RF positive or RF negative. They found that the RF-negative patients had higher scores on scales reporting negative life events before the onset of disease, whereas RF-positive patients did not exhibit such a strong association. In addition, objective measures of disease activity correlated with stress levels in the RF-negative group but not in the RF-positive group. This work suggests that stress may influence the onset and course of disease in different subgroups of patients. Furthermore, the role of stress may vary depending on one's predisposition to the disease, which may be determined by genetic or other constitutional factors. It may be that the RF-positive patients have a lower threshold for development of the disease and therefore stress is not required for the development of the disorder. For patients who are RF negative, however, larger amounts of stress may be necessary to drive disease activity.

Other research evaluating the effects of stress on the course of RA has found no clear answer regarding the role of stress in the illness. A study by Thomason and colleagues (1992) examined major and minor stressors, pain, disability, and erythrocyte sedimentation rate, a common serologic marker of inflammation. The researchers found no association between major stressors and RA status. However, after controlling for global disease status and major stressors, they found that minor stress did correlate with inflammation.

It is believed that RA is related to dysregulation of negative feedback by glucocorticoid hormones (cortisol) on the immune system (see below). Chikanza and colleagues (1992) compared hormonal and immune responses to the physical stress of surgery in patients with RA, osteoarthritis, and osteomyelitis. Patients with osteomyelitis exhibited increases in IL-1β, IL-6, and cortisol after surgery. In contrast, although surgery was associated with elevations in IL-1β and IL-6 in RA patients, there was no corresponding increase of cortisol. Both groups of patients exhibited similarly elevated erythrocyte sedimentation rate values, suggesting that, although both had inflammation, the adrenal production of cortisol was not appropriately elevated given the level of inflammation in the patients with RA. A similar finding was reported by Kanik et al. (2000), who found a lack of relationship between inflammatory indices and cortisol levels in RA patients at baseline.

Depression is commonly comorbid with RA and may relate to psychosocial factors such as pain and disability. It may also be related to circulating immune factors released as part of the inflammatory process of the illness. In fact, studies have reported increases in the proinflammatory cytokines IL-1, IL-6, and TNF-α in the joint spaces and serum of RA patients, which may mediate the depression that commonly occurs in RA (see below). The soluble IL-2-receptor (sIL-2R) is a marker for immune activation, and its presence has been correlated with increased disease activity in rheumatoid arthritis. A study by Harrington and colleagues (1993) examined the relationships among joint inflammation, mood, and levels of sIL-2R. Although the researchers found that joint swelling corresponded to increased sIL-2R levels, disturbed mood was surprisingly associated with decreased sIL-2R levels. More work is needed to explore the relationships among stress, depression, and disease activity in RA, paying attention to immune and HPA axis alterations that mediate these relationships.

## Systemic Lupus Erythematosus

SLE is an autoimmune disorder with multiple systemic manifestations. The pathology of SLE has been identified as primarily antibody mediated, resulting in deposition of antigen-antibody immune complexes in tissues. Because SLE is approximately ten times more common in women than in men, hormonal mechanisms are thought to play a critical role in the initiation and perpetuation of the illness. The proinflammatory effect of estrogen seems to influence the course of disease, as flares of the disease increase during pregnancy and drop off after menopause. Pregnancy is accompanied by a shift from Th1 to Th2 activity that seems to exacerbate SLE. Estrogen replacement therapy also increases the risk of development of SLE. The question of stress or other psychosocial factors in exacerbating the illness has been of interest to clinicians and researchers over the years. A recently reported study by DaCosta and colleagues (1999) found that a history of stressful life events in the 6 months before evaluation correlated with reduced functional ability 8 months after evaluation. Increasing severity of depression scores was also correlated with changes in functional ability 8 months after evaluation. Research by Ward and colleagues (1999) on a large cohort of patients with SLE also has found that greater disease activity in SLE patients was associated with less social support, and that increased physical disability was associated with depression in these patients. Thus, the evidence suggests that stress and depression play a role in the clinical course of SLE.

## Graves' Disease

Graves' disease is an antibody-mediated autoimmune disorder in which antibody to the thyroid-stimulating hormone (TSH) receptor stimulates the gland to produce thyroid hormone. Despite markedly increased levels of circulating thyroid hormones and accompanying decreases in thyrotropin-releasing hormone and TSH, the thyroid gland continues to produce hormone. The illness is accompanied by an increased likelihood of possessing the HLA type DR3. As with other autoimmune illnesses, clinicians have been interested in investigating the role of stress and psychological functioning in precipitating or exacerbating the illness. One factor that must be considered in these studies is that elevated thyroid hormone levels may alter retrospective recall of stressful events, perception of current stress, or behavior that might precipitate stressful events. Some studies have found an increase in stressful life events to be associated with the onset of the disease. Sonino and colleagues (1993) reported that an increase in multiple types of life events—positive and negative, controlled and uncontrolled—was associated with the onset of the illness. One strength of this study was that the patients were interviewed regarding stressful events after they were in remission from the disease. In recently reported work, Yoshiuchi et al. (1998) found that stressful life events and smoking were both associated with the development of Graves' disease in women but not in men. Because the disease is more prevalent in women and estrogen is thought to play a role because of its immunostimulant effects (similar to what occurs in SLE), it is possible that development of the disease in men is associated with a stronger genetic predisposition than in women. Thus,

although the disease is multifactorial, there is evidence for the role of stress and psychological factors in its onset, especially in women.

### Pediatric Autoimmune Neuropsychiatric Disorder Associated With Streptococcus Infections

An immune-related disorder with neuropsychiatric manifestations occurring in children has recently been identified, called pediatric autoimmune neuropsychiatric disorder associated with streptococcus infections (PANDAS). The disorder is associated with the immune response to infection with group A β-hemolytic streptococcus (GABHS) and involves the development of neuropsychiatric syndromes, including obsessive-compulsive disorder and tic disorder, following a primary infection with GABHS (Swedo et al. 1998). The symptom course is relapsing and remitting with exacerbations on reinfection with GABHS. The pathophysiology of this disorder is thought to be the result of antibodies against the GABHS, which cross-react with neuronal antigens, particularly in the basal ganglia. Both intravenous immunoglobulin and plasma exchange have been shown to produce clinical improvement. These intriguing data suggest that brain antigens may become direct targets of autoimmune processes, leading to neuropsychiatric disorders with protean manifestations.

## Psychiatric Illness and Immune Function

During the past several decades, a tremendous amount of information has been amassed from investigations of immune parameters in the major psychiatric illnesses. The research falls into the two broad categories of enumerative and functional studies as noted above. Cell numbers, lymphocyte proliferation, and cytokine production have been examined in patient populations. NK cell activity and cytokine and acute phase protein levels in the blood have also been measured. Finally, DTH and antibody production against vaccines or latent viruses have been evaluated. These measures have been used in efforts to understand immune functioning in psychiatric disorders such as major depression, schizophrenia, bipolar disorder, and anxiety disorders.

## Depression

The question of altered immunity in major depression has received the most attention with regard to the relationship among the nervous, endocrine, and immune systems in psychiatric disorders. Early work suggested that major depression is accompanied by impaired immunity, but subsequent studies present a more complicated picture. Findings of immune changes accompanying depression have included decreased lymphocyte count, increased neutrophil number, decreased mitogen responses of peripheral blood lymphocytes, and decreased NK cell activity (Table 4–5). At least two meta-analyses have confirmed these findings. Nevertheless, although the results in toto suggest immune alterations in depressed patients, important exceptions are apparent, indicating that the findings are not reproducible across studies. For example, Schleifer et al. (1989) and Andreoli et al. (1993) failed to detect differences in immune function in depressed patients who were compared with carefully matched control subjects. These two studies controlled for a number of relevant variables, including age, gender, severity of depression, level of physical activity, and ethanol and tobacco use. Although no mean differences between groups of depressed and nondepressed patients were found, particular subgroups of depressed patients in these and other studies have been shown to exhibit immune abnormalities. When immune changes are found in depression, they typically accompany other characteristics of depressed patients. For example, although Schleifer and colleagues found no differences in mean values of immune measures between depressed and nondepressed groups, greater age and more severe depression were associated with decreases in CD4+ cell numbers and mitogen responsiveness of peripheral blood lymphocytes. Cover and Irwin (1994) reported that decreased NK cell activity in depressed patients was associated with sleep disturbance. Several studies have reported that male patients with depression are more likely to exhibit NK cell decreases than are female patients with depression (Evans et al. 1992). Decreased circulating levels of NK cells have also been associated with greater severity of depression (Evans et al. 1992). Thus, although depression as a factor in itself may not explain alterations in immune parameters, depression in the context of greater age, altered sleep, male gender, or more severe symptoms may be most likely to be associated with decreased immune parameters.

More recent research has addressed the possibility that depressed patients may exhibit activation of certain aspects of the immune response, particularly innate immunity as measured by acute phase proteins and proinflammatory cytokines. This possibility is consistent with the clinical observation of a high rate of depression in autoimmune and other immune-related diseases, demonstrating that depression can coexist with immune activation. Moreover, a syndrome of "sickness behavior"

**TABLE 4–5.** Summary of immune changes in major depression

**Peripheral blood**
  Decreased lymphocyte number
  Increased neutrophil number
  Decreased peripheral blood lymphocyte responses to mitogens
  Decreased natural killer cell activity
  Increased IL-6, soluble IL-6-receptor, soluble IL-2-receptor
  Decreased IL-2
  Increased acute phase proteins (C-reactive protein, $\alpha_1$-acid glycoprotein, haptoglobin, $\alpha_1$-antitrypsin, complement protein C4)

**Cerebrospinal fluid**
  Decreased IL-6, soluble IL-6-receptor
  Increased IL-1$\beta$

*Note.* IL=interleukin.

resembling major depression occurs with the administration of cytokine therapies such as IFN-$\alpha$ and IL-2 (Dantzer et al. 1999). Prominent features of this syndrome include depressed mood, anhedonia, sleep and appetite disturbances, malaise, and poor concentration. Because of the resemblance of the syndrome of sickness behavior to major depression, levels of serum cytokines and acute phase proteins in depressed patients have received special attention. A variety of results have subsequently been reported regarding abnormalities in serum levels of cytokines and acute phase proteins in major depression (see Table 4–5). Overall patterns found in serum cytokine levels include increases in the proinflammatory cytokine IL-6, increases in soluble IL-6 receptor (sIL-6R) and sIL-2R, and a decrease in IL-2. Increases in acute phase proteins such as C-reactive protein, serum haptoglobin, the complement protein C4, $\alpha_1$-acid glycoprotein, and $\alpha_1$-antitrypsin have also been reported in several well-controlled studies. Not all studies have confirmed the findings of serum cytokine alterations, however. A large study by Haack and colleagues (1999) examined serum cytokine levels in 361 psychiatric inpatients with a variety of diagnoses compared with healthy control subjects. After accounting for many individual variables such as gender, smoking status, and body mass index, the only differences found in major depression were slightly decreased serum levels of TNF-$\alpha$ and soluble TNF-$\alpha$ receptor p55.

In recent work, Stubner and colleagues (1999) measured cytokine levels in the CSF of patients with depression and compared these levels with those measured in control subjects. They studied 20 elderly patients and

20 matched control subjects. It should be noted that all patients except one were taking psychotropic medication. This study found decreased levels of IL-6 and sIL-6R in the CSF of depressed patients compared with control subjects. Levine and colleagues (1999) assayed CSF of hospitalized depressed patients compared with 10 control subjects and found higher levels of IL-1β, lower levels of IL-6, and no change in TNF-α levels in the CSF.

A few studies have examined measures of immune activation following recovery from depression. Seidel and colleagues (1995) found significantly higher mitogen-induced production of IFN-γ and sIL-2R in inpatients with depression compared with control subjects. These parameters normalized over six weeks of successful treatment. Initially increased serum levels of C-reactive protein, haptoglobin, and $\alpha_2$-macroglobulin also normalized over this time period.

## Schizophrenia

The search for a cause of schizophrenia has led to the immune system for several reasons. First, the possibility of a viral (or bacterial) infection (superinfection) during neural development has been suggested by several epidemiologic studies (Yolken and Torrey 1995). Findings include 1) an increased likelihood in schizophrenic patients of having been born in late winter or spring; 2) an association between viral epidemics during pregnancy and later development of schizophrenia in the offspring; and 3) an increased presence of older siblings in the household (thought to be a potential source for viral infections) during pregnancies resulting in schizophrenic offspring. Moreover, the clinical presentation of schizophrenia, particularly the early prodromal symptoms, neurological "soft signs," and the global dysfunction caused by the disease suggest the possibility of early disruption in brain development.

Specific measures of immune function in schizophrenia have presented an overall pattern of immune activation in this illness. Table 4–6 summarizes immune alterations that have been reported in schizophrenia. Increased numbers of immune cells such as B cells, CD4+ lymphocytes, and monocytes have been reported in multiple studies. In at least two studies, a subset of patients have exhibited increased numbers of CD5+ B cells, a B cell subset associated with autoimmune disease (McAllister et al. 1989; Printz et al. 1999).

Despite the changes in cell numbers, there have been conflicting reports regarding alterations in lymphocyte responses to mitogens and NK cell activity. Studies have reported increases (Yovel et al. 2000), decreases (Abdeljaber et al. 1994; Ganguli et al. 1995; Sasaki et al. 1994),

**TABLE 4–6.** Summary of immune changes in schizophrenia

**Peripheral blood**

Increased number of B cells, CD4+ lymphocytes, monocytes

Increased number of CD5+ cells

Increased soluble IL-2-receptor

Increased IL-2 levels in serum

Decreased IL-2 production by mitogen-stimulated lymphocytes

Increased levels of haptoglobin, fibrinogen, complement proteins C3C and C4, $\alpha_1$-acid glycoprotein, hemopexin

**Cerebrospinal fluid**

Increased IL-2

Increased soluble IL-6-receptor

Increased IL-10

Increased $\alpha_2$-haptoglobin

Increased soluble intercellular adhesion molecule

Increased albumin

*Note.* IL = interleukin.

and no change (Caldwell et al. 1991). Factors such as smoking status may confound the results of these functional studies, particularly NK cell activity.

Several specific cytokines have been implicated in schizophrenia, including IL-6 and IL-2. Increases in serum IL-6 levels have been reported in schizophrenic patients, particularly in those with longer duration of illness or more severe symptomatology. Increases in serum sIL-2R concentrations have also been found, possibly representing a state marker for schizophrenia, because the increases were seen only in the affected twin of nonconcordant twin pairs (Ganguli and Rabin 1989). The involvement of IL-2 in schizophrenia is further suggested by the observation that IL-2 administration can provoke psychotic symptoms and cognitive impairment in nonpsychiatric patients. An increased IL-2 level in the serum was also reported by Kim et al. (2000); however, in vitro production of IL-2 by stimulated lymphocytes was decreased, possibly representing lymphocyte "exhaustion" due to sustained in vivo IL-2 production versus a decreased capacity of lymphocytes to produce IL-2. In contrast to these abnormalities, Haack and colleagues (1999), in their large study of immune factors in psychiatric inpatients and psychiatrically healthy control subjects, found that the only abnormality in schizophrenia was a slightly decreased soluble TNF-α receptor p55 subunit.

Elevations in serum acute phase proteins, which are nonspecific accompaniments to inflammation, also have been reported in schizophrenia. Maes and colleagues (1997) reported elevations in haptoglobin, fibrinogen, the complement proteins C3C and C4, $\alpha_1$-acid glycoprotein, and hemopexin in schizophrenia. Other groups have found similar elevations in multiple acute phase proteins. A small postmortem study of brain tissue from schizophrenic patients found elevated levels of fibrinogen split products (Korschenhausen et al. 1996).

Studies of immune measures, including cytokines and their receptors and acute phase proteins, in the CSF of schizophrenic patients have produced inconsistent results, but taken together they suggest the presence of immune activation. An increase in CSF IL-2 has been reported in untreated schizophrenic patients (Licinio et al. 1993), although no change has been found in other studies. Increase in soluble IL-6 receptors in the CSF suggests immune activation, as the IL-6 receptor when bound to IL-6 increases its activity. A relationship has been suggested between high levels of sIL-6R in the CSF and positive symptoms of psychosis. Increased IL-10 in the CSF has been correlated to an increase in negative symptoms of psychosis. Other cytokines studied that have yielded conflicting results include IL-1 and TNF. An increase in the acute phase protein $\alpha_2$-haptoglobin has been found in CSF of schizophrenics. Elevated CSF levels of soluble intercellular adhesion molecule and albumin in schizophrenic patients suggest an impairment of the integrity of the blood-brain barrier in at least a subset of patients with schizophrenia. Impairment of blood-brain barrier integrity can accompany a process of immune activation.

The evidence of activation of aspects of the immune system, particularly the elevations in proinflammatory cytokines and IL-2, suggests that inflammation in response to infection or as part of an autoimmune process may contribute to schizophrenia. However, neither infectious agents nor autoantibodies to CNS antigens have been consistently identified in schizophrenia (Yolken and Torrey 1995). Other possible explanations for the development of schizophrenia include exposure to a viral infection early in development that disrupts neural development and is subsequently cleared from the body. In addition, an environmental stimulus may trigger a temporary autoimmune response similar to the cardiac injury that occurs in rheumatic fever after infection with β-hemolytic streptococci (Delves and Roitt 2000b). Clearly, more research in this area is required before any role of the immune system can be substantiated.

## Bipolar Disorder

Bipolar disorder has not received as much attention as depression or schizophrenia in the search for immune alterations. Presentations of the illness vary dramatically, and studies similarly vary in clinical status of the patients studied. The relapsing and remitting, chronic nature of the disorder highlights the question of state versus trait abnormalities in this illness in particular and in psychiatric illnesses in general.

A recently reported study by Tsai and colleagues (1999) used a case-control design to investigate several functional measures of immunity in patients with bipolar disorder during mania and after remission. Lymphocyte proliferative responses to the mitogen phytohemagglutinin were increased during the manic phase, as were plasma sIL-2R levels. These findings normalized after remission of the disease. Rapaport and colleagues (1999) reported increased levels of sIL-2R and sIL-6R in symptomatic patients with rapid-cycling bipolar disorder, which normalized after 30 days of treatment with lithium. Interestingly, levels of IL-2, sIL-2R, and sIL-6R were also increased in psychiatrically healthy volunteers who took lithium. These findings suggest that immune abnormalities occur in bipolar disorder, perhaps during acute phases of the illness. More work is needed in this area to determine what, if any, immune alterations occur in this disease and if these alterations represent state or trait changes.

# Mechanisms of Brain-Immune Interactions

There are many pathways through which the immune system and brain interact and mediate the complex relationships observed in various clinical conditions. These pathways involve nervous system innervation of lymphoid tissue, the expression of relevant receptors on immune cells for transmitters derived from the nervous system, and access to and presence of cytokines and their receptors in the brain.

## Neural Innervation of Immune Tissues

A primary mechanism by which the nervous and immune systems interact is via autonomic nervous system innervation of lymphoid tissues. Nerve fibers of the sympathetic branch of the autonomic nervous system have been best described and are found in the bone marrow, thymus, spleen, and lymph nodes (Felten et al. 1984; Giron et al. 1980; Williams et al. 1981). Nerve fibers arising from the vagus, phrenic, and recurrent laryngeal nerves with contributions from the stellate ganglia of the thoracic sympathetic chain innervate the thymus gland. The celiac ganglion provides sympathetic nerves to the spleen, and the bone marrow is innervated by nerve fibers arising from the level of the spinal cord associated with the location of the bone. Autonomic nervous system innervation of the lymph nodes is not as dense or as uniquely distributed as noted for the spleen or thymus. In general, sympathetic nerve fibers enter lymphoid tissues in association with the vascular supply. Although autonomic nerve fibers play an important role in regulating vascular tone, sympathetic (noradrenergic) nerve terminals as identified by tyrosine hydroxylase staining have been found deep in the parenchyma of immune tissues in close association with immune cells (Figure 4–3). Aside from catecholamines, other relevant neurotransmitters (neuropeptides) are expressed in nerve fibers innervating immune tissues, including neuropeptide Y, substance P, vasoactive intestinal peptide, calcitonin gene-related peptide, and corticotropin-releasing hormone. Interruption of autonomic nervous system fibers by pharmacologic or surgical means has been shown to release immune responses from the inhibitory influences of catecholamines and to block the effects of stress on immune function in the spleen. As an example of the bidirectional nature of nervous-immune system interactions, data suggest that locally released cytokines can influence neurotransmitter release from nerve fibers in immune tissues. Finally, stimulation of the vagus nerve has been shown to reduce the release of inflammatory cytokines in response to immune stimulation (Borovikova et al. 2000). These immunoregulatory effects of vagal nerve stimulation may be relevant to the recently described effects of vagus nerve stimulation on mood.

## Immune Cell Receptors for Neurally Derived Molecules

Cells of the immune system express receptors for a variety of molecules that are regulated or produced by the nervous system. The β-adrenergic receptor was one of the first receptors identified on lymphocytes, and over the years receptors for virtually all of the major neurotransmitters, hormones, and neuropeptides have been characterized on immune cells (Table 4–7).

Several important concepts are relevant to understanding the effects of neurally derived molecules on immune function. First, the expression of receptors is heterogeneous. For example, of the two types of receptors for adrenal steroids—mineralocorticoid receptors and glucocorticoid receptors—only glucocorticoid receptors are expressed in the thymus, whereas both glucocorticoid and mineralocorticoid receptors are expressed in the spleen. Related to heterogeneity in receptor expression in immune cells and tissues is heterogeneity in

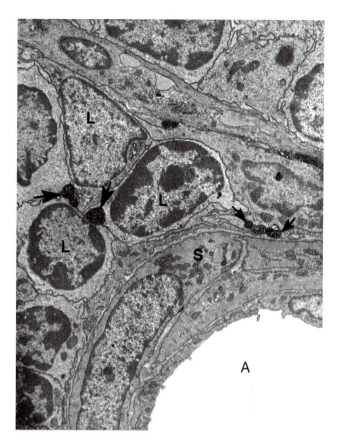

**FIGURE 4–3.** Sympathetic nervous system innervation of lymphoid tissue. Tyrosine hydroxylase-immunoreactive nerve processes (small arrowheads) in contact with the smooth muscle (S) of the central arteriole (A), and nerve processes (large arrowheads) in direct contact with lymphocytes (L) in the periarteriolar lymphatic sheath of the rat spleen. (Transmission electron micrograph, 6732×.)

*Source.* Courtesy of Denise L. Bellinger, Department of Neurology and Anatomy, University of Rochester School of Medicine and Dentistry, Rochester, NY. Reprinted with permission from Miller AH, Pariante CM, Pearce BD: "Immune System and Central Nervous System Interactions," in *Comprehensive Textbook of Psychiatry/VII.* Edited by Kaplan HI, Saddock BJ. Philadelphia, PA, Lippincott Williams & Wilkins, 2000, p. 123.

receptor density. For example, of the three subsets of T cells, the number of β-adrenergic receptors is highest for T suppressor cells, followed by T cytotoxic cells and then T helper cells.

Heterogeneity of both receptor expression and receptor density is important for understanding the sensitivities of the various immune cells and tissues to circulating hormones and is important for determining the net effect of those agents on immune function in vivo.

A second important concept is that the microenvironment of any given tissue is critical in determining hormonal or neurotransmitter influences on immune function. This concept even applies to circulating factors

**TABLE 4–7.** Receptors expressed on immune cells for neurotransmitters, hormones, and peptides

| Neurotransmitters | Hormones | Peptides |
|---|---|---|
| Acetylcholine | Corticosteroids | ACTH |
| Dopamine | (glucocorticoids, | α-MSH |
| Histamine | mineralocorticoids) | AVP |
| Norepinephrine | Gonadal steroids | Calcitonin |
| Serotonin | (estrogen, | CGRP |
|  | progesterone, | CRH |
|  | testosterone) | GHRH |
|  | Growth hormone | GnRH |
|  | Prolactin | IGF-I |
|  | Opioids (endorphins, | Melatonin |
|  | enkephalins) | NPY |
|  | Thyroid hormone | PTH |
|  |  | Somatostatin |
|  |  | Substance P |
|  |  | TRH |
|  |  | TSH |
|  |  | VIP |

*Note.* ACTH = adrenocorticotropin; α-MSH = α-melanocyte-stimulating hormone; AVP = arginine vasopressin; CGRP = calcitonin gene-related peptide; CRH = corticotropin-releasing hormone; GHRH = growth hormone–releasing hormone; GnRH = gonadotropin-releasing hormone; IGF-I = insulin-like growth factor I; NPY = neuropeptide Y; PTH = parathyroid hormone; TRH = thyrotropin-releasing hormone; TSH = thyroid-stimulating hormone; VIP = vasoactive intestinal peptide.

whose access to receptors of local immune cells is dependent on a host of tissue enzymes and binding proteins. Thus, the influence of any given molecule on the immune system is a function of 1) the type of cell that exhibits the relevant receptor, 2) the density of the receptors on that cell, and 3) whether that cell is located in an immune compartment that allows access of the relevant molecule to the receptor under the conditions being studied. Finally, crosstalk between receptor-associated signal transduction pathways is an important biochemical mechanism by which neurally derived or regulated molecules influence the immune response.

## Major Pathways of Brain to Immune Signaling

Given the above-noted capacity of the immune system to receive signals from the nervous and endocrine systems, investigators have begun to tease apart the relative contributions of the two major outflow pathways activated by stress: the hypothalamic-pituitary-adrenal (HPA) axis and the sympathetic nervous system (SNS) (Figure 4–4).

## Hypothalamic-Pituitary-Adrenal Axis

Glucocorticoids, the final product of HPA axis activation, have well-documented effects on multiple aspects of the immune system (Dhabhar and McEwen 2001; McEwen et al. 1997; Schleimer and Claman 1989; Wilckens and DeRijk 1997). Glucocorticoids influence the immune response by (1) modulating the trafficking of immune cells throughout the body (Dhabhar et al. 1995, 1996; A.H. Miller et al. 1994); (2) inhibiting cytokine production and function through interaction of glucocorticoid receptors with transcription factors (e.g., AP-1, NF-kappa B), which in turn regulate cytokine gene expression and/or the expression of cytokine-inducible genes (Almawi et al. 1990, Auphan et al. 1995; Vacca et al. 1992); (3) inhibiting the generation of products of the arachidonic acid pathway, which mediate inflammation (Goldstein et al. 1992; Schleimer et al. 1989); (4) inhibiting T cell–mediated and NK cell–mediated cytotoxicity (Nair and Schwartz 1984); (5) modulating cell death pathways in immature and mature cell types (J.J. Cohen 1989; Gonzalo et al. 1993; McEwen et al. 1997; Wyllie 1980); and (6) modulating the Th1/Th2 phenotype of the immune response by inhibiting Th1 (cell-mediated) responses and enhancing Th2 (antibody) responses (see Figure 4–2C).

Glucocorticoids mediate some of the acute effects of stress on the immune system, including the effects of stress on peripheral blood immune cell distribution and lymphocyte proliferative responses to mitogens in rodents and the inhibitory effects of stress on lymph node cellularity during viral infections in mice (Cunnick et al. 1990; Dhabhar et al. 1995, 1996; Hermann et al. 1995). Finally, as discussed below, glucocorticoids appear to mediate some of the effects of corticotropin-releasing hormone (CRH) on immune responses.

Although glucocorticoids are best known for their ability to mediate the immunosuppressive effects of stress (discussed below), it is important to mention that glucocorticoid hormones also play an important role in maintaining bodily homeostasis and protecting the body against an overshoot of potentially damaging immune activation (Munck and Guyre 1991). For example, neutralization of endogenous glucocorticoid function results in increases in pathologic symptoms and mortality rate in animals exposed to endotoxin (e.g., lipopolysaccharide) and autoimmunity-inducing stimuli (e.g., streptococcal cell wall antigen or myelin basic protein) (Bertini et al. 1988; Sternberg et al. 1989). Similar increases in pathologic symptoms have been found to occur after viral infections in the absence of glucocorticoids (A.H. Miller et al. 2000; Price et al. 1996; Ruzek et al. 1999). These

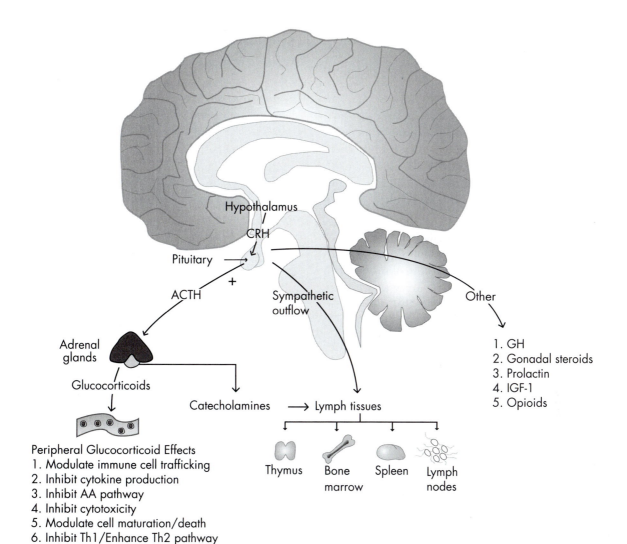

**FIGURE 4–4.** Neuroendocrine mechanisms by which the brain influences the immune system. Activation of the hypothalamic-pituitary-adrenal (HPA) axis and the sympathetic nervous system (SNS) by corticotropin-releasing hormone (CRH) results in the release of glucocorticoids and catecholamines by the adrenal glands and norepinephrine by SNS fibers that innervate immune tissues. Glucocorticoids have multiple immune-mediating effects: mobilizing cells to peripheral immune compartments (e.g., the skin), shaping the relative balance between helper T cell (Th) subtypes, and containing inflammation. Glucocorticoids also provide negative feedback on the HPA axis at several levels, including CRH. Activation of SNS fibers in lymphoid tissues also influences cellular migration and function and helps shape Th cell development. Opioids, sexually dimorphic hormones, growth hormone (GH), and insulin-like growth factor-1 (IGF-1) released from the brain and pituitary also have multiple effects on immunity and in turn can interact with HPA axis and SNS influences.

*Note.* AA = arachidonic acid.

data support the notions that glucocorticoids are immunomodulators and that the ultimate effects of stress-induced elevations in glucocorticoids are a function of the context within which they occur.

## Sympathetic Nervous System

As might be anticipated by the pattern of nervous innervation of lymphoid tissues, abrogation of stress-induced immune changes by antagonizing the SNS (as noted

above) is most apparent in solid immune tissues such as the spleen. For example, Cunnick et al. (1990) showed that stress-induced suppression of splenic lymphocyte proliferation to polyclonal mitogens is not influenced by adrenalectomy but is markedly attenuated by β-adrenergic receptor antagonists. Based on this and other studies (Cunnick et al. 1992; A.H. Miller et al. 1990), it is apparent that different neuroendocrine mechanisms can be operative in different immune compartments. Specifically, immune responses in the peripheral blood seem to be more influenced by glucocorticoids, whereas immune responses in the spleen seem to be more sensitive to catecholamines.

In humans, the SNS appears to play an important role in the immune changes induced by brief experimental stressors, as suggested by the rapid onset of these changes and the higher sensitivity of subjects with increased cardiovascular responses (Herbert et al. 1994). Moreover, the majority of the effects of acute laboratory stressors are blocked by pretreatment with β-adrenergic receptor antagonists (Bachen et al. 1995). Administration of catecholamines to humans transiently produces immune changes similar both qualitatively and quantitatively to those observed with acute stress (Benschop et al. 1996; Crary et al. 1983; Landmann et al. 1984; Maisel et al. 1989). Catecholamines also have been shown to decrease the number of adhesion molecules on lymphocytes (Mills and Dimsdale 1996; Rogers et al. 1999), suggesting that increased SNS activity may alter numbers of circulating lymphocytes by decreasing endothelial adhesion of these cells. Interestingly, acute stress has likewise been shown to decrease the adhesion molecule L-selectin on lymphocytes (Mills and Dimsdale 1996). Evidence of increased sympathetic activity has also been described in subjects experiencing chronic life stress (Uchino et al. 1992), and therefore it is likely that the SNS plays a role in certain of the immune changes occurring in association with naturalistic stressors as well.

## Corticotropin-Releasing Hormone

CRH is one of the major factors that regulate interactions between the nervous and immune systems during stress and neuropsychiatric disorders, including both affective and anxiety disorders. CRH released from the paraventricular nucleus in the hypothalamus is a central regulatory neuropeptide in the coordination of the neuroendocrine response to stress and in turn activates both the pituitary-adrenal axis and the SNS. Figure 4–5 presents an overview of feedback pathways among the HPA axis, the sympathetic nervous system, and the immune system. The immunologic effects of CRH on a wide range of immune functions have been extensively characterized (Irwin 1993; Irwin et al. 1988, 1990). Intracerebroventricular administration of CRH to laboratory animals has been found to suppress NK cell activity (Irwin et al. 1988) in the spleen and inhibit in vivo and in vitro antibody formation, including the generation of an immunoglobulin G response to immunization with keyhole-limpet hemocyanin (Irwin 1993; Leu and Singh 1993).

CRH-overproducing mice also exhibit immune deficits characterized by a profound decrease in the number of B cells and severely diminished primary and memory antibody responses (Stenzel-Poore et al. 1996). Long-term intracerebroventricular administration of CRH and short-term infusion of CRH into the locus coeruleus have been shown to suppress lymphocyte proliferative responses to nonspecific mitogens and T cell responses to T cell receptor antibody (Caroleo et al. 1993; Labeur et al. 1995; Rassnick et al. 1994).

CRH also has been found to stimulate the release of proinflammatory cytokines in both laboratory animals and humans. For example, long-term intracerebroventricular administration of CRH to rats led to induction of IL-1β mRNA in splenocytes, and short-term intravenous infusion of CRH in humans led to an almost fourfold induction of IL-1α (Labeur et al. 1995; Schulte et al. 1994). Both treatments also led to significant increases in the immunoregulatory cytokine IL-2 (Labeur et al. 1995; Schulte et al. 1994). In addition, CRH has also been found to induce the release of IL-1 and IL-6 from human mononuclear cells in vitro (Leu and Singh 1992; Paez Pereda et al. 1995).

In the periphery, CRH may play a role in inflammatory responses (Karalis et al. 1991, 1997). Local production of CRH has been demonstrated in inflammatory diseases such as ulcerative colitis (Kawahito et al. 1995) and arthritis, in which it has been suggested that it acts as a local proinflammatory agent (Nishioka et al. 1996). Recent evidence also suggests that CRH may act as a protective factor against inflammation-induced pain (Lariviere and Melzack 2000; Schafer et al. 1994) and plasma extravasation (Yoshihara et al. 1995).

Taken together, these results indicate that CRH has immunosuppressive effects on in vivo cellular and humoral responses while having a stimulatory effect on cytokine production and local inflammation.

As for mechanisms by which CRH influences immune responses, the sympathetic ganglionic blocker chlorisondamine has been shown to reverse CRH-induced inhibition of NK cell activity in the spleen (Irwin et al. 1988), indicating that the SNS plays a major role in this effect. The HPA axis is also involved, as was shown by Labeur and colleagues (1995), who demonstrated that the effects of long-term intracerebroventricular CRH administration on splenocyte proliferative responses are eliminated by adrenalectomy. In addition, the B cell decreases found in CRH-overproducing mice are very consistent with the marked reduction in rodent B cells found after long-term exposure to glucocorticoids (A.H. Miller et al. 1994).

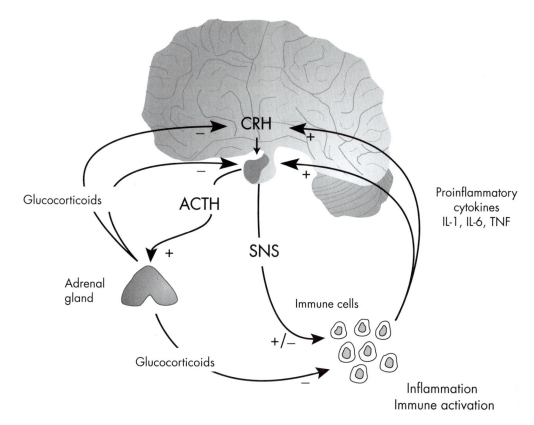

**FIGURE 4–5.** Bidirectional interactions between the immune system and brain. Immune cells produce cytokines, which stimulate the hypothalamic-pituitary-adrenal (HPA) axis at both the hypothalamus and pituitary. HPA activation results in glucocorticoid release by the adrenal glands via stimulation of pituitary ACTH. Glucocorticoids, in turn, provide negative feedback to the HPA axis and generally inhibit inflammation. Sympathetic nervous system (SNS) outflow—particularly to lymph tissues such as spleen, bone marrow, and lymph nodes—has a variety of effects on immune cell trafficking and function.

## Other Factors

Aside from glucocorticoids and catecholamines, there are numerous other mediators that have been examined for their relevance to interactions among the nervous, endocrine, and immune systems. Of these, opioids, the gonadal steroids, prolactin, and growth hormone are briefly described below.

Opioids have well-known effects on the immune system as determined both in vitro and in vivo (Eisenstein and Hilburger 1998; Hall et al. 1998; Mellon and Bayer 1998; Sharp et al. 1998). Some of the most compelling findings are the profound suppression of a wide range of immune parameters after in vivo administration of morphine (Eisenstein and Hilburger 1998). Morphine inhibits several peripheral immune functions, including NK cell activity, mitogen-induced lymphocyte proliferation, and phagocytic cell function, and these effects are mediated by activation of central opioid receptors (primarily the μ receptor) (Eisenstein and Hilburger 1998; Hall et al. 1998; Mellon and Bayer 1998; Sharp et al. 1998).

Short-term effects of morphine are mediated in large part by the SNS, whereas more chronic effects are mediated by activation of the HPA axis (Mellon and Bayer 1998). Direct effects of morphine on immune cell function are also involved (Sharp et al. 1998). In addition, endogenous opioids appear to play a role in modulating immune responses following stress (Sharp et al. 1998). For example, rats subjected to a foot-shock paradigm known to be associated with opioid analgesia exhibited decreased NK cell activity that was prevented by administration of the opioid antagonist naltrexone (Shavit et al. 1984). Of note, Yin et al. (2000) recently reported that the effects of endogenous opioids in mediating the immunologic effects of stress were independent of the HPA axis and occurred through induction of increased cell loss (apoptosis) in the spleen.

The role of gonadal steroids in regulating immune responses is exemplified by the sexual dimorphism in immune function (Martin 2000; Whitacre et al. 1999). Adult women have more exuberant antibody responses to immune challenge, reject transplanted tissues more vigorously, are more susceptible to allergies, and live longer than adult men (Martin 2000). The majority of the approximately 40 autoimmune disorders are more common in women. In part, it is believed that the differences in immune responsiveness are secondary to a greater propensity in women to develop a Th1 response after infectious challenge or antigen exposure (except during pregnancy, when a Th2 propensity prevails) (Whitacre et al. 1999). The etiology of these sex differences in immune function is secondary to a combination of the direct effects of sexually dimorphic hormones, including estrogens, progesterone, androgens, prolactin, growth hormone, and insulin-like growth factor I on immune function and the influence of gonadal steroids on the development of nervous and immune system cells and tissues (Martin 2000). As noted, immune cells express receptors for these sexually dimorphic hormones, and evidence suggests that the enzymes that synthesize gonadal steroids are expressed in immune tissues (Martin 2000). Estrogens tend to promote Th1-type responses, whereas progesterone tends to promote Th2-type responses (Whitacre et al. 1999) (see Figure 4–2C). Testosterone exhibits anti-inflammatory and immunosuppressive properties, as determined in animal models of autoimmunity (Whitacre et al. 1999). During pregnancy, when progesterone predominates, Th2-type immune responses prevail and autoimmune disorders related to excessive Th1-like activity (MS and RA) improve (Whitacre et al. 1999). Diseases related to Th2-like activity (SLE) are exacerbated during pregnancy (Martin 2000; Whitacre et al. 1999). In a related fashion, studies indicate that periods of high estrogen level correlate with increased susceptibility to stress-induced lung tumor colonization in laboratory animals. This increased vulnerability to a tumor challenge is mediated by an increased sensitivity to adrenergic (catecholamine) suppression of NK cell activity (Ben-Eliyahu et al. 2000).

In addition to direct effects on the immune system, gonadal steroids also have been shown to modulate the HPA axis response to stress (Torpy and Chrousos 1996). Thus, gonadal hormones also may influence immune responses indirectly through effects on HPA axis–immune pathways.

Finally, studies conducted on hypophysectomized rats show that the stress-induced suppression of peripheral blood lymphocyte proliferative responses to the mitogen phytohemagglutinin is more pronounced in stressed, hypophysectomized animals than in stressed intact animals (controls) (Keller et al. 1988). These findings suggest that pituitary hormones may be involved in counteracting stress-induced immunosuppressive mechanisms. The specific pituitary-dependent mitigating or

compensating hormones are not known, but they likely include growth hormone or prolactin, both of which have been shown to have immune-enhancing properties and maintain basal immunocompetence (Ader et al. 2001; Venters et al. 2001; Yu-Lee 1997). Other endogenous hormones, including dehydroepiandrosterone (DHEA) and its metabolite androstenediol, may also be involved in counteracting stress-induced immune changes (Padgett and Sheridan 1999; Padgett et al. 1997; Regelson et al. 1994).

## Biochemical Pathways

As far as the biochemical mechanisms of the effects of stress on the immune system are concerned, it is important to note that nitric oxide (NO) has been shown to be involved in the physiologic and pathologic responses to stress in various tissues, including tissues of the immune system. NO is a ubiquitous molecule that is involved in very different phenomena (e.g., blood vessel tone, gastric mucosa protection, neurotoxicity, and macrophage function) and acts mainly by forming covalent linkages to several targets such as enzymes. NO production in the immune system has been shown to be induced in acutely stressed rats (Persoons et al. 1995). Moreover, it has been found that stress-induced NO production by macrophages is involved in stress-induced decreases in the lymphocyte proliferative response, since both the depletion of macrophages and the addition of the NO synthesis inhibitor $N(G)$-methyl-L-arginine acetate (L-NMMA) attenuate stress-induced immune changes (Coussons-Read et al. 1994).

## Pathways of Immune to Brain Signaling

Research lending support to the importance of interactions between the immune system and the CNS includes the discovery that cytokines are capable of exerting profound effects on the nervous and endocrine systems. Since cytokines do not freely cross the blood-brain barrier under usual circumstances (i.e., in the absence of CNS infection), considerable attention has been paid to how peripheral immune signals are transmitted to the brain (Watkins et al. 1995). Several mechanisms have been proposed (Table 4–8). For example, it has been suggested that local (peripheral) production of proinflammatory cytokines can stimulate visceral afferent nerve fibers, which in turn communicate with the brain through the vagus nerve. Ultimately, this mechanism modulates CNS function (e.g., CRH release for the hypothalamus) through interconnected neuronal circuits involving ascending catecholaminergic fibers (A2 and C2 cell groups) of the nucleus of the solitary tract, which project to the parvocellular division of the paraventricular nucleus of the hypothalamus (Cunningham et al. 1990; Ericsson et al. 1994; Watkins et al. 1995). Lending support to the idea that the vagus nerve mediates communication between peripheral cytokines and the CNS is the observation that the hyperthermia induced by intraperitoneally administered IL-1β can be blocked by transection of the subdiaphragmatic vagus nerve (Watkins et al. 1995). Moreover, data indicate that afferent signals traveling through the vagus nerve may also mediate in part the effects of local cytokines on hyperalgesia, increased HPA axis activation, and conditioned taste aversion (Maier et al. 1998). Circulating cytokines also may enter the brain in regions where the blood-brain barrier is leaky, allowing passive diffusion into the brain parenchyma and entry into CSF flow pathways (Rivest et al. 2000; Schobitz et al. 1994). For example, a high dose of IL-1 causes the induction of the early immediate gene, *c-fos*, in two such leaky regions, the area postrema and the vascular organ of the lamina terminalis (Brady et al. 1994; Ericsson et al. 1994). Cytokines can also communicate with the brain through intermediates without themselves entering the CNS parenchyma, for example, by acting on cells of the brain endothelium or choroid plexus and inducing the release of secondary messengers, including prostaglandins and nitric oxide (Schobitz et al. 1994). Active transport mechanisms for proinflammatory cytokines provide another mechanism by which small quantities of proinflammatory cytokines may reach neuroendocrine regulatory circuits (Banks and Kastin 1991; Banks et al. 1995; Plotkin et al. 1996). Finally, immune activation and possibly stress can disrupt the blood-brain barrier and may upregulate the active transport of proinflammatory cytokines into the brain, thereby facilitating the communication of peripheral immune signals with CNS targets.

---

**TABLE 4–8.** Mechanisms by which cytokines signal the brain

Local cytokines (in periphery) stimulate peripheral afferent nerve fibers

Passive diffusion at leaky regions in the blood-brain barrier

Active transport across blood-brain barrier

Stimulation of endothelium or choroid plexus to produce secondary messengers

---

Once cytokines enter the brain, the signals can be transmitted and amplified within the context of the cytokine network in the brain (Benveniste 1998; Quan et al. 1999; Rothwell et al. 1996). Receptors for proinflam-

matory cytokines are located in the brain, including brain regions that play important roles in vegetative functions, emotional regulation, and memory (Benveniste 1998; Besedovsky and del Rey 1996; Schobitz et al. 1994). IL-1β and its mRNA have been found in nerve cell bodies and nerve fibers within the hypothalamus, the hippocampus, and other regions in human and rodent brains. Furthermore, there is accumulating evidence that several cytokines derived from neural cells may act as intermediaries in communicating peripheral inflammatory signals to the brain. For example, peripheral injection of lipopolysaccharide and circulating cytokines such as IL-1 have been shown to induce neural cells within the hypothalamus and other brain regions to produce proinflammatory cytokines such as IL-1, IL-6, and TNF (Gatti and Bartfai 1993; Laye et al. 1994; Quan et al. 1994; Spangelo et al. 1990; van Dam et al. 1992). Furthermore, recent studies suggest that such autoinduction of cytokines can be transmitted indirectly through vagal pathways discussed above (Laye et al. 1995; Watkins et al. 1995). For example, direct stimulation of the vagus nerve has been shown to induce IL-1β mRNA in the hypothalamus and hippocampus (Hosoi et al. 2000). Thus, during immune activation, peripherally released cytokines could either cross the blood-brain barrier (e.g., at leaky sites or through active transport mechanisms) or activate peripheral afferents and consequently recruit local neural cells to produce other cytokines such as IL-1, IL-6 or TNF, thereby amplifying cytokine signals in relevant brain areas. Among neural cells, activated glia (especially microglia) are rich sources of proinflammatory cytokines. Activated microglia and astrocytes can produce large quantities of IL-1, and virus-induced proinflammatory cytokines are potent stimulants of glial activation (Schobitz et al. 1994). Finally, recent data suggest that nonimmunologic stressors can induce cytokine expression in the brain, suggesting that the behavioral and neuroendocrine responses to stress may involve cytokine signaling pathways (Nguyen et al. 1998).

The impact of cytokines on CNS function has been examined in numerous in vitro and in vivo studies. Cytokines have been shown to influence neurotransmitter turnover and electrophysiologic responses in the CNS (Brebner et al. 2000; Dunn 2001; Dunn and Wang 1995; Dunn et al. 1999). For example, after short-term administration, IL-1 has been shown to increase the release and metabolism of several monoamines, including norepinephrine and serotonin. In addition, both IL-2 and IFN-α have been shown to alter dopamine metabolism. Most studies have focused on short-term administration of cytokines, and therefore very little is known about the long-term effects of cytokine exposure (as might occur in chronic inflammatory disorders). Of note, cytokines also appear to have significant effects on long-term potentiation (Jankowsky and Patterson 1999), raising the intriguing hypothesis that cytokines can have lasting influences on memory, behavior, and endocrine responses by affecting the synaptic plasticity of relevant neuronal circuits.

Acting at the level of the hypothalamus, the pituitary, and the adrenal glands, immune system products—including IL-1, IL-2, IL-6, leukemia inhibitory factor, and TNF—appear to play a role in the regulation of sleep, temperature, feeding behavior, and the secretion of multiple hormones, most notably glucocorticoids (Besedovsky and del Rey 1996, Chesnokova and Melmed 2000). Based on a series of studies examining the mechanisms by which proinflammatory cytokines such as IL-1 and IL-6 lead to HPA axis activation, a major final common pathway involves cytokine induction of CRH in the paraventricular nucleus of the hypothalamus (Berkenbosch et al. 1987; Besedovsky and del Rey 1996; Bethin et al. 2000; Kovacs and Elenkov 1995; Matta et al. 1992; Naitoh et al. 1988; Rivier 1995; Schmidt et al. 1995; Spinedi et al. 1992; Suda et al. 1990). In addition to actions through CRH secretion, cytokines may regulate glucocorticoid release through multiple alternate pathways, including direct effects on the pituitary or adrenal glands (Besedovsky and del Rey 1996; Callahan and Piekut 1997; Kovacs and Elenkov 1995; Matta et al. 1992; Naitoh et al. 1988; Pearce et al. 1999a, 1999b; Perlstein et al. 1993; Spinedi et al. 1992). The simultaneous release of adrenocorticotropic hormone (ACTH)-like and $\beta$ endorphin–like products in response to a variety of stimuli, including CRH, indicates that immunocytes (probably macrophages), like pituitary cells, are capable of transcribing the proopiomelanocortin gene, which is responsible for coding the precursor protein from which ACTH and $\beta$ endorphin are derived. Other hormones found to be secreted by immunocytes include somatostatin, vasoactive intestinal polypeptide, thyrotropin, and prolactin. Lymphocyte production of an ACTH-like hormone suggests that immunocytes may be capable of tapping directly into the HPA axis at the level of the adrenal gland, giving rise to a so-called lymphoid-adrenal axis.

Behavioral effects of cytokines include the induction of a syndrome referred to as "sickness behavior" in humans and laboratory animals that has many features in common with major depression, including anhedonia, listlessness, altered sleep patterns, reduced appetite, and social withdrawal (see below) (Bluthe et al. 1997; Connor and Leonard 1998; Kelley et al. 1997; Kent et al. 1992; Krueger et al. 1995; Plata-Salaman et al. 1996). There are several pathways by which cytokines (especially proinflammatory cytokines) could contribute to the development of major depression during cytokine therapies or medical illnesses associated with significant inflammatory processes (Figure 4–6). First, IL-1, IL-6, and TNF-$\alpha$ have all been shown to be potent inducers of CRH (Besedovsky and del Rey 1996; Besedovsky et al. 1986; Ericsson et al. 1994; Rivier 1995; Schobitz et al. 1994). CRH hypersecretion is believed to play a central role in the pathophysiology of depression, both in terms of the effects of CRH on behaviors that are known to be altered in depression (including activity, sleep, and feeding) and in terms of the role of CRH in the hyperactivity of the HPA axis, which characterizes a significant proportion of depressed patients (Owens and Nemeroff 1993). Second, proinflammatory cytokines have been shown to have significant effects on monamine turnover in key brain regions believed to be involved in mood disorders, including the hippocampus and hypothalamus (Brebner et al. 2000; Dunn and Wang 1995; Dunn et al. 1999). Third, cytokines have the capacity to induce the euthyroid sick syndrome that is characterized by normal TSH and T4 levels but reduced T3 level in the early stage and a normal TSH level but reduced T4 and T3 levels in the later stage (Papanicolaou 2000). Fourth, activation of the immune system by cytokines has been associated with activation of the enzyme indolamine 2,3-dioxygenase (IDO), which metabolizes tryptophan and leads to reduced tryptophan availability (Brown et al. 1991; Song et al. 1998). Depletion of tryptophan has been shown to precipitate depressive symptoms in vulnerable individuals (Moore et al. 2000). Finally, cytokines (especially IL-1) have been shown to disrupt glucocorticoid receptor function, which in turn could disrupt negative feedback pathways on CRH (contributing to CRH hypersecretion) and further release of cytokines (contributing to runaway inflammation) (A.H. Miller et al. 1999; Pariante and Miller, in press; Pariante et al. 1999).

## Immune to Brain: Clinical Effects of Cytokines

Cytokines such as IFN-$\alpha$, IFN-$\gamma$, and IL-2 are used to treat viral illnesses, including chronic hepatitis B and C, and malignancies such as malignant melanoma and renal cell carcinoma (Table 4–9) (Lerner et al. 1999; Meyers and Valentine 1995). These cytokines are known for a variety of constitutional and psychiatric side effects that frequently limit the dose and duration of treatment. Human recombinant forms of these immune mediators are typically administered in doses that are much higher than physiological doses. The pattern of their side effects may be divided into acute and chronic phases. The acute phase follows a single pattern of symptoms for different cytokines. Often described as a "flu-like" syndrome,

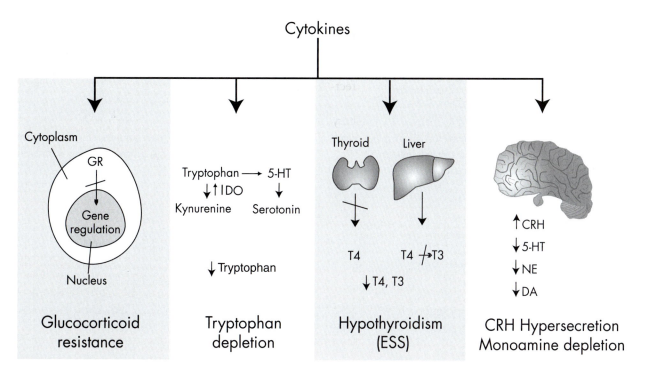

**FIGURE 4–6.** Potential mechanisms by which cytokines cause sickness behavior/depression. There are several potential mechanisms by which cytokines may induce behavioral symptoms in humans. At a cellular level, cytokines can induce glucocorticoid resistance by inhibiting glucocorticoid receptor (GR) translocation. Glucocorticoid resistance in turn releases corticotropin-releasing hormone (CRH) and proinflammatory cytokines from negative regulation by glucocorticoids. Cytokines can deplete tryptophan by increasing its conversion into kynurenine by the enzyme indolamine 2,3-dioxygenase (IDO). Tryptophan is the primary precursor of serotonin, and tryptophan depletion has been shown to precipitate depression in vulnerable individuals. Cytokines can inhibit production of T4 by the thyroid gland and the conversion of T4 to active T3 by the liver, leading to the euthyroid sick syndrome (ESS). In the brain, cytokines can stimulate secretion of CRH (which is elevated in the brains of patients with depression) and cause depletion of the monoamine neurotransmitters norepinephrine (NE), dopamine (DA), and 5-hydroxytryptophan (5-HT).

these effects are characterized by fever, chills, myalgias, nausea, vomiting, and malaise. The group of symptoms in the later phase of toxicity for the interferons is referred to as "sickness behavior," a syndrome of behavioral manifestations that resembles depression in humans (Dantzer et al. 1999). Symptoms can include psychomotor slowing, depressed mood, decreased concentration, fatigue, and altered sleep. This syndrome has become of interest to psychiatry because it so closely resembles major depression and suggests some potential mechanisms involved in depression, especially in medically ill patients who have multiple sources of inflammation (and inflammatory cytokines) and high rates of depressive disorders. Other side effects of the therapeutic cytokines have included mania, psychotic symptoms, and disorientation occasionally to the point of delirium (Meyers 1999). Research into the effects of therapeutic cytokines and ways to mitigate their toxicity is ongoing.

## Psychopharmacology and Immune Function

Given the presence of relevant neurotransmitter receptors on immune cells, there logically has been interest in the relative impact on the immune system of psychopharmacologic agents that alter neurotransmitter availability and function.

### Antidepressants

A number of investigators have examined in vitro and in vivo immune function following treatment with antidepressants. In vitro studies indicate that antidepressants generally reduce immune responsiveness (Maes et al. 1999). For example, tricyclic antidepressants (TCAs) have been found to inhibit mitogen-induced lymphocyte

**TABLE 4–9.** Therapeutic uses of cytokines

| Cytokine | Clinical uses | Side effects |
|---|---|---|
| Granulocyte-macro-phage colony-stimu-lating factor (GM-CSF) | Neutropenia from cancer, chemotherapy, or bone marrow transplantation<br>AIDS | |
| IFN-α | Malignancies—malignant melanoma, Kaposi's sarcoma, hairy cell leukemia<br>Chronic hepatitis B and C | Fatigue, malaise, psychomotor slowing, cognitive changes—decreased concentration, decreased memory<br>Mania (rare) |
| IFN-β | Multiple sclerosis<br>Malignancies | Fatigue, malaise, psychomotor slowing |
| IFN-γ | Chronic granulomatous disease<br>Malignancies | Mild fatigue, malaise, dizziness, confusion |
| IL-2 | Malignancies—renal cell carcinoma, malignant melanoma<br>HIV | Fatigue, malaise, depression, neurotoxicity, somnolence, disorientation |
| Transforming growth factor beta | Multiple sclerosis<br>Myasthenia gravis | |

*Note.* IFN = interferon; IL = interleukin.

proliferation and NK cell activity (A.H. Miller et al. 1986), although at least one report has suggested that selective serotonin reuptake inhibitors (SSRIs) may increase NK cell function (Frank et al. 1999). Both TCAs and SSRIs have been associated with decreased monocyte or lymphocyte production of several cytokines, including TNF-α, IL-1β, IL-2, and IFN-γ. Release of the inhibitory cytokine IL-10 has been shown to be increased after in vitro administration of antidepressant.

In vivo studies have given more mixed results, likely due to the fact that immune changes during antidepressant therapy are a conglomeration of the direct effects of drugs on immune cell activity and the indirect effects of drugs on physiology and mood. Results of in vivo studies have ranged from no immunologic effect of antidepressant treatment (Brambilla and Maggioni 1998; Landmann et al. 1997; Schleifer et al. 1999) to normalization of altered immune parameters (Frank et al. 1999; Maes et al. 1997; Pariante and Miller 1995; Ravindran et al. 1998; Sluzewska et al. 1995) to decreases/increases in immune function during treatment. For example, Weizman et al. (1994) reported that IL-1β production increased during antidepressant treatment, whereas Seidel et al. (1995) reported that initially increased levels of acute phase proteins did not change during treatment, although initially increased levels of IL-2, IL-10, and IFN-γ returned to normal. Interestingly, recent data from both humans and laboratory animals indicate that pretreatment with antidepressants can block the development of sickness behavior during cytokine administration. Whether these clinical effects are mediated by direct effects of antidepressants on the release of proinflammatory cytokines remains to be determined.

## Antipsychotics

The most well-known effect of antipsychotic drugs on the immune system is clozapine-induced agranulocytosis, which is believed to be related to alterations in granulocyte-macrophage colony-stimulating factor (GM-CSF), an important signaling molecule in cell development in the bone marrow. Nevertheless, altered peripheral blood cytokine and cytokine receptor levels associated with antipsychotic treatment suggests that these agents have an effect on the cytokine network. Examples include an association between antipsychotics and decreased TNF concentrations and decreased concentrations of sIL-6R. In contrast to the effects on TNF and sIL-6R, increased levels of sIL-2R have been reported with antipsychotic administration. In a study by van Kammen et al. (1999), schizophrenic patients exhibited no statistically significant changes in concentrations of CSF IL-6 at baseline and no effects of antipsychotic drugs on CSF IL-6 levels during treatment.

## Conclusions

This chapter has provided a necessarily simplified overview of the fundamental concepts regarding interactions among the nervous, endocrine, and immune systems. The immune system has a documented capacity to receive signals from nervous system–derived transmitters, and more recent data indicate that immune signaling molecules (cytokines) have a profound impact on the CNS and endocrine system. Data from clinical studies indicate that these pathways of communication between the brain and immune system are relevant to the development, course, and outcome of both immunologically based diseases and neuropsychiatric disorders. Stress and depression have been shown to alter the development and course of cancer, infectious diseases, and autoimmune disorders, and activation of the immune system has been associated with depression and schizophrenia.

Nervous and immune system interactions represent an exciting new frontier in the understanding of the influence of the environment (internal and external) on the expression of genetic vulnerability to disease. New concepts of gene regulation coupled with elucidation of the specific neuroendocrine-immune pathways involved will undoubtedly lead to novel approaches to the prevention and treatment of immune and nervous system diseases. Appreciation of the complex interactions between bodily systems that mediate internal regulation is a critical component to understanding the development and outcome of all diseases.

# References

Abbas AK, Lichtman AH, Pober JS: Cellular and Molecular Immunology. Philadelphia, PA, WB Saunders, 2000

Abdeljaber MH, Nair MP, Schork MA, et al: Depressed natural killer cell activity in schizophrenic patients. Immunol Invest 23:259–268, 1994

Ader R, Friedman SB: Differential early experiences and susceptibility to transplanted tumors in the rat. J Comp Physiol 59:361–364, 1965

Ader R, Felten D, Cohen N (eds): Psychoneuroimmunology, 3rd Edition. New York, Academic Press, 2001

Almawi WY, Sewell KL, Hadro ET, et al: Mode of action of the glucocorticosteroids as immunosuppressive agents, in Molecular and Cellular Biology of Cytokines, Progress in Leukocyte Biology, Vol 10A. Edited by Oppenheim J, Powanda MC, Kluger MJ, et al. New York, Wiley-Liss, 1990, pp 321–326

Andreoli AV, Keller SE, Rabaeus M, et al: Depression and immunity: age, severity, and clinical course. Brain Behav Immun 7:279–292, 1993

Auphan N, DiDonato JA, Rosette C, et al: Immunosuppression by glucocorticoids: inhibition of NF-kappa B activity through induction of I kappa B synthesis. Science 270:286–290, 1995

Bachen EA, Manuck SB, Cohen S, et al: Adrenergic blockade ameliorates cellular immune responses to mental stress in humans. Psychosom Med 57:366–372, 1995

Banks WA, Kastin AJ: Blood to brain transport of interleukin links the immune and central nervous systems. Life Sci 48:PL117–PL121, 1991

Banks WA, Kastin AJ, Broadwell RD: Passage of cytokines across the blood-brain barrier. Neuroimmunomodulation 2:241–248, 1995

Baumann H, Gauldie J: The acute phase response. Immunol Today 15:74–80, 1994

Ben-Eliyahu S, Shakhar G, Shakhar K, et al: Timing within the oestrous cycle modulates adrenergic suppression of NK activity and resistance to metastasis: possible clinical implications. Br J Cancer 83:1747–1754, 2000

Benschop RJ, Godaert GL, Geenen R, et al: Relationships between cardiovascular and immunological changes in an experimental stress model. Psychol Med 25:323–327, 1995

Benschop RJ, Rodriguez-Feuerhahn M, Schedlowski M: Catecholamine-induced leukocytosis: early observations, current research, and future directions. Brain Behav Immun 10:77–91, 1996

Benveniste EN: Cytokine actions in the central nervous system. Cytokine Growth Factor Rev 9:259–275, 1998

Berkenbosch F, van Oers J, del Rey A, et al: Corticotropin-releasing factor–producing neurons in the rat activated by interleukin-1. Science 238:524–526, 1987

Bertini R, Bianchi M, Ghezzi P: Adrenalectomy sensitizes mice to the lethal effects of interleukin 1 and tumor necrosis factor. J Exp Med 167:1708–1712, 1988

Besedovsky HO, del Rey A: Immune-neuro-endocrine interactions: facts and hypotheses. Endocr Rev 17:64–102, 1996

Besedovsky H, del Rey A, Sorkin E, et al: Immunoregulatory feedback between interleukin-1 and glucocorticoid hormones. Science 233:652–654, 1986

Bethin KE, Vogt SK, Muglia LJ: Interleukin-6 is an essential, corticotropin-releasing hormone–independent stimulator of the adrenal axis during immune system activation. Proc Natl Acad Sci U S A 97:9317–9322, 2000

Bluthe RM, Dantzer R, Kelley KW: Central mediation of the effects of interleukin-1 on social exploration and body weight in mice. Psychoneuroendocrinology 22:1–11, 1997

Borovikova LV, Ivanova S, Zhang M, et al: Vagus nerve stimulation attenuates the systemic inflammatory response to endotoxin. Nature 405:458–462, 2000

Brady LS, Lynn AB, Herkenham M, et al: Systemic interleukin-1 induces early and late patterns of c-fos mRNA expression in brain. J Neurosci 14:4951–4964, 1994

Brambilla F, Maggioni M: Blood levels of cytokines in elderly patients with major depressive disorder. Acta Psychiatr Scand 97:309–313, 1998

Brebner K, Hayley S, Zacharko R, et al: Synergistic effects of interleukin-1 beta, interleukin-6, and tumor necrosis factor-alpha: central monoamine, corticosterone, and behavioral variations. Neuropsychopharmacology 22:566–580, 2000

Brown RR, Ozaki Y, Datta SP, et al: Implications of interferon-induced tryptophan catabolism in cancer, auto-immune diseases and AIDS. Adv Exp Med Biol 294:425–435, 1991

Buccheri G: Depressive reactions to lung cancer are common and often followed by a poor outcome. Eur Respir J 11:173–178, 1998

Burack JH, Barrett DC, Stall RD, et al: Depressive symptoms and CD4 lymphocyte decline among HIV-infected men. JAMA 270:2568–2573, 1993

Caldwell CL, Irwin M, Lohr J: Reduced natural killer cell cytotoxicity in depression but not in schizophrenia. Biol Psychiatry 30:1131–1138, 1991

Callahan TA, Piekut DT: Differential fos expression induced by IL-1 beta and IL-6 in rat hypothalamus and pituitary gland. J Neuroimmunol 73:207–211, 1997

Caroleo MC, Pulvirenti L, Arbitrio M, et al: Evidence that CRH microinfused into the locus coeruleus decreases cell-mediated immune response in rats. Funct Neurol 8:271–277, 1993

Chesnokova V, Melmed S: Leukemia inhibitory factor mediates the hypothalamic pituitary adrenal axis response to inflammation. Endocrinology 141:4032–4040, 2000

Chikanza IC, Petrou P, Kingsley G, et al: Defective hypothalamic response to immune and inflammatory stimuli in patients with rheumatoid arthritis. Arthritis Rheum 35:1281–1288, 1992

Chrousos GP, Gold PW: The concepts of stress and stress system disorders. Overview of physical and behavioral homeostasis. JAMA 267:1244–1252, 1992

Cohen F, Kemeny ME, Kearney KA, et al: Persistent stress as a predictor of genital herpes recurrence. Arch Intern Med 159:2430–2436, 1999

Cohen JJ: Lymphocyte death induced by glucocorticoids, in Anti-inflammatory Steroid Action, Basic and Clinical Aspects. Edited by Schleimer RP CH, Oronsky A. San Diego, CA, Academic Press, 1989, pp 110–131

Cohen S, Tyrrell DA, Smith AP: Psychological stress and susceptibility to the common cold. N Engl J Med 325:606–612, 1991

Cole SW, Kemeny ME: Psychosocial influences on the progression of HIV infection, in Psychoneuroimmunology. Edited by Ader R, Felton DL, Cohen N. San Diego, CA, Academic Press, 2001, pp 583–612

Connor TJ, Leonard BE: Depression, stress and immunological activation: the role of cytokines in depressive disorders. Life Sci 62:583–606, 1998

Courtney JG, Longnecker MP, Theorell T, et al: Stressful life events and the risk of colorectal cancer. Epidemiology 4:407–414, 1993

Coussons-Read ME, Maslonek KA, Fecho K, et al: Evidence for the involvement of macrophage-derived nitric oxide in the modulation of immune status by a conditioned aversive stimulus. J Neuroimmunol 50:51–58, 1994

Cover H, Irwin M: Immunity and depression: insomnia, retardation, and reduction of natural killer cell activity. J Behav Med 17:217–223, 1994

Crary B, Borysenko M, Sutherland DC, et al: Decrease in mitogen responsiveness of mononuclear cells from peripheral blood after epinephrine administration in humans. J Immunol 130:694–697, 1983

Cunnick JE, Lysle DT, Kucinski BJ, et al: Evidence that shock-induced immune suppression is mediated by adrenal hormones and peripheral beta-adrenergic receptors. Pharmacol Biochem Behav 36:645–651, 1990

Cunnick JE, Lysle DT, Kucinski BJ, et al: Stress-induced alteration of immune function. Diversity of effects and mechanisms. Ann N Y Acad Sci 650:283–287, 1992

Cunningham AJ, Edmonds CV, Jenkins GP, et al: A randomized controlled trial of the effects of group psychological therapy on survival in women with metastatic breast cancer. Psychooncology 7:508–517, 1998

Cunningham ET Jr, Bohn MC, Sawchenko PE: Organization of adrenergic inputs to the paraventricular and supraoptic nuclei of the hypothalamus in the rat. J Comp Neurol 292:651–667, 1990

DaCosta D, Dobkin PL, Pinard L, et al: The role of stress in functional disability among women with systemic lupus erythematosus: a prospective study. Arthritis Care Research 12:112–119, 1999

Dantzer R, Aubert A, Bluthe RM, et al: Mechanisms of the behavioural effects of cytokines. Adv Exp Med Biol 461:83–106, 1999

Delves PJ, Roitt IM: The immune system. First of two parts. N Engl J Med 343:37–49, 2000a

Delves PJ, Roitt IM: The immune system. Second of two parts. N Engl J Med 343:108–117, 2000b

Dhabhar FS, McEwen BS: Stress-induced enhancement of antigen-specific cell-mediated immunity. J Immunol 156:2608–2615, 1996

Dhabhar FS, McEwen BS: Bidirectional effects of stress and glucocorticoid hormones on immune function: possible explanations for paradoxical observations, in Psychoneuroimmunology, 2nd Edition. Edited by Ader R, Felten D, Cohen N. New York, Academic Press, 2001, pp 301–338

Dhabhar FS, Miller AH, McEwen BS, et al: Effects of stress on immune cell distribution: dynamics and hormonal mechanisms. J Immunol 154:5511–5527, 1995

Dhabhar FS, Miller AH, McEwen BS, et al: Stress-induced changes in blood leukocyte distribution. Role of adrenal steroid hormones. J Immunol 157:1638–1644, 1996

Dhabhar FS, Satoskar AR, Bluethmann H, et al: Stress-induced enhancement of skin immune function: a role for gamma interferon. Proc Natl Acad Sci U S A 97:2846–2851, 2000

Dunn AJ: Effects of cytokines and infections on brain neurochemistry, in Psychoneuroimmunology. Edited by Ader R, Felten DL, Cohen N. San Diego, CA, Academic Press, 2001, pp 649–666

Dunn AJ, Wang J: Cytokine effects on CNS biogenic amines. Neuroimmunomodulation 2:319–328, 1995

Dunn AJ, Wang J, Ando T: Effects of cytokines on cerebral neurotransmission. Comparison with the effects of stress. Adv Exp Med Biol 461:117–127, 1999

Edelman S, Lemon J, Bell DR, et al: Effects of group CBT on the survival time of patients with metastatic breast cancer. Psychooncology 8:474–481, 1999

Eisenstein TK, Hilburger ME: Opioid modulation of immune responses: effects on phagocyte and lymphoid cell populations. J Neuroimmunol 83:36–44, 1998

Ericsson A, Kovacs KJ, Sawchenko PE: A functional anatomical analysis of central pathways subserving the effects of interleukin-1 on stress-related neuroendocrine neurons. J Neurosci 14:897–913, 1994

Esterling BA, Kiecolt-Glaser JK, Glaser R: Psychosocial modulation of cytokine-induced natural killer cell activity in older adults. Psychosom Med 58:264–272, 1996

Evans DL, McCartney CF, Nemeroff CB, et al: Depression in women treated for gynecological cancer: clinical and neuroendocrine assessment. Am J Psychiatry 143:447–451, 1986

Evans DL, Folds JD, Petitto J, et al: Circulating natural killer cell phenotypes in males and females with major depression: relation to cytotoxic activity and severity of depression. Arch Gen Psychiatry 49:388–395, 1992

Evans DL, Leserman J, Perkins DO, et al: Stress-associated reductions of cytotoxic T lymphocytes and natural killer cells in asymptomatic HIV infection. Am J Psychiatry 152:543–550, 1995

Evans DL, Leserman J, Perkins DO, et al: Severe life stress as a predictor of early disease progression in HIV infection. Am J Psychiatry 154:630–634, 1997

Evans DL, Mason K, Bauer R, et al: Neuropsychiatric manifestations of HIV-1 infection and AIDS, in Psychopharmacology: The Fifth Generation of Progress. Edited by Charney D, Coyle J, Davis K, et al. New York, Raven Press (in press)

Everson SA, Goldberg DE, Kaplan GA, et al: Hopelessness and risk of mortality and incidence of myocardial infarction and cancer. Psychosom Med 58:113–121, 1996

Faller H, Bulzebruck H, Drings P, et al: Coping, distress, and survival among patients with lung cancer. Arch Gen Psychiatry 56:756–762, 1999

Fawzy FI, Fawzy NW, Hyun CS, et al: Malignant melanoma. Effects of an early structured psychiatric intervention, coping, and affective state on recurrence and survival 6 years later. Arch Gen Psychiatry 50:681–689, 1993

Felten DL, Livnats, Felten SY, et al: Sympathetic innervation of lymph nodes in mice. Brain Res Bull 13:693–699, 1984

Frank MG, Hendricks SE, Johnson DR, et al: Antidepressants augment natural killer cell activity: in vivo and in vitro. Neuropsychobiology 39:18–24, 1999

Ganguli R, Rabin BS: Increased serum interleukin 2 receptor concentration in schizophrenic and brain-damaged subjects. Arch Gen Psychiatry 46:292, 1989

Ganguli R, Brar JS, Chengappa KR, et al: Mitogen-stimulated interleukin-2 production in never-medicated, first-episode schizophrenic patients. The influence of age at onset and negative symptoms. Arch Gen Psychiatry 52:668–672, 1995

Gatti S, Bartfai T: Induction of tumor necrosis factor-alpha mRNA in the brain after peripheral endotoxin treatment: comparison with interleukin-1 family and interleukin-6. Brain Res 624:291–294, 1993

Giron LT Jr, Crutcher KA, Davis JN: Lymph nodes—a possible site for sympathetic neuronal regulation of immune responses. Ann Neurol 8:520–525, 1980

Glaser R, Kiecolt-Glaser JK, Bonneau RH, et al: Stress-induced modulation of the immune response to recombinant hepatitis B vaccine. Psychosom Med 54:22–29, 1992

Goldstein RA, Bowen DL, Fauci AS: Adrenal corticosteroids, in Inflammation: Basic Principles and Clinical Correlates. Edited by Gallin JI, Snyderman R. New York, Raven, 1992, pp 1061–1081

Gonzalo JA, Gonzalez-Garcia A, Martinez C, et al: Glucocorticoid-mediated control of the activation and clonal deletion of peripheral T cells in vivo. J Exp Med 177:1239–1246, 1993

Grant I, Brown GW, Harris T, et al: Severely threatening events and marked life difficulties preceding onset or exacerbation of multiple sclerosis. J Neurol Neurosurg Psychiatry 52:8–13, 1989

Haack M, Hinze-Selch D, Fenzel T, et al: Plasma levels of cytokines and soluble cytokine receptors in psychiatric patients upon hospital admission: effects of confounding factors and diagnosis. J Psychiatr Res 33:407–418, 1999

Hall DM, Suo JL, Weber RJ: Opioid mediated effects on the immune system: sympathetic nervous system involvement. J Neuroimmunol 83:29–35, 1998

Harrington L, Affleck G, Urrows S, et al: Temporal covariation of soluble interleukin-2 receptor levels, daily stress, and disease activity in rheumatoid arthritis. Arthritis Rheum 36:199–203, 1993

Herbert TB, Cohen S: Depression and immunity: a meta-analytic review. Psychological Bull 113:472–486, 1993

Herbert TB, Cohen S, Marsland AL: Cardiovascular reactivity and the course of immune response to an acute psychological stressor. Psychosom Med 56:337–344, 1994

Hermann G, Beck FM, Sheridan JF: Stress-induced glucocorticoid response modulates mononuclear cell trafficking during an experimental influenza viral infection. J Neuroimmunol 56:179–186, 1995

Hosoi T, Okuma Y, Nomura Y: Electrical stimulation of afferent vagus nerve induces IL-1 beta expression in the brain and activates HPA axis. Am J Physiol Regul Integr Comp Physiol 279:R141–147, 2000

Irwin M: Brain corticotropin-releasing-hormone- and interleukin-1-beta-induced suppression of specific antibody production. Endocrinology 133:1352–1360, 1993

Irwin M: Immune correlates of depression. Adv Exp Med Biol 461:1–24, 1999

Irwin M, Hauger RL, Brown M, et al: CRF activates autonomic nervous system and reduces natural killer cell cytotoxicity. Am J Physiol Regul Integr Comp Physiol 255:R744–R747, 1988

Irwin M, Vale W, Rivier C: Central corticotropin-releasing factor mediates the suppressive effect of stress on natural killer cell cytotoxicity. Endocrinology 126:2837–2844, 1990

Irwin M, Costlow C, Williams H, et al: Cellular immunity to varicella-zoster virus in patients with major depression. J Infect Dis 178 (suppl):S104–S108, 1998

Jankowsky JL, Patterson PH: Cytokine and growth factor involvement in long-term potentiation [corrected and republished in Mol Cell Neurosci 14(6):273–286, 1999]

Johansen C, Olsen JH: Psychological stress, cancer incidence and mortality from non-malignant diseases. Br J Cancer 75:144–148, 1997

Kanik KS, Chrousos GP, Schumacher HR, et al: Adrenocorticotropin, glucocorticoid, and androgen secretion in patients with new onset synovitis/rheumatoid arthritis: relations with indices of inflammation. J Clin Endocrinol Metab 85:1461–1466, 2000

Karalis K, Sano H, Redwine J, et al: Autocrine or paracrine inflammatory actions of corticotropin-releasing hormone in vivo. Science 254:421–423, 1991

Karalis K, Muglia LJ, Bae D, et al: CRH and the immune system. J Neuroimmunol 72:131–136, 1997

Kawahito Y, Sano H, Mukai S, et al: Corticotropin releasing hormone in colonic mucosa in patients with ulcerative colitis. Gut 37:544–551, 1995

Keller SE, Weiss JM, Schleifer SJ, et al: Suppression of immunity by stress: effect of a graded series of stressors on lymphocyte stimulation in the rat. Science 213:1397–1400, 1981

Keller SE, Schleifer SJ, Liotta AS, et al: Stress-induced alterations of immunity in hypophysectomized rats. Proc Natl Acad Sci U S A 85:9297–9301, 1988

Kelley KW, Hutchison K, French R, et al: Central interleukin-1 receptors as mediators of sickness. Ann N Y Acad Sci 823:234–246, 1997

Kent S, Bluthe RM, Kelley KW, et al: Sickness behavior as a new target for drug development. Trends Pharmacol Sci 13:24–28, 1992

Kiecolt-Glaser JK, Marucha PT, Malarkey WB, et al: Slowing of wound healing by psychological stress. Lancet 346:1194–1196, 1995

Kiecolt-Glaser JK, Glaser R, Gravenstein S, et al: Chronic stress alters the immune response to influenza virus vaccine in older adults. Proc Natl Acad Sci U S A 93:3043–3047, 1996

Kim YK, Kim L, Lee MS: Relationships between interleukins, neurotransmitters and psychopathology in drug-free male schizophrenics. Schizophr Res 44:165–175, 2000

Knekt P, Raitasalo R, Heliovaara M, et al: Elevated lung cancer risk among persons with depressed mood. Am J Epidemiol 144:1096–1103, 1996

Korschenhausen DA, Hampel HJ, Ackenheil M, et al: Fibrin degradation products in postmortem brain tissue of schizophrenics: a possible marker for underlying inflammatory processes. Schizophr Res 19:103–109, 1996

Kovacs KJ, Elenkov IJ: Differential dependence of ACTH secretion induced by various cytokines on the integrity of the paraventricular nucleus. J Neuroendocrinol 7:15–23, 1995

Krueger JM, Takahashi S, Kapas L, et al: Cytokines in sleep regulation. Advances in Neuroimmunology 5:171–188, 1995

Labeur MS, Arzt E, Wiegers GJ, et al: Long-term intracerebroventricular corticotropin-releasing hormone administration induces distinct changes in rat splenocyte activation and cytokine expression. Endocrinology 136:2678–2688, 1995

Landmann RM, Muller FB, Perini C, et al: Changes of immunoregulatory cells induced by psychological and physical stress: relationship to plasma catecholamines. Clin Exp Immunol 58:127–135, 1984

Landmann R, Schaub B, Link S, et al: Unaltered monocyte function in patients with major depression before and after three months of antidepressive therapy. Biol Psychiatry 41:675–681, 1997

Lariviere WR, Melzack R: The role of corticotropin-releasing factor in pain and analgesia. Pain 84:1–12, 2000

Laye S, Parnet P, Goujon E, et al: Peripheral administration of lipopolysaccharide induces the expression of cytokine transcripts in the brain and pituitary of mice. Brain Res Mol Brain Res 27:157–162, 1994

Laye S, Bluthe RM, Kent S, et al: Subdiaphragmatic vagotomy blocks induction of IL-1 beta mRNA in mice brain in response to peripheral LPS. Am J Physiol 268:R1327–1331, 1995

LeMay LG, Vander AJ, Kluger MJ: The effects of psychological stress on plasma interleukin-6 activity in rats. Physiol Behav 47:957–961, 1990

Lerner DM, Stoudemire A, Rosenstein DL: Neuropsychiatric toxicity associated with cytokine therapies. Psychosomatics 40:428–435, 1999

Leserman J, Petitto JM, Perkins DO, et al: Severe stress, depressive symptoms, and changes in lymphocyte subsets in human immunodeficiency virus–infected men. A 2-year follow-up study. Arch Gen Psychiatry 54:279–285, 1997

Leserman J, Jackson ED, Petitto JM, et al: Progression to AIDS: the effects of stress, depressive symptoms, and social support. Psychosom Med 61:397–406, 1999

Leserman J, Petitto JM, Golden RN, et al: Impact of stressful life events, depression, social support, coping, and cortisol on progression to AIDS. Am J Psychiatry 157:1221–1228, 2000

Leu SJ, Singh VK: Stimulation of interleukin-6 production by corticotropin-releasing factor. Cell Immunol 143:220–227, 1992

Leu SJ, Singh VK: Suppression of in vitro antibody production by corticotropin-releasing factor neurohormone. J Neuroimmunol 45:23–29, 1993

Levine J, Barak Y, Chengappa KN, et al: Cerebrospinal cytokine levels in patients with acute depression. Neuropsychobiology 40:171–176, 1999

Licinio J, Seibyl JP, Altemus M, et al: Elevated CSF levels of interleukin-2 in neuroleptic-free schizophrenic patients. Am J Psychiatry 150:1408–1410, 1993

Linkins RW, Comstock GW: Depressed mood and development of cancer. Am J Epidemiol 132:962–972, 1990

Lyketsos CG, Hoover DR, Guccione M, et al: Depressive symptoms as predictors of medical outcomes in HIV infection. Multicenter AIDS Cohort Study. JAMA 270:2563–2567, 1993

Lyketsos CG, Hoover DR, Guccione M: Depression and survival among HIV-infected persons. JAMA 275:35–36, 1996

Maes M, Meltzer HY, Bosmans E, et al: Increased plasma concentrations of interleukin-6, soluble interleukin-6, soluble interleukin-2, and transferrin receptor in major depression. J Affect Disord 34:301–309, 1995

Maes M, Delange J, Ranjan R, et al: Acute phase proteins in schizophrenia, mania and major depression: modulation by psychotropic drugs. Psychiatry Res 66:1–11, 1997

Maes M, Song C, Lin AH, et al: Negative immunoregulatory effects of antidepressants: inhibition of interferon-gamma and stimulation of interleukin-10 secretion. Neuropsychopharmacology 20:370–379, 1999

Maier SF, Watkins LR: Cytokines for psychologists: implications of bidirectional immune-to-brain communication for understanding behavior, mood, and cognition. Psychol Rev 105:83–107, 1998

Maisel AS, Wright CM, Carter SM, et al: Tachyphylaxis with amrinone therapy: association with sequestration and down-regulation of lymphocyte beta-adrenergic receptors. Ann Intern Med 110:195–201, 1989

Martin J: Sexual dimorphism in immune function: the role of prenatal exposure to androgens and estrogens. Eur J Pharmacol 405:251–261, 2000

Matta SG, Weatherbee J, Sharp BM: A central mechanism is involved in the secretion of ACTH in response to IL-6 in rats: comparison to and interaction with IL-1b. Neuroendocrinology 56:516–525, 1992

Mayne TJ, Vittinghoff E, Chesney MA, et al: Depressive affect and survival among gay and bisexual men infected with HIV. Arch Intern Med 156:2233–2238, 1996

McAllister CG, Rapaport MH, Pickar D, et al: Increased numbers of CD5+ B lymphocytes in schizophrenic patients. Arch Gen Psychiatry 46:890–894, 1989

McEwen BS, Biron CA, Brunson KW, et al: The role of adrenocorticoids as modulators of immune function in health and disease: neural, endocrine and immune interactions. Brain Res Brain Res Rev 23:79–133, 1997

McGee R, Williams S, Elwood M: Depression and the development of cancer: a meta-analysis. Soc Sci Med 38:187–192, 1994

Mellon RD, Bayer BM: Evidence for central opioid receptors in the immunomodulatory effects of morphine: review of potential mechanism(s) of action. J Neuroimmunol 83:19–28, 1998

Meyers CA: Mood and cognitive disorders in cancer patients receiving cytokine therapy. Adv Exp Med Biol 461:75–81, 1999

Meyers CA, Valentine AD: Neurological and psychiatric adverse effects of immunological therapy. CNS Drugs 3:56–68, 1995

Miller AH, Asnis GM, van Praag HM, et al: Influence of desmethylimipramine on natural killer cell activity. Psychiatry Res 19:9–15, 1986

Miller AH, Spencer RL, Stein M, et al: Adrenal steroid receptor binding in spleen and thymus after stress or dexamethasone. Am J Physiol Endo Metab 259:E405–412, 1990

Miller AH, Spencer RL, Hassett J, et al: Effects of selective type I and II adrenal steroid agonists on immune cell distribution. Endocrinology 135:1934–1944, 1994

Miller AH, Pariante CM, Pearce BD: Effects of cytokines on glucocorticoid receptor expression and function. Glucocorticoid resistance and relevance to depression. Adv Exp Med Biol 461:107–116, 1999

Miller AH, Pearce BD, Ruzek MC, et al: Interactions between the hypothalamic-pituitary-adrenal axis and immune system during viral infection: pathways for environmental effects on disease expression, in Handbook of Physiology, Vol IV. New York, Oxford University Press, 2000, pp 425–450

Miller GE, Cohen S, Rabin BS, et al: Personality and tonic cardiovascular, neuroendocrine, and immune parameters. Brain Behav Immun 13:109–123, 1999a

Miller GE, Dopp JM, Myers HF, et al: Psychosocial predictors of natural killer cell mobilization during marital conflict. Health Psychol 18:262–271, 1999b

Mills PJ, Dimsdale JE: The effects of acute psychologic stress on cellular adhesion molecules. J Psychosom Res 41:49–53, 1996

Mohr DC, Goodkin DE, Bacchetti P, et al: Psychological stress and the subsequent appearance of new brain MRI lesions in MS. Neurology 55:55–61, 2000

Moore P, Landolt H, Seifritz E, et al: Clinical and physiological consequences of rapid tryptophan depletion. Neuropsychopharmacology 23:601–622, 2000

Nair MP, Schwartz SA: Immunomodulatory effects of corticosteroids on natural killer and antibody-dependent cellular cytotoxic activities of human lymphocytes. J Immunol 132:2876–2882, 1984

Naitoh Y, Fukata J, Tominaga T, et al: Interleukin-6 stimulates the secretion of adrenocorticotropic hormone in conscious, freely moving rats. Biochem Biophys Res Commun 155:1459–1463, 1988

Nguyen KT, Deak T, Owens SM, et al: Exposure to acute stress induces brain interleukin-1 beta protein in the rat. J Neurosci 18:2239–2246, 1998

Nishioka T, Kurokawa H, Takao T, et al: Differential changes of corticotropin releasing hormone (CRH) concentrations in plasma and synovial fluids of patients with rheumatoid arthritis (RA). Endocr J 43:241–247, 1996

Nisipeanu P, Korczyn AD: Psychological stress as risk factor for exacerbations in multiple sclerosis. Neurology 43:1311–1312, 1993

Owens MJ, Nemeroff CB: The role of corticotropin-releasing factor in the pathophysiology of affective and anxiety disorders: laboratory and clinical studies. Ciba Foundation Symposium 172:296–308, 1993; discussion 308–316, 1993

Padgett DA, Sheridan JF: Androstenediol (AED) prevents neuroendocrine-mediated suppression of the immune response to an influenza viral infection. J Neuroimmunol 98:121–129, 1999

Padgett DA, Loria RM, Sheridan JF: Endocrine regulation of the immune response to influenza virus infection with a metabolite of DHEA-androstenediol. J Neuroimmunol 78:203–211, 1997

Paez Pereda M, Sauer J, Perez Castro C, et al: Corticotropin-releasing hormone differentially modulates the interleukin-1 system according to the level of monocyte activation by endotoxin. Endocrinology 136:5504–5510, 1995

Page-Schafer K, Delorenze GN, Satariano WA, et al: Comorbidity and survival in HIV-infected men in the San Francisco Men's Health Survey. Ann Epidemiol 6:420–430, 1996

Papanicolaou D: Euthyroid sick syndrome and the role of cytokines. Reviews in Endocrine and Metabolic Disorders 1:43–48, 2000

Pariante CM, Miller AH: Natural killer cell activity in major depression: a prospective study of the in vivo effects of desmethylimipramine treatment. Eur Neuropsychopharmacol 5 (suppl):83–88, 1995

Pariante CM, Miller AH: Glucocorticoid receptors in major depression: relevance to pathophysiology and treatment. Biol Psychiatry 49:391–404, 2001

Pariante CM, Carpiniello B, Orru MG, et al: Chronic caregiving stress alters peripheral blood immune parameters: the role of age and severity of stress. Psychother Psychosom 66:199–207, 1997

Pearce BD, Po CL, Pisell TL, et al: Lymphocytic responses and the gradual hippocampal neuron loss following infection with lymphocytic choriomeningitis virus (LCMV). J Neuroimmunol 101:137–147, 1999a

Pariante CM, Pearce BD, Pisell TL, et al: The proinflammatory cytokine, interleukin-1 alpha, reduces glucocorticoid receptor translocation and function. Endocrinology 140:4359–4366, 1999b

Pearce BD, Ruzek MC, Karalis K, et al: CRH-independent activation of corticosterone release during viral infection. Abstracts of the Society for Neuroscience 29,580.13, 1999a

Perlstein RS, Whitnall MH, Abrams JS, et al: Synergistic roles of interleukin-6, interleukin-1, and tumor necrosis factor in the adrenocorticotropin response to bacterial lipopolysaccharide in vivo. Endocrinology 132:946–952, 1993

Perry S, Fishman B, Jacobsberg L, et al: Relationships over 1 year between lymphocyte subsets and psychosocial variables among adults with infection by human immunodeficiency virus. Arch Gen Psychiatry 49:396–401, 1992

Persoons JH, Schornagel K, Breve J, et al: Acute stress affects cytokines and nitric oxide production by alveolar macrophages differently. Am J Respir Crit Care Med 152:619–624, 1995

Peters ML, Godaert GL, Ballieux RE, et al: Immune responses to experimental stress: effects of mental effort and uncontrollability. Psychosom Med 61:513–524, 1999

Petitto JM, Leserman J, Perkins DO, et al: High versus low basal cortisol secretion in asymptomatic, medication-free HIV-infected men: differential effects of severe life stress on parameters of immune status. Behav Med 25:143–151, 2000

Pike JL, Smith TL, Hauger RL, et al: Chronic life stress alters sympathetic, neuroendocrine, and immune responsivity to an acute psychological stressor in humans. Psychosom Med 59:447–457, 1997

Plata-Salaman CR, Sonti G, Borkoski JP, et al: Anorexia induced by chronic central administration of cytokines at estimated pathophysiological concentrations. Physiol Behav 60:867–875, 1996

Plotkin SR, Banks WA, Kastin AJ: Comparison of saturable transport and extracellular pathways in the passage of interleukin-1 alpha across the blood-brain barrier. J Neuroimmunol 67:41–47, 1996

Price P, Olver SD, Silich M, et al: Adrenalitis and the adrenocortical response of resistant and susceptible mice to acute murine cytomegalovirus infection. Eur J Clin Invest 26:811–819, 1996

Printz DJ, Strauss DH, Goetz R, et al: Elevation of CD5+ B lymphocytes in schizophrenia. Biol Psychiatry 46:110–118, 1999

Quan N, Sundar SK, Weiss JM: Induction of interleukin-1 in various brain regions after peripheral and central injections of lipopolysaccharide. J Neuroimmunol 49:125–134, 1994

Quan N, Stern EL, Whiteside MB, et al: Induction of pro-inflammatory cytokine mRNAs in the brain after peripheral injection of subseptic doses of lipopolysaccharide in the rat. J Neuroimmunology 93:72–80, 1999

Rabkin JG, Williams JB, Remien RH, et al: Depression, distress, lymphocyte subsets, and human immunodeficiency virus symptoms on two occasions in HIV-positive homosexual men. Arch Gen Psychiatry 48:111–119, 1991

Ramirez AJ, Craig TK, Watson JP, et al: Stress and relapse of breast cancer. BMJ 298:291–293, 1989

Rapaport MH, Guylai L, Whybrow P: Immune parameters in rapid cycling bipolar patients before and after lithium treatment. J Psychiatr Res 33:335–340, 1999

Rasmussen AF Jr, Marsh JT, Brill NQ: Increased susceptibility to herpes simplex in mice subjected to avoidance-learning stress or restraint. Proc Soc Exp Biol Med 96:183–189, 1957

Rassnick S, Sved AF, Rabin BS: Locus coeruleus stimulation by corticotropin-releasing hormone suppresses in vitro cellular immune responses. J Neurosci 14:6033–6040, 1994

Ravindran AV, Griffiths J, Merali Z, et al: Circulating lymphocyte subsets in major depression and dysthymia with typical or atypical features. Psychosom Med 60:283–289, 1998

Reed GM, Kemeny ME, Taylor SE, et al: Negative HIV-specific expectancies and AIDS-related bereavement as predictors of symptom onset in asymptomatic HIV-positive gay men. Health Psychol 18:354–363, 1999

Regelson W, Loria R, Kalimi M: Dehydroepiandrosterone (DHEA)—the "mother steroid." I. immunologic action. Ann N Y Acad Sci 719:553–563, 1994

Rivest S, Lacroix S, Vallieres L, et al: How the blood talks to the brain parenchyma and the paraventricular nucleus of the hypothalamus during systemic inflammatory and infectious stimuli. Proc Soc Exp Biol Med 223:22–38, 2000

Rivier C: Influence of immune signals on the hypothalamic-pituitary axis of the rodent. Front Neuroendocrinol 16:151–182, 1995

Roberts FD, Newcomb PA, Trentham-Dietz A, et al: Self-reported stress and risk of breast cancer. Cancer 77:1089–1093, 1996

Rogers CJ, Brissette-Storkus CS, Chambers WH, et al: Acute stress impairs NK cell adhesion and cytotoxicity through CD2, but not LFA-1. J Neuroimmunol 99:230–241, 1999

Roitt I, Brostoff J, Male D (eds): Immunology. London, CV Mosby, 1996

Rothwell NJ, Luheshi G, Toulmond S: Cytokines and their receptors in the central nervous system: physiology, pharmacology, and pathology. Pharmacol Ther 69:85–95, 1996

Ruzek MC, Pearce BD, Miller AH, et al: Endogenous glucocorticoids protect against cytokine-mediated lethality during viral infection. J Immunol 162:3527–3533, 1999

Sasaki T, Nanko S, Fukuda R, et al: Changes of immunological functions after acute exacerbation in schizophrenia. Biol Psychiatry 35:173–178, 1994

Schafer M, Carter L, Stein C: Interleukin 1 beta and corticotropin-releasing factor inhibit pain by releasing opioids from immune cells in inflamed tissue. Proc Natl Acad Sci U S A 91:4219–4223, 1994

Schleifer SJ, Keller SE, Bond RN, et al: Major depressive disorder and immunity. Role of age, sex, severity, and hospitalization. Arch Gen Psychiatry 46:81–87, 1989

Schleifer SJ, Keller SE, Bartlett JA: Depression and immunity: clinical factors and therapeutic course. Psychiatry Res 85:63–69, 1999

Schleimer RP, Claman HN, Oronsky A: Anti-inflammatory Steroid Action: Basic and Clinical Aspects. San Diego, CA, Academic Press, 1989

Schmidt ED, Janszen AW, Wouterlood FG, et al: Interleukin-1–induced long-lasting changes in hypothalamic corticotropin-releasing hormone (CRH)-neurons and hyperresponsiveness of the hypothalamus-pituitary-adrenal axis. J Neurosci 15:7417–7426, 1995

Schobitz B, De Kloet ER, Holsboer F: Gene expression and function of interleukin 1, interleukin 6 and tumor necrosis factor in the brain. Prog Neurobiol 44:397–432, 1994

Schulte HM, Bamberger CM, Elsen H, et al: Systemic interleukin-1 alpha and interleukin-2 secretion in response to acute stress and to corticotropin-releasing hormone in humans. Eur J Clin Invest 24:773–777, 1994

Segerstrom SC, Taylor SE, Kemeny ME, et al: Optimism is associated with mood, coping, and immune change in response to stress. J Pers Soc Psychol 74:1646–1655, 1998

Seidel A, Arolt V, Hunstiger M, et al: Cytokine production and serum proteins in depression. Scand J Immunol 41:534–538, 1995

Sharp BM, Roy S, Bidlack JM: Evidence for opioid receptors on cells involved in host defense and the immune system. J Neuroimmunol 83:45–56, 1998

Shavit Y, Lewis JW, Terman GW, et al: Opioid peptides mediate the suppressive effect of stress on natural killer cell cytotoxicity. Science 223:188–190, 1984

Sluzewska A, Rybakowski JK, Laciak M, et al: Interleukin-6 serum levels in depressed patients before and after treatment with fluoxetine. Ann N Y Acad Sci 762:474–476, 1995

Song C, Lin A, Bonaccorso S, et al: The inflammatory response system and the availability of plasma tryptophan in patients with primary sleep disorders and major depression. J Affect Disord 49:211–219, 1998

Sonino N, Girelli ME, Boscaro M, et al: Life events in the pathogenesis of Graves' disease. A controlled study. Acta Endocrinology (Copenhagen) 128:293–296, 1993

Spangelo BL, Judd AM, MacLeod RM, et al: Endotoxin-induced release of interleukin-6 from rat medial basal hypothalami. Endocrinology 127:1779–1785, 1990

Spiegel D, Bloom JR, Kraemer HC, et al: Effect of psychosocial treatment on survival of patients with metastatic breast cancer. Lancet 2:888–891, 1989

Spinedi E, Hadid R, Daneva T, et al: Cytokines stimulate the CRH but not the vasopressin neuronal system: evidence for a median eminence site of interleukin-6 action. Neuroendocrinology 56:46–53, 1992

Stenzel-Poore MP, Duncan JE, Rittenberg MB, et al: CRH overproduction in transgenic mice: behavioral and immune system modulation. Ann N Y Acad Sci 780:36–48, 1996

Sternberg EM, Hill JM, Chrousos GP, et al: Inflammatory mediator-induced hypothalamic-pituitary-adrenal axis activation is defective in streptococcal cell wall arthritis-susceptible Lewis rats. Proc Natl Acad Sci U S A 86:2374–2378, 1989

Stewart MW, Knight RG, Palmer DG, et al: Differential relationships between stress and disease activity for immunologically distinct subgroups of people with rheumatoid arthritis. J Abnorm Psychol 103:251–258, 1994

Stubner S, Schon T, Padberg F, et al: Interleukin-6 and the soluble IL-6 receptor are decreased in cerebrospinal fluid of geriatric patients with major depression: no alteration of soluble gp130. Neurosci Lett 259:145–148, 1999

Suda T, Tozawa F, Ushiyama T, et al: Interleukin-1 stimulates corticotropin-releasing factor gene expression in rat hypothalamus. Endocrinology 126:1223–1228, 1990

Swedo SE, Leonard HL, Garvey M, et al: Pediatric autoimmune neuropsychiatric disorders associated with streptococcal infections: clinical description of the first 50 cases. Am J Psychiatry 155:264–271, 1998

Then Bergh F, Kumpfel T, Trenkwalder C, et al: Dysregulation of the hypothalamo-pituitary-adrenal axis is related to the clinical course of MS. Neurology 53:772–777, 1999

Thomason BT, Brantley PJ, Jones GN, et al: The relation between stress and disease activity in rheumatoid arthritis. J Behav Med 15:215–220, 1992

Torpy DJ, Chrousos GP: The three-way interactions between the hypothalamic-pituitary-adrenal and gonadal axes and the immune system. Bailliere's Clinical Rheumatology 10:181–198, 1996

Tsai SY, Chen KP, Yang YY, et al: Activation of indices of cell-mediated immunity in bipolar mania. Biol Psychiatry 45:989–994, 1999

Uchino BN, Kiecolt-Glaser JK, Cacioppo JT: Age-related changes in cardiovascular response as a function of a chronic stressor and social support. J Pers Soc Psychol 63:839–846, 1992

Vacca A, Felli MP, Farina AR, et al: Glucocorticoid receptor-mediated suppression of the interleukin 2 gene expression through impairment of the cooperativity between nuclear factor of activated T cells and AP-1 enhancer elements. J Exp Med 175:637–646, 1992

van Dam AM, Brouns M, Louisse S, et al: Appearance of interleukin-1 in macrophages and in ramified microglia in the brain of endotoxin-treated rats: a pathway for the induction of non-specific symptoms of sickness? Brain Res 588:291–296, 1992

van Kammen DP, McAllister-Sistilli CG, Kelley ME, et al: Elevated interleukin-6 in schizophrenia. Psychiatry Res 87:129–136, 1999

Venters HD, Dantzer R, Freund GG, et al: Growth hormone and insulin-like growth factor as cytokines in the immune system, in Psychoneuroimmunology, 3rd Edition. Edited by Alder R, Felten D, Cohen N. New York, Academic Press, 2001, pp 339–362

Walker LG, Heys SD, Walker MB, et al: Psychological factors can predict the response to primary chemotherapy in patients with locally advanced breast cancer. Eur J Cancer 35:1783–1788, 1999

Ward MM, Lotstein DS, Bush TM, et al: Psychosocial correlates of morbidity in women with systemic lupus erythematosus. J Rheumatol 26:2153–2158, 1999

Watkins LR, Goehler LE, Relton JK, et al: Blockade of interleukin-1 induced hyperthermia by subdiaphragmatic vagotomy: evidence for vagal mediation of immune-brain communication. Neurosci Lett 183:27–31, 1995

Watson M, Haviland JS, Greer S, et al: Influence of psychological response on survival in breast cancer: a population-based cohort study. Lancet 354:1331–1336, 1999

Weiss JM, Sundar S: Effects of stress on cellular immune responses in animals, in American Psychiatric Association Annual Review, Vol 11. Edited by Tasman A, Riba MB. Washington, DC, American Psychiatric Press, 1992, pp 145–168

Weizman R, Laor N, Podliszewski E, et al: Cytokine production in major depressed patients before and after clomipramine treatment. Biol Psychiatry 35:42–47, 1994

Whitacre CC, Reingold SC, O'Looney PA: A gender gap in autoimmunity. Science 283:1277–1278, 1999

Wilckens T, DeRijk R: Glucocorticoids and immune function: unknown dimensions and new frontiers. Immunol Today 18:418–424, 1997

Williams JM, Peterson RG, Shea PA: Sympathetic innervation of murine thymus and spleen: evidence for a functional link between the nervous and immune systems. Brain Res Bull 6:83–94, 1981

Wulsin LR, Vaillant GE, Wells VE: A systematic review of the mortality of depression. Psychosom Med 61:6–17, 1999

Wyllie AH: Glucocorticoid-induced thymocyte apoptosis is associated with endogenous endonuclease activation. Nature 284:555–556, 1980

Yin D, Tuthill D, Mufson RA, et al: Chronic restraint stress promotes lymphocyte apoptosis by modulating CD95 expression. J Exp Med 191:1423–1428, 2000

Yolken RH, Torrey EF: Viruses, schizophrenia, and bipolar disorder. Clin Microbiol Rev 8:131–145, 1995

Yoshihara S, Ricciardolo FL, Geppetti P, et al: Corticotropin-releasing factor inhibits antigen-induced plasma extravasation in airways. Eur J Pharmacol 280:113–118, 1995

Yoshiuchi K, Kumano H, Nomura S, et al: Stressful life events and smoking were associated with Graves' disease in women, but not in men. Psychosom Med 60:182–185, 1998

Yovel G, Sirota P, Mazeh D, et al: Higher natural killer cell activity in schizophrenic patients: the impact of serum factors, medication, and smoking. Brain Behav Immun 14:153–169, 2000

Yu-Lee LY: Molecular actions of prolactin in the immune system. Exp Biol Med 215:35–52, 1997

Zhou D, Kusnecov AW, Shurin MR, et al: Exposure to physical and psychological stressors elevates plasma interleukin 6: relationship to the activation of hypothalamic-pituitary-adrenal axis. Endocrinology 133:2523–2530, 1993

PART

II

# Neuropsychiatric Assessment

# Bedside Neuropsychiatry

*Eliciting the Clinical Phenomena*
*of Neuropsychiatric Illness*

Fred Ovsiew, M.D.

Unless we take pains to be accurate in our examinations as to the question propounded, our observations will be of little value. The investigator who simply asks leading questions…is not accumulating "facts," but is "organising confusion." He will make errors enough without adopting a clumsy plan of investigating which renders blundering certain.

—*John Hughlings-Jackson (1880/1881)*

In this chapter, I aim to provide the neuropsychiatric clinician with a method for data gathering at the bedside. To this end, I review the tools offered by history taking and examination for discovering the contribution of cerebral dysfunction to psychological abnormality and behavioral disturbance. The data available at the bedside are rich, and they are the touchstone for data gathered elsewhere. The focus is on the methods of filling in a matrix of clinical information. The clinical correlates of the symptoms and signs discussed are mentioned but not comprehensively reviewed.

Likewise, the localizing significance of the phenomena is not unduly emphasized. Localization as a paradigm for neuropsychiatric thinking has had great successes, and no doubt more are to come (H. Damasio and Damasio 1989; Kertesz 1994). In what is, so to speak, a best-case scenario for neuropsychiatric phenomenology, understanding of psychopathology would provide "clues as to the cerebral location of functional pathology.…The challenge for neuropsychiatry is to develop the neurobiology of the auditory system, of delusion formation and of disordered thinking to interpret the associations between psychotic symptoms encountered clinically" (Santhouse

et al. 2000, p. 2062). However, localization has its limits (Knopman and Rubens 1986; Ward 1990). Some of the syndromes of classical behavioral neurology may be invalid (Rizzo 1993). Moreover, even valid syndromes merely reflecting anatomical proximity of disparate functions are unlikely to lead to greater understanding of brain organization (Benton 1992), especially because localizing information is available through powerful imaging methods without reliance on clinical signs.

Furthermore, neuropsychologically defined behavioral disturbances may not fully reflect performance in real-world contexts. In particular, tests of executive cognitive function may incompletely capture disabling impairments in everyday life. Patients with deficits in planning and prospective memory—those with "strategy application disorder"—may perform fully normally on a broad array of traditional neuropsychological measures (Burgess 2000; Eslinger and Damasio 1985). More commonly, the disturbance is disproportionately more evident in daily life, even in the social interaction of the clinical encounter, than in the neuropsychological laboratory, which is designed to be quiet, free of interruptions and social pressures, and oriented to unambiguous judgments of external reality rather than adaptive decision making in the context of personal priorities (E. Goldberg and Podell 2000; Statish et al. 1999). Disturbances of affect may not be reflected in neuropsychological measures at all (Burgess et al. 1998).

In neuropsychiatry, attention to cerebral organization must not be matched by neglect of psychosocial variables, for these may have substantial impact on symptom expression, impairment, and disability. Thus, the more naturalistic clinical examination cannot lose its relevance, even in the era of brain imaging and cognitive neuropsychology. Ideally, the clinical approach will be guided by the best available understanding of the fundamental principles of brain organization, but the rubrics provided below cannot be claimed as such elementary modules of cognition and behavior.

## Taking the History

Obtaining a history is an active process on the part of the interviewer, who must have in mind a matrix to be filled in with information. The excuse "the patient is a poor historian" has no place in neuropsychiatry. The examiner must realize that it is he or she, and not the patient, who is the "historian," responsible for gathering information from all necessary sources and forming a coherent narrative. Discovering that the patient is unable to give an adequate account of his or her life and illness should prompt, first, a search for other informants and, second, a search for an explanation of the incapacity.

### Birth

The neuropsychiatric history begins with events that took place even before the birth of the patient. Maternal illness in pregnancy and the process of labor and delivery must be reviewed for untoward events associated with fetal maldevelopment, including bleeding and substance abuse during pregnancy, the course of labor, and fetal distress at birth and in the immediate postnatal period. Obstetric complications are associated with schizophrenia (Cannon et al. 2000; McNeil et al. 2000; Rosso et al. 2000b) and perhaps with mood disorder (Kinney et al. 1993a; Preti et al. 2000) and other psychiatric conditions (Capstick and Seldrup 1977; Raine et al. 1994; Schachar 1991).

### Development

At times, the historian can gather information from the first minutes of extrauterine life, for example when Apgar scores are available in hospital records. More commonly, parental recollection of milestones must be relied on. The ages at which the child crawled, walked, spoke words, spoke sentences, went to school, and so on can often be elicited from parents. Parents may be able to compare the patient with a "control" sibling. The infant's temperament—shy, active, cuddly, fussy, and so on—may give clues to persisting traits. School performance is an important marker of both the intellectual and the social competence of the child and often is the only information available about premorbid intellectual level. Childhood illness, including febrile convulsions, head injury, and central nervous system infection, is sometimes the precursor of adult neuropsychiatric disorder.

### Handedness

The simplest and most obvious indicator of cerebral dominance is handedness. Several questionnaires are available (Bryden 1977; McMeekan and Lishman 1975). Fortunately, a few simple inquiries—asking the patient which hand he or she uses to write, throw, draw, and use a scissors or toothbrush—serve well to establish handedness (Bryden 1977). With some nonverbal patients (e.g., the severely mentally retarded), watching the patient catch a thrown ball or crumpled piece of paper is a simple examination for handedness. The "torque test" of drawing circles (Demarest and Demarest 1980), examination of the angle formed by the opposed thumb and little finger (Metzig et al. 1975, 1976), and observation of handwriting (J. Levy and Reid 1976) have their advocates as ways to establish cerebral dominance beyond simple handedness.

### Ictal Events

Many "spells" or "attacks" occur in neuropsychiatric patients, and taking the history of a paroxysmal event has certain requirements regardless of the nature of the event. The clinician must be concerned with the phases of the paroxysm, starting with the prodrome, then the aura, then the remainder of the ictus (the aura being the onset or core of the ictus), then the aftermath. For any attack disorder, how frequent and how stereotyped the events are must be determined. Rapidity of onset and cessation; disturbance of consciousness or of language; occurrence of autochthonous sensations, ideas, and emotions and of lateralized motor or cognitive dysfunction; purposefulness and coordination of actions; memory for the spell; and duration of the recovery period must be ascertained. Beginning an inquiry about seizures by asking if the patient has just one sort of spell or more than one reduces confusion as history taking proceeds with a patient who has both partial and generalized seizures. Some patients with pseudoseizures will say that they have epileptic spells and then another sort that happens when they are upset.

Prodromal phases of epileptic attacks were formerly well known, when epileptic patients resided in colonies and were under observation as they "built up" to a seizure. Adverse mood changes commonly occur on the days preceding a seizure (Blanchet and Frommer 1986). Prodromes occur in migraine as well (Sacks 1971).

Hermann et al. (1982) reported that patients with fear as a part of the seizure ictus are at greater risk for psychopathology. The nature of the aura in complex partial epilepsy is correlated with age at onset, IQ, laterality, and temporal lobe pathology (Taylor and Lochery 1987). Some of the abnormal experiences well known in temporal lobe epilepsy—the "elaborate" mental state described by Hughlings-Jackson (Bancaud et al. 1994; Gloor et al. 1982)—occur in mood disorders and in other psychiatric states as a putative marker of limbic dysfunction (Ardila et al. 1993; Atre-Vaidya et al. 1994; Persinger and Makarec 1993; Roberts et al. 1990; Silberman et al. 1985, 1994; Teicher et al. 1993). These phenomena in nonepileptic populations are associated with markers of brain injury, such as a history of perinatal hypoxia, fever with delirium, or head trauma (Ardila et al. 1993, Roberts et al. 1990), and with childhood abuse (Teicher et al. 1993). The phenomena can be elicited by questions about déjà vu and *jamais vu*, episodic sensory experiences such as visual illusions, paranormal experiences such as clairvoyance, and other paroxysmal experiences.

## Head Injury

Discerning the role of cerebral dysfunction in posttraumatic states is a common diagnostic challenge. The length of the anterograde amnesia, from the moment of trauma to the recovery of the capacity for consecutive memory, can be learned either from the patient or from hospital records. The patient can say what the last memories before the accident are; from last memory to injury is the period of retrograde amnesia. The lengths of these intervals and the duration of coma are correlated with the severity of brain damage (Lishman 1998). Usually, posttraumatic amnesia is the best indicator. The nature of the trauma, including its psychosocial setting and whether impulsive or reckless behavior led to the injury, should be learned.

## Alcohol and Drug Use

A substance abuse history must be taken from all patients. Questions about vocational, family, and medical impairment attributable to abuse; shame and guilt over abuse and efforts to control it; morning or secret drinking; blackouts; and other familiar issues help the clinician identify pathological behavior in this sphere. Cocaine and alcohol abuse in particular are associated with a variety of neuropsychiatric consequences, including cognitive impairment, movement disorders, seizures, and stroke (Marshall 1999).

## Mild Cognitive Impairment

One commonly encounters patients with mild, chronic, stable, global cognitive disturbance not meeting the criteria for a diagnosis of dementia; no doubt the most frequent condition giving rise to this state is traumatic brain injury (M.P. Alexander 1995; Gutierrez et al. 1993, 1994). Lezak (1978) emphasized the patient's experience of perplexity, distractibility, and fatigue in mild and severe brain injury. In my experience, some cognitive symptoms reported by patients are so characteristic that they are nearly diagnostic of organic illness. Other features, such as emotional lability and irritability, are characteristic of, but less specific to, organic states.

For example, before undergoing resection of an arteriovenous malformation, a successful businesswoman had been accustomed to reading the newspaper carefully over breakfast. After the procedure, she discovered that although she was able to read a newspaper and absorb its import adequately, she was not able to do so while eating breakfast. She could do only one thing at a time. This loss of the capacity for divided attention is highly characteristic of mild cerebral disease. Distractibility is heightened, and automatic tasks require attention and effort. An interesting possible example is the "stops walking when talking" phenomenon in the elderly (Bloem et al. 2000; Lundin-Olsson et al. 1997). These symptoms were clearly described and experimentally demonstrated many years ago (Brodal 1973; Chapman and Wolff 1958; Chapman et al. 1958). The features of focal lesions producing disturbances of "multitasking" have recently come under scrutiny (Burgess et al. 2000).

## Appetitive Functions

Appetitive functions include sleep, eating, and sexual interest and performance. Disturbed sleep is common in patients with psychiatric disorders of any origin and in the general population as well. In a search for clues to organic factors in psychiatric illness, the clinician inquires about the pattern of disturbance: early waking in depressive illness, nighttime wakings related to pain or nocturnal myoclonus, excessive daytime sleepiness in narcolepsy and sleep apnea, sleep attacks in narcolepsy, and periodic excessive somnolence in Kleine-Levin syndrome and related disorders. Simple observation of a hospitalized patient by night nursing staff, or at home by family members, can reveal apneas or abnormal movements. Some neuropsychiatrists take an interest in the patient's dreams. Solms (1997) analyzed dreaming in a large series of brain-injured patients. He found that loss of dreaming occurs with parietal lesions in either hemisphere and with deep bifrontal injury. Dreams devoid of visual imagery occur with ventral occipitotemporal lesions. Patterns of abnormal eating behavior can be recognized beyond the anorexia of depressive illness and food-avoidance in anorexia nervosa: the hyperphagia of hypothalamic disease, in which food exerts an irresistible attraction; the mouthing and eating of nonfood objects in bilateral amygdalar disease (part of the Klüver-Bucy syndrome); and the impulsive stuffing of food into the mouth irrespective of hunger in frontal disease (Mendez et al. 1995; G. Smith et al. 1998).

Sexual interest and performance are commonly disturbed in brain disease. Helping a patient discuss these matters can be a great relief to the patient. Once the subject is broached, the details of abnormal sexual performance can usually be elicited (Boller and Frank 1982). Hyposexuality seems to be a feature of epilepsy, although its mechanism is controversial (Morrell et al. 1994; Toone et al. 1989). A change in a person's habitual sexual interests, either quantitative or qualitative, occurring de novo in adult life, suggests organic disease (Cummings 1999).

## Aggression

Patterns of aggressive behavior in brain disease have been described and related to the locus of injury (Benjamin 1999a), and epileptic violence has been delineated (Fenwick 1989). Features of aggressive behavior such as its onset and cessation; the patient's mental state and especially clarity of consciousness during the violent period; the patient's capacity for planned, coordinated, and well-organized action as displayed in the act; the patient's regret, or otherwise, afterward; and any associated symptoms may yield clues about the contribution of cerebral dysfunction to the behavior.

## Personality Change

Changes in sexual preference with onset in adult life have already been mentioned as pointers to organic mental disorder. Persisting alterations in or exaggerations of other personality traits, if not related to an abnormal mood

state or psychosis, may be important indicators of the development of cerebral disease. Lability and shallowness of emotion, irritability, aggressiveness, loss of sense of humor, and coarsening of the sensibilities are often mentioned. However, the warning of Syz (1937) written more than 60 years ago still applies:

> Whenever those nervous structures which control the personality-organization are damaged it may become particularly difficult to discriminate between alterations of function due to organic lesions and alterations due to reactive tendencies of the total organism in its adaptation to the environment. So that we may be confronted with combinations or fusions of the two types of processes which are difficult to untangle. (p. 374)

A particular set of personality traits is said to be distinctive in temporal lobe epilepsy, including mystical or religious interests, "humorless sobriety," tendency toward rage, interpersonal stickiness or "viscosity," and hyposexuality. Whether these traits are related to epilepsy, to the temporal lobe injury underlying epilepsy, or merely to psychopathology remains controversial (Bear et al. 1989).

## Occupation

The relationship of occupational hazards to illness is an entire medical specialty, and an outline for eliciting relevant information has been prepared (Occupational and Environmental Health Committee 1983). Exposures to heavy metals or volatile hydrocarbons and repeated blows to the head in boxers are examples of occupational causes of neuropsychiatric illness. Apart from etiological information, the clinician needs to know about the patient's work in order to gauge premorbid capacities and to assess disability.

## Family History

Genetic contributions to many neuropsychiatric illnesses are well delineated (e.g., in Huntington's disease); in other illnesses, the contribution is probable but its nature less clear (e.g., in Tourette syndrome). Genetic transmission of a seizure threshold makes the family history of seizures relevant not only in idiopathic epilepsy but even after certain precipitating brain insults (Schaumann et al. 1994). Inquiring about the family history of neuropsychiatric illness relative by relative, even constructing a family tree with the assistance of collateral informants, is more revealing than asking questions such as "Is there any mental illness in the family?"

## Examining the Patient

The British neurologist Henry Miller (1975) referred to psychiatry as "neurology without physical signs" (p. 462). Geoffrey Lloyd (1983) called psychosomatics "medicine without signs" (p. 539). We may consider neuropsychiatry to be "psychiatry with signs." Unfortunately, the sensitivity and specificity of many findings are unknown, even for signs that are routine or traditional in the clinical examination. Too often, the clinical examination proceeds by ritual. The clinician who asks the patient with right-hemisphere stroke to interpret proverbs but not to copy figures, or asks him or her to remember three words but not three shapes, is bowing to tradition and ignoring the physiology of the brain disease. Moreover, the tasks may lack discernible relation to cognitive or anatomic systems: what underlies the ability to recall the names of the last four presidents? Probes should be chosen with reference to the structure of the mind, as best understood.

Sometimes, clinicians attempt to elicit not signs of brain disease but so-called positive signs of nonorganic states. Vibratory sensation that shows lateralized deficit on the sternum is an example. These signs are of limited utility, not because they are uncommon in hysteria but because suggestibility is common in organic mental states as well (Gould et al. 1986; Rolak 1988). They cannot be relied on for differential diagnosis.

## Asymmetry and Minor Physical Anomalies

Abnormal development of a hemisphere may be betrayed by slight differences in the size of the thumbs or thumbnails. A postcentral location of cortical lesions causing asymmetry is characteristic (Penfield and Robertson 1943). A small hemiface or hemicranium is usually ipsilateral to an epileptic focus (Tinuper et al. 1992).

Other physical anomalies are stable through childhood and give clues to abnormal neurodevelopment even in adulthood. The Waldrop scale is in common use (Table 5–1), but minor anomalies not included in that scale may be relevant (Ismail et al. 1998a). They may occur in healthy individuals, and no individual anomaly, except perhaps abnormal head circumference (Lainhart et al. 1997; Steg and Rapoport 1975), has a correlation with psychopathology. The deviant development can be traced to the first four months of fetal life, and either genetic or environmental factors can give rise to the disturbance of gestation (McNeil et al. 2000). Presumably, the relationship of the anomalies to the brain disorder lies in a disturbance of contemporaneous cerebral development.

**TABLE 5–1.** Waldrop scale of minor physical anomalies

**Head**
Head circumference outside the normal range[a]
Fine, "electric" hair that will not comb down
More than one hair whorl
Abnormal epicanthal folds of the eyes
Hypertelorism or hypotelorism
Low-set ears (entirely below the plane of the pupils)
Malformed or asymmetrical ears
High palate
Furrowed tongue

**Hands and feet**
Curved fifth finger (clinodactyly)
Single palmar crease
Wide gap between first and second toes
Partial syndactyly of the toes
Third toe longer than second

[a]The normal range of head circumference in adults is governed by a complex relation to height, weight, and sex. Roughly, for males the range is 54–60 cm (21.25–23.5 inches) and for females, 52–58 cm (20.5–22.75 inches) (Bushby et al. 1992).

Such anomalies are associated with schizophrenia (McNeil et al. 2000), even late-onset schizophrenia (Lohr et al. 1997). They may also be associated with mood disorder (Lohr et al. 1997), as well as tardive dyskinesia (Waddington et al. 1995), autism (Gualtieri et al. 1982; Steg and Rapoport 1975), schizotypal personality disorder (Weinstein et al. 1999), violent delinquency in boys (Arseneault et al. 2000) and perhaps inhibited behavior in girls (C.A. Fogel et al. 1985), and violent behavior in criminals (Kandel et al. 1989). Thus they are best regarded as a nonspecific indicator of abnormal neurodevelopment (Ismail et al. 2000; Tarrant and Jones 1999), maldevelopment that may interact with psychosocial factors in the genesis of psychopathology (Pine et al. 1997). Dysmorphic features in a mentally retarded patient should lead to investigations to identify the cause of the retardation (Ryan and Sunada 1997).

## Olfaction

Hyposmia or anosmia can be detected in Alzheimer's disease, Parkinson's disease, normal aging, schizophrenia, multiple sclerosis, subfrontal tumor, human immunodeficiency virus (HIV) infection, migraine, and traumatic brain injury (Brody et al. 1991; Eslinger et al. 1982; Harrison and Pearson 1989; Hirsch 1992; Kopala et al. 1994; Pinching 1977). The most common cause of hyposmia, however, is local disease of the nasal mucosa, and the examiner must exclude local disease before regarding the finding as having neuropsychiatric significance.

Pinching (1977) provided an assessment of what test odors are most sensitive and specific for olfactory defects. Stimuli that cause trigeminal irritation (e.g., ammonia) are not suitable. Floral and musk odors provide the greatest sensitivity. I use raspberry and cherry scented lip balm to test for olfactory defects; these scents are simple and strong, and the containers can be easily carried in a coat pocket. More sophisticated equipment is available for clinical use and may be of diagnostic value (Savic et al. 1997).

## Eyes

Dilated pupils associated with anticholinergic toxicity may be a clue to the cause of delirium, and small pupils associated with opiate intoxication may be a clue to substance abuse. Argyll Robertson pupils—bilaterally small, irregular, and reactive to accommodation but not to light—characteristically accompany neurosyphilis (Burke and Schaberg 1985; Luxon et al. 1979), but they also occur in sarcoidosis and other conditions (Dasco and Bortz 1989). Pupillary abnormalities other than Argyll Robertson pupils, such as bilateral tonic pupils, also may occur in neurosyphilis (Fletcher and Sharpe 1986).

A Kayser-Fleischer ring is nearly always present when Wilson's disease affects the brain (Demirkiran et al. 1996). This brownish-green discoloration of the cornea begins at the limbus, at 12 o'clock then 6 o'clock, spreading from each location medially and laterally until a complete ring is formed. It can be difficult to discern in patients with dark irises, so slit-lamp examination should supplement bedside inspection (Marsden 1987; Walshe 1986).

Korein (1981) reported that pale (blue, green, gray, or hazel) irises are more common in patients with dystonia than in control subjects. An attempt to replicate the finding failed (Lang et al. 1982). Iris pigmentation also may be linked to the temperamental trait of behavioral inhibition; inhibited children are more apt to be blue-eyed than their uninhibited peers (Reznick et al. 1989; Rosenberg and Kagan 1987, 1989; Rubin and Both 1989).

## Visual Fields

When lesions disrupt the white matter of the temporal lobe, a congruent homonymous upper quadrantanopsia or even a full homonymous hemianopsia can result from involvement of Meyer's loop, the portion of the optic radiation that dips into the temporal lobe (Falconer and Wilson 1958; Tecoma et al. 1993). Such an abnormality can be seen in some patients with temporal lobe epilepsy. In cases of delirium from posterior cerebral or right mid-dle cerebral artery infarction, hemianopsia may be the only pointer to a structural cause rather than a toxic-metabolic encephalopathy (L.R. Caplan et al. 1986; Devinsky et al. 1988).

## Blinking

The normal response to regular one-per-second taps on the glabella (with the examiner behind the patient so that the striking finger is not within the patient's visual field and the patient is not responding to visual threat) is blinking to the first few taps, followed by habituation and no blinking. The normal spontaneous blink rate increases through childhood but is stable in adulthood at a rate of about $16 \pm 8$ (Zametkin et al. 1979).

Stevens (1978a) drew attention to abnormalities of blinking in schizophrenic patients and reminded us that Kraepelin, among other early investigators, had already commented on them. She found high rates of spontaneous blinking, paroxysms of rapid rhythmic blinking during episodes of abnormal behavior, and abnormal responses to glabellar tap. On glabellar tap, Stevens's patients either failed to blink, produced a shower of blinks, or failed to habituate. Although Stevens's patients were drug free, few were neuroleptic-naïve, so she could not distinguish between an abnormality intrinsic to schizophrenia and tardive dyskinesia (Stevens 1978b). Others confirmed the finding (Helms and Godwin 1985; Karson 1979).

The matter is of particular interest because the rate of spontaneous blinking is quite insensitive to peripheral stimuli (ambient light, humidity, even deafferentation of the fifth nerve) but is under dopaminergic control (Ellsworth et al. 1991; Freed et al. 1980). Clinically, this process is manifested by a low blink rate in parkinsonism and the increase of blink rate with effective levodopa treatment (Karson et al. 1984). Thus, blink rate provides a simple, quantitative index of central dopamine activity. Low blink rates in mentally retarded adults with stereotypies (Bodfish et al. 1995) and in children with schizophrenia (R. Caplan and Guthrie 1994) suggest hypodopaminergia in these patients. Failure to habituate to glabellar tap also is seen in parkinsonism and is called Myerson's sign.

## Eye Movements

Stevens (1978a) also called attention to early observations by Kraepelin and others of a number of abnormal eye movements seen in psychotic patients. She noted gaze abnormalities, abnormality in eye contact with the examiner (e.g., fixed staring or no eye contact), impaired convergence movements, and irregular smooth pursuit movements. Clinicians' descriptions of eye movement are often inferential (e.g., "looking at the voices"), but it is useful to attempt a phenomenological description (e.g., "unexplained episodic lateral glances").

Stevens's finding of irregular smooth pursuit movements in schizophrenic patients can be compared with laboratory investigations of abnormal smooth pursuit movements in psychotic patients. This abnormality is thought to be a trait under genetic control and related to abnormal attentional function and vulnerability to psychosis (D.L. Levy et al. 1993). However, jerky smooth pursuit movements are a common and nonspecific finding on bedside examination and do not reliably distinguish schizophrenic patients from healthy control subjects (E.Y.H. Chen et al. 1995).

Elucidating abnormalities of eye movement in neuropsychiatric patients requires separate examination of voluntary eye movements without fixation ("look to the left"), generation of saccades to a target ("look at my finger, now at my fist," with one hand on each side of the patient), and smooth pursuit ("follow my finger"). Failure of voluntary downgaze is a hallmark of progressive supranuclear palsy but is not always present early in the course (Collins et al. 1995). Limitation of voluntary upgaze is common in the healthy elderly. Inability to inhibit reflexive saccades to a target is characteristic of frontal disease and is seen in schizophrenia (Kennard et al. 1994); in its extreme, when any moving object captures the patient's gaze, this phenomenon is visual grasping (Ghika et al. 1995b). Milder manifestations can be elicited by instructing the patient to look at the examiner's finger when the fist moves, and vice versa, with one hand on each side of the patient (Shaunak et al. 1995). Slowed saccades, inability to make a saccade without moving the head or blinking, and other eye movement abnormalities are common in Huntington's disease (Leigh et al. 1983). Head-eye synkinesia occurs in schizophrenia (E.Y.H. Chen et al. 1995; Kolada and Pitman 1983) and in dementia. Abnormalities of eye movement (nystagmus, a VI [sixth nerve] palsy, or a gaze palsy) in a confused patient may indicate Wernicke's encephalopathy (Victor et al. 1989).

Apraxia of gaze (also called psychic paralysis of gaze and ocular apraxia) is, like other apraxias, a failure of voluntary movement with the preserved capacity for spontaneous movement (Rizzo 1993). Congenital ocular motor apraxia can be associated with other neurodevelopmental abnormalities (PeBenito and Cracco 1988). Patients with gaze apraxia may have difficulty with searching or scanning arrays or scenes. Gaze apraxia is a feature of Balint's syndrome (see the discussion on disordered reaching and simultanagnosia below). In so-called apraxia of eyelid opening, patients have difficulty in initiating lid elevation. This disorder occurs in extrapyramidal disease, notably progressive supranuclear palsy (Grandas and Esteban 1994); with frontal lesions, especially right-hemisphere infarction (Algoed et al. 1992); and as an isolated finding (Defazio et al. 1998). Ptosis is absent, and eye closure and reflex eye opening are normal. In apraxia of lid opening, as distinct from blepharospasm, the orbicularis oculi are not excessively contracted; in blepharospasm, the brows are lowered below the superior orbital margins (Grandas and Esteban 1994). Sensory tricks may be effective in initiating eye opening (Defazio et al. 1998), probably an indicator of extrapyramidal dysfunction in the disorder (thus making the term *apraxia* incorrect). Supranuclear disorders of eyelid closure may occur with bilateral frontal lesions, either structural (Ghika et al. 1988) or functional, as in the case of progressive supranuclear palsy (Grandas and Esteban 1994). Spontaneous blinking is intact. Often, other bulbar musculature is involved (Ross Russell 1980).

## Facial Movement

A double dissociation in the realm of facial movement demonstrates that emotional movements and volitional movements are separately organized (Monrad-Krohn 1924; Wilson 1924). A paresis seen in movements in response to a command ("show me your teeth") is sometimes overcome in spontaneous smiling; this indicates disease in pyramidal pathways (Hopf et al. 1992). A severe impairment of voluntary control of the bulbar musculature with preservation of automatic movements is seen in bilateral opercular lesions, the anterior opercular or Foix-Chavany-Marie syndrome (Mao et al. 1989; Weller 1993). The inverse phenomenon—normal movement in response to a command but asymmetry of spontaneous emotional movements—is seen with disease in the supplementary motor area (Laplane et al. 1976), thalamus (Bogousslavsky et al. 1988; Graff-Radford et al. 1984; Hopf et al. 1992), temporal lobe (Remillard et al. 1977), and striatum and internal capsule (Trosch et al. 1990). A.R. Damasio and Maurer (1978) reported the occurrence of this sign in autism and argued that it indicates disease in limbic regions. Emotional facial weakness is contralateral to the seizure focus in temporal lobe epilepsy and may relate to brain injury early in life (Cascino et al. 1993; Remillard et al. 1977).

# Speech

## Dysarthria

Disorders of articulation are difficult to describe, although they often are easily recognized when heard. In pyramidal disorders, the speech output is slow, strained, and slurred. Often accompanying the speech disorder are other features of pseudobulbar palsy, including dysphagia, drooling, and disturbance of the expression of emotions. Usually, the causative lesions are bilateral. Bulbar, or flaccid, dysarthria is marked by breathiness and nasality, as well as impaired articulation. Signs of lower motor neuron involvement can be found in the bulbar musculature. The lesion is in the lower brain stem. Scanning speech is a characteristic sign of disease of the cerebellum and its connections; the rate of speech output is irregular, with equalized stress on the syllables. In extrapyramidal disorders and in depression, speech is hypophonic and monotonous, often tailing off with longer phrases.

Darley et al. (1975) described in detail a scheme for examining the motor aspects of speech. It begins with assessment of the elements of speech production (facial musculature, tongue, palate, and so on) at rest and during voluntary movement. The patient is asked to produce the vowel "ah" steadily for as long as possible; the performance is assessed for voice quality, duration, pitch, steadiness, and loudness. Production of strings of individual consonants (e.g., "puh-puh-puh-puh") and alternated consonants (e.g., "puh-tuh-kuh-puh-tuh-kuh") is assessed for rate and rhythm. Extended utterances also are examined to observe the effects of fatigue and context.

## Stuttering and Cluttering

Common developmental stuttering, or stammering, is familiar to everyone's ear. The rhythm of speech is disturbed by the repetition, prolongation, or arrest of sounds. Acquired stuttering, subtly different from the developmental variety (Helm-Estabrooks 1999), is unusual but can be caused by stroke (Carluer et al. 2000; Grant et al. 1999), traumatic brain injury (Ardila et al. 1999), psychotropic drugs (Brady 1998), and extrapyramidal disease (Benke et al. 2000; Leder 1996). In developmental but not acquired stuttering, involuntary movements of the face and head resembling those of cranial dystonia—such as excessive blinking, forced eye closure, clonic jaw movements, and head tilt—are characteristically seen (Kiziltan and Akalin 1996). Alternatively, such movements can be interpreted as being akin to tics; this view is supported by an increased prevalence of obses-

sive-compulsive behaviors in persons with developmental stuttering (Abwender et al. 1998). Rarely, developmental stuttering that had been overcome returns after a brain injury, or developmental stuttering disappears after a brain injury (Helm-Estabrooks 1999).

Cluttering is a disorder of fluency in which discourse, rather than purely articulation, is disturbed by a range of deficits in speech pragmatics, motor control, and attention (Daly and Burnett 1999). Speech output is abnormal because of rapid rate, disturbed prosody, sound transpositions or slips of the tongue, poor narrative skills, and impaired management of the social interaction encompassing speech. Thoughts may be expressed in fragments; words or phrases may be repeated. In sharp contrast to developmental stuttering, patients are characteristically unconcerned about their impairment. Stuttering may be mistakenly diagnosed or occur in association. Rare instances of acquired cluttering have been reported (Thacker and De Nil 1996).

## Foreign Accent Syndrome

In 1947, the Scandinavian neurologist Monrad-Krohn (1947) described "dysprosody or altered 'melody of language'" in a patient with a wartime missile injury of the left frontotemporal region. She was a noncombatant, in fact a woman who had never been out of her small Norwegian town. She showed aphasic troubles, mild right-sided signs, and slight personality change. Most strikingly, her speech pattern had changed so that she sounded like a German when she spoke her native Norwegian. A number of similar cases of "foreign accent syndrome" have been described (tabulated in Carbary and Patterson 2000). All showed pathology in the language-dominant hemisphere involving motor or premotor cortex or subjacent white matter; one dextral patient had a foreign accent after a crossed aphemia with right-hemisphere infarction (Berthier et al. 1991). What distinguishes these patients from those with cortical dysarthria or apraxia of speech seems to be that the phonetic and prosodic alterations lead to characteristics that occur in natural languages. Thus, listeners hear the speech as "foreign" rather than abnormal, although often the foreign accent is generic and listeners cannot agree on its apparent provenance (Kurowski et al. 1996).

## Aprosodia

Ross and Mesulam (1979), following the work of Heilman et al. (1975) and Tucker et al. (1977) on "auditory affective agnosia," reported cases in which right hemisphere lesions led to loss of the affective elements of speech. Analysis of the cases led to recognition of syndromes of loss of prosody in expression and of impaired decoding of prosodic information in speech. Ross (1981) later schematized these syndromes—the "aprosodias"—as mirror images of left-hemisphere aphasic syndromes, although others failed to confirm this schema (Cancelliere and Kertesz 1990; Wertz et al. 1998).

Thus, lesions of either the left or the right hemisphere may disturb prosody. Left-hemisphere lesions may be marked by dysprosody along with aphasia and cortical dysarthria; right-hemisphere lesions may produce alterations in the affective component of speech, sometimes with dysarthria as well (Wertz et al. 1998). Often, disturbed recognition of the affective component of material presented visually is also present in cases of right-hemisphere lesions, and the disturbance can be detected with appropriate test materials. At times, the aprosodias present as disturbances in mood or social relatedness. The examiner must listen to spontaneous speech for prosodic elements; ask the patient to produce statements in various emotional tones, for example, anger, sadness, surprise, and joy; produce such emotional phrasings himself or herself, using a neutral sentence (e.g., "I am going to the store") while turning his or her face away from the patient, and ask the patient to identify the emotion; and ask the patient to reproduce an emotional phrasing the examiner has generated (Ross 1993).

## Echolalia

In this phenomenon, the patient repeats the speech of another person automatically, without communicative intent or effect (Ford 1989). Often, the speech repeated is the examiner's, and the phenomenon is immediately apparent, without being specifically elicited. However, at times other verbalizations in the environment are repeated; for example, patients may repeat words overheard from the corridor or the television. Sometimes the patient repeats only the last portion of what he or she hears, beginning with a natural break in the utterance. Sometimes grammatical corrections are made when the examiner deliberately utters an ungrammatical sentence. The patient may reverse pronouns (e.g., "I" for "you"), altering the sentence in a grammatically appropriate way. These corrections and alterations evince intactness of the patient's syntactic capabilities. The completion phenomenon also may be seen, whereby the patient automatically completes a well-known phrase uttered by the examiner: "Roses are red," says the examiner. "Roses are red, violets are blue," responds the patient. Speaking to the patient in a foreign language may elicit obviously automatic echolalic speech (Lecours et al. 1983).

Echolalia is a normal phenomenon in the learning of language in infancy (Lecours et al. 1983). Echolalia in transcortical aphasia marks the intactness of primary language areas in the frontal and temporal lobes, with syntax thus unimpaired but disconnected from control by other language functions. Other underlying disorders include autism, Tourette syndrome, dementia of the frontal type and other degenerative disorders, and startle-reaction disorders (Comings and Comings 1987; Howard and Ford 1992; Snowden and Neary 1993; Stengel 1947). Echolalia in a nonfluent aphasic patient may represent an environmental dependency reaction, akin to imitation behavior (see below) (Hadano et al. 1998).

## Palilalia

Palilalia is the patient's automatic repetition of his or her own final word or phrase. The volume of the patient's voice trails off, and the rate of speech is festinant. Palilalia occurs with basal ganglion disease (Boller et al. 1973), including progressive supranuclear palsy (Kluin et al. 1993) and postencephalitic or idiopathic parkinsonism (Benke et al. 2000; Critchley 1927), but midbrain and thalamic lesions (Stracciari et al. 1993; Yasuda et al. 1990), general paresis (Geschwind 1964), Tourette syndrome (Comings and Comings 1987), traumatic brain injury (Ardila et al. 1999), and epilepsy with a supplementary motor area focus (Alajouanine et al. 1959) have been implicated as well.

## "Blurting"

I have seen a few patients whose speech was marked by impulsive utterances of stereotyped or simple responses with no aphasic or echolalic features. For example, an elderly woman had the clinical features of progressive supranuclear palsy with no evident elementary cognitive abnormality. When questioned, she often replied "yes, yes" or "no, no" even before the questioner finished speaking and regardless of her intended answer to the question. She could then correct herself and give the reply she wished to give. She was unable to explain the behavior. These personal cases evinced disease in the frontostriatal circuit. The phenomenon seems to be related to echolalia and palilalia as well as to the environment-driven, impulsive but not stereotyped utterances of patients with frontal lobe disease (Ghika et al. 1995b). The phenomenon was recorded in dementia of the frontal type (Snowden and Neary 1993), and a similar or identical phenomenon was called "echoing approval" by Ghika et al. (1996).

## Mutism

The term *mutism* should be reserved for the situation "in which a person does not speak and does not make any attempt at spoken communication despite preservation of an adequate level of consciousness" (Departments of Psychiatry and Child Psychiatry 1987, p. 33). The first order of business in examining an alert patient who does not speak is to discover whether the disorder is due to elementary sensorimotor abnormalities involving the apparatus of speech. Such disturbances can be recognized by examining phonation, articulation, and nonspeech movements of the relevant musculature (e.g., swallowing and coughing).

If an elementary disorder is not at fault, the examination proceeds to a search for specific disturbances of verbal communication. Does the patient make any spontaneous attempt at communication through means other than speech? Does the patient gesture? Can the patient write, or, if hemiplegic, can he or she write with the nondominant hand? Can he or she arrange cut-out paper letters or letters from a child's set of spelling toys? Or, if familiar with sign language, can he or she sign?

Some patients with acute vascular lesions restricted to the lower primary motor cortex and the adjacent frontal operculum have transient mutism then recover through severe dysarthria without agrammatism, a disorder known as aphemia (Schiff et al. 1983). Transcortical motor aphasia features a prominent disturbance of spontaneous speech, occasionally beginning as mutism (M.P. Alexander 1989). A.R. Damasio and Van Hoesen (1983) described such a patient with a lesion in the dominant supplementary motor area; after recovery, the patient reported that she lacked the urge to speak. Mutism commonly develops in patients with frontotemporal dementia or primary progressive aphasia (Snowden et al. 1992). A restricted disturbance of verbal communication must be distinguished from a more global disorder of the initiation of activity. At its extreme, the latter is the state of akinetic mutism. M.P. Alexander (1999) pointed out that mutism has its "lesser forms": long latencies, terseness, and simplification of utterances.

# Abnormalities of Movement

## Weakness

The findings associated with lesions of the pyramidal tracts, spinal cord, peripheral nerves, and muscles are described in texts of neurology (Duus 1998). Greater awareness of the findings in nonpyramidal syndromes may help the clinician identify neurobehavioral syndromes associated with cerebral disease outside the primary motor regions. L.R. Caplan et al. (1990) described the features of a "nonpyramidal hemimotor" syndrome with caudate nucleus lesions. Patients show clumsiness and decreased spontaneous use of the affected limbs; associated movements are decreased as well. What appears at first glance to be paresis proves to be a slow development of full strength; if coaxed and given time, the patient shows mild weakness at worst. Freund and Hummelsheim (1985) explored the motor consequences of lesions of the premotor cortex. They observed a decrease in spontaneous use of the arm and attributed it to a failure of postural fixation; when supported, the arm showed at worst mild slowing of finger movements. The defect in elevation and abduction of the arm was best demonstrated by asking the patient to swing the arms in a windmill movement, both arms rotating forward or backward; the same defect can be found in cycling movements of the legs, especially backward cycling (Freund 1992). Movement rapidly decomposed when such coordination was required. Pyramidal signs—increased tendon jerks, Babinski's sign, and spasticity—may be absent in patients with these findings. In acute parietal lesions, "motor helplessness" due to loss of sensory input is regularly seen (Ghika et al. 1998).

## Disordered Gait

In evaluating gait, attention should be paid to rising from a chair, standing posture, postural reflexes, initiation of gait, stride length and base, and turning (Nutt et al. 1993). Frontal gait disorder is characterized by short, shuffling steps on either a wide or a narrow base, with hesitation at starts and turns. Postural equilibrium is impaired, although not as much as in Parkinson's disease, and the trunk is held upright on stiff, straight legs. Festination is not a feature. This is the gait disorder of subcortical vascular dementia (FitzGerald and Jankovic 1989a; Thompson and Marsden 1987), and it must be distinguished from Parkinson's disease (Kurlan et al. 2000). Stressed gait (e.g., walking heel to toe or on the outer aspects of the feet) may reveal asymmetric posturing of the upper extremity in patients without other signs.

## Akinesia

Akinesia has several aspects: delay in the initiation of movement, slowness in the execution of movement, and special difficulty with complex movements. The disturbance is demonstrated by requiring the patient to perform a repeated action, such as tapping thumb to forefinger, or two actions at once. A decrement in amplitude or freezing in the midst of the act is observed. When established, akinesia is unmistakable in the patient's visage and demeanor and in the way he or she sits motionlessly and has trouble arising from the chair. A distinction between parkinsonian akinesia and depressive psychomotor retardation is not easy to make, but the associated features of tremor, rigidity, and postural instability are generally absent in depressive illness (Rogers et al. 1987).

## Agitation

The term *agitation* is often misused to refer to the behavior of aggression or the affect of anxiety. "The preferred definition of psychomotor agitation is of a disorder of motor activity associated with mental distress which is characterized by a restricted range of repetitive, non-progressive ('to-and-fro'), non-goal directed activity" (Day 1999, p. 95). In distinction from akathisia, the excessive movement characteristically involves the upper extremities. In some patients with Alzheimer's disease, wandering is associated with depressive and anxiety symptoms and may represent agitation in this cognitively impaired population (Klein et al. 1999; Logsdon et al. 1998). Why certain causes of confusion commonly produce agitation—alcohol withdrawal, hypoxemia, post-ictal twilight state, and infarction in the territory of the left posterior cerebral artery—and others do not is uncertain. Hyperactivity in childhood, when pervasive rather than situational, seems to be linked to neurodevelopmental disorder, low IQ, clumsiness, and language delay, often against a background of obstetric complications (Schachar 1991).

Roaming, differentiated from wandering by being purposeful and exploratory, is characteristic of frontotemporal dementia (Mendez et al. 1993). In my experience, the excessive activity may be stereotyped, as, for example, the patient who roamed the hospital unit in rectilinear fashion, just so far from each wall with precise turns at each corner.

## Akathisia

Motor restlessness accompanied by an urge to move is referred to as akathisia (Sachdev 1995). Although akathisia is most familiar as a side effect of psychotropic drugs, the phenomenon occurs often in idiopathic Parkinson's disease (Comella and Goetz 1994) and occasionally with extensive destruction of the orbitofrontal cortex, as in traumatic brain injury (Stewart 1991) or herpes simplex encephalitis (Brazzelli et al. 1994). In a few cases it has been associated with restricted basal ganglion lesions, even occurring unilaterally with a contralateral lesion (Carrazana et al. 1989; Hermesh and Munitz 1990; Stuppaeck et al. 1995). Akathisia also may occur after withdrawal from dopamine-blocking drugs or as a tardive

movement disorder (Lang 1994; Sachdev 1995).

Eliciting the account of subjective restlessness from a psychotic patient may be difficult, but recognizing akathisia and distinguishing it from agitation are important. Complaints specifically referable to the legs are more characteristic of akathisia than of anxiety (Sachdev and Kruk 1994). Although by derivation the term refers to an inability to sit, its objective manifestations are most prominent when the patient attempts to stand still. The patient "marches in place," shifting weight from foot to foot. Seated, the patient may shuffle or tap his or her feet or repeatedly cross his or her legs. When the disorder is severe, the recumbent patient may show myoclonic jerks or a coarse tremor of the legs. One patient of mine with severe withdrawal akathisia caused an ulcer of the heel of her foot by constantly rubbing it against the bedsheets.

## Hypertonus

There are three forms of increased muscle tone as it concerns the neuropsychiatrist. In spasticity, tone is increased in flexors in the upper extremity and extensors in the lower, but not in the antagonists. The hypertonus shows an increase in resistance followed by an immediate decrease (the clasp-knife phenomenon) and depends on the velocity of the passive movement. This is the typical hemiplegic pattern of hemisphere stroke, universally called pyramidal, which indicates a lesion actually not in the pyramidal tract but in the corticoreticulospinal tract (G.E. Alexander and DeLong 1992; Brodal 1981). In rigidity, tone is increased in both agonists and antagonists throughout the range of motion; the increase is not velocity dependent. This is the characteristic hypertonus of extrapyramidal disease. In paratonia, or *gegenhalten*, increased tone is erratic and depends on the intensity of the imposed movement. This pattern of hypertonus is usually related to extensive brain dysfunction, typically with frontosubcortical involvement. The erratic quality is related to the presence of both oppositional and facilitatory aspects of the patient's motor performance. Beversdorf and Heilman (1998) described a test for facilitatory paratonia: the patient's arm is repeatedly flexed fully at the elbow and extended to 90°, then the examiner's hand is withdrawn at the point of arm extension. In the abnormal response, the patient lifts or even continues to flex and extend the arm. A cogwheel feel to increased muscle tone is not intrinsic to the hypertonus; the cogwheeling in parkinsonism is imparted by postural (not rest) tremor superimposed on rigidity (Findley et al. 1981). In delirium and dementia, the paratonia of diffuse brain dysfunction can be mistaken for extrapyramidal rigidity when the examiner feels cogwheeling, which actually indicates the additional presence of the common tremor of metabolic encephalopathy or postural tremor of some other etiology (Kurlan et al. 2000).

## Dystonia

Dystonia has been defined by Fahn et al. (1987) as "sustained muscle contractions, frequently causing twisting and repetitive movements, or abnormal postures" (p. 335). The contractions may be generalized or focal. Typically, the dystonic arm hyperpronates, with a flexed wrist and extended fingers; the dystonic lower extremity shows an inverted foot with plantar flexion. A number of syndromes of focal dystonia are well recognized, such as torticollis, writer's cramp, and blepharospasm with jaw and mouth movements (Meige syndrome). A dystonic pattern of particular interest is oculogyric crisis, in which forced thinking or other psychological disturbance accompanies forced deviation of the eyes (Benjamin 1999b; Leigh et al. 1987). Dystonia, including oculogyric crisis, can occur as an acute or tardive effect of dopamine blockade (FitzGerald and Jankovic 1989b; Sachdev 1993; Wojcik et al. 1991). Dystonic movements characteristically worsen with voluntary action and may be evoked only by very specific action patterns. Dystonic movements, especially in an early stage or mild form of the illness, can produce apparently bizarre symptoms, such as a patient who cannot walk because of twisting feet and legs but who is able to run or a patient who can do everything with his or her hands except write. Adding to the oddness is the frequent capacity of the patient to reduce the involuntary movement by using "sensory tricks" (*le geste antagoniste*); in torticollis, for example, the neck contractions that are violent enough to break restraining devices may yield to the patient's simply touching the chin with his or her own finger. Eliciting a history of such tricks or observing the patient's use of them is diagnostic.

## Tremor

All tremors are rhythmic, regular oscillating movements around a joint. Three major forms of tremor are distinguished. In rest tremor, the movement is present distally when the limb is supported and relaxed; action reduces the intensity of the tremor. The frequency is usually low, about 4–8 cps. This is the well-known tremor of parkinsonism. Because the amplitude of the tremor diminishes with action, rest tremor is usually less disabling than it might appear. In postural tremor, the outstretched limb oscillates. At times, this can be better visualized by placing a piece of paper over the outstretched hand. Postural tremor is produced by anxiety, by certain drugs (e.g., caf-

feine, lithium, steroids, and adrenergic agonists), and by hereditary essential tremor. A coarse, irregular, rapid postural tremor is frequently seen in metabolic encephalopathy (Plum and Posner 1980). In intention tremor, the active limb oscillates more prominently as the limb approaches its target during goal-directed movements. This tremor is seen in disease of the cerebellum and its connections. Rubral, or midbrain, tremor is a low-frequency, predominantly unilateral tremor with rest, postural, and intention components (Samie et al. 1990). Tardive tremor has been rarely recognized (Stacy and Jankovic 1992).

Observing the patient with arms supported and fully at rest, then with arms outstretched, and then with arms abducted to 90° at the shoulders and bent at the elbows, while the hands are held palms down with the fingers pointing at each other in front of the chest, will demonstrate most upper-extremity tremors (Lang 2000). A given patient's organic tremor may vary in amplitude, for example, with anxiety when the patient is aware of being observed. However, anxiety and other factors do not alter tremor frequency. Thus, if the patient's tremor slows or accelerates when the examiner asks him or her to tap slowly or quickly with the opposite limb, hysteria should be suspected (Koller et al. 1989).

## Chorea

Chorea is the occurrence of "brief, random, sudden, rapid, arrhythmic, involuntary movements" (Padberg and Bruyn 1986, p. 549) that dance over the patient's body. The patient may incorporate these movements into purposeful ones in an effort to hide the chorea when it is mild. As with dystonia, chorea may become more evident when elicited by gait or other activity. Choreic disturbance of respiratory movements is probably underrecognized, especially in tardive dyskinesia (Ivanovich et al. 1993; Rich and Radwany 1994). Predominantly proximal movements, large in amplitude and violent in force, are called ballistic. Usually, ballism is unilateral and is caused by lesions in the subthalamic nucleus, but it can be bilateral (Lodder and Baard 1981), and lesions elsewhere in the basal ganglia can be culpable (Dewey and Jankovic 1989).

The differential diagnosis of chorea is wide (Hyde et al. 1991). Late-onset abnormal movements due to dopamine-blocking drugs—tardive dyskinesia—may be choreic, although the oral movements are best considered stereotypies (Stacy et al. 1993). If the patient has psychosis, the clinician must not assume that chorea is tardive dyskinesia but must consider a differential diagnosis of diseases that can produce both chorea and psychosis (e.g., Wilson's disease, systemic lupus erythematosus, Huntington's disease, and Fahr's syndrome). Furthermore, abnormal movements similar to those of tardive dyskinesia can be seen in untreated severe psychiatric illness (Fenton et al. 1997; Turner 1992). Antiepileptic drugs and antidepressants also can produce abnormal movements, and not all antidopaminergic drugs are antipsychotic agents, so the clinician must inquire about use of metoclopramide and prochlorperazine (Lang 1990; Sewell and Jeste 1992).

Many elderly dyskinetic patients are edentulous. Koller (1983) reported differences between edentulous dyskinesia and tardive dyskinesia. In the former, abnormal movements of the upper face and limbs were absent, and the tongue lay still in the mouth; tongue protrusion was unimpaired. In contrast, vermicular (wormlike) movements of the tongue inside the mouth are prominent in tardive dyskinesia, and patients are often unable to maintain the tongue protruded. Lang (2000) tabulated the differential diagnostic features between Huntington's disease and tardive dyskinesia (Table 5–2).

**TABLE 5–2.** Tardive dyskinesia (TD) versus Huntington's disease (HD)

|  | TD | HD |
| --- | --- | --- |
| **Nature of the movements** | | |
| Repetitive stereotypic movements | + + | – |
| Flowing choreic movements | ± | + + |
| **Sites** | | |
| Forehead | – | + |
| Blepharospasm | ± | ± |
| Oro-buccolingual | + + | ± |
| Platysma | ± | ± |
| Nuchal muscles | ± | + |
| Respiratory | + | ± |
| Trunk, legs | + | + + |
| **Additional features** | | |
| Oculomotor disturbances, head thrusts | – | + + |
| Impersistence of tongue protrusion | – | + + |
| Improvement of facial movements with tongue protrusion | + + | – |
| Facial dyspraxia | – | + + |
| Dysarthria | – | + + |
| Milkmaid grip | – | + + |
| Body rocking movements | + | ± |
| Marching in place | + | – |
| Bizarre ataxic gait | – | + + |
| Postural instability | – | + + |

*Note.* + + = common or characteristic; + = sometimes present; ± = occasionally present; – = generally absent.
*Source.* Adapted from Lang 2000.

## Myoclonus

Myoclonus is the occurrence of sudden, jerky, shocklike movements arising from the central nervous system (Brown 1999). Certain forms of myoclonus are within normal experience; the hiccup and the jerk that awakens one just as one drifts off to sleep (the hypnic jerk) are myoclonic phenomena. Myoclonus does not show the continuous, dancelike flow of movement that characterizes chorea. When myoclonus is rhythmic, it differs from tremor in having an interval between individual movements, a "square wave" rather than a "sine wave." The distinction of myoclonus from tic is partly based on subjective features: the tiqueur reports a wish to move, a sense of relief after the movement, and the ability to delay the movement (albeit at the cost of increasing subjective tension) (Lang 1992). Also, tics can be more complex and stereotyped than myoclonic jerks. Myoclonus can accompany dystonia (Obeso et al. 1983), including tardive dystonia (Abad and Ovsiew 1993), and tardive myoclonus without dystonia is also recognized (Little and Jankovic 1987). Myoclonus occurring in a confused patient is usually a feature of toxic-metabolic encephalopathy but should raise the question of nonconvulsive status epilepticus (Rohr-Le Floch et al. 1988; Thomas et al. 1992; Tomson et al. 1992).

## Asterixis

Repeated momentary loss of postural tone produces a flapping movement of the outstretched hands originally described in the setting of liver failure but subsequently recognized in many or all states of metabolic encephalopathy and in all muscle groups. Young and Shahani (1986) recommended eliciting it by asking the patient to dorsiflex the index fingers for 30 seconds while the hands and arms are outstretched, with the patient watching to ensure maximum voluntary contraction. Physiologically, asterixis is the inverse of multifocal myoclonus; the electromyogram shows brief silence on the background of sustained discharge (Young and Shahani 1986). The coarse tremor of delirium is a slower version of asterixis. Bilateral asterixis is a valuable sign because it points reliably to a toxic-metabolic confusional state. Asterixis, to my knowledge, has never been described in the "functional" psychoses and is thus pathognomonic for an organic encephalopathy. Occasionally, asterixis is unilateral and reflects a lesion of the contralateral thalamic, parietal, or medial frontal structures (usually thalamic) (Tatu et al. 2000); rarely, bilateral asterixis is of structural origin (Rio et al. 1995).

## Startle

Brown et al. (1991b) reviewed the physiology of the normal reaction to sudden unexpected auditory stimuli. The clinician produces an auditory stimulus with an unexpected handclap outside the patient's field of vision. Clinically, the reflex invariably involves eye blink, although this is physiologically distinct from the rest of the phenomenon (Brown et al. 1991a). The muscle jerks are most intense cranially, taper caudally, and are predominantly flexor. A rare, usually familial, disorder in which this reflex is disturbed is called hyperexplexia; it features hyperreflexia, hypertonus, and abnormal gait in infancy; myoclonus; and exaggerated startle, frequently causing falls (Brown 1999). Abnormal startle reactions are also seen in posttraumatic stress disorder, Tourette syndrome, some epilepsies, certain culture-bound syndromes such as latah and the "jumping Frenchmen of Maine," brain stem encephalitis, post-anoxic encephalopathy, and hexosaminidase A deficiency (Brown 1999). The stimulus-sensitive myoclonus seen in Creutzfeldt-Jakob disease may not be a true disorder of the startle mechanism (Howard and Ford 1992).

## Tic and Compulsions

Some of the key features of tics have been described earlier in this chapter in differentiating them from myoclonus. Tics are sudden jerks, sometimes simple (a blink or a grunt) but sometimes as complex as a well-organized voluntary movement (repeatedly touching an object or speaking a word) (Lees 1985; Lennox 1999). In addition to the important subjective differences noted previously, tics differ from many other abnormal movements in that they may persist during sleep (Lang 2000). (Some myoclonic disorders and some dyskinetic movements may also persist during sleep [Sawle 1999].) Despite the quasi-voluntary quality of some tics, electrophysiological evidence shows that tics differ from identical movements produced voluntarily by the same person in that they lack the readiness potential *(Bereitschaftspotential)* that normally precedes a voluntary movement (Obeso et al. 1981).

A distinction between complex tics and compulsions rests partly on the subjective experience of the patient (Holzer et al. 1994). Compulsions are taken to be voluntary, but tics may be experienced as deliberate responses to an urge (like scratching because of an itch) or be given a post hoc meaning by the patient, so the distinction may be obscured. Obsessions and compulsions can occur in organic disease (Berthier et al. 1996; Laplane 1994; Weiss and Jenike 2000). Some compulsive behavior may represent utilization behavior rather than activity driven by anxiety (Destée et al. 1990).

## Stereotypy and Mannerism

Stereotypies are purposeless and repetitive movements that may be performed in lieu of other motor activity for long periods of time (Lees 1988). Ridley (1994) distinguished stereotypy from perseveration, noting that in the former the amount of one type of behavior is excessive and in the latter the range of behavior is reduced so that behavior is repetitive but not excessive. Stereotypies include movements such as crossing and uncrossing the legs, clasping and unclasping the hands, picking at clothes or at the nails or skin, head banging, and rocking. In schizophrenia, a delusional idea associated with stereotyped movements can sometimes, but not always, be elicited (I.H. Jones 1965).

Stereotyped movements are seen in schizophrenia, autism, mental retardation, Rett syndrome, Tourette syndrome, neuroacanthocytosis, congenital blindness (but not in those whose blindness is acquired late [Frith and Done 1990; Ridley and Baker 1982]), and numerous other psychopathological states (Stein et al. 1998). They are particularly characteristic of frontotemporal dementia (Neary and Snowden 1996). For example, one such patient over and over again tapped a complex rhythm on his knee, using both hands. In nonpsychotic, intellectually normal subjects, they may be associated with obsessive and compulsive symptoms (Niehaus et al. 2000). At times, especially in the mentally retarded, a distinction from epileptic events may be difficult (Paul 1997). Many of the abnormal movements of tardive dyskinesia (chewing movements and pelvic rocking) are patterned and repetitive, not random as is chorea, and are best described as stereotypies (Kaneko et al. 1993; Stacy et al. 1993). Amphetamine intoxication is a well-recognized cause of stereotypy, known in this setting as *punding*, a Swedish word introduced during a Scandinavian epidemic of amphetamine abuse (Rylander 1972). Similarly, cocaine and levodopa can cause stereotyped movements (Friedman 1994). Stereotypies occur occasionally ipsilateral or contralateral to a motor deficit during the acute phase of stroke (Ghika et al. 1995a; Ghika-Schmidt et al. 1997).

Manneristic movements are purposeful movements carried out in a bizarre way. They may result from the incorporation of stereotypies into goal-directed movements (Lees 1985, 1988).

## Catatonia

The syndrome described by Kahlbaum in the last century and incorporated into the concept of dementia praecox by Kraepelin occurs in a wide variety of organic states as well as in the classic functional psychoses (Rogers 1991,

**TABLE 5–3.** Primitive reflexes

| Name | Stimulus | Abnormal response |
| --- | --- | --- |
| Suck | Examiner's knuckle between patient's lips | Any sucking motion |
| Snout | Minimal pressure of examiner's finger on patient's lips, then drawing away | Puckering of lips |
| Grasp | Stroking of patient's palm toward fingers while patient is distracted | Flexion of fingers |
| Avoidance | Same as grasp | Extension of wrist and fingers |
| Palmomental | Noxious stroking of thenar eminence | Contraction of ipsilateral mentalis muscle |
| Nuchocephalic | Shoulders of standing patient are briskly turned while eyes are closed | Head remains in initial position |
| Mouth-opening/ finger-spreading | Patient opens mouth while extended arms are supported by examiner | Spreading and extension of fingers |

1992). The syndrome can be defined broadly as abnormality of movement or muscle tone associated with psychosis (C.M. Fisher 1989), or more narrowly as "at least one motor sign (catalepsy, posturing, or waxy flexibility) in combination with at least one sign of psychosocial withdrawal or excitement and/or bizarre repetitive movement (mutism, negativism, impulsiveness, grimacing, stereotypies, mannerisms, command automatism, echopraxia/echolalia or verbigeration)" (Barnes et al. 1986, p. 991). Such signs are common in severe mental disorder (Rogers 1985), and several scales for their assessment have been formalized and validated (Braunig et al. 2000; Bush et al. 1996; McKenna et al. 1991; Northoff et al. 1999). Cataleptic postures (waxy flexibility) can occur with contralateral parietal lesions (Ghika et al. 1998; Saver et al. 1993).

## Synkinesia and Mirror Movements

Normal movement requires that certain automatic movements take place along with intended ones. Excessive synkinesia occurs in a variety of states (Zulch and Muller 1969). Obligatory, congenital bimanual synkinesia ("mirror movements") persisting into adulthood occurs with cervical spine disease, such as Klippel-Feil syndrome, as well as with agenesis of the corpus callosum (Schott and Wyke 1981). The pathophysiology involves abnormal ipsilateral motor pathways (L.G. Cohen et al. 1991). When not due to such a malformation, persistent mirror movements are commonly associated with neuropsychiatric disorder, and tests for mirror movements appear in inventories of soft signs (E.Y.H. Chen et al. 1995; Rasmussen 1993). The phenomenon is easily observed by asking the patient to touch, repeatedly and in turn, the fingers to the thumb of each hand; along with watching the active hand for fine motor coordination, the examiner watches the contralateral hand for mirror movements.

## Primitive Reflexes

The received wisdom about the grasp, suck, snout, and palmomental reflexes (Table 5–3) is that these are signs brought about by cortical disease, especially frontal, which disinhibits primitive reflexes (Paulson and Gottleib 1968). However, there is considerable doubt that all signs of this sort are of pathological significance (Landau 1989). For example, Jacobs and Grossman (1980) found that the palmomental sign could be elicited in more than 20% of healthy subjects in their third and fourth decades and in more than 50% in their ninth decade; the snout sign could be found in more than 30% of subjects older than age 60. Similarly, Koller et al. (1982) found the snout sign in more than half, and Vreeling et al. (1995) in just fewer than half, of healthy elderly subjects.

Primitive reflexes may be of clinical importance in specific circumstances. E.Y.H. Chen et al. (1995) found the grasp, snout, and palmomental signs infrequently in schizophrenic patients but significantly more commonly than in healthy control subjects. Other investigators also found primitive reflexes more commonly in schizophrenic patients than in control subjects and suggested that the developmental brain abnormality indicated by primitive reflexes and soft signs (see the discussion following) interacts with neuroleptic medication to bring about extrapyramidal side effects (Gupta et al. 1995; Khanna et al. 1994; Youssef and Waddington 1988). Primitive reflexes in demented patients may be associated with poorer functional capacity at a given level of cognitive impairment and indicate poor prognosis (Molloy et al. 1991; Mölsä et al. 1995). They are commonly present in patients with cerebrovascular disease (Rao et al. 1999), but they may be more common in frontotemporal dementia than in comparably severe vascular dementia with frontal predominance (Sjögren et al. 1997).

The localizing value of these signs is also incompletely understood. To consider them all equally as "frontal release signs" would seem to go beyond the available evidence. The grasp reflex is associated with damage to the supplementary motor area; when the damage is more extensive in the medial frontal cortex, involving the anterior cingulate gyrus, a grope reflex may appear (Hashimoto and Tanaka 1998). Often, it occurs bilaterally with a unilateral lesion (De Renzi and Barbieri 1992). Some less familiar signs such as the nuchocephalic (Jenkyn et al. 1975), avoidance (Denny-Brown 1958), mouth-opening/finger-spreading (Touwen and Prechtl 1970), and self-grasping (Ropper 1982) signs may prove to be relatively specific or of localizing value.

## Soft Signs

Under the rubric of soft signs is grouped a varied set of findings taken to demonstrate impairment in sensorimotor integration and motor control. Unfortunately, the many studies of these signs have not used the same test batteries, so comparisons from one study to another are not always easy (Sanders and Keshavan 1998) (Table 5–4). A focus on soft signs in psychiatric patients should not blind the examiner to "hard signs" and extrapyramidal signs unrelated to medication in patients with idiopathic psychiatric illness (Caligiuri et al. 1993; Griffiths et al. 1998; Kinney et al. 1993b).

Schizophrenia is unquestionably associated with the finding of an excess of abnormal signs. Such signs seen in adulthood may represent the residua of childhood motor abnormalities (Neumann and Walker 1996; Rosso et al. 2000a). They are independent of neuroleptic treatment (Wolff and O'Driscoll 1999) and are associated with neuropsychological deficits (Arango et al. 1999; Wong et al. 1997), poor treatment response (R.C. Smith et al. 1999), and adverse effects of neuroleptics (Convit et al. 1994). They are present in siblings of schizophrenic persons, implying a relation to genetic risk for the illness (Y.L.R. Chen et al. 2000; Ismail et al. 1998b; Niethammer et al. 2000), although a relation to perinatal injury is possible as well (Cantor-Graae et al. 2000). Although the bulk of studies examine the occurrence of soft signs in schizophrenia, they are not specific for this disorder, being found inter alia in homeless persons (Douyon et al. 1998) as well as in mood disorder (Boks et al. 2000), obsessive-compulsive disorder (Hollander et al. 1990), borderline personality disorder (Gardner et al. 1987), and posttraumatic stress disorder (Gurvits et al. 2000). Thus, the presence of soft signs should be taken as a nonspecific indicator of cerebral dysfunction.

## Signs of Callosal Disconnection

Bogen (1993) showed that many of the crucial elements of the disconnection syndrome can be found by simple maneuvers. The history may disclose features typical of disconnection. Most remarkably, the patient reports behavioral conflict between the hands or merely a sense that the left hand behaves in an "alien" fashion. Brion and Jedynak (1972) described *"le signe de la main étrangère,"* translated in the English summary of the article as the "strange hand sign" but subsequently (and better) as the "alien hand sign." The original description clearly conveyed a sensory phenomenon, akin to neglect and in fact considered a "hemisomatagnosia specific for touch" (Brion and Jedynak 1972, p. 262). For example, one patient felt his left hand with his right behind his back while dressing. He recognized it as a hand but not as his own hand. The authors emphasized the unawareness specifically of ownership of the hand, that is, the sense of "strangeness" or alienation. In all four cases reported by Brion and Jedynak (1972), the patients had posterior callosal lesions. However, not all patients with the alien hand phenomenon have callosal disconnection. A posterior alien hand syndrome seen after noncallosal lesions producing a disturbance of the body schema in addition to abnormal movements has been described (Ay et al. 1998; Bundick and Spinella 2000). The alien hand seen in corticobasal degeneration (Thompson and Marsden 1992) may fit this pattern in some instances; in others it may be more closely akin to the levitation of the upper extremity seen with contralateral parietal lesions (Barclay et al. 1999; Denny-Brown et al. 1952; Mori and Yamadori 1989). Other patients with neurodegenerative disorders and without callosal lesions may have the alien hand syndrome through a combination of deficits involving praxis and proprioception (MacGowan et al. 1997). The phenomenon of directed though unwilled behavior by the hand—the "anarchic hand"—associated with frontal lobe pathology is described later in this chapter.

On examination, the patient with callosal lesions shows an inability to name odors presented to the right nostril. In visual field testing, a hemianopsia appears to be present in each hemifield alternately, opposite to the hand the patient uses to point to stimuli. Thus, when the patient is using the right hand, he or she responds only to stimuli in the right hemifield but when using the left, only to the left hemifield.

An apraxia of the left hand can be shown by the usual testing maneuvers. Because verbal information processed in the left hemisphere cannot be transferred to the right, and because the right hemisphere has limited capacity to understand spoken commands, the

**TABLE 5–4.** Comparison of batteries of soft signs

| Element | NES | Modified NES | CNI | Griffiths |
|---|---|---|---|---|
| **Gait and balance** | | | | |
| Casual gait | | | ✓ | |
| Tandem gait | ✓ | ✓ | ✓ | ✓ |
| Romberg | ✓ | ✓ | ✓ | ✓ |
| **Complex movements** | | | | |
| Ring/fist | ✓ | ✓ | | ✓ |
| Fist/edge/palm | ✓ | ✓ | ✓ | ✓ |
| Oseretsky (alternating fists) | ✓ | ✓ | ✓ | ✓ |
| Finger/thumb opposition | ✓ | | ✓ | ✓ |
| Rhythm tapping | ✓ | | ✓ | |
| Tap reproduction | ✓ | ✓ | | |
| Dysdiadochokinesia | ✓ | ✓ | ✓ | ✓ |
| **Extraocular movements** | | | | |
| Visual tracking | | | ✓ | ✓ |
| Convergence | ✓ | | | ✓ |
| Gaze persistence | ✓ | | ✓ | |
| **Other motor** | | | | |
| Drift | | | ✓ | |
| Motor persistence | | | ✓ | |
| Finger-nose | ✓ | | ✓ | ✓ |
| Mirror movements | ✓ | | ✓ | ✓ |
| Synkinesia of head | ✓ | | ✓ | |
| Tremor | ✓ | | ✓ | ✓ |
| Choreoathetosis | ✓ | | ✓ | ✓ |
| **Sensory** | | | | |
| Audiovisual integration | ✓ | ✓ | | ✓ |
| Stereognosis | ✓ | | ✓ | ✓ |
| Graphesthesia | ✓ | ✓ | ✓ | ✓ |
| Face-hand test | ✓ | ✓ | ✓ | ✓ |
| **Two-point discrimination** | | | | |
| Right-left orientation | ✓ | ✓ | ✓ | ✓ |
| **Primitive reflexes** | | | | |
| Glabellar | ✓ | | ✓ | ✓ |
| Snout | ✓ | | ✓ | ✓ |
| Palmomental | | ✓ | ✓ | |
| Grasp | ✓ | | ✓ | ✓ |
| Suck | ✓ | | | ✓ |

*Note.* NES = Neurological Evaluation Scale, see Buchanan and Heinrichs 1989. Modified NES, see Sanders et al. 1998. CNI = Cambridge Neurological Inventory, see E.Y.H. Chen et al. 1995. Griffiths, see Griffiths et al. 1998.

patient is not able to produce appropriate responses with the left hand to spoken commands. Similarly, writing with the left hand is impossible. These features were emphasized in the "deconnection syndrome" reported by Geschwind and Kaplan (1962) in their work (which initiated the modern era of clinical disconnection studies and in considerable measure initiated the current development of behavioral neurology [Absher and Benson 1993]). For reciprocal reasons, the right hand shows a constructional disorder.

The patient has an anomia for unseen objects felt with the left hand. If the examiner places one of the patient's hands (again unseen) into a given posture, the patient is unable to match the posture with the other hand. Similarly, the patient cannot touch with the left thumb the finger of the left hand that corresponds to the finger of the right hand touched by the examiner, and vice versa.

## Orientation

Disorientation is the shibboleth of the nonneuropsychiatrist's cognitive examination. In common psychiatric parlance, disorientation means organic disease, but the shortcomings of this definition are twofold. First, many patients have organic cognitive disorders without disorientation—particularly focal cognitive disorders such as alexia or constructional disorder. Even in the syndromes of delirium and dementia, disorientation is far from invariable. Cutting (1980) found in his series of 74 cases of "acute organic reaction" that only 36% were disoriented to the year, 43% to the month, and 34% to the name of the hospital. By contrast, 85% had abnormalities of mood and 46% had abnormal beliefs. Similarly, in a study of disorientation after stroke, the sensitivity of disorientation for dementia was only 59% and for defective attention by neuropsychological assessment only 34% (Desmond et al. 1994). Second, disorientation is a nonspecific indicator. A patient may be unable to give the date or place because of impairment in attention, memory, language, or content of thought. The neuropsychiatrist probes these mechanisms by using more specific tasks.

The pattern of disorientation can have diagnostic significance. Disorientation to place can carry an entirely different significance from disorientation to date (see below). Delirious disorientation was distinguished from delusional disorientation in Jacksonian terms by M. Levin (1951, 1956), who pointed out that the delirious patient mistakes the unfamiliar for the familiar—reducing the novel to the automatic—as when the patient reports that the hospital is "a factory," where he or she formerly worked. By contrast, the schizophrenic patient mistakes the familiar for the unfamiliar, as when the patient identifies his or her location as Mars. Schnider et al. (1996) argued that in amnestic patients disorientation reflects confusion in temporal context due to orbitofrontal dysfunction.

## Attention

Full alertness with normal attention lies at one end of a continuum, the other end of which is coma. Where the patient is on this continuum can be assessed by observing the reaction to a graded series of probes: entering the room, speaking the patient's name, touching the patient without speaking, shouting, and so on through painful stimulation. The proper recording of the response is by specific notation of the probe and the reaction (e.g., "makes no response to examiner's entrance but orients to examiner's voice; speaks only when shaken by the shoulder").

Deficits occur in the capacity to maintain attention to external stimuli (vigilance), the capacity to attend consistently to internal stimuli (concentration), and the capacity to shift attention from one stimulus to another. Vigilance can be assessed by the patient's capacity to carry out a continuous-performance task; such tasks have been extensively used in the psychological laboratory. In a bedside adaptation, the "A test," the patient is presented with a string of letters, one per second, and is required to signal at each occurrence of the letter *A* (Strub and Black 1988). A single error of omission or of commission is considered an abnormal response. Concentration can be assessed by the patient's capacity to recite the numbers from 20 to 1 or to give the days of the week or the months of the year in reverse order. A pathognomonic error is the intrusion of the ordinary forward order: "20, 19, 18, 17, 18, 19, …." This amounts to a failure to inhibit the intrusion of the more familiar "set."

Digit span is a classic psychological test of attention, easily performed at the bedside. The examiner recites strings of numbers, slowly, clearly, and without phrasing into chunks. The patient is required to repeat them immediately. Subsequently, the patient can be asked to repeat strings of digits after reversing them in his or her head. The normal forward digit span is usually considered to be a minimum of five. The backward digit span may depend on visuospatial processing as well as attention (Black 1986). A related task of working memory is asking the patient to alphabetize the letters of the word *world* (Leopold and Borson 1997). Testing working memory by number-letter alternation is discussed below.

## Neglect

The patient who pays no attention to the left side of his or her body and the left side of space is one of the most dramatic phenomena in neuropsychiatry. Bisiach (1993) used the term *dyschiria* to refer to neglect and related phenomena such as extinction (unresponsiveness to stimuli when concurrent with contralateral stimuli) and allochiria (mislocation of stimuli as contralateral to their true location). The bedside clinician can readily identify the patient who entirely ignores one half of space, leaving his or her left arm out of the sleeve of a gown, leaving the left side of breakfast uneaten, and so on. Milder degrees of neglect can be recognized using a line-bisection task (the patient must place an X at the midpoint of a line drawn by the examiner) or a cancellation task (in which the patient crosses out letters or other items for which he or she must search in an array) (Mesulam 2000). Neglect may occur not only in external space but in "representational space" (i.e., the patient may neglect the left half of an imagined object). Bisiach and Luzzatti (1978) demonstrated this by asking patients to describe a well-known piazza as it appeared from one direction, thereby eliciting a description that neglected the left side of the piazza, and then asking the patients to describe the piazza as it appeared from the opposite direction, thereby eliciting a description that neglected the previously described side of the piazza and included the previously neglected side. Using a less picturesque approach, Baxter and Warrington (1983) found the same phenomenon by asking a patient to spell words forward and backward. This patient with neglect dysgraphia neglected the left half of the word as it appeared in the mind's eye, whether that was the first half or the second half of the word. In a related, simple but telling demonstration of hemineglect in the internal representation of the external world, Poizner et al. (1987) found that deaf patients fluent in sign language who develop left hemineglect from right-hemisphere stroke do not neglect left hemispace syntactically in sign even while they do so visuospatially.

Mesulam (1981) constructed a network theory in which the parietal cortex, frontal cortex, and cingulate cortex interact to generate attention to the opposite side of space. Lesions in these cortices produce distinguishable contralateral sensory neglect, directional hypokinesia, and reduced motivational value, respectively. Thus, Daffner et al. (1990) described a patient whose capacity for spatial exploration in left hemispace was reduced after a right frontal infarction, as shown by failure on a letter-cancellation task, despite the absence of sensory abnormality. Following a subsequent right parietal lesion, visual and auditory extinction on the left emerged and the exploratory defect was accentuated. Inventive experimental paradigms confirmed this distinction between the input and output ends of a sensorimotor-processing continuum (Bisiach 1993; Tegnér and Levander 1991). Neglect is a transient feature after right-hemisphere stroke, usually disappearing after a few months (Hier et al. 1983). Rarely, neglect occurs not on the left-right axis but on a vertical or radial (near-far) axis (Adair et al. 1995).

Posner et al. (1988) found right hemineglect in schizophrenic patients by means of methods to demonstrate neglect not applicable at the bedside. In their view, the right-hand agraphesthesia that can be found in schizophrenic patients is a clinical manifestation of the "disengage deficit"—the inability to detach attention from ipsilateral hemispace—which results, in schizophrenia, from dysfunction of the left cingulate gyrus. Voeller and Heilman (1988) found left neglect on a letter-cancellation task in children with attention deficit disorder.

An inverse syndrome of "acute hemiconcern" was described as occurring after right parietal stroke producing pseudothalamic sensory loss without neglect. The patients transiently concentrated attention on the left side of the body and manipulated it actively (Bogousslavsky et al. 1995).

## Hypermetamorphosis

Wernicke coined the term *hypermetamorphosis* to refer to an excessive and automatic attention to environmental stimuli. Klüver and Bucy (1937, 1939) demonstrated this phenomenon in monkeys with bilateral temporal lobectomy; a Klüver-Bucy syndrome can be seen in humans as well (Poeck 1985a). One of my patients, an elderly man, presented to the hospital with serial seizures. On awakening, he showed a post-ictal twilight state. In this period, he compulsively attended to elements of the environment and kept up a remarkable running commentary on them: "You're wearing a tie, there's a picture on the wall," and so on. Electroencephalography showed bilateral posterior temporal spike foci. Perhaps this is related to the Schneiderian symptom of auditory hallucinations that provide a running commentary on the schizophrenic patient's activity.

# Memory

Bedside testing of verbal memory can be done briefly and validly (Kopelman 1986). Recall of paragraph-length material after a 45-minute delay may be an ideal test, but recall of a name and address or three words after several minutes is simple and satisfactory (Bowers et al. 1989; Katzman et al. 1983; Kopelman 1986). The improvement of verbal recall with semantic cues implies a disorder of retrieval mechanisms, such as is seen in frontal-subcortical disease (Yuspeh et al. 1998). Similar testing of figural memory at the bedside is also easily done. For example, the "three words–three shapes" test of Weintraub and Mesulam (Weintraub 2000; Weintraub and Mesulam 1985) quickly and simply compares verbal and figural memory side by side. I sometimes ask patients to recall three pointed directions (e.g., up at a 45° angle, to the right, and to the left). Memory failure is a sensitive indicator of attentional dysfunction, in which case the basis is not in memory systems proper.

The testing of verbal and nonverbal short-term memory does not cover all the memory subroutines that have been identified by neuropsychologists. Whether remote memory can be validly assessed at the bedside is uncertain. Can we briefly and validly, without specialized materials, make assessments of memory for source and temporal context, functions especially impaired in frontal lobe lesions? In frontal amnesia, recognition memory is relatively spared for a given level of memory by free recall. Can we reliably discern this disparity at the bedside? Can we assess procedural memory, for example, the learning of a motor task? Developing and validating bedside methods for these domains are goals for the future.

# Language and Praxis

## Aphasia

This discussion is a review of what the clinician examines in the patient with an acquired disorder of language (Goodglass and Kaplan 1983).

**Spontaneous speech.**   Although the clinician hears the patient's spontaneous speech during the interview, it is nonetheless essential to listen for a period of time with an ear to language abnormalities. One listens for both fluency—melody, effortfulness, rate, and phrase length—and errors, both of syntax and of word choice (lexicon).

**Repetition.**   Language disorders with spared repetition (or even excessive echolalic repetition) and disproportionately affected repetition both occur. Repetition is tested by offering the patient phrases of increasing length and grammatical complexity. For example, one may start with single words and continue with simple phrases, then invert the phrases into questions, then make up phrases of grammatical function words (e.g., "no ifs, ands, or buts").

**Naming.**   One has already listened for paraphasic errors in the course of the patient's spontaneous speech. Ordinarily, more detailed testing by confrontation naming can be performed by using items at hand: a watch and its parts; parts of the body; shirt, sleeve, or cuff; and so on. Naming is dependent on the frequency of occurrence of the target word in the vocabulary, so testing must employ less frequently used items to detect mild but clinically meaningful deficits. Occasionally, alternative methods are required, as with a blind patient (or a patient with optic aphasia or visual agnosia), for whom tactile naming can be employed. One also can ask the patient to name items based on a description (e.g., "What do you call the four-legged animal that barks? What is the vehicle that travels underwater?"). Some patients have extraordinary domain-specific dissociations in naming ability ("category-specific anomia"); for example, the ability to name vegetables may be intact but the ability to name animals devastated (Gainotti 2000).

**Comprehension.**   Preferably the output demands are minimized in testing comprehension, so motor responses should not be required. Asking yes-no questions of progressive difficulty (e.g., "Am I wearing a hat, is there a tree in the room, does lunch come before dinner, is ice cream hotter than coffee?") is simple and is systematized in the Boston Diagnostic Aphasia Examination (BDAE) (Goodglass and Kaplan 1983). Patients with anterior aphasia often have mild disorders of comprehension of syntactically complex material. This can be observed by asking patients to interpret sentences using the passive voice and similarly difficult constructions (e.g., "The lion was killed by the tiger. Which animal was dead?")

**Reading.**   Reading comprehension can be tested conveniently by offering the same stimuli as were used orally. Before diagnosing alexia, one must establish the patient's premorbid literacy. Alexia can be present with no other abnormality of language (alexia without agraphia).

**Writing.**   Writing is most conveniently tested by asking the patient to spontaneously write a short paragraph about his or her illness or being in the hospital. Agraphia is a constant accompaniment of aphasic syndromes, so the writing sample is a good screening test of language function (assuming premorbid literacy). It is a particularly sensitive test in revealing confusional states (Chédru and Geschwind 1972a, 1972b). Similarly, agraphic errors can be seen in writing samples of patients with Alzheimer's disease earlier in the course than aphasic errors in spontaneous speech (Faber-Langendoen et al. 1988; Horner et al. 1988).

## Ideomotor Apraxia

Incapacity to perform skilled movements in the absence of elementary sensory or motor dysfunction that explains the defect is known as *apraxia*. Limb-kinetic apraxia amounts to a nonpyramidal clumsiness (Freund and Hummelsheim 1985). Ideational apraxia is discussed later in this chapter. Ideomotor apraxia is discussed here because of its close relationship to language disorders.

Oral apraxia and the left-hand apraxia seen with left-hemisphere lesions are revealed by requiring the patient to perform learned movements to command. This means that in the presence of auditory comprehension difficulties, the presence of apraxia is hard to establish. Deficits in motor performance may differ across a number of dimensions: transitive versus intransitive, meaningful versus nonmeaningful, outward-directed versus self-directed, or novel versus overlearned (Leiguarda and Marsden 2000). Furthermore, performance of axial, orofacial, and limb movements may be differentially affected (M.P. Alexander et al. 1992). Thus, a screening examination should utilize several tasks that differ in these respects. Performance in imitation of the examiner or utilization of actual objects does not test the same pathway from verbal input to movement engram to motor output as does performance to command. Disorders of performance of pantomime of transitive movements are predominantly seen in patients with left-hemisphere lesions (Leiguarda and Marsden 2000).

For oral apraxia, suitable tests are "Show me how you would blow out a match" or "How do you lick a postage stamp?" For limb apraxia, the patient should demonstrate such movements as waving good-bye, thumbing a ride, using a hammer, comb, or toothbrush, and imitating the examiner's hand positions. Responses in which the patient uses a body part in lieu of the pantomimed object are often considered defective. Thus, if the patient continues to use his or her fingers as the comb despite instruction to pretend he or she is holding a comb, the body-part-as-object response is taken as parapraxic. However, this determination may be erroneous (Duffy and Duffy 1989). As with other tasks in the cognitive examination, errors in performing skilled movements are more telling than simple failures, and the patient who shows how to hammer with a flat palm is unequivocally apraxic. For some forms of apraxia, patients do not complain of apraxic deficits and are not disabled by them, because the deficits do not appear in a natural context. However, this may not always be so, and exploration of the motor performance deficit across contexts is appropriate (Cubelli and Della Sala 1996).

## Visuospatial Function

### Visuospatial Analysis

Abnormalities of visual memory and emotional prosody have already been mentioned as signs of right-hemisphere dysfunction. The traditional probes for impairment with regard to spatial relations are drawing and copying tasks. Copying a Greek cross, intersecting pentagons, a figure from the Bender-Gestalt test, or the figures in Mesulam's and Weintraub's three-shapes test (Weintraub 2000), or drawing a clock face serves as a suitable screen; more subtle abnormality may be sought using the Rey Complex Figure (see Chapter 7, Figure 7–5). Copying performance is impaired (although differently) by both left- and right-sided lesions. The complexity of the Rey figure offers the opportunity to assess not only the final performance, but also the patient's strategy. Having the patient change the color of ink several times during the copying process shows the steps taken to produce the final drawing (Milberg et al. 1996). The difference between a piecemeal approach (the patient slavishly cop-

ies element by element) and a gestalt approach (the patient grasps the major structures, such as the large rectangle) can be noted, with the former suggesting right-sided disease. Neglect of the left side of the figure likewise strongly suggests right-hemisphere disease.

Other tasks probe visuospatial analysis without the same output demand. Elements of neuropsychological instruments can be used, for example, in asking the patient to discern overlapping figures or to identify objects photographed from noncanonical views. Even if vision is impaired, it is possible to test related functions by topographical skills: "If I go from Chicago to New York, is the Atlantic Ocean in front of me, behind me, to my left or right?"

### Disorders of Complex Visual Processing

Defects of color vision due to cerebral disease (central achromatopsia) are caused by inferior occipital damage contralateral to the defective field (A. Damasio et al. 1980). Presenting colored stimuli in each hemifield is essential to their detection; patients with hemiachromatopsia may not report a loss of color vision and may do well at naming colors in central vision (Rizzo 2000). Acquired defects of facial recognition are called prosopagnosia (De Renzi et al. 1994; Ettlin et al. 1992). Equipped with photographs of a few famous people, the bedside examiner can identify clinical cases of prosopagnosia. Some prosopagnostic patients show not only an inability to recognize specific faces (while knowing that they are looking at a face), but also an inability to recognize individual exemplars of other classes of items; such a patient may not be able to identify his or her own car or farm animal (Rizzo 2000). Developmental prosopagnosia is less well studied but may be of relevance in Asperger's syndrome as part of a wider right-hemisphere deficit (Kracke 1994).

Isolated defects of topographical skill occur, either on an amnesic or an agnosic basis (Barrash 1998; Luzzi et al. 2000); but usually when one hears of a patient who gets lost in his or her neighborhood or observes a patient having difficulty finding the way to his or her hospital room the impairment is only one element of broader right-hemisphere or bilateral dysfunction.

### Visual Agnosia

The relative importance of perceptual processes in the agnosias has been debated; certainly, in many cases (the apperceptive agnosias), subtle defects of visual processing can be identified (Farah 1990). The bedside clinician can seek evidence of relatively intact elementary visual processing (e.g., copying the picture of an object may be possible). Although the patient's language is intact (e.g., he or she is able to name the object in the picture from a description or from tactile data), his or her capacity to recognize the object visually—either by naming it or by using it—is strikingly abnormal. Such patients are often markedly impaired in activities of daily living. Like the disorders of complex visual processing described above, visual agnosia results from a ventral lesion of the "what" stream of processing.

## Disordered Reaching and Simultanagnosia

Rare patients are unable to guide the movements of the hand and arm by vision (A.R. Damasio and Benton 1979; Rondot 1989). This phenomenon, known as optic ataxia, is seen along with apraxia of voluntary gaze (ocular apraxia) and an impairment of the simultaneous perception of multiple objects (simultanagnosia) as Balint's syndrome. If the patient's reaching under visual guidance (within a field of normal vision) is disturbed, arm movement without visual guidance must be examined (e.g., observing the patient, with the patient's eyes closed, dressing, pointing to parts of his or her body, or reaching with the right hand to grasp the outstretched left thumb and vice versa).

Simultanagnosia is detected by asking the patient to describe a visually complex array; the Cookie Theft picture from the BDAE is suitable (Rizzo 2000). Simultanagnosia is a rare and incompletely characterized defect, and its association with optic ataxia and psychic paralysis of gaze is inconstant. Thus, Balint's "syndrome" probably lacks syndromal validity (Rizzo 1993). These disorders result from dorsal lesions of the "where" processing stream. Focal cortical degenerations or Alzheimer's disease may produce dysfunction of posterodorsal or posteroventral cortices with disturbed spatial processing or object recognition (Caselli 2000; Fujimori et al. 1997; Levine et al. 1993; Mendez et al. 1990).

## Form of Thought

### Thought Disorder

Features of thought disorder in the functional psychoses—poverty of speech, pressure of speech, derailment, tangentiality, incoherence, and so on—have been carefully defined (Andreasen 1979). Cutting and Murphy (1988) differentiated between intrinsic thinking disturbances, including loose associations, concreteness, overinclusiveness, and illogicality; disorders of the expression of thought, including disturbed pragmatics of language; and deficits in real-world knowledge, which can produce odd conversational interchange. They argued that the dis-

tinctive pattern of schizophrenic thought is suggestive of right-hemisphere dysfunction. However, the thought impairments found in schizophrenic patients may differ (Kuperberg et al. 2000), and lesions elsewhere may produce abnormal expression of thought (Chatterjee et al. 1997). Semantic systems may be damaged in schizophrenic patients with thought disorder (Spitzer 1997), and category-specific semantic impairments have been shown in case studies (Laws et al. 1999). Many authors have noted the similarity between the "negative" features of thought disorder and the characteristics of the frontal lobe syndrome. Cutting (1987) contrasted the "positive" features of thought disorder in schizophrenia with the thinking process of delirious patients. The latter was prominently illogical or slowed and impoverished in output; more distinctively, delirious patients gave occasional irrelevant replies amid competent responses. The form of thought in mentally retarded and demented patients has not been well characterized.

### Confabulation

The confabulating patient fabricates material in response to the examiner's queries and may tell tales spontaneously as well. Although this disorder is linked with amnesia, elaborate or spontaneous confabulation betokens additional disease outside memory systems, particularly the disturbance of the temporal context of memories that is characteristic of orbitofrontal lesions (Fischer et al. 1995; Kopelman 1999; Ptak and Schnider 1999; Schnider 2000; Schnider and Ptak 1999). Schizophrenic patients produce confabulations in narrative speech, probably because of difficulty suppressing abnormal ideas and insensitivity to context and the listener's expectations (Kramer et al. 1998; Nathaniel-James et al. 1996). Akin to confabulation is a phenomenon Geschwind (1964) called "wild paraphasia." He offered the example of a patient who calls an intravenous pole a Christmas tree decoration. In this case, the failure lies not within language systems but in impaired visual perception as well as in the cerebral apparatus for self-monitoring; disruption of attention in a confusional state is the usual setting (Wallesch and Hundsalz 1994). Delusional memories in psychotic patients appear to be neuropsychologically distinct from confabulation (Kopelman 1999; Kopelman et al. 1995).

### Vorbeireden (Vorbeigehen)

*Vorbeireden* (*Vorbeigehen*), the symptom of approximate answers, is the defining feature of the Ganser state (Sigal et al. 1992). The patient's responses show that he or she understands the questions, but the lack of knowledge implied by the mistaken replies is implausible (e.g., the patient reports that a horse has three legs). This phenomenon is rare. Whether it rests on organic foundations has been controversial from the outset. Ganser (1974) described three patients (of four he had seen); two had suffered head injury and one was recovering from typhus. Subsequently, some regarded the behavior as dissociative (Feinstein and Hattersley 1988; Heron et al. 1991), and others emphasized the neuropsychological underpinnings (Cutting 1990).

## Narrative Process in the Interview Setting

Patients who do not have elementary disorders of language function may nonetheless have macrolinguistic deficits. Where words and sentences—lexicon and syntax—are normal, paragraphs and discourse may not be. Patients with right-hemisphere disease, despite the adequacy of their lexical-semantic and syntactical performance, have deficits in the capacity to tell a story or recognize the point of a joke (Brownell and Martino 1998; Paradis 1998). These patients rarely give "I don't know" responses, rather they contrive some answer even if implausible; they fail to draw appropriate inferences, especially from emotional data, so that incongruity is not recognized; and the sense of humor is impaired (Wapner et al. 1981). People with temporal lobe epilepsy or who have had traumatic brain injury show deficits in planning, producing, and monitoring discourse; their narratives may be verbose and inefficient or contain insufficient or irrelevant information, requiring the listener to expend extra effort to understand them (Biddle et al. 1996; Field et al. 2000).

These findings emphasize the value of open-ended inquiries (e.g., "What brings you to the hospital?"), with attention to the patient's discourse taken as a whole as a sign of cerebral function. Disorders at the level of discourse are well recognized phenomenologically in psychiatry. One patient with compulsive personality disorder, who had an advanced degree in linguistics, acknowledged to me that people had a hard time talking with her because she "violated the Gricean maxims," referring to the work of the logician Grice, who postulated rules of inference in social interaction. How verbosity and circumstantiality (in this instance) are organized neurobiologically has not been carefully considered.

# Content of Thought

## Delusions

Cutting (1987) pointed out that themes of "imminent misadventure to others" and "bizarre happenings in the immediate vicinity" characterize delirium rather than acute schizophrenic psychosis. Misidentification symptoms such as Capgras' and Frégoli's syndromes suggest focal brain dysfunction, especially impairment of facial recognition, and many patients with misidentifications will have right or bilateral frontolimbic lesions (Feinberg 1997). Carefully studied patients with Capgras' and Frégoli's syndromes have shown prominent memory and executive cognitive dysfunction (Feinberg et al. 1999). However, not all patients with misidentification syndromes (or nonsyndromal misidentification phenomena, which are quite common in nonorganic psychosis [Mojtabai 1998]) have a recognizable organic contribution to the disorder (Signer 1994). A number of terms describe patients who, with delusional intensity, mistake their location, including reduplicative paramnesia (Pick 1903), disorientation for place (C.M. Fisher 1982), and *délire spatial* (spatial delusion) (Vighetto et al. 1985). One of my patients, for example, insisted that he was in his own house, thanked me for bringing all the doctors to visit him at home, and when skeptically confronted with features of the environment explained that he kept poles for intravenous lines and the like at home in case he needed them. These patients generally have defects of visuospatial analysis and executive function (Sellal et al. 1996).

Fleminger and Burns (1993) found that the presence of persecutory delusions before the advent of misidentification spoke against evident organic factors, whereas misidentification of place was characteristically of organic origin. Malloy and Richardson (1994) argued that delusions confined to a single topic suggest frontal lobe disorder, but again, as Kopelman et al. (1995) emphasized, by no means can organic disease always be identified. Complex psychotic phenomena, such as first-rank symptoms, are associated with preservation of cognitive capacity (Almeida et al. 1995); patients with dementia show unsystematized abnormal beliefs that often arise ad hoc from situations of cognitive failure.

## Hallucinations

Visual hallucinations suggest organic states, especially if auditory hallucinations are absent, but visual hallucinations are common in idiopathic schizophrenia (Bracha et al. 1989; Goodwin et al. 1971). Visual hallucinations without other psychopathology, usually in the presence of ocular disease with visual loss, known as the Charles Bonnet syndrome, are also common, especially in the elderly (Manford and Andermann 1998). The hallucinations are usually vivid images of animals or human beings, and the patient is aware of their unreality. Visual hallucinations in a hemifield blind from cerebral disease are well described

(Kölmel 1993). Vivid, elaborate, and well-formed visual hallucinations may occur with disease in the upper brain stem or thalamus (so-called peduncular hallucinosis) (Kölmel 1991). Such hallucinations are often worse in the evening (crepuscular) or when the patient is sleepy, and again the patient is generally aware of their unreality. A dreamlike state may accompany the hallucinosis. Similar hallucinations occur as hypnagogic phenomena in narcolepsy and in response to dopaminergic drugs in Parkinson's disease, and the brainstem mechanism may be related (C.M. Fisher 1991; Manford and Andermann 1998). Visual hallucinations early in a degenerative dementia suggest a diagnosis of dementia with Lewy bodies (Ballard et al. 1999). A lilliputian character is present in visual hallucinations of various etiologies without apparent specificity (M.A.A. Cohen et al. 1994).

Auditory hallucinations have resulted from pontine lesions (Cambier et al. 1988; Cascino and Adams 1986; Douen and Bourque 1997), with characteristics in some ways similar to peduncular visual hallucinations. Musical hallucinations are associated with hearing impairment, especially in depressed elderly women, and possibly right-hemisphere lesions (Keshavan et al. 1992; Pasquini and Cole 1997). Musical hallucinations also occur in schizophrenia (Baba and Hamada 1999). Unilateral auditory hallucinations are characteristically ipsilateral to a deaf (or the more deaf) ear (Almeida et al. 1993).

Olfactory hallucinations, often taken to imply epilepsy or temporal lobe disease, are common in nonorganic psychiatric disorders (Kopala et al. 1994). Palinopsia refers to persisting or recurrent visual images after the stimulus is gone. Responsible lesions are typically parieto-occipital (Norton and Corbett 2000). The physiology of this phenomenon may be epilepsy or disinhibition of the short-term visual memory system (Maillot et al. 1993). The analogous phenomenon in auditory experience is palinacousis, which is due to temporal-lobe lesions on either side (Jacobs et al. 1973). David (1994) proposed that thought-echo is due to a disturbance in short-term auditory verbal memory (the phonological loop).

## Emotion

Assessment of emotion and its modulation is performed by the clinician as a natural part of observing the patient during the examination; in addition, the examiner asks questions about the patient's emotional experience. There is no substitute for extended and sensitive conversation.

Pathological laughter and crying are defined not only by the lack of congruent inner experience but also by their elicitation through nonemotional stimuli (e.g., waving a hand before the patient's face) and by the all-or-none character of the response (Poeck 1985b). These signs, produced by lesions of the descending tracts modulating brainstem centers (Asfora et al. 1989; Ceccaldi et al. 1994), may be on a continuum with the affective dyscontrol, lability, and shallowness that occur in frontal disease or dementia. This latter finding, also called emotionalism, can be defined by increased tearfulness (or, more rarely, laughter) and sudden, unexpected, and uncontrollable tears (Allman 1991; Allman et al. 1990; House et al. 1989). So defined, emotionalism is common, associated with cognitive impairment, and related to left frontal and temporal lesions, but it is not dissociated from the patient's emotional experience or situation. Allman et al. (1992) and Robinson et al. (1993) developed scales for clinician rating of pathological emotion, and Moore et al. (1997) provided a self-report measure. Ross and Stewart (1987) suggested that pathological affect might screen a major depressive syndrome. Thus, faced with pathological affect the examiner should seek not only the signs of pseudobulbar palsy but also the symptoms and signs of melancholia.

A sudden display of laughter—*le fou rire prodromique*—is a rare prodrome to a catastrophic vascular event in the brain stem or thalamus (Ceccaldi and Milandre 1994; Couderq et al. 2000; Wali 1993). Laughing (gelastic) and crying (dacrystic) seizures are unusual (Luciano et al. 1993), although ictal emotion, especially fear, is common (Williams 1956). Gelastic epilepsy is associated with hypothalamic hamartomas and left-sided lesions (Arroyo et al. 1993), and dacrystic epilepsy is associated with right-sided lesions. Although crying is more common than laughter in pathological affect, laughing seizures are more common than crying seizures (Sackeim et al. 1982). Weeping during an ictus, in fact, suggests pseudoseizure (Walczak and Bogolioubov 1996).

Apathy is the absence or quantitative reduction of affect. It differs from depression; even the slowed, unexpressive depressed patient reports unpleasant emotional experience if carefully questioned. The term *apathy* has been in recent use for the phenomenon called abulia in this chapter. Euphoria, a persistent and unreasonable sense of well-being without the increased mental and motor rates of a manic state, is often alluded to in connection with multiple sclerosis. Actually, euphoria is unusual, and its occurrence almost always signals extensive disease and cognitive impairment (Ron and Logsdail 1989).

## Initiation and Organization of Action

The capacity for initiation and organization of action corresponds to a major aspect of the developing concept of executive cognitive function in neuropsychology (Tranel et al. 1994). Disorders of activation, planning, sequencing, self-monitoring, and flexible attention are important causes of functional disability (B.S. Fogel 1994). Moreover, such disturbances may be more evident during clinical examination than during formal neuropsychometric assessment because the structure of the formal assessment replaces the missing capacity of the patient to ignore distracting stimuli and direct and organize action toward adaptive goals. Elucidating deficits in the patient's planning and organizing adaptive behavior may require inventive testing methods, such as those described by Shallice and Burgess (Burgess 2000; Shallice and Burgess 1991). An interesting verbal bedside probe is asking the patient to estimate unfamiliar quantities (e.g., the length of a person's spine or the cost of a refrigerator) (Shallice and Evans 1978; M.L. Smith and Milner 1984). Unable to draw on rote knowledge, the patient with executive dysfunction may generate implausible responses that he or she is unable to monitor and correct.

## Abulia

C.M. Fisher (1984) resurrected the old term *abulia* (Berrios and Gili 1995) to describe loss of spontaneity due to cerebral disease, of which the extreme case is akinetic mutism. In a less severe form of abulia, the phenomena include slowness, delayed response, laconic speech, and reduced initiative and effort, the patient perhaps performing only one of a series of requested actions. C.M. Fisher (1968) described a transient but repeated lack of response as "intermittent interruption of behavior." Apathy often accompanies abulia, and in recent years the term *apathy* has come to subsume the disorder of action to which *abulia* has referred as well as the disorder of affect to which *apathy* primarily refers. Other terms used for this phenomenon are pure psychic akinesia (Laplane et al. 1984), loss of psychic self-activation (Laplane 1990), and athymhormia (Poncet and Habib 1994). Laplane and colleagues (Laplane 1994; Laplane et al. 1989) emphasized its occurrence after basal ganglia lesions, with a subjective sense of mental emptiness, in which context obsessive-compulsive phenomena commonly co-occur.

At times, even severe abulia can be overcome by stimuli that elicit automatic responses. For example, in the "telephone test," the clinician whose hospital patient is making no response to queries goes to a nearby room and telephones the patient, who astonishingly may be capable of having a conversation on the telephone (L.R. Caplan, personal communication, 1981). One of my patients who replied to no more than one question out of

a dozen, not even to simple inquiries as to the place or her name, readily recited a whole stanza of *The Rubáiyát of Omar Khayyám*, her favorite poem.

Generating lists of words by categories (e.g., "Name all the animals you can think of," or all modes of transportation, or items one might buy in a supermarket) requires sustained attention to a task, ability to organize an effective search of memory, intact language, and, of course, a certain amount of real-world knowledge. In Alzheimer's disease, generating exemplars for categories is more impaired than generating words beginning with a given letter. This finding represents the breakdown of semantic memory in Alzheimer's disease (Monsch et al. 1992, 1994). At the bedside, quantitative scoring—BDAE data suggest 12 animals in 1 minute as a cutoff for normal performance (Goodglass and Kaplan 1983)—can be supplemented by assessing the strategy the patient applies. Normally, a patient names all the animals that come to mind from one class (e.g., barnyard animals), then switches to another class (e.g., jungle animals). The patient with a disorder of spontaneity and flexible attention has trouble picking a productive strategy and switching it when necessary.

## Perseveration

Perseveration refers to the patient's continuing into present activity the elements of previous actions. Luria (1965) devised a number of bedside tasks to probe the programming of action and to reveal perseveration. For example, the patient is asked to form alternately a ring and a fist with his or her hand. Luria noted that in the most characteristic form of abnormality the patient perseverates on one position or the other, even while he or she is correctly saying aloud, "ring-fist-ring-fist." Luria and Homskaya (1963) regarded this disconnection of action from verbal mediation as the essence of frontal dysfunction. A similar but harder task is alternating from fist to edge of hand to palm, or the patient can be asked to alternate repeatedly from outstretched left fist and right palm to outstretched right fist and left palm (the Oseretsky test).

If similar tasks in the graphomotor sphere are given to the patient, a permanent record of the patient's performance results. Simply obtaining a writing sample often elicits perseveration. In Figure 5–1, a patient's response to the request to write a note to a family member is shown. She looked at the upper line, wondered aloud why she kept repeating things, and produced the lower line. Other tasks include asking for repeated sequences of two crosses and a circle or three triangles and two squares.

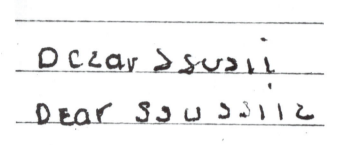

**FIGURE 5–1.** Perseveration. The patient was asked to write a note to a family member. She wrote the first line, wondered aloud why she hadn't gotten it right, then tried again on the second line.

Sandson and Albert (1987), following Luria, described several forms of perseveration. In recurrent perseveration, a prior response occurs in the context of a new set or demand for action (e.g., the patient names a pen correctly, then calls the point a pen, a watch a pen, and so on). In stuck-in-set perseveration, the patient maintains a category or set inappropriately, demonstrating a disorder of conceptual shifting or flexibility. The task posed by Sandson and Albert involved asking the patient to shift from responding with a circle or square to specified stimuli, to responding with a square or circle to those stimuli (i.e., to reverse the response). Others have used tasks of reciprocal action programs. For example, the patient is asked to point with one finger when the examiner points with two, and vice versa. Continuous perseveration, in the Sandson and Albert terminology, entails continuation or prolongation of a response without cessation. Asking the patient to repetitively produce the cursive letters *m* and *n* may test this continuation.

Perseveration can be seen in diseases of various brain regions, but when related to diseases outside frontal regions, it is characteristically limited to a specific modality of processing or response (E. Goldberg and Bilder 1987). For example, a patient with disease in the temporoparietal language area may make perseverative errors in naming. Ghika-Schmidt and Bogousslavsky (2000) described palipsychism, a phenomenon seen in anterior thalamic infarction in which perseveration led to overlapping of categories of thought ordinarily easily kept separate. As an example they cited a woman who ascribed her illness to "a triangle," which she had just been shown. Sandson and Albert (1987) claimed that continuous per-

severation is related to nondominant hemisphere disease, but this finding has not been confirmed (Annoni et al. 1998). Motor perseveration may take the form of stereotyped abnormal movements reminiscent of focal motor status epilepticus (Fung et al. 1997).

## Disinhibition

Loss of the capacity for planful action leaves the patient with organic cerebral disease prey to impulses; impulsive behavior is the reverse of the coin of which perseveration is the obverse. The clinician learns about such deficits primarily from the history. The questions often used to examine the patient's judgment (i.e., "What would you do if you found a stamped, addressed envelope in the street?") are not useful, in my opinion. The issue under examination is not the patient's knowledge of social norms; rather, it is his or her ability to use this knowledge to direct behavior. Eslinger and Damasio (1985) argued that in frontal disease a disconnection between the two is characteristic—so-called acquired sociopathy.

Usually, but not always, the structure of the interview and examination prevents display of impulsive behavior. For example, one middle-aged patient, being interviewed in his wife's presence, took advantage of my attention to his wife as she spoke to remove chewing gum from his mouth and carefully place it underneath the radiator cover. Few formal tests demonstrate this functional defect. Failure to inhibit reflexive gaze is discussed above. Go/no-go tasks are commonly used to explore the effects of frontal lesions in animals (Drewe 1975). A simple bedside adaptation is a tapping task in which the patient is instructed to tap for one stimulus and to refrain for another: "When I tap once, I want you to tap twice; when I tap twice, you do nothing at all." After a practice trial, a single error of commission represents a failure (Leimkuhler and Mesulam 1985). Heilman and Watson (1991) described other ways of specifying deficits in various forms of "defective response inhibition."

## Ideational Apraxia

The phenomenon of ideational apraxia is the incapacity to carry out a sequential or ordered set of actions toward a unitary goal in the presence of the necessary objects (Leiguarda and Marsden 2000). For example, the patient may be able to carry out the individual acts involved in preparing a letter to be sent—folding the letter, placing it in the envelope, sealing the envelope—but not be able to do them in the proper order to produce a useful result. Although focal lesions involving the left parietal and frontal cortex may produce ideational apraxia, more often it occurs in association with confusional states or dementia and represents a global disorder of the organization of behavior.

## Impersistence

M. Fisher (1956) described the incapacity of certain patients to sustain activities they were quite capable of beginning. The patient with impersistence peeks when asked to do tasks requiring the eyes to be closed or the gaze to be averted. Maintaining eyelid closure, tongue protrusion, mouth opening, and lateral gaze to the left may be the tasks most sensitive to this incapacity (Jenkyn et al. 1977; Kertesz et al. 1985). In most but not all studies, impersistence has been an indicator of right-hemisphere disease (De Renzi et al. 1986; Jenkyn et al. 1977; Joynt et al. 1962; Kertesz et al. 1985).

## Environment-Driven Responses

An important concept in thinking about dysexecutive syndromes is environmental dependency (Bindschaedler and Assal 1992; Lhermitte 1986). When the organism cannot generate plans for behavior toward self-initiated goals, behavior directed by the environment results. Blurting, echolalia, disinhibition, and hypermetamorphosis are discussed above, as is the tendency of the patient with frontal disease to stuff food into the mouth. Visual grasping, manual groping, and the "rush toward rewarding objects" are related "environment-driven responses" (Ghika et al. 1995b). Compulsive reading (Assal 1985), writing (Cambier et al. 1988), and speaking (Tanaka et al. 2000) also fall into this category, but hyperlexia and hypergraphia of this type bear an uncertain relationship to similar phenomena described in limbic epilepsy (Okamura et al. 1993), mental retardation (Jancar and Kettle 1984), and autism (Tirosh and Canby 1993).

Lhermitte et al. (1986) described utilization behavior as an automatic tendency to make use of objects in the environment. Further analysis of this phenomenon demonstrated that unprovoked utilization behavior is unusual (Brazzelli et al. 1994; Shallice et al. 1989). Nonetheless, Lhermitte (1993) found this behavior to be associated with major depression.

## Anarchic Hand

The sense of "alienation" of the hand seen in posterior callosal injury is described above. Sometimes, the dramatic manifestation of unwilled acts undertaken by the limb is anatomically and physiologically different. The acts of the "wayward" (G. Goldberg 1987) or "anarchic" (Della Sala et al. 1994) hand are elicited by the environment; they are well organized and recognized as abnormal by the patient. This phenomenon may be due to medial frontal injury with or without callosal involvement and may represent a complex form of grasping or groping; in another sense, it is unilateral utilization behavior (Della Sala et al. 1994; Gasquoine 1993).

# Awareness of Deficit

The patient who lacks awareness of a deficit obvious to everyone else is a common phenomenon in neuropsychiatry, one with important implications for treatment. In right-parietal lesions, denial of a left hemiparesis commonly occurs and is called anosognosia (Levine et al. 1991; McGlynn and Schacter 1989; Starkstein et al. 1992). A range of states can be seen, from minimization of the gravity of the deficit (anosodiaphoria) to bizarre denial of ownership of the affected body part or delusional beliefs about it (somatoparaphrenia) (Halligan et al. 1995). More broadly, psychotic patients are regularly unaware of the pathological nature of their perceptions and beliefs and resent attempts to intervene (Amador and David 1998), and the patient with Alzheimer's disease often lacks awareness of the reason his or her spouse wants to visit the doctor (Migliorelli et al. 1995). In Anton's syndrome, the patient is unaware of blindness, typically cortical blindness (Förstl et al. 1993). Patients with tardive dyskinesia are often unaware of the abnormal movements, probably because of a schizophrenic defect state (Collis and Macpherson 1992). The bedside examiner should repeatedly explore the patient's understanding of the nature of the symptoms.

# Psychological Management in the Neuropsychiatric Examination

In neuropsychiatry—as in all of medicine—the diagnostic evaluation is also part of the psychological treatment. The interest shown by the examiner, the rapport formed with the patient and the family, and the laying on of hands all form the basis of subsequent treatment and must be attended to from the beginning of the consultation.

A common difficulty for beginners is how to introduce the formal cognitive inquiry. All too often, one hears the examiner apologize for the "silly but routine" questions he or she is about to ask. (One never hears a cardiologist apologize for the silly but routine instrument being applied to the patient's precordium.) This is rarely the best way to gain the patient's full cooperation and best effort. Most of the time, patients report symptoms that can lead naturally (i.e., naturally from the patient's point of view) to a cognitive examination. For example, a patient with depressive symptoms may report trouble concentrating. If the examiner then says, "Let me ask you some questions to check your concentration," the patient is more likely to collaborate and less likely to be offended. Nearly any tasks can then be introduced.

At what point in the interview should this be done? If the initial few minutes of history-taking give reason to suspect substantial cognitive difficulty, one may wish to do at least some of the testing promptly. Not all of the cognitive examination needs to be done at once. Fatigue is an important factor in the cognitive performance of many patients, and long examinations may not elicit their best performance. L.R. Caplan (1978) pointed out that variability in performance is characteristic of patients with cerebral lesions and that perseveration may lead to drastic declines as tasks proceed. For this reason, short periods of probing may yield new perspectives on a patient's capacities. Shorter periods of questioning also may help prevent the catastrophic reaction that ensues when a patient's capacities are exceeded. This reaction of agitation and disorganization (Goldstein 1952; Reinhold 1953) is suggestive of organic disease but certainly counterproductive for emotional rapport. Moreover, for a period after such a reaction, the patient is incapable of tasks that are otherwise within his or her capacities, so the data subsequently collected are limited in their significance.

Who should be present for the diagnostic inquiry? Usually, it is necessary to interview ancillary informants to gather a neuropsychiatric history. Frequently, one discovers that a family member has misjudged the nature or severity of the patient's impairment. Testing the patient in front of the family to reveal impairments allows consensual validation and mutual discussion. This testing requires tact and occasionally requires that the examination be discontinued.

## Screening Batteries and Rating Scales

Several investigators have developed brief screening tests of cognitive functioning (Malloy et al. 1997; Nelson et al. 1986; van Gorp et al. 1999). These have the advantages of being repeatable, quantitative, and reliable. They are most useful for the recognition of dementia; focal cognitive syndromes may easily escape detection. The widely used Mini-Mental State Exam (MMSE) (Folstein et al. 1975) has important limitations, notably that executive cognitive dysfunction is not tested. An expansion of the MMSE, called the Modified Mini-Mental State (3MS) (Teng and Chui 1987), which includes elements of exec-

utive function, may be more sensitive and specific (Grace et al. 1995). Supplementing the memory item of the MMSE by a cued-recall procedure provides the benefit of distinguishing between retrieval and storage deficits (Yuspeh et al. 1998). Katzman et al. (1983) offered a particularly simple screening examination for dementia; it consists of questions probing orientation, attention, and memory. Like the MMSE, it serves best as a screen for cortical dementing disorders.

Other instruments may be more appropriate as screens for subcortical disorders. Power et al. (1995) devised a screening test for HIV-related dementia. Along with a memory task and a test of inhibition of reflexive saccades, it contains timed construction and writing tasks. Even the memory and the timed tasks, without the inhibition task, can identify HIV-related cognitive impairment (Berghuis et al. 1999). A particularly simple screen, also validated in a population of patients with acquired immunodeficiency syndrome (AIDS), is an oral modification of the Trail Making B Test, called the Mental Alternation Test (B.N. Jones et al. 1993). The patient is asked to alternate between numbers and letters: "1-A, 2-B, 3-C, …." The number of correct alternations in 30 seconds is the score; incorrect items are not counted. A maximum score would be 52; a cutoff of 14/15 gave a sensitivity of 95% and a specificity of 93% in a population of HIV-positive patients being evaluated for encephalopathy. Grigsby and his colleagues reported on the utility of this measure for assessing information processing and working memory in various other populations (Grigsby and Kaye 1995; Grigsby et al. 1994).

The choice of an appropriate screening instrument thus depends on the population being screened. However, the assessment of executive cognitive dysfunction is of paramount importance in neuropsychiatry, and in all neuropsychiatric populations a screen for cognitive deficit is incomplete without attention to this domain. The sole use of the MMSE or a comparable instrument is insufficient for assessment of the skills required for independent functioning. The Executive Interview (EXIT) is a screening test for executive cognitive dysfunction (Royall et al. 1992). A similar and simpler scale is the Behavioral Dyscontrol Scale (Table 5–5). Both scales show better correlation with functional status, such as the ability to live independently, than the MMSE (Grigsby et al. 1993, 1998; Royall et al. 1993, 2000). Dubois et al. (2000) devised the Frontal Assessment Battery (Figure 5–2) for identifying executive dysfunction at the bedside in several domains in patients with extrapyramidal disorders. Individual items of the scale address motor sequencing, verbal fluency, response inhibition, and other executive functions; the scale requires less than 5 min-

**TABLE 5–5.** Behavioral Dyscontrol Scale

1. Patient taps twice with the dominant hand and once with the nondominant hand, repetitively.
2. Patient taps twice with the nondominant hand and once with the dominant hand, repetitively.
3. Patient squeezes examiner's hand when examiner says "red," does nothing when examiner says "green."
4. If examiner taps twice, patient taps once; if examiner taps once, patient taps twice.
5. Patient alternates between touching the thumb and each finger of dominant hand, in succession, to table top, repetitively.
6. Patient makes a fist with knuckles turned down, places the edge of the extended hand on the table, places the palm on the table, repetitively.
7. Facing the examiner, patient duplicates positions of the examiner's hands, using the same hand as the examiner (i.e., without mirroring). Positions include left fist beside left ear, right index finger pointing to right eye, "T" with left hand vertical and right hand horizontal, left hand on left ear, and fingers of right hand under chin with fingers bent at 90°
8. Patient alternates counting with recitation of the alphabet through the letter L.
9. Examiner rates patient's insight.

*Note.* All items except rating of insight scored 0 points (failure), 1 point (impaired), or 2 points (normal). Insight is given 0 points (complete inability to judge own performance) to 3 points (intact insight).
*Source.* Adapted from Grigsby et al. 1992 and Grigsby et al. 1998.

utes to administer. Although not yet well validated, it appears promising as a complement to the MMSE or other measures of elementary cognitive functions. Royall and colleagues (Royall et al. 1998, 1999) showed that freehand drawing of a clock is sensitive to executive cognitive dysfunction and can be used as a screening instrument.

Scales for quantifying noncognitive aspects of organic dysfunction also exist. Two instruments of particular interest for neuropsychiatric practice are the Neuropsychiatric Inventory and the Neurobehavioral Rating Scale. The Neuropsychiatric Inventory assesses disturbances, including psychosis, mood and affective disorders, aggression, disinhibition, and aberrant motor activity (Cummings et al. 1994). A screen and metric approach is used; there are 10 screening questions, and supplementary questions to rate frequency and severity are invoked if the screening question is answered affirmatively. A modification allows its use as a questionnaire for relatives or caregivers (Kaufer et al. 2000). The Neurobehavioral Rating Scale (Figure 5–3) is a modification of the well-known Brief Psychiatric Rating Scale, with the addition of items thought relevant initially for a population

with head injuries but also appropriate for patients with dementia and other disorders (H.S. Levin et al. 1987; Sultzer et al. 1995). Of interest is a compendium of rating scales for a variety of functional disabilities, many relevant to the neuropsychiatrist (Wade 1992).

## Conclusions

The "complete examination" is a figment. No practical examination can include all possible elements. The expert clinician is constantly generating hypotheses and constructing an examination to confirm or refute them (L.R. Caplan 1990). The diagnostician as historian constantly strives to write the patient's biography: how did this person arrive at this predicament at this time? This biographical endeavor is far more complex than attaching a DSM-IV-TR label to a patient. Diagnosis in neuropsychiatry does not mean the search only for cause, or only for localization, or only for functional capacity. It means, along with those aims, constructing a pathophysiological and psychopathological formulation from cause to effect, from etiological factor to symptomatic complaint or performance. This formulation of pathogenetic mechanisms provides a rational framework for intervention.

Cognitive examination is the traditional psychiatric method for making a nonidiopathic mental diagnosis, and reliance on hard signs on physical examination is the traditional neurological method. The material reviewed in this chapter shows the broad array of tools that can implicate brain impairment in the pathogenesis of mental disorder. The clinician should maximize use of the means available in this difficult task, ideally without interference from disciplinary boundaries.

## References

Abad V, Ovsiew F: Treatment of persistent myoclonic tardive dystonia with verapamil. Br J Psychiatry 162:554–556, 1993

Absher JR, Benson DF: Disconnection syndromes: an overview of Geschwind's contributions. Neurology 43:862–867, 1993

Abwender DA, Trinidad KS, Jones KR, et al: Features resembling Tourette syndrome in developmental stutterers. Brain Lang 62:455–464, 1998

Adair JC, Williamson DJ, Jacobs DH, et al: Neglect of radial and vertical space: importance of the retinotopic reference frame. J Neurol Neurosurg Psychiatry 58:724–728, 1995

Alajouanine T, Castaigne P, Sabouraud O, et al: Palilalie paroxystique et vocalisations itératives au cours de crises épilep-

**Similarities:** "In what way are they alike?"

- banana and orange (in the event of total failure, e.g., "they are not alike," or partial failure, e.g., "both have peel," help the patient by saying, "both a banana and an orange are" but credit 0 for the item; do not help the patient for the two following items)
- table and chair
- tulip, rose, and daisy

Score only category response (fruits, furniture, flower) correct:

    3 correct = 3

    2 correct = 2

    1 correct = 1                       [___]

    0 correct = 0

**Lexical fluency:** "Say as many words as you can beginning with the letter *S*, any words except surnames or proper nouns." If the patient gives no response during the first 5 seconds, say, "for instance, snake." If the patient pauses 10 seconds, stimulate him by saying, "any word beginning with the letter *S*." The time allowed is 60 seconds.

Score (word repetitions or variations, surnames, or proper nouns are not counted)

    More than nine words = 3

    Six to nine = 2

    Three to five = 1                    [___]

    Fewer than three = 0

**Motor series:** "Look carefully at what I'm doing." The examiner, seated in front of the patient, performs alone three times with his left hand the series of Luria "fist-edge-palm." "Now, with your right hand do the same series, first with me, then alone." The examiner performs the series three times with the patient, then says to him or her: "Now, do it on your own."

    Six correct consecutive series alone = 3

    At least three correct consecutive series alone = 2

    Fails alone, but performs three correct consecutive series with the examiner = 1

    Cannot perform three correct consecutive series even with the examiner = 0    [___]

**Conflicting instructions:** "Tap twice when I tap once." To be sure that the patient has understood the instruction, a series of three trials is run: 1-1-1. "Tap once when I tap twice." To be sure that the patient has understood the instruction, a series of three trials is run: 2-2-2. The examiner performs the following series 1-1-2-1-2-2-2-1-1-2.

    No error = 3

    One or two errors = 2

    More than two errors = 1

    Patient taps like the examiner at least four consecutive times = 0        [___]

**Go/no-go:** "Tap once when I tap once." To be sure that the patient has understood the instruction, a series of three trials is run: 1-1-1. "Do not tap when I tap twice." To be sure that the patient has understood the instruction, a series of three trials is run: 2-2-2. The examiner performs the following series: 1-1-2-1-2-2-2-1-1-2.

    No error = 3

    One or two errors = 2

    More than two errors = 1

    Patient taps like the examiner at least four consecutive times = 0        [___]

**Prehension behavior:** The examiner is seated in front of the patient. Place the patient's hands palm up on his or her knees. Without saying anything or looking at the patient, the examiner brings his or her hands close to the patient's hands and touches the palms of both the patient's hands, to see if he or she will spontaneously take them. If the patient takes the hands, the examiner will try again after asking him or her: "Now do not take my hands."

    Patient does not take the examiner's hands = 3

    Patient hesitates and asks what he or she has to do = 2

    Patient takes the hands without hesitation = 1

    Patient takes the examiner's hand even after being told not to do so = 0      [___]

                                                 Total = ____

**FIGURE 5–2.** Frontal Assessment Battery.

*Source.* Reprinted with permission from Dubois B, Slachevsky A, Litvan I, et al.: "The FAB: A Frontal Assessment Battery at Bedside." *Neurology* 55:1621–1626, 2000.

**DIRECTIONS: Place an X in the appropriate box to represent level of severity of each symptom.**

| | Not present | Very mild | Mild | Moderate | Mod. severe | Severe | Extremely severe |
|---|---|---|---|---|---|---|---|
| 1. INATTENTION/REDUCED ALERTNESS—fails to sustain attention, easily distracted, fails to notice aspects of environment, difficulty directing attention, decreased alertness. | ☐ | ☐ | ☐ | ☐ | ☐ | ☐ | ☐ |
| 2. SOMATIC CONCERN—volunteers complaints or elaborates about somatic symptoms (e.g., headache, dizziness, blurred vision), and about physical health in general. | ☐ | ☐ | ☐ | ☐ | ☐ | ☐ | ☐ |
| 3. DISORIENTATION—confusion or lack of proper association for person, place, or time. | ☐ | ☐ | ☐ | ☐ | ☐ | ☐ | ☐ |
| 4. ANXIETY—worry, fear, overconcern for present or future. | ☐ | ☐ | ☐ | ☐ | ☐ | ☐ | ☐ |
| 5. EXPRESSIVE DEFICIT—word-finding disturbance, anomia, pauses in speech, effortful and agrammatic speech, circumlocution. | ☐ | ☐ | ☐ | ☐ | ☐ | ☐ | ☐ |
| 6. EMOTIONAL WITHDRAWAL—lack of spontaneous interaction, isolation, deficiency in relating to others. | ☐ | ☐ | ☐ | ☐ | ☐ | ☐ | ☐ |
| 7. CONCEPTUAL DISORGANIZATION—thought processes confused, disconnected, disorganized, disrupted; tangential social communication; perseverative. | ☐ | ☐ | ☐ | ☐ | ☐ | ☐ | ☐ |
| 8. DISINHIBITION—socially inappropriate comments and/or actions, including aggressive/sexual content, or inappropriate to the situation, outbursts of temper. | ☐ | ☐ | ☐ | ☐ | ☐ | ☐ | ☐ |
| 9. GUILT FEELINGS—self-blame, shame, remorse for past behavior. | ☐ | ☐ | ☐ | ☐ | ☐ | ☐ | ☐ |
| 10. MEMORY DEFICIT—difficulty learning new information, rapidly forgets recent events, although immediate recall (forward digit span) may be intact. | ☐ | ☐ | ☐ | ☐ | ☐ | ☐ | ☐ |
| 11. AGITATION—motor manifestations of overactivation (e.g., kicking, arm flailing, picking, roaming, restlessness, talkativeness). | ☐ | ☐ | ☐ | ☐ | ☐ | ☐ | ☐ |
| 12. INACCURATE INSIGHT AND SELF-APPRAISAL—poor insight, exaggerated self-opinion, overrates level of ability and underrates personality change in comparison with evaluation by clinicians and family. | ☐ | ☐ | ☐ | ☐ | ☐ | ☐ | ☐ |
| 13. DEPRESSIVE MOOD—sorrow, sadness, despondency, pessimism. | ☐ | ☐ | ☐ | ☐ | ☐ | ☐ | ☐ |
| 14. HOSTILITY/UNCOOPERATIVENESS—animosity, irritability, belligerence, disdain for others, defiance of authority. | ☐ | ☐ | ☐ | ☐ | ☐ | ☐ | ☐ |
| 15. DECREASED INITIATIVE/MOTIVATION—lacks normal initiative in work or leisure, fails to persist in tasks, is reluctant to accept new challenges. | ☐ | ☐ | ☐ | ☐ | ☐ | ☐ | ☐ |
| 16. SUSPICIOUSNESS—mistrust, belief that others harbor malicious or discriminatory intent. | ☐ | ☐ | ☐ | ☐ | ☐ | ☐ | ☐ |
| 17. FATIGABILITY—rapidly fatigues on challenging cognitive tasks or complex activities, lethargic. | ☐ | ☐ | ☐ | ☐ | ☐ | ☐ | ☐ |
| 18. HALLUCINATORY BEHAVIOR—perceptions without normal external stimulus correspondence. | ☐ | ☐ | ☐ | ☐ | ☐ | ☐ | ☐ |
| 19. MOTOR RETARDATION—slowed movements or speech (excluding primary weakness). | ☐ | ☐ | ☐ | ☐ | ☐ | ☐ | ☐ |
| 20. UNUSUAL THOUGHT CONTENT—unusual, odd, strange, or bizarre thought content. | ☐ | ☐ | ☐ | ☐ | ☐ | ☐ | ☐ |
| 21. BLUNTED AFFECT—reduced emotional tone, reduction in normal intensity of feelings, flatness. | ☐ | ☐ | ☐ | ☐ | ☐ | ☐ | ☐ |
| 22. EXCITEMENT—heightened emotional tone, increased reactivity. | ☐ | ☐ | ☐ | ☐ | ☐ | ☐ | ☐ |
| 23. POOR PLANNING—unrealistic goals, poorly formulated plans for the future, disregards prerequisites (e.g., training), fails to take disability into account. | ☐ | ☐ | ☐ | ☐ | ☐ | ☐ | ☐ |
| 24. LABILITY OF MOOD—sudden change in mood which is disproportionate to the situation. | ☐ | ☐ | ☐ | ☐ | ☐ | ☐ | ☐ |
| 25. TENSION—postural and facial expression of heightened tension, without the necessity of excessive activity involving the limbs or trunk. | ☐ | ☐ | ☐ | ☐ | ☐ | ☐ | ☐ |
| 26. COMPREHENSION DEFICIT—difficulty in understanding oral instructions on single or multistage commands. | ☐ | ☐ | ☐ | ☐ | ☐ | ☐ | ☐ |
| 27. SPEECH ARTICULATION DEFECT—misarticulation, slurring or substitution of sounds which affect intelligibility (rating is independent of linguistic content). | ☐ | ☐ | ☐ | ☐ | ☐ | ☐ | ☐ |

**FIGURE 5–3.** The Neurobehavioral Rating Scale.

*Source.* Reprinted with permission from Levin HS, High WM, Goethe KE, et al.: "The Neurobehavioural Rating Scale: Assessment of the Behavioural Sequelae of Head Injury by the Clinician." *Journal of Neurology, Neurosurgery and Psychiatry* 50:183–193, 1987.

tiques par lésion intéressant l'aire motrice supplémentaire. Rev Neurol (Paris) 101:685–697, 1959

Alexander GE, DeLong MR: Central mechanisms of initiation and control of movement, in Diseases of the Nervous System/Clinical Neurobiology, 2nd Edition. Edited by Asbury AK, McKhann GM, McDonald WI. Philadelphia, PA, WB Saunders, 1992, pp 285–308

Alexander MP: Frontal lobes and language. Brain Lang 37:656–691, 1989

Alexander MP: Mild traumatic brain injury: pathophysiology, natural history, and clinical management. Neurology 45:1253–1260, 1995

Alexander MP: Disturbances in language initiation: mutism and its lesser forms, in Movement Disorders in Neurology and Psychiatry, 2nd Edition. Edited by Joseph AB, Young RR. Oxford, UK, Blackwell Science, 1999, pp 366–371

Alexander MP, Baker E, Naeser MA, et al: Neuropsychological and neuroanatomical dimensions of ideomotor apraxia. Brain 115:87–107, 1992

Algoed L, Janssens J, Vanhooren G: Apraxia of eyelid opening secondary to right frontal infarction. Acta Neurol Belg 92:228–233, 1992

Allman P: Depressive disorders and emotionalism following stroke. Int J Geriatr Psychiatry 6:377–383, 1991

Allman P, Hope RA, Fairburn CG: Emotionalism following brain damage: a complex phenomenon. Postgrad Med J 66:818–823, 1990

Allman P, Marshall M, Hope T, et al: Emotionalism following stroke: development and reliability of a semi-structured interview. International Journal of Methods in Psychiatric Research 2:125–131, 1992

Almeida OP, Förstl H, Howard R, et al: Unilateral auditory hallucinations. Br J Psychiatry 162:262–264, 1993

Almeida OP, Howard RJ, Levy R, et al: Psychotic states arising in late life (late paraphrenia): the role of risk factors. Br J Psychiatry 166:215–228, 1995

Amador XF, David AS (eds): Insight and Psychosis. Oxford, UK, Oxford University Press, 1998

Andreasen NC: Thought, language, and communication disorders. Arch Gen Psychiatry 36:1315–1321, 1979

Annoni GM, Pegna AJ, Michel CM, et al: Motor perseverations: a function of the side and the site of a cerebral lesion. Eur Neurol 40:84–90, 1998

Arango C, Bartko JJ, Gold JM, et al: Prediction of neuropsychological performance by neurological signs in schizophrenia. Am J Psychiatry 156:1349–1357, 1999

Ardila A, Niño CR, Pulido E, et al: Episodic psychic symptoms in the general population. Epilepsia 34:133–140, 1993

Ardila A, Rosselli M, Surloff C, et al: Transient paligraphia associated with severe palilalia and stuttering: a single case report. Neurocase 5:435–440, 1999

Arroyo S, Lesser RP, Gordon B, et al: Mirth, laughter and gelastic seizures. Brain 116:757–780, 1993

Arseneault L, Tremblay RE, Boulerice B, et al: Minor physical anomalies and family adversity as risk factors for violent delinquency in adolescence. Am J Psychiatry 157:917–923, 2000

Asfora WT, DeSalles AAF, Abe M, et al: Is the syndrome of pathological laughing and crying a manifestation of pseudobulbar palsy? J Neurol Neurosurg Psychiatry 52:523–525, 1989

Assal G: Un aspect du comportement d'utilisation: la dépendance vis-à-vis du langage écrit. Rev Neurol (Paris) 141:493–495, 1985

Atre-Vaidya N, Taylor MA, Jampala VC, et al: Psychosensory features in mood disorder: a preliminary report. Compr Psychiatry 35:286–289, 1994

Ay H, Buonanno FS, Price BH, et al: Sensory alien hand syndrome: case report and review of the literature. J Neurol Neurosurg Psychiatry 65:366–369, 1998

Baba A, Hamada H: Musical hallucinations in schizophrenia. Psychopathology 32:242–251, 1999

Ballard C, Holmes C, McKeith I, et al: Psychiatric morbidity in dementia with Lewy bodies: a prospective clinical and neuropathological comparative study with Alzheimer's disease. Am J Psychiatry 156:1039–1045, 1999

Bancaud J, Brunet-Bourgin F, Chauvel P, et al: Anatomic origin of déjà vu and vivid "memories" in human temporal lobe epilepsy. Brain 117:71–90, 1994

Barclay CL, Bergeron C, Lang AE: Arm levitation in progressive supranuclear palsy. Neurology 52:879–882, 1999

Barnes MP, Saunders M, Walls TJ, et al: The syndrome of Karl Ludwig Kahlbaum. J Neurol Neurosurg Psychiatry 49:991–996, 1986

Barrash J: A historical review of topographical disorientation and its neuroanatomical correlates. J Clin Exp Neuropsychol 20:807–827, 1998

Baxter DM, Warrington EK: Neglect dysgraphia. J Neurol Neurosurg Psychiatry 46:1073–1078, 1983

Bear D, Hermann B, Fogel B: Interictal behavior syndrome in temporal lobe epilepsy: the views of three experts. J Neuropsychiatry Clin Neurosci 1:308–318, 1989

Benjamin S: A neuropsychiatric approach to aggressive behavior, in Neuropsychiatry and Mental Health Services. Edited by Ovsiew F. Washington, DC, American Psychiatric Press, 1999a, pp 149–196

Benjamin S: Oculogyric crisis, in Movement Disorders in Neurology and Neuropsychiatry, 2nd Edition. Edited by Joseph AB, Young RR. Boston, MA, Blackwell Scientific, 1999b, pp 92–103

Benke T, Hohenstein C, Poewe W, et al: Repetitive speech phenomena in Parkinson's disease. J Neurol Neurosurg Psychiatry 69:319–325, 2000

Benton AL: Gerstmann's syndrome. Arch Neurol 49:445–447, 1992

Berghuis JP, Uldall KK, Lalonde B: Validity of two scales in identifying HIV-associated dementia. J Acquir Immune Defic Syndr 21:134–140, 1999

Berrios GE, Gili M: Abulia and impulsiveness revisited: a conceptual history. Acta Psychiatr Scand 92:161–167, 1995

Berthier ML, Ruiz A, Massone MI, et al: Foreign accent syndrome: behavioural and anatomic findings in recovered and non-recovered patients. Aphasiology 5:129–147, 1991

Berthier ML, Kulisevsky J, Gironell A, et al: Obsessive-compulsive disorder associated with brain lesions: clinical phenomenology, cognitive function, and anatomic correlates. Neurology 47:353–361, 1996

Beversdorf DQ, Heilman KM: Facilatory paratonia and frontal lobe functioning. Neurology 51:968–971, 1998

Biddle KR, McCabe A, Bliss LS: Narrative skills following traumatic brain injury in children and adults. J Commun Disord 29:447–469, 1996

Bindschaedler C, Assal G: La dépendance à l'égard de l'environnement lors de lésions cérébrales: conduites d'imitation, de préhension et d'utilisation. Schweizer Archiv fur Neurologie und Psychiatrie 143(2):175–187, 1992

Bisiach E: Mental representation in unilateral neglect and related disorders: the twentieth Barlett Memorial Lecture. Q J Exp Psychol 46A:435–461, 1993

Bisiach E, Luzzatti C: Unilateral neglect of representational space. Cortex 14:129–133, 1978

Black FW: Digit repetition in brain-damaged adults: clinical and theoretical implications. J Clin Psychol 42:770–782, 1986

Blanchet P, Frommer GP: Mood change preceding epileptic seizures. J Nerv Ment Dis 174:471–476, 1986

Bloem BR, Grimbergen YAM, Cramer M, et al: "Stops walking when talking" does not predict falls in Parkinson's disease (letter). Ann Neurol 48:268, 2000

Bodfish JW, Powell SB, Golden RN, et al: Blink rate as an index of dopamine function in adults with mental retardation and repetitive behavior disorders. Am J Ment Retard 99:335–344, 1995

Bogen JE: The callosal syndromes, in Clinical Neuropsychology, 3rd Edition. Edited by Heilman KM, Valenstein E. New York, Oxford University Press, 1993, pp 337–407

Bogousslavsky J, Regli F, Uske A: Thalamic infarcts: clinical syndromes, etiology, and prognosis. Neurology 38:837–848, 1988

Bogousslavsky J, Kumral E, Regli F, et al: Acute hemiconcern: a right anterior parietotemporal syndrome. J Neurol Neurosurg Psychiatry 58:428–432, 1995

Boks MPM, Russo S, Knegtering R, et al: The specificity of neurological signs in schizophrenia: a review. Schizophr Res 43:109–116, 2000

Boller F, Frank E: Sexual Dysfunction in Neurological Disorders: Diagnosis, Management, and Rehabilitation. New York, Raven, 1982

Boller F, Boller M, Denes G, et al: Familial palilalia. Neurology 23:1117–1125, 1973

Bowers D, White T, Bauer RM: Recall of three words after 5 minutes: its relationship to performance on neuropsychological memory tests [abstract]. Neurology 39 (suppl 1):176, 1989

Bracha HS, Wolkowitz OM, Lohr JB, et al: High prevalence of visual hallucinations in research subjects with chronic schizophrenia. Am J Psychiatry 146:526–528, 1989

Brady JP: Drug-induced stuttering: a review of the literature. J Clin Psychopharmacol 18:50–54, 1998

Braunig P, Kruger S, Shugar G, et al: The catatonia rating scale I: development, reliability and use. Compr Psychiatry 41:147–158, 2000

Brazzelli M, Colombo N, Della Sala S, et al: Spared and impaired cognitive abilities after bilateral frontal damage. Cortex 30:27–51, 1994

Brion S, Jedynak C-P: Troubles du transfert interhémisphérique. À propos de trois observations de tumeurs du corps calleux. Le signe de la main étrangère. Rev Neurol (Paris) 126:257–266, 1972

Brodal A: Self-observations and neuro-anatomical considerations after a stroke. Brain 96:675–694, 1973

Brodal A: Neurological Anatomy in Relation to Clinical Medicine, 3rd Edition. New York, Oxford University Press, 1981

Brody D, Serby M, Etienne N, et al: Olfactory identification deficits in HIV infection. Am J Psychiatry 148:248–250, 1991

Brown P: Myoclonus, in Movement Disorders in Clinical Practice. Edited by Sawle G. Oxford, UK, Isis Medical Media, 1999, pp 147–157

Brown P, Rothwell JC, Thompson PD, et al: The hyperekplexias and their relationship to the normal startle reflex. Brain 114:1903–1928, 1991a

Brown P, Rothwell JC, Thompson PD, et al: New observations on the normal auditory startle reflex in man. Brain 114:1891–1902, 1991b

Brownell H, Martino G: Deficits in inference and social cognition: the effects of right hemisphere brain damage on discourse, in Right Hemisphere Language Comprehension: Perspectives from Cognitive Neuroscience. Edited by Beeman M, Chiarello C. Mahwah, NJ, Erlbaum, 1998, pp 309–328

Bryden MP: Measuring handedness with questionnaires. Neuropsychologia 15:617–624, 1977

Buchanan RW, Heinrichs DW: The Neurological Evaluation Scale (NES): a structured instrument for the assessment of neurological signs in schizophrenia. Psychiatry Res 27:335–350, 1989

Bundick T, Spinella M: Subjective experience, involuntary movement, and posterior alien hand syndrome. J Neurol Neurosurg Psychiatry 68:83–85, 2000

Burgess PW: Strategy application disorder: the role of the frontal lobes in human multitasking. Psychol Res 63:279–288, 2000

Burgess PW, Alderman N, Evans J, et al: The ecological validity of tests of executive function. J Int Neuropsychol Soc 4:547–558, 1998

Burgess PW, Veitch E, de Lacy Costello A, et al: The cognitive and neuroanatomical correlates of multitasking. Neuropsychologia 38(6):848–863, 2000

Burke JM, Schaberg DR: Neurosyphilis in the antibiotic era. Neurology 35:1368–1371, 1985

Bush G, Fink M, Petrides G, et al: Catatonia, I: rating scale and standardized examination. Acta Psychiatr Scand 93:129–136, 1996

Bushby KMD, Cole T, Matthews JNS, et al: Centiles for adult head circumference. Arch Dis Child 67:1286–1287, 1992

Caligiuri MP, Lohr JB, Jeste DV: Parkinsonism in neuroleptic-naive schizophrenic patients. Am J Psychiatry 150:1343–1348, 1993

Cambier J, Masson C, Benammou S, et al: La graphomanie. Activité graphique compulsive manifestation d'un gliome fronto-calleux. Rev Neurol (Paris) 144:158–164, 1988

Cancelliere AEB, Kertesz A: Lesion localization in acquired deficits of emotional expression and comprehension. Brain Cogn 13:133–147, 1990

Cannon TD, Rosso IM, Hollister JM, et al: A prospective cohort study of genetic and perinatal influences in the etiology of schizophrenia. Schizophr Bull 26:351–366, 2000

Cantor-Graae E, Ismail B, McNeil TF: Are neurological abnormalities in schizophrenic patients and their siblings the result of perinatal trauma? Acta Psychiatr Scand 101:142–147, 2000

Caplan LR: Variability of perceptual function: the sensory cortex as a "categorizer" and "deducer." Brain Lang 6:1–13, 1978

Caplan LR: The Effective Clinical Neurologist. Cambridge, MA, Blackwell, Scientific, 1990

Caplan LR, Kelly M, Kase CS, et al: Infarcts of the inferior division of the right middle cerebral artery: mirror image of Wernicke's aphasia. Neurology 36:1015–1020, 1986

Caplan LR, Schmahmann JD, Kase CS, et al: Caudate infarcts. Arch Neurol 47:133–143, 1990

Caplan R, Guthrie D: Blink rate in childhood schizophrenia spectrum disorder. Biol Psychiatry 35:228–234, 1994

Capstick N, Seldrup J: Obsessional states: a study in the relationship between abnormalities occurring at the time of birth and the subsequent development of obsessional symptoms. Acta Psychiatr Scand 56:427–431, 1977

Carbary TJ, Patterson JP: Foreign accent syndrome following a catastophic second injury: MRI correlates, linguistic and voice pattern analysis. Brain Cogn 43:78–85, 2000

Carluer L, Marié R-M, Lambert J, et al: Acquired and persistent stuttering as the main symptom of striatal infarction. Mov Disord 15:343–346, 2000

Carrazana E, Rossitch E, Martinez J: Unilateral "akathisia" in a patient with AIDS and a toxoplasmosis subthalamic abscess. Neurology 39:449–450, 1989

Cascino GD, Adams RD: Brainstem auditory hallucinosis. Neurology 36:1042–1047, 1986

Cascino GD, Luckstein RR, Sharbrough FW, et al: Facial asymmetry, hippocampal pathology, and remote symptomatic seizures: a temporal lobe epileptic syndrome. Neurology 43:725–727, 1993

Caselli RJ: Visual syndromes as the presenting feature of degenerative brain disease. Semin Neurol 20:139–144, 2000

Ceccaldi M, Milandre L: A transient fit of laughter as the inaugural symptom of capsular-thalamic infarction. Neurology 44:1762, 1994

Ceccaldi M, Poncet M, Milandre L, et al: Temporary forced laughter after unilateral strokes. Eur Neurol 34:36–39, 1994

Chapman LF, Wolff HG: Disease of the neopallium and impairment of the highest integrative functions. Med Clin North Am 677–689, 1958

Chapman LF, Thetford WN, Berlin L, et al: Highest integrative functions in man during stress, in Brain and Human Behavior. Edited by Solomon HC, Cobb S, Penfield W. Baltimore, MD, Williams & Wilkins, 1958, pp 491–534

Chatterjee A, Yapundich R, Mennemeier M, et al: Thalamic thought disorder: on being "a bit addled." Cortex 33:419–440, 1997

Chédru F, Geschwind N: Disorders of higher cortical functions in acute confusional states. Cortex 8:395–411, 1972a

Chédru F, Geschwind N: Writing disturbances in acute confusional states. Neuropsychologia 10:343–353, 1972b

Chen EYH, Shapleske J, Luque R, et al: The Cambridge Neurological Inventory: a clinical instrument for assessment of soft neurological signs in psychiatric patients. Psychiatry Res 56:183–204, 1995

Chen YLR, Chen YHE, Mak FL: Soft neurological signs in schizophrenic patients and their nonpsychotic siblings. J Nerv Ment Dis 188:84–89, 2000

Cohen LG, Meer J, Tarkka I, et al: Congenital mirror movements: abnormal organization of motor pathways in two patients. Brain 114:381–403, 1991

Cohen MAA, Alfonso CA, Haque MM: Lilliputian hallucinations and medical illness. Gen Hosp Psychiatry 16:141–143, 1994

Collins SJ, Ahlskog JE, Parisi JE, et al: Progressive supranuclear palsy: neuropathologically based diagnostic clinical criteria. J Neurol Neurosurg Psychiatry 58:167–173, 1995

Collis RJ, Macpherson R: Tardive dyskinesia: patients' lack of awareness of movement disorder. Br J Psychiatry 160:110–112, 1992

Comella CL, Goetz CG: Akathisia in Parkinson's disease. Mov Disord 9:545–549, 1994

Comings DE, Comings BG: A controlled study of Tourette syndrome, IV: obsessions, compulsions, and schizoid behaviors. Am J Med Genet 41:782–803, 1987

Convit A, Volavka J, Czobor P, et al: Effect of subtle neurological dysfunction on response to haloperidol treatment in schizophrenia. Am J Psychiatry 151:49–56, 1994

Couderq C, Drouineau J, Rosier M-P, et al: Fou rire prodromique d'une occlusion du tronc basilaire. Rev Neurol (Paris) 156:281–284, 2000

Critchley M: On palilalia. Journal of Neurology and Psychopathology 8:23–31, 1927

Cubelli R, Della Sala S: The legacy of automatic/voluntary dissociations in apraxia. Neurocase 2:449–454, 1996

Cummings JL: Neuropsychiatry of sexual deviations, in Neuropsychiatry and Mental Health Services. Edited by Ovsiew F. Washington, DC, American Psychiatric Press, 1999, pp 363–384

Cummings JL, Mega M, Gray K, et al: The Neuropsychiatric Inventory: comprehensive assessment of psychopathology in dementia. Neurology 44:2308–2314, 1994

Cutting J: Physical illness and psychosis. Br J Psychiatry 136:109–119, 1980

Cutting J: The phenomenology of acute organic psychosis: comparison with acute schizophrenia. Br J Psychiatry 151:324–332, 1987

Cutting J: The Right Cerebral Hemisphere and Psychiatric Disorders. Oxford, UK, Oxford University Press, 1990

Cutting J, Murphy D: Schizophrenic thought disorder: a psychological and organic interpretation. Br J Psychiatry 152:310–319, 1988

Daffner KR, Ahern GL, Weintraub S, et al: Dissociated neglect behavior following sequential strokes in the right hemisphere. Neurology 28:97–101, 1990

Daly DA, Burnett ML: Cluttering: traditional views and new perspectives, in Stuttering and Related Disorders of Fluency, 2nd Edition. Edited by Curlee RF. New York, Thieme, 1999, pp 222–254

Damasio A, Yamada T, Damasio H, et al: Central achromatopsia: behavioral, anatomic, and physiologic aspects. Neurology 30:1064–1071, 1980

Damasio AR, Benton AL: Impairment of hand movements under visual guidance. Neurology 29:170–178, 1979

Damasio AR, Maurer RG: A neurological model for childhood autism. Arch Neurol 35:777–786, 1978

Damasio AR, Van Hoesen GW: Emotional disturbances associated with focal lesions of the limbic frontal lobe, in Neuropsychology of Human Emotion. Edited by Heilman KM, Satz P. New York, Guilford, 1983, pp 85–110

Damasio H, Damasio AR: Lesion Analysis in Neuropsychology. New York, Oxford University Press, 1989

Darley FL, Aronson AE, Brown JR: Motor Speech Disorders. Philadelphia, PA, WB Saunders, 1975

Dasco CC, Bortz DL: Significance of the Argyll Robertson pupil in clinical medicine. Am J Med 86:199–202, 1989

David AS: Thought echo reflects the activity of the phonological loop. Br J Clin Psychol 33:81–83, 1994

Day RK: Psychomotor agitation: poorly defined and badly measured. J Affect Disord 55:89–98, 1999

Defazio G, Livrea P, Lamberti P, et al: Isolated so-called apraxia of eyelid opening: report of 10 cases and a review of the literature. Eur Neurol 39:204–210, 1998

Della Sala S, Marchetti C, Spinnler H: The anarchic hand: a fronto-mesial sign, in Handbook of Neuropsychology, Vol 9. Edited by Boller F, Grafman J. Amsterdam, Elsevier, 1994, pp 233–255

Demarest J, Demarest L: Does the "torque test" measure cerebral dominance in adults? Percept Mot Skills 50:155–158, 1980

Demirkiran M, Jankovic J, Lewis RA, et al: Neurological presentation of Wilson disease without Kayser-Fleischer rings. Neurology 46:1040–1043, 1996

Denny-Brown D: The nature of apraxia. J Nerv Ment Dis 126:9–32, 1958

Denny-Brown D, Meyer JS, Horenstein S: The significance of perceptual rivalry resulting from parietal lesion. Brain 75:433–471, 1952

De Renzi E, Barbieri C: The incidence of the grasp reflex following hemispheric lesion and its relation to frontal damage. Brain 115:243–313, 1992

De Renzi E, Gentilini M, Bazolli M: Eyelid movement disorders and motor impersistence in acute hemisphere disease. Neurology 36:414–418, 1986

De Renzi E, Perani D, Carlesimo GA, et al: Prosopagnosia can be associated with damage confined to the right hemisphere: an MRI and PET study and a review of the literature. Neuropsychologia 32:893–902, 1994

Departments of Psychiatry and Child Psychiatry, The Institute of Psychiatry and The Maudsley Hospital London: Psychiatric Examination: Notes on Eliciting and Recording Clinical Information in Psychiatric Patients, 2nd Edition. Oxford, Oxford University Press, 1987

Desmond DW, Tatemichi TK, Figueroa M, et al: Disorientation following stroke: frequency, course, and clinical correlates. J Neurol 241:585–591, 1994

Destée A, Gray F, Parent M, et al: Comportement compulsif d'allure obsesionnelle et paralysie supranucléaire progressive. Rev Neurol (Paris) 146:12–18, 1990

Devinsky O, Bear D, Volpe BT: Confusional states following posterior cerebral artery infarction. Arch Neurol 45:160–163, 1988

Dewey RB, Jankovic J: Hemiballism-hemichorea: clinical and pharmacologic findings in 21 patients. Arch Neurol 46:862–867, 1989

Douen AG, Bourque PR: Musical auditory hallucinations from Listeria rhombencephalitis. Can J Neurol Sci 24:70–72, 1997

Douyon R, Guzman P, Romain G, et al: Subtle neurological deficits and psychopathological findings in substance-abusing homeless and non-homeless veterans. J Neuropsychiatry Clin Neurosci 10:210–215, 1998

Drewe EA: Go–no go learning after frontal lobe lesions in humans. Cortex 11:8–16, 1975

Dubois B, Slachevsky A, Litvan I, et al: The FAB: a frontal assessment battery at bedside. Neurology 55:1621–1626, 2000

Duffy RJ, Duffy JR: An investigation of Body Part as Object (BPO) responses in normal and brain-damaged adults. Brain Cogn 10:220–236, 1989

Duus P: Topical Diagnosis in Neurology, 3rd Edition. New York, Thieme, 1998

Ellsworth JD, Lawrence MS, Roth RH, et al: $D_1$ and $D_2$ dopamine receptors independently regulate spontaneous blink rate in the vervet monkey. J Pharmacol Exp Ther 259:595–600, 1991

Eslinger PJ, Damasio AR: Severe disturbance of higher cognition after bilateral frontal lobe ablation: patient EVR. Neurology 35:1731–1741, 1985

Eslinger PJ, Damasio AR, Van Hoesen GW: Olfactory dysfunction in man: anatomical and behavioral aspects. Brain Cogn 1:259–285, 1982

Ettlin TM, Beckson M, Benson DF, et al: Prosopagnosia: a bihemispheric disorder. Cortex 28:129–134, 1992

Faber-Langendoen K, Morris JC, Knesevich JW, et al: Aphasia in senile dementia of the Alzheimer type. Neurology 23:365–370, 1988

Fahn S, Marsden CD, Calne DB: Classification and investigation of dystonia, in Movement Disorders 2. Edited by Marsden CD, Fahn S. London, Butterworths, 1987, pp 332–358

Falconer MA, Wilson JL: Visual field changes following anterior temporal lobectomy: their significance in relation to "Meyer's loop" of the optic radiation. Brain 81:1–14, 1958

Farah MJ: Visual Agnosia: Disorders of Object Recognition and What They Tell Us about Normal Vision. Cambridge, MA, MIT Press, 1990

Feinberg TE: Some interesting perturbations of the self in neurology. Semin Neurol 17:129–135, 1997

Feinberg TE, Eaton LA, Roane DM, et al: Multiple Fregoli delusions after traumatic brain injury. Cortex 35:373–387, 1999

Feinstein A, Hattersley A: Ganser symptoms, dissociation, and dysprosody. J Nerv Ment Dis 176:692–693, 1988

Fenton WS, Blyler CR, Wyatt RJ, et al: Prevalence of spontaneous dyskinesia in schizophrenic and non-schizophrenic psychiatric patients. Br J Psychiatry 171:265–268, 1997

Fenwick P: The nature and management of aggression in epilepsy. J Neuropsychiatry Clin Neurosci 1:418–425, 1989

Field SJ, Saling MM, Berkovic SF: Interictal discourse production in temporal lobe epilepsy. Brain Lang 74:213–222, 2000

Findley LJ, Gresty MA, Halmagyi GM: Tremor, the cogwheel phenomenon and clonus in Parkinson's disease. J Neurol Neurosurg Psychiatry 44:534–546, 1981

Fischer RS, Alexander MP, D'Esposito M, et al: Neuropsychological and neuroanatomical correlates of confabulation. J Clin Exp Neuropsychol 17:20–28, 1995

Fisher CM: Intermittent interruption of behavior. Transactions of the American Neurological Association 93:209–210, 1968

Fisher CM: Disorientation for place. Arch Neurol 39:33–36, 1982

Fisher CM: Abulia minor vs. agitated behavior. Clin Neurosurg 31:9–31, 1984

Fisher CM: "Catatonia" due to disulfiram toxicity. Arch Neurol 46:798–804, 1989

Fisher CM: Visual hallucinations on eye closure associated with atropine toxicity. A neurological analysis and comparison with other visual hallucinations. Can J Neurol Sci 18:18–27, 1991

Fisher M: Left hemiplegia and motor impersistence. J Nerv Ment Dis 123:201–218, 1956

FitzGerald PM, Jankovic J: Lower body parkinsonism: evidence for vascular etiology. Mov Disord 4:249–260, 1989a

FitzGerald PM, Jankovic J: Tardive oculogyric crises. Neurology 39:1434–1437, 1989b

Fleminger S, Burns A: The delusional misidentification syndromes in patients with and without evidence of organic cerebral disorder: a structured review of case reports. Biol Psychiatry 33:22–32, 1993

Fletcher WA, Sharpe JA: Tonic pupils in neurosyphilis. Neurology 36:188–192, 1986

Fogel BS: The significance of frontal system disorders for medical practice and health policy. J Neuropsychiatry Clin Neurosci 6:343–347, 1994

Fogel CA, Mednick SA, Michelsen N: Hyperactive behavior and minor physical anomalies. Acta Psychiatr Scand 72:551–556, 1985

Folstein MF, Folstein SE, McHugh PR: Mini-Mental State: a practical method for grading the cognitive state of patients for the clinician. J Psychiatr Res 12:189–198, 1975

Ford RA: The psychopathology of echophenomena. Psychol Med 19:627–635, 1989

Förstl H, Owen AM, David AS: Gabriel Anton and "Anton's symptom": on focal diseases of the brain which are not perceived by the patient (1898). Neuropsychiatry Neuropsychol Behav Neurol 6:1–8, 1993

Freed WJ, Kleinman JE, Karson CN, et al: Eye-blink rates and platelet monoamine oxidase activity in chronic schizophrenic patients. Biol Psychiatry 15:329–332, 1980

Freund H-J: Apraxia, in Diseases of the Nervous System/Clinical Neurobiology, 2nd Edition. Edited by Asbury AK, McKhann GM, McDonald WI. Philadelphia, PA, WB Saunders, 1992, pp 751–767

Freund H-J, Hummelsheim H: Lesions of premotor cortex in man. Brain 108:697–733, 1985

Friedman JH: Punding on levodopa. Biol Psychiatry 36:350–351, 1994

Frith CD, Done DJ: Stereotyped behaviour in madness and in health, in Neurobiology of Stereotyped Behaviour. Edited by Cooper SJ, Dourish CT. Oxford, UK, Clarendon, 1990, pp 232–259

Fujimori M, Imamura T, Yamashita H, et al: The disturbances of object vision and spatial vision in Alzheimer's disease. Dement Geriatr Cogn Disord 8:228–231, 1997

Fung VSC, Morris JGL, Leicester J, et al: Clonic perseveration following thalamofrontal disconnection: a distinctive movement disorder. Mov Disord 12:378–385, 1997

Gainotti G: What the locus of brain lesion tells us about the nature of the cognitive defect underlying category-specific disorders: a review. Cortex 36:539–559, 2000

Ganser SJM: A peculiar hysterical state [1898], in Themes and Variations in European Psychiatry. Edited by Hirsch SR, Shepherd M. Bristol, UK, John Wright & Sons, 1974, pp 67–73

Gardner D, Lucas PB, Cowdry RW: Soft sign neurological abnormalities in borderline personality disorder and normal control subjects. J Nerv Ment Dis 175:177–180, 1987

Gasquoine PG: Alien hand sign. J Clin Exp Neuropsychol 15:653–667, 1993

Geschwind N: Non-aphasic disorders of speech. Int J Neurol 4:207–214, 1964

Geschwind N, Kaplan E: A human cerebral deconnection syndrome: a preliminary report. Neurology 12:675–685, 1962

Ghika J, Regli F, Assal G, et al: Impossibilité à la fermeture volontaire des paupières: discussion sur les troubles supranucléaires de la fermeture palpébrale à partir de 2 cas, avec revue de la littérature. Schweizer Archiv fur Neurologie und Psychiatrie 139(6):5–21, 1988

Ghika J, Bogousslavsky J, van Melle G, et al: Hyperkinetic motor behaviors contralateral to hemiplegia in acute stroke. Eur Neurol 35:27–32, 1995a

Ghika J, Tennis M, Growden J, et al: Environment-driven responses in progressive supranuclear palsy. J Neurol Sci 130:104–111, 1995b

Ghika J, Bogousslavsky J, Ghika-Schmidt F, et al: "Echoing approval": a new speech disorder. J Neurol 243:633–637, 1996

Ghika J, Ghika-Schmidt F, Bogousslavsky J: Parietal motor syndrome: a clinical description in 32 patients in the acute phase of pure parietal strokes studied prospectively. Clin Neurol Neurosurg 100:271–282, 1998

Ghika-Schmidt F, Bogousslavsky J: The acute behavioral syndrome of anterior thalamic infarction: a prospective study of 12 cases. Ann Neurol 48:220–227, 2000

Ghika-Schmidt F, Ghika J, Regli F, et al: Hyperkinetic movement disorders during and after acute stroke: the Lausanne Stroke Registry. J Neurol Sci 146:109–116, 1997

Gloor P, Olivier A, Quesny LF, et al: The role of the limbic system in experiential phenomena of temporal lobe epilepsy. Ann Neurol 12:129–140, 1982

Goldberg E, Bilder RM: The frontal lobes and hierarchical organization of cognitive control, in The Frontal Lobes Revisited. Edited by Perecman E. Hillsdale, NJ, Erlbaum, 1987, pp 159–187

Goldberg E, Podell K: Adaptive decision making, ecological validity, and the frontal lobes. J Clin Exp Neuropsychol 22:56–68, 2000

Goldberg G: From intent to action: evolution and function of the premotor systems of the frontal lobe, in The Frontal Lobes Revisited. Edited by Perecman E. Hillsdale, NJ, Erlbaum, 1987, pp 273–306

Goldstein K: The effect of brain damage on the personality. Psychiatry 15:245–260, 1952

Goodglass H, Kaplan E: The Assessment of Aphasia and Related Disorders, 2nd Edition. Philadelphia, PA, Lea & Febiger, 1983

Goodwin DW, Alderson P, Rosenthal R: Clinical significance of hallucinations in psychiatric disorders: a study of 116 hallucinatory patients. Arch Gen Psychiatry 24:76–80, 1971

Gould R, Miller BL, Goldberg MA, et al: The validity of hysterical signs and symptoms. J Nerv Ment Dis 174:593–597, 1986

Grace J, Nadler JD, White DA, et al: Folstein vs Modified Mini-Mental State Examination in geriatric stroke. Arch Neurol 52:477–484, 1995

Graff-Radford NR, Eslinger PJ, Damasio AR, et al: Nonhemorrhagic infarction of the thalamus: behavioral, anatomic, and physiologic correlates. Neurology 34:14–23, 1984

Grandas F, Esteban A: Eyelid motor abnormalities in progressive supranuclear palsy. J Neural Transm 42 (suppl):33–41, 1994

Grant AC, Biousse V, Cook AA, et al: Stroke-associated stuttering. Arch Neurol 56:624–627, 1999

Griffiths TD, Sigmundsson T, Takei N, et al: Neurological abnormalities in familial and sporadic schizophrenia. Brain 121:191–203, 1998

Grigsby J, Kaye K: Alphanumeric sequencing and cognitive impairment among elderly persons. Percept Mot Skills 80:732–734, 1995

Grigsby J, Kaye K, Robbins LJ: Reliabilities, norms and factor structure of the Behavioral Dyscontrol Scale. Percept Mot Skills 74:883–892, 1992

Grigsby J, Kravcisin N, Ayarbe SD, et al: Prediction of deficits in behavioral self-regulation among persons with multiple sclerosis. Arch Phys Med Rehabil 74:1350–1353, 1993

Grigsby J, Kaye K, Busenbark D: Alphanumeric sequencing: a report on a brief measure of information processing used among persons with multiple sclerosis. Percept Mot Skills 78:883–887, 1994

Grigsby J, Kaye K, Baxter J, et al: Executive cognitive abilities and functional status among community-dwelling older persons in the San Luis Valley Health and Aging Study. J Am Geriatr Soc 46:590–596, 1998

Gualtieri CT, Adams A, Shen CD, et al: Minor physical anomalies in alcoholic and schizophrenic adults and hyperactive and autistic children. Am J Psychiatry 139:640–643, 1982

Gupta S, Andreasen NC, Arndt S, et al: Neurological soft signs in neuroleptic-naive and neuroleptic-treated schizophrenic patients and in normal comparison subjects. Am J Psychiatry 152:191–196, 1995

Gurvits TV, Gilbertson MW, Lasko NB, et al: Neurologic soft signs in chronic posttraumatic stress disorder. Arch Gen Psychiatry 57:181–186, 2000

Gutierrez R, Atkinson JH, Grant I: Mild neurocognitive disorder: needed addition to the nosology of cognitive impairment (organic mental) disorders. J Neuropsychiatry Clin Neurosci 5:161–177, 1993

Gutierrez R, Atkinson JH, Grant I: Corrected tables. J Neuropsychiatry Clin Neurosci 6:76–86, 1994

Hadano K, Nakamura H, Hamanaka T: Effortful echolalia. Cortex 34:67–82, 1998

Halligan PW, Marshall JC, Wade DT: Unilateral somatoparaphrenia after right hemisphere stroke: a case description. Cortex 31:173–182, 1995

Harrison PJ, Pearson RCA: Olfaction and psychiatry. Br J Psychiatry 155:822–828, 1989

Hashimoto R, Tanaka Y: Contribution of the supplementary motor area and anterior cingulate gyrus to pathological grasping phenomena. Eur Neurol 40:151–158, 1998

Heilman KM, Watson RT: Intentional motor disorders, in Frontal Lobe Function and Dysfunction. Edited by Levin HS, Eisenberg HM, Benton AL. New York, Oxford University Press, 1991, pp 199–213

Heilman KM, Scholes R, Watson RT: Auditory affective agnosia: disturbed comprehension of affective speech. J Neurol Neurosurg Psychiatry 38:69–72, 1975

Helm-Estabrooks N: Stuttering associated with acquired neurological disorders, in Stuttering and Related Disorders of Fluency, 2nd Edition. Edited by Curlee RF. New York, Thieme, 1999, pp 255–268

Helms PM, Godwin CD: Abnormalities of blink rate in psychoses: a preliminary report. Biol Psychiatry 20:103–106, 1985

Hermann BP, Dikmen S, Schwartz MS, et al: Interictal psychopathology in patients with ictal fear: a quantitative investigation. Neurology 32:7–11, 1982

Hermesh H, Munitz H: Unilateral neuroleptic-induced akathisia. Clin Neuropharmacol 13:253–258, 1990

Heron EA, Kritchevsky M, Delis DC: Neuropsychological presentation of Ganser symptoms. J Clin Exp Neuropsychol 13:652–666, 1991

Hier DB, Mondlock J, Caplan LR: Recovery of behavioral abnormalities after right hemisphere stroke. Neurology 33:345–350, 1983

Hirsch AR: Olfaction in migraineurs. Headache 32:233–236, 1992

Hollander E, Schiffman E, Cohen B, et al: Signs of central nervous system dysfunction in obsessive-compulsive disorder. Arch Gen Psychiatry 47:27–32, 1990

Holzer JC, Goodman WK, McDougle CJ, et al: Obsessive-compulsive disorder with and without a chronic tic disorder: a comparison of symptoms in 70 patients. Br J Psychiatry 164:469–473, 1994

Hopf HC, Müller-Forell W, Hopf NJ: Localization of emotional and volitional facial paresis. Neurology 42:1918–1923, 1992

Horner J, Heyman A, Dawson D, et al: The relationship of agraphia to the severity of dementia in Alzheimer's disease. Arch Neurol 45:760–763, 1988

House A, Dennis M, Molyneux A, et al: Emotionalism after stroke. BMJ 298:991–994, 1989

Howard R, Ford R: From the jumping Frenchmen of Maine to post-traumatic stress disorder: the startle response in neuropsychiatry. Psychol Med 22:695–707, 1992

Hughlings-Jackson J: On right- or left-sided spasm at the onset of epileptic paroxysms, and on crude sensation warnings and elaborate mental states. Brain 3:192–214, 1880/1881

Hyde TM, Hotson JR, Kleinman JE: Differential diagnosis of choreiform tardive dyskinesia. J Neuropsychiatry Clin Neurosci 3:255–268, 1991

Ismail B, Cantor-Graae E, McNeil TF: Minor physical anomalies in schizophrenic patients and their siblings. Am J Psychiatry 155:1695–1702, 1998a

Ismail B, Cantor-Graae E, McNeil TF: Neurological abnormalities in schizophrenic patients and their siblings. Am J Psychiatry 155:84–89, 1998b

Ismail B, Cantor-Graae E, McNeil TF: Minor physical anomalies in schizophrenia: cognitive, neurological and other clinical correlates. J Psychiatr Res 34:45–56, 2000

Ivanovich M, Glantz R, Bone RC, et al: Respiratory dyskinesia presenting as acute respiratory distress. Chest 103:314–316, 1993

Jacobs L, Grossman MD: Three primitive reflexes in normal adults. Neurology 30:184–188, 1980

Jacobs L, Feldman M, Diamond SP, et al: Palinacousis: persistent or recurring auditory sensations. Cortex 9:275–287, 1973

Jancar J, Kettle LB: Hypergraphia and mental handicap. Journal of Mental Deficiency Research 28:151–158, 1984

Jenkyn LR, Walsh DB, Walsh BT, et al: The nuchocephalic reflex. J Neurol Neurosurg Psychiatry 38:561–566, 1975

Jenkyn LR, Walsh DB, Culver CM, et al: Clinical signs in diffuse cerebral dysfunction. J Neurol Neurosurg Psychiatry 40:956–966, 1977

Jones BN, Teng EL, Folstein MF, et al: A new bedside test of cognition for patients with HIV infection. Ann Intern Med 119:1001–1004, 1993

Jones IH: Observations on schizophrenic stereotypies. Compr Psychiatry 6:323–335, 1965

Joynt RJ, Benton AL, Fogel ML: Behavioral and pathological correlates of motor impersistence. Neurology 12:876–881, 1962

Kandel E, Brennan PA, Mednick SA, et al: Minor physical anomalies and recidivistic adult criminal behavior. Acta Psychiatr Scand 79:103–107, 1989

Kaneko K, Yuasa T, Miyatake T, et al: Stereotyped hand clasping: an unusual tardive movement disorder. Mov Disord 8:230–231, 1993

Karson CN: Oculomotor signs in a psychiatric population: a preliminary report. Am J Psychiatry 136:1057–1060, 1979

Karson CN, Burns RS, LeWitt PA, et al: Blink rates and disorders of movement. Neurology 34:677–678, 1984

Katzman R, Brown T, Fuld P, et al: Validation of a short orientation-memory-concentration test of cognitive impairment. Am J Psychiatry 140:734–739, 1983

Kaufer DI, Cummings JL, Ketchel P, et al: Validation of the NPI-Q, a brief clinical form of the Neuropsychiatric Inventory. J Neuropsychiatry Clin Neurosci 12:233–239, 2000

Kennard C, Crawford TJ, Henderson I: A pathophysiological approach to saccadic eye movements in neurological and psychiatric disease. J Neurol Neurosurg Psychiatry 57:881–885, 1994

Kertesz A (ed): Localization and Neuroimaging in Neuropsychology. San Diego, CA, Academic Press, 1994

Kertesz A, Nicholson I, Cancelliere A, et al: Motor impersistence: a right-hemisphere syndrome. Neurology 35:662–666, 1985

Keshavan MS, David AS, Steingard S, et al: Musical hallucinations: a review and synthesis. Neuropsychiatry Neuropsychol Behav Neurol 5:211–223, 1992

Khanna R, Damodaran SS, Chakraborty SP: Overflow movements may predict neuroleptic-induced dystonia. Biol Psychiatry 35:491–492, 1994

Kinney DK, Yurgelun-Todd DA, Levy DL, et al: Obstetrical complications in patients with bipolar disorder and their siblings. Psychiatry Res 48:45–56, 1993a

Kinney DK, Yurgelun-Todd DA, Woods BT: Neurological hard signs in schizophrenia and major mood disorders. J Nerv Ment Dis 181:202–204, 1993b

Kiziltan G, Akalin MA: Stuttering may be a type of action dystonia. Mov Disord 11:278–282, 1996

Klein DA, Steinberg M, Galik E, et al: Wandering behavior in community-residing persons with dementia. Int J Geriatr Psychiatry 14(4):272–279, 1999

Kluin KJ, Foster NL, Berent S, et al: Perceptual analysis of speech disorders in progressive supranuclear palsy. Neurology 43:563–566, 1993

Klüver H, Bucy PC: Psychic blindness and other symptoms following bilateral temporal lobectomy in rhesus monkeys. Am J Physiol 119:352–353, 1937

Klüver H, Bucy PC: Preliminary analysis of functions of the temporal lobes in monkeys. AMA Archives of Neurology and Psychiatry 42:979–1000, 1939

Knopman DS, Rubens AB: The validity of computed tomographic scan findings for the localization of cerebral functions: the relationship between computed tomography and hemiparesis. Arch Neurol 43:328–332, 1986

Kolada SJ, Pitman RK: Eye-head synkinesia in schizophrenic adults during a repetitive visual search task. Biol Psychiatry 18:675–684, 1983

Koller WC: Edentulous orodyskinesia. Neurology 13:97–99, 1983

Koller WC, Glatt S, Wilson RS, et al: Primitive reflexes and cognitive function in the elderly. Ann Neurol 12:302–304, 1982

Koller W, Lang A, Vetere-Overfield B, et al: Psychogenic tremors. Neurology 39:1094–1099, 1989

Kölmel HW: Peduncular hallucinations. J Neurol 238:457–459, 1991

Kölmel HW: Visual illusions and hallucinations. Baillière's Clinical Neurology 2:243–264, 1993

Kopala LC, Good KP, Honer WG: Olfactory hallucinations and olfactory identification ability in patients with schizophrenia and other psychiatric disorders. Schizophr Res 12:205–211, 1994

Kopelman MD: Clinical tests of memory. Br J Psychiatry 148:517–525, 1986

Kopelman MD: Varieties of false memory. Cognitive Neuropsychology 16:197–214, 1999

Kopelman MD, Guinan EM, Lewis PDR: Delusional memory, confabulation, and frontal lobe dysfunction: a case study in De Clérambault's syndrome. Neurocase 1:71–77, 1995

Korein J: Iris pigmentation (melanin) in idiopathic dystonic syndromes including torticollis. Ann Neurol 10:53–55, 1981

Kracke I: Developmental prosopagnosia in Asperger syndrome: presentation and discussion of an individual case. Dev Med Child Neurol 36:873–886, 1994

Kramer S, Bryan KL, Frith CD: "Confabulation" in narrative discourse by schizophrenic patients. Int J Lang Commun Disord 33 (suppl):202–207, 1998

Kuperberg GR, McGuire PK, David AS: Sensitivity to linguistic anomalies in spoken sentences: a case study approach to understanding thought disorder in schizophrenia. Psychol Med 30:345–357, 2000

Kurlan R, Richard IH, Papka M, et al: Movement disorders in Alzheimer's disease: more rigidity of definitions is needed. Mov Disord 15:24–29, 2000

Kurowski KM, Blumstein SE, Alexander M: The foreign accent syndrome: a reconsideration. Brain Lang 54:1–25, 1996

Lainhart JE, Piven J, Wzorek M, et al: Macrocephaly in children and adults with autism. J Am Acad Child Adolesc Psychiatry 36:282–290, 1997

Landau WM: Reflex dementia: disinhibited primitive thinking. Neurology 39:133–137, 1989

Lang AE: Clinical differences between metoclopramide- and antipsychotic-induced tardive dyskinesias. Can J Neurol Sci 17:137–139, 1990

Lang AE: Clinical phenomenology of tic disorders: selected aspects. Adv Neurol 58:25–32, 1992

Lang AE: Withdrawal akathisia: case reports and a proposed classification of chronic akathisia. Mov Disord 9:188–192, 1994

Lang AE: Movement disorders: symptoms, in Neurology in Clinical Practice, 3rd Edition. Edited by Bradley WG, Daroff RB, Fenichel GM, et al. Boston, MA, Butterworth-Heinemann, 2000, pp 319–340

Lang AE, Ellis C, Kingon H, et al: Iris pigmentation in idiopathic dystonia. Ann Neurol 12:585–586, 1982

Laplane D: La perte d'auto-activation psychique. Rev Neurol (Paris) 146:397–404, 1990

Laplane D: Obsessions et compulsions par lésions des noyaux gris centraux. Rev Neurol (Paris) 150:594–598, 1994

Laplane D, Orgogozo JM, Meininger V, et al: Paralysie faciale avec dissociation automatico-volontaire inverse par lesion frontale: son origine corticale. Ses relations avec l'A. M. S. Rev Neurol (Paris) 132:725–734, 1976

Laplane D, Baulac M, Widlöcher D, et al: Pure psychic akinesia with bilateral lesions of basal ganglia. J Neurol Neurosurg Psychiatry 47:377–385, 1984

Laplane D, Levasseur M, Pillon B, et al: Obsessive-compulsive and other behavioural changes with bilateral basal ganglia lesions: a neuropsychological, magnetic resonance imaging and positron tomographic study. Brain 112:699–725, 1989

Laws KR, Kondel TK, McKenna PJ: A receptive language deficit in schizophrenic thought disorder: evidence for impaired semantic access and monitoring. Cognitive Neuropsychology 4:89–105, 1999

Lecours AR, Lhermitte F, Bryans B: Aphasiology. London, Baillière Tindall, 1983

Leder SB: Adult onset of stuttering as a presenting sign in a parkinsonian-like syndrome: a case report. J Commun Disord 29:471–478, 1996

Lees AJ: Tics and Related Disorders. Edinburgh, UK, Churchill Livingstone, 1985

Lees AJ: Facial mannerisms and tics. Adv Neurol 49:255–261, 1988

Leigh RJ, Newman SA, Folstein SE, et al: Abnormal ocular motor control in Huntington's disease. Neurology 33:1268–1275, 1983

Leigh RJ, Foley JM, Remler BF, et al: Oculogyric crisis: a syndrome of thought disorder and ocular deviation. Ann Neurol 22:13–17, 1987

Leiguarda RC, Marsden CD: Limb apraxias: higher-order disorders of sensorimotor integration. Brain 123:860–879, 2000

Leimkuhler ME, Mesulam M-M: Reversible go–no go deficits in a case of frontal lobe tumor. Ann Neurol 18:617–619, 1985

Lennox G: Tics and related disorders, in Movement Disorders in Clinical Practice. Edited by Sawle G. Oxford, UK, Isis Medical Media, 1999, pp 135–146

Leopold NA, Borson AJ: An alphabetical "WORLD": a new version of an old test. Neurology 49:1521–1524, 1997

Levin HS, High WM, Goethe KE, et al: The Neurobehavioural Rating Scale: assessment of the behavioural sequelae of head injury by the clinician. J Neurol Neurosurg Psychiatry 50:183–193, 1987

Levin M: Delirium: a gap in psychiatric teaching. Am J Psychiatry 107:689–694, 1951

Levin M: Thinking disturbances in delirium. AMA Archives of Neurology and Psychiatry 75:62–66, 1956

Levine DN, Calvanio R, Rinn WE: The pathogenesis of anosognosia for hemiplegia. Neurology 41:1770–1781, 1991

Levine DN, Lee JM, Fisher CM: The visual variant of Alzheimer's disease: a clinicopathologic case study. Neurology 43:305–313, 1993

Levy DL, Holzman PS, Matthysse S, et al: Eye tracking dysfunction and schizophrenia: a critical perspective. Schizophr Bull 19:461–536, 1993

Levy J, Reid M: Variations in writing posture and cerebral organization. Science 194:614–615, 1976

Lezak MD: Subtle sequelae of brain damage: perplexity, distractibility, and fatigue. American Journal of Physical Medicine 57:9–15, 1978

Lhermitte F: Human autonomy and the frontal lobes, II: patient behavior in complex and social situations: the "environmental dependency syndrome." Ann Neurol 19:335–343, 1986

Lhermitte F: Les comportements d'imitation et d'utilisation dans les états dépressifs majeurs. Bull Acad Natl Med 177:883–892, 1993

Lhermitte F, Pillon B, Serdaru M: Human autonomy and the frontal lobes, I: imitation and utilization behavior: a neuropsychological study of 75 patients. Ann Neurol 19:326–334, 1986

Lishman WA: Organic Psychiatry: The Psychological Consequences of Cerebral Disorder, 3rd Edition. Oxford, UK, Blackwell Science, 1998

Little JT, Jankovic J: Tardive myoclonus: a case report. Mov Disord 2:307–311, 1987

Lloyd G: Medicine without signs. BMJ 287:539–542, 1983

Lodder J, Baard WC: Paraballism caused by bilateral hemorrhagic infarction in basal ganglia. Neurology 31:484–486, 1981

Logsdon RG, Teri L, McCurry SM, et al: Wandering: a significant problem among community-residing individuals with Alzheimer's disease. J Gerontol 53B:294–299, 1998

Lohr JB, Alder M, Flynn K, et al: Minor physical anomalies in older patients with late-onset schizophrenia, early-onset schizophrenia, depression, and Alzheimer's disease. Am J Geriatr Psychiatry 5:318–323, 1997

Luciano D, Devinsky O, Perrine K: Crying seizures. Neurology 43:2113–2117, 1993

Lundin-Olsson L, Nyberg L, Gustafson Y: "Stops walking when talking" as a predictor of falls in elderly people [letter]. Lancet 349:617, 1997

Luria AR: Two kinds of motor perseveration in massive injury of the frontal lobes. Brain 88:1–10, 1965

Luria AR, Homskaya ED: Le trouble du role régulateur du langage au cours des lésions du lobe frontal. Neuropsychologia 1:9–26, 1963

Luxon L, Lees AJ, Greenwood RJ: Neurosyphilis today. Lancet 1:90–93, 1979

Luzzi S, Pucci E, Di Bella P, et al: Topographical disorientation consequent to amnesia of spatial location in a patient with right parahippocampal damage. Cortex 36:437–434, 2000

MacGowan DJL, Delanty N, Petito F, et al: Isolated myoclonic alien hand as the sole presentation of pathologically established Creutzfeldt-Jakob disease: a report of two patients. J Neurol Neurosurg Psychiatry 63:404–407, 1997

Maillot F, Belin C, Perrier D, et al: Persévération visuelle et palinopsie: une pathologie de la mémoire visuelle? Rev Neurol (Paris) 149:794–796, 1993

Malloy PF, Richardson ED: The frontal lobes and content-specific delusions. J Neuropsychiatry Clin Neurosci 6:455–466, 1994

Malloy PF, Cummings JL, Coffey CE, et al: Cognitive screening instruments in neuropsychiatry: a report of the Committee on Research of the American Neuropsychiatric Association. J Neuropsychiatry Clin Neurosci 9:189–197, 1997

Manford M, Andermann F: Complex visual hallucinations. Clinical and neurobiological insights. Brain 121:1819–1840, 1998

Mao C-C, Coull BM, Golper LAC, et al: Anterior operculum syndrome. Neurology 39:1169–1172, 1989

Marsden CD: Wilson's disease. Q J Med 65:959–966, 1987

Marshall EJ: Neuropsychiatry of substance abuse, in Neuropsychiatry and Mental Health Services. Edited by Ovsiew F. Washington, DC, American Psychiatric Press, 1999, pp 105–148

McGlynn SM, Schacter DL: Unawareness of deficits in neuropsychological syndromes. J Clin Exp Neuropsychol 11:143–205, 1989

McKenna PJ, Lund CE, Mortimer AM, et al: Motor, volitional and behavioural disorders in schizophrenia, 2: the "conflict of paradigms" hypothesis. Br J Psychiatry 158:328–336, 1991

McMeekan ERL, Lishman WA: Retest reliabilities and interrelationship of the Annett Hand Preference Questionnaire and the Edinburgh Handedness Inventory. Br J Psychol 66:53–59, 1975

McNeil TF, Cantor-Graae E, Ismail B: Obstetric complications and congenital malformation in schizophrenia. Brain Res Rev 31:166–178, 2000

Mendez MF, Mendez MA, Martin R, et al: Complex visual disturbances in Alzheimer's disease. Neurology 40:439–443, 1990

Mendez MF, Selwood A, Mastri AR, et al: Pick's disease versus Alzheimer's disease: a comparison of clinical characteristics. Neurology 43:289–292, 1993

Mendez MF, Foti DJ, Cummings JL: Abnormal oral behaviors in neurological and psychiatric syndromes [abstract]. J Neuropsychiatry Clin Neurosci 7:397, 1995

Mesulam M-M: A cortical network for directed attention and unilateral neglect. Ann Neurol 10:309–325, 1981

Mesulam M-M: Attentional networks, confusional states and neglect syndromes, in Principles of Behavioral and Cognitive Neurology, 2nd Edition. Edited by Mesulam M-M. Oxford, UK, Oxford University Press, 2000, pp 174–256

Metzig E, Rosenberg S, Ast M: Lateral asymmetry in patients with nervous and mental disease: a preliminary study. Neuropsychobiology 1:197–202, 1975

Metzig E, Rosenberg S, Ast M, et al: Bipolar manic-depressives and unipolar depressives distinguished by tests of lateral asymmetry. Biol Psychiatry 11:313–323, 1976

Migliorelli R, Tesón A, Sabe L, et al: Anosognosia in Alzheimer's disease: a study of associated factors. J Neuropsychiatry Clin Neurosci 7:338–344, 1995

Milberg WP, Hebben N, Kaplan E: The Boston Process Approach to neuropsychological assessment, in Neuropsychological Assessment of Neuropsychiatric Disorders, 2nd Edition. Edited by Grant I, Adams KM. New York, Oxford University Press, 1996, pp 65–86

Miller H: Psychiatry—medicine or magic?, in Contemporary Psychiatry: Selected Reviews from the British Journal of Hospital Medicine. Edited by Silverstone T, Barraclough B. London, Ashford, Kent, Headley, 1975, pp 462–466

Mojtabai R: Identifying misidentifications: a phenomenological study. Psychopathology 31:90–95, 1998

Molloy DW, Clarnette RM, McIlroy WE, et al: Clinical significance of primitive reflexes in Alzheimer's disease. J Am Geriatr Soc 39:1160–1163, 1991

Mölsä PK, Marrila RJ, Rinne UK: Long-term survival and predictors of mortality in Alzheimer's disease and multi-infarct dementia. Acta Neurol Scand 91:159–164, 1995

Monrad-Krohn GH: On the dissociation of voluntary and emotional innervation in facial paresis of central origin. Brain 47:22–35, 1924

Monrad-Krohn GH: Dysprosody or altered "melody of language." Brain 70:405–415, 1947

Monsch AU, Bondi MW, Butters N, et al: Comparisons of verbal fluency tasks in the detection of dementia of the Alzheimer type. Arch Neurol 49:1253–1258, 1992

Monsch AU, Bondi MW, Butters N, et al: A comparison of category and letter fluency in Alzheimer's disease and Huntington's disease. Neuropsychology 8:25–30, 1994

Moore SR, Gresham LS, Bromberg MB, et al: A self report measure of affective lability. J Neurol Neurosurg Psychiatry 63:89–93, 1997

Mori E, Yamadori A: Rejection behaviour: a human homologue of the abnormal behaviour of Denny-Brown and Chambers' monkey with bilateral parietal ablation. J Neurol Neurosurg Psychiatry 52:1260–1266, 1989

Morrell MJ, Sperling MR, Stecker M, et al: Sexual dysfunction in partial epilepsy: a deficit in physiological sexual arousal. Neurology 44:243–247, 1994

Nathaniel-James DA, Foong J, Frith CD: The mechanism of confabulation in schizophrenia. Neurocase 2:475–483, 1996

Neary D, Snowden JS: Fronto-temporal dementia: nosology, neuropsychology, and neuropathology. Brain Cogn 31:176–187, 1996

Nelson A, Fogel BS, Faust D: Bedside cognitive screening instruments: a critical assessment. J Nerv Ment Dis 174:73–83, 1986

Neumann CS, Walker EF: Childhood neuromotor soft signs, behavior problems, and adult psychopathology, in Advances in Clinical Child Psychology. Edited by Ollendick TH, Prinz RJ. New York, Plenum, 1996, pp 173–203

Niehaus DJ, Emsley RA, Brink P, et al: Stereotypies: prevalence and association with compulsive and impulsive symptoms in college students. Psychopathology 33:31–35, 2000

Niethammer R, Weisbrod M, Schiesser S, et al: Genetic influence on laterality in schizophrenia? A twin study of neurological soft signs. Am J Psychiatry 157:272–274, 2000

Northoff G, Koch A, Wenke J, et al: Catatonia as a psychomotor syndrome: a rating scale and extrapyramidal motor symptoms. Mov Disord 14:404–416, 1999

Norton JW, Corbett JJ: Visual perceptual abnormalities: hallucinations and illusions. Semin Neurol 20:111–121, 2000

Nutt JG, Marsden CD, Thompson PD: Human walking and higher-level gait disorders, particularly in the elderly. Neurology 43:268–279, 1993

Obeso JA, Rothwell JC, Marsden CD: Simple tics in Gilles de la Tourette's syndrome are not prefaced by a normal premovement EEG potential. J Neurol Neurosurg Psychiatry 44:735–738, 1981

Obeso JA, Rothwell JC, Lang AE, et al: Myoclonic dystonia. Neurology 33:825–830, 1983

Occupational and Environmental Health Committee of the American Lung Association of San Diego and Imperial Counties: Taking the occupational history. Ann Intern Med 99:641–651, 1983

Okamura T, Fukai M, Yamadori A, et al: A clinical study of hypergraphia in epilepsy. J Neurol Neurosurg Psychiatry 56:556–559, 1993

Padberg GW, Bruyn GW: Chorea: differential diagnosis, in Handbook of Neurology, Vol 49: Extrapyramidal Disorders. Edited by Vinken PJ, Bruyn GW, Klawans HL. Amsterdam, Elsevier, 1986, pp 549–564

Paradis M: The other side of language: pragmatic competence. Journal of Neurolinguistics 11:1–10, 1998

Pasquini F, Cole MG: Idiopathic musical hallucinations in the elderly. J Geriatr Psychiatry Neurol 10:11–14, 1997

Paul A: Epilepsy or stereotypy? diagnostic issues in learning disabilities. Seizure 6:111–120, 1997

Paulson G, Gottleib G: Developmental reflexes: the reappearance of foetal and neonatal reflexes in aged patients. Brain 91:37–52, 1968

PeBenito R, Cracco JB: Congenital ocular motor apraxia. Clin Pediatr 27:27–31, 1988

Penfield W, Robertson JSM: Growth asymmetry due to lesions of the postcentral cerebral cortex. AMA Archives of Neurology and Psychiatry 50:405–430, 1943

Persinger MA, Makarec K: Complex partial epileptic signs as a continuum from normals to epileptics: normative data and clinical populations. J Clin Psychol 49:33–45, 1993

Pick A: Clinical studies, III: on reduplicative paramnesia. Brain 26:260–267, 1903

Pinching AJ: Clinical testing of olfaction reassessed. Brain 100:377–388, 1977

Pine DS, Shaffer D, Schonfeld IS, et al: Minor physical anomalies: modifiers of environmental risks for psychiatric impairment? J Am Acad Child Adolesc Psychiatry 36:395–403, 1997

Plum F, Posner JB: The Diagnosis of Stupor and Coma, 3rd Edition. Philadelphia, PA, FA Davis, 1980

Poeck K: The Kluver-Bucy syndrome in man, in Handbook of Clinical Neurology, Vol 45: Clinical Neuropsychology. Edited by Frederiks JAM. Amsterdam, Elsevier, 1985a, pp 257–263

Poeck K: Pathological laughter and crying, in Handbook of Clinical Neurology, Vol 45: Clinical Neuropsychology. Edited by Frederiks JAM. Amsterdam, Elsevier, 1985b, pp 219–225

Poizner H, Klima ES, Bellugi U: What the Hands Reveal about the Brain. Cambridge, MA, MIT Press, 1987

Poncet M, Habib M: Atteinte isolée des comportements motivés et lésions des noyaux gris centraux. Rev Neurol (Paris) 150:588–593, 1994

Posner MI, Early TS, Reiman E, et al: Asymmetries in hemispheric control of attention in schizophrenia. Arch Gen Psychiatry 45:814–821, 1988

Power C, Selnes OA, Grim JA, et al: HIV Dementia Scale: a rapid screening test. J Acquir Immune Defic Syndr 8:273–278, 1995

Preti A, Cardascia L, Zen T, et al: Obstetric complications in patients with depression—a population-based case-control study. J Affect Disord 61:101–106, 2000

Ptak R, Schnider A: Spontaneous confabulations after orbitofrontal damage: the role of temporal context confusion and self-monitoring. Neurocase 5:243–250, 1999

Raine A, Brennan P, Mednick SA: Birth complications combined with early maternal rejection at age 1 year predispose to violent crime at age 18 years. Arch Gen Psychiatry 51:984–988, 1994

Rao R, Jackson S, Howard R: Primitive reflexes in cerebrovascular disease: a community study of older people with stroke and carotid stenosis. Int J Geriatr Psychiatry 14: 964–972, 1999

Rasmussen P: Persistent mirror movements: a clinical study of 17 children, adolescents and young adults. Dev Med Child Neurol 35:699–707, 1993

Reinhold M: Human behaviour reactions to organic cerebral disease. Journal of Mental Science 99:130–135, 1953

Remillard GM, Andermann F, Rhi-Sausi A, et al: Facial asymmetry in patients with temporal lobe epilepsy: a clinical sign useful in the lateralization of temporal epileptogenic foci. Neurology 27:109–114, 1977

Reznick JS, Gibbons JL, Johnson MO, et al: Behavioral inhibition in a normative sample, in Perspectives on Behavioral Inhibition. Edited by Reznick JS. Chicago, IL, University of Chicago Press, 1989, pp 25–49

Rich MW, Radwany SM: Respiratory dyskinesia: an underrecognized phenomenon. Chest 105:1826–1832, 1994

Ridley RM: The psychology of perseverative and stereotyped behaviour. Prog Neurobiol 44:221–231, 1994

Ridley RM, Baker HF: Stereotypy in monkeys and humans. Psychol Med 12:61–72, 1982

Rio J, Montalbán J, Pujadas F, et al: Asterixis associated with anatomic cerebral lesions: a study of 45 cases. Acta Neurol Scand 91:377–381, 1995

Rizzo M: "Balint's syndrome" and associated visuospatial disorders. Baillière's Clinical Neurology 2:415–437, 1993

Rizzo M: Clinical assessment of complex visual dysfunction. Semin Neurol 20:75–87, 2000

Roberts RJ, Varney NR, Hulbert JR, et al: The neuropathology of everyday life: the frequency of partial seizure symptoms among normals. Neuropsychology 4:65–85, 1990

Robinson RG, Parikh RM, Lipsey JR, et al: Pathological laughing and crying following stroke: validation of a measurement scale and a double-blind treatment study. Am J Psychiatry 150:286–293, 1993

Rogers D: The motor disorders of severe psychiatric illness: a conflict of paradigms. Br J Psychiatry 147:221–232, 1985

Rogers D: Catatonia: a contemporary approach. J Neuropsychiatry Clin Neurosci 3:334–340, 1991

Rogers D: Motor Disorder in Psychiatry: Toward a Neurological Psychiatry. Chichester, UK, Wiley, 1992

Rogers D, Lees AJ, Smith E, et al: Bradyphrenia in Parkinson's disease and psychomotor retardation in depressive illness. Brain 110:761–776, 1987

Rohr-Le Floch J, Gauthier G, Beaumanoir A: États confusionnels d'origine épileptique: intérêt de l'EEG fait en urgence. Rev Neurol (Paris) 144:425–436, 1988

Rolak LA: Psychogenic sensory loss. J Nerv Ment Dis 176:686–687, 1988

Ron MA, Logsdail SJ: Psychiatric morbidity in multiple sclerosis: a clinical and MRI study. Psychol Med 19:887–895, 1989

Rondot P: Visuomotor ataxia, in Neuropsychology of Visual Perception. Edited by Brown JW. Hillside, NJ, Erlbaum, 1989, pp 105–119

Ropper AH: Self-grasping: a focal neurological sign. Ann Neurol 12:575–577, 1982

Rosenberg A, Kagan J: Iris pigmentation and behavioral inhibition. Dev Psychobiol 20:377–392, 1987

Rosenberg AA, Kagan J: Physical and physiological correlates of behavioral inhibition. Dev Psychobiol 22:753–770, 1989

Ross ED: The aprosodias: functional-anatomic organization of the affective components of language in the right hemisphere. Arch Neurol 38:561–569, 1981

Ross ED: Nonverbal aspects of language. Neurol Clin 11:9–23, 1993

Ross ED, Mesulam M-M: Dominant language functions of the right hemisphere? Arch Neurol 36:144–148, 1979

Ross ED, Stewart RS: Pathological display of affect in patients with depression and right frontal brain damage: an alternative mechanism. J Nerv Ment Dis 175:165–172, 1987

Ross Russell RW: Supranuclear palsy of eyelid closure. Brain 103:71–82, 1980

Rosso IM, Bearden CE, Hollister JM, et al: Childhood neuromotor dysfunction in schizophrenia patients and their unaffected siblings: a prospective cohort study. Schizophr Bull 26:367–378, 2000a

Rosso IM, Cannon TD, Huttunen T, et al: Obstetric risk factors for early onset schizophrenia in a Finnish birth cohort. Am J Psychiatry 157:801–807, 2000b

Royall DR, Mahurin RK, Gray KF: Bedside assessment of executive cognitive impairment: the executive interview. J Am Geriatr Soc 40:1221–1226, 1992

Royall DR, Mahurin RK, True JE, et al: Executive impairment among the functionally dependent: comparisons between schizophrenic and elderly subjects. Am J Psychiatry 150:1813–1819, 1993

Royall DR, Cordes JA, Polk MJ: CLOX: an executive clock drawing test. J Neurol Neurosurg Psychiatry 64:588–594, 1998

Royall DR, Mulroy AR, Chiodo LK, et al: Clock drawing is sensitive to executive control: a comparison of six methods. J Gerontol 54B:P328–P333, 1999

Royall DR, Chiodo LK, Polk MJ: Correlates of disability among elderly retirees with "subclinical" cognitive impairment. J Gerontol 55A:M541–M546, 2000

Rubin KH, Both L: Iris pigmentation and sociability in childhood: a re-examination. Dev Psychobiol 22:717–725, 1989

Ryan R, Sunada K: Medical evaluation of persons with mental retardation referred for psychiatric assessment. Gen Hosp Psychiatry 19:274–280, 1997

Rylander G: Psychoses and the punding and choreiform syndromes in addiction to central stimulant drugs. Psychiatria, Neurologia, Neurochirurgia 75:203–212, 1972

Sachdev P: Clinical characteristics of 15 patients with tardive dystonia. Am J Psychiatry 150:498–500, 1993

Sachdev P: Akathisia and Restless Legs. Cambridge, UK, Cambridge University Press, 1995

Sachdev P, Kruk J: Clinical characteristics and predisposing factors in acute drug-induced akathisia. Arch Gen Psychiatry 51:963–974, 1994

Sackeim HA, Greenberg MS, Weiman AL, et al: Hemispheric asymmetry in the expression of positive and negative emotions. Arch Neurol 39:210–218, 1982

Sacks O: Migraine: Evolution of a Common Disorder. London, Faber & Faber, 1971

Samie MR, Selhorst JB, Koller WC: Post-traumatic midbrain tremor. Neurology 40:62–66, 1990

Sanders RD, Keshavan MS: The neurologic examination in adult psychiatry: from soft signs to hard science. J Neuropsychiatry Clin Neurosci 10:395–404, 1998

Sanders RD, Forman SD, Pierri JN, et al: Inter-rater reliability of the neurological examination in schizophrenia. Schizophr Res 29(3):287–292, 1998

Sandson J, Albert ML: Perseveration in behavioral neurology. Neurology 37:1736–1741, 1987

Santhouse AM, Howard RJ, ffytche DH: Visual hallucinatory syndromes and the anatomy of the visual brain. Brain 123:2055–2064, 2000

Saver J, Greenstein P, Ronthal M, et al: Asymmetric catalepsy after right hemisphere stroke. Mov Disord 8:69–73, 1993

Savic I, Bookheimer SY, Fried I, et al: Olfactory bedside test: a simple approach to identify temporo-orbitofrontal dysfunction. Arch Neurol 54:162–168, 1997

Sawle G: Movement disorders during sleep, in Movement Disorders in Clinical Practice. Edited by Sawle G. Oxford, UK, Isis Medical Media, 1999, pp 159–163

Schachar R: Childhood hyperactivity. J Child Psychol Psychiatry 32:155–191, 1991

Schaumann BA, Annegers JF, Johnson B, et al: Family history of seizures in posttraumatic and alcohol-associated seizure disorders. Epilepsia 35:48–52, 1994

Schiff HB, Alexander MP, Naeser MA, et al: Aphemia: clinical-anatomic correlations. Arch Neurol 40:720–727, 1983

Schnider A: Spontaneous confabulations, disorientation, and the processing of "now." Neuropsychologia 38:175–185, 2000

Schnider A, Ptak R: Spontaneous confabulators fail to suppress currently irrelevant memory traces. Nat Neurosci 2:677–681, 1999

Schnider A, von Däniken C, Gutbrod K: Disorientation in amnesia: a confusion of memory traces. Brain 119:1627–1632, 1996

Schott GD, Wyke MA: Congenital mirror movements. J Neurol Neurosurg Psychiatry 44:586–599, 1981

Sellal F, Fontaine SF, Van Der Linden M, et al: To be or not to be at home? A neuropsychological approach to delusion for place. J Clin Exp Neuropsychol 18:234–248, 1996

Sewell DD, Jeste DV: Metoclopramide-associated tardive dyskinesia: an analysis of 67 cases. Arch Fam Med 1:271–278, 1992

Shallice T, Burgess PW: Deficits in strategy application following frontal lobe damage in man. Brain 114:727–741, 1991

Shallice T, Evans ME: The involvement of the frontal lobes in cognitive estimation. Cortex 4:294–303, 1978

Shallice T, Burgess PW, Schon F, et al: The origins of utilization behavior. Brain 112:1587–1598, 1989

Shaunak S, O'Sullivan E, Kennard C: Eye movements. J Neurol Neurosurg Psychiatry 59:115–125, 1995

Sigal M, Altmark D, Alfici S, et al: Ganser syndrome: a review of 15 cases. Compr Psychiatry 33:124–138, 1992

Signer SF: Localization and lateralization in the delusion of substitution: Capgras symptom and its variants. Psychopathology 27:168–176, 1994

Silberman EK, Post RM, Nurnberger J, et al: Transient sensory, cognitive and affective phenomena in affective illness: a comparison with complex partial epilepsy. Br J Psychiatry 146:81–89, 1985

Silberman EK, Sussman N, Skillings G, et al: Aura phenomena and psychopathology: a pilot investigation. Epilepsia 35:778–784, 1994

Sjögren M, Wallin A, Edman A: Symptomatological characteristics distinguish between frontotemporal dementia and vascular dementia with a dominant frontal lobe syndrome. Int J Geriatr Psychiatry 12:656–661, 1997

Skolasky RI, Esposito DR, Selncs OA, et al: Modified HIV Dementia Scale: accurate staging of HIV-associated dementia. J Neurovirol 4:366, 1998

Smith G, Vigen V, Evans J, et al: Patterns and associates of hyperphagia in patients with dementia. Neuropsychiatry Neuropsychol Behav Neurol 11:97–102, 1998

Smith ML, Milner B: Differential effects of frontal-lobe lesions on cognitive estimation and spatial memory. Neuropsychologia 22:697–705, 1984

Smith RC, Kadewari RP, Rosenberger JR, et al: Nonresponding schizophrenia: differentiation by neurological soft signs and neuropsychological tests. Schizophr Bull 25:813–825, 1999

Snowden JS, Neary D: Progressive language dysfunction and lobar atrophy. Dementia 4:226–231, 1993

Snowden JS, Neary D, Mann DM, et al: Progressive language disorder due to lobar atrophy. Ann Neurol 31:174–183, 1992

Solms M: The Neuropsychology of Dreams: A Clinico-Anatomical Study. Mahwah, NJ, Erlbaum, 1997

Spitzer M: A cognitive neuroscience view of schizophrenic thought disorder. Schizophr Bull 23:29–50, 1997

Stacy M, Jankovic J: Tardive tremor. Mov Disord 7:53–57, 1992

Stacy M, Cardoso F, Jankovic J: Tardive stereotypy and other movement disorders in tardive dyskinesias. Neurology 43:937–941, 1993

Starkstein SE, Federoff JP, Price TR, et al: Anosognosia in patients with cerebrovascular lesions: a study of causative factors. Stroke 23:1446–1453, 1992

Statish U, Streufert S, Eslinger PJ: Complex decision making after orbitofrontal damage: neuropsychological and strategic management simulation assessment. Neurocase 5:355–364, 1999

Steg JP, Rapoport JL: Minor physical anomalies in normal, neurotic, learning disabled, and severely disturbed children. Journal of Autism and Childhood Schizophrenia 5:299–307, 1975

Stein DJ, Niehaus DJH, Seedat S, et al: Phenomenology of stereotypic movement disorder. Psychiatric Annals 28: 297–312, 1998

Stengel E: A clinical and psychological study of echo-reactions. Journal of Mental Science 93:27–41, 1947

Stevens JR: Disturbances of ocular movements and blinking in schizophrenia. J Neurol Neurosurg Psychiatry 41:1024–1030, 1978a

Stevens JR: Eye blink and schizophrenia: psychosis or tardive dyskinesia. Am J Psychiatry 135:223–226, 1978b

Stewart JT: Akathisia following traumatic brain injury: treatment with bromocriptine. J Neurol Neurosurg Psychiatry 52:1200–1201, 1991

Stracciari A, Guarino M, Cirignotta F, et al: Development of palilalia after stereotaxic thalamotomy in Parkinson's disease. Eur Neurol 33:275–276, 1993

Strub RL, Black FW: The bedside mental status examination, in Handbook of Neuropsychology, Vol I. Edited by Boller F, Grafman J. Amsterdam, Elsevier, 1988, pp 29–46

Stuppaeck CH, Miller CH, Ehrmann H, et al: Akathisia induced by necrosis of the basal ganglia after carbon monoxide intoxication. Mov Disord 10:229–231, 1995

Sultzer DL, Berisford MA, Gunay I: The neurobehavioral rating scale: reliability in patients with dementia. J Psychiatr Res 29:185–191, 1995

Syz H: Recovery from loss of mnemic retention after head trauma. J Gen Psychol 17:355–387, 1937

Tanaka Y, Albert ML, Hara H, et al: Forced hyperphasia and environmental dependency syndrome. J Neurol Neurosurg Psychiatry 68:224–226, 2000

Tarrant CJ, Jones PB: Precursors to schizophrenia: do biological markers have specificity? Can J Psychiatry 44:335–349, 1999

Tatu L, Moulin T, Monnier G, et al: Unilateral pure thalamic asterixis: clinical, electromyographic, and topographic patterns. Neurology 54:2339–2342, 2000

Taylor DC, Lochery M: Temporal lobe epilepsy: origin and significance of simple and complex auras. J Neurol Neurosurg Psychiatry 50:673–681, 1987

Tecoma ES, Laxer KD, Barbaro NM, et al: Frequency and characteristics of visual field deficits after surgery for mesial temporal sclerosis. Neurology 43:1235–1238, 1993

Tegnér R, Levander M: Through a looking glass: a new technique to demonstrate directional hypokinesia in unilateral neglect. Brain 114:1943–1951, 1991

Teicher MH, Glod CA, Surrey J, et al: Early childhood abuse and limbic system ratings in adult psychiatric outpatients. J Neuropsychiatry Clin Neurosci 5:301–306, 1993

Teng EL, Chui HC: The Modified Mini-Mental State (3MS) Examination. J Clin Psychiatry 48:314–318, 1987

Thacker RC, De Nil LF: Neurogenic cluttering. Journal of Fluency Disorders 21:227–238, 1996

Thomas P, Beaumanoir A, Genton P, et al: "De novo" absence status of late onset: report of 11 cases. Neurology 42:104–110, 1992

Thompson PD, Marsden CD: Gait disorder of subcortical arteriosclerotic encephalopathy: Binswanger's disease. Mov Disord 2:1–8, 1987

Thompson PD, Marsden CD: Corticobasal degeneration. Baillière's Clinical Neurology 1:677–686, 1992

Tinuper P, Plazzi G, Provini F, et al: Facial asymmetry in partial epilepsies. Epilepsia 33:1097–1100, 1992

Tirosh E, Canby J: Autism with hyperlexia: a distinct syndrome? Am J Ment Retard 98:84–92, 1993

Tomson T, Lindbom U, Nilsson BY: Nonconvulsive status epilepticus in adults: thirty-two consecutive patients from a general hospital population. Epilepsia 33:829–835, 1992

Toone BK, Edeh J, Nanjee MN, et al: Hyposexuality and epilepsy: a community survey of hormonal and behavioural changes in male epileptics. Psychol Med 19:937–943, 1989

Touwen BCL, Prechtl HFR: The Neurological Examination of the Child With Minor Nervous Dysfunction. London, Heinemann Medical Books, 1970

Tranel D, Anderson SW, Benton A: Development of the concept of "executive function" and its relationship to the frontal lobes, in Handbook of Neuropsychology, Vol 9. Edited by Boller F, Grafman J. Amsterdam, Elsevier, 1994, pp 125–148

Trosch RM, Sze G, Brass LM, et al: Emotional facial paresis with striatocapsular infarction. J Neurol Sci 98:195–201, 1990

Tucker DM, Watson RT, Heilman KM: Discrimination and evocation of affectively intoned speech in patients with right parietal disease. Neurology 27:947–950, 1977

Turner TH: A diagnostic analysis of the Casebooks of Ticehurst House Asylum, 1845–1890. Psychological Medicine Monograph Supplement 21:1–70, 1992

van Gorp WG, Marcotte TD, Sultzer DL, et al: Screening for dementia: comparison of three commonly used instruments. J Clin Exp Neuropsychol 21:29–38, 1999

Victor M, Adams RD, Collins GH: The Wernicke-Korsakoff Syndrome and Related Neurological Diseases Due to Alcoholism and Malnutrition, 2nd Edition. Philadelphia, PA, FA Davis, 1989

Vighetto A, Henry E, Garde P, et al: Le délire spatial: une manifestation des lésions de l'hémisphère mineur. Rev Neurol (Paris) 141:476–481, 1985

Voeller KKS, Heilman KM: Attention deficit disorder in children: a neglect syndrome? Neurology 38:806–808, 1988

Vreeling FW, Houx PJ, Jolles J, et al: Primitive reflexes in Alzheimer's disease and vascular dementia. J Geriatr Psychiatry Neurol 8:111–117, 1995

Waddington JL, O'Callaghan E, Buckley P, et al: Tardive dyskinesia in schizophrenia: relationship to minor physical anomalies, frontal lobe dysfunction and cerebral structure on magnetic resonance imaging. Br J Psychiatry 167:41–45, 1995

Wade DT: Measurement in Neurological Rehabilitation. Oxford, UK, Oxford University Press, 1992

Walczak TS, Bogolioubov A: Weeping during psychogenic nonepileptic seizures. Epilepsia 37:208–210, 1996

Wali GM: "Fou rire prodromique" heralding a brainstem stroke. J Neurol Neurosurg Psychiatry 56:209–210, 1993

Wallesch C-W, Hundsalz A: Language function in delirium: a comparison of single word processing in acute confusional states and probable Alzheimer's disease. Brain Lang 46:592–606, 1994

Walshe JM: Wilson's disease, in Handbook of Clinical Neurology, Vol 49: Extrapyramidal Disorders. Edited by Vinken PJ, Bruyn GW, Klawans HL. Amsterdam, Elsevier Science, 1986, pp 223–238

Wapner W, Hamby S, Gardner H: The role of the right hemisphere in the apprehension of complex linguistic materials. Brain Lang 14:15–33, 1981

Ward CD: Neuropsychiatry and the modularity of mind. J Neuropsychiatry Clin Neurosci 2:443–449, 1990

Weinstein DD, Diforio D, Schiffman J, et al: Minor physical anomalies, dermatoglyphic asymmetries, and cortisol levels in adolescents with schizotypal personality disorder. Am J Psychiatry 156:617–623, 1999

Weintraub S: Neuropsychological assessment of mental state, in Principles of Cognitive and Behavioral Neurology, 2nd Edition. Edited by Mesulam M-M. Oxford, UK, Oxford University Press, 2000, pp 121–173

Weintraub S, Mesulam M-M: Mental state assessment of young and elderly adults in behavioral neurology, in Principles of Behavioral Neurology. Edited by Mesulam M-M. Philadelphia, PA, FA Davis, 1985, pp 71–123

Weiss AP, Jenike MA: Late-onset obsessive-compulsive disorder: a case series. J Neuropsychiatry Clin Neurosci 12:265–268, 2000

Weller M: Anterior opercular cortex lesions cause dissociated lower cranial nerve palsies and anarthria but no aphasia: Foix-Chavany-Marie syndrome and "automatic voluntary dissociation" revisited. J Neurol 240:199–208, 1993

Wertz RT, Henschel CR, Auther LL, et al: Affective prosodic disturbance subsequent to right hemisphere stroke: a clinical application. Journal of Neurolinguistics 11:89–102, 1998

Williams D: The structure of emotions reflected in epileptic experiences. Brain 79:29–67, 1956

Wilson SAK: Some problems in neurology: no. 11: pathological laughing and crying. Journal of Neurology and Psychopathology 4:299–333, 1924

Wojcik JD, Falk WE, Fink JS, et al: A review of 32 cases of tardive dystonia. Am J Psychiatry 148:1055–1059, 1991

Wolff A-L, O'Driscoll GA: Motor deficits and schizophrenia: the evidence from neuroleptic-naïve patients and populations at risk. J Psychiatry Neurosci 24:304–314, 1999

Wong AHC, Voruganti LNP, Heslegrave RJ, et al: Neurocognitive deficits and neurological signs in schizophrenia. Schizophr Res 23:139–146, 1997

Yasuda Y, Akiguchi I, Ino M, et al: Paramedian thalamic and midbrain infarcts associated with palilalia. J Neurol Neurosurg Psychiatry 53:797–799, 1990

Young RR, Shahani BT: Asterixis: one type of negative myoclonus. Adv Neurol 43:137–156, 1986

Youssef HA, Waddington JL: Primitive (developmental) reflexes and diffuse cerebral dysfunction in schizophrenia and bipolar affective disorder: overrepresentation in patients with tardive dyskinesia. Biol Psychiatry 23:791–796, 1988

Yuspeh RL, Vanderploeg RD, Kershaw DA: Validity of a semantically cued recall procedure for the Mini-Mental State Examination. Neuropsychiatry Neuropsychol Behav Neurol 11:207–211, 1998

Zametkin AJ, Stevens JR, Pittman R: Ontogeny of spontaneous blinking and of habituation of the blink reflex. Ann Neurol 5:453–457, 1979

Zulch KJ, Muller N: Associated movements in man, in Handbook of Clinical Neurology, Vol 1. Edited by Vinken PJ, Bruyn GW. Amsterdam, North-Holland, 1969, pp 404–426

# CHAPTER 6

# Electrodiagnostic Techniques in Neuropsychiatry

Thomas C. Neylan, M.D.

Charles F. Reynolds III, M.D.

David J. Kupfer, M.D.

Electrophysiologic techniques are powerful tools for measuring brain dysfunction that cannot be detected by anatomic brain imaging. They complement positron emission tomography and functional and anatomic magnetic resonance imaging techniques by providing a noninvasive measure of physiology with exquisite temporal resolution. The main clinical use of electrophysiologic tests is to rule out epilepsy and gross brain pathology. However, advances in computer analysis have led to an expanded clinical role of electrophysiologic tests in the diagnosis and management of patients. Electrophysiology continues to be a powerful research tool in the exploration of the biological substrate for neuropsychiatric disorders. This chapter provides a broad overview of the clinical and research uses of electrophysiologic tests.

## Electroencephalography

### History With Respect to Neuropsychiatry

Electrical brain signals were first discovered in 1875 in England by Richard Caton, who demonstrated that oscil-

lating electrical potentials could be detected by electrodes placed on the cerebral cortex of animal brains (Brazier 1986). Caton demonstrated that the cerebral cortex has a baseline or tonic level of electrical activity. He also showed that phasic electrical activity could be evoked in response to sensory stimulation (Caton 1875). In 1912 in Russia, Kaufman discovered abnormal electroencephalographic discharges in experimentally induced epilepsy in animals (Kaufman 1912). Years later, the use of the electroencephalogram in humans was pioneered in Germany by Hans Berger (1929). In his original report, Berger described the posterior alpha rhythm and its disappearance with eye opening. Soon thereafter, spike and wave discharges were described in epileptic patients, heralding the rapid growth of the field of epileptology (Gibbs et al. 1935) and the wide use of electroencephalography (EEG) in clinical practice (Table 6–1).

### Theoretical Overview of Electroencephalographic Activity

The electrical signal detected by the electroencephalograph is the final summation of a multitude of potentials generated by the cerebral cortex. The structural organi-

Supported in part from the following grants: MH57157 (T.C.N.), MH37869 (C.F.R.), MH52247 (C.F.R.), and MH24652 (D.J.K.).

**TABLE 6–1.**  History of electroencephalography in neuropsychiatry

| | |
|---|---|
| 1791 | Galvani experiments with frog nerve preparations and speculates that nervous tissue has intrinsic electrical activity. |
| 1848 | Du Bois-Reymond discovers the action potential of nerve tissue. |
| 1875 | Caton demonstrates the presence of electrical brain signals in animals. He shows that the brain is electrically active at rest and that sensory stimulation evokes cortical potential changes. |
| 1912 | Kaufman reports abnormal electroencephalographic discharges in experimentally induced epilepsy in animals. |
| 1929 | Berger presents the first human electroencephalographic study. |
| 1935 | Biggs and colleagues describe the spike and wave discharge in human epilepsy. |

*Source.*  Adapted from Brazier 1986.

zation of the cerebral cortex can be conceptualized as a mosaic of vertical columns with apical dendrites oriented toward the surface and axons projecting to deeper structures (Fenton 1989). Thus, the signal detected by the scalp electrode is predominated by the excitatory and inhibitory postsynaptic potentials on dendrites and neuronal cell bodies, and not the deeper axon action potentials (Goff et al. 1978; Goldensohn 1979). The superficial cortical layers are influenced by projections from the thalamus, which in turn receive input from the reticular activating system. Thus, the cortical electroencephalographic signal is regulated by brainstem structures controlling arousal and sleep. For example, during waking, the brisk tonic activity of the reticular activating system leads to the desynchronization of the cortical electroencephalographic signal. At sleep onset, the thalamocortical rhythms are unmasked and synchronized, leading to a slower, higher-amplitude signal (Andersen and Andersson 1968; Fenton 1989).

Although brain potentials may range in frequency from 0.1 to 1,000 Hz (Niedermeyer 1990; Rodin et al. 1971), the scalp electroencephalographic signal has an upper frequency range of approximately 70 Hz. This range is subdivided into frequency bands defined as beta (>14 Hz), alpha (8–14 Hz), theta (4–8 Hz), and delta (≤4.0 Hz). When the brain is at rest, large areas of cortex may fire in relative synchrony. Therefore, lower frequencies, such as the alpha rhythm, are better detected than higher frequencies, which are highly asynchronous and are attenuated by transmission through the skull and scalp (Cooper et al. 1965) (Figure 6–1).

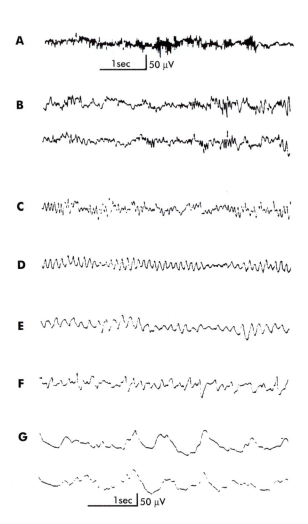

**FIGURE 6–1.**  The electroencephalographic frequencies. *Panel A.* Fast activity, around 30–35 per second: fast beta range. *Panel B.* Mixed activity with beta waves in the 20–25 per second range. *Panel C.* Mixed activity with beta waves in the 14–18 per second range. *Panel D.* Alpha rhythm, 9 per second. *Panel E.* Theta rhythm, 5–6 per second. *Panel F.* Mixed delta and theta activity, mainly in the 2.5–5 per second range. *Panel G.* Predominant delta activity, mostly in the 1–1.5 per second range.
*Source.*  Reprinted with permission from Niedermeyer E: "Introduction to Electroencephalography," in *The Epilepsies: Diagnosis and Management.* Baltimore, MD, Urban & Schwarzenberg, 1990, pp. 35–49.

## Clinical Electroencephalography

Routine EEG is performed when the subject is awake and at rest. Activation procedures such as hyperventilation and photic stimulation may be used to elicit abnormal activity. Sleep deprivation can increase the sensitivity for detecting epileptiform activity. The electrode placement generally follows the standard 10–20 montage (Jasper 1958) (Figure 6–2). Special electrodes such as nasopha-

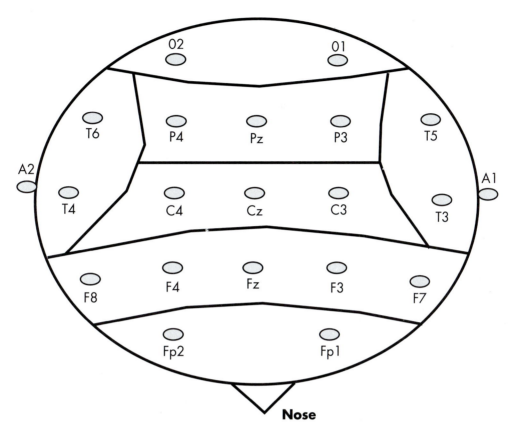

**FIGURE 6–2.** Standard 10–20 clinical electroencephalogram montage.

ryngeal or ethmoid electrodes may be used to increase sensitivity or further enhance localization of abnormal discharges.

The most prevalent method of analysis of the electroencephalogram in the clinical setting remains visual analysis by the electroencephalographer. The record is first examined for focal abnormalities, slowing of normal rhythms, epileptiform activity, paroxysmal activity, asymmetries, and artifact. (The human visual association cortex remains far superior to any computer method of detection of epileptiform or paroxysmal activity.) After the visual examination, the background activity is quantified with respect to frequency and amplitude. It is perhaps this aspect of electroencephalographic analysis that holds the most promise in electrophysiologic research in neuropsychiatry. Because there are no specific waveforms seen in neuropsychiatric disorders, electrophysiologic differentiation of patients from control subjects may be obtainable only by demonstrating a quantitative difference between the two groups (Pfefferbaum et al. 1995; Shagass 1977).

The electroencephalogram is a nonspecific indicator of cerebral function. Any pathophysiological insult to the central nervous system can result in alterations in electro-

physiology. For example, a large variety of pharmacologic, metabolic, or neurodegenerative processes can result in diffuse slowing of electroencephalographic rhythms. Thus, with few exceptions (Table 6–2), EEG does little to provide a precise diagnosis. Electroencephalographic abnormalities are most pronounced with acute injuries of the outer cortex. Disorders that affect deep brain structures or result in a chronic indolent loss of neurons may show little to no electroencephalographic changes (Fenton 1989).

## Evoked Potentials

The earliest studies of electroencephalograms demonstrated that sensory stimuli provoked a measurable electrophysiologic response (Caton 1875). Event-related potentials (ERPs) are measured by signal averaging techniques, in which the potentials elicited from repeated stimulation are superimposed by computer analysis. This enhances the stimulus-specific response, or evoked potential, and causes the background activity to average to zero (Knight 1985). The development of these techniques quickly led to the characterization of the soma-

**TABLE 6–2.** Electroencephalographic findings in a sample of neuropsychiatric disorders

| Disorder | Electroencephalographic findings |
|---|---|
| Epilepsy | Focal and generalized spikes, sharp waves, polyspikes, and spike-wave complexes |
| Delirium | Generalized slowing and irregular high-voltage delta activity |
| Encephalitis | Background slowing, diffuse epileptiform activity, and periodic lateralized epileptiform discharges (PLEDs) |
| Barbiturate or benzodiazepine intoxication | Background slowing and diffuse superimposed beta activity |
| Tumor or infarction | Focal slowing at border of infarction or tumor; necrotic tissue is electrically silent |
| Aging | Generalized slowing of alpha rhythm, diffuse theta and delta activity, decline of low-voltage beta activity, and focal delta activity in temporal areas |
| Dementia | Accelerated development of electroencephalographic changes of normal aging, paroxysmal bifrontal delta activity, and asymmetry between hemispheres |
| Creutzfeldt-Jakob disease and subacute sclerosing panencephalitis | Periodic complexes |
| Uremic or hepatic encephalopathy | Triphasic waves |

*Source.* Adapted from Fenton 1989.

tosensory, visual, and brainstem auditory evoked potentials. These potentials have well-defined positive and negative peaks and occur within the first 50 msec after the stimulus. They represent the electrical activity of the primary neural pathway from sensory receptor to the cortex. The primary sensory evoked potentials are useful for determining if the sensory pathways are intact. Structural damage, as may result from multiple sclerosis (R.A. Levine et al. 1994), or functional impairment, as may result from delirium (Trzepacz et al. 1989), will result in abnormal primary sensory evoked potentials.

The middle (50–250 msec) and late (250–500 msec) potentials are of particular interest in neuropsychiatry because they represent higher cognitive processes and hence are sensitive to psychological factors such as attention and vigilance. Cognitions take place in milliseconds

and are often manifested electrophysiologically in high-frequency cortical activity (Knight 1985). ERPs index the electrical activity of the neural pathways involved in attention and cognition (Pfefferbaum et al. 1995) and therefore have advantages in the study of information processing. Several are named in reference to the experimental condition that elicits the response, such as the contingent negative variation and selective attention effect, whereas others are named for electrophysiologic characteristics, such as the P300 (positive wave, 300 msec).

## P50

The P50 wave of the auditory evoked response is particularly useful in studying the phenomenon of sensory gating because it involves a hardwired process that does not vary with voluntary attention or levels of wakeful alertness (Cardenas et al. 1997; Jerger et al. 1992). Healthy subjects presented with two closely paired clicks will have a reduction in amplitude of the P50 wave to the second click. The reduced amplitude is thought to result from inhibitory interneurons involved in habituation and sensory gating (Freedman et al. 1996). P50 is usually studied in a conditioning/testing paradigm in which responses to pairs of stimuli are recorded, with long intervals between stimulus pairs (e.g., >7 sec) and shorter intervals within stimulus pairs (e.g., 0.5 sec). The conditioning/testing paradigm allows separate measurement of P50 generation and P50 gating, which have been shown to involve separable neural mechanisms.

Suppression of P50 has been extensively studied in schizophrenia. Freedman and others have used the conditioning/testing paradigm to demonstrate that schizophrenia is associated with impaired sensory gating (Freedman et al. 1996). Some evidence suggests that nicotinic receptor desensitization may cause the sensory gating deficits found in schizophrenia (Griffith et al. 1998). Of interest are studies that show that transient increases in noradrenergic activity are associated with reduced P50 suppression (Waldo et al. 1992). Cold stress, which increases sympathetic arousal, is associated with reduced P50 suppression (M.R. Johnson and Adler 1993). This raises the possibility that elevated noradrenergic tone, which is a well-established finding in schizophrenia (Neylan et al. 1992; van Kammen et al. 1990), may explain some of the variability in P50 suppression. Recent data have found that posttraumatic stress disorder (PTSD), which is also associated with elevated noradrenergic tone (Southwick et al. 1993), is associated with reduced P50 suppression (Neylan et al. 1999) (Figure 6–3).

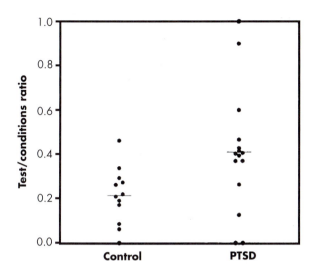

**FIGURE 6–3.** Singular value decomposition analysis of P50 showed a significantly increased T/C ratio in posttraumatic stress disorder subjects (mean=0.407, standard deviation=0.275) compared with control subjects (mean=0.213; standard deviation=0.126; two-tailed *t*, *P*=0.0239). Horizontal bars=mean.

## P300

The P300 potential has received a great deal of attention in psychiatric electrophysiology. It is elicited when a subject is presented a rare target stimulus interspersed with frequent nontarget stimuli. P300 is typically measured in a three-stimulus "oddball" task in which subjects are instructed to respond to an infrequent target auditory or visual stimulus that is presented interspersed with frequent nontarget stimuli and infrequent nontarget distractors (Donchin and Coles 1988). The evidence to date suggest that P300 has several subcomponents generated by multiple neural sources (R. Johnson 1993; Polich and Kok 1995). For example, the P3a is seen when a novel unexpected stimulus is presented. It is thought to be an orienting response that is mediated by frontal structures (Courchesne et al. 1975; Ritter et al. 1968; Snyder and Hillyard 1976; Squires et al. 1975). The P3a is decreased in subjects with lesions in the prefrontal cortex (Knight 1984), subjects with human immunodeficiency virus (HIV) disease with cognitive impairment (Fein et al. 1995b), and subjects with chronic drug (C. Biggins et al., unpublished observations, 2001) or alcohol abuse (Fein et al. 1995a). The P3b is seen with attended target stimuli and is mediated by central and parietal structures (Knight et al. 1989). Most studies have reported changes in latency and amplitude associated with different patient groups. P3 latency and amplitude conceptually represent the speed and magnitude of information pro-

cessing handled by the brain in response to a stimulus.

Multiple studies have found that schizophrenic patients have abnormal P300 potentials. The most consistent finding is a reduction in amplitude (Javitt et al. 1995; Levit 1973; Roth et al. 1980) (Figure 6–4). P300 abnormalities are evident in both medicated and drug-free patients and are associated with negative symptoms (Hirayasu et al. 1998; Pfefferbaum et al. 1989). Of interest, Kutcher et al. (1987) found that P300 abnormalities were prevalent in patients with borderline personality disorder and could distinguish this group of patients from those with other personality disorders; however, the P300 abnormalities were indistinguishable from those of schizophrenic patients. O'Donnell et al. (1995) reported that prolongation of P300 latency, which is normally associated with aging, is exaggerated in schizophrenic subjects. They suggest that this is electrophysiologic evidence that schizophrenia is a neurodegenerative disorder. Recently, Mathalon and colleagues reported that P300 latency is delayed as a function of duration of illness (Mathalon et al. 2000) (Figure 6–5). The P300 latency is a possible measure of cognitive processing speed (Polich 1996). Javitt et al. (1995) found a reduced amplitude of the mismatch negativity (MMN) component of the auditory ERP preceding the P300. Since the MMN is the earliest cortical response to stimulus novelty (Kazmerski et al. 1997) and requires frontal lobe involvement, abnormal information processing in schizophrenia may be related to impaired functioning of the frontal cortex.

These findings, which are not unique to schizophrenia, have been linked to deficits in cognition. For example, evoked potential studies of information processing using the P300 response have shown that schizophrenic patients have difficulties in screening out distracting stimuli (Grillon et al. 1990). This is strong support for the hypothesis that persons with schizophrenia have impaired sensorimotor gating or filtering of internal and external stimuli (Braff and Geyer 1990; McGhie and Chapman 1961). P300 abnormalities in schizophrenic patients have been found to be correlated with left sylvian fissure enlargement on computed tomographic scans as well as with positive symptoms (McCarley et al. 1989). Additional studies are needed to validate the correlational data so far obtained in addition to clarifying inconsistencies in the reported findings.

The relationship between PTSD and P300 has been studied in several reports. Studies have found P300 amplitude to be both increased and decreased in subjects with PTSD relative to control subjects without PTSD. The studies finding P300 amplitude decreases attributed their results to concentration and memory impairment (McFarlane et al. 1993) or attention deficits (Charles et

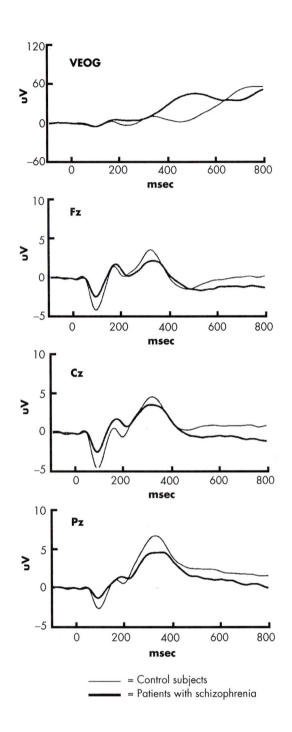

**FIGURE 6–4.** Grand averages of event-related potentials elicited by target tones from healthy control subjects (*n*=26) and patients with schizophrenia (*n*=35). Waveforms are shown for vertical electroencephalogram (VEOG) and Fz, Cz, and Pz standard EEG leads. VEOG activity was removed from the event-related potentials mathematically but is shown here for illustrative purposes. Positive voltages at the scalp are plotted up. The *x* axis reflects time in milliseconds, and the *y* axis reflects amplitude in microvolts.

al. 1995; Metzger et al. 1997). Those finding P300 amplitude increases suggest that their results are due to altered selective attention (Attias et al. 1996), heightened neurophysiological response (Kounios et al. 1997), or a heightened orienting response (Kimble et al. 2000). Except for Kimball et al. (2000), all of the studies that found a reduced P300 in PTSD utilized the auditory modality (Charles et al. 1995; McFarlane et al. 1993; Metzger et al. 1997), whereas those finding an increased P300 with PTSD were conducted in the visual modality (Attias et al. 1996; Kounios et al. 1997). This raises the question of whether information processing abnormalities, as indexed by the P300 component, are modality specific.

Middle and late evoked potentials may provide important insights to the physiology of attention, categorization, and filtering of sensory stimuli. However, unlike the earlier peaks, they are more prone to experimental artifact. Motivation, level of consciousness, medications, sensory acuity, and movement artifact all can confound the data (Rosse et al. 1989).

## Contingent Negative Variation

The contingent negative variation (CNV), often referred to as the readiness potential, is a negative potential that occurs after a warning stimulus alerts the subject that a second stimulus demanding a response is forthcoming (Verleger et al. 1999). It represents a preparation or priming of the cortex to facilitate an expected activity and reflects functioning of the prefrontal cortex (Klein et al. 2000). Subjects with a history of closed head injury and frontal lobe damage show an impaired readiness potential compared with age-matched control subjects (Rugg et al. 1989). Reduced CNV amplitude is correlated with negative symptoms in schizophrenic subjects (Oke et al. 1994).

## Magnetoencephalography

Magnetoencephalography (MEG) is the recording of the magnetic fields generated by intraneuronal electric current. The "right-hand rule" of electromagnetism is that magnetic fields occur at right angles to the direction of current flow (Zimmerman 1983). Thus the magnetoencephalographic signal, which is a billionfold weaker than the earth's magnetic field (Reeve et al. 1989), can be conceptualized as the magnetic counterpart to the electroencephalographic or evoked potential signal. MEG naturally complements EEG and has potential advantages in localization and a broader range in frequency resolution

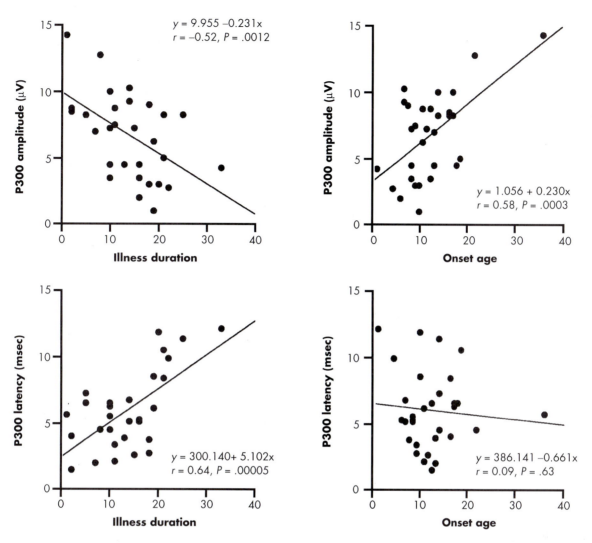

**FIGURE 6–5.** *Top panel.* Relationships between P300 amplitude at Pz and (left) illness duration in years and (right) age at onset of illness for patients with schizophrenia. *Bottom panel.* Same as upper panel but for P300 latency at Pz. Regression equations, Pearson correlation coefficients, and two-tailed significance levels are shown.

(Cuffin and Cohen 1979; Rose et al. 1987). Magnetic fields are not appreciably affected by the scalp and skull. For example, high frequencies are poorly resolved by scalp EEG electrodes (Pfurtscheller and Cooper 1975) but may be better detected with MEG. MEG is also more accurate in detecting deep-brain sources and can detect tangential current sources such as from neurons in the sulci, whose axial orientation is parallel to the scalp (Reite 1989). The recent availability of large-array super-conducting biomagnetometer systems has made MEG a feasible diagnostic test to perform (Gallen et al. 1995). Perhaps its greatest promise is to accurately detect the neuronal sources of known electroencephalographic and evoked potential signals (Reeve 1989; Reite et al. 1989) and to more precisely localize epileptic foci in the brain (Baumgartner et al. 2000). Magnetic source imaging,

which combines MEG with anatomic magnetic resonance imaging, has been used to produce neuromagnetic maps of somatosensory and auditory evoked potentials in healthy subjects (Gallen et al. 1993). Magnetic source imaging is also used to evaluate seizure foci in patients who are neurosurgical candidates (Aung et al. 1995). The principal disadvantage of MEG is that the magnetometer must contend with a low signal-to-noise ratio, necessitating the use of expensive shielding to eliminate ambient magnetic noise.

## Epilepsy and Epileptiform Activity

The most important use of EEG continues to be in the diagnosis of seizure disorders. No other brain abnormality has an electrophysiologic pattern as distinctive as epilepsy (Duffy 1988). Epilepsy is found in approximately 0.3%–0.6% of adults in the general population (Anderson et al. 1999). The presence of spikes (defined as a potential with a duration less than 70 msec), sharp waves (duration of 70–200 msec) and polyspikes, frequently followed by a slow wave, are often seen interictally in epileptic patients (Aminoff 1986; Goodin and Aminoff 1984). The study of the behavioral consequences of epilepsy has a rich history and is discussed in detail in Chapter 19 in this volume.

Epileptiform activity is found in 1%–10% of the nonepileptic general population (Zivin et al. 1968). Epileptiform electroencephalographic variants are seen in approximately 30% of patients with schizophrenia and psychotic mood disorders (Inui et al. 1998). Electroencephalographic spikes are occasionally seen in nonepileptic patients who are taking antidepressant or antipsychotic medications (Fenton 1989). For example, 13% of schizophrenic patients in one sample developed electroencephalographic spikes after initiating clozapine therapy (Freudenreich et al. 1997). More frequently, nonepileptic patients may have paroxysmal electroencephalographic activity during sedative-hypnotic withdrawal states.

## Age, Dementia, and Delirium

The background alpha rhythm changes very little with normal aging (Visser 1985) and is extremely useful in longitudinal studies. A drop of 1 Hz over a short period of time may indicate a significant encephalopathic process even though the alpha rhythm remains in the normal range (Pro and Wells 1977). Low-voltage beta activity increases in adults up to age 60 and declines thereafter. Mild diffuse slowing is found in approximately 20% of healthy elders over age 75. Focal delta activity, particularly in the anterior temporal areas, is seen in 30%–40% of the normal population over age 60 (Fenton 1989).

The electroencephalogram is useful in the study and diagnosis of cognitive disorders. For example, electroencephalographic slowing has been found to be correlated with the severity of dementia (Fenton 1986) and the number of senile plaques (Deisenhammer and Jellinger 1974) in Alzheimer's disease. Robinson et al. (1994) reported that 92% of subjects with Alzheimer's disease, confirmed prospectively by histopathology, had abnormal electroencephalograms, in contrast to 35% of age-matched control subjects. Similarly, the severity of delirium has been found to be correlated with electroenceph-

alographic abnormalities (Matsushima et al. 1997). The electroencephalogram is a valuable tool in hospital psychiatry in that it can help distinguish a mild delirium from major depression.

## Schizophrenia

Although there are no specific electroencephalographic findings in schizophrenia, most studies do show that these patients have more abnormalities than are found in healthy control subjects. Abnormal electroencephalograms have been described in up to 80% of schizophrenic patients. Studies that include adequate numbers of control subjects report a much lower rate (McKenna et al. 1985). Despite the large number of reported electroencephalographic abnormalities, middle-aged schizophrenic subjects do not appear to have more clinical seizures than age-matched control subjects (Gelisse et al. 1999). Several studies have documented electroencephalographic asymmetries, particularly in the left hemisphere (Abrams and Taylor 1979; Nasrallah 1986). The lack of a family history of schizophrenia is associated with an increased likelihood of abnormal electroencephalographic activity in schizophrenic patients (Kendler and Hays 1982). Although an abnormal electroencephalogram may be a predictor of resistance to neuroleptic medications (Itil 1982), the principal clinical utility of the electroencephalogram in schizophrenia is as a screening tool for gross neuropathology or seizure disorder.

## Screening Electroencephalograms

The routine use of screening EEG in psychiatric patients remains controversial. Data from the 1989 National Hospital Discharge Survey (Pokras 1990) showed that 2.8% of the 1.51 million patients discharged from general hospitals with a primary diagnosis of mental disorder undergo an electroencephalogram (Olfson 1992). In contrast, 18%–33% of patients with mental disorders treated at university hospitals undergo an electroencephalogram (Lam et al. 1988; van Sweden et al. 1986). Van Sweden et al. (1986) reported that 42.5% of patients with mental disorders referred for EEG have significant abnormalities. Unsuspected abnormal electroencephalograms have been found in approximately 20% of psychiatric patients (Struve 1976, 1984). However, an abnormal electroencephalogram may not redirect treatment choices or lead to an improvement in clinical outcome. A retrospective study of 698 psychiatric inpatients found that a screening of electroencephalogram altered the clinical diagnosis in only 1.7% of cases (Warner et al. 1990).

# Quantitative Electroencephalography

The electroencephalographer makes a visual inspection of the background electroencephalographic rhythm. However, it is impossible to appreciate or analyze, unaided, the time-dependent changes in frequency content, particularly when there are multiple leads. Techniques of quantitative EEG (QEEG) include power spectral analysis and period-amplitude analysis. Often, electroencephalographic parameters are assigned a visual analog, such as color, which allows for formation of a topographical maps. All quantitative electroencephalographic techniques effectively make the enormous amount of data that is contained in a typical electrophysiologic recording more accessible.

QEEG has been successfully used to detect age-related changes in electroencephalographic activity in normal and clinical populations (Bresnahan et al. 1999), brain ischemia during surgery (Edmonds et al. 1992), subtle cerebral anomalies in carbon monoxide poisoning (Denays et al. 1994), and cerebral manifestations of systemic lupus erythematosus (Ritchlin et al. 1992). Adams et al. (1995) conducted a controlled reliability study measuring quantitative electroencephalographic versus standard electroencephalographic measures of cerebral ischemia in surgical procedures. QEEG showed anomalies suggestive of ischemia during control procedures that were presumed to have little risk for ischemia. This study illustrates a pervasive problem in the clinical applicability of QEEG to neuropsychiatry; that is, issues of sensitivity, specificity, reliability, and validity have yet to be clearly established. In addition, the transformation of extremely complex data into a simple image can distort the underlying data and present features that appear grounded in fact (Brodie 1996).

Other forms of EEG-derived data can be condensed into a topographical map. For example, derivative statistics such as the coefficient of variation can be topographically mapped, giving the neurophysiologist an immediate visual impression of the variability of spectral content (Duffy 1986). Electrophysiologic data from multiple subjects can be summarized into a consolidated group map. Group maps of various patient groups and control subjects can be visually and statistically compared (Rosse et al. 1987). Finally, maps demonstrating the functional activation of electrical activity secondary to performing specific neuropsychological tasks can be compared to the resting state (Gruzelier and Liddiard 1989).

QEEG has been used in clinical research to determine whether patients with psychiatric disorders can be distinguished electrophysiologically from healthy control subjects. For example, several studies have shown that schizophrenic patients have more delta activity, particularly over the frontal cortex, compared with control subjects (Guenther et al. 1986; Morihisa et al. 1983; Morstyn et al. 1983). Subsequent studies that have controlled for eye movement artifact have replicated the finding of increased diffuse delta activity in schizophrenic patients but have failed to find a tendency for frontal localization (Karson et al. 1987). Preliminary findings in studies of dementia have shown significant differences in alpha power between presenile and senile-onset patients, whereas little difference is seen between healthy young and old subjects (Gueguen et al. 1989). Alpha and beta power during photic stimulation is significantly decreased in patients with presenile dementia compared with age-matched control subjects (Wada et al. 1997). Quantitative electroencephalographic studies have shown regional asymmetries in alpha power in depressed and anxious subjects (Bruder et al. 1997). Frontal asymmetry is associated with trait-like fearful temperament and increased activity of brain corticotropin-releasing factor (Kalin et al. 2000). Multiple studies have reported increased delta activity in intoxication, delirium, and dementia. Hence, quantitative electroencephalographic measures are indicative of both state and trait characteristics of brain function.

Another potential use of electroencephalographic topography is to determine whether particular medications produce a characteristic profile (Itil and Itil 1986). Although the fact that psychotropic drugs can affect the electroencephalogram has been known since 1933 (Berger 1933), the search for specific drug-related electroencephalographic patterns did not begin until the 1950s (Saletu 1989). The advent of electroencephalographic mapping has greatly accelerated this work. For example, imipramine causes a decrease in alpha power and an increase in delta activity in the posterior regions. Acute tryptophan depletion in healthy control subjects results in electroencephalographic slowing with an increase in delta activity (Knott et al. 1999). In contrast, diazepam decreases delta activity in the posterior regions and increases beta activity in the vertex and frontal regions (Saletu et al. 1987). Of interest, these techniques have been used to study the pharmacodynamic effect of midazolam and its reversal by flumazenil (Fiset et al. 1995). Although these reports are intriguing, to date no drug has been found to have a specific electroencephalographic signature. At present, pharmacologic electroencephalographic topography has been used predominantly by anesthesiologists to study and predict the level of central nervous system sedation by various agents (Leslie et al. 1996; Liu et al. 1996).

Spectral analysis is a computer-based method of analyzing the electroencephalographic frequency spectrum over time (Bickford et al. 1973). It allows for the determination of the relative predominance or power of any frequency band. It takes advantage of the analytic power of the computer and its ability to translate an enormous quantity of background electroencephalographic frequency data into concise parameters by a method called the fast Fourier transform (Press et al. 1986). The correlation between the spectra of contralateral or adjacent leads provides a measure of electroencephalographic coherence. A subtle neuropathologic process may be detected only from observing a change in coherence or relative electroencephalographic power of specific frequency bands. For example, Leuchter et al. (1987) found that analysis of electroencephalographic spectra and coherence could distinguish patients with Alzheimer's disease from those with multi-infarct dementia, as well as from healthy control subjects.

## Polysomnography

Among neuropsychiatrists, interest in the study of sleep began with a fascination with dreams. In 1868, Griesinger speculated that dreams were occurring when sleeping subjects had eye movements. Freud (1895/1954) suggested that dreaming was associated with profound relaxation to prevent the physical expression of dreams. Eight years after the first published human electroencephalographic study, the first all-night electroencephalographic study showed that sleep was composed of discrete stages (Loomis et al. 1937). Finally, in 1953, Aserinsky and Kleitman discovered and electrographically characterized rapid eye movement (REM) sleep. Since that time there has been a tremendous growth in sleep research as well as the emergence of the field of sleep medicine. Perhaps the most important result of this development has been the recognition that symptoms of insomnia and excessive sleepiness have broad differential diagnoses and warrant a thorough assessment.

Polysomnography remains the principal diagnostic tool in the field of sleep medicine. The term *polysomnography* is progressively becoming ambiguous because the physiologic variables that can be measured during all-night recordings are numerous (Table 6–3). A thorough polysomnographic study provides data on sleep continuity, sleep architecture, REM sleep physiology, sleep-

**TABLE 6–3.** Physiologic variables frequently recorded during polysomnography

| Physiologic variable | Recording medium (utility) |
|---|---|
| Sleep stage | Electroencephalogram (multiple leads may be used to diagnose sleep-associated seizures) |
| Eye movements | Electro-oculogram (helpful in defining stage I and rapid eye movement sleep and in detecting eye movement artifact in the electroencephalographic signal) |
| Muscle contractions | Electromyogram<br>Submentalis (detects muscle atonia seen in rapid eye movement sleep)<br>Anterior tibialis (detects periodic leg movements [nocturnal myoclonus])<br>Intercostal and diaphragm (detects respiratory effort) |
| Respiratory effort | Thoracic or abdominal strain gauge<br>Esophageal pressure balloon |
| Nasal and oral airflow | Throat microphone (detects snoring)<br>Nasal or oral thermistors (helps in diagnosing sleep apnea) |
| Oxygen saturation | Oximetry |
| Carbon dioxide content | Transcutaneous carbon dioxide monitor |
| Cardiac rate and arrhythmias | Electrocardiogram |
| Sleeping position | Video camera (documents presence of abnormal movements) |
| Nocturnal penile tumescence | Penile strain gauges |
| Gastroesophageal reflux | Esophageal pH probe |

related respiratory impairment, oxygen desaturation, cardiac arrhythmias, and periodic movements. Additional measures may include nocturnal penile tumescence and temperature and infrared video monitoring. For a detailed discussion of sleep disorders, please refer to Chapter 20 in this volume.

Quantitative analysis of sleep EEG has been utilized to characterize sleep microarchitecture in depressed subjects (Armitage et al. 1992; C.F. Reynolds and Kupfer 1987). These studies have utilized spectral analysis and period amplitude analysis to describe differences in delta wave activity in depressed subjects compared with healthy and psychiatric control subjects (Armitage 1995). These two techniques complement each other by yielding different quantitative information about the electroencephalographic signal. Fast Fourier transform is

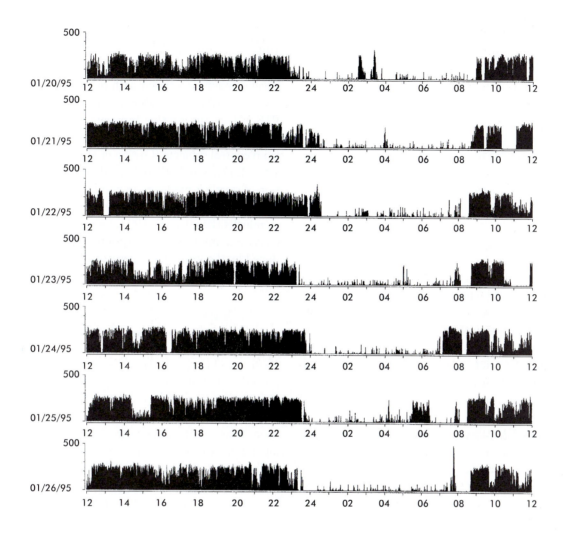

**FIGURE 6–6.** Sleep-wake activity over 7 days in a healthy 39-year-old man.

a frequency-domain technique that combines information about wave amplitude and incidence into power spectra for all frequency components. Period amplitude analysis is a time-domain technique that measures amplitude and counts EEG within predetermined bandwidths (Armitage 1995; C.F. Reynolds and Brunner 1995). Both techniques have a high degree of overlap (Pigeau et al. 1981). Quantitative electroencephalographic studies in the sleep electroencephalogram have shown that diminished interhemispheric and intrahemispheric coherence is associated with major depression, suggesting an underlying disturbance of ultradian regulation of electroencephalographic rhythms (Fulton et al. 2000).

## Activity Monitoring

Motion activity monitoring (actigraphy) is increasingly being used in studies of sleep-wake patterns (Figure 6–

6). Wrist-worn activity monitors provide continuous activity data using a battery-operated wristwatch-size microprocessor that senses motion and detects movement in all three axes. A signal is generated that is processed and stored in the unit's memory. Frequency, sensitivity, and threshold parameters are adjustable, and data can be stored in an ASCII file according to specified time intervals that range from 1 second to 1 hour. There is also an event marker for participants to indicate "lights out" and "lights on" time, as well as other salient events. The unit weighs 2 ounces and is worn comfortably around the wrist. Data can be presented in the form of percentage of time spent awake and asleep for a variety of time frames.

There is an excellent correlation (0.89–0.98) between polysomnographic and actigraphic estimates of sleep time in healthy persons (Kripke et al. 1978; Mullaney et al. 1980). Furthermore, actigraphy allows for an extended period of data collection in the home environment. In addition, actigraphy is excellent for detecting longitudinal changes or treatment effects (Brooks et al. 1993; Chambers 1994). A principal disadvantage is that it is not a true measure of sleep and does not give information about sleep architecture. Furthermore, its accuracy in estimating sleep time diminishes the more disturbed the sleep (Hauri and Wisbey 1994; B. Levine et al. 1986), and it may have some disadvantages in disorders associated with increased nocturnal locomotor activity. Sadeh et al. (1995) have emphasized the need to conduct validation studies of actigraph sleep assessment in specific populations in their natural environments.

## Electrodermal Activity

The conductance of electricity through skin is dependent on sweat gland activity, which in turn is controlled by the sympathetic nervous system (Rosse et al. 1987). However, other factors may influence electrodermal activity, such as skin thickness, number of sweat glands (Venables and Christie 1980), and age of the subject (Drory and Korczyn 1993). Measuring skin conductance therefore provides an indirect measure of arousal. For example, subjects with PTSD, which by definition is associated with hyperarousal, have exaggerated skin conductance in response to trauma-related script imagery, compared with non-PTSD control subjects (Shalev et al. 1992, 1993). Subjects with generalized anxiety disorder show an increase in skin conductance in response to oral caffeine administration compared with control subjects (Bruce et al. 1992). Decreased electrodermal activity has been found in antisocial adolescents (Raine and Venables 1984). In one of the few prospective studies, Raine et al. (1990) found that low arousal as measured by electrodermal activity predicted future criminal behavior. Furthermore, antisocial adolescents with high psychophysiologic arousal were more likely to desist from criminal behavior than were adolescents with low arousal (Raine et al. 1995). These findings support a theory that criminality is associated with decreased central and autonomic arousal (Eysenck 1977).

## Electromyography: Startle Responses

Electromyography (EMG) has been used to study the central nervous system primarily in studies of the startle response to abrupt stimuli. Typically, these studies examine the magnitude of the eyeblink response to loud sounds. Studies have found that the amplitude of elec-

tromyographic responses to loud sound is increased with fear states and diminished with pleasure (Lang et al. 1998). Morgan and Grillon have suggested that variability in baseline startle may be related to the greater conditioned anxiety associated with unfamiliar contexts (e.g., the psychophysiology laboratory) found in subjects with PTSD. They suggest that fear-potentiation of startle may be a better method for distinguishing PTSD subjects from control subjects (Grillon et al. 1998a; Morgan et al. 1995a). Davis and others have shown that fear-potentiation of startle is mediated in part by corticotropin-releasing factor (CRF) activity in the bed nucleus of the stria terminalis (Fendt et al. 1997; Lee and Davis 1997). The increased amplitude of response is thought to be produced by the immediate increase in release of CRF during fear-provoking stimuli.

## Conclusions

Neuropsychiatric electrophysiology continues to be a powerful clinical and research tool. It remains one of the few noninvasive probes of brain function. The future advances in this field will likely come from combining quantitative electrophysiologic data with anatomic imaging obtained from well-defined clinical populations and well-selected control groups. The clinical applicability of quantitative electroencephalographic and electrophysiologic techniques continues to hold much promise.

## References

Abrams R, Taylor MA: Laboratory studies in the validation of psychiatric diagnoses, in Hemisphere Asymmetries of Function in Psychopathology. Edited by Gruzelier JH, Flor-Henry P. New York, Elsevier North-Holland, 1979, pp 363–372

Adams DC, Heyer EJ, Emerson RG, et al: The reliability of quantitative electroencephalography as an indicator of cerebral ischemia. Anesth Analg 81:80–83, 1995

Aminoff MJ: Electroencephalography: general principles and clinical applications, in Electrodiagnosis in Clinical Neurology. Edited by Aminoff MJ. New York, Churchill Livingstone, 1986, pp 21–75

Andersen P, Andersson SA: Physiologic Basis of the Alpha Rhythm. New York, Appleton-Century-Crofts, 1968

Anderson VE, Hauser WA, Rich SS: Genetic heterogeneity and epidemiology of the epilepsies. Adv Neurol 79:59–73, 1999

Armitage R: Microarchitectural findings in sleep EEG in depression: diagnostic implications. Biol Psychiatry 37:72–84, 1995

Armitage R, Roffwarg HP, Rush AJ, et al: Digital period analysis of sleep EEG in depression. Biol Psychiatry 31(1):52–68, 1992

Aserinsky E, Kleitman N: Regularly occurring periods of eye motility and concomitant phenomena during sleep. Science 118:273–274, 1953

Attias J, Bleich A, Furman V, et al: Event-related potentials in post-traumatic stress disorder of combat origin. Biol Psychiatry 40(5):373–381, 1996

Aung M, Sobel DF, Gallen CC, et al: Potential contribution of bilateral magnetic source imaging to the evaluation of epilepsy surgery candidates. Neurosurgery 37(6):1113–1120, 1995

Baumgartner C, Pataraia E, Lindinger G, et al: Magnetoencephalography in focal epilepsy. Epilepsia 41 (suppl 3):S39–S47, 2000

Berger H: Uber das Elektrenkephalogramm des Menschen. Archiv fur Psychiatrie und Nervenkrankheiten 87:527–570, 1929

Berger H: Uber das Elektroencephalogramm des Menschen. VIII. Mitteilung. Archiv fur Psychiatrie und Nervenkrankheiten 101:452–469, 1933

Bickford RG, Brimmer J, Berger L: Application of a Compressed Spectral Array in Clinical EEG. New York, Raven, 1973

Braff DL, Geyer MA: Sensorimotor gating and schizophrenia. Arch Gen Psychiatry 47:181–188, 1990

Brazier MAB: The emergence of electrophysiology as an aid to neurology, in Electrodiagnosis in Clinical Neurology. Edited by Aminoff MJ. New York, Churchill Livingstone, 1986, pp 1–19

Bresnahan SM, Anderson JW, Barry RJ: Age-related changes in quantitative EEG in attention-deficit/hyperactivity disorder. Biol Psychiatry 46(12):1690–1697, 1999

Brodie JD: Imaging for the clinical psychiatrist: facts, fantasies, and other musings. Am J Psychiatry 153:145–149, 1996

Brooks JO III, Friedman L, Bliwise DL, et al: Use of the wrist actigraph to study insomnia in older adults. Sleep 16:151–155, 1993

Bruce M, Scott N, Shine P, et al: Anxiogenic effects of caffeine in patients with anxiety disorders. Arch Gen Psychiatry 49:867–869, 1992

Bruder GE, Fong R, Tenke CE, et al: Regional brain asymmetries in major depression with or without an anxiety disorder: a quantitative electroencephalographic study. Biol Psychiatry 41(9):939–948, 1997

Cardenas VA, Gill P, Fein G: Human P50 suppression is not affected by variations in wakeful alertness. Biol Psychiatry 41(8):891–901, 1997

Caton R: The electric currents of the brain. BMJ 2:278, 1875

Chambers MJ: Actigraphy and insomnia: a closer look. Part 1. Sleep 17:405–408, 1994

Charles G, Hansenne M, Ansseau M, et al: P300 in posttraumatic stress disorder. Neuropsychobiology 32(2):72–74, 1995

Cooper R, Winter AL, Crow HJ, et al: Comparison of subcortical, cortical and scalp activity using chronically indwelling electrodes in man. Electroencephalogr Clin Neurophysiol 18:217–228, 1965

Courchesne E, Hillyard SA, Galambos R: Stimulus novelty, task relevance and the visual evoked potential in man. Electroencephalogr Clin Neurophysiol 39:131–143, 1975

Cuffin BN, Cohen D: Comparison of the magnetoencephalogram and electroencephalogram. Electroencephalogr Clin Neurophysiol 47:132–146, 1979

Deisenhammer E, Jellinger K: EEG in senile dementia. Electroencephalogr Clin Neurophysiol 36:91, 1974

Denays R, Makhoul E, Dachy B, et al: Electroencephalographic mapping and 99mTc HMPAO single-photon emission computed tomography in carbon monoxide poisoning. Ann Emerg Med 24:947–952, 1994

Donchin E, Coles MG: Is the P300 component a manifestation of context updating? Behav Brain Sci 11(3):357–427, 1988

Drory VE, Korczyn AD: Sympathetic skin response: age effect. Neurology 43:1818–1820, 1993

Duffy FH: Topographic Mapping of Brain Electrical Activity. Boston, MA, Butterworths, 1986

Duffy FH: Issues facing the clinical use of brain electrical activity mapping, in Functional Brain Imaging. Edited by Pfurtscheller G, Lopes da Silva FH. Toronto, ON, Hans Huber, 1988, pp 149–160

Edmonds HL Jr, Griffiths LK, van der Laken J, et al: Quantitative electroencephalographic monitoring during myocardial revascularization predicts postoperative disorientation and improves outcome (comments). J Thorac Cardiovasc Surg 103:555–563, 1992

Eysenck HJ: Crime and Personality. St. Albans, UK, Paladin Frogmore, 1977

Fein G, Biggins CA, MacKay S: Alcohol abuse and HIV infection have additive effects on frontal cortex function as measured by auditory evoked potential P3A latency. Biol Psychiatry 37:183–195, 1995a

Fein G, Biggins CA, MacKay S: Delayed latency of the event-related brain potential P3A component in HIV disease. Progressive effects with increasing cognitive impairment. Arch Neurol 52:1109–1118, 1995b

Fendt M, Koch M, Schnitzler HU: Corticotropin-releasing factor in the caudal pontine reticular nucleus mediates the expression of fear-potentiated startle in the rat. Eur J Neurosci 9:299–305, 1997

Fenton GW: The electrophysiology of Alzheimer's disease. Br Med Bull 42:29–33, 1986

Fenton GW: The EEG in neuropsychiatry, in The Bridge Between Neurology and Psychiatry. Edited by Reynolds EH, Trimble MR. Edinburgh, UK, Churchill Livingstone, 1989, pp 302–333

Fiset P, Lemmens HL, Egan TE, et al: Pharmacodynamic modeling of the electroencephalographic effects of flumazenil in healthy volunteers sedated with midazolam. Clin Pharmacol Ther 58:567–582, 1995

Freedman R, Adler LE, Myles-Worsley M, et al: Inhibitory gating of an evoked response to repeated auditory stimuli in schizophrenic and normal subjects. Arch Gen Psychiatry 53:1114–1121, 1996

Freud S: Project for a scientific psychology (1895), in The Origins of Psychoanalysis: Letters to Wilhelm Fliess, Drafts and Notes, 1887–1902. Edited by Bonaparte M, Freud A, Kres E. New York, Basic Books, 1954, p 400

Freudenreich O, Weiner RD, McEvoy JP: Clozapine-induced electroencephalogram changes as a function of clozapine serum levels. Biol Psychiatry 42(2):132–137, 1997

Fulton MK, Armitage R, Rush AJ: Sleep electroencephalographic coherence abnormalities in individuals at high risk for depression: a pilot study. Biol Psychiatry 47(7):618–625, 2000

Gallen CC, Sobel DF, Lewine JD, et al: Neuromagnetic mapping of brain function. Radiology 187:863–867, 1993

Gallen CC, Hirschkoff EC, Buchanan DS: Magnetoencephalography and magnetic source imaging. Capabilities and limitations. Neuroimaging Clin N Am 5:227–249, 1995

Gelisse P, Samuelian JC, Genton P: Is schizophrenia a risk factor for epilepsy or acute symptomatic seizures? Epilepsia 40(11):1566–1571, 1999

Gibbs FA, Davis H, Lennox WG: The electroencephalogram in epilepsy and in conditions of impaired consciousness. Arch Neurol Psychiatry 34:1133–1135, 1935

Goff WR, Allison T, Vaughan HG: The functional neuroanatomy of event-related potentials, in Event-Related Brain Potentials in Man. Edited by Callaway E, Tueting P, Koslow SH. New York, Academic Press, 1978, pp 1–79

Goldensohn ES: Neurophysiologic substrates of EEG activity, in Current Practice of Electroencephalography. New York, Raven Press, 1979, pp 421–439

Goodin DS, Aminoff MJ: Does the interictal EEG have a role in the diagnosis of epilepsy? Lancet 1:837, 1984

Griesinger W: Berliner medicinisch-psychologische Gesellschaft. Archiv fur Psychiatrie und Nervenkrankeiten 1:200–204, 1868

Griffith JM, O'Neill JE, Petty F, et al: Nicotinic receptor desensitization and sensory gating deficits in schizophrenia. Biol Psychiatry 1998 44(2):98–106, 1998

Grillon C, Courchesne E, Ameli R, et al: Increased distractibility in schizophrenic patients. Arch Gen Psychiatry 47:171–179, 1990

Grillon C, Morgan CA III, Davis M, et al: Effects of experimental context and explicit threat cues on acoustic startle in Vietnam veterans with posttraumatic stress disorder. Biol Psychiatry 44:1027–1036, 1998

Gruzelier J, Liddiard D: The neuropsychology of schizophrenia in the context of topographical mapping of electrocortical activity, in Topographic Brain Mapping of EEG and Evoked Potentials. Edited by Maurer K. Berlin, Springer-Verlag, 1989, pp 421–437

Gueguen B, Etevenon P, Plancon D, et al: EEG mapping in pathological aging and dementia: utility for diagnosis and therapeutic evaluation, in Topographic Brain Mapping of EEG and Evoked Potentials. Edited by Maurer K. Berlin, Springer-Verlag, 1989, pp 219–225

Guenther W, Breitling D, Banquet JP, et al: EEG mapping of left hemisphere dysfunction during motor performance in schizophrenia. Biol Psychiatry 21:249–262, 1986

Hauri PJ, Wisbey J: Actigraphy and insomnia: a closer look. Part 2. Sleep 17:408–410, 1994

Hirayasu Y, Asato N, Ohta H, et al: Abnormalities of auditory event-related potentials in schizophrenia prior to treatment. Biol Psychiatry 1998 43(4):244–253, 1998

Inui K, Motomura E, Okushima R, et al: Electroencephalographic findings in patients with DSM-IV mood disorder, schizophrenia, and other psychotic disorders. Biol Psychiatry 43(1):69–75, 1998

Itil TM: The use of electroencephalography in the practice of psychiatry. Psychosomatics 23:799–813, 1982

Itil TM, Itil KZ: The significance of pharmacodynamic measurement in the assessment of bioavailability and bioequivalence of psychotropic drugs using CEEG and dynamic brain mapping. J Clin Psychiatry 47 (suppl):20–27, 1986

Jasper HH: The ten-twenty electrode system of the International Federation. Electroencephalogr Clin Neurophysiol 10:371–375, 1958

Javitt DC, Doneshka P, Grochowski S, et al: Impaired mismatch negativity generation reflects widespread dysfunction of working memory in schizophrenia. Arch Gen Psychiatry 52:550–558, 1995

Jerger K, Biggins C, Fein G: P50 suppression is not affected by attentional manipulations. Biol Psychiatry 31(4):365–377, 1992

Johnson MR, Adler LE: Transient impairment in P50 auditory sensory gating induced by a cold-pressor test. Biol Psychiatry 33(5):380–387, 1993

Johnson R: On the neural generators of the P300 component of the event-related potential. Psychophysiology 30:90–97, 1993

Kalin NH, Shelton SE, Davidson RJ: Cerebrospinal fluid corticotropin-releasing hormone levels are elevated in monkeys with patterns of brain activity associated with fearful temperament. Biol Psychiatry 47(7):579–585, 2000

Karson CN, Coppola R, Morihisa JM, et al: Computed electroencephalographic activity mapping in schizophrenia. Arch Gen Psychiatry 44:514–517, 1987

Kaufman PY: Electrical phenomenon in cerebral cortex. Obzory Psikhiatrii Nevrologii i Eksperimental'noi Psikhologii 7–8:403, 1912

Kazmerski VA, Friedman D, Ritter W: Mismatch negativity during attend and ignore conditions in Alzheimer's disease. Biol Psychiatry 42:382–402, 1997

Kendler KS, Hays P: Familial and sporadic schizophrenia: a symptomatic, prognostic and EEG comparison. Am J Psychiatry 139:1557–1562, 1982

Kimble M, Kaloupek D, Kaufman M, et al: Stimulus novelty differentially affects attentional allocation in PTSD. Biol Psychiatry 47(10):880–890, 2000

Klein C, Heinks T, Andresen B, et al: Impaired modulation of the saccadic contingent negative variation preceding antisaccades in schizophrenia. Biol Psychiatry 47(11):978–990, 2000

Knight RT: Decreased response to novel stimuli after prefrontal lesions in man. Electroencephalogr Clin Neurophysiol 59:9–20, 1984

Knight RT: Electrophysiology in behavioral neurology, in Principles of Behavioral Neurology. Edited by Mesulam M-M. Philadelphia, PA, FA Davis, 1985, pp 327–346

Knight R, Scabini D, Woods D, et al: Contributions of temporal-parietal junction to the human auditory P3. Brain Res 502:109–116, 1989

Knott VJ, Howson AL, Perugini M, et al: The effect of acute tryptophan depletion and fenfluramine on quantitative EEG and mood in healthy male subjects. Biol Psychiatry 46(2):229–238, 1999

Kounios J, Litz B, Kaloupek D, et al: Electrophysiology of combat-related PTSD. Ann N Y Acad Sci 821:504–507, 1997

Kripke DF, Mullaney DJ, Messin S, et al: Wrist actigraphic measures of sleep and rhythms. Electroencephalogr Clin Neurophysiol 44:674–676, 1978

Kutcher SP, Blackwood DHR, St Clair D, et al: Auditory P300 in borderline personality disorder and schizophrenia. Arch Gen Psychiatry 44:645–650, 1987

Lam RW, Hurwitz TA, Wada JA: The clinical use of EEG in a general psychiatric setting. Hospital and Community Psychiatry 39:533–536, 1988

Lang PJ, Bradley MM, Cuthbert BN: Emotion, motivation, and anxiety: brain mechanisms and psychophysiology. Biol Psychiatry 44(12):1248–1263, 1998

Lee Y, Davis M: Role of the septum in the excitatory effect of corticotropin-releasing hormone on the acoustic startle reflex. J Neurosci 17:6424–6433, 1997

Leslie K, Sessler DI, Smith WD, et al: Prediction of movement during propofol/nitrous oxide anesthesia. Performance of concentration, electroencephalographic, pupillary, and hemodynamic indicators. Anesthesiology 84:52–63, 1996

Leuchter AF, Spar JE, Walter DO, et al: Electroencephalographic spectra and coherence in the diagnosis of Alzheimer's type and multi-infarct dementia. Arch Gen Psychiatry 44:993–998, 1987

Levine B, Moyles T, Roehrs T, et al: Actigraphic monitoring and polygraphic recording in determination of sleep and wake, in Sleep Research, Vol 15. Edited by Chase MH, McGinty DJ, Crane G. Los Angeles, CA, UCLA Brain Information Service/Brain Research Institute, 1986, p 247

Levine RA, Gardner JC, Fullerton BC, et al: Multiple sclerosis lesions of the auditory pons are not silent. Brain 117:1127–1141, 1994

Levit AL, Sutton S, Zubin J: Evoked potential correlates of information processing in psychiatric patients. Psychol Med 3:487–494, 1973

Liu J, Singh H, White PF: Electroencephalogram bispectral analysis predicts the depth of midazolam-induced sedation. Anesthesiology 84:64–69, 1996

Loomis AL, Harvey EN, Hobart GA: Cerebral states during sleep, as studied by human brain potentials. Journal of Experimental Psychology 21:127–144, 1937

Mathalon DH, Ford JM, Rosenbloom M, et al: P300 reduction and prolongation with illness duration in schizophrenia. Biol Psychiatry 47(5):413–427, 2000

Matsushima E, Nakajima K, Moriya H, et al: A psychophysiological study of the development of delirium in coronary care units. Biol Psychiatry 41(12):1211–1217, 1997

McCarley RW, Faux SF, Shenton M, et al: CT abnormalities in schizophrenia: a preliminary study of their correlations with P300/P200 electrophysiological features and positive/negative symptoms. Arch Gen Psychiatry 46:698–708, 1989

McFarlane AC, Weber DL, Clark CR: Abnormal stimulus processing in posttraumatic stress disorder. Biol Psychiatry 34(5):311–320, 1993

McGhie A, Chapman J: Disorders of attention and perception in early schizophrenia. Br J Med Psychol 34:103–116, 1961

McKenna PJ, Kane JM, Parrish K: Psychotic syndromes in epilepsy. Am J Psychiatry 142:895–904, 1985

Metzger LJ, Orr SP, Lasko NB, et al: Auditory event-related potentials to tone stimuli in combat-related posttraumatic stress disorder. Biol Psychiatry 42(11):1006–1015, 1997

Morgan CA III, Grillon C, Southwick SM, et al: Fear-potentiated startle in posttraumatic stress disorder. Biol Psychiatry 38:378–385, 1995

Morihisa JM, Duffy FH, Wyatt RJ: Brain electrical activity mapping in schizophrenic patients. Arch Gen Psychiatry 40:719–728, 1983

Morstyn R, Duffy FH, McCarley RW: Altered topography of EEG spectral content in schizophrenia. Electroencephalogr Clin Neurophysiol 56(4):263–271, 1983

Mullaney DJ, Kripke DF, Messin S: Wrist-actigraphic estimation of sleep time. Sleep 3:83–92, 1980

Nasrallah HA: Is schizophrenia a left hemisphere disease?, in Can Schizophrenia Be Localized in the Brain? Edited by Andreasan NC. Washington, DC, American Psychiatric Press, 1986, pp 55–74

Neylan TC, Van Kammen DP, Kelley ME, et al: Sleep in schizophrenic patients on and off haloperidol therapy: clinically stable vs relapsed patients. Arch Gen Psychiatry 49:643–649, 1992

Neylan TC, Fletcher DJ, Lenoci M, et al: Sensory gating in chronic posttraumatic stress disorder: reduced auditory P50 suppression in combat veterans. Biol Psychiatry 46(12):1656–1664, 1999

Niedermeyer E: Introduction to electroencephalography, in The Epilepsies: Diagnosis and Management. Baltimore, MD, Urban & Schwarzenberg, 1990, pp 35–49

O'Donnell BF, Faux SF, McCarley RW, et al: Increased rate of P300 latency prolongation with age in schizophrenia. Electrophysiological evidence for a neurodegenerative process. Arch Gen Psychiatry 52:544–549, 1995

Oke S, Saatchi R, Allen E, et al: The contingent negative variation in positive and negative types of schizophrenia. Am J Psychiatry 151:432–433, 1994

Olfson M: Utilization of neuropsychiatric diagnostic tests for general hospital patients with mental disorders. Am J Psychiatry 149:1711–1717, 1992

Pfefferbaum A, Ford JM, White PM, et al: P3 in schizophrenia is affected by stimulus modality, response requirements, medication status, and negative symptoms. Arch Gen Psychiatry 46:1035–1044, 1989

Pfefferbaum A, Roth WT, Ford JM: Event-related potentials in the study of psychiatric disorders. Arch Gen Psychiatry 52:559–563, 1995

Pfurtscheller G, Cooper R: Frequency dependence of the transmission of the EEG from cortex to scalp. Electroencephalogr Clin Neurophysiol 38:93–96, 1975

Pigeau RA, Hoffmann RF, Moffitt AR: A multivariate comparison between two EEG analysis techniques: period analysis and Fast Fourier Transform. Electroencephalogr Clin Neurophysiol 52:656–658, 1981

Pokras R: National Hospital Discharge Survey Data Tape Documentation, 1989. Hyattsville, MD, National Center for Health Statistics, 1990

Polich J: Meta-analysis of P300 normative aging studies. Psychophysiology 33(4):334–353, 1996

Polich J, Kok A: Cognitive and biological determinants of P300: an integrative review. Biol Psychology 41(2):103–146, 1995

Press WH, Flannery BP, Teukolsky SA, et al: Numerical Recipes: The Art of Scientific Computing. New York, Cambridge University Press, 1986

Pro JD, Wells CE: The use of the electroencephalogram in the diagnosis of delirium. Diseases of the Nervous System 38:804–808, 1977

Raine A, Venables PH: Electrodermal nonresponding, antisocial behavior, and schizoid tendencies in adolescents. Psychophysiology 21:424–433, 1984

Raine A, Venables PH, Williams M: Relationships between central and autonomic measures of arousal at age 15 years and criminality at age 24 years. Arch Gen Psychiatry 47:1003–1007, 1990

Raine A, Venables PH, Williams M: High autonomic arousal and electrodermal orienting at age 15 years as protective factors against criminal behavior at age 29 years. Am J Psychiatry 152:1595–1600, 1995

Reeve A, Rose DF, Weinberger DR: Magnetoencephalography: applications in psychiatry. Arch Gen Psychiatry 46:573–576, 1989

Reite M, Teale P, Goldstein L, et al: Late auditory magnetic sources may differ in the left hemisphere of schizophrenic patients. Arch Gen Psychiatry 46:565–572, 1989

Reynolds CF, Brunner D: Sleep microarchitecture in depression: commentary. Biol Psychiatry 37:71, 1995

Reynolds CF, Kupfer DJ: Sleep research in affective illness: State of the art circa 1987. Sleep 10:199–215, 1987

Ritchlin CT, Chabot RJ, Alper K, et al: Quantitative electroencephalography. A new approach to the diagnosis of cerebral dysfunction in systemic lupus erythematosus. Arthritis Rheum 35:1330–1342, 1992

Ritter W, Vaughan HG, Costa LD: Orienting and habituation to auditory stimuli: a study of short term changes in averaged evoked responses. Electroencephalogr Clin Neurophysiol 25:550, 1968

Robinson DJ, Merskey H, Blume WT, et al: Electroencephalography as an aid in the exclusion of Alzheimer's disease. Arch Neurol 51:280–284, 1994

Rodin E, Onuma T, Wasson S, et al: Neurophysiological mechanism involved in grand mal seizures induced by metrazol and megimide. Electroencephalogr Clin Neurophysiol 30:62–72, 1971

Rose DF, Smith PD, Sato S: Magnetoencephalography and epilepsy research. Science 238:329–335, 1987

Rosse RB, Owen CM, Morihisa JM: Brain imaging and laboratory testing in neuropsychiatry, in The American Psychiatric Press Textbook of Neuropsychiatry. Edited by Hales RE, Yudofsky SC. Washington DC, American Psychiatric Press, 1987, pp 17–39

Rosse RB, Warden DL, Morihisa JM: Applied electrophysiology, in Comprehensive Textbook of Psychiatry, 5th Edition. Edited by Kaplan HI, Sadock BJ. Baltimore, MD, Williams & Wilkins, 1989, pp 74–85

Roth WT, Horvath TB, Pfefferbaum A, et al: Event related potentials in schizophrenics. Electroencephalogr Clin Neurophysiol 48:127–139, 1980

Rugg MD, Cowan CP, Nagy ME, et al: CNV abnormalities following closed head injury. Brain 112:489–506, 1989

Sadeh A, Hauri PJ, Kripke DF, et al: The role of actigraphy in the evaluation of sleep disorders. Sleep 18:288–302, 1995

Saletu B: EEG imaging of brain activity in clinical psychopharmacology, in Topographic Brain Mapping of EEG and Evoked Potentials. Edited by Maurer K. Berlin, Springer-Verlag, 1989, pp 482–506

Saletu B, Anderer P, Kinsperger K, et al: Topographic brain mapping of EEG in neuropsychopharmacology, part II: clinical applications (pharmaco-EEG imaging). Methods Find Exp Clin Pharmacol 9:385–408, 1987

Shagass C: Twisted thoughts, twisted brain waves?, in Psychopathology and Brain Dysfunction. Edited by Shagass C, Gershon S, Friedhoff AJ. New York, Raven, 1977, pp 353–378

Shalev AY, Orr SP, Peri T, et al: Physiologic responses to loud tones in Israeli patients with posttraumatic stress disorder. Arch Gen Psychiatry 49:870–875, 1992

Shalev AY, Orr SP, Pitman RK: Psychophysiologic assessment of traumatic imagery in Israeli civilian patients with posttraumatic stress disorder. Am J Psychiatry 150:620–624, 1993

Snyder E, Hillyard SA: Long-latency evoked potentials to irrelevant, deviant stimuli. Behavioral Biology 16:319, 1976

Southwick SM, Krystal JH, Morgan CA, et al: Abnormal noradrenergic function in posttraumatic stress disorder. Arch Gen Psychiatry 50(4):266–274, 1993

Squires NK, Squires KC, Hillyard SA: Two varieties of long-latency positive waves evoked by unpredictable auditory stimuli in man. Electroencephalogr Clin Neurophysiol 38(4):387–401, 1975

Struve FA: The necessity and value of screening routine EEG in psychiatric patients: a preliminary report on the issues of referrals. Clin Electroencephalogr 7:115–130, 1976

Struve FA: Selective referral versus routine screening of clinical EEG assessment of psychiatric inpatients. Psychiatric Medicine 1:317–343, 1984

Trzepacz PT, Sclabassi RJ, Van Thiel DH: Delirium: a subcortical phenomenon? J Neuropsychiatry Clin Neurosci 1:283–290, 1989

van Kammen DP, Peters J, Yao J, et al: Norepinephrine in acute exacerbations of chronic schizophrenia. Negative symptoms revisited. Arch Gen Psychiatry 47:161–168, 1990

van Sweden B, de Bruecker G: Patterns of EEG dysfunction in general hospital psychiatry. Neuropsychobiology 16:131–134, 1986

Venables PH, Christie MJ: Electrodermal activity, in Techniques in Psychophysiology. Edited by Martin I, Venables PH. New York, Wiley, 1980, pp 3–67

Verleger R, Wascher E, Arolt V, et al: Slow EEG potentials (contingent negative variation and post-imperative negative variation) in schizophrenia: their association to the present state and to Parkinsonian medication effects. Clin Neurophysiol 110(7):1175–1192, 1999

Visser SL: EEG and evoked potentials in the diagnosis of dementia, in Senile Dementia of the Alzheimer Type. Edited by Traber J, Gispen WH. Berlin, Springer, 1985, pp 102–116

Wada Y, Nanbu Y, Jiang ZY, et al: Electroencephalographic abnormalities in patients with presenile dementia of the Alzheimer type: quantitative analysis at rest and during photic stimulation. Biol Psychiatry 41(2):217–225, 1997

Waldo M, Gerhardt G, Baker N, et al: Auditory sensory gating and catecholamine metabolism in schizophrenic and normal subjects. Psychiatry Res 44(1):21–32, 1992

Warner MD, Boutros NN, Peabody CA: Usefulness of screening EEGs in a psychiatric inpatient population. J Clin Psychiatry 51:363–364, 1990

Zimmerman JE: Magnetic quantities, units, materials, and measurements, in Biomagnetism: An Interdisciplinary Approach. Edited by Williamson SJ, Romani GL, Kaufman L, et al. New York, Plenum, 1983, pp 17–42

Zivin L, Ajmone Marsan C: Incidence and prognostic significance of "epileptiform" activity in the EEG of non-epileptic subjects. Brain 91:751–779, 1968

# CHAPTER 7

# The Neuropsychological Evaluation

Diane B. Howieson, Ph.D.

Muriel D. Lezak, Ph.D.

Neuropsychologists assess brain function by making inferences from an individual's cognitive, sensorimotor, emotional, and social behavior. During the early history of neuropsychology, these assessments were often the most direct measure of brain integrity in persons who did not have localizing neurologic signs and symptoms and who had problems confined to higher mental functions (Hebb 1942; Teuber 1948). Neuropsychological measures are useful diagnostic indicators of brain dysfunction for many conditions and will remain the major diagnostic modality for some (Bigler 1999; Farah and Feinberg 2000; Jernigan and Hesselink 1987; Lezak 1995; Mesulam 2000). However, diagnosis of brain damage has become increasingly accurate in recent decades as a result of improved visualization of brain structure by computed tomography (CT), magnetic resonance imaging (MRI), and angiography (Frith and Friston 1997; Theodore 1988). Advances in electrophysiologic examination techniques (Caccioppo et al. 2000; Daube 1996; Johnson 1995) and in quantitative and functional neuroimaging have further enriched our understanding of pathological disturbances of the brain (Aine 1995; Binder et al. 1995; Ernst et al. 1999; Frith and Grasby 1995; J.M. Levin et al. 1996; Menon and Kim 1999; Papanicolaou 1999). It is even possible to produce precisely placed, reversible "lesions" to study how the remainder of the brain functions without a designated cortical area (Grafman and Wassermann 1999; V. Walsh and Rushworth 1999). These developments have allowed a shift in the focus of neuropsychological assessment from the diagnosis of pos-sible brain damage to a better understanding of specific brain-behavior relationships and the psychosocial consequences of brain damage.

## Indications for Neuropsychological Evaluation

Patients referred to a neuropsychologist for assessment typically fall into one of three groups. The first, and probably largest, group consists of patients with known brain disorders. The more common neurological disorders are cerebrovascular disorders, developmental disorders, traumatic brain injury, Alzheimer's disease and related disorders, Parkinson's disease, multiple sclerosis, Huntington's chorea, tumors, seizures, and infections. Psychiatric disorders also may be associated with brain dysfunction; chief among them are schizophrenia, obsessive-compulsive disorder, and depression.

A neuropsychological evaluation can be useful in defining the nature and severity of resulting behavioral and emotional problems. The assessment provides information about the patient's cognition, personality characteristics, social behavior, emotional status, and adaptation to limitations. The individual's potential for independent living and productive activity can be inferred from these data. Information about the patient's behavioral strengths and weaknesses provides a foundation for treatment planning, vocational training, competency determination, and counseling for both patients and their families

217

(Acker 1989; Diller 2000; Newcombe 1987; Sloan and Ponsford 1995).

> A 52-year-old real estate agent had a left-hemisphere stroke producing mild aphasia and right-sided hemiparesis. A neuropsychological examination conducted several months later showed that she had good language comprehension and reading skills, mild word-finding problems, mild visuospatial deficits, and moderate impairment in verbal memory. Like many patients who have had strokes (Astrom et al. 1993; Cullum and Bigler 1991; Niemi et al. 1988; Robinson 1998), she was also depressed. Information from the examination was used to make decisions about the likelihood of returning successfully to her previous job, for planning rehabilitation and strategies to help her compensate for persistent cognitive deficits, for recommendations regarding treatment of her depression, and for family counseling.

The second group of patients is composed of persons with a known risk factor for brain disorder in whom a change in behavior might be the result of such a disorder. In these cases a neuropsychological evaluation might be used both to provide evidence of brain dysfunction and to describe the nature and severity of problems. An individual who has sustained a blow to the head from an automobile accident that produces a brief loss of consciousness, even with no apparent further neurological complications, might experience disruption in cognitive efficiency. On returning to work after 1 week, this individual might be unable to keep up with job demands. After several weeks of on-the-job difficulties, the physician may refer the patient to a neuropsychologist for evaluation of possible brain injury from the accident. The examiner would look for evidence of problems with divided attention, sustained concentration and mental tracking, and memory, all of which are common findings in the weeks or months following mild head injury (Bennett and Raymonds 1997; Varney and Roberts 1999; Wrightson and Gronwall 1999). The neuropsychologist can advise the patient that these problems frequently occur after head injury and that considerable improvement might be expected during the next month or two. Recommendations about how to structure work activities to minimize both these difficulties and the equally common problem of fatigue provide both aid and comfort to the concerned patient. The neuropsychologist might repeat the examination several months after the injury to see if these predictions held true and to assess the individual's adjustment and possible need for further counseling or other treatment.

A depressed older individual may complain of poor memory, raising concern about a possible illness producing dementia.

> A 55-year-old rancher noticed problems remembering to carry out activities and difficulty retaining information. He had an aunt with Alzheimer's disease and was worried that he might have this disease. His emotional stressors included concern about his son's substance abuse. His cognitive testing showed memory performance typical of his age and argued for a diagnosis of anxiety and depression rather than dementia.

It is not unusual to observe attention and memory problems in patients such as this based on depression alone. In most cases, the nature and degree of cognitive problems would differentiate the diagnoses.

Many medical conditions can affect brain function (Lezak 1995; Tarter et al. 1988). Brain function can be disrupted by systemic illnesses: endocrinopathies; metabolic and electrolyte disturbances; diseases of the kidney, liver, and pancreas; nutritional deficiencies; and conditions producing decreased blood supply to the brain. The latter include vascular disorders, cardiac disease, pulmonary disease, anemia, and complications of anesthesia or surgery. Age and health habits also must be taken into consideration when evaluating a person's behavioral alterations, since they affect the probability of cerebral disorder (Dubois et al. 1990; Kolb 1989; Perfect and Maylor 2000). In addition, many medicines can disrupt cognition through their subtle effects on alertness, attention, and memory (Blain and Lane 1991; Davison and Hassanyck 1991; Pagliaro and Pagliaro 1998; Stein and Strickland 1998).

In the last group, brain disease or dysfunction is often suspected based on the observation of a change in a person's behavior without an identifiable cause: that is, the patient has no known risk factors for brain disorder and this diagnosis is considered on the basis of exclusion of other diagnoses. Frequently, psychiatrists are asked to evaluate an adult with no previous psychiatric history who has had an uncharacteristic change in behavior or personality and for whom no obvious sources of current emotional distress can be identified. An explanation is sought, since behavior patterns and personality are relatively stable characteristics of adults. The list of differential diagnoses is long and may include a wide variety of brain disorders ranging from metabolic disturbance, vitamin deficiency, endocrine disorder, and heavy metal poisoning to neoplasm, infection, and multiple small strokes. The psychiatric literature contains numerous examples of individuals who were being treated for psychiatric illness before it was discovered that they had brain disease, such as a frontal lobe tumor (R.A. Berg 1988; Fahy et al. 1995; Lesser 1985).

The most common application of the neuropsychological evaluation of older adults without obvious risk factors for brain disease is in the early detection of progressive dementia, such as Alzheimer's disease (Howieson et al. 1997; Jacobs et al. 1995; Masur et al. 1994; Morris et al. 1991; Petersen et al. 1994; Rentz and Weintraub 2000). Most persons have symptoms associated with dementia for at least 1 year before they see a health care provider because the problems initially are minor and easily attributed to factors such as aging or recent emotional stress. The progression of these symptoms is insidious, and people have "good" as well as "bad" days during the early course of this illness. Neuropsychological assessment is useful in evaluating whether problems noted by the family or the individual are age related, are attributable to other factors such as depression, or are suggestive of early dementia. During the past decade, human immunodeficiency virus (HIV) infection and the complications of drug abuse have been added as conditions that can produce an insidious dementia in younger persons (I. Grant et al. 1995; Kelly et al. 1996; Van Gorp et al. 1989).

Another clinical condition that produces no clinical clues for brain damage except for a change in behavior is the so-called silent stroke. Without obvious sensory, motor, or speech problems, a stroke may go undetected yet produce a persistent change in behavior or abilities. Silent stokes can produce subtle cognitive impairment (Armstrong et al. 1996; Pohjasvaara et al. 1999), or a series of small strokes may produce an insidious dementia (O'Connell et al. 1998). Silent strokes and white matter hyperintensities observed on MRI scans can also predispose elderly persons to depression (Alexopoulos et al. 1997).

Environmental toxins constitute another class of hidden conditions that present general patterns of neuropsychological impairment (Anger 1992; Feldman and White 1996; Freed and Kandel 1988; Grattan et al. 1998; Ryan et al. 1988; White et al. 1992).

In such cases with no known cause to explain mental deterioration, a search for possible risk factors or other evidence for brain disease is conducted through history taking, performing physical examination, conducting laboratory tests, and interviewing the patient's family or close associates. Even if this search produces no evidence of disease, a diagnostic neuropsychological study might be useful.

The neuropsychological examination of persons with or without known risk factors for brain damage is diagnostically useful if a meaningful pattern of deficits is found. A pattern considered meaningful would be one that may be specific to one, or only a few, diagnoses, such as a pattern of cognitive disruption suggestive of a lateralized or focal brain lesion.

A man with HIV infection had a two-week history of "feeling odd." He became easily lost, even in familiar settings, and complained of an inability to perform a task as simple as making his sheets "fit the bed." He said that he could not read because he was unable to follow a line consistently across the page. He had stopped working as a barber after giving a poor haircut. He had no established symptoms of his infection. Although he was known to have an appropriate reactive depression related to his infection, his complaints were atypical for depression. A neuropsychological evaluation showed that he had severe and circumscribed visuospatial and constructional deficits, a pattern of cognitive deficits usually associated with right parietal dysfunction. A subsequent MRI scan showed white matter disease involving a large area of the right parietal lobe and several small areas elsewhere in the right hemisphere. A biopsy confirmed the diagnosis of multifocal progressive leukoencephalopathy.

Neuropsychological signs and symptoms that are possible indicators of a pathological brain process are presented in Table 7–1. Positive neuropsychological diagnoses are much more likely to be made when risk factors for brain dysfunction exist or signs and symptoms of brain dysfunction are observed than when neuropsychological diagnoses are considered on the basis solely of exclusion of other diagnoses.

One of the greatest challenges for a neuropsychologist is to assess whether patients with psychiatric illness have evidence of an independent underlying brain disorder. Many psychiatric patients without neurological disease have cognitive disruption and behavioral or emotional aberrations. Conversely, neurological disease can present as a psychiatric disorder (Cummings 1999; Skuster et al. 1992). Depressed patients often underperform compared with control subjects on measures of speed of processing, mental flexibility, and executive function (Veiel 1997). Memory impairment is less consistently observed (Basso and Bornstein 1999b; Boone et al. 1995; Palmer et al. 1996), and memory performance may be intact even when memory complaints are present (Dalgleish and Cox 2000; Kalska et al. 1999). Cognitive deficits, including memory, are more common in depressed patients with psychotic features than in those with no psychotic features (Basso and Bornstein 1999a; McKenna et al. 2000). Compared with control subjects, euthymic bipolar patients may have difficulty with attention, memory, abstraction (Denicoff et al. 1999), and executive functions (Ferrier et al. 1999). The degree of cognitive impairment appears to be related to the number of prior episodes (Denicoff et al. 1999; Van Gorp et al. 1998). Although a number of psychological explanations have been proposed, such as self-focused rumination associated with dysphoria (Hertel 1998), the

**TABLE 7–1.** Neuropsychological signs and symptoms that are possible indicators of a pathological brain process

| Functional class | Symptoms and signs |
|---|---|
| Speech and language | Dysarthria |
| | Dysfluency |
| | Marked change in amount of speech output |
| | Paraphasias |
| | Word-finding problems |
| Academic skills | Alterations in reading, writing, frequent letter or number reversals, calculating, and number abilities |
| Thinking | Perseveration of speech |
| | Simplified or confused mental racking, reasoning, and concept formation |
| Motor | Weakness or clumsiness, particularly if lateralized |
| | Impaired fine motor coordination (e.g., changes in handwriting) |
| | Apraxias |
| | Perseveration of action components |
| Memory[a] | Impaired recent memory for verbal or visuospatial material or both |
| | Disorientation |
| Perception | Diplopia or visual field alterations |
| | Inattention (usually left-sided) |
| | Somatosensory alterations (particularly if lateralized) |
| | Inability to recognize familiar stimuli (agnosia) |
| Visuospatial abilities | Diminished ability to perform manual skills (e.g., mechanical repairs and sewing) |
| | Spatial disorientation |
| | Left-right disorientation |
| | Impaired spatial judgment (e.g., angulation of distances) |
| Emotions[b] | Diminished emotional control with temper outburst and antisocial behavior |
| | Diminished empathy or interest in interpersonal relationships |
| | Affective changes |
| | Irritability without evident precipitating factors |
| | Personality change |
| Comportment[b] | Altered appetites and appetitive activities |
| | Altered grooming habits (excessive fastidiousness and carelessness) |
| | Hyperactivity or hypoactivity |
| | Social inappropriateness |

[a]Many emotionally disturbed persons complain of memory deficits, which most typically reflect the person's self-preoccupation, distractibility, or anxiety rather than a dysfunctional brain. Thus, memory complaints in themselves do not necessarily warrant neuropsychological evaluation.
[b]Some of these changes are most likely to be neuropsychologically relevant in the absence of depression, although they can also be mistaken for depression.

possibility has been raised of an underlying structural abnormality in the neural pathways that modulate mood (Ali et al. 2000; Strakowski et al. 1999).

Numerous studies (Heaton et al. 1978; Lenzer 1980) have shown that neuropsychological test scores alone often fail to discriminate between schizophrenic and neurologically impaired patients. Broad cognitive impairment is highly prevalent in schizophrenia (Heinrichs and Zakzanis 1998), particularly for attention, processing speed, memory, problem solving, cognitive flexibility, organization, and planning (Goldman et al. 1996). As for all symptoms of schizophrenia, considerable heterogeneity exists (Binks and Gold 1998; Goldstein et al. 1998), and some individuals appear cognitively normal (Palmer

et al. 1997). Obsessive-compulsive disorders are often accompanied by mild cognitive impairment. Areas of difficulty may include nonverbal memory, use of strategies, visuospatial skills, and selected executive functions (Deckersbach et al. 2000; Mataix-Cols et al. 1999; Savage et al. 2000; Tallis 1997; K.D. Wilson 1998). Both schizophrenia and obsessive-compulsive behavior have been linked to dysfunction of frontal-subcortical circuits (Abbruzzese et al. 1995; Cummings 1999), and temporal lobe structures also have been implicated (Post 2000; Strange 1992).

Although neuropsychological assessment provides a measure of the type and degree of cognitive disorder, it often cannot specify the cause of the disturbance. In the absence of known or suspected brain disorder, a patient diagnosed with a psychiatric condition and nonspecific cognitive impairment is most likely experiencing cognitive disruption on the basis of the psychiatric condition. On the other hand, cognitive deficits appearing in an adult patient who previously functioned well and has no history of psychiatric illness or recent stress should raise suspicions of a neurological disorder.

## Role of the Referring Psychiatrist

The referring psychiatrist has the tasks of identifying patients who might benefit from an evaluation, preparing the patient, and formulating referral questions that best define the needed neuropsychological information. A valid evaluation depends on obtaining the patient's best performance. It is nearly impossible to obtain satisfactory evaluations of patients who are uncooperative, fatigued, actively psychotic, seriously depressed, or highly anxious. For example, seriously depressed patients may appear to have dementia and the evaluation may underestimate the individual's full potential (Chaves and Izquierdo 1992; King and Caine 1996; Marcopulos 1989; Yousef et al. 1998). Whenever possible, severely depressed or actively psychotic patients should be referred after there has been clinical improvement, when the results may be more representative of the patient's true ability uncontaminated by reversible emotional or behavioral disturbances.

To obtain the patient's cooperation and alleviate unnecessary anxiety, it is important to prepare the patient for the evaluation (Lezak 1995). The patient should understand the purpose and nature of the evaluation. The explanation usually includes a statement that the evaluation is requested to assess how the brain is functioning by looking at activities that the brain processes such as mental abilities. In most cases, patients should know that the purpose of the evaluation is to look for mental and emotional strengths as well as problem areas to obtain information that will assist in counseling and planning.

The more explicit the referral question, the more likely it is that the evaluation will be conducted to provide the needed information. The referral question should include

- Identifying information about the patient
- The reasons why the evaluation is requested
- A description of the problem to be assessed
- Pertinent history

The neuropsychologist will design a different examination when the referral question asks whether the patient is a candidate for psychotherapy than when an evaluation is requested for a personal injury lawsuit. Some appropriate referrals seek behavioral descriptions, such as "Does this individual who has multiple sclerosis show evidence of cognitive deficits and, if so, what are they? Could they interfere with treatment compliance?" Other referral questions may be framed around problems with patient management, counseling, and educational or vocational planning. In some instances, the neuropsychologist may identify a problem—or competencies—that negates the referral question, in which case the experienced neuropsychologist will reformulate the examination goals to conform to the needs of the patient in the light of the original referral question (e.g., Lezak 1995, pp 125–126).

## The Assessment Process

Interview and observation are the chief means by which neuropsychological evaluations are conducted. The interview provides the basis of the evaluation (Christensen 1979; Lezak 1995; Luria 1980; Sbordone 2000). The main purposes are to elicit the patient's and family's complaints, understand the circumstances in which these problems occur, and evaluate the patient's attitude toward these problems. Understanding the range of the patient's complaints, as well as which ones the patient views as most troublesome, contributes to the framework on which the assessment and recommendations are based. A thorough history of complaints and pertinent background is essential.

The presenting problems and the patient's attitude toward them also may provide important diagnostic information. Patients with certain neuropsychological conditions lack awareness of their problems or belittle their significance (Markova and Berrios 2000; Prigatano and Schacter 1991). Many patients with right hemisphere stroke, Alzheimer's disease, and frontal lobe damage are unaware of or unable to appreciate the problems resulting from their brain injury. In the extreme form of right hemisphere stroke, some patients with hemiplegia are unable to comprehend that the left side of their body is part of them, let alone that they cannot use it. In a more muted form, many patients with dementia attribute their memory problems to aging and minimize their significance (see Strub and Black 2000). Conversely, patients, families, or caregivers sometimes attribute problems to brain damage when a careful history suggests otherwise.

The interview provides an opportunity to observe the patient's appearance, attention, speech, thought content, and motor abilities and to evaluate affect, appropriateness of behavior, orientation, insight, and judgment. The interview can provide information about the patient's premorbid intellectual ability and personality, occupational and school background, social situation, and ability to use leisure time.

The tests used by neuropsychologists are simply standardized observation tools that, in many instances, have the added advantage of providing normative data that aid in interpreting the observations. A variety of assessment approaches are available, but they all have in common the goals of determining whether the patient shows evidence of brain dysfunction and identifying the nature of problems detected. The two main approaches are individually tailored examinations and fixed assessment procedures. The former is often referred to as the *hypothesis-testing* approach, because test selection is based on hypotheses about the cause and nature of the brain dysfunction from information acquired before and during the assessment (Kaplan 1988; Lezak 1995; Milberg et al. 1996). Using this approach, information is obtained about the individual's medical and psychological background and about the patient's activities from the individual and other knowledgeable sources. Hypotheses regarding neuropsychological deficits are generated and tested. For example, the case may involve an individual known to have had a heart attack who sustained brief and unremarked hypoxia. The family reports that the individual appears depressed, as he sits all day without showing an interest in other people or activities. Several hypotheses could be generated from this information to explain the behavior. The patient may indeed be depressed. Alternatively, the individual may have inertia secondary to cerebral damage. The examiner may decide to include tests that are relatively unstructured and require the patient's initiation and de novo organization. Other hypotheses that might be considered and tested include that the patient is confused and unable to respond to the situations that the family describe; or that the patient has serious memory difficulties that interfere with his intention to initiate or maintain ongoing activities.

The more information that can be gained before the assessment procedure begins, the more efficiently specific hypotheses can be generated. Moreover, hypothesis testing continues throughout the assessment. When a problem is observed on a particular test, new hypotheses are generated or old ones are modified with regard to the nature of the observed problem. Typically the examination focuses on the problem areas while briefly screening other areas that appear to be relatively intact, except when detailed information about residual competencies is required, as when developing a remediation program.

A second approach to neuropsychological testing is to use a fixed battery of tests (Broshek and Barth 2000; Reitan and Wolfson 1993). This approach involves examining the same range of cognitive and behavioral functioning in every individual. It is analogous to a physician conducting a standard physical examination on all patients. These fixed battery examinations frequently last from 6 to 8 hours. The advantage of fixed batteries is that the patient has a fairly broad-based examination. The consistency of the administration procedures and normative data, and the relatively wide range of data, make batteries useful for research purposes. Although these advantages might lure the examiner, this fixed approach does not focus on specific areas of difficulty. In some cases it might be unclear why performance is impaired without additional testing outside of the battery. Time may be wasted in testing areas of cognition or sensorimotor functioning that are not problems, and subtle problems can be overlooked. Moreover, aspects of neuropsychological functioning not included in a fixed battery will not be examined. In this era of tightening health care budgets, it is necessary that good neuropsychological service be provided at reasonable cost. Tailoring the examination to the patient's requirements rather than using a fixed battery allows the examiner to learn what is needed about the patient with a minimum of time and cost.

Cognitive performance is only one aspect of an assessment. A full evaluation of the individual assesses emotional and social characteristics as well. Many patients with brain injuries have changes in personality, mood, or ability to control emotional states (Heilman et al. 1993; Lishman 1997) and problems with social relationships (Dikmen et al. 1996; Lezak 1988a). Depression is a common and sometimes serious complication of brain disease. An unusually high incidence of depression occurs with certain neurodegenerative disorders, such as Parkinson's disease and Huntington's disease (see Lerner and Whitehouse, Chapter 28, in this volume). Other neurological diseases in which depression is common are tumors (particularly those of the orbitofrontal and temporoparietal cortex), multiple sclerosis, Wilson's disease, HIV encephalopathy, Alzheimer's disease, vascular dementia, and Lewy body dementia (Cummings 1994). At least 30% of stroke patients experience depression (Paradiso et al. 1997; Pohjasvaara et al. 1998). Factors that appear to determine the presence of depression include the location of the brain injury, degree of disability, and level of social activity (Gustafson et al. 1995; Robinson 1998). In some cases these changes may be secondary to cognitive impairment (Andersen et al. 1995). Patients who have had a right hemisphere stroke may show impaired processing of emotional material and complex social situations, which leads to interpersonal problems (Lezak 1994). Although the history and observers' reports will inform the examiner of changes in these characteristics, current emotional status and personality can also be evaluated by standard psychological tests (Gass 1992; Lezak 1995).

As computers have become valuable aids in many fields, there has been increasing interest in using computerized testing procedures (Adams and Brown 1986; Curtis-Prior 1996; Kane and Kay 1992; Lezak 1988c). This technology offers the possibility of obtaining test results under highly standardized conditions with minimal time expenditure by the examiner. These features make it valuable in circumstances where large numbers of individuals need to be screened for potential problems. Computers also have timing and scoring features and can plot the data graphically. In addition, computer programs are available in some cases for interpreting test responses. The Minnesota Multiphasic Personality Inventory–2 (MMPI-2) is available with computer scoring and, if purchased separately, interpretation (Butcher 1989). Computerized interpretations of the MMPI-2 and other tests presumably provide the most common interpretations of test patterns but are not applicable to every case, especially for individuals with brain disorders (Cripe 1999). Therefore, they should be used only as a source of hypotheses about individuals to be confirmed or negated by data from other sources (Butcher et al. 2000).

Although many adults with brain injuries can tolerate responding to the computer format, and some may even enjoy it, these methods lose important information about the way the individual approaches cognitive tasks or why errors are made unless the examiner monitors the process (Lezak 1995). Some brain-damaged patients are impulsive and others overly cautious. Either factor could greatly alter a test score without providing information about the particular function that is the object of investigation.

## The Nature of Neuropsychological Tests

An important component of neuropsychological evaluations is psychological testing, in which an individual's cognitive and often emotional status and executive functioning are assessed. Neuropsychological assessment differs from psychological assessment in its basic assumptions. The latter compares the individual's responses with normative data from a sample of healthy individuals taking the same test (Anastasi and Urbina 1997). The neuropsychological assessment of adults relies on compari-

sons between the patient's present level of functioning and the known or estimated level of premorbid functioning based on demographically similar individuals and current performance on tests of functions less likely to be affected by brain disorders. Thus, much of clinical neuropsychological assessment involves *intraindividual* comparisons of the abilities and skills under consideration.

Two types of standardized neuropsychological tests are available. Some tests are constructed of cognitive or sensorimotor tasks that can be accomplished by all intact adults within the culture. They are designed so that all individuals are expected to be able to perform the task, and thus failure to do so may be interpreted as impairment. Examples of this approach include many aphasia tests of basic language skills. Anyone from English-speaking, Western cultural backgrounds would be expected to name, describe, and demonstrate the use of common objects as tested by the Porch Index of Communicative Ability (Porch 1983). The Dementia Rating Scale (Mattis 1988) is based on the assumption that adults will be able to perform most of the cognitive tasks used in this test. The manual specifies the small number of errors considered normal. Most individuals achieve a nearly perfect score on the Mini-Mental State Examination (MMSE) (Folstein et al. 1975).

However, most tests of cognitive abilities are designed with the expectation that only very few persons will obtain a perfect score and most scores will cluster in a middle range. For these tests, scores are conceptualized as continuous variables. The scores of many persons taking the test can be plotted as a distribution curve. Most scores on tests of complex learned behaviors fall into a characteristic bell-shaped curve called a normal distribution curve (Figure 7–1). The statistical descriptors of the curve are the *mean* or average score; the degree of spread of scores about the mean, expressed as the *standard deviation;* and the *range*, or the distance from the highest to the lowest scores.

The level of competence in different cognitive functions as well as other behaviors varies from individual to individual and also within the same individual at different times. This variability also has the characteristics of a normal curve, as in Figure 7–1. Because of the normal variability of performance on cognitive tests, any single score can be considered only as representative of a normal performance range and must not be taken as a precise value. For example, the statistical properties of a score at the 75th percentile (the equivalent of a scaled score of 12 on a test in the Wechsler Intelligence Scale battery) must be understood as likely representing a range of scores from the 50th to the 90th percentile. For this reason, many

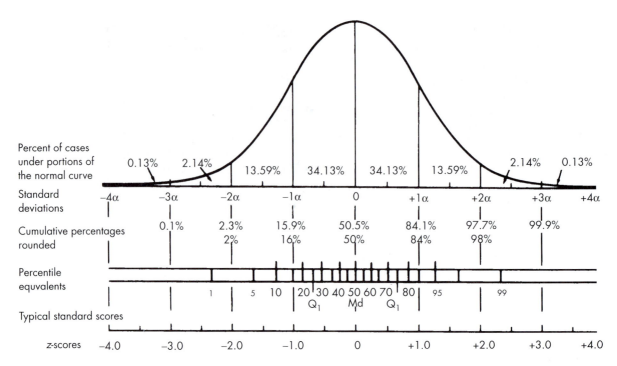

**FIGURE 7–1.**    A normal distribution curve showing the percentage of cases between −4 standard deviation (−σ) and +4 standard deviation (+σ). The average range is defined as −0.6 to +0.6 standard deviation or the 25th to the 75th percentiles.

**TABLE 7–2.**    Ability test classifications expressed as deviations from the mean calculated from the normative sample

| Z score range | Percentile | Classification |
|---|---|---|
| > +2.0 | 98–100 | Very superior |
| +1.3 to +2.0 | 91–97 | Superior |
| +0.67 to +1.3 | 75–90 | High average |
| −0.66 to +0.66 | 26–74 | Average |
| −0.67 to −1.3 | 10–25 | Low average |
| −1.3 to −2.0 | 3–9 | Borderline |
| < −2.0 | 0–2 | Mentally retarded |

neuropsychologists are reluctant to report scores, but rather describe their findings in terms of ability levels. See Table 7–2 for interpretations of ability levels based on deviations from the mean of the normative sample.

An individual's score is compared with the normative data, often by calculating a standard or z score, which describes the individual's performance in terms of statistically regular distances (i.e., standard deviations). In this framework, scores within ±0.66 standard deviation are considered average, since 50% of a normative sample scores within this range. The z scores are used to describe the probability that a deviant response occurs by chance or because of an impairment. A performance in the

below-average direction that is greater than two standard deviations from the mean is usually described as falling in the impaired range because 98% of the normative sample taking the test achieve better scores. Figure 7–2 shows the performance of 34 men with schizophrenia on a set of neuropsychological tests. The z scores are calculated based on the performance of a control group (the 0 line). The patients group had poorer performance than the control group on all measures.

Some test makers recommend "cut" or "cutoff" scores to evaluate certain test performances. The cutoff scores represent those exceeded by most neuropsychologically intact persons; scores below the cutoff point are typically achieved by persons with impairment in the relevant abilities (e.g., Benton et al. 1994). Cutoff scores are usually derived on the basis of the distribution of scores of a healthy control sample. The threshold for normal is typically set at 1.5 standard deviations below the mean to include the top 95% of the normal sample. One difficulty with many fixed cutoff scores is that they are not based on normative samples that are appropriate for the individual being studied. For example, calculation of the cutoff score may not take into account level of education or age (Bornstein 1986; Prigatano and Parsons 1976). A score that is satisfactory for a person of average ability may be unsatisfactory for a person of superior abil-

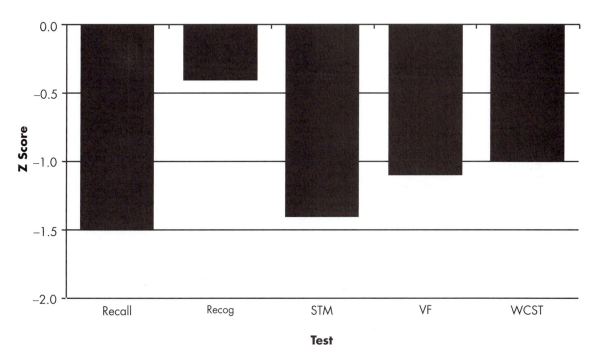

**FIGURE 7–2.** Mean performance of patients with schizophrenia compared with control subjects on cognitive tests: delayed recall of words and stories (Recall); recognition of words when targets were mixed with distractors (Recog); short-term memory (STM) measured by the Brown-Peterson technique; verbal fluency (VF); and Wisconsin Card Sorting Test (WCST) categories achieved.

*Source.* Adapted from Sullivan et al. 1994.

ity. Or the cutoff score may derive from a biased sample, such as unselected psychiatric patients, in whom brain impairment occurs more frequently than in a healthy control group. The use of cutoff scores imposes an artificial dichotomy in describing a performance or ability that is actually a continuous distribution (Dwyer 1996). Cutoff scores work best on tests of abilities normally expected in all adults, such as basic language or motor skills.

Psychological tests should be constructed to have both reliability and validity (Anastasi and Urbina 1997). The reliability of a test refers to the consistency of test scores when the test is given to the same individual at different times or with different sets of equivalent items. As perfect reliability cannot be achieved for any test, each individual score represents a range of variability, which narrows to the degree that the test's reliability approaches the ideal (Anastasi and Urbina 1997). Tests have validity when they measure what they purport to measure. If a test is designed to measure attention disorders, then patient groups known to have attention deficits should perform more poorly on the test than persons from the population at large. Tests also should be constructed with large normative samples of individuals with similar demographic characteristics, particularly for age

and education (Gade et al. 1985; Heaton et al. 1991; Malec et al. 1992). For example, the Wechsler Adult Intelligence Scale–III has normative data for 2,450 adults stratified for age, sex, race, geographic region, occupation, and education according to United States census information (Psychological Corporation 1997). Most tests have much smaller normative samples in the range of 30 to 200 individuals.

Some psychological tests detect subtle deficits better than others. A simple signal detection test of attention, such as crossing out all the letters *A* on a page, is less sensitive a test of attention than a divided attention task, such as crossing out all letters *A* and C. Tests involving complex tasks, such as problem solving requiring abstract thinking and cognitive flexibility, are more sensitive than many other cognitive tests at reflecting brain damage, because a wide variety of brain disorders can easily disrupt performance on them. However, other factors such as depression, anxiety, medicine side effects, and low energy level due to systemic illness may also disrupt cognition on these sensitive tests. Therefore, they are sensitive to cognitive disruption but not specific to one type of cognitive disturbance. The specificity of a test in detecting a disorder depends on the overlap between the distributions of the scores of persons who are intact and of the

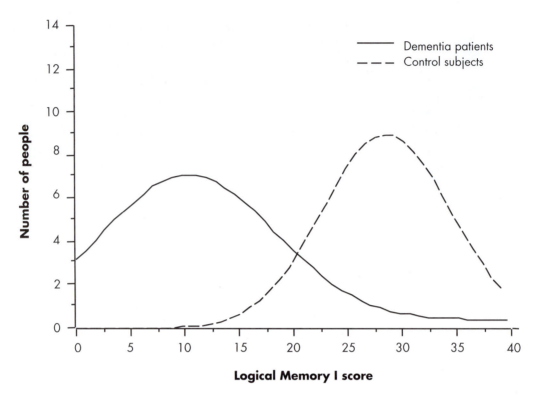

**FIGURE 7–3.**    Distribution of test scores by a group with mild dementia and age-matched control subjects on the Wechsler Memory Scale–Revised Logical Memory I, a story-recall test. Scores ranging from 15 to 39 occurred in both groups, whereas scores below 15 occurred in only the dementia group. The smaller the areas of overlapping curves, the higher the test specificity.

scores of persons who have the disorder (Figure 7–3). The less overlap there is, the more diagnostic the test result. A test that is highly specific, such as the Token Test (Boller and Vignolo 1966; De Renzi and Vignolo 1962), which assesses language comprehension, produces few abnormal test results in nonaphasic persons, that is, few false-positive results. Many neuropsychological tests offer a tradeoff between sensitivity and specificity.

Test selection involves a careful consideration of which tests are most likely to provide useful information. Performance on any test may yield false-positive or false-negative information. Interpretation of neuropsychological tests involves consideration of response patterns by experienced clinicians who can evaluate the data in light of meaningful patterns and inconsistencies.

Indications of brain dysfunction come from qualitative features of the patient's performance as well as from test scores (Lezak 1995; Pankratz and Taplin 1982; K.W. Walsh 1985). There are many ways of failing a test, and a poor score does not tell the means to the end (K.W. Walsh 1987). Occasionally a patient gives a "far out" response to a question. The examiner asks the patient to repeat the question and, often in this circumstance, finds that the patient has misunderstood the question or

instruction rather than lacked the ability to produce a correct response. Some features of behavioral disturbance are best recognized by the manner in which the patient approaches the testing situation or behaves with the examiner. Brain-injured patients are prone to problems with short attention span, distractibility, impulsivity, poor self-monitoring, disorganization, irritability, perplexity, and suspiciousness.

## Interpretation Principles and Cautions

The interpretation of test performance is based on an assumption that the patient is expected to perform in a particular way on tasks; deviations from expectation require evaluation (Lezak 1986, 1995). Most healthy people perform within a statistically definable range on cognitive tests, and this range of performance levels is considered to be characteristic of healthy people. Deviations below this expected range raise the question of an impairment. A person may have scores in the high average range on many tests except for low average performance in one functional area.

A 91-year-old former artist was referred by her family, who asked whether her gradual functional decline was related to aging or to a progressive dementia. Her performance, expressed in z scores, was compared with the scores of neuropsychologically normal persons of her age and educational background. Her scores were within expectation on some tests, including reasoning, constructions, and fund of information, but were deficient on tests of memory and confrontational naming. The deviations were significantly below expectations for her age group. The impaired performance and history were interpreted as supporting a diagnosis of mild dementia. She eventually progressed to show a full dementia syndrome with broad cognitive impairment.

The assumption of deficit is valid in most instances in which one or a set of scores fall significantly below expectations, although a few persons show an unusual variability on cognitive tasks (Matarazzo and Prifitera 1989). Multiple measures involving similar or related abilities increase the reliability of findings. Thus, if a deviant score shows up on one task, other tests requiring similar skills are used to see if the deviant finding persists across tasks. If so, the finding is considered reliable. If similar tasks do not elicit a deviant performance, either the finding was spurious or the additional tasks varied in important features that did not involve the patient's problem area. The need to have multiple measures of many cognitive functions is the reason why neuropsychological examinations may be lengthy.

Interpretation of test performances also must take into account demographic variables. When estimating the premorbid ability levels necessary for making intraindividual comparisons, the patients' educational and occupational background, sex, and race must be considered along with their level of test performance (Lezak 1995; Vanderploeg et al. 1996). The more severely impaired the patients, the more unlikely it is that they will be performing at premorbid levels on any of the tests. This increases the examiner's reliance on demographic and historical data to estimate premorbid functioning. Some tests are fairly resistant to disruption by brain damage and may offer the best estimates of premorbid ability. Good examples are fund of information and reading vocabulary, such as the National Adult Reading Test (NART) (Nelson 1982) and a revision for American English, the NAART (Spreen and Strauss 1998). For meaningful interpretations of neuropsychological test performance, not only do examiners rely on many tests but they search for a performance pattern (test scores plus qualitative features) that makes neuropsychological sense. Because there are few pathognomonic findings in neuropsychology, or in most other branches of medical science for that matter (Sox et al. 1988), a performance

pattern often can suggest several diagnoses. For example, a cluster of documented deficits including slowed thinking and mild impairment of concentration and memory is a nonspecific finding associated with a number of conditions: very mild dementia, a mild post-concussion syndrome, mild toxic encephalopathy, depression, and fatigue, to name a few. Other patterns may be highly specific for certain conditions. The finding of left-sided neglect and visuospatial distortions is highly suggestive of brain dysfunction and specifically occurs with right hemisphere damage. For many neuropsychological conditions, typical deficit patterns are known, allowing the examiner to evaluate the patient's performances in light of these known patterns for a possible match.

The quality of a neuropsychological evaluation depends on many factors. In general, one should beware of conclusions from evaluations in which test scores alone (that is, without information from history, interview, and observations of examination behavior) are used to make diagnostic decisions and of dogmatic statements offered without strongly supportive evidence. It is also important to remember that neuropsychological tests do not measure "brain damage." Rather, the finding of impaired mental functioning implies an underlying brain disorder. It is important to keep in mind that poor performance on neuropsychological tests does not necessarily mean that the patient has a brain disorder. Other possible interpretations may exist.

## Major Test Categories

This section presents a brief review of tests used for assessment of major areas of cognition and personality. Many useful neuropsychological tests are not described in this summary. Please refer to *Neuropsychological Assessment*, 3rd edition (Lezak 1995) for a relatively complete review.

### Mental Ability

The most commonly used set of tests of general intellectual function of adults in the Western world is contained in the various versions of the Wechsler Intelligence Scales (WIS) (Wechsler 1944, 1955, 1981, 1997a). These batteries of brief tests provide scores on a variety of cognitive tasks covering a range of skills. Each version was originally developed as an "intelligence" test to predict academic and vocational performance of neurologically intact adults by giving an IQ (intelligence quotient) score, which is based on the mean performance on the tests in this battery. The entire test battery is frequently among the tests included in a neuropsychological examination. The individual tests were designed to assess relatively distinct areas of cognition, such as arithmetic, abstract thinking, and visuospatial organization, and thus are differentially sensitive to dysfunction of various areas of the brain. Therefore, this test is often used to screen for specific areas of cognitive deficits. When given to neuropsychologically impaired persons, the summary IQ scores can be very misleading because individual test scores lowered by specific cognitive deficits, when averaged in with scores relatively unaffected by the brain dysfunction, can result in IQ scores associated with ability levels that represent neither the severity of deficits nor the patient's residual competencies (Lezak 1988b).

For example, a patient with a visuospatial deficit consisting of an inability to appreciate the structure of visual patterns would have difficulty performing the Block Design test, which requires copying pictured designs with blocks. When such a patient performs well above average on other tests, a summation of all the scores would both hide the important data and be lower than the other test scores in the battery would warrant. Therefore, neuropsychologists focus on the pattern of the Wechsler scores rather than the summed or average performance on all the tests in the battery.

In some cases neuropsychologists have used discrepancies between summed scores on what Wechsler called the Verbal scale of the WIS (i.e., Verbal IQ) and summed scores on the so-called Performance scale (Performance IQ) to indicate a specific area of cognitive deficit. The procedure has developed because there is a tendency for left-hemisphere lesions to produce a relatively depressed Verbal IQ, whereas both right-hemisphere lesions and diffuse damage, as in dementia or any problem resulting in response slowing, produce a depressed Performance IQ. Even this amount of summation can mask important data (Bornstein 1983; Crawford 1992, pp 31–32; Grossman 1983; Larrabee 1986). In the example above, impaired performance on one subtest would not be likely to produce sufficient relative lowering of the Performance IQ to detect the cognitive deficit. Moreover, the Arithmetic and Digit Span tests of the Verbal scale are very sensitive to attentional deficits, and only three of the Performance Scale measures involve motor response: one (Picture Completion) calls for a purely verbal response and loads significantly on the verbal factor in factor analytic studies. Many neuropsychologists use and interpret these tests discretely, administering only those deemed relevant for each patient and treating the findings as they treat data obtained from individually developed tests.

A similar battery for assessing children is the Wechsler Intelligence Scale for Children–III (WISC-III) (Wechsler 1991). It contains tests similar to those in the Wechsler Adult Intelligence Scale–III but appropriate for ages 6–16 years.

## Language

Lesions to the hemisphere dominant for speech and language, which is the left hemisphere in 95%–97% of right-handed persons and 60%–70% of left-handed persons (Corballis 1991; Strauss and Goldsmith 1987), can produce any of a variety of disorders of symbol formulation and use, the aphasias (see Cummings and Mendez, Chapter 15, in this volume). Although many aphasiologists argue against attempting to classify all patients into one of the standard aphasia syndromes because of individual differences, persons with aphasia tend to be grouped according to whether the main disorder is in language comprehension (receptive aphasia), expression (expressive aphasia), repetition (conduction aphasia), or naming (anomic aphasia). Many comprehensive language assessment tests are available, such as the Multilingual Aphasia Examination (Benton and Hamsher 1989). Comprehensive aphasia test batteries are best administered by speech pathologists or other clinicians with special training in this field. These batteries usually include measures of spontaneous speech, speech comprehension, repetition, naming, reading, and writing.

Test selection may be based on whether the information is to be used for diagnostic, prognostic, or rehabilitation purposes. For example, the Boston Diagnostic Aphasia Examination (BDAE) (Goodglass and Kaplan 1987) might be selected as an aid for treatment planning because of its wide scope and sensitivity to different aphasic characteristics. The Porch Index of Communicative Ability (PICA) (Porch 1983) best measures treatment progress because of its sensitivity to small changes in performance. A language screening examination is the Bedside Evaluation Screening Test, 2nd Edition (BEST-2) (West et al. 1998). This approximately 20-minute examination provides measures of comprehension, talking, and reading.

## Attention and Mental Tracking

A frequent consequence of brain disorders is slowed thinking and impaired ability for focused behavior (Gronwall and Sampson 1974; Van Zomeren and Brouwer 1994). Damage to the brain stem or diffuse damage involving the cerebral hemispheres can produce a variety of attentional deficits, and attentional deficits are common in neuropsychiatric disorders. Many neuropsychological assessments will include measures of these abilities. The Wechsler scales contain several. The Digit Span test measures attention span or short-term memory for numbers by assessing forward digit repetition. The task also measures backward digit repetition, which is a more demanding task requiring concentration and mental tracking. It is not uncommon for severely brain damaged patients to perform poorly only on the backward repetition portion of this test. Because Digits Forward and Digits Backward measure different functions, assessment data for each should be given separately. The Digit Symbol test also requires concentration and both motor and mental speed for successful performance. The patient must accurately and rapidly code numbers into symbols. Another commonly used measure of concentration and mental tracking is the Trail Making Test (Armitage 1946). In the first part of this test (part A), the patient is asked to draw rapidly and accurately a line connecting in sequence a random display of numbered circles on a page. The level of difficulty is increased in the second part (part B) by having the patient again sequence a random display of circles, this time alternating numbers and letters (Figure 7–4). This test requires concentration, visual scanning, and flexibility in shifting cognitive sets and, as such, it is among those that are most sensitive to the presence of brain injury (Crockett et al. 1988; Spreen and Benton 1965; Van Zomeren and Brouwer 1994). However, it shares with other highly sensitive tests vulnerability to many other kinds of deficits such as motor slowing, which could be based on peripheral factors such as nerve damage, and diminished visual acuity. It is also sensitive to educational deprivation and cannot be used with persons not accustomed to the alphabet as known in Western countries.

In cases of subtle brain injury, assessment sensitivity can be increased by selecting a more difficult measure of concentration and mental tracking in which material must be held in mind while information is manipulated for the performance of such complex cognitive activities as comprehension, learning, and reasoning. Performance on the orally administered Arithmetic test provides information about attention deficits, as it requires intact auditory attention span and mental tracking for success. When patients perform poorly on the WIS Arithmetic test, the examiner must determine whether the failure results from attentional deficits or lack of arithmetic skills. The ability to hold information in mind while performing a mental task is called working memory (Baddeley 1994). As such, working memory requires attention and short-term memory. The Self Ordered Pointing Task (Petrides and Milner 1982; Spreen and Strauss 1998) instructs patients to point to one item in a set ranging from 6 to 18 varied items. On each trial, in which the

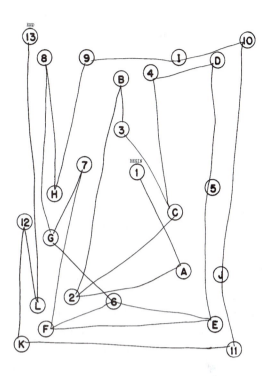

**FIGURE 7–4.** Trail Making Test (Armitage 1946) part B performance by a 61-year-old man with normal-pressure hydrocephalus. Two types of errors are demonstrated: erroneous sequencing (1→A→2→C) and failure to alternate between numbers and letters (D→5→E→F).

positions of the items are randomly changed, patients are told to point to a different item that they had not previously pointed to, and then another, until they had pointed to all the items. The successful performance of this working memory task depends on keeping in mind which items have already been eliminated. Another example of a difficult attentional task is the Paced Auditory Serial Addition Test (PASAT) (Gronwall 1977; Gronwall and Sampson 1974). The patient is required to add consecutive pairs of numbers rapidly under an interference condition. As numbers are presented at a fixed rate, the patient must always add the last two numbers presented and ignore the number that represents the last summation. For example, if the numbers "3–5–2–7" are presented, the patient must respond "8" after the number 5, and then "7" after the number 2, and then "9." It is a difficult test of divided attention because of the strong tendency to add the last number presented to the last summation. The level of difficulty can be heightened by speeding up the rate of presentation of numbers.

## Memory

Memory is another cognitive function frequently impaired by brain disorders (see Stern and Sackeim,

Chapter 17, in this volume). Many diffuse brain injuries produce general impairments in abilities for new learning and retention. Many focal brain injuries also produce memory impairment; left-hemisphere lesions are most likely to produce primarily verbal memory deficits, whereas visuospatial memory impairments tend to be associated with right-hemisphere lesions (Milner 1978; Ojemann and Dodrill 1985). Memory impairment often is a prominent feature of herpes encephalitis, Huntington's chorea, Korsakoff's syndrome, hypoxia, closed head injury, and a variety of neurological degenerative diseases such as Alzheimer's disease (Baddeley et al. 1995; Butters and Miliotis 1985; Kapur 1988; Mayes 2000).

In most cases of brain injury, memory for information learned before the injury is relatively preserved compared with new learning. For this reason, many patients with memory impairment will perform relatively well on tests of fund of information or recall of remote events. However, amnesic disorders can produce a retrograde amnesia, with loss of memory extending weeks, months, or years before the onset of the injury. Electroconvulsive therapy can also produce retrograde amnesia (Squire et al. 1975). The retrograde amnesia of Huntington's chorea or Korsakoff's syndrome can go back for decades (Butters and Miliotis 1985; Cermak 1982). In rare cases, a patient will have retrograde amnesia without significant anterograde amnesia, that is, new learning ability remains intact (Kapur et al. 1996; Reed and Squire 1998). Isolated retrograde amnesia may include amnesia for autobiographical events (Della Sala et al. 1993; Evans et al. 1996; Kapur 1997; Levine et al. 1998). However, cases of amnesia for personal identity often have a psychogenic cause (Hodges 1991).

The Wechsler Memory Scale (WMS) batteries (Wechsler 1987, 1997b) are the most commonly used set of tests of new learning and retention in the United States. These batteries are composed of a variety of tests measuring free recall or recognition of both verbal and visual material. In addition, these tests include measures of recall of personal information and attention, concentration, and mental tracking. Several of the tests provide measures of both immediate and delayed (approximately 30 minutes) recall.

Other memory tests frequently used include word-list learning tasks, such as the Rey Auditory Verbal Learning Test (Lezak 1995; Rey 1964; Schmidt 1996) or the California Verbal Learning Test (Delis et al. 1983, 1986, 1987), and visuospatial tasks such the Complex Figure Test (Mitrushina et al. 1999; Osterrieth 1944; Rey 1941; Spreen and Strauss 1998). When patients are unable to produce verbal responses or use their preferred hand for producing drawings, recognition memory tests requiring a simple "yes" or "no" response are useful. Representative of these learning tests are the Continuous Visual Memory Test (Trahan and Larrabee 1988) and the Recognition Memory Test (Warrington 1984).

## Perception

Perception arising from any of the sensory modalities can be affected by brain disease. Perceptional inattention (sometimes called neglect) is one of the major perceptual syndromes because of its frequency in association with focal brain damage (Bisiach and Vallar 1988; Heilman et al. 2000b; Rafal 2000; Lezak 1994). This phenomenon involves diminished or absent awareness of stimuli in one side of personal space by a patient with an intact sensory system. Unilateral inattention is often most prominent immediately after acute-onset brain injury such as stroke. Most commonly seen is left-sided inattention associated with right-hemisphere stroke.

Several techniques can be used to detect unilateral inattention. Visual inattention can be assessed by using a Line Bisection Test (Schenkenberg et al. 1980), in which the patient is asked to bisect a series of lines on a page, or by using a cancellation task requiring the patient to cross out a designated symbol distributed among other similar symbols on a page (Bisiach and Vallar 1988; Mesulam 2000). A commonly used test for tactile inattention is the Face-Hand Test (G. Berg et al. 1987; Smith 1983). The patient is instructed to indicate with the eyes closed whether points on the face (cheeks) or hands or both are touched by the examiner. Each side is touched singly and then in combination with the other side, such as left cheek and right hand. The patient should have no difficulty reporting a single point of stimulation. Failure to report stimulation to one side when both sides are stimulated is referred to as tactile inattention or double simultaneous extinction.

The most commonly used forms of perceptual tests assess perceptual discrimination among similar stimuli. These visual tests may include discrimination of geometric forms, angulation, color, faces, or familiar objects (Lezak 1995; McCarthy and Warrington 1990; Newcombe and Ratcliff 1989). Some perceptual tasks assess the patient's perceptual synthesis ability. The Hooper Visual Organization Test (Hooper 1958) presents line drawings of familiar objects in fragmented, disarranged pieces and asks for the name of each object. Many of these tests can also be administered in tactile version (Craig 1985; Van Lancker et al. 1989; Varney 1986). Frequently used tactile tests include form recognition and letter or number recognition (Reitan and Wolfson 1993).

Another important area of perceptual assessment is recognition of familiar visual stimuli. Although the syndromes are rare and often occur independently of one another, a brain injury can produce an inability to recognize visually familiar objects (visual object agnosia) or faces (prosopagnosia) (Benson 1989; Damasio et al. 1989; McCarthy and Warrington 1990). Assessment involves testing the recognition—often in the form of naming—of real objects or representations of objects, sometimes in a masked or distorted form. The WIS batteries include a perceptual task in which the subject must identify missing features of line drawings of familiar objects.

Some patients with brain injury have difficulty discriminating sounds even without primary auditory deficits or aphasia. Therefore, tests have been devised to measure discrimination of speech sound (Benton et al. 1994; Wepman and Reynolds 1987) and nonsymbolic sound patterns (Seashore et al. 1960). Discrimination of speech tends to be associated with left temporal lobe lesions, whereas nonsymbolic sounds such as sirens, bells, and doors closing seem to be associated with right temporal lobe lesions (Milner 1971; Polster and Rose 1998). In interpreting patients' performances on certain tests involving auditory discrimination, the examiner must be sensitive to the possible effects of attentional deficits, as low scores on these tests can result from a constricted auditory span or compromised ability to concentrate. This potential for misinterpretation of examination findings is always present and is one of the reasons that valid neuropsychological assessment requires knowledgeable and experienced examiners.

## Praxis

Many patients with left-hemisphere damage have at least one form of apraxia, and apraxia is common in progressed stages of Alzheimer's disease, Parkinson's disease, Pick's disease, and progressive supranuclear palsy (Dobigny-Roman et al. 1998; Fukui et al. 1996; Leiguarda et al. 1997). Inability to perform the required sequence of motor activities is not based on motor weakness. Rather, the deficit is in planning and carrying out the required activities (De Renzi et al. 1983; Heilman et al. 2000a; Jason 1990) and is associated with disruption of neural representations for extrapersonal (e.g., spatial location) and intrapersonal (e.g., hand position) features of movement (Haaland et al. 1999). Tests for apraxia assess the patient's ability to reproduce learned movements of the face or limbs. These learned movements can include the use of objects (usually pantomime use of objects) and gestures (Goodglass and Kaplan 1987; Rothi et al. 1997;

Strub and Black 2000), or sequences of movements demonstrated by the examiner (Christensen 1979; Haaland and Flaherty 1984).

## Constructional Ability

Although constructional problems were once considered a form of apraxia, more recent analysis has shown that the underlying deficits involve impaired appreciation of one or more aspects of spatial relationships. These can include distortions in perspective, angulation, size, and distance judgment. Thus, unlike apraxias, the problem is not an inability to draw lines or assemble constructions, but rather misperceptions and misjudgments involving spatial relationships. Neuropsychological assessments may include any of a number of measures of visuospatial processing. Patients may be asked to copy geometric designs, such as the Complex Figure (Mitrushina et al. 1999; Osterrieth 1944; Rey 1941; Spreen and Strauss 1998) presented in Figure 7–5 or one of the alternate forms (Loring et al. 1988; Meador et al. 1993; Taylor 1979). The WIS battery includes constructional tasks involving reconstructing designs with blocks and assembling puzzle pieces (Wechsler 1944, 1955, 1981, 1997a). Lesions of the posterior cerebral cortex cause the greatest difficulty with constructions, and right-hemisphere lesions produce greater deficits than left-hemisphere lesions (Benton and Tranel 1993).

## Conceptual Functions

Tests of concept formation measure aspects of thinking including reasoning, abstraction, and problem solving. Conceptual dysfunction tends to occur with serious brain injury regardless of site. Most neuropsychological tests require that simple conceptual functioning be intact. For example, reasoning skills are required for the successful performance of most WIS tests: Comprehension assesses commonsense verbal reasoning and interpretation of proverbs; Similarities measures ability to make verbal abstractions by asking for similarities between objects or concepts; Arithmetic involves arithmetic problem solving; Picture Completion requires perceptual reasoning; Picture Arrangement examines sequential reasoning for thematic pictures; Block Design and Object Assembly test visuospatial analysis and problem solving of block designs and puzzles; and Matrix Reasoning depends on pattern, spatial, and numerical relationships.

Other commonly used tests of concept formation include the Category Test (Halstead 1947) and the Wisconsin Card Sorting Test (WCST) (E.A. Berg 1948; D.A. Grant and Berg 1948; Spreen and Strauss 1998). These

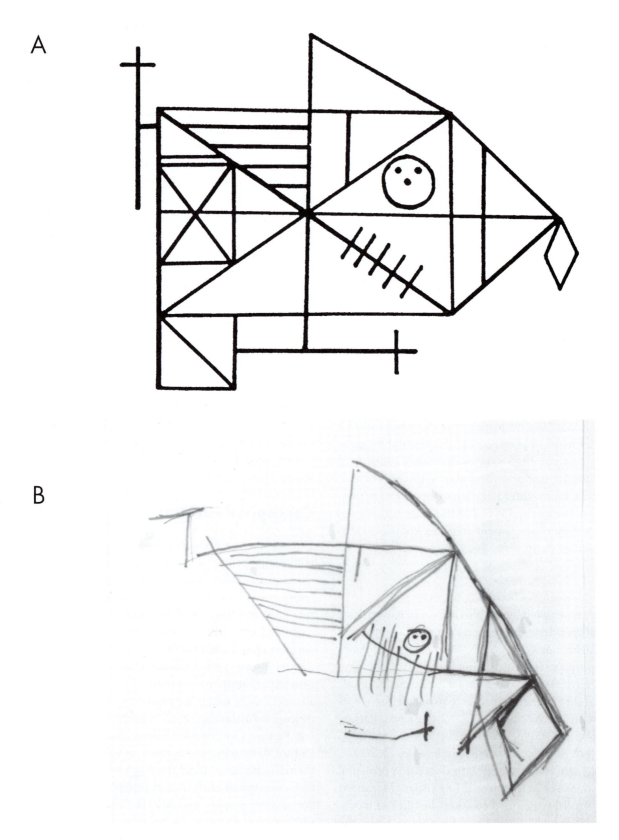

**FIGURE 7–5.**    Rey Complex Figure (*Panel A*) and copy (*Panel B*) drawn by a 42-year-old, right-handed man who had a right frontoparietal stroke 4 days before this examination. The copy shows the patient's neglect of the left and lower portions of the figure, a strong perseverative tendency, and visuospatial fragmentation.

tests measure concept formation, hypothesis testing, problem solving, and flexibility of thinking. The Category Test presents patterns of stimuli and requires the patient to figure out a principle or concept that is true for each item within the set based on feedback about the correctness of each response. The patient is told that the correct principle may be the same for all sets or different for each set. For example, the correct principle in one set is position (first, second, etc.) of the stimulus on the page, whereas for another it is the number of items on the page.

The WCST is similar to the Category Test in requiring the patient to figure out a principle that is true for items within a set. This test differs in several ways. One of the main ways is that without warning the patient, the examiner changes the correct principle as the test proceeds. Therefore, the patient must figure out independently that a shift in principles has occurred and act accordingly.

Tests of conceptualization and reasoning illustrate some of the interpretation problems inherent in most neuropsychological tests because they require complex mental activity. Thus, patients with recent memory disorders and those who are highly distractible may be able to solve the conceptual problems presented by these tests but fail because of inability to keep the correct solution in mind (e.g., see Parsons 1975).

## Executive Functions

Executive functions include abilities to formulate a goal, to plan, to carry out goal-directed plans effectively, and to monitor and self-correct spontaneously and reliably (Lezak 1982). These are difficult tasks for many patients with frontal lobe or diffuse brain injuries (Luria 1980). Yet they are essential for fulfilling most adult responsibilities and maintaining socially appropriate conduct. Tasks that best assess executive functions are tests of planning and/or are open-ended tests that permit the patient to decide how to perform the task and when it is complete. The Bender-Gestalt (Bender 1938), a favorite old neuropsychological test, requires foresight to arrange nine drawings on a single page so that space is well used. Another type of test that requires planning is a maze. The patient must plan an exit from the maze, which involves foresight to minimize trial-and-error behavior. The Tower of London (Shallice 1982) and Tower of Hanoi tests also assess planning and foresight, as disks are moved from stack to stack to reach a stated goal. Patients with frontal lobe lesions have particular difficulty with planning tests (Carlin et al. 2000; Goel and Grafman 1995). Other tasks that rely heavily on planning for successful comple-

tion are multistep tasks calling for decision making or priority-setting abilities. Few neuropsychological tests are specifically designed to assess these aspects of behavior, yet many complex tasks depend on this analysis.

One example of a priority-setting task is the Twenty Questions test, which is known as a popular game. In the test version (Laine and Butters 1982), the patient is shown an array of 48 drawings of familiar objects and told to identify the one the examiner is thinking of by asking only "yes/no" questions. The goal is to identify the specified objects with as few questions as possible. The quality of the questions asked varies according to the number of objects they include or exclude as a possible target. Many patients with frontal-lobe injuries begin questioning with low-priority questions or even by asking whether the target is a specific object (Upton and Thompson 1999). Frontal-lobe injury patients also can have difficulty with the conceptual requirement of the test, because high-priority questions are more abstract. Detoxified alcoholics also have difficulty on this task (Laine and Butters 1982).

Inertia presents one of the most difficult assessment problems for neuropsychologists. There are few open-ended tests that measure initiation or ability to carry out purposeful behavior. By their very nature, most tests are structured and require little initiation by the patient (Lezak 1982). Examples of less structured tests include the Tinkertoy Test, in which the patient decides what to build and how to design it (Bayless et al. 1989; Lezak 1982). Because there are few rules, the patient's level of productivity on this task typically reflects his or her level of productivity in the real world (Lezak 1995). Tests of verbal fluency are used to measure initiation of concepts and persistence on a task. Patients are asked to name as many items as they can in a category, such as animals, or produce as many words as they can beginning with a specified letter of the alphabet (Mitrushina et al. 1999; Spreen and Strauss 1998). These tasks are performed best if the examinee initiates effective and varied strategies.

## Motor Functions

Neuropsychological tests can supplement the neurological examination of motor functions by providing standardized measures of motor activities. Normative data have been acquired for commonly measured functions such as grip strength and finger tapping; more complex tests of fine motor coordination include tests that require patients to rapidly place pegs in holes, such as the Grooved Pegboard Test (Mitrushina et al. 1999) and the Purdue Pegboard Test (Spreen and Strauss 1998). These tests examine absolute performance as well as comparing the preferred hand against the nonpreferred hand to measure the possibility of lateralized motor deficit.

## Personality and Emotional Status

Numerous questionnaires have been devised to measure symptoms of physical and emotional distress of patients with neurological or medical problems (Lezak 1989). As examples, the Neurobehavioral Rating Scale (H.S. Levin et al. 1987) is an examiner-rated measure of problems commonly associated with head trauma, and the Mayo-Portland Adaptability Inventory (MPAI) provides for ratings from clinicians, the patient, and patient family members (Malec et al. 2000).

Many tests devised to measure psychological distress or psychiatric illness have been used with persons with brain disorders. The Symptom Check List (SCL-90-R) (Derogatis 1983) is a self-report of symptoms associated with psychiatric disorders when they occur at high frequency levels. The MMPI (Dahlstrom et al. 1975; Hathaway and McKinley 1951; G.S. Welsh and Dahlstrom 1956) and the revised version, called the MMPI-2 (Butcher 1989; Butcher and Pope 1990; Butcher et al. 1989), have been used extensively with patients with brain disorders (Chelune et al. 1986; Dahlstrom et al. 1975; Mueller and Girace 1988). In general, these patients tend to have elevated MMPI and MMPI-2 profiles, which may reflect the relatively frequent incidence of emotional disturbance (Filskov and Leli 1981), their accurate reporting of symptoms and deficits (Lezak 1995), or their compromised ability to read or understand the test questions. Elevations in scales Hs, Hy, and Sc are common because many "neurological" symptoms appear on these scales (Alfano et al. 1990; Cripe 1999; Gass 1992; Gass and Apple 1997). The interpretation of data from persons with brain disorders must take into account the contributions of neurological symptoms, the patient's emotional reactions to the condition, and the patient's premorbid personality.

Many attempts have been made to use the MMPI to differentiate diagnoses of psychiatric and neurological illness. Results generally have been unsatisfactory, probably because of the extreme variety of brain disorders and their associated problems (Alfano et al. 1990; Lezak 1995; Mueller and Girace 1988). Not surprisingly, the MMPI also has been an inefficient instrument for localizing cerebral lesions (Lezak 1995).

Neuropsychologists are frequently asked to evaluate "psychological overlay" or functional complaints. The diagnostic problem occurs because some individuals may be financially motivated to establish injuries related to work or accidents for which financial compensation may be sought. In addition, some individuals receive emotional or social rewards for invalidism, leading to malingering and functional disabilities. It is difficult to establish with complete certainty that a person's complaints are functional. To add to the complexity of the diagnosis, patients with established brain injury sometime embellish their symptoms, wittingly or unwittingly, so that the range of problems may represent a combination of true deficits and exaggeration. The clinician usually must search for a combination of factors that would support or discredit a functional diagnosis. General factors include evidence of inconsistency in history, reporting of symptoms, or test performance; the individual's emotional predisposition; the probability of secondary gain; and the patient's emotional reactions to his or her complaints, such as the classic *la belle indifférence.*

Psychological tests may be helpful in establishing evidence of exaggeration of symptoms. Responses to the MMPI and MMPI-2 validity scales (L, F, and K) can provide information about the patient's cooperativeness while taking this test and the likelihood that symptoms are exaggerated—or minimized. Because people faking brain damage tend to exaggerate poor performance on testing, another useful diagnostic approach has been The Symptom Validity Test (Pankratz 1979). The fundamental procedure is that the patient's complaints are examined by forcing a response to a simple, two-alternative problem. Using many trials, the examiner can calculate the likelihood that the performance deviates from chance. The validity of memory complaints is tested by the Hiscock and Hiscock Digit Memory Test (Hiscock et al. 1994) by requiring the patient to recall a short series of numbers using a forced-choice, two item recognition task and by the Test of Memory Malingering (TOMM) by asking the patient to choose which pictures had been shown to them previously using a similar forced-choice technique (Spreen and Strauss 1998; Tombaugh 1996).

## Special Assessment Tools

### Batteries

Many neuropsychologists use a formalized battery of tests, in which case they may develop considerable skill and familiarity with this preselected set of tests. The WIS battery of tests, described earlier, is commonly used for this purpose.

Of the commercial batteries designed for neuropsychological evaluations, by far the most popular in the United States is the Halstead-Reitan Battery. This battery was designed to assess frontal lobe disorders by Ward C. Halstead (1947) and was subsequently taken on by Ralph Reitan (1969), who added some tests and recommended this battery as a diagnostic test for all kinds of brain damage. The tests include the Category Test, described earlier; the Tactual Performance Test, a tactile spatial performance and memory test; the Rhythm Test, a nonverbal auditory perception test; the Speech Sounds Perception Test, a phoneme discrimination test; the Finger Tapping Test, a motor speed test; the Trail Making Test, described earlier; the Aphasia Screening Test; a sensory examination; and a measure of grip strength. Examiners using this battery currently administer it with one of the forms of the WIS, the WMS, and the MMPI-2.

A newer "all-purpose" batteries is the Luria-Nebraska Neuropsychological Battery (Golden et al. 1978, 1980), which has generated the greatest controversy because of its many psychometric flaws (Lezak 1988c). It derives its name from the takeover of test items used by the late Russian neurologist and neuropsychologist A.R. Luria and published by A-L Christensen (1979). However, neither Luria nor Christensen advocated the use of a fixed battery. The examiner must be extremely cautious about drawing conclusions based on the scores and indices of this battery (Lezak 1995).

Examinations designed to address specific diagnostic questions are available. Several dementia examinations have been devised. The Dementia Rating Scale (Mattis 1976, 1988) contains items assessing attention, initiation/perseveration, construction, conceptualization, and memory and is useful in distinguishing dementia from cognitive decline associated with aging. A brief examination for dementia by the Consortium to Establish a Registry for Alzheimer's Disease (CERAD) uses the MMSE and tests of category fluency, confrontational naming, verbal learning, and design copy (K.A. Welsh et al. 1992). Batteries designed to assess executive deficits include the Behavioral Assessment of the Dysexecutive Syndrome (BADS) (B.A. Wilson et al. 1998), the Behavioral Dyscontrol Scale (Grigsby et al. 1992), and the Executive Interview (EXIT) (Royall et al. 1992).

## Screening Tests

Many clinicians would like to have a brief, reliable screening examination with good sensitivity for brain damage of unknown cause or when it is only suspected. However, there is a tradeoff between the amount of information obtained in an assessment and its actual usefulness in the detection of brain dysfunction. Brief examinations are often too restricted in range or too simple to be sensitive to subtle or circumscribed areas of dysfunction. The commonly used MMSE contains only 11 simple tasks. It is useful for examining patients with global confusion, poor memory, or dementia. However, many brain-injured patients, such as those with stroke, mild to moderate head injury, and even early dementia, perform adequately on this examination (Benedict and Brandt 1992).

The Neurobehavioral Cognitive Status Examination (NCSE) (Kiernan et al. 1987; Mysiw et al. 1989; Schwamm et al. 1987) takes approximately 30 minutes and contains reasonably difficult items of attention, language comprehension, repetition and naming, constructional ability, memory, calculations, reasoning, and judgment, thereby increasing its sensitivity. It is a screening examination, however, and not a substitute for a thorough neuropsychological examination. It may be used to acquire information to decide whether further evaluation is warranted. As with any screening examination, intact performance does not exclude the possibility of brain dysfunction.

## Competency

A cognitive competency determination is usually based on a specialized interview in which a patient's ability to handle financial matters and/or make decisions regarding his or her well-being is assessed by asking questions about the individual's personal situation. The patient's understanding of his or her personal needs is more relevant to a competency determination than a score on a formal test. Nevertheless, the Cognitive Competency Test (Wang et al. 1986) is a useful component of a competency examination of patients with brain disorders because it evaluates cognitive skills that are required to maintain safe and independent living. The test samples a wide range of cognitive skills varying from overlearned, basic living skills to memory, abstract problem solving, and safety judgment. However, it omits areas that need to be assessed, such as awareness of personal needs and basic current events. A method for assessing patients' consent to medical treatment under different legal standards asks patients to make decisions based their evaluation of the associated risks and benefits of hypothetical medical problems and treatment alternatives (Marson et al. 1995a, 1995b).

## Treatment and Planning

Examination findings are used to assess an individual's strengths and weaknesses and to formulate treatment interventions (Lezak 1987; Raskin and Mateer 1999; Sohlberg and Mateer 1989). Clinical interventions vary according to the individual's specific needs. Many patients with brain disorders have primary or secondary emotional problems for which psychotherapy or counseling is advisable. However, brain-injured patients frequently have problems that require special consideration. Foremost among these problems are cognitive rigidity, impaired learning ability, and diminished self-awareness, any one of which may limit the patient's adaptability and capacity to benefit from rehabilitation. Therefore, neuropsychological evaluations provide important information about treatment possibilities and strategies. The evaluation is also used to consider patients' ability for independence in society and their educational or vocational potential.

## Qualifications for Performing Neuropsychological Evaluations

The field of neuropsychology is enriched by the diversity of areas of expertise of those interested in the study of brain-behavior relationships. Professionals in this field come from backgrounds in psychology, psychiatry, neurology, neurosurgery, and language pathology, to name the most common contributing disciplines. In psychology alone, practitioners come from backgrounds in clinical, cognitive, developmental, and physiological psychology.

Professionals qualified to provide clinical evaluations have both expertise in brain-behaviors relationships and skills in diagnostic assessment and counseling (Bornstein 1988a, 1988b). A growing number of neuropsychologists have qualified for proficiency in this subspecialty area, earning the American Board of Professional Psychology's award of Diploma in Clinical Neuropsychology (Bieliauskas and Matthews 1987).

## References

Abbruzzese M, Bellodi L, Ferri S, et al: Frontal lobe dysfunction in schizophrenia and obsessive-compulsive disorder: a neuropsychological study. Brain Cogn 27:202–212, 1995

Acker MB: A review of the ecological validity of neuropsychological tests, in The Neuropsychology of Everyday Life: Assessment and Basic Competencies. Edited by Tuppert DE, Cicerone KD. Boston, MA, Kluwer, 1989, pp 19–55

Adams KM, Brown GG: The role of the computer in neuropsychological assessment, in Neuropsychological Assessment of Neuropsychiatric Disorders. Edited by Grant I, Adams, KM. New York, Oxford University Press, 1986, pp 87–99

Aine CJ: A conceptual overview and critiques of functional neuroimaging techniques in humans, I: MRI/FMRI and PET. Crit Rev Neurobiol 9:229–309, 1995

Alexopoulos GS, Meyers BS, Young RC, et al: "Vascular depression" hypothesis. Arch Gen Psychiatry 54:915–922, 1997

Alfano DP, Finlayson AJ, Stearns GM, et al: The MMPI and neurologic dysfunction: profile configuration and analysis. Clin Neuropsychol 4:69–79, 1990

Ali SO, Denicoff KD, Altshuler LL, et al: A preliminary study of the relation of neuropsychological performance to neuroanatomic structures in bipolar disorder. Neuropsychiatry Neuropsychol Behav Neurol 13:20–28, 2000

Anastasi A: Psychological Testing, 6th Edition. New York, Macmillan, 1988

Anastasi A, Urbina S: Psychological Testing. Upper Saddle River, NJ, Prentice-Hall, 1997

Andersen G, Vestergaard K, Ingemann-Nielsen M, et al: Risk factors for post-stroke depression. Acta Psychiatr Scand 92:193–198, 1995

Anger WK: Assessment of neurotoxicity in humans, in Neurotoxicology. Edited by Tilson H, Mitchell C. New York, Raven, 1992, pp 363–386

Armitage SG: An analysis of certain psychological tests used for the evaluation of brain injury. Psychological Monographs (No 277) 60:1–48, 1946

Armstrong FD, Thompson RJ Jr, Wang W, et al: Cognitive functioning and brain magnetic resonance imaging in children with sickle cell disease. Neuropsychology Committee of the Cooperative Study of Sickle Cell Disease. Pediatrics 97:864–870, 1996

Astrom M, Adolfsson R, Asplund K: Major depression in stroke patients. A 3-year longitudinal study. Stroke 24:976–982, 1993

Baddeley A: Working memory: the interface between memory and cognition, in Memory Systems 1994. Edited by Schacter DL, Tulving E. Cambridge, MA, MIT Press, 1994, pp 351–367

Baddeley AD, Wilson BA, Watts FN (eds): Handbook of Memory Disorders. Chichester, UK, Wiley, 1995

Basso MR, Bornstein RA: Neuropsychological deficits in psychotic versus nonpsychotic unipolar depression. Neuropsychology 13:69–75, 1999a

Basso MR, Bornstein RA: Relative memory deficits in recurrent versus first-episode major depression on a word-list learning task. Neuropsychology 13:557–563, 1999b

Bayless JD, Varney NR, Roberts RJ: Tinker Toy Test performance and vocational outcome in patients with closed head injuries. J Clin Exp Neuropsychol 11:913–917, 1989

Bender L: A visual motor gestalt test and its clinical use. American Orthopsychiatric Association Research Monographs (No 3), 1938

Benedict RH, Brandt J: Limitation of the Mini-Mental State Examination for the detection of amnesia. J Geriatr Psychiatry Neurol 5:233–237, 1992

Bennett T L, Raymonds MJ: Special issue: mild brain injury. Appl Neuropsychol 4, 1997

Benson DF: Disorders of visual gnosis, in Neuropsychology of Visual Perception. Edited by Brown JW. New York, IRBN Press, 1989, pp 59–76

Benton AL, Hamsher K de S: Multilingual Aphasia Examination. Iowa City, IO, AJA Associates, 1989

Benton AL, Tranel D: Visuoperceptual, visuospatial, and visuoconstructive disorders, in Clinical Neuropsychology. Edited by Heilman KM, Valenstein E. New York, Oxford University Press, 1993, pp 461–497

Benton AL, Silvan AB, Hamsher K de S, et al: Contributions to Neuropsychological Assessment. New York, Oxford University Press, 1994

Berg EA: A simple objective test for measuring flexibility in thinking. J Gen Psychol 39:15–22, 1948

Berg G, Edwards DR, Danzinger WL, et al: Longitudinal change in three brief assessments of SDAT. J Am Geriatr Soc 35:205–212, 1987

Berg RA: Cancer, in Medical Neuropsychology. Edited by Tarter RE, Van Thiel DH, Edwards KL. New York, Plenum, 1988, pp 265–290

Bieliauskas LA, Matthews CG: American Board of Clinical Neuropsychology: policies and procedures. Clin Neuropsychol 1:21–28, 1987

Bigler ED: Neuroimaging in mild TBI, in The Evaluation and Treatment of Mild Traumatic Brain Injury. Edited by Varney NR, Roberts RJ. Hillsdale, NJ, Erlbaum, 1999, pp 63–80

Binder JR, Rao SM, Hammeke TA, et al: Lateralized human brain language systems demonstrated by task subtraction functional magnetic resonance imaging. Arch Neurol 52:593–601, 1995

Binks SW, Gold JJ: Differential cognitive deficits in the neuropsychology of schizophrenia. Clin Neuropsychol 12:8–20, 1998

Bisiach E, Vallar G: Hemineglect in humans, in Handbook of Neuropsychology, Vol 1. Edited by Boller F, Grafman J. Amsterdam, The Netherlands, Elsevier, 1988, pp 195–222

Blain PG, Lane RJM: Neurological disorders, in Textbook of Adverse Drug Reactions, 4th Edition. Edited by Davies DM. Oxford, UK, Oxford University Press, 1991, pp 535–566

Boller F, Vignolo LA: Latent sensory aphasia in hemisphere-damaged patients: an experimental study with the Token Test. Brain 89:815–831, 1966

Boone KB, Lesser IM, Miller BL, et al: Cognitive functioning in older depressed outpatients: relationship of presence and severity of depression to neuropsychological test scores. Neuropsychology 9:390–398, 1995

Bornstein RA: Verbal IQ–Performance IQ discrepancies on the Wechsler Adult Intelligence Scale–Revised in patients with unilateral or bilateral cerebral dysfunction. J Consult Clin Psychol 51:779–780, 1983

Bornstein RA: Classification rates obtained with "standard" cut-off scores on selected neuropsychological measures. J Clin Exp Neuropsychol 8:413–420, 1986

Bornstein RA: Entry into clinical neuropsychology: graduate, undergraduate, and beyond. Clin Neuropsychol 2:213–220, 1988a

Bornstein RA: Reports at the Division 40 Task Force on education, accreditation, and credentialing. Clin Neuropsychol 2:25–29, 1988b

Broshek DK, Barth JT: The Halstead-Reitan Neuropsychological Test Battery, in Neuropsychological Assessment in Clinical Practice. Edited by Groth-Marnet G. New York, Wiley, 2000, pp 223–262

Butcher JN: User's Guide for the MMPI-2 Minnesota Report: Adult Clinical System. Minneapolis, MN, National Computer Systems, 1989

Butcher JN, Pope KS: MMPI-2: a practical guide to clinical, psychometric, and ethical issues. Independent Practitioner 10:20–25, 1990

Butcher JN, Dahlstrom WG, Graham JR, et al: Minnesota Multiphasic Personality Inventory: (MMPI-2): Manual for Administration and Scoring. Minneapolis, MN, University Minnesota Press, 1989

Butcher JN, Perry JN, Atlis MM: Validity and utility of computer-based test interpretation. Psychological Assessment 12:6–18, 2000

Butters J, Miliotis P: Amnesic disorders, in Clinical Neuropsychology, 2nd Edition. Edited by Heilman KM, Valenstein E. New York, Oxford University Press, 1985, pp 403–451

Caccioppo JT, Tassinary LG, Bernston GG: Handbook of Psychophysiology. New York, Cambridge University Press, 2000

Carlin D, Bonerba J, Phipps M, et al: Planning impairments in frontal lobe dementia and frontal lobe lesion patients. Neuropsychologia 38:655–665, 2000

Cermak LS (ed): Human Memory and Amnesia. Hillsdale, NJ, Erlbaum, 1982

Chaves ML, Izquierdo I: Differential diagnosis between dementia and depression: a study of efficiency increment. Acta Neurol Scand 85:378–382, 1992

Chelune GJ, Ferguson W, Moehle K: The role of standard cognitive and personality tests in neuropsychological assessment, in Clinical Application of Neuropsychological Test Batteries. Edited by Incagnoli T, Goldstein G, Golden CJ. New York, Plenum, 1986, pp 75–119

Christensen A-L: Luria's Neuropsychological Investigation Test, 2nd Edition. Copenhagen, Denmark, Munksgaard, 1979

Corballis MC: The Lopsided Ape. New York, Oxford University Press, 1991

Craig JC: Tactile pattern perception and its perturbations. J Acoust Soc Am 77:238–246, 1985

Crawford JR: Current and premorbid intelligence measures in neuropsychological assessment, in A Handbook of Neuropsychological Assessment. Edited by Crawford JR, Parker DM, McKinlay WW. Hove, UK, Erlbaum, 1992, pp 21–49

Cripe LI: Use of the MMPI with mild closed head injury, in The Evaluation and Treatment of Mild Traumatic Brain Injury.

Edited by Varney NR, Roberts RJ. Hillsdale, NJ, Erlbaum, 1999, pp 291–314

Crockett D, Tallman K, Hurwitz T, et al: Neuropsychological performance in psychiatric patients with or without documented brain dysfunction. Int J Neurosci 41:71–79, 1988

Cullum CM, Bigler ED: Short- and long-term psychological status following stroke: short form MMPI results. J Nerv Ment Dis 179:274–278, 1991

Cummings JL: Depression in neurologic diseases. Psychiatric Annals 24:525–531, 1994

Cummings JL: Principles of neuropsychiatry: towards a neuropsychiatric epistemology. Neurocase: Case Studies in Neuropsychology, Neuropsychiatry, and Behavioral Neurology 5:181–188, 1999

Curtis-Prior PB: Computerized methods of neuropsychological assessment. British Journal of Hospital Medicine 56:445–449, 1996

Dahlstrom WG, Welsh GS, Dahlstrom LE: An MMPI Handbook, Vol 1: Clinical Interpretation, Revised. Minneapolis, MN, University Minnesota Press, 1975

Dalgleish R, Cox SG: Mood and memory, in Memory Disorders in Psychiatric Practice. Edited by Berrios GE, Hodges JR. New York, Cambridge University Press, 2000, pp 34–46

Damasio AR, Tranel D, Damasio H: Disorders of visual recognition, in Handbook of Neuropsychology, Vol 2. Edited by Boller F, Grafman J. Amsterdam, The Netherlands, Elsevier, 1989, pp 317–332

Daube J: Clinical Neurophysiology. Philadelphia, PA, FA Davis, 1996

Davison K, Hassanyck F: Psychiatric disorders, in Textbook of Adverse Drug Reactions, 4th Edition. Edited by Davies DM. Oxford, Oxford University Press, 1991, pp 601–642

Deckersbach T, Otto MW, Savage CR, et al: The relationship between semantic organization and memory in obsessive-compulsive disorder. Psychother Psychosom 69:101–107, 2000

Delis DC, Kramer JH, Kaplan E, et al: California Verbal Learning Test, Form II (Research Edition). San Antonio, TX, Psychological Corporation, 1983

Delis DC, Kramer JH, Kaplan E, et al: California Verbal Learning Test. San Antonio, TX, Psychological Corporation, 1986

Delis DC, Kramer JH, Kaplan E, et al: California Verbal Learning Test, Form II (Research Edition). San Antonio, TX, Psychological Corporation, 1987

Della Sala S, Laiacona M, Spinnler H, et al: Autobiographical recollection and frontal damage. Neuropsychologia 31:823–839, 1993

Denicoff KD, Ali SO, Mirsky AF, et al: Relationship between prior course of illness and neuropsychological functioning in patients with bipolar disorder. J Affect Disord 56:67–73, 1999

De Renzi E, Vignolo LA: The Token Test: a sensitive test to detect disturbances in aphasics. Brain 85:665–678, 1962

De Renzi E, Faglioni P, Lodesani M, et al: Performance of left brain–damaged patients on imitation of single movements and motor sequences. Cortex 19:333–343, 1983

Derogatis LR: Symptom Checklist 90–Revised (SCL-90-R). Towson, MD, Clinical Psychometric Research, 1983

Dikmen S, Machamer J, Savoie T, et al: Life quality outcome in head injury, in Neuropsychological Assessment of Neuropsychiatric Disorders, 2nd Edition. Edited by Grant I, Adams KM. New York, Oxford University Press, 1996, pp 552–576

Diller L: Poststroke rehabilitation practice guidelines, in International Handbook of Neuropsychological Rehabilitation. Edited by Christensen A-L, Uzzell BP. New York, Kluwer Academic/Plenum, 2000, pp 167–182

Dobigny-Roman N, Dieudonne-Moinet B, Verny M, et al: Ideomotor apraxia test: a new test of imitation of gestures for elderly people. Eur J Neurol 5:571–578, 1998

Dubois B, Pillon B, Sternic N, et al: Age-induced cognitive deficit in Parkinson's disease. Neurology 40:38–41, 1990

Dwyer CA: Cut scores and testing: statistics, judgment, truth, and error. Psychological Assessment 8:360–362, 1996

Ernst T, Chang L, Itti L, et al: Correlation of regional cerebral blood flow from perfusion MRI and spect in normal subjects. Magn Reson Imaging 17:349–354, 1999

Evans JJ, Breen EK, Antoun N, et al: Focal retrograde amnesia for autobiographical events following cerebral vasculitis: a connectionist account. Neurocase: Case Studies in Neuropsychology, Neuropsychiatry, and Behavioral Neurology 2:1–11, 1996

Fahy ST, Carey TG, Oswens JM, et al: Psychiatric presentation of frontal meningiomas. Irish Journal of Psychological Medicine 12:61–63, 1995

Farah MJ, Feinberg TE (eds): Patient-Based Approaches to Cognitive Neuroscience. Cambridge, MA, MIT Press, 2000

Feldman RG, White RF: Role of the neurologist in hazard identification and risk assessment. Environ Health Perspect 104 (suppl 2):227–237, 1996

Ferrier IN, Stanton BR, Kelly TP, et al: Neuropsychological function in euthymic patients with bipolar disorder. Br J Psychiatry 175:246–251, 1999

Filskov SB, Leli DA: Assessment of the individual in neuropsychological practice, in Handbook of Clinical Neuropsychology. Edited by Filskov SB, Boll TJ. New York, Wiley-Interscience, 1981, pp 545–576

Folstein MF, Folstein SE, McHugh PR: Mini-Mental State: a practical method for grading the cognitive state of patients for the clinician. J Psychiatr Res 12:189–198, 1975

Freed DM, Kandel E: Long-term occupational exposure and the diagnosis of dementia. Neurotoxicology 9:391–400, 1988

Frith CD, Friston KJ: Studying brain function with neuroimaging, in Cognitive Neuroscience. Edited by Rugg MD. Cambridge, MA, Cambridge University Press, 1997, pp 169–195

Frith CD, Grasby PM: rCBF studies of prefrontal function and their relevance to psychosis, in Positron Emission Tomography and Neurobehavior. Edited by Baron JC. Amsterdam, The Netherlands, Elsevier, 1995, pp 383–403

Fukui T, Sugita K, Kawamura M, et al: Primary progressive apraxia in Pick's disease: a clinicopathologic study. Neurology 47:467–473, 1996

Gade A, Mortensen EL, Udensen H, et al: On the importance of control data and background variables in the evaluation of neuropsychological aspects of brain functioning, in Neurobehavioral Methods in Occupational and Environmental Health. Environmental Health Series. Copenhagen, World Health Organization, 1985, pp 91–96

Gass CS: MMPI-2 interpretation of patients with cerebrovascular disease: a correction factor. Archives of Clinical Neuropsychology 7:17–27, 1992

Gass CS, Apple C: Cognitive complaints in closed-head injury: relationship to memory test performance and emotional disturbance. J Clin Exp Neuropsychol 19:290–299, 1997

Goel V, Grafman J: Are the frontal lobes implicated in "planning" functions? interpreting data from the Tower of Hanoi. Neuropsychologia 33:623–642, 1995

Golden CJ, Hammeke TA, Purisch AD: Diagnostic validity of a standardized neuropsychological battery derived from Luria's neuropsychological tests. J Consult Clin Psychol 46:1258–1265, 1978

Golden CJ, Hammeke TA, Purisch AD: Manual for the Luria-Nebraska Neuropsychological Battery. Los Angeles, CA, Western Psychological Services, 1980

Goldman RS, Axelrod BN, Taylor SF: Neuropsychological aspects of schizophrenia, in Neuropsychological Assessment of Neuropsychiatric Disorders. Edited by Grant I, Adams KM. New York, Oxford University Press, 1996, pp 504–528

Goldstein G, Allen DN, Seaton BE: A comparison of clustering solutions for cognitive heterogeneity in schizophrenia. J Int Neuropsychol Soc 4:353–362, 1998

Goodglass H, Kaplan E: Boston Diagnostic Aphasia Examination (BDAE), 2nd Edition. Philadelphia, PA, Lea & Febiger, 1987

Grafman J, Wassermann E: Transcranial magnetic stimulation can measure and modulate learning and memory. Neuropsychologia 37:159–167, 1999

Grant DA, Berg EA: A behavioral analysis of degree of reinforcement and ease of shifting to new responses on a Weigl-type card-sorting problem. J Exp Psychol 38:404–411, 1948

Grant I, Heaton RK, Atkinson JH: Neurocognitive disorders in HIV-1 infection. HNRC Group. HIV Neurobehavioral Research Center. Curr Top Microbiol Immunol 202:11–32, 1995

Grattan LM, Oldach D, Perl TM, et al: Learning and memory difficulties after environmental exposure to waterways containing toxin-producing Pfiesteria or Pfiesteria-like dinoflagellates. Lancet 352:532–539, 1998

Grigsby J, Kaye K, Robbins LJ: Reliabilities, norms and factor structure of the Behavioral Dyscontrol Scale. Percept Mot Skills 74:883–892, 1992

Gronwall DMA: Paced auditory serial-addition task: a measure of recovery from concussion. Percept Mot Skills 44:367–373, 1977

Gronwall DMA, Sampson H: The Psychological Effects of Concussion. Auckland, New Zealand, University Press, 1974

Grossman FM: Percentage of WAIS-R standardization sample obtaining verbal-performance discrepancies. J Consult Clin Psychol 51:641–642, 1983

Gustafson Y, Nilsson I, Mattsson M, et al: Epidemiology and treatment of post-stroke depression. Drugs Aging 7:298–309, 1995

Haaland KY, Flaherty D: The different types of limb apraxia made by patients with left vs. right hemisphere damage. Brain Cogn 3:370–384, 1984

Haaland KY, Harrington DL, Kneight RT: Spatial deficits in ideomotor limb apraxia. A kinematic analysis of aiming movements. Brain 122:1169–1182, 1999

Halstead WC: Brain and Intelligence. Chicago, IL, University of Chicago Press, 1947

Hathaway SR, McKinley JC: The Minnesota Multiphasic Personality Inventory Manual, Revised. New York, Psychological Corporation, 1951

Heaton RK, Baade LE, Johnson KL: Neuropsychological test results associated with psychiatric disorders in adults. Psychol Bull 85:141–162, 1978

Heaton RK, Grant I, Matthews CG: Comprehensive Norms for an Expanded Halstead-Reitan Battery: Demographic Corrections, Research Findings, and Clinical Applications. Odessa, FL, Psychological Assessment Resources, 1991

Heilman KM, Bowers D, Valenstein E: Emotional disorders associated with neurological disease, in Clinical Neuropsychology. Edited by Heilman KM, Valenstein E. New York, Oxford University Press, 1993, pp 461–497

Heilman KM, Watson RT, Rothi LJG: Disorders of skilled movement, in Patient-Based Approaches to Cognitive Neuroscience. Edited by Farah MJ, Feinberg TE. Cambridge, MA, MIT Press, 2000a, pp 335–343

Heilman KM, Watson RT, Valenstein E: Neglect I: clinical and anatomic issues, in Patient-Based Approaches to Cognitive Neuroscience. Edited by Farah MJ, Feinberg TE. Cambridge, MA, MIT Press, 2000b, pp 115–123

Heinrichs RW, Zakzanis KK: Neurocognitive deficit in schizophrenia: a quantitative review of the evidence. Neuropsychology 12:426–445, 1998

Hertel PT: Relation between rumination and impaired memory in dysphoric moods. J Abnorm Psychol 107:166–172, 1998

Hiscock CK, Branham JD, Hiscock M: Detection of feigned cognitive impairment: the two-alternative forced-choice method compared with selected conventional tests. Journal of Psychopathology and Behavioral Assessment 16:95–110, 1994

Hodges JR: Transient Amnesia: Clinical and Neuropsychological Aspects. London, WB Saunders, 1991

Hooper HE: The Hooper Visual Organization Test Manual. Los Angeles, CA, Western Psychological Services, 1958

Howieson DB, Dame A, Camicioli R, et al: Cognitive markers preceding Alzheimer's dementia in the healthy oldest old. J Am Geriatr Soc 45:584–589, 1997

Jacobs D, Sana M, Dooneief G, et al: Neuropsychological detection and characterization of preclinical Alzheimer's disease. Neurology 45:957–962, 1995

Jason GW: Disorders of motor function following cortical lesions: review and theoretical considerations, in Cerebral Control of Speech and Limb Movements. Edited by Hammond GR. Amsterdam, The Netherlands, Elsevier, 1990, pp 141–168

Jernigan TL, Hesselink JR: Human brain-imaging: basic principles and applications in psychiatry, in Psychiatry. Edited by Michels R, Cavenar JO. Philadelphia, PA, JB Lippincott, 1987, pp 1–9

Johnson RJ: Event-related brain potentials and cognition, in Handbook of Neuropsychology, Vol 10. Edited by Boller F, Grafman J. Amsterdam, The Netherlands, Elsevier, 1995, pp 3–327

Kalska H, Punamaki RL, Makinen-Belli T, et al: Memory and metamemory functioning among depressed patients. Appl Neuropsychol 6:96–107, 1999

Kane RL, Kay GG: Computerized assessment in neuropsychology: a review of tests and test batteries. Neuropsychol Rev 3:1–117, 1992

Kaplan E: A process approach to neuropsychological assessment, in Clinical Neuropsychological and Brain Function: Research, Measurement, and Practice. Edited by Boll T, Bryant BK. Washington, DC, American Psychological Association, 1988, pp 125–167

Kapur N: Memory Disorders in Clinical Practice. London, Butterworth, 1988

Kapur N: How can we best explain retrograde amnesia in human memory disorder? Memory 5:115–129, 1997

Kapur N, Scholey K, Moore E, et al: Long-term retention deficits in two cases of disproportionate retrograde amnesia. J Cogn Neurosci 8:416–434, 1996

Kelly MD, Grant I, Heaton RK: Neuropsychological findings in HIV infection and AIDS, in Neuropsychological Assessment of Psychiatric Disorders. Edited by Grant I, Adams KM. New York, Oxford University Press, 1996, pp 403–422

Kiernan RJ, Mueller J, Langston JW, et al: The Neurobehavioral Cognitive Status Examination: a brief but differentiated approach to cognitive assessment. Ann Intern Med 107:481–485, 1987

King DA, Caine ED: Cognitive impairment and major depression: beyond the pseudodementia syndrome, in Neuropsychological Assessment of Neuropsychiatric Disorders, 2nd Edition. Edited by Grant I, Adams KM. New York, Oxford University Press, 1996, pp 200–217

Kolb B: Preoperative events and brain damage: a commentary, in Preoperative Events: Their Effects on Behavior Following Brain Damage. Edited by Schulkin J. New York, Erlbaum, 1989, pp 305–311

Laine M, Butters N: A preliminary study of problem solving strategies of detoxified long-term alcoholics. Drug Alcohol Depend 10:235–242, 1982

Larrabee GJ: Another look at VIQ-PIQ scores and unilateral brain damage. Int J Neurosci 29:141–148, 1986

Leiguarda RC, Pramstaller PP, Merello M, et al: Apraxia in Parkinson's disease, progressive supranuclear palsy, multiple system atrophy and neuroleptic-induced parkinsonism. Brain 120:75–90, 1997

Lenzer I: Halstead-Reitan Test Battery: a problem of differential diagnosis. Percept Mot Skills 50:611–630, 1980

Lesser RP: Psychogenic seizures, in Recent Advances in Epilepsy. Edited by Pedley TA, Meldrum BS. New York, Churchill Livingstone, 1985, pp 273–293

Levin HS, High WM, Goethe KE, et al: The Neurobehavioral Rating Scale assessment of behavioural sequelae of head injury by the clinician. J Neurol Neurosurg Psychiatry 50:183–193, 1987

Levin JM, Ross MH, Harris G, et al: Applications of dynamic susceptibility contrast magnetic resonance imaging in neuropsychiatry. Neuroimage 4:S147–162, 1996

Levine B, Black SE, Cabeza R, et al: Episodic memory and the self in a case of isolated retrograde amnesia. Brain 121:1951–1973, 1998

Lezak MD: The problem of assessing executive functions. International Journal of Psychology 17:281–297, 1982

Lezak MD: An individual approach to neuropsychological assessment, in Clinical Neuropsychology. Edited by Logue PE, Schear JM. Springfield, IL, Charles C Thomas, 1986, pp 29–49

Lezak MD: Assessment for rehabilitation planning, in Neuropsychological Rehabilitation. Edited by Meier M, Benton AL, Diller L. Edinburgh, Churchill Livingstone, 1987, pp 41–58

Lezak MD: Brain damage is a family affair. J Clin Exp Neuropsychol 10:111–123, 1988a

Lezak MD: IQ: R.I.P. J Clin Exp Neuropsychol 10:351–361, 1988b

Lezak MD: Neuropsychological tests and assessment techniques, in Handbook of Neuropsychology, Vol 1. Edited by Boller F, Grafman J. Amsterdam, Elsevier, 1988c, pp 47–68

Lezak MD: Assessment of psychosocial dysfunctions resulting from head trauma, in Assessment of the Behavioral Consequences of Head Trauma, Vol 7. Frontiers of Clinical Neuroscience. Edited by Lezak MD. New York, Alan R Liss, 1989, pp 113–144

Lezak MD: Domains of behavior from a neuropsychological perspective: the whole story, in Integrative Views of Motivation, Cognition, and Emotion. Nebraska Symposium on

Motivation. Edited by Spaulding WD. Lincoln, NE, University of Nebraska Press, 1994, pp 23–55

Lezak MD: Neuropsychological Assessment, 3rd Edition. New York, Oxford University Press, 1995

Lishman WA: Organic Psychiatry, 3rd Edition. Oxford, UK, Blackwell Scientific, 1997

Loring DW, Lee GP, Meador KJ: Revising the Rey-Osterrieth: rating right hemisphere recall. Archives of Clinical Neuropsychology 3:239–247, 1988

Luria AR: Higher Cortical Functions in Man, 2nd Edition. New York, Basic Books, 1980

Malec JF, Ivnik R, Smith G, et al: Mayo's older Americans' normative studies: utility of corrections for age and education for the WAIS-R. Clin Neuropsychol 6:31–47, 1992

Malec JF, Moessner AM, Kragness M, et al: Refining a measure of brain injury sequelae to predict postacute rehabilitation outcome: rating scale analysis of the Mayo-Portland Adaptability Inventory. J Head Trauma Rehabil 15:670–682, 2000

Marcopulos BA: Pseudodementia, dementia, and depression: test differentiation, in Testing Older Adults: A Reference Guide for Geropsychological Assessments. Edited by Hunt T, Lindley CJ. Austin, TX, Pro-Ed, 1989, pp 70–91

Markova IS, Berrios GE: Insight into memory deficits, in Memory Disorders in Psychiatric Practice. Edited by Berrios GE, Hodges JR. New York, Cambridge University Press, 2000, pp 34–46

Marson DC, Ingram KK, Cody HA, et al: Assessing the competency of patients with Alzheimer's disease under different legal standards. A prototype instrument. Arch Neurol 52:949–954, 1995a

Marson DC, Cody HA, Ingram KK, et al: Neuropsychologic predictors of competency in Alzheimer's disease using a rational reasons legal standard. Arch Neurol 52:955–959, 1995b

Masur D, Sliwinsi M, Lipton R, et al: Neuropsychological prediction of dementia and the absence of dementia in healthy elderly persons. Neurology 44:1427–1432, 1994

Mataix-Cols D, Junque C, Sanchez-Turet M, et al: Neuropsychological functioning in a subclinical obsessive-compulsive sample. Biol Psychiatry 45:898–904, 1999

Matarazzo JD, Prifitera A: Subtest scatter and premorbid intelligence: lessons from the WAIS-R standardization sample. J Consult Clin Psychol 1:186–191, 1989

Mattis S: Mental status examination for organic mental syndrome in the elderly patient, in Geriatric Psychiatry. Edited by Bellak L, Karasu TB. New York, Grune & Stratton, 1976, pp 77–121

Mattis S: Dementia Rating Scale (DRS) Manual. Odessa, FL, Psychological Assessment Resources, 1988

Mayes AR: Selective memory disorders, in The Oxford Handbook of Memory. Edited by Tulving E, Craik FIM. Oxford, UK, Oxford University Press, 2000, pp 427–440

McCarthy RA, Warrington EK: Cognitive Neuropsychology: A Clinical Introduction. San Diego, CA, Academic Press, 1990

McKenna PJ, McKay AP, Laws K: Memory in functional psychosis, in Memory Disorders in Psychiatric Practice. Edited by Berrios GE, Hodges JR. New York, Cambridge University Press, 2000, pp 234–267

Meador KJ, Moore EE, Nichols OL: The role of cholinergic systems in visuospatial processing and memory. J Clin Exp Neuropsychol 15:832–842, 1993

Menon RS, Kim SG: Spatial and temporal limits in cognitive neuroimaging with fMRI. Trends in Cognitive Science 3:207–216, 1999

Mesulam M-M: Principles of Behavioral and Cognitive Neurology, 2nd Edition. New York, Oxford University Press, 2000

Milberg WP, Hebben N, Kaplan E: The Boston approach to neuropsychological assessment, in Neuropsychological Assessment of Neuropsychiatric Disorders. Edited by Grant I, Adams KM. New York, Oxford University Press, 1996, pp 58–80

Milner B: Interhemispheric differences in the localization of psychological processes in man. Br Med Bull 27:272–277, 1971

Milner B: Clues to the cerebral organization of memory, in Cerebral Correlates of Conscious Experience. Edited by Buser PA, Raugeul-Buser A. INSERM Symposium No 6. Amsterdam, The Netherlands, Elsevier North-Holland, 1978, pp 139–153

Mitrushina MN, Boone KB, D'Elia LF: Handbook of Normative Data for Neuropsychological Assessment. New York, Oxford University Press, 1999

Morris J, McKeel D Jr, Storandt M, et al: Very mild Alzheimer's disease: informant-based clinical, psychometric, and pathologic distinction for normal aging. Neurology 41:469–478, 1991

Mueller SR, Girace M: Use and misuse of the MMPI, a reconsideration. Psychol Rep 63:483–491, 1988

Mysiw WJ, Beegan JG, Gatens PF: Prospective cognitive assessment of stroke patients before inpatient rehabilitation: the relationship of the Neurobehavioral Cognitive Status Examination to functional improvement. Am J Phys Med Rehabil 68:168–171, 1989

Nelson HE: The National Adult Reading Test (NART): Test Manual. Windsor, UK, UK:NFER-Nelson, 1982

Newcombe F: Psychometric and behavioral evidence: scope, limitations, and ecological validity, in Neurobehavioral Recovery From Head Injury. Edited by Levin HS, Grafman J, Eisenberg HM. New York, Oxford University Press, 1987, pp 129–145

Newcombe F, Ratcliff G: Disorders of visuospatial analysis, in Handbook of Neuropsychology, Vol 2. Edited by Boller F, Grafman J. Amsterdam, The Netherlands, Elsevier, 1989, pp 333–356

Niemi M-L, Laaksonen R, Kotila M, et al: Quality of life 4 years after stroke. Stroke 19:1101–1107, 1988

O'Connell JE, Gray CS, French JM, et al: Atrial fibrillation and cognitive function: case-control study. J Neurol Neurosurg Psychiatry 65:386–389, 1998

Ojemann GA, Dodrill CB: Verbal memory deficits after left temporal lobectomy for epilepsy. J Neurosurg 62:101–107, 1985

Osterrieth PA: Le test de copie d'une figure complex. Archives de Psychologie 30:206–356, 1944

Pagliaro LA, Pagliaro AM: Psychologists' Neuropsychotropic Drug Reference. Philadelphia, PA, Brunner/Mazel, 1998

Palmer BW, Boone KB, Lesser IM, et al: Neuropsychological deficits among older depressed patients with predominantly psychological or vegetative symptoms. J Affect Disord 41:17–24, 1996

Palmer BW, Heaton RK, Paulsen JS, et al: Is it possible to be schizophrenic yet neuropsychologically normal? Neuropsychology 11:437–446, 1997

Pankratz L: Symptom validity testing and symptom retraining: procedures for the assessment and treatment of functional sensory deficits. J Consult Clin Psychol 47:409–410, 1979

Pankratz LD, Taplin JD: Issues in psychological assessment, in Critical Issues, Developments, and Trends in Professional Psychology. Edited by McNamara JR, Barclay AG. New York, Praeger, 1982, pp 115–151

Papanicolaou AC: Fundamentals of Functional Brain Imaging. Lisse, The Netherlands, Swets & Zeitlinger, 1999

Paradiso S, Ohkubo T, Robinson RG: Vegetative and psychological symptoms associated with depressed mood over the first two years after stroke. Int J Psychiatry Med 27:137–157, 1997

Parsons OA: Brain damage in alcoholics: altered states of unconsciousness, in Alcohol Intoxication and Withdrawal. Experimental Studies No 2. Edited by Gross MM. New York, Plenum, 1975, pp 569–584

Perfect TJ, Maylor EA (eds): Models of Cognitive Aging. Oxford, UK, Oxford University Press, 2000

Petersen R, Smith G, Ivnik R, et al: Memory function in very early Alzheimer's disease. Neurology 42:867–872, 1994

Petrides M, Milner B: Deficits on subject-ordered tasks after frontal- and temporal-lobe lesions in man. Neuropsychologia 20:249–262, 1982

Pohjasvaara T, Leppavuori A, Siira I, et al: Frequency and clinical determinants of poststroke depression. Stroke 29:2311–2317, 1998

Pohjasvaara T, Mantyla R, Aronen HJ, et al: Clinical and radiological determinants of prestroke cognitive decline in a stroke cohort. J Neurol Neurosurg Psychiatry 67:742–748, 1999

Polster MR, Rose SB: Disorders of auditory processing: evidence for modularity in audition. Cortex 34:47–65, 1998

Porch BE: Porch Index of Communicative Ability. Manual. Palo Alto, CA, Consulting Psychologists Press, 1983

Post RM: Neural substrates of psychiatric syndromes, in Principles of Behavioral and Cognitive Neurology. Edited by Mesulam M-M. New York, Oxford University Press, 2000, pp 406–438

Prigatano GP, Parsons OA: Relationship of age and education to Halstead test performance in different patient populations. J Consult Clin Psychol 44:527–533, 1976

Prigatano GP, Schacter DL (eds): Awareness of Deficit After Brain Injury. New York, Oxford University Press, 1991

Psychological Corporation: WAIS-III and WMS-III Technical Manual. San Antonio, TX, Psychological Corporation, 1997

Rafal RD: Neglect II: cognitive neuropsychological issues, in Patient-Based Approaches to Cognitive Neuroscience. Edited by Farah MJ, Feinberg TE. Cambridge, MA, MIT Press, 2000, pp 115–123

Raskin SA, Mateer CA: Neuropsychological Management of Mild Traumatic Brain Injury. New York, Oxford University Press, 1999

Reed JM, Squire LR: Retrograde amnesia for facts and events: findings from four new cases. J Neurosci 18:3943–3954, 1998

Reitan RM: Manual for the Administration of Neuropsychological Test Batteries for Adults and Children. Indianapolis, IN, Author, 1969

Reitan RM, Wolfson D: The Halstead-Reitan Neuropsychological Test Battery: Theory and Clinical Interpretation, 2nd Edition. Tucson, AZ, Neuropsychology Press, 1993

Rentz DM, Weintraub S: Neuropsychological detection of early probable Alzheimer's disease, in Early Diagnosis of Alzheimer's Disease. Edited by Scinto LFM, Daffner KR. Totowa, NJ, Humana Press, 2000, pp 169–189

Rey A: L'examen psychologique dans les cas d'encephalopathie traumatique. Archives de Psychologie 28(112):286–340, 1941

Rey A: L'examen clinique en psychologie. Paris, Presses Universitaries de France, 1964

Robinson RG: The Clinical Neuropsychiatry of Stroke. New York, Cambridge University Press, 1998

Rothi LJG, Raymer AM, Heilman KM: Limb praxis assessment, in Apraxia: The Neuropsychology of Action. Edited by Rothi LJG, Heilman KM. Hove, UK, Psychology Press, 1997, pp 61–73

Royall DR, Mahurin RK, Gray KF: Bedside assessment of executive cognitive impairment: the executive interview. J Am Geriatr Soc 40:1221–1226, 1992

Ryan CM, Morrow LA, Hodgson M: Cacosmia and neurobehavioral dysfunction associated with occupational exposure to mixtures of organic solvents. Am J Psychiatry 145:1442–1445, 1988

Savage CR, Deckersbach T, Wilhelm S, et al: Strategic processing and episodic memory impairment in obsessive compulsive disorder. Neuropsychology 14:141–151, 2000

Sbordone RJ: The assessment interview in clinical neuropsychology, in Neuropsychological Assessment in Clinical Practice. Edited by Groth-Marnat G. New York, Wiley, 2000, pp 94–126

Schenkenberg T, Bradford DC, Ajax ET: Line bisection and unilateral visual neglect in patients with neurologic impairment. Neurology 30:509–517, 1980

Schmidt M: Rey Auditory Verbal Learning Test (RAVLT): A Handbook. Los Angeles, CA, Western Psychological Services, 1996

Schwamm LH, Van Dyke C, Kiernan RJ, et al: The Neurobehavioral Cognitive Status Examination: comparison with the Cognitive Capacity Screening Examination and the Mini-Mental State Examination in a neurosurgical population. Ann Intern Med 107:486–491, 1987

Seashore CE, Lewis D, Saetveit DL: Seashore Measures of Musical Talents, Revised. New York, Psychological Corporation, 1960

Shallice T: Specific impairments of planning. Philos Trans R Soc Lond B Biol Sci 298:199–209, 1982

Skuster DZ, Digre KB, Corbett JJ: Neurologic conditions presenting as psychiatric disorders. Psychiatr Clin North Am 15:311–333, 1992

Sloan S, Ponsford J: Assessment of cognitive difficulties following TBI, in Traumatic Brain Injury. Rehabilitation for Everyday Adaptive Living. Edited by Ponsford J. Hillsdale, NJ, Erlbaum, 1995, pp 65–101

Smith A: Clinical psychological practice and principles of neuropsychological assessment, in Handbook of Clinical Psychology: Theory, Research and Practice. Edited by Walker CE. Homewood, IL, Dorsey Press, 1983, pp 445–500

Sohlberg MM, Mateer CA: Introduction to Cognitive Rehabilitation. New York, Guilford, 1989

Sox HC, Blatt MA, Higgins MC, et al: Medical Decision Making. Boston, MA, Butterworths, 1988

Spreen O, Benton AL: Comparative studies of some neuropsychological tests for cerebral damage. J Nerv Ment Dis 140:323–333, 1965

Spreen O, Strauss E: A Compendium of Neuropsychological Tests, 2nd Edition. New York, Oxford University Press, 1998

Squire LR, Slater PC, Chase PM: Retrograde amnesia: temporal gradient in very long-term memory following electroconvulsive therapy. Science 187:77–79, 1975

Stein RA, Strickland TL: A review of the neuropsychological effects of commonly used prescription medicines. Archives of Clinical Neuropsychology 13:259–284, 1998

Strakowski SM, Del Bello MP, Sax KW, et al: Brain magnetic resonance imaging of structural abnormalities in bipolar disorder. Arch Gen Psychiatry 56:254–260, 1999

Strange PG: Brain Biochemistry and Brain Disorders. Oxford, Oxford University Press, 1992

Strauss E, Goldsmith SM: Lateral preferences and performance on non-verbal laterality tests in a normal population. Cortex 23:495–503, 1987

Strub RL, Black FW: The Mental Status Examination in Neurology. Philadelphia, PA, FA Davis, 2000

Sullivan EV, Shear PK, Zipursky RB, et al: A deficit profile of executive, memory, and motor functions in schizophrenia. Biol Psychiatry 36:641–653, 1994

Tallis F: The neuropsychology of obsessive-compulsive disorder: a review and consideration of clinical implications. Br J Clin Psychol 36:3–20, 1997

Tarter RE, Edwards KL, Van Thiel DH: Perspective and rationale for neuropsychological assessment of medical disease, in Medical Neuropsychology. Edited by Tarter RE, Van Thiel DH, Edwards KL. New York, Plenum 1988, pp 1–10

Taylor LB: Psychological assessment of neurosurgical patients, in Functional Neurosurgery. Edited by Rasmussen T, Marino R. New York, Raven, 1979, pp 165–180

Teuber H-L: Neuropsychology, in Recent Advances in Diagnostic Psychological Testing. Edited by Harrower MR. Springfield, IL, Charles C Thomas, 1948

Theodore WH: Clinical neuroimaging, in Frontiers of Neuroscience, Vol 4. Edited by Theodore WH. New York, Alan R Liss, 1988, pp 1–9

Tombaugh TN: Test of Memory Malingering (TOMM). New York, Multi Health Systems, 1996

Trahan DE, Larrabee GJ: Continuous Visual Memory Test. Odessa, FL, Psychological Assessment Resources, 1988

Upton D, Thompson PJ: Twenty questions task and frontal lobe dysfunction. Archives of Clinical Neuropsychology 14:203–216, 1999

Vanderploeg RD, Schinka JA, Axelrod BN, et al: Estimation of WAIS-R premorbid intelligence: current ability and demographic data used in a best-performance fashion. Psychological Assessment 8:404–411, 1996

Van Gorp WG, Miller EN, Satz P, et al: Neuropsychological performance in HIV-1 immunocompromised patients. J Clin Exp Neuropsychol 11:763–773, 1989

Van Gorp WG, Altshuler L, Theberge DC, et al: Cognitive impairment in euthymic bipolar patients with and without prior alcohol dependence. A preliminary study. Arch Gen Psychiatry 55:41–46, 1998

Van Lancker DR, Dreiman J, Cummings J: Voice perception deficits: neuroanatomical correlates of phonagnosia. J Clin Exp Neuropsychol 11:665–674, 1989

Van Zomeren AH, Brouwer WH: Clinical Neuropsychology of Attention. New York, Oxford University Press, 1994

Varney NR: Somesthesis, in Experimental Techniques in Human Neuropsychology. Edited by Hannay HJ. New York, Oxford University Press, 1986, pp 212–237

Varney NR, Roberts RJ (eds): The Evaluation and Treatment of Mild Traumatic Brain Injury. Hillsdale, NJ, Erlbaum, 1999

Veiel HO: A preliminary profile of neuropsychological deficits associated with major depression. J Clin Exp Neuropsychol 19:587–603, 1997

Walsh KW: Understanding Brain Damage. Edinburgh, UK, Churchill Livingstone, 1985

Walsh KW: Neuropsychology, 2nd Edition. Edinburgh, UK, Churchill Livingstone, 1987

Walsh V, Rushworth M: A primer of magnetic stimulation as a tool for neuropsychology. Neuropsychologia 37:125–135, 1999

Wang PL, Ennis KE, Copland SL: CCT: Cognitive Competency Test Manual. Department of Psychology, Mount Sinai Hospital, Toronto, ON, Canada, 1986

Warrington EK: Recognition Memory Test. Windsor, UK, NFER-Nelson, 1984

Wechsler D: The Measurement of Adult Intelligence, 3rd Edition. Baltimore, MD, Williams & Wilkins, 1944

Wechsler D: WAIS Manual. New York, Psychological Corporation, 1955

Wechsler D: WAIS-R Manual. New York, Psychological Corporation, 1981

Wechsler D: Wechsler Memory Scale–Revised Manual. San Antonio, TX, Psychological Corporation, 1987

Wechsler D: WISC-III Manual. Wechsler Intelligence Scale for Children–III. New York, Psychological Corporation, 1991

Wechsler D: WAIS-III. Administration and Scoring Manual. San Antonio, TX, Psychological Corporation, 1997a

Wechsler D: WMS-III. Administration and Scoring Manual. San Antonio, TX, Psychological Corporation, 1997b

Welsh GS, Dahlstrom WG (eds): Basic Readings on the MMPI in Psychology and Medicine. Minneapolis, MN, University of Minnesota Press, 1956

Welsh KA, Butters N, Hughes JP, et al: Detection and staging of dementia in Alzheimer's disease. Use of the neuropsychological measures developed for the Consortium to Establish a Registry for Alzheimer's Disease. Arch Neurol 49:448–452, 1992

Wepman JM, Reynolds WM: Wepman's Auditory Discrimination Test, 2nd Edition. Los Angeles, CA, Western Psychological Services, 1987

West JF, Sands E, Ross-Swain D: Bedside Evaluation Screening Test, Austin, TX, Pro-Ed, 1998

White RF, Feldman RG, Proctor SP: Neurobehavioral effects of toxic exposures, in Clinical Syndromes in Adult Neuropsychology: The Practitioner's Handbook. Edited by White RF. New York, Elsevier, 1992, pp 1–51

Wilson BA, Evans JJ, Emslie H, et al: The development of an ecologically valid test for assessing patients with a dysexecutive syndrome. Neuropsychological Rehabilitation 8:213–228, 1998

Wilson KD: Issues surrounding the cognitive neuroscience of obsessive-compulsive disorder. Psychonomic Bulletin and Review 5:161–172, 1998

Wrightson P, Gronwall D: Mild Head Injury. Oxford, Oxford University Press, 1999

Yousef G, Ryan WJ, Lambert T, et al: A preliminary report: a new scale to identify the pseudodementia syndrome. Int J Geriatr Psychiatry 13:389–399, 1998

# CHAPTER 8

# Clinical Imaging in Neuropsychiatry

Robin A. Hurley, M.D.

L. Anne Hayman, M.D.

Katherine H. Taber, Ph.D.

Psychiatry as a medical specialty has a tumultuous past. There have been entanglements with philosophy, religion, politics, and science since the beginning of time. Concepts to explain human behavior that have been well accepted by the public and leaders of civilizations have included demonic possession, the wandering uterus, anger of the gods, witchcraft, and sins of the parents. Psychiatry, as a twenty-first-century concept, includes the idea that human behavior is a product of our genetics, our brain structure and function, and our experiences from the past and interpretation of the present. Neuropsychiatry, as a subspecialty, developed to assess and treat patients with cognitive or emotional disturbances due to brain dysfunction. This concept could not have evolved without the influence of brain imaging. In the short time span of one century, imaging technology has advanced from a primitive skull X ray to real-time pictures of brain changes as we perform a task or feel an emotion such as sadness or happiness. Future imaging contributions will not only be in the diagnostic arena but also in estimating the course of illness and treatment response and in the development of new neurotransmitter-specific medications.

Currently, brain imaging is divided into two categories: functional and structural (Table 8–1). Functional imaging of the brain measures changes related to neuronal activity. The most common functional imaging techniques utilize indirect measures, such as blood flow, metabolism, or oxygen extraction. Functional imaging techniques include single photon emission computed tomography (SPECT), positron emission tomography (PET), functional magnetic resonance imaging (fMRI), magnetic resonance spectroscopy (MRS), and magnetoencephalography (MEG). These techniques and their application to neuropsychiatry are discussed in Chapter 9 of this book. Structural imaging is defined as information gathered regarding the physical constitution of the brain at any one point in time and is not dependent on thought, motor activity, or mood. It includes both anatomic and pathologic studies. Computed tomography (CT) and magnetic resonance imaging (MRI) are the standard tools. However, recent advances have broadened the range of information that can be obtained clinically. For example, xenon-enhanced computed tomography (Xe/CT) is available on the newer CT scanners, providing a way to identify structural lesions once hidden from view.

## What Can Be Learned From Structural Imaging

Soon after the advent of CT and MRI, scientists began to image patients with psychotic and mood disorders hoping to demonstrate concrete proof that these illnesses were indeed brain disorders and not conditions of "weak personalities" or "poor parenting." Initial studies in the classic conditions of bipolar disorder, major depression, and

**TABLE 8–1.** Brain imaging modalities

| Type of imaging | Parameter measured |
| --- | --- |
| **Anatomic and pathologic** | |
| Computed tomography (CT) | Tissue density |
| Xenon-enhanced computed tomography (Xe/CT) | Xenon concentration in blood |
| Magnetic resonance imaging (MRI) | Many properties of tissue (T1 and T2 relaxation times, spin density, magnetic susceptibility, water diffusion, blood flow) |
| **Functional (brain activation)** | |
| Positron emission tomography (PET) | Radioactive tracers in blood or tissue |
| Single photon emission computed tomography (SPECT) | Radioactive tracers in blood or tissue |
| Functional magnetic resonance imaging (fMRI) | Deoxyhemoglobin levels in blood |
| Magnetoencephalography (MEG) | Magnetic fields induced by neuronal discharges |
| Magnetic resonance spectroscopy (MRS) | Metabolite concentrations in tissue |
| Tomographic electroencephalography (EEG) | Summed neuronal discharges |

schizophrenia met with disappointing results—with, at most, nonspecific findings that occur in many disease states (i.e., ventricular enlargement or generalized atrophy). As neuropsychiatry matures, so is the knowledge that can be attained from structural images. Researchers studying conditions such as cerebral vascular accidents, ruptured aneurysms, traumatic brain injury, and multiple sclerosis were among the first to document that psychiatric symptoms do occur as a result of brain injury; that emotion, memory, and thought processing happen by way of tracts or circuits (Mega and Cummings 1994); and that indeed many patients do have subtle lesions that account for their symptoms. Not only has this information led to a further understanding of brain function, but it has provided prognostic information for patients and has led to treatment plan changes.

In an era when cost containment and third-party review has restricted the physician's ability to provide service, it is imperative that the practicing neuropsychiatrist understand structural imaging as a helpful tool and be able to explain why it is *essential* in the workup of a patient with psychiatric symptoms. This chapter focuses on the basic concepts of CT and MRI, advancing technology, and normal imaging anatomy related to the "brain circuits" that affect one's emotion or thought processing. The chapter also contains selected examples to illustrate where structural imaging can provide valuable clinical information. The chapter does not cover all psychiatric conditions in which there are imaging findings, but it does provide the tools to understand the available scientific literature that documents those conditions. (Examples of recent review articles that cover selected neuropsychiatric conditions and their imaging findings are Chakos et al. 1998; Weight and Bigler 1998.)

## General Principles for Neuropsychiatric Imaging

Early studies in the 1980s promoted the limited use of CT scanning in psychiatric patients only after focal neurological findings had been developed (Larson et al. 1981). Studies of the late 1980s and 1990s encouraged a wider use of diagnostic CT in psychiatric patients (Beresford et al. 1986; Kaplan et al. 1994; Weinberger 1984). With the advent of utilization review and cost containment in the late 1990s, once again more narrow criteria were proposed that recommended use of CT only when reversible pathology was suspected (Branton 1999; Schemmer et al. 1999). Others strongly debate these criteria, including the authors of this chapter.

An excellent review of this controversy can be found in an article by Rauch and Renshaw (1995). They propose six categories of psychiatric patients in whom imaging should be performed: those with new-onset psychosis; those with delirium or dementia of unknown cause; and those with acute mental status changes associated with either abnormal findings on neurological examination, brain injury of any kind (traumatic or "organic"), or age greater than 50. We propose slightly wider criteria (Table 8–2). These are based on several factors: 1) rapid advances in clinical imaging allow identification of once-hidden lesions; 2) clinical experience indicates that patients with symptoms outside the "clinical norms" for a working diagnosis often have brain lesions that will explain the presentation; and 3) an identified brain lesion can change treatment plans, medication choices for targeted symptoms, and prognosis. For example, a patient with poststroke mania might best be treated with sodium valproate rather than lithium, as lithium could increase confusion or cognitive impairment in such a patient.

**TABLE 8–2.** Clinical indications for imaging in psychiatric patients

Psychiatric symptoms outside "clinical norms"
Dementia or cognitive decline
Traumatic brain injury
New-onset mental illness after age 50
Initial psychotic break
Alcohol abuse
Seizure disorders with psychiatric symptoms
Movement disorders
Autoimmune disorders
Eating disorders
Poison or toxin exposure
Catatonia
Focal neurological signs

## Practical Considerations

### Ordering the Examination

The neuroradiologist needs very clear clinical information on the imaging request form (not just "rule out pathology" or "new-onset mental status changes"). If a lesion is suspected in a particular location, the neuroradiologist should be informed of this or given enough clinical data for selection of the best imaging method and parameters to view suspicious areas. The clinician should ask the neuroradiologist about any special imaging techniques that may enhance visualization of the limbic circuits (see "Common Pulse Sequences," below, in this chapter). The neuroradiologist and technical staff also need information on the patient's current condition (e.g., delirious, psychotic, easily agitated, paranoid). This may eliminate difficulties with patient management during the scan.

### Contrast-Enhanced Studies

When ordering CT or MRI, the physician can request that an additional set of images be gathered after intravenous administration of a contrast agent. This process, although using different physical principles for CT or MRI (see later sections for full discussion), is required for identification of lesions that are the same signal intensity as surrounding brain tissue. Contrast agents travel in the vascular system and normally do not cross into the brain parenchyma because they cannot pass through the blood-brain barrier (BBB). The BBB is formed by tight junctions in the capillaries that serve as a structural barrier and function like a plasma membrane. The ability of a substance to pass through these junctions depends on several factors, including the substance's affinity for plasma proteins, its lipophilic nature, and its size. (An excellent review of the physiology of the blood-brain barrier and the basics of contrast enhancement can be found in Sage et al. 1998.)

In some disease processes, the BBB is broken or damaged. As a result, contrast agents can diffuse into brain tissue. Pathologic processes in which the BBB is disrupted include autoimmune diseases, infections, and tumors. Contrast enhancement can also be useful in the case of vascular abnormalities (such as arteriovenous malformations and aneurysms), although the contrast agent remains intravascular. When ordering the imaging procedure, the neuropsychiatrist should be mindful to request a study with contrast enhancement if one of the above disease states is suspected.

### Patient Preparation

The psychiatrist should always explain the procedure to the patient shortly beforehand, being mindful to mention the loud noises of the scanner (MRI), the tightly enclosing imaging coil (MRI), and the requirement for absolute immobility during the test (MRI and CT). Both the body and head are secured with tight wraps to minimize movement during scanning. If the psychiatrist suspects that the patient may become agitated or be unable to remain still for the length of the examination, then sedation may be necessary. A clinician may select a regimen that he or she is familiar and comfortable with. We have found that for patients with agitation and psychosis, a sedating antipsychotic with lorazepam 1–2 mg intramuscularly 30 minutes before scanning usually works well in a physically healthy nongeriatric adult.

### Understanding the Scan

The neuropsychiatrist should review the scan and radiology report with the neuroradiologist. It is important to remember that the radiographic view places the patient's right on the reader's left and the patient's left on the reader's right. The first points to observe on a scan are the demographics: the hospital name; the date; the scanner number; and the patient's name, age, sex, and identification number. It is also important to note whether the scan was done with or without contrast enhancement. If an MRI has been obtained, the weighting parameters are important. The locations of these factors on CT and MRI scans are illustrated later in the chapter. Next, the neuropsychiatrist should ask the neuroradiologist to point out the normal anatomical markers and any pathology observed on the films. Prior understanding of the limbic system anatomy is essential and is reviewed later in this chapter.

## Computed Tomographic Imaging

The first computed tomographic image, obtained in 1972, required 9 days to collect the data and more than 2 hours to process on a mainframe computer (Orrison 1995). The scanners of today can capture a slice in one half second (Figure 8–1). With the use of multiple detectors, several slices can be acquired simultaneously. Thus, with multislice imaging, CT scans of the entire brain can be completed in less than 17 seconds (B.R. Westerman, unpublished communication, May 2000). Newer CT technologies that are just beginning to be applied to neuropsychiatric patients include three-dimensional helical (spiral) CT and xenon-enhanced CT (Xe/CT).

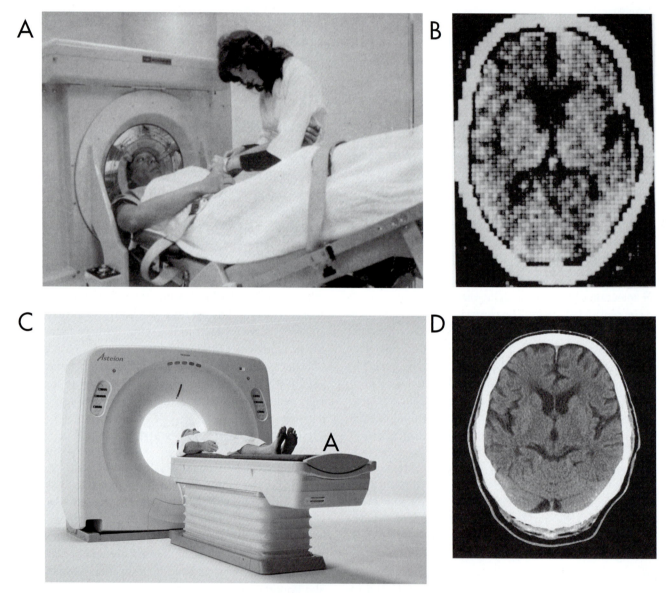

**FIGURE 8–1.** Computed tomography then and now. A first-generation computed tomography (CT) scanner (*Panel A*), circa 1975, created crude brain images (*Panel B*) that still were superior to other imaging techniques available at the time. In 1986, helical (or spiral) CT was patented. This technique significantly increased scan speed and expanded the application of CT into new areas. In 1998, the multislice CT scanner (*Panel C*) was introduced. Multislice CT opens new possibilities for more efficient health care, better diagnoses, earlier disease detection, and cost reduction. Multislice CT has been hailed as the biggest advancement in medical imaging of the 1990s (Diagnostic Imaging January 2000). Modern CT scanners produce images of much higher resolution (*Panel D*) than early CT images.

*Source.* Panel C, photograph of Aquilion Multi scanner courtesy of Toshiba America Medical Systems, Inc. Panel D, image courtesy of Toshiba America Medical Systems, Inc., and Delta County Memorial Hospital, Delta, CO.

## Technical Considerations

### Standard Two-Dimensional CT

Like a conventional radiograph, CT uses an X-ray tube as a source of photons. When a conventional radiograph is acquired, the photons directly expose X-ray film. When a CT image is acquired, the photons are collected by detectors. The latest generation of CT scanners split the X-ray beam and add multiple detectors, allowing collection of multiple slices simultaneously ("multislice scanners"). These data are relayed to a computer that places the data in a two-dimensional grid that is then printed on X-ray film or viewed on monitor (Rauch and Renshaw 1995). CT scans deliver a clinically insignificant cumulative dose of about 5 rads localized to the head. To avoid even this small dose of radiation to the lens of the eye, CT scans are angled parallel to a line drawn between the orbit and the external auditory meatus (referred to as the *orbitomeatal line*). Although there is no appreciable radiation deposited outside the head, a lead apron is often placed over the abdomen of a pregnant woman during a head CT.

The patient lies on a table that is advanced between acquisition of each CT slice. To acquire each CT slice, a beam of photons rotates around the head. As the photons pass through the head, some are absorbed by the tissues of the head. Detectors located opposite the beam source measure the attenuation of the photons (Figure 8–2). Thus, the CT images of the brain record tissue density as measured by the variable attenuation of X-ray photons. High-density tissues such as bone appear white, indicating an almost complete absorption of the X rays (high attenuation). Air has the lowest rate of attenuation (or absorption of radiation) and appears black. The appearance of other tissues is given in Table 8–3.

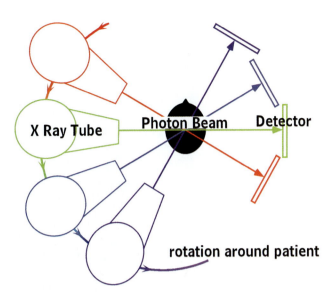

**FIGURE 8–2.** Schematic of conventional computed tomography X-ray tube and detector. Note the simultaneous circular movement of both devices about the head.

Modern CT scanners can generate brain images that range from 0.5 to 10 mm in thickness, with 3–5 mm used most commonly. The slice thickness of a CT image is an important variable in clinical scanning. Thinner slices allow visualization of smaller lesions. However, the thinnest sections have less contrast (i.e., the signal intensity difference between gray and white matter is less) because the signal:noise ratio is lower. It also takes longer to complete the examination because more slices must be acquired. Thus there is more chance of patient motion degrading the images. The longer scan time also decreases the number of patients that can be examined in a day. Thicker sections (or slices) have greater contrast, but smaller lesions may be missed. There is also a greater incidence of artifacts due to increased volume averaging. This is particularly true in the base of the skull, and this may obscure brain stem and mesial temporal structures. See Figure 8–3 for other scan parameters that affect image quality.

### Three-Dimensional CT (Single-Slice and Multislice Helical CT)

As CT imaging became an integral part of medical diagnostics, faster and more advanced technologies were invented. The 1990s brought the clinical introduction of helical (spiral) CT, in which slip rings allow continuous scanning of a patient. This is much faster than the older "scan—stop—move the table and reset the detector—scan again" sequence used for standard two-dimensional CT (Figure 8–4). In addition, there is

**TABLE 8–3.** Relative gray-scale appearance on a noncontrast computed tomography scan

| Tissue | Appearance |
| --- | --- |
| Bone | White |
| Calcified tissue | White |
| Clotted blood | White[a] |
| Gray matter | Light gray |
| White matter | Medium gray |
| Cerebrospinal fluid | Nearly black |
| Water | Nearly black |
| Air | Black |

[a]Becomes isointense to brain as clot ages approximately 1–2 weeks.

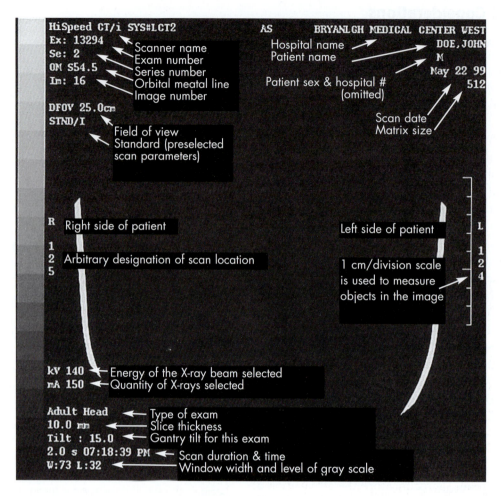

**FIGURE 8–3.** Computed tomography header information and arbitrary gray scale. Explanations for abbreviations used on the image are also included.

less radiation exposure, and less contrast agent is needed. More images can be collected before the X-ray beam must be shut down for cooling. Two-dimensional images can be reconstructed in any plane of section from the acquired three-dimensional data set. Three-dimensional reconstructions can also be done in as little as 2 minutes (Figure 8–5).

Initially, single-slice helical CT was principally useful in body scanning. It had limited use in the brain due to skull thickness (i.e., it produced grainy images that did not discriminate between gray and white matter very well) (Bahner et al. 1998; Coleman and Zimmerman 1994). Applications for the head included evaluations of pediatric patients (thinner cranium), adult carotid stenosis, aneurysms, arteriovenous malformations, vessel occlusions in acute stroke, and as a tool for intravenous angiography (Coleman and Zimmerman 1994; Kuszyk et al. 1998; Schwartz 1995). The newest helical CT scanners provide images of similar quality to the standard single-slice CT (Kuntz et al. 1998). Three-dimensional

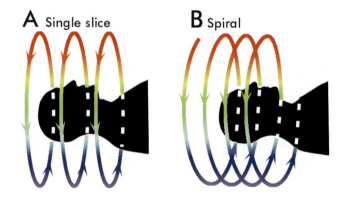

**FIGURE 8–4.** Schematic of computed tomography (CT) scanning path. *Panel A.* Conventional CT. *Panel B.* Helical (spiral) CT. Note the continuous overlapping helical path in spiral CT.

reconstruction is still available for use in stereotactic neurosurgery planning and vascular evaluations (Katada 1999; Moringlane et al. 1997).

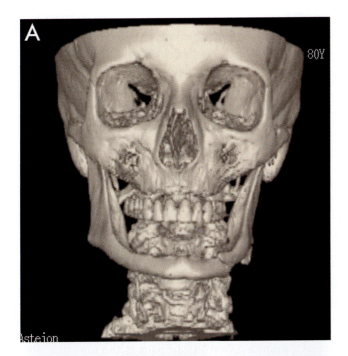

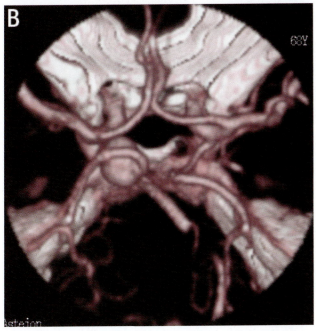

**FIGURE 8–5.** Three-dimensional reconstruction from helical computed tomography (CT). Current CT scanners can acquire extremely detailed data sets in a matter of seconds. The data can be viewed as three-dimensional volume images from any desired angle. Reconstructions of bone (*Panel A*) are valuable both for diagnosis and for surgical planning. CT angiography, such as this view of an aneurysm in the circle of Willis (*Panel B*), is capable of displaying vessels from any angle. Since scanning is very rapid and noninvasive, such examinations may be performed in place of conventional angiograms.

*Source.* Images courtesy of Toshiba America Medical Systems, Inc.

## Xenon-Enhanced CT

Although officially labeled a functional imaging technique, xenon-enhanced CT (Xe/CT) allows identification of structural lesions that may be invisible on CT and MRI. Xe/CT uses stable xenon gas as a contrast agent because it is radiodense and lipid soluble. After obtaining baseline standard CT images, the patient inhales a mixture of xenon (26%–33%) and oxygen. A second set of images is then collected in which the distribution of the xenon shows regional blood flow, allowing areas of abnormality to be identified.

Xe/CT has evolved to allow more routine clinical use as technical advances have lessened the side effects and permit repeated imaging. Currently, the images can be computed in seconds. At the diluted concentration mentioned above, transient side effects of xenon inhalation include euphoria, dysphoria, sedation, nausea, and apnea (reversible with instructions to breathe). Advantages of Xe/CT over other methods of imaging blood flow include lack of radiation or radiotracer exposure, good image resolution, and direct anatomical correlation. It is inexpensive (the technique adds less than $100 per study), can be repeated frequently (for example after a drug challenge), and adds no more than 10 minutes to the total examination time.

Clinical indications for Xe/CT are slowly emerging. Currently, the technique has proved advantageous in discovering hidden lesions not evident on standard imaging. Patients whose clinical symptoms do not fit the classic historical picture for the working diagnosis should therefore be considered for Xe/CT. Taber et al. reported a case of a patient whose diagnoses were changed from probable Alzheimer's disease and major depression to dementia secondary to a cerebrovascular accident. In that particular case, treatment plans were then altered (Taber et al. 1999). Examples of a normal CT and companion Xe/CT scan in a different stroke patient are given in Figure 8–6.

## Contrast Agents

The administration of intravenous iodinated contrast medium immediately before obtaining a CT scan greatly improves the detection of many brain lesions that are isodense on noncontrast CT. Contrast agents are useful when there is a breakdown of the BBB. Under normal circumstances, the BBB does not allow passage of contrast medium into the extravascular spaces of the brain. When there is a break in this barrier, the contrast agent enters the damaged area and collects in or around the lesion. The *increased* density of the contrast agent will appear as a white area on the scan. Without a companion noncon-

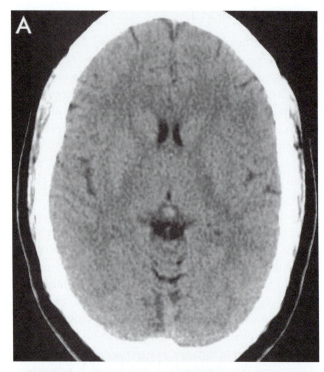

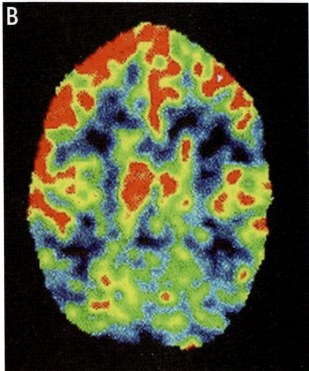

**FIGURE 8–6.** Imaging of acute stroke in a fifty-two-year-old woman who presented with left-sided weakness. Computed tomographic (CT) images acquired 1.5 hours after onset (*Panel A*) were normal. Companion xenon-enhanced CT images (*Panel B*) showed luxury perfusion on the right (arrows), indicating that the area of the stroke had already reperfused. Magnetic resonance images acquired the next day were normal.

*Source.* Images courtesy of Ben Taub General Hospital, Houston, TX.

trast CT scan, preexisting dense areas (calcified or hemorrhagic) might be mistaken for contrast-enhanced lesions. In difficult cases, a double dose of contrast agent may be used to improve detection of lesions with minimal BBB impairment.

Currently there are two types of iodinated CT contrast agents: ionic or high osmolality and nonionic or low osmolality. Both types are associated with allergic reactions, and contraindications for both exist. Allergic reactions to contrast agents are defined by two types in two time frames: anaphylactoid or nonanaphylactoid (chemotoxic) and immediate or delayed. The recent literature debates the true incidence of all of these (Federle et al. 1998; Jacobs et al. 1998; Oi et al. 1997; Yasuda and Munechika 1998). Immediate reactions occur within 1 hour of injection; delayed reactions occur within 7 days but usually within 24 hours. Anaphylactoid reactions include hives, rhinitis, bronchospasm, laryngeal edema, hypotension, and death. Chemotoxic reactions include nausea, vomiting, warmth or pain at the injection site, hypotension, tachycardia, and arrhythmias (Cohan et al. 1998a; Federle et al. 1998). The overall mortality rate from ionic dyes is reported to be 1 per 12,000–170,000 (average is 1/100,000), with severe reactions occurring in 1 per 1,000 patients (Cohan et al. 1998b; Jacobs et al. 1998). The rates for severe reactions to nonionic dyes are significantly lower (1–2 per 10,000 examinations) (Cohan et al. 1998c). Currently, average rates for milder reactions are 5%–25% for ionic agents and 1%–5% for nonionic agents (Federle et al. 1998; Jacobs et al. 1998; Yasuda and Munechika 1998). The ionic agents are significantly less expensive, but they are very rarely used because of the greater risk of allergic reactions (see Table 8–6 for the cost of both the scan and contrast media).

The American College of Radiology standards recommend the use of nonionic dye in patients with histories of previous significant contrast media reactions; any previous serious allergic reaction to any material; asthma; sickle cell disease; diabetes; renal insufficiency (creatinine ≥ 1.5 mg/dL); cardiac diseases; inability to communicate; geriatric age; or other debilitating health problems (Cohan et al. 1998d; Halpern et al. 1996). Patients who are receiving dialysis or who have histories of milder reactions to shellfish require the use of nonionic dyes when contrast CT is unavoidable. The older ionic agents are not used in these patients.

Extravasation (leakage of the contrast dye at the injection site) is generally a mild problem associated with some stinging or burning. However, in infrequent cases, patients have developed tissue ulceration or necrosis. If a patient has had a previous episode of extravasation, then nonionic dye should be used, as it is associated with fewer reactions.

Other areas of caution include patients with histories of anaphylaxis. These patients should be considered for other types of imaging, rather than contrast-enhanced CT. If contrast-enhanced CT is necessary, then premedication with steroids and antihistamines and the use of nonionic dye are recommended. Metformin, an oral anti-hyperglycemic agent, must be withheld before iodinated dye is given. It can be restarted after 48 hours with laboratory evidence of normal renal function. Metformin can cause lactic acidosis, especially in patients with a history of renal or hepatic dysfunction, alcohol abuse, or cardiac disease (Cohan et al. 1998d).

## Magnetic Resonance Imaging

In 1946, the phenomenon of nuclear magnetic resonance was discovered. The discovery led to the development of a powerful new technique for studying matter by using radio waves together with a static magnetic field. This development, combined with other important insights and emerging technologies in the 1970s, led to the first magnetic resonance image of a living patient. By the 1980s, commercial MRI scanners were becoming more common. Although the physics that make MRI possible are complex, a grasp of the basic principles will help the clinician understand the results of the imaging examination and explain this procedure to anxious patients.

## Physical Principles

### Reconstructing an Image

Clinical MRI is based on manipulating the small magnetic field around the nucleus of the hydrogen atom (proton), a major component of water in soft tissue. To make a magnetic resonance image of a patient's soft tissues, the patient must be placed inside a large magnet. The strength of the magnet is measured in teslas (T). A high-field clinical system has a field strength of 1.5 T. (More powerful systems are often used in research settings.) A mid-field system is generally 0.5 T, and low-field units range from 0.1 to 0.5 T.

The magnetic field of the MRI scanner slightly magnetizes the hydrogen atoms in the body, changing their alignment. The stronger the magnetic field, the more magnetized the hydrogen atoms in tissue become and the more signal they will produce. The stronger signal available with 1.5-T systems allows higher-resolution images to be collected. However, this increased detail is costly, because high-field systems are more expensive than mid- or low-field systems. Also, many patients feel uncomfort-

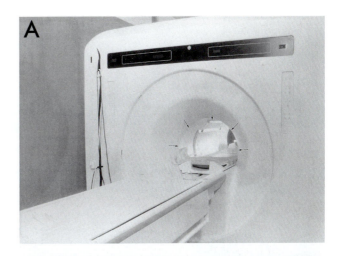

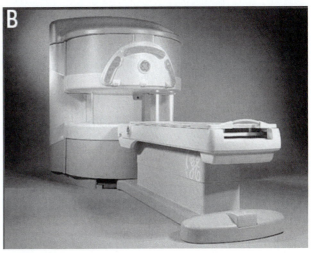

**FIGURE 8–7.** Magnetic resonance scanners. *Panel A.* High-field (1.5-T) magnetic resonance scanner. Note the relatively small circular opening (arrows). *Panel B.* An open-design scanner allows greater access to the patient and reduces the likelihood of claustrophobia.

*Source.* Photographs of Signa scanner (panel A) and Signa OpenSpeed scanner (panel B) courtesy of GE Medical Systems.

able while lying inside these huge enclosing magnets (Figure 8–7A). Open-design magnets are now available that help the patient feel less confined (Figure 8–7B).

To create a magnetic resonance image, the patient's hydrogen atoms are exposed to a carefully calculated series of radio frequency (RF) pulses while the patient is within the scanner's magnetic field. These RF pulses cause changes in the magnetization of the hydrogen atoms. This changing magnetic field generates tiny electric signals that are picked up by a receiver placed close to the area being scanned (the imaging coil). A head coil that closely encloses the head, allowing maximal signal reception, is used to obtain brain images.

The scanner's computer converts these signals into a spatial map, the magnetic resonance image. This conver-

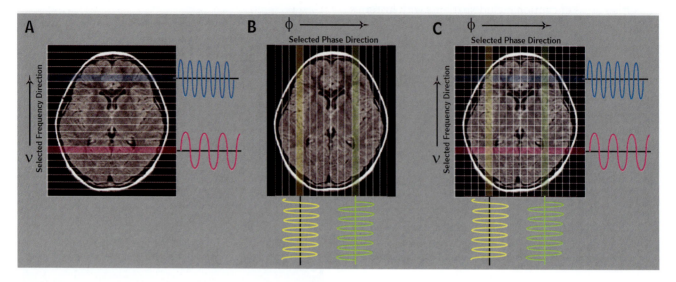

**FIGURE 8–8.** Origin of the imaging grid. *Panel A.* Sample magnetic resonance image is overlaid with rows created by a read (frequency-encoding) gradient. *Panel B.* Sample magnetic resonance image is overlaid with columns created by a phase gradient. *Panel C.* Sample magnetic resonance image is overlaid with the grid created by the frequency and phase gradients. The computer uses the combination of frequency and phase to identify the signal from each block in the grid.

sion requires parceling information into blocks that form a square (or sometimes rectangular) grid. The size of each block (commonly called a voxel or a pixel in the final two-dimensional image) in the grid is important. If the blocks are too large, they will contain many types of tissue and will not have the desired spatial resolution. If the blocks are too small, there will not be enough signal in each to form an image.

The scanner's computer places signals in each block using a two-step process that makes each block slightly different from all other blocks. First the computer alters the magnetic field strength in each succeeding row of blocks by applying a magnetic field gradient across the tissue (the *read gradient*). This difference in magnetic field strength changes the frequency of the signal from each row in the image, hence the term *frequency-encoding direction* (Figure 8–8A). The number of frequency bands the computer divides the signal into determines the number of rows that will form the image (most commonly 256 or 512). Thus, each row represents a different frequency (measured in hertz).

The second step separates the signals in the other direction to superimpose columns over the rows (Figure 8–8B). A *phase gradient* is applied across the columns to speed up (or slow down) the radio waves that form the signal, hence the term *phase-encoding direction*. The individual measurement, called a *view*, has to be repeated multiple times, with the phase gradient increased each time. This process takes up most of the scan time. The number of *phase-encoding steps* determines the number

of columns in the image. It is selectable and is usually set at 192 or 256. The computer uses the combination of the exact frequency and phase of each component radio wave from the signal to assign it to the correct block within the grid, thus forming the image (Figure 8–8C). The technologist can apply read and phase gradients in any direction, but they must remain perpendicular to each other to form a grid and thereby create the magnetic resonance image.

The magnetic field gradients needed to acquire the image are created by huge coils of wire embedded in the magnet. These are driven with large-current audio amplifiers similar to those used for musical concerts. The gradients must be switched on and off very rapidly. This creates loud noises during the scan and may distress the unprepared patient.

## Common Pulse Sequences

The combination of RF and magnetic field pulses used by the computer to create the image is called the *pulse sequence*. Pulse sequences have been developed that result in images sensitive to different aspects of the hydrogen atom's behavior in a high magnetic field. Thus each image type contains unique information about the tissue. A pulse sequence is repeated many times to form an image (see previous section).

The pulse sequence used most commonly in clinical MRI is the *spin echo* (SE) sequence. Many centers now use a faster variant of this sequence, the *fast spin echo* (FSE). These pulse sequences emphasize different tissue

**TABLE 8–4.** Acquisition parameter ranges for different pulse sequences (given in milliseconds)

| Acquisition parameter | Pulse sequence | | |
|---|---|---|---|
| | T1-weighted | T2-weighted | Spin density–weighted |
| Repetition time (TR) | 400–800 | 3,000–5,000 | 3,000–5,000 |
| Echo time (TE) | 10–20 | 60–120 | 10–20 |

**TABLE 8–5.** Relative gray scale values present in tissues visible on magnetic resonance imaging scans (non-contrast-enhanced)

| Tissue | Pulse sequence | | |
|---|---|---|---|
| | T1-weighted | T2-weighted | Spin density–weighted |
| Bone | Black | Black | Black |
| Calcified tissue | Variable, usually gray | Variable, usually gray | Variable, usually gray |
| Gray matter | Medium gray | Medium gray | Light gray |
| White matter | Light gray | Dark gray | Medium gray |
| Cerebrospinal fluid | Black | White | Gray |
| Water | Black | White | Gray |
| Air | Black | Black | Black |
| Pathology (excluding blood) | Gray | White | White |
| Blood | | | |
| Acute | Dark gray | Black | Light gray |
| Subacute | White | White | White |

properties by varying two factors. One is the time between applying each repetition of the sequence, referred to as the *repetition time* or *time to recovery* (TR). The other is the time at which the receiver coil collects signal after the RF pulses have been given. This is called the *echo time* or *time until the echo* (TE). The ranges of TR and TE that result in commonly used types of magnetic resonance images are listed in Table 8–4. A summary of the expected imaging appearance of various tissues on commonly used types of magnetic resonance images is given in Table 8–5.

Images collected using a short TR and short TE are most heavily influenced by the T1 relaxation times of the tissues and so are called *T1 weighted* (T1W). Figure 8–9 shows a T1-weighted set of brain images. Note the sharply margined boundaries between the brain (light gray) and cerebrospinal fluid (CSF) (black). Traditionally, this type of image is considered best for displaying anatomy.

Images collected using a long TR and a long TE are most heavily influenced by the T2 relaxation times of tissues and so are called *T2 weighted* (T2W). Figure 8–10 shows a set of T2-weighted images of the same brain. This type of image is best for displaying pathology, which most commonly appears bright, often similar in intensity to CSF. A very useful variant on the T2-weighted scan, called a *fluid-attenuated inversion recovery* (FLAIR)

image, allows the intense signal from CSF to be nullified. This makes pathology near CSF-filled spaces much easier to see (Arakia et al. 1999; Bergin et al. 1995; Brant-Zawadzki et al. 1996; Rydberg et al. 1994). Figure 8–11 shows a set of FLAIR images. We have found this method of MRI to be extremely useful in neuropsychiatric imaging (Figure 8–12).

If a long TR and a short TE are used, the image is most sensitive to the concentration of hydrogen atoms, also called the proton density or spin density. Thus, these images are called *spin density weighted* (SDW). Figure 8–13 shows a set of spin density–weighted images of the same brain. The striking contrast between brain tissue and CSF seen on the T1-weighted and T2-weighted images is not present. The mild T2 weighting of this type of image makes fiber tracts easy to see.

The next most commonly used pulse sequence in clinical imaging is the *gradient echo* (GE or GRE) sequence. In this type of image acquisition, a gradient reversal rather than an RF pulse is used to generate the echo. As a result, this technique is very sensitive to anything in the tissue causing magnetic field inhomogeneity, such as hemorrhage or calcium. These images are sometimes called *susceptibility weighted* because differences in magnetic susceptibility between tissues cause magnetic field inhomogeneity and signal loss. As a result, gradient echo images have artifacts at the interfaces

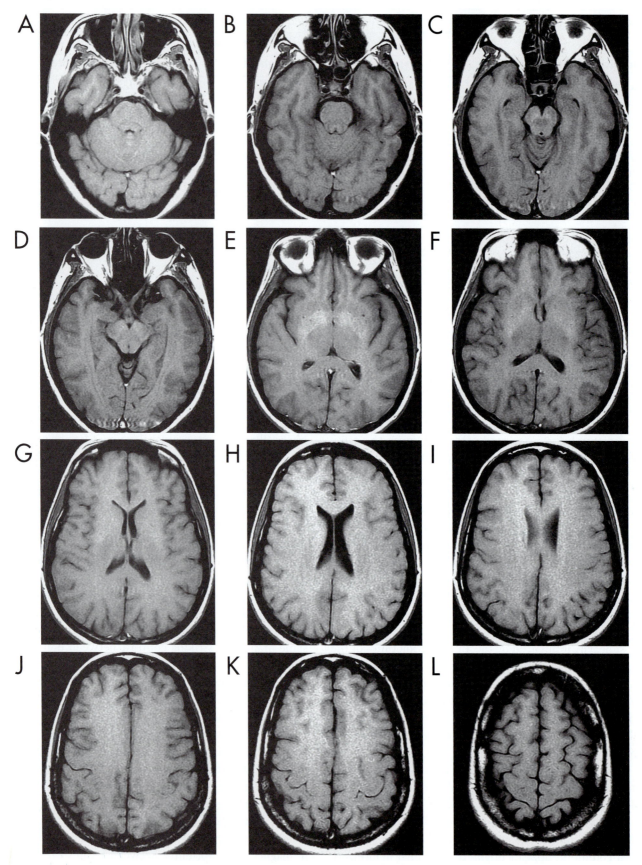

**FIGURE 8–9.** Serial axial T1-weighted magnetic resonance images of a normal adult brain.

*Source.* Images courtesy of GE Medical Systems.

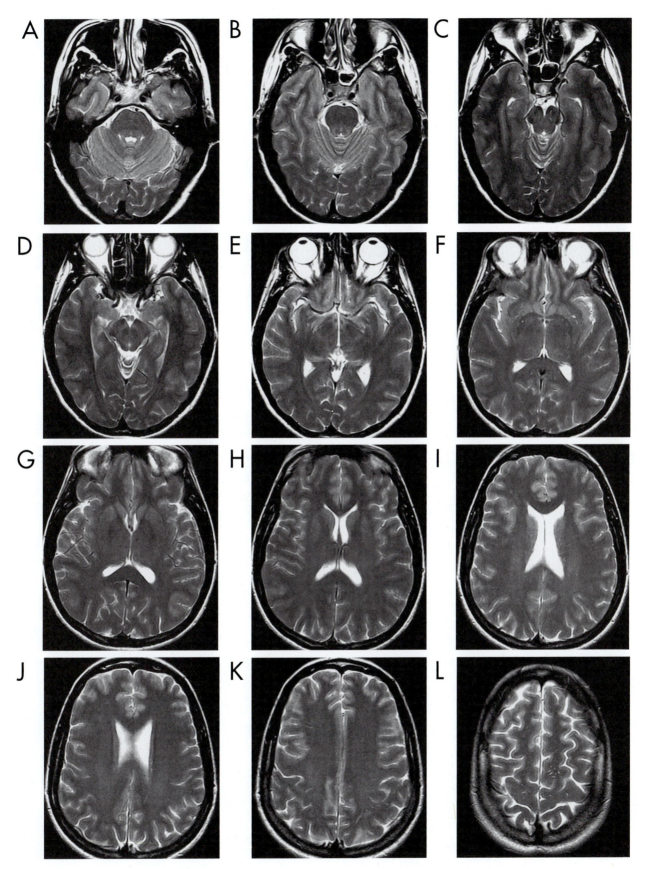

**FIGURE 8–10.** Serial axial T2-weighted magnetic resonance images of a normal adult brain.

*Source.* Images courtesy of GE Medical Systems.

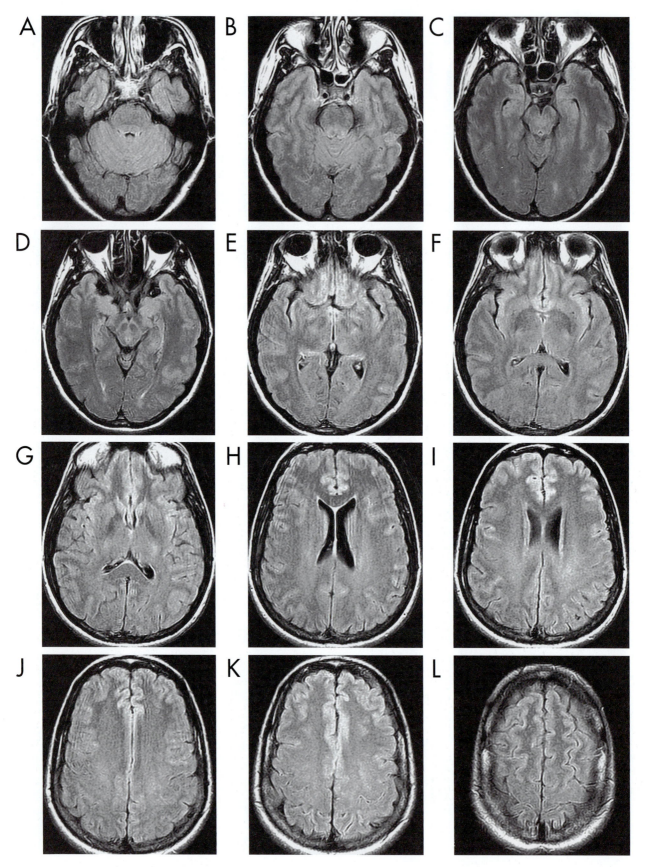

**FIGURE 8–11.** Serial axial fluid-attenuated inversion recovery (FLAIR) magnetic resonance images of a normal adult brain.

*Source.* Images courtesy of GE Medical Systems.

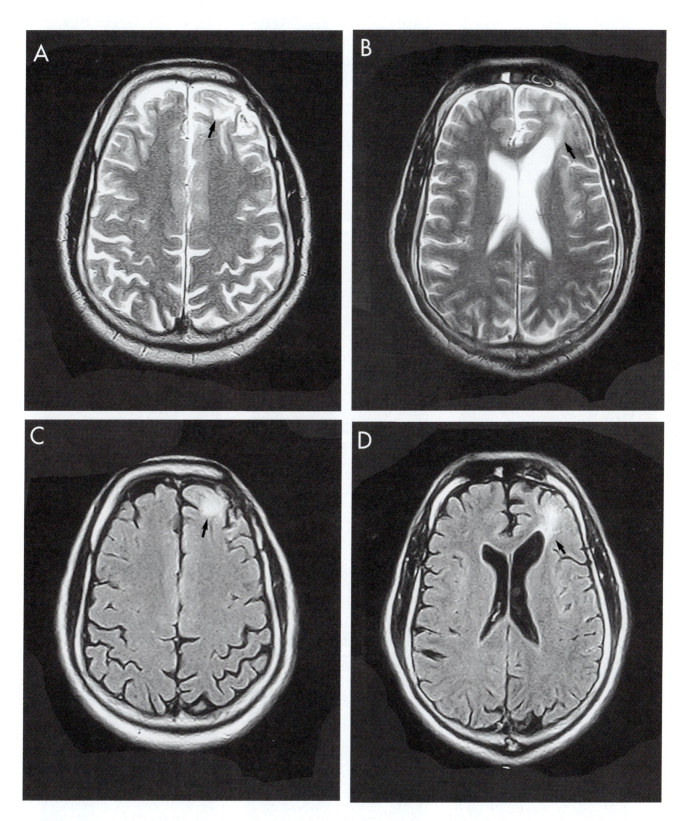

**FIGURE 8–12.** Comparison of T2-weighted and fluid-attenuated inversion recovery (FLAIR) magnetic resonance imaging (MRI). MRI scans of a 36-year-old man who presented for admission with nausea, vomiting, and hyponatremia. Two days later the patient was agitated, sexually inappropriate, and wandering incoherently. Neuropsychiatric workup revealed status epilepticus. Subsequent MRI demonstrated a previous left frontal traumatic brain injury. Although the injury is visible on T2-weighted images (*A* and *B*), the extent of the injury is much more easily appreciated on the FLAIR images (*C* and *D*).

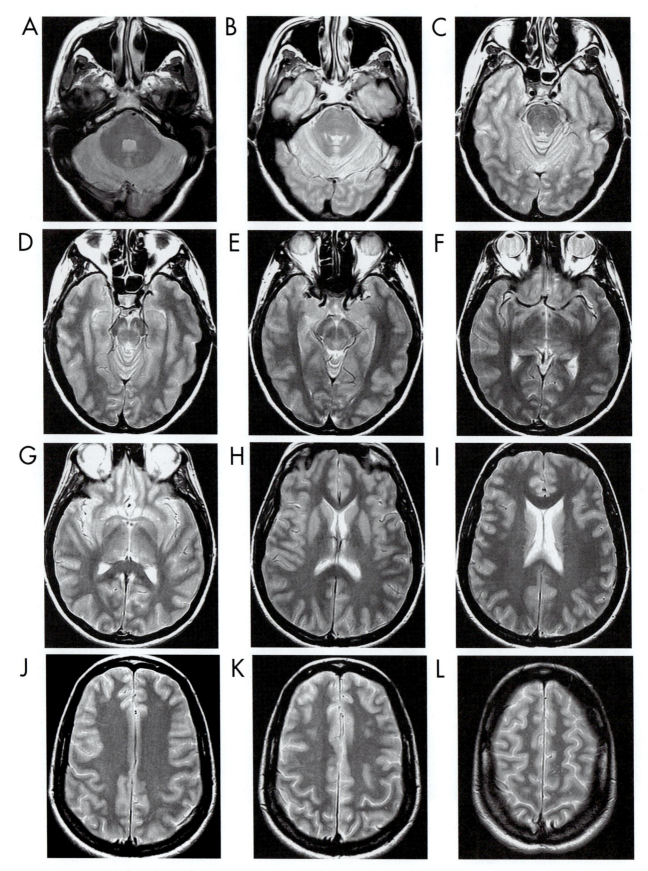

**FIGURE 8–13.** Serial axial spin density–weighted magnetic resonance images of a normal adult brain.

*Source.* Images courtesy of GE Medical Systems.

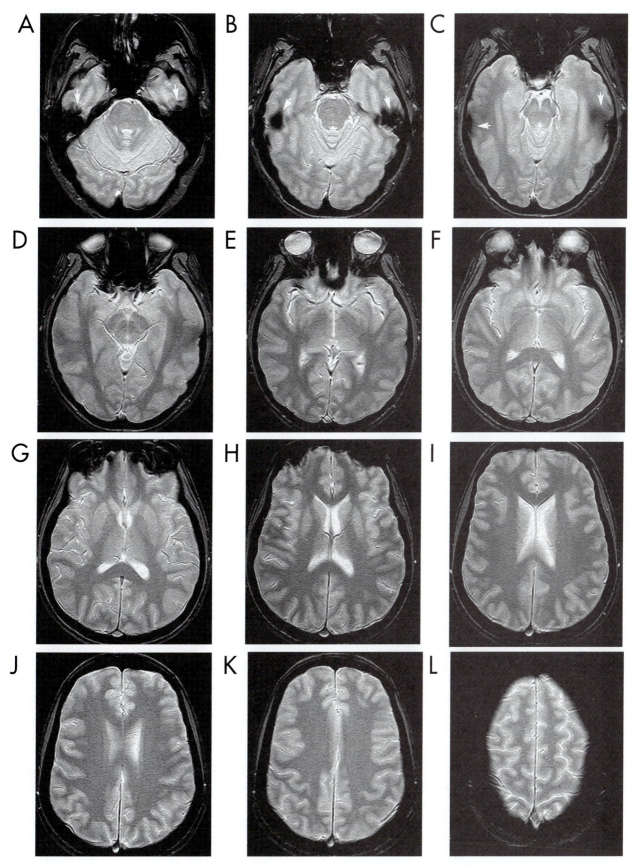

**FIGURE 8–14.** Serial axial gradient echo magnetic resonance images of a normal adult brain.

*Source.* Images courtesy of GE Medical Systems.

between tissues with very different magnetic susceptibility, such as bone and brain. The artifacts at the skull base are sometimes severe (see arrows on Figure 8–14). Figure 8–14 shows a set of gradient echo images of the same brain. Other scan parameters also affect image quality. These parameters are indicated in Figure 8–15.

## New Pulse Sequences

Several types of pulse sequences that are sensitive to other aspects of tissue state are being tested for clinical work. One method is sensitive to interactions between free protons (unbound water in tissue) and bound protons (water bound to macromolecules such as those in myelin membranes) (Hanyu et al. 1999; Tanabe et al. 1999). This type of magnetic resonance image, called a magnetization transfer (MT) image, may be able to differentiate white matter lesions due to different causes and thus provide insight into pathological processes (Hanyu et al. 1999; Tanabe et al. 1999). Another method of MRI is sensitive to the speed of water diffusion. Diffusion-weighted (DW) MRI may be able to visualize areas of stroke in the critical first few hours after onset. It may be that in the future, a combination of some of these newer methods of MRI will provide important information for differential diagnosis.

## Contrast Agents

The first experimental contrast-enhanced magnetic resonance image was made in 1982 using a gadolinium complex, gadolinium-diethylenetriamine pentaacetic acid (Gd-DTPA), now called gadopentetate dimeglumine. Six years later gadopentetate dimeglumine was approved as an intravenous contrast agent for human clinical MRI scans (Wolf 1991). See Table 8–6 for the cost of both MRI and contrast agent.

Metal ions such as gadolinium are quite toxic to the body if they are in a free state. To make an MRI contrast agent, the metal ion is attached to a very strong ligand (such as DTPA) that prevents any interaction with surrounding tissue. This allows the gadolinium complex to be excreted intact by the kidneys. Three gadolinium-based contrast agents are currently in common use: gadopentetate dimeglumine (Magnevist, Berlex Laboratories), gadodiamide (Omniscan, Nycomed Amersham), and gadoteridol (ProHance, Bracco Diagnostics) (Shellock and Kanal 1999). These agents are administered intravenously, whereupon they distribute to the vascular compartment and then diffuse throughout the extracellular compartment (Mitchell 1997).

Gadolinium is a metal ion that is highly paramagnetic, with a natural magnetic field 657 times greater than that of the hydrogen atom. Unlike the iodinated contrast agents used in CT, the currently used clinical MRI contrast agents are not imaged directly. Rather, the presence of the contrast agent changes the T1 and T2 properties of hydrogen atoms (protons) in nearby tissue (Runge et al. 1997). Like CT contrast agents, MRI contrast agents do not enter the brain under normal conditions because they cannot pass through the BBB. When there is damage to the BBB, these agents accumulate in tissue around the breakdown. The effect of this accumulation is most easily seen on a T1-weighted scan, where it results in an increase in signal (seen as a white or bright area; see Figure 8–16) (Runge et al. 1997).

On a worldwide basis, 30%–40% of MRI studies include contrast enhancement (Shellock and Kanal 1999). The total incidence of adverse side effects appears to be less than 3%–5%, with any single type of side effect occurring in fewer than 1% of patients (Runge et al. 1997; Shellock and Kanal 1999). Immediate reactions at the injection site include warmth or a burning sensation, pain, and local edema. Delayed reactions (including erythema, swelling, and pain) appear 1–4 days after the injection. Immediate systemic reactions include nausea (sometimes vomiting) and headache. Anaphylactoid reactions have been reported, particularly in patients with a history of allergic respiratory disease. The incidence of these reactions appears to be somewhere between 1 and 5 in 500,000. These agents can be used even in a patient with severe renal disease, provided there is some renal output. This allows contrast-enhanced MRI scans to be obtained in dialysis patients. (For a more extensive review of the biosafety aspects of MRI contrast agents, see Shellock and Kanal 1999.)

Many new MRI contrast agents are under development (Earls and Bluemke 1999; Mitchell 1997). Some link metal ions (gadolinium, manganese) with a structure that allows them to be directed toward specific tissues. Another approach uses specially formulated iron oxide particles (superparamagnetic iron oxide). These alter T2 relaxation more than T1 and are imaged using T2-weighted and gradient echo sequences. Still other efforts are directed toward developing MRI of specific receptors (Nunn et al. 1997). As new contrast agents become available for MRI of the brain, the range of applications in neuropsychiatry may well expand.

## Safety and Contraindications

To date, there appear to be no permanent hazardous effects from short-term exposure to magnetic fields and RF pulses generated in clinical MRI scanners (Price

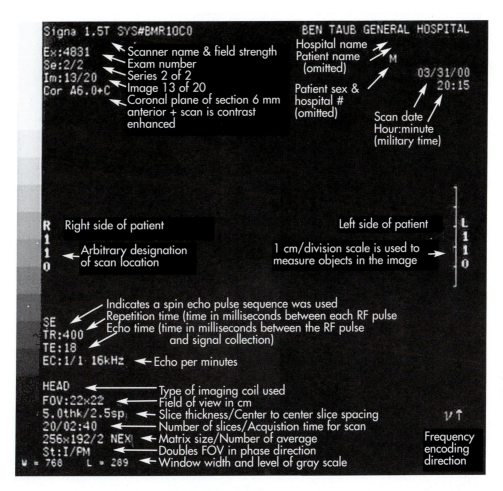

**FIGURE 8–15.** Magnetic resonance imaging header information and arbitrary gray scale. Explanations for abbreviations used on the image are also included.

1999). Volunteers scanned using systems with very high field strength (4 T) have reported effects including headaches, dizziness, and nausea (Shellock and Kanal 1991). With very intense gradients it is possible to directly stimulate peripheral nerves, but this is not a concern at clinical field strengths (Bourland et al. 1999; Hoffmann et al. 2000).

There are, however, important contraindications to the use of MRI (see Table 8–6 for summary). The magnetic field can damage electrical, mechanical, or magnetic devices implanted in or attached to the patient. Pacemakers can be damaged by programming changes, possibly inducing arrhythmias. Currents can develop within the wires, leading to burns, fibrillation, or movement of the wires or the pacemaker unit itself. Cochlear implants, dental implants, magnetic stoma plugs, bone-growth stimulators, and implanted medication-infusion pumps can all be demagnetized or injure the patient by movement during exposure to the scanner's magnetic field. In addition, metallic implants, shrapnel, bullets, or metal shavings within the eye (e.g., from welding) can

conduct a current and/or move, injuring the eye. All of these devices distort the magnetic resonance image locally and may decrease diagnostic accuracy. Metallic objects near the magnet can be drawn into the magnet at high speed, injuring the patient or staff (Price 1999; Shellock and Kanal 1991).

Although there is no evidence of damage to the developing fetus, most authorities recommend caution. Judgment should be exercised when considering MRI of a pregnant woman. When possible, express written consent might be obtained from the patient, especially in the first trimester (Shellock and Kanal 1991).

Difficulties have also been encountered when a patient requires physiologic monitoring during the procedure. Several manufacturers have developed MRI-compatible respirators and monitors for blood pressure and heart rate. If these are not available, then the standard monitoring devices must be placed at least 8 feet from the magnet. Otherwise, the readout may be altered or the devices may interfere with obtaining the MRI scan.

**TABLE 8–6.** Factors considered when choosing computed tomography (CT) or magnetic resonance imaging (MRI) examination

| Clinical considerations | CT | MRI |
|---|---|---|
| Availability | Universal | Limited |
| Sensitivity | Good | Superior |
| Resolution | 1.5 mm | 1.5 mm |
| Average examination time | 1 minute | 30–45 minutes |
| Plane of section | Axial only | Any plane of section |
| Conditions for which it is the preferred procedure | Acute hemorrhage<br>Calcified lesions<br>Screening examination<br>Bone injury | All subcortical lesions<br>Poison or toxin exposure<br>Demyelinating disorders<br>Eating disorders<br>Examination requiring anatomical detail, especially temporal lobe<br>Any condition best viewed in nonaxial plane |
| Contraindications | History of anaphylaxis or severe allergic reaction (contrast-enhanced CT)<br>Creatinine ≥ 1.5 mg/dL (contrast-enhanced CT)<br>Metformin administration on day of scan (contrast-enhanced CT) | Any magnetic metal in the body, including surgical clips and sutures<br>Implanted electrical, mechanical, or magnetic devices<br>Claustrophobia<br>History of welding (requires skull films before MRI)<br>Pregnancy (legal contraindication) |
| Cost to patient per scan without contrast medium[a] | ~$230 | ~$550 |
| Cost to patient per single dose of contrast medium[a] | ~$60 nonionic | ~$110 |

[a]Costs are regionally variable. Please consult imaging sources in your area for current figures.

## MRI Versus CT

The choice of imaging modality should be based on the anatomy and/or pathology that one desires to view (see Table 8–6). CT is used as an inexpensive screening examination. There are also a few conditions best viewed with CT. These include calcification, acute hemorrhage, and any bone injury, as these pathologies are not yet reliably imaged with MRI (Figure 8–17). However, in the vast majority of cases, MRI is the preferred modality. The image resolution is much higher, more types of pathology are visible, and the brain can be imaged in any plane of section. For example, subcortical lesions are consistently better visualized with MRI because of the greater gray-white contrast and the ability to image in planes other than axial (Figure 8–18). Demyelination due to poison exposure or autoimmune disease (such as multiple sclerosis) is also seen significantly better on MRI, especially when many small lesions are present (Figure 8–19). MRI does not produce the artifacts from bone that are seen in CT, so all lesions near bone (i.e., brain stem, posterior

fossa, pituitary, hypothalamus) are better visualized on MRI. Most temporal lobe structures, especially the hippocampal formation and amygdala, are most easily evaluated using the coronal and sagittal planes of section, rather than axial.

## Normal Imaging Anatomy

It is essential for the practicing neuropsychiatrist to have a basic understanding of the cortical and subcortical anatomy involved in thought, memory, and emotion if he or she is to use information gathered from imaging. This includes sufficient knowledge to identify these structures on CT and MRI in the various planes of section. In addition, the neuropsychiatrist must have the ability to identify clinical scenarios that warrant imaging investigation for lesions (e.g., traumatic brain injury, stroke, poison/toxin exposure).

The following section presents an introductory overview of the functional neuroanatomy of executive function, memory, and emotion, as well as clinical examples

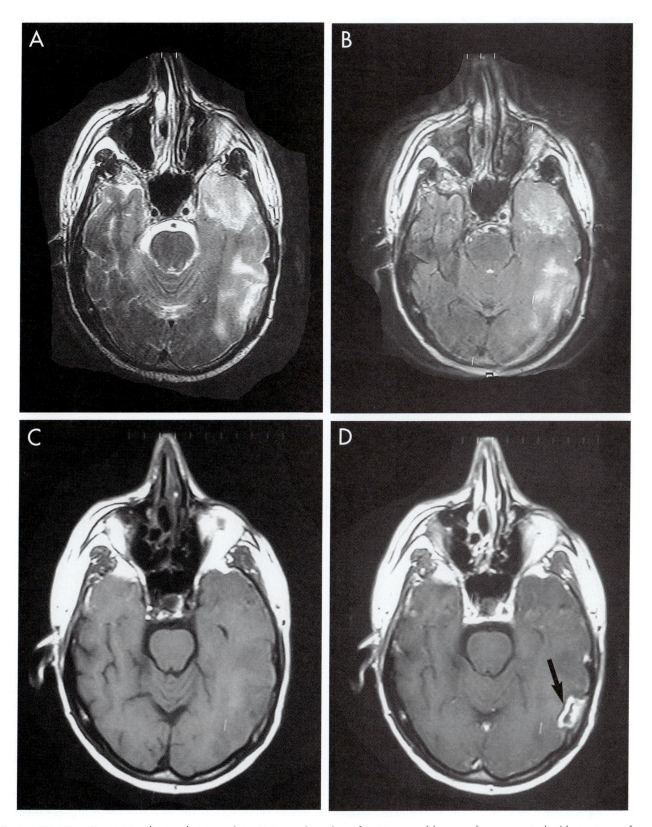

**FIGURE 8–16.** Contrast-enhanced magnetic resonance imaging of a 69-year-old man who presented with acute confusion and status post a generalized tonic-clonic seizure. Sequential imaging revealed a left temporal mass, most probably an astrocytoma (infiltrating type). The tumor is more easily seen on T2-weighted (*Panel A*) and fluid-attenuated inversion recovery (*Panel B*) images than on T1-weighted images (*Panel C*). After administration of contrast medium (*Panel D*), an area of blood-brain barrier breakdown within the tumor becomes visible *(arrow)*.

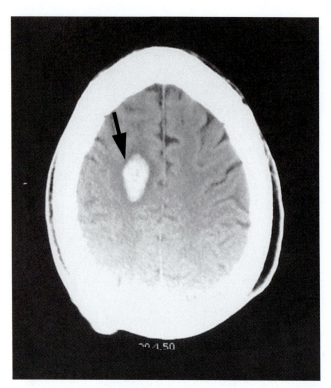

**FIGURE 8–17.** Computed tomographic image of a 56-year-old man taking warfarin who presented with left-sided weakness a few hours after being involved in a motorcycle accident. He experienced a brief loss of consciousness after the accident. Note the well-visualized area of hyperdense hemorrhage (arrow).

and references for further reading. An illustration of the subcortical structures is given in Figure 8–20. The imaging atlas combines normal CT, normal MRI, and diagrammatic representations of color-coded key structures to promote understanding (Figures 8–21 through 8–32). It is important to realize that in many cases, lesions within these structures are best viewed in the coronal and sagittal planes of section—thus MRI is often preferable to CT. In addition, both T2-weighted sagittal and FLAIR sequences may provide details of lesions not seen on other sequences. However, in most cases the attending physician must specifically request these pulse sequences before imaging. This atlas and the accompanying brief descriptive material can not only familiarize the clinician with normal imaging anatomy pertinent to a neuropsychiatrist, but it can also serve as a base for further study. The cranial nerves, motor pathways, and peripheral sensory tracts are not discussed. Although T1-weighted images are generally considered the best for displaying anatomy, proton density–weighted images are used in the atlas because they reproduce better.

Thought, memory, and emotion are believed to occur by way of complicated circuits or networks of interconnected areas of brain. Lesions at any point in a circuit can potentially give rise to identical symptoms (Burruss et al. 2000; Masterman and Cummings 1997; Mega and Cummings 1994). The reader should be mindful that although the larger brain structures are mentioned in the following discussion, any lesion along the small tracts between regions can also produce similar deficits. A comprehensive review of these circuits is beyond the scope of this chapter (the interested reader may consult the following articles: Hurley et al. 1995; Mega et al. 1997; Trimble et al. 1997). With the advent of graphic programs and computer technology, there are many three-dimensional models available that make these circuits easier to understand (e.g., Hayman et al. 1995; Hurley et al. 1995; Interactive Atlas of Human Anatomy 1995; Naumescu et al. 1999; Nowinski et al. 1997).

The major neuropsychiatric symptoms associated with damage to various subcortical structures are summarized below. These summaries were derived from a more comprehensive review, which can be consulted for more detail (Naumescu et al. 1999).

## Cerebral Cortex

The largest division of the human brain is the cerebral cortex. Anatomists divide the cerebral cortex into either four or five lobes. All recognize the frontal, temporal, parietal, and occipital lobes. Some consider the limbic lobe a fifth lobe; others consider it to be contained within the temporal and frontal lobes and diencephalon (see Figures 8–26, 8–27, 8–31, and 8–32). The cerebral cortex and its associated functions are discussed in Chapter 3 of this book.

## Basal Ganglia

The basal ganglia are a group of small, interconnected subcortical nuclei made up of the caudate nucleus, putamen, globus pallidus, claustrum, subthalamus, and substantia nigra (see Figures 8–24 and 8–25). The caudate nucleus and putamen are often called the *corpus striatum*, and the globus pallidus and putamen are called the *lentiform nucleus*. Together, the structures of the basal ganglia are familiar to neuropsychiatrists from disorders such as Huntington's chorea and Parkinson's disease, or as the targets of many poison/toxin exposures. These nuclei serve a key role as a site for bringing emotion, executive function, motivation, and motor activity together. There are many input and output circuits that traverse these areas, including the three frontal lobe circuits of dorsolateral, orbitofrontal, and anterior cingulate gyrus (Burruss et al. 2000). Lesions within these struc-

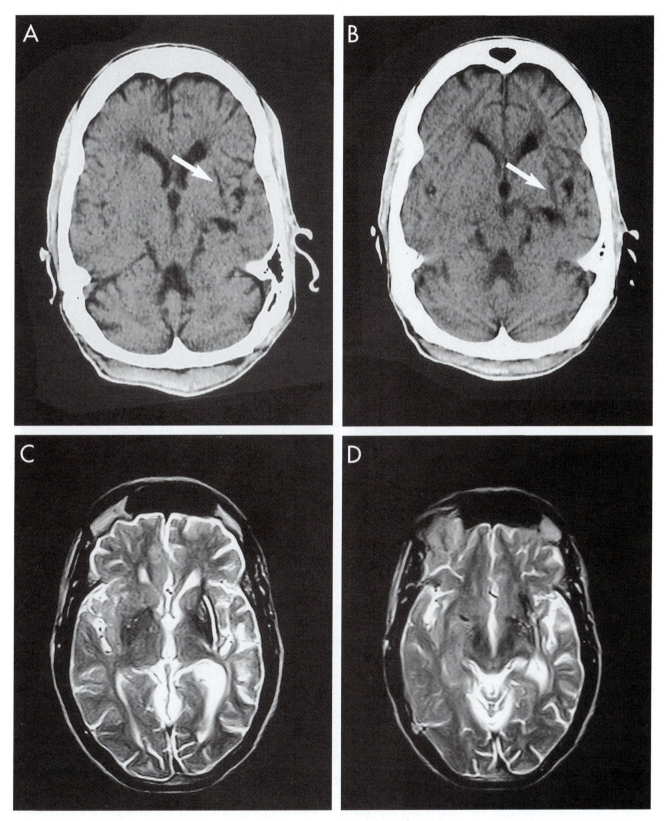

**FIGURE 8–18.** Comparison of computed tomography and T2-weighted magnetic resonance imaging. Images of a 69-year-old man who presented status post a generalized tonic-clonic seizure. Abnormal areas indicative of subcortical ischemia are evident on the conventional CT images (*Panel A* and *Panel B*, arrows). Areas of ischemic injury and old hemorrhage as well as normal anatomy are much better visualized on T2-weighted magnetic resonance images (*Panel C* and *Panel D*).

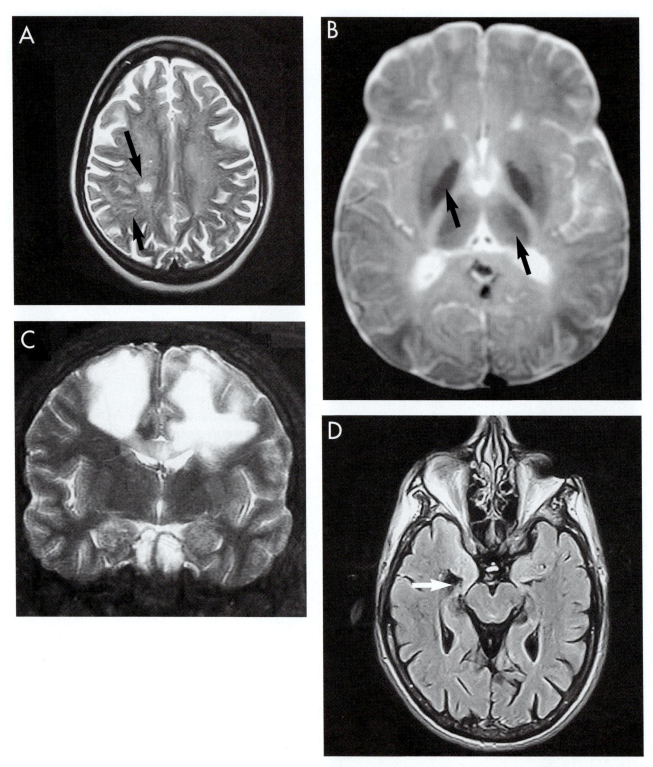

**FIGURE 8–19.** Representative examples of clinical applications of magnetic resonance imaging (MRI). *Panel A.* MRI of a 23-year-old woman with multiple sclerosis. Note the characteristic ovoid, hyperintense demyelinating lesions (arrows). *Panel B.* MRI of an 18-year-old woman with chronic severe toluene abuse. Note the global demyelination and hypointense signal in the globus pallidus and to a lesser extent in the thalamus (arrows). *Panel C.* MRI of a 10-year-old girl with acute disseminated encephalomyelitis. Note the extensive white matter damage as indicated by the hyperintense signal in both medial frontal lobes. *Panel D.* MRI of a 49-year-old man with mesial temporal sclerosis secondary to traumatic brain injury. Note the dilation of the tip of the right temporal horn due to volume loss in the surrounding temporal lobe structures (arrow).

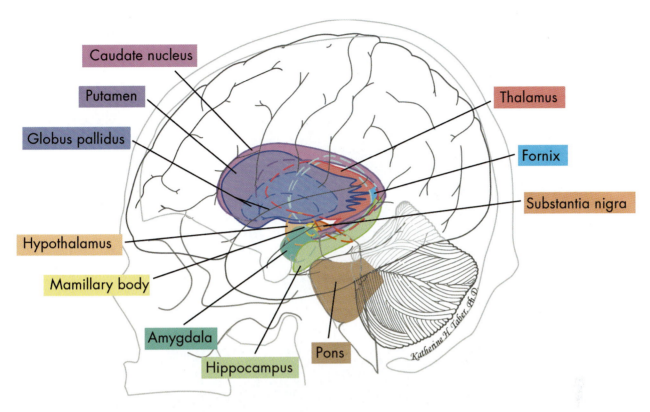

**FIGURE 8–20.** Schematic (lateral sagittal view) illustrating the positioning of the major subcortical structures in relationship to cortex and skull.

*Source.* Modified with permission from "Neuropsychiatric Symptoms Associated with Subcortical Injury," Smart Charts, 1999.

tures result in syndromes of hypokinetic or hyperkinetic movements as well as cognitive and emotional dysfunction. The basal ganglia contain significant acetylcholine, dopamine, γ-aminobutyric acid (GABA) and neuropeptide projections (Mello and Villares 1997). The dopaminergic projections have been pharmacologic targets for schizophrenia and Parkinson's disease.

## Caudate Nucleus

The caudate nuclei are C-shaped structures, each having a head, body, and tail. They arch to follow the walls of the lateral ventricles and terminate into the amygdaloid nuclei bilaterally (see Figures 8–25, 8–26, and 8–29). The caudate nucleus and putamen together are thought of as the input nuclei receiving projections from the cerebral cortex, thalamus, and substantia nigra pars compacta. The major outputs for the caudate nucleus and putamen are the globus pallidus and substantia nigra pars reticulata. Neuropsychiatric symptoms of damage to the caudate nucleus are numerous and can be divided into behavioral, emotional, memory, language, and other symptoms. More commonly reported deficits include disinhibition, disorganization, executive dysfunction, apathy, depression, memory loss, atypical aphasia, psy-

chosis, personality changes, and predisposition for delirium.

## Putamen

The putamen is the most lateral of the basal ganglia structures. It is separated from the caudate nucleus by the anterior limb of the internal capsule (see Figures 8–25, 8–29, and 8–30). The putamen and the caudate nucleus are considered input nuclei. See "Caudate Nucleus" above for afferent and efferent projections. Neuropsychiatric symptoms of lesions to the putamen include primarily language and behavioral deficits (i.e., atypical aphasia, obsessive-compulsive traits, executive dysfunction). However, hemineglect, depression, and memory loss have been reported.

## Globus Pallidus

The globus pallidus lies medial to the putamen and has two divisions (internal and external) (see Figures 8–25 and 8–29). The globus pallidus is functionally considered an output nucleus. Primary output is to the subthalamus and thalamus via GABAergic pathways. (For a further discussion of the afferent and efferent connections of the globus pallidus, see Crossman 1995b.) Neuropsychiatric

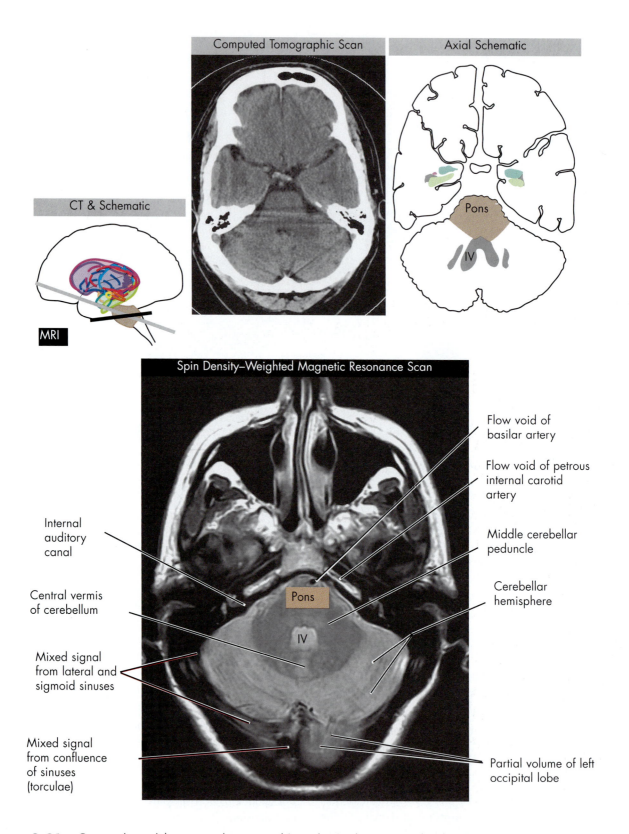

**FIGURE 8–21.** Companion axial computed tomographic and spin density–weighted magnetic resonance brain images. Color-coded schematics with major subcortical structures illustrated are included to show the level and angle of the sections and to assist in structure identification.

*Source.* Magnetic resonance image courtesy of GE Medical Systems. Color-coded schematics reprinted with permission from "Neuropsychiatric Symptoms Associated with Subcortical Injury," Smart Charts, 1999.

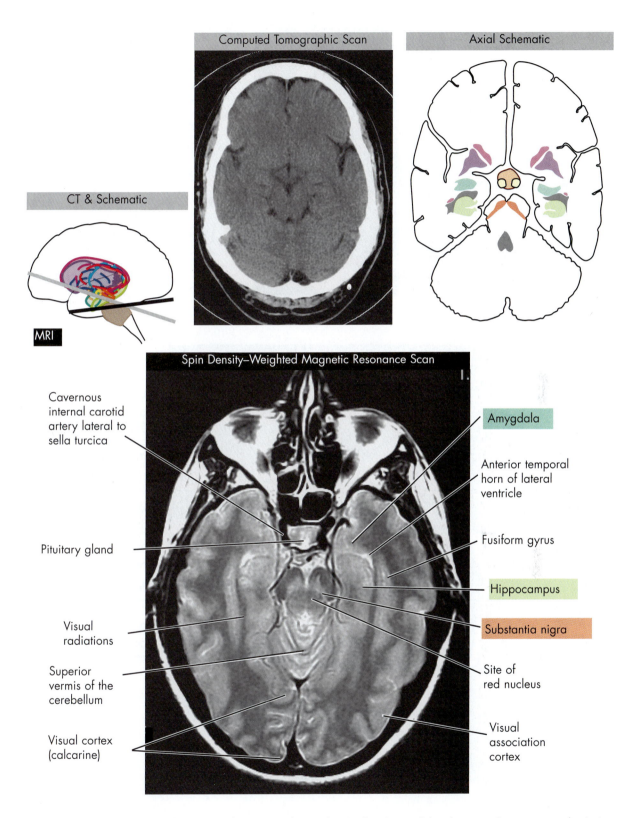

**FIGURE 8–22.** Companion axial computed tomographic and spin density–weighted magnetic resonance brain images. Color-coded schematics with major subcortical structures illustrated are included to show the level and angle of the sections and to assist in structure identification.

*Source.* Magnetic resonance image courtesy of GE Medical Systems. Color-coded schematics reprinted with permission from "Neuropsychiatric Symptoms Associated with Subcortical Injury," Smart Charts, 1999.

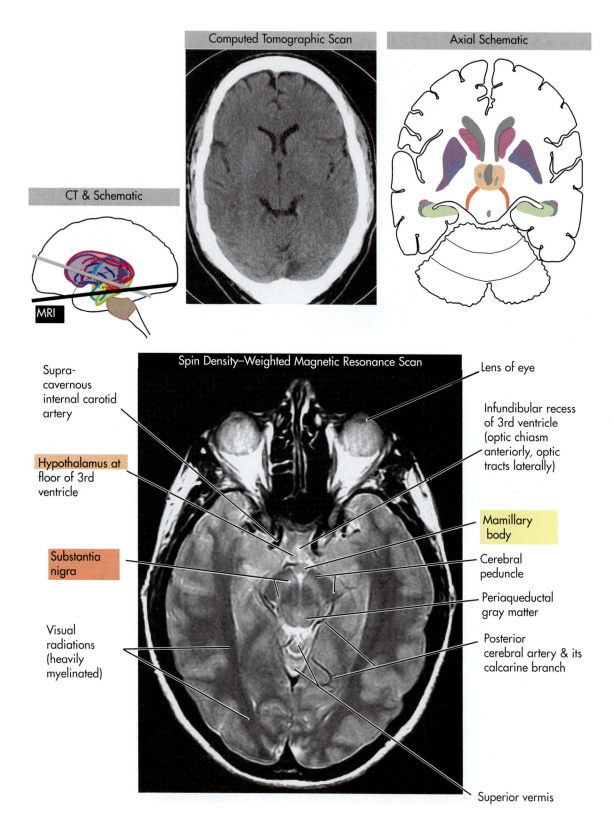

**FIGURE 8–23.** Companion axial computed tomographic and spin density–weighted magnetic resonance brain images. Color-coded schematics with major subcortical structures illustrated are included to show the level and angle of the sections and to assist in structure identification.

*Source.* Magnetic resonance image courtesy of GE Medical Systems. Color-coded schematics reprinted with permission from "Neuropsychiatric Symptoms Associated with Subcortical Injury," Smart Charts, 1999.

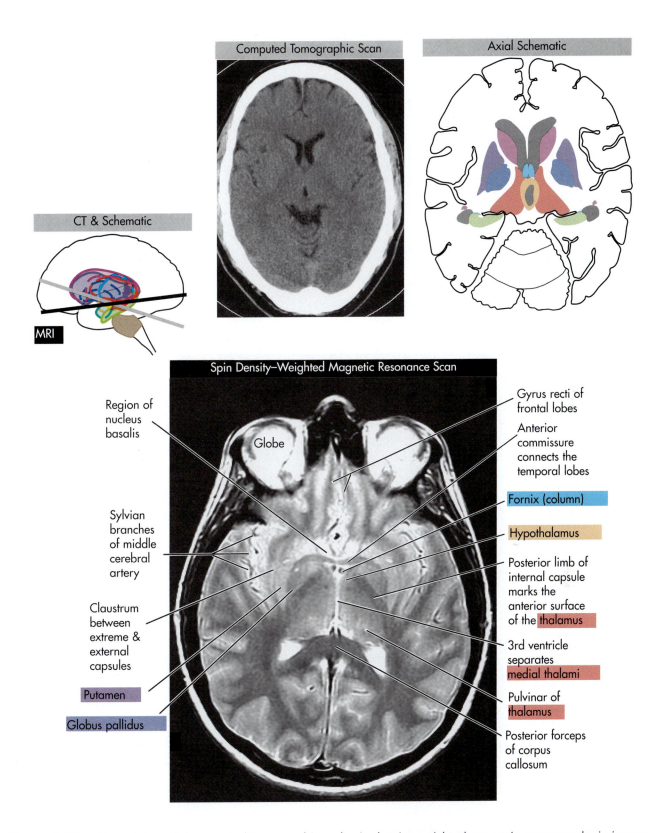

**FIGURE 8–24.** Companion axial computed tomographic and spin density–weighted magnetic resonance brain images. Color-coded schematics with major subcortical structures illustrated are included to show the level and angle of the sections and to assist in structure identification.

*Source.* Magnetic resonance image courtesy of GE Medical Systems. Color-coded schematics reprinted with permission from "Neuropsychiatric Symptoms Associated with Subcortical Injury," Smart Charts, 1999.

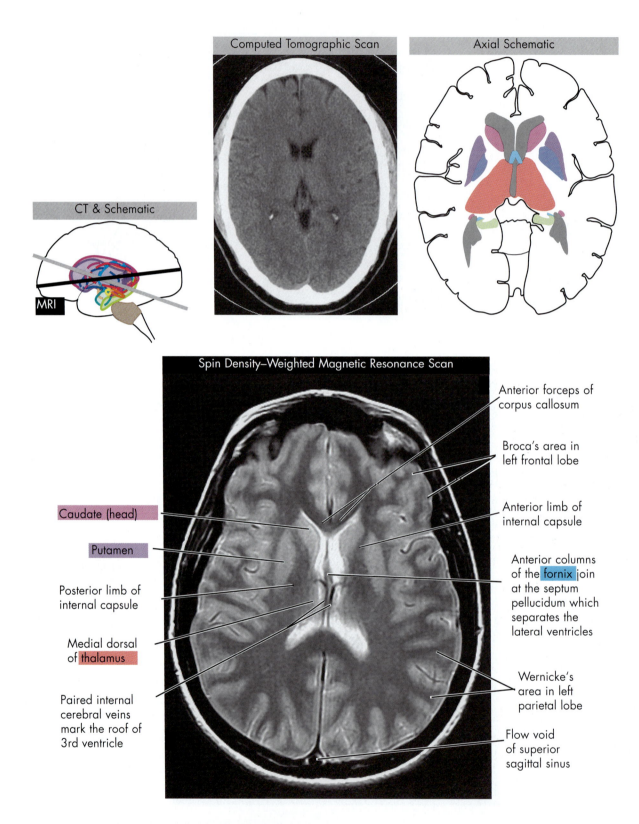

**FIGURE 8–25.** Companion axial computed tomographic and spin density–weighted magnetic resonance brain images. Color-coded schematics with major subcortical structures illustrated are included to show the level and angle of the sections and to assist in structure identification.

*Source.* Magnetic resonance image courtesy of GE Medical Systems. Color-coded schematics reprinted with permission from "Neuropsychiatric Symptoms Associated with Subcortical Injury," Smart Charts, 1999.

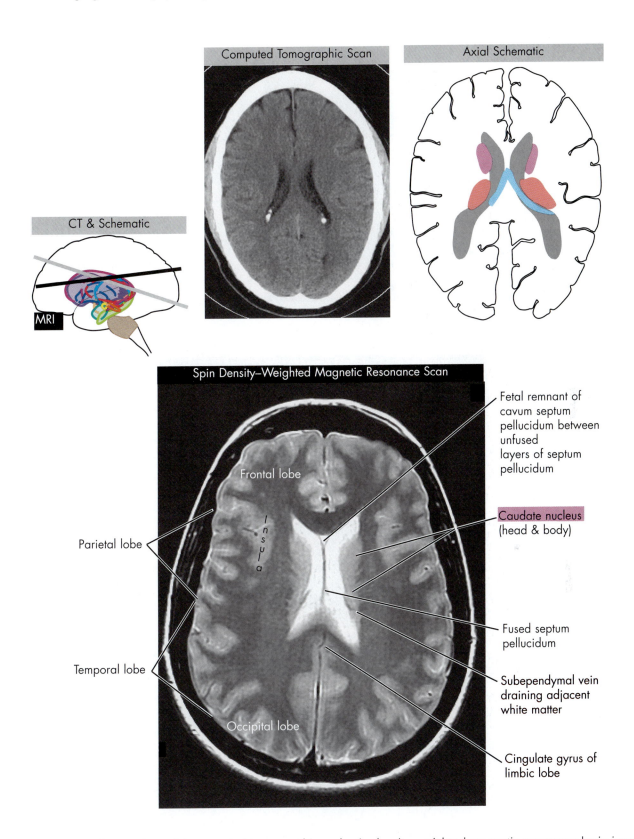

**FIGURE 8–26.** Companion axial computed tomographic and spin density–weighted magnetic resonance brain images. Color-coded schematics with major subcortical structures illustrated are included to show the level and angle of the sections and to assist in structure identification.

*Source.* Magnetic resonance image courtesy of GE Medical Systems. Color-coded schematics reprinted with permission from "Neuropsychiatric Symptoms Associated with Subcortical Injury," Smart Charts, 1999.

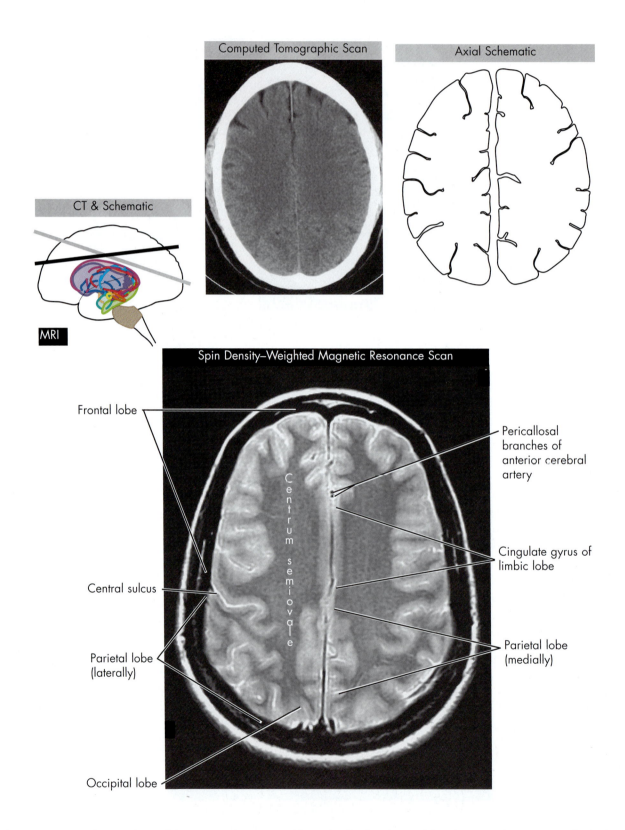

**FIGURE 8–27.** Companion axial computed tomographic and spin density–weighted magnetic resonance brain images. Color-coded schematics with major subcortical structures illustrated are included to show the level and angle of the sections and to assist in structure identification.

*Source.* Magnetic resonance image courtesy of GE Medical Systems. Color-coded schematics reprinted with permission from "Neuropsychiatric Symptoms Associated with Subcortical Injury," Smart Charts, 1999.

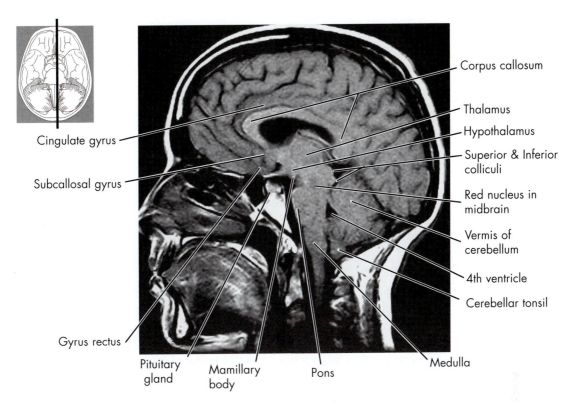

Cingulate gyrus

Subcallosal gyrus

Gyrus rectus

Pituitary gland

Mamillary body

Pons

Corpus callosum

Thalamus

Hypothalamus

Superior & Inferior colliculi

Red nucleus in midbrain

Vermis of cerebellum

4th ventricle

Cerebellar tonsil

Medulla

**FIGURE 8–28.** Sagittal spin density–weighted magnetic resonance brain image.

*Source.* Image courtesy of GE Medical Systems.

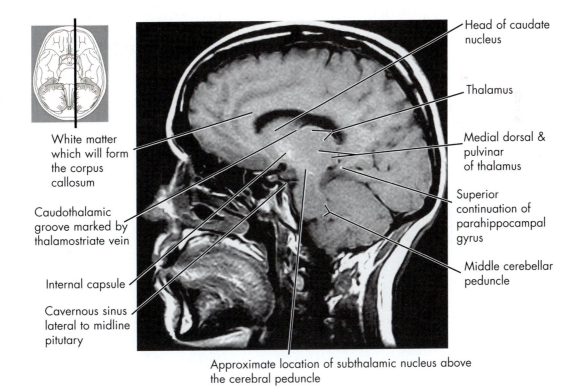

White matter which will form the corpus callosum

Caudothalamic groove marked by thalamostriate vein

Internal capsule

Cavernous sinus lateral to midline pituitary

Head of caudate nucleus

Thalamus

Medial dorsal & pulvinar of thalamus

Superior continuation of parahippocampal gyrus

Middle cerebellar peduncle

Approximate location of subthalamic nucleus above the cerebral peduncle

**FIGURE 8–29.** Sagittal spin density–weighted magnetic resonance brain image.

*Source.* Image courtesy of GE Medical Systems.

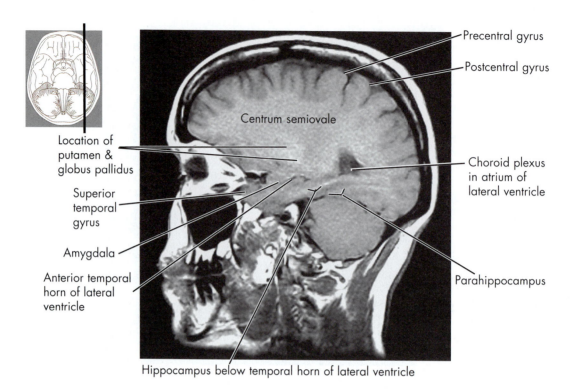

**FIGURE 8–30.** Sagittal spin density–weighted magnetic resonance brain image.
*Source.* Image courtesy of GE Medical Systems.

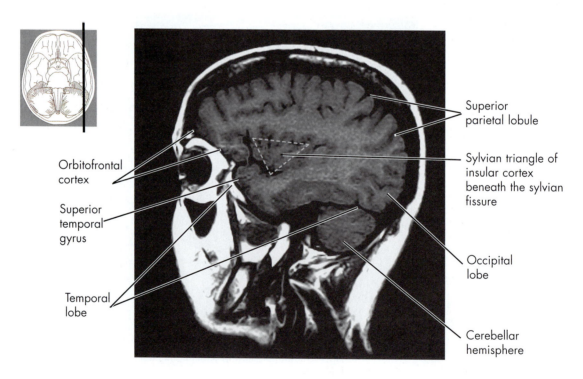

**FIGURE 8–31.** Sagittal spin density–weighted magnetic resonance brain image.
*Source.* Image courtesy of GE Medical Systems.

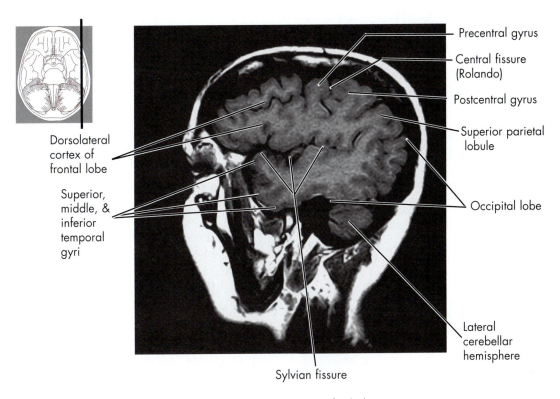

Dorsolateral cortex of frontal lobe

Superior, middle, & inferior temporal gyri

Precentral gyrus

Central fissure (Rolando)

Postcentral gyrus

Superior parietal lobule

Occipital lobe

Lateral cerebellar hemisphere

Sylvian fissure

**FIGURE 8–32.** Sagittal spin density–weighted magnetic resonance brain image.
*Source.* Image courtesy of GE Medical Systems.

symptoms of lesions to the globus pallidus include primarily emotional, and other (i.e., anxiety, depression, apathy, psychosis, and central pain). Other less often reported symptoms include amnesia and cognitive deficits.

## Substantia Nigra

The substantia nigra nuclei of the midbrain are dark because they contain melanin. They are divided into the pars compacta and pars reticulata. The first sends dopaminergic projections to the caudate nucleus and putamen. The latter receives input from the striatum and sends efferents to the thalamus, subthalamus, and reticular formation (see Figures 8–22 and 8–23). Reported neuropsychiatric symptoms of lesions to the substantia nigra include primarily behavioral and emotional deficits (i.e., apraxia, ataxia, aggression, and depression), with less frequent reports of memory and cognitive deficits.

## Limbic System

The term *limbic system* is most often used to describe the areas of brain involved in the production of emotion, memory, or aggression (Lopes Da Silva et al. 1990; Sitoh and Tien 1997). Originally suggested by Broca ("*le grand lobe limbique*"), the name is purely descriptive of the anatomic location of these structures (*limbus* means

"border," and these structures border the neocortex). Papez suggested that these areas were important for memory and emotion, rather than just smell, as had been previously believed. MacLean applied the name "limbic system" to the circuit of Papez, reasoning that these structures are placed to integrate signals from the external and internal worlds (Figure 8–33). Commonly, these structures are divided into an outer and an inner lobe (Figure 8–34). The outer lobe is composed of the cingulate, subcallosal, parahippocampal, and uncal cortices. The inner lobe consists of the paraterminal gyrus, the indusium griseum (supracallosal gyrus), and the hippocampal complex. Other areas closely associated with these and often considered part of the limbic system include the mamillary bodies and parts of the thalamus. Some authors also include other areas, such as the orbitofrontal cortex and hypothalamus. (See Mega et al. 1997 for an excellent review of the anatomic and phylogenetic development of the limbic system.)

## Hippocampal Formation and Parahippocampal Cortex

The hippocampal formation and parahippocampal cortex (or gyrus) are collectively considered to be the "memory structures." They function in essence to form and direct the storage of memories. The parahippocampus extends

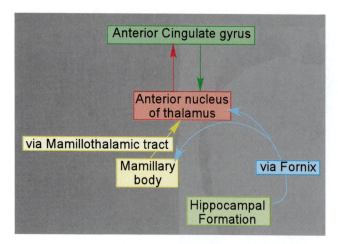

**FIGURE 8–33.** Schematic of the emotion and memory circuit of Papez.

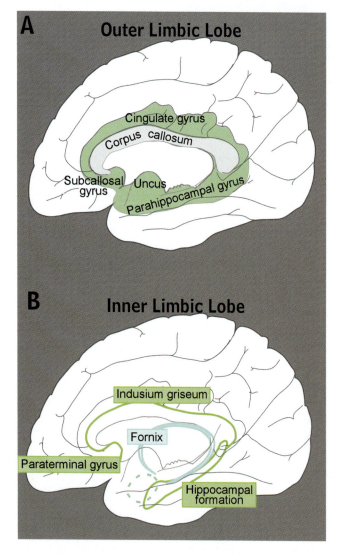

**FIGURE 8–34.** Schematic diagrams of the medial surface of the right cerebral hemisphere showing the outer (*Panel A*) and inner (*Panel B*) limbic lobes.

from the cingulate cortex to the amygdala (see Figure 8–34). The main body of the hippocampal formation extends from the crus of the fornix to the amygdala located in the medial temporal lobe. The fornix is the major fiber tract of the hippocampal formation (see Figures 8–22 and 8–30). Neuropsychiatric symptoms of lesions to the hippocampal formation are primarily memory deficits. These include anterograde and retrograde amnesia, inability to form new memories, and temporally graded amnesia.

The fornix is made up of afferent and efferent hippocampal fibers. It forms from the fibers (fimbria) that course on the ventricular surface of the hippocampus. The fimbria become the crus of the fornix. The crus join to form the body of the fornix. The body then passes between the lateral ventricles in the septum pellucidum. The body divides around the anterior commissure to form the anterior (precommissural) and posterior (postcommissural) columns of the fornix (see Figures 8–25 and 8–26). Neuropsychiatric symptoms of lesions to the fornix are memory deficits and overlap those following damage to the hippocampal formation. They include impaired recent memory, syndrome of transitory amnesia, and long-term anterograde amnesia.

## Amygdala

The amygdala lies at the juncture of the tail of the caudate nucleus and the anterior-most ends of the parahippocampus and hippocampus. It sends projections to the basal forebrain and striatum via the anterior portion of the ventral amygdalofugal pathway. The caudal portion of this pathway carries the projection from the amygdala to the thalamus. The amygdala also sends projections to the hypothalamus via both the stria terminalis and ventral amygdalofugal pathway. A component continues on to the midbrain and brain stem (see Figures 8–22 and 8–30). Neuropsychiatric symptoms of lesions to the amygdala are primarily behavioral and emotional. These include passivity or aggression, hypersexuality, hyperorality, hyperphagia, decreased fear, anxiety or startle, and decreased link between emotion and memory.

## Mamillary Body

The mamillary bodies are two small round nuclei that lie in the posterior portion of the diencephalon. They receive afferents from the hippocampus and send efferents to the brain stem and thalamus (see Figures 8–23 and 8–28). The mamillothalamic tract is the projection from the mamillary bodies to the anterior nucleus of the thalamus. Neuropsychiatric symptoms with lesions of the mamillary body or its tract are primarily memory deficits and psychosis. Confabulation and anterograde memory loss are most common.

## Thalamus

The thalamus is medial to the caudate nucleus and putamen and lateral to the third ventricle. The superior and medial portions contain the anterior nucleus, the medial dorsal nucleus, and the lateral dorsal nucleus (see Figures 8–24, 8–25, 8–28, and 8–29) (Armstrong 1990; Bentivoglio et al. 1993). These nuclei have intimate interconnections with the limbic system (Yakovlev et al. 1960). Damage to the medial portion of the left thalamus is associated with deficits in language, verbal intellect, and verbal memory. Damage to the right is associated with deficits in visuospatial and nonverbal intellect and visual memory. Medial thalamus may be important for temporal aspects of memory. Bilateral damage is associated with severe memory impairment ("thalamic amnesia") as well as dementia. The memory deficits may result from destruction of the tracts (mamillothalamic tract, amygdalofugal tract) connecting these thalamic nuclei with limbic structures. Damage to the anterior and medial thalamus can also result in disturbances of autonomic functions, mood, and the sleep/waking cycle (Bassetti et al. 1996; Lovblad et al. 1997).

## Hypothalamus

The hypothalamus lies ventral to the thalamus around the third ventricle. It has projections to and from the orbitofrontal cortex, the limbic circuits, the thalamus, the reticular formation, and the autonomic and endocrine systems. Thus it is a key structure in bridging internal homeostasis and the outside environment (see Figures 8–23 and 8–28). Behavioral, emotional, and memory symptoms as well as other deficits are associated with damage to the hypothalamus. Examples of commonly reported symptoms are aggression, violence, anorexia, depression, impaired short-term memory, dementia, gelastic seizures, and altered sleep/wake cycle.

## Pons

The pons lies in the posterior fossa between the midbrain and the medulla oblongata. It contains nuclei and tracts that are necessary for arousal (reticular formation) and affective stability (see Figures 8–21, 8–28, and 8–29). The raphe nuclei (found at the midline along the entire brainstem) send serotonergic projections to structures throughout the brain, including the thalamus, hippocampus, basal ganglia, and frontal cortex. The locus coeruleus is also found in the pons. It sends noradrenergic projec-

tions to the limbic system, hypothalamus, thalamus, cerebellum, and cerebral cortex (Crossman 1995a). Neuropsychiatric symptoms from pontine lesions include behavioral, emotional, language, memory, and other deficits. Commonly reported deficits include disinhibition, disturbed sleep/wake cycles, anxiety, depression, emotional lability, cognitive deficits, central pain, personality changes, and psychosis.

## References

Arakia Y, Ashikaga R, Fujii K, et al: MR fluid-attenuated inversion recovery imaging as routine brain T2-weighted imaging. Eur J Radiol 32:136–143, 1999

Armstrong E: Limbic thalamus: anterior and mediodorsal nuclei, in The Human Nervous System. Edited by Paxinos G. San Diego, CA, Academic Press, 1990, pp 469–481

Bahner ML, Reith W, Zuna I, et al: Spiral CT vs incremental CT: is spiral CT superior in imaging of the brain? Eur Radiol 8:416–420, 1998

Bassetti C, Mathis J, Gugger M, et al: Hypersomnia following paramedian thalamic stroke: a report of 12 patients. Ann Neurol 39:471–480, 1996

Bentivoglio M, Kultas-Ilinsky K, Ilinsky I: Limbic thalamus: structure, intrinsic organization, and connections, in Neurobiology of Cingulate Cortex and Limbic Thalamus: A Comprehensive Handbook. Edited by Vogt BA, Gabriel M. Boston, MA, Birkhauser, 1993, pp 71–122

Beresford TP, Blow FC, Hall RCW, et al: CT scanning in psychiatric inpatients: clinical yield. Psychosomatics 27:105–112, 1986

Bergin PS, Fish DR, Shorvon SD, et al: Magnetic resonance imaging in partial epilepsy: additional abnormalities shown with the fluid attenuated inversion recovery (FLAIR) pulse sequence. J Neurol Neurosurg Psychiatry 58:439–443, 1995

Bourland JD, Nyenhuis JA, Schaefer DJ: Physiologic effects of intense MR imaging gradient fields. Neuroimaging Clin N Am 9:363–377, 1999

Brant-Zawadzki M, Atkinson D, Detrick M, et al: Fluid-attenuated inversion recovery (FLAIR) for assessment of cerebral infarction. Initial clinical experience in 50 patients. Stroke 27:1187–1191, 1996

Branton T: Use of computerized tomography by old age psychiatrists: an examination of criteria for investigation of cognitive impairment. Int J Geriatr Psychiatry 14:567–571, 1999

Brice J: The Excellence in Diagnostic Imaging Awards. Diagn Imaging 22(1), 2000

Burruss JW, Hurley RA, Taber KH, et al: Functional neuroanatomy of the frontal lobe circuits. Radiology 214(1):227–230, 2000

Chakos MH, Esposito S, Charles C, et al: Clinical applications of neuroimaging in psychiatry. Magn Reson Imaging Clin N Am 6:155–164, 1998

Cohan RH, Matsumoto JS, Quagliano PV: Adverse effects, in Manual on Contrast Media, 4th Edition. Edited by Cohan RH, Matsumoto JS, Quagliano PV. American College of Radiology, 1998a, pp 4–7

Cohan RH, Matsumoto JS, Quagliano PV: Incidence, in Manual on Contrast Media, 4th Edition. Edited by Cohan RH, Matsumoto JS, Quagliano PV. American College of Radiology, 1998b, p 8

Cohan RH, Matsumoto JS, Quaglianao PV: Letter of correction for incidence, in Manual on Contrast Media, 4th Edition. Edited by Cohan RH, Matsumoto JS, Quaglianao PV. American College of Radiology, 1998c

Cohan RH, Matsumoto JS, Quagliano PV: Manual on Contrast Media, 4th Edition. Reston, VA, American College of Radiology, 1998d

Coleman LT, Zimmerman RA: Pediatric craniospinal spiral CT: current applications and future potential. Semin Ultrasound CT MR 15:148–155, 1994

Crossman AR: Neuroanatomy: An Illustrated Colour Text. Edited by Crossman AR, Neary D. Edinburgh, UK, Churchill Livingstone, 1995a, pp 69

Crossman AR: Neuroanatomy: An Illustrated Colour Text. Edited by Crossman AR, Neary D. Edinburgh, UK, Churchill Livingstone, 1995b, pp 119–125

Earls JP, Bluemke DA: New MR imaging contrast agents. Magn Reson Imaging Clin N Am 7:255–273, 1999

Federle MP, Willis LL, Swanson DP: Ionic versus nonionic contrast media: a prospective study of the effect of rapid bolus injection on nausea and anaphylactoid reactions. J Comput Assist Tomogr 22:341–345, 1998

Halpern JD, Hopper KD, Arredondo MG, et al: Patient allergies: role in selective use of nonionic contrast material. Radiology 199:359–362, 1996

Hanyu H, Asano T, Sakurai H, et al: Magnetization transfer ratio in cerebral white matter lesions of Binswanger's disease. J Neurol Sci 166:85–90, 1999

Hayman LA, Hurley RA, Puryear L: Pathways for declarative memory and emotion, I: a three- dimensional model of the limbic, diencephalic and brainstem circuits. International Journal of Neuroradiology 1:87–89, 1995

Hoffmann A, Faber SC, Werhahn KJ, et al: Electromyography in MRI—first recordings of peripheral nerve activation caused by fast magnetic field gradients. Magn Reson Med 43(4):534–539, 2000

Hurley RA, Hayman LA, Puryear LJ, et al: Pathways for declarative memory and emotion, II: clinical brain imaging. International Journal of Neuroradiology 1:90–101, 1995

Interactive Atlas of Human Anatomy: Summit, NJ, Ciba-Geigy Medical Education, 1995

Jacobs JE, Birnbaum BA, Langlotz CP: Contrast media reactions and extravasation: relationship to intravenous injection rates. Radiology 209:411–416, 1998

Kaplan H, Sadock B, Grebb J: The brain and behavior, in Kaplan and Sadock's Synopsis of Psychiatry. Behavioral Sciences Clinical Psychiatry, 7th Edition. Edited by Kaplan H, Sadock BJ, Graff JA. Baltimore, MD, Williams & Wilkins, 1994, pp 112–125

Katada K: Current status and future prospects of multislice CT; moving toward the ideal x-ray CT system. Toshiba Medical Review 71:1–11, 1999

Kuntz R, Skalej M, Stefanou A: Image quality of spiral CT versus conventional CT in routine brain imaging. Eur J Radiol 26:235–240, 1998

Kuszyk BS, Beauchamp NJJ, Fishman EK: Neurovascular applications of CT angiography. Semin Ultrasound CT MR 19:394–404, 1998

Larson EB, Mack LA, Watts B, et al: Computed tomography in patients with psychiatric illnesses: advantage of a "rule-in" approach. Ann Intern Med 95:360–364, 1981

Lopes Da Silva FH, Witer MP, Boeijinga PH, et al: Anatomic organization and physiology of the limbic cortex. Physiol Rev 70:453–511, 1990

Lovblad KO, Bassetti C, Mathis J, et al: MRI of paramedian thalamic stroke with sleep disturbance. Neuroradiology 39:693–698, 1997

Masterman DL, Cummings JL: Frontal-subcortical circuits: the anatomic basis of executive, social and motivated behaviors. J Psychopharmacol 11:107–114, 1997

Mega MS, Cummings JL: Frontal-subcortical circuits and neuropsychiatric disorders. J Neuropsychiatry Clin Neurosci 6:358–370, 1994

Mega MS, Cummings JL, Salloway S, et al: The limbic system: an anatomic, phylogenetic, and clinical perspective (comments). J Neuropsychiatry Clin Neurosci 9:315–330, 1997

Mello LEAM, Villares J: Neuroanatomy of the basal ganglia. Psychiatr Clin North Am 20:691–704, 1997

Mitchell DG: MR imaging contrast agents—what's in a name? J Magn Reson Imaging 7:1–4, 1997

Moringlane JR, Bartylla K, Hagen T, et al: Stereotactic neurosurgery planning with 3-D spiral CT-angiography. Minim Invasive Neurosurg 40:83–86, 1997

Naumescu I, Hurley RA, Hayman LA, et al: Neuropsychiatric symptoms associated with subcortical brain injuries. International Journal of Neuroradiology 5:51–59, 1999

Nowinski WL, Bryan RN, Raghavan R: The Electronic Blinical Brain Atlas: Multiplanar Navigation of the Human Brain, CD-ROM Edition. New York, Thieme, 1997

Nunn AD, Linder KE, Tweedle MF: Can receptors be imaged with MRI agents? Q J Nucl Med 41:155–162, 1997

Oi H, Yamazaki H, Matsushita M: Delayed vs immediate adverse reactions to ionic and non-ionic low-osmolality contrast media. Radiat Med 15:23–27, 1997

Orrison WW: Introduction to brain imaging, in Functional Brain Imaging. Edited by Orrison WW Jr, Levine JD, Sanders JA, et al. St. Louis, MO, Mosby-Year–Book, 1995, pp 1–12

Price RR: The AAPM/RSNA physics tutorial for residents. MR imaging safety considerations. Radiological Society of North America. Radiographics 19:1641–1651, 1999

Rauch SL, Renshaw PF: Clinical neuroimaging in psychiatry. Harv Rev Psychiatry 2:297–312, 1995

Runge VM, Muroff LR, Wells JW: Principles of contrast enhancement in the evaluation of brain diseases: an overview. J Magn Reson Imaging 7:5–13, 1997

Rydberg JN, Hammond CA, Grimm RC, et al: Initial clinical experience in MR imaging of the brain with a fast fluid-attenuated inversion-recovery pulse sequence. Radiology 193:173–180, 1994

Sage MR, Wilson AJ, Scroop R: Contrast media and the brain. The basis of CT and MR imaging enhancement. Neuroimaging Clin N Am 8:695–707, 1998

Schemmer DS, Siekierski M, Steiner M: CT of the brain: how useful is it in general psychiatry? (letter). Can J Psychiatry 44:929, 1999

Schwartz RB: Helical (spiral) CT in neuroradiologic diagnosis. Radiol Clin North Am 33:981–995, 1995

Shellock FG, Kanal E: Policies, guidelines, and recommendations for MR imaging safety and patient management. SMRI Safety Committee. J Magn Reson Imaging 1:97–101, 1991

Shellock FG, Kanal E: Safety of magnetic resonance imaging contrast agents. J Magn Reson Imaging 10:477–484, 1999

Sitoh YY, Tien RD: The limbic system. An overview of the anatomy and its development. Neuroimaging Clin N Am 7:1–10, 1997

Taber KH, Zimmerman JG, Yonas H, et al: Applications of xenon CT in clinical practice: detection of hidden lesions. J Neuropsychiatry Clin Neurosci 11:423–425, 1999

Tanabe JL, Ezekiel F, Jagust WJ, et al: Magnetization transfer ratio of white matter hyperintensities in subcortical ischemic vascular dementia. AJNR Am J Neuroradiol 20:839–844, 1999

Trimble MR, Mendez MF, Cummings JL: Neuropsychiatric symptoms from the temporolimbic lobes. J Neuropsychiatry Clin Neurosci 9:429–438, 1997

Weight DG, Bigler ED: Neuroimaging in psychiatry. Psychiatr Clin North Am 21:725–759, 1998

Weinberger DR: Brain disease and psychiatric illness: when should a psychiatrist order a CAT scan? Am J Psychiatry 141:1521–1527, 1984

Wolf GL: Paramagnetic contrast agents for MR imaging of the brain, in MR and CT Imaging of the Head, Neck, and Spine. Edited by Latchaw RE. St. Louis, MO, Mosby-Year–Book, 1991, pp 95–108

Yakovlev PI, Locke S, Koskoff DY, et al: Limbic nuclei of thalamus and connections of limbic cortex. Arch Neurol 3:620–641, 1960

Yasuda R, Munechika H: Delayed adverse reactions to nonionic monomeric contrast-enhanced media. Invest Radiol 33:1–5, 1998

# CHAPTER 9

# Functional Neuroimaging in Psychiatry

James C. Patterson II, M.D., Ph.D.

Kathryn J. Kotrla, M.D.

The practice of psychiatry alleviates a staggering array of symptoms that result from disorders of thought, mood, and behavior. The pathophysiologic processes producing these symptoms are poorly understood, making it difficult to understand the neurobiological basis for psychiatric illnesses, or predict the best treatment intervention. Fortunately, functional neuroimaging techniques allow scientists and clinicians to look inside the human brain and attempt to see the human mind.

Currently, functional neuroimaging methods are mostly restricted to scientific investigations. Day-to-day clinical practice, with a few exceptions, is unlikely to benefit from any of the functional imaging techniques outlined below. Nevertheless, results from functional neuroimaging are shaping our understanding about many neuropsychiatric conditions.

Abnormal activity in specific brain areas that is associated with any psychiatric symptom or disorder that results in abnormal behavior is theoretically measurable. In addition, the changes in concentration of various brain chemicals associated with these disorders can be determined, specific neurotransmitter receptors can be labeled, and the effects of psychotropic medication can be studied in vivo, all with functional neuroimaging. Such results lead to hypotheses about the neuroanatomic and neurochemical substrate for psychiatric conditions.

This chapter provides an overview of the techniques themselves, how they are used to understand normal brain functioning, and what has been learned about neuropsychiatric disorders. It provides a foundation to evalu-

ate the information from functional neuroimaging, so that the practicing psychiatrist can assess research findings that affect clinical practice.

## Functional Neuroimaging Concepts

There are various ways to image the functional activity of the living human brain. One approach uses radioactivity to measure brain metabolism, blood flow, or neurotransmitter receptors via positron emission tomography (PET) or single photon emission computed tomography (SPECT). Another avenue to investigate the brain's function applies magnetic resonance imaging techniques to produce various types of functional images without the use of radioactivity. Functional magnetic resonance imaging (fMRI) uses blood oxygenation levels to estimate neural activation, whereas a technique known as arterial spin tagging (AST) can estimate cerebral blood flow. Local chemical concentrations can be examined with magnetic resonance spectroscopy (MRS), and evaluation of white matter integrity is done via a process known as diffusion-weighted imaging. Yet another technique, magnetoencephalography (MEG), involves looking at the minute magnetic fluctuations associated with regional brain activity.

All these techniques give us a general idea of neuronal activity in localized regions of the brain. Active neurons expend maximal energy at their synapses, causing localized increases in metabolic demands and

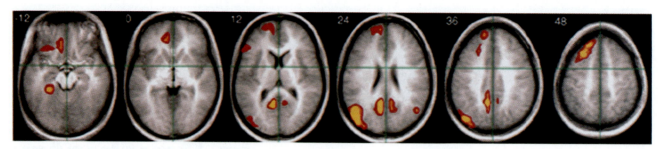

**FIGURE 9–1.** The resting state compared with a tone discrimination task. Regions of significant activation difference (*P* < 0.00001) are shown in red-yellow superimposed on averaged anatomical brain images in axial orientation. Stereotaxic *x* and *y* axes are shown in green, and *z* coordinates are given above each image. The left hemisphere is on the reader's left. Areas more active during rest include the left parahippocampus, orbital frontal and rostral-ventral anterior cingulate cortex, angular gyrus, posterior cingulate/retrosplenial cortex, and left dorsal prefrontal cortex.

*Source.* Reprinted with permission from Binder JR, Frost JA, Hammeke TS, et al.: "Conceptual Processing During the Conscious Resting State: a Functional MRI Study." *Journal of Cognitive Neuroscience* 11(1):80–93, 1999.

glucose consumption (Schwartz et al. 1979). As metabolism increases, blood flow increases concordant with (or greater than) the increased energy demand (Fox et al. 1988). PET using radiolabeled glucose images changes in synaptic metabolism, whereas PET using ($^{15}$O)water, SPECT, fMRI, and AST use direct and indirect measures of blood flow to follow changes in synaptic activity.

When a functional brain image shows changes in regional metabolism or blood flow, this is due to the activity of afferent synapses in that area. The neuronal cell bodies that have altered their firing rate may lie in nearby cortex or in distant locations. The afferent input may come from inhibitory or excitatory synapses, so it is possible that decreased blood flow to a region in the frontal cortex, for example, may be due to decreased inhibitory inputs, leading to increased firing of those frontal output neurons. Conversely, increased blood flow may reflect increased inhibitory inputs, functionally quieting the area's output (Nadeau and Crosson 1995). This means that when a change in activity in an area is reported, this is a composite picture of the firing of local and distant afferent neurons. How this alters the area's output is an unknown. Because of this, studies that examine the connectivity of regions are important. Various types of statistical analyses are beginning to be used to examine connectivity. These techniques look at not just what changes occur in a given location, but how the regions are related to one another in terms of activity within a network.

Functional neuroimaging provides a way to examine patterns of brain activity during complex cognitive processes and emotions. In fact, its remarkable sensitivity is both an advantage and a disadvantage. Although virtually

any brain function can be imaged, uncontrolled (and undesired) mental activities and moods compose part of that functional image. This is particularly troublesome in studies done at rest, in which results reflect incoming sensory stimuli and internal thoughts and feelings (Andreasen et al. 1995a). The rest state may differ significantly between neuropsychiatrically ill patients and healthy volunteers, as the baseline mood, thoughts, or response to scanning may be distinct for the two populations. To control for the rest state, many functional neuroimaging studies are performed while the participant is doing a task, thereby engaging specific brain systems or neural networks. In addition, recent work in studies of "rest" show that there is a consistent network that is active when the body is not expressing behavior (Binder et al. 1999), and this network overlaps significantly with brain regions that are pathologic in many psychiatric disorders (Figure 9–1).

Each functional neuroimaging technique has advantages and limitations. The techniques differ in repeatability, which determines whether participants are imaged at rest or during tasks. They differ in spatial resolution, which limits how easily activity is localized to specific brain regions. They differ in sensitivity, and this influences which brain processes are observable. Of practical importance, they differ in price and availability, which affects who gets imaged. PET imaging has been the most expensive and difficult to find outside an academic research institution; however, it is becoming more prevalent as the technology becomes less expensive and more common and as clinical uses expand. A review of the techniques allows the practicing psychiatrist to understand what conclusions can be drawn from each one.

# Functional Neuroimaging Techniques

## Positron Emission Tomography

### Theory

PET is named from its use of positron-emitting isotopes to image brain functioning. Positron-emitting isotopes are very short-lived radioactive entities including oxygen 15 ($^{15}O$), nitrogen 13 ($^{13}N$), carbon 11 ($^{11}C$), and fluorine 18 ($^{18}F$). The radioactive isotopes are incorporated into specific molecules to study cerebral metabolism, blood flow, and neuroreceptors. Most commonly used are ($^{15}O$)water for cerebral blood flow studies or [$^{18}F$]fluoro-deoxyglucose (FDG) to image metabolism (Berman and Weinberger 1991; Nadeau and Crosson 1995).

Radioactive agents are intravenously injected into the subject, whose head is positioned within a radiation detector. The radioactive isotope decays within the brain, releasing a positron. The positron travels a short distance and collides with an electron, resulting in the emission of two photons that travel at 180° to each other at the speed of light. The photons are detected at the opposite sides of the head simultaneously, and the location of the emitting positron can thus be calculated (Berman and Weinberger 1991).

### Cerebral Blood Flow and Metabolism

($^{15}O$)water and FDG are the two mainstays of PET and have quite different properties. ($^{15}O$)water provides a measure of cerebral blood flow and has a half-life of about 2 minutes (Saha et al. 1994). Because of the short half-life, up to 8–10 scans can be performed during a single imaging session. This allows experimenters to image multiple conditions, as participants can perform different tasks during the 8–10 scans (Nadeau and Crosson 1995).

FDG is actively taken up by the glucose transport mechanism into cells and is phosphorylated to FDG-6-phosphate by hexokinase. This remains trapped intracellularly because it is not a glycolytic substrate. Scanning produces a measure of glucose metabolism; because most brain energy use is synaptic, a map of regional glucose use indicates neural activity (Saha et al. 1994).

FDG uptake requires about 30 minutes, a relatively long time for functional neuroimaging. Often, brain images are obtained during a resting state or during the same task lasting 30 minutes. The relatively long imaging time limits the number of brain states imaged. Because of radiation exposure, each participant can be studied only two to four times a year (Berman and Weinberger 1991).

### Neurotransmitters and Receptors

PET also images neurotransmitters and their receptors. See Table 9–1 for a listing of various ligands and their use. Although they are not specifically listed in the table, PET radiotracers have also been made by attaching a radioactive carbon to pharmacologically active compounds like deprenyl and fluoxetine (George et al. 1996).

### Advantages and Limitations

PET imaging is extremely valuable to clinical neuroscience. ($^{15}O$)water PET has been used extensively to understand normal brain functioning because participants are imaged during several conditions. Both ($^{15}O$)water and FDG PET are widely used for research on neuropsychiatric illnesses. Such usefulness has led to the development of sophisticated methods for data acquisition and analysis, which improve the reliability and credibility of PET information.

However, PET images lack the spatial resolution and anatomical details needed to specifically identify smaller areas of brain activity. Technical constraints limit the theoretical resolution of PET to about 4 mm (Messa et al. 1995), although data are often blurred 1.5 to 2 times the spatial resolution of the image (Friston et al. 1995) to diminish the influence of individual neuroanatomic variability. To localize brain activity, the image from an individual may be converted into a standardized, stereotactic space such as Talairach space (Talairach and Tournoux 1988). Data from many individuals are grouped to uncover areas of activation. Alternatively, computer programs can register PET scans with high-resolution MRI scans of the same participant. Areas of PET activation are then localized using the structural brain image. Each of these techniques has its own pitfalls, and it is best to consider whether one wants across-subject examinations that can be generalized to a population, or within-subject analyses that have more internal accuracy. For example, if a patient with an ill-defined brain tumor has a functional image study done to locate regions of neoplasm or inflammation in the brain, this can be overlaid on the subject's MRI to provide precise localization of the functional changes. However, if a population of schizophrenic patients was the topic of study, across-subject analysis would be optimal.

Because of the short-half lives of positron-emitting isotopes, PET must be performed near the cyclotron that produces them. Thus, PET has been exclusively performed near research centers and therefore has not enjoyed wide clinical use. However, regional cyclotrons that can deliver isotopes (with the exception of the short-half-life $^{15}O$-labeled isotopes) to nearby PET

**TABLE 9–1.** Radio ligands used in positron emission tomography

| Common name | Radiolabel | Labeling target | Citation |
|---|---|---|---|
| Water | $^{15}O$ | Cerebral blood flow | |
| Fluorodeoxyglucose (FDG) | $^{18}F$ | Cerebral metabolism | |
| Dihydrotetrabenazine (DTBZ) | $^{11}C$ | Vesicular monoamine transporter | Henry and Scherman 1989 |
| Fluorodopa | $^{18}F$ | Dopamine neurons | Seeman and Seeman 1988 |
| β-CIT | $^{11}C$ | Dopamine transporter | Muller et al. 1993 |
| RTI-32 | $^{11}C$ | Dopamine transporter | Wilson et al. 1996 |
| NNC112 | $^{11}C$ | $D_1$ receptor | Halldin et al. 1998 |
| NNC756 | $^{11}C$ | $D_1$ receptor | Rinne et al. 1996 |
| SCH23390 | $^{11}C$ or $^{76}Br$ | $D_1$ receptor | Seeman and Seeman 1988 |
| Spiperone | $^{18}F$, $^{11}C$, $^{76}Br$ | $D_2$ receptor | Seeman and Seeman 1988 |
| Fluorethylspiperone | $^{18}F$ | $D_2$ receptor | Seeman and Seeman 1988 |
| Raclopride | $^{11}C$ | $D_2$ receptor | Seeman and Seeman 1988 |
| Benperidol, bromperidol, brombenperidol | $^{18}F$, $^{75}Br$ | $D_2$ receptor | Seeman and Seeman 1988 |
| Haloperidol | $^{18}F$ | $D_2$ receptor | Seeman and Seeman 1988 |
| Pimozide | $^{11}C$ | $D_2$ receptor | Seeman and Seeman 1988 |
| N-methylspiroperidol | $^{18}F$ or $^{11}C$ | $D_2$ receptor | Seeman and Seeman 1988 |
| Epidepride | $^{11}C$ | $D_2$ receptor | Langer et al. 1999 |
| FLB 457 | $^{11}C$ | $D_2$ receptor | Farde et al. 1997 |
| Nemonapride YM-09151–2 | $^{11}C$ | $D_2$ receptor | Tanji et al. 1998 |
| N-methylspiperone | $^{11}C$ | 5-$HT_2$ and $D_2$ receptors | Berman and Weinberger 1991 |
| Deprenyl | $^{11}C$ | Monoamine oxidase | George et al. 1996 |
| Fluoxetine | $^{11}C$ | Serotonin transporter | George et al. 1996 |
| (+)McN-5652 | $^{11}C$ | Serotonin transporter | Szabo et al. 1996 |
| α-Methyl-tryptophan | $^{11}C$ | Serotonin synthesis rate | Muzik et al. 1997 |
| WAY-100635 | $^{11}C$ | 5-$HT_{1A}$ receptor | Pike et al. 1996 |
| CPC0222 | $^{11}C$ | 5-$HT_{1A}$ receptor | Houle et al. 1997 |
| Setoperone | $^{18}F$ | 5-$HT_{2A}$ receptor | Blin et al. 1990 |
| Altanserin | $^{18}F$ | 5-$HT_{2A}$ receptor | Crouzel et al. 1992 |
| Flumazenil | $^{11}C$ | Benzodiazepine receptor | Saha et al. 1994 |
| N1'-(methyl) naltrindole | $^{11}C$ | Delta opioid receptor | Madar et al. 1996 |
| 6-deoxy-6-β-fluoronaltrexone | $^{18}F$ | Opioid receptor | Cohen et al. 1997 |
| Carfentanil | $^{11}C$ | μ-selective opioid receptor | Frost et al 1985 |
| Diprenorphine | $^{11}C$ | Non-μ opioid receptor | Jones et al 1988 |
| PMP | $^{11}C$ | Acetylcholinesterase | Kuhl et al. 1999 |
| Nicotine | $^{11}C$ | Nicotinic cholinergic receptor | Cumming et al. 1999 |
| NMPB | $^{11}C$ | Muscarinic cholinergic receptor | Asahina et al. 1998 |
| Xanomeline, and the analog butylthio-TZTP | $^{11}C$ | Muscarinic cholinergic receptor | Farde et al. 1996 |

scanners are becoming more common, making it possible to have a PET scanner at regional and private hospitals. Many types of clinical PET scans are now covered by some health insurance plans, mainly for cancer evaluations.

Also, the use of radioactivity inherently limits the number of scans that can be done within a single individual, so longitudinal studies or studies in children are ethically difficult. Despite these limitations, PET has made substantial inroads into understanding normal brain functioning and investigating abnormalities in neuropsychiatric populations.

# Single Photon Emission Computed Tomography

## Theory

SPECT also uses radioactive compounds to image brain activity. Like PET, SPECT derives its name from the type of radioisotope involved, compounds that produce only one photon per disintegration. The radioisotopes are readily available from commercial sources. This makes SPECT available in most clinical centers. However, because SPECT imaging depends on a single photon

**TABLE 9–2.** Radioligands used in single photon emission computed tomography

| Common Name | Radiolabel | Labeling Target | Citation |
|---|---|---|---|
| β-CIT | $^{123}$I | Dopamine transporter | Brucke et al. 1993 |
| Fluoroalkyl analogs of β-CIT | $^{123}$I | Dopamine transporter | Abi-Dargha et al. 1996 |
| TRODAT-1 | $^{99m}$Tc | Dopamine transporter | Kung et al. 1996 |
| TISCH | $^{123}$I | D$_1$ receptor | Saha et al. 1994 |
| IBZM | $^{123}$I | D$_2$ receptor | Saha et al. 1994 |
| Bromospiperone | $^{77}$Br | D$_2$ receptor | Saha et al. 1994 |
| IBF | $^{123}$I | D$_2$ receptor | Ichise et al. 1996 |
| NCQ298 | $^{123}$I | D$_2$ receptor | Ryding et al 1998 |
| Iodolisuride | $^{123}$I | D$_2$ receptor | Saha et al. 1994 |
| Epidepride | $^{123}$I | D$_2$ receptor | Kornhuber et al. 1995 |
| Iodoketanserine | $^{123}$I | 5-HT$_2$ receptor | Saha et al. 1994 |
| R93274 | $^{123}$I | 5-HT$_2$ receptor | Busatto et al. 1997 |
| MK-801 | $^{123}$I | Glutamate (NMDA) receptor | Owens et al. 1997 |
| Iomazenil Ro16–0154 | $^{123}$I | GABA$_A$ receptor | Saha et al. 1994 |
| QNB | $^{123}$I | Muscarinic cholinergic receptor | Saha et al. 1994 |
| Iododexitimide (IDEX) | $^{123}$I | Muscarinic cholinergic receptor | Saha et al. 1994 |

being released, its spatial resolution is less than that of PET.

## Cerebral Blood Flow

SPECT produces both quantitative and qualitative measures of cerebral blood flow. The most common radioligand used to produce qualitative measures of brain perfusion is [$^{99m}$Tc]hexamethylpropylene amine oxime (HMPAO). After it is intravenously injected, it is accumulated by endothelial cell membranes within several minutes. It concentrates in proportion to regional cerebral blood flow (Reba 1993), and its activity may remain constant for up to 24 hours (Saha et al. 1994). Because of this, participants can be injected during very controlled conditions, away from the noise and anxiety of the scanning room. A snapshot of the relative cerebral perfusion during this controlled period is obtained when the participant is scanned up to several hours later (Saha et al. 1994). Another available radioligand is [$^{99m}$Tc]ethyl cysteinate dimer (ECD). Although this ligand produces less extracerebral uptake, it also has some dramatically different patterns of uptake within the cerebrum compared with HMPAO (Patterson et al. 1997). Many other studies also find differences between these two tracers. This indicates that there may be differences in uptake based on the ligand, and therefore variance in activity patterns may result not only from changes in brain activity but also from the radioligand being used.

SPECT resolution is limited to around 10 mm by the technique itself. Also, for perfusion studies with HMPAO, only a limited number of scans can be done in a subject because of the relatively long half-life of the

radioisotope. Likewise, if multiple scans are desired, for example during multiple tasks, they must be performed after delays of several days to allow for isotope washout (Nadeau and Crosson 1995).

## Neuroreceptors

SPECT now has a number of radiolabeled receptor binding agents available for imaging studies. These agents are outlined in Table 9–2. The use of receptor binding agents is generally limited to research studies.

## Advantages and Limitations

SPECT is clinically available for a qualitative measure of cerebral perfusion. It may be beneficial in diagnosing dementing illnesses. Areas of relative hypoperfusion, corresponding to neuronal degeneration, are visually apparent. SPECT is also used for research. Many studies done in the late 1980s and early 1990s analyzed SPECT scans using regions of interest (ROIs) and used a cerebellar region as the "control" region. This is because it was thought at the time that the cerebellum had little to do with cognition. Over the past few years, it has become apparent that the cerebellum is very actively involved in cognitive processes (see for example Gao et al. 1996). Many new studies find either cerebellar activity in normal subjects, or cerebellar pathology in studies of mental disorders, thus older SPECT evaluations that use the cerebellum as a control site must be interpreted with this in mind. Even older studies that used $^{133}$Xe SPECT (one of the original radiolabeled tracers used for brain imaging) suffer from very limited spatial resolution, making localization of brain activity difficult. [$^{99m}$Tc]HMPAO SPECT has limited repeatability, so many studies are done at rest. Although SPECT has contributed to the understanding of neuropsychiatric illnesses, it is a less precise tool than PET due to its significantly lower temporal and spatial resolution.

## Functional Magnetic Resonance Imaging

### Theory

Functional MRI couples the exquisite spatial resolution of structural MRI with the ability to image areas related to neural activity. It does this noninvasively, without the use of radioactive agents. When a localized region of brain tissue becomes active, it uses oxygen and glucose and produces certain metabolic byproducts. In these areas of increased neural activity, the metabolism and blood flow increase with the increased energy demands. The cerebrovascular physiology of the brain is such that local blood flow and volume increase to supply the needed fuel and remove the metabolic waste products. Although the exact mechanism remains to be determined, many scientists believe that the supply of oxygen is much greater than what neurons utilize. This results in an actual increase in the concentration of oxygenated hemoglobin compared with deoxygenated hemoglobin in areas of neural activity. Oxygenated hemoglobin is less paramagnetic and has increased intensity (looks brighter) compared with deoxygenated hemoglobin on images created with $T_2$-weighted pulse sequences. fMRI uses this blood-oxygen level dependent (BOLD) effect to image changes in neural activity (Kwong et al. 1992).

### Advantages and Limitations

Because fMRI requires no radiation and can be completely noninvasive, a participant can be imaged multiple times. This allows patients to be imaged during different clinical states, or before and after pharmacologic, psychotherapeutic, or behavioral treatments to determine how treatment interventions affect cerebral functioning. It also removes ethical constraints about imaging children and adolescents with psychiatric illnesses. In addition, fMRI is performed in standard, clinically available 1.5-T magnetic resonance scanners. In theory, it can be implemented at any of the numerous sites that have a magnetic resonance scanner

Although fMRI provides precise neuroanatomic localization, it also means that minor subject movements introduce artifacts that impair the ability to appreciate neural activity. Moreover, relying on the oxygenation status of endogenous hemoglobin molecules produces very small changes in signal intensity, on the order of 1%–5%. This makes it very difficult to appreciate the true signal associated with neural activity above the background noise of ongoing brain activity.

## Magnetic Resonance Spectroscopy

### Theory

MRS is performed in the same scanners as structural and functional MRI. However, by altering the scanning parameters, the signal represents chemical entities from brain areas. The response of an atom in a magnetic field is characteristic, based on the number and nature of its subatomic particles, as well as its unique molecular environment. Spectra are obtained that are characteristic for nuclei within certain molecules (McClure et al. 1995). This principle is employed in MRS to study the concentration of brain metabolites. Typically, spectra are obtained from a number of nuclei, including $^1$H, $^{13}$C, $^{23}$Na, $^7$Li, and $^{31}$P.

In psychiatry, investigators are primarily using $^1$H and $^{31}$P MRS. Proton ($^1$H) spectroscopy can distinguish N-acetyl aspartate (NAA), creatine and phosphocreatine, and phosphatidylcholine. Signals can be obtained from glutamate, glutamine, γ-aminobutyric acid, lactate, and inositol phosphates, although these signals may be difficult to adequately resolve (Narayana and Jackson 1991). NAA is found in neurons and is absent in most glial cell lines. Decreases in NAA may reflect a diminished number or density of neurons; NAA levels decrease proportionate to the brain loss in neurodegenerative disorders (Maier 1995; Renshaw et al. 1995). Creatine and phosphocreatine are important energy substrates, and phosphatidylcholine is an important component of cell membranes (Narayana and Jackson 1991).

MRS with $^{31}$P detects the relative tissue concentrations of certain phosphorous metabolites, including those involved in energy and phospholipid metabolism (Waddington et al. 1990). Resonances are obtained from the precursors and breakdown products of membrane phospholipids (phosphomonoesters and phosphodiesters, respectively), which uncover potential abnormalities in membrane turnover. To reflect energy metabolism, $^{31}$P MRS senses phosphocreatine, adenosine triphosphate, adenosine diphosphate, and inorganic orthophosphate; intracellular pH can also be assessed (Pettegrew et al. 1991).

### Advantages and Limitations

MRS is notable for its noninvasiveness, repeatability, and ability to provide information about membrane and metabolic moieties. It has successfully imaged abnormalities in areas of tumor growth and ischemia. Comparisons have been made of the concentrations of substances between healthy brains and brains with neuropsychiatric abnormalities. It may prove ideal for longitudinal studies. However, it has limited spatial resolution, although this is improving. Also, for molecules present in low concentration, like receptor sites, PET is superior because it uses radiolabeled ligands (Moonen et al. 1990).

**Cerebral blood flow evaluation with MRI.** Nonradioactive paramagnetic agents (like gadolinium) can be given to participants in an intravenous bolus, and the decreased signal intensity can be mapped to produce an image of relative cerebral perfusion (Mattay et al. 1995). Perfusion can also now be imaged without the use of intravenous contrast material by using arterial spin labeling (ASL). This is a relatively new technology that holds great promise as an easy means to visualize blood flow. This technique is based on the ability to "label" arterial blood in a region proximal to the brain (typically the neck) by using an electromagnetic pulse, and then measuring the appearance of the labeled blood in different brain regions (Wong et al. 1999). By varying the parameters, either quantitative or qualitative measurements of cerebral blood flow can be performed (Detre and Alsop 1999). To date, no studies using this new technique have been carried out in psychiatric patients, although it shows promise, and it has been used to evaluate other disorders such as stroke and epilepsy.

## Normal Brain Functioning

Functional neuroimaging allows visualization of brain activities ranging from the simple to the complex. PET is notably successful in localizing the neuroanatomic regions influenced by a task. fMRI has even better temporal and spatial resolution. The brain utilizes distributed neuronal networks during any task or state, and each node within the network serves a specific function. These networks are as dynamic as the brain itself, changing with experience even during the course of an imaging session. Knowing the normal location of brain functions builds a foundation for understanding neuropsychiatric symptoms.

The field of cognitive neuroscience has been extremely productive within the last 10 years, both with regard to normal brain functioning and with regard to abnormal function related to pathological states. It is therefore difficult to summarize these findings, and the following sections on normal brain function provide only

a brief overview and a few highlights of the voluminous literature available.

## Vision

The visual system is often the first place to validate functional neuroimaging techniques. The pathway leading from the retina to calcarine cortex is well established; there are clear expectations for primary visual cortical activation when humans look at light. Many PET, SPECT, and fMRI studies have documented increased metabolism and/or perfusion in striate cortex in response to light. However, vision is more than a simple light response. To appreciate a scene's complexities, the brain is specialized to sense certain attributes. There has been much functional imaging work that elucidates the more complex aspects of visual processing. PET reveals localized activations with the perception of color, movement, shape, faces, and spatial locations (Haxby et al. 1994; Watson et al. 1993). Electrophysiological primate work predicts a specific cortical area sensitive to moving stimuli; fMRI confirms this in humans (Tootell et al. 1995). Likewise, ($^{15}$O)water PET or fMRI during facial recognition shows increased blood flow in the occipitotemporal area (Haxby et al. 1994; Puce et al. 1995); spatial recognition requires increased blood flow in the superior parietal cortex. This is consistent with primate work showing two distinct visual pathways specialized for identifying what an object is separate from where it is (Haxby et al. 1991, 1994). Another more recent fMRI study examined the perception of three-dimensional structure by showing subjects a curved surface rotating in depth, and found activity in specific areas of visual association cortex (Paradis et al. 2000).

## Movement

Even a simple action like moving fingers activates a distributed network of cortical and subcortical areas. Functional imaging studies invariably show that the sensorimotor cortex is involved (Figure 9–2). However, depending on the nature of the task, activity may also be seen in the basal ganglia, thalamus, supplementary motor area, cerebellum, premotor, or parietal areas. For example, sequences (Mazziotta et al. 1991) of self-initiated actions (Passingham et al. 1989) require the supplementary motor area.

In addition, with a relatively repeatable technique like PET blood flow, or more readily with fMRI, investigators can watch the brain learn. As the brain becomes more proficient while the subject performs a movement, blood flow within the motor circuit and primary motor

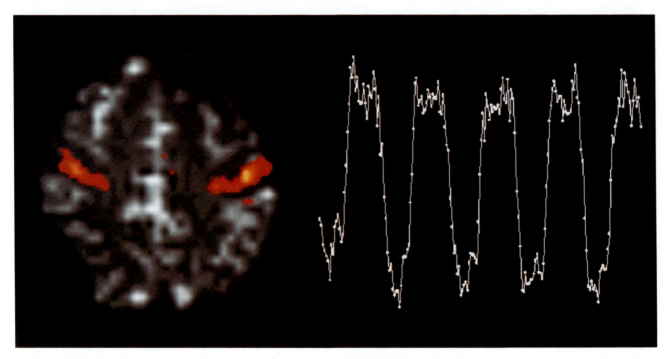

**FIGURE 9–2.** Bilateral motor cortical activation with finger tapping during functional magnetic resonance imaging. This figure shows an axial slice from an echo-planar magnetic resonance image with regions of significant activation overlaid in color. The graph to the right depicts the change in intensity of a voxel at the focus of activity. This was an alternating finger tap/rest paradigm, with one-minute periods of finger tapping interposed with periods of rest.

*Source.* Image from Peter Bandettini with permission.

cortex changes (Friston et al. 1992; Grafton et al. 1992; Karni et al. 1998; Seitz et al. 1990).

fMRI results provide an explanation for motor recovery after a stroke. Because fMRI is so repeatable, participants can move both right and left hands during scanning. The right motor cortex is activated primarily during left hand movements; the left motor cortex is somewhat activated even during ipsilateral finger movements (Kim et al. 1993; Rao et al. 1993), consistent with anatomical evidence for 10%–15% of uncrossed fibers in the lateral cortical spinal tract. fMRI also shows activation of the motor network when the participant is only imagining finger movements (Rao et al. 1993). The somatotopic organization of the motor cortex is also evident to some extent in the basal ganglia as well. One recent fMRI study found distinct hand, foot, and facial representations in the putamen (Maillard et al. 2000).

## Attention

Attention involves a distributed neural network linking the prefrontal, parietal, and cingulate cortices, with connections to the thalamus and striatum (Mesulam 1990). Each area makes a specific contribution to attention, so the requirements of each task determine which distributed brain areas are needed (Petersen et al. 1994).

With simple attention to sensory or visual stimulation, ($^{15}$O)water PET shows increased blood flow in the frontal and parietal areas (Pardo et al. 1991). During sustained visual attention, fMRI localizes signal changes in primary and secondary visual cortex, the dorsolateral prefrontal, inferior parietal, and anterior cingulate cortices (Simpson et al. 1995). If participants must discriminate between auditory stimuli, FDG PET also reveals metabolic changes in the frontal, parietal, and cingulate cortices (R.M. Cohen et al. 1988b).

However, with more complicated tasks, additional brain regions show blood flow changes as measured by ($^{15}$O)water PET. If a participant must determine changes in the color, shape, or movement speed of a complex target, blood flow changes depend on which target characteristic is being monitored (Corbetta et al. 1991). If the stimulus is visual, blood flow increases in brain areas involved in visual processing. At the same time, blood flow decreases to areas involved in processing other sensory information, like primary auditory and auditory association cortices (Haxby et al. 1994). Likewise, attending to an expected touch on the fingers is associated with reduced blood flow to the areas of somatosensory cortex from other body regions (Drevets et al. 1995).

Certain aspects of attention require specific nodes

within the network. For example, the superior parietal cortex is activated when a shift in attention occurs, regardless of whether this shift is driven by external or internal stimuli, or the nature of the required response. In contrast, when attention is tonically maintained, this area does not evidence increased blood flow (Petersen et al. 1994). A PET study done to examine the effects of attention on cortical activation in a tactile task found that attending to various features of a tactile stimulus enhanced activation in the S2 region of the somatosensory cortex over that when there was no attention (Burton et al. 1999).

## Learning and Memory

Functional neuroimaging can capture the location of memory and monitor how the brain changes when it learns or forgets. Like attention, learning and memory depend on tightly linked, distributed neural networks. Which nodes within the network are activated depends on the nature of the task, including the information given to the subject, and the response required. As learning takes place, the brain alters its activity patterns.

Learning and memory are diverse functions. Certain brain areas encode unconscious material such as motor skills, habits, stimulus-response associations, and priming (Squire and Zola-Morgan 1991). A different network involving frontal, parietal, and temporal cortices appears necessary for the conscious memories of events and facts (Mesulam 1990). The hippocampus and overlying cortical areas are required for the transition from short-term to long-term memory (Squire and Zola-Morgan 1991). Prefrontal cortex is required for working memory, the process by which fragments of information, like telephone numbers, are kept in mind for short periods of time (Figure 9–3) (Goldman-Rakic et al. 1990).

Classical conditioning, the unconscious process in which a neutral stimulus is linked to a response, can be seen using ($^{15}$O)water PET. When volunteers hear a tone followed by an air puff to the eye, the air puff causes a blink. With repetition, subjects will blink at the tone alone; unconscious learning has occurred. Activity changes in a network involving the primary auditory, prefrontal, parietal, cingulate, and insular cortices and the striatum and cerebellum (Molchan et al. 1994). Blood flow changes are influenced by whether participants are learning the task or forgetting the association.

The brain's dynamic nature can be visualized during conscious tasks too. When participants generate an action verb to match a noun, like saying "throw" to the word "ball," ($^{15}$O)water PET shows activity increases in the left prefrontal, left posterior temporal, anterior cingulate, and

bilateral sylvian-insular cortices and the right cerebellar hemisphere. After repeating the same verb to the same nouns for 15 minutes, the response is learned, like a habit. At that time, blood flow in the left prefrontal and anterior cingulate cortices and the right cerebellar hemisphere decreases. Activity increases in the sylvian-insular cortices and appears in the left medial extrastriate cortex (Raichle et al. 1994). The frontal cortex is implicated in generating a novel response; the cingulate cortex plays a role in selecting a response. When the verb named is automatic, or learned, these brain areas are not required as much, as reflected by their decreased blood flow.

When working memory is used during PET scanning, a network involving the dorsolateral prefrontal, anterior cingulate, and parietal cortices is activated (Petrides et al. 1993a, 1993b). fMRI likewise shows activation in the prefrontal cortex during working memory tasks (J.D. Cohen et al. 1993); this particular scanning technique did not image other nodes within the network. Using an fMRI technique that images the whole brain, a spatial working memory task did find activity in the frontal, anterior cingulate, and parietal cortices (Stein et al. 1995).

Prefrontal cortex is also active when conscious memories are evoked during PET scanning (Buckner et al. 1995; Squire et al. 1992). When participants are asked to recall the memory of a specific personal event (episodic memory) during ($^{15}$O)water PET scanning, a network including the left frontal operculum, inferior bitemporal regions, anterior cingulate cortex, thalamus, and cerebellum is activated (Andreasen et al. 1995a).

Different brain regions activate depending on the test requirements (Jonides et al. 1993; Raichle 1993). If an auditory stimulus is presented, brain areas involved in auditory processing will be involved. If the volunteer speaks, areas involved in speech production will show blood flow changes (Paulesu et al. 1993; Petrides et al. 1993b; Raichle 1991). A working memory test of visuospatial location will activate the right side of the brain (Jonides et al. 1993), while rehearsing letters will induce changes in the left hemisphere (Paulesu et al. 1993). During fMRI, remembering the location of an object activated parietal areas, whereas remembering the shape of an object selectively activated the inferior temporal regions (Belger et al. 1998). Likewise, memories must be made and remembered. In one study, left dorsolateral prefrontal and posterior cingulate cortices increase blood flow while encoding information. During information retrieval, right prefrontal and precuneus cortices and the thalamus are activated. Some regions, like the anterior cingulate cortex, are required for both functions (Fletcher et al. 1995).

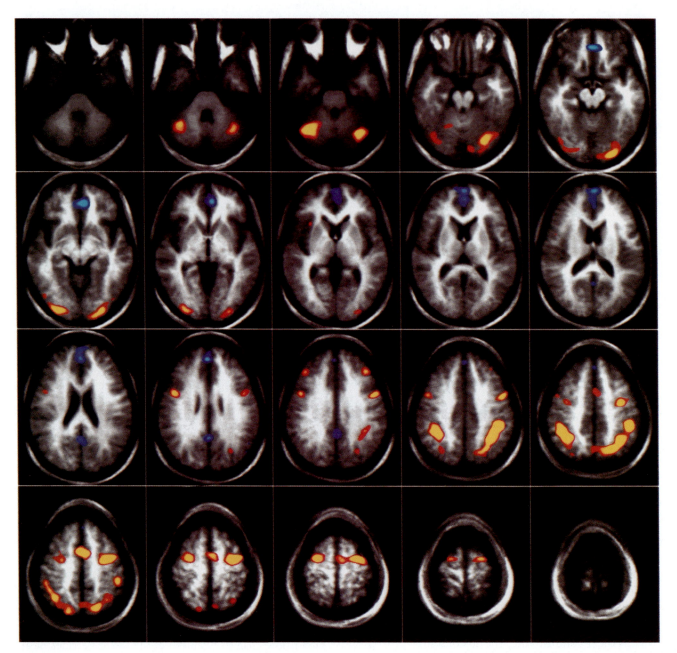

**FIGURE 9–3.** Working memory versus rest. These are results from the author's own research of a functional magnetic resonance imaging experiment during a "two-back" working memory task, in which the subject has to keep a moving sequence of objects in memory and report the object seen two trials previously. Red and yellow represent significant regions of increased activity in working memory versus the resting state, and blue represents regions of significantly decreased activity. The task is presented visually and is reported with button press, thus both the visual and motor cortices are active. Bilateral parietal and dorsolateral prefrontal regions are consistently seen with this type of working memory task. Note the decreased activity in the ventromedial prefrontal and posterior cingulate cortices, regions previously reported to be active at rest (see Figure 9–1).

## Language

Functional neuroimaging allows an elegant dissection of the neuroanatomic basis of language. As with other complex functions, language is encoded in the brain in distributed areas. Activation depends on the way words are experimentally presented, and the demands placed on processing those words.

When participants simply look at words during a ($^{15}$O)water PET scan, striate, lateral extrastriate, and medial extrastriate cortices show increased blood flow (Petersen and Fiez 1993). These reflect the response to any visual activation (striate) as well as areas involved in understanding words (extrastriate). For words presented auditorily, activation is seen in primary auditory cortex, bilaterally along the superior temporal gyrus, and in the left temporoparietal cortex (Petersen and Fiez 1993).

To read words aloud requires mouth movements. PET shows the activation of the motor circuit, including sensorimotor cortex, supplementary motor areas, and bilateral sylvian fissure regions near Broca's area. And when participants must generate a verb to match each presented noun, or must generate words beginning with the letter A or generate names of occupations, left frontal and cingulate cortices showed increased blood flow, consistent with the role of these brain areas in generating and choosing a response (Frith et al. 1991; Petersen et al. 1988).

## Emotion

The neural basis of emotion has long been debated. Modern medicine has postulated a limbic basis for emotions with the awareness that cortical-subcortical circuits of neurons will also be involved (George et al. 1996). To understand the neuroanatomy of mood, several groups have used multiple techniques to image affective states. Studies of emotion, conditioning, and reward learning have further mapped the cortical networks involved in emotion and emotion-laden processes. Much of this work centers on evaluation of the orbitofrontal and ventromedial cortices, insula, cingulate lobe, amygdala, and anterior temporal lobe. The anterior temporal, orbitofrontal, and ventromedial prefrontal cortex form part of an important link between the phylogenetically more primitive limbic and subcortical regions and the heteromodal, polysensory cortical regions from which they receive the majority of their input. It is here that emotions and cognition come together for decision making and planning of things such as social behavior. Mood, anxiety, and addictive disorders are typically found to affect the activity of this network, and the imaging of emotional processes has shed light on these disorders.

Much of the work done on emotions has been carried out with examinations of those of the negative type: fear, anger, anxiety, disgust, and so on. In a study of normal volunteers in which PET was used to examine anticipatory anxiety, increased regional cerebral blood flow (rCBF) was found in the left insula and ventrolateral prefrontal/orbitofrontal regions (Chua et al. 1999), consistent with previous reports examining this phenomenon. Other investigators have asked healthy volunteers to remember a personal event that evokes sadness. Self-induced dysphoria was associated with increased blood flow to the inferior and orbitofrontal cortices, more prominently in the left hemisphere (Pardo et al. 1993). Further studies replicated this and additionally found increased blood flow in the amygdala and anterior temporal lobes, components of the limbic system (George et al. 1994a). Interestingly, transient happiness caused a limited activation in the anterior cingulate cortex but decreased blood flow in temporal-parietal and frontal cortices (George et al. 1994b). These findings suggest that sad feelings originate from a circuit linking the orbital and prefrontal cortex with the amygdala and anterior temporal lobes. Activity in the orbitofrontal cortex, subgenual cingulate cortex, and ventral anterior cingulate cortex was found in a verbal go/no-go task with affect-laden words (Elliott et al. 2000). This fMRI-based task required subjects to make a decision based on affective content (sad, happy, or neutral). Another study examined brain activity in normal subjects who were generating words with affective content (Crosson et al. 1999). This study examined only the left side of the brain in right-handed subjects. Activation was found in regions consistent with their hypothesis that generation of emotion-laden words involves both limbic and perilimbic regions as well as verbal processing regions (Broca's area).

## Limitations of Functional Neuroimaging

Many neuropsychiatric conditions are investigated with functional neuroimaging techniques, and general themes are emerging about the neuroanatomic location of these illnesses. However, much work remains to be done to clarify the neurobiology of psychiatric symptoms. Currently, seeking global differences in brain blood flow or metabolism between patients and control subjects yields mixed results. The most consistent finding in this regard is in patients with thyroid abnormalities. In this population, thyroid-stimulating hormone levels have been found to inversely correlate with global flow. More consistent findings emerge by imaging the participant during a task that taps into a particular neural network.

Many factors can produce inconsistent findings when evaluating brain activity in a given patient population. First, patients sharing a diagnostic label can be very heterogeneous. For example, patients with schizophrenia can have paranoid schizophrenia with mainly positive symptoms, or disorganized schizophrenia with mainly negative symptoms. The same can be said of a diagnosis of major depressive disorder. It is also possible that distinct pathophysiologic processes (with different patterns of brain activity) can lead to expression of very similar symptoms. Other biases can easily affect results as well. Different research sites may attract particular subtypes of psychiatric disorders, and different criteria for inclusion and exclusion may bias the population. Often, studies are done with small numbers of subjects. When this is combined with several of the confounds listed above, as well as a small main effect within the data, results can vary significantly and thus may not be representative of the population being studied. The subjects' medication state, whether they are imaged during an acutely or chronically ill state or during a state or remission, even what time of day they are imaged, can all affect the resulting patterns of brain activity. Also, many studies of neuropsychiatric patients are performed at rest, which means that thoughts and feelings during the scan are imaged. Individuals respond idiosyncratically to the scanning environment; this may be more pronounced when comparing patients with volunteers. Different research groups allow variable stimuli during a resting scan. Some participants are imaged with their eyes closed and their ears plugged; others can see and hear the ambient environment. As mentioned earlier, recent work has shown consistent patterns of activity during rest (Binder et al. 1999) as well as in sleep (Nofzinger et al. 1999, 2000), and this activity is present in some of the same regions that are affected in many psychiatric disorders.

Lastly, independent research groups differ in the techniques used. PET, SPECT, fMRI, and MRS have all been applied to neuropsychiatric populations, and these methods have variable anatomical resolution and repeatability. Even when groups use the same general method, the scanners used vary in their resolution, sensitivity, and quality of images. Once the data are acquired, researchers choose a variety of methods for data analysis. All these variables can result in conflicting neuroimaging results.

Despite these problems, functional neuroimaging has provided tantalizing insights into neuropsychiatric conditions. Perhaps as the technology advances further, it will be possible to image an individual, understand the function and dysfunction within specific neural networks, and determine how the brain responds to treatment interventions.

## State Versus Trait Markers in Neuroimaging Studies of Mental Disorders

From the standpoint of longitudinal studies of brain function in a given disorder, it is difficult to know whether there are brain perfusion changes before there is phenotypic expression (disease symptoms) of those changes. Most patients do not have functional brain imaging done *before* they get sick; they get scans as a result of the disease process being expressed. Thus, little is known about what changes in perfusion might be occurring before diagnosis. Some studies are beginning to look at family members of mentally ill patients to look for possible "trait" markers, but this type of study is in its infancy (Blackwood et al. 1999). After an ill patient has had functional imaging performed, and has then been treated and gotten well, additional scans can be obtained. Comparison of these brain scans in two different *states* within the same patient or patient population is quite useful. This provides information about brain regions or networks that are affected by the disease process. Regions of abnormal activity during illness that normalize during remission are generally considered to be "state" markers, whereas regions that remain constantly abnormal irrespective of the wellness of the subject are "trait" markers of the illness being studied. A good example of this is the subgenual anterior cingulate cortex in familial depression, which remains hypoperfused even during states of remission from depression (Figure 9–4) (Drevets et al. 1997). It is possible, at least in theory, that trait markers like these can predict illness, if subjects at risk are screened for the disease.

## Neuropsychiatric Disorders

### Autism

Children with pervasive developmental disorder exhibit many problematic symptoms. Social interaction is impaired, language is delayed, and stereotyped motor behaviors and a marked need for sameness are common. Although structural neuroanatomic abnormalities are reported in autism, results from functional neuroimaging studies to date have been inconsistent. This may be due to technical limitations, difficulty conceptualizing the illness, or the heterogeneity of the disorder itself. Fortunately, with SPECT ligand studies, fMRI, and MRS, there is every reason to hope for clearer answers about the neuroanatomic and neurobiological basis of autism.

Using FDG PET, the resting cerebral metabolism of autistic men was higher than that of control subjects (Horwitz et al. 1988; Rumsey et al. 1985). In contrast, [$^{99m}$Tc]HMPAO SPECT of four autistic adult men showed decreased perfusion throughout the brain and focal decreases in the right temporal and bilateral frontal lobes. However, the control volunteers were not

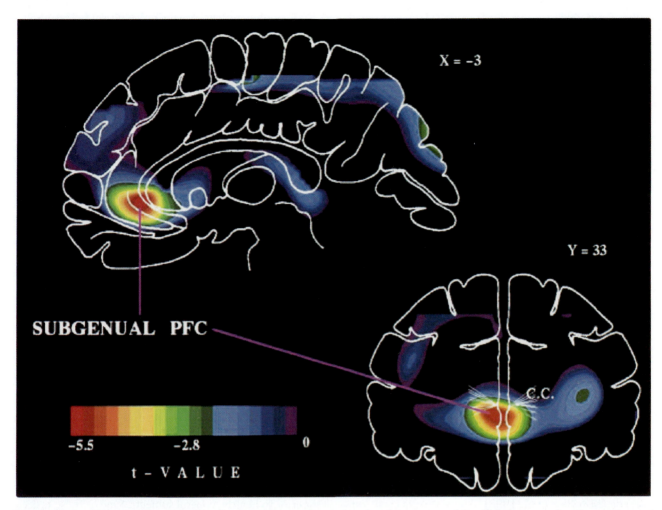

**FIGURE 9–4.** Decreased metabolism in the subgenual anterior cingulate cortex of familial depressed patients. Coronal and sagittal sections show negative voxel *t* values where metabolism is decreased in depressive patients relative to control subjects. This figure depicts the results of a PET study of patients diagnosed with major depressive disorder or bipolar affective disorder, depressed, compared with control subjects during the resting state. This region of the cortex in patients with mood disorders has less activity than in the nondepressed control group.

*Source.*   Reprinted by permission from Drevets WC, Price JL, Simpson JR, et al.: "Subgenual Prefrontal Cortex Abnormalities in Mood Disorders." *Nature* 386:824–827, 1997.

matched for IQ or gender to the autistic patients (George et al. 1992). In six autistic children, reduced perfusion was noted in the temporal and parietal lobes, but again, control subjects were not IQ matched to the patients (Mountz et al. 1995). In addition, in resting PET and SPECT studies, no abnormalities in cerebral blood flow or metabolism were found in autistic children (De Volder et al. 1987; Zilbovicius et al. 1992) or adults (Herold et al. 1988).

Such conflicting findings may arise from a number of variables. For example, in one intriguing $^{133}$Xe SPECT study, autistic children were studied longitudinally at age 3–4 years and again at age 6–7 years. Compared with age-matched control subjects, the younger autistic children showed frontal hypoperfusion; at the older age, frontal blood flow had normalized (Zilbovicius et al. 1995). In a

qualitative SPECT study on 23 children with autism, ranging from age 2 to age 7, multiple areas of hypoperfusion were noted in individual scans, including the cerebellum, thalami, parietal, and temporal regions (Ryu et al. 1999). These two studies suggest that participants' age may influence whether abnormalities are found.

In addition, matching on IQ is critical, since any abnormalities noted should be associated with autism as opposed to general mental retardation. For example, when children with autism were compared with age-matched control subjects with developmental disabilities and attention deficit/hyperactivity disorder (ADHD), blood flow to the frontal and temporal lobes in the autistic children was reduced. The blood flow to these areas was positively correlated with the developmental level (and IQ), underscoring the need to assess IQ when evaluating functional neuroimaging results (Hashimoto et al. 2000).

When SPECT was used to compare autistic children with nonautistic children of similar age and IQ, decreased perfusion was found in the bilateral insula, superior temporal gyri, left inferior frontal gyrus, and left middle frontal gyrus. Moreover, specific symptoms were associated with blood flow patterns. Impairments in communication and social interaction were positively correlated with blood flow in the left medial prefrontal cortex and the anterior cingulate gyrus, whereas an obsessive desire for sameness was positively correlated with blood flow in the right medial temporal region (Ohnishi et al. 2000). Abnormalities in the anterior cingulate gyrus were also noted in an MRI and PET study of autistic adults comparing them with gender- and age-matched control subjects, in which the dorsal anterior cingulate gyrus was reduced in volume and metabolism in autism (Haznedar et al. 1997).

MRS can also be utilized to explore abnormalities in specific brain areas. For example, the dorsolateral prefrontal cortex has been studied using phosphorus MRS in high-functioning autistic adolescent and adult men compared with age-, IQ-, and gender-matched control subjects. Although there were no abnormalities of phosphomonoesters or phosphodiesters (the building blocks and breakdown products of cell membranes), there were differences in high-energy phosphate compounds (Minshew et al. 1993). These results await replication, and the meaning of the abnormality is unclear. Using proton MRS, reduced NAA was found in the cerebellums of children with autism, consistent with neuropathological reports of reduced cerebellar Purkinje and granules cells in the cerebellar cortex in autism (Chugani et al. 1999).

The serotonin system has been investigated in autistic children using a PET tracer for serotonin synthesis. Neurochemical abnormalities were seen in boys with autism in the network connecting the dentate nucleus of the cerebellum, the thalamus, and the prefrontal cortex (Chugani et al. 1997). This pathway is important in motor learning and higher cognitive functions, including language (R.A. Muller et al. 1998).

However, the studies mentioned above were done at rest, which fails to control for the participants' affective or cognitive state. It is possible that consistent brain differences in autism would emerge if patients were imaged performing a task that differentiates them from healthy control subjects, or during tasks involving brain systems implicated in autism, such as language or social emotional processing.

Two pilot studies investigated auditory functions and language in a small number of autistic adults compared with non-IQ-matched control subjects. ($^{15}$O)water PET revealed a trend toward reduced auditory cortex but increased left anterior cingulate gyrus activations in autism when listening to tones. Autistic individuals showed a significant reversal of normal left dominance and cerebellar dentate nuclear activation when listening to sentences. Repeating sentences caused reduced blood flow in the prefrontal cortex of healthy individuals but not in autistic individuals. When required to generate sentences, the autism group showed reduced activation of the left thalamus and possibly the prefrontal cortex, again implicating abnormalities in the dentate-thalamo-cortical pathway that had been implicated in disordered serotonin synthesis (R.A. Muller et al. 1998, 1999).

Since social interactions are universally impaired in autism, even with spared IQ, a recent fMRI study imaged nine males with Asperger's syndrome and autism, and compared them with age-, gender-, and IQ-matched control subjects. Participants viewed faces with neutral, happy, or angry expressions. Individuals with autism did not activate the right fusiform gyrus (the cortical area that processes faces), left amygdala, or left cerebellum when processing emotional expressions (Critchley et al. 2000).

One novel approach has been to use fMRI to study individuals with autism during a task at which they are superior to healthy control subjects. One of these tasks is the Embedded Figures Task, in which a participant is asked to find a simple shape embedded in a more complex one. Six individuals with autism or Asperger's syndrome were matched to control subjects by age, gender, handedness, and IQ. Both groups activated the middle and inferior temporal gyri, the supramarginal gyrus, inferior frontal gyrus, and middle occipital gyrus to perform the task. However, the control subjects showed significantly greater response in bilateral dorsal parietal cortex and right dorsolateral prefrontal cortex, whereas the autistic group showed more activation in the right occipital cortex extending to the inferior temporal gyrus (Ring et al. 1999). This suggests that individuals with autism use a more posterior and "local" approach to processing complex visual information, rather than at the global level by activating the prefrontal cortex.

These recent studies offer the potential to explore specific neural networks linking the cerebellum, thalamus, striatum, limbic system, and prefrontal cortex, and to determine the association between discrete networks and the symptoms expressed under the global diagnosis of autism.

## Attention Deficit/Hyperactivity Disorder

ADHD is characterized by hyperactivity, disordered attention, and impulsivity. Although this disorder begins in childhood, symptoms may persist into adulthood. In adults with ADHD performing an auditory continuous-attention task, brain metabolism showed a generalized reduction, with focal decreases in the premotor and superior prefrontal areas (Zametkin et al. 1990). In adolescents with ADHD, regional metabolic decreases were uncovered in the left anterior frontal and right temporal lobes (Zametkin et al. 1993). A more recent study evaluated adult patients with ADHD during a working memory task (Schweitzer et al. 2000). The data found that patients had a relative lack of task-related activity in frontal regions while having more extrastriate activity. This indicates a defect in engaging frontal regions for use in difficult executive tasks, while having to use more visual imagery to make up for this. The cerebral basis of attention has been fairly well studied with PET and fMRI (see previous section on Attention). Brains areas with abnormal metabolism in ADHD correspond to regions involved in attention in healthy volunteers. This was remarkably well demonstrated by two studies done using fMRI. In the first, adult ADHD patients failed to activate the cognitive/attention division of the anterior cingulate gyrus during the Counting Stroop task compared with a group of matched control subjects. Instead the patients with ADHD activated a different network, including the insula, striatum, and thalamus (Bush et al. 1999). The second study examined children with ADHD during a motor response inhibition task and found less activity in regions of the medial prefrontal cortex bordering the cingulate attentional region (Figure 9–5). This region is important in directing motor responses (Rubia et al. 1999).

One of the fundamental underlying dysfunctions in ADHD is thought to be within the dopamine system. Most drugs that are effective in treating ADHD (e.g., stimulants) work by blocking reuptake of dopamine by the dopamine transporter. Two studies done with radiolabeled ligands have been performed to evaluate dopamine's involvement in this disorder. The first was a SPECT study that used [$^{123}$I]Altropane to examine dopamine transporter density in adults with ADHD. Doughtery and colleagues saw a 70% increase in dopamine transporter density in the striatum of adults with ADHD compared with control subjects (Dougherty et al. 1999). Another study done using the PET radioligand [$^{18}$F]fluorodopa found a 48% increase of dopa accumulation in the right midbrain of children (medication-free for two weeks) with ADHD compared with control sub-

jects. Furthermore, the degree of accumulation of radiolabeled dopa in the right midbrain correlated with the severity of ADHD symptoms in the patients (Ernst et al. 1999). These studies are complementary, as overproduction of dopamine in the midbrain could be related to increased reuptake of dopamine in the striatum.

## Anxiety and Panic Disorders

Panic disorder is defined by spontaneous panic attacks, discrete episodes of intense fear with accompanying somatic symptoms. A review of the functional imaging literature related to panic disorder has been published (Goddard and Charney 1997). In panic disorder, the intravenous infusion of sodium lactate can precipitate a panic attack, and patients with panic disorder produce excessive amounts of blood lactate in response to a variety of metabolic challenges. MRS offers a noninvasive measure of brain lactate. It was used to compare a small number of panic disorder patients with healthy control subjects during hyperventilation. Brain lactate level rose significantly more in patients with panic disorder (Dager et al. 1995). Another MRS investigation used $^{31}$P MRS to examine high-energy phosphate metabolism in the frontal lobes of patients with panic disorder (Shioiri et al. 1996). This study found phosphocreatine asymmetry with levels on the left greater than those on the right, consistent with previous findings of perfusion asymmetry in this disorder. In another resting state examination, unmedicated females with panic disorder were compared with control subjects in a PET study of metabolism using FDG. This work found increased activity at rest in the hippocampus and the parahippocampal gyrus on the left side, but decreased activity in the inferior parietal and posterior temporal regions on the right (Bisaga et al. 1998). The presence of panic disorder was confirmed after performance of the scan by measuring lactate level. Other studies have also found abnormalities in the hippocampus. Another PET study that also used FDG examined metabolism in medicated, stable responders and found abnormal asymmetry in the orbitofrontal and hippocampal regions (Nordahl et al. 1998). To summarize, many studies of panic disorder implicate the limbic system as playing a role in this disease.

## Obsessive-Compulsive Disorder

Obsessive-compulsive disorder (OCD) is characterized by unwanted, persistent, repetitive thoughts and the performance of ritualistic behaviors. This disorder is associated with a number of neurological conditions, including Sydenham's chorea, Tourette syndrome, postencephal-

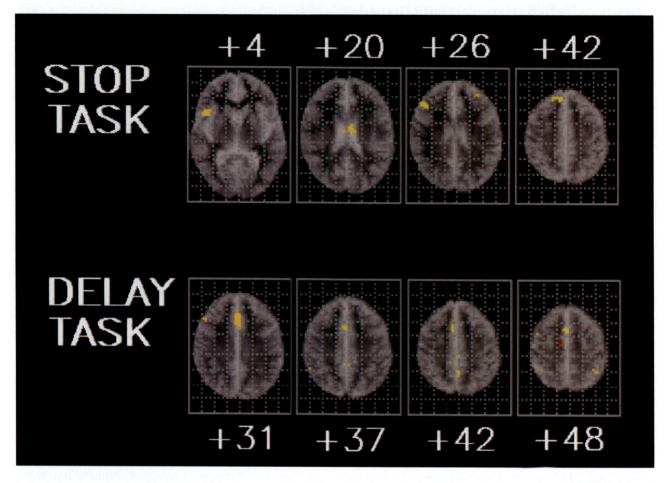

**FIGURE 9–5.** Areas of significant difference in power of brain activation between seven adolescent boys with attention deficit/hyperactivity disorder (ADHD) and nine healthy comparison subjects during performance of a motor response inhibition task and a motor timing task. Yellow voxels show greater mean signal power in the control subjects; red voxels show greater mean signal power in the adolescents with ADHD.

*Source.* Reprinted with permission from Rubia K, Overmeyer S, Taylor E, et al.: "Hypofrontality in Attention Deficit Hyperactivity Disorder During Higher-Order Motor Control: A Study With Functional MRI." *American Journal of Psychiatry* 156:891–896, 1999.

itic Parkinson's disease, and bilateral globus pallidus lesions (Insel 1992). These conditions all involve dysfunction in the basal ganglia, suggesting a neuroanatomic basis for OCD.

The basal ganglia are involved in fine motor control, habit learning, and behavior selection. Five separate parallel circuits connect areas of cortex with the striatum and thalamus. The role these circuits play in behavior and cognition depends on their unique cortical connections. Functional neuroimaging has implicated dysfunction in three of these circuits in OCD. There is a dorsolateral prefrontal circuit that may play a role in memory functions. A lateral orbitofrontal circuit projects to the ventral caudate nucleus; lesions in animals result in an inability to switch behavioral routines. An anterior cingulate circuit involves cortex, ventral striatum, and limbic structures such as the hippocampus, amygdala, and overlying mesial temporal cortex. Animal studies have been insuf-

ficient to delineate a role for this circuit (Alexander et al. 1986), although the limbic connections suggest an affective component.

Using resting FDG PET, OCD patients were shown to have increased metabolism in the caudate and orbital frontal gyri (Baxter et al. 1987, 1988). Patients with childhood-onset OCD shared this abnormality and additionally had evidence of increased prefrontal and cingulate metabolism (Swedo et al. 1989).

Treatment interventions alter the abnormal metabolic patterns. FDG PET during a continuous-performance task was performed on OCD patients before and after treatment with clomipramine. With clomipramine, metabolism in the basal ganglia and orbital frontal cortex decreased to a level comparable to that seen in healthy volunteers; clinical improvement correlated with the normalized caudate and orbital frontal metabolism (Benkelfat et al. 1990).

In a resting SPECT study, OCD patients had increased mesial-frontal perfusion, which normalized with fluoxetine treatment (Hoehn-Saric et al. 1991). A resting FDG PET study looked at changes in cerebral metabolism after OCD patients responded to treatment with either fluoxetine or behavior therapy. With either intervention, responders showed normalized caudate metabolism (Baxter et al. 1992). In a group of patients with childhood-onset OCD, successful treatment was associated with normalization of metabolism in the orbitofrontal cortex (Swedo et al. 1992).

In one of the earliest fMRI studies of this disorder, symptom provocation was used to induce pathological activity in patients with OCD. Abnormally increased brain activity was found in the orbitofrontal cortex and in the anterior cingulate, anterior temporal, and insular regions (H.C. Breiter et al. 1996). A further symptom-provocation study was done using PET to examine regional cerebral blood flow in three different anxiety disorders (OCD, simple phobia, and posttraumatic stress disorder). In compiling the results of this evaluation, the researchers looked at pooled data from all three diagnoses and again found increased orbitofrontal and insular activity. However, they also found increased rCBF in the striatum and brain stem, and the brain stem foci correlated with subjective anxiety scores (Rauch et al. 1997).

## Gilles de la Tourette Syndrome

Tourette syndrome is defined by intrusive, impulsive motor acts, including tics and vocalizations. The association between Tourette syndrome and OCD is well established. The two have a high comorbidity and may result from the same genetic basis. Recently, SPECT scans were performed at rest on 50 patients with Tourette syndrome, who were compared with healthy participants. Patients showed reduced perfusion in the left caudate nucleus, anterior cingulate cortex, and left dorsolateral prefrontal cortex, although the latter hypoperfusion was likely associated with depression (Moriarty et al. 1995). In this initial study, the neural circuits that are abnormal in Tourette syndrome are those involved in the initiation, continuation, and inhibition of actions, similar to findings in OCD. Another study performed in twins discordant for severity of Tourette syndrome symptoms found that there was a high correlation between a symptom index and the degree of $[^{123}I]$3-iodo-6-methoxybenzamine (IBZM) binding in the head of the caudate nucleus (Wolf et al. 1996). This indicated that the quantity of $D_2$ receptor binding in the head of the caudate nucleus may be related to the severity of Tourette syndrome.

Within this group of studies, there are inconsisten-

cies. Not every research group finds altered metabolism or perfusion in the same brain region. Such inconsistencies are perhaps not surprising in that these groups use different scanning methods with different spatial resolution. In addition, some groups have participants rest with eyes open, others with eyes closed; some groups have participants performing a sustained-attention task. Also, for the before-and-after-treatment studies, OCD patients were studied while taking different medications and after treatments that ranged in duration from 10 weeks to one year. These differences, too, could significantly affect the functional neuroimaging results (Insel 1992). What is remarkable is the consistency with which specific cortico-basal ganglia-thalamo-cortical circuits are implicated, particularly those involving the orbitofrontal, cingulate, and prefrontal cortices and the caudate nucleus.

## Mood Disorders

Mood disorders are particularly heterogeneous. Mood states encompass a wide range of severity and may or may not include psychosis. Some patients experience significant cognitive impairment, whereas others do not. Some patients do not respond to intervention; others experience discrete episodes of illness and return to premorbid functioning after treatment. The etiologic bases for these different types of illness may be varied and likely involve both genetic vulnerability and responses to difficult life events.

Coupled with the heterogeneity of the illnesses is the variability in patient populations recruited, length and stage of illness, number of patients in a given study, medication state, imaging technique, imaging state (resting versus performing a task), and method of data analysis. Some studies have taken the approach of looking at mood disorders across diagnostic categories to search for common abnormalities. Others examine not just a specific illness but a subset of patients within that illness, for example, unmedicated patients with major depressive disorder, acute onset, without cognitive deficits. Both approaches provide useful information about brain regions related to pathological mood states.

Despite these many variables, there is some consensus about the cerebral basis of mood disorders. There have been several recent reviews of the functional imaging findings in mood disorders (Drevets 1998, 1999; Soares and Mann 1997). There seems to be an underlying network of regions implicated in most studies of depressed patients. Although this network is almost always involved, the actual regions and the direction of change in a given region vary based on several factors.

This network includes the medial prefrontal cortex, orbitofrontal cortex, perigenual cingulate cortex, posterior cingulate cortex, amygdala, and extended amygdala. Of note, this same network of cortical and subcortical regions is involved in many anxiety disorders. Furthermore, another network that is active in executive functioning includes the dorsolateral prefrontal cortex; this network is frequently involved in mood disorders.

When unipolar depressed patients with similar severity of depressive symptoms were compared based on the presence or absence of pseudodementia, patients with cognitive impairment showed reduced flow in the left medial prefrontal cortex and increased flow in the cerebellum. Compared with healthy control subjects, depressed patients showed decreased flow in the dorsolateral prefrontal cortex, left anterior cingulate cortex, and right insula (Dolan et al. 1992).

Likewise, specific symptom complexes are associated with blood flow patterns. Psychomotor agitation was associated with increased flow in the posterior cingulate and inferior parietal cortices. Psychomotor retardation and mood disturbance were correlated with decreased flow in the left dorsolateral prefrontal cortex and left angular gyrus. Decreased blood flow in the medial prefrontal cortex was associated with increasing cognitive impairment (Bench et al. 1993), and decreased metabolism in the nearby subgenual anterior cingulate cortex has been related to familial mood disorders, both unipolar and bipolar (see Figure 9–4) (Drevets et al. 1997).

The involvement of the frontal cortex in depression is strengthened by a study in which 10 unipolar depressed patients were imaged using resting FDG PET before and after treatment. Improved mood was associated with increases in metabolism in the prefrontal and anterior cingulate cortices (Mayberg et al. 1997). A follow-up study showed that nondepressed patients with provoked dysphoric mood and depressed patients recovered from depression had inverse relationships with brain activity in the subgenual anterior cingulate and dorsolateral prefrontal cortices (Mayberg et al. 1999).

Regional differences between depressed and nondepressed participants included decreased [99mTc]HMPAO uptake in bilateral orbital frontal, inferotemporal, and parietal areas (Lesser et al. 1994). A PET comparison between predominantly unipolar depressed patients and healthy volunteers showed that the depressed group had decreased flow in specific brain regions, including the left dorsolateral prefrontal cortex, the left angular gyrus, and the left anterior cingulate gyrus; increased flow was found in the left posterior cingulate gyrus (Bench et al. 1993). A more recent [99mTc]HMPAO resting SPECT study found hypoperfusion in the inferior frontal, anterior temporal, and anterior cingulate cortices in patients with refractory depression (Mayberg et al. 1994).

Not all studies find reductions in frontal blood flow or metabolism. In fact, many recent studies show relative increases in flow in the ventral and medial orbitofrontal regions of patients with acute untreated, unmedicated major depression, coupled with changes in activity in the dorsolateral prefrontal cortex. The majority of studies examining this illness report changes either bilaterally or localized to the left side. Using ($^{15}$O)water PET, it was shown that depressed patients had increased left ventrolateral frontal blood flow and increased blood flow in the left amygdala (Drevets et al. 1992). Interestingly, patients in remission showed normalized frontal flow but continued elevations in the amygdala (Drevets et al. 1992), indicating possible state versus trait differences. FDG PET likewise found increased metabolism in the orbital frontal lobes, along with decreased metabolism in the dorsolateral frontal and parietal cortices of unipolar depressed patients (Biver et al. 1994). This study suggests that distinct regions of frontal cortex may play different roles in depression.

Furthermore, an fMRI study of depressed patients and nondepressed control subjects measured brain activity in a task viewing sadness-laden film clips (Beauregard et al. 1998). Patients with depression had significantly greater activity in the left medial prefrontal cortex and right cingulate gyrus than did control subjects. Another report of pathology in this same network came from an examination of regional perfusion using PET. Depressed patients were compared with healthy control subjects in a study examining flow changes in response to performance feedback on a task. Unlike the nondepressed subjects, the depressed patients did not activate the ventromedial orbitofrontal cortex and medial caudate nucleus (Elliott et al. 1998).

There has also been recent work on receptor activity and function in depression. Both the serotonin receptor and transporter have been studied. The 5-hydroxytryptamine (serotonin) type 1A (5-HT$_{1A}$) receptor has been of interest to psychiatrists, as modulation of this presynaptic autoreceptor may play a role in both anxiolytic and antidepressant efficacy. A study that examined this receptor in depressed patients found significantly decreased binding potential for the PET radioligand [$^{11}$C]WAY-100635 in both regions examined (dorsal raphe, mesiotemporal cortex). However, more widespread decreases were thought to be present, as post hoc examination revealed decreased binding potential in other regions as well (Figure 9–6) (Drevets et al. 1999). Another study did look at the 5-HT$_{1A}$ receptor across the

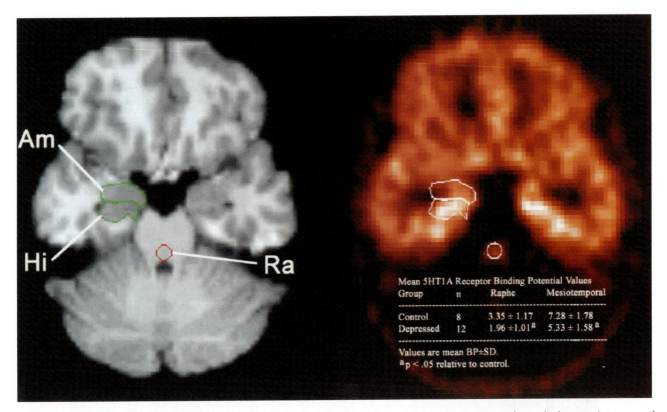

**FIGURE 9–6.** Coregistered magnetic resonance and positron emission tomographic sections through the mesiotemporal cortex and midbrain to show placement of the mesiotemporal cortex and raphe regions of interest. Am=amygdala; Hi=hippocampus; Ra=raphe. The inset table details the significant differences between the depressed and control groups overall.

*Source.* Reprinted with permission from Drevets WC, Frank E, Price JC, et al.: "PET Imaging of Serotonin 1A Receptor Binding in Depression." *Biological Psychiatry* 46(10):1375–1387, 1999.

entire brain, and indeed found significantly decreased binding potential (Sargent et al. 2000). This study also examined the effect of antidepressant treatment, and surprisingly found no difference in binding potential between patients treated with antidepressant (paroxetine) and those who were not treated. Furthermore, the study found no difference between those who responded to treatment and those who did not.

An evaluation of the brain stem serotonin transporter was carried out with [$^{123}$I]2β-carbomethoxy-3β-(4-iodophenyl)tropane, a cocaine analog with specific binding to the serotonin and dopamine transporters (Malison et al. 1998). Because there appear to be no dopamine transporters in the brain stem, this radioligand was used to study the serotonin reuptake pump in this region. Decreased specific binding of the radioligand to the serotonin transporter was found in the brain stem, indicating likely decreased numbers of receptors there. The serotonin type 2 (5-HT$_2$) receptor has also been examined with PET. [$^{18}$F]setoperone was used to examine this receptor in patients with depression before treatment and 3 weeks after treatment with a tricyclic antidepressant (Attar-

Levy et al. 1999). These researchers found a trend toward lower specific binding in untreated depressed patients compared with control subjects. Specific binding also decreased with antidepressant treatment, coincident with binding of the receptor by the antidepressant and/or modulation.

## Bipolar Disorder

Patients in the manic phase of bipolar disorder are often difficult to study due to their illness, and thus there are only a few examinations of patients in this state. However, those that report on this disorder also find pathological activity in may of the same regions found in unipolar depression. Two recent PET studies examined regional cerebral perfusion in three groups of subjects: medicated patients with bipolar mania, medicated euthymic patients with bipolar disorder, and healthy control subjects. The researchers examined activity across these three groups during the resting state and during a word-generation task (word generation minus word repetition) (Figure 9–7) (Blumberg et al. 1999, 2000). During the

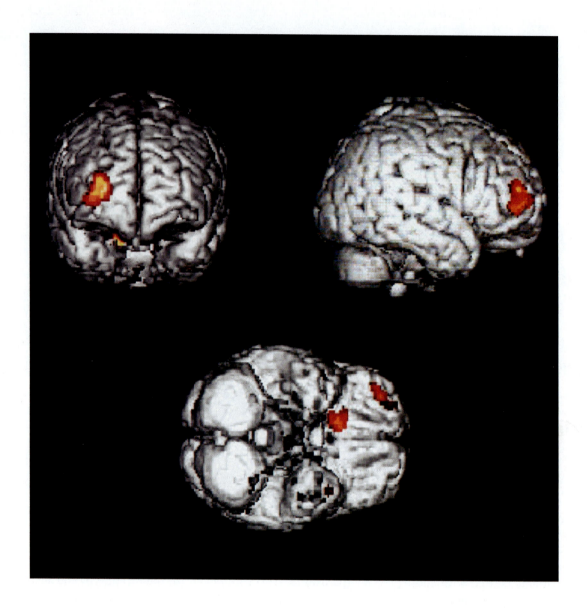

**FIGURE 9–7.** Areas of decreased activity in patients with bipolar mania compared with bipolar patients in a euthymic state during a word-generation task. Frontal (left), right lateral (right), and ventral (bottom) brain surface renderings demonstrate these areas of decreased regional cerebral blood flow (*P*<0.005).

*Source.* Reprinted with permission from Blumberg HP, Stern E, Ricketts S, et al.: "Rostral and Orbital Prefrontal Cortex Dysfunction in the Manic State of Bipolar Disorder." *American Journal of Psychiatry* 156:1986–1988, 1999.

word-generation task, the researchers found decreased activity in the right prefrontal cortex of the manic patients compared with either the euthymic patients or control subjects. In addition, manic patients compared with euthymic patients at rest had decreased activity in the right posterior orbitofrontal cortex and decreased activity in the left ventromedial prefrontal cortex compared with the psychiatrically healthy subjects. In the manic patients compared with euthymic patients,

increased activity was found in the left caudate nucleus and left dorsal anterior cingulate gyrus, with trends to increased activity in the right dorsal and ventral anterior cingulate gyrus. Another examination of patients with familial mood disorders (either unipolar or bipolar) found decreased subgenual anterior cingulate activity, regardless of the mood state (Drevets et al. 1997). Medicated patients with stable bipolar disorder who were withdrawn from lithium treatment and then became manic developed relative increases in the dorsal anterior cingulate gyrus and the left orbitofrontal cortex (Goodwin et al. 1997).

In summary, mood disorders appear to be associated with changes in specific networks involving prefrontal cortical and limbic regions. The specific regions affected may be linked to specific clinical symptoms. Different regions or subsections of the affected networks are likely involved in different diagnoses and/or stages of the illness. Interestingly, inducing transient sadness in healthy volunteers increases blood flow to orbitofrontal regions, areas that show flow decreases in some depressed patients and flow increases in others. This further implicates the orbitofrontal cortex as being an integral part of a network that controls mood.

## Schizophrenia

Functional neuroimaging studies in schizophrenia are arguably the most advanced in neuropsychiatry. These techniques are used to explore many aspects of the illness, including schizophrenia subtypes, response to antipsychotic treatment, neurotransmitter systems involved, cognitive networks affected, symptom-related pathology, and others. There have been reviews of functional imaging in schizophrenia recently published (Berman and Weinberger 1999; Soares et al. 1999). Techniques that examine patients during a baseline state can help researchers find some differences between a group of patients and control subjects but may not fully evaluate regions that are not active or pathological at baseline. Techniques capable of brain imaging during various tasks can help researchers determine whether brain activity (as estimated by perfusion, blood oxygenation, or metabolism) is dysfunctional in certain regions and networks involved in those tasks. Further examination of these data in larger samples can help researchers examine how different affected regions are interacting within the network. What appears likely is that schizophrenia is not caused by dysfunction in one brain area. Rather, there is abnormal modulation of, and/or abnormal activity in, the networks linking subcortical regions, the cerebellum, and frontal, parietal, and temporal cortices.

### The Dopamine Hypothesis

Functional neuroimaging allows direct and indirect tests of hypotheses about the etiology of schizophrenia. PET is particularly well suited to obtaining images that show the distribution and density of dopamine and other receptors. The dopamine hypothesis of schizophrenia maintains that the illness results from an abnormality of the brain dopaminergic system. This is suggested because all antipsychotic medications have the ability to block $D_2$ receptors, and their efficacy as antipsychotics is typically correlated with the degree of $D_2$ blockade, at least with the typical antipsychotics. This has been directly investigated using PET and dopaminergic ligands in many studies. Although a twofold to threefold increase in $D_2$ receptor density in the striatum has been reported in neuroleptic-naïve schizophrenic patients (Wong et al. 1986), this finding has not been replicated in several studies in which normal densities of $D_2$ receptors were found in schizophrenic patients (Farde et al. 1987, 1990; Nordstrom et al. 1995a). A more recent study was done after a 3-week medication washout in patients classified as treatment nonresponders and in treatment-responsive patients. The cerebral metabolic response induced by a single dose of antipsychotic medication distinguished between treatment responders and nonresponders (Bartlett et al. 1998). Kapur and others examined this issue as well, using [$^{11}$C]raclopride as a probe of $D_2$ receptor occupancy (Kapur et al. 2000a). Patients with schizophrenia were given either 1.0 or 2.5 mg of haloperidol in a double-blind fashion, and measurements were taken 2 weeks later. The relationship between occupancy at the $D_2$ receptor and clinical response, extrapyramidal side effects, and prolactin levels in 22 patients with first-episode schizophrenia was examined. The patients showed a wide range of $D_2$ receptor occupancy, from 38% to 87%. However, the magnitude of receptor binding was directly related to clinical response, side effects, and serum prolactin levels. A clinical response was found when receptor occupancy was greater than 65%, but extrapyramidal side effects were not apparent until 78% occupancy. Hyperprolactinemia was intermediate between these two levels, associated with 72% occupancy. Given the wide range in variability in $D_2$ receptor binding and this narrow therapeutic window, this PET study demonstrates the difficulty in optimal titration of haloperidol dose across a patient population. This may not be true for the newer atypical antipsychotics, however. One SPECT study using [$^{123}$I]IBZM examined dopamine receptor binding in the presence of either a low dose (5 mg) or a high dose (20 mg) of olanzapine. The researchers found significant differences in $D_2$ binding at the two doses, but no clinically significant differences in ratings, symptoms, or extrapyramidal symptoms (Raedler et al. 1999). Quetiapine, on the other hand, had markedly different patterns of $D_2$ blockade. Using [$^{11}$C]raclopride as a measure of $D_2$ binding, quetiapine was found to cause transient blockade of the $D_2$ receptor 2–3 hours after administration, at levels up to approximately 60%, that would then slowly decrease over time (Figure 9–8) (Kapur et al. 2000b).

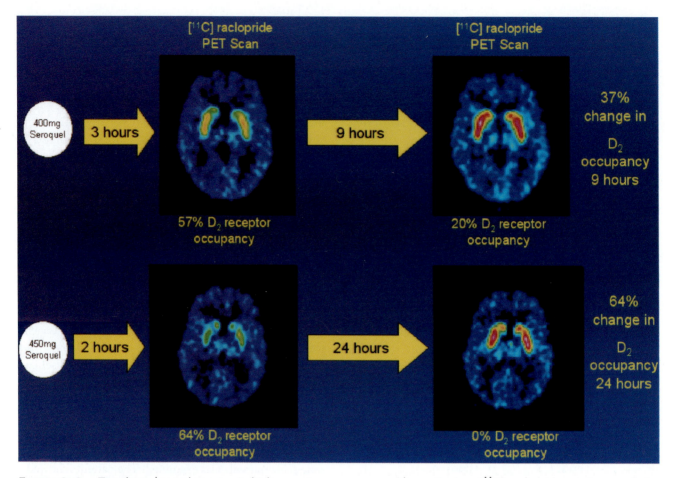

**FIGURE 9–8.** Transient dopamine type 2 (D$_2$) receptor occupancy with quetiapine. [$^{11}$C]-raclopride positron emission tomography (PET) scans were obtained in patients who were scanned twice after their last dose of quetiapine. *Top panel.* The patient received a dose of 400 mg of quetiapine. *Bottom panel.* The patient received a dose of 450 mg of quetiapine.
*Source.* Reprinted with permission from Kapur S, Zipursky R, Jones C, et al.: "A Positron Emission Tomography Study of Quetiapine in Schizophrenia." *Archives of General Psychiatry* 57:553–559, 2000.

In summary, it appears likely from all these reports that dopamine plays a central role in schizophrenia. Radioligand studies like these reviewed here are helping to shed light on clinically relevant questions regarding this disorder.

## The Neurodevelopmental Hypothesis

The neurodevelopmental hypothesis views schizophrenia as resulting from abnormal brain development, with a focus on the interconnections between the frontal, parietal, temporal, and limbic cortices (Weinberger 1987). There have been multiple recent studies that find pathology in both the neurons of these regions and the white matter tracts that connect them. Other theories of abnormal connectivity have also been put forth, including the disconnection hypothesis (Friston et al. 1998) and the reduced neuropil hypothesis (Selemon and Goldman-Rakic 1999). The former has to do with abnormal plasticity in systems having to do with emotional learning and memory, whereas the latter relates to a decrease in the synaptic connections that cells make, without a decrease in cell numbers. Reports relevant to these ideas are presented in later sections (MRS in Schizophrenia, White Matter Integrity: Diffusion Tensor Imaging).

## Cognitive Dysmetria

One recent model of schizophrenia attempts to unify rather than divide the disorder based on varied presentations and is founded on the common thread that all individuals with schizophrenia have cognitive deficits. This model implicates cerebellar abnormalities in schizophrenia and is consistent with increasing information about the role of the cerebellum in cognitive function. The idea of "cognitive" dysmetria posits that cerebellar dysfunction is involved in the schizophrenic patient's uncoordinated thought processes, similar to the uncoordinated motor deficits seen with lesions in motor-related portions of the cerebellum (Andreasen et al. 1999).

There have been multiple recent studies that indicate the cerebellum is involved in the pathophysiology of schizophrenia. Functional MRI using an injected contrast agent showed increased cerebellar blood flow in persons with schizophrenia, and lower than normal flow in patients with bipolar disorder (Loeber et al. 1999).

## Functional Studies Done During the Resting State

The first functional cerebral abnormality reported in older schizophrenic patients was a reduction in frontal blood flow, or hypofrontality (Ingvar and Franzen 1974). This finding spawned a number of studies, with techniques including $^{133}$Xe SPECT, ($^{15}$O)water PET, and FDG PET. Patient populations have ranged from acutely ill, never-medicated adolescents to patients receiving long-term medication. Hypofrontality is an inconsistent finding and probably depends on many factors (for review, see Berman and Weinberger 1991, 1999; Chabrol et al. 1986; Cleghorn et al. 1989; Early et al. 1987; Gur et al. 1995; Paulman et al. 1990; Tamminga et al. 1992). In fact, some investigators find hyperfrontality in unmedicated schizophrenic patients (Ebmeier et al. 1993).

It has been argued that hypofrontality is an artifact from medicating patients. Although neuroleptics reliably increase metabolism and blood flow in the basal ganglia (Szechtman et al. 1988), they do not appear to cause hypofrontality (Andreasen et al. 1992; Berman et al. 1992; Buchsbaum et al. 1987), and it has been suggested that they normalize (by increasing) perfusion to the frontal lobes (Vita et al. 1995). What is more likely is that looking for resting differences in brain function is insufficient to capture the dysfunction of schizophrenia. As mentioned earlier in the chapter, the resting state is not well defined, and thus is not an optimal task by itself.

## Studies Linking Symptoms With Brain Function

Where resting studies have yielded information is in attempting to understand the heterogeneity of schizophrenia. For example, patients with paranoid schizophrenia may be extremely delusional, yet have clear thought processes. Other patients are so disorganized as to be incoherent. Patients may be free of delusions and hallucinations, yet be incapacitated by social withdrawal and apathy. Numerous studies find that the symptoms of schizophrenia cluster along three dimensions that may be somewhat independent of each other. These are negative symptoms (apathy, flat affect, social withdrawal, amotivation), psychoticism (delusions and hallucinations), and disorganization (Andreasen et al. 1995b). Functional neuroimaging has begun to search for the neurobiological underpinnings of these symptom complexes. To do this,

most studies image schizophrenic patients during a resting state, and blood flow or metabolism is correlated with clinical symptoms. Certain brain regions are implicated in particular symptoms. Unfortunately, perhaps due to differences in imaging methods, patient populations, or even resting-state variability, whether activity increases or decreases in specific brain regions differs across studies.

**Negative symptoms.**   Negative symptoms in patients with schizophrenia can arise from several sources, including comorbid mood disorders and the effect of antipsychotic medication. However, it has been recognized that there are core negative symptoms of schizophrenia termed the *deficit syndrome*. This syndrome, and negative symptoms in general, are difficult to treat and have been the subject of multiple functional imaging studies.

In 20 medication-free schizophrenic patients, negative symptoms were associated with decreased metabolism in the right dorsolateral prefrontal cortex (Wolkin et al. 1992). Similarly, SPECT showed a negative correlation between negative symptoms and frontal perfusion (Ebmeier et al. 1993). In a different group of unmedicated patients, 4 patients with predominantly negative symptoms were compared with 7 nondeficit patients. Patients with negative symptoms showed reduced metabolism in the frontal and parietal cortices and the thalamus (Tamminga et al. 1992). Using $^{15}$O PET, negative symptoms were associated with decreased blood flow in a large area of the prefrontal cortex, extending from the dorsolateral to the medial aspect and into the anterior cingulate gyrus and the left parietal cortex. Greater negative symptoms were associated with increasing blood flow in the caudate nucleus (Liddle et al. 1992).

In contrast, FDG PET of 20 unmedicated patients with recent-onset schizophrenia revealed a positive correlation between negative symptoms and metabolism in the left dorsal prefrontal and dorsal parietal regions (Kaplan et al. 1993). In a relatively large FDG PET study, negative symptoms had no association with dorsolateral prefrontal cortical metabolism. Instead, patients with severe negative symptoms had increased relative metabolism in the mesial frontal and left midtemporal areas (Gur et al. 1995).

Thus, reminiscent of depression, the frontal lobe is implicated in negative symptoms, although the exact location and meaning of the dysfunction requires further study. In fact, it is unclear whether the frontal deficits are specific to negative symptoms in schizophrenia, or whether frontal dysfunction reflects symptoms and not the illness. For example, large groups of patients with schizophrenia and major depression were studied using $^{15}O$ PET at rest. Patients with poverty of speech, regardless of whether they had schizophrenia or major depression, had reduced blood flow in the left dorsolateral prefrontal cortex (Dolan et al. 1993).

All the studies mentioned in this section on negative symptoms examined patients in the resting state and searched for correlates with negative symptoms. Studies done on patients with the deficit syndrome performing cognitive tasks are presented later in this section.

**Psychoticism.**    Psychoticism includes hallucinations and delusions. In 20 unmedicated patients with recent-onset schizophrenia, psychoticism was positively correlated with metabolism in the left temporal, inferior parietal, and occipitotemporal regions and was negatively correlated in the right posterior frontal/anterior parietal area (Kaplan et al. 1993).

In a $^{15}O$ PET blood flow study, increasing psychoticism in long-term medicated patients was associated with increasing blood flow in the left mesial temporal area, superior temporal pole, and lateral prefrontal cortex. Negative correlations were found between psychoticism and flow in the right caudate nucleus, posterior cingulate gyrus, posterior superior temporal regions, and adjacent supramarginal gyrus (Liddle et al. 1992). A SPECT study likewise found a correlation between psychoticism and perfusion in the left anterior temporal lobe; however, in this case, as psychoticism increased, perfusion decreased (Ebmeier et al. 1993).

The neural basis for hallucinations alone has been investigated. Using FDG PET at rest, 12 schizophrenic patients experiencing hallucinations were compared with 10 patients without hallucinations during the procedure. All patients were free of medication, and most had never received neuroleptics. Hallucinations were correlated with metabolism in the anterior cingulate cortex and the striatum (Cleghorn et al. 1992). Hallucinating patients also showed decreased metabolism in the posterior temporal region. However, patients with hallucinations were more symptomatic, with more positive and negative symptoms as well as greater cognitive impairment. Also, using ($^{15}O$)water PET, 5 schizophrenic patients were studied. Their blood flow patterns at rest were compared with the patterns seen when the patients were experiencing auditory hallucinations. Auditory hallucinations were associated with activity in the mesial temporal lobes, right anterior cingulate and left orbitofrontal cortices, and the right ventral striatum and thalamus (Silbersweig et al. 1995). Another study done recently used event-related fMRI to examine what regions of the brain were active during actual auditory hallucinations (Sukhwinder

et al. 2000). The researchers found activity correlated with auditory hallucinations in many regions, including bilateral temporal (Brodmann's areas [BA] 21, 22, and 39), superior frontal (BA 8, 9, 46), inferior frontal (BA 44), and insular areas.

**Disorganization.**    In a resting $^{15}O$ PET blood flow study of long-term medicated patients, increasing disorganization was associated with increasing blood flow in the anterior cingulate cortex and contiguous medial prefrontal cortex, the left superior temporal lobe, and the thalamus (Liddle et al. 1992). In 20 unmedicated patients with recent-onset disease, disorganization scores correlated negatively with metabolism in the left superior temporal and inferior parietal areas (Kaplan et al. 1993).

## Tests of Benzodiazepine Function

A study of 15 patients with schizophrenia was done with [$^{123}$I]iomazenil using SPECT, comparing them with 12 healthy control subjects (Busatto et al. 1997). The purpose of the study was to look at benzodiazepine receptor ($\gamma$-aminobutyric acid type A [GABA$_A$]) abnormalities in patients with schizophrenia. Although the researchers found no overall difference between patients and control subjects, they discovered an inverse relationship between receptor binding and positive symptom scores in the left medial temporal lobe, and an inverse relationship between negative symptoms and binding in the medial prefrontal cortex. These findings are consistent with corticolimbic involvement in schizophrenia pathophysiology and indicate that there may be abnormalities in the GABA system in patients with schizophrenia.

## Studies Performed Using Cognitive Tasks

By imaging participants during the performance of tasks, cerebral activity patterns reflect a state with less variability due to random, task-independent thought processes. Schizophrenic individuals invariably show dysfunction within frontal-parietal-temporal networks, regardless of the task used.

**Visual system.**    One preliminary fMRI study reported that schizophrenic patients have increased signal intensity changes in the primary visual cortex in response to light when compared with healthy control subjects (Renshaw et al. 1994). However, visual tasks are often used as controls in PET or SPECT studies of executive function; schizophrenic patients do not differ from healthy volunteers in primary visual cortical activity (Andreasen et al. 1992; Berman et al. 1988; Nakashima et al. 1994) An advantage of the visual system is that its pathways and functions are very well characterized in humans and in nonhuman primates.

The primary visual cortex has connections with visual association areas, which then connect to the prefrontal, executive function cortices that contribute to attention and eye tracking. In a study of eye tracking, relatives of schizophrenic individuals were categorized into two groups: those who had eye-tracking deficits and those who did not. These subjects, along with healthy control subjects, underwent ($^{15}$O)water PET scans while performing a task involving smooth pursuit and fixation. The relatives with eye-tracking deficits had significantly less activation of the frontal eye fields than either control subjects or relatives with no deficits in tracking (O'Driscoll et al. 1999). This adds further support for a genetic, heritable basis of schizophrenia.

**Motor.** One preliminary $^{133}$Xe SPECT study compared schizophrenic patients with predominantly positive or negative symptoms to healthy control subjects during a hand-movement task. Patients with positive symptoms had diffuse increases in activity in contrast to the expected circumscribed increases in contralateral sensorimotor cortex seen in healthy volunteers; patients with negative symptoms show decreased activation (Guenther et al. 1991). Likewise, a small fMRI study found reduced sensorimotor cortex activation in schizophrenic patients during finger movements (Wenz et al. 1994). However, it is unclear how these results are related to schizophrenia, as similar results were reported by the same investigators in patients with depression (both bipolar and unipolar) (Guenther et al. 1986). A recent review of fMRI studies of the human motor system, including examination during psychiatric illnesses, provides further details on this topic (Mattay and Weinberger 1999).

**Attention.** Schizophrenic patients have difficulty with sustained attention, and they have been studied with FDG PET during an auditory continuous discrimination test. Healthy volunteers increase metabolism in the prefrontal cortex and lower metabolism in the cingulate and superior parietal cortices, areas implicated in the network responsible for attention. Compared with the volunteers, schizophrenic patients had reduced prefrontal metabolism and increased metabolism in the cingulate and parietal cortices (R.M. Cohen et al. 1988a), as if patients were unable to appropriately modulate the network responsible for sustained attention. In never-medicated patients scanned during a visual continuous-performance task, lower metabolic rates in the lateral and medial prefrontal and cingulate cortices and basal ganglia were found (Buchsbaum et al. 1992). Cohen's group further examined attention in another auditory discrimina-

tion task and found patterns of metabolism that correlated with response to antipsychotic mediation (R.M. Cohen et al. 1998b). This study discovered that patients who responded to neuroleptics had lower prefrontal cortex metabolism on the right than those who did not respond, whereas lower rates of metabolism in the midcingulate cortex and higher basal ganglia predicted a poor response to treatment.

In a group of 79 medication-free schizophrenic patients, FDG PET was done during a continuous-performance test. The PET results were then compared with clinical symptoms. Patients with reality distortion and patients with negative symptoms had decreased activity in the anterior cingulum/mesial frontal area. Negative symptoms were associated with hyperfrontality (Schroder et al. 1995).

In another PET study done using ($^{15}$O)water, performance on a single-trial Stroop task was used to measure attention in 14 patients compared with 15 healthy subjects. The researchers found that patients with schizophrenia (chronic, stable, medicated) made more errors and had less activation in the right anterior cingulate gyrus during color naming in the color-incongruent part of the task (Carter et al. 1997). This was consistent with their hypothesis of deficits of attention in schizophrenic patients, as well as the many other studies that find pathophysiology in this subsystem.

**Memory.** Unmedicated schizophrenic patients were compared with matched healthy volunteers during $^{133}$Xe SPECT while performing verbal and facial recognition tasks. Although the control subjects showed areas of specific regional activation during both tasks, patients with schizophrenia showed diffuse increases in the task. During the facial task, control subjects showed activation in the frontal pole and in the precentral, postcentral, and anterior temporal regions; during the verbal task, control subjects had increased blood flow in the dorsolateral prefrontal, premotor, precentral, and postcentral regions (Gur et al. 1994). Patients did not activate as much as control subjects and showed activation in different brain regions, namely the left frontal pole and the anterior temporal and occipital temporal regions.

A recent study of memory retrieval examined three sets of subjects: control subjects, schizophrenic individuals with the deficit syndrome, and schizophrenic individuals without the deficit syndrome (Heckers et al. 1999). They found that patients with primary negative symptoms recruited hippocampal regions equally as well as patients without deficit symptoms. The difference was found in bilateral regions of the prefrontal cortex, where there was significantly less activity in schizophrenic patients with deficit syndrome, consistent with many of the previous studies that found decreased prefrontal cortex activity with this disorder. It is interesting to note here that, despite the difference in prefrontal rCBF, performance in the recall task was not different between the deficit and nondeficit subtypes of schizophrenia.

**Language.** During a PET cerebral blood flow study, healthy control subjects and schizophrenic patients were imaged during verbal tasks. In one task, words beginning with a certain letter (e.g., *A*, apple) were generated by the participant every 5 seconds; in another, given words were simply repeated. From work with healthy control subjects during word generation, activation was expected in the dorsolateral prefrontal cortex, cingulate cortex, and superior temporal cortex. Schizophrenic patients showed activation in the same areas as the control subjects; however, they may have needed to activate a greater region of the dorsolateral prefrontal cortex to perform the task and did not show the expected decrease in the superior temporal cortex (Frith et al. 1995). This supports the idea that the neural networks linking the frontal and temporal cortices function abnormally in schizophrenia.

**Executive function.** Executive functions include assessment of the environment, planning behavior, and generating novel responses, areas of particular difficulty for schizophrenic individuals. The Wisconsin Card Sorting Test (WCST) is an abstract reasoning test that taps executive functions. In it, a card is matched to one of four possible choices; participants must decide whether to match on color, object shape, or number of objects on the card. They must remember which responses are correct and periodically alter which aspect of the card is the right response. Healthy volunteers performing the WCST during [133]Xe SPECT activated a neural network including the frontal, parietal, and temporal cortices (Weinberger et al. 1992). Chronic schizophrenic patients, whether medication free or taking medications, did not increase blood flow to the prefrontal cortex (Weinberger et al. 1988). This was also true when newly diagnosed patients with schizophrenia or schizophreniform disorder were compared with healthy volunteers using [99mTc]HMPAO SPECT. To underscore the advantage of imaging during a task, no perfusion differences were seen at rest (Rubin et al. 1991). Conversely, in an fMRI working memory task (Sternberg Item Recognition Paradigm), schizophrenic patients showed greater activation in the left dorsolateral prefrontal cortex than did a group of healthy control subjects, despite worse performance on the task per se (Manoach et al. 1999). Further examination by the same group revealed striatal activation only in the patients,

indicating possible frontostriatal dysfunction (Manoach et al. 2000).

Likewise, monozygotic twins discordant for schizophrenia were compared during rest and during performance of number matching and the WCST using [133]Xe SPECT. During rest and number matching, there were no blood flow differences between the ill and well twin. During the WCST, however, every twin with schizophrenia had reduced blood flow to the dorsolateral prefrontal cortex. This suggests that dysfunction in the prefrontal cortex is ubiquitous in schizophrenia (Berman et al. 1992). The failure of prefrontal cortical activation was not found in a small group of patients with affective disorder (Berman et al. 1993).

The Tower of London is also a task requiring prefrontal cortical activation (Andreasen et al. 1992). The participant must devise a plan to move colored balls from one stick to a predetermined pattern on three different sticks. For the control task, participants watched moving, colored shapes. Using [133]Xe SPECT, never-medicated patients with first-episode schizophrenia and medication-free patients with chronic schizophrenia were compared with healthy control subjects. Volunteers and patients both globally increased blood flow during performance of the Tower of London. However, regional differences were evident; patients did not show normal increases in the left mesial frontal or right parietal areas. This is true in patients with recent-onset and chronic disease, again suggesting that abnormalities in frontally linked networks are a primary problem in schizophrenia. Interestingly, patients with fewer negative symptoms were better able to increase perfusion to the mesial frontal region than were patients with more negative symptoms (Andreasen et al. 1992).

Importantly, it does not appear to be an abstract task per se that results in abnormal blood flow patterns. Rather, it appears to be dependent on which neural network is involved in the task. A different abstract reasoning task, the Ravens Progressive Matrices (RPM), requires participants to complete missing parts of abstract designs. Using [133]Xe SPECT, healthy volunteers show increased blood flow primarily to posterior cortical areas, including parietal and parieto-occipital cortices. The same pattern is seen in medication-free chronic schizophrenic patients (Berman et al. 1988).

Additional work in schizophrenic individuals performing a working memory task evaluated changes in brain activity related to switching from classic to atypical antipsychotic medication (Honey et al. 2000). This fMRI study found increased prefrontal and parietal cortical activation in patients taking risperidone on a verbal working memory task compared with a group of patients taking classic antipsychotics, consistent with less mesocortical $D_2$ blockade with this drug.

## MRS in Schizophrenia

MRS provides information about the chemical composition of brain areas with functional abnormalities in schizophrenia. $^{31}P$ MRS has been used to investigate membrane components and high-energy phosphate compounds in the left dorsolateral prefrontal cortex of drug naïve patients with first-episode schizophrenia, patients with chronic schizophrenia, and healthy control subjects. All patients with schizophrenia, whether acute, drug-naïve, or chronic, showed decreased levels of phosphomonoesters, building blocks for cell membranes. First-episode, drug-naïve schizophrenic patients had increased levels of phosphodiesters, membrane breakdown products (Pettegrew et al. 1991), which were not found in newly diagnosed medicated or long-term medicated patients (Stanley et al. 1995). It appears that membrane breakdown products are increased early in the course of schizophrenia, whereas membrane precursors are reduced throughout the illness (Pettegrew et al. 1993; Stanley et al. 1995). This leads to speculation that schizophrenia involves an exaggeration of normal dendritic remodeling and pruning (Maier 1995). However, other groups have reported increased phosphodiesters even in chronic patients and have not replicated the reduction in phosphomonoesters (Deicken et al. 1994).

Using $^{1}H$ MRS, abnormalities were found in the ratio of NAA, a marker of neuronal integrity to either creatine or choline in chronic schizophrenic patients. Regions of interest were drawn in multiple brain regions, but only in the mesial temporal lobe and dorsolateral prefrontal cortices did patients show reduced NAA (Bertolino et al. 1995). This has been replicated in both temporal lobes in patients with schizophrenia and in a mixed group of bipolar and schizophrenic patients (Renshaw et al. 1995; Yurgelun-Todd et al. 1993). This fits well with PET and SPECT results finding abnormalities in the neural networks linking the frontal, parietal, and temporal lobes. However, as with many of these techniques, there are inconsistencies. One study investigated the left frontal and temporal lobes of a mixed group of patients with first-episode and chronic schizophrenia; differences in NAA were found only in the left frontal lobes of male patients (Buckley et al. 1994). A recent study involving a cognitive-activation task in schizophrenic patients discovered a strong correlation between dorsolateral prefrontal NAA and activation of the cortical network involved in working memory (Figure 9–9) (Bertolino et al. 2000). Further work with this technique in the dorsolateral pre-

frontal cortex has found that patients with the deficit syndrome of schizophrenia have lower NAA in this region than do other patients or control subjects (Delamillieure et al. 2000). Another study looking only at the thalamus found significantly decreased NAA bilaterally in patients with schizophrenia (Deicken et al. 2000). In summary, these MRS studies of schizophrenia are consistent with brain areas implicated in schizophrenia, both from postmortem and other in vivo imaging studies.

## White Matter Integrity: Diffusion Tensor Imaging

New technological advances in MRI make it possible to study white matter tracks with MRI. By studying the diffusion anisotropy in water around white matter, these tracts can be traced. There have been several studies in schizophrenic individuals indicating that white matter regions of the brain are pathological. A study looked at this property of white matter in a group of five patients with schizophrenia and also in six control subjects (Figure 9–10) (Buchsbaum et al. 1998). The researchers studied the prefrontal cortex and striatum using PET, and found that the patients had less correlation between metabolic rates in the two regions than the control subjects, indicating less connectivity. Indeed, the white matter tracks connecting the two regions also had significantly lower diffusion anisotropy, agreeing with the PET findings, supplying twofold evidence for decreased connectivity between the striatum and prefrontal cortex. Another study used magnetization transfer imaging as an indicator of myelin and axonal integrity (Foong et al. 2000). In this study, white matter abnormalities were found in the temporal lobes of patients with schizophrenia. In contrast to these two studies, an evaluation of white matter integrity using diffusion tensor imaging found widespread differences in a group of schizophrenic patients (Lim et al. 1999).

## Conclusions

The various functional neuroimaging modalities make possible the study of the activity of the living human brain. With these techniques, we are able to determine the neural networks underlying the psychiatric illnesses that afflict our patients and families. The future holds great promises for this field and provides an open door to investigate the neurobiological bases for these disorders, disease and symptom heterogeneity, and treatment responsiveness. Many of these studies are going on now, and the mysteries of the mind and brain's function may someday be understood with much more clarity.

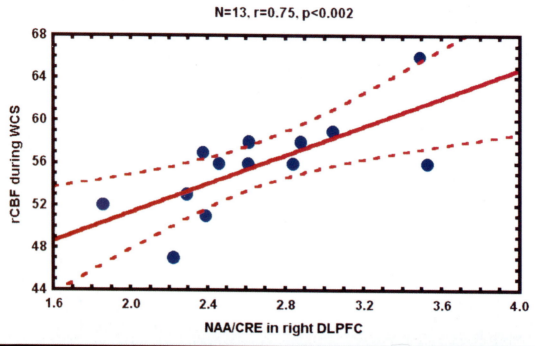

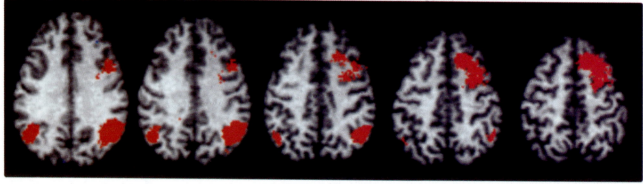

**FIGURE 9–9.** Correlations between metabolite ratios for the dorsolateral prefrontal cortex of 13 schizophrenic patients and blood flow activation during performance of the Wisconsin Card Sorting Test (WCST). The bottom part of the figure shows the brain locations of maximal positive correlations between blood flow activation during the WCST and the ratio of *N*-acetyl aspartate to creatine (NAA/CRE). The top portion shows the correlations between NAA/CRE and regional cerebral blood flow (rCBF) in the dorsolateral prefrontal cortex.

*Source.* Reprinted with permission from Bertolino A, Esposito G, Callicott JH, et al.: "Specific Relationship Between Prefrontal Neuronal *N*-Acetylaspartate and Activation of the Working Memory Cortical Network in Schizophrenia." *American Journal of Psychiatry* 157:26–33, 2000.

# References

Abi-Dargham A, Gandelman MS, DeErausquin GA, et al: SPECT imaging of dopamine transporters in human brain with iodine-123-fluoroalkyl analogs of beta-CIT. J Nucl Med 37:1129–1133, 1996

Ahlfors SP, Simpson GV, Dale AM, et al: Spatiotemporal activity of a cortical network for processing visual motion revealed by MEG and fMRI. J Neurophysiol 82:2545–2555, 1999

Alexander GE, DeLong MR, Strick PL: Parallel organization of functionally segregated circuits linking basal ganglia and cortex. Annu Rev Neurosci 9:357–381, 1986

Andreasen NC, Rezai K, Alliger R, et al: Hypofrontality in neuroleptic-naive patients and in patients with chronic schizophrenia. Arch Gen Psychiatry 49:943–958, 1992

Andreasen NC, O'Leary DX, Cizadlo T, et al: Remembering the past: two facets of episodic memory explored with positron emission tomography. Am J Psychiatry 152:1576–1585, 1995a

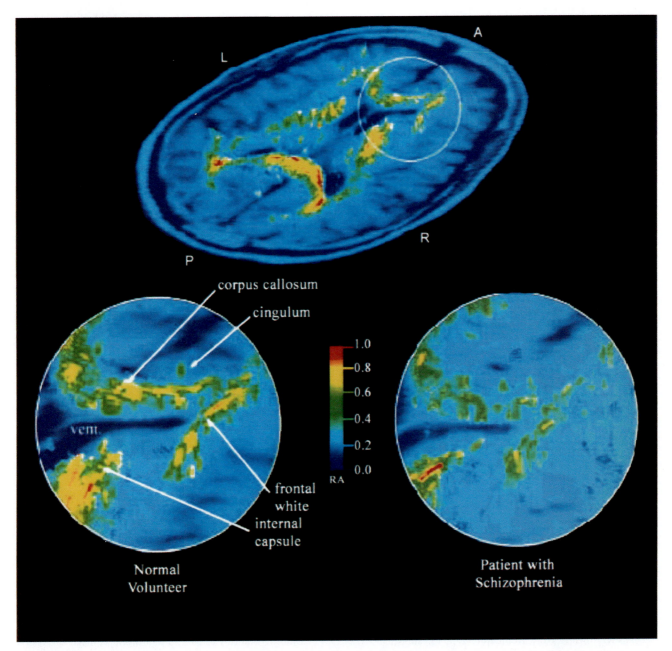

**FIGURE 9–10.** Diffusion white matter anisotropy in schizophrenia. Two diffusion tensor images of individual subjects were interpolated and represented as a three-dimensional volume. The eigenvectors were represented as small three-dimensional tubes (axon masses) colored using the relative anisotropy measure (color scale). The top image shows a perspective view of the tubes rendered and superimposed on the corresponding structural magnetic resonance image. L=left; A=anterior; R=right; P=posterior. Bottom left and right images show close-ups, in a healthy volunteer and a schizophrenic patient, respectively, of the right frontal region where statistically significant anisotropy differences were found.

*Source.* Reprinted with permission from Buchsbaum MS, Tang CY, Peled S, et al.: "MRI White Matter Diffusion Anisotropy and PET Metabolic Rate in Schizophrenia." *Neuroreport* 9:425–430, 1998.

Andreasen NC, Arndt S, Alliger R, et al: Symptoms of schizophrenia. Methods, meanings and mechanisms. Arch Gen Psychiatry 52:341–351, 1995b

Andreasen NC, Nopoulos P, O'Leary DS, et al: Defining the phenotype of schizophrenia: cognitive dysmetria and its neural mechanisms. Biol Psychiatry 46:908–920, 1999

Asahina M., Suhara T, Shinotoh H, et al: Brain muscarinic receptors in progressive supranuclear palsy and Parkinson's disease: a positron emission tomographic study. J Neurol Neurosurg Psychiatry 65:155–163, 1998

Attar-Levy D, Martinot JL, Blin J, et al: The cortical serotonin2 receptors studied with positron-emission tomography and

[18F]-setoperone during depressive illness and antidepressant treatment with clomipramine. Biol Psychiatry 45(2):180–186, 1999

Bartlett EJ, Brodie JD, Simkowitz P, et al: Effect of a haloperidol challenge on regional brain metabolism in neuroleptic-responsive and nonresponsive schizophrenic patients. Am J Psychiatry 155:337–343, 1998

Baxter LR Jr, Phelps ME, Mazziotta JC, et al: Local cerebral glucose metabolism rates in obsessive-compulsive disorder. Arch Gen Psychiatry 44:211–218, 1987

Baxter LR Jr, Schwartz JM, Mazziotta JC, et al: Cerebral glucose metabolic rates in nondepressed patients with obsessive-compulsive disorder. Am J Psychiatry 145:1560–1563, 1988

Baxter LR Jr, Schwartz JM, Bergman KS, et al: Caudate glucose metabolic rate changes with both drug and behavior therapy for obsessive-compulsive disorder. Arch Gen Psychiatry 49:681–689, 1992

Beauregard M, Leroux JM, Bergman S, et al: The functional neuroanatomy of major depression: an fMRI study using an emotional activation paradigm. Neuroreport 9:3253–3258, 1998

Belger A, Puce A, Krystal JH, et al: Dissociation of mnemonic and perceptual processes during spatial and nonspatial working memory using fMRI. Hum Brain Mapp, 6(1):14–32, 1998

Bench CJ, Friston KJ, Brown RG, et al: Regional cerebral blood flow in depression measured by positron emission tomography: the relationship with clinical dimensions. Psychol Med 23:579–590, 1993

Benkelfat C, Thomas TE, Semple WE, et al: Local cerebral glucose metabolic rates in obsessive-compulsive disorder. Arch Gen Psychiatry 47:840–848, 1990

Berman KF, Weinberger DR: Functional localization in the brain schizophrenia, in American Psychiatric Press Review of Psychiatry, Vol 10. Edited by Tasman A, Goldfinger SM. Washington, DC, American Psychiatric Press, 1991, pp 24–59

Berman KF, Illowsky BP, Weinberger DR: Physiological dysfunction of dorsolateral prefrontal cortex in schizophrenia, IV: further evidence for regional and behavioral specificity. Arch Gen Psychiatry 45:616–622, 1988

Berman KF, Torrey EF, Daniel DG, et al: Regional cerebral blood flow in monozygotic twins discordant and concordant for schizophrenia. Arch Gen Psychiatry 49:927–934, 1992

Berman KF, Doran AR, Pickar D, et al: Is the mechanism of prefrontal hypofunction in depression the same as in schizophrenia? Regional cerebral blood flow during cognitive activation. Br J Psychiatry 162:183–192, 1993

Berman KF, Weinberger DR: Functional brain imaging studies in schizophrenia, in Neurobiology of Mental Illness. Edited by Charney DS, Nestler EJ, Bunney BS. New York, Oxford University Press, 1999, pp 2246–2257

Bertolino A, Nawroz S, Mattay VS, et al: Multislice proton magnetic resonance spectroscopic imaging in schizophrenia: regional reduction of a marker of neuronal density (abstract). Society of Neuroscience 21:260, 1995

Bertolino A, Esposito G, Callicott JH, et al: Specific relationship between prefrontal neuronal N-acetylaspartate and activation of the working memory cortical network in schizophrenia. Am J Psychiatry 157:26–33, 2000

Binder JR, Frost JA, Hammeke TS, et al: Conceptual processing during the conscious resting state: a functional MRI study. J Cogn Neurosci 11(1):80–93, 1999

Bisaga A, Katz JL, Antonini A, et al: Cerebral glucose metabolism in women with panic disorder. Am J Psychiatry 155:1178–1183, 1998

Biver F, Goldman S, Delvenne V, et al: Frontal and parietal metabolic disturbances in unipolar depression. Biol Psychiatry 36:381–388, 1994

Blackwood DH, Glabus MF, Dunan J, et al: Altered cerebral perfusion measured by SPECT in relatives of patients with schizophrenia. Correlations with memory and P300. Br J Psychiatry 175:357–366, 1999

Blin J, Sette G, Fiorelli M, et al: A method for the in vivo investigation of the serotonergic 5-HT2 receptors in the human cerebral cortex using positron emission tomography and 18F-labeled setoperone. J Neurochem 54:1744–1754, 1990

Blumberg HP, Stern E, Ricketts S, et al: Rostral and orbital prefrontal cortex dysfunction in the manic state of bipolar disorder. Am J Psychiatry 156:1986–1988, 1999

Blumberg HP, Stern E, Martinez D, et al: Increased anterior cingulate and caudate activity in bipolar mania. Biol Psychiatry 48(11):1045–1052, 2000

Breiter HC, Rauch SL, Kwong KK, et al: Functional magnetic resonance imaging of symptom provocation in obsessive-compulsive disorder. Arch Gen Psychiatry 53:595–606, 1996

Brucke T, Kornhuber J, Angelberger P, et al: SPECT imaging of dopamine and serotonin transporters with [123I]beta-CIT. Binding kinetics in the human brain. Journal of Neural Transmission, General Section 94:137–146, 1993

Buchsbaum MS, Wu J, DeLisi LE, et al: Positron emission tomography studies of basal ganglia and somatosensory cortex neuroleptic drug effects: differences between normal controls and schizophrenic patients. Biol Psychiatry 22:479–494, 1987

Buchsbaum MS, Haier RJ, Potkin SG, et al: Frontostriatal disorder of cerebral metabolism in never-medicated schizophrenics. Arch Gen Psychiatry 49:935–942, 1992

Buchsbaum MS, Tang CY, Peled S, et al: MRI white matter diffusion anisotropy and PET metabolic rate in schizophrenia. Neuroreport 9:425–430, 1998

Buckley PF, Moore C, Long H, et al: [1]H-Magnetic resonance spectroscopy of the left temporal and frontal lobes in schizophrenia: clinical, neurodevelopmental, and cognitive correlates. Biol Psychiatry 36:792–800, 1994

Buckner RL, Petersen SE, Ojemann JG, et al: Functional anatomical studies of explicit and implicit memory retrieval tasks. J Neurosci 15:12–29, 1995

Burton H, Abend NS, MacLeod AM, et al: Tactile attention tasks enhance activation in somatosensory regions of parietal cortex: a positron emission tomography study. Cerebral Cortex 9:662–674, 1999

Busatto GF, Pilowsky LS, Costa DC, et al: Initial evaluation of 123I-5-I-R91150, a selective 5-HT2A ligand for single-photon emission tomography, in healthy human subjects. Eur J Nucl Med 24:119–124, 1997

Bush G, Frazier JA, Rauch SL, et al: Anterior cingulate cortex dysfunction in attention-deficit/hyperactivity disorder revealed by fMRI and the Counting Stroop. Biol Psych 45:1542–1552, 1999

Carter CS, Mintun M, Nichols T, et al: Anterior cingulate gyrus dysfunction and selective attention deficits in schizophrenia: [$^{15}$O]H$_2$O PET study during single-trial Stroop task performance. Am J Psychiatry 154:1670–1675, 1997

Chabrol H, Guell A, Bes A, et al: Cerebral blood flow in schizophrenic adolescents (letter). Am J Psychiatry 143: 130, 1986

Chua P, Krams M, Toni I, et al: A functional anatomy of anticipatory anxiety. Neuroimage 9:563–571, 1999

Chugani DC, Muzik O, Rothermel R, et al: Altered serotonin synthesis in the dentatothalamocortical pathway in autistic boys. Ann Neurol 42:666–669, 1997

Chugani DC, Sundram BS, Behen M, et al: Evidence of altered energy metabolism in autistic children. Prog Neuropsychopharmacol Biol Psychiatry 23:635–641, 1999

Cleghorn JM, Garnett ES, Nahmias C, et al: Increased frontal and reduced parietal glucose metabolism in acute untreated schizophrenia. Psychiatry Res 28:119–133, 1989

Cleghorn JM, Franco S, Szechtman B, et al: Toward a brain map of auditory hallucinations. Am J Psychiatry 149:1062–1069, 1992

Cohen JD, Forman SD, Casey BJ, et al: Spiral-scan imaging of dorsolateral prefrontal cortex during a working memory task (abstract). Society for Magnetic Resonance in Medicine Twelfth Annual Meeting 3:1405, 1993

Cohen RM, Semple WE, Gross M, et al: From syndrome to illness: delineating the pathophysiology of schizophrenia with PET. Schizophr Bull 14:169–176, 1988a

Cohen RM, Semple WE, Gross M, et al: Functional localization of sustained attention: comparison to sensory stimulation in the absence of instruction. Neuropsychiatry Neuropsychol Behav Neurol 1:3–20, 1988b

Cohen RM, Andreason PJ, Doudet DJ, et al: Opiate receptor avidity and cerebral blood flow in Alzheimer's disease. J Neurol Sci 148:171–180, 1997

Corbetta M, Miezin FM, Dobmeyer S, et al: Selective and divided attention during visual discriminations of shape, color, and speed: functional anatomy by positron emission tomography. J Neurosci 11:2383–2402, 1991

Critchley HD, Daly EM, Bullmore ET, et al: The functional neuroanatomy of social behavior. Changes in cerebral blood flow when people with autistic disorder process facial expressions. Brain 123:2203–2212, 2000

Crosson B, Radonovich K, Saek JR, et al: Left-hemisphere processing of emotional connotation during word generation. Neuroreport 10:2449–2455, 1999

Crouzel C, Guillaume M, Barre L, et al: Ligands and tracers for PET studies of the 5-HT system—current status. International Journal of Radiation Applications and Instrumentation. Part B, Nuclear Medicine and Biology 19: 857–870, 1992

Cumming P, Yokoi F, Chen A, et al: Pharmacokinetics of radiotracers in human plasma during positron emission tomography. Synapse 34:124–134, 1999

Dager SR, Strauss WL, Marro KI, et al: Proton magnetic resonance spectroscopy investigation of hyperventilation in subjects with panic disorder and comparison subjects. Am J Psychiatry 152:666–672, 1995

Deicken RF, Calabrese G, Merrin EL, et al: $^{31}$Phosphorus magnetic resonance spectroscopy of the frontal and parietal lobes in chronic schizophrenia. Biol Psychiatry 36:503–510, 1994

Deicken RF, Johnson C, Eliaz Y, et al: Reduced concentrations of thalamic N-acetylaspartate in male patients with schizophrenia. Am J Psychiatry 157:644–647, 2000

Delamillieure P, Fernandez J, Constans JM, et al: Proton magnetic resonance spectroscopy of the medial prefrontal cortex in patients with deficit schizophrenia: preliminary report. Am J Psychiatry 157:641–643, 2000

Detre JA, Alsop DC: Perfusion magnetic resonance imaging with continuous arterial spin labeling: methods and clinical applications in the central nervous system. Eur J Radiol 30:115–124, 1999

De Volder A, Bol A, Michel C, et al: Brain glucose metabolism in children with the autistic syndrome: positron tomography analysis. Brain Dev 9:581–587, 1987

Dolan RJ, Bench CJ, Brown RG, et al: Regional cerebral blood flow abnormalities in depressed patients with cognitive impairment. J Neurol Neurosurg Psychiatry 55:768–773, 1992

Dolan RJ, Bench CJ, Liddle PF, et al: Dorsolateral prefrontal cortex dysfunction in the major psychoses: symptom or disease specificity? J Neurol Neurosurg Psychiatry 56: 1290–1294, 1993

Dougherty DD, Bonab AA, Spencer TJ, et al: Dopamine transporter density in patients with attention deficit hyperactivity disorder. Lancet 354:2132–2133, 1999

Drevets WC: Functional neuroimaging studies of depression: the anatomy of melancholia. Annu Rev Med 49:341–361, 1998

Drevets WC: Prefrontal cortical-amygdalar metabolism in major depression. Ann N Y Acad Sci 877:614–637, 1999

Drevets WC, Videen TO, Price JL, et al: A functional anatomical study of unipolar depression. J Neurosci 12:3628–3641, 1992

Drevets WC, Burton H, Videen TO, et al: Blood flow changes in human somatosensory cortex during anticipated stimulation. Nature 373:249–252, 1995

Drevets WC, Price JL, Simpson JR, et al: Subgenual prefrontal cortex abnormalities in mood disorders. Nature 386:824–827, 1997

Drevets WC, Frank E, Price JC, et al: PET imaging of serotonin 1A receptor binding in depression. Biol Psychiatry 46(10):1375–1387, 1999

Early TS, Reiman EM, Raichle ME, et al: Left globus pallidus abnormalities in never-medicated patients with schizophrenia. Proc Natl Acad Sci U S A 84:561–563, 1987

Ebmeier KP, Blackwood DHR, Murray C, et al: Single-photon emission computed tomography with $^{99m}$Tc-exametazime in unmedicated schizophrenic patients. Biol Psychiatry 33:487–495, 1993

Elliott R, Sahakian BJ, Michael A, et al: Abnormal neural response to feedback on planning and guessing tasks in patients with unipolar depression. Psychol Med 28:559–571, 1998

Elliott R, Rubinsztein JS, Sahakian BJ, et al: Selective attention to emotional stimuli in a verbal go/no-go task: an fMRI study. Neuroreport 11:1739–1744, 2000

Ernst M, Zametkin AJ, Matochik JA, Pascualvaca D et al: High midbrain [18F]DOPA accumulation in children with attention deficit hyperactivity disorder. Am J Psychiatry 156:1209–1215, 1999

Farde L, Wiesel F, Hall H, et al: No $D_2$ receptor increase in PET study of schizophrenia. Arch Gen Psychiatry 44:671–672, 1987

Farde L, Wiesel F-A, Stone-Elander S, et al: $D_2$ dopamine receptors in neuroleptic-naive schizophrenic patients. Arch Gen Psychiatry 47:213–219, 1990

Farde L, Suhara T, Halldin C, et al: PET study of the M1-agonists [11C]xanomeline and [11C]butylthio-TZTP in monkey and man. Dementia 7:187–195, 1996

Farde L, Suhara T, Nyberg S, et al: A PET-study of [11C]FLB 457 binding to extrastriatal D2-dopamine receptors in healthy subjects and antipsychotic drug-treated patients. Psychopharmacology 133:396–404, 1997

Fletcher PC, Frith CD, Grasby PM, et al: Brain systems for encoding and retrieval of auditory-verbal memory: an in vivo study in humans. Brain 118:401–416, 1995

Foong J, Maier M, Barker GJ, et al: In vivo investigation of white matter pathology in schizophrenia with magnetisation transfer imaging. J Neurol Neurosurg Psychiatry 68:70–74, 2000

Fox PT, Raichle ME, Mintun MA, et al: Nonoxidative glucose consumption during focal physiologic neural activity. Science 241:462–464, 1988

Friston KJ, Frith CD, Passingham RE, et al: Motor practice and neurophysiological adaptation in the cerebellum: a positron tomography study. Proc R Soc Lond B Biol Sci 248:223–228, 1992

Friston KJ, Holmes A, Poline J-B, et al: Detecting activations in PET and fMRI: levels of inference and power. Neuroimage 4:223–235, 1995

Friston KJ: The disconnection hypothesis. Schizophr Res 30:115–125, 1998

Frith CD, Friston KJ, Liddle PF, et al: A PET study of word finding. Neuropsychologia 29:1137–1148, 1991

Frith CD, Friston KJ, Herold S, et al: Regional brain activity in chronic schizophrenic patients during the performance of a verbal fluency task. Br J Psychiatry 167:343–349, 1995

Frost JJ, Wagner HN, Dannals RF, et al: Imaging opiate receptors in the human brain by positron tomography. J Comp Assist Tomogr 9:231–236, 1985

Gao JH, Parsons LM, Bower JM, et al: Cerebellum implicated in sensory acquisition rather than motor control. Science 272:545–547, 1996

George MS, Costa DC, Kouris K, et al: Cerebral blood flow abnormalities in adults with infantile autism. J Nerv Ment Dis 180:413–417, 1992

George MS, Ketter TA, Parekh P, et al: Spatial ability in affective illness: differences in regional brain activation during a spatial matching task ($H_2^{15}O$ PET). Neuropsychiatry Neuropsychol Behav Neurol 7:143–153, 1994a

George MS, Ketter TA, Post RM: Activation studies in mood disorders. Psychiatric Annals 24:648–652, 1994b

George MS, Ketter TA, Kimbrell TA, et al: What functional imaging has revealed about the brain basis of mood and emotion, in Advances in Biological Psychiatry, Vol 2. Edited by Panksepp J. Greenwich, CT, JAI Press, 1996, pp 63–113

Goddard AW, Charney DS: Toward an integrated neurobiology of panic disorder. J Clin Psychiatry 58 (suppl 2):4–11, 1997

Goldman-Rakic PS, Funahashi S, Bruce CJ: Neocortical memory circuits. Cold Spring Harb Symp Quant Biol 55:1025–1038, 1990

Goodwin GM, Cavanagh JTO, Glabus MF, et al: Uptake of 99mTc-exametazime shown by single photon emission computed tomography before and after lithium withdrawal in bipolar patients: associations with mania. Br J Psychiatry 170:426–430, 1997

Grafton ST, Mazziotta JC, Presty S, et al: Functional anatomy of human procedural learning determined with regional cerebral blood flow and PET. J Neurosci 12:2542–2548, 1992

Guenther W, Moser E, Mueller-Spahn F, et al: Pathological cerebral blood flow during motor function in schizophrenic and endogenous depressed patients. Biol Psychiatry 21:889–899, 1986

Guenther W, Petsch R, Steinberg R, et al: Brain dysfunction during motor activation and corpus callosum alterations in schizophrenia measured by cerebral blood flow and magnetic resonance imaging. Biol Psychiatry 29:535–555, 1991

Gur RE, Jaggi JL, Shtasel DL, et al: Cerebral blood flow in schizophrenia: effects of memory processing on regional activation. Biol Psychiatry 35:3–15, 1994

Gur RE, Mozley D, Resmick SM, et al: Resting cerebral glucose metabolism in first-episode and previously treated patients with schizophrenia relates to clinical features. Arch Gen Psychiatry 52:657–667, 1995

Halldin C, Foged C, Chou YH, et al: Carbon-11-NNC 112: a radioligand for PET examination of striatal and neocortical D1-dopamine receptors. J Nucl Med 39:2061–2068, 1998

Hashimoto T, Sasaki M, Fukumizu M, et al: Single-photon emission computed tomography of the brain in autism: effect of the developmental level. Pediatr Neurol 23:416–420, 2000

Haxby JV, Grady CL, Horwitz B, et al: Dissociation of object and spatial visual processing pathways in human extrastriate cortex. Proc Natl Acad Sci U S A 88:1621–1625, 1991

Haxby JV, Horwitz B, Ungerleider LG, et al: The functional organization of human extrastriate cortex: a PET-rCBF study of selective attention to faces and locations. J Neurosci 14:6336–6353, 1994

Haznedar MM, Buchsbaum MS, Metzger M, et al: Anterior cingulated gyrus volume and glucose metabolism in autistic disorder. Am J Psychiatry 154:1047–1050, 1997

Heckers S, Goff D, Schacter DL, et al: Functional imaging of memory retrieval in deficit vs nondeficit schizophrenia. Arch Gen Psychiatry 56:1117–1123, 1999

Henry JP, Scherman D: Radioligands of the vesicular monoamine transporter and their use as markers of monoamine storage vesicles. Biochem Pharmacol 38:2395–2404, 1989

Herold S, Frackowiak RSJ, LeCouteur A, et al: Cerebral blood flow and metabolism of oxygen and glucose in young autistic adults. Psychol Med 18:823–831, 1988

Hoehn-Saric R, Pearlson GD, Harris GJ, et al: Effects of fluoxetine on regional cerebral blood flow in obsessive-compulsive patients. Am J Psychiatry 148:1243–1245, 1991

Honey GD, Bullmore ET, Soni W, et al: Differences in frontal cortical activation by a working memory task after substitution of risperidone for typical antipsychotic drugs in patients with schizophrenia. Proc Natl Acad Sci U S A 96:13432–13437, 2000

Horwitz B, Rumsey JM, Grady CL, et al: The cerebral metabolic landscape in autism: intercorrelations of regional glucose utilization. Arch Neurol 45:749–755, 1988

Houle S, Wilson AA, Inaba T, et al: Imaging 5-HT1A receptors with positron emission tomography: initial human studies with [11C]CPC-222. Nucl Med Commun 18:1130–1134, 1997

Ichise M, Ballinger JR, Golan H, et al: Noninvasive quantification of dopamine D2 receptors with iodine-123-IBF SPECT. J Nucl Med 37:513–520, 1996

Ingvar DH, Franzen G: Abnormalities of cerebral blood flow distribution in patients with chronic schizophrenia. Acta Psychiatr Scand 50:425–462, 1974

Insel TR: Toward a neuroanatomy of obsessive-compulsive disorder. Arch Gen Psychiatry 49:739–744, 1992

Jones AK, Luthra SK, Maziere B, et al: Regional cerebral opioid receptor studies with [11]C diprenorphine in normal volunteers. J Neurosci Methods 23:121–129, 1988

Jonides J, Smith EE, Koeppe RA, et al: Spatial working memory in humans as revealed by PET. Nature 363:623–625, 1993

Kaplan RD, Szechtman H, Franco S, et al: Three clinical syndromes of schizophrenia in untreated subjects: relation to brain glucose activity measured by positron emission tomography (PET). Schizophr Res 11:47–54, 1993

Kapur S, Zipursky R, Jones C, et al: A positron emission tomography study of quetiapine in schizophrenia. Arch Gen Psychiatry 57:553–559, 2000a

Kapur S, Zipursky R, Jones C, et al: Relationship between dopamine D2 occupancy, clinical response, and side effects: a double-blind PET study of first-episode schizophrenia. Am J Psychiatry 157:514–520, 2000b

Karni A, Meyer G, Rey-Hipolito C, et al: The acquisition of skilled motor performance: fast and slow experience-driven changes in primary motor cortex. Proc Natl Acad Sci U S A 95(3):861–868, 1998

Kim S-G, Ashe J, Hendrich K, et al: Functional magnetic resonance imaging of motor cortex: hemispheric asymmetry and handedness. Science 261:615–617, 1993

Kornhuber J, Brucke T, Angelberger P, et al: SPECT imaging of dopamine receptors with [123I]epidepride: characterization of uptake in the human brain. Journal of Neural Transmission, General Section 101(1–3):95–103, 1995

Kuhl DE, Koeppe RA, Minoshima S, et al: In vivo mapping of cerebral acetylcholinesterase activity in aging and Alzheimer's disease. Neurology 52:691–699, 1999

Kung HF, Kim HJ, Kung MP, et al: Imaging of dopamine transporters in humans with technetium-99m TRODAT-1. Eur J Nucl Med 23:1527–1530, 1996

Kwong KK, Belliveau JW, Chesler DA, et al: Dynamic magnetic resonance imaging of human brain activity during primary sensory stimulation. Proc Natl Acad Sci U S A 89:5675–5679, 1992

Langer O, Halldin C, Dolle F, et al: Carbon-11 epidepride: a suitable radioligand for PET investigation of striatal and extrastriatal dopamine D2 receptors. Nucl Med Biol 26:509–518, 1999

Lesser IM, Mena I, Boone KB, et al: Reduction of cerebral blood flow in older depressed patients. Arch Gen Psychiatry 51:677–686, 1994

Liddle PF, Friston KJ, Frith CD, et al: Patterns of cerebral blood flow in schizophrenia. Br J Psychiatry 160:179–186, 1992

Lim KO, Hedehus M, Moseley M, et al: Compromised white matter tract integrity in schizophrenia inferred from diffusion tensor imaging. Arch Gen Psychiatry 56:367–374, 1999

Loeber RT, Sherwood AR, Renshaw PF, et al: Differences in cerebellar blood volume in schizophrenia and bipolar disorder. Schizphr Res 37:81–89, 1999

Madar I, Lever JR, Kinter CM, et al: Imaging of delta opioid receptors in human brain by N1'-([11C]methyl)naltrindole and PET. Synapse 24:19–28, 1996

Maier M: In vivo magnetic resonance spectroscopy: applications in psychiatry. Br J Psychiatry 167:299–306, 1995

Maillard L, Ishii K, Bushara K, et al: Mapping the basal ganglia: fMRI evidence for somatotopic representation of face, hand, and foot. Neurology 55:377–383, 2000

Malison RT, Price LH, Berman R, et al: Reduced brain serotonin transporter availability in major depression as measured by [123I]-2 beta-carbomethoxy-3 beta-(4-iodophenyl)tropane and single photon emission computed tomography. Biol Psychiatry 44(11):1090–1098, 1998

Manoach DS, Press DZ, Thangaraj V, et al: Schizophrenic subjects activate dorsolateral prefrontal cortex during a working memory task, as measured by fMRI. Biol Psychiatry 45:1128–1137, 1999

Manoach DS, Gollub RL, Benson ES, et al: Schizophrenic subjects show aberrant fMRI activation of dorsolateral prefrontal cortex and basal ganglia during working memory performance. Biol Psychiatry 48:99–109, 2000

Mattay VS, Weinberger DR, Barrios FA, et al: Brain mapping with functional MR imaging: comparison of gradient-echo–based exogenous and endogenous contrast techniques. Radiology 194(3):687–691, 1995

Mattay VS, Weinberger DR: Organization of the human motor system as studied by functional magnetic resonance imaging. Eur J Radiol 30:105–114, 1999

Mayberg HS, Lewis PJ, Regenold W, et al: Paralimbic hypoperfusion in unipolar depression. J Nucl Med 35:929–934, 1994

Mayberg HS, Brannan SK, Mahurin RK, et al: Cingulate function in depression: a potential predictor of treatment response. Neuroreport 8:1057–1061, 1997

Mayberg HS, Liotti M, Brannan SK, et al: Reciprocal limbic-cortical function and negative mood: converging PET findings in depression and normal sadness. Am J Psychiatry 156(5):675–682, 1999

Mazziotta JC, Grafton ST, Woods RC: The human motor system studied with PET measurements of cerebral blood flow: topography and motor learning, in Brain Work and Mental Activity, Alfred Benzon Symposium 31. Edited by Lassen NA, Ingvar DH, Raichle ME, et al. Copenhagen, Munksgaard, 1991, pp 280–290

McCarthy G, Blamire AM, Puce A, et al: Functional magnetic resonance imaging of human prefrontal cortex activation during a spatial working memory task. Proc Natl Acad Sci U S A 91:8690–8694, 1994

McCarthy G, Puce A, Constable RT, et al: Activation of human prefrontal cortex during spatial and nonspatial working memory tasks measured by functional MRI. Cereb Cortex 6:600–611, 1996

McClure RJ, Kanfer JN, Panchalingam K, et al: Magnetic resonance spectroscopy and its application to aging and Alzheimer's disease. Neuroimaging Clin N Am 5:69–86, 1995

Messa C, Fazio F, Costa DC, et al: Clinical brain radionuclide imaging studies. Semin Nucl Med 25:111–143, 1995

Mesulam M-M: Large-scale neurocognitive networks and distributed processing for attention, language, and memory. Ann Neurol 28:597–613, 1990

Minshew NJ, Goldstein G, Dombrowski SM, et al: A preliminary 31P MRS study of autism: evidence for undersynthesis and increased degradation of brain membranes. Biol Psychiatry 33:762–773, 1993

Molchan SE, Sunderland T, McIntosh AR, et al: A functional anatomic study of associative learning in humans. Proc Natl Acad Sci U S A 91:8122–8126, 1994

Moonen CTW, van Zijl PCM, Frank JA, et al: Functional magnetic resonance imaging in medicine and physiology. Science 250:53–61, 1990

Moriarty J, Campos Costa D, Schmitz B, et al: Brain perfusion abnormalities in Gilles de la Tourette's syndrome. Br J Psychiatry 167:249–254, 1995

Mountz JM, Tolbert LC, Lill DW, et al: Functional deficits in autistic disorder: characterization by technetium-99m-HMAO and SPECT. J Nucl Med 36:1156–1162, 1995

Muller L, Halldin C, Farde L, et al: [11C] beta-CIT, a cocaine analogue. Preparation, autoradiography and preliminary PET investigations. Nucl Med Biol 20(3):249–255, 1993

Muller RA, Chugani DC, Behen ME, et al: Impairment of dentate-thalamo-cortical pathway in autistic men: language activation data from positron emission tomography. Neurosci Lett 245:1–4, 1998

Muller RA, Behen ME, Rothermel RD, et al: Brain mapping of language and auditory perception in high-functioning autistic adults: a PET study. J Autism Dev Disord 29:19–31, 1999

Muzik O, Chugani DC, Chakraborty P, et al: Analysis of [C-11]alpha-methyl-tryptophan kinetics for the estimation of serotonin synthesis rate in vivo. J Cereb Blood Flow Metab 17:659–669, 1997

Nadeau SE, Crosson B: A guide to the functional imaging of cognitive processes. Neuropsychiatry Neuropsychol Behav Neurol 8:143–162, 1995

Nakashima Y, Momose T, Sano I, et al: Cortical control of saccade in normal and schizophrenic subjects: a PET study using a task-evoked rCBF paradigm. Schizophr Res 12:259–264, 1994

Narayana PA, Jackson EF: Image-guided in vivo proton magnetic resonance spectroscopy in human brain. Current Science 61:340–351, 1991

Nofzinger EA, Nichols TE, Meltzer CC, et al: Changes in forebrain function from waking to REM sleep in depression: preliminary analyses of [18F]FDG PET studies. Psychiatry Res 91:59–78, 1999

Nofzinger EA, Price JC, Meltzer CC, et al: Towards a neurobiology of dysfunctional arousal in depression: the relationship between beta EEG power and regional cerebral glucose metabolism during NREM sleep. Psychiatry Res 98:71–91, 2000

Nordahl TE, Stein MB, Belkelfat C, et al: Regional cerebral metabolic asymmetries replicated in an independent group of patients with panic disorder. Biol Psychiatry 44:998–1006, 1998

Nordstrom A-L, Farde L, Eriksson L, et al: No elevated $D_2$ dopamine receptors in neuroleptic-naive schizophrenic patients revealed by positron emission tomography and [$^{11}$C]N-methylspiperone. Psychiatry Res 61:67–83, 1995a

Nordstrom A-L, Farde L, Nyberg S, et al: $D_1$, $D_2$, and 5-HT$_2$ receptor occupancy in relation to clozapine serum concentration: a PET study of schizophrenic patients. Am J Psychiatry 152:1444–1449, 1995b

O'Driscoll GA, Benkelfat C, Florencio PS, et al: Neural correlates of eye tracking deficits in first-degree relatives of schizophrenic patients: a positron emission tomography study. Arch Gen Psych, 56(12):1127-1134, 1999

Ohnishi T, Matsuda H, Hashimoto T, et al: Abnormal regional cerebral blood flow in childhood autism. Brain 123:1838–1844, 2000

Owens J, Wyper DJ, Patterson J, et al: First SPET images of glutamate (NMDA) receptor activation in vivo in cerebral ischaemia. Nucl Med Commun 18:149–158, 1997

Paradis AL, Cornilleau-Peres V, Droulez J, et al: Visual perception of motion and 3D structure from motion: an fMRI study. Cerebral Cortex 10:772–783, 2000

Pardo JV, Fox PT, Raichle ME: Localization of a human system for sustained attention by positron emission tomography. Nature 349:61–64, 1991

Pardo JV, Pardo PJ, Raichle ME: Neural correlates of self-induced dysphoria. Am J Psychiatry 150:713–719, 1993

Passingham RE, Chen YC, Thaler D: Supplementary motor cortex and self-initiated movement, in Neural Programming. Edited by Ito M. Basel, Switzerland, Karger, 1989, pp 13–24

Patterson JC, Early TS, Martin A, et al: Computerized SPECT image analysis using statistical parametric mapping: comparison of $^{99m}$Tc-radiolabeled exametazime and bicisate tracers. J Nucl Med 38:1721–1725, 1997

Paulesu E, Frith CD, Frackowiak RSJ: The neural correlates of the verbal component of working memory. Nature 362:342–344, 1993

Paulman RG, Devous MD, Gregory RR, et al: Hypofrontality and cognitive impairment in schizophrenia: dynamic single-photon tomography and neuropsychological assessment of schizophrenic brain function. Biol Psychiatry 27:377–399, 1990

Petersen SE, Fiez JA: The processing of single words studied with positron emission tomography. Annu Rev Neurosci 16:509–530, 1993

Petersen SE, Fox PT, Posner MI, et al: Positron emission tomographic studies of the cortical anatomy of single-word processing. Nature 331:585–589, 1988

Petersen SE, Corbetta M, Miezin FM, et al: PET studies of parietal involvement in spatial attention: comparison of different task types. Can J Exp Psychol 48:319–338, 1994

Petrides M, Alivisatos B, Evans AC, et al: Dissociation of human mid-dorsolateral from posterior dorsolateral frontal cortex in memory processing. Proc Natl Acad Sci U S A 90:873–877, 1993a

Petrides M, Alivisatos B, Meyer E, et al: Functional activation of the human frontal cortex during the performance of verbal working memory tasks. Proc Natl Acad Sci U S A 90:878–882, 1993b

Pettegrew JW, Keshavan MS, Panchalingam K, et al: Alterations in brain high-energy phosphate and membrane phospholipid metabolism in first-episode, drug-naive schizophrenics. Arch Gen Psychiatry 48:563–568, 1991

Pettegrew JW, Keshavan MS, Minshew NJ: 31P nuclear magnetic resonance spectroscopy: neurodevelopment and schizophrenia. Schizophr Bull 19:35–53, 1993

Pike VW, McCarron JA, Lammertsma AA, et al: Exquisite delineation of 5-HT1A receptors in human brain with PET and [carbonyl-11 C]WAY-100635. Eur J Pharmacol 301:R5–R7, 1996

Puce A, Allison T, Gore JC, et al: Face-sensitive regions in human extrastriate cortex studied by functional MRI. J Neurophysiol 74:1192–1199, 1995

Raedler TJ, Knable MB, Lafargue T, et al: In vivo determination of striatal dopamine D2 receptor occupancy in patients treated with olanzapine. Psychiatry Res 90:81–90, 1999

Raichle ME: Memory mechanisms in the processing of words and word-like symbols, in Exploring Brain Functional Anatomy With Positron Tomography (Ciba Foundation Symposium). Edited by Chadwick D, Whelan J. Chichester, UK, Wiley, 1991, pp 198–217

Raichle ME: The scratchpad of the mind. Nature 363:583–584, 1993

Raichle ME, Fiez JA, Videen TO, et al: Practice-related changes in human brain functional anatomy during nonmotor learning. Cereb Cortex 4:8–26, 1994

Rao SM, Binder JR, Bandettini PA, et al: Functional magnetic resonance imaging of complex human movements. Neurology 43:2311–2318, 1993

Rauch SL, Savage CR, Alpert NM, et al: The functional neuroanatomy of anxiety: a study of three disorders using positron emission tomography and symptom provocation. Biol Psychiatry 42:446–452, 1997

Reba RC: PET and SPECT: opportunities and challenges for psychiatry. J Clin Psychiatry 54 (11 suppl):26–32, 1993

Renshaw PF, Yurgelun-Todd DA, Cohen BM: Greater hemodynamic response to photic stimulation in schizophrenic patients: an echo planar MRI study. Am J Psychiatry 151:1493–1495, 1994

Renshaw PF, Yurgelun-Todd DA, Tohen M, et al: Temporal lobe proton magnetic resonance spectroscopy of patients with first-episode psychosis. Am J Psychiatry 152:444–446, 1995

Ring HA, Baron-Cohen S, Wheelwright S, et al: Cerebral correlates of preserved cognitive skills in autism: a functional

MRI study of embedded figures task performance. Brain 122:1305–1315, 1999

Rinne JO, Hublin C, Partinen M, et al: Striatal dopamine D1 receptors in narcolepsy: a PET study with [11C]NNC 756. J Sleep Res 5:262–264, 1996

Rubia K, Overmeyer S, Taylor E, et al: Hypofrontality in attention deficit hyperactivity disorder during higher-order motor control: a study with functional MRI. Am J Psychiatry 156:891–896, 1999

Rubin P, Holm S, Friberg L, et al: Altered modulation of prefrontal and subcortical brain activity in newly diagnosed schizophrenia and schizophreniform disorder. Arch Gen Psychiatry 48:987–995, 1991

Rumsey JM, Duara R, Grady C, et al: Brain metabolism in autism. Resting cerebral glucose utilization rates as measured with positron emission tomography. Arch Gen Psychiatry 42:448–455, 1985

Ryding E, Tuninger E, Ohlsson T, et al: Dopamine D2-receptor density in humans as assessed with SPET and the new high-affinity ligand 123I-NCQ298: a pilot study. Nucl Med Commun 19:263–270, 1998

Ryu YH, Lee JD, Yoon PH, et al: Perfusion impairments in infantile autism on technetium-99m ethyl cysteinate dimer brain single-photon emission tomography: comparison with findings on magnetic resonance imaging. Eur J Nucl Med 26:253–259, 1999

Saha GB, MacIntyre WJ, Go RT: Radiopharmaceuticals for brain imaging. Semin Nucl Med 24:324–349, 1994

Sargent PA, Kjaer KH, Bench CJ, et al: Brain serotonin1A receptor binding measured by positron emission tomography with [11C]WAY-100635: effects of depression and antidepressant treatment. Arch Gen Psychiatry 57:174–180, 2000

Schroder J, Buchsbaum MS, Siegel BV, et al: Structural and functional correlates of subsyndromes in chronic schizophrenia. Psychopathology 28:38–45, 1995

Schwartz WJ, Smith CB, Davidsen L, et al: Metabolic mapping of functional activity in the hypothalamo-neurohypophysial system of the rat. Science 205:723–725, 1979

Schweitzer JB, Faber TL, Grafton ST, et al: Alterations in the functional anatomy of working memory in adult attention deficit hyperactivity disorder. Am J Psychiatry 157:278–280, 2000

Seeman MV, Seeman P: Psychosis and positron tomography. Can J Psychiatry 33:299–306, 1988

Seitz RJ, Roland PE, Bohm C, et al: Motor learning in man: a positron emission tomographic study. Neuroreport 1:57–66, 1990

Selemon LD, Goldman-Rakic PS: The reduced neuropil hypothesis: a circuit based model of schizophrenia. Biol Psychiatry 45:17–25, 1999

Shioiri T, Tadafumi K, Murashita J, et al: High-energy phosphate metabolism in the frontal lobes of patients with panic disorder detected by phase-encoded 31P-MRS. Biol Psychiatry 40:785–793, 1996

Silbersweig DA, Stern E, Frith S, et al: A functional neuroanatomy of hallucinations in schizophrenia. Nature 378:176–179, 1995

Soares JC, Mann JJ: The functional neuroanatomy of mood disorders. J Psychiatr Res 31:393–432, 1997

Soares JC, Innis RB: Neurochemical brain imaging investigations of schizophrenia. Biol Psychiatry 46:600–615, 1999

Squire LR, Zola-Morgan S: The medial temporal lobe memory system. Science 253:1380–1385, 1991

Squire LR, Ojemann JG, Miezin FM, et al: Activation of the hippocampus in normal humans: a functional anatomical study of memory. Proc Natl Acad Sci U S A 89:1837–1841, 1992

Stanley JA, Williamson PC, Drost DJ, et al: An in vivo study of the prefrontal cortex of schizophrenic patients at different stages of illness via phosphorus magnetic resonance spectroscopy. Arch Gen Psychiatry 52:399–406, 1995

Sukhwinder SS, Brammer MJ, Williams SCR, et al: Mapping auditory hallucinations in schizophrenia using functional magnetic resonance imaging. Arch Gen Psychiatry 57:1033–1038, 2000

Swedo SE, Schapiro MB, Grady CL, et al: Cerebral glucose metabolism in childhood-onset obsessive-compulsive disorder. Arch Gen Psychiatry 46:518–523, 1989

Swedo SE, Pietrini P, Leonard HL, et al: Cerebral glucose metabolism in childhood-onset obsessive-compulsive disorder. Revisualization during pharmacotherapy. Arch Gen Psychiatry 49:690–694, 1992

Szabo Z, Kao PF, Mathews WB, et al: Positron emission tomography of 5-HT reuptake sites in the human brain with C-11 McN5652 extraction of characteristic images by artificial neural network analysis. Behav Brain Res 73:221–224, 1996

Szechtman H, Nahmias C, Garnett ES, et al: Effect of neuroleptics on altered cerebral glucose metabolism in schizophrenia. Arch Gen Psychiatry 45:523–532, 1988

Talairach J, Tournoux P: Co-planar Stereotaxic Atlas of the Human Brain. Stuttgart, Thieme, 1988

Tamminga CA, Thaker GK, Buchanan R, et al: Limbic system abnormalities identified in schizophrenia using positron emission tomography with fluorodeoxyglucose and neocortical alterations with deficit syndrome. Arch Gen Psychiatry 49:522–530, 1992

Tanji H, Nagasawa H, Araki T, et al: PET study of striatal fluorodopa uptake and dopamine D2 receptor binding in a patient with juvenile parkinsonism. Eur J Neurol 5:243–248, 1998

Tootell RBH, Reppas JB, Kwong KK, et al: Functional analysis of human MT and related visual cortical areas using magnetic resonance imaging. J Neurosci 15:3215–3230, 1995

Vita A, Bressi S, Perani D, et al: High-resolution SPECT study of regional cerebral blood flow in drug-free and drug-naive schizophrenic patients. Am J Psychiatry 152:876–882, 1995

Waddington JL, O'Callaghan E, Larkin C, et al: Magnetic resonance imaging and spectroscopy in schizophrenia. Br J Psychiatry 157:56–65, 1990

Watson JDG, Myers R, Frackowiak RSJ, et al: Area V5 of the human brain: evidence from a combined study using positron emission tomography and magnetic resonance imaging. Cereb Cortex 3:79–94, 1993

Weinberger DR: Implications of normal brain development for the pathogenesis of schizophrenia. Arch Gen Psychiatry 44:660–669, 1987

Weinberger DR, Berman KF, Illowsky BP: Physiological dysfunction of dorsolateral prefrontal cortex in schizophrenia, III: a new cohort and evidence for a monoaminergic mechanism. Arch Gen Psychiatry 45:609–615, 1988

Weinberger DR, Berman KF, Suddath R, et al: Evidence of dysfunction of a prefrontal-limbic network in schizophrenia: a magnetic resonance imaging and regional cerebral blood flow study of discordant monozygotic twins. Am J Psychiatry 149:890–897, 1992

Wenz F, Schad LR, Knopp MV, et al: Functional magnetic resonance imaging at 1.5 T: activation pattern in schizophrenic patients receiving neuroleptic medication. Magn Reson Imaging 12:975–982, 1994

Wolf SS, Jones DW, Knable MB, et al: Tourette syndrome: prediction of phenotypic variation in monozygotic twins by caudate nucleus D2 receptor binding. Science 273(5279):1225–1227, 1996

Wolkin A, Sanfilipo M, Wolf AP, et al: Negative symptoms and hypofrontality in chronic schizophrenia. Arch Gen Psychiatry 49:959–965, 1992

Wong DF, Wagner HN Jr, Tune LE, et al: Positron emission tomography reveals elevated $D_2$-dopamine receptors in drug-naive schizophrenics. Science 234:1558–1563, 1986

Wong EC, Buxton RB, Frank LR: Implementation of quantitative perfusion imaging techniques for functional brain mapping using pulsed arterial spin labeling. NMR Biomed 10:237–249, 1997

Yurgelun-Todd DA, Renshaw PF, Waternaux CM, et al: $^1$H spectroscopy of the temporal lobes in schizophrenic and bipolar patients. Society of Magnetic Resonance in Medicine 12th Annual Meeting Abstracts 3:1539, 1993

Zametkin AJ, Nordahl TE, Gross M, et al: Cerebral glucose metabolism in adults with hyperactivity of childhood onset. N Engl J Med 323:1361–1366, 1990

Zametkin AJ, Liebenauer LL, Fitzgerald GA, et al: Brain metabolism in teenagers with attention-deficit hyperactivity disorder. Arch Gen Psychiatry 50:333–340, 1993

Zilbovicius M, Garreau B, Tzourio N, et al: Regional cerebral blood flow in childhood autism: a SPECT study. Am J Psychiatry 149:924–930, 1992

Zilbovicius M, Garreau B, Samson Y, et al: Delayed maturation of the frontal cortex in childhood autism. Am J Psychiatry 152:248–252, 1995

# Epidemiologic and Genetic Aspects of Neuropsychiatric Disorders

Dolores Malaspina, M.D., M.S.P.H.

Cheryl Corcoran, M.D.

Steven P. Hamilton, M.D., Ph.D.

The last decade has witnessed a revolution in our understanding of the etiology of many neuropsychiatric disorders. Advances in statistical genetics, genetic epidemiology, and molecular methodology have provided new insights and avenues for conducting genetic and epidemiologic studies and for analyzing gene-environment interactions. The recent mapping of the human genome now sets the stage for even greater progress in the coming years. In this chapter, we focus on some of the findings of these disciplines in the study of neuropsychiatric disorders.

## Epidemiologic Studies

Epidemiology is based on the fundamental assumption that factors causal to human disease can be identified through the systematic examination of different populations, or of subgroups within a population, in different places or at different times (Hennekens and Buring 1987). Epidemiologic research may be viewed as directed at a series of questions:

- What is the frequency of a disorder?
- Are there subgroups in which the disorder is more frequent?
- What specific risk factors are associated with the disorder?
- Are these risk factors consistently and specifically related to the disorder?
- Does exposure to these factors precede the development of disease?

A variety of epidemiologic strategies have been developed to address these questions.

### Measures of Disease Frequency

Measures of disease frequency serve as the basis for formulating and testing etiologic hypotheses because they permit a comparison of frequencies between different populations or among individuals within a population with particular exposures or characteristics. The two measures of disease frequency used most often are *prevalence* and *incidence*. The former refers to the number of

The authors would like to thank Charles A. Kaufman, M.D., Scott Yale, M.S.W., David Leitman, B.S., Eileen Alexander, B.S., and Marc Benor for their assistance in the preparation of this chapter.

existing cases of a disease at a given point in time as a proportion of the total population. The latter refers to the number of new cases of a disease during a given period as a proportion of the total population at risk. The two measures are interrelated: the prevalence of a disease depends on both its incidence and its duration. One can compare two populations with and without a factor suspected of contributing to the development of disease through the calculation of the ratio of disease frequency in the two populations; this is known as the *relative risk*.

Disease incidence can be defined in several ways. *Risk* refers to the probability that an individual will develop a disease over a specified time and thus can vary from zero to unity. A common difficulty in long-term studies is that subjects become lost to follow-up. The alternative measure of incidence, called the *rate*, is used to address this problem. The rate is the instantaneous measure of individuals newly developing the disease in relation to the subject number that remain at risk (i.e., new cases per person-years of follow-up).

## Descriptive Studies

Correlational studies of populations, and descriptive studies of single individuals or groups of individuals, also contribute to formulating etiologic hypotheses by showing a statistical association between exposure to specific risk factors and occurrence of the disease. Descriptive studies are conducted when little is known about the occurrence or antecedents of a disease. Hypotheses regarding risk factors then may emerge from studying several characteristics of affected individuals (e.g., sex, age, birth cohort), their place of residence, or the timing of their exposure. Descriptive studies, however, cannot be used to test etiologic hypotheses: they lack adequate comparison groups, making it difficult to determine the specificity of exposure to the disease, and they are cross-sectional, making it difficult to determine the temporal relation between an exposure and the development of disease.

## Analytic Studies

An analytic study commences when enough is known about a disease that specific a priori hypotheses can be examined. Such etiologic hypotheses may be tested through various analytic strategies. In a prospective cohort study, information is obtained about exposure status at the time the study begins. New cases of illness are then identified from among those who did and those who did not have the exposure. This contrasts with retrospective cohort studies, in which prior exposure status is

established on the basis of available information and disease incidence is determined from then until the end of the study. Case-control studies begin with the designation of disease status and then compare past exposure to a risk factor in those individuals who have a disease (case subjects) with that of the appropriate control subjects. Procedures for matching control subjects to case subjects involve attempting to control for confounding variables and other biases.

## Genetic Studies

Genetic research is concerned with identifying inherited factors that contribute to the development of disease. It, too, may be conceptualized as directed at a series of questions:

- Is the disorder familial?
- Is it inherited?
- What is being inherited in the disorder; that is, what constitutes predisposition to the disorder, and what are the earliest manifestations of such predisposition?
- What additional ("epigenetic") variables increase or decrease the chances of genetically predisposed individuals developing the disorder?
- How is the disorder inherited?
- Where and what are the abnormal genes conferring genetic risk?
- What are the molecular and, ultimately, the pathologic consequences of these abnormal genes?

A variety of genetic strategies have been developed to address these questions (Table 10–1)

**TABLE 10–1.** Genetics of neuropsychiatric disorders: questions and strategies

| Question | Strategy |
| --- | --- |
| Is the disorder familial? | Family studies |
| Is it inherited? | Twin studies |
| | Adoption studies |
| What is being inherited in the disorder? | High-risk studies |
| What "epigenetic" factors influence development of the disorder? | High-risk studies |
| How is the disorder inherited? | Segregation analysis |
| | Pedigree analysis |
| Where is (are) the abnormal gene(s)? | Linkage analysis |
| What is (are) the abnormal gene(s)? | Molecular approaches |
| What is (are) its (their) molecular and pathologic effect(s)? | Molecular approaches |

**TABLE 10–2.**   Relative risk for neuropsychiatric disorders

| Disease | Population prevalence per 100,000 | Morbid risk in first-degree relatives (%) | Relative risk |
|---|---|---|---|
| Gertsmann-Sträussler syndrome | 0.01 | 50 | 5,000,000 |
| Acute intermittent porphyria | 2 | 50 | 25,000 |
| Metachromatic leukodystrophy | 2.5 | 25–50 | 20,000 |
| Myotonic dystrophy | 5.5 | 50 | 9,090 |
| Narcolepsy | 10–100 | 30–50 | 5,000 |
| Huntington's disease | 19 | 50 | 2,630 |
| Lesch-Nyhan syndrome | 10 | 25 | 2,500 |
| Wilson's disease | 10 | 25 | 2,500 |
| Pick's disease | 24 | 17 | 708 |
| Gilles de la Tourette's syndrome | 28.7 | 3.6 | 125 |
| Parkinson's disease | 133 | 8.3 | 62.4 |
| Bipolar disorder | 500 | 8 | 16 |
| Schizophrenia | 900 | 12.8 | 14.2 |
| Dyslexia | 5,000–10,000 | 45 | 9.0 |
| Epilepsy | 1,700 | 4.1 | 2.4 |
| Alzheimer's disease | 7,700 | 14.4 | 1.90 |

## Family, Twin, and Adoption Studies

Family studies are a type of relative-risk study in which patterns of disease distributions within families are examined and the variability of the disease within families is compared with the variability between families. These studies may show an elevated risk for an illness in first-degree relatives of an affected individual in comparison with that in the general population (Table 10–2), but they cannot distinguish whether this elevated risk is due primarily to shared genetic or environmental factors.

Twin studies can further be used to resolve the genetic contribution to a disorder. Although they are exposed to the same familial environment, monozygotic (MZ) and dizygotic (DZ) twin pairs differ in their genetic endowment (sharing 100% and 50% of their genes, respectively). Thus, when genetic factors are important in etiology, the MZ and DZ co-twins of probands differ in their risk for the disorder. As a result, the comparison of relative concordance rates for MZ and DZ twins is an index of the disorder's heritability, or the proportion of variability that can be attributed to genetic, as opposed to environmental and stochastic, factors. It is still conceivable that environmental as well as genetic differences may influence the relative risk of diseases in MZ and DZ twins.

Adoption studies offer still another strategy for disentangling genetic and environmental influences, and they are particularly useful for the study of psychiatric disorders, in which cultural influences might otherwise allow for vertical transmission of behaviors. There are several types of adoption studies. In the adoptee study method, offspring separated at birth from their affected mothers are compared with the adopted-away offspring of control mothers. This can be considered a special form of cohort study. Cross-fostering studies examine adoptees whose biologic parents are without illness and contrast the rates of illness in those reared by affected and unaffected adoptive parents. In the adoptee's family method, the biologic relatives of affected adoptees are matched with the biologic relatives of control adoptees, and their rates of illness are compared. Such studies are examples of the case-control paradigm.

## High-Risk Studies

The high-risk approach represents another form of cohort study. Individuals who are at genetic risk for a disorder (e.g., those with affected parents) are followed up prospectively, from early in life through the period of maximum risk for the disorder. This strategy permits the identification of features that are of primary pathogenic significance to the disorder, in contrast to those that are secondary to the illness or to its treatment. Moreover, by contrasting characteristics of at-risk individuals who go on to develop the disorder with characteristics of those who do not, this strategy allows for the identification of additional genetic and environmental influences that contribute to disease expression.

## Birth-Cohort Studies

Another important type of epidemologic study is the birth-cohort study, in which all individuals born in a certain location at a certain time are followed up. Correlations between hypothetical causes and disease expression then can be explored.

## Identifying Mode of Inheritance

Even when family, twin, and adoption studies suggest a role for genetic factors, they say nothing of which, or even how many, genes are involved. Single-gene mutations are inherited in a mendelian dominant, recessive, or sex-linked manner. They can produce thousands of *monogenic* disorders, many of which affect mental functioning, but any particular monogenic disorder is rare, and common diseases are likely to be *polygenic*—representing the combined small effects of many genes. Even with genetic liability, environmental influences may be necessary for an illness to be expressed.

Segregation analysis tests explicit models about the inheritance of disease genes on existing family data by comparing the distribution of illness observed in family members with that predicted by a given genetic hypothesis. The detection of mendelian ratios in a sibship can provide support for single-locus inheritance of the genes that confer susceptibility to a disease. Segregation analysis also can be conducted in other pedigree structures, including complex genealogies, to test models of inheritance from single-gene to polygenic inheritance. Segregation analysis (of nuclear family data) allows estimation of model parameters (such as gene frequency and penetrance) by treating each family as a separate observation (Kidd 1981). Its power is limited because it assumes that the same genetic disorder is present in all families. Pedigree analysis, on the other hand, examines more (multigenerational) relationships and is less likely to result in a type II error (a falsely attributed relationship to disease) but is more likely to result in a type I error (an overlooked relationship to disease) because an individual pedigree may manifest an idiosyncratic form of the disorder. Examination of *multiplex* sibships, in which two or more sibs are affected, represents a compromise approach.

## Complex Disorders

Genetic causation can range from a point mutation in single genes to polygenic causes that entail epistasis (interaction) among the several genes involved and/or environmental factors. Many of the neuropsychiatric disorders have a complex pattern of inheritance. Qualities of complex disorders include the following:

1. An unknown mode of inheritance
2. Incomplete penetrance, wherein additional environ-

mental factors may be necessary for the final expression of even genetic forms of the disorder
3. Epistasis, whereby the disorder may result from the interaction of several major genes
4. Variable expressivity, in which a single form of the disorder may have several phenotypic expressions, making it difficult to define who is affected
5. Diagnostic instability, such that a subject's affection status may change over time
6. Etiologic heterogeneity, under which an ordinarily genetic syndrome may have sporadic (environmentally produced) forms—known as *phenocopies*—as well as a variety of genetic forms resulting from disruption in a number of different genes—a condition known as *nonallelic heterogeneity*

The enormous growth in elucidating the genetics of some neuropsychiatric disorders in the last decade is chiefly the result of recent advances in statistical methods and molecular approaches designed to overcome these complexities.

## Linkage Analysis

Linkage analysis, also called positional cloning, is a strategy for isolating a gene of unknown structure or function based on its chromosomal location. It is based on establishing, within pedigrees, the coinheritance of the disorder with identifiable genetic markers of known chromosomal location. Mendel's second law (the law of independent assortment) implies that the disease gene, and hence the disorder, will not be consistently coinherited with a marker allele derived from a different chromosome. Moreover, even if the disease and marker alleles originally lie on the same parental chromosome (are *syntenic*), they may become separated during gametogenesis through the process of recombination or crossing-over, wherein genetic material on homologous chromosomes is exchanged (Figure 10–1). These rearranged chromosomes are ultimately passed on to the offspring.

Disease genes are mapped to the human chromosomes with linkage maps of the human genome. A sequence map of about 90% of the DNA in the human genome was completed in June 2000, several years ahead of schedule, by the Human Genome Project (HGP) and the biotechnology company Celera, with the final map of the human genome expected by the year 2003. These maps were constructed based on DNA polymorphisms, which are the large number of loci in the genome that vary in sequence among individuals, which can be identified by simple laboratory techniques. Types of polymorphisms that are used for genetic studies include restric-

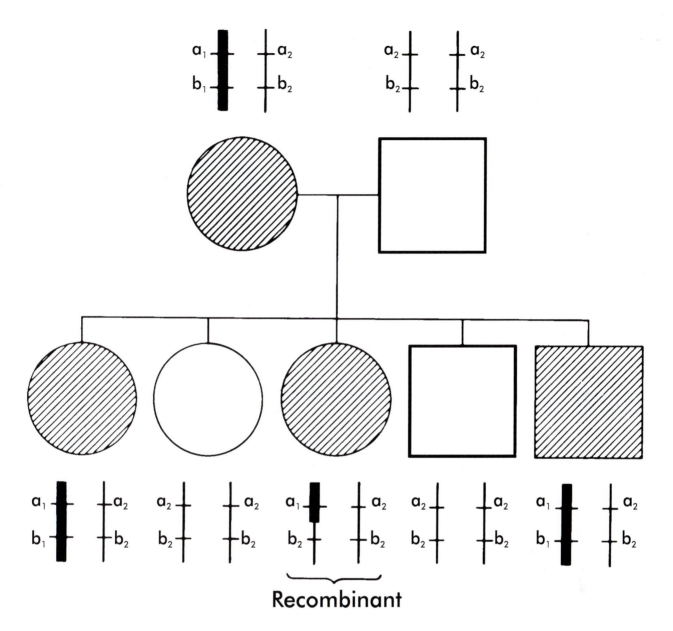

**Recombinant**

**FIGURE 10–1.** Genetic linkage and recombination. Depicted is a hypothetical family (*circles*=females, *squares*=males) segregating an autosomal dominant disease. The disease locus *a* (containing either the defective allele, $a_1$, or its normal counterpart, $a_2$) lies close to a polymorphic marker locus *b* (containing marker alleles $b_1$ and $b_2$). The mother is affected with the disease (*top shaded circle*) and is heterozygous at both the disease and the marker loci. The father is unaffected (*top unshaded square*) and is homozygous at both loci. Because the disease and marker loci are genetically linked (i.e., they lie near one another), crossing over rarely occurs between them. Most children who inherit the disease allele, $a_1$, will also receive the $b_1$ allele from their mother. Occasionally, a recombination event will occur in the mother, and she will transfer a chromosome bearing the $b_2$ marker allele along with the disease allele (as has occurred in the daughter labeled "Recombinant").

*Source.* Reprinted from Rieder RO, Kaufmann CA: "Genetics," in *The American Psychiatric Press Textbook of Psychiatry,* 2nd Edition. Edited by Talbott JA, Hales RE, Yudofsky SC. Washington, DC, American Psychiatric Press, 1994, pp. 35–79. Used with permission.

tion fragment length polymorphisms (RFLPs), which result from a mutation in a restriction enzyme site (Botstein et al. 1980), and variable number tandem repeat sequences (Nakamura et al. 1987). Both forms of these polymorphisms are typically found in noncoded regions

of DNA. Single-nucleotide polymorphisms (SNPs) are also used in genetic studies (D.G. Wang et al. 1998). SNPs are DNA sequence variations that occur when a single nucleotide (A, T, C, or G) in the genome sequence is altered. SNPs can be in noncoding regions or in genes that affect disease susceptibility or drug response.

When the polymorphism and disease gene are close to each other on the chromosome, there is a low chance of their being separated by recombination at meiosis (i.e., they are linked). The probability that a disease and marker allele will recombine depends on their distance from each other. In fact, the frequency with which the two alleles recombine (the recombination rate, or θ [theta]) can be used as a measure of the distance between their respective loci: 1% recombination is synonymous with a genetic distance of 1 centimorgan (cM) and roughly corresponds to a physical distance of $10^6$ base pairs (bp) of DNA.

If disease and marker alleles lie near one another, crossing over will occur only rarely, and parental gametes will be overrepresented. The disease and marker loci are then said to be *linked*. Statistical support for linkage is obtained by examining the cosegregation of disease and marker phenotypes within a pedigree, determining the likelihood (Z) of achieving the observed distribution of phenotypes given estimates for the recombination fraction, θ, ranging from 0.00 to 0.50 (the latter representing no linkage), and calculating the odds ratio [defined as the ratio $Z(\theta)/Z(\theta = 0.50)$], that is, the relative likelihood of there being linkage versus no linkage. This odds ratio depends on the particular genetic parameters chosen in determining the likelihood. These parameters include the mode of inheritance, the frequency of the disease allele, and the probability of the disease given the presence of 0, 1, or 2 disease alleles. To the extent that evidence for linkage depends on such parameters, likelihood-based calculations are referred to as *parametric* linkage analyses. By convention, the odds ratio is expressed as its base 10 logarithm and is known as a *lod score*. In this way, the linkage data from several pedigrees can be pooled and their respective contributions added to obtain a combined probability of linkage. Also by convention, when the lod score at the best estimate of θ (defined as that estimate yielding the highest lod score) is greater than +3, linkage is confirmed; when it is less than −2, linkage is rejected for the data set supported for that set of pedigrees.

The thousands of DNA markers that encompass the genetic map of the entire genome can be used to complete the "whole genome" search for disease genes. When markers are examined that have been systematically drawn from throughout the genome, they may suggest linkage between a disorder and specific chromosomal regions. Conversely, they may reject linkage to these regions, thereby contributing to an *exclusion map* for the disorder. Markers from several regions may be examined concurrently; such a simultaneous search of the genome may detect multiple loci that contribute to a disorder. Of note, because several loci are tested as candidates with whole genome scans, *P* values must be made lower than 0.05 to reject the null hypothesis.

It is worth emphasizing that linkage refers to the two loci and not to their associated alleles. Even if crossing over is rare and certain allele pairs are disproportionately represented within any given pedigree, recombination does occasionally occur and eventually results in a more random distribution of allele combinations within the population at large. Thus, linkage of two loci does not necessarily imply an association of specific disease and marker phenotypes in the general population. An exception occurs when disease and marker loci lie so near to each other that it takes many generations for the allele combinations to equilibrate. For example, if the two loci are separated by 1 cM, it will take 69 generations, or about 2,000 years, until the frequency of an allele combination goes halfway to its equilibrium value (J. Ott 1985).

## Nonparametric Approaches

Genetic linkage studies have been successful in identifying genes that have a large effect on illness risk. But such studies are problematic when several genes of small effect cause a disorder, as is true in most psychiatric conditions. It is also difficult to find enough large families with members who are willing to take part in the study. In addition, when the mode of inheritance is unknown, then many different models and assumptions must be applied to the data, leading to significant statistical problems.

Nonparametric analyses represent alternative methods for evaluating genetic linkage. These studies can be conducted without making assumptions about the mode of inheritance. One commonly used nonparametric approach is the *affected sib pair* strategy (McCarthy et al. 1998). This method compares siblings who are definitely affected or unaffected, so the boundary of the condition does not need to be defined. It examines the frequency with which two siblings, both affected with the disorder of interest, share 0, 1, or 2 alleles coinherited from a common ancestor at the locus of interest; such alleles are said to be *identical by descent*. Under the null hypothesis of no linkage, these frequencies are 1/4, 1/2, and 1/4, respectively. Statistically significant deviations from this distribution of frequencies suggest linkage.

Association studies can examine if a particular DNA polymorphism is associated with a disorder by comparing unrelated affected and unaffected individuals. Association studies can even identify genes of very small effect or those that participate in gene-environment interactions. A candidate gene study is a type of association study. Hypothesis-dependent candidate genes (those nominated by neurobiologic clues to disease pathogenesis) and hypothesis-independent candidate genes (those put forward without regard to pathogenic hypotheses) may be explored. A method that is widely used to test candidate genes is allelic association, also called linkage disequilibrium. It can be used when most of the individuals with the disease are descended from a common ancestor in whom the disease mutation originated. There will be different allele frequencies between individuals with the disease and the general population for markers that are very close to the disease gene. An etiologic role for the candidate gene or nearby regions of the genome can be excluded with as few as one or two recombinants.

## Anticipation, Imprinting, and Mitochondrial Inheritance

A clinical phenomenon called *anticipation*, wherein the age at onset of disease decreases and the severity of disease increases in successive generations, has been recognized for many decades. With the discovery of expanding trinucleotide repeats in the early 1990s (Richards and Sutherland 1992), a convincing molecular mechanism was provided for this phenomenon. The phenomenon is now well described for several neuropsychiatric disorders, including myotonic dystrophy, fragile X syndrome, and Huntington's disease (HD), and there has been some evidence for anticipation in schizophrenia and bipolar disorder. Differences in the offspring's liability for illness due to the sex of the transmitting parent may be the result of genomic imprinting (Langlois 1994) or of mitochondrial inheritance. Genomic imprinting is the selective methylation of inherited chromosomes. Methylation affects the likelihood that genes will be transcribed and that correlating proteins will be made.

## Molecular Approaches

Once linkage analysis has implicated a particular chromosomal region in the etiology of a disorder, a variety of molecular genetic approaches may be used for identifying the disease gene and its pathologic consequences. Thus, markers in linkage disequilibrium with, and thus in close proximity to, the disease gene may be identified. Genetic markers flanking the disease gene also may be recognized, thereby defining the minimal genetic region containing the disease gene. Overlapping cytogenetic anomalies producing the disease may then narrow this minimal genetic region. Alternatively, a more refined location for the

putative disease locus may be provided by multilocus marker *haplotypes* surrounding the locus in genetically isolated populations (through a strategy known as *shared segment mapping*). The sequencing of the gene requires advanced gene sequencing and analytic technology. Specific molecular abnormalities (insertions, deletions, and base substitutions) within the disease gene then may be discovered, and research then focuses on determining how the genetic malfunction causes disease. Genetically modified animals, particularly mice, which breed rapidly, have been used to study human genetics. Introducing the normal or disease gene into appropriate in vitro and in vivo model systems may determine the pathologic consequences of the disease mutation (see Figure 10–2). Although there are no clear animal models for human psychiatric diseases, certain traits that vary continuously (and are likely polygenic) can be studied with quantitative trait loci analysis.

## Joint Effects of Genes and Environmental Exposures on Illness Risk

Multiple genes and environmental exposures influence the risk for many neuropsychiatric disorders. What then is the relation between these causes and, in particular, between the genetic causes on the one hand and the environmental causes on the other? The simplest view is that either genes—albeit multiple genes—or environment can be sufficient to cause the illness and that most cases are either primarily genetic or primarily environmental in origin. This model is implicit in genetic studies that consider environmentally induced cases as phenocopies (also termed *sporadics*, i.e., genetically nonsusceptible but nonetheless affected individuals). Another model is that of multifactorial causation. In its most general form, this view holds that numerous factors confer an increased risk for a disease, but these factors are not related to the disease in a one-to-one fashion. In most cases, the disease results from the interaction of several risk factors.

Multifactorial causation is not, however, a single model of causation. Rather, it encompasses several distinct models, each of which has been found to apply to some diseases. Genes and environmental exposures can combine to produce disease in many ways, and no consensus exists as to the most useful conceptual framework for categorizing these processes. One framework that has emerged from a synthesis of the concepts used in epidemiology and genetics includes three generally accepted models of multifactorial causation and a fourth model,

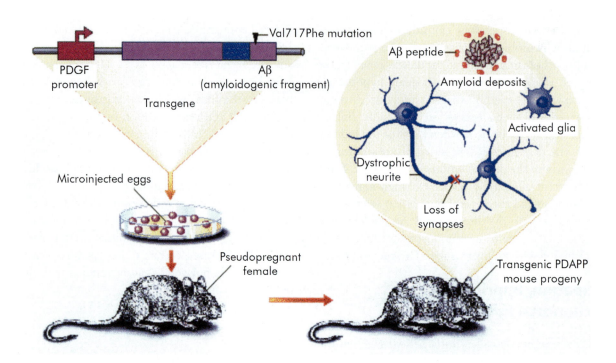

**FIGURE 10–2.** Animal model of Alzheimer's disease. The transgene consists of the human amyloid precursor protein (APP) gene containing a mutation causing a rare form of early-onset familial Alzheimer's disease (Val717Phe). The transgene, with expression that is driven by the platelet-derived growth factor (PDGF) promoter, is microinjected into mouse eggs and implanted in a pseudopregnant female mouse. After the progeny are screened for the presence of the transgene, they are bred and their offspring analyzed for pathologic features characteristic of Alzheimer's disease. The brains of the transgenic PDAPP mice (i.e., those with the PDGF promoter expressing APP) have abundant β-amyloid deposits (made up of the Aβ peptide), dystrophic neurites, activated glia, and overall decrease in synaptic density.

*Source.* Reprinted from Tanzi RE: "A Promising Animal Model of Alzheimer's Disease." *New England Journal of Medicine* 332:1512–1513, 1995. Copyright 1995, Massachusetts Medical Society. Used with permission.

which is commonly adopted but which is controversial (Malaspina et al. 1999). More complex circumstances generally can be subsumed by an elaboration of these models.

The first is an "additive model"; when an individual is exposed to both a genetic and an environmental factor, the effect on risk of schizophrenia is simply the sum of the individual effects. An additive model may apply when the relevant genetic and environmental factors act at the same point in the causal path, that is, they are alternative means to the same end. For instance, if either a genetic defect or a prenatal insult can increase the risk of disrupted neuronal migration during early gestation, and if disrupted neuronal migration increases the risk of schizophrenia, then the gene and the prenatal insult may combine in an additive fashion to increase the risk of the disease. An additive model also may apply when a large number of genes and environmental exposures can increase the liability to a disease, such as

epilepsy. The risk of disease may be a function of the total number of these susceptibility factors that are present in an individual because each factor adds to the risk in an individual.

Another model is that of "effect modification," wherein one factor modifies the effect of the other. The effect of the genetic exposure is different in persons with and without the environmental exposure. Conversely, the effect of the environmental exposure is different in persons with and without the genetic exposure. To illustrate this scenario, assume that the lifetime risk of a disease is influenced by a specific gene and by a specific prenatal exposure. A gene would cause disease in the presence of an exposure but not cause the disease in the absence of the exposure. Among individuals with both the gene and the prenatal exposure, the disease risk could be dramatically increased. Among individuals with only the gene, however, the risk of disease would be quite low. Effect modification is common in nature. Type 1 diabetes mellitus provides a well-known illustration. Some cases have been shown to result from a human leukocyte antigen (HLA) haplotype that is expressed as disease following an autoimmune response to coxsackie virus infection. Neural tube defects such as spina bifida and anencephaly also provide an example of effect modification for a neurodevelopmental disorder. Recent reports suggest that fetal neural tube defects can be caused by a genetic defect combined with low maternal intake of folate in early gestation. The genetic defect impedes the metabolism of homocysteine, whereas folate has the opposite effect. In the presence of a high folate intake in early gestation, the effect of the genetic defect on the risk of a neural tube defect in the fetus may be minimal. On the other hand, in the presence of low folate intake in early gestation, the genetic defect may confer a high risk of a neural tube defect in the fetus.

Another model is "effect mediation," in which the gene does not directly influence the risk of disease, but rather, the gene influences the chances of exposure to an environmental risk factor, which in turn influences the risk of disease. The risk of disease is a function of the environmental exposure. This would be exemplified by a circumstance in which a gene is associated with an individual's risk of sustaining head trauma, and head trauma increases the risk of the individual's developing epilepsy.

A fourth "multiplicative" model also might apply to some disorders. Under a multiplicative model, when an individual is exposed to both a genetic and an environmental factor, the effect on risk of a disease is obtained by multiplying the individual effects. For instance, given a threefold increase in risk for a gene and a threefold increase in risk for an environmental exposure, an individual with both risk factors would have a nine times greater risk for a disease than an individual with neither risk factor. This model tends to conform well to the data for cancers, which may require several stages or "hits" to transform normal cells into carcinogenic cells, and for other diseases that require several sequential steps to produce the disease.

In what follows, we discuss epidemiologic and genetic studies of selected neuropsychiatric illnesses. For didactic purposes, we have chosen disorders, which affect diverse functions of the nervous system and which have diverse degrees of heritability, modes of inheritance, and molecular mechanisms. We use the organization of Baraitser (1990), dividing these disorders into those affecting the basal ganglia, those occurring in childhood, those resulting in dementia, those associated with seizures, those involving the neuromuscular system, those resulting in psychiatric disorders, and others.

# Basal Ganglia Disease

## Huntington's Disease

In 1872, George Huntington described a familial illness he found in his Long Island, New York, practice: it was characterized by dancelike movements and "insanity." The illness appeared in midlife, afflicted men and women equally, did not skip generations, and led to early death. In 1908, the famed physician William Osler described HD as having an autosomal dominant mode of inheritance with complete penetrance: he noted that affected individuals usually had an affected parent, and conversely, approximately one-half of the offspring of affected parents were themselves affected. As early as 1932, Vessie noted that HD was prevalent throughout the world. Over the ensuing century, HD has been more completely described and its mutant gene and gene product identified, isolated, and well studied.

HD is characterized by progressive dementia, chorea, and psychiatric symptoms. The mean age at onset is about 40 years, but its symptoms can occur as early as age 2 and as late as age 80–90. HD usually causes death within 10–20 years of onset (J.B. Martin and Gusella 1986). In about 10% of the individuals with HD, the onset of symptoms occurs before age 20 (Gusella et al. 1993). Juvenile-onset HD or the "Westphal variant" is characterized by akinesia and rigidity instead of chorea, as well as a more rapid and severe course of illness.

Psychiatric symptoms occur in 70%–80% of the patients (Harper 1996) and can include a change in personality, paranoia, psychosis, and depression. About 40% of the patients develop an affective disorder; 25% of these have bipolar disorder (Peyser and Folstein 1990). Affective disorder may antedate other symptoms by 2–20 years (Folstein et al. 1983). In HD, the suicide rate is estimated to be as high as 12% (Harper 1996).

### Epidemiologic Studies

HD has an overall prevalence of 1 in 10,000 in Caucasian populations (Harper 1992), although the disease exists worldwide. In fact, prevalence is higher in some places because of a large concentration of affected families; for example, the prevalence is more than 100 per 100,000 in a specific region of Venezuela (Conneally 1984). In the United States, 25,000–30,000 people are affected with HD. Because of the age structure of the affected population and the late onset of the disease, about five times as many individuals are at risk for HD, and about 40% of these individuals will eventually prove to possess the defective HD gene (Gusella et al. 1993). The incidence of HD from 1950 through 1989 in Minnesota was reported to be 0.4 for women and 0.2 for men per 100,000 person-years (Kokmen et al. 1994).

## Family Studies

The age at onset of HD is variable and depends on the sex and the age at onset of the transmitting parent. Anticipation occurs, which means that each successive generation tends to develop HD at an earlier age than did the previous one; this phenomenon is most striking with paternal inheritance. Many individuals with early-onset disease inherit the HD gene from their father and show anticipation, that is, a significantly earlier age at onset than their father (Ridley et al. 1988), whereas many individuals with late-onset disease inherit the gene from their mother.

## High-Risk Studies

Several studies have examined whether subtle, slowly progressive neuropsychologic impairments in patients with HD might be present before chorea is clinically evident, providing support for a continuous model of cognitive deterioration. Studies done before genetic testing was available suggested that at-risk relatives of HD patients had cognitive impairment before the onset of overt disease (Jason et al. 1988; Lyle and Gottesman 1977; Strauss and Brandt 1986).

With the advent of genetic testing, it became possible to stratify at-risk relatives into gene-positive and gene-negative subgroups. A well-designed longitudinal study with multiple comparisons showed no cognitive differences between these two groups, suggesting that factors other than genetic susceptibility to HD account for differences in cognition between nominally at-risk individuals and healthy control subjects (Giordani et al. 1995). However, genetic testing enables study of putative preclinical HD: asymptomatic gene carriers have declines in putamen volume (G.J. Harris 1999) and mean annual striatal loss of dopamine receptors (T.C. Andrews et al. 1999) intermediate between HD patients and gene-negative at-risk individuals.

## Mode of Inheritance

HD is transmitted in an autosomal dominant fashion. Individuals who carry two defective copies of the HD gene (homozygotes) do not differ clinically from those who carry only one copy of the defective HD gene (heterozygotes) (R.H. Myers et al. 1989; Wexler et al. 1987). Heterozygous inactivation of the HD gene as a result of chromosomal translocation is not associated with an abnormal phenotype (Ambrose et al. 1994).

## Molecular Approaches

In 1983, the gene responsible for HD was mapped to the short arm of chromosome 4 by the use of a linked polymorphic marker (Gusella et al. 1983). This evidence made it possible to detect HD allele carriers presymptomatically and also confirmed that HD is truly a dominant genetic condition (R.H. Myers et al. 1989; Wexler et al. 1987). Ten years later, in 1993, the genetic abnormality responsible for HD was identified as a CAG trinucleotide-repeat expansion in the first exon of a novel gene (Huntington Disease Collaborative Research Group 1993). No other known mutations in this gene cause the HD phenotype. The gene, *IT15*, is located on 4p16.3; it spans approximately 210 kilobases (kb), comprises 67 exons, and encodes two messenger RNA (mRNA) species with a predicted protein product of 348 kilodaltons (kd), known as huntingtin (see next section).

Possible explanations for the "parental origin effect" include 1) maternally inherited extrachromosomal factors and 2) genomic imprinting, whereby a gene is differentially methylated (and therefore expressed) depending on whether it passed through the maternal or the paternal germline (Reik 1988). However, the explanation for the parental origin effect became clear when the *HD* gene was identified and cloned and its nature of mutation understood. Age at onset was found to be related to the length of trinucleotide repeats in the gene (see Figure 10–3). The sex of the transmitting parent is a major factor influencing the trinucleotide expansion (Telenius et al. 1993). CAG repeats tend to expand modestly from one generation to the next but can double in length when passed from father to child. These dramatic expansions occur during spermatogenesis; examination of sperm DNA shows variation in trinucleotide repeat length among individual sperm (Leeflang et al. 1995; MacDonald et al. 1993). CAG expansions likely propagate through the formation of stable hairpin structures and mismatched duplexes during gametogenesis (Mariappan et al. 1998).

The CAG repeat is highly polymorphic in the general population and ranges from 8 to 37 copies; 99% of people have fewer than 30 repeats. Individuals with HD, however, have a trinucleotide repeat size of 36–121 and a median of 44 repeats (Kremer et al. 1994). Almost all individuals (>99%) with a clinical diagnosis of HD have CAG trinucleotide expansion of the *HD* gene. Adult-onset HD (ages 35–55) is associated with 40–50 CAG repeats; juvenile-onset HD is associated with repeat lengths of more than 64 CAG units. Spontaneous HD occurs when trinucleotide repeats expand beyond a threshold length of about 37 copies. In a recent report, an

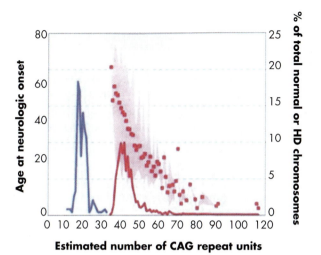

**FIGURE 10–3.** CAG repeat length on normal and Huntington's disease (HD) chromosomes and age at onset in HD. The CAG repeat length distribution of alleles found on normal (*blue line*) and HD (*red line*) chromosomes are expressed as a percentage of each type of chromosome (right axis). The mean age at onset associated with each CAG repeat length is plotted as a red square (against the left axis). The pink area surrounding the mean age at onset denotes the range of ages at onset associated with any given repeat length, with deviations presumably being due to the effects of genetic, environmental, or stochastic modifiers.

unaffected woman with 36 CAG repeats had two daughters with HD, with CAG repeats of 66 and 57; gonadal mosaicism of CAG repeat length was found in the unaffected mother (Laccone and Christian 2000).

Multiple studies have shown that the CAG repeat size and the age at onset of HD are inversely correlated but that for a given repeat size, there is a wide range of onset ages (see Figure 10–3). Thus, the use of repeat size to predict the age at onset is not particularly useful (Gusella et al. 1993). This suggests the influence of as-yet-unknown genetic, environmental, and stochastic modifying factors, as does the fact that individuals with 36–39 CAG repeats may develop the disease late in life or not at all. CAG repeat lengths also are associated with the age at onset of psychiatric symptoms and the presence of intranuclear inclusions but not with disease duration, which is invariably 15–20 years. The CAG expansion within the *HD* gene is thus a highly sensitive and specific marker for the inheritance of the HD mutation (Kremer et al. 1994). Rapid and accurate diagnosis can be made with polymerase chain reaction–based tests, even in utero (Alford et al. 1996).

**Huntingtin.** The *HD* gene codes for huntingtin, a protein that bears no significant similarity to any known protein and has not been ascribed a specific function. It is highly conserved across species and is expressed broadly across the organism during all stages of development. It does not appear to affect cellular transcription or translation (Ambrose et al. 1994), but it has been hypothesized to play a role in neurogenesis. The lack of transcriptional and translational effects suggests that the HD defect acts by altering the structure of huntingtin, producing an expanded polyglutamine stretch near the N terminus and making the HD huntingtin larger than its normal counterpart (Persichetti et al. 1995). A gain of function is likely; in other words, the polyglutamine segment confers new properties that may be unrelated to huntingtin's normal activity (see Figure 10–4). Duyao et al. (1995) tested these models by generating an inactivation mutation of the mouse huntingtin gene *Hdh*. Heterozygous Hdh inactivation did not mimic adult neuropathology, suggesting that HD involves a gain of function. Also, homozygous inactivation of huntingtin in mouse models were lethal: embryos did not develop organs and died before embryonic day 8.5. Neuropathologic analysis of these embryos showed apoptotic cell death in the embryonic ectoderm.

There have been efforts to test the gain in function theory by developing transgenic animal models, in which complementary DNA (cDNA) of the mutant huntingtin gene has been introduced. An introduction of the full-length cDNA with 44 CAG repeats into mice yielded no expression of abnormal huntingtin protein or any behavioral or other abnormalities (Goldberg et al. 1996). In another investigation (Mangiarini et al. 1996), a mouse model with a transgene of the huntingtin gene with 115–150 CAG repeats yielded a phenotype that included progressive involuntary stereotypies, tremors, seizures, reduction in brain and body weight, and early death. These mice did not show neurodegeneration but had early signs of neural apoptosis and selective reductions in receptors (dopamine, acetylcholine, and glutamate receptors) in the brain. In a third attempt, transgenic mice were created with full huntingtin cDNA with 89 CAG repeats. The phenotype of these mice more closely resembled human HD, with initial hyperactivity yielding to hypoactivity, subsequent akinesia, and death; neuropathologic analysis showed selective neurodegeneration in the striatum and cortex, gliosis, and neuronal loss of about 20% (Reddy et al. 1999).

The critical pathogenic event in HD may be accelerated apoptosis. Apoptotic DNA fragments have been found in postmortem striatal tissue of HD patients (Butterworth et al. 1998). Mutant huntingtin is cleaved by caspase-3, an apoptotic enzyme, and this cleavage is

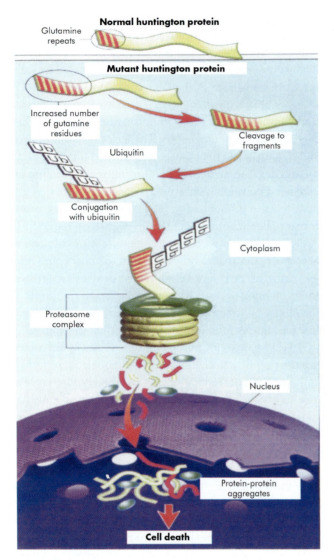

**FIGURE 10–4.** Proposed mechanism of huntingtin-induced death of neuronal cells. The mutant huntingtin protein produced by an increase in the number of CAG repeats in the *HD* gene is cleaved to fragments that retain the increased number of glutamine residues. These fragments are conjugated with ubiquitin and carried to the proteasome complex. Subsequent cleavage is incomplete, and components of both huntingtin and the proteasome are translocated to the nucleus, where aggregates form, resulting in intranuclear inclusions. Over time, this process leads to cell death.

enhanced by polyglutamate length (Martindale et al. 1998; Wellington et al. 1998). Mutant huntingtin is expressed abundantly by presynaptic cholinergic interneurons and cortical pyramidal cells that activate the striatal neurons that die (Fusco et al. 1999). This lends credence to the idea that excessive synaptic release of glutamate leads to excitotoxic striatal cell death (Sapp et al. 1999).

## Potential Treatment

Thus far, only palliative treatment of symptoms exists for HD. A novel approach to therapy is to introduce trophic factors that may delay or retard excitotoxic damage of striatal neurons. In a nongenetic animal model for HD, in which rodents received intrastriatal injection of excitatory amino acids, selective destruction of medium spiny neurons and motor and cognitive changes resulted, similar to what occurs in HD. When these animals received fibroblast grafts that secrete trophic factors, degeneration of striatal neurons was retarded and motor and cognitive defects were prevented (Kordower et al. 1999). Small grafts induce widespread expression of catalase, a free radical scavenger, throughout the striatum. Neuroprotection is likely conferred by nerve growth factors' antioxidative properties or their effect on adenosine triphosphate (ATP) production. Simple infusion of trophic factors themselves was not effective.

Another potential therapy is the use of antioxidants (such as coenzyme Q10 and ubiquinone) that protect against glutamate toxicity and rescue mitochondrial metabolism and administration of creatine to buffer against energy depletion (Grunewald and Beal 1999). Others have proposed antiapoptosis agents, immunosuppressants, and fetal cell transplant as possible therapeutic approaches for this fatal disease that as yet has no clear treatment.

## Lesch-Nyhan Syndrome

Lesch-Nyhan syndrome (LNS) results from deficient purine nucleotide synthesis. It is an X-linked, "genetically lethal" disorder. The clinical diagnosis of LNS is based on developmental delay, spastic movements, postural tremors, and retardation in a male child after the first year of life. Affected patients also often have blood and uric acid in the urine. Later, self-mutilation, seizures, severe neurologic abnormalities, and impaired renal function occur. The most curious symptom evidenced in LNS is self-mutilation, particularly biting of the lips, mouth, and fingers, and head banging. There is no effective treatment for the central nervous system (CNS) damage, and death usually ensues in the second or third decade from infection and renal failure. There is one report of decline in self-mutilation in an open trial of carbamazepine (Roach et al. 1996). Biochemically, the uric acid level is elevated from a deficiency of the enzyme hypoxanthine guanine phosphoribosyltransferase (HPRT).

The neurologic symptoms of LNS are thought to derive from early failure of dopaminergic neurons to undergo growth-factor-induced differentiation in the context of reduced purine synthesis (Yeh et al. 1998). Positron-emission tomographic imaging suggested fewer dopaminergic nerve terminals in the brain (Ernst et al. 1996) and decreased dopamine transporter concentration in the basal ganglia (D.F. Wong et al. 1996). Postmortem neurochemical studies revealed a 60%–90% decrease of dopamine content in the basal ganglia (Visser et al. 2000), and magnetic resonance imaging (MRI) showed volume reduction in the basal ganglia (J.C. Harris et al. 1998). HPRT-deficient mice have an age-dependent decrease in dopamine in the basal ganglia (Jinnah et al. 1999). The anatomic locus of toxicity has been thought to be similar in LNS and in Parkinson's disease (PD), with the difference in symptoms being attributed to the timing in development of the insult.

The *HPRT* gene is very vulnerable to mutation. In fact, the HPRT locus has been used extensively to study mammalian mutation and reversion events. Individuals with a partial deficiency do not incur CNS abnormalities, but they do acquire early adulthood gouty arthritis and uric acid renal stones, which are treatable with allopurinol, a xanthine oxidase inhibitor. Somatic cell gene therapy may be a potential treatment for LNS (i.e., the introduction of a normal *HPRT* gene to correct a deficiency of the enzyme).

## Epidemiologic Studies

The prevalence of LNS is 10 in 100,000 males. Male LNS patients have carrier mothers in more than two-thirds of cases. There are two reports of female LNS patients (van Bogaert et al. 1992; Ogasawara et al. 1989) who have de novo mutations in the maternally derived HPRT, with nonrandom inactivation of the genetically normal paternal X chromosome. A third female patient inherited the HPRT mutation from her mother and also had nonrandom inactivation of the paternal X chromosome carrying the normal *HPRT* gene (De Gregorio 2000).

## Molecular Approaches

Extensive knowledge of the structure, the organization, and the entire nucleotide sequence of the *HPRT* gene has aided the molecular analysis of the genetic alterations involved in LNS. The gene for HPRT has been cloned (Jolly et al. 1983; Patel et al. 1984), and 57 kb of DNA sequence at the locus, including the entire *HPRT* gene, has been determined (Edwards et al. 1990). The *HPRT* gene is encoded as a single structural gene localized to Xq26–27, with nine exons and eight introns totaling 44 kb (Patel et al. 1986). Mutations at aspartate 206 are common in LNS; this is the only amino acid site that directly contacts magnesium, suggesting that magnesium

is an important cofactor for the activity of HPRT (Heroux et al. 1999).

Affected males usually have unique genetic backgrounds and have not inherited a common founder chromosome (Gibbs et al. 1989; Igarashi et al. 1989; Wilson et al. 1986). The HPRT locus is apparently quite vulnerable to mutation: CpG dinucleotides are the most frequent site of mutations in vivo (O'Neill and Finette 1998). The mutations at the *HPRT* gene include base substitutions, deletions, single base insertions, and RNA splicing errors; these have been characterized with polymerase chain reaction amplification of cDNA (Davidson et al. 1991; Gibbs et al. 1989) and individual exons (Gibbs et al. 1990). More than 100 HPRT mutations have been identified in patients with LNS, and they are seemingly all heterogeneous (Davidson et al. 1989; Yang et al. 1984). About 15% of the LNS mutations are large deletions of part or all of the *HPRT* gene and are detectable by Southern blot analysis (Yang et al. 1984). Only a few cases of gene duplication have been identified (Monnat et al. 1992; Yang et al. 1988); they are thought to result from nonhomologous recombination.

Disease status in males can be diagnosed easily by enzyme assay; there are now also reports of genetic prenatal testing (Ray et al. 1999). Determination of carrier status in females has been more challenging. Enzyme assay is unreliable because of varying patterns of X inactivation that cause an overlap of ranges of enzyme activity in carrier and genetically normal females. Use of RFLP analysis is an alternative for detecting carrier status, but DNA must be available from key family members, and marker homozygosity may interfere with accurate determination of carrier status. A better alternative for carrier detection is heteroduplex detection with hydrolink gel electrophoresis (Keen et al. 1991). When this method was applied to 12 LNS families, female carrier status and all 12 mutations were determined in the affected families (Boyd et al. 1993).

## Parkinson's Disease

PD was first described in 1817 as a "shaking palsy." It is a progressive movement disorder characterized by resting tremor, rigidity, bradykinesia (slowness of movement), gait disturbance, and postural changes. It is the second most common neurodegenerative disease (after Alzheimer's dementia), and it affects 6–7 million people worldwide (Goedert 1999). In PD, neuropathologic changes primarily include a loss of pigmented (dopaminergic) neurons in the zona compacta of the substantia nigra, but other brain regions may be affected, including the locus coeruleus, hypothalamus, dorsal medial nucleus

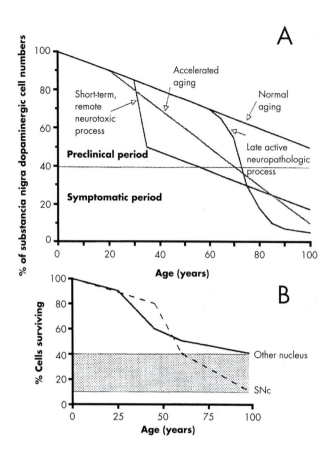

**FIGURE 10–5.** Hypothetical models for neural degeneration in Parkinson's disease. *Panel A.* Different models of the rate of progression of substantia nigra cell (SNc) neurodegeneration (from Gerlach and Riederer 1997; based on Mcgreer et al. 1988). *Panel B.* Model illustrating differential rates of neurodegeneration in different nuclei of the IP brain. The shaded region represents the period in which SNc neuronal loss is great enough to produce the classic idiopathic Parkinson's symptomology but in which sufficient cells remain to make neuroprotection a viable strategy. The degree of neuronal loss in other nuclei that produce clinically detectable symptoms will, of course, be different, as will the window of opportunity for neuroprotective strategy.

of the vagus, and nucleus basalis of Meynert. See Figure 10–5 for an illustration of hypothetical models of the neurodegenerative nature of PD.

PD may be associated with a variety of psychiatric syndromes, including cognitive and affective disturbances, personality changes, and psychosis. Some studies have found an excess of depression and anxiety in PD patients as compared with control subjects (Henderson et al. 1992), but others have not (Hantz et al. 1994). Psychosis increases in prevalence in PD with advanced age and severity of cognitive impairment (Naimark et al. 1996). Hallucinations have not been found to be related to L-dopa dose (Sanchez-Ramos et al. 1996) or to be

exacerbated by intravenous L-dopa (Goetz et al. 1998). Psychosis in PD responds to clozapine in doses lower than 50 mg/day (French Clozapine Parkinson Study Group 1999).

## Epidemiologic Studies

The prevalence of PD has been estimated as 133 in 100,000; the average age at onset is 63 years (Bekkelund et al. 1989). The incidence of the disorder has been reported as 11 in 100,000 person-years (Hofman et al. 1989a). Other studies have found similar statistics (reviewed in Checkoway and Nelson 1999). The lifetime risk of developing PD is about 1 in 40 (Ben-Shlomo and Sieradzan 1995). Studies of temporal trends in incidence in the nonindustrialized community of Rochester, Minnesota suggested virtually no change over the preceding 35 years (Schoenberg 1987). However, mortality data suggest increasing death rates from PD in persons aged 75 and older in the United States, Europe, and Japan (Checkoway and Nelson 1999); perhaps individuals are simply living longer and are less likely to die from other causes. Age is the greatest risk factor for PD: incidence and prevalence rise sharply at age 50 and continue to increase thereafter (Checkoway and Nelson 1999). A prevalence study in France in 1994 showed that age-specific prevalence ratios increased with age, from 0.5% in the age group 65–69 to 6.1% in individuals older than 90, a finding that is consistent with other population-based studies (Tison et al. 1994).

Some authors have found that PD death rates vary according to race/ethnicity and sex (Kurtzke and Goldberg 1988); however, mortality rate data are limited by incomplete information on death certificates and the fact that PD is often not fatal (Checkoway and Nelson 1999). Some population-based surveys have shown a male preponderance of 20%–30% (Fall et al. 1996; Mayeux et al. 1995a), although others have not found gender differences in PD. In the United States, whites have higher PD prevalence and mortality than do African Americans, although racial differences are not evident in international comparisons (Lanska 1997; Mayeux et al. 1995a). Differences in case ascertainment and diagnostic criteria may impede efforts to compare PD rates and may substantially influence estimates of prevalence (De Rijk et al. 1997). Nonetheless, the broad geographic distribution of PD suggests that it is caused by either a wide variety of factors or a few very common factors. The relatively low prevalence of PD suggests that exposures alone do not cause illness but interact with genetic vulnerability to the disorder.

In a cross-sectional survey in Israel, spatial clustering

of PD was found in three adjacent kibbutzim (prevalence = 2.2%) and was thought to be the result of a common environmental factor, such as agricultural chemicals or drinking water (Goldsmith et al. 1990). Temporal clustering of PD also has been noted in six families with the disease and has been interpreted as consistent with an environmental cause (Calne et al. 1987).

Nearly all forms of PD, both familial and sporadic, are characterized by the presence of Lewy bodies and Lewy neurites, which are intracellular aggregates composed of α-synuclein (Figure 10–6). Many patients with familial PD have mutations in the α-synuclein gene. But even sporadic PD patients with normal α-synuclein genes have Lewy bodies that are composed of α-synuclein. It is not clear what leads to the formation of Lewy bodies and neurites in the more common, sporadic forms of PD; several environmental agents are being studied.

**Pesticides and toxins.** Research on environmental toxins has been strongly influenced by the example of 1-methyl-4-phenyl-1,2,3,6-tetrahydropyridine (MPTP), a recreational drug that was found in the 1980s to cause a near replica of PD in very young substance abusers. MPTP also causes a lasting PD-like syndrome in higher primates (Marsden and Jenner 1987); investigation of animal models has yielded hypotheses about the etiology and pathophysiology of sporadic PD. 1-methyl-4-phenylpyridine (MPP+), a metabolite of MPTP, inhibits the nicotinamide adenine dinucleotide (NADH) dehydrogenase of mitochondrial complex I, leading to a decline in ATP and an accumulation of free radicals, which both lead to oxidative damage. Of note, the chemical structure of paraquat is similar to that of MPTP.

In North America and Europe, early-onset PD appears to be associated with rural residence, perhaps reflecting exposure to pesticides, well water, or wood pulp (Hubble et al. 1993; Semchuk et al. 1992; Tanner 1989; G.F. Wong et al. 1991; reviewed in Langston 1998; Olanow and Tatton 1999). Prevalence of PD has been reported to correlate with volume of pesticides sold in nine regions of Canada (Barbeau et al. 1987). Preclinical parkinsonian symptoms are more common in regions of Israel where carbamates and organophosphates are detected (Herishanu et al. 1998). Cohort studies of subjects with pesticide exposures have not found increased PD; this may be because the sample sizes have been too small and, thus, the power limited (reviewed in Le Couteur et al. 1999).

More than half of all the case-control studies examining PD prevalence and pesticide exposure have shown significant associations (reviewed in Le Couteur et al. 1999); these studies have been done throughout the

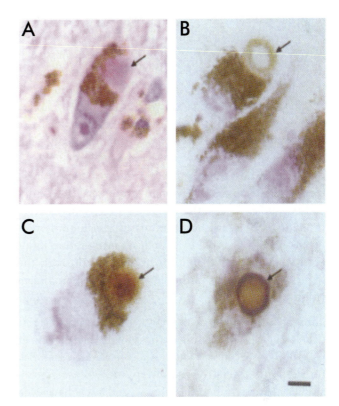

**FIGURE 10–6.** Lewy bodies in pigmented neurons of the substantia nigra from a Parkinson's disease patient, seen as large spherical inclusions in the cell cytoplasm (arrows). *Panel A.* Hematoxylin-eosin stain. *Panel B.* Ubiquitin immunohistochemistry, which stains predominantly the halo of the Lewy body. *Panel C.* α-Synuclein immunohistochemistry, in which the core of the Lewy body is most densely stained. *Panel D.* Double staining with ubiquitin (blue) and α-synuclein (brown) showing additive staining of the two markers in the halo and core, respectively, of the Lewy body. The granular brown deposits in the cytoplasm of cells in each micrograph indicate the melanin pigmentation of nigral neurons, not all of which contain Lewy bodies (see *Panel B*). Scale bar=10 mm.

*Source.* Micrographs provided by M.G. Spillantini, University of Cambridge, United Kingdom.

world. However, many studies have not shown a clear association (reviewed in Checkoway and Nelson 1999). Three studies suggested increasing gradients of risk of PD with years of pesticide exposure (Gorell et al. 1998; Liou et al. 1997; Seidler et al. 1996), although one did not (Jimenez-Jimenez et al. 1992). There are several case reports of PD following exposure to pesticides, such as organophosphates, paraquat, diquat, and maneb (reviewed in Le Couteur et al. 1999). Also, dieldrin, an organochlorine, is more commonly found postmortem in PD patients than in control subjects (Fleming et al. 1994). Dieldrin is one of the only pesticides that accumulates in human tissue; therefore, it may be a marker of more general pesticide exposure. Identifying exposure to specific pesticides is often compromised by poor recall (reviewed in Le Couteur et al. 1999). The greatest evidence for association with a specific pesticide may be for paraquat (Hertzmann et al. 1990; Liou et al. 1997).

PD has been associated with a number of toxins other than pesticides, including trace metals, cyanide, lacquer thinner, organic solvents, carbon monoxide, and carbon disulfide (Olanow and Tatton 1999). Increased risk (odds ratio = 21) also has been described with high blood mercury levels (Ngim and Devathasan 1989). Population studies suggest that the risk for PD is increased in individuals born in the years of influenza epidemics (1890–1930), possibly explained by intrauterine influenza virus exposure predisposing to PD through the depletion of neurons in the developing substantia nigra (Mattock et al. 1988).

**Tobacco.**  Tobacco may exert a protective effect against developing PD. In a case-control study by Hertzmann et al. (1990), tobacco was found to confer a decreased risk for PD, with a relative risk of 0.6. Other case-control studies have confirmed this finding, and a few have even found strong inverse dose-response relations; prospective cohort studies also found a negative association between smoking and PD (reviewed in Checkoway and Nelson 1999). This association has been found to be related to neither selective survival of nonsmoking PD patients (Morens et al. 1996) nor premorbid personality (Paulson and Dadmehr 1991). However, a case-control study in New York suggested that cigarette smoking does not protect against PD, but rather that PD reduces smoking (Mayeux et al. 1994; see also Riggs 1992). If tobacco does protect against PD, it may do so by inducing cytochromes that detoxify pesticides and other exogenous toxins.

**Diet.**  There are no consistent findings regarding PD and diet, despite expectations that vitamins A, C, and E would be protective given their antioxidant properties and that a high-fat diet would increase risk because of the potential for free radical generation (Checkoway and Nelson 1999). One study found an odds ratio of 9.0 for very high intake of animal fat (Logroscino et al. 1998). Of note, a recent study suggested that coffee intake is associated with a decreased risk for PD (Ross et al. 2000).

## Family Studies

Since the time of Gowers (1903), the observation that patients with PD often have affected relatives has suggested a role for genetic factors in the disease. Subsequent case-control studies found a 2- to 14-fold increase in PD in close relatives of affected individuals (Gasser 1998). Payami et al. (1994) examined the incidence of PD in 586 first-degree relatives of 114 randomly ascertained caucasian patients with idiopathic PD and in 522 first-degree relatives of 114 age-matched caucasian control subjects and found that 16% of the patients had a family history, in comparison with 4% of the control subjects. W.E. Martin et al. (1973) examined the aggregation of illness among the first-degree, second-degree, and third-degree relatives of patients with PD in comparison with the relatives of spouse control subjects; 26.8% of the probands and 14.8% of the control subjects reported at least one affected relative. The greatest risk was found for the relatives of young probands; thus, 8.3% of the sibs of probands aged 35–44 were affected compared with 1.4% of the sibs of probands aged 65–74. That younger-onset probands have a more familial form of PD, however, has not been universally found (Marttila and Rinne 1988), and young-onset and later-onset forms of the disorder may not be clinically or pathologically distinguished. Young-onset PD, however, should be distinguished from juvenile PD (onset before age 21 years), which is invariably familial (Quinn et al. 1987; Yokochi et al. 1984). Of interest is that PD may be three times more common in the relatives of probands with Alzheimer's disease (AD) than in control subjects, suggesting an etiologic overlap between these disorders (Hofman et al. 1989b). An increased frequency of PD among the first-degree relatives of patients with lymphoreticular malignancies in comparison with the relatives of hospital control subjects (relative risk = 3.0) suggests a shared pathophysiology, perhaps through immune dysfunction (Grufferman et al. 1989).

## Twin Studies

A Department of Veterans Affairs twin study showed similar rates of concordance in MZ and DZ twins of PD patients older than 60 (Tanner et al. 1999); however, for PD with an age at onset of 50 or younger, increased concordance in MZ twins was found (Tanner et al. 1999). This suggests that, as in other diseases, there may be an early-onset form that is more familial. Of note, twin studies in PD are limited by uncertainty regarding the affection status of "asymptomatic" co-twins: 80% of basal ganglia dopamine may need to be lost before symptoms of PD become overt. Subclinical loss of dopamine neurons seen with positron-emission tomographic scanning has an MZ concordance rate of 53%, compared with 13% in DZ twins (Brooks 1998), suggesting a more sensitive means than clinical examination for evaluating co-twins (Johnson et al. 1990).

**TABLE 10–3.**  Gene mutations identified in familial Parkinson's disease (PD)

| Gene | Chromosome | Inheritance | Phenotype | Pathology | Reference |
|------|-----------|-------------|-----------|-----------|-----------|
| α-Synuclein | 4 | Autosomal dominant | L-Dopa responsive, early-onset PD | Lewy bodies | Polymeropoulos et al. 1997 |
| Parkin | 6 | Autosomal recessive | L-Dopa responsive, juvenile-onset PD | No Lewy bodies | Kitada et al. 1998 |
| *UCH-L1* | 4 | Incomplete penetrance | Typical PD | Not reported | Leroy et al. 1998 |
| 4p Haplotype | 4 | Autosomal dominant | L-Dopa responsive, PD or postural tremor | Lewy bodies | Farrer et al. 1998 |
| *PARK3* | 2 | Autosomal dominant | Similar to sporadic PD | Lewy bodies | Gasser et al. 1998 |

## Mode of Inheritance

Familial PD may prove to be etiologically heterogeneous; family members not only share genes but also may have common environmental exposures. Apparent autosomal dominant inheritance with reduced penetrance is found in some families (Farrer et al. 1989; Golbe et al. 1993; Lazzarini et al. 1994; Maraganore et al. 1991; Waters and Miller 1994), although the presence of atypical features, such as cerebellar signs, has suggested that some of these families may have olivopontocerebellar atrophy. Autosomal recessive inheritance may characterize juvenile-onset PD (Yamamura et al. 1973). W. E. Martin et al. (1973) suggested a multifactorial polygenic mode of inheritance; this model is consistent with the observation that the risk for an individual to develop familial PD increases with the number of affected individuals in the at-risk person's family. Studies examining intergenerational differences in age at onset of PD have found a significantly earlier age at onset in the proband generation than in the parental generation, a finding that is consistent with genetic anticipation (Payami et al. 1995; see also Bonifati et al. 1994).

## Molecular Approaches

A number of loci have been linked to PD (Table 10–3). Some cases of early-onset PD have been linked to mutations in a gene in the q21–23 region of chromosome 4 that encodes α-synuclein, a small protein of unclear function that is abundantly produced in the brain and localized to presynaptic nerve terminals. α-Synuclein may be involved in plasticity and learning; it is similar to synelfin, an avian homologue that is upregulated during song learning in birds (George et al. 1995). There are two known missense mutations in the α-synuclein gene that lead to

disease in humans: they are substitutions for alanine by threonine (A53T) and by proline (A30P). A53T was first found in the Contursi kindred, a large Italian-American family, and then in Greek pedigrees with autosomal dominant inheritance (Polymeropoulos et al. 1997): 85% of the individuals with the mutation developed PD, whereas the mutation was not seen in any control subjects. A53T can be traced to a founder on the western coast of Greece. A53T is associated with an age at onset in the sixth decade and has near complete penetrance. A30P was found in a single large German pedigree with early-onset PD (Kruger et al. 1998).

A second gene, parkin, on chromosome 6, has been identified in a large Japanese pedigree with autosomal recessive inheritance of juvenile-onset PD without Lewy bodies (Kitada et al. 1998). It is a large gene with 500 kb and 12 exons; its product is expressed abundantly in the brain, including the substantia nigra, but its activity is not known. Deletions have been found in this gene in affected individuals in unrelated Japanese families. A third putative locus, designated *PARK3*, on 2p13, has been identified in a series of northern German and southern Danish families in which transmission was autosomal dominant but not fully penetrant (Gasser et al. 1998). No candidate gene has been found in this identified region.

Other than α-synuclein, other loci on chromosome 4 have been linked to PD in different pedigrees. Mutations in a ubiquitin processing pathway gene, thiol protease UCH-L1, have been identified in a small German pedigree; its presumed pathophysiology is through increased protein aggregation and ubiquitination of α-synuclein in Lewy bodies (Leroy et al. 1998). Also, there is evidence for association of a 4p haplotype with either PD or essential tremor in some families (Farrer et al. 1998). Ubiquitin hydrolase, a candidate gene for PD in this region, was not linked to disease status.

**Candidate genes.** Many genes have been screened that have not been found to be associated with an increased risk of PD: brain-derived neurotrophic factor (BDNF), amyloid precursor protein (APP), ε4 type of apolipoprotein E (APOE4), tyrosine hydroxylase, glutathione peroxidase, catalase, superoxide dismutase, and the dopamine 2, 3, and 4 receptors (Gasser et al. 1994). Of these, many were excluded from linkage in a series of autosomal dominant PD families. However, some studies implicate the monoamine oxidase genes as hereditary factors that influence the susceptibility of individuals to PD (Hotamisligil et al. 1994; Kurth et al. 1993; reviewed in Olanow and Tatton 1999). No clear linkage has been found for PD and mitochondrial genes (Maraganore et al. 1991).

Some authors have hypothesized that PD is related to diminished detoxification of external agents by endogenous enzymes (Kuhn and Muller 1997; Langston 1996). This is a two-hit gene-environment interaction model in which disease presence is determined by both genetic vulnerability and the exposure to a toxin. There are reports of linkage of PD to polymorphisms in cytochrome P450 D6 (CYP450D6), a hepatic enzyme; variants in CYP450D6 alone are associated with only a weak increase in risk, but together with a variant of GSTM1, a glutathione S-transferase, leads to a risk 11–14 times that of the general population (Foley and Riederer 1999). Some preliminary evidence indicates an association between slow acetylation (*N*-acetyltransferase) and PD (Bandmann et al. 1997); slow acetylators may metabolize toxins more slowly, therefore potentiating their effect on vulnerable neurons. Also, in individuals with pesticide exposure, an association was found between PD and polymorphisms in a glutathione transferase (GSTP) locus (Menegon et al. 1998); the glutathione pathway plays a role in scavenging free radicals.

## Hypotheses for Pathophysiology of Sporadic Parkinson's Disease

Complex I, a mitochondrial protein involved in energy generation, is inhibited by MPP+, a metabolite of MPTP, which is a known cause of PD that is selectively toxic to dopaminergic neurons. Idiopathic or sporadic PD also has been associated with a systematic defect in complex I (Schapira 1996). This defect may be mediated by mutation of DNA or by direct organelle toxicity. Complex I deficiency in PD has been linked to mutations in mitochondrial DNA in some patients, but no disease-specific mutation has been found (Ikebe et al. 1995). Transfer of PD platelet mitochondrial DNA into normal platelets that contain only nuclear DNA (see Figure 10–7) yields

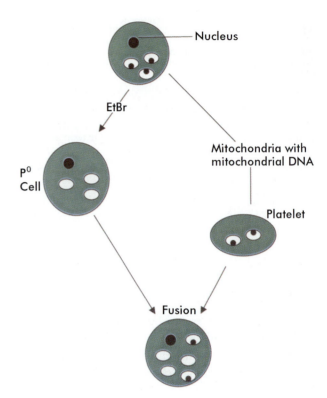

**FIGURE 10–7.** Generation of cybrids using p[0] cells (which lack mitochondrial DNA [mtDNA]) and platelets of Parkinson's disease patients who carry mtDNA point mutations to study functional aspects of these mutations. p[0] cells are generated by incubation with ethidium bromide (EtBr). EtBr removes mtDNA from the cells, which are then cultured in a uridine-supplemented medium. Following the fusion of p[0] cells with the patients' platelets, the mitochondrial functional phenotype of the patients is expressed by the cybrid cell line.

transfected platelets that have the reduced complex I function that is consistent with PD (Swerdlow et al. 1996). It is not known whether the mitochondrial DNA mutation arises somatically or is inherited, or even whether it plays a role in PD pathogenesis (Schapira 1999).

Correspondingly, sporadic PD has been hypothesized to arise from prolonged low-level exposure to toxins such as pesticides, which can poison the mitochondria of neurons, interfere with bioenergetics, and lead to oxidant damage. These toxins need not be selective for dopaminergic neurons, as dopaminergic neurons may be comparatively more vulnerable than others in the brain. In sporadic PD, it may be that oxidant damage interferes with proteasomal cleavage of normal α-synuclein, therefore leading to Lewy body formation (Jenner and Olanow 1998). Some individuals may have a genetic vulnerability for increased disease risk from toxin exposure. There are several models for the mechanisms by which neurodegeneration may lead to expression of clinical symptoms (see Figure 10–7).

## Potential Treatment

Genetic discoveries may inform treatment of PD in the future. Thus far, combined L-dopa/carbidopa has been the standard treatment for PD, especially akinesia and rigidity early in treatment. However, efficacy declines over time with increased severity of side effects, especially disabling dyskinesias. Other dopaminergic agents have been investigated, including catechol-O-methyl-transferase (COMT), monoamine oxidase inhibitors, and dopamine transport blockers. Because PD is thought to be mediated by oxidative damage, investigators have studied the protective effect of antioxidants, especially early in illness. Vitamin E had no effect, but selegiline slowed the progression of the disease (Shoulson 1998). Putative treatments that remain to be studied include other antioxidants, glutamate receptor antagonists, and antiapoptotic factors. Other potential treatments include the creation of lesions through surgery or through high-frequency stimulation. Transplants of human and porcine fetal dopaminergic cells have been tested, but results have been mixed. Another area of investigation is the transplant of neurotrophin-secreting fibroblasts; neurotrophic factors have been shown in rodents and monkeys to reverse MPTP damage to the substantia nigra (Tomac et al. 1995; Zhang et al. 1997).

# Wilson's Disease

In 1912, Wilson described a familial nervous disease associated with cirrhosis of the liver. Patients with this disorder (which is also known as hepatolenticular degeneration) may present with the triad of liver dysfunction, neuropsychiatric deterioration, and Kayser-Fleischer rings of the cornea. Renal impairment in patients with Wilson's disease (WD) may also be present.

WD occurs as a result of excessive copper accumulation and failure of copper excretion. Normally, copper is extracted from the portal circulation by hepatocytes and then either used for cellular metabolism, incorporated into ceruloplasmin, or excreted into bile. These last two pathways are impaired in WD. WD is diagnosed by measuring ceruloplasmin oxidase activity and hepatic copper content. A standard for disease diagnosis is the presence of more than 250 μg of copper per gram of liver (dry weight).

In WD, toxic amounts of copper accumulate first in the liver, where it leads to impaired protein synthesis, lipid peroxidation of membranes, DNA oxidative damage, and reduced amount of cellular antioxidants. Mitochondria are especially vulnerable to this free radical damage and show early structural damage. Hepatocellular necrosis and apoptosis occur. Excess copper then spills out from damaged hepatocytes into the serum to infiltrate the brain, kidneys, and corneas. The basal ganglia are especially susceptible to the toxic effects of copper, although the reasons for this are unclear.

Neurologic features in WD can include spasticity, rigidity, dysarthria, dysphagia, and a flapping tremor of the wrist and shoulder. Psychiatric manifestations are frequent and include personality changes, depressive episodes, cognitive dysfunction, and psychosis (Akil et al. 1991; Dening 1991). At least 20% of the patients have psychiatric symptoms at the time of initial diagnosis (Dening and Berrios 1990), and 10% of the patients present initially with only psychiatric symptoms (Akil et al. 1991). In WD, neurologic and psychiatric symptoms frequently co-occur, but they have not been found to be correlated with either serum copper levels (Rathbun 1996) or MRI abnormalities (Akil et al. 1991). Interestingly, psychiatric symptoms are often exacerbated with the onset of chelation therapy of excess copper (Dening 1991; McDonald and Lake 1995). Findings suggest that psychiatric symptoms may reflect active neurotoxicity rather than total copper load (Estrov et al. 2000).

WD is progressive and fatal if untreated; death can occur from hemolytic crisis or liver failure if diagnosis is delayed. Treatment of WD involves removal of excess copper by administering a chelating agent such as penicillamine (Walshe 1956) or trientine or by blocking intestinal copper absorption with zinc salts (Hoogenraad et al. 1979). Liver transplant is also an effective treatment and cure for end-stage WD. Possible therapies in the future include liver cell transplantation and gene therapy with adenoviral vectors carrying the normal *WD* gene.

## Epidemiologic Studies

The prevalence of WD is 10 in 100,000. Onset may be as early as age 4 or as late as the fifth decade. Presentation of the disease appears to depend in part on age at onset. Thus, patients with an early age at onset are more likely to present with hepatic rather than neuropsychiatric signs (Cox et al. 1972). Nonetheless, many patients with signs of intellectual deterioration and movement disorder may present before age 10.

## Family Studies

Sibs affected with WD have been described (Bearn 1960; Bickel et al. 1957; Walshe 1967). High rates of consanguinity, for example, among Indian and Arab patients, have suggested autosomal recessive inheritance (Dastur et al. 1969; Passwell et al. 1977).

## High-Risk Studies

Sibs of patients with WD have a 25% risk for developing the disorder. Because most families are complete by the time the diagnosis is made in the first sib, this information is mostly helpful in directing secondary prevention. Early recognition of biochemical evidence of illness in at-risk individuals may allow for treatment to begin earlier with dietary copper restriction, zinc, and penicillamine administered before overt disease can develop.

## Mode of Inheritance

WD is an autosomal recessive disorder.

## Linkage Analysis

The *WD* locus (*WND*) was assigned to the long arm of chromosome 13 by close linkage with the red cell esterase D locus in a large Israeli-Arab kindred with affected members in two generations (Frydman et al. 1985). The authors of that study found a lod score of 3.21 at 6% recombination with the chromosome 13 marker esterase D. Combining these results with those of a second unrelated 10-member sibship gave a lod score of 4.55. Bonne-Tamir et al. (1986) confirmed this linkage in two unrelated Druze kindreds, reporting a maximum lod score of 5.49. Subsequent study with DNA markers on chromosome 13 placed the *WND* locus distal to esterase D (Bonne-Tamir et al. 1986).

Multipoint linkage analysis led to the construction of a long-range restriction map of the region (Bull and Cox 1993). Thomas et al. (1994) studied DNA haplotypes of dinucleotide repeat polymorphisms (CA repeats) in the 13q14.3 region for 51 families with WD. Three new highly polymorphic markers (*D13S314*, *D13S315*, and *D13S316*) were developed close to the *WND* locus.

## Molecular Approaches

Identification of the gene for another disorder, Menkes' syndrome, led to the identification of the *WD* locus. Like WD, Menkes' syndrome is a rare inherited disorder of copper metabolism. However, its pathophysiology is characterized not by copper excess but by copper deficiency. In Menkes' syndrome, transport of copper into the gut, across the placenta, and across the blood-brain barrier is inadequate, leading to deficient activity of essential copper-dependent enzymes. Analysis of a balanced translocation in an affected individual led to the physical mapping of the Menkes' gene, which, when cloned, was found to be similar to an adenosine triphosphatase (ATPase) essential for copper metabolism in bacteria. It was hypothesized that the affected proteins in

Menkes' syndrome and WD might be similar, given that in both disorders, copper transport is impaired. Molecular screening for genes homologous to the Menkes' gene in the *WND* locus led to the isolation and identification of the gene for WD, named *ATP7B*. Petrukhin et al. (1994) reported the complete exon/intron structure of the *WD* gene. Individuals with WD were then confirmed to have mutations at this locus.

The *WD* gene, *ATP7B*, has itself been cloned and found to encode a putative copper-transporting P-type ATPase (see Figure 10–8) that has 55% amino acid identity to the Menkes' ATPase (Bull et al. 1993; Tanzi et al. 1993; Yamaguchi et al. 1993). Alternative splicing patterns in human brain and liver have been found to lead to differential regional expression of the WD ATPase. Some authors hypothesized that the difference in clinical expression of Menkes' syndrome and WD may result more from tissue-specific differences in expression than from differences in the actual proteins affected (Schaefer and Gitlin 1999). The most common mutation in WD, a replacement of histidine with glutamine, when applied to the Menkes' protein, also disrupts copper transport. Furthermore, normal WD protein can rescue the phenotype of Menkes' syndrome protein-deficient cells. Schaefer and Gitlin (1999) proposed that inducing expression of *ATP7B* early in development of Menkes' syndrome may be therapeutic.

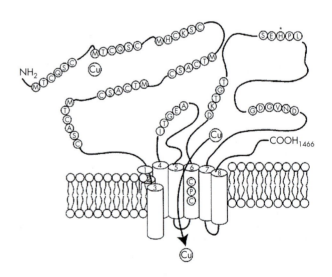

**FIGURE 10–8.** Proposed topographic model of human Wilson's disease P-type adenosine triphosphatase (ATPase). The directed movement of copper (Cu) from cytoplasm into the secretion is shown. Conserved amino acid motifs are indicated in circles. *Histidine residue 1069, which is the site of common disease mutation.

*Source.* Adapted from http://www.medscape.com.

The amino acid composition of *ATP7B* highly resembles that of other ATP-dependent metal ion transporters found across species, with domains identified for phosphorylation, ATP binding, and potential conformational changes. Specifically, an intramembranous sequence of cysteine-proline-cysteine is highly conserved in metal-transporting ATPases (Bacon and Schilsky 1999). The most common site of mutation in WD is in a histidine residue of an intracytoplasmic ATP-binding domain that is conserved in all known copper-transporting P-type ATPases (see also Figure 10–8).

## Pathophysiologic Mechanisms in Wilson's Disease

The ATP7B protein has been localized to the trans-Golgi complex. Studies in yeast deficient for copper-transporting ATPase and in an animal model for WD, the Long-Evans cinnamon (LEC) rat, provide evidence that ATP7B transports copper from the cytoplasm to the vesicular system, where it is incorporated into ceruloplasmin and prepared for excretion.

Interestingly, although both the Menkes' syndrome and the WD ATPases normally are located in the trans-Golgi complex, they are themselves transported to a cytoplasmic vesicular compartment in the presence of increased copper. This relocation of the enzymes occurs within minutes, and the ATPases are recycled back to the trans-Golgi complex when copper levels decline.

## Identification and Diagnosis

Abnormalities in the *WD* gene arise frequently. More than 60 disease-specific mutations have been identified; most are point mutations, although deletions, insertions, and missense and splice site mutations also have been found. Most mutations occur either in transmembranous regions of the protein or at a site thought to be involved in ATP binding. The most frequent mutation is a point mutation at position 1069, in which glutamine replaces histamine (H1069Q); it is found in 30% of the patients of European descent. The large number of putative mutations reduces the feasibility of a general screening test at this time. However, newer sequence analysis methodologies that screen the entire coding system of *ATP7B* may make such general screening plausible in the future. This will depend on differentiating disease-specific mutations from normal polymorphisms of the gene. At this time, haplotype analysis can be used for screening family members of patients with WD. At-risk siblings can have genetic and biochemical testing as toddlers; if they are characterized as likely to develop the disorder, minimally toxic zinc therapy can begin as early as age 3 years to reduce copper absorption.

There has been some effort to correlate specific genotypes with clinical manifestations. Maier-Dobersberger et al. (1997) reported that patients with the H1069Q mutation presented later and had primarily neurologic manifestations, but other investigators were unable to confirm this finding (Shah et al. 1997).

# Illnesses of Childhood

## Autism

Autism is an uncommon neuropsychiatric disorder that is manifested by profound impairments in verbal and nonverbal communication and reciprocal social interrelationships and by interests and behaviors that are often repetitive and restrictive (American Psychiatric Association 2000). Onset of autism typically occurs before age 3 years, and the disorder persists throughout the life of the patient. Estimates of the population prevalence of autism are on the order of 5–10 per 10,000 (Bryson et al. 1988; Fombonne 1999). A consistently observed male-to-female ratio of 3–4:1 has been noted, with females often having more severe impairment, particularly in IQ (Volkmar et al. 1993).

### Family Studies

Beginning in the 1980s, family studies in which siblings of autistic probands were directly assessed showed rates of autism in the siblings of 2%–6% (August et al. 1981; Ritvo et al. 1989; Tsai et al. 1981). Another 20 subsequent studies continued to support these findings (Bailey et al. 1998). Szatmari (1999) pooled many such studies and estimated the risk to siblings as 2.2% (95% confidence interval = 1.1%–3.3%). Second- and third-degree relatives of autistic probands also have been assessed (DeLong and Dwyer 1988; Jorde et al. 1991; Pickles et al. 1995; Szatmari et al. 1995). These studies suggested an overall rate of autism of 0.2% in second-degree relatives and 0.1% in third-degree relatives. This dramatic decline in relative risk compared with that of first-degree relatives suggests a polygenic complex disorder. Family study data have been examined to determine whether a broader phenotype of pervasive developmental disorders (PDDs), of which autism is one, or other traits that occur in the relatives of autistic probands should be considered as phenotypes. On the whole, this research indicated that relatives of autistic probands can have a spectrum of behavioral traits from isolated communication impairments and social difficulties to more severe disorders in the PDD spectrum (reviewed in Bailey et al. 1998). Although suggestive, this area of investigation has not been completely resolved, and it is clear that there is no evidence for "a behavioral or cognitive profile that is either universal or specific" (Bailey et al. 1998).

## Twin Studies

To determine whether the familial component of autism is genetic, several twin studies have been performed (Bailey et al. 1995; Folstein et al. 1977; Ritvo et al. 1985; Steffenburg et al. 1989). These investigations, with a total of 108 twin pairs, reported a concordance rate of 36%–91% for MZ twins and 0%–24% for DZ twins. Only one group saw any concordance between DZ pairs (Ritvo et al. 1985). The observed nonconcordance in the DZ twins was probably secondary to the small sample number and low recurrence rate seen in siblings in family studies. These concordance rates yield heritability estimates in the range of 90%. This suggests that a substantial portion of the liability to autism is genetic in origin. These data also highlight the nonmendelian nature of its inheritance, implying multiple genes and epistatic gene interactions. Twin studies also support the inheritance of a broader phenotype. In an early study involving 21 twin pairs, concordance for cognitive and social abnormalities was 82% for MZ pairs and 10% for DZ pairs (Folstein et al. 1977). In a follow-up study that included the original group plus 28 new twin pairs, concordance for cognitive and social disorders was 92% for MZ pairs and again 10% for DZ pairs (Bailey et al. 1995).

## Adoption Studies

There are no known adoption studies for autistic disorder.

## High-Risk Studies

For several decades, clinicians have described the co-incidence of autism and various medical disorders. Depending on the stringency of the diagnostic criteria for autism and the comprehensiveness of the medical workup, this association is between 10% and 37% (Barton and Volkmar 1998; Gillberg and Coleman 1996; Rutter et al. 1994). Despite this variability in estimates and the ongoing debate on how they are derived, it is clear that the likelihood of a coexisting medical condition is related to a decreasing IQ (Ritvo et al. 1990; Steffenburg 1991). For example, one retrospective study that assessed 211 autistic subjects found that 24% of the subjects with an IQ greater than 50 had a broadly defined medical condition, whereas a full 40% of the individuals with an IQ less than 50 met the broad criteria for a medical condition (Barton and Volkmar 1998). Steffenburg (1991) used this association to propose potentially etiologic subgroups

of autism based on the associated medical condition. Her groupings included 1) pure hereditary autism, 2) other hereditary conditions (e.g., neurofibromatosis, tuberous sclerosis, fragile X syndrome), 3) other specific brain damage conditions (e.g., Möbius' syndrome, Rett's disorder), 4) nonspecific brain damage (e.g., epilepsy; hearing deficiencies; altered cerebrospinal fluid [CSF], electroencephalogram [EEG], computed tomography [CT] scan), and 5) unknown brain damage or genetic factors. One well-documented disease association occurs with tuberous sclerosis. This condition is an autosomal dominant disorder involving the growth of hamartomas, which are abnormal benign lesions, in several organs, including the brain. The CNS involvement is characterized by cortical and subependymal lesions, as well as seizures and mental retardation. Twenty-five percent of the patients with tuberous sclerosis also have autism, and up to 40% have a disorder in the PDD spectrum (Smalley et al. 1998). Tuberous sclerosis has been reported to occur in 1%–2% of the patients with autism (Smalley et al. 1992), and the rate is even higher in autistic individuals with a seizure disorder (Gillberg 1991). This co-occurrence between autism and tuberous sclerosis is much higher than would be predicted by prevalence rates of both of these rare disorders. Two genes have been identified, *TSC1* (Kandt et al. 1992) and *TSC2* (van Slegtenhorst et al. 1997), whose gene products are known as hamartin and tuberin, respectively. The gene products of both genes are thought to be tumor suppressors (A.J. Green et al. 1994; van Slegtenhorst et al. 1997). Smalley et al. (1998) developed several hypotheses that may explain why genes thought to govern regulation of growth and differentiation could be associated with autism. First, and most favored, loss of TSC protein function may lead to abnormal neural development in regions possibly related to autism. Second, TSC genes may actually be in close proximity, or linkage disequilibrium, to true autism genes. Finally, neuroanatomic and neuropsychologic sequelae of tuberous sclerosis gene dysfunction, like seizures or tubers, may indirectly damage areas of the brain associated with autism. Further investigation of TSC gene products in neurogenesis is warranted and may provide intriguing insights into one of a potential number of etiologies of autism.

## Mode of Inheritance

Several patterns of inheritance have been offered for autism, most deriving from particular clinical findings. The observation that the prevalence among girls is lower than among boys, yet female probands often have more autistic relatives, suggested a multifactorial hypothesis composed of genetic and nongenetic factors (Tsai et al.

1981). Likewise, the high male-to-female ratio and association with fragile X syndrome have suggested X-linked mechanisms, although enthusiasm for this theory has been tempered by the lack of linkage findings on the X chromosome (see next section). Genomic imprinting also has been suggested as a mode of inheritance that attempts to solve the problem of unequal sex prevalence (Skuse 2000). More formal attempts at understanding the mode of inheritance have had varied results. Ritvo et al. (1985) performed a classical segregation analysis on 46 multiple nuclear families (i.e., two or three autistic probands per family) and reported a segregation ratio close to that expected for an autosomal recessive mode of inheritance. They rejected both dominant and polygenic inheritance in these families. These data must be interpreted in light of the multiply affected ascertainment bias of the study. The same group produced different conclusions when they carried out a segregation analysis on all cases in a "well-defined" population (Jorde et al. 1991). Jorde et al. used a mixed model in 185 families and determined that the only inconsistent model was a single major locus model. Pickles et al. (1995) used an analytic strategy that focused on the decrease in relative risk with degree of relatedness and estimated that three loci were most likely involved (range = 2–10). Together, these studies suggested that the interaction of multiple genes is more likely to cause autism than is a single major locus. The issues of selection due to low reproduction rates, phenotypic uncertainty, and genetic heterogeneity all complicate the elucidation of the mode of inheritance of autism. Attempts to determine clinical markers of heterogeneity have proven frustrating. One group found no obvious indicators of heterogeneity with estimations of clinical variability between and within MZ twin pairs (Le Couteur et al. 1996). A similar approach was used in 37 multiplex families, and again there was no concordance for IQ or specific autistic symptoms, although some repetitive and ritualistic behaviors seemed to show some intrafamily concordance (Spiker et al. 1994).

## Linkage Analysis

The last decade has seen the first attempts to identify susceptibility loci for autism. Four international multicenter genome scans have been published. The first, performed by the International Molecular Genetic Study of Autism Consortium (1998; IMGSAC), was a two-stage screen of 87 British, German, and Dutch affected sibling pairs and 12 nonsibling relative pairs. In the first stage, 39 families were typed with 354 markers, yielding 62 markers with maximum lod scores greater than 1.0. Sixty additional families were then typed in the second stage with 175 markers that were derived from the regions of

interest from the first stage. The combined results identified six chromosomal regions with maximum lod scores greater than 1.0 (chromosomes 4, 7, 10, 16, 19, 22). The highest score observed, 2.53, was seen on 7q, with the score increasing to 3.55 in a subgroup of 56 of 66 families from the United Kingdom.

In the second study, 51 multiplex families from seven countries were genotyped with 264 microsatellite markers (Philippe et al. 1999). Based on two-point affected sib-pair analysis, 12 markers showed maximum lod scores greater than 0.6 (nominal $P<0.05$) on chromosomes 2, 4, 5, 6, 10, 15, 16, 18, 19, and X, the highest scores being on 6, 18, and 19. When subjected to multipoint analysis, the regions on 2, 18, and X became nonsignificant, and a region of 7 reached significance. This study showed regions of overlap with the IMGSAC study at 2q, 7q, 16p, and 19p.

The third genome scan comprised the largest sample, totaling 147 affected sib pairs in 139 sibships (Risch et al. 1999). In the first stage, 97 independent affected sib pairs in 90 multiplex sibships were screened with a set of 362 markers. These same families were also genotyped with a second set of 157 new markers that were in the 7q region derived from the IMGSAC or in regions of large gaps of chromosomal coverage. In the second stage, 50 affected sib pairs from 49 families were genotyped with the first set of markers and 89 markers from the second set. The maximum multipoint lod score occurred on 1p, with a score of 2.15 for the entire sample. Regions on 7p, 17p, and 18q also showed scores greater than 1.0, whereas the regions from the two earlier published genome scans showed only "modestly" positive lod scores.

The fourth study, performed by the Collaborative Linkage Study of Autism, used 75 multiplex families and 416 markers (Barrett et al. 1999). In contrast to the nonparametric approaches of the previous scans, Barrett et al. used parametric analyses. They found maximum multipoint heterogeneity lod scores of 3.0 and 2.3 for two markers on chromosomes 13 and 2.2 for a 7q marker. These were found under a recessive model, with 35%, 33%, and 29% of the families being linked, respectively.

From these four studies, the region of 7q is clearly the most interesting. Combining these observations with the discovery of a paracentric inversion in the 7q22–q31.2 region in a multiply affected sibship, Ashley-Koch et al. (1999) went on to genotype 76 multiplex families with nine microsatellite markers covering a 35-cM region of 7q. Two markers in this region showed maximum lod scores of 2.01 and 1.77. Other studies have focused linkage analyses on a region of common chromosomal abnormalities in autism and are discussed later in this chapter.

The lack of robust linkage findings on the X chromosome in the above genome scans is of interest given the noted sex imbalance in prevalence. One study in which 38 multiplex families were genotyped with 35 X chromosome markers showed no significant findings, with a single marker showing a maximum lod score of 1.24 (Hallmayer et al. 1996). In summary, these studies suggest evidence for an autism susceptibility locus on 7q. Positional cloning of candidate genes and higher-density marker scans will determine whether these remarkable findings hold true.

## Molecular Approaches

**Chromosomal abnormalities.** Chromosomal abnormalities have long been associated with autism. In a thorough review, Gillberg (1998) catalogs much of what has been described. Based on diagnostic criteria from DSM-III, DSM-III-R, DSM-IV (American Psychiatric Association 1980, 1987, 1994), and ICD-10 (World Health Organization 1992), some 49 individuals with autism have been reported to have abnormalities of 16 of 22 autosomes and both sex chromosomes. With less stringent criteria, only chromosomes 14 and 20 have not been associated with autism (Gillberg 1998). One survey found that 5% of autistic individuals had a major chromosomal abnormality (Ritvo et al. 1990). Anomalies occur most often in patients with mental retardation, with chromosome 15 abnormalities being particularly common and showing deletions and partial trisomy or tetrasomy in the 15q11–13 region. There appears to be some specificity to this region, as one study showed that 20 of 29 individuals selected for inverted duplications of chromosome 15 had "a high probability" of being autistic (Rineer et al. 1998). This is especially interesting in that deletions in this region are also implicated in Angelman syndrome, a behavioral syndrome that is characterized by prominent mental retardation, ataxic gait, and episodic smiling and laughing. In one survey of a population of 49,000 children, all 4 children diagnosed with Angelman syndrome also met the criteria for autism (Steffenburg et al. 1996). Interest in this region has spawned focused linkage studies, which have produced promising results (Bass et al. 1999; Cook et al. 1998), as well as successful efforts in physical mapping of the region (Maddox et al. 1999). Although it is still unclear what role chromosomal anomalies may play in autism, the strength of their association appears strong and thus will catalyze further investigation.

**Candidate genes.** The region of chromosome 15q11–13 harbors several genes that may be interesting autism candidate genes (Lamb et al. 2000). A cluster of genes comprising the $\alpha_5$, $\beta_3$, and $\gamma_3$ subunits of the $\gamma$-aminobutyric acid (GABA) receptor lies in the region. GABA is the chief inhibitory neurotransmitter in the CNS, and the GABA system is thought to be involved in seizure disorders. Mice deficient for the $\beta_3$ subunit show abnormal EEG findings, experience seizures, and engage in behavior reported to be similar to that in patients with Angelman syndrome (learning deficits, hyperactivity, poor motor coordination, and disturbed rest-activity patterns) (DeLorey et al. 1998). Cook et al. (1998) used a microsatellite marker located in the third intron of the human $\beta_3$ gene (*GABRB3*), as well as eight other markers in the region, to genotype 140 autistic families. The *GABRB3* marker was in significant linkage disequilibrium with autism. The markers immediately adjacent to the *GABRB3* marker showed no such signal, raising some concern that this might be a false-positive result. Another group used five of the same markers, including the *GABRB3* microsatellite, plus two others in the region to genotype 94 families from the IMGSAC dataset and was unable to replicate this finding (Maestrini et al. 1999). Another gene in this region, *UBE3A*, which encodes E6-AP ubiquitin-protein ligase, has been found to be causative for a proportion of persons with Angelman syndrome (Kishino et al. 1997). The promoter and coding region of this gene were sequenced from DNA from 10 autistic individuals, and no functional mutations were identified (Veenstra-VanderWeele et al. 1999). These studies, although initially promising and etiologically appealing, do not currently provide strong evidence for involvement of this region in autism.

A second avenue of research stems from investigations that showed elevated blood serotonin levels in autistic individuals, when compared with control subjects (Abramson et al. 1989; J.C. Anderson et al. 1987). Serotonin levels were higher in autistic persons with autistic siblings, compared with autistic probands with no affected siblings, suggesting a relation between serotonin and a genetic diathesis for autism (Piven et al. 1991). The utility of serotonergic drugs in autism has rekindled interest in the serotonin system. A family-based study of 86 parent-proband trios showed significant linkage disequilibrium with a functional promoter polymorphism in the serotonin transporter gene (*SLC6A4*), the protein responsible for recycling synaptic serotonin and the target of many psychoactive medications (Cook et al. 1997). A similar approach was used by another group in 52 parent-proband trios, and the same association was not found (Klauck et al. 1997). Ninety families in the IMGSAC dataset likewise showed no association between the serotonin transporter and autism (Maestrini et al. 1999) nor did a case-control study with 72 autistic individuals (Zhong et al. 1999). Polymorphisms in the serotonin type 2A and type 7 (5-HT$_{2A}$ and 5-HT$_7$) receptor genes, *HTR2A* and *HTR7*, respectively, also have failed to be associated with autism (Herault et al. 1996; Lassig et al. 1999).

# Metachromatic Leukodystrophy

Leukodystrophies are degenerative disorders that involve the white matter of the brain. They are characterized by deterioration following a period of normal development, motor impairment, and lack of seizures. Metachromatic leukodystrophy (MLD) is a disorder characterized by diffuse demyelination and progressive neurologic symptoms. This disease is fatal if untreated. In MLD, cerebroside sulfate, an important component of myelin, is sequestered in lysosomes because of a deficiency in arylsulfatase A (EC 3.1.6.1 [sulfuric ester hydrolase]). The enzyme defect leads to the accumulation of cerebroside sulfate, a metachromatic sphingolipid, in the peripheral and central white matter and in peripheral organs. Some rarer cases may result from multiple sulfatase deficiencies. Three clinical types are described: late infantile, juvenile, and adult arylsulfatase A deficiency. Psychosis may be the first manifestation of the adult form (Alves et al. 1986; Cerizza et al. 1987; Finelli 1985; Skomer et al. 1983).

## Clinical Types of Metachromatic Leukodystrophy and Associated Conditions

The infantile form of MLD presents at age 1–2 years and is characterized by loss of acquired motor skills, gait disturbance, and ataxia. Mental deterioration accompanies disease progression. The EEG shows marked cerebral slowing, and electromyography shows peripheral nerve involvement (decreased motor and sensory nerve conduction velocities). Spasticity and myoclonic jerks also become prominent as the illness progresses, and deep tendon reflexes are lost. This form of MLD has a short course, and death usually occurs about 1–7 years after onset.

The juvenile-onset type of MLD presents between ages 3 and 16 years. Gait disturbance and movement disorders are seen, concomitant with behavior problems and subtle mental deterioration. Progression of symptoms occurs more slowly than in the infantile form. Most of these cases are fatal, but in a few cases the course of disease can be up to 20 years.

The adult-onset form of MLD manifests after age 16 but is not clearly demarcated from the juvenile form. Adult-onset MLD also can begin in very late life. Presentation can include personality changes and intellectual deterioration, and it must be considered in the etiology of psychotic and dementing disorders, especially presenile dementia. Psychiatric symptoms often precede neurologic symptoms. Juvenile- and adult-onset MLD are often mistakenly diagnosed as attention-deficit/hyperactivity disorder (ADHD), family problems, or early schizophrenia. The CNS process can be detected by white matter changes on CT and MRI. This form of MLD has a slow progression and a 5- to 10-year survival period.

In addition to these three clinical forms of MLD, which result from deficiencies in arylsulfatase A activity due to mutations in the arylsulfatase A gene, there are three associated conditions. The first is termed *arylsulfatase A pseudodeficiency* and is characterized by low arylsulfatase A activity in healthy persons. These people do not store metachromatic material and have normal excretion of urinary sulfatidate (Barth et al. 1994a). Arylsulfatase A pseudodeficiency has been found in psychiatric patients, although any causal relationship is quite speculative. Two of 295 psychiatric and neurologic patients studied by Herska et al. (1987) and 13 of 99 chronic psychiatric patients evaluated by Galbraith et al. (1989) had arylsulfatase A deficiency, with the normal allele and intact enzyme kinetic features.

The second associated condition is a nonallelic variant of MLD known as *multiple sulfatase deficiency*. This is an autosomal recessive disorder with at least seven different deficient sulfatases, one of which is arylsulfatase A (Kolodny 1989).

The third condition is another nonallelic condition—*sphingolipid activator protein B–deficient MLD*. In this condition, the arylsulfatase A gene is normal. The mutation is located in the gene that codes for sphingolipid activator protein B, which makes the cerebroside sulfate accessible to the enzyme (Kolodny 1989) and which is necessary for arylsulfatase A to function correctly.

## Prenatal Diagnosis and Possible Treatment

Prenatal diagnosis of MLD is based on identification of reduced arylsulfatase A in the fetus by either amniocentesis or chorionic villus sampling. Presymptomatic diagnosis can be made in apparently unaffected families by reduced arylsulfatase A enzyme activity and diminished nerve conduction velocity. In years past, MLD was an untreatable disease that inexorably led to death. However, some investigators have reported success in bone marrow transplantation early in the course of juvenile- and adult-onset MLD (Krivit et al. 1999) (see Figure 10–9). Asymptomatic siblings who screen positive for MLD (through measurement of urinary sulfatide) have been

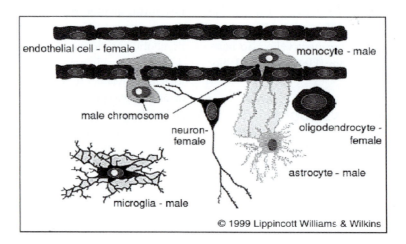

**FIGURE 10–9.** Entry of monocytes into the central nervous system.

*Source.* Krivit W, Peters C, Shapiro EG: "Bone Marrow Transplantation as Effective Treatment of Central Nervous System Disease in Globoid Cell Leukodystrophy, Metachromatic Leukodystrophy, Adrenoleukodystrophy, Mannosidosis, Fucosidosis, Aspartylglucosaminuria, Hurler, Maroteaux-Lamy, and Sly Syndromes, and Gaucher Disease Type III." *Current Opinion in Neurology* 12:167–176, 1999.

given bone marrow transplantation and have remained asymptomatic.

## Epidemiologic Studies

The incidence of the late-infantile form of MLD is 2.5 in 100,000 (Gustavson and Hagberg 1971); the juvenile form has an incidence of 6 in 100,000. Disease frequency differs across racial/ethnic groups. Molecular studies illustrate that different alleles exist in different populations, providing evidence for a series of founder effects. MLD is most prevalent among Habbanite Jews, among whom 1 in every 75 newborns is found to be affected (Zlotogora et al. 1995).

## Family Studies

Siblings with MLD who have identical biochemical profiles and dramatically different clinical courses have been described (Clark et al. 1989). Usually, however, the clinical picture is comparable within a family. Yet intrafamilial variation in clinical expression in MLD, as in other lysosomal storage diseases, is common. This can include dissimilarity in age at onset, severity, and neurologic involvement. The variation may be secondary to genetic heterogeneity or related to genetic factors (Zlotogora 1987).

## Mode of Inheritance

Most MLD is considered to be autosomal recessive; this was suggested by the proportion of affected siblings with the juvenile type (Schutta et al. 1966). Also, heterozygotes usually have a normal phenotype. However, dominant forms of MLD have been described in some family studies. In one study (Kohn et al. 1988), MLD heterozygotes showed normal neurologic and EEG examinations but had impaired performance on tests involving spatial and constructional components.

## Molecular Approaches

The arylsulfatase A gene is located on 22q. Stein et al. (1989) cloned and sequenced a full-length cDNA for human arylsulfatase A, which is polymorphic. Kreysing et al. (1990) determined the structure of the arylsulfatase A gene, which includes 3.2 kb of genomic DNA divided into eight exons. Three splice variants of mRNA are transcribed from the gene. The arylsulfatase A protein contains 506 residues with three potential $N$-glycosylation sites. Arylsulfatase A is a 62-kd peptide that acts to remove the sulfate from cerebroside sulfate, initiating degradation. In arylsulfatase A–deficient individuals, the cerebroside accumulates in a variety of tissues, including kidney, gallbladder, and bile ducts, but only oligodendrocytes seem to be affected functionally (Gieselmann et al. 1998).

More than 40 mutations of the arylsulfatase A gene have been identified, and MLD appears to be genetically heterogeneous. Most mutations are confined to discrete subpopulations; however, two mutations that are prevalent in Caucasian populations each account for about 25%, and thus for about half, of all MLD alleles (Gieselmann et al. 1991; Polten et al. 1991). One is a splice donor site mutation and the other is an amino acid substitution (proline426 to leucine [Pro426Leu]). These two mutations are uncommon in Japanese patients, who more frequently have a glycine99 to aspartic acid (Gly99Asp) substitution allele (Kondo et al. 1991).

Affected Habbanite Jews are homozygous for Pro377Leu substitution (Zlotogora et al. 1995). Ethnically Arabic individuals in Australia who have MLD tend to have a threonine274 to methionine (Thr274Met) substitution (Harvey et al. 1993; Heinisch et al. 1995), whereas a splice donor site mutation in intron 4 is common in affected Navajo Indians (Pastor-Soler et al. 1994).

There seems to be evidence of genotype-phenotype correlation in Caucasian populations because the two most common alleles in this group are associated with two different clinical forms of the disease. Gieselmann et al. (1994) found that among Caucasians, all patients who were homozygous for a splice donor site allele that causes a complete loss of enzyme activity had the more severe early-onset late-infantile form of the disease; patients who were homozygous for an allele associated with low amounts of residual enzyme activity mainly had the adult form of MLD; and all patients who were compound heterozygotes (i.e., having one of each of these two alleles) had the intermediate juvenile form.

In addition to normal and mutant alleles, there is a arylsulfatase A pseudodeficiency allele; its enzyme lacks a glycosylation site but has sufficient residual activity to function (Ameen et al. 1990). A level of 10% or more of arylsulfatase A activity is consistent with a normal phenotype (Aicardi 1993). The pseudodeficiency allele has a high frequency in general populations and is estimated to have a range of 7%–15% (Barth et al. 1994b; Hohenschutz et al. 1989; P.V. Nelson et al. 1991). The differential diagnosis between arylsulfatase A pseudodeficiency is important in genetic counseling because arylsulfatase A pseudodeficiency may coexist in families carrying MLD mutations (Barth et al. 1993a, 1993b; Gieselmann et al. 1991).

**Mouse models.** Arylsulfatase A–deficient mice have been generated; like human MLD patients, they are unable to degrade sulfatide and accumulate the substance intralysosomally in both neuronal and nonneuronal tissues. Both knockout mice and affected humans have astrogliosis and reduction of axonal diameter (Hess et al. 1996); they also share gait abnormalities and imbalance (Hess et al. 1996). Unlike human MLD patients, knockout mice have a relatively minor phenotype with less demyelination; also, unlike humans, these mice are deaf. Interestingly, although deafness is not a feature of human MLD, affected patients show changes in brain-stem auditory evoked potentials early in the course of illness (F.R. Brown et al. 1981).

Arylsulfatase A–deficient mice have been successfully transplanted with bone marrow cells containing a retroviral vector that expresses arylsulfatase A; arylsulfatase A is then expressed for up to 5 months, but storage material is not reduced (Gieselmann et al. 1998). It is thought that monocytes in the donor bone marrow transverse the blood-brain barrier and become perivascular microglia that secrete arylsulfatase A, which is then endocytosed and used by deficient host glial cells (see Figure 10–9). Based on this work, bone marrow transplantation has been used in MLD patients with some success, depending on the type of MLD and the stage of illness.

## Dyslexia

Dyslexia was first described about a century ago as "congenital word blindness." It is composed of reading and spelling deficits that cannot be accounted for by mental retardation, emotional disturbance, neurologic disorder, hearing deficits, or visual problems. Reading and spelling abilities in dyslexia are inconsistent with a child's mental age, educational exposure, and apparent intellectual potential (Vandenberg et al. 1986). One standard definition is that age-expected reading and spelling levels are 1 to 2 standard deviations below IQ.

Dyslexia usually becomes evident during first grade, when affected children may have difficulty reciting the alphabet, naming letters, or reciting rhymes. However, dyslexia may not be identified in some children with high IQs until as late as the fourth grade because of compensatory strategies. Dyslexia is not transitional or confined to a phase in development; children who have difficulty reading in the second grade tend to remain in the lowest strata of reading ability by the eighth grade (reviewed in Warnke 1999).

Some theories about dyslexia have focused on visual processing deficits; individuals with dyslexia have been found to have abnormal eye movements, lack of eye dominance, deficits in processing fast visual sequences, abnormal visual evoked potentials, and abnormalities in the lateral geniculate nuclei, a part of the thalamus that connects with the visual cortex (reviewed in Warnke 1999). Also, functional brain imaging shows abnormal visual processing in dyslexia (Eden et al. 1996).

In recent years, data have emerged that support the idea that dyslexia stems from deficits in timing precision and coordination that affect the visual, auditory, and motor systems. Motor incoordination has been found to aggregate with affected status in a subset of dyslexic families and is highly correlated with slow syllable repetition (Wolff 1999). Shaywitz (1998) argued that the central deficit in dyslexia is phonologic: dyslexic individuals have trouble breaking down both written and spoken words into smaller units of sound. At-risk children can then be identified by reading-readiness tests that assess language delays and difficulty in attending to the sound of words.

## Epidemiologic Studies

Reading ability occurs along a continuum, with reading disability representing the lower tail of a normal distribution (Shaywitz et al. 1992). Estimates of the prevalence of dyslexia typically range from 5% to 10% of schoolchildren (Benton and Pearl 1978) and 80% of the children who are identified as learning disabled (Lerner 1989). Although earlier studies suggested a preponderance of boys with dyslexia (Vandenberg et al. 1986), more recent studies show that the prevalence is about equal in boys and girls (Shaywitz et al. 1990; Wadsworth et al. 1992). An increased risk of dyslexia has been associated with season of birth patterns; proposed explanations include weather-related fetal stress, variations in nutrition, and viral illness (Livingston et al. 1993). However, the discrepancy also has been accounted for by age at school entrance and kindergarten entrance cutoff dates (Flynn et al. 1996). Children at risk for dyslexia have delays in literacy at age 6 years; early speech and language skills, specifically letter knowledge at 45 months, predict later reading difficulties (Gallagher et al. 2000). Dyslexic children are at risk for behavioral and other difficulties; among 8-year-old German dyslexic children, 25% underwent criminal proceedings by age 18 and 26% were unemployed at age 25 (compared with 4% of control subjects) (Esser and Schmidt 1994). In one study, 41% of Swedish prison inmates were found to have dyslexia (Jenner et al. 1999).

## Family Studies

That reading disability aggregates in families was noted as early as 1907 (Stephenson 1907). Subsequently, numerous reports of dyslexia in several generations of extended pedigrees appeared (Finucci et al. 1976; Marshall and Ferguson 1939). In one series, 45% (29 of 65) of the families of reading-disabled probands had secondary cases of dyslexia (Zahalkova et al. 1972). Male relatives of affected individuals appear to be affected more often than do female relatives (Wolf 1967). In the Colorado Family Reading Study, the families of 125 dyslexic probands were systematically compared with those of 125 control subjects. A variety of deficits (e.g., in both reading recognition and reading comprehension) in the parents and siblings of probands conclusively confirmed the familial nature of the disorder (DeFries et al. 1978).

The prevalence of dyslexia is 38%–62% in siblings and 20%–49% in parents of dyslexic children (reviewed in Warnke 1999) and 23%–65% in children of those with

dyslexia (Shaywitz 1998). Wolff and Melngailis (1994) found that sibs of dyslexic subjects had a greater risk for reading difficulties when one parent was affected than when neither parent was affected. Sibs also were at greater risk for academic problems and were more severely impaired when the father, rather than the mother, was the affected parent or when both parents were affected. This study found indirect evidence that assortative mating may codetermine patterns of affectation in families with dyslexia.

Geschwind and Behan (1982, 1984) and Geschwind and Galaburda (1985a, 1985b) suggested associations among learning disorders, immune disorders, and non-right-handedness, theorizing that prenatal testosterone acted independently on the developing thymus and the brain. In family and twin samples, Gilger et al. (1992a) found an association between reading disorders and immune disorders in only two of four samples. An autoimmune basis to dyslexia remains possible, especially given that linkage has been found between dyslexia and a region of chromosome 6 that includes an HLA locus (Cardon et al. 1994).

## Twin Studies

Concordance rates for dyslexia in MZ twin pairs have ranged from 84% to 100%; rates in these studies for same-sex DZ twin pairs have ranged from 21% to 29% (Bakwin 1973; Hermann and Norrie 1958). These results further support the importance of genetic factors in the etiology of reading disability.

Twin studies in Colorado found that genetic factors account for about half of the observed deficits in word recognition, orthographic coding, and phonologic decoding and awareness (Gayan and Olson 1999). Furthermore, genetic factors that influence phonologic decoding and verbal IQ have been found to account for approximately 82% of the observed correlation between reading and math performance in affected twins (Light et al. 1998). Twin studies also show that the heritability of spelling is maybe greater than that of reading (Stevenson et al. 1987).

In a study of MZ and DZ twin pairs in which at least one member had a reading disability, Gilger et al. (1992b) found that ADHD and reading disabilities occurred more frequently together than would be expected by chance, but it was unclear whether this was due to genetic vulnerability.

## Mode of Inheritance

In an extensive (but nonblinded) study of the families of 116 dyslexic probands, Hallgren (1950) found evidence to support an autosomal dominant mode of inheritance; a probable direct line of descent through three generations was seen in 29 families, and at least one affected parent was present in 83% of the cases. Conversely, the absence of consanguinity in these families argued against recessive inheritance. Statistical analyses of families in which one parent was affected gave mendelian ratios for males that were consistent with single-gene effects, whereas the results for females did not fit such a hypothesis. These data were thought to be compatible with sex-related differences in disease penetrance, the illness affecting or less frequently being diagnosed in females (Hallgren 1950). In later reanalyses, Hallgren's data were thought to be consistent with autosomal dominant inheritance with reduced penetrance in males but essentially autosomal recessive inheritance in females (Sladen 1970). Similarly, formal segregation analysis of the Colorado Family Reading Study was consistent with autosomal recessive inheritance in the families of female probands (Lewitter et al. 1980).

Alternatively, other authors, such as Finucci (1976), contend that the variation in severity of illness among individuals and the unequal distribution in illness between the sexes are consistent with a polygenic mode of inheritance. The "mixed-model" hypothesis is yet another theory, presented by Pennington et al. (1991). In the mixed model, the major gene and polygenic hypotheses can be combined, and major genes are thought to operate in the context of a multifactorial background. This complex segregation analysis study found evidence for a single major locus transmission in three families and polygenic transmission in the fourth sample. These findings suggest the potential of using linkage techniques to identify potential major loci for dyslexia.

### Linkage Analysis

Reading is such a complex process that it might be expected that several genes would contribute to reading skills; support for genetic heterogeneity in subjects with dyslexia has come from linkage analysis.

In an examination of 9 pedigrees with 50 affected and 34 unaffected individuals, linkage was established to variations in banding patterns (heteromorphisms) on 15q, with a maximum lod score of 3.24 (S. Smith et al. 1983). Of note, one pedigree showed a very large negative lod score, suggesting a different genetic form of disorder in that family. Linkage to 15q21 has been confirmed (Grigorenko et al. 1997) and has specifically been linked to spelling disability (Nothen et al. 1999; Schulte-Korne et al. 1998). Evidence of linkage also has been reported for markers in the Rh region of chromosome 1

(1p34–36) (Rabin et al. 1993) and for a translocation between 1p and 2q (Froster et al. 1993).

Interval mapping of data from two independent samples of sib pairs, with at least one affected sib, found evidence for a quantitative trait locus for dyslexia at 6p21.3 (see Figure 10–10) (Cardon et al. 1994). This linkage was confirmed in further studies (Fisher et al. 1999; Gayan et al. 1999), especially with phonologic awareness (Grigorenko et al. 1997). However, linkage was not established when phonologic coding (spelling) was identified as the prime deficit in the dyslexia phenotype (Field and Kaplan 1998).

A genomewide search for linkage was done in an extended Norwegian family in which a relatively mild form of dyslexia was inherited as an autosomal dominant trait (Fagerheim et al. 1999); a region on 2p15–2p16 was found to cosegregate with dyslexia, with observed lod scores of 3.54, 2.92, and 4.32 (with three different diagnostic models).

In conclusion, children younger than 2 years whose language centers are injured often go on to develop adequate language ability; teenagers with similar injuries usually never regain normal language function. Understanding the genetics of dyslexia may enable the identification of at-risk toddlers, who may especially benefit from intervention, given their enormous neuroplasticity (Fagerheim et al. 1999).

## Dementia

### Alzheimer's Disease

AD is the most common form of dementia, accounting for about 70% of all cases (Morris 1994). AD usually begins after age 45 with a progressive clinical course leading over years to death; it is characterized by a gradual loss of memory and language. Psychiatric and behavioral symptoms are among the earliest signs and are accompanied by a slow decline in activities of daily living. As the illness progresses, more overtly neurologic signs may appear, such as upgoing toes, rigid limbs, frontal release findings, and seizures.

Currently, AD is a clinical diagnosis of exclusion and can be detected with certainty only at autopsy, when senile plaques, neurofibrillary tangles, and granulovacuolar degeneration are seen, mostly in the temporoparieto-occipital association cortex and hippocampal formation. Senile plaques consist largely of amyloid, whereas neurofibrillary tangles are composed of abnormally phosphorylated tau protein (Peskind 1996). The genes associated with familial AD are known to affect the formation and

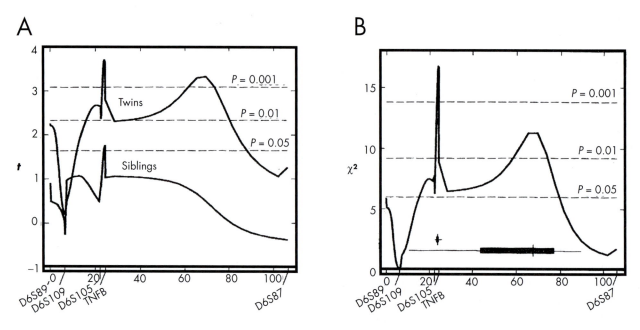

**FIGURE 10–10.**   Evidence for a quantitative trait locus (QTL) for dyslexia on 6p21.3. Interval mapping results for five DNA markers on chromosome 6 in kindred siblings and dizygotic (DZ) twins. *Panel A. t* Test statistic for each group. The predicted QTL is situated at position 24.2 cM in kindred siblings and at 23.8 cM in DZ twins. *Panel B.* Approximate $\chi^2$ statistics for the combined samples were computed by summing the squared *t* test values for siblings and twins in graph A. The maximal peak corresponds to QTL 0.4 cM distal to the tumore necrosis factor β (TNFB) marker. The solid bars represent the one-lod support interval for the primary and secondary peaks; the odds ratios decrease by a factor of 10 within these regions. The lines extending from the solid bars indicate two-lod support intervals, representing a decrease of 100 in the odds ratio. The two-lod support interval for the combined sample is fully contained within the *D6S105*-TNFB interval. The corresponding support interval for the secondary peak between TNFB and *D6S105* overlaps with that of the putative QTL between *D6S105* and TNFB, suggesting that the secondary peak is a "ghost image" of the major peak.
*Source.*   Adapted from Cardon LR, Smith SS, Fulkner DW, et al.: "Quantitative Trait Locus for Reading Disability on Chromosome 6." *Science* 266:276–279, 1994. Used with permission.

deposition of amyloid but not that of the tau protein. However, cognitive impairment in AD is more closely associated with the presence of tau-composed tangles and not the presence of amyloid plaques. This suggests that amyloid may play a primary role in pathogenesis but that tau may be a marker of disease progression.

In AD, primary motor and sensory areas are relatively spared, although subcortical structures also are affected. There is a loss of acetylcholinergic neurotransmitter cells from the nucleus basalis of Meynert (Whitehouse et al. 1981), a nucleus that projects widely to the cerebral cortex, hippocampus, and limbic formation. This loss of cholinergic axons underlies the cognitive deficits of AD, and the decrement of the enzyme choline acetyltransferase correlates with the extent of dementia (Coyle et al. 1983).

A score of 25 or less on Folstein's Mini-Mental State Exam (MMSE) in an elderly individual with a high school education should alert caregivers to the possibility of dementia (Farlow 1998). Test results that suggest AD in

the live patient include low β-amyloid protein and high tau protein levels in the CSF, as well as hypometabolism of the posterior parietal lobes seen with functional imaging, but these tests are controversial and costly (Farlow 1998). Structural imaging may show only nonspecific cortical atrophy and ventriculomegaly.

AD is a disease process and not a part of the normal process of brain aging. Age at onset before 60 distinguishes presenile from senile dementia, although this is debatable. The neuropathology is the same, although population studies suggest that the presenile group has more language dysfunction and a more rapid clinical course (Seltzer and Sherwin 1983).

## Epidemiologic Studies

The prevalence estimates of AD vary depending on the population sampled (community samples or nursing home residents), diagnostic criteria (different definitions of "significant impairment"), and age. A conservative estimate is that 1%–2% of the population between ages

65 and 74 and about a quarter of the population older than 85 are afflicted with AD (Hendrie 1998). The rate of AD has been found to approximately double every 5.1 years after age 40 (Hendrie 1998). In the United States, approximately 4 million people have AD, although this figure will likely triple over the next 50 years as people live longer and demographics shift toward a larger percentage of the population being elderly (Geldmacher and Whitehouse 1997). AD is said to be relatively more common in women, whereas multi-infarct dementia may be more common in men (Jorm et al. 1987).

AD has a lower prevalence in non-Western (Japan) and developing countries (India and Nigeria). This could be because different research methods are used in different studies, or it may reflect real differences among populations in prevalence of AD. Studies of migrant populations suggested that differences between groups may be more a function of environmental exposure than of genetic vulnerability because groups with similar genetic backgrounds who live in different parts of the world have different prevalence rates of AD. Also, AD prevalence rates are similar among different ethnic groups living in the same region. For example, the prevalence of AD in Japan is 1.5%, whereas ethnic Japanese in Honolulu, Hawaii, have a prevalence of AD of 5.4%, a rate comparable to that of Caucasians in Hawaii (White et al. 1996). Likewise, the prevalence of AD is much higher among African Americans in Indianapolis, Indiana (8.2%) than it is in Nigeria (2.3%) (Hendrie et al. 1995). The prevalence of AD in African Americans in Indianapolis, however, is close to the prevalence of AD in Japanese Americans in Seattle (6.3%), and to the prevalence of AD in mostly white Canadians (8.0%) (Canadian Study of Health and Aging 1994; Graves et al. 1996). These studies support the idea of the role of environment in the etiology of AD (however, different geographic mortality rates cannot absolutely be ruled out as a cause of differential AD prevalence in genetically similar groups). A possible mediating environmental factor may be diet: an association between AD and a susceptibility gene involved in lipid metabolism appears strongest in populations that have high-cholesterol, high-fat diets (see the Molecular Approaches section later in this chapter).

In addition to diet, many environmental factors have been theorized to play a role in the etiology of AD; they include metal intoxication (notably aluminum), head trauma, and others. Education, estrogen, smoking, and nonsteroidal anti-inflammatory agents have been studied as possible protective factors. Risk factor research in AD (Hendrie 1998) has been complicated by variations in methodology and problems inherent to each method (see Epidemiologic Studies section at the beginning of this chapter).

Aluminum has long been considered as a possible etiologic factor in AD, especially given that aluminum has been found to be associated with AD neuropathology. Case-control studies yield mixed results as to the association of AD with aluminum in the drinking water (Forster et al. 1995; Martyn et al. 1997; McLachlan et al. 1996). One study showed an association between dietary aluminum and AD risk (Rogers and Simon 1999). Many studies have failed to show any association between occupational exposure to aluminum and AD risk (Graves et al. 1998; Gun et al. 1997; Salib and Hillier 1996).

Evidence for traumatic brain injury as a risk factor for AD is mixed, with some studies showing an association and others not (Harwood et al. 1999a; Hendrie 1998; Launer et al. 1999; Mehta et al. 1999; O'Meara et al. 1997; Salib and Hillier 1997). A rare prospective study of AD incidence showed that traumatic brain injury leads to a relative risk of AD of 4.1 (1.3–12.7) for 5 years after traumatic brain injury occurs. A few studies (Mayeux et al. 1995b; Tang et al. 1996) have shown that increased risk for AD in patients with prior traumatic brain injury was significant only for individuals who had a specific polymorphism (apo e4) at an AD susceptibility gene that encodes apolipoprotein E (see Molecular Approaches section later in this chapter). However, another study found exactly the opposite—namely, that an association existed only in individuals lacking this specific polymorphism (Guo et al. 2000). Yet a third found that the association of traumatic brain injury and AD was entirely independent of the presence of this polymorphism (O'Meara et al. 1997). The association between traumatic brain injury and AD risk may be affected also by the severity of traumatic brain injury (loss of consciousness or not) and by family history of AD (Guo et al. 2000). One study suggested that traumatic brain injury does not increase absolute risk but shortens time to onset in those patients destined to have developed AD anyway (Nemetz et al. 1999).

More education may be protective against AD or at least delay the onset of obvious symptoms (Katzman 1993). Many studies have shown an association between lower level of education and AD (Callahan et al. 1996; Launer et al. 1999; Mortel et al. 1995). However, in an Italian study, this association was no longer significant when adjusted for age and sex (Bonaiuto et al. 1995). Another study found that education was associated only with non-Alzheimer's dementia (Cobb et al. 1995). In a rare prospective study of at-risk individuals, low education level was associated with a doubling of AD incidence (Stern et al. 1994). In one model, higher education level either causes or reflects greater cognitive reserve and adaptation, so that such individuals appear less symptomatic in the face of equivalent neuropathology. This is supported by findings from brain imaging that, given the same level of symptom severity, more educated individuals have greater perfusion deficits than do those with little schooling (Stern et al. 1992). However, it cannot be ruled out that education may be an indicator of socioeconomic status or may be linked to other factors that influence risk of AD, such as diet, occupation, or toxic exposures (Canadian Study of Health and Aging 1994). For example, education level is associated with AD risk in white non-Hispanics but not in white Hispanics (Harwood et al. 1999a). Furthermore, an apparent association between AD and education may be spurious and reflect a lack of sensitivity in determining disease status in more educated individuals with current methods (Hendrie 1998). It is important to determine whether education may directly play a protective role because this has implications for prevention and treatment of AD. At this time, trials of cognitive training are under way in individuals identified as at risk for AD (Hendrie 1998).

Case-control studies yield results that suggest that estrogen replacement therapy (ERT) may play a protective role in the etiology of AD. ERT is more common in control subjects than in AD patients; among AD patients, ERT is associated with better cognition (V.W. Henderson et al. 1994). In a cohort of retired women in southern California, a case-control study showed that AD was less prevalent among women who had ERT than among women who did not (Paganini-Hill and Henderson 1996). In the Baltimore Longitudinal Study on Aging, a prospective study, ERT users had a relative risk for AD of 0.46 (95% confidence interval = 0.21–1.00). In the Italian Longitudinal Study on Aging, women with AD were significantly less likely to have had ERT (odds ratio = 0.24; 95% confidence interval = 0.07–0.77) (Baldereschi et al. 1998). This association remained significant even after adjustment for age, education, age at menarche, age at menopause, smoking, alcohol use, body weight, and number of children. Although these studies are suggestive, use of ERT was not random among subjects, so that women who are less likely to develop AD also may be more likely to use ERT, for whatever reason. Although double-blind, placebo-controlled ERT studies have been done in mild to moderate AD (Mulnard et al. 2000), no such studies have yet been done to assess AD prevention.

Smoking has been found in different studies to be positively correlated, negatively correlated, and not at all associated with AD risk. Meta-analyses of series of case-control studies strongly suggest that smoking has a pro-

tective role in AD (Graves et al. 1991; P.N. Lee 1994). However, a prospective cohort study of more than 30,000 British physicians found no correlation between smoking and AD (Doll et al. 2000). A pooled analysis of four prospective studies showed that smoking increases AD risk, especially in men (Launer et al. 1999). Of note, two independent longitudinal follow-up studies of community-based samples of individuals older than 55 found very similar results: a doubling of AD risk for smoking overall and an interaction with apolipoprotein E polymorphism in risk, with the normally disease-promoting APOE*E4 actually being protective against increased risk from smoking (Merchant et al. 1999; A. Ott et al. 1998).

Several large epidemiologic studies showed that exposure to either corticosteroids or nonsteroidal anti-inflammatory drugs is associated with a lower risk of AD (Breitner et al. 1994; J.B. Rich et al. 1995). This may not be surprising because amyloid is a proinflammatory substance, and neuropathologic examination shows that plaques are surrounded by signs of inflammation.

## Family Studies

Early epidemiologic studies reported an increased prevalence of dementia in the family members of AD patients: 25%–40% of the patients with AD had at least one affected first-degree relative (Davies 1986). Family studies of AD have been well reviewed by St. George-Hyslop et al. (1989). These studies are hindered by the late age at onset because individuals can die from other conditions or develop a dementia from a different etiology. The increased family prevalence of AD occurs predominantly in those with early-onset disease (Heston 1981), although such cases may be just more easily ascertained, and both early- and late-onset cases often occur within a single family.

The estimates of increased risk for first-degree relatives are variable and small: 10%–14.4% for parents and 3.8%–13.9% for siblings (Amaducci et al. 1986; Constantinidis et al. 1962; Heston and Mastri 1977; Heston et al. 1981; Heyman et al. 1983; Whalley et al. 1982). Life table studies that adjust for non-AD deaths, however, indicate that the risk of AD may be as high as 50% in family members by age 90, compared with 10% for control subjects (Breitner et al. 1986; Huff et al. 1988; Mohs et al. 1987). These analyses support a common autosomal gene for AD, with an age-dependent penetrance. Another study (Farrer et al. 1989), factoring in diagnostic uncertainties, found a risk of only 24% to first-degree relatives by age 93 and of 16% to control subjects by age 90. These and other estimates of the increase in AD risk to family members vary widely.

## Twin Studies

Twin studies have shown consistently higher concordance rates for MZ twin pairs than for DZ twin pairs, ranging from 21% to 67% for MZ twin pairs and 8% to 50% for DZ twin pairs (Breitner et al. 1995; Gatz et al. 1997; L.F. Jarvik et al. 1980; Kallmann 1956; Nee et al. 1987; Raiha et al. 1996). One study found that MZ twins concordant for AD had a significantly higher frequency of a positive family history than did discordant MZ twins (Rapoport et al. 1991). These results suggest heritability in at least some forms of AD (although common exposures to environmental risks cannot be entirely ruled out). Discordant twins may have disease that results either from variation in environmental influences or from a somatic chromosomal change following zygotic division. They also could have heritable disease with variation in ages at onset; concordant MZ twin pairs can differ in age at onset by as many as 20 years (Chandra et al. 1998). For example, a study of an 81-year-old female discordant MZ twin pair with clinical assessments, standardized rating scales, and brain imaging studies suggested that the unaffected twin was developing the prodrome of AD and that varied life histories may have explained the discordance and/or possible delay in onset for the apparently unaffected twin (Small et al. 1993). Furthermore, variation in ages at onset of AD in twins has been linked to both hysterectomy and infection (Nee and Lippa 1999).

## High-Risk Studies

About one half of elderly individuals found to have cognitive impairment will progress to clinical dementia within 4–5 years (Devanand et al. 1997; Petersen et al. 1995). Prospective studies have shown that depressed mood in late life may herald the onset of a progressive dementia, either by increasing risk for AD or as part of an AD prodrome (Devanand et al. 1996). Depressive episodes double the risk for AD even 20 years later (Speck et al. 1995).

## Mode of Inheritance

Clearly familial forms of early-onset AD have an autosomal dominant mode of inheritance and age-dependent penetrance. A "susceptibility gene" for AD has been found that may act as a modifier of other genotypes and as a modifier of environmental exposures. This gene, the apolipoprotein E (APOE) gene, appears to play a role in all forms of AD, both early-onset and late-onset familial and sporadic AD. Familial forms of late-onset AD have a less clear inheritance pattern and may result from a more complex interaction of genes and environment. The apolipoprotein E protein is neither necessary nor sufficient to produce AD, and its effect on phenotype is nonmendelian. Its modifying effect is likely age-dependent and population-specific.

## Molecular Approaches

The involvement of three loci in early-onset familial AD has been identified through linkage studies: the APP gene on chromosome 21 (Goate et al. 1991), the presenilin 1 gene on chromosome 14 (Sherrington et al. 1995), and the presenilin 2 gene on chromosome 1 (Levy-Lehad et al. 1995; Rogaev et al. 1995). Five percent of all early-onset AD cases are accounted for by mutations in APP, 18%–50% in presenilin 1, and fewer than 1% in presenilin 2 (Cruts et al. 1998). Although these three loci are responsible for fewer than 5% of all cases of AD, their identification has shed light on the biochemistry of amyloid formation and deposition in the human brain, which may have implications for treatment of AD. Interestingly, although tau protein is involved in the neuropathology of AD, mutations in the TAU gene are not associated with AD but instead with frontotemporal dementia and progressive supranuclear palsy.

The first gene to be linked to early-onset familial AD was the APP gene. Because patients with Down syndrome or trisomy 21 have neuropathology similar to that seen in patients with AD, the first segregation analyses in familial AD were done on polymorphic markers from chromosome 21 (Mann 1988). A natural candidate gene was the APP gene, located at 21q21.2, because it codes for a precursor of β-amyloid, a major component in the senile plaques of AD (Kang et al. 1987; Tanzi et al. 1987). Positive linkage was found in only a subset of families with familial AD, implying genetic heterogeneity in AD. APP is a large protein that is cleaved to form β-amyloid peptides that range in length from 39 to 43 amino acids. All known APP mutations are near proteolytic cleavage sites involved in the formation of β-amyloid. Some AD-associated mutations lead to a greater relative concentration of longer β-amyloid proteins (42 or 43 amino acids), which are less soluble and more prone to aggregation than shorter β-amyloid proteins (Hardy 1996). Other APP mutations shift protein processing from one pathway to another, which also may augment amyloid deposition. A common mutation is at codon 717, which has been found in families of a variety of ethnic backgrounds. APP mutations are associated with onset between ages 55 and 60 (Cruts et al. 1998).

In 1992, a disease locus (AD3) was mapped to 14q24.3; linkage data suggested that this locus might account for many early-onset cases of familial AD (Schellenberg et al. 1992; St. George-Hyslop et al. 1992; Van Broeckhoven et al. 1992). The autosomal dominant gene at this locus, named presenilin 1, was identified and sequenced (Sherrington et al. 1995). Presenilin 1 has since been linked to familial AD in tens of families from diverse ethnic groups; more than 40 different mutations have been found (St. George-Hyslop 2000). Because dementia results from one of several identified missense mutations scattered across the gene, it is thought that this gene must have a high de novo mutation frequency and may account for apparently sporadic cases of AD (Cruts et al. 1998). Presenilin 1 mutations are associated with a very early age at onset, from ages 30 to 55 (Cruts et al. 1998).

In a series of Volga German families with autosomal dominant, early-onset AD, illness was associated with a locus on 1q31–42 (Lahad et al. 1995a). Cloning of this locus in yeast artificial chromosomes yielded sequences that were homologous to presenilin 1, with 67% identity. Disease-associated mutations at this locus, named presenilin 2, also were found to be missense mutations, although only four have thus far been identified. Presenilin 2 mutations are associated with a wide range of ages at onset (Sherrington et al. 1996). Both presenilins are expressed throughout the body, including the brain, heart, placenta, lungs, and liver; both encode transmembranous proteins whose function remains unknown. However, studies in vitro suggest that disease-associated mutations in each gene increase the production and deposition of amyloid (Farlow 1998). Specifically, presenilin 2 mutations have been shown in vivo and in vitro to lead to a greater relative amount of longer β-amyloid peptides (Cruts et al. 1998). Of note, some evidence indicates that a mutation in the promoter region of presenilin 2 may be associated with late-onset familial AD (Cruts et al. 1998).

Unlike the genes for APP and the presenilins, which account for fewer than 5% of all AD cases, the *APOE* locus on 19q13.2 has a major effect in 20%–40% of all AD cases (Pericak-Vance et al. 1991; Plassman and Breitner 1996; Schellenberg et al. 1987). The *APOE* locus was found by a genomewide search for markers in late-onset AD with the "affected pedigree members" method. The *APOE* locus encodes apolipoprotein E, which in the central and peripheral nervous systems is involved in the mobilization and redistribution of lipids in the repair, growth, and maintenance of myelin and axonal membranes during development or after injury (Boyles et al. 1989). The *APOE* gene locus has multiple alleles that give rise to protein polymorphism; among western European populations, they exist in the following frequencies: *APOE2* (10%), *APOE3* (75%), and *APOE4* (15%).

*APOE4* occurs in fewer than 5% of the Amish and in about a quarter of individuals of African descent (Hendrie 1998).

Several case-control studies have shown that the *APOE4* allele is overrepresented in all types of AD, including early-onset AD, both familial and sporadic (Okuizumi et al. 1994; Van Duijn et al. 1994), and late-onset AD, both familial and sporadic (Saunders et al. 1993; Strittmatter et al. 1993). In AD patients, 65% have been found to carry at least one copy of the *APOE4* allele (Farlow 1997). The inheritance of the *APOE4* allele is associated with an increased risk of disease expression and a younger age at onset in a dose-dependent manner in both familial and sporadic AD (Corder et al. 1993, 1994). In familial AD, homozygosity for *APOE4* relative to absence of the *APOE4* allele was associated with an increase in risk from 20% to 90% and a decrease in mean age at onset from 84 to 68 (Corder et al. 1993).

In a population study by the National Institute on Aging, the number of *APOE4* alleles present in an individual (0, 1, or 2) correlated in a dose-dependent manner with absolute risk for AD. The odds ratio for AD for 1 *APOE4* allele was 2.2–4.4; for 2 *APOE4* alleles, the odds ratio increased to a range of 5.1–17.9 (National Insitute on Aging/Alzheimer's Association Working Group 1996). Odds ratios in these ranges have been found in both case-control (high-end) and population (low-end) studies (D.A. Evans et al. 1997; A.S. Henderson et al. 1995). Of note, the modifying effect of *APOE4* on AD risk has been found to be age dependent (50–75), sex dependent (women more than men), and population dependent (white more than nonwhite) (Blacker et al. 1997; Corder et al. 1993; Duara et al. 1996; Hendrie 1998; G.P. Jarvik et al. 1995; Payami et al. 1996; Sahota et al. 1997; Saunders et al. 1993; Tang et al. 1996). *APOE4* increased the odds of AD by 3.5-fold in white non-Hispanics but not in Hispanics (Harwood et al. 1999b). No associations at all between *APOE4* and AD have been found in specific groups, including native Swedish, Nigerian, and Amish populations (Lannfelt et al. 1994; Osuntokun et al. 1995; Pericak-Vance et al. 1996). Although *APOE4* is highly prevalent in Nigeria, the prevalence of AD is quite low (Chandra et al. 1998).

Several studies have shown that homozygosity for *APOE4* is not sufficient to cause AD (A.S. Henderson et al. 1995); only 55% of the homozygotes in the Framingham study developed AD by age 80 (R.H. Myers et al. 1996). In a large population study in Kansas, 85% of the *APOE4* homozygotes (average age of 81) had no cognitive impairment (Hyman 1996). These results suggest that *APOE4* interacts with other genetic factors and/or environmental factors to cause illness. It has been hypothesized that the association between *APOE4* and AD may depend on diet, with high-fat, high-cholesterol diets strengthening the association; this is supported by international differences in prevalence across populations (Chandra et al. 1998).

In contrast to *APOE4*, the *APOE2* allele has been found in some studies to reduce the risk for AD and increase the age at onset of the disorder (Corder et al. 1994). In this same study, the inheritance of the *APOE4* allele was associated with 65% of the AD expression. The absence of the *APOE2* allele accounted for 23% of the cases of AD, further supporting the role of *APOE* in the pathogenesis of AD. However, some authors have not found a protective role for *APOE2* (Harwood et al. 1999b; Van Duijn et al. 1995).

There are many possible mechanisms for the modifying effect of the *APOE* locus on the expression of AD. Apolipoprotein isoforms may modify disease expression through differential binding to disease-associated proteins. Apolipoprotein E binds with both the β-amyloid of senile plaques and the tau protein of neurofibrillary tangles; *APOE4* has been found to bind amyloid more readily than do the other isoforms (Strittmatter et al. 1993) but to bind tau less readily than the others (Strittmatter et al. 1994). Evidence that supports the role of this binding in pathogenesis comes from transgenic mice with APP mutations; abundant amyloid plaque formation ceases in mice with apolipoprotein gene knockouts (Bales et al. 1997).

Apolipoprotein isoforms may influence AD expression through effects on cholinergic neurons. Choline acetyltransferase (ChAT) activity measured in the postmortem frontal cortex of 32 AD patients with different *APOE* genotypes showed that the ChAT activities of AD patients with two *APOE4* alleles were significantly lower than those in patients without *APOE4* alleles (Soininen et al. 1995). These results suggest that AD patients with the *APOE4* allele have a more severe cholinergic deficit than do AD patients without the *APOE4* allele. Consistent with this, tacrine, a cholinesterase inhibitor, has been found to be more effective among patients without the *APOE4* allele (Farlow 1997); however, no interaction has been found between apolipoprotein genotype and the efficacy of another cholinesterase inhibitor, metrifonate (Farlow 1998).

Other preliminary evidence exists for associations between AD and other genes, such as the $\alpha_1$-antichymotrypsin gene (Kamboh et al. 1995), the very-low-density lipoprotein receptor gene (Okuizumi et al. 1995), the apolipoprotein J gene, the serotonin transporter gene, major histocompatibility genes, CYP450 genes (CYP2D6), and the gene encoding the nonamyloid component of senile plaques (NACP) (reviewed in Cruts et al. 1998). Some forms of late-onset AD have been linked to a susceptibility gene in the pericentromeric region of chromosome 12 (Pericak-Vance et al. 1997; Rogaev et al. 1998; J. Stephenson 1997) and to mutations in the mitochondrial cytochrome c oxidase gene (Davis et al. 1997).

Several groups have developed transgenic mice that carry mutations in the APP and that have neuropathologic features characteristic of AD. One example is the PDAPP transgenic mouse (platelet-derived growth factor promoter expressing APP) (Games et al. 1995) (see Figure 10–2). Study of the PDAPP transgenic mouse has yielded a great deal of information about the neuropathology of AD, including plaque formation, alterations in synaptic transmission, and changes in long-term potentiation. Interestingly, immunization of these transgenic mice with β-amyloid leads to an attenuation of AD pathology (Schenk et al. 1999). Now there are other transgenic mice have different mutations in the *APP* gene, variations in *APOE* polymorphisms, and even mutations in the presenilin genes. These mice offer an opportunity to fully characterize AD and to develop effective forms of treatment for AD.

## Prion Diseases

The prion diseases have been referred to as the "slow and unconventional virus diseases" and as "spongiform encephalopathies." However, it is unlikely that these diseases are caused by viruses (Aiken and Marsh 1990; Meyer et al. 1991; Prusiner 1982), and they do not consistently yield a spongiform pathology (noninflammatory vacuolation). The unifying characteristic of the prion diseases is that they are caused by prions, or proteinaceous infectious particles, which are abnormal forms of a human gene product. Through some form of posttranslational modification, prions induce normal protein to change shape (Prusiner et al. 1990) from an α-helix to a β-pleated sheet (Liberski 1995), which then aggregates intracellularly. Abnormal isoforms are thought to derive either from infection from an exogenous source (consumed human flesh or beef, human endocrine injections, or dura mater transplants), from germline or somatic mutations in the *PRNP* gene, or from chance errors in *PRNP* gene expression. Of note, prion diseases are invariably fatal, and no treatment is available.

### Creutzfeldt-Jakob Disease

Creutzfeldt-Jakob disease (CJD) is the most common of the prion diseases. It may be sporadic (with no clear cause), familial, or acquired (iatrogenic or ingested). All forms of CJD are transmissible, including the familial or genetic types. Kuru is infectious in cause, transmitted by cannibalism in New Guinea, and is now nearly extinct in humans. Familial prion diseases include Gerstmann-Sträussler-Scheinker syndrome and fatal familial insomnia; they are also transmissible in laboratory settings.

The classic sporadic form of CJD accounts for approximately 85% of all cases and has an average age at onset of 60 years (Brown et al. 1994). Seventy-five percent of the patients die within 6 months; some die within a few weeks (Knight 1998). It usually begins with a rapidly progressive dementia, although abnormal behavior or gait imbalance are the presenting symptoms in about one-third of the patients. Abnormal movements are also common (including myoclonus, spasticity, tremors, rigidity, and choreoathetoid movements), as are dementia, visual problems (cortical blindness), and speech abnormalities. Patients deteriorate rapidly and develop akinetic mutism. A distinct triphasic EEG with periodic complexes is nearly pathognomonic and is seen in 75%–85% of the patients (Brown et al. 1986). Diagnosis also can be established by detection of a protein 14-3-3 in the CSF that is different from prion protein; this test has a sensitivity of 96% and a specificity of 96%–99% (Hsich et al. 1996). Autopsy shows gliosis, neuron loss, and spongiform change. Prion-containing amyloid deposits are identified by immunochemical staining.

The clinical presentation of familial CJD varies, depending on the site of mutation within the *PRNP* gene. It can closely resemble the classic sporadic form of CJD or present a variant phenotype. Iatrogenic CJD by definition depends on human-to-human transmission. Its period of incubation depends on the route of transmission: 12 years for peripheral hormone administration and 6 years for direct transplant of brain tissue. Unlike in other forms of CJD, iatrogenic CJD patients develop only mild dementia late in the course of illness; presenting symptoms are more commonly ataxia and gait abnormalities (Belay 1999).

## New Variant CJD

New variant, or nvCJD, is a new disease in Europe that is thought to have derived from the infectious agent of bovine spongiform encephalopathy (BSE), more popularly known as "mad cow disease." Transmission across species has occurred before with BSE, with house cats (Pearson et al. 1991), ungulates (Kirkwood et al. 1990), and primates in French zoos contracting spongiform encephalopathies after presumably eating products derived from contaminated beef. Furthermore, BSE is thought to have originated about 20 years ago when Brit-

ish cows ate sheep products contaminated with scrapie. The average age at onset of nvCJD is much younger—27 years—than that of sporadic CJD. The duration of illness (14 months) is longer than in classic sporadic CJD, and the characteristic triphasic EEG pattern does not occur. CSF 14-3-3 is not consistently found. Common presenting symptoms are psychiatric, such as agitation, aggression, anxiety, depression, lability, and social withdrawal. Hallucinations, delusions, insomnia, and sensory distortions are not uncommon. Most patients do not have clear neurologic signs until months after initial presentation. Many have had upgaze paresis, a symptom uncommon in sporadic CJD. Progressive dementia, ataxia, and myoclonus do occur but later in the illness and then in the context of delusions. Neuropathologically, nvCJD also differs from the classic sporadic form: it has "daisy" or "florid" amyloid plaques surrounded by "petals" of spongiosis, which is also typical of sheep scrapie (see Figure 10–11). Of note, nvCJD can be detected in tonsils, appendix, spleen, and lymph nodes, as well as in the brain.

## Gerstmann-Sträussler-Sheinker Syndrome

Gerstmann-Sträussler-Sheinker syndrome (GSS) is a rare familial neurodegenerative disorder with an age at onset in the fourth to seventh decade. Patients initially present with ataxia and later develop dementia; they also have dysarthria, oculodysmetria, and hyporeflexia. Death ensues within 1–10 years. Neuropathologic examination reveals neuronal vacuolation, astrocytic gliosis, and deposition of amyloid plaques. Although GSS is familial, it is a member of the prion disease family. It can be transmitted to subhuman primates and rodents via intracerebral inoculation as an infectious disease; infectivity is associated with the 27- to 30-kd protein known as the *scrapie prion protein* (PrPSc). Antibodies to PrPSc react with the amyloid plaques seen in GSS.

## Fatal Familial Insomnia

Fatal familial insomnia is a prion disease characterized by progressive insomnia, severe dementia, and autonomic dysfunction; it can also include panic attacks, phobias, hallucinations, ataxia, dysphagia, dysarthria, tremor, and myoclonus. Late symptoms include primitive reflexes, breathing disorders, weight loss, mutism, and coma. Both slow-wave and rapid eye movement (REM) phases of sleep are lost, patients have enacted dream states, and insomnia is near-total. Autonomic dysfunction includes profuse sweating, fever, and elevated heart rate and blood pressure. The mean age at onset in fatal familial insomnia is 49, and the disease lasts about a year. No characteristic

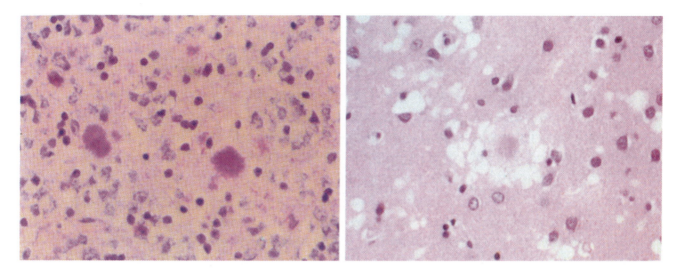

**FIGURE 10–11.** Histologic sections of amyloid plaques in sporadic Creutzfeldt-Jakob disease (*left*) and new variant Creutzfeldt-Jakob disease (*right*). Note the absence of surrounding vacuolation in the sporadic case and its presence in the new variant case (original magnification, 40×).

*Source.* Reprinted from Brown P: "The Risk of Bovine Spongiform Encephalopathy ('Mad Cow Disease') to Human Health." *Journal of the American Medical Association.* 278:1008–1011, 1997. Used with permission.

triphasic EEG pattern is seen. Fatal familial insomnia involves nearly exclusive bilateral degeneration of the thalamus without spongiform changes or amyloid seen at postmortem. Abnormal prion protein is seen in the brain, confirming the inclusion of fatal familial insomnia in the family of prion diseases, despite its atypical presentation (Medori et al. 1992).

## Epidemiologic Studies

CJD is the most common prion disease; its prevalence is 1 in 1 million. Sex ratios are nearly equal, although there may be a preponderance of men older than 60. Death rates remained stable from 1979 through 1994. CJD death rates are higher for whites than for African Americans (Belay 1999).

Epidemiologic studies have been done to explore the etiology of classic sporadic CJD. Case-control studies have not shown any link of sporadic CJD to consumption of meat or organs; exposure to blood and blood products (transfusion or surgery); head trauma; or employment as a health professional, butcher, farmer, or slaughterhouse worker (reviewed in Belay 1999). None of the Centers for Disease Control and Prevention cohort of CJD patients who died between 1979 and 1996 were found to have had hemophilia A or B, thalassemia, or sickle cell anemia. Surveillance of deaths among patients from 120 United States hemophilia centers did not detect any evidence of CJD, even with random postmortem survey (Holman et al. 1996). A cohort of patients known to have received blood from a CJD donor did not have CJD themselves at long-term follow-up (Heye et al. 1994).

Also, of 196 patients known to have received blood products from CJD donors, none were known to contract CJD over long-term follow-up (Belay 1999).

Iatrogenic CJD was first described in 1974 in the recipient of a corneal transplant (Duffy et al. 1974). Other reports of modes of human-to-human transmission include use of contaminated EEG electrodes (Bernoulli et al. 1977) and neurosurgical instruments (Will and Matthews 1982), as well as human-derived hormones (Cochius et al. 1990) and dura mater grafts (Thadani et al. 1988). More than 84 cases of CJD resulting from contaminated human growth hormone have been described worldwide; this mode of transmission should cease now that synthetic hormone is used instead (Belay 1999). By the end of 1998, dura mater grafts accounted for 64 cases of CJD worldwide (Belay 1999).

In Great Britain, nvCJD began to appear 10 years after BSE was first identified in cows in 1984. By 1996, nvCJD was reported based on the clinical presentation of 10 young individuals with a seemingly atypical presentation of CJD who had no prion protein mutations or known risk exposures. The geographic location of both nvCJD and BSE supported a link, as did a number of other findings. The introduction of BSE-infected brain tissue into primates produces the same "daisy" plaque pathology seen postmortem in nvCJD patients (Lasmezas et al. 1996) (see Figure 10–11). Western blot analysis of nvCJD plaque shows a pattern similar to that in BSE but different from that of sporadic CJD (Collinge et al. 1996). Also, mice injected with either nvCJD or BSE neural tissue develop nearly identical disease processes (incubation periods and lesion profiles) that are quite different from that seen in mice injected with sporadic CJD tissue (Bruce et al. 1997).

Regarding the link between BSE and nvCJD, three inexplicable facts remain (Brown 1997):

1. It is postulated that scrapie in sheep led to BSE in cows, which then led to nvCJD in humans. However, there is no evidence of humans contracting a prion disease from sheep.
2. No infectivity has been noted in muscle or milk of cattle.
3. Beef was eaten nearly universally in Britain, but nvCJD occurred only in young people.

As for the first point, kuru can be transmitted from humans to ferrets only indirectly, through nonhuman primates; BSE can only be transmitted from cows to hamsters through the intermediate host of mice. As for the second point, BSE prions may be in muscle or milk in amounts lower than what can now be detected. As for the third point, meat products intended for babies and children may have had different processing that may have increased transmissibility. Also, younger people may have some increased susceptibility or a shorter incubation period; in the future, nvCJD may be seen in older individuals.

In the wake of the appearance of nvCJD in Great Britain, other countries have closely monitored the appearance of any cases among their populations. Despite rigorous detection programs, there have been reports of only three very recent cases of nvCJD outside of Britain: three in France and one in Ireland. No other cases of nvCJD have been found, including in the United States. No BSE has been seen in the United States, despite extensive surveys of beef brains and tonsils.

The prevalence of GSS is estimated to be about 5 in 100 million (Belay 1999). Fatal familial insomnia is extremely rare and has been identified in fewer than 20 families.

## Mode of Inheritance

Familial CJD, GSS, and fatal familial insomnia all have an autosomal dominant mode of inheritance.

## Molecular Approaches

The infectious agent of scrapie was identified as a 27- to 30-kd protease-resistant polypeptide in hamsters (Bolton et al. 1982; McKinley et al. 1983; Prusiner 1982); no clear evidence of nucleic acids could be found. Unusually, infectivity was not abolished by ultraviolet or ionizing radiation, nucleases, proteases, or other agents. The gene for this protein was found not in the infectious agent but in the host DNA. Disease expression does not occur in the absence of this protein, which was found to share molecular characteristics with a common cellular glycoprotein (Oesch et al. 1985). The pathogenic form of this protein, called a prion, differs from the normal variant in its three-dimensional structure, being more likely to form a β-pleated sheet that will aggregate (Pan et al. 1993). The crucial event in the occurrence of disease is the induction of conformational changes in normal protein by abnormal protein (Prusiner and DeArmond 1990; Telling et al. 1996). With the new conformation, the protein is resistant to heat, radiation, proteases, and solvents such as alcohol, formalin, and phenol (Belay 1999). The conformational change likely represents a gain of function; introduction of abnormal prion protein (Prusiner et al. 1993) into mice without normal PrP will not lead to disease. Also, PRNP knockout mice appear entirely normal.

The normal prion protein gene *PRNP* is located on the short arm of chromosome 20; its entire open reading frame is contained in one exon. It is expressed in a variety of tissues in mammals, with its highest level in the brain. The normal protein encoded by *PRNP* is 33–35 kd and is localized to cell membranes; its function is not known. *PRNP* is the only locus known to influence prion disease expression, either through mutations causing familial prion diseases or by polymorphisms that increase vulnerability or shape disease expression.

GSS results most commonly from mutations in codon 102 but is also associated with mutations in 105, 117, 145, 198, and 217 (Doh-ura et al. 1989). The age at onset, duration of illness, and clinical picture can vary greatly according to the specific gene mutation involved. Codon 102 GSS has been identified in Europe, North America, Israel, and Japan; affected individuals generally are in their 40s, present with ataxia, and have the disease for up to 5 years. Codon 105 GSS, which has been seen in Japan, is largely characterized by spastic paraparesis, ataxia, and dementia; it has an early age at onset (38–48) and lasts about 9 years. At postmortem, codon 105 GSS is marked by amyloid plaques in the absence of spongiform changes. One variant of codon 117 GSS has marked dementia with little ataxia; it has been found among ethnic French and Germans. Another variant has prominent ataxia instead; both can present with parkinsonian signs. Codon 198 GSS was found in an Indiana kindred; its mean age at onset is 52, and it is characterized by dementia, ataxia, and parkinsonian symptoms (all reviewed in Belay 1999). Affected individuals have the usual amyloid plaques that contain PrP and also have widespread Alzheimer's-type neurofibrillary tangles. Additionally, insert mutations have been reported that consist of extra copies of a repeating octapeptide sequence in the region between codons 51 and 91 (Goldfarb et al. 1992).

Familial CJD most commonly stems from mutations in codon 200 of the PrP gene, although mutations in other codons also have been implicated (reviewed in Belay 1999). The phenotype of codon 200 familial CJD is nearly identical to that of sporadic CJD; it has been found in geographic clusters in Libya, Chile, and Slovakia and episodically seen in other parts of the world (Brown et al. 1991; Meiner et al. 1997). Codon 183 CJD has been seen in Brazil; it is marked by parkinsonian symptoms in addition to dementia and usually does not demonstrate a triphasic EEG (Nitrini et al. 1997). Codon 178 familial CJD has been found mostly in Europe; it is similar to sporadic CJD but lacks the triphasic EEG, has an earlier age at onset (40s), and has a longer duration of illness (about 2 years) (Brown et al. 1992).

Interestingly, polymorphisms in codon 129 of the PrP gene influence disease expression in familial, iatrogenic, and sporadic illness. In familial prion disease, polymorphisms in codon 129 influence the phenotypic expression of disease resulting from mutations in codon 178 (Goldfarb et al. 1992); in the presence of a mutation at codon 178, a valine (Val) at 129 will lead to a CJD picture, whereas a Met at 129 will lead to fatal familial insomnia. It is thought that these polymorphisms may influence distribution of protein accumulation, with Val favoring cortical and Met favoring subcortical localization. In fact, nearly all cases of fatal familial insomnia (a thalamic disease) have the combination of codon 178 mutation and codon 129 Met polymorphism. In both iatrogenic and sporadic CJD, more than 90% of the individuals have homozygosity at codon 129 (Met/Met or Val/Val), as compared with about 50% of the non-CJD control subjects (Belay 1999). In the United Kingdom, 37% of the healthy population has Met/Met at 129 compared with 79% of the patients with classic sporadic CJD (Knight 1998). Furthermore, individuals with nvCJD are almost all Met/Met homozygotes at codon 129 (Will et al. 1996). These findings suggest that heterozygosity at codon 129 (Met/Val) may confer some protection against developing CJD. Of note, homozygosity at codon 129 is associated with a more rapid deterioration in both fatal familial insomnia and familial CJD and with a lower age at onset in familial CJD patients.

In sporadic CJD, clinicopathologic profiles depend on both the haplotype at codon 129 in the PrP gene and the size of the abnormal prion protein fragment. Most sporadic CJD patients have Met/Met (or occasionally Met/Val) at codon 129 and have a type 1 prion fragment. These patients primarily have dementia and myoclonus, triphasic EEG, and a short duration of illness (4.4

months). Patients with the same type 1 fragment who instead have Val/Val at codon 129 also show predominantly dementia but develop the illness at a younger age, have a longer duration of illness, and typically do not have a triphasic EEG. A much smaller group, CJD patients with Met/Val at codon 129, have more ataxia, no triphasic EEG, and a preponderance of amyloid plaque at postmortem if they also have a different prion fragment (type 2) (Parchi et al. 1998).

It is unclear what accounts for different types of prion activity, which have been described as strains that modify the course of illness. Some investigators hypothesize that an informational molecular component in addition to prion protein, perhaps a nucleic acid, accounts for different strains (the "virino hypothesis") (Almond 1998). Investigators have reported evidence for the presence of nucleic acids that are not homologous to host DNA, which may account in part for infectivity (Dron and Manuelidis 1996; Manuelidis and Fritch 1996). Lasmezas et al. (1997) reported that mice transfected with BSE-contaminated bovine brain tissue developed illness without any demonstrable deposition of abnormal prion protein. The question of the presence of nucleic acids that might account for infectivity remains.

## Epilepsy

Epilepsy is one of the most common neurologic disorders, affecting about 4% of the population. It is defined by the presence of repeated seizures that do not have an immediate precipitant such as acute structural or metabolic CNS insults. More than 40 different types of epilepsy have been delineated based on phenomenology, etiology, and electroencephalographic features. Epilepsy is subclassified into *generalized seizures*, which involve the entire brain from the outset, and *partial seizures*, which have a localized onset. Recurrent seizures that follow a CNS event such as head trauma, stroke, or infection are *secondary epilepsy*. Epilepsy occurring in the absence of neurologic lesions and presumed to have a genetic etiology is termed *idiopathic epilepsy*. The term *cryptogenic* is used to describe recurrent seizures that are presumed to be nongenetic based on presentation or neuropathology, although distinguishing cryptogenic epilepsy from idiopathic epilepsy may be imprecise. Approximately 40% of the risk for epilepsy is related to genetic factors (Gardiner 1999). Recent research has found associations between epilepsy and mutations in genes for CNS ion- and neurotransmitter-gated voltage channels; these epilepsies are called *channelopathies*. Epilepsy also may result from mutations in genes related to neurodevelopment. Other known genetic causes of epilepsy are rare mendelian disorders in which mental retardation and notable physical manifestations typically accompany seizures.

## Epidemiologic Studies

A recent population-based study identified a prevalence of self-reported epilepsy as 5.8 per 1,000 population (Wiebe et al. 1999). A more accurate overall estimate for the prevalence of epilepsy is probably 1%–2% because patients significantly underreport seizures (Dalrymple and Appleby 2000), and most series include only patients who have been evaluated at medical facilities. The type of seizure studied and the means of ascertaining cases also influence prevalence estimates. The cumulative risk of repeated seizures increases with age: estimates are 0.7% by age 10, 1.7% by age 40, and 4.1% by age 80. Although the age-specific incidence for epilepsy is highest in the first year of life, Hauser et al. (1982) found that the greatest incidence of epilepsy occurs after age 60 years.

Febrile seizures are the most common form of seizures, with a reported cumulative incidence of 2%–5%, although a prospective population-based study (Berg et al. 1999) yielded a higher rate of febrile seizure onset—13.9% of 524 children. Ninety percent of febrile seizures present in the first 3 years of life (Verity et al. 1985). Although only a small proportion of patients with febrile seizures go on to have epilepsy, 20% of the adults with epilepsy report having had childhood febrile seizures (Shinnar et al. 1990). Many patients with febrile seizures (or other early-onset epilepsy) have a spontaneous remission by age 10 because of the increase in seizure threshold that occurs with maturation.

A trend toward increased incidence of epilepsy in males may be explained by the higher incidence of seizures secondary to head trauma, although there may be an interaction of genetic vulnerability and exogenous precipitants (Evans 1962; Jennett 1975). Stressful, unpleasant life events increased the occurrence of seizures in only male patients with epilepsy (Neugebauer et al. 1994). There are also reports of racial/ethnic variation in the expression of seizures, although differences in diet, exposures to toxins, or other exogenous factors may explain this divergence. Of note, individuals with generalized-onset or partial-onset epilepsy are 2.4 times more likely than their relatives without epilepsy to develop migraine (Lipton et al. 1994).

## Family Studies

Epilepsy is increased in the relatives of epilepsy probands, even though most affected people do not have affected relatives. Good estimates of familial aggregation were reported from the Rochester-Olmsted County Record Linkage Project that considered probands with idiopathic or cryptogenic epilepsy who had onset before age 16. The risk of developing epilepsy by age 40 was 3.6% in siblings and 10.6% in offspring, compared with 1.7% in the Rochester population. Overall, the risk of epilepsy was increased 2.5-fold in siblings and 6.7-fold in offspring. The risk of epilepsy was not increased in more distant relatives (e.g., nieces and nephews, grandchildren).

As seen in other disorders, an earlier age at onset in a proband predicts an increased recurrence of epilepsy within families (Eisner et al. 1959). Callenbach et al. (1998) recently found that 10% of children with newly diagnosed multiple seizures had at least one first-degree relative with seizures. The type of epilepsy also affects the familial recurrence rates. Idiopathic seizures have a 1.5-fold higher prevalence of family history than do secondary seizures (Eisner et al. 1959; Lennox and Lennox 1960; Tsuboi and Endo 1977). Complex partial seizures (also called temporal lobe and psychomotor seizures) are less hereditary than are other types of epilepsy (Ottman 1989). Juvenile myoclonic epilepsy is particularly specific in transmission; its incidence in family members of patients with epilepsy is increased some 20-fold over that in families without a history of epilepsy.

Febrile seizures, which by definition are associated with an environmental precipitant, are nonetheless highly heritable (Fukuyama et al. 1979; Tsuboi 1987). The recurrence risk for febrile seizures decreases by the degree of relationship of the relative. Tsuboi and Endo (1991) found recurrence risks of 17% in parents and 23% in siblings, which declined to 6.1% in second-degree relatives and to 4.6% in third-degree relatives. Berg et al. (1999) found that children with febrile seizures had increased febrile seizures in their relatives, but they were not more likely to have family histories of absence or localized epilepsies. Additionally, the offspring of epileptic mothers may have increased rates of febrile seizures (Janz and Beck-Managetta 1982).

## Twin Studies

The early twin studies of epilepsy (reviewed by V.E. Anderson et al. 1989) showed an MZ concordance of 0.58 and a DZ concordance of 0.11. This reduced penetrance suggests that environmental factors affect illness expression. Even lower concordance rates were found when the affected discordant MZ twin had brain damage (Lennox and Jolly 1954). Tsuboi and Endo (1991) studied twins with febrile seizures and found MZ pairwise concordance of 69% (18 of 26 pairs) and DZ concordance of 20% (4 of 20 pairs).

Although DZ twins have different EEGs, those of MZ twins are as similar as those taken from the same individual on separate occasions, even when the twins are reared apart (Lykken et al. 1982). Thus, EEG patterns may be closer to gene abnormalities than are seizures themselves. Particular EEG features have been examined in epileptic families, and the overall incidence of abnormal EEG findings in relatives of those with seizures is quite high at 37%—five times the recurrence risk of seizure disorder.

## Mode of Inheritance

Epilepsy is a highly complex genetic disorder. There is evidence for locus and allelic heterogeneity, variable expression (pleiotropy), and the interaction of several genes (epistasis). Loci responsible for particular types of seizures can differ among families, and different types of seizures may be linked to the same mutation within a family. There is also etiologic heterogeneity with an important role for environmental factors and for gene-environment interaction. This heterogeneity of epilepsies makes genetic modeling difficult. Autosomal dominant models with reduced penetrance have been suggested for epilepsy, especially when the diagnosis includes the presence of abnormal EEG findings. Other family data best conform to a polygenic multifactorial model, wherein an undetermined number of genetic and environmental variables contribute to the expression of the illness. Family data on febrile seizures have suggested several different modes of inheritance, including autosomal dominant with incomplete penetrance and multifactorial inheritance (see Kugler and Johnson 1998; Tsuboi and Endo 1991).

A higher risk of seizures is found in the offspring of women with epilepsy than in those of men with epilepsy, supporting the existence of a maternally derived influence (mitochondrial, intrauterine, or imprinting of a susceptibility gene) (Ottman 1990). A point mutation in the mitochondrial transfer RNA lysine (Lys) coding gene has been found to cause progressive myoclonic epilepsy in children and adults (Delgado-Escueta et al. 1994).

### Genetic Studies

Even though genetic epilepsies are variably penetrant, age-dependent disorders with heterogeneous clinical phenotypes, several epilepsies have now been successfully mapped to specific chromosomes. Indeed, more than a dozen single gene mutations have been linked to epilepsy phenotypes, and many more gene findings are anticipated in the coming years.

Most identified loci are for generalized seizures, which affect up to one-half of those with epilepsy. Juvenile myoclonic epilepsy, the most common of the generalized epilepsies, may be solely explained by genetic causes. Two chromosomal loci on 6p and 15q14 have been found for the disorder (Elmslie et al. 1997; Liu et al. 1995); these linkages have been replicated, although not in all families (Delgado-Escueta et al. 1994; Durner et al. 2000; Elmslie et al. 1996). The 6p loci are distinct from the HLA region. Preliminary evidence implicates a mutation in the gene for the $\alpha_7$ subunit of the neuronal nicotinic acetylcholine receptor in some families.

Childhood absence epilepsy is another predominantly genetic seizure disorder for which loci have been found on 1p and 8q24 (Delgado-Escueta et al. 1999; Mikami et al. 1999). A gene responsible for an unusual EEG pattern of delta bursts has been mapped to chromosome 3 (3p14.2–p12.1) (Zara et al. 1998), and a putative susceptibility loci for idiopathic generalized epilepsies also is on 8q24 (see Plaster et al. 1999). Febrile convulsions do not appear to be linked to the loci identified for generalized seizures (Racacho et al. 2000). However, loci on 2q (23–24 and 21–33) and 19q have been linked to febrile seizures (Baulac et al. 1999; Peiffer et al. 1999), possibly in the region encoding genes for the $\alpha$ subunit of voltage-gated sodium channels, which may result in persistent sodium ion influx and neuronal hyperexcitability.

A rare subtype of epilepsy called autosomal dominant nocturnal frontal lobe epilepsy has been linked to mutations on 20q13.2–13.3, the location of the $\alpha_4$ subunit of the neuronal nicotinic acetylcholine receptor. This mutation has been localized to a part of the gene that encodes a transmembrane channel. The mutation alters the receptor function in several ways, including loss of calcium ion permeability. Evidence suggests that mutations in this gene have independently arisen on numerous occasions because a second mutation affecting this same transmembrane domain has also been identified in a Norwegian pedigree (see Steinlein 2000).

In addition to the evidence for other seizure loci (6p21.2, 6q23–25, 8q24, 8p, 10q), a mitochondrial gene related to epilepsy has been identified and cloned. As described by Arcos-Burgos et al. (2000), these findings have complications, including the linking of a single locus to different types of epilepsy and the linking of a single form of disease to several loci.

Table 10–4 summarizes some of the findings of seizure loci. Five susceptibility genes have been identified in families with mendelian forms of epilepsy not associated with other severe medical problems (i.e., excluding progressive myoclonic epilepsy of Unverricht-Lundborg

**TABLE 10–4.** Linkage to loci in various epilepsy syndromes

| Epilepsy syndrome | Chromosomal location | Gene |
|---|---|---|
| Benign familial neonatal convulsions | 20q13 | KCNQ2 |
| | 8q24 | KCNQ3 |
| | | (potassium channels) |
| Benign familial infantile convulsions | 19q | ? |
| Progressive myoclonic epilepsy (Unverricht-Lundborg type) | 21q22 | Cystatin B (cysteine protease inhibitor) |
| Lafora's disease | 6q24 | EPM2A (protein tyrosine phosphatase) |
| Progressive epilepsy with mental retardation | 8p | CLN8 (transmembrane protein) |
| Juvenile myoclonic epilepsy | 6p | ? |
| | 15q14 | ? |
| Autosomal dominant partial epilepsy with auditory features | 10q22–24 | ? |
| Autosomal dominant nocturnal frontal lobe epilepsy | 20q13 | CHRNA4 (nicotinic acetylcholine receptor) |
| Benign epilepsy of childhood with centrotemporal spikes | 15q14 | ? |
| Generalized epilepsy with febrile seizures plus other seizure types | 19q13 | SCN1B |
| | 2q24 | SCN1A |
| | | (voltage-gated sodium channels) |
| Autosomal dominant febrile convulsions | 8q | ? |
| | 19p | ? |
| Familial partial epilepsy with variable foci | 22q11–12 | ? |

*Source.* Adapted from Ruth Ottman, personal communication, 2000.

type, progressive epilepsy with mental retardation, and Lafora's disease). All encode ion channels, which are known to be critical to propagation of neural stimuli: two potassium channels, two sodium channels, and one neuronal nicotinic acetylcholine receptor, which interacts with a calcium channel.

## Molecular Approaches

The genetic research on epilepsy is currently focused on linkage analysis aimed at positional cloning of susceptibility genes. The goal of neurogenetic studies is to understand the localization and developmental expression of these gene products and how they may control or modify neural excitability.

Recent molecular data suggest that idiopathic epilepsies with autosomal dominant inheritance may be caused by gene defects in ion channel subunits, either ligand-gated or voltage-gated (Berkovic and Scheffer 1999). Candidate genes for generalized epilepsy include the GABA receptor gene, the potassium channel gene, and the human homologue of the mouse jerky gene, which is in 8q24 and 6p11 (Delgado-Escueta et al. 1999). Generalized epilepsy with febrile seizures has been linked to a point mutation in chromosome 19 at band 13.1 for the β subunit of a voltage-gated sodium channel (SCN1B). Another candidate gene is the potassium channel gene of the cardiac long–Q-T family.

Seizures also may result from mutations in genes involved in cortical neurodevelopment that produce small heterotopias or defects in cortical development (Pennacchio et al. 1996). The X-linked lissencephaly/subcortical band heterotopia (XLIS) gene causes neuronal migration defects in human brain, which can manifest as a thickened cortex, deficient white matter, and gray matter heterotopias. Mutations in "doublecortin" can lead to the double cortex syndrome and to a lissencephaly that is accompanied by seizures (see Allen and Walsh 1999). Other genes related to epilepsy may be involved in energy metabolism (mitochondrial genes) or may be related to diseases that result in progressive neurodegeneration.

Although seizures often can be controlled, epilepsy is not curable and can be associated with significant physical and psychosocial morbidity. The identification of epilepsy susceptibility genes, even those that account for only a small percentage of cases (such as potassium ion channels and the $\alpha_4$ subunit of the nicotinic receptor), may lead us to novel drug discovery strategies that have broad utility in treating the epilepsies.

# Muscle Disorders

## Myotonic Dystrophy

Myotonic dystrophy is the most frequent genetic muscle disease in adults. It is a multisystem disease that is usually typified by muscle wasting and weakness, particularly in the face and neck and in the muscles of mastication and the distal legs and arms. The muscle weakness occurs in combination with "myotonia," the delayed relaxation of skeletal muscle after a voluntary contraction, as typified by difficulty releasing the hand from a grasp. Other associated features can include cataracts, frontal baldness, testicular atrophy, menstrual irregularities or infertility, cardiac and gastrointestinal symptoms, immunoglobulin abnormalities, and intellectual impairment. The mutation causing myotonic dystrophy is in the protein kinase *DMPK* gene on chromosome 19, although mutations in several other loci can cause very similar disorders.

The age at onset, extent of muscular disability, and the degree of cerebral abnormality vary greatly among individuals and are related to the length of the expanding trinucleotide repeat. A congenital form of the disorder includes feeding and respiratory difficulties, which can be fatal. This form of myotonic dystrophy is almost always accompanied by maternal inheritance. Seventy five percent of those with the congenital form have nonprogressive mental retardation, which can be accompanied by ventricular dilation. The CNS disturbances are unrelated to the repeat expansion length in the congenital form (Martinello et al. 1999), although the mild cognitive impairments in the noncongenital forms do correlate with CTG expansion length.

Other neural abnormalities in myotonic dystrophy patients include defects in primary sensory systems and higher-level cognitive dysfunction, evidenced by abnormal event-related potential studies (Ragazzoni et al. 1991). The most frequent child psychiatric diagnosis is ADHD (Steyaert et al. 1997). Other common features include emotional deficits, anhedonia, apathy, and hypersomnolence (Bungener et al. 1998; Rubinsztein et al. 1998).

### Epidemiologic Studies

The prevalence of myotonic dystrophy has been estimated at 5.5 in 100,000 (Grimm 1975; Mostacciuolo et al. 1987) and 1 in 8,000 (Aslanidis 1992).

### Twin Studies

The first study of MZ twins with myotonic dystrophy in whom monozygosity was confirmed found that there was strong phenotypic concordance, with the exception of discordant findings in lens opacities (Dubel et al. 1992). This concordance was found despite neonatal complications that were more severe in one twin than in the other in the first twin set and despite the fact that the second twin set had lived separately since age 13 years. The results suggested that genetic factors (i.e., repeat length) are primarily responsible for modulating the expression of the myotonic dystrophy gene, although the expression of the gene may be altered by developmental factors.

### Mode of Inheritance

Myotonic dystrophy is an autosomal dominant condition with a highly variable clinical phenotype. The inheritance of myotonic dystrophy displays anticipation that can be defined on two levels. On the clinical level, the onset of myotonic dystrophy appears to be earlier and its form more severe with each succeeding generation (Howeler et al. 1989). It is a cascade of late-onset (mild), classical, or adult-onset (moderate to severe) type and congenital type (very severe) in subsequent generations. At the molecular level, anticipation can be defined as an increase in the number of CTG repeats (Carpenter 1994).

The long-term effects of anticipation were examined in a study of an extended family with myotonic dystrophy. de Die-Smulders et al. (1994) reported that the transmission from the mild to the adult-onset type of myotonic dystrophy was associated with transmission through a male parent. Alternatively, there was a female transmission bias in the stable transmission of the asymptomatic or mild phenotype.

Of interest is the transmission of the congenital and most severe form of the phenotype, congenital myotonic dystrophy, which results in significant fetal loss and death in the perinatal period. Because the transmission of congenital myotonic dystrophy is reported to be mainly maternal, it was hypothesized to reflect either genomic imprinting or a maternal intrauterine factor. It has been shown, however, that the mouse homologue of the myotonic dystrophy gene does not undergo imprinting (Jansen et al. 1993), and a newly reported case of paternally inherited congenital myotonic dystrophy rules out the requirement of an intrauterine factor in the etiology of this form of myotonic dystrophy (Nakagawa et al. 1994).

### Molecular Approaches

Myotonic dystrophy has been found to be caused by an expanded trinucleotide repeat. A DNA trinucleotide, or triplet, repeat expansion mutation consists of three nucleotides consecutively repeated within a region of DNA expansion mutation, in which the number of triplets in a repeat increases and the length becomes unstable. In 1992, three groups independently reported the genetic mechanism that causes myotonic dystrophy to be the expansion of an unstable CTG repeat (Aslanidis et al. 1992; Buxton et al. 1992; Harley et al. 1992). The unstable repeat is located in the 3'-untranslated region of the myotonin protein kinase gene (Brook et al. 1992; Fu et al. 1993; Mahadevan et al. 1992). The number of CTG repeats in healthy individuals ranges from 5 to about 37 copies. Patients who carry the myotonic dystrophy mutation have about 50–2,000 copies, and those with the congenital form have more than 500 copies (Brunner et al. 1992). The number of CTG repeats tends to increase in successive generations, although a few cases of reductions have been reported (Abeliovich et al. 1993; Hunter et al. 1993; O'Hoy et al. 1993).

The sex of the affected parent influences the repeat size in the offspring with myotonic dystrophy in a manner similar to that affecting clinical presentation (Ashizawa et al. 1992; Tsilfidis et al. 1992). In a family study to assess the relation between the CTG repeat number and the clinical phenotype, it was concluded that the length of the triplet expansion is influenced by the sex of the transmitting parent and is related to the clinical onset of features of the disease (Redman et al. 1993). Ashizawa et al. (1994) concluded that the stability of the CTG repeat in myotonic dystrophy offspring differs between maternally and paternally transmitted cases. Although congenital myotonic dystrophy almost always occurs in the offspring of affected mothers, an accurate prediction of congenital myotonic dystrophy by the analysis of repeat sizes in mothers with myotonic dystrophy and their fetuses is currently not possible. For fathers, small expansions resulted in larger repeat size expansions in their offspring, whereas large paternal repeat sizes resulted in less size change in their offspring.

Diagnosis can now depend on a DNA test for the expanded CTG repeat, which is more reliable and less invasive than electromyography or muscle biopsy. Prenatal measurement of the CTG repeat is an accurate means of detecting the myotonic dystrophy mutation in patients at risk because the mutant and normal repeats are distinguishable and the length of the mutant repeat alleles is associated with clinical severity.

Because mutation in the myotonic dystrophy gene can be readily identified, variant syndromes have been detected that are not linked to chromosome 19. Mutations in at least three different genes can cause myotonic dystrophy syndromes. Disorders associated with this allelic heterogeneity include myotonic dystrophy type 2 (linked to chromosome 3) (Day et al. 1999) and proximal myotonic myopathy (Kohler et al. 2000).

## Psychiatric Disorders

## Attention-Deficit/Hyperactivity Disorder

ADHD is a common disorder with onset during childhood that is characterized by hyperactive, inattentive, and impulsive behaviors (American Psychiatric Association 2000). Population prevalence has been estimated to be 6% (J.C. Anderson et al. 1987; Bird et al. 1988; Szatmari et al. 1989), with a fivefold greater prevalence among boys when compared with girls. This disorder results in substantial social, academic, and psychologic impairment.

### Family Studies

Several types of family studies have established the familial nature of ADHD. Studies of first-degree relatives, siblings, and parents were started in the 1970s. When siblings of children with ADHD were assessed, 15%–25% also were found to have ADHD, whereas the rate for the siblings of control subjects was 5%–8%, which is near the expected population prevalence (Biederman et al. 1990; Pauls et al. 1984; Welner et al. 1977). Male gender increased, decreased, or did not affect the relative risk, depending on the study. A more dramatic finding was seen when the siblings of adults with ADHD were analyzed, with 41% having ADHD themselves compared with 0% of the siblings of control subjects (Manshadi et al. 1983). The larger morbid risk to the siblings of adult probands suggests a highly familial form of ADHD associated with persistent illness. Although ADHD is more prevalent in boys, family studies have shown that siblings of girls with ADHD have more attentional and learning problems than do siblings of boys with ADHD (Pauls et al. 1984) and that psychiatric disorders were more common in the parents of girls with ADHD.

The parents of ADHD probands also had elevated rates of ADHD when compared with the parents of control subjects (15%–44% vs. 2%–19% for fathers, 4%–38% vs. 0%–13% for mothers), resulting in paternal and maternal relative risks of about 2–8, respectively (Biederman et al. 1990; Cantwell 1972; Morrison and Stewart 1971). Exceptions to these findings have been noted, reporting no significantly elevated relative risk of ADHD in the parents of ADHD probands (Reeves et al. 1987).

Studies of second-degree relatives also support a familial component to ADHD. Assessment of pairs of half-siblings showed less concordance for minimal brain dysfunction, a diagnostic precursor to ADHD, than for pairs of full siblings (Safer 1973). Uncles and aunts (Morrison and Stewart 1971), cousins (Cantwell 1972), and grandparents (Faraone et al. 1994) of probands with ADHD are at higher risk for ADHD, although aunts seem to have a comparatively lower risk.

## Twin Studies

As with other putative genetic disorders, twin studies can be used to determine whether familial transmission is due to genetic factors or shared environmental factors. Early small-scale studies of hyperactive probands suggested higher concordance between MZ twins when compared with DZ twins, which was confirmed with larger reports (R. Goodman and Stevenson 1989). Studies have reported estimates of heritability of ADHD of about 0.80 (Eaves et al. 1997; Gilger et al. 1992b; F. Levy et al. 1997; Nadder et al. 1998; Sherman et al. 1997); and even as high as 0.98 (Gillis et al. 1992). Population-based twin studies assessing attentional problems and hyperactivity posited heritabilities of 0.71–0.76 and 0.88, respectively (Gjone et al. 1996; Thapar et al. 1995).

## Adoption Studies

Much like twin studies, adoption studies allow the differentiation of environmental from genetic factors in familial disorders. Morrison and Stewart (1973) showed that the biologic parents and aunts and uncles of hyperactive children were more likely to have been hyperactive as children when compared with their adoptive parents. The biologic relatives of children with ADHD also show cognitive measures of attentional dysfunction when compared with the adoptive relatives of other children with ADHD (Alberts-Corush et al. 1986). Unfortunately, the probands are separate groups of children, making definitive conclusions tentative, at best.

## High-Risk Studies

Among the early hypotheses about ADHD was one in which it was posited that ADHD-like behavior was a result of brain injury secondary to birth complications, which was partially confirmed by several retrospective studies in the 1950s and 1960s. A more recent report involved the examination of 129 referrals for hyperactivity among a birth cohort of more than 24,000 persons in Wales. Chandola et al. (1992) found that antepartum hemorrhage, length of second stage of labor, and 1-minute Apgar scores were risk factors in referral for hyperactivity and that those factors were not due to socioeconomic factors.

## Mode of Inheritance

Relatively few studies have sought to determine the genetic model for the inheritance of ADHD. Two separate studies totaling some 185 ADHD pedigrees suggested a dominant or codominant single major locus (Deutsch et al. 1990; Faraone et al. 1992), as did a limited linkage analysis study of a candidate locus on chromosome 20 (E.J. Hess et al. 1995). These studies contrast with an older study that ruled out a dominant model and supported a polygenic transmission (Morrison and Stewart 1974). The low statistical power and the modest recurrence rate of ADHD in siblings in these studies make their conclusions nondefinitive, and the relatively common occurrence of ADHD in the population provides an argument for a complex polygenic disorder.

## Linkage Analysis

Although studies assessing linkage in sibling pairs have been performed, no linkage studies with multigenerational multiplex ADHD pedigrees have been reported.

## Molecular Approaches

In the absence of linkage to provide direction for the positional cloning of a putative ADHD gene or genes, hypothesis-oriented candidate gene approaches have been used. The pharmacologic treatment of ADHD has guided candidate gene studies. Methylphenidate, a psychostimulant known to effectively treat hyperactivity since the 1930s, has led to interest in the role of dopaminergic genes. The dopamine transporter (SLC6A3, also DAT1) is inhibited by methylphenidate, and polymorphisms in this gene have been analyzed in children with ADHD. The first report described an association between ADHD and an allele of a 40-bp repeat in the 3'-untranslated region of the SLC6A3 gene (Cook et al. 1995). This study of 57 parent and proband trios calculated the haplotype-based relative risk statistic and found a significant association between the 480-bp allele and ADHD ($P = 0.006$). This finding was replicated in Irish children with a similar study design (Gill et al. 1997). A third study that used both family-based and population-based designs provided further evidence for an association (Waldman et al. 1998). There is no evidence that the repeat region itself alters protein function, although the associated allele may be in linkage disequilibrium with a mutation elsewhere in SLC6A3, or even in a nearby gene. Nevertheless, the dopamine transporter remains an interesting candidate gene, especially in light of a mouse model in which the SLC6A3 gene is rendered nonfunctional. SLC6A3-deficient mice evidence hyperlocomotion and insensitivity to amphetamines (Giros et al. 1996).

Similar interest has been generated by investigations of the $D_4$ dopamine receptor gene (DRD4). This grew out of reports of the association between a polymorphic region of the *DRD4* gene encoding the third cytoplasmic loop of the protein and novelty seeking, as measured by the Tridimensional Personality Questionnaire (Benjamin et al. 1996; Ebstein et al. 1996). This finding was replicated (Ebstein et al. 1997; Ekelund et al. 1999) but has not been found by other groups (Gelernter et al. 1997; Malhotra et al. 1996; Pogue-Geile et al. 1998; Sullivan et al. 1998; Vandenbergh et al. 1997). This behavioral construct, described as excitement following novel stimuli, was extrapolated to describe the behavioral characteristics of ADHD. Initial studies showed an association between ADHD and the 7-repeat allele of *DRD4* (LaHoste et al. 1996; Swanson et al. 1998), and family-based studies replicated this finding (Faraone et al. 1999; Smalley et al. 1998). Other studies, however, have shown little to no support (Castellanos et al. 1998), and three more recent family-based studies all found no association (Eisenberg et al. 2000; Hawi et al. 2000; Kotler et al. 2000). Although this polymorphism results in a variable number of repeated 16–amino acid segments, no functional difference has been noted (Asghari et al. 1994; Jovanovic et al. 1999). Mice with the deletion of the *DRD4* gene show less approach behavior to novel objects (Dulawa et al. 1999). So, at present, approximately half of the *DRD4* studies are positive and half are negative. This might mean that the gene does not play a role in the development of ADHD, but it is most consistent with a gene that contributes only a minor risk for developing this complex genetic disorder.

A third dopamine system gene, the $D_2$ dopamine receptor (*DRD2*), also has been investigated. One study described an association between ADHD and a single nucleotide polymorphism 10,000 bp distal to the *DRD2* gene (Comings et al. 1991a). A later study did not see the same association (Rowe et al. 1998). Similarly, no association has been found for other dopamine-related genes, the $D_3$ dopamine receptor (*DRD3*) and COMT (Barr et al. 1999, 2000). An intriguing family-based study, albeit small and needing replication, found an association between ADHD in a Chinese population and an X-chromosome marker near the genes for monoamine oxidase A and B (Jiang et al. 2000). The role of these enzymes in dopamine metabolism and the usefulness of medications that inhibit them suggest that further work is warranted.

ADHD is without question a familial disorder. Numerous family, twin, and adoption studies support a genetic component, although the mode of inheritance is not clear, and evidence that a single major gene is responsible is not strong. As with other complex disorders, development of larger, well-characterized samples and

the exploitation of the almost-certain genetic heterogeneity of this disorder for subtyping are called for. Indeed, current efforts involve developing approaches for standardizing diagnosis (Curran et al. 2000) and optimizing pedigree composition for genetic studies by using ADHD populations with comorbid disorders (Faraone et al. 2000).

## Bipolar Disorder

Bipolar I disorder is an episodic disturbance in mood characterized by mania (elevated or irritable mood, increased psychomotor activity, distractibility, diminished need for sleep, and often psychosis) alternating with depression (dysphoric mood, diminished psychomotor activity, decreased concentration, sleep and appetite disturbances, and often suicidality). Bipolar II disorder consists of hypomanic rather than manic episodes; hypomania is a discrete change in mood observable by others that is less severe than mania and does not require hospitalization.

### Epidemiologic Studies

Estimates of the general population risk (lifetime prevalence) of bipolar disorder range from 1% to 1.6% in the United States (Kessler et al. 1994; Robins and Price 1991) and from 0.3% to 1.5% worldwide (Weissman et al. 1996). The risk for bipolar and other affective disorders has increased in successive cohorts over the course of the century; this increase may be due to a "period effect" (the effect of some exogenous pathogenic factor over a limited period) (Lavori et al. 1986).

### Family Studies

A recent meta-analysis of eight studies in which family members were directly interviewed found that family members of bipolar probands have a sevenfold increase in lifetime risk for bipolar disorder compared with family members of control subjects. Twenty-one studies of family members of bipolar probands all found increased risk as compared with control subjects or the general population, with relative risk ranging from 2 to 18 (Craddock and Jones 1999).

The risk for bipolar disorder appears to be especially elevated for the relatives of probands with early-onset disorder (the fewer than 5% of patients who have prepubertal onset of mood disturbance) (Fogarty et al. 1994; Geller et al. 1994; Strober et al. 1988); this observation cannot be attributed exclusively to the period effect mentioned previously (Tsuang and Faraone 1990). Risk for bipolar disorder increases with the number of psychiatrically ill relatives (Gershon et al. 1982) but does not vary with gender, either of the relative or bipolar proband (Heun and Maier 1993).

In addition to bipolar disorder, several other psychiatric conditions aggregate in the relatives of probands with bipolar disorder, including bipolar II disorder (Simpson et al. 1993), recurrent unipolar disorder, schizoaffective disorder (bipolar type), and suicide. Preliminary results indicated that bipolar II disorder breeds true (Heun and Maier 1993), although it is also seen among the relatives of bipolar I probands. Some studies have suggested that alcoholism is also part of the bipolar disorder "spectrum," whereas others have not (reviewed in Gershon 1990).

Family studies not only provide evidence for the familial nature of bipolar disorder and for the phenotypic boundaries of putative bipolar susceptibility genes but also provide clues to the identity of these genes. Bipolar families evince intergenerational differences in age at onset and severity of disease that are consistent with the genetic phenomenon of anticipation. Thus, the age at onset of the first manic or depressive episode has been shown to be earlier, and the frequency of episodes greater, in the younger generation of two generations of affected relative pairs (McInnis et al. 1993; Nylander et al. 1994). As reviewed elsewhere in this chapter (see the discussions of myotonic dystrophy and HD), anticipation has been associated with the pathogenic expansion of trinucleotide repeat sequences in several neuropsychiatric disorders. Observed anticipation in bipolar disorder may be the result of such genetic factors, environmental changes, or ascertainment issues.

Furthermore, it has been observed that some pedigrees have primarily paternal transmission, whereas others have mostly maternal transmission of the illness to offspring. Sex differences in transmission may implicate vulnerability genes on sex chromosomes, mitochondrial inheritance in some families, or the role of genomic imprinting, in which genes are differentially methylated depending on which parent they are inherited from.

## Twin Studies

Ten twin studies of mood disorders that have been conducted since 1928, in which affected twins have either bipolar or unipolar disorder, have suggested higher concordance rates in MZ pairs (58%–74%) than in same-sex DZ pairs (17%–29%) (reviewed in Tsuang and Faraone 1990). A relative scarcity of unipolar-bipolar pairs argues against these disorders being genotypically identical, although a relation between the two disorders seems to exist. Six twin studies have focused on bipolar disorder

alone; each showed greater concordance among MZ than among DZ twins. Pooling of data from these studies yielded an MZ concordance rate of about 50% (Craddock and Jones 1999). Interestingly, as in schizophrenia, among discordant MZ twin pairs, offspring of the affected and nonaffected twin have identical risk of developing bipolar disorder; this supports the role of environmental factors in the expression of the bipolar phenotype for those who are genetically vulnerable.

## Adoption Studies

A significantly greater risk of affective disorder (unipolar, bipolar, and schizoaffective) was found in the biologic parents (18%) than in the adoptive parents (7%) of adopted bipolar probands (Mendlewicz and Rainer 1977). The risk for illness in biologic parents of adopted and nonadopted bipolar probands was similar. Another study of biologic and adopted relatives of probands with mood disorders and control probands also showed that the biologic relatives of affected probands had increased risk for the same broad spectrum of affective disorder; the biologic relatives of affected probands were 8 times more likely to have unipolar depression and 15 times more likely to have completed suicide (Wender et al. 1986). Wender's study also found that several environmental factors in an adoptive family appear to play a role in the development of mood disorders, including parental alcohol problems, other parental psychiatric problems, and parental death (Cadoret et al. 1985).

## High-Risk Studies

Structured diagnostic interview of 60 offspring who had at least one parent with bipolar disorder yielded a 51% prevalence of psychiatric disorder, predominantly attention-deficit, unipolar, and bipolar disorders (Chang et al. 2000). The risk of bipolar disorder in offspring was associated with early age at onset of bipolar disorder in the parent. Bilineal risk was associated in affected children with greater severity of depression and irritability. In a single extended pedigree identified by a bipolar proband, the risk of early-onset affective disorder was correlated with degree of relatedness to affected adults (Todd et al. 1994). In a series of National Institute of Mental Health (NIMH) bipolar pedigrees, children of parents with affective disorder were five times more likely to have an affective disorder than were children of healthy parents (Todd et al. 1996).

Children of bipolar parents may have greater degrees of aggressiveness, obsessionality, and affective expression than do age-matched control subjects (reviewed in Goodwin and Jamison 1990). High-risk children have been found to have cognitive deficits, especially on performance subtests of the Wechsler Intelligence Scale for Children, that are suggestive of right-hemisphere dysfunction and also are reminiscent of deficits seen in adult bipolar patients (Kestenbaum 1979).

## Mode of Inheritance

It is unlikely that a single gene confers susceptibility to bipolar disorder; complete scans of the entire genome in many affected individuals have not identified any major bipolar locus (Berrettini 1998). Also, a single major gene model is inconsistent with the very rapid decrease in recurrence risk observed with decreases in genetic relatedness: MZ twins (50%) to first-degree relatives (5%–10%) to the general population (1%). Single-gene inheritance may play a role in only select pedigrees, such as the Old-Order Amish (Rice et al. 1987; Spence et al. 1995). At present, bipolar disorder is considered a genetically complex illness that is characterized by phenotypic variability, probable locus heterogeneity, and possible interlocus interactions (epistasis). There are likely a number of susceptibility loci for bipolar disorder, which are neither necessary nor sufficient for disease expression but which increase the risk for illness (Berrettini 1998).

The observed absence of male-to-male transmission of bipolar disorder in many families suggested a dominant X-linked transmission (Winokur et al. 1969). Many kindreds show an excess of maternal transmission (McMahon et al. 1995). However, other possible explanations for this, other than sex chromosome transmission, include mitochondrial inheritance and genomic imprinting. Autosomal loci might result in an apparent absence of male-to-male transmission, given that affected males have an earlier age at onset, greater morbidity, and, consequently, significantly fewer offspring than affected females (Hebebrand and Hennighausen 1992).

Studying the genetics of bipolar disorder presents several potential difficulties: phenotypic variability (some bipolar disorder may be phenocopies originating from environmental factors), diagnostic boundaries (variable inclusion of schizoaffective and unipolar disorder into a broad spectrum), incomplete penetrance (obligate carriers may appear unaffected), locus heterogeneity, and epistasis. Furthermore, there is a birth cohort effect, in which successive generations have earlier ages at onset. Nonetheless, there is reason for guarded optimism that genes for susceptibility to bipolar disorder soon may be identified; genes for other complex disorders showing phenotypic variability (such as malignant melanoma), locus heterogeneity (such as Hirschsprung's disease), and epistasis (such as type 1 diabetes mellitus) all have been identified.

## Linkage Analysis

**Chromosome 18.** A genomewide scan of 22 North American extended pedigrees of families with affective disorder showed an association between illness status and markers in the pericentromeric region of chromosome 18 (Berretini et al. 1994). Two affected sib pair studies also showed evidence for linkage of this region to bipolar disorder (Berrettini et al. 1997; Stine et al. 1995). A parent-of-origin effect was found in these data sets: greatest linkage was seen in those pedigrees in which affected fathers transmitted the illness (Gershon et al. 1996).

Other studies have shown linkage of bipolar disorder with other areas of chromosome 18; a systematic genomic screen in two large isolated Costa Rican pedigrees with 24 severely ill bipolar I members yielded lod scores of 3.70 and 4.06, respectively, for two markers at 18q21–q23 (Freimer et al. 1996). Both pedigrees derived from a common eighteenth-century ancestral couple and thus were appropriately examined for haplotype sharing among affected individuals (Houwen et al. 1994); an identical four-marker haplotype was observed in 22 of the 23 affected individuals descended from this couple, strongly suggesting that a chromosome 18 susceptibility locus was contained therein.

Not all studies have corroborated findings of linkage of bipolar disorder with chromosome 18 loci (Detera-Wadleigh et al. 1997; Kalsi et al. 1997; Maier et al. 1995; Mynett-Johnson et al. 1997), but examples of nonreplication do not necessarily disprove linkage because there are difficulties in replicating linkage results for oligogenic disorders (Suarez et al. 1994), and different susceptibility loci may be important in different populations. For example, two studies in a genetically isolated population, the Old-Order Amish, also did not find linkage between bipolar disorder and chromosome 18 (Kelsoe et al. 1995; Pauls et al. 1995b). An association between schizophrenia and loci on chromosome 18 has been found (Berrettini 2000), suggesting a common susceptibility locus for bipolar disorder and schizophrenia. A candidate gene in this area is Golf, which is a subunit of a G protein expressed in the brain. There is a report of possible segregation distortion for Golf with bipolar disorder (Bickeboller et al. 1997) that has not been replicated in other bipolar populations (Turecki et al. 1996). Another candidate gene, a novel human inositol monophosphatase gene (IMP.18), maps near 18p11.2 in the pericentromeric region of chromosome 18; it is of interest because the gene product is potently inhibited by lithium (Yoshikawa et al. 1997).

**Chromosome 21.** It has been observed that bipolar disorder and trisomy 21 (Down syndrome) rarely co-occur, certainly less frequently than expected by chance. This has led to the hypothesis that there may be a susceptibility gene for bipolar disorder on chromosome 21. In a genome scan of 47 pedigrees, Straub et al. (1994) reported linkage between affective disorder and 21q22.3. Smyth et al. (1997) used a more narrowly defined phenotype and also found linkage, with an overall lod score of 3.87 when an oligogenic two-locus model was used (adding the tyrosine hydroxylase locus on chromosome 11). Detera-Wadleigh et al. (1996) used affected sib-pair analysis and found a high proportion of 21q markers that were shared identically by descent with excessive allele sharing; the same group recently confirmed linkage at 21q22. There are, however, a few negative reports of linkage of 21q with bipolar disorder from studies done in six large North American pedigrees (Byerley et al. 1995), two Danish families (Ewald et al. 1996), and 180 individuals in large multigenerational bipolar pedigrees from eastern Quebec (Merette et al. 1995). As mentioned earlier, this does not disprove linkage. Interestingly, maternal inheritance pedigrees contribute more to the observed linkage on chromosome 21, converse to the association of paternal transmission and chromosome 18. Thus, there may be different loci on different chromosomes that confer risk differently depending on the sex of the transmitting parent (Berrettini 1998).

**X chromosome.** In the 1980s, evidence was published for linkage of bipolar disorder in Israeli pedigrees to color blindness and glucose-6-phosphate dehydrogenase (G6PD) deficiency, traits known to be linked to the X chromosome. However, updating and review of the original data and the use of molecular methods to study linkage (specific Xq28 markers) have shown linkage in this region to be unlikely. Linkage of another region on the X chromosome that spans Xq24–27.1 was found with bipolar disorder in an extended Finnish pedigree; the largest lod score was 3.54. All pedigree members with bipolar or schizoaffective disorder had the identical haplotype in this region (Pekkarinen et al. 1995). There were also reports of linkage with another locus in this region, factor IX (Craddock and Owen 1992; Gill et al. 1992); this region is near the hypoxanthine phosphoribosyl transferase (HPRT) locus. Stine et al. (1997) found increased allele sharing near HPRT for sister-sister bipolar pairs. Evidence for linkage to HPRT (Xq26) does not provide evidence for linkage to the X markers of color blindness and G6PD, which are located at Xq28. Also, although evidence for Xq26 is accumulating, it cannot explain susceptibility in the subset of families in which male-to-male transmission occurs.

**Chromosome 4.** Linkage of bipolar disorder to chromosome 4 was found during a genome scan in a large multigeneration Scottish pedigree, yielding a lod score of 4.09 for one marker, 4p16 (Blackwood et al. 1996). Haplotype analysis was consistent with a haplotype being passed from the founder to affected individuals. Linkage was not found to candidate genes on chromosome 4, which include the $D_5$ receptor and a GABA receptor, *GABRB1*.

**Chromosome 11.** Linkage studies in an Old-Order Amish pedigree initially provided evidence for a bipolar locus on chromosome 11 (lod score>4.0); however, this was not replicated in other populations, and an extension of the original Amish pedigree weakened the evidence (lod score of about 2.0). Therefore, there may be an 11p15.5 locus of only small effect in this population (Berrettini 1998). Cosegregation of balanced translocations involving chromosome 11 and psychopathology has been described in three independent pedigrees. St. Clair et al. (1990) described a 77-member family in which 16 of 34 individuals carrying a t(1;11)(q42.2;q21) translocation had several severe psychiatric illnesses, including schizoaffective disorder and recurrent major depression; the translocation breakpoint has now been cloned (Muir et al. 1995). Similarly, a second 24-member family has been described in which 6 of the 7 individuals carrying a t(9;11)(p24;q23.1) translocation had bipolar I disorder or recurrent major depression (M. Smith et al. 1989). This translocation breakpoint has now been refined to a region of 150 kb that excludes the *DRD2* gene (Baysal et al. 1995).

**Chromosome 12.** Affective disorder has been found to cosegregate with Darier's disease, a dominantly inherited skin disorder that maps to 12q23–q24 (Dawson et al. 1995). Forty-five bipolar families without Darier's disease were found to have linkage in this region, with maximum evidence at a trinucleotide repeat marker within an intron of phospholipase $A_{2a}$ (Jacobsen et al. 1999). Linkage to 12q23–24 also was established within a homogeneous population in Quebec (Morisette et al. 1999). Detera-Wadleigh et al. (1999) confirmed linkage in this region.

**Other chromosomes.** A recent high-density genome scan of nearly 400 individuals from 22 multiplex pedigrees showed strongest linkage at 13q32, with a lod score of 3.5 ($P = 0.000028$) with a broad bipolar phenotype that includes unipolar depression and schizoaffective disorder (Detera-Wadleigh 1999).

## Molecular Approaches

**Candidate genes.** A leading theory of pathophysiology in bipolar disorder is the catecholamine hypothesis, in which mania is caused by an excess, and depression caused by a deficit, of catecholamines; roles for norepinephrine and dopamine are supported by the pharmacologic effects on mood of antidepressants, L-dopa, amphetamines, and antipsychotics. Therefore, candidate gene studies in bipolar disorder have focused on genes involved in catecholamine synthesis, degradation, and transduction.

Tyrosine hydroxylase is the rate-limiting enzyme in catecholamine synthesis. It is located near 11p15.5, a region that may have a susceptibility locus of small effect in some populations. Many investigators have searched in vain for linkage between tyrosine hydroxylase and bipolar disorder; there are only rare reports of linkage (Malafosse et al. 1997). The $D_4$ dopamine receptor also maps to this region. Lim et al. (1994a) provided preliminary evidence that bipolar patients, when compared with control subjects, had an excess of one variant (allele 7) and a deficiency of another (allele 3) of the $D_4$ dopamine receptor. Unfortunately, this observation has not been corroborated. The $D_2$ dopamine receptor also is located on chromosome 11; extensive efforts to detect linkage between this locus and bipolar disorder have not been fruitful. No evidence indicates linkage between bipolar disorder and the $D_1$ dopamine receptor, the dopamine transporter (chromosome 5), or the $D_3$ dopamine receptor (chromosome 3) (Kirov et al. 1999).

Two case-control studies showed an allelic association between monoamine oxidase A (on the X chromosome) and bipolar disorder (Kawada et al. 1995; Lim et al. 1994b), but a third study that used a more conservative, within-family control (haplotype relative risk) design did not confirm this association (Nothen et al. 1995). Finally, candidate gene studies have examined the distal portion of 5q, a region containing the $\beta_2$-adrenergic receptor gene; linkage was not shown (Mirow et al. 1994).

COMT is an important candidate gene because its protein methylates and inactivates dopamine and norepinephrine. COMT maps to 22q11, a region associated with velocardiofacial syndrome and increased incidence of schizophrenia and bipolar disorder. Some suggestive but not conclusive evidence indicates that COMT may be linked to bipolar disorder in select populations, such as Irish women (Mynett-Johnson et al. 1998), Han Chinese (Li et al. 1997), and patients with velocardiofacial syndrome (Lachman et al. 1996). It also may be a modifying gene for susceptibility to ultrarapid cycling in bipolar disorder in adults (Kirov et al. 1998; Papolos et al. 1998). However, several studies found no linkage between bipolar disorder and COMT in either general Caucasian or other subpopulations.

Other theories of pathogenesis in bipolar disorder inform the choice of candidate genes. For example, in the "permissive hypothesis" of serotonin activity in bipolar disorder, there is defective dampening by serotonin of other neurotransmitters, leading to fluctuations in mood (Hilty 1999). No association between bipolar disorder and the serotonin transporter has been found (Bocchetta et al. 1999; Ewald et al. 1998; Liu et al. 1999). Also, desynchronization of circadian rhythms also has been implicated in bipolar disorder (Brady 1999). Genes have been identified that influence seasonal variation in mood; these may play a role in bipolar disorder (Craddock and Jones 1999). Also, bipolar disorder in women frequently begins with a manic episode in the postpartum period; this trigger may be familial, implicating genetic influences of steroid hormone pathways (Craddock and Jones 1999).

**Anticipation.** In the light of intergenerational differences in disease expression that are consistent with anticipation, several groups have sought evidence for trinucleotide repeat expansion in bipolar disorder. O'Donovan et al. (1995) used a repeat expansion detection assay and reported significantly larger CAG repeats among 49 unrelated bipolar subjects than among 74 control subjects. The finding of expanded repeats has been replicated by some investigators (Lindblad et al. 1995; Oruc et al. 1997) but not others (Vincent et al. 1995). Lindblad's group found that most of the repeats occurred in two specific loci, one of which has a modest association with bipolar disorder: *CTG18.1*. Of note, the number of repeats is not associated with age at onset or disease severity (Craddock et al. 1997). However, the number of repeats has been found to be associated with change in phenotype from unipolar depression to bipolar disorder across generations (Mendlewicz et al. 1997). The identification of four folate-sensitive chromosomal fragile/breakage sites in patients with bipolar disorder, and the recognition that large expansions of the trinucleotide repeat CGG underlie such fragile sites in fragile X syndrome, are guiding efforts to identify CGG repeat–containing sequences that might be amplified in some bipolar patients (Kapalanga et al. 1995).

# Panic Disorder

Panic disorder is a common anxiety disorder that has come under increasing scrutiny by neuropsychiatric geneticists. Panic disorder is characterized by panic attacks, the spontaneous occurrence of intense anxiety accompanied by somatic symptoms, including dyspnea, palpitations, sweating, and chest pain. Panic disorder is currently diagnosed in the setting of recurrent panic attacks, with 1 month of anticipatory anxiety, worry about the implications of the attacks, or significant attack-related behavior changes (American Psychiatric Association 2000). Understanding of the genetics of panic disorder was initially hampered by earlier approaches of studying anxiety disorders as a class. Only with the pharmacologic dissection of anxiety syndromes (Klein 1964) and the development of operational criteria for panic disorder (DSM-III) could reliable diagnoses be made and thus grant genetic studies more phenotypic certainty.

## Epidemiologic Studies

An international epidemiologic study of 40,000 persons reported a lifetime prevalence of panic disorder of 1.4%–2.9% (Weissman et al. 1997). This study found an exception to this in Taiwan, where the rate was 0.4%, where the rates of other psychiatric disorders were equally reduced. The prevalence of panic disorder in females is about twice that in males (Eaton et al. 1994). The age of highest risk is 25–44 years (Robins et al. 1984), with a mean age at onset of 24; the hazard rates are highest at 25–34 for females and 30–44 for males (Burke et al. 1990).

## Family Studies

Investigations from the first half of the twentieth century focusing on the diagnostic precursors to modern panic disorder suggested a familial component to panic (Cohen et al. 1951; Oppenheimer and Rothschild 1918; Wood 1941). Subsequent studies have relied on two advances in family genetic studies—criteria-based diagnoses and direct interview of relatives. The first study to use DSM-III diagnoses showed that 31% of the first-degree relatives of panic probands were affected, compared with 4% of the relatives of control subjects (Crowe et al. 1980) (relative risk = 7.8). An extension of this study with twice the number of probands and relatives confirmed this finding, with a relative risk on the order of 9.9–10.7, depending on the diagnostic criteria used (Crowe et al. 1983). Among 41 families with panic disorder, 25 (61%) had at least one affected relative, compared with 4 of 41 (10%) in control families. The risk was double for female relatives compared with male relatives. Several subsequent studies confirmed these findings (Fyer et al. 1995; Hopper et al. 1987; Maier et al. 1993; Mendlewicz et al.

1993; Noyes et al. 1986; Weissman 1993). One group found that specific smothering symptoms increased the risk of panic disorder (Horwath et al. 1997) and that early age at onset increased the risk of panic in the first-degree relatives of panic probands to 17 (Goldstein et al. 1997). On the whole, family studies of first-degree relatives of panic disorder probands suggested a relative risk of 2.6–20 (mean = 7.8) (Knowles and Weissman 1995). Similar work in second-degree relatives of panic probands showed a sevenfold relative risk (Pauls et al. 1979b), similar to studies in first-degree relatives. Also consistent with the first-degree relative studies, female second-degree relatives were at higher risk for panic disorder. Overall, these studies indicate that panic disorder clearly aggregates in a familial pattern, but whether that pattern is due to genetic factors is undetermined.

## Twin Studies

Before 1970, six twin studies were published in which the clinical entity "neurosis" was investigated. The largest found that the ICD diagnosis of "anxiety state" led to concordance rates of 41% for MZ twin and 4% for DZ twin pairs (Slater and Shields 1969). It was not until the 1980s that twin studies that used rigorous diagnostic criteria were published. Torgerson (1983) used DSM-III diagnostic criteria and interviewed 299 Norwegian twin pairs; in 11 twin pairs, one co-twin had panic disorder, and in 18 twin pairs, one person had panic disorder with agoraphobia. No co-twin shared the same diagnosis in this group, although in two MZ twin pairs, one twin had panic disorder and the other twin had panic disorder with agoraphobia. When criteria were loosened to include any anxiety disorder with panic attacks, concordances of 31% and 0% were found for MZ and DZ pairs, respectively. A larger study that used DSM-III-R diagnoses ascertained 49 twin pairs in which one twin had an anxiety disorder and 32 comparison pairs without an anxiety disorder. When the co-twins were assessed, 5 of 20 (25%) of the MZ co-twins and 3 of 29 (10%) of the DZ twins were found to have panic disorder (Skre et al. 1993). The concordance rates for the comparison group were 8% and 10% in MZ and DZ twin pairs, respectively.

A much larger analysis of 1,030 female twin pairs derived from the Virginia Twin Registry was carried out by Kendler's group (Kendler et al. 1993). DSM-III-R diagnoses were made with varying levels of certainty, and 5.8% of the 2,163 interviewed twins met lifetime criteria for panic disorder. The concordance rates were 24% and 11% for MZ and DZ twins, respectively. The best fitting model for the narrowest diagnostic scheme implied that the variance in susceptibility to panic disorder was due to individual-specific environment and additive genes, and the heritability was estimated at 46%. This estimate lies at the lower end of the 30%–62% heritabilities extrapolated from the Norwegian twin studies. One potential explanation for this discrepancy is the ascertainment methods used in the different sets of studies. Kendler and colleagues (1993) used a population-based approach, whereas the work of Torgersen (1983) and Skre and colleagues (1993) relied on treatment samples, which conceivably can be considered more severe and potentially more genetically liable. An argument against this notion was offered in a study in which familial rates of panic disorder did not differ when probands were ascertained from a specialty anxiety clinic, specialty depression clinic, or population survey (Wickramaratne et al. 1994). Indeed, a recent study that used population-recruited twin pairs found high concordance rates for MZ twins (73%), but not for DZ pairs (0%) (Perna et al. 1997). Other explanations include differences in clinician blindedness and the sex difference between studies (i.e., all female vs. female/male twin pairs). Another observation that comes from the twin literature involves the low DZ concordance rate. DZ twins should have a morbid risk similar to that of other first-degree relatives. Across the twin studies of panic disorder, risk to a DZ co-twin of a panic proband is 0%–11%, much lower than the 8%–41% reported in family studies for first-degree relatives. The nature of this inconsistency is unclear, but it certainly warrants caution in attempting to estimate heritability of panic disorder. Despite this caveat, twin studies support a modest genetic component of panic disorder.

## Adoption Studies

There are no known adoption studies for panic disorder.

## High-Risk Studies

Panic disorder is often comorbid with other psychiatric conditions, raising an interest in whether these comorbidities may provide insight into the genetics of panic disorder. Depression occurs in at least one-third of the persons with panic disorder (Markowitz et al. 1989). Investigation of the families of depressed patients showed evidence for (Weissman et al. 1984) and against (Coryell et al. 1988) the hypothesis that panic disorder would increase the risk of depression in relatives. A family study that collected patients from treatment clinics and population-based surveys showed that panic disorder itself did not increase risk for depression in relatives per se, and vice versa, whereas comorbid panic and depression increased the risk of both panic alone and depression alone, as well as comorbid panic and depression, in rela-

tives (Weissman et al. 1993). These authors concluded that depression and panic are separate disorders, agreeing with many of the existing family studies (Crowe et al. 1983; Mendlewicz et al. 1993) and twin studies (Skre et al. 1993) of panic disorder.

Comorbidity between alcohol disorder and panic is a well-known clinical phenomenon. Relatives of panic probands have been reported to be at higher risk for alcohol or substance abuse (E.L. Harris et al. 1983). Other family investigations indicate that panic does not increase risk for an alcohol disorder any more than do several other psychiatric disorders (Coryell et al. 1988; Mendlewicz et al. 1993).

Another interesting observation about comorbid conditions derives from linkage studies in bipolar disorder. In one study, 57 bipolar families collected for linkage analysis were found to have 41 persons with panic disorder among 528 relatives. Of these 41 persons, 36 also had bipolar disorder (MacKinnon et al. 1997). Nearly 18% of the original bipolar probands and relatives who received diagnoses of bipolar disorder had panic disorder as well, suggesting a potential familial subtype of panic disorder and/or bipolar disorder. The same group stratified 28 of the families by whether the identified bipolar proband had panic disorder (5 families), panic attacks (6 families), or no panic attacks or disorder (17 families) and performed a linkage study with 31 markers on chromosome 18, where previous evidence of linkage for bipolar disorder had been detected (Stine et al. 1995). Multipoint nonparametric linkage analysis determined that the five bipolar/panic *disorder* families showed z scores of greater than 4.0 ($P \leq 0.0001$) over five consecutive markers on chromosome 18, whereas the bipolar/panic *attack* families showed intermediate scores, and the bipolar/no panic group showed low or negative scores (MacKinnon et al. 1998). These data provide intriguing, but limited, evidence for a subgroup of both disorders that may share a common genetic mechanism.

Another avenue of research has identified a potential biologic marker for panic disorder in high-risk individuals. Numerous groups have used inhaled carbon dioxide ($CO_2$) or infused lactate, among other compounds, to induce panic attacks in persons with panic disorder (Balon et al. 1988; Gorman et al. 1990). Subsequent work has shown that when family histories of healthy subjects are taken, subjects with a high prevalence of anxiety disorders in their first-degree relatives had panic attacks after lactate infusion, whereas those who did not panic showed a lower risk in their relatives (Balon et al. 1989). One group showed that the psychiatrically healthy first-degree relatives of panic probands had $CO_2$-induced panic attacks at significantly higher rates than did control subjects with no family history of panic disorder, although at rates lower than the identified probands (Perna et al. 1995). The same group studied the prevalence rates of panic disorder in 895 first-degree relatives of 203 panic probands. A positive reaction to $CO_2$ inhalation in the proband conferred a morbid risk of 14.4% among first-degree relatives, whereas the rate in the families of probands with negative responses was 3.9% (Perna et al. 1996). In another study (Coryell 1997), a total of 39 persons with and without family histories of panic disorder had $CO_2$ inhalation; those with a positive family history were more likely to experience panic attacks. Bellodi et al. (1998) evaluated 20 MZ and 25 DZ twin pairs obtained from an Italian twin registry to test for concordance of the panic response to $CO_2$ inhalation and found concordance rates of 55.6% and 12.5% for MZ and DZ pairs, respectively. A segregation analysis of 165 families found that the 134 families in which a panic proband was hypersensitive to $CO_2$ fit a dominant single major locus model of inheritance (Cavallini et al. 1999b). Overall, these data suggest that genetic mechanisms may determine the link between $CO_2$, and possibly lactate, hypersensitivity and panic disorder. Challenges with these agents thus may provide a tool to identify more familial forms of panic disorder.

## Mode of Inheritance

The first attempt to define the mode of inheritance of panic disorder came from an early family study of 139 patients, mostly servicemen, with neurocirculatory asthenia (Cohen et al. 1951). Family histories were obtained from the probands, and the observed rates of neurocirculatory asthenia were compared with the expected rates under several genetic models. The data fit a so-called double-dominant inheritance pattern, in which two dominant genes of equal frequency occurred. Simple dominant, recessive, and sex-linked models of inheritance were ruled out. This syndrome, characterized by nervousness, dyspnea (in 99% of the individuals), palpitations, fatigability, and a host of other somatic symptoms (Cohen et al. 1948), is clearly a precursor diagnosis to the modern conception of panic disorder. But the imprecision of the diagnosis and the method of data collection limit useful conclusions from the data.

The Iowa group was the first to address the mode of inheritance of panic disorder based on DSM criteria. By comparing rates of unilineal and bilineal inheritance in their family data, Pauls and colleagues (1979a) suggested a single-gene dominant model, a finding supported by additional data showing a dropoff in risk in second-degree relatives (Pauls et al. 1979b). The Iowa group carried out

a segregation analysis on their dataset, which also suggested a dominant model, albeit with an unrealistic phenocopy rate of zero (Pauls et al. 1980), whereas further model-fitting work on their expanding family collection determined that neither dominant nor polygenic models could be ruled out (Crowe et al. 1983). A segregation analysis by a group at Columbia University in New York City estimated that dominant and recessive models were equally likely, and more important, the phenocopy rate of 1% suggested that a quarter to half of all cases would be nongenetic, depicting a complex, heterogeneous picture (Vieland et al. 1993). This finding was replicated in an independent sample (Vieland et al. 1996) and predicted the twin concordance rate observed by Kendler et al. (1993). Overall, segregation analyses agree on the genetic contribution to panic disorder but have not resolved the specific model of inheritance, giving weight to autosomal dominant, autosomal recessive, and polygenic etiologies.

## Linkage Analysis

In the setting of positive evidence from family studies for a familial component to panic disorder, and confirmation from twin studies and segregation analyses that the familial factor is genetic, a number of genetic linkage studies of panic disorder have been performed. The first tested 26 families comprising 198 interviewed relatives with 29 polymorphic red cell antigens and blood proteins, covering 10 chromosomes (Crowe et al. 1987b). Crowe et al. used a dominant model derived from their earlier segregation analysis and found that one marker, α-haptoglobin (16q22), had a maximum lod score of 2.27 at a recombination fraction of zero. Nonparametric sib-pair analysis supported this finding ($P = 0.022$). The same group followed up this suggestive, although nonsignificant, linkage finding (Crowe et al. 1990). Ten new families were tested for linkage at the α-haptoglobin locus, this time with a DNA-based RFLP to detect two polymorphisms with the locus, and linkage was excluded. When the 10 families were combined with the previous 26 and analyzed, the maximum lod score was 0.67, effectively excluding the α-haptoglobin locus in panic disorder.

The Columbia University group procured a large collection of multiply affected pedigrees, in which almost half of the family members in whom DNA was collected were affected, with 2–12 affected members per family (Fyer and Weissman 1999). This group performed a two-stage genome scan on 23 families with 540 microsatellite markers. Thirteen families were scanned in the first stage with 394 markers, yielding 48 markers with lod scores greater than 1.0 in either dominant or recessive genetic models (Knowles et al. 1998). Ten additional families were then typed with additional markers in the regions of interest, and six were found to have lod scores between 1.0 and 2.0 for the entire sample. One of these, *D20S27* on chromosome 20, also had shown positive scores in the work of Crowe and colleagues. While collecting these pedigrees, the Columbia University group observed that certain medical conditions, particularly renal and bladder problems, thyroid conditions, and mitral valve prolapse, seemed to be enriched in these families. Considering these families a potential subgroup, they carried out a linkage analysis comparing 19 families with this "syndrome" with 15 families without the "syndrome" (Weissman et al. 2000). A maximum lod score was 3.3 for a chromosome 13 marker in a model of heterogeneity; this score rose to 4.22 when observing the families with bladder involvement and setting any bladder proband as affected. Although preliminary, this study shows the utility of developing potential syndromic subtypes for sharpening genetic analysis.

Finally, a separate genome scan of 105 alcoholic pedigrees focusing on personality traits as assessed by the Tridimensional Personality Questionnaire found that several loci were linked to harm avoidance, a trait thought to be related to the susceptibility to anxiety (Cloninger et al. 1998). Of interest, one marker in this scan was in the region of 20p, where a positive lod score greater than 1.0 was reported in the work of Knowles and colleagues (1998).

In summary, linkage studies have not provided strong evidence of genomic regions that are highly likely to be related to panic disorder, possibly reflective of the lower sensitivity of parametric linkage studies in diseases of uncertain mode of inheritance and in which multiple genes of small effect may be operative.

## Molecular Approaches

Several lines of evidence provide theoretical candidate genes for panic disorder. The pharmacologic efficacy of drugs that affect various neurotransmitter receptors, transporters, and catabolic enzymes, as well as challenge studies with specific panicogens and pathways investigated in animal models of fear and anxiety, all point toward several genes of neuropsychiatric interest. Unfortunately, most investigations attempting to associate panic disorder with variants on these genes have provided little support for the candidates. Early linkage studies focusing on the polymorphic genes for tyrosine hydroxylase, $\alpha$- and $\beta$-adrenergic receptors, GABA receptors, and pro-opiomelanocortin did not support the association of these genes with panic disorder (Crowe et al. 1987a; Mutchler et al. 1990; Schmidt et al. 1993; Z.W. Wang et

al. 1992). Similarly, negative results were found for the $D_2$ and $D_4$ dopamine receptors and the dopamine transporter (Crawford et al. 1995; Hamilton et al. 2000). Several case-control studies and one family-based association and linkage study of the serotonin system found no role for the serotonin transporter in panic disorder (Deckert et al. 1997; Hamilton et al. 1999; Ishiguro et al. 1997; Matsushita et al. 1997). Likewise, polymorphisms in the serotonin type 1D$\alpha$ (5-HT$_{1D\alpha}$) and 5-HT$_{1D\beta}$ receptor genes were not associated (Ohara et al. 1996). Positive and negative associations have been reported with the adenosine$_{2A}$ receptor and the $\alpha_4$ subunit of the neuronal acetylcholine receptor, respectively (Deckert et al. 1998; Steinlein et al. 1997). Finally, although positive associations have been reported with case-control studies investigating genes for monoamine oxidase A, cholecystokinin, and the cholecystokinin B receptor (Deckert et al. 1999; Kennedy et al. 1999; Z. Wang et al. 1998), similar studies that used a family-based design had negative associations (Hamilton et al., in press a, in press b).

This rather uneven history of candidate gene studies in panic disorder points to several problems plaguing psychiatric genetics in general: 1) low power from limited sample sizes for detecting genes of small effect; 2) low prior probability and multiple testing; 3) population admixture, affecting case-control studies; and 4) phenotypic heterogeneity. As in studies of other disorders, an ideal solution would include a very large, family-based sample with a subtype population (e.g., those with $CO_2$ hypersensitivity or an endophenotypic medical syndrome) such as that described above.

## Obsessive-Compulsive Disorder

Obsessive-compulsive disorder (OCD) is a common anxiety disorder in which the patient has persistent intrusive thoughts, or obsessions, typically involving concerns about contamination, symmetry, or checking. Patients with OCD also perform ritualistic tasks, or compulsions, that interfere with normal daily function. OCD has been well characterized in children and adolescents and has been found to lead to substantial impairment and social isolation.

## Epidemiologic Studies

Prior to the large epidemiologic studies of the 1980s, OCD was thought to be relatively uncommon, with a prevalence of about 0.05% (Rasmussen and Eisen 1992). It is likely that the traditional study of inpatients and, to a lesser extent, outpatients led to the dramatic underestimation of prevalence of a disorder for which treatment was often not sought or was provided by nonpsychiatric physicians (S. Shapiro et al. 1984).

As part of the Epidemiologic Catchment Area (ECA) study, more than 9,500 persons across three sites in the United States were interviewed for 15 DSM-III disorders, for which lifetime and 6-month prevalence data were obtained. OCD was found to have a lifetime prevalence of 1.9%–3.0% among the three sites (Robins et al. 1984), whereas 6-month prevalence was estimated to be 1.3%–2.0% (Myers et al. 1984). A subsequent study extended the ECA findings to more than 18,500 persons across all five ECA sites and confirmed a lifetime prevalence of 1.9%–3.3% (Karno et al. 1988). Some caution is warranted regarding these results. Analysis of the temporal stability of the diagnosis of OCD with the ECA data reported that only 19.2% of those meeting diagnostic criteria for OCD continued to do so when reinterviewed 1 year later (E. Nelson and Rice 1997). Those persons whose diagnosis remained stable reported an earlier age at onset and had stable comorbid conditions (particularly other anxiety disorders). The authors interpreted these results as a combination of false-positives and false-negatives and questioned the validity of the instrument used, the Diagnostic Interview Schedule.

In a population-based study of 356 adolescents selected from an original screening set of 5,600, the DSM-III diagnosis of OCD had current and lifetime prevalences of 1.0% and 1.9%, respectively (Flament et al. 1988). Community survey data from seven countries obtained by the Cross National Collaborative Group indicated an annual prevalence rate of 1.1%–1.8% and a lifetime rate of 1.9%–2.5% (Weissman et al. 1994). One country, Taiwan, was clearly an outlier, with corresponding rates of 0.4% and 0.7%, respectively. This finding was consonant with the observed low rates of all psychiatric disorders in Taiwan.

There appears to be a slight excess of females with OCD compared with males. In a review of 11 studies performed before 1970 of treatment populations totaling 1,336 persons, 51% of the patients were women (Black 1974). More recent epidemiologic evidence suggests a larger female-to-male ratio, with five of the seven countries in the Cross National Collaborative Group having ratios of 1.2–1.6, with two outlying countries with proportions of 0.8 and 3.8 (Weissman et al. 1994). The difference between the epidemiologic and treatment populations, possibly reflecting gender difference in treatment-seeking behaviors, may explain the discrepancy between the estimates. One striking finding has been the reversal of the sex ratio in children. In one clinic-based sample, 76% (13 of 17) of the patients were boys (Hollingsworth et al. 1980), and a cohort of 70

patients followed up at the NIMH showed a male-to-female ratio of 2:1 (Swedo et al. 1989b). The ratio during adolescence seems to revert to that seen with adults (Flament et al. 1988). The mean age at onset is 20.9 years, with a significant difference between sexes (male 19.5, female 22.0, $P<0.003$) (Rasmussen and Eisen 1992).

## Family Studies

Until the 1930s, very little was known about the heredity of OCD. Beginning with 50 obsessional patients from the Maudsley Hospital in London, Lewis (1936) collected detailed information about 100 parents and 206 siblings. Thirty-seven parents had "obsessional traits" (e.g., methodical, strong religious feelings, strictness), as did 20 of the siblings. Another British study, comparing first-degree relatives of probands with several psychoneurotic states with control subjects, found a prevalence of obsessional states of 7.1%–7.5% in the 96 relatives of the 20 probands with obsessional states (F.W. Brown 1942). The prevalence in the 189 relatives of the 31 control subjects was 0%.

More than a dozen family studies have been published since the 1960s and have been comprehensively reviewed (Pauls and Alsobrook 1999; Sobin and Karayiorgou 2000). Methodologic considerations distinguish many of these studies. The use of the family history method, in which a proband provides historical information about relatives, predominated among the older studies. The family study method, in which direct interviews of all first-degree relatives are used, came to the fore in more recent studies. Some studies combine both approaches. Because persons with OCD may be less forthcoming about embarrassing or shameful symptoms in a direct interview, the family history method may identify affected relatives. Conversely, direct interview may detect affected relatives with symptoms unknown to the family history informant. One review of 11 OCD family studies published since 1965 illustrates this methodologic problem (Sobin and Karayiorgou 2000). Nine adult studies with 686 probands and 2,427 first-degree relatives showed OCD or obsessive-compulsive symptoms at rates ranging from 0% to 20%. Two child and adolescent studies with a total of 66 probands and 186 first-degree relatives showed OCD rates of 9.5%–25%. Sobin and Karayiorgou noted that the studies that used more direct interviews reported high morbid risk rates, although several of those also were family studies of children and adolescents, enriching for the early-onset form of the disorder. This is important in the context of studies indicating that the age at onset modifies risk of OCD in relatives (Pauls et al. 1995a). Despite the wide range of estimates of morbid risk to first-degree relatives from studies facing a variety of methodologic challenges, family studies suggest a familial aggregation of OCD.

## Twin Studies

The number of twin studies focusing on OCD is not large. In 1936, Lewis described three sets of MZ twins with concordant obsessional traits but drew few conclusions from his data, opining "two or three pairs tell very little: it is a pity that twins are so rare" (pp. 325–326). A later review of the largely anecdotal intervening literature calculated a concordance of 57% (29 of 51) among MZ pairs, with an adjusted rate of 65% (13 of 20) after removing 30 pairs with questionable zygosity (Rasmussen and Tsuang 1984). Unfortunately, data for direct comparison to DZ twin rates were not presented, preventing any conclusions about the contribution of genetic factors.

Three subsequent studies have been published, all including DZ twins and totaling 233 MZ and 328 DZ pairs (G. Andrews et al. 1990; Carey and Gottesman 1981; Torgersen 1983). In 30 twin pairs with pre-DSM-III diagnoses (15 MZ and 15 DZ), one group found MZ and DZ concordances of 87% and 47%, respectively, for obsessional symptoms but no difference for OCD (Carey and Gottesman 1981). A twin registry-based study (446 pairs, 186 MZ and 260 DZ) and a clinically derived sample (85 pairs, 32 MZ and 53 DZ) both looked at concordance of a variety of anxiety disorders among twins (G. Andrews et al. 1990; Torgersen 1983). Both found no concordant DSM-III OCD, but both did note higher concordances when OCD was grouped together with other anxiety and affective disorders. For example, Torgersen observed in his clinical sample that when OCD was grouped with agoraphobia, panic disorder, and social phobia, but not with generalized anxiety disorder, respective MZ and DZ concordances of 45% (9 of 20) and 15% (5 of 33) were seen. This effect was lost when generalized anxiety disorder was added to the diagnostic grouping. In the population-based study, 19 of 186 (10.2%) MZ twins were concordant for a "neurotic" cluster of disorders, including depression, dysthymia, generalized anxiety disorder, panic disorder, and OCD, compared with 25 of 260 (9.6%) DZ pairs (G. Andrews et al. 1990). This difference was not significant. The authors still concluded that their twin study suggested a genetic component to these disorders because their population prevalences predicted a nongenetic concordance rate on the order of 7%.

One group used a different diagnostic approach to assess obsessional traits and symptoms with the Leyton Obsessional Inventory (Clifford et al. 1984). They studied 419 twin pairs derived from a British normal twin registry and found heritabilities of 44% and 47% for obses-

sional traits and symptoms, respectively. It is difficult to draw firm conclusions from the OCD twin literature. As a group, these studies are characterized by heterogeneous diagnostic schemes, interviewer knowledge of co-twin diagnosis and zygosity, and analytic strategies often based on combining diagnostic entities into larger groups. Despite all of these differences, this literature does argue that OCD has a genetic component.

## Adoption Studies

There are no known adoption studies for OCD.

## High-Risk Studies

The striking differences in male-to-female ratios in OCD patients with prepubertal childhood-onset (3:1) and postpubertal adolescent-onset (1:1) disorder derive from the wide differences in age at onset between males and females. Males with early-onset OCD have been reported to have persistent and severe symptoms (Flament et al. 1990) as well as a higher incidence of birth complications than did females (Lensi et al. 1996), suggesting that males may be more vulnerable to CNS damage resulting in OCD than are females.

The study of OCD in children and adolescents has provided other useful insights into high-risk populations and the heterogeneous nature of the disorder (Leonard et al. 1999). It has long been observed that OCD co-occurs with tics and Tourette's disorder (Pauls et al. 1986), particularly in males and those with early-onset OCD (Leonard et al. 1992). Early-onset OCD also predicts Tourette's disorder and tics in relatives, suggesting a distinct risk group for OCD (Pauls et al. 1995a).

Studies of children with Sydenham's chorea, a neurologic manifestation of rheumatic fever, led to the discovery that many children with this poststreptococcal autoimmune syndrome showed higher rates of obsessive-compulsive symptoms (Swedo et al. 1989a). In cohorts of children with OCD some children were described as having acute and dramatic development of symptoms, associated with choreiform movements and other neurologic abnormalities, prepubertal onset, and frequent streptococcal infections (Leonard et al. 1993; Swedo et al. 1989b). Continued investigation into this phenomenon has resulted in the definition of PANDAS (pediatric autoimmune neuropsychiatric disorder associated with streptococcal infections) (Swedo et al. 1998). Swedo's group used a monoclonal antibody (D8/17) against a B cell antigen previously found to identify probands with rheumatic fever (Khanna et al. 1989) to assay children with PANDAS, children with Sydenham's chorea, and 24 control children (Swedo et al. 1997). They found that the PANDAS and Sydenham's chorea groups were D8/17-positive significantly more often than were control subjects (85% and 89%, respectively, vs. 17%). These data suggest that being D8/17-positive may increase susceptibility to these two disorders. A subsequent study appears to generalize this finding to early-onset OCD and Tourette's disorder, showing that these groups also expressed the D8/17 antigen more frequently than did control samples (Murphy et al. 1997). The original description of this marker suggested the intriguing possibility that the increased susceptibility to PANDAS, OCD, and Tourette's disorder may be genetically mediated. Khanna et al. found that 100% of the rheumatic fever probands were D8/17-positive, expressing the antigen on 33% of their B cells. Unaffected siblings and parents expressed the marker on 15% and 13% of their cells, respectively, a rate approximately twice that of control subjects (Khanna et al. 1989). The authors assessed the pattern of marker expression in their pedigrees and concluded that this was consistent with autosomal recessive inheritance.

## Mode of Inheritance

Only recently have efforts focused on the mode of transmission in OCD. Cavallini et al. (1999a) performed a segregation analysis of 107 Italian families with DSM-III-R OCD and focused on the phenotypes of OCD or OCD plus Tourette's disorder and tics. For the OCD-only analysis, the model of no genetic transmission was rejected but general mendelian inheritance was not. Within the mendelian model, the dominant model was the best-fitting using Akaike's Information Content. Interestingly, the analysis of the OCD plus Tourette's disorder and tics group rejected both the no genetic transmission and the general mendelian models. More than half (54 of 107) of the families used in this study had a single member affected with OCD, a finding noted consistently in family studies. The importance of this observation was addressed in another segregation analysis of 96 DSM-III-R OCD probands and their 453 first-degree relatives (Alsobrook et al. 1999). Fifty-one families had a family history of OCD, meaning an affected member besides the index proband, whereas 45 of 96 (47%) did not. In all of the families, segregation analysis rejected only the model of no genetic transmission. When analyzing only those with a positive family history of OCD, all models were rejected except for a mixed model. This group then stratified their families with a four-factor structure for obsessive symptoms (Leckman et al. 1997). Segregation analysis was performed on the subsets of families in which the proband scored in one of the four

factors, and all analyses rejected the no genetic transmission model. In the analysis that used factor 3, corresponding to symmetry, ordering, counting, and ritual obsessions and compulsions, polygenic transmission also was rejected, suggesting a general mendelian model. Although a single major locus model appears possible, the prominent clinical heterogeneity seen in OCD, as well as the limited set of genetic models tested in these segregation analyses, argues for a more complicated mode of transmission. The factor analysis approach of Alsobrook and colleagues (1999), the use of potential biologic markers such as D8/17, and the development of more sophisticated modeling may provide further insights into the genetic mode of inheritance for OCD.

## Linkage Analysis

No linkage studies have been performed for OCD. It is not clear that current approaches in linkage analysis will be useful in understanding the genetic basis of OCD. Traditional linkage studies are most powerful for detecting disorders in which a gene of major effect occurs in a substantial portion of families and in which fairly accurate parameters are known for the mode of inheritance. This is clearly not the situation for OCD. Less powerful methods that forgo models of transmission, such as sib-pair analysis, may prove useful but will require the collection of families far larger than most extant studies, providing a rationale for collaborative genetic studies.

## Molecular Approaches

Several candidate gene association studies, mostly case-control, have been carried out with OCD populations. Most of these studies investigated genes involved with serotonin and dopamine function, a result of hypotheses derived from pharmacologic studies and clinical observations (W.K. Goodman et al. 1990a, 1990b).

Genes involved in serotonin function have received the most attention. The serotonin transporter (SLC6A4), the molecular target for serotonin reuptake inhibitors, has been studied extensively. Sequence analysis of cDNAs isolated from 22 OCD patients and 4 control subjects showed no changes in amino acid sequence at this locus (Altemus et al. 1996). The coding sequence of SLC6A4 was scanned with denaturing gradient gel electrophoresis in 45 OCD patients, and again no variants were seen (Di Bella et al. 1996a). The next study (Billett et al. 1997) used a repeat sequence (5HTTLPR) in the promoter region of SLC6A4 that altered transcription activity depending on the number of repeats (Lesch et al. 1996). Billett and colleagues (1997) assayed this polymorphism in 72 OCD patients in a case-control study.

No difference in allele frequency was noted between cases and control subjects nor was there any association between the promoter polymorphism and response to medication in the patient group. In a study of 34 parent and proband trios, McDougle et al. (1998) detected a marginally significant preferential transmission of the long allele of the 5HTTLPR polymorphism ($P<0.03$). This result was not corrected for multiple testing, and the finding of the long allele being associated ran counter to positive associations in other disorders, in which the short allele is involved.

Serotonin receptors also have been studied. Two groups reported on polymorphisms in the 5-HT$_{2A}$ receptor (HTR2A). Nicolini et al. (1996) found no association between OCD and a silent coding sequence variant in HTR2A in 67 patients compared with 54 control subjects. A group studying 62 OCD patients in a case-control design found marginal association with an HTR2A promoter polymorphism, although this was not corrected for multiple testing (Enoch et al. 1998). Association studies of modest sizes reported negative results for the 5-HT$_{2C}$ receptor (HTR2C) (Cavallini et al. 1998) and positive results for the 5-HT$_{1D\beta}$ receptor (HTR1D) (Mundo et al. 2000).

The first candidate gene studies in OCD involved genes for dopamine receptors, given the association between OCD and Tourette's disorder, a disorder commonly treated with dopamine receptor antagonists. Four case-control studies found no association between OCD and the *DRD2* and *DRD3* genes (Billett et al. 1998; Catalano et al. 1994; Nicolini et al. 1996; Novelli et al. 1994). Likewise, negative associations have been reported with *DRD4* (Billett et al. 1998; Cruz et al. 1997; Di Bella et al. 1996b) and the dopamine transporter (Billett et al. 1998).

The final candidate gene, COMT, is an enzyme involved in the catabolism of several neurotransmitters, including dopamine. This gene was studied in light of data suggesting that persons with a microdeletion of 22q11 frequently had obsessive and compulsive symptoms (Papolos et al. 1996). COMT lies within this region and is commonly deleted in persons with this chromosomal aberration (Karayiorgou et al. 1995). Karayiorgou et al. studied a common single-nucleotide polymorphism in the coding region of COMT that led to a change in amino acid sequence and three- to fourfold difference in enzyme activity (Karayiorgou et al. 1997). Seventy-three OCD probands were compared with 148 control subjects, and the low-activity allele of COMT was associated with OCD in males but not in females. The strong association in particular with the homozygous low-activity genotype suggested a recessive effect. This finding was replicated in a follow-up family-based study that used 110 probands (Karayiorgou et al. 1999). Furthermore, this study reported similar significant male-specific associations between OCD and a polymorphism in the monoamine oxidase A gene, a gene on the X chromosome whose protein product also is involved with the enzymatic degradation of neurotransmitters and is the target of one class of medications.

As with other complex disorders discussed in this chapter, association studies like many of those described above present some problems. Often, candidate genes are chosen based on hypotheses derived from the indirect evidence of psychopharmacologic treatment studies. The role of pharmacologically relevant candidate genes may prove to be an epiphenomenon and not shed light on the etiologies of these disorders. Problems of disease heterogeneity, without the judicious use of clinical or biologic subtypes, may only ensure false-negative results, whereas issues of population admixture in case-control studies will continue to foster false-positive results. Nevertheless, linkage and candidate gene studies still hold promise.

## Schizophrenia

Schizophrenia comprises a group of serious psychiatric disorders that are characterized by "positive" (psychotic) symptoms, "negative" (deficit) symptoms, and cognitive impairment. Most patients are initially affected in young adulthood; 50% go on to experience some disability throughout their lives, and an additional 25% never recover and require lifelong care.

### Epidemiologic Studies

The lifetime morbid risk for schizophrenia is 0.9% (Gottesman and Shields 1982). The sex ratio of schizophrenia is about equal over the life course, although women tend to have a later onset by about 5 years. Accumulating data suggest that both genetic and environmental factors play a role in the etiology of the disorder. A widely accepted model is that schizophrenia results in part from an early, most likely prenatal, abnormality in neural development that remains latent until the affected region matures and is required to function optimally (Weinberger 1987). Follow-up studies of large birth cohorts provide evidence supporting a neurodevelopmental etiology because persons who later develop schizophrenia often have cognitive abnormalities that are detectable in the first years of life (Done et al. 1994; Jones et al. 1994). Also, minor physical anomalies, which originate in utero, are in excess for patients with schizophrenia as compared with control subjects (M.F. Green 1994; Lohr and Flynn 1993).

The environmental factors most likely responsible for neurodevelopmentally related schizophrenia are prenatal and early life exposures. A role for infections is supported by the well-documented excess of schizophrenic births in the winter and early spring on the order of 8%–10% (Bradbury and Miller 1985; Torrey et al. 1977), suggesting that seasonally varying agents, acting at or near the time of birth, influence the subsequent development of schizophrenia. Infections with characteristic seasonal variations are likely agents (Adams et al. 1993), particularly rubella (Brown et al. 2001) and influenza (Mednick et al. 1988; O'Callaghan et al. 1991; Takei et al. 1996).

Other reported maternal pregnancy exposures include low birthweight, cigarette smoking (O'Dwyer 1997; Sacker et al. 1995), Rh incompatibility (Hollister et al. 1996), and stress (Huttunen and Niskanen 1978; Van Os and Selten 1998). Also, exposure to famine or malnutrition early in gestation (i.e., the Dutch Hunger Winter of 1944–1945) was associated with a doubling of the risk of schizophrenia in offspring (Susser et al. 1996). An association of malnutrition with schizophrenia in offspring was confirmed by Dalman et al. (1999).

Obstetric complications that lead to oxygen deprivation or trauma also are hypothesized to be relevant to schizophrenia (Magrath et al. 1995; McNeil 1988; Parnas et al. 1982). These include unusual length of labor (McNeil and Kaij 1987), premature delivery (Woerner et al. 1971), preeclampsia (Kendell et al. 1996; McNeil and Kaij 1987), umbilical cord complications (Gunther-Genta et al. 1994), and malpresentation (Gunther-Genta et al. 1994; Parnas et al. 1982). Because of sample size limitations, most of these investigations have aggregated individual obstetric complications into summary score measures. Jones et al. (1998) recently was able to separate maternal, prenatal, obstetric, and neonatal factors. An important finding was that characteristics of the child (birthweight and early birth) were more related to later schizophrenia than were characteristics of the delivery.

Postnatal events also may affect schizophrenia risk. For example, CNS infection (especially neonatal coxsackie B meningitis) is associated with later schizophrenia (Rantakallio et al. 1997). Imigration from poor countries in Africa, Asia, and the Caribbean to wealthy countries such as England and the Netherlands is associated with a 3- to 10-fold increase in schizophrenia risk, compared with both the host country and the country of origin (reviewed in Jones and Cannon 1998). This finding has been multiply replicated, and the effect is greater for second-generation than for first-generation migrants, arguing against selective migration of at-risk individuals. Sug-arman and Craufurd (1994) found increased rates of illness among siblings of Afro-Caribbean probands living in Britain (and born in the United Kingdom) but not in the Afro-Caribbean–born parents, a finding consistent with the effect of some common environmental exposure precipitating schizophrenia in genetically vulnerable individuals. It is not clear whether this finding reflects the effect of urbanization, stress, racism, or exposure to some new infectious or other environmental agent.

Some data support models of interaction between genetic vulnerability and the environment. For adopted-away children of mothers with schizophrenia, adversity and poor family functioning in the adoptive home increases the risk of schizophrenia; however, no such effect is seen for adopted-away children of healthy mothers (Tienari 1991). In an Israeli study, children of mothers with schizophrenia had a higher risk of developing the illness themselves if raised in a kibbutz instead of a family home; again, this effect was not seen for children without genetic risk (Mirsky et al. 1985). Likewise, obstetric complications greatly augment schizophrenia risk in those who already have genetic vulnerability but not in low-risk groups (reviewed in Jones and Cannon 1998). Of interest, rheumatoid arthritis rarely co-occurs with schizophrenia (Oken and Schulzer 1999), suggesting that immunologic mechanisms may play a role in disease expression.

## Family Studies

Family studies consistently report an elevated morbid risk for schizophrenia in the first-degree relatives of schizophrenic probands in comparison with the risk in the general population (0.9%), suggesting that schizophrenia is familial. A review of 40 studies up until 1987 yielded risk rates of 6% for parents, 10% for siblings, and 13% and 46% for children with, respectively, one or two affected parents (Gottesman 1991). Relatives of probands also have elevated risks for other nonaffective psychoses (Tsuang et al. 1999) and for schizotypal personality disorder (Battaglia and Torgersen 1996; Siever et al. 1993). The variability in expression of schizophrenia among family members also may extend to nonpsychotic symptoms (Tsuang 1991) and psychophysiologic abnormalities. The latter are elevated in both probands and their relatives and include smooth-pursuit eye movement abnormalities (D.L. Levy et al. 1994), neurologic soft signs (Kinney et al. 1986; Quitkin et al. 1976; Rieder and Nichols 1979), psychometric deviation (Moldin et al. 1990), and psychophysiologic gating impairments (Myles-Worsley et al. 1999; Waldo et al. 1991).

## Twin Studies

Comparisons of relative concordance rates for MZ and DZ twins (53% vs. 15%; Kendler and Gardner 1997) showed that 60%–90% of the liability to schizophrenia can be attributed to genes (Cannon et al. 1998; Jones and Cannon 1998; NIMH Genetics Workshop 1998). As in bipolar disorder, a follow-up study of the offspring of MZ twins with a diagnosis of schizophrenia and of unaffected MZ co-twins showed equal rates of schizophrenia in the offspring (about 16%–18%); hence, each group of offspring carried equal genetic vulnerability for schizophrenia (Fisher 1971; Gottesman and Bertelsen 1989; Kringlen and Cramer 1989). In contrast, the risk of schizophrenia in the offspring of an affected DZ twin is 17.4% but only 2.1% in a nonaffected DZ twin. A mechanism for differential environmental exposure of MZ twins to maternal blood-borne factors in utero was suggested in a study by Davis and Phelps (1995). They used handedness as a retrospective marker of placentation status and found higher concordance in presumed monochorionic MZ twin pairs (60%) than in dichorionic pairs (32%), a finding consistent with presumed differential environmental effects during gestation.

## Adoption Studies

Adoption studies also consistently report increased schizophrenia risk in the biologic relatives of probands (Heston 1966; Kety et al. 1994; Rosenthal et al. 1968). A potential criticism of adoption studies is that offspring may be exposed in utero to an illness-causing factor in mothers with schizophrenia. One way to address this concern is to study paternal half-siblings, who have the same father but different mothers. Kety (1988) found that 13% of the paternal half-siblings of adoptees with schizophrenia themselves developed the illness, as compared with only 2% of the paternal half-siblings of nonaffected adoptees. Adoption studies also provide evidence for gene-environment interaction. Adopted-away children of biologic mothers with schizophrenia are more likely to develop schizophrenia if they are raised by adoptive mothers with high "communication deviance" (Wahlberg et al. 1997). No such increased risk with communication deviance is seen in adopted-away children of unaffected biologic mothers.

## High-Risk Studies

High-risk studies were initiated in the 1950s, when it was recognized that children who went on to develop schizophrenia as adults were neurologically different from their peers (O'Neal and Robins 1958). Fish (1977), and Fish and colleagues (1992), found signs of abnormal development in many spheres of the CNS, including motor, sensory, cognitive, and cerebellar function, in children who went on to develop schizophrenia; they labeled this as "pandevelopmental retardation." Other studies also found early neurologic abnormalities in both children at risk and those who actually go on to develop the disorder. In an Israeli study, at-risk children had compromised psychomotor performance as infants and cognitive and motor dysfunction by age 10 (J. Marcus et al. 1981). An innovative blinded review of home videos showed that raters could accurately identify which children would later develop schizophrenia, based on motor skills (Walker et al. 1994). General population birth-cohort studies also have confirmed that children who go on to develop schizophrenia have delays in developmental milestones during infancy (such as walking and talking), more isolated play at ages 4 and 6, speech problems and clumsiness at ages 7 and 11, and poor school performance and social anxiety during the teenaged years (reviewed in Jones and Cannon 1998; Tarrant and Jones 1999).

Deficits on the Continuous Performance Task (Erlenmeyer-Kimling and Cornblatt 1978) are estimated to exist in approximately 40% of schizophrenic patients, whereas similar deficits, when found, exist at a lower rate in other psychiatric patients (Nuechterlein and Dawson 1984). In another study, Erlenmeyer-Kimling and Cornblatt (1992) examined attentional impairment in the offspring of parents with schizophrenia followed up as part of the New York High-Risk Project. Their results provided support for the hypothesis that global attentional dysfunction may be a biobehavioral marker for genetic liability to schizophrenia. Abnormal social behavior also may be an indicator of risk for schizophrenia. In a study conducted in Copenhagen, teenagers who went on to develop schizophrenia had trouble making friends, disciplinary problems, and unusual behavior (Parnas et al. 1982a, 1982b).

## Mode of Inheritance

Despite the overwhelming evidence that schizophrenia is a genetic disorder, the nature of the genetic diathesis remains unclear. Schizophrenia does not show a clear mendelian mode of inheritance, and various segregation analyses have suggested dominant, recessive, additive, sex-linked, and oligogenic inheritance (see Book 1953; DeLisi and Crow 1989; Elston and Campbell 1970; Garrone 1962; Karlsson 1972; Kendler and Diehl 1993; Slater 1958; Slater and Cowie 1971; Stewart et al. 1980; Zerbin-Rudin 1967). A three-locus epistasis model was found to optimally account for the rapidly decreasing recurrence risk data for individuals with lowering degrees of relatedness to probands with schizophrenia (Risch 1990). Many different genes may increase schizophrenia vulnerability (Kaufmann et al. 1998), and the several replicated loci that have been linked to schizophrenia may together account for only a small proportion of the genetic risk. Recent studies that used parametric linkage analysis in large multiply affected pedigrees or allele-sharing methods of linkage to schizophrenia indicated that single-gene transmission in schizophrenia is extremely unlikely (O'Donovan and Owen 1999). As described, schizophrenia is probably etiologically heterogeneous, with various genetic, environmental, and interactive etiologies resulting in a common phenotype.

Earlier age at onset of schizophrenia in successive generations of multiply affected pedigrees has been shown to occur in schizophrenia, consistent with trinucleotide repeat expansions, as is seen in disorders such as HD (Petronis and Kennedy 1995). Patients with schizophrenia had generally longer CAG/CTG repeats than did nonschizophrenic persons (Morris et al. 1995; O'Donovan et al. 1995). However, it has not been determined which genes had these longer repeats and whether such genes are involved in the pathogenesis of schizophrenia (O'Donovan and Owen 1999).

Recently, Malaspina and colleagues (2000) identified a strong increase in schizophrenia risk related to the age of the father, consistent with a possible role for de novo mutations in schizophrenia vulnerability genes.

## Linkage and Association Studies

Schizophrenia is a heterogeneous disorder that likely results from the cumulative effects of many genes. Studies have yielded some evidence of linkage to schizophrenia in more than half of all human chromosomes (Pulver 2000). Alleles that confer risk may be highly prevalent in the population, and illness may result from some constellation of disease genes, where none or few may be sufficient by themselves. Because the phenotype of schizophrenia is heterogeneous, some studies have focused on examining putative "endophenotypes" of schizophrenia genes. These may be of more use than the diagnosis itself in linkage and association studies because they are easier to define, simpler, more objective, and may have a higher penetrance. Such studies require fewer subjects and may enable investigators to identify genes of small effect. Promising candidate endophenotypes include aberrant smooth-pursuit eye movement (Crawford et al. 1998; O'Driscoll et al. 1998; Ross et al. 1998), N-acetyl aspartate concentrations in the hippocampus (Callicott et al. 1998), abnormal hippocampal morphology (Csernansky

et al. 1998), and the P50 gating deficit (see "Chromosome 15" subsection below).

**Chromosome 15.** Common in schizophrenia is a failure in sensory gating—namely, the failure to inhibit the P50 auditory evoked response to repeated stimuli, which appears to be inherited in an autosomal dominant fashion in schizophrenia pedigrees (C. Siegel et al. 1984). The auditory evoked potential deficit has been linked to the $\alpha_7$ subunit of the nicotinic acetylcholine receptor gene on 15q14, with a lod score of 5.3 in nine families (reviewed in Freedman et al. 1999). Conversely, the lod score for linkage of this allele to schizophrenia in these same pedigrees was only 1.3, which is not unexpected given the nonmendelian transmission of the illness and the low power for detection of the study (only nine families). However, the NIMH Genetics Initiative for Schizophrenia found linkage between schizophrenia and this locus with affected sib-pair analysis, yielding $P < 0.0024$, which is adequate for replication of previous findings (Leonard et al. 1998). Also, 15q14 is linked to other diseases such as Prader-Willi syndrome and Andersmann's agenesis of the corpus callosum, which can entail schizophrenia-like psychoses (Freedman et al. 1999).

**Chromosome 13.** Complete genome scans for susceptibility loci in schizophrenia pedigree sets have only rarely yielded significant linkage results. Nonetheless, Blouin et al. (1998) found significant linkage of schizophrenia to 13q32 in a genomewide scan of European families, with a lod score of 3.19 under a recessive inheritance model. Interestingly, linkage of this same region to bipolar illness also has been found (Detera-Wadleigh et al. 1999). Linkage also was found when using a narrow phenotype definition when additional Caucasian families were added but not when they were combined with Asian pedigrees (M.W. Lin et al. 1997). Overall, there is suggestive but not conclusive evidence for linkage at 13q32.

**Chromosome 8.** Suggestive but not yet definitive evidence exists for a susceptibility locus on 8p (Blouin et al. 1998; Kendler et al. 1996; Pulver et al. 1995; Shaw et al. 1998). In families with both schizophrenia and schizophrenia spectrum disorders, a lod score of 5.04 was found for 8p21–22 (Pulver 2000). Nonparametric analysis of a genome scan in NIMH families yielded evidence for another susceptibility locus in the region, 8pter–8q12, but only in African American, not European American, schizophrenia pedigrees (Kaufmann et al. 1998).

**Chromosome 22.** The search for possible linkage of schizophrenia to 22q11 by Pulver et al. (1994) was prompted by observations of phenotypic similarity between schizophrenia and velocardiofacial syndrome, the latter being due to microdeletions on 22q11. Twenty-two percent of patients with velocardiofacial syndrome are estimated to also have schizophrenia. Because 22q11 microdeletions were found in 2% (1 in 50) of a random sample of schizophrenic patients from an epidemiologic study, compared with 0.025% (1 in 4,000) of the general population, it has been concluded that 22q11 deletions may confer susceptibility to schizophrenia. Multiple studies have yielded weak positive findings for regions on chromosome 22, but no significant linkage has yet been established; there may be a minor susceptibility locus in this region (Pulver 2000).

**Chromosome 6.**  Extending the database and findings of S. Wang et al. (1995), Straub et al. (1995) found that the 6p22–25 region was linked to schizophrenia in 265 pedigrees, yielding a maximum heterogeneity lod score of 3.51 for one locus. This locus appeared to influence the susceptibility to schizophrenia in 15%–30% of the pedigrees studied, showing the maximal effect when an intermediate phenotypic definition was used. Schwab et al. (1995) used affected sib-pair analysis and found a lod score of 2.2 at 6p22. Other investigators also have found suggestive linkage to schizophrenia in this region (Antonarakis et al. 1995; Kaufmann et al. 1998; Moises et al. 1995) as well as linkage to bipolar disorder in Amish pedigrees (Ginns et al. 1996). It may be that a locus in this region may confer susceptibility to symptoms common to both bipolar disorder and schizophrenia. Maziade et al. (1997) found linkage between the 6p24–22 locus and illness in one lare mixed bipolar-schizophrenia pedigree. This area of 6p is close to the HLA region. There has been interest in this region because of the association of schizophrenia with prenatal infections. Many years ago, there had been a suggestion of linkage between schizophrenia spectrum disorders and the HLA region on 6p in six informative pedigrees (Turner 1979), but the finding was not replicated in subsequent studies (Andrew et al. 1987; Chada et al. 1986; Goldin et al. 1987; McGuffin et al. 1983). However, centromeric to the HLA region, at 6p21–23, lie two loci that yielded lod scores greater than 3.0 in eight German pedigrees in studies of linkage to eye-tracking abnormalities, which, like sensory gating deficits, are common in schizophrenia (Arolt et al. 1996). As with other endophenotypes, no significant linkage was found to schizophrenia itself, although this again may be because the number of subjects was too small to detect linkage.

**Other chromosomes.**  A recent genome scan in 22 densely affected families yielded the impressively high lod score of 6.50 for 1q21–q22 (Brzustowicz et al. 2000); this new and exciting finding has yet to be replicated. In addition to 13q32 and 6p, there is preliminary evidence for linkage of schizophrenia to loci on 18p that also have been linked to bipolar disorder (Berrettini et al. 1994; Schwab et al. 1998). Linkage to chromosome 10 has been found in Caucasian but not African American schizophrenia pedigrees (Faraone et al. 1998). There is some additional evidence for linkage to schizophrenia on chromosomes 10, 3, 4, 7, 9, 14, and 20 (Pulver 2000). Cytogenetic anomalies had suggested linkage between schizophrenia and chromosomes 2, 5, and X, but these have not been supported by further studies.

## Candidate Genes

Candidate gene studies in schizophrenia are informed by theories of pathophysiology and focus largely, but not exclusively, on monoamine neurotransmission. The results of these investigations have largely been disappointing (although many of the studies have likely been underpowered). The most promising findings have been for two candidate genes: the 5-HT$_{2A}$ receptor gene and the *DRD3*.

A Japanese group first found an association between a polymorphism in the 5-HT$_{2A}$ receptor gene and schizophrenia (Inayama et al. 1996); this finding was replicated by a European study that had 571 patients and 639 control subjects (Williams et al. 1996). Negative reports of association were found by others, although these studies may have been underpowered. A meta-analysis of data on 3,000 subjects confirmed the original finding, with $P = 0.0009$, and publication bias was found to be unlikely (Williams et al. 1997). The evidence for a real association between this polymorphism and schizophrenia is substantial, although the polymorphism neither changes the amino acid sequence of the receptor nor has any appreciable effect on transcription, so it is difficult to know what this association reflects at the molecular level (O'Donovan and Owen 1999).

Studies of the association between schizophrenia and the *DRD3* follow a similar pattern to that of the 5-HT$_{2A}$ receptor gene: an initial finding, some replications, some negative reports (perhaps underpowered), and then a meta-analysis that provides support for the initial finding (O'Donovan and Owen 1999; Williams et al. 1998). So, there is a balance of evidence for an association between a polymorphism in this gene and schizophrenia but no definitive proof and no molecular biologic model for disease expression to explain the association.

Of note, several candidate genes have been studied in depth and have yielded little or no evidence of any association; these include APP (important in AD) and glutamate receptors and other proteins important in monoamine synthesis, activity, and catabolism (transporters and other receptors for serotonin and dopamine, monoamine oxidases, and COMT).

# Narcolepsy

The hallmark features of classic narcolepsy are excessive daytime sleepiness and cataplexy, or the sudden weakening of the muscles on the experience of strong emotions. Other common features include hypnagogic hallucinations and sleep paralysis, with blackouts and automatic behaviors occurring less frequently. The definitive clinical diagnosis of narcolepsy is made from polysomnographic evidence of abnormal REM sleep on the Multiple Sleep Latency Test. In a triumph of positional cloning, Mignot's group (L. Lin et al. 1999) recently identified an autosomal recessive mutation that accounted for narcolepsy in a well-established canine colony. This linkage finding led directly to the identification of a candidate gene for human narcolepsy, orexin (hypocretin), and the possibility of new insights into the neurophysiology of sleep and wakefulness.

## Epidemiologic Studies

Narcolepsy is a lifelong disorder that can begin at any age, although onset peaks in late adolescence, and most cases begin before age 25. The prevalence of narcolepsy with cataplexy is approximately 1 in 2,000 individuals, with estimates varying from 10–100 in 100,000 in the United States and Europe to 160 in 100,000 in Japan. Previous evidence of a genetic susceptibility for narcolepsy derived from the correlation between the frequency of narcolepsy and geographic variation of class II HLA antigens on chromosome 6. Almost all caucasian narcolepsy patients are *HLA-DR2* positive, whereas African-American patients frequently have the *HLA-DQB1* allele. This association between narcolepsy and HLA haplotypes is among the highest known for HLA-linked syndromes. HLA types serve as markers for the predisposition to pathologic immune responses in various diseases (Charon 1990; Nepom and Erlich 1991; Singha et al. 1990). Despite this association, attempts to show that narcolepsy was an autoimmune disease proved unsuccessful (Frederikson et al. 1990; Matsuki et al. 1988; Mignot et al. 1991; Parkes et al. 1986; Rubin et al. 1988). Other factors were presumed to be involved because exactly the same alleles are found in healthy subjects (Uryu et al. 1989). Models being explored for immune functions and narcolepsy include CNS cytokines and microglia. The gene that was recently identified for narcolepsy is distinct from the HLA alleles.

## Family Studies

Familial transmission of narcolepsy is uncommon (Aldrich 1990). However, the first-degree relatives of affected individuals are 10–40 times more likely to have narcolepsy than is the general population, consistent with genetic transmissibility (Mignot 1998). It is of note that the clinical expression of narcolepsy can vary markedly, even within the same family.

## Mode of Inheritance

Both an autosomal dominant model with variable expressivity and low penetrance (Baraitser and Parkes 1987) and a high-heritability multifactorial model with multiple thresholds fit well with family recurrence data (Guilleminault et al. 1989; Honda et al. 1983; S. Kessler et al. 1974). Also, environmental factors likely contribute to narcolepsy risk (Guilleminault et al. 1989) because identical twins have low concordance rates (Douglass et al. 1989; Montplaisir and Poirier 1987), and about one-half of patients experience a precipitating illness, head injury, or stressful psychologic factor prior to the onset of the narcolepsy (Passouant and Billiard 1976). Although the association with precipitating events may be coincidental, it would be consistent with a disease model in which onset is triggered by an exogenous event in those who have an underlying genetic predisposition.

## Linkage Analysis

In their groundbreaking study, Mignot and colleagues (L. Lin et al. 1999) used positional cloning to identify carnac-1, an autosomal recessive gene for canine narcolepsy. The gene was cloned in bacterial artificial chromosomes, and the homologous human gene was identified. The susceptibility allele was a mutation in the G-protein-coupled orexin-2 receptor. A role for this gene in narcolepsy was further confirmed when Yanagisawa and colleagues reported narcoleptic-like attacks in mice with an orexin knockout mutation (Chemelli et al. 1999).

## Molecular Approaches

Abnormalities in the orexin gene or its physiologic pathways can cause human narcolepsy. Orexin neurons arise in the lateral and posterior hypothalamus and project to regions that include the limbic system, thalamus, brain stem, and spinal cord (Reid et al. 1998). Orexin neurotransmission participates in regulation of feeding behaviors (Sakurai et al. 1998), and much research is under way to elucidate its role in sleep mechanisms and narcolepsy. There is hope that these efforts also may lead to novel therapeutic agents for the treatment of this chronic and disabling disorder.

## Conclusions

In this chapter, we have focused on identifying some of the environmental and hereditary factors that may contribute to certain neuropsychiatric diseases. These reviews are not exhaustive; rather, they have been chosen to illustrate current thinking and the methodologies that are available to examine the etiology of disease. As is apparent, these factors are often not clearly distinguishable from one another as to their role in disease production. Nonetheless, the role of environmental factors may be large in some illnesses, such as PD, and smaller in others, such as HD. Traditionally, epidemiology has focused on exogenous influences, whereas genetics has focused on endogenous influences. In practice, the fields often overlap, genetic epidemiology being a discipline within epidemiology.

In defining environmental effects on disease, epidemiology proceeds in a stepwise manner. First, an association is established between exposure to a particular factor and development of the disease. Next, it is determined whether this association is valid or is the consequence of chance, bias, or confounds by the introduction of suitable control subjects and blinds. Finally, it is judged whether this association represents a cause-and-effect relation by its magnitude, consistency, and biologic plausibility (Hennekens and Buring 1987).

Likewise, genetic studies proceed to uncover heritable effects, first by establishing the association between familial and genetic exposure to the disorder and then by validating this association, again with appropriate control subjects and blinds. Subsequently, genetic studies specify the genes mediating these effects. With some disorders, the abnormal gene product (e.g., a defective enzyme or reduction in enzyme quantities) may be known, and the disease gene coding for that product may thereby be isolated. This has been the case for several disorders, such as metochromatic leukodystrophy, WD, and LNS. For other disorders, the abnormal gene product is unknown and may be coded by any of the estimated 50,000 genes that are thought to be involved in CNS function. In these disorders, the search for the disease gene begins with establishing its chromosomal location (linkage). The gene then may be isolated through the rapidly evolving techniques of molecular genetics.

The initial successes in molecular genetics were achieved with genetically simple disorders. These are relatively rare illnesses demonstrating clear mendelian modes of inheritance, such as the autosomal recessive disorder cystic fibrosis, the autosomal dominant disorder neurofibromatosis, and the X-linked recessive disorder Duchenne type muscular dystrophy. More recently, major genes have been localized for genetically complex disorders, including major genes for Hirschsprung's disease, familial breast cancer, and type I diabetes mellitus. Unfortunately, success in the application of positional cloning strategies to the study of complex illnesses, notably the neuropsychiatric disorders, has been more difficult. Still, there are some remarkable and exciting findings, as described herein.

Broad advances in human genetics have had significant effects on the theory and practice of medicine, and we expect that its influence will expand with the increase in genetic knowledge. Neuropsychiatry is no exception: clinical, molecular, and statistical genetic strategies promise to reveal much about the etiology, pathogenesis, and treatment of mental illness. In the foreseeable future, we hope to discover how the disposition to neuropsychiatric illness is transmitted, the biologic nature of the inherited factors, and the ways in which these genetic factors interact with environmental exposures. Yet to be determined are the full implications of these developments for etiology, prevention, and treatment.

Advances in molecular genetics techniques also will increase the accuracy of the detection of at-risk individuals. In HD, for example, molecular genetic techniques can be used to assess the number of CAG trinucleotide repeats at the huntingtin locus to determine who is at risk for developing the disorder. Careful consideration needs to be given to the potential ethical, legal, and social effects of these technologies and discoveries.

## References

Abeliovich D, Lerer I, Pashut-Lavon I, et al: Negative expansion of the myotonic dystrophy unstable sequence. Am J Hum Genet 52:1175–1181, 1993

Abramson RK, Wright HH, Carpenter R, et al: Elevated blood serotonin in autistic probands and their first-degree relatives. J Autism Dev Disord 19:397–407, 1989

Adams W, Kendell RE, Hare EH, et al: Epidemiological evidence that maternal influenza contributes to the aetiology of schizophrenia: an analysis of Scottish, English, and Danish data. Br J Psychiatry 163:522–534, 1993

Aicardi J: The inherited leukodystrophies: a clinical overview. J Inherit Metab Dis 16:733–743, 1993

Aiken JM, Marsh RF: The search for scrapie agent nucleic acid. Microbiology Reviews 54:242–246, 1990

Akil M, Schwartz JA, Dutchak D, et al: The psychiatric presentations of Wilson's disease [see comments]. J Neuropsychiatry Clin Neurosci 3:377–382, 1991

Alberts-Corush J, Firestone P, Goodman JT: Attention and impulsivity characteristics of the biological and adoptive parents of hyperactive and normal control children. Am J Orthopsychiatry 56:413–423, 1986

Aldrich MS: Narcolepsy. N Engl J Med 323:389–394, 1990

Alford RL, Ashizawa T, Jankovic J, et al: Molecular detection of new mutations, resolution of ambiguous results and complex genetic counseling issues in Huntington disease. Am J Med Genet 66:281–286, 1996

Allen KM, Walsh CA: Genes that regulate neuronal migration in the cerebral cortex. Epilepsy Res 36(2–3):143–154, 1999

Almond JW: Bovine spongiform encephalopathy and new variant Creutzfeldt-Jakob disease. Br Med Bull 54:749–759, 1998

Alsobrook II JP, Leckman JF, Goodman WK, et al: Segregation analysis of obsessive-compulsive disorder using symptom-based factor scores. Am J Med Genet 88:669–675, 1999

Altemus M, Murphy DL, Greenberg B, et al: Intact coding region of the serotonin transporter gene in obsessive-compulsive disorder. Am J Med Genet 67:409–441, 1996

Alves D, Pieres MM, Guimaraes A, et al: Four cases of metachromatic leukodystrophy in a family: clinical, biochemical and neuropathological studies. J Neurol Neurosurg Psychiatry 49:1417–1422, 1986

Amaducci LA, Fratiglioni L, Rocca WA, et al: Risk factors for clinically diagnosed Alzheimer's disease: a case study of an Italian population. Neurology 36:922–931, 1986

Ambrose CM, Duyao MP, Barnes G, et al: Structure and expression of the Huntington's disease gene: evidence against simple inactivation due to an expanded CAG repeat. Somat Cell Mol Genet 20:27–38, 1994

Ameen M, Lazzarino DA, Kelly BM, et al: Deficient glycosylation of arylsulfatase A in pseudoarylsulfatase A deficiency. Mol Cell Biochem 92:117–127, 1990

American Psychiatric Association: Diagnostic and Statistical Manual of Mental Disorders, 3rd Edition. Washington, DC, American Psychiatric Association, 1980

American Psychiatric Association: Diagnostic and Statistical Manual of Mental Disorders, 3rd Edition, Revised. Washington, DC, American Psychiatric Association, 1987

American Psychiatric Association: Diagnostic and Statistical Manual of Mental Disorders, 4th Edition. Washington, DC, American Psychiatric Association, 1994

American Psychiatric Association: Diagnostic and Statistical Manual of Mental Disorders, 4th Edition, Text Revision. Washington, DC, American Psychiatric Association, 2000

Anderson JC, Williams S, McGee R, et al: DSM-III disorders in preadolescent children: prevalence in a large sample from the general population. Arch Gen Psychiatry 44:69–76, 1987

Anderson VE, Wilcox KJJ, Rich SS, et al: Twin studies in epilepsy, in Genetics of the Epilepsies. Edited by Beck-Mannagetta G, Anderson VE, Doose H, et al. Berlin, Germany, Springer-Verlag, 1989, pp 145–155

Andrew B, Watt DC, Gillespie C, et al: A study of genetic linkage in schizophrenia. Psychol Med 17:363–370, 1987

Andrews G, Stewart G, Allen R, et al: The genetics of six neurotic disorders: a twin study. J Affect Disord 19:23–29, 1990

Andrews TC, Weeks RA, Turjanski N, et al: Huntington's disease progression: PET and clinical observations. Brain 122 (pt 12):2353–2363, 1999

Antonarakis SE, Blouin JL, Pulver AE, et al: Schizophrenia susceptibility and chromosome 6p24–22 (letter; comment). Nat Genet 11:235–236, 1995

Arcos-Burgos M, Palacio LG, Mora O, et al: Aspectos geneticomoleculares de la susceptibilidad para desarrollar epilepsia idiopatica. Rev Neurol 30:173–177, 2000

Arolt V, Lencer R, Nolte A, et al: Eye tracking dysfunction is a putative phenotypic susceptibility marker of schizophrenia and maps to a locus on chromosome 6p in families with multiple occurrence of the disease. Am J Med Genet 67:564–579, 1996

Asghari V, Schoots O, van Kats S, et al: Dopamine D4 receptor repeat: analysis of different native and mutant forms of the human and rat genes. Mol Pharmacol 46:364–373, 1994

Ashizawa T, Dubel JR, Dunne PW, et al: Anticipation in myotonic dystrophy, II: complex relationships between clinical findings and structure of the GCT repeat. Neurology 42:1877–1883, 1992

Ashizawa T, Dunne PW, Ward PA, et al: Effects of the sex of myotonic dystrophy patients on the unstable triplet repeat in their affected offspring. Neurology 44:120–122, 1994

Aslanidis C, Jansen G, Amemiya C, et al: Cloning of the essential myotonic dystrophy region: mapping of the putative defect. Nature 355:548–551, 1992

Ashley-Koch A, Wolpert CM, Menold MM, et al: Genetic studies of autistic disorder and chromosome 7. Genomics 61:227–236, 1999

August GJ, Stewart MA, Tsai L: The incidence of cognitive disabilities in the siblings of autistic children. Br J Psychiatry 138:416–422, 1981

Bacon BR, Schilsky ML: New knowledge of genetic pathogenesis of hemochromatosis and Wilson's disease. Adv Intern Med 44:91–116, 1999

Bailey A, Le Couteur A, Gottesman I, et al: Autism as a strongly genetic disorder: evidence from a British twin study. Psychol Med 25:63–77, 1995

Bailey A, Palferman S, Heavey L, et al: Autism: the phenotype in relatives. J Autism Dev Disord 28:369–392, 1998

Bakwin H: Reading disability in twins. Dev Med Child Neurol 15:184–187, 1973

Baldereschi M, Di Carlo A, Lepore V, et al: Estrogen-replacement therapy and Alzheimer's disease in the Italian Longitudinal Study on Aging. Neurology 50:996–1002, 1998

Bales KR, Verina T, Dodel RC, et al: Lack of apolipoprotein E dramatically reduces amyloid beta-peptide deposition (letter) [see comments]. Nat Genet 17:263–264, 1997

Balon R, Pohl R, Yeragani VK, et al: Lactate- and isoproterenol-induced panic attacks in panic disorder patients and controls. Psychiatry Res 23:153–160, 1988

Balon R, Jordan M, Pohl R, et al: Family history of anxiety disorders in control subjects with lactate-induced panic attacks. Am J Psychiatry 146:1304–1306, 1989

Bandmann O, Vaughan J, Holmans P, et al: Association of slow acetylator genotype for N-acetyltransferase 2 with familial Parkinson's disease [see comments]. Lancet 350:1136–1139, 1997

Baraitser M: The Genetics of Neurological Disorders, 2nd Edition. New York, Oxford Medical Publications, 1990

Barbeau A, Roy M, Bernier G, et al: Ecogenetics of Parkinson's disease: prevalence and environmental aspects in rural areas. Can J Neurol Sci 14:36–41, 1987

Barr CL, Wigg K, Malone M, et al: Linkage study of catechol-O-methyltransferase and attention-deficit hyperactivity disorder. Am J Med Genet 88:710–713, 1999

Barr CL, Wigg KG, Wu J, et al: Linkage study of two polymorphisms at the dopamine D3 receptor gene and attention-deficit hyperactivity disorder. Am J Med Genet 96:114–117, 2000

Barrett S, Beck JC, Bernier R, et al: An autosomal genomic screen for autism. Collaborative linkage study of autism. Am J Med Genet 88:609–615, 1999

Barth ML, Fensom A, Harris A: Missense mutations in the arylsulphatase A gene of metachromatic leukodystrophy patients. Hum Mol Genet 2:2117–2121, 1993a

Barth ML, Fensom A, Harris A: Prevalence of common mutations in the arylsulphatase A gene in metachromatic leukodystrophy patients diagnosed in Britain. Hum Genet 91:73–77, 1993b

Barth ML, Fensom A, Harris A: The arylsulphatase A gene and molecular genetics of metachromatic leukodystrophy. J Med Genet 31:663–666, 1994a

Barth ML, Ward C, Harris A, et al: Frequency of arylsulphatase A pseudodeficiency associated mutations in a health population. J Med Genet 3:667–671, 1994b

Barton M, Volkmar F: How commonly are known medical conditions associated with autism? J Autism Dev Disord 28:273–278, 1998

Battaglia M, Torgersen S: Schizotypal disorder: at the crossroads of genetics and nosology. Acta Psychiatr Scand 94:303–310, 1996

Baulac S, Gourfinkel-An I, Picard F, et al: A second locus for familial generalized epilepsy with febrile seizures plus maps to chromosome 2q21-q33. Am J Hum Genet 65:1078–1085, 1999

Baysal BE, Potkin SG, Farr JE, et al: Cloning a balanced t(9;11)(p24;q23.1) chromosomal translocation breakpoint segregating with bipolar affective disorder in a small pedigree. Am J Hum Genet 57:A256, 1995

Bearn AG: A genetical analysis of thirty families with Wilson's disease (hepatolenticular degeneration). Ann Hum Genet 24:33–43, 1960

Bekkelund SI, Selseth B, Mellgren SI: Parkinson's disease in a population group in northern Norway. Tidsskr Nor Laegeforen 109:561–563, 1989

Belay ED: Transmissible spongiform encephalopathies in humans. Annu Rev Microbiol 53:283–314, 1999

Bellodi L, Perna G, Caldirola D, et al: CO2-induced panic attacks: a twin study. Am J Psychiatry 155:1184–1188, 1998

Benjamin J, Li L, Patterson C, et al: Population and familial association between the D4 dopamine receptor gene and measures of novelty seeking. Nat Genet 12:81–84, 1996

Ben-Shlomo Y, Sieradzan K: Idiopathic Parkinson's disease: epidemiology, diagnosis and management. Br J Gen Pract 45:261–268, 1995

Berg AT, Shinnar S, Levy SR, et al: Childhood-onset epilepsy with and without preceding febrile seizures. Neurology 53:1742–1748, 1999

Berkovic SF, Scheffer IE: Genetics of the epilepsies. Curr Opin Neurol 12:177–182, 1999

Bernoulli C, Siegfried J, Baumgartner G, et al: Danger of accidental person-to-person transmission of Creutzfeldt-Jakob disease by surgery (letter). Lancet 1:478–479, 1977

Berrettini W: Progress and pitfalls: bipolar molecular linkage studies. J Affect Disord 50:287–297, 1998

Berrettini WH: Susceptibility loci for bipolar disorder: overlap with inherited vulnerability to schizophrenia. Biol Psychiatry 47:245–251, 2000

Berrettini WH, Ferraro TN, Goldin LR, et al: Chromosome 18 DNA markers and manic-depressive illness: evidence for a susceptibility gene. Proc Natl Acad Sci U S A 91:5918–5921, 1994

Berrettini WH, Ferraro TN, Goldin LR, et al: A linkage study of bipolar illness. Arch Gen Psychiatry 54:27–35, 1997

Bickeboller H, Kistler M, Scholz M: Investigation of the candidate genes ACTHR and golf for bipolar illness by the transmission/disequilibrium test. Genet Epidemiol 14:575–580, 1997

Bickel H, Neale FC, Hall G: A clinical and biochemical study of hepatolenticular degeneration (Wilson's disease.) QJM 26:527–558, 1957

Biederman J, Faraone SV, Keenan K, et al: Family genetic and psychosocial risk factors in DSM-III attention deficit disorder. J Am Acad Child Adolesc Psychiatry 29:526–533, 1990

Billett EA, Richter MA, King N, et al: Obsessive compulsive disorder, response to serotonin reuptake inhibitors and the serotonin transporter gene. Mol Psychiatry 2:403–406, 1997

Billett EA, Richter MA, Sam F, et al: Investigation of dopamine system genes in obsessive-compulsive disorder. Psychiatr Genet 8:163–169, 1998

Bird HR, Canino G, Rubio-Stipec M, et al: Estimates of the prevalence of childhood maladjustment in a community survey in Puerto Rico: the use of combined measures [published erratum appears in Arch Gen Psychiatry 51:429, 1994]. Arch Gen Psychiatry 45:1120–1126, 1988

Black A: The natural history of obsessional neurosis, in Obsessional States. Edited by Beech HR. London, UK, Methuen, 1974

Blacker D, Haines JL, Rodes L, et al: ApoE-4 and age at onset of Alzheimer's disease: the NIMH genetics initiative. Neurology 48:139–147, 1997

Blackwood DH, He L, Morris SW, et al: A locus for bipolar affective disorder on chromosome 4p. Nat Genet 12:427–430, 1996

Blouin JL, Dombroski BA, Nath SK, et al: Schizophrenia susceptibility loci on chromosomes 13q32 and 8p21. Nat Genet 20:70–73, 1998

Bocchetta A, Piccardi MP, Palmas MA, et al: Family based association study between bipolar disorder and DRD2, DRD4, DAT, and SERT in Sardinia. Am J Med Genet 88:522–526, 1999

Bolton DC, McKinley MP, Prusiner SB: Identification of a protein that purifies with the scrapie prion. Science 218:1309–1311, 1982

Bonaiuto S, Rocca WA, Lippi A, et al: Education and occupation as risk factors for dementia: a population-based case-control study. Neuroepidemiology 14:101–109, 1995

Bonifati V, Vanacore N, Meco G: Anticipation of onset age in familial Parkinson's disease. Neurology 44:1978–1979, 1994

Bonne-Tamir B, Farrer LA, Frydman M, et al: Evidence for linkage between Wilson disease and esterase D in three kindreds: detection of linkage for an autosomal recessive disorder by the family study method. Genet Epidemiol 3:201–209, 1986

Book JA: A genetic and psychiatric investigation of a north Swedish population with special regard to schizophrenia and mental deficiency. Acta Genet 4:1–139, 1953

Botstein D, White RL, Skolnick M, et al: Construction of a genetic linkage map using restriction fragment length polymorphisms. Am J Hum Genet 32:314–331, 1980

Boyd M, Lanyon WG, Connor JM: Screening for molecular pathologies in Lesch-Nyhan syndrome. Hum Mutat 2:127–130, 1993

Boyles JK, Zoellner CD, Anderson LJ, et al: A role for apolipoprotein A-I and low density lipoprotein receptors in cholesterol transport during regeneration and remyelination of the rat sciatic nerve. J Clin Invest 83:1015–1031, 1989

Bradbury TN, Miller GA: Season of birth in schizophrenia: a review of evidence, methodology, and etiology. Psychol Bull 98:569–594, 1985

Breitner JCS, Murphey EA, Folstein MF: Familial aggregation of Alzheimer dementia, II: clinical genetic implications of age dependent onset. J Psychiatry Res 20:45–55, 1986

Breitner JC, Gau BA, Welsh KA, et al: Inverse association of anti-inflammatory treatments and Alzheimer's disease: initial results of a co-twin control study. Neurology 44:227–232, 1994

Breitner JC, Welsh KA, Gau BA, et al: Alzheimer's disease in the National Academy of Sciences-National Research Council Registry of Aging Twin Veterans, III: detection of cases, longitudinal results, and observations on twin concordance. Arch Neurol 52:763–771, 1995

Brook JD, McCurrack ME, Harley HG, et al: Molecular basis of myotonic dystrophy: expansion of a trinucleotide (CTG) repeat at the 3´ end of a transcript encoding a protein kinase family member. Cell 68:799–808, 1992

Brooks DJ: The early diagnosis of Parkinson's disease. Ann Neurol 44:S10–S18, 1998

Brown AS, Cohen P, Harkavy-Friedman J, et al: A.E. Bennett Research Award: prenatal rubella, premorbid abnormalities, and adult schizophrenia. Biol Psychiatry 49:473–486, 2001

Brown FR III, Shimizu H, McDonald JM, et al: Auditory evoked brainstem response and high-performance liquid chromatography sulfatide assay as early indices of metachromatic leukodystrophy. Neurology 31:980–985, 1981

Brown FW: Heredity in the psychoneuroses. Proceedings of the Royal Society of Medicine 35:785–790, 1942

Brown P: The risk of bovine spongiform encephalopathy ('mad cow disease') to human health. JAMA 278:1008–1011, 1997

Brown P, Cathala F, Castaigne P, et al: Creutzfeldt-Jakob disease: clinical analysis of a consecutive series of 230 neuropathologically verified cases. Ann Neurol 20:597–602, 1986

Brown P, Goldfarb LG, Cathala F, et al: The molecular genetics of familial Creutzfeldt-Jakob disease in France. J Neurol Sci 105:240–246, 1991

Brown P, Goldfarb LG, Kovanen J, et al: Phenotypic characteristics of familial Creutzfeldt-Jakob disease associated with the codon 178Asn PRNP mutation. Ann Neurol 31:282–285, 1992

Brown P, Gibbs CJ Jr, Rodgers-Johnson P, et al: Human spongiform encephalopathy: the National Institutes of Health series of 300 cases of experimentally transmitted disease. Ann Neurol 35:513–529, 1994

Bruce ME, Will RG, Ironside JW, et al: Transmissions to mice indicate that 'new variant' CJD is caused by the BSE agent [see comments]. Nature 389:498–501, 1997

Brunner HG, Nilesen W, van-Oost BA, et al: Presymptomatic diagnosis of myotonic dystrophy. J Med Genet 29:780–784, 1992

Bryson SE, Clark BS, Smith IM: First report of a Canadian epidemiological study of autistic syndromes. J Child Psychol Psychiatry 29:433–445, 1988

Brzustowicz LM, Hodgkinson KA, Chow EW, et al: Location of a major susceptibility locus for familial schizophrenia on chromosome 1q21-q22. Science 288:678–682, 2000

Bull PC, Cox DW: Long range restriction mapping of 13q14.3 focused on the Wilson disease region. Genomics 16:593–598, 1993

Bull PC, Thomas GR, Rommens M, et al: The Wilson disease gene is a putative copper transporting ATPase similar to the Menkes disease gene. Nat Genet 5:327–337, 1993

Bungener C, Jouvent R, Delaporte C: Psychopathological and emotional deficits in myotonic dystrophy. J Neurol Neurosurg Psychiatry 65:353–356, 1998

Burke KC, Burke JD Jr, Regier DA, et al: Age at onset of selected mental disorders in five community populations. Arch Gen Psychiatry 47:511–518, 1990

Butterworth NJ, Williams L, Bullock JY, et al: Trinucleotide (CAG) repeat length is positively correlated with the degree of DNA fragmentation in Huntington's disease striatum. Neuroscience 87:49–53, 1998

Buxton J, Shelbourne P, Davies J, et al: Detection of an unstable fragment of DNA specific to individuals with myotonic dystrophy. Nature 355:547–548, 1992

Byerley W, Holik J, Hoff M, et al: Search for a gene predisposing to manic-depression on chromosome 21. Am J Med Genet 60:231–233, 1995

Cadoret RJ, O'Gorman TW, Heywood E, et al: Genetic and environmental factors in major depression. J Affect Disord 9:155–164, 1985

Callahan CM, Hall KS, Hui SL, et al: Relationship of age, education, and occupation with dementia among a community-based sample of African Americans. Arch Neurol 53:134–140, 1996

Callenbach PM, Geerts AT, Arts WF, et al: Familial occurrence of epilepsy in children with newly diagnosed multiple seizures: Dutch Study of Epilepsy in Childhood. Epilepsia 39:331–336, 1998

Callicott JH, Egan MF, Bertolino A, et al: Hippocampal N-acetyl aspartate in unaffected siblings of patients with schizophrenia: a possible intermediate neurobiological phenotype. Biol Psychiatry 44:941–950, 1998

Calne S, Schoenberg B, Martin W, et al: Familial Parkinson's disease: possible role of environmental factors. Can J Neurol Sci 14:303–305, 1987

Canadian Study of Health and Aging: Risk factors for Alzheimer's disease in Canada. Neurology 44:2073–2080, 1994

Cannon TD, Kaprio J, Lonnqvist J, et al: The genetic epidemiology of schizophrenia in a Finnish twin cohort: a population-based modeling study. Arch Gen Psychiatry 55:67–74, 1998

Cantwell DP: Psychiatric illness in the families of hyperactive children. Arch Gen Psychiatry 27:414–417, 1972

Cardon LR, Smith SS, Fulkner DW, et al: Quantitative trait locus for reading disability on chromosome 6. Science 266:276–279, 1994

Carey G, Gottesman II: Twin and family studies of anxiety, phobic, and obsessive disorders, in Anxiety: New Research and Changing Concepts. Edited by Klein DF, Rabkin JD. New York, Raven, 1981

Carpenter NJ: Genetic anticipation: expanding tandem repeats. Neurol Clin 12:683–697, 1994

Castellanos FX, Lau E, Tayebi N, et al: Lack of an association between a dopamine-4 receptor polymorphism and atten-tion-deficit/hyperactivity disorder: genetic and brain morphometric analyses. Mol Psychiatry 3:431–434, 1998

Catalano M, Sciuto G, Di Bella D, et al: Lack of association between obsessive-compulsive disorder and the dopamine D3 receptor gene: some preliminary considerations. Am J Med Genet 54:253–255, 1994

Cavallini MC, Di Bella D, Pasquale L, et al: 5HT2C CYS23/SER23 polymorphism is not associated with obsessive-compulsive disorder. Psychiatry Res 77:97–104, 1998

Cavallini MC, Pasquale L, Bellodi L, et al: Complex segregation analysis for obsessive compulsive disorder and related disorders. Am J Med Genet 88:38–43, 1999a

Cavallini MC, Perna G, Caldirola D, et al: A segregation study of panic disorder in families of panic patients responsive to the 35% CO2 challenge. Biol Psychiatry 46:815–820, 1999b

Cerizza M, Nemni R, Tamma F: Adult metachromatic leukodystrophy: an underdiagnosed disease. J Neurol Neurosurg Psychiatry 50:1710–1712, 1987

Chada R, Kulhara P, Singh T, et al: HLA antigens in schizophrenia: a family study. Br J Psychiatry 149:612–615, 1986

Chandola CA, Robling MR, Peters TJ, et al: Pre- and perinatal factors and the risk of subsequent referral for hyperactivity. J Child Psychol Psychiatry 33:1077–1090, 1992

Chandra V, Ganguli M, Pandav R, et al: Prevalence of Alzheimer's disease and other dementias in rural India: the Indo-US study [see comments]. Neurology 51:1000–1008, 1998

Chang KD, Steiner H, Ketter TA: Psychiatric phenomenology of child and adolescent bipolar offspring. J Am Acad Child Adolesc Psychiatry 39:453–460, 2000

Charon D: Molecular basis of human leucocyte antigen class II disease associations. Adv Immunol 18:107–159, 1990

Checkoway H, Nelson LM: Epidemiologic approaches to the study of Parkinson's disease etiology. Epidemiology 10:327–336, 1999

Chemelli RM, Willie JT, Sinton CM, et al: Narcolepsy in orexin knockout mice: molecular genetics of sleep regulation. Cell 98:437–451, 1999

Clark J, Skomorowski MA, Chang PL: Marked clinical difference between 2 sibs affected with juvenile MRA. Am J Med Genet 33:10–13, 1989

Clifford CA, Murray RM, Fulker DW: Genetic and environmental influences on obsessional traits and symptoms. Psychol Med 14:791–800, 1984

Cloninger CR, Van Eerdewegh P, Goate A, et al: Anxiety proneness linked to epistatic loci in genome scan of human personality traits. Am J Med Genet 81:313–317, 1998

Cobb JL, Wolf PA, Au R, et al: The effect of education on the incidence of dementia and Alzheimer's disease in the Framingham Study. Neurology 45:1707–1712, 1995

Cochius JI, Burns RJ, Blumbergs PC, et al: Creutzfeldt-Jakob disease in a recipient of human pituitary-derived gonadotrophin. Aust N Z J Med 20:592–593, 1990

Cohen ME, White PD, Johnson RE: Neurocirculatory asthenia, anxiety neurosis, or the effort syndrome. Arch Intern Med 81:260–281, 1948

Cohen ME, Badal DW, Kilpatrick A, et al: The high familial prevalence of neurocirculatory asthenia (anxiety neurosis, effort syndrome). Am J Hum Genet 3:126–158, 1951

Collinge J, Sidle KC, Meads J, et al: Molecular analysis of prion strain variation and the aetiology of 'new variant' CJD [see comments]. Nature 383:685–690, 1996

Comings DE, Comings BG, Muhleman D, et al: The dopamine D2 receptor locus as a modifying gene in neuropsychiatric disorders [see comments]. JAMA 266:1793–1800, 1991a

Conneally PM: Huntington disease: genetics and epidemiology. Am J Hum Genet 36:506–526, 1984

Constantinidis J, Garrone G, de Ajuriaguerra J: L'Hérédité des démences de l'âge avancé. Encephale 51:301–344, 1962

Cook EH Jr, Stein MA, Krasowski MD, et al: Association of attention-deficit disorder and the dopamine transporter gene. Am J Hum Genet 56:993–998, 1995

Cook EH Jr, Courchesne R, Lord C, et al: Evidence of linkage between the serotonin transporter and autistic disorder. Mol Psychiatry 2:247–250, 1997

Cook EH Jr, Courchesne RY, Cox NJ, et al: Linkage-disequilibrium mapping of autistic disorder, with 15q11–13 markers. Am J Hum Genet 62:1077–1083, 1998

Corder EH, Saunders AM, Strittmatter WJ, et al: Gene dose of apolipoprotein E type 4 allele and the risk of Alzheimer's disease in late onset families. Science 261:921–923, 1993

Corder EH, Saunders AM, Risch NJ, et al: Apolipoprotein E type 2 allele decreases the risk of late-onset Alzheimer's disease. Nat Genet 7:180–184, 1994

Coryell W: Hypersensitivity to carbon dioxide as a disease-specific trait marker. Biol Psychiatry 41:259–263, 1997

Coryell WJ, Endicott NC, Andreasen MB, et al: Depression and panic attacks: the significance of overlap as reflected in follow-up and family study data. Am J Psychiatry 145:293–300, 1988

Cox DW, Fraser FC, Sass-Kortsak A: A genetic study of Wilson's disease: evidence for heterogeneity. Am J Hum Genet 24:646–666, 1972

Coyle JT, Price DL, Delong MR: Alzheimer's disease: a disorder of the cholinergic innervation of cortex. Science 219:1184–1190, 1983

Craddock N, Jones I: Genetics of bipolar disorder. J Med Genet 36:585–594, 1999

Craddock N, Owen M: Christmas disease and major affective disorder (letter; comment). Br J Psychiatry 160:715, 1992

Craddock N, McKeon P, Moorhead S, et al: Expanded CAG/CTG repeats in bipolar disorder: no correlation with phenotypic measures of illness severity. Biol Psychiatry 42:876–881, 1997

Crawford TJ, Hoyne P, Diaz A, et al: Occurrence of the Cys311 DRD2 variant in a pedigree multiply affected with panic disorder. Am J Med Genet 60:332–334, 1995

Crawford TJ, Sharma T, Puri BK, et al: Saccadic eye movements in families multiply affected with schizophrenia: the Maudsley Family Study. Am J Psychiatry 155:1703–1710, 1998

Crowe RC, Pauls DL, Slymen DJ, et al: A family study of anxiety neurosis: morbidity risk in families of patients with and without mitral valve prolapse. Arch Gen Psychiatry 37:77–79, 1980

Crowe RR Jr, Noyes R, Pauls DL, et al: A family study of panic disorder. Arch Gen Psychiatry 40:1065–1069, 1983

Crowe RR, Noyes R Jr, Persico AM: Pro-opiomelanocortin (POMC) gene excluded as a cause of panic disorder in a large family. J Affect Disord 12:23–27, 1987a

Crowe RR, Noyes R Jr, Wilson AF, et al: A linkage study of panic disorder. Arch Gen Psychiatry 44:933–937, 1987b

Crowe RR, Noyes R Jr, Samuelson S, et al: Close linkage between panic disorder and alpha-haptoglobin excluded in 10 families. Arch Gen Psychiatry 47:377–380, 1990

Cruts M, van Duijn CM, Backhovens H, et al: Estimation of the genetic contribution of presenilin-1 and -2 mutations in a population-based study of presenile Alzheimer disease. Hum Mol Genet 7:43–51, 1998

Cruz C, Camarena B, King N, et al: Increased prevalence of the seven-repeat variant of the dopamine D4 receptor gene in patients with obsessive-compulsive disorder with tics. Neurosci Lett 231:1–4, 1997

Csernansky JG, Joshi S, Wang L, et al: Hippocampal morphometry in schizophrenia by high dimensional brain mapping. Proc Natl Acad Sci U S A 95:11406–11411, 1998

Curran S, Newman S, Taylor E, et al: Hypescheme: an operational criteria checklist and minimum data set for molecular genetic studies of attention deficit and hyperactivity disorders. Am J Med Genet 96:244–250, 2000

Dalman C, Allebeck P, Cullberg J, et al: Obstetric complications and the risk of schizophrenia: a longitudinal study of a national birth cohort. Arch Gen Psychiatry 56:234–240, 1999

Dalrymple J, Appleby J: Cross sectional study of reporting of epileptic seizures to general practitioners. BMJ 320(7227):94–97, 2000

Dastur DK, Manghani DK, Wadia NH: Wilson's disease in India, in Progress in Neurogenetics. Edited by Barbeau A, Brunette JR. Amsterdam, The Netherlands, Excepta Medical, 1969, pp 615–621

Davidson BL, Tarle SA, Patella TD, et al: Molecular basis of hypoxanthine-guanine phosphoribosyltransferase deficiency in ten subjects determined by direct sequencing of amplified transcripts. J Clin Invest 84:342–346, 1989

Davidson BL, Tarle SA, van Antwerp M, et al: Identifications of 17 independent mutations responsible for human hypoxanthine-guanine phosphoribosyltransferase. Am J Hum Genet 48:951–958, 1991

Davies P: The genetics of Alzheimer's disease: a review and a discussion of the implications. Neurobiol Aging 7:459–466, 1986

Davis JO, Phelps JA: Twins with schizophrenia: genes or germs? Schizophr Bull 21:13–18, 1995

Davis RE, Miller S, Herrnstadt C, et al: Mutations in mitochondrial cytochrome c oxidase genes segregate with late-onset Alzheimer disease. Proc Natl Acad Sci U S A 94:4526–4531, 1997

Dawson E, Parfitt E, Roberts Q, et al: Linkage studies of bipolar disorder in the region of the Darier's disease gene on chromosome 12q23–24.1. Am J Med Genet 60:94–102, 1995

Day JW, Roelofs R, Leroy B, et al: Clinical and genetic characteristics of a five-generation family with a novel form of myotonic dystrophy (DM2). Neuromuscul Disord 9:19–27, 1999

Deckert J, Catalano M, Heils A, et al: Functional promoter polymorphism of the human serotonin transporter: lack of association with panic disorder. Psychiatr Genet 7:45–47, 1997

Deckert J, Nothen MM, Franke P, et al: Systematic mutation screening and association study of the A1 and A2a adenosine receptor genes in panic disorder suggest a contribution of the A2a gene to the development of disease. Mol Psychiatry 3:81–85, 1998

Deckert J, Catalano M, Syagailo YV, et al: Excess of high activity monoamine oxidase A gene promoter alleles in female patients with panic disorder. Hum Mol Genet 8:621–624, 1999

de Die-Smulders, Howeler CJ, Mirandolle JF, et al: Anticipation resulting in elimination of the myotonic dystrophy gene: a follow up study of one extended family. J Med Genet 31:595–601, 1994

DeFries J, Singer S, Foch T, et al: Familial nature of reading disability. Br J Psychiatry 132:361–367, 1978

De Gregorio L, Nyhan WL, Serafin E, et al: An unexpected affected female patient in a classical Lesch-Nyhan family. Mol Genet Metab 69:263–268, 2000

Delgado-Escueta AV, Serratosa JM, Liu A, et al: Progress in mapping human epilepsy genes. Epilepsia 35 (suppl 1):S29–S40, 1994

Delgado-Escueta AV, Medina MT, Serratosa JM, et al: Mapping and positional cloning of common idiopathic generalized epilepsies: juvenile myoclonus epilepsy and childhood absence epilepsy. Adv Neurol 79:351–374, 1999

DeLisi LE, Crow TJ: Evidence for a sex chromosome locus for schizophrenia. Schizophr Bull 15:431–440, 1989

DeLong GR, Dwyer JT: Correlation of family history with specific autistic subgroups: Asperger's syndrome and bipolar affective disease. J Autism Dev Disord 18:593–600, 1988

DeLorey TM, Handforth A, Anagnostaras SG, et al: Mice lacking the beta3 subunit of the GABAA receptor have the epilepsy phenotype and many of the behavioral characteristics of Angelman syndrome. J Neurosci 18:8505–8514, 1998

Dening TR: The neuropsychiatry of Wilson's disease: a review. Int J Psychiatry Med 21:135–148, 1991

Dening TR, Berrios GE: Wilson's disease: a longitudinal study of psychiatric symptoms. Biol Psychiatry 28:255–265, 1990

De Rijk MC, Rocca WA, Anderson DW, et al: A population perspective on diagnostic criteria for Parkinson's disease. Neurology 48:1277–1281, 1997

Detera-Wadleigh SD: Chromosomes 12 and 16 workshop. Am J Med Genet 88:255–259, 1999

Detera-Wadleigh SD, Badner JA, Goldin LR, et al: Affected-sib-pair analyses reveal support of prior evidence for a susceptibility locus for bipolar disorder, on 21q. Am J Hum Genet 58:1279–1285, 1996

Detera-Wadleigh SD, Badner JA, Yoshikawa T, et al: Initial genome scan of the NIMH genetics initiative bipolar pedigrees: chromosomes 4, 7, 9, 18, 19, 20, and 21q. Am J Med Genet 74:254–262, 1997

Detera-Wadleigh SD, Badner JA, Berrettini WH, et al: A high-density genome scan detects evidence for a bipolar-disorder susceptibility locus on 13q32 and other potential loci on 1q32 and 18p11.2. Proc Natl Acad Sci U S A 96:5604–5609, 1999

Deutsch CK, Matthysse S, Swanson JM, et al: Genetic latent structure analysis of dysmorphology in attention deficit disorder. J Am Acad Child Adolesc Psychiatry 29:189–194, 1990

Devanand DP, Sano M, Tang MX, et al: Depressed mood and the incidence of Alzheimer's disease in the elderly living in the community. Arch Gen Psychiatry 53:175–182, 1996

Devanand DP, Jacobs DM, Tang MX, et al: The course of psychopathologic features in mild to moderate Alzheimer disease. Arch Gen Psychiatry 54:257–263, 1997

Di Bella D, Catalano M, Balling U, et al: Systematic screening for mutations in the coding region of the human serotonin transporter (5-HTT) gene using PCR and DGGE. Am J Med Genet 67:541–545, 1996a

Di Bella D, Catalano M, Cichon S, et al: Association study of a null mutation in the dopamine D4 receptor gene in Italian patients with obsessive-compulsive disorder, bipolar mood disorder and schizophrenia. Psychiatr Genet 6:119–121, 1996b

Doh-ura K, Tateishi J, Sasaki H, et al: Pro-leu change at the position 102 of the prion protein is the most common but not the sole mutation related to Gerstmann-Straussler-Scheinker disease syndrome. Biochem Biophys Res Commun 163:974–979, 1989

Doll R, Peto R, Boreham J, et al: Smoking and dementia in male British doctors: prospective study [see comments]. BMJ 320:1097–1102, 2000

Done DJ, Crow TJ, Johnstone EC, et al: Childhood antecedents of schizophrenia and affective illness: social adjustment at ages 7 and 11. BMJ 309:699–703, 1994

Douglass AB, Harris L, Pazderka F: Monozygotic twins concordant for the narcoleptic syndrome. Neurology 39:140–141, 1989

Dron M, Manuelidis L: Visualization of viral candidate cDNAs in infectious brain fractions from Creutzfeldt-Jakob disease by representational difference analysis. J Neurovirol 2:240–248, 1996

Duara R, Barker WW, Lopez-Alberola R, et al: Alzheimer's disease: interaction of apolipoprotein E genotype, family history of dementia, gender, education, ethnicity, and age of onset. Neurology 46:1575–1579, 1996

Dubel JR, Armstrong RM, Perryman MB, et al: Phenotypic expression of the myotonic dystrophy gene in monozygotic twins. Neurology 42:1815–1817, 1992

Duffy P, Wolf J, Collins G, et al: Letter: possible person-to-person transmission of Creutzfeldt-Jakob disease. N Engl J Med 290:692–693, 1974

Dulawa SC, Grandy DK, Low MJ, et al: Dopamine D4 receptor-knock-out mice exhibit reduced exploration of novel stimuli. J Neurosci 19:9550–9556, 1999

Durner M, Shinnar S, Resor SR, et al: No evidence for a major susceptibility locus for juvenile myoclonic epilepsy on chromosome 15q. Am J Med Genet 96:49–52, 2000

Duyao MP, Auerbach AB, Ryan A, et al: Inactivation of the mouse Huntington's disease gene homolog Hdh. Science 269:407–410, 1995

Eaton WW, Kessler RC, Wittchen HU, et al: Panic and panic disorder in the United States. Am J Psychiatry 151:413–420, 1994

Eaves LJ, Silberg JL, Meyer JM, et al: Genetics and developmental psychopathology: the main effects of genes and environment on behavioral problems in the Virginia Twin Study of Adolescent Behavioral Development. J Child Psychol Psychiatry 38:965–980, 1997

Ebstein RP, Novick O, Umansky R, et al: Dopamine D4 receptor (D4DR) exon III polymorphism associated with the human personality trait of Novelty Seeking. Nat Genet 12:78–80, 1996

Ebstein RP, Nemanov L, Klotz I, et al: Additional evidence for an association between the dopamine D4 receptor (D4DR) exon III repeat polymorphism and the human personality trait of novelty seeking. Mol Psychiatry 2:472–477, 1997

Eden GF, VanMeter JW, Rumsey JM, et al: Abnormal processing of visual motion in dyslexia revealed by functional brain imaging [see comments]. Nature 382:66–69, 1996

Edwards A, Voss H, Rice P, et al: Automated DNA sequencing of the human hprt locus. Genomics 6:593–608, 1990

Eisenberg J, Zohar A, Mei-Tal G, et al: A haplotype relative risk study of the dopamine D4 receptor (DRD4) exon III repeat polymorphism and attention deficit hyperactivity disorder (ADHD). Am J Med Genet 96:258–261, 2000

Eisner V, Pauli LL, Livingston S: Heredity aspects of epilepsy. Johns Hopkins Hospital Bulletin 105:245–271, 1959

Ekelund J, Lichtermann D, Jarvelin MR, et al: Association between novelty seeking and the type 4 dopamine receptor gene in a large Finnish cohort sample. Am J Psychiatry 156:1453–1455, 1999

Elmslie FV, Williamson MP, Rees M, et al: Linkage analysis of juvenile myoclonic epilepsy and microsatellite loci spanning 61 cM of human chromosome 6p in 19 nuclear pedigrees provides no evidence for a susceptibility locus in this region. Am J Hum Genet 59:653–663, 1996

Elmslie FV, Rees M, Williamson MP, et al: Genetic mapping of a major susceptibility locus for juvenile myoclonic epilepsy on chromosome 15q. Hum Mol Genet 6:1329–1334, 1997

Elston RC, Campbell MA: Schizophrenia: evidence for the major gene hypothesis. Behav Genet 1:3–10, 1970

Enoch MA, Kaye WH, Rotondo A, et al: 5-HT2A promoter polymorphism—1438G/A, anorexia nervosa, and obsessive-compulsive disorder (letter). Lancet 351(9118):1785–1786, 1998

Erlenmeyer-Kimling L, Cornblatt B: Attentional measure in the study of children at high risk for schizophrenia. J Psychiatr Res 114:93–98, 1978

Erlenmeyer-Kimling L, Cornblatt BA: A summary of attentional findings in the New York High-Risk Project. J Psychiatr Res 26:405–426, 1992

Ernst M, Zametkin AJ, Matochik JA, et al: Presynaptic dopaminergic deficits in Lesch-Nyhan disease. N Engl J Med 334:1568–1572, 1996

Esser G, Schmidt MH: Children with specific reading retardation—early determinants and long-term outcome. Acta Paedopsychiatrica 56:229–237, 1994

Estrov Y, Scaglia F, Bodamer OA: Psychiatric symptoms of inherited metabolic disease. J Inherit Metab Dis 23:2–6, 2000

Evans DA, Beckett LA, Field TS, et al: Apolipoprotein E epsilon4 and incidence of Alzheimer disease in a community population of older persons [see comments]. JAMA 277:822–824, 1997

Evans JH: Post-traumatic epilepsy. Neurology 12:665–674, 1962

Ewald H, Eiberg H, Mors O, et al: Linkage study between manic-depressive illness and chromosome 21. Am J Med Genet 67:218–224, 1996

Ewald H, Flint T, Degn B, et al: A functional variant of the serotonin transporter gene in families with bipolar affective disorder. J Affect Disord 48:135–144, 1998

Fagerheim T, Raeymaekers P, Tonnessen FE, et al: A new gene (DYX3) for dyslexia is located on chromosome 2. J Med Genet 36:664–669, 1999

Fall PA, Axelson O, Fredriksson M, et al: Age-standardized incidence and prevalence of Parkinson's disease in a Swedish community. J Clin Epidemiol 49:637–641, 1996

Faraone SV, Biederman J, Chen WJ, et al: Segregation analysis of attention deficit hyperactivity disorder. Psychiatr Genet 2:257–275, 1992

Faraone SV, Biederman J, Milberger S: An exploratory study of ADHD among second-degree relatives of ADHD children. Biol Psychiatry 35:398–402, 1994

Faraone SV, Matise T, Svrakic D, et al: Genome scan of European-American schizophrenia pedigrees: results of the NIMH Genetics Initiative and Millennium Consortium. Am J Med Genet 81:290–295, 1998

Faraone SV, Biederman J, Weiffenbach B, et al: Dopamine D4 gene 7-repeat allele and attention deficit hyperactivity disorder. Am J Psychiatry 156:768–770, 1999

Faraone SV, Biederman J, Monuteaux MC: Toward guidelines for pedigree selection in genetic studies of attention deficit hyperactivity disorder. Genet Epidemiol 18:1–16, 2000

Farlow MR: Alzheimer's disease: clinical implications of the apolipoprotein E genotype. Neurology 48:S30–S34, 1997

Farlow MR: Etiology and pathogenesis of Alzheimer's disease [published erratum appears in Am J Health Syst Pharm 55(24):2640, 1998]. Am J Health Syst Pharm 55 (suppl 2):S5–10, 1998

Farlow MR, Lahiri DK, Poirier J, et al: Treatment outcome of tacrine therapy depends on apolipoprotein genotype and gender of the subjects with Alzheimer's disease. Neurology 50:669–677, 1998

Farrer LA, O'Sullivan DM, Cupples A, et al: Assessment of genetic risk for Alzheimer's disease among first-degree relatives. Ann Neurol 25:485–493, 1989

Farrer M, Wavrant-De Vrieze F, Crook R, et al: Low frequency of alpha-synuclein mutations in familial Parkinson's disease. Ann Neurol 43:394–397, 1998

Field LL, Kaplan BJ: Absence of linkage of phonological coding dyslexia to chromosome 6p23-p21.3 in a large family data set [published erratum appears in Am J Hum Genet 64:334, 1999]. Am J Hum Genet 63:1448–1456, 1998

Finelli PF: Metachromatic leukodystrophy manifesting as a schizophrenic disorder: computed tomographic correlation. Ann Neurol 18:94–95, 1985

Finucci JM, Guthrie JT, Childs AL, et al: The genetics of specific reading disability. Ann Hum Genet 40:1–23, 1976

Fish B: Neurobiologic antecedents of schizophrenia in children: evidence for an inherited, congenital neurointegrative defect. Arch Gen Psychiatry 34:1297–1313, 1977

Fish B, Marcus J, Hans SL, et al: Infants at risk for schizophrenia: sequelae of a genetic neurointegrative defect: a review and replication analysis of pandysmaturation in the Jerusalem Infant Development Study. Arch Gen Psychiatry 49:221–235, 1992

Fisher BK: Neurotic excoriations. CMAJ 105:937–938, 1971

Fisher SE, Marlow AJ, Lamb J, et al: A quantitative-trait locus on chromosome 6p influences different aspects of developmental dyslexia. Am J Hum Genet 64:146–156, 1999

Flament MF, Whitaker A, Rapoport JL, et al: Obsessive-compulsive disorder in adolescence: an epidemiological study. J Am Acad Child Adolesc Psychiatry 27:764–771, 1988

Flament MF, Koby E, Rapoport JL, et al: Childhood obsessive-compulsive disorder: a prospective follow-up study. J Child Psychol Psychiatry 31:363–380, 1990

Fleming L, Mann JB, Bean J, et al: Parkinson's disease and brain levels of organochlorine pesticides. Ann Neurol 36:100–103, 1994

Flynn JM, Rahbar MH, Bernstein AJ: Is there an association between season of birth and reading disability? J Dev Behav Pediatr 17:22–26, 1996

Fogarty F, Russell JM, Newman SC, et al: Epidemiology of psychiatric disorders in Edmonton: mania. Acta Psychiatr Scand Suppl 376:16–23, 1994

Foley P, Riederer P: Pathogenesis and preclinical course of Parkinson's disease. J Neural Transm Suppl 56:31–74, 1999

Folstein S, Rutter M: Infantile autism: a genetic study of 21 twin pairs. J Child Psychol Psychiatry 18:297–321, 1977

Folstein SE, Abbott MH, Chase GA, et al: The association of affective disorder with Huntington's disease in a case series and in families. Psychol Med 13:537–542, 1983

Fombonne E: The epidemiology of autism: a review. Psychol Med 29:769–786, 1999

Forster DP, Newens AJ, Kay DW, et al: Risk factors in clinically diagnosed presenile dementia of the Alzheimer type: a case-control study in northern England [see comments]. J Epidemiol Community Health 49:253–258, 1995

Frederikson S, Carlander B, Billiard M, et al: CSF immune variable in patients with narcolepsy. Acta Neurol Scand 81:253–254, 1990

Freedman R, Adler LE, Leonard S: Alternative phenotypes for the complex genetics of schizophrenia. Biol Psychiatry 45:551–558, 1999

Freimer NB, Reus VI, Escamilla MA, et al: Genetic mapping using haplotype, association and linkage methods suggests a locus for severe bipolar (BPI) at 18q22-q23. Nat Genet 12:436–441, 1996

French Clozapine Parkinson Study Group: Clozapine in drug-induced psychosis in Parkinson's disease. Lancet 353:2041–2042, 1999

Froster U, Schulte-Korne G, Hebebrand J, et al: Cosegregation of balanced translocation (1;2) with retarded speech development and dyslexia. Lancet 342:178–179, 1993

Frydman M, Bonne-Tamir B, Farrer LA, et al: Assignment of the gene for Wilson disease to chromosome 13: linkage to esterase D locus. Proc Natl Acad Sci U S A 82:1819–1821, 1985

Fu YH, Friedman DL, Richards S, et al: Decreased expression of myotonin-protein kinase messenger RNA and protein in adult form of myotonic dystrophy. Science 260:235–238, 1993

Fukuyama Y, Kagawa K, Tanaka K: A genetic study of febrile convulsions. Eur Neurol 18:166–182, 1979

Fusco FR, Chen Q, Lamoreaux WJ, et al: Cellular localization of huntingtin in striatal and cortical neurons in rats: lack of correlation with neuronal vulnerability in Huntington's disease. J Neurosci 19:1189–1202, 1999

Fyer AJ, Weissman MM: Genetic linkage study of panic: clinical methodology and description of pedigrees. Am J Med Genet 88:173–181, 1999

Fyer AJ, Mannuzza S, Chapman TF, et al: Specificity in familial aggregation of phobic disorders. Arch Gen Psychiatry 52:564–573, 1995

Galbraith DA, Gordon BA, Feleki V, et al: Metachromatic leukodystrophy in hospitalized adult psychiatric patients resistant to drug treatment. Can J Psychiatry 34:299–302, 1989

Gallagher A, Frith U, Snowling MJ: Precursors of literacy delay among children at genetic risk of dyslexia (In Process Citation). J Child Psychol Psychiatry 41:203–213, 2000

Games D, Adams D, Alessandrini R, et al: Alzheimer-type neuropathology in transgenic mice overexpressing V717F b-amyloid precursor protein. Nature 373:523ñ527, 1995

Gardiner RM: Genetic basis of the human epilepsies. Epilepsy Res 36(2–3):91–95, 1999

Garrone G: Etude statistique et génétique de la schizophrénie à Genève de 1901 à 1950. J Genet Hum 11:89–219, 1962

Gasser T: Genetics of Parkinson's disease. Ann Neurol 44:S53–S57, 1998

Gasser T, Wszolek ZK, Trofatter J, et al: Genetic linkage studies in autosomal dominant parkinsonism: evaluation of seven candidate genes. Ann Neurol 36:387–396, 1994

Gasser T, Muller-Myhsok B, Wszolek ZK, et al: A susceptibility locus for Parkinson's disease maps to chromosome 2p13. Nat Genet 18:262–265, 1998

Gatz M, Pedersen NL, Berg S, et al: Heritability for Alzheimer's disease: the study of dementia in Swedish twins. J Gerontol A Biol Sci Med Sci 52:M117–M125, 1997

Gayan J, Olson RK: Reading disability: evidence for a genetic etiology. Eur Child Adolesc Psychiatry 8 (suppl 3):52–55, 1999

Gayan J, Smith SD, Cherny SS, et al: Quantitative-trait locus for specific language and reading deficits on chromosome 6p. Am J Hum Genet 64:157–164, 1999

Geldmacher DS, Whitehouse PJ Jr. Differential diagnosis of Alzheimer's disease. Neurology 48:S2–S9, 1997

Gelernter J, Kranzler H, Coccaro E, et al: D4 dopamine-receptor (DRD4) alleles and novelty seeking in substance-dependent, personality-disorder, and control subjects. Am J Hum Genet 61:1144–1152, 1997

Geller B, Fox LW, Clark KA, et al: Rate and predictors of prepubertal bipolarity during follow-up of 6- to 12-year-old depressed children. J Am Acad Child Adolesc Psychiatry 33:461–468, 1994

George JM, Jin H, Woods WS, et al: Characterization of a novel protein regulated during the critical period for song learning in the zebra finch. Neuron 15:361–372, 1995

Gershon E: Genetics, in Manic-Depressive Illness. Edited by Goodwin FK, Jamison KR. New York, Oxford University Press, 1990, pp 373–401

Gershon ES, Hamovit J, Guroff JJ, et al: A family study of schizoaffective, bipolar I, bipolar II, unipolar, and normal control probands. Arch Gen Psychiatry 39:1157–1167, 1982

Gershon ES, Badner JA, Detera-Wadleigh SD, et al: Maternal inheritance and chromosome 18 allele sharing in unilineal bipolar illness pedigrees. Am J Med Genet 67:202–207, 1996

Geschwind N, Behan PO: Left-handedness: association with immune disease, migraine, and developmental learning disorder. Proc Natl Acad Sci U S A 79:5097–5100, 1982

Geschwind N, Behan PO: Laterality, hormones, and immunity, in Cerebral Dominance: The Biological Foundations. Edited by Geschwind N, Galaburda A. Cambridge, MA, Harvard University Press, 1984, pp 211–224

Geschwind N, Galaburda A: Cerebral lateralization: biological mechanisms, associations, and pathology, I: a hypothesis and a program for research. Arch Neurol 42:428–459, 1985a

Geschwind N, Galaburda A: Cerebral lateralization: biological mechanisms, associations, and pathology, II: a hypothesis and a program for research. Arch Neurol 42:521–552, 1985b

Gibbs RA, Nguyen P, McBride LJ, et al: Identification of mutations leading to the Lesch-Nyhan syndrome by automated direct DNA sequencing of in vitro amplified cDNA. Proc Natl Acad Sci U S A 86:1919–1923, 1989

Gibbs RA, Nguyen PN, Edwards A, et al: Multiplex DNA deletion detection and exon sequencing of the hypoxanthine phosphoribosyltransferase gene in Lesch-Nyhan families. Genomics 7:1–10, 1990

Gieselmann V, Fluharty AL, Tonnesen T, et al: Mutations in the arylsulfatase A pseudodeficiency allele causing metachromatic leukodystrophy. Am J Hum Genet 49:407–413, 1991

Gieselmann V, Polten A, Kreysing J, et al: Molecular genetics of metachromatic leukodystrophy. J Inherit Metab Dis 17:500–509, 1994

Gieselmann V, Matzner U, Hess B, et al: Metachromatic leukodystrophy: molecular genetics and an animal model. J Inherit Metab Dis 21:564–574, 1998

Gilger JW, Pennington BF, DeFries JC: A twin study of the etiology of comorbidity: attention-deficit hyperactivity disorder and dyslexia. J Am Acad Child Adolesc Psychiatry 31:343–348, 1992a

Gilger JW, Pennington BF, Green P, et al: Reading disability, immune disorders and non-right-handedness: twin and family studies of their relations. Neuropsychologia 30:209–227, 1992b

Gill M, Castle D, Duggan C: Cosegregation of Christmas disease and major affective disorder in a pedigree [see comments]. Br J Psychiatry 160:112–114, 1992

Gill M, Daly G, Heron S, et al: Confirmation of association between attention deficit hyperactivity disorder and a dopamine transporter polymorphism. Mol Psychiatry 2:311–313, 1997

Gillberg C: Outcome in autism and autistic-like conditions. J Am Acad Child Adolesc Psychiatry 30:375–382, 1991

Gillberg C, Coleman M: Autism and medical disorders: a review of the literature. Dev Med Child Neurol 38:191–202, 1996

Gillis JJ, Gilger JW, Pennington BF, et al: Attention deficit disorder in reading-disabled twins: evidence for a genetic etiology. J Abnorm Child Psychol 20:303–315, 1992

Ginns EI, Ott J, Egeland JA, et al: A genome-wide search for chromosomal loci linked to bipolar affective disorder in the Old Order Amish. Nat Genet 12:431–435, 1996

Giordani B, Berent S, Boivin MJ, et al: Longitudinal neuropsychological and genetic linkage analysis of persons at risk for Huntington's disease. Arch Neurol 52:59–64, 1995

Giros B, Jaber M, Jones SR, et al: Hyperlocomotion and indifference to cocaine and amphetamine in mice lacking the dopamine transporter. Nature 379:606–612, 1996

Gjone H, Stevenson J, Sundet JM: Genetic influence on parent-reported attention-related problems in a Norwegian general population twin sample. J Am Acad Child Adolesc Psychiatry 35:588–596, 1996

Goate A, Chartier-Harlin MC, Mullan M, et al: Segregation of a missense mutation in the amyloid precursor protein gene with familial Alzheimer's disease. Nature 349:704–706, 1991

Goedert M: Filamentous nerve cell inclusions in neurodegenerative diseases: tauopathies and alpha-synucleinopathies. Philos Trans R Soc Lond B Biol Sci 354:1101–1118, 1999

Goetz CG, Pappert EJ, Blasucci LM, et al: Intravenous levodopa in hallucinating Parkinson's disease patients: high-dose challenge does not precipitate hallucinations [see comments]. Neurology 50:515–517, 1998

Golbe LI, Lazzarini AM, Schwarz KO, et al: Autosomal dominant parkinsonism with benign course and typical Lewy-body pathology. Neurology 43:2222–2227, 1993

Goldberg YP, Kalchman MA, Metzler M, et al: Absence of disease phenotype and intergenerational stability of the CAG repeat in transgenic mice expressing the human Huntington disease transcript. Hum Mol Genet 5:177–185, 1996

Goldfarb LG, Brown P, Vrbovska A, et al: An insert mutation in the chromosome 20 amyloid precursor gene in a Gerstmann-Straussler-Scheinker family. J Neurol Sci 111:189–194, 1992

Goldin LR, DeLisi LE, Gershon ES: Relationship of HLA to schizophrenia in 10 nuclear families. Psychiatry Res 20:69–77, 1987

Goldsmith JR, Herishanu Y, Abarbanel JM, ET AL: Clustering of Parkinson's disease points to environmental etiology. Arch Environ Health 45:88–94, 1990

Goldstein RB, Wickramaratne PJ, Horwath E, et al: Familial aggregation and phenomenology of 'early onset' (at or before age 20 years) panic disorder. Arch Gen Psychiatry 54:271–278, 1997

Goodman R, Stevenson J: A twin study of hyperactivity—II: the aetiological role of genes, family relationships and perinatal adversity. J Child Psychol Psychiatry 30:691–709, 1989

Goodman WK, McDougle CJ, Price LH, et al: Beyond the serotonin hypothesis: a role for dopamine in some forms of obsessive compulsive disorder? J Clin Psychiatry 51 (suppl 8):36–43, 1990a

Goodman WK, Price LH, Delgado PL, et al: Specificity of serotonin reuptake inhibitors in the treatment of obsessive-compulsive disorder: comparison of fluvoxamine and desipramine [see comments]. Arch Gen Psychiatry 47:577–585, 1990b

Goodwin FK, Jamison KR: Manic-Depressive Illness. New York, Oxford University Press, 1990

Gorell JM, Johnson CC, Rybicki BA, et al: The risk of Parkinson's disease with exposure to pesticides, farming, well water, and rural living. Neurology 50:1346–1350, 1998

Gorman JM, Papp LA, Martinez J, et al: High-dose carbon dioxide challenge test in anxiety disorder patients. Biol Psychiatry 28:743–757, 1990

Gottesman II, Bertelsen A: Confirming unexpressed genotypes for schizophrenia: risks in the offspring of Fischer's Danish identical and fraternal discordant twins [see comments]. Arch Gen Psychiatry 46:867–872, 1989

Gottesman II, Shields J: Schizophrenia: The Epigenetic Puzzle. Cambridge, MA, Cambridge University Press, 1982

Gowers WR: A Manual of Diseases of the Nervous System, 2nd Edition. Philadelphia, PA, Blakiston, 1903, p 636

Graves AB, van Duijn CM, Chandra V, et al: Alcohol and tobacco consumption as risk factors for Alzheimer's disease: a collaborative re-analysis of case-control studies. EURODEM Risk Factors Research Group. Int J Epidemiol 20 (suppl 2):S48–S57, 1991

Graves AB, Larson EB, Edland SD, et al: Prevalence of dementia and its subtypes in the Japanese American population of King County, Washington State: the Kame Project. Am J Epidemiol 144:760–771, 1996

Graves AB, Rosner D, Echeverria D, et al: Occupational exposures to solvents and aluminum and estimated risk of Alzheimer's disease. Occup Environ Med 55:627–633, 1998

Green AJ, Johnson PH, Yates JR: The tuberous sclerosis gene on chromosome 9q34 acts as a growth suppressor. Hum Mol Genet 3:1833–1834, 1994

Green MF, Bracha HS, Satz P, et al: Preliminary evidence for an association between minor physical anomalies and second trimester neurodevelopment in schizophrenia. Psychiatry Res 53:119–127, 1994

Grigorenko EL, Wood FB, Meyer MS, et al: Susceptibility loci for distinct components of developmental dyslexia on chromosomes 6 and 15 [see comments]. Am J Hum Genet 60:27–39, 1997

Grimm T: The ages of onset and at death in dystrophia myotonica. J Hum Genet 23 (suppl):301–308, 1975

Grufferman S, Cohen HJ, Delzell ES, et al: Familial aggregation of multiple myeloma and central nervous system diseases. J Am Geriatr Soc 37:303–309, 1989

Grunewald T, Beal MF: Bioenergetics in Huntington's disease. Ann N Y Acad Sci 893:203–213, 1999

Guilleminault C, Mignot E, Grumet FC: Familial patterns of narcolepsy. Lancet 2:1376–1379, 1989

Gun RT, Korten AE, Jorm AF, et al: Occupational risk factors for Alzheimer disease: a case-control study. Alzheimer Dis Assoc Disord 11:21–27, 1997

Gunther-Genta F, Bovet P, Hohlfeld P: Obstetric complications and schizophrenia: a case-control study [see comments]. Br J Psychiatry 164:165–170, 1994

Guo Z, Cupples LA, Kurz A, et al: Head injury and the risk of AD in the MIRAGE study (In Process Citation). Neurology 54:1316–1323, 2000

Gusella JF, Wexler NS, Conneally PM, et al: A polymorphic DNA marker genetically linked to Huntington's disease. Nature 306:234–238, 1983

Gusella JF, MacDonald ME, Ambrose CM, et al: Molecular genetics of Huntington's disease. Arch Neurol 50:1157–1163, 1993

Gustavson KH, Hagberg B: The incidence and genetics of metachromatic leukodystrophy in northern Sweden. Acta Paediatrica Scandinavica 60:585–590, 1971

Hallgren B: Specific dyslexia: a clinical and genetic study. Acta Psychiatrica et Neurologica Scandinavica 65 (suppl):1–287, 1950

Hallmayer J, Hebert JM, Spiker D, et al: Autism and the X chromosome: multipoint sib-pair analysis. Arch Gen Psychiatry 53:985–989, 1996

Hamilton SP, Heiman GA, Haghighi F, et al: Lack of genetic linkage or association between a functional serotonin transporter polymorphism and panic disorder. Psychiatr Genet 9:1–6, 1999

Hamilton SP, Haghighi F, Heiman GA, et al: Investigation of dopamine receptor (DRD4) and dopamine transporter (DAT) polymorphisms for genetic linkage or association to panic disorder. Am J Med Genet 96:324–330, 2000

Hamilton SP, Slager SL, Heiman GA, et al: No genetic linkage or association between a functional promoter polymorphism in the monoamine oxidase-A gene and panic disorder. Mol Psychiatry (in press a)

Hamilton SP, Slager SL, Helleby L, et al: No association or linkage between polymorphisms in the genes encoding cholecystokinin and cholecystokinin B receptor and panic disorder. Mol Psychiatry (in press b)

Hantz P, Caradoc-Davies G, Caradoc-Davies T, et al: Depression in Parkinson's disease. Am J Psychiatry 151:1010–1014, 1994

Hardy J: Molecular genetics of Alzheimer's disease. Acta Neurol Scand Suppl 165:13–17, 1996

Harley HG, Brook JD, Rundle SH, et al: Expansion of an unstable DNA region and phenotypic variation in myotonic dystrophy. Nature 355:545–546, 1992

Harper PS: The epidemiology of Huntington's disease. Hum Genet 89:365–376, 1992

Harper PS: New genes for old diseases: the molecular basis of myotonic dystrophy and Huntington's disease: the Lumleian Lecture 1995. J R Coll Physicians Lond 30:221–231, 1996

Harris EL, Noyes R Jr, Crowe RR, et al: Family study of agoraphobia: report of a pilot study. Arch Gen Psychiatry 40:1061–1064, 1983

Harris GJ, Codori AM, Lewis RF, et al: Reduced basal ganglia blood flow and volume in pre-symptomatic, gene-tested persons at-risk for Huntington's disease. Brain 122 (pt 9):1667–1678, 1999

Harris JC, Lee RR, Jinnah HA, et al: Craniocerebral magnetic resonance imaging measurement and findings in Lesch-Nyhan syndrome. Arch Neurol 55:547–553, 1998

Harvey JS, Nelson PV, Carey WF, et al: An arylsulfatase A (ARSA) missense mutation (T274M) causing late-infantile metachromatic leukodystrophy. Hum Mutat 2:261–267, 1993

Harwood DG, Barker WW, Loewenstein DA, et al: A cross-ethnic analysis of risk factors for AD in white Hispanics and white non-Hispanics. Neurology 52:551–556, 1999a

Harwood DG, Barker WW, Ownby RL, et al: Apolipoprotein-E (APO-E) genotype and symptoms of psychosis in Alzheimer's disease. Am J Geriatr Psychiatry 7:119–123, 1999b

Hauser WA, Anderson VE, Loewenson RB, et al: Seizure recurrence after a first unprovoked seizure. N Engl J Med 307: 522–528, 1982

Hawi Z, McCarron M, Kirley A, et al: No association of the dopamine DRD4 receptor (DRD4) gene polymorphism with attention deficit hyperactivity disorder (ADHD) in the Irish population. Am J Med Genet 96:268–272, 2000

Hebebrand J, Hennighausen K: A critical analysis of data presented in eight studies favouring X-linkage of bipolar illness with special emphasis on formal genetic aspects. Hum Genet 90:289–293, 1992

Heinisch U, Zlotogora J, Kafert S, et al: Multiple mutations are responsible for the high frequency of metachromatic leukodystrophy in a small geographic area. Am J Hum Genet 56:51–57, 1995

Henderson AS, Easteal S, Jorm AF, et al: Apolipoprotein E allele epsilon 4, dementia, and cognitive decline in a population sample [see comments]. Lancet 346:1387–1390, 1995

Henderson R, Kurlan R, Kersun JM, et al: Preliminary examination of the comorbidity of anxiety and depression in Parkinson's disease. J Neuropsychiatry Clin Neurosci 4:257–264, 1992

Henderson VW, Paganini-Hill A, Emanuel CK, et al: Estrogen replacement therapy in older women: comparisons between Alzheimer's disease cases and nondemented control subjects. Arch Neurol 51:896–900, 1994

Hendrie HC: Epidemiology of dementia and Alzheimer's disease. Am J Geriatr Psychiatry 6:S3–18, 1998

Hendrie HC, Osuntokun BO, Hall KS, et al: Prevalence of Alzheimer's disease and dementia in two communities: Nigerian Africans and African Americans [see comments]. Am J Psychiatry 152:1485–1492, 1995

Hennekens CH, Buring JE: Epidemiology in Medicine. Boston, MA, Little, Brown, 1987

Herault J, Petit E, Martineau J, et al: Serotonin and autism: biochemical and molecular biology features. Psychiatry Res 65:33–43, 1996

Herishanu YO, Kordysh E, Goldsmith JR: A case-referent study of extrapyramidal signs (preparkinsonism) in rural communities of Israel. Can J Neurol Sci 25:127–133, 1998

Hermann K, Norrie E: Is congenital word-blindness an hereditary type of Gerstmann's syndrome? Psychiatria et Neurologia 136:59–73, 1958

Heroux A, White EL, Ross LJ, et al: Crystal structure of Toxoplasma gondii hypoxanthine-guanine phosphoribosyltransferase with XMP, pyrophosphate, and two Mg(2+) ions bound: insights into the catalytic mechanism. Biochemistry 38:14495–14506, 1999

Herska M, Moscovich DG, Kalian, et al: Aryl sulfatase A deficiency in psychiatric and neurologic patients. Am J Med Genet 26:629–635, 1987

Hertzmann C, Wiens M, Bowering D, et al: Parkinson's disease: a case-control study of occupational and environmental risk factors. Am J Ind Med 17:349–355, 1990

Hess B, Saftig P, Hartmann D, et al: Phenotype of arylsulfatase A-deficient mice: relationship to human metachromatic leukodystrophy. Proc Natl Acad Sci U S A 93:14821–14826, 1996

Hess EJ, Rogan PK, Domoto M, et al: Absence of linkage of apparently single gene mediated ADHD with the human syntenic region of the mouse mutant Coloboma. Am J Med Genet 60:573–579, 1995

Heston LL: Psychiatric disorders in foster home reared children of schizophrenic mothers. Br J Psychiatry 112:819–825, 1966

Heston LL: Genetic studies of dementia: with emphasis on Parkinson's disease and Alzheimer's neuropathology, in The Epidemiology of Dementia. Edited by Mortimer JA, Schuman LM. New York, Oxford University Press, 1981, pp 107–117

Heston LL, Mastri AR: The genetics of Alzheimer's disease: associations with hematologic malignancy and Down's syndrome. Arch Gen Psychiatry 34:976–981, 1977

Heston LL, Mastri AR, Anderson E, et al: Dementia of the Alzheimer type: clinical genetics, natural history, and associated conditions. Arch Gen Psychiatry 38:1085–1090, 1981

Heun R, Maier W: The distinction of bipolar II disorder from bipolar I and recurrent unipolar depression: results of a controlled family study. Acta Psychiatr Scand 87:279–284, 1993

Heye N, Hensen S, Muller N: Creutzfeldt-Jakob disease and blood transfusion (letter; comment). Lancet 343:298–299, 1994

Heyman A, Wilkinson WEE, Hurwitz BJ, et al: Alzheimer's disease: genetic aspects and associated clinical disorder. Ann Neurol 14:507–515, 1983

Hilty DM, Brady KT, Hales RE: A review of bipolar disorder among adults. Psychiatr Serv 50:201–213, 1999

Hofman A, Collette HJ, Bartelds AI: Incidence and risk factors of Parkinson's disease in the Netherlands. Neuroepidemiology 8:296–299, 1989a

Hofman A, Schulte W, Tanja TA, et al: History of dementia and Parkinson's disease in 1st-degree relatives of patients with Alzheimer's disease. Neurology 39:1589–1592, 1989b

Hohenschutz C, Eich P, Friedl W, et al: Pseudodeficiency of arylsulfatase A: a common genetic polymorphism with possible disease implications. Hum Genet 82:45–48, 1989

Hollingsworth CE, Tanguay PE, Grossman L, et al: Long-term outcome of obsessive-compulsive disorder in childhood. J Am Acad Child Adolesc Psychiatry 19:134–144, 1980

Hollister JM, Laing P, Mednick SA: Rhesus incompatibility as a risk factor for schizophrenia in male adults. Arch Gen Psychiatry 53:19–24, 1996

Holman RC, Khan AS, Belay ED, et al: Creutzfeldt-Jakob disease in the United States, 1979–1994: using national mortality data to assess the possible occurrence of variant cases. Emerg Infect Dis 2:333–337, 1996

Honda Y, Asaka A, Tanimura M, et al: A genetic study of narcolepsy and excessive daytime sleepiness in 308 families with narcolepsy or hypersomnia proband, in Sleep/Wake Disorders. Edited by Guilleminault C, Lugaresi E. New York, Raven, 1983, pp 187–199

Hoogenraad HU, Koevoet R, de Ruyter Korver EGWM: Oral zinc sulphate as long term treatment in Wilson's disease. Eur Neurol 18:205–211, 1979

Hopper JL, Judd FK, Derrick PL, et al: A family study of panic disorder. Genet Epidemiol 4:33–41, 1987

Horwath E, Adams P, Wickramaratne P, et al: Panic disorder with smothering symptoms: evidence for increased risk in first-degree relatives. Depress Anxiety 6:147–153, 1997

Hotamisligil GS, Girmen AS, Fink JS, et al: Hereditary variations in monoamine oxidase as a risk factor for Parkinson's disease. Mov Disord 9:305–310, 1994

Houwen RHJ, Baharloo S, Blankenship K, et al: Genome screening by searching for shared segments: mapping a gene for benign recurrent intrahepatic cholestasis. Nat Genet 8:380–386, 1994

Howeler CJ, Busch HF, Geraedts JP, et al: Anticipation in myotonic dystrophy: fact or fiction? Brain 112 (part 3):779–797, 1989

Hsich G, Kenney K, Gibbs CJ, et al: The 14–3–3 brain protein in cerebrospinal fluid as a marker for transmissible spongiform encephalopathies [see comments]. N Engl J Med 335:924–930, 1996

Hubble JP, Cao T, Hassanein RE, et al: Risk factors for Parkinson's disease. Neurology 43:1693–1697, 1993

Huff FJ, Auerbach J, Chakravarti A, et al: Risk of dementia in relatives of patients with Alzheimer's disease. Neurology 38:786–790, 1988

Hunter AGW, Jacob P, O'Hoy K, et al: Decrease in the size of the myotonic dystrophy CTG repeat during transmission from parent to child: implications for genetic counseling and genetic anticipation. Am J Med Genet 45:401–407, 1993

Huntington Disease Collaborative Research Group: A novel gene containing a trinucleotide repeat that is expanded and unstable on Huntington disease chromosomes. Cell 72:971–983, 1993

Huttunen MO, Niskanen P: Prenatal loss of father and psychiatric disorders. Arch Gen Psychiatry 35:429–431, 1978

Hyman BT: Alzheimer's disease or Alzheimer's diseases? Clues from molecular epidemiology (editorial). Ann Neurol 40:135–136, 1996

Iacono WG, Bassett AS, Jones BD: Eye tracking dysfunction is associated with partial trisomy chromosome 5 and schizophrenia. Arch Gen Psychiatry 45:1140–1141, 1988

Igarashi T, Minami M, Nisheda Y: Molecular analysis of hypoxanthine guanine phosphoribosyl transferase mutations in 5 unrelated Japanese patients. Acta Paediatr Jpn 31:303–313, 1989

Ikebe S, Tanaka M, Ozawa T: Point mutations of mitochondrial genome in Parkinson's disease. Brain Res Mol Brain Res 28:281–295, 1995

Inayama Y, Yoneda H, Sakai T, et al: Positive association between a DNA sequence variant in the serotonin 2A receptor gene and schizophrenia. Am J Med Genet 67:103–105, 1996

International Molecular Genetic Study of Autism Consortium: A full genome screen for autism with evidence for linkage to a region on chromosome 7q. Hum Mol Genet 7:571–578, 1998

Ishiguro H, Arinami T, Yamada K, et al: An association study between a transcriptional polymorphism in the serotonin transporter gene and panic disorder in a Japanese population. Psychiatry Clin Neurosci 51:333–335, 1997

Jacobsen NJ, Franks EK, Owen MJ, et al: Mutational analysis of phospholipase A2A: a positional candidate susceptibility gene for bipolar disorder. Mol Psychiatry 4:274–279, 1999

Janjua NA, Andermann E, Eeg-Olofsson O, et al: Plasma amino acid and genetic studies in epilepsy, in Genetics of the Epilepsies. Edited by Beck-Managetta G, Anderson VE, Doose H, et al. New York, Springer-Verlag, 1989, pp 162–174

Jansen G, Bartolomei M, Kalscheuer V, et al: No imprinting involved in the expression of the DM-kinase mRNAs in mouse and human tissues. Hum Mol Genet 2:1221–1227, 1993

Janz D, Beck-Managetta G: Epilepsy and neonatal seizures in the offspring of parents with epilepsy, in Genetic Basis of the Epilepsies. Edited by Anderson VE, Hauser WA, Penry JK, et al. New York, Raven, 1982, pp 135–144

Jarvik GP, Wijsman EM, Kukull WA, et al: Interactions of apolipoprotein E genotype, total cholesterol level, age, and sex in prediction of Alzheimer's disease: a case-control study. Neurology 45:1092–1096, 1995

Jarvik LF, Ruth V, Matsuyama SS: Organic brain syndrome and aging: a six year follow up of surviving twins. Arch Gen Psychiatry 37:280–286, 1980

Jason GW, Pajurkova E, Suchowersky O, et al: Presymptomatic neuropsychological impairment in Huntington's disease. Arch Neurol 45:769–773, 1988

Jenner AR, Rosen GD, Galaburda AM: Neuronal asymmetries in primary visual cortex of dyslexic and nondyslexic brains. Ann Neurol 46:189–196, 1999

Jenner P, Olanow CW: Understanding cell death in Parkinson's disease. Ann Neurol 44:S72–S84, 1998

Jennett B: Epilepsy and acute traumatic intracranial haematoma. J Neurol Neurosurg Psychiatry 38:378–381, 1975

Jiang S, Xin R, Wu X, et al: Association between attention deficit hyperactivity disorder and the DXS7 locus. Am J Med Genet 96:289–292, 2000

Jimenez-Jimenez FJ, Mateo D, Gimenez-Roldan S: Exposure to well water and pesticides in Parkinson's disease: a case-control study in the Madrid area. Mov Disord 7:149–152, 1992

Jinnah HA, Jones MD, Wojcik BE, et al: Influence of age and strain on striatal dopamine loss in a genetic mouse model of Lesch-Nyhan disease. J Neurochem 72:225–229, 1999

Johnson WG, Hodge SE, Duvoisin R: Twin studies and the genetics of Parkinson's disease—a reappraisal. Mov Disord 5:187–194, 1990

Jolly DJ, Okayama H, Berg P, et al: Isolation and characterization of a full-length expressible cDNA for human hypoxanthine phosphoribosyltransferase. Proc Natl Acad Sci U S A 80:477–481, 1983

Jones P, Cannon M: The new epidemiology of schizophrenia. Psychiatr Clin North Am 21:1–25, 1998

Jones P, Rodgers B, Murray R, et al: Child development risk factors for adult schizophrenia in the British 1946 birth cohort. Lancet 344:1398–1402, 1994

Jones PB, Rantakallio P, Hartikainen AL, et al: Schizophrenia as a long-term outcome of pregnancy, delivery, and perinatal complications: a 28-year follow-up of the 1966 north Finland general population birth cohort. Am J Psychiatry 155:355–364, 1998

Jorde LB, Hasstedt SJ, Ritvo ER, et al: Complex segregation analysis of autism. Am J Hum Genet 49:932–938, 1991

Jorm AF, Korten AE, Henderson AS: The prevalence of dementia: a quantitative integration of the literature [see comments]. Acta Psychiatr Scand 76:465–479, 1987

Jovanovic V, Guan HC, Van Tol HH: Comparative pharmacological and functional analysis of the human dopamine D4.2 and D4.10 receptor variants. Pharmacogenetics 9:561–568, 1999

Kallmann FJ: Genetic aspects of mental disorders in later life, in Mental Disorders in Later Life, 2nd Edition. Edited by Kaplan OJ. Stanford, CA, Stanford University Press, 1956, pp 26–46

Kalsi G, Smyth C, Brynjolfsson J, et al: Linkage analysis of manic depression (bipolar affective disorder) in Icelandic and British kindreds using markers on the short arm of chromosome 18. Hum Hered 47:268–278, 1997

Kamboh MI, Sanghera DK, Ferrell RE, et al: APOE*4-associated Alzheimer's disease risk is modified by alpha 1-antichymotrypsin polymorphism [published erratum appears in Nat Genet 11:104, 1995]. Nat Genet 10:486–488, 1995

Kandt RS, Haines JL, Smith M, et al: Linkage of an important gene locus for tuberous sclerosis to a chromosome 16 marker for polycystic kidney disease. Nat Genet 2:37–41, 1992

Kang J, Lemaire H, Unterbeck A, et al: The precursor of Alzheimer's disease amyloid A4 protein resembles a cell-surface receptor. Nature 325:733–736, 1987

Kapalanga J, Zhang H, Wing M, et al: Chromosomal fragile sites in patients with bipolar affective disorder. Am J Hum Genet 57:A118, 1995

Karayiorgou M, Morris MA, Morrow B, et al: Schizophrenia susceptibility associated with interstitial deletions of chromosome 22q11. Proc Natl Acad Sci U S A 92:7612–7616, 1995

Karayiorgou M, Altemus M, Galke BL, et al: Genotype determining low catechol-O-methyltransferase activity as a risk factor for obsessive-compulsive disorder. Proc Natl Acad Sci U S A 94:4572–4575, 1997

Karayiorgou M, Sobin C, Blundell ML, et al: Family based association studies support a sexually dimorphic effect of COMT and MAOA on genetic susceptibility to obsessive-compulsive disorder. Biol Psychiatry 45:1178–1189, 1999

Karlsson JL: A two-locus hypothesis for inheritance of schizophrenia, in Genetic Factors in Schizophrenia. Edited by Kaplan AR. Springfield, IL, Charles C Thomas, 1972, pp 246–255

Karno M, Golding JM, Sorenson SB, et al: The epidemiology of obsessive-compulsive disorder in five US communities. Arch Gen Psychiatry 45:1094–1099, 1988

Katzman R: Education and the prevalence of dementia and Alzheimer's disease. Neurology 43:13–20, 1993

Kaufmann CA, Suarez B, Malaspina D, et al: NIMH Genetics Initiative Millenium Schizophrenia Consortium: linkage analysis of African-American pedigrees. Am J Med Genet 81:282–289, 1998

Kawada Y, Hattori M, Dai XY, et al: Possible association between monoamine oxidase A gene and bipolar affective disorder. Am J Med Genet 56:335–336, 1995

Keen J, Lester DH, Inglehearn CF, et al: Rapid detection of single base mismatches as heteroduplexes on Hydrolink gels. Trends Genet 7:5, 1991

Kelsoe JR, Sadovnick AD, Kristbjanarson H, et al: Genetic linkage studies of bipolar disorder and chromosome 18 markers in North American, Icelandic, and Amish pedigrees. Psychiatr Genet 5:S17, 1995

Kendell RE, Juszczak E, Cole SK: Obstetric complications and schizophrenia: a case control study based on standardised obstetric records [see comments]. Br J Psychiatry 168:556–561, 1996

Kendler K, Diehl S: The genetics of schizophrenia: a current genetic-epidemiologic perspective. Schizophr Bull 19:261–285, 1993

Kendler KS, Gardner CO: The risk for psychiatric disorders in relatives of schizophrenic and control probands: a comparison of three independent studies. Psychol Med 27:411–419, 1997

Kendler KS, Neale MC, Kessler RC, et al: Panic disorder in women: a population-based twin study. Psychol Med 23:397–406, 1993

Kendler KS, MacLean CJ, O'Neill FA, et al: Evidence for a schizophrenia vulnerability locus on chromosome 8p in the Irish Study of High-Density Schizophrenia Families. Am J Psychiatry 153:1534–1540, 1996

Kennedy JL, Bradwejn J, Koszycki D, et al: Investigation of cholecystokinin system genes in panic disorder. Mol Psychiatry 4:284–285, 1999

Kessler RC, McGonagle KA, Zhao S, et al: Lifetime and 12-month prevalence of DSM-III-R psychiatric disorders in the United States: results from the National Comorbidity Survey. Arch Gen Psychiatry 51:8–19, 1994

Kessler S, Guilleminault C, Dement W: A family study of 50 REM narcoleptics. Acta Neurol Scand 50:503–512, 1974

Kestenbaum CJ: Children at risk for manic-depressive illness: possible predictors. Am J Psychiatry 136:1206–1208, 1979

Kety SS: Schizophrenic illness in the families of schizophrenic adoptees: findings from the Danish national sample. Schizophr Bull 14:217–222, 1988

Kety SS, Wender PH, Jacobsen B, et al: Mental illness in the biological and adoptive relatives of schizophrenic adoptees: replication of the Copenhagen Study in the rest of Denmark. Arch Gen Psychiatry 51:442–455, 1994

Khanna AK, Buskirk DR, Williams RC Jr, et al: Presence of a non-HLA B cell antigen in rheumatic fever patients and their families as defined by a monoclonal antibody. J Clin Invest 83:1710–1716, 1989

Kidd KK: Genetic models for psychiatric disorders, in Genetic Research Strategies for Psychobiology and Psychiatry. Edited by Gershon ES, Matthysse S, Breakefield XO, et al. Pacific Grove, CA, Boxwood Press, 1981, pp 369–382

Kinney DK, Woods BT, Yurgelun-Todd D: Neurologic abnormalities in schizophrenic patients and their families; II: neurologic and psychiatric findings in relatives. Arch Gen Psychiatry 43:665–668, 1986

Kirkwood JK, Wells GA, Wilesmith JW, et al: Spongiform encephalopathy in an Arabian oryx (Oryx leucoryx) and a greater kudu (Tragelaphus strepsiceros) [see comments]. Vet Rec 127:418–420, 1990

Kirov G, Murphy KC, Arranz MJ, et al: Low activity allele of catechol-O-methyltransferase gene associated with rapid cycling bipolar disorder. Mol Psychiatry 3:342–345, 1998

Kirov G, Jones I, McCandless F, et al: Family based association studies of bipolar disorder with candidate genes involved in dopamine neurotransmission: DBH, DAT1, COMT, DRD2, DRD3 and DRD5. Mol Psychiatry 4:558–565, 1999

Kishino T, Lalande M, Wagstaff J: UBE3A/E6-AP mutations cause Angelman syndrome. Nat Genet 15:70–73, 1997

Kitada T, Asakawa S, Hattori N, et al: Mutations in the parkin gene cause autosomal recessive juvenile parkinsonism [see comments]. Nature 392:605–608, 1998

Klauck SM, Poustka F, Benner A, et al: Serotonin transporter (5-HTT) gene variants associated with autism? Hum Mol Genet 6:2233–2238, 1997

Klein DF: Delineation of two drug-responsive anxiety syndromes. Psychopharmacology 5:397–408, 1964

Knight R: Creutzfeldt-Jakob disease: clinical features, epidemiology and tests. Electrophoresis 19:1306–1310, 1998

Knowles JA, Weissman MM: Panic disorder and agoraphobia, in American Psychiatric Press Review of Psychiatry, Vol 14. Edited by Oldham JM, Riba MB. Washington, DC, American Psychiatric Press, 1995, pp 383–404

Knowles JA, Fyer AJ, Vieland VJ, et al: Results of a genome-wide genetic screen for panic disorder. Am J Med Genet 81:139–147, 1998

Kohler A, Burkhard P, Hefft S, et al: Proximal myotonic myopathy: clinical, electrophysiological and pathological findings in a family. Eur Neurol 43:50–53, 2000

Kohn H, Manowitz P, Miller M, et al: Neuropsychological deficits in obligatory heterozygotes for metachromatic leucodystrophy. Hum Genet 79:8–12, 1988

Kokmen E, Ozekmekci S, Beard M, et al: Incidence and prevalence of Huntington's disease in Olmstead County, Minnesota (1950 through 1989). Arch Neurol 51:696–698, 1994

Kolodny EH: Metachromatic leukodystrophy and multiple sulfatase deficiency, in The Metabolic Basis of Inherited Disease, 6th Edition. Edited by Scriver CR, Beaudet AL, Sly WS, et al. New York, McGraw-Hill, 1989, pp 1721–1750

Kondo R, Wakamatsu N, Yoshino H, et al: Identification of a mutation in the arylsulfatase A gene of a patient with adult-type metachromatic leukodystrophy. Am J Hum Genet 48:971–978, 1991

Kordower JH, Isacson O, Emerich DF: Cellular delivery of trophic factors for the treatment of Huntington's disease: is neuroprotection possible? Exp Neurol 159:4–20, 1999

Kotler M, Manor I, Sever Y, et al: Failure to replicate an excess of the long dopamine D4 exon III repeat polymorphism in ADHD in a family based study. Am J Med Genet 96:278–281, 2000

Kremer HPH, Goldberg YP, Andrew SE, et al: Worldwide study of the Huntington's disease mutation: the sensitivity and specificity of the repeated CAG sequences. N Engl J Med 330:1401–1406, 1994

Kreysing J, von Figura K, Gieselmann V: The structure of the arylsulfatase A gene. Eur J Biochem 191:627–631, 1990

Kringlen E, Cramer G: Offspring of monozygotic twins discordant for schizophrenia. Arch Gen Psychiatry 46:873–877, 1989

Krivit W, Peters C, Shapiro EG: Bone marrow transplantation as effective treatment of central nervous system disease in globoid cell leukodystrophy, metachromatic leukodystrophy, adrenoleukodystrophy, mannosidosis, fucosidosis, aspartylglucosaminuria, Hurler, Maroteaux-Lamy, and Sly syndromes, and Gaucher disease type III. Curr Opin Neurol 12:167–176, 1999

Kruger R, Kuhn W, Muller T, et al: Ala30Pro mutation in the gene encoding alpha-synuclein in Parkinson's disease (letter). Nat Genet 18:106–108, 1998

Kugler SL, Johnson WG: Genetics of the febrile seizure susceptibility trait. Brain Dev 20:265–274, 1998

Kuhn W, Muller T: [Therapy of Parkinson disease, 2: new therapy concepts for treating motor symptoms]. Fortschr Neurol Psychiatr 65:375–385, 1997

Kurth JH, Kurth MC, Poduslo SE, et al: Association of a monoamine oxidase B allele with Parkinson's disease. Ann Neurol 33:368–372, 1993

Kurtzke JF, Goldberg ID: Parkinsonism death rates by race, sex, and geography. Neurology 38:1558–1561, 1988

Laccone F, ChristianW: A recurrent expansion of a maternal allele with 36 CAG repeats causes Huntington disease in two sisters. Am J Hum Genet 66:1145–1148, 2000

Lachman HM, Morrow B, Shprintzen R, et al: Association of codon 108/158 catechol-O-methyltransferase gene polymorphism with the psychiatric manifestations of velo-cardio-facial syndrome. Am J Med Genet 67:468–472, 1996

LaHoste GJ, Swanson JM, Wigal SB, et al: Dopamine D4 receptor gene polymorphism is associated with attention deficit hyperactivity disorder [see comments]. Mol Psychiatry 1:121–124, 1996

Lamb JA, Moore J, Bailey A, et al: Autism: recent molecular genetic advances. Hum Mol Genet 9:861–868, 2000

Langlois S: Genomic imprinting: a new mechanism for disease. Pediatr Pathol 14:161–165, 1994

Langston JW: The etiology of Parkinson's disease with emphasis on the MPTP story. Neurology 47:S153–S160, 1996

Langston JW: Epidemiology versus genetics in Parkinson's disease: progress in resolving an age-old debate. Ann Neurol 44:S45-S52, 1998

Lannfelt L, Bogdanovic N, Appelgren H, et al: Amyloid precursor protein mutation causes Alzheimer's disease in a Swedish family (letter). Neurosci Lett 168:254–256, 1994

Lanska DJ: The geographic distribution of Parkinson's disease mortality in the United States. J Neurol Sci 150:63–70, 1997

Lasmezas CI, Deslys JP, Demaimay R, et al: BSE transmission to macaques (letter). Nature 381:743–744, 1996

Lasmezas CI, Deslys JP, Robain O, et al: Transmission of the BSE agent to mice in the absence of detectable abnormal prion protein. Science 275:402–405, 1997

Lassig JP, Vachirasomtoon K, Hartzell K, et al: Physical mapping of the serotonin 5-HT(7) receptor gene (HTR7) to chromosome 10 and pseudogene (HTR7P) to chromosome 12, and testing of linkage disequilibrium between HTR7 and autistic disorder. Am J Med Genet 88:472–475, 1999

Launer LJ, Andersen K, Dewey ME, et al: Rates and risk factors for dementia and Alzheimer's disease: results from EURODEM pooled analyses. EURODEM Incidence Research Group and Work Groups. European Studies of Dementia. Neurology 52:78–84, 1999

Lavori PW, Klerman GL, Keller MB, et al: Age-period-cohort analysis of secular trends in onset of major depression: findings in siblings of patients with major affective disorder. J Psychiatr Res 21:23–35, 1986

Lazzarini AM, Myers RH, Zimmerman TR Jr, et al: A clinical genetic study of Parkinson's disease: evidence for dominant transmission. Neurology 44:499–506, 1994

Leckman JF, Grice DE, Boardman J, et al: Symptoms of obsessive-compulsive disorder. Am J Psychiatry 154:911–917, 1997

Le Couteur A, Bailey A, Goode S, et al: A broader phenotype of autism: the clinical spectrum in twins. J Child Psychol Psychiatry 37:785–801, 1996

Le Couteur DG, McLean AJ, Taylor MC, et al: Pesticides and Parkinson's disease. Biomed Pharmacother 53:122–130, 1999

Lee PN: Smoking and Alzheimer's disease: a review of the epidemiological evidence. Neuroepidemiology 13:131–144, 1994

Leeflang EP, Zhang L, Tavare S, et al: Single sperm analysis of the trinucleotide repeats in the Huntington's disease gene: quantification of the mutation frequency spectrum. Hum Mol Genet 4:1519–1526, 1995

Lennox WG, Jolly DH: Seizures, brain waves and intelligence tests of epileptic twins. Res Publ Assoc Res Nerv Ment Dis 33:325–345, 1954

Lennox WG, Lennox M: Epilepsy and Related Disorders, Vol 1. Boston, MA, Little, Brown, 1960

Lensi P, Cassano GB, Correddu G, et al: Obsessive-compulsive disorder: familial-developmental history, symptomatology, comorbidity and course with special reference to gender-related differences. Br J Psychiatry 169:101–107, 1996

Leonard HL, Lenane MC, Swedo SE, et al: Tics and Tourette's disorder: a 2- to 7-year follow-up of 54 obsessive-compulsive children. Am J Psychiatry 149:1244–1251, 1992

Leonard HL, Swedo SE, Lenane MC, et al: A 2- to 7-year follow-up study of 54 obsessive-compulsive children and adolescents. Arch Gen Psychiatry 50:429–439, 1993

Leonard S, Gault J, Moore T, et al: Further investigation of a chromosome 15 locus in schizophrenia: analysis of affected sibpairs from the NIMH Genetics Initiative. Am J Med Genet 81:308–312, 1998

Leonard HL, Swedo SE, Garvey M, et al: Postinfectious and other forms of obsessive-compulsive disorder. Child Adolesc Psychiatr Clin N Am 8:497–511, 1999

Lerner JW: Educational interventions in learning disabilities. J Am Acad Child Adolesc Psychiatry 28:326–331, 1989

Leroy E, Boyer R, Auburger G, et al: The ubiquitin pathway in Parkinson's disease (letter). Nature 395:451–452, 1998

Lesch K-P, Bengel D, Heils A, et al: Association of anxiety-related traits with a polymorphism in the serotonin transporter gene regulatory region. Science 274:1527–1531, 1996

Levy DL, Holzman PS, Matthysse S, et al: Eye tracking and schizophrenia. Schizophr Bull 20:47–62, 1994

Levy F, Hay DA, McStephen M, et al: Attention-deficit hyperactivity disorder: a category or a continuum? Genetic analysis of a large-scale twin study. J Am Acad Child Adolesc Psychiatry 36:737–744, 1997

Levy-Lehad E, Lahad A, Wijsman EM, et al: Apolipoprotein E genotypes and age of onset in early onset familial Alzheimer's disease. Ann Neurol 38:678–680, 1995

Lewis A: Problems of obsessional illness. Proceedings of the Royal Society of Medicine 29:325–336, 1936

Lewitter F, De Fries JC, Elston RC: Genetic models of reading disability. Behav Genet 10:9–30, 1980

Li T, Vallada H, Curtis D, et al: Catechol-O-methyltransferase Val158Met polymorphism: frequency analysis in Han Chinese subjects and allelic association of the low activity allele with bipolar affective disorder. Pharmacogenetics 7:349–353, 1997

Liberski PP: Prions, beta-sheets and transmissible dementias: is there still something missing? Acta Neuropathol (Berl) 90:113–125, 1995

Light JG, DeFries JC, Olson RK: Multivariate behavioral genetic analysis of achievement and cognitive measures in reading-disabled and control twin pairs. Hum Biol 70:215–237, 1998

Lim LC, Nothen MM, Korner J, et al: No evidence of association between dopamine D4 receptor variants and bipolar affective disorder. Am J Med Genet 54:259–263, 1994a

Lim LC, Powell JF, Murray R, et al: Monoamine oxidase A gene and bipolar affective disorder. Am J Hum Genet 54:1122–1124, 1994b

Lin L, Faraco J, Li R, et al: The sleep disorder canine narcolepsy is caused by a mutation in the hypocretin (orexin) receptor 2 gene. Cell 98:365–376, 1999

Lin MW, Sham P, Hwu HG, et al: Suggestive evidence for linkage of schizophrenia to markers on chromosome 13 in Caucasian but not Oriental populations. Hum Genet 99:417–420, 1997

Lindblad K, Nylander PO, De Bruyn A, et al: Detection of expanded CAG repeats in bipolar affective disorder using the repeat expansion detection (RED) method. Neurobiol Dis 2:55–62, 1995

Liou HH, Tsai MC, Chen CJ, et al: Environmental risk factors and Parkinson's disease: a case-control study in Taiwan. Neurology 48:1583–1588, 1997

Lipton RB, Ottman R, Ehrenberg BL, et al: Comorbidity of migraine: the connection between migraine and epilepsy. Neurology 44 (10 suppl 7):S28–S32, 1994

Liu AW, Delgado-Escueta AV, Serratosa JM, et al: Juvenile myoclonic epilepsy locus in chromosome 6p21.2-p11: linkage to convulsions and electroencephalography trait. Am J Hum Genet 57:368–381, 1995

Liu W, Gu N, Feng G, et al: Tentative association of the serotonin transporter with schizophrenia and unipolar depression but not with bipolar disorder in Han Chinese (In Process Citation). Pharmacogenetics 9:491–495, 1999

Livingston R, Adam BS, Bracha HS: Season of birth and neurodevelopmental disorders: summer birth is associated with dyslexia. J Am Acad Child Adolesc Psychiatry 32:612–616, 1993

Logroscino G, Marder K, Graziano J, et al: Dietary iron, animal fats, and risk of Parkinson's disease. Mov Disord 13 (suppl 1):13–16, 1998

Lohr JB, Flynn K: Minor physical anomalies in schizophrenia and mood disorders. Schizophr Bull 19:551–556, 1993

Lykken DT, Tellegen A, Iacono WG: EEG spectra in twins: evidence for a neglected mechanism of genetic determination. Physiol Psychol 10:60–65, 1982

Lyle OE, Gottesman II: Premorbid psychometric indicators of the gene for Huntington's disease. J Consult Clin Psychol 45:1011–1022, 1977

MacDonald ME, Barnes G, Srinidhi J, et al: Gametic but not somatic instability of CAG repeat length in Huntington's disease. J Med Genet 30:982–986, 1993

MacKinnon DF, McMahon FJ, Simpson SG, et al: Panic disorder with familial bipolar disorder. Biol Psychiatry 42:90–95, 1997

MacKinnon DF, Xu J, McMahon FJ, et al: Bipolar disorder and panic disorder in families: an analysis of chromosome 18 data. Am J Psychiatry 155:829–831, 1998

Maddox LO, Menold MM, Bass MP, et al: Autistic disorder and chromosome 15q11-q13: construction and analysis of a BAC/PAC contig. Genomics 62:325–331, 1999

Maestrini E, Lai C, Marlow A, et al: Serotonin transporter (5-HTT) and gamma-aminobutyric acid receptor subunit beta3 (GABRB3) gene polymorphisms are not associated with autism in the IMGSA families: the International Molecular Genetic Study of Autism Consortium. Am J Med Genet 88:492–496, 1999

Mahadevan M, Tsilfidis C, Sabourin L, et al: Myotonic dystrophy mutation: an unstable CTG repeat in the 3′ untranslated region of the gene. Science 255:1253–1255, 1992

Maier W, Lichtermann D, Minges J, et al: A controlled family study in panic disorder. J Psychiatr Res 27 (suppl 1):79–87, 1993

Maier W, Hallmayer J, Zill P, et al: Linkage analysis between pericentrometric markers on chromosome 18 and bipolar disorder: a replication test. Psychiatry Res 59:7–15, 1995

Maier-Dobersberger T, Ferenci P, Polli C, et al: Detection of the His1069Gln mutation in Wilson disease by rapid polymerase chain reaction [see comments]. Ann Intern Med 127:21–26, 1997

Malafosse A, Leboyer M, d'Amato T, et al: Manic depressive illness and tyrosine hydroxylase gene: linkage heterogeneity and association. Neurobiol Dis 4:337–349, 1997

Malaspina D, Sohler NL, Susser E: Interaction of genes and prenatal exposures in schizophrenia, in Prenatal Exposures in Schizophrenia. Edited by Susser E, Brown AS, Gorman JM. Washington, DC, American Psychiatric Press, 1999, pp 35–61

Malhotra AK, Virkkunen M, Rooney W, et al: The association between the dopamine D4 receptor (D4DR) 16 amino acid repeat polymorphism and novelty seeking. Mol Psychiatry 1:388–391, 1996

Mangiarini L, Sathasivam K, Seller M, et al: Exon 1 of the HD gene with an expanded CAG repeat is sufficient to cause a progressive neurological phenotype in transgenic mice. Cell 87:493–506, 1996

Mann DAM: The pathologic association between Down syndrome and Alzheimer's disease. Mech Ageing Dev 43:99–136, 1988

Manshadi M, Lippmann S, O'Daniel RG, et al: Alcohol abuse and attention deficit disorder. J Clin Psychiatry 44:379–380, 1983

Manuelidis L, Fritch W: Infectivity and host responses in Creutzfeldt-Jakob disease. Virology 216:46–59, 1996

Maraganore DM, Harding AE, Marsden CD: A clinical and genetic study of familial Parkinson's disease. Mov Disord 6:205–211, 1991

Marcus J, Auerbach J, Wilkinson L, et al: Infants at risk for schizophrenia: the Jerusalem Infant Development Study. Arch Gen Psychiatry 38:703–713, 1981

Mariappan SV, Silks LA III, Chen X, et al: Solution structures of the Huntington's disease DNA triplets, (CAG)n. J Biomol Struct Dyn 15:723–744, 1998

Markowitz JS, Weissman MM, Ouellette R, et al: Quality of life in panic disorder. Arch Gen Psychiatry 46:984–992, 1989

Marsden CD, Jenner PG: The significance of 1-methyl-4-phenyl-1,2,3,6-tetrahydropyridine. Ciba Found Symp 126:239–256, 1987

Marshall W, Ferguson J: Hereditary word blindness as a defect of selective attention. J Nerv Ment Dis 89:164–173, 1939

Martin JB, Gusella JF: Huntington's disease: pathogenesis and management. N Engl J Med 315:1267–1276, 1986

Martin WE, Young WI, Anderson VE: Parkinson's disease—a genetic study. Brain 96:495–506, 1973

Martindale D, Hackam A, Wieczorek A, et al: Length of huntingtin and its polyglutamine tract influences localization and frequency of intracellular aggregates. Nat Genet 18:150–154, 1998

Martinello F, Piazza A, Pastorello E, et al: Clinical and neuroimaging study of central nervous system in congenital myotonic dystrophy. J Neurol 246:186–192, 1999

Marttila RJ, Rinne UK: Parkinson's disease and essential tremor in families of patients with early onset Parkinson's disease. J Neurol Neurosurg Psychiatry 51:429–431, 1988

Martyn CN, Coggon DN, Inskip H, et al: Aluminum concentrations in drinking water and risk of Alzheimer's disease. Epidemiology 8:281–286, 1997

Matsuki K, Honda Y, Satake M, et al: HLA in narcolepsy in Japan, in HLA in Narcolepsy. Edited by Honda Y, Juji T. Berlin, Germany, Springer-Verlag, 1988, pp 58–75

Matsushita S, Muramatsu T, Kimura M, et al: Serotonin transporter gene regulatory region polymorphism and panic disorder. Mol Psychiatry 2:390–392, 1997

Mattock C, Marmot M, Stern G: Could Parkinson's disease follow intra-uterine influenza? A speculative hypothesis. J Neurol Neurosurg Psychiatry 51:753–756, 1988

Mayeux R, Tang MX, Marder K, et al: Smoking and Parkinson's disease. Mov Disord 9:207–212, 1994

Mayeux R, Marder K, Cote LJ, et al: The frequency of idiopathic Parkinson's disease by age, ethnic group, and sex in northern Manhattan, 1988–1993 [see comments] [published erratum appears in Am J Epidemiol 143:528, 1996]. Am J Epidemiol 142:820–827, 1995a

Mayeux R, Ottman R, Maestre G, et al: Synergistic effects of traumatic head injury and apolipoprotein-epsilon 4 in patients with Alzheimer's disease [see comments]. Neurology 45:555–557, 1995b

Maziade M, Bissonnette L, Rouillard E, et al: 6p24–22 region and major psychoses in the Eastern Quebec population. Le Groupe IREP. Am J Med Genet 74:311–318, 1997

McCarthy MI, Kruglyak L, Lander ES: Sib-pair collection strategies for complex diseases. Genet Epidemiol 15:317–340, 1998

McDonald LV, Lake CR: Psychosis in an adolescent patient with Wilson's disease: effects of chelation therapy. Psychosom Med 57:202–204, 1995

McDougle CJ, Epperson CN, Price LH, et al: Evidence for linkage disequilibrium between serotonin transporter protein gene (SLC6A4) and obsessive compulsive disorder. Mol Psychiatry 3:270–273, 1998

McGuffin P, Festenstein H, Murray R: A family study of HLA antigens and other genetic markers in schizophrenia. Psychol Med 13:31–43, 1983

McInnis MG, McMahon FJ, Chase GA, et al: Anticipation in bipolar affective disorder. Am J Hum Genet 53:385–390, 1993

McKinley MP, Bolton DC, Prusiner SB: A protease-resistant protein is a structural component of the scrapie prion. Cell 35:57–62, 1983

McLachlan DR, Bergeron C, Smith JE, et al: Risk for neuropathologically confirmed Alzheimer's disease and residual aluminum in municipal drinking water employing weighted residential histories [see comments]. Neurology 46:401–405, 1996

McMahon FJ, Stine OC, Meyers DA, et al: Patterns of maternal transmission in bipolar affective disorder. Am J Hum Genet 56:1277–1286, 1995

McNeil TF: Women with nonorganic psychosis: psychiatric and demographic characteristics of cases with versus without postpartum psychotic episodes. Acta Psychiatr Scand 78:603–609, 1988

McNeil TF, Kaij L: Swedish high-risk study: sample characteristics at age 6. Schizophr Bull 13:373–381, 1987

Mednick SA, Machon RA, Huttunen MO, et al: Adult schizophrenia following prenatal exposure to an influenza epidemic. Arch Gen Psychiatry 45:189–192, 1988

Medori R, Tritschler HJ, LeBlanc A, et al: Fatal familial insomnia, a prion disease with a mutation at codon 178 of the prion protein gene [see comments]. N Engl J Med 326:444–449, 1992

Mehta KM, Ott A, Kalmijn S, et al: Head trauma and risk of dementia and Alzheimer's disease: the Rotterdam Study. Neurology 53:1959–1962, 1999

Meiner Z, Gabizon R, Prusiner SB: Familial Creutzfeldt-Jakob disease: codon 200 prion disease in Libyan Jews. Medicine (Baltimore) 76:227–237, 1997

Mendlewicz J, Rainer JD: Adoption study supporting genetic transmission in manic-depressive illness. Nature 268:327–329, 1977

Mendlewicz J, Papadimitriou G, Wilmotte J: Family study of panic disorder: comparison with generalized anxiety disorder, major depression and normal subjects. Psychiatr Genet 3:73–78, 1993

Mendlewicz J, Lindbald K, Souery D, et al: Expanded trinucleotide CAG repeats in families with bipolar affective disorder. Biol Psychiatry 42:1115–1122, 1997

Menegon A, Board PG, Blackburn AC, et al: Parkinson's disease, pesticides, and glutathione transferase polymorphisms [see comments]. Lancet 352:1344–1346, 1998

Merchant C, Tang MX, Albert S, et al: The influence of smoking on the risk of Alzheimer's disease. Neurology 52:1408–1412, 1999

Merette C, Rowllard E, Cliche D, et al: No conclusive evidence of susceptibility loci for bipolar disorder on 18p11 and 21q22 in extended pedigrees of Eastern Quebec. Psychiatr Genet 5:S18, 1995

Meyer N, Rosenbaum V, Schmidt B, et al: Search for a putative scrapie genome in purified prion fractions reveals a paucity of nucleic acids. J Gen Virol 72 (pt 1):37–49, 1991

Mignot E: Genetic and familial aspects of narcolepsy. Neurology 50 (2 suppl 1):S16–22, 1998

Mignot E, Guilleminault C, Grumet FC, et al: Is narcolepsy an autoimmune disease? Paper presented at the Proceedings of the Third Milano International Symposium on Sleep: Hormones and Immunological System, Milan, Italy, September 1991

Mikami M, Yasuda T, Terao A, et al: Localization of a gene for benign adult familial myoclonic epilepsy to chromosome 8q23.3-q24.1. Am J Hum Genet 65:745–751, 1999

Mirow AL, Kristbjanarson H, Egeland JA, et al: A linkage study of distal chromosome 5q and bipolar disorder. Biol Psychiatry 36:223–229, 1994

Mirsky AF, Silberman EK, Latz A, et al: Adult outcomes of high-risk children: differential effects of town and kibbutz rearing. Schizophr Bull 11:150–154, 1985

Mohs RC, Breitner JCS, Silverman JM, et al: Alzheimer's disease: morbid risk in relatives approximates 50% by age 90. Arch Gen Psychiatry 44:405–408, 1987

Moises HW, Yang L, Kristbjarnarson H, et al: An international two-stage genome-wide search for schizophrenia susceptibility genes. Nat Genet 11:321–324, 1995

Moldin SO, Gottesman II, Erlenmeyer-Kimling L, et al: Psychometric deviance in offspring at risk for schizophrenia, I: initial delineation of a distinct subgroup. Psychiatry Res 32:297–310, 1990

Monnat RJ, Chiaverotti TA, Hackman AFM, et al: Molecular structure and genetic stability of human hypoxanthine phosphoribosyltransferase gene duplications. Genomics 13:758–796, 1992

Montplaisir J, Poirier G: Narcolepsy in monozygotic twins. Neurology 37:1089, 1987

Morens DM, Grandinetti A, Davis JW, et al: Evidence against the operation of selective mortality in explaining the association between cigarette smoking and reduced occurrence of idiopathic Parkinson disease. Am J Epidemiol 144:400–404, 1996

Morris AG, Gaitonde E, McKenna PJ, et al: CAG repeat expansions and schizophrenia: association with disease in females and with early age-at-onset. Hum Mol Genet 4:1957–1961, 1995

Morris JC: Differential diagnosis of Alzheimer's disease. Clin Geriatr Med 10:257–276, 1994

Morrison JR, Stewart MA: A family study of the hyperactive child syndrome. Biol Psychiatry 3:189–195, 1971

Morrison JR, Stewart MA: The psychiatric status of the legal families of adopted hyperactive children. Arch Gen Psychiatry 28:888–891, 1973

Morrison JR, Stewart MA: Bilateral inheritance as evidence for polygenicity in the hyperactive child syndrome. J Nerv Ment Dis 158:226–228, 1974

Mortel KF, Meyer JS, Herod B, et al: Education and occupation as risk factors for dementias of the Alzheimer and ischemic vascular types. Dementia 6:55–62, 1995

Mostacciuolo ML, Lombardi A, Cambissa V, et al: Population data on benign and severe forms of X-linked muscular dystrophy. Hum Genet 75:217–220, 1987

Muir WJ, Gosden CM, Brookes AJ, et al: Direct microdissection and microcloning of a translocation breakpoint region, t(111)(q42.2q21), associated with schizophrenia. Cytogenet Cell Genet 70:35–40, 1995

Mulnard RA, Cotman CW, Kawas C, et al: Estrogen replacement therapy for treatment of mild to moderate Alzheimer disease: a randomized controlled trial. Alzheimer's Disease Cooperative Study [see comments]. JAMA 283:1007–1015, 2000

Mundo E, Richter MA, Sam F, et al: Is the 5-HT(1Dbeta) receptor gene implicated in the pathogenesis of obsessive-compulsive disorder? (In Process Citation). Am J Psychiatry 157:1160–1161, 2000

Murphy TK, Goodman WK, Fudge MW, et al: B lymphocyte antigen D8/17: a peripheral marker for childhood-onset obsessive-compulsive disorder and Tourette's syndrome? Am J Psychiatry 154:402–407, 1997

Mutchler K, Crowe RR, Noyes R Jr, et al: Exclusion of the tyrosine hydroxylase gene in 14 panic disorder pedigrees. Am J Psychiatry 147:1367–1369, 1990

Myers JK, Weissman MM, Tischler GL, et al: Six-month prevalence of psychiatric disorders in three communities 1980 to 1982. Arch Gen Psychiatry 41:959–967, 1984

Myers RH, Leavitt J, Farrer LA, et al: Homosygotes for Huntington's disease. Am J Hum Genet 45:614–618, 1989

Myers RH, Schaefer EJ, Wilson PW, et al: Apolipoprotein E epsilon4 association with dementia in a population-based study: the Framingham study. Neurology 46:673–677, 1996

Myles-Worsley M, Coon H, Tiobech J, et al: Genetic epidemiological study of schizophrenia in Palau, Micronesia: prevalence and familiality. Am J Med Genet 88:4–10, 1999

Mynett-Johnson LA, Murphy VE, Manley P, et al: Lack of evidence for a major locus for bipolar disorder in the pericentromeric region of chromosome 18 in Irish pedigrees. Biol Psychiatry 42:486–494, 1997

Mynett-Johnson LA, Murphy VE, Claffey E, et al: Preliminary evidence of an association between bipolar disorder in females and the catechol-O-methyltransferase gene. Psychiatr Genet 8:221–225, 1998

Nadder TS, Silberg JL, Eaves LJ, et al: Genetic effects on ADHD symptomatology in 7- to 13-year old twins: results from a telephone survey. Behav Genet 28:83–99, 1998

Naimark D, Jackson E, Rockwell E, et al: Psychotic symptoms in Parkinson's disease patients with dementia [see comments]. J Am Geriatr Soc 44:296–299, 1996

Nakagawa M, Yamada H, Higuchi I, et al: A case of paternally inherited congenital myotonic dystrophy. J Med Genet 31:397–400, 1994

Nakamura Y, Leppert M, O'Connell P, et al: Variable number of tandem repeat (VNTR) markers for human gene mapping. Science 235:1616–1622, 1987

National Institute on Aging/Alzheimer's Association Working Group: Apolipoprotein E genotyping in Alzheimer's disease. Lancet 347:1091–1095, 1996

Nee LE, Lippa CF: Alzheimer's disease in 22 twin pairs—13-year follow-up: hormonal, infectious and traumatic factors. Dement Geriatr Cogn Disord 10:148–151, 1999

Nee LE, Eldridge R, Sunderland T, et al: Dementia of the Alzheimer type: clinical and family study of 22 twin pairs. Neurology 37:359–363, 1987

Nelson E, Rice J: Stability of diagnosis of obsessive-compulsive disorder in the Epidemiologic Catchment Area study. Am J Psychiatry 154:826–831, 1997

Nelson PV, Carey WF, Morris CP: Population frequency of the arylsulphatase A pseudo-deficiency allele. Hum Genet 87:87–88, 1991

Nemetz PN, Leibson C, Naessens JM, et al: Traumatic brain injury and time to onset of Alzheimer's disease: a population-based study. Am J Epidemiol 149:32–40, 1999

Nepom GT, Erlich H: MHC class II molecules and autoimmunity. Annu Rev Immunol 9:493–525, 1991

Neugebauer R, Paik M, Hauser WA, et al: Stressful life events and seizure frequency in patients with epilepsy. Epilepsia 35:336–343, 1994

Ngim CH, Devathasan G: Epidemiologic study on the association between body burden mercury level and idiopathic Parkinson's disease. Neuroepidemiology 8:128–141, 1989

Nicolini H, Cruz C, Camarena B, et al: DRD2, DRD3 and 5HT2A receptor genes polymorphisms in obsessive-compulsive disorder. Mol Psychiatry 1:461–465, 1996

Nitrini R, Rosemberg S, Passos-Bueno MR, et al: Familial spongiform encephalopathy associated with a novel prion protein gene mutation. Ann Neurol 42:138–146, 1997

Nothen MM, Eggerman K, Albus M, et al: Association analysis of the monoamine oxidase A gene in bipolar affective disorder by using family based internal controls. Am J Hum Genet 57:975–977, 1995

Nothen MM, Schulte-Korne G, Grimm T, et al: Genetic linkage analysis with dyslexia: evidence for linkage of spelling disability to chromosome 15. Eur Child Adolesc Psychiatry 8 (suppl 3):56–59, 1999

Novelli E, Nobile M, Diaferia G, et al: A molecular investigation suggests no relationship between obsessive-compulsive disorder and the dopamine D2 receptor. Neuropsychobiology 29:61–63, 1994

Noyes R Jr, Crowe RR, Harris EL, et al: Relationship between panic disorder and agoraphobia: a family study. Arch Gen Psychiatry 43:227–232, 1986

Nuechterlein KH, Dawson ME: Information processing and attentional functioning in the developmental course of schizophrenic disorders. Schizophr Bull 10:160–203, 1984

Nylander PO, Engstrom C, Chotai J, et al: Anticipation in Swedish families with bipolar affective disorder. J Med Genet 31:686–689, 1994

O'Callaghan E, Sham P, Takei N, et al: Schizophrenia after prenatal exposure to 1957 A2 influenza epidemic [see comments]. Lancet 337:1248–1250, 1991

O'Donovan MC, Owen MJ: Candidate-gene association studies of schizophrenia. Am J Hum Genet 65:587–592, 1999

O'Donovan MC, Guy C, Craddock N, et al: Expanded CAG repeats in schizophrenia and bipolar disorder. Nat Genet 10:380–381, 1995

O'Driscoll GA, Lenzenweger MF, Holzman PS: Antisaccades and smooth pursuit eye tracking and schizotypy. Arch Gen Psychiatry 55:837–843, 1998

O'Dwyer JM: Schizophrenia in people with intellectual disability: the role of pregnancy and birth complications. J Intellect Disabil Res 41 (pt 3):238–251, 1997

Oesch B, Westaway D, Walchli M, et al: A cellular gene encodes scrapie PrP 27–30 protein. Cell 40:735–746, 1985

Ogasawara N, Stout JT, Goto H, et al: Molecular analysis of a female Lesch-Nyhan patient. J Clin Invest 84:1024–1027, 1989

Ohara K, Xie DW, Ishigaki T, et al: The genes encoding the 5HT1D alpha and 5HT1D beta receptors are unchanged in patients with panic disorder. Biol Psychiatry 39:5–10, 1996

O'Hoy KL, Tsilfidis C, Mahadevan MS, et al: Reduction in the size of the myotonic dystrophy trinucleotide repeat mutation during transmission. Science 259:809–812, 1993

Oken RJ, Schulzer M: At issue: schizophrenia and rheumatoid arthritis: the negative association revisited. Schizophr Bull 25:625–638, 1999

Okuizumi K, Onodera O, Tanaka H, et al: ApoE-epsilon 4 and early onset Alzheimer's (letter). Nat Genet 7:10–11, 1994

Okuizumi K, Onodera O, Namba Y, et al: Genetic association of the very low density lipoprotein (VLDL) receptor gene with sporadic Alzheimer's disease. Nat Genet 11:207–209, 1995

Olanow CW, Tatton WG: Etiology and pathogenesis of Parkinson's disease. Annu Rev Neurosci 22:123–144, 1999

O'Meara ES, Kukull WA, Sheppard L, et al: Head injury and risk of Alzheimer's disease by apolipoprotein E genotype. Am J Epidemiol 146:373–384, 1997

O'Neill JP, Finette BA: Transition mutations at CpG dinucleotides are the most frequent in vivo spontaneous single-based substitution mutation in the human HPRT gene. Environ Mol Mutagen 32:188–191, 1998

Oppenheimer BS, Rothschild MA: The psychoneurotic factor in the irritable heart of soldiers. JAMA 70:1919–1922, 1918

Oruc L, Lindblad K, Verheyen GR, et al: CAG repeat expansions in bipolar and unipolar disorders (letter). Am J Hum Genet 60:730–732, 1997

Osuntokun BO, Sahota A, Ogunniyi AO, et al: Lack of an association between apolipoprotein E epsilon 4 and Alzheimer's disease in elderly Nigerians. Ann Neurol 38:463–465, 1995

Ott A, Slooter AJ, Hofman A, et al: Smoking and risk of dementia and Alzheimer's disease in a population-based cohort study: the Rotterdam Study [see comments]. Lancet 351:1840–1843, 1998

Ott J: Analysis of Human Genetic Linkage. Baltimore, MD, Johns Hopkins University Press, 1985

Ottman R: Genetics of the partial epilepsies: a review. Epilepsia 30:107–111, 1989

Ottman R: Sex specific recurrence risks and the maternal effect in epilepsy. Am J Hum Genet 47 (suppl):A142, 1990

Paganini-Hill A, Henderson VW: Estrogen replacement therapy and risk of Alzheimer disease. Arch Intern Med 156:2213–2217, 1996

Pan KM, Baldwin M, Nguyen J, et al: Conversion of alpha-helices into beta-sheets features in the formation of the scrapie prion proteins. Proc Natl Acad Sci U S A 90:10962–10966, 1993

Papolos DF, Faedda GL, Veit S, et al: Bipolar spectrum disorders in patients diagnosed with velo-cardio-facial syndrome: does a hemizygous deletion of chromosome 22q11 result in bipolar affective disorder? Am J Psychiatry 153:1541–1547, 1996

Papolos DF, Veit S, Faedda GL, et al: Ultra-ultra rapid cycling bipolar disorder is associated with the low activity catecholamine-O-methyltransferase allele. Mol Psychiatry 3:346–349, 1998

Parchi P, Petersen RB, Chen SG, et al: Molecular pathology of fatal familial insomnia. Brain Pathol 8:539–548, 1998

Parkes JD, Langdon N, Lock C: Narcolepsy and immunity. BMJ 292:359–360, 1986

Parnas J, Schulsinger F, Schulsinger H, et al: Behavioral precursors of schizophrenia spectrum: a prospective study. Arch Gen Psychiatry 39:658–664, 1982a

Parnas J, Schulsinger F, Teasdale TW, et al: Perinatal complications and clinical outcome within the schizophrenia spectrum. Br J Psychiatry 140:416–420, 1982b

Passouant P, Billiard M: The evolution of narcolepsy with age, in Narcolepsy. Edited by Guilleminault C, Dement WC, Passouant P. New York, Spectrum, 1976, pp 179–196

Passwell J, Adam A, Garfinkel D, et al: Heterogeneity of Wilson's disease in Israel. Isr J Med Sci 13:15–19, 1977

Pastor-Soler NM, Rafi MA, Hoffman JD, et al: Metachromatic leukodystrophy in the Navajo Indian population: a splice site mutation in intron 4 of the arylsulfatase A gene. Hum Mutat 4:199–207, 1994

Patel PI, Nussbaum RL, Framson PE, et al: Organisation of the HPRT gene and related sequences in the human genome. Somat Cell Mol Genet 10:483–493, 1984

Patel PI, Framson PE, Caskey CT, et al: Fine structure of the human hypoxanthine phosphoribosyltransferase gene. Mol Cell Biol 6:393–403, 1986

Pauls DL, Alsobrook JP: The inheritance of obsessive-compulsive disorder. Child Adolesc Psychiatr Clin N Am 8:481–496, 1999

Pauls DL, Crowe RR, Noyes R Jr: Distribution of ancestral secondary cases in anxiety neurosis (panic disorder). J Affect Disord 1:387–390, 1979a

Pauls DL, Noyes R Jr, Crowe RR: The familial prevalence in second-degree relatives of patients with anxiety neurosis (panic disorder). J Affect Disord 1:279–285, 1979b

Pauls DL, Bucher KD, Crowe RR, et al: A genetic study of panic disorder pedigrees. Am J Hum Genet 32:639–644, 1980

Pauls DL, Shaywitz SE, Kramer PL, et al: Demonstration of vertical transmission of attention deficit disorder. Ann Neurol 14:363, 1984

Pauls DL, Towbin KE, Leckman JF, et al: Gilles de la Tourette's syndrome and obsessive-compulsive disorder: evidence supporting a genetic relationship. Arch Gen Psychiatry 43:1180–1182, 1986

Pauls DL, Alsobrook JP, Goodman W, et al: A family study of obsessive-compulsive disorder. Am J Psychiatry 152:76–84, 1995a

Pauls DL, Ott J, Paul SM, et al: Linkage analyses of chromosome 18 markers do not identify a major susceptibility locus for bipolar affective disorder in the Old Order Amish. Am J Hum Genet 57:636–643, 1995b

Paulson GW, Dadmehr N: Is there a premorbid personality typical for Parkinson's disease? Neurology 41:73–76, 1991

Payami H, Larsen K, Bernard S, et al: Increased risk of Parkinson's disease in parents and siblings of patients. Ann Neurol 36:659–661, 1994

Payami H, Bernard S, Larsen K, et al: Genetic anticipation in Parkinson's disease. Neurology 45:135–138, 1995

Payami H, Zareparsi S, Montee KR, et al: Gender difference in apolipoprotein E-associated risk for familial Alzheimer disease: a possible clue to the higher incidence of Alzheimer disease in women. Am J Hum Genet 58:803–811, 1996

Pearson GR, Gruffydd-Jones TJ, Wyatt JM, et al: Feline spongiform encephalopathy (letter). Vet Rec 128:532, 1991

Peiffer A, Thompson J, Charlier C, et al: A locus for febrile seizures (FEB3) maps to chromosome 2q23–24. Ann Neurol 46:671–678, 1999

Pekkarinen P, Terwilliger J, Bredbacka PE, et al: Evidence of a predisposing locus to bipolar disorder on Xq24-q27.1 in an extended Finnish pedigree. Genome Res 5:105–115, 1995

Pennacchio LA, Lehesjoki AE, Stone NE, et al: Mutations in the gene encoding cystatin B in progressive myoclonus epilepsy (EPM1) [see comments]. Science 271:1731–1734, 1996

Pennington BF, Gilger JW, Pauls D, et al: Evidence for major gene transmission of developmental dyslexia. JAMA 266:1527–1534, 1991

Pericak-Vance MA, Bebout JL, Gaskell PC Jr, et al: Linkage studies in familial Alzheimer disease: evidence for chromosome 19 linkage. Am J Hum Genet 48:1034–1050, 1991

Pericak-Vance MA, Johnson CC, Rimmler JB, et al: Alzheimer's disease and apolipoprotein E-4 allele in an Amish population. Ann Neurol 39:700–704, 1996

Pericak-Vance MA, Bass MP, Yamaoka LH, et al: Complete genomic screen in late-onset familial Alzheimer disease: evidence for a new locus on chromosome 12. JAMA 278:1237–1241, 1997

Perna G, Cocchi S, Bertani A, et al: Sensitivity to 35% CO2 in healthy first-degree relatives of patients with panic disorder. Am J Psychiatry 152:623–625, 1995

Perna G, Bertani A, Caldirola D, et al: Family history of panic disorder and hypersensitivity to CO2 in patients with panic disorder. Am J Psychiatry 153:1060–1064, 1996

Perna G, Caldirola D, Arancio C, et al: Panic attacks: a twin study. Psychiatry Res 66:69–71, 1997

Persichetti F, Ambrose CM, Ge P, et al: Normal and expanded Huntington's disease gene alleles produce distinguishable proteins due to translation across the CAG repeat. Mol Med 1:374–383, 1995

Peskind ER: Neurobiology of Alzheimer's disease. J Clin Psychiatry 57 (suppl 14):5–8, 1996

Petersen RC, Smith GE, Ivnik RJ, et al: Apolipoprotein E status as a predictor of the development of Alzheimer's disease in memory-impaired individuals [published erratum appears in JAMA 274:538, 1995]. JAMA 273:1274–1278, 1995

Petronis A, Kennedy JL: Unstable genes—unstable mind? Am J Psychiatry 152:164–172, 1995

Petrukhin K, Lutsenko S, Chernov I, et al: Characterization of the Wilson disease gene encoding a P-type copper transporting ATPase: genomic organization, alternative splicing, and structure/function predictions. Hum Mol Genet 3:1647–1656, 1994

Peyser CE, Folstein SE: Huntington's disease as a model for mood disorders: clues from neuropathology and neurochemistry. Mol Chem Neuropathol 12:99–119, 1990

Philippe A, Martinez M, Guilloud-Bataille M, et al: Genome-wide scan for autism susceptibility genes. Paris Autism Research International Sibpair Study. Hum Mol Genet 8:805–812, 1999

Pickles A, Bolton P, Macdonald H, et al: Latent-class analysis of recurrence risks for complex phenotypes with selection and measurement error: a twin and family history study of autism. Am J Hum Genet 57:717–726, 1995

Piven J, Tsai GC, Nehme E, et al: Platelet serotonin, a possible marker for familial autism. J Autism Dev Disord 21:51–59, 1991

Plassman BL, Breitner JC: Recent advances in the genetics of Alzheimer's disease and vascular dementia with an emphasis on gene-environment interactions [see comments]. J Am Geriatr Soc 44:1242–1250, 1996

Plaster NM, Uyama E, Uchino M, et al: Genetic localization of the familial adult myoclonic epilepsy (FAME) gene to chromosome 8q24. Neurology 53:1180–1183, 1999

Pogue-Geile M, Ferrell R, Deka R, et al: Human novelty-seeking personality traits and dopamine D4 receptor polymorphisms: a twin and genetic association study. Am J Med Genet 81:44–48, 1998

Polten A, Fluharty AL, Fluharty CB, et al: Molecular basis of different forms of metachromatic leukodystrophy. N Engl J Med 324:18–22, 1991

Polymeropoulos MH, Lavedan C, Leroy E, et al: Mutation in the alpha-synuclein gene identified in families with Parkinson's disease [see comments]. Science 276:2045–2047, 1997

Prusiner SB: Novel proteinaceous infectious particles cause scrapie. Science 216:136–144, 1982

Prusiner SB, DeArmond SJ: Prion diseases of the central nervous system. Monogr Pathol 32:86–122, 1990

Prusiner SB, Scott M, Foster D, et al: Transgenetic studies implicate interactions between homologous PrP isoforms in scrapie prion replication. Cell 63:673–686, 1990

Prusiner SB, Groth D, Serban A, et al: Ablation of the prion protein (PrP) gene in mice prevents scrapie and facilitates production of anti-PrP antibodies. Proc Natl Acad Sci U S A 90:10608–10612, 1993

Pulver AE: Search for schizophrenia susceptibility genes. Biol Psychiatry 47:221–230, 2000

Pulver AE, Karayiorgou M, Wolyniec PS, et al: Sequential strategy to identify a susceptibility gene for schizophrenia: report of potential linkage on chromosome 22q12-q13.1: part 1. Am J Med Genet 54:36–43, 1994

Pulver AE, Lasseter VK, Kasch L, et al: Schizophrenia: a genome scan targets chromosomes 3p and 8p as potential sites of susceptibility genes. Am J Med Genet 60:252–260, 1995

Quinn N, Critchley P, Marsden CD: Young onset Parkinson's disease. Mov Disord 2:73–91, 1987

Quitkin F, Rifkin A, Klein D: Neurologic soft signs in schizophrenia and character disorders. Arch Gen Psychiatry 33:845–853, 1976

Rabin M, Wen XL, Hepburn M, et al: Suggestive linkage of developmental dyslexia to chromosome 1p24-p36. Lancet 342:178, 1993

Racacho LJ, McLachlan RS, Ebers GC, et al: Evidence favoring genetic heterogeneity for febrile convulsions. Epilepsia 41:132–139, 2000

Ragazzoni A, Pinto F, Taiuti R, et al: Myotonic dystrophy: an electrophysiological study of cognitive deficits. Can J Neurol Sci 18:300–306, 1991

Raiha I, Kaprio J, Koskenvuo M, et al: Alzheimer's disease in Finnish twins [see comments]. Lancet 347:573–578, 1996

Rantakallio P, Jones P, Moring J, et al: Association between central nervous system infections during childhood and adult onset schizophrenia and other psychoses: a 28-year follow-up. Int J Epidemiol 26:837–843, 1997

Rapoport SI, Pettigrew KD, Schapiro MB: Discordance and concordance of dementia of the Alzheimer type (DAT) in monozygotic twins indicate heritable and sporadic forms of Alzheimer's disease. Neurology 41:1549–1553, 1991

Rasmussen SA, Eisen JL: The epidemiology and clinical features of obsessive compulsive disorder. Psychiatr Clin North Am 15:743–758, 1992

Rasmussen SA, Tsuang MT: The epidemiology of obsessive compulsive disorder. J Clin Psychiatry 45:450–457, 1984

Rathbun JK: Neuropsychological aspects of Wilson's disease. Int J Neurosci 85:221–229, 1996

Ray PF, Harper JC, Ao A, et al: Successful preimplantation genetic diagnosis for sex Link Lesch—Nyhan Syndrome using specific diagnosis. Prenat Diagn 19:1237–1241, 1999

Reddy PH, Charles V, Williams M, et al: Transgenic mice expressing mutated full-length HD cDNA: a paradigm for locomotor changes and selective neuronal loss in Huntington's disease. Philos Trans R Soc Lond B Biol Sci 354:1035–1045, 1999

Redman JB, Fenwick RG, Fu YH, et al: Relationship between parental trinucleotide GCT repeat length and severity of myotonic dystrophy in offspring. JAMA 269:1960–1965, 1993

Reeves JC, Werry JS, Elkind GS, et al: Attention deficit, conduct, oppositional, and anxiety disorders in children, II: clinical characteristics. J Am Acad Child Adolesc Psychiatry 26:144–155, 1987

Reid MS, Nishino S, Tafti M, et al: Neuropharmacological characterization of basal forebrain cholinergic stimulated cataplexy in narcoleptic canines. Exp Neurol 151:89–104, 1998

Reik W: Genomic imprinting: a possible mechanism for the parental origin effect in Huntington's chorea. J Med Genet 25:805–808, 1988

Rice J, Reich T, Andreasen NC, et al: The familial transmission of bipolar illness. Arch Gen Psychiatry 44:441–447, 1987

Rich JB, Rasmusson DX, Folstein MF, et al: Nonsteroidal anti-inflammatory drugs in Alzheimer's disease [see comments]. Neurology 45:51–55, 1995

Richards RI, Sutherland GR: Dynamic mutations: a new class of mutations causing human disease. Cell 70:709–712, 1992

Ridley RM, Frith CD, Crow TJ, et al: Anticipation in Huntington's disease is inherited through the male line but may originate in the female. J Med Genet 25:589–595, 1988

Rieder RO, Nichols PL: Offspring of schizophrenics; III: hyperactivity and neurological soft signs. Arch Gen Psychiatry 36:665–674, 1979

Riggs JE: Cigarette smoking and Parkinson disease: the illusion of a neuroprotective effect. Clin Neuropharmacol 15:88–99, 1992

Rineer S, Finucane B, Simon EW: Autistic symptoms among children and young adults with isodicentric chromosome 15. Am J Med Genet 81:428–433, 1998

Risch N: Linkage strategies for genetically complex traits, I: multilocus models. Am J Hum Genet 46:222–228, 1990

Risch N, Spiker D, Lotspeich L, et al: A genomic screen of autism: evidence for a multilocus etiology. Am J Hum Genet 65:493–507, 1999

Ritvo ER, Spence MA, Freeman BJ, et al: Evidence for autosomal recessive inheritance in 46 families with multiple incidences of autism. Am J Psychiatry 142:187–192, 1985

Ritvo ER, Jorde LB, Mason-Brothers A, et al: The UCLA-University of Utah epidemiologic survey of autism: recurrence risk estimates and genetic counseling. Am J Psychiatry 146:1032–1036, 1989

Ritvo ER, Mason-Brothers A, Freeman BJ, et al: The UCLA-University of Utah epidemiologic survey of autism: the etiologic role of rare diseases. Am J Psychiatry 147:1614–1621, 1990

Roach ES, Delgado M, Anderson L, et al: Carbamazepine trial for Lesch-Nyhan self-mutilation. J Child Neurol 11:476–478, 1996

Robins LN, Price RK: Adult disorders predicted by childhood conduct problems: results from the NIMH Epidemiologic Catchment Area project. Psychiatry 54:116–132, 1991

Robins LN, Helzer JE, Weissman MM, et al: Lifetime prevalence of specific psychiatric disorders in three sites. Arch Gen Psychiatry 41:949–958, 1984

Rogaev EI, Sherrington R, Rogaeva EA, et al: Familial Alzheimer's disease in kindreds with missense mutations in a gene on chromosome 1 related to the Alzheimer's disease type 3 gene. Nature 376:775–778, 1995

Rogaev E, Premkumar S, Song Y, et al: Evidence for an Alzheimer disease susceptibility locus on chromosome 12 and for further locus heterogeneity. JAMA 280:614–618, 1998

Rogers MA, Simon DG: A preliminary study of dietary aluminum intake and risk of Alzheimer's disease. Age Ageing 28:205–209, 1999

Rosenthal D, Wender PH, Kety SS, et al: Schizophrenics' offspring reared in adoptive homes. J Psychiatr Res 6:377–391, 1968

Ross GW, Abbott RD, Petrovitch H, et al: Association of coffee and caffeine intake with the risk of Parkinson disease. JAMA 283:2674–2679, 2000

Ross RG, Olincy A, Harris JG, et al: Anticipatory saccades during smooth pursuit eye movements and familial transmission of schizophrenia. Biol Psychiatry 44:690–697, 1998

Rowe DC, Stever C, Giedinghagen LN, et al: Dopamine DRD4 receptor polymorphism and attention deficit hyperactivity disorder. Mol Psychiatry 3:419–426, 1998

Rubin RL, Hajdukovitch RM, Mitler MM: HLA DR2 association with excessive somnolence in narcolepsy does not generalize to sleep apnea and is not accompanied by systematic autoimmune abnormalities. Clin Immunol Immunopathol 49:149–158, 1988

Rubinsztein JS, Rubinsztein DC, Goodburn S, et al: Apathy and hypersomnia are common features of myotonic dystrophy. J Neurol Neurosurg Psychiatry 64:510–515, 1998

Rutter M, Bailey A, Bolton P, et al: Autism and known medical conditions: myth and substance. J Child Psychol Psychiatry 35:311–322, 1994

Sacker A, Done DJ, Crow TJ, et al: Antecedents of schizophrenia and affective illness: obstetric complications [see comments]. Br J Psychiatry 166:734–741, 1995

Safer DJ: A familial factor in minimal brain dysfunction. Behav Genet 3:175–186, 1973

Sahota A, Yang M, Gao S, et al: Apolipoprotein E-associated risk for Alzheimer's disease in the African-American population is genotype dependent. Ann Neurol 42:659–661, 1997

Sakurai T, Amemiya A, Ishii M, et al: Orexins and orexin receptors: a family of hypothalamic neuropeptides and G protein-coupled receptors that regulate feeding behavior. Cell 92:573–585, 1998

Salib E, Hillier V: A case-control study of Alzheimer's disease and aluminium occupation. Br J Psychiatry 168:244–249, 1996

Salib E, Hillier V: Head injury and the risk of Alzheimer's disease: a case control study. Int J Geriatr Psychiatry 12:363–368, 1997

Sanchez-Ramos JR, Ortoll R, Paulson GW: Visual hallucinations associated with Parkinson disease [see comments]. Arch Neurol 53:1265–1268, 1996

Sapp E, Penney J, Young A, et al: Axonal transport of N-terminal huntingtin suggests early pathology of corticostriatal projections in Huntington disease. J Neuropathol Exp Neurol 58:165–173, 1999

Saunders AM, Strittmatter WJ, Schmechel D, et al: Association of apolipoprotein E allele e4 with late-onset familial and sporadic Alzheimer's disease. Neurology 43:1467–1472, 1993

Schaefer M, Gitlin JD: Genetic disorders of membrane transport, IV: Wilson's disease and Menkes disease. Am J Physiol 276:G311–G314, 1999

Schapira AH: Neurotoxicity and the mechanisms of cell death in Parkinson's disease. Adv Neurol 69:161–165, 1996

Schapira AH: Mitochondrial involvement in Parkinson's disease, Huntington's disease, hereditary spastic paraplegia and Friedreich's ataxia [see comments]. Biochim Biophys Acta 1410:159–170, 1999

Schellenberg GD, Boehnke M, Bryant EM, et al: Association of apolipoprotein CII allele with familial dementia of the Alzheimer's type. J Neurogenet 4:97–108, 1987

Schellenberg GD, Bird TD, Wijsman EM, et al: Genetic linkage evidence for a familial Alzheimer's disease locus on chromosome 14. Science 258:668–671, 1992

Schenk D, Barbour R, Dunn W, et al: Immunization with amyloid-beta attenuates Alzheimer-disease-like pathology in the PDAPP mouse [see comments]. Nature 400:173–177, 1999

Schmidt SM, Zoega T, Crowe RR: Excluding linkage between panic disorder and the gamma-aminobutyric acid beta 1 receptor locus in five Icelandic pedigrees. Acta Psychiatr Scand 88:225–228, 1993

Schoenberg BS: Descriptive epidemiology of Parkinson's disease: disease distribution and hypothesis formulation. Adv Neurol 45:277–283, 1987

Schulte-Korne G, Grimm T, Nothen MM, et al: Evidence for linkage of spelling disability to chromosome 15 (letter). Am J Hum Genet 63:279–282, 1998

Schutta HS, Pratt RTC, Metz H, et al: A family study of the late infantile and juvenile forms of metachromatic leucodystrophy. J Med Genet 3:86–90, 1966

Schwab SG, Albus M, Hallmayer J, et al: Evaluation of a susceptibility gene for schizophrenia on chromosome 6p by multipoint affected sib-pair linkage analysis. Nat Genet 11:325–327, 1995

Schwab SG, Hallmayer J, Lerer B, et al: Support for a chromosome 18p locus conferring susceptibility to functional psychoses in families with schizophrenia, by association and linkage analysis. Am J Hum Genet 63:1139–1152, 1998

Seidler A, Hellenbrand W, Robra BP, et al: Possible environmental, occupational, and other etiologic factors for Parkinson's disease: a case-control study in Germany. Neurology 46:1275–1284, 1996

Seltzer B, Sherwin I: A comparison of clinical features in early and late onset primary degenerative dementia: one entity or two? Arch Neurol 40:143–146, 1983

Semchuk KM, Love EJ, Lee RG: Parkinson's disease and exposure to agricultural work and pesticide chemicals. Neurology 42:1328–1335, 1992

Shah AB, Chernov I, Zhang HT, et al: Identification and analysis of mutations in the Wilson disease gene (ATP7B): population frequencies, genotype-phenotype correlation, and functional analyses. Am J Hum Genet 61:317–328, 1997

Shapiro S, Skinner EA, Kessler LG, et al: Utilization of health and mental health services; three Epidemiologic Catchment Area sites. Arch Gen Psychiatry 41:971–978, 1984

Shaw SH, Kelly M, Smith AB, et al: A genome-wide search for schizophrenia susceptibility genes. Am J Med Genet 81:364–376, 1998

Shaywitz SE: Dyslexia [see comments]. N Engl J Med 338:307–312, 1998

Shaywitz SE, Shaywitz BA, Fletcher JM, et al: Prevalence of reading disability in boys and girls: results of the Connecticut Longitudinal Study [see comments]. JAMA 264:998–1002, 1990

Shaywitz SE, Escobar MD, Shaywitz BA, et al: Evidence that dyslexia may represent the lower tail of a normal distribution of reading ability [see comments]. N Engl J Med 326:145–150, 1992

Sherman DK, Iacono WG, McGue MK: Attention-deficit hyperactivity disorder dimensions: a twin study of inattention and impulsivity-hyperactivity. J Am Acad Child Adolesc Psychiatry 36:745–753, 1997

Sherrington R, Rogaev EI, Liang Y, et al: Cloning of a gene bearing missense mutations in early onset familial Alzheimer's disease. Nature 375:754–760, 1995

Sherrington R, Froelich S, Sorbi S, et al: Alzheimer's disease associated with mutations in presenilin 2 is rare and variably penetrant. Hum Mol Genet 5:985–988, 1996

Shinnar S, Berg AT, Moshe SL, et al: Risk of seizure recurrence following a first unprovoked seizure in childhood: a prospective study. Pediatrics 85:1076–1085, 1990

Shoulson I: DATATOP: a decade of neuroprotective inquiry, Parkinson Study Group: deprenyl and tocopherol antioxidative therapy of parkinsonism. Ann Neurol 44:S160–S166, 1998

Siegel C, Waldo M, Mizner G, et al: Deficits in sensory gating in schizophrenic patients and their relatives: evidence obtained with auditory evoked responses. Arch Gen Psychiatry 41:607–612, 1984

Siever LJ, Kalus OF, Keefe RS: The boundaries of schizophrenia. Psychiatr Clin North Am 16:217–244, 1993

Simpson SG, Folstein SE, Meyers DA, et al: Bipolar II: the most common bipolar phenotype? Am J Psychiatry 150:901–903, 1993

Singha AA, Lopez MT, McDevitt HO: Autoimmune diseases: the failure of self tolerance. Science 248:1380–1388, 1990

Skomer C, Stears JU, Austin J: Metachromatic leucodystrophy (MLD); XV: adult MLD with focal lesions by computed tomography. Arch Neurol 40:354–355, 1983

Skre I, Onstad S, Torgersen S, et al: A twin study of DSM-III-R anxiety disorders. Acta Psychiatr Scand 88:85–92, 1993

Skuse DH: Imprinting, the X-chromosome, and the male brain: explaining sex differences in the liability to autism. Pediatr Res 47:9–16, 2000

Sladen B: Inheritance of dyslexia. Bulletin of the Orton Society 20:30–40, 1970

Slater E: The monogenic theory of schizophrenia. Acta Genetica et Statistica Medica 8:50–56, 1958

Slater E, Cowie V: The Genetics of Mental Disorders. London, England, Oxford University Press, 1971

Slater E, Shields J: Genetical aspects of anxiety, in Studies of Anxiety. Edited by Lader MH. London, Headly Brothers, 1969

Small GW, Leuchter AF, Mandelkern MA, et al: Clinical, neuroimaging, and environmental risk differences in monozygotic female twins appearing discordant for dementia of the Alzheimer type. Arch Neurol 50:209–219, 1993

Smalley SL, Tanguay PE, Smith M, et al: Autism and tuberous sclerosis. J Autism Dev Disord 22:339–355, 1992

Smalley SL, Bailey JN, Palmer CG, et al: Evidence that the dopamine D4 receptor is a susceptibility gene in attention deficit hyperactivity disorder [see comments] [published erratum appears in Mol Psychiatry 4:100, 1999]. Mol Psychiatry 3:427–430, 1998

Smith M, Wasmuth J, McPherson D, et al: Cosegregation of an 11q22.3–9p22 translocation with affective disorder: proximity of the dopamine D2 receptor gene relative to the translocation breakpoint. Am J Hum Genet 45:A220, 1989

Smith S, Kimberling W, Pennington B, et al: Specific reading disability: identification of an inherited form through linkage analysis. Science 219:1345–1347, 1983

Smyth C, Kalsi G, Curtis D, et al: Two-locus admixture linkage analysis of bipolar and unipolar affective disorder supports the presence of susceptibility loci on chromosomes 11p15 and 21q22. Genomics 39:271–278, 1997

Sobin C, Karayiorgou M: The genetic basis and neurobiological characteristics of obsessive-compulsive disorder, in Genetic Influences on Neural and Behavioral Functions. Edited by Pfaff DW, Berrettini WH, Joh TH, et al. Boca Raton, FL, CRC Press, 2000

Soininen H, Kosunen O, Helisalmi S, et al: A severe loss of choline acetyltransferase in the frontal cortex of Alzheimer patients carrying apolipoprotein e4 allele. Neurosci Lett 187:79–82, 1995

Speck CE, Kukull WA, Brenner DE, et al: History of depression as a risk factor for Alzheimer's disease. Epidemiology 6:366–369, 1995

Spence MA, Flodman PL, Sadovnick AD, et al: Bipolar disorder: evidence for a major locus [see comments]. Am J Med Genet 60:370–376, 1995

Spiker D, Lotspeich L, Kraemer HC, et al: Genetics of autism: characteristics of affected and unaffected children from 37 multiplex families. Am J Med Genet 54:27–35, 1994

St. Clair D, Blackwood D, Muir W, et al: Association within a family of a balanced autosomal translocation with major mental illness. Lancet 336:13–16, 1990

St. George-Hyslop PH: Molecular genetics of Alzheimer's disease. Biol Psychiatry 47:183–199, 2000

St. George-Hyslop PH, Myers R, Haines JL, et al: Familial Alzheimer's disease: progress and problems. Neurobiol Aging 10:417–425, 1989

St. George-Hyslop P, Haines J, Rogaev E, et al: Genetic evidence for a novel familial Alzheimer's disease locus on chromosome 14. Nat Genet 2:330–334, 1992

Steffenburg S, Gillberg C, Hellgren L, et al: A twin study of autism in Denmark, Finland, Iceland, Norway, and Sweden. J Child Psychol Psychiatry 30:405–416, 1989

Steffenburg S: Neuropsychiatric assessment of children with autism: a population-based study. Dev Med Child Neurol 33:495–511, 1991

Steffenburg S, Gillberg CL, Steffenburg U, Kyllerman M: Autism in Angelman syndrome: a population-based study. Pediatr Neurol 14:131–136, 1996

Stein C, Gieselman V, Kreysing J, et al: Cloning and expression of human arylsulfatase A. J Biol Chem 264:1252–1259, 1989

Steinlein OK: Neuronal nicotinic receptors in human epilepsy. Eur J Pharmacol 393:243–247, 2000

Steinlein OK, Deckert J, Nothen MM, et al: Neuronal nicotinic acetylcholine receptor alpha 4 subunit (CHRNA4) and panic disorder: an association study. Am J Med Genet 74:199–201, 1997

Stephenson J: Researchers find evidence of a new gene for late-onset Alzheimer disease (news). JAMA 277:775, 1997

Stephenson S: Six cases of congenital word blindness affecting three generations of one family. Ophthalmoscope 5:482–484, 1907

Stern Y, Alexander GE, Prohovnik I, et al: Inverse relationship between education and parietotemporal perfusion deficit in Alzheimer's disease. Ann Neurol 32:371–375, 1992

Stern Y, Gurland B, Tatemichi TK, et al: Influence of education and occupation on the incidence of Alzheimer's disease [see comments]. JAMA 271:1004–1010, 1994

Stevenson J, Graham P, Fredman G, et al: A twin study of genetic influences on reading and spelling ability and disability. J Child Psychol Psychiatry 28:229–247, 1987

Stewart J, Debray Q, Caillard V: Schizophrenia: the testing of genetic models. Am J Hum Genet 32:55–63, 1980

Steyaert J, Umans S, Willekens D, et al: A study of the cognitive and psychological profile in 16 children with congenital or juvenile myotonic dystrophy. Clin Genet 52:135–141, 1997

Stine OC, Xu J, Koskela R, et al: Evidence for linkage of bipolar disorder to chromosome 18 with a parent-of-origin effect. Am J Hum Genet 57:1384–1394, 1995

Stine OC, McMahon FJ, Chen L, et al: Initial genome screen for bipolar disorder in the NIMH genetics initiative pedigrees: chromosomes 2, 11, 13, 14, and X. Am J Med Genet 74:263–269, 1997

Straub RE, Lehner T, Luo Y, et al: A possible vulnerability locus for bipolar affective disorder on chromosome 21q22.3. Nat Genet 8:291–296, 1994

Straub RE, MacLean CJ, O'Neill FA, et al: A potential vulnerability locus for schizophrenia on chromosome 6p24–22: evidence for genetic heterogeneity. Nat Genet 11:287–293, 1995

Strauss ME, Brandt J: An attempt at preclinical identification of Huntington's disease using the WAIS. J Clin Exp Neuropsychol 8:210–218, 1986

Strittmatter WJ, Saunders AM, Schmechel DE, et al: Apolipoprotein E: high affinity binding to betaA amyloid and increased frequency of type 4 allele in familial Alzheimer's. Proc Natl Acad Sci U S A 90:1977–1981, 1993

Strittmatter WJ, Saunders AM, Goedert M, et al: Isoform-specific interactions of apolipoprotein E with microtubule-associated protein tau: implications for Alzheimer disease. Proc Natl Acad Sci U S A 91:11183–11186, 1994

Strober M, Morrell W, Burroughs J, et al: A family study of bipolar I disorder in adolescence: early onset of symptoms linked to increased family loading and lithium resistance. J Affect Disord 15:255–268, 1988

Suarez BK, Hampe CL, Van Eerdewegh P: Problems of replicating linkage claims in psychiatry, in Genetic Approaches to Mental Disorders. Edited by Gershon ES, Cloninger CR. Washington, DC, American Psychiatric Press, 1994, pp 23–46

Sugarman PA, Craufurd D: Schizophrenia in the Afro-Caribbean community. Br J Psychiatry 164:474–480, 1994

Sullivan PF, Fifield WJ, Kennedy MA, et al: No association between novelty seeking and the type 4 dopamine receptor gene (DRD4) in two New Zealand samples. Am J Psychiatry 155:98–101, 1998

Susser E, Neugebauer R, Hoek HW, et al: Schizophrenia after prenatal famine: further evidence [see comments]. Arch Gen Psychiatry 53:25–31, 1996

Swanson JM, Sunohara GA, Kennedy JL, et al: Association of the dopamine receptor D4 (DRD4) gene with a refined phenotype of attention deficit hyperactivity disorder (ADHD): a family based approach. Mol Psychiatry 3:38–41, 1998

Swedo SE, Rapoport JL, Cheslow DL, et al: High prevalence of obsessive-compulsive symptoms in patients with Sydenham's chorea. Am J Psychiatry 146:246–249, 1989a

Swedo SE, Rapoport JL, Leonard H, et al: Obsessive-compulsive disorder in children and adolescents: clinical phenomenology of 70 consecutive cases. Arch Gen Psychiatry 46:335–341, 1989b

Swedo SE, Leonard HL, Mittleman BB, et al: Identification of children with pediatric autoimmune neuropsychiatric disorders associated with streptococcal infections by a marker associated with rheumatic fever [see comments]. Am J Psychiatry 154:110–112, 1997

Swedo SE, Leonard HL, Garvey M, et al: Pediatric autoimmune neuropsychiatric disorders associated with streptococcal infections: clinical description of the first 50 cases [published erratum appears in Am J Psychiatry 155:578, 1998]. Am J Psychiatry 155:264–271, 1998

Swerdlow RH, Parks JK, Miller SW, et al: Origin and functional consequences of the complex I defect in Parkinson's disease. Ann Neurol 40:663–671, 1996

Szatmari P, Offord DR, Boyle MH: Ontario Child Health Study: prevalence of attention deficit disorder with hyperactivity. J Child Psychol Psychiatry 30:219–230, 1989

Szatmari P, Archer L, Fisman S, et al: Asperger's syndrome and autism: differences in behavior, cognition, and adaptive functioning. J Am Acad Child Adolesc Psychiatry 34:1662–1671, 1995

Szatmari P: Heterogeneity and the genetics of autism. J Psychiatry Neurosci 24:159–165, 1999

Takei N, Mortensen PB, Klaening U, et al: Relationship between in utero exposure to influenza epidemics and risk of schizophrenia in Denmark. Biol Psychiatry 40:817–824, 1996

Tang MX, Maestre G, Tsai WY, et al: Effect of age, ethnicity, and head injury on the association between APOE genotypes and Alzheimer's disease. Ann N Y Acad Sci 802:6–15, 1996

Tanner CM: The role of environmental toxins in the etiology of Parkinson's disease. Trends Neurosci 12:49–54, 1989

Tanner CM, Ottman R, Goldman SM, et al: Parkinson disease in twins: an etiologic study. JAMA 281:341–346, 1999

Tanzi RE: A promising animal model of Alzheimer's disease. N Engl J Med 332:1512–1513, 1995

Tanzi RE, St. George-Hyslop PH, Haines JL, et al: The genetic defect in familial Alzheimer's disease is not tightly linked to the amyloid b-protein gene. Nature 329:156–157, 1987

Tanzi RE, Petrukhin K, Chernov I, et al: The Wilson disease gene is a copper transporting ATPase with homology to the Menkes disease gene. Nat Genet 5:344–350, 1993

Tarrant CJ, Jones PB: Precursors to schizophrenia: do biological markers have specificity? [see comments]. Can J Psychiatry 44:335–349, 1999

Telenius H, Kremer HPH, Theilmann J, et al: Molecular analysis of juvenile Huntington's disease: the major influence on (CAG)n repeat length is the sex of the affected parent. Hum Mol Genet 2:1535–1540, 1993

Telling GC, Parchi P, DeArmond SJ, et al: Evidence for the conformation of the pathologic isoform of the prion protein enciphering and propagating prion diversity [see comments]. Science 274:2079–2082, 1996

Thadani V, Penar PL, Partington J, et al: Creutzfeldt-Jakob disease probably acquired from a cadaveric dura mater graft: case report [see comments]. J Neurosurg 69:766–769, 1988

Thapar A, Hervas A, McGuffin P: Childhood hyperactivity scores are highly heritable and show sibling competition effects: twin study evidence. Behav Genet 25:537–544, 1995

Thomas GR, Bull PC, Roberts EA, et al: Haplotype studies in Wilson disease. Am J Hum Genet 54:71–78, 1994

Tienari P: Interaction between genetic vulnerability and family environment: the Finnish adoptive family study of schizophrenia. Acta Psychiatr Scand 84:460–465, 1991

Tison F, Dartigues JF, Dubes L, et al: Prevalence of Parkinson's disease in the elderly: a population study in Gironde, France. Acta Neurol Scand 90:111–115, 1994

Todd RD, Reich W, Reich T: Prevalence of affective disorder in the child and adolescent offspring of a single kindred: a pilot study. J Am Acad Child Adolesc Psychiatry 33:198–207, 1994

Todd RD, Reich W, Petti TA, et al: Psychiatric diagnoses in the child and adolescent members of extended families identified through adult bipolar affective disorder probands. J Am Acad Child Adolesc Psychiatry 35:664–671, 1996

Tomac A, Lindqvist E, Lin LF, et al: Protection and repair of the nigrostriatal dopaminergic system by GDNF in vivo [see comments]. Nature 373:335–339, 1995

Torgersen S: Genetic factors in anxiety disorders. Arch Gen Psychiatry 40:1085–1089, 1983

Torrey EF, Torrey BB, Peterson MR: Seasonality of schizophrenic births in the United States. Arch Gen Psychiatry 34:1065–1070, 1977

Tsai L, Stewart MA, August G: Implication of sex differences in the familial transmission of infantile autism. J Autism Dev Disord 11:165–173, 1981

Tsilfidis C, MacKenzie AE, Mettler G, et al: Correlation between CTG repeat length and frequency of severe congenital myotonic dystrophy. Nat Genet 328:471–475, 1992

Tsuang MT: Morbidity risks of schizophrenia and affective disorders among first-degree relatives of patients with schizoaffective disorders. Br J Psychiatry 158:165–170, 1991

Tsuang MT, Faraone SV: The Genetics of Mood Disorders. Baltimore, MD, Johns Hopkins University Press, 1990

Tsuang MT, Stone WS, Faraone SV: The genetics of schizophrenia. Curr Psychiatry Rep 1:20–24, 1999

Tsuboi T: Genetic analysis of febrile convulsions: twin and family studies. Hum Genet 75:7–14, 1987

Tsuboi T, Endo S: Incidence of seizures and EEG abnormality among offspring of epileptic patients. Hum Genet 36:173–189, 1977

Tsuboi T, Endo S: Genetic studies of febrile convulsions: analysis of twin and family data. Epilepsy Res 4 (suppl):119–128, 1991

Turecki G, Alda M, Grof P, et al: No association between chromosome-18 markers and lithium-responsive affective disorders. Psychiatry Res 63:17–23, 1996

Turner WD: Genetic markers for schizotaxia. Biol Psychiatry 14:177–205, 1979

Uryu N, Maeda M, Nagata Y, et al: No difference in the nucleotide sequence of the DQB B1 domain between narcoleptic and healthy individuals with DR2, DW2. Hum Immunol 24:175–181, 1989

van Bogaert P, Ceballos I, Desguerre I, et al: Lesch-Nyhan in a girl. J Inherit Metab Dis 15:790–791, 1992

Van Broeckhoven C, Backhovens H, Cruts M, et al: Mapping of a gene predisposing to early onset Alzheimer's disease to chromosome 14q24.3. Nat Genet 2:335–339, 1992

Vandenberg SG, Singer SM, Pauls DL: The Heredity of Behavior Disorders in Adults and Children. New York, Plenum, 1986

Vandenbergh DJ, Zonderman AB, Wang J, et al: No association between novelty seeking and dopamine D4 receptor (D4DR) exon III seven repeat alleles in Baltimore Longitudinal Study of Aging participants. Mol Psychiatry 2:417–419, 1997

Van Duijn CM, de Knijff P, Cruts M, et al: Apolipoprotein E4 allele in a population-based study of early onset Alzheimer's disease [see comments]. Nat Genet 7:74–78, 1994

Van Duijn CM, de Knijff P, Wehnert A, et al: The apolipoprotein E epsilon 2 allele is associated with an increased risk of early onset Alzheimer's disease and a reduced survival. Ann Neurol 37:605–610, 1995

Van Os J, Selten JP: Prenatal exposure to maternal stress and subsequent schizophrenia: the May 1940 invasion of The

Netherlands [see comments]. Br J Psychiatry 172:324–326, 1998

van Slegtenhorst M, de Hoogt R, Hermans C, et al: Identification of the tuberous sclerosis gene TSC1 on chromosome 9q34. Science 277:805–808, 1997

Veenstra-VanderWeele J, Gonen D, Leventhal BL, et al: Mutation screening of the UBE3A/E6-AP gene in autistic disorder. Mol Psychiatry 4:64–67, 1999

Verity CM, Butler NR, Golding J: Febrile convulsions in a national cohort followed up from birth. I—prevalence and recurrence in the first five years of life. BMJ 290(6478): 1307–1310, 1985

Vieland VJ, Hodge SE, Lish JD, et al: Segregation analysis of panic disorder. Psychiatr Genet 3:63–71, 1993

Vieland VJ, Goodman DW, Chapman T, et al: New segregation analysis of panic disorder. Am J Med Genet 67:147–153, 1996

Vincent JB, Petronis A, Klempan T, et al: Repeat expansion detection in manic depression and schizophrenia. Am J Hum Genet 57:A335, 1995

Visser JE, Bar PR, Jinnah HA: Lesch-Nyhan disease and the basal ganglia. Brain Res Brain Res Rev 32(2–3):449–475, 2000

Volkmar FR, Szatmari P, Sparrow SS: Sex differences in pervasive developmental disorders. J Autism Dev Disord 23:579–591, 1993

Wadsworth SJ, DeFries JC, Stevenson J, et al: Gender ratios among reading-disabled children and their siblings as a function of parental impairment. J Child Psychol Psychiatry 33:1229–1239, 1992

Wahlberg KE, Wynne LC, Oja H, et al: Gene-environment interaction in vulnerability to schizophrenia: findings from the Finnish Adoptive Family Study of Schizophrenia. Am J Psychiatry 154:355–362, 1997

Waldman ID, Rowe DC, Abramowitz A, et al: Association and linkage of the dopamine transporter gene and attention-deficit hyperactivity disorder in children: heterogeneity owing to diagnostic subtype and severity. Am J Hum Genet 63:1767–1776, 1998

Waldo MC, Carey G, Myles-Worsley M, et al: Codistribution of a sensory gating deficit and schizophrenia in multi-affected families. Psychiatry Res 39:257–268, 1991

Walker EF, Savoie T, Davis D: Neuromotor precursors of schizophrenia. Schizophr Bull 20:441–451, 1994

Walshe JM: Penicillamine: a new oral therapy for Wilson's disease. Am J Med 21:487–495, 1956

Walshe JM: The physiology of copper in man and its relation to Wilson's disease. Brain 90:149–176, 1967

Wang DG, Fan JB, Siao CJ, et al: Large-scale identification, mapping, and genotyping of single-nucleotide polymorphisms in the human genome. Science 280(5366):1077–1082, 1998

Wang S, Sun CE, Walczak CA, et al: Evidence for a susceptibility locus for schizophrenia on chromosome 6pter-p22. Nat Genet 10:41–46, 1995

Wang ZW, Crowe RR, Noyes R Jr: Adrenergic receptor genes as candidate genes for panic disorder: a linkage study. Am J Psychiatry 149:470–474, 1992

Wang Z, Valdes J, Noyes R, et al: Possible association of a cholecystokinin promotor polymorphism (CCK-36CT) with panic disorder. Am J Med Genet 81:228–234, 1998

Warnke A: Reading and spelling disorders: clinical features and causes. Eur Child Adolesc Psychiatry 8 (suppl 3):2–12, 1999

Waters CH, Miller CA: Autosomal dominant Lewy body parkinsonism in a four-generation family. Ann Neurol 35:59–64, 1994

Weinberger DR: Implications of normal brain development for the pathogenesis of schizophrenia. Arch Gen Psychiatry 44:660–669, 1987

Weissman MM: Family genetic studies of panic disorder. J Psychiatr Res 27 (suppl 1):69–78, 1993

Weissman MM, Leckman JF, Merikangas KR, et al: Depression and anxiety disorders in parents and children: results from the Yale family study. Arch Gen Psychiatry 41:845–852, 1984

Weissman MM, Wickramaratne PJ, Adams PB, et al: The relationship between panic disorder and major depression. Arch Gen Psychiatry 50:767–780, 1993

Weissman MM, Bland RC, Canino GJ, et al: The cross national epidemiology of obsessive compulsive disorder: the Cross National Collaborative Group. J Clin Psychiatry 55 (suppl):5–10, 1994

Weissman MM, Bland RC, Canino GJ, et al: Cross-national epidemiology of major depression and bipolar disorder. JAMA 276:293–299, 1996

Weissman MM, Bland RC, Canino GJ, et al: The cross-national epidemiology of panic disorder. Arch Gen Psychiatry 54:305–309, 1997

Weissman MM, Fyer AJ, Haghighi F, et al: Potential panic disorder syndrome: clinical and genetic linkage evidence. Am J Med Genet 96:24–35, 2000

Wellington CL, Ellerby LM, Hackam AS, et al: Caspase cleavage of gene products associated with triplet expansion disorders generates truncated fragments containing the polyglutamine tract. J Biol Chem 273:9158–9167, 1998

Welner Z, Welner A, Stewart M, et al: A controlled study of siblings of hyperactive children. J Nerv Ment Dis 165:110–117, 1977

Wender PH, Kety SS, Rosenthal D, et al: Psychiatric disorders in the biological and adoptive families of adopted individuals with affective disorders. Arch Gen Psychiatry 43:923–929, 1986

Wexler NS, Young AB, Tanzi R, et al: Homosygotes for Huntington's disease. Nature 3326:194–197, 1987

Whalley LJ, Carothers AD, Collyer S, et al: A study of familial factors in Alzheimer's disease. Br J Psychiatry 140:249–256, 1982

White L, Petrovitch H, Ross GW, et al: Prevalence of dementia in older Japanese-American men in Hawaii: the Honolulu-Asia Aging Study [see comments]. JAMA 276:955–960, 1996

Whitehouse PJ, Price DL, Clark JT, et al: Alzheimer disease: evidence for selective loss of cholinergic neurons in the nucleus basalis. Ann Neurol 10:122–126, 1981

Wickramaratne PJ, Weissman MM, Horwath E, et al: The familial aggregation of panic disorder by source of proband ascertainment. Psychiatr Genet 4:125–133, 1994

Wiebe S, Bellhouse DR, Fallahay C, et al: Burden of epilepsy: the Ontario Health Survey. Can J Neurol Sci 26:263–270, 1999

Will RG, Matthews WB: Evidence for case-to-case transmission of Creutzfeldt-Jakob disease. J Neurol Neurosurg Psychiatry 45:235–238, 1982

Williams J, Spurlock G, McGuffin P, et al: Association between schizophrenia and T102C polymorphism of the 5-hydroxytryptamine type 2a-receptor gene. European Multicentre Association Study of Schizophrenia (EMASS) Group [see comments]. Lancet 347:1294–1296, 1996

Williams J, McGuffin P, Nothen M, et al: Meta-analysis of association between the 5-HT2a receptor T102C polymorphism and schizophrenia. EMASS Collaborative Group. European Multicentre Association Study of Schizophrenia (letter). Lancet 349:1221, 1997

Wilson JM, Stout JT, Palella TD, et al: A molecular survey of hypoxanthine-guanine phosphoribosyltransferase deficiency in man. J Clin Invest 77:188–195, 1986

Winokur G, Clayton PJ, Reich T: Manic Depressive Illness. St. Louis, MO, CV Mosby, 1969

Woerner MG, Pollack M, Klein DF: Birth weight and length in schizophrenics personality disorders and their siblings. Br J Psychiatry 118:461–464, 1971

Wolf C: An experimental investigation of specific language disability. Bulletin of the Orton Society 17:32–38, 1967

Wolff PH: A candidate phenotype for familial dyslexia. Eur Child Adolesc Psychiatry 8 (suppl 3):21–27, 1999

Wolff PH, Melngailis I: Family patterns of developmental dyslexia: clinical findings. Am J Med Genet 54:122–131, 1994

Wong DF, Harris JC, Naidu S, et al: Dopamine transporters are markedly reduced in Lesch-Nyhan disease in vivo. Proc Natl Acad Sci U S A 93:5539–5543, 1996

Wong GF, Gray CS, Hassanein RS, et al: Environmental risk factors in siblings with Parkinson's disease. Arch Neurol 48:287–289, 1991

Wood P: Etiology of Da Costa's syndrome. BMJ 1:845–851, 1941

World Health Organization: The ICD-10 Classification of Mental and Behavioural Disorders. Geneva, Switzerland, World Health Organization, 1992

Yamaguchi Y, Heiny ME, Gitlin JD: Isolation and characterization of a human liver cDNA as a candidate gene Wilson disease. Biochem Biophys Res Commun 197:271–277, 1993

Yamamura Y, Sobue I, Ando K, et al: Paralysis agitans of early onset with marked diurnal fluctuation of symptoms. Neurology 23:239–244, 1973

Yang TP, Patel PI, Stout JT, et al: Molecular evidence for new mutations in the HPRT locus in Lesch-Nyhan patients. Nature 310:412–414, 1984

Yang TP, Stout JT, Konecki DS, et al: Spontaneous reversion of novel Lesch-Nyhan mutations by HPRT gene rearrangement. Somat Cell Mol Genet 14:293–303, 1988

Yeh J, Zheng S, Howard BD: Impaired differentiation of HPRT-deficient dopaminergic neurons: a possible mechanism underlying neuronal dysfunction in Lesch-Nyhan syndrome. J Neurosci Res 53:78–85, 1998

Yokochi M, Narabayashi H, Iizuka R, et al: Juvenile parkinsonism—some clinical, pharmacological and neuropathological aspects. Adv Neurol 40:407–413, 1984

Yoshikawa T, Turner G, Esterling LE, et al: A novel human myo-inositol monophosphatase gene, IMP.18p, maps to a susceptibility region for bipolar disorder. Mol Psychiatry 2:393–397, 1997

Zahalkova M, Vrzal V, Kloboukova E: Genetical investigations in dyslexia. J Med Genet 9:48–52, 1972

Zara F, Labuda M, Garofalo PG, et al: Unusual EEG pattern linked to chromosome 3p in a family with idiopathic generalized epilepsy. Neurology 51:493–498, 1998

Zerbin-Rudin E: [What are the implications of the current findings in twins for schizophrenia research?]. Dtsch Med Wochenschr 92:2121–2122, 1967

Zhang Z, Miyoshi Y, Lapchak PA, et al: Dose response to intraventricular glial cell line-derived neurotrophic factor administration in parkinsonian monkeys. J Pharmacol Exp Ther 282:1396–1401, 1997

Zhong N, Ye L, Ju W, et al: 5-HTTLPR variants not associated with autistic spectrum disorders. Neurogenetics 2:129–131, 1999

Zlotogora J: Intrafamilial variability in lysosomal storage diseases. Am J Med Genet 27:633–638, 1987

Zlotogora J, Bach G, Bosenberg C, et al: Molecular basis of late infantile metachromatic leukodystrophy in the Habbanite Jews. Hum Mutat 5:137–143, 1995

PART

III

# Neuropsychiatric Symptomatologies

# CHAPTER 11

# Neuropsychiatric Aspects of Pain Management

William G. Brose, M.D.

Raymond Gaeta, M.D.

David Spiegel, M.D.

Pain is a common, frustrating, and—though often undertreated—treatable problem. Because pain is affected by all the neural processes that modulate perception, it is a fascinating neuropsychiatric phenomenon.

## Prevalence

Approximately one-third of all Americans, it is estimated, have some form of chronic pain. Back pain, arthritis, headaches, and musculoskeletal disorders, as well as pain due to neurological, cardiac, or oncological disease combined affect an estimated 97 million people (Bonica 1990). Cancer pain affects approximately one-third of cancer patients with primary disease and two-thirds of those with metastatic disease. Chronic pain is a common symptom among patients seeking medical care and is often associated with frequent and costly treatments. During 1992, the chronic pain patients of the Group Health Cooperative of Puget Sound accounted for more annual costs than patients with other chronic conditions, including heart disease, hypertension, and diabetes. The costs of chronic pain are not limited to medical care, however. Disability payments and lost productivity associated with chronic pain create even more of a financial impact. A 1996 Louis Harris poll indicated that pain was the third leading cause of workplace absenteeism in the United States in the previous year. The same poll showed that 75% of the population use over-the-counter medications for pain and 35% of the population use prescribed

medications for pain. A chronic pain study performed in Michigan in 1997 concluded that 20% of all adults have chronic pain. In addition, 70% of these Michigan pain patients reported that they continued to have pain despite treatment. When we attempt to include the cost of lost productivity, the additive economic impact of pain is absolutely staggering. The monetary cost of pain is not the only issue. From a social perspective, pain is a tremendous burden. The level of continued human suffering is unacceptable to all of us. The opportunities and dreams that every pain sufferer loses have a tremendous impact on each and every one of us. Pain is a leading reason patients seek alternative and complementary treatments (Astin 1998; D. Spiegel et al. 1998), a practice now engaged in by some 40% of Americans (Eisenberg et al. 1998).

## Cortical Modulation of Pain

Pain is the ultimate psychosomatic phenomenon. It is composed of both a somatic signal that something is wrong with the body and a message or interpretation of that signal involving attentional, cognitive, affective, and social factors. The limbic system and the cortex provide means of modulating pain signals (Melzack 1982)—either amplifying them through excessive attention or affective dysregulation or minimizing them through denial, inattention, relaxation, or attention-control techniques. Like any other perceptual phenomenon, pain is modulated by attentional processes. Novelty tends to enhance pain perception (as with an acute injury, chronic pain is often reported to be greater during evenings and weekends, when people are not distracted by routine activities). Although pain during sleep is reported less frequently than pain while awake, pain often interferes with sleep; severe pain can substantially reduce sleep efficiency. In addition, the medications that are employed to treat pain often reduce alertness and arousal, compounding the effects of sleep interference. This and other undesired effects of analgesic medications—including the potential for abuse of opioid analgesics—further increase the suffering of those experiencing chronic pain.

In 1979, after much consideration, the International Association for the Study of Pain (IASP) defined pain as "an unpleasant sensory and emotional experience associated with actual or potential tissue damage or described in terms of such damage." The operational word *experience* in this definition places pain outside the realm of simple sensation. Unlike sight, smell, taste, hearing, and touch, pain has a more complicated perceptual foundation. The capacity for any of the five senses to provide the sensory component to pain further differentiates pain from a simple sensation. Functional brain imaging research has confirmed the in vivo presence of neurochemical changes of chronic pain states (Craig et al. 1996; Kwan et al. 2000; Tolle et al. 1999). Whether these changes are uniquely associated with affective, sensory, cognitive, motor, inhibitory, learned, or autonomic responses to a painful stimulus is unclear. New and exciting research holds the promise of elucidating the specific connections between the sensory and experiential components of pain. It is well known that many athletes and soldiers incur serious injuries in the height of sport or combat and are unaware of the injury until someone points out bleeding or swelling. Even overwhelming and serious injury may sometimes be accompanied by a surprising absence of pain perception until hours after the injury. This traumatic dissociation has been observed in victims of natural disaster, combat, and motor vehicle accidents (D. Spiegel et al. 1988). On the other hand, some individuals with comparatively minor physical disturbance report being totally immobilized and demoralized by pain. Certain genetic phenotypes have been found recurrently in patients with certain chronic pain conditions (A. Mailis, personal communication, October 2000). Even with promising new research tools, the mysteries of the perception of pain are likely to remain for many years to come. Fortunately, our understanding of these interconnections is not required to observe the wonders of the integrated neurochemistry. A single parent with a sarcoma complained of severe, unremitting pain that was interlaced with tearful concern about her failure to discuss her terminal prognosis with her adolescent son. When an appropriate meeting was arranged in which she could discuss her prognosis with him and plan for his future, the pain resolved (Kuhn and Bradnan 1979).

## Cognitive Factors Influencing Pain

### Attention to Pain

Health perception is modulated by the cortex, which enhances or diminishes awareness of incoming signals. Neuropsychological and brain imaging research have demonstrated at least three attentional centers that modulate perception: a posterior parieto-occipital orienting system, a focusing system localized to the anterior cingulate gyrus, and an arousal-vigilance system in the right frontal lobe (Posner and Petersen 1990). These systems provide, among other things, for selective attention to incoming stimuli, allowing competing stimuli to be relegated to the periphery of awareness (Price 2000). Recent brain imaging research indicates that reduced pain perception produced through hypnotic analgesia is associated with activation of the anterior cingulate gyrus (Crawford et al. 1993; Rainville et al. 1997). Other studies indicate that alteration of perception with hypnosis also produces consonant changes in the primary association cortex (D. Spiegel et al. 1989).

Thus, both naturally occurring and therapeutic factors that modulate attention may modulate pain perception via activation of brain centers of selective attention and modulating activity of the sensory cortex.

When Melzack and Wall (1965) postulated the gate control theory of pain, they observed that higher cortical input could inhibit pain signals as well. They cited Pavlov's observation that repeated shocks to dogs eventually failed to elicit pain behavior; that is, the dogs habituated to the painful signals, and this response could be explained only as cortical inhibition of pain response. Thus, in Melzack and Wall's model, there is room for descending inhibition of pain via the substantia gelatinosa as well as competitive inhibition at the gate (Melzack 1982; Wall 1972). The original formulation of the gate control theory has been substantially modified, and extensive revisions of the hypothesis have been provided involving endogenous opiates and other mechanisms of pain modulation (Melzack 1982, 1999; Wall 1972). The important concept we gain from this theory is the interaction between central processing and the perception of noxious stimuli at the periphery.

## Meaning of Pain

It has been known for half a century that the meaning structure in which pain is embedded influences the intensity of pain experienced. Beecher (1956) had noted with initial surprise that soldiers on the Anzio beachhead in World War II who had been quite badly wounded seemed to require very little in the way of analgesic medication. In a classic study, he examined a matched set of surgical patients at Massachusetts General Hospital with equal or less serious surgically induced wounds. These patients demanded far higher levels of analgesic medication than did the combat soldiers, despite less serious injury. Beecher concluded that this difference was based on a difference in the meaning of the pain. To combat soldiers, the pain was almost welcome as an indication that they were likely to get out of combat alive, whereas to the surgical patients, pain represented an interference with life and a threat to survival. This means that patients who interpret pain signals as an ominous sign of the worsening of their disease are likely to experience a greater intensity of pain. This hypothesis has been confirmed, for example, among cancer patients. Those who believe that the pain represents a worsening of their disease report more pain (D. Spiegel and Bloom 1983b).

## Mood Disorders

Descending influence of cortical function on pain is related to mood and anxiety disorders as well. As described below, serotoninergic and noradrenergic function influences pain processing (Yaksh 1988), and these neurotransmitter systems are involved in depression and anxiety disorders and are modulated by antidepressants. Bond and Pearson (1969) reported a correlation between neuroticism on the Maudsley Personality Inventory (Eysenck and Eysenck 1964) and pain among patients who had cervical carcinoma. This result was confirmed by Woodforde and Fielding (1970), who reported that cancer patients who sought treatment in a pain clinic were rated as more depressed and having more psychosomatic, gastrointestinal, and hypochondriacal symptoms than cancer patients who did not seek pain treatment. Several other studies (Ahles et al. 1983; Derogatis et al. 1983; Lansky et al. 1985; Massie and Holland 1987; D. Spiegel and Bloom 1983b) have reported that patients with pain score higher on measures of depression, anxiety, and other signs of mood disturbance than do those with little or no pain. In particular, depression and anxiety are frequent concomitants of pain (Blumer and Heilbronn 1982; Bond 1973; Bond and Pearson 1969; Wood-

forde and Fielding 1970). This earlier work implied that patients with psychopathology complained more about pain than did psychiatrically healthy patients. Later work suggested that there is an interaction and that perhaps chronic pain amplifies or even produces depression (Peteet et al. 1986; D. Spiegel and Sands 1988). Indeed, the presence of significant pain among cancer patients is more strongly associated with major depressive symptoms than is a prior life history of depression (D. Spiegel et al. 1994).

Depression is the most frequently reported psychiatric diagnosis among chronic pain patients. Reports of depression among chronic pain populations range from 10% to 87% (Dworkin et al. 1990; Pilowski et al. 1977; Reich et al. 1983). The relative severity of the depression observed in chronic pain patients is illustrated by the finding by Katon et al. (1985) that 32% of a sample of 37 pain patients met criteria for major depression and 43% had a past episode of major depression.

In a large sample of health maintenance organization (HMO) patients (Dworkin et al. 1990), patients with two or more pain conditions were found to be at elevated risk for major depression, whereas patients with only one pain condition did not show such an elevated rate of mood disorder. Although pain patients referred for psychiatric treatment are clearly selected for a higher prevalence of depression and anxiety (Lansky et al. 1985), there is general agreement in the literature that pain and mood disorder co-occur and that therefore the treatment of pain from a neuropsychiatric point of view must include appropriate treatment of depression and anxiety.

Anxiety is a frequent concomitant of acute pain. It may be an appropriate response to serious trauma, injury, or illness. Pain may serve a signal function or may be part of an anxious preoccupation, as in the case of the woman with the sarcoma cited earlier. Similarly, anxiety and pain may reinforce each other, producing a snowball effect of escalating and mutually reinforcing central and peripheral symptoms.

## Neurological Mechanisms of Pain

The classic teaching of a simple pathway for pain transmission still exists in the minds of many practicing medical professionals. The understated sophistication of a dedicated spinothalamic tract that relays all pain messages received from peripheral nerves arising on the contralateral side of the body supported the concepts of pain and analgesia prevalent even in the mid- to later 1900s. An ever-increasing body of knowledge has now displaced this simple explanation of pain transmission. Highly complex interactions of many different peripheral and central nervous system (CNS) structures, from the skin surface to the cerebral cortex, are now known to be involved in the processing of pain. Blockade of any of these pathways and/or antagonism of involved neurotransmitters may now be rationally considered in the treatment of specific pain problems. Presentation of these various treatment options is best preceded by a brief discussion of certain established parts of this complex pathway for pain transmission. Yaksh (1988), in a review that referenced more than 700 reports, summarized detailed neurophysiological and neuropharmacological findings from 1913 until 1986. Even more intriguing than exploration of the afferent nociceptive sensory pathways is the recognition of descending controls from the cortex. In 1986, Wall and Mac Mahon wrote, "The discovery that descending controls from the highest reaches of the brain affect the messages transmitted to the brain had a revolutionary impact. It is no longer possible to propose a separate system continuously delivering an accurate account of events in the periphery and generating innocent sensation without value judgement." Although many of the specifics of this descending control remain elusive, the clinical experience of pain modification has integrated these concepts in rationalizing therapies.

## Peripheral Sensory Receptors

Each individual can appreciate that when a potentially damaging stimulus is applied to a sensitive area of the body such as the skin, a chain of signals is initiated that results in identifying the stimulus as painful. Early descriptions of peripheral nerves indicated that they were modality specific and that each class of nerve fiber was responsible for only one sensory modality (Müller 1844). This concept was not supported by anatomical studies of skin surface, which demonstrated that not every class of nerve ending is present in all skin areas. More recent neurophysiological work has established the existence of specific primary afferent nerves for signaling noxious stimulation. These nerves are termed nociceptors.

Nociceptors are activated by some form of energy (mechanical, thermal, or chemical) (Figure 11–1). They transduce that energy into an electrical impulse, which is conducted through the nerve axon toward the brain. The reflex response and the subjective reporting of pain associated with a noxious stimulus are the results of processing by the spinal cord, brain stem, midbrain, and higher cortex of signals from the numerous primary afferent nociceptors that were activated by the stimulus. Nociceptors are characterized by 1) having a high threshold for all naturally occurring stimuli compared with other

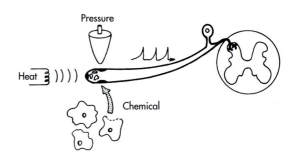

**FIGURE 11–1.** Sensitivity range of the polymodal C fiber nociceptor. Available evidence suggests that the terminals are sensitive to direct heat or mechanical distortion; thus, transduction can occur at the terminal. The terminals are also sensitive to chemicals released from damaged cells. In this manner, any tissue cell can serve as an intermediate in the transduction process. In a sense, all tissue cells are "receptors" for injury.

*Source.* Reprinted from Fields HL: *Pain.* New York, McGraw-Hill, 1987, p. 27. Used with permission.

receptors in the same tissue and 2) progressively augmenting response to repeated or increasingly noxious stimuli (sensitization).

## Cutaneous Pain Sensation

Mechanosensory nociceptors respond when the pressure necessary for producing tissue damage has been achieved. Most of these receptors initiate impulses carried by thinly myelinated fibers (Aδ fibers). The responses increase in proportion to the magnitude of the pressure applied. These receptors in the trunk have fairly large receptive fields, whereas those in the face have smaller fields.

*Thermoreceptive* nociceptors respond to normal heating or cooling with sensitivity near 1°C when the temperature is 30°–40°C; they also respond to noxious thermal stimuli with an increasing frequency of discharge. High-frequency discharge can be seen in C fiber afferents after the application of intense heat (47°–51°C) to the small receptive fields near these receptors.

*Mechanothermal* nociceptors are activated by high-intensity heat or pressure sensation. They have small receptive fields and are probably responsible for the "first pain" transmitted by small myelinated Aδ fibers.

Polymodal C fiber nociceptors respond to many different noxious stimuli. These are the most common of all nociceptors. They are activated by pressure, temperature, and chemical stimuli supplied to their small receptive fields. These small unmyelinated fibers transmit at slower conduction velocities and are probably responsible for the phenomenon of "second pain."

## Skeletal Muscle Pain

Nociceptors found in skeletal muscle respond to chemical agents that are released locally during muscle contraction. Metabolic by-products alone do not trigger these receptors. There appears to be a need for other algogenic agents, perhaps prostaglandins released during intense muscle contraction, to be present as well.

## Cardiac Muscle Pain

Cardiac muscle afferents are activated by high-intensity mechanical stimulation, heat, and chemical agents. Humoral agents released locally may be responsible for the pain experienced in angina. Prostaglandins are released after myocardial hypoxia. Prostaglandins, histamine, bradykinin, and serotonin have each been shown to stimulate these receptors.

## Joint Pain

Joint nociceptors activated by deformation or expansion within the joint relay pain messages via Aδ fiber afferents. These receptors also appear to be sensitized by certain chemical substances injected into the joint (e.g., urate crystals, endotoxin, and prostaglandins).

## Visceral Pain

These nociceptors have not been well identified. Pain is seen in response to mechanical (distention) as well as thermal and chemical stimuli. These receptors also appear to be sensitized by the presence of certain chemicals (e.g., prostaglandins).

As stated previously, particular nociceptors respond only to particular types of stimuli. Although the exact pathways involved in the transduction of noxious-information nociceptors have not yet been elucidated, it appears that the peripheral terminal of the Aδ mechanical nociceptor is likely to function as a receptor (Fields 1987). Whether this is true for other nociceptors remains the subject of speculation. The presence of vesicles in primary nociceptive afferent terminals has been determined by electron microscopy. These vesicles probably provide the substrate for various peripherally active agents.

Substance P is an undecapeptide found in small-diameter primary afferent neurons. This peptide has been shown to be transmitted to the periphery by these nerves, and stimulation of these primary afferents leads to the release of substance P from the distal terminus of the nerve. However, local application of exogenous substance P to these nerve terminals does not induce a painful response. It does appear to activate local vasculature

to cause extravasation of fluid into the tissues. Other chemicals present in the blood and tissues have been demonstrated to be algesic. Serotonin, histamine, acetylcholine, bradykinin, slow-reacting substance of anaphylaxis (SRS-A), calcitonin gene-related peptide (CGRP), and potassium all excite primary noxious afferents. At this time the definition of pain neuropeptide has not been specified. Prostaglandins alone do not excite pain fibers; however, they do appear to sensitize primary afferents to painful substances.

Direct tissue trauma results in potassium release, synthesis of bradykinin in plasma, and synthesis of prostaglandins in the region of damaged tissue (Figure 11–2A). Antidromic impulses in primary nociceptor afferents result in an increase in production of substance P from nerve endings. This increase is associated with an increase in vascular permeability and, in turn, results in the marked release of bradykinin. There is also an increase in histamine production from mast cells and an increase in serotonin production from platelets; both of these substances are capable of powerful activation of nociceptors (Figure 11–2B). Histamine release combines with substance P release to increase vascular permeability. Local increases in histamine and serotonin, via activation of nociceptors, result in a further increase in substance P; thus, a self-perpetuating cycle can be seen to develop at each region of the nociceptive afferent nerve fiber in the damaged tissue. In surrounding extracellular fluid, increases in histamine and serotonin result in activation of nearby nociceptors, which is one reason for secondary hyperalgesia (Figure 11–2C). Superimposed on all these events are the effects of the increased release of catecholamines from sympathetic nerve endings, which results in sensitization of nociceptors. Evidence from animal models of arthritis and various human data point to the sympathetic postganglionic neuron as being integral in the changes seen in vascular permeability in response to the activation of primary afferent nociceptors (Levine et al. 1985).

# Primary Afferent Transmission

After a noxious stimulus has been detected by a nociceptor, the resultant impulse travels away from the point of origin via the primary afferent nerve. The primary afferent nerves that carry pain impulses are almost exclusively unmyelinated C fibers and finely myelinated Aδ fibers. Most C fiber afferents originate from polymodal nociceptors, which are activated by mechanical, chemical, and thermal noxious stimuli. The conduction velocity of these C fibers is approximately 1 m/s, which probably explains the "slow pain" felt 1–2 seconds after the application of a

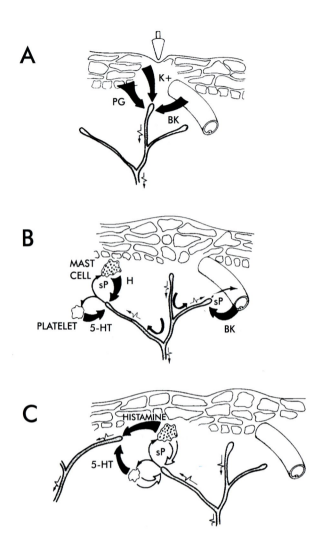

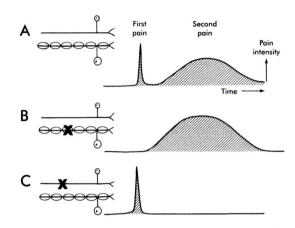

**FIGURE 11–3.** First and second pain fibers. *Panel A.* First pain and second pain are carried by two different primary afferent axons. *Panel B.* First pain is abolished by selective blockade of myelinated axons. *Panel C.* Second pain is abolished by blocking C fibers.
*Source.* Reprinted from Fields HL: *Pain.* New York, McGraw-Hill, 1987, p. 26. Used with permission.

noxious stimulus (Figure 11–3). The finely myelinated Aδ fibers also transmit pain impulses, but the conduction velocity of these neurons is much faster (12–30 m/s). Aδ fibers are particularly sensitive to stimulation with sharp instruments. In addition, 20%–50% of Aδ fibers respond to heat as well as to mechanical stimulation. These fiber types carry the impulses that initially report a noxious stimulus. These primary afferent nociceptors make up the majority of fibers in any peripheral nerve.

Lesion of these peripheral nerves does not necessarily correlate with the presence or absence of pain. The loss of large-fiber input in these cases still creates activation of cortical neurons, allowing transmission of noxious stimuli that might otherwise be blocked by large-fiber afferent transmission when it remains intact. Pain that occurs in Fabry's disease—in which congenital absence of small-fiber afferents would predict abolition of painful sensation—also requires a more expansive definition of pain than a simple primary pain pathway. This is probably explained by altered modulation at high-processing centers. Thus it appears that single balance of large-fiber and small-fiber activity is far too simplistic a view of pain modulation.

Peripheral nerve injuries can also lead to pain. The proposed pathways by which such an injury could evoke a pain response include

- Increased activity in sympathetic fibers near the damaged area

**FIGURE 11–2.** Events leading to activation, sensitization, and spread of sensitization of primary afferent nociceptor terminals. *Panel A.* Direct activation by intense pressure and consequent cell damage. Cell damage leads to release of potassium (K⁺) and to synthesis of prostaglandins (PG) and bradykinin (BK). Prostaglandins increase the sensitivity of the terminal to bradykinin and other pain-producing substances. *Panel B.* Secondary activation. Impulses generated in the stimulated terminal propagate not only to the spinal cord, but into other terminal branches, where they induce the release of peptides, including substance P (sP), which causes vasodilation and neurogenic edema with further accumulation of bradykinin. In addition, substance P causes the release of histamine (H) from mast cells and serotonin (5-HT) from platelets. *Panel C.* Histamine and serotonin levels rise in the extracellular space, secondarily sensitizing nearby nociceptors. This leads to a gradual spread of hyperalgesia and/or tenderness.
*Source.* Reprinted from Fields HL: *Pain.* New York, McGraw-Hill, 1987, p. 36. Used with permission.

- Neuroma formation due to sprouting from damaged axons
- Collaterals sprouting from intact neighboring fibers
- Changes in dorsal root ganglion cells or in central terminals of damaged axons that have lost part of their dorsal input
- Stimulation of nociceptive nervi nervorum of peripheral nerves

Molecular genetics and cellular physiology research have led to a tremendous growth in knowledge about the structure and function of primary nociceptors (Wood et al. 2000). The presence of multiple receptors and various ion channels has suggested that a therapeutic target for analgesics could be elucidated within the primary afferent. Adenosine triphosphate–gated channels, proton-gated channels, heat-operated capsaicin-gated channels, and sensory-specific sodium channels join a plethora of receptors—including serotonins 5-$HT_{1A}$, 5-$HT_{1D}$, 5-$HT_2$, and 5-$HT_3$—that influence primary neuron activity.

## Spinal Cord Terminals of Primary Afferents

### Dorsal and Ventral Roots

The cell bodies of all somatic primary afferent fibers are in the dorsal root ganglia adjacent to the spinal cord. The only primary afferent cell body outside this position is the trigeminal ganglia, which is the rostral continuation of the dorsal root ganglia. Fibers from the dorsal root are organized within the root according to diameter. The large-diameter afferents enter the spinal cord in the dorsal region of the entry zone, whereas the small-diameter afferents enter in the lateral region of the cord. Having entered the spinal cord, the nociceptive primary afferent fibers (Aδ and C fibers) bifurcate into both cephalad- and caudad-projecting branches traveling in Lissauer's tract (the dorsolateral tract). These fibers terminate primarily in the ipsilateral dorsal gray matter, but a small number of the fibers cross dorsal to the central canal to terminate in the dorsal gray matter of the contralateral side. The majority of sensory afferents enter the spinal cord through the dorsal root entry zone. However, nonmyelinated C fiber afferents have also been discovered in the ventral root. The clinical relevance of the fibers that cross or those that enter the ventral root is not known. This heterogeneity in the pathway of the primary afferents associated with pain transmission helps explain the incomplete pain relief that is seen after ablation of a unilateral dorsal root entry zone.

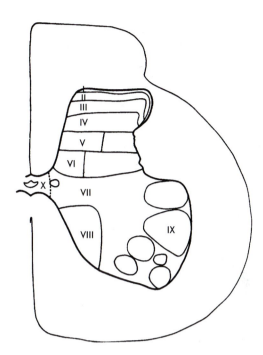

**FIGURE 11–4.**  Schematic drawing of the lamination of the ventral cell column of the seventh lumbar spinal cord segment in the full-grown cat.
*Source.*  Reprinted from Rexed B: "Cytoarchitectonic Organization of the Spinal Cord in the Cat." *Journal of Comparative Neurology* 96:415–495, 1952. Used with permission.

### Dorsal Horn

Once the impulses have entered the spinal cord via the dorsal or ventral roots, they terminate in the ipsilateral dorsal horn of the spinal cord. The dorsal horn is organized into distinct laminae, with specific primary afferent terminals found in individual laminae (Figure 11–4). Aδ fibers terminate primarily in lamina I, in ventral portions in lamina II, and through most of lamina III. Unmyelinated C fibers terminate in lamina II.

### Lamina I

Lamina I is a thin, superficial layer of neurons that make up the marginal zone. The neurons with cell bodies in lamina I are termed *marginal cells*. These marginal cells receive projections from Aδ and C fiber afferents responsive to noxious mechanical stimuli. In addition, they respond to some polymodal C fiber afferents as well as Aδ temperature impulses. The neurons that respond to Aδ and C fiber noxious stimuli also show response to group III and group IV muscle afferents. This dual response accounts for a convergence of pain impulses from both skin and muscle. These neurons then project to one of several areas: to the thalamus by way of the contralateral spinothalamic tracts, to the ipsilateral dorsal white matter, or to the ipsilateral dorsal gray matter for an area of several segments.

## Lamina II

Lamina II is also known as the substantia gelatinosa, owing to the clear appearance of this section of spinal matter in comparison with the surrounding marginal layer and nucleus proprius. This region has undergone extensive evaluation. The neurons of lamina II act as a modulating center for afferent impulses of small and large fibers that terminate in this region. Afferent input is from noxious stimulation, as well as from light touch and pressure sensations. The area is densely packed with cells that make extensive synaptic connections with other cells in the area. The axons of most of these cells are short, and only a few of them project to the thalamus through the contralateral-anterolateral columns. The clinical phenomenon of selective spinal cord opiate analgesia is mediated through opioid receptors found in lamina II (Yaksh 1988). Stimulation of these receptors leads to inhibition of marginal cell firing in response to primary afferent signals. Similar inhibition has been postulated with other neurochemicals acting on this lamina, but much more work needs to be done to delineate the complex interactions involved in processing noxious stimuli here.

## Laminae III and IV

The nucleus proprius is made up of the neurons located in laminae III and IV. One of the predominant populations of cells in the nucleus proprius responds to Aβ, Aδ, and C fiber input; these are termed *wide dynamic range neurons* (WDRs). Although the receptive fields of the individual afferents may be quite small, the corresponding WDR has a larger receptive field. Afferent input from closely related somatotopic fields is typically seen on a single WDR, accounting for the somatotopic convergence seen in stimulation of different areas. In addition to somatotopic convergence, there is also evidence that visceral afferents traveling with sympathetic neurons also converge on WDRs. WDRs project throughout the anterolateral funiculus to the thalamus.

The convergence of somatic nociceptive afferents and visceral nociceptive afferents on the same neuron in the dorsal horn probably explains the phenomenon of referred pain. The presence of viscero-somatic, muscle-somatic, and viscero-viscero convergence seen in the various laminae of the dorsal horn and the development of fairly large receptive fields in some of these second-order neurons also helps to explain some of the peculiar characteristics of

nonsomatic pain. Hyperexcitability in these dorsal horn neurons is proposed as one potential mechanism to account for central sensitivity seen in chronic pain states. The presence of N-methyl-D-aspartate (NMDA) receptor activity on these cell bodies shows increased participation in experimental models of nerve injury pain. These are shown schematically in Figure 11–5.

## Lamina X (Central Canal)

The central canal has also been identified as receiving input from the Aδ fibers associated with noxious stimulation. These fibers terminate on cells with small receptive fields, like those seen in the marginal zone. The afferents are sensitive to temperature and pinch stimuli. The cells of the central canal are subsequently known to ascend ipsilaterally and contralaterally in the ventrolateral tract to the reticular formation.

## Ascending Sensory Pathways

The second-order neurons that arise in the respective laminae of the dorsal horn of the spinal cord subsequently use several specific routes to carry their messages to higher brain centers (Figure 11–6). The specific routes are characterized as tracts and systems that include the neospinothalamic, paleospinothalamic, and spinoreticular systems and dorsal columns. The names given to these nociceptive pathways are derived from the point of origin and termination of their respective fibers. The spinothalamic and spinoreticular systems represent the most important tracts associated with pain transmission in humans. The fibers from these tracts make up the anterolateral funiculus.

Axons from laminae I, IV, V, VII, and VIII make up the spinothalamic tract. These axons ascend predominantly in the contralateral ventral quadrant of the spinal cord. Crossed fibers predominate, but neuroanatomic studies have indicated that perhaps 25% of all fibers ascend in the ipsilateral ventral quadrant (Yaksh 1988). These spinothalamic fibers subsequently ascend to the thalamus.

Numerous other systems are also involved in the rostral projection of nociceptive information. Important among these other systems would be the dorsal funicular systems and intersegmental systems, which are probably involved in descending inhibitory transmission as well.

## Brainstem Processing

The brain stem is involved in transmission of all ascending and descending information. Nociceptive afferent fibers relay to projection neurons in the dorsal horn, which ascend in the anterolateral funiculus to end in the thala-

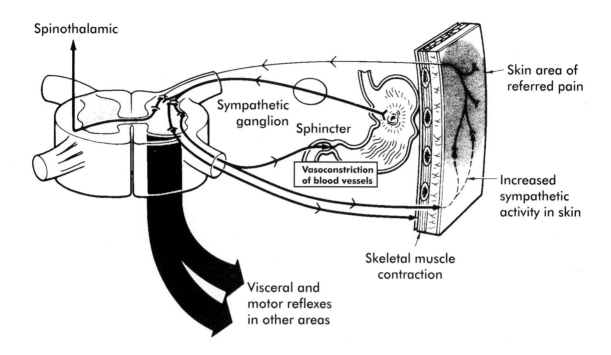

**FIGURE 11–5.** Visceral pain: convergence of visceral and somatic nociceptive afferents. Visceral sympathetic afferents converge on the same dorsal horn neuron as do somatic nociceptive afferents. Visceral noxious stimuli are then conveyed, together with somatic noxious stimuli, via the spinothalamic pathways to the brain.

*Note.* 1) Referred pain is felt in the cutaneous area corresponding to the dorsal horn neurons on which visceral afferents converge; this is accompanied by allodynia and hyperalgesia in this skin area. 2) Reflex somatic motor activity results in muscle spasm, which may stimulate parietal peritoneum and initiate somatic noxious input to the dorsal horn. 3) Reflex sympathetic efferent activity may result in spasm of sphincters of viscera over a wide area, causing pain remote from the original stimulus. 4) Reflex sympathetic efferent activity may result in visceral ischemia and further noxious stimulation; also, visceral nociceptors may be sensitized by norepinephrine release and microcirculatory changes. 5) Increased sympathetic activity may influence cutaneous nociceptors, which may be at least partly responsible for referred pain. 6) Peripheral visceral afferents branch considerably, causing much overlap in the territory of individual dorsal roots; only a small number of visceral afferent fibers converge on dorsal horn neurons compared with somatic nociceptive fibers. Also, visceral afferents converge on the dorsal horn over a large number of segments. This dull, vague visceral pain is very poorly localized and is often called *deep visceral pain.*

*Source.* Reprinted from Cousins MJ, Bridenbaugh PO (eds.): *Neural Blockade in Clinical Anesthesia and Management of Pain,* 2nd Edition. Philadelphia, PA, JB Lippincott, 1988, p. 743. Used with permission.

mus. During the rostral conduction of these impulses, collaterals activate the nucleus reticularis gigantocellularis, which in turn sends projections to the thalamus, as well as to the periaqueductal gray matter (Figure 11–6).

## Thalamic Relays

Several nuclear groups of the thalamus are associated with the relay of nociceptive afferent impulses (Figure 11–7). Included among these are the posterior nuclear complex, the ventrobasilar complex, and the medial intralaminar nuclear complex. In the thalamus, spinothalamic neurons terminate largely on the ventroposterolateral and centromedian nuclei. The ventrobasilar complex also receives input from the dorsal columns. The ventroposterolateral nucleus projects to areas 1, 2, and 3 of the parietal lobe, but these areas have not been found to be involved with aversive or emotional aspects of nociception. Consequently, it is currently believed that the ventroposterolateral nucleus is involved with localization of the impulse rather than with its qualitative aspects (Besson and Chaouch 1987; Willis 1985). The centromedian nucleus is believed to be involved in the qualitative aspects of nociception in that stimulation of this region triggers the unpleasantness associated with tissue damage (Besson and Chaouch 1987). The projections of the centromedian nucleus are poorly understood, but presumably they activate the aversive centers in the limbic system. The nucleus submedius has also been implicated in nociceptive processing, because it receives all of its input from terminals of marginal projection neurons in the spinal cord. However, the physiological functions and connections of this nucleus are unknown.

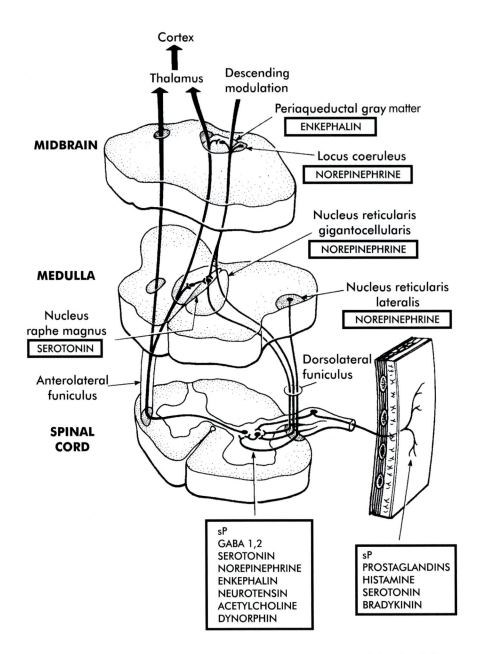

**FIGURE 11–6.** Schematic drawing of nociceptive processing, outlining ascending *(left side of diagram)* and descending *(right side of diagram)* pathways. Stimulation of nociceptors in the skin surface leads to impulse generation in the primary afferent. Concomitant with this impulse generation, increased levels of various endogenous algesic agents (substance P [sP], prostaglandins, histamine, serotonin, and bradykinin) are detected near the area of stimulation in the periphery. The noxious impulse is conducted to the dorsal horn of the spinal cord, where it is subjected to local factors and descending modulation. The endogenous neurochemical mediators of this interaction at the dorsal horn that have been characterized are listed in the figure. Primary nociceptive afferents relay to projection neurons in the dorsal horn that ascend in the anterolateral funiculus to end in the thalamus. En route, collaterals of the projection neurons activate the nucleus reticularis gigantocellularis, whose neurons project to the thalamus and also activate the periaqueductal gray matter of the midbrain. Enkephalinergic neurons from the periaqueductal gray matter and noradrenergic neurons from the nucleus reticularis gigantocellularis activate descending serotoninergic neurons of the nucleus raphe magnus. These fibers join with noradrenergic fibers from the locus coeruleus reticularis lateralis to project descending modulatory impulses to the dorsal horn via the dorsolateral funiculus.

*Note.* GABA = γ-aminobutyric acid.

*Source.* Reprinted from Brose WG, Cousins MJ: "Gynecologic Pain," in *Gynecologic Oncology.* Edited by Coppelson M. Edinburgh, Churchill Livingstone, 1992, pp. 1439–1479. Used with permission.

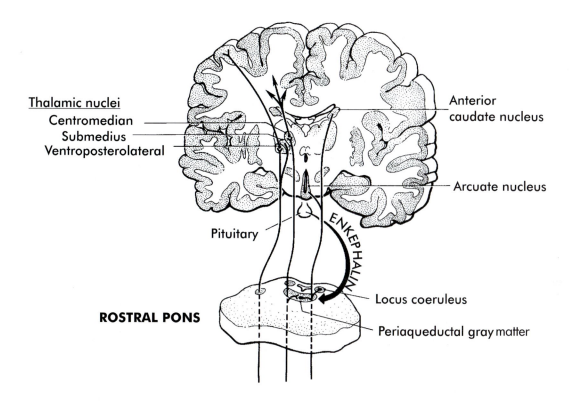

Thalamic nuclei
Centromedian
Submedius
Ventroposterolateral

Anterior
caudate nucleus

Arcuate nucleus

Pituitary

ENKEPHALIN

Locus coeruleus

**ROSTRAL PONS**

Periaqueductal gray matter

**FIGURE 11–7.** Rostral projections of nociceptive processing. Ascending stimuli *(left side of diagram)* traveling in the anterolateral funiculus—as well as impulses relayed from the medulla, pons, and midbrain—are projected to the thalamic nuclear complex. The centromedian, submedius, and ventroposterolateral nuclei receive nociceptive information. The ventroposterolateral nucleus projects discretely to the cortex. The centromedian nucleus projects more diffusely, particularly to the limbic region. The descending fibers *(right side of the diagram)* inhibit the transmission of nociceptive information between primary afferents and the projection neurons in the dorsal horn. The periaqueductal gray matter is controlled by projections from the anterior caudate nucleus, the midline limbic nuclei, and the arcuate nucleus of the hypothalamus. In addition to direct neural connection, endorphins synthesized in the pituitary are released into the cerebrospinal fluid and the blood, where they can exert an inhibitory effect at multiple centers, including the periaqueductal gray matter.

## Cerebral Cortex

The somatosensory cortex receives processed input from spinothalamic, spinoreticular, and dorsal column systems, as outlined earlier. Initially, the majority of attention was focused on SII as the principal cortical region involved with the reception and perception of noxious information. The anterior portion of SII receives input from the ventrobasilar thalamus, whereas the posterior portion of SII receives input from the posterior thalamus. Berkley and Palmer (1974) demonstrated that bilateral ablation of the posterior region of SII produces an increase in nociceptive threshold. The application of non-invasive neural imaging techniques has created a new interest in this area of nociceptive processing. The current neuromatrix for pain expands beyond SI and SII to include the midbrain region and the periaqueductal gray matter, the lenticular complex, the insula, and the orbitofrontal, prefrontal, and motor areas (Kwan et al. 2000).

## Descending Modulation

Up to this point, the discussion of pain pathways has been limited to the rostral projection of primary noxious stimuli. The failure of a particular painful stimulus to provoke given behavior in different individuals points out the uncoupling of a simple stimulus-response concept of pain processing. The uncoupling of pain stimulus and response is perhaps best identified by observing the absence of pain in some individuals who are injured in battle or in a sporting event. One of the primary focuses of research during the past two decades has been to delineate the physiological explanations for these observed differences in pain response. Through this investigation it has become apparent that the discussion of the afferent limb of the pain pathway mandates consideration of the modulating influences on that pain transmission.

Modulation of pain stimuli can occur at many different levels in the pathway. In their proposal of the gate control theory, Melzack and Wall (1965) predicted modulation of small-fiber activity by the presence of large-fiber activity in the same region of the dorsal horn. Cutaneous activation of large-fiber afferents through transcutaneous nerve stimulation supports this peripheral modulation at the dorsal horn. In addition, the stimulation of dorsal columns that mimics the activation of descending inhibition has also been shown to inhibit the discharge of dorsal horn interneuron nociceptors. Although this work has been proved incorrect, the subsequent evolution and acceptance of a descending control system are well accepted.

Earlier work by Hagbarth and Kerr (1954) demonstrated the existence of descending long-tract systems to modulate spinal evoked activity. Virtually every pathway carrying nociceptive information, including the spinothalamic and spinoreticular tracts, is under modulatory control from supraspinal systems. Experimental evidence of this supraspinal influence includes inhibition of nociceptive reflexes by electrical stimulation or microinjections of opioid at brain-stem sites, both of which are naloxone reversible. Various nuclei of the medulla oblongata and the pons project caudally to the spinal gray matter and the spinal nucleus of the trigeminal nerve. Serotoninergic neurons in the nucleus raphe magnus, the catecholaminergic neurons of the lateral reticular formation, and the locus coeruleus are all believed to play a role in descending modulation (Basbaum and Fields 1978; Besson and Chaouch 1987; Fields and Basbaum 1984). Axons from these centers project to all levels of the spinal cord through the dorsolateral funiculus (Figure 11–6).

Stimulation of the medullary centers prevents the activation of second-order neurons in the dorsal horn or trigeminal gray matter by primary afferent fibers through this descending inhibition (Basbaum 1985; Basbaum and Fields 1978; Besson and Chaouch 1987). The exact mechanism of this inhibition has not been characterized, but several models have been proposed (Basbaum 1985; Dubner 1985). In addition to the different modulating pathways that have been partially characterized (Figure 11–8), there are undoubtedly additional descending inhibitory influences that have yet to be evaluated. The depression of spinothalamic neurons by cortical and pyramidal stimulation is an example of such an uncharacterized pathway. Continued research in this area will help to unravel the complex reaction between pain stimulus and response and perhaps suggest additional therapeutic modalities that may be applied to the treatment of pain.

# Neuropharmacology

## Pharmacology of Pain

Basic research on the processing of nociceptive information by the CNS has led to an improved understanding of pain and pain treatment. Figure 11–6 also summarizes the site of action of several of the chemical substances that have been identified with nociceptive processing. Using this simplified picture of the pain pathway, we can focus on pharmacological interventions at different points in the pathway and determine a clinical effect on the relief of pain.

## Peripheral Desensitization

A rough schematic drawing of the local circuitry involved in the detection of a noxious stimulus from the periphery is shown in Figure 11–9. As discussed previously, after trauma to a peripheral site, an inflammatory reaction, including the activation of complement and coagulation-fibrinolytic pathways, begins. Local release of histamine, serotonin, prostaglandins, and substance P occurs. Subsequent changes in the local environment such as decreased tissue pH, changes in the microcirculation, and an increase in efferent sympathetic activity all appear to increase the response of peripheral nociceptors.

Attempts have been made through numerous drug therapies to interrupt these peripheral processes. Blockade of pain by aspirin-like drugs is one such peripheral action. Aspirin, indomethacin, ibuprofen, diclofenac, and ketorolac are all cyclooxygenase inhibitors. Cyclooxygenase is the enzyme responsible for the synthesis of prostaglandins, prostacyclins, and thromboxanes. All these endogenous substances have been proposed as mediators of the local pain response (Juan 1978). Clinical trials with topical capsaicin are also focused on peripheral action. This drug has been shown to deplete substance P from cutaneous nerve endings (Gamse et al. 1980). The initial effect is a burning pain, followed by insensitivity to subsequent painful stimuli.

The involvement of the sympathetic nervous system is also suspect. It is known that sympathetic fibers are present in large numbers near cutaneous nociceptors. Blockade of these sympathetic fibers can eliminate the pain of causalgia in some patients. The burning dysesthetic pain and hyperalgesia that are seen with this syndrome, which may be eliminated by sympathetic blockade, can be made to reappear with local application of norepinephrine, the sympathetic neurotransmitter.

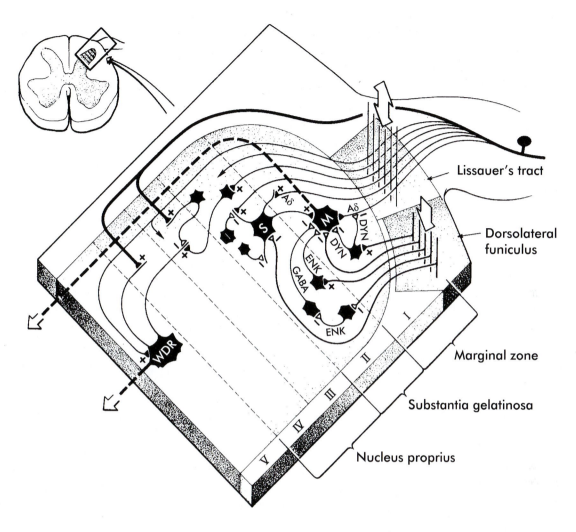

**FIGURE 11–8.** Dorsal horn processing. Large- and small-diameter primary neurons have their cell bodies in the dorsal root ganglia. These fibers segregate as they approach the spinal cord. Large-diameter afferents *(thick solid lines)* travel in the medial portion, whereas small-diameter afferents *(thin solid lines:* C and Aδ) segregate to the lateral portions of the entry zone. The spinal terminals of the small fibers enter the cord, where they may ascend or descend for several segments in the dorsolateral tract (Lissauer's tract) and subsequently terminate throughout the dorsal horn of the spinal cord. Aδ fiber afferents terminate primarily in lamina I (marginal zone), whereas C fiber afferents terminate in lamina II (substantia gelatinosa). In lamina I, nociceptive fibers synapse on dendrites of the large marginal (M) neurons. Smaller neurons in lamina I may exert presynapse inhibition of the marginal neuron. Other nociceptive fibers (Aδ) synapse with stalked (S) neurons in lamina II. These S neurons stimulate M neurons in lamina I. The relay between primary afferent fibers and S neurons is also subject to modulation by inhibitory islet (I) neurons in lamina II. Central transmission is accomplished by M neurons directly, wide dynamic range neurons (WDRs) directly, or S neurons indirectly. M neurons are subject to inhibition by neurons in lamina II. Descending serotoninergic neurons from the nucleus raphe magnus, which travel in the dorsolateral funiculus, are also shown. These neurons terminate throughout the spinal cord on interneurons (γ-aminobutyric acid [GABA] and enkephalins [ENK]) to provide inhibition of nociceptive transmission.
*Note.* DYN = dynorphin.

## Neural Blockade

In the early part of the twentieth century, Cushing (1902) presented his theory that nerve blockade could prevent the pain and shock of amputation. Later, Crile (1910) proposed that disruption of the pain pathway might improve outcome from trauma. Indeed, a multitude of investigations have proved the beneficial effect of neural blockade with respect to neuroendocrine function after trauma and/or surgery (Kehlet 1988).

Neural blockade can occur at any point along the pain pathway. The most common sites of neural blockade

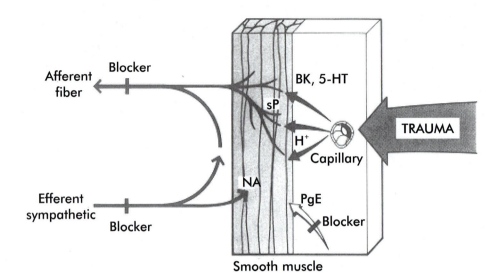

**FIGURE 11–9.** Local tissue factors and peripheral pain receptors. The physical stimuli of "trauma," the chemical environment (e.g., H$^+$), algesic substances (e.g., serotonin [5-HT] and bradykinin [BK]), and microcirculatory changes may all modify peripheral receptor activity. Efferent sympathetic activity may increase the sensitivity of receptors by means of noradrenaline (NA) (norepinephrine) release. Substance P (sP) may be the peripheral pain transmitter. Points of potential blockade of nociception are shown as "Blocker"; other potential sites involve bradykinin, serotonin, noradrenaline, and substance P.

*Note.*   PgE = prostaglandin E.

*Source.*   Reprinted from Cousins MJ, Phillips GD (eds): *Acute Pain Management.* London, Churchill Livingstone, 1986, p. 742. Used with permission.

are peripheral nerves, somatic plexuses, and dorsal roots. These blockages can be performed with relatively short-acting agents such as local anesthetics for acute pain, whereas long-acting (permanent) blockade with alcohol or phenol may be more appropriate for chronic pain. Surgical lesions at any of these points have also been suggested to provide long-lasting interruption of specific pain pathways. The disadvantage of permanent techniques is that they are neither specific to pain fibers nor reliable for protracted pain problems. The lack of anatomical separation of fibers carrying pain, motor, and other sensory information exposes the patient in whom neural blockade is employed to varying amounts of sympathetic, somatic, and perhaps motor dysfunction. Although these side effects may be well tolerated in certain situations—for example, in treatment of acute pain when the patient is expected to improve rapidly or in treatment of chronic cancer pain when the life expectancy of the patient is less than 12 months—the use of these techniques in chronic pain management situations is inappropriate.

## Opioid Analgesia

In recent years, researchers have identified multiple endogenous opioid chemicals that have analgesic effects (Yaksh 1988). Included among these are the enkephalins and β endorphin. At least four different types of opioid receptors have also been located in the brain and spinal cord. Table 11–1 summarizes the pharmacodynamic effects obtained when each of these opioid receptors is stimulated. Pert and Snyder (1973) demonstrated opioid receptors in the brain and the brain stem. Later, Yaksh and Rudy (1976) reported long-lasting analgesia after the introduction of intrathecal opioids. The discovery that spinally administered opioids produced dose-dependent, stereospecific, naloxone-reversible analgesia has led to the development of an important clinical tool to combat pain.

### Brain Receptors

It has been known for centuries that opium possesses analgesic properties. Despite the wide recognition of these properties, the location of the active sites for opium was not known. Microinjection techniques used in the 1960s identified the periaqueductal gray matter of the midbrain and the midline medullary nuclei to be the most sensitive sites. Through descending serotoninergic and/or noradrenergic links with the spinal cord, morphine microinjections into these centers have been shown to inhibit spinal reflexes. This analgesic effect has also been shown to be similar to the effect achieved by

**TABLE 11–1.** Pharmacodynamic effects obtained when an opioid agonist interacts with the various types of opioid receptors

| | Receptor subtype | | | |
|---|---|---|---|---|
| **Effect** | μ | κ | σ | δ |
| Pain relief | Yes | Yes, especially at spinal cord level | Yes | Yes |
| Sedation | Yes | Yes | — | — |
| Respiratory effects | Depression | Depression, but not as much as for μ (may reach plateau) | Stimulation | Depression |
| Affect | Euphoria | — | Dysphoria | — |
| Physical dependence | Marked | Less severe than with μ | — | Yes |
| Prototype agonist (other drugs with predominantly agonist activity) | Morphine (meperidine, methadone, fentanyl, heroin, codeine, propoxyphene, buprenorphine) | Ketocyclazocine (nalbuphine, dynorphin, butorphanol, nalorphine, pentazocine) | SKF 10,047 | Enkephalins |

*Note.* SKF = Smith, Kline & French.
*Source.* Adapted from Gourlay et al. 1987b.

systemically administered morphine. Further research has documented dose dependency, stereospecificity, naloxone reversibility, and well-defined structure activity relationships of these centers to other opiate agonists.

## Spinal Cord Receptors

As interesting as the delineation of the descending inhibition of nociception initiated by centrally administered opioids is the growing appreciation of opioid systems in spinal function. Opioids administered systemically produce inhibition of nociceptive reflexes in animals with transected spinal cords. Also, administration of opioids to the dorsal horn of the spinal cord inhibits the discharge of nociceptive neurons. Multiple discrete populations of opioid receptors have been identified. Stimulation of μ and κ systems present in the spinal cord depresses the response to noxious stimulation (Yaksh 1981).

Opiate systems appear to be active in the modulation of noxious impulses presented to the substantia gelatinosa by both direct action and indirect descending inhibition via serotoninergic and noradrenergic systems (Yaksh 1988). In addition, other nonopioid systems appear to be functioning at this level to produce analgesic effects. Baclofen and clonidine also rely on both ascending and descending effects for antinociception (Sawynok and Labella 1981). Newer work has focused on the NMDA receptor ion channel complex. Improved understanding of the complex interaction of the excitatory amino acids glutamate and NMDA with glycine activity and the nitric oxide intercellular pathways may yield novel agents that can be used in the future management of difficult painful syndromes.

In summary, it appears that the substantia gelatinosa receives collaterals of nociceptive information and that that information is subject to extensive modulation at the spinal level. Chemical mediators shown to be associated with analgesia at this level include opioids, serotonin, norepinephrine, γ-aminobutyric acid (GABA), neurotensin, and acetylcholine. Some of the proposed endogenous and exogenous ligands for these neurotransmitter systems are shown in Table 11–2.

## Electrical Stimulation

The prediction that large-fiber activity could block certain noxious information at the level of the dorsal horn resulted in the introduction of transcutaneous electrical nerve stimulation (TENS). The clinical utility of TENS has yet to be established for individual pain syndromes. Dorsal column stimulation (DCS) excites descending inhibitory pathways with electricity to provide analgesia. The success of DCS has been mixed, but it may have a place in certain deafferentation pain syndromes.

The success of central morphine microinjection techniques to provide analgesia may have prompted Reynolds (1969) to demonstrate similar results in animals by means of electrical stimulation of the periaqueductal gray matter.

**TABLE 11–2.** Spinal neurotransmitters, receptors, and ligands

| Neurotransmitter system | Proposed receptor | Endogenous ligand | Exogenous ligand |
|---|---|---|---|
| Opioid | $\mu$ | β Endorphin; Met/Leuen-kephalin | Morphine |
| | $\delta$ | Met/Leuenkephalin | |
| | $\kappa$ | Dynorphin | |
| Adrenergic | $\alpha_1$ | Norepinephrine | Methoxamine |
| | $\alpha_2$ | Norepinephrine | Clonidine |
| | $\beta$ | Epinephrine | Isoproterenol |
| Serotoninergic | 5-HT | Serotonin | Serotonin |
| GABAergic | A | GABA | Baclofen |
| | B | GABA | Muscimol |
| Neurotensin | — | Neurotensin | Neurotensin |
| Cholinergic | Muscarinic | Acetylcholine | Oxotremorine |

*Note.*   GABA = γ-aminobutyric acid; 5-HT = 5-hydroxytryptamine (serotonin); — = unidentified.
*Source.*   Adapted from Yaksh 1988.

Hosobuchi subsequently demonstrated naloxone-reversible analgesia in humans after implantation of brain-stem electrodes (Bonica and Ventafridda 1979). Each of these applications of electrical stimulation was predicted on the basis of improved understanding of the pain pathway. Electrical stimulation seems to have found a place in pain management by exciting intrinsic mechanisms used for the modulation of nociceptive information.

## Nonsteroidal Anti-inflammatory Drugs

The effect of nonsteroidal anti-inflammatory drugs (NSAIDs) in inhibiting the synthesis of prostaglandins is currently thought to be the explanation of their pain-relieving properties. The prostaglandins, leukotrienes, and thromboxanes are oxygenated derivatives of arachidonic acid, an essential polyunsaturated fat. The term *eicosanoids* is often used to describe all the products of arachidonic acid metabolism. This inhibition occurs by the inactivation of cyclooxygenase, which catalyzes the formation of cyclic endoperoxides from arachidonic acid. Anti-inflammatory steroids act at an earlier step in the arachidonic acid metabolism pathway (Raja et al. 1988). As discussed earlier, prostaglandins are formed in damaged tissue and appear to be involved in sensitizing the peripheral nociceptors to painful stimuli.

The indications for NSAIDs range from the treatment of aches and sprains to dysmenorrhea to long-term therapy for rheumatoid arthritis and osteoarthritis, as well as degenerative joint diseases (e.g., ankylosing spondylitis and gout). Their anti-inflammatory activities have also been shown to relieve pain in cancer patients with bone metastases. In contrast to the opioid drugs, there has not been a clear demonstration of a relationship between blood levels of NSAIDs and pain relief. The majority of NSAIDs can be classified into one of two groups based on their elimination half-lives (Table 11–3). The NSAIDs in the first group have half-lives between 2 and 4 hours. Acetaminophen is also included in this group, despite its lack of anti-inflammatory properties. The drugs in the second group have longer half-lives, ranging from 6 to 60 hours. Patients with renal insufficiency are thought to be at risk for toxicity due to these agents because they are excreted through the kidney.

The use of NSAIDs alone has been supported through years of clinical practice. However, the different sites of action found with NSAIDs and opioids would also suggest additive or possibly even synergistic effects. The continued evolution of NSAID pharmacology has led to the release and widespread use of refecocoxib (Vioxx) and celecoxib (Celebrex) as more selective agents of this type. The Cox-2 inhibitors, as they are described, work selectively in a position within the arachidonic acid cascade to prevent the elaboration of prostanoids associated with inflammation while still allowing important functions outside the peripheral injury area. The reduced side-effect profile of these two drugs has resulted in their being widely prescribed by multiple providers.

Dosing of the individual agents is covered in Table 11–3. These doses have been derived from long-term therapy of rheumatological disease and represent near-maximal anti-inflammatory activity. Although these doses are considered safe for long-term therapy, careful monitoring of side effects is appropriate. Side effects of NSAIDs include gastric irritation, salt and fluid retention, platelet inhibition, and tinnitus. The gastric damage is caused by decreased prostaglandin levels, which cause reduced production of gastric

**TABLE 11–3.** Terminal half-life, recommended dosage, influence of food on absorption, and incidence of gastric erosion from nonsteroidal anti-inflammatory drugs (NSAIDs)

| Drug | Terminal half-life (hours) | Oral dosage (mg/hour) | Effect of food on absorption[a] | Incidence of gastric erosion (gastritis) |
|---|---|---|---|---|
| Aspirin | 0.2–0.3 | 600–900/4 | 1 | High |
| Salicylate | 2–3 | 600/4 | 1 | Intermediate |
| Diflunisal | 8–12 | 500/12 | 1 | Low |
| Diclofenac | 1.5–2 | 25–50/8 | 1 | Low |
| Ibuprofen | 2–3 | 200–400/8 | 1 | Low |
| Naproxen | 12–15 | 250–375/12 | 3 | Low |
| Fenoprofen | 2–3 | 400–600/6 | 2 | Low |
| Indomethacin | 6–8 | 50–75/8 | 1 | Intermediate |
| Sulindac | 6–8 | 100–200/12 | 2 | Low |
| Piroxicam | 30–60 | 20–30/24 | 1 | Low |
| Flufenamic acid | 8–10 | 500/6 | 1 | — |
| Mefenamic acid | 3–4 | 250/6 | 1 | Intermediate |
| Ketoprofen | 1–4 | 50/6 | 1 | Low |
| Ketorolac[b] | 5 | 10–30/6 | ? | ? |

[a]1 = decrease in rate of absorption; no change in oral bioavailability; 2 = decrease in rate of absorption and oral bioavailability; 3 = no change in rate of absorption and oral bioavailability.

[b]Not currently available for clinical use; dosages based on review of scientific literature.

*Source.* Adapted from Gourlay et al. 1987b.

mucus, increased acid secretion, and decreased gastric mucosal blood supply. Acetaminophen does not share the potential for these prostaglandin-mediated side effects, but it carries the potential for liver damage with excessive doses.

## Antidepressants

The possible involvement of neurotransmitters in the transmission of pain is discussed above. Many of the antidepressant drugs act by blocking the uptake of noradrenaline and serotonin in the CNS. This effect may also occur in the medulla and increase the concentrations of these neurotransmitters at the synapses involved in the descending inhibition of dorsal horn cells. Table 11–4 lists the names and properties of some of these antidepressants. Secondary amines are thought to be more effective blockers of norepinephrine, whereas the tertiary amines appear to be more effective in blocking serotonin reuptake.

Oral tricyclic antidepressants (TCAs) are well absorbed from the gastrointestinal tract. There is conflicting information regarding the existence of therapeutic ranges for antidepressants. All the currently available pharmacokinetic information refers to the antidepressant activity of these drugs. The time taken for the perception of pain relief after the institution of these drugs is only 2–7 days, compared with the accepted time for antidepressant effect of 3–4 weeks. This observation suggests that different mechanisms may be involved in their analgesic effect and their antidepressant action.

Side effects from TCA use include autonomic, anticholinergic, and adrenergic effects. Dry mouth, the most common side effect, can be relieved by increased fluid intake and salivary stimulants such as sugarless candy. Blurring of vision is also common and usually interferes with reading. Orthostatic hypotension is also common. Patients should be warned to rise slowly and watch for dizziness. Constipation has also been described in association with these agents.

More recently, selective serotonin reuptake inhibitors (SSRIs) have been introduced in the management of depression. They have similar efficacy in treating depression but reduced side effects. As selective serotonin blockers, they have a side-effect profile that does not include sedation or anticholinergic symptoms, unlike the TCAs, which have a mixed norepinephrine/serotonin profile. The SSRIs are effective in reducing comorbid depression, as are the new combined serotonin/norepinephrine reuptake inhibitors.

Although serotoninergic pathways have been described in the context of descending modulation, the efficacy of these agents in chronic painful conditions has not yet been established. Anecdotal reports suggest a role in the management of muscular as well as neuropathic conditions. Clearly, the management of depression, with its high comorbidity in chronic pain, is essential. The nonsedating aspect of these agents is advantageous when

**TABLE 11–4.** Terminal half-life, recommended daily dose, and other properties of antidepressant drugs

| Drug | Amine group | Terminal half-life (hours) | Inhibitor concentration[a] NA | Inhibitor concentration[a] 5-HT | Recommended daily dose (mg)[b] |
|---|---|---|---|---|---|
| Amitriptyline | Tertiary | 20–30 | 4.6 | 4.4 | 50–150 |
| Nortriptyline | Secondary | 18–36 | 0.9 | 17.0 | 50–150 |
| Protriptyline | Secondary | 50–90 | — | — | 10–50 |
| Clomipramine | Tertiary | 20–30 | 4.6 | 0.5 | 50–75 |
| Imipramine | Tertiary | 20–30 | 4.6 | 0.5 | 50–75 |
| Desipramine | Secondary | 12–24 | 0.2 | 35.0 | 75–150 |
| Doxepin | Tertiary | 10–25 | 6.5 | 20.0 | 75–150 |
| Dothiepin | Tertiary | 20–30 | — | — | 50–100 |
| Mianserin | Tertiary | 10–20 | 20.0 | 130.0 | 20–50 |
| Nomifensine | Primary and tertiary | 2–4 | 2.0 | 120.0 | 75–150 |
| Zimelidine | Tertiary | 5–10 | 630.0 | 14.0 | 200–300 |

[a]Inhibitor concentration (IC50) represents the antidepressant concentration ($\times 10^{-8}$ M) required to inhibit the uptake of either noradrenaline (NA) or serotonin (5-hydroxytryptamine [5-HT]) by 50% using rat midbrain synaptosomes.

[b]It is generally recommended that the antidepressant be administered as a single dose at night, unless significant side effects occur, in which case a night and a morning dose (divided dose) may be appropriate.

*Source.* Adapted from Gourlay et al. 1987b.

setting exceptions of increased daytime function in patients with chronic pain. Although there is some indication of moderate selective efficacy (e.g., in diabetic neuropathy but not other neuropathic pain [Kishore-Kumar et al. 1990]), there is evidence of analgesic effects of SSRIs (Boyer 1992; Finley 1994). However, a specific role in pain reduction similar to that of TCAs is not yet clear.

## Analgesic Adjuvants

A multitude of agents have been purported to have analgesic qualities. The majority of these agents are thought to potentiate the analgesia provided by opioid and non-opioid analgesics. Although the data in support of the use of such compounds may be anecdotal, a small number of these drugs do appear to have clinical utility in the management of cancer pain. Table 11–5 summarizes some of the currently available co-analgesics.

Corticosteroids are the first group of drugs to be considered as coanalgesics. These drugs have been used successfully for the management of neuropathic pain from direct neural compression and from pain due to increased intracranial pressure. Systemic steroids are thought to reduce perineural edema and lymphatic edema that may be contributing to pain by compressing individual nerves. This treatment appears to be especially helpful in cases of spinal cord compression. Treatment of such neural compression involves relatively high doses of dexamethasone

(near 30 mg/day). Steroids are best employed on a trial basis. A single morning dosage or twice-daily dosage of 2–4 mg/day of dexamethasone can be used over a 10- to 14-day period. An additional benefit of corticosteroids is that they often stimulate appetite; this effect may aid in the nutritional support of patients with malignancy. The use of steroids is not without problems, however. Attention needs to be focused on the possible development of oral and vaginal candidiasis; in addition, this treatment may worsen peripheral edema.

Anticonvulsants are also often advocated as analgesic adjuvants. They suppress neuronal firing and have been successfully employed for the treatment of neuropathic pain states, including trigeminal neuralgia and peripheral neuropathies. Anticonvulsant drugs probably exert their effects by blocking voltage-dependent sodium channels and thereby interfering with the transduction and perhaps spontaneous depolarization seen in damaged neurons. Carbamazepine and phenytoin have been helpful in managing cancer pain with dysesthetic components. These drugs need to be started slowly and increased gradually, with particular attention to the development of possible side effects. Common side effects can include dizziness, ataxia, drowsiness, blurred vision, and gastrointestinal irritation. In addition, carbamazepine has associated bone marrow toxicity, and sodium valproate is known to produce hepatic toxicity.

A newer agent in the class of anticonvulsants is gabapentin (Neurontin). This agent has only recently been

**TABLE 11–5.** Coanalgesic medications

| Drugs, by classification | Indications | Comments |
| --- | --- | --- |
| **Antidepressant**<br>Amitriptyline<br>Imipramine<br>Mianserin<br>Clomipramine<br>Doxepin | Chronic pain, neuropathic pain associated with neuropathy and headache | Improves sleep, may improve appetite |
| **Corticosteroid**<br>Dexamethasone<br>Prednisolone<br>Fludrocortisone | Neuropathic pain secondary to direct neural compression; pain secondary to increased intracranial pressure | May stimulate appetite; limit trial to 2 weeks and reassess efficacy |
| **Anticonvulsant**<br>Carbamazepine<br>Phenytoin<br>Valproate<br>Clonazepam | Neuropathic pain with paroxysmal character | Start slowly, increase gradually while observing for side effects |
| **Membrane stabilizer**<br>Lidocaine<br>2-Chloroprocaine<br>Tocainide<br>Mexiletine | Neuropathic pain associated with peripheral neuropathy | Efficacy of oral preparations is not established |
| **Phenothiazine**<br>Levomepromazine | Insomnia unresponsive to antidepressant or short-acting benzodiazepines | Increase dose slowly to achieve desired effect |
| **Butyrophenone**<br>**haloperidol** | Acute confusion, nausea, and vomiting | Prolonged use may be complicated by tardive dyskinesia |
| **Antihistamine**<br>Hydroxyzine | Nausea, pruritus, and anxiety | Anticholinergic side effects |
| **CNS stimulant**<br>Dextroamphetamine<br>Cocaine<br>Caffeine | Opioid-induced sedation, potentiation of NSAID, potentiation of opioid analgesia not proven in cancer | Should only be used as short-term therapeutic trial |

*Note.* CNS = central nervous system; NSAID = nonsteroidal anti-inflammatory drug.

used in the management of neuropathic pain states. Controlled clinical trials are lacking, although case reports have suggested quite good results in the management of reflex sympathetic dystrophy and other neuropathic pain states. The side-effect profile of gabapentin is low, and therefore many patients tolerate very high dose ranges.

The use of lidocaine and 2-chloroprocaine in the treatment of certain peripheral neuropathies that have been refractory to other analgesic medications has led to the investigation of another group of drugs, which may be loosely classified as membrane stabilizers. In addition to intermittent intravenous infusion of these two local anesthetics, oral administration of the lidocaine congeners mexiletine and tocainide has been reported as useful in certain patients (Dejard et al. 1988; Lindstrom and Lindblom 1987). Typically, it is thought, these patients' pain has neuropathic components. In comparison to patients

with episodic lancinating neuropathic pain, who benefit from antiepileptics, patients who benefit from membrane stabilizers may have a more constant pain.

Antipsychotics have long been purported to potentiate the analgesic effect of opioids. Most studies employing these drugs are uncontrolled, however, and the enthusiasm for their continued use is in contrast to available literature. The phenothiazines are the most commonly employed antipsychotics for analgesia. Dundee and colleagues (Dundee et al. 1963; Moore and Dundee 1961a, 1961b) published data regarding the analgesic potency of 14 different phenothiazines in an uncontrolled trial of experimental pain. The results of these studies suggested that the action of a few potentially analgesic phenothiazines was initially antianalgesic and after 2–3 hours only mildly analgesic (Atkison et al. 1985).

Review of phenothiazines in both experimental and

clinical pain reveals that only levomepromazine (methotrimeprazine) has established analgesic properties. Levomepromazine appears to have analgesic potency about half that of morphine in patients with cancer pain (Beaver et al. 1966). Haloperidol is a butyrophenone antipsychotic that has found a useful position in the management of acute confusional states associated with terminal cancer. Haloperidol also has useful antiemetic properties, which can be helpful in the management of cancer pain. The appropriate use of antipsychotics in the management of chronic cancer pain has not been established. Care must be taken in the long-term administration of these drugs because of the potential for tardive dyskinesia.

Benzodiazepines are often discussed as coanalgesics. These drugs do not have any demonstrated analgesic effect. Diazepam has been studied extensively with respect to analgesic activity, and it does not alter sensitivity to pain or potentiate the analgesic activity of opioids. These drugs do decrease affective responses to acute pain, however, and they may produce extended relief in chronic pain due to musculoskeletal disorders, perhaps as a result of their muscle-relaxant properties. Judicious use of benzodiazepines in cancer pain is appropriate for short-term relief of anxiety, but superior analgesic effects and nighttime sedation can be achieved by employing a TCA.

The more general class of agents known as muscle relaxants is a diverse group with varied profiles, but with the specific intent of providing muscle relaxation and hence relief from painful muscular conditions. The utility of these agents in the treatment of painful muscular conditions, however, is questionable; they may in general provide a nonspecific benefit from poorly characterized central effects.

The most specific of these agents is baclofen—an agent known to interact with the $GABA_B$ receptor, in distinction to the benzodiazepines, which interact with both the $GABA_A$ and the $GABA_B$ receptor sites. Although baclofen does have demonstrated efficacy in patients with spasticity from spinal cord injury or cerebral injury, the evidence that baclofen improves outcomes in chronic muscular syndromes such as fibromyalgia and myofascial pain is less convincing. Anecdotal reports suggest that baclofen may be a useful agent when used adjunctively with other agents in the management of chronic pain. Sedation is the primary limiting side effect. However, most patients acclimate rapidly.

Other agents in this class are more nonspecific in their actions, including cyclobenzaprine (Flexeril) and carisoprodol (Soma). These agents have CNS effects that allow skeletal muscle relaxation and hence reduction to

the TCAs. Cyclobenzaprine has a higher side-effect profile with sedation, whereas carisoprodol is better tolerated.

Hydroxyzine is an antihistaminic agent. It has proven analgesic properties at high doses. It does not consistently improve analgesia obtained with opioids, but it does potentiate the effect of opioids on the affective components of pain. It appears that hydroxyzine administered intramuscularly has analgesic properties similar to those of low doses of morphine (Beaver and Feise 1976). In addition, the sedative and antipruritic properties of this drug are useful in the setting of chronic cancer pain.

The final group of analgesic adjuvants to be considered are the stimulants. This group includes amphetamines, cocaine, and caffeine. Chronic cancer pain has been treated for nearly a century with combinations of opioid and stimulant in Brompton's cocktail. This mixture contains morphine, cocaine, and a phenothiazine. Despite years of clinical experience with such a mixture, no controlled studies have demonstrated superior analgesia with this combination compared with opioid alone. Potentiation of analgesia by sympathomimetics has been well described. Caffeine is known to increase the analgesic effects of aspirin and acetaminophen, and one study suggested that dextroamphetamine doubled the analgesic potency of morphine (Forrest et al. 1977). The long-term use of these stimulants in pain has not been systematically evaluated. The use of these drugs should probably be limited to a therapeutic trial period of several days to determine efficacy for individual patients.

## Opioids

Opioids are extremely effective agents in the treatment of nociceptive components of acute pain. Many misconceptions surround the use of opioid drugs, which results in a marked tendency toward inadequate doses and inappropriately long dosing intervals. Once a decision has been made to use opioid medications, it is both logical and essential to use an effective dosage regimen.

Although vast sums of money have been invested during the last decade in the development of new opioids, an increased understanding of the pharmacokinetics and pharmacodynamics involved in opioid administration has done more to improve the treatment of pain than has any new drug. The introduction of concepts such as the minimum effective analgesic concentration (MEC) has helped health care providers conceptualize the association between blood opioid concentrations and analgesic effect. Equally important to effective pain treatment has been the realization that there may be as much as a fivefold to sixfold interpatient variability in the value of

MEC for any one agent. Many factors, both physical and psychological, influence MEC. It is impossible to predict the value of MEC for any patient-opioid combination. It is therefore necessary that the dose for each individual be adjusted to the desired effect. Although MEC and other pharmacokinetic variables cannot be used ahead of time to predict the exact analgesic doses of opioids necessary for obtaining analgesia, these concepts provide a good starting point. They also allow the prediction of the effect of certain disease states on opioid requirements.

In addition to planning effective analgesic therapy by individualizing opioids to a particular patient, the use of opioids often involves the management of side effects. The major side effects limiting the effectiveness of opioid therapy are nausea, vomiting, sedation, and respiratory depression. The incidence and severity of the side effects seen with the various μ agonists are probably similar at equianalgesic doses. Rather than restricting the dose of opioids to the point at which a patient is free from side effects but is experiencing pain, one should consider administering other medications to treat the side effects.

## Delivery Systems

The continued reports of inadequate pain relief, despite the vast numbers of newly developed opioids, point to the problems associated with opioid delivery rather than to any defect in the individual drugs per se. There are many different delivery systems and dosing regimens that can provide good pain relief when used properly. The association between stable blood levels of opioids and continuous analgesia must be remembered when planning any systemic opioid therapy. The effective dose of opioid medication is the minimum dose that provides acceptable pain relief with a low incidence of side effects.

### Oral Opioids

The rapid clearance of the majority of opioids, combined with their extensive hepatic metabolism, has important implications for oral dosing. Drugs are absorbed from the gastrointestinal tract directly into the portal circulation, where they travel to the liver. Therefore, with oral dosing, a significant percentage of the dose is metabolized to inactive products before the opioids reach the systemic circulation (Mather and Gourlay 1984). This phenomenon is referred to as the *hepatic first-pass effect*. This effect and the poor bioavailability seen with certain opioids lead to perceptions that the oral administration of opioids is ineffective.

Oral bioavailability ranges from zero for heroin to 80% for methadone. The oral bioavailability of morphine ranges from 10% to 40%, leading to very wide fluctuations in oral dosing requirements between different patients. Similar variability is seen in meperidine (pethidine) and other opioids (Table 11–6). The high bioavailability of methadone and the long terminal half-life suggest that stable blood levels of the drug could be obtained from oral dosing.

Much attention has also been focused on the development of effective sustained-release preparations of morphine. Although the concept of sustained release is fairly simple, obtaining a pharmacologic preparation that maintains a steady dose release without tendency toward dose dumping, which can lead to a bolus effect, has proved more difficult. Currently, sustained-release morphine products are available in many countries. The actual changes in the pharmacokinetics of these sustained-release preparations with regard to food intake, activity, and posture have not been evaluated. As continued progress is made in this area, the availability of a reliable sustained-release preparation should be forthcoming.

In summary, satisfactory analgesia with oral dosing can be obtained if attention is focused on the pharmacokinetics of the particular opioid to be administered, the oral bioavailability of the drug, and titration of the drug to achieve adequate analgesia in each patient.

### Sublingual Administration

Ongoing interest in the improved pain management of patients with terminal malignancy has led to the investigation of sublingual administration. The sublingual route is particularly useful in patients who cannot tolerate oral medication because it causes nausea, vomiting, or dysphagia. This method of administration has theoretical advantages in that the oral cavity is well perfused, providing rapid onset of action; subsequent absorption results in systemic rather than portal drug delivery. The sublingual absorption of lipid-soluble drugs (methadone, fentanyl, and buprenorphine) from alkaline solution was shown to provide analgesic concentrations very quickly (Weinberg et al. 1988). The utility of this technique in comparison with other methods of administration still needs to be assessed.

### Rectal Administration

Rectal administration of opioids has been advocated for patients who cannot swallow or those who have a high incidence of nausea or vomiting with oral administration. Studies of rectal administration of meperidine have indicated a bioavailability similar to that seen with oral dosing: 50% (Ripamonti and Bruera 1991). Prolonged pain

**TABLE 11–6.** Doses, pharmacokinetic parameters, minimum effective concentration, and duration of pain relief for various opioid drugs

| Opioid | Dose (mg) im/iv | Dose (mg) po | Terminal half-life (hours) | Bioavailability (%) | MEC (ng/mL) | Duration of pain relief (hours) | Comments |
|---|---|---|---|---|---|---|---|
| Codeine | 130 | 250 | 2–3 | 50 | — | 3–4 | Weak opiate, frequently combined with aspirin. Useful for pain with visceral and integumentary components. |
| Propoxyphene | 240 | 500 | 8–24 | 40 | — | 4–6 | Weak opioid. Unacceptable incidence of side effects. |
| Oxycodone | 10 | 30 | — | 30–50 | — | 4–6 | Suppository (30 mg) can provide pain relief for 8–10 hours. |
| Diamorphine | 5 | 15 | 0.05 | — | — | 2–3 | Very soluble, rapidly converted to 6-mono-acetyl morphine and morphine in vivo. No oral bioavailability. |
| Morphine | 10 | 40 | 2–4 | 10–40 | 10–40 | 3–4 | Standard opiate to which new opioids are compared. New sustained-release formulation available in some countries is of considerable benefit in chronic cancer pain. |
| Methadone | 10 | 10–15 | 10–80 | 70–95 | 20–80 | 10–60 | Duration of pain relief ranges from 10 to 60 hours both postoperatively and for cancer pain. Variable half-life. Requires initial care to establish dose for each patient to avoid accumulation. Otherwise of great value. |
| Hydromorphone | 2 | 4–6 | 2–3 | 50–60 | 4 | 3–4 | More potent but shorter acting than morphine. |
| Levorphanol | 2 | 4 | 12–16 | 40–60 | — | 4–6 | Good oral availability, but long half-life compared to analgesia may lead to accumulation. |
| Phenazocine | 3 | 10–20 | — | 20–30 | — | 4–6 | Similar to morphine, only more potent. |
| Oxymorphone | 1 | 6 | — | 10–40 | — | 3–4 | Similar to morphine, only more potent. |
| Meperidine | 100 | 300 | 3–5 | 30–60 | 200–800 | 2–4 | Not as effective in relieving anxiety as morphine. Suppositories (200–400 mg) have slow onset (2–3 hours) but can last for 6–8 hours. Normeperidine toxicity. |
| Dextromoramide | 7.5 | 10 | — | 75 | — | 2–3 | Methadone-like chemical structure. Short acting. Useful in covering exacerbation pain. Supposed as iv form. |

**TABLE 11–6.** Doses, pharmacokinetic parameters, minimum effective concentration, and duration of pain relief for various opioid drugs (continued)

| Opioid | Dose (mg) | | Pharmacokinetic parameters (range) | | | Duration of pain relief (hours) | Comments |
| | im/iv | po | Terminal half-life (hours) | Bioavailability (%) | MEC (ng/mL) | | |
|---|---|---|---|---|---|---|---|
| Buprenorphine | 0.3 | 0.2–1.2 | 2–3 | 30 | — | 6–8 | Available in many countries as a sublingual tablet, which appears useful in treatment of cancer pain. Ceiling in analgesic effect at dose near 5 mg/day. Should not be used with a pure opioid agonist. |
| Butorphanol | 22 | — | 2.5–3.5 | — | — | 3–6 | Oral form unavailable in many countries. Value in treatment of chronic pain not established. |
| Nalbuphine | 10 | 40 | 4–6 | 20 | — | 3–6 | Oral form unavailable in many countries. Value in treatment of chronic pain not established. |

*Note.* Data presented are estimates obtained from the literature. MEC = minimum effective analgesic concentration; — = not available.
*Source.* Adapted from Gourlay et al. 1987b.

relief of 6–8 hours is observed after large doses (400 mg) of rectal meperidine, but a significant latency of 2–3 hours after administration can be seen. Rectal oxycodone has also been shown to have clinical utility, providing pain relief for up to 8 hours.

## Intramuscular Administration

The most commonly used approach to managing postoperative pain is intramuscular administration of morphine or meperidine. The typical prescription would read, "Morphine 10 mg (or meperidine 100 mg) intramuscularly every 3–4 hours as needed for pain." This approach has been shown to provide inadequate analgesia for many reasons: the patient may not request medication despite experiencing severe pain, the nurse may not administer the medication, the dose may not be adequate for the patient's needs. Even controlling all these potential problems, the variable blood levels seen after intramuscular dosing usually results in periods of pain alternating with periods of toxicity (Austin et al. 1980).

## Subcutaneous Administration

Subcutaneous administration of opioids has been used for decades to provide analgesia. More recent attention has been focused on this technique with the availability of small infusion pumps for delivering continuous opioids

to ambulatory patients. Recent applications include subcutaneous infusion for cancer pain and subcutaneous patient-controlled analgesia (PCA). Bruera et al. (1988b) presented data confirming the efficacy of subcutaneous infusion in treating patients with severe pain due to malignancy, both at home and in the hospital. The pharmacokinetic information available for subcutaneous administration of opioids is extremely limited. Continuous infusion of subcutaneous morphine has been demonstrated to provide analgesia and blood levels equivalent to those of intravenous infusion in postoperative patients (Waldeman et al. 1984). Other drugs have been delivered by this route, but no definitive information is available on blood levels achieved. Subcutaneous infusion appears to act clinically like a continuous infusion, but more carefully controlled trials need to be carried out to determine whether this similarity is true for all opioids.

## Intravenous Administration

The use of intravenous opioids, by intermittent injection as well as continuous infusion, has been known for years to provide more rapid and effective analgesia. The clinical utility of this technique in the management of cancer pain was reviewed by the Sloan-Kettering Group (Portenoy et al. 1986). The pharmacokinetic support for this clinical observation has been developed over the last several years. Intravenous administration of opioids can maintain analgesia as long as the blood opioid concentration is kept above the MEC in a given patient. Knowledge of the systemic clearance of a drug allows close approximation of the MEC value for a specific opioid to be delivered via continuous infusion. Using infusion alone, however, requires approximately four times the terminal half-life to achieve stable concentrations. The clinical use of continuous-infusion opioids is best simplified by providing a loading dose followed by a continuous infusion. The amount of the loading dose and the initial infusion can be predicted if the MEC, volume of distribution ($V_d$), and clearance (Cl) are known. The practical steps in calculating such an analgesic infusion are

1. Loading dose = $V_d \times$ MEC
2. Maintenance infusion = Cl $\times$ MEC

Providing the loading dose as an infusion over 10–15 minutes (followed by the maintenance rate) will allow good analgesia to be rapidly established with a minimum of toxicity. Subsequently, the maintenance infusion rate should be adjusted to patient comfort.

## Patient-Controlled Analgesia

The wide interpatient variability of the pharmacokinetic parameters discussed thus far is a primary reason that individual titration of opioid dosing is required in order to achieve adequate analgesia. Although the physician can do this by evaluating patients at a given time after the therapy has been initiated, the option of PCA is well suited to accommodating the differences between the theory and practice of pain relief. Using PCA, the physician decides the drug to be employed and the dose to be given. The patient can decide when a dose should be administered and the timing between doses.

Although there are several variants of PCA, the most commonly employed is a bolus demand form. With this type of PCA, the physician prescribes the drug on the basis of his or her personal preferences. The usual practice is to prescribe a bolus dose range that can be adjusted if toxicity or inadequate analgesia develops from a single demand. In addition, the minimum time between doses is also prescribed by the physician; this practice avoids potential toxicity from repeated demands being provided before the peak effect of each bolus has been seen.

The majority of pharmacokinetic information that has been applied to PCA has been inferred from the single-dose or continuous infusion of opioids. The applicability of this information to the multiple-dose system of PCA has yet to be investigated. Despite this theoretical uncertainty, the clinical practice of PCA is successful. Several investigators have reported higher patient satisfaction and lower pain scores with therapy, compared with other forms of parenteral opioid analgesia in acute pain management. The efficacy of short-term subcutaneous PCA was also demonstrated in cancer pain management (Bruera et al. 1988a).

## Spinal Administration

The use of spinal opioids for acute pain management dates back only into the last decade. Compared with all the delivery systems discussed above, which use indirect delivery of the opioid to the receptor site via the systemic circulation, spinal delivery is a system in which the opioids are delivered directly to the receptors in the spinal cord via local mechanisms. The presence of opioid receptors in the dorsal horn of the spinal cord was suggested by Calvillo et al. (1974). The localization of high concentrations of opioid receptors in the substantia gelatinosa followed (Atweh and Kuhar 1977). Behavioral analgesia from intrathecal administration of morphine in rats was reported by Yaksh and Rudy (1976). Large numbers of clinical reports of long-lasting analgesia obtained with spinal opioids followed, but these were also accompanied by frequent reports of side effects. These side effects included nausea, vomiting, sedation, pruritus, urinary retention, and respiratory depression. Fortunately, the identification of these side effects tempered the rampant application of this technique. Meanwhile, fundamental knowledge about the use of spinal opioids was obtained through extensive animal studies (Yaksh 1981; Yaksh and Noueihed 1985).

The term spinal opioid as applied in this section is used to describe intrathecal, epidural, and intracerebroventricular administration of opioids. In an effort to present some of the data concerning spinal opioids, the remainder of this section deals with the epidural opioids, except where specifically stated.

The pharmacokinetics of epidurally administered morphine applied in the lumbar epidural space are still incompletely studied. It appears that after epidural injection of morphine, only low concentrations of lipid-soluble, un-ionized drug are present in the epidural space. Movement of the drug into the cerebrospinal fluid (CSF) by diffusion across the dura mater and transfer across the arachnoid granulation, as well as vascular uptake by spinal arteries and the epidural venous system, all regulate the distribution of epidural morphine (Figure 11–10). Because only small concentrations of the morphine present in the CSF are un-ionized, the transfer across the spinal cord to the dorsal horn receptors is slow. Morphine is also available to move upward with the flow of CSF

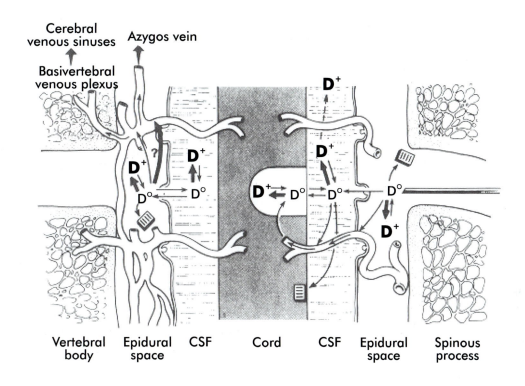

Cerebral venous sinuses  Azygos vein

Basivertebral venous plexus

D⁺

D⁺

D⁺

D⁺    D°

D⁺ ⇌ D°    D°    D°

D⁺

Vertebral body  Epidural space  CSF  Cord  CSF  Epidural space  Spinous process

**FIGURE 11–10.** Pharmacokinetics model of an epidural injection of a hydrophilic opioid such as morphine. An epidural needle is shown delivering drug to the epidural space. The role of absorption by way of the radicular arteries remains speculative. The *shaded squares* represent nonspecific binding sites.

*Note.* $D^{\circ}$ = un-ionized, lipophilic drug; $D^{+}$ = ionized hydrophilic drug; CSF = cerebrospinal fluid.

*Source.* Reprinted from Cousins MJ, Bridenbaugh PO (eds.): *Neural Blockade in Clinical Anesthesia and Management of Pain,* 2nd Edition. Philadelphia, PA, JB Lippincott, 1988, p. 987. Used with permission.

toward the brain. This explanation of epidural morphine distribution correlates well with the delayed onset of analgesia and the late respiratory depression seen.

Much of the existing concern about the use of spinal opioids has focused on concern for respiratory depression. This can be early (associated with the peak blood levels after epidural administration) or late (perhaps due to the rostral migration of morphine into sensitive respiratory centers). Outcome studies (Rawal et al. 1987) generated from large groups of patients in Sweden who received spinal opioids indicate that the incidence of severe delayed respiratory depression after epidural morphine administration is approximately 1/1,000 patients. Although certain demographic characteristics of at-risk populations have been identified, the inability to predict the occurrence of delayed respiratory depression in healthy patients points out the need for increased surveillance of all patients who are receiving opioid analgesia.

The spinal administration of opioids is appropriate for pain in virtually any region of the body. Spinally administered morphine has been shown to migrate over the entire distance of the spinal cord, even when injected in the lumbar epidural space (Gourlay et al. 1985,

1987a). Pain relief from such spinal opioid systems has been demonstrated for pain in cervical dermatomes and even in the trigeminal system.

Continued efforts to refine and evaluate spinal opioids should help to determine the appropriate use of this therapy. The high quality of analgesia and the tremendous reports of patient satisfaction seen after epidural morphine analgesia provide ample support for research in this field.

As mentioned above, multiple endogenous chemicals, which are thought to modulate nociceptive processing, have been identified in the region of the dorsal horn of the spinal cord. The clinical success of opioids in providing selective spinal analgesia has prompted the evaluation of analgesic agents other than morphine. Clonidine has recently been approved by the U.S. Food and Drug Administration for intraspinal administration. This adrenergic agonist appears to have selective benefits for certain patients, particularly when coadministered with opioids. Baclofen is the third of the intraspinal medications available for use. Although the approval for baclofen is uniquely related to the spinal injury muscle spasm, this medication is receiving widespread use as an adjunct in intraspinal medication trials. As further research and development of intraspinal medications is encouraged, the release of newer agents—including the selective *N*-type calcium channel blocker ziconotide—is likely. These medications, used alone or in combination with opioids, will provide new therapeutic alternatives for those experiencing chronic pain.

## Electrical Stimulation

### Transcutaneous Electrical Nerve Stimulation

The origin of TENS in Western medical society dates back to Roman times, when the use of electric fish was ascribed analgesic properties. Publication of the gate theory of pain by Melzack and Wall (1965) renewed interest in electrical stimulation to produce analgesia. The excitation of large-fiber peripheral afferents by electrical stimulation at the periphery has been successful in treating nociceptive pain. TENS is a low-intensity stimulation, stimulating skin and muscle afferents in a specific segmental distribution. Numerous studies have documented the efficacy of TENS in certain pathological pain states. In addition, when used as an adjunct for postoperative analgesia, TENS has been shown to decrease the amount of opioid analgesia required.

### Acupuncture

Classical acupuncture differs from modern concepts of acupuncture analgesia in that the techniques for the former evolved initially for the management of disease. Acupuncture analgesia uses stimulation of designated body sites by manual rotation of needles to produce a sensation known as *chi*. The stimulation provided in classical acupuncture has been modernized more recently by the application of low-frequency (<5 Hz) stimulation of the needles, which also produces powerful muscle contractions. Acupuncture produces a high-intensity stimulation that is believed to induce a chemical modulation of pain, which explains why the relief is not confined to a local segmental distribution.

### Dorsal Column Stimulation

Many patients with deafferentation pain are candidates for dorsal column stimulation. This technique uses percutaneously positioned electrical leads that deliver a high-frequency current over the dorsal spinal cord in an effort to stimulate descending analgesic pathways. Effective electrical stimulation suggests that implantation of a self-contained battery-powered device may be efficacious in selected patients. There have been no prospective trials of this therapy in the management of neuropathic terminal cancer pain, but the responses achieved with other deafferentation pain syndromes point to possible efficacy in this difficult problem.

## Neural Blockade

Patients who exhaust the analgesics or who develop toxicity problems from other medications may benefit from techniques of neurolytic blockade. The most common approach is to proceed from the least invasive to the more invasive techniques, as required for pain management. In one major study (Ventafridda et al. 1987) undertaken in a comprehensive cancer care center, only 20% of patients required treatment with neurolytic blocks or other neurodestructive techniques. The continued advancement of spinal opioid techniques, as well as the success of continuous subcutaneous opioid infusions, will probably continue to decrease the need for neurodestructive techniques. In cancer pain, local anesthetics may be used for diagnostic, prognostic, and therapeutic blocks.

Diagnostic blocks are used to localize the pain pathway and to pharmacologically differentiate the fiber type involved in mediating the pain. It is difficult to be certain that only a specific fiber type will be blocked by using differing concentrations of local anesthetics. Therefore, many pain clinicians prefer to use blockade at sites where the fibers are anatomically separated (e.g., lumbar sympathetic block and individual somatic nerve blocks). The interpretation of diagnostic neural blockade is both difficult and crucial to the appropriate use of these techniques. This interpretation is discussed in detail by Boas and Cousins (1988).

Prognostic blockades should always be carried out at least twice before neurolytic or surgical ablation. This permits confirmation that the pain is relieved and also gives the patient an opportunity to decide whether any side effects are acceptable.

Therapeutic blocks with local anesthetic cannot be expected to relieve pain permanently. However, pain may be due to muscle spasms, postoperative neuralgia, denervation phenomena, or neuroma formation. In some of these cases, a series of long-acting local anesthetic blocks will produce long-lasting or permanent pain relief.

## Neurodestructive Procedures

Continued progress in pain management with multidisciplinary therapies has decreased the use of neurodestructive procedures. Despite the continued success of less invasive and nondestructive techniques, however, neurolytic blockade still provides valuable adjunctive treatment of nociceptive and neuropathic pain in terminal cancer (Cousins 1988). Often, a properly performed neurodestructive procedure can markedly decrease medication use and control the unwanted side effects associated with high doses of analgesics. Virtually all neurodestructive techniques should be confined to the treatment of nociceptive pain. Not only are the CNS and peripheral changes associated with neuropathic pain never relieved by neurodestructive techniques; they are often aggravated by such procedures. Neurolytic blocks are mainly indicated for localized unilateral pain, except for pituitary ablation, which is suitable for diffuse areas of pain.

## Hypnosis

Central psychological approaches to pain control can also be effective and are underused (Holroyd 1996). It has been known since the middle of the 1800s that hypnosis is effective in controlling even severe surgical pain (Esdaile 1846/1957). Hypnosis and similar techniques work through two primary mechanisms: peripheral muscle relaxation and a central combination of perceptual alteration and cognitive distraction. Pain is not infrequently accompanied by reactive muscle tension. Patients frequently splint the part of their body that hurts. Yet, because muscle tension can by itself cause pain in normal tissue and because traction on a painful part of the body can produce more pain, techniques that induce greater physical relaxation can reduce pain in the periphery. Therefore, having patients enter a state of hypnosis so they can concentrate on an image connoting physical relaxation such as floating or lightness often produces physical relaxation and reduces pain.

The second major component of hypnotic analgesia is perceptual alteration. Patients can be taught to imagine that the affected body part is numb. This is especially useful for extremely hypnotizable individuals who can, for example, relive an experience of dental anesthesia and reproduce the drug-induced sensations of numbness in their cheek, which they can then transfer to the painful part of their body. They can also simply switch off perception of the pain with surprising effectiveness (Hargadon et al. 1995; Miller and Bowers 1993). Temperature

metaphors are often especially useful, which is not surprising, given the fact that pain and temperature sensations are part of the same sensory system, as noted above. Thus, imagining that an affected body part is cooler or warmer (through an image of dipping it in ice water or heating it in the sun) can often help transform pain signals. Some patients prefer to imagine that the pain is a substance with dimensions that can be moved or that it can flow out of the body as if it were a viscous liquid. Others like to imagine that they can step outside their body—to, for example, visit another room in the house. Less hypnotizable individuals often do better with distraction techniques that help them focus on competing sensations in another part of the body.

Hypnotic techniques can easily be taught to patients for self-administration (D. Spiegel 1994). Pain patients can be taught to enter a state of self-hypnosis in a matter of seconds with some simple induction strategies such as looking up while slowly closing their eyes; taking a deep breath and then letting the breath out; relaxing the eyes; imagining the body floating; and letting one hand float up in the air like a balloon. The patients are then instructed in the pain control exercise and are taught to bring themselves out by reversing the induction procedure, again looking up, letting the eyes open, and letting the raised hand float back down. Patients can use this exercise every 1–2 hours initially and anytime they experience an attack of pain. Patients can then evaluate their effectiveness in conducting the pain control exercise by rating on a scale from 0 to 10 the intensity of their pain before and after the self-hypnosis session. As with any pain treatment technique, hypnosis is more effective when employed early in the pain cycle, before the pain has become so overwhelming it impairs concentration. Patients should be encouraged to use this technique early and often because it is simple and effective (D. Spiegel and Bloom 1983a) and has no side effects (D. Spiegel 1986). Indeed, it has been shown, in a randomized trial in interventional radiology, to produce better analgesia than that resulting from PCA with midazolam and fentanyl, with less anxiety, fewer side effects, and fewer procedural interruptions (Lang and Hamilton 1994; Lang et al. 1996). A large randomized trial demonstrated that patients taught self-hypnosis used half as much patient-controlled analgesic medication and had less pain and anxiety and fewer episodes of autonomic instability. In addition, the technique resulted in shortening procedure time by 18 minutes (Lang et al. 2000). Thus, hypnosis was not only an effective analgesic, but it resulted in fewer procedural complications and was cost-effective as well.

Although not all patients are sufficiently hypnotizable to benefit from these techniques, two out of three adults are at least somewhat hypnotizable (H. Spiegel and Spiegel 1987), and it has been estimated that hypnotic capacity is correlated at a level of 0.5 with effectiveness in medical pain reduction (E.R. Hilgard and Hilgard 1975). Highly hypnotizable individuals can use hypnosis as analgesia for surgery (Levitan and Harbaugh 1992), but clinically effective hypnotic analgesia is not confined to those with high hypnotizability (Holroyd 1996).

Hypnosis is especially effective in comforting children who are in pain (Kuttner et al. 1988). Several good studies have shown greater efficacy than placebo attention control (Ellis and Spanos 1994; J.R. Hilgard and LeBaron 1982; Kellerman et al. 1983; Zeltzer and LeBaron 1982). This is probably due to the fact that children as a group are more hypnotizable than adults (Morgan and Hilgard 1973). Their imaginative capacities are so intense that separate relaxation exercises are not necessary. Children naturally relax when they mobilize their imagination during the sensory alteration component of hypnotic analgesia (Niven 1996).

Other research indicates cortical effects of hypnotic alteration of perceptions, including reduced event-related potential (ERP) amplitude in response to somatosensory (D. Spiegel et al. 1989) and visual (Jasiukaitis et al. 1996) stimuli, and increased frontal and parietal blood flow (Crawford et al. 1993). Positron emission tomography (PET) studies have demonstrated activation of the anterior cingulate gyrus during hypnotic analgesia (Faymonville et al. 2000; Rainville et al. 1997), and there is also PET evidence of alteration in activation of primary sensory cortex in the visual system (color vision) in response to hypnotic modulation of perception (Kosslyn et al. 2000). Thus, hypnotic alteration of nociception seems to involve cortical modulation of attentional processes and pain perception.

## Secondary Gain

Secondary gain is a major problem with chronic pain. The term refers to the secondary reinforcements that accompany a primary loss involving physical function, ability to work, ability to engage in sexual activity, or other concomitants of injury and illness. A pain syndrome can set off a downward social spiral in which a patient loses the ordinary reinforcement that comes from contact with colleagues at work and the self-esteem that comes from being productive. Increasing depression can result in a loss of energy and an inability to interact rewardingly with others, leading to social withdrawal. Social contact becomes increasingly organized around pain complaints. Patients who seem to lose the ability to elicit enjoyable and rewarding social interactions increasingly coerce attention from health care providers, family members, and friends over their disabilities, a process that contributes part of the secondary gain. Additional secondary gain may come in the form of being able to avoid unwanted responsibilities, such as the pressures of work, or unwelcome aspects of social interaction, such as sexual activity.

Another major form of secondary gain is financial reinforcement. Disability systems frequently intensify this form of secondary gain by creating an adversarial system in which any evidence of the patient's ability to return to normal function endangers financial support—a system that in essence requires complete disability. Thus, disability systems designed to provide a reasonable level of financial support for persons who have physical and psychiatric illness have become rather rigid and end up providing financial reinforcement for continued disability. In such an adversarial system, efforts at rehabilitation are used as evidence that there was never any serious disability in the first place. Furthermore, attaining disability status is often a protracted and unpleasant process. During a consolidation phase after an acute injury when patients might be able to return to some level of functioning despite continuing symptoms, they are instead engaged in a battle to prove the extent of their disability. Any improvement results in the reduction or elimination of disability payment.

Many patients are victims of this system. Others manipulate it, exaggerating their disability to obtain financial benefits, further reinforcing the system's adversarial nature. On the other hand, many more patients are accused of such exaggeration than actually commit it—in part because it is extremely difficult to communicate pain complaints in a rational and believable manner to others. Pain, after all, is not directly observable. It can only be interpreted through the reports, both verbal and nonverbal, of the patient. In their own desire to control their pain, patients tend to either overmodulate or undermodulate it. At times they seem perfectly composed and comfortable when in fact they are suffering; at other times they appear histrionic and disruptive and apparently exaggerating the extent of their discomfort.

Secondary-gain factors, both social and financial, substantially complicate treatment, and it is best to do everything possible to minimize them. Useful social strategies include the behavior therapy principle of requesting health care personnel and family members to provide attention and positive reinforcement for non-pain-related behaviors (Fordyce et al. 1973) while diminishing reinforcement for pain-related interactions. For example, a nurse would be encouraged to walk up to a patient and say, "How nice to see you walking around," and to engage him or her in other conversation when the patient does in fact walk, but to minimize social contact when responding to a demand for more pain medication.

Many chronic pain patients seek multiple surgeries and other procedures in a vain hope of returning themselves to a pre-injury, pain-free state. It is often important to help them change their goals from this all-or-none type of thinking to a more realistic goal of substantial pain reduction and improved function. This often involves helping them to accept the damage done to their lives by the injury or illness and to think more in terms of rehabilitation than restitution.

Interactions with the legal system can be handled by advising patients to discuss with their attorney the ways to obtain the largest lump-sum settlement possible as quickly as possible to prevent losing years in an emotionally and physically depleting struggle to prove how damaged they really are. Direct contact with attorneys (after a patient's permission has been obtained) is also a good way to reinforce the urgency of settling the complaint before the situation deteriorates further.

## Conclusions

As we continue to enrich the knowledge base from which we understand the causes, transmission, and processing of pain signals, we can make pain treatment more comprehensive, humane, and effective. There are multiple levels at which the pain problem can be approached, including

- Removing the cause of the pain at the periphery
- Reducing muscle tension that exacerbates pain input
- Blocking pain transmission through competitive electrical stimulation or acupuncture
- Administering drugs through infusions into the CNS
- Administering drugs that block pain transmission or perception or the disorders of mood that accompany and exacerbate it
- Using important cognitive interventions such as hypnosis that can help reduce patients' focus on pain and ameliorate their reaction to it
- Treating comorbid depression and anxiety with antidepressant and other psychoactive medication and appropriate psychotherapy

In addition, there are interventions that can reduce the social reinforcement of pain perception and behavior. The old dichotomy between peripheral and central pain

is being replaced by a more complex and comprehensive analysis that evaluates the central and the peripheral components of pain and that designs interventions taking advantage of therapeutic opportunities at all levels of pain perception processing. This point of view is important because it underscores the fact that successful psychosocial interventions for reducing pain may occur via understandable neurological mechanisms and do not prove that the pain is largely functional. In the same way, successful pharmacological intervention does not prove that the pain is completely peripheral in origin. Most pain syndromes are a combination of physical and neuropsychiatric distress and dysfunction and require a combination of biological and psychosocial intervention to be optimally effective. The strain in pain lies mainly in the brain.

## References

Ahles TA, Blanchard EB, Ruckdeschel JC: Multidimensional nature of cancer-related pain. Pain 17:277–288, 1983

Astin JA: Why patients use alternative medicine: results of a national study. JAMA 279(19):1548–1552, 1998

Atkison JH, Kremer EF, Garfin SR: Current concepts review: psychopharmacologic agents in the treatment of pain. J Bone Joint Surg Am 67:337–339, 1985

Atweh SF, Kuhar MJ: Autoradiographic localization of opiate receptors in rat brain, I: spinal cord and lower medulla. Brain Res 124:53–67, 1977

Austin KL, Stapleton JV, Mather LE: Multiple intramuscular injections: a major source of variability in analgesic response to pethidine. Pain 8:4–19, 1980

Basbaum AI: Functional analysis of the cytochemistry of the spinal dorsal horn, in Advances in Pain Research and Therapy, Vol 9. Edited by Fields HL, Dubner R, Cervero F. New York, Raven, 1985, pp 149–171

Basbaum AI, Fields HL: Endogenous pain control mechanisms: review and hypothesis. Ann Neurol 4:451–462, 1978

Beaver WT, Feise G: Comparison of the analgesic effects of morphine, hydroxyzine, and their combination in patients with postoperative pain, in Advances in Pain Research and Therapy, Vol 1. Edited by Bonica JJ, Albe-Fessard DG. New York, Raven, 1976, pp 553–565

Beaver WT, Wallenstein SL, Houde RW, et al: A comparison of the analgesic effects of methotrimeprazine and morphine in patients with cancer. Clin Pharmacol Ther 7:436–446, 1966

Beecher HK: Relationship of significance of wound to pain experienced. JAMA 161:1609–1616, 1956

Berkley KJ, Palmer R: Somatosensory cortical involvement in response to noxious stimulation in the cat. Exp Brain Res 20:363–374, 1974

Besson JM, Chaouch A: Peripheral and spinal mechanisms of nociception. Physiol Rev 67:67–186, 1987

Blumer D, Heilbronn M: Chronic pains as a variant of depressive disease: the pain prone disorder. J Nerv Ment Dis 170:381–406, 1982

Boas RA, Cousins MJ: Diagnostic neural blockade, in Neural Blockade in Clinical Anesthesia, 2nd Edition. Edited by Cousins MJ, Bridenbaugh PO. Philadelphia, PA, JB Lippincott, 1988, p 885

Bond MR: Personality studies in patients with pain secondary to organic disease. J Psychosom Res 17:257–263, 1973

Bond MR, Pearson IB: Psychological aspects of pain in women with advanced cancer of the cervix. J Psychosom Res 13:13–19, 1969

Bonica JJ: Evolution and current status of pain programs. J Pain Symptom Manage 5:368–374, 1990

Bonica JJ, Ventafridda V: Advances in Pain Research and Therapy: International Symposium on Pain of Advanced Cancer. New York, Raven, 1979

Boyer WF: Potential indications for the selective serotonin reuptake inhibitors. Int Clin Psychopharmacol 6 (suppl 5):5–12, 1992

Brose WG, Cousins MJ: Gynecologic pain, in Gynecologic Oncology. Edited by Coppelson M, Monaghan JM, Morrow CP, et al. Edinburgh, UK, Churchill Livingstone 1992, pp 1439–1479

Bruera E, Brenneis C, Michaud M, et al: Patient controlled subcutaneous hydromorphone versus continuous subcutaneous infusion for the treatment of cancer pain. J Natl Cancer Inst 80:1152–1154, 1988a

Bruera E, Brenneis C, Michaud M, et al: Use of subcutaneous route for the administration of narcotics in patients with cancer pain. Cancer 62:407–411, 1988b

Calvillo O, Henry JL, Newman RS: Effects of morphine and naloxone on dorsal horn neurons in the cat. Can J Physiol Pharmacol 52:1207–1211, 1974

Cousins MJ: Chronic pain and neurolytic blockade, in Neural Blockade in Clinical Anesthesia and Management of Pain, 2nd Edition. Edited by Cousins MJ, Bridenbaugh PO. Philadelphia, PA, JB Lippincott, 1988, pp 1053–1084

Cousins MJ, Bridenbaugh PO (eds): Neural Blockade in Clinical Anesthesia and Management of Pain, 2nd Edition. Philadelphia, PA, JB Lippincott, 1988

Cousins MJ, Phillips GD (eds): Acute Pain Management. London, Churchill Livingstone, 1986

Craig AD, Reiman EM, Evans A, et al: Functional brain imaging of an illusion of pain. Nature 384:120–126, 1996

Crawford HJ, Gur RC, Skolnick B, et al: Effects of hypnosis on regional cerebral blood flow during ischemic pain with and without suggested hypnotic analgesia. Int J Psychophysiol 3:181–195, 1993

Crile GW: Phylogenetic association in relation to certain medical problems. Boston Medical and Surgical Journal 163:893, 1910

Cushing H: On the avoidance of shock in major amputations by cocainization of large nerve-trunks preliminary to their division. Ann Surg 36:321–345, 1902

Dejard A, Peterson P, Kestrup J: Mexiletine for the treatment of chronic painful diabetic neuropathy. Lancet 1:9–11, 1988

Derogatis LR, Morrow GR, Fetting J, et al: The prevalence of psychiatric disorders among cancer patients. JAMA 249:751–757, 1983

Dubner R: Specialization of nociceptive pathways: sensory discrimination, sensory modulation, and neural connectivity, in Advances in Pain Research and Therapy, Vol 9. Edited by Fields HL, Dubner R, Cervero F. New York, Raven, 1985, pp 111–117

Dundee JW, Love WJ, Moore J: Alterations in response to somatic pain associated with anesthesia, XV: further studies with phenothiazine derivatives and similar drugs. Br J Anaesth 35:597–610, 1963

Dworkin SF, Von Koroff M, LeResche L: Multiple pains and psychiatric disturbance: an epidemiologic investigation. Arch Gen Psychiatry 47:239–244, 1990

Eisenberg DM, Davis RB, Ettner SL et al: Trends in alternative medicine use in the United States, 1990–1997: results of a follow-up national survey. JAMA 280:1569–1575, 1998

Ellis JA, Spanos NP: Cognitive-behavioral interventions for children's distress bone marrow aspirations and lumbar punctures: a critical review. J Pain Symptom Manage 9:96–108, 1994

Esdaile J: Hypnosis in Medicine and Surgery (1846). New York, Julian Press, 1957

Eysenck HJ, Eysenck BG: Manual of the Eysenck Personality Inventory. London, University of London Press, 1964

Faymonville ME, Laureys S, Degueldre C, et al: Neural mechanisms of antinociceptive effects of hypnosis. Anesthesiology 92:1257–1267, 2000

Fields HL: Pain. New York, McGraw-Hill, 1987

Fields HL, Basbaum AI: Endogenous pain control mechanisms, in Textbook of Pain. Edited by Wall PD, Melzack R. Edinburgh, UK, Churchill-Livingstone, 1984, pp 142–153

Finley PR: Selective serotonin reuptake inhibitors: pharmacologic profiles and potential therapeutic distinctions. Annals of Pharmacology 12:1359–1369, 1994

Fordyce WE, Fowler RS, Lehmann JR, et al: Operant conditioning in the treatment of chronic pain. Arch Phys Med Rehabil 54:399–408, 1973

Forrest WH, Brown BW, Brown CR, et al: Dextroamphetamine with morphine for the treatment of postoperative pain. N Engl J Med 296:712–715, 1977

Gamse R, Holzer P, Lembeck F: Decrease of substance P in primary afferent neurones and impairment of neurogenic plasma extravasation by capsaicin. Br J Pharmacol 68:207–213, 1980

Gourlay GK, Cherry DA, Cousins MJ: Cephalad migration of morphine in CSF following lumbar epidural administration in patients with cancer pain. Pain 23:317–326, 1985

Gourlay GK, Cherry DA, Plummer JL, et al: The influence of drug polarity on the absorption of opioid drugs into the CSF and subsequent cephalad migration following lumbar epidural administration: application to morphine and pethidine. Pain 31:297–305, 1987a

Gourlay GK, Cousins MJ, Cherry DA: Drug therapy, in Handbook of Chronic Pain Management. Edited by Burrows GD, Elton D, Stanley GV. Amsterdam, The Netherlands, Elsevier, 1987b, pp 20–24

Hagbarth KE, Kerr DIB: Central influences on spinal afferent conduction. J Neurophysiol 17:295–300, 1954

Hargadon R, Bowers KS, Woody EZ: Does counterpain imagery mediate hypnotic analgesia? J Abnorm Psychol 104:508–516, 1995

Hilgard ER, Hilgard JR: Hypnosis in the Relief of Pain. Los Altos, CA, William Kaufmann, 1975

Hilgard JR, LeBaron S: Relief of anxiety and pain in children and adolescents with cancer: quantitative measures and clinical observations. Int J Clin Exp Hypn 4:417–442, 1982

Holroyd J: Hypnosis treatment of clinical pain: understanding why hypnosis is useful. Int J Clin Exp Hypn 441:33–151, 1996

Jasiukaitis P, Nouriani B, Spiegel D: Left hemisphere superiority for event-related potential effects of hypnotic obstruction. Neuropsychologia 34:661–668, 1996

Juan H: Prostaglandins as modulators of pain. Journal of General Pharmacology 9:403–409, 1978

Katon W, Egan K, Miller D: Chronic pain: lifetime psychiatric diagnosis and family history. Am J Psychiatry 142:1156–1160, 1985

Kehlet H: Modification of responses to surgery by neural blockade: clinical implications, in Neural Blockade in Clinical Anesthesia and Management of Pain, 2nd Edition. Edited by Cousins MJ, Bridenbaugh PO. Philadelphia, PA, JB Lippincott, 1988, pp 145–188

Kellerman J, Zeltzer L, Ellenberg L, et al: Adolescents with cancer: hypnosis for the reduction of the acute pain and anxiety associated with medical procedures. J Adolesc Health Care 4:35–90, 1983

Kishore-Kumar R, Max MB, Schafer SC, et al: Desipramine relieves postherpetic neuralgia. Clin Pharmacol Ther 47:305–312, 1990

Kosslyn SM, Thompson WL, Costantini-Ferrando MF, et al: Hypnotic visual illusion alters color processing in the brain. Am J Psychiatry 157(8):1279–1284, 2000

Kuhn CC, Bradnan WA: Pain as a substitute for fear of death. Psychosomatics 20:494–495, 1979

Kuttner L, Bowman M, Teasdale M: Psychological treatment of distress, pain, and anxiety for young children with cancer. J Dev Behav Pediatr 9(6):374–381, 1988

Kwan CL, Crawley AP, Mikulis DJ, et al: An fMRI study of the anterior cingulate cortex and surrounding medial wall activations evoked by noxious cutaneous heat and cold stimuli. Pain 85:359–374, 2000

Lang EV, Hamilton D: Anodyne imagery: an alternative to iv sedation in interventional radiology. AJR Am J Roentgenol 162:1221–1226, 1994

Lang EV, Joyce JS, Spiegel D, et al: Self-hypnotic relaxation during interventional radiological procedures: effects on pain perception and intravenous drug use. Int J Clin Exp Hypn 44:106–119, 1996

Lang EV, Benotsch EG, Fick LJ, et al: Adjunctive non-pharmacological analgesia for invasive medical procedures: a randomised trial. Lancet 355:1486–1490, 2000

Lansky SB, List MA, Herrmann CA, et al: Absence of major depressive disorder in female cancer patients. J Clin Oncol 3:1553–1560, 1985

Levine JD, Dardick SJ, Basbaum AI, et al: Reflex neurogenic inflammation, I: contribution of the peripheral nervous system to spatially remote inflammatory responses that follow injury. J Neurosci 5:1380–1386, 1985

Levitan AA, Harbaugh TE: Hypnotizability and hypnoanalgesia: hypnotizability of patients using hypnoanalgesia during surgery. Am J Clin Hypn 34:223–226, 1992

Lindstrom P, Lindblom U: The analgesic effect of tocainide in trigeminal neuralgia. Pain 28:45–50, 1987

Massie MJ, Holland JC: The cancer patient with pain: psychiatric complications and their management. Cancer Pain 71:243–258, 1987

Mather LE, Gourlay GK: The biotransformation of opioids, in Opioid Agonist/Antagonist Drugs in Clinical Practice. Edited by Nimmo WS, Smith G. Amsterdam, The Netherlands, Excerpta Medica, 1984, pp 120–133

Melzack R: Recent concepts of pain. J Med 13:147–160, 1982

Melzack R: From the gate to the neuromatrix. Pain (suppl 6): S121–S126, 1999

Melzack R, Wall PD: Pain mechanisms: a new theory. Science 150:971–979, 1965

Miller ME, Bowers KS: Hypnotic analgesia: dissociated experience or dissociated control? J Abnorm Psychol 102:29–39, 1993

Moore J, Dundee JW: Alterations in response to somatic pain associated with anesthesia, V: the effect of promethazine. Br J Anaesth 33:3–8, 1961a

Moore J, Dundee JW: Alterations in response to somatic pain associated with anesthesia, VII: the effects of nine phenothiazine derivatives. Br J Anaesth 33:422–431, 1961b

Morgan AH, Hilgard ER: Age differences in susceptibility to hypnosis. Int J Clin Exp Hypn 21:78–85, 1973

Müller J: Von den Ergentumlichkeiten der ein zelnen Nerve, in Handbuch der Physiologie der Menschen. Edited by Kobling L. Coblenz, Germany, Holscher, 1844

Niven N: Theoretical concepts and practical applications of hypnosis in the treatment of children and adolescents with dental fear and anxiety. Br Dent J 180:11–16, 1996

Pert CB, Snyder SH: Opiate receptors: demonstration in nervous tissue. Science 179:1011–1014, 1973

Peteet J, Tay V, Cohen G, et al: Pain characteristics and treatment in an outpatient cancer population. Cancer 57:1259–1265, 1986

Pilowski I, Chapman CR, Bonica JJ: Pain, depression and illness behavior in a pain clinic population. Pain 4:183–192, 1977

Portenoy RK, Moulin DE, Rodgers A, et al: IV infusion of opioids for cancer pain: clinical review and guidelines for use. Cancer Treat Rev 70:575–580, 1986

Posner MI, Petersen SE: The attention system of the human brain. Annu Rev Neurosci 13:125–142, 1990

Price DD: Psychological and neural mechanisms of the affective dimension of pain. Science 288:1769–1772, 2000

Rainville P, Duncan GH, Price DD, et al: Pain affect encoded in human anterior cingulate but not somatosensory cortex. Science 277:968–971, 1997

Raja SN, Meyer RA, Campbell JN: Peripheral mechanisms of somatic pain. Anesthesiology 68:571–590, 1988

Rawal N, Arner S, Gustaffson LL, et al: Present state of extradural and intrathecal opioid analgesia in Sweden: a nationwide follow-up survey. Br J Anaesth 59:791–799, 1987

Reich J, Tupin JP, Abramowitz SI: Psychiatric diagnosis of chronic pain patients. Am J Psychiatry 140:1495–1498, 1983

Rexed B: Cytoarchitectonic organization of the spinal cord in the cat. J Comp Neurol 96:415–495, 1952

Reynolds DV: Surgery in the rat during electrical analgesia induced by focal brain stimulation. Science 164:444–445, 1969

Ripamonti C, Bruera E: Rectal, buccal and sublingual narcotics for the management of cancer pain. J Palliat Care 7:30–35, 1991

Sawynok J, Labella L: GABA and baclofen potentiate the $K^+$-evoked release of methionine-enkephalin from rat striatal slices. Eur J Pharmacol 70:103–110, 1981

Spiegel D: Oncological and pain syndromes, in Psychiatry Update: The American Psychiatric Association Annual Review, Vol 5. Edited by Frances AJ, Hales RE. Washington, DC, American Psychiatric Press, 1986, pp 561–579

Spiegel D: Hypnosis, in The American Psychiatric Press Textbook of Psychiatry, 2nd Edition. Edited by Hales RE, Yudofsky SC, Talbott JA. Washington, DC, American Psychiatric Press, 1994, pp 1115–1142

Spiegel D, Bloom JR: Group therapy and hypnosis reduce metastatic breast carcinoma pain. Psychosom Med 45:333–339, 1983a

Spiegel D, Bloom JR: Pain in metastatic breast cancer. Cancer 52:341–345, 1983b

Spiegel D, Sands S: Pain management in the cancer patient. Journal of Psychosocial Oncology 6:205–216, 1988

Spiegel D, Hunt T, Dondershine H: Dissociation and hypnotizability in posttraumatic stress disorder. Am J Psychiatry 145:301–355, 1988

Spiegel D, Bierre P, Rootenberg J: Hypnotic alteration of somatosensory perception. Am J Psychiatry 146:749–754, 1989

Spiegel D, Sands S, Koopman C: Pain and depression in patients with cancer. Cancer 74:2570–2578, 1994

Spiegel D, Stroud P, Fyfe A: Complementary medicine. West J Med 168:241–247, 1998

Spiegel H, Spiegel D: Trance and Treatment: Clinical Uses of Hypnosis. Washington, DC, American Psychiatric Press, 1987

Tolle TR, Kaufmann T, Seissmeier T, et al: Region-specific encoding of sensory and affective components of pain in the human brain: a positron emission tomography correlation analysis. Ann Neurol 45:40–47, 1999

Ventafridda V, Tamburini M, Carceni A, et al: A validation study of the WHO method for cancer relief. Cancer 59:850–856, 1987

Waldeman C, Eason J, Rambohui E, et al: Serum morphine levels: a comparison between continuous subcutaneous and intravenous infusions in post-operative patients. Cancer Treat Rev 71:953–956, 1984

Wall PD: An eye on the needle. New Scientist July:129–131, 1972

Weinberg DS, Inturrisi CE, Reidenberg B, et al: Sublingual absorption of selected opioid analgesics. Clin Pharmacol Ther 44:335–342, 1988

Willis WD: Thalamocortical mechanisms of pain, in Advances in Pain Research and Therapy, Vol 9. Edited by Fields HL, Dubner R, Cervero F. New York, Raven, 1985, pp 175–200

Wood JN, Akopian AN, Cesare P, et al: The primary nociceptor: special functions, special receptors, in Proceedings of the 9th World Congress on Pain, Vienna, 1999. Edited by Devor M, Rowbotham MC, Wiesenfeld-Hallin Z. Seattle, WA, IASP Press, 2000, pp 47–62

Woodforde JM, Fielding JR: Pain and cancer. J Psychosom Res 14:365–370, 1970

Yaksh TL: Spinal opiates analgesia: characteristics and principles of action. Pain 11:293–346, 1981

Yaksh TL: Neurologic mechanisms of pain, in Neural Blockade in Clinical Anesthesia and Management of Pain, 2nd Edition. Edited by Cousins MJ, Bridenbaugh PO. Philadelphia, PA, JB Lippincott, 1988, pp 791–844

Yaksh TL, Noueihed R: The physiology and pharmacology of spinal opiates. Annu Rev Pharmacol Toxicol 25:433–462, 1985

Yaksh TL, Rudy TA: Narcotic analgesia produced by a direct action on the spinal cord. Science 192:1357–1358, 1976

Zeltzer L, LeBaron S: Hypnosis and nonhypnotic techniques for reduction of pain and anxiety during painful procedures in children and adolescents with cancer. J Pediatr 101:1032–1035, 1982

# Neuropsychiatric Aspects of Primary Headache Disorders

Stephen D. Silberstein, M.D., F.A.C.P.

Richard B. Lipton, M.D.

Naomi Breslau, Ph.D.

Headache and psychiatric disorders have many links and parallels in their classification, diagnosis, comorbidity, mechanisms, and treatment. The classification system for headache disorders developed by the International Headache Society (IHS) in 1988 (Headache Classification Committee of the International Headache Society 1988) was modeled on the DSM-III classification system for psychiatric disorders (American Psychiatric Association 1980).

Both headache and psychiatric disorder can be divided into primary and secondary disorders. In primary headache (migraine, cluster headache, and tension-type headache [TTH]) (Table 12–1, categories 1–4), the headache disorder itself is the problem. These headache disorders are analogous to the major idiopathic psychiatric disorders. In secondary headache, the symptoms are due to an underlying condition, such as a metabolic derangement, a brain tumor, a stroke, or other forms of structural brain disease (Table 12–1, categories 5–13). Secondary headache disorders are therefore analogous to the organic psychiatric syndromes.

Primary headache classification is based on the associated symptoms that accompany headache attacks and the pattern of pain. Diagnosis relies on the patients' retrospective reporting of their headache experiences. Physical examination and laboratory tests serve primarily to exclude other, more ominous, causes of headache. Like that of many psychiatric disorders, headache classification uses symptom-based criteria in the absence of a truly objective diagnostic gold standard. The IHS system (Headache Classification Committee 1988) provides clear operational rules for headache diagnosis. These rules have replaced an older system (Ad Hoc Committee on Classification of Headache 1962) that provided descriptions and causal theories but not explicit diagnostic rules. Extensive efforts are now under way to field test the IHS system to provide an empirical basis for proposing revisions. The fundamental demarcation of the primary headache disorders is the subject of ongoing debate. The headache disorders differ in symptom profiles, severity, and response to treatment. The IHS system separates migraine from TTH, but this distinction is not universally accepted. In psychiatry, there are similar arguments about the relationship between major depression and anxiety disorders.

Some people argue that migraine and TTH are closely related disorders on opposite ends of a continuum (Silberstein 1993). Population-based studies have not yet resolved this issue. Waters (1988) examined the association between pain intensity and the three cardinal features he considered essential to a diagnosis of migraine: 1) unilateral pain, 2) a warning in the form of a prodrome or aura, and 3) nausea or vomiting. Waters reached the following conclusion:

> The distribution of headache severity extends as a continuous spectrum from mild attacks, which usually

**TABLE 12–1.** International Headache Society classification

1. Migraine
2. Tension-type headache
3. Cluster headache and chronic paroxysmal hemicrania
4. Miscellaneous headaches unassociated with structural lesion
5. Headache associated with head trauma
6. Headache associated with vascular disorders
7. Headache associated with nonvascular intracranial disorder
8. Headache associated with substances or their withdrawal
9. Headache associated with noncephalic infection
10. Headache associated with metabolic disorder
11. Headache or facial pain associated with disorder of cranium, neck, eyes, ears, nose, sinuses, teeth, mouth, or other facial or cranial structures
12. Cranial neuralgias, nerve trunk pain, and deafferentation pain
13. Headache not classifiable

*Source.* Reprinted from Headache Classification Committee of the International Headache Society: "Classification and Diagnostic Criteria for Headache Disorders, Cranial Neuralgias and Facial Pain." *Cephalalgia* 8 (suppl 7):1–96, 1988. Used with permission.

have neither unilateral distribution nor warning, nor nausea, to severe headaches, which are frequently accompanied by the three migraine features. (Waters 1988, p. 65)

In this chapter, we explore the neuropsychiatry of the primary headaches. We begin with a discussion of TTH, the most common of the primary headache disorders and the one most likely to be viewed as psychogenic. We then discuss migraine, a disabling headache disorder that is highly comorbid with depression, anxiety disorders, and a number of other conditions. We discuss the overlapping mechanisms that may operate in headache disorders and psychiatric disease and then consider some of the elements of treatment. We conclude with a discussion of cluster headache.

# Tension-Type Headache and Chronic Daily Headache

Tension-type headaches (TTHs) are the headaches of everyday life. Older terms include tension headache, muscle contraction headache, and psychogenic headache. The old definition of tension headache was

an ache or a sensation of tightness, pressure, or constriction, widely varying in intensity, frequency, and

**TABLE 12–2.** International Headache Society diagnostic criteria for episodic tension-type headache (2.1)

A. At least 10 previous headache episodes fulfilling criteria B–D listed below. Number of days with such headache <180 per year (<15 per month)
B. Headache lasting from 30 minutes to 7 days
C. At least two of the following pain characteristics:
    1. Pressing/tightening (nonpulsating) quality
    2. Mild or moderate intensity (may inhibit but does not prohibit activities)
    3. Bilateral location
    4. No aggravation by walking stairs or similar routine physical activity
D. Both of the following:
    1. No nausea or vomiting (anorexia may occur)
    2. Photophobia and phonophobia are absent, or one but not the other is present

*Source.* Reprinted from Headache Classification Committee of the International Headache Society: "Classification and Diagnostic Criteria for Headache Disorders, Cranial Neuralgias and Facial Pain." *Cephalalgia* 8 (suppl 7):1–96, 1988. Used with permission.

duration, long-lasting, commonly occipital, and associated with sustained contraction of skeletal muscles, usually as a part of the individual's reaction during life stress. (Ad Hoc Committee on Classification of Headache 1962, pp. 14–15)

This definition assumes that a reaction to stress causes sustained muscle contraction that gives rise to pain, an assumption that has no scientific support. In contrast, the IHS system defines TTH according to the headache symptom features, distinguishing between two varieties of TTH, episodic tension-type headache (ETTH) (Table 12–2) and chronic tension-type headache (CTTH) (Table 12–3). These are divided into two groups: those that are and those that are not associated with a disorder of the pericranial muscles (Ad Hoc Committee on Classification of Headache 1962; Silberstein 1993). In the IHS system, TTH is defined in contrast with migraine. Both migraine and TTH are characterized by episodic pain, but the pain characteristics and associated features differ (Table 12–4).

The IHS system notwithstanding, some believe that migraine and TTH vary in degree rather than kind (Marcus 1992). The severity model postulates that TTH is a mild, benign, recurring headache and that migraine is a more severe form of the same basic disorder (Bakal 1982; Featherstone 1985; Raskin 1988; Waters 1988). In this model, the migraine attack may begin with features of a TTH that develops migrainous features as it increases in severity. Iversen et al. (1990) examined the clinical characteristics of headache in three groups of patients: those

**TABLE 12–3.** International Headache Society diagnostic criteria for chronic tension-type headache (2.2)

A. Average headache frequency >15 days per month (180 days per year) for >6 months, fulfilling criteria B–D
B. At least two of the following pain characteristics:
   1. Pressing/tightening quality
   2. Mild or moderate severity (may inhibit but does not prohibit activities)
   3. Bilateral location
   4. No aggravation by walking stairs or similar routine physical activity
C. Both of the following:
   1. No vomiting
   2. No more than one of the following: nausea, photophobia, or phonophobia

*Source.* Reprinted from Headache Classification Committee of the International Headache Society: "Classification and Diagnostic Criteria for Headache Disorders, Cranial Neuralgias and Facial Pain." *Cephalalgia* 8 (suppl 7):1–96, 1988. Used with permission.

**TABLE 12–4.** International Headache Society diagnostic criteria for migraine without aura (1.1)

A. At least five attacks fulfilling B–D
B. Headache lasting 4–72 hours (untreated or unsuccessfully treated)
C. Headache has at least two of the following characteristics:
   1. Unilateral location
   2. Pulsating quality
   3. Moderate or severe intensity (inhibits or prohibits daily activities)
   4. Aggravation by walking stairs or similar routine physical activity
D. During headache, at least one of the following:
   1. Nausea and/or vomiting
   2. Photophobia and phonophobia
E. At least one of the following:
   1. History, physical, and neurologic examinations do not suggest an organic disorder
   2. History and/or physical and/or neurologic examinations do suggest such disorder, but it is ruled out by appropriate investigations
   3. Such disorder is present, but migraine attacks do not occur for the first time in close temporal relation to the disorder

*Source.* Reprinted from Headache Classification Committee of the International Headache Society: "Classification and Diagnostic Criteria for Headache Disorders, Cranial Neuralgias and Facial Pain." *Cephalalgia* 8 (suppl 7):1–96, 1988. Used with permission.

who had only migraine, those who had only TTH, and those who had both migraine and TTH. Patients with only TTH had nonthrobbing headaches that were not aggravated by routine physical activity, whereas patients with both TTH and migraine had TTHs that were aggravated by routine physical activity. This finding suggests that the definition of TTH may encompass two distinct disorders: 1) attacks of mild migraine and 2) pure TTH that is not associated with other features or attacks of migraine (Silberstein 1993). Further substantiating this concept is the observation that TTH in migraineurs responds to sumatriptan, while TTH occurring alone does not (Lipton et al. 1999). The IHS (Headache Classification Committee 1988) has delineated specific diagnostic criteria for CTTH (Table 12–3). This disorder is characterized by TTH that occurs on more than 15 days a month for more than 180 days a year. It afflicts about 3% of the population (Rasmussen et al. 1991). Although the term is often used as a synonym for chronic daily headache (CDH), CTTH is best regarded as a distinct clinical entity (Silberstein et al. 1994). We divide CDH (that is, headache occurring for at least 4 hours/day for at least 15 days/month) into CTTH, chronic (transformed) migraine (CM), new daily persistent headache (NDPH), and hemicrania continua (HC). Episodic headache is relatively easy to diagnose, but as headache frequency increases, the specific characteristics that enable us to classify headaches become blurred. With chronic daily headache (the most common problem seen in headache clinics in the United States and most often due to CM), a difficult-to-define headache continuum develops. Treatment often fails, and many patients overuse one or several treatments for acute headache. CM occurs in childhood, adolescence, middle adult life, and advanced age (Silberstein et al. 1994).

The most common cause of intractable headache is the overuse of acute-headache medication, including analgesics, opioids, ergotamine, and triptans. Patients with frequent headaches are likely to overuse one or both of these medications. Overuse occurs when patients take simple analgesics on a daily basis, combination analgesics or triptans more than three times a week, or ergotamine tartrate or opioids more than twice a week. Overuse may produce drug-induced CDH, dependence on symptomatic medications, and refractoriness to preventive drugs. If the overused medications are discontinued, withdrawal symptoms, including increased headache, frequently occur, followed by an "analgesic washout" period and, finally, improvement (Silberstein 1993; Silberstein and Lipton 2001).

Escalation of headache may occur without drug overuse or may continue even after medication overuse ceases; therefore, overuse is not always the cause of CDH. Medication overuse may be a consequence rather than a cause of CDH in some patients. It may also arise as a form of self-treatment for a comorbid mood disorder. For example, patients with bipolar disorder may overmedicate themselves with a caffeine-barbiturate combination to treat their mood disturbance, in effect treating their depression with the caffeine and their mania with the barbiturate. In other instances, patients with anxiety disorders may be predisposed to using sedative-containing medication.

## Epidemiology

Primary headache disorders—that is, headaches that are not due to an underlying condition—are very common by any standard. There have been few epidemiologic studies of TTH in which IHS criteria were used. Rasmussen et al. (1991) examined a random sample of 740 subjects who were identified through a population registry in Copenhagen, Denmark. ETTH affected 78% of the subjects at some time in their lives. The lifetime prevalence of TTH was higher in women (88%) than in men (69%) (Rasmussen et al. 1991). Data from the Danish study on the frequency of attacks indicate that 35% of patients with TTH have one to seven attacks yearly. In population-based surveys, primary CDH occurs in 4.1% of Americans, 4.35% of Greeks, 3.9% of elderly Chinese, and 4.7% of Spaniards. Population-based estimates for the 1-year period prevalence of CTTH are 1.7% in Ethiopia (Tekle Haimanot et al. 1995), 3% in Denmark (Rasmussen 1995), 2.2% in Spain (Castillo et al. 1999), 2.7% in China (Wang et al. 2000), and 2.2% in the United States (Scher et al. 1998). Wang et al. (2000) looked at the characteristics of primary CDH in a population of elderly Chinese. CDH was diagnosed as a headache that occurred more than 15 days a month for at least 6 months in the previous year and was subclassified into CTTH, CM, and other primary CDH. Person-to-person biannual follow-up of the primary CDH patients was done in June 1995 and August 1997. Sixty patients (3.9%) had CDH. Significantly more women than men had primary CDH (5.6% and 1.8%, $P < 0.001$). Of the primary CDH patients, 42 (70%) had CTTH (2.7% of the total population), 15 (25%) had CM (1% of the total), and 3 (5%) had other CDH. Significant risk factors of primary CDH included overuse of analgesic medications (odds ratio [OR] = 79), a history of migraine (OR = 6.6), and a score of 8 or above on the Geriatric Depression Scale–Short Form (OR = 2.6). At follow-up in 1995 and 1997, approximately two-thirds of patients still had CDH. Compared with the patients in remission, the patients with persistent primary CDH in 1997 had a significantly higher frequency of overuse of analgesics (33% vs. 0%, $P = 0.03$) and major depression (38% vs. 0%, $P = 0.04$).

## Comorbidity

### ETTH and Psychopathology

Many people have attempted to portray ETTH as a psychological disorder (Ad Hoc Committee on Classification of Headache 1962; Friedman et al. 1954; Merikangas et al. 1993a; Silberstein 1993). Their conclusions, based on studies of patients with CDH frequently complicated by medication overuse, may not be relevant to ETTH. Merikangas et al. (1993b), studying a cohort of ETTH patients from Zurich, Switzerland, found no evidence of associated anxiety or depression, in contrast to the association of anxiety and depression with migraine and the association of psychological distress with CDH. However, severity of headache was not taken into account in that study, and persons with ETTH whose headaches were milder than the typical headache of migraine were not excluded from the comparison. Based on a large sample of the general population, Breslau et al (2000) reported that most persons who met IHS criteria for ETTH (89%) scored below the 30th percentile of the distribution of impairment/severity scores of those with migraine. These researchers reported that among a group of persons with severe nonmigraine headache, of whom approximately 60% met criteria for ETTH, there was a higher lifetime prevalence for major depression, compared with control subjects with no headache (Breslau et al. 2000).

### CTTH and CDH

A persistent, vague headache is often attributed to underlying psychic distress, and some believe that CTTH (or CDH) can mask depression or other serious emotional disorders. However, depression may be a result, not a cause, of chronic pain. Additionally, depression, anxiety, and chronic headache may be comorbid conditions with a common biological basis. Diamond (1987) found that 84% of depressed patients complained of headache. The source of his population is not clear, nor is it clear whether the headache preceded the depression, followed it, or occurred simultaneously. Persons with either migraine or CTTH report higher rates of stressful life events occurring before the onset of their attacks, compared with headache-free control subjects (DeBenedittis et al. 1990).

Anxiety, depression, panic disorder, and bipolar disorder occur more frequently in migraineurs than in control subjects who do not have migraine (Breslau and Davis 1993; Merikangas et al. 1990). Since CM evolves from migraine, one would expect to find psychiatric comorbidity in CM. In fact, depression occurs in 80% of CM patients (Mathew 1990, 1991; Mathew et al. 1990; Saper 1987). Comorbid depression often improves when the cycle of daily head pain is broken. Mongini et al. (1997) found that after headache improved, several scores decreased on the Minnesota Multiphasic Personality Inventory (MMPI) and on the State-Trait Anxiety Inventory–2, but 12 of 20 patients continued to have a conversion V configuration on the MMPI. Mitsikostas and Thomas (1999) found that patients with CTTH, mixed headache, or drug abuse headache had the highest scores for depression and anxiety on the Hamilton Rating Scale for Depression. Verri et al. (1998) found current psychiatric comorbidity in 90% of primary CDH patients, in 81% of migraineurs, and in 83% of chronic low back pain patients (no significant differences). Generalized anxiety disorders were the most common in each group (primary CDH, 69.3%, $P \leq 0.001$; migraine, 59.5%, $P \leq 0.05$). The most common mood disorder in primary CDH was major depressive disorder (25%). Somatoform disorders (including somatization, conversion disorder, and hypochondriasis) were found in 5.7% of primary CDH patients, always concomitant with anxiety and mood disorders. Psychiatric comorbidity is a predictor of intractability. Curioso et al. (1999) found that 31 of 69 (45%) primary CDH patients had an adjustment disorder, 16 (23%) had major depression, 12 (17%) were dysthymic, 6 (9%) had generalized anxiety disorder, 1 (2%) was bipolar, and 3 (4%) were normal. The risk of a bad outcome after treatment was significantly greater for patients with major depression than for those without. Primary CDH patients who have major depression or have abnormal Beck Depression Inventory scores have worse outcomes at 3 to 6 months compared with patients who are not depressed. Puca et al. (1999) evaluated 234 adult CDH patients using a structured clinical interview, the Structured Clinical Interview for DSM-IV, and the Symptom Checklist–90–Revised. At least one psychiatric disorder was detected in 66% of the CDH patients (anxiety disorders, 45%; mood disorders, 33%). The prevalence of psychopathologic symptoms was more than 78%. At least one psychosocial stress factor was found in 42% of cases. Sixty-four percent of patients overused symptomatic drugs.

## Mechanisms of TTH

Although TTH was long believed to arise from the sustained contraction of the pericranial muscles, recent studies do not support this notion. This theory suggested that emotional tension gives rise to tonic muscle contraction, relative tissue ischemia, and pain (Silberstein 1993; Wolff 1963). However, there may be as much, if not more, muscle contraction in patients with migraine as in patients with TTH. No correlation exists between muscle contraction, tenderness, and the presence of headache. There is no evidence of muscle ischemia in patients with TTH. Temporal muscle blood flow is normal at rest and during teeth clenching (Langemark et al. 1990).

Olesen (1991) proposed a "vascular-supraspinal-myogenic" model for migraine and TTH. The nucleus caudalis of the trigeminal complex is the major relay nucleus for head and face pain. It receives nociceptive input from cephalic blood vessels and pericranial muscles and dual supraspinal input, both inhibitory and facilitatory (Fields and Heinricher 1989; Hupp et al. 1989). Recent evidence suggests that there are central pain facilitatory neurons in the ventromedial medulla (Fields and Heinricher 1989). In addition, nucleus caudalis neurons can be sensitized as a result of intense neuronal activation (Silberstein 1993). In both migraine and TTH, there may be increased supraspinal facilitation of the nucleus caudalis neurons. In migraine, the vascular nociceptor may be hypersensitive. In TTH associated with a disorder of the pericranial muscles, the myofascial nociceptor may be more hypersensitive, whereas in TTH not associated with a disorder of the pericranial muscles, there may be less myofascial nociceptor hypersensitivity and a general increase in nociception. Sensitization of nucleus caudalis neurons can cause normal, nonpainful stimuli to become painful, producing trigger spots, an overlap in the symptoms of migraine and TTH, and activation of the trigeminal vascular system.

## Treatment

### ETTH

Treatment of ETTH is relatively easy with pharmacotherapy and psychophysiological and physical modalities. Short-term therapy to stop or reduce the severity of the individual attack consists of nonsteroidal anti-inflammatory drugs (NSAIDs) or simple analgesics, alone or in combination with caffeine, anxiolytics, or codeine. Because of the potential for drug-induced headache, however, these drugs must be limited (Silberstein 1993).

Preventive treatment for ETTH is designed to reduce the frequency and severity of headache attacks and is indicated in patients with 3 or more days of headache-related disability per month. Our preference is to begin preventive treatment with antidepressants, but one can try any of the migraine-preventive drugs, particularly in patients who have both migraine and ETTH (Silberstein 1993).

### CDH

Because they often have physical and emotional dependency, low frustration tolerance, sleep disturbance, and depression, patients with CDH are the most difficult headache patients to treat. Interrupting the cycle of medication overuse is crucial, as is recognizing the patient's lifestyle and emotional and psychological needs. One has to be wary of all the coexistent and comorbid conditions, including drug toxicity and dependency, fear of another headache, depression, mania, and personality disorders (especially borderline personality disorder and dissociative disorders). Appropriate psychological intervention may be necessary for treatment to succeed. We recommend the following steps: First, exclude secondary headache disorders; second, diagnose the specific primary headache disorder (i.e., CM, HC); and third, identify comorbid medical and psychiatric conditions, as well as exacerbating factors, especially medication overuse. Limit all symptomatic medications (with the possible exception of the long-acting NSAIDs). Patients should be started on a program of preventive medication (to decrease reliance on symptomatic medication), with the explicit understanding that the drugs may not become fully effective until medication overuse has been eliminated and detoxification (the washout period) completed (Silberstein and Saper 1993). Patients need education and continuous support during this process.

Patients who are overusing medication may not become fully responsive to acute and preventive treatment for 2 to 10 weeks after medication overuse is eliminated. Withdrawal symptoms include severely exacerbated headaches accompanied by nausea, vomiting, agitation, restlessness, sleep disorder, and (rarely) seizures. Barbiturates and benzodiazepine must be tapered gradually to avoid a serious withdrawal syndrome. The washout period may last 3 to 8 weeks; once it is over, there is frequently considerable headache improvement (Baumgartner et al. 1989; Mathew et al. 1990; Raskin 1986; Silberstein et al. 1990).

Inpatient infusion (in an ambulatory infusion unit) and outpatient detoxification options are available. If outpatient detoxification proves difficult or is dangerous, hospitalization may be required. Diener et al. (1988) were able to detoxify only 1.5% of 200 patients on an outpatient basis. A recent consensus paper by the German Migraine Society recommends outpatient withdrawal for highly motivated patients who do not take barbiturates or tranquilizers with their analgesics. Inpatient treatment is recommended for patients who do not improve with outpatient treatment; have high depression scores; or take tranquilizers, codeine, or barbiturates (Diener et al. 1992).

Disturbances in mood and function are common and require management with behavioral methods of pain management and supportive psychotherapy (including biofeedback, stress management, and cognitive behavioral therapy). Treatment of the comorbid psychiatric illness is often necessary before the primary CDH comes under control. "Chronobiological interventions," such as encouraging regular habits of sleep, exercise, and meals, are often useful (Silberstein and Saper 1993).

Psychophysiological therapy involves reassurance, counseling, stress management, relaxation therapy, and biofeedback. The use of traditional acupuncture is controversial and has not proved more effective than placebo (Tavola et al. 1992). Physical therapy consists of modality treatments (heat, cold packs, ultrasound, and electrical stimulation); improvement of posture through stretching, exercise, and traction; trigger point injections; occipital nerve blocks; and a program of regular exercise, stretching, balanced meals, and adequate sleep (Silberstein 1984). It has been our experience that treating painful trigger areas in the neck can result in the improvement of intractable primary CDH.

Choice of acute pharmacotherapy depends on the diagnosis. Patients with chronic migraine who do not overuse symptomatic medication can treat acute migrainous headache exacerbations with antimigraine drugs, including triptans, dihydroergotamine (DHE), and NSAIDs. These drugs must be strictly limited to prevent superimposed rebound headache that will complicate treatment and require detoxification. The risk of rebound is much lower for DHE and triptans than for analgesics, opioids, and ergotamine. CTTH and NDPH can be treated with nonspecific headache medications, and HC can be treated with supplemental doses of indomethacin.

Patients with very frequent headaches should be treated primarily with preventive medications, with the explicit understanding that their medications may not become fully effective until the overused medication has been eliminated. It may take 3 to 6 weeks for treatment effects to develop. The following principles guide the use of preventive treatment: 1) Preventive agents should be chosen from among the first-line drugs based on their side-effect profiles, comorbid conditions, and specific indications (e.g., indomethacin for HC); 2) Drugs should be started at a low dose; 3) The dose should be gradually increased until efficacy is achieved, until the patient develops side effects, or until the ceiling dose for the drug in question is reached; 4) Treatment effects develop over weeks, and treatment may not become fully effective until rebound is eliminated; 5) If one agent fails and if all other things are equal, an agent should be chosen from another therapeutic class; 6) Monotherapy is to be preferred, but combination therapy should not be ruled out; 7) Realistic expectations should be communicated to the patient (Silberstein and Lipton 1994).

Antidepressants are attractive agents for use in primary CDH (CM, CTTH, and NDPH), since many patients have comorbid depression and anxiety. β-Blockers (propranolol, nadolol) remain a mainstay of therapy for migraine and have been used for CDH. Antiepileptic drugs have also been used for migraine and mania have been used for CDH. They include divalproex, gabapentin, and topiramate.

## Treatment of Medication Overuse

### Outpatient

There are two general outpatient strategies. One approach is to taper the overused medication, gradually substituting a long-acting NSAID as effective preventive therapy is established. The alternative strategy is to abruptly discontinue the overused drug, substitute a transitional medication to replace the overused drug, and subsequently taper the transitional drug. Outpatient treatment is preferred for motivated patients but is not always safe or effective. Patients who do not need hospital-level care but cannot be safely or adequately treated as outpatients can be considered for ambulatory infusion treatment. Contraindications to outpatient ambulatory infusion include the likelihood of withdrawal symptoms at night when patients are withdrawn from long-acting or potent drugs; psychiatric disorders that interfere with treatment (these patients cannot be treated as aggressively as outpatients); and comorbid medical illness that requires prolonged monitoring. No long-term observation is available, and many problems manifest themselves in an intensely monitored interactive environment.

### Inpatient

If outpatient treatment fails or is not safe, or if there is significant medical or psychiatric comorbidity present, inpatient treatment may be needed (Silberstein and Saper 1993). The goals of inpatient headache treatment include 1) medication withdrawal and rehydration; 2) pain control with parenteral therapy; 3) establishment of effective preventive treatment; 4) interruption of the pain cycle; 5) patient education; and 6) establishment of outpatient methods of pain control. Many workers have shown that an inpatient regimen consisting of repetitive intravenous DHE can help during this period (Raskin 1986). When this protocol is used, the headache is brought under control more easily, the detoxification process is accelerated, and the withdrawal symptoms are made more tolerable. Patients who are not candidates for DHE treatment or who do not respond can use repetitive

intravenous neuroleptics, such as chlorpromazine, droperidol, and prochlorperazine, and/or corticosteroids. These agents may also supplement repetitive intravenous DHE in refractory patients (Silberstein et al. 1990). Hospitalization is also used as a time for patient education, for introducing behavioral methods of pain control, and for adjusting preventive medication.

In one study, 90% of hospitalized patients became headache free, usually within 2–3 days, and 80% continued to show significant improvement in the long term (Silberstein 1993; Silberstein and Silberstein 1992).

Approximately 10%–20% of patients with CDH do not respond to aggressive management. Some have idiopathic intracranial hypertension (requiring a lumbar puncture for diagnosis), dissociative disorders, bipolar disorders, or refractory depression. Some have a demeanor that does not suggest severe pain, despite their complaint of severe, invariant headache. In patients with chronic pain, pain behavior and the level of pain may be dissociated; this small group may contain what has in the past been labeled *psychogenic headache* (Silberstein and Silberstein 1992).

## Migraine

Migraine is an episodic headache disorder often accompanied by neurologic, gastrointestinal, autonomic, and psychological changes. The IHS distinguishes seven categories of migraine, the most important of which are *migraine without aura* (formerly *common migraine*) (Table 12–4) and *migraine with aura* (formerly *classic migraine*) (Table 12–5). The aura is the complex of focal neurologic symptoms that initiates or accompanies an attack (Headache Classification Committee 1988). The same patient may have headache without aura, headache with aura, and aura without headache.

## Phases of Migraine

The migraine attack can be divided into four phases :

1. The premonitory phase, which occurs hours or days before the headache
2. The *aura*, which occurs immediately before or with the headache
3. The headache itself
4. The *postdrome*

Although most people experience more than one of these phases, no one particular phase is required for a diagnosis of migraine (Blau 1980). A description of these

**TABLE 12–5.** International Headache Society diagnostic criteria for migraine with aura (1.2)

A. At least two attacks fulfilling B

B. At least three of the following four characteristics:
   1. One or more fully reversible aura symptoms indicating focal cerebral cortical, brain stem dysfunction, or both.
   2. At least one aura symptom develops gradually over more than 4 minutes, or two or more symptoms occur in succession.
   3. No aura symptom lasts more than 60 minutes. If more than one aura symptom is present, accepted duration is proportionally increased.
   4. Headache follows aura with a free interval of less than 60 minutes. (It may also begin before or simultaneously with the aura.)

C. At least one of the following:
   1. History, physical, and neurologic examinations do not suggest one of the disorders listed in groups 5–11.[a]
   2. History, physical, or neurologic examinations or all do suggest such disorder, but it is ruled out by appropriate investigations.
   3. Such disorder is present, but migraine attacks do not occur for the first time in close temporal relation to the disorder.

[a]See groups listed in Table 12–1.

*Source.* Reprinted from Headache Classification Committee of the International Headache Society: "Classification and Diagnostic Criteria for Headache Disorders, Cranial Neuralgias and Facial Pain." *Cephalalgia* 8 (suppl 7):1–96, 1988. Used with permission.

---

four phases provides a convenient way of reviewing the diverse manifestations of migraine.

## Premonitory Phase

Premonitory (prodromal) phenomena occur in approximately 60% of patients with migraine, or migraineurs, often hours to days before the onset of headache (Amery et al. 1986a, 1986b; Blau 1980). These phenomena include psychological, neurologic, constitutional, and autonomic features. Psychological symptoms include depression, euphoria, irritability, restlessness, mental slowness, hyperactivity, fatigue, and drowsiness. Neurologic phenomena include photophobia, phonophobia, and hyperosmia. Constitutional symptoms include a stiff neck, a cold feeling, sluggishness, increased thirst, increased urination, anorexia, diarrhea, constipation, fluid retention, and food cravings. Some patients report a poorly characterized feeling that a migraine attack is coming.

Although prodromal features vary widely among individuals, they are often consistent within an individual. Two types of migraine prodromes are described: 1) nonevolutive prodromes, which precede the attack by up to 48 hours; and 2) evolutive prodromes, which start approximately 6 hours before the attack, gradually increasing in intensity and culminating in the attack (Amery et al. 1986a, 1986b; Isler 1986).

The features of the prodrome, such as depression, cognitive dysfunction, and episodic bouts of food cravings, may be difficult to diagnose as part of the migraine complex if they occur in isolation or with a mild headache, or if a careful headache history is not taken. A diary may be helpful to show the relationship of these periodic events to migraine (Silberstein and Saper 1993).

The periodicity of migraine and the flow of symptoms from prodrome to aura to headache suggest that the prodrome may be regulated by the hypothalamus and mediated by dopamine and serotonin (Silberstein and Saper 1993). Antidopaminergic drugs such as domperidone prevented 66% of headache attacks in a double-blind, placebo-controlled trial (Waelkens et al. 1986). Metoclopramide may be as effective as domperidone (Spierings 1989).

## Aura

The migraine aura is characterized by focal neurologic symptoms that typically precede but sometimes accompany an attack. Approximately 20% of patients with migraine experience auras. Most aura symptoms evolve slowly over 5–20 minutes and usually last less than 60 minutes. The aura can be characterized by visual, sensory, or motor phenomena, either alone or in combination. Auras may also involve language or brainstem disturbances (Table 12–6). Headache usually occurs within 60 minutes of the end of the aura.

Aura and headache are dissociable neurobiological events. Although auras typically precede the onset of headache, they may begin during the headache. In one prospective study, headache followed the aura only 80% of the time (K. Jensen et al. 1986); in other words, an aura may occur without a headache. Occasionally the period between the aura and headache is as long as 5 hours (Blau 1992). Most patients do not feel normal during this period. Alterations in mood, detachment from the environment or other people, fears, disturbances of speech or thought, or somatic complaints may occur. Patients may feel very strange or unusually removed from reality and may not tell anyone about these "funny spells" because of their fear of being "insane" (Blau 1992; Silberstein and Young 1995). If the aura is prolonged, it may meet the criteria for what was formerly called *complicated migraine* (Silberstein and Young 1995). Patients

**TABLE 12–6.** Characteristics of the visual aura

1. **Positive phenomena, negative phenomena, or both:** Either may occur alone; positive phenomena often occur first and are followed by negative phenomena.
2. **Visual field:** Scotomata often start centrally and migrate peripherally.
3. **Shape:** Fortification spectra often "C" shaped; scotomata bean shaped.
4. **Motion:** Objects may rotate, oscillate, or "boil."
5. **Flicker:** Rate = 10 cycles per second; may change during the course of the aura.
6. **Color:** Usually black and white.
7. **Clarity:** May be blurry or fuzzy.
8. **Brightness:** Intense.
9. **Expansion:** Buildup occurs in both fortification spectra and scotomata.
10. **Migration:** Spectra may "march" from the central area to periphery or sometimes vice versa.

*Source.* Reprinted from Silberstein SD, Young WB: "Migraine Aura and Prodrome." *Seminars in Neurology* 45:175–182, 1995. Used with permission.

can have more than one type of aura, with a progression from one symptom to another. Most patients who have a sensory aura also have a visual aura (Ziegler and Hassanein 1990).

The aura of migraine can be either an illusion or an organic pseudohallucination. Illusions result from and depend on transformation of external stimuli, whereas hallucinations are independent of perception. Genuine hallucinations are present if the patient treats the experience as reality. If the patient recognizes that the experiences are subjective phenomena that originate in his or her own mind rather than in the surroundings, they are termed *pseudohallucinations* (Jaspers 1973; Kandinsky 1981). Migraine auras are recognized as not real and are therefore pseudohallucinations.

The most common type of migraine aura is visual. The visual aura often has a hemianoptic distribution and includes both positive (scintillations, fortification spectra, photopsia [the sensation of unformed flashes of light or sparkles before the eyes]) and negative (scotomata [loss of vision]) visual features that often occur together. Elementary visual disturbances can occur; these include colorless scotomata or positive visual phenomena such as photopsia or phosphene (an objective visual sensation that appears with the eyes closed and in the absence of light). Simple flashes, specks, or crude or uniform pseudohallucinations of geometric forms (points, stars, lines, curves, circles, sparks, flashes, or flames) may occur and may be single or may number in the hundreds. They may move rapidly across the visual field; they sometimes cross the midline and often precede a scotoma. Shimmering or undulations in the visual field may also occur.

Selby and Lance (1960) found these minor visual disorders in 42 of 500 patients. Interestingly, these were more likely to occur during, rather than before, the headache (Selby and Lance 1960). More complicated pseudohallucinations include teichopsia, or fortification spectrum, which is the most characteristic visual aura and is diagnostic of migraine. An arc of scintillating lights often begins in central vision, sometimes forms a herringbone pattern, and may expand to encompass an increasing portion of a visual hemifield. Other complex positive features, such as bright geometric lights, may also occur. Objects may occasionally appear to change in size or shape (Table 12–6) (Silberstein and Saper 1993; Silberstein and Young 1995).

Retinal auras are rare; they are characterized by monocular, not hemianoptic, visual disturbances. Transient monocular visual loss, the most frequent presentation of retinal migraine, usually occurs in adults younger than age 40. Patients describe a "black-out," "gray-out," or "white-out" of vision; at times a shade covering the field of vision is reported (Alvarez 1960; Hupp et al. 1989; O'Sullivan et al. 1992). Photopsias or phosphenes are also common. The duration of visual loss ranges from seconds to hours, but most scotomata last less than 30 minutes (Alvarez 1960; Carroll 1970; Hedges and Lackman 1976). In some patients, attacks cluster over several months.

Numbness or tingling (paresthesia) over one side of the face and in the ipsilateral hand or arm are the most common of the somatosensory phenomena. Hemiparesis may occur, and if the dominant hemisphere is involved, dysphasia or aphasia may develop (K. Jensen et al. 1986; Manzoni et al. 1985). Olfactory hallucinations have been reported preceding migraine. Odors tend to be unpleasant and can last from 5 minutes to 24 hours. This may be preceded or followed by other aura symptoms. Anxiety, déjà vu, and *jamais vu* have been reported and are presumably of temporal lobe origin (Sacks 1985). Transient global amnesia has been postulated to be due to migraine (Bruyn 1986; Caplan et al. 1981; Sacks 1985).

In some instances, one type of aura may follow another. For example, sensory phenomena may develop as visual phenomena fade, or motor features may develop as sensory features subside. Although auras are relatively specific for migraine, related phenomena may occur in cerebrovascular disease, including carotid dissection, and in epilepsy, especially of the occipital lobes. When a prolonged or atypical aura is present, the possibility of a hypercoagulable state (due to antiphospholipid antibody syndrome, for example) should be considered.

Auras may occur repeatedly, even many times an hour for several months. This condition is termed *migraine aura status* (Haas 1982). Scotomata may occur repeatedly, even alternating sides, and closely repeating cycles of migrating sensory auras may occur for hours on end (Sacks 1985). Auras may have a sudden onset. Some characteristics of the aura are listed in Table 12–6 (Silberstein and Young 1995).

## Headache Phase

An individual can experience enormous variations in the symptoms and severity of headache (Schneider et al. 1994). The typical migraine headache is unilateral and throbbing. The severity ranges from moderate to marked, and the pain is often aggravated by routine physical activity or simple head movement (Ad Hoc Committee on Classification of Headache 1962). Not all of these features, however, are required to be diagnostic of migraine: the pain may be bilateral at its onset (which it is in 40% of patients) and may remain bilateral throughout the attack or begin on one side and become generalized (Selby and Lance 1960). The headache can occur at any time of the day or night, but it occurs most frequently on arising (Selby and Lance 1960). The onset is usually gradual; the pain peaks and then subsides, usually lasting 4–72 hours in adults and 2–48 hours in children (Silberstein and Saper 1993).

The pain of migraine headache varies greatly in intensity in different attacks and between attacks, although most people who have migraine report pain ratings of 5 or greater on a 0–10 scale (Stewart et al. 1994). The pain is described as throbbing in 85% of patients, although throbbing pain is often a feature of other types of headache (Stewart et al. 1994).

Other features invariably accompany the pain of migraine. Anorexia is common, although food cravings can also occur. Nausea occurs in as many as 90% of migraineurs, and vomiting occurs in about one-third (Lipton et al. 1992; Silberstein 1995). Many patients experience sensory hyperexcitability manifested by photophobia, phonophobia, and osmophobia and seek a dark, quiet room (Drummond 1986; Selby and Lance 1960). Other systemic symptoms, including blurry vision, nasal stuffiness, anorexia, hunger, tenesmus, diarrhea, abdominal cramps, polyuria (followed by decreased urinary output after the attack), facial pallor (or, less commonly, redness), sweating, and sensations of heat or cold, may be noted during the headache phase. Localized edema of the scalp, face, or periorbital regions may occur; scalp tenderness, unusual prominence of a vein or artery in the tem-

ple, or stiffness and tenderness of the neck are not uncommon. Impaired concentration is common; memory impairment occurs less frequently. Depression, fatigue, anxiety, nervousness, and irritability are also common. Lightheadedness, rather than true vertigo, and a feeling of faintness may occur. The extremities tend to be cold and moist. The IHS selects particular associated features as cardinal manifestations for diagnosis (Silberstein and Lipton 1994).

## Postdrome

The headache of migraine is often followed by the postdrome, during which patients may have many of the symptoms that occurred during the prodrome. The patient may feel tired, washed out, irritable, and listless and may have impaired concentration, scalp tenderness, or mood changes. Some people feel unusually refreshed or euphoric after an attack, whereas others note depression and malaise. Recurrent psychosis has been reported; so-called migraine madness may last up to 4 weeks and may be manifested by morbid visual hallucinations and delusions, including the belief that homes or people have been replaced by exact doubles (reduplicative paramnesia or Capgras syndrome) (Silberstein and Young 1995).

# Formal IHS Classification

## Migraine Without Aura (Common Migraine)

To establish a diagnosis of IHS migraine without aura (1.1) (Headache Classification Committee 1988) (Table 12–4), five attacks must occur. Each attack must last 4–72 hours and have at least two of the following four pain characteristics:

1. Unilateral location
2. Pulsating quality
3. Moderate to severe intensity
4. Aggravation by routine physical activity

In addition, the attacks must be associated either with nausea or vomiting, or with photophobia and phonophobia. No single characteristic is mandatory for a diagnosis of migraine. A patient with photophobia, phonophobia, and severe pain that is aggravated by routine activity meets these criteria, as does the more typical patient with unilateral throbbing pain and nausea (Silberstein and Lipton 1994).

Migraine usually lasts several hours or all day; when it persists for longer than 3 days, the term *status migrainosus* is applied. Although migraine often begins in the morning, sometimes awakening the patient at dawn, it can begin at any time of the day or night. The frequency of attacks varies widely, from a few in a lifetime to several a week. The average migraineur experiences one to three headaches a month. Migraine is, by definition, a recurrent phenomenon. The requirement of at least five attacks is imposed because headaches simulating migraine may be caused by organic diseases such as brain tumors, sinusitis, and glaucoma (Silberstein and Lipton 1994).

The IHS also requires that secondary headache disorders be excluded. Thus, migraine is both a diagnosis of inclusion, because specific combinations of features are required, and a diagnosis of exclusion, because alternative causes of headache must be systematically eliminated.

## Migraine With Aura (Classic Migraine)

An IHS diagnosis of migraine with aura (1.2) (Table 12–5) requires at least two attacks with any three of the following four features:

1. One or more fully reversible aura symptoms
2. Aura developing over a course of more than 4 minutes
3. Aura lasting less than 60 minutes
4. Headache following the aura within 60 minutes

Fewer attacks are required to make a diagnosis of migraine with aura because a typical aura is assumed to be a highly specific feature of migraine. However, other causes of headache must still be excluded (Ad Hoc Committee on Classification of Headache 1962; Silberstein and Lipton 1994).

Migraine with aura is subclassified into migraine with typical aura (1.2.1) (homonymous visual disturbance, unilateral numbness or weakness, or aphasia); migraine with prolonged aura (1.2.2) (aura lasting longer than 60 minutes); familial hemiplegic migraine (1.2.3); basilar migraine (1.2.4); migraine aura without headache (1.2.5); and migraine with acute-onset aura (1.2.6). Other varieties of migraine include ophthalmoplegic migraine (1.3), retinal migraine (1.4), and childhood periodic syndromes (1.5).

The headache and associated symptoms of migraine with aura are similar to those of migraine without aura but may be less severe and/or of shorter duration. Most people who have migraine with aura also have migraine without aura. In those who do experience aura, the aura usually lasts 20–30 minutes and typically precedes the headache, but occasionally it occurs only during the headache. In contrast to that of a transient ischemic attack, the aura of migraine evolves gradually and consists of both positive features, such as scintillations or tingling,

and negative features, such as scotomata or numbness (Headache Classification Committee 1988; Silberstein and Lipton 1994; Silberstein and Saper 1993).

# Migraine Variants

## Basilar Migraine

Originally called *basilar artery migraine* (Ad Hoc Committee on Classification of Headache 1962) or *Bickerstaff's migraine* (Bickerstaff 1987), basilar migraine was originally believed to be mainly a disorder of adolescent girls. However, it has been identified in all age groups and in both sexes, although it is more common in women than in men. The aura often lasts less than 1 hour and is usually followed by a headache. A distinguishing characteristic of basilar migraine is the bilateral nature of many of the associated neurologic events, which helps differentiate it from more typical migraine. Visual symptoms often start with a hemianoptic field disturbance, which can rapidly involve both visual fields, leading at times to temporary blindness. The visual aura is usually followed by at least one of the following:

- Ataxia
- Vertigo
- Tinnitus
- Diplopia
- Nausea and vomiting
- Nystagmus
- Dysarthria
- Bilateral paresthesia
- Changes in levels of consciousness and cognition

Spells of basilar migraine can present a confusing picture. This disorder should be considered in patients with paroxysmal brainstem disturbances.

## Confusional Migraine

Confusional migraine (Ad Hoc Committee on Classification of Headache 1962; Hosking 1988) is characterized by a typical migraine aura; a headache (which may not be significant); and confusion, which may precede or follow the headache. During the period of confusion, the patient is inattentive and distracted and has difficulty maintaining speech and other motor activities. The electroencephalogram may be abnormal during the attack. Agitation, memory disturbances, obscene utterances, and violent behavior are not uncommon. Single attacks are most common, and multiple attacks are rare. Both may be triggered by mild head trauma. If the level of consciousness is more profoundly disturbed, migraine stupor lasting 2–5 days can occur. The differential diagnosis includes drug ingestion, metabolic encephalopathies (Reye's syndrome, hypoglycemia), viral encephalitis, postictal state, and acute psychosis. Confusional migraine may be difficult to diagnose. Confusional migraine is part of the syndrome of migraine with white matter abnormality linked to chromosome 19 (Chabriat et al. 1995).

## Unusual Migraine Auras

The visions of Hildegard of Bingen, an eleventh-century mystic, have been attributed in part to her migrainous scintillating scotomata. Characteristic of the visions that she and other visionary prophets saw were working, boiling, or fermenting lights. Hildegard's visions often contained elements of blinding lights (Silberstein and Young 1995):

> I saw a great star most splendid and beautiful, and with it an exceeding multitude of falling sparks which with the star followed southward…. But sometimes I behold within this light another light which I name "the living light itself." (p. 178)

In the book of the visionary prophet Ezekiel, he describes his vision (Silberstein and Young 1995):

> I saw a storm wind coming from the north, a vast cloud with flashes of fire and brilliant light about it; and within was a radiance like brass, glowing in the heart of the flames…. As I looked at the living creatures, I saw wheels on the ground, one beside each of the four. The wheels sparkled like topaz, and they were all alike: in form and working they were like a wheel inside a wheel, and when they moved in any of the four directions they never swerved in their course. (p. 178)

Perhaps mysticism is common among migraineurs.

### Association Cortex Auras

Association cortex auras include visual distortions and hallucinations. Such auras may have been the source of some of Lewis Carroll's descriptions in his book *Alice in Wonderland*. These attacks occur more commonly in children, are usually followed by a headache, and are characterized by a complex disorder of visual perception that may include metamorphopsia, micropsia, macropsia, zoom vision (opening up or closing down in the size of objects), or mosaic vision (fracturing of images into facets) (Golden 1979; Hosking 1988). An auditory analog of zoom vision characterized by cyclical oscillation in the amplitude of ambient sound (oscillocusis) has been described in patients with migraine aura (Whitman and

Lipton 1995). Nonvisual association cortex symptoms also often occur. These include complex difficulties in the perception and use of the body (apraxia and agnosia); speech and language disturbances; states of double or multiple consciousness associated with déjà vu or jamais vu; and elaborate, dreamy, nightmarish, trance-like, or delirious states. In addition to "Alice in Wonderland" syndrome, migraine aura may lead to isolated disorders of visual perception. Patients have reported many complex disorders of visual perception, including alexia, micropsia, macropsia, zoom vision, mosaic vision, cinematographic vision (illusion of motion lost), achromatopsia (loss of color), and palinopsia (persistence or recurrence of visual images after the stimulus object has been removed) (Klee and Willanger 1966; Lippman 1952; Sacks 1985; Selby and Lance 1960).

### Aura Without Headache

Periodic neurologic dysfunction, which may be part of the migraine aura, can occur in isolation, without the headache (Whitty 1967). These phenomena (scintillating scotomata or recurrent sensory, motor, or mental phenomena) can be a part of migraine, but they are accepted as migraine only after a full investigation and prolonged follow-up. Headache occurring in association with aura symptoms helps confirm the diagnosis (Silberstein and Silberstein 1990). Ziegler and Hassanein (1990) reported that 44% of their patients who had headache with aura had aura without headache at some time.

Levy (1988) looked at the incidence of transient (<24 hours) neurologic loss in a group of Cornell University neurologists. Thirty-two percent had transient central nervous system (CNS) dysfunction, most commonly visual phenomena (field cuts, obscurations, or scotomata). Nonvisual symptoms included hemiparesis, clumsiness, paresthesias, and dysarthria. Migraine was reported in 29%. Forty-four percent reporting transient CNS dysfunction had migraine, whereas 22% of those not reporting such dysfunction had migraine. Follow-up for up to 5 years showed that none of the responders developed any residual deficit or chronic neurologic disorder, suggesting that these symptoms are benign migrainous accompaniments ("funny spells").

Fisher (1980, 1986) described late-life migrainous accompaniments, which are transient neurologic phenomena that are frequently not associated with headache. He reported on 188 patients older than age 40; 60% were men, and 57% had a history of recurrent headache. They had one or more attacks of episodic neurologic dysfunction, lasting 1 minute to 72 hours, with variable recurrence (27% had 1 attack, 45% had 2 to 10 attacks, and 28% had more than 10 attacks). Fisher considered a scintillating scotoma to be diagnostic of migraine, even when it occurred in isolation, whereas other episodic neurologic symptoms (paresthesia, aphasia, and sensory and motor symptoms) needed more careful evaluation (Table 12–7). Wijman et al. (1998) determined the frequency, characteristics, and stroke outcome of subjects with migrainous visual symptoms in the Framingham study. Visual symptoms occurred in 186 subjects. Visual symptoms that corresponded to the visual aura of migraine were reported by 26 of 186 subjects (14%), with a prevalence of 1.23% overall (1.33% in women and 1.08% in men). The episodes were never accompanied by headaches in 58%, and 42% had no headache history. Three of 26 subjects (11.5%) had a stroke one or more years later; one had a subarachnoid hemorrhage 1 year later; one had a brainstem infarct 3 years later; and one had a cardioembolic stroke secondary to atrial fibrillation 27 years later. This stroke incidence rate of 11.5% was significantly lower than the stroke incidence rate of 33.3% in subjects with transient ischemic attacks in the same cohort ($P = 0.030$) (these usually occurred within 6 months) and did not differ from the stroke incidence rate of 13.6% of those without migrainous phenomena or transient ischemic attacks. Mattsson and Lundberg (1999) estimated the prevalence and characteristics of transient visual disturbances of possible migraine origin in both a clinical and a general population. Lifetime prevalence was 37% in migraine patients and 13% in the general population. Headache following transient visual disturbances had more migrainous features in patients than in control subjects. The transient visual disturbances that did not fulfill the IHS criteria for migraine with aura probably represented abortive migraine phenomena. These transient migrainous accompaniments have profiles that are similar to those of the migraine aura (such as scintillating scotomata, numbness, aphasia, dysarthria, and motor weakness). When they occur for the first time after age 45, they can easily be confused with transient ischemic attacks of cerebrovascular origin. Fischer pointed out that migraine is the most likely mechanism for these episodes because they are gradual in onset and evolution and have a mixture of positive and negative symptomatic features. He also wisely stated that transient migraine accompaniment remains a diagnosis of exclusion in all but the most classic cases (Fisher 1986).

## Epidemiology

Several recent population-based studies have examined the prevalence of IHS-defined migraine (Lipton et al. 1994). The three largest of these studies yielded remark-

**TABLE 12–7.** Main criteria for the diagnosis of late-life migrainous accompaniments

1. Scintillations (or other visual display), paresthesias, aphasia, dysarthria, and paralysis
2. Buildup of scintillations (not seen in cerebrovascular disease)
3. "March" of paresthesias (not seen in cerebrovascular disease)
4. Progression from one accompaniment to another, often with a delay
5. Two or more similar attacks (helps exclude embolism)
6. Headache occurring in 50% of attacks
7. Episodes lasting 15–25 minutes
8. Characteristic midlife "flurry" of attacks
9. Generally benign course
10. Normal angiography (excludes thrombosis)
11. Cerebral thrombosis, embolism and dissection, epilepsy, thrombocythemia, polycythemia, and thrombotic thrombocytopenia ruled out

*Source.* Adapted from Fisher 1980 and Fisher 1986.

ably consistent estimates; the 1-year period prevalence was about 6% in men and 15%–18% in women (Lipton et al. 1994; Silberstein and Lipton 1993). Most studies find that migraine is about three times more common in women than in men (Henry et al. 1992; Lipton et al. 1994; Rasmussen et al. 1991; Silberstein and Lipton 1993; Stewart et al. 1992a).

The American Migraine Study (Stewart et al. 1992a) showed increasing migraine prevalence in both men and women from age 12 until approximately age 40, after which prevalence decreased (Figure 12–1). The gender ratio (ratio of migraine prevalence in women to that in men) also varied with age, increasing from menarche to about age 42, at which time it began to decline. Cyclical hormonal changes associated with menses may account for some aspects of the migraine prevalence ratio.

Physician- and clinic-based studies have suggested that migraine is associated with high intelligence and social class (Lipton et al. 1994). Epidemiologic studies in adults, using intelligence testing and occupation as measures of socioeconomic status, revealed no evidence to connect migraine with either social class or intelligence. In the American Migraine Study (Stewart et al. 1992a), migraine prevalence was found to be lower at higher income levels. An analysis of 1981–1989 data from the National Health Interview Survey confirmed that migraine prevalence is highest in low-income groups (Lipton and Stewart 1993). In the American Migraine Study, individuals in high-income groups were much more likely to report a medical diagnosis of migraine than were those with lower incomes (Stewart et al. 1992a). As

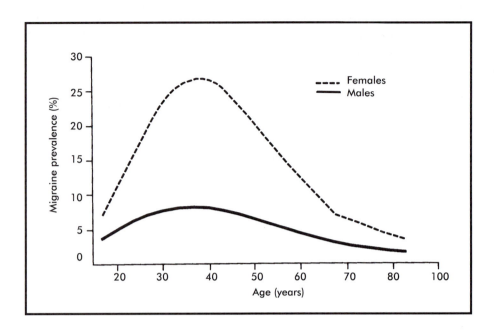

**FIGURE 12–1.** Prevalence of migraine in females and males by age. Migraine prevalence increased from ages 12 to 38 in both females and males. The peak prevalence was considerably higher in females.

*Source.* Reprinted from Lipton RB, Stewart WF: "Migraine in the United States: Epidemiology and Healthcare Use." *Neurology* 43:6–10, 1993. Used with permission.

Waters (1988) suggested, people from higher-income households are more likely to consult physicians and are therefore disproportionately represented in clinic-based samples.

Migraine is a public health problem of enormous scope that has an impact on both the individual patient and society. The American Migraine Study estimates that there are 23 million Americans who get severe migraine headaches (Stewart et al. 1992a). Twenty-five percent of women experience four or more severe attacks per month, 35% experience one to three severe attacks per month, and 40% experience one or fewer severe attacks per month. Similar frequency patterns were observed in men. In the American Migraine Study, more than 85% of women and more than 82% of men who had severe migraine had some headache-related disability (Stewart et al. 1992a). About one-third were severely disabled or needed bed rest. In addition to the disability related to attacks, many migraineurs live in fear, knowing that at any time an attack could disrupt their ability to work, to care for their families, or to meet social obligations.

## Comorbidity of Migraine

Migraine is associated with a number of neurologic diseases (epilepsy and stroke) and psychiatric disorders (depression, mania, anxiety, and panic). The term *comorbidity*, coined by Feinstein (1970), originally referred to

coexistent conditions in clinical trials. For our purposes, *comorbidity* refers to a more-than-coincidental association between two disorders (Lipton and Silberstein 1994).

Migraine comorbidity is important for a number of reasons, as discussed elsewhere (Lipton and Silberstein 1994). Co-occurring diseases can complicate diagnosis, inform choices about treatment, and give clues about pathophysiology. For example, depression, anxiety disorders, or epilepsy can all cause headaches, whereas headaches can change mood and behavior (Ottman and Lipton 1994; Welch 1994).

Comorbidity, however, is more than a problem of differential diagnosis; the real challenge for the neuropsychiatrist is recognizing that more than one disease is present (Lipton and Silberstein 1994). Because of the high rate of comorbid disorders in migraine, the principle of diagnostic parsimony does not apply: the presence of migraine should increase the suspicion that another disorder may be present. Conversely, patients with depressive disorders often have medically undiagnosed migraine, and there may be a tendency to attribute the migrainous manifestations to the depressive disorder (Lipton and Stewart 1993).

It is important to consider comorbidity when developing treatment strategies (Lipton and Silberstein 1994) because there may be opportunities to treat two conditions with a single drug. Antidepressants can be used to treat both migraine and depression (Breslau et al. 1994a; Merikangas et al. 1993a). When migraine occurs with manic-depressive illness or epilepsy, divalproex sodium can be used to treat both conditions (Bowden et al. 1994; Hering and Kuritzky 1992; Saper et al. 1993). However, comorbid illnesses also may impose therapeutic limitations. Some treatments may be relatively contraindicated in individuals who have more than one disease. For example, β-blockers may be a less desirable option when treating a migraine patient who also has depression.

In addition to the diagnostic and therapeutic implications, the presence of comorbidity may provide clues to the pathophysiology of migraine. When two conditions occur in the same person, there are a number of alternative causal explanations (Lipton and Silberstein 1994). First, the apparent associations may arise by coincidence or because of the method of subject ascertainment (Berkson 1949). Second, one condition may cause the other. For example, it has been suggested that depression may cause migrainelike headaches as a form of masked depression. Third, shared environmental or genetic risk factors might account for the co-occurrence of two disorders. For example, head injury is a risk factor for both migraine and epilepsy and may account for part of the relationship between the disorders. Shared genetic risk factors may also account for the association between comorbid disorders (Ottman and Lipton 1994). Finally, independent genetic or environmental risk factors may produce a brain state that gives rise to both migraine and a comorbid condition (Lipton and Silberstein 1994). For example, migraine and depression have each been attributed to a brain state characterized by serotonergic dysregulation.

## Migraine and Epilepsy

Migraine and epilepsy are chronic neurologic disorders with neuropsychiatric manifestations. Attacks are episodic, and features include hallucinations, changes in mood and behavior, alterations of consciousness, and focal sensory or motor symptoms. The relationships between migraine and epilepsy are complex. Headaches have been associated with seizures as ictal or postictal phenomena, particularly in occipital-lobe epilepsies (Andermann and Andermann 1987; Lennox and Lenox 1960; Marks and Ehrenberg 1993; Ottman and Lipton 1994). Migraine aura may trigger seizures, producing a condition sometimes referred to as *migralepsy* (Andermann and Andermann 1987; Lennox and Lenox 1960; Marks and Ehrenberg 1993).

The Epilepsy Family Study of Columbia University (Ottman and Lipton 1994; Ottman and Susser 1992) demonstrated that migraine and epilepsy are associated. The risk of migraine is more than twice as high in persons with epilepsy than in those without epilepsy. This increased risk of migraine was greatest in persons whose epilepsy was caused by head trauma, but it occurred in every subgroup of epilepsy defined by seizure type, age at onset, etiology, and family history of epilepsy (Ottman and Lipton 1994).

Differentiating migraine from epilepsy can be difficult (Andermann and Andermann 1987; Ehrenberg 1991; Marks and Ehrenberg 1993). The most helpful clinical features are the duration of the aura—an aura lasting more than 5 minutes suggests a migraine aura, and an aura of less than 5 minutes suggests an epileptic aura—and the aura symptom profile. Alteration of consciousness, automatism, and positive motor features suggest an epileptic aura, and a mix of positive and negative features, such as a scintillating scotoma, suggest migraine.

The comorbidity of migraine and epilepsy also has implications for diagnosis and treatment. For example, before a tricyclic antidepressant or a neuroleptic is prescribed for a patient with migraine, it should be determined that there is no history of epilepsy, because these medications may lower seizure thresholds. In the selection of prophylactic drugs for migraine, it is sometimes advantageous to treat comorbid conditions with a single agent; for example, when migraine and hypertension occur concomitantly, a β-blocker or a calcium channel blocker is often appropriate (G. D. Solomon 1989). Similarly, agents that are potentially useful for both migraine and epilepsy, such as divalproex (Hering and Kuritzky 1992; R. Jensen et al. 1994; Saper et al. 1993), should be considered in patients with comorbid migraine and epilepsy.

## Psychopathology of Migraine and Psychiatric Disorders

A number of studies have examined the relationship of migraine to specific psychiatric disorders (Silberstein et al. 1995). Several clinic-based studies have reported an increased prevalence of migraine in patients with major depression and an increased prevalence of major depression in patients with migraine (Marchesi et al. 1989; Merikangas et al. 1988; Morrison and Price 1989). Three population-based studies have examined a wide range of psychiatric disorders in addition to major depression (Breslau et al. 1991; Merikangas et al. 1990, 1993b; Silberstein et al. 1995; Stewart et al. 1989, 1992b).

## Affective Disorders

Merikangas et al. (1990) reported on the association of migraine with specific psychiatric disorders in a random sample of 457 adults ages 27–28 in Zurich, Switzerland. Persons with migraine ($n = 61$) were found to have increased 1-year rates of affective and anxiety disorders. Specifically, the odds ratio (OR) for major depression (OR = 2.2; 95% confidence interval [CI] = 1.1–4.8), bipolar spectrum disorders (OR = 2.9; 95% CI = 1.1–8.6), generalized anxiety disorder (OR = 2.7; 95% CI = 1.5–5.1), panic disorder (OR = 3.3; 95% CI = 0.8–13.8), simple phobia (OR = 2.4; 95% CI = 1.1–5.1), and social phobia (OR = 3.4; 95% CI = 1.1–10.9) were significantly higher in persons with migraine than in persons without migraine.

Migraine with major depression was frequently complicated by an anxiety disorder. In persons with all three disorders, Merikangas et al. (1990) suggest that the onset of anxiety generally precedes the onset of migraine, whereas the onset of major depression most often follows the onset of migraine (Silberstein et al. 1995).

## Panic

Stewart et al. (1989) studied the relationship of migraine to panic disorder and panic attacks in a population-based telephone interview survey of 10,000 residents of Washington County, Maryland, ages 12–29. The highest rates of migraine headaches occurring in the preceding week were reported by men and women with a history of panic disorder. The relative risk of migraine headache occurring during the previous week and associated with a history of panic disorder was 6.96 in men and 3.70 in women.

In a follow-up analysis of the same sample, Stewart et al. (1992b) found that 14.2% of women and 5.8% of men who had experienced headache in the previous 12 months had consulted a physician for the problem. An unexpectedly high proportion of those who had consulted a physician for headache had a history of panic disorder. Of those who had recently seen a physician, 15% of women and 12.8% of men between ages 24 and 29 had a panic disorder. This suggests that comorbid psychiatric disease is associated with seeking care for headache disorders.

## Psychiatric Disorders

Breslau et al. (1991) studied the association of IHS-defined migraine with specific psychiatric disorders in a sample of 1,007 young adults ages 21–30 in southeast Michigan. Persons with a history of migraine ($n = 128$) had significantly higher lifetime rates of affective disorder, anxiety disorder, illicit drug use disorder, and nico-

tine dependence. The sex-adjusted ORs were 4.5 for major depression (95% CI = 3.0–6.9), 6.0 for manic episode (95% CI = 2.0–18.0), 3.2 for any anxiety disorder (95% CI = 2.2–4.6), and 6.6 for panic disorder (95% CI = 3.2–13.9) (Breslau and Davis 1993). The psychiatric comorbidity odds associated with migraine with aura were generally higher than those associated with migraine without aura (Breslau et al. 1991). Migraine with aura was associated with an increased lifetime prevalence of both suicidal ideation and suicide attempts, after the factors of sex, major depression, and other co-occurring psychiatric disorders were controlled for (Breslau 1992).

Using follow-up data gathered 3.5 years after baseline, Breslau et al. (1994b) reported on the prospective relationship between migraine and major depression in a cohort of young adults. The relative risk for the first onset of major depression during the follow-up period in persons with prior migraine versus no prior migraine was 4.1 (95% CI = 2.2–7.4). The relative risk for the first onset of migraine during the follow-up period in persons with prior major depression versus no history of major depression was 3.3 (95% CI = 1.6–6.6) (Table 12–8).

In summary, recent epidemiologic studies support the association between migraine and major depression previously reported in clinic-based studies. The prospective data indicate that the observed cross-sectional or lifetime association between migraine and major depression could result from a bidirectional influence, from migraine to subsequent onset of major depression and from major depression to first migraine attack. Furthermore, these epidemiologic studies indicate that persons with migraine have increased prevalence of bipolar disorder, panic disorder, and one or more anxiety disorders (Breslau and Davis 1992; Breslau et al. 1994a, 1994b; Silberstein et al. 1995).

It has been proposed that major depression in persons with migraine might represent a psychological reaction to repeated, disabling migraine attacks. Migraine has an earlier mean age at onset than major depression, both in the general population and in persons with comorbid disease. Nonetheless, the bidirectional influence of each condition on the risk for the onset of the other is incompatible with the simple causal model (Silberstein et al. 1995). Furthermore, Breslau and Davis (1992) reported that the increased risk for the first episode of major depression (and/or panic disorder) did not vary by the proximity of migraine attacks. These findings dampen the plausibility that the migraine-depression association results from the demoralizing experience of recurrent and disabling headaches, suggesting instead that their association might reflect shared etiologies.

**TABLE 12–8.** Relative risk (RR) estimates from two Cox-proportional hazards models (Detroit area)

| | Risk of migraine in patients with major depression | | |
| --- | --- | --- | --- |
| | RR | 95% CI | P |
| Migraine | 3.2 | 2.3–4.6 | 0.0001 |
| Sex (female) | 1.7 | 1.2–2.5 | 0.0014 |
| Education (<college) | 1.2 | 0.9–1.7 | 0.183 |
| | Risk of major depression in patients with migraine | | |
| | RR | 95% CI | P |
| Major depression | 3.1 | 2.0–5.0 | 0.0001 |
| Sex (female) | 2.7 | 1.8–4.1 | 0.0001 |
| Education (<college) | 1.8 | 1.3–2.6 | 0.0014 |

*Note.* CI=confidence interval.
*Source.* Adapted from Breslau et al. 1994b.

Depression has also been linked to other pain conditions. The evidence of the association between depression and pain calls into question the specificity of the migraine–major depression connection. A previous report of a higher prevalence of major depression in persons with migraine but no ETTH did not address the specificity issue, because the difference in the rates of depression between the two headache conditions might have been explained by differences in severity.

In a recent study, Breslau et al. (2000) examined the migraine-depression comorbidity in a large-scale epidemiologic study, the Detroit Area Study of Headache. The study comprised three groups: persons with migraine (*n*=536), persons with other severe headaches of comparable pain severity and disability (*n*=162), and matched control subjects with no history of severe headache (*n*=586). These three representative samples of the population were identified by a random-digit dialing telephone survey of 4,765 persons ages 25–55. The lifetime prevalence of major depression in persons with migraine was 40.7%; in those with other severe headaches, 35.8%; and in control subjects, 16.0%. Sex-adjusted odds ratios in the two headache groups, relative to control subjects, were approximately of the same magnitude, 3.5 and 3.2. However, examination of the bidirectional relationship between major depression and each headache type yielded different results. With respect to migraine, a bidirectional relationship was observed: migraine signaled an increased risk for the first onset of major depression, and major depression signaled an increased risk for the first-time occurrence of migraine; sex-adjusted hazard ratios were 2.4 and 2.8, respectively (both statistically significant). In contrast, severe nonmigraine headache signaled an increased risk for major depression, but there was no evidence of a significant influence in the reverse direction, that is, from major

depression to severe headache; sex-adjusted hazard ratios were 3.6 and 1.6, respectively (only the first is statistically significant).

The pattern of the results suggests the possibility that different causal pathways might account for the comorbidity of major depression in these two headache categories. The results for migraine suggest shared causes, whereas those for other headache of comparable severity suggest a causal effect of headache on depression.

Another line of evidence comes from a study of a biological marker of depression in migraineurs. Jarman et al. (1990) administered the tyramine test to 40 migraine patients, 16 of whom had a lifetime history of major depression. Low tyramine conjugation, a trait marker for endogenous depression, was strongly associated with a lifetime history of major depression in subjects with comorbid disease, regardless of their current psychiatric status. The authors argue that the association of the trait marker with major depression in migraineurs rules out the possibility that the depression is a psychological reaction to migraine attacks (Silberstein et al. 1995).

## Psychopathology of Migraine and Personality Characteristics

The relationship between migraine and psychopathology has been discussed far more often than it has been systematically studied (Silberstein et al. 1995). Over the years, many studies have focused on particular personality traits of migraineurs. The basic assumptions are that 1) migraineurs share common personality traits, 2) these traits are enduring and measurable, and 3) these traits differentiate migraineurs from control subjects (Schmidt et al. 1986). The notion of a "migraine personality" first grew out of clinical observations of the highly selected patients seen in subspecialty clinics (Silberstein et al. 1995).

**TABLE 12–9.**    Migraine and personality: epidemiologic studies (community)[a]

| Author and year | Subjects (*N*, diagnosis) and response rate | Age (years) | Source | Control subjects (*N*, characteristics) | Instrument | Findings |
|---|---|---|---|---|---|---|
| | **Sample** | | | | | |
| Brandt et al. 1990 | 162, migraine 94.2% | 12–29 | Community telephone survey of 10,169 | 162, matched for sex and age; no headache | EPQ | EPQ—neuroticism scale scores were higher in both female and male migraine subjects than in control subjects EPQ—psychoticism scale scores were higher in female subjects than in control subjects |
| Rasmussen 1992 | 77, migraine 167, TTH 76% | 25–64 | Random sample of 1,000 selected from the National Central Person Registry | 496, nonheadache | EPQ | EPQ—neuroticism scale scores were higher in TTH and migraine subjects versus others; no difference between "pure" migraine versus rest |
| Merikangas et al. 1993b | 11, classic migraine 91, common migraine 63, TTH 56, symptoms only | 28–29 | Community survey in Zurich—longitudinal | 158, nonheadache | Freiburg Personality Inventory[b] | Subjects with classic migraine scored higher than other groups on nervousness, depressiveness, inhibition, decreased levels of resilience |

[a]Abbreviations: EPQ = Eysenck Personality Questionnaire; TTH = tension-type headache.
[b]Göllner and Salvini 1971.
*Source.*    Reprinted from Silberstein SD, Lipton RB, Breslau N: "Migraine: Association With Personality Characteristics and Psychopathology." *Cephalalgia* 15:1–15, 1995. Used with permission.

Touraine and Draper (1934) reported that migraineurs were deliberate, hesitant, insecure, detailed, perfectionistic, sensitive to criticism, and deeply frustrated emotionally. They were said to lack warmth and to have difficulty making social contacts. Wolff (1937) found migraineurs to be rigid, compulsive, perfectionistic, ambitious, competitive, chronically resentful, and unable to delegate responsibility.

Most investigations have used psychometric instruments such as the MMPI (Hathaway and McKinley 1943) or the Eysenck Personality Questionnaire (EPQ) (Eysenck and Eysenck 1975). The EPQ is a well-standardized measure that includes four scales: 1) psychoticism (P), 2) extroversion (E), 3) neuroticism (N), and 4) lie (L) (Table 12–9).

Brandt et al. (1990) used the Washington County Migraine Prevalence Study to conduct the first population-based case-control study of personality in patients with migraine (Table 12–9). More than 10,000 12- to 29-year-olds who were selected through random-digit dialing

received a diagnostic telephone interview. A sample of subjects who met the criteria for migraine with or without aura (*n* = 162) were compared with subjects without migraine. Each subject received the EPQ, the 28-item version of the General Health Questionnaire (Goldberg 1975), and a question about headache laterality.

Subjects with migraine scored significantly higher than control subjects on the neuroticism scale of the EPQ, indicating that they were more tense, anxious, and depressed than the control group. In addition, women with migraine scored significantly higher than control subjects on the psychoticism scale of the EPQ, indicating that they were more hostile, less interpersonally sensitive, and out of step with their peers. Rasmussen (1992) screened a population-based sample to identify patients with migraine and those with TTH. TTH occurring alone was associated with high neuroticism scores on the EPQ. Persons with pure migraine (that is, without TTH) did not score above the norms on the neuroticism scale, although persons with migraine, with and without TTH, showed a tendency to score above the norms on the neuroticism scale.

Merikangas et al. (1993b) investigated the cross-sectional association between personality, symptoms, and headache subtypes as part of a prospective longitudinal study of 19- and 20-year-olds in Zurich, Switzerland. Subjects with migraine scored higher on indicators of neuroticism than did subjects without migraine.

In summary, studies that used the EPQ or similar personality measures and compared persons with migraine with control subjects without migraine have generally reported an association between migraine and neuroticism (Passchier and Orlebeke 1985; Passchier et al. 1984; Phillips 1976; Rasmussen 1992; Silberstein et al. 1995).

Many investigators (Invernizzi et al. 1989; Kudrow and Sutkus 1979; Sternbach et al. 1980; Weeks et al. 1983) have used the MMPI to investigate the personalities of subjects with migraine. These studies have been limited by several factors (Stewart et al. 1991). MMPI studies have usually been clinic based, limiting their generalizability and creating opportunities for selection bias. Most have not used control groups, relying instead on historical norms. Many have not used explicit diagnostic criteria for migraine. Despite these limitations, most studies show elevation of the neurotic triad, although this is not statistically significant (Table 12–10) (Silberstein et al. 1995).

Studies of migraine and personality have generally not controlled for drug use, headache frequency, and headache-related disability. Furthermore, they have not controlled for major psychiatric disorders (such as major depression or panic disorder), which occur more commonly in migraineurs. The association between major psychiatric disorders and personality disorders may confound the assessment of the relationships between these disorders and migraine. Neuroticism, in particular, is associated with depression and anxiety, which occur with increased prevalence in migraineurs. Differences in neuroticism across studies might reflect variations in the role of comorbid psychiatric disease. The available data suggest that subjects with migraine may be more neurotic than those without migraine. The stereotypical rigid, obsessional migraine personality might reflect the selection bias of a distinct subtype of migraine that is more likely to be seen in the clinic.

Breslau and Andreski (1995) examined the association between migraine and personality, taking into account a history of co-occurring psychiatric disorders. Data came from their epidemiologic study of young adults in the Detroit, Michigan, metropolitan area. Migraine was associated with neuroticism, but not with extroversion or psychoticism, as measured by the EPQ. The association remained significant when the authors controlled for sex and history of major depression and anxiety disorders. More than 25% of persons with migraine alone that was uncomplicated by psychiatric comorbidity scored in the highest quartile of neuroticism. The results suggest that subjects with migraine might be more likely to have psychopathology and to adjust poorly to their medical condition. The findings also suggest that the association between migraine and neuroticism is not attributable to comorbid depression or anxiety disorders. In a later report, Breslau et al. (1996) presented findings from prospective data on the migraine-neuroticism association from their epidemiologic study of young adults. In women, neuroticism measured at baseline predicted the first incidence of migraine during the 5-year follow-up. Specifically, controlling for major depression and anxiety disorders at baseline, women scoring in the highest quartile of the neuroticism scale were nearly three times more likely to develop migraine than those scoring in the lowest quartile. In men, neuroticism did not predict migraine, although the small number of incidence cases in men precluded reliable estimates of the risk for migraine associated with neuroticism.

## Mechanisms of the Visual System in Subjects With Migraine

The human visual system is sensitive to stripe patterns, mediated by cortical pattern sensitivity detectors. The visual cortex breaks the stripe pattern down to its primitive features. Certain square-wave gratings can induce visual illusions of color, shape, and motion. Migraineurs are particularly susceptible to these illusions. Persons who experience frequent headaches report numerous stripe-induced illusions (Wilkins et al. 1984). Patients with unilateral headaches are likely to report asymmetric illusions in a 4-cycles-per-degree grating pattern (Wilkins et al. 1984).

Certain stripe patterns are unpleasant to look at, and migraineurs are extremely sensitive to the adverse effects of stripe patterns. Their discomfort is further aggravated by illuminating the stripes with red light. Marcus and Soso (1989) found 82% of subjects with migraine to be stripe sensitive, compared with 6.2% of those without migraine. Migraineurs had a strong aversion (significantly more than control subjects) to viewing escalator treads, narrow-slat venetian blinds, striped clothing, and striped wall coverings. Visual discomfort was measured by recording the number of aversive movements (wincing, head turning, etc.) that the subjects made.

**TABLE 12–10.** Migraine and personality: MMPI (neurotic triad[a]) studies

| Author and year | Sample | | | | Findings |
| | Subjects (*N*, diagnosis) | Age (years) | Source | Control subjects | |
| --- | --- | --- | --- | --- | --- |
| Sternbach et al. 1980 | 83, vascular<br>41, muscle contraction<br>58, mixed | 20–70 | Patients seen for headache at pain treatment center | Data on MMPI from 50,000 patients, compared on age and sex | Vascular subjects were less depressed and less neurotic than muscle-contraction and mixed subjects.<br>All groups combined versus control subjects scored significantly higher on Hs, D, and Hy scales.<br>Males with muscle contraction scored higher than females on paranoid scale.<br>Females in all headache groups scored higher than males on Hy and Hs scales. |
| Andrasik et al. 1982 | 26, migraine<br>39, muscle contraction<br>12, cluster headache<br>22, migraine plus muscle contraction | 18–68 | Physician referral or self-referral | 30 friends or relatives of patients matched on age, sex, socioeconomic status, and marital status | Control subjects showed no meaningful elevations on any scale.<br>None of headache types showed significant elevations on any scale.<br>Significant $\chi^2$ tests for *t*-score elevations ≥70 versus <70 by the five headache groups for Hs and Hy scales. |
| Weeks et al. 1983 | 50, migraine<br>50, combination | Not specified | Outpatients evaluated for treatment at headache center | | Subjects with combination headache scored significantly higher than those with migraine on Hy, D, and Hs scales. |
| Levor et al. 1986 | 20, common migraine<br>9, classic migraine<br>5, mixed | 23–63 | Patients recruited from physicians specializing in treatment of headache | Data from days prior to a migraine day were matched with the same person's data prior to headache-free days. | Mild, subclinical elevations on Hs, D, and Hy scales for all headache subjects versus control subjects. |
| Ellertsen and Kløve 1987 | 12, TTH<br>33, migraine | 16–70 | Neurology patients | 34 headache-free patients with muscle pain in neck/shoulder recruited by advertisements | Muscle pain subjects: males scored higher than females on Hs scale.<br>TTH: Males and females had elevated scores on Hs and D scales (no significant differences between males and females).<br>Female migraine and TTH subjects had similar profiles. |
| Dieter and Swerdlow 1988 | 82, migraine<br>48, scalp muscle contraction<br>58, posttrauma<br>61, mixed<br>53, cluster headache | Not specified | Random selection from general practice population | 68 headache-free people solicited from hospital staff | Scalp muscle contraction, migraine/cluster, mixed/posttrauma subjects were each significantly different from control subjects on Hs, D, and Hy scales.<br>Mixed and posttrauma subjects (both males and females) had clinically elevated scores on Hs scale.<br>Mixed and posttrauma subjects (males only) had clinically elevated scores on D scale.<br>Mixed and posttrauma subjects (both males and females) had clinically elevated scores on Hy scale. |

**TABLE 12–10.** Migraine and personality: MMPI (neurotic triad[a]) studies *(continued)*

| Author and year | Subjects (*N*, diagnosis) | Sample Age (years) | Source | Control subjects | Findings |
|---|---|---|---|---|---|
| Invernizzi et al. 1989 | 148, migraine 183, TTH 87, mixed | 16–70 | Patients referred to headache center | None | Mixed versus migraine and mixed versus TTH subjects had significantly different scores on Hs, D, and Hy scales. |
| Inan et al. 1994 | 44, migraine 36, TTH | Not specified | Patients referred to clinical psychologist | 36 healthy control subjects | Female TTH subjects scored higher than control subjects on Hs, D, and Hy scales. Female migraine subjects had higher scores than female control subjects on Hy scale. No significant differences between TTH and migraine groups. |

[a]The Minnesota Multiphasic Personality Inventory (MMPI) Neurotic Triad consists of the following scales: depression (D), hypochondriasis (Hs), and hysteria (Hy).

*Note.* TTH = tension-type headache.

*Source.* Reprinted from Silberstein SD, Lipton RB, Breslau N: "Migraine: Association With Personality Characteristics and Psychopathology." *Cephalalgia* 15:1–15, 1995. Used with permission.

Migraineurs also see more illusions and experience more discomfort in viewing grating patterns than do control subjects (Khalil 1991; Khalil and Legg 1989). The illusions and discomfort are frequent and more intense in migraineurs with aura (Coleston and Kennard 1993; Khalil 1991; Khalil and Legg 1989). Subjects who experience unilateral headache are likely to have asymmetrical illusions. Those who experience frequent migraine attacks (more than 1 a week) tend to see more illusions than do those with infrequent attacks (5–10 per year) (Khalil 1991; Khalil and Legg 1989).

At least 32 distinct visual areas with different functional properties process visual information in the brain (Fellerman and VanEssen 1991). These differences make it possible to distinguish between low-level and high-level vision. Low-level visual processing is concerned with finding edges, organizing texture or color, and establishing depth to help segregate a figure from its background. High-level visual processing uses previously stored information about objects or events to navigate, identify objects, and form and process mental images (Kosslyn 1994).

Migraine with aura may be associated with changes in low-level visual processing. Wray et al. (1995) tested (between migraine attacks) 12 subjects who experienced migraine with aura and 12 matched control subjects on computerized visual tasks. Two tasks, orientation detection and temporal order judgment, were devised to examine low-level visual processes. Picture-naming and word-priming tasks were devised to examine high-level visual processes. The migraineurs were faster than the control subjects in the two low-level tasks, suggesting a psychophysical basis for their enhanced sensitivity to visual stimuli. The remaining two tasks, picture naming and word priming, which involve the use of previously stored information, did not distinguish migraineurs from matched control subjects (Wray et al. 1995). Migraineurs have a clear superiority in tasks that rely only on low-level visual processing (utilizing the primary visual cortex). The two low-level tasks used, orientation detection and temporal order judgment, required focused attention and a visual search for detection of target features. Migraineurs were not superior in the two high-level visual tasks, which relied on matching input to stored representations, namely picture-name verification and word reading. The high speed of the migraineur's brain in discerning a single target—the key characteristic of low-level visual processing—is a new observation made by Wray et al. (1995) and is consistent with the hypothesis that migraine patients have greater sensitivity in low-level vision.

## Pathogenesis of Migraine

There are two major theories of migraine pathogenesis (Silberstein 1992). The older (vascular) theory, first proposed by Harold Wolff (1948), postulated that the aura of migraine is a consequence of vasoconstriction and brain ischemia and that the headache phase of migraine is due to painful vasodilatation of cranial blood vessels.

Emerging evidence has challenged these ideas and has given rise to the neural hypothesis of migraine (Dalessio 1987; Moskowitz 1984). This hypothesis holds that the primary events in a migraine attack take place in the brain, that these neural events activate the trigeminal nerve to produce neurogenic inflammation of the cranial blood vessels, and that it is inflammation, not just dilatation of blood vessels, that is the fundamental substrate of migraine pain (Moskowitz 1984).

A complete theory of migraine pathogenesis must account for all four phases of the migraine attack and their interrelationships. Although the vascular theory accounts for the throbbing quality of the pain and the treatment response to vasoconstrictor drugs, it does not account for many other aspects of the migraine attack. Because prodromal features such as changes in mood and food craving occur well before the changes in blood flow that develop during the migraine attack, these are best explained by derangements in the CNS. Similarly, the photophobia, phonophobia, and cognitive symptoms of migraine suggest the involvement of higher cortical centers and are difficult to explain on a vascular basis. The timing of the blood flow changes that occur during the migraine attack is incompatible with the vascular theory. Finally, some of the drugs used to treat migraine have no effect on blood vessels (Dalessio 1987; Goadsby and Gundlach 1991; Lance 1993; Moskowitz 1984).

The best-supported elements of the neural hypothesis pertain to the role of the trigeminovascular system in mediating neurogenic inflammation. Moskowitz (1984) demonstrated direct connections between the trigeminal nerve and the cerebral blood vessels. Trigeminal C fibers contain substance P, calcitonin gene–related peptide (CGRP), and vasoactive intestinal peptide (VIP), among other neurotransmitters. Activation of the trigeminal nerve leads to the release of these sensory neuropeptides, which in turn induce inflammatory changes in the cranial blood vessels. These changes include vascular dilatation, plasma extravasation, and sterile inflammation. This process also activates platelets, helping to account for the well-described platelet changes that occur during the migraine attack.

The role of the trigeminovascular system is supported by a convergence of evidence from studies in humans and animals (Moskowitz 1984). In animal models, stimulation of the trigeminal nerve produces the cascade of events just described. In human subjects with migraine, CGRP is measurably elevated in jugular blood during the attack, suggesting that trigeminal activation is part of the migraine process (Goadsby and Gundlach 1991). In animal models, administration of acute migraine treatment such as the triptans and ergots blocks

the development of neurogenic inflammation (Moskowitz 1984). This family of drugs blocks the release of CGRP in human migraineurs. Many of the drugs that block neurogenic inflammation are agonists at the 5-hydroxytryptamine (serotonin) subtype 1 (5-HT$_1$) receptor. This class of receptors is found in the trigeminal nerve endings and provides a site of action for many exigent treatments. In aggregate, these data suggest that neurogenic inflammation is the substrate of migraine pain and that exigent treatments can work at the trigeminovascular junction to block migraine pain.

The central events of migraine (which activate the trigeminovascular system) are less well understood. Emerging evidence suggests that spreading depression is the substrate of the migraine aura and that central perturbations in serotonin and other transmitters may play a role in the pathogenesis of migraine.

Olesen and Edvinsson (1988) assessed changes in cerebral blood flow during migraine and found that cerebral blood flow decreased during migraine with aura but did not change in migraine without aura. While the aura developed, blood flow progressively decreased as a wave of spreading oligemia began in the occipital cortex and moved forward at a rate of 2–3 mm/minute. Oligemia began with the aura and persisted into the headache phase; the headache itself began during the period of decreased cerebral blood flow. These blood flow changes are consistent with a primary neuronal event producing secondary vascular changes but are not consistent with reactive vasodilation as a cause of headache.

In migraine with aura, a wave of oligemia spreads forward from the occipital area before the aura and persists into the headache phase (Olesen and Edvinsson 1988). The rate of progression of the oligemia is the same as the rate of the cortical spreading depression measured by Leão (1944). Leão electrically stimulated exposed rabbit cortices and monitored the induced changes in electrical activity, which spread over the cortex at a rate of 2–3 mm/minute. Magnetoencephalographic studies suggest the existence of spreading depression in humans with migraine (Simkins et al. 1989), implying that spreading depression may be the mechanism that produces the aura (Blau 1984; Lance 1993; Pearce 1984; Raskin 1990; Welch et al. 1990).

Wolff (1963) suggested that the migraine aura was caused by arterial vasoconstriction, which could be overridden by the administration of the potent vasodilator $CO_2$. However, experimental studies on cortical spreading depression offer another explanation: Hypercapnic hyperoxia inhibits the propagation of cortical spreading depression. Thus, the effects of hypercapnia on the migraine aura may be mediated by the inhibition of cortical spreading depression (Lauritzen 1986).

Several lines of indirect evidence suggest a relationship between serotonin and migraine. The 5-HT receptors consist of at least three distinct types of molecular structures: guanine nucleotide G protein–coupled receptors, ligand-gated ion channels, and transporters. At least seven 5-HT receptors have been identified: $5\text{-HT}_1$, $5\text{-HT}_2$, $5\text{-HT}_3$, $5\text{-HT}_4$, $5\text{-HT}_6$, and $5\text{-HT}_7$ (Silberstein 1994b). At least five $5\text{-HT}_1$ receptor subtypes are present in humans: $5\text{-HT}_{1A}$, $5\text{-HT}_{1B}$, $5\text{-HT}_{1D}$, $5\text{-HT}_{1E}$, and $5\text{-HT}_{1F}$. The search to characterize serotonin receptors in the vasculature led to the identification of the $5\text{-HT}_1$-like receptor (Humphrey et al. 1990a). Serotonin is intimately involved in the affective disorders. $5\text{-HT}_{1A}$ receptors may be involved in anxiety, whereas $5\text{-HT}_2$ receptors may be involved in depression.

Headaches similar to migraine can be triggered by serotoninergic drugs, such as reserpine (which releases and depletes 5-HT) and $m$-chlorophenylpiperazine (a serotoninergic agonist) (Silberstein and Lipton 1994). Agents that are effective in the exigent treatment of migraine—the triptans, a serotonin analog (Humphrey et al. 1990a; Peroutka 1990a, 1990b), and DHE, an ergot derivative (Callaham and Raskin 1986; Silberstein and Lipton 1994)—are agonists at the $5\text{-HT}_{1A}$, $5\text{-HT}_{1B}$, $5\text{-HT}_{1D}$, and $5\text{-HT}_{1F}$ receptors. They block the development of neurogenically induced inflammation in rat dura mater, presumably by activating prejunctional 5-HT1D heteroreceptors on the trigeminal nerve. This, in turn, blocks the release of neuropeptides, including substance P and CGRP, preventing neurogenic inflammation. The NSAIDs may also block neurogenic inflammation; the mechanism of this action is less certain, but it may involve inhibition of prostaglandin synthesis (Silberstein and Lipton 1994).

In cats, intravenous radiolabeled DHE passes through the blood-brain barrier and labels nuclei in the brain stem and spinal cord, which are intimately involved in the transmission and modulation of pain (Goadsby and Gundlach 1991). In addition, stimulation of the sagittal sinus activates one of these nuclei, the caudal trigeminal nucleus, and this activity is transmitted to the thalamus (Lance 1986). In clinically active doses, ergotamine, DHE, and centrally penetrating triptans suppressed this activation. These data suggest that the ergot alkaloids— ergotamine, DHE, and the centrally penetrating triptans—exert their antimigraine effects by a receptor-mediated neural pathway in both the CNS and the trigeminal nerve, where they block neurogenic inflammation.

Drugs used for migraine prevention include $5\text{-HT}_2$ receptor antagonists, such as methysergide maleate and cyproheptadine hydrochloride. Antidepressants block 5-HT reuptake and downregulate the $5\text{-HT}_2$ receptor antagonists. Calcium channel blockers inhibit 5-HT release, and β-blockers modulate serotoninergic neurons. Valproic acid (divalproex), an anticonvulsant that is effective for migraine prophylaxis, turns off the serotoninergic raphe neurons in the brain stem and may block neurogenic inflammation.

Clearly, a number of systems are involved in a migraine attack. If migraine is described as a decrease in the activation threshold of these systems, it is easy to see how stress or fatigue can trigger an attack. Migraine may begin centrally and secondarily affect the trigeminal vascular system, which may enhance or generate pain and produce secondary blood vessel changes. The medications used to treat migraine can work either centrally or through the trigeminal system.

## Treatment

Effective migraine treatment depends on several factors. First, the physician must make an accurate diagnosis. This should be followed by teaching the patient how to identify and avoid headache triggers and then providing a treatment plan that reduces the impact of migraine and targets the symptoms that are most disturbing to the individual patient. Although behavioral interventions are often useful, drugs are the mainstay of treatment for most patients (Silberstein and Lipton 1994).

Pharmacologic treatment of migraine may be acute (abortive, symptomatic) or preventive (prophylactic). Patients experiencing frequent severe headaches often require both approaches. Symptomatic treatment attempts to abort (i.e., stop the progression of) or reverse a headache once it has started. Preventive therapy is given on a daily basis, even in the absence of a headache, to reduce the frequency and severity of anticipated attacks. Symptomatic treatment is appropriate for most acute attacks and should be used no more than 2–3 days a week. If attacks occur more frequently, treatment strategies should focus on decreasing the frequency of attacks.

Medications used for the treatment of acute headache include analgesics, antiemetics, anxiolytics, NSAIDs, ergots, steroids, major tranquilizers, narcotics, and, more recently, selective $5\text{-HT}_1$ (serotonin) agonists (triptans) (Table 12–11). One or more of these medications can be used for headaches of differing severities (Silberstein and Saper 1993). Preventive treatments include a broad range of medications, most notably β-blockers, calcium channel blockers, antidepressants, serotonin antagonists, and anticonvulsants (Table 12–12).

**TABLE 12–11.**　Abortive medications: efficacy, side effects, and relative contraindications and indications[a]

| Drug | Efficacy | Side effects | Comorbid conditions | |
|---|---|---|---|---|
| | | | Relative contraindications[b] | Relative indications |
| Aspirin | 1+ | 1+ | Kidney disease, ulcer disease, PVD, gastritis (age <15) | CAD, TIA |
| Acetaminophen | 1+ | 1+ | Liver disease | Pregnancy |
| Caffeine adjuvant | 2+ | 1+ | Frequent headache | |
| Butalbital, caffeine, and analgesics | 2+ | 2+ | Use of other sedative; history of medication overuse | |
| Isometheptene | 2+ | 1+ | Uncontrolled HTN, CAD, PVD | |
| NSAIDs | 2+ | 1+ | Kidney disease, ulcer disease, gastritis | |
| Narcotics | 3+ | 3+ | Drug or substance abuse | Pregnancy; rescue medication[c] |
| Ergotamine | | | | |
|   Tablets | 2+ | 2+ | Prominent nausea or vomiting, CAD, PVD, uncontrolled HTN | |
|   Suppositories | 3+ | 3+ | | |
| Dihydroergotamine | | | | |
|   Injections | 4+ | 2+ | CAD, PVD, uncontrolled HTN | Orthostatic hypotension |
|   Intranasal | 3+ | 1+ | | |
| Triptans | | | | |
|   Sumatriptan | | | | |
|     *SC injection* | 4+ | 1+ | CAD, PVD, HTN | Nausea or vomiting |
|     *Nasal spray* | 3+ | 1+ | CAD, PVD, HTN | Nausea or vomiting |
|     *Tablets* | 3+ | 1+ | CAD, PVD, HTN | Nausea |
|   Zolmitriptan | 3+ | 1+ | CAD, PVD, HTN | Nausea |
|   Rizatriptan | 3+ | 1+ | CAD, PVD, HTN | Nausea |
|   Naratriptan | 2+ | +/– | CAD, PVD, HTN | Nausea |
|   Almotriptan | 3+ | 1+ | CAD, PVD, HTN | Nausea |

[a]Ratings of efficacy and side effects are given on a scale from 1+ (lowest) to 4+ (highest). Abbreviations: PVD = peripheral vascular disease; CAD = coronary artery disease; TIA = transient ischemic attack; HTN = hypertension; NSAIDs = nonsteroidal anti-inflammatory drugs.
[b]Caution is required in patients with frequent headaches.
[c]Narcotics are indicated as rescue medication when other medications fail.
*Source.*　Adapted from Silberstein et al. 1994.

**TABLE 12–12.**　Preventive medications: efficacy, side effects, and relative contraindications and indications[a]

| Drug | Efficacy | Side effects | Comorbid conditions | |
|---|---|---|---|---|
| | | | Relative contraindications | Relative indications |
| β-Blockers | 4+ | 2+ | Asthma, depression, CHF, Raynaud's disease, diabetes | HTN, angina |
| Antiserotonin: methysergide | 4+ | 4+ | Angina, PVD | Orthostatic hypotension |
| Calcium channel blockers: verapamil | 2+ | 1+ | Constipation, hypotension | Migraine with aura, HTN, angina, asthma |
| Antidepressants: amitriptyline | 4+ | 2+ | Urinary retention, heart block | Other pain disorders, depression, anxiety disorders, insomnia |
| Anticonvulsants: divalproex | 4+ | 3+ | Liver disease, bleeding disorders | Mania, epilepsy, anxiety disorders |
| NSAIDs: naproxen | 2+ | 2+ | Ulcer disease, gastritis | Arthritis, other pain disorders |

[a]Ratings of efficacy and side effects are given on a scale from 1+ (lowest) to 4+ (highest). Abbreviations: CHF = congestive heart failure; HTN = hypertension; PVD = peripheral vascular disease; NSAIDs = nonsteroidal anti-inflammatory drugs.
*Source.*　Adapted from Silberstein et al. 1994.

## Treatment of the Aura

Subjects who had a spontaneous migraine visual aura have been studied with functional magnetic resonance imaging (MRI) (Cutrer et al. 1998). Interictally, using perfusion-weighted imaging, cerebral blood flow, cerebral blood volume, and mean transit time were normal and symmetrical. During visual auras, cerebral blood flow decreased 15%–53%, cerebral blood volume decreased 6%–33%, and mean transit time increased 10%–54% in the occipital cortex gray matter contralateral to the affected visual hemifield. When multiple perfusion images were obtained during the same aura, the margin of the perfusion defect moved anteriorly. The absence of diffusion abnormalities in these patients suggests that ischemia does not occur during the migraine aura (Cutrer and O'Donnell 1999). Recent positron-emission tomographic and functional MRI studies, and older magnetoencephalographic studies, support the existence of the spreading phenomenon in humans with migraine (Simkins et al. 1989). This evidence suggests that spreading depression may be the mechanism that produces spreading oligemia and the aura (Blau 1984; Pearce 1984; Welch et al. 1990).

Uncontrolled studies demonstrated that the inhalation of 10% $CO_2$ in air for 5 minutes was temporarily effective in decreasing the visual aura of migraine, whereas the inhalation of 10% $CO_2$ with 90% $O_2$ was always effective in abolishing the aura of migraine and preventing the development of the expected headache (Dalessio 1980). When headache was present, the effect of 10% $CO_2$ with 90% $O_2$ was unpredictable. As a practical matter, patients can sometimes successfully abort an aura by breathing into and out of a paper bag. In one study (Alvarez 1934), the inhalation of 100% $O_2$ for 15–120 minutes produced relief in fewer than half of patients.

We preferentially use the calcium channel blockers, especially verapamil, as preventive treatment in patients with migraine auras, with or without headache, especially if the auras are prolonged or are associated with hemiparesis. Although there is no scientific evidence for doing so, some avoid the use of β-blockers in patients who have migraine with prolonged aura. The use of aspirin has also been suggested for patients who have migraine with frequent or prolonged aura to prevent migraine stroke (Silberstein and Saper 1993; Silberstein et al. 1998).

## Treatment of the Headache

**Acute treatment.** There are many treatments available for acute migraine. The choice of treatment depends on the severity and frequency of headaches, the pattern of associated symptoms, the presence or absence of comorbid illnesses, and the patient's treatment response profile (Table 12–11) (Tfelt-Hansen and Lipton 1993). We start with nonspecific oral medications, such as analgesics, NSAIDs, or a caffeine adjuvant compound for patients who have mild to moderate headaches. If that treatment fails, or if the headache is moderate to severe, we move on to triptans or DHE. If prominent nausea or vomiting is present, we recommend an antiemetic and nonoral treatment. If oral medication is ineffective or cannot be used because of gastrointestinal symptoms, we recommend suppositories, nasal sprays, or injections, depending on the patient's preferred route of administration. Suppositories include ergotamine, indomethacin, and prochlorperazine. Nasal sprays include transnasal butorphanol, DHE, and sumatriptan A. Injections include subcutaneous sumatriptan and intramuscular DHE, among others. We often prescribe more than one exigent treatment at the time of the initial visit. For example, we may advise patients to use naproxen sodium for mild to moderate headaches and a triptan for more severe headaches (Silberstein and Lipton 1994; Silberstein et al. 1998).

**Simple and combination analgesics and NSAIDs.** We often begin with simple analgesics for patients with mild to moderate headaches. Many individuals find headache relief with a simple analgesic such as aspirin or acetaminophen, either alone or in combination with caffeine. Butalbital is another effective analgesic adjuvant. We also use the combination of acetaminophen, isometheptene (a sympathomimetic), and dichloralphenazone (a chloral hydrate derivative). For patients who are nauseated, we use the antiemetic metoclopramide. We often try naproxen sodium first, but we use all the NSAIDs, often in combination with metoclopramide. Indomethacin, available as a 50-mg rectal suppository, and intramuscular ketorolac are useful in patients with severe nausea and vomiting (Silberstein and Lipton 1994; Silberstein et al. 1998).

**Opioids.** More potent opioid analgesics, such as propoxyphene, meperidine, morphine, hydromorphone, and oxycodone are available alone and in combination with simple analgesics. Because medication overuse and rebound headache pose a threat, these agents are most appropriate for patients who experience infrequent headaches. There is less potential for abuse of agonist-antagonist opioids than of receptor agonists. Transnasal butorphanol tartrate, given in a dose of 1 mg followed by 1 mg 1 hour later, has been shown to be effective for the exigent treatment of migraine headache (Bowdle and Galer 1993; Silberstein et al. 1998).

**Ergotamine and DHE.** We use ergotamine and its derivative, DHE, to treat moderate to severe migraine if analgesics do not provide satisfactory headache relief or if they produce significant side effects. Because rectal absorption is more reliable than oral absorption, we prefer to use ergotamine by suppository. Patients who cannot tolerate ergotamine because of nausea are pretreated with metoclopramide, prochlorperazine, promethazine, or a mixture of a barbiturate and a belladonna alkaloid. Metoclopramide may enhance the absorption of oral ergotamine (Silberstein 1990; Silberstein and Lipton 1994; Volans 1978).

DHE has fewer side effects than ergotamine and can be administered intramuscularly, intranasally, subcutaneously, or intravenously. DHE is given in intramuscular or intravenous doses up to 1 mg per treatment, with a maximum of 3 mg/day. We typically limit monthly use to 18 ampules or 12 events. DHE is a mainstay of treatment because it is effective in most patients, it is associated with a low (less than 20%) headache recurrence rate, and it is less likely than ergotamine to exacerbate nausea or to produce rebound headache (Silberstein and Lipton 1994).

We avoid using ergotamine and DHE in women who are attempting to become pregnant and in patients with uncontrolled hypertension; sepsis; renal or hepatic failure; or coronary, cerebral, or peripheral vascular disease. Although nausea is a common side effect with ergotamine, it is less common with DHE (unless it is given intravenously). Other side effects include dizziness, paresthesias, abdominal cramps, and chest tightness; rare idiosyncratic arterial and coronary vasospasm can also occur. We recommend that all patients have an electrocardiogram before receiving their first dose of DHE, particularly if there are any cardiac risk factors (including age greater than 40 years) (Silberstein and Lipton 1994).

**Serotonin receptor agonists (triptans).** The first selective 5-HT$_{1B/1D}$ agonist to be developed and tested was sumatriptan, followed by zolmitriptan, naratriptan, rizatriptan, almotriptan, eletriptan, and frovatriptan (the latter two agents are still in clinical development). Sumatriptan is available both as an injection (6 mg subcutaneously) and as tablets (25- and 50-mg oral tablets). Sumatriptan has a more rapid onset of action when given subcutaneously than when given orally. Sumatriptan relieves headache pain, nausea, photophobia, and phonophobia and restores the patient's ability to function normally (Cady et al. 1991; Subcutaneous Sumatriptan International Study Group 1991). We often prescribe a triptan at the initial consultation as a first-line drug for severe attacks and as an escape medication for less severe attacks that do not adequately respond to simple or combination analgesics. We prefer subcutaneous injection for patients who need rapid relief or have severe nausea or vomiting. Although 80% of patients experience pain relief from an initial dose of sumatriptan, headache recurs in about 40%. Recurrences—most likely in patients with long-duration headaches—respond well to a second dose of sumatriptan or to simple and combination analgesics (Silberstein and Lipton 1994; Silberstein et al. 1998).

None of the triptans should be used for patients who have clinical ischemic heart disease, Prinzmetal's angina, uncontrolled hypertension, or strictly vertebrobasilar migraine or who are at high risk for these conditions. Common side effects of sumatriptan administration include pain at the injection site, tingling, flushing, burning, and warm or hot sensations. Dizziness, heaviness, neck pain, and dysphoria can also occur. These side effects generally abate within 45 minutes. Sumatriptan causes noncardiac chest pressure in approximately 4% of patients. These side effects generally abate within 45 minutes. We obtain an electrocardiogram for patients over age 40 and those who have risk factors for heart disease before using any of the triptans. We often give the first dose of sumatriptan in the office at a time when the patient does not have a headache (Silberstein and Lipton 1994; Silberstein et al. 1998).

**Second-generation triptans.** Oral naratriptan differs from sumatriptan primarily in its longer half-life, longer time of maximal concentration, higher oral bioavailability (70%), and lipophilicity. Studies of more than 4,000 patients indicate that the drug has a well-defined dose-response relationship for headache relief, with a mean response of 48% at 2 hours after administration, but therapeutic gains are comparatively modest (21%) (Humphrey et al. 1990b). Rates of relief with naratriptan were lower than with the other oral 5-HT$_{1B/1D}$ agonists. In a direct comparative crossover study with sumatriptan in patients prone to headache recurrence, about one-third fewer experienced recurrence when they used naratriptan compared with sumatriptan. However, 24-hour comparisons of naratriptan and sumatriptan found relief rates to be similar. The studies showed excellent tolerability for the 2.5-mg dose of naratriptan, with an adverse event rate close to that of placebo.

Oral eletriptan is rapidly absorbed, with high bioavailability (50%) and a long half-life (5 hours). There is some concern, however, regarding eletriptan's possible interaction with other compounds that are metabolized at the cytochrome P450 site. In a dose-ranging comparative trial, 2-hour responses were 67% at 40 mg and 77%

at 80 mg with excellent therapeutic gains. In this study, headache recurrences were about one-third, similar to sumatriptan (Färkkilä 1996; Jackson 1996). Rizatriptan has rapid oral absorption and high oral bioavailability at 45% for the 10-mg dose. Four trials found that rizatriptan was significantly better than placebo for headache relief and complete relief at 2 hours; doses tested ranged from 5 mg to 40 mg, with higher rates of relief reported with the higher doses (doses of rizatriptan currently available in the United States are 5 mg and 10 mg) (Cutler et al. 1996; Gijsman et al. 1997; Teall et al. 1998; Visser et al. 1996b). Rizatriptan has high consistency from attack to attack in formal blinded consistency studies and a useful wafer (melt) formulation that many patients (particularly those with nausea as a prominent feature) find convenient, as it dissolves on the tongue and requires no water. Rizatriptan has a significant interaction with propranolol, which requires that the dose be halved to 5 mg, and is contraindicated with monoamine oxidase inhibitors (MAOIs) because of its route of metabolism. Zolmitriptan was the second selective $5\text{-}HT_{1B/1D}$ agent marketed in the United States. It has high oral bioavailability (40%), a time of maximal concentration of about 2.5 hours, and metabolism by the cytochrome P450 system to an active metabolite that is degraded by monoamine oxidase A. Therefore, patients taking MAOIs are limited to a total zolmitriptan dose of 5 mg/day. Zolmitriptan (2.5 or 5 mg) was shown in three trials to be significantly more effective than placebo for headache relief and complete relief at 2 and 4 hours (Rapoport et al. 1997; Solomon et al. 1997; Visser et al. 1996a). In studies, zolmitriptan demonstrated a headache response of 64% with a therapeutic gain of 34% for the 2.5-mg dose and a headache response of 65% and a 37% therapeutic gain for the 5-mg dose. The recommended starting dose of 2.5 mg provides the best balance of benefit and side effects, although some patients may benefit from the 5-mg dose. It is now available as an oral disintegrating tablet. Frovatriptan is a $5\text{-}HT_{1B/1D}$ receptor agonist with a high affinity for the $5\text{-}HT_{1B/1D}$ receptors, potent agonism in human isolated cerebral arteries, functional selectivity for isolated cerebral arteries compared with coronary arteries, and limited coronary constrictor activity relative to sumatriptan. A randomized, double-blind, placebo-controlled, parallel-group, outpatient study of placebo, 2.5 mg, 5 mg, 10 mg, 20 mg, and 40 mg frovatriptan allocated in a 1:1:1:2:2:2 ratio was performed in 38 centers in the United States. At 2 hours there was a twofold significant difference in response rates between all doses of frovatriptan (40%–48%) and placebo (22%) ($P \le 0.012$). Frovatriptan was effective and well tolerated across a wide range of doses. In a follow-up study, a dose response

was observed for both efficacy, and, to a lesser extent, safety. At 2 hours, headache response for 2.5 mg was statistically significantly superior to placebo.

**Almotriptan.** The newest $5\text{-}HT_{1B/1D}$ agonist is almotriptan. Placebo-controlled, randomized trials in migraine patients suggest clinically significant migraine relief with oral almotriptan (Cabarrocas and Zayas 1998). In one study (Robert et al. 1999), a single oral dose of 6.25 mg or 12.5 mg of almotriptan or placebo was administered during three different migraine attacks. The overall percentages of attacks were 38.4%, 59.9%, and 70.3% for placebo, 6.25 mg and 12.5 mg, respectively. Pain-free values at 2 hours were 15.5%, 29.9%, and 38.8% for placebo, 6.25 mg and 12.5 mg, respectively.

**Adjunctive treatment.** The symptoms associated with migraine, such as nausea and vomiting, can be as disabling as the actual headache pain. The gastric stasis and delayed gastric emptying associated with migraine can decrease the effectiveness of oral medication. As a result, antiemetics such as metoclopramide—available in tablet, syrup, and injectable forms (in doses of 10–20 mg)—are extremely useful for the treatment of migraine. In addition, metoclopramide decreases gastric atony and enhances the absorption of coadministered medications (Albibi and McCallum 1983). Promethazine—available in tablet, liquid, suppository, and injectable forms (in doses of 25–50 mg)—is also useful to control nausea and vomiting, but unlike metoclopramide, it does not enhance gastric emptying. Ondansetron, a selective $5\text{-}HT_3$ receptor antagonist approved for chemotherapy-related emesis, can be used as an antiemetic and can be administered as an intravenous infusion (0.15 mg/kg diluted in 50 mL of 5% dextrose or normal saline) or as an 8-mg tablet (Albibi and McCallum 1983; Boyle et al. 1990; Tfelt-Hansen et al. 1980; Volans 1978).

**Preventive treatment.** Preventive medication should be considered under any of the following circumstances:

1. Recurring migraine that, in the patient's opinion, significantly interferes with his or her daily routine despite acute treatment (e.g., *two or more attacks a month produce disability lasting 3 or more days* or headache attacks that are infrequent but produce profound disability)

2. Failure of, contraindication to, or troublesome side effects from acute medications

3. Overuse of acute medications (required more than twice a week)

4. Presence of special circumstances—such as hemiplegic migraine or attacks with a risk of permanent neu-

rologic injury; or headache attacks that are rare but produce profound disruption (Silberstein and Lipton 1994)

5. Very frequent headaches (more than two per week) with the risk of rebound headache development

6. Patient preference, that is, the desire to have as few acute attacks as possible

These rules are stricter during pregnancy, during which time severe disabling attacks accompanied by nausea, vomiting, and possibly dehydration are required for long-term treatment to be prescribed (Silberstein 1997).

The major medication groups that are currently used for migraine preventive treatment include β-adrenergic blockers, antidepressants, calcium channel antagonists, serotonin antagonists, and anticonvulsants. Many of these agents interact with serotonergic neural systems, either by binding to 5-HT$_2$ receptor sites, downregulating the 5-HT$_2$ receptor, or modulating the discharge of serotonergic neurons (Silberstein and Lipton 1994).

If preventive medication is indicated, the agent should be chosen from one of the major categories based on side effect profiles and comorbid conditions (Table 12–12) (Tfelt-Hansen and Welch 1993). The drug should be started at a low dose and increased slowly until therapeutic effects or side effects develop or until the ceiling dose for the agent in question is reached. A full therapeutic trial may take 2–6 months. To obtain the maximum benefit from preventive medications, the patient should not overuse analgesics or ergot derivatives. Migraine headache may improve with time independent of treatment; if the headaches are well controlled, a drug holiday can be undertaken after a slow taper program.

**β-Blockers.** β-blockers, the most widely used class of drugs in the prophylactic treatment of migraine, are 60%–80% effective in producing a reduction in attack frequency greater than 50%. All β-blockers can produce behavioral side effects, such as drowsiness, fatigue, lethargy, sleep disorders, nightmares, depression, memory disturbance, and hallucinations, indicating that they affect the CNS (Andersson and Vinge 1990).

**Antidepressants.** The tricyclic antidepressants and atypical antidepressants, such as selective serotonin reuptake inhibitors, are used in the preventive treatment of migraine. These antidepressants are especially useful in patients with comorbid depression and anxiety disorders (Silberstein and Lipton 1994; Silberstein and Saper 1993).

**Anticonvulsant medications.** Valproic acid, the most useful anticonvulsant for migraine prophylaxis, is often used in the form of divalproex (Silberstein and Lipton 1994). Its efficacy in prophylaxis of headache, including migraine, has been supported in recent studies (Hering and Kuritzky 1992; R. Jensen et al. 1994; Klapper 1995; Mathew et al. 1995). The results of several open studies support its role in the treatment of migraine (Sorensen 1988) and transformed migraine (Mathew 1990). Migraine prevention may be correlated with plasma level, with suggested target plasma levels of 70 and 90 units (Sianard-Gainko et al. 1993). Divalproex is especially useful when migraine occurs in patients with epilepsy, anxiety disorders, or manic-depressive illness. Because of its safety, divalproex can be administered to patients with depression, Raynaud's disease, asthma, and diabetes, circumventing the contraindications to β-blockers (Silberstein and Lipton 1994). Gabapentin (600 to 1,800 mg) was effective in episodic migraine in a randomized, placebo-controlled, double-blind trial (Mathew et al. 1998). The most common adverse effects were dizziness or giddiness and drowsiness. Topiramate is a structurally unique anticonvulsant that was discovered by serendipity. Topiramate is a derivative of the naturally occurring monosaccharide D-fructose and contains a sulfamate functionality. Topiramate has been associated with weight loss, not weight gain (a common reason to discontinue preventive medication) with long-term use. Squab et al. (1999) found that topiramate (25 to 100 mg/day) was effective for frequent migraine.

## Setting Treatment Priorities

The goals of treatment are to relieve or prevent the pain and associated symptoms of migraine and to optimize the patient's ability to function normally. To achieve these goals, patients must learn to identify and avoid headache triggers. Acute treatment is almost always indicated, but preventive treatment should be used more selectively and should be limited to patients with frequent or severe headaches. The choice of treatment should be based on the presence of comorbid conditions. A concurrent illness should be treated with a single agent when possible, and agents that might aggravate a comorbid illness should be avoided. Biofeedback, relaxation techniques, and other behavioral interventions can also be used (Silberstein and Lipton 1994; Silberstein et al. 1998).

## Cluster Headache

Although it was once classified together with migraine as a vascular headache, cluster headache is a distinct clinical and epidemiologic entity (Horton et al. 1939; Silberstein

1994a). The image of the tortured individual rocking or pacing in the dark, with tears streaming from one eye and face contorted in exquisite pain, is distinct and unique in medicine. Attacks occur in series that last for weeks or months (cluster periods), separated by remission periods that usually last months or years.

The IHS criteria for cluster headache require at least five attacks of severe, unilateral, orbital, supraorbital, and/or temporal pain lasting 15–180 minutes if untreated (Table 12–13). The pain must be associated with at least one of the following: conjunctival injection, lacrimation, nasal congestion, rhinorrhea, forehead and facial sweating, miosis, ptosis, or eyelid edema. The attack frequency ranges from one attack every other day to eight attacks a day. Cluster headache can be divided into two clinical entities based on the remission pattern. Episodic cluster headache (IHS 3.1.2) periods last 7 days to 1 year, separated by pain-free periods lasting 14 days or more. Typical patients with cluster headache have one or two cluster periods a year, each lasting about 2–3 months. In patients with chronic cluster headache (IHS 3.1.3), attacks occur on a near-daily basis for at least 1 year, although remissions lasting fewer than 14 days are permissible. Chronic cluster headache may arise de novo or develop in a patient with episodic cluster headache. Chronic cluster headaches occur in fewer than 20% of patients with cluster headache (Horton et al. 1939; Mathew 1992; Silberstein 1994a; S.S. Solomon et al. 1991). About 10% of patients have chronic symptoms with no remission periods.

---

**TABLE 12–13.** Diagnostic criteria for cluster headache (3.1)

A. At least five attacks fulfilling B–D
B. Severe unilateral orbital, supraorbital, and/or temporal pain lasting 15–180 minutes if untreated
C. Headache is associated with at least one of the following signs, which have to be present on the pain side:
   1. Conjunctival injection
   2. Lacrimation
   3. Nasal congestion
   4. Rhinorrhea
   5. Forehead and facial sweating
   6. Miosis
   7. Ptosis
   8. Eyelid edema
D. Frequency of attacks: from one every other day to eight per day

*Source.* Reprinted from Headache Classification Committee of the International Headache Society: "Classification and Diagnostic Criteria for Headache Disorders, Cranial Neuralgias and Facial Pain." *Cephalalgia* 8 (suppl 7):1–96, 1988. Used with permission.

## Epidemiology

Cluster headache is a distinct clinical and epidemiologic entity. A study conducted in Minnesota found an age-adjusted incidence of cluster headache of 15.6 per 100,000 person-years for men and 4.0 per 100,000 person-years for women (Swanson et al. 1994).

## Comorbidity

Graham (1972) believed that cluster headache patients have a distinct personality, which he called the *leonine-mouse syndrome.* He described these individuals as timid people with increased dependency needs who needed to appear powerful. He further characterized them as ambitious, efficient, goal oriented, hard driving, and compulsive, but insecure and lacking in self-confidence. Patients with cluster headache usually have normal MMPI and Self-Rating Depression Scale scores (Mathew 1992). They often work despite their suffering, enduring four or five severe attacks a day (Mathew 1992). There have been no studies of psychopathology in representative samples of these patients.

## Pathophysiology

Cluster headache involves the first and second divisions of the trigeminal nerve. The strictly unilateral pain that precedes the onset of increased blood flow and the associated autonomic features provide evidence for involvement of the trigeminal system (Drummond and Lance 1984). Additional evidence is asymmetry in the blink reflex (Pavesi et al. 1987) and the fact that radiofrequency thermocoagulation of the trigeminal rootlets or ganglion produces pain relief (Mathew and Hurt 1988). The trigeminovascular system may be the common final pathway for cluster headache pain. Moskowitz (1988) believes that all clinical features of cluster headache, except for the periodicity, can be explained by a lesion in and around the cavernous portion of the carotid artery, the only anatomic area in which all the nociceptive, sympathetic, and parasympathetic fibers that innervate the eye come together. But recent positron-emission tomographic data establish that blood flow changes in that region are not limited to cluster headache. Positron-emission tomographic studies indicate that the pathophysiology is driven partially or entirely from the central nervous system with the demonstration of activation in the posterior hypothalamic gray matter in acute cluster headache. The episodic nature of cluster headache, in which the headaches turn on and off like clockwork, seems to respect some daily (circadian) rhythm. Moreover, the remarkable half-yearly, yearly, or even biennial cycling of the bouts is one of the most fascinating cycling processes of human biology. The increase in attacks associated with the summer and winter solstices and the relative reduction of attacks around the equinoxes is remarkable. Cluster headache may be regarded as a dysfunction of neurons in the pacemaker or clock regions of the brain (posterior hypothalamus) that allows activation of a trigeminal-autonomic loop in the brain stem that leads to pain with autonomic features in the pattern of cluster headache.

The cluster period may be caused by a cyclically occurring dysfunction of the biological-clock mechanisms of the suprachiasmatic nuclei of the hypothalamus. Secretory patterns of melatonin, cortisol, β-endorphin, and prolactin differ in cluster periods and remissions (Chazot et al. 1984; Mathew 1992).

## Treatment

Pharmacologic treatment for cluster headache can be acute (abortive) therapy, preventive (prophylactic) treatment, or a combination of both methods (Silberstein 1994b; S.S. Solomon et al. 1991).

### Acute Treatment

Treatments for sudden-onset, short-duration, acute attacks of cluster headache include oxygen inhalation, sumatriptan, DHE, and local anesthetics (Silberstein 1994b; S.S. Solomon et al. 1991).

Oxygen given by face mask (7–10 L/minute for 15 minutes) is effective in approximately 70% of patients, usually within 10 minutes (Kudrow 1981). Sumatriptan given subcutaneously is another highly effective exigent treatment for cluster headache, also providing a response within 10 minutes (Sumatriptan Cluster Headache Study Group 1991). It is most useful in patients who experience fewer than two attacks a day. DHE (given intramuscularly or subcutaneously) is also effective. Intranasal lidocaine is occasionally effective.

### Preventive Treatment

Patients with cluster headache usually require preventive therapy, the goal of which is to produce rapid remission and maintain it with minimal adverse effects until the cluster period is over. Effective medications include ergotamine, methysergide, corticosteroids, verapamil, lithium, and valproic acid. Indomethacin is also occasionally effective (Mathew 1992; Silberstein 1994b; S.S. Solomon et al. 1991).

We start treatment early in the cluster period and continue it until the patient is headache free for at least 2 weeks, then gradually taper the drug until the next cluster period. Treatment must be individualized. We often initiate preventive treatment with a combination of prednisone (60–100 mg daily) and verapamil (240 mg daily). Prednisone often produces a rapid remission, but it also produces side effects, which are cumulative. Verapamil has a favorable side effect profile but a delayed onset of action. By the time the prednisone taper is complete, the verapamil usually becomes effective. The verapamil dose may need to be increased (Kudrow 1980; Mather et al. 1991); however, if this is done and there is still no relief, methysergide (Kudrow 1980) (2 mg three to four times daily) is an effective alternative, especially in younger patients. If methysergide is ineffective, lithium (Ekbom 1981) or divalproex (Hering and Kuritzky 1989) can be used, either alone or in combination with verapamil. While waiting for the other drugs to take effect, we use corticosteroids and intramuscular DHE daily to break the headache cycle or to treat severe exacerbations. In patients with exclusively nocturnal attacks, we use ergotamine alone at bedtime.

Lithium carbonate was first tried in patients with cluster headache because of its demonstrated efficacy in manic-depressive illness, another cyclical disorder. Lithium carbonate is the preventive treatment of choice for chronic cluster headache and a treatment of second choice for the episodic variant. The mode of action of lithium in patients with cluster headache (and in those with manic-depressive illness) is unknown. It alters many circadian rhythms and reduces the frequency of rapid eye movement sleep. It has been suggested that a lithium-induced depletion of inositol results in decreased production of inositol triphosphate (a second messenger) and reduction of neuronal activity (Silberstein and Saper 1993).

Divalproex sodium (600–2,000 mg/day in two or three divided doses) has been reported to be effective; treatment is well tolerated and nausea is the only reported side effect (Hering and Kuritzky 1989). Lethargy, tremor, weight gain, and hair loss are some of the common adverse effects. In patients with refractory illness, combination preventive treatments are used; verapamil is commonly administered with lithium or divalproex. Like lithium, divalproex is also an effective therapy for mania and bipolar disorder. This overlap of therapies may suggest a common mechanism involving these cyclical disorders.

Chronic cluster headache can be treated with verapamil or lithium, alone or in combination. Divalproex, alone or in combination with verapamil, is often very effective. Patients with episodic cluster headache may become resistant to a previously successful prophylactic medication. These patients may require polypharmacy and (rarely) inpatient treatment. We use DHE given intravenously every 8 hours (in an inpatient setting) for the rare patient with intractable cluster headache (Mather et al. 1991). If hospitalization and all efforts at prevention fail, a neuroablative procedure may be necessary.

Newer treatments for cluster headache include the use of 10 mg of melatonin at bedtime and the use of topiramate.

## Conclusions

The primary headache disorders are linked to traditional psychiatric diseases on many levels. In both neurology and psychiatry, in the absence of true diagnostic gold standards, diagnosis depends on self-reported symptoms and other clinical features. Both families of disorders produce changes in mood, thought, and behavior that are attributed to poorly specified alterations of brain function. In both fields, neurochemical, neuroendocrine, and neuroimaging strategies are being used to better characterize the pathophysiologic substrates of the disorders. In both fields, there is strong evidence for genetic contributions, but the mechanisms have remained elusive. As the revolution in neuroscience and neurogenetics continues, we predict that the fundamental connections between headache and psychiatric disease will become increasingly apparent.

Both epidemiologic evidence and treatment response profiles suggest that headache disorders and psychiatric disease may have a common brain mechanism. Epidemiologic studies show a powerful association between migraine and mood disorders. The bidirectionality of risk is incompatible with simple causal models; depression cannot merely be a response to pain, because the onset of depression may precede the onset of migraine. Comorbidity is most likely to be, at least in part, a consequence of overlapping neural mechanisms. This notion is supported by the fact that there are many drugs that are effective in the treatment of both headache and psychiatric disease. Antidepressants, anticonvulsants, lithium carbonate, and neuroleptics are part of this shared therapeutic armamentarium. Many of the drugs developed in psychiatry may find application in the treatment of headache, especially in patients with comorbid disease.

The important clinical implication of comorbidity is that clinicians in neurology and psychiatry need to have a heightened index of suspicion for clinical conditions linked to each other's discipline. There is a burden of undiagnosed and untreated psychiatric disease in patients presenting with headache, and a burden of headache in patients presenting with psychiatric disease. As the fundamental biochemical and pharmacologic links between headache and psychiatric disease increase, so should the opportunities to effectively treat comorbid illnesses.

## References

Ad Hoc Committee on Classification of Headache: Classification of headache. Arch Neurol 6:13–16, 1962

Albibi R, McCallum RW: Metoclopramide: pharmacology and clinical application. Ann Intern Med 98:86–95, 1983

Alvarez WC: The present day treatment of migraine. Mayo Clin Proc 9:22, 1934

Alvarez WC: The migrainous scotoma as studied in 618 persons. Am J Ophthalmol 49:489–504, 1960

American Psychiatric Association: Diagnostic and Statistical Manual of Mental Disorders, 3rd Edition. Washington, DC, American Psychiatric Association, 1980

Amery WK, Waelkens J, Caers I: Dopaminergic mechanisms in premonitory phenomena, in The Prelude to the Migraine Attack. Edited by Amery WK, Wauquier A. London, Bailliere Tindall, 1986a, pp 64–77

Amery WK, Waelkens J, Van den Bergh V: Migraine warnings. Headache 26:60–66, 1986b

Andermann E, Andermann FA: Migraine-epilepsy relationships: epidemiological and genetic aspects, in Migraine and Epilepsy. Edited by Andermann FA, Lugaresi E. Boston, MA, Butterworths, 1987, pp 281–291

Andersson K, Vinge E: Alpha-adrenoceptor blockers and calcium antagonists in the prophylaxis and treatment of migraine. Drugs 39:355–373, 1990

Andrasik F, Blanchard EB, Arena JG, et al: Psychologic functioning in headache sufferers. Psychosom Med 44:171–182, 1982

Bakal DA: The Psychobiology of Chronic Headache. New York, Springer, 1982

Baumgartner C, Wessly P, Bingol C, et al: Long-term prognosis of analgesic withdrawal in patients with drug-induced headaches. Headache 29:510–514, 1989

Berkson J: Limitations of the application of fourfold table analysis to hospital data. Biometrics 2:47–53, 1949

Bickerstaff ER: Migraine variants and complications, in Migraine: Clinical and Research Aspects. Edited by Blau JN. Baltimore, MD, Johns Hopkins University Press, 1987, pp 55–75

Blau JN: Migraine prodromes separated from the aura: complete migraine. BMJ 281:658–660, 1980

Blau JN: Migraine pathogenesis: the neural hypothesis reexamined. J Neurol Neurosurg Psychiatry 47:437–442, 1984

Blau JN: Classical migraine: symptoms between visual aura and headache onset. Lancet 340:355–356, 1992

Bowden CL, Brugger AM, Swann AC, et al: Efficacy of divalproex vs lithium and placebo in the treatment of mania. JAMA 271:918–924, 1994

Bowdle TA, Galer BS: Agonist-antagonist and partial agonist opioids: pharmacologic mechanisms and clinical application in the treatment of headache. Headache 4:322–336, 1993

Boyle R, Behan PO, Sutton JA: A correlation between severity of migraine and delayed emptying measured by an epigastric impedance method. Br J Clin Pharmacol 30:405–409, 1990

Brandt J, Celentano D, Stewart WF, et al: Personality and emotional disorder in a community sample of migraine headache sufferers. Am J Psychiatry 147:303–308, 1990

Breslau N: Migraine, suicidal ideation, and suicide attempts. Neurology 42:392–395, 1992

Breslau N, Andreski P: Migraine, personality, and psychiatric comorbidity. Headache 35:382–386, 1995

Breslau N, Davis GC: Migraine, major depression and panic disorder: a prospective epidemiologic study of young adults. Cephalalgia 12:85–89, 1992

Breslau N, Davis GC: Migraine, physical health and psychiatric disorders: a prospective epidemiologic study of young adults. J Psychiatr Res 27:211–221, 1993

Breslau N, Davis GC, Andreski P: Migraine, psychiatric disorders and suicide attempts: an epidemiological study of young adults. Psychiatry Res 37:11–23, 1991

Breslau N, Merikangas K, Bowden CL: Comorbidity of migraine and major affective disorders. Neurology 44:17–22, 1994a

Breslau N, Davis GC, Schultz LR, et al: Migraine and major depression: a longitudinal study. Headache 7:387–393, 1994b

Breslau N, Chilcoat HD, Andreski P: Further evidence on the link between migraine and neuroticism. Neurology 47:663–667, 1996

Breslau N, Schultz LR, Stewart WF, et al: Headache and major depression: is the association specific to migraine? Neurology 54(2):308–313, 2000

Bruyn GW: Migraine equivalents, in Handbook of Clinical Neurology. Edited by Rose FC. New York, Elsevier, 1986, pp 155–171

Cabarrocas X, Zayas JM: Efficacy data on oral almotriptan, a novel 5HT1B/1D agonist. Headache 38:377, 1998

Cady BK, Wendt JK, Kirchner JR, et al: Treatment of acute migraine with subcutaneous sumatriptan. JAMA 265:2831–2835, 1991

Callaham M, Raskin N: A controlled study of dihydroergotamine in the treatment of acute migraine headache. Headache 26:168–171, 1986

Caplan L, Chedru F, Lhermitte F, et al: Transient global amnesia and migraine. Neurology 31:1167–1170, 1981

Carroll D: Retinal migraine. Headache 10:9–13, 1970

Castillo J, Munoz P, Guitera V, et al: Epidemiology of chronic daily headache in the general population. Headache 39:190–196, 1999

Chabriat H, Vahedi K, Iba-Zizen MT, et al: Clinical spectrum of CADASIL: a study of seven families. Lancet 346:934–939, 1995

Chazot C, Claustrat B, Brun J, et al: A chronologic study of melatonin cortisol, growth hormone and prolactin secretion in cluster headache. Cephalalgia 4:213–220, 1984

Coleston DM, Kennard C: Visual changes in migraine: indications of cortical dysfunction (abstract). Cephalalgia 13 (suppl 13):11, 1993

Curioso EP, Young WB, Shechter AL, et al: Psychiatric comorbidity predicts outcome in chronic daily headache patients. Neurology 52:A471, 1999

Cutler NR, Claghorn J, Sramek JJ, et al: Pilot study of MK-462 in migraine. Cephalalgia 16:113–116, 1996

Cutrer FM, O'Donnell A: Recent advances in functional neuroimaging. Curr Opin Neurol 12:255–259, 1999

Cutrer FM, Sorenson AG, Weisskoff RM, et al: Perfusion-weighted imaging defects during spontaneous migrainous aura. Ann Neurol 43:25–31, 1998

Dalessio DJ (ed): Wolff's Headache and Other Head Pain, 4th Edition. Oxford, UK, Oxford University Press, 1980

Dalessio DJ (ed): Wolff's Headache and Other Head Pain, 5th Edition. New York, Oxford University Press, 1987

DeBenedittis G, Lorenzetti A, Pieri A: The role of stressful life events in the onset of chronic primary headache. Pain 40:65–75, 1990

Diamond S: Muscle contraction headache, in Wolff's Headache and Other Head Pain, 5th Edition. Edited by Dalessio DJ. New York, Oxford University Press, 1987, pp 172–189

Diener HC, Gerber WD, Geiselhart S: Short and long-term effects of withdrawal therapy in drug-induced headache, in Drug-Induced Headache. Edited by Diener HC, Wilkinson M. Berlin, Germany, Springer-Verlag, 1988, pp 133–142

Diener HC, Pfaffenrath V, Soyka D, et al: Therapie des medikamenten-induzierten dauerkopfschmerzes. Munchener medizinische Wochenschrift 134:159–162, 1992

Dieter JN, Swerdlow B: A replicative investigation of the reliability of the MMPI in the classification of chronic headaches. Headache 28:212–222, 1988

Drummond PD: A quantitative assessment of photophobia in migraine and tension headache. Headache 26:465–469, 1986

Drummond PD, Lance JW: Thermographic changes in cluster headache. Neurology 34:1292–1298, 1984

Ehrenberg BL: Unusual clinical manifestations of migraine, and "the borderland of epilepsy" re-explored. Semin Neurol 11:118–127, 1991

Ekbom K: Lithium for cluster headache: review of the literature and preliminary results of long-term treatment. Headache 21:132–139, 1981

Ellertsen B, Kløve H: MMPI patterns in chronic muscle pain, tension headache, and migraine. Cephalalgia 7:65–71, 1987

Eysenck HJ, Eysenck SBG: Manual of the Eysenck Personality Questionnaire. San Diego, CA, EdITS/Educational and Industrial Testing Service, 1975

Färkkilä M: A dose-finding study of eletriptan (UK-116,044) (5–30 mg) for the acute treatment of migraine. Cephalalgia 16:387–388, 1996

Featherstone HJ: Migraine and muscle contraction headaches: a continuum. Headache 25:194–198, 1985

Feinstein AR: The pretherapeutic classification of comorbidity in chronic disease. Journal of Chronic Diseases 23:455–468, 1970

Fellerman DJ, VanEssen DC: Distributed hierarchical processing in the primate cerebral cortex (review). Cereb Cortex 1:1–47, 1991

Fields HL, Heinricher M: Brainstem modulation of nociceptor-driven withdrawal reflexes. Ann N Y Acad Sci 563:34–44, 1989

Fisher CM: Late-life migraine accompaniments as a cause of unexplained transient ischemic attacks. Can J Neurol Sci 7:9–17, 1980

Fisher CM: Late-life migraine accompaniments: further experience. Stroke 17:1033–1042, 1986

Friedman AP, VonStorch TJC, Merritt HH: Migraine and tension headaches: a clinical study: 2000 cases. Neurology 4:773–788, 1954

Gijsman H, Kramer MS, Sargent J, et al: Double-blind, placebo-controlled, dose-finding study of rizatriptan (MK-462) in the acute treatment of migraine. Cephalalgia 17:647–651, 1997

Goadsby PJ, Gundlach AL: Localization of 3H-dihydroergotamine-binding sites in the cat central nervous system: relevance to migraine. Ann Neurol 29:91–94, 1991

Goldberg D: Manual of the General Health Questionnaire. San Diego, CA, EdITS/Educational and Industrial Testing Service, 1975

Golden GS: The Alice in Wonderland syndrome in juvenile migraine. Pediatrics 63:517–519, 1979

Göllner VR, Salvini D: Untersuchungen mit dem Freiburger Persnlichkeitsinventar bei stationren Psychotherapie-Patienten. Zeitschrift fur Psychosomatische Medizin und Psychoanalyse 17:179–186, 1971

Graham JR: Cluster headache. Headache 11:175–185, 1972

Haas DC: Prolonged migraine aura status. Ann Neurol 11:197–199, 1982

Hathaway SR, McKinley JC: Minnesota Multiphasic Personality Inventory. Minneapolis, MN, University of Minnesota, 1943

Headache Classification Committee of the International Headache Society: Classification and diagnostic criteria for headache disorders, cranial neuralgias and facial pain. Cephalalgia 8:1–96, 1988

Hedges TR, Lackman RD: Isolated ophthalmic migraine in the differential diagnosis of cerebro-ocular ischemia. Stroke 7:379–381, 1976

Henry P, Michel P, Brochet B, et al: A nationwide survey of migraine in France: prevalence and clinical features in adults. Cephalalgia 12:229–237, 1992

Hering R, Kuritzky A: Sodium valproate in the treatment of cluster headache: an open clinical trial. Cephalalgia 9:195–198, 1989

Hering R, Kuritzky A: Sodium valproate in the prophylactic treatment of migraine: a double-blind study versus placebo. Cephalalgia 12:81–84, 1992

Horton BT, MacLean AR, Craig WM: A new syndrome of vascular headache: results of treatment with histamine: preliminary report. Mayo Clin Proc 14:257–260, 1939

Hosking G: Special forms: variants of migraine in childhood, in Migraine in Childhood. Edited by Hockaday JM. Boston, MA, Butterworths, 1988, pp 35–53

Humphrey PP, Feniuk W, Perren MJ: Antimigraine drugs in development: advances in serotonin receptor pharmacology. Headache 30:12–16, 1990a

Humphrey PP, Apperley E, Feniuk W, et al: A rational approach to identifying a fundamentally new drug for the treatment of migraine, in Cardiovascular Pharmacology of 5-Hydroxytryptamine: Prospective Therapeutic Applications. Edited by Saxena PR, Wallis DI, Wouters W, et al. Boston, MA, Kluwer Academic Publishers, 1990b, pp 416–431

Hupp SL, Kline LB, Corbett JJ: Visual disturbances of migraine. Surv Ophthalmol 33:221–236, 1989

Inan L, Soykan C, Tulunay FC: MMPI profiles of Turkish headache sufferers. Headache 34:152–154, 1994

Invernizzi G, Gala C, Buono M, et al: Neurotic traits and disease duration in headache patients. Cephalalgia 9:173–178, 1989

Isler H: Frequency and time course of premonitory phenomena, in The Prelude to the Migraine Attack. Edited by Amery WK, Wauquier A. London, Bailliere Tindall, 1986, pp 44–53

Iversen HK, Langemark M, Andersson PG, et al: Clinical characteristics of migraine and episodic tension-type headache in relation to old and new diagnostic criteria. Headache 30:514–519, 1990

Jackson NC: A comparison of oral eletriptan (UK-116,044) (20–80 mg) and oral sumatriptan (100 mg) in the acute treatment of migraine, for the Eletriptan Steering Committee (anstract). Cephalalgia 16:368–369, 1996

Jarman J, Fernandez M, Davies PTG, et al: High incidence of endogenous depression in migraine: confirmation by tyramine test. J Neurol Neurosurg Psychiatry 53:573–575, 1990

Jaspers K: Allemiene Psychopathologie. New York, Springer, 1973

Jensen K, Tfelt-Hansen P, Lauritzen M, et al: Classic migraine, a prospective recording of symptoms. Acta Neurol Scand 73:359–362, 1986

Jensen R, Brinck T, Olesen J: Sodium valproate has a prophylactic effect in migraine without aura. Neurology 44:647–651, 1994

Kandinsky V: Zur lehr von den Hallucinationen. Archiv fur Psychiatrie und Nervenkrankheiten 11:453–464, 1981

Kanto J, Allonen H, Koski K, et al: Pharmacokinetics of dihydroergotamine in healthy volunteers and in neurologic patients after a single intravenous injection. International Journal of Clinical Pharmacology, Therapy, and Toxicology 19:127–130, 1981

Khalil NM: Investigations of visual function in migraine using visual evoked potentials and visual psychophysical tests. Ph.D. dissertation, University of London, 1991

Khalil NM, Legg NJ: Pathophysiology of migraine: a study using VEP and contrast sensitivity, in New Advances in Headache Research: Proceedings of the 7th Migraine Trust International Symposium, London, September 1988. Edited by Rose FC. London, Smith-Gordon, 1989, pp 57–61

Klapper J: Divalproex sodium in the prophylactic treatment of migraine (abstract). Headache 35:290, 1995

Klee A, Willanger R: Disturbances of visual perception in migraine. Acta Neurol Scand 42:400–414, 1966

Kosslyn SM: Image and Brain: The Resolution of the Imagery Debate. Cambridge, MA, MIT Press, 1994

Kudrow L: Cluster Headache: Mechanisms and Management. New York, Oxford University Press, 1980

Kudrow L: Response of cluster headache attacks to oxygen inhalation. Headache 21:1–4, 1981

Kudrow L, Sutkus GJ: MMPI pattern specificity in primary headache disorders. Headache 19:18–24, 1979

Lance JW: The pharmacotherapy of migraine. Med J Aust 144:85–88, 1986

Lance JW: The pathophysiology of migraine, in Wolff's Headache and Other Head Pain, 6th Edition. Edited by Dalessio DJ, Silberstein SD. New York, Oxford University Press, 1993, pp 59–95

Langemark M, Jensen K, Olesen J: Temporal muscle blood flow in chronic tension-type headache. Arch Neurol 47:654–658, 1990

Lauritzen M: Spreading cortical depression as a mechanism of the aura in classic migraine, in The Prelude to the Migraine Attack. Edited by Amery WK, Wauquier A. London, Bailliere Tindall, 1986, pp 134–141

Leão AAP: Spreading depression of activity in the cerebral cortex. J Neurophysiol 2:438–440, 1944

Lennox WG, Lenox MA: Epilepsy and Related Disorders. Boston, MA, Little, Brown, 1960

Levor RM, Cohen MJ, Naliboff BD, et al: Psychosocial precursors and correlates of migraine headache. J Consult Clin Psychol 54:347–353, 1986

Levy DE: Transient CNS deficits: a common, benign syndrome in young adults. Neurology 38:831–836, 1988

Lippman CV: Certain hallucinations peculiar to migraine. J Nerv Ment Dis 116:346–351, 1952

Lipton RB, Silberstein SD: Why study the comorbidity of migraine? Neurology 44:4–5, 1994

Lipton RB, Stewart WF: Migraine in the United States: epidemiology and healthcare use. Neurology 43:6–10, 1993

Lipton RB, Stewart WF, Celentano DD, et al: Undiagnosed migraine: a comparison of symptom-based and self-reported physician diagnosis. Arch Intern Med 156:1–6, 1992

Lipton RB, Silberstein SD, Stewart WF: An update on the epidemiology of migraine. Headache 34:319–328, 1994

Lipton RB, Cady RK, Stewart WF, et al.: Sumatriptan treats the full spectrum of headache in individuals with disabling IHS migraine (abstract). Neurology 52 (suppl 2):256, 1999

Manzoni G, Farina S, Lanfranchi M, et al: Classic migraine-clinical findings in 164 patients. Eur Neurol 24:163–169, 1985

Marchesi C, De Ferri A, Petrolini N, et al: Prevalence of migraine and muscle tension headache in depressive disorders. J Affect Disord 16:33–36, 1989

Marcus DA: Migraine and tension-type headaches: the questionable validity of current classification systems. Clin J Pain 8:28–36, 1992

Marcus DA, Soso MJ: Migraine and stripe-induced visual discomfort. Arch Neurol 46:1129–1132, 1989

Marks DA, Ehrenberg BL: Migraine-related seizures in adults with epilepsy, with EEG correlation. Neurology 43:2476–2483, 1993

Mather P, Silberstein SD, Schulman E, et al: The treatment of cluster headache with repetitive intravenous dihydroergotamine. Headache 31:525–532, 1991

Mathew NT: Drug induced headache. Neurol Clin 8:903–912, 1990

Mathew NT: Chronic daily headache: clinical features and natural history, in Headache and Depression: Serotonin Pathways as a Common Clue. Edited by Nappi G, Bono G, Sandrini G, et al. New York, Raven, 1991, pp 49–58

Mathew NT: Cluster headache. Neurology 42:22–30, 1992

Mathew NT, Hurt W: Percutaneous radiofrequency trigeminal gangliorhizolysis in intractable cluster headache. Headache 28:328–331, 1988

Mathew NT, Kurman R, Perez F: Drug induced refractory headache—clinical features and management. Headache 30:634–638, 1990

Mathew NT, Saper JR, Silberstein SD, et al: Migraine prophylaxis with divalproex. Arch Neurol 52:281–286, 1995

Mathew NT, Saper JR, Magnus-Miller L: Efficacy and safety of gabapentin (Neurontin®) in migraine prophylaxis (abstract). 17th Annual Meeting of the American Pain Society, San Diego, CA, 1998

Mattsson P, Lundberg PO: Characteristics and prevalence of transient visual disturbances indicative of migraine visual aura. Cephalalgia 19:479–484, 1999

Merikangas KR, Risch NJ, Merikangas JR, et al: Migraine and depression: association and familial transmission. J Psychiatr Res 22:119–129, 1988

Merikangas KR, Angst J, Isler H: Migraine and psychopathology. Results of the Zurich cohort study of young adults. Arch Gen Psychiatry 47:849–853, 1990

Merikangas KR, Merikangas JR, Angst J: Headache syndromes and psychiatric disorders: association and familial transmission. J Psychiatr Res 27:197–210, 1993a

Merikangas KR, Stevens DE, Angst J: Headache and personality: results of a community sample of young adults. J Psychiatr Res 27:187–196, 1993b

Mitsikostas DD, Thomas AM: Comorbidity of headache and depressive disorders. Cephalalgia 19:211–217, 1999

Mongini F, Defilippi N, Negro C: Chronic daily headache. A clinical and psychologic profile before and after treatment. Headache 37:83–87, 1997

Morrison DP, Price WH: The prevalence of psychiatric disorder among female new referrals to a migraine clinic. Psychol Med 19:919–925, 1989

Moskowitz MA: The neurobiology of vascular head pain. Ann Neurol 16:157–168, 1984

Moskowitz MA: Cluster headache: evidence for a pathophysiologic focus in the superior pericarotid cavernous sinus plexus. Headache 28:584–586, 1988

Muller SE: Ergot alkaloids in migraine: is the effect via 5-HT receptors?, in 5- Hydroxytryptamine Mechanisms in Primary Headaches. Edited by Olesen J, Saxena PR. New York, Raven, 1992, pp 297–304

Olesen J: Clinical and pathophysiologic observations in migraine and tension-type headache explained by integration of vascular, supraspinal and myofascial inputs. Pain 46:125–132, 1991

Olesen J, Edvinsson L: Basic Mechanisms of Headache. Amsterdam, The Netherlands, Elsevier North-Holland, 1988

O'Sullivan F, Rossor M, Elston JS: Amaurosis fugax in young people. Br J Ophthalmol 76:660–662, 1992

Ottman R, Lipton RB: Comorbidity of migraine and epilepsy. Neurology 44:2105–2110, 1994

Ottman R, Susser ML: Strategies for data collection in genetic epidemiology: the Epilepsy Family Study of Columbia University. J Clin Epidemiol 45:721–727, 1992

Passchier J, Orlebeke JF: Headaches and stress in schoolchildren: an epidemiological study. Cephalalgia 5:167–176, 1985

Passchier J, Hylkema H, Orlebeke JF: Personality and headache type: a controlled study. Headache 24:140–146, 1984

Pavesi A, Granelia F, Brambila S, et al: Blink reflex in cluster headache: evidence of a trigeminal system dysfunction (abstract). Cephalalgia 7:100–101, 1987

Pearce JMS: Migraine: a cerebral disorder. Lancet 11:86–89, 1984

Peroutka SJ: Developments in 5-hydroxytryptamine receptor pharmacology in migraine. Neurol Clin 8:829–383, 1990a

Peroutka SJ: The pharmacology of current antimigraine drugs. Headache 30:5–11, 1990b

Phillips C: Headache and personality. J Psychosom Res 20:535–542, 1976

Puca F, Genco S, Prudenzano MP, et al: Psychiatric comorbidity and psychosocial stress in patients with tension-type headache from headache centers in Italy. The Italian Collaborative Group for the Study of Psychopathological Factors in Primary Headaches. Cephalalgia 19:159–164, 1999

Rapoport AM, Ramadan NM, Adelman JU, et al: Optimizing the dose of zolmitriptan (Zomig, 311C90) for the acute treatment of migraine: a multicenter, double-blind, placebo-controlled, dose range-finding study—The 017 Clinical Trial Study Group. Neurology 49:1210–1218, 1997

Raskin NH: Repetitive intravenous dihydroergotamine as therapy for intractable migraine. Neurology 36:995–997, 1986

Raskin NH: Headache, 2nd Edition. New York, Churchill-Livingstone, 1988

Raskin NH: Conclusions. Headache 30:24–28, 1990

Rasmussen BK: Migraine and tension-type headache in a general population: psychosocial factors. Int J Epidemiol 21:1138–1143, 1992

Rasmussen BK: Epidemiology of headache. Cephalalgia 15:45–68, 1995

Rasmussen BK, Jensen R, Schroll M, et al: Epidemiology of headache in a general population—a prevalence study. J Clin Epidemiol 44:1147–1157, 1991

Robert M, Cabarrocas X, Zayas JM, et al: Overall response of oral almotriptan in the treatment of three migraine attacks: on behalf of the Almotriptan Multiple Attacks Study Group. Cephalalgia 19:363, 1999

Sacks O: Migraine: Understanding a Common Disorder. Berkeley, CA, University of California Press, 1985

Saper JR: Ergotamine dependency—a review. Headache 27:435–438, 1987

Saper J, Matthew N, Silberstein S, et al: Safety and efficacy of divalproex sodium in the prophylaxis of migraine headache: a multicentered double-blind, placebo-controlled study (abstract). Neurology 43:401, 1993

Scher AI, Stewart WF, Liberman J, et al: Prevalence of frequent headache in a population sample. Headache 38:497–506, 1998

Schmidt FN, Carney P, Fitzsimmons G: An empirical assessment of the migraine personality type. J Psychosom Res 30:189–197, 1986

Schneider KA, Johannes CB, Linet MF, et al: Spectrum of headache in women with migraine with aura (abstract). Headache 5:301, 1994

Selby G, Lance JW: Observations on 500 cases of migraine and allied vascular headache. J Neurol Neurosurg Psychiatry 23:23–32, 1960

Sianard-Gainko J, Lenaerts M, Bastings E, et al: Sodium valproate in severe migraine and tension-type headache: clinical efficacy and correlations with blood levels (abstract). Cephalalgia 13 (suppl 13):252, 1993

Silberstein SD: Treatment of headache in primary care practice. Am J Med 77:65–72, 1984

Silberstein SD: Twenty questions about headaches in children and adolescents. Headache 30:716–724, 1990

Silberstein SD: Advances in understanding the pathophysiology of headache. Neurology 42 (suppl 2):6–10, 1992

Silberstein SD: Tension-type and chronic daily headache. Neurology 43:1644–1649, 1993

Silberstein SD: Pharmacologic management of cluster headache. CNS Drugs 2:199–207, 1994a

Silberstein SD: Review: serotonin 5-HT and migraine. Headache 34:408–417, 1994b

Silberstein SD: Migraine symptoms: survey of 500 self-reported migraineurs. Headache 35:287–396, 1995

Silberstein SD: Migraine and pregnancy. Neurol Clin 15:209–231, 1997

Silberstein SD, Lipton RB: The epidemiology of migraine. Neuroepidemiology 12:179–194, 1993

Silberstein SD, Lipton RB: Overview of diagnosis and treatment of migraine. Neurology 44:S6–S16, 1994

Silberstein SD, Lipton RB: Chronic daily headache, in Wolff's Headache and Other Head Pain, 7th Edition. Edited by Silberstein SD, Lipton RB, Dalessio DJ. New York, Oxford University Press, 2001, pp 247–282

Silberstein SD, Saper J: Migraine: diagnosis and treatment, in Wolff's Headache and Other Head Pain, 6th Edition. Edited by Dalessio D, Silberstein SD. New York, Oxford University Press, 1993, pp 96–170

Silberstein SD, Silberstein MM: New concepts in the pathogenesis of headache, II: mechanisms and treatment. Pain Management 3:334–342, 1990

Silberstein SD, Silberstein JR: Chronic daily headache: prognosis following inpatient treatment with repetitive IV DHE. Headache 32:439–445, 1992

Silberstein SD, Young WB: Migraine aura and prodrome. Semin Neurol 45:175–182, 1995

Silberstein SD, Schulman EA, Hopkins MM: Repetitive intravenous DHE in the treatment of refractory headache. Headache 30:334–339, 1990

Silberstein SD, Lipton R, Solomon S, et al: Classification of daily and near daily headaches: proposed revisions to the IHS classification. Headache 34:1–7, 1994

Silberstein SD, Lipton RB, Breslau N: Migraine: association with personality characteristics and psychopathology. Cephalalgia 15:1–15, 1995

Silberstein SD, Lipton RB, Goadsby PJ: Headache in Clinical Practice. Oxford, UK, Isis Medical Media, 1998

Simkins RT, Tepley N, Barkley GL: Spontaneous neuromagnetic fields in migraine: possible link to spreading cortical depression. Neurology 39:325, 1989

Solomon GD: Management of the headache patient with medical illness. Clin J Pain 5:95–99, 1989

Solomon SS, Lipton RB, Newman LC: Prophylactic therapy of cluster headaches: review. Clin Neuropharmacol 14:116–130, 1991

Solomon GD, Cady RK, Klapper JA, et al: Clinical efficacy and tolerability of 2.5 mg zolmitriptan for the acute treatment of migraine: the 042 Clinical Trial Study Group. Neurology 49:1193–1195, 1997

Sorensen KV: Valproate: a new drug in migraine prophylaxis. Acta Neurol Scand 78:346–348, 1988

Spierings ELH: Treatment of the migraine attack, in Migraine and Other Headaches. Edited by Ferrari MD, Lataste X. Park Ridge, NJ, Parthenon, 1989, pp 241–248

Sternbach RA, Dalessio DJ, Kunzel M, et al: MMPI patterns in common headache disorders. Headache 20:311–315, 1980

Stewart WF, Linet MS, Celentano DD: Migraine headaches and panic attacks. Psychosom Med 51:559–569, 1989

Stewart WF, Linet MS, Celentano DD, et al: Age and sex-specific incidence rates of migraine with and without visual aura. Am J Epidemiol 34:1111–1120, 1991

Stewart WF, Lipton RB, Celentano DD, et al: Prevalence of migraine headache in the United States. JAMA 267:64–69, 1992a

Stewart WF, Shechter A, Liberman J: Physician consultation for headache pain and history of panic: results from a population-based study. Am J Med 92:35S–40S, 1992b

Stewart WF, Schecter A, Lipton RB: Migraine heterogeneity: disability, pain intensity, attack frequency, and duration. Neurology 44:S24–S39, 1994

Subcutaneous Sumatriptan International Study Group: Treatment of migraine attacks with sumatriptan. N Engl J Med 325:316–321, 1991

Sumatriptan Cluster Headache Study Group: Treatment of acute cluster headache with sumatriptan. N Engl J Med 325:322–326, 1991

Swanson JW, Yanagihara T, Stang PE: Incidence of cluster headache: a population-based study in Olmstead County, Minnesota. Neurology 44:433–437, 1994

Tavola T, Gala C, Conte G, et al: Traditional Chinese acupuncture in tension-type headache: a controlled study. Pain 48:325–329, 1992

Teall J, Tuchman M, Cutler N, et al: Rizatriptan (MAXALT) for the acute treatment of migraine and migraine recurrence: a placebo-controlled, outpatient study—Rizatriptan 022 Study Group. Headache 38:281–287, 1998

Tekle Haimanot R, Seraw B, Forsgren L, et al: Migraine, chronic tension-type headache, and cluster headache in an Ethiopian rural community. Cephalalgia 15:482–488, 1995

Tfelt-Hansen P, Lipton RB: Prioritizing treatment, in The Headaches. Edited by Olesen J, Tfelt-Hansen P, Welch KMA. New York, Raven, 1993, pp 359–362

Tfelt-Hansen P, Welch KMA: Prioritizing prophylactic treatment, in The Headaches. Edited by Olesen J, Tfelt-Hansen P, Welch KMA. New York, Raven, 1993, pp 403–404

Tfelt-Hansen P, Olesen J, Aebelholt-Krabbe A, et al: A double blind study of metoclopramide in the treatment of migraine attacks. J Neurol Neurosurg Psychiatry 43:369–371, 1980

Touraine GA, Draper G: The migrainous patient: a constitutional study. J Nerv Ment Dis 80:183–204, 1934

Verri AP, Cecchini P, Galli C, et al: Psychiatric comorbidity in chronic daily headache. Cephalalgia 18:45–49, 1998

Visser WH, Klein KB, Cox RC, et al: 311C90, a new central and peripherally acting 5-HT1D receptor agonist in the acute oral treatment of migraine: a double-blind, placebo-controlled, dose-range finding study. Neurology 46:522–526, 1996a

Visser WH, Terwindt GM, Reines SA, et al: Rizatriptan vs sumatriptan in the acute treatment of migraine: a placebo-controlled, dose-ranging study—Dutch/US Rizatriptan Study Group. Arch Neurol 53:1132–1137, 1996b

Volans GN: Research review: migraine and drug absorption. Clin Pharmacokinet 3:313–318, 1978

Waelkens J, Caers I, Amery WK: Effects of therapeutic measures taken during the premonitory phase, in The Prelude to the Migraine Attack. Edited by Amery WK, Wauquier A. London, Bailliere Tindall, 1986, pp 78–83

Wang SJ, Fuh JL, Lu SR, et al: Chronic daily headache in Chinese elderly: prevalence, risk factors, and biannual follow-up. Neurology 54(2):314–319, 2000

Waters WE: Series in Clinical Epidemiology: Headache. Littleton, MA, PSG Publishing, 1988

Weeks R, Baskin S, Sheftell F, et al: A comparison of MMPI personality data and frontalis electromyographic readings in migraine and combination headache patients. Headache 23:75–82, 1983

Welch KMA: Relationship of stroke and migraine. Neurology 44 (suppl 7):33–36, 1994

Welch KMA, D'Andrea G, Tepley N, et al: The concept of migraine as a state of central neuronal hyperexcitability. Neurol Clin 8:817–828, 1990

Whitman B, Lipton RB: Oscillocusis: an unusual manifestation of migraine aura. Headache 35:430–431, 1995

Whitty CWM: Migraine without headache. Lancet 2:283–285, 1967

Wijman C, Wolf PA, Kase CS, et al: Migrainous visual accompaniments are not rare in late life: the Framingham Study. Stroke 29:1539–1543, 1998

Wilkins AJ, Nimmo-Smith I, Tait A, et al: A neurologic basis for visual discomfort. Brain 107:989–1017, 1984

Wolff HG: Personality features and reactions of subjects with migraine. Archives of Neurology and Psychiatry 37:895–921, 1937

Wolff HG: Headache in the migraine syndrome, in Headache and Other Head Pain. Edited by Wolff HG. New York, Oxford University Press, 1948, pp 255–318

Wolff HG: Muscles of the head and neck as sources of headache and other pain, in Headache and Other Head Pain, 2nd Edition. Edited by Wolff HG, Dalessio DJ. New York, Oxford University Press, 1963, pp 582–616

Wray SH, Prelec DM, Kosslyn SM: Visual processing in migraineurs. Brain 118:25–35, 1995

Ziegler DK, Hassanein RS: Specific headache phenomena: their frequency and coincidence. Headache 30:152–156, 1990

# CHAPTER 13

# Neuropsychiatric Aspects of Disorders of Attention

Ronald A. Cohen, Ph.D.

Stephen Salloway, M.D.

Tricia Zawacki, Ph.D.

Disorders of attention and consciousness often lead to requests for neuropsychiatric consultation. Attention-deficit/hyperactivity disorder (ADHD) in particular has become prominently featured in public awareness. At the same time, advances in understanding attentional systems and treating attentional disorders are moving rapidly forward. Neuropsychiatrists need to understand the neural systems and neurochemistry involved in the mediation of attention and need to be familiar with assessment techniques and treatment strategies for attentional disorders.

In the first section of this chapter, we review the conceptual models of attentional systems in the brain and define terms that are commonly associated with attention and consciousness. In the second section, we review the assessment of attention, and in the third section, we discuss the clinical features and management of attentional disturbance seen in clinical practice with adults.

## Importance of Attention in the Practice of Neuropsychiatry

William James described attention in this way (James 1890):

> Everyone knows what attention is. It is the taking possession by the mind, in clear vivid form, of one out of

what seems several simultaneous possible objects or trains of thought. Focalization, concentration of consciousness are of its essence. It implies withdrawal from some things in order to deal effectively with others.

Because the human mind cannot process at any one time all of the stimuli it receives from internal and external sources, processes must be present that can select, filter, and organize information into manageable and meaningful units. The term *attention* refers to that part of the cognitive apparatus that allows an individual to focus on selected features of sensory stimuli and ideas while keeping potentially distracting stimuli at bay.

The work of attention is essential to everyday existence and is part of our common vocabulary. At a cocktail party, people attempt to converse while simultaneously eating, drinking, listening to music, and being aware of other conversations and people nearby. Teachers instruct their students to "pay attention" in school, soldiers are ordered "to attention," and athletes may attribute a poor performance to a lack of concentration.

The terms *attention* and *consciousness* are closely related. Consciousness has been described as an alert state in which individuals are "aware of self and environment" (Adams and Victor 1981), whereas impaired consciousness implies diminished awareness and reactivity. The determination of an individual's level of consciousness is essential to the evaluation of attention. The neu-

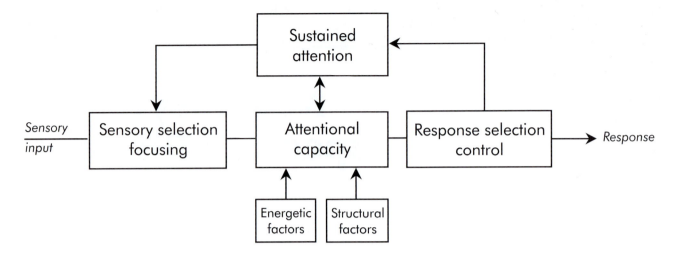

**FIGURE 13–1.** Primary factors underlying attention. This model depicts the flow of information through the four major components of attention: 1) sensory selection, 2) response selection control, 3) capacity, and 4) sustained attention. Attentional capacity is influenced by energetic and structural components. Sustained attention is the product of the information flow through the system and the resulting feedback, which affects each factor.
*Source.* Reprinted from Cohen RA: *Neuropsychology of Attention.* New York, Plenum, 1993. Used with permission.

robiology of consciousness is currently an area of active research. The interested reader should consult recent reviews by Crick and Koch (1990), Hill (1989), and Picton and Stuss (1994).

## Elements of Attention

Many terms have been used to describe aspects of attention. For the purpose of this review, attention depends on the interaction of four component processes: 1) *attentional capacity,* 2) *selective attention,* 3) *response selection and executive control,* and 4) *sustained attention.* These functional units are defined and discussed in the following paragraphs (R.A. Cohen 1993; Mirsky 1989; Posner and Boies 1971). A model depicting the flow of information through these four major components of attention is shown in Figure 13–1.

## Attentional Capacity and Focus

Humans have a limited capacity for attention. We are able to perform only a small number of tasks concurrently. The intensity of attentional focus that can be allocated at one point in time is limited. Attentional capacity governs both the amount of information that can be handled and the intensity of cognitive processing that can be performed on that information.

Capacity limitations constrain other attentional processes, influencing the efficiency of both sensory and response selection in addition to control. In the light of

this fact, some cognitive scientists have developed entire theories of attention based on the construct of a limited-capacity attentional system (Kahneman 1973).

Attentional capacity is not constant over time but fluctuates as a function of both extrinsic factors, such as the perceived value of stimuli and prevailing response demands, and intrinsic processes, such as energetic and structural factors (R.A. Cohen 1993; Kahneman 1973). Energetic factors include arousal, affective state, and drive and motivation. Structural factors include processing speed (e.g., reaction times), memory capacity, spatial dynamics, and temporal dynamics of the system. Structural capacity also varies in accordance with the individual's ability to perform specific cognitive operations. For instance, a chess expert is likely to find it easier than a novice to attend to a chess game. Structural factors represent more stable resource limitations that vary among individuals, whereas energetic factors fluctuate dramatically as a normal part of human functioning.

Focused attention is strongly dependent on attentional capacity. Attentional focus requires the ongoing allocation of available processing resources to a particular task or object. The intensity of focus is a function of requirements of the task but is constrained by capacity limitations.

It is relatively easy to identify examples of focused attention in everyday life. For instance, when one attempts to solve a mathematical problem, one may initially experience difficulty if one's abilities are not fully allocated to the task. Only when concentrated effort is directed toward the problem does a solution emerge.

Focused attention is strongly associated with the subjective experience of concentration.

Processing speed is a function of the amount of information that an individual can register, integrate, and respond to per unit of time. The relationship between information-processing speed and capacity is so dramatic that some investigators have argued that processing speed is a direct correlate of "intelligence." Correlations between reaction time and intelligence quotient (IQ) are between 0.6 and 0.9, depending on the sample characteristics and the type of IQ test utilized (Brand 1981; Vernon 1987). Information processing rate is therefore an important constraint on the capacity of attention as well as other aspects of cognition.

Reaction time reflects the time required to make an attentional selection or a response on tasks requiring attentional focus (Posner 1986). Tasks with greater processing demands tend to be associated with increased reaction times. From the standpoint of classic information-processing theory, a system's information-processing capacity is directly related to the rate of processing within the system: faster rates of processing are characteristic of larger-capacity systems (Broadbent 1958; Shannon and Weaver 1949).

Processing rate might be especially critical for tasks requiring manipulation of information within working memory (W. Schneider and Shiffrin 1977). Because the contents of working memory rapidly decay, information must be encoded into "chunks" and stored in long-term memory before further information can be accepted into working memory. If the rate of stimulus presentation exceeds this processing capacity, the new information will not be processed adequately. Because the perceiver usually does not control the rate of information presentation, this is a relatively common occurrence. Most people have had the experience of finding a classroom lecture going too quickly for note-taking or assimilation. After asking for directions from a local person, we receive a rapid-paced description of distances, turns, and landmarks that becomes irretrievably jumbled by the time we take to the road again. In both cases, the rate of information presentation has exceeded the working memory's capacity and rate of processing, resulting in degradation of the information.

The capacity for focused attention is directly related to the difficulty of the task and the number of operations that must be performed simultaneously. Even under ordinary conditions, attention is subject to division among a multitude of processes and potential stimuli. A teenager who does homework while watching television is engaging in divided attention, as is someone who drives while listening to the radio.

Engaging in divided attention is difficult because of interference created by the competing stimuli. Attending to one object often makes focusing on another object impossible. Cognitive studies indicate that people have a limited capacity for divided attention that is dependent on the same factors that influence attentional capacity. As the number of simultaneous information sources to be processed increases, attentional performance declines markedly, especially when task demands are made more difficult (Hasher and Zacks 1979; Kahneman and Treisman 1984; Navon 1985).

The quality of attentional performance on multiple simultaneous tasks is strongly dependent on how automatically the tasks can be performed. For instance, typists who are able to talk with people or carry out other activities while typing are demonstrating automatic attentional capacity for typing.

Cognitive scientists have demonstrated that automatic and controlled attentional processes can be dissociated by manipulating the parameters of particular tasks (W. Schneider and Shiffrin 1977). Memory load, spatial frame size, and number of targets to be detected are among the variables that influence an individual's ability to perform tasks automatically.

Some types of attention require much more effort than others. Tasks that require high levels of attentional effort have been characterized as *controlled-effortful attention*. Such tasks are also more apt to demand conscious awareness (Hasher and Zacks 1979; Kahneman and Treisman 1984). Effortful demands strongly influence the divided attentional capacity. This is obvious in cases of extreme physical exertion. It is not difficult to listen to a radio while engaging in moderate physical exercise, such as walking. However, it becomes increasingly difficult to maintain attentional focus when extreme physical exertion is required. At such times, people become increasingly aware of the signals being given out by the body (e.g., a pounding heartbeat), so that continued attention to other information becomes impossible. Interference effects associated with performing simultaneous tasks with effortful demands are also evident in more subtle neuropsychological tasks. Concurrent task demands, such as simultaneous finger tapping and verbal fluency, typically produce subtle decrements in performance on both tasks in normal subjects and produce dramatic impairments in patients with brain injury.

A central feature of the physiology of attention is the orienting response (Pavlov 1927; Siddle et al. 1983). The orienting response is the initial reaction of an animal to a novel stimulus and is characterized by activation in autonomic and motoric responses and brain electrical activity. Orienting responses are subject to decreases in response strength through a process of habituation. Habituation, an important element of attention, shifts attention and behavioral readiness away from stimuli that do not possess high levels of intrinsic salience to new stimuli. Sensitization is a process that opposes habituation and reflects an increased orienting response. Sensitization may occur due to an increase in generalized arousal or as a result of the introduction of other stimuli that increase the general readiness to respond to the habituated stimulus. There are now considerable data regarding the neural mechanisms underlying these responses (Kandel and Schwartz 1982), and it is likely that some of the mechanisms mediating these responses reflect brain events associated with attentional allocation.

## Selective Attention

Perhaps the most fundamental quality of all attentional processes is selectivity. Attention enables the selective deployment of cognitive resources toward salient information from either the external environment or the internal milieu. Attention also requires a shift from less salient information. Processes that enable or facilitate the selection of salient information for further cognitive processing are collectively referred to as *selective attention* (Treisman 1969; Triesman and Geffen 1967).

Selective attention influences the selection of particular target stimuli from the environment. Although selective attention is usually considered a phenomenon closely aligned with sensory processing and perception, it also facilitates the selection and control of response alternatives (R.A. Cohen and Waters 1985; J.A. Deutsch and Deutsch 1963; Jennings et al. 1980; Verfaellie et al. 1988). As a result of selective attention, some stimuli are given priority over others.

Selective attention always occurs relative to a temporal-spatial frame of reference. Information that is processed is selected from a broad spatial array over a specified period of time (M.R. Jones and Boltz 1989; Meck 1984; Neisser and Becklen 1975; Parasuraman 1984). Even when there is no predetermined basis for the selections, attention is pulled by events in the environment. If we see a police car's flashing light in the distance, our attention is likely to be pulled to that spatial location. Therefore, selective attention is governed by both intrinsic factors and the external milieu.

Selective attention is also facilitative. Attention enhances the capacity to process and respond to salient, task-relevant information, helping to optimize cognitive and behavioral performance (Desimone and Gross 1979; Goldberg and Bushnell 1981; Goldberg and Wurtz 1972). Although attentional facilitation serves many beneficial

functions, there are costs associated with attending. By attending to a particular stimulus, the likelihood of detecting other potentially relevant stimuli or choosing an alternative response strategy is reduced. Of course, this outcome is also adaptive. Individuals are constantly flooded with an infinite number of signals from both outside and within. By reducing the amount of information that will receive additional processing, attention constrains incoming information to the individual's available capacity at a given point in time, thereby keeping the level of information to be processed at a manageable level. Metaphorically, attention has often been compared to the aperture and lens system of a camera. By changing the depth of field and focal point, attention enables humans to direct themselves to appropriate aspects of external environmental events and internal operations. Attention thereby serves as a gating mechanism for the flow of information processing and the control of behavior.

## Response Selection and Executive Control

Although attention is often thought of as a process that prepares the individual for optimal sensory intake, perceptual analysis, and integration, it is also involved in response selection and control. Even when a task primarily requires selective attention, there are usually coexisting response demands (Heilman et al. 1985, 1988; Parasuraman 1975). To attend to information on the television, for example, we must first respond by turning on the television and then sitting down in a chair to look and listen. Although sensory selection may be elicited by the characteristics of the stimuli reaching our senses, more often than not the act of attending is linked to a planned, goal-directed course of action. We direct our behavior to obtain information that will allow us to select the most salient stimuli and optimal responses from available alternatives.

A wide variety of processes are associated with response selection and control, ranging from simple behavioral orienting (e.g., turning one's head in the direction of an auditory stimulus) to more complex cognitive processes involving intention, planning, and decision making. Response selection and control also form the basis for volitional action, as when a person who prepares to select and execute a response acts with deliberate focus in choosing the best response alternative.

Before responding, individuals generate a large number of response alternatives. The quality of these response alternatives is evaluated through trial and error or cognitively, without making an actual motor response. These responses form a response bias, which influences the probability of selecting specific responses. The process of establishing a response bias forms the attentional component of response intention (R.A. Cohen 1993; Heilman et al. 1988). Intention is influenced by the intrinsic salience of stimuli as well as the value placed on information or response alternatives within a specific context. In turn, intention influences the direction of attention, providing an impetus for both sensory and response selection.

The act of looking is an example of an intentional behavior. Looking not only involves the act of orienting one's head and eyes but is also associated with a readiness and preparation for future action (Neisser and Becklen 1975). For instance, a hunter who goes into the woods uses a wide range of tracking behaviors that may increase the likelihood of finding the target. The hunter's intentions guide his overt and covert responses and ultimately prime his level of vigilance to his target.

The attentional processes involved in response selection and control are related to a broader class of cognitive processes, commonly referred to as *executive functions* (Fuster 1989; Luria 1966). Several processes associated with response generation underlie executive control: intention, selection, initiation, inhibition, facilitation, and switching. Not only do these processes account for the control of simple motor responses, they also provide the foundation for more complex cognitive processes, such as planning, problem solving, and decision making, as well as conceptual processes such as categorization, organization, and abstraction. Executive control is strongly dependent on the actions of prefrontal-subcortical systems.

Attention is facilitated by neural mechanisms that suppress the probability of response to nontarget stimuli (inhibition) as well as by processes that increase the probability of response to targets (enhancement). Executive control is dependent on the ability to efficiently shift from one response alternative to another in accordance with changing environmental demands (switching).

## Sustained Attention

Attention is also strongly influenced by the temporal dynamics of the prevailing task demands and is characterized by performance variability over time (M.R. Jones and Boltz 1989; Meck 1984; Parasuraman 1984). The centrality of temporal factors to attention distinguishes attentional processes from other cognitive operations. Attention is more variable than sensory processes, primary perception, and memory, which are characterized by relative consistency over time. We assume that if a perceptual system is working properly, it will always detect and recognize stimuli that meet certain psycho-

physical conditions. In contrast, attention is inherently inconsistent because the likelihood that a particular stimulus will be detected or will receive additional focused processing is constantly changing and depends on prevailing task conditions and the person's momentary disposition. The tendency for performance to vary as a function of the temporal characteristics of tasks is often a result of demands for sustained attention. Problems with sustained attention are commonly associated with tasks requiring attentional persistence for long durations, because sustained performance is accompanied by considerable processing demands. Although sustained attention varies as a function of the relationship between target stimuli and distracters as well as the cognitive operations that are required, time is by itself a central determinant of attention. Sustained attention depends on the cyclical reprocessing of information that provides positive and negative feedback from the results of prior action.

All people have limits in their capacity for sustained attention. Sitting in a 1-hour lecture is not a problem for most bright college students, but even the brightest students would encounter tremendous difficulties sustaining their focus for a lecture that lasted 12 consecutive hours.

Vigilance is sustained attention directed toward specific targets. It requires a state of readiness to detect and respond to small changes occurring at random intervals in the environment (Colquhoun and Baddeley 1967; Corcoran et al. 1977; Jerison 1967). Detecting rare targets with lengthy intervals between responses can be difficult. This type of sustained attention, which is usually referred to as *vigilance*, is actually quite common in everyday life. For example, a watchman may spend the entire night attending to the possibility of an intruder without this event ever occurring. Attention to low-frequency events has different processing requirements than responding to high-frequency events and, for many people, is more difficult. Vigilance and sustained attention are under the influence of sustained motivational level, boredom, and fatigue, which are sensitive to the dynamics of temporal tasks.

## Models of Attention

Attention is not a unitary process; it spans multiple psychological domains and includes many neural systems. The boundaries of attention intersect with other constructs in common usage: memory, consciousness, vigilance, motivation, and alertness. Using examples of patients with distinctive lesions and information from basic neuroscience and neuroanatomy, a number of researchers have developed conceptual models of the cognitive constructs and neural systems involved in attention. There is considerable agreement among these conceptual systems (for greater detail, see R.A. Cohen 1993). There appears to be a consensus that attention is mediated through the interaction of neural networks (Mesulam 1981). The key structures involved in these neural networks are the reticular activating system (RAS), the thalamus and striatum, the nondominant posterior parietal cortex, the prefrontal cortex, and the anterior cingulate gyrus and limbic system.

Mesulam (1985) subdivided attention into two major categories: a matrix or state function and a vector or channel function. Matrix functions regulate overall information-processing capacity, detection efficiency, focusing power, and vigilance, which he associated primarily with the RAS. The vector function regulates the direction or target of attention. This is analogous to selective attention and is associated with neocortical systems. In practice, these two systems are integrated (Figure 13–2).

Heilman et al. (1993) developed a model of a corticolimbic-reticular formation network. This model accounts for hemiattention associated with neglect syndrome and provides a general neuroanatomical framework for attention. In this model, selective attention is considered to be dependent on arousal, sensory transmission, intact sensory association area projections, projections to the nucleus reticularis of the thalamus, sensory convergence to a heteromodal cortex, a supramodal cortex such as the inferior parietal lobule, and limbic connections. Neglect is considered to be an arousal-attentional disorder created by dysfunction of this network. Unilateral lesions affecting any part of the network may result in neglect (Figure 13–3).

A two-process model of attention has also been proposed by Posner and Cohen (1984) and Posner et al. (1987), who consider the parietal cortex and cingulate region to be the brain's two primary attentional systems. These researchers maintain that these two systems influence different attentional processes. The parietal cortex is involved in the covert disengagement of attention that is necessary for sensory selection, whereas the cingulate cortex is responsible for the intensity of attentional focus. In the next section, we briefly describe the role of each of these systems in attention.

The RAS plays a major role in modulating arousal and provides global regulation of attentional tone for the forebrain (Moruzzi and Magoun 1949). Lesions of the midbrain reticular core may cause permanent stupor or coma. The midbrain reticular core projects to the intralaminar nuclei of the thalamus, which in turn project

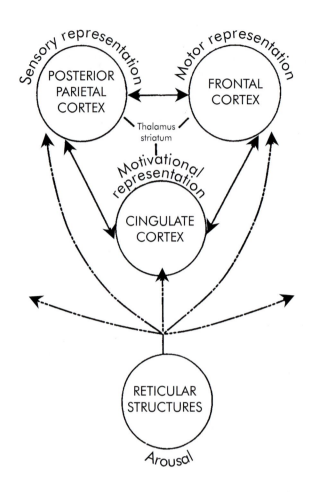

**FIGURE 13–2.** A network involved in the distribution of attention to extrapersonal targets.
*Source.* Reprinted from Mesulam M-M: *Principles of Behavioral Neurology.* Philadelphia, PA, FA Davis, 1985. Used with permission.

to the caudate nucleus, prefrontal cortex, and many other cortical regions but not to the primary sensory areas (E.G. Jones and Leavitt 1974; E.G. Jones et al. 1979; Steriade and Glenn 1982). The RAS-thalamic input to the cortex provides nonspecific priming for attention. The reticular nucleus of the thalamus has reciprocal connections with the midbrain RAS, the prefrontal cortex, and the sensory nuclei of the thalamus. The reticular nucleus appears to inhibit thalamic relay to the cortex, and Scheibel (1981) has proposed that the reticular nucleus acts as an attentional gate or filter for sensory stimuli. Increased arousal or behavioral activation inhibits the reticular nucleus, facilitating transmission of sensory information to the cortex.

The intensity of arousal and direction of attention is strongly influenced by the hypothalamus through its regulation of the daily circadian rhythm and its role in the modulation of appetitive function (Folkard 1979; Hockey and Colquhoun 1972). Each individual has an internal circadian clock, which regulates the sleep-wake

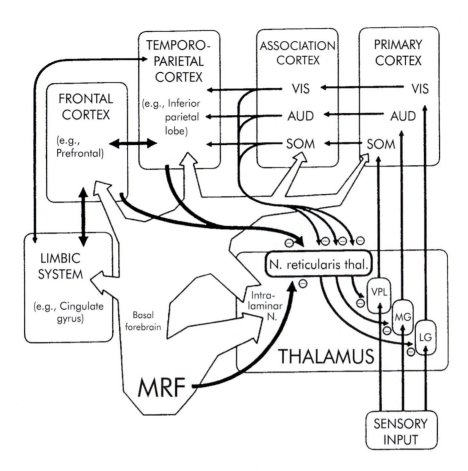

**FIGURE 13–3.** Schematic representation of pathways important in sensory attention and tonic arousal.

*Note.* MRF = mesencephalic reticular formation; VIS = visual; AUD = auditory; SOM = somasthetic. The thalamic sensory relay nuclei are VPL = ventralis posterolateralis; MG = medial geniculate; LG = lateral geniculate.

*Source.* Reprinted from Heilman KM, Watson RT, Valenstein E: "Neglect and Related Disorders," in *Clinical Neuropsychology*, 3rd Edition. Edited by Heilman KM, Valenstein E. New York, Oxford University Press, 1993, pp 279–336. Used with permission.

rhythm that is primarily under the control of the suprachiasmatic nucleus of the hypothalamus. Some individuals describe themselves as "morning persons" or "night persons" on the basis of consistently higher levels of alertness, energy, and attentional capacity at certain times of the day. This phenomenon is probably related to interactions between the RAS and the suprachiasmatic nucleus/ extended circadian network. The circadian rhythm is a dynamic process that changes throughout the life cycle. Understanding the relationship between the circadian rhythm and attention is important for optimizing educational and occupational activities. This relationship is also important in clinical practice when a clinician advises patients with attentional disturbance regarding remedial academic and work programs and patients with Alzheimer's disease who experience disruption of the circadian rhythm and are vulnerable to attentional disturbance and confusion in the late afternoon and evening.

The frontal lobe is an essential component of the

attentional matrix. The prefrontal cortex is linked with subcortical structures in three behaviorally relevant circuits (Alexander et al. 1986; Cummings 1993; Mega and Cummings 1994; Salloway and Cummings 1994). The dorsolateral prefrontal cortex circuit is involved in maintaining response flexibility and generating response alternatives, the working memory, and the temporal sequencing of information. Lesions affecting this system are associated with perseveration, distractibility, impersistence, slowing of cognitive speed, impairments in abstraction and memory retrieval, cognitive disorganization, and flatness of affect. The orbitomedial prefrontal circuit modulates impulses and participates in the regulation of mood and working memory. Patients with lesions in this circuit tend to be impulsive and disinhibited, with prominent mood lability. These patients have poor self-monitoring and have trouble inhibiting responses on attentional tasks. The anterior cingulate circuit plays a major role in drive and motivation. Lesions in this system lead to apathy and poor motivation (R.A. Cohen et al. 1990, 1994; Salloway 1994). Dysfunction in this system may be associated with the easy boredom seen in patients with ADHD.

The dorsolateral prefrontal cortex and the orbitomedial prefrontal region are involved in the executive control of attention and cognition. These functions include intention and response initiation, inhibition, persistence, and switching, processes that are central to the planning and generation of behavior and to the direction of responding relative to goals. Executive control depends on the ability to inhibit responding to irrelevant stimuli and to facilitate goal-appropriate responses. A mechanism whereby "switching" between response alternatives can occur is necessary for executive control.

The clinical disorder of hemispatial inattention associated with hemineglect syndrome provides evidence that the nondominant parietal cortex plays a central role in visual selective attention. Subsequent neurophysiological investigations expand on these observations, yielding information about underlying mechanisms confirming that neurons in the inferior parietal lobule have specialized attentional functions. Single-unit neuron activity from inferior parietal cells of awake primates show increased firing rates when attention is directed toward motivationally salient stimuli (Bushnell et al. 1981; Hyvarinen et al. 1980; Mountcastle et al. 1975). Neurons in area PG (angular gyrus) of the right inferior parietal lobule have the ability to facilitate future responding to expected stimuli at a particular spatial location. Neuronal activation of inferior parietal neurons occurs in the absence of motoric responding, including eye movements, but is associated with the task demands for future responding. Furthermore, firing rates of inferior parietal neurons can be modified by changing attentional and motivational parameters. These neurons in monkeys appear to activate before actual sensory analysis (Bushnell et al. 1981; Desimone and Gross 1979; Goldberg and Bushnell 1981; Goldberg and Wurtz 1972; Hyvarinen et al. 1980).

Many investigators have demonstrated that the right parietal lobe is dominant for directed attention to extrapersonal space. The posterior parietal cortex maintains a sensory representation of extrapersonal space, whereas the frontal eyefields and associated cortex maintain a motor representation. These areas are influenced by projections from the cingulate cortex, which provide motivational input, and from the RAS, which modulates arousal. These structures are interconnected with the thalamus and striatum.

Limbic areas provide inputs to the sensory association cortex that modulate the attentional response of sensory association areas such as the inferior parietal lobules. The mesial temporal cortex controls memory processes, emotional experience, and the binding of informational value to stimuli. These inputs inhibit or facilitate attentional response in accordance with information pertaining to stimulus significance, motivational state, and the goal orientation of the animal (Hyvarinen et al. 1980; Nauta 1986; Pribram 1969).

The anterior cingulate gyrus, a component of the limbic circuit, plays a pivotal role in attention by contributing important energetic components of drive and motivation. Bilateral lesions of the anterior cingulate region can produce a profound apathetic state of akinetic mutism. Such lesions may be seen after infarction of the bilateral anterior cerebral artery caused by rupture of an aneurysm of the anterior communicating artery. Individuals in this state are alert but demonstrate little interest in interacting with stimuli in the environment.

Evidence for the role of the cingulate gyrus in attention comes from cognitive studies in normal adults using functional imaging and from the evaluation of patients after cingulotomy (R.A. Cohen et al. 1990, 1994). The cingulate gyrus activates as a function of the intensity of attentional focus and effort. In two studies (Pardo et al. 1991; Petersen et al. 1989) of regional cerebral blood flow with positron emission tomography in subjects completing the Stroop task and a semantic activation task, the anterior cingulate region was found to activate during tasks that involve scrutinizing stimuli and selecting the correct response (Figure 13–4).

Obsessive-compulsive disorder may be a disorder of excessive vigilance involving dysregulation in frontostriatothalamic circuits (Baxter 1992; Baxter et al. 1992; Modell et al. 1989). Functional imaging studies have found increased activity in the orbital frontal gyrus, the cingulate gyrus, and the head of the caudate nucleus, particularly in the left hemisphere (Benkelfat et al. 1990; Swedo et al. 1992). Metabolism normalizes in these areas when symptoms are reduced after successful drug and behavioral treatments. This disorder highlights the role that the basal ganglia and thalamus play in modulating components of attention such as arousal, vigilance, executive control, and response selection (Mindus et al. 1994; Rapoport 1991; Salloway et al. 1995).

Although the neurochemistry underlying attention systems is not well understood, there is evidence that catecholaminergic, cholinergic, and, indirectly, serotonergic systems are important in attentional processes (McCormick 1989; Sato et al. 1987; Shute and Lewis 1967). The RAS comprises a network of monoaminergic (norepinephrine, dopamine, and serotonin) and cholinergic neurotransmitters. Stimulation or blockade of these

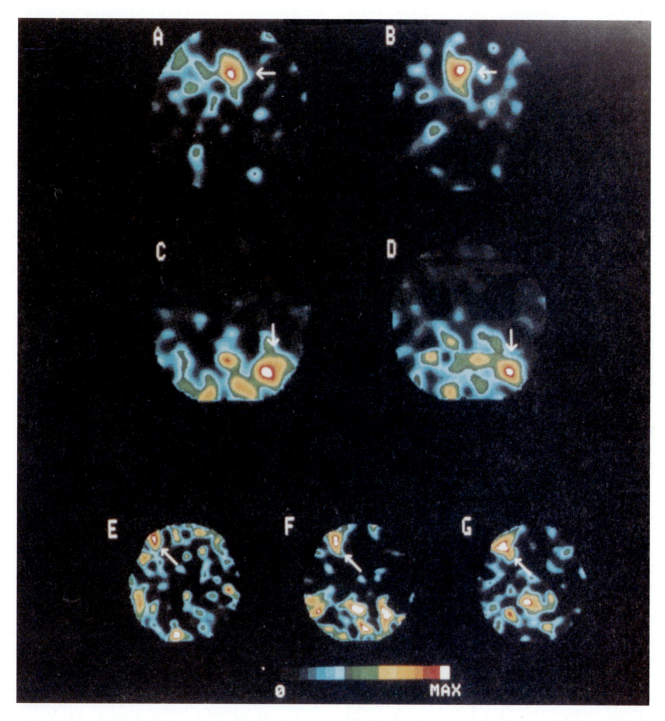

**FIGURE 13–4.** Positron-emission tomographic imaging of visual (A, C, F) versus auditory (B, D, G) presentation of a semantic association task. These slices (except E) represent blood flow changes when blood flow response during repetition of presented words is subtracted from the subject's verbal statement of a use for the presented word (e.g., "cake"—"eat"). Slices A and B show activation near the midline in anterior cingulate cortex. Slices C and D show activation in right lateral cerebellum. Slices E, F, and G show activation in left anterior, inferior frontal cortex. Slices F and G are from the vocalize use association task; slice E is from a different semantic association task, in which subjects were asked to silently monitor a list of words for members of a semantic category. These findings demonstrate the role of anterior brain systems on tasks requiring focused semantic processing and increased attentional demands.

*Source.* Reprinted from Pardo JV, Fox PT, Raichle ME: "Localization of a Human System for Sustained Attention by Positron Emission Tomography." *Nature* 349:61–64, 1991. Used with permission.

neurotransmitters can have a prominent effect on arousal and neuronal responsiveness to sensory input. The clinical efficacy of stimulant medication in treating ADHD provides indirect evidence for the role of catecholamines in attention. These medications promote catecholaminergic activity by increasing the presynaptic release and blocking the reuptake of dopamine and norepinephrine (Clemens and Fuller 1979; Shekim et al. 1994; Shenker 1992).

In a recent report (Ebstein et al. 1996), individuals with high levels of novelty-seeking behavior were found to have abnormalities in the gene for the dopamine type 4 ($D_4$) receptor, suggesting that dopamine systems play a role in novelty seeking and reinforcement. In contrast, patients with Parkinson's disease have low levels of exploratory behavior (J.S. Schneider et al. 1994). In addition, dopamine has an effect on cognitive speed and reaction time. Patients with untreated Parkinson's disease have slower cognitive speed than patients taking levodopa, even after controlling for motor dysfunction (Lange et al. 1992; Owens et al. 1992). This effect is probably mediated through mesencephalic-prefrontal dopaminergic pathways.

A recent study of monkeys treated with 1-methyl-4-phenyl-1,2,3,6-tetrahydropyridine (MPTP), a drug toxic to dopaminergic neurons, demonstrated that dopamine agonists and stimulants increase task persistence (J.S. Schneider et al. 1994). Dopamine and norepinephrine also participate in prefrontal memory systems (Arnstein and Goldman-Rakic 1985). Serotoninergic systems probably modulate the impulsive and hyperactive symptoms associated with attentional disturbance by directly affecting mood and by interacting with catecholaminergic systems in the nucleus accumbens and prefrontal cortex (Costall et al. 1979; Halperin et al. 1994).

## Assessing Disorders of Attention

Although it is an essential part of human experience, attention is difficult to directly observe or measure. Attention fluctuates with changes in task conditions and in the processing capacity of the subject. Attentional performance is often situationally dependent. Patients may demonstrate good attentional ability in a structured office setting but be quite impaired in a school, work, or home environment with high stimulation and less structure. Consequently, attention is less amenable than many other cognitive functions to assessment by traditional, standardized, paper-and-pencil testing.

The ability to pay attention is fundamental to effective cognitive performance. When attentional processes are impaired, assessment of the mental status examination may be unreliable. Clinicians often reach conclusions regarding the presence of attentional disturbance by default. When reduced cognitive performance is observed in the absence of consistent deficits of memory, language, visual integration, or other cognitive functions, attentional problems are implicated. Yet methodological advances such as the advent of computer-based assessment paradigms, as well as increased knowledge regarding underlying attentional processes, have led to better methods for the assessment of attention.

In clinical practice, the evaluation of attention is often made quickly, at the bedside or in the office. Three sources of information are typically used in the assessment of attention: 1) clinical interview and self-report inventories, 2) direct behavioral observation, and 3) standardized tests of cognitive functions. In this section, we summarize these approaches to the clinical evaluation of attention. The reader is encouraged to review Lezak (1995) for a more detailed account of the actual test procedures and norms and R.A. Cohen (1993) for methodological issues in the assessment of attention.

The clinical interview and medical history can provide important information regarding possible attentional disturbance. DSM-IV-TR (American Psychiatric Association 2000) provides a foundation for the clinical interview and describes the criteria for a diagnosis of ADHD.

ADHD researchers have developed a number of specific inventories for rating attention and behavioral disturbances. Conners (1969) developed a teacher's rating system for measuring behavioral problems, including ADHD in children. (See Barkley et al. 1990 for a complete review of such inventories.)

Inventories developed for rating the cognitive and behavioral impairments of patients with brain damage may also prove useful. The Neurobehavioral Rating Scale (Levin et al. 1987) was developed for rating symptoms of closed head injury (CHI) and contains items pertaining to attention impairment. Although structured interview and inventories provide useful clinical information about possible attentional disturbance, data from these sources must be considered with caution. These methods often require ratings from a family member or someone who may lack objectivity. ADHD is such a popular disorder that patients may be very quick to describe problems concentrating when their behavior is within normal limits. An adequate assessment of attention, therefore, requires data from multiple sources.

Clinical inferences regarding possible attentional disturbance are often based on behavioral observation. A patient who is well directed with eye contact and orientation toward a task is usually considered to be attending.

Restlessness and an inability to stay seated during tasks are strong indicators of hyperactivity. Initial clinical judgments regarding attentional disturbance are often made on the basis of such observations. If greater measurement validity is desired, however, a number of methods for structured behavioral observation and quantification are available. These include event recording (frequency of undesirable behavior) and interval recording (duration of behaviors). Several excellent texts are available for a more detailed review of behavioral assessment methods (see Bellack and Hersen 1988).

Unlike most other cognitive processes, attention primarily serves a facilitative function (R.A. Cohen et al. 1998). Attention enhances or inhibits perception, memory, motor output, and executive functions, including problem solving. The following must be considered when assessing attention (R.A. Cohen et al. 1998):

- Pure tests of attention do not exist.
- Attention usually must be assessed within the context of performance on tasks that load on one or more these other domains.
- Attentional performance is often a function of a derived measure obtained by comparing performance across tasks that load differentially with respect to key attentional parameters (e.g., target-distractor ratio).
- Absolute performance is often less informative than measures of performance inconsistencies in the assessment of attention. For example, how performance varies as a function of time, spatial characteristics, or memory load provides more information about attentional dynamics than simply considering total errors on a visual detection task.
- Attentional assessment requires a multifactorial approach. Given that attention is not the by-product of a unitary process, it cannot be adequately assessed on the basis of findings from one specific test. For example, conclusions about attention solely based on Digit Span performance are misguided.

## Neuropsychological Tests of Attention

Neuropsychiatrists often request neuropsychological assessment to help in the evaluation of attentional disturbance. It is important for clinicians to be familiar with the tests commonly used to assess attention and the specific features of attention that they are designed to measure.

Attention comprises multiple processes, and the clinical evaluation of attention requires that data from multiple tasks be considered. Each task should be sensitive to a specific manifestation of attention. Although at times possible attentional disturbance can be inferred

**TABLE 13–1.** Neuropsychological measures of attentional domains

**Sensory selective attention**
    Double simultaneous stimulation
    Letter or symbol cancellation
    Line bisection
    Spatial cueing paradigms
    Dichotic listening
    Wechsler Adult Intelligence Scale—Revised (WAIS-R): picture completion
    Orienting response
    Event-related potential (ERP) tasks

**Response selection and control (executive control)**
    Motor impersistence task
    Go/no-go task
    Reciprocal motor programs
    Trail Making Test
    Wisconsin Card Sorting Test
    Porteus Mazes Test
    Controlled word generation
    Design fluency
    Spontaneous verbal generation

**Attentional capacity—focus**
    Digit Span Forward, Digit Span Backwards
    Corsi Blocks
    Serial addition/subtraction
    Consonant Trigrams
    Symbol-digit tasks
    Stroop Test
    Reaction time paradigms
    Paced Auditory Serial Addition Task (PASAT)
    Dichotic Listening Test

**Sustained performance and vigilance**
    Continuous Performance Test (CPT)
    Motor continuation
    Cancellation tasks

from the findings of single test, a thorough assessment of attention requires the use of more than one test. A comprehensive assessment of attention necessitates the use of a neuropsychological battery containing several standardized paradigms that are capable of measuring specific impairments of attention. Table 13–1 lists the domains that should be evaluated in a comprehensive assessment of attention.

Many tests are designed to assess other cognitive functions but are also sensitive to attentional disturbance. The Mental Control and Digit Span subtests of the Wechsler Memory Scale (Wechsler 1945), as well as other memory measures, also provide indirect measures of attention. Comparison of the recall on Trial 1 relative to subsequent learning trials on word list learning tasks, such as Paired Associated Learning, indicates how well the patient is attending initially. Possible attentional problems may also be identified on the basis of the subject's response characteristics during testing. Excessive interitem variability may reflect fluctuations in attentional focus and problems with sustained attention. Intertest variability, particularly when inconsistencies are noted between subtests measuring the same cognitive function, may also suggest impaired attention. However, caution should be used when interpreting performance variability, because some variability may reflect the standard error of measurement and subtle differences in the nature of certain tasks.

When considering tests sensitive to specific processes of attention, it is important to recognize that the attentional components measured by these tests are not completely distinct. Tests that are particularly sensitive to impairments of sustained attention may also require executive control and attentional focus. Impairments affecting one element of attention may be associated with impairments of other attentional functions.

## Attentional Capacity and Focus

A variety of structural and energetic factors influence attentional capacity. Tasks that tax energetic or structural capacity limitations typically require effortful, focused attention. Many tests are available for the assessment of attentional capacity and focus. Although these tasks are similar in requiring attentional focus, the actual cognitive operation necessary to perform the task may vary. Subjects may therefore exhibit performance inconsistencies across tasks according to their ability to perform certain cognitive operations.

Among the standard measures used to assess attentional focus are tests that require mental arithmetic and control. Digit Span Backwards, Backwards Spelling, the Arithmetic subtest of the Wechsler Adult Intelligence Scale—Revised (WAIS-R) (Wechsler 1981), serial addition and subtraction tests, and asking the patient to recite the months of the year backwards are examples of such tasks. All of these tasks are also very sensitive to brain dysfunction.

The Digit Span test of the WAIS-R (Wechsler 1981) asks subjects to repeat digits. The length of the digit sequence is increased across trials until there has been a failure across two consecutive trials of a particular length. The average number of digits that normal adults can repeat is five to seven. In the Digit Span Backwards test, subjects are asked to repeat digits in reverse. This test requires attentional focus and controlled effort. The discrepancy between Digit Span Forward and Digit Span

Backwards normally does not exceed two digits.

The Digit Span Forward test is often described as a test of attention. Yet performance on this test is strongly associated with short-term memory, working memory, and the language requirement of repetition. Performance is dependent on the ability to hold a string of items in mind for a short period of time until a response is requested. Encoding of the information into a more permanent memory storage is not necessary for completion of these tasks. Typically, individuals are unable to recall information from such tasks soon after initial recall. Therefore, tests of brief attention span bridge the functions of attention and short-term memory.

A weak score on the Digit Span test alone is not diagnostic of attentional disturbance. When analyzed in relation to other findings, however, this measure may provide useful clinical information. If performance on the digits backwards test exceeds that on the digits forward test, the possibility of inattention or motivational factors should be considered. Considerable interitem variability, such as missing some short sequences but then correctly repeating longer sequences, is significant because it suggests a lapse of attention.

The Corsi Blocks Test (Milner 1971) is a visual-spatial variation of the Digit Span test. The subject observes while the examiner points to a sequence of spatially distributed blocks. The subject is then asked to point to block sequences of various lengths in forward and reverse order. The normal nonverbal attention span should be equivalent to that seen in the Digit Span test. However, poor performance on spatial span tests may also reflect spatial attentional deficits (De Renzi et al. 1977).

The Consonant Trigrams Test (L.R. Peterson and Peterson 1959) is another test of attentional focus. Subjects are asked to repeat a string of three consonants. On some trials, the consonants are repeated immediately after they are presented, whereas on others, delays of 3, 9, and 18 seconds are used, during which subjects perform an interference task requiring mental arithmetic.

Slowed processing speed is a common manifestation of the attentional disturbance associated with brain damage, usually reflected by increased reaction times across a variety of information-processing tasks (Gronwall and Sampson 1974; Gronwall and Wrightson 1974). Deficits in reaction times are strongly associated with the neuropsychological impairments of multiple sclerosis (MS), Parkinson's disease, and CHI, as discussed in the next section. Slowed processing speed and attentional disturbance often coexist in patients with relatively intact cognitive functions across other domains.

Measurement of reaction time is most easily

# KEY

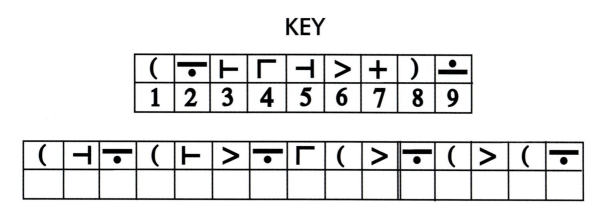

**FIGURE 13–5.** Symbol Digit Modality Test. Subjects are required to transcribe symbols to digits in accordance with the template at top. The total number of digits coded in 90 seconds is determined.

*Source.* Reprinted with permission of the publisher, Western Psychological Services, 12031 Wilshire Boulevard, Los Angeles, CA 90025. Copyright 1973 by Western Psychological Services.

achieved by computerized calculation of the time required to respond, via key press, to an auditory or visual stimulus. The complexity of reaction time can be increased by measuring the time required for an individual to make differential responses to different targets (e.g., right-hand key press to light, left-hand key press to sound). This test is referred to as choice reaction time.

The Paced Auditory Serial Addition Task (PASAT) (Gronwall and Sampson 1974; Gronwall and Wrightson 1974) is an example of a highly controlled test of attention that requires both focused and sustained attention. The PASAT is a variation of a serial arithmetic task. The subject is asked to add the first number presented to the second, the second number to the third, and so forth. Subjects must inhibit their tendency to add the new number to the prior sum. Performance is a function of the number of errors in calculation. The level of difficulty can be altered by varying the interstimulus interval.

The PASAT is sensitive to subtle attentional impairments. However, considerable effort is required for adequate performance, and the PASAT is difficult for patients with severe brain dysfunction. Poor motivation and reduced arousal also greatly affect performance on the PASAT.

The Symbol Digit Modality Test (SDMT) (Smith 1973) and the Digit Symbol subtests of the WAIS-R are also excellent measures of focused attentional capacity. These tasks require rapid processing of symbolic information and the coding of symbol-number pairs. Collectively, they can be considered as symbol-coding tests. Subjects are presented with a template containing nine number and symbol pairs. Below the template is a random array of the symbols without numbers. The task is to write the appropriate number above the symbol, using the template as a

guide. Performance is determined by the number of correct numbers transcribed in 90 seconds. Focused attention is required because the number-symbol pairs to be coded are not familiar to the subject (Figure 13–5).

A number of tasks place demands on attentional capacity and focus because of the requirement to divide attention or to inhibit interfering stimuli or responses. An example is the Stroop Test, in which the subject is required to name the color of a word while ignoring the actual word (Nehemkis and Lewinsohn 1972; Stroop 1935). Interference is created because the color and the meaning of the word are mismatched. The score is based on the number of colors named in 45 seconds and the number of errors produced by reading the word instead of naming the color (Figure 13–6). This test places strong demands on inhibitory systems, which must suppress both the other stimulus feature and a strong response tendency.

Concurrent production tasks (e.g., finger tapping while performing verbal fluency) provide a vehicle for assessing capacity limitations associated with divided attention. Such tasks are extremely effortful and require controlled, focused attention. The task of finger tapping with fluency is useful for assessing demands associated with two forms of response production. Dichotic listening paradigms provide another test for assessing focused attention in the context of sensory selective attention.

## Sensory Selective Attention

Tests used in the assessment of neglect syndrome provide a foundation for the assessment of sensory selective attention. For instance, letter and symbol cancellation tasks are useful for detecting abnormalities in both the spatial distribution of visual attention and general signal detection capacity. On the symbol cancellation task, the

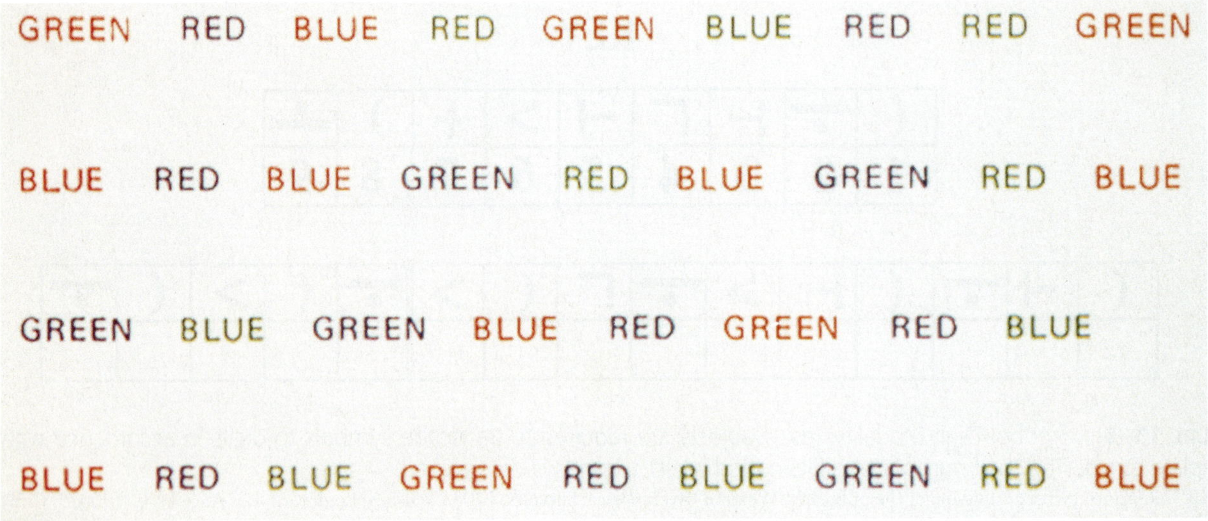

**GREEN** RED BLUE RED GREEN BLUE RED RED GREEN

BLUE RED BLUE GREEN RED BLUE GREEN RED BLUE

GREEN BLUE GREEN BLUE RED GREEN RED BLUE

BLUE RED BLUE GREEN RED BLUE GREEN RED BLUE

**FIGURE 13–6.** Stroop task-interference trial. The patient is required to scan down each column, naming the actual color of the word while ignoring the word itself. Each stimulus contains a mismatch between word and color, which creates distraction and demands for attentional focus. The number of colors named in 45 seconds is determined, as is the number of breaks in response set (i.e., reading the word).
*Source.* Adapted from Stroop 1935.

subject scans an array of letters or symbols and marks a line through or circles all of the A's, or any other designated target symbol (Kaplan et al. 1989) (Figure 13–7). The total time for detection and cancellation of all targets, along with the number of misses and false-positive errors, are determined. Information can also be obtained about the subject's ability to carry out a consistent detection strategy.

Line bisection may also provide evidence for a hemispatial attentional disturbance (Albert 1973). The paradigm of double simultaneous stimulation provides a method for detecting extinction and neglect of stimuli in the impaired hemispace. The analysis of the spontaneous drawings of objects and copying of figures may point to lateral differences in attention to detail or spatial quality. All of these techniques are standard methods for assessing visual selective attention.

A number of experimental paradigms also exist that may facilitate the assessment of selective attention. For instance, dichotic listening paradigms that involve the presentation of different information to the two ears provides a way of assessing auditory attentional selection under different conditions of discrimination and response bias (Kimura 1967; Springer 1986). However, this paradigm also involves divided attention and reflects capacity limitations. Dichotic listening has been employed in shadowing paradigms, which require the subject to repeat material being presented in one ear (the shadowed ear) while processing a competing message in the other ear. Subjects typically have great difficulty extracting information from the

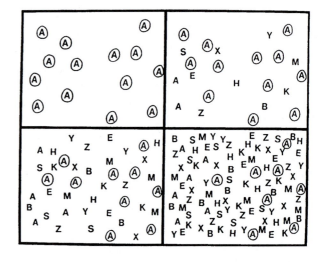

**FIGURE 13–7.** Letter cancellation. A subject with right subcortical infarction was asked to circle all the A's. Performance declined with increase in stimulus load. Note the relative inattention to the left side of each box.
*Source.* Reprinted from Kaplan RF, Verfaellie M, Meadows ME, et al.: "Changing Attentional Demands in Left Hemispatial Neglect." *Archives of Neurology* 48:1263–1266, 1991. Used with permission.

nonshadowed ear during dichotic listening but can detect physical changes in the stimuli to that ear (Cherry 1953). Subjects also show little memory of material presented to the nonshadowed ear, although they attend better to the nonshadowed channel when different modalities are used (Treisman and Davies 1986) and after they have learned to attend to the nonshadowed channel (Underwood 1976).

A comprehensive assessment of selective attention requires the incorporation of signal detection and reaction time methods, either explicitly or implicitly (Green and Swets 1966). Signal detection methods enable the determination of attentional accuracy under different task conditions. A discriminability index (D´) can be derived on the basis of errors due to missing a target and false-positive errors due to responding to nontargets. A response bias (beta) can also be determined that indicates the systematic errors and response tendencies of the subject. Other indices can also be determined, which enable a parametric analysis of attentional performance.

## Response Selection and Executive Control

Tests of executive functioning can be characterized by four factors: 1) the capacity to inhibit interference and maintain a pattern of responding; 2) the ability to alternate between response sets; 3) the ability to plan, organize, and derive solutions on tasks requiring hypothesis testing; and 4) the capacity for response generation. A large number of measures of response selection and executive functions are available. Double alternating movements, graphemic sequences (e.g., Rampart figures), motor impersistence, and the go/no-go paradigm (Christensen 1989; Stuss and Benson 1986) are useful for the assessment of simple motoric response control. Tests such as the Trail Making Test (Armitage 1946), the Stroop tasks (Stroop 1935), the Wisconsin Card Sorting Test (Heaton 1985), and the Porteus Mazes Test provide a means of assessing higher-order executive functions, such as goal-directed behavior, response planning, and active switching of response set (Armitage 1946; Christensen 1989; Porteus 1965; Stuss and Benson 1986).

Intentionality is often inferred rather than measured directly, but there are ways of assessing impairments of intentionality. A failure to spontaneously initiate behaviors despite a capacity to respond on command suggest an intentional problem. Failure to persist with motor responding in the neglected hemispace is thought to reflect an intentional disturbance as well. However, more tests of intention need to be developed.

A subject's capacity for initiation, generation, and persistence can be measured in a number of ways. On the Controlled Word Association Test, subjects produce as many words as possible that start with a particular letter (F, A, or S) or that belong to a semantic category (animals) in 60 seconds (Benton et al. 1983; Spreen and Strauss 1991). The total number of words generated is then scored. The response norms vary with age and level of education. Normal young adults can generate 36 F, A, or S words in 3 minutes and the names of more than 20

animals in 1 minute. Normal geriatric subjects should be able to generate the names of more than 13 animals. Information about the subject's tendency to perseverate and self-monitoring capacity can be gained from this task.

Design fluency is a nonverbal alternative to the Controlled Word Association Test (Jones-Gotman and Milner 1977). This task requires subjects to draw as many different designs as possible using a set of dots, and the number of figures produced in a set time period is determined. Verbal and design fluency indicate not only the total quantity of response output for a circumscribed time period but also can point to problems with initiation and persistence.

Simple and choice reaction time may be helpful in characterizing latencies for response initiation. Tests of motor functioning such as the Grooved Pegboard Test (Klove 1963) measure the generation of fine motor responses. This test measures the time required for the sequential rotation and placement of 25 pegs in holes on a grooved board. Scores are calculated separately for both the right and left hand. Although motor speed and dexterity may be intact in patients with severe impairments of spontaneous response generation, impairment on pure motor tasks may correlate in some subjects with executive dysfunction, which affects other aspects of response generation. Motor system deficits need to be considered when assessing whether response generation deficits relate to attentional-executive impairments. Occasionally, problems in the motor domain may be a confounding variable in the interpretation of neuropsychological results. However, deficits in the ability to persist on motor tasks may also reflect secondary problems with executive functioning.

This capacity can be measured by interference tasks such as the Stroop Test. Intrusion errors across other cognitive tests may also point to problems with response inhibition. The go/no-go paradigm is a simple test in which the subject is asked to place a hand on the table and raise the index finger in response to a single tap while holding still in response to two taps. The taps should be made on the undersurface of the table to avoid the use of visual cues. Patients with prefrontal lesions have difficulty inhibiting the raising of the finger.

Several tasks require the alternation of response pattern. The Trail Making Test (Armitage 1946) is one of the most commonly used tests of response switching ability and mental control. Subjects are initially required to connect a sequence of numbers by drawing a line between numbers that are placed randomly on a sheet of paper (Trails A). On Trails B, subjects are required to alternate between numbers and letters in ascending order (Figure 13–8). Errors occur when the patient fails to alternate

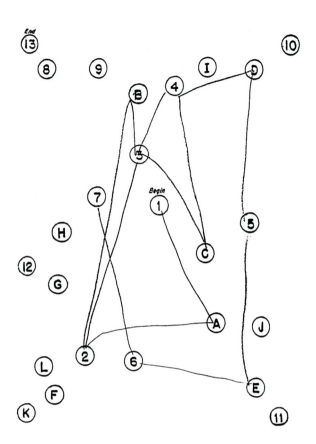

**FIGURE 13–8.**    Trail Making Test. This test requires the patient to connect the numbers and letters in alternating sequence. In this example, the patient, a 52-year-old man with a right thalamic stroke, failed to maintain the sequence (at numbers 2 and 3), indicating breaks in response set. Impersistence, with neglect of the left side of the page, is also evident.

and connects two letters or numbers or when there is a break in the sequence and a particular item is omitted. Each task is timed.

Sorting tasks, such as the Wisconsin Card Sorting Test, measure concept formation and hypothesis testing (Stuss and Benson 1986). Subjects are presented with cards containing features for color, shape, and number. The task is to determine the correct category for a response based on feedback provided by the examiner. Subjects sort cards to the appropriate category but must switch to a new category when the response criteria change. Failure on the Wisconsin Card Sorting Test is often associated with impairments of conceptual flexibility and switching and perseveration secondary to frontal lobe damage affecting the dorsolateral region.

## Sustained Attention and Vigilance

Tests that measure performance over time provide a means of assessing sustained attention and vigilance. Cur-

rently, the task most widely used for this type of assessment is the Continuous Performance Test (CPT) (Rosvold et al. 1956), which measures signal detection performance over blocks of trials. There are many versions of the CPT, all consisting of the same basic paradigm. Visual or auditory stimuli (usually letters) are presented sequentially. Intermixed among distracter stimuli are particular target stimuli, such as the letter A. The task is to respond to the target and not to the distracters. The attentional demands of the task can be modified on many CPT versions by changing the ratio of targets to distracters, the total number of stimuli, the total time of the test, the perceptual complexity of the stimuli and background, the interstimulus interval, and the use of anticipatory stimuli. A variety of signal detection measures—such as misses, false-positives, inconsistency, and vigilance decrement—can be determined to help quantify impairments of sustained attention.

Symbol coding tasks, such as the Digit Symbol subtest, may also be used to assess sustained attention by comparing performance during the early and late stages of the task. Similar task modifications can also be sensitive to tests requiring sustained attentional performance in completion of a task involving other cognitive operations. On the Sustained Motor Tapping Test (R. A. Cohen 1993), the subject is required to tap a finger on key for an extended period. Decrement in responding is measured as a function of the number of taps per 10-second interval. The Motor Continuation Task (Wing and Kristofferson 1973) requires the subject to maintain a set tapping rate for a given interval. Performance is determined on the basis of the variance in interbeat interval.

Many sustained attentional tasks, such as the CPT and Symbol Cancellation, can be modified to increase the demand for focused attention and effort. On the CPT, this can be done by increasing the complexity of target selection (e.g., respond to x only when preceded by an *A*). By adjusting parameters such as memory load, interstimulus times, and the presence of more than one stimulus in a target field on a trial, other attentional factors in addition to sustained attention can be examined. This is particularly useful in experimental studies although somewhat problematic for clinical use, because modifying task demands changes the norms for these tests.

## Steps in Decision Making When Assessing Attention

Regardless of the battery that is chosen, the assessment of attention depends on a logical, stepwise decision process (R. A. Cohen et al. 1998):

1. Is the patient fully alert? Is lethargy or fatigue evident?

2. Is activity level within normal limits, or is the patient slow or agitated?

3. Does the patient seem to exert adequate effort?

4. Are sensory, perceptual, and motor functions intact? If not, it is essential to factor in the contribution of these impairments.

5. Is attentional capacity reduced? Do impairments consistently appear on tasks requiring high levels of focus, working memory, or effort?

6. Is reduced capacity general or limited to specific operations or modalities? If it is operation specific, attentional effects may be secondary to the greater effort required for tasks that are more difficult cognitively for the patient.

7. If a general capacity problem is present, limiting factors should be examined in detail. This involves assessing factors such as processing speed and memory influence.

8. Is attentional performance temporally inconsistent? Is there a performance decrement? If so, a more thorough assessment of sustained attention is in order.

9. Is the attention problem limited to sensory selection or to response selection and control?

10. If sensory selective attention impairment is suggested, is spatial distribution of attention abnormal? Is attention also impaired in nonspatial visual or auditory tasks?

11. Are response selection problems related to specific problems with intention, initiation, inhibition, persistence, switching, or other executive functions?

## Current Assessment Trends

Technological advances have provided the opportunity to overcome some of the primary disadvantages of reliance on a "paper-and-pencil" methodology. Although traditional neuropsychological methods typically provide useful data about error characteristics, they are not well suited for response time measurement, nor do such measures provide adequate information about interitem variability or change in performance across the task duration (R.A. Cohen et al. 1998). Therefore, employing computerized attention tasks allows for better control of stimulus and response parameters and provides more specific response characteristics. Optimally, signal detection and reaction time measures are analyzed simultaneously as a function of different attentional task demands to provide a more complete profile of attentional performance (R.A. Cohen et al. 1998).

## Psychophysiological Methods

Psychophysiological testing provides a potentially rich source of information about the neurobiological substrates of attention. Demonstration of physiological reactivity associated with attention helps localize the brain regions involved in attentional processes and measures the intensity of attention. Although these methods are not widely used in standard clinical assessment, physiological methods are useful for studying normal attentional responses and characterizing disturbances of attention in patients with neuropsychiatric illness.

The two physiological methods most commonly used involve the measurement of either autonomic or central nervous system indices. Autonomic studies use skin conductance response and cardiovascular measures, such as changes in heart rate. Other peripheral responses, such as muscle activity (electromyography), have also been used (Coles and Duncan-Johnson 1975; Kahneman and Beatty 1966; Oscar-Berman and Gade 1979). Heart rate deceleration during sensory processing and selective attention versus heart rate acceleration during effortful attentional processing has been well demonstrated. Other autonomic measures, such as pupil dilation, skin conductance, and electromyographic changes, also reflect task-specific attentional activation. Studies of the central nervous system use electroencephalographic (EEG) measurement in conjunction with sensory or cognitive tasks leading to a sensory evoked potential response (Hansch et al. 1982; Hansen et al. 1983; Hillyard and Hansen 1986; Hillyard et al. 1973; Squires et al. 1980). The small EEG activation associated with a series of stimulus presentations is averaged to produce an event-related potential (ERP) that can be localized to specific brain regions. Both autonomic and ERP indices provide excellent measures of attentional allocation.

The ERP consists of a series of specific positive (P) and negative (N) voltage deflections. On attentional tasks, the first deflection occurs at approximately 100 milliseconds (N1) and is associated with passive attention to rare events (automatic selective attention). The most widely studied deflection usually occurs at approximately 300 milliseconds (P3 or P300) in normal subjects and reflects task-dependent factors such as stimulus probability, expectancy, and task relevance. The P300 has been linked to conscious deployment of limited-capacity attentional resources.

The N2 and P300 components have been studied extensively in relation to normal aging, psychopathology, and neurologic brain disorders. Slowing of the P300 component is seen in patients with dementia and other brain diseases, whereas psychiatric disorders most often result in decreased amplitude of particular ERP components (R.A. Cohen et al. 1995; O'Donnell et al. 1990). The measurement of changes in ERP in conjunction with different tasks provides a direct means of determining the effect of changing attentional task demands on brain activity.

## Neuroimaging Techniques

Technological advances in functional neuroimaging using positron emission tomography and functional magnetic resonance imaging continue to provide exciting advances in the cognitive and affective neurosciences (Baron et al. 1994; Binder et al. 1994; Hinke et al. 1993; Rao et al. 1994; Roland 1993). The paradigms used in these studies are similar to those employed for both autonomic and ERP studies, although specific tasks are modified in accordance with the temporal parameters of the specific imaging methods. The background resting activity on positron emission tomography or functional magnetic resonance imaging is subtracted from the activation response to specific sensory or cognitive tasks to isolate and measure the brain systems involved in specific cognitive operations, including attention.

Recurrent themes in the neuroimaging literature support the presence of multiple attention neural subsystems that improve distinct attentional processes and task performance (Cabeza and Nyberg 2000; O'Craven et al. 1999; B.S. Peterson et al. 1999). The thalamus is suggested to play a role in mediating the interaction of attention and arousal (Kinomura et al. 1996; Portas et al. 1998). Corbetta and colleagues (2000) demonstrated that distinct parietal region activations mediate different attentional processes using event-related functional magnetic resonance imaging. In addition, Badgaiyan and Posner (1998) illustrated distinct areas of cingulate cortex activation on a correct and error-feedback task compared with a generate and repeat task, suggesting functional heterogeneity in this region. Anterior cingulate cortex activity also has been associated with detecting and signaling the occurrence of conflicts in informational processing (Botvinick et al. 1999). The anterior cingulate cortex displays greater activity on incompatible compared with compatible trials (Botvinick et al. 1999). Sequentially presented stimuli evoke stronger activations than simultaneously presented stimuli unless the participant's attention is directed to one of the stimuli (Kastner et al. 1998). In the context of directed attention task, the authors interpreted the reduced response to simultaneous compared with sequentially presented stimuli as illustrating an increased suppressive mechanism from competitive interactions or a filtering of irrelevant information that corresponds with ventral extrastriate cortex activation (Kastner et al. 1998).

# Clinical Disorders of Attention

In this section, we provide clinical examples of attentional disturbance seen in neurologic and psychiatric disorders (see R.A. Cohen 1993).

Impairments of attention may present as relatively specific and well localized or as diffuse and nonlocalizing deficits. Both types of attentional disturbance provide insights into the cognitive processes of attention and the brain mechanisms that underlie these processes. Although localized lesions provide the best vehicle for analysis of the role of specific brain structures in attentional control, nonspecific attentional impairments associated with nonlocalized brain disorders illustrate the influence of metabolic and neurochemical abnormalities on information processing rate, arousal, and a host of other energetic and structural factors that may affect attentional capacity.

## Levels of Consciousness

A subject's level of consciousness must be determined before attention can be adequately assessed. Levels of consciousness range from normal consciousness to coma. A patient with normal consciousness is awake, alert, fully responsive, and aware of self and environment. Individuals in deep coma appear to be asleep, unarousable, and unresponsive to external and internal stimuli. With less severe forms of coma, brainstem reflexes are present, and posturing of the limbs may be seen. In a persistent vegetative state, patients may open their eyes spontaneously and in response to pain. They may have roving eye movements and may blink in response to threat. They may fix their gaze on an individual or an object in the environment, giving the false impression of conscious cognition. There is arousal or wakefulness without awareness or meaningful responsiveness. The locked-in syndrome is characterized by intact consciousness and awareness but inability to generate verbal and motor responses. This condition is usually caused by basilar artery infarction in the pons, causing quadriparesis and mutism while sparing most cortical function. Akinetic mutism, which is usually caused by bilateral infarction in the territory of the anterior cerebral artery, is characterized by a profound amotivational state in which the individual is alert but remains motionless and mute and reacts only minimally to environmental stimuli. Stupor is a level of consciousness in which the patient shows minimal cognitive or behavioral activity yet is arousable. With repeated stimulation, a stuporous patient will open his or her eyes and may even vocalize, but responses to verbal commands are minimal.

Abnormal reflexes, tremor, restlessness, or other movement problems are common, and the patient is often described as "obtunded." With stupor, as with all deeper levels of coma, minimal awareness is evident.

Between normal consciousness and stupor, there are many levels of impaired consciousness, usually referred to as *confusional states, lethargy,* or *delirium.* The term *confusion* lacks precision but usually refers to a state of decreased clarity and speed of thinking. Confused patients may be able to engage in conversation but exhibit slowness and incoherence, disorientation, and extreme distractibility. Psychosis, agitation, irritability, and a fluctuating level of arousal is common. At higher levels of consciousness, patients may be responsive and able to communicate and may show no evidence of disorientation or confusion yet exhibit inattention or alteration in their quality of awareness.

## Metabolic Encephalopathy

Alterations in level and quality of consciousness and attention are hallmark features of metabolic encephalopathy. Metabolic disorders are typically associated with diffuse neuronal dysregulation rather than structural brain lesions and often arise from systemic problems outside the brain. Metabolic disorders affect consciousness and attention by altering levels of oxygen, $CO_2$, glucose, electrolyte balance, proteins, or other biochemicals in the brain. The specific attentional disturbance depends on the type and severity of metabolic disturbance. Metabolic problems that produce activation are likely to produce restlessness in addition to distractibility and prominent shifting of attention. Psychomotor retardation and lethargy may occur with impaired sustained attention, decreased generative ability, and errors of omission of selective attention. Attentional performance is often quite variable because of the waxing and waning of consciousness.

## Attentional Disturbance in Neurologic Disorders

### Stroke

Stroke has long been considered one of the best neurologic disorders for the study of brain-behavior relationships because of its rapid onset and well-localized neuroanatomic involvement. Neglect syndrome is the most well known and dramatic disorder of attention resulting from stroke. Most patients with neglect exhibit impairments of sensory selective attention, although some may have primary problems with response selection and control. Regardless of which attentional process is most affected, all patients with neglect syndrome have a fundamental disorder involving the spatial distribution and allocation of attention.

The defining feature of neglect syndrome is the failure to attend to, respond to, or be aware of stimuli on one side of space. Many variants of neglect syndrome may be observed clinically. Patients may fail to draw the left side of an object when copying figures or when producing spontaneous drawings. Drawings may also contain a shift of the object to the extreme right side of the page. Visual scanning is typically impaired because the patient looks only to the right hemispace, missing information on the left. On testing, patients with neglect often miss targets on cancellation tasks or fail at line bisection, even though they are capable of adequately perceiving these stimuli.

The underlying attentional disturbance of neglect can be demonstrated in a number of ways. Patients with primary sensory disturbances such as hemianopia usually direct their gaze to compensate for their field cut. In contrast, patients with neglect may have normal visual fields yet fail to look at certain spatial positions (i.e., spatial inattention). There is often a failure to direct visual search to one hemispace. In extreme cases, patients may appear to actively direct their gaze or even their entire body position away from the hemispace contralateral to the side of the lesion. They may be able to perceive the entire field but do not consistently attend to all stimuli that are perceived. Hemispatial neglect can be dissociated from primary sensory and perceptual disturbances, such as hemianopia or visual agnosia, on this basis.

Although visual-spatial neglect is most common, patients may exhibit inattention to stimuli presented across different modalities. Somatosensory neglect with inattention to tactile or proprioceptive stimulation to one side of the body is relatively common. Inaccurate reporting of spatial orientation, body position, or direction of movement may be given. Some patients exhibit neglect of one side of their own body, acting as though their left arm or leg does not belong to them. Others may report that their limb ipsilateral to the lesion site has been touched when stimulation was to the contralateral limb (allesthesia). Auditory neglect has also been reported in certain patients. Patients with allokinesia turn to the ipsilesional hemispace when addressed from the side contralateral to the lesion. These phenomena demonstrate that neglect syndrome is not only a disorder of spatial inattention but often is also a disorder of altered awareness of spatial experience.

It is not uncommon for patients with neglect syndrome to exhibit disturbed emotional experience relative to their neglected side of space. A patient who was monitored in our clinic responded appropriately when approached from his intact side but became hostile and verbally combative when social interactions were attempted from the impaired side. Most patients, however, exhibit indifference toward the neglected hemispace, as well as apathy and denial or lack of awareness of their symptoms (anosognosia). Patients may confabulate and produce elaborate descriptions that are complete fabrications about their neglected side. This may even take the form of a depersonalization of the affected body part. Alterations in affective response and awareness in patients with neglect reflect important relationships among emotional experience, awareness, and attention.

Neglect was once attributed to impairments of sensory or perceptual processes, as well as body schema disturbance (Battersby et al. 1956; Brain 1941; Denny-Brown and Chambers 1958). Sensory hypotheses have been refuted by cases of neglect resulting from lesions outside of primary sensory pathways. Perceptual and body schema hypotheses appear somewhat more viable, because patients with neglect often exhibit coexisting perceptual or spatial impairments. Neglect cannot be explained fully on the basis of a perceptual defect alone but may result from lesions in brain regions directly involved in perception and in the absence of other sensory or perceptual impairments. The fact that neglect across different sensory modalities may coexist in a single patient tends to argue against a perceptual hypothesis, because perception is usually modality specific.

Experimental investigations have confirmed the role of attention in hemineglect syndrome. Manipulation of attentional parameters demonstrates that symptoms of hemineglect change as task demands are modified. For example, symbol detection performance in patients with right-hemisphere lesions depends on both the relationship of the targets to distracters and the hemispace to be searched (Rapczak et al. 1989). Patients have greatest difficulty when they must both explore the left hemispace and also perform difficult visual discriminations. Increasing the number of distracters relative to targets increases the severity of hemineglect on cancellation tasks (Kaplan et al. 1989) (see Figure 13–8).

The following are summary points for hemineglect, extinction, and hemi-inattention syndromes (R.A. Cohen et al. 1998):

1. Hemi-inattention and neglect are manifestations of unilateral brain lesions. Striking spatial asymmetry in attentional performance is a central feature of these syndromes.
2. Neglect usually occurs relative to the left side of space, which illustrates the importance of the non-dominant hemisphere in spatial attention.

3. Although most patients with neglect have a number of common symptoms, the specific attentional disturbance depends on the exact location of the lesion.
   a. Lesions affecting the reticular system that produce neglect also involve significant arousal and activation impairments.
   b. Unilateral basal ganglia damage often results in both hemiattention and intention impairments, reflecting the importance of this system to sensorimotor integration.
   c. Cingulate lesions are more likely to affect intention than sensory selective attention.

Although hemineglect syndrome is one of the most dramatic forms of attentional disturbance, focal lesions secondary to stroke commonly produce disorders that do not involve hemineglect (R.A. Cohen et al. 1998):

1. Focal frontal lesions may produce impairments of focused attention in addition to the common finding of attentional impairments of response selection and control.
2. Thalamic lesions may result in problems with informational gating and selection regardless of whether unilateral neglect is present.
3. Subcortical lesions often produce impairments of arousal, activation, and information-processing speed, which in turn may limit attentional capacity.
4. Subcortical small vessel disease secondary to cerebral hypoperfusion may result in dementia; this type of dementia seems to affect attention and information-processing efficiency most dramatically.

## Other Neurologic Disorders

Although impairments of attention are common sequelae of neurologic diseases, attention has generally received less emphasis than other cognitive functions in neuropsychological investigations of brain disorders. This probably reflects the fact that attention cannot be localized to an individual brain system in the same way as can disorders of language or vision. Attention may be more difficult to measure in the normal clinical context than aphasia, apraxia, or other major neurobehavioral syndromes. However, attentional dysfunction is a defining characteristic of some neurologic diseases and is an important feature in others, as outlined below.

**Multiple sclerosis.**    MS, one of the most common neurologic diseases affecting young adults, is characterized by multifocal areas of demyelination. Studies of MS have focused primarily on the sensorimotor symptoms, although cognitive dysfunction is common. Approximately 10% of patients with MS exhibit a progressive decline in cognitive abilities that is indicative of subcortical dementia (Rao 1986). These patients have great difficulty on a wide range of neuropsychological tasks, including major problems with learning and memory.

Ten percent of patients with MS develop subcortical dementia, and more than 40% demonstrate cognitive impairment (Heaton et al. 1985). Learning, memory, and executive control are most commonly affected, and impairments of these functions are usually associated with reduced perceptual-motor speed, psychomotor slowing, and attentional difficulties. Many of the problems with learning and memory found in MS patients may be attributable to attentional factors (Kessler et al. 1992).

Patients with MS experience difficulty maintaining consistent effort on tasks. Under conditions of increased information load, they typically show performance decrements. They also experience slowing of processing and psychomotor speed. Although MS patients often have primary motor deficits that may partially account for their psychomotor slowing, it is unlikely that gross motor slowing alone explains the decrease in information-processing speed. R.A. Cohen and Fisher (1988) found that the motor impairments of MS patients could be dissociated from the attentional difficulties of these patients.

Of the cognitive impairments that often accompany MS, the most common disorders involve attention (R.A. Cohen 1993; R.A. Cohen et al. 1998):

1. Fatigue is the most common of all symptoms in MS. Fatigue is associated not only with motor effort but also with attending to and performing cognitive tasks.
2. Subcortical lesions secondary to demyelination may disrupt attentional control.
3. Subcortical white matter lesions also reduce neural transmission speed. Slowed processing time reduces attentional capacity and creates processing bottlenecks.

## Case Example

A 40-year-old man with a 5-year history of chronic progressive MS experiences waxing and symptoms of chronic fatigue. When fatigue is worse, his thinking slows down and he becomes confused. In this state, it is difficult for him to process information and to interpret events, particularly of an emotional nature. Attentional capacity is easily overwhelmed, which leads to frustration, irritability, and angry outbursts.

Magnetic resonance imaging reveals extensive areas of high signal intensity on $T_2$-weighted scans in the midline frontal lobe white matter (Figure 13–9). The MS plaques interrupt pathways involved in speed

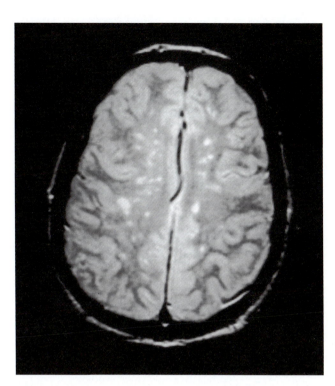

**FIGURE 13–9.** $T_2$-weighted axial magnetic resonance imaging scan above the level of the lateral ventricles demonstrates multiple areas of high signal in the frontal subcortical white matter in a 40-year-old with multiple sclerosis and attentional disturbance.

of processing, focusing, and sustaining attention. Systems involved in regulation of mood and impulses are also affected.

**Closed head injury.** Primary brain damage associated with CHI is usually the result of contusions and diffuse axonal injury. Contusions, which are caused by the impact of the brain on the surface of the skull, occur most often on the basal surfaces of the frontal lobes and the poles of the temporal lobes, regardless of the site of the external impact on the head. Diffuse axonal damage occurs due to shearing of axons as they are stretched by the movement of surrounding brain tissue. Axons of the brain stem and cerebral hemispheres are both affected by rotational forces associated with CHI.

The cognitive processes most likely to be affected after CHI are attention and executive functions (Levin and Kraus 1994). Persistent distractibility, poor concentration, apathy, and fatigability are prominent sequelae of CHI (Gronwall 1987; Van Zomeren and Van Den Burg 1985). Patients with CHI may perform poorly on tests of mental control, concentration, and performance speed. Timed tests are particularly sensitive to head trauma. Vigilance performance is often impaired. The classic tests of attention from the Wechsler Intelligence and Memory scales, Digit Symbol, Digit Span, and Mental Control, are often depressed (Gronwall 1987). Deficits of arousal, selective attention, divided attention, processing speed, and executive functions may contribute to poor performance on these measures. Problems with divided attention may reflect reduced information-processing capacity and speed in addition to decreased ability to inhibit interference (Stuss 1987; Stuss et al. 1989; Van Zomeren and Van Den Burg 1985; Van Zomeren et al. 1984).

The attention and executive impairments of CHI usually reflect subcortical and frontal lobe dysfunction. Damage to subcortical midbrain systems impairs arousal. Damage to white matter pathways from shearing forces disrupts the spread of activation from the midbrain systems to higher cortical areas and contributes to slowing of information processing. Contusion and hematoma involving the frontal cortex may contribute to attentional impairment in patients with CHI. Frontal lobe damage is associated with executive dysfunction, including response intention selection and control, as discussed previously.

**Epilepsy.** Transient changes in the level and quality of consciousness are a common feature of seizure disorders. The acute impairment of awareness and attention is often seen in the ictal or postictal state. Cognitive impairments observed in the interictal state are highly variable and are influenced by a variety of factors, including location of the seizure focus, seizure frequency, and side effects of anticonvulsant medications. Memory impairment is common and may be related to mesial temporal and limbic system dysfunction (C.P. Deutsch 1953; Loiseau et al. 1980; Rausch et al. 1978).

Determination of attentional disturbance in epileptic patients is confounded by problems of seizure frequency and control, etiology of the seizures, and side effects of medication. There is considerable heterogeneity in the brain disorders that can cause seizures, and attentional performance is not consistent in patients with epilepsy. In a recent study that sought to minimize methodological confounding factors, Piccirilli et al. (1994) found that children with rolandic epilepsy who had right-sided or bilateral spikes had impairments on a letter cancellation task, whereas children with left-sided foci did as well as control subjects. Mirsky et al. (1960) found that patients with generalized epilepsy had greater problems than those with focal seizures on a test of sustained attention. Several studies have found that patients with epilepsy are more impaired than control subjects on tests of divided attention (Glowinsky 1973). This impairment appears to be related to slowed speed of cognitive processing, which affects attentional capacity (Bruhn and Parsons 1977).

## Case Example

An 8-year-old boy was doing poorly in English and mathematics classes. His teacher felt that he was a "daydreamer" because he often stared off into space and had trouble paying attention. She thought that he might have ADHD. His parents became frustrated because he had trouble explaining what went on in school and he was often confused about his homework assignments. Neurologic evaluation was unremarkable. Electroencephalography revealed intermittent 3-Hz spike and wave discharges lasting 3–10 seconds, consistent with absence epilepsy.

This is a case of occult absence epilepsy presenting with learning problems caused by brief intermittent disturbances in awareness and attention. Making the diagnosis was crucial in this patient because his seizures were well controlled with sodium valproate, resulting in a marked improvement in school performance.

**Alzheimer's disease.** Alzheimer's disease involves a progressive deterioration of most cognitive abilities, with impairments of learning and memory as cardinal features. By the time a patient with Alzheimer's disease is brought to medical attention, a marked anterograde amnesia is apparent. Attentional disturbance is not usually described as a primary feature of Alzheimer's disease, and some authors have emphasized that attention is largely spared in patients with this disorder. However, this conclusion may be somewhat misleading.

Patients with early-stage Alzheimer's disease typically do not exhibit overt behaviors indicative of inattention, such as restlessness, failure to look at the examiner, or diminished attention span on tasks such as Digit Span Forward. Patients with early Alzheimer's disease are usually alert, energetic, and motivated. Yet relatively early in the disease course, problems are evident in the areas of focused attention, capacity, and executive control.

Patients with Alzheimer's disease have difficulty performing concurrent tasks and consequently perform poorly on tasks such as the Stroop Test (R.A. Cohen 1993; Storandt et al. 1984). They also encounter great difficulty on tasks requiring concentration and focus, such as Digit Span Backwards and Symbol Coding Tasks. Simple executive control abilities may be adequate (e.g., double alternating movements), but failure occurs on more complex tasks requiring switching, such as Trail Making. Abnormal responses involving sudden lapses in accuracy are quite common, even on tasks involving sensory selective attention. Patients also show deficits of sustained attention early in the disease course, which may be secondary both to response impersistence caused by frontal lobe damage and to amnesia. Such a patient will begin a task or sentence, suffer a distraction or pause to find a word, and then forget the task requirements or the thread of discourse.

As the disease progresses, performance becomes impaired on most tasks requiring effortful attentional processing (Storandt et al. 1984). Pervasive disturbance eventually develops, affecting all attentional processes. Perhaps the only aspect of attention that is not greatly affected until the latest stages of Alzheimer's disease is arousal and automatic orienting to stimuli. Eventually, all areas of higher cognitive function deteriorate, and the patient is rendered mute and unresponsive with no capacity to attend and with minimal self-awareness.

## Attentional Disturbance Associated With Psychiatric Illness

### Affective Disorders

Difficulties with concentration and sustained attention are commonly reported by patients with affective disorders and constitute key determinants for making the diagnosis of both major depression and bipolar affective disorder (American Psychiatric Association 1994). The opposing energetic and motivational states associated with major depression and mania have considerable bearing on the attentional disturbances that accompany these disorders. Depressed patients tend to exhibit behavioral withdrawal and anhedonia, with reduced verbal output, psychomotor speed, and motivation, as well as loss of interest. They have diminished goal-directed behavior and quickly fatigue on tasks that normally require little effort. In contrast, manic patients are usually very energized, with flight of ideas, pressured speech, and increases in goal-directed behaviors. Although the depressed patient has difficulty initiating and sustaining behaviors, the manic patient may have problems with response inhibition across a wide range of behavioral and social contexts.

Early neuropsychological studies of affective disorders found that cognitive impairments are associated with affective disorders. Learning problems are easily demonstrated in depressed patients, but the basis for these impairments has not been entirely clear (R.A. Cohen and Lohr 1995; R.M. Cohen et al. 1982). There is a strong relationship between expenditure of effort and memory performance in patients with affective disorders (R.M. Cohen et al. 1982). Difficulty exerting sufficient effort may account for problems in performance across a range of tasks, from difficulties with learning and memory to actual decrements in motor strength.

Impairments on tests of verbal and nonverbal memory also tend to coexist with problems in the area of mental control and attention (Breslow et al. 1977; Stromgren 1977). Depressed patients typically exhibit considerable variability in memory performance. For instance, Breslow et al. (1977) found that depressed patients did not differ from control subjects in performance on paired associate learning tasks, even though performance on the mental control subtest of the Wechsler Memory Scale was significantly weaker for the affective patients. Such findings argue against a primary amnestic disorder in these patients and for an inefficient learning process.

The most consistently demonstrated attentional impairment in patients with affective disorders is in the area of sustained attention and vigilance. Sustained attention performance is proportional to the level of depression and improves when depression resolves (Byrne 1977; Malone and Hemsley 1977). Therefore, the deficits in sustained attention in patients with affective disorders are state dependent (Firth et al. 1983).

Diminished attentional capacity is particularly evident on tasks that require psychomotor speed, attentional focus, and effortful demands for mental control. Deficits are common on Digit Span Backwards, serial arithmetic tasks such as the PASAT, Digit Symbol Substitution, and other tasks that require focused attention and concentration (R.A. Cohen and Lohr 1995; R.M. Cohen et al. 1982). Impaired attentional capacity in depressed patients is most likely a by-product of alterations in behavioral energetics, including arousal, appetitive, and motivational states.

Slowing on the finger-tapping test has been shown to correlate with impaired performance on the Stroop interference test and on other measures of mental control (Raskin et al. 1969). Sustained effort, attention, and cognitive flexibility were found to be impaired in these patients. A relationship between psychomotor, executive, and attentional functioning has also been reported by other investigators (Breslow et al. 1977; R.M. Cohen et al. 1982).

Although effortful expenditure is clearly a problem for depressed patients, a paradoxical relationship between effort and performance has occasionally been described. Depressed patients occasionally fail to show an advantage on Digit Span Forward over Digit Span Backwards, which has been interpreted as evidence that depressed patients fail to exert sufficient effort on less demanding tasks. The assumption is that easier tasks are not sufficiently motivating to activate the depressed patient's attention. Although undoubtedly some depressed patients may benefit from attentional activation by increasing the motivating quality of tasks, most studies do not support the hypothesis that depressed patients perform better on effortful tasks. To the contrary, the performance of depressed patients usually decreases as effortful task demands increase (R.A. Cohen and Lohr 1995; R.M. Cohen et al. 1982). Although diminished psychomotor speed may result in slowed scanning and response times, depressed patients do not typically exhibit major impairments on most sensory selective-attention paradigms. Such patients may occasionally miss targets, particularly over sustained periods of time, but neglect or inattention to specific spatial locations is not usually evident. Problems with selective attention are most likely to be related to response bias rather than actual sensory selection difficulties.

Attentional disturbance is the most common cognitive symptom associated with major affective disorders (R.A. Cohen et al. 1998):

1. Subjective complaints of problems with concentration and focus are among the symptoms that are considered in a diagnosis of depression.
2. Problems with reduced energetic capacity (focused attention) and sustained attention are most common. Response selection and control is often more moderately impaired. Sensory selective attention is usually less affected.
3. Attentional performance is often quite variable over time.
4. The quality of attentional impairments varies as a function of affective state. Manic patients tend to make more errors of commission and failure to inhibit responding, whereas depressed patients make more errors of omission and are likely to show low levels of arousal with psychomotor slowing. Great effort is often required for attention.
5. Given the strong likelihood of attentional disturbance in patients with affective disorders, it is essential that depression be ruled out or factored in when one is assessing attention associated with other brain disorders.

## Schizophrenia

The early researchers of schizophrenia, Kraepelin and Bleuler, reported attentional disturbances in their patients (Kraepelin 1931). They noted perseveration in thought and action, tangentiality, inability to initiate actions or sustain attention, rapid fatigue, and orienting to trivial stimuli. Bleuler (1911/1950) noted that autistically withdrawn patients had disturbances of passive attention, seemed to have little awareness of the outside world, and attended to stimuli in the environment in an almost random manner. These findings suggested to Bleuler that schizophrenia consisted of problems in both the inhibiting and the facilitating components of attention. Bleuler also concluded that these patients had a fundamental disruption of the associative organization of mental activity, which interfered with the person's capacity for purposeful behavior, organized thought, and discourse.

There is now general agreement that abnormal attention is a central feature of schizophrenia. Deficits across all domains of attention can be demonstrated in patients with this disorder. Filtering of irrelevant information is a major problem, as evidenced by the occurrence of hallucinations, thought insertions, and other positive symptoms. Schizophrenic patients often encounter difficulties on tests of sensory selective attention because of their susceptibility to distraction, which in turn is correlated with the presence and severity of thought disorder (Oltmanns et al. 1978; Wielgus and Harvey 1988). Slowing of reaction time is a ubiquitous feature in schizophrenic patients and may be related to distractibility caused by intrinsic factors such as auditory hallucinations and transient loss of set (Nuechterlein 1977; Nuechterlein and Dawson 1984; Schwartz et al. 1989). Performance deficits are seen on tests of divided attention when concurrent task performance is required. People with schizophrenia encounter great difficulty on tests requiring suppression of interfering information (e.g., the Stroop Test). Attentional capacity and focus, as measured by Digit Symbol Substitution, the PASAT, and other tests that require mental control, are usually impaired. Furthermore, people with schizophrenia have great difficulty with sustained attention, probably as a result of the combined interaction of all attentional problems, particularly distractibility.

Contemporary models of attention deficit in patients with schizophrenia can be broadly categorized into those that emphasize disturbances of information processing and those that focus on disturbances of arousal. Both factors appear to be important in schizophrenia. Behavioral abnormalities develop when the person with schizophrenia is confronted with excessive task demands or becomes overloaded with either internal signals or external information that tax his or her limited available attentional capacity. This is most apparent when tasks require effortful controlled attentional processing. People with schizophrenia show better performance on tasks that are well practiced and involve automatic forms of attention (Callaway and Naghdi 1982; Neale and Oltmanns 1980). These deficits may be directly associated with disturbances of informational gating in dopaminergic brain systems.

## Attention-Deficit/Hyperactivity Disorder

ADHD is characterized by difficulty paying attention to internal and external stimuli, impaired ability to organize and complete tasks, and problems controlling behaviors, emotions, and impulses (Shaffer 1994). Individuals with ADHD often do not achieve their academic, occupational, and social potential (Barkley et al. 1993; Rutter 1983; Shaywitz and Shaywitz 1987). ADHD has become one of the most widely diagnosed disorders of childhood. DSM-IV-TR distinguishes between symptoms of attentional disturbance and hyperactivity/impulsivity and provides criteria for ADHD, combined type, predominantly inattentive type, and predominantly hyperactive-impulsive type (American Psychiatric Association 2000). To meet DSM-IV-TR criteria, symptoms must be present for at least 6 months; must cause impairment in social, occupational, or academic functioning; and must be present in two or more settings (Table 13–2).

Although attentional symptoms improve with age in people with ADHD, approximately 11%–31% of children with the disorder continue to be disabled by it in adulthood (Gittelman et al. 1985; Mannuzza et al. 1993). The diagnosis of ADHD in adults is now a common reason for neuropsychiatric evaluation, but there is not a separate category for the diagnosis of ADHD in adults. To meet criteria for ADHD in adults, some hyperactive-impulsive or inattentive symptoms must have been present and must have caused impairment before age 7.

The essential features of ADHD are inattention, impulsiveness, and hyperactivity that are developmentally inappropriate. Diagnosis of ADHD is age related, because behavioral norms change across the life span. For example, the DSM-IV-TR criteria for restlessness change from physical evidence of motor restlessness in childhood to a subjective sense of restlessness in adolescents and adults. The diagnosis of ADHD is also strongly influenced by cultural expectations of what constitutes the range of age-appropriate behavior. ADHD is most evident in cultures requiring attendance in schools for long periods of the day, during which a child must stay seated and sustain attention on highly abstract tasks with minimal ongoing reinforcement. Even in cultures as similar as the United States and Great Britain, the frequency with which this syndrome is diagnosed shows surprising variability. Rutter (1983) cites evidence that the diagnosis of hyperactivity is made nearly 50 times as often in North America as in Britain.

ADHD is more common in first- and second-degree relatives of patients with ADHD (Biederman et al. 1990; Faraone et al. 1993, 1994). Male relatives may be at

**TABLE 13–2.** Criteria for attention-deficit/hyperactivity disorder

**Inattention (six or more symptoms)**
Makes careless mistakes, has poor attention to detail
Has difficulty sustaining attention
Does not seem to listen
Does not follow through or finish tasks
Has difficulty organizing tasks
Avoids activities that require sustained mental effort
Loses things easily
Is easily distracted
Is forgetful

**Hyperactivity/impulsivity (six or more symptoms)**
*Hyperactivity*
Fidgets, squirms
Has difficulty remaining seated
Runs or climbs excessively (children), experiences subjective restlessness (adults)
Has difficulty with quiet activities
Is "on the go," "driven by a motor"
Talks excessively
*Impulsivity*
Blurts out answers before questions are completed
Is impatient
Often interrupts others

greater risk, although results from gender studies in ADHD vary. Family members of ADHD probands also appear to have a higher incidence of comorbid psychiatric disorders, such as antisocial personality disorder, major depression, substance abuse, and anxiety disorder (Shaywitz and Shaywitz 1987).

Comorbid conditions commonly accompany ADHD in children and adults. Chang et al. (1995) assessed the presence of comorbid conditions in a retrospective chart review of 130 adults referred for evaluation of attentional disturbance and found that substance abuse, mood disorder, and learning disability were present in a large percentage of the sample. Biederman et al. (1992, 1993b) found a high incidence of conduct, mood, and anxiety disorders in children and adults with ADHD.

Structural and functional imaging studies have implicated frontal system dysfunction in persons with ADHD (Castellanos et al. 1994; Ciedd et al. 1994; Lou et al. 1984; Matochik et al. 1994; Zametkin et al. 1993). Deficits in dopaminergic and noradrenergic function have also been implicated in patients with ADHD (Kostrzewa et al. 1994; Satterfield et al. 1994). The ability of stimulants to ameliorate symptoms of ADHD lends further support to the involvement of catecholamines in this disorder. Serotonin may play a modulatory role in ADHD, particularly in relationship to symptoms of mood, aggression, and impulse control (Costall et al. 1979; Halperin et al. 1994). Functional imaging studies have also found prefrontal and anterior temporal hypometabolism in patients with secondary depression (Mayberg 1994). Dysfunction in dopaminergic systems in the nucleus accumbens appears to play a central role in substance abuse. One possible explanation for the high incidence of comorbidity between attentional symptoms and mood, impulse control, and substance abuse is that these systems share a close anatomic, neurochemical, and functional composition in the basal forebrain and anteromedial frontal lobe.

The diagnosis of ADHD can be difficult and is based primarily on subjective reports by patients and family members. It is important to obtain historical information about the attentional complaint from multiple sources (Ward et al. 1993). Situational variations in the behavioral manifestation of an attention deficit poses another diagnostic challenge. Behavior in the office and performance on cognitive tasks in a structured setting may be normal. However, the same individual may be impaired in a less structured environment with competing demands for attention.

For the most part, patients with ADHD have normal intelligence and do not exhibit major cognitive dysfunction. However, certain deficit patterns are observed on standardized tests. Poor performance on three WAIS-R subscales (Digit Span, Arithmetic, and Digit Symbol) are associated with ADHD when general verbal and visual-spatial performance are at normal or nearly normal levels (Kaufman 1979). This pattern is not unique to ADHD; other disorders that affect concentration, working memory, or processing speed also produce this profile.

Impaired sustained attention is a primary feature of ADHD. Impairments are greatest when vigilance is required to detect infrequent information, particularly when this information is not motivationally salient. Hyperactive children exhibit more errors of both omission and commission on the CPT than do children without ADHD, and they also show more rapid deterioration of task performance over time (Sykes et al. 1973). In other studies (Barkley 1977; Rapoport et al. 1978), CPT performance often improved after the administration of stimulants.

Errors of omission and commission on motor tasks requiring selective inhibition of responses (e.g., go/no-go paradigms) provide other markers for ADHD (Risser and Bowers 1993; Trommer et al. 1988). Furthermore, differences in performance between children with ADHD with and without hyperactivity may exist on this paradigm. These impairments on the go/no-go paradigm may reflect general problems with impulsivity (Barkley et al.

1992). Additional research is needed to better characterize the nature of impulsivity in persons with ADHD.

One long-standing hypothesis regarding the nature of ADHD is that the attention deficit results from susceptibility to distraction. Children with ADHD were thought to have an impairment related to the filtering of task-irrelevant stimuli. Yet children with ADHD rarely show problems with performance in the presence of distracting information on laboratory tests (Douglas and Peters 1981). Attentional filtering may not be the major problem in most cases of ADHD.

The primary symptoms of ADHD, inattentiveness and impulsiveness, cause a wide range of behaviors that vary greatly among children. Barkley (1988) has argued that this suggests a more fundamental impairment involving the use of rule-governed behavior, including the ability to use language as a discriminative stimulus for behavior control. If this is true, many of the attentional impairments of ADHD reflect difficulties in the compliance that is necessary for sustained attention in the absence of strong immediate reinforcement (Douglas 1983). Ultimately, ADHD may result from a failure of normal reinforcement in interaction with defective processes of attention and response inhibition.

## Case Example: Adult ADHD, Case 1

A 38-year-old male nursing student was evaluated for complaints of difficulty paying attention. He stated that he had done poorly in school and "was ignored by the teachers and allowed to graduate from high school without doing the work." He found it difficult to pay attention to what people were saying, because his thoughts were jumping quickly from one topic to another. Sitting still to read required tremendous effort. He always had a very high energy level. He became convinced that he was a failure as a student and that he was fit only for manual labor. He also suffered from significant mood lability and heavily abused cocaine and alcohol. He reported that cocaine made him feel normal. His substance abuse habit became severe, and he admitted himself for inpatient substance abuse treatment 10 years ago. He has been drug free since that time. He has gradually resumed his education but has found that he has to work twice as hard as other students to cover the material.

Neuropsychological testing revealed his intelligence to be in the normal range, but his Verbal IQ was 23 points higher than his Performance IQ. Scores on tests requiring complex attention were moderately impaired. Achievement test scores revealed performance below expectations in spelling, reading, and arithmetic.

He was begun on methylphenidate, 10 mg in the morning and 10 mg at noon, with an excellent response. He became able to read for longer periods of time without losing his concentration or having to get up and pace. He no longer had to get up in the middle of the night to complete his assignments. He began to take tests without time limitations in a separate room and began taping lectures to review at home. His class average increased from C+ to A.

Methylphenidate was tolerated without side effects. The dose was increased to 10 mg, morning, noon, and late afternoon, to help with schoolwork in the evening. Supportive counseling has helped him improve his self-image, and he now plans to pursue graduate work in health care.

This case demonstrates a profound example of attentional disturbance that was not addressed in childhood. Subsequent academic performance and self-image were poor. This patient also showed the common comorbid features of mood lability, substance abuse, and poor academic performance. Successful treatment first required discontinuation of substance abuse. Medication, modifications to his academic environment (Table 13–3), and counseling to help with self-esteem provided significant benefits.

## Case Example: Adult ADHD, Case 2

A 45-year-old woman was evaluated for difficulties paying attention and problems with short-term memory. Her son had recently been diagnosed with and treated for ADHD. She was a college graduate who throughout school had struggled with reading, processing lecture material, and keeping her work organized. She felt that she had to work twice as hard as her peers. She had no evidence of hyperactivity, mood disturbance, or substance abuse. Neuropsychological testing revealed superior intelligence with impairment of complex attention and difficulty with sustained reading and reading comprehension.

She was begun on methylphenidate, 10 mg in the morning and at noon, with a good initial response. The dose has since been increased to 20 mg in the morning and at noon, with an occasional 10-mg dose in the afternoon if she needs to work in the early evening.

This case demonstrates an example of a long-standing disturbance of attention and organization in an adult without hyperactivity, learning disability, or another psychiatric diagnosis. There appears to be a familial pattern. Treatment with methylphenidate increased attention and organization, which led to considerable improvement in her daily functioning.

The diagnosis of ADHD should be made carefully, with special attention to the identification of comorbid conditions. In a retrospective sample (Chang et al. 1995), 50% of adults referred for evaluation of ADHD did not meet the diagnostic criteria for ADHD. Historical information about the attentional disturbance should be gathered from the patient, family, and additional sources.

**TABLE 13–3.** Academic recommendations for patients with attention deficit disorder and learning disabilities

1. Modified test format, including open-book exams, short-answer questions, or multiple-choice evaluations, with a simplified verbal structure for the questions and answers. Having a reader available to interpret questions may be necessary.
2. Access in class to notes of another student or the instructor
3. Permission to tape lectures or workshops
4. Use of a word processor for all written assignments, including essay tests, with spelling and grammar checks
5. Untimed testing because of slow reading rate and difficulty accessing information under pressure
6. Books on tape or the assignment of a study partner who can help in getting the material from the reading assignments
7. Tutoring in coursework if the study partner is not available
8. Testing in a separate room to eliminate distractions
9. Use of a calculator and the ability to bring formulas or to have open-book exams when math is required
10. Waiver of the math requirement in academic settings if accommodations and tutoring are not successful
11. Waiver of the foreign-language requirement if accommodations and tutoring are not successful
12. Limit to one the number of courses with heavy reading requirements

**Individualized tutoring is suggested to work on the following skills:**

1. Basic written-language skills, including reading decoding, reading comprehension, spelling, grammar, phonetics, and punctuation
2. Advanced reading skills, including comprehension efficiency, main idea identification, and key terms scanning
3. Advanced writing skills, including syntax, use of an outline for term papers, idea development in written form, organization, and proofreading. The use of capitalization should also be addressed.
4. Study skills, including planning how to attack reading and writing assignments, memorization, scheduling, organizational strategies, and self-monitoring for comprehension
5. Test-taking skills, including how to read multiple-choice questions, organization of essay questions, strategies for deciding which questions to answer first, and how to recognize the material studied in the format of the test questions
6. Cognitive strategies to improve organization and to help overcome procrastination. Efforts to enhance concentration for listening and reading should be attempted.

Adults who were referred for evaluation of ADHD and who had a history of childhood ADHD had a different pattern of cognitive performance than did adults without a childhood history of ADHD. (Recommendations for the office evaluation of ADHD are provided in Table 13–4.) Neuropsychological testing can help highlight cognitive strengths and weaknesses, diagnose the presence of learning disabilities, and help distinguish attentional disturbance from an underlying memory disorder. Although cognitive testing can help document attentional disturbance, normal attentional performance on neuropsychological testing does not exclude the diagnosis of ADHD.

The first step in the treatment of ADHD is to develop a problem list in which each problem is weighted by severity. A treatment plan is then constructed that targets symptom clusters one at a time. If substance abuse is present it must be treated before attentional symptoms can be reliably evaluated and treated. If attentional symptoms are the primary problem, then a trial of treatment with a stimulant should be initiated. If depression is the primary symptom with secondary attentional complaints, then treatment with an antidepressant should be initiated first.

In a limited number of carefully controlled medication trials for ADHD, methylphenidate and other stimulants were superior to placebo (Elia 1993; Hechtman et al. 1984; Matochik et al. 1994; Mattes et al. 1984; Pelham et al. 1990; Rapoport et al. 1994; Wender et al. 1985; Wilens and Biederman 1992). Response rates up to 70% have been reported. Responders often report feeling more composed, with improvement in symptoms of irritability, impatience, mood lability, and impulsivity in addition to improved attention, concentration, and organization.

The usual starting dose of methylphenidate is 10 mg in the morning and at noon. The usual dose range is 20–90 mg/day in two to three divided doses. Most patients do well on 20–30 mg/day. The therapeutic effect lasts approximately 3–4 hours. Some patients notice a wearing-off effect with dysphoria. The medication is usually well tolerated. Jitteriness is a common side effect, and methylphenidate should not be taken together with caffeinated beverages. Insomnia, headache, nausea, irritability, moodiness, agitation, tics, and rebound phenomena occur infrequently. For patients with milder symptoms or those who experience a wearing-off effect, a sustained-release preparation (Ritalin SR) may be tried. This preparation tends to have a smoother onset and less of a wearing-off effect. The sustained-release form is given as a 20-mg dose in the morning and at noon. Patients and physicians need to adjust the timing and the dose of the stimulants to find the optimum regimen, particularly for individuals who work second and third shifts. Comparable effectiveness of methylphenidate sustained-release and standard preparations has been reported in patients with ADHD (Fitzpatrick et al. 1992; Lawrence et al. 1997; Pelham et al. 1990). A once-daily dose of methylphenidate was recently introduced for treatment of ADHD

**TABLE 13–4.** Office evaluation of attention-deficit/hyperactivity disorder

**History of attentional complaints**

Duration, primary symptoms

Are symptoms diffuse or specific to modality or setting?

Is there evidence of hyperactivity? Can they sit in class or through dinner or a movie without getting up?

Do they read for pleasure? Do they have problems reading (decoding, comprehension)? How long do they read at one time? Can they recall what they read?

Can they take effective notes in class and follow what is said?

Do they have trouble being organized, misplacing things?

Do they keep their room and belongings in good order?

Do they daydream? Do their thoughts jump around?

Are they forgetful? Do they feel frequently overwhelmed?

Do they have trouble completing tasks?

Do they lose interest quickly and shift from one activity to another?

Can they listen to others and keep track of conversations?

Are they easily distracted, impulsive, impatient? Can they wait in line? Are they short-tempered, irritable, and easily angered?

Do they blurt out answers and interrupt others?

Do their moods change frequently?

**History from patient and informant**

Developmental history; history of brain injury, tics, conduct disturbance

Academic history—highest educational level, grades at each level, best and worst subjects, resource help, special education, repetition of a grade, history of hyperactivity in school

History of depression, mood lability, or substance abuse

Family history of ADHD symptoms

**Office tests**

Recitation of months of the year backwards, Digit Span

Repetition of a short story

Letter cancellation task

Arithmetic problems: addition, multiplication, subtraction, division

Reading: fluency, comprehension, educational level

Test-free articulation of ideas by asking patients to describe a paragraph that they read or to answer other open-ended questions

Brief writing sample

Verbal fluency

Abstraction

Figure copying

Memory

General information

General intelligence estimation

Observation of problem-solving strategy—carefulness, consistency, frustration and anxiety levels

(Modi et al. 2000a, 2000b); however, controlled treatment trials comparing effectiveness of these preparations have not been published to date. Most patients take stimulants 7 days a week, but some prefer to take them only during the work or school week, and a few patients take them only as needed before an examination or when projects require sustained attention.

There has been a great deal of interest in other medications to treat ADHD. Patients who do not respond satisfactorily or have unacceptable side effects with one medication may do well with another drug. Other stimulant medications that may be tried are dextroamphetamine and pemoline (Sallee et al. 1992). Methylphenidate and dextroamphetamine are controlled substances, and prescribing these agents can be cumbersome. Only a 1-month supply can be given at a time, and prescriptions cannot be renewed over the telephone. Pemoline and the antidepressants are not subject to these restrictions. However, it is important to note that liver toxicity has been reported in a small number of patients prescribed pemoline (Marotta and Roberts 1998), raising concerns about its prescription. The controversial role of pemoline in the treatment of ADHD was debated at a recent consensus conference (Pliszka et al. 2000). Subsequent recommendations stated that if neither methylphenidate nor amphetamine treatment is successful, a trial of pemoline may be considered (Pliszka et al. 2000). Given the potential dangers of liver toxicity, liver function tests are warranted every 2 weeks (Pliszka et al. 2000). Desipramine, in doses used to treat depression, and bupropion may also be helpful (Biederman et al. 1986, 1989, 1993a; Casat et al. 1989; Pataki et al. 1993; Simeon et al. 1986; Wender and Reimher 1990). These drugs may be particularly useful in patients with a history of substance abuse who are at risk for abusing stimulant medication. There are scarce controlled data on the use of selective serotonin reuptake inhibitors in the treatment of ADHD (Barrickman et al. 1991; Jankovic 1993; Spencer et al. 1993a, 1993b; Wilens et al. 1993). Patients with ADHD and comorbid depression may require treatment with both a stimulant and an antidepressant.

Behavioral treatments for attentional disturbance can be an extremely helpful adjunct to medication. Identifying the time of day when the patient is most productive and advising him or her to concentrate on the most demanding attentional activities during that period will optimize daily performance. Academic tutoring and modifications to the academic program—such as taking untimed tests; taking tests in a separate, quiet room; and taping lectures for later review—are often recommended (Table 13–4). Limiting the number of courses and making

realistic career choices will increase the likelihood of academic success. Supportive counseling and education about the illness for the patient and the family can help improve self-esteem. Coaching services that work on organizational skills can help with the development of productive new habits.

# References

Adams RD, Victor M: Principles of Neurology, 2nd Edition. New York, McGraw-Hill, 1981

Albert ML: A simple test of visual neglect. Neurology 23:658–664, 1973

Alexander GE, DeLong MR, Strick PL: Parallel organization of functionally segregated circuits linking basal ganglia and cortex. Annu Rev Neurosci 9:357–381, 1986

American Psychiatric Association: Diagnostic and Statistical Manual of Mental Disorders, 4th Edition, Text Revision. Washington, DC, American Psychiatric Association, 2000

Armitage SG: An analysis of certain psychological tests used for the evaluation of brain injury. Psychological Monographs 60:1–23, 1946

Arnstein A, Goldman-Rakic P: Alpha$_2$-adrenergic mechanisms in prefrontal cortex associated with cognitive decline in aged nonhuman primates. Science 230:1273–1276, 1985

Badgaiyan RD, Posner MI: Mapping the cingulated cortex in response selection and monitoring. Neuroimage 7:255–260, 1998

Barkley RA: The effect of methylphenidate on various measures of activity level and attention in hyperkinetic children. J Abnorm Child Psychol 5:351–369, 1977

Barkley RA: Attention deficit disorder with hyperactivity, in Behavioral Assessment of Childhood Disorders. Edited by Barkley RA, Mash EJ, Terdal LG. New York, Guilford, 1988, pp 69–104

Barkley RA, DuPaul GJ, McMurray MB: Comprehensive evaluation of attention deficit disorder with and without hyperactivity as defined by research criteria. J Consult Clin Psychol 58:775–789, 1990

Barkley RA, Grodzinsky G, DuPaul GJ: Frontal lobe functions in attention deficit disorder with and without hyperactivity: a review and research report. J Abnorm Child Psychol 20:163–188, 1992

Barkley RA, Guevremont DC, Anastopoulos AD, et al: Driving-related risks and outcomes of attention deficit hyperactivity disorder in adolescents and young adults: a 3- to 5-year follow-up survey. Pediatrics 92:212–218, 1993

Baron JC, Petit-Taboue MC, LeDoze F: Right frontal hypometabolism in transient global amnesia: a PET study. Brain 117:593–606, 1994

Barrickman L, Noyes R, Kuperman S, et al: Treatment of ADHD with fluoxetine: a preliminary trial. J Am Acad Child Adolesc Psychiatry 30:762–767, 1991

Battersby WS, Bender MB, Pollack M: Unilateral spatial agnosia (inattention) in patients with cerebral lesions. Brain 79:68–93, 1956

Baxter LR: Neuroimaging studies of obsessive compulsive disorder. Psychiatr Clin North Am 15:871–884, 1992

Baxter LR, Schwartz JM, Bergman KS, et al: Caudate glucose metabolic rate changes with both drug and behavior therapy for obsessive compulsive disorder. Arch Gen Psychiatry 49:681–689, 1992

Bellack AS, Hersen M: Behavioral Assessment, 3rd Edition. New York, Pergamon, 1988

Benkelfat C, Nordhal TE, Semple WE, et al: Local cerebral glucose metabolic rates in obsessive compulsive disorder: patients treated with clomipramine. Arch Gen Psychiatry 47:840–848, 1990

Benton A, Hamsher K, Varney NR, et al: Contributions to Neuropsychological Assessment. New York, Oxford University Press, 1983

Biederman J, Gastfriend DR, Jellinek MS: Desipramine in the treatment of children with ADD. J Clin Psychopharmacol 6:359–363, 1986

Biederman J, Baldessarini RJ, Wright V, et al: A double-blind placebo controlled study of desipramine in the treatment of ADD: efficacy. J Am Acad Child Adolesc Psychiatry 32:199–204, 1989

Biederman J, Faraone SV, Keenan K, et al: Family genetic and psychosocial risk factors in DSM-III attention deficit disorder. J Am Acad Child Adolesc Psychiatry 29:526–533, 1990

Biederman J, Faraone SV, Keenan K, et al: Further evidence for family genetic risk factors in attention deficit hyperactivity disorder: patterns of comorbidity in probands and relatives in psychiatrically and pediatrically referred samples. Arch Gen Psychiatry 49:728–738, 1992

Biederman J, Baldessarini RJ, Wright V, et al: A double-blind placebo controlled study of desipramine in the treatment of ADD, III: lack of impact of comorbidity and family history factors on clinical response. J Am Acad Child Adolesc Psychiatry 32:199–204, 1993a

Biederman J, Faraone SV, Spencer T, et al: Patterns of psychiatric comorbidity, cognition, and psychosocial functioning in adults with attention deficit hyperactivity disorder. Am J Psychiatry 150:1792–1798, 1993b

Binder JR, Rao SM, Hammeke TA, et al: Functional magnetic resonance imaging of human auditory cortex. Ann Neurol 35:662–672, 1994

Bleuler E: Dementia Praecox or the Group of Schizophrenias (1911). New York, International Universities Press, 1950

Botvinick M, Nystrom LE, Fissell K, et al: Conflict monitoring versus selection for action in anterior cingulate cortex. Nature 402:179–181, 1999

Brain WR: Visual disorientation with special reference to lesions of the right cerebral hemisphere. Brain 64:224–272, 1941

Brand C: General intelligence and mental speed: their relationship and development, in Intelligence and Learning. Edited by Friedman MP, Das JP, O'Connor N. New York, Plenum, 1981, pp 589–593

Breslow R, Kocsis J, Belkin B: Memory deficits in depressive illness. J Psychiatr Res 185–191, 1977

Broadbent DE: Perception and Communication. New York, Pergamon, 1958

Bruhn P, Parsons OA: Reaction time variability in epileptic and brain-damaged patients. Cortex 13:373–384, 1977

Bushnell MC, Goldberg ME, Robinson DL: Behavioral enhancement of visual responses in monkey cerebral cortex, I: modulation in posterior parietal cortex related to selective visual attention. J Neurophysiol 46:755–772, 1981

Byrne DC: Affect and vigilance performance in depressive illness. J Psychiatr Res 13:185–191, 1977

Cabeza R, Nyberg L: Imaging cognition II: an empirical review of 275 PET and fMRI studies. J Cogn Neurosci 12:1–47, 2000

Callaway E, Naghdi S: An information processing model for schizophrenia. Arch Gen Psychiatry 39:339–347, 1982

Casat CD, Pleasants DZ, Schroeder DH, et al: Bupropion in children with attention deficit disorder. Psychopharmacology Bulletin 25:198–201, 1989

Castellanos FX, Giedd JN, Eckburg P, et al: Quantitative morphology of the caudate nucleus in attention deficit hyperactivity disorder. Am J Psychiatry 151:1791–1796, 1994

Chang K, Neeper R, Jenkins M, et al: Clinical profile of patients referred for evaluation of adult attention deficit hyperactivity disorder. J Neuropsychiatry Clin Neurosci 7:400–401, 1995

Cherry EC: Some experiments on the recognition of speech, with one and with two ears. J Acoust Soc Am 26:975–979, 1953

Christensen AL: Luria's Neuropsychological Investigation, 2nd Edition. Copenhagen, Denmark, Munksgaard, 1989

Ciedd JN, Castellanos FX, Casey BJ, et al: Quantitative morphology of the corpus callosum in attention deficit hyperactivity disorder. Am J Psychiatry 151:665–669, 1994

Clemens JA, Fuller RW: Differences in the effects of amphetamine and methylphenidate on brain dopamine turnover and serum prolactin concentration in reserpine-treated rats. Life Sci 24:2077–2081, 1979

Cohen RA: Neuropsychology of Attention. New York, Plenum, 1993

Cohen RA, Fisher M: Neuropsychological correlates of fatigue associated with multiple sclerosis. J Clin Exp Neuropsychol 10:48–52, 1988

Cohen RA, Lohr I: The influence of effort on impairments of attention associated with major affective disorders (abstract). Journal of the International Neuropsychological Society 1:122, 1995

Cohen RA, Waters W: Psychophysiological correlates of levels and states of cognitive processing. Neuropsychologia 23:243–256, 1985

Cohen RA, McCrae V, Phillips K, et al: Neurobehavioral consequences of bilateral medial cingulotomy (abstract). Neurology 40:198, 1990

Cohen RA, Kaplan RF, Meadow ME, et al: Habituation and sensitization of the orienting response following bilateral anterior cingulotomy. Neuropsychologia 132:609–617, 1994

Cohen RA, O'Donnell BF, Meadows M-E, et al: ERP indices and neuropsychological performance as predictors of functional outcome in dementia. J Geriatr Psychiatry Neurol 8:217–225, 1995

Cohen RA, Malloy PF, Jenkins MA: Disorders of attention, in Clinical Neuropsychology: A Pocket Handbook for Assessment. Edited by Snyder PJ, Nussbaum PD. Washington DC, American Psychological Association, 1998, pp 541–572

Cohen RM, Weingartner H, Smallberg SA, et al: Effort and cognition in depression. Arch Gen Psychiatry 39:593–597, 1982

Coles MGH, Duncan-Johnson CC: Cardiac activity and information processing: the effects of stimulus significance, and detection and response requirement. J Exp Psychol Hum Percept Perform 1:418–428, 1975

Colquhoun WP, Baddeley AD: Influence of signal probability during pretraining on vigilance decrement. Journal of Experimental Psychology 73:153–155, 1967

Conners CK: A teacher rating scale for use with children. Am J Psychiatry 126:884–888, 1969

Corbetta M, Kincad JM, Ollinger JM, et al: Voluntary orienting is dissociated from target detection in human posterior parietal cortex. Nat Neurosci 3:292–297, 2000

Corcoran DW, Mullin J, Rainey MT, et al: The effects of raised signal and noise amplitude during the course of vigilance tasks, in Vigilance: Theory, Operational Performance, and Psychological Correlates. Edited by Mackie R. New York, Academic Press, 1977

Costall B, Hui SC, Naylor RJ: The importance of serotonergic mechanisms for the induction of hyperactivity by amphetamine. Neuropharmacology 18:605–609, 1979

Crick F, Koch C: Towards a neurobiological theory of consciousness. Seminars in the Neurosciences 2:263–275, 1990

Cummings JL: Frontal-subcortical circuits and human behavior. Arch Neurol 50:873–880, 1993

Denny-Brown D, Chambers RA: The parietal lobe and behavior. Research Publication of the Association for the Research of Nervous and Mental Diseases 36:35–117, 1958

De Renzi E, Faglioni P, Previdi P: Spatial memory and hemispheric locus of lesion. Cortex 13:424–433, 1977

Desimone R, Gross CG: Visual areas in the temporal cortex of the macaque. Brain Res 178:363–380, 1979

Deutsch CP: Differences among epileptics and between epileptics and nonepileptics in terms of some learning and memory variables. Arch Neurol Psychiatry 70:474–482, 1953

Deutsch JA, Deutsch D: Attention: some theoretical considerations. Psychol Rev 70:80–90, 1963

Douglas VI: Attentional and cognitive problems, in Developmental Neuropsychiatry. Edited by Rutter M. New York, Guilford, 1983, pp 280–329

Douglas VI, Peters KG: Towards a clearer definition of the attention deficit of hyperactive children, in Attention and Cognitive Development. Edited by Hale GA, Lewis M. New York, Plenum, 1981, pp 173–246

Ebstein R, Novick O, Umansky R, et al: Dopamine D4 receptor exon III polymorphism associated with the human personality trait of novelty seeking. Nat Genet 12:78–80, 1996

Elia J: Drug treatment of hyperactive children: therapeutic guidelines. Drugs 46:863–871, 1993

Faraone SV, Biederman J, Lehman BK, et al: Evidence for the independent familial transmission of attention deficit hyperactivity disorder and learning disabilities: results from a family genetic study. Am J Psychiatry 150:891–895, 1993

Faraone SV, Biederman J, Milberger S: An exploratory study of ADHD among second degree relatives of ADHD children. Biol Psychiatry 35:398–402, 1994

Firth CD, Stevens M, Johnstone EC, et al: Effects of ECT and depression on various aspects of memory. Br J Psychiatry 142:610–617, 1983

Fitzpatrick PA, Klorman R, Brumaghim JT, et al: Effects of sustained release and standard preparations of methylphenidate on attention deficit disorder. J Am Acad Child Adolesc Psychiatry 31:226–234, 1992

Folkard S: Time of day and level of processing. Memory and Cognition 7:247–252, 1979

Fuster JM: The Prefrontal Cortex: Anatomy, Physiology, and Neuropsychology of the Frontal Lobe. New York, Raven, 1989

Gittelman R, Mannuzza S, Shenker R, et al: Hyperactive boys almost grown up, I: psychiatric status. Arch Gen Psychiatry 42:937–947, 1985

Glowinsky H: Cognitive deficits in temporal lobe epilepsy: an investigation of memory functioning. J Nerv Ment Dis 157:129–137, 1973

Goldberg ME, Bushnell MD: Behavioral enhancement of visual response in monkey cerebral cortex, II: modulation in frontal eye fields specifically related to saccades. J Neurophysiol 46:773–787, 1981

Goldberg ME, Wurtz RH: Activity of superior colliculus in behaving monkey, I: visual receptive fields of single neurons. J Neurophysiol 35:542–559, 1972

Green DM, Swets JA: Signal detection theory and psychophysics. New York, Wiley, 1966

Gronwall D: Advances in the assessment of attention and information processing after head injury, in Neurobehavioral Recovery From Head Injury. Edited by Levin HS, Grafman

J, Eisenberg HM. New York, Oxford University Press, 1987, pp 355–371

Gronwall DMA, Sampson H: The Psychological Effects of Concussion. Auckland, New Zealand, Auckland University Press/Oxford University Press, 1974

Gronwall DMA, Wrightson P: Delayed recovery of intellectual function after minor head injury. Lancet 4:605–609, 1974

Halperin JM, Sharma V, Siever LJ, et al: Serotonergic function in aggressive and nonaggressive boys with attention deficit hyperactivity disorder. Am J Psychiatry 151:243–248, 1994

Hansch EC, Syndulko K, Cohen SN, et al: Cognition in Parkinson disease: an event-related potential perspective. Ann Neurol 11:599–607, 1982

Hansen JC, Dickstein PW, Berlin C, et al: Event-related potentials during selective attention to speech sounds. Biol Psychol 16:211–229, 1983

Hasher L, Zacks RT: Automatic and effortful processes in memory. J Exp Psychol Gen 108:356–388, 1979

Heaton RK: Wisconsin Card Sorting Test. Odessa, FL, Psychological Assessment Resources, 1985

Heaton RK, Nelson LM, Thompson DS, et al: Neuropsychological findings in relapsing/remitting and chronic/progressive multiple sclerosis. J Consult Clin Psychol 53:103–110, 1985

Hechtman L, Weiss G, Perlman T: Young adult outcome in hyperactive children who received long-term stimulant treatment. Journal of the American Academy of Child Psychiatry 23:261–269, 1984

Heilman KM, Bowers D, Coslett HB, et al: Directional hypokinesia in neglect. Neurology 35:855–860, 1985

Heilman KM, Watson RT, Valenstein E, et al: Attention: behavior and neural mechanisms. Attention 11:461–481, 1988

Heilman KM, Watson RT, Valenstein E: Neglect and related disorders, in Clinical Neuropsychology, 3rd Edition. Edited by Heilman KM, Valenstein E. New York, Oxford University Press, 1993, pp 279–336

Hill D: On states of consciousness, in The Bridge Between Neurology and Psychiatry. Edited by Reynolds EH, Trimble MR. London, Churchill Livingstone, 1989, pp 56–71

Hillyard SA, Hansen JC: Attention: electrophysiological approaches, in Psychophysiology: Systems, Processes and Applications. Edited by Coles M, Donchin E, Porges S. New York, Guilford, 1986, pp 227–243

Hillyard SA, Hink RF, Schwent VL, et al: Electrical signs of selective attention in the human brain. Science 182:177–180, 1973

Hinke RM, Stillman AE, Kim SG: Functional magnetic imaging of Broca's area during internal speech. Neuroreport 4:675–678, 1993

Hockey GRJ, Colquhoun WP: Diurnal variation in human performance: a review, in Aspects of Human Efficiency: Diurnal Rhythm and Loss of Sleep. Edited by Colquhoun WP. London, English Universities Press, 1972

Hyvarinen J, Poranen A, Jokinen Y: Influence of attentive behavior on neuronal responses to vibration in primary somatosensory cortex of the monkey. J Neurophysiol 43:870–882, 1980

James W: Principles of Psychology. New York, Holt, 1890

Jankovic J: Deprenyl in attention deficit associated with Tourette's syndrome. Arch Neurol 9:181–189, 1993

Jennings JR, Averill RJ, Opton ME, et al: Some parameters of heart rate change: perceptual versus motor task requirements, noxiousness, and uncertainty. Psychophysiology 7:194–212, 1980

Jerison HJ: Signal detection theory in the analysis of human vigilance. Hum Factors 9:285–288, 1967

Jones EG, Leavitt RY: Retrograde axonal transport and demonstration of nonspecific projections to the cerebral cortex and striatum from thalamic intralaminar nuclei in the rat, cat and monkey. J Comp Neurol 154:349–378, 1974

Jones EG, Wise SP, Coulter JD: Differential thalamic relationships of sensory-motor and parietal cortical fields in monkeys. J Comp Neurol 183:833–882, 1979

Jones MR, Boltz M: Dynamic attending and responses to time. Psychol Rev 96:459–491, 1989

Jones-Gotman M, Milner B: Design fluency: the invention of nonsense drawings after focal cortical lesions. Neuropsychologia 15:61–71, 1977

Kahneman D: Attention and Effort. Englewood Cliffs, NJ, Prentice-Hall, 1973

Kahneman D, Beatty J: Pupil diameter and load on memory. Science 154:1583–1585, 1966

Kahneman D, Treisman A: Changing views of attention and automaticity, in Varieties of Attention. Edited by Parasuraman R, Davies DR. New York, Academic Press, 1984, pp 286–294

Kandel ER, Schwartz JH: Molecular biology of memory: modulation of transmitter release. Science 218:433–443, 1982

Kaplan RF, Verfaellie M, DeWitt L, et al: Effects of changes in stimulus continency on visual extinction. Neurology 40:1299–1301, 1989

Kaplan RF, Verfaellie M, Meadows ME, et al: Changing attentional demands in left hemi-spatial neglect. Arch Neurol 48:1263–1266, 1991

Kastner S, de Weerd P, Desimone R, et al: Mechanisms of directed attention in the human extrastriate cortex as revealed by functional MRI. Science 282:108–111, 1998

Kaufman AS: Intelligence Testing With the WISC-R. New York, Wiley, 1979

Kessler HR, Cohen RA, Lauer K, et al: The relationship between disability and memory dysfunction in multiple sclerosis. Int J Neurosci 62:17–34, 1992

Kimura D: Functional asymmetry of the brain in dichotic listening. Cortex 3:163–178, 1967

Kinomura S, Larsson J, Gulyas B, et al: Activation by attention of the human reticular formation and thalamic intralaminar nuclei. Science 271:512–515, 1996

Klove H: Clinical neuropsychology, in The Medical Clinics of North America. Edited by Forster FM. New York, WB Saunders, 1963

Kostrzewa RM, Brus R, Kalbfleisch JH, et al: Proposed animal model of attention deficit hyperactivity disorder. Brain Res Bull 34:161–167, 1994

Kraepelin E: Dementia Praecox and Paraphrenia. Edinburgh, UK, Livingstone, 1931

Lange KW, Robbins TW, Marsden CD, et al: L-Dopa withdrawal selectively impairs performance in tests of frontal lobe function in Parkinson's disease. Psychopharmacology 107:394–404, 1992

Lawrence JD, Lawrence DB, Carson DS: Optimizing ADHD therapy with sustained-release methylphenidate. Am Fam Physician 55:1705–1709, 1997

Levin H, Kraus M: The frontal lobes and traumatic brain injury. J Neuropsychiatry Clin Neurosci 6:443–454, 1994

Levin HS, Mattis S, Ruff RM, et al: Neurobehavioral outcome of minor closed head injury: a three center study. J Neurosurgery 66:234–243, 1987

Lezak MD: Neuropsychological Assessment, 3rd Edition. New York, Oxford University Press, 1995

Loiseau P, Stube E, Broustet D, et al: Evaluation of memory function in a population of epileptic patients and matched controls. Acta Neurol Scand 62:58–61, 1980

Lou HC, Henriksen L, Bruhn P: Focal cerebral hypoperfusion in children with dysphasia and/or attention deficit disorder. Arch Neurol 41:825–829, 1984

Luria AR: Higher Cortical Functions in Man. New York, Basic Books, 1966

Malone JRL, Hemsley DR: Lowered responsiveness and auditory signal detectability during depression. Psychol Med 7:717–722, 1977

Mannuzza S, Klein RG, Bessler A, et al: Adult outcome of hyperactive boys: educational achievement, occupational rank, and psychiatric status. Arch Gen Psychiatry 50:565–576, 1993

Marotta PJ, Roberts EA: Pemoline hepatotoxicity in children. J Pediatr 132:894–897, 1998

Matochik JA, Liebenauer II, King AC, et al: Cerebral glucose metabolism in adults with attention deficit hyperactivity disorder after chronic stimulant treatment. Am J Psychiatry 151:658–664, 1994

Mattes JA, Boswell L, Oliver H: Methylphenidate effects on symptoms of attention deficit disorder in adults. Arch Gen Psychiatry 41:1059–1063, 1984

Mayberg HS: Frontal lobe dysfunction in secondary depression. J Neuropsychiatry Clin Neurosci 6:428–442, 1994

McCormick DA: Cholinergic and noradrenergic modulation of thalamocortical processing. Trends in Neurology 12:215–221, 1989

Meck WH: Attentional bias between modalities: effect on the internal clock, memory, and decision stages used in animal time discrimination, in Timing and Time Perception. Edited by Gibbon J, Allan L. New York, Annals of the New York Academy of Sciences, New York Academy of Sciences, 1984, pp 528–541

Mega MS, Cummings JL: Frontal-subcortical circuits and neuropsychiatric disorders. J Neuropsychiatry Clin Neurosci 6:358–370, 1994

Mesulam M-M: A cortical network for directed attention and unilateral neglect. Ann Neurol 10:309–325, 1981

Mesulam M-M: Principles of Behavioral Neurology. Philadelphia, PA, FA Davis, 1985

Milner B: Interhemispheric differences in the localization of psychological processes in man. Br Med Bull 27:272–277, 1971

Mindus P, Rasmussen S, Lindquist C: Neurosurgical treatment for refractory obsessive compulsive disorder: implications for understanding frontal lobe function. J Neuropsychiatry Clin Neurosci 6:467–477, 1994

Mirsky AF: The neuropsychology of attention: elements of a complex behavior, in Integrating Theory and Practice in Clinical Neuropsychology. Edited by Perelman E. Hillsdale, NJ, Erlbaum, 1989

Mirsky AF, Primac DW, Marsan CA, et al: A comparison of the psychological test performance of patients with focal and nonfocal epilepsy. Exp Neurol 2:75–89, 1960

Modell JG, Mountz JM, Curtis GC, et al: Neurophysiological dysfunction in basal ganglia/limbic striatal and thalamocortical circuits as a pathogenetic mechanism of obsessive-compulsive disorder. J Neuropsychiatry Clin Neurosci 1:27–36, 1989

Modi NB, Lindemulder B, Gupta SK: Single- and multiple-dose pharmacokinetics of an oral once-a-day osmotic controlled release OROS (methylphenidate HCI) formulation. J Clin Pharmacol 40:379–388, 2000a

Modi NB, Wang B, Noveck RJ, et al: Dose-proportional and stereospecific pharmacokinetics of methylphenidate delivered using an osmotic, controlled-release oral delivery system. J Clin Pharmacol 40:1141–1149, 2000b

Moruzzi G, Magoun HW: Brainstem reticular formation and activation of the EEG. Electroencephalogr Clin Neurophysiol 1:455–473, 1949

Mountcastle VB, Lynch JC, Georgopoulos A, et al: Posterior parietal association cortex of the monkey: command function from operations within extrapersonal space. J Neurophysiol 38:871–908, 1975

Nauta HJ: The relationship of the basal ganglia to the limbic system, in Handbook of Clinical Neurology, Vol 5: Extrapyramidal Disorders. Edited by Vinken PJ, Bruyn GW, Klawans HL. New York, Elsevier, 1986, pp 19–29

Navon D: Attention division or attention sharing?, in Attention and Performance XI. Edited by Posner MI, Marin OSM. Hillsdale, NJ, Erlbaum, 1985, pp 133–146

Neale JM, Oltmanns TF: Schizophrenia. New York, Wiley, 1980

Nehemkis AM, Lewinsohn PM: Effects of left and right cerebral lesions in the naming process. Percept Mot Skills 35:787–798, 1972

Neisser U, Becklen R: Selective looking: attending to visually specified events. Cognitive Psychology 7:480–494, 1975

Nuechterlein KH: Reaction time and attention in schizophrenia: a critical evaluation of the data and theories. Schizophr Bull 3:373–428, 1977

Nuechterlein KH, Dawson ME: Information processing and attentional functioning in the developmental course of schizophrenic disorders. Schizophr Bull 10:160–203, 1984

O'Craven KM, Downing PE, Kanwisher N: fMRI evidence for objects as the units of attentional selection. Nature 401:584–587, 1999

O'Donnell BF, Friedman S, Squires NK, et al: Active and passive P3 latency in dementia: relationship to psychometric, EEG, and CT measures. Neuropsychiatry, Neuropsychology and Behavioral Neurology 3:164–179, 1990

Oltmanns TF, Ohayon J, Neale JM: The effect of anti-psychotic medication and diagnostic criteria on distractibility in schizophrenia. J Psychiatr Res 14:81–91, 1978

Oscar-Berman M, Gade A: Electrodermal measures of arousal in humans with cortical or subcortical brain damage, in The Orienting Reflex in Humans. Edited by Kimmel H, Van Olst E, Orlebeke J. Hillsdale, NJ, Erlbaum, 1979, pp 665–676

Owens A, James M, Leigh PN, et al: Fronto-striatal cognitive deficits at different stages of Parkinson's disease. Brain 115:1727–1751, 1992

Parasuraman R: Response bias and physiological reactivity. J Psychol 91:309–313, 1975

Parasuraman R: Sustained attention in detection and discrimination, in Varieties of Attention. Edited by Parasuraman R, Davies DR. New York, Academic Press, 1984, pp 243–289

Pardo JV, Fox PT, Raichle ME: Localization of a human system for sustained attention by positron emission topography. Nature 349:61–64, 1991

Pataki CS, Carlson GA, Kelly KL, et al: Side effects of methylphenidate and desipramine alone and in combination in children. J Am Acad Child Adolesc Psychiatry 32:1065–1072, 1993

Pavlov IP: Conditioned Reflexes. London, Oxford University Press, 1927

Pelham WE, Greenslade KE, Vodde-Hamilton M, et al: Relative efficacy of long-acting stimulants on children with attention deficit–hyperactivity disorder: a comparison of standard methylphenidate, sustained-release methylphenidate, sustained-release dextroamphetamine, and pemoline. Pediatrics 86:226–237, 1990

Petersen SE, Fox PT, Posner MI, et al: Positron emission tomographic studies of the processing of single words. Journal of Cognitive Neuroscience 1:153–170, 1989

Peterson BS, Skudlarski P, Gatneby JC, et al: An fMRI study of Stroop word-color interference: evidence for cingulate subregions subserving multiple distributed attentional systems. Biol Psychiatry 15:1237–1258, 1999

Peterson LR, Peterson MJ: Short-term retention of individual verbal items. Journal of Experimental Psychology 58:193–198, 1959

Piccirilli M, Alessandro P, Sciarma T, et al: Attention problems in epilepsy: possible significance of the epileptogenic focus. Epilepsia 35:1091–1096, 1994

Picton T, Stuss D: Neurobiology of conscious experience. Curr Opin Neurobiol 4:256–265, 1994

Pliszka SR, Greenhill LL, Crismon ML, et al and the Texas Consensus Conference Panel on Medication Treatment of Childhood Attention-Deficit/Hyperactivity Disorder: The Texas Children's Medication Algorithm Project: Report of the Texas Consensus Conference Panel on Medication Treatment of Childhood Attention Deficit/Hyperactivity Disorder, Part 1. J Am Acad Child Adolesc Psychiatry 39:908–919, 2000

Portas CM, Rees G, Howseman AM, et al: A specific role for the thalamus in mediating the interaction of attention and arousal in humans. J Neurosci 18:8979–8989, 1998

Porteus SD: Fifty Years' Application. New York, Psychological Corporation, 1965

Posner MI: Chronometric explorations of the mind. New York, Oxford University Press, 1986

Posner MI, Boies SJ: Components of attention. Psychol Rev 78:391–408, 1971

Posner MI, Cohen Y: Facilitation and inhibition in shifts of visual attention, in Attention and Performance X. Edited by Bouma H, Bowhuis D. Hillsdale, NJ, Erlbaum, 1984

Posner MI, Walker JA, Friedrich FA, et al: How do the parietal lobes direct covert attention? Neuropsychologia 25:135–145, 1987

Pribram KH: The neurobehavioral analysis of limbic forebrain mechanisms: revision and progress report, in Advances in the Study of Behavior, Vol 2. New York, Academic Press, 1969

Rao SM: Neuropsychology of multiple sclerosis: a critical review. J Clin Exp Neuropsychol 8:503–542, 1986

Rao SM, Binder JR, Bandettini PA, et al: Functional magnetic resonance imaging of complex human movements. Neurology 43:2311–2318, 1994

Rapczak S, Verfaellie M, Fleet WS, et al: Selective attention in hemispatial neglect. Arch Neurol 46:178–182, 1989

Rapoport JL: Basal ganglia dysfunction as a proposed cause of obsessive compulsive disorder, in Psychopathology and the Brain. Edited by Carroll BJ, Barrett JE. New York, Raven, 1991, pp 77–95

Rapoport JL, Buchsbaum MS, Zahn TP, et al: Dextroamphetamine: cognitive and behavioral effects in normal prepubertal boys. Science 199:560–563, 1978

Rapport MD, Denney C, DuPaul GJ, et al: Attention deficit disorder and methylphenidate: normalization rates, clinical effectiveness and response prediction in 76 children. J Am Acad Child Adolesc Psychiatry 33:882–893, 1994

Raskin DC, Kotses H, Bever J: Autonomic indicators of orienting and defensive reflexes. Journal of Experimental Psychology 80:423–433, 1969

Rausch R, Lieb JP, Crandall PH: Neuropsychologic correlates of depth spike activity in epileptic patients. Arch Neurol 35:699–705, 1978

Risser MG, Bowers TG: Cognitive and neuropsychological characteristics of attention deficit hyperactivity disorder in children receiving stimulant medications. Percept Mot Skills 77:1023–1031, 1993

Roland P: Brain Activation. New York, Wiley, 1993

Rosvold HE, Mirsky AF, Sarandon I, et al: A continuous performance test of brain damage. J Consult Clin Psychol 20:343–350, 1956

Rutter M: Issues and prospects in developmental neuropsychiatry, in Developmental Neuropsychiatry. Edited by Rutter M. New York, Guilford, 1983, pp 577–598

Sallee FR, Stiller KL, Perel IM: Pharmaco-dynamics of pemoline in attention deficit disorder with hyperactivity. J Am Acad Child Adolesc Psychiatry 31:244–251, 1992

Salloway S: Diagnosis and treatment of patients with frontal lobe syndromes. J Neuropsychiatry Clin Neurosci 6:388–398, 1994

Salloway S, Cummings J: Subcortical disease and neuropsychiatric illness. J Neuropsychiatry Clin Neurosci 6:93–99, 1994

Salloway S, Rasmussen S, Malloy P: Resolution of long-standing obsessive compulsive disorder following left anteromedial thalamic infarction. Neurology 45 (suppl 14):A167, 1995

Sato H, Hata Y, Hagihara K, et al: Effects of cholinergic depletion on neuron activities in the cat visual cortex. J Neurophysiol 58:781–794, 1987

Satterfield JH, Schell AM, Nicholas T: Preferential neural processing of attended stimuli in attention-deficit hyperactivity disorder and normal boys. Psychophysiology 31:1–10, 1994

Scheibel AB: The problem of selective attention: a possible structural substrate, in Brain Mechanisms and Perceptual Awareness. Edited by Pompeiano O, Marsan CA. New York, Raven, 1981

Schneider JS, Sun ZQ, Roeltgen DP: Effects of dopamine agonists on delayed response performance in chronic low-dose MPTP-treated monkeys. Pharmacol Biochem Behav 48:235–240, 1994

Schneider W, Shiffrin RM: Controlled and automatic human information processing, I: detection, search, and attention. Psychol Rev 84:1–66, 1977

Schwartz F, Carr AC, Munich RL, et al: Reaction time impairment in schizophrenia and affective illness: the role of attention. Biol Psychiatry 25:540–548, 1989

Shaffer D: Attention deficit hyperactivity disorder in adults. Am J Psychiatry 151:633–637, 1994

Shannon CE, Weaver W: The Mathematical Theory of Communication. Urbana, IL, University of Illinois Press, 1949

Shaywitz SE, Shaywitz BA: Attention deficit disorder: current perspectives. Pediatr Neurol 3:129–135, 1987

Shekim WO, Bylund DB, Hodges K, et al: Platelet alpha 2–adrenergic receptor binding and the effects of d-amphetamine in boys with attention deficit hyperactivity disorder. Neuropsychobiology 29:120–124, 1994

Shenker A: The mechanism of action of drugs used to treat attention-deficit hyperactivity disorder: focus on catecholamine receptor pharmacology. Advances in Psychiatry 30:337–381, 1992

Shute CC, Lewis PR: The ascending cholinergic reticular system, neocortical, olfactory and subcortical projections. Brain 90:497–520, 1967

Siddle D, Stephenson D, Spinks JA: Elicitation and habituation of the orienting response, in Orienting and Habituation: Perspectives in Human Research. Edited by Siddle D. New York, Wiley, 1983, pp 109–182

Simeon JG, Ferguson HB, Van Wyck Fleet J: Bupropion effects in attention deficit and conduct disorders. Can J Psychiatry 31:581–585, 1986

Smith A: Symbol Digit Modalities Test Manual. Los Angeles, CA, Western Psychological Service, 1973

Spencer T, Biederman J, Kerman K, et al: Desipramine treatment of children with attention-deficit hyperactivity disorder and tic disorder or Tourette's syndrome. J Am Acad Child Adolesc Psychiatry 32:354–360, 1993a

Spencer T, Biederman J, Steingard R, et al: Bupropion exacerbates tics in children with attention-deficit hyperactivity disorder and Tourette's syndrome. J Am Acad Child Adolesc Psychiatry 32:205–210, 1993b

Spreen O, Strauss E: A Compendium of Neuropsychological Tests. New York, Oxford University Press, 1991

Springer SP: Dichotic listening, in Experimental Techniques in Human Neuropsychology. Edited by Hannay J. New York, Oxford University Press, 1986, pp 138–166

Squires KC, Chippendale TJ, Wrege KS, et al: Electrophysiological assessment of mental function in aging and dementia, in Aging in the 1980s. Edited by Poon LW. Washington, DC, American Psychological Association, 1980, pp 82–94

Steriade M, Glenn M: The neocortical and caudate projections of intralaminal thalamic neurons and their synaptic excitation from the thalamic reticular core. J Neurophysiol 48:352–371, 1982

Storandt M, Botwinick J, Danzinger WL, et al: Psychometric differentiation of mild senile dementia of the Alzheimer type. Arch Neurol 41:497–499, 1984

Stromgren LS: The influence of depression on memory. Acta Psychiatr Scand 109–128, 1977

Stroop JR: Studies of interference in serial verbal reactions. Journal of Experimental Psychology 18:643–662, 1935

Stuss DT: Contribution of frontal lobe injury to cognitive impairment after closed head injury: methods of assessment and recent findings, in Neurobehavioral Recovery From Head Injury. Edited by Levin HS, Grafman J, Eisenberg HM. New York, Oxford University Press, 1987, pp 166–177

Stuss DT, Benson DF: The Frontal Lobes. New York, Raven, 1986

Stuss DT, Stethem LL, Hugenholtz H, et al: Reaction time after head injury: fatigue, divided and focused attention, and consistency of performance. J Neurol Neurosurg Psychiatry 52: 742–748, 1989

Swedo SE, Pietrini P, Leonard HL, et al: Cerebral glucose metabolism in childhood-onset obsessive compulsive disorder: revisualization during pharmacotherapy. Arch Gen Psychiatry 49:690–694, 1992

Sykes DH, Douglas VI, Morgenstern G: Sustained attention in hyperactive children. J Child Psychol Psychiatry 14:213–220, 1973

Treisman AM: Strategies and models of selective attention. Psychol Rev 76:282–299, 1969

Treisman AM, Davies A: Divided attention to ear and eye, in Attention and Performance IV. Edited by Kornblum S. New York, Academic Press, 1986

Treisman AM, Geffen G: Selective attention: perception or response? Q J Exp Psychol 19:1–18, 1967

Trommer BL, Hoeppner JB, Lorber R, et al: The go–no-go paradigm in attention deficit disorder. Ann Neurol 24:610–614, 1988

Underwood G: Attention and Memory. New York, Pergamon, 1976

Van Zomeren AH, Van Den Burg W: Residual complaints of patients 2 years after severe head injury. J Neurol Neurosurg Psychiatry 48:21–28, 1985

Van Zomeren AH, Brouwer WH, Deelman BG: Attentional deficits: the riddles of selectivity, speed and alertness, in Closed Head Injury: Psychological, Social and Family Con-

sequences. Edited by Brooks N. New York, Oxford University Press, 1984, pp 74–107

Verfaellie M, Bowers D, Heilman KM: Attentional factors in the occurrence of stimulus-response compatibility effects. Neuropsychologia 26:435–444, 1988

Vernon PA: Speed of Information Processing and Intelligence. Norwood, NJ, Ablex, 1987

Ward MF, Wender PH, Reimherr FW: The Wender Utah Rating Scale: an aid in the retrospective diagnosis of childhood attention deficit hyperactivity disorder. Am J Psychiatry 150:885–890, 1993

Wechsler D: A standardized memory scale for clinical use. J Psychol 19:87–95, 1945

Wechsler D: Wechsler Adult Intelligence Scale—Revised. San Antonio, TX, Psychological Corporation, 1981

Wender PH, Reimher FW: Bupropion treatment of ADHD in adults. Am J Psychiatry 147:1018–1020, 1990

Wender PH, Reimherr FW, Wood D, et al: A controlled study of methylphenidate in the treatment of attention deficit disorder, residual type, in adults. Am J Psychiatry 142: 547–552, 1985

Wielgus MS, Harvey PD: Dichotic listening and recall in schizophrenia and mania. Schizophr Bull 14:689–700, 1988

Wilens TE, Biederman J: The stimulants. Psychiatr Clin North Am 15:191–222, 1992

Wilens TE, Biederman J, Geist DE, et al: Nortriptyline in the treatment of ADHD: a chart review of 58 cases. J Am Acad Child Adolesc Psychiatry 32:343–349, 1993

Wing AN, Kristofferson AB: Response delays and the timing of discrete motor responses. Perception and Psychophymology 14:5–12, 1973

Zametkin AJ, Liebenauer M, Fitzgerald GA, et al: Brain metabolism in teenagers with attention deficit hyperactivity disorder. Arch Gen Psychiatry 50:333–340, 1993

# CHAPTER 14

# Neuropsychiatric Aspects of Delirium

Paula T. Trzepacz, M.D.

David J. Meagher, M.D.,
M.R.C.Psych., M.Sc. (Neuroscience)

Michael G. Wise, M.D.

Delirium is a commonly occurring neuropsychiatric syndrome primarily, but not exclusively, characterized by impairment in cognition, which causes a "confusional state." Delirium is a state of consciousness between normal alertness and awakeness and stupor or coma (Figure 14–1). Delirium may have a rapid, robust onset replete with many symptoms or it may be preceded by subclinical delirium with more insidious changes such as alterations in sleep or aspects of cognition. Precise clinical delineation between severe delirium and stupor is difficult when the delirium presents hypomotorically. It is generally believed that coming out of coma involves a period of delirium before normalcy is achieved.

Because there is a wide variety of underlying etiologies for delirium—identification of which is part of clinical management—it is considered a syndrome and not a unitary disorder. It may, however, represent dysfunction of a final common neural pathway that leads to its characteristic symptoms (see below). Its broad constellation of symptoms includes not only the diffuse cognitive deficits implicit for its diagnosis but also delusions, perceptual disturbances, affective lability, language abnormalities, disordered thought processes, sleep-wake cycle disturbance, and psychomotor changes.

Unlike most other psychiatric disorders, delirium symptoms typically fluctuate in intensity over a 24-hour period. During this characteristic waxing and waning of symptoms, relative lucid or quiescent periods often occur. In milder cases, such periods involve a significant diminution of delirium symptoms or even a seeming res-

olution of symptoms, although the latter has not been carefully studied. In addition, fluctuation in the level of symptom severity may relate to shifts between hypoactive and hyperactive periods or disruption of the sleep-wake cycle. Table 14–1 presents details of symptoms of delirium and highlights characteristic features that help differentiate delirium from other psychiatric disorders.

Although delirium in children has not been as well studied as delirium in adults, the symptoms appear to be the same (Platt et al. 1994b; Prugh et al. 1980). Documentation of delirium symptoms in preverbal children or noncommunicative adults is difficult. In these patients, there is a need for more reliance on inference and observation of changed or unusual behaviors, for example, inferring hallucinations or recording changes in the sleep-wake cycle.

*Delirium* is the accepted term to denote acute disturbances of global cognitive function as defined in both DSM-IV and ICD-10 research classification systems (American Psychiatric Association 1994; World Health Organization 1992). Nevertheless, myriad synonyms exist in clinical practice, reflecting the diversity of potential etiologies and settings in which delirium is encountered (Table 14–2). Unfortunately, different terms are used by physicians from different disciplines, who associate its occurrence with specific clinical settings. Examples of these terms are *intensive care unit (ICU) psychosis*, *hepatic encephalopathy*, *toxic psychosis*, and *posttraumatic amnesia*. These terms inappropriately suggest the existence of independent psychiatric disorders

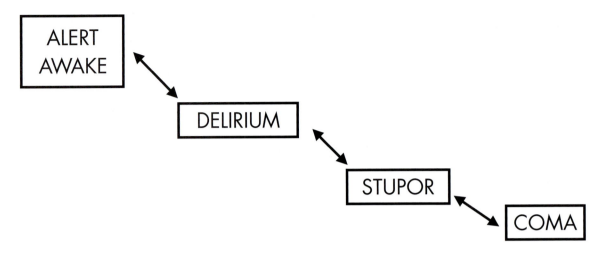

**FIGURE 14–1.** Continuum of level of consciousness.

for each etiology rather than acknowledging delirium as a unitary syndrome. Terms such as *acute brain failure* and *acute organic brain syndrome* more accurately highlight the global nature and acute onset of cerebral cortical deficits in patients with delirium, although they lack specificity from other cognitive mental disorders. The term *delirium* subsumes these many other terms, and its use will enhance medical communication and diagnosis as well as research.

## Differential Diagnosis

The presence of delirium is frequently not detected in clinical practice. Between one-third and two-thirds of cases are missed across a range of therapeutic settings and by a variety of specialists, including psychiatrists and neurologists (Johnson et al. 1992). Nonrecognition is not merely the result of labeling delirium using one of its synonyms (e.g., "acute confusion") but represents an actual failure to recognize both the symptoms and diagnosis of delirium and is reflected in poorer outcomes (Rockwood et al. 1994). Poor detection rates in part reflect that delirium is an inherently fluctuating neuropsychiatric disorder involving multiple cognitive and noncognitive disturbances that confer great clinical variability.

The stereotyped image of delirium in an agitated psychotic patient does not represent the majority of patients with delirium, who have either mixed or hypoactive symptom profiles (Meagher and Trzepacz 2000). The hypoactive presentation is less appreciated because the quiet, untroublesome patient is often presumed to have intact cognition and is more easily overlooked in the time-pressurized technological environment of modern medicine. It is not surprising that nursing staff, who have

the greatest amount of contact with patients and relatives, can have better detection rates than physicians (Gustafson et al. 1991a). Detection can be improved by routinely assessing cognitive function, improving awareness of the varied presentations of delirium, and using one of the screening instruments for delirium currently available (Rockwood et al. 1994 ), such as the Confusion Assessment Method (CAM) (Inouye et al. 1990) (see below).

Delirium has a wide differential diagnosis. It can be mistaken for dementia, depression, primary or secondary psychosis, anxiety and somatoform disorders, and, particularly in children, behavioral disturbance (Table 14–3). Accurate diagnosis requires close attention to symptom profile, temporal onset, and results of tests (e.g., cognitive, laboratory, electroencephalographic). Given that delirium can be the presenting feature of serious medical illness, any patient experiencing a sudden deterioration in cognitive function should be investigated for possible delirium. Urinary tract infections in nursing home patients commonly present as delirium.

The most difficult differential diagnosis for delirium is dementia, the other cause of generalized cognitive impairment. Indeed, end-stage dementia has been described as a chronic delirious state. The distinction is clouded by the increasing recognition of a form of dementia that bears close resemblance to delirium: Lewy body dementia, which fluctuates in severity and involves prominent psychotic symptoms (e.g., visual hallucinations). The overlap between delirium and dementia extends beyond symptom profile; any cognitive impairment, including dementia, is a potent predisposing factor for the development of delirium. Consequently, delirium and dementia have high comorbidity rates, especially in the elderly, and up to two-thirds of cases of delirium

**TABLE 14–1.** Signs and symptoms of delirium

**Diffuse cognitive deficits**
Attention
Orientation (time, place, person)
Memory (short- and long-term; verbal and visual)
Visuoconstructional ability
Executive functions

**Temporal course**
Acute/abrupt onset
Fluctuating severity of symptoms over 24-hour period
Usually reversible
Subclinical syndrome may precede and/or follow the episode

**Psychosis**
Perceptual disturbances (especially visual), including illusions, hallucinations, metamorphosias
Delusions (usually paranoid and poorly formed)
Thought disorder (tangentiality, circumstantiality, loose associations)

**Sleep-wake disturbance**
Fragmented throughout 24-hour period
Reversal of normal cycle
Sleeplessness

**Psychomotor behavior**
Hyperactive
Hypoactive
Mixed

**Language impairment**
Word-finding difficulty/dysnomia/paraphasia
Dysgraphia
Altered semantic content
Severe forms can mimic expressive or receptive aphasia

**Altered or labile affect**
Any mood can occur, usually incongruent to context
Anger or increased irritability common
Hypoactive delirium often mislabeled as depression
Lability (rapid shifts) common
Unrelated to mood preceding delirium

**TABLE 14–2.** Terms used to denote delirium

Acute brain failure
Acute brain syndrome
Acute brain syndrome with psychosis
Acute dementia
Acute organic psychosis
Acute organic reaction
Acute organic syndrome
Acute reversible psychosis
Acute secondary psychosis
Cerebral insufficiency
Confusional state
Dysergastic reaction
Encephalopathy
Exogenous psychosis
Infective-exhaustive psychosis
Intensive care unit (ICU) psychosis
Metabolic encephalopathy
Oneiric state
Organic brain syndrome
Posttraumatic amnesia
Reversible cerebral dysfunction
Reversible cognitive dysfunction
Reversible dementia
Reversible toxic psychosis
Toxic confusion state
Toxic encephalopathy

occur superimposed on preexisting cognitive impairment (Wahlund and Bjorland 1999). Delirium is 2–3.5 times more common in patients with dementia than in nondemented control subjects (Erkinjuntti et al. 1986; Jitapunkul et al. 1992). The risk of delirium appears to be greater in Alzheimer's disease of late onset and in dementia of vascular origin compared with other dementias, perhaps reflecting the relatively widespread neuronal disturbance associated with these conditions (Robertsson et al. 1998).

Despite this substantial overlap, delirium and dementia can be reliably distinguished by a combination of careful history taking and interviewing for onset of the symptom profile and clinical investigation. The tendency for abrupt onset and fluctuating course are highly characteristic of delirium. In addition, level of consciousness and attention are markedly disturbed in delirium but remain relatively intact in uncomplicated dementia. Dementia patients often have nocturnal disturbances of sleep, whereas in delirium there are varying degrees of disruption of the sleep-wake cycle, including fragmentation and sleeplessness. Overall, the presentation of delirium does not seem to be greatly altered by the presence of dementia, and delirium symptoms dominate the clinical picture when they co-occur (Trzepacz et al. 1998a).

A range of investigative tools can facilitate the differentiation of delirium and dementia in clinical practice. Both the Delirium Rating Scale (DRS) (Trzepacz and Dew 1995), which allows assessment of delirium symptom severity, and the Cognitive Test for Delirium (CTD) (Hart et al. 1996), an instrument specifically designed to assess cognition in delirious ICU patients, can be used to help differentiate the conditions. Although abnormalities of the electroencephalogram (EEG) are common to both delirium and dementia, diffuse slowing occurs more frequently (81% vs. 33%) and favors a diagnosis of delirium. Electroencephalographic slowing occurs later in the

**TABLE 14–3.** Differential diagnosis of delirium

|  | **Delirium** | **Dementia** | **Depression** | **Schizophrenia** |
|---|---|---|---|---|
| Onset | Acute | Insidious[a] | Variable | Variable |
| Course | Fluctuating | Often progressive | Diurnal variation | Variable |
| Reversibility | Usually[b] | Not usually | Usually but can be recurrent | No but has exacerbations |
| Level of consciousness | Impaired | Clear until late stages | Generally unimpaired | Unimpaired (perplexity in acute stage) |
| Attention/memory | Inattention, poor memory | Poor memory without marked inattention | Poor attention, memory intact | Poor attention, memory intact |
| Hallucinations | Usually visual; can be auditory, tactile, gustatory, olfactory | Can be visual or auditory | Usually auditory | Usually auditory |
| Delusions | Fleeting, fragmented, and usually persecutory | Paranoid, often fixed | Complex and mood congruent | Frequent, complex, systematized, and often paranoid |

[a]Except for large strokes.

[b]Can be chronic (paraneoplastic syndrome, central nervous system adverse events of medications, severe brain damage).

course of most degenerative dementias, although slowing occurs sooner with viral and prion dementias. The percentage of theta activity on quantitative EEGs allows differentiation of delirium from dementia (Jacobson and Jerrier 2000).

Often the early behavioral changes of delirium are mistaken for adjustment reactions to adverse events, particularly in patients who have experienced major trauma or have cancer. Hypoactive delirium is frequently mistaken for depression (Nicholas and Lindsey 1995). Some symptoms of major depression occur in delirium (e.g., psychomotor slowing, sleep disturbances, irritability). It has been estimated that 7% of delirious patients attempt self harm during an episode. However, in major depression, symptom onset tends to be less acute and mood disturbances typically dominate the clinical picture, with any cognitive impairments of depression resembling a mild subcortical dementia: "depressive pseudodementia." Delirium can be precipitated by dehydration or malnutrition in severely depressed patients who are unable to maintain food or fluid intake. The distinction of delirium from depression is particularly important because, in addition to delayed treatment, some antidepressants have anticholinergic activity (paroxetine and tricyclics) that can aggravate delirium. Conversely, the overactive, disinhibited profile of some delirious patients can closely mimic similar disturbances encountered in patients with agitated depression or mania. The most severe mania ("Bell's mania") includes cognitive impairment and mimics delirium.

Abnormalities of thought and perception can occur in both delirium and schizophrenia, but they are more fluctuant and fragmentary in delirium. Delusions in delirium are rarely as fixed or complex as in schizophrenia, and first-rank symptoms are uncommon (Cutting 1987). Unlike in schizophrenia, hallucinations in delirium tend to be visual rather than auditory. Consciousness, attention, and memory are generally less impaired in schizophrenia, with the exception of the pseudodelirious picture that can occur due to marked perplexity in the acute stage of illness. Careful physical examination, coupled with EEG and/or an instrument such as the DRS, generally distinguishes delirium from these functional disorders.

# Epidemiology

Delirium can occur at any age, although it is unfortunately understudied in children and adolescents. In contrast, most epidemiologic studies focus on the elderly, who are at higher risk to develop delirium than younger adults. This is likely because of changes that occur in the brain with aging. These changes include decreased cholinergic activity, often referred to as "reduced brain reserve." The frequent occurrence of central nervous system (CNS) disorders (e.g., stroke, hypertensive and diabetic vessel changes, tumor, dementia) in the elderly further increases their vulnerability to delirium. These facts will also present a serious challenge for physicians and medical personnel in the future because the world's population is aging at a dramatic rate.

During the next three decades, the population who are 60 and older will increase by 159% in less developed countries and by 59% in more developed countries (Jackson 1999). In the United States, in 1994 only 10% of the elderly were older than 85 years. By 2050, almost 25% of elderly persons will be over 85 (Jackson 1999). This is particularly worrisome because dementia affects 5%–8% of those over age 65, 15%–20% of those over 75, and 25%–50% of those older than 85 (American Psychiatric Association 1997). Dementia increases the risk for delirium.

Most studies of the incidence and prevalence of delirium report general hospital populations consisting of either referral samples or consecutive admissions to a given service. A wide range of percentages has been found in studies. Specific patient populations (e.g., elderly patients who have undergone hip surgery) may be responsible for disparate rates reported in studies. In addition, not all studies employ sensitive and specific diagnostic and measurement techniques, possibly resulting in overestimates or underestimates of the true occurrence of delirium. The review by Fann (2000) of (mostly) prospective studies found an incidence range from 3% to 42% and a prevalence range from 5% to 44% in hospitalized patients. Up to 60% of nursing home patients over 65 years old may be delirious when assessed cross-sectionally (Sandberg et al. 1998). In addition, 10%–15% of elderly persons are delirious when admitted to a hospital and another 10%–40% are diagnosed with delirium during the hospitalization. Table 14–4 describes several studies of the incidence and prevalence of delirium in which DSM diagnostic criteria or rating scales were used. A clinical rule of thumb seems to be that, on average, approximately a fifth of general hospital patients have delirium sometime during hospitalization.

## Morbidity and Mortality

Delirium is associated with high rates of morbidity and mortality. Whether the mortality risk is increased during the index admission, at long-term follow-up, or both is not completely clear. It is not known whether the increased mortality rate is 1) solely attributable to the physiological perturbations due to the underlying causes of delirium, 2) attributable to indirect effects on the body related to perturbations of neuronal (or neuronal-endocrine-immunological) function during delirium, or 3) attributable to damaging effects on the brain from neurochemical abnormalities associated with delirium (e.g., similar to glutamate surges after stroke). Furthermore, delirious patients cannot fully cooperate with their medical care or participate in rehabilitative programs during hospitalization. Their behaviors can even directly reduce the effectiveness of procedures meant to treat

their medical problems (e.g., removing tubes and intravenous lines, climbing out of bed), which adds to morbidity and possibly to further physiological injury and mortality. Figure 14–2 summarizes outcomes and key factors for delirium.

Methodological inconsistencies and shortcomings affect the interpretation of studies of mortality risk associated with delirium. Some do not compare delirium to control groups, most do not address the effects of treatment, many include comorbid dementia, many do not control for severity differences in medical comorbidity, most do not address effects of advanced age as a separate risk factor, and rarely are specific delirium rating instruments utilized. Prospective application of DSM criteria by qualified clinicians, attention to whether the sample is incident or prevalent, identification of biases related to referral samples, and whether or not follow-up mortality rates are cumulative to include the original sample size are also important issues that vary across study designs.

Mortality rates during index hospitalization for a delirium episode range from 4% to 65% (Cameron et al. 1987; Gustafson et al. 1988) depending on the study design and population. One study found significant differences in index mortality rate among motoric subtypes, with the lowest rate (10%) in hyperalert patients compared with hypoalert patients (38%) and mixed cases (30%) (Olofsson et al. 1996). When delirium present on admission was excluded, the index mortality rate for incident cases was as low as about 1.5% (Inouye et al. 1999). Index mortality rates for delirium did not differ significantly from those of nondelirious control subjects in some studies (Forman et al. 1995; George et al. 1997; Gustafson et al. 1988; Inouye et al. 1998, 1999; Kishi et al. 1995), whereas it did in others (Cameron et al. 1987; Jitapunkul et al. 1992; Pompeii et al. 1994; Rabins and Folstein 1982; van Hemert et al. 1994). Many studies of longer-term follow-up of delirium mortality rates (more than 3 months after discharge) do find worse mortality rates in delirium groups. Excessive mortality in some reports was attributed to greater age (Gustafson et al. 1988; Huang et al. 1998; Kishi et al. 1995; Trzepacz et al. 1985; Weddington 1982), more serious medical problems (Cole and Primeau 1993; Jitapunkul et al. 1992; Magaziner et al. 1989; Trzepacz et al. 1985), and dementia (Cole and Primeau 1993; Gustafson et al. 1988). Other researchers did not find cancer as an explanation for higher mortality rates (Rabins and Folstein 1982), whereas studies comparing only cancer inpatients did find significantly poorer survival in delirium patients compared with control subjects (Lawlor et al. 2000; Minagawa et al. 1996). Manos and Wu (1997) found no differences in delirium mortality rates between medical

**TABLE 14–4.** Epidemiology of delirium using established criteria[a]

| Reference | N | Type of patient | Frequency, % | Prevalence, % | Incidence, % |
|---|---|---|---|---|---|
| Erkinjuntti et al. 1986 | 2,000 | Medical, age 55 or older | | 15 | |
| Cameron et al. 1987 | 133 | Medical, age 32–97 | | 11.3 | 4.2 |
| Gustafson et al. 1988 | 111 | Femoral neck fracture, age 65 or older | | | |
| | | Before surgery | 33 | | |
| | | After surgery | 42 | | |
| Rockwood 1989 | 80 | Medical, age 65 or older | | 16 | 10.4 |
| Johnson et al. 1990 | 235 | Medical, age 70 or older | | 16 | 5 |
| Francis et al. 1990 | 229 | Medical, age 70 or older | | 15.7 | 7.3 |
| Schor et al. 1992 | 325 | Medical/surgical, age 65 or older | | 11 | 31 |
| Rockwood 1993 | 168 | Geriatric | | 18 | 7 |
| Marcantonio et al. 1994a | 134 | Postsurgical (elective noncardiac) | | | 9 |
| Pompeii et al. 1994[b] | 432 | Medical/surgical, age 65 or older | | 5 | 10 |
| | 323 | Medical/surgical, age 70 or older | | 15 | 12 |
| Inouye and Charpentier 1996 | 196 | Consecutive admissions, age 70 or older | | 5 | 18 |
| | 312 | Consecutive admissions, age 70 or older | | 2 | 15 |
| O'Keeffe and Lavan 1997 | 225 | Acute case geriatric | | 18 | 29 |
| Inouye et al. 1998 | 727 | Consecutive admissions, age 65 or older | | 12 | |
| Lawlor et al. 2000 | 104 | Consecutive admissions with advanced cancer, age 62 ± 11.9 years | | 42.3 | 45 |
| Brauer et al. 2000 | 571 | Admissions with hip fracture, age 69–101 | | | |
| | | Delirium at time of admission (4) | | 1 | |
| | | Developed delirium before surgery (16) | | | 4 |
| | | Delirium day of surgery (5) | | | 1 |
| | | Developed delirium after surgery (29) | | | 5 |

[a]DSM-III, DSM-III-R, DSM-IV criteria or delirium assessment instruments.

[b]Lower rates in this study may be explained by exclusion of patients with severe cognitive impairment.

*Source.* Reprinted from Wise MG, Gray KF, Seltzer B: "Delirium, Dementia, and Amnestic Disorders," in *American Psychiatric Press Textbook of Psychiatry*, 3rd Edition. Edited by Hales RE, Yudofsky SC, Talbott JA. Washington, DC, American Psychiatric Press, 1999, p. 31. Used with permission.

and postoperative groups after 3.5 years. Inouye et al. (1998) found that delirium significantly increased mortality risk even after controlling for age, sex, dementia, activities of daily living (ADL) level, and APACHE II (Knaus et al. 1985) scores in a prospective study of medically hospitalized elderly persons when using the CAM for delirium diagnosis.

Morbidity associated with delirium during an index episode is easily appreciated in terms of human suffering by patients and caregivers, although this is less easily measured. One study found more complications in the delirium group during index hospitalization, including decubitus ulcers, feeding problems, and urinary incontinence (Gustafson et al. 1988). Effects on hospital length of stay (LOS), "persistence" of cognitive impairment, increased rate of institutionalization, and reduced ambulation and/or ADL level have been reported.

Significantly increased LOS associated with delirium has been reported in many studies (Forman et al. 1995; Francis et al. 1990; Gustafson et al. 1988; Hales et al. 1988; Levkoff et al. 1992; Pompeii et al. 1994; R.I. Thomas et al. 1988) and as a trend toward significance in one (Inouye et al. 1998). In contrast, others have not found an increased LOS (Cole et al. 1994; George et al. 1997; Jitapunkul et al. 1992; Rockwood 1989). However, a meta-analysis of eight studies (Cole and Primeau 1993) does support both numerical and statistical differences between delirium and control groups' LOS.

Decreased independent living status and increased rate of institutionalization during follow-up after a delirium episode were found in many studies (Cole and Primeau 1993; George et al. 1997; Inouye et al. 1998). Reduction in ambulation and/or ADL level at follow-up is also commonly reported (Francis and Kapoor 1992; Gustafson et al. 1988; Inouye et al. 1998; Minagawa et al. 1996; Murray et al. 1993). Delirium also has an impact in nursing home settings, where incident cases are associated with poor 6-month outcome including behavioral decline, initiation of physical restraints, greater risk of hospitalization, and increased mortality rate (Murphy 1999).

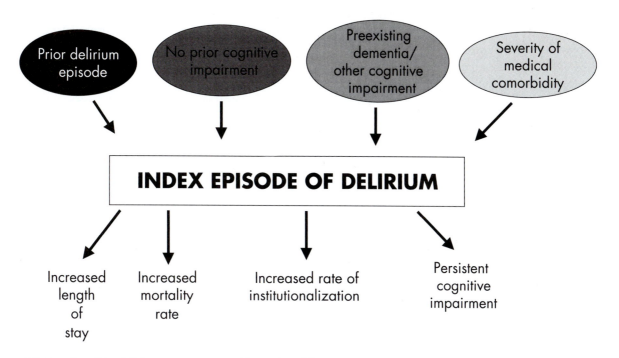

**FIGURE 14–2.** Possible delirium outcomes and key related factors.

One controversial matter is so-called persistent cognitive impairment at longer-term follow-up, which some (Levkoff et al. 1992) suggest represents damage from the delirium episode affecting future brain function. Many interpret persisting cognitive deficits as being more related to "diminished brain reserve" or preexisting dementia that has simply progressed over time (Frances and Kapoor 1992; Koponen et al. 1994). Dementia may go unrecognized at the time of the delirium index episode and is a key risk factor for the occurrence of delirium; often they are comorbid. In nursing home patients, better cognitive function at baseline was associated with better outcome from delirium (Murphy 1999). This finding lends support to the notion that impaired brain reserve is an important predelirium factor that needs to be taken into account in any longitudinal outcome assessments. Therefore, carefully designed longitudinal research is needed to help clarify this issue. It is necessary to gather premorbid cognitive functioning data and to administer neuropsychological tests over time that are designed to detect and differentiate patterns of dementia that could have existed before the delirium and may be progressive. Detection of cognitive deficit patterns among elderly persons that do not match those associated with either Alzheimer's disease or vascular, frontal, or other dementing processes or the medical insults experienced could then suggest separate delirium-induced damage. Alternatively, longitudinal postdelirium cognitive assessments of younger adults who are not at risk for

dementia could help answer this question.

In summary, although the mechanism is not understood, the presence of delirium does indeed appear to be an adverse prognostic sign that is associated with substantial morbidity and an increased risk for mortality, extending well beyond the index hospitalization. To what extent aggressive treatment of both the delirium and its comorbid medical problems would reduce morbidity and mortality is not well studied, but such treatment makes good clinical sense.

## Reversibility of a Delirium Episode

Delirium has traditionally been distinguished from dementia by virtue of acute onset, fluctuating severity level, symptom profile, and reversibility. In most cases it is reversible, except in terminal illness or particular examples of severe brain injury. Whether delirium itself causes permanent damage is under debate.

Bedford's (1957) landmark study of delirium indicated that approximately 5% of patients were still "confused" at 6-month follow-up, but more recent studies suggest that persistent disturbances may be more frequent following an episode of delirium. Levkoff et al. (1994), in a 6-month longitudinal study of DSM-III-R diagnosed delirium in elderly patients, found that almost one-third of patients still had delirium, with a majority still having some of its features (orientation difficulties, emotional lability, and sleep disturbances). However, dementia patients had not been excluded from this study. Full resolution of delirium symptoms at hospital discharge of elderly patients may be the exception rather than the rule (Levkoff et al. 1992; Rockwood et al. 1993). However, these studies do not fully account for the role of underlying etiologies, treatment received, preexisting cognitive impairment, or even fiscal constraints promoting premature discharge. Kopnonen et al.'s (1994) 5-year longitudinal study of delirium in the elderly found persistence and progression of symptoms to be attributed more to the underlying dementia than to the previous delirium episode. Camus et al. (2000b) found that preexisting dementia was associated with partial or no recovery from delirium in hospitalized elderly persons at 3-week follow-up. Kolbeinsson and Jonsson (1993) found that delirium was complicated by dementia at follow-up in 70% of cases. Thus, "persistent" deficits may instead reflect an underlying disorder and not the delirium.

Individual delirium symptoms may predict the duration of an episode. Wada and Yamaguchi (1993), in a study of elderly neuropsychiatry consults, found that a longer duration of delirium (≥1 week) was predicted by the severity of cognitive disturbance, mood lability, and sleep-wake cycle disruption. Treloar and MacDonald (1997) found that the degree of "reversibility" of an index episode of delirium was predicted by motor activity, speech and thought disturbances, and a fluctuating course. However, their definition of reversibility was defined conservatively as a 5-point or 2% improvement on the Mini-Mental State Exam (MMSE) (Folstein et al. 1975), far less than what most clinicians would expect.

Biological measures may correlate with reversibility of delirium. Mach et al. (1995) found that higher levels of serum anticholinergic activity were associated with greater propensity for full resolution of delirium, perhaps reflecting an association between higher levels and more reversible causes of delirium such as anticholinergic toxicity, although this was not specifically addressed in this study.

The relationship between delirium and "persistent symptoms" at follow-up may be explained by an index episode of delirium being an actual risk factor, rather than a cause or marker, for other causes of cognitive impairment. Rockwood et al. (1999) reported an 18% annual incidence of dementia in patients with delirium—more than 3 times higher risk than incidence in nondelirious patients when the confounding effects of comorbid illness severity and age were adjusted for. Camus et al. (2000b), in a cross-sectional study of consecutive psychogeriatric admissions, found that the only factor significantly linked to incomplete symptom resolution in delirium was the presence of preexisting cognitive impairment.

To date, the roles of unrecognized prior cognitive impairment, delirium treatment exposure, and the possibility that certain etiologies may be associated with persistence of cognitive impairment have not been fully accounted for in studies. Nonetheless, the concept of delirium as an inherently reversible condition is being increasingly questioned. Given that many older patients experience "persistent symptoms," at the very least, these studies highlight the need for careful planning of postdischarge treatment plans for delirious patients irrespective of the cause of any symptoms detected at long-term follow-up. This is especially true for elderly patients. Terminology is also difficult regarding when chronic delirium becomes dementia and whether the experience of an index episode of delirium, perhaps by virtue of a neurotoxic or kindling effect, may alter the threshold for further episodes of delirium or contribute to the development of dementia.

## Risk Factors for Delirium

Delirium is particularly common during hospitalization when there is a confluence of both predisposing factors (vulnerabilities) and precipitating factors. A number of patient-related, illness, pharmacologic, and environmental factors have been identified as being relevant risk factors for delirium, as illustrated in Figure 14–3. Although certain factors are more relevant in certain settings, age, preexisting cognitive impairment, severe comorbid illness, and medication exposure are particularly robust predictors of delirium risk across a range of populations (Inouye et al. 1999).

Stress-vulnerability models for the occurrence of delirium have been long recognized. Henry and Mann (1965) described "delirium readiness." More recent models of causation involve cumulative interactions between predisposing (vulnerability) factors and precipitating insults (Inouye and Charpentier 1996; O'Keeffe and Lavan 1996). Baseline risk is a more potent predictor of the likelihood of delirium: If baseline vulnerability is low, patients are very resistant to the development of delirium despite exposure to significant precipitating factors, whereas if baseline vulnerability is high, delirium is likely even in response to minor precipitants (Figure 14–4). Tsutsui et al. (1996), for example, found that in patients over 80 years old, delirium occurred in 52% after emergency surgery and in 20% after elective procedures, whereas no case of delirium was noted in patients under

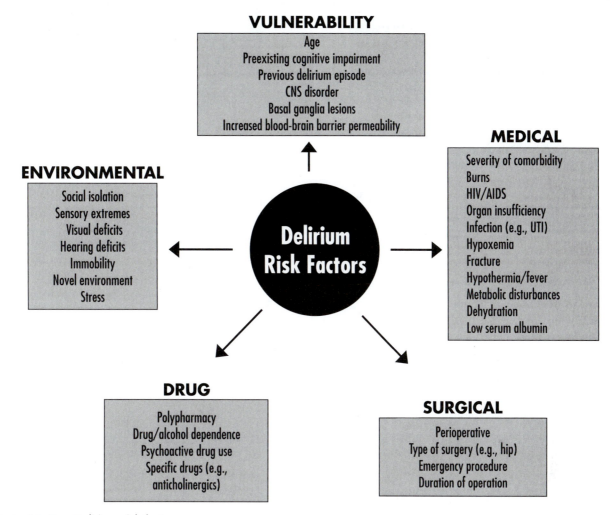

**FIGURE 14–3.** Delirium risk factors.

*Note.* AIDS = acquired immune deficiency syndrome; CNS = central nervous system; HIV = human immunodeficiency virus; UTI = urinary tract infection.

age 50 undergoing either elective or emergency procedures. It is generally believed that the aged brain is more vulnerable to delirium, in part related to structural/degenerative changes as well as altered neurochemical flexibility. Children are also considered to be at higher risk for delirium, possibly related to brain structural and chemical development.

O'Keeffe and Lavan (1996) stratified patients into four levels of delirium risk based on the presence of three factors (chronic cognitive impairment, severe illness, elevated serum urea level) and found that the risk of delirium increased as these factors accumulated. Similarly, Inouye and Charpentier (1996) developed a predictive model that included four predisposing factors (cognitive impairment, severe illness, visual impairment, and dehydration) and five precipitating factors (more than three medications added, catheterization, use of restraints, malnutrition, any iatrogenic event). These predicted a

17-fold variation in the relative risk of developing delirium. Although the value of reducing risk factors appears self-evident, many risk factors may simply be markers of general morbidity, and therefore studies demonstrating preventive impact are important.

Some risk factors are potentially modifiable and thus are targets for preventive interventions. Even just closer observation of patients at high risk for delirium could mean more prompt intervention in emergent delirium. Medication exposure is probably the most readily modifiable risk factor for delirium, being implicated as a cause in 20%–40% of cases of delirium. Inouye et al. (1999) studied the impact of preventive measures aimed at minimizing six of the risk factors identified in their previous work with hospitalized elderly persons (Inouye et al. 1993). Standardized protocols to address cognitive impairment, sleep deprivation, immobility, visual impairment, hearing impairment, and dehydration resulted in

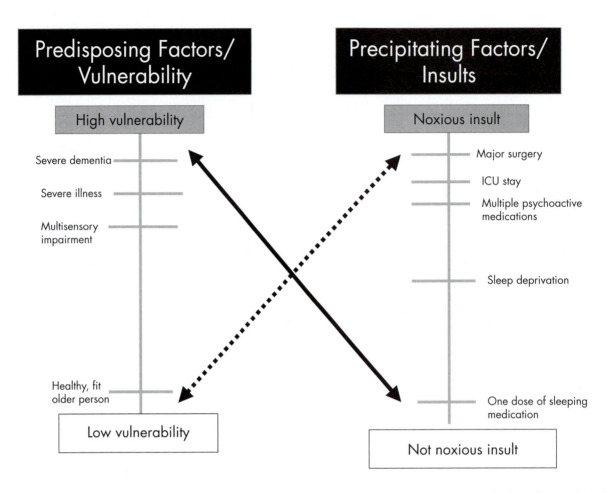

**FIGURE 14–4.** The relationship between an individual person's health status in combination with the effects of insults determines the threshhold for the occurrence of delirium.

*Note.* ICU = intensive care unit.

*Source.* Adapted from Inouye and Charpentier 1996.

significant reductions in the number and duration of delirium episodes. Others demonstrated the potential preventive impact of using preoperative psychological interventions to reduce anxiety and optimizing perioperative management with medical involvement (Owens et al. 1982; Schindler et al. 1989).

Polypharmacy and drug intoxication/withdrawal may be the most common causes of delirium, and drug use is also a risk factor (Hales et al. 1988; Trzepacz et al. 1985). Benzodiazepines, opiates, and drugs with anticholinergic activity have a particular association with delirium (T.M. Brown 2000; Marcantonio et al. 1994b). Many drugs (and their metabolites) can unexpectedly contribute to delirium due to unrecognized anticholinergic effects. Ten of the 25 most commonly prescribed drugs for the elderly had sufficient in vitro anticholinergic activity identified by radioreceptor assay to cause memory and attention impairment in normal elderly subjects (Tune et al. 1992) (Table 14–5). It is therefore important to minimize drug exposure, especially when

facing high-risk periods such as the perioperative phase.

There has been relatively little study of risk factors for delirium in children and adolescents despite a general belief that children are especially vulnerable to delirium. Thiamine deficiency is an underappreciated cause of and/or risk factor for delirium in pediatric intensive care and oncology patients (Seear et al. 1992) and nonalcoholic elderly patients (O'Keeffe et al. 1994).

The temporal relationship between exposure to risk factors and development of delirium requires further study. Postoperative delirium (excluding emergence from anesthesia) appears most frequently at day 3, suggesting that the intervening interval is high risk. Van der Mast (2000) proposed that surgery induces immune activation and a physical stress response. This is composed of increased limbic-hypothalamic-pituitary-adrenocortical axis activity, low T3 syndrome, and alterations of blood-brain barrier permeability. Increased blood-brain barrier permeability is a risk factor for delirium, as occurs in uremia. A large multicenter study found age, duration of

**TABLE 14–5.** Anticholinergic drug levels in 25 medications ranked by the frequency of their prescription for elderly patients

| Medication[a] | Anticholinergic drug level (ng/mL) of atropine equivalents |
|---|---|
| Furosemide | 0.22 |
| Digoxin | 0.25 |
| Dyazide (hydrochlorothiazide and triamterene) | 0.08 |
| Lanoxin[b] | 0.25 |
| Hydrochlorothiazide | 0.00 |
| Propranolol | 0.00 |
| Salicylic acid | 0.00 |
| Dipyridamole | 0.11 |
| Theophylline anhydrous | 0.44 |
| Nitroglycerin | 0.00 |
| Insulin | 0.00 |
| Warfarin | 0.12 |
| Prednisolone | 0.55 |
| Methyldopa | 0.00 |
| Nifedipine | 0.22 |
| Isosorbide dinitrate | 0.15 |
| Ibuprofen | 0.00 |
| Codeine | 0.11 |
| Cimetidine | 0.86 |
| Diltiazem hydrochloride | 0.00 |
| Captopril | 0.02 |
| Atenolol | 0.00 |
| Metoprolol | 0.00 |
| Timolol | 0.00 |
| Ranitidine | 0.22 |

[a]Drug concentration: $10^{-8}$ M.
[b]A digoxin compound.

*Source.* Reprinted from Tune L, Carr S, Hoag E, et al.: "Anticholinergic Effects of Drugs Commonly Prescribed for the Elderly: Potential Means for Assessing Risk of Delirium." *American Journal of Psychiatry* 149:1393–1394, 1992. Used with permission.

anesthesia, lower educational level, second operation, postoperative infection, and respiratory complications to be predictors of postoperative cognitive impairment. However, this study revealed little about possible pathophysiological mechanisms for impairment because delirium risk was not linked to hypoxemia, hypotension, or use of specific anesthetic agents or procedures (Moller et al. 1998).

Low serum albumin is an important risk factor at any age and may signify poor nutrition, chronic disease, or liver or renal insufficiency. Hypoalbuminemia results in a greater bioavailability of many drugs that are transported in the bloodstream by albumin, which in turn is associated with an increased risk of side effects including delir-

ium (Dickson 1991; Trzepacz and Francis 1990). This increased biological drug activity occurs within the therapeutic range and is not recognized because increased levels of free drug are not separately reported in assays. Serum albumin was identified by discriminant analysis, along with Trailmaking Test Part B and EEG dominant posterior rhythm, to sensitively distinguish delirious from nondelirious liver transplant candidates (Trzepacz et al. 1988b).

## Diagnosis and Assessment

### Diagnosis

Specific diagnostic criteria for delirium did not appear in the first two editions of the *Diagnostic and Statistical Manual of Mental Disorders* (DSM and DSM-II) (American Psychiatric Association 1952, 1968) or in Research Diagnostic Criteria (RDC). Diagnostic criteria for delirium first appeared in DSM-III (American Psychiatric Association 1980). Thus, early clinical reports and research were affected by this lack of diagnostic specificity. Symptom rating scales for delirium began to appear around the time of DSM-III.

DSM was first published in 1952 and described acute and chronic brain syndromes. Most forms of delirium were encompassed within the acute, reversible category and were characterized by impairments of orientation, memory, all intellectual functions, and judgment, as well as lability and shallowness of affect. Other disturbances, such as hallucinations and delusions, were considered secondary to the disturbance of the sensorium. Causes of delirium were specifically noted, for example, "acute brain syndrome associated with cerebrovascular accident" (this notation of medical etiology returned in DSM-IV).

DSM-II described two organic brain syndromes, psychotic and nonpsychotic types, each with an acute or chronic delineation. DSM-II maintained the same five symptoms as DSM. DSM-III first described symptoms and diagnostic criteria for the syndrome termed *delirium*. Delirium was distinguished from dementia and other organic mental disorders; each was identified by its own explicit criteria. Some revisions were made in DSM-III-R (American Psychiatric Association 1987), especially to the major criterion involving inattention and altered consciousness.

DSM-IV (American Psychiatric Association 1994) has five categories of delirium; the criteria are the same for each category except the one for etiology. The categories are delirium due to 1) a general medical condition

**TABLE 14–6.** DSM-IV-TR criteria for diagnosis of delirium due to a general medical condition

A. Disturbance of consciousness (i.e., reduced clarity of awareness of the environment) with reduced ability to focus, sustain, or shift attention.

B. A change in cognition (such as memory deficit, disorientation, language disturbance) or the development of a perceptual disturbance that is not better accounted for by a preexisting, established, or evolving dementia.

C. The disturbance develops over a short period of time (usually hours to days) and tends to fluctuate during the course of the day.

D. There is evidence from the history, physical examination, or laboratory findings that the disturbance is caused by the direct physiological consequences of a general medical condition.

(Table 14–6), 2) substance intoxication, 3) substance withdrawal, 4) multiple etiologies, and 5) not otherwise specified. This notation of etiology in DSM-IV is reminiscent of the first DSM.

DSM-III, DSM-III-R, and DSM-IV include efforts to further clarify the major criterion describing altered state of consciousness. This criterion has been considered as either inattention or "clouding of consciousness." The latter term is obfuscating because the elements of consciousness that are altered are not specified, nor is it clear how "clouding" differs from "level" of consciousness. Attentional disturbance distinguishes delirium from dementia where the first criterion is memory impairment. Attentional disturbances in delirium range from general, nonspecific reduction in alertness (may be nicotinic cholinergic, histaminergic, or adrenergic) to decreased selective focusing or sustaining of attention (may be muscarinic cholinergic). The contribution of attentional deficits to the altered awareness that occurs in delirium is insufficient by itself to account for other prominent symptoms—formal thought disorder, language and sleep-wake cycle disturbances, and other cognitive-perceptual deficits.

The characteristic features of the temporal course of delirium—acute onset and fluctuation of symptoms—have constituted a separate criterion in each of the last three editions of DSM. Temporal features assist in distinguishing delirium from dementia, and most clinicians consider them to be important in making a diagnosis.

Despite the breadth of the symptoms of delirium, not all have been emphasized in the various editions of DSM. Dysexecutive symptoms (impairment of prefrontal executive cognition) are not mentioned in any DSM edition, despite the importance of prefrontal involvement in delirium (Trzepacz 1994a). Psychosis has not received much attention except in DSM-II, despite the occurrence of delusions in about a fifth of patients (Ross et al. 1991; Sirois 1988; Webster and Holroyd 2000). Characteristic features of delusions (usually paranoid and poorly formed) and hallucinations (often visual) have not been specified in DSM criteria, despite their usefulness to the clinician.

The World Health Organization's (1992) ICD-10 research diagnostic criteria for delirium are similar to DSM-IV criteria A, C, and D (see Table 14–6). However, ICD-10 diverges from DSM-IV in that cognitive dysfunction is manifested by both "(1) impairment of immediate recall and recent memory, with intact remote memory; (2) disorientation in time, place or person." In addition, a disturbance in sleep is present and is manifested by insomnia, nocturnal worsening of symptoms, or disturbing dreams or nightmares that may continue as hallucinations or illusions when awake, which seems to indicate an etiologic link between perceptual disturbances and sleep mechanisms. Despite these differences, a study of 80 delirious patients showed 100% concordance for diagnosis between DSM-III-R and ICD-10 research criteria for delirium systems (Treloar and Mac-Donald 1997).

## Cognitive Assessment

Because delirium is primarily a cognitive disorder, bedside assessment of cognition is critical to proper diagnosis. All cognitive domains are affected—orientation, attention, short-term and long-term memory, visuoconstructional ability, and executive functions (the latter are poorly studied in delirium)—even though attentional deficits are most specifically emphasized in DSM. Pattern and timing of deficits assist in differential diagnosis from dementias and amnestic disorders. Use of bedside screening tests such as the MMSE is clinically important to document the presence of a cognitive disorder, although the MMSE alone is insufficient to distinguish delirium from dementia (Trzepacz et al. 1988a). The MMSE is easy for many people (ceiling effect) and has a limited breadth of items, particularly for prefrontal executive and right-hemisphere functions.

The CTD (Hart et al. 1996) is a more recent bedside test designed specifically for delirious patients, who are often unable to speak or write in a medical setting. The CTD correlates highly with the MMSE ($r=0.82$) in delirium patients and was performable in 42% of ICU patients in whom the MMSE was not. It has two equivalent forms that correlate highly ($r=0.90$) in dementia patients, which makes it better suited for repeated measurements. However, it correlates less well with symptom rating scales for delirium that also include noncognitive symptoms—for example, the Medical College of Virginia (MCV) Nurses Rating Scale for Delirium (Hart et al. 1996) ($r=-0.02$) or the Delirium Rating Scale–Revised-98 (DRS-R-98) (Trzepacz et al. 2001) ($r=-0.62$). The CTD has many nonverbal (nondominant hemisphere) items and includes abstraction questions.

It has been theorized that prefrontal and right hemisphere circuits are especially important in delirium neuropathophysiology (Trzepacz 1994a, 1999b, 2000). Two studies found that just a few cognitive tests (e.g., similarities and Digit Span Forward) were able to discriminate delirious from nondelirious medical patients. One assessed only right hemisphere functions—visual attention span forward and recognition memory for pictures (Hart et al. 1997)—and the other assessed prefrontal functions (Bettin et al. 1998).

Manos (1997) found that the clock drawing test is a useful screen for cognitive impairment in medically ill patients, but it does not discriminate between delirium and dementia. A global rating of attentiveness, Digit Span Backward and cancellation tests, differentiated delirium from dementia among elderly medical inpatients, whereas the vigilance test, MMSE, and Digit Span Forward did not (O'Keeffe and Gosney 1997). However, patients were excluded from the study if their MMSE score was 10 points or less, which effectively rules out applicability to many delirium patients.

## Delirium Assessment Instruments

Diagnostic criteria are important in diagnosing delirium, and cognitive tests are useful to document cognitive impairment. Rating a range of delirium symptoms, however, requires other methods. More than 10 instruments have been proposed to assess symptoms of delirium (Trzepacz 1994b) for screening, diagnosis, or symptom severity rating. However, only a few of these have been used broadly (see descriptions below). Three instruments operationalized DSM-III criteria: the Saskatoon Delirium Checklist (Miller et al. 1988), the Organic Brain Syndrome Scale (Berggren et al. 1987), and the Delirium Assessment Scale (O'Keeffe 1994). In these, DSM-III–derived items are rated along a continuum of mild, moderate, and severe. None has been well described or validated. The Delirium Assessment Scale could not distinguish delirium from dementia patients. A more recently developed severity scale, the Confusional State Evaluation (Robertsson 1999), assessed 22 items, but 12 were determined a priori to be "key symptoms." It was not validated against control groups, and dementia

patients were included in the delirium group.

The CAM is probably the most widely used delirium screening tool in general hospitals (Inouye et al. 1990). It is based on DSM-III-R criteria and requires the presence of three of four cardinal symptoms of delirium. It is intended for use by nonpsychiatric clinicians in hospital settings and is useful for case finding, although nurses' ratings were much less sensitive than those done by physicians (1.00 vs. 0.13) when compared with an independent physician's DSM-III-R diagnosis (Rolfson et al. 1999). One study (Rockwood 1993) suggested that lower specificity and sensitivity are a trade-off for its simplicity, although in other studies it performed well compared with physicians' diagnoses in short-term hospital settings. It has not been well studied for its ability to distinguish delirium from dementia, depression, or other psychiatric disorders. The CAM appears to be useful to screen elderly emergency room patients for delirium (Monette et al. 2001). Based on a geriatrician's interview, comparison between ratings from the geriatrician interviewer and an observing lay person revealed interrater reliability of 0.91, sensitivity of 0.86, and specificity of 1.00. A recent extension of the CAM is the CAM-ICU (Ely et al. 2001), aimed at use in severely medically ill patients. It uses specific adjunctive tests and standardized administration to enhance reliability and validity.

Fanjiang and Folstein (2001) recently piloted a simple screener scale, the Three Item Delirium Scale (TIDS), for bedside detection of delirium by medical students. It requires the presence of altered consciousness plus either cognitive impairment or hallucinations. An initial report suggests that it has high sensitivity (0.89) and specificity (1.00) compared with an attending psychiatrist diagnosis, although the medical students were not blind to patient history at the time of the ratings.

The DRS (Trzepacz et al. 1988a) is a 10-item scale assessing a breadth of delirium features and can function both to clarify diagnosis and to assess symptom severity, due to its hierarchical nature (Trzepacz 1999a; van der Mast 1994). It is probably the most widely used delirium rating scale and has been translated into Italian, French, Spanish, Korean, Japanese, Mandarin Chinese, Dutch, Swedish, German, Portuguese, and a language of India for international use. It is generally used by those who have some psychiatric training. The DRS has high interrater reliability and validity even compared with other psychiatric patient groups, and it distinguishes delirium from dementia. However, because of some of its items it does not function as well for frequent repeated measurements, and thus it has been modified by some researchers to a 7- or 8-item subscale. In one study (Treloar and Mac-

**TABLE 14–7.** Recommended delirium assessment instruments (see text for descriptions)

| Instrument | Type | Rater |
|---|---|---|
| Confusion Assessment Method (Inouye et al. 1990) | 4-item diagnostic screener | Nonpsychiatric clinician |
| Delirium Rating Scale (Trzepacz et al. 1998) | 10-item severity/diagnostic | Psychiatrically trained clinician |
| Memorial Delirium Assessment Scale (Smith et al. 1994) | 10-item severity scale | Clinician |
| Delirium Rating Scale–Revised-98 (Trzepacz et al. 2001) | 16-item scale (includes severity subscale) | Psychiatrically trained clinician |

Donald 1997), the DRS and CAM diagnosed delirium patients with a high level of agreement ($\kappa = 0.81$).

The Memorial Delirium Assessment Scale (MDAS) is a 10-item severity rating scale for use after a diagnosis of delirium has been made (Breitbart et al. 1997). It was intended for repeated ratings within a 24-hour period, as occurs in treatment studies. The MDAS does not include items for temporal onset and fluctuation of symptoms, which are characteristic symptoms that help to distinguish delirium from dementia. The MDAS correlated highly with the DRS ($r = 0.88$) and the MMSE ($r = -0.91$). The Japanese version of the MDAS was validated in 37 elderly patients with either delirium, dementia, mood disorder, or schizophrenia and was found to distinguish among them ($p < 0.0001$), with a mean score of 18 in the delirium group (Matsuoka et al. 2001). It correlated reasonably well with the DRS Japanese version ($r = -0.74$) and the Clinician's Global Rating of Delirium ($r = 0.67$), and less well with the MMSE ($r = 0.54$).

The Delirium Rating Scale–Revised-98 (DRS-R-98) is a substantially revised version of the DRS that addresses the shortcomings of the DRS (Trzepacz et al. 2001). It allows for repeated measurements and includes separate/new items for language, thought processes, motor agitation, motor retardation, and five cognitive domains. The DRS-R-98 has 16 items, with 3 diagnostic items separable from 13 severity items. Severity for a broad range of symptoms known to occur in delirium is described using standard phenomenological definitions, without a priori assumptions about which symptoms occur more frequently. The total scale is used for initial evaluation of delirium to allow discrimination from other disorders. The DRS-R-98 total score ($P < 0.001$) distinguished delirium from dementia, schizophrenia, depression, and other medical conditions during blind ratings, with sensitivities ranging from 91% to 100% and specificities from 85% to 100%, depending on the cutoff score chosen. It has high internal consistency (Cronbach's

alpha = 0.90), correlates well with the DRS ($r = 0.83$) and the CTD ($r = -0.62$), and has high interrater reliability (intraclass correlation coefficient [ICC] = 0.99). Translations are already under way for Japanese, Korean, Greek, Portuguese, Danish, Dutch, German, and Spanish versions.

Based on issues such as instrument design, purpose, and experience, a few of the available instruments are recommended (Table 14–7). They can be used together or separately depending on the clinical or research need. For example, a screening tool can be used for case detection, followed by application of DSM criteria and then a more thorough rating for symptom severity.

# Electroencephalography

In the 1940s, Engel and Romano (1944, 1959; Romano and Engel 1944) first wrote a series of classic papers that described the relationship of delirium, as measured by cognitive impairment, to electroencephalographic slowing. In their seminal work, they showed an association between abnormal electrical activity of the brain and the psychiatric symptoms of delirium; the reversibility of both of these conditions; the ubiquity of electroencephalographic changes for different underlying disease states; and improvement in electroencephalography (EEG) background rhythm that paralleled clinical improvement. Figure 14–5 demonstrates the progression of cognitive impairment, using the clock drawing test, coupled with increasing degree of electroencephalographic slowing to illustrate this relationship.

Working with burn patients, Andreasen et al. (1977) showed that the time course of electroencephalographic slowing could precede or lag behind overt clinical symptoms of delirium, although sensitive delirium symptom ratings were not used. EEG dominant posterior rhythm, along with serum albumin and the Trailmaking Test Part B, distinguished delirious from nondelirious cirrhosis patients in another study (Trzepacz et al. 1988b).

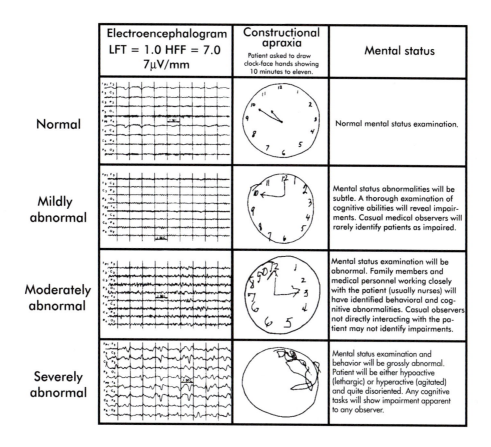

**FIGURE 14–5.** Comparison of electroencephalogram, constructional apraxia, and mental status.

**TABLE 14–8.** Electroencephalographic patterns in patients with delirium

| Electroencephalographic finding | Comment | Causes |
|---|---|---|
| Diffuse slowing | Most typical delirium pattern | Many causes, including anticholinergicity, posttraumatic brain injury, hepatic encephalopathy, hypoxia |
| Low-voltage fast activity | Typical of delirium tremens | Alcohol withdrawal; benzodiazepine intoxication |
| Spikes/polyspikes, frontocentral | Toxic ictal pattern (nonconvulsive) | Hypnosedative drug withdrawal; tricyclic and phenothiazine intoxication |
| Left/bilateral slowing or delta bursts; frontal intermittent rhythmic delta | Acute confusional migraine | Usually in adolescents |
| Epileptiform activity, frontotemporal or generalized | Status with prolonged confusional states | Nonconvulsive status and complex partial status epilepticus |

Although generalized slowing is the typical EEG pattern for both hypoactive and hyperactive presentations of delirium and for most etiologies of delirium, delirium tremens is associated with low-voltage fast activity (Kennard et al. 1945), making it an important exception. An animal model for delirium using atropine found similar EEG slowing in rats as in humans that were associated over time with worsened cognitive function (maze performance) (Leavitt et al. 1994; Trzepacz et al. 1992).

EEG characteristics in delirium include slowing/dropout of the dominant posterior rhythm, diffuse theta or delta waves (i.e., slowing), poor organization of background rhythm, and loss of reactivity of the EEG to eye opening and closing (Jacobson and Jerrier 2000). Similarly, quantitative EEG (QEEG) in delirium shows parallel findings affecting slowing of power bands' mean frequency.

Table 14–8 describes different EEG patterns that can

be seen clinically in delirium. Although diffuse slowing is the most common presentation, false-negative results occur when a person's characteristic dominant posterior rhythm does not slow sufficiently to drop from the alpha to the theta range, thereby being read as normal despite the presence of abnormal slowing for that individual. (Generally, a change of more than 1 Hz from an individual's baseline is considered abnormal.) Comparison with prior baseline EEGs is often helpful to document that slowing has in fact occurred. Less commonly, but nonetheless important, an EEG may detect focal problems, such as ictal and subictal states or a previously unsuspected tumor that presents with prominent confusion. These include toxic ictal psychosis, nonconvulsive status, and complex partial status epilepticus (Drake and Coffey 1983; Trzepacz 1994a) or focal lesions (Jacobson and Jerrier 2000). New-onset complex partial seizures are underappreciated in the elderly, related to ischemic damage (Sundaram and Dostrow 1995). Jacobson and Jerrier (2000) warn that it can be difficult to distinguish delirium from drowsiness and light sleep unless the technologist includes standard alerting procedures during the EEG. In most cases, EEGs are not needed to make a clinical diagnosis of delirium, instead being used when seizures are suspected or differential diagnosis is difficult, such as in schizophrenic patients with medical illness.

More recent advances in electroencephalographic technologies have expanded our knowledge. Using spectral analysis of delirious elderly patients (about 75% of whom also had dementia), Koponen et al. (1989b) found significant reductions of alpha percentage, increased theta and delta activity, and slowing of the peak and mean frequencies. All of these findings are consistent with electroencephalographic slowing. The study also found a correlation between the severity of cognitive decline and the length of the patient's hospital stay, on one hand, and the degree of electroencephalographic slowing, on the other. Using QEEG, Jacobson et al. (1993a) could distinguish delirious from nondelirious individuals using the relative power of the alpha frequency band and could distinguish delirious from demented patients using theta activity and the relative power of the delta band. Serial EEGs of delirious patients showed associations between the relative power of the alpha band and cognitive ability, whereas in demented patients, the absolute power of the delta band was associated with cognitive changes (Jacobson et al. 1993b). QEEG could replace conventional EEG for delirium assessment in the future (Jacobson and Jerrier 2000).

Evoked potentials may also be abnormal in delirium, suggesting thalamic or subcortical involvement in the production of symptoms. Metabolic causes of delirium precipitate abnormalities in visual, auditory, and somatosensory evoked potentials (Kullmann et al. 1995; Trzepacz 1994a), whereas somatosensory evoked potentials are abnormal in patients whose delirium is due to posttraumatic brain injury, suggesting damage to the medial lemniscus. In general, normalization of evoked potentials parallels clinical improvement, although evoked potentials are not routinely recorded for clinical purposes.

EEGs and evoked potentials in children with delirium show patterns similar to those in adults, with diffuse slowing on EEG and increased latencies of evoked potentials (Katz et al. 1988; Prugh et al. 1980; Ruijs et al. 1993, 1994). The degree of slowing on EEGs and evoked potentials recorded serially over time in children and adolescents correlates with the severity of delirium and with recovery from delirium (Foley et al. 1981; Montgomery et al. 1991; Onofrj et al. 1991).

## Phenomenology

### Symptoms

Wolff and Curran's (1935) classic descriptive study of 106 consecutive dysergastic reaction (delirium) patients is still consistent with modern notions of delirium symptoms. More recent reports, however, suffer from inconsistent terminology, unclear definitions of symptoms, and underutilization of standardized symptom assessment tools. This makes it difficult to compare symptom incidences across studies and patient etiologic populations. Nearly all studies are cross-sectional, so we lack an understanding of how various symptoms change over the course of an episode. Even whether sleep disruption occurs as a heralding symptom of delirium is not clear from the limited work in this area.

Relationships between symptoms have also not been studied, except through factor analyses in a few reports (Trzepacz and Dew 1995; Trzepacz et al. 1998; van der Mast 1994). Although the studies involved different populations, these factor analyses had some striking similarities regarding which symptoms clustered together in factors, and they also suggested that delirium symptoms overshadow dementia symptoms when they are comorbid.

The presence or absence of certain symptoms might also be predictive of certain aspects of delirium. For example, Wada and Yamaguchi (1993) found greater cognitive impairment, disturbance of sleep-wake cycle, mood lability, and hallucinations in elderly patients whose delirium episodes lasted more than 1 week.

**TABLE 14–9.** Delirium symptom frequencies reported in studies (not all symptoms reported in all studies)

| Symptom | Frequencies from various studies (%) |
| --- | --- |
| Disorientation | 43, 78, 80, 88, 100 |
| Attentional deficits | 17, 62, 100 |
| Clouded consciousness | 58, 65, 100 |
| Diffuse cognitive deficits | 77 |
| Memory impairment | 64, 90 |
| Language deficits | 41, 47, 62, 76, 93 |
| Disorganized thinking | 95 |
| Sleep-wake cycle disturbance | 25, 49, 77, 95, 96 |
| Hallucinations/perceptual disturbance | 24, 35, 41 |
| Delusions | 18, 19, 25, 68 |
| Affective lability | 43, 63 |
| Psychomotor changes | 38, 53, 55, 92, 93 |

Despite across-study inconsistencies (Table 14–9) for symptom frequencies, it does appear that certain symptoms appear more often than others, consistent with the proposal that there are core symptoms in delirium irrespective of etiology (Trzepacz 1999b, 2000). Figure 14–6 illustrates how multiple etiologies for delirium may "funnel" into a final common neural pathway (Trzepacz 1999b, 2000) so that the phenomenological expression becomes similar despite a breadth of different physiologies. This also implies that certain brain circuits and neurotransmitter systems are more affected (see Neuropathophysiology, below) (Trzepacz 1994a, 1999b, 2000). Candidates for "core" symptoms include attentional deficits, memory impairment, disorientation, sleep-wake cycle disturbance, thought process abnormalities, motoric alterations, and language disturbances, whereas "associated" or noncore symptoms would include perceptual disturbances (illusions, hallucinations), delusions, and affective changes (Trzepacz 1999b). The presence of associated symptoms might suggest the involvement of specific etiologies that are associated with specific physiologies or with individual differences in brain circuitry and vulnerability. Characteristic diagnostic features of delirium, such as altered state of consciousness (called "clouding" by some) and fluctuation of symptom severity over a 24-hour period, may be epiphenomena and not symptoms per se. These may be more related to *how* the symptoms are expressed in combination to affect the observed outward appearance of delirium patients.

Historically, delirium has been viewed by some neurologists primarily as a disturbance of attention; less importance has been attributed to its other cognitive deficits and behavioral symptoms. Attentional disturbance is

a key symptom required for the diagnosis of delirium, yet it is unlikely to explain the breadth of impairment of higher cortical functions. The parietal and prefrontal cortices, as well as the brain stem and thalamus, play roles in subserving attention, although other brain regions are likely to be involved in other symptoms of delirium.

Memory impairment occurs often in delirium, affecting both short-term and long-term memory, although most reports have not distinguished between types of memory impairment. In subclinical hepatic encephalopathy, attention is intact whereas nonverbal memory is impaired, suggesting that these cognitive functions may be differentially affected with delirium (Tarter et al. 1988). In delirium due to posttraumatic brain injury, procedural and declarative memory are impaired, and procedural memory improves first (Ewert et al. 1985). Patients are usually amnestic for some or all of their delirium episodes.

Language disturbances in delirium include dysnomia, paraphasias, impaired comprehension, dysgraphia, and word-finding difficulties. In extreme cases, language resembles a fluent dysphasia. Incoherent speech or speech disturbance is reported commonly. Dysgraphia was once believed to be specific to delirium (Chedru and Geschwind 1972). A more recent comparison with writing samples from patients with other psychiatric disorders revealed that dysgraphia was not specific (Patten and Lamarre 1989). It appears that the semantic content of language is a more differentiating feature of delirium.

Disorganized thinking was found in 95% of patients in one study (Rockwood 1993) and was also noted by Cutting (1987) to be different from schizophrenic thought processes. However, very little work has been done to characterize thought process disorder in patients with delirium, which clinically ranges from tangentiality and circumstantiality to loose associations.

Disturbances of the sleep-wake cycle are common in patients with delirium. Sleep-wake cycle disturbances may underlie fluctuations in the severity of symptoms during a 24-hour period. Sleep disturbances range from napping and nocturnal disruptions to a more severe disintegration of the normal circadian cycle. The extent to which sleep-wake cycle disturbance confounds the hyperactive-hypoactive subtyping of delirium is not known.

The type of perceptual disturbance and delusion distinguishes delirium from schizophrenia (Cutting 1987). Hallucinations, illusions, other misperceptions, and delusions occur less frequently in delirium than do "core" symptoms. Clinically, the occurrence of visual (as well as tactile, olfactory, and gustatory) hallucinations heightens the likelihood of an identifiable medical problem,

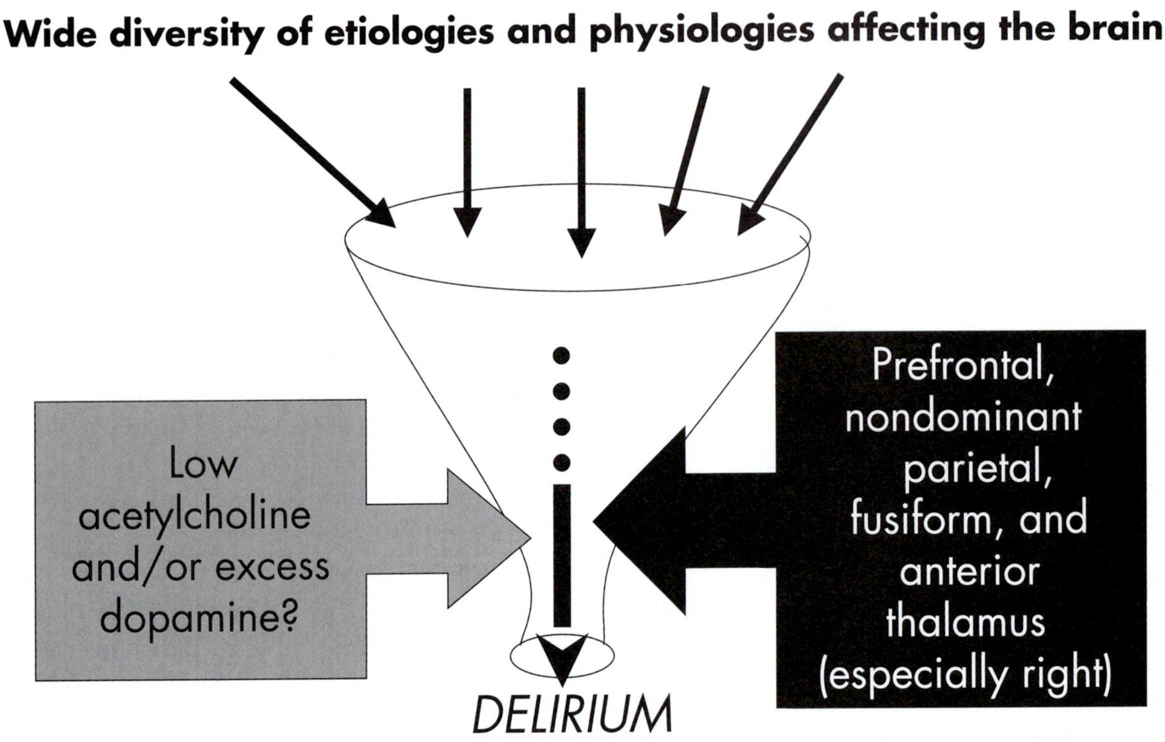

# Wide diversity of etiologies and physiologies affecting the brain

**FIGURE 14–6.** Delirium final common pathway.

although primary psychiatric disorders occasionally present with visual misperceptions. Visual hallucinations range from patterns or shapes to complex and vivid animations, which may vary according to which part of the brain is being affected (Trzepacz 1994a). Persecutory delusions that are poorly formed (not systematized) are the most common type in delirium, although other types can occur (e.g., somatic or grandiose). Delusions do not seem to be a result of cognitive impairment per se.

Affective lability that changes within minutes is characteristic of delirium. It takes many forms (e.g., anxious, apathetic, angry, dysphoric), changes from one type to another without obvious relationship to the context (i.e., incongruent), and is usually not under good self-control.

## Motoric Subtypes

Numerous delirium subtyping schema have been suggested, including those based on putative underlying neuropathophysiology, etiology, and symptom profile (Trzepacz 1994a). Motorically defined subgroups have been most studied. Although not all delirious patients express a motoric change, different presentations of psychomotor activity have been recognized for centuries. Disorientation with reduced motor activity has been

called "acute confusion," whereas hyperactive disoriented patients have been labeled "delirious" (Mesulam 1985; Mori and Yamadori 1987). Based on a study of infarctions of the right middle cerebral artery, Mori and Yamadori (1987) suggested that acute confusional states are disturbances of attention resulting from frontostriatal damage, whereas acute agitated deliria are disturbances of emotion and affect resulting from injury to the middle temporal gyrus. However, these distinctions are not supported by data. There is a comparable degree of diffuse cognitive impairment in hyperactive and hypoactive subtypes (Koponen et al. 1989b; Ross et al. 1991), electroencephalographic patterns of diffuse slowing occur in both subtypes (Trzepacz 1994a), and temporal-limbic information is linked to prefrontal cortex via the basotemporal-limbic pathways and the thalamo-frontalstriatal circuits. Thus, delirium likely relates to frontal and temporal-limbic dysfunction.

Lipowski (1990) combined these concepts under the umbrella of delirium and described three motoric subtypes: "hyperactive," "hypoactive," and "mixed." Definitions of motoric subtypes are subjectively described, not standardized, and include nonmotoric behavioral features such as disturbances of speech, emotion, thinking, and perception (Table 14–10). Using such definitions, motoric subtypes have similar

**TABLE 14–10.** Features of psychomotoric subtypes of delirium[a]

|  | Hyperactive | Hypoactive |
|---|---|---|
| Motoric symptoms | Increased activity levels | Decreased activity levels |
|  | Increased speed of actions | Decreased speed of actions |
|  | Loss of control of activity | Apathy/listlessness |
|  | Restlessness/wandering |  |
| Nonmotoric symptoms | Increased amount, speed, and volume of speech | Decreased amount, speed, and volume of speech |
|  | Altered content of verbal output (singing, shouting, laughing, etc.) | Hypoalertness |
|  | Aggression, combativeness, uncooperativeness | Hypersomnolence |
|  | Hallucinations | Social withdrawal |
|  | Hyperalertness, increased startle |  |
| Electroencephalogram | Diffuse slowing | Diffuse slowing |
| Cognition | Diffuse deficits | Diffuse deficits |
| Treatment | Neuroleptic responsive | Neuroleptic responsive |
| Outcome | ? lower mortality rate | ? increased mortality rate and closer to stupor |

[a]Mixed subtype requires evidence of both hyperactive and hypoactive delirium.

**TABLE 14–11.** Studies of frequency of motoric subtypes in delirium[a]

| Study | Motoric definition | Hyper % | Hypo % | Mixed % | None % |
|---|---|---|---|---|---|
| Koponen et al. 1989a | Lipowski description | 38 | 13 | 49 | — |
| Koponen et al. 1989b | Lipowski description | 31 | 14 | 55 | — |
| Ross et al. 1991 | Visual analog scale | 68 | 32 | — | — |
| Liptzin and Levkoff 1992 | Liptzin and Levkoff criteria | 15 | 19 | 52 | 14 |
| Kobayashi et al. 1992 | Lipowski description | 79 | 6 | 15 | — |
| Platt et al. 1994a | Psychomotor item of DRS | 37 | 46 | 17 | — |
| Uchiyama et al. 1996 | Clinical observation | 80 | 20 | — | — |
| Meagher et al. 1996 | Liptzin and Levkoff criteria | 30 | 24 | 46 | — |
| Olofsson et al. 1996 | Clinical observation | 71 | 18 | 11 | — |
| O'Keeffe and Lavan 1999 | DAS score during initial 48 hours | 21 | 29 | 43 | 7 |
| Okamoto et al. 1999 | DSI item | 73 | — | 27 | — |
| Camus et al. 2000b | Own checklist | 46 | 26 | 27 | — |

*Note.* DRS = Delirium Rating Scale; DAS = Delirium Assessment Scale; DSI = Delirium Symptom Inventory.
[a]Comorbid dementia was not excluded, nor was effect of drug treatment accounted for in most of these studies.

degrees of overall cognitive impairment and electroencephalographic slowing (Koponen et al. 1989b; Ross 1991), but they differ for some nonmotoric symptoms. Delusions, hallucinations, mood lability, speech incoherence, and sleep disturbances may be more frequent in hyperactive patients (Meagher and Trzepacz 2000; Ross et al. 1991). Waxing and waning of symptom severity and sleep-wake cycle abnormalities complicate understanding motoric subtypes, as well as reliance on subjective and retrospective reports of behavior over 24-hour periods. There is wide variation among reports of relative frequencies of motoric subtypes (Table 14–11), even when alcohol withdrawal cases are excluded.

Objective motor activity level monitoring is needed.

In many reports, up to half of patients present as a mixed motoric subtype during their episode (see Table 14–11). These mixed cases may reflect different impacts over time of multiple etiological effects on motoric behavior or may be a hybrid state. Detailed longitudinal study of delirium symptoms is necessary before any definitive conclusion can be reached regarding the stability of motoric subtypes.

A recent factor analysis supports the distinction of separate hyperactive and hypoactive symptom clusters (Camus et al. 2000a). However, the symptoms included in this analysis were restricted to psychomotoric ones and did not include cognition, sleep, language, etc. Therefore, the conclusions were circular and simply confirmed that symptoms from an a priori defined symptom list clustered according to opposite features but do little to address the core issue of defining delirium subtypes or whether motoric subtypes even exist beyond the motoric behavior itself.

To date, clinical studies have not provided convincing evidence that motoric subtypes have distinct neurobiological underpinnings. The delirium symptom profile of patients with localized cerebral insults does not reliably link specific motoric subtypes to lesions at particular cerebral sites. Moreover, studies of cognition and EEG indicate that both hypoactive and hyperactive delirium are associated with comparable disturbances. Alcohol withdrawal delirium, which is generally hyperactive, is associated with increased beta electroencephalographic activity, but all other causes of delirium are typically associated with diffuse electroencephalographic slowing, regardless of motoric presentation (Trzepacz 1994a). Similarly, functional neuroimaging studies of delirium indicate increased cerebral blood flow in alcohol withdrawal delirium (Hemmingsen et al. 1988), whereas other causes are associated with reductions in global or frontal cerebral blood flow irrespective of motoric subtype (Trzepacz 1994a).

Disturbances of cholinergic systems are the neurochemical aberration most consistently linked to delirium. Evidence from animal studies and normal human volunteers suggests that reduced cholinergic activity is associated with relative hyperactivity, but studies measuring possible markers of CNS cholinergic function in delirium, such as serum anticholinergic activity and cerebrospinal fluid (CSF) somatostatin-like immunoreactivity, have not supported this possibility. Similarly, arguments have been made for involvement of other neurochemical systems (dopamine, serotonin, γ-aminobutyric acid [GABA], histamine), but more study is needed (Meagher and Trzepacz 2000).

Studies of etiology, treatment, and outcome suggest that motoric subtypes of delirium may have clinically important distinctions. Studies indicate that motoric profile is influenced by etiology; delirium due to drug-related causes is most commonly hyperactive, whereas delirium due to metabolic disturbances, including hypoxia, is more frequently hypoactive in presentation (Meagher et al. 1996; O'Keeffe and Lavan 1999; Olofsson et al. 1996; Ross et al. 1991).

Patients with a hyperactive subtype experience better outcomes after an episode of delirium in the form of shorter LOS, lower mortality rates, and a higher rate of full recovery (Kobayashi et al. 1992; Liptzin and Levkoff

1992; Olofsson et al. 1996; Reyes et al. 1981). However, these differences may reflect neuropathophysiological underpinnings, underlying causes, recognition rates, and/or treatment practices. Underdetection is especially common in hypoactive patients. Even when the influence of earlier detection or more active investigation is negated by active screening, hypoactive cases may still have a poorer outcome (O'Keeffe and Lavan 1999). Meagher et al. (1996) found that use of psychotropic medication and supportive environmental ward strategies were more closely linked to level of hyperactivity rather than to the degree of cognitive disturbance. In contrast, Olofsson et al. (1996) reported better outcome in patients with hyperactive delirium but noted that they received less haloperidol than nonhyperactive patients. O'Keeffe and Lavan (1999) reported greater use of neuroleptics and shorter hospital stays in hyperactive patients but linked this to less severe illness at the onset of delirium and a lower incidence of hospital-acquired infections and bed sores in those who were hyperactive. Still other work has found similar outcomes in the different motoric groups (Camus et al. 2000b). The precise relationship between motoric subtype, treatment exposure, and outcome therefore remains uncertain.

Studies investigating effectiveness of delirium treatment for different motoric subtypes are scarce. It is often (unfortunately) presumed that psychotropic agents are useful in delirium solely for sedative or antipsychotic purposes and thus are more effective for hyperactive patients. Clinical experience and one study found comparable efficacy for haloperidol in treating both hypoactive and hyperactive delirious medical patients (Platt et al. 1994a). Uchiyama et al. (1996) found better rates of response to mianserin in delirium with hyperactive motoric presentation compared with hypoactive motoric profile, perhaps related to its sedating effects.

## Etiologies of Delirium

Delirium can be caused by a wide variety of etiologies alone or in combination (Table 14–12). These include primary cerebral disorders, systemic disturbances that affect cerebral function, drug/toxin exposure (including intoxication and withdrawal), and a range of factors that can contribute to delirium but have an uncertain role as etiological factors by themselves (psychological/environmental factors). In DSM-IV, delirium is categorized according to etiology rather than other aspects of its clinical profile. Categories described include delirium due to a general medical condition, to substance use or withdrawal, and to multiple causes and cases in which

**TABLE 14–12.** Etiologies of delirium

**Drug intoxication**
- Alcohol
- Sedative-hypnotic
- Opiate
- Psychostimulant
- Hallucinogenic
- Inhalants
- Industrial poisons
- Prescribed or over-the-counter drug

**Drug withdrawal**
- Alcohol
- Sedative-hypnotic
- Opiate
- Psychostimulants
- Prescribed drug

**Metabolic/endocrine disturbance**
- Volume depletion/volume overload
- Acidosis/alkalosis
- Hypoxia
- Uremia
- Anemia
- Avitaminosis ($B_1$, $B_6$, $B_{12}$, folate)/hypervitaminosis (A, D)
- Hypoglycemia/hyperglycemia
- Hypoalbuminemia/hyperalbuminemia
- Bilirubinemia
- Hypocalcemia/hypercalcemia
- Hypokalemia/hyperkalemia
- Hyponatremia/hypernatremia
- Hypomagnesemia/hypermagnesemia
- Hypophosphatemia
- Hypothyroidism/hyperthyroidism
- Hypoparathyroidism/hyperparathyroidism
- Cushing's syndrome
- Addison's disease
- Hypopituitarism
- Hyperinsulinoma
- Metabolic disorders (porphyria, carcinoid syndrome)

**Traumatic brain injury**

**Seizures**

**Neoplastic disease**
- Intracranial primary/metastasis/meningeal
- Carcinomatosis
- Extracranial primary/paraneoplastic syndrome

**Intracranial infection**
- Meningitis
- Encephalitis
- Abscess
- Neurosyphilis
- HIV

**Systemic infection**
- Bacteremia
- Sepsis
- Fungal
- Protozoal
- Viral

**Cerebrovascular disorder**
- Transient ischemic attack
- Subarachnoid hemorrhage
- Stroke
- Subdural hemorrhage
- Subdural hematoma
- Cerebral edema
- Cerebral aneurysm
- Hypertensive encephalopathy
- Intraparenchymal hemorrhage
- Cerebral vasculitis

**Organ insufficiency**
- Cardiac/pulmonary/hepatic/renal/pancreatic

**Other CNS etiologies**
- Parkinson's disease
- Huntington's disease
- Multiple sclerosis
- Wilson's disease
- Hydrocephalus

**Other systemic etiologies**
- Heatstroke
- Hypothermia
- Radiation
- Electrocution
- Postoperative state
- Immunosuppression
- Fractures

no apparent cause has been identified. For an etiology to be considered causal, it should be a recognized possible cause of delirium and should be temporally related in onset and course to delirium presentation, and the delirium should not be better accounted for by other factors. No clear cause is found in approximately 10% of patients, and these cases are categorized as delirium not otherwise specified (NOS) in DSM-IV.

In studies in which the possibility of multiple etiologies has been considered, between two and six possible causes are typically identified (Breitbart et al. 1996; Francis et al. 1990; Meagher et al. 1996; O'Keeffe 1999; Trzepacz et al. 1985), with a single etiology identified in fewer than 50% of cases (Camus et al. 2000b; O'Keeffe

1999; Olofsson et al. 1996). Multiple-etiology delirium is more frequent in the elderly and those with terminal illness. For example, delirium in cancer patients can be due to the direct effect of the primary tumor or indirect via effects of metastases, metabolic problems (organ failure or electrolyte disturbance), chemotherapy, radiation and other treatments, infections, vascular complications, nutritional deficits, and paraneoplastic syndromes. This multifactorial nature has been underemphasized in research—etiologic attribution is typically based on clinical impressions that are not standardized (e.g., the most likely cause identified by the referring physician) or oversimplified by documenting a single etiology for each case. That delirium due to a single etiology is the exception rather than the rule highlights the importance of multidisciplinary approaches to management and the need for continued vigilance to the possibility of further etiological inputs even when a cause has been identified.

Some causes are more frequently encountered in particular populations. Drugs and polypharmacy commonly cause or contribute to delirium, especially in the elderly (T.M. Brown 2000). Drug-related causes are more commonly reported in psychiatric populations. (See Table 14–13 for a list of implicated drugs.) Delirium in children and adolescents involves the same categories of etiologies as in adults, although specific causes may differ. Delirium related to illicit drugs is more common in younger populations, whereas that due to prescribed drugs and polypharmacy is more common in older populations. Cerebral hypoxia is common at age extremes, with chronic obstructive airway disease, myocardial infarction, and stroke common in older patients and hypoxia due to foreign body inhalation, drowning, and asthma more frequent in younger patients. Poisonings are also more common in children than in adults, whereas children and the elderly both have high rates of delirium related to head trauma—bicycle accidents in children and falls in the elderly.

Delirium has historically been viewed as a nonspecific CNS response to a variety of causative insults. More recently, specific etiologies are being recognized as possibly affecting symptom profile. Delirium due to drug-related causes and traumatic brain injury tend to be present with motor hyperactivity, disturbances of sleep-wake cycle, and prominent psychotic symptoms. In contrast, delirium due to metabolic causes typically involves reduced psychomotor activity with psychomotor slowing and reduced vigilance (for review, see Meagher and Trzepacz 1998). The mode of onset of delirium (acute or subacute) may also be related to underlying cause of delirium, with a prodromal phase more likely in delirium of less acute onset that occurs due to metabolic causes.

An implication of distinct symptom patterns for certain etiologies is whether they reflect pathophysiological processes. It has been suggested that delirium due to traumatic brain injury, stroke, hypoxia, thiamine deficiency, or hypoglycemia is associated with reduced cholinergic activity in the CNS (Trzepacz 1996a, 2000). In contrast, delirium due to sedative-hypnotic or alcohol withdrawal has been linked to disturbances of GABA metabolism (Meagher and Trzepacz 1998). Reduced plasma tryptophan in post–cardiac surgery patients has linked delirium to reduced serotonin metabolism (van der Mast 1998).

Once the diagnosis of delirium is made, a careful and thorough, though prioritized, search for causes must be conducted. Ameliorations of specific underlying causes are important in resolving delirium, although this should not preclude treatment of the delirium itself, which can reduce symptoms even before underlying medical causes are rectified (Breitbart et al. 1996).

## Treatment of Delirium

After the diagnosis of delirium is made, the process of identifying and reversing suspected causes begins. Rapid treatment is important because of the high morbidity and mortality rates associated with delirium. Treatments include medication, environmental manipulation, and patient and family psychosocial support (American Psychiatric Association 1999). However, there is no drug with a U.S. Food and Drug Administration (FDA) indication for the treatment of delirium, and double-blind, placebo-controlled studies are lacking. The American Psychiatric Association (APA) Practice Guidelines on treatment of delirium note the need for such research (American Psychiatric Association 1999).

The use of orienting techniques (e.g., calendars, night lights, and reorientation by staff) and familiarizing the patient with the environment (e.g., with photographs of family members) are sometimes comforting, although it is important to remember that environmental manipulations alone do not reverse delirium (S.D. Anderson 1995; American Psychiatric Association 1999). It has also been suggested that diurnal cues from natural lighting reduce sensory deprivation and incidence of delirium (Wilson 1972), although sensory deprivation alone is insufficient to cause delirium (Frances 1993).

Pharmacologic treatment with a neuroleptic agent (dopamine $D_2$ antagonist) is the clinical standard of delirium treatment. Benzodiazepines are generally reserved for delirium due to ethanol or sedative-hypnotic withdrawal; lorazepam or clonazepam (the latter for alprazo-

**TABLE 14–13.** Drugs implicated in the etiology of delirium

**Analgesics**
- Meperidine
- Opiates
- Pentazocine
- Salicylates

**Antibiotics**
- Acyclovir, ganciclovir
- Aminoglycosides
- Amodiaquine
- Amphotericin B
- Cephalexin
- Cephalosporins
- Chloramphenicol
- Chloroquine
- Ethambutol
- Gentamicin
- Interferon
- Sulfonamides
- Tetracycline
- Ticarcillin
- Vancomycin

**Anticholinergic drugs**
- Antihistamines (chlorpheniramine)
- Antispasmodics
- Atropine/homatropine
- Belladonna alkaloids
- Benztropine
- Biperiden
- Diphenhydramine
- Phenothiazines (especially thioridazine)
- Promethazine
- Scopolamine
- Tricyclics (especially amitriptyline)
- Trihexyphenidyl

**Anticonvulsants**
- Phenobarbital
- Phenytoin
- Valproic acid

**Anti-inflammatory drugs**
- Adrenocorticotropic hormone
- Corticosteroids
- Ibuprofen
- Indomethacin
- Naproxen
- Phenylbutazone
- Steroids

**Antineoplastic drugs**
- Aminoglutethimide
- Asparaginase
- Dacarbazine (DTIC)
- 5-Fluorouracil
- Hexamethylenamine
- Methotrexate (high dose)
- Tamoxifen
- Vinblastine
- Vincristine

**Antiparkinsonism drugs**
- Amantadine
- Bromocriptine
- Carbidopa
- Levodopa

**Antituberculous drugs**
- Isoniazid
- Rifampin

**Cardiac drugs**
- β-Blockers (propranolol)
- Captopril
- Clonidine
- Digitalis
- Disopyramide
- Lidocaine
- Methyldopa
- Mexiletine
- Procainamide
- Quinidine
- Tocainide

**Drug withdrawal**
- Alcohol
- Barbiturates
- Benzodiazepines

**Sedative-hypnotics**
- Barbiturates
- Benzodiazepines
- Glutethimide

**Sympathomimetics**
- Aminophylline
- Amphetamines
- Cocaine
- Ephedrine
- Epinephrine
- Phenylephrine
- Phenylpropanolamine
- Theophylline

**Miscellaneous drugs**
- Baclofen
- Bromides
- Chlorpropamide
- Cimetidine
- Disulfiram
- Ergotamines
- Lithium
- Metrizamide
- Metronidazole
- Phenelzine
- Podophyllin (by absorption)
- Procarbazine
- Propylthiouracil
- Quinacrine
- Ranitidine
- Timolol ophthalmic

lam withdrawal) is often used. Some use lorazepam as an adjunctive medication with haloperidol in severe cases of delirium or when extra assistance with sleep is needed.

The cholinergic deficiency hypothesis of delirium suggests that treatment with a cholinergic enhancer drug could be therapeutic. Physostigmine reverses anticholinergic delirium (Stern 1983), but its side effects (seizures) and short half-life make it unsuitable for routine clinical treatment of delirium. Tacrine was also shown to reverse central anticholinergic syndrome (Mendelson 1977), although it has not been studied formally. Three case reports found that donepezil improved delirium in postoperative state, comorbid Lewy body dementia, and comorbid alcohol dementia (Burke et al. 1999; Wengel et al. 1998, 1999).

Psychostimulants can worsen delirium—probably via increased dopaminergic activity—and have not been recommended when a depressed mood is present (J.A. Levenson 1992; Rosenberg et al. 1991). Whether a combination of a $D_2$ blocker and a stimulant could treat hypoactive delirium is under study.

Mianserin, a serotonergic tetracyclic antidepressant, has been used in Japan for delirium in elderly medical and postsurgical cohorts, administered either orally or as a suppository. Several open-label studies found reductions in DRS scores similar to those seen when using haloperidol (J. Nakamura et al. 1995, 1997a, 1997b; Uchiyama et al. 1996). The efficacy of mianserin was theorized to be due to its effect on the sleep-wake cycle and/or to its weak $D_2$ receptor antagonism in conjunction with blockade of postsynaptic serotonin type 2, presynaptic α-adrenergic, and histamine type 1 ($H_1$) and type 2 ($H_2$) receptor blockade.

A single 8-mg intravenous dose of odansetron, a 5-$HT_3$ antagonist, was reported to reduce agitation in delirium patients when a 4-point rating scale was applied prospectively in 35 postcardiotomy patients (mean age = 51 years) (Bayindir et al. 2000). Further research is needed to more carefully assess cognitive and other behavioral effects of this agent.

Haloperidol is the neuroleptic agent most often chosen for the treatment of delirium. It can be administered orally, intramuscularly, or intravenously (Adams 1984, 1988; Dudley et al. 1979; Gelfand et al. 1992; Moulaert 1989; Sanders and Stern 1993; Tesar et al. 1985), although the intravenous route has not been approved by the FDA. Intravenously administered haloperidol is twice as potent as that taken orally (Gelfand et al. 1992). Bolus intravenous doses usually range from 0.5 to 20 mg, although larger doses are sometimes given. In severe, refractory cases, continuous intravenous infusions of 15–25 mg/hr (up to 1,000 mg/day) can be given (Fernandez et al. 1988; J.L. Levenson 1995; Riker et al. 1994; Stern 1994).

The specific brain effects of haloperidol in alleviating delirium are not known, but positron emission tomographic scans show reduced glucose utilization in the limbic cortex, thalamus, caudate nucleus, and frontal and anterior cingulate cortices (Bartlett et al. 1994). These regions are important for behavior and cognition and have been implicated in the neuropathogenesis of delirium.

Based on clinical usage, haloperidol has been considered to be relatively safe in the seriously medically ill and does not cause as much hypotension as droperidol (Gelfand et al. 1992; Moulaert 1989; Tesar et al. 1985). Haloperidol does not antagonize dopamine-induced increases in renal blood flow (Armstrong et al. 1986). When haloperidol is given intravenously, extrapyramidal symptoms have been considered unusual (Menza et al. 1987; Tesar et al. 1986), except in human immunodeficiency virus (HIV) and Lewy body dementia (Fernandez et al. 1989; McKeith et al. 1992; Swenson et al. 1989). In a case series of five ICU patients receiving 250–500 mg/day of continuous or intermittent intravenous haloperidol, patients had self-limited withdrawal dyskinesia after receiving high-dose haloperidol (Riker et al. 1997). Intravenous lorazepam is sometimes combined with intravenous haloperidol in critically ill cancer patients to lessen extrapyramidal symptoms and produces a deeply sedated state for several days (Menza et al. 1988).

Cases of prolonged $QT_c$ interval on electrocardiogram (ECG) and torsades de pointes tachyarrhythmia (multifocal ventricular tachycardia) have been attributed to intravenously administered haloperidol (Hatta et al. 2001; Huyse 1988; Kriwisky et al. 1990; Metzger and Friedman 1993; O'Brien et al. 1999; Perrault et al. 2000; Wilt et al. 1993; Zee-Cheng et al. 1985). This is a potentially life-threatening event. Risk factors for this arrhythmia are not clearly identified, but prolonged $QT_c$ increases its risk (Sanders et al. 1991). The APA Treatment Guidelines for Delirium (American Psychiatric Association 1999) recommend that $QT_c$ prolongation greater than 450 msec or to greater than 25% over a previous ECG may warrant telemetry, cardiological consultation, dose reduction, or discontinuation. They also recommend monitoring serum magnesium and potassium in critically ill delirious patients whose $QT_c$ is ≥450 msec because of the common use of concomittant drugs and/or electrolyte disturbances that also can prolong the $QT_c$ interval. Wilt et al. (1993) found only 4 cases of torsades de pointes in 1,100 consecutive cases of haloperidol-treated patients admitted to an ICU, and cases who have severe cardiac disease have been reported to tolerate intravenous haloperidol without complication (Tesar et al. 1985), even at daily doses exceeding 1,000 mg (Sanders et al. 1991). In pigs, intravenous haloperidol (50-mg boluses) does not alter mean heart rate, QRS duration, or $QT_c$ interval; in fact, it raises the ventricular fibrillation threshold (Tisdale et al. 1991). However, large intravenous doses of haloperidol were implicated in causing torsades de pointes tachycardia in a delirious post-CABG patient in the absence of $QT_c$ prolongation (Perrault et al. 2000). High-dose intravenous haloperidol (80 mg) was reported to cause torsades de pointes in an agitated 41-year-old woman without predisposing factors at the first hour of treatment when her $QT_c$ was noted to be 610 msec (O'Brien et al. 1999). A cross-sectional cohort study compared 34 patients receiving intravenous haloperidol plus flunitrazepam to 13 receiving intravenous flunitrazepam for emergency treatment of agitation alone while the ECG was continuously monitored (Hatta et al. 2001). They found mean $QT_c$ was significantly prolonged at 8 hours in the haloperidol group ($P < 0.001$), including 4 patients with $QT_c > 500$ msec, and there was a modest correlation between $QT_c$ prolongation and haloperidol dose. These authors note that during agitation the myocardium receives adrenergic stimulation that can trigger automatic ventricular activity and facilitate the onset of reeentrant arrhythmias.

Empirical evidence for neuroleptic benefits in treating delirium is substantial, but treatment studies are rare. Itil and Fink (1966) found that chlorpromazine reversed anticholinergic delirium. Using standardized assessment methods and a double-blind, randomized controlled design, Breitbart et al. (1996) found that delirium in acquired immune deficiency syndrome (AIDS) patients significantly improved with haloperidol or chlorpromazine, but not with lorazepam. In addition, both hypoactive and hyperactive subtypes responded to treatment with haloperidol or chlorpromazine (Platt et al. 1994a). Improvement was noted within hours of treatment, even before the underlying medical causes were addressed (Platt et al. 1994a). Thus, delirium irrespective of motoric presentation should be treated in parallel to identifying and managing comorbid medical conditions.

Haloperidol use in pediatric patients with delirium is not well documented, despite its use in adult delirium and in many other childhood psychiatric disorders (Teicher and Gold 1990). Its efficacy in children for delusions, hallucinations, thought disorder, aggressivity, stereotypies, hyperactivity, social withdrawal, and learning ability (Teicher and Gold 1990) suggests that it may have a potentially beneficial role in pediatric delirium. Clinical experience with haloperidol in pediatric delirium supports its beneficial effects, although there are no controlled studies. A retrospective report of 30 children

(mean age, $7 \pm 1.0$ years; range 8 months to 18 years) with burn injuries supports the use of haloperidol for agitation, disorientation, hallucinations, delusions, and insomnia (R.L. Brown et al. 1996). The mean dose of haloperidol was $0.47 \pm 0.002$ mg/kg, with a mean maximum dose in 24 hours of 0.455 mg/kg, administered intravenously, orally, and intramuscularly. Mean efficacy, as scored on a 0–3 point scale (3 = excellent), was $2.3 \pm 0.21$, but the drug was not efficacious in 17% of cases (4 of 5 of these failures were via the oral route). Extrapyramidal symptoms were not observed, and there was one episode of hypotension with the intravenous route.

In other psychiatric disorders, pediatric haloperidol doses range from 0.25 to 10 mg/day or from 0.04 to 0.06 mg/kg per day (Locasio et al. 1991; Malone et al. 1991; Spencer et al. 1992). Side effects are similar to those in adults. Sedation and extrapyramidal symptoms occur frequently (Spencer et al. 1992), except in preschool-age children (Teicher and Gold 1990). Dystonias occur more often in adolescents than in children (Teicher and Gold 1990).

Droperidol is sometimes used to treat patients with acute agitation and confusion from a variety of causes, including mania and delirium (Hooper and Minter 1983; Resnick and Burton 1984; H. Thomas et al. 1992), and is superior to placebo (van Leeuwen et al. 1977). After initial use in patients with severe agitated delirium, droperidol can be replaced by haloperidol for continued treatment. Compared with haloperidol, droperidol is more sedating, has a faster onset of action, can only be used parenterally, and is very hypotensive due to potent $\alpha$-adrenergic antagonism, although continuous intravenous to infusion of 1–10 mg/hr causes less hypotension than do intravenous boluses (Moulaert 1989). Having the patient lie supine is helpful. Dosing is similar to haloperidol, although it may have less antipsychotic activity and fewer extrapyramidal symptoms (Frye et al. 1995). Prolonged $QT_c$ intervals can occur with droperidol (Lawrence and Nasraway 1997; Lischke et al. 1994), although there were no associated ventricular arrhythmias noted in a small series of patients with cardiac conditions (Frye et al. 1995). However, oral droperidol (and thioridazine) was recently reported in Europe to significantly prolong the $QT_c$ interval in a dose-related manner in a study of 495 patients and 101 healthy volunteers (Reilly et al. 2000). Droperidol has been recently withdrawn from the market in several European countries because of risk-benefit issues.

So-called atypical antipsychotic agents—more novel neuroleptic drugs—differ from haloperidol and other conventional neuroleptics in a variety of neurotransmitter activities, in particular serotonin. Some are being used to treat delirium, also mentioned in a few case reports. Receptor activities and adverse event profiles differ among the atypical agents, and extrapyramidal symptoms, $QT_c$ prolongation, and effects on cognition are particularly relevant to any use in delirium.

Clozapine, the first atypical antipsychotic agent, is clinically distinct from the others. It is very sedating, has significant anticholinergic side effects, causes sinus tachycardia, lowers seizure threshold, and is associated with causing agranulocytosis. Clozapine has been reported to cause delirium in 8% of 315 psychiatric inpatients, and in 7 of these 33 delirium cases it was the only drug used (Gaertner et al. 1989). Cholinergic agents were reported to reverse treatment-emergent delirium during clozapine therapy (Schuster et al. 1977).

Risperidone (mean dose, $1.59 \pm 0.8$ mg/day) has been reported to reduce delirium severity in 8 of 11 patients as measured on the Clinical Global Impression scale in an open-label case series, with the maximum response on the 5th day (Sipahimalani and Masand 1997). However, in four cases, risperidone use was reported to cause delirium (Chen and Cardasis 1996; Ravona-Springer et al. 1998). Risperidone has dose-related extrapyramidal symptoms beginning at about 2 mg/day based on double-blind placebo-controlled studies (Katz et al. 1999).

Eleven delirious patients treated with olanzapine (mean dose, $8.2 \pm 3.4$ mg at bedtime) were compared with 11 delirious patients treated with haloperidol (mean dose, $5.1 \pm 3.5$ mg at bedtime) in an open-label nonrandomized case series (Masand and Sipahimalani 1998). Drug efficacy was comparable when measured as a greater than 50% reduction on the DRS, although 5 haloperidol patients had extrapyramidal symptoms or excessive sedation versus none in the olanzapine group. Delirium in a medically ill cancer patient responded to olanzapine 10 mg without adverse effects (Passik and Cooper 1999). Breitbart (2000) described 82 consecutive delirious cancer inpatients (mean age = 60 years)—81% of whom had metastases (20% in the brain)—who were treated with olanzapine (dose range = 2.5–20 mg) for delirium. Using standardized measures, the researchers found olanzapine to have a high degree of efficacy (in more than three-fourths of patients) and tolerability, without extrapyramidal symptoms. Olanzapine has a favorable extrapyramidal symptom profile and does not appear to have a clinically significant effect on the $QT_c$ interval at therapeutic doses in schizophrenia patients (Czekalla et al. 2001). Olanzapine significantly improved cognitive function to a greater extent than either risperidone or haloperidol, which did not significantly differ

from each other, in a head-to-head trial in early-phase schizophrenic patients as measured by sensitive neuropsychological tests (Purdon et al. 2000). Olanzapine increases acetylcholine release measured by in vivo microdialysis in both rat prefrontal cortex (Meltzer 1999) and hippocampus (Schirazi et al. 2000), consistent with procholinergic activity that may improve cognition. Kennedy and colleagues (in press) theorized that presynaptic effects of olanzapine at 5-HT$_3$, 5-HT$_6$, and m2 receptors may account for this increased acetylcholine release.

A retrospective study of remoxipride (median dose, 75 mg; range, 50–300 mg) in 103 elderly persons, 73 of whom had delirium (comorbid with dementia in 70 of 73) using DSM-III-R criteria, reported efficacy for 65% of patients with side effects in 25% (tiredness, extrapyramidal symptoms, aggressiveness) (Robertsson et al. 1996). Although it may have had some efficacy for delirium, remoxipride was withdrawn from the market due to an association with aplastic anemia.

There are no reports for ziprasidone or quetiapine use for delirium at this time. However, quetiapine 300 mg bid has been reported to cause delirium in a 62-year-old man, which was associated with a change on his EEG (slowing) compared with a prior normal EEG (Sim et al. 2000). A previous right thalamic lacunar infarct may have increased his risk for delirium. The delirium cleared when quetiapine was discontinued.

Further delirium treatment research is needed, especially randomized, double-blind, placebo-controlled trials. Unlike haloperidol and droperidol, atypical agents have not been available in parenteral forms in the United States, which are often useful in confused patients. Intramuscular forms of olanzapine and ziprasidone are under FDA consideration for agitation in psychiatric patients. Olanzapine has a rapidly dissolving oral formulation that is placed on the tongue, although it has not yet been reported for use in delirium.

## Neuropathophysiology

### The Final Common Neural Pathway in Delirium

Delirium is considered to result from a generalized disturbance of higher cerebral cortical processes, as reflected by diffuse slowing on the EEG and a breadth of symptoms (cognition, perception, sleep, motor, language, and thought). However, it is not accompanied by primary motor or sensory deficits except when related to a specific etiology (e.g., asterixis). Thus, not all brain regions

**TABLE 14–14.** Lesions associated with delirium in structural neuroimaging studies

| Authors | Lesions associated with delirium |
| --- | --- |
| Mesulam 1976; Price and Mesulam 1985 | CVA in R posterior parietal, R prefrontal, ventromedial temporal, or occipital cortex |
| Horenstein et al. 1967 | CVAs in fusiform and calcarine cortices |
| Medina et al. 1977 | L or bilateral mesial temporal-occipital CVA |
| Medina et al. 1974 | L hippocampal or fusiform CVA |
| Vaphiades et al. 1996 | R mesial occipital, parahippocampal, and hippocampus (with visual hallucinations) |
| Nighoghossian et al. 1992 | R subcortical CVA (with frontal deactivation) |
| Bogousslavsky et al. 1988 | R anterior thalamus CVA on preexisting L caudate lesion (with ↓ frontal perfusion on SPECT) |
| Figiel et al. 1989; Martin et al. 1992 | Lesions in caudate nucleus (in depressed patients treated with ECT or medications) |
| Figiel et al. 1991 | Parkinson's disease patients (depressed and treated with ECT or medications) |
| Koponen et al. 1989a | R prefrontal or posterior parietal cortex CVA (many with comorbid dementia) |
| Dunne et al. 1986 | R temporoparietal CVA |
| Mullaly et al. 1982 | R temporal or parietal CVA |
| Boiten and Lodder 1989 | R inferior parietal lobule CVA |
| Santamaria et al. 1984; Friedman 1985 | R anteromedial thalamus CVA |
| Henon et al. 1999 | R superficial CVA (prospective sample) |

*Note.* ECT = electroconvulsive therapy; CVA = cerebrovascular accident (stroke); L = left; R = right; SPECT = single photon emission computed tomography.

*Source.* Reprinted from Trzepacz PT: "Is There a Final Common Neural Pathway in Delirium? Focus on Acetylcholine and Dopamine." *Seminars in Clinical Neuropsychiatry* 5:132–148, 2000. Used with permission.

are equally affected in delirium. Certain regions, circuits, and neurochemistry may be integral in the neuropathogenesis of delirium (Trzepacz 1994a, 1999b, 2000). Henon et al. (1999) found that laterality of lesion location and not metabolic factors accounted for the differences in delirium incidence for superficial cortical lesions.

Even though delirium has many different etiologies, each with its own physiological effects on the body, its constellation of symptoms is largely stereotyped, with some considered "core" symptoms. Somehow this diversity of physiological perturbations translates into a common clinical expression that may well relate to dysfunction of certain neural circuits (as well as neurotransmitters)—that is, a final common neural pathway (Trzepacz 1999b, 2000). An analogy of a funnel (see Figure 14–6) can be used to represent this common neural circuitry. Studies support certain pathways being involved. Specifically, bilateral or right prefrontal cortex, superficial right posterior parietal cortex, basal ganglia, either fusiform cortex (ventromesial temporoparietal) and lingual gyrus, and right anterior thalamus appear to be particularly associated with delirium (Trzepacz 2000). In addition, the pathways linking them (thalamic-frontal-subcortical and temporolimbic-frontal/subcortical) are likely involved. This hypothesis is largely based on struc-

tural neuroimaging reports (Table 14–14), only a few of which are consecutive and prospective in design, and a limited number of functional neuroimaging studies.

Lateralization to more right-sided circuitry involvement in delirium is also supported by evidence besides lesion studies. The right prefrontal cortex cognitively processes novel situations, in contrast to the left (which processes familiar situations), and this may account for delirium patients' difficulties with comprehending new environments (E.L. Goldberg 1998). The right posterior parietal cortex subserves sustained attention and attention to the environment (Posner and Boies 1971), and both are often impaired in delirium. Bipolar patients had the highest incidence of delirium (35.5%) among 199 psychiatric inpatients (Ritchie et al. 1996), and because right-sided anterior and subcortical pathways have been implicated in mania (Blumberg et al. 1999), this suggests a predisposition to delirium possibly based on neuroanatomy. Bell's mania is a severe form of mania that causes pseudodelirium. Visual attention and visual memory tests—assessing nondominant hemisphere cognitive functions—distinguished delirious from nondelirious patients (Hart et al. 1997). Dopamine neurotransmission is lateralized such that activity is normally higher in the left prefrontal cortex (Glick et al. 1982), and this difference may become more extreme if right-sided pathways are affected in delirium.

Lesions of the right posterior parietal cortex may be present with severe delirium that overshadows sensory deficits (Boiten and Lodder 1989; Koponen et al. 1989a; Mesulam et al. 1976; Price and Mesulam 1985). Infarctions distributed in the right middle cerebral artery produce fewer localizing neurologic signs when they are accompanied by agitated delirium (Schmidley and Messing 1984). Lesions of the fusiform region may be associated with an acute, agitated delirium accompanied by visual impairment (Horenstein et al. 1967; Medina et al. 1974, 1977). Despite their posterior location, lesions in this basal temporal region also may affect functions of the prefrontal cortex via temporal-limbic-frontal pathways.

The thalamus is uniquely positioned to filter, integrate, and regulate information among the brain stem, cortex, and subcortex. The anterior, medial, and dorsal thalamic nuclei have important interconnections with prefrontal, subcortical, and limbic areas that are involved in cognitive and behavioral functions. Because the thalamus is extensively and reciprocally interconnected with all areas of the cerebral cortex, a relatively small thalamic lesion can cause delirium. The thalamus is rich in GABA-ergic interneurons and glutamatergic neurons (Sherman and Kock 1990) and receives cholinergic, noradrenergic, and serotonergic afferents from brainstem nuclei. Muscarinic influences at the thalamus affect baseline electroencephalographic rhythm. Strokes in the right paramedian and anteromedial thalamus (Bogousslavsky et al. 1988; Friedman 1985; Santamaria et al. 1984) can cause delirium.

Basal ganglia lesions are also associated with delirium. Preexisting lesions of the caudate nucleus (Figiel et al. 1989; Martin et al. 1992) and Parkinson's disease (Figiel et al. 1991) increase the risk of delirium during electroconvulsive therapy and with the use of tricyclic antidepressants. From a study of delirium incidence among 175 consecutive dementia patients, Robertsson et al. (1998) concluded that subcortical damage increased delirium risk and that patients with vascular dementia were more at risk than were those with early Alzheimer's or frontotemporal dementia.

A retrospective study of 661 stroke patients found 33% to be acutely confused on presentation (Dunne et al. 1986). The 19 patients diagnosed as having delirium almost exclusively had right-sided temporoparietal cortex lesions, although another 26 patients with similar lesions were not classified as having delirium because they lacked "clouded consciousness," which likely underdiagnosed the frequency of delirium associated with such lesions. A retrospective study of 309 neurology consultations found 60 patients with acute confusional state; those with focal lesions had mostly right temporal or parietal locations (Mullaly et al. 1982).

There are a few prospective studies of stroke location and delirium incidence. Using DSM-IV criteria and a DRS score of 10 or more points to define cases, 202 consecutive stroke patients had a 25% incidence of delirium (Henon et al. 1999). Right-sided superficial cortical lesions were more associated with delirium than were left-sided lesions ($P = 0.009$), whereas deep lesions did not show laterality. Computed tomographic scans for 69 consecutively admitted delirious (DSM-III diagnosis) elderly patients, many of whom had comorbid dementia, were compared with 31 age-matched control subjects with other neurological disorders (Koponen et al. 1989a). Delirious patients had more generalized atrophy and focal changes, in particular right hemisphere lesions in the parieto-occipital association area. Using DSM-III-R criteria, 48% of 155 consecutive stroke patients were acutely confused (Gustafson et al. 1991b). Among these, more patients with left-sided lesions were confused (58%) than those with right-sided lesions (38%), although the study was not designed to assess effects of laterality. Thus, many patients with strokes can become delirious, through a variety of chemical or structural mechanisms—for example, glutamatergic surges and cholinergic deficiency—but the majority of evidence supports laterality for cortical and thalamic lesions.

Findings from single photon emission computed tomography (SPECT) and positron emission tomography (PET) scans also support the relevance of the prefrontal cortex and subcortical regions in patients with delirium (Trzepacz 1994a). These tests usually show reduced flow or metabolism in the frontal cortex and either increased or decreased flow in subcortical regions. Dysfunction in both cortical and subcortical regions in delirium is also supported by slowing of EEG and evoked potentials (see Electroencephalography above, in this chapter).

## Neurotransmission

A final common neural pathway for delirium could have neuroanatomical and neurochemical components. The predominance of evidence in the literature supports a low cholinergic excess dopaminergic state in this final common neural theory (Trzepacz 1996a, 2000). Although other neurotransmitter systems are known to be involved for certain etiologies (e.g., hepatic insufficiency or alcohol withdrawal deliria), the activity of cholinergic and dopaminergic pathways can be regulated and affected by these neurotransmitters, including serotoninergic, opiatergic, GABAergic, and glutamatergic systems. Thus, alterations of these other neurotransmitters may interact with the final common pathway to produce delirium.

Neurotransmission may be altered in many ways, including through widespread effects on oxidative metabolism. Metabolic pathways for the oxidation of glucose involve oxygen, vitamins (cofactors for enzymes), and substrates related to neurotransmission (e.g., amino acids and acetyl coenzyme A). During severe illness, surgery, and trauma, ratios of plasma amino acids may affect synthesis in the brain of neurotransmitters that are associated with immune activation and adaptive metabolic changes that redirect energy consumption (van der Mast and Fekkes 2000).

Whereas some etiologies of delirium alter neurotransmission via general metabolism, others may antagonize or interfere with specific receptors and transmitters. There is evidence for both specific and widespread effects on neurotransmission in delirium. In addition to changes in major neurotransmitter systems, neurotoxic metabolites, such as quinolinic acid from tryptophan metabolism (Basile et al. 1995), and false transmitters, such as octopamine in patients with liver failure, can alter neurotransmission and also have been implicated in the neuropathogenesis of delirium. Because glia regulate neurotransmitter amounts in the synapse, glial dysfunction may also be involved.

A wide variety of medications and their metabolites have anticholinergic activity and cause delirium. Some act postsynaptically; others act presynaptically; and still others, such as norfentanyl and normeperidine, have anticholinergic metabolites (Coffman and Dilsaver 1988). Tune et al. (1992) studied and measured the anticholinergic activity of many medications in "atropine equivalents." They identified medications usually not recognized as being anticholinergic (e.g., digoxin, nifedipine, cimetidine, and codeine). However, the assay used did not discriminate among the muscarinic receptor subtypes, activity at which can result in opposite effects in the brain depending on location in the synapse. Delirium induced by anticholinergic drugs is associated with generalized electroencephalographic slowing and is reversed by treatment with physostigmine or neuroleptics (Itil and Fink 1966; Stern 1983). Centrally active anticholinergic agents can cause electroencephalographic slowing and reduced verbal memory (Sloan et al. 1992).

A rat model of delirium using a range of atropine doses demonstrated similar features as human delirium: cognitive impairment, electroencephalographic slowing, and hyperactivity during objective motor monitoring (Leavitt et al. 1994; Trzepacz et al. 1992). A different rat model using lower atropine doses showed cognitive impairment, but because EEGs were not recorded, intoxication but not delirium per se was shown (O'Hare et al. 1997).

In addition, several medical conditions have anticholinergic effects, including thiamine deficiency, hypoxia, and hypoglycemia, all of which may reduce acetylcholine by affecting the oxidative metabolism of glucose and the production of acetyl coenzyme A, the rate-limiting step for acetylcholine synthesis (Trzepacz 1994a, 1996a). Consistent with these findings, glucose has been shown to enhance memory performance via a CNS muscarinic mechanism (Kopf and Baratti 1994). Parietal cortex levels of choline are reduced in chronic hepatic encephalopathy, as measured by magnetic resonance imaging (MRI) spectroscopy (Kreis et al. 1991).

Serum levels of anticholinergic activity are elevated in patients with postoperative delirium and correlate with severity of cognitive impairment (Tune et al. 1981), improving with resolution of the delirium (Mach et al. 1995). Post–electroconvulsive therapy delirium is also associated with higher serum anticholinergic levels (Mondimore et al. 1983). High serum anticholinergic activity levels were associated with reduced self-care ability among nursing home patients (Rovner et al. 1988). A double-blind intervention study in a nursing home showed that reduction of anticholinergic drugs improved cognitive status in those who had had elevated serum anticholinergic levels (Tollefson et al. 1991).

Alzheimer's and vascular dementias reduce cholinergic activity and are associated with increased risk for delirium. Lewy body dementia mimics delirium with its fluctuating symptom severity, confusion, hallucinations (especially visual), delusions, and electroencephalographic slowing and is associated with significant loss of cholinergic nucleus basalis neurons. Its delirium symptoms respond to donepezil (Kaufer et al. 1998). Age-associated changes in cholinergic function also increase delirium propensity.

Stroke and traumatic brain injury are associated with decreased cholinergic activity—especially in the thalamus, amygdala, frontal cortex, hippocampus, and basal forebrain (Yamamoto et al. 1988)—and with increased vulnerability to antimuscarinic drugs (Dixon et al. 1994). The low cholinergic state seems to correlate temporally with delirium following the acute event. Thus, there is broad support for an anticholinergic mechanism for many seemingly diverse mechanisms of delirium.

On the other hand, cholinergic toxicity from organophosphate insecticides, nerve poisons, and tacrine (Trzepacz et al. 1996) can also cause delirium, although this is not as well described as anticholinergic delirium. Perhaps delirium results from extreme imbalances of cholinergic neurotransmitter activity levels.

Increased dopamine activity may occur as a result of reduced cholinergic activity, conceptualized as an imbalance of the activities of dopamine and acetylcholine relative to each other. Hypoxia is associated with increased release of dopamine while decreasing the release of acetylcholine (Broderick and Gibson 1989). In striatum, $D_2$ receptor stimulation reduces acetylcholine release, whereas $D_1$ stimulation increases it (Ikarashi et al. 1997).

Delirium can occur from intoxication with dopaminergic drugs, including levodopa, dopamine, and bupropion (Ames et al. 1992), and from cocaine binges (Wetli et al. 1996). Patients with alcohol withdrawal delirium are more likely to have the A-9 allele of the dopamine transporter gene compared with matched control subjects without delirium (Sander et al. 1997), suggesting a role for dopamine in delirium propensity. Delirium from opiates may be mediated by increased dopamine and glutamate activity in addition to decreased acetylcholine. Hypoxia increases the release of dopamine (Broderick and Gibson 1989), in addition to decreasing acetylcholine (Gibson et al. 1975). Excess dopamine levels occur during hepatic encephalopathy, presumably owing to increased levels of tyrosine and phenylalanine in CSF (Knell et al. 1974) or to changes in dopamine regulation by altered serotonin activity. Dopamine agonists (active at $D_1$ and $D_2$ receptors) have been shown to cause electroencephalographic slowing and behavioral arousal in rats (Ongini et al. 1985), findings similar to those seen in rats treated with atropine (Leavitt et al. 1994; Trzepacz et al. 1992). A rat model for delirium using apomorphine (a direct $D_1$ and $D_2$ agonist) in a choice reaction task showed reversal of performance deficits by administration of haloperidol and aniracetam, a cholinomimetic, but not by administration of tacrine, which worsened them (K. Nakamura et al. 1998). The investigators concluded that cognitive deficits were mediated by a $D_2$ mechanism, but because EEGs were not recorded, it is not clear if this could be a delirium animal model.

Little is known about which dopamine receptor subtypes are involved in the neuropathogenesis of delirium, although those related to mesolimbic and mesofrontal dopaminergic pathways are probably involved. Antidopaminergic agents, particularly neuroleptics, can be successfully used to treat delirium, including that arising from anticholinergic causes (Itil and Fink 1966; Platt et al. 1994a). Traditional neuroleptics that are effective in treating delirium are not subtype specific; haloperidol predominantly affects $D_2$ receptors, although it also affects $D_1$, $D_3$, and $D_4$ receptors (Piercey et al. 1995). Use of selective dopamine antagonists might shed light on the mechanism underlying delirium. For example, differential effects on $D_1$, $D_2$, and $D_3$ receptors might

underlie different motoric presentations during an individual delirium episode (Trzepacz 2000).

Both increased and decreased GABA have been implicated in causing delirium. Increased GABAergic activity, in addition to reduced glutamate and increased serotonin activity, is one of several putative mechanisms implicated in hepatic encephalopathy (Mousseau and Butterworth 1994). Increased GABA activity may result from elevated ammonia levels, which increase levels of glutamate and glutamine, which are then converted into GABA (B. Anderson 1984; Schafer and Jones 1982). Consistent with this hypothesis is the improvement observed in some patients with hepatic encephalopathy using flumazenil, which blocks $GABA_A$-benzodiazepine receptors. Glutamine levels have been shown to be elevated in hepatic encephalopathy as measured by MRI spectroscopy, although the chemical relationships among glutamine, GABA, and glutamate confound the meaning of this measurement (Kreis et al. 1991). Reduced GABA activity occurs during delirium due to withdrawal from ethanol and sedative-hypnotic drugs. Decreased GABA activity is also implicated in the mechanism of antibiotic delirium caused by penicillins, cephalosporins, and quinolones (Akaike et al. 1991; Mathers 1987).

Both low and excessive levels of serotonin are associated with delirium (van der Mast and Fekkes 2000). Serotonin activity may be increased in patients with hepatic encephalopathy—related to increased tryptophan uptake in the brain (Mousseau and Butterworth 1994; van der Mast and Fekkes 2000)—as well as in sepsis (Mizock et al. 1990) and serotoninergic syndromes (R.J. Goldberg and Huk 1992). The precursor of serotonin, tryptophan, is also implicated in delirium. Increases in free tryptophan levels in plasma correlate with reductions in cerebral blood flow on xenon computed tomographic scans in patients with subclinical hepatic encephalopathy (Rodriguez et al. 1987), and $l$-5-hydroxytryptophan induces delirium (Irwin et al. 1986). In contrast, tryptophan is decreased in patients with postcardiotomy delirium (van der Mast et al. 1994). Serotonin regulates dopamine activity in some brain regions, including the striatum and limbic system (Meltzer 1993), which may explain why neuroleptics are useful in treating serotonergic deliria.

Histamine may play a role in delirium through its effects on arousal and hypothalamic regulation of sleep-wake circadian rhythms. $H_1$ agonists and $H_3$ antagonists increase wakefulness (Monti 1993), whereas antihistamines ($H_1$ antagonists) reduce arousal and are associated with rapid eye movement (REM) sleep (Marzanatti et al. 1989) and delirium (Tejera et al. 1994). $H_1$ antagonists increase catechols and serotonin levels and have anticholinergic properties (Jones et al. 1986), possibly mediating delirium. H$_2$ antagonists also cause delirium, possibly related to their anticholinergic properties (Picotte-Prillmayer et al. 1995), although they do not affect brain sleep centers.

Glutamate release is increased during hypoxia, and glutamatergic receptors may be activated by quinolone antibiotics (Williams and Helton 1991). Activation of glutamatergic receptors is a possible mechanism for quinolones causing delirium. Dopamine and glutamate are both neurotransmitters at the thalamus, a region potentially important in the neuropathogenesis of delirium.

Cytokines have been implicated as causes of inflammatory or infectious-induced delirium, and they also may have a role in sleep (Moldofsky et al. 1986). They are polypeptide hormones secreted in the CNS by glia and macrophages, whose normally low extracellular levels are increased during stress, rapid growth, inflammation, tumor, trauma, and infection (Hopkins and Rothwell 1995; Rothwell and Hopkins 1995; Stefano et al. 1994). Although cytokines not yet identified as neurotransmitters per se, they may influence the activities of catecholamines, indolamines, GABA, and acetylcholine (Rothwell and Hopkins 1995) and cause increased release and turnover of dopamine and norepinephrine (Stefano et al. 1994), thereby causing delirium. Cytokines acting as neurotoxins, as in HIV dementia, is another mechanism for causing brain dysfunction (Lipton and Gendelman 1995).

## Conclusions

Delirium is a common neuropsychiatric disorder affecting cognition, thinking, perception, sleep, language, and other behaviors. It is associated with an increased mortality rate, the attribution of which to delirium itself or underlying medical problems is unclear. It affects persons of any age, although elderly patients may be particularly vulnerable, especially if demented. Research on delirium in children is sorely needed. The assessment of delirium can be aided through the use of diagnostic criteria and rating scales, as well as knowledge of which populations are at risk.

Certain symptoms of delirium may represent "core" symptoms, whereas others may be associated symptoms that occur under certain conditions. Core symptoms may reflect dysfunction of certain brain regions and neurotransmitter systems that constitute a "final common neural pathway" that is responsible for the presentation of the syndrome of delirium. Regions implicated include prefrontal cortex, thalamus, basal ganglia, right temporoparietal cortex, and fusiform and lingual gyri. A diversity of physiologies related to the wide variety of etiologies may funnel into a common neurofunctional expression for delirium via elevated brain dopaminergic and reduced cholinergic activity, or a relative imbalance of these. Other neurochemical candidates include serotonin, GABA, and glutamate, although these may interact to regulate and alter activity of acetylcholine and dopamine.

The clinical standard of treatment involves a dopamine antagonist medication—usually haloperidol—although, theoretically, procholinergic drugs should help. There is a dearth of drug treatment studies for delirium, in particular double-blind, and there are none with placebo controls. Newer agents deserve more study as well. It is important to initiate treatment even before medical causes have been rectified, for both hypoactive and hyperactive psychomotoric subtypes.

## References

Adams F: Neuropsychiatric evaluation and treatment of delirium in the critically ill cancer patient. Cancer Bulletin 36:156–160, 1984

Adams F: Emergency intravenous sedation of the delirious medically ill patient. J Clin Psychiatry 49 (suppl):22–26, 1988

Akaike N, Shirasaki T, Yakushiji T: Quinolone and fenbufen interact with GABA-A receptors in dissociated hippocampal cells of rats. J Neurophysiol 66:497–504, 1991

American Psychiatric Association: Diagnostic and Statistical Manual: Mental Disorders. Washington, DC, American Psychiatric Association, 1952

American Psychiatric Association: Diagnostic and Statistical Manual of Mental Disorders, 2nd Edition. Washington, DC, American Psychiatric Association, 1968

American Psychiatric Association: Diagnostic and Statistical Manual of Mental Disorders, 3rd Edition. Washington, DC, American Psychiatric Association, 1980

American Psychiatric Association: Diagnostic and Statistical Manual of Mental Disorders, 3rd Edition, Revised. Washington, DC, American Psychiatric Association, 1987

American Psychiatric Association: Diagnostic and Statistical Manual of Mental Disorders, 4th Edition. Washington, DC, American Psychiatric Association, 1994

American Psychiatric Association: Practice guidelines for treatment of patients with Alzheimer's disease and other dementias of late life. Am J Psychiatry 154 (suppl):1–39, 1997

American Psychiatric Association: Practice guidelines for the treatment of patients with delirium. Am J Psychiatry 156 (suppl):1–20, 1999

American Psychiatric Association: Diagnostic and Statistical Manual of Mental Disorders, 4th Edition, Text Revision Washington, DC, American Psychiatric Association, 2000

Ames D, Wirshing WC, Szuba MP: Organic mental disorders associated with bupropion in three patients. J Clin Psychiatry 53:53–55, 1992

Anderson B: A proposed theory for the encephalopathies of Reye's syndrome and hepatic encephalopathy. Med Hypotheses 15:415–420, 1984

Anderson SD: Treatment of elderly patients with delirium. Canadian Medical Association Journal 152:323–324, 1995

Andreasen NJC, Hartford CE, Knott JR, et al: EEG changes associated with burn delirium. Diseases of the Nervous System 38:27–31, 1977

Armstrong DH, Dasts JF, Reilly TE, et al: Effect of haloperidol on dopamine-induced increase in renal blood flow. Drug Intelligence and Clinical Pharmacy 20:543–546, 1986

Bartlett EJ, Brodie JD, Simkowitz P, et al: Effects of haloperidol challenge on regional cerebral glucose utilization in normal human subjects. Am J Psychiatry 151:681–686, 1994

Basile AS, Saito K, Li Y, et al: The relationship between plasma and brain quinolinic acid levels and the severity of hepatic encephalopathy in animal models of fulminant hepatic failure. J Neurochem 64:2607–2614, 1995

Bayinder O, Akpinar B, Can E, et al: The use of the 5-HT$_3$ antagonist odansetron for the treatment of post-cardiotomy delirium. Journal of Cardiothoracic Vascular Anesthesia 14:288–292, 2000

Bedford PD: General medical aspects of confusional states in elderly people. BMJ 2:185–188, 1957

Berggren D, Gustafson Y, Eriksson B, et al: Postoperative confusion following anesthesia in elderly patients treated for femoral neck fractures. Anesth Analg 66:497–504, 1987

Bettin KM, Maletta GJ, Dysken MW, et al: Measuring delirium severity in older general hospital inpatients without dementia. Am J Geriatr Psychiatry 6:296–301, 1998

Blumberg HP, Stern E, Ricketts S, et al: Rostral orbitofrontal prefrontal cortex dysfunction in the manic state of bipolar disorder. Am J Psychiatry 156:1986–1988, 1999

Bogousslavsky J, Ferranzzini M, Regli F, et al: Manic delirium and frontal-like syndrome with paramedian infarction of the right thalamus. J Neurol Neurosurg Psychiatry 51:116–119, 1988

Boiten J, Lodder J: An unusual sequela of a frequently occurring neurologic disorder: delirium caused by brain infarct. Ned Tijdschr Geneeskd 133:617–620, 1989

Brauer C, Morrison S, Silberzweig SB, et al: The cause of delirium in patients with hip fracture. Arch Intern Med 160:1856–1860, 2000

Breitbart W: Consecutive case series of olanzapine treatment of delirium. Symposium presented at the annual meeting of the Academy of Psychosomatic Medicine, Palm Springs, CA, November 2000

Breitbart W, Marotta R, Platt MM, et al: A double-blind trial of haloperidol, chlorpromazine, and lorazepam in the treatment of delirium in hospitalized AIDS patients. Am J Psychiatry 153:231–237, 1996

Breitbart W, Rosenfeld B, Roth A, et al: The Memorial Delirium Assessment Scale. J Pain Symptom Manage 13:128–137, 1997

Broderick PA, Gibson GE: Dopamine and serotonin in rat striatum during in vivo hypoxic-hypoxia. Metab Brain Dis 4:143–153, 1989

Brown RL, Henke A, Greenhalgh DG, et al: The use of haloperidol in the agitated, critically ill pediatric patient with burns. J Burn Care Rehabil 17:34–38, 1996

Brown TM: Drug-induced delirium. Semin Clin Neuropsychiatry 5:113–125, 2000

Burke WJ, Roccaforte WH, Wengel SP: Treating visual hallucinations with donepezil. Am J Psychiatry 156:1117–1118, 1999

Cameron DJ, Thomas RI, Mulvihill M, et al: Delirium: a test of DSM-III criteria on medical inpatients. J Am Geriatr Soc 35:1007–1010, 1987

Camus V, Burtin B, Simeone I, et al: Factor analysis supports evidence of existing hyperactive and hypoactive subtypes of delirium. Int J Geriatr Psychiatry 115:313–316, 2000a

Camus V, Gonthier R, Dubos G, et al: Etiologic and outcome profiles in hypoactive and hyperactive subtypes of delirium. J Geriatr Psychiatry Neurol 13:38–42, 2000b

Chedru F, Geschwind N: Writing disturbances in acute confusional states. Neuropsychologia 10:343–353, 1972

Chen B, Cardasis W: Delirium induced by lithium and risperidone combination. Am J Psychiatry 153:1233–1234, 1996

Coffman JA, Dilsaver SC: Cholinergic mechanisms in delirium. Am J Psychiatry 145:382–383, 1988

Cole MG, Primeau FJ: Prognosis of delirium in elderly hospital patients. Canadian Medical Association Journal 149:41–46, 1993

Cole MG, Primean FJ, Bailey RF, et al: Systematic intervention for elderly inpatients with delirium: a randomized trial. Can Med Assoc J 151:965–970, 1994

Cutting J: The phenomenology of acute organic psychosis: comparison with acute schizophrenia. Br J Psychiatry 151:324–332, 1987

Czekalla J, Beasley CM Jr, Dellva MA, et al: Analysis of the QTc interval during olanzapine treatment of patients with schizophrenia and related psychoses. J Clin Psychiatry 62:191–198, 2001

Dickson LR: Hypoalbuminemia in delirium. Psychosomatics 32:317–323, 1991

Dixon CE, Hamm RJ, Taft WC, et al: Increased anticholinergic sensitivity following closed skull impact and controlled cortical impact traumatic brain injury in the rat. J Neurotrauma 11:275–287, 1994

Drake ME, Coffey CE: Complex partial status epilepticus simulating psychogenic unresponsiveness. Am J Psychiatry 140:800–801, 1983

Dudley DL, Rowlett DB, Loebel PJ: Emergency use of intravenous haloperidol. Gen Hosp Psychiatry 1:240–246, 1979

Dunne JW, Leedman PJ, Edis RH: Inobvious stroke: a cause of delirium and dementia. Aust N Z J Med 16:771–778, 1986

Ely EW, Gordan S, Francis J, et al: Evaluation of delirium in critically ill patients: validation of the Confusion Assessment Method for the intensive care unit (CAM-ICU). Crit Care Med 29:1370–1379, 2001

Engel GL, Romano J: Delirium, II: reversibility of electroencephalogram with experimental procedures. Archives of Neurological Psychiatry 51:378–392, 1944

Engel GL, Romano J: Delirium, a syndrome of cerebral insufficiency. Journal of Chronic Disease 9:260–277, 1959

Erkinjuntti T, Wikstrom J, Parlo J, et al: Dementia among medical inpatients: evaluation of 2000 consecutive admissions. Arch Intern Med 146:1923–1926, 1986

Ewert J, Levin HS, Watson MG, et al: Procedural memory during posttraumatic amnesia in survivors of severe closed head injury: implications for rehabilitation. Arch Neurol 46:911–916, 1985

Fanjiang G, Folstein MF: The three-item delirium scale (abstract). Psychosomatics 42:172, 2001

Fann JR: The epidemiology of delirium: a review of studies and methodological issues. Semin Clin Neuropsychiatry 5:86–92, 2000

Fernandez F, Holmes VF, Adams F, et al: Treatment of severe, refractory agitation with a haloperidol drip. J Clin Psychiatry 49:239–241, 1988

Fernandez F, Levy JK, Mansell PWA: Management of delirium in terminally ill AIDS patients. Int J Psychiatry Med 19:165–172, 1989

Figiel GS, Krishman KR, Breitner JC, et al: Radiologic correlates of antidepressant-induced delirium: the possible significance of basal ganglia lesions. J Neuropsychiatry Clin Neurosci 1:188–190, 1989

Figiel GS, Hassen MA, Zorumski C, et al: ECT-induced delirium in depressed patients with Parkinson's disease. J Neuropsychiatry Clin Neurosci 3:405–411, 1991

Foley CM, Polinsky MS, Gruskin AB, et al: Encephalopathy in infants and children with chronic renal disease. Arch Neurol 38:656–658, 1981

Folstein MF, Folstein SE, McHugh PR: Mini-Mental State: a practical method for grading the cognitive state of patients for the clinician. J Psychiatr Res 12:189–198, 1975

Forman LJ, Cavalieri TA, Galski T, et al: Occurrence and impact of suspected delirium in hospitalized elderly patients. J Am Osteopath Assoc 95:588–591, 1995

Frances J: Sensory and environmental factors in delirium. Paper presented at Delirium: Current Advancements in Diagnosis, Treatment and Research, Geriatric Research, Education, and Clinical Center (GRECC), Veterans Administration Medical Center, Minneapolis, MN, September 13–14, 1993

Francis J, Kapoor WN: Prognosis after hospital discharge of older medical patients with delirium. J Am Geriatr Soc 40:601–606, 1992

Francis J, Martin D, Kapoor WN: A prospective study of delirium in hospitalized elderly. JAMA 263:1097–1101, 1990

Friedman JH: Syndrome of diffuse encephalopathy due to nondominant thalamic infarction. Neurology 35:1524–1526, 1985

Frye MA, Coudreaut MF, Hakeman SM, et al: Continuous droperidol infusion for management of agitated delirium in an ICU. Psychosomatics 36:301–305, 1995

Gaertner HJ, Fischer E, Hoss J: Side effects of clozapine. Psychopharmacology 99:S97–S100, 1989

Gelfand SB, Indelicato J, Benjamin J: Using intravenous haloperidol to control delirium (abstract). Hospital and Community Psychiatry 43:215, 1992

George J, Bleasdale S, Singleton SJ: Causes and prognosis of delirium in elderly patients admitted to a district general hospital. Age Ageing 26:423–427, 1997

Gibson GE, Jope R, Blass JP: Decreased synthesis of acetylcholine accompanying impaired oxidation of pyruvate in rat brain slices. Biochem J 26:17–23, 1975

Glick SD, Ross DA, Hough LB: Lateral asymmetry of neurotransmitters in human brain. Brain Res 234:53–63, 1982

Goldberg EL: Lateralization of frontal lobe functions and cognitive novelty. J Neurospychiatry Clin Neurosci 6:371–378, 1998

Goldberg RJ, Huk M: Serotonergic syndrome from trazodone and buspirone (letter). Psychosomatics 33:235–236, 1992

Gustafson Y, Berggren D, Brahnstrom B, et al: Acute confusional states in elderly patients treated for femoral neck fracture. J Am Geriatr Soc 36:525–530, 1988

Gustafson Y, Brannstrom B, Norberg A, et al: Underdiagnosis and poor documentation of acute confusional states in the elderly hip fracture patient. J Am Geriatr Soc 39:760–765, 1991a

Gustafson Y, Olsson T, Eriksson S, et al: Acute confusional state (delirium) in stroke patients. Cerebrovasc Dis 1:257–264, 1991b

Hales RE, Polly S, Orman D: An evaluation of patients who received an organic mental disorder diagnosis on a psychiatric consultation-liaison service. Gen Hosp Psychiatry 11:88–94, 1988

Hart RP, Levenson JL, Sessler CN, et al: Validation of a cognitive test for delirium in medical ICU patients. Psychosomatics 37:533–546, 1996

Hart RP, Best AM, Sessler CN, et al: Abbreviated Cognitive Test for Delirium. J Psychosom Res 43:417–423, 1997

Hatta K, Takahashi T, Nakamura H, et al: The association between intravenous haloperidol and prolonged QT interval. J Clin Psychopharmacol 21:257–261, 2001

Hemmingsen R, Vorstrup S, Clemmesen L, et al: Cerebral blood flow during delirium tremens and related clinical states studied with xenon-133 inhalation tomography. Am J Psychiatry 145:1384–1390, 1988

Henon H, Lebert F, Durieu I, et al: Confusional state in stroke. Relation to preexisting dementia, patient characteristics and outcome. Stroke 30:773–779, 1999

Henry WD, Mann AM: Diagnosis and treatment of delirium. Can Med Assoc J 93:1156–1166, 1965

Hooper JF, Minter G: Droperidol in the management of psychiatric emergencies. J Clin Psychopharmacol 3:262–263, 1983

Hopkins SJ, Rothwell NJ: Cytokines and the nervous system, I: expression and recognition. Trends Neurosci 18:83–88, 1995

Horenstein S, Chamberlin W, Conomy J: Infarction of the fusiform and calcarine regions: agitated delirium and hemianopia, in Translations of the American Neurological Association 1967, Vol 92. Edited by Yahr MD. New York, Springer, 1967, pp 85–89

Huang S-C, Tsai S-J, Chan C-H, et al: Characteristics and outcome of delirium in psychiatric inpatients. Psychiatry Clin Neurosci 52:47–50, 1998

Huyse F: Haloperidol and cardiac arrest. Lancet 2:568–569, 1988

Ikarashi Y, Takahashi A, Ishimaru H, et al: Regulation of dopamine D1 and D2 receptors on striatal acetylcholine release in rats. Brain Res Bull 43:107–115, 1997

Inouye SK, Charpentier PA: Precipitating factors for delirium in hospitalized elderly patients: predictive model and interrelationships with baseline vulnerability. JAMA 275:852–857, 1996

Inouye SK, van Dyke CH, Alessi CA, et al: Clarifying confusion: the Confusion Assessment Method. Ann Intern Med 113:941–948, 1990

Inouye SK, Viscoli CM, Horwitz RI, et al: A predictive model for delirium in hospitalized elderly medical patients based on admission characteristics. Arch Intern Med 119:474–481, 1993

Inouye SK, Rushing JT, Foreman MD, et al: Does delirium contribute to poor hospital outcome? J Gen Intern Med 13:234–242, 1998

Inouye SK, Bogardus ST, Charpentier PA, et al: A multicomponent intervention to prevent delirium in hospitalized older patients. N Engl J Med 340:669–676, 1999

Irwin M, Fuentenebro F, Marder SR, et al: L-5-Hydroxytryptophan-induced delirium. Biol Psychiatry 21:673–676, 1986

Itil T, Fink M: Anticholinergic drug-induced delirium: experimental modification, quantitative EEG, and behavioral correlations. J Nerv Ment Dis 143:492–507, 1966

Jackson SA: The epidemiology of aging, in Principles of Geriatric Medicine and Gerontology. Edited by Hazzard WR, Blass JP, Ettinger WH, et al. New York, McGraw-Hill, 1999, p 203

Jacobson SA, Jerrier S: EEG in delirium. Semin Clin Neuropsychiatry 5:86–93, 2000

Jacobson SA, Leuchter AF, Walter DO: Conventional and quantitative EEG diagnosis of delirium among the elderly. J Neurol Neurosurg Psychiatry 56:153–158, 1993a

Jacobson SA, Leuchter AF, Walter DO, et al: Serial quantitative EEG among elderly subjects with delirium. Biol Psychiatry 34:135–140, 1993b

Jitapunkul S, Pillay I, Ebrahim S: Delirium in newly admitted elderly patients: a prospective study. Quarterly Journal of Medicine 83:307–314, 1992

Johnson JC, Gottlieb GL, Sullivan E, et al: Using DSM-III criteria to diagnose delirium in elderly general medical patients. Journal of Gerontology 45:M113–M119, 1990

Johnson JC, Kerse NM, Gottlieb G, et al: Prospective versus retrospective methods of identifying patients with delirium. J Am Geriatr Soc 40:316–319, 1992

Jones J, Dougherty J, Cannon L: Diphenhydramine-induced toxic psychosis. Am J Emerg Med 4:369–371, 1986

Katz IR, Jeste DV, Mintzer JE, et al: Comparison of risperidone and placebo for psychosis and behavioral disturbances associated with dementia: a randomized double-blind trial. J Clin Psychiatry 60:107–115, 1999

Katz JA, Mahoney DH, Fernbach DJ: Human leukocyte alpha-interferon induced transient neurotoxicity in children. Invest New Drugs 6:115–120, 1988

Kaufer DI, Catt KE, Lopez OL, et al: Dementia with Lewy bodies: response of delirium-like features to donepezil. Neurology 51:1512–1513, 1998

Kennard MA, Bueding E, Wortis WB: Some biochemical and electroencephalographic changes in delirium tremens. Quarterly Journal of Studies on Alcohol 6:4–14, 1945

Kennedy JS, Zagar A, Bymaster F, et al: The central cholinergic system profile of olanzapine compared with placebo in Alzheimer's disease. International Journal of Geriatric Psychiatry (in press)

Kishi Y, Iwasaki Y, Takezawa K, et al: Delirium in critical care unit patients admitted through an emergency room. Gen Hosp Psychiatry 17:371–379, 1995

Knaus WA, Draper EA, Wagner DP, et al: APACHE II: a severity of disease classification system. Crit Care Med 13:818–829, 1985

Knell AJ, Davidson AR, Williams R, et al: Dopamine and serotonin metabolism in hepatic encephalopathy. BMJ 1:549–551, 1974

Kobayashi K, Takeuchi O, Suzuki M, et al: A retrospective study on delirium type. Japanese Journal of Psychiatry and Neurology 46:911–917, 1992

Kolbeinsson H, Jonsson A: Delirium and dementia in acute medical admissions of elderly patients in Iceland. Acta Psychiatr Scand 87:123–127, 1993

Kopf SR, Baratti CM: Memory-improving actions of glucose: involvement of a central cholinergic muscarinic mechanism. Behavioral and Neural Biology 62:237–243, 1994

Koponen H, Hurri L, Stenback U, et al: Computed tomography findings in delirium. J Nerv Ment Dis 177:226–231, 1989a

Koponen H, Partanen J, Paakkonen A, et al: EEG spectral analysis in delirium. J Neurol Neurosurg Psychiatry 52:980–985, 1989b

Koponen H, Stenbach U, Mattila E, et al: Delirium among elderly persons admitted to a psychiatric hospital: clinical course during the acute stage and one year follow-up. Acta Psychiatr Scand 79:579–585, 1989c

Koponen H, Sirvio J, Lepola U, et al: A long-term follow-up study of cerebrospinal fluid acetylcholinesterase in delirium. Eur Arch Psychiatry Clin Neurosci 243:347–351, 1994

Kreis R, Farrow N, Ross BN: Localized NMR spectroscopy in patients with chronic hepatic encephalopathy: analysis of changes in cerebral glutamine, choline, and inositols. NMR Biomed 4:109–116, 1991

Kriwisky M, Perry GY, Tarchitsky, et al: Haloperidol-induced torsades de pointes. Chest 98:482–484, 1990

Kullmann F, Hollerbach S, Holstege A, et al: Subclinical hepatic encephalopathy: the diagnostic value of evoked potentials. J Hepatol 22:101–110, 1995

Lawlor PG, Gagnon B, Mancini IL, et al: Occurrence, causes and outcome of delirium in patients with advanced cancer. Arch Intern Med 160:786–794, 2000

Lawrence KR, Nasraway SA: Conduction disturbances associated with administration of butyrophenone antipsychotics in the critically ill: a review of the literature. Pharmacotherapy 17:531–537, 1997

Leavitt M, Trzepacz PT, Ciongoli K: Rat model of delirium: atropine dose-response relationships. J Neuropsychiatry Clin Neurosci 6:279–284, 1994

Levenson JA: Should psychostimulants be used to treat delirious patients with depressed mood? (letter). J Clin Psychiatry 53:69, 1992

Levenson JL: High-dose intravenous haloperidol for agitated delirium following lung transplantation. Psychosomatics 36:66–68, 1995

Levkoff SE, Evans DA, Liptzin B, et al: Delirium: the occurrence and persistence of symptoms among elderly hospitalized patients. Arch Intern Med 152:334–340, 1992

Levkoff SE, Liptzin B, Evans D, et al: Progression and resolution of delirium in elderly patients hospitalized for acute care. Am J Geriatr Psychiatry 2:230–238, 1994

Lipowski ZJ: Delirium: Acute Confusional States. New York, Oxford University Press, 1990

Lipton SA, Gendelman HE: Dementia associated with the acquired immunodeficiency syndrome. N Engl J Med 332:934–940, 1995

Liptzin B, Levkoff SE: An empirical study of delirium subtypes. Br J Psychiatry 161:843–845, 1992

Lischke V, Behne M, Doelken P, et al: Droperidol causes a dose-dependent prolongation of the QT interval. Anesth Analg 79:983–986, 1994

Locasio JJ, Malone RP, Small AM, et al: Factors related to haloperidol response and dyskinesias in autistic children. Psychopharmacol Bull 27:119–125, 1991

Mach J, Dysken M, Kuskowski M, et al: Serum anticholinergic activity in hospitalized older persons with delirium: a preliminary study. J Am Geriatr Soc 43:491–495, 1995

Magaziner J, Simonsick EM, Kashner M, et al: Survival experience of aged hip fracture patients. Am J Public Health 79:274–278, 1989

Malone RP, Ernst M, Godfrey KA, et al: Repeated episodes of neuroleptic-related dyskinesias in autistic children. Psychopharmacol Bull 27:113–117, 1991

Manos PJ: The utility of the ten-point clock test as a screen for cognitive impairment in general hospital patients. Gen Hosp Psychiatry 19:439–444, 1997

Manos PJ, Wu R: The duration of delirium in medical and postoperative patients referred for psychiatric consultation. Ann Clin Psychiatry 9:219–225, 1997

Marcantonio ER, Goldman L, Mangione CM, et al: A clinical prediction rule for delirium after elective noncardiac surgery. JAMA 271:134–139, 1994a

Marcantonio ER, Juarez G, Goldman L, et al: The relationship of postoperative delirium with psychoactive medications. JAMA 272:1518–1522, 1994b

Martin M, Figiel G, Mattingly G, et al: ECT-induced interictal delirium in patients with a history of a CVA. J Geriatr Psychiatry Neurol 5:149–155, 1992

Marzanatti M, Monopoli A, Trampus M, et al: Effects of nonsedating histamine H-1 antagonists on EEG activity and behavior in the cat. Pharmacol Biochem Behav 32:861–866, 1989

Masand PS, Sipahimalani A: Olanzapine in the treatment of delirium. Psychosomatics 39:422–430, 1998

Mathers DA: The GABA-A receptor: new insights from single channel recording. Synapse 1:96–101, 1987

Matsuoka Y, Miyake Y, Arakaki H, et al: Clinical utility and validation of the Japanese version of the Memorial Delirium Assessment Scale in a psychogeriatric inpatient setting. Gen Hosp Psychiatry 23:36–40, 2001

McKeith I, Fairbairn A, Perry R, et al: Neuroleptic sensitivity in patients with senile dementia of Lewy body type. BMJ 305:673–678, 1992

Meagher DJ, Trzepacz PT: Delirium phenomenology illuminates pathophysiology, management and course. J Geriatr Psychiatry Neurol 11:150–157, 1998

Meagher DJ, Trzepacz PT: Motoric subtypes of delirium. Semin Clin Neuropsychiatry 5:76–86, 2000

Meagher DJ, O'Hanlon D, O'Mahony E, et al: Use of environmental strategies and psychotropic medication in the management of delirium. Br J Psychiatry 168:512–515, 1996

Medina JL, Rubino FA, Ross E: Agitated delirium caused by infarctions of the hippocampal formation and fusiform and lingual gyri. Neurology 24:1181–1183, 1974

Medina JL, Sudhansu C, Rubino FA: Syndrome of agitated delirium and visual impairment: a manifestation of medial temporo-occipital infarction. J Neurol Neurosurg Psychiatry 40:861–864, 1977

Meltzer HY: Serotonin-dopamine interactions and atypical antipsychotic drugs. Psychiatric Annals 23:193–200, 1993

Meltzer HY, O'Laughlin IA, Dai J, et al: Atypical antipsychotic drugs but not typical increased extracellular acetylcholine levels in rat medial prefrontal cortex in the absence of acetylcholinesterase inhibition. Society of Neuroscience Abstracts 25:452, 1999

Mendelson G: Pheniramine aminosalicylate overdose. Reversal of delirium and choreiform movements with tacrine treatment. Arch Neurol 34:313, 1977

Menza MA, Murray GB, Holmes VF, et al: Decreased extrapyramidal symptoms with intravenous haloperidol. J Clin Psychiatry 48:278–280, 1987

Menza MA, Murray GB, Holmes VF, et al: Controlled study of extrapyramidal reactions in the management of delirious, medically ill patients: intravenous haloperidol versus intravenous haloperidol plus benzodiazepines. Heart Lung 17:238–241, 1988

Mesulam M-M: Attention, confusional states, and neglect, in Principles of Behavioral Neurology. Edited by Mesulam M-M. Philadelphia, PA, FA Davis, 1985, pp 125–168

Mesulam M-M, Waxman SG, Geschwind N, et al: Acute confusional states with right middle cerebral artery infarction. J Neurol Neurosurg Psychiatry 39:84–89, 1979

Metzger E, Friedman R: Prolongation of the corrected QT and torsades de pointes cardiac arrhythmia associated with intravenous haloperidol in the medically ill. J Clin Psychopharmacol 13:128–132, 1993

Miller PS, Richardson JS, Jyu CA, et al: Association of low serum anticholinergic levels and cognitive impairment in elderly presurgical patients. Am J Psychiatry 145:342–345, 1988

Minagawa H, Uchitomi Y, Yamawaki S, et al: Psychiatric morbidity in terminally ill cancer patients: a prospective study. Cancer 78:1131–1137, 1996

Mizock BA, Sabelli HC, Dubin A, et al: Septic encephalopathy: evidence for altered phenylalanine metabolism and comparison with hepatic encephalopathy. Arch Intern Med 150:443–449, 1990

Moldofsky H, Lue FA, Eisen J, et al: The relationship of interleukin-1 and immune functions to sleep in humans. Psychosom Med 48:309–318, 1986

Moller JT, Cluitmans P, Rasmussen LS, et al: Long-term postoperative cognitive dysfunction in the elderly ISPOCD1 study. ISPOCD investigators. International Study of Post-Operative Cognitive Dysfunction. Lancet 351:857–861, 1998

Mondimore FM, Damlouji N, Folstein MF, et al: Post-ECT confusional states associated with elevated serum anticholinergic levels. Am J Psychiatry 140:930–931, 1983

Monette J, Galbaud du Fort G, Fung SH, et al: Evaluation of the Confusion Assessment Method (CAM) as a screening tool for delirium in the emergency room. Gen Hosp Psychiatry 23:20–25, 2001

Montgomery EA, Fenton GW, McClelland RJ, et al: Psychobiology of minor head injury. Psychosom Med 21:375–384, 1991

Monti JM: Involvement of histamine in the control of the waking state. Life Sci 53:1331–1338, 1993

Mori E, Yamadori A: Acute confusional state and acute agitated delirium. Arch Neurol 44:1139–1143, 1987

Moulaert P: Treatment of acute nonspecific delirium with IV haloperidol in surgical intensive care patients. Acta Anaesthesiol Belg 40:183–186, 1989

Mousseau DD, Butterworth RF: Current theories on the pathogenesis of hepatic encephalopathy. Proc Soc Exp Biol Med 206:329–344, 1994

Mullaly W, Huff K, Ronthal M, et al: Frequency of acute confusional states with lesions of the right hemisphere (abstract). Ann Neurol 12:113, 1982

Murphy KM: The baseline predictors and 6-month outcomes of incident delirium in nursing home residents: a study using the minimum data set. Psychosomatics 40:164–165, 1999

Murray AM, Levkoff SE, Wetle TT, et al: Acute delirium and functional decline in the hospitalized elderly patient. Journal of Gerontology 48:M181–M186, 1993

Nakamura J, Uchimura N, Yamada S, et al: The effect of mianserin hydrochloride on delirium. Human Psychopharmacology 10:289–297, 1995

Nakamura J, Uchimura N, Yamada S, et al: Does plasma free-3-methoxy-4-hydroxyphenyl(ethylene)glycol increase the delirious state? A comparison of the effects of mianserin and haloperidol on delirium. Int Clin Psychopharmacol 12:147–152, 1997a

Nakamura J, Uchimura N, Yamada S, et al: Mianersin suppositories in the treatment of post-operative delirium. Human Psychopharmacology 12:595–599, 1997b

Nakamura K, Kurasawa M, Tanaka Y: Apomorphine-induced hypoattention in rat and reversal of the choice performance impairment by aniracetam. Eur J Pharmacol 342:127–138, 1998

Nicholas LM, Lindsey BA: Delirium presenting with symptoms of depression. Psychosomatics 36:471–479, 1995

Nighoghossian N, Trouillas P, Vighetto A, et al: Spatial delirium following a right subcortical infarct with frontal deactivation. J Neurol Neurosurg Psychiatry 55:334–335, 1992

O'Brien JM, Rockwood RP, Suh KI: Haloperidol-induced torsades de pointes. Ann Pharmacother 33:1046–1050, 1999

O'Hare E, Weldon DT, Bettin K, et al: Serum anticholinergic activity and behavior following atropine sulfate administration in the rat. Pharmacol Biochem Behavior 56:151–154, 1997

O'Keeffe ST: Rating the severity of delirium: the Delirium Assessment Scale. Int J Geriatr Psychiatry 9:551–556, 1994

O'Keeffe ST: Clinical subtypes of delirium in the elderly. Dement Geriatr Cogn Disord 10:380–385, 1999

O'Keeffe ST, Gosney MA: Assessing attentiveness in older hospitalized patients: global assessment vs. test of attention. J Am Geriatr Soc 45:470–473, 1997

O'Keeffe ST, Lavan JN: Predicting delirium in elderly patients: development and validation of a risk-stratification model. Age Ageing 25:317–321, 1996

O'Keeffe S, Lavan J: The prognostic significance of delirium in older hospital patients. J Am Geriatr Soc 45:174–178, 1997

O'Keeffe ST, Lavan JN: Clinical significance of delirium subtypes in older people. Age Ageing 28:115–119, 1999

O'Keeffe ST, Tormey WP, Glasgow R, et al: Thiamine deficiency in hospitalized elderly patients. Gerontology 40:18–24, 1994

Okamato Y, Matsuoka Y, Sasaki T, et al: Trazodone in the treatment of delirium. J Clin Psychopharmacol 19:280–282, 1999

Olofsson SM, Weitzner MA, Valentine AD, et al: A retrospective study of the psychiatric management and outcome of delirium in the cancer patient. Support Care Cancer 4:351–357, 1996

Ongini E, Caporali MG, Massotti M: Stimulation of dopamine D-1 receptors by SKF 38393 induces EEG desynchronization and behavioral arousal. Life Sci 37:2327–2333, 1985

Onofrj M, Curatola L, Malatesta G, et al: Reduction of P3 latency during outcome from post-traumatic amnesia. Acta Neurol Scand 83:273–279, 1991

Owens JF, Hutelmyer CM: The effect of postoperative intervention on delirium in cardiac surgical patients. Nurs Res 31:60–62, 1982

Passik SD, Cooper M: Complicated delirium in a cancer patient successfully treated with olanzapine. J Pain Symptom Manage 17:219–223, 1999

Patten SB, Lamarre CJ: Dysgraphia (letter). Can J Psychiatry 34:746, 1989

Perrault LP, Denault AY, Carrier M, et al: Torsades de pointes secondary to intravenous haloperidol after coronary artery bypass graft surgery. Can J Anesth 47:251–254, 2000

Picotte-Prillmayer D, DiMaggio JR, Baile WF: H-2 blocker delirium. Psychosomatics 36:74–77, 1995

Piercey MF, Camacho-Ochoa M, Smith MW: Functional roles for dopamine-receptor subtypes. Clin Neuropharmacol 18:S34–S42, 1995

Platt MM, Breitbart W, Smith M, et al: Efficacy of neuroleptics for hypoactive delirium. J Neuropsychiatry Clin Neurosci 6:66–67, 1994a

Platt MM, Trautman P, Frager G, et al: Pediatric delirium: research update. Paper presented at the annual meeting of the Academy of Psychosomatic Medicine, Phoenix, AZ, November 1994b

Pompeii P, Foreman M, Rudberg MA, et al: Delirium in hospitalized older persons: outcomes and predictors. J Am Geriatr Soc 42:809–815, 1994

Posner ML, Boies SJ: Components of attention. Psychol Rev 78:391–408, 1971

Price BH, Mesulam M: Psychiatric manifestations of right hemisphere infarctions. J Nerv Ment Dis 173:610–614, 1985

Prugh DG, Wagonfeld S, Metcalf D, et al: A clinical study of delirium in children and adolescents. Psychosom Med 42:177–195, 1980

Purdon SE, Jones BDW, Stip E, et al: Neuropsychological change in early phase schizophrenia during 12 months of treatment with olanzapine, risperidone, or haloperidol. Arch Gen Psychiatry 57:249–258, 2000

Rabins PV, Folstein MF: Delirium and dementia; diagnostic criteria and fatality rates. Br J Psychiatry 140:149–153, 1982

Ravona-Springer R, Dohlberg OT, Hirschman S, et al: Delirium in elderly patients treated with risperidone: a report of three cases. J Clin Psychopharmacol 18:171–172, 1998

Reilly JG, Ayis AS, Ferrier IN, et al: $QT_c$-interval abnormalities and psychotropic drug therapy in psychiatric patients. Lancet 355:1048–1052, 2000

Resnick M, Burton BT: Droperidol versus haloperidol in the initial management of acutely agitated patients. J Clin Psychiatry 45:298–299, 1984

Reyes RL, Bhattacharyya AK, Heller D: Traumatic head injury: restlessness and agitation as prognosticators of physical and psychological improvement in patients. Arch Phys Med Rehabil 62:20–23, 1981

Riker RR, Fraser GL, Cox PM: Continuous infusion of haloperidol controls agitation in critically ill patients. Crit Care Med 22:433–440, 1994

Riker RR, Fraser GL, Richen P: Movement disorders associated with withdrawal from high-dose intravenous haloperidol therapy in delirious ICU patients. Chest 111:1778–1781, 1997

Ritchie J, Steiner W, Abrahamowicz M: Incidence of and risk factors for delirium among psychiatric patients. Psychiatric Services 47:727–730, 1996

Robertsson B: Assessment scales in delirium. Dement Geriatr Cogn Disord 10:368–379, 1999

Robertsson B, Karlsson I, Eriksson L, et al: An atypical neuroleptic drug in the treatment of behavioral disturbances and psychotic symptoms in elderly people. Dementia 7:142–146, 1996

Robertsson B, Blennow K, Gottfries CG, et al: Delirium in dementia. Int J Geriatr Psychiarty 13:49–56, 1998

Rockwood K: Acute confusion in elderly medical patients. J Am Geriatr Soc 37:150–154, 1989

Rockwood K: The occurrence and duration of symptoms in elderly patients with delirium. Journal of Gerontological Medical Science 48:M162–M166, 1993

Rockwood K, Cosway S, Stolee P, et al: Increasing the recognition of delirium in elderly patients. J Am Geriatr Soc 42:252–256, 1994

Rockwood K, Cosway S, Carver D, et al: The risk of dementia and death after delirium. Age Ageing 28:551–556, 1999

Rodriguez G, Testa R, Celle G, et al: Reduction of cerebral blood flow in subclinical hepatic encephalopathy and its correlation with plasma-free tryptophan. J Cereb Blood Flow Metab 7:768–772, 1987

Rolfson DB, McElhaney JE, Jhangri GS, et al: Validity of the Confusion Assessment Method in detecting post-operative delirium in the elderly. Int Psychogeriatr 11:431–438, 1999

Romano J, Engel GL: Delirium, I: electroencephalographic data. Archives of Neurology and Psychiatry 51:356–377, 1944

Rosenberg PB, Ahmed I, Hurwitz S: Methylphenidate in depressed medically ill patients. J Clin Psychiatry 52:263–267, 1991

Ross CA, Peyser CE, Shapiro I, et al: Delirium: phenomenologic and etiologic subtypes. Int Psychogeriatr 3:135–147, 1991

Rothwell NJ, Hopkins SJ: Cytokines and the nervous system, II: actions and mechanisms of action. Trends Neurosci 18:130–136, 1995

Rovner BW, David A, Lucas-Blaustein MJ, et al: Self-care capacity and anticholinergic drug levels in nursing home patients. Am J Psychiatry 145:107–109, 1988

Ruijs MB, Keyser A, Gabreels FJ, et al: Somatosensory evoked potentials and cognitive sequelae in children with closed head injury. Neuropediatrics 24:307–312, 1993

Ruijs MB, Gabreels FJ, Thijssen HM: The utility of electroencephalography and cerebral CT in children with mild and moderately severe closed head injuries. Neuropediatrics 25:73–77, 1994

Sandberg O, Gustafson Y, Brannstrom B, et al: Prevalence of dementia, delirium and psychiatric symptoms in various care settings for the elderly. Scandinavian Journal of Social Medicine 26:56–62, 1998

Sander T, Harms H, Podschus J, et al: Alleleic association of a dopamine transporter gene polymorphism in alcohol dependence with withdrawal seizures or delirium. Biol Psychiatry 41:299–304, 1997

Sanders KM, Stern TA: Management of delirium associated with use of the intra-aortic balloon pump. Am J Crit Care 2:371–377, 1993

Sanders KM, Murray GB, Cassem NH: High-dose intravenous haloperidol for agitated delirium in a cardiac patient on intra-aortic balloon pump. J Clin Psychopharmacol 11:146–147, 1991

Santamaria J, Blesa R, Tolosa ES: Confusional syndrome in thalamic stroke. Neurology 34:1618–1619, 1984

Schafer DF, Jones EA: Hepatic encephalopathy and the gamma-aminobutyric acid neurotransmitter system. Lancet 1:18–20, 1982

Schirazi S, Rodriguez D, Nomikos GG: Effects of typical and atypical antipsychotic drugs on acetylcholine release in the hippocampus. Society of Neuroscience Abstracts 26:2144, 2000

Schmidley JW, Messing RO: Agitated confusional states with right hemisphere infarctions. Stroke 5:883–885, 1984

Schor JD, Levkoff SE, Lipsitz LA, et al: Risk factors for delirium in hospitalized elderly. JAMA 267:827–831, 1992

Schuster P, Gabriel E, Kufferle B, et al: Reversal by physostigmine of clozapine-induced delirium. Clin Toxicology 10:437–441, 1977

Seear M, Lockitch G, Jacobson B, et al: Thiamine, riboflavin and pyridoxine deficiency in a population of critically ill children. J Pediatr 121:533–538, 1992

Sherman SM, Kock C: Thalamus, in The Synaptic Organization of the Brain, 3rd Edition. Edited by Shepherd GM. New York, Oxford University Press, 1990, pp 246–278

Sim FH, Brunet DG, Conacher GN: Quetiapine associated with acute mental status changes (letter). Can J Psychiatry 3:299, 2000

Sipahimalani A, Masand PS: Use of risperidone in delirium: case reports. Ann Clin Psychiatry 9:105–107, 1997

Sirois F: Delirium: 100 cases. Can J Psychiatry 33:375–378, 1988

Sloan EP, Fenton GW, Standage KP: Anticholinergic drug effects on quantitative EEG, visual evoked potentials, and verbal memory. Biol Psychiatry 31:600–606, 1992

Spencer EK, Kafantaris V, Padron-Gayol MV, et al: Haloperidol in schizophrenic children: early findings from a study in progress. Psychopharmacol Bull 28:183–186, 1992

Stefano GB, Bilfinger TV, Fricchione GL: The immune-neuro-link and the macrophage: post-cardiotomy delirium, HIV-associated dementia and psychiatry. Prog Neurobiol 42:475–488, 1994

Stern TA: Continuous infusion of physostigmine in anticholinergic delirium: a case report. J Clin Psychiatry 44:463–464, 1983

Stern TA: Continuous infusion of haloperidol in agitated critically ill patients. Crit Care Med 22:378–379, 1994

Sundaram M, Dostrow V: Epilepsy in the elderly. The Neurologist 1:232–239, 1995

Swenson JR, Erman M, Labelle J, et al: Extrapyramidal reactions: neuropsychiatric mimics in patients with AIDS. Gen Hosp Psychiatry 11:248–253, 1989

Tarter RE, van Thiel DH, Arria AM, et al: Impact of cirrhosis on the neuropsychological test performance of alcoholics. Alcohol Clin Exp Res 12:619–621, 1988

Teicher MH, Gold CA: Neuroleptic drugs: indications and guidelines for their rational use in children and adolescents. Journal of Child and Adolescent Psychopharmacology 1:33–56, 1990

Tejera CA, Saravay SM, Goldman E, et al: Diphenhydramine-induced delirium in elderly hospitalized patients with mild dementia. Psychosomatics 35:399–402, 1994

Tesar GE, Murray GB, Cassem NH: Use of high-dose intravenous haloperidol in the treatment of agitated cardiac patients. J Clin Psychopharmacol 5:344–347, 1985

Tesar GE, Murray GB, Cassem NH: Response to Dr. Weiden (letter). J Clin Psychopharmacol 6:375, 1986

Thomas H, Schwartz E, Petrilli R: Droperidol versus haloperidol for chemical restraint of agitated and combative patients. Ann Emerg Med 21:407–413, 1992

Thomas RI, Cameron DJ, Fahs MC: A prospective study of delirium and prolonged hospital stay. Arch Gen Psychiatry 45:937–946, 1988

Tisdale JE, Kambe JC, Chow MSS, et al: The effect of haloperidol on ventricular fibrillation threshold in pigs. Pharmacol Toxicol 69:327–329, 1991

Tollefson GD, Montagne-Clouse J, Lancaster SP: The relationship of serum anticholinergic activity to mental status performance in an elderly nursing home population. J Neuropsychiatry Clin Neurosci 3:314–319, 1991

Treloar AJ, MacDonald AJ: Outcome of delirium, I: outcome of delirium diagnosed by DSM III-R, ICD-10 and CAMDEX and derivation of the Reversible Cognitive Dysfunction Scale among acute geriatric inpatients. Int J Geriatr Psychiatry 12:609–613, 1997

Trzepacz PT: Neuropathogenesis of delirium: a need to focus our research. Psychosomatics 35:374–391, 1994a

Trzepacz PT: A review of delirium assessment instruments. Gen Hosp Psychiatry 16:397–405, 1994b

Trzepacz PT: Anticholinergic model for delirium. Semin Clin Neuropsychiatry 1:294–303, 1996a

Trzepacz PT: Delirium: advances in diagnosis, assessment, and treatment. Psychiatr Clin North Am 19:429–448, 1996b

Trzepacz PT: The Delirium Rating Scale: its use in consultation/liaison research. Psychosomatics 40:193–204, 1999a

Trzepacz PT: Update on the neuropathogenesis of delirium. Dement Geriatr Cogn Disord 10:330–334, 1999b

Trzepacz PT: Is there a final common neural pathway in delirium? focus on acetylcholine and dopamine. Semin Clin Neuropsychiatry 5:132–148, 2000

Trzepacz PT, Francis J: Low serum albumin and risk of delirium (letter). Am J Psychiatry 147:675, 1990

Trzepacz PT, Dew MA: Further analyses of the Delirium Rating Scale. Gen Hosp Psychiatry 17:75–79, 1995

Trzepacz PT, Teague GB, Lipowski ZJ: Delirium and other organic mental disorders in a general hospital. Gen Hosp Psychiatry 7:101–106, 1985

Trzepacz PT, Baker RW, Greenhouse J: A symptom rating scale for delirium. Psychiatry Res 23:89–97, 1988a

Trzepacz PT, Brenner R, Coffman G, et al: Delirium in liver transplantation candidates: discriminant analysis of multiple test variables. Biol Psychiatry 24:3–14, 1988b

Trzepacz PT, Leavitt M, Ciongoli K: An animal model for delirium. Psychosomatics 33:404–415, 1992

Trzepacz PT, Ho V, Mallavarapu H: Cholinergic delirium and neurotoxicity associated with tacrine for Alzheimer's dementia. Psychosomatics 37:299–301, 1996

Trzepacz PT, Mulsant BH, Dew MA, et al: Is delirium different when it occurs in dementia? A study using the Delirium Rating Scale. J Neuropsychiatry Clin Neurosci 10:199–204, 1998

Trzepacz PT, Mittal D, Torres R, et al: Validation of the Delirium Rating Scale–Revised-98: comparison to the Delirium Rating Scale and Cognitive Test for Delirium. J Neuropsychiatry Clin Neurosci 13:229–242, 2001

Tsutsui S, Kitamura M, Higachi H, et al: Development of postoperative delirium in relation to a room change in the general surgical unit. Surg Today 26:292–294, 1996

Tune LE, Dainloth NF, Holland A, et al: Association of postoperative delirium with raised serum levels of anticholinergic drugs. Lancet 2:651–653, 1981

Tune L, Carr S, Hoag E, et al: Anticholinergic effects of drugs commonly prescribed for the elderly: potential means for assessing risk of delirium. Am J Psychiatry 149:1393–1394, 1992

Uchiyama M, Tanaka K, Isse K, et al: Efficacy of mianserin on symptoms of delirium in the aged: an open trial study. Prog Neuropsychopharmacol Biol Psychiatry 20:651–656, 1996

Vaphiades MS, Celesia GG, Brigell MG: Positive spontaneous visual phenomena limited to the hemianopic field in lesions of central visual pathways. Neurology 47:408–417, 1996

van der Mast RC: Detecting and measuring the severity of delirium with the symptom rating scale for delirium, in Delirium After Cardiac Surgery. Thesis, Erasmus University Rotterdam, Benecke Consultants, Amsterdam, The Netherlands, 1994, pp 78–89

van der Mast RC: Pathophysiology of delirium. J Geriatr Psychiatry Neurol 11:138–146, 1998

van der Mast RC, Fekkes D: Serotonin and amino acids: partners in delirium pathophysiology? Semin Clin Neuropsychiatry 5:125–131, 2000

van der Mast RC, Fekkes D, van den Broek WW, et al: Reduced cerebral tryptophan availability as a possible cause for postcardiotomy delirium. Psychosomatics 35:195, 1994

van Hemert AM, van der Mast RC, Hengeveld MW, et al: Excess mortality in general hospital patients with delirium: a 5-year follow-up study of 519 patients seen in psychiatric consultation. J Psychosom Res 38:339–346, 1994

van Leeuwen AMH, Molders J, Sterkmans P, et al: Droperidol in acutely agitated patients: a double-blind placebo-controlled study. J Nerv Ment Dis 164:280–283, 1977

Wada Y, Yamaguchi N: Delirium in the elderly: relationship of clinical symptoms to outcome. Dementia 4:113–116, 1993

Wahlund LA, Bjorlin GA: Delirium in clinical practice: experiences from a specialized delirium ward. Dement Geriatr Cogn Disord 10:389–392, 1999

Webster R, Holroyd S: Prevalence of psychotic symptoms in delirium. Psychosomatics 41:519–522, 2000

Weddington WW: The mortality of delirium: an underappreciated problem? Psychosomatics 23:1232–1235, 1982

Wengel SP, Roccaforte WH, Burke WJ: Donepezil improves symptoms of delirium in dementia: implications for future research. J Geriatr Psychiatry Neurol 11:159–161, 1998

Wengel SP, Burke WJ, Roccaforte WH: Donepezil for postoperative delirium associated with Alzheimer's disease. J Am Geriatr Soc 47:379–380, 1999

Wetli CV, Mash D, Karch SB: Cocaine-associated agitated delirium and the neuroleptic malignant syndrome. Am J Emerg Med 14:425–428, 1996

Williams PD, Helton DR: The proconvulsive activity of quinolone antibiotics in an animal model. Toxicol Lett 58:23–28, 1991

Wilson LM: Intensive care delirium: the effect of outside deprivation in a windowless unit. Arch Intern Med 130:225–226, 1972

Wilt JL, Minnema AM, Johnson RF, et al: Torsades de pointes associated with the use of intravenous haloperidol. Ann Intern Med 119:391–394, 1993

Wolff HG, Curran D: Nature of delirium and allied states: the dysergastic reaction. Archives of Neurology and Psychiatry 33:1175–1215, 1935

World Health Organization: International Statistical Classification of Diseases and Related Health Problems, 10th Revision. Geneva, World Health Organization, 1992

Yamamoto T, Lyeth BG, Dixon CE, et al: Changes in regional brain acetylcholine content in rats following unilateral and bilateral brainstem lesions. J Neurotrauma 5:69–79, 1988

Zee-Cheng C-S, Mueller CE, Siefert CF, et al: Haloperidol and torsades de pointes (letter). Ann Intern Med 102:418, 1985

# CHAPTER 15

# Neuropsychiatric Aspects of Aphasia and Related Disorders

Mario F. Mendez, M.D., Ph.D.

Jeffrey L. Cummings, M.D.

Aphasia is the loss or impairment of language caused by brain dysfunction. Language is the unique human ability to communicate through symbols, whether these are in the form of spoken or written language, braille, musical notation, or sign language. Normal language requires the ability to decode, encode, and interrupt these symbols for the exchange of information. In aphasic patients, some or all of these language functions become disturbed, usually as a consequence of acquired brain damage in the language structures of the left hemisphere.

The aphasic syndromes disturb communication and can be severely disabling. In addition to disturbances in linguistic processing, the aphasic syndromes are associated with other neuropsychiatric manifestations. Aphasic patients are prone to psychiatric problems, including depression or paranoid ideation, cognitive abnormalities, and psychosocial challenges in adjusting to the impact of their disorder. These complications may cause more disability than the aphasia itself.

Despite interest in aphasia, clinicians have paid relatively little attention to the behavioral complications of aphasic syndromes. In some cases, aphasic disorders may be misinterpreted as the speech abnormalities associated with psychiatric diseases such as schizophrenia or depression.

## Background

Aphasia is a common manifestation of brain disease. The annual incidence of stroke in the United States is about 500,000, and about 20% of these stroke patients have aphasia or a related disorder (Pedersen et al. 1995). Dementia, intracranial neoplasms, traumatic brain injury, and many other neurological disorders can also produce language disturbances. Aphasia is particularly prominent in Alzheimer's disease, frontotemporal dementia, and the specific language degenerations known as primary progressive aphasia.

Current approaches to aphasia stem from early work on the localization of language to discrete, interconnected areas in the left hemisphere. In 1861, Paul Broca inaugurated the modern study of aphasia with his description of a patient who had lost the ability to speak and had a focal brain injury in the frontal region. This early work established the dominance of the human left hemisphere for language function and demonstrated an anterior-posterior dichotomy of language processing (Broca 1865). Later, Karl Wernicke and others described a group of specialized and interconnected language regions in the brain (Kleist 1934; Lichtheim 1885; Wernicke 1874). The two major centers for this model were Broca's area in the anterior frontal region for language production and Wernicke's area in the superior temporal gyrus for language decoding. The elaboration of this model led to a view that language functions were localized in neuroanatomic regions in the left perisylvian region (Figure 15–1).

Many prominent neuroscientists and clinicians challenged this view of localization of language functions and proposed that language is not a single, unitary function.

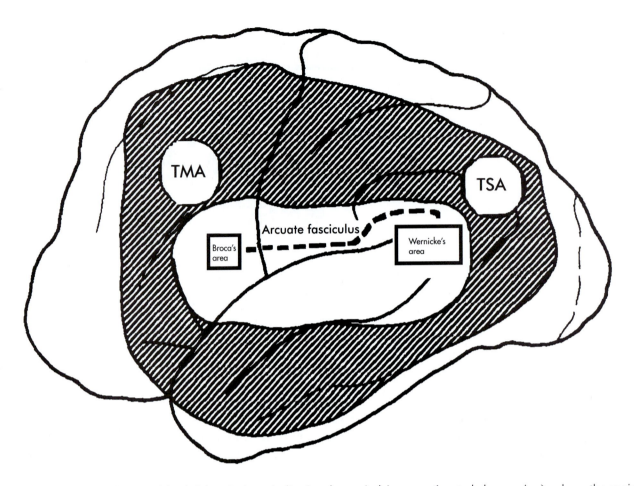

**FIGURE 15–1.**   Lateral view of the left hemisphere indicating the perisylvian area (central clear region), where the major language centers are located. Broca's area in the frontal operculum, Wernicke's area in the superior temporal gyrus, and the arcuate fasciculus are indicated. Lesions in these corresponding structures result in Broca's aphasia, Wernicke's aphasia, and conduction aphasia, respectively. These perisylvian aphasia syndromes include disturbances in the ability to repeat spoken language. Lesions in the surrounding border zone area (cross-hatched region) may result in transcortical aphasia syndromes characterized by sparing of repetition. TMA=region where a lesser lesion may result in transcortical motor aphasia; TSA=region where a lesion may result in transcortical sensory aphasia.

This holistic view reached its acme in the 1960s, with the belief in a central language area, vaguely localized to the thalamus (Bay 1964b). The original views of Broca and Wernicke were restored, however, when Norman Geschwind demonstrated that separation (disconnection) of cortical foci could produce distinct language impairments (Geschwind 1965). Investigators have since used improved clinical and laboratory studies to confirm the clinicoanatomic syndromes formulated by the nineteenth-century French and German aphasiologists. The reborn localization concept is embodied in the current Wernicke-Geschwind model of language and aphasia (Benson and Ardila 1996) (Figure 15–2).

In recent years, many disciplines have added to our understanding of aphasia (Benson and Ardila 1996; A.R. Damasio 1992). Linguists applied the analysis of elements of language (phonemes, morphemes, grammar or syntax, semantics, and pragmatics) to disorders of language. For example, Noam Chomsky's (1972) emphasis on a universal grammar further suggested a common brain substrate for language. Anatomists and others reported a larger planum temporale containing Wernicke's area in the left hemisphere in adults, in fetal brains by about 30 weeks of gestation, and in human skull imprints at least 40,000 years old. Neuropsychologists noted greater bilaterality of language in the brains of most left-handed individuals and therefore decreased value and localization of the classic aphasia syndromes in those individuals. Computer scientists clarified the parallel distributed nature of brain-behavior systems such as language. Finally, the recent advances in positron emission tomography, single photon emission computed tomography, and functional magnetic resonance imaging have expanded our view of the anatomic relationships and

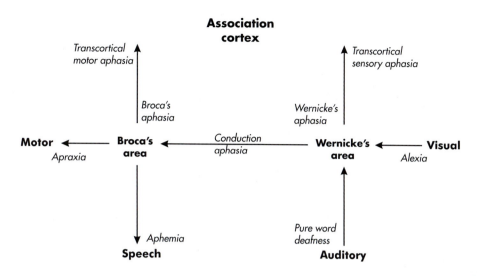

**FIGURE 15–2.** Wernicke-Geschwind model. The diagram illustrates the organization of language and corresponding aphasia syndromes in the left hemisphere. The perisylvian language region receives auditory and visual input and produces speech and motor output. Disturbances in the corresponding regions are indicated in italics. Aphemia and pure word deafness are disturbances at the prelanguage and postlanguage levels, respectively. Alexia and apraxia reflect disorders of visual language input and nonspeech motor output, respectively. Language symbols must be interpreted by relating to other associations in higher association cortex. Lesions outside the perisylvian language region may result in the transcortical aphasias, sparing the direct perisylvian pathway mediating repetition.

functional connectivity of language organization in the brain (Muller et al. 1997).

## Classification and Diagnosis of Aphasia

### The Language Examination

The syndrome classification based on the Wernicke-Geschwind model remains the core of both clinical and academic studies of aphasia. Classification of aphasia syndromes by this model requires the examination of six major language areas: 1) fluency, 2) auditory comprehension, 3) confrontational naming, 4) repetition, 5) reading (aloud and for comprehension), and 6) writing. Six additional and helpful areas of examination are 1) word-list generation, 2) automatic speech, 3) content of speech, 4) presence of language errors (paraphasias and neologisms), 5) prosody, and 6) speech mechanics. Table 15–1 presents an abridged version of this classification with the major language abnormalities, basic neurologic dysfunctions, and characteristic anatomic findings associated with each syndrome (Benson and Ardila 1996; A.R. Damasio 1992; Kertesz 1979; Kirshner 1995).

Fluency evaluation requires an assessment of the generation and ease of production of language. The examiner elicits language in spontaneous conversation, listening for sev-

eral elements of potential dysfluency. These include a decrease in the number of words generated per minute (usually fewer than 50 in English), shortened phrase length (no more than a few words per phrase), a drop-out of grammatic words such as prepositions or conjunctions (agrammatic or "telegraphic" speech), and effort or struggle in speech production. In addition, aphasic patients often have a dysarthric or poorly articulated verbal output with loss of the normal components of prosody or intonation. Often, their verbal output is brief and strained, but succinct and informative. In the assessment of fluency, it is also valuable to have the patient generate a list of words, such as animal names, in a 1-minute timed sample (normal is 12 or more). The patient's ability to produce automatic speech, such as counting numbers or reciting the days of the week, also reflects his or her ability to generate and produce language.

A second step in the language examination is an assessment of auditory comprehension. This is achieved by giving the patient simple commands or asking yes/no questions. Commands such as "close your eyes" or "open your mouth" can be escalated to more complex pointing commands such as "first touch your chin and then touch your right shoulder." The patient should be able to comprehend and follow these instructions. Additional bedside tasks include syntactically difficult questions, for example, "If a lion was killed by a tiger, which animal is dead?"

The ability to produce names is probably the most commonly impaired language function in aphasia. The

**TABLE 15–1.** Principal aphasia syndromes

| Aphasia syndrome | Fluency | Auditory comprehension | Repetition | Naming | Reading | Writing comprehension |
|---|---|---|---|---|---|---|
| Broca's | Abnormal | Relatively normal | Abnormal | Abnormal | Normal or abnormal | Abnormal |
| Wernicke's | Normal, paraphasic | Abnormal | Abnormal | Abnormal | Abnormal | Abnormal |
| Global | Abnormal | Abnormal | Abnormal | Abnormal | Abnormal | Abnormal |
| Conduction | Normal, paraphasic | Relatively normal | Abnormal | Usually abnormal | Relatively normal | Abnormal |
| Transcortical motor | Abnormal | Relatively normal | Relatively normal | Abnormal | Relatively normal | Abnormal |
| Transcortical sensory | Normal, echolalic | Abnormal | Relatively normal | Abnormal | Abnormal | Abnormal |
| Anomic | Normal | Relatively normal | Normal | Abnormal | Normal or abnormal | Normal or abnormal |

evaluation of confrontational naming requires the patient to name objects or pictures. The examiner initially asks the patient to name common items present in his or her environment, such as pen, watch, ring, tie, keys. Subsequently, the examiner asks the patient to name less common items and parts of objects, such as face of a watch, heels of shoes, cuff of sleeve.

In addition to fluency, auditory comprehension, and confrontational naming, the examiner must evaluate repetition, reading, writing, and the presence or absence of paraphasic errors. The examiner asks the patient to repeat sentences or phrases such as "no ifs, ands, or buts" and listens for the presence of literal paraphasias (language errors involving the substitution of incorrect syllables in a word). The patient must read a brief written passage aloud and is then queried for his or her comprehension of the passage. A brief written sample, preferably a sentence of their own composition and a dictated sentence, screens for agraphias or acquired writing disturbances. Finally, the examiner carefully assesses the patient's language output for paraphasic errors, not only literal but also semantic paraphasias (the substitution of an incorrect word) and neologisms (the production of "new" or made-up-sounding words).

## Syndromes of Abnormal Verbal Output

### Broca's Aphasia

Nonfluent verbal output characterizes Broca's aphasia. Spontaneous speech is sparse, effortful, dysarthric, dysprosodic, short in phrase length, and agrammatic. Decreased fluency occurs in the presence of relatively preserved comprehension (although relational words such as "above" and "behind" may be poorly understood),

abnormal repetition and naming, a disturbance in reading (particularly for relational and syntactic words), and disturbed writing. Most patients with Broca's aphasia have right-sided weakness varying from mild paresis to total hemiplegia, and some have sensory loss as well. Apraxia of the left limb and buccal-lingual apraxia are common. The neuropathology involves the left hemisphere frontal operculum containing Broca's area (Figure 15–3). If the lesion is superficial and involves only the cortex, the prognosis for improvement is good. However, if the lesion extends sufficiently deep to involve the basal ganglia and internal capsule, the language defect tends to be permanent.

### Wernicke's Aphasia

The most striking abnormality of Wernicke's aphasia is a disturbance of comprehension, which may range from a total inability to understand spoken language to a partial difficulty in decoding the spoken word. The characteristics of Wernicke's aphasia include fluent verbal output with normal word count and phrase length; no abnormal effort, articulatory problems, or prosodic difficulties; and difficulty in repetition and in word finding. The verbal output is often empty of content words and full of paraphasic substitutions and neologisms. *Jargon aphasia* refers to this output when it is extreme and unintelligible, and it must be distinguished from the "word salad" of schizophrenia (Table 15–2). Often there are no basic neurologic defects, but a superior quadrantanopsia may be present. The neuropathology involves the posterior superior temporal lobe of the left hemisphere (the auditory association cortex) and, in some cases, the primary auditory sensory area as well (Figure 15–4).

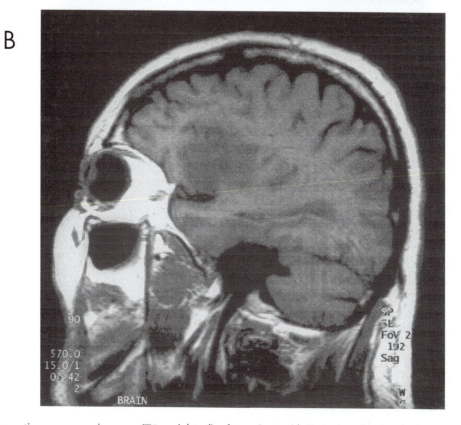

**FIGURE 15–3.** Magnetic resonance images (T1 weighted) of a patient with Broca's aphasia. The horizontal (*Panel A*) and sagittal (*Panel B*) views show a stroke involving the left inferior frontal region and encompassing Broca's area.

**TABLE 15–2.** Comparison of language characteristics for Wernicke's aphasia, delirium, schizophrenia, and mania

| | Wernicke's aphasia | Delirium | Schizophrenia | Mania |
|---|---|---|---|---|
| **Basic language** | | | | |
| Fluency | Normal | Mildly abnormal | Extended | Logorrheic |
| Comprehension | Abnormal | Variable | Intact | Normal |
| Repetition | Abnormal | Mildly abnormal | Intact | Normal |
| Naming | Abnormal | Nonaphasic | Intact | Normal |
| Reading comprehension | Abnormal | | Intact | Normal |
| Writing | Abnormal | Abnormal | Resembles spoken output | Normal |
| **Other examination** | | | | |
| Word list generation | Diminished | Abnormal | Diminished on average, bizarre | Increased |
| Automatic speech | Paraphasic | Normal | Normal, bizarre | Normal |
| Content | Empty | Incoherent | Impoverished, bizarre, restricted | Grandiose |
| Neologisms and paraphasias | Common | Absent | Rare (stable meaning) | |
| Prosody | Normal | Mildly abnormal | Mildly abnormal | Mildly abnormal |
| Motor speech | Normal | Dysarthric and incoherent | Possible clanging | Press of speech |
| **Associated features** | | | | |
| Thinking | | Confused | Special productions | Rapid, flight of ideas |
| Awareness of deficit | Present | Partial | Absent | Absent |
| Neurological examination | Possibly abnormal | Possibly abnormal | Normal | Normal |

## Conduction Aphasia

Conduction aphasia features a prominent disturbance in repetition out of proportion to any other language disturbance. Patients with conduction aphasia have fluent verbal output and a preserved ability to comprehend. Paraphasias are common, particularly substitutions of phonemes, and confrontational naming is often limited by these paraphasic intrusions. Reading aloud and writing are disturbed, but reading comprehension can be entirely normal. Apraxia of both the right and the left limb is often present, and cortical sensory loss of the left hand or the left side of the face is common. Most cases of conduction aphasia have neuropathology involving the anterior inferior parietal lobe, including the supramarginal gyrus and the arcuate fasciculus (H. Damasio and Damasio 1980), but exceptions are recognized (Mendez and Benson 1985).

## Global Aphasia

A severe language impairment in which all modalities—verbal fluency, comprehension, repetition, naming, reading, and writing—are impaired is known as *global aphasia* or *total aphasia*. Most patients have a right hemiparesis or hemiplegia, a right hemisensory deficit, and a right homonymous hemianopsia. Global aphasia is usually caused by a complete infarction in the territory of the middle cerebral artery. Exceptions are noted, however, including some in which there is global aphasia without hemiparesis due to multiple cerebral emboli to the left hemisphere.

## Transcortical Aphasias

The major factor underlying transcortical aphasias is the relative preservation of the ability to repeat spoken language in the presence of other language impairments. Transcortical motor aphasia resembles Broca's aphasia in its decreased verbal fluency but differs in the normal or nearly normal ability to repeat. Patients with this disorder present the strange picture of struggling to utter words in spontaneous conversation but of easily saying the same words on repetition.

The neuropathologic lesions underlying transcortical aphasias are most often located in the supplementary motor area of the left hemisphere or between that area and the frontal operculum. Transcortical sensory aphasia resembles Wernicke's aphasia in its fluent paraphasic out-

A

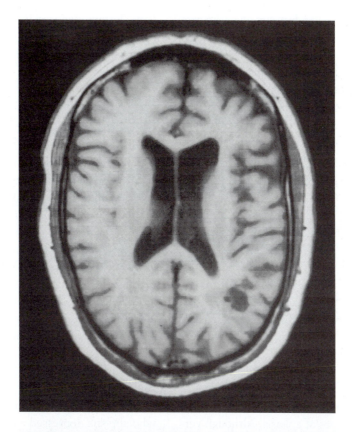

B

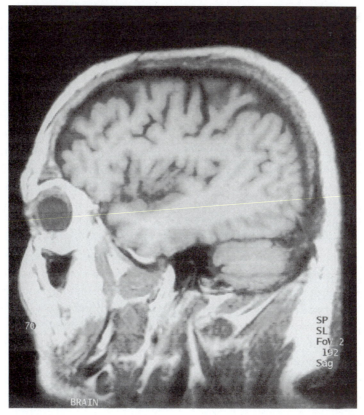

**FIGURE 15–4.** Magnetic resonance images (T1 weighted) of a patient with Wernicke's aphasia. The horizontal (*Panel A*) and sagittal (*Panel B*) views show an embolic stroke involving the left temporal lobe and encompassing Wernicke's area.

put and decreased comprehension but differs in the preserved ability to repeat. When extreme, there is a tendency to exhibit echolalia. Patients with this disorder may manifest the peculiar tendency to repeat everything that the examiner says, as if mimicking them. This tendency to echolalia can lead to the misdiagnosis of the aphasia as a factitious or primary psychiatric condition.

The most common site of neuropathology in transcortical sensory aphasia is in the angular gyrus in the left parietal region. Mixed transcortical aphasia, also known as isolation of the speech area, is the transcortical equivalent of global aphasia. Patients with this disorder may be entirely unable to speak or to comprehend language, but they are able to repeat spoken words. The neuropathology in the mixed transcortical syndrome involves the vascular border zone or watershed areas in both the frontal and parietal lobes. Some patients with transcortical aphasia have widespread pathology with involvement of the frontal lobes. In these cases, the echolalia is a manifestation of environmental dependency.

## Anomic Aphasia

Anomic aphasia is a common residual effect following improvement from other types of aphasia. Although verbal output is fluent and repetition and comprehension are intact, naming to confrontation is significantly disturbed. There are multiple word-finding pauses, a tendency to circumlocution, and a somewhat stumbling verbal output. Many individuals with anomic aphasia also have reading and writing disturbances (alexia and agraphia). There is no specific causative location, although neuropathology often involves the left hemisphere angular gyrus. Anomic aphasia has also been reported with lesions of the left temporal pole.

## Subcortical Aphasia

With the advent of brain imaging, it became apparent that predominant subcortical lesions (hemorrhage or infarction) could produce acute aphasia syndromes or variable symptomatology (Nadeau and Crosson 1997). Subcortical aphasias characteristically begin with a period of mutism followed by a period of abnormal motor speech, usually hypophonia and articulatory difficulty. As recovery ensues, patients regain much of their speech but are left with paraphasic errors. Similar to the transcortical aphasias, repetition is near normal, and comprehension, naming, reading, and writing may or may not show abnormality. If the lesion is entirely subcortical, recovery usually ensues; many individuals recover totally from the aphasia but are left with residual speech impairments. Recent studies suggest that basal ganglia or tha-

lamic lesions alone are insufficient to produce permanent aphasia and that cortical involvement is necessary to produce permanent language changes (Bhatia and Marsden 1994).

## Amelodia/Aprosodia

In addition to the classic aphasia syndromes from left-hemisphere damage, several related disturbances of communication result from right-hemisphere lesions. The right hemisphere has a dominant role for emotional features, including emotional prosodic aspects of communication (Borod 1992). Amelodia (also called affective motor aprosodia) is a disturbance characterized by loss of melody, prosody, or emotional intonation in verbal output (Ross 1981). There is a flat, monotonous verbal output, inability to produce a melody when singing (expressive amusia), decreased facial grimacing, and sparse use of gestures. The result is a seemingly emotionless response easily misinterpreted as depression.

The neuropathology of amelodia involves the right frontal opercular area or its connection, the right-hemisphere equivalent of Broca's area. Inasmuch as the causative lesion may be small and otherwise silent, the patient who appears depressed and is unable to produce melody deserves special consideration for neuroimaging. In addition, receptive amusias and other disorders of music appreciation are related disturbances predominantly associated with right-hemisphere lesions.

## Verbal Dysdecorum

Verbal dysdecorum is characterized by a decreased ability to monitor and control the content of verbal output (Alexander et al. 1989). Although language itself is not defective in verbal dysdecorum, the serious psychosocial problems caused by poorly monitored output have a neurobiological source. Individuals with verbal dysdecorum speak too freely, discuss improper topics, make snide or cruel (but often true) remarks about themselves and others, argue, and are otherwise disagreeable without realizing the social consequences of their actions. Often these patients' presenting complaint is an inability to maintain friendships, and even a short exposure to such an individual identifies the problem. Verbal dysdecorum may or may not be associated with confabulation or with physical impropriety, and it must be distinguished from manic verbal output with press of speech (see Table 15–2). Current evidence suggests a right-hemisphere frontal, probably lateral convexity, site of neuropathology (Alexander et al. 1989), although the disorder may also be seen in the disinhibition syndrome associated with orbitofrontal lesions and with right anterior temporal disorders. The most common causes of verbal dysdecorum are trauma and other focal lesions affecting the frontal lobes, and frontotemporal dementia.

## Miscellaneous Disorders

Several other disorders of communication may have neuropsychiatric manifestations. The alexias are language disturbances characterized by the inability to read and may or may not be accompanied by agraphia, the inability to write. Pure word deafness is a disturbance of language comprehension at the prelanguage level (see Figure 15–3). Aphemia is a disturbance of language production at the postlanguage level. Unless preserved language ability is demonstrated in the written modality, clinicians may mistake pure word deafness, aphemia, and even auditory agnosia for the aphasia syndromes. The apraxias, or disturbances in the execution of learned motor acts, often accompany aphasias and require the interpretation of a language command prior to the execution of a motor response. Disorders of speech, or the neuromotor aspects of verbal communication, involve not only the dysarthrias and mutism but also reiterative speech disorders such as palilalia (repetition of one's own words or phrases), acquired stuttering (repetition of syllables), and logoclonia (specific repetition of the end syllables of words). In addition, the verbal output of delirium includes incoherence and nonaphasic misnaming, and clinicians must be able to distinguish the language of delirium from jargon aphasia and the language of psychiatric disorders (see Table 15–2).

Aphasia is an integral part of the multiple cognitive deficits that characterize the dementias (Kramer and Duffy 1996). Patients with Alzheimer's disease usually progress from early word-finding difficulty to a transcortical sensory aphasia. In patients with vascular dementia, there may be a range of aphasia syndromes, given the variability in stroke location. The frontotemporal dementias, such as Pick's disease, are characterized by early verbal dysdecorum and decreased word-list generation that gradually progress to reiterative speech disturbances such as echolalia, decreased verbal output, and eventual mutism. In most other dementias, patients have decreased word-list generation and poor confrontational naming.

Asymmetric neurodegeneration of the cortex can result in a primary progressive aphasia syndrome. These language disorders usually result as prolonged asymmetric presentations of frontotemporal dementia, but they may also result from Alzheimer's disease or other dementias. There are two main types; one is progressive nonfluent aphasia, a disorder characterized by the insidious onset and progression of a loss of verbal fluency (Westbury and Bud 1997). These patients

have left inferior frontal atrophy. A second type is often described as "semantic dementia" (Hodges et al. 1992). This condition results from loss of the meaning or understanding of words. Despite apparent fluency, patients have difficulty not only in confrontational naming but also in passive naming or responding to cues. These patients may also have an agnosia, or loss of knowledge, for objects and are unable to recognize or describe their use. Semantic dementia results from disproportionate involvement of the temporal lobes. After a period of two or more years of predominant language impairment, patients with these progressive aphasia syndromes usually progress into the clinical syndrome of frontotemporal dementia, Alzheimer's disease, or some other dementing disease (Green et al. 1990).

Apraxia, agnosia, and Gerstmann's syndrome may accompany a language disorder and could contribute to the neuropsychiatric consequences of aphasia. Apraxia is an acquired impairment in learned motor movements not due to primarily motor or sensory deficits. The examination for apraxia involves asking the patient to perform learned movements such as waving good-bye and pantomiming brushing his or her teeth. If the patient fails a task, the examiner should demonstrate the movement and ask the patient to imitate it. Apraxia may result from damage to motor programs, disconnection of language from the areas for motor control, or the inability to understand concepts. The agnosias are disorders of recognition that may complicate aphasia. Agnosias may be visual or auditory or involve another modality, and they are often classified as either associative or apperceptive. Associative agnosia refers to a normal perception that is disconnected from its other associations and meanings. Apperceptive agnosia implies a problem with recognition because of subtle disturbances in perceptual processing. Finally, some patients may have Gerstsmann's syndrome from involvement of the left angular gyrus. In addition to agraphia, these patients have right-left confusion and difficulty with finger recognition ("finger agnosia"). Another component of Gerstmann's syndrome is difficulty manipulating numbers or numerical concepts ("acalculia"). All of these cognitive disturbances can contribute to the neuropsychiatric consequences of a language impairment.

## Neuropsychiatric Aspects of Aphasia

Patients with aphasias or related disorders often have neuropsychiatric disturbances that may be more debilitating than the language impairment itself. Lack of awareness of these disturbances stems in part from the fact that the language disorder interferes with communication and with the psychiatric assessment of patients. The behavioral assessment of aphasic patients through their language impairment requires a great deal of skill and expertise. In the following sections, we discuss the neuropsychiatric aspects of aphasia as psychiatric aspects, cognitive aspects, and psychosocial aspects.

## Psychiatric Aspects

Two distinct, long-term behavioral syndromes accompany aphasia syndromes. One accompanies nonfluent (anterior) aphasia, and the other appears in cases of fluent (posterior) aphasia (Benson 1973).

### Anterior Aphasia Behavioral Syndrome

Persons with Broca's aphasia or transcortical motor aphasia know exactly what they wish to say, but their verbal output is restricted and barely intelligible. This inability to explain their wishes or thoughts in other than telegraphic words can cause intense frustration. These nonfluent aphasic patients may manifest their attempts to communicate with agitated gestures and expletives.

Depression is another aspect of the anterior aphasia behavioral reaction. Nonfluent aphasic patients develop intense feelings of personal worthlessness and hopelessness. Depression is considerably more common and intense in patients with anterior aphasia than in those with posterior aphasia (Robinson 1997). This is due in part to the patient's ability to recognize the disability and the frustration of not being able to express thoughts and desires, but there are neurobiological causes for the depression as well.

The occurrence of depression correlates with acute strokes in the left prefrontal region and surrounding areas (Robinson and Szetela 1981). The depressive reaction typically starts with feelings of futility that lead to an unwillingness to participate in self-care or in rehabilitation activities. During the depressed period, aphasic patients may sink deep within themselves; stop eating; refuse social interaction with therapists, other patients, or even family members; and manifest a strong but passive noncooperation. In rare instances, the negative reaction may become intense and explosive, a catastrophic reaction (Goldstein 1948). Although the depression, frustration, and catastrophic reaction of the patient with anterior aphasia suggest a strong potential for suicide, it is rarely reported in this group.

### Posterior Aphasia Behavioral Syndrome

Most patients with posterior aphasia have difficulty comprehending spoken language and remain unaware of their deficit, producing a persistent unconcern that is pathologic. Because they are unable to monitor their own verbal output, they often fail to realize that they are producing an incomprehensible jargon. In fact, when tape recordings of such jargon have been made and then replayed immediately, many patients with posterior aphasia deny that it is their own speech. The persistent unawareness and unconcern in patients with posterior aphasia stands in sharp contrast to the frustrated, depressed condition in individuals with anterior aphasia.

Paranoia with agitation, another aspect of posterior aphasia behavioral syndrome, occurs when damage is limited to the posterior temporal lobe (Wernicke's aphasia). This feature is much less common in patients with transcortical sensory aphasia and is virtually unknown in those with anterior aphasia. Paranoid behavior is also universally present in the prelanguage disorder of pure word deafness. Unaware of their own comprehension disturbance, individuals with posterior aphasia or pure word deafness tend to blame their communication difficulties on others. They suggest that the person they are talking to is not speaking clearly or is not paying sufficient attention. Some of these patients come to believe that persons they observe talking together must be using a special code because their conversation cannot be understood. This reaction is similar to the paranoid reaction of acquired deafness, but there are also neurobiological causes for the paranoia. A paranoid reaction correlates with lesions in the left temporal lobe, suggesting that damage to this anatomic region facilitates the perception of threat.

In addition, some patients with posterior aphasia display impulsive behavior. The combination of unawareness, paranoia, and impulsiveness makes them potentially dangerous to others. Physical attacks against medical personnel, family members, or other patients can occur, particularly when the patients misinterpret the behaviors of others. Almost all aphasic patients who need custodial management because of dangerous behavior have a posterior, fluent aphasia (Benson and Geschwind 1985). Moreover, compared with patients having anterior aphasia with depression, those having posterior aphasia with both paranoia and impulsiveness tend to commit suicide more often, particularly as self-awareness of their deficit occurs.

## Cognitive Aspects

Aphasic patients often present initially with delirium followed by a period of decreased insight into the existence of their language deficit. If the brain insult is sufficiently large, the patient with aphasia is lethargic or has a clouding of consciousness from the cerebral edema, diaschisis, and other acute neuropathologic changes. After resolution of the initial delirium, in days to weeks, a more prolonged period ensues in which the aphasic patient fails to fully realize the alterations that have occurred. Although alert and responsive, the patient does not yet grasp the significance of the language defect. At this stage, the patient cannot participate rationally in plans for the future because of a decreased appreciation of reality. As previously discussed, some patients with posterior aphasia have a permanent impairment in awareness and concern, but for most, the insight that they are language impaired eventually dawns on them, sometimes rather acutely, and can lead directly to reactive depression.

Language facilitates thought. Among aphasic individuals, thinking processes are less efficient, due to language deficits. Following Bastian (1898), who declared that humans think in words, many experts have emphasized the symbolic nature of cognition and have concluded that defective use of language symbols produces defective thinking. Both Goldstein (1948) and Bay (1964a) accepted aphasia as proof that thinking was abnormal, either regressed or concrete. Furthermore, pathology of the posterior language area may be more likely than anterior damage to interfere with intellectual competency (Benson 1979).

Despite these observations, the studies of intelligence in aphasic patients have provided somewhat nebulous results (Basso et al. 1981; Hamsher 1981; Lebrun 1974; Zangwill 1964). Most aphasic patients perform poorly on standard tests of intellectual competency, sometimes in both verbal and nonverbal portions, but many retain considerable nonverbal capability. Standard IQ tests, however, emphasize language skills and thus exaggerate intellectual deficits among aphasic patients. Moreover, most intelligence studies treat aphasia as a single, unitary disturbance, failing to note that intellectual dysfunction varies considerably with the specific aphasia syndrome and the locus of neuropathology. In real life, the examiner must base a decision about the intellectual competence of an aphasic patient on observations; test results alone are not sufficient. Important information, such as the retention of social graces; counting; making change; exhibiting appropriate concern about family, business, and personal activities; finding their way about; socializing; and showing self-concern, may provide valuable indications of residual intelligence in individuals with aphasia.

## Psychosocial Aspects

An important but easily overlooked factor affecting most individuals with acquired aphasia stems from the sudden, unexpected, and truly calamitous alteration of lifestyle produced by the language disorder. In many aphasic patients, the magnitude of the loss of language is overwhelming. Language is such a basic human function that, in shock value, its acute loss ranks with sudden blindness, quadriplegia, or the diagnosis of an incurable disease. Along with the sudden loss of this critical function, many of the stabilizing factors of personal existence are lost. Because of the losses incurred, aphasic patients may enter a period of bereavement, grief reaction, or reactive depression. As a rule, however, such feelings are delayed after the onset of acquired language impairment and may build over weeks, months, or even years.

The onset of aphasia disrupts previously secure patterns of interaction and communication in both social activities and employment. The changes in social status do not occur immediately, and realization of the degree of change may not occur for some time after its onset. If the language disturbance is relatively mild, the aphasic individual may retain or eventually regain his or her previous status within the family, but when the language disturbance is more severe, the spouse or some other family member must assume much of the decision-making role. Aphasia can place an individual in a passive, childlike position within the family, and he or she may need help to carry out even basic, everyday activities. Not infrequently, the reaction to this downgrading of family status is violent, with negative, hostile, and sometimes cruel behavior directed toward close family members. Some families are incapable of successfully managing this transition. The spouse often feels and expresses anger and hostility because of decreased income, altered social position, and numerous added responsibilities.

Physical limitations may aggravate the adjustment to the language disorder. Aphasia usually occurs in the context of stroke or other brain disorder, resulting in additional neurological impairments. Hemiparesis, balance insecurity, visual field defect, unilateral attention disorder, pain, paresthesias, epileptic seizures, the need for major medical or surgical treatments, and many other physical problems plague these patients. Among aphasia patients, sexual maladjustment is a potential problem that can be missed by physicians and therapists. A major degree of paralysis, an inability to communicate accurately, and an underlying uncertainty of residual sexual competency can hinder healthy sexual relationships. In most instances, however, the acquired lack of sexuality is physiologically unfounded.

Legal capacity for decision making is another psychosocial consideration for aphasic patients. Many aphasic patients can manage their own affairs, whereas others are obviously unable to make decisions and deserve the protection of a conservator or a guardian. Informed medical opinion is often needed to determine whether an aphasic patient has sufficient language and comprehension to sign checks or business papers, to dispense money, to manage property or other holdings, to make a will or other testamentary documents, and so forth. A physician should evaluate and carefully record the patient's ability to comprehend both spoken and written language and to express personal decisions. Special procedures are necessary if a legal act (e.g., signing a will or entering into a contract) is to be performed by an aphasic patient. In addition to receiving added explanations, the document in question should be reviewed with the patient until both the physician and the attorney are satisfied that the patient understands its basic meaning. Such a procedure may require several sessions and, for practical reasons, the document should be kept short, simple, and as free as possible of legal jargon. An even more difficult problem arises when a physician is asked to provide retrospective testimony about an aphasic patient's legal competency, such as the question of whether a patient did or did not understand a legal document consummated after the onset of aphasia. A physician's testimony can relate only to a description of the patient's ability to understand spoken and written language and the ability to express ideas.

## Prognosis and Treatment

Most poststroke aphasia patients recover significant language function (Basso 1992; Benson and Ardila 1996; Robey 1998). Patients with anomic or conduction aphasia have an excellent recovery and are often left with some more minor degree of language impairment. Many patients with initial Broca's or Wernicke's aphasia recover to anomic or conduction aphasia. The exception is patients with initial global aphasia. In general, these patients have a poor prognosis for recovery of functional language. In addition, patients with aphasia due to dementia or primary progressive aphasia continue to have a slowly progressive deterioration in their language ability, eventually complicated by deficits in other areas of cognition.

The treatment for aphasia requires a careful assessment, usually performed by a speech-language pathologist. The assessment includes evaluation with one of the commonly used aphasia tests, such as the Boston Diagnostic Aphasia Examination, the Psycholinguistic Assessment of Language Processing in Aphasia, or the Communicative Abilities of Daily Living (Lezak 1994). The therapist then formulates a therapy program based on specific goals. In addition to traditional rote repetition

and rehearsal, a range of other language therapy techniques are available. These include stimulation-facilitation techniques such as melodic intonation therapy and emotional speech techniques (Benson and Ardila 1996; Reuterskiold 1991). Some techniques focus on modular treatments aimed at specific deficits, such as verbal fluency. Other techniques focus on functional improvement, caregiver interventions, manual or visual symbol systems, use of communication aids, or more recent neurocognitive and psycholinguistic approaches. Whatever the program, a significant emphasis is directed toward positive language competency, allowing few failures and rewarding all successes.

Drug treatments for language disturbances have had little success. Although bromocriptine, bupropion, and methylamphetamine have improved fluency in some nonfluent patients, more rigorous studies have failed to show significant benefits (Gupta et al. 1995). In addition, some aphasic patients need extensive rehabilitation measures other than speech and language therapy. These include physical therapy, gait training, mechanical aids such as crutches and leg braces, recreational therapy, and occupational therapy, including instruction and training in activities of daily living.

Despite the language disturbance, many forms of psychotherapy may be useful for aphasic patients, not the least of which is the support provided by family members, nursing staff, therapists, physicians, and others in contact with the patient. There is almost always a positive transference between the patient with aphasia and the speech-language pathologist, a phenomenon that can be used therapeutically. Most language therapists, however, are not formally trained in psychotherapy, and they may become discouraged, for example, if the patient's psychiatric manifestations obviate good language rehabilitation. Moreover, the comprehension deficit of patients with posterior aphasia precludes more traditional insight-oriented psychotherapy. These barriers need to be considered and overcome. Group psychotherapy, when possible, can decrease feelings of isolation and provide encouragement as patients observe improvements in others. Finally, family counseling often represents a crucial factor in the successful management of an aphasic patient's neuropsychiatric problems.

Among patients with an aphasia syndrome, the early recognition of a mood disorder is critical to the treatment of depression. Awareness of the onset of depression in an aphasic patient should be immediately followed by supportive measures. Challenging therapies (e.g., language, occupational, and physical) should be halted and replaced with activities that the patient can perform successfully. The patient should not be allowed to fail, particularly at tasks that would be considered simple and mundane in normal life. Careful monitoring is needed, and suicide precautions may become necessary, particularly for patients with posterior aphasia. Physicians often use antidepressant medications, particularly for the depression of patients with anterior aphasia. Because aphasic patients are often elderly and have cardiovascular disease, selective serotonin reuptake inhibitors are usually the medications of choice. Drugs such as sertraline and paroxetine have been beneficial in relieving symptoms of depression in these patients.

In addition to antidepressants, a range of psychoactive medications can be useful in the management of aphasic patients. Benzodiazepines can help alleviate anxiety and hyperactivity, but their potential suppression of learning and memory may impede rehabilitation. Atypical antipsychotics, such as quetiapine, olanzapine, or risperidone, are useful in selected aphasic patients, especially those with posterior aphasia who have impulsive, paranoid behavior. Patients with Wernicke's aphasia and pure word deafness who are treated with these psychotropic medications appear to have less agitation and are more compliant with rehabilitation measures. Doses should be kept low to avoid interference with residual mental functions. When brain damage causes apathy, lethargy, and decreased drive, judicious use of a stimulant such as methylphenidate could be beneficial. Again, these drugs need to be monitored carefully because of the increased susceptibility of brain-damaged patients to potential complications.

## Conclusions

Patients with aphasia and related disorders often suffer significant psychiatric, cognitive, and psychosocial complications. These changes result from their altered ability to communicate, from their compromised personal and social status, and directly from the brain lesion itself. The neuropsychiatric aspects of aphasia hamper language rehabilitation and may produce serious dysfunction. The optimal management of aphasic patients does not stop with language therapy but also requires competence in the management of the neuropsychiatric aspects of these syndromes.

## References

Alexander MP, Benson DE, Stuss DT: Frontal lobes and language. Brain Lang 37:641–691, 1989

Basso A: Prognostic factors in aphasia. Aphasiology 6:337–348, 1992

Basso A, Capitani E, Luzzatti C, et al: Intelligence and left hemisphere disease: role of aphasia, apraxia and size of lesion. Brain 104:721–734, 1981

Bastian HC: Aphasia and Other Speech Defects. London, HK Lewis, 1898

Bay E: Aphasia and intelligence. International Journal of Neurology 4:252–264, 1964a

Bay E: Principles of classification and their influence on our concepts of aphasia, in Disorders of Language. Edited by De Renck AV, O'Connor M. Boston, MA, Little, Brown, 1964b, pp 122–139

Benson DF: Psychiatric aspects of aphasia. Br J Psychiatry 123:555–566, 1973

Benson DF: Aphasia, Alexia, and Agraphia. New York, Churchill Livingstone, 1979

Benson DF, Ardila A: Aphasia: A Clinical Approach. New York, Oxford University Press, 1996

Benson DF, Geschwind N: The aphasias and related disturbances, in Clinical Neurology, Vol 1. Edited by Baker AB, Joynt R. Philadelphia, PA, Harper & Row, 1985, pp 1–34

Bhatia KP, Marsden CD: The behavioural and motor consequences of focal lesions of the basal ganglia in man. Brain 117:859–876, 1994

Borod JC: Interhemispheric and intrahemispheric control of emotion: a focus on unilateral brain damage. J Consult Clin Psychol 60:339–348, 1992

Broca P: Remarques sur le siège de la faculté du langage articulé, suivies d'une observation d'aphémie. Bulletin de la Societé Anatomique de Paris 2:330–357, 1861

Broca P: Sur la faculté du langage articulé. Bulletin de la Societé Anthropologie 6:337–393, 1865

Chomsky N: Language and Mind, 2nd Edition. New York, Harcourt Brace Jovanovich, 1972

Damasio AR: Aphasia. N Engl J Med 326:531–539, 1992

Damasio H, Damasio A: The anatomical basis of conduction aphasia. Brain 103:337–350, 1980

Geschwind N: Disconnexion syndromes in animals and man. Brain 88:237–294, 585–644, 1965

Goldstein K: Language and Language Disturbances: Aphasic Symptom Complexes and Their Significance for Medicine and Theory of Language. New York, Grune & Stratton, 1948

Green J, Morris JC, Sandson J, et al: Progressive aphasia: a precursor of global dementia? Neurology 40:423–429, 1990

Gupta SR, Mlcoch G, Scolaro C, et al: Bromocriptine treatment of nonfluent aphasia. Neurology 45:2170–2173, 1995

Hamsher K: Intelligence and aphasia, in Acquired Aphasia. Edited by Sarno MT. New York, Academic Press, 1981, pp 327–359

Hodges JR, Patterson K, Oxbury S, et al: Semantic dementia. Brain 115:1783–1806, 1992

Kertesz A: Aphasia and Associated Disorders. New York, Grune & Stratton, 1979

Kirschner HS (ed): Handbook of Neurological Speech and Language Disorders. New York, Marcel Dekker, 1995

Kleist K: Gehirnpathologie. Leipzig, Barth, 1934

Kramer JH, Duffy JM: Aphasia, apraxia, and agnosia in the diagnosis of dementia. Dementia 7:23–26, 1996

Lebrun Y: Intelligence and Aphasia. Amsterdam, The Netherlands, Swets & Zeitlinger, 1974

Lezak M: Neuropsychological Assessment, 3rd Edition. New York, Oxford University Press, 1994

Lichtheim L: On aphasia. Brain 7:434–484, 1885

Mendez MF, Benson DE: Atypical conduction aphasia: a disconnection syndrome. Arch Neurol 42:886–891, 1985

Muller R-A, Rothermel RD, Behen ME, et al: Receptive and expressive language activation for sentences. Neuroreport 8:3767–3770, 1997

Nadeau SE, Crosson B: Subcortical aphasia. Brain Lang 58:355–402, 1997

Pedersen PM, Jorgensen HS, Nakayama H, et al: Aphasia in acute stroke: incidence, determinants, and recovery. Ann Neurol 38:659–666, 1995

Reuterskiold C: The effects of emotionality on auditory comprehension in aphasia. Cortex 27:595–604, 1991

Robey RR: A meta-analysis of clinical outcomes in the treatment of aphasia. J Speech Lang Hear Res 41:172–187, 1998

Robinson RG: Neuropsychiatric consequences of stroke. Annu Rev Med 48:217–229, 1997

Robinson R, Szetela B: Mood change following left hemisphere brain injury. Ann Neurol 9:447–453, 1981

Ross ED: The aprosodias: functional-anatomic organization of the affective components of language in the right hemisphere. Arch Neurol 38:561–569, 1981

Wernicke C: Das Aphasiche Symptomenkomplex. Breslau, Poland, Kohn & Neigart, 1874

Westbury C, Bud D: Primary progressive aphasia: a review of 112 cases. Brain Lang 60:381–406, 1997

Zangwill OL: Intelligence in aphasia, in Disorders of Language. Edited by De Renck AV, O'Connor M. Boston, MA, Little, Brown, 1964, pp 261–274

# CHAPTER 16

# Neuropsychiatric Aspects of Aggression and Impulse Control Disorders

Eric Hollander, M.D.

Nicole Posner, M.D.

Scott Cherkasky, M.D.

The concepts of impulsivity and aggression play important roles not only in clinical psychiatry but also in everyday life. *Impulsivity* is defined as the failure to resist an impulse, drive, or temptation that is harmful to oneself or others. An impulse is impetuous and lacks deliberation. It may be sudden in onset and transitory, or a gradual increase in tension may reach a crescendo in an explosive expression of the impulse, resulting in violence without regard for self or others. What makes an impulse pathologic is an inability to resist it and its expression in an inappropriate environment.

*Aggression* is any form of behavior directed toward harm or injury of another person. It constitutes a multidetermined act that often results in physical (or verbal) injury to others, self, or objects. The behavioral manifestations of aggression are characterized by heightened vigilance and enhanced readiness to attack. Aggressive acts may be classified as defensive, premeditated, or impulsive. *Impulsive aggression* refers to impulsive and aggressive behavior occurring simultaneously. Sometimes impulsivity has been confused with aggression. Pathological gamblers, for example, are impulsive but not necessarily aggressive. Likewise, a premeditated, well-planned assassination attempt is aggressive but not necessarily impulsive. Impulsive aggression correlates more clearly with biological indices of neurotransmitter function than does premeditated aggression. Often impulsivity and aggression are expressed together, as in antisocial personality disorder.

Impulsivity and aggression may be part of the defining characteristics of many psychiatric illnesses, including personality disorders such as borderline and antisocial personality, neurologic disorders characterized by disinhibited behavior, attention-deficit/hyperactivity disorder, substance and alcohol abuse, bulimia, and impulse control disorders such as intermittent explosive disorder. Impulsivity is also a significant correlate of suicide and violent behavior.

The concepts of impulsivity and aggression are diagnostically nonspecific but may be viewed as dimensional constructs. A closer look at clinical syndromes characterized by these behaviors may also help elucidate the biological underpinnings of impulsivity and aggression.

Impulsive aggressive behaviors are severe behavioral disturbances with substantial associated morbidity and mortality. These behaviors may also lead to prolonged social, vocational, and family dysfunction; violent crimes (including murder, rape, robbery, and assault); accidents (including reckless driving); and injuries. Individuals who manifest impulsivity and aggression often become involved in the legal system and need repeated psychiatric evaluation and treatment and government financial assistance.

Clearly, the causes of impulsivity and aggression are complex and involve a combination of biological, developmental, psychosocial, and cultural factors (Figure 16–1). This chapter focuses on the neuropsychiatry and neurobiology of impulsivity and aggression, discusses specific disorders of impulse control, and highlights treatment strategies for managing impulsive and aggressive behavior.

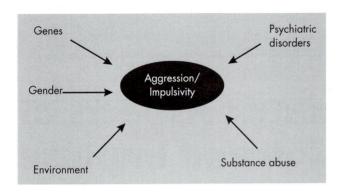

**FIGURE 16–1.** Factors contributing to aggression and impulsivity.

## Epidemiology

We live in a violent society. In the United States, homicide is the second leading cause of death among those 15–24 years of age. The four crimes classified as violent by the Federal Bureau of Investigation (FBI) are homicide, armed robbery, rape, and assault. Impulsivity and aggression are often the causes of crime, violence, homicide, suicide, substance abuse, and accidents and injuries. A greater percentage of the aggression in our society is associated with the young, and half of all homicides are committed by those younger than age 25. A 1995 study by the U.S. Department of Justice revealed that 23% of people who have handguns are younger than age 18. The highest rates of death and homicide are among young, poor, urban men. Overall, rates of death by homicide are about three times greater for men than for women. Homicide remains the leading cause of death of black men and women between ages 15 and 34. The fact that homicide is the leading cause of death for young blacks is partly explained by the low rate of natural deaths in the young in general and partly by high rates of poverty and concentration in large central cities protecting them from the leading cause of death for young whites—motor vehicle accidents. Much lower rates of homicide have been reported in countries such as England, Sweden, and Japan, which all have strict gun control laws.

There are more than 20,000 homicides in the United States each year, and men are three times more likely than women to be killed. In 90% of homicides, the perpetrator and victim involved are the same race, and a handgun is used in more than 50% of the murders. Alcohol use is associated with 25%–75% of homicides. Homicide often occurs in families in the context of domestic quarrels and when members have access to firearms. In domestic violence, women are more likely to attack their husbands than vice versa. The Epidemiologic Catchment Area (ECA) project suggested that the rate of family violence was increasing among both blacks and whites, particularly in the younger populations (Federal Bureau of Investigation 1991).

Aggression and impulsivity are clearly linked to violence in our society. The etiology of violence, impulsivity, and aggression is multifactorial and not fully understood. A better understanding of the biological underpinnings of violence and aggression is only a part of the remedy, and these statistics help convey the depth of the problem and the degree to which it affects our culture.

## Measurements of Impulsivity and Aggression

Direct in vitro laboratory tests of impulsivity and aggression are currently unavailable. This discussion focuses on instruments that have been specifically designed to quantify aggressive, impulsive behavior. All studies examining the biological basis of impulsivity and aggression in humans have used either interview or self-reported assessments of anger or aggressive behavior. Rating scales measuring aggressive or impulsive behavior have been developed, covering both personality dimensions and clinical syndromes. These rating scales have been used as tools for measuring prognosis and outcome. The scales can be specific or comprehensive, and they can measure both internally experienced variables (e.g., mood) and externally observable variables (e.g., behavior).

One of the problems in measuring aggression is the potential for discrepancies between self-rating scales and observer scales. Verbal aggression is difficult to assess because it may be a function of social class and clinical status. Some patients threaten others but are not aggressive in person, whereas others store their rage and ultimately explode in anger. How a patient handles aggressive urges requires evaluation of not only what he or she says but also of past behavior. On the other hand, the measurement of severe aggressive behavior (i.e., physical aggression) is often limited to observer scales because data based on the patients' own reports are likely to be biased on the basis of social desirability. Because there is social stigma attached to violent, aggressive behavior, few patients will honestly report their true behavior. In addition, patients with reduced verbal capacity or cognitive impairments (i.e., dementia) are often limited in their self-reporting. Observer scales are mainly used in moderately to severely aggressive hospitalized or institutionalized patients and are limited in distinguishing between chronic baseline aggression and exacerbations or heightened states of sporadic verbal or physical aggression.

Traditionally, before more valid and reliable instruments were developed, projective tests such as the Rorschach test or Thematic Apperception Test (TAT) were used to quantify aggression. Currently the most commonly used aggression questionnaire is the Buss-Durkee Hostility Inventory. Below is a brief summary of the various strategies used to assess aggression in humans.

## Self-Report Assessments

### Buss-Durkee Hostility Inventory

The Buss-Durkee Hostility Inventory (BDHI) (Buss and Durkee 1957) is the most widely used self-report assessment. It is a 75-item true/false questionnaire that measures different aspects of hostility, aggression, and danger (e.g., "I seldom strike back, even if someone hits me first: true or false"). There are eight subscales: assault, indirect hostility, irritability, negativism, resentment, suspicion, verbal hostility, and guilt. The BDHI has good test-retest reliability and good reports of positive, concurrent validity.

### Hostility and Direction of Hostility Questionnaire

The Hostility and Direction of Hostility Questionnaire (HDHQ) (Philip 1969) is a true/false questionnaire containing 51 items derived from the Minnesota Multiphasic Personality Inventory (Hathaway and McKinley 1989). It contains five subscales, of which only one, "acting out hostility," is relevant to aggressive behavior. The HDHQ has modest to good test-retest reliability for its subscales.

### Spielberger State-Trait Anger Expression Inventory

The Spielberger State-Trait Anger Expression Inventory (STAEI) (Spielberger 1988) takes about 15 minutes to complete. It is a 44-item scale that divides behavior into state anger (i.e., current feelings) and trait anger (i.e., disposition toward angry reactions). (Sample items: "How I feel right now: I feel irritated"; "How I generally feel: I fly off the handle.")

## Interview Assessments

### Life History Assessments: The Brown-Goodwin Assessment for Life History of Aggression

The Brown-Goodwin Assessment (BGA) (G. Brown et al. 1979) is one of the most commonly used assessments of aggressive behavior. It is rated by a clinician based on direct interview with the patient and/or review of medical records and other information about the patient (including information from informants). The BGA has 11 assessments of aggression: temper, fighting, assault, school discipline, civilian discipline, antisocial behavior not involving police, antisocial behavior involving police, military discipline, military judicial discipline, property damage, and verbal aggression.

## Direct Laboratory Assessments

The direct laboratory assessments assess the extent to which a subject responds aggressively to an opponent in a simulated "game" involving the subject giving an electric shock to his "opponent" or another measure of aggression. The three major direct laboratory assessments are listed below.

### Buss "Aggression Machine" Paradigm

In the Buss "Aggression Machine" (BAM) (Buss 1961), the experimental subject's task is to teach his or her opponent a concept by showing an example of the concept. If the opponent is correct, a feedback button notifies the experimental subject, who is instructed beforehand not to deliver a shock in this circumstance. If the opponent is incorrect, the experimental subject has to press one of 10 buttons that that deliver increasing intensities of electric shock.

### Taylor Competitive Reaction Time-Task

The Taylor Competitive Reaction Time-Task (TCRTT) (Taylor 1987) is a modification of the BAM. The experimental subject is engaged in a reaction-time task with an opponent.

### Cherek Point Subtraction Aggression Paradigm

The Cherek Point Subtraction Aggression Paradigm (PSAP) (Kelly and Cherek 1993) is a modification of the TCRTT, whereby the investigator is able to set the level of preoccupation for each session.

Although these rating measurements are useful, it is helpful to consider their limitations in the evaluation of dangerousness. Assessment of release from prison or hospital depends more on subjective parameters, such as the patients' alliance or compliance with medication, than on several tests, and the patients' history is still the most important determinant in the process of risk assessment.

## Neurobiology and Neuropsychiatry

In this section, we review neuroanatomical and neurotransmitter research that has focused on aggression and impulsivity as underlying personality or behavioral traits. Much of this work has used aggression and suicidality as indices of impulsivity. Although not all aggressive and suicidal behaviors are impulsive, these behaviors can arguably be seen as constituting a measure of the tendency to be impulsive (i.e., impulsive aggression). In addition, we discuss neuroendocrine and genetic correlates of impulsivity and aggression. Impulsivity and aggression are likely to be the result of several different independent factors interacting to modulate an individual's behavior.

# Neurologic Structures Involved in Aggression

A vast body of literature exists linking specific brain structures to aggressive behavior in mammals and nonhuman primates (Hess 1957). Clinicians have also commonly observed that patients with neurologic lesions may present with symptoms of aggression (Weiger and Bear 1988). A number of investigators hypothesize that for a subgroup of chronically aggressive persons, the root of the aggressive behavior is brain damage. D.O. Lewis et al. (1982) reported that every death row inmate studied by her team had a history of head injury, often inflicted by abusive parents. Her study concluded that death row inmates constitute an especially neuropsychiatrically impaired prison population. Although the connection between physical abuse, head injury, and aggression is uncertain, many studies do show an association between physical abuse and later aggressive behavior. Clinical reports of aggressive patients with specific neurologic lesions may help delineate the structures that mediate these symptoms. In patients who present with aggressive symptoms, researchers have demonstrated neurologic "soft signs," a marker of subtle neurologic dysfunction (Shaffer et al. 1985). Research on the major brain structures involved in mediating aggression have focused on the hypothalamus, amygdala, and prefrontal cortex. We briefly review the relationships between impulsive, aggressive behavior and these three structures.

## Hypothalamus

The hypothalamus monitors internal status and orchestrates neuroendocrine responses via sympathetic arousal. It is involved in the regulation of the sleep-wake cycle, appetite, body temperature, and sexual activity. In combination with the pituitary, it is the major regulator of the autonomic nervous system. The mesolimbic dopamine pathway and the ascending serotonergic, noradrenergic, and cholinergic pathways from the brain stem have terminations in the hypothalamus.

The hypothalamus plays a major role in the expression of aggression in animals (Eichelman 1971; Wasman and Flynn 1962). Stimulation of the anterior hypothalamus causes predatory attacks in cats, whereas activation of the dorsomedial aspect produces aggression in which the animal ignores the presence of a rat and attacks the experimenter. Destruction of aggression-inhibitory areas, such as the ventromedial nucleus of the hypothalamus, produces permanently aggressive cats and rats (Bard 1928; Reeves and Plum 1969). After cortical ablation, stimulation of the posterior lateral hypothalamus of the cat elicits sham-rage, a posture of preparation for attack. Stimulation of the posterior lateral portion of the hypothalamus shortens the latency of the attack, whereas stimulation of the medial ventral area prolongs the latency of attack (Eichelman 1971; Wasman and Flynn 1962). Hamsters tested for offensive aggression after microinjections of arginine vasopressin (AVP) directly within the anterior hypothalamus in combination with a 5-hydroxytryptamine (5-HT) (serotonin) type 1B (5-$HT_{1B}$) receptor agonist have increased aggression, whereas those injected with AVP and a serotonin type 1A (5-$HT_{1A}$) receptor agonist have a dose-dependent inhibition of AVP-affiliated offensive aggression (Ferris et al. 1999). Structural lesions of the hypothalamus in humans may be associated with unplanned and undirected aggressive symptoms that often appear unprovoked but may be in response to physical discomfort (Haugh and Markesbery 1983; Killeffer and Stern 1970; Ovsiew and Yudofsky 1983; Reeves and Plum 1969).

## Amygdala

The limbic system encompasses the amygdala and temporal cortex. The amygdala activates and/or suppresses the hypothalamus and modulates input from the neocortex. It also has efferents to the extrapyramidal system. The amygdala may have a role in associating sensory experience with (hypothalamically directed) affects and behaviors, including anger (Bear 1991). In a study using positron emission tomography, the amygdala was shown to be more activated during the processing of visually presented linguistic threats than during the processing of neutral words (Isenberg et al. 1999).

Bilateral lesions of the amygdala tame a variety of hostile and vicious animals (Klüver and Bucy 1939), whereas irritative lesions or electrical stimulation can lead to rage outbursts. Removal of the amygdala from monkeys results in decreased aggression (Downer 1961). However, amygdalectomy in submissive monkeys may result in increased aggression (Dicks et al. 1969). Aggressive behavior following stimulation of the amygdala in cats varies according to their preexisting temperament (Adamac 1990). These findings suggest that the amygdala may not simply function to increase regulatory affects and behaviors, but rather it may mediate and balance their control.

In monkeys, bilateral temporal lobectomy leads to hyperorality, hypersexuality, absence of fear response, increased touching, and visual agnosia (Klüver-Bucy syndrome). Bilateral temporal lobe damage in humans leads to similar symptoms, including hypersexuality and visual and auditory agnosias. In addition, humans exhibit placidity, apathy, bulimia, and aphasia (Isern 1987; Marlowe et al. 1975; Terzian and Ore 1955). This syndrome appears to be a disconnection between sensory information about the environment and the regulation of affects and behaviors (e.g., aggression, sex, food) that usually help the person or animal negotiate that environment.

Seizure studies of the limbic area in humans give insight into the possible neuroanatomical underpinnings of aggression. Whereas bilateral temporal lobe damage in humans may lead to Klüver-Bucy syndrome with a decrease in regulatory affects and behaviors, disorders of temporal lobe excitation may result in increased affect and aggression (Nachson 1988; Serafetinides 1965). Researchers have noted associations between aggression and temporal lobe epilepsy. Elliot (1992) found that 30% of 286 patients with intermittent violent outbursts had temporal lobe epilepsy (TLE). D.O. Lewis (1982) found psychomotor epilepsy in 18 of 97 (19%) incarcerated delinquent boys with a history of violence. Patients with TLE may demonstrate hyperemotionality and increased aggression. Interictal aggression is much more common than ictal or postictal aggression in TLE. Interictal aggression is often characterized by intense affect in response to environmental stimuli, whereas ictal and postictal aggression are spontaneous and unfocused.

In humans, reports of surgical intervention for the relief of mental or structural brain disease or epilepsy have shown that both the amygdala and other temporal lobe and limbic system structures contribute to aggression modulation. Two patients who underwent bilateral amygdalotomy for intractable aggression showed a reduction in autonomic arousal in response to stressful stimuli and a decrease in aggressive outbursts (Lee et al. 1998). Limbic system tumors, infections, and blood vessel abnormalities have also been associated with violence. Although it is clear that various limbic system structures have an inhibitory or excitatory effect on aggression, the precise mechanism of the aggression pathway is still far from established.

## Prefrontal Cortex

The prefrontal cortex modulates limbic and hypothalamic activity and is associated with the social and judgment aspects of aggression. The frontal cortex coordinates timing of social cues, often before the expression of associated emotions. Lesions in this area give rise to disinhibited anger after minimal provocation, characterized by an individual showing little regard for the consequences of affect and behavior. Weiger and Bear (1988) suggest that whereas TLE patients may express deep remorse over an aggressive act, patients with prefrontal lesions often indicate indifference. Patients with violent behavior have been found to have a high frequency of frontal lobe lesions (Kandel and Freed 1989; Lishman 1968). In a study of Vietnam veterans with a history of penetrating head injuries, patients with ventromedial lesions had higher verbal aggression scores than control subjects and those with lesions in other brain areas (Grafman et al. 1996). Frontal lesions may result in the sudden discharge of limbic- and/or amygdala-generated affects no longer modulated, processed, or inhibited by the frontal lobe. Individuals consequently respond with rage or aggression on feelings that would have ordinarily been modulated. Prefrontal damage may cause aggression by a secondary process involving lack of inhibition of the limbic area. Dorsal lesions of the prefrontal cortex are associated with impairment in long-term planning and increased apathy. Orbital lesions of the prefrontal cortex are associated with increases in reflexive emotional responses to environmental stimuli (Luria 1980).

Positron emission tomography has allowed researchers to explore whether reduced serotonergic functioning occurs in specific brain regions in individuals with increased aggression and impulsivity. One imaging study showed that in contrast to control subjects, patients with borderline personality disorder have diminished response to serotonergic stimulation (*dl*-fenfluramine) in areas of prefrontal cortex associated with impulsive behavior regulation, specifically the medial and orbital regions of the right prefrontal cortex, left middle and superior temporal gyri, left parietal lobe, and left caudate body (Soloff et al. 2000). Siever et al. (1999) found that impulsive-aggressive patients had significantly blunted metabolic responses in orbital frontal, adjacent ventral medial, and cingulate cortex compared with control subjects. Finally, impulsive murderers have been shown to have lower left and right prefrontal functioning and higher right subcortical functioning in comparison to predatory murderers (Raine et al. 1998).

Other areas implicated in impulsivity and aggression include the midline thalamus, lateral preoptic region, mamillary bodies, hippocampus, and basal ganglia.

**TABLE 16–1.** Studies of serotonin and aggression and impulsivity

| | Study | Findings |
|---|---|---|
| Animal studies | Higley et al. 1996b | Lower CSF concentration of 5-HIAA in primates correlated with greater alcohol consumption |
| | Depue and Spoont 1987 | Decreased brain 5-HT found in the brain stems of aggressive rats |
| 5-HIAA in CSF | Lidberg et al. 2000 | Low 5-HIAA concentration in CSF in homicide offenders with history of suicide attempts |
| | Stanley et al. 2000 | Low 5-HIAA concentration in CSF in aggressive population independent of suicidal behavior |
| | G. Brown et al. 1982 | Low 5-HIAA concentration in CSF of patients with personality disorders: decrease correlating with scores on lifetime aggression scale |
| | Lidberg et al. 1984 Linnoila et al. 1983 G. Brown et al. 1982 Bioulac 1980 | Inverse relationship between CSF levels of 5-HIAA and impulsive/violent behaviors |
| 5-HT platelet studies | Coccaro et al. 1996 | Reduced numbers of platelet 5-HT transporter sites is associated with history of aggressive behavior in patients with personality disorder |
| | Mann et al. 1992 | Increased platelet 5-HT content correlates with lifetime aggression in patients with borderline personality disorder |
| | Marazziti and Conti 1991 Biegon et al. 1990 | Abnormal 5-HT levels in platelets correlated with impassivity and aggression |
| | Stoff et al. 1987 | Decreased numbers of platelet 5-HT transporter sites found in aggressive institutionalized subjects |
| | C.S. Brown et al. 1989 | Platelet 5-HT uptake is inversely correlated with Barratt Impulsivity score in aggressive males |
| Serum tryptophan | C.E. Lewis 1991 | Low serum ratio of tryptophan to other neutral amino acids is seen in alcoholics arrested for assaultive behaviors compared with other alcoholics |

*Note.* CSF = cerebrospinal fluid; 5-HIAA = 5-hydroxyindoleacetic acid; 5-HT = serotonin.

# Neuropharmacology of Impulsivity and Aggression

## Decreased Serotonin Function

There is significant evidence for the role of serotonergic dysregulation in impulsive aggression in both animals and humans (Table 16–1) (Åsberg et al. 1976; G. Brown et al. 1979, 1982; Sabrie 1986). This association has been shown using varied measures of serotonergic function. A decrease in brain serotonin is found in the brain stems of muricidal rats (aggressive rats that spontaneously kill mice introduced into their cages) and other animals made aggressive by isolation. The administration of tryptophan, a serotonin precursor, reduces or abolishes the violence (Depue and Spoont 1987). In primate studies, researchers have noted higher blood levels of serotonin and higher cerebrospinal fluid (CSF) levels of 5-hydroxyindoleacetic acid (5-HIAA) in monkeys who tend to be dominant and high-ranking in their colonies (Higley et al. 1992) and have noted lower CSF concentration of 5-HIAA as an antecedent to greater alcohol consumption (Higley et al. 1996b).

In humans, Åsberg et al. (1976) initially noted an inverse relationship between violent/lethal suicidal behavior and CSF concentration of the serotonin metabolite 5-HIAA in depressed patients. Subsequent studies on populations in eight different countries confirmed that suicidal depressed patients have lower CSF concentration of 5-HIAA than nonsuicidal depressed patients. For example, Lidberg et al. (2000) found that homicide offenders with a history of suicide attempts had a lower CSF concentration of 5-HIAA than the remaining murderers. This correlation is particularly strong in those with violent suicide attempts. Low CSF concentration of 5-HIAA has also been shown to be related to aggressive behavior independent of suicidal behavior in patients with Axis I disorders (Stanley et al. 2000). In addition, G. Brown et al. (1982) demonstrated a decrease in CSF concentration of 5-HIAA in patients with personality disorders and found that this decrease correlated with scores on a lifetime aggression scale. Many studies have confirmed an inverse relationship between CSF 5-HIAA level and impulsive and violent behaviors (Biolac 1980; Brown et al. 1982; Lidberg et al.

1984; Linnoila et al. 1983). The individual cases and small populations studied include psychopathic military personnel, arsonists, murderers, violent suicidal patients, and behaviorally disrupted children and adolescents. Linnoila et al. (1983) have reported reduced CSF 5-HIAA concentration in both impulsive violent offenders and impulsive arsonists compared with those who commit premeditated violence, suggesting that it is nonpremeditated ("impulsive") aggression, specifically, that correlates with reduced central serotonin function in these individuals.

Suicidal behavior can be conceptualized as aggressive behavior directed toward the self, and studies have found that decreased brainstem levels of serotonin and 5-HIAA are consistent postmortem findings in suicide victims. Investigators have also correlated abnormal serotonin platelet studies with impulsivity and aggression (Biegon et al. 1990; Marazziti and Conti 1991). Platelets bind and transport serotonin. Decreased numbers of platelet serotonin transporter sites are found in aggressive conduct-disordered subjects and in "aggressive" institutionalized psychiatric subjects (Stoff et al. 1987). In addition, an inverse correlation between platelet serotonin uptake and Barratt "Impulsivity" score has been reported in aggressive adult males (C.S. Brown et al. 1989). In children and adolescents with conduct disorder, there is a negative correlation between platelet imipramine binding and impulsive aggression (Stoff et al. 1987). In individuals with personality disorders, platelet-titrated paroxetine binding has been shown to be inversely correlated with the Life History of Aggression total score and aggression score and with the Buss-Durkee Hostility Inventory Assault score (Coccaro et al. 1996).

Researchers have noted consistently reduced imipramine binding (C.S. Brown et al. 1989) and increased platelet serotonin type 2 (5-HT$_2$) binding in suicide victims (Biegon et al. 1990). Reduced numbers of platelet serotonin transporter sites are associated with life history of aggressive behavior in patients with personality disorder (Coccaro et al. 1996). The reduced imipramine binding may reflect decreased serotonin release. Increased 5-HT$_2$ binding may reflect the brain's compensatory response to a decrease in functional serotonergic neurons, with consequent upregulation of postsynaptic 5-HT$_2$ binding sites. Additional findings that suggest the role of serotonin in impulsivity and aggression include reports of low serum ratios of tryptophan to other neutral amino acids in alcoholic subjects arrested for assaultive behaviors compared with other alcoholic subjects or nonalcoholic control subjects (C.E. Lewis 1991). Type 2 alcoholism is associated with both violent behavior and serotonergic deficit (LeMarquand et al. 1994; Virkkunen

and Linnoila 1990). Individuals with a family history of alcoholism may be more sensitive to impulsivity in response to low serotonin levels, as tryptophan-depleted individuals with a family history of alcoholism made more errors in a modified Taylor task than did those with no family history of alcoholism (LeMarquand et al. 1999).

Neurotransmitters other than serotonin likely influence aggressive and impulsive behavior, for example, γ-aminobutyric acid (GABA), norepinephrine, and dopamine (Figure 16–2) (Oquendo and Mann 2000). An α-amino-3-hydroxy-5-methylisoxadole-4-propionate (AMPA) receptor antagonist, NBQX, was found to increase impulsivity in rats. Normal behavior was restored by injection of a positive allosteric modulator of AMPA receptors, which indicated that the AMPA receptor, a type of glutamate receptor, is involved in the regulation of impulsivity (Nakamura et al. 2000).

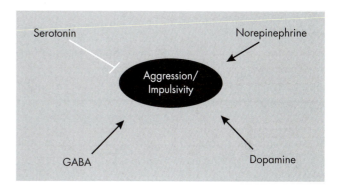

**FIGURE 16–2.** Neurochemistry of aggression and impulsivity. GABA=γ-aminobutyric acid.

One way to study the biology of impulsivity and aggression is to study the traits that cut across personality disorder diagnoses. For example, borderline and antisocial personality disorders are characterized by impulsivity and aggression, behavioral dimensions that are hypothesized to have specific neurobiological correlates. Studies of patients with borderline personality disorder (BPD) have found increased platelet serotonin content that correlated with hostility and lifetime aggression, whereas platelet serotonin content was decreased in depressed patients (Mann et al. 1992). Platelet monoamine oxidase (MAO) has been described as a peripheral marker of cerebral MAO activity and has been found to be lower in individuals with a high level of impulsiveness, for example, in bullfighters (Carrasco et al. 1999) and bulimic patients (Carrasco et al. 2000). One study found platelet MAO significantly decreased in BPD patients compared with control subjects (Yehuda et al. 1989). However, another study (Soloff et al. 1991) did not find this association. These contradictory results suggest the complexity of neuronal mechanisms in producing behavior. One point to consider is that MAO is relatively nonspecific, as it is involved in the breakdown of a number of monoamines, and the activity of MAO in platelets may not reflect MAO activity in the central nervous system.

## Pharmacologic Challenge Studies

Pharmacologic challenges have confirmed a role for serotonin in impulsivity and aggression. The hypothalamic-pituitary-adrenal axis is involved in regulating the interaction between various neurotransmitters that appear, in part, to be stimulated by serotonin. Serotonin stimulation of the hypothalamus causes release of an unidentified prolactin-releasing factor (Ben-Jonathan et al. 1989) that acts on the pituitary, resulting in increased prolactin release. One way that impulsive, aggressive behavior has been linked to serotonergic abnormalities is via measurement of prolactin response to serotonin agonists. Serotonin agonists such as *m*-chlorophenylpiperazine (m-CPP) and fenfluramine stimulate serotonin release through the limbic-hypothalamic-pituitary axis and thereby increase plasma prolactin levels. This action is blocked by serotonin antagonists.

Pharmacologic studies provide insight into the possible mechanisms of impulsivity and aggression. In animal studies, monkeys that have a low prolactin response to fenfluramine display more aggressive gestures when shown a slide of a threatening human being than do those with a high prolactin response (Kyes et al. 1995). Researchers have administered m-CPP and fenfluramine to aggressive subjects, assaultive borderline and antisocial personality disorder patients, and patients who attempted suicide, and found a blunted prolactin response that correlated inversely with impulsive aggression (Coccaro et al. 1997; Lopez-Ibor et al. 1990; Moss et al. 1990; O'Keane et al. 1992). In personality-disordered patients, the prolactin response to these agents was inversely correlated with self-reported irritability and aggression, possibly reflecting decreased receptor sensitivity (Coccaro and Murphy 1990; Coccaro et al. 1989). This blunted prolactin response to selective and nonselective serotonergic agents may reflect multiple abnormalities at different functional levels of the serotonergic system. Rinne et al. (2000) found that the cortisol and prolactin responses to an m-CPP challenge in BPD patients was significantly lower than in control subjects and was inversely correlated with frequency of physical and sexual abuse. These data suggest that severe and traumatic stress during childhood affects the serotonergic system. Another line of evidence for serotonin dysregulation in impulsive, aggressive BPD patients stems from the fact that serotonergic drugs have been shown to improve these symptoms. Lithium, for example, has been reported to enhance presynaptic transmission of serotonin via second messenger systems (Coccaro et al. 1991), and it has been shown to produce global improvement in BPD patients (Links et al. 1990). Fluoxetine, a selective serotonin reuptake inhibitor (SSRI), has been reported to decrease impulsivity and aggression in BPD patients (Coccaro and Murphy 1990; Cornelius et al. 1989; Norden 1989). On the other hand, MAO inhibitors (MAOIs) have been shown to increase agitation and irritability in some BPD patients (Cowdry and Gardner 1988; Soloff et al. 1986). These studies support the hypothesis that increases in noradrenergic function, which in part are influenced by serotonergic mechanisms, may be associated with the tendency to act aggressively. Although studies are limited, the association between pharmacologic enhancement of serotonin neurotransmission and reduced impulsivity in BPD patients supports the hypothesis that a decrease in serotonin transmission may underlie impulsivity in BPD patients.

However, a few studies failed to replicate the finding of blunted prolactin response in selected disorders of impulsivity and found augmented neuroendocrine response to serotonin agonists in impulsive substance abusers (Moss et al. 1990), patients with BPD (Hollander et al. 1994), and pathological gamblers. Patients with alcohol abuse (Moss et al. 1990), trichotillomania (Stein et al. 1993), and pathological gambling (DeCaria 1996) experienced a "high" compared with control subjects after receiving m-CPP. This high was characterized by feelings of "spaciness" and feelings of mild derealization or depersonalization and was described as similar to the highs reported when these patients were actually pulling hair (Stein et al. 1995) or gambling (DeCaria et al. 1996). In addition, male patients with BPD had greater increases in cortisol levels and marginally blunted prolactin responses compared with control subjects after receiving m-CPP (Hollander et al. 1994). The blunted prolactin response to serotonin agonists and the reported feeling of being high in impulsive and aggressive patients suggests aberrant serotonergic functioning in this population.

Although most of the research in impulsivity and aggression has focused on serotonergic function, there is also limited evidence for the role of norepinephrine. In fact, the serotonergic, noradrenergic, and dopaminergic systems are highly connected, and it is difficult to stimulate one without affecting the other. Animal studies support the hypothesis that the norepinephrine system has a direct effect on aggression. For example, MAOIs and tricyclic antidepressants, which increase the amount of central norepinephrine in the synaptic cleft, increase shock-induced fighting in rodents (Kantak et al. 1981). One study involving humans found that CSF concentration of 3-methoxy-4-hydroxyphenylglycol (MHPG) correlated with aggressive behavior in a sample of personality-disorder subjects (G. Brown et al. 1979). Another study found a correlation between irritability and growth hormone response to the α-noradrenergic agonist clonidine in personality-disordered patients (Coccaro et al. 1991). Norepinephrine may modulate serotonergically mediated impulsive aggression. Decreases in norepinephrine, for example, may mediate depression, suicide, and inwardly directed aggression, whereas increases in norepinephrine may mediate outwardly directed aggression and irritability (Siever and Davis 1991). Overall, however, the role of norepinephrine is less studied and is not as clear as the role of serotonin in impulsivity and aggression. Nonserotonergic medications have been useful in treating impulsivity and aggression in BPD patients. These include neuroleptics (Soloff et al. 1986), carbamazepine (Cowdry and Gardner 1988), and valproic acid (Hollander et al. 2001; Stein et al. 1995). The reason for the effectiveness of these agents has not been established and lends support to the role of multiple neurotransmitters in the mediation of aggression and impulsivity.

## Genetic Studies

Genetic studies in humans and animals have not yet supported a definitive association among impulsivity, aggression, and reduced serotonin activity. The Maudsley rat study, however, was an example of genetic breeding for aggressive behavior. Two groups of rats were bred. The first group (MNR) included rats that had low measures of impulsivity and high measures of inhibition. The second group (MR) had the opposite features. The MR strains bred from the second group were significantly more impulsive and demonstrated increased aggressive behavior compared with the MNR rats (Eichelman 1971). Neurochemically, the MNR strain showed lower limbic brain serotonin levels than the MR strain (Sudak and Maas 1964).

At the synaptic level, reuptake of serotonin is accomplished by a plasma membrane carrier called serotonin transporter (5-HTT). The gene for 5-HTT has been mapped to chromosome 17 (Collier et al. 1996). Preliminary evidence for a genetic disturbance in serotonergic function that might predispose individuals to impulsive-aggressive behavior include a study of the gene for the rate-limiting enzyme for serotonin synthesis, tryptophan

hydroxylase (TPH). The gene for TPH has been mapped to the short arm of chromosome 11 and is one of the major candidate genes for psychiatric and behavioral disorders. Part of the gene for TPH has been discovered to exist as two alleles, U and L, with certain genotypes (UL and LL) being associated with impulsive aggressive behavior and suicidal behavior and low CSF levels of 5-HIAA in violent offenders (Nielson et al. 1994). Persons having the TPH U allele scored significantly higher on measures of aggression than did individuals homozygous for the L allele. Also, peak prolactin response was attenuated among male subjects, but not female subjects, having any U allele relative to LL homozygotes (Manuck et al. 1999). In another study, TPH genotype was found to be associated with impulsive-aggressive behaviors in male patients with personality disorders, but not in female patients with the same disorders (New et al. 1998). Further studies are needed to clarify the role of TPH alleles in aggression and the differences between genders. In summary, serotonin synthesis and regulation are at least partially controlled by genetic factors that likely contribute to an individual's propensity for impulsive and aggressive behaviors.

Currently, there are no controlled family history studies of individuals with impulse control disorders (i.e., intermittent explosive disorder, kleptomania, pyromania, pathological gambling, and trichotillomania). There are studies supporting associations between major mood disorder and alcohol and substance abuse in first-degree relatives of individuals with kleptomania and in first-degree relatives of pathological gamblers (Linden et al. 1986; Ramirez et al. 1983; Saiz et al. 1992). Other findings include associations between anxiety disorders in the families of individuals with kleptomania and violent behavior and attention-deficit/hyperactivity disorder in families of individuals with intermittent explosive disorder (McElroy et al. 1991).

Research involving monozygotic twins supports a hereditary aspect to aggressive behavior, with concordance rates for monozygotic twins being greater than those for dizygotic twins. Twin studies suggest that antisocial behavior in adult life is related more to genetic factors than to environmental factors (Cadoret et al. 1995).

Chromosomal studies have looked at the influence of chromosomal abnormalities in aggression, particularly the XYY syndrome (Bioulac et al. 1980). However, the link between XYY syndrome and violence has not been confirmed. Inborn metabolic disorders that affect the nervous system can be associated with aggressive personalities. These disorders, which diffusely affect the central nervous system and are inherited, include phenylketonuria, Lesch-Nyhan syndrome, Prader-Willi syndrome,

Vogt's syndrome (a neuronal storage disorder), and Sanfilippo's syndrome (increased mucopolysaccharide storage).

## Evidence for the Role of the 5-HT$_{1B}$ Receptor in Aggression

Animal models have been used to define more clearly the role of specific serotonin receptors in impulsivity and aggression. To define the contribution of serotonin receptor subtypes to behavior, mutant mice lacking the 5-HT$_{1B}$ receptor were generated by homologous recombination. These mice did not exhibit any obvious developmental or cognitive defects. However, they were noted to be extremely aggressive and attacked intruders faster and more intensely than did wild-type mice (Hen 1994). They also had increased impulsive aggression, more rapidly acquired cocaine self-administration, and had increased alcohol consumption (Brunner 1997). These findings suggest a role for the 5-HT$_{1B}$ receptors in modulating aggressive, impulsive, and addiction behavior (Hen 1994).

Genetic studies involving the 5-HT$_{1B}$ receptor gene in human subjects have been equivocal. In one study, a polymorphism of the 5-HT$_{1B}$ receptor gene was linked to aggressive and impulsive behavior in alcoholic individuals (Lappalainen et al. 1998). However, Huang et al. (1999) found no relationship between suicide, alcoholism, or pathological aggression with 5-HT$_{1B}$ receptor binding indices or genotype using two common polymorphisms.

Hollander et al. (1992) observed that a subgroup of patients with obsessive-compulsive disorder (OCD) experienced exacerbation of obsessive symptoms following m-CPP challenge studies. m-CPP has affinity for the 5-HT$_{1A}$, 5-HT$_{2C}$, and 5-HT$_{1D}$ receptor subtypes. Patients who underwent challenge studies with MK212, a serotonin agonist with affinity for the 5-HT$_{1A}$ and 5-HT$_{2C}$ receptor subtypes but not for the 5-HT$_{1D}$ subtype, did not manifest exacerbation of obsessions and compulsions. Because there are behavioral changes in a subgroup of OCD patients after administration of m-CPP but not of MK212, and because the activity of these two agonists differ with regard to only one receptor subtype, the 5-HT$_{1D}$ receptor, there is a suggestion that this receptor may modulate obsessions, of which sexual and aggressive symptoms may be prominent.

## Endocrine Studies

Animal studies show that testosterone levels of male rhesus monkeys correlate positively with behavioral dominance and aggression. If a single male monkey is placed with other aggressive males, he becomes submissive and shows a decrease in plasma testosterone, revealing that endogenous hormone production can be affected by behavioral variables. The connection between the endocrine system and aggression and impulsivity is not clear. Some researchers have hypothesized that androgens may play a role in aggression. They suggest that the androgen insensitivity syndrome and the androgenital syndrome are examples of androgen excesses and deficiencies associated with aggressive and inhibited behavior, respectively. In one study, plasma testosterone levels were elevated in juvenile prisoners who had committed violent crimes. CSF free testosterone has been shown to be correlated with overall aggressiveness but not with measures of impulsivity (Higley et al. 1996a). Estrogens and antiandrogens have been used to reduce aggressiveness effectively in some violent sex offenders, although these agents clearly need to be better studied. Low salivary cortisol levels have been associated with persistence and early onset of aggression in school-age boys, suggesting that low hypothalamic-pituitary-adrenal axis activity correlates with aggressive activity (McBurnett et al. 2000).

## Neuropsychiatric/Neuropsychological Studies of Impulsivity and Aggression

Because aggression and impulsivity appear to be core features of both BPD and antisocial personality disorder (ASPD), much of the neuropsychiatric research in this area has focused on patients who meet criteria for these disorders. Researchers have suggested that impaired neuropsychiatric development could lead to personality pathology and that individuals with aggressive symptoms manifest subtle neuropsychiatric impairment. In this section, we review the neuropsychiatric and neuropsychological aspects of BPD and ASPD that give greater insight into the biological basis of impulsivity and aggression in these disorders.

### Borderline Personality Disorder

BPD patients are often in a state of crisis. Their behavior is unpredictable, sometimes dangerous to self or others, and they rarely are able to achieve up to the level of their abilities. The painful nature of their lives is reflected in repetitive, self-destructive acts that may include impulsive wrist slashing, self-mutilation, or suicide. There are fewer neuropsychological studies of BPD patients than of ASPD patients. BPD patients have commonly been thought, however, to have cognitive impairment on the basis of clinical observation of "ego deficits" (Kernberg

1975). BPD patients show no impairments in performance on structured psychological tests, such as the Wechsler Adult Intelligence Scale, but they have disturbed performance on unstructured, projective tests such as the Rorschach (Singer 1977). Although there is limited support for cognitive impairment in BPD, these studies support the idea that cognitive capacities in BPD are vulnerable to affective disruption and that patients lack stable self-organizing strategies. Neuropsychological studies of BPD patients support the association with impairment in complex information processing. Researchers have shown that, compared with control subjects, BPD patients had deficits on tests requiring the ability to plan multiple operations, to maintain a prolonged response over time, and to perform complex auditory and visual memory tasks (Burgess 1991). In addition, BPD patients also had significant impairment on tests of visual filtering and discrimination. These neuropsychological disturbances, particularly defects of memory, have been linked to the unstable, chaotic interactions characterized by impulsivity that are often seen in BPD patients.

Researchers have also studied neurologic soft signs in BPD patients. The term *neurologic soft signs* refers to nonlocalizing abnormalities not indicative of gross neurologic disease. Soft signs are associated with a wide variety of developmental disabilities and include involuntary movements, a variety of apraxias, difficulties in performing rapid alternate movements, difficulties in discerning double simultaneous stimulation, and dysgraphesthesia. The assessment of neurologic soft signs appears reliable and stable.

Work on patients with personality disorders characterized by impulsivity supports an association between these disorders and increased soft signs. Gardner et al. (1987) found significantly more soft sign neurologic abnormalities in BPD patients compared with control subjects. Vitiello et al. (1990) found that increased soft signs were associated with impulsive responding on cognitive tests but not with global cognitive functioning.

Our group (Stein et al. 1993) found that patients with DSM-III-R–diagnosed BPD (American Psychiatric Association 1987) had significantly more left-sided soft signs than did control subjects. These left-sided soft signs correlated with lowered neuropsychological test performance of visuospatial tasks. There was also a significant association between history of aggression and right-sided soft signs. These findings are consistent with an association between impulsive aggression and left-hemisphere dysfunction. Evidence of neuropsychiatric abnormalities in personality disorders characterized by impulsivity have a number of clinical implications. Impairment in tasks of complex information processing, which appears to be associated with increased neurologic soft signs, may contribute to difficulties in building and maintaining a coherent and stable sense of self and in using past experiences to organize present behavior and to predict future consequences. Impairment on verbal functions mediated by the left hemisphere may also contribute to impaired regulation of impulsivity and aggression insofar as verbal processing facilitates mental exploration before motor enactment, allowing greater appreciation of consequences and alternatives. In view of their nonspecificity and unclear etiology, however, neurologic soft signs provide only a limited view of the neuropsychiatry of impulsivity and aggression.

Electroencephalographic abnormalities have been associated with impulsive aggression, although definitive results have been inconclusive. An early study of BPD found that a small percentage of these patients have nonspecific electroencephalographic abnormalities (Andrulonis et al. 1981). Some investigators have found significantly more electroencephalographic dysrhythmias in BPD patients compared with depressed control subjects (Cowdry et al. 1985), but others have found no significant differences between these groups (Archer et al. 1988; Cornelius et al. 1986).

Neither gross inspection nor quantitative measures have revealed computed tomographic abnormalities in BPD patients more frequently than in normal control subjects (Lucas et al. 1989; Snyder et al. 1983). One positron emission tomographic study did show an inverse correlation of global cerebral glucose metabolic rate and aggression. This finding was specific to the BPD group compared with other personality disorders. Regional metabolic glucose rates in the frontal and parietal lobes were also depressed in BPD patients (Goyer et al. 1994). These studies are small and require further investigation.

## Antisocial Personality Disorder

ASPD is characterized by continued antisocial or criminal acts, but it is not synonymous with criminality. Rather, it is an inability to conform to social norms and a pervasive pattern of disregard for and violation of the rights of others. A notable finding is patients' lack of remorse for their behavior. Persons with ASPD repeatedly get into fights or are assaultive. Impulsivity in ASPD may manifest itself in a failure to show normal cautions and in increased recklessness. Impulsive behaviors may be driven by a need for excitement that expresses a disregard for the person's own safety and an intolerance for the feelings that he or she would otherwise experience. Conduct disorder is associated with ASPD later in life. Both ASPD and conduct disorder are associated with an increased use of illicit substances. Substance use and abuse is often impulsive, is frequently characterized by behavioral disinhibition, and commonly results in harm to oneself or others. The neurobiological association between certain behavioral characteristics of substance abuse, ASPD, and impulsive-aggressive behavior in other contexts is beyond the scope of this chapter.

Neuropsychological testing of patients with ASPD has yielded mixed results. Using the Halstead-Reitan battery, Yeudall and Fromm-Auch (1979) studied laterality of cerebral dysfunction in various subject groups. They found impairments on variables sensitive primarily to left-hemisphere dysfunction in violent criminals, alcoholic persons with personality disorders, and adolescents with conduct disorders, but predominantly right-hemisphere dysfunction in nonviolent criminals, alcoholic individuals with affective disorders, and individuals with affective personality disorders. Fedora and Fedora (1983) also found that prisoners with impulsive behaviors had evidence of left-hemisphere impairment, particularly of the anterior regions.

Electroencephalograms and brainstem auditory evoked potentials of ASPD patients are not significantly different from those of control subjects (Fishbein et al. 1989). Conduct disorder in some children appears to be associated with later ASPD. Both disorders are characterized by impulsivity, aggression toward others, and violation of the rights of others. Our group has shown that patients with conduct disorder have greater neuropsychological impairment compared with control subjects (Aronowitz 1994). Conduct disorder patients have greater visuospatial, visuoperceptual, and visuoconstructional impairments compared with non–conduct-disordered patients (Aronowitz 1994). Socially appropriate behavior requires modulation of activity, self-restraint, flexibility, adaptation, and planning and anticipation of consequences. These abilities may be difficult for individuals with ASPD and conduct disorder, perhaps because of their neuropsychological deficits.

## Impulse Control Disorders

The five impulse control disorders listed in DSM-IV-TR are intermittent explosive disorder, kleptomania, pathological gambling, pyromania, and trichotillomania (American Psychiatric Association 2000). Self-mutilation and sexual impulsivity are considered impulse control disorders not otherwise specified and include behavioral characteristics that overlap with a number of other DSM-IV-TR disorders. There have been few studies examining the neurobiological underpinnings of DSM-IV-TR impulse

control disorders. Most of the studies involve controlled pharmacotherapy studies for the treatment of impulsivity, which is discussed in the treatment section of this chapter. Pathological gamblers have higher CSF MHPG levels but similar CSF 5-HIAA levels compared with control subjects. Pharmacologic challenge with intravenous clomipramine revealed blunted prolactin response in pathological gamblers. Our group demonstrated augmented neuroendocrine and behavioral response to m-CPP in pathological gamblers (DeCaria et al. 1996). Some investigators have found clomipramine (Hollander et al. 1992) and fluvoxamine (Hollander et al. 1998, 2000) useful in the treatment of pathological gambling. There are also reports of the use of lithium in this disorder. Virkkunen et al. (1987) found lower CSF 5-HIAA and MHPG concentrations in fire setters compared with control subjects. All of the arsonists in the study met DSM-III criteria for borderline personality disorder, and many demonstrated explosive behavior. Very little neurobiological research has been done on kleptomania and trichotillomania. There is some anecdotal evidence that kleptomania responds to various antidepressants, including SSRIs. Self-mutilation has been studied in patients with personality disorders, and one study showed a negative correlation between impulsive self-mutilation and the number of platelet imipramine-binding receptor sites (Stoff et al. 1987). Self-mutilators did not differ from nonmutilators in CSF 5-HIAA level or in platelet imipramine binding (Simeon et al. 1992). Case reports have noted the usefulness of lithium, SSRIs, and opiate antagonists, again suggesting the heterogeneous nature of self-mutilation and the complexity of its underlying neurobiology.

# Treatment of Impulsivity and Aggression

Impulsivity and aggression are behavioral characteristics that encompass a broad range of clinical problems. Studies on impulsivity and aggression have focused on a heterogeneous group of disorders with varied responses to pharmacotherapeutic interventions. In this section we do not focus on the treatment of patients with epilepsy and patients with drug-induced aggression. These areas are reviewed elsewhere.

Controlled studies suggest that a number of medications may be useful in the treatment of impulsivity and aggression. Given the evidence for decreased serotonergic function in impulsive and aggressive behaviors, many, but not all, of these medications involve direct serotonergic mechanisms. SSRIs have been shown to reduce impulsive, aggressive behaviors in different psychiatric disorders. For example, fluvoxamine resulted in improvement in gambling severity in patients with pathological gambling compared with placebo in one double-blind study (Hollander et al. 2000). However, in some disorders characterized by impulsivity, SSRIs have a quick onset, but these effects may be transient and some patients may require additional augmentation with compounds such as lithium, buspirone, and anticonvulsants (Hollander and Wong 1995). The neurotransmitter effects of lithium are complex and include an effect on second-messenger systems related to the serotonergic system. Medications that are not serotonergically mediated such as carbamazepine have also been useful. Although evidence suggests that impulsivity and aggression are serotonergically mediated, a serotonergic hypothesis of impulsivity is not a definitive model. The complete role of serotonin activity and its complex interactions with other neurotransmitters and receptors in impulsivity and aggression has not yet been fully delineated.

BPD is a common clinical problem whereby researchers have used pharmacologic interventions to target the characteristic symptoms of impulsivity, aggression, lability, and hostility. Fluoxetine is the best-studied SSRI for the treatment of impulsivity and aggression. A number of open trials of fluoxetine in BPD suggest its efficacy in the treatment of impulsivity and aggression in BPD. Markowitz (1990) reported that BPD patients showed significant decreases in self-injurious behavior after treatment with fluoxetine 80 mg/day for 12 weeks. Three subsequent double-blind, placebo-controlled trials of fluoxetine confirmed the findings of the open trials (Markowitz 1992). Overall, controlled studies of fluoxetine, sertraline, and fluvoxamine suggest that these medications are of benefit to patients with impulsivity and aggression in the context of BPD. More studies are needed to assess further which behaviors are associated with responsivity to an SSRI, appropriate dosage, and longitudinal efficacy of those agents.

Researchers and clinicians have used lithium, carbamazepine, valproic acid, and more recently gabapentin, lamotrigine, and topiramate to treat the impulsivity, aggression, and mood instability seen in bipolar patients, and they subsequently reasoned that it might stabilize these same symptoms in BPD. In a double-blind, placebo-controlled trial (Cowdry and Gardner 1988), carbamazepine decreased impulsivity in a group of BPD patients. MAOIs have not been shown to decrease the behavioral dyscontrol or impulsivity seen in BPD. Furthermore, in BPD patients, overdosing on psychotropic agents is a common form of suicide, and MAOIs are

clearly dangerous in these situations.

The tricyclic antidepressants have been extensively studied in BPD for their effects on depression in BPD patients. Although they are clearly effective for depressive symptoms, tricyclic antidepressants have not been shown to be particularly helpful in decreasing aggression and impulsivity in BPD (Soloff et al. 1986). Some BPD patients actually experienced increased anger, hostility, and aggression while taking imipramine (Klein 1968) and amitriptyline (Soloff et al. 1986). There are case reports of using desipramine and clomipramine effectively to treat violent outbursts in some patients and of using amitriptyline, trazodone, and fluoxetine for aggression associated with brain injury and anoxic encephalopathy. The potential for worsening impulsive, aggressive symptoms and the danger of overdose in patients who have impaired self-control may limit the use of tricyclic antidepressants.

Neuroleptics are among the most studied medications for treatment of BPD, and they have been effective in treating violence associated with psychosis. Although they are the most commonly used medications for violence and aggression related to psychosis, neuroleptics are often chronically misused as sedatives. In BPD patients, however, neuroleptics were not well tolerated and were statistically no better than placebo in the reduction of hostility, anger, and aggression (Goldberg et al. 1986; Soloff et al. 1986). In one 8-week open-label pilot study, BPD patients treated with olanzapine had decreased Barratt Impulsivity Scale and Buss-Durkee Hostility Inventory scores compared with those treated with placebo (Schultz et al. 1999). Neuroleptics may result in a number of adverse side effects. They may cause tolerance to sedation and lead to increased doses and thereby increased side effects such as akathisia, extrapyramidal side effects, and anticholinergic toxicity. These specific side effects can worsen aggression in predisposed patients, particularly those with organic brain injury.

Our group (Stein et al. 1995) found that valproate led to significant overall improvement in 50% of a small sample of BPD patients who completed an 8-week open-label trial. Also, in a 10-week double-blind study, we found that valproate may be more effective than placebo (Hollander et al. 1998; Hollander et al. 2001). The medication was helpful for impulsivity, anger, and irritability as well as for mood instability and anxiety. The potential efficacy of valproate in the treatment of BPD raises the question of the neurobiological underpinnings of the core features of BPD, namely impulsivity and aggression. A number of points are relevant. First, a link between impulsive aggression and limbic abnormality has long been postulated. Although only a small percentage of BPD patients have seizure activity, more subtle neuropsychiatric abnormalities have been found in this population, including increased neurologic soft signs. The hypothesis that valproate alters limbic dysfunction by interrupting neuronal kindling is therefore of interest. Second, there is increasing evidence that serotonin hypofunction may play a role in the mediation of BPD symptoms. Although valproate has multiple effects on neurotransmission, it is notable that valproate increases 5-HIAA levels. Further studies and larger sample sizes for the use of valproate in the treatment of BPD are warranted.

## Treatment in the Developmentally Disabled

Autistic disorder and mental retardation are often associated with impulsive outbursts, emotional lability, rage episodes, and aggression toward self and others. Treatment with fluoxetine has decreased aggression, self-injury, and agitation in profoundly mentally retarded patients (Markowitz 1992). Lithium has been shown to be beneficial in a subset of children with rage, aggression, and irritability (DeLong 1978) and in mentally retarded patients with repeated, uncontrolled aggression and self-injury (Craft 1987). β-Blockers, which also bind to 5-$HT_1$-like receptors, have been found in open trials to lead to improvements in aggressive patients with neuropsychological disorders and in patients with impulsive aggression (Silver and Yudofsky 1995). Williams et al. (1982) documented the efficacy of propranolol in a diagnostically diverse population sharing the problem of rage outbursts. A series of case reports has indicated that carbamazepine treatment decreased rage outbursts and aggression in a group of patients demonstrating heterogeneous behaviors associated with aggression. Our group reported that valproate resulted in improvement in impulsive-aggressive symptoms and affective instability in autism spectrum disorders (Hollander et al. 2001). Buspirone, a nonbenzodiazepine, nonsedating 5-$HT_{1A}$ agonist, may be effective in the treatment of patients with developmental disabilities and head injury. These findings need further controlled trials. Eltoprazine, a phenylpiperazine derivative and mixed 5-$HT_1$ agonist, has shown antiaggressive properties in animal models. Eltoprazine-like compounds may be used in future treatment strategies and as a probe to further study the basis of impulsivity and aggression (Mak et al. 1995).

## References

Adamac R: Does the kindling model reveal anything clinically significant? Biol Psychiatry 27:249–279, 1990

American Psychiatric Association: Diagnostic and Statistical Manual of Mental Disorders, 3rd Edition, Revised. Washington, DC, American Psychiatric Association, 1987

American Psychiatric Association: Diagnostic and Statistical Manual of Mental Disorders, 4th Edition. Washington, DC, American Psychiatric Association, 1994

American Psychiatric Association: Diagnostic and Statistical Manual of Mental Disorders, 4th Edition, Text Revision. Washington, DC, American Psychiatric Association, 2000

Andrulonis PA, Glueck BC, Stroebel CF, et al: Organic brain dysfunction and the borderline syndrome. Psychiatr Clin North Am 4:47–66, 1981

Archer RP, Struve FA, Ball JD, et al: EEG in borderline personality disorder. Biol Psychiatry 24:731–732, 1988

Aronowitz B: Neuropsychiatric and neuropsychological findings in conduct disorder and attention-deficit hyperactivity disorder. J Neuropsychiatry Clin Neurosci 6:245–249, 1994

Åsberg M, Träskman L, Thorén P: 5-HIAA in the cerebrospinal fluid: a biochemical suicide predictor? Arch Gen Psychiatry 33:1193–1197, 1976

Bard P: A diencephalic mechanism for the expression of rage with special reference to the sympathetic nervous system. Am J Psychol 84:490–515, 1928

Bear DM: Neurological perspectives on aggression. J Neuropsychiatry Clin Neurosci 3 (suppl 1):3–8, 1991

Ben-Jonathan N, Abbogast LA, Hyde JF: Neuroendocrine regulation of prolactin release. Prog Neurobiol 33:399–447, 1989

Biegon A, Grinspoon A, Blumfeld R, et al: Increased serotonin 5-$HT_2$ receptor binding on blood platelets of suicidal men. Psychopharmacology (Berl) 100:165–167, 1990

Bioulac B, Benezech M, Renaud B, et al: Biogenic amines in 47 XYY syndrome. Biol Psychiatry 15:917–923, 1980

Brown CS, Kent TA, Bryant SG, et al: Blood platelet uptake of serotonin in episodic aggression. Psychiatry Res 27:5–12, 1989

Brown G, Goodwin F, Ballenger J, et al: Aggression in humans correlates with cerebrospinal fluid amine metabolites. Psychiatry Res 1:131–139, 1979

Brown G, Ebert M, Grayer P, et al: Aggression, suicide, and serotonin. Am J Psychiatry 139:741–746, 1982

Brunner D, Hen R: Insights into the neurobiology of impulsive behavior from serotonin receptor knockout mice. Ann N Y Acad Sci 836:81–105, 1997

Burgess JW: Relationship of depression and cognitive impairment to self-injury in borderline personality disorder, major depression, and schizophrenia. Psychiatry Res 38:77–87, 1991

Buss AH: The Psychology of Aggression. New York, Wiley, 1961

Buss AH, Durkee A: An inventory for assessing different kinds of hostility. J Consult Clin Psychol 21:343–349, 1957

Cadoret RJ, Yates WR, Troughton E, et al: Adoption study demonstrating two genetic pathways to drug abuse. Arch Gen Psychiatry 52:42–52, 1995

Carrasco JL, Saiz-Ruiz J, Diaz-Marsa M, et al: Low platelet monoamine oxidase activity in sensation-seeking bullfighters. CNS Spectrums 4(12):21–24, 1999

Carrasco JL, Diaz-Marsa M, Hollander E, et al: Decreased platelet monoamine oxidase activity in female bulimia nervosa. Eur Neuropsychopharmacol 10(2):113–117, 2000

Coccaro EF, Murphy DL (eds): Serotonin in Major Psychiatric Disorders. Washington, DC, American Psychiatric Press, 1990

Coccaro EF, Siever LJ, Klar H, et al: Serotonergic studies in affective and personality disorder patients: correlates with suicidal and impulsive aggressive behavior. Arch Gen Psychiatry 46:587–599, 1989

Coccaro EF, Lawrence T, Trestman R, et al: Growth hormone responses to intravenous clonidine challenge correlates with behavioral irritability in psychiatric patients and in healthy volunteers. Psychiatry Res 39:129–139, 1991

Coccaro EF, Kavoussi RJ, Sheline YI, et al: Impulsive aggression in personality disorders correlates with tritiated paroxetine binding in the platelet. Arch Gen Psychiatry 53:531–536, 1996

Coccaro EF, Kavoussi RJ, Cooper TB, et al: Central serotonin activity and aggression: inverse relationship with prolactin response to d-fenfluramine, but not CSF 5-HIAA concentration, in human subjects. Am J Psychiatry 154:1430–1435, 1997

Collier DA, Stober G, Li T et al: A novel functional polymorphism within the promoter of the serotonin transporter gene: possible role in susceptibility to affective disorders. Mol Psychiatry 1:453–460, 1996

Cornelius JR, Brenner RP, Soloff PH, et al: EEG abnormalities in borderline personality disorder: specific or nonspecific. Biol Psychiatry 21:974–977, 1986

Cornelius JR, Soloff PH, George AWA, et al: An evaluation of the significance of selected neuropsychiatric abnormalities in the etiology of borderline personality disorder. J Personal Disord 3:19–25, 1989

Cowdry RW, Gardner DL: Pharmacotherapy of borderline personality disorder: alprazolam, carbamazepine, trifluoperazine, and tranylcypromine. Arch Gen Psychiatry 45:111–119, 1988

Cowdry RW, Pickar D, Davies R: Symptoms and EEG findings in the borderline syndrome. Int J Psychiatry Med 15:201–211, 1985

Craft M, Ismail IA, Krishnamurti D, et al: Lithium in the treatment of aggression in mentally handicapped patients: a double blind trial. Br J Psychiatry 150:685–689, 1987

DeCaria CM: Diagnosis, neurobiology and treatment of pathological gambling. J Clin Psychiatry 57 (suppl 8):80–83, 1996

DeLong GR: Lithium carbonate treatment of select behavior disorders in children suggesting manic-depressive illness. J Pediatr 93:689–694, 1978

Depue RA, Spoont MR: Conceptualizing a serotonin trait: a behavioral dimension of constraint, in Psychobiology of Suicidal Behavior. Edited by Mann JJ, Stanley M. New York, New York Academy of Sciences, 1987, pp 71–73

Dicks P, Meyers RE, Kling A: Uncus and amygdala lesions: effects on social behavior in the free-ranging monkey. Science 165:69–71, 1969

Downer JL: Changes in visual gnostic functions and emotional behavior following unilateral temporal pole damage in the "split brain" monkey. Nature 191:50–51, 1961

Eichelman B: Effect of subcortical lesions on shock-induced aggression in the rat. Journal of Comparative and Physiological Psychology 74:331–339, 1971

Elliot FA: Violence: the neurological contribution: an overview. Arch Neurol 49:595–603, 1992

Federal Bureau of Investigation: Crime in the United States: Uniform Crime Reports, 1990. Washington, DC, U.S. Government Printing Office, 1991

Fedora O, Fedora S: Some neuropsychological and psychophysiological aspects of psychopathic and nonpsychopathic criminals, in Laterality and Psychopathology. Edited by Flor-Henry P, Gruzelier J. Amsterdam, The Netherlands, Elsevier, 1983, pp 20–25

Ferris CF, Stolberg T, Delville Y: Serotonin regulation of aggressive behavior in male golden hamsters (Mesocricetus auratus). Behav Neurosci 113(4):804–815, 1999

Fishbein DH, Lozovsky D, Jaffe JH: Impulsivity, aggression, and neuroendocrine responses to serotonergic stimulation in substance abusers. Biol Psychiatry 25:1049–1066, 1989

Gardner D, Lucas PB, Cowdry RW: Soft sign neurological abnormalities in borderline personality disorder and normal control subjects. J Nerv Ment Dis 3:177–180, 1987

Goldberg SC, Schulz SC, Schulz PM, et al: Borderline and schizotypal personality disorders treated with low-dose thiothixene vs. placebo. Arch Gen Psychiatry 43:680–686, 1986

Goyer PF, Andreason PJ, Semple WE, et al: Positron emission tomography and personality disorders. Neuropsychopharmacology 10:21–28, 1994

Grafman J, Schwab K, Warden D, et al: Frontal lobe injuries, violence, and aggression: a report of the Vietnam Head Injury Study. Neurology 46:1231–1238, 1996

Hathaway SR, McKinley JC: Minnesota Multiphasic Personality Inventory–2. Minneapolis, MN, University of Minnesota, 1989

Haugh RM, Markesbery WR: Hypothalamic astrocytoma: syndrome of hyperphagia, obesity, and disturbances of behavior and endocrine and autonomic function. Arch Neurol 40:560–563, 1983

Hen R: Enhanced aggressive behavior in mice lacking HT$_{1B}$ receptor. Science 265:119–123, 1994

Hess WR: The Functional Organization of the Diencephalon. New York, Grune & Stratton, 1957, p 180

Higley JD, Mehlman PT, Taub PM, et al: Cerebrospinal fluid monoamine and adrenal correlates of aggression in free-ranging rhesus monkeys. Arch Gen Psychiatry 48:437–441, 1992

Higley JD, Mehlman PT, Poland RE, et al: CSF testosterone and 5-HIAA correlate with different types of aggressive behaviors. Biol Psychiatry 40(11):1067–1082, 1996a

Higley JD, Suomi SJ, Linnoila M: A nonhuman primate model of type II excessive alcohol consumption?, I: low cerebrospinal fluid 5-hydroxindoleacetic acid concentrations and diminished social competence correlate with excessive alcohol consumption. Alcohol Clin Exp Res 20:629–642, 1996b

Hollander E, Wong CM: Obsessive-compulsive spectrum disorders. J Clin Psychiatry 56 (suppl 4):3–6, 53–55, 1995

Hollander E, Frenkel M, DeCaria C, et al: Treatment of pathological gambling with clomipramine (letter). Am J Psychiatry 149:710–711, 1992

Hollander E, Stein DJ, DeCaria CM, et al: Serotonergic sensitivity in borderline personality disorder: preliminary findings. Am J Psychiatry 151:277–280, 1994

Hollander E, DeCaria CM, Mari E, et al: Short-term single-blind fluvoxamine treatment of pathological gambling. Am J Psychiatry 155(12):1781–1783, 1998

Hollander E, DeCaria CM, Finkell J, et al: A randomized double-blind fluvoxamine/placebo crossover trial in pathological gambling. Biol Psychiatry 47:813–817, 2000

Hollander E, Allen A, Lopez, RP, et al: A preliminary double-blind placebo controlled trial of divalproex sodium in borderline personality disorder. J Clin Psychiatry 62:199–203, 2001

Hollander E, Dolgoff-Kaspar R, Cartwright C, et al: An open trial of divalproex sodium in autism spectrum disorders. J Clin Psychiatry 62:530–534, 2001

Huang YY, Grailhe R, Arango V, et al: Relationship of psychopathology to the human serotonin1B genotype and receptor binding kinetics in postmortem brain tissue. Neuropsychopharmacology 21(2):238–246, 1999

Isenberg N, Silbersweig D, Engelien A, et al: Linguistic threat activates the human amygdala. PNAS Online 96(18):10456–10459, 1999

Isern R: Family violence and the Klüver-Bucy syndrome. South Med J 80:373–377, 1987

Kandel E, Freed D: Frontal-lobe dysfunction and antisocial behavior: a review. J Clin Psychol 45:404–413, 1989

Kantak RM, Hegstrand LR, Eichelman B: Facilitation of shock-induced fighting following intraventricular 5,7-dihydroxy-tryptamine and 6-hydroxydopa. Psychopharmacology (Berl) 74:157–160, 1981

Kelly TH, Cherek DR: The effects of alcohol on free-operant aggressive behavior. J Stud Alcohol Suppl 11:40–52, 1993

Kernberg O: Borderline Conditions and Pathological Narcissism. Dunmore, PA, Jason Aronson, 1975

Killeffer FA, Stern WE: Chronic effects of hypothalamic injury. Arch Neurol 22:419–429, 1970

Klein DF: Psychiatric diagnosis and a typology of clinical drug effects. Psychopharmacologia 13:359–386, 1968

Klüver H, Bucy PC: Preliminary analysis of functions of the temporal lobes in monkeys. Archives of Neurological Psychiatry 42:979–1000, 1939

Kyes RC, Botchin MB, Kaplan JR, et al: Aggression and brain serotonergic responsivity: response to slides in male macaques. Physiol Behav 57:205–208, 1995

Lappalainen J, Long JC, Eggert M, et al: Linkage of antisocial alcoholism to the serotonin 5-HT$_{1B}$ receptor gene in two populations. Arch Gen Psychiatry 55:989–994, 1998

Lee GP, Bechara A, Adolphs R, et al: Clinical and physiological effects of stereotaxic bilateral amygdalotomy for intractable aggression. J Neuropsychiatry Clin Neurosci 10(4):413–420, 1998

LeMarquand D, Pihl RO, Benkelfat C: Serotonin and alcohol intake, abuse, and dependence: clinical evidence. Biol Psychiatry 36:326–337, 1994

LeMarquand DG, Benkelfat C, Pihl RO, et al: Behavioral disinhibition induced by tryptophan depletion in nonalcoholic young men with multigenerational family histories of paternal alcoholism. Am J Psychiatry 156(11):1771–1779, 1999

Lewis CE: Neurochemical mechanisms of chronic antisocial behavior: a literature review. J Nerv Ment Dis 179:720–729, 1991

Lewis DO, Pincus JH, Sharok SS, et al: Psychomotor epilepsy and violence in a group of incarcerated adolescent boys. Am J Psychiatry 139:882–887, 1982

Lidberg L, Åsberg M, Sundguist-Stensman UB: 5-Hydroxindoleacetic acid levels in attempted suicides who have killed their children (letter). Lancet 2:928, 1984

Lidberg L, Belfrage H, Bertilsson L, et al: Suicide attempts and impulse control disorder are related to low cerebrospinal fluid 5-HIAA in mentally disordered violent offenders. Acta Psychiatr Scand 101(5):395–402, 2000

Linden RD, Pope HG Jr, Jonas JM: Pathological gambling and major affective disorder: preliminary findings. J Clin Psychiatry 47:201–203, 1986

Links PS, Steiner M, Boiago I, et al: Lithium therapy for borderline patients: preliminary findings. J Clin Psychopharmacol 4:173–181, 1990

Linnoila M, Virkkunen M, Scheinin M, et al: Low cerebrospinal fluid 5-hydroxyindoleacetic acid concentration differentiates impulsive from nonimpulsive violent behavior. Life Sci 33:2609–2614, 1983

Lishman WA: Brain damage in relation to psychiatric disability after head injury. Br J Psychiatry 114:373–410, 1968

Lopez-Ibor JJ, Lana F, Saiz Ruiz J: Conductas autoliticas impulsivas y serotonina. Actas Luso-Espanolas de Neurologia, Psiquiatria y Ciencias Afines 18:316–325, 1990

Lucas PB, Gardner DL, Cowdry RW, et al: Cerebral structure in borderline personality disorder. Psychiatry Res 27:111–115, 1989

Luria AR: Higher Cortical Functions in Man. New York, Basic Books, 1980

Mak M, DeKoning P, Mos J, et al: Preclinical and clinical studies on the role of the 5-HT₁ receptors in aggression, in Impulsivity and Aggression. Edited by Hollander E, Stein DJ. New York, Wiley, 1995, pp 289–311

Mann JJ, McBride PA, Anderson GM, et al: Platelet and whole blood serotonin content in depressed inpatients: correlations with acute and lifetime psychopathology. Biol Psychiatry 32:243–257, 1992

Manuck SB, Flory JD, Ferrell RE, et al: Aggression and anger-related traits associated with a polymorphism of the tryptophan hydroxylase gene. Biol Psychiatry 45(5):603–614, 1999

Marazziti D, Conti L: Aggression, hyperactivity, and platelet IMI-binding. Acta Psychiatr Scand 84:209–211, 1991

Markowitz PI: Fluoxetine treatment of self-injurious behavior in the mentally retarded (letter). J Clin Psychopharmacol 10:299–300, 1990

Markowitz PI: Effect of fluoxetine on self-injurious behavior in the developmentally disabled: a preliminary study. J Clin Psychopharmacol 12:27–31, 1992

Marlowe WB, Mancall EL, Thomas JJ: Complete Klüver-Bucy syndrome in man. Cortex 11:53–59, 1975

McBurnett K, Lahey BB, Rathouz PJ, et al: Low salivary cortisol and persistent aggression in boys referred for disruptive behavior. Arch Gen Psychiatry 57(1):38–43, 2000

McElroy SC, Hudson JI, Pope HG Jr, et al: Kleptomania: clinical characteristics and associated psychopathology. Psychol Med 21:93–108, 1991

Moss HB, Yao YK, Panzak GL: Serotonergic responsivity and behavioral dimensions in antisocial personality disorder with substance abuse. Biol Psychiatry 28:325–338, 1990

Nachson I: Hemisphere function in violent offenders, in Biological Contributions to Crime Causation. Edited by Moffitt TE, Mednick SA. Dordrecht, Germany, Martinus Nijhoff, 1988, pp 55–67

Nakamura K, Kurasawa M, Shirane M: Impulsivity and AMPA receptors: aniracetam ameliorates impulsive behavior induced by a blockade of AMPA receptors in rats. Brain Res 862:266–269, 2000

New AS, Gelernter J, Yovell Y, et al: Tryptophan hydroxylase genotype is associated with impulsive-aggression measures: a preliminary study. Am J Med Genet 81:13–17, 1998

Nielson DA, Goldman D, Virkkunen M, et al: Suicidality and 5-hydroxyindoleacetic acid concentration associated with a tryptophan hydroxylase polymorphism. Arch Gen Psychiatry 51:34–38, 1994

Norden MJ: Fluoxetine in borderline personality disorder. Prog Neuropsychopharmacol Biol Psychiatry 13:885–893, 1989

O'Keane V, Moloney E, O'Neill H, et al: Blunted prolactin responses to d-fenfluramine in sociopathy: evidence for subsensitivity of central serotonergic function. Br J Psychiatry 160:643–646, 1992

Oquendo MA, Mann JJ: The biology of impulsivity and suicidality. Psychiatr Clin North Am 23(1):11–25, 2000

Ovsiew F, Yudofsky S: Aggression: a neuropsychiatric perspective, in Rage, Power, and Aggression: The Role of Affect in Motivation, Development and Adaptation. Edited by Glick RA, Roose SP. New Haven, CT, Yale University Press, 1983, pp 213–230

Philip A: The development and use of the Hostility and Direction of Hostility Questionnaire. J Psychosom Res 13:283–287, 1969

Raine A, Melroy JR, Bihrle S, et al: Reduced prefrontal and increased subcortical brain functioning assessed using positron emission tomography in predatory and affective murderers. Behav Sci Law 16(3):319–332, 1998

Ramirez LF, McCormick RA, Russo AM, et al: Patterns of substance abuse in pathological gamblers undergoing treatment. Addict Behav 8:425–428, 1983

Reeves AG, Plum F: Hyperphasia, rage, and dementia accompanying a ventromedial hypothalamus neoplasm. Arch Neurol 20:616–624, 1969

Rinne T, Westenberg HG, den Boer JA, et al: Serotonergic blunting to meta-chlorophenylpiperazine (m-CPP) highly correlates with sustained childhood abuse in impulsive and autoaggressive female borderline patients. Biol Psychiatry 47(6):548–556, 2000

Sabrie P: Reconciling the role of central serotonin neurons in human and animal behavior. Behav Brain Sci 9:319–364, 1986

Saiz J, Moreno I, Lopez-Ibor JJ: Ludopatia: estudio clinico y terapeutico-evolutivo de un grupo de jugadores patologicos. Actas Luso-Espanolas de Neurologia, Psiquiatrica y Ciencias Afines 20:189–197, 1992

Schultz SC, Camlin KL, Berry SA, et al: Olanzapine safety and efficacy in patients with borderline personality disorder and comorbid dysthymia. Biol Psychiatry 46:1429–1435, 1999

Serafetinides EA: Aggressiveness in temporal lobe epileptics and its relation to cerebral dysfunction and environmental factors. Epilepsia 6:33–42, 1965

Shaffer D, Schonfeld IS, O'Connor PA, et al: Neurological soft signs and their relationship to psychiatric disorder and intelligence in childhood and adolescence. Arch Gen Psychiatry 42:342–351, 1985

Siever LJ, Davis KL: A psychological perspective on the personality disorders. Am J Psychiatry 148:1647–1658, 1991

Siever LJ, Buchsbaum MS, New AS, et al: d,l-Fenfluramine response in impulsive personality disorder assessed with [18F]fluorodeoxyglucose positron emission tomography. Neuropsychopharmacology 20(5):413–423, 1999

Silver JM, Yudofsky SC: Organic mental disorder and impulsive aggression, in Impulsivity and Aggression. Edited by Hollander E, Stein D. New York, Wiley, 1995, pp 243–259

Simeon D, Stanley B, Frances A, et al: Self-mutilation in personality disorders: psychological and biological correlates. Am J Psychiatry 149:221–226, 1992

Singer MT: The borderline diagnosis and psychological tests: review and research, in Borderline Personality Disorder. Edited by Harticollis P. New York, International Universities Press, 1977, pp 193–212

Snyder S, Pitts WM, Gustin Q: CT scans of patients with borderline personality disorder (letter). Am J Psychiatry 140:272, 1983

Soloff PH, George A, Nathan RS, et al: Progress in pharmacology of borderline disorders. Arch Gen Psychiatry 43:691–697, 1986

Soloff PH, Cornelius J, Foglia J, et al: Platelet MAO in borderline personality disorder. Biol Psychiatry 29:499–502, 1991

Soloff PH, Meltzer CC, Greer PJ, et al: A fenfluramine-activated FDG-PET study of borderline personality disorder. Biol Psychiatry 47(6):540–547, 2000

Spielberger CD: Anger Expression Inventory. Odessa, FL, Psychological Assessment Resources, 1988

Stanley B, Molcho A, Stanley M, et al: Association of aggressive behavior with altered serotinergic function in patients who are not suicidal. Am J Psychiatry 157(4):609–614, 2000

Stein DJ: Trichotillomania and obsessive-compulsive disorder. J Clin Psychiatry 56 (suppl 4):28–34, 1995

Stein DJ, Hollander E, Liebowitz MR: Neurobiology of impulsivity and the impulse control disorders. J Neuropsychiatry Clin Neurosci 5:9–17, 1993

Stein DJ, Simeon D, Frenkel M, et al: An open trial of valproate in borderline personality disorder. J Clin Psychiatry 56:506–510, 1995

Stoff DM, Pollack L, Vitello B, et al: Reduction of (3H)-imipramine binding sites on platelets of conduct disordered children. Neuropsychopharmacology 1:55–62, 1987

Sudak HW, Maas JW: Behavioral neurochemical correlation in reactive and nonreactive strains of rats. Science 146:418–420, 1964

Taylor SP: Aggressive behavior and physiological arousal as a function of provocation and the tendency to inhibit aggression. J Pers 35:297–310, 1987

Terzian H, Ore JD: Syndrome of Klüver and Bucy reproduced in man by bilateral removal of the temporal lobes. Neurology 5:373–380, 1955

Virkkunen M, Linnoila M: Serotonin in early onset, male alcoholics with violent behaviour. Ann Med 22:327–331, 1990

Virkkunen M, Narvanen S: Plasma insulin, tryptophan and serotonin levels during the glucose tolerance test among habitually violent and impulsive offenders. Neuropsychobiology 17:19–23, 1987

Vitiello B, Stoff D, Atkins M, et al: Soft neurological signs and impulsivity in children. J Dev Behav Pediatr 11:112–115, 1990

Wasman M, Flynn JP: Directed attack elicited from the hypothalamus. Arch Neurol 6:220–227, 1962

Weiger WE, Bear DM: An approach to the neurology of aggression. J Psychiatr Res 22:85–98, 1988

Williams DT, Mehl R, Yudofsky S, et al: The effect of propranolol on uncontrolled rage outbursts in children and adolescents with organic brain dysfunction. Journal of the American Academy of Child Psychiatry 21:129–135, 1982

Yehuda R, Southwick SM, Edell WS, et al: Low platelet monoamine oxidase activity in borderline personality disorder. Psychiatry Res 30:265–273, 1989

Yeudall LT, Fromm-Auch D: Neuropsychological impairments in various psychopathological populations, in Hemisphere Asymmetries of Function in Psychopathology. Edited by Gruzelier J, Flor-Henry P. Amsterdam, The Netherlands, Elsevier, 1979, pp 81–83

# CHAPTER 17

# Neuropsychiatric Aspects of Memory and Amnesia

Yaakov Stern, Ph.D.

Harold A. Sackeim, Ph.D.

## Memory Systems

Our understanding of memory has increased dramatically during the past decade. Three related lines of research have demonstrated that memory is not a unitary entity and have outlined the nature of different memory "systems." First, in experimental cognitive research with healthy individuals, comparisons of different types of tasks have dissected memory into interrelated, but discriminable, processes. Second, studies of abilities that are differentially affected and retained in patients with discrete brain lesions have also supported the concept of distinct memory systems. Third, functional brain imaging studies, using cognitive challenge procedures with positron emission tomography (PET) or functional magnetic resonance imaging (fMRI) have contributed to the separation of memory processes and contributed to our understanding of the neural network mediating memory performance. For some memory systems, there is relatively good evidence that they are subserved by specific areas of the brain or by specific neural networks. Other systems without clear-cut anatomical correlates have been identified experimentally on the basis of the type of information they process or how they operate. Thus, whether some distinct memory systems actually represent different brain systems remains to be seen. In this section, we review the different aspects of memory that have been identified. The various systems are summarized in Figure 17–1.

Most memory researchers make an initial separation of memory into two categories: *declarative* and *non-declarative* (Cohen and Squire 1980; Squire 1992). Declarative memory describes the conscious recollection of words, scenes, faces, stories, and events. It is the type of memory assessed by traditional tests of recall and recognition, which rely on what has been called the *explicit* retrieval of information (Graf and Schacter 1985). Nondeclarative memory is best described in the negative—as a collection of memory processes that are not declarative. The hallmark of nondeclarative memory is evidence that some types of life experience can result in behavioral change without requiring conscious access to the experience—that is, without explicit recall. Tests of nondeclarative memory typically rely on what has been called *implicit* retrieval, and they attempt to demonstrate that a particular type of experience has resulted in a later change in behavior. Several types of memory are subsumed under the heading of nondeclarative memory. These include procedural memory, classical conditioning, simple associative learning, and priming. Separate from the declarative-nondeclarative distinction is working memory, which is viewed as an active memory buffer that can serve either as a scratch pad for newly acquired information or as a locus/mechanism for retrieving and operating on already stored information.

### Declarative Memory

Declarative memory is the aspect of memory that is most often assessed clinically with tests of recall or recognition. It is usually subdivided into two compo-

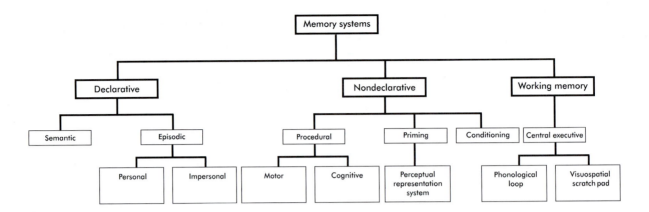

**FIGURE 17–1.** An outline of the components of memory.
*Source.* Adapted from Squire 1992.

nents: *semantic* and *episodic* memory (Tulving 1972, 1983). Semantic memory refers to the acquisition of factual information about the world. Typically, semantic memories cannot be fixed as having been acquired at a specific time. For example, although most people know that Shakespeare is the author of *Hamlet*, few can recall when they first acquired this information. Episodic memory refers to the recording and conscious recollection of personal experiences. Semantic memory is required for episodic memory. However, our typical recollections are more than simple facts. They include the spatial and temporal context of events as well as other associated features, such as the emotions associated with life events and the specific details that encompass life events. Episodic memory encompasses personal or autobiographical memories as well as memories for public events. Most standard clinical assessments of memory evaluate episodic memory. It is important to recognize that personal or autobiographical events may become episodic memories, losing any associated recall of spatial or temporal context. As a fact, we may remember that we graduated from college in a particular year but have no recall of the events surrounding the graduation.

A key observation underlying the current memory taxonomy is the view that declarative memory is dependent on the integrity of the hippocampus and its related structures. This was demonstrated most dramatically by the famous case of H.M., who underwent surgery for severe epilepsy (Milner 1959). The medial temporal region of this individual's brain was removed bilaterally, including the uncus, amygdala, anterior two-thirds of the hippocampus, and hippocampal gyrus. After the operation, H.M. was unable to retain new information if he was distracted for more than a few seconds from rehearsing the material. Thus, his performance on standard tests of recall was impaired, and he could not learn new vocabulary words. On the other hand, his recall of events remote from the operation was close to normal (Corkin 1984; Marslen-Wilson and Teuber 1975). Other intellectual functions, including IQ, were spared. H.M. remains densely amnesic to this day. H.M.'s case provided compelling evidence for the importance of the hippocampus and related structures to the process of memory formation and storage that underlies the laying down of new declarative memories. Indeed, the strongest argument for the existence of a memory system can be made for declarative memory, which can be convincingly demonstrated to rely, at least in part, on a specific set of brain structures.

## Nondeclarative Memory

The concept of nondeclarative memory stems from the observation that several types of memory tasks can be performed successfully even by patients who have sustained damage to the hippocampus and its associated structures (Cohen and Squire 1980) with marked deficits in declarative memory. The fact that studies of healthy control subjects have also demonstrated dissociations in task performance suggests that some tasks do not require declarative memory. Unlike declarative memory, nondeclarative memory cannot be considered a system. Rather, the term is simply a general classification for a disparate group of tasks (and presumably memory processes) whose performance is not mediated by conscious recall. Some of these tasks have been grouped into hypothetical systems, and these are described in the following sections. One unifying feature of nondeclarative memory tasks is that they demand implicit recall, in which there is no need for conscious storage or recall of material.

## Procedural Memory

The term *procedural memory* is typically applied to tasks that assess the acquisition of motor or cognitive skills. One can describe procedural memory as "knowing how," as opposed to declarative memory's "knowing that" (Cohen and Squire 1980).

A well-investigated test of procedural memory is the Tower of Hanoi task. In this task, which is based on an old puzzle, the subject is given a board with three posts. On one of the posts is a pile of disks of graduated sizes, so that each disk is smaller than the one below it. The subject's task is to move all of the disks from one post to another, following two rules: only one disk can be moved at a time, and a larger disk can never be put on top of a smaller disk. The key to solving this puzzle is to develop the optimal sequence of moves needed to move the disks. With practice, an amnesic patient can improve his or her performance on this task to the optimal level (Cohen 1984; Cohen and Corkin 1981). When given the task again at a later date, the amnesic patient does not remember ever having performed it and needs to be taught the rules as if this were his or her first exposure. However, once the patient begins to perform the task, it is clear that the performance level is far better than at the first exposure to the task. Thus, although the individual has no episodic memory for the task or its rules, the procedures or strategies that contribute to task performance have been retained. This procedural memory is thought to be not dependent on the parahippocampal structures and is *implicit*.

Procedural memory has also been demonstrated for motor tasks. One example is the pursuit rotor task, in which the subject must learn to keep a stylus touching a spot on a revolving turntable. As with the more cognitively based Tower of Hanoi task, amnesic patients can learn and retain this skill (Corkin 1968). Other tests of procedural learning include mirror reading and jigsaw puzzle assembly.

The brain areas that mediate procedural memory have not been identified. However, because several studies have suggested that learning the pursuit rotor task depends on the integrity of the basal ganglia, the possibility exists that procedural memory for motor tasks depends on areas of the brain associated with initial task acquisition and performance (Butters et al. 1990). Similarly, it has been suggested that the brain structures that mediate the acquisition and initial performance of nonmotor tasks also mediate procedural memory for these cognitive skills.

## Simple Conditioning and Simple Associative Learning

Amnesic patients can acquire new conditioned responses. In one early study, Weiskrantz and Warrington (1979) assessed classical conditioning of the blink response in two amnesic patients. These patients retained conditioned responses for as long as 24 hours even though they did not recognize the conditioning apparatus. Other simple associative learning is also intact in amnesic patients.

## Priming

Priming is another type of nondeclarative memory that requires implicit recall. Some investigators have suggested that distinct memory systems may underlie performance on priming tasks. *Priming* can be defined as the facilitated identification of perceptual objects from reduced cues as a consequence of prior exposure to those objects (Tulving and Schacter 1990).

In a typical priming task, the subject studies some material but is not told that he or she will be expected to recall it. For example, the subject may be given a list of words and asked to identify those that contain a particular letter or to make some judgment about the words (e.g., degree of pleasantness). A key feature of the subsequent retrieval task is that it is also implicit. For example, in one typical retrieval task, the subject is given the first three letters of words (i.e., word stems) and is asked to generate words that begin with those stems as quickly as possible. Half of the word stems are the beginnings of words to which the subject was previously exposed, whereas the other half correspond to new words. In this experiment, the subject will generate words more rapidly for stems of previously studied words. This priming effect is not dependent on explicit recall and is present in amnesic patients (Graf and Schacter 1985). In addition, this priming experiment includes an explicit-recall component, usually a recognition task in which the subject is given a list of words containing both previously studied and new words. Typically, the subject's ability to discriminate the "old" from the "new" words is quite poor, thus demonstrating that exposure to the words was not sufficient for retrieval in a standard explicit recall task.

A wide range of priming paradigms have been used. The studied material has included words, shapes, and sounds. The mode of exposure of the studied list has also been extensively varied, and these studies have provided insight into the memory processes underlying priming. An important feature of the subject's initial exposure to the list is the "level of processing." A distinction can be made between instructions that call attention to the perceptual features of items (e.g., their shape, constituent letters) and those that require a deeper or more conceptual level of processing (e.g., making judgments about whether words belong to specific categories). In general, the more the mode of study is perceptual in nature (a quality some call "data driven"), the better the priming performance. In contrast, deeper conceptual study is more beneficial to declarative modes of recall (Blaxton 1995).

Some priming tasks benefit from deeper levels of processing. These tasks, known as conceptual priming tasks, require semantic processing of the task stimuli and often require responses that are conceptually or semantically related to a stimulus. For example, subjects are given the name of a category (e.g., animal) and asked to produce the first instance that comes to mind (e.g., bear). It has been argued that these conceptual priming tasks differ from standard perceptual priming and rely on semantic learning (Tulving and Schacter 1990).

The sensitivity of priming performance to perceptual manipulation, as well as its lack of reliance on hippocampal systems, has led some theorists to suggest that priming is an expression of *perceptual representation systems* (PRSs)— a group of domain-specific subsystems that process and represent information about the form and structure, but not the meaning or other associative properties, of words and objects (Tulving and Schacter 1990). PRSs are thought to involve the brain areas responsible for the initial perception and processing of material. Schacter and colleagues have proposed three such systems: *visual word form* (Schacter 1990), *auditory word form* (Schacter and Church 1992), and *structural description* (Schacter et al. 1990). The most carefully worked out of these hypothesized systems is the visual word form PRS, which presumably mediates most of the visually presented verbal priming tasks. This system would include areas in the occipital cortex and elsewhere that are important for visual processing, but would exclude both those areas involved in the semantic processing of words and those implicated in explicit recall.

# Working Memory

Working memory is typically viewed as distinct from the declarative and nondeclarative memory systems. In one sense, working memory is similar to what in the past has been called short-term memory. It provides a repository for briefly holding on to information such as a telephone number or the name of a newly met person. It is also important in tasks that require mental manipulation of information, such as multistep arithmetic problems. However, for many theorists (e.g., Goldman-Rakic 1992), working memory also has a more important role as the work space where recalled information is actually used, manipulated, and related to other information, thus allowing complex cognitive processes such as comprehension, learning, and reasoning to take place.

A detailed model of working memory was proposed by Baddeley and colleagues (Baddeley 1986). In this model, working memory is viewed not as a single memory buffer, but instead as three interrelated components: an attentional controller termed the central executive, which is aided by two active slave subsystems, the articulatory or phonological loop and the visuospatial scratch pad or sketch pad.

The phonological loop maintains speech-based information. Without any intervention, this information would fade rapidly. However, the information can be maintained for longer periods in the loop by an articulatory control process, which in effect recycles or rehearses the information. Thus, one way to hold on to a telephone number until it is dialed is to mentally repeat it continuously. Similar to the phonological loop, the visuospatial scratch pad briefly stores and rehearses visuospatial information.

Although the central executive is presumably the most important component of working memory, its role is the least well defined. One function of the central executive is to coordinate information from the separate subsystems. In one study of this function, subjects were asked to simultaneously perform pursuit-tracking and digit-span tasks, the latter of which involves remembering a newly presented string of numbers. Because these two tasks rely on the phonological loop and the visuospatial scratch pad, a subject's relative ability or inability to perform them simultaneously may reflect the capacity of the central executive. Another function attributed to the central executive is the organization and generation of new strategies for the retrieval or processing of information.

## Memory Consolidation

Studies of amnesic patients, as well as of nonamnesic humans and animals treated with electroconvulsive shock or specific medications, suggest that there is a difference between how memory is stored for short and for longer periods of time. The short-term memory store has limited capacity and persists for just a few minutes without rehearsal. This level of storage is probably comparable to that described in the working memory system. The short-term memory store is thought to be based on either short-term changes in synaptic transmission or on some form of ongoing neural activity that maintains the information. Manipulations that silence neuronal activity, such as cooling or anoxia, can disrupt short-term memory but not long-term memory.

If memory is to persist longer, it must be transferred into a long-term memory store. However, the long-term memory store can also be subdivided into an earlier phase that is relatively sensitive to disruption and a later phase that is more insensitive to disruption. As reviewed below, immediately following a treatment course with electroconvulsive therapy (ECT), deficits in the recall or recognition of both personal and public information learned before treatment are common; that is, retrograde amnesia (Lisanby et al. 2000; Sackeim 1992; Sackeim et al. 1993, 2000). These deficits are greatest for events that occurred temporally closest to the treatment (i.e., typically within weeks or months) (Lisanby et al. 2000; McElhiney et al. 1995; Squire 1986). Thus, whereas memory for more remote events is intact, patients may have difficulty recalling events that occurred during and several months—or, in some cases, a few years—before the ECT course. This observation is consistent with the idea that the more recent memories are more easily disrupted because they have not yet been stored in their final long-term memory form. In classic amnesia, the retrograde amnesia can also have a temporal gradient, with poorer recall for more recent information (Russell and Nathan 1946). The observation that ECT-caused retrograde amnesia is mostly transitory argues that the memory stores themselves are not affected by ECT, but rather the ability to retrieve these memories (Sackeim 1992).

Animal studies using agents designed to block protein or mRNA synthesis have shown that long-term memory is selectively impaired and short-term memory is unaffected (Davis and Squire 1984). In this case, the actual long-term storage of the material may be affected, rather than the retrieval from long-term storage. Thus, memories in the later phase of long-term storage are probably in the form of actual protein changes that alter the connections between neurons.

## System Versus Process Concepts

Some investigators have preferred to categorize memory tasks in a way that does not rely on the concept of systems. Thus, for example, the dissociations between performance on a task that requires implicit retrieval (such as priming) and one that requires explicit retrieval (such as a word recognition test) might not be a function of the use of separate memory systems. Rather, a *process-based* view of memory would posit that these dissociations are a function of the type of processing performed on the test material at study and test. In general, to the degree that the type of processing at study is recapitulated at test, memory performance will improve (Blaxton 1995; Gabrieli 1995). Two types of processing are typically considered: conceptually driven, which is based on the semantic meaning of stimuli, and data driven, which is based on perceptual features of stimuli. Often, the study phase of priming tests is data driven, with the subject

instructed to attend to some perceptual feature of the studied material. This procedure creates an advantage in a data-driven test such as the word-fragment technique sometimes used in priming tasks (as described above) and a disadvantage in a more conceptually driven task such as word recognition. Alternatively, when material is studied at a conceptually driven level—for example, by generating synonyms to the studied words—an advantage is created in tests that also require this type of processing. Thus, the process-based approach argues that it is not necessary to posit that implicit and explicit retrieval reflect two distinct memory systems. Rather, processing matches or mismatches can be introduced into tasks requiring either type of retrieval with predictable results.

Proponents of the process-based approach most often study healthy subjects, although predictions from this approach have been supported in some studies of populations with brain damage, including left temporal lobe epilepsy and Alzheimer's disease (Blaxton 1992). The process-based predictions are not completely upheld, however, in individuals with diencephalic/bilateral medial temporal amnesia (Keane et al. 1993). These patients appear to have normal priming on implicit conceptual memory tasks but are impaired on explicit conceptual tasks. This pattern supports the argument that these patients have a deficit in explicit recall, as systems theorists would predict. Most theorists now agree that systems-based and process-based approaches are not mutually exclusive and that manipulations of processing type can enrich insights about the nature of memory systems.

## Coordinating Memory Systems

Although experimental manipulations and careful observation of patients with brain lesions support the concept of dissociable memory systems, it should be emphasized that these systems do not usually operate independently. For example, in a healthy subject, a priming task probably does not measure implicit recall only, because performance might also be aided by explicit recall. Consequently, most experimenters design priming studies to minimize the influence of explicit recall. Others, however, have developed techniques that attempt to evaluate the relative contribution of explicit (or conscious) and explicit (or unconscious) recall during the performance of a memory task (Jacoby et al. 1992).

More importantly, memory theorists have proposed models of memory that suggest how the different memory systems are normally integrated. Presented here is a simplification of one such model, proposed by Moscovitch (1994). Modules similar to the PRS previously described are responsible for the perception and encoding of information. Other associated central systems semantically encode the perceptual information. These systems operate automatically (without awareness) and may subserve implicit recall. The information from these systems can be delivered to working memory, where it can be briefly stored or processed. According to Moscovitch, information in working memory that receives full conscious attention is automatically processed by the hippocampus and related structures. Storage in these structures is in the form of simple association, in which a cue in working memory will produce the associated memories from the hippocampal structures regardless of whether they are relevant. Input to the hippocampus from working memory and output from the hippocampus to working memory can be guided, organized, and evaluated by executive systems, most likely located in prefrontal cortex. In this model, "the frontal lobes are necessary for converting remembering from a stupid reflexive act triggered by a cue to an intelligent, reflective, goal-directed activity under voluntary control" (Moscovitch 1994, pp. 278–279). Acquisition and retention of skills in procedural memory tasks may be mediated by modification of the same structures that are involved in task performance, similar to the operation of PRSs in priming tasks. This model integrates the reviewed declarative and nondeclarative memory systems, as well as the components of working memory, into a coordinated system and provides a framework for how these systems interact. Clearly, in the course of day-to-day activities, all of these systems must work together to allow us to store, recall, and use memories.

## Amnesia

*Amnesia* is the generic term for severe memory deficit, regardless of cause. Table 17–1 summarizes the DSM-IV-TR (American Psychiatric Association 2000) criteria for amnesia.

**TABLE 17–1.** DSM-IV-TR criteria for amnestic disorder

A. The development of memory impairment as manifested in the inability to learn new information or the inability to recall previously learned information.

B. The memory disturbance causes significant impairment in social or occupational functioning and represents a significant decline from a previous level of functioning.

C. The memory disturbance does not occur exclusively during the course of a delirium or a dementia.

Four clinical characteristics are typical of most amnesic patients: anterograde amnesia, retrograde amnesia, confabulation, and intact intellectual function. Anterograde amnesia is the hallmark of an amnesic disorder; it refers to the inability after the onset of the disorder to acquire new information for explicit retrieval. Retrograde amnesia refers to difficulty in retrieving events that occurred before the onset of the amnesic disorder, often demarcated as the time of head trauma, stroke, or other injury. It is more variably present in different amnesias. When amnesic patients are asked to recall information and cannot, they may confabulate, providing made-up or inaccurate information without having any apparent awareness that their responses are incorrect. Again, confabulation does not occur in all amnesias, and it is often more common in the acute stage of the neuropsychiatric illness. Finally, in the classic amnesic disorders, the patients' intellectual function remains relatively intact even though some specific secondary cognitive defects may be noted on careful neuropsychological testing.

## Lesions of the Mesial Regions of the Temporal Lobes

The classic case of bilateral mesial temporal lobe (MTL) ablation is the patient H.M., who was described earlier in this chapter. Since his surgery, H.M. has had severe anterograde amnesia and essentially cannot recall or recognize virtually any newly learned information. He can remember events from his early childhood but has difficulty with events that occurred just before his operation, indicating a restricted retrograde amnesia. His IQ is in the normal range.

Although bilateral temporal lobectomies are rare, unilateral temporal lobectomies are commonly performed to treat intractable seizure disorders. This operation is usually effective in treating the seizure disorder, and patients may have no obvious memory deficits. However, careful testing often demonstrates subtle memory impairments, with removal of the left temporal lobe commonly producing relative deficits in verbal memory and removal of the right temporal lobe producing relative deficits in remembering nonverbal information, indicating material-specific amnesia. A similar pattern has often been demonstrated in the acute postictal state following ECT, where unilateral treatment with electrodes on the left side produces greater persistence of postictal confusion and verbal anterograde and retrograde memory deficits, whereas stimulation over the right hemisphere produces greater anterograde and retrograde memory deficits for nonverbal material (Sackeim 1992). Likewise, left and right medial temporal lobe sclerosis due to epilepsy has been associated with material-specific amnesia.

## Wernicke-Korsakoff Syndrome

Wernicke-Korsakoff syndrome is the prototypical example of diencephalic amnesia, given that the memory disorders seen in this condition are attributed to lesions of mesial diencephalic brain structures, including the dorsomedial nucleus of the thalamus and/or the mamillary bodies (Victor et al. 1989). The syndrome is typically observed in nutritionally depleted alcoholic patients. When the diet is insufficient, neuronal injury occurs in thiamine-dependent areas of the brain and can lead to the characteristic lesions associated with this condition. In the acute phase, Wernicke's encephalopathy, common presenting complaints include mental confusion, staggering gait, ocular symptoms, and polyneuropathy. The chronic phase of the disease, Korsakoff's psychosis, is characterized by both anterograde and retrograde memory deficits. The anterograde amnesia is dense, with the patient unable to recall events that are no longer in working memory. Retrograde amnesia consists of difficulty recalling past personal or public events. Recall is poorest for events that are closest to the onset of the amnesia and improves for events in the more distant past. This pattern of retrograde amnesia is called a temporal gradient (Albert et al. 1979). Performance on IQ tests is comparable to that of chronic alcoholic individuals without amnesia. Deficits can be demonstrated, however, on tests that require speed and visuoperceptual and spatial organization components. The neuropathology of this syndrome consists of lesions to the paraventricular regions of the thalamus, the hypothalamus, the mamillary bodies, the periaqueductal region of the midbrain, the floor of the fourth ventricle, and the superior vermis (Victor et al. 1989).

## Frontal Lobe Lesions and the Role of the Frontal Lobes in Memory

Most of the literature investigating frontal lobe lesions has concentrated on cognitive functions other than memory. Although the frontal lobes are complex structures with many differentiated areas and functions, the consensus had long been that lesions to the frontal lobes do not produce the kinds of memory deficits that are seen in amnesia. Memory performance is affected in patients with frontal lobe lesions, but this has been attributed to the role of frontal structures in the placement of information into spatial and temporal contexts and in the execution of complex mnemonic strategies (Baddeley 1986; Milner et al. 1985). Without context, it is difficult to organize information for storage or retrieval. Some patients with frontal lobe lesions have been described as not being able to remember to remember; that is, they do not spontaneously initiate the activity required to retrieve information or to identify a retrieval strategy. This view of the frontal lobes in memory loss is concordant with the model of memory systems set forth above.

However, a recent meta-analysis of studies relating frontal lobe lesions to tests of recognition, cued recall, and free recall suggests that all three types of performance are disrupted in patients with frontal lobe lesions (Wheeler et al. 1995). In many published studies, there was a nonsignificant trend toward better performance in the control groups, and the failure to obtain statistically significant differences was often attributed to a lack of statistical power. This weakness is eliminated with meta-analysis. The review found that these patients performed more poorly on recall than on recognition tests, which again may implicate the processes involved in the organization of information and the initiation of recall as the primary reasons for the memory deficit. However, the patients' performances were also poorer than those of control subjects on recognition tasks, which may suggest that the frontal lobes have a more primary role in episodic memory.

Nonetheless, the role of the frontal lobe in memory processes is undergoing substantial reevaluation. This stems principally from several sources of evidence. First, frontal lobe damage can result in a profound, temporally graded retrograde amnesia (Kopelman 1992; Kopelman et al. 1999; Moscovitch 1994; Shimamura 1994; Stuss and Benson 1986), in some comparisons as great as MTL pathology (Kopelman et al. 1999) and presumably due to the disruption of retrieval processes. In amnesic patients, anterograde and retrograde amnesia are often weakly associated, and there is evidence that tests of frontal lobe (executive) function covary with the magnitude of retrograde amnesia (Kopelman 1992).

Markowitsch (1995, 2000) conducted a careful analysis of the sites of injury in brain-damaged patients with preserved anterograde memory but marked retrograde amnesia. He proposed that ventrolateral (orbital) prefrontal cortex and temporopolar cortex, interconnected through the ventral branch of the uncinate fasciculus, are essential for the retrieval of declarative information from long-term memory, with the caveat that right-side damage was especially associated with retrograde amnesia. A host of imaging studies in normal samples have shown activation of ventrolateral prefrontal cortex and anterolateral portions of the temporal cortex during episodic memory retrieval (Buckner 1996; Buckner et al. 1995, 1998a, 1998b, 1999, 2000; S. Kapur et al. 1995; Lepage et al. 2000; Shallice et al. 1994; Tulving and Markowitsch 1997; Tulving et al. 1994a, 1994b, 1999). Thus, the evidence from focal retrograde amnesia (N. Kapur 1999) and imaging studies of normal recall or recognition of newly learned information emphasizes a key contribution of the ventrolateral prefrontal cortex and the temporal pole.

More generally and surprisingly, early imaging studies of the retrieval of newly learned information had difficulty in showing MTL activation (Schacter and Wagner 1999). However, recent work has suggested that there may be differential encoding/retrieval activation within the hippocampus along the rostral-caudal axis (Lepage et al. 1998). In addition, the novelty of stimuli may strongly affect the nature of MTL activation. Saykin et al. (1999) and Johnson et al. (2001), using fMRI, in normal participants, found that the processing of novel words led to activation of the left anterior hippocampus, whereas recognition of familiar words activated the left posterior parahippocampal gyrus and right dorsolateral prefrontal cortex. In particular, retrieval success was strongly associated with activation of the right dorsolateral prefrontal cortex (Johnson et al. 2001).

Overall, it is more firmly established from imaging studies that dorsal prefrontal cortical regions participate in retrieval of newly learned information. Tulving and colleagues offered the hemispheric encoding/retrieval asymmetry (HERA) model (S. Kapur et al. 1995; Nyberg et al. 1996a, 1996b, 1996c, 1998, 2000; Tulving and Markowitsch 1997, 1998; Tulving et al. 1994a, 1994b), which posits that the left prefrontal cortex (particularly the dorsolateral prefrontal cortex) is critical to the encoding of novel information in episodic memory and retrieval from semantic memory. In contrast, the right prefrontal cortex (particularly the dorsolateral prefrontal cortex) is critical in episodic memory retrieval. HERA has been carefully critiqued (Buckner 1996; Nyberg et al. 1996a), and regions involved in encoding/retrieval have been refined. For instance, S. Kapur et al. (1995) distinguished between general retrieval attempt and successful retrieval of stored memories ("ecphory"). Although the former was associated with primarily right prefrontal (Brodmann's area[s] [BA] 9/10/46) activation, the latter was characterized by activation of more posterior right-sided regions (right cuneus-precuneus). Subsequently, Lepage et al. (2000) made the distinction between episodic retrieval mode and ecphory. Retrieval mode was associated with right greater than left prefrontal cortical activation, including BA 9/10. They concluded that the retrieval asymmetry in HERA is explained by the asym-

metry in retrieval mode, but that the new findings did not necessitate reformulation of the encoding asymmetry aspect of HERA (left greater than right). In other work, this group has used partial least squares analyses of imaging data and identified a functional network involving the right prefrontal cortex, left MTL, and left parietal regions (cuneus-precuneus) in episodic retrieval (Nyberg et al. 2000). Thus, beyond the MTL, recent work on memory retrieval of newly learned information in normal subjects has generally emphasized right-sided dorsal prefrontal (typically dorsolateral) structures, as well as ventromedial and temporopolar regions. Of note, the left dorsolateral prefrontal cortex is thought to be critical in the retrieval of semantic memories (facts about the world).

This imaging work with normal participants has focused on retrieval of (impersonal) newly learned information (e.g., word lists). Relevance to our understanding of retrograde amnesia in patients with lesions (or who have received ECT) or for the processes mediating memories of our own past may be questionable. Only a small set of studies has examined activation patterns during recall of autobiographical memories in healthy subjects (with only case studies of patients with retrograde amnesia), and, in general, this literature is methodologically compromised (e.g., no control over the age of events recalled, no verification of accuracy of recall, etc.). Andreasen et al. (1995) found left dorsolateral prefrontal activation during recall of autobiographical or personal memories. Because their procedure involved verbalization during scanning, the researchers repeated the experiment with silent recall (Andreasen et al. 1999), finding activation of medial and orbital frontal cortex, anterior cingulate gyrus, left parietal regions, and left thalamus. In line with HERA, Fink et al. (1996) found that retrieval of autobiographical memories activated multiple right hemisphere regions, including dorsal prefrontal cortex (BA 6), temporomedial, temporoparietal, and temporolateral cortex, and posterior cingulate gyrus. There was also activation of MTL structures, including amygdala, hippocampus, and parahippocampus. In contrast, Conway et al. (1999) found activation predominantly of the left side (frontal BA 6/44/45) and the inferior temporal lobe (BA 20) in response to recall of both recent and remote autobiographical memories. These researchers also detected hippocampal activation under both conditions, implying that even if remote memory storage extends beyond MTL regions, intact hippocampal function may be necessary for successful retrieval. Finally, Maguire and Mummery (1999) found evidence of activation of the left temporal pole, left medial frontal cortex (BA 10), and the left hippocampus during retrieval of autobiographical memories. Taken together, these studies indicate that there is great uncertainty about the exact region(s) necessary for retrieval of autobiographical memories in normal participants. Furthermore, unlike the larger literature on retrieval of newly learned information, this handful of imaging studies of autobiographical memory has not explicitly examined the consequences of unsuccessful ecphory of events, that is, amnesia. Finally, aside from Conway et al. (1999), no study has examined differential activation of recent versus remote autobiographical memories, despite the fact that most theories suggest a time-limited role for events to be stored in the MTL before being permanently transferred to cortical representations (e.g., Moscovitch 1994).

## Alzheimer's Disease

Alzheimer's disease is a progressive dementing disorder that affects a wide range of intellectual functions. The hallmark of all dementias is acquired amnesia, along with deficits in other cognitive functions. Patients with Alzheimer's disease have difficulty learning new material. In addition, their memory deficit is characterized by rapid forgetting of newly acquired material (Welsh et al. 1992). In addition, as the disease progresses, there is a growing retrograde amnesia, typically manifesting a classic temporal gradient, with greatest preservation of remote memories. Recent studies suggest that the memory deficit of Alzheimer's disease is actually present years before the clinical diagnosis becomes apparent (Jacobs et al. 1995). The histopathologic manifestations of Alzheimer's disease—cell loss, senile plaques, and neurofibrillary tangles—are relatively widespread but early in the disease are primarily present in the hippocampus and surrounding entorhinal cortex (Ball et al. 1985).

Twelve elderly persons who had documented isolated memory decline over 3 years but no dementia were studied with an fMRI paradigm in which they studied pictured faces for later recall (Small et al. 1999). The subjects were dichotomized into two subgroups: four with diminished entorhinal activation (i.e., entorhinal activation at least 2 standard deviations below that of the normal elderly) and eight with normal entorhinal activation. The diminished entorhinal activation subgroup had diminished activation in the hippocampus proper and the subiculum compared with healthy elderly persons. This group may have preclinical Alzheimer's disease. The normal-activation subgroup had diminished activation restricted to the subiculum. This subgroup of subjects is unlikely to have early Alzheimer's disease, but may have memory decline for some other reason. Thus, diminished activation of the entorhinal cortex and hippocampus may

be an early marker of Alzheimer's disease. This is compatible with the evidence that atropy of the hippocampus and surrounding entorhinal cortex is an early marker of Alzheimer's disease.

Recent imaging work suggests that some patients with early Alzheimer's disease utilize the same neural networks as matched elderly control subjects when performing memory tasks (Stern et al. 2000). In contrast, other patients appear to utilize different and apparently compensatory networks. The use of compensatory networks is associated with poorer memory performance and may mark a stage of disease progression in which pharmacologic attempts to arrest the disease process may be less successful.

## Psychiatric Disorders and Normal Aging

The major psychiatric disorders—schizophrenia, mania, and major depression—almost invariably compromise aspects of attention and concentration (Goldberg and Gold 1995; Sackeim and Steif 1988). Because the ability to focus and sustain attention is central to the acquisition of new information in general and declarative memory in particular, deficits in acquiring new information are common among these patients.

### Mood Disorders

Since the classic work of Cronholm and Ottosson (1961), it has been repeatedly demonstrated that although patients experiencing an episode of major depression or mania have a reduced capacity to learn new, unstructured information, they are usually less impaired in retaining whatever information they do learn. For example, in verbal and nonverbal paired-associate tasks, depressed patients will typically recall fewer items than will matched control subjects when tested immediately after stimulus presentation, with the extent of this deficit often associated with measures of depression severity and reversing with successful treatment (Bornstein et al. 1991; Steif et al. 1986; Sternberg and Jarvik 1976). In contrast, after controlling for the amount of information learned, researchers have found that depressed patients and control subjects typically do not differ in the percentage of the material recalled after a delay. Thus, in general, depression appears to have a greater influence on the acquisition than the retention of information (D.B. Burt et al. 1995). This is not to say that memory impairments cannot be identified in mood disorder samples. In a meta-analysis, Zakzanis et al. (1998) found that anterograde memory tests were among the most discriminative neuropsychological measures in distinguishing patients with major depression and matched control subjects. In part, this may be due to the contribution of attentional deficits to memory performance.

This acquisition impairment is most marked for material that is unstructured and that exceeds the capacity of working memory. Healthy individuals are capable of recalling or recognizing 7 ± 2 items immediately after presentation, and this aspect of short-term memory is often assessed with digit-span tests. The evidence is mixed that digit-span performance is impaired in the major mood disorders (Breslow et al. 1980; Gass and Russell 1986; Whitehead 1973). When deficits on this measure are observed in mood disorder patients, it is generally thought that the deficits reflect not an inherent limitation in the capacity of working memory, but rather an attentional dysfunction, with difficulties in concentration leading to greater distractibility and interference effects.

Other sources support the notion that attentional dysfunction and, more generally, impaired executive skills commonly form the basis for memory deficits in mood disorders (Sackeim and Steif 1988). Calev and Erwin (1985) compared depressed patients and healthy control subjects on a verbal memory task in which the difficulty of recall and recognition was matched. Depressed patients demonstrated deficits in recall but not in recognition. This finding suggested that there were no deficits in the consolidation and storage of information, but that depressed patients had a reduced ability to organize effective retrieval strategies. Furthermore, the deficits in episodic memory seen in depressed patients are most pronounced when the material to be learned is unstructured. For example, when given a list of words to remember that are drawn from semantic categories (e.g., pants, shirt, shoe) in which the order of words is clustered by category, depressed patients are typically equivalent to healthy control subjects in recall. However, when overt clustering is not provided, patients manifest a recall deficit (Backman and Forsell 1994; Channon et al. 1993; Weingartner et al. 1981). This finding suggests that depressed patients are less likely both to spontaneously impose organization on new information and to link that information to preexisting knowledge. Consequently, the depth of encoding is more shallow, resulting in impaired learning and retrieval.

Cognitive psychologists have distinguished between *automatic* and *effortful* processing (Hasher and Zacks 1979). Similar to the notion of nondeclarative memory, automatic operations place limited demands on attentional capacity and occur without intention or awareness.

Our learning and retaining what we had for breakfast—that is, *incidental* learning—is an example of automatic processing. In contrast, effortful processing requires the use of limited attentional capacity, is initiated intentionally, and benefits from rehearsal. Committing to memory a long shopping list is an example of effortful processing. In general, depressed patients are more likely to manifest deficits on tasks that require effort or greater depth of processing but not on tasks that can be completed automatically (Roy-Byrne et al. 1986; Weingartner et al. 1981). Similarly, most studies that have compared implicit and explicit memory in major depression have noted deficits in the declarative, explicit domain but not in the nondeclarative, implicit domain (Bazin et al. 1994; Watkins et al. 1996). This overall pattern may be useful clinically in distinguishing depressed patients from those with Alzheimer's disease. Anterograde memory deficits in Alzheimer's disease are expected even when tasks call for shallow processing and minimal effort. Furthermore, a conservative response bias is commonly observed in major depression, where recognition errors tend to be of the sort in which patients fail to recognize a previously learned stimulus (false-negative errors) (Corwin et al. 1990). In contrast, patients with Alzheimer's disease are often more prone to false-positive errors, misidentifying a novel stimulus as part of a learning set (Gainotti and Marra 1994; Lachner and Engel 1994).

Often, depressed patients not only are impaired in their capacity for effortful learning but also manifest changes in the content of memory. In clinical interviews, it is evident that much of the recollection of depressed patients involves autobiographical events with negative emotional valence. The concept of the effects of *mood congruence* on memory stipulates that the efficiency of mnemonic processing is influenced by the match between an existing mood state and the affective tone of the material to be remembered (Blaney 1986; Singer and Salovey 1988). There will be greater access to memories whose affective valence is congruent with the current mood state. For example, some evidence exists that depressed psychiatric patients are more likely to recall experiences of failure relative to experiences of success (DeMonbreun and Craighead 1977). Furthermore, this biasing of memory may extend beyond explicit, conscious recall. Watkins et al. (1996) recently found that whereas healthy control subjects showed greater implicit priming effects for positively emotionally toned words than for negative words, the opposite characterized depressed patients. The concept of mood congruence is attractive in helping to account for the apparent bias in accessibility of personal memories among depressed patients. However, in clinical samples, such mood-congruence effects have been observed mostly in memory tests for experimenter-presented material (Breslow et al. 1981). When effects have been obtained for "real life" autobiographical memories, they have often pertained to the latency of recall (e.g., Lloyd and Lishman 1975) or to the extent of detail in the reported memories (Brittlebank et al. 1993). In addition, there is evidence that mood-congruence effects are most readily obtained when the recall of autobiographical memories is relatively unstructured (Eich et al. 1994). Typical procedures involve presentation of cue words as free-association stimuli for recalling autobiographical events. In contrast, when using procedures that required a deliberate memory search for specific classes of events, McElhiney et al. (1995) found no difference between severely depressed patients and healthy control subjects in capacity to recall negatively versus positively charged autobiographical memories. If this formulation is correct, it suggests that the spontaneous trains of thought of depressed patients are biased to retrieve negative affective memories, but that no abnormalities are seen when retrieval is guided or structured.

There is increasing evidence that the neuropsychological impairments—and, in particular, memory disturbance—in mood disorder patients may not fully reverse with resolution of the depressive or manic episode and may intensify with repeated episodes. T. Burt et al. (2000) compared young and elderly unipolar and bipolar patients in an episode of major depression on a variety of anterograde memory tasks. Elderly bipolar patients, even though free of psychotropic medication, had the poorest performance of all groups, suggesting a particular iatrogenic effect of a long-term history of bipolar disorder. This is all the more impressive because in evaluations of neuropsychological differences between young adults with unipolar and bipolar illness, those with bipolar illness have generally fared better (Donnelly et al. 1982; Mason 1956; McKay et al. 1995; Overall et al. 1978). In a meta-analysis of 40 studies, Kindermann and Brown (1997) reported that studies that examined both bipolar and unipolar patients found greater dysfunction of moderate effect size compared with studies examining only unipolar depressed patients. The larger differences were found for 1) figural (vs. verbal) memory, 2) delayed (vs. immediate) memory, and 3) recognition (vs. free and cued recall). Similarly, D.B. Burt et al. (1995) in another meta-analysis noted that recall deficits were of greater magnitude in samples that contained both bipolar and unipolar depressed patients compared with samples restricted only to unipolar major depression.

Several studies have shown that bipolar patients in the euthymic state manifest neuropsychological deficits relative to matched control subjects, but the characterization of these deficits is still unclear, with the exception possibly of impairments in verbal learning and executive functions (Coffman et al. 1990; Kessing 1998; van Gorp et al. 1998) and the suggestion that greater frequency of episodes or duration of illness may be related to greater impairment. Of particular note, Shelline and colleagues (1999) examined euthymic women with a history of unipolar major depression and reported that the number of days lifetime in a depressive episode was inversely related to hippocampal volume. The interpretation offered is that excessive glucocorticoids (e.g., hypercortisolemia) during the episode have an atrophic effect on hippocampal volume. Of note, reduced hippocampal size was associated with inferior performance on a verbal memory test. Thus, in the last several years, there has been a major change in perspective. Memory deficits in mood disorders were largely seen as a state-dependent phenomenon, mainly attributable to attentional disturbance and difficulties with effortful processing. There is incomplete, but increasing, evidence that learning and memory abnormalities may persist during euthymia and may reflect structural brain abnormalities induced by the mood-disorder episodes.

## Schizophrenia

Schizophrenia is associated with disturbance in attention, motor behavior, speed of processing, abstraction, learning, and memory. Indeed, patients with schizophrenia perform poorly on a wide variety of cognitive and behavioral tasks. This generalized intellectual decline seems to be present early in the illness and, in most cases, does not appear to be subsequently progressive (Hyde et al. 1994; Nopoulos et al. 1994). Given the multiple dimensions of deficit, one goal of neuropsychological investigation has been to determine whether certain cognitive domains are especially impaired in schizophrenia. The belief has been that identifying such differential deficits may provide leads regarding the cognitive dysfunction that plays a more primary role in the disorder's pathoetiology (Blanchard and Neale 1994; Chapman and Chapman 1973). Related goals have been to determine whether subgroups of patients differ in their profiles of cognitive disability and to relate findings of cognitive impairment to functional and structural brain abnormalities (Goldberg and Gold 1995).

In recent years, the focus of research on memory impairment in schizophrenia has been to improve characterization of the deficits in working and declarative memory. In line with imaging studies of function and structure, the most characteristic neuropsychological profile in schizophrenia is compatible with deficits in systems mediated by the prefrontal and temporohippocampal cortices (M.A. Taylor and Abrams 1984), with relative sparing of language and visuospatial processing mediated by the posterior cortex.

There is debate concerning whether the deficits in working memory and associated executive functions in schizophrenia are less or more profound than those in verbal, declarative memory (Goldberg and Gold 1995; Saykin et al. 1994). In a large study of first-episode, never-medicated patients; medication-free, previously treated patients; and healthy control subjects, Saykin et al. (1994) reported that verbal memory impairment was the most profound deficit and was present early in the course of the illness. The magnitude of impairment in this domain was extensive even after the investigators controlled for impairments in executive functions (i.e., attention-vigilance, abstraction-flexibility). Similarly, in a recent community-based study of 138 patients with schizophrenia, Kelly et al. (2000) found that 15% had significant global cognitive impairment, 81% had impaired memory, 25% had executive dyscontrol, and 49% had impaired verbal fluency. Elvevag et al. (2000) attempted to examine how various manipulations of paired-associate learning would interfere with the memory performance of schizophrenic patients in a manner akin to the interference seen with patients with frontal lobe damage. They concluded that that susceptibility to interference effects was not a specific problem in patients with schizophrenia but reflected a more general disturbance in memory. Verdoux and Liraud (2000) compared the memory and executive abilities of patients with schizophrenia, other nonschizophrenic psychoses, bipolar disorder, and major depression. Memory deficits were most discriminatory between patients with schizophrenia and those with other psychotic or mood disorders.

The verbal memory deficit seen in patients with schizophrenia is compatible with left temporohippocampal dysfunction and has been observed in patients with schizotypal personality disorder (Voglmaier et al. 2000). Related imaging research with fluorodeoxyglucose positron emission tomography in the resting state revealed that increased metabolic activity in the left inferior frontal and left midtemporal regions was associated with increased verbal memory deficits (Mozley et al. 1996). This finding was interpreted as indicating dysfunction in the circuitry subserving declarative verbal memory and, in particular, excessive activation in these regions. Compatible with these findings are a highly consistent set of observations of volume reduction in the left temporal lobe of patients with schizotypal personality disorder, first-episode schizophrenia, and chronic schizo-

phrenia (Gur et al. 2000; McCarley et al. 1999) and reduced P300 evoked potential amplitudes over the left temporal lobe in patients with schizophrenia (O'Donnell et al. 1999; Salisbury et al. 1999). Compared with control subjects and patients with manic psychosis, patients with first-episode schizophrenia have smaller gray matter left planum temporale and Heschl gyrus volume (Hirayasu et al. 2000). Patients with chronic schizophrenia may be more likely to show volume reductions in MTL structures, particularly the hippocampus (Dickey et al. 1999).

However, Gold et al. (1995) compared neuropsychological profiles in patients with schizophrenia and patients with left or right temporal lobe epilepsy. Among the epileptic patients, particularly those with left temporal lobe epilepsy, memory was selectively impaired relative to other domains, particularly attention. Among schizophrenic patients, the magnitude of attentional and memory impairments was relatively equal. Other research has suggested that individual patients may differ in the extent to which they manifest neuropsychological impairments characteristic of frontal lobe (executive function) or temporal lobe (episodic memory) dysfunction (Harvey et al. 1995) and that impairments in each domain may have distinct clinical correlates (Sullivan et al. 1994). Indeed, in a recent study, Weickert et al. (2000) examined neuropsychological profiles in a large group of patients with chronic schizophrenia in relation to estimates of current and premorbid intellectual level. Across the subgroups, they concluded that executive function and attention deficits may be core cognitive features of the disorder, independent of variations in intelligence. In examining patients with schizophrenia, healthy siblings, and control subjects, Staal et al. (2000) found that executive function deficits and, to some extent, sensorimotor impairments characterized both the patients and siblings, suggesting that these cognitive abnormalities may be related to the schizophrenia genotype.

The focus on executive function and working memory impairments suggests disruption of prefrontal cortical function. Compatible physiological and biochemical data have been obtained. Callicott et al. (2000) reported that during the performance of a working memory task (N-Back), patients with schizophrenia manifested abnormal activation in the dorsolateral prefrontal cortex, with the correlation between the degree of activation response and performance opposite in direction in patients and control subjects. Furthermore, N-acetylasparate (NAA) concentrations, measured by proton magnetic resonance spectroscopy, were lower in this region (BA 9, 46) in patients compared with controls, suggesting prefrontal neuronal pathology, and the NAA levels predicted the fMRI response to the working memory challenge. Thus, in addition to the substantial evidence for a (verbal) declarative memory deficit in schizophrenia, it is evident that many patients also manifest deficits in working memory and other executive functions.

The nature of the declarative memory deficits in schizophrenia has been further specified. Deficits are usually more pronounced in tests of recall than in tests of recognition (Beatty et al. 1993; Calev 1984). The deficits in explicit recall have often been attributed to shallow or inefficient encoding of information, disorganized or inefficient retrieval strategies, and rapid forgetting (Goldberg and Gold 1995; McKenna et al. 1990). Of note, a growing number of studies report that schizophrenic patients evidence little or no deficits in nondeclarative memory tasks, including procedural memory (as reflected in motor skill learning) and implicit memory (as reflected in various tests of perceptual and conceptual priming) (Clare et al. 1993; Gras-Vincendon et al. 1994; Perry et al. 2000).

As indicated, schizophrenia is also associated with often profound impairments in aspects of working memory. Primate and human research has indicated that various prefrontal areas are critical to the capacity to hold information in consciousness, update past and current information based on a changing environment, and guide behavior on the basis of these representations (Goldman-Rakic 1994). Lesions in selective prefrontal areas in primates result in characteristic deficits in modality-specific aspects of working memory. Neuropsychological tests designed to sample analogous functions in humans have repeatedly shown marked deficits in patients with schizophrenia (Keefe et al. 1995; Park and Holzman 1993). Indeed, a diverse number of deficits is subsumed under the concept of "working memory" or "executive function." The central executive is responsible for selecting stimuli for further processing (i.e., allocating attention). Deficits in this function will be reflected in increased distractibility and inability to maintain vigilance. In line with decades of research suggesting increased distractibility, Fleming et al. (1995) demonstrated that even a simple concurrent task will interfere with short-term memory performance in patients with schizophrenia. Furthermore, the central executive is responsible for shifting sets (i.e., changing strategies and behavior when they no longer meet environmental demands). A deficit in this domain would be expressed as perseveration and as difficulty with rule learning and concept formation. Impairments in these domains are characteristic, as reflected in performance deficits on the Wisconsin Card Sorting Test (Heaton et al. 1993) or the Category Test from the Halstead-Reitan Battery (Reitan

and Wolfson 1985). Nonetheless, it has still not been established that dysfunction of specific prefrontal areas is responsible for the working-memory deficits seen in schizophrenia. Indeed, there is preliminary evidence that schizophrenic patients may have marked deficits in aspects of working memory that are less reliant on the prefrontal cortex. Using a remarkably simple task, Strous et al. (1995) demonstrated that schizophrenic patients were impaired in matching two tones after a brief delay of only 300 milliseconds but were unimpaired when there was no intertone interval. This aspect of auditory sensory (echoic) memory is thought to be subserved by nonassociation cortex outside the frontal lobes (superior temporal plane). Thus, both prefrontal and nonprefrontal components of working memory may be preferentially disturbed in schizophrenia.

## Dissociative Amnesia

Table 17–2 provides the DSM-IV-TR diagnostic criteria for dissociative amnesia (formerly called psychogenic amnesia). Dissociative amnesia is a disorder in which memory loss is attributed to functional factors. The memory loss may be localized in time, may be selective for elements of history, and, most rarely, may be generalized and continuous. In the generalized form, patients may have amnesia for their own identity and history.

Dissociative amnesia is rarely diagnosed. Several factors may account for its low incidence. First, even among patients who at one time received diagnoses of hysteric disorders, amnesia was a relatively uncommon symptom. Perley and Guze (1962) examined the frequency of a wide range of symptoms in a sample of patients with "hysterical neurosis." (At that time, dissociative disorders were included in this grouping.) First, whereas symptoms such as dizziness, headache, fatigue, and abdominal pain occurred at high rates (all in more than 70% of patients), amnesia was found in only 8% of cases. Second, patients presenting with forms of functional amnesia typically have a number of other psychiatric disorders or manifest the amnesia after trauma—as may occur, for instance, in combat situations. Current nosology excludes diagnosis of dissociative amnesia in many such instances. Third, functional amnesia does not necessarily interfere with social or occupational functioning. The most common varieties involve forgetting of isolated events. Furthermore, patients with dissociative amnesia may display indifference to their symptoms and thus may be unlikely to present for treatment.

Dissociative amnesia may be more common among females, and it is thought to occur more often in adolescents and young adults than in elderly persons. Most

**TABLE 17–2.** DSM-IV-TR criteria for dissociative amnesia

A. The predominant disturbance is one or more episodes of inability to recall important personal information, usually of a traumatic or stressful nature, that is too extensive to be explained by ordinary forgetfulness.

B. The disturbance does not occur exclusively during the course of dissociative identity disorder, dissociative fugue, posttraumatic stress disorder, acute stress disorder, or somatization disorder and is not due to the direct physiological effects of a substance (e.g., a drug of abuse, a medication) or a neurological or other general medical condition (e.g., amnestic disorder due to head trauma).

C. The symptoms cause clinically significant distress or impairment in social, occupational, or other important areas of functioning.

patients demonstrate rapid recovery of memory, and therefore the disorder is usually transient. Abeles and Schilder (1935) and Herman (1938) reported on 63 cases of dissociative amnesia (they also included fugue states in this categorization). Of these individuals, 27 recovered within 24 hours; 21, within 5 days; 7, within a week; and 4, within 3 weeks or more.

Problems of differential diagnosis usually involve distinguishing dissociative amnesia from two other types of conditions: trauma to the brain, which may produce similar syndromes, and malingering.

The DSM-IV-TR grouping of dissociative disorders is an attempt to categorize disturbances of higher cognitive functions that resemble effects of neurologic dysfunction but that are believed to be functional in origin. If a patient's amnesia can be related to a neurologic disorder, the diagnosis of dissociative disorder is inappropriate. To date, no studies have examined the frequency with which patients with dissociative disorder diagnoses concurrently or ultimately show signs of neurologic disease. However, such work in the case of hysterical conversion reactions indicates that a disturbingly large number of patients thus diagnosed manifested neurologic disorders (at the time or shortly thereafter) that in some proved fatal (Slater and Glithero 1965; Whitlock 1967).

The difficulties of differential diagnosis in this area can be illustrated with the syndrome of transient global amnesia (Fisher and Adams 1964; Pantoni et al. 2000). Without warning, individuals, usually middle-aged, display retrograde amnesia for events that occurred in the previous days, weeks, or years and a dense anterograde amnesia. The amnesia is typically transient, lasting from minutes to several hours. When memory returns, there is typically a progressive recall of distant events, with memory of the most recent past returning last. Retrograde amnesia may resolve before the anterograde component

(N. Kapur et al. 1998). During the amnesia, the individual is usually well oriented, with perception, sense of identity, and other higher cognitive functions intact. There is typically considerable concern and upset on the part of the individual about the memory loss. The attacks may strike only once or may be recurrent (Heathfield et al. 1973).

The transient nature of the amnesia and its occurrence in individuals who appear medically healthy might suggest a dissociative reaction. Heathfield et al. (1973) reported on 31 patients who were referred for transient loss of memory. Of the 31 patients, memory loss was associated with epilepsy in 6 patients (19%), with migraine in 1 patient (3%), and with temporal lobe encephalitis in 2 patients (6%). Three patients (10%) received the diagnosis of dissociative (psychogenic) amnesia. The remaining 19 patients (61%) were considered as presenting the syndrome of transient global amnesia. The age of these 19 patients (13 men, 6 women) ranged from 46 to 68 years; amnesic episodes lasted from 30 minutes to 5 days; 11 had only one attack during the period of study. Cerebrovascular dysfunction was suggested in 9 of the 19 patients. Heathfield et al. (1973) concluded, "It is probable that most episodes of transient global amnesia result from bilateral temporal lobe or thalamic lesions. In some of our patients there was clear evidence of ischemia in the territory of the posterior cerebral circulation, and we consider that such ischemia is the cause of this syndrome" (p. 735). However, recent investigations have suggested that etiologies based on migraine, seizures, transient cerebral arterial ischemia, or a thromboembolic pathogenesis are unlikely to account for transient global amnesia (Lauria et al. 1998; Lewis 1998). Receiving greater attention is the possibility that a blockage of venous return (such as in a Valsalva maneuver) results in high venous retrograde pressure to the cerebral venous system and produces venous ischemia in the diencephalon and MTL (Lewis 1998; Sander et al. 2000). Regardless, several imaging studies, using single photon emission computed tomography (SPECT), PET, or diffusion-weighted magnetic resonance imaging have reported decreased activity in MTL structures during transient global amnesia with normalization on recovery (Jovin et al. 2000; Strupp et al. 1998; Tanabe et al. 1999).

Some general guidelines may be useful in distinguishing dissociative amnesia from the memory loss that accompanies neurologic disease. Typically, the memory loss associated with head trauma, Korsakoff's psychosis, temporal lobe dysfunction, and ECT has both retrograde and anterograde components, whereas patients with dissociative amnesia will often show unaltered ability to acquire and retain new information (as also opposed to transient global amnesia). It is rare in the context of neurologic disease for a patient to manifest global amnesia across the life span, and personal identity and early memories are typically preserved. Dissociative amnesia may selectively affect autobiographical memory, whereas both personal and impersonal memory is disturbed in amnesia associated with neurologic insult.

Contributing to differential diagnosis is the collateral behavior of the patient and the nature of the recovery of memory. Patients who present with amnesia accompanied by clouded consciousness, disorientation, and/or mood change are likely manifesting neurologic disturbance. Indifference to amnesia concerning events that would ordinarily be associated with guilt and shame for the patient suggests a dissociative basis. Dissociative amnesia usually pertains to traumatic events, and amnesia for the ordinary events of life would suggest a neurologic disturbance. Amnesia during or after a stressful experience is not, however, a reliable sign of dissociative origin (it is excluded by DSM-IV-TR). Stress may precipitate a transient ischemic attack (TIA) or epileptic event, resulting in amnesia. Retrograde amnesia associated with known neurologic insult typically also has a standard course of recovery. Events in the most distant past are recovered before more recent events. In dissociative amnesia, there is usually a sudden return of memory (Nemiah 1979). Interviews employing hypnotism and/or sodium amobarbital may be useful to distinguish dissociative amnesia from neurologic disturbance. A number of reports exist of patients who recovered memory with either procedure, and in some cases the recovery was permanent (e.g., Herman 1938). Recovery of memory with the use of hypnosis or amobarbital should not occur in cases of neurologic disturbance.

*Malingering* refers to deliberate and voluntary simulation of psychological or physical disorder. The assumption in a diagnosis of dissociative amnesia is that the loss of memory and its subsequent recovery are not under voluntary control. It should be noted that some clinicians with considerable exposure to amnesia of psychological origin question whether a distinction between malingering and dissociative amnesia can or should be made. Differentiating between dissociative amnesia and malingering is difficult. The degree to which a malingerer is successful at simulation likely depends on the sophistication of the patient with regard to manifestations of psychological and neurologic disease. In a somewhat similar context, it should be noted that experienced hypnotists cannot reliably distinguish hypnotized subjects from individuals simulating the effects of hypnosis (Orne 1979). It should be noted that in recent years, psychometric instruments have been validated that appear to be successful in distinguishing between the malingering of anterograde amnesia and a true amnestic syndrome. The basis of this approach is to use memory tests that are subjectively experienced as difficult, but in which patients with amnesia show high performance accuracy. In contrast, individuals who are malingering generate low scores (Rees et al. 1998; Tombaugh 1996).

# Normal Aging

Complaints about memory loss are common in the elderly, and normal aging is accompanied by characteristic decrements in memory performance (Parkin et al. 1995; West 1996). However, the decline in memory with aging is selective, affecting some cognitive processes more than others. The capacity to deliberately acquire and retain new information (declarative episodic memory) is often impaired by age 50, particularly when the material to be learned is unstructured, such as random lists of words (Albert et al. 1987). This deficit seems to reflect not a more rapid forgetting with aging, but rather the use of less-efficient encoding and retrieval strategies. In part, this deficit, as in major depression, may reflect limited attentional capacity and reduced capacity for "effortful processing." Aging also exerts greater negative effects on memory for the context in which information was learned as opposed to memory for the information itself. For example, age-related changes have been demonstrated in memory for the temporal order (Parkin et al. 1995) and the source (Craik et al. 1990) of information. This pattern of memory deficits, with decrements in source memory and in the acquisition and retention of unstructured, but not highly structured, material is suggestive of an age-related decline in the memory processes supported by prefrontal cortex (West 1996). Indeed, the age-related impairment in source memory has been found to covary with other measures of frontal lobe function, the Wisconsin Card Sorting Test, and verbal fluency (Craik et al. 1990; Parkin et al. 1995). There is also evidence that with aging, the frontal lobe undergoes greater reductions in volume and in resting functional activity than do other brain areas (West 1996).

The literature on the effects of aging on nondeclarative memory is inconsistent. Although it appears that many of the cognitive processes that underlie these aspects of learning and memory are unaltered by age (Light and La Voie 1993), age-related deficits have been reported, particularly for priming tasks. Indeed, there is also evidence linking impaired implicit memory to age-related frontal lobe dysfunction (Winokur et al. 1996).

# The Subjective Evaluation of Memory: Metamemory

In clinical circumstances, we often obtain individuals' assessments of their own memory functioning, a domain referred to as *metamemory*. The perception of memory decline may be the first indication of valid incipient changes in cognitive function. A large number of studies, conducted in neurologic, psychiatric, and healthy populations, have examined the relationships between self-evaluations of memory and objective test results.

The most consistent finding in this literature is that the strongest predictor of memory self-evaluation is current mood state (Bennett-Levy and Powell 1980; Coleman et al. 1996; Hinkin et al. 1996; Larrabee and Levin 1986). Almost invariably, depressed mood, whether assessed by observers or by self-report, is associated with self-evaluations of impaired cognitive function (Prudic et al. 2000). In contrast, although significant associations between objective neuropsychological and subjective cognitive evaluations have been occasionally reported (Riege 1982), for the most part such associations are either small in magnitude or nonexistent. Furthermore, when associations have been reported, they have not always been in the expected direction. Hinkin et al. (1996) found that men who were seropositive for human immunodeficiency virus type 1 (HIV-1) with a low level of memory complaints performed worse on memory testing than did those with a higher level of complaints.

It is sobering that, independent of neurologic or psychiatric illness, we are generally poor judges of the quality of our memory. To some extent, this lack of association might be attributed to the limited ecological validity of standard memory-assessment batteries, which may fail to capture the type of memory failures experienced in everyday life (e.g., incidental learning and forgetting). Furthermore, it is clear that a variety of neurologic and psychiatric conditions, including but not limited to Alzheimer's disease and schizophrenia, may be associated with distinct deficits in metamemory, such that patients are particularly likely to deny or be unaware of cognitive deficits. However, the fact that current mood state is a consistent predictor of memory functioning strongly implies that factors other than actual memory performance influence self-evaluations. Figure 17–2 illustrates changes on the Squire Subjective Memory Questionnaire (Squire et al. 1979) in patients with major depression who did and did not respond to ECT (Coleman et al. 1996). Both at baseline and shortly after the ECT course, patient scores on this metamemory measure were

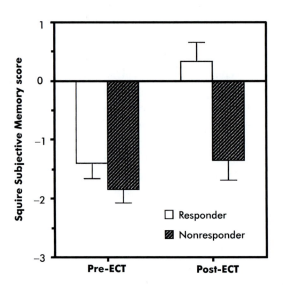

**FIGURE 17–2.** Scores on the Squire Subjective Memory Questionnaire in depressed patients treated with electroconvulsive therapy (ECT). A score of 0 indicates that the patient assesses memory function to be the same as it was before the episode of depressive illness, whereas a negative score indicates that the patient considers current memory function to be impaired. Before receiving ECT, patients report marked impairment, the magnitude of which covaries with the severity of depressive symptoms. Patients who respond to ECT report marked improvement even though objective tests indicate memory deficits.

*Source.*　Adapted from Coleman et al. 1996.

strongly associated with depression-severity scores. Despite the fact that patients had characteristic anterograde and retrograde memory disturbances at the time of post-ECT metamemory evaluation, approximately 80% of patients reported improved memory functioning after ECT relative to before ECT. Although the magnitude of these memory deficits were generally equivalent in ECT responders and nonresponders, the improvement in the metamemory measure was particularly pronounced in patients whose depression responded to ECT.

Little consensus exists about the theoretical underpinnings of metamemory or subjective memory judgments. The field is largely driven by empirical interest in the relationship of objective memory performance to subjective complaints, and, in particular, the disjunction between the two, that is, why reports of memory performance deviate so markedly from actual performance, a common occurrence. For example, it was hypothesized that there exists an internal memory monitor that reviews memory contents in an unbiased manner and forms judgments about the retrievability of memories (Burke et al. 1991). A later view suggested that judgments about memory are highly inferential, and that evaluations of the objective status of memory must be made based on sources of information other than access to a review of memory content. Other sources of information that affect subjective judgments may include retrieval fluency, the amounts of related and unrelated information activated by attempts to remember (Koriat 1993), and feelings about memory, such as the feeling of familiarity (Schwartz et al. 1997).

As a result, there are likely to be multiple dimensions to assess when evaluating subjective memory. An inclusive conceptual approach offered four dimensions: 1) memory knowledge, which involves factual knowledge about memory and its processes; 2) memory monitoring, which includes awareness of the current state of one's memory and of how one uses memory; 3) memory-related affect; and 4) memory self-efficacy, a set of beliefs about one's memory, including changes in memory status (Hultsch et al. 1988). Evaluations of the psychometric properties of questionnaires developed to examine subjective assessments of memory indicated that assessments of memory capacity and change in memory status were best related to beliefs about memory, which were, in turn, subject to a variety of influences, including mood and locus of control (Cavanaugh and Green 1990). In a meta-analysis of the effects of memory training on subjective memory assessment, Floyd and Scoggin (1997) found that memory training and improvement in performance did not alter subjective memory assessment in normal elderly adults. Instead, techniques such as relaxation training, which may alter affect or mood, and interventions directed at changing participants' beliefs about the effects of aging on memory significantly improved subjective assessment of memory. This suggests that interventions that improve objective memory performance have less impact on subjective evaluations than do interventions targeted either at beliefs about memory or affective state.

## Effects of Somatic Treatments on Learning and Memory

### Psychotropic Agents

In addition to the deleterious effects of benzodiazepines on psychomotor performance, this class of medications can produce consistent adverse effects on memory. The most characteristic deficit is diminished delayed recall for newly learned information (J.L. Taylor and Tinklenberg 1987). This deficit is most evident acutely after ingestion and is most marked in the first hour or two

postingestion for diazepam and the third or fourth hour postingestion for lorazepam. Despite producing this deficit in anterograde declarative memory, benzodiazepines do not appear to impair retrograde memory. Indeed, lists of words learned before benzodiazepine administration may be better recalled in the postingestion period, a phenomenon termed retrograde facilitation. This effect may be more pronounced at higher benzodiazepine dosages and has been interpreted as reflecting reduced retroactive interference due to diminished learning after drug ingestion. The capacity of short-term or working memory does not appear to be altered by benzodiazepine use, although the speed at which information is processed may be slowed. Contrary to the case for psychomotor performance, there is evidence that tolerance to adverse acute effects of benzodiazepines on memory functions may not develop with long-term use (Gorenstein et al. 1994) and that elderly individuals are particularly sensitive to the amnesic effects of benzodiazepines.

A wide range of medications have anticholinergic properties, including heterocyclic antidepressants (e.g., amitriptyline, imipramine, and nortriptyline), neuroleptics (e.g., chlorpromazine), antiparkinsonism agents (e.g., benztropine), and sleep and cold preparations that contain antihistamines. Anticholinergics can produce sedation, attentional impairment, memory disturbance, and, in extreme cases, an anticholinergic delirium. There is compelling evidence that psychotropic medications that differ in anticholinergic properties also differ in their effects on learning and memory. For example, despite equivalent clinical improvement, patients with major depression will show superior performance on declarative memory measures when treated with fluoxetine relative to amitriptyline (Richardson et al. 1994). In a double-blind, crossover study in chronic schizophrenic patients, Silver and Geraisy (1995) found that biperiden (an anticholinergic) but not amantadine (a dopamine agonist) produced detectable deficits in both working and declarative memory. As with the benzodiazepines, vulnerability to the adverse cognitive effects of anticholinergic agents may be augmented in the elderly. There is evidence that tolerance develops to the adverse cognitive effects of anticholinergics, but there is no such evidence for benzodiazepines. Nonetheless, all else being equal, avoidance of agents with pronounced anticholinergic effects may be advisable, particularly in patients with preexisting memory impairment.

Aside from the anticholinergic properties of antidepressants or neuroleptics, there is not convincing evidence that standard antidepressants or traditional neuroleptics exert intrinsic detrimental effects on learning and memory. For example, differences among the selective serotonin reuptake inhibitors (SSRIs) in neuropsychological effects are largely attributable to differences among their anticholinergic properties. Although excessive dosages can produce sedation with traditional neuroleptic treatment, most studies comparing patients with schizophrenia with themselves in unmedicated and neuroleptic-treated states have found no change or slight improvement in the medicated state, particularly in measures of attention. This pattern also appears to hold for atypical neuroleptics such as clozapine (Goldberg et al. 1993).

At present, considerable attention is being paid to the possibility that atypical antipsychotic medications have an ameliorative effect on cognitive deficits in schizophrenia (Purdon 1999). Currently, much of the evidence is circumstantial and tentative. At least 12 studies have examined the effects of clozapine on cognitive parameters, with the most general finding being an improvement in measures of attention and verbal fluency, with some additional evidence for improved executive function. However, as reviewed by Meltzer and McGurk (1999), effects of clozapine on working memory and standard measures of verbal and nonverbal learning and memory are inconclusive. Somewhat similarly, risperidone appears to exert positive effects on working memory, executive function, and attention, whereas effects on standard measures of learning and memory are inconsistent. There is preliminary evidence that olanzapine may have a different profile, improving verbal learning and memory, verbal fluency, and executive function, but not attention, working memory, or visual (nonverbal) learning and memory (e.g., Purdon et al. 2000). Thus, the possibility has been raised that atypical antipsychotics differ in their effects on memory, with risperidone having stronger beneficial effects on working (short-term) memory and olanzapine exerting stronger action on verbal learning and memory.

## Electroconvulsive Therapy and Other Brain Stimulation Treatments

ECT is a remarkably effective treatment for specific psychiatric disorders (American Psychiatric Association et al. 2001; Sackeim et al. 1995). However, its cognitive side effects are the major factor limiting its use. As with spontaneous seizures, in the immediate postictal period, patients may manifest transient neurologic abnormalities, alterations of consciousness (disorientation, attentional dysfunction), sensorimotor abnormalities, and disturbances in higher cognitive functions, particularly learning and memory (Sackeim 1992). Technical factors in ECT administration, including electrode placement (bilateral

versus unilateral), stimulus dosage, and electrical waveform, strongly determine the severity and persistence of these acute effects. Indeed, these factors determine whether patients require on average a few minutes or several hours to achieve full reorientation after seizure termination (Sackeim 1992; Sackeim et al. 1993, 2000; Weiner et al. 1986).

There is rapid recovery of cognitive function after a single treatment. However, with forms of ECT that exert more severe acute cognitive effects, recovery may be incomplete by the time of the next treatment. In such cases, deterioration may occur over the treatment course, particularly when treatments are closely spaced in time. Some patients may develop an organic mental syndrome with marked disorientation during the ECT course. With milder forms of ECT, cumulative deterioration in cognitive functions need not occur. Indeed, with specific alterations of ECT technique, cumulative *improvement* in some acute cognitive measures has been demonstrated (Sackeim 1992).

Associations between the magnitude of cognitive effects and ECT treatment parameters diminish with time after ECT treatment. Differences between bilateral and unilateral electrode placement are difficult to detect after more than a few months have elapsed since the end of the ECT course (Lisanby et al. 2000; Sackeim 1992; Sackeim et al. 1993, 2000; Weiner et al. 1986). Within days of the end of an ECT course, depressed patients manifest superior performance in most cognitive domains relative to their pretreatment baseline. On tests of intelligence, patients' scores shortly after ECT will typically be superior to those produced in the untreated depressed state (Sackeim et al. 1992). Similarly, before treatment, depressed patients usually manifest deficits in the acquisition of information, as revealed by tests of immediate recall or recognition of item lists. Within days after an ECT course, patients are typically unchanged or improved in these measures of learning, with the change in clinical state being the critical predictor of the magnitude of improvement. In contrast, patients often manifest impaired ability to retain information over a delay. This impairment reflects a double dissociation between the effects of depression and ECT on anterograde learning and memory (Steif et al. 1986). ECT introduces a new deficit in consolidation or retention, so that information that is newly learned is rapidly forgotten.

During and shortly after a course of ECT, patients also display retrograde amnesia. Deficits in the recall or recognition of both personal and public information learned before ECT are common, and there is evidence that these deficits are greatest for events that occurred temporally closest to the treatment (McElhiney et al.

1995; Squire 1986). Thus, whereas memory for more remote events is intact, patients may have difficulty recalling events that occurred during and several months to years before the ECT course. The retrograde amnesia is rarely dense, as patients typically show spottiness in memory for recent events. It has typically been thought that the amnesia is most dense for autobiographical information (Weiner 1984). However, careful analysis of the extent of amnesia for public and personal events, and the details of those events, indicates that information about the world (public events) is subject to greater memory loss (Lisanby et al. 2000). This is in contrast to the pattern often seen with MTL brain damage, in which retrograde amnesia for personal information is greater than that for impersonal or public events (Nadel and Moscovitch 1997).

As time from treatment increases, there is improved retrograde functioning, with a return of more distant memories (Lisanby et al. 2000; McElhiney et al. 1995). This temporally graded pattern is compatible with similar findings of the effects of repeated electroconvulsive shock in animals (Krueger et al. 1992). Both the anterograde and the retrograde amnesia are most marked for explicit or declarative memory, whereas no effects of ECT have been seen on measures of implicit or procedural memory (Squire et al. 1985). In this respect, the effects of ECT on memory are similar to those associated with MTL dysfunction. In general, there is no relation between the magnitude of the adverse effects of ECT on memory and its therapeutic properties (McElhiney et al. 1995).

Within a few weeks after the end of ECT, objective evidence of persistent cognitive deficits is difficult to document. The anterograde amnesia typically resolves rapidly after ECT termination (Sackeim et al. 1993, 2000). The retrograde amnesia will often show a more gradual reduction, with substantial return of memory for events that were seemingly "forgotten" when assessed immediately after the treatment course. However, ECT can result in persistent deficits (McElhiney et al. 1995; Sackeim 2000a; Weiner et al. 1986), most likely due to a combination of retrograde and anterograde effects. Even when tested at substantial time periods after treatment, patients may manifest persistent amnesia for some events that occurred several months immediately before and after ECT. Recent work suggests that the patients most vulnerable to persistent retrograde amnesia are those with preexisting cognitive impairment and those who manifest the most prolonged disorientation immediately after seizure induction (Sobin et al. 1995). In rare patients, the extent of persistent or permanent retrograde amnesia may extend several years into the past (Sackeim 2000a).

In recent years, other brain stimulation treatments have been developed. There have been more than 20 reports on the use of repetitive transcranial magnetic stimulation (rTMS) in the treatment of major depression, as well as application to other neuropsychiatric conditions (George et al. 1999). This noninvasive technique, which involves inducing focal current flow in cortical tissue by imposing a time-varying magnetic field, has shown remarkable promise as a method to map brain function (through transitory disruption of local activity) and brain connectivity, when combined with functional imaging techniques. Although neuropsychological investigation has been limited in the standard treatment trials in neuropsychiatric disorders (usually at least 10 days of stimulation, each for 15–20 periods), initial impressions are that rTMS (either at slow or fast frequencies) is benign in cognitive effects. Of greater uncertainty, at least in the treatment of major depression, is whether nonconvulsive rTMS will have a significant clinical role. Therapeutic properties have been highly variable in effect size, and there is little information on the persistence of clinical benefit (Sackeim 2000b). Using similar technology, an alternative that is being developed is the deliberate induction of seizure activity under general anesthesia with rTMS, termed magnetic seizure therapy (MST). Due to the greater control magnetic stimulation affords over the site of seizure initiation and electrical dosage in the brain, MST may have advantages over ECT in reducing adverse amnestic effects (Lisanby et al. 2001).

Finally, another new brain stimulation approach is the use of vagus nerve stimulation (VNS) in the therapy of treatment-resistant major depressive episodes. VNS is approved for treatment-resistant epilepsy, with approximately 10,000 implants having been performed. The procedure involves inserting a stimulator in the chest wall and running leads to electrodes attached to the left vagus nerve in the neck. Stimulation is continuous with the 24-hour cycle usually involving 30 seconds of stimulation followed by a 5-minute off period. Intensity of the current administered is the primary variable adjusted, and it is usually varied in relation to tolerability. An initial open-label pilot study suggested that a substantial number of patients with treatment-resistant depression showed marked and sustained clinical improvement (Rush et al. 2000). Neuropsychological investigation in this sample before and after the acute VNS treatment phase did not reveal any deleterious effects. Indeed, there was improvement in a variety of neurocognitive measures, including memory, but especially executive functions, that tended to covary with the extent of clinical improvement (Sackeim et al. 2001).

# References

Abeles M, Schilder P: Psychogenic loss of personal identity. Archives of Neurology and Psychiatry 34:587–604, 1935

Albert MS, Butters N, Levin J: Temporal gradients in the retrograde amnesia of patients with alcoholic Korsakoff's disease. Arch Neurol 36:211–216, 1979

Albert MS, Duffy FH, Naeser MA: Nonlinear changes in cognition and their neurophysiologic correlates. Canadian Journal of Psychology 41:141–157, 1987

American Psychiatric Association: Diagnostic and Statistical Manual of Mental Disorders, 4th Edition, Text Revision. Washington, DC, American Psychiatric Association, 2000

American Psychiatric Association and Weiner RD, Coffey CE, Fochtmann L, et al: The Practice of ECT: Recommendations for Treatment, Training and Privileging, 2nd Edition. Washington, DC, American Psychiatric Press, 2001

Andreasen NC, O'Leary DS, Cizadlo T, et al: Remembering the past: two facets of episodic memory explored with positron emission tomography. Am J Psychiatry 152:1576–1585, 1995

Andreasen NC, O'Leary DS, Paradiso S, et al: The cerebellum plays a role in conscious episodic memory retrieval. Hum Brain Mapp 8:226–234, 1999

Backman L, Forsell Y: Episodic memory functioning in a community-based sample of old adults with major depression: utilization of cognitive support. J Abnorm Psychol 103:361–370, 1994

Baddeley AD: Working Memory. Oxford, UK, Oxford University Press, 1986

Ball MJ, Fishman M, Hachinski V, et al: A new definition of Alzheimer's disease: a hippocampal dementia. Lancet 1:14–16, 1985

Bazin N, Perruchet P, De Bonis M, et al: The dissociation of explicit and implicit memory in depressed patients. Psychol Med 24:239–245, 1994

Beatty WW, Jocic Z, Monson N, et al: Memory and frontal lobe dysfunction in schizophrenia and schizoaffective disorder. J Nerv Ment Dis 181:448–453, 1993

Bennett-Levy J, Powell GE: The Subjective Memory Questionnaire (SMQ): an investigation into the self-reporting of "real-life" memory skills. British Journal of Social and Clinical Psychology 19:177–188, 1980

Blanchard JJ, Neale JM: The neuropsychological signature of schizophrenia: generalized or differential deficit? Am J Psychiatry 151:40–48, 1994

Blaney PH: Affect and memory: a review. Psychol Bull 99:229–246, 1986

Blaxton TA: Dissociations among memory measures in memory-impaired subjects: evidence for a processing account of memory. Mem Cognit 20:549–562, 1992

Blaxton TA: A process-based view of memory. J Int Neuropsychol Soc 1:112–114, 1995

Bornstein RA, Baker GB, Douglass AB: Depression and memory in major depressive disorder. J Neuropsychiatry Clin Neurosci 3:78–80, 1991

Breslow R, Kocsis J, Belkin B: Memory deficits in depression: evidence utilizing the Wechsler Memory Scale. Percept Mot Skills 51:541–542, 1980

Breslow R, Kocsis J, Belkin B: Contribution of the depressive perspective to memory function in depression. Am J Psychiatry 138:227–230, 1981

Brittlebank AD, Scott J, Williams JM, et al: Autobiographical memory in depression: state or trait marker? Br J Psychiatry 162:118–121, 1993

Buckner RL: Beyond HERA: contributions of specific prefrontal brain areas to long-term memory retrieval. Psychonomic Bulletin and Review 3:149–158, 1996

Buckner RL, Petersen SE, Ojemann JG, et al: Functional anatomical studies of explicit and implicit memory retrieval tasks. J Neurosci 15:12–29, 1995

Buckner RL, Koutstaal W, Schacter DL, et al: Functional-anatomic study of episodic retrieval, II: selective averaging of event-related fMRI trials to test the retrieval success hypothesis. Neuroimage 7:163–175, 1998a

Buckner RL, Koutstaal W, Schacter DL, et al: Functional-anatomic study of episodic retrieval using fMRI, I: retrieval effort versus retrieval success. Neuroimage 7:151–162, 1998b

Buckner RL, Kelley WM, Petersen SE: Frontal cortex contributes to human memory formation. Nat Neurosci 2:311–314, 1999

Buckner RL, Koutstaal W, Schacter DL, et al: Functional MRI evidence for a role of frontal and inferior temporal cortex in amodal components of priming. Brain 123 Pt 3:620–640, 2000

Burke D, MacKay DG, Worthley JS, et al: On the tip of the tongue: what causes word findings failures in young and older adults. Journal of Memory and Language 30:542–579, 1991

Burt DB, Zembar MJ, Niederehe G: Depression and memory impairment: a meta-analysis of the association, its pattern, and specificity. Psychol Bull 117:285–305, 1995

Burt T, Prudic J, Peyser S, et al: Learning and memory in bipolar and unipolar major depression: effects of aging. Neuropsychiatry, Neuropsychology, and Behavioral Neurology 13(4):246–253, 2000

Butters N, Heindel WC, Salmon DP: Dissociation of implicit memory in dementia: neurological implications. Bulletin of the Psychonomic Society 28:230–246, 1990

Calev A: Recall and recognition in mildly disturbed schizophrenics: the use of matched tasks. Psychol Med 14:425–429, 1984

Calev A, Erwin P: Recall and recognition in depressives: use of matched tasks. Br J Clin Psychol 24:127–128, 1985

Callicott JH, Bertolino A, Mattay VS, et al: Physiological dysfunction of the dorsolateral prefrontal cortex in schizophrenia revisited. Cereb Cortex 10:1078–1092, 2000

Cavanaugh JC, Green EE: I believe, therefore I can: self-efficacy beliefs in memory aging, in Aging and Cognition: Mental Processes, Self-Awareness and Interventions. Edited by Lovelace EA. New York, Elsevier, 1990, pp 189–230

Channon S, Baker JE, Robertson MM: Effects of structure and clustering on recall and recognition memory in clinical depression. J Abnorm Psychol 102:323–326, 1993

Chapman LJ, Chapman JP: Disordered Thought in Schizophrenia. Englewood Cliffs, NJ, Prentice-Hall, 1973

Clare L, McKenna PJ, Mortimer AM, et al: Memory in schizophrenia: what is impaired and what is preserved? Neuropsychologia 31:1225–1241, 1993

Coffman JA, Bornstein RA, Olson SC, et al: Cognitive impairment and cerebral structure by MRI in bipolar disorder. Biol Psychiatry 27:1188–1196, 1990

Cohen NJ: Preserved learning capacity in amnesia: evidence for multiple memory systems, in The Neuropsychology of Memory. Edited by Squire LR, Butters N. New York, Guilford, 1984, pp 83–103

Cohen NJ, Corkin S: The amnesic patient H.M.: learning and retention of a cognitive skill (abstract). Society of Neuroscience Abstracts 7:235, 1981

Cohen NJ, Squire LR: Preserved learning and retention of pattern analyzing skill in amnesia: dissociation of knowing how and knowing that. Science 210:207–209, 1980

Coleman EA, Sackeim HA, Prudic J, et al: Subjective memory complaints before and after electroconvulsive therapy. Biol Psychiatry 39:346–356, 1996

Conway MA, Turk DJ, Miller SL, et al: A positron emission tomography (PET) study of autobiographical memory retrieval. Memory 7:679–702, 1999

Corkin S: Acquisition of motor skill after bilateral medial temporal lobe excision. Neuropsychologia 6:225–265, 1968

Corkin S: Lasting consequences of bilateral medial temporal lobectomy: clinical course and experimental findings in H.M. Semin Neurol 4:249–259, 1984

Corwin J, Peselow E, Feenan K, et al: Disorders of decision in affective disease: an effect of beta-adrenergic dysfunction? Biol Psychiatry 27:813–833, 1990

Craik FIM, Morris LW, Morris RG, et al: Relations between source amnesia and frontal lobe functioning in older adults. Psychol Aging 5:148–151, 1990

Cronholm B, Ottosson J-O: Memory functions in endogenous depression: before and after electroconvulsive therapy. Arch Gen Psychiatry 5:193–199, 1961

Davis H, Squire L: Protein synthesis and memory. Psychol Bull 96:518–559, 1984

DeMonbreun B, Craighead W: Selective recall of positive and neutral feedback. Cognitive Therapy and Research 1:311–329, 1977

Dickey CC, McCarley RW, Voglmaier MM, et al: Schizotypal personality disorder and MRI abnormalities of temporal lobe gray matter. Biol Psychiatry 45:1393–1402, 1999

Donnelly EF, Murphy DL, Goodwin FK, et al: Intellectual function in primary affective disorder. Br J Psychiatry 140:633–636, 1982

Eich E, Macaulay D, Ryan L: Mood dependent memory for events of the personal past. J Exp Psychol Gen 123:201–215, 1994

Elvevag B, Egan MF, Goldberg TE: Paired-associate learning and memory interference in schizophrenia. Neuropsychologia 38:1565–1575, 2000

Fink GR, Markowitsch HJ, Reinkemeier M, et al: Cerebral representation of one's own past: neural networks involved in autobiographical memory. J Neurosci 16:4275–4282, 1996

Fisher C, Adams R: Transient global amnesia. Acta Neurol Scand 40 (suppl 9):1–83, 1964

Fleming K, Goldberg TE, Gold JM, et al: Verbal working memory dysfunction in schizophrenia: use of a Brown-Peterson paradigm. Psychiatry Res 56:155–161, 1995

Floyd M, Scoggin F: Effects of memory training on the subjective memory functioning and mental health of older adults: a meta-analysis. Psychol Aging 12:150–161, 1997

Gabrieli JDE: A systematic view of human memory processes. J Int Neuropsychol Soc 1:115–118, 1995

Gainotti G, Marra C: Some aspects of memory disorders clearly distinguish dementia of the Alzheimer's type from depressive pseudo-dementia. J Clin Exp Neuropsychol 16:65–78, 1994

Gass C, Russell E: Differential impact of brain damage and depression on memory test performance. J Consult Clin Psychol 54:261–263, 1986

George MS, Lisanby SH, Sackeim HA: Transcranial magnetic stimulation: applications in psychiatry. Arch Gen Psychiatry 56:300–311, 1999

Gold JM, Blaxton TA, Hermann BP, et al: Memory and intelligence in lateralized temporal lobe epilepsy and schizophrenia. Schizophr Res 17:59–65, 1995

Goldberg TE, Gold JM: Neurocognitive deficits in schizophrenia, in Schizophrenia. Edited by Hirsch SR, Weinberger DR. Oxford, UK, Blackwell, 1995, pp 146–162

Goldberg TE, Greenberg R, Griffin S: The impact of clozapine on cognition and psychiatric symptoms in patients with schizophrenia. Br J Psychiatry 162:43–48, 1993

Goldman-Rakic PS: Working memory and the mind. Sci Am 267:110–117, 1992

Goldman-Rakic PS: Working memory dysfunction in schizophrenia. J Neuropsychiatry Clin Neurosci 6:348–357, 1994

Gorenstein C, Bernik MA, Pompeia S: Differential acute psychomotor and cognitive effects of diazepam on long-term benzodiazepine users. Int Clin Psychopharmacol 9:145–153, 1994

Graf P, Schacter DL: Implicit and explicit memory for new associations in normal and amnesic patients. J Exp Psychol Learn Mem Cogn 11:501–518, 1985

Gras-Vincendon A, Danion JM, Grange D, et al: Explicit memory, repetition priming and cognitive skill learning in schizophrenia. Schizophr Res 13:117–126, 1994

Gur RE, Turetsky BI, Cowell PE, et al: Temporolimbic volume reductions in schizophrenia. Arch Gen Psychiatry 57:769–775, 2000

Harvey PD, Powchik P, Mohs RC, et al: Memory functions in geriatric chronic schizophrenic patients: a neuropsychological study. J Neuropsychiatry Clin Neurosci 7:207–212, 1995

Hasher L, Zacks R: Automatic and effortful processes in memory. J Exp Psychol Gen 108:356–388, 1979

Heathfield K, Croft P, Swash M: The syndrome of transient global amnesia. Brain 96:729–736, 1973

Heaton R, Chelune G, Talley J, et al: Wisconsin Card Sorting Test (WCST) Manual, Revised and Expanded. Odessa, FL, Psychological Resources, 1993

Herman M: The use of intravenous sodium amytal in psychogenic amnesic states. Psychiatr Q 12:738–742, 1938

Hinkin CH, van Gorp WG, Satz P, et al: Actual versus self-reported cognitive dysfunction in HIV-1 infection: memory-metamemory dissociations. J Clin Exp Neuropsychol 18:431–443, 1996

Hirayasu Y, McCarley RW, Salisbury DF, et al: Planum temporale and Heschl gyrus volume reduction in schizophrenia: a magnetic resonance imaging study of first-episode patients. Arch Gen Psychiatry 57:692–699, 2000

Hultsch DF, Hertzog C, Dixon RA, et al: Memory self-knowledge in the aged, in Cognitive Development in Adulthood: Progress in Cognitive Development Research. Edited by Howe ML, Brainerd CJ. New York, Springer, 1988, pp 65–92

Hyde TM, Nawroz S, Goldberg TE, et al: Is there cognitive decline in schizophrenia? a cross-sectional study. Br J Psychiatry 164:494–500, 1994

Jacobs DM, Sano M, Dooneief G, et al: Neuropsychological detection and characterization of preclinical Alzheimer's disease. Neurology 45:957–962, 1995

Jacoby LL, Lindsay DS, Toth JP: Unconscious influences revealed: attention, awareness, and control. Am Psychol 47:802–809, 1992

Johnson SD, Saykin AJ, Flashman LA, et al: Brain activation on fMRI and verbal memory ability: functional neuroanatomic correlates of CVLT performance. J Int Neuropsychol Soc 7:55–62, 2001

Jovin TG, Vitti RA, McCluskey LF: Evolution of temporal lobe hypoperfusion in transient global amnesia: a serial single photon emission computed tomography study. J Neuroimaging 10:238–241, 2000

Kapur N: Syndromes of retrograde amnesia: a conceptual and empirical synthesis. Psychol Bull 125:800–825, 1999

Kapur N, Millar J, Abbott P, et al: Recovery of function processes in human amnesia: evidence from transient global amnesia. Neuropsychologia 36:99–107, 1998

Kapur S, Craik FI, Jones C, et al: Functional role of the prefrontal cortex in retrieval of memories: a PET study. Neuroreport 6:1880–1884, 1995

Keane MM, Gabrieli JDE, Monti LA, et al: Amnesic patients show normal priming and a normal depth-of-processing effect in a conceptually driven implicit task (abstract). Society of Neuroscience Abstracts 19:1079, 1993

Keefe RS, Roitman SE, Harvey PD, et al: A pen-and-paper human analogue of a monkey prefrontal cortex activation task: spatial working memory in patients with schizophrenia. Schizophr Res 17:25–33, 1995

Kelly C, Sharkey V, Morrison G, et al: Nithsdale Schizophrenia Surveys. 20. Cognitive function in a catchment-area-based population of patients with schizophrenia. Br J Psychiatry 177:348–353, 2000

Kessing LV: Cognitive impairment in the euthymic phase of affective disorder. Psychol Med 28:1027–1038, 1998

Kindermann SS, Brown GG: Depression and memory in the elderly: a meta-analysis. J Clin Exp Neuropsychol 19:625–642, 1997

Kopelman MD: The "new" and the "old": components of the anterograde and retrograde memory loss in Korsakoff and Alzheimer patients, in Neuropsychology of Memory, 2nd Edition. Edited by Squire LR, Butters N. New York, Guilford, 1992, pp 130–146

Kopelman MD, Stanhope N, Kingsley D: Retrograde amnesia in patients with diencephalic, temporal lobe or frontal lesions. Neuropsychologia 37:939–958, 1999

Koriat A: How do we know that we know? The accessibility model of the feeling of knowing. Psychol Rev 100:609–639, 1993

Krueger RB, Sackeim HA, Gamzu ER: Pharmacological treatment of the cognitive side effects of ECT: a review. Psychopharmacol Bull 28:409–424, 1992

Lachner G, Engel RR: Differentiation of dementia and depression by memory tests: a meta-analysis. J Nerv Ment Dis 182:34–39, 1994

Larrabee GJ, Levin HS: Memory self-ratings and objective test performance in a normal elderly sample. J Clin Exp Neuropsychol 8:275–284, 1986

Lauria G, Gentile M, Fassetta G, et al: Transient global amnesia and transient ischemic attack: a community-based case-control study. Acta Neurol Scand 97:381–385, 1998

Lepage M, Habib R, Tulving E: Hippocampal PET activations of memory encoding and retrieval: the HIPER model. Hippocampus 8:313–322, 1998

Lepage M, Ghaffar O, Nyberg L, et al: Prefrontal cortex and episodic memory retrieval mode. Proc Natl Acad Sci U S A 97:506–511, 2000

Lewis SL: Aetiology of transient global amnesia. Lancet 352:397–399, 1998

Light LL, La Voie D: Direct and indirect measures of memory in old age, in Implicit Memory. Edited by Graf P, Masson MEJ. Hillsdale, NJ, Erlbaum, 1993, pp 207–230

Lisanby SH, Maddox JH, Prudic J, et al: The effects of electroconvulsive therapy on memory of autobiographical and public events. Arch Gen Psychiatry 57:581–590, 2000

Lisanby SH, Schlaepfer TE, Fisch H-U, et al: Magnetic seizure therapy of major depression. Arch Gen Psychiatry 58(3): 303–305, 2001

Lloyd GG, Lishman WA: Effect of depression on the speed of recall of pleasant and unpleasant experiences. Psychol Med 5:173–180, 1975

Maguire EA, Mummery CJ: Differential modulation of a common memory retrieval network revealed by positron emission tomography. Hippocampus 9:54–61, 1999

Markowitsch HJ: Which brain regions are critically involved in the retrieval of old episodic memory? Brain Res Brain Res Rev 21:117–127, 1995

Markowitsch HJ: The neuroanatomy of memory, in The Oxford Handbook of Memory. Edited by Tulving E, Craik FIM. New York, Oxford University Press, 2000, pp 465–484

Marslen-Wilson WD, Teuber H: Memory for remote events in anterograde amnesia: recognition of public figures from news photographs. Neuropsychologia 13:353–364, 1975

Mason CF: Pre-illness intelligence of mental hospital patients. Journal of Consulting Psychology 20:297–300, 1956

McCarley RW, Wible CG, Frumin M, et al: MRI anatomy of schizophrenia. Biol Psychiatry 45:1099–1119, 1999

McElhiney MC, Moody BJ, Steif BL, et al: Autobiographical memory and mood: effects of electroconvulsive therapy. Neuropsychology 9:501–507, 1995

McKay AP, Tarbuck AF, Shapleske J, et al: Neuropsychological function in manic-depressive psychosis. Evidence for persistent deficits in patients with chronic, severe illness. Br J Psychiatry 167:51–57, 1995

McKenna PJ, Tamlyn D, Lund CE, et al: Amnesic syndrome in schizophrenia. Psychol Med 20:967–972, 1990

Meltzer HY, McGurk SR: The effects of clozapine, risperidone, and olanzapine on cognitive function in schizophrenia. Schizophr Bull 25:233–255, 1999

Milner B: The memory defect in bilateral hippocampal lesions. Psychiatric Research Reports of the American Psychiatric Association 11:43–52, 1959

Milner B, Petrides M, Smith ML: Frontal lobes and the temporal organization of memory. Human Neurobiology 4:137–142, 1985

Moscovitch M: Memory and working with memory: evaluation of a component process model and comparisons with other models, in Memory Systems 1994. Edited by Schacter D, Tulving E. Cambridge, MA, MIT Press, 1994, pp 269–310

Mozley LH, Gur RC, Gur RE, et al: Relationships between verbal memory performance and the cerebral distribution of fluorodeoxyglucose in patients with schizophrenia. Biol Psychiatry 40:443–451, 1996

Nadel L, Moscovitch M: Memory consolidation, retrograde amnesia and the hippocampal complex. Curr Opin Neurol 7:217–227, 1997

Nemiah J: Dissociative amnesia: a clinical and theoretical reconsideration, in Functional Disorders of Memory. Edited by Kihlstrom J, Evans F. Hillsdale, NJ, Erlbaum, 1979, pp 303–323

Nopoulos P, Flashman L, Flaum M, et al: Stability of cognitive functioning early in the course of schizophrenia. Schizophr Res 14:29–37, 1994

Nyberg L, Cabeza R, Tulving E: PET studies of encoding and retrieval: the HERA model. Psychonomic Bulletin and Review 3:135–148, 1996a

Nyberg L, McIntosh AR, Cabeza R, et al: General and specific brain regions involved in encoding and retrieval of events: what, where, and when. Proc Natl Acad Sci U S A 93: 11280–11285, 1996b

Nyberg L, McIntosh AR, Houle S, et al: Activation of medial temporal structures during episodic memory retrieval. Nature 380:715–717, 1996c

Nyberg L, McIntosh AR, Tulving E: Functional brain imaging of episodic and semantic memory with positron emission tomography. J Mol Med 76:48–53, 1998

Nyberg L, Persson J, Habib R, et al: Large scale neurocognitive networks underlying episodic memory. J Cogn Neurosci 12:163–173, 2000

O'Donnell BF, McCarley RW, Potts GF, et al: Identification of neural circuits underlying P300 abnormalities in schizophrenia. Psychophysiology 36:388–398, 1999

Orne M: On the simulating subjects as a quasi-control group in hypnosis research: what, why, and how, in Hypnosis: Developments in Research and New Perspectives. Edited by Fromm E, Shor R. New York, Aldine, 1979, pp 519–565

Overall JE, Hoffmann NG, Levin H: Effects of aging, organicity, alcoholism, and functional psychopathology on WAIS subtest profiles. J Consult Clin Psychol 46:1315–1322, 1978

Pantoni L, Lamassa M, Inzitari D: Transient global amnesia: a review emphasizing pathogenic aspects. Acta Neurol Scand 102:275–283, 2000

Park S, Holzman PS: Association of working memory deficit and eye tracking dysfunction in schizophrenia. Schizophr Res 11:55–61, 1993

Parkin AJ, Walter BM, Hunkin NM: Relationships between normal aging, frontal lobe function, and memory for temporal and spatial information. Neuropsychology 9:304–312, 1995

Perley M, Guze S: Hysteria—the stability and usefulness of clinical criteria. N Engl J Med 266:421–426, 1962

Perry W, Light GA, Davis H, et al: Schizophrenia patients demonstrate a dissociation on declarative and non-declarative memory tests. Schizophr Res 46:167–174, 2000

Prudic J, Peyser S, Sackeim HA: Subjective memory complaints: a review of patient self-assessment of memory after electroconvulsive therapy. J ECT 16:121–132, 2000

Purdon SE: Cognitive improvement in schizophrenia with novel antipsychotic medications. Schizophr Res 35 (suppl):S51–60, 1999

Purdon SE, Jones BD, Stip E, et al: Neuropsychological change in early phase schizophrenia during 12 months of treatment with olanzapine, risperidone, or haloperidol. The Canadian Collaborative Group for Research in Schizophrenia. Arch Gen Psychiatry 57:249–258, 2000

Rees LM, Tombaugh TN, Gansler DA, et al: Five validation experiments of the Test of Memory Malingering (TOMM). Psychol Assess 10:10–20, 1998

Reitan R, Wolfoson D: The Halstead-Reitan Neuropsychological Test Battery: Theory and Clinical Interpretation. Tuscon, AZ, Neuropsychology Press, 1985

Richardson JS, Keegan DL, Bowen RC, et al: Verbal learning by major depressive disorder patients during treatment with fluoxetine or amitriptyline. Int Clin Psychopharmacol 9:35–40, 1994

Riege WH: Self-report and tests of memory aging. Clinical Gerontologist 1:23–36, 1982

Roy-Byrne PP, Weingartner H, Bierer LM, et al: Effortful and automatic cognitive processes in depression. Arch Gen Psychiatry 43:265–267, 1986

Rush AJ, George MS, Sackeim HA, et al: Vagus nerve stimulation (VNS) for treatment-resistant depressions: a multicenter study. Biol Psychiatry 47:276–286, 2000

Russell WR, Nathan PW: Traumatic amnesia. Brain 69:280–300, 1946

Sackeim HA: The cognitive effects of electroconvulsive therapy, in Cognitive Disorders: Pathophysiology and Treatment. Edited by Moos WH, Gamzu ER, Thal LJ. New York, Marcel Dekker, 1992, pp 183–228

Sackeim HA: Memory and ECT: from polarization to reconciliation. J ECT 16:87–96, 2000a

Sackeim HA: Repetitive transcranial magnetic stimulation: what are the next steps? Biol Psychiatry 48:959–961, 2000b

Sackeim HA, Steif BL: The neuropsychology of depression and mania, in Depression and Mania. Edited by Georgotas A, Cancro R. New York, Elsevier, 1988, pp 265–289

Sackeim HA, Freeman J, McElhiney M, et al: Effects of major depression on estimates of intelligence. J Clin Exp Neuropsychol 14:268–288, 1992

Sackeim HA, Prudic J, Devanand DP, et al: Effects of stimulus intensity and electrode placement on the efficacy and cognitive effects of electroconvulsive therapy. N Engl J Med 328:839–846, 1993

Sackeim HA, Devanand DP, Nobler MS: Electroconvulsive therapy, in Psychopharmacology: The Fourth Generation of Progress. Edited by Bloom F, Kupfer D. New York, Raven, 1995, pp 1123–1142

Sackeim HA, Prudic J, Devanand DP, et al: A prospective, randomized, double-blind comparison of bilateral and right unilateral electroconvulsive therapy at different stimulus intensities. Arch Gen Psychiatry 57:425–434, 2000

Sackeim HA, Keilp JG, Rush AJ, et al: The effects of vagus nerve stimulation on cognitive performance in patients with treatment-resistant depression. Neuropsychiatry, Neuropsychology, and Behavioral Neurology 14(1):53–62, 2001

Salisbury DF, Shenton ME, McCarley RW: P300 topography differs in schizophrenia and manic psychosis. Biol Psychiatry 45:98–106, 1999

Sander D, Winbeck K, Etgen T, et al: Disturbance of venous flow patterns in patients with transient global amnesia. Lancet 356:1982–1984, 2000

Saykin AJ, Shtasel DL, Gur RE, et al: Neuropsychological deficits in neuroleptic naive patients with first-episode schizophrenia. Arch Gen Psychiatry 51:124–131, 1994

Saykin AJ, Johnson SC, Flashman LA, et al: Functional differentiation of medial temporal and frontal regions involved in processing novel and familiar words: an fMRI study. Brain 122:1963–1971, 1999

Schacter DL: Perceptual representation systems and implicit memory: toward a resolution of the multiple memory systems debate. Ann N Y Acad Sci 1990:608:543–571

Schacter DL, Church B: Auditory priming: implicit and explicit memory for words and voices. J Exp Psychol Learn Mem Cogn 18:915–930, 1992

Schacter DL, Wagner AD: Medial temporal lobe activations in fMRI and PET studies of episodic encoding and retrieval. Hippocampus 9:7–24, 1999

Schacter DL, Cooper LA, Delaney SM: Implicit memory for unfamiliar objects depends on access to structural descriptions. J Exp Psychol Gen 119:5–24, 1990

Schwartz BL, Benjamin AS, Bjork RA: The inferential and experiential bases of metamemory. Current Directions in Psychological Science 6:132–137, 1997

Shallice T, Fletcher P, Frith CD, et al: Brain regions associated with acquisition and retrieval of verbal episodic memory. Nature 368:633–635, 1994

Shelline YI, Sanghavi M, Mintun MA, et al: Depression duration but not age predicts hippocampal volume loss in medically healthy women with recurrent major depression. J Neurosci 19:5034–5043, 1999

Shimamura AP: Memory and frontal lobe function, in The Cognitive Neurosciences. Edited by Gazzaniga MS. Cambridge, MA, MIT Press, 1994, pp 803–813

Silver H, Geraisy N: Effects of biperiden and amantadine on memory in medicated chronic schizophrenic patients: a double-blind cross-over study. Br J Psychiatry 166:241–243, 1995

Singer JA, Salovey P: Mood and memory: evaluating the network theory of affect. Clin Psychol Rev 8:211–251, 1988

Slater E, Glithero E: A follow-up of patients diagnosed as suffering from "hysteria." J Psychosom Res 9:9–13, 1965

Small SA, Perera GM, DeLaPaz R, et al: Differential regional dysfunction of the hippocampal formation among elderly with memory decline and Alzheimer's disease. Ann Neurol 45:466–472, 1999

Sobin C, Sackeim HA, Prudic J, et al: Predictors of retrograde amnesia following ECT. Am J Psychiatry 152:995–1001, 1995

Squire LR: Memory functions as affected by electroconvulsive therapy. Ann N Y Acad Sci 462:307–314, 1986

Squire LR: Declarative and nondeclarative memory: multiple brain systems supporting learning and memory. Journal of Cognitive Neuroscience 99:195–231, 1992

Squire LR, Wetzel CD, Slater PC: Memory complaint after electroconvulsive therapy: assessment with a new self-rating instrument. Biol Psychiatry 14:791–801, 1979

Squire L, Shimamura A, Graf P: Independence of recognition memory and priming effects: a neuropsychological analysis. J Exp Psychol Learn Mem Cogn 11:37–44, 1985

Staal WG, Hijman R, Hulshoff Pol HE, et al: Neuropsychological dysfunctions in siblings discordant for schizophrenia. Psychiatry Res 95:227–235, 2000

Steif BL, Sackeim HA, Portnoy S, et al: Effects of depression and ECT on anterograde memory. Biol Psychiatry 21:921–930, 1986

Stern Y, Moeller JR., Anderson, KE, et al: Different brain networks mediate task performance in normal aging and AD: defining compensation. Neurology 55:1291–1297, 2000

Sternberg DE, Jarvik ME: Memory function in depression: improvement with antidepressant medication. Arch Gen Psychiatry 33:219–224, 1976

Strous RD, Cowan N, Ritter W, et al: Auditory sensory (echoic) memory dysfunction in schizophrenia. Am J Psychiatry 152:1517–1519, 1995

Strupp M, Bruning R, Wu RH, et al: Diffusion-weighted MRI in transient global amnesia: elevated signal intensity in the left mesial temporal lobe in 7 of 10 patients. Ann Neurol 43:164–170, 1998

Stuss DT, Benson DF: The Frontal Lobes. New York, Raven, 1986

Sullivan EV, Shear PK, Zipursky RB, et al: A deficit profile of executive, memory, and motor functions in schizophrenia. Biol Psychiatry 36:641–653, 1994

Tanabe M, Watanabe T, Ishibashi M, et al: Hippocampal ischemia in a patient who experienced transient global amnesia after undergoing cerebral angiography: case illustration. J Neurosurg 91:347, 1999

Taylor JL, Tinklenberg JR: Cognitive impairment and benzodiazepines, in Psychopharmacology: The Third Generation of Progress. Edited by Meltzer H. New York, Raven, 1987, pp 1449–1454

Taylor MA, Abrams R: Cognitive dysfunction in schizophrenia. Am J Psychiatry 141:196–201, 1984

Tombaugh T: Test of Memory Malingering (TOMM). New York, Multi Health Systems, 1996

Tulving E: Episodic and semantic memory, in Organization of Memory. Edited by Tulving E, Donaldson W. New York, Academic Press, 1972, pp 381–403

Tulving E: Elements of Episodic Memory. Oxford, UK, Oxford University Press, 1983

Tulving E, Markowitsch HJ: Memory beyond the hippocampus. Curr Opin Neurobiol 7:209–216, 1997

Tulving E, Markowitsch HJ: Episodic and declarative memory: role of the hippocampus. Hippocampus 8:198–204, 1998

Tulving E, Schacter DL: Priming and human memory systems. Science 247:301–306, 1990

Tulving E, Kapur S, Craik FI, et al: Hemispheric encoding/retrieval asymmetry in episodic memory: positron emission tomography findings. Proc Natl Acad Sci U S A 91:2016–2020, 1994a

Tulving E, Kapur S, Markowitsch HJ, et al: Neuroanatomical correlates of retrieval in episodic memory: auditory sentence recognition. Proc Natl Acad Sci U S A 91:2012–2015, 1994b

Tulving E, Habib R, Nyberg L, et al: Positron emission tomography correlations in and beyond medial temporal lobes. Hippocampus 9:71–82, 1999

van Gorp WG, Altshuler L, Theberge DC, et al: Cognitive impairment in euthymic bipolar patients with and without prior alcohol dependence. A preliminary study. Arch Gen Psychiatry 55:41–46, 1998

Verdoux H, Liraud F: Neuropsychological function in subjects with psychotic and affective disorders. Relationship to diagnostic category and duration of illness. Eur Psychiatry 15:236–243, 2000

Victor M, Adams RD, Collins GH: The Wernicke-Korsakoff Syndrome, 2nd Edition. Philadelphia, PA, FA Davis, 1989

Voglmaier MM, Seidman LJ, Niznikiewicz MA, et al: Verbal and nonverbal neuropsychological test performance in subjects with schizotypal personality disorder. Am J Psychiatry 157:787–793, 2000

Watkins PC, Vache K, Verney SP, et al: Unconscious mood-congruent memory bias in depression. J Abnorm Psychol 105:34–41, 1996

Weickert TW, Goldberg TE, Gold JM, et al: Cognitive impairments in patients with schizophrenia displaying preserved and compromised intellect. Arch Gen Psychiatry 57:907–913, 2000

Weiner RD: Does ECT cause brain damage? Behavioral Brain Science 7:1–53, 1984

Weiner RD, Rogers HJ, Davidson JR, et al: Effects of stimulus parameters on cognitive side effects. Ann N Y Acad Sci 462:315–325, 1986

Weingartner H, Cohen R, Murphy D, et al: Cognitive processes in depression. Arch Gen Psychiatry 38:42–47, 1981

Weiskrantz L, Warrington EK: Conditioning in amnesic patients. Neuropsychologia 17:187–194, 1979

Welsh KA, Butters N, Hughes JP, et al: Detection and staging of dementia in Alzheimer's disease: use of the neuropsychological measures developed for the Consortium to Establish a Registry for Alzheimer's Disease. Arch Neurol 49:448–452, 1992

West RL: An application of prefrontal cortex function theory to cognitive aging. Psychol Bull 120:272–292, 1996

Wheeler MA, Stuss DT, Tulving E: Frontal lobe damage produces episodic memory impairment. J Int Neuropsychol Soc 1:525–536, 1995

Whitehead A: Verbal learning and memory in elderly depressives. Br J Psychiatry 123:203–208, 1973

Whitlock F: The etiology of hysteria. Acta Psychiatr Scand 43:144–162, 1967

Winokur G, Moscovitch M, Stuss DT: Explicit and implicit memory in the elderly: evidence for double dissociation involving medial temporal- and frontal-lobe functions. Neuropsychology 10:57–65, 1996

Zakzanis KK, Leach L, Kaplan E: On the nature and pattern of neurocognitive function in major depressive disorder. Neuropsychiatry, Neuropsychology, and Behavioral Neurology 11:111–119, 1998

PART

**IV**

# Neuropsychiatric Disorders

# Neuropsychiatric Aspects of Traumatic Brain Injury

Jonathan M. Silver, M.D.

Robert E. Hales, M.D., M.B.A.

Stuart C. Yudofsky, M.D.

Each year in the United States, more than 2 million people sustain a traumatic brain injury (TBI); 300,000 of these persons require hospitalization, and more than 80,000 of the survivors are afflicted with the chronic sequelae of such injuries (J.F. Kraus and Sorenson 1994). In this population, psychosocial and psychological deficits are commonly the major source of disability to the victims and of stress to their families. The psychiatrist, neurologist, and neuropsychologist are often called on by other medical specialists or the families to treat these patients. In this chapter, we review the role these professionals play in the prevention, diagnosis, and treatment of the cognitive, behavioral, and emotional aspects of TBI.

## Epidemiology

It is commonly taught in introductory courses in psychiatry that suicide is the second most common cause of death among persons under age 35. What is often not stated is that the most common cause is injuries incurred during motor vehicle accidents. TBI accounts for 2% of all deaths and 26% of all injury deaths (Sosin et al. 1989). A conservative estimate of the annual incidence of TBI (including brain trauma and transient and persistent postconcussion syndromes) is 200 per 100,000 per year (J.F. Kraus and Sorenson 1994). In the United States, between 2.5 million and 6.5 million individuals live with

the long-term consequences of TBI (NIH Consensus Development Panel 1999). Disorders arising from traumatic injuries to the brain are more common than any other neurologic disease, with the exception of headaches (Kurtzke 1984).

Those at the highest risk for brain injury are men 15–24 years old. Alcohol use is common in brain injury; a positive blood alcohol concentration was demonstrated in 56% of one sample of victims (J.F. Kraus et al. 1989). Motor vehicle accidents account for approximately one-half of traumatic injuries; other common causes are falls (21%), assaults and violence (20%), and accidents associated with sports and recreation (3%) (although as many as 90% of injuries in this category may be unreported) (NIH Consensus Development Panel 1999). Children are highly vulnerable to accidents as passengers, to falls as pedestrians, to impact from moving objects (e.g., rocks or baseballs), and to sports injuries. In the United States, as many as 5 million children sustain head injuries each year, and of this group 200,000 are hospitalized (Raphaely et al. 1980). As a result of bicycle accidents alone, 50,000 children sustain head injuries, and 400 children die each year (U.S. Department of Health and Human Services 1989). Tragically, among infants, most head injuries are the result of child abuse (64%) (U.S. Department of Health and Human Services 1989).

The total economic cost of brain injury is staggeringly high: an estimated $37.8 billion per year for the United

States alone to treat 328,000 victims of brain injury (W. Max et al. 1991). The average lifetime cost of treatment per person ranges from $600,000 to $1,875,000 (NIH Consensus Development Panel 1999). Because the victims of TBI most commonly are young adults, they may require prolonged rehabilitation.

Statistics form only a piece of the picture of the cost of TBI. Mental health professionals must deal with individuals and families who have endured these tragic events. The psychological and social disability after brain injury can be dramatic. As with patients who have many psychiatric illnesses, and in distinction to patients with neurologic disorders such as stroke and Parkinson's disease, many survivors of TBI appear to be physically well (without sensorimotor impairment). In addition to the neurologic consequences of TBI, the cognitive, social, and behavioral problems result in significant impairment. Studies examining the psychosocial functioning and adjustment at 1 month, 2 years, or 7 years after severe TBI have shown that patients have extreme difficulty in numerous critical areas of functioning, including work, school, familial, interpersonal, and avocational activities (Crawford 1983; McLean et al. 1984; Oddy et al. 1985; Weddell et al. 1980).

## Neuroanatomy and Pathophysiology of Traumatic Brain Injury

### Neuroanatomy

The patient who sustains brain injury from trauma may incur damage through several mechanisms, which are listed in Table 18–1. Contusions affect specific areas of the brain and usually occur as the result of low-velocity injuries, such as falls. Courville (1945) examined the neuroanatomic sites of contusions and found that most injuries were in the basal and polar portions of the temporal and frontal lobes. Most of these lesions were the result of the location of bony prominences that surround the orbital, frontal, and temporal areas along the base of the skull. Coup injuries occur at the site of impact due to local tissue strain. Contrecoup injuries occur away from the site of impact during sudden deceleration and translational and angular movements of the head. Impact is not required for contrecoup injuries to occur, and they usually occur in frontal and temporal areas (Gennarelli and Graham 1998).

*Diffuse axonal injury* refers to mechanical or chemical damage to the axons in cerebral white matter that commonly occurs with lateral angular or rotational acceleration. The axon is vulnerable to injury during high-

**TABLE 18–1.** Mechanisms of neuronal damage in traumatic brain injury

**Primary effects**
    Contusions
    Diffuse axonal injury
**Secondary effects**
    Hematomas
        *Epidural effects*
        *Subdural effects*
        *Intracerebral effects*
    Cerebral edema
    Hydrocephalus
    Increased intracranial pressure
    Infection
    Hypoxia
    Neurotoxicity
    Inflammatory response
    Protease activation
    Calcium influx
    Excitotoxin and free radical release
    Lipid peroxidation
    Phospholipase activation

velocity accidents when there is twisting and turning of the brain around the brain stem (as can occur in "whiplash" car accidents). Axons are stretched, causing disruption of the cytoskeleton and impaired axoplasm transport. This results in axoplasmic swelling and detachment and in wallerian degeneration of the distal stump of the axon (Cassidy 1994). The disruption of axons can occur as long as 2 weeks after the injury (Gennarelli and Graham 1998). Chemically, metabolic changes occur, leading to axonal damage (discussion follows). The most vulnerable sites in the brain to axonal injury are the reticular formation, superior cerebellar peduncles, regions of the basal ganglia, hypothalamus, limbic fornices, and corpus callosum (Cassidy 1994).

Diffuse axonal injury often results in sudden loss of consciousness (LOC) and can occur in minor brain injury or *concussion* (Jane et al. 1985; Povlishock et al. 1983). Among cases of TBI without diffuse axonal injury, there is a lower incidence of skull fractures, contusions, and intracranial hematomas (Adams et al. 1982).

Subdural hematomas (acute, subacute, and chronic) and intracerebral hematomas have effects that are specific to their locations and degree of neuronal damage. In general, subdural hematomas affect arousal and cognition.

### Pathophysiology

After TBI, the damaged neurons have an increased demand for energy. However, a decrease in cerebral blood flow occurs, which results in a mismatch between needed and available energy supply. These injured cells are more vulnerable to hypoxia, resulting in further neuronal damage (DeKosky et al. 1998). Secondary neurotoxicity is caused by calcium influx, phospholipase activation, inflammatory response, protease activation, excitotoxin release, and lipid peroxidation that further damage axons and neuronal systems (DeKosky et al. 1998; Honig and Albers 1994). During hypoxia, free radicals and excitotoxic neurotransmitters, such as glutamate, are released and result in further neuronal damage (Becker et al. 1988; Faden et al. 1989), especially hippocampal damage to the CA1 neurons (Gennarelli and Graham 1998). Palmer et al. (1994) found that the brain concentration of aspartate, glutamate, glycine, and γ-aminobutyric acid (GABA) significantly increased in 5 patients with severe TBI. In evaluating the concentrations of glutamate in the cerebrospinal fluid (CSF) of 12 brain-injured patients, elevations were found that persisted for days after the injury (A.J. Baker et al. 1993).

Studies in animals suggest that the hippocampal formation is differentially sensitive to injury relative to other regions of the brain, that the CA1 and CA3 subfields and the dentate hilar region are most commonly affected, that such injury can occur even in the absence of hypoxia or elevated intracranial pressure (Hicks et al. 1993; Lowenstein et al. 1992; D.H. Smith et al. 1991; Toulmond et al. 1993), and that functional alterations may occur without actual neuronal cell death (Reeves et al. 1995). Furthermore, these lesions correlate with decrements in memory performance (Hamm et al. 1992; Hicks et al. 1993; Lowenstein et al. 1992; D.H. Smith et al. 1991).

Animal models of TBI, including fluid percussion models in cats and rodents and controlled angular acceleration devices in nonhuman primates, suggest that even mild TBI can result in neuronal injury with the appearance of axonal edema, separation of proximal and distal portions of the injured axons, and subsequent wallerian degeneration of the distal axonal segment (Jane et al. 1985; Povlishock and Coburn 1989). This is accompanied by disruption of axoplasmic transport and by secondary deafferentation. These changes evolve over a broad period of time—for example, from hours to weeks in the cat model (Povlishock and Coburn 1989)—perhaps providing some rationale for evolving symptoms in the days and weeks following a mild TBI. Although there is a general correlation between the length of unconsciousness and the amount of diffuse axonal injury, neuropathological changes characteristic of those seen in brain injury have been shown in cases of very mild TBI in humans, even those in whom there was no LOC (Blum-

bergs et al. 1994; Gennarelli et al. 1982; Oppenheimer 1968).

There have been several studies of neurochemical changes after TBI. From these studies, it is evident that TBI can affect the neurotransmitter systems that mediate mood and affect, including norepinephrine, serotonin, dopamine, and acetylcholine. In two studies (Clifton et al. 1981; Hamill et al. 1987), markedly elevated plasma norepinephrine levels were found after acute head injury. Elevated plasma levels of norepinephrine were correlated with more severe injury and poorer clinical outcome. However, animal studies of contusion have found widespread decrease in brain norepinephrine turnover (Dunn-Meynell et al. 1994).

The results of four studies of serotonin activity after TBI are inconsistent. Whereas Vecht et al. (1975) found that lumbar CSF levels of 5-hydroxyindoleacetic acid (5-HIAA) were below normal in conscious patients and normal in patients who were unconscious, Bareggi et al. (1975) found normal 5-HIAA levels in patients after severe TBI. Ventricular CSF 5-HIAA levels were elevated in patients within days of severe TBI (Bareggi et al. 1975). Patients with frontotemporal contusions and patients with diffuse contusions were investigated by Van Woerkom et al. (1977). Decreased levels of 5-HIAA were found in patients with frontotemporal contusions, but those with more diffuse contusions had increased 5-HIAA levels.

Two groups of investigators (Bareggi et al. 1975; Vecht et al. 1975) found a decrease in lumbar CSF homovanillic acid (HVA) levels, whereas Porta et al. (1975) demonstrated elevated ventricular CSF HVA levels after severe TBI. Elevated serum dopamine level may be related to the severity of the injury and to poor outcome (Hamill et al. 1987). Finally, patients with TBI had elevated acetylcholine levels in fluid obtained from intraventricular catheters or lumbar puncture (Grossman et al. 1975).

Specific lesions may deplete norepinephrine and serotonin by interrupting the nerve tracts of these pathways (Morrison et al. 1979). The norepinephrine nerve tracts course from the brain stem anteriorly to curve around the hypothalamus, the basal ganglia, and the frontal cortex. Similarly, the serotonin system has projections to the frontal cortex. Diffuse axonal injury or contusions can affect both of these systems.

Cholinergic changes, including increased levels of acetylcholine and decreased binding at cholinergic receptors, have been shown to occur after TBI (DeAngelis et al. 1994; Lyeth et al. 1994). This has been interpreted as increased activity of the cholinergic system (DeKosky et al. 1998).

# Neuropsychiatric Assessment of Traumatic Brain Injury

## History Taking

Although brain injuries subsequent to serious automobile, occupational, or sports accidents may not result in diagnostic enigmas for the psychiatrist, less severe trauma may first present as relatively subtle behavioral or affective change. Patients may fail to associate the traumatic event with subsequent symptoms. Prototypic examples include the alcoholic man who is amnestic for a fall that occurred while he was inebriated, the 10-year-old boy who falls from his bicycle and hits his head but fails to inform his parents, or the wife who was beaten by her husband but who is either fearful or ashamed to report the injury to her family physician. Confusion, intellectual changes, affective lability, or psychosis may occur directly after the trauma or as long as many years afterward. Individuals who present for emergency treatment for blunt trauma may not be adequately screened for TBI (Chambers et al. 1996). Even individuals who have identified themselves as "nondisabled" but who had experienced a blow to the head that left them at a minimum dazed and confused had symptoms and emotional distress similar to a group of individuals with known mild TBI (Gordon et al. 1998).

For all psychiatric patients, the clinician must specifically inquire whether the patient has been involved in situations that are associated with head trauma. The practitioner should ask about automobile, bicycle, or motorcycle accidents; falls; assaults; playground accidents; and participation in sports that are frequently associated with brain injury (e.g., football, soccer, rugby, and boxing). Patients must be asked whether there was any alteration in consciousness after they were injured, including feeling dazed or confused, losing consciousness, or experiencing a period of amnesia after the accident. The clinician should inquire as to whether the patients were hospitalized and whether they had posttraumatic symptoms, such as headache, dizziness, irritability, problems with concentration, and sensitivity to noise or light. Most patients will not volunteer this information without direct inquiry. Patients are usually unaware of the phenomenon of posttraumatic amnesia and may confuse posttraumatic amnesia with LOC. They assume that if they are unable to recall events, they must have been unconscious. Therefore, care must be taken to document the source of this observation (e.g., whether there were observers who witnessed the period of unconsciousness).

Because many patients either are unaware of, mini-mize, or deny the severity of behavioral changes that occur after TBI, family members also must be asked about the effects of injury on the behavior of their relative. For example, in evaluating the social adjustment of patients years after severe brain injury, Oddy et al. (1985) compared symptoms reported by both patients and their relatives. Forty percent of relatives of 28 patients with TBI reported that their relative behaved childishly. However, this symptom was not reported by the patients themselves. Although 28% of the patients complained of problems with their vision after the injury, this difficulty was not reported by relatives. Patients overestimate their level of functioning compared with the reporting of relatives, and they report more physical than nonphysical impairment (Sherer et al. 1998).

Family members also are more aware of emotional changes than are the victims of brain injury. Whereas individuals with TBI tend to view the cognitive difficulties as being more severe than the emotional changes (Hendryx 1989), mood disorders and frustration intolerance are viewed by family members as being more disabling than cognitive disabilities (Rappaport et al. 1989).

## Documentation and Rating of Symptoms

Symptom rating scales, electrophysiological imaging, and neuropsychiatric assessments should be used to define symptoms and signs that result from TBI (Table 18–2). The severity of injury may be determined by several parameters, including duration of unconsciousness, initial score on the Glasgow Coma Scale (GCS) (Teasdale and Jennett 1974), and degree of posttraumatic amnesia. The GCS (Table 18–3) is a 15-point scale that documents eye opening, verbal responsiveness, and motor response to stimuli and may be used to measure the depth of coma, both initially and longitudinally. The Galveston Orientation and Amnesia Test (GOAT) (Levin et al. 1979) measures the extent of posttraumatic amnesia and can be used serially to document recovery of memory (Figure 18–1). Overall cognitive and behavioral recovery may be documented using the Rancho Los Amigos Cognitive Scale (Table 18–4).

In severe TBI, posttraumatic amnesia or LOC may persist for at least 1 week or longer or, in extreme cases, may last weeks to months. GCS scores for severe TBI are less than 10. Mild head injury is usually defined as LOC for less than 15–20 minutes, a GCS score of 13–15, brief or no hospitalization, and no prominent residual neurobehavioral deficits. LOC is not required for the diagnosis of traumatic brain injury; however, there must be some evidence of alteration in consciousness, including feeling

**TABLE 18–2.** Assessment of traumatic brain injury

**Behavioral assessment**
Structured interviews (e.g., Structured Clinical Interview for DSM-IV Diagnoses [SCID], Multinational Neuropsychiatric Inventory [MINI])
Neurobehavioral Rating Scale (NBRS)
Positive and Negative Symptom Scale (PANSS)
Glasgow Coma Scale (GCS)
Galveston Orientation and Amnesia Test (GOAT)
Rancho Los Amigos Cognitive Scale
Rating scales for depression (Hamilton)
Rating scales for aggression (Overt Aggression Scale/Agitated Behavior Scale)
Neuropsychiatric Inventory/Neuropsychiatric Inventory Questionnaire
Brain Injury Symptom Questionnaire
Rivermead Postconcussion Questionnaire

**Brain imaging**
Computed tomography (CT)
Magnetic resonance imaging (MRI) with fluid-attenuated inversion recovery (FLAIR)
Functional magnetic resonance imaging (fMRI)
Single photon emission computed tomography (SPECT)
Regional cerebral blood flow (rCBF)
Positron emission tomography (PET)
Proton magnetic resonance spectroscopy (MRS)

**Electrophysiological assessment**
Electroencephalogram (EEG), including special leads
Computerized EEG
Brain electrical activity mapping (BEAM)

**Neuropsychological assessment**
Attention and concentration
Premorbid intelligence
Memory
Executive functioning
Verbal capacity
Problem-solving skills

**TABLE 18–3.** Glasgow Coma Scale

**Eye opening**

| | | |
|---|---|---|
| None | 1. | Not attributable to ocular swelling |
| To pain | 2. | Pain stimulus is applied to chest or limbs |
| To speech | 3. | Nonspecific response to speech or shout, does not imply the patient obeys command to open eyes |
| Spontaneous | 4. | Eyes are open, but this does not imply intact awareness |

**Motor response**

| | | |
|---|---|---|
| No response | 1. | Flaccid |
| Extension | 2. | "Decerebrate." Adduction, internal rotation of shoulder, and pronation of the forearm |
| Abnormal flexion | 3. | "Decorticate." Abnormal flexion, adduction of the shoulder |
| Withdrawal | 4. | Normal flexor response; withdraws from pain stimulus with adduction of the shoulder |
| Localizes pain | 5. | Pain stimulus applied to supraocular region or fingertip causes limb to move so as to attempt to remove it |
| Obeys commands | 6. | Follows simple commands |

**Verbal response**

| | | |
|---|---|---|
| No response | 1. | (Self-explanatory) |
| Incomprehensible | 2. | Moaning and groaning, but no recognizable words |
| Inappropriate | 3. | Intelligible speech (e.g., shouting or swearing), but no sustained or coherent conversation |
| Confused | 4. | Patient responds to questions in a conversational manner, but the responses indicate varying degrees of disorientation and confusion |
| Oriented | 5. | Normal orientation to time, place, and person |

*Source.* Adapted from Teasdale and Jennett 1974.

dazed or experiencing a period of posttraumatic amnesia (Committee on Head Injury Nomenclature 1966; Quality Standards Subcommittee 1997). In fact, in analysis of 1,142 patients assessed after hospitalization for TBI, the simple presence or absence of LOC was not significantly related to performance on neuropsychological tests (Smith-Seemiller et al. 1996). Operationalized diagnostic criteria for mild TBI have been proposed (Table 18–5) (Mild Traumatic Brain Injury Committee 1993). A specific grading scale has been developed for concussions that occur during sports: Grade 1—confusion without amnesia and no LOC; Grade 2—confusion with amnesia and no LOC; and Grade 3—LOC (Kelly 1995).

The use of structured clinical interviews and rating scales will assist the clinician in the determination of the

presence of symptoms and in rating their severity. For example, the Structured Clinical Interview for DSM-IV Diagnoses (SCID) (Spitzer et al. 1997) or the Multinational Neuropsychiatric Inventory (MINI) (Sheehan 1998) may be used to evaluate psychiatric diagnoses, whether or not they are associated with brain injury. Scales such as the Neurobehavioral Rating Scale (NBRS) (Levin et al. 1987b) and the Positive and Negative Symptom Scale (PANSS) (S.R. Kay et al. 1987) may be used to document the presence and severity of many emotional and cognitive symptoms. The Brain Injury Screening Questionnaire (Department of Rehabilitation Medicine 2000) or the Rivermead Postconcussion Questionnaire (King et

**TABLE 18–4.** Rancho Los Amigos Cognitive Scale

I. **No response:** Unresponsive to any stimulus

II. **Generalized response:** Limited, inconsistent, nonpurposeful responses, often to pain only

III. **Localized response:** Purposeful responses; may follow simple commands; may focus on presented object

IV. **Confused, agitated:** Heightened state of activity; confusion, disorientation; aggressive behavior; unable to do self-care; unaware of present events; agitation appears related to internal confusion

V. **Confused, inappropriate:** Nonagitated; appears alert; responds to commands; distractible; does not concentrate on task; agitated responses to external stimuli; verbally inappropriate; does not learn new information

VI. **Confused, appropriate:** Good directed behavior, needs cueing; can relearn old skills as activities of daily living (ADLs); serious memory problems; some awareness of self and others

VII. **Automatic, appropriate:** Appears appropriate, oriented; frequently robotlike in daily routine; minimal or absent confusion; shallow recall; increased awareness of self, interaction in environment; lacks insight into condition; decreased judgment and problem solving; lacks realistic planning for future

VIII. **Purposeful, appropriate:** Alert, oriented; recalls and integrates past events; learns new activities and can continue without supervision; independent in home and living skills; capable of driving; defects in stress tolerance, judgment, abstract reasoning persist; many function at reduced levels in society

*Source.* Reprinted with permission of the Adult Brain Injury Service of the Rancho Los Amigos Medical Center, Downey, California.

**TABLE 18–5.** Definition of mild traumatic brain injury

A patient with mild traumatic brain injury is a person who has had a traumatically induced physiological disruption of brain function, as manifested by **at least** one of the following:

1. Any period of loss of consciousness.
2. Any loss of memory for events immediately before or after the accident;
3. Any alteration in mental state at the time of the accident (e.g., feeling dazed, disoriented, or confused); and
4. Focal neurological deficit(s) that may or may not be transient; but where the severity of the injury does not exceed the following: loss of consciousness of approximately 30 minutes or less; after 30 minutes, an initial Glasgow Coma Scale (GCS) score of 13–15; and posttraumatic amnesia (PTA) not greater than 24 hours.

*Source.* Reprinted from Mild Traumatic Brain Injury Committee of the Head Injury Interdisciplinary Special Interest Group of the American Congress of Rehabilitation Medicine: "Definition of Mild Traumatic Brain Injury." *Journal of Head Trauma Rehabilitation* 8(3):86–87, 1993. Used with permission.

al. 1995) can be used to monitor the presence of multiple symptoms that often occur after TBI. The Neuropsychiatric Inventory (NPI) (Cummings et al. 1994) or the abbreviated NPI Questionnaire (Kaufer et al. 2000) will enable the examiner to review symptoms with relatives or caregivers. The Overt Aggression Scale (OAS) (Yudofsky et al. 1986) and Overt Agitation Severity Scale (OASS) (Yudofsky et al. 1997) can be used to document the frequency and severity of aggressive outbursts and agitation that are so commonly associated with brain injury (Silver and Yudofsky 1987, 1991). In addition, the Agitated Behavior Scale (Bogner 1999) may be helpful.

## Laboratory Evaluation

### Imaging Techniques

Brain imaging techniques are frequently used to demonstrate the location and extent of brain lesions. Computed tomography (CT) is now widely available and may document contusions and hematomas and fractures. The timing of such imaging is important because lesions may be visualized months after the injury that cannot be seen during the acute phase. Thus, for a significant number of patients with severe brain injury, initial CT evaluations may not detect lesions that are observable on CT scans performed 1 and 3 months after the injury (Cope et al. 1988).

Magnetic resonance imaging (MRI) has been shown to detect clinically meaningful lesions in patients with severe brain injury when CT scans have not demonstrated anatomical bases for the degree of coma (Levin et al. 1987a; Wilberger et al. 1987). MRI is especially sensitive in detecting lesions in the frontal and temporal lobes that are not visualized by CT, and these loci are frequently related to the neuropsychiatric consequences of the injury (Levin et al. 1987a). MRI has been found to be more sensitive for the detection of contusions, shearing injury, and subdural and epidural hematomas (Orrison et al. 1994), and it has been able to document evidence of diffuse axonal injury in patients who have a normal CT scan after experiencing mild TBI (Mittl et al. 1994). When MRI is used, fluid-attenuated inversion recovery (FLAIR) is superior to T2-weighted spin-echo technique, especially in visualizing central diffuse axonal injury of the fornix and corpus callosum (Ashikaga et al. 1997). Morphometric analyses of individuals with TBI have revealed decreased thalamic volume (Anderson et al. 1996) and hippocampal atrophy (Bigler et al. 1997).

Functional techniques in brain imaging, such as regional cerebral blood flow (rCBF) and positron emission tomography (PET), can detect areas of abnormal

Name_____          Date of test ___/___/___/
Age _____  Sex  M  F                                Day of the week:
                                                        s  m  t  w  t  f  s
Date of birth ___/___/___/                            Time  A.M.  P.M.
Diagnosis _____           Date of injury ___/___/___/

**Galveston Orientation and Amnesia Test (GOAT)**     **Error points**

1. What is your name? (2) _____            ___/___/
   When were you born? (4) _____           ___/___/
   Where do you live? (4) _____             ___/___/
2. Where are you now? (5) city _____        ___/___/
   (5) hospital _____                       ___/___/
   (unnecessary to state name of hospital)
3. On what date were you admitted to this hospital? (5) _____   ___/___/
   How did you get here? (5) _____          ___/___/
4. What is the first event you can remember after the injury? (5) _____   ___/___/
   Can you describe in detail (e.g., date, time, companions) the first event you can recall after injury?   ___/___/
   (5) _____
5. Can you describe the last event you recall before the accident? (5) _____   ___/___/
   Can you describe in detail (e.g., date, time, companions) the first event you can recall before the   ___/___/
   injury? (5) _____
6. What time is it now? _____ (–1 for each ¾ hour removed from correct time to maximum of –5)   ___/___/
7. What day of the week is it? _____ (–1 for each day removed from correct one) _____   ___/___/
8. What day of the month is it? _____ (–1 for each day removed from correct date to maximum   ___/___/
   of –5) _____
9. What is the month? _____ (–5 for each month removed from correct one to maximum of –15)   ___/___/
   _____
10. What is the year? _____ (–10 for each year removed from correct one to maximum of –30)   ___/___/
   _____

**Total error points**                                ___/___/
**Total GOAT Score (100 points minus total error points)**   ___/___/

**FIGURE 18–1.**  The Galveston Orientation and Amnesia Test (GOAT).
*Source.*  Reprinted from Levin HS, O'Donnell VM, Grossman RG: "The Galveston Orientation and Amnesia Test: A Practical Scale to Assess Cognition After Head Injury." *Journal of Nervous and Mental Disease* 167:675–684, 1979. Used with permission.

function, when even CT and MRI scans fail to show any abnormalities of structure (Langfitt et al. 1987; Ruff et al. 1989). Single photon emission computed tomography (SPECT) also shows promise in documenting brain damage after TBI. Abnormalities are visualized in patients who have experienced mild TBI (Gross et al. 1996; Masdeu et al. 1994; Nedd et al. 1993) or who have chronic TBI (Nagamachi et al. 1995), even in the presence of normally appearing areas on CT scans. Abnormalities on SPECT appear to correlate with the severity of trauma (Jacobs et al. 1994). These techniques were utilized in examining a group of individuals with late whiplash syndrome (Bicik et al. 1998). Although there was significant frontopolar hypometabolism, it correlated significantly with scores on the Beck Depression Inventory. However, in individual cases, the reliability of the depiction of hypometabolism was low.

Proton magnetic resonance spectroscopy (MRS) has been investigated for the detection of abnormalities in TBI. Cech and colleagues (1998) examined 35 patients with TBI and found that a majority of those with mild TBI as well as severe TBI demonstrated abnormal levels of *N*-acetyl aspartate (NAA) in the splenium, consistent with diffuse axonal injury. Early changes in NAA concentrations in the gray matter were predictive of outcome in a group of 14 patients after TBI (S.D. Friedman et al. 1999).

McAllister and colleagues (1999) used functional MRI (fMRI) to assess patterns of regional brain activation in response to working memory loads in a group of individuals 1 month after they had sustained mild TBI. This group demonstrated significantly increased activation during a high-load task, particularly in the right parietal and right dorsolateral frontal regions. However, there were no differences in task performance compared with the control group. This study appears to correlate with the complaints of patients who state that they have to "work harder" to recall things, but in whom no deficits are found on objective testing.

Caution must be observed in applying the findings in this literature to a clinical population. We are unable to determine the presence of abnormalities before the accident. Abnormalities on SPECT or PET have been demonstrated in individuals with psychiatric disorders who have no history of brain injury, including posttraumatic stress disorder (PTSD) (Rauch et al. 1996), somatization disorder (Lazarus and Cotterell 1989), major depression (Dolan et al. 1992), and chronic alcoholism (Kuruoglu et al. 1996). The American Academy of Neurology has concluded that there currently is insufficient evidence for the use of SPECT to diagnose TBI, and its use in this condition should be considered investigational (Therapeutics and Technology Assessment Subcommittee 1996). With the present state of the art, functional imaging results can only be used as part of an overall evaluation to confirm findings documented elsewhere (Silver and McAllister 1997).

## Electrophysiological Techniques

Electrophysiological assessment of the patient after TBI may also assist in the evaluation. Electroencephalography can detect the presence of seizures or abnormal areas of functioning. To enhance the sensitivity of this technique, the electroencephalogram (EEG) should be performed after sleep deprivation, with photic stimulation and hyperventilation and with anterotemporal and/or nasopharyngeal leads (Goodin et al. 1990). Computed interpretation of the EEG and brain electrical activity mapping (BEAM) may be useful in detecting areas of dysfunction not shown in the routine EEG (Watson et al. 1995). There is controversy regarding the usefulness of these techniques. The American Academy of Neurology and the American Clinical Neurophysiology Society have concluded that "the evidence of clinical usefulness or consistency of results are not considered sufficient for us to support [the] use [of quantitative electroencephalography] in diagnosis of patients with postconcussion syndrome, or minor or moderate head injury" (Nuwer 1997). However, the EEG and Clinical Neuroscience Society addressed significant concerns regarding the interpretation of this report (Thatcher et al. 1999). In their opinion, there is significant scientific literature on the use and interpretation of quantitative electroencephalography and that several findings have been consistent (reduced amplitude of high-frequency electroencephalography, especially in the frontal lobes, a shift toward lower increased electroencephalographic frequencies,

and changes in electroencephalographic coherence) (Thatcher et al. 1999). This area requires further examination.

## Neuropsychological Testing

Neuropsychological assessment of the patient with TBI is essential to document cognitive and intellectual deficits and strengths. Tests are administered to assess the patient's attention, concentration, memory, verbal capacity, and executive functioning. This latter capacity is the most difficult to assess and includes problem-solving skills, abstract thinking, planning, and reasoning abilities. A valid interpretation of these tests includes assessment of the patient's preinjury intelligence and other higher levels of functioning. Because multiple factors affect the results of testing (Table 18–6), tests must be performed and interpreted by a clinician with skill and experience.

Patients' complaints may not be easily or accurately categorized as either functional (i.e., primarily due to a psychiatric disorder) or neurologic (i.e., primarily caused by the brain injury). Nonetheless, outside agencies (e.g., insurance companies and lawyers) may request a neuropsychiatric evaluation to assist with this "differential." In reality, most symptoms result from the interaction of many factors, including neurologic, social, emotional, educational, and vocational. Because important insurance and other reimbursement decisions may hinge on whether or not disabilities stem from brain injury, the clinician should take care that his or her impressions are based on data and are not misapplied to deprive the patient of deserved benefits. For example, mood disorders and cognitive sequelae of brain injury are often miscategorized as "mental illnesses" that are not covered by some insurance policies.

**TABLE 18–6.** Major factors affecting neuropsychological test findings

Original endowment
Environment
Motivation (effort)
Physical health
Psychological distress
Psychiatric disorders
Medications
Qualifications and experience of neuropsychologist
Errors in scoring
Errors in interpretation

*Source.* Reprinted from Simon RI: "Ethical and Legal Issues," in *Neuropsychiatry of Traumatic Brain Injury.* Edited by Silver JM, Yudofsky SC, Hales RE. Washington, DC, American Psychiatric Press, 1994, pp. 569–630. Used with permission.

## Clinical Features

The neuropsychiatric sequelae of TBI include problems with attention and arousal, concentration, and executive functioning; intellectual changes; memory impairment; personality changes; affective disorders; anxiety disorders; psychosis; posttraumatic epilepsy; sleep disorders; aggression; and irritability. Physical problems such as headache, chronic pain, vision impairment, and dizziness complicate recovery. The severity of the neuropsychiatric sequelae of the brain injury is determined by multiple factors existing before, during, and after the injury (Dikmen and Machamer 1995) (Table 18–7). In general, prognosis is associated with the severity of injury. The duration of posttraumatic amnesia correlates with subsequent cognitive recovery (Levin et al. 1982). In addition, the symptoms of injury are correlated with the type of damage sustained. For example, those with diffuse axonal injury often experience problems with arousal, attention, and slow cognitive processing. The presence of total anosmia in a group of patients with closed head injury predicted major vocational problems at least 2 years after these patients had been given medical clearance to return to work (Varney 1988). Posttraumatic anosmia may occur as a result of damage to the olfactory nerve, which is located adjacent to the orbitofrontal cortex, although there may be peripheral nerve involvement that results in anosmia (Hirsch and Wyse 1993). Impairment in olfactory naming and recognition frequently occurs in patients with moderate or severe brain injury and is related to frontal and temporal lobe damage (Levin et al. 1985a).

In a review by J.D. Corrigan (1995), victims of TBI who were intoxicated with alcohol at the time of the injury had longer periods of hospitalization, had more complications during hospitalization, and had a lower level of functioning at the time of discharge from the hospital compared with patients with TBI who had no detectable blood alcohol level at the time of hospitalization. One factor complicating the interpretation of these data is the fact that intoxication may produce decreased responsivity even without TBI, which can result in a GCS score that indicates greater severity of injury than is actually present. Furthermore, even a history of substance abuse is associated with increased morbidity and mortality rates.

Morbidity and mortality rates after brain injury increase with age. Elderly persons who experience TBI have longer periods of agitation and greater cognitive impairment and are more likely to develop mass lesions and permanent disability than are younger victims (Fogel and Duffy 1994; F.C. Goldstein and Levin 1995; Katz

**TABLE 18–7.** Factors influencing outcome after brain injury

- Severity of injury
- Type of injury
- Anosmia
- Intellectual functioning
- Psychiatric diagnosis
- Sociopathy
- Premorbid behavioral problems (children)
- Social support
- Substance use
- Neurologic disorder
- Age
- Apolipoprotein E status

and Alexander 1994; Rakier et al. 1995). Individuals who have a previous brain injury do not recover as well from subsequent injuries (Carlsson et al. 1987).

The interaction between the brain injury and the psychosocial factors cannot be underestimated. Demographic factors have been found to predict cognitive dysfunction after TBI (Smith-Seemiller et al. 1996). Preexisting emotional and behavioral problems are exacerbated after injury. Although many victims of TBI may not have a history of previous psychiatric problems, a significant percentage of patients do have histories of learning disabilities, attentional deficits, behavioral problems, and drug or alcohol abuse. Social conditions and support networks that existed before the injury affect the symptoms and course of recovery. In general, individuals with greater preinjury intelligence recover better after injury (G. Brown et al. 1981). Factors such as level of education, level of income, and socioeconomic status are positive factors in the ability to return to work after minor head injury (Rimel et al. 1981).

There have been several studies that have associated the presence of apolipoprotein E (ApoE) e4 with prognosis of recovery from TBI. Examining recovery in professional boxers, Jordan and colleagues (1997) found that the presence of ApoE e4 was associated with chronic neurologic deficits in "high-exposure" boxers. In individuals with TBI who were admitted to a neurosurgical unit, the presence of ApoE e4 predicted poor recovery after 6 months, even after controlling for severity of injury (Teasdale et al. 1997). Among individuals who were in a rehabilitation program subsequent to TBI, G. Friedman et al. (1999) found that ApoE e4 predicted poorer recovery. Although these results need additional confirmation, especially in those with mild TBI, they emphasize the fact that there are prognostic factors that influence recovery that we do not assess or that have not yet been determined. We must avoid "blaming the victim" or concluding that the individual does not "want" to improve (for psychological or monetary reasons), when there may be biological factors that influence recovery. Our belief is that many more biological factors will be discovered that significantly affect recovery from TBI.

## Personality Changes

Unlike many primary psychiatric illnesses that have gradual onset, TBI often occurs suddenly and devastatingly. Although some patients recognize that they no longer have the same abilities and potential that they had before the injury, many others with significant disabilities deny that there have been any changes. Prominent behavioral traits such as disorderliness, suspiciousness, argumentativeness, isolativeness, disruptiveness, and anxiousness often become more pronounced after brain injury.

In a study of children with head injury, G. Brown et al. (1981) found that disinhibition, social inappropriateness, restlessness, and stealing were associated with injuries in which there was a LOC extending for more than 7 days. In a survey of the relatives of victims of severe TBI, McKinlay et al. (1981) found that 49% of 55 patients developed personality changes 3 months after the injury. After 5 years, 74% of these patients were reported to have changes in their personality (Brooks et al. 1986). More than one-third of these patients had problems of "childishness" and "talking too much" (Brooks et al. 1986; McKinlay et al. 1981).

Thomsen (1984) found that 80% of 40 patients with severe TBI had personality changes that persisted 2–5 years, and 65% had changes lasting 10–15 years after the injury. These changes included childishness (60% and 25%, respectively), emotional lability (40% and 35%, respectively), and restlessness (25% and 38%, respectively). Approximately two-thirds of patients had less social contact, and one-half had loss of spontaneity and poverty of interests after 10–15 years.

Because of the vulnerability of the prefrontal and frontal regions of the cortex to contusions, injury to these regions is common and gives rise to changes in personality known as the frontal lobe syndrome. For the prototypic patient with frontal lobe syndrome, the cognitive functions are preserved while personality changes abound. Psychiatric disturbances associated with frontal lobe injury commonly include impaired social judgment, labile affect, uncharacteristic lewdness, inability to appreciate the effects of one's behavior or remarks on others, a loss of social graces (such as eating manners), a diminution of attention to personal appearance and hygiene, and boisterousness. Impaired judgment may take the form of

diminished concern for the future, increased risk taking, unrestrained drinking of alcohol, and indiscriminate selection of food. Patients may appear shallow, indifferent, or apathetic, with a global lack of concern for the consequences of their behavior.

Certain behavioral syndromes have been related to damage to specific areas of the frontal lobe (Auerbach 1986). The orbitofrontal syndrome is associated with behavioral excesses, such as impulsivity, disinhibition, hyperactivity, distractibility, and mood lability. Injury to the dorsolateral frontal cortex may result in slowness, apathy, and perseveration. This may be considered similar to the negative (deficit) symptoms associated with schizophrenia, wherein the patient may exhibit blunted affect, emotional withdrawal, social withdrawal, passivity, and lack of spontaneity (S.R. Kay et al. 1987). As with TBI, deficit symptoms in patients with schizophrenia are thought to result from disordered functioning of the dorsolateral frontal cortex (Berman et al. 1988). Outbursts of rage and violent behavior occur after damage to the inferior orbital surface of the frontal lobe and anterior temporal lobes.

Patients also develop changes in sexual behavior after brain injury, most commonly decreased sex drive, erectile function, and frequency of intercourse (Zasler 1994). Kleine-Levin syndrome—characterized by periodic hypersomnolence, hyperphagia, and behavioral disturbances that include hypersexuality—has also been reported to occur subsequent to brain injury (Will et al. 1988).

Although there have been studies examining personality changes after TBI, few have focused on Axis II psychopathology in individuals with TBI. In utilizing a structured clinical interview to diagnose personality disorders in 100 individuals with TBI, Hibbard and colleagues (2000) found that several personality disorders developed after TBI that were reflective of persistent challenges and compensatory coping strategies facing these individuals. Whereas before TBI, 24% of the sample population had personality disorders, 66% of the sample met criteria for personality disorders after TBI. The most common disorders were borderline, avoidant, paranoid, obsessive-compulsive, and narcissistic.

In DSM-IV-TR (American Psychiatric Association 2000), these personality changes would be diagnosed as personality change due to traumatic brain injury. Specific subtypes are provided as the most significant clinical problems (Table 18–8).

## Intellectual Changes

Problems with intellectual functioning may be among the most subtle manifestations of brain injury. Changes can

**TABLE 18–8.** DSM-IV-TR diagnostic criteria for personality change due to traumatic brain injury

A. A persistent personality disturbance that represents a change from the individual's previous characteristic personality pattern. (In children, the disturbance involves a marked deviation from normal development or a significant change in the child's usual behavior patterns lasting at least 1 year.)

B. There is evidence from the history, physical examination, or laboratory findings that the disturbance is the direct physiological consequence of a general medical condition.

C. The disturbance is not better accounted for by another mental disorder (including other mental disorders due to a general medical condition).

D. The disturbance does not occur exclusively during the course of a delirium and does not meet criteria for a dementia.

E. The disturbance causes clinically significant distress or impairment in social, occupational, or other important areas of functioning.

Specify type:

**Labile type:** if the predominant feature is affective lability

**Disinhibited type:** if the predominant feature is poor impulse control as evidenced by sexual indiscretions, etc.

**Aggressive type:** if the predominant feature is aggressive behavior

**Apathetic type:** if the predominant feature is marked apathy and indifference

**Paranoid type:** if the predominant feature is suspiciousness or paranoid ideation

**Other type:** if the predominant feature is not one of the above, e.g., personality change associated with a seizure disorder

**Combined type:** if more than one feature predominates in the clinical picture

**Unspecified type**

---

**TABLE 18–9.** Executive functions

- Setting goals
- Assessing strengths and weaknesses
- Planning and/or directing activity
- Initiating and/or inhibiting behavior
- Monitoring current activity
- Evaluating results

*Source.* Reprinted from O'Shanick GJ, O'Shanick AM: "Personality and Intellectual Changes," in *Neuropsychiatry of Traumatic Brain Injury.* Edited by Silver JM, Yudofsky SC, Hales RE. Washington, DC, American Psychiatric Press, 1994, pp. 163–188. Used with permission.

---

Studies suggest that among the long-term sequelae of brain trauma is Alzheimer's disease (Amaducci et al. 1986; Graves et al. 1990). Amyloid protein deposition has been found in the brains of patients who experienced severe TBI (Roberts et al. 1994; Sheriff et al. 1994). Several investigators have found this association in elderly persons who have brain injury (Mayeux et al. 1993; Van Duijn et al. 1992). Sustaining TBI reduced the time to onset of Alzheimer's disease among those who were at risk (Nemetz et al. 1999). There have been several studies that have examined the influence of ApoE status on the risk of developing Alzheimer's disease subsequent to TBI. Mayeux et al. (1995) found that the presence of the ApoE e4 allele combined with a history of head injury results in synergistic effect, increasing the risk from 2-fold with ApoE e4 alone to a 10-fold increase in risk with ApoE e4 and TBI. Katzman and colleagues (1996) determined that in their population, there was an additive effect. However, in another large family study, the influence of TBI on the development of Alzheimer's disease was greater among persons lacking ApoE e4 (Guo et al. 2000). This connection between these disorders is logical, given the pathological features of these disorders, and must be considered when reviewing the lifelong implications of recovery from TBI.

Children who survive head trauma often return to school with behavioral and learning problems (Mahoney et al. 1983). Children with behavioral disorders are much more likely to have a history of prior head injury (Michaud et al. 1993). In addition, children who sustained injury at or before age 2 years had significantly lower IQ scores (Michaud et al. 1993). The sequelae of mild TBI in children are controversial (Birmaher and Williams 1994). In a study of 43 children and adolescents who had sustained TBI, J.E. Max et al. (1998b) found that preinjury family functioning was a significant predictor of psychiatric disorders after 1 year. Whereas some investigators have demonstrated neuropsychological sequelae after mild TBI when carefully tested (Gul-

occur in the capacity to concentrate, use language, abstract, calculate, reason, remember, plan, and process information (Barth et al. 1983; Levin et al. 1985b; Stuss et al. 1985). Problems with arousal can take the form of inattentiveness, distractibility, and difficulty switching and dividing attention (Ponsford and Kinsella 1992). Mental sluggishness, poor concentration, and memory problems are common complaints of both patients and relatives (Brooks et al. 1986; McKinlay et al. 1981; Thomsen 1984). High-level cognitive functions, termed executive functions, are frequently impaired, although such impairments are difficult to detect and diagnose with cursory cognitive testing (Table 18–9) (O'Shanick and O'Shanick 1994). Only specific tests that mimic real-life decision-making situations may objectively demonstrate the problems encountered in daily life (Bechara et al. 1994).

brandsen 1984), others have shown that mild TBI produces virtually no clinically significant long-term deficits (Fay et al. 1993). In patients who survive moderate to severe brain injury, the degree of memory impairment often exceeds the level of intellectual dysfunction (Levin et al. 1988). The following case example illustrates a typical presentation of an adolescent with TBI presenting with behavioral and academic problems.

## Case Example

A 17-year-old girl was referred by her father for neuropsychiatric evaluation because of many changes that were observed in her personality during the past 2 years. Whereas she had been an A student and had been involved in many extracurricular activities during her sophomore year in high school, there had been a substantial change in her behavior during the past 2 years. She was barely able to maintain a C average, was "hanging around with the bad kids," and was frequently using marijuana and alcohol. A careful history revealed that 2 years earlier, her older brother had hit her in the forehead with a rake, which stunned her, but she did not lose consciousness. Although she had had a headache after the accident, no psychiatric or neurologic follow-up was pursued.

Neuropsychological testing at the time of evaluation revealed a significant decline in intellectual functioning from her "preinjury" state. Testing revealed poor concentration, attention, memory, and reasoning abilities. Academically, she was unable to "keep up" with the friends she had before her injury, and she began to socialize with a group of students with little interest in academics and began to conceptualize herself as being a rebel. When neuropsychological testing results were explained to the patient and her family as a consequence of the brain injury, she and her family were able to understand the "defensive" reaction to her changed social behavior.

## Psychiatric Disorders

Recent studies that utilize standard psychiatric diagnostic criteria have found that several psychiatric disorders are common in individuals with TBI (Deb et al. 1999; Fann et al. 1995; Hibbard et al. 1998a; Jorge et al. 1993; van Reekum et al. 2000). In a group of patients referred to a brain injury rehabilitation center, Fann and colleagues (1995) found that 26% had current major depression, 14% had current dysthymia, 24% had current generalized anxiety disorder, and 8% had current substance abuse. There was a 12% occurrence of pre-TBI depression. Deb and colleagues (1999) performed a psychiatric evaluation of 196 individuals who were hospitalized after TBI. They found that a psychiatric disorder was found in 21.7% versus 16.4% of a control population of individuals hospitalized for other reasons. Compared with the control group,

the individuals with TBI had a higher rate of depression (13.9% versus 2.1%) and panic disorder (9.0% versus 0.8%). Factors associated with these psychiatric disorders included a history of psychiatric illness, preinjury alcohol use, unfavorable outcome, lower Mini-Mental State Exam scores, and fewer years of education. Hibbard and colleagues (1998a) administered a structured psychiatric interview to 100 individuals with TBI. Major depression (61%), substance use disorder (28%), and PTSD (19%) were the most common psychiatric diagnoses elicited. Jorge and colleagues (1993) found that 26% of individuals had major depression 1 month after injury; 11% had comorbid generalized anxiety disorder.

In the New Haven portion of the National Institute of Mental Health Epidemiologic Catchment Area (ECA) program, individuals were administered standardized and validated structured interviews (Silver et al., in press). Among 5,034 individuals interviewed, 361 admitted to a history of severe brain trauma with LOC or confusion (weighted rate of 8.5/100). When controlling for sociodemographic factors, quality-of-life indicators, and alcohol use, risk was increased for major depression, dysthymia, panic disorder, obsessive-compulsive disorder, phobic disorder, and drug abuse/dependence.

Several studies suggest that individuals who experience TBI have a higher than expected rate of preinjury psychiatric disorders. Histories of prior psychiatric disorders in individuals with TBI have varied between 17% and 44%, and pre-TBI substance use figures have ranged from 22% to 30% (Jorge et al. 1994; van Reekum et al. 1996). Fann and colleagues (1995) found that 50% of individuals who had sustained TBI reported a history of psychiatric problems prior to the injury. The Research and Training Center for the Community Integration of Individuals with TBI at Mt. Sinai Medical Center in New York found that in a group of 100 individuals with TBI, 51% had pre-TBI psychiatric disorders, most commonly major depression or substance use disorders, that occurred at rates more than twice those reported in community samples (Hibbard et al. 1998a).

## Affective Changes

Depression occurs frequently after TBI (Rosenthal et al. 1998). There are several diagnostic issues that must be considered in the evaluation of the patient who appears depressed after TBI. Sadness is a common reaction after TBI, as patients describe "mourning" the loss of their "former selves," often a reflection of deficits in intellectual functioning and motoric abilities. Careful psychiatric evaluation is required to distinguish grief reactions, sadness, and demoralization from major depression.

Although scales such as the Hamilton Rating Scale for Depression (Hamilton 1960) or the Beck Depression Inventory (Beck et al. 1961) are useful in evaluating the severity of depression in patients with major depressive disorder, these are not substitutes for careful and thorough clinical evaluation. When the relationship between Beck Depression Inventory scores and the current diagnosis of depression was examined, high scores on the Beck Depression Inventory appeared to represent hyperreactivity to post-TBI symptoms rather than clinical depression (Sliwinski et al. 1998). Patients with depressed mood may not experience the somatic symptoms required for the diagnosis of major depressive disorder. The clinician must distinguish mood lability that occurs commonly after brain injury from major depression. Lability of mood and affect may be caused by temporal limbic and basal forebrain lesions (Ross and Stewart 1987) and has been shown to be responsive to standard pharmacologic interventions of depression (discussion follows). In addition, apathy secondary to brain injury (which includes decreased motivation and pursuit of pleasurable activities or schizoid behavior) and complaints of slowness in thought and cognitive processing may resemble depression.

The clinician should endeavor to determine whether a patient may have been having an episode of major depression before an accident. Traumatic injury may occur as a result of the depression and suicidal ideation. Alcohol use, which frequently occurs with and complicates depressive illness, is also a known risk factor for motor vehicle accidents. One common scenario is depression leading to poor concentration, to substance abuse, and to risk taking (or even overt suicidal behavior), which together contribute to the motor vehicle accident and brain injury.

## Prevalence of Depression After TBI

The prevalence of depression after brain injury has been assessed through self-report questionnaires, rating scales, and assessments by relatives. For mild TBI, estimates of depressive complaints range from 6% to 39%. For depression after severe TBI, in which patients often have concomitant cognitive impairments, reported rates of depression vary from 10% to 77%.

Robert Robinson and his colleagues have performed prospective studies of the occurrence of depression after brain injury (Federoff et al. 1992; Jorge et al. 1993). They evaluated 66 hospitalized patients who sustained acute TBI and followed the course of their mood over 1 year. Diagnoses were made using structured interviews and DSM-III-R criteria. Patients were evaluated at

1 month, 3 months, 6 months, and 1 year after injury. At each period, approximately 25% of patients fulfilled criteria for major depressive disorder. The mean duration of depression was 4.7 months, with a range of 1.5–12 months. Of the entire group of patients, 42% developed major depression during the first year after injury. The researchers also found that patients with generalized anxiety disorder and comorbid major depression have longer lasting mood problems than do those patients with depression and no anxiety (Jorge et al. 1993). In an unselected population sample, major depression was found in 11.1% of those with a history of brain injury (Silver et al. 1998). Deb and colleagues (1999) found 13.9% of individuals developed depression after TBI. Major depression occurred in 61% of a sample of individuals with TBI who were administered a structured psychiatric interview (Hibbard et al. 1998a). In a group of patients referred to a brain injury rehabilitation center, Fann and colleagues (1995) found that 26% had current major depression, and 14% had current dysthymia.

Studies consistently report increased risk of suicide subsequent to TBI (Tate et al. 1997). Data from a follow-up study (N. Brooks, personal communication, 1990) of 42 patients with severe TBI showed that 1 year after injury, 10% of those surveyed had spoken about suicide and 2% had made suicide attempts. Five years after the traumatic event, 15% of the patients had made suicide attempts. In addition, many other patients expressed hopelessness about their condition and a belief that life was not worth living. Silver et al. (2001) found that those with brain injury reported a higher frequency of suicide attempts than individuals without TBI (8.1% versus 1.9%). This remained significant even after controlling for sociodemographic factors, quality-of-life variables, and the presence of any coexisting psychiatric disorder. Mann and colleagues (1999) found an increased occurrence of TBI in individuals who have made suicide attempts.

We believe that the high incidence of suicide attempts in this population is due to the combination of major depression with disinhibition secondary to frontal lobe injury. The medical team, family, and other caregivers must work closely together to gauge suicide risk on a regular and ongoing basis.

The incidence and severity of depression have not been found to be related to the duration of LOC (Bornstein et al. 1989; Levin and Grossman 1978), to the duration of posttraumatic amnesia (Bornstein et al. 1988), or to the presence or absence of skull fracture (Bornstein et al. 1988). However, depression may be related to the extent of neuropsychological impairment as documented by neuropsychological testing (Bornstein et al. 1989;

Dikmen and Reitan 1977). Patients with post-TBI depression had a greater incidence of poor social adjustment and dissatisfaction before the injury (Federoff et al. 1992). Those who experienced an early transient depressive episode had left frontodorsolateral and left basal ganglia lesions. Depression that lasted longer than 6 months was associated with poorer social functioning and activities of daily living (Jorge et al. 1994). Fann et al. (1995) have shown that individuals with coexistent anxiety and depression had a greater severity of postconcussive symptoms and rated themselves as having a lesser degree of recovery. Satz et al. (1998) found that individuals with depressive symptoms and TBI had poorer outcome as related on the Glasgow Outcome Scale but not on neuropsychological measures.

### Mania After Traumatic Brain Injury

Manic episodes and bipolar disorder have also been reported to occur after TBI (Burstein 1993), although the occurrence is less frequent than that of depression after brain injury (Bakchine et al. 1989; Bamrah and Johnson 1991; Bracken 1987; Clark and Davison 1987; Nizamie et al. 1988). In the New Haven ECA sample, bipolar disorder occurred in 1.6% of those with brain injury, although the odds ratio was no longer significant when sociodemographic factors and quality of life were controlled (Silver et al., in press). Predisposing factors for the development of mania after brain injury include damage to the basal region of the right temporal lobe (Starkstein et al. 1990) and right orbitofrontal cortex (Starkstein et al. 1988) in patients who have family histories of bipolar disorder.

## Delirium

When a psychiatrist is consulted during the period when a patient with a brain injury is emerging from coma, the usual clinical picture is one of delirium with restlessness, agitation, confusion, disorientation, delusions, and/or hallucinations. As Trzepacz (1994) observed, this period of recovery is often termed posttraumatic amnesia in the brain injury literature and is classified as Rancho Los Amigos Cognitive Scale Level IV or V (see Table 18–4). Although delirium in patients with TBI is most often the result of the effects of the injury on brain tissue chemistry, the psychiatrist should be aware that there may be other causes for the delirium (such as side effects of medication, withdrawal, or intoxication from drugs ingested before the traumatic event) and environmental factors (such as sensory monotony). Table 18–10 lists common factors that can result in posttraumatic delirium.

**TABLE 18–10.** Causes of delirium in patients with traumatic brain injury

- Mechanical effects (acceleration or deceleration, contusion, and others)
- Cerebral edema
- Hemorrhage
- Infection
- Subdural hematoma
- Seizure
- Hypoxia (cardiopulmonary or local ischemia)
- Increased intracranial pressure
- Alcohol intoxication or withdrawal, Wernicke's encephalopathy
- Reduced hemoperfusion related to multiple trauma
- Fat embolism
- Change in pH
- Electrolyte imbalance
- Medications (barbiturates, steroids, opioids, and anticholinergics)

*Source.* Reprinted from Trzepacz P: "Delirium," in *Neuropsychiatry of Traumatic Brain Injury.* Edited by Silver JM, Yudofsky SC, Hales RE. Washington, DC, American Psychiatric Press, 1994, pp. 189–218. Used with permission.

Stuss et al. (1999) examined patients recovering from acute TBI using tests of attention and memory. Attention improved before performance on memory tasks, especially in individuals with mild TBI. The researchers concluded that the phenomenon currently termed posttraumatic amnesia is actually a confusional state and that the term *posttraumatic confusional state* should be used instead.

## Psychotic Disorders

Psychosis can occur either immediately after brain injury or after a latency of many months of normal functioning. Smeltzer et al. (1994) reviewed the literature regarding the reports of the occurrence of psychosis in patients who had TBI and noted that a major difficulty in this literature was the absence of a standard definition of psychosis; therefore, comparison of studies is problematic. McAllister (1998) observes that psychotic symptoms may result from a number of different post-TBI disorders, including mania, depression, and epilepsy. Lishman (1987) reported schizophrenic-like symptoms of patients after TBI that were "indistinguishable" from symptoms of the "naturally occurring" disorder. The psychotic symptoms may persist despite improvement in the cognitive deficits caused by trauma (Nasrallah et al. 1981). Review of the literature published between 1917 and 1964 (Davison and Bagley 1969) revealed that 1%–15% of schizophrenic inpatients have histories of brain injury.

Violon and De Mol (1987) found that of 530 head injury patients, 3.4% developed psychosis 1–10 years after the injury. Wilcox and Nasrallah (1987) found that a group of patients diagnosed with schizophrenia had a significantly greater history of brain injury with LOC before age 10 than did patients who were diagnosed with mania or depression or patients who were hospitalized for surgery. Achte et al. (1991) reported on a sample of 2,907 war veterans in Finland who sustained brain injury. They found that 26% of these veterans had psychotic disorders. In a detailed evaluation of 100 of these veterans, the authors found that 14% had paranoid schizophrenia. In a comparison of patients who developed symptoms of schizophrenia or schizoaffective disorder subsequent to TBI, left temporal lobe abnormalities were found only in the group who developed schizophrenia (Buckley et al. 1993). The rate of schizophrenia in the group of individuals with a history of TBI in the New Haven group in the ECA study was 3.4% (Silver et al., in press). However, after controlling for alcohol abuse and dependence, the risk for the occurrence of schizophrenia was of borderline significance.

Patients with schizophrenia may have had brain injury that remains undetected unless the clinician actively elicits a history specific for the occurrence of brain trauma. One high-risk group is homeless mentally ill individuals. To examine the relationship of TBI to schizophrenia and homelessness, Silver et al. (1993) conducted a case-control study of 100 literally homeless and 100 never-homeless indigent schizophrenic men, and a similar population of women. In the group of men, 55 patients had a prior TBI (36 literally homeless, 19 domiciled, $P << 0.01$). In the group of women, 35 had previous TBI (16 literally homeless, 19 domiciled, $P =$ not significant). We believe that the cognitive deficits subsequent to TBI in conjunction with psychosis increase the risk for becoming homeless; in addition, being homeless, and living in a shelter, carries a definite risk for trauma (Kass and Silver 1990).

## Posttraumatic Epilepsy

A varying percentage of patients, depending on the location and severity of injury, will have seizures during the acute period after the trauma. Posttraumatic epilepsy, with repeated seizures and the requirement for anticonvulsant medication, occurs in approximately 12%, 2%, and 1% of patients with severe, moderate, and mild head injuries, respectively, within 5 years of the injury (Annegers et al. 1980). Risk factors for posttraumatic epilepsy include skull fractures and wounds that penetrate the brain, a history of chronic alcohol use, intracra-nial hemorrhage, and increased severity of injury (Yablon 1993).

Salazar et al. (1985) studied 421 Vietnam veterans who had sustained brain-penetrating injuries and found that 53% had posttraumatic epilepsy. In 18% of these patients, the first seizure occurred after 5 years; in 7%, the first seizure occurred after 10 years. In addition, 26% of the patients with epilepsy had an organic mental syndrome as defined in DSM-III. In a study of World War II veterans (Corkin et al. 1984), patients with brain-penetrating injuries who developed posttraumatic epilepsy had a decreased life expectancy compared with patients with brain-penetrating injuries without epilepsy or compared with patients with peripheral nerve injuries. Patients who develop posttraumatic epilepsy have also been shown to have more difficulties with physical and social functioning and to require more intensive rehabilitation efforts (Armstrong et al. 1990).

Posttraumatic epilepsy is associated with psychosis, especially when seizures arise from the temporal lobes. Brief episodic psychoses may occur with epilepsy; about 7% of patients with epilepsy have persistent psychoses (McKenna et al. 1985). These psychoses exhibit a number of atypical features, including confusion and rapid fluctuations in mood. Psychiatric evaluation of 101 patients with epilepsy revealed that 8% had organic delusional disorder that, at times, was difficult to differentiate symptomatically from schizophrenia (Garyfallos et al. 1988).

Anticonvulsant drugs can produce cognitive and emotional symptoms (Reynolds and Trimble 1985; Rivinus 1992; M.C. Smith and Bleck 1991). Phenytoin has more profound effects on cognition than does carbamazepine (Gallassi et al. 1988), and negative effects on cognition have been found in patients who received phenytoin after traumatic injury (Dikmen et al. 1991). Minimal impairment in cognition was found with both valproate and carbamazepine in a group of patients with epilepsy (Prevey et al. 1996). Dikmen et al. (2000) found no adverse cognitive effects of valproate when it was administered for 12 months after TBI. The effects of phenytoin and carbamazepine in patients recovering from TBI were compared by K.R. Smith et al. (1994). They found that both phenytoin and carbamazepine had negative effects on cognitive performance, especially those that involved motor and speed performance. Although in the patient group as a whole, the effects were of questionable clinical significance, some individual patients experienced significant effects. Intellectual deterioration in children undergoing long-term treatment with phenytoin or phenobarbital also has been documented (Corbett et al. 1985). Treatment with more than one anticonvulsant (polytherapy) has been associated with increased adverse neuropsychiatric reactions (Reynolds and Trimble 1985). Of the newer anticonvulsant medications, topiramate, but not gabapentin or lamotrigine, demonstrated adverse cognitive effects in healthy young adults (Martin et al. 1999). Hoare (1984) found that the use of multiple anticonvulsant drugs to control seizures resulted in an increase in disturbed behavior in children.

Patients who have a seizure immediately after brain injury are often given an anticonvulsant drug for seizure prophylaxis. Temkin et al. (1990) showed that the administration of phenytoin soon after traumatic injury had no prophylactic effect on seizures that occurred subsequent to the first week after injury. Similarly, valproate did not demonstrate any efficacy in preventing late posttraumatic seizures (Temkin et al. 1999). It should be noted that there was a nonsignificant trend toward a higher mortality rate. Anticonvulsant medications are not recommended after 1 week of injury for prevention of posttraumatic seizures (Brain Injury Special Interest Group 1998) Any patient with TBI who is treated with anticonvulsant medication requires regular reevaluations to substantiate continued clinical necessity.

## Anxiety Disorders

Several anxiety disorders may develop after TBI. Epstein and Ursano (1994) compiled the results of 12 studies conducted from 1942 to 1990. Out of a group of 1,199 patients, 29% were diagnosed with clinical anxiety after TBI. Jorge et al. (1993) found that 11% of 66 patients with TBI developed generalized anxiety disorder in addition to major depression. Fann et al. (1995) evaluated 50 outpatients with TBI and found that 24% had generalized anxiety disorder. Deb et al. (1999) evaluated 196 individuals who were hospitalized after TBI. Panic disorder developed in 9%. Hibbard et al. (1998a) found that 18% developed PTSD, 14% developed obsessive-compulsive disorder, 11% developed panic disorder, 8% developed generalized anxiety disorder, and 6% developed phobic disorder. All of these were more frequent after TBI compared with before TBI. In analysis of data from the New Haven portion of the ECA study, Silver et al. (in press) found that of individuals with a history of brain injury during their lifetime, the incidences of anxiety disorders were 4.7% for obsessive-compulsive disorder, 11.2% for phobic disorder, and 3.2% for panic disorder. Dissociative disorders, including depersonalization (Grigsby and Kaye 1993) and dissociative identity disorder (Sandel et al. 1990), may occur. It is our clinical observation that patients with histories of prior trauma are at higher risk for developing these disorders.

Because of the potential life-threatening nature of many of the causes of TBI, including motor vehicle accidents and assaults, one would expect that these patients are at increased risk of developing PTSD. There is a 9.2% risk of developing PTSD after exposure to trauma, highest for assaultive violence (Breslau et al. 1998). PTSD and acute stress response are not uncommon after serious motor vehicle accidents (Koren et al. 1999; Ursano et al. 1999a), including symptoms of peritraumatic dissociation (Ursano et al. 1999b).

PTSD has been found in individuals with TBI (Bryant 1996; McMillan 1996; Ohry et al. 1996; Parker and Rosenblum 1996; Rattok 1996; Silver et al. 1997). In utilizing the SCID in evaluating 100 individuals with a history of TBI, Hibbard and colleagues found that 18% met criteria for PTSD (Hibbard et al. 1998a). Harvey and Bryant conducted a 2-year study of 79 survivors of motor vehicle accidents who sustained mild TBI. They found that acute stress disorder developed in 14% of these patients at 1 month. After 2 years, 73% of the group with acute stress disorder developed PTSD (Harvey and Bryant 2000). Six months after severe TBI, 26 of 96 individuals (27.1%) developed PTSD (Bryant et al. 2000). Although few patients had intrusive memories (19.2%), 96.2% reported emotional reactivity. The authors suggested that traumatic experiences may be mediated at an implicit level. Similarly, in 47 subjects with moderate TBI who were amnestic for the traumatic event, Warden et al. (1995) found that no patients met the full criteria for the diagnosis of PTSD, which includes reexperiencing the event. However, 14% of patients had avoidance and arousal symptoms. Not all investigators have found that PTSD occurs with TBI. In evaluating a group of 70 patients diagnosed with PTSD or mild TBI, Sbordone and Liter (1995) found that no patients had both disorders (although the presence of subsyndromal PTSD was not assessed). Children are also susceptible to the development of PTSD after TBI. J.E. Max et al. (1998a) evaluated 50 children who were hospitalized after TBI. Although only 4% of subjects developed PTSD, 68% had one PTSD symptom after 3 months, suggesting subsyndromal PTSD despite neurogenic amnesia.

Because of the overlap among symptoms of PTSD and mild TBI, it can be difficult to ascribe specific symptoms to the brain injury or to the circumstances of the accident. In studies of patients with PTSD, memory deficits consistent with temporal lobe injury have been demonstrated (Bremner et al. 1993). Imaging studies have shown smaller hippocampal volumes with PTSD (Bremner et al. 1995, 1997). It is therefore apparent that exposure to extreme stressors results in brain dysfunction that may be similar to that found after TBI.

We present the following case as an illustration:

## Case Example

While Mr. A was working, a machine was activated accidentally, and his head was crushed. He had full recall of the sound of his skull cracking and the sensation of blood coming down his forehead. It was several hours before he was transported to a hospital, but he never lost consciousness. His EEG revealed irregular right cerebral activity, and MRI was compatible with contusion and infarction of the right temporal parietal region.

Since the accident, Mr. A developed the full syndrome of PTSD; he experienced flashbacks, mood lability, sensitivity to noise, decreased interest, distress when looking at pictures of the accident, and problems with concentration.

## Sleep Disorders

It is common for individuals with TBI to complain of disrupted sleep patterns, ranging from hypersomnia to difficulty maintaining sleep. Fichtenberg and colleagues (2000) assessed 91 individuals with TBI who were admitted to an outpatient neurorehabilitation clinic. The presence of depression (as indicated by score on the Beck Depression Inventory) and mild severity of the TBI were correlated with the occurrence of insomnia. Guilleminault and colleagues (2000) assessed 184 patients with head trauma and hypersomnia. Abnormalities were demonstrated on the Multiple Sleep Latency Test (MSLT). Sleep-disordered breathing was common (59/184 patients). Hypersomnia must be differentiated from lack of motivation and apathy. In addition, the contribution of pain to disruption of sleep must be considered. Although depression and sleep disorders can be related and have similarities in the sleep-endocrine changes (Frieboes et al. 1999), in our experience with depressed individuals after TBI, the sleep difficulties persist after successful treatment of the mood disorder. In addition, we have seen patients who have developed sleep apnea or nocturnal myoclonus subsequent to TBI.

## Mild Traumatic Brain Injury and the Postconcussion Syndrome

Patients with mild TBI may present with somatic, perceptual, cognitive, and emotional symptoms that have been characterized as the postconcussion syndrome (Table 18–11). By definition, mild TBI is associated with a brief duration of LOC (less than 20 minutes) or no LOC, and posttraumatic amnesia of less than 24 hours; the patient usually does not require hospitalization after

**TABLE 18–11.** Postconcussion syndrome

**Somatic symptoms**
  Headache
  Dizziness
  Fatigue
  Insomnia
**Cognitive symptoms**
  Memory difficulties
  Impaired concentration
**Perceptual symptoms**
  Tinnitus
  Sensitivity to noise
  Sensitivity to light
**Emotional symptoms**
  Depression
  Anxiety
  Irritability

*Source.* Adapted from Lishman 1988.

the injury (see Table 18–5). For each patient hospitalized with mild TBI, probably four to five others sustain mild TBIs but receive treatment as outpatients or perhaps get no treatment at all. The psychiatrist is often called to assess the patient years after the injury, and the patient may not associate brain-related symptoms such as depression and cognitive dysfunction with the injury. The results of laboratory tests, such as structural brain imaging studies, often do not reveal significant abnormalities. However, as discussed previously, functional imaging studies such as SPECT (Masdeu et al. 1994; Nedd et al. 1993) and computerized electroencephalography and brainstem auditory evoked potential recordings have demonstrated abnormal findings (Watson et al. 1995). Diffuse axonal injury occurs with mild TBI, as demonstrated in the pathological examination of brains from patients who have died from systemic injuries (Oppenheimer 1968), as well as in nonhuman primates (Gennarelli et al. 1982).

Most studies of cognitive function subsequent to mild TBI suggest that patients report trouble with memory, attention, concentration, and speed of information processing, and patients can in fact be shown to have deficits in these areas shortly after their injury (1 week to 1 month) (S.J. Brown et al. 1994; McAllister 1994; McMillan and Glucksman 1987). In an evaluation of neuropsychological deficits in 53 patients who were experiencing postconcussive problems from 1 to 22 months after injury, Leininger et al. (1990) detected significantly poorer performance ($P < 0.05$) on tests of reasoning, information processing, and verbal learning than that found in a control population. Hugenholtz et al. (1988)

reported that significant attentional and information processing impairment ($P < 0.01$) occurred in a group of adults after mild concussion. Although there was improvement over time, the patient group continued to have abnormalities 3 months after the injury.

Individuals with mild TBI have an increased incidence of somatic complaints, including headache, dizziness, fatigue, sleep disturbance, and sensitivity to noise and light (S.J. Brown et al. 1994; Dikmen et al. 1986; Levin et al. 1987c; Rimel et al. 1981). In the behavioral domain, the most common problems include irritability, anxiety, and depression (Dikmen et al. 1986; Fann et al. 1995; Hibbard et al. 1998a).

The majority of individuals with mild TBI recover quickly, with significant and progressive reduction of complaints in all three domains (cognitive, somatic, and behavioral) at 1, 3, and certainly 6 months from the injury (Bernstein 1999). Unfortunately good recovery is not universal. A significant number of patients continue to complain of persistent difficulties 6–12 months and even longer after their injury. For example, Keshavan et al. (1981) found that 40% of their patients had significant symptoms 3 months after injury. Levin et al. (1987c), in a multicenter study, found that 3 months postinjury, 47% complained of headache, 22% of decreased energy, and 22% of dizziness. In a review of this topic, Bohnen et al. (1992) found a range of 16%–49% of patients with persistent symptoms at 6 months, and 1%–50% with persistent symptoms at 1 year. Those with persistent symptoms have been found to have impaired cognitive function (Leininger et al. 1990). S.J. Brown et al. (1994) suggest that if symptoms are present at 3–6 months subsequent to injury, they tend to persist. Alves et al. (1993) prospectively assessed 587 patients with uncomplicated mild TBI for 1 year. The most frequent symptoms were headache and dizziness. The researchers found that fewer than 6% of these subjects complained of multiple symptoms consistent with postconcussion syndrome.

Therefore, there may be two groups of mild TBI patients: those who recover by 3 months and those who have persistent symptoms. It is not known whether the persistent symptoms are part of a cohesive syndrome or simply represent a collection of loosely related symptoms resulting from the vagaries of an individual injury (Alves et al. 1986). However, it is increasingly recognized that "mild" TBI and concussions that occur in sports injuries result in clinically significant neuropsychological impairment (Collins et al. 1999; Matser et al. 1999; J.W. Powell and Barber-Foss 1999).

Compensation and litigation do not appear to affect the course of recovery after "mild" brain injury (Born-stein et al. 1988), and many patients return to work despite the continuation of psychiatric symptoms (Hugenholtz et al. 1988). In fact, professional athletes who sustain mild TBI and have a negative financial incentive to stop playing have the same symptoms of postconcussion syndrome as do individuals who sustain mild TBI at work or in motor vehicle accidents. As McAllister (1994) has pointed out,

> there may be times when a patient's attorney gives clear encouragement to maintain symptoms when litigation extends over a period of several years.... [However,] there is virtually no evidence at this point to suggest that it is the primary factor in the overwhelming majority of patients with mild brain injury. (p. 375)

In an extensive review of the literature, Alexander (1995) highlighted several important aspects regarding patients who develop prolonged postconcussion syndrome: 1) they are more likely to have been under stress at the time of the accident, 2) they develop depression and/or anxiety soon after the accident, 3) they have extensive social disruption after the accident, and 4) they have problems with physical symptoms such as headache and dizziness.

The treatment of patients with mild TBI involves initiating several key interventions (T. Kay 1993). In the early phase of treatment, the major goal is prevention of the postconcussion syndrome. This involves providing information and education about understanding and predicting symptoms and their resolution and actively managing a gradual process of return to functioning. Education about the postconcussion syndrome and its natural history improves prognosis (Wade et al. 1998). It is important to involve the patient's family or significant other, so that they understand the disorder and predicted recovery. After the postconcussion syndrome has developed, the clinician must develop an alliance with the patient and validate his or her experience of cognitive and emotional difficulties while not prematurely confronting emotional factors as primary. A combined treatment strategy is required that addresses the emotional problems along with cognitive problems.

As discussed in the previous section, patients with mild TBI may have vivid recollections of the traumatic event; this may contribute to the development of PTSD in addition to postconcussive symptoms. There is overlap between these two syndromes, and determining the predominant diagnosis may be difficult. In general, postconcussion symptoms should decrease within 3 months, whereas symptoms of PTSD may not diminish until 3–6 months after the trauma. Reexperiencing the traumatic event (e.g., in flashbacks or nightmares) is characteristic of PTSD.

## Aggression

Individuals who have traumatic brain injury may experience irritability, agitation, and aggressive behavior (Silver and Yudofsky 1994a). These episodes range in severity from irritability to outbursts that result in damage to property or assaults on others. In severe cases, affected individuals cannot remain in the community or with their families and often are referred to long-term psychiatric or neurobehavioral facilities. Increased isolation and separation from others often occur.

In the acute recovery period, 35%–96% of patients are reported to have exhibited agitated behavior (Silver and Yudofsky 1994a). After the acute recovery phase, irritability or bad temper is common. There has been only one prospective study of the occurrence of agitation and restlessness that has been monitored by an objective rating instrument, the OAS (Figure 18–2) (Brooke et al. 1992b). These authors found that of 100 patients with severe TBI (GCS score less than 8, more than 1 hour of coma, and more than 1 week of hospitalization), only 11 patients exhibited agitated behavior. Only 3 patients manifested these behaviors for more than 1 week. However, 35 patients were observed to be restless but not agitated. In a prospective sample of 100 patients admitted to a brain injury rehabilitation unit, 42% exhibited agitated behavior during at least one nursing shift (Bogner and Corrigan 1995). In follow-up periods ranging from 1 to 15 years after injury, these behaviors occurred in 31%–71% of patients who experienced severe TBI (Silver and Yudofsky 1994a). Studies of mild TBI have evaluated patients for much briefer periods of time; 1-year estimates from these studies range from 5% to 70% (Silver and Yudofsky 1994a). Carlsson et al. (1987) examined the relationship between the number of traumatic brain injuries associated with LOC and various symptoms, and they demonstrated that irritability increases with subsequent injuries. Of the men who did not have head injuries with LOC, 21% reported irritability, whereas 31% of men with one injury with LOC and 33% of men with two or more injuries with LOC admitted to this symptom ($P < 0.0001$).

Explosive and violent behaviors have long been associated with focal brain lesions as well as with diffuse damage to the central nervous system (Anderson and Silver 1999). The current diagnostic category in DSM-IV is personality change due to a general medical condition (American Psychiatric Association 1994) (see Table 18–8). Patients with aggressive behavior would be specified as aggressive type, whereas those with mood lability are specified as labile type. Characteristic behavioral features occur in many individuals who exhibit aggressive behavior after brain injury (Yudofsky et al. 1990). Typically, violence seen in these patients is *reactive* (i.e., triggered by modest or trivial stimuli). It is *nonreflective*, in that it does not involve premeditation of planning, and *nonpurposeful*, in the sense that the aggression severs no obvious long-term aims or goals. The violence is *periodic*, with brief outbursts of rage and aggression, interspersed between long periods of relatively calm behavior. The aggression is *ego-dystonic*, such that the individual is often upset or embarrassed after the episode. Finally, it is generally *explosive*, occurring suddenly with no apparent buildup.

## Physical Problems

### Coldness

Complaints of feeling cold, without actual alteration in body temperature, are occasionally seen in patients who have sustained brain injury. This feeling can be distressing to those who experience it. Patients may wear excessive amounts of clothing and may adjust the thermostat so that other members of the family are uncomfortable. Although this is not a commonly reported symptom of TBI, Hibbard et al. (1998b) found that in a sample of 331 individuals with TBI, 27.9% complained of changes in body temperature, and 13% persistently felt cold. Eames (1996), while conducting a study of the cognitive effects of vasopressin nasal spray in patients with TBI, reported incidentally that 13 patients had the persistent feeling of coldness, despite normal sublingual temperature. All were treated with nasal vasopressin spray for 1 month. Eleven of these patients stopped complaining of feeling cold after 1 month of treatment, and 1 other patient had improvement in the symptom, without complete relief. We describe below a series of 6 patients with brain injury whose subsequent complaints of feeling cold were treated with 1-desamino-8-D-arginine vasopressin (DDAVP) (intranasal vasopressin or desmopressin acetate).

In a pilot study, six patients who complained of persisting coldness after brain injury were treated with intranasal vasopressin (DDAVP) twice daily for 1 month (Silver and Anderson 1999). Response was assessed after 1 month of treatment. DDAVP was discontinued, and reassessment was done 1 month later. Five of the six patients had a dramatic response to DDAVP, as soon as 1 week after initiating treatment and no longer complained of feeling cold. Response persisted even after discontinuation of treatment. Patients denied any side

## Overt Aggression Scale (OAS)

Stuart Yudofsky, M.D., Jonathan Silver, M.D., Wynn Jackson M.D., and Jean Endicott, Ph.D.

### Identifying Data

| Name of patient | Name of rater |
|---|---|
| Sex of patient:  1 male   2 female | Date     /     /          (mo/da/yr)<br>Shift: 1 night     2 day     3 evening |

☐ No aggressive incident(s) (verbal or physical) against self, others, or objects during the shift (check here).

### Aggressive Behavior (check all that apply)

| Verbal aggression | Physical aggression against self |
|---|---|
| ☐ Makes loud noises, shouts angrily | ☐ Picks or scratches skin, hits self, pulls hair (with no or minor injury only) |
| ☐ Yells mild personal insults (e.g., "You're stupid!") | ☐ Bangs head, hits fist into objects, throws self onto floor or into objects (hurts self without serious injury) |
| ☐ Curses viciously, uses foul language in anger, makes moderate threats to others or self | ☐ Small cuts or bruises, minor burns |
| ☐ Makes clear threats of violence toward others or self (I'm going to kill you.) or requests to help to control self | ☐ Mutilates self, makes deep cuts, bites that bleed, internal injury, fracture, loss of consciousness, loss of teeth |

| Physical aggression against objects | Physical aggression against other people |
|---|---|
| ☐ Slams door, scatters clothing, makes a mess | ☐ Makes threatening gesture, swings at people, grabs at clothes |
| ☐ Throws objects down, kicks furniture without breaking it, marks the wall | ☐ Strikes, kicks, pushes, pulls hair (without injury to them) |
| ☐ Breaks objects, smashes windows | ☐ Attacks others, causing mild to moderate physical injury (bruises, sprain, welts) |
| ☐ Sets fires, throws objects dangerously | ☐ Attacks others, causing severe physical injury (broken bones, deep lacerations, internal injury) |

| Time incident began: ___ ___ : ___ ___ am/pm | Duration of incident: ___ ___ : ___ ___ (hours/minutes) |
|---|---|

### Intervention (check all that apply)

| | | |
|---|---|---|
| ☐ None<br>☐ Talking to patient<br>☐ Closer observation<br>☐ Holding patient | ☐ Immediate medication given by mouth<br>☐ Immediate medication given by injection<br>☐ Isolation without seclusion (time out)<br>☐ Seclusion | ☐ Use of restraints<br>☐ Injury requires immediate medical treatment for patient<br>☐ Injury requires immediate treatment for other person |

### Comments

**FIGURE 18–2.**   The Overt Aggression Scale (OAS).

*Source.*   Reprinted from Yudofsky SC, Silver JM, Jackson W, et al.: "The Overt Aggression Scale for the Objective Rating of Verbal and Physical Aggression." *American Journal of Psychiatry* 143:35–39, 1986. Used with permission.

effects from treatment with DDAVP. The experience of persisting coldness can respond dramatically to brief treatment with intranasal DDAVP. It is striking that the beneficial effects of DDAVP persisted after the treatment period ended. DDAVP may reverse physiologic effects of a relative deficit in vasopressin in the hypothalamus, caused by injury to the vasopressin precursor producing cells in the anterior hypothalamus, and corrects an internal temperature set point disrupted by the brain injury.

## Other Somatic Problems

The psychiatrist treating an individual who has sustained TBI should be aware of many other somatic problems that interfere with functioning and may exacerbate emotional problems (Horn and Zasler 1996). This includes chronic pain and headaches (including recurrence of migraines), dizziness from vestibular disorders, and visual problems. There are specific modalities (such as vestibular therapy and vision therapy) that can alleviate these problems and improve quality of life.

# Treatment

There are many useful therapeutic approaches available for people who have brain injuries. Brain-injured patients may develop neuropsychiatric symptoms based on the location of their injury, the emotional reaction to their injury, their preexisting strengths and difficulties, and social expectations and supports. Comprehensive rehabilitation centers address many of these issues with therapeutic strategies that are developed specifically for this population (Ben-Yishay and Lakin 1989; Binder and Rattok 1989; Pollack 1989; Prigatano 1989).

Although these programs meet many of the needs of patients with TBI, comprehensive neuropsychiatric evaluation (including the daily evaluation and treatment of the patient by a psychiatrist) is rarely available. Although we propose a multifactorial, multidisciplinary, collaborative approach to treatment, for purposes of exposition we have divided treatment into psychopharmacologic, behavioral, psychological, and social interventions.

## Psychopharmacologic Treatment

It is critical to conduct a thorough assessment of the patient before any intervention is initiated. Two issues require particular attention in the evaluation of the potential use of medication. First, the presenting complaints must be carefully assessed and defined. Second, the current treatment must be reevaluated. Although

consultation may be requested to decide whether medication would be helpful, it is often the case that 1) other treatment modalities have not been properly applied, 2) there has been misdiagnosis of the problem, or 3) there has been poor communication among treating professionals. On occasion, a potentially effective medication has not been beneficial because it has been prescribed in a dose that is too low or for a period of time that is too brief. In other instances, the most appropriate pharmacologic recommendation is that no medication is required and that other therapeutic modalities need to be reassessed. In reviewing the patient's current medication regimen, two key issues should be addressed: 1) the indications for all drugs prescribed and whether they are still necessary, and 2) the potential side effects of these medications. Patients who have had a severe brain trauma may be receiving many medications that result in psychiatric symptoms such as depression, mania, hallucinations, insomnia, nightmares, cognitive impairments, restlessness, paranoia, or aggression.

There are several general principles that should be followed in the pharmacologic treatment of the psychiatric syndromes that occur after TBI. Patients with brain injury of any type are far more sensitive to the side effects of medications than are patients who are not brain injured. Doses of psychotropic medications must be raised and lowered in small increments over protracted periods of time, although patients ultimately may require the same doses and serum levels that are used for patients without brain injury to achieve therapeutic response (Silver and Yudofsky 1994b).

When medications are prescribed, it is important that they are given in a manner to enhance the probability of benefit and to reduce the possibility of adverse reactions. Medications should be initiated at dosages that are lower than those usually administered to patients without brain injury. Dose increments should be made gradually, to minimize side effects and enable the clinician to observe adverse consequences. However, it is also critical that the medications be given sufficient time to work. Thus, when a decision to administer a medication is made, the patient must receive an adequate therapeutic trial of that medication in terms of dosage and duration of treatment.

Due to frequent changes in clinical status of patients after TBI, continuous reassessment is necessary to determine whether or not the medication is required. For conditions such as depression, the standard guidelines for the treatment of major depression should be used (i.e., continuation of medication for a minimum of 6 months after remission of symptoms). For other psychiatric conditions, the guidelines may not be so clear. For example, agitation that occurs during the early phases of recovery from TBI may last days, weeks, or months. The periods of underarousal and unresponsiveness may have similar variability of symptom duration. In general, if the patient has responded favorably to medication treatment, the clinician must use clinical judgment and apply risk/benefit determinations to each specific case in deciding just when to taper and attempt to discontinue the medication following TBI. There may be spontaneous remission or a carryover effect of the medication (i.e., its effects last longer than the duration of treatment).

Although individuals after TBI may be experiencing multiple neuropsychiatric symptoms (such as depressed mood, irritability, poor attention, fatigue, and sleep disturbances) that may all appear to result from a single "psychiatric diagnosis" such as major depression, we have found that many symptoms persist after the major "diagnosis" has been treated. Therefore, several medications may be required to alleviate distinct symptoms. However, medications must be initiated one at a time to determine the efficacy and side effects of each prescribed drug.

Studies of the effects of psychotropic medications in patients with TBI are few, and rigorous double-blind, placebo-controlled studies are rare (see Arciniegas et al. 2000a). Therefore, many of the recommendations are extensions of the known uses of these medications in the non-brain-injured psychiatric population or from studies on other types of brain injury (stroke, multiple sclerosis, etc.).

## Affective Illness

### Depression

Affective disorders subsequent to brain damage are common and are usually highly detrimental to a patient's rehabilitation and socialization. However, the published literature is sparse regarding the effects of antidepressant agents and/or electroconvulsive therapy (ECT) in the treatment of patients with brain damage in general and TBI in particular (Arciniegas et al. 1999; Bessette and Peterson 1992; Cassidy 1989; Saran 1985; Varney et al. 1987; see Silver and Yudofsky 1994b for review).

**Guidelines for using antidepressants for patients with TBI.** The choice of an antidepressant depends predominantly on the desired side-effect profile. Usually, antidepressants with the fewest sedative, hypotensive, and anticholinergic side effects are preferred. Thus, the selective serotonin reuptake inhibitors (SSRIs) are usually the first-line medications prescribed. These would be initiated at low dosages (e.g., fluoxetine starting at 10 mg/

day, sertraline starting at 25 mg/day, or citalopram starting at 10 mg/day). Fann and colleagues performed a single-blind placebo run-in trial of sertraline in 15 patients with major depression after TBI. Two-thirds of these patients achieved a Hamilton Rating Scale score consistent with remission by 2 months (Fann et al. 2000). In addition, those patients showed improvements in psychomotor speed, recent verbal memory, recent visual memory, and general cognitive efficiency (Fann et al. 2001). Other SSRIs, such as paroxetine and fluvoxamine, as well as venlafaxine and nefazodone, also appear effective. In a study comparing nortriptyline and fluoxetine in poststroke depression, nortriptyline was superior in efficacy to fluoxetine, and fluoxetine demonstrated no benefit above placebo (Robinson et al. 2000). If a heterocyclic antidepressant (HCA) is chosen, we suggest nortriptyline (initial doses of 10 mg/day) or desipramine (initial doses of 10 mg tid) and careful plasma monitoring to achieve plasma levels in the therapeutic range for the parent compound and its major metabolites (e.g., nortriptyline levels 50–100 ng/mL; desipramine levels greater than 125 ng/mL) (American Psychiatric Association Task Force 1985). Should the patient become sedated, confused, or severely hypotensive, the dosage of these drugs should be reduced.

ECT remains a highly effective and underused modality for the treatment of depression overall, and ECT can be used effectively after acute or severe TBI (Kant et al. 1999; Ruedrich et al. 1983). We recommend using treatment with the lowest possible energy levels that will generate a seizure of adequate duration (greater than 20 seconds), using pulsatile currents, increased spacing of treatments (2–5 days between each treatment), and fewer treatments in an entire course (four to six). If there is preexisting memory impairment, nondominant unilateral ECT should be used.

**Side effects.** The most common and disabling antidepressant side effects in patients with TBI, especially with the older HCAs, are the anticholinergic effects. These medications may impair attention, concentration, and memory, especially in patients with brain lesions. The antidepressants amitriptyline, trimipramine, doxepin, and protriptyline have high affinities for the muscarinic receptors and thus are highly anticholinergic and should be used only after careful consideration of alternative medications. Fluoxetine, sertraline, citalopram, mirtazepine, trazodone, venlafaxine, nefazodone, and bupropion all have minimal or no anticholinergic action. Several antidepressants (e.g., mirtazepine, doxepin, amitriptyline, trimipramine, imipramine, maprotiline, trazodone) are highly sedating and may result in significant problems of arousal in the TBI patient.

In some individuals, SSRIs may result in word-finding problems or apathy. This may be due to the effects of SSRIs on decreasing dopaminergic functioning, and it may be reversible with the addition of a dopaminergic or stimulant medication.

The available evidence suggests that, overall, antidepressants may be associated with a greater frequency of seizures in patients with brain injury. The antidepressants maprotiline and bupropion may be associated with a higher incidence of seizures (Davidson 1989; Pinder et al. 1977). Wroblewski et al. (1990) reviewed the records of 68 patients with TBI who received HCA treatment for at least 3 months. The frequencies of seizures were compared for the 3 months before treatment, during treatment, and after treatment. Seizures occurred in 6 patients (9%) during the baseline period, in 16 (24%) during HCA treatment, and in 4 (6%) after treatment was discontinued. Fourteen patients (19%) had seizures shortly after the initiation of HCA treatment. For 12 of these patients, no seizures occurred after HCA treatment was discontinued. Importantly, 7 of these patients were receiving anticonvulsant medication before and during HCA treatment. The occurrence of seizures was related to greater severity of brain injury. However, Zimmer et al. (1992) treated 17 patients with neurologic disorders (e.g., TBI, stroke, degenerative disease) with bupropion at an average dosage of 200 mg/day. No seizures occurred in this group of patients. Other investigations have found that seizure control does not appear to worsen if psychotropic medication is introduced cautiously and if the patient is on an effective anticonvulsant regimen (Ojemann et al. 1987). Although there have been reports of seizures occurring with fluoxetine, Favale et al. (1995) demonstrated an anticonvulsant effect in patients with seizures. In our experience, few patients have experienced seizures during treatment with SSRIs and other newer antidepressants. Although antidepressants should be used with continuous monitoring in patients with severe TBI, we also believe that antidepressants can be used safely and effectively in patients with TBI.

## Mania

Manic episodes that occur after TBI have been successfully treated with lithium carbonate, carbamazepine (Stewart and Nemsath 1988), valproic acid (Pope et al. 1988), clonidine (Bakchine et al. 1989), and ECT (Clark and Davison 1987). Because of the increased incidence of side effects when lithium is used in patients with brain lesions, we limit the use of lithium in patients with TBI to those with mania or with recurrent depressive illness

that preceded their brain damage. Furthermore, to minimize lithium-related side effects, we begin with low doses (300 mg/day) and assess the response to low therapeutic blood levels (e.g., 0.2–0.5 mEq/L).

Lithium has been reported to aggravate confusion in patients with brain damage (Schiff et al. 1982), as well as to induce nausea, tremor, ataxia, and lethargy in this population. In addition, lithium may lower seizure threshold (Massey and Folger 1984). Hornstein and Seliger (1989) reported a patient with preexisting bipolar disorder who experienced a recurrence of mania after experiencing closed head injury. Before the injury, this patient's mania was controlled with lithium carbonate without side effects. However, after the brain injury, dysfunctions of attention and concentration emerged that reversed with lowering of the lithium dosage.

For patients with mania subsequent to TBI, valproic acid is begun at a dosage of 250 mg twice daily and is gradually increased to obtain plasma levels of 50–100 mg/mL. Tremor and weight gain are common side effects. Hepatotoxicity is rare and usually occurs in children who are treated with multiple anticonvulsants (Dreifuss et al. 1987). Carbamazepine should be initiated at a dosage of 200 mg twice daily and adjusted to obtain plasma levels of 8–12 g/mL. As for patients without histories of TBI, the clinician should be aware of the potential risks associated with carbamazepine treatment, particularly bone marrow suppression (including aplastic anemia) and hepatotoxicity. The most common signs of neurotoxicity include lethargy, confusion, drowsiness, weakness, ataxia, nystagmus, and increased seizures. Lamotrigine and gabapentin are other options, although evidence as to efficacy, especially in individuals with TBI, is sparse.

## Lability of Mood and Affect

Antidepressants may be used to treat the labile mood that frequently occurs with neurologic disease. However, it appears that the control of lability of mood and affect may differ from that of depression, and the mechanism of action of antidepressants in treating mood lability in those with brain injuries may differ from that in the treatment of patients with "uncomplicated" depression (Lauterbach and Schweri 1991; Panzer and Mellow 1992; Ross and Rush 1981; Schiffer et al. 1985; Seliger et al. 1992; Sloan et al. 1992). Schiffer et al. (1985) conducted a double-blind crossover study with amitriptyline and placebo in 12 patients with pathologic laughing and weeping secondary to multiple sclerosis. Eight patients experienced a dramatic response to amitriptyline at a maximum dose of 75 mg/day.

There have been several reports of the beneficial effects of fluoxetine for "emotional incontinence" secondary to several neurologic disorders (K.W. Brown et al. 1998; Nahas et al. 1998; Panzer and Mellow 1992; Seliger et al. 1992; Sloan et al. 1992). K.W. Brown and colleagues (1998) treated 20 patients with poststroke emotionalism with fluoxetine in a double-blind, placebo-controlled study. The individuals receiving fluoxetine exhibited statistically and clinically significant improvement. In our experience, all SSRIs can be effective, and the dosage guidelines are similar to those used in the treatment of depression. In addition, other antidepressants, such as nortriptyline, can also be effective for emotional lability. We emphasize that for many patients it may be necessary to administer these medications at standard antidepressant dosages to obtain full therapeutic effects, although response may occur for others within days of initiating treatment at relatively low doses.

## Cognitive Function and Arousal

Stimulants, such as dextroamphetamine and methylphenidate, and dopamine agonists, such as amantadine and bromocriptine, may be beneficial in treating the patient with apathy and impaired concentration to increase arousal and to diminish fatigue. These medications all act on the catecholaminergic system but in different ways. Dextroamphetamine blocks the reuptake of norepinephrine and, in higher doses, also blocks the reuptake of dopamine. Methylphenidate has a similar mechanism of action. Amantadine acts both presynaptically and postsynaptically at the dopamine receptor and may also increase cholinergic and GABAergic activity (Cowell and Cohen 1995). In addition, amantadine is an N-methyl-D-aspartate (NMDA) glutamate receptor antagonist (Weller and Kornhuber 1992). Bromocriptine is a dopamine type 1 receptor antagonist and a dopamine type 2 receptor agonist. It appears to be a dopamine agonist at midrange doses (Berg et al. 1987). Assessment of improvement in attention and arousal may be difficult (Whyte 1992), and further work needs to be conducted in this area to determine whether these medications affect outcome. Therefore, careful objective assessment with appropriate neuropsychological tests may be helpful in determining response to treatment.

### Dextroamphetamine and Methylphenidate

Several reports have indicated that impairments in verbal memory and learning, attention, and behavior are alleviated with either dextroamphetamine or methylphenidate (Bleiberg et al. 1993; R.W. Evans et al. 1987; Kaelin

et al. 1996; Lipper and Tuchman 1976; Weinberg et al. 1987; Weinstein and Wells 1981). In a double-blind, placebo-controlled crossover study, C.T. Gualtieri and Evans (1988) studied 15 patients with TBI who were currently functioning at a Rancho Los Amigos Scale level of VII or VIII. Patients received a 2-week treatment with either placebo, methylphenidate 0.15 mg/kg body weight twice daily, or methylphenidate 0.30 mg/kg body weight twice daily. Of the 15 patients treated, 14 improved with active medication and had increased scores on ratings of mood and performance. The authors observed that this short-term response was not sustained over time. In a double-blind, placebo-controlled trial the administration of methylphenidate in the subacute setting to individuals with moderate to moderately severe TBI, Plenger and colleagues (1996) found that attention and performance were improved at 30 days but did not differ from a control group at 90 days. Therefore, the rate, but not the extent, of recovery was improved with stimulants. Speech et al. (1993) conducted a double-blind, placebo-controlled study of the effects of methylphenidate in 10 patients with chronic TBI. They found no significant increase in measures of attention, arousal, learning, cognitive processing speed, or behavior. Mooney and Haas (1993) found that methylphenidate improved anger and other personality problems after TBI. Whyte et al. (1997) performed a randomized, placebo-controlled trial of methylphenidate on 19 patients who exhibited attentional deficits after TBI. Although there was improvement in speed of mental processing, there were no improvements noted in orienting to distractions, sustained attention, and motor speed.

When used, methylphenidate should be initiated at 5 mg twice daily and dextroamphetamine at 2.5 mg twice daily. Maximum dosage of each medication is usually 60 mg/day, administered twice daily or three times daily. However, we have seen some patients who have required higher dosages of methylphenidate to obtain a reasonable serum level of 15 mg/mL.

### Sinemet and Bromocriptine

Lal et al. (1988) reported on the use of L-dopa/carbidopa (Sinemet) in the treatment of 12 patients with brain injury (including anoxic damage). With treatment, patients exhibited improved alertness and concentration; decreased fatigue, hypomania, and sialorrhea; and improved memory, mobility, posture, and speech. Dosages administered ranged from 10/100 to 25/250 four times daily. Eames (1989) suggests that bromocriptine may be useful in treating cognitive initiation problems of brain-injured patients at least 1 year after injury. He recommended starting at 2.5 mg/day and administering treatment for at least 2 months at the highest dose tolerated (up to 100 mg/day). Other investigators have found that patients with nonfluent aphasia (Gupta and Mlcoch 1992), akinetic mutism (Echiverri et al. 1988), and apathy (Catsman-Berrevoets and Harskamp 1988) have improved after treatment with bromocriptine. Parks et al. (1992) suggest that bromocriptine exerts specific effects on the frontal lobe and increases goal-directed behaviors.

## Amantadine

Amantadine may be beneficial in the treatment of anergia, abulia, mutism, and anhedonia subsequent to brain injury (Chandler et al. 1988; Cowell and Cohen 1995; T. Gualtieri et al. 1989; Nickels et al. 1994). M.F. Kraus and Maki (1997) administered amantadine 400 mg/day to six patients with TBI. Improvement was found in motivation, attention, and alertness, as well as executive function and dyscontrol. Dosages should initially be 50 mg twice daily and should be increased every week by 100 mg/day to a maximum dosage of 400 mg/day.

## Tricyclic Antidepressants

Although the drugs involved are not in the category of stimulants or dopamine agonists, Reinhard and colleagues (1996) administered amitriptyline (1 patient) and desipramine (2 patients) and found improvement in arousal and initiation after TBI. The authors hypothesize that the improvement is from the noradrenergic effects of the HCA.

## Side Effects of Medications for Impaired Concentration and Arousal

Adverse reactions to medications for impaired concentration and arousal are most often related to increases in dopamine activity. Dexedrine and methylphenidate may lead to paranoia, dysphoria, agitation, and irritability. Depression often occurs on discontinuation, so stimulants should be discontinued using a slow regimen. Interestingly, there may be a role for stimulants to increase neuronal recovery subsequent to brain injury (Crisostomo et al. 1988). Side effects of bromocriptine include sedation, nausea, psychosis, headaches, and delirium. Amantadine may cause confusion, hallucinations, edema, and hypotension; these reactions occur more often in elderly patients.

There is often concern that stimulant medications may lower seizure threshold in patients with TBI who are at increased risk for posttraumatic seizures. Wroblewski

et al. (1992) reviewed their experience with methylphenidate in 30 patients with severe brain injury and seizures and examined changes in seizure frequency after initiation of methylphenidate. The number of seizures was monitored for 3 months before treatment with methylphenidate, for 3 months during treatment, and for 3 months after treatment was discontinued. The researchers found that whereas only 4 patients experienced more seizures during methylphenidate treatment, 26 had either fewer or the same number of seizures during treatment. The authors concluded that there is no significant risk in lowering seizure threshold with methylphenidate treatment in this high-risk group. Although many patients in this study were treated concomitantly with anticonvulsant medications that may have conferred some protection against the development of seizures, this does not explain why 13 patients had fewer seizures when treated with methylphenidate. In a double-blind, placebo-controlled study of the effects of methylphenidate (0.3 mg/kg twice daily) in 10 children with well-controlled seizures and attention-deficit/hyperactivity disorder, no seizures occurred during the 4 weeks of treatment either with active drug or with placebo (Feldman et al. 1989). Dextroamphetamine has been used adjunctively in the treatment of refractory seizures (S. Livingston and Pauli 1975), and bromocriptine may also have some anticonvulsant properties (Rothman et al. 1990). Amantadine may lower seizure threshold (T. Gualtieri et al. 1989). We have also observed several patients who had not experienced seizures for months before the administration of amantadine to have had a seizure weeks after it was prescribed.

**Problems with processing multiple stimuli.** Although individuals with TBI may have difficulty with maintaining attention on single tasks, they can also have difficulty in processing multiple stimuli. This difficulty has been called an abnormality in auditory gating, and it is consistent with an abnormal response in processing auditory stimuli that are given 50 milliseconds apart (P50 response) (Arciniegas et al. 2000b). Preliminary evidence suggests that this response normalizes after treatment with donepezil 5 mg, which also results in symptomatic improvement (Arciniegas 2001).

# Fatigue

Stimulants (methylphenidate and dextroamphetamine) and amantadine can diminish the profound daytime fatigue experienced by patients with TBI. Dosages utilized would be similar to those used for treatment of diminished arousal and concentration. Modafinil, a medication recently approved for the treatment of excessive daytime somnolence in patients with narcolepsy, also may have a role in treatment of post-TBI fatigue. There have been studies specifically in patients with multiple sclerosis that have shown benefit (Rammahan et al. 2000; Terzoudi et al. 2000). Dosages should start with 100 mg in the morning and can be increased to up to 600 mg/day administered in two doses (i.e., 400 mg in the morning and 200 mg in the afternoon).

## Cognition

### Cholinesterase Inhibitors

TBI may produce cognitive impairments via disruption of cholinergic function (Arciniegas et al. 1999), and the relative sensitivity of TBI patients to medications with anticholinergic agents has prompted speculation that cognitively impaired TBI patients may have a relatively reduced reserve of cholinergic function. This has prompted trials of procholinergic agents, and in particular physostigmine, to treat behavioral dyscontrol and impaired cognition in TBI survivors (Eames and Sutton 1995). However, the significant peripheral effects and narrow margin of safety of physostigmine have made treatment with this agent impractical. With the advent of relatively centrally selective acetylcholinesterase inhibitors such as donepezil, the issue of cholinergic augmentation strategies in the treatment of cognitive impairment following TBI is currently being revisited, and preliminary reports suggest that donepezil may improve memory and global functioning (Taverni et al. 1998). Doses of donepezil range from 5–10 mg/day. The most common side effects include sedation, insomnia, diarrhea, and dizziness, which are minimized by starting with the lower dosage and adjusting upward slowly. Although these adverse effects are generally transient, a few patients will be unable to tolerate the medication due to persistent, severe diarrhea.

## Psychosis

The psychotic ideation resulting from TBI is generally responsive to treatment with antipsychotic medications. However, side effects such as hypotension, sedation, and confusion are common. Also, brain-injured patients are particularly subject to dystonia, akathisia, and other parkinsonian side effects—even at relatively low doses of antipsychotic medications (Wolf et al. 1989). Antipsychotic medications have also been reported to impede neuronal recovery after brain injury (Feeney et al. 1982). Therefore, we advise that antipsychotics should be used sparingly during the acute phases of recovery after the injury. Risperidone, olanzapine, and quetiapine have preferred therapeutic profiles over the conventional high-potency neuroleptics (such as haloperidol) because of decreased extrapyramidal effects. Therapeutic effect may not be evident for 3 weeks after treatment at each dosage. In general, we recommend a low-dose neuroleptic strategy for all patients with neuropsychiatric disorders. Clozapine is a novel and effective antipsychotic medication that does not produce extrapyramidal side effects. Although its use in patients with neuropsychiatric disorders has yet to be investigated fully, its side-effect profile poses many potential disadvantages. It is highly anticholinergic, produces significant sedation and hypotension, lowers seizure threshold profoundly, and is associated with a 1% risk of agranulocytosis that requires lifetime weekly monitoring of blood counts.

Among all the first-generation antipsychotic drugs, molindone and fluphenazine have consistently demonstrated the lowest potential for lowering the seizure threshold (Oliver et al. 1982). Clozapine treatment is associated with a significant dose-related incidence of seizures (ranging from 1% to 2% of patients who receive doses below 300 mg/day and 5% of patients who receive 600–900 mg/day); thus, in patients with TBI it must be used with extreme caution and for most carefully considered indications (Lieberman et al. 1989).

## Sleep

Sleep patterns of patients with brain damage are often disordered, with impaired rapid eye movement (REM) recovery and multiple nocturnal awakenings (Prigatano et al. 1982). Hypersomnia that occurs after severe missile head injury most often resolves within the first year after injury, whereas insomnia that occurs in patients with long periods of coma and diffuse injury has a more chronic course (Askenasy et al. 1989). Barbiturates and long-acting benzodiazepines should be prescribed for sedation with great caution, if at all. These drugs interfere with REM and stage 4 sleep patterns and may contribute to persistent insomnia (Buysse and Reynolds 1990). Clinicians should warn patients of the dangers of using over-the-counter preparations for sleeping and for colds because of the prominent anticholinergic side effects of these agents.

Trazodone, a sedating antidepressant medication that is devoid of anticholinergic side effects, may be used for nighttime sedation. A dose of 50 mg should be administered initially; if this is ineffective, doses up to 150 mg may be prescribed. Nonpharmacologic approaches should be considered. These include minimizing daytime

# CHAPTER 19

# Neuropsychiatric Aspects of Seizure Disorders

Gary J. Tucker, M.D.

Before the development of the electroencephalogram (EEG) by Dr. Hans Berger in the 1930s, all seizure disorders were classified with mental disorders (Berger 1929–1938). Indeed, a strong link between epilepsy and psychiatry has been known for a century. In the late nineteenth century, the noted neuropsychiatrist Emil Kraepelin (1922/1968) described three types of psychoses: dementia praecox, manic depressive illness, and psychosis associated with epilepsy. Until recently, the conception that epilepsy is a mental disorder was held in many countries.

Epilepsy represents one of the more interesting aspects of brain-behavior relationships. Not only is epilepsy an important medical condition, it is also important in the differential diagnosis of behavioral disorders. Epilepsy—and its ability to cause behavioral symptoms without overt classical seizures—make it an important natural model of behavioral disturbance.

The behavioral symptoms associated with either insults to the central nervous system (CNS) or diseases of the CNS are actually very few; consequently, a wide variety of etiologies can cause the same symptoms (Table 19–1). Epilepsy can cause both chronic and episodic behavioral disorders. However, as with all disturbances of the CNS, when there is clear evidence of pathology, either by EEG or imaging, the possible etiological diagnosis of behavioral disturbance is enhanced. Unfortunately, with various epileptic conditions, clear laboratory diagnostic evidence is often not present and the hypothesis about etiology is based solely on the clinical picture.

## Seizure Disorders

### Seizures and Epilepsy

*Epilepsy* is a term applied to a broad group of disorders. The defining feature of any of the epilepsies is the seizure. A seizure can have almost protean manifestations, and it is usually defined as having all or parts of the following: an impairment of consciousness, involuntary movements, behavioral changes, and/or altered perceptual experiences (Table 19–2).

The diagnosis of epilepsy is made only when a person has recurrent seizures. A seizure involves paroxysmal cerebral neuronal firing, which may or may not produce disturbed consciousness and/or perceptual or motor alterations. The classic image of a seizure is that of the *grand mal* or generalized tonic-clonic seizure. These seizures usually involve relatively short (10–30 seconds) tonic movements, with marked extension and flexion of muscles, without shaking. A longer phase (15–60 seconds) involving clonic movements, manifesting as rhythmic muscle group shaking, follows the tonic phase. Tonic phase movements may be associated with laryngeal stridor manifested as a high-pitched screaming sound. Urinary, and occasionally fecal, incontinence may occur due to sphincteric relaxation, and the seizures are almost invariably followed by headache, sleepiness, and confusion. Seizures preceded by perceptual, autonomic, affective, or cognitive alterations (aura) usually indicate a focal onset with secondary generalization. There are many types of seizures that vary markedly from the above description (Chadwick 1993; Engel 1992).

**TABLE 19–1.** Primary symptoms and dysfunctions of central nervous system disturbances

**Cognitive**
    Affect modulation
    Intellectual function
    Judgment
    Memory
    Orientation
**Behavioral**
    Anxiety
    Arousal
    Mood
    Motor
    Personality traits
**Perceptions**
    Auditory
    Kinesthetic pain
    Olfactory
    Taste
    Visual

**TABLE 19–2.** Modified International League Against Epilepsy revised classification of epileptic seizures

1. Partial (focal, local) seizures
    A. Simple: motor, somatosensory, autonomic, or psychic
    B. Complex
        1) Impaired consciousness at outset
        2) Simple partial followed by impaired consciousness
    C. Partial seizures evolving to generalized tonic-clonic (GTC)
        1) Simple to GTC
        2) Complex to GTC
2. Generalized seizures (convulsive or nonconvulsive)
    A. Absence seizures
    B. Myoclonic
    C. Clonic
    D. Tonic
    E. Tonic-clonic
    F. Atonic
    G. Combinations
3. Unclassified epileptic seizures

*Source.* Adapted from International League Against Epilepsy Commission 1981.

# Classification of Seizures

The classification of seizures and epilepsy has changed over time. It has shifted away from terms such as grand mal to an attempt to correlate clinical seizure type with electroencephalographic ictal (i.e., during the seizure) and interictal (i.e., between seizures) changes. The latest classification of epileptic seizures, as recognized by the International League Against Epilepsy (ILAE) in 1981, ignores anatomical aspects; for example, the term *temporal lobe epilepsy* technically no longer exists (International League Against Epilepsy Commission 1981). Furthermore, the classification ignores attempts at explaining pathology and does not take into account age and sex (see Table 19–2). It makes a descriptive attempt at classifying epilepsy as generalized or partial and describes the progression of firing; for example, seizures may begin as simple partial, progress to complex partial, and then secondarily generalize. The number of permutations is very large. Because these seizure types are somewhat perplexing, we describe them here briefly.

## Generalized Seizures

*Generalized seizures* (or generalized attacks) are epileptic seizures that manifest immediately and spread bilaterally through the cerebral cortex. They are generalized in that subcortical fibers may be involved, and there is simultaneous spread throughout the cerebral cortex. There are no preceding motor or perceptual experiences, and there is almost invariably total loss of consciousness.

## Partial (Focal) Seizures

In *partial (focal) seizures* (or partial focal attacks), epileptic firing starts in a specific focus in the brain (usually the cerebral cortex). This evokes a physiological experience that stimulating that focus would produce. When such seizures involve no alteration in consciousness, they are called *simple partial seizures* (previously called *elementary partial seizures)*. When there is a defect in consciousness (i.e., confusion, dizziness), they are called *complex partial seizures* (CPSs). Some authors further subdivide CPSs into type 1 (temporal lobe) and type 2 (extratemporal). It is important to note that 40% of all patients with epilepsy will have CPSs (International League Against Epilepsy Commission 1985).

## Tonic-Clonic Seizures

*Tonic-clonic seizures* (or grand mal seizures) are the most common form of generalized seizure. They manifest as total loss of consciousness with a tetanic muscular phase, usually several seconds (tonic), followed by a phase of repetitive jerking, usually 1–2 minutes (clonic). These seizures may be generalized from the start or begin as partial seizures and secondarily generalize.

Partial seizures secondarily generalized are seizures that start as partial seizures. This phase may or may not be remembered. They then spread bilaterally throughout the cerebral cortex, producing secondary generalization. This terminology is different from a previous classification that spoke of secondary generalized epilepsy, which referred to a kind of epilepsy generalized from the start, with features of a diffuse cerebral pathology.

## Absence Seizures

Typical *absence seizures* (or *petit mal* seizures) are a common seizure type that occur primarily in children. These are generalized from the start, with loss of consciousness for a few seconds without any motor phase. Typical electroencephalographic findings are bilateral and synchronous and have spike waves of 3–4 Hz.

## Status Epilepticus

Tonic-clonic seizure *status epilepticus* involves two or more seizures superimposed on each other without total recovery of consciousness and is a true medical emergency. With CPSs and absence seizures status, consciousness is often preserved, and the diagnosis is often made by EEG (Novak et al. 1971). The latter forms are not necessarily emergencies and can be treated in a more leisurely fashion. However, they could eventually generalize if left untreated.

# Temporal Lobe Epilepsy

In this chapter, we use the term *temporal lobe epilepsy*, which is no longer recognized by the ILAE, but we emphasize that the term is used in the descriptive sense, implying both complex and simple partial seizures, including psychomotor automatisms and tonic-clonic seizures that may originate from the temporal lobe. Many such phenomena interpreted as having originated in the temporal lobe may, in fact, be extratemporal.

Although the term *temporal lobe epilepsy* has formally become an anachronism, in practice it is still commonly used in the absence of an adequate alternative. The phenomena of temporal lobe epilepsy are *not* synonymous with those of its proposed, nonanatomical replacement, CPSs, because CPSs are restricted to patients who have focal firing with defects of consciousness.

In practice, many patients with temporal lobe epilepsy have no defect of consciousness and have simple partial seizures (e.g., olfactory hallucinations), which may derive from the temporal lobes. In addition, they may have simple partial seizures with psychic symptomatology (e.g., cognitive alterations, such as flashbacks or déjà vu experiences occurring in clear consciousness). Temporal lobe epilepsy may also manifest with the *temporal lobe absence* or behavioral arrest that is associated with a brief loss of consciousness of 10–30 seconds. These episodes may be associated with minor automatisms (e.g., chewing movements) and at times with "drop attacks" (the falling associated with loss of muscle tone). Patients with temporal lobe epilepsy often appear to be staring and after the episode may be aware that there was a loss of consciousness. They may experience postictal features such as headache and sleepiness. Thus, the temporal lobe absence differs from petit mal, as the latter is a shorter episode, without muscle movements and postictal features (Fenton 1986).

Temporal lobe epilepsy may also manifest with psychomotor automatisms alone, which are no longer regarded as a form of CPS. Psychomotor automatisms may involve a psychic (cognitive-affective, somatosensory, or perceptual) phase followed by a motor phase. The psychic phase may be very brief and not recognized by the patient, who may be amnestic for it. It may be associated with many perceptual alterations, such as an auditory buzz or hum, complex verbalizations, or aphasias. Visual abnormalities include diplopia, misperceptions of movement, and changes in perceived object size or shape. Other alterations may include illusions, tactile distortions, olfactory phenomena (e.g., generally unpleasant, burning, or rotting smells), gustatory phenomena (e.g., metallic tastes), and somatosensory autonomic symptoms (e.g., piloerection, gastric sensations, or nausea). Flashbacks and alterations of consciousness (*jamais vu*, depersonalization, derealization, and déjà vu) may occur. These are followed by automatisms of various degrees of complexity. There may be simple buttoning or unbuttoning or masticatory movements, more complex "wandering" fugue states, furor-type anger (which is very rare), or speech automatisms (which are far more common than is recognized).

The features of temporal lobe epilepsy are varied and protean (Bear 1986; Blumer 1975). Table 19–3 describes some of the symptoms that have often been associated with temporal lobe disturbances.

# Epilepsy Syndromes

How the various types of seizures represent themselves clinically allows for grouping into syndromes. There have been many groupings that often cause confusion, and

**TABLE 19–3.** Behavioral symptoms often associated with seizures, particularly temporal lobe epilepsy

Hallucinations: all sensory modalities
Illusions
Déjà vu
Jamais vu
Depersonalization
Repetitive thoughts and nightmares
Flashbacks and visual distortions
Epigastric sensations
Automatisms
Affective and mood changes
Catatonia
Cataplexy
Amnestic episodes

most overlap. Consequently, terms in common usage are: *focal-* or *localization-related syndromes*, *idiopathic syndromes*, *secondary* or *symptomatic epilepsies*, and *progressive* and *nonprogressive syndromes* (International League Against Epilepsy Commission 1985).

The idiopathic or genetic epilepsies, in which there is no evident CNS pathology, are usually childhood syndromes. In patients older than age 30, the onset of epilepsy or recurrent seizures is usually associated with CNS pathology and a search must be made for the cause of the seizures. Where CNS pathology is present, these syndromes are usually described as symptomatic or secondary seizure disorders, or epilepsy. Conditions such as head injury, encephalitis, birth trauma, or hyperpyrexia represent rather static and permanent lesions that can cause epilepsy or seizures. Conditions that can be progressive and that change over time include medication overdose or withdrawal, tumor, infections, metabolic disease (e.g., hypoglycemia and uremia), and endocrine diseases. Alzheimer's disease and other dementias, multiple sclerosis, cerebral arteriopathy, and other degenerative or infiltrative conditions can all lead to a progressive and changing picture of seizures.

Seizures can also be a reaction to various medical or physiological stresses. This fact is particularly evident at both ends of the age spectrum. For example, febrile conditions are more likely to cause seizures in young people and older people. The tendency to have seizures is related to an inherited predisposition for variations in the seizure threshold, as not all young or older patients with the same fever will have a seizure.

## Epidemiology of Seizure Disorders

As can be seen from the variety of seizures and syndromes that constitute epilepsy, it is often difficult to get a clear idea of the epidemiology. However, most researchers seem to agree that the prevalence of active epilepsy is in the range of 4–10 in 1,000 people. A large study (Hauser et al. 1993) from Rochester, Minnesota, showed that the highest prevalence of epilepsy was before age 10 and after age 65, with a cumulative incidence of epilepsy at age 70 as high as 2%–3% of the population. The disparity between the cumulative incidence and the prevalence raises interesting questions concerning the natural history and prognosis of epilepsy. Shovron and Reynolds (1986) present convincing data that the majority of patients developing seizures enter long-term remission. Annegers et al. (1979) indicate that of 475 patients, 76% experienced at least one seizure-free period for 5 or more years. Seventy percent of the patients were in continual remission 20 years after the diagnosis. Another community survey by Goodridge and Shovron (1983) reported that 122 patients from a sample of 6,000 suffered at least one epileptic seizure (excluding febrile seizures), and 70% of these patients, after 15 years following the initial diagnosis, were in long-term remission. The earlier the remission of seizures after onset, the more likely it was that the patient would have a permanent remission. Those whose seizures continued beyond 2 years were more likely to have seizures at the end of the longitudinal study. A recent study by Sillanpaa et al. (1995) confirms these findings. Many of the patients in remission were able to be withdrawn completely from medication. Consequently, the image of epilepsy as a chronic condition is not necessarily a valid one; however, in a condition that consists of so many different manifestations and causes, it is often difficult to generalize beyond the individual case. Unfortunately, there are no good long-term studies of the behavioral disturbances associated with seizure disorders. It would be of some interest, considering the high remission rate of epilepsy, to see if the behavior also ceased.

## Psychosocial Facets of Epilepsy

The epileptic patient encounters major psychosocial stressors. First is the stress of having a chronic illness. Studies comparing the epileptic patient with groups of patients with other chronic illnesses, such as rheumatic heart disease, diabetes mellitus, and cancer, have concluded that each of these conditions has its own special stressors (Dodrill and Batzel 1986). However, when comparing any of these populations to patients with organic brain disease, there are specific problems in that damage to the CNS, in and of itself, leads to unique consequences (Szatmari 1985).

A special difficulty of the epileptic patient is the

often paroxysmal (or episodic) element to the illness. Between episodes, the person with epilepsy may be functioning normally. There is a substantial covert stress that leads the person with epilepsy to be afraid of performing normal social activities, such as dating during adolescence. The fear of a seizure is greater than the occurrence. In addition, the witnessing of an actual tonic-clonic seizure is a frightening experience for many members of the general population, and there is much folklore associated with seizures (Temkin 1979). Consequently, conceptions of epilepsy may be distorted thereafter, and even an isolated seizure may have grave consequences on interpersonal relations.

Within American culture, persons with epilepsy are, at times, perceived as an inferior minority group. In some preliterate subcultures, an epileptic seizure is often regarded as a type of communication with ancestors or with higher beings, and epileptic individuals may be perceived as having special powers. Many of them become shamans or witch doctors and are highly respected members of their culture (Temkin 1979). Also, the disorders create limitations on the patient's activities (i.e., epileptic individuals cannot operate complex machinery, work in jobs that expose them to dangers, swim alone, or, in some instances, even bathe autonomously). The consequences of not being allowed to drive are a major obstacle in our society, particularly in rural areas. These functional limitations can be considerable, particularly because they are often disregarded by the patient (e.g., driving), which may create additional guilt, moral and ethical consequences, and legal complications. Frequently, in families with epileptic members, abnormal relationships develop that may lead to increased dependency or isolation. Patterns of dependency can be difficult to dislodge, and it is sometimes easier to remain ill than to become seizure free and healthy. The epileptic patient needs to learn to develop independence and a sense of self-care and to create constructive relationships that promote health. The degree of influence that apparent psychological factors may have on the course of epilepsy should not be underestimated (Hoare 1984; Stevens 1988; Ziegler 1982).

## Diagnosis

The diagnosis of epilepsy is basically a clinical one, much as is the diagnosis of schizophrenia. Although an EEG can often be confirmatory, 20% of patients with epilepsy will have normal EEGs and 2% of patients without epilepsy will have spike and wave formations (Engel 1992). The best diagnostic test for seizures is the observation of the patient or the report of someone who has observed the patient having a seizure. Thus, the history taken from the patient and the family is crucial. Key factors important in the history of these patients are the age at onset of seizures, any history of illness or trauma to the nervous system that could cause seizures, a family history of epilepsy, and some idea of whether the condition is progressive or static. Attempts should be made to determine whether the seizures are idiopathic or secondary. Certainly, these descriptions are most helpful in the diagnosis of major motor seizures or generalized seizures. They are also useful in attempting to determine the relationship between the seizures and various behavioral disturbances. As the seizure focus can reside in any location in the brain, as well as affecting various circuits within the brain, the number of behavioral symptoms associated with seizures are considerable (see Table 19–3).

### Laboratory

Finding an elevated prolactin level is the only major chemical diagnostic test for the diagnosis of seizures. After a seizure, usually within 15–20 minutes after a generalized tonic-clonic seizure, there will be an abrupt rise in prolactin levels. As a rule, the prolactin level decreases to normal within 60 minutes; therefore, blood should be drawn 15–20 minutes after the seizure. These levels are typically three to four times the patient's baseline prolactin level. This response of prolactin is seen more often in major motor seizures and less frequently in partial complex seizures. Widespread activation of the temporal lobe structures, however, is often associated with increasing prolactin levels. There are some data indicating that repeated seizures and the frequency of seizure decreases the prolactin response (Malkowicz et al. 1995). It is also important to remember that neuroleptics can also raise prolactin levels.

### Imaging

Magnetic resonance imaging (MRI) and computed tomography (CT) scans are crucial for the evaluation of symptomatic epilepsies. Another important use of these imaging modalities is to evaluate presurgical patients to determine the locations of lesions. Functional imaging such as single photon emission computed tomography (SPECT) and positron emission tomography (PET) has been valuable in evaluating ictal events and blood flow to focal lesions during a seizure. However, postictal and interictal evaluations are much less informative. SPECT studies are very reliable for localizing ictal events. PET is somewhat better in the detection of interictal temporal lobe hypermetabolism (Ho et al. 1995). Undoubtedly, as these instruments become more sensitive, they will be used more frequently in the evaluation of seizure disorders.

## Electroencephalogram

The EEG is one of the most important tests in the evaluation of seizures, suspected seizures, or episodic behavioral disturbances. In this day of major advances in imaging, the EEG is also frequently overlooked and often, when it is used, it is misinterpreted. The paroxysmal interictal EEG with spikes and wave complexes can confirm the clinical diagnosis of a seizure disorder. It can, when positive, differentiate between seizure types (e.g., absence seizures from generalized seizures) and indicate the possibility of a structural lesion when there are focal findings in the EEG. However, a normal EEG cannot eliminate the possibility of a seizure disorder being present in a particular patient. The EEG is a reflection of surface activity in the cortex and may not reflect seizure activity deep in the brain. Most clinicians, when confronted with a behavior disorder that does not fit the usual clinical picture of a schizophrenic psychosis (particularly if the disorder is episodic), will obtain an EEG. If the EEG is negative, the clinicians may then be deterred from further pursuing the idea that this episodic behavior may represent a seizure disorder. It is important to remember that the diagnosis of epilepsy (as with schizophrenia) is a clinical one and that although the EEG can confirm the diagnosis, it cannot exclude it. Even with elaborate recordings (i.e., 24-hour EEGs) and concomitant videotaping, a diagnosis of a seizure disorder cannot always be made.

Special techniques have been used to help with EEG diagnosis. One commonly used technique is the use of nasopharyngeal electrodes. However, the increased yield with nasopharyngeal electrodes is not substantial—some studies indicate less than 10% detection (Bickford 1979). On the other hand, the yield with sphenoidal electrodes is greatly increased (Ebersole and Leroy 1983). Unfortunately, placement of sphenoidal electrodes requires time and expertise, which are not readily available.

One suggestion has been the placement of electrodes on the buccal skin surface in the area of the submandibular notch. It appears that these placements may entirely eclipse the use of nasopharyngeal electrodes because they are almost as effective at picking up foci as sphenoidal placements (Sadler and Goodwin 1986). Much more definitive, however, is the use of cerebral cortical placements during neurosurgery procedures. These may show firing (e.g., in patients with temporal lobe epilepsy and psychosis) in the region of the hippocampus (Heath 1982). The improvement in signal detection gained from the direct placement of intracranial electrodes underscores the insensitivity of the scalp electrode placement commonly used in surface EEGs.

There are several methods that are used for evoking electroencephalographic abnormalities. One very common method is the usage of sleep records. In this method, the yield of actual ictal-related events is not substantially increased. However, the potential for detecting a particular focus or focal abnormality may increase because of the extra synchronization that may occur. Phases of sleep may differ in threshold for inducing seizures (i.e., less potentiality for seizures), and it is during such phases that focal abnormalities may be more evident (Brodsky et al. 1983). This fact explains the apparent paradox of the usage, for many years, of barbiturates such as secobarbital sodium in sleep records.

The preferred means of evaluating brain wave activity during sleep is the natural induction of sleep. However, in a laboratory situation this is often not practical, and at times (e.g., overnight) the patient is sleep deprived so that no medication need be given. Such a practice is a good one but is not applicable to the psychiatric patient who is generally disturbed enough to require a sedative. The alternative is the administration of chloral hydrate, 1–3 g as premedication before the sleep record. The chloral hydrate has little effect on the EEG and does not prevent the demonstration of focal abnormalities. Overall, a sleep electroencephalographic record increases the chances of picking up a focal abnormality, such as a temporal lobe focus, approximately fourfold. For example, Gibbs and Gibbs (1952) found only 20% interseizure waking electroencephalographic abnormalities in temporal lobe epilepsy; this figure went up to 80% in sleep records in a nonhomogeneous neurological population. A recent study by Cendes et al. (2000) demonstrated that when the EEG showed lateralization, there was also evidence of hippocampal atrophy on the MRI. Thus, in those suspected of having temporal lobe epilepsy, the lateralized EEG was very helpful in making the diagnosis.

Certain medications should be particularly avoided when obtaining electroencephalographic studies. The first are those in the benzodiazepine group, which may have, by virtue of their strong antiepileptic effects, profound effects in normalizing the EEG. Because effects on receptor activity may last weeks, even with the short-acting benzodiazepines, the yield of demonstrating abnormal activity after administration of benzodiazepines may decrease substantially. The second medication to avoid for sleep is L-tryptophan. Adamec and Stark (1983) demonstrated that L-tryptophan has some effect in raising the seizure threshold during electroconvulsive therapy (ECT). Some psychotropic medications, such as neuroleptics, the tricyclic and heteropsychic antidepressants, and the benzodiazepines (Pincus and Tucker 1985), may also increase synchronization of the EEG (leading to a seizurelike pattern). One report (Ryback and Gardner 1991) describes a small series in which procaine activation of the EEG was useful in identifying patients with episodic behavioral disorders responsive to anticonvulsants.

Recent advances in electroencephalographic technology may ultimately change the whole perspective of its use in psychiatry. Computer electroencephalographic monitoring allows breakdown of waveforms and allows correlation with evoked potentials, including cognitive evoked potentials. It also facilitates the demonstration of changes in particular areas of the brain that can be easily delineated at a visual level. This application could prove to be a useful psychophysiological correlate of psychopathology.

## Differential Diagnosis of Behavioral Symptoms Associated With Epilepsy

There is a range of medical conditions that must be distinguished from seizures: panic disorder, hyperventilation, hypoglycemia, various transient cerebral ischemias, migraine, narcolepsy, malingering, and conversion reactions. The defining characteristics of temporal lobe epilepsy are typically subjective experiences or feelings, automatisms, and, more rarely, catatonia or cataplexy. Because the symptoms are usually related to a focal electrical discharge in the brain, they are usually consistent and few in number. Although the list of possible symptoms may be quite large (see Table 19–3), each patient will have a limited number of specific symptoms, for example, auditory hallucinations (usually voices), repetitive sounds, or visual hallucinations and misperceptions that are of a consistent type that include a visual disturbance. The automatisms, as related previously, are simple (e.g., chewing, swallowing, pursing of the lips, looking around, smiling, grimacing, crying). Other types of automatisms are attempting to sit up, examining or fumbling with objects, and buttoning or unbuttoning clothes. Complex, goal-directed behavior is unusual during these episodes. Aggressive behavior is also rare. The only time the patient will sometimes become aggressive is when there is an attempt to restrain or prevent ambulation (Rodin 1973). Typical attacks usually consist of a cessation of activity, followed by automatism and impairment of consciousness. The entire episode usually lasts from 10 seconds to as long as 30 minutes. The motor phenomena and postural changes, such as catatonia, are more rare (Fenton 1986; Kirubakaran et al. 1987).

The profile of patients who present primarily with behavioral symptoms is usually of episodic "brief" disturbances lasting for variable periods of time (hours to

**TABLE 19–4.** Factors helpful in the diagnosis of temporal lobe epilepsy

Does the patient describe typical subjective alterations?

Has the patient been observed performing characteristic automatisms?

Was the patient confused during the episode?

Is the patient's memory for events that occurred impaired?

Did the patient experience postictal depression?

Has the patient had other lapses during which he or she engaged in nearly identical behavior?

days). Historically, the patient often states that such episodes have occurred mainly once a month or once every 3 months. The patient seeks psychiatric attention when the frequency of the episodes increases to daily or several times per day and, as a result, functioning becomes impaired. Critical factors helpful in the diagnosis of temporal lobe epilepsy are shown in Table 19–4.

A final term that requires clarification does not refer to epileptic seizures at all. The term *pseudoseizures* is used synonymously with *hysteroepilepsy* and *nonepileptic seizure* or *conversion reaction*. The differentiation of these conditions from true seizures is, at times, extremely difficult (Table 19–5), often complicated by the fact that the person who is suspected of having "seizures," primarily related to psychological reasons, often has a history of seizures. Devinsky and Gordon (1998) noted that nonepileptic seizures can often follow epileptic seizures. They postulate that the epileptic seizure, particularly the complex partial seizure, leads to possible loss of inhibition of impulses and emotions. The patients with nonepileptic seizures differ from seizure disorder patients in that they may have significantly more stress, more negative life events, and a history of child abuse, and they often have more somatic symptoms and awareness of their bodies (Arnold and Privitera 1996; Tojek et al. 2000). Most of the nonepileptic seizure patients demonstrate somatoform disorders, particularly conversion, rather than dissociative disorders. Interestingly, in the patients with nonepileptic seizures who did not fit the criteria for conversion, there was a high incidence of anxiety and psychotic disorders (Alper et al. 1995; Kuyk et al. 1999).

However, patients will at times have episodes that are extremely difficult to interpret. These episodes may be very short-lived, lasting seconds or minutes, but on occasion can last for days. Such patients behave out of character and usually exhibit a profound lability of affect, with disturbances ranging from depression through mania. The patients may appear markedly thought disordered, delusional, or to be hallucinating. Very often,

**TABLE 19–5.** General features of nonepileptic seizures ("pseudoseizures")

**Setting**

    Environmental gain (audience usually present)

    Seldom sleep related

    Often triggered (e.g., by stress)

    Suggestive profile on Minnesota Multiphasic Personality
       Inventory (Hathaway and McKinley 1989)

**Attack**

    Atypical movements, often bizarre or purposeful

    Seldom results in injury

    Often starts and ends gradually

    Out-of-phase movements of extremities

    Pelvic thrusting or side-to-side movements

**Examination**

    Restraint accentuates the seizure

    Inattention decreases over time

    Plantar flexor reflexes

    Reflexes intact (corneal, pupillary, and blink)

    Consciousness preserved

    Autonomic system uninvolved

    Autonomically intact

**After attack**

    No postictal features (lethargy, tiredness, abnormal elec-
       troencephalogram)

    Prolactin normal (after 30 minutes)

    No or little amnesia

    Memory exists (hypnosis or amobarbital sodium)

these episodes are repetitive and of the same quality each time. These patients may exhibit behavioral alterations perceived as characterological disorders. Clinically these nonepileptic seizures often occur in young women and consist of significant amounts of staring, shaking, blacking out without falling, and stiffening without loss of consciousness (Devinsky et al. 1996). Pelvic thrusting can occur in many types of seizures and is not typical of nonepileptic seizures (Geyer et al. 2000)

In such episodes, EEGs or 24-hour monitoring may not reveal any additional information. However, if the patients have temporal spikes, even if they do not correlate with video monitoring, they may respond to anticonvulsant medication. But in most cases the patient will be left with the label of having nonepileptic seizures. Twenty percent of intractable seizures remain as nonepileptic seizures (Krumholz 1999). Kanner et al. (1999) studied 45 patients with the diagnosis of nonepileptic seizures. Interestingly, 29% of the patients stopped having seizures after being told that the seizures were psychogenic. Twenty-seven percent had only brief recurrences, and in 44% the seizures persisted. The patients in whom the seizures persisted often had psychiatric diagnoses of recur-

rent affective disorder, dissociative disorders, or personality disorders. However, an abnormal MRI predicted the recurrence of seizures with 75% accuracy, which may indicate some covert biological basis for the nonepileptic seizure.

Frontal lobe epilepsy can also present with bizarre behavioral symptoms and can be confused with nonepileptic seizures. Laskowitz et al. (1995) noted that the symptoms often appear as spells with an aura of panic symptoms, with weird vocalizations and with bilateral limb movements but no periods of postictal tiredness and no confusion; there are also no oral or alimentary movements. These spells last about 60–70 seconds. Fortunately, most of these seizures are symptomatic of a CNS lesion, and usually the correct diagnosis is made with the EEG or imaging studies. Thomas et al. (1999) described a form of nonconvulsive status epilepticus of frontal origin. These patients often presented with a mood disturbance similar to hypomania, subtle cognitive impairments, some disinhibition, and some indifference.

## Etiological Links of Seizures to Psychopathology

The increased incidence of psychopathology and seizure disorders is clear and evident, but the exact etiology of this increased incidence is unclear. There have been two major theories historically. One is an affinity theory, best exemplified by the classic articles of Slater et al. (1963), which described a group of patients with epilepsy and psychosis. An opposing theory was first postulated by Von Meduna (1937), who observed (incorrectly) that the schizophrenic patients under his care had few epileptic conditions (Fink 1984). He then hypothesized that the induction of a seizure in a psychotic patient might be therapeutic. Landolt (1958) observed a group of patients whose EEGs seemed to normalize during a psychotic episode. This has been called "forced normalization," and Pakalinis et al. (1987) observed seven patients who had this pattern. This antagonistic relationship between seizures and behavioral disturbances has been noted by many clinicians. For example, it is not uncommon for a patient with epilepsy to have a marked decrease in seizures for a prolonged period of time and then later to have an increase in behavioral disturbances. After a seizure, the behavior seems to normalize again. Although these observations are clinically and statistically apparent (Schiffer 1987), their exact etiological importance to all patients with epilepsy and behavior disturbance is unclear. The relationship between psychopathology and seizures is not clear and is complicated by whether the behavior disturbance is a preictal event, an ictal event, or a postictal event. Many hypothesize the existence of subictal electrical events in the brain that are pathological, leading to disturbances of CNS function, manifesting as behavior disturbance. *Kindling*, a pathophysiological event, is the sequence whereby repetitive subthreshold electrical or chemical stimuli to specific brain areas eventually induce a seizure or a behavior disturbance that persists. This process has been hypothesized as one of the possible causes of psychopathology. However, kindling remains only a tantalizing hypothesis, and it has never been demonstrated in humans (Adamec and Stark 1983).

Other hypotheses about the cause of the psychopathology have been that seizures create a type of organic brain syndrome related to some underlying diffuse process or are caused by active focal damage (Pincus and Tucker 1985). Toxicity of the medicines used to treat seizure disorders has also been implicated, and although most anticonvulsant drugs cause significant cognitive impairment, they do not seem to be associated with the development of major psychopathology (Dodrill and Troupin 1991; Meador et al. 1993; Moehle et al. 1984; Trimble 1988). Overmedication with anticonvulsant medications before the availability of blood level monitoring was a likely cause of confusion and behavioral disturbance in some of these patients; however, with present-day monitoring, these disturbances occur much less frequently.

## Temporal Lobe Specificity and Psychopathology

A major question about the behavioral changes in epilepsy is whether behavior disturbances occur more commonly in patients with temporal lobe epilepsy specifically or whether the behavior disturbance is related to seizure disorders in general.

This issue is complex, with many confounding variables. For example, more complicated patients gravitate toward university hospitals, where studies are usually undertaken. In the hospital study by Currie et al. (1970) in London, 25% of the 2,664 patients seen in a university hospital clinic had a history of psychiatric hospitalization, whereas only 5%–9% of 678 patients in a private clinic in the same city had a similar history of psychiatric hospitalization. Another confounding variable is the age at onset of psychomotor epilepsy, which is similar to that of schizophrenia. Moreover, three-quarters of patients with psychomotor seizures or CPSs are older than age 16 at the onset of the seizure disorder (Stevens 1988).

The vast majority of patients with seizure disorders will have temporal lobe foci on electroencephalographic examination at some point during their illness. Kris-

tensen and Sindrup (1978) compared patients with CPSs and psychosis to CPS patients without psychosis and could find little difference in the two groups with regard to age at onset, laterality of focus, and interval between epilepsy onset and time of examination. The patients with psychosis had significantly more neurological signs, spike EEGs, a history of brain damage, and no family history of seizure disorders, suggesting that these patients may have had other associated organic brain syndromes. The increased incidence of psychosocial problems in these groups may further confound the relationship to behavior disturbances.

Additionally, patients with CPSs and secondary generalization are often more difficult to keep seizure free than those with generalized seizures. Consequently, they are often taking high doses of anticonvulsants and/or anticonvulsant polytherapy. Their greater number of seizures and the frequent evidence of associated organic brain syndromes further confound the relationship to behavior disturbance.

The incidence of psychoses associated with temporal lobe epilepsy (compared with non–temporal lobe epilepsy) is usually noted as being four to seven times greater (McKenna et al. 1985; Sengoku et al. 1983). The confounding variables include increased seizures, increased amounts of anticonvulsants, and increased numbers of different types of seizures. The temporal lobe constitutes 40% of the cerebral cortex (Stevens 1988). These factors could differentially be perceived as important causal, predisposing, or incidental features. However, patients with temporal lobe epilepsy have increased difficulties with seizure control and medication, and this may be related to the more primitive embryological structure of the archipallium. The relative degree of encephalization in this area is less than that in other areas of the brain. This primitive structure could predispose to psychopathology.

## Comorbid Psychiatric Syndromes

The relationship of psychopathology and seizure disorders is difficult to establish. Most of the studies rest at the level of case report, and even large-scale studies usually deal with populations that have come to psychiatric attention rather than community-based samples (Popkin and Tucker 1994). The question constantly arises: Are we dealing with behavior associated with a seizure disorder or is the behavior associated with another underlying disease of the CNS that can cause seizures? Comparison of symptoms between patients with seizure disorders and those with other disturbances of the CNS demonstrates a considerable overlap. For example, symptoms of impulsiveness and irritability, emotional lability, paranoia, changes in sexual behavior, regression, and poor sleep have been noted in patients with seizure disorders, head trauma, and tumors, and in patients with abnormal EEGs as the only finding. Therefore, at the symptom level, we are frequently dealing with general symptoms related to damage of the CNS and not specific to any one condition or region of the brain. The symptoms can be episodic changes in mood, irritability/impulsiveness, psychosis, anxiety disorders, or confusional syndromes. The other major types of symptoms usually seen with CNS dysfunction are related to more insidious disorders, such as dementia, depression, various motor diseases, or distinctive personality changes, such as those seen after head trauma (Popkin and Tucker 1994). Consequently, when we talk about psychopathology associated with seizure disorders, we see a wide range of syndromes. The etiologies of these syndromes may be related to the seizure specifically or to the underlying damage to the CNS. The various symptom patterns may be related to individual genetic predispositions, environmental influences, or genetic/environmental interactions.

## Psychosis

It is clear that *all* of the symptoms described in schizophrenic patients can occur in patients with seizure disorders (Toone et al. 1982). The classic study by Slater et al. (1963) conducted at Maudsley Hospital in London evaluated patients hospitalized for psychosis who had seizure disorders. These patients had all the symptoms associated with schizophrenia. A community sample studied by Perez and Trimble (1980) showed that 50% of the patients with epilepsy and psychosis met diagnostic criteria for schizophrenia by standardized rating scales. However, the question of definition remains. There are similarities in the cognitive deficits noted in both epileptic patients and schizophrenic patients. Mellers et al. (2000) compared a group of patients with epilepsy and psychosis, epilepsy alone, and schizophrenia with a group of neuropsychologically healthy control subjects using neuropsychological testing. Patients with psychosis and epilepsy had almost identical neuropsychological test patterns. Often, what patients with seizure disorders and behavioral problems describe is a single complaint such as auditory hallucinations or a solitary perceptual change. The patients with these single symptoms are frequently classified by clinicians as psychotic. Conversely, psychiatric patients with several symptoms are sometimes dubiously labeled as epileptic based on a history of a seizure disorder, a solitary seizure, seizures associated with alcohol or other substance withdrawal, or vaguely described and poorly characterized "blackouts." Such cases are difficult to interpret, but there seems to be no denying the relationship of seizures to psychopathology. Kanner et al. (1996) studied patients admitted to a video electroencephalographic monitoring unit for evaluation of their seizures. As part of the evaluation, all anticonvulsants were stopped. The researchers found that of the 140 patients admitted to the unit, there was a 7.8% incidence of postictal psychiatric events; 6.4% were psychotic and 1.4% were nonpsychotic. The psychotic events were mostly depressive, hypomanic, or delusional, and all seemed to take place in a confused state. These episodes responded to psychotropic medication and lasted about 69 hours on average. A similar finding was noted by Ketter et al. (1994), who described increased anxiety and depressive symptoms in 38% of 32 patients withdrawn from their anticonvulsant medications in order to enter a controlled trial.

There are many empirical similarities between seizure disorders and schizophrenia that also make the differential diagnosis difficult. Both disorders are also phenomenologically based constructs presenting primarily as behavioral disturbances, and there are often no specific pathological changes evident in either of these conditions. Furthermore, the peak age at onset is similar. Both disorders may occur in early to late adolescence, although epilepsy often presents in childhood and may occur at any age. The neurotransmitter dopamine is somehow related in both conditions, as dopamine antagonists are antipsychotic and mildly epileptogenic. Dopamine agonists are psychotogenic and mildly antiepileptic (Trimble 1977). Perhaps most significantly, both conditions require a team approach to rehabilitate patients. However, they do differ in that many seizure disorders go into complete remission, whereas most schizophrenic disorders do not. The family history can be of help in that the genetic frequencies are similar for both conditions, with 10%–13% of the offspring of parents with either schizophrenia or epilepsy having the same condition (Metrakos and Metrakos 1961), but this leaves the majority of cases without a family history of either condition.

Despite more than 100 publications in the scientific literature dealing with core issues of epilepsy in relation to psychosis, the cause of the increased psychopathology in epileptic conditions remains unclear, and a precise clinical picture has not been established (Diehl 1989; McKenna et al. 1985; Neppe 1986). Betts (1974), Ey (1954), Gibbs and Gibbs (1952), Gudmundsson (1966), Krohn (1961), Lindsay et al. (1979), Sengoku et al. (1983), Slater et al. (1963), and Wilensky and Neppe

(1986) have all described a clear association between these two conditions. These diverse studies come from several different countries and range from national surveys of unselected populations to studies of patients in outpatient clinics as well as psychiatric hospital populations. These studies suggest that the incidence of psychosis in relation to epilepsy ranges from 4% (Trimble 1977) to 27% (average, about 7%) (Dongier 1959–1960).

Clinically, there seem to be three psychotic presentations that one sees with seizure disorders. One is an episodic course usually manifested by perceptual changes, alterations in consciousness, and poor memory for the events. A chronic psychotic condition also occurs in which the patient may have simple auditory hallucinations, paranoia, or other perceptual changes. The third type is simply a variation in which the patient usually has some type of persistent experience of depersonalization or visual distortion that, for lack of a better name, is usually labeled as psychotic. The latter is probably a variant of the chronic psychotic state.

Although Slater et al. (1963) postulated a long period between the onset of seizures and subsequent psychosis, it is not uncommon for a clinician to treat a patient for "schizophrenia" who is often completely unresponsive to antipsychotic medications. During the course of this treatment, the patient has a grand mal seizure. An EEG is then obtained that confirms the diagnosis of epilepsy.[1] The patient is then treated with anticonvulsant medication, and there is a marked decrease in the "psychotic" symptoms.

In retrospect, patients with a seizure disorder and psychosis, such as the one noted above, have subtly different clinical characteristics than the typical schizophrenic patient. Patients with a seizure disorder and psychosis often talk about their symptoms in almost a detached manner. Some might say the patients view the symptoms as ego-dystonic—the symptoms are not part of them, as though something was imposed on them such as a physical illness. Second, most of these patients seem quite intact even when experiencing the symptoms, particularly so between episodes. Their mental status examinations seem to show no evidence of other schizophrenic symptoms. During the episode, what is often seen is a confusional state and an alteration in consciousness rather than an inability to communicate. It is not uncommon to talk to one of these patients on the telephone, have a fairly normal conversation, and then, at the end,

ask if the hallucinations are still present. These patients will note that the hallucinations are still occurring on a frequent basis. Additionally, many of these patients have good premorbid social histories. What they and their families describe is an abrupt change in personality, mood, or ability to function. It is important to remain suspicious of altered perceptual experiences that do not completely meet DSM-IV-TR (American Psychiatric Association 2000) criteria for schizophrenia and to reevaluate patients who do not respond to antipsychotic medication (Table 19–6).

## Possibly Related Seizure Disorders

An interesting area of speculation involves the concept of so-called atypical psychosis. Clinicians have often noted that the distinctions made by classification systems are more distinct in theory than in practice. Consequently, although there are clear cases that are unambiguously labeled as either schizophrenia or affective disorder, there is a large group of patients that do not fit neatly into either category. These patients are frequently diagnosed as having schizoaffective disorder or atypical psychosis. In an excellent review, Procci (1976) noted that the atypical psychotic patients usually have an acute onset, more frequent remissions, good premorbid functioning (often with symptoms of schizophrenia), affective symptoms, and/or confusion and agitation. Mitsuda (1967) also described a group of atypical psychotic patients while doing a large genetic study of schizophrenia and affective disorder. The schizophrenic patients had few children with atypical psychosis, bipolar patients had rare occurrences of atypical psychosis in their children, and the atypical psychotic patients seemed to produce children exclusively with atypical psychosis. Mitsuda also noted that patients with atypical psychosis seemed to have marked disturbance in their EEGs and that the incidence of epilepsy was higher among them than among the patients with schizophrenia or bipolar disorder.

Monroe (1982) extended this concept by delineating a group he called "episodic psychotics," and he related this to a limbic ictal disorder that was unresponsive to antidepressants and neuroleptics. He noted that these patients' psychoses were of a precipitous onset, with intense affects, and had an intermittent course characterized by symptom-free intervals. He postulated that this represented some type of limbic seizure disorder. As an extension of these studies, Tucker et al. (1986) described

---

[1] It is important to note that although neuroleptics may lower the seizure threshold, they do not usually cause seizures in patients who are not predisposed to them. A recent study showed that among inpatients taking psychotropic medication, seizures were infrequent, occurring in 0.03% of psychiatric inpatients (Popli et al. 1995).

**TABLE 19–6.** Diagnostic clues indicating psychosis may be due to lesion of the central nervous system or seizures

1. Presentation that does not meet DSM-IV criteria
2. Good premorbid social history
3. Abrupt change in personality, mood, or ability to function
4. Rapid fluctuations in mental status
5. Unresponsiveness to usual biological or psychological interventions

a series of patients who had documented temporal lobe dysfunction on EEGs with symptomatology very similar to the group described by Procci (1976) and the episodic psychosis described by Monroe (1982). All of the patients described had spell-type episodes. They also experienced marked mood lability, often with suicidal ideation and suicide attempts, as well as psychotic phenomena and cognitive changes. All patients returned to normal baseline with symptom-free intervals. It is extremely important that many of these conditions occur in a state of clear consciousness and do not necessarily present with either a clouding of consciousness or symptoms of disorientation.

Such studies of patients with possible temporolimbic dysfunction have been continued from other sources (Wells and Duneau 1980), including chronic nonepileptic psychiatric patients with electroencephalographic temporal lobe foci, violent patients with refractory schizophrenia (Hakola and Laulumaa 1982), patients with borderline personality disorder (Cowdry and Gardner 1988), and patients who become dysphoric when taking neuroleptics and have abnormal EEGs (Brodsky et al. 1983). Although many of these patients respond to carbamazepine in particular, it should not be seen as a panacea. If carbamazepine is used inappropriately, some patients appear to deteriorate, and response to anticonvulsants does not imply the presence of seizure disorder.

## Treatment of Psychotic Conditions

The major treatment of the episodic psychotic conditions is usually the appropriate use of anticonvulsant medications. The treatment of chronic conditions involves not only anticonvulsant medications but neuroleptics and other antipsychotic medications as well. In general, the use of medication in these patients is difficult in that very small doses of any medication often cause an increase in symptoms that diminishes over time. Consequently, very small doses and infrequent changes seem to be the major guidelines in treating these patients. For example, when adding a neuroleptic to the anticonvulsant medications, a clinician often begins with a small dose, such as 1 mg of

haloperidol, and waits 6–8 weeks before changing the dose. Although all of the neuroleptics can lower the seizure threshold, haloperidol, fluphenazine, molindone, pimozide, and trifluoperazine seem to lower the seizure threshold the least. The propensity for clozapine to lower the seizure threshold is quite well known. Although seizures have been reported with the use of risperidone, quetiapine, and olanzapine, the rate is quite low, and it would seem safe to use these new atypical neuroleptics in patients with seizures and psychosis (Alldredge 1999).

With anticonvulsant drugs, it is best to adjust their doses as far as possible to the top range of the therapeutic window. Because all of the anticonvulsants can cause cognitive side effects, it is important to distinguish between toxicity from the drugs and a worsening in behavior (Armon et al. 1996; Hamer et al. 2000; Martin et al. 1999; Meador et al. 1995). Vigabatrin has been reported to have a side-effect profile that shows a 2.5% incidence of psychotic symptoms and a 17.1% incidence of affective symptoms (Levinson and Devinsky 1999).

## Anxiety Disorders

The correspondence between seizure disorders and anxiety disorders is a fascinating topic, and the substantial overlapping of symptoms often makes differentiation between these classes of disorders complex. Either type of syndrome can be confused with the other, and the same class of medications (benzodiazepines) helps to reduce the symptoms and subsequent impairment of both types. Panic disorder and CPSs are each included in the differential diagnosis of the other. Although many symptoms overlap, evidence of neurophysiological linkage between anxiety and seizure disorder remains tenuous, except that both involve underlying limbic dysfunction (Fontaine et al. 1990). This connection appears to be more relevant between partial seizure and CPS than other seizure disorders, and it has been speculated that there is a subgroup of patients who have panic disorder that has a pathophysiological relation to epilepsy (Dantendorfer et al. 1995). This relationship is not surprising given that modulation of fear is associated with the temporal lobes; others have hypothesized relationships between the parietal and frontal lobe neural circuits and panic attacks (Alemayehu et al. 1995; McNamara and Fogel 1990).

Little is known about the prevalence of comorbidity. A post hoc analysis of the Epidemiologic Catchment Area data suggested a mild association between panic disorder and seizures (Neugebauer et al. 1993). On the other hand, Spitz (1991) reported that in a clinical sample there was no association between panic disorder and

**TABLE 19–7.** Anxiety disorder symptoms that overlap with those of seizure disorder

**Panic disorder**
    Fear
    Depersonalization
    Derealization
    Déjà vu
    Jamais vu
    Misperceptions
    Illusions
    Dizziness
    Paresthesias
    Chills or hot flashes

**Obsessive-compulsive disorder**
    Obsessions, forced or intrusive

**Posttraumatic stress disorder**
    Recurrent memories or distressing recollections
    Flashbacklike episodes
    Irritability
    Difficulty concentrating

**Agoraphobia**
    Fear of recurrent episodes that leads to restriction of activities

CPS. The relationship between posttraumatic stress disorder, obsessive-compulsive disorder, generalized anxiety, social phobia, and simple phobias has not been articulated. As is the case with panic disorder, there are overlapping symptoms. Table 19–7 lists many of the symptoms that overlap between CPS and anxiety disorders.

Roth and Harper (1962) have pointed out some of the similarities between epilepsy and anxiety disorders. Both are episodic disorders with sudden onset without a precipitating event; both sometimes present with dissociative symptoms: depersonalization, derealization, and déjà vu; both often present with abnormal perceptual and emotional disturbance, such as intense fear and terror; and both have associated physical symptoms. There are significant clinical differences between panic disorder and CPS that help to differentiate the two: in panic disorders consciousness is usually preserved, olfactory hallucinations are unusual, there is a positive family history; electroencephalographic results are usually normal, and many patients do not respond well to anticonvulsants (Handal et al. 1995). Individuals with CPS do not generally have agoraphobia, they may have automatisms, their attacks are generally shorter, they often have abnormal brain scans, and antidepressants may worsen the course of their illness (Roth and Harper 1962). Patients with refractory anxiety, in particular panic disorder, and

patients who have atypical responses to psychotropic medications should be reevaluated for a seizure disorder. A pilot study by Weilburg et al. (1995) found that in patients with atypical panic attacks, ambulatory electroencephalographic monitoring helped to identify an underlying seizure disorder. Electroencephalographic changes occurred in 33% of the subjects ($N = 15$), and among subjects with "captured" panic attacks, 45% showed focal paroxysmal electroencephalographic changes. Two of these five subjects previously had a normal routine EEG.

## Treatment of Comorbid Anxiety

Patients with seizure disorders and comorbid anxiety disorder should receive treatment for their anxiety. Most anxiety disorders can be treated using psychotherapeutic approaches, for example, behavioral, cognitive-behavioral, and short-term symptom-focused therapies. Patients with more severe or refractory anxiety disorders may require pharmacological intervention. Most antianxiety agents and selective serotonin reuptake inhibitors (SSRIs) and other newer antidepressants are tolerated by patients with seizure disorders. The principal reason for not treating epileptic patients with benzodiazepines (although they can be used if needed) is the concern of developing tolerance and dependence and promoting withdrawal-related seizures.

# Mood Disorders

CNS disorders and chronic medical illnesses are frequently associated with increased incidence of mood disorders (Silver et al. 1990); however, there seems to be a distinct relationship between mood disorders and epilepsy. Suicide is of special concern because its prevalence is more common than in the general population (Gehlert 1994; Robertson 1986). Barraclough (1981) reported a 25-fold increase in suicide risk for patients with temporal lobe epilepsy. Most studies of major depression from clinical samples suggest an increase in depressive symptoms using self-report measures (Guze and Gitlin 1994; Robertson et al. 1994), but there are some exceptions (Fiordelli et al. 1993). Little is known about the prevalence of bipolar disorder and dysthymia and comorbid seizure disorders. It is also unknown whether there is an increased vulnerability to depression due to type, frequency, or age at onset of seizures. Several studies have identified a link between left-sided epileptogenic lesions and depression (Mendez et al. 1994; Victoroff et al. 1994). Partial seizures, male gender, and depressive symptoms have also been associated with a left epileptogenic focus (Altshuler et al. 1990; Septien et al. 1993; Strauss et al. 1992). Blumer et al. (1995) evaluated 97 patients admitted to a neurodiagnostic electroencephalographic/video monitoring unit and noted that 34% had atypical depression and 22% had nonepileptic seizures. He defined eight key symptoms that he thought were characteristic of the affective disorders of these patients: depressed mood, anergy, irritability, euphoria, pain, insomnia, fear, and anxiety. These patients also had a history of suicide attempts and hallucinations. Blumer believes this is an epilepsy-specific syndrome, but again many of these symptoms are associated with many types of insult to the CNS. Altshuler et al. (1999) did a 10-year follow-up of 49 patients who had undergone surgery for refractory temporal lobe seizures. The incidence of affective disorder in these patients was quite high: 45% had a lifetime history of depression, 77% had a prior history of depression, 10% developed depression for the first time after surgery, and 50% showed complete remission of their depression after surgery. Forty-seven percent had no recurrence of their depression after surgery. This study certainly implicates the temporal lobes as an anatomical area of some interest in affective disorder.

There are several features of depression in epilepsy that require special consideration before one diagnoses a patient as having a comorbid affective disorder. Sometimes it can be difficult to distinguish affective symptoms from symptoms related to the seizure disorder or the underlying pathology. For example, depressive symptoms for some patients may represent an aura preceding an ictal event or a characteristic postictal phase (Robertson 1986). Similarly, emotional lability or affective instability are symptoms that span both the "neurologic" and "psychiatric" spectrum of epilepsy.

In evaluating depression in a patient with epilepsy, it is very important to examine the medications the patient is taking. Anticonvulsants have been identified as causal agents of depression and cognitive impairments; phenobarbital, the anticonvulsant vigabatrin, and multiple combinations of anticonvulsants appear to contribute to mood disturbance (Bauer and Elger 1995; Brent et al. 1990; Levinson and Devinsky 1999; Mendez et al. 1993). Other anticonvulsants have minimal effect, and some, such as carbamazepine and lamotrigine, may have beneficial effects on mood.

## Treatment of Comorbid Mood Disorders

The role of psychotherapeutic approaches seems intuitively beneficial, but there are few empirical studies that have evaluated this topic. Several studies have suggested that psychological interventions help children and adults with seizure disorders to comply with medications, accept and manage the illness, cope with stressful events, and develop improved self-esteem (Fenwick 1994; Mathers 1992; Regan et al. 1993). A study by Gillham (1990) demonstrated that psychological intervention with education to improve coping skills could be helpful in reducing seizure frequency and psychological symptoms (as well as depressive symptoms) in patients with refractory seizures.

Some patients with seizure disorders and comorbid depression are frequently taking many medications and may respond to careful anticonvulsant monotherapy, especially with carbamazepine (Carrieri et al. 1993). An open study of partial seizure patients with depression refractory to tricyclic antidepressants demonstrated that a subgroup responded very well to carbamazepine (Varney et al. 1993). For patients with a bipolar diathesis or suspected mood lability, monotherapy using carbamazepine or valproic acid (or now lamotrigine) may suffice to prevent episodes, decrease severity of symptoms, and minimize overall decompensation.

It has been well documented that most of the tricyclic antidepressants lower the seizure threshold. This is particularly true of amitriptyline, maprotiline, and clomipramine. Bupropion is also very likely to cause seizures. However, doxepin, trazodone, and the monoamine oxidase inhibitors have less of a tendency to lower the seizure threshold (Rosenstein 1988). All of the SSRIs and other new antidepressants (nefazodone and mirtazapine; venlafaxine and fluvoxamine have slightly higher incidences of seizures) have had seizures reported with their use, but the incidence is low (Alldredge 1999). Most of the seizures reported with any of these medications are dose related; therefore, blood level monitoring in these patients can be quite useful. Consequently, it is important to start any medication with smaller doses than are conventionally given, with gradual increases over time. In most cases, treating the depression often improves seizure control. In an open study evaluating the use of fluoxetine as an adjunctive medication in patients with CPSs, six patients showed a dramatic improvement, and the others had a 30% reduction in their seizure frequency over 14 months (Favale et al. 1995). To date there is no evidence that any one particular antidepressant is more effective than another, and the choice should be made on clinical grounds. Patients with refractory or severe depression should be considered for ECT, but this is another area lacking data from well-designed studies (Zwil and Pelchat 1994). Blumer (1997) reported a series of depressed epileptic patients who responded to a combination of a tricyclic antidepressant and an SSRI; he advocates this regimen for psychotic epileptic patients as well, because he sees the psychosis as an interictal dysphoric disorder (Blumer et al. 2000).

## Behavioral and Personality Disturbances

The literature and clinical experience clearly point to an association between seizure disorders and behavioral disturbances, particularly in patients who have had a chronic course (Neppe and Tucker 1988). Evidence for personality pathology with seizure disorders is sparse because of methodological constraints, but many case reports cite personality disturbance (Blumer 1999; Blumer et al. 1995). Hermann and Riel (1981) underscored the issues that have perpetuated misunderstanding of the relationship between personality and seizures. Methods of measuring personality pathology and comparisons among epilepsy and control groups have not been uniform. There are no longitudinal studies that have assessed behavior and personality before the onset of a seizure disorder. Most of our knowledge in this area comes from cross-sectional case control studies, case reports, and tertiary centers that treat the most severe cases. As a result, it is difficult to extricate the relationship between personality formation and the course of a seizure disorder. Several factors such as stigma of the illness, adverse social factors, level of social support, cultural acceptability, consequences of the illness on psychosocial adaptation, and interpersonal relationships play an important role in shaping patterns of behavior and have a significant impact on the integrity of personality development. Factors that may assume a role in the pathogenesis of personality and behavioral disturbance are the age at onset of the seizure disorder, the type of seizure disorder, the location and the laterality, the frequency of the seizures, the etiology, the presence of a structural lesion, the presence of another medical illness or behavior dysfunction, and the ongoing administration of anticonvulsants.

It is unlikely that there is an epileptic personality (Dam and Dam 1986; Devinsky and Najjar 1999), and there is only a tenuous link between any formal DSM-IV-TR personality disorders and seizure disorders. Some have suggested that neurologic dysfunction, including epilepsy, may play a role in the development of symptoms in subtypes of borderline personality disorder (Andrulonis et al. 1982; Gunderson and Zanarini 1989). Maladaptive personality characteristics and specific personality profiles have been described—preoccupation with philosophical and moral concerns; a belief in a personal destiny; dependency; and traits such as humorlessness (circumstantially), hypergraphia, hyposexuality, religiosity, viscosity, and paranoia

(Bear and Fedio 1977; Hermann and Riel 1981; Waxman and Geschwind 1975)— but large-scale studies do not confirm these case reports or even that there is a specific personality type associated with seizure disorders (Mungus 1982; Rodin and Schmaltz 1984; Stark-Adamec et al. 1985; Stevens 1975).

An increase in episodic and impulsive aggression has also been associated with seizure disorders, particularly CPS (Blake et al. 1995; Mann 1995). Following the postictal period, uncooperative and aggressive behavior may occur when a confused patient is restrained or may occur in a patient who develops a postictal paranoid psychosis (Rodin 1973). Aggressive behavior during a seizure is very unusual, and aggressive activity is usually carried out in a disordered, uncoordinated, and nondirected way (Fenwick 1986). The relationship between aggression and seizure disorders has traditionally been controversial because of methodological concerns. The prevalence of interictal aggression is increased in some seizure disorders, CPS, and generalized seizure disorders but may be an epiphenomenon of epilepsy. This probably can be accounted for by other factors associated with violence and aggression: exposure to violence as a child, male sex, low IQ, low socioeconomic status, adverse social factors, focal or diffuse neurologic lesions, refractory seizures, cognitive impairment, history of institutionalization, and drug use (Devinsky and Vazquez 1993).

The manner in which a particular seizure disorder promotes psychopathic behavioral syndromes is not well understood. Auras have been hypothesized as manifestations of an underlying mechanism that contributes to the development of personality disturbance (Mendez et al. 1993). There is evidence that patients with chronic seizure disorders develop brain neuropathology, and histologic studies of the temporal lobes in CPS demonstrate neuronal loss (Sloviter and Tamminga 1995).

Devinsky and Vazquez (1993) emphasized the diversity of symptoms, behaviors, and profiles, and that the most important characteristic of patients with a seizure disorder is the tendency for extremes of behavior to be accentuated in numerous manners. Not all of the symptoms and consequences of a seizure disorder are debilitating, and some may play an even positive role. It is the maladaptive consequences and dysfunctional traits that should be of paramount importance in treatment.

## Overall Guidelines for the Treatment of Comorbid Psychiatric Syndromes

With any chronic illness, there are basic principles that should be applied in developing a treatment plan. Seizure disorders are no exception, and guidelines for treatment are summarized in Table 19–8. A thorough assessment of premorbid functioning, past episodes, previous trials and responses, duration of current episode, and level of impairment and psychosocial dysfunction facilitates proper intervention and guides subsequent management. Patients with seizure disorders vary greatly in their degree of functioning and coping with life's vicissitudes. Careful attention to ongoing interpersonal and psychosocial impairment, stigmatization, and the effects of the illness on self-esteem and behavior will aid in strengthening the therapeutic alliance and promote psychoeducational and psychopharmacologic interventions. Given that insults to the CNS only produce a limited amount of symptom expression, as a general principle, it behooves the clinician not to be too procrustean about insisting that mood, anxiety, psychotic, cognitive, or behavioral symptoms and signs fit neatly into the DSM-IV psychiatric categories (Tucker 1996). The protean nature of the manifestations of various types of seizure disorders may make diagnostic confirmation difficult, especially if there are no electroencephalographic abnormalities or if, after neurologic consultation, there are reservations about the diagnosis. Under such conditions, the neuropsychiatrist may elect to treat patients with a suspected seizure disorder empirically. These patients, and some patients with refractory psychiatric illness, may find benefit with the addition of an anticonvulsant (Post et al. 1985). In a small number of patients with concomitant psychiatric illness, anticonvulsant monotherapy for the seizure disorder may suffice. The degree of seizure control is not associated with an increase in the number of anticonvulsants (Neppe et al. 1988). Patients taking anticonvulsants should have serum blood levels checked at the first indication of incipient or worsening psychiatric symptoms or signs. Increase in the dosage of an anticonvulsant may be all that is necessary to diminish symptoms and prevent decompensation. Conversely, patients with complex medication regimens may realize symptom improvement after dosage reduction (Trimble and Thompson 1983).

Most patients will require treatment of psychiatric syndromes. Individual, group, family, or couple therapies can provide specific syndrome-focused treatments. Psychotherapeutic approaches have many advantages. They avoid drug interactions, circumvent the tendency of psychotropic medications to alter seizure thresholds, and can teach patients behavior and coping skills that can have a positive impact on symptoms and dysfunction.

Many patients will require pharmacotherapy, either combined with psychotherapeutic approaches or alone. Patients with temporal lobe epilepsy display a wide variety of mood, anxiety, dissociative, psychotic, and behav-

**TABLE 19–8.** Basic principles of treating patients with a seizure disorder and concomitant psychiatric symptoms

Perform a thorough assessment of biopsychosocial factors that aggravate neuropsychiatric symptoms.

Evaluate the need for adjustment of the anticonvulsant.

Consider psychotherapeutic approaches (individual, group, family) that are specific for the syndrome or that target behaviors or stressors.

Preferably—but not always—use anticonvulsant monotherapy.

Optimize the addition of psychotropic medication by targeting specific psychiatric symptoms.

Start with smaller than usual dose and wait until symptoms stabilize (often weeks) before changing doses.

Anticipate interactions between anticonvulsant and psychotropic medications.

Collaborate with other caregivers.

ioral disturbances that frequently resemble psychiatric disorders. Discriminating the symptoms of previous seizures from target psychiatric symptoms will ensure a greater likelihood of response to medication.

Although we recommend an aggressive approach for the treatment of comorbid psychiatric syndromes, we are judicious with the dosing of psychotropics and prefer gradual increases. Clinical experience shows that many patients with seizure disorders seem to respond to smaller doses. Given the concern about anticonvulsant and psychotropic drug interactions, such an approach is warranted. Any time a new drug is added it is mandatory for the clinician to be aware of potential drug interactions. Many anticonvulsants will lower the serum drug level of psychotropics through enzyme induction (Perucca et al. 1985), and psychotropics may increase the levels of anticonvulsants secondary to increased P450 hepatic enzyme competition (Cloyd et al. 1986). For patients receiving tricyclic antidepressants, monitoring of serum levels is recommended, and avoiding elevated blood levels may prevent seizure promotion (Preskorn and Fast 1992). Initially, anticonvulsant blood levels should be monitored weekly and then monthly, after the addition of a psychotropic. After a few months, serum levels can be checked less frequently. Thereafter, any changes in the dosage of medications require reexamination of serum blood levels.

Finally, the importance of coordinating care with other professionals and health care providers cannot be overemphasized. It behooves the psychiatrist to work with a neurologist (if available) to develop a long-term strategy. Often, psychiatrists will assume the role of supervising all treatment planning (Schoenenberger et al. 1995).

# Specific Aspects of Anticonvulsant Use

It is important to recognize that in many of the patients who have suspected seizure disorders, the psychiatrist will be left to manage the anticonvulsants. Often, even when the patient has a documented seizure disorder and the major persistent symptoms are behavioral, the psychiatrist will also be managing these medications alone. Until the psychiatrist is comfortable with these medications, collaboration with a neurologist is not only helpful but is a good learning technique. However, as valproic acid and carbamazepine have become more common in the treatment of bipolar illness, the basic principles are known to most psychiatrists (McElroy et al. 1988; Neppe et al. 1988).

## Pharmacokinetic Interactions

Anticonvulsant administration is particularly important and particularly difficult by virtue of enzyme induction and inhibition occurring in the liver. This enzyme induction tends to affect predominantly the P450 cytochrome enzyme system in the liver. This implies that both the metabolism of anticonvulsants (particularly carbamazepine) and the metabolism of other lipid-soluble compounds are accelerated (Alldredge 1999; Post et al. 1985). However, some of the new anticonvulsants—oxcarbazepine, gabapentin, and vigabatrin—have few drug interactions (Dichter and Brodie 1996).

Of the major anticonvulsants, phenobarbital, phenytoin, carbamazepine, lamotrigine, topiramate, and tiagabine have potent drug interactions. Table 19–9 indicates what is known about some interactions and demonstrates the complexity of these drug interactions (Bertilsson 1978; Birkhimer et al. 1985; Bramhall and Levine 1988; Dichter and Brodie 1996; Dorn 1986; Jann et al. 1985; Kidron et al. 1985; Shukla et al. 1984; Zimmerman 1986).

### Phenobarbital

Phenobarbital is the most potent of the enzyme inducers; when it is used in combination, levels of other anticonvulsants are commonly reduced because of the extensive enzyme induction. In addition, phenobarbital causes psychological depression, has the potential for addiction (although this is generally low among patients receiving phenobarbital for seizures), and is potentially lethal in overdose. Indeed, it was the major cause of death due to overdose during the 1950s. It also produces a cognitive impairment, which may explain the rigidity of personality that was at times seen with patients with

**TABLE 19–9.** Known interactions between carbamazepine and other drugs

**Drugs that increase carbamazepine level**
Isoniazid
Valproic acid (increased free carbamazepine in vitro)
Carbamazepine epoxide only
Troleandomycin
Propoxyphene
Erythromycin
Nicotinamide
Cimetidine
Viloxazine

**Drugs that decrease carbamazepine level**
Phenobarbital
Phenytoin
Primidone and phenobarbital
Carbamazepine itself (autoinduction)
Alcohol (chronic use)
Cigarettes

**Conditions caused by carbamazepine**
Pregnancy test failure
Escape from dexamethasone suppression
Oral contraceptive failure

**Substances whose effects are decreased by carbamazepine**
Vitamin D, calcium, and folate; causes possible hyponatremia
Clonazepam
Dicumarol
Doxycycline
Phenytoin
Sodium valproate
Theophylline
Ethosuximide
Haloperidol
Isoniazid

*Note.* Because enzyme induction is the mechanism in most of these interactions, it can be hypothesized that there are similar effects with phenytoin, phenobarbital, and primidone.

seizure disorders taking phenobarbital.

We see little role for barbiturates in the outpatient management of seizure disorders today; their only place is with patients who are already taking them and who do not have significant side effects. In our experience, most patients have side effects such as CNS depression, psychological depression, or cognitive impairments of one kind or another. It is extremely difficult to taper off barbiturates without producing an epileptic seizure in the patients.

### Phenytoin

Although not as problematic as phenobarbital, diphenylhydantoin sodium (or phenytoin) is now less popular than it was and has limited use in the neuropsychiatric patient, despite being an outstanding anticonvulsant in controlling generalized tonic-clonic and some partial seizures. Its problem, like phenobarbital, is its side-effect profile (Pulliainen and Jokelainen 1994). Mild cognitive impairment occurs, particularly in higher doses. Because phenytoin has a small therapeutic range, patients can easily become drug toxic, and (ironically) one of the side effects of significant toxicity is seizures. Additionally, it can make petit mal seizures worse. Gum hyperplasia is a particular problem with the long-term use of phenytoin, producing an appearance that can, at times, be unsightly (Trimble 1979, 1988). Phenytoin is a potent enzyme inducer but is weaker than phenobarbital.

## Carbamazepine

There has been an increasing trend to use carbamazepine rather than phenytoin, because it has fewer side effects, may have some psychotropic properties, and has proven value in severe disorders and bipolar illness. It is as effective as phenytoin in both generalized tonic-clonic seizures and partial seizures and thus is the drug of choice for such conditions. It is ineffective in petit mal absences, where sodium valproate or ethosuximide are generally used.

A possible further role for carbamazepine is its use in treating nonresponsive psychotic patients or atypical psychotic patients with any electroencephalographic temporal lobe abnormalities, with episodic hostility, or with affective lability (Blumer et al. 1988; Cowdry and Gardner 1988; Neppe et al. 1991).

Carbamazepine and the other anticonvulsants involved in enzyme induction can cause many unanticipated side effects (Cloyd et al. 1986) (e.g., patients taking oral contraceptives may have their steroid levels lowered, patients may become vitamin D deficient, folic acid may be depleted). Finally, there is commonly a slight elevation in hepatic enzyme levels such as glutamyl transferase; this does not imply that the anticonvulsant drugs should be stopped.

The rate of onset of the induction process appears to be between 24 and 72 hours for carbamazepine (Neppe and Friel 1987). Thus, in the early phase, patients taking neuroleptics who are given carbamazepine may well have more side effects as a consequence of raised levels from competition at enzyme system pathways.

Because of induction by the neuroleptic, the levels of all anticonvulsants can be higher. Consequently, the necessary doses of anticonvulsant for monotherapy are lower when the anticonvulsant is given in conjunction with psychotropic agents, partly because of competition and partly because the additive pharmacodynamics produce sedation.

In addition to the phenomenon of induction of hepatic enzymes, a second phenomenon of deinduction of hepatic enzyme systems also occurs (Neppe and Kaplan 1988). It is probable that patients going off anticonvulsant medication will experience a reverse process, whereby the rate of liver metabolism will decrease, with the consequence that there may be an accumulation of psychotropic agents.

## Valproate

Sodium valproate is particularly useful in combined tonic-clonic and petit mal seizures. It also appears to be effective against CPSs.

Valproate does not induce enzymes but metabolically competes; thus, theoretically, it raises levels of psychotropics and has its own level raised. It is safe, relatively nontoxic, and generally well tolerated. The major concern with its use is potentially fatal, primarily rare hepatotoxicity in young children, particularly when they are taking other anticonvulsants (McElroy et al. 1988).

## New Antiepileptic Drugs

There are many new antiepileptic drugs (AEDs): gabapentin, felbamate, oxcarbazepine, tiagabine, topiramate, vigabatrin, and lamotrigine. Most of these drugs for which the actions are known affect either the inhibitory γ-aminobutyric acid system (gabapentin, tiagabine, vigabatrin) or the excitatory glutaminergic system (felbamate, lamotrigine). Many of these have been well studied throughout the world and in the United States, and all have various mild to serious side effects (Table 19–10) (Dichter and Brodie 1996; Ketter et al. 1999). Gabapentin, lamotrigine, and topiramate have been increasingly used in psychiatry for bipolar disorder and anxiety disorders and may have uses for similar disorders in seizure disorder patients (Ghaemi and Gaughan 2000; Ketter et al. 1999).

## Conclusions

Psychopathology occurs only in a minority of persons with epilepsy. Attempted etiologic explanations such as kindling, lateralization, localization, and biochemical changes are all, therefore, explanations for a small proportion of the epileptic population. Medications used to treat seizure disorders often do not alleviate behavior changes, and at times agents such as neuroleptics and antidepressants help behavior change but not seizure disturbances. The exact etiology of these conditions remains to be determined. Clinical judgment in the individual

**TABLE 19–10.** Selected clinical aspects of the new anticonvulsants

**Felbamate**[a,b]
Irritability, insomnia, stimulant effects
Aplastic anemia, hepatitis

**Gabapentin**
Weight gain
Few drug interactions
Anxiolytic

**Lamotrigine**[a,b]
No weight gain
Occasional tourettism
Rash
Does not induce P450 system
Can increase neurotoxicity of carbamazepine

**Oxcarbazepine**
Few drug interactions (not affected by enzyme inducers)
Induces 3A family of P450 system weakly
Hyponatremia

**Tiagabine**
Confusion, fatigue
Does not induce P450 system

**Topiramate**[a]
Hyperammonemic encephalopathy when combined with valproate
Cognitive impairments
Weak effect on P450 system

**Vigabatrin**[a]
Increased incidence of depression and psychosis
Weight gain
Possible retinal damage
No drug interactions

[a]Can affect phenytoin, carbamazepine, or phenobarbital levels.
[b]Valproate decreases levels of this compound.

case remains the essential standard of care in the absence of solid evidence for specific indications and protocols for the use of anticonvulsant/psychotropic combinations in specific populations.

# References

Adamec RE, Stark AC: Limbic kindling and animal behavior: implications for human psychopathology associated with complex partial seizures. Biol Psychiatry 18:269–293, 1983

Alemayehu S, Bergey GK, Barry E, et al: Panic attacks as ictal manifestations of parietal lobe seizures. Epilepsia 36:824–830, 1995

Alldredge BK: Seizure risk associated with psychotropic drugs: clinical and pharmacokinetic considerations. Neurology 53 (suppl 2):S68–S75, 1999

Alper K, Devinsky O, Perrine K, et al: Psychiatric classification of nonconversion nonepileptic seizures. Arch Neurol 52:199–201, 1995

Altshuler LL, Devinsky O, Post RM, et al: Depression, anxiety, and temporal lobe epilepsy: laterality of focus and symptoms. Arch Neurol 47:284–288, 1990

Altshuler LL, Rausch R, Delrahim S, et al: Temporal lobe epilepsy, temporal lobectomy, major depression. J Neuropsychiatry Clin Neurosci 11:436–443, 1999

American Psychiatric Association: Diagnostic and Statistical Manual of Mental Disorders, 4th Edition. Washington, DC, American Psychiatric Association, 1994

American Psychiatric Association: Diagnostic and Statistical Manual of Mental Disorders, 4th Edition, Text Revision. Washington, DC, American Psychiatric Association, 2000

Andrulonis PA, Glueck BC, Stroebel CF, et al: Borderline personality subcategories. J Nerv Ment Dis 170:670–679, 1982

Annegers JF, Hauser WA, Elveback LR: Remission of seizures and relapse in patients with epilepsy. Epilepsia 10:729–737, 1979

Armon C, Shin M, Miller P, et al: Reversible parkinsonism and cognitive impairment with chronic valproate use. Neurology 47:626–635, 1996

Arnold LM, Privtera MD: Psychopathology and trauma in epileptic and psychogenic seizure patients. Psychosomatics 37:438–443, 1996

Barraclough B: Suicide and epilepsy, in Epilepsy and Psychiatry. Edited by Reynolds EH, Trimble MR. Edinburgh, UK, Churchill Livingstone, 1981, pp 72–76

Bauer J, Elger CE: Anticonvulsive drug therapy: historical and current aspects. Nervenarzt 66:403–411, 1995

Bear DM: Behavioural changes in temporal lobe epilepsy: conflict, confusion challenge, in Aspects of Epilepsy and Psychiatry. Edited by Trimble ME, Bolwig TG. London, Wiley, 1986, pp 19–29

Bear DM, Fedio P: Quantitative analysis of interictal behavior in temporal lobe epilepsy. Arch Neurol 34:454–467, 1977

Berger H: Ueber das Elektrenkephalogramm des Menschen. Archives of Psychiatry I–XIV:87–108, 1929–1938

Bertilsson L: Clinical pharmacokinetics of carbamazepine. Clin Pharmacokinet 3:128–143, 1978

Betts TA: A follow-up study of a cohort of patients with epilepsy admitted to psychiatric care in an English city, in Epilepsy: Proceedings of the Hans Berger Centenary Symposium, Edinburgh, 1973. Edited by Harris P, Mawdsley C. New York, Churchill Livingstone, 1974

Bickford RG: Activation procedures and special electrodes, in Current Practice of Unusual Electroencephalography. Edited by Kass D, Daly DD. New York, Raven, 1979, pp 269–306

Birkhimer LJ, Curtis JL, Jann MW: Use of carbamazepine in psychiatric disorders. Clinical Pharmacology 4:425–434, 1985

Blake P, Pincus J, Buckner C: Neurologic abnormalities in murderers. Neurology 45:1641–1647, 1995

Blumer D: Temporal lobe epilepsy and its psychiatric significance, in Psychiatric Aspects of Neurological Disease. Edited by Benson FD, Blumer D. New York, Grune & Stratton, 1975, pp 171–198

Blumer D: Antidepressant and double antidepressant treatment for the affective disorder of epilepsy. J Clin Psychiatry 58:3–11, 1997

Blumer D: Evidence supporting the temporal lobe epilepsy personality syndrome: Neurology 53 (suppl 2):S9–S12, 1999

Blumer D, Heilbronn M, Himmelhoch J: Indications for carbamazepine in mental illness: atypical psychiatric disorder or temporal lobe syndrome? Compr Psychiatry 29:108–122, 1988

Blumer D, Montouris G, Hermann B: Psychiatric morbidity in seizure patients on a neurodiagnostic monitoring unit. J Neuropsychiatry Clin Neurosci 7:445–456, 1995

Blumer D, Wakhulu S, Montouris G, et al: Treatment of the interictal psychoses. J Clin Psychiatry 61:110–122, 2000

Bramhall D, Levine M: Possible interaction of ranitidine with phenytoin. Drug Intelligence and Clinical Pharmacy 22:979–980, 1988

Brent DA, Crumrine PK, Varma R, et al: Phenobarbital treatment and major depressive disorder in children with epilepsy: a naturalistic follow-up. Pediatrics 85:1086–1091, 1990

Brodsky L, Zuniga JG, Casenas ER, et al: Refractory anxiety: a masked epileptiform disorder. Psychiatric Journal of the University of Ottawa 8:42–45, 1983

Carrieri PB, Provitera V, Iacovitti B, et al: Mood disorders in epilepsy. Acta Neurologica Napoli 15:62–67, 1993

Cendes F, Li LM, Watson C, et al: Is ictal recording mandatory in temporal lobe epilepsy? Arch Neurol 57:497–500, 2000

Chadwick D: Seizures, epilepsy, and other episodic disorders, in Brain's Diseases of the Nervous System, 10th Edition. Edited by Walton J. London, Oxford University Press, 1993, pp 697–733

Cloyd JC, Levy RH, Wedlund RH: Relationship between carbamazepine concentration and extent of enzyme autoinduction (abstract). Epilepsia 27:592, 1986

Cowdry R, Gardner DL: Pharmacotherapy of borderline personality disorder. Arch Gen Psychiatry 45:111–119, 1988

Currie S, Heathfield RWG, Henson RA, et al: Clinical course and prognosis of temporal lobe epilepsy: a survey of 666 patients. Brain 94:173–190, 1970

Dam M, Dam AM: Is there an epileptic personality? in Aspects of Epilepsy and Psychiatry. Edited by Trimble MR, Bolwig TG. New York, Wiley, 1986, pp 9–18

Dantendorfer K, Amering M, Baischer W, et al: Is there a pathophysiological and therapeutic link between panic disorder and epilepsy? Acta Psychiatr Scand 91:430–432, 1995

Devinsky O, Gordon E: Epileptic seizures progressing into nonepileptic conversion seizures. Neurology 51:1293–1296 1998

Devinsky O, Najjar S: Evidence against the existence of a temporal lobe epilepsy personality syndrome. Neurology 53 (suppl 2):S12–S25, 1999

Devinsky O, Vazquez B: Behavioral changes associated with epilepsy. Neurol Clin 11:127–149, 1993

Devinsky O, Sanchez-Villasenor F, Vazquez B, et al: Clinical profile of patients with epileptic and nonepileptic seizures. Neurology 46:1530–1533, 1996

Dichter M, Brodie M: New antiepileptic drugs. N Engl J Med 334:1583–1590, 1996

Diehl LW: Schizophrenic syndromes in epilepsies. Psychopathology 22:65–140, 1989

Dodrill CB, Batzel LW: Interictal behavioral features of patients with epilepsy. Epilepsia 27 (suppl 2):S64–S76, 1986

Dodrill CB, Troupin AS: Neuropsychological effects of carbamazepine and phenytoin. Neurology 41:141–143, 1991

Dongier S: Statistical study of clinical and electroencephalographic manifestations of 536 psychotic episodes occurring in 516 epileptics between clinical seizures. Epilepsia 1:117–142, 1959–1960

Dorn JM: A case of phenytoin toxicity possibly precipitated by trazodone. J Clin Psychiatry 47:89–90, 1986

Ebersole JS, Leroy RJ: Evaluation of ambulatory EEG monitoring. Neurology 33:853–860, 1983

Engel J: The epilepsies, in Cecil's Textbook of Medicine, 19th Edition. Edited by Wyngoorden J, Smith L, Bennet C. Philadelphia, PA, WB Saunders, 1992, pp 2202–2213

Ey H: Etudes psychiatriques. Paris, Desclee de Brouwer, 1954

Favale E, Rubino P, Mainardi P, et al: Anticonvulsant effect of fluoxetine in humans. Neurology 45:1926–1927, 1995

Fenton GW: The EEG, epilepsy and psychiatry, in What Is Epilepsy? Edited by Trimble MR, Reynolds EH. Edinburgh, UK, Churchill Livingstone, 1986, pp 139–160

Fenwick P: In dyscontrol epilepsy, in What Is Epilepsy? Edited by Trimble MR, Reynolds EH. Edinburgh, UK, Churchill Livingstone, 1986, pp 161–182

Fenwick P: The behavioral treatment of epilepsy generation and inhibition of seizures. Neurol Clin 12:175–202, 1994

Fink M: Meduna and the origins of convulsive therapy. Am J Psychiatry 141:1034–1041, 1984

Fiordelli E, Beghi E, Bogliun G, et al: Epilepsy and psychiatric disturbance: a cross-sectional study. Br J Psychiatry 163: 446–450, 1993

Fontaine R, Breton G, D'ery R, et al: Temporal lobe abnormalities in panic disorder: an MRI study. Biol Psychiatry 27:304–310, 1990

Gehlert S: Perceptions of control in adults with epilepsy. Epilepsia 35:81–88, 1994

Geyer J, Payne T, Drury I: The value of pelvic thrusting in the diagnosis of seizures and pseudoseizures. Neurology 54:227–229, 2000

Ghaemi S, Gaughan S: Novel anticonvulsants: a new generation of mood stabilizers. Harv Rev Psychiatry 8:1–7, 2000

Gibbs FA, Gibbs EL: Atlas of Electroencephalography. Cambridge, MA, Addison-Wesley, 1952

Gillham RA: Refractory epilepsy: an evaluation of psychological methods in outpatient management. Epilepsia 31:427–432, 1990

Goodridge DMG, Shovron SD: Epileptic seizures in a population of 6000. BMJ 287:641–644, 1983

Gudmundsson G: Epilepsy in Iceland. Acta Neurol Scand 43 (suppl 25):1–124, 1966

Gunderson JG, Zanarini MC: Pathogenesis of borderline personality, in American Psychiatric Press Review of Psychiatry, Vol 8. Edited by Tasman A, Hales RE, Frances AJ. Washington, DC, American Psychiatric Press, 1989, pp 25–48

Guze BH, Gitlin M: The neuropathologic basis of major affective disorders: neuroanatomic insights. J Neuropsychiatry Clin Neurosci 6:114–121, 1994

Hakola HP, Laulumaa VA: Carbamazepine in treatment of violent schizophrenics (letter). Lancet 1:1358, 1982

Hamer H, Knake S, Schomburg M, et al: Valproate induced hyperammonemic encephalopathy in the presence of topiramate. Neurology 54:230–232, 2000

Handal N, Masand P, Weilburg J: Panic disorder and complex partial seizures: a truly complex relationship. Psychosomatics 36:498–502, 1995

Hathaway SR, McKinley JC: Minnesota Multiphasic Personality Inventory—2. Minneapolis, MN, University of Minnesota, 1989

Hauser WA, Annegers J, Kurland L: Incidence of epilepsy and unprovoked seizures in Rochester, MN. Epilepsia 34:453–468, 1993

Heath RG: Psychosis and epilepsy: similarities and differences in the anatomic-physiologic substrate. Advances in Biological Psychiatry 8:106–116, 1982

Hermann BP, Riel P: Interictal personality and behavioral traits in temporal lobe and generalized epilepsy. Cortex 17:125–128, 1981

Ho S, Berkovic S, Berlangieri S, et al: Comparison of ictal SPECT and interictal PET in the presurgical evaluation of TLE. Ann Neurol 37:738–745, 1995

Hoare P: Does illness foster dependency? Dev Med Child Neurol 26:20–24, 1984

International League Against Epilepsy Commission: Proposal for revised clinical and electroencephalographic classification of epileptic seizures. Epilepsia 22:489–501, 1981

International League Against Epilepsy Commission: Proposal for classification of epilepsies and epileptic syndromes. Epilepsia 26:268–278, 1985

Jann MW, Ereshefsky L, Saklad SR, et al: Effects of carbamazepine on plasma haloperidol levels. J Clin Psychopharmacol 5:106–109, 1985

Kanner A, Stagno S, Kotagal P, et al: Postictal psychiatric events during prolonged video-EEG monitoring studies. Arch Neurol 53:258–263, 1996

Kanner A, Parra J, Frey M, et al: Psychiatric and neurologic predictors of psychogenic seizure outcome. Neurology 53:933–938, 1999

Ketter T, Malow B, Flamini R, et al: Anticonvulsant withdrawal emergent psychopathology. Neurology 44:55–61, 1994

Ketter T, Post R, Theodore W: Positive and negative psychiatric effects of antiepileptic drugs in patients with seizure disorders. Neurology 53 (suppl 2):S53–S67, 1999

Kidron R, Averbuch I, Klein E, et al: Carbamazepine-induced reduction of blood levels of haloperidol in chronic schizophrenia. Biol Psychiatry 20:219–222, 1985

Kirubakaran V, Sen S, Wilkinson C: Catatonic stupor: unusual manifestation of TLE. Psychiatric Journal of the University of Ottawa 12:244–246, 1987

Kraepelin E: Lecture VI: epileptic insanity (1922), in Lectures in Clinical Psychiatry. Translated by Johnstone T. New York, Hafner, 1968, pp 48–57

Kristensen O, Sindrup EH: Psychomotor epilepsy and psychosis, II: electroencephalographic findings. Acta Neurol Scand 57:370–379, 1978

Krohn W: A study of epilepsy in Northern Norway: its frequency and character. Acta Psychiatr Scand (suppl 150):215–225, 1961

Krumholz A: Nonepileptic seizures: diagnosis and management. Neurology 53 (suppl 2):S76–S83, 1999

Kuyk J, Spinhoven P, Boas W, et al: Dissociation in temporal lobe epilepsy and pseudo-epileptic seizure patients. J Nerv Ment Dis 187:713–720, 1999

Landolt H: Serial encephalographic investigations during psychotic episodes in epileptic patients and during schizophrenic attacks, in Lectures on Epilepsy. Edited by Lorentz de Haas AM. London, Elsevier, 1958, pp 91–133

Laskowitz D, Sperling M, French J, et al: The syndrome of frontal lobe epilepsy. Neurology 45:780–787, 1995

Levinson D, Devinsky O: Psychiatric events during vigabatrin therapy. Neurology 53:1503–1511, 1999

Lindsay J, Ounstead C, Richards P: Long-term outcome in children with temporal lobe seizures, III: psychiatric aspects in childhood and adult life. Dev Med Child Neurol 21:630–636, 1979

Malkowicz D, Legido A, Jackel R, et al: Prolactin secretion following repetitive seizures. Neurology 45:448–452, 1995

Mann JJ: Violence and aggression, in Psychopharmacology: The Fourth Generation of Progress. Edited by Bloom FE, Kupfer DJ. New York, Raven, 1995, pp 1919–1928

Martin R, Kuzniecky R, Ho S, et al: Cognitive effects of topiramate, gabapentin, and lamotrigine in healthy young adults. Neurology 52:321–327, 1999

Mathers CB: Group therapy in the management of epilepsy. Br J Med Psychol 65:279–287, 1992

McElroy S, Keck P, Pope H, et al: Valproate in primary psychiatric disorders, in Use of Anticonvulsants in Psychiatry. Edited by McElroy S, Pope H. Clifton, NJ, Oxford Health Care, 1988, pp 25–42

McKenna PJ, Kane JM, Parrish K: Psychotic syndromes in epilepsy. Am J Psychiatry 142:895–904, 1985

McNamara ME, Fogel BS: Anticonvulsant-responsive panic attacks with temporal lobe EEG abnormalities. J Neuropsychiatry Clin Neurosci 2:193–196, 1990

Meador KJ, Loring DW, Abney OL, et al: Effects of carbamazepine and phenytoin on EEG and memory in healthy adults. Epilepsia 34:153–157, 1993

Meador KJ, Loring D, Moore E, et al: Comparative effects of phenobarbital, phenytoin, and valproate in healthy adults. Neurology 45:1494–1499, 1995

Mellers J, Toone B, Lishman A: A neuropsychological comparison of schizophrenia and schizophrenia-like psychosis of epilepsy. Psychol Med 30:325–335, 2000

Mendez MF, Doss RC, Taylor JL, et al: Depression in epilepsy: relationship to seizures and anticonvulsant therapy. J Nerv Ment Dis 181:444–447, 1993

Mendez MF, Taylor JL, Doss RC, et al: Depression in secondary epilepsy: relation to lesion laterality. J Neurol Neurosurg Psychiatry 57:232–233, 1994

Metrakos K, Metrakos JD: Genetics of convulsive disorders, II: genetics and encephalographic studies in centrencephalic epilepsy. Neurology 11:454–483, 1961

Mitsuda H: Clinical genetics in psychiatry. Bulletin of the Osaka Medical School (suppl 12):23–261, 1967

Moehle KA, Bolter JF, Long CJ: The relationship between neuropsychological functioning and psychopathology in temporal lobe epileptic patients. Epilepsia 25:418–422, 1984

Monroe RR: Limbic ictus and atypical psychoses. J Nerv Ment Dis 170:711–716, 1982

Mungus D: Interictal behavior abnormality in temporal lobe epilepsy. Arch Gen Psychiatry 39:108–111, 1982

Neppe VM: Epileptic psychosis: a heterogeneous condition (letter). Epilepsia 27:634, 1986

Neppe VM, Friel P: Carbamazepine, clinical and pharmacokinetic variation with psychotropics, in Proceedings of Epilepsy International Congress, Jerusalem, Israel, September 1987, p 85

Neppe VM, Kaplan C: Short-term treatment of atypical spells with carbamazepine. Clin Neuropharmacol 11:287–289, 1988

Neppe VM, Tucker GJ: Modern perspectives on epilepsy in relation to psychiatry: behavioral disturbances of epilepsy. Hospital and Community Psychiatry 39:389–396, 1988

Neppe VM, Tucker GJ, Wilensky AJ: Fundamentals of carbamazepine use in neuropsychiatry. J Clin Psychiatry 49 (suppl 4):4–6, 1988

Neppe VM, Bowman B, Sawchuk KSLJ: Carbamazepine for atypical psychosis with episodic hostility: a preliminary study. J Nerv Ment Dis 179:339–340, 1991

Neugebauer R, Weissman MM, Ouellette R, et al: Comorbidity of panic disorder and seizures: affinity or artifact? J Anxiety Disord 7:21–35, 1993

Novak J, Corke P, Fairley N: Petit mal status in adults. Diseases of the Nervous System 32:245–248, 1971

Pakalinis A, Drake M, Kellum J: Forced normalization: acute psychosis after seizure control in seven patients. Arch Neurol 44:289–292, 1987

Perez MM, Trimble MR: Epileptic psychosis: psychopathological comparison with process schizophrenia. Br J Psychiatry 137:245–249, 1980

Perucca E, Manzo L, Crema A: Pharmacokinetic interactions between antiepileptic and psychotropic drugs, in The Psychopharmacology of Epilepsy. Edited by Trimble M. Chichester, UK, Wiley, 1985, pp 95–105

Pincus JH, Tucker GJ: Behavioral Neurology, 3rd Edition. New York, Oxford University Press, 1985

Popkin M, Tucker GJ: Mental disorders due to a general medical condition and substance-induced disorders: mood, anxiety, psychotic, catatonic, and personality disorders, in DSM-IV Source Book. Edited by Widiger T, Frances J, Pincus HA, et al. Washington, DC, American Psychiatric Press, 1994, pp 243–276

Popli A, Kando J, Pillay S, et al: Occurrence of seizures related to psychotropic medication among psychiatric inpatients. Psychiatr Serv 46:486–488, 1995

Post RM, Uhde TW, Joffe RT, et al: Anticonvulsant drugs in psychiatric illness: new treatment alternatives and theoretical implications, in The Psychopharmacology of Epilepsy. Edited by Trimble MR. Chichester, UK, Wiley, 1985, pp 141–171

Preskorn SH, Fast GA: Tricyclic antidepressant-induced seizures and plasma drug concentration. J Clin Psychiatry 53:160–162, 1992

Procci WR: Schizo-affective psychosis: fact or fiction? A survey of the literature. Arch Gen Psychiatry 33:1167–1178, 1976

Pulliainen V, Jokelainen M: Effects of phenytoin and carbamazepine on cognitive functions in newly diagnosed epileptic patients. Acta Neurol Scand 89:81–86, 1994

Regan KJ, Banks GK, Beran RG: Therapeutic recreation programmes for children with epilepsy. Seizure 2:195–200, 1993

Robertson MM: Ictal and interictal depression in patients with epilepsy, in Aspects of Epilepsy and Psychiatry. Edited by Trimble MR, Bolwig TG. Chichester, UK, Wiley, 1986, pp 213–234

Robertson MM, Channon S, Baker J: Depressive symptomatology in a general hospital sample of outpatients with temporal lobe epilepsy: a controlled study. Epilepsia 35:771–777, 1994

Rodin EA: Psychomotor epilepsy and aggressive behavior. Arch Gen Psychiatry 28:210–213, 1973

Rodin EA, Schmaltz S: The Bear-Fedio personality inventory and temporal lobe epilepsy. Neurology 34:591–596, 1984

Rosenstein DL, Nelson JC, Jacobs SC, et al: Seizures associated with antidepressants: a review. J Clin Psychiatry 54:289–299, 1993

Roth M, Harper M: Temporal lobe epilepsy and the phobic anxiety-depersonalization syndrome, II: practical and theoretical considerations. Compr Psychiatry 3:215–226, 1962

Ryback R, Gardner E: Limbic system dysrhythmia: a diagnostic EEG procedure utilizing procaine activation. J Neuropsychiatry Clin Neurosci 3:321–329, 1991

Sadler M, Goodwin J: The sensitivity of various electrodes in the detection of epilepsy from potential patients with partial complex seizures (letter). Epilepsia 27:627, 1986

Schiffer R: Epilepsy, psychosis, and forced normalization (editorial). Arch Neurol 44:253, 1987

Schoenenberger R, Tonasijevic M, Jha A, et al: Appropriateness of antiepileptic drug level monitoring. JAMA 274:1622–1626, 1995

Sengoku A, Yagi K, Seino M, et al: Risks of occurrence of psychoses in relation to the types of epilepsies and epileptic seizures. Folia Psychiatrica et Neurologica Japonica 37:221–225, 1983

Septien L, Giroud M, Didi-Roy R, et al: Depression and partial epilepsy: relevance of laterality of the epileptic focus. Neurol Res 15:136–138, 1993

Shovron SD, Reynolds EH: The nature of epilepsy: evidence from studies of epidemiology, temporal patterns of seizures, prognosis and treatment, in What Is Epilepsy? Edited by Trimble MR, Reynolds EH. Edinburgh, UK, Churchill Livingstone, 1986, pp 36–45

Shukla S, Godwin CD, Long LE, et al: Lithium-carbamazepine neurotoxicity and risk factors. Am J Psychiatry 141:1604–1606, 1984

Sillanpaa M, Camfield P, Camfield C: Predicting long-term outcome of childhood epilepsy in Nova Scotia, Canada and Turku, Finland. Arch Neurol 52:589–592, 1995

Silver JM, Hales RE, Yudofsky SC: Psychopharmacology of depression in neurologic disorders. J Clin Psychiatry 51:33–39, 1990

Slater E, Beard AW, Glithero E: The schizophrenia-like psychoses of epilepsy. Br J Psychiatry 109:95–150, 1963

Sloviter RS, Tamminga CA: Cortex, VII: the hippocampus in epilepsy (letter). Am J Psychiatry 152:659, 1995

Spitz MC: Panic disorder in seizure patients: a diagnostic pitfall. Epilepsia 32:33–38, 1991

Stark-Adamec C, Adamec RE, Graham JM, et al: Complexities in the complex partial seizures personality controversy. Psychiatric Journal of the University of Ottawa 10:231–236, 1985

Stevens JR: Interictal clinical manifestations of complex partial seizures, in Advances in Neurology. Edited by Penry JK, Daly DD. New York, Raven, 1975, pp 85–107

Stevens JR: Psychiatric aspects of epilepsy. J Clin Psychiatry 49 (suppl 4):49–57, 1988

Strauss E, Wada J, Moll A: Depression in male and female subjects with complex partial seizures. Arch Neurol 49:391–392, 1992

Szatmari P: Some methodologic criteria for studies in developmental neuropsychiatry. Psychiatric Developments 3:153–170, 1985

Temkin O: The Falling Sickness, 2nd Edition. Baltimore, MD, Johns Hopkins University Press, 1979

Thomas P, Zifkin B, Migneco O, et al: Nonconvulsive status epilepticus of frontal origin. Neurology 52:1174–1183, 1999

Tojek TM, Lumley M, Barkley G, et al: Stress and other psychosocial characteristics of patients with psychogenic nonepileptic seizures. Psychosomatics 41:221–226, 2000

Toone BK, Garralda ME, Ron MA: The psychoses of epilepsy and the functional psychoses: a clinical and phenomenological comparison. Br J Psychiatry 141:256–261, 1982

Trimble MR: The relationship between epilepsy and schizophrenia: a biochemical hypothesis. Biol Psychiatry 12:299–304, 1977

Trimble MR: The effects of anticonvulsant drugs on cognitive abilities. Pharmacol Ther 4:677–685, 1979

Trimble MR: Cognitive hazards of seizure disorders. Epilepsia 29 (suppl 1):S19–S24, 1988

Trimble MR, Thompson PJ: Anticonvulsant drugs, cognitive impairment, and behavior. Epilepsia 24 (suppl):S55–S63, 1983

Tucker GJ: Current diagnostic issues in neuropsychiatry, in Neuropsychiatry. Edited by Fogel BS, Schiffer RB. Baltimore, MD, Williams & Wilkins, 1996, pp 1009–1014

Tucker GJ, Price TP, Johnson VB, et al: Phenomenology of temporal lobe dysfunction: a link to atypical psychosis—a series of cases. J Nerv Ment Dis 174:348–356, 1986

Varney NR, Garvey MJ, Cook BL, et al: Identification of treatment-resistant depressives who respond favorably to carbamazepine. Ann Clin Psychiatry 5:117–122, 1993

Victoroff JI, Benson F, Grafton ST, et al: Depression in complex partial seizures. Arch Neurol 51:155–163, 1994

Von Meduna L: Die Konvulsionstherapie der Schizophrenia. Halle, Germany, Marhold, 1937

Waxman SG, Geschwind N: The interictal behavior syndrome of temporal lobe epilepsy. Arch Gen Psychiatry 32:1580–1586, 1975

Weilburg JB, Schacter S, Worth J, et al: EEG abnormalities in patients with atypical panic attacks. J Clin Psychiatry 56:358–362, 1995

Wells C, Duneau GW: Neurology for Psychiatrists. Philadelphia, PA, FA Davis, 1980

Wilensky AJ, Neppe VM: Acute interictal psychoses in epileptic patients (letter). Epilepsia 27:634, 1986

Ziegler R: Epilepsy: individual illness, human prediscontent and family dilemma. Family Relations 31:435–444, 1982

Zimmerman AW: Hormones and epilepsy. Neurol Clin 4:853–861, 1986

Zwil AS, Pelchat RJ: ECT in the treatment of patients with neurological and somatic disease. Int J Psychiatry Med 24:1–29, 1994

# CHAPTER 20

# Neuropsychiatric Aspects of Sleep and Sleep Disorders

Max Hirshkowitz, Ph.D., A.B.S.M.

As a scientific field, sleep was first studied by psychiatrists, neurologists, and psychologists. More recently, sleep research has attracted the attention of internists and pulmonologists. This growing interdisciplinary interest has allowed sleep medicine to emerge as a subspecialty in its own right. Human sleep, however, is a very broad topic. I therefore restrict this chapter's scope to eight main topics, beginning with a general overview and background information concerning the study of human sleep. This is followed by a review of the physiology of normal human sleep that includes a description of the stages of sleep, their characteristics, their correlates, and their pattern. A description of the basic underlying mechanisms that regulate sleep follows, and sleep in patients with psychiatric conditions is considered. Clinical sleep medicine topics begin with an overview of sleep disorder classification systems and continues with characterization of the most common sleep disorders presenting as insomnia, hypersomnia, and parasomnia.

The most fundamental concept for understanding sleep is realizing that sleep is a brain process. Furthermore, it is not one process. There are several sleep states, each having distinctly different neuronal generators, regulatory mechanisms, and electroencephalographic correlates. Moreover, some of the sleep processes involve cortical activation. Thus, at times sleep is active rather than passive (Chase 1972; Kleitman 1972).

When considering basic states of neurologic organization, sleep versus wakefulness usually marks the first conceptual division. Hans Berger (1930), the grandfather of electroencephalography, used his string galvanometer to make the first electroencephalographic recordings during sleep. He described the disappearance of the alpha rhythm when his subject fell asleep. Cessation of alpha rhythm in an individual with closed eyes who is not engaged in mental activity (for example, solving arithmetic equations) is essentially the definition still used today for defining sleep onset.

The first continuous overnight electroencephalographic recordings in humans were published by Loomis et al. (1937). Using the tracings from their giant 8-foot-long drum polygraph, they developed a sleep stage classification system (stages A, B, C, D, and E) and graphically illustrated sleep stages in a manner remarkably similar to that currently used. They defined sleep stages according to sleep electroencephalogram (EEG) frequency bands, including beta activity (>13 Hz), sleep spindles (bursts of 12–14 Hz), alpha rhythm (8–13 Hz, sometimes slower), theta rhythm (4–7 Hz, more common in adolescents than adults), sawtooth theta waves (4–7 Hz, with notched appearance), delta rhythm (<4 Hz), and slow waves (≤2 Hz).

The next major milestone was Eugene Aserinsky's discovery (while a graduate student working with Nathaniel Kleitman) of periodic electro-oculographic activity episodes during sleep. These activity episodes occurred approximately every 90–120 minutes. At first the electro-oculographic activation was thought to be a recording artifact, but continued research verified that actual eye movements were occurring. At first called jerky eye movements (JEMs), the phenomenon was renamed rapid eye movement (REM) sleep, reportedly by William C. Dement (a medical student at that time).

Subsequent studies revealed that individuals awakened from REM sleep reported dreaming on 20 of the 27 instances (Aserinsky and Kleitman 1953).

The discovery of a connection between REM sleep and dreaming generated tremendous excitement in the psychiatric community. Freud had characterized dreams as "the royal road to the unconscious" (Freud 1950). The sleep EEG-electro-oculogram (EOG) recording technique held promise as an objective way to explore the mysteries of the unconscious mind. Hundreds of studies attempted to exploit this paradigm; however, no unified "dream theory" emerged. Many of the concepts forwarded by Freud were verified (for example, daytime residue), whereas others were not. Modern theoretical framework varies widely. The neurophysiologically grounded "activation-synthesis hypothesis" casts dreams as epiphenomena arising from the cortex making its best attempt to interpret random subcortical activation. By contrast, the cognitive theories consider dreaming an extension of daytime thought, albeit governed by a different grammar and looser rules (Foulkes 1982; Hobson and McCarley 1977).

In the late 1950s, Michel Jouvet introduced the concept that REM sleep was a third state of consciousness and not just another component of the basic rest activity cycle (BRAC) (Jouvet et al. 1959). He observed postural changes in the cat associated with different states of sleep, and using electromyographic recordings he found muscle atonia accompanying REM sleep in normal animals. This discovery of "functional paralysis" using electromyographic recording was the final step toward development of what is now standard recording practice. The final transition step that helped launch modern sleep research was the development and publication of *A Manual of Standardized Terminology, Techniques and Scoring System for Sleep Stages of Human Subjects*. This manual was the result of efforts by leading sleep researchers throughout the world. An ad hoc standardization committee was formed, chaired by Allan Rechtschaffen and Anthony Kales (1968), and the stages of sleep were defined. The project's success derives, in no small measure, from the chairmen's insistence on consensus. The R&K system, as it is often called, remains *the system* for recording and classifying sleep stages in humans. It provides a common language for sleep researchers and clinicians.

## Physiology of Normal Human Sleep

### Stages of Sleep

In humans, sleep stages are differentiated on the basis of activity occurring in central (C3 or C4) and occipital (O3 or O4) EEGs, right and left eye EOGs (recorded from the outer canthi), and submental electromyograms (EMGs). Traditional sleep recordings were paper polygraphic tracings usually made at a chart speed of 10 mm/ second. The resulting polysomnogram (PSG) represented each 30 seconds of recording (1 epoch) as one polygraph page. It is for this reason that standard practice was designed to classify each 30-second epoch as either awake or one or another of the stages of sleep. The practice of epoch classification according to sleep stage continues even though computerized polygraph systems allow page resizing and temporal resolution alteration (Rechtschaffen and Kales 1968).

Stage W (also called wakefulness or stage 0), is characterized by an EEG containing predominantly alpha activity and/or low-voltage, mixed-frequency activity. Muscle activity is fairly high, and both rapid and slow eye movements may occur. The sleep-onset epoch is determined when the duration of alpha activity decreases below 50% of an epoch and/or a vertex wave, a K complex, a sleep spindle, or delta activity occurs. The K complex is a high-voltage biphasic slow or sharply contoured wave that begins with a negative component and is followed by a positive component. The sleep spindle is a burst of 11.5–16 Hz waves with a duration greater than 0.5 seconds. If a sleep spindle or K complex occurs and high-amplitude (75 $\mu$V or greater) delta electroencephalographic activity occupies less than 20% of an epoch, Stage II is scored. If there is 20%–50% delta activity, Stage III is designated, and if there is more than 50% delta activity the epoch is classified as sleep Stage IV. Stage I is an intermediate, non-alpha state that has low-voltage, mixed-frequency electroencephalographic activity that is a deltaless, spindleless stage that does not have K complexes. Rapid eye movements and muscle atonia accompanying stage 1 EEG define REM sleep. Sawtooth theta is another common electroencephalographic feature of REM sleep. Table 20–1 shows the electroencephalographic, electro-oculographic, and electromyographic characteristics of the different sleep stages, and Figure 20–1 shows an example of each stage.

Stages I, II, III, and IV are sometimes collectively referred to as non-REM (NREM) sleep. Stages III and IV are often combined and called slow-wave sleep. NREM and REM sleep differ for a wide variety of physiologic measures (Table 20–2).

## Normal Sleep Pattern: Generalizations

In a good sleeper, 5% or less of total time in bed should be spent awake. Sleep onset should be swift (less than 15 minutes) and nocturnal awakenings brief. Under normal

**TABLE 20–1.** Sleep stage electroencephalographic, electro-oculographic, and electromyographic characteristics

| Stage | Electroencephalographic characteristics | EOG | Electromyographic muscle activity |
|-------|------------------------------------------|------|-----------------------------------|
| 1 | Low voltage, mixed frequency | Slow | Decreased from awake |
| 2 | Sleep spindles and K complexes | None | Decreased from awake |
| 3 | Sleep spindles and slow waves | None | Decreased from awake |
| 4 | Mostly slow waves | None | Decreased from awake |
| REM | Low voltage, mixed frequency | Rapid | Nearly absent |

*Note.* EOG = electro-oculogram.

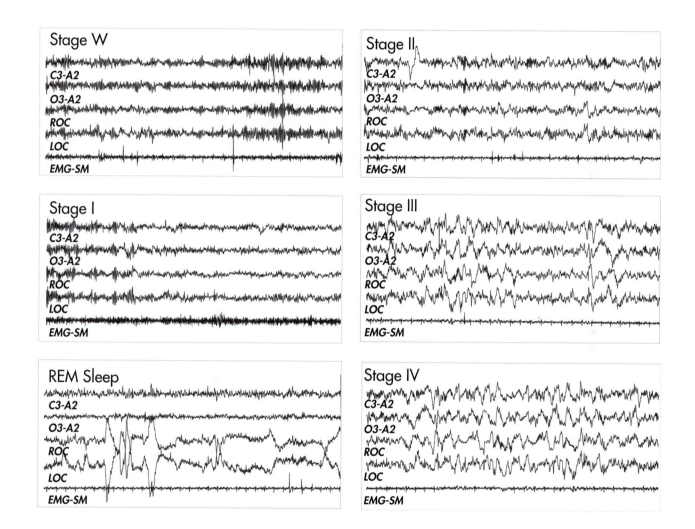

**FIGURE 20–1.** Polysomnographic recordings of the stages of sleep.

circumstances, Stage II sleep comprises approximately half of a night's sleep in a healthy young adult. About one-quarter is REM sleep, and the remainder is distributed between slow-wave sleep and Stage I. Figure 20–2 shows the nightly percentages for each stage. Sleeping for the first time in a new environment (for example, a sleep laboratory) is usually associated with delayed sleep onset, general disruption, and decreased percentages of REM and/or slow-wave sleep. This adaptation-related phe-

nomenon is termed the *first-night effect*. Nonetheless, age-specific normative values have been derived empirically for both first and succeeding nights. Such data are useful for clinical sleep assessments (Hirshkowitz et al. 1992; Roffwarg et al. 1966; R.L. Williams et al. 1974).

Sleep architecture refers to the progression and continuity of sleep through a given night. One does not have single blocks of each sleep stage, but rather there is a repeating cycle of NREM and REM sleep. There are also

**TABLE 20–2.** Comparison of NREM and REM sleep activity

| Physiologic measure | NREM sleep | REM sleep |
|---|---|---|
| Heart and breathing rate | Regular, slow | Variable |
| Oxygen consumption | Low | High |
| Cerebral blood flow | Low | High |
| Penile blood flow (erections) | Absent | Present |
| Vaginal blood flow and uterine activity | Low | Increased |
| Breathing response to $O_2$ | Similar to awake | Similar to awake |
| Breathing response to $CO_2$ | Similar to awake | Depressed |
| Electrodermal activity | Present, active | Absent |
| Temperature regulation | Homeothermic | Poikilothermic |
| Mental activity | Thoughtlike | Dreamlike |

*Note.* REM=rapid eye movement; NREM=non–rapid eye movement.

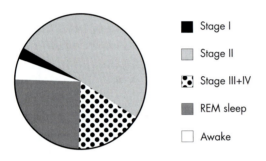

**FIGURE 20–2.** Sleep stage percentages in a healthy young adult.

systematic alterations in cycle properties as the night progresses. Figure 20–3 is a graphical representation of a typical night with normal sleep architecture in a healthy young adult. The following five generalizations can be made about sleep architecture: 1) sleep is entered through NREM sleep; 2) NREM and REM sleep alternate approximately every 90 minutes; 3) slow-wave sleep predominates in the first third of the night; 4) REM sleep predominates in the last third of the night; and 5) REM sleep occurs in 4–6 discrete episodes each night, with episodes generally being longer later in the sleep period.

Aging-related sleep pattern changes occur across the lifespan; the most global is the gradual decline in overall total sleep time. REM sleep percentage (of total sleep time) decreases from birth to adolescence and then stabilizes at 20%–25%; however, some additional decline may occur after age 65. By contrast, slow-wave sleep begins to decline after adolescence and continues that trend with age, disappearing completely in some elderly individuals. Aging, especially after middle age, is associated with greater wakefulness intermixed with sleep (fragmentation) and increased incidence of sleep-related breathing and movement disorders. Figure 20–4 shows changes in sleep stage composition from adulthood to old age.

## Mechanisms Regulating Sleep

There are significant individual differences that produce variation in normal human sleep. Some of us are naturally long sleepers, whereas others are short sleepers. No correlation has been found between intelligence and sleep need; however, personality differences are noted. Short sleepers tend to be more outgoing and extroverted. Long sleepers tend to be more introverted and possibly creative (Hartmann et al. 1972). There are three basic factors involved in the general coordination of sleep and wakefulness: 1) autonomic nervous system balance, 2) homeostatic sleep drive, and 3) circadian rhythms (Hirshkowitz et al. 1997).

### Autonomic Nervous System Balance

In general, sleep depends on decreasing sympathetic activation and increasing parasympathetic balance. Consequently, activities and influences that increase sympathetic outflow have the potential to disturb sleep. It does not matter whether the cause of sympathetic activation is exogenous or endogenous. That is, ingesting stimulants before bedtime (exogenous) and anxious rumination when trying to sleep (endogenous) work via the same autonomic mechanism. Table 20–3 shows some common endogenous and exogenous sources of arousal that can cause sleep disruption. Sometimes an exogenous stimulus can trigger and be amplified by an internal source of arousal. For example, an unfamiliar noise in the house can provoke an anxiety or fear response that will prevent an individual from falling asleep.

Another property of autonomic activation is that it commences rapidly but dissipates slowly. Thus, if one gets "worked up" about an issue right before bedtime, it is unrealistic to expect the arousal to cease immediately

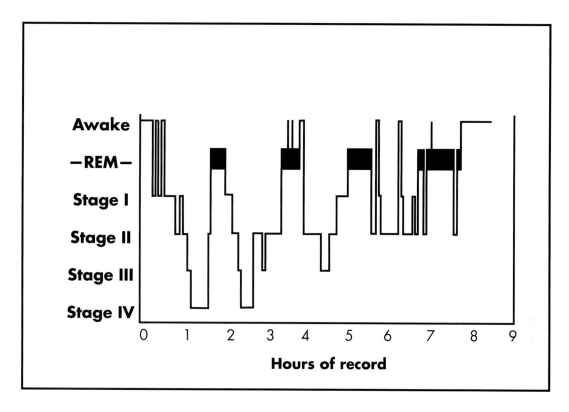

**FIGURE 20–3.** Sleep stage histogram for a healthy young adult.

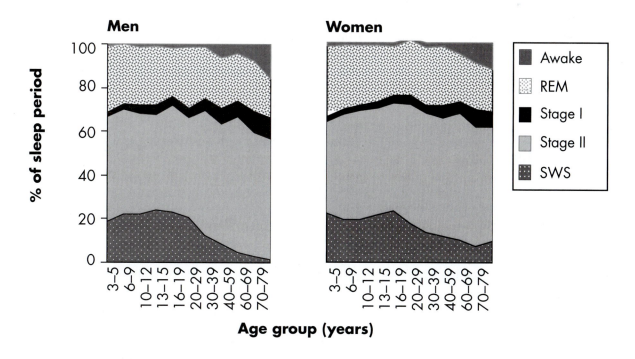

**FIGURE 20–4.** Sleep macroarchitecture (stages) as a function of age. SWS=slow-wave sleep.

**TABLE 20–3.** Autonomic nervous system (ANS) roles in precipitating and perpetuating insomnia

| Exogenous ANS activation sources | Endogenous ANS activation sources | Autonomic conditioning sources |
|---|---|---|
| Caffeine | Worry | Inappropriate associations that promote sleep can be involved in producing sleep-onset association disorder |
| Nicotine | Hunger | |
| Exercise | Fear | Stimulus cues that impede sleep can be involved in producing psychophysiological insomnia |
| Heat | Pain | |
| Unfamiliar sounds | Struggling to sleep | |
| Noise | Sleep performance anxiety | |

because one retires for the night. Rituals are often helpful during the presleep period to promote progressive relaxation and gradual reorientation away from daytime stressors and toward nocturnal tranquility. In children who sleep well, elaborate presleep rituals are common. Such rituals may include bedtime stories, a light snack, teeth brushing, prayers, and having a favorite stuffed animal, toy, pillow, and blanket. The latter act as sleep-onset association stimuli and likely also play a role in respondent conditioning.

Autonomic activities are susceptible to classical conditioning (also known as respondent or Pavlovian conditioning). Pavlov was able to condition a dog to salivate by ringing a bell that had been paired with presenting food (which will automatically produce canine salivation). Conditioning sleep onset, or the autonomic properties surrounding it, is therefore possible. The bed can become a conditioned stimulus for falling asleep, or in some cases it can become a cue for becoming aroused and alert (as in psychophysiological insomnia). Similarly, if a parent becomes the infant's conditioned stimulus for sleep onset, the parent may find himself or herself having to rock the baby back to sleep at any and all times of the night.

## Homeostatic Sleep Drive

In general, the longer an individual remains awake, the sleepier he or she becomes. Such are the dynamics of sleep debt. Homeostatic regulation of sleepiness is similar to that for thirst, hunger, and sex. These motivated states direct behavior to perform actions to reduce drive. The hypothalamus is implicated in all of these physiologic drive states. If one attempts continuous, uninterrupted prolonged wakefulness, sleep eventually becomes irresistible.

Sleep deprivation studies explore changes resulting from stretching the homeostatic mechanism beyond its normal limits. Such studies ultimately hope to gain insight into the role or function of sleep by examining deficits produced by its loss. Sleep deprivation can be total, partial, or stage specific. Sleep loss not only increases sleepiness, it adversely affects a variety of coping mechanisms. Sleep-deprived individuals become irritable and easily frustrated. As sleep deprivation continues, attention becomes impaired and performance lapses occur on tasks that challenge the ability to remain vigilant. Psychomotor impairment may occur, and mood suffers. Longer-term sleep deprivation can, in some individuals, produce hallucinations and on rare occasions seizures. Psychological stability and affect diminish, and there may be episodes of paranoia, disorientation, and mood swings. After 72 hours of total sleep deprivation, executive function may deteriorate. Similar failure in "frontal lobe" abilities is found in patients whose sleep is disturbed long-term by sleep-disordered breathing. Because sleep deprivation is stressful, catecholamine turnover increases and cortisol concentration rises. The drive to sleep increases but may be self-reported as fatigue, tiredness, exhaustion, or weariness. Moreover, some individuals and most children lose their impulse control and suffer attention deficits when sleepy (Binks et al. 1999; Dinges 1992; Horne 1988).

However, in your own experience you may have noticed that during an extended wakeful vigil, sleepiness waxes and wanes. Sometimes after staying up all night, the chronobiological self-abuser will note a surge of energy at daybreak. This indicates the presence of another sleep-wake mechanism: the circadian rhythm.

## Circadian Rhythms

An approximate daylong or 24-hour rhythm is called a circadian rhythm (from the Latin *circa*, around + *dias*, day). There are many circadian rhythms; however, the one that regulates the sleep-wake cycle is superimposed on the homeostatic mechanisms. The biological clock believed to regulate the sleep-wake circadian rhythm is located in the suprachiasmatic nucleus (SCN). SCN firing patterns oscillate in concert and persist even in isole preparations (in vitro). Because the daily core body temperature cycle is entrained to this sleep-wake oscillator, the temperature cycle is commonly used as a marker of circadian rhythm. In general, 1) when temperature is at its peak, there is maximum alertness; 2) when temperature starts to fall, drowsiness ensues; 3) when temperature reaches nadir, sleepiness can be overwhelming; 4) as temperature starts to rise, sleepiness decreases and alertness increases; and 5) when temperature reaches maximal level, the cycle begins again. Lack of synchrony between scheduled bedtime and the sleepiness biological rhythm could mean less than optimal sleep and/or less than optimal daytime alertness (some degree of daytime drowsiness) (Aschoff 1965; Borbely and Achermann 1992; Moore-Ede 1982).

## Sleep in Patients With Psychiatric Conditions

Thirty-five percent of patients seen in sleep disorders centers with a chief complaint of insomnia had a psychiatric disorder (Coleman et al. 1982). Half of these patients had a major depressive disorder (MDD). Moreover, 90% of patients with MDD have insomnia (Reynolds and Kupfer 1987). Sleep problems are a risk factor (or marker) for worsening or recurrence of depression episodes. Sleep disturbances identified using electroencephalographic criteria in MDD include 1) generalized sleep disturbance (increase sleep latency, increased nocturnal awakenings, and early-morning awakenings), 2) slow-wave sleep decrease in the first NREM-REM cycle with delta activity shifts to the second NREM period, 3) latency to REM sleep shortened, 4) REM sleep occurring earlier in the night, and 5) REM density increase (especially early in the night). Selective REM sleep deprivation alleviates depression. Furthermore, this antidepressant action can persist for several days or more. Interestingly, most antidepressant medications suppress REM sleep (including selective serotonin reuptake inhibitors, tricyclic antidepressants, and monoamine oxidase inhibitors). Arecoline (a cholinergic agonist) infusion will induce REM sleep in depressed patients, and scopolamine withdrawal mimics depression in normal subjects (including electroencephalographic sleep changes). These data support the cholinergic-aminergic imbalance theory of major depression. Although it still holds that any drug capable of suppressing REM sleep has potential antidepressant properties, a couple of newer antidepressants do not suppress REM sleep (i.e., bupropion and nefazodone). Thus, a piece is missing from the theory. Restated, REM suppression is sufficient but not necessary for antidepressant action (Benca et al. 1992; Ford

and Kamerow 1989; Hirshkowitz, in press; Vogel et al. 1980).

Patients with *mania* and *hypomania* seldom complain of sleep problems even though they sleep only a short time (2–4 hours per night), have very prolonged latency to sleep, and sometimes have reduced slow-wave sleep. Patients with *schizophrenia* have no consistent electroencephalographic sleep changes except that they do not have REM sleep rebound in response to REM sleep deprivation. The only other consistent finding is that patients with schizophrenia frequently deny having slept even though sleep appears normal on the EEG-EOG-EMG. Patients with *anxiety* and *personality* disorders often have sleep-onset and sleep-maintenance insomnia (Culebras 1996; Joseph et al. 1989; Zarcone 1989).

## Sleep Disorders Overview and Classification Systems

The seriousness of sleep disorders and their contribution to diminished quality of life are poorly recognized. Although individuals afflicted with sleep problems may desperately seek help, often they are met with indifference on the part of health care providers. Medical education for sleep disorders is inadequate, amounting usually to an hour or two in the curriculum. This level of ignorance—coupled with an attitude jaded by a sleepless, overworked internship or residency—leaves many practitioners with little empathy for those with sleep disorders. It is easy to forget that sleep disorders can be life threatening either directly (e.g., obstructive sleep apnea) or indirectly as a result of sleep-related accidents.

Several classification systems have been developed to categorize sleep disorders, including the International Classification of Diseases (ICD), the Diagnostic and Statistical Manual of Mental Disorders (DSM), and the International Classification of Sleep Disorders (ICSD). The most complete nosology is ICSD, which details 84 individual sleep disorders and is organized into four sections: dyssomnias, parasomnias, sleep disorders associated with medical and psychiatric disorders, and proposed sleep disorders. Table 20–4 outlines the ICSD (American Sleep Disorders Association 1997).

For instructional purposes, however, it is useful to consider sleep disorders categorized according to presenting complaint; that is, insomnia (disorders of initiating or maintaining sleep), hypersomnia (disorders of excessive sleepiness), and parasomnias (disorders of arousal [things that go bump in the night]). The national

**TABLE 20–4.** International Classification of Sleep Disorders

1. **Dyssomnias**
A. Intrinsic Sleep Disorders
   307.42-0 Psychophysiological Insomnia
   307.49-1 Sleep State Misperception
   780.52-7 Idiopathic Insomnia
   347 Narcolepsy
   780.54-2 Recurrent Hypersomnia
   780.54-8 Posttraumatic Hypersomnia
   780.54-7 Idiopathic Hypersomnia
   780.53-0 Obstructive Sleep Apnea Syndrome
   780.51-0 Central Sleep Apnea Syndrome
   780.51-1 Central Alveolar Hypoventilation Syndrome
   780.52-4 Periodic Limb Movement Disorder
   780.52-5 Restless Legs Syndrome
   780.52-9 Intrinsic Sleep Disorders NOS
B. Extrinsic Sleep Disorders
   307.41-1 Inadequate Sleep Hygiene
   780.52-6 Environmental Sleep Disorder
   289.0 Altitude Insomnia
   307.41-0 Adjustment Sleep Disorder
   307.49-4 Insufficient Sleep Syndrome
   307.42-4 Limit-Setting Sleep Disorder
   307.42-5 Sleep-Onset Association Disorder
   780.52-2 Food Allergy Insomnia
   780.52-8 Nocturnal Eating (Drinking) Syndrome
   780.52-0 Hypnotic-Dependent Sleep Disorder
   780.52.1 Stimulant-Dependent Sleep Disorder
   780.52-3 Alcohol-Dependent Sleep Disorder
   780.54-6 Toxin-Induced Sleep Disorder
   780.52-9 Extrinsic Sleep Disorder NOS
C. Circadian Rhythm Sleep Disorders
   307.45-0 Time-Zone Change (Jet-Lag) Syndrome
   307.45-1 Shift Work Sleep Disorder
   307.45-3 Irregular Sleep-Wake Pattern
   780.55-0 Delayed Sleep Phase Syndrome
   780.55-1 Advanced Sleep Phase Syndrome
   780.55-2 Non–24 Hour Sleep-Wake Disorder
   780.55-9 Circadian Rhythm Sleep Disorder NOS
2. **Parasomnias**
A. Arousal Disorders
   307.46-2 Confusional Arousals
   307.46-0 Sleepwalking
   307.46-1 Sleep Terrors
B. Sleep-Wake Transition Disorders
   307.3 Rhythmic Movement Disorder
   307.47-2 Sleep Starts
   307.47-3 Sleep Talking
   729.82 Nocturnal Leg Cramps
C. Parasomnias Usually Associated With REM Sleep
   307.47-0 Nightmares
   780.56-2 Sleep Paralysis

   780.56-3 Impaired Sleep-Related Penile Erections
   780.56-4 Sleep-Related Painful Erections
   780.56-8 REM Sleep-Related Sinus Arrest
   780.59-0 REM Sleep Behavior Disorder
D. Other Parasomnias
   306.8 Sleep Bruxism
   780.56-0 Sleep Enuresis
   780.56-6 Sleep-Related Abnormal Swallowing Syndrome
   780.59-1 Nocturnal Paroxysmal Dystonia
   780.59-3 Sudden Unexplained Nocturnal Death Syndrome
   780.53-1 Primary Snoring
   770.80 Infant Sleep Apnea
   770.81 Congenital Central Hypoventilation Syndrome
   798.0 Sudden Infant Death Syndrome
   780.59-5 Benign Neonatal Sleep Myoclonus
   780.59-9 Other Parasomnia NOS
3. **Sleep Disorders Associated With Medical/Psychiatric Disorders**
A. Associated With Mental Disorders
   292–299 Psychoses
   296–301 Mood Disorders
   300 Anxiety Disorders
   300 Panic Disorder
   303 Alcoholism
B. Associated With Neurological Disorders
   330-337 Cerebral Degenerative Disorders
   331 Dementia
   332–333 Parkinsonism
   337.9 Fatal Familial Insomnia
   345 Sleep-Related Epilepsy
   345.8 Electrical Status Epilepticus of Sleep
   346 Sleep-Related Headaches
C. Associated With Other Medical Disorders
   086 Sleeping Sickness
   411–414 Nocturnal Cardiac Ischemia
   490–494 Chronic Obstructive Pulmonary Disease
   493 Sleep-Related Asthma
   530.1 Sleep-Related Gastroesophageal Reflux
   531–534 Peptic Ulcer Disease
   729.1 Fibrositis Syndrome
4. **Proposed Sleep Disorders**
   307.49-0 Short Sleeper
   307.49-2 Long Sleeper
   307.47-1 Subwakefulness Syndrome
   780.59-7 Fragmentary Myoclonus
   780.8 Sleep Hyperhidrosis
   780.54-3 Menstrual-Associated Sleep Disorder
   780.59-6 Pregnancy-Associated Sleep Disorder
   307.47-4 Terrifying Hypnagogic Hallucinations
   780.53-2 Sleep-Related Neurogenic Tachypnea
   780.59-4 Sleep-Related Laryngospasm
   307.42-1 Sleep Choking Syndrome

*Source.* Reprinted from American Sleep Disorders Association: *The International Classification of Sleep Disorders, Revised: Diagnostic and Coding Manual.* American Sleep Disorders Association, Rochester, MN, 1997. Used with permission.

cooperative study (Coleman et al. 1982) of patients ($N = 5,000$) seen in accredited sleep disorders centers found that 31% of patients had insomnias, 51% had hypersomnias, and 15% had parasomnias. In addition, 3% of patients had disorders of the sleep-wake schedule (circadian dysrhythmia).

## Insomnia

According to DSM-IV (American Psychiatric Association 1994), insomnia is difficulty initiating sleep or maintaining sleep, or experiencing nonrestorative sleep for one month or more. The insomnia or resulting sleepiness must cause clinically significant impairment or distress. To be considered primary insomnia, the etiology of the insomnia must not be rooted in psychiatric conditions, parasomnias, substance use or abuse, sleep-disordered breathing, or circadian rhythm disorders. However, insomnia usually has multiple and overlapping causes, and ruling in the assorted contributors is more helpful clinically for devising a treatment plan than is ruling out factors for the sake of diagnostic purity.

Essentially, insomnia is a symptom. It is neither a disease nor a specific condition. Insomnia can accompany a wide variety of sleep, medical, and psychiatric disorders. When possible, the goal is to treat the cause(s); however, in some cases, symptomatic relief is desirable while therapeutic modalities progress. Descriptively, insomnia is sometimes categorized in terms of how it affects sleep (e.g., sleep-onset insomnia, sleep maintenance insomnia, or early morning awakening). It is also classified according to its duration (e.g., transient, short-term, and long-term). Approximately a third of the American population has several serious bouts of insomnia yearly, and in 9% insomnia is a chronic condition. Individuals with chronic insomnia have more than twice as many motor vehicle accidents as the general population, but only 5% of those with chronic insomnia will see a health care provider to seek help for sleeplessness. Nonetheless, more than 40% of individuals with chronic insomnia will self-medicate with over-the-counter drugs, alcohol, or both (Gallup Organization 1991; Mellinger et al. 1985).

Spielman et al. (1987a) conceptualized insomnia in terms of the dynamic model depicted in Figure 20–5. In this model, an individual's generalized threshold for sleeplessness acts in conjunction with three factors: 1) predisposition, 2) precipitating event, and 3) perpetuating factors. In the preclinical state, every person falls within some range from being a very *sound sleeper* to a *light sleeper*. A light sleeper may have a lower sleeplessness threshold such that even minor changes in routine or mildly disquieting daytime events will trigger insomnia. The sound sleeper may be conceptualized as having a high threshold for sleeplessness and thus has no difficulty sleeping even in novel or environmentally adverse conditions. Nonetheless, a precipitating factor may usher in an episode of insomnia regardless of the individual trait disposition for sound or light sleep. Precipitating factors can vary widely. Examples include job stress, relocation, anxiety about taking an examination, undergoing a tax audit, being sued, development of a medical condition, change in medication, separation or divorce, or grief reaction. Over time, the impact of most of these factors will wane and one would expect the sleeplessness to follow suit; however, the insomnia often persists. The persistence of sleeplessness, notwithstanding diminution of the influence of the original causes (for example, having taken the examination and passed), is considered to result from perpetuating factors. Examples of perpetuating factors are ongoing use of alcohol as a sleep aid, developing habits that are inconsistent with good quality sleep (e.g., watching television in bed), or having a grief reaction evolve into depression. In some cases, the bed and bedroom become conditioned stimuli for wakefulness, and psychophysiological insomnia is the perpetuating factor.

According to the multicenter cooperative study (Coleman et al. 1982), the most common types of insomnia (primary diagnosis) in patients seen at sleep disorders centers were psychiatric disorders, psychophysiological insomnia, drug and alcohol dependence, periodic limb movement disorder or restless legs syndrome, sleep-state misperception, and sleep-disordered breathing (Figure 20–6A). In the following paragraphs, each of these conditions is reviewed along with several other important etiologies for insomnia that are less frequently seen at sleep centers; that is, inadequate sleep hygiene, idiopathic insomnia, and circadian rhythm dyssomnia.

## Psychophysiological Insomnia

Psychophysiological insomnia often occurs in combination with stress and anxiety disorders, delayed sleep phase syndrome, and hypnotic drug use and withdrawal. The patient with psychophysiological insomnia has developed a conditioned arousal associated with the thought of sleeping. Objects related to sleep (e.g., the bed, the bedroom) likewise have become conditioned stimuli that evoke insomnia. Daytime adaptation is usually good. Work and relationships are satisfying; however, there can be extreme tiredness and the individual can become desperate. By contrast, daytime adaptation in patients with psychiatrically related insomnia is often impaired. Other

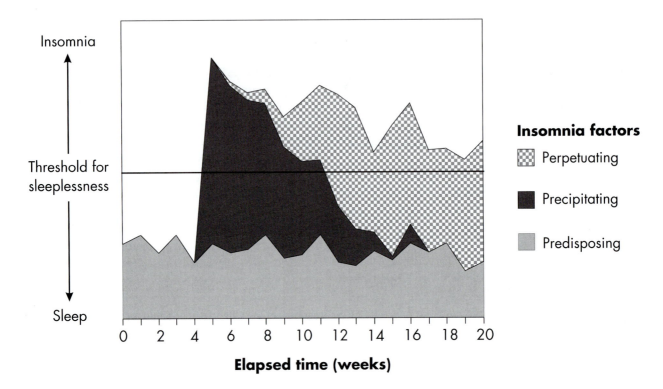

**FIGURE 20–5.** Spielman's dynamic model of insomnia.
*Source.* Adapted from Spiegelman et al. 1987a.

features of psychophysiological insomnia include 1) excessive worry about not being able to sleep, 2) trying too hard to sleep, 3) rumination, inability to clear one's mind while trying to sleep, 4) increased muscle tension when getting into bed, 5) other somatic manifestations of anxiety, 6) ability to fall asleep when not trying to (e.g., while watching television), and 7) sleeping better away from one's own bedroom (including in the sleep laboratory). In one sense, the individual has developed a performance anxiety concerning the ability to sleep, and autonomic nervous system conditioning reinforces the situation. Stimulus control therapy is well suited for treating psychophysiological insomnia (see Behavioral Treatments, below) (American Sleep Disorders Association 1997; Hauri and Fisher 1986).

## Drug and Alcohol Dependence

Use of alcohol and hypnotic drugs initially promotes sleep onset because of the sedating properties of these substances. The problem is that the sleep, although apparently greater in quantity, is poorer in quality. Alcohol may relax a tense person and thereby decrease his or her latency to sleep. Sleep later in the night, however, is fragmented by arousals. As tolerance develops to the

alcohol, greater amounts are needed to sustain the effects. Furthermore, during withdrawal or after tolerance has developed, the sleep disturbance can rebound to a level more severe than the initial problem. If sleep is considered a behavior, and this behavior is dependent on the use of alcohol, then by definition this is a form of alcoholism. Interestingly, one of the earliest effective hypnotic drugs was chloral hydrate, which may be considered essentially alcohol in pill form (because it is metabolized to alcohol).

Barbiturates and, later, benzodiazepines represent the most commonly used prescription medications for insomnia during the twentieth century. Both have potential for abuse and dependency, especially those producing euphoria. Except in rare cases, sedative-hypnotic medicines are not recommended for long-term use. Benzodiazepines that alter sleep architecture and produce rebound insomnia on withdrawal tend to be habit-forming and can act as a perpetuating factor for insomnia. Abnormally increased electroencephalographic beta and sleep spindle activity commonly develop with long-term or high-dose benzodiazepine ingestion (for further discussion, see Drug Treatment, below) (American Sleep Disorders Association 1997; Hirshkowitz, in press).

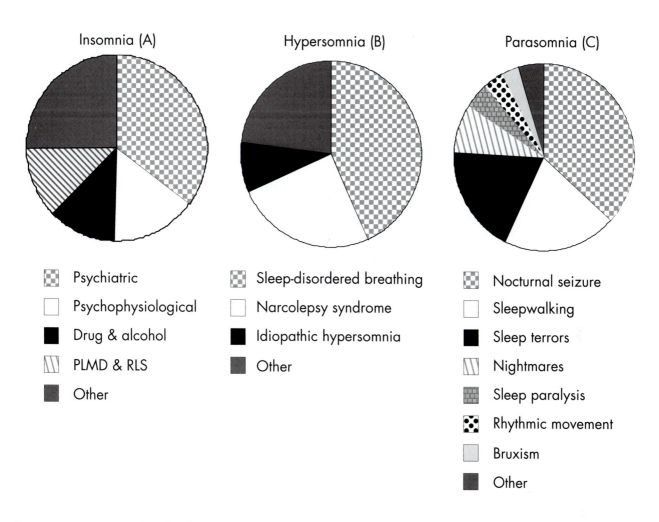

**FIGURE 20–6.** Proportions for the most common insomnias (A), hypersomnias (B), and parasomnias (C) seen in sleep disorders centers. PLMD=periodic limb movement disorder; RLS=restless legs syndrome.
*Source.* Adapted from Coleman et al. 1982.

## Restless Legs Syndrome and Periodic Limb Movement Disorder

Restless legs syndrome is characterized by the irresistible urge to move the legs when at rest or while trying to fall asleep. Patients often report crawling feelings in their legs. Moving the legs or walking around helps alleviate the discomfort. Thus, as the individual is lying in bed and relaxing, he or she is disturbed by these sensations. The individual then moves the legs and again tries to fall asleep. This cycle sometimes continues for hours and results in profound insomnia.

Another type of leg movement disorder associated with insomnia is periodic limb movement disorder (PLMD) (previously called nocturnal myoclonus). PLMD involves brief, stereotypic, repetitive, nonepileptiform movements of the limbs, usually the legs. It occurs primarily in NREM sleep and involves an extension of the big toe. Partial flexion of the ankle, knee, and hip may also occur. These movements range from 0.5 to 5 seconds in duration and occur every 20–40 seconds. The leg movements are frequently associated with brief arousals from sleep and as a result can (but do not always) disturb sleep architecture. The prevalence of PLMD increases with age and can occur in association with folate deficiency, renal disease, anemia, and the use of antidepressants (American Sleep Disorders Association 1997; Ekbom 1960; Lugaresi et al. 1986; Walters 1995; Walters et al. 1991).

## Sleep-State Misperception

Most individuals are under the mistaken impression that mental activity necessarily ceases during sleep. One might arrive at this conclusion because of the inability to recall anything between retiring to bed and arising in the morning. However, this confuses the amnesic property of sleep with lack of mentation. Most people readily acknowledge dreaming and understand that dreams constitute mental activity. Nonetheless, under normal circumstances sleep and unconsciousness are coupled; however, they can dissociate. Anxiety can provoke sleep-state misperception, and ruminative worry about not sleeping adds fuel to the fire. Thus, if one lies in bed attempting to sleep and has ruminative thoughts, it is perceived as insomnia even if brain physiology indicates sleep (American Sleep Disorders Association 1997; Carskadon et al. 1976).

This type of insomnia has previously been called pseudoinsomnia or insomnia without objective findings. Both of these appellations imply invalidation of the complaint and place the clinician at odds with the patient. Often a psychoeducational approach that attempts to explain the dissociability between physiological brain correlates of sleep and the perception of sleep is more helpful. Furthermore, the ruminations (which seem so urgent at the time but lose their importance or may not even be remembered in the morning) may actually be a useful marker of sleep onset. If individuals can interpret the rumination as an indicator that they *are* asleep and it belays their worrying about not being able to sleep, the sleep-state misperception often diminishes or disappears.

## Sleep-Disordered Breathing

Sleep-related breathing disorders are more commonly associated with excessive daytime sleepiness than with insomnia. In some individuals, particularly if the breathing disorder is mild or at an early stage of development, the predominant complaint will be insomnia. Similarly, in obstructive forms of sleep apnea, sleep disruption results from awakenings that return ventilation to voluntary control and thus allow breathing to resume. These recurrent awakenings produce (sometimes severe) sleep maintenance insomnia. Further details of sleep-disordered breathing follows in discussion of conditions associated with hypersomnolence.

## Idiopathic Insomnia

Persons with idiopathic insomnia have a lifelong inability to obtain adequate sleep. The insomnia must predate any psychiatric condition, and other etiologies must be ruled out or treated, including psychophysiological insomnia, environmental sleep disturbances, and practices that would constitute poor sleep hygiene. If the insomnia persists, then it is assumed that there is a defect in the neurological mechanisms that govern the sleep-wake system. That is, the sleep homeostatic process is dysfunctional. Sleep restriction therapy may provide some benefit and

will also give the clinician a clue to the limits of the patient's homeostatic process. Sleep restriction is a technique by which homeostatic drive is maximized by sleep schedule compression (see Behavioral Treatments, below). Unfortunately, patients with idiopathic insomnia never slept well and will likely never have normal sleep. Although it is controversial, this group may require long-term pharmacotherapeutic intervention.

## Circadian Rhythm Dyssomnias

In an optimal schedule, hours in bed must coincide with the sleepy phase of the circadian cycle. *Advanced sleep phase* is when the circadian rhythm cycle is shifted earlier. Therefore, the sleepiness cycle is advanced with respect to clock time. Individuals with advanced sleep phase are drowsy in the evening, want to retire to bed earlier, awaken earlier, and are more alert in the early morning. Individuals with this pattern of advanced sleep phase are sometimes called "larks" (sometimes called "surgeons" in the medical center). By contrast, the biological clock may run slow or be shifted later than the desired schedule. This produces a *phase delay* in the sleepiness-alertness cycle. Individuals with delayed sleep phase are more alert in the evening and early nighttime, stay up later, and are more tired in the morning. These individuals are referred to as "owls" (Moore-Ede et al. 1982; Zammit 1997).

Under the extreme condition of time isolation, most adults exhibit features of delayed sleep phase. In the absence of time cues, the sleep-wake cycle will drift later and later on each successive day. Furthermore, there can be a dissociation of the sleep-wake and temperature rhythms. Under normal circumstances, however, the biological clock is reset each day by bright light, social cues, stimulants, and activity. In cases when these factors are unable to reentrain the circadian rhythm, the advanced sleep phase and delayed sleep phase disorders of the sleep-wake cycle may occur associated with complaints of early morning awakening insomnia and sleep-onset insomnia, respectively. In the past, chronotherapy was used to reentrain the circadian rhythm; however, it has largely been replaced by bright light therapy (see Behavioral Treatments, below) (Czeisler et al. 1989).

## Insomnia Treatment Options

### Behavioral Treatments

Behavioral treatments for insomnia include universal sleep hygiene, relaxation training, stimulus control therapy, sleep restriction therapy, and bright light therapy.

**Universal sleep hygiene.**   Many individuals with insomnia, regardless of the underlying cause, make things worse with poor sleep hygiene. Essentially, they have developed bad habits with respect to sleep. These habits may operate through autonomic, homeostatic, or circadian mechanisms. When these habits are a primary etiology, inadequate sleep hygiene can be diagnosed. Universal sleep hygiene essentially involves recommending that the individual promote sleep-enhancing habits and avoid sleep-destroying behaviors. Table 20–5 lists some recommendations to improve sleep hygiene. In applying this approach, the clinician should review the patient's day-to-day habits and obtain an appreciation of the sleep environment. From the assortment of potential sleep-impeding activities, the clinician must judiciously choose one or two items (three at the most) to initially address. The reason for limiting the scope is that most of these directives amount to asking the patient to change an element of his or her lifestyle. Such changes are difficult at best, and therapy that overloads a person is doomed to fail. Continued follow-up with monitoring progress is essential. As goals are achieved, additional sleep hygiene issues can be addressed. Often a few simple alterations can produce dramatic results. In addition, improving sleep hygiene usually enhances sleep even when the etiology of the insomnia is clearly psychiatric or physical. Presumably, adopting good sleep hygienic practices optimizes sleep, and for most people there is room for improvement (Lacks and Rotert 1986; Morgan and Closs 1999b).

**Relaxation training.**   This type of behavioral therapy takes many forms, including progressive relaxation, breathing exercises (or yoga), biofeedback, and guided visualization. The goal of relaxation training is twofold. Primarily, it provides a systematic technique for reducing tension and stress. Thus, it acts through the autonomic mechanisms that can enhance or impede sleep. Additionally, however, it provides a distraction such that the individual thinks about something other than his or her inability to sleep. The therapy must be properly performed and overlearned before it is applied. Many individuals immediately reject relaxation therapy when it is suggested on the basis that they have tried it and it did not work. Questioning typically reveals that the patient purchased a self-help tape and listened to it when in bed unable to sleep. Such an approach indeed does not work. Whatever the approach, be it biofeedback or listening to an instructional tape, the technique must first be mastered. Practicing during the daytime, sometimes for weeks, is needed so that the individual can immediately move through the technique and become relaxed. Trying to learn a method while struggling to sleep must be

**TABLE 20–5.**   Sleep hygiene and affected systems

| Presumed mechanism of action | Sleep hygiene recommendation |
| --- | --- |
| Strengthens circadian rhythm | Maintain a regular sleep-wake schedule |
| | Get a steady daily amount of exercise |
| Avoids endogenous ANS activation | Do not try to fall asleep, let sleep come |
| | A light snack before bedtime may be helpful |
| Avoids exogenous ANS activation | Insulate the bedroom against loud noises |
| | Make sure bedroom is not excessively warm |
| | Do not eat a heavy meal close to bedtime |
| | Avoid caffeine in the evening |
| | Quit smoking or avoid smoking near bedtime |
| Avoids developing dependence | Avoid ongoing use of sleeping pills as a sleep aid |
| | Avoid ongoing use of alcohol as a sleep aid |

*Note.*   ANS = autonomic nervous system.

avoided because it creates an adverse conditioning paradigm. Moreover, if the person starts to fall asleep, he or she will arouse himself or herself to finish the exercise. The clinician should monitor the progress during training to ensure that the technique is performed correctly and to judge when it is time for it to be applied in the sleepless bed. Finally, relaxation techniques are readily combined with other behavioral therapies (Espie et al. 1989; Lichstein and Riedel 1994).

**Stimulus control therapy.**   For individuals with psychophysiological insomnia, stimulus control directly addresses the underlying autonomic conditioning. Secondarily it arranges homeostatic and circadian factors so that they will work in concert with attempts to recondition sleep onset. Stimulus control therapy directives attempt to enhance stimulus cues for sleeping and diminish bedroom stimulus associations with sleeplessness. The instructions are simple; however, following them consistently and keeping sleep diaries are the keys to success. The first rule is to go to bed only when sleepy. Second, use the bed only for sleeping. That is, in bed one should not eat, read, talk on the telephone, watch television, do paperwork, write letters, exercise, argue with one's spouse, or worry about things that happened in the past or are expected to happen in the future. If the indi-

**TABLE 20–6.**    Medications used to treat periodic limb movement disorder and restless legs syndrome

| Medication class | Drug name | Cautionary notes |
|---|---|---|
| Dopaminergic | Carbidopa-levodopa<br>Bromocriptine<br>Pergolide<br>Pramipexole<br>Ropinirole | Drugs can have blood pressure effects and produce rebound movement disorders. Contraindicated in patients taking monoamine oxidase inhibitors, with history of melanoma, and with narrow-angle glaucoma. |
| Benzodiazepine | Clonazepam<br>Triazolam<br>Temazepam | Daytime sedation, tolerance, and alcohol interaction. |
| Narcotic | Propoxyphene<br>Codeine<br>Methadone<br>Oxycodone<br>Hydrocodone | Drugs have addiction liability and a high abuse potential. |
| Other | Selegiline<br>Carbamazepine<br>Gabapentin | Efficacy not determined. |

vidual is unable to sleep, rule three instructs him or her to get up, go to another room, and do something nonarousing until he or she becomes sleepy. One should not watch the clock; in fact, the clock should be hidden from view so that when nocturnal arousals occur the time is not known. Nonetheless, if one feels that he or she has been unable to sleep for more than a few minutes, getting out of bed avoids increasing frustration with the inability to sleep. Ultimately, the goal is to associate the bed and bedroom with rapid sleep onset. Rule three should be repeated as often as needed. A diary should be kept indicating how many times getting out of bed was necessary. This information can be correlated with specific daytime events to promote insight into the precipitating factors for the individual's insomnia. In addition, it will serve as a memory aid because results may not be seen for the first few weeks or month. Having a record can show that bouts of insomnia are diminishing in both frequency and severity. This provides reinforcement and hope when a sudden sleeplessness recurrence prompts a patient to become discouraged and wants to try something else. The final stimulus control therapy instructions address circadian and homeostatic factors to increase sleep pressure. Patients are instructed to awaken at the same time every morning, regardless of bedtime, total sleep time, or day of the week, and to totally avoid napping (Bootzin 1972, 1977).

**Sleep restriction therapy.**    Sleep restriction therapy is designed to enhance sleep through the homeostatic mechanism. In cases in which the patient spends a diminished percentage of his or her time in bed actually sleeping, sleep restriction therapy attempts to compress the sleep episode and enhance sleep drive. The initial step is to have a patient keep a diary of bedtimes, arising times, and the amount of time spent actually sleeping. From this, the total sleep time can be estimated. Sometimes, patients will spend an inordinate amount of time in bed in an attempt to increase their sleep time, only to find their sleep becoming more and more fragmented. I have seen patients who spend 11 hours in bed to attain a reported 6 hours of sleep. The second step in sleep restriction therapy is to compress the sleep schedule to the reported sleep time. Thus, in a patient reporting 6 hours of sleep in an 11-hour total bedtime, I set arising time at 6 hours after retiring time. It should be noted that restricting bedtime schedule to less than four hours per night is not advised. In addition, patients must be advised that they will likely be very sleepy the next day and must exercise extreme care, especially when performing potentially dangerous actions (e.g., driving). Sleep at other times during the day must be avoided, except in elderly persons, who may take a 30-minute nap. Each night, the amount of time spent asleep is reported and the clinician calculates sleep efficiency (the ratio of total sleep time to total bed time). If the patient attains a five-night moving average sleep efficiency of 0.85 or greater, time in bed is increased by 15 minutes (some clinicians use a three-night average). In this manner, time awake in bed is controlled while time asleep gradually and steadily increases. Moreover, when the sleep efficiency plateaus, the clinician has an empirical estimate of the patient's homeostatic drive limit and can better judge if idiopathic insomnia is present. Nonetheless, greater sleep consolidation is achieved and the patient spends less time lying in bed becoming frustrated by his or her inability to sleep (Morin et al. 1994; Spielman et al. 1987b).

**Bright light therapy.** Bright light appears to be the critical factor in controlling the biological clock. With precise timing of bright light exposure, the biological clock may be phase advanced, phase delayed, or even stopped and reset. The use of bright light exposure to overcome desynchrony between environmental and biological clocks produced by rapid time zone change (jet lag), shift work, and space travel is an exciting frontier in sleep research. In general, bright light in the evening will delay the sleep phase, and bright light in the morning will advance the sleep phase. Thus, the phase-delayed "owl" who stays up surfing the Internet until 2:00 A.M. with his or her face less than a meter from a 19-inch video monitor is probably further phase delaying the sleep-wake cycle. What the phase-delaying "owl" needs to do is avoid bright light in the evening and replace it with bright light in the early morning (Czeisler et al. 1989; Zammit 1997).

## Drug Treatments

Specific drug therapies have been applied for periodic limb movement disorder and restless legs syndrome. Table 20–6 lists medications used in the different compound classes. Currently, the most popular pharmacotherapy is with the dopaminergic agents carbidopa-levodopa, pramipexole, and ropinirole. However, clonazepam and narcotics are in common use and are quite effective (Chockroverty 2000).

It should go without saying that antidepressants are indicated if depression is comorbid. Most antidepressants, however, alter sleep architecture and exacerbate the leg movement disorders. Tricyclic antidepressants and selective serotonin reuptake inhibitors suppress REM sleep (especially clomipramine and amitriptyline). Amitriptyline, doxepin, and trazodone have strong sedative properties. Most tricyclics increase slow-wave sleep, whereas serotonin reuptake inhibitors generally decrease or do not change slow-wave activity. Monoamine oxidase inhibitors are powerful REM-sleep suppressors and also diminish slow-wave sleep. By contrast, nefazodone and bupropion are not associated with decreased REM sleep (Hirshkowitz, in press).

The more general, nonspecific, drug-therapy approach to insomnia involves using sedative-hypnotic medications. The profile for an ideal hypnotic is shown in Table 20–7. Sleep-promoting substances have been used since antiquity (e.g., opium and alcohol), but in the 1860s chloral hydrate was formulated as a sleeping pill. In essence it represented alcohol in pill form, and it

**TABLE 20–7.** Profile for an ideal hypnotic

| Desired effect | Parameter |
| --- | --- |
| Increase | Sleep efficiency |
| | Total sleep time |
| Decrease | Latency to sleep onset |
| | Wake after sleep onset time |
| | Number of awakenings |
| Remain unchanged | Sleep macroarchitecture (stages) |
| | Sleep microarchitecture |
| Avoid producing | Carryover—hangover |
| | Early morning rebound insomnia |
| | Withdrawal rebound insomnia |
| | Psychomotor impairment |
| | Cognitive impairment |
| | Dependency |

gained widespread acceptance. At the turn of the last century, barbiturates became available. As strong partial γ-aminobutyric acid (GABA) agonists, barbiturates were very effective at producing sedation and immediately became popular, notwithstanding their toxic liability. Most of the barbiturates have a large REM sleep suppression effect and a smaller slow-wave sleep suppression effect. Sleep latency decreases, sleep efficiency increases, and there are fewer awakenings after sleep onset. The toxic liability, however, spurred further development, and in the 1960s a new class of GABA partial agonists, the benzodiazepines, largely replaced barbiturates for treating insomnia. Their wide dose safety range, minimum side effects, and milder abstinence syndrome on withdrawal made benzodiazepines far more attractive than previously available medications. Perhaps the most clinically salient advantage of benzodiazepines compared with barbiturates was the increased dose-range margin of safety (that is, a much wider effective dose to lethal dose [ED:LD] ratio). The safety range for toxicity is critically important because of the number of patients with MDD who present with a complaint of insomnia. Barbiturates have a long legacy of lethality. Nonetheless, even with benzodiazepines, long-term use is considered problematic. Pharmaceutical companies developed a wide variety of benzodiazepines, differing in speed of onset, half-life, and presence or absence of active metabolites (Table 20–8). Benzodiazepines are very effective at decreasing sleep latency, increasing sleep efficiency, and decreasing awakenings after sleep onset; however, they also alter sleep macroarchitecture with suppression of slow-wave sleep and, to a lesser extent, REM sleep. Sleep macroarchitecture is also altered in that benzodiazepines can powerfully increase sleep spindle activity. Longer-acting benzodiazepines (especially those with active metabolites) often have carryover effects (hangover) in terms of both residual sedation and diminished psychomotor performance. The efficacy of shorter-acting benzodiazepine is marred by early morning rebound and withdrawal rebound insomnia.

Pharmaceutical development continued, and a class of more specific benzodiazepine receptor agonists was developed, cyclopyrrolones (zopiclone) and imadazopyridine (zolpidem) in the 1980s and pyrazolopyrimidine (zaleplon) in the 1990s. These further pharmacological strides have been made because the newer medications target specific GABA receptor subtypes. These hypnotics now dominate the market. These drugs are effective hypnotics and appear to produce fewer rebound problems. The newer drugs tend to have very rapid onset, be short acting, and have little or no effect on sleep macroarchitecture. Zolpidem and zaleplon are also associated with fewer side effects, most notably the lack of residual sedation (due to their short half-lives and nonactive metabolites). Amnesia, however, persists as a side effect (less in zaleplon than zolpidem, but present in both). There is evidence that memory effects may be related to sleep induction (inasmuch as sleep itself produces amnesia). Consequently, it may not be possible to entirely eliminate amnesia as an undesirable effect of sleep-promoting substances (Morgan and Closs 1999a; Shneerson 2000).

## Current Recommendations

Short-term insomnia treatment recommendations include several areas of intervention. First, it is important to review and address any behaviors or habits that are counterproductive to a good night's sleep by initiating a sleep hygiene program. Next, if other factors are identified as contributory to perpetuating sleeplessness (for example, psychophysiological insomnia), they should be treated aggressively. If pharmacotherapy is intended, the lowest effective dose of a short-acting sedative-hypnotic should be used. Finally, treatment course should usually be less than 3 weeks in duration, and intermittent dosing is preferred.

Treatment is more difficult for chronic insomnia. First, the underlying condition(s), if present, that predispose the individual to sleeplessness must be identified and treated. For example, if underlying depression exists, treating only the insomnia is ill-advised. Similarly, any perpetuating factors (e.g., inadequate sleep hygiene, ongoing use of alcohol, conditioned insomnia) should be a main therapeutic target. In chronic insomnia it is important to improve sleep behaviorally as much as possible even if other treatments are planned. Thus, combined behavioral, psychological, and pharmacologic treatment can be used concurrently. In chronic insomnia resulting from restless legs syndrome and periodic limb movement disorder, sedative-hypnotics, dopaminergic, and opioid medications have been used successfully. If a vitamin or mineral deficiency is found, its cause should be determined and nutritional supplementation should commence. For primary insomnia, when selecting medication the clinician should consider the etiology of the insomnia and pharmacokinetic factors (duration of action, half-life, and whether or not metabolites are psychoactive). In insomnia from causes other than periodic limb movement disorder and restless legs syndrome, time-limited and intermittent dosing is usually preferred. Nonetheless, there will be patients who require continuing pharmacotherapy.

**TABLE 20–8.** Pharmacokinetics of sedative-hypnotic medications

| Generic name | Brand name | Manufacturer | Dose (mg) | Onset time (minutes) | Half-life (hours) | Active metabolite |
|---|---|---|---|---|---|---|
| Clorazepate | Tranxene | Abbott | 3.75–15.0 | 30–60 | 30–200 | Nordiazepam |
| Flurazepam | Dalmane | Roche | 15–30 | 30–60 | 47–100 | N-desalkyl-flurazepam |
| Diazepam | Valium | Roche | 2–5 | 15 | 20–100 | Nordiazepam |
| Quazepam | Doral | Baker-Cummins | 7.5–15 | 20–45 | 15–70 | N-desalkyl-flurazepam |
| Clonazepam | Klonopin | Roche | 0.5–2.0 | 20–60 | 18–60 | None |
| Estazolam | ProSom | Abbott | 1–2 | 15–30 | 10–24 | None |
| Lorazepam | Ativan | Wyeth-Ayerst | 0.5–4 | 30–60 | 9–24 | None |
| Temazepam | Restoril | Sandoz | 7.5–30 | 45–120 | 10–20 | None |
| Oxazepam | Serax | Wyeth-Ayerst | 10–30 | 30–60 | 3–21 | None |
| Triazolam | Halcion | Upjohn | 0.125–0.25 | 15–30 | 1.5–5.4 | None |
| Zolpidem | Ambien | Searle | 5–10 | 30 | 1.4–4.5 | None |
| Zaleplon | Sonata | Wyeth-Ayerst | 10–20 | 30–60 | 1–2 | None |

Clinicians should be cautious when prescribing hypnotic medications for patient who are elderly; who have a history of heavy snoring; who have renal, hepatic, or pulmonary disease; or who are using concomitant psychoactive medications (especially depressants). Caution is also warranted when prescribing sedating drugs for patients who use alcohol regularly, have suicidal tendencies, or work in hazardous occupations. If a person needs to be able to become alert rapidly during their usual sleep period (for example, a physician on call), sedative-hypnotics are generally contraindicated unless they are ultra-short-acting. Sedative-hypnotic medications are clearly contraindicated during pregnancy and in patients who have sleep-disordered breathing or who use alcohol to excess.

## Hypersomnia

Excessive sleepiness is a serious, debilitating, potentially life-threatening, noncommunicable condition. It affects not only the afflicted individuals but also their families and co-workers and the public at large. Sleepiness can be a consequence of insufficient sleep, disrupted sleep, or nonrestorative sleep. The sleep debt produced by insufficient sleep is cumulative. If one reduces sleep duration by 1–2 hours per night and continues this regimen for a week, sleepiness will reach pathological levels. When sleep debt is added to sleep disruption or nonrestorative sleep, there is increasing risk that an individual will lapse unexpectedly into sleep. Sleep onset in such circumstances characteristically occurs without warning. Sleepiness can be episodic and can occur as irresistible sleep attacks, can occur in the morning as sleep drunkenness, or be chronic. Fatigue, tiredness, and sleepiness are terms that are used by most people synonymously; however, one can be tired but not sleepy, sleepy but not tired, or sleepy and tired.

Sleepiness adversely affects attention, concentration, memory, and higher-order cognitive processes. Serious results of sleepiness include failure at school, loss of employment, motor vehicle accidents, and industrial disasters. The transportation industry—including trucking, rail, shipping, and aviation—is particularly susceptible to sleep-related accidents (National Commission on Sleep Disorders Research 1993). Determinants of daytime sleepiness include insufficient sleep, drug use, aging, circadian phase, and sleep disorders. Although *insufficient sleep syndrome* is a diagnostic entity, most individuals are aware of the cause; therefore, medical help is seldom sought. Disregard for the sleep-wake schedule has reached nearly epidemic proportions in some segments of the population, especially among teenagers and young professionals. Insufficient sleep is an insidious killer of otherwise healthy individuals in its role as the underlying cause of countless vehicular accidents. Alcohol ingestion, sedentary situations, a warm room, or a heavy meal unmask and worsen sleepiness, sometimes making it difficult to maintain concentration or remain alert (Dinges and Kribbs 1991; Horne 1991; Lubin 1967; Williams et al. 1959).

There are many sleep disorders associated with excessive daytime sleepiness; however, sleep-disordered breathing is by far the most common dyssomnia seen in sleep disorders centers. In the cooperative study by Coleman and colleagues (1982), sleep apnea syndromes accounted for 43.2% of sleepy patients. More recent statistics estimate that sleep-disordered breathing accounts for 67.8% of all patients seen in sleep disorders centers (Punjabi et al. 2000). The two next most common sleep disorders producing hypersomnia are narcolepsy and idiopathic hypersomnia (see Figure 20–6B). Other disorders of excessive sleepiness include recurrent hypersomnia (Klein-Levin syndrome) and posttraumatic hypersomnia (resulting from brain or brain stem injury).

## Sleep-Disordered Breathing

Sleep-disordered breathing includes disorders ranging from upper-airway resistance syndrome to severe obstructive sleep apnea. An episode of sleep apnea is defined as a cessation of breathing for 10 seconds or more during sleep. A reduction in breathing is termed *hypopnea*. These sleep-related breathing impairments are most often caused by airway obstruction; however, sometimes respiratory reduction results from central (brain stem) changes in ventilatory control, metabolic factors, or heart failure. I classify each sleep-disordered breathing event as either *central*, *obstructive*, or *mixed*. Central apnea or hypopnea is the absence of breathing due to lack of respiratory effort. In obstructive events, respiratory effort continues but airflow stops due to reduction in or loss of airway patency. Mixed apnea or hypopnea episodes contain components of both, often beginning as central apnea and progressing to obstructive apnea.

Sleep-disordered breathing events may be accompanied by oxygen desaturation and cardiac arrhythmias. Clinical features associated with obstructive sleep apnea (the most common form of sleep-disordered breathing) include 1) excessive daytime sleepiness, 2) loud snoring with frequent awakenings, 3) awakening with choking and/or gasping for breath, 4) morning dry mouth, and 5) witnessed apnea. Predisposing factors include 1) being male, 2) reaching middle age, 3) obesity, 4) micrognathia or retrognathia and nasal pharyngeal abnormalities, and 5) hypothyroidism and acromegaly. Other features and comorbidities include sleep choking, morning headaches, nocturnal sweating, sleepwalking, sleep talking, nocturia, enuresis, impotence, memory impairment, impaired quality of life, depression, hearing loss, automatic behaviors, hypertension, polycythemia, and right-sided heart failure (Flemons and Tsai 1997; Guilleminault et al. 1988; Robinson and Guilleminault 1999).

## Treatment

Many treatments are available for sleep-disordered breathing, including weight loss, positive airway pressure therapy, use of oral appliances, and surgery. Weight loss is difficult to achieve and maintain; therefore, it is recommended but not relied on (Fairbanks et al. 1987; Loube et al. 1999; Sanders 2000; Thorpy and Ledereich 1990).

**Continuous positive airway pressure.** Currently, the most popular therapy is positive airway pressure. Positive airway pressure comes in three varieties: continuous, bilevel, and sleep-adjusting. Continuous positive airway pressure (CPAP) is the most common and represents the preferred treatment. It delivers fan-generated flow at a set pressure to the nares, usually via a nasal mask. In so doing it creates a "pneumatic splint" and thereby maintains airway patency. It is highly effective in most patients; however, it requires nightly utilization. Patients who have more severe sleep-disordered breathing or who are sleepier at baseline are the most compliant with this therapy. It is important that the proper pressure be selected. If pressure is too low, then airway obstructions continue; if pressure is too high, sleep is disturbed. Pressures are usually adjusted during a sleep study. Often a rebound in REM and/or slow-wave sleep will occur when an effective pressure is reached. Sleep normalization is impressive. Sleep-disordered breathing is marked by frequent brief arousals. These arousals are needed to return ventilatory control to the voluntary system so that breathing will resume after airway closure. Once airway patency is achieved, these constant sleep disruptions disappear, permitting the patient to have the first good night of sleep he or she has had, possibly in decades.

**Bilevel and self-adjusting positive airway pressure.** Some patients have difficulty exhaling against the constant pressure of CPAP. In such cases, a variant of CPAP, bilevel positive airway pressure (bilevel PAP), can be used. Bilevel PAP allows differential setting of inspiratory and expiratory pressures and is sometimes also used as a nasal ventilatory assist for central sleep apnea. Another variant of CPAP is self-adjusting CPAP, or AutoCPAP. In

AutoCPAP devices, a sensor tries to detect sleep-disordered breathing events and compensate by changing airflow pressure. Several such devices are being marketed, and clinical trials are being performed to test their efficacy and safety.

**Oral appliances.** For patients who cannot tolerate positive airway pressure, other options include oral appliances or surgery. Oral appliances were developed to treat snoring and have also been found to be sometimes effective for upper-airway resistance syndrome and mild to moderate obstructive sleep apnea. Most appliances in current use either manipulate the position of the mandible, retain the tongue, or both. Breathing, although improved, may not reach satisfactory levels; therefore, follow-up sleep studies are needed.

**Surgery.** The earliest surgical intervention for severe obstructive sleep apnea was tracheostomy. There was little doubt that tracheostomy succeeded in creating an airway. Although it is no longer a preferred treatment, it remains a standard against which newer therapies are judged. The next generation of surgical intervention was uvulopalatopharyngoplasty (UPPP). Initial results indicated that this modification of the soft palate was effective. More recent studies have tempered the initial enthusiasm. Clinically significant improvement is attained with UPPP in approximately 50% of patients with sleep apnea. The soft palate surgeries are also sometimes performed using a laser. Nonetheless, predicting success is difficult, and complications may occur. Another surgical intervention includes maxillomandibular advancement. This procedure seems particularly effective in retrognathic patients or in patients with cephalometrics revealing compromised posterior airway space. Finally, the most recent anatomic alteration performed for sleep-disordered breathing, called somnoplasty, uses radiofrequency ablation.

**Other treatments.** Position-dependent sleep-disordered breathing, although rare, is sometimes encountered. Typically, breathing will be impaired when the patient sleeps supine. In such cases, tennis balls sewn onto or placed into pockets on the back of the nightshirt may prevent the patient from sleeping on his or her back. Finally, it would be a great advantage if a medication to treat sleep apnea were discovered. Methoxyprogesterone acetate was once thought to be helpful but is seldom used now. Similarly, tricyclic antidepressants (e.g., protriptyline) may decrease apnea severity by increasing upperairway tone and/or reducing REM sleep (the sleep stage in which the worst sleep-disordered breathing usually occurs). Theophylline also reportedly reduces sleep-disordered breathing; however, further study is needed.

# Narcolepsy

The origin of narcolepsy is not known. It is characterized by a tetrad of symptoms: 1) excessive daytime sleepiness, 2) cataplexy, 3) sleep paralysis, and 4) hypnagogic hallucinations. Patients with narcolepsy often have an abnormal sleep architecture in which REM sleep occurs soon after sleep onset both at night and during daytime naps. This, in connection with the symptom tetrad, makes narcolepsy appear to be a REM sleep intrusion syndrome, presumably resulting from dysfunction of REM sleep generator gating mechanisms. The features of the tetrad match REM sleep characteristics. The sleep paralysis is similar to the muscle atonia that occurs during REM sleep. The hypnagogic hallucinations are vivid "dreams" that occur while the patient is still conscious or partially conscious. However, not all patients have the full constellation of symptoms. Narcolepsy is estimated to afflict 10–60 individuals per 10,000. Symptoms commonly appear in the second decade of life. Strong emotions usually act as the "trigger" for cataplexy. Common emotional triggers include laughter and anger. The severity of cataplexy ranges widely from transient weakness in the knees to total paralysis while the patient is fully conscious. Episodes may last from several seconds to minutes. Usually, the patient is unable to speak and may fall to the floor. Nocturnal sleep is often fragmented, and there can be considerable sleep disturbance (Aldrich 1996; Fry 1998; Standards of Practice Committee 1994).

Narcolepsy is diagnosed with an overnight sleep study followed by a multiple sleep latency test (MSLT). The overnight sleep study helps rule out sleep-disordered breathing, PLMD, or other identifiable pathophysiologies that could be responsible for the sleepiness and other symptoms. The MSLT is a series of four to six 20-minute nap opportunities provided at 2-hour intervals on the day after the sleep study, commencing 2 hours from morning arising. On the clinical version of the MSLT, if a patient falls asleep within the 20-minute limit, he or she is allowed to sleep for an additional 15 minutes. The MSLT provides two categories of important diagnostic data. First, it objectively documents sleepiness. If the mean latency to sleep across all nap sessions is 5 minutes or less, then sleepiness is considered pathological. A mean sleep latency in the 6- to 10-minute range is borderline. The MSLT also measures REM sleep coordination and pressure. If REM sleep occurs on two or more naps in a symptomatic patient, then the diagnosis is confirmed. Alternatively, a sleep-onset REM period on the previous night's sleep study and one MSLT nap with REM sleep also confirm the diagnosis. Current standard of practice and regulations in many states require diagnostic validation of

narcolepsy with the MSLT if stimulants are used for treatment (Carskadon et al. 1986).

## Treatment

In general, the ancillary symptoms of narcolepsy (cataplexy, sleep paralysis, and hypnagogia) are treated with REM-suppressing medications. For years, tricyclic antidepressants (especially imipramine and protriptyline) were widely used. In the past decade, however, the use of selective serotonin reuptake inhibitors has become commonplace for controlling daytime cataplexy.

The excessive daytime sleepiness associated with narcolepsy presents a greater challenge. Stimulant medications are used palliatively to provide symptom relief. Until recently, methylphenidate was the usual first-line treatment, followed by amphetamines if it was ineffective. Pemoline was used with some success but has fallen out of favor due to increasing reports of serious adverse events. The introduction of modafinil, a nonstimulant somnolytic, provides clinicians with an alternative option for treating sleepiness in narcolepsy. Modafinil's benign side-effect profile makes it more attractive for long-term use than traditional stimulants. Other strategies to help offset the loss of effectiveness of these medications in combating sleepiness is to have the patient take prophylactic naps to replace a scheduled stimulant dose. Periodic withdrawals from medication, so-called drug holidays, are also used when sleepiness increases to uncontrollable levels notwithstanding increased dosing. The abstinence period usually restores efficacy of the drug when it is readministered.

# Idiopathic Hypersomnia

Idiopathic hypersomnia is another disorder of excessive sleepiness; however, patients do not have the ancillary symptoms associated with narcolepsy. Unlike in narcolepsy, sleep is usually well preserved, and sleep efficiency remains high even with very extended sleep schedules (12 hours or more). Furthermore, the patient readily falls asleep if given an opportunity to nap the following day. The proportion of slow-wave sleep is often increased; however, the electroencephalographic sleep pattern is essentially the same as that seen in healthy individuals who are sleep deprived. Unlike a sleep-deprived individual, however, the sleep pattern continues in this profile even after several nights of extended sleep. As the name indicates, the etiology of idiopathic hypersomnia is not known; however, a central nervous system cause is presumed. Three general categories have been developed to attempt classification in hopes of furthering our understanding of whether this is one dyssomnia or a collection of several disorders. *Subgroup 1* includes individuals who are human lymphocyte antigen (HLA) Cw2 positive, have autonomic nervous system dysfunctions, and have other affected family members. *Subgroup 2* includes patients who are status postviral infection (e.g., Guillain-Barré syndrome [ascending polyneuropathy], mononucleosis, and atypical viral pneumonia). *Subgroup 3* patients do not have other affected family members and have not had viral infections (i.e., truly idiopathic hypersomnia). Age at onset is characteristically between 15 and 30 years, and the dyssomnia becomes a lifelong problem. In addition to the prolonged, undisturbed, and unrefreshing sleep, idiopathic hypersomnia is associated with long nonrefreshing naps, difficulty awakening, sleep drunkenness, and automatic behaviors with amnesia. Other symptoms suggesting autonomic nervous system dysfunction, including migraine-like headaches, fainting spells, syncope, orthostatic hypotension, and Raynaud's-type phenomena with cold hands and feet, are typical (Aldrich 1996; Guilleminault and Pelayo 2000).

### Treatment

The sleepiness is treated palliatively in a similar fashion to the approach used in narcolepsy. However, the stimulants are usually less effective than in narcolepsy, and prophylactic napping does not seem to be as beneficial. Modafinil has not been tested in patients with idiopathic hypersomnia. However, in pivotal clinical trials in the United States, modafinil was equally effective for patients with and without cataplexy who nonetheless were diagnosed with narcolepsy.

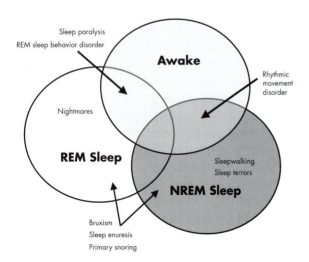

**FIGURE 20–7.**  The relationship of common parasomnias to REM sleep, NREM sleep, and the awake state.

## Parasomnia

Parasomnias are sometimes referred to as disorders of partial arousal. In general, the parasomnias are a large and diverse collection of sleep disorders characterized by physiological or behavioral phenomena that occur during or that are potentiated by sleep. One conceptual framework posits many parasomnias as overlapping or intrusion of one basic sleep-wake state into another (Figure 20–7). Wakefulness, NREM sleep, and REM sleep can be characterized as the three basic states that differ in their neurologic organization. In the awake state, both the body and brain are active, whereas in NREM sleep, both the body and brain are inactive. REM sleep involves an inactive body (atonic, in fact) and an active brain (capable of creating elaborate dream fantasies). Regional cerebral blood flow studies have confirmed increased brain activation during REM sleep. It certainly appears that in some parasomnias there are state boundary violations. For example, all of the arousal disorders (confusional arousals, sleepwalking, and sleep terrors) involve momentary or partial wakeful behaviors suddenly occurring in NREM (slow-wave) sleep. Similarly, isolated sleep paralysis is the persistence of REM sleep atonia into the wakefulness transition, whereas REM sleep behavior disorder is the failure of the mechanism creating paralytic atonia such that individuals literally act out their dreams (American Sleep Disorders Association 1997).

Significant parasomnia can occur frequently or rarely. The clinical significance has more to do with the medical consequences or the distress than with how often it occurs. REM sleep behavior disorder that occurs infrequently but during which the patient is seriously injured while enacting a dream constitutes a more urgent scenario than weekly bruxism. Similarly, monthly recurrent nightmares that provoke severe insomnia and fear of sleeping can be more distressing than night terrors with the same frequency (at least to the patient). The irregularities of occurrence of most parasomnias make them difficult to document in the sleep laboratory. Sleep studies, however, are often conducted to make a differential diagnosis and ensure that the unusual behavior is not secondary to seizure, sleep-disordered breathing, or another sleep disorder.

The nosologic classification for parasomnias has evolved over the years and the system used in the multicenter cooperative study differed from today's nosology. Figure 20–6C shows recalculated percentages of occurrence of different parasomnias among patients seen at sleep disorders centers using the cooperative study data (Coleman et al. 1982). According to this study, the most commonly encountered parasomnias are secondary to nocturnal seizure activity (33.7%). After that, the most common conditions currently classified as parasomnias include sleepwalking, sleep terrors, sleep-related enuresis, nightmares, familial sleep paralysis, head banging (rhythmic movement disorder), bruxism, and other parasomnias.

## Sleepwalking

Sleepwalking in its classic form is, as the name implies, a condition in which an individual arises from bed and ambulates without awakening. Sleepwalking individuals can engage in a variety of complex behaviors while unconscious. Sometimes called somnambulism, sleepwalking usually occurs during slow-wave sleep and lies in the middle of a parasomnia continuum that ranges from confused arousal to sleep terror. Sleepwalks characteristically begin toward the end of the first or second slow-wave sleep episode. Sleep deprivation and interruption of slow-wave sleep appear to exacerbate, or even provoke, sleepwalking in susceptible individuals. Sleepwalking episodes may range from sitting up and attempting to walk to conducting an involved sequence of semipurposeful actions. The sleepwalker can often successfully interact with the environment (for example, avoiding tripping over objects in his or her path). However, the sleepwalker will often interact with the environment inappropriately, which sometimes results in injury (for example, stepping out of an upstairs window or walking into the roadway). There are cases in which sleepwalkers have committed acts of violence. An individual who is sleepwalking is difficult to awaken. Once awake, the sleepwalker will usually appear confused. It is best to gently attempt to lead a sleepwalker back to bed rather than attempt to awaken him or her by grabbing, shaking, or shouting. In their confused state, sleepwalkers may think they are being attacked and may react violently to defend themselves. Sleepwalking in adults is rare, has a familial pattern, and may occur as a primary parasomnia or secondary to another sleep disorder (for example, sleep apnea). By contrast, sleepwalking is very common in children, with peak prevalence between ages 4 and 8 years. After adolescence it usually disappears spontaneously. Nightly to weekly sleepwalking episodes associated with physical injury to the patient and others are considered severe (American Sleep Disorders Association 1997; Kales et al. 1966, 1980b).

## Sleep Terrors

Sleep terror (sometimes called pavor nocturnus, incubus, or night terror) is characterized by a sudden arousal with intense fearfulness. It may begin with a piercing scream or cry. Autonomic and behavioral correlates of fright typically mark the experience. An individual experiencing a sleep terror usually sits up in bed, is unresponsive to stimuli, and if awakened is confused or disoriented. Vocalizations may occur, but they are usually incoherent. Notwithstanding the intensity of these events, amnesia for the episodes usually occurs. Like sleepwalking, these episodes usually arise from slow-wave sleep. Fever and withdrawal from central nervous system depressants can potentiate sleep terror episodes. Unlike nightmares in which an elaborate dream sequence unfolds, sleep terrors may be devoid of images or contain only fragments of very brief and frighteningly vivid but sometimes static images. A familial pattern has been reported. Like other slow-wave sleep parasomnias, sleep terrors can be provoked or exacerbated by sleep deprivation. Psychopathology is seldom associated with sleep terrors in children; however, a history of traumatic experience or frank psychiatric problems is often comorbid in adults with this disorder. Severity ranges from less than once per month to almost nightly occurrence (with injury to patient or others) (American Sleep Disorders Association 1997; Fisher et al. 1973; Hartmann 1988).

## Sleep Enuresis

Sleep enuresis is a disorder in which the individual urinates during sleep while in bed. Bedwetting, as it is commonly called, has primary and secondary forms. In children, primary sleep enuresis is the continuance of bedwetting since infancy. Secondary enuresis refers to relapse after toilet training was complete and there was a period when the child remained dry. Usually, after toilet training bedwetting spontaneously resolves before age 6 years. Prevalence progressively declines from 30% at age 4 to 10% at age 6 to 5% at age 10 and 3% at age 12 years. If a parent had primary enuresis, it increases the likelihood that the children will be enuretic. A single recessive gene is suspected. Secondary enuresis in children may occur with the birth of a sibling and represent a "cry for attention." Secondary enuresis can also be associated with nocturnal seizures, sleep deprivation, and urologic anomalies. In adults, sleep enuresis is occasionally seen in patients with sleep-disordered breathing. In most cases, embarrassment is the most serious consequence. Nonetheless, if sleep enuresis is not addressed, it may leave psychosocial scars. A variety of medications have also been used to treat sleep enuresis and include imipramine, oxybutynin chloride, and synthetic vasopressin. Behavioral treatments—including bladder training, use of conditioning devices (bell and pad), and fluid restriction—

reportedly have good success when properly administered. Other treatments include psychotherapy, motivational strategies, and hypnotherapy. Frequency ranges from nightly to monthly, and severity ranges from mild embarrassment to severe shame and guilt (Nino-Murcia and Keenan 1987; Scharf et al. 1987).

## Nightmares

Nightmares are frightening or terrifying dreams. Sometimes called dream anxiety attacks, they produce sympathetic activation and ultimately awaken the dreamer. Nightmares occur in REM sleep and usually evolve from a long, complicated dream that becomes increasingly frightening. Having aroused to wakefulness, the individual typically remembers the dream content (in contrast to sleep terrors). Some nightmares are recurrent, and—reportedly when occurring in association with posttraumatic stress disorder—they may be recollections of actual events. Common in children ages 3–6 (prevalence estimates range from 10%–50%), nightmares are rare in adults (1% or less). Frequent and distressing nightmares are sometimes responsible for insomnia because the individual is afraid to sleep. In Freudian terms, the nightmare is an example of the failure of the dream process that defuses the emotional content of the dream by disguising it symbolically, thus preserving sleep. Most patients who experience nightmares are free from psychiatric conditions. Nonetheless, individuals at risk for nightmares include those with schizotypal personality, borderline personality disorder, schizoid personality disorder, and schizophrenia. Hartmann (1984) posits that nightmares are more common in individuals with "thin boundaries," who are open and trusting, and who often have creative or artistic inclinations. Having thin boundaries makes these individuals more vulnerable; furthermore, they may be at risk for schizophrenia. Traumatic events are known to induce nightmares, sometimes immediately but at other times delayed. The nightmares can persist for many years. Several medications, including levodopa, β adrenergic blockers, and withdrawal from REM suppressant medications, are known to sometimes provoke nightmares. Finally, drug or alcohol abuse are associated with nightmares (Ermin 1987; Hartmann 1984, 1998; Kales et al. 1980a)

Frequently occurring nightmares often produce a "fear of sleeping" type of insomnia. In turn, the insomnia may provoke sleep deprivation, which is known to exacerbate nightmares. In this manner, a vicious cycle is created. Treatment using behavioral techniques can be helpful. Universal sleep hygiene, stimulus control therapy, lucid dream therapy, and cognitive therapy reportedly

improve sleep and reduce nightmares. In patients with nightmares related to posttraumatic stress disorder, nefazodone (an atypical antidepressant) reportedly provides therapeutic benefit. Benzodiazepines may also be helpful; however, systematic controlled trials are lacking (Hirshkowitz and Moore 2000).

## Sleep Paralysis

Sleep paralysis is, as the name implies, an inability to make voluntary movements during sleep. It becomes a parasomnia when it occurs at sleep onset or on awakening, a time when the individual is partially conscious and aware of his or her surroundings. This inability to move can be extremely distressing, especially when it is coupled with the feeling that there is an intruder in the house or when hypnagogic hallucinations are occurring. Sleep paralysis is one of the tetrad of symptoms associated with narcolepsy; however, it is known to occur (with or without hypnagogia) in individuals who have neither cataplexy nor excessive daytime sleepiness. Although it is sometimes frightening, sleep paralysis is a feature of normal REM sleep briefly intruding into wakefulness. The paralysis may last from one to several minutes. It is interesting that the occurrence of sleep paralysis with hypnagogia may account for a variety of experiences in which the sleeper is confronted or attacked by some sort of creature. The common description is that a "presence" is felt to be near; the individual is paralyzed; and the creature talks, attacks, or sits on the sleeper's chest and then vanishes. Whether it is called incubus, "Old Hag," vampire, ghost oppression (*kanashibari*), witch riding, or alien encounter, elements common to sleep paralysis are seen. Irregular sleep, sleep deprivation, psychological stress, and shift work are thought to increase the likelihood of sleep paralysis occurring. Occasional sleep paralysis occurs in 7%–8% of young adults. Estimates of at least one experience of sleep paralysis during the lifetime range from 25% to 50%. Improving sleep hygiene and ensuring sufficient sleep are first-line therapies. Sometimes, if the individual voluntarily makes very rapid eye movements or is touched by another person, the episode will terminate (Broughton 1982; Ness 1978; Wing et al. 1994).

## Rhythmic Movement Disorder

More commonly known as head banging, rhythmic movement disorder is characterized by stereotypic, repetitive movements that most often occur at the transition from wakefulness to sleep. Large muscle groups produce a movement that is rhythmic, most commonly involving the head and neck. The majority of infants will sometimes move rhythmically at sleep onset; however, prevalence drops from 66% to 8% by age 4 years. Estimates indicate a 4-to-1 male-to-female ratio. One theory posits that the infant or child is creating vestibular stimulation, which has a soothing effect and helps promote sleep (like the rocking of a cradle). Other names for rhythmic movement disorder include *jactatio capitis nocturna*, head banging, head rolling, body rocking, and *rhythmie du sommeil*. Onset after adolescence is rare. In most cases, rhythmic movement disorder is benign; however, it is sometimes associated with drug abuse and withdrawal. The consequence of the movements can cause injury, and this is the manner by which this parasomnia becomes a serious condition. Particularly with head banging, precautions must be taken to avoid injury (padding and wearing a helmet if necessary). When the condition occurs in an adult, a full neurological evaluation is important to determine if the movements are secondary to seizures or other central nervous system dysfunction (Thorpy 1990).

## Sleep Bruxism

Sleep bruxism is a parasomnia in which individuals grind or clench their teeth during sleep. Sleep bruxism can produce abnormal wear on the teeth, damage teeth, provoke tooth and jaw pain, and/or make loud, unpleasant sounds that disturb the bed partner. Sometimes atypical facial pain and headache also result. It is estimated that more than 85% of the population will have sleep bruxism at some time during their lives; however, it is clinically significant in only about 5%. Sleep bruxism can occur in any stage of sleep but appears to be most common at transition to sleep, during stage 2, and during REM sleep. Some evidence indicates that teeth grinding during REM sleep is more commonly associated with dental wear or damage. Sleep bruxism does not appear to be exacerbated by dental malocclusion but rather worsens during periods of stress. Researchers studying sleep bruxism find that many patients seem to have less frequent teeth grinding when sleeping in the laboratory; therefore, repeated study may be needed to document the disorder. By contrast, bruxism frequently appears on polysomnographic recordings made for other purposes. Sleep bruxism can occur secondary to sleep-related breathing disorders, the use of monoaminergic stimulants (e.g., amphetamine, cocaine), alcohol ingestion, and treatment with selective serotonin reuptake inhibitors. Differential diagnosis should rule out nocturnal seizure. Sleep bruxism can occur infrequently (monthly), regularly (weekly), or frequently (nightly). Severity is judged on the basis of dental injury, consequent pain, and sleep disruption. Usual treatment involves having the patient wear an oral appliance to protect the teeth during sleep. There are two basic types of appliances used. The soft one (mouth guard) is typically used in the short term, whereas the hard acrylic one (bite splint) is used for a longer term and requires regular follow-up. Relaxation, biofeedback, hypnosis, physical therapy, and stress management are also used to treat sleep bruxism. A variety of drug therapies (benzodiazepines, muscle relaxants, dopaminergic agonists, and propranolol) have been tried; however, outcome data are not available (Rugh and Harlan 1988; Ware and Rugh 1988).

## REM Sleep Behavior Disorder

REM sleep behavior disorder involves a failure of the atonia mechanism (sleep paralysis) during stage REM sleep. The result is that the patient literally enacts his or her dreams. Under normal circumstances, the dreamer is immobilized by REM-related hypopolarization of alpha and gamma motor neurons. Without this paralysis or with intermittent atonia, punching, kicking, leaping, and running from bed occur during attempted dream enactment. The activity has been correlated with dream imagery, and unlike during sleepwalking, the individual seems unaware of the actual environment. Although complex behaviors can be performed, the individual is acting on the dream sensorium. Thus, a sleepwalker may calmly go to a bedroom window, open it, and step out. By contrast, a person with REM sleep behavior disorder would more likely dive through the window thinking it to be a dream-visualized lake. Patients and bed partners frequently sustain injuries, sometimes serious ones (e.g., lacerations, fractures). Animal research ascribes REM sleep atonia to the peri–locus coeruleus exerting an excitatory influence on the medulla (reticularis magnocellularis nucleus), which in turn paralyzes spinal motor neurons. Cats with pontine tegmental lesions perform a variety of behaviors during REM sleep. Neurologic examinations of patients with REM sleep behavior disorder suggest diffuse lesions of the hemispheres, bilateral thalamic abnormalities, or primary brainstem lesions. Biperiden, tricyclic antidepressants, monoamine oxidase inhibitors, caffeine, venlafaxine, selegiline, and serotonin agonists can precipitate or exacerbate REM behavior disorder. In addition, REM behavior disorder may occur during withdrawal from alcohol, meprobamate, pentazocine, and nitrazepam. A variety of neurologic conditions, including Parkinson's disease, dementia, progressive supranuclear palsy, Shy-Drager syndrome, and narcolepsy, have been associated with this parasomnia. Other conditions that may provoke a secondary REM sleep behavior disorder include sleepwalking, sleep terrors, sleep-disordered breathing, post-traumatic stress disorder, and nocturnal seizures. REM sleep behavior disorder is rare. Severity ranges from a mild form in which nonviolent episodes occur less than once a month to a severe form in which injury-associated episodes occur more than once a week (Schenck et al. 1986, 1989).

## Primary Snoring

Primary snoring is snoring in the absence of obstructive sleep apnea, upper-airway resistance syndrome, or other sleep-related breathing disorders. To be classified as primary or benign snoring, it must not be associated with excessive sleepiness. Primary snoring, like sleep-disordered breathing, is more common in men than in women, and the prevalence increases with age. The noise from the snoring may cause the bed partner to sleep in another room. Snoring may be louder and more frequent during REM sleep or while the patient sleeps supine. It is not known whether primary snoring progresses to other sleep-disordered breathing with advancing age. Soft palate surgery and oral appliances are sometimes helpful to decrease the snoring sounds. Snoring is the cardinal symptom of sleep-disordered breathing; therefore, it is critical to rule out sleep-related breathing disorders before beginning symptomatic treatment of the snoring. Because sleep apnea is potentially life-threatening, symptom masking can be dangerous (American Sleep Disorders Association 1997; Hoffstein 2000).

## References

Aldrich M: The clinical spectrum of narcolepsy and idiopathic hypersomnia. Neurology 46:393–401, 1996

American Psychiatric Association: Diagnostic and Statistical Manual of Mental Disorders, 4th Edition. Washington, DC, American Psychiatric Association, 1994

American Sleep Disorders Association: The International Classification of Sleep Disorders, Revised: Diagnostic and Coding Manual. Rochester, MN, American Sleep Disorders Association, 1997

Aschoff J: Circadian rhythms in man. Science 148:1427–1432, 1965

Aserinsky E, Kleitman N: Regularly occurring periods of eye motility, and concomitant phenomena. Science 118:273–274, 1953

Benca RM, Obermeyer WH, Thisted RA, et al: Sleep and psychiatric disorders: a meta-analysis. Arch Gen Psychiatry 49:651–668, 1992

Berger H: Ueber das elektroenkephalogramm des menschen. Journal of Psychology and Neurology 40:160–179, 1930

Binks GP, Waters FW, Hurry M: Short-term total sleep deprivations does not selectively impair higher cortical functioning. Sleep 22:328–334, 1999

Bootzin RR: A stimulus control treatment for insomnia. Proceedings of the American Psychological Association 7:395–396, 1972

Bootzin RR: Effects of self-control procedures for insomnia, in Behavioral Self-Management: Strategies, Techniques, and Outcomes. Edited by Stuart RB. New York, Brunner/Mazel, 1977, pp 176–195

Borbely AA, Achermann P: Concepts and models of sleep regulation: an overview. J Sleep Res 1:63–79, 1992

Broughton RJ: Neurology and dreaming. Psychiatric Journal of the University of Ottawa 7:101–110, 1982

Carskadon M, Dement WC, Mitler M, et al: Sleep report versus sleep laboratory findings in 122 drug free subjects with the complaint of chronic insomnia. Am J Psychiatry 133:1382–1388, 1976

Carskadon MA, Dement WC, Mitler MM, et al: Guidelines for the Multiple Sleep Latency Test (MSLT): a standard measure of sleepiness. Sleep 9:519–524, 1986

Chase MH (ed): The Sleeping Brain. Los Angeles, CA, Brain Information Service/Brain Research Institute, University of California–Los Angeles, 1972

Chockroverty S: Clinical Companion to Sleep Disorders Medicine, 2nd Edition. Boston, MA, Butterworth-Heinemann, 2000

Coleman RM, Roffwarg HP, Kennedy SJ, et al: Sleep-wake disorders based on a polysomnographic diagnosis. A national cooperative study. JAMA 247:997–1003, 1982

Culebras A: Sleep disorders associated with psychiatric, medical and neurologic disorders, in Clinical Handbook of Sleep Disorders. Edited by Culebras A. Boston, MA, Butterworth-Heinemann, 1996, pp 233–282

Czeisler CA, Kronauer RE, Allan JS, et al: Bright light induction of strong (type 0) resetting of the human circadian pacemaker. Science 244:1328–1333, 1989

Dinges D: Proving the limits of functional capability: the effects of sleep loss on short-duration tasks, in Sleep, Arousal, and Performance. Edited by Broughton RJ, Ogilvie RD. Boston, MA, Birkhauser, 1992, pp 177–188

Dinges DF, Kribbs NB: Performing while sleepy: effects of experimentally induced sleepiness, in Sleep, Sleepiness and Performance. Edited by Monk TM. Chichester, UK, Wiley, 1991, pp 97–128

Ekbom KA: Restless legs syndrome. Neurology 10:868–873, 1960

Ermin MK: Dream anxiety attacks (nightmares). Psychiatr Clin North Am 10:667–674, 1987

Espie CA, Lindsay WR, Brooks DN, et al: A controlled comparative investigation of psychological treatments for chronic sleep-onset insomnia. Behav Res Ther 27:79–88, 1989

Fairbanks DNF, Fujita S, Ikematsu T, et al: Snoring and Obstructive Sleep Apnea. New York, Raven, 1987

Fisher C, Kahn E, Edwards A: A psychophysiological study of nightmares and night terrors, I: psychophysiological aspects of the stage 4 terror. J Nerv Ment Dis 157:75–98, 1973

Flemons WW, Tsai W: Quality of life consequences of sleep-disordered breathing. J Allergy Clin Immunol 99: S750–S756, 1997

Ford DE, Kamerow DB: Epidemiologic study of sleep disturbances and psychiatric disorders: an opportunity for prevention? JAMA 262:1479–1484, 1989

Foulkes D: A cognitive-psychological model of REM dream production. Sleep 5:169–187, 1982

Freud S: The Interpretation of Dreams. New York, Random House, 1950

Fry JM: Treatment modalities for narcolepsy. Neurology 50: S43–48, 1998

Gallup Organization: Sleep in America. Princeton, NJ, Gallup, 1991

Guilleminault C, Pelayo R: Idiopathic central nervous system hypersomnia, in Principles and Practice of Sleep Medicine. Edited by Kryger MH, Roth T, Dement WC. Philadelphia, PA, WB Saunders, 2000, pp 687–692

Guilleminault C, Partinen MD, Quera-Salva MA, et al: Determinants of daytime sleepiness in obstructive sleep apnea. Chest 9 (1):32–37, 1988

Hartmann E: The Nightmare: The Psychology and Biology of Terrifying Dreams. New York, Basic Books, 1984

Hartmann E: Two case reports: night terrors with sleep-walking a potentially lethal disorder. J Nerv Ment Dis 171:503–550, 1988

Hartmann E: Dreams and Nightmares. New York, Plenum, 1998

Hartmann E, Baekeland R, Zwilling G: Psychological differences between long and short sleepers. Arch Gen Psychiatry 26:463–468, 1972

Hauri PJ, Fisher J: Persistent psychophysiological (learned) insomnia. Sleep 2:38–53, 1986

Hirshkowitz M: Somnopharmacology. J Am Osteopath Assoc (in press)

Hirshkowitz M, Moore CA: Nightmares, in Encyclopedia of Stress, Vol 3. Edited by Fink G. San Diego, CA, Academic Press, 2000, pp 49–53

Hirshkowitz M, Moore CA, Hamilton CR, et al: Polysomnography of adults and elderly: sleep architecture, respiration, and leg movements. J Clin Neurophysiol 9:56–63, 1992

Hirshkowitz M, Moore CA, Minhoto G: The basics of sleep, in Understanding Sleep: The Evaluation and Treatment of Sleep Disorders. Edited by Pressman MR, Orr WC. Washington, DC, American Psychological Association, 1997, pp 11–34

Hobson JA, McCarley R: The brain as a dream stage generator: an activation-synthesis hypothesis of the dream process. Am J Psychiatry 134:1335–1348, 1977

Hoffstein V: Snoring, in Principles and Practice of Sleep Medicine. Edited by Kryger MH, Roth T, Dement WC. Philadelphia, PA, WB Saunders, 2000, pp 813–826

Horne J: Why We Sleep. Oxford, UK, Oxford University Press, 1988

Horne J: Dimensions to sleepiness, in Sleep, Sleepiness and Performance. Edited by Monk TM. Chichester, UK, Wiley, 1991, pp 169–196

Joseph KC, Dube D, Sitaram N: Sleep electroencephalographic characteristics of anxiety disorders, in Principles and Practice of Sleep Medicine. Edited by Kryger MH, Roth T, Dement WC. Philadelphia, PA, WB Saunders, 1989, pp 424–425

Jouvet M, Michel F, Courjon J: Sur un stade d'activite electrique cerebrale rapide au cours du sommeil physiologique. C R Seances Soc Biol Fil 153:1024–1028, 1959

Kales A, Jacobson A, Paulson MJ, et al: Somnambulism: psychophysiological correlates, I: all-night EEG studies. Arch Gen Psychiatry 14:586–594, 1966

Kales A, Soldatos C, Caldwell A, et al: Nightmares: clinical characteristics and personality patterns. Am J Psychiatry 137:1197–1201, 1980a

Kales A, Soldatos CR, Caldwell AB, et al: Sleepwalking. Arch Gen Psychiatry 37:1406–1410, 1980b

Kleitman N: Sleep and Wakefulness, 2nd Edition. Chicago, IL, University of Chicago, 1972

Lacks P, Rotert M: Knowledge and practice of sleep hygiene techniques in insomniacs and good sleepers. Behav Res Ther 24:365–368, 1986

Lichstein KL, Riedel BW: Behavioral assessment and treatment of insomnia: a review with an emphasis on clinical application. Behavior Therapy 25:659–688, 1994

Loomis AL, Harvey N, Hobart GA: Cerebral states during sleep, as studied by human brain potentials. Journal of Experimental Psychology 21:127–144, 1937

Loube DI, Gay PC, Strohl KP, et al: Indications for positive airway pressure treatment of adult obstructive sleep apnea patients: a consensus statement. Chest 115:863–866, 1999

Lubin A: Performance under sleep loss and fatigue, in Sleep and Altered States of Consciousness. Edited by Kety SS, Evarts EV, Williams HL. Baltimore, MD, Williams & Wilkins, 1967, pp 506–513

Lugaresi E, Cirgnotta F, Coccagna G, et al: Nocturnal myoclonus and restless legs syndrome. Adv Neurol 43:295–306, 1986

Mellinger GD, Balter MB, Uhlenhuth EH: Insomnia and its treatment: prevalence and correlates. Arch Gen Psychiatry 42:225–232, 1985

Moore-Ede MC, Sulzman FM, Fuller CA: The Clocks That Time Us. Cambridge, MA, Harvard University Press, 1982

Morgan K, Closs SJ: Hypnotic drugs in the treatment of insomnia, in Sleep Management in Nursing Practice. Edinburgh, UK, Churchill Livingstone, 1999a, pp 143–159

Morgan K, Closs SJ: Sleep hygiene, in Sleep Management in Nursing Practice. Edinburgh, UK, Churchill Livingstone, 1999b, pp 95–104

Morin CM, Culbert JP, Schwartz SM: Nonpharmacological interventions for insomnia: a meta-analysis of treatment efficacy. Am J Psychiatry 151:1172–1180, 1994

National Commission on Sleep Disorders Research: Wake Up America: A National Sleep Alert, Vol 1: Executive Summary and Executive Report, Report of the National Commission on Sleep Disorders Research, National Institutes of Health. Washington, DC, U.S. Government Printing Office, 1993

Ness RC: The old hag phenomenon as sleep paralysis: a biocultural interpretation. Cult Med Psychiatry 2:15–39, 1978

Nino-Murcia G, Keenan SA: Enuresis and sleep, in Sleep and Its Disorders in Children. Edited by Guilleminault C. New York, Raven, 1987, pp 253–267

Punjabi NM, Welch D, Strohl K: Sleep disorders in regional sleep centers: a national cooperative study. Sleep 23:471–480, 2000

Rechtschaffen A, Kales A (eds): A manual of standardized terminology, techniques and scoring system for sleep stages of human subjects (NIH Publ No 204). Washington, DC, U.S. Government Printing Office, 1968

Reynolds CF, Kupfer DJ: Sleep research in affective illness: state of the art circa 1987. Sleep 10:199–215, 1987

Robinson A, Guilleminault C: Obstructive sleep apnea syndrome, in Sleep Disorders Medicine. Edited by Chokroverty S. Boston, MA, Butterworth-Heinemann, 1999, pp 331–354

Roffwarg HP, Muzio JN, Dement WC: Ontogenetic development of the human sleep-dream cycle. Science 152:604–619, 1966

Rugh JD, Harlan J: Nocturnal bruxism and temporomandibular disorders. Adv Neurol 49:329–341, 1988

Sanders MH: Medical therapy for obstructive sleep apnea-hypopnea syndrome, in Principles and Practice of Sleep Medicine. Edited by Kryger MH, Roth T, Dement WC. Philadelphia, PA, WB Saunders, 2000, pp 879–893

Scharf MB, Pravda MF, Jennings SW, et al: Childhood enuresis: a comprehensive treatment program. Psychiatr Clin North Am 10:655–674, 1987

Schenck CH, Bundlie SR, Ettinger MG, et al: Chronic behavioral disorders of human REM sleep: a new category of parasomnia. Sleep 9:293–308, 1986

Schenck CH, Hurwitz TD, Bundlie SR, et al: Sleep-related injury in 100 adult patients: a polysomnographic and clinical report. Am J Psychiatry 146:1166–1173, 1989

Shneerson JM: Handbook of Sleep Medicine. Oxford, UK, Blackwell Science, 2000

Spielman AJ, Caruso LS, Glovinsky PB: A behavioral perspective on insomnia treatment. Psychiatr Clin North Am 10:541–553, 1987a

Spielman AJ, Saskin P, Thorpy MJ: Treatment of chronic insomnia by restriction of time in bed. Sleep 10:45–65, 1987b

Standards of Practice Committee of the American Sleep Disorders Association: Practice parameters for the use of stimulants in the treatment of narcolepsy. Sleep 17:348–351, 1994

Thorpy MJ: Rhythmic movement disorder, in Handbook of Sleep Disorders. Edited by Thorpy MJ. New York, Marcel Dekker, 1990, pp 609–629

Thorpy MJ, Ledereich PS: Medical treatment of obstructive sleep apnea, in Handbook of Sleep Disorders. Edited by Thorpy MJ. New York, Marcel Dekker, 1990, pp 285–309

Vogel GW, Vogel F, McAbee RS, et al: Improvement of depression by REM sleep deprivation. Arch Gen Psychiatry 37:247–253, 1980

Walters AS: Toward a better definition of the restless legs syndrome. International Restless Legs Syndrome Study Group. Mov Disord 10:634–642, 1995

Walters AS, Hening W, Rubinstein, et al: A clinical and polysomnographic comparison of neuroleptic-induced akathisia and the idiopathic restless legs syndrome. Sleep 14:339–345, 1991

Ware JC, Rugh JD: Destructive bruxism: sleep stage relationship. Sleep 11:172–181, 1988

Williams HL, Lubin A, Goodnow JJ: Impaired performance and acute sleep loss. Psychological Monographs 73 (part 14):1–26, 1959

Williams RL, Karacan I, Hursch CJ: EEG of Human Sleep: Clinical Applications. New York, Wiley, 1974

Wing YK, Lee ST, Chen CN: Sleep paralysis in Chinese: ghost oppression phenomenon in Hong Kong. Sleep 17:609–613, 1994

Zammit GK: Delayed sleep phase syndrome and related conditions, in Understanding Sleep: The Evaluation and Treatment of Sleep Disorders. Edited by Pressman MR, Orr WC. Washington, DC, American Psychological Association, 1997, pp 229–248

Zarcone V: Sleep abnormalities in schizophrenia, in Principles and Practice of Sleep Medicine. Edited by Kryger MH, Roth T, Dement WC. Philadelphia, PA, WB Saunders, 1989, pp 422–423

# CHAPTER 21

# Neuropsychiatric Aspects of Cerebrovascular Disorders

Robert G. Robinson, M.D.

Sergio E. Starkstein, M.D., Ph.D.

Cerebrovascular disease includes a wide range of disorders, from atherosclerotic narrowing of cerebral blood vessels to transitory permanent infarction to hemorrhagic phenomena caused by weakness of the vascular wall. This chapter focuses on stroke, which is defined as a sudden loss of blood supply to the brain leading to permanent tissue damage.

Stroke is the most common serious neurologic disorder in the world and accounts for half of all the exigent hospitalizations for neurologic disease. The age-specific incidence of stroke varies dramatically over the life course (Figure 21–1). In Rochester, Minnesota, the annual incidence in those under age 35 was 1 per 10,000 population, whereas among those over age 85 the incidence was almost 200 per 10,000 population (Bonita 1992).

The neuropsychiatric complications of cerebrovascular disease include a wide range of emotional and cognitive disturbances. Although studies providing empirical data about individual neuropsychiatric disorders and their relationship to specific types of cerebrovascular disease have been published over the last 20 years, many more of these kinds of investigations are essential before we will have a firm empirical database for our understanding of the clinical manifestations, treatments, and mechanisms of these disorders.

This chapter is organized into three sections: the historical development of concepts in neuropsychiatry related to cerebrovascular disease, the classification of types of cerebrovascular disease, and the description and classification of clinical psychiatric disorders associated with cerebrovascular disease.

## Historical Perspective

The first reports of emotional reactions after brain damage (usually caused by cerebrovascular disease) were made by neurologists and psychiatrists in case descriptions. Meyer (1904) warned that new discoveries of cerebral localization in the early 1900s of such capacities as language function led to an overhasty identification of centers and functions. He identified several disorders such as delirium, dementia, and aphasia that were the direct result of brain injury. In keeping with his view of biopsychosocial causes of most mental "reactions," however, he saw manic-depressive illness and paranoiac conditions as arising from a combination of head injury (specifically citing left frontal lobe and cortical convexities) along with a family history of psychiatric disorder and premorbid personal psychiatric disorders, thus producing the specific mental reaction. Bleuler (1951) noted that after stroke, "melancholic moods lasting for months and sometimes longer appear frequently" (p. 230). Kraepelin (1921) recognized an association between manic-depressive insanity and cerebrovascular disease. He stated that the diagnosis of states of depression may offer difficulties, especially when arteriosclerosis is involved. Cere-

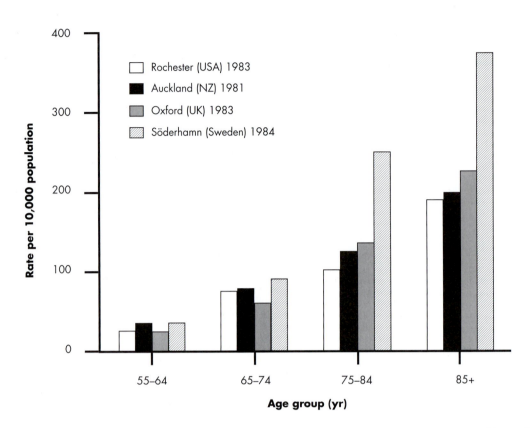

**FIGURE 21–1.**    Average annual age-specific incidence of stroke in selected studies around the world. In all studies, the incidence of stroke increased with increasing age.

*Source.*    Reprinted from Bonita R: "Epidemiology of Stroke." *Lancet* 339:342–344, 1992. Used with permission. The Rochester 1983 study refers to Broderick et al. 1989; the Auckland 1981 study to Bonita et al. 1984; the Oxford 1983 study to Bamford et al. 1988; and the Söderhamn 1984 study to Terent 1988.

brovascular disorder may be an accompanying phenomenon of manic-depressive illness or may itself engender states of depression.

In contrast to psychiatric disorders seen in patients with or without brain injury, Goldstein (1939) described an emotional disorder thought to be uniquely associated with brain disease. He termed this disorder *catastrophic reaction*, which is an emotional outburst characterized by various degrees of anger, frustration, depression, tearfulness, refusal, shouting, swearing, and sometimes aggressive behavior. Goldstein ascribed this reaction to the inability of the subject to cope when faced with a serious defect in physical or cognitive functions. In his extensive studies of brain injuries in war, Goldstein (1942) described two symptom clusters: those related directly to physical damage of a circumscribed area of the brain and those related secondarily to the subject's psychological response to injury. Emotional symptoms, therefore, represented the latter category (i.e., the psychological response of a subject struggling with physical or cognitive impairments). (Catastrophic reaction is also discussed later in this chapter under "Neuropsychiatric Syndromes

Associated With Cerebrovascular Disease.")

A second emotional abnormality, also thought to be characteristic of brain injury, was the indifference reaction Babinski (1914) noted that patients with right-hemisphere disease often displayed the symptoms of anosognosia, euphoria, and indifference. The indifference reaction, associated with right-hemisphere lesions, consisted of symptoms of indifference toward failures, lack of interest in family and friends, enjoyment of foolish jokes, and minimization of physical difficulties (Denny-Brown et al. 1952; Haecen et al. 1951).

A third emotional disorder that has been historically associated with brain injury, such as cerebral infarction, is pathologic laughter or crying. Ironside (1956) described the clinical manifestations of this disorder. Patients' emotional displays were characteristically unrelated to their inner emotional state. Crying, for example, may have occurred spontaneously or after some seemingly minor provocation. This phenomenon has been given various names, including emotional incontinence, emotional lability, pseudobulbar affect, and pathologic emotionalism. Some investigators have differentiated pseudobulbar disorder, which is characterized by bilateral brain lesions and subjective feelings of being forced to laugh or cry, from emotional lability, in which there is an easy and sometimes rapid vacillation between laughter and crying. These disorders, however, have never been systematically examined or classified into subcategories on the basis of reliable features such as a characteristic clinical presentation, etiology, or response to treatment. (This disorder is also discussed under "Neuropsychiatric Syndromes Associated With Cerebrovascular Disease.")

The first systematic study to contrast the emotional reactions of patients with right- and left-hemisphere brain damage was done by Gainotti (1972). He reported that catastrophic reaction was more frequent among 80 patients with left-hemisphere brain damage, particularly those with aphasia, than were indifference reactions, which occurred more frequently among 80 patients with right-hemisphere brain damage. Indifference reactions were also associated with neglect of the opposite half of the body and space. Gainotti agreed with Goldstein's (1942) explanation of catastrophic reaction as the desperate reaction of the subject confronted with severe physical disability. Indifference reaction, on the other hand, was not as easy to understand. Gainotti suggested that denial of illness and disorganization of the nonverbal type of synthesis may have been responsible for this emotional symptom.

Despite the assertions by Kraepelin (1921) and others that emotional disorder may be produced directly by focal brain injury, many investigators have adopted "psychological" explanations for the emotional symptoms associated with brain injury. Studies in which the emotional symptoms specifically associated with cerebrovascular disease were examined began to appear in the early 1960s. Ullman and Gruen (1960) reported that stroke was a particularly severe stress to the patient, as Goldstein (1942) had suggested, because the organ governing the emotional response to injury had itself been damaged. G.F. Adams and Hurwitz (1963) noted that discouragement and frustration caused by disability could themselves impede recovery from stroke. Fisher (1961) described depression associated with cerebrovascular disease as reactive and understandable because "the brain is the most cherished organ of humanity" (p. 379). Thus, depression was viewed as a natural emotional response to a decrease in self-esteem from a life-threatening injury and the resulting disability and dependence.

Systematic studies, however, led other investigators, impressed by the frequency of association between brain injury and emotional disorders, to hypothesize more direct causal links. In a study of 100 elderly patients with affective disorder, Post (1962) stated that the high fre-

quency of brain ischemia associated with first episodes of depressive disorder suggested that the causes for atherosclerosis and depression may be linked. Folstein et al. (1977) compared 20 stroke patients with 10 orthopedic patients and found that, although the functional disability in both groups was comparable, more of the stroke patients were depressed. These authors concluded that "mood disorder was a more specific complication of stroke than simply a response to motor disability" (p. 1018).

Two primary lines of thought have emerged in the study of emotional disorders associated with cerebrovascular disease. One attributes emotional disorders to an understandable psychological reaction to the associated impairment; the other, based on a lack of association between severity of impairment and severity of emotional disorder, suggests a direct causal connection between cerebrovascular disease and neuropsychiatric disorders.

## Classification of Cerebrovascular Disease

There are many ways to classify the wide range of disorders that constitute the spectrum of cerebrovascular disease. On the one hand, cerebrovascular disease can be understood as an anatomic-pathologic process of the blood vessels that perfuse the brain. This perspective leads to a classification based on the etiologies of underlying anatomic-pathologic processes. Such a classification would include an extensive list of diseases, including infectious, connective tissue, neoplastic, hematologic, pharmacologic, and trauma-related. Alternatively, one could examine the mechanisms by which these pathologic processes are manifested: for example, the interactive effects of systemic hypertension and atherosclerosis on the resilience of large arteries, the integrity of vessel lumina, and the production of end-organ ischemia; the formation of aneurysmal dilatations or vascular disease; or the effect of cardiac arrhythmias on the propagation of thromboemboli.

From the perspective of schematizing its neuropsychiatric complications, however, probably the most pragmatic way of classifying cerebrovascular disease is not to focus on the anatomic-pathologic processes or the interactive mechanisms but to examine the means by which parenchymal changes in the brain occur. The first of these, ischemia, may occur either with or without infarction of parenchyma and includes transient ischemic attacks (TIAs), atherosclerotic thrombosis, cerebral embolism, and hemorrhage. The last of these may cause either direct parenchymal damage by extravasation of blood into the surrounding brain tissue, as in intracerebral hemorrhage (ICH), or indirect damage by hemorrhage into the ventricles, subarachnoid space, extradural area, or subdural area. These changes result in a common mode of expression, defined by R.D. Adams and Victor (1985) as a sudden, convulsive, focal neurologic deficit, or stroke.

To expand slightly on this categorization (i.e., the means by which parenchymal changes occur), there are two categories of ischemic disorders and three categories of hemorrhagic disorders (Table 21–1). These include atherosclerotic thrombosis, cerebral embolism, lacunae, and ICH. In various studies of the incidence of cerebrovascular disease (e.g., Wolf et al. 1977), the ratio of infarcts to hemorrhages has been shown to be about 5:1. Atherosclerotic thrombosis and cerebral embolism each accounts for approximately one-third of all incidents of stroke. Finally, there are several less common types of intracranial disease. These may lead to intraparenchymal damage, but frequently bleeds on the surface of the brain (e.g., subdural hematoma) do not produce permanent parenchymal damage.

## Atherosclerotic Thrombosis

Atherosclerotic thrombosis is often the result of a dynamic interaction between hypertension and the atherosclerotic deposition of hyaline-lipid material in the walls of peripheral, coronary, and cerebral arteries. Risk factors in the development of atherosclerosis include hyperlipidemia, diabetes mellitus, hypertension, and cigarette smoking. Atheromatous plaques tend to propagate at the branchings and curves of the internal carotid artery or the carotid sinus, in the cervical part of the vertebral arteries and their junction to form the basilar artery, in the posterior cerebral arteries as they wind around the midbrain, and in the anterior cerebral arteries as they curve over the corpus callosum. These plaques may lead to stenosis of one or more of these cerebral arteries or to complete occlusion. TIAs, defined as periods of transient focal ischemia associated with reversible neurologic deficits, almost always indicate that a thrombotic process is occurring. Only rarely is embolism or ICH preceded by transient neurologic deficits. Thrombosis of virtually any cerebral or cerebellar artery can be associated with TIAs.

TIAs, therefore, although not listed among the main causes of stroke, may precede, accompany, or follow the development of stroke or may occur by themselves without leading to complete occlusion of a cerebral or cerebellar artery. Most commonly, TIAs have a duration of 2–15 minutes, with a range from a few seconds to 24 hours.

**TABLE 21–1.** Classification of cerebrovascular disease

**Ischemic phenomena (85%)**
*Infarction*
    Atherosclerotic thrombosis
    Cerebral embolism
    Lacunae
    Other causes (arteritis [e.g., infectious or connective tissue disease], cerebral thrombophlebitis, fibromuscular dysplasia, venous occlusions)
*Transient ischemic attacks*
**Hemorrhagic phenomena (15%)**
*Intraparenchymal hemorrhage*
    Primary (hypertensive) intracerebral hemorrhage
    Other causes (hemorrhagic disorders [e.g., thrombocytopenia, clotting disorders], trauma)
*Subarachnoid or intraventricular hemorrhage*
    Ruptured saccular aneurysm or arteriovenous malformation
    Other causes
*Subdural or epidural hematoma*

Whereas the neurologic findings between successive episodes of this thrombotic process are entirely normal, the permanent neurologic deficits of atherosclerotic thrombosis indicate that infarction has occurred. The progression of events leading to the completed thrombotic stroke, however, can be quite variable.

## Cerebral Embolism

Cerebral embolism, which like atherosclerotic thrombosis accounts for approximately one-third of all strokes, is usually caused by a fragment breaking away from a thrombus within the heart and traveling up the carotid artery. Less often, the source of the embolism may be an atheromatous plaque within the lumen of the carotid sinus or the distal end of a thrombus within the internal carotid artery, or it may represent a fat, tumor, or air embolus within the internal carotid artery. The possible causes of thrombus formation within the heart include cardiac arrhythmias, congenital heart disease, infectious processes (e.g., syphilitic heart disease, rheumatic valvular disease, or endocarditis), valve prostheses, postsurgical complications, or myocardial infarction with mural thrombus.

Of all the types of stroke, those due to cerebral embolism develop most rapidly. In general, there are no warning episodes; embolism can occur at any time. A large embolus may occlude the internal carotid artery or the stem of the middle cerebral artery, producing a severe hemiplegia. More often, however, the embolus is smaller and passes into one of the branches of the middle cerebral artery. This may produce infarction distal to the site of the arterial occlusion, which is characterized by a pattern of neurologic deficits consistent with that vascular distribution, or may result in a transient neurologic deficit that resolves as the embolus fragments and travels into smaller, more distal arteries.

## Lacunae

Lacunae, which account for nearly one-fifth of strokes, are the result of occlusion of small penetrating cerebral arteries. They are infarcts that may be so small as to produce no recognizable deficits or, depending on their location, may be associated with pure motor or sensory deficits. Lacunae are strongly associated with both atherosclerosis and hypertension, suggesting that lacunar infarction is the result of the extension of the atherosclerotic process into small-diameter vessels.

## Intracerebral Hemorrhage

ICH is the fourth most frequent cause of stroke. The main causes of ICH that present as acute stroke include hypertension, rupture of saccular aneurysms or arteriovenous malformations (AVMs), a variety of hemorrhagic disorders of assorted etiologies, and trauma. Primary (hypertensive) ICH occurs within the brain tissue when the extravasation of blood forms a roughly circular or oval-shaped mass that disrupts and displaces the parenchyma. Adjacent tissue is compressed, and seepage into the ventricular system usually occurs, producing bloody cerebrospinal fluid in more than 90% of cases.

ICHs can range in size from massive bleeds of several centimeters in diameter to petechial hemorrhages of a millimeter or less, most commonly occurring within the putamen, in the adjacent internal capsule, or in various portions of the white matter underlying the cortex. Hemorrhages of the thalamus, cerebellar hemispheres, or pons are also common. Severe headache is generally considered to be a constant accompaniment of ICH, but this occurs in only about 50% of cases. The prognosis for ICH is grave: 70%–75% of patients die within 30 days (R.D. Adams and Victor 1985).

## Aneurysms and Arteriovenous Malformations

Ruptured aneurysms and AVMs are the next most common type of cerebrovascular disease after thrombosis, embolism, lacunae, and ICH. Aneurysms are usually located at arterial bifurcations and are presumed to result from developmental defects in the formation of the arterial wall. Rupture occurs when the intima bulges outward

and eventually breaks through the adventitia. AVMs consist of a tangle of dilated vessels that form an abnormal communication between the arterial and venous systems. They are developmental abnormalities consisting of embryonic patterns of blood vessels. Most AVMs are clinically silent but ultimately bleed. Hemorrhage from aneurysms or AVMs may occur within the subarachnoid space, leading to an identifiable presentation as a bleeding vessel anomaly, or may occur within the parenchyma, leading to hemiplegia or death.

## Subdural and Epidural Hematomas

Although it could be contended that subdural hematomas (SDHs) and epidural hematomas do not represent forms of cerebrovascular disease, their behavior as vascular space-occupying lesions that produce many of the signs and symptoms of stroke nonetheless warrants a brief description here.

Chronic SDHs are frequently (60%), but not exclusively, caused by head trauma, followed by a gradual progression of signs and symptoms during the subsequent days to weeks. Traumatic chronic SDH may be caused by tears of bridging veins in the subdural space. Nontraumatic causes include ruptured aneurysms or AVMs of the pial surface or rapid deceleration injuries. The most common symptom of chronic SDH is headache that has a variety of neuropsychiatric manifestations paralleling the gradual increase in intracranial pressure. These manifestations include confusion, inattention, apathy, memory loss, drowsiness, and coma. Chronic SDH is also one of the many conditions in the differential diagnosis of treatable causes of dementia. Fluctuations in the level of consciousness predominate over any focal or lateralizing signs, which may include hemiparesis, hemianopsia, cranial nerve abnormalities, aphasia, or seizures. If left unchecked, chronic SDH may continue to expand or may reabsorb spontaneously.

Acute SDH and epidural hematomas, although frequently manifested by similar changes in level of consciousness and focal neurologic deficits (as in chronic SDH), are associated with severe head trauma, may occur in combination with cerebral laceration or contusion, and may progress rapidly over a period of a few hours to days, rather than days to weeks. Epidural hematomas usually follow a temporal or parietal skull fracture that causes a laceration or avulsion of the middle meningeal artery or vein or a tear of the aural venous sinus. Acute SDH is usually caused by the avulsion of bridging veins or laceration of pial arteries. Both conditions produce loss of consciousness or a brief period of lucidity followed by a loss of consciousness, hemiparesis, cranial nerve palsies, and death, usually secondary to respiratory compromise, if the hematoma is not emergently evacuated.

## Other Types of Cerebrovascular Disease

Another cause of cerebrovascular disease is fibromuscular dysplasia, which leads to narrowed arterial segments caused by degeneration of elastic tissue, disruption and loss of the arterial muscular coat, and an increase in fibrous tissue. Inflammatory diseases of the arterial system can also lead to stroke. These diseases include meningovascular syphilis, pyogenic or tuberculous meningitis, temporal arteritis, and systemic lupus erythematosus.

Many other less common causes of cerebrovascular disease have not been cited here due to lack of space. It appears obvious, however, that examining the many causes and types of cerebrovascular disease in relation to specific neuropsychiatric disorders is a formidable task. In studies comparing traumatic brain injury with thromboembolic stroke, or hemorrhagic with ischemic infarcts, it has been found that the associated moods share many characteristics, depending on the size and location of the lesion and the time that has elapsed since the injury (Jorge et al. 1993; Robinson and Szetela 1981; Robinson et al. 1983b). As indicated previously, however, the type or pattern of neuronal damage may be different, depending on the cause of the cerebrovascular disease, and resultant neuropsychiatric disorders must be systematically examined.

## Neuropsychiatric Syndromes Associated With Cerebrovascular Disease

A number of emotional disorders, many of which are discussed in this section, have been associated with cerebrovascular disease (Table 21–2). The neuropsychiatric disorder that has received the greatest amount of investigation, however, is poststroke depression (PSD).

## Poststroke Depression

### Diagnosis

Although strict diagnostic criteria have not been used in some studies of emotional disorders associated with cerebrovascular disease (Andersen et al. 1993), most studies have used structured interviews and diagnostic criteria defined by DSM-III-R or DSM-IV (American Psychiatric Association 1987, 1994) or Research Diagnostic Criteria (Eastwood et al. 1989; Morris et al. 1990; Robinson et al. 1983a; Spitzer et al. 1978). Poststroke major depression is now categorized in DSM-IV-TR (American Psychiatric Association 2000) as "mood disorder due to stroke with major depressive-like episode" (p. 370). For patients with less severe forms of depression, there are "research criteria" in DSM-IV for minor depression (i.e., subsyndromal major depression; depression or anhedonia with at least one but fewer than four additional symptoms of major depression) or, alternatively, a diagnosis of mood disorder due to stroke with depressive features.

Investigators of depression associated with physical illness have debated the most appropriate method for diagnosis of depression when some symptoms (e.g., sleep or appetite disturbance) could result from the physical illness. Cohen-Cole and Stoudemire (1987) reported that four approaches have been used to assess depression in the physically ill. These approaches are the "inclusive approach," in which depressive diagnostic symptoms are counted regardless of whether they may be related to physical illness (Rifkin et al. 1985); the "etiological approach," in which a symptom is counted only if the diagnostician feels that it is not caused by the physical illness (Rapp and Vrana 1989); the "substitutive approach" of Endicott (1984), in which other psychological symptoms of depression replace the vegetative symptoms; and the "exclusive approach," in which symptoms are removed from the diagnostic criteria if they are not found to be more frequent in depressed than nondepressed patients (Bukberg et al. 1984).

Paradiso et al. (1997) recently examined the utility of these methods in the diagnosis of PSD during the first 2 years following stroke. Among 205 patients with acute stroke, 142 were followed up for examination at 3, 6, 12, or 24 months following stroke. The patients who were not included in the follow-up either had died, could not be located, or refused to attend follow-up evaluations. Of 142 patients with follow-up, 60 (42%) reported the presence of a depressed mood (depressed group) while they were in hospital, and the remaining 82 patients (58%) were nondepressed. There were no significant differences in the background characteristics between the depressed and nondepressed group except that the depressed group was significantly younger ($P=0.006$) and had a significantly higher frequency of personal history of psychiatric disorder ($P=0.04$).

The frequencies of vegetative symptoms in hospital and at each of the follow-up visits are shown in Figure 21–2. Throughout the 2-year follow-up, depressed patients showed a higher frequency of both vegetative and psychological symptoms compared with the nondepressed patients. The only vegetative symptoms that

**TABLE 21–2.** Clinical syndromes associated with cerebrovascular disease

| Syndrome | Prevalence | Clinical symptoms | Associated lesion location |
|---|---|---|---|
| Major depression | 20% | Depressed mood, diurnal mood variation, loss of energy, anxiety, restlessness, worry, weight loss, decreased appetite, early-morning awakening, delayed sleep onset, social withdrawal, and irritability | Left frontal lobe and left basal ganglia during the acute period after stroke |
| Minor depression | 10%–40% | Depressed mood, anxiety, restlessness, worry, diurnal mood variation, hopelessness, loss of energy, delayed sleep onset, early-morning awakening, social withdrawal, weight loss, and decreased appetite | Left posterior parietal and occipital regions during the acute post-stroke period |
| Mania | Unknown, rare | Elevated mood, increased energy, increased appetite, decreased sleep, feeling of well-being, pressured speech, flight of ideas, grandiose thoughts | Right basotemporal or right orbito-frontal lesions |
| Bipolar mood disorder | Unknown, rare | Symptoms of major depression alternating with mania | Right basal ganglia or right thalamic lesions |
| Anxiety disorder | 27% | Symptoms of major depression plus intense worry and anxious foreboding in addition to depression, associated light-headedness or palpitations and muscle tension or restlessness, and difficulty concentrating or falling asleep | Left cortical lesions, usually dorso-lateral frontal lobe |
| Psychotic disorder | Unknown, rare | Hallucinations or delusions | Right temporoparietal-occipital junction |
| **Apathy** | | | |
| Without depression | 22% | Loss of drive, motivation, interest, low energy, unconcern | Posterior internal capsule |
| With depression | 11% | | |
| Pathological laughing and crying | 20% | Frequent, usually brief laughing and/or crying; crying not caused by sadness or out of proportion to it; and social withdrawal secondary to emotional outbursts | Frequently, bilateral hemispheric lesions; can occur with almost any lesion location |
| Anosognosia | 24%–43% | Denial of impairment related to motor function, sensory perception, visual perception, or other modality with an apparent lack of concern | Right hemisphere and enlarged ventricles |
| Catastrophic reaction | 19% | Anxiety reaction, tears, aggressive behavior, swearing, displacement, refusal, renouncement, and compensatory boasting | Left anterior-subcortical region |
| **Aprosodias** | | | |
| Motor | Unknown | Poor expression of emotional prosody and gesturing, good prosodic comprehension and gesturing, and denial of feelings of depression | Right hemisphere posterior inferior frontal lobe and basal ganglia |
| Sensory | 32%–49% | Good expression of emotional prosody and gesturing, poor prosodic comprehension and gesturing, and difficulty empathizing with others | Right hemisphere posterior inferior parietal lobe and posterior superior temporal lobe |

were not more frequent in the depressed than in the nondepressed patients were weight loss and early awakening at the initial evaluation; weight loss and early-morning awakening at 6 months; weight loss, early-morning awakening, anxious foreboding, and loss of libido at 1 year; and weight loss and loss of libido at 2 years. Among the psychological symptoms, the depressed patients had a higher frequency of most psychological symptoms throughout the 2-year follow-up. The only psychological symptoms that were not significantly more frequent in the depressed than in the nondepressed group were suicide plans, simple ideas of reference, and pathological guilt at 3 months; pathological guilt at 6 months; pathological guilt, suicide plans, guilty ideas of reference, and irritability at 1 year; and pathological guilt and self-depreciation at 2 years.

The effect of using each of the proposed alternative diagnostic methods for PSD using DSM-IV criteria was

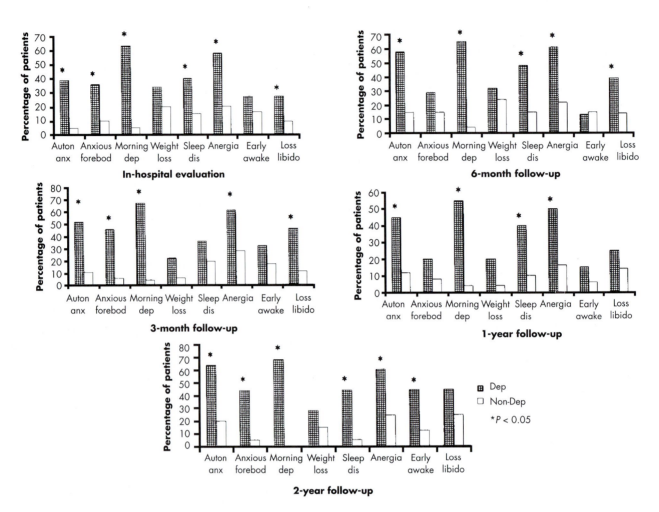

**FIGURE 21–2.** The frequency of vegetative symptoms of depression in patients with depressed mood (Dep) and without depressed mood (Non-Dep) following stroke. Symptom frequency is shown over the 2-year follow-up. Morning depression (i.e., diurnal mood variation) and anergia were associated with depression throughout the entire 2-year period. Loss of libido was only seen early in the follow-up, whereas early-morning awakening was only seen late in the follow-up. These findings suggest changes over time in both the effects of chronic medical illness and the phenomenology of depression following stroke.

*Note.* Abbreviations: Auton anx = autonomic anxiety; Anxious forebod = anxious foreboding; Morning dep = morning depression; Sleep dis = sleep disturbance; Early awake = early-morning awakening; Loss libido = loss of libido.

*Source.* Reprinted from Robinson RG: *The Clinical Neuropsychiatry of Stroke.* New York, Cambridge University Press, 1998 (data taken from Paradiso et al. 1997). Used with permission.

examined. The symptoms were obtained using the inclusive approach (i.e., symptoms that the patients acknowledged were included as positive even if there was some suspicion that the symptom may have been related to the physical illness). Thus, the initial diagnoses were based on the inclusive criteria. During the in-hospital evaluation, 26 patients (18%) met DSM-IV diagnostic criteria for major depression. Modified DSM-IV diagnostic criteria required five or more specific symptoms (i.e., we excluded weight loss and early-morning awakening from DSM-IV diagnostic criteria because they were not significantly more frequent in the depressed than in the nondepressed patients). Of 27 patients with major depres-

sion, 3 were excluded. Compared with diagnoses based solely on the existence of five or more specific symptoms for the diagnosis of DSM-IV major depression, diagnoses based on unmodified symptoms (i.e., early awakening and weight loss included) had a specificity of 98% and a sensitivity of 100%.

Modified DSM-IV criteria were then used to examine the substitutive approach (i.e., all vegetative symptoms were eliminated and the presence of four psychological symptoms plus depressed mood was required for the diagnosis of major depression). Using this approach, none of the original 27 patients with major depression was excluded. There were, in addition, four patients who presented with four or more specific symptoms of major depression but denied the presence of a depressed mood. These cases may represent "masked" depression.

Similar results were found at 3, 6, 12, and 24 months follow-up. The sensitivity of unmodified DSM-IV criteria consistently showed a sensitivity of 100% and a specificity that ranged from 95% to 98% compared with criteria using only specific symptoms. Thus, one could reasonably conclude that modifying DSM-IV criteria because of the existence of an acute medical illness is probably unnecessary.

These findings also suggest that the nature of PSD may change over time. Since the symptoms that were specific to depression changed over time, this may reflect an alteration in the underling etiology of PSD associated with early-onset depression compared with the late or chronic poststroke period (see Figure 21–2).

## Phenomenology

Lipsey et al. (1986) examined the frequency of depressive symptoms in a group of 43 patients with major PSD compared with that in a group of 43 age-matched patients with "functional" (i.e., no known brain pathology) depression. The main finding was that both groups showed almost identical profiles of symptoms, including those that were not part of the diagnostic criteria (Figure 21–3). More than 50% of the patients who met the diagnostic criteria for major PSD reported sadness, anxiety, tension, loss of interest and concentration, sleep disturbances with early-morning awakening, loss of appetite with weight loss, difficulty concentrating and thinking, and thoughts of death.

Gainotti et al. (1999) examined the phenomenology of PSD using their own Poststroke Depression Rating Scale (PSDRS). The scale includes 10 items: depressed mood, guilt feelings, thoughts of death or suicide, vegetative symptoms, apathy and loss of interest, anxiety, catastrophic reaction, hyperemotionalism, anhedonia, and diurnal mood variations. The last section on diurnal mood variations is scored in a range between +2 and –2, with +2 indicating a motivated depression associated with situational stresses, handicaps, or disabilities, and –2 indicating a lack of associated motivation, with depression being more prominent in the early morning. This scale was used to compare patients with poststroke major depression less than 2 months ($n=58$), 2–4 months ($n=52$), and more than 4 months ($n=43$) after stroke with 30 patients who were admitted to the psychiatric hospital with a diagnosis of endogenous major depression. Although statistical adjustment controlling for the large number of comparisons was not provided, the data

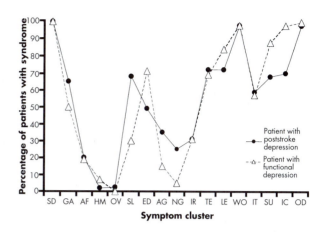

**FIGURE 21–3.** Patients with major depression after acute stroke ($n=43$) were compared with age-comparable patients hospitalized for functional primary depression ($n=43$). The symptom clusters are "syndromes" derived from the semistructured interview of the present state examination (PSE). SD=simple depression; GA=general anxiety; AF=affective flattening; HM=hypomania; OV=overactivity; SL=slowness; ED=special features of depression; AG=agitation; NG=self-neglect; IR=ideas of reference; TE=tension; LE=lack of energy; WO=worrying; IT=irritability; SU=social unease; IC=loss of interest and concentration; OD=other symptoms of depression. Patients with primary and poststroke depression showed the same frequency of all syndromes except slowness (stroke patients showed a higher frequency) and loss of interest and concentration (primary depression patients showed a higher frequency).

*Source.* Reprinted from Robinson RG: *The Clinical Neuropsychiatry of Stroke.* New York, Cambridge University Press, 1998 (modified from Lipsey et al. 1986). Used with permission.

were interpreted to indicate that poststroke patients with endogenous depression had higher scores on suicide and anhedonia, whereas patients with PSD had higher scores on catastrophic reaction, hyperemotionalism, and diurnal mood variation, which indicates an association with disability.

These authors asserted that failure to assess these aspects of depression (included in the PSDRS) indicates methodological errors in the assessment of depression by Robinson et al. (1983b; Gainotti et al. 1999). There are, however, clearly established criteria for the diagnosis of major depression as validated through numerous studies supporting DSM-IV-TR (American Psychiatric Association 2000). The inclusion of catastrophic reaction, hyperemotionalism, and diurnal variations (which are scored based on the patients' attribution of their depression to life stressors and disability) are clearly idiosyncratic criteria for the diagnosis of depression arbitrarily added to the diagnostic criteria to show differences with primary depression. As is shown later in this chapter, catastrophic reaction and hyperemotionalism are commonly seen in patients with stroke and are often associated with depression. Both catastrophic reaction and hyperemotionalism, however, occur in patients without depression, indicating that these conditions are comorbid in nature and are not symptoms that are integral to the diagnosis of depression. The addition of symptoms to the widely accepted criteria for depression must be validated as defining a specific population of patients with a unique poststroke depressive disorder. Validation of this new form of depressive disorder should include demonstration of predictable duration of disorder, specific associated clinical and pathological correlates, and response to treatment that are not found when "standard" criteria are used. As they stand, the Gainotti criteria do not further the phenomenology of PSD; they only support a preconceived hypothesis about the etiology of PSD. The only evidence available in the literature comparing primary depression and PSD using standard criteria indicates a very close correspondence between PSD and primary depression in the elderly (Lipsey et al. 1986).

## Prevalence

During the past 10 years, there have been a large number of studies around the world examining the prevalence of PSD. These publications indicate an increasing interest among clinicians caring for poststroke patients in the frequency and significance of depression following stroke. The findings of many of these studies are shown in Table 21–3. In general, these studies have found similar rates of major and minor depression among patients hospitalized for acute stroke, in rehabilitation hospitals, and in outpatient clinics. The mean frequency of major depression among patients in acute and rehabilitation hospitals was 22% for major depression and 17% for minor depression. Among patients studied in community settings, however, the mean prevalence of major depression was 13% and the mean prevalence of minor depression was 10%. Thus, PSD is common both among patients who are receiving treatment for stroke and among community samples. The higher rates of depression among patients who were receiving treatment for stroke is probably related to the greater severity of stroke seen in treatment settings compared with community settings, in which many patients have no physical or intellectual impairment.

## Duration

A consecutive series of 103 acute stroke patients was prospectively studied in a 2-year longitudinal study of PSD (Robinson et al. 1987). At the time of the initial in-hospital evaluation, 26% of the patients had the symptom cluster of major depression, whereas 20% had the symptom cluster of minor depression. Although both major and minor depressive disorders were still present in 86% of patients with in-hospital major or minor depression at a 6-month follow-up evaluation, only 1 of 5 patients with major depression continued to have major depression at 1-year follow-up (2 patients had minor depression). Patients with minor depression had a less favorable prognosis; only 40% had no depression at 1-year follow-up, and 30% had no depression at 2-year follow-up. In addition, about 30% of patients who were not depressed in the hospital became depressed after discharge. Thus, the natural course of major depression appeared to be between 6 months and 1 year, whereas the duration of minor depression was more variable, and in many cases the patients appeared to be chronically depressed.

Morris et al. (1990) found that among a group of 99 patients in a stroke rehabilitation hospital in Australia, those with major depression had a duration of major depression of 40 weeks, whereas those with adjustment disorders (minor depression) had a duration of depression of only 12 weeks. These findings confirm that major depression has a duration of approximately 9 months to 1 year but suggest that less severe depressive disorders may be more variable in their duration. Astrom et al. (1993a, 1993b) found that, among 80 patients with acute stroke, 27 (34%) developed major depression in hospital or at 3-month follow-up. Of these patients with major depression, 15 (60%) had recovered by 1-year follow-up, but by 3-year follow-up, only 1 more patient had recovered. This finding indicates that there may be a minority of patients with either major or minor depression who develop prolonged PSD.

The percentage of patients with major depression who had recovered by 1-year follow-up is shown in Figure 21–4. Although all studies found that the majority of depressions were less than 1 year in duration, the mean frequency of major depression that was persistent beyond 1 year was 26%.

Two factors have been identified that can influence the natural course of PSD. One is treatment of depression with antidepressant medications (discussed below). The second factor is lesion location. Starkstein et al. (1988c) compared two groups of depressed patients: one group ($n = 6$) had spontaneously recovered from depression by 6 months after stroke, whereas the other group ($n = 10$) remained depressed at this point. There were no significant between-group differences in important demographic variables, such as age, sex, and education, and both groups had similar levels of social functioning

**TABLE 21–3.** Prevalence studies of poststroke depression

| Investigators | Patient population | N | Criteria | % Major | % Minor | Total % |
|---|---|---|---|---|---|---|
| Folstein et al. 1977 | Rehab hospital | 20 | PSE & items | | | 45 |
| Finklestein et al. 1982 | Rehab hospital | 25 | Cutoff score | | | 48 |
| Sinyor et al. 1986 | Rehab hospital | 35 | Cutoff score | | | 36 |
| Finset et al. 1989 | Rehab hospital | 42 | Cutoff score | | | 36 |
| Eastwood et al. 1989 | Rehab hospital | 87 | SADS, RDC | 10 | 40 | 50 |
| Morris et al. 1990 | Rehab hospital | 99 | CIDI, DSM-III | 14 | 21 | 35 |
| Schubert et al. 1992 | Rehab hospital | 18 | DSM-III-R | 28 | 44 | 72 |
| Gainotti et al. 1999 | Rehab hospital | 153 | DSM-III-R | 31 | NR | 31+ |
| Schwartz et al. 1993 | Rehab hospital | 91 | DSM-III | 40 | | 40[a] |
| Feibel et al. 1982 | Outpatient (6 months) | 91 | Nursing evaluation | | | 26 |
| Robinson and Price 1982 | Outpatient (6 months–10 years) | 103 | Cutoff score | | | 29 |
| Collin et al. 1987 | Outpatient | 111 | Cutoff score | | | 42 |
| Astrom et al. 1993a, 1993b | Outpatient (3 months) | 73 | DSM-III | 31 | NR | 31[a] |
| | (1 year) | 73 | DSM-III | 16 | NR | 16[a] |
| | (2 years) | 57 | DSM-III | 19 | NR | 19[a] |
| | (3 years) | 49 | DSM-III | 29 | NR | 29[a] |
| Robinson 1998 | Outpatient (3 months) | 77 | PSE, DSM-III | 20 | 13 | 33 |
| | (6 months) | 80 | PSE, DSM-III | 21 | 21 | 42 |
| | (1 year) | 70 | PSE, DSM-III | 11 | 16 | 27 |
| | (2 years) | 67 | PSE, DSM-III | 18 | 17 | 35 |
| Pohjasvaara et al. 1998 | Outpatient | 277 | DSM-III-R | 26 | 14 | 40 |
| Dennis et al. 2000 | Outpatient (6 months) | 309 | Cutoff score | | | 38 |
| N. Herrmann et al. 1998 | Outpatient (3 months) | 150 | Cutoff score | | | 27 |
| | (1 year) | 136 | | | | 22 |
| Kotila et al. 1998 | Outpatient (3 months) | 321 | Cutoff score | | | 47 |
| | (1 year) | 311 | | | | 48 |
| Wade et al. 1987 | Community | 379 | Cutoff score | | | 30 |
| House et al. 1991 | Community | 89 | PSE, DSM-III | 11 | 12 | 23 |
| Burvill et al. 1995 | Community | 294 | PSE, DSM-III | 15 | 8 | 23 |
| Robinson et al. 1983b | Acute hospital | 103 | PSE, DSM-III | 27 | 20 | 47 |
| Ebrahim et al. 1987 | Acute hospital | 149 | Cutoff score | | | 23 |
| Fedoroff et al. 1991 | Acute hospital | 205 | PSE, DSM-III | 22 | 19 | 41 |
| Castillo et al. 1995 | Acute hospital | 291 | PSE, DSM-III | 20 | 18 | 38 |
| Starkstein et al. 1992 | Acute hospital | 80 | PSE, DSM-III | 16 | 13 | 29 |
| Astrom et al. 1993a, 1993b | Acute hospital | 80 | DSM-III | 25 | NR | 25[a] |
| M. Herrmann et al. 1993 | Acute hospital | 21 | RDC | 24 | 14 | 38 |
| Andersen et al. 1994 | Acute hospital or outpatient | 285 | Ham-D cutoff | 10 | 11 | 21 |
| | Mean | | | 20 | 21 | 34[a] |

[a]Because minor depression was not included, these values may be low.

*Note.* PSE = Present State Examination; SADS = Schedule for Affective Disorders and Schizophrenia; RDC = Research Diagnostic Criteria; CIDI = Composite International Diagnostic Interview; DSM-III = Diagnostic and Statistical Manual of Mental Disorders, 3rd Edition; DSM-III-R = Diagnostic and Statistical Manual of Mental Disorders, 3rd Edition, Revised; NR = not reported; Ham-D = Hamilton Rating Scale for Depression.

*Source.* Reprinted from Robinson RG: *The Clinical Neuropsychiatry of Stroke.* New York, Cambridge University Press, 1998. Used with permission.

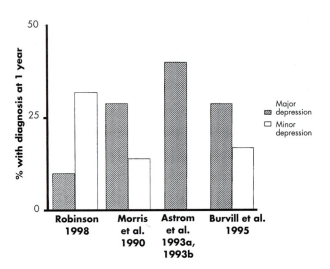

**FIGURE 21–4.** The percentage of patients with an initial assessment diagnosis of major poststroke depression who continued to have a diagnosis of major depression or who had improved to a diagnosis of minor depression at 1-year follow-up. Note that the number of chronic cases varies between studies, probably reflecting a mixture of etiologies among the group with an in-hospital diagnosis of major poststroke depression. The mean frequency of persistent major depression at 1-year follow-up across all studies was 26%.

*Source.* Reprinted from Robinson RG: *The Clinical Neuropsychiatry of Stroke.* New York, Cambridge University Press, 1998. Used with permission.

and degrees of cognitive dysfunction. There were, however, two significant between-group differences. One was lesion location: the recovered group had a higher frequency of subcortical and cerebellar–brain stem lesions; the nonrecovered group had a higher frequency of cortical lesions ($P < 0.01$). Impairments in activities of daily living (ADL) were also significantly different between the two groups: the nonrecovered group had significantly more severe impairments in ADL in hospital than did the recovered group ($P < 0.01$).

The available data suggest that PSD is not transient but is usually a long-standing disorder with a natural course of approximately 9–10 months for most cases of major depression. Depression lasting more than 2 years, however, does occur in some patients with major or minor depression. Lesion location and severity of associated impairments may influence the longitudinal evolution of PSD.

## Relationship to Lesion Variables

Relationship between depressive disorder and lesion location has perhaps been the most controversial area of research in the field of poststroke mood disorder. Although establishing an association between specific clinical symptoms and lesion location is one of the fundamental goals of clinical practice in neurology, this has rarely been the case with psychiatric disorders. Cognitive functions, speech, impairment, and the extent and severity of motor or sensory impairment are all symptoms of stroke that are commonly used by clinicians to localize lesions to particular brain regions. There is, however, no known neuropathology consistently associated with primary mood disorders (i.e., mood disorders without known brain injury) or secondary mood disorders (i.e., mood disorders associated with a physical illness). The idea that there may be a neuropathology associated with development of major depression has led to both surprise and skepticism.

The first study to report a significant clinical-pathologic correlation in PSD was an investigation by Robinson and Szetela (1981) of 29 patients with left-hemisphere brain injury secondary to stroke ($n = 18$) or to traumatic brain injury ($n = 11$). Based on localization of the lesion by computed tomography, there was a significant inverse correlation between the severity of depression and the distance of the anterior border of the lesion from the frontal pole ($r = 0.76$). This surprising finding led to a number of subsequent examinations of this phenomenon in other populations. Robinson et al. (1984) found a significant correlation in 10 patients with left-frontal acute stroke who were right-handed and had no known risk factors for depression ($r = 0.92$; $P < 0.05$). Thus, the location of the lesion along the anterior-posterior dimension appears to be an important variable in the severity of depression after stroke.

In addition, however, lesion location also influences the frequency of depression. In a study of 45 patients with single lesions restricted to either cortical or subcortical structures in the left or right hemisphere, Starkstein et al. (1987b) found that 44% of patients with left cortical lesions were depressed, whereas 39% of patients with left subcortical lesions, 11% of patients with right cortical lesions, and 14% of patients with right subcortical lesions were depressed. Thus, patients with lesions in the left hemisphere had significantly higher rates of depression than did those with lesions in the right hemisphere, regardless of the cortical or subcortical location of the lesion. These findings supported the hypothesis that depressive disorders after stroke are more frequent among patients with acute left-hemisphere lesions than in those with right-hemisphere lesions ($P < 0.05$).

When patients were further divided into those with anterior and those with posterior lesions, 5 of 5 patients with left cortical lesions involving the frontal lobe had depression, compared with 2 of 11 patients with left cortical-posterior lesions. Moreover, 4 of the 6 patients with left subcortical anterior lesions had depression, compared with 1 of 7 patients with left subcortical posterior lesions. Finally, correlations between depression scores and the distance of the lesion from the frontal pole were significant for patients with left cortical lesions and patients with left subcortical lesions. These relationships were not significant for patients with right-hemisphere lesions.

In a subsequent study, Starkstein et al. (1988a) examined the relationship between lesions of specific subcortical nuclei and depression. Basal ganglia (caudate and/or putamen) lesions produced major PSD in 7 of 8 patients with left-sided lesions, compared with only 1 of 7 patients with right-sided lesions and 0 of 10 with thalamic lesions ($P < 0.001$).

Astrom et al. (1993a, 1993b) similarly found that among patients with acute stroke, 12 of 14 with left anterior lesions had major depression, compared with only 2 of 7 patients with left posterior lesions ($P = 0.017$) and 2 of 23 with right-hemisphere lesions ($P < 0.001$). House et al. (1990a, 1990b) found only 4 cases of major depression among 40 patients with acute stroke in a community survey and did not find an association with left anterior lesions. M. Herrmann et al. (1993), however, found major depression in 7 of 10 patients with nonfluent aphasia and left anterior lesions, compared with 0 of 7 patients with fluent aphasia and left posterior lesions ($P = 0.0014$), but only during the acute poststroke period.

Numerous studies, however, have failed to replicate these findings. Some of these findings are shown in Figure 21–5. For example, Gainotti et al. (1999) examined lesion location in 53 patients using magnetic resonance or computed tomographic scans. Among patients with left anterior lesions who were less than 2 months poststroke, only 1 of 9 patients had major depression, although 3 of 7 patients with right anterior lesions had major depression. Among patients 2–4 months poststroke, 2 of 6 patients with left anterior lesions had major depression compared with 3 of 7 with right anterior lesions. Among patients who were more than 4 months poststroke, 5 of 9 patients with left anterior lesions had major depression compared with 2 of 3 with right anterior lesions.

This failure to replicate findings that were reported in at least four other studies was referred to by Gainotti as a "factual error of Robinson et al." (Gainotti et al. 1999). Negative findings, of course, happen all the time, and failure to replicate others' findings is far from proving the null hypothesis. Shimoda and Robinson (1999) examined the relationship between lesion location and time since stroke using a longitudinally studied patient population. This study examined 60 patients with single

lesions involving either the right or left middle cerebral artery distribution that were visible on computed tomographic scan and who had follow-up at 3 or 6 months (short-term follow-up) and at 12 or 24 months (long-term follow-up). There were no statistically significant differences between the patients with right and left hemisphere lesions in their age, gender, race, marital status, or other background characteristics. The frequency of depression in patients during the initial evaluation was significantly higher for both major and minor depression among patients with left-hemisphere stroke compared with patients with right-hemisphere stroke ($P = 0.0006$) (Figure 21–6). At short- and long-term follow-up, however, there were no significant differences between groups with right-hemisphere and left-hemisphere lesions in terms of the frequency of major or minor depression.

This study suggests that the failure of other investigators to replicate the association of left anterior lesion location with increased frequency of depression may in most cases be related to time since stroke. The lateralized effect of left anterior lesions on both major and minor depression is a phenomenon of the acute poststroke period (less than a month or two after the stroke). This lateralized effect is lost after these first few weeks, and subsequently there is an equal likelihood of patients with right- or left-hemisphere lesions having PSD.

Perhaps the most consistent finding from the studies of lesion location in patients with PSD is the statistically significant correlation between the severity of depression and the proximity of lesions to the frontal pole. As indicated previously, this correlation was first reported by Robinson and Szetela in 1981 and does not appear to be as sensitive to time since stroke as the association of left frontal and left basal ganglia lesion location with increased frequency of major depression during the acute poststroke period. The studies that have found a significant correlation between severity of depression and proximity of the lesion of the frontal pole are shown in Figure 21–7. In the previous follow-up study by Shimoda and Robinson (1999), there was a significant correlation between the severity of depression and proximity of the lesion to the left frontal pole during the acute poststroke period (Figure 21–8). There was, however, no significant correlation between the proximity of the right-hemisphere lesion to the frontal pole and severity of depressive symptoms. At short-term follow-up (3–6 months), patients with right-hemisphere lesions, as well as patients with left-hemisphere lesions, showed a significant correlation between severity of depression and proximity of the lesion to the frontal pole.

At long-term follow-up (12–24 months) there was

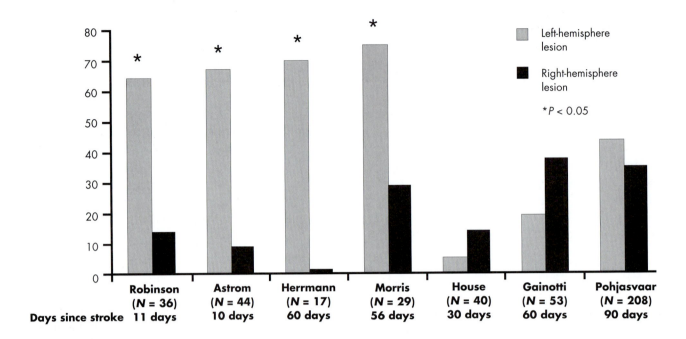

**FIGURE 21–5.** The frequency of major depression among patients with single lesions of left or right hemisphere. The association of left (anterior) lesions with major depression was found among patients who were studied within 2 months of their acute stroke. Numerous studies have not found this association with left-hemisphere lesions. Most, but not all, of these studies examined patients more than 2 months following stroke. Longitudinal follow-up in the Robinson et al. and Astrom et al. studies found no lateralized differences in frequency of depression at 3-month follow-up.

*Source.* Reprinted from Robinson RG: *The Clinical Neuropsychiatry of Stroke.* New York, Cambridge University Press, 1998. Used with permission.

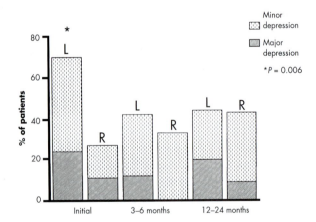

**FIGURE 21–6.** The frequency of major and minor depression defined by DSM-IV criteria associated with single lesions of the right (R) or left (L) hemisphere during the acute stroke period and at follow-up. The lateralized effect of left-hemisphere lesions on both major and minor depression was found only during the acute stroke period. At short-term and long-term follow-up, there were no hemispheric lesion effects on the frequency of depression.

*Source.* Reprinted from Robinson RG: *The Clinical Neuropsychiatry of Stroke.* New York, Cambridge University Press, 1998. Used with permission.

no significant correlation between severity of depression as measured by the Hamilton Rating Scale for Depression (Ham-D) (Hamilton 1960) or the Present State Examination (Wing et al. 1974) and the proximity of the lesion to the frontal pole among patients with left-hemisphere lesions ($n=25$). Among patients with right-hemisphere stroke ($n=21$), however, severity of depression was significantly correlated with proximity of the lesion to the occipital pole (i.e., lesions farther from the frontal pole were associated with more severe depression). This study found an intriguing, temporally dependent relationship between depression and lesion location. The association of depression with left anterior lesions was present only during the acute stroke period. By 3–6 months poststroke, depression was correlated with proximity of the lesion to the frontal pole for both patients with right-hemisphere lesions and patients with left-hemisphere lesions and, at long-term follow-up, depression was associated with proximity of the lesion to the occipital pole but only among patients with right-hemisphere stroke.

Although it is uncertain why this temporal dynamic occurs in the relationship between severity of depression and lesion location, it suggests that if physiologic changes such as depletion of biogenic amines occur in patients

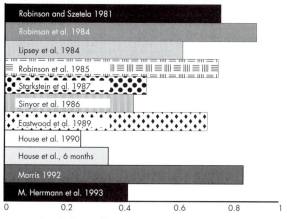

**FIGURE 21–7.** Magnitude of correlation coefficients between severity of depression and proximity of the lesion to the frontal pole (left-hemisphere or combined left- and right-hemisphere lesion data) for all studies that have examined this correlation. All correlations were statistically significant and ranged in magnitude so that between 8% and 80% of the variance in depression severity can be explained. "House et al. 1990, 6 months" refers to findings from examination of patients 6 months poststroke.

*Source.* Reprinted from Robinson RG: *The Clinical Neuropsychiatry of Stroke.* New York, Cambridge University Press, 1998. Used with permission.

with left anterior lesions that lead to depression, these changes are hemisphere-specific for only a few weeks. By 2–3 months after stroke (i.e., short-term follow-up) similar alternative mechanisms occur in patients with right frontal lesions that lead to correlation of depression severity with proximity of the lesion to the frontal pole.

## Premorbid Risk Factors

The studies reviewed above indicate that although a significant proportion of patients with left anterior or right posterior lesions develop PSD, not every patient with a lesion in these locations develops a depressive mood. This observation raises the question of why clinical variability occurs and why some but not all patients with lesions in these locations develop depression.

Starkstein et al. (1988b) examined these questions by comparing 13 patients with major PSD with 13 stroke patients without depression, all of whom had lesions of the same size and location. Eleven pairs of patients had left-hemisphere lesions, and two pairs had right-hemisphere lesions. Damage was cortical in 10 pairs and subcortical in 3 pairs. The groups did not differ on important demographic variables, such as age, sex, socioeconomic status, or education. They also did not differ on family or personal history of psychiatric disorders or neurologic

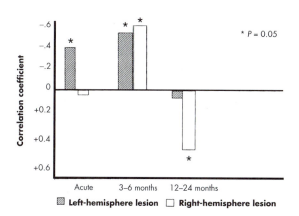

**FIGURE 21–8.** Spearman correlation coefficients between severity of depression, as measured by Present State Examination total score, and distance of the lesion from the frontal pole, as measured by computed tomographic scan. A negative correlation indicates that depression increased with proximity of the lesion to the frontal pole, and a positive correlation indicates that depression increased with the proximity of the lesion to the occipital pole. During the acute stroke period, depression severity correlated with the proximity of the lesion to the frontal pole but only among patients with left-hemisphere lesions. During short-term follow-up, the proximity of the lesion to the frontal pole was correlated with more severe depression for both right- and left-hemisphere lesions. At long-term follow-up, severity of depression was significantly correlated with the proximity of the lesion to the occipital pole (i.e., lesions farther away from the frontal pole) but only for patients with right-hemisphere lesions. These findings demonstrate the dynamic nature of clinical-pathological correlations to poststroke depression.

*Source.* Reprinted from Robinson RG: *The Clinical Neuropsychiatry of Stroke.* New York, Cambridge University Press, 1998. Used with permission.

deficits. Patients with major PSD, however, had significantly more subcortical atrophy ($P < 0.05$), as measured both by the ratio of third ventricle to brain (i.e., the area of the third ventricle divided by the area of the brain at the same level) and by the ratio of lateral ventricle to brain (i.e., the area of the body of the lateral ventricle contralateral to the brain lesion divided by the brain area at the same level). It is likely that the subcortical atrophy preceded the stroke. Thus, a mild degree of subcortical atrophy may be a premorbid risk factor that increases the risk of developing major depression following a stroke.

In the previously described study of patients with right-hemisphere lesions, Starkstein et al. (1989b) found that patients who developed major depression after the occurrence of a right-hemisphere lesion had a significantly higher frequency of family history of psychiatric disorders than did either nondepressed patients with right-hemisphere lesions or patients with major depression following the occurrence of left-hemisphere lesions. This finding suggests that a genetic predisposition for depression may play an important role after the occurrence of right-hemisphere lesions. Eastwood et al. (1989) and Morris et al. (1990) also reported that depressed patients were more likely than nondepressed patients to have either a personal or a family history of psychiatric disorders.

In summary, lesion location is not the only factor that influences the development of PSD. Subcortical atrophy that probably precedes the stroke and a family or personal history of affective disorders also seem to play an important role.

## Relationship to Physical Impairment

Numerous investigators, including Robinson et al. (1983b), Eastwood et al. (1989), and N. Herrmann et al. (1998), have reported a low but significant correlation between depression and functional physical impairment (i.e., ADL). This association, however, might be construed as the severe functional impairment producing depression or, alternatively, the severity of depression influencing the severity of functional impairment. Several studies lend support to the latter suggestion.

Sinyor et al. (1986) reported that, although nondepressed stroke patients showed either a slight increase or no change in functional status over time, depressed patients had significant decreases in function during the first month after stroke ($P < 0.05$). In another study, Parikh et al. (1990) compared a consecutive series of 63 stroke patients who had major or minor depression with nondepressed stroke patients during a 2-year follow-up. Although both groups had similar impairments in ADL during the time they were in hospital, the depressed patients had significantly less improvement by 2-year follow-up than did the nondepressed patients. This finding held true after the authors controlled for important variables such as the type and extent of in-hospital and rehabilitation treatment, the size and location of the lesion, the patients' demographic characteristics, the nature of the stroke, the occurrence of another stroke during the follow-up period, and medical history.

A recent study by Chemerinski and Robinson (2000) included a consecutive series of patients with PSD ($N = 55$) divided into those whose mood improved at 3- to 6-month follow-up and those who had not improved ($n = 34$). This study found significantly greater improvement in ADL scores among patients whose major or minor depression improved compared with those whose depression did not. There were no significant differences in the background characteristics of patients whose mood did and did not improve, including lesion characteristics, neurologic symptoms, and background characteristics such as age and education. In addition, patients with minor depression showed the same degree of improvement with remission of their depression as did patients with major depression. The fact that patients with major and minor depression showed an equal degree of recovery in ADL with remission of their depression suggests that the effect of depression on physical impairment may be mediated by psychological mechanisms rather than by physiological mechanisms. For example, depressed patients may be hopeless about the future and thus less motivated to put an effort into rehabilitation exercises. This could lead to slowed recovery among depressed patients.

## Relationship to Cognitive Impairment

Numerous investigators have reported that elderly patients with functional major depression have intellectual deficits that improve with treatment of depression (Wells 1979). This issue was first examined in patients with PSD by Robinson et al. (1986). Patients with major depression after a left-hemisphere infarct were found to have significantly lower (i.e., more impaired) scores on the Mini-Mental State Exam (MMSE) (Folstein et al. 1975) than did a comparable group of nondepressed patients. Both the size of the patients' lesions and their depression scores correlated independently with severity of cognitive impairment.

In a second study (Starkstein et al. 1988b), stroke patients with and without major depression were matched for lesion location and volume. Of 13 patients with major PSD, 10 had an MMSE score lower than that of their matched control subjects, 2 had the same score, and only 1 patient had a higher score ($P < 0.001$). Thus, even when patients were matched for lesion size and location, depressed patients were more cognitively impaired.

In a follow-up study, Bolla-Wilson et al. (1989) administered a comprehensive neuropsychological battery and found that patients with major depression and left-hemisphere lesions had significantly greater cognitive impairments than did nondepressed patients with comparable left-hemisphere lesions ($P < 0.05$). These cognitive deficits primarily involved tasks of temporal orientation, language, and executive motor and frontal lobe functions. On the other hand, among patients with right-hemisphere lesions, patients with major depression did not differ from nondepressed patients on any of the measures of cognitive impairment.

Downhill and Robinson (1994) conducted a 2-year follow-up study of 140 patients after the occurrence of stroke. They found that major depression was associated with a greater degree of cognitive impairment, as measured by the MMSE, than were minor depression or no depression for 1 year after stroke. The intellectual deficit, however, was most prominent among patients with major depression after a left-hemisphere lesion. Patients who had major depression following a right-hemisphere stroke or patients with minor depression, or patients in whom stroke had occurred 2 years previously, did not show an effect of major depression on cognitive impairment.

Treatment studies of PSD have consistently failed to show an improvement in cognitive function even when poststroke mood disorders responded to antidepressant therapy (Andersen et al. 1996). Kimura et al. (2000) examined this issue in a study comparing nortriptyline and placebo using a double-blind treatment methodology among patients with major ($n = 33$) or minor ($n = 14$) PSD. Although the groups treated with nortriptyline and with placebo showed no significant differences in the change in MMSE scores from beginning to end of the treatment study, when patients were divided into those who responded to treatment (i.e., greater than 50% decline in Ham-D score and no longer meeting depression diagnosis criteria) and those who did not respond, there was a significantly greater improvement in MMSE score among patients who responded to treatment ($n = 24$) compared with patients who did not respond to treatment ($n = 23$) (Figure 21–9). The responding group included 16 patients treated with nortriptyline and 9 treated with placebo, whereas the nonresponding group included 5 patients treated with nortriptyline and 18 treated with placebo. There were no significant differences between the two groups in baseline Ham-D scores, demographic characteristics, stroke characteristics, or neurologic findings. A repeated measures analysis of variance (ANOVA) demonstrated a significant group by time interaction ($P = 0.005$), and planned post hoc comparisons demonstrated that the responders had significantly less impaired MMSE scores than did the nonresponders, at nortriptyline doses of 75 mg ($P = 0.036$) and 100 mg ($P = 0.024$). If only nortriptyline-treated patients were used in the treatment response group compared with all placebo-treated patients in the treatment failure group, there was still a significant group by time interaction ($P = 0.036$), which indicates that the failure to demonstrate cognitive improvement in earlier studies was not the result of nortriptyline drug effects such as sedation or impaired attention due to anticholinergic effects. When

the effect of major versus minor depression was examined, patients with major depression who responded to treatment ($n = 15$) showed significantly greater improvement in MMSE scores than did patients with major depression who did not respond ($n = 18$) ($P = 0.0087$) (Figure 21–9). Among patients with minor depression (9 responders and 5 nonresponders), repeated measures ANOVA of MMSE scores showed no significant group by time interaction.

The fact that earlier treatment studies did not show a significant effect of treatment of depression on cognitive function was the result of effect size. When patients treated with nortriptyline (some of whom responded to treatment and some of whom did not) were compared with patients treated with placebo (some of whom responded to treatment some of whom did not), the effect size was only 0.16. When patients were divided into those who responded and those who did not respond, the effect size increased to 0.96, thus allowing a significant difference to be demonstrated with a much smaller group size.

## Mechanism of PSD

Although the cause of PSD remains unknown, one of the mechanisms that has been hypothesized to play an etiologic role is dysfunction of the biogenic amine system. The noradrenergic and serotonergic cell bodies are located in the brain stem and send ascending projections through the median forebrain bundle to the frontal cortex. The ascending axons then arc posteriorly and run longitudinally through the deep layers of the cortex, arborizing and sending terminal projections into the superficial cortical layers (Morrison et al. 1979). Lesions that disrupt these pathways in the frontal cortex or the basal ganglia may affect many downstream fibers. Based on these neuroanatomic facts and the clinical findings that the severity of depression correlates with the proximity of the lesion to the frontal pole, Robinson et al. (1984) suggested that PSD may be the consequence of depletions of norepinephrine and/or serotonin produced by lesions in the frontal lobe or basal ganglia.

In support of this hypothesis, laboratory investigations in rats have demonstrated that the biochemical response to ischemic lesions is lateralized. Right-hemisphere lesions produce depletions of norepinephrine and spontaneous hyperactivity, whereas comparable lesions of the left hemisphere do not (Robinson 1979). More recently, a similar lateralized biochemical response to ischemia in human subjects was reported by Mayberg et al. (1988). Patients with stroke lesions in the right hemisphere had significantly higher ratios of ipsilateral to con-

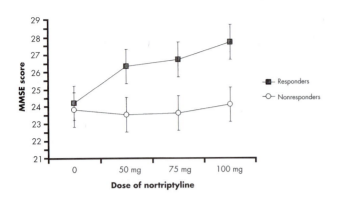

**FIGURE 21–9.** Change in Mini-Mental State Exam (MMSE) scores in patients with poststroke major depression during a double-blind treatment study of nortriptyline versus placebo. Treatment responders ($n=15$) showed significantly greater improvement in cognitive function than nonresponders ($n=18$) ($P=0.0087$). Error bars represent standard errors of mean (SE).

*Source.* Reprinted from Kimura M, Robinson RG, Kosier T: "Treatment of Cognitive Impairment After Poststroke Depression." *Stroke* 31(7):1482–1486, 2000. Used with permission.

tralateral spiperone binding (presumably serotonin type 2 receptor binding) in noninjured temporal and parietal cortex than did patients with comparable left-hemisphere strokes. Patients with left-hemisphere lesions, on the other hand, showed a significant inverse correlation between the amount of spiperone binding in the left temporal cortex and depression scores (i.e., higher depression scores were associated with lower serotonin receptor binding).

Thus, a greater depletion of biogenic amines in patients with right-hemisphere lesions than in those with left-hemisphere lesions could lead to a compensatory upregulation of receptors that might protect against depression. On the other hand, patients with left-hemisphere lesions may have moderate depletions of biogenic amines but without a compensatory upregulation of serotonin receptors and, therefore, a dysfunction of biogenic amine systems in the left hemisphere. This dysfunction may ultimately lead to the clinical manifestations of depression.

## Treatment of PSD

At the present time, there have been four placebo-controlled, randomized, double-blind treatment studies on the efficacy of single-antidepressant treatment of PSD. In the first study, Lipsey et al. (1984) examined 14 patients treated with nortriptyline and 20 patients given placebo. The 11 patients treated with nortriptyline who completed the 6-week study showed significantly greater improvement in their Ham-D scores than did 15 placebo-treated patients ($P<0.01$). Successfully treated patients had serum nortriptyline levels of 50–150 ng/mL. Three patients experienced side effects (including delirium, confusion, drowsiness, and agitation) that were severe enough to require the discontinuation of nortriptyline. Similarly, Reding et al. (1986) reported that patients with PSD (defined as having an abnormal dexamethasone suppression test) taking trazodone had greater improvement in Barthel ADL scores (Granger et al. 1979) than did placebo-treated control subjects ($P<0.05$). In another double-blind controlled trial in which the selective serotonin reuptake inhibitor (SSRI) citalopram was used, it was found that Ham-D scores were significantly more improved over 6 weeks in patients receiving active treatment ($n=27$) than in those receiving placebo ($n=32$) (Andersen et al. 1994). At both 3 and 6 weeks, the group receiving active treatment had significantly lower Ham-D scores than did the group receiving placebo. This study established for the first time the efficacy of an SSRI in the treatment of PSD.

The most recent treatment study, however, was conducted by Robinson et al. (2000). This study compared depressed patients treated with fluoxetine ($n=23$), nortriptyline ($n=16$), or placebo ($n=17$) in a double-blind, randomized treatment design. Patients were enrolled if they had a diagnosis of either major or minor PSD and had no contraindication to the use of fluoxetine or nortriptyline such as intracerebral hemorrhage (fluoxetine) or cardiac induction abnormalities (nortriptyline). Patients in the fluoxetine group were treated with 10-mg doses for the first 3 weeks, 20 mg for weeks 4–6, 30 mg for weeks 6–9, and 40 mg for weeks 9–12. The patients in the nortriptyline group were given 25 mg for the first week, 50 mg for weeks 2 and 3, 75 mg for weeks 3–6, and 100 mg for weeks 6–12. Patients treated with placebo were given identical capsules in the same number used for the actively treated patients. Intention-to-treat analysis demonstrated significant time by treatment interaction, with patients treated with nortriptyline showing a significantly greater decline in Ham-D scores than either the placebo-treated or the fluoxetine-treated patients at 12 weeks of treatment. There were no significant differences between the fluoxetine and the placebo groups (Figure 21–10).

Nortriptyline led to a significantly higher response rate (with response defined as more than 50% drop in Ham-D score and the patient no longer meeting diagnostic criteria for major or minor depression) (10 of 16, 62%) than either fluoxetine (2 of 23, 9%) or placebo (4 of 17, 24%) (Fisher exact $P=0.001$). In addition, fluox-

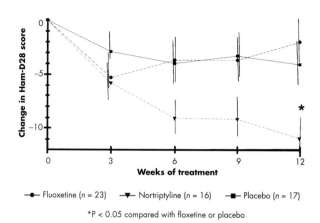

**FIGURE 21–10.** Intention-to-treat analysis. Change in (28-item) Hamilton Rating Scale for Depression score over 12 weeks of treatment for all patients who were entered in the study.

*Source.* Reprinted from Robinson RG, Schultz SK, Castillo C, et al.: "Nortriptyline Versus Fluoxetine in the Treatment of Depression and in Short Term Recovery After Stroke: A Placebo Controlled, Double-Blind Study." *American Journal of Psychiatry* 157:351–359, 2000. Used with permission.

etine treatment was associated with a mean weight loss of 15.1 lb or 8.5% of initial body weight from beginning to end of the 12-week treatment trial, which was not seen among patients treated with either placebo or nortriptyline. Of the 12 patients treated with fluoxetine, 10 lost 10 or more pounds, whereas only 2 of 13 nortriptyline patients and 1 of 11 placebo patients lost this amount of weight (Fisher exact $P=0.004$).

Based on the available data, if there are no contraindications to nortriptyline such as heart block, cardiac arrhythmia, narrow-angle glaucoma, sedation, or orthostatic hypotension, nortriptyline remains the first-line treatment for PSD. Doses of nortriptyline should be increased slowly and blood levels should be monitored with a goal of achieving serum concentrations between 50 and 150 ng/mL. If there are contraindications to the use of nortriptyline, citalopram (20 mg under age 66, 10 mg age 66 and over) would be the next choice. Electroconvulsive therapy has also been reported to be effective for treating PSD (Murray et al. 1987). It causes few side effects and no neurologic deterioration. Psychostimulants have also been reported in open-label trials to be effective for the treatment of PSD. Finally, psychological treatment—including cognitive-behavioral therapy (Hibbard et al. 1990), group therapy, and family therapy—has also been reported to be useful (Oradei and Waite 1974; Watzlawick and Coyne 1980). However, controlled stud-

ies for these treatment modalities have not been conducted.

## Psychosocial Adjustment

Psychosocial adjustment after stroke is an important issue to consider. Thompson et al. (1989) examined 40 stroke patients and their caregivers at an average of 9 months after the occurrence of stroke. They found that a lack of meaningfulness in life and overprotection by the caregiver were independent predictors of depression. Kotila et al. (1998) examined depression after stroke in the Finnstroke study. This study examined the effect of active rehabilitation programs after discharge together with support and social activities on the frequency of depression among patients and caregivers at 3 months and 1 year after stroke. At both 3 months and 1 year, the frequency of depression was significantly lower among patients receiving active outpatient treatment than among patients without active rehabilitation programs (41% vs. 54% at 3 months and 42% vs. 55% at 1 year). Although there were no significant differences between districts with and without active programs in the rate of depression among caregivers at 3 months, at 12 months there were significantly more severely depressed caregivers in districts without active programs ($P=0.036$). Greater severity of impairment, as measured by the Rankin Scale (Rankin 1957), was also associated with increased depression among caregivers at 3 months after stroke.

## Poststroke Mania

Although poststroke mania occurs much less frequently than depression (we have observed only three cases among a consecutive series of more than 300 stroke patients), manic syndromes are sometimes associated with stroke.

### Phenomenology of Secondary Mania

Starkstein et al. (1988a) examined a series of 12 consecutive patients who met DSM-III criteria for an organic affective syndrome, manic type. These patients, who developed mania after a stroke, traumatic brain injury, or tumors, were compared with patients with functional (i.e., no known neuropathology) mania (Starkstein et al. 1987a). Both groups of patients showed similar frequencies of elation, pressured speech, flight of ideas, grandiose thoughts, insomnia, hallucinations, and paranoid delusions. Thus, the symptoms of mania that occurred after brain damage (secondary mania) appeared to be the same as those found in patients with mania without brain damage (primary mania).

## Lesion Location

Several studies of patients with brain damage have found that patients who develop secondary mania have a significantly greater frequency of lesions in the right hemisphere than patients with depression or no mood disturbance. The right-hemisphere lesions that lead to mania tend to be in specific right-hemisphere structures that have connections to the limbic system. The right basotemporal cortex appears to be particularly important, because direct lesions as well as distant hypometabolic effects (diaschisis) of this cortical region are frequently associated with secondary mania.

Cummings and Mendez (1984) reported on two patients who developed mania after right thalamic stroke lesions. After a review of the literature, these authors suggested a specific association between secondary mania and lesions in the limbic system or in limbic-related areas of the right hemisphere.

Robinson et al. (1988) reported on 17 patients with secondary mania. Most of the patients had right-hemisphere lesions involving either cortical limbic areas, such as the orbitofrontal cortex and the basotemporal cortex, or subcortical nuclei, such as the head of the caudate nucleus or the thalamus. The frequency of right-hemisphere lesions was significantly greater than it was among patients with major depression, who tended to have left-frontal or basal ganglia lesions.

These findings have been replicated in another study of eight patients with secondary mania (Starkstein et al. 1990b). All eight patients had right-hemisphere lesions (seven unilateral and one bilateral injury). Lesions were either cortical (basotemporal cortex in four patients and orbitofrontal cortex in one patient) or subcortical (frontal white matter, head of the caudate nucleus, and anterior limb of the internal capsule in one patient each). Positron emission tomography scans with ($^{18}$F)fluorodeoxyglucose were carried out in the three patients with purely subcortical lesions. They all showed a focal hypometabolic deficit in the right basotemporal cortex.

## Risk Factors

Not every patient with a lesion in limbic areas of the right hemisphere will develop secondary mania. Therefore, there must be risk factors for this disorder.

In one study (Robinson et al. 1988), patients with secondary mania were compared with patients with secondary major depression. Results indicated that patients with secondary mania had a significantly higher frequency of positive family history of affective disorders than did depressed patients or patients with no mood disturbance ($P < 0.05$). Therefore, it appears that genetic predisposition to affective disorders may constitute a risk factor for mania.

In another study (Starkstein et al. 1987a), patients with secondary mania were compared with patients with no mood disturbance who were matched for size, location, and etiology of brain lesion. The groups were also compared with patients with primary mania and control subjects. No significant between-group differences were found either in demographic variables or neurologic evaluation. Patients with secondary mania, however, had a significantly greater degree of subcortical atrophy, as measured by bifrontal-to-brain ratio and third ventricle-to-brain ratio ($P < 0.001$). Moreover, of the patients who developed secondary mania, those with a positive family history of psychiatric disorders had significantly less atrophy than those without such a family history ($P < 0.05$), suggesting that genetic predisposition to affective disorders and brain atrophy may be independent risk factors.

The relatively rare occurrence of mania after stroke suggests that there are premorbid risk factors that have an impact on the expression of this disorder. Studies thus far have identified two such factors. One is a genetic vulnerability for affective disorder and the other is a mild degree of subcortical atrophy. The subcortical atrophy probably preceded the stroke, but its cause remains unknown.

## Mechanism of Secondary Mania

Several studies have demonstrated that the amygdala (located in the medial portion of the temporal lobe) has an important role in the production of instinctive reactions and the association between stimulus and emotional response (Gloor 1986). The amygdala receives its main afferents from the basal diencephalon (which in turn receives psychosensory and psychomotor information from the reticular formation) and the temporopolar and basolateral cortices (which receive main afferents from heteromodal association areas) (Beck 1949; Crosby et al. 1962). The basotemporal cortex receives afferents from association cortical areas and the orbitofrontal cortex and sends efferent projections to the entorhinal cortex, hippocampus, and amygdala. By virtue of these connections, the basotemporal cortex may represent a cortical link between sensory afferents and instinctive reactions (Goldar and Outes 1972).

The orbitofrontal cortex may be subdivided into two regions: a posterior one, which is restricted to limbic functions and should be considered part of the limbic system, and an anterior one, which exerts tonic inhibitory control over the amygdala by means of its connection through the uncinate fasciculus with the basotemporal cortex (Nauta 1971). Thus, the uncinate fasciculus and the basotemporal cortex may mediate connections between psychomotor and volitional processes, generated in the frontal lobe, and vital processes and instinctive behaviors, generated in the amygdala (Starkstein et al. 1988a).

A case report by Starkstein et al. (1989a) suggested that the mechanism of secondary mania is not related to the release of transcallosal inhibitory fibers (i.e., the release of left limbic areas from tonic inhibition due to a right-hemisphere lesion). A patient who developed secondary mania after bleeding from a right basotemporal arteriovenous malformation underwent a Wada test before the therapeutic embolization of the malformation. Injection of amobarbital in the left carotid artery did not abolish the manic symptoms (which would be expected if the "release" theory were correct).

Although the mechanism of secondary mania remains unknown, both lesion studies and metabolic studies suggest that the right basotemporal cortex may play an important role. A combination of biogenic amine system dysfunction and release of tonic inhibitory input into the basotemporal cortex and lateral limbic system may lead to the production of mania.

## Treatment of Secondary Mania

Although no systematic treatment studies of secondary mania have been conducted, one report suggested several potentially useful treatment modalities. Bakchine et al. (1989) carried out a double-blind, placebo-controlled treatment study in a single patient with secondary mania. Clonidine (0.6 mg/day) rapidly reversed the manic symptoms, whereas carbamazepine (1,200 mg/day) was associated with no mood changes and levodopa (375 mg/day) was associated with an increase in manic symptoms. In other treatment studies, however, the anticonvulsants valproic acid and carbamazepine as well as neuroleptics and lithium therapy have been reported to be useful in treating secondary mania (Starkstein et al. 1991). None of these treatments, however, have been evaluated in double-blind, placebo-controlled studies.

## Poststroke Bipolar Disorder

Although some patients have one or more manic episodes after brain injury, other manic patients also have depression after brain injury. In an effort to examine the crucial factors in determining which patients have bipolar as opposed to unipolar disorder, Starkstein et al. (1991) examined 19 patients with the diagnosis of secondary mania. The bipolar (manic-depressive) group consisted of patients who, after the occurrence of the brain lesion,

met DSM-III-R criteria for organic mood syndrome, mania, followed or preceded by organic mood syndrome, depressed. The unipolar-mania group consisted of patients who met the criteria for mania described previously (i.e., DSM-III-R organic mood syndrome, mania), not followed or preceded by depression. All the patients had computed tomographic scan evidence of vascular, neoplastic, or traumatic brain lesion and no history of other neurologic, toxic, or metabolic conditions.

Patients in the bipolar group were found to have significantly greater intellectual impairment as measured by MMSE scores ($P < 0.05$). Almost half of the patients in the bipolar group had recurrent episodes of depression, whereas approximately one-fourth of patients in both the unipolar and bipolar groups had recurrent episodes of mania.

Of the 7 patients with bipolar disorder, 6 had lesions restricted to the right hemisphere, which involved the head of the caudate nucleus (2 patients); the thalamus (3 patients); and the head of the caudate nucleus, the dorsolateral frontal cortex, and the basotemporal cortex (1 patient). The remaining patient developed bipolar illness after surgical removal of a pituitary adenoma. In contrast to the primarily subcortical lesions in the bipolar group, 8 of 12 patients in the unipolar mania group had lesions restricted to the right hemisphere, which involved the basotemporal cortex (6 patients), the orbitofrontal cortex (1 patient), and the head of the caudate nucleus (1 patient). The remaining 4 patients had bilateral lesions involving the orbitofrontal cortex (3 patients) and the orbitofrontal white matter (1 patient).

This study suggests that a prior episode of depression may have occurred in about one-third of patients with secondary mania. Patients with bipolar disorder tend to have subcortical lesions (mainly involving the right head of the caudate nucleus or the right thalamus), whereas patients with pure mania tend to show a higher frequency of cortical lesions (particularly in the right orbitofrontal and right basotemporal cortices). Finally, bipolar patients tend to have greater cognitive impairment than do patients with unipolar mania, which may either reflect differences in lesion location or suggest that the presence of a previous episode of depression may produce residual cognitive effects.

How might subcortical lesions produce bipolar disorder? Subcortical lesions have been reported to produce hypometabolic effects in widespread regions, including contralateral brain areas (i.e., crossed-hemisphere and crossed-cerebellar diaschisis) (Pappata et al. 1987). Thus, it is possible that subcortical lesions may have induced metabolic changes in left frontocortical regions, which (as noted above) are associated with depression.

Mania may develop at a later stage, when these metabolic changes become restricted to the orbitofrontal and/or basotemporal cortices of the right hemisphere.

## Poststroke Anxiety Disorder

Studies of patients with functional depression (i.e., of no known neuropathologic origin) have demonstrated that it is important to distinguish depression associated with significant anxiety symptoms (i.e., agitated depression) from depression without these symptoms (i.e., retarded depression), because their cause and course may be different (Stravakaki and Vargo 1986). This finding raises questions not only about the frequency and correlates of anxiety in stroke victims, but also about the nature of the relationship between anxiety and depression among patients with brain injury.

Starkstein et al. (1990a) examined a consecutive series of patients with acute stroke lesions for the presence of both anxiety and depressive symptoms. Slightly modified DSM-III criteria for generalized anxiety disorder (GAD) (i.e., excluding 6-month duration criteria) were used for the diagnosis of anxiety disorder. The presence of anxious foreboding and excessive worry were required, as were one or more symptoms of motor tension (i.e., muscle tension, restlessness, and easy fatigability), one or more symptoms of autonomic hyperactivity, and one or more symptoms of vigilance and scanning (i.e., feeling keyed up or on edge, difficulty concentrating because of anxiety, trouble falling or staying asleep, and irritability). Of a consecutive series of 98 patients with first-episode acute stroke lesions, only 6 met the criteria for GAD in the absence of any other mood disorder. On the other hand, 23 of 47 patients with major depression also met the criteria for GAD. Patients were then divided into those with anxiety only ($n=6$), anxiety and depression ($n=23$), depression only ($n=24$), and no mood disorder ($n=45$).

The only significant between-group difference in demographic variables was the presence of a higher frequency of alcoholism in patients with anxiety only. No significant between-group differences were found on neurologic examination. Examination of patients with positive computed tomographic scans revealed that anxious-depressed patients had a significantly higher frequency of cortical lesions (16 of 19 patients) than did either the depression-only group (7 of 15 patients) or the control group (13 of 27 patients) (Figure 21–11). On the other hand, the depression-only group showed a significantly higher frequency of subcortical lesions than did the anxious-depressed group.

Castillo et al. (1993, 1995) found that 78 (27%) of a

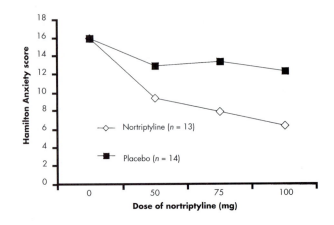

**FIGURE 21–11.** Mean Hamilton Anxiety Scale scores in patients with generalized anxiety disorder with comorbid depression after stroke following treatment with nortriptyline or placebo

group of 288 patients hospitalized with an acute stroke met DSM-III-R criteria for GAD (excluding the 6-month duration criteria). Most patients with GAD also had major or minor depression (i.e., 58 of 78 patients with GAD also had depression). Depression plus anxiety was associated with left cortical lesions, whereas anxiety alone was associated with right-hemisphere lesions. In a 2-year follow-up in a subgroup of 142 of these 288 patients, it was found that 32 patients (23%) developed GAD after the initial in-hospital evaluation (i.e., between 3 and 24 months after stroke). Early-onset but not late-onset GAD was associated with a history of psychiatric disorder, including alcohol abuse, and early-onset anxiety had a mean duration of 1.5 months, whereas delayed-onset GAD had a mean duration of 3.0 months (Castillo et al. 1995).

Astrom (1996) examined 71 acute stroke patients for anxiety disorder and observed these patients over 3 years. The strongest correlates of GAD were the absence of social contacts outside the family and dependence of patients on others to perform their primary activities of daily living. These factors were significantly more common in the GAD population than in the non-GAD population at 3 months, 1 year, 2 years, and 3 years after stroke. No other impairment or demographic factors distinguished the GAD patients from the non-GAD patients throughout the follow-up period. At 3-year follow-up, however, GAD was associated with both cortical atrophy (7 of 7 GAD patients had cortical atrophy vs. 19 of 39 non-GAD patients) and greater subcortical atrophy (as measured by frontal horn ratios on computed tomographic scan, $P=0.03$).

A recent study by Shimoda and Robinson (1998a,

1998b) examined the effect of GAD on outcome in patients with stroke. A group of 142 patients examined during hospitalization for acute stroke and followed up for 2 years were diagnosed with either GAD ($n = 9$), major depressive disorder alone ($n = 10$), both GAD and major depression ($n = 10$), or neither GAD nor depression ($n = 36$). An examination of the effect of GAD and major depression at the time of the initial hospital evaluation on recovery in ADL at short-term follow-up (i.e., 3–6 months) demonstrated a significant effect of major depression but no significant effect of GAD and no interaction. At long-term follow-up (1–2 years), however, there was a significant interaction between major depression and GAD to inhibit recovery in ADL.

Similarly, an analysis of social functioning at short-term follow-up showed significant main effects of both major depression and GAD but no interaction. At long-term follow-up there were significant interactions between GAD and time as well as between major depression, GAD, and time. These findings indicate that patients with GAD were more impaired in their social functioning over the entire 2-year follow-up period and that patients with major depression plus GAD had the most severe impairment in social functioning of any group. Perhaps the most significant finding from this study, however, was that major depressive disorder and anxiety disorder diagnosed at the time of the initial in-hospital evaluation had a greater effect on impairment in ADL at 1-year and 2-year follow-up than did major depression alone, anxiety disorder alone, or no mood or anxiety disturbance. These findings suggest that anxiety disorder is an important variable affecting long-term prognosis following stroke.

Another interesting finding from this study was that patients with major depression plus GAD had depression that was significantly longer in duration and greater in severity than patients with major depression alone.

A recent treatment study examined the effect of nortriptyline on GAD that is comorbid with PSD (Kimura and Robinson, unpublished observations, 2001). The study included 29 patients who met criteria for GAD (17 with comorbid major depression, 10 with minor depression, and 2 with no depression). Analysis of the 27 GAD patients with comorbid depression used an intention-to-treat analysis that included 4 patients who dropped out of the study. There were no significant differences between the patients treated with nortriptyline and the patients treated with placebo in background characteristics including age, education, and time since stroke. There were also no significant differences between actively treated and placebo-treated patients in their neurologic findings or the nature of the stroke

lesion. In the group treated with nortriptyline, 54% of the patients had right-hemisphere lesions; 64% of the placebo group had similar lesions. Motor impairments were present in 77% of the nortriptyline-treated patients and in 86% of the placebo-treated patients. Aphasia was found in 23% of the nortriptyline-treated patients and in 14% of the placebo patients. Because some patients in the study had been treated for 6 weeks whereas others had been treated for 12 weeks, they were combined based on the dose of nortriptyline that they were receiving.

A repeated measures ANOVA of Hamilton Anxiety Scale (Ham-A) scores using an intention-to-treat analysis demonstrated a significant group by time interaction ($P = 0.002$) (i.e., the nortriptyline group improved more quickly than the placebo group) (see Figure 21–11). Planned comparisons revealed that the nortriptyline group was significantly more improved than the placebo group at nortriptyline doses of 50 mg, 75 mg, and 100 mg. Nine of 13 (69%) of the nortriptyline-treated group had more than a 50% reduction in Ham-A scores, whereas only 3 of 14 placebo-treated patients (21%) had a similar reduction ($P = 0.017$). When patients were divided into those with GAD plus major depression ($n = 6$ treated with nortriptyline; $n = 11$ treated with placebo) and those with GAD plus minor depression, there were too few patients with minor depression treated with placebo ($n = 3$) to analyze the data on the patients with minor depression. However, repeated measures ANOVA of Ham-A scores for the patients with major depression showed a significant group by time interaction ($P = 0.022$). The patients treated with nortriptyline improved significantly more quickly than patients treated with placebo. To determine whether depression and anxiety symptoms were responding independently, the rate of change in symptom severity was compared between a Ham-A and a Ham-D measurement. At 50 mg of nortriptyline (i.e., 2–3 weeks), there was a 39% improvement in Ham-A scores and only a 14% improvement in Ham-D scores ($P = 0.03$). This suggests that anxiety symptoms were responding more rapidly than depressive symptoms with nortriptyline therapy. This was the first study using double-blind, placebo-controlled methodology to demonstrate that generalized anxiety disorder following stroke can be effectively treated with the tricyclic antidepressant nortriptyline.

## Poststroke Psychosis

The phenomenon of hallucinations and delusions in patients who have experienced stroke has been called agitated delirium, acute atypical psychosis, peduncular hallucinosis, release hallucinations, and acute organic psychosis. In a study of acute organic psychosis occurring after stroke lesions, Rabins et al. (1991) found a very low prevalence of psychosis among stroke patients (only 5 in more than 300 consecutive admissions). All 5 of these patients, however, had right-hemisphere lesions, primarily involving frontoparietal regions. When compared with 5 age-matched patients with cerebrovascular lesions in similar locations but no psychosis, patients with secondary psychosis had significantly greater subcortical atrophy, as manifested by significantly larger areas of both the frontal horn of the lateral ventricle and the body of the lateral ventricle (measured on the side contralateral to the brain lesion). Several investigators have also reported a high frequency of seizures among patients with secondary psychosis (Levine and Finklestein 1982). These seizures usually started after the occurrence of the brain lesion but before the onset of psychosis. The study by Rabins et al. (1991) found seizures in 3 of 5 patients with poststroke psychosis, compared with none of 5 poststroke, nonpsychiatric control subjects.

It has been hypothesized that three factors may be important in the mechanism of organic hallucinations: 1) a right-hemisphere lesion involving the temporoparietal cortex, 2) seizures, and/or 3) subcortical brain atrophy (Starkstein et al. 1992).

Secondary psychosis is a rare finding in patients with brain injury and is frequently associated with lesions involving the temporoparietal junction in the right hemisphere as well as subcortical atrophy or seizure disorder. Treatment has been primarily pharmacologic, with either neuroleptic medication or antiseizure drugs. The mechanism resulting in hallucinations and delusions has not been determined.

## Apathy

Apathy is the absence or lack of feeling, emotion, interest, or concern and has been reported frequently among patients with brain injury. Using the Apathy Scale, Starkstein et al. (1993a) examined a consecutive series of 80 patients with single-stroke lesions and no significant impairment in comprehension. Of 80 patients, 9 (11%) showed apathy as their only psychiatric disorder, whereas another 11% had both apathy and depression. The only demographic correlate of apathy was age, as apathetic patients (with or without depression) were significantly older than nonapathetic patients. In addition, apathetic patients showed significantly more severe deficits in ADL, and a significant interaction was noted between depression and apathy on ADL scores, with the greatest impairment found in patients who were both apathetic and depressed.

Patients with apathy (without depression) showed a significantly higher frequency of lesions involving the posterior limb of the internal capsule than did patients without apathy (Starkstein et al. 1993a). Lesions in the internal globus pallidus and the posterior limb of the internal capsule have been reported to produce behavioral changes, such as motor neglect, psychic akinesia, and akinetic mutism (Helgason et al. 1988). The ansa lenticularis is one of the main internal pallidal outputs, and it ends in the pedunculopontine nucleus after going through the posterior limb of the internal capsule (Nauta 1989). In rodents, this pathway has a prominent role in goal-oriented behavior (Bechara and van der Kooy 1989), and dysfunction of this system may explain the presence of apathy in patients with lesions of the posterior limb of the internal capsule.

## Catastrophic Reaction

As described under Historical Perspective earlier in this chapter, *catastrophic reaction* is a term coined by Goldstein (1939) to describe the "inability of the organism to cope when faced with physical or cognitive deficits." Catastrophic reaction is expressed by anxiety, tears, aggressive behavior, swearing, displacement, refusal, renouncement, and sometimes compensatory boasting. Starkstein et al. (1993b) assessed a consecutive series of 62 patients, using the Catastrophic Reaction Scale, which was developed to assess the existence and severity of catastrophic reaction. The Catastrophic Reaction Scale has been demonstrated to be a reliable instrument in the measurement of symptoms of catastrophic reaction.

Catastrophic reactions occurred in 12 of 62 (19%) consecutive patients with acute stroke lesions (Starkstein et al. 1993b). Three major findings emerged from this study. First, patients with catastrophic reaction were found to have a significantly higher frequency of familial and personal history of psychiatric disorders (mostly depression) than were patients without catastrophic reaction. Second, catastrophic reaction was not significantly more frequent among aphasic (33%) than among nonaphasic (66%) patients. This finding does not support the contention that catastrophic reaction is an understandable psychological response of "frustrated" aphasic patients (Gainotti 1972). Third, 9 of the 12 patients with catastrophic reaction also had major depression, 2 had minor depression, and only 1 was not depressed. On the other hand, among the 50 patients without catastrophic reaction, 7 had major depression, 6 had minor depression, and 37 were not depressed. Thus, catastrophic reaction was significantly associated with major depression, but it does not support the proposal by Gainotti et al.

(1999) that the catastrophic reaction is an integral part of PSD. It is rather a comorbid condition that occurs in some but not all patients with PSD or may characterize a subgroup of patients with PSD.

In addition to its association with depression, patients with catastrophic reaction had a significantly higher frequency of lesions involving the basal ganglia (Starkstein et al. 1993b). When 10 depressed patients with catastrophic reaction were compared with 10 depressed patients without catastrophic reaction, the group with catastrophic reaction showed significantly more anterior lesions, which were mostly located in subcortical regions (8 of 9 depressed patients with catastrophic reaction had subcortical lesions, and 3 of 9 depressed patients without catastrophic reaction had subcortical lesions) ($P = 0.01$).

One may conclude from the evidence presented above that catastrophic reaction may have a neurophysiologic underpinning, rather than being just a behavioral response of patients confronted with their limitations. Catastrophic reactions seem to be associated with a specific type of poststroke major depression (i.e., major depression associated with anterior subcortical lesions). Although anterior brain lesions (both cortical and subcortical) have been associated with PSD, subcortical damage has usually been hypothesized to underlie the "release" of emotional display by removing inhibitory input to the limbic areas of the cortex (Ross and Stewart 1987).

Catastrophic reaction occurs in about 20% of stroke patients (Starkstein et al. 1993b) and is associated with a family or personal history of psychiatric disorders. Catastrophic reaction is significantly associated with major depression and may be mediated by a release of emotional display produced by anterior subcortical lesions. Thus, catastrophic reaction may or may not represent an independent clinical syndrome. Catastrophic reaction may be a behavioral symptom of a subgroup of depression provoked by anterior subcortical damage.

## Pathologic Emotions

Emotional lability is a common complication of stroke lesions. It is characterized by sudden, easily provoked episodes of crying that, although frequent, generally occur in appropriate situations and are accompanied by a congruent mood change. Pathologic laughing and crying is a more severe form of emotional lability and is characterized by episodes of laughing and/or crying that are not appropriate to the context. They may appear spontaneously or may be elicited by nonemotional events and do not correspond to underlying emotional feelings. These disorders have also been termed *emo-*

*tional incontinence* and *pathologic emotions.*

Robinson et al. (1993) examined the clinical correlates and treatment of emotional lability (including pathologic laughter and crying) in 28 patients with either acute or chronic stroke. A Pathologic Laughter and Crying Scale (PLACS) (Robinson et al. 1993) was developed to assess the existence and severity of emotional lability. The reliability and validity of this instrument were assessed in 18 patients receiving treatment for emotional lability and 54 other patients who had experienced acute stroke. Furthermore, PLACS scores did not correlate with Ham-D scores, MMSE scores, or ADL scores, indicating that the PLACS was assessing a factor other than the ones being measured by the other instruments.

A double-blind treatment trial of nortriptyline versus placebo was conducted. The doses of nortriptyline were 25 mg for 1 week, 50 mg for 2 weeks, 70 mg for 1 week, and 100 mg for the last 2 weeks of the study. One patient dropped out during the study, 2 patients withdrew before initiation of the study, and 28 completed the 6-week protocol. Patients receiving nortriptyline showed significant improvements in PLACS scores compared with the placebo-treated patients. These differences became statistically significant at 4 and 6 weeks. Although a significant improvement in depression scores was also observed, improvements in PLACS scores were significant for both depressed and nondepressed patients with pathologic laughing and crying, indicating that treatment response was not simply related to an improvement in depression (Robinson et al. 1993).

Andersen et al. (1993) also conducted a double-blind study using the SSRI citalopram to treat pathological crying. This study evaluated 16 patients using a crossover design. Three of the patients were dropped from the study—1 was given placebo because of a generalized seizure on day 28, and 2 others who are also taking placebo because of a lack of response to treatment after the first week. The protocol consisted of 1 week as a baseline, 3 weeks of treatment, and 1 week of washout, followed by 1 week as a second baseline, then 3 weeks of the crossover treatment. The number of crying episodes was recorded daily by the patients in their journals as the measure of treatment efficacy. Their response to treatment is shown in Figure 21–12. Although the Robinson et al. (1993) study used PLACS scores to measure outcome, the two studies were compared by examining the percentage reduction in baseline measure following treatment. All 13 of the patients treated with citalopram in the Andersen study responded by reduction in the number of crying episodes by at least 50%, and 2 of the patients also responded while receiving placebo. None of the patients had major depression at the start of the

Andersen study, but their mean Ham-D scores decreased from 8.9 to 5.3 during the 3 weeks of treatment with citalopram ($P = 0.005$). The response to citalopram was nearly immediate, with patients reporting a 50% or greater reduction in the frequency of crying episodes during the first week of treatment; 8 patients reported response within 24 hours, 3 patients reported response within 3 days, and only 4 patients took more than a week to respond. This appears to be a more rapid response to treatment than that noted among the patients treated with nortriptyline. Citalopram was given in a once-daily dose of 20 mg except for patients over age 65, who were given 10 mg. In both the Andersen study and the Robinson study, it was possible to show that although a significant number of the patients had comorbid depressive disorder, the response of pathological crying to treatment with either nortriptyline or citalopram was independent of the effect of depression.

## Aprosody

Ross and Mesulam (1979) described aprosody as abnormalities in the affective components of language, encompassing prosody and emotional gesturing. Prosody can be defined as the "variation of pitch, rhythm, and stress of pronunciation that bestows certain semantic and emotional meaning to speech" (Ross and Mesulam 1979, p. 144).

Motor aprosody consists of marked difficulty in spontaneous use of emotional inflection in language (e.g., an absence of normal prosodic variations in speech) or emotional gesturing, whereas comprehension of emotional inflection or gesturing remains intact. Sensory aprosody, on the other hand, is manifested by intact spontaneous emotional inflection in language and gesturing, whereas comprehension of emotional inflection or gesturing is markedly impaired. In a manner analogous to the organization of propositional language in the left hemisphere, expression and comprehension of emotional inflection have been associated respectively with frontal and temporoparietal regions of the right hemisphere (Ross and Mesulam 1979).

Starkstein et al. (1994) examined prosody comprehension in 59 patients with acute stroke lesions. With the use of tapes expressing verbal emotion and photographs of emotional facial expressions, impaired comprehension of emotion was found in a mild form in 10 patients (17%) and in a severe form in 19 patients (32%). Severe aprosody was associated with the following three clinical variables: 1) neglect for tactile stimulation, 2) lesions of the right hemisphere, including the basal ganglia and temporoparietal cortex, and 3) significantly larger third ven-

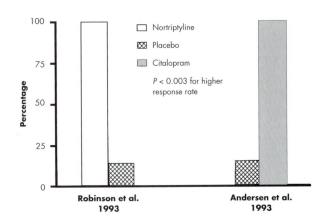

**FIGURE 21–12.** Comparison of double-blind treatment studies using nortriptyline or citalopram in patients with pathological crying. Both nortriptyline and citalopram produced improvement in 100% of the cases, whereas placebo treatment produced improvement in about 15% of the cases. These findings suggest that nortriptyline and citalopram produce similar reductions in severity measures as well as similar response rates for pathological crying.
*Source.* Reprinted from Robinson RG: *The Clinical Neuropsychiatry of Stroke.* New York, Cambridge University Press, 1998. Used with permission.

tricle to brain ratio. Although Ross and Rush (1981) suggested that patients with sensory aprosody might not be able to recognize their own depressed mood, major depression was found in 2 of 19 patients (11%) with severe aprosody and 7 of 30 patients (23%) without aprosody ($P$ not significant).

Impairment in the ability to comprehend emotion was found in about one-third of patients. It was strongly associated with right-hemisphere lesions, subcortical atrophy, and neglect but did not preclude patients from recognizing their own depression.

## Conclusions

There are numerous emotional and behavioral disorders that occur after cerebrovascular lesions (see Table 21–2). Depression occurs in about 40% of stroke patients, with approximately equal distributions of major depression and minor depression. Major depression is significantly associated with left frontal and left basal ganglia lesions during the acute stroke period and may be successfully treated with nortriptyline or citalopram. Treatment of depression has also been shown to improve poststroke cognitive function.

Mania is a rare complication of stroke and is strongly associated with right-hemisphere damage involving the orbitofrontal cortex, basal temporal cortex, thalamus, or basal ganglia. Risk factors for mania include a family history of psychiatric disorders and subcortical atrophy. Bipolar disorders are associated with subcortical lesions of the right hemisphere, whereas right cortical lesions lead to mania without depression.

Generalized anxiety disorder, which is present in about 27% of stroke patients, is associated with depression in the vast majority of cases. Among the few patients with poststroke anxiety and no depression, there is a high frequency of alcoholism and lesions of the right hemisphere. Apathy is present in about 20% of stroke patients. It is associated with older age, more severe deficits in ADL, and a significantly higher frequency of lesions involving the posterior limb of the internal capsule. A recent treatment study demonstrated that a generalized anxiety disorder can be treated effectively with nortriptyline.

Psychotic disorders are rare complications of stroke lesions. Poststroke hallucinations are associated with right-hemisphere temporoparietal lesions, subcortical brain atrophy, and seizures.

Catastrophic reactions occur in about 20% of stroke patients. These reactions are not related to the severity of impairments or the presence of aphasia but may represent a symptom for one clinical type of poststroke major depression. Catastrophic reactions are associated with anterior subcortical lesions and may result from a "release" of emotional display in a subgroup of depressed patients. Pathologic laughing and crying is another common complication of stroke lesions that may sometimes coexist with depression and may be successfully treated with nortriptyline or citalopram.

# References

Adams GF, Hurwitz LM: Mental barriers to recovery from strokes. Lancet 2:533–537, 1963

Adams RD, Victor M: Principles of Neurology. New York, McGraw-Hill, 1985

American Psychiatric Association: Diagnostic and Statistical Manual of Mental Disorders, 3rd Edition, Revised. Washington, DC, American Psychiatric Association, 1987

American Psychiatric Association: Diagnostic and Statistical Manual of Mental Disorders, 4th Edition. Washington, DC, American Psychiatric Association, 1994

American Psychiatric Association: Diagnostic and Statistical Manual of Mental Disorders, 4th Edition, Text Revision. Washington, DC, American Psychiatric Association, 2000

Andersen G, Vestergaard K, Riis J: Citalopram for poststroke pathological crying. Lancet 342(8875):837–839, 1993

Andersen G, Vestergaard K, Lauritzen L: Effective treatment of poststroke depression with the selective serotonin reuptake inhibitor citalopram. Stroke 25:1099–1104, 1994

Andersen G, Vestergaard K, Riis JO, et al: Dementia of depression or depression of dementia in stroke? Acta Psychiatr Scand 94:272–278, 1996

Astrom M: Generalized anxiety disorder in stroke patients: a 3-year longitudinal study. Stroke 27:270–275, 1996

Astrom M, Adolfsson R, Asplund K: Major depression in stroke patients: a 3-year longitudinal study. Stroke 24:976–982, 1993a

Astrom M, Olsson T, Asplund K: Different linkage of depression to hypercortisolism early versus late after stroke: a 3-year longitudinal study. Stroke 24:52–57, 1993b

Babinski J: Contribution a l'etude des troubles mentaux dans l'hemiplegic organique cerebrale (anosognosie). Rev Neurol (Paris) 27:845–848, 1914

Bakchine S, Lacomblez L, Benoit N, et al: Manic-like state after orbitofrontal and right temporoparietal injury: efficacy of clonidine. Neurology 39:778–781, 1989

Bamford J, Sandercock P, Dennis M, et al: A prospective study of acute cerebrovascular disease in the community: the Oxfordshire Community Stroke Project 1981–86, 1: methodology, demography and incident cases of first-ever stroke. J Neurol Neurosurg Psychiatry 51(11):1373–1380, 1988

Bechara A, van der Kooy D: The tegmental pedunculopontine nucleus: a brainstem output of the limbic system critical for the conditioned place preferences produced by morphine and amphetamine. J Neurosci 9:3440–3449, 1989

Beck E: A cytoarchitectural investigation into the boundaries of cortical areas 13 and 14 in the human brain. J Anat 83:145–147, 1949

Bleuler EP: Textbook of Psychiatry. New York, Macmillan, 1951

Bolla-Wilson K, Robinson RG, Starkstein SE, et al: Lateralization of dementia of depression in stroke patients. Am J Psychiatry 146:627–634, 1989

Bonita R: Epidemiology of stroke. Lancet 339:342–344, 1992

Bonita R, Beaglehole R, North JD: Event, incidence and case fatality rates of cerebrovascular disease in Auckland, New Zealand. Am J Epidemiol 120(2):236–243, 1984

Broderick JP, Phillips SJ, Whisnant JP, et al: Incidence rates of stroke in the eighties: the end of the decline in stroke? Stroke 20(5):577–582, 1989

Bukberg J, Penman D, Holland JC: Depression in hospitalized cancer patients. Psychosom Med 46:199–212, 1984

Burvill PW, Johnson GA, Jamrozik KD, et al: Prevalence of depression after stroke: the Perth Community Stroke Study. Br J Psychiatry 166(3):320–327, 1995

Castillo CS, Starkstein SE, Fedoroff JP, et al: Generalized anxiety disorder following stroke. J Nerv Ment Dis 181:100–106, 1993

Castillo CS, Schultz SK, Robinson RG: Clinical correlates of early onset and late-onset poststroke generalized anxiety. Am J Psychiatry 152:1174–1179, 1995

Chemerinski E, Robinson RG: The neuropsychiatry of stroke. Psychosomatics 41(1):5–14, 2000

Cohen-Cole SA, Stoudemire A: Major depression and physical illness: special considerations in diagnosis and biologic treatment. Psychiatr Clin North Am 10:1–17, 1987

Collin SJ, Tinson D, Lincoln NB: Depression after stroke. Clin Rehabil 1:27–32, 1987

Crosby E, Humphrey T, Laner E: Correlative Anatomy of the Nervous System. New York, Macmillan, 1962

Cummings JL, Mendez MF: Secondary mania with focal cerebrovascular lesions. Am J Psychiatry 141:1084–1087, 1984

Dennis M, O'Rourke S, Lewis S, et al: Emotional outcomes after stroke: factors associated with poor outcome. J Neurol Neurosurg Psychiatry 68(1):47–52, 2000

Denny-Brown D, Meyer JS, Horenstein S: The significance of perceptual rivalry resulting from parietal lesions. Brain 75:434–471, 1952

Downhill JE Jr, Robinson RG: Longitudinal assessment of depression and cognitive impairment following stroke. J Nerv Ment Dis 182:425–431, 1994

Eastwood MR, Rifat SL Nobbs H, et al: Mood disorder following cerebrovascular accident. Br J Psychiatry 154:195–200, 1989

Ebrahim S, Barer D, Nouri F: Affective illness after stroke. Br J Psychiatry 151:52–56, 1987

Endicott J: Measurement of depression in patients with cancer. Cancer 53 (suppl):2243–2248, 1984

Fedoroff JP, Lipsey JR, Starkstein SE, et al: Phenomenological comparisons of major depression following stroke, myocardial infarction or spinal cord lesions. J Affect Disord 22(1–2):83–89, 1991

Feibel JH, Springer CJ: Depression and failure to resume social activities after stroke. Arch Phys Med Rehabil 63(6):276–277, 1982

Finklestein S, Benowitz LI, Baldessarini RJ, et al: Mood, vegetative disturbance, and dexamethasone suppression test after stroke. Ann Neurol 12(5):463–468, 1982

Finset A, Goffeng L, Landro NI, et al: Depressed mood and intra-hemispheric location of lesion in right hemisphere stroke patients. Scand J Rehabil Med 21(1):1–6, 1989

Fisher SH: Psychiatric considerations of cerebral vascular disease. Am J Cardiol 7:379–385, 1961

Folstein MF, Folstein SE, McHugh PR: Mini-Mental State: a practical method for grading the cognitive state of patients for the clinician. J Psychiatr Res 12:189–198, 1975

Folstein MF, Maiberger R, McHugh PR: Mood disorder as a specific complication of stroke. J Neurol Neurosurg Psychiatry 40(10):1018–1020, 1977

Gainotti G: Emotional behavior and hemispheric side of the brain. Cortex 8:41–55, 1972

Gainotti G, Azzoni A, Marra C: Frequency, phenomenology and anatomical-clinical correlates of major poststroke depression. Br J Psychiatry 175:163–167, 1999

Gloor P: Role of the human limbic system in perception, memory, and affect: lessons from temporal lobe epilepsy, in The Limbic System: Functional Organization and Clinical Disorders. Edited by Doane BK, Livingston KE. New York, Raven, 1986, pp 159–169

Goldar JC, Outes DL: Fisiopatologia de la desinhibicion instintiva. Acta Psiquiatrica y Psicologica de America Latina 18: 177–185, 1972

Goldstein K: The Organism: A Holistic Approach to Biology Derived From Pathological Data in Man. New York, American Books, 1939

Goldstein K: After Effects of Brain Injuries in War. New York, Grune & Stratton, 1942

Granger CV, Denis LS, Peters NC, et al: Stroke rehabilitation: analysis of repeated Barthel Index measures. Arch Phys Med Rehabil 60:14–17, 1979

Haecen H, de Ajuriaguerra J, Massoner J: Les troubles visoconstructifs para lesion parieto occipitale droit. Encephale 40:122–179, 1951

Hamilton MA: A rating scale for depression. J Neurol Neurosurg Psychiatry 23:56–62, 1960

Helgason C, Wilbur A, Weiss A, et al: Acute pseudobulbar mutism due to discrete bilateral capsular infarction in the territory of the anterior choroidal artery. Brain 111:507–519, 1988

Herrmann M, Bartles C, Wallesch C-W: Depression in acute and chronic aphasia: symptoms, pathoanatomical-clinical correlations and functional implications. J Neurol Neurosurg Psychiatry 56:672–678, 1993

Herrmann N, Black SE, Lawrence J, et al: The Sunnybrook Stroke Study: a prospective study of depressive symptoms and functional outcome. Stroke 29:618–624, 1998

Hibbard MR, Grober SE, Gordon WA, et al: Modification of cognitive psychotherapy for the treatment of poststroke depression. Behavior Therapy 13:15–17, 1990

House A, Dennis M, Warlow C, et al: Mood disorders after stroke and their relation to lesion location: a CT scan study. Brain 113:1113–1130, 1990a

House A, Dennis M, Warlow C, et al: The relationship between intellectual impairment and mood disorder in the first year after stroke. Psychol Med 20(4):805–814, 1990b

House A, Dennis M, Mogridge L, et al: Mood disorders in the year after first stroke. Br J Psychiatry 158:83–92, 1991

Ironside R: Disorders of laughter due to brain lesions. Brain 79:589–609, 1956

Jorge RE, Robinson RG, Arndt SV, et al: Depression following traumatic brain injury: a 1 year longitudinal study. J Affect Disord 27:233–243, 1993

Kimura M, Robinson RG, Kosier T: Treatment of cognitive impairment after poststroke depression. Stroke 31(7):1482–1486, 2000

Kotila M, Numminen H, Waltimo O, et al: Depression after stroke: results of the FINNSTROKE Study. Stroke 29:368–372, 1998

Kraepelin E: Manic Depressive Insanity and Paranoia. Edinburgh, Scotland, E & S Livingstone, 1921

Levine DN, Finklestein S: Delayed psychosis after right temporoparietal stroke or trauma: relation to epilepsy. Neurology 32:267–273, 1982

Lipsey JR, Robinson RG, Pearlson GD, et al: Nortriptyline treatment of poststroke depression: a double-blind study. Lancet 2:297–300, 1984

Lipsey JR, Spencer WC, Rabins PV, et al: Phenomenological comparison of functional and poststroke depression. Am J Psychiatry 143:527–529, 1986

Mayberg HS, Robinson RG, Wong DF, et al: PET imaging of cortical S2-serotonin receptors after stroke: lateralized changes and relationship to depression. Am J Psychiatry 145:937–943, 1988

Meyer A: The anatomical facts and clinical varieties of traumatic insanity. American Journal of Insanity 60:373, 1904

Morris PLP, Robinson RG, Raphael B: Prevalence and course of depressive disorders in hospitalized stroke patients. Int J Psychiatry Med 20:349–364, 1990

Morrison JR, Molliver ME, Grzanna R: Noradrenergic innervation of the cerebral cortex: widespread effects of local cortical lesions. Science 205:313–316, 1979

Murray GB, Shea V, Conn DR: Electroconvulsive therapy for poststroke depression. J Clin Psychiatry 47:258–260, 1987

Nauta WJH: The problem of the frontal lobe: a reinterpretation. Journal of Psychological Research 8:167–187, 1971

Nauta WJH: Reciprocal links of the corpus striatum with the cerebral cortex and the limbic system: a common substrate for movement and thought?, in Neurology and Psychiatry: A Meeting of Minds. Edited by Mueller J. Basel, Switzerland, Karger, 1989, pp 43–63

Oradei CM, Waite NS: Group psychotherapy with stroke patients during the immediate recovery phase. Am J Orthopsychiatry 44:386–395, 1974

Pappata S, Dinh ST, Baron JC, et al: Remote metabolic effects of cerebrovascular lesions: magnetic resonance and positron tomography imaging. Neuroradiology 29:1–6, 1987

Paradiso S, Ohkubo T, Robinson RG: Vegetative and psychological symptoms associated with depressed mood over the first two years after stroke. Int J Psychiatry Med 27:137–157, 1997

Parikh RM, Robinson RG, Lipsey JR, et al: The impact of poststroke depression on recovery in activities of daily living over two year follow-up. Arch Neurol 47:785–789, 1990

Pohjasvaara T, Leppavuori A, Siira I, et al: Frequency and clinical determinants of poststroke depression. Stroke 29(11):2311–2317, 1998

Post F: The Significance of Affective Symptoms in Old Age, Vol 10. Maudsley Monograph. London, Oxford University Press, 1962

Rabins PV, Starkstein SE, Robinson RG: Risk factors for developing atypical (schizophreniform) psychosis following stroke. J Neuropsychiatry Clin Neurosci 3:6–9, 1991

Rankin J: Cerebral vascular accidents in patients over the age of 60, II: prognosis. Scott Med J 2:200–215, 1957

Rapp SR, Vrana S: Substituting nonsomatic for somatic symptoms in the diagnosis of depression in elderly male medical patients. Am J Psychiatry 146:1197–1200, 1989

Reding MJ, Orto LA, Winter SW, et al: Antidepressant therapy after stroke: a double-blind trial. Arch Neurol 43:763–765, 1986

Rifkin A, Reardon G, Siris S, et al: Trimipramine in physical illness with depression. J Clin Psychiatry 46(2):4–8, 1985

Robinson RG: Differential behavioral and biochemical effects of right and left hemispheric cerebral infarction in the rat. Science 105:707–710, 1979

Robinson RG: The Clinical Neuropsychiatry of Stroke. New York, Cambridge University Press, 1998

Robinson RG, Price TR: Post-stroke depressive disorders: a follow-up study of 103 patients. Stroke 13(5):635–641, 1982

Robinson RG, Szetela B: Mood change following left hemispheric brain injury. Ann Neurol 9:447–453, 1981

Robinson RG, Kubos KL, Starr LG, et al: Mood changes in stroke patients: relationship to lesion location. Compr Psychiatry 24:555–566, 1983a

Robinson RG, Starr LB, Kubos KL, et al: A two year longitudinal study of poststroke mood disorders: findings during the initial evaluation. Stroke 14:736–744, 1983b

Robinson RG, Kubos KL, Starr LB, et al: Mood disorders in stroke patients: importance of location of lesion. Brain 107:81–93, 1984

Robinson RG, Bolla-Wilson K, Kaplan E, et al: Depression influences intellectual impairment in stroke patients. Br J Psychiatry 148:541–547, 1986

Robinson RG, Bolduc P, Price TR: A two year longitudinal study of poststroke depression: diagnosis and outcome at one and two year follow-up. Stroke 18:837–843, 1987

Robinson RG, Boston JD, Starkstein SE, et al: Comparison of mania with depression following brain injury: causal factors. Am J Psychiatry 145:172–178, 1988

Robinson RG, Parikh RM, Lipsey JR, et al: Pathological laughing and crying following stroke: validation of measurement scale and double-blind treatment study. Am J Psychiatry 150:286–293, 1993

Robinson RG, Schultz SK, Castillo C, et al: Nortriptyline versus fluoxetine in the treatment of depression and in short term recovery after stroke: a placebo controlled, double-blind study. Am J Psychiatry 157:351–359, 2000

Ross ED, Mesulam MM: Dominant language functions of the right hemisphere: prosody and emotional gesturing. Arch Neurol 36:144–148, 1979

Ross ED, Rush AJ: Diagnosis and neuroanatomical correlates of depression in brain-damaged patients. Arch Gen Psychiatry 38:1344–1354, 1981

Ross ED, Stewart RS: Pathological display of affect in patients with depression and right frontal brain damage. J Nerv Ment Dis 175:165–172, 1987

Schwartz JA, Speed NM, Brunberg JA, et al: Depression in stroke rehabilitation. Biol Psychiatry 33(10):694–699, 1993

Schubert DS, Burns R, Paras W, et al: Increase of medical hospital length of stay by depression in stroke and amputation patients: a pilot study. Psychother Psychosom 57(1–2):61–66, 1992

Shimoda K, Robinson RG: Effect of anxiety disorder in impairment and recovery from stroke. J Neuropsychiatry Clin Neurosci 10:34–40, 1998a

Shimoda K, Robinson RG: The relationship between social impairment and recovery from stroke. Psychiatry 61(2):101–111, 1998b

Shimoda K, Robinson RG: The relationship between poststroke depression and lesion location in long-term follow-up. Biol Psychiatry 45:187–192, 1999

Sinyor D, Jacques P, Kaloupek DG, et al: Poststroke depression and lesion location: an attempted replication. Brain 109:539–546, 1986

Spitzer RL, Endicott J, Robins E: Research diagnostic criteria: rationale and reliability. Arch Gen Psychiatry 35:773–782, 1978

Starkstein SE, Pearlson GD, Boston J, et al: Mania after brain injury: a controlled study of causative factors. Arch Neurol 44:1069–1073, 1987a

Starkstein SE, Robinson RG, Price TR: Comparison of cortical and subcortical lesions in the production of poststroke mood disorders. Brain 110:1045–1059, 1987b

Starkstein SE, Boston JD, Robinson RG: Mechanisms of mania after brain injury: 12 case reports and review of the literature. J Nerv Ment Dis 176:87–100, 1988a

Starkstein SE, Robinson RG, Price TR: Comparison of patients with and without poststroke major depression matched for size and location of lesion. Arch Gen Psychiatry 45:247–252, 1988b

Starkstein SE, Robinson RG, Price TR: Comparison of spontaneously recovered versus non-recovered patients with poststroke depression. Stroke 19:1491–1496, 1988c

Starkstein SE, Berthier PL, Lylyk A, et al: Emotional behavior after a WADA test in a patient with secondary mania. J Neuropsychiatry Clin Neurosci 1:408–412, 1989a

Starkstein SE, Robinson RG, Honig MA, et al: Mood changes after right hemisphere lesion. Br J Psychiatry 155:79–85, 1989b

Starkstein SE, Cohen BS, Fedoroff P, et al: Relationship between anxiety disorders and depressive disorders in patients with cerebrovascular injury. Arch Gen Psychiatry 47:785–789, 1990a

Starkstein SE, Mayberg HS, Berthier ML, et al: Secondary mania: neuroradiological and metabolic findings. Ann Neurol 27:652–659, 1990b

Starkstein SE, Fedoroff JP, Berthier MD, et al: Manic depressive and pure manic states after brain lesions. Biol Psychiatry 29:149–158, 1991

Starkstein SE, Robinson RG, Berthier ML: Post-stroke delusional and hallucinatory syndromes. J Neuropsychiatry Neuropsychol Behav Neurol 5:114–118, 1992

Starkstein SE, Fedoroff JP, Price TR, et al: Apathy following cerebrovascular lesions. Stroke 24:1625–1630, 1993a

Starkstein SE, Fedoroff JP, Price TR, et al: Catastrophic reaction after cerebrovascular lesions: frequency, correlates, and validation of a scale. J Neurol Neurosurg Psychiatry 5:189–194, 1993b

Starkstein SE, Fedoroff JP, Price TR, et al: Neuropsychological and neuroradiological correlates of emotional prosody comprehension. Neurology 44:515–522, 1994

Stravakaki C, Vargo B: The relationship of anxiety and depression: a review of the literature. Br J Psychiatry 149:7–16, 1986

Terent A: Increasing incidence of stroke among Swedish women. Stroke 19(5):598–603, 1988

Thompson SC, Sobolew-Shobin A, Graham MA, et al: Psychosocial adjustment following stroke. Soc Sci Med 28:239–247, 1989

Ullman M, Gruen A: Behavioral changes in patients with stroke. Am J Psychiatry 117:1004–1009, 1960

Wade DT, Legh-Smith J, Hewer RA: Depressed mood after stroke. A community study of its frequency. Br J Psychiatry 151:200–205, 1987

Watzlawick P, Coyne JC: Depression following stroke: brief, problem-focused family treatment. Fam Process 19(1):13–18, 1980

Wells CE: Pseudodementia. Am J Psychiatry 136:895–900, 1979

Wing JK, Cooper JE, Sartorius N: The Measurement and Classification of Psychiatric Symptoms. An Instruction Manual for the PSE and CATEGO Program. New York, Cambridge University Press, 1974

Wolf PA, Dawber TR, Thomas HE, et al: Epidemiology of stroke, in Advances in Neurology. Edited by Thompson RA, Green JR. New York, Raven, 1977, pp 5–19

# CHAPTER 22

# Neuropsychiatric Aspects of Brain Tumors

Trevor R.P. Price, M.D.

Kenneth L. Goetz, M.D.

Mark R. Lovell, Ph.D.

Tumors involving the central nervous system (CNS) are common. The annual incidence of primary brain tumors is 9.0 per 100,000, and that of metastatic brain tumors is 8.3 per 100,000. There is evidence suggesting that the overall incidence of brain tumors and the proportion of brain tumors that are malignant have been increasing over the past two decades in industrialized countries (Olney et al. 1996). Brain tumors are second only to stroke as the leading cause of death from neurologic diseases (Radhakrishnan et al. 1994).

Brain tumors are typically classified according to whether they are primary or metastatic, as well as according to location and histologic cell type. Most primary tumors are either gliomas or meningiomas, gliomas being found more frequently (Table 22–1). The most common metastatic lesions are from lung and breast primary lesions (Table 22–2). Seventy percent of all tumors are supratentorial, with distribution by lobe as indicated in Figure 22–1. This distribution is influenced to some degree by tumor histology (Figure 22–2).

Age is also a determining factor for the frequency of various cell types. In children, astrocytomas are the most commonly seen CNS tumors, followed by medulloblastomas (Radhakrishnan et al. 1994). Gliomas are more often seen in the middle-aged population, and meningio-mas increase in incidence in the elderly (Radhakrishnan et al. 1994). Furthermore, metastatic disease is more frequent in the elderly and occurs with higher incidence than primary brain tumors.

It has been reported that primary brain tumors are up to 10 times more common among psychiatric patients than in psychiatrically healthy control subjects and that mental changes and behavioral symptoms, including confusion and various other neuropsychiatric symptoms, are more frequent early indicators of primary brain tumors than are classic physical manifestations such as headaches, seizures, and focal neurologic signs (Kocher et al. 1984).

Although the various tumor classifications may eventually turn out to be important in understanding the occurrence of neuropsychiatric symptoms associated with brain tumors, there have been as yet no large-scale, detailed studies carefully examining correlations between clinical phenomenology and various tumor parameters. Our knowledge of the neuropsychiatric and neuropsychological aspects of brain tumors is based on a relatively small number of clinical case reports and larger, uncontrolled case series from the older neurologic and neurosurgical literature. Much of the discussion that follows draws on this database.

**TABLE 22–1.** Relative frequencies of common histologic types of brain tumors

| Tumor type | Frequency (%) |
|---|---|
| **Primary** | |
| Gliomas | 40–55 |
|    *Astrocytomas* | 10–15 |
|    *Glioblastomas* | 20–25 |
|    *Others* | 10–15 |
| Meningiomas | 10–20 |
| Pituitary adenomas | 10 |
| Neurilemmomas (mainly acoustic neuromas) | 5–8 |
| Medulloblastomas and pinealomas | 5 |
| Miscellaneous primary tumors | 5 |
| **Metastatic** | 15–25 |

*Source.* Reprinted from Lohr JB, Cadet JL: "Neuropsychiatric Aspects of Brain Tumors," in *The American Psychiatric Press Textbook of Neuropsychiatry.* Edited by Talbott JA, Hales RE, Yudofsky SC. Washington, DC, American Psychiatric Press, 1987, p. 356. Used with permission.

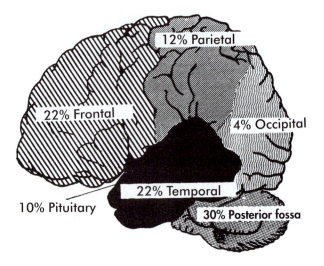

**FIGURE 22–1.** Relative frequency of intracranial brain tumors according to location in the adult.

*Source.* Reprinted from Lohr JB, Cadet JL: "Neuropsychiatric Aspects of Brain Tumors," in The American Psychiatric Press Textbook of Neuropsychiatry. Edited by Talbott JA, Hales RE, Yudofsky SC. Washington, DC, American Psychiatric Press, 1987, p. 355. Used with permission.

**TABLE 22–2.** Relative frequencies of metastatic brain tumors by site of the primary lesion

| Tumor | Frequency (%) |
|---|---|
| Lung | 35–45 |
| Breast | 10–20 |
| Kidney | 5–10 |
| Gastrointestinal tract | 5–10 |
| Melanoma | 2–5 |
| Others (including thyroid, pancreas, ovary, uterus, prostate, testes, bladder, and sarcoma) | 25–30 |

*Source.* Reprinted from Lohr JB, Cadet JL: "Neuropsychiatric Aspects of Brain Tumors," in *The American Psychiatric Press Textbook of Neuropsychiatry.* Edited by Talbott JA, Hales RE, Yudofsky SC. Washington, DC, American Psychiatric Press, 1987, p. 356. Used with permission.

## Frequency of Neuropsychiatric Symptoms in Patients With Brain Tumors

Unfortunately, and surprisingly, there is a paucity of recent studies examining the frequency of psychiatric symptoms in patients with brain tumors. This is probably because of modern imaging and neurosurgical techniques, which make early diagnosis and treatment commonplace but also prevent the opportunity to study the behavioral consequences of tumors. The studies that are available tend to be large autopsy studies, predominantly from the first half of the century.

For example, Keschner et al. (1938) noted psychiatric symptoms in 413 (78%) of 530 patients with brain tumors, and Schlesinger (1950) found behavioral changes in 301 (51%) of his series of 591 patients. Although tumor-associated, complex neuropsychiatric symptoms may occur along with focal neurologic signs and symptoms, often they may be the first clinical indication of a tumor, as was the case in 18% of patients examined by Keschner et al. (1938). This, of course, also suggests that with modern technologies, 82% of this population would have had medical or surgical intervention before the advent of behavioral symptoms. On the other hand, in a more recent report of 4 patients with intracranial tumors, Ko and Kok (1989) noted that 3 patients had initially presented to psychiatrists for diagnosis and treatment, emphasizing the need to be alert to indications of neurologic abnormalities.

Minski (1933) studied 58 patients with cerebral tumors and, in addition to reporting that the psychiatric symptomatology of 25 of these patients simulated "functional psychoses," noted that 19 actually attributed the onset of their behavioral symptoms to a number of stresses, including financial worries and the deaths of relatives. This underscores the difficulty that clinicians face in making an appropriate diagnosis early in the course of disease: It may be impossible on purely clinical grounds to determine the organic basis of the patient's complaints until progression of the tumor has resulted in the emergence of more typical and unmistakable neurologic signs and symptoms.

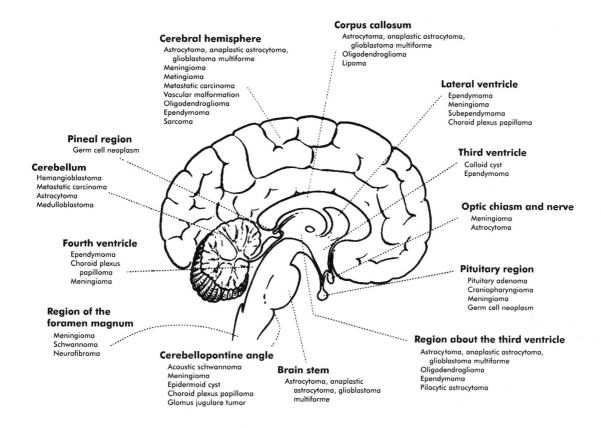

**Cerebral hemisphere**
Astrocytoma, anaplastic astrocytoma,
glioblastoma multiforme
Meningioma
Metingioma
Metastatic carcinoma
Vascular malformation
Oligodendroglioma
Ependymoma
Sarcoma

**Corpus callosum**
Astrocytoma, anaplastic astrocytoma,
glioblastoma multiforme
Oligodendroglioma
Lipoma

**Lateral ventricle**
Ependymoma
Meningioma
Subependymoma
Choroid plexus papilloma

**Pineal region**
Germ cell neoplasm

**Cerebellum**
Hemangioblastoma
Metastatic carcinoma
Astrocytoma
Medulloblastoma

**Third ventricle**
Colloid cyst
Ependymoma

**Optic chiasm and nerve**
Meningioma
Astrocytoma

**Fourth ventricle**
Ependymoma
Choroid plexus
papilloma
Meningioma

**Pituitary region**
Pituitary adenoma
Craniopharyngioma
Meningioma
Germ cell neoplasm

**Region of the
foramen magnum**
Meningioma
Schwannoma
Neurofibroma

**Cerebellopontine angle**
Acoustic schwannoma
Meningioma
Epidermoid cyst
Choroid plexus papilloma
Glomus jugulare tumor

**Brain stem**
Astrocytoma, anaplastic
astrocytoma, glioblastoma
multiforme

**Region about the third ventricle**
Astrocytoma, anaplastic astrocytoma,
glioblastoma multiforme
Oligodendroglioma
Ependymoma
Pilocytic astrocytoma

**FIGURE 22–2.** Topographic distribution of intracranial tumors in the adult.
*Source.* Reprinted from Burger PC, Scheithauer BW, Vogel FS: *Surgical Pathology of the Nervous System and Its Coverings,* 3rd Edition. New York, Churchill Livingstone, 1991. Used with permission.

Despite the high prevalence of psychiatric symptoms in patients with brain tumors, the prevalence of intracranial tumors in psychiatric patients, compiled from autopsy data from mental hospitals, is only about 3%. This rate is similar to that found in autopsy series in general hospitals (Galasko et al. 1988). In a recent study by J.K.A. Roberts and Lishman (1984), only 1 of 323 psychiatric patients who had computed tomography (CT) scans done as part of their diagnostic evaluations was found to have a tumor. Hollister and Boutros (1991) evaluated CT or magnetic resonance imaging (MRI) studies performed on 337 psychiatric patients. Only 2 patients were found to have brain tumors, and both had significant neurologic findings on physical examination. Other studies suggest that the risk of an occult neoplasm in patients presenting with purely psychiatric complaints may be as low as 0.1% (Hobbs 1963; Remington and Robert 1962).

Two large autopsy studies (Klotz 1957; Selecki 1965) of psychiatric patients have suggested that approximately half of all tumors go undiagnosed before postmortem examination. However, these studies do not necessarily establish that brain pathology was not suspected in patients who turned out to have unrecognized brain

tumors at postmortem examination, nor that these tumors were necessarily responsible for any or all of the psychiatric and behavioral symptoms the patients had exhibited during their lifetimes. Of interest is another autopsy study, by Percy et al. (1972), which demonstrated that before the advent of modern imaging techniques, 37% of brain tumors in an unselected population were first diagnosed at autopsy. Most of these patients were asymptomatic during their lifetimes. Undoubtedly, sophisticated brain imaging, which was unavailable at the time these series were done, would have diminished the likelihood of missing a tumor.

## General Neuropsychiatric and Neuropsychological Considerations in Relation to Brain Tumors

### General Neuropsychiatric Considerations

Patients with CNS tumors can present with mental symptoms that are virtually identical to those found in patients with primary functional psychiatric disorders. These symptoms run the gamut from major depression and schizophrenia to personality disorders and conversion disorders. Over the years, many clinicians and researchers have hypothesized the existence of a predictable relationship between tumor location and neuropsychiatric phenomenology. Smaller series have supported the generally held belief that depression is more common in frontal lobe tumors and psychosis is more common with temporal lobe neoplasms (Filley and Kleinschmidt-DeMasters 1995). Most of the older, autopsy-related studies do not strongly support this hypothesis and often concluded that observed behavioral changes were of no localizing value (Keschner et al. 1938; Selecki 1965). Unfortunately, these studies were performed with little understanding of localizing phenomena, and we now are better able to recognize the role of anatomic location in determining psychiatric and neuropsychological symptomatology. Nevertheless, the nature and severity of psychiatric dysfunction accompanying tumors is determined by a number of other factors that are of as great or even greater importance than anatomic location. The reason for this may be the fact that neuroanatomic substrates of particular behaviors tend not to be localized to single lobes or specific anatomic locations.

The best examples of this are behaviors mediated by tumors involving the limbic system, which includes the temporal lobes and portions of the frontal lobes, the hypothalamus, and the midbrain. Tumors affecting any of these structures may produce similar psychopathology. Furthermore, even lesions outside the limbic system may produce similar behavioral changes, attributable to limbic release or disinhibition, through diaschisis or disconnection syndromes (see General Neuropsychological Considerations below). Limbic tumors have often been associated with depression, affective flattening, apathy, agitation, assaultive behavior, and even a variety of psychotic symptoms. In one study (Malamud 1967) of patients with tumors in or near limbic system structures who had initially been admitted to psychiatric hospitals, it was found that the patients shared similar psychopathology regardless of the actual structures involved.

A study (Starkstein et al. 1988) of patients who developed mania after a variety of brain lesions, including tumors, also illustrates the difficulty of trying to associate specific kinds of psychiatric symptoms with the anatomic location of tumors. Although there was an overall predominance of right-sided involvement, lesions occurred in the frontal, temporoparietal, and temporo-occipital lobes, as well as in the cerebellum, thalamus, and pituitary. The authors concluded that the unifying aspect in all of these lesions was not their anatomic location but rather the interconnection of the involved structures with the orbitofrontal cortex. This underscores the need for formulating more sophisticated localization models in which a combination of both neuroanatomic location and connectivity are considered as they relate to focal brain lesions.

Other factors may also influence presenting symptoms and thereby diminish the localizing value of a particular behavioral change. Increased intracranial pressure is a nonspecific consequence of CNS tumors in general and has been implicated in behavioral changes such as apathy, depression, irritability, agitation, and changes in consciousness. In a study of lesions involving the occipital lobes, Allen (1930) concluded that most observed mental changes were due to increases in intracranial pressure rather than to effects of the tumors themselves.

Another factor is the patient's premorbid level of functioning, which often has a significant impact on the nature of the clinical presentation. Tumors often cause an exaggeration of the individual's previous predominant character traits and coping styles. The behavioral changes associated with a brain tumor usually represent a complex combination of the patient's premorbid psychiatric status, tumor-associated mental symptoms, and adaptive or maladaptive responses to the psychological stress of having been diagnosed with a brain tumor.

It has been noted that rapidly growing tumors are more commonly associated with severe, acute psychiatric symptoms, such as agitation or psychosis, as well as with more obvious cognitive dysfunctions. Patients with slow-growing tumors are more likely to present with vague personality changes, apathy, or depression, often without associated cognitive changes (Lishman 1987). Multiple tumor foci also tend to produce behavioral symptoms with greater frequency than single lesions.

The relationship between tumor type and neuropsychiatric symptoms is also complex. Several large studies (Frazier 1935; Keschner et al. 1938) have shown no association between histologic type of tumor and associated behavioral changes. Early reports suggested that meningiomas produced neuropsychiatric symptoms more often than other tumors (McIntyre and McIntyre 1942). Davison and Bagley (1969) reviewed the literature on numerous patients with psychosis secondary to brain tumors and found no significant predominance of one tumor type over another. This should not be surprising, given the variability of tumor classification systems used by different pathologists (Reitan and Wolfson 1985). Schirmer and Bock (1984) found no differences in symptoms between primary brain tumors and intracranial metastases. Lishman (1987), however, has suggested that gliomas may be more likely than benign tumors to produce behavioral changes, possibly because of the rapidity of growth or the multiplicity of tumor sites that may be involved. One study found more anxiety and depression in patients with meningiomas than with any other tumor type (Pringle et al. 1999). Patton and Sheppard (1956) noted a greater incidence of meningiomas among psychiatric patients than among general hospital patients, whereas gliomas were equally common in both groups. Perhaps this is because meningiomas have a greater predilection to occur in proximity to the frontal lobes, where lesions are often associated with behavioral changes. Furthermore, because of their location and slow growth, meningiomas often produce few focal signs and less obvious symptoms and therefore are associated with an increased likelihood that the patient will first present to a psychiatrist. For the most part, however, tumor type seems to be less important than other factors in determining the presence and nature of neuropsychiatric symptoms.

In general, the factors that most significantly influence symptom formation appear to be the extent of tumor involvement, the rapidity of its growth, and its propensity to cause increased intracranial pressure. In addition, the patient's premorbid psychiatric history, level of functioning, and characteristic psychological coping mechanisms may play a significant contributing role in determining the nature of a patient's particular symptoms. Lesion location may often, in fact, play a relatively minor role.

Nonetheless, there remains among many physicians a tendency to search for certain neuropsychiatric syndromes that are characteristic of lesions located in specific neuroanatomic regions. One reason for this may be the fact that much of what we now know about tumors and their associated psychopathology is based on retrospective, uncontrolled, single case reports and clinical series. These studies often describe the nature of the symptoms associated with mass lesions occurring in particular locations, rather than prospectively comparing the relative frequencies of behavioral changes associated with tumors occurring in various regions of the brain. One older study (Keschner et al. 1936) examined the comparative types of psychiatric symptoms in patients with tumors of the frontal and temporal lobes and found few differences (Figure 22–3). Of course, this should not be very surprising, given the intimate anatomic interconnections between these two brain regions. Nonetheless, many of the earlier autopsy studies have supported the conclusion that the types of behavioral changes observed with brain tumors tend to be similar, regardless of the specific anatomic brain region involved (Keschner et al. 1936; Schlesinger 1950; Selecki 1965).

Overall, then, lesion location is probably not the most important factor in determining the occurrence of specific types of neuropsychiatric symptoms. However, there have been some reports that brain lesions in certain locations may be associated with an increased frequency of psychiatric symptoms. For example, although Keschner et al. (1936) found no overall difference in the types of behavioral symptoms associated with tumors of the frontal and temporal lobes, they did find that, to a small degree, complex visual and auditory hallucinations were more common among patients with tumors of the temporal lobe and that "facetiousness" was more frequently found among those with tumors of the frontal lobe. Perhaps more significantly, they found that mental changes were twice as likely to occur among patients with supratentorial tumors than among those with infratentorial tumors (Keschner et al. 1938). Likewise, mental changes tended to be early symptoms in 18% of the patients with supratentorial tumors but in only 5% of those with infratentorial tumors. Psychiatric disturbances were also found to be more common among patients with tumors of the frontal and temporal lobes than in those with tumors of the parietal or occipital lobes.

Psychotic symptoms tend to be particularly frequent among patients with tumors of the temporal lobes and pituitary gland and much less common among those with occipital and cerebellar tumors, although this finding seems to depend on the particular study being reviewed (Davison and Bagley 1969). This underscores one of the major difficulties in comparing clinical series, especially when they were conducted during different time periods. Most of the available literature antedates the development of our current diagnostic system for classifying psychiatric clinical phenomenology, and therefore significant nosologic and methodological problems result when one attempts to compare the conclusions of such older series either with each other or with more recent studies.

Despite these limitations, the literature taken as a whole seems to support a higher frequency of behavioral changes among patients with lesions of the frontal and temporal lobes, as well as those with lesions involving deep midline structures. Similarly, bilateral tumors and those with multifocal involvement appear to be more frequently associated with neuropsychiatric symptoms.

# General Neuropsychological Considerations

Neuropsychological testing is often useful in patients with CNS neoplasms. Although neuropsychological testing was initially used to provide diagnostic information

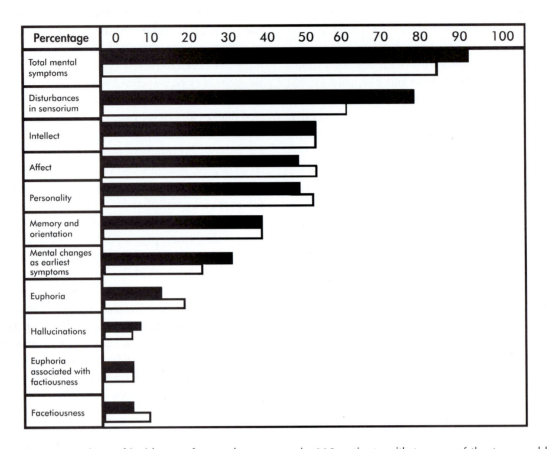

**FIGURE 22–3.** Comparison of incidence of mental symptoms in 110 patients with tumors of the temporal lobe (*solid bars*) and in 64 patients with tumors of the frontal lobe (*open bars*).

*Source.* Reprinted from Keschner M, Bender MB, Strauss I: "Mental Symptoms in Cases of Tumor of the Temporal Lobe." *Archives of Neurology and Psychiatry* 35:572–596, 1936. Copyright 1936, American Medical Association. Used with permission.

about the location and nature of brain tumors, the current widespread availability of CT and MRI, and the consequent greater capacity for precise anatomic localization, has lessened the use of neuropsychological testing for diagnostic purposes. Currently, neuropsychological testing is most often used to determine the extent of cognitive dysfunction associated with a tumor, to provide a preoperative baseline measure of cognitive or memory functioning, or to monitor the efficacy and progress of cognitive rehabilitation efforts after treatment.

The histologic type and rate of growth of a tumor may affect the nature and severity of cognitive symptoms. For example, rapidly growing, invasive tumors, such as glioblastoma multiforme, have long been thought to cause obvious cognitive dysfunction, whereas slower-growing, noninvasive tumors, such as meningiomas, have not as frequently been associated with obvious cognitive changes or with focal neurologic deficits at all (Reitan and Wolfson 1985). However, a more recent, well-controlled study did not find significant differences between patients with glioblastomas and those without glioblastomas on a battery of neuropsychological tests (Scheibel et

al. 1996). In patients with slower-growing tumors, the degree to which cognitive deficits will become clinically apparent is substantially affected by the individual's level of intelligence and adaptive functioning before the development of the tumor. Thus, patients with higher premorbid IQs tend to have greater cognitive and intellectual reserves, as well as a broader range of coping and adaptive skills, which allow them to compensate for and conceal emerging cognitive impairments more successfully for longer periods of time. In addition, younger patients may be less likely than older patients to manifest cognitive and behavioral deficits (Bigler 1984).

In addition to the diffuse disruption of cognitive functioning secondary to these tumor-associated phenomena, other factors may result in cognitive deficits that do not reflect the anatomic location of the tumor. Specific patterns of deficits may be linked to anatomic location (Scheibel et al. 1996), and the tumor may also produce disruption of brain function in nonadjacent regions. According to Lezak (1995), several types of "distance effects" may be important in determining the types of deficits found on neuropsychological testing. First, diaschisis refers to impairment of neuronal activity in a functionally related but distant region of the brain (von Monakow 1914). Second, disconnection of a given region of the brain from a more distant region by a structural lesion can also affect the cognitive expression of the symptom. This has been dramatically demonstrated in patients who have undergone surgical sectioning of the corpus callosum as treatment for intractable seizures (Sperry 1974).

Despite its methodological and nosologic limitations, the large body of descriptive literature addressing neuropsychiatric and neuropsychological symptoms associated with brain tumors over the past several decades has clearly documented that a broad array of behavioral and cognitive changes may result from tumors of the brain. Thus, it underscores the need for psychiatrists to consider the possibility of an underlying brain tumor when initially evaluating any psychiatric patient. It also helps the psychiatrist in better understanding, evaluating, and treating patients with known brain tumors who have neuropsychiatric and neuropsychological symptoms. Finally, despite the generally weak association between lesion location and specific psychiatric, behavioral, and cognitive symptomatology, the literature does describe selected constellations of neuropsychiatric symptoms that are seen more frequently in patients with tumors involving certain brain regions. Recognition of the localizing value of these associations may lead the clinician to consider organic pathology more strongly in certain patients and perhaps to pursue more vigorously the diagnosis of a previously unsuspected brain tumor.

## Specific Neuropsychiatric and Neuropsychological Symptoms and Brain Tumor Location

In the discussion that follows, we review the range of neuropsychiatric and neuropsychological signs and symptoms that have been observed to co-occur preferentially with brain tumors involving various anatomic structures, including the frontal, temporal, parietal, and occipital lobes; the diencephalon; the corpus callosum; the pituitary; and the posterior fossa.

### Tumors of the Frontal Lobe

#### Neuropsychiatric and Behavioral Manifestations

Tumors of the frontal lobes are frequently associated with behavioral symptoms. One study reported mental changes in as many as 90% of cases (Strauss and Keschner

1935). Of these patients, 43% manifested such changes early in the course of their illness. This is not surprising when one considers that higher-level executive and cognitive functions are mediated by this region of the cortex. Rather than being homogeneous and unidimensional in their functions, the frontal lobes are made up of a variety of functionally distinct subregions. These areas are involved in a number of related and unrelated tasks, such as the mediation of problem-solving behavior, the regulation of attentional processes, the temporal organization of behavior, and the modulation of affective states (McAllister and Price 1987).

Injuries to the frontal lobes have been associated with three kinds of clinical syndromes (Cummings 1993). The orbitofrontal syndrome is characterized by changes in personality. These patients typically present with irritability and lability. Cognitively, patients with this syndrome often demonstrate poor judgment and a lack of insight into their behavior. These patients have sometimes been referred to as pseudopsychopathic (McAllister and Price 1987).

Conversely, patients with injury to the frontal convexities, the so-called dorsolateral prefrontal syndrome, often present with apathy, indifference, and psychomotor retardation. Cognitively, such patients have difficulty initiating or persisting in behavioral activities and have problems with sustained attention and/or sequencing, and they may demonstrate perseverative behavior (Goldberg 1986). These deficits may not be especially apparent on standard intellectual or neuropsychological assessments, but they usually become apparent with more specific tests of executive functioning, such as the Wisconsin Card Sorting Test (Goldberg 1986; Heaton 1985). Patients with this syndrome have been referred to as being pseudodepressed because the apathy, aspontaneity, and abulia with which they often present resemble the classic symptoms of major depression (McAllister and Price 1987).

Finally, an anterior cingulate syndrome has also been described. Patients with this syndrome may be akinetic with mutism and inability to respond to commands.

Despite the occurrence of these three syndromes as relatively distinct entities compared with other types of disorders of the frontal lobe, most patients with tumors of the frontal lobe present with a combination of symptoms. This is probably due in part to the fact that tumors of the frontal lobe are rarely confined to a single subregion of the frontal lobe and may be causing effects on other areas, both directly and indirectly via pressure effects and edema, as well as by diaschisis and disconnection. It is therefore difficult to find clear descriptions of these three syndromes in pure form when reviewing the literature on neoplasms of the frontal lobe. Psychiatric symptoms also appear to be more common in patients with lesions of the anterior frontal lobe than in those with lesions of the posterior frontal lobe, suggesting that tumor location on the anteroposterior gradient within the frontal lobe may play a significant role in determining clinical presentation (Gautier-Smith 1970).

Psychiatric and behavioral presentations of frontal lobe tumors can be quite variable. Anxiety has been described and has been noted to increase with tumor progression (Kaplan and Miner 1997). Affective symptoms are common and can include depression, irritability, apathy, and euphoria. Often psychomotor retardation with aspontaneity, hypokinesia, or akinesia is present. In one study of 25 patients with frontal lobe tumors (Direkze et al. 1971), 5 had initially presented to psychiatric units with what appeared to be mood disturbances. In their study of 85 patients, Strauss and Keschner (1935) reported affective symptoms in 63%, of whom 30% presented with euphoria and 4% presented with hypomania. Although these authors found no correlation between clinical presentations and laterality of lesions, Belyi (1987) noted a tendency for patients with right frontal lesions to present with euphoria, whereas those with left frontal lesions tended to present with akinesia, abulia, and depressed affect. Another study reported psychiatric symptoms only in patients with right frontal as opposed to left frontal meningiomas (Lampl et al. 1995).

Changes in personality have been found in as many as 70% of patients with frontal lobe tumors (Strauss and Keschner 1935). These changes, which have been described as "characteristic" of frontal lobe disease (Pincus and Tucker 1978), include irresponsibility, childishness, facetiousness, disinhibition, and indifference toward others, as well as inappropriate sexual behavior. The term *witzelsucht* has been used to describe the tendency of patients with frontal lobe lesions to make light of everything. This humorous bent often has an angry, sarcastic, cutting quality to it. Although these behaviors are consistent with descriptions of the characteristic features of orbitofrontal syndrome, it should be noted that similar "frontal lobe" personality changes have been described in patients with temporal lobe and diencephalic lesions, probably as a result of the rich, reciprocal interconnections that link the temporal, limbic, and frontal regions.

Psychotic symptoms occur with some regularity in patients with frontal lobe tumors. Strauss and Keschner (1935) reported a 10% incidence of both delusions and hallucinations in their series. Other psychotic symptoms reported in patients with frontal lobe tumors have included paranoid ideation and ideas of reference. Typi-

cally, delusions secondary to intracranial tumors are less complex than those that occur as part of the delusional systems of schizophrenic patients. Likewise, simple rather than complex hallucinations and visual rather than auditory hallucinations tend to occur in patients with brain tumors.

Hypersomnolence has also been reported in these patients (Frazier 1935). A careful psychiatric assessment and evaluation of mental status may be needed to clearly differentiate this symptom from the lethargy and fatigue often encountered in patients with major depression. The presence of leg weakness, gait abnormalities, or urinary incontinence with psychiatric and behavioral symptoms should strongly indicate the need for a thorough search for frontal lobe pathology.

## Neuropsychological Manifestations

Cognitively, patients with tumors of the frontal region of the brain, and of the prefrontal area in particular, often present with significant behavioral changes in the absence of obvious intellectual decline or focal neurologic dysfunction. In such patients, previously acquired cognitive skills are often preserved and performance on formal intelligence testing may be quite adequate. More sophisticated neuropsychological assessment of executive functioning, however, often reveals profound deficits in the individual's ability to organize, initiate, and direct personal behavior (Lezak 1995; Teuber 1972). Deficits in executive functioning, which disrupt the very core of an individual's drive, initiative, and integration as well as the ability to carry out critical higher cognitive functions, are often the most devastating and disabling types of cognitive dysfunction encountered in neurologic, neurosurgical, and psychiatric patients (Luria 1980).

Tumors of the frontal lobes can also result in significant deficits in attentional processes (Luria 1973). In addition, tumors of the posterior frontal lobe can lead to expressive (Broca's) aphasia, when the lesion is localized to the dominant hemisphere (Benson 1979), or aprosody, when it is localized to the anterior nondominant hemisphere (Ross 1988).

## Tumors of the Temporal Lobe

### Neuropsychiatric and Behavioral Manifestations

In any discussion of the psychiatric and behavioral symptoms associated with tumors of the temporal lobe, it is important to distinguish between seizure-associated and non-seizure-associated symptoms and, within the former category, ictal and interictal phenomena. Ictal phenomena are discussed in Chapter 19 of this book. In this section, we confine ourselves to non-seizure-associated and interictal symptoms due to temporal lobe tumors.

Patients with temporal lobe tumors have been noted to have a high frequency of schizophrenia-like illnesses. Malamud (1967) reported that 6 of 11 patients (55%) with temporal lobe tumors initially presented with a diagnosis of schizophrenia. Selecki (1965) reported that an initial diagnosis of schizophrenia had been made in 2 of his 9 patients with temporal lobe tumors, and he reported auditory hallucinations in 5. More recently, G.W. Roberts et al. (1990) reported that gangliogliomas, neoplastic hamartomatous lesions that preferentially involve the left medial temporal lobes, are frequently found in patients with delayed-onset, schizophrenia-like psychoses associated with chronic temporal lobe epilepsy.

Again, it must be borne in mind that many of these studies were published before the advent of DSM-IV diagnostic criteria (American Psychiatric Association 1994) and that therefore there may have been a tendency to overdiagnose schizophrenia. In fact, many of the case descriptions of Malamud (1967) do not indicate that the patients had clear evidence of psychotic symptoms such as delusions, hallucinations, or formal thought disorder. Patients with temporal lobe dysfunction due to tumors or other causes often present with psychotic symptoms that are somewhat atypical for classic schizophrenia. These symptoms include episodic mood swings with suicidal ideation or attempts and visual, olfactory, and tactile hallucinations, as well as the auditory hallucinations more typically seen in schizophrenic patients (Tucker et al. 1986). Patients with schizophrenia-like psychoses due to temporal lobe disease often report having "spells" or dreamlike episodes, as well as "staring" behavior or "dazed feelings" (Tucker et al. 1986). Unlike schizophrenic patients with notably flat or inappropriate affect and a markedly diminished capacity to interact with and relate appropriately to others, patients with psychoses associated with temporal lobe disease often manifest broad-range and appropriate affect and interact with and relate to others in a relatively normal fashion. Supporting the association between psychotic symptomatology and temporal lobe tumors is the work of Davison and Bagley (1969), who reviewed 77 psychotic patients with known brain neoplasms and found that tumors of the temporal lobes were most frequent.

Other studies, however, have not confirmed the apparent high frequency of psychotic syndromes in patients with temporal lobe tumors. Keschner et al. (1936) studied 110 such patients and found that only 2 had complex hallucinations. In another study (Mulder and Daly 1952), only 4 of 100 patients with temporal lobe tumors had psychotic symptoms. Strobos (1953) noted complex auditory hallucinations in only 1 (1%) of his 62 patients with temporal lobe tumors. He found complex visual hallucinations in 5 (8%) and simple olfactory or gustatory hallucinations in approximately 19 (30%), although these almost invariably immediately preceded the onset of seizures.

Regardless of how often specific psychotic symptoms may occur with temporal lobe tumors, these lesions are commonly associated with behavioral disturbances. Neuropsychiatric symptoms associated with temporal lobe tumors tend to be similar to those seen in patients with frontal lobe tumors and may include depressed mood with apathy and irritability or euphoric, expansive mood with hypomania or mania. As noted previously, this probably results from the complex interconnections among the frontal lobes, temporal lobes, and related structures within the limbic system.

Personality change has been described in more than 50% of patients with temporal lobe tumors and may be an early symptom thereof (Keschner et al. 1936). Research by Bear and Fedio (1977) suggests that characteristic interictal personality traits occur in patients with temporal lobe epilepsy and, furthermore, that the presence or absence of certain traits depends on whether the seizure focus is in the right or the left temporal lobe. More recent studies (Mungas 1982; Rodin and Schmaltz 1984), however, have failed to confirm these initial findings. Thus, there do not appear to be specific interictal personality traits that are characteristic of temporal lobe lesions. Often patients present with an intensification of premorbid character traits or with symptoms similar to those seen in conjunction with frontal lobe tumors. Personality changes due to brain tumors, including affective lability, episodic behavioral dyscontrol, intermittent anger, irritability, euphoria, and facetiousness, are also commonly seen (Lishman 1987).

Anxiety symptoms appear to be quite commonly associated with temporal lobe tumors. Mulder and Daly (1952) noted anxiety in 36 of their 100 patients. Two cases of panic attacks in patients with right temporal lobe tumors have been reported (Drubach and Kelly 1989; Ghadirian et al. 1986), although the number of cases is obviously too small to draw any conclusions about the influence of laterality on the appearance of such phenomena. However, these case reports are consistent with work by Reiman et al. (1986) demonstrating abnormally low ratios of left-to-right parahippocampal blood flow in patients with panic disorder who were vulnerable to lactate-induced panic. The authors suggested that this asymmetry could be secondary to increases in neuronal activity, anatomic asymmetry, or an increase in blood-brain barrier permeability in the right parahippocampal region. Such mechanisms could also occur in conjunction with temporal lobe tumors.

## Neuropsychological Manifestations

Tumors of the temporal lobes can also result in neuropsychological and cognitive deficits. First, verbal or nonverbal memory functioning may be affected, depending on the cerebral hemisphere involved. Dysfunction of the dominant temporal lobe is often associated with deficits in the ability to learn and remember verbal information, whereas that of the nondominant temporal lobe is often associated with deficits in acquiring and retaining nonverbal (i.e., visuospatial) information (Bauer et al. 1993; Butters and Milotis 1979). Tumors of the dominant temporal lobe may also result in receptive (Wernicke's) aphasia, whereas tumors of the nondominant lobe may lead to disruption of the discrimination of nonspeech sounds (Spreen et al. 1965).

Because of the high incidence of seizure disorders in patients with tumors of the temporal lobes (Strobos 1953), cognitive dysfunction in such patients may result directly from seizure activity; indirectly from dysfunction in other areas of the brain through diaschisis or disconnection; or from the administration of certain anticonvulsants, especially when they are used in high doses, for long periods, or as part of multidrug regimens.

## Tumors of the Parietal Lobe

### Neuropsychiatric and Behavioral Manifestations

In general, tumors of the parietal lobe are less likely to cause behavioral changes than are tumors in other locations; they are relatively "silent" with respect to psychiatric symptoms. This has been well documented in large, comparative studies of psychiatric and behavioral phenomenology as a function of the anatomic location of various brain tumors. Schlesinger (1950) found affective symptoms in only 5 (16%) of 31 patients with parietal lobe tumors. The affective symptoms in these patients were predominantly depression and apathy, rather than euphoria or mania, a finding consistent with the previous report of Keschner et al. (1938). More recently, two case studies have reported mania in patients with right parietal tumors (Khouzam et al. 1994; Salazar-Calderon Perriggo et al. 1993).

Psychotic symptoms also appear to be less common in patients with parietal lobe tumors than in those with other types of lesions. Selecki (1965), however, reported episodes of "paranoid psychosis" in two of the seven patients with parietal lobe tumors in his series. Cotard's

syndrome, involving the denial of one's own existence, has recently been reported in a patient with a left parietal astrocytoma (Bhatia 1993).

## Neuropsychological Manifestations

Of greater significance than the psychiatric and behavioral symptoms associated with parietal lobe tumors are the complex sensory and motor abnormalities that may accompany them. In general, parietal lobe tumors are more likely to lead to cognitive rather than psychiatric symptoms. Depending on the location of a neoplasm within the parietal lobes, a variety of neuropsychological abnormalities may be observed.

Tumors of the anterior parietal lobes may result in abnormalities of sensory perception in the contralateral hand. Inability of the individual to perceive objects placed in the hand (astereognosis) is common and may have localizing value to the contralateral parietal cortex. Difficulty in recognizing shapes, letters, and numbers drawn on the hand (agraphesthesia) is common and may aid in localizing neoplasms to the parietal lobes. Apraxias may also be present. Parietal lobe tumors may interfere with the ability to decipher visuospatial information, particularly when they are localized to the nondominant hemisphere (Warrington and Rabin 1970).

Tumors of the dominant parietal lobe may lead to dysgraphia, acalculia, finger agnosia, and right-left confusion (Gerstmann's syndrome) and often affect reading and spelling. Individuals with parietal lobe tumors often present with a marked lack of awareness or even frank denial of their neurologic and/or neuropsychiatric difficulties, even in the face of rather obvious dysfunctions, such as hemiparesis (Critchley 1964a). Such phenomena are referred to as anosognosia or neglect syndromes. Because of the often bizarre neurologic complaints and atypical symptoms that may accompany parietal lobe tumors, patients with these lesions are often thought to have psychiatric problems and are often initially misdiagnosed as having either a conversion disorder or some other type of somatization disorder (Critchley 1964b; Jones and Barklage 1990).

## Tumors of the Occipital Lobe

### Neuropsychiatric and Behavioral Manifestations

Patients with tumors of the occipital lobe may also present with psychiatric symptoms, but like patients with tumors involving the parietal lobes, they have been reported to be less likely to do so than those with tumors of the frontal or temporal lobes (Keschner et al. 1938). In 1930, Allen found psychiatric symptoms in 55% of a large series ($N = 40$) of patients with occipital lobe tumors. In 17% of these patients, behavioral symptoms had been the presenting complaint. The most characteristic finding was visual hallucinations, which were present in 25% of the patients. These hallucinations tended to be simple and unformed and were frequently merely flashes of light. In only two patients were there complex visual hallucinations.

Other symptoms that have been observed in patients with occipital lobe tumors include agitation, irritability, suspiciousness, and fatigue, although Allen (1930) felt that many of these symptoms (other than the visual hallucinations) were nonspecific effects of increased intracranial pressure. Keschner et al. (1938) observed affective symptoms in 5 of 11 patients with occipital lobe tumors. Three of these patients were dysphoric, and 2 presented with euphoria or facetiousness.

## Neuropsychological Manifestations

Tumors of the occipital lobes may cause significant and characteristic difficulties in cognitive and perceptual functions. A typical finding in patients with occipital lobe neoplasms is homonymous hemianopsia, the loss of one-half of the visual field in each eye. Inability to recognize items visually (visual agnosia) may also be seen (Lezak 1995). Inability to recognize familiar faces, a condition known as prosopagnosia, may also accompany neoplastic lesions in the occipital lobes, particularly when they are bilateral (Meadows 1974).

# Diencephalic Tumors

## Neuropsychiatric and Behavioral Manifestations

Tumors of the diencephalon (i.e., the thalamus, the hypothalamus, and the structures surrounding the third ventricle) typically involve regions that are part of or closely contiguous to the limbic system. These lesions also interrupt the various cortical-striatal-pallidal-thalamic-cortical loops, which affect many frontal lobe functions (Alexander and Crutcher 1990). It is therefore not surprising that these lesions are often associated with psychiatric and behavioral disturbances. For example, Malamud (1967) reported diagnoses of schizophrenia in four of seven patients with tumors involving structures near the third ventricle. Cairns and Mosberg (1951) reported "emotional instability" and psychosis in patients with colloid cysts of the third ventricle. Burkle and Lipowski (1978) also reported depression, affective flattening, and withdrawal in a patient with a colloid cyst of the third ventricle. Personality changes similar to those seen in patients with frontal lobe disease (Alpers 1937; Gut-

mann et al. 1990), akinetic mutism (Cairns et al. 1941), or catatonia (Neuman et al. 1996) have also been reported in patients with diencephalic or deep midline tumors.

Hypothalamic tumors have been associated with disorders of eating behavior, including hyperphagia (Coffey 1989), and with symptoms indistinguishable from those of anorexia nervosa. Chipkevitch (1994) reported on 21 cases in the literature in which patients with brain lesions presented with symptoms consistent with a diagnosis of anorexia nervosa. Eleven of these patients had tumors of the hypothalamus. In eight of these patients, surgical resection or radiation treatment led to improvement in the symptoms of anorexia. Patients with lesions of the hypothalamus can also present with hypersomnia and daytime somnolence.

## Neuropsychological Manifestations

Neoplasms originating in subcortical brain regions often have their most dramatic effects on memory. These lesions often result in significant impairment in the retrieval of learned material, whereas other aspects of neuropsychological functioning may appear to be relatively intact on initial evaluation (Lishman 1987). However, detailed neuropsychological evaluation of a patient with a subcortical tumor may reveal a pattern of "subcortical dementia" characterized by a general slowing of thought processes, forgetfulness, apathy, abulia, and depression and an impaired ability to manipulate acquired knowledge (Albert et al. 1974; Cummings 1990). Tumors in this area may also lead indirectly to more diffuse, generalized cognitive dysfunction by interfering with the normal circulation of cerebrospinal fluid, causing hydrocephalus.

# Tumors of the Corpus Callosum

Tumors of the corpus callosum have been associated with behavioral symptoms in as many as 90% of patients (Selecki 1964). Such symptoms appear to be most common in patients with tumors of the genu and splenium (Schlesinger 1950), probably because of involvement of adjacent structures (i.e., the frontal lobes and deep midline and limbic structures). Although a broad array of behavioral changes have been reported, including psychosis and personality changes, affective symptoms appear to be particularly common with tumors involving this area. In a recent study, patients with corpus callosum tumors were compared with patients with other types of tumors. Significantly more depression was found in the group with tumors of the corpus callosum (Nasrallah and

McChesney 1981). One of these patients had received a trial of tricyclic antidepressants (TCAs) for a presumed primary affective disorder before emerging neurologic symptoms led to the correct diagnosis. Tanaghow et al. (1989) also described a patient with a corpus callosum tumor without focal neurologic findings who had initially presented with atypical features of depression and prominent cognitive deficits.

## Pituitary Tumors

Patients with pituitary tumors often present with behavioral changes resulting from upward extension of the tumor to other structures, particularly those in the diencephalon. This is a common occurrence in patients with craniopharyngiomas, who sometimes present with disorders of sleep or temperature regulation, clinical phenomena that are ordinarily more common with tumors of the hypothalamus. Anorexia nervosa syndromes have also been reported in patients with craniopharyngiomas (Chipkevitch 1994).

Tumors of the pituitary can also result in endocrine disturbances, which can cause neuropsychiatric symptoms. Basophilic adenomas are commonly associated with Cushing's syndrome, which is likewise often associated with affective lability, depression, or psychotic symptoms. Patients with acidophilic adenomas often present with acromegaly, which has been associated, though infrequently, with both anxiety and depression (Avery 1973).

As with brain tumors involving other anatomic locations, the entire spectrum of psychiatric symptoms, from depression and apathy to paranoia, has been reported to occur in patients with pituitary tumors. One review of 5 patients with pituitary lesions reported delusions and hallucinations in 3 (White and Cobb 1955). In a study by Russell and Pennybacker (1961), 8 (33%) of 24 patients had severe mental disturbances that dominated their clinical picture, and 3 (13%) had initially presented to psychiatric hospitals for diagnosis and treatment. The broad spectrum of psychiatric and behavioral symptoms associated with pituitary tumors probably reflects the direct and indirect involvement of diencephalic and hypothalamic structures, as well as the effects of various endocrine dysfunctions.

## Tumors of the Posterior Fossa

Patients with infratentorial tumors present with psychiatric symptoms less often than those with other types of tumors. The wide variety of behavioral symptoms that may occur in patients with such tumors again under-

scores the difficulty of localizing lesions on the basis of the typology of associated psychiatric symptoms. Although they are less common overall, all of the psychiatric and behavioral disturbances that have been described in patients with supratentorial tumors have also been reported in patients with infratentorial and posterior fossa lesions.

In one series, psychiatric and behavioral symptoms were found in 76% of patients with lesions of the posterior fossa and included paranoid delusions and affective disorders (Wilson and Rupp 1946). Pollack et al. (1996) also reported affective disorders, psychosis, personality change, and somatization in their small series. Cases of mania have also been noted (e.g., Greenberg and Brown 1985). Tumors of the posterior fossa have been reported to be associated with irritability, apathy, hypersomnolence, and auditory hallucinations (Cairns 1950). Visual hallucinations have been reported in conjunction with tumors compressing the midbrain (Dunn and Weisberg 1983; Nadvi and van Dellen 1994), and manic or mixed states have been described in three adults with acoustic neuroma (Kalayam et al. 1994). Overanxious disorder of childhood with school phobia was reported in a 12-year-old boy with a fourth-ventricle tumor (Blackman and Wheler 1987). The anxiety symptoms were alleviated by surgical removal of the tumor. Overall, however, no convincing correlation has been established between tumors involving particular anatomic structures within the posterior fossa and the occurrence of specific psychiatric or behavioral symptomatology.

## Laterality of Brain Tumors and Clinical Manifestations

Despite the fact that many older studies reported no consistent differences in the psychiatric and behavioral symptoms associated with left- and right-sided tumors, more recent studies have raised questions about this. The importance of cerebral hemispheric lateralization was elegantly demonstrated by Robinson et al. (1984) in their work with stroke patients. This work indicates an increased frequency of depression in patients with left anterior lesions and a tendency toward inappropriate cheerfulness in patients with right anterior lesions. Although there have been few reports specifically addressing these findings in cohorts of patients with brain tumors, studies reviewing cases of mania secondary to mixed CNS lesions, including tumors, have found a preponderance of right-hemisphere lesions (Cummings and Mendez 1984; Jamieson and Wells 1979; Starkstein et al.

1988). A recent study of unilateral frontal tumors (Belyi 1987) reported that left-sided lesions were commonly associated with akinesia and depression, whereas right-sided lesions were more often associated with euphoria and underestimation by the patients of the seriousness of their illnesses. Pringle et al. (1999) also reported higher incidence of psychiatric disturbances overall in women with left-sided lesions.

These studies suggest that lesion laterality may be a more important factor in symptom formation than had previously been thought. In addition, overall the available literature suggests the need to reevaluate tumor location and its implications for neuropsychiatric and neuropsychological symptomatology from a different, more topographic perspective. There is a need to consider not only specific regional anatomic localization but also factors such as laterality, anterior/posterior and cortical/subcortical location, and afferent and efferent projections between the region directly involved with the tumor and distant anatomic regions. More important, such a perspective will provide a more clinically relevant, though necessarily more complex, theoretical framework from which to approach the study of psychopathologic symptoms and syndromes associated with brain tumors. Future studies of brain tumor-associated psychopathology patterned after the work of Robinson et al. (1984) should further enhance our understanding not only of these secondary psychiatric and behavioral symptoms and syndromes but also of the anatomic substrates of many primary psychiatric disorders.

## Clinical Diagnosis and Treatment

### General Clinical Characteristics of Brain Tumors

For clinicians, especially psychiatrists, prompt and accurate diagnosis of brain tumors rests on awareness of the many clinical manifestations they may produce. A high index of suspicion and willingness to vigorously pursue appropriate specialty consultations and diagnostic studies are critical to early diagnosis.

The most characteristic clinical feature of CNS tumors is the progressive appearance of focal neurologic signs and symptoms in addition to neuropsychiatric symptoms. These are actually more frequent than the neurologic signs and symptoms in early brain tumors and may include changes in personality and affect, altered sensorium, and cognitive and memory dysfunction. The specific constellation of clinical phenomena encountered and how rapidly they progress depend on the type, size,

location, and rate of growth of the tumor; whether it is benign or malignant; and, if the latter, how aggressive it is and whether there are associated cerebral edema, increased intracranial pressure, and/or hydrocephalus.

Typical neurologic signs and symptoms associated with brain tumors include headaches (25%–35%), nausea and vomiting (33%), seizures (20%–50%), papilledema, and visual changes, including field cuts and diplopia. Focal motor and sensory changes are of considerable value in localizing the tumor (Table 22–3).

### When to Suspect a Brain Tumor in a Psychiatric Patient

Although recognition of brain tumors in patients presenting with characteristic focal neurologic signs and symptoms should not ordinarily be problematic, it may be quite difficult to promptly and accurately diagnose a brain tumor in a patient presenting with predominantly psychiatric and behavioral symptoms. However, the occurrence of one or more of the following five signs and symptoms in a known psychiatric patient or in a patient presenting for the first time with psychiatric symptoms should heighten the clinician's index of suspicion regarding the possibility of a brain tumor:

1. Seizures, especially if of new onset in an adult and if they are focal or partial seizures, with or without secondary generalization; seizures may be the initial neurologic manifestation of a tumor in as many as 50% of cases
2. Headaches, especially if of new onset; generalized and dull (i.e., nonspecific); of increasing severity and/or frequency; or positional, nocturnal, or present immediately on awakening
3. Nausea and vomiting, especially in conjunction with headaches
4. Sensory changes: visual changes such as loss or diminution of vision, visual field defects, or diplopia; auditory changes such as tinnitus or hearing loss, especially when unilateral; and vertigo
5. Other focal neurologic signs and symptoms, such as localized weakness, localized sensory loss, paresthesias or dysesthesias, ataxia, and incoordination

The clinician should bear in mind that nausea and vomiting, visual field defects, papilledema, and other focal neurologic signs and symptoms often are not seen early in the course of many brain tumors. These signs may not be seen until very late, especially with "silent" tumors, such as meningiomas or slow-growing astrocytomas, and other kinds of tumors occurring in relatively

**TABLE 22–3.** Neurologic and neuropsychologic findings with localizing value

| Brain region | Neurologic and neuropsychological findings |
| --- | --- |
| **Frontal lobes** | |
| Prefrontal | Contralateral grasp reflex, executive functioning deficits (inability to formulate goals, to plan, and to effectively carry out these plans), decreased oral fluency (dominant hemisphere), decreased design fluency (nondominant hemisphere), motor perseveration or impersistence, and inability to hold set |
| Posterior | Contralateral hemiparesis; decreased motor strength, speed, and coordination; and Broca's aphasia |
| **Temporal lobes** | Partial complex seizures, contralateral homonymous inferior quadrantanopsia, Wernicke's aphasia, decreased learning and retention of verbal material (dominant hemisphere), decreased learning and retention of nonverbal material (nondominant hemisphere), amusia (nondominant hemisphere), and auditory agnosia |
| **Parietal lobes** | Partial sensory seizures, agraphesthesia, astereognosis, anosognosia, Gerstmann's syndrome (acalculia, agraphia, finger agnosia, and right-left confusion), ideomotor and ideational apraxia, constructional apraxia, agraphia with alexia, dressing apraxia, prosopagnosia, and visuospatial problems |
| **Occipital lobes** | Partial sensory seizures with visual phenomena, homonymous hemianopsia, alexia, agraphia, prosopagnosia, color agnosia, and construction apraxia |
| **Corpus callosum** | Callosal apraxia |
| **Thalamus** | Contralateral hemisensory loss and pain |
| **Basal ganglia** | Contralateral choreoathetosis, dystonia, rigidity, motor perseveration, and parkinsonian tremor |
| **Pituitary** | Bitemporal hemianopia, optic atrophy, hypopituitarism, and hypothalamus and diabetes insipidus |
| **Pineal** | Loss of upward gaze (Parinaud's syndrome) |
| **Cerebellum** | Ipsilateral hypotonia, ataxia, dysmetria, intention tremor, and nystagmus toward side of tumor |
| **Brain stem** | |
| Midbrain | Pupillary and extraocular muscle abnormalities and contralateral hemiparesis |
| Pons | Sixth and seventh nerve involvement (diplopia and ipsilateral facial paralysis) |

*Source.* Reprinted from Lohr JB, Cadet JL: "Neuropsychiatric Aspects of Brain Tumors," in *The American Psychiatric Press Textbook of Neuropsychiatry.* Edited by Talbott JA, Hales RE, Yudofsky SC. Washington, DC, American Psychiatric Press, 1987, p. 354. Used with permission.

"silent" locations (see Physical and Neurologic Examinations below).

## Diagnostic Evaluation

A comprehensive, careful, and detailed history of the nature and time course of both psychiatric and neurologic signs and symptoms is the cornerstone of diagnosis. This should be supplemented by careful physical and neurologic examinations, appropriate brain imaging and electrodiagnostic studies, and bedside neurocognitive assessment, including the Mini-Mental State Exam (MMSE) (Folstein et al. 1975), as well as formal neuropsychological testing.

### Physical and Neurologic Examinations

All psychiatric patients, and particularly those in whom the psychiatrist is considering a brain tumor in the differential diagnosis, should have full and careful physical, neurologic, and mental status examinations. Patients with brain tumors often manifest focal neurologic findings as well as abnormalities in cognitive functioning on careful bedside neurocognitive testing. Table 22–3 highlights some of the more important and common localizing neurologic findings that are found in association with brain tumors in various locations. It is important to be aware that, even despite repeated careful clinical examinations, some brain tumors may not become clinically apparent until relatively late in their course. Such tumors often involve the anterior frontal lobes, corpus callosum, nondominant parietal and temporal lobes, and posterior fossa, the so-called silent regions. Thus, in patients with negative clinical examinations for focal neurologic findings, other diagnostic studies are essential to conclusively rule out the presence of a tumor.

### Computed Tomography Scans

In the 1970s, the CT scan largely replaced plain skull films, radioisotope brain scans, electroencephalography, echoencephalography, and pneumoencephalography in the diagnosis of brain tumors, because it provided far greater resolution of anatomic brain structures and was much more able to identify small soft-tissue mass lesions. The capacity of the CT scan to reveal neoplasms has been further enhanced by the concomitant use of intravenous iodinated contrast materials, such as iohexol, that highlight tumors when they are present. CT scans can also suggest the presence of tumors by revealing calcifications, cerebral edema, obstructive hydrocephalus, a shift in midline structures, or other abnormal changes in the ventricular system. Although they are extremely useful, CT scans may not reveal very small tumors, tumors in the posterior fossa, tumors that are isodense with respect to brain tissue and/or cerebrospinal fluid, and tumors diffusely involving the meninges (i.e., carcinomatosis).

## MRI Scans

In general, MRI is superior to CT scanning in the diagnosis of brain tumors and other soft-tissue lesions in the brain because of its higher degree of resolution and resultant greater ability to detect very small lesions (Figures 22–4 and 22–5). In addition, MRI does not involve exposure to radiation. Its chief drawbacks are its cost and its inability to reveal calcified lesions. It also cannot be used in patients in whom ferrometallic foreign objects are present. Enhancement of MRI with gadolinium further enhances its diagnostic sensitivity (Figure 22–6).

## Cisternography

CT cisternography, a radiographic technique for evaluating the ventricular system, subarachnoid spaces, and basilar cisterns, may be helpful in the differential diagnosis of intraventricular tumors as well as tumor-associated hydrocephalus. This technique has largely replaced pneumoencephalography, an older air-contrast imaging technique that provided limited diagnostic information and was poorly tolerated by patients because of associated severe headaches and nausea and vomiting.

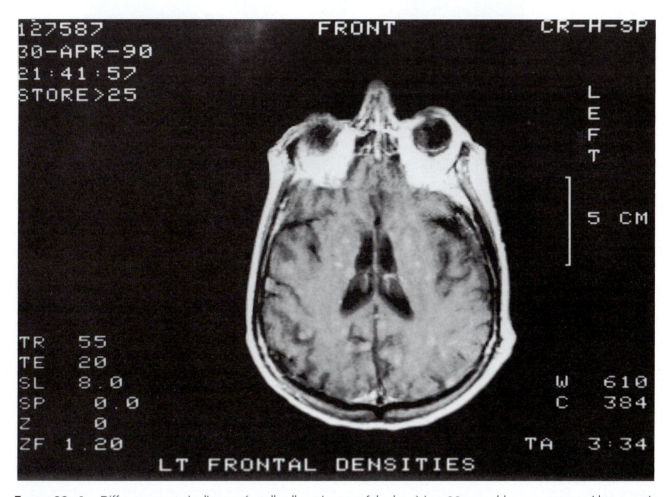

**FIGURE 22–4.** Diffuse metastatic disease (small cell carcinoma of the lung) in a 66-year-old man, as seen with magnetic resonance imaging. A computed tomography scan had not shown any metastatic lesions.

*Source.* Image courtesy of Dr. A. Goldberg, Department of Radiology, Allegheny General Hospital, Pittsburgh, Pennsylvania.

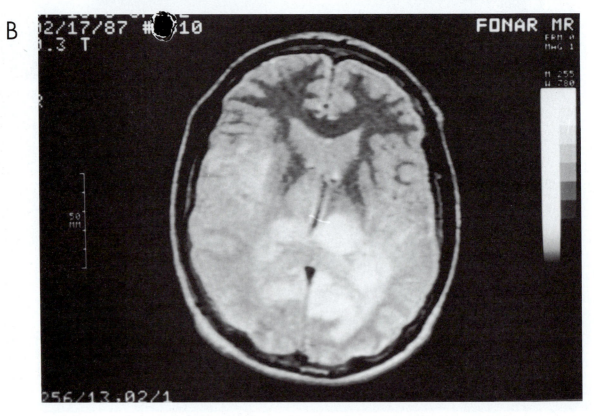

**FIGURE 22–5.** Brain images of a 50-year-old man with a multicentric glioma. A computed tomography scan shows no evidence of tumor (*Panel A*). In a magnetic resonance imaging scan, the tumor is clearly evident (*Panel B*).

*Source.* Figure courtesy of Dr. A. Goldberg, Department of Radiology, Allegheny General Hospital, Pittsburgh, Pennsylvania.

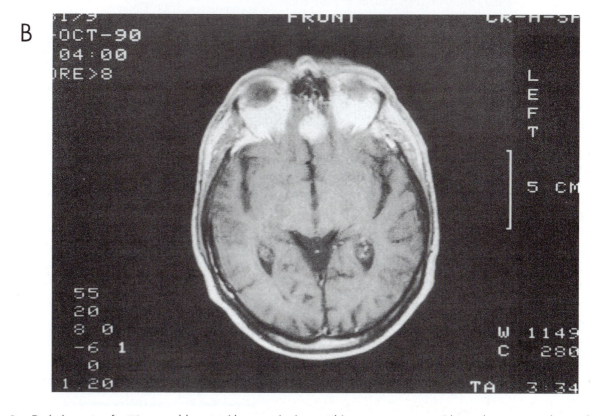

**Figure 22–6.** Brain images of a 70-year-old man with a meningioma. This tumor was not evidenced on an unenhanced magnetic resonance imaging (MRI) scan (*Panel A*) but was seen clearly with a gadolinium-enhanced MRI scan (*Panel B*).

*Source.* Figure courtesy of Dr. A. Goldberg, Department of Radiology, Allegheny General Hospital, Pittsburgh, Pennsylvania.

## Skull Films

Although plain skull films are no longer routinely used in the diagnosis of brain tumors, tomographs of the sella turcica may be helpful in the diagnosis of pituitary tumors, craniopharyngiomas, and the so-called empty sella syndrome. Plain skull films may also be helpful in the diagnosis of bone (skull) metastases, but bone scans are generally superior in this regard.

## Cerebral Angiography

In some cases, cerebral angiography may be important in delineating the vascular supply to a brain tumor before surgery.

## Neuropsychological Testing

As mentioned previously, neuropsychological testing was often used in the diagnosis and localization of brain tumors before the advent of CT and MRI. Although it is no longer used for these purposes, it still plays an important role in the overall management of patients with cerebral tumors. It can be very helpful in determining the extent of tumor-associated cognitive dysfunction and in providing baseline, preoperative, and/or preradiation measures of cognitive functioning. It may also be helpful in assessing the efficacy of surgery with respect to improvements in tumor-associated, preoperative, and preradiation cognitive and neuropsychological dysfunction. It is also helpful in documenting postoperative and postradiation cognitive changes and monitoring the effectiveness of rehabilitative efforts with respect to them.

## Lumbar Puncture

Given the range of other, more sensitive, specific, and less invasive diagnostic studies currently available, lumbar puncture is now used less frequently than in the past in the diagnosis of brain tumors. Brain tumors may be associated with elevated cerebrospinal fluid protein and increased intracranial pressure, but these findings are diagnostically nonspecific, and in the presence of the latter, there is a potential danger of herniation after a lumbar puncture. Therefore, before proceeding with a lumbar puncture in a patient with a brain tumor, the clinician should carefully examine the eyegrounds for indications of papilledema, and a CT or MRI scan should be done to rule out increased intracranial pressure. With certain types of neoplastic diseases of the CNS, such as meningeal carcinomatosis and leukemia, however, lumbar puncture may play an important diagnostic role when other neurodiagnostic studies have been unrevealing.

## Electroencephalography

Electroencephalograms in patients with brain tumors may reveal nonspecific electrical abnormalities, such as spikes and slow waves, either diffuse or focal and paroxysmal or continuous. Frequently, however, the electroencephalogram is normal in such patients. It is not a very specific or sensitive test and thus is not very helpful in differentiating brain tumors from other localized structural cerebral lesions.

## Other Testing

Obtaining a chest radiograph is important in evaluating brain tumors because they may often be metastatic from primary lung neoplasms. Single photon emission computed tomography (SPECT), positron emission tomography (PET), and brain electrical activity mapping (BEAM) are newly emerging quantitative, computer-based techniques for evaluating various aspects of brain structure and metabolic and neurophysiologic functioning. At present, none of these techniques appears to have major advantages over the more standard approaches discussed previously in the routine diagnostic evaluation of brain tumors, but this may change as experience with them accumulates. SPECT may have some utility in differentiating tumor recurrence from radiation necrosis in brain tumor patients who have received radiation therapy (Figures 22–7 and 22–8), or in the differentiation of CNS lymphoma from toxoplasma encephalitis in AIDS patients (Ruiz et al. 1994).

Magnetoencephalography (MEG), a newly emerging technology in the assessment of brain function, relies on measurement of magnetic fields to localize neuronal cells producing abnormal electrical activity. MEG is more precise than electroencephalography in localizing sources of abnormal electrical activity in the brain and has the potential additional advantage of being able to be used sequentially in assessing brain activity over time without radiation exposure. The role MEG may play in the evaluation of brain tumors is unclear at present, but it may prove useful in the assessment of tumor-associated diaschisis and disconnection syndromes.

# Treatment of Psychiatric and Behavioral Symptoms Associated With Cerebral Tumors

## General Considerations

Psychiatric and behavioral symptoms may be completely relieved after removal of the cerebral tumor with which

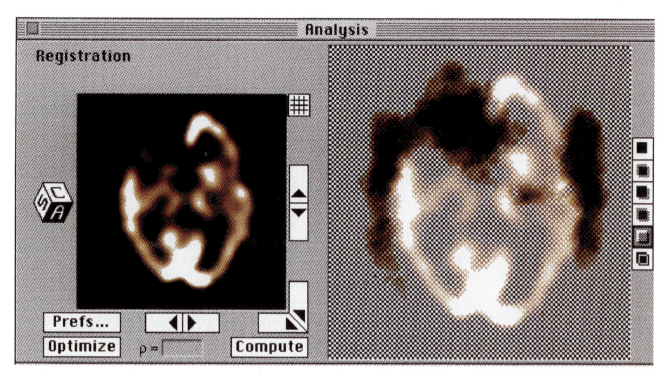

**FIGURE 22–7.** Single photon emission computed tomography scans of a patient with recurrent glioblastoma. [⁹⁹ᵐTc]Hexamethylpropylene amine oxime (HMPAO) scan (*left*) indicates decreased tracer uptake in the right frontal area. Superimposed thallium scan (*right*) shows increased tracer uptake in the same area, indicating recurrent tumor.
*Source.* Figure courtesy of Dr. M. Adatepe, Department of Nuclear Medicine, Allegheny General Hospital, Pittsburgh, Pennsylvania.

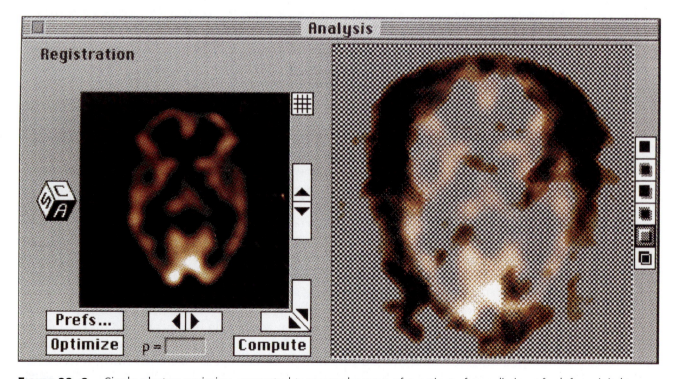

**FIGURE 22–8.** Single photon emission computed tomography scan of a patient after radiation of a left occipital tumor. Decreased uptake on [⁹⁹ᵐTc]hexamethylpropylene amine oxime (HMPAO) scan (*left*) combined with decreased uptake on superimposed thallium scan (*right*) suggests an area of postradiation necrosis rather than recurrent tumor.
*Source.* Figure courtesy of Dr. M. Adatepe, Department of Nuclear Medicine, Allegheny General Hospital, Pittsburgh, Pennsylvania.

they are associated. When this does not happen, as is often the case, decreasing the size or interfering with the growth of the tumor through surgery, chemotherapy, or radiation therapy (alone, sequentially, or in combination) may significantly ameliorate the severity of associated behavioral symptoms. Improvement in cognitive and behavioral symptoms may be rapid and dramatic with treatments that diminish increased intracranial pressure or relieve hydrocephalus associated with brain tumors.

In cases where neuropsychiatric or behavioral symptoms persist or worsen after optimal surgical and nonsurgical interventions, psychopharmacologic, psychotherapeutic, and psychosocial interventions become a major treatment focus. The persistence of such psychiatric, behavioral, and neurocognitive symptoms should lead the neurosurgeon or neurologist to seek psychiatric consultation because these symptoms are distressing, cause functional impairment and disability, and have a very negative effect on the patient's overall quality of life (Weitzner 1999). It is at this juncture that the psychiatrist or neuropsychiatrist can provide the greatest assistance by providing supportive psychotherapeutic interventions to the patient and family and recommending effective somatic treatments for specific psychiatric symptoms to the patient's doctor.

The interventions of the consulting psychiatrist—who works closely with the attending neurosurgeon—may significantly enhance the patient's level of functioning and overall quality of life (Fox 1998). Ameliorating the disabling dysphoria and anergia of severe depression, alleviating the distress caused by overwhelming anxiety, or simply providing consistent supportive contacts to fearful patients and their families may make an enormous difference to all concerned. Often such interventions also lead to improved treatment outcome through increased patient motivation and improved treatment compliance, which may substantially enhance the efficacy of the neurosurgeon's clinical management of the patient's brain tumor.

Although patients with cerebral tumors often have psychiatric and behavioral symptoms, only a portion of these are due to a mental disorder directly related to the tumor. Patients may also have persistent or recurrent symptoms of affective or anxiety disorders that were present premorbidly and were uncovered or exacerbated by the stress of having to live with a brain tumor. Anxiety and depressive symptoms may arise de novo in any brain tumor patient, with or without a history of a psychiatric disorder, as a result of psychological reactions to the stress of the initial diagnosis of a brain tumor, concerns about how it will be treated, fears about the potential adverse effects of surgery, radiation therapy, and/or chemotherapy, and worries about long-term prognosis.

Other psychiatric symptoms may emerge later in reaction to the difficulties of adjusting to functional disabilities or distressing life changes that may result from the tumor itself or from the side effects and complications of the various therapeutic interventions brought to bear on it. It is important for the consulting psychiatrist to differentiate as precisely as possible among symptoms that are specifically tumor related (i.e., symptoms due to an organic mental syndrome); those that result from preexisting primary psychiatric disorders; and those that are predominantly reactive in nature and secondary to psychological stresses. This is because optimal pharmacologic and psychotherapeutic interventions, individually or in combination, depend on which of these are the primary cause of the patient's symptoms.

## Pharmacologic Management of Patients With Primary Psychiatric Disorders Who Develop Brain Tumors

The psychopharmacologic management of patients with preexisting primary psychiatric illnesses that persist or recur in the context of the diagnosis and treatment of cerebral tumors should follow the same general therapeutic principles that apply to tumor-free patients with similar disorders. However, it is important for the psychiatrist to be cognizant of the potential need to make downward adjustments in medication dose and to use drugs that are less likely to cause delirium in patients with brain tumors, as a result of the increased susceptibility of these patients to side effects of psychotropic medications. This is especially true of patients who are in the immediate postoperative period or are receiving chemotherapy or radiation therapy. Lithium, low-potency antipsychotic drugs, tertiary amine TCAs, and antiparkinsonian agents all have significant, dose-related deliriogenic potential when given individually, and this is even more true when they are given in combination with each other or other potentially deliriogenic agents. Thus, these agents should be used with care in known psychiatric patients with brain tumors. It may be necessary to substitute an atypical antipsychotic, carbamazepine, valproic acid, and/or a benzodiazepine, such as lorazepam or clonazepam, for lithium in patients with mania; a newer-generation heterocyclic or secondary amine TCA, a selective serotonin reuptake inhibitor (SSRI), or one of the newer, novel-structured antidepressants for tertiary amine TCAs in patients with depression; or one of the atypical antipsychotics for old-line, standard neuroleptics in patients with schizophrenia.

Another significant concern is the potential for precipitating seizures through the use of these drugs, especially in patients with brain tumors in whom seizures may be more likely to occur anyway. Neuroleptics, antidepressants, and lithium all lower seizure threshold, although to varying degrees. Although the available data are inconclusive, standard neuroleptics such as molindone and fluphenazine (Oliver et al. 1982), and possibly haloperidol (Mendez et al. 1984), are among the older antipsychotic drugs that are believed to carry the smallest risk for seizures; whereas low-potency agents like chlorpromazine and clozapine are associated with an increased frequency of seizures (Stoudemire et al. 1993). In general, the newer atypical antipsychotics, as a class, are believed to have a lower likelihood of precipitating seizures and thus offer an important therapeutic advantage over the old-line antipsychotics. Among the antidepressants, maprotiline and bupropion appear to have the greatest seizure-inducing potential (Dubovsky 1992). Clinical and animal studies report variable effects of TCAs on seizure threshold (Edwards et al. 1986), and the evidence is unclear as to which antidepressants carry the smallest overall risk, although the SSRIs in general have been reported to have low potential to precipitate seizures. In acutely manic patients with brain tumors, for whom lithium—which lowers seizure threshold and may therefore induce seizures (Massey and Folger 1984)— might otherwise be the drug of choice, carbamazepine, valproic acid, lorazepam, clonazepam, and gabapentin— all of which have anticonvulsant properties—may be preferable alternatives.

The psychiatrist should also bear in mind that patients with brain tumors who have psychiatric disorders and are also taking anticonvulsants for a known seizure diathesis should be monitored carefully for the adequacy of anticonvulsant blood levels and should have their anticonvulsant dose increased or decreased as appropriate when psychotropic agents are given. This is because of the epileptogenic effects of certain of these medications, as well as their potential for decreasing or increasing anticonvulsant blood levels through drug-drug interactions affecting protein binding and/or hepatic metabolism involving the cytochrome P450 system, which may lead either to recrudescence of previously controlled seizures or the development of signs of anticonvulsant toxicity.

## Psychotherapeutic Management of Syndromes Associated With Brain Tumors

Supportive psychotherapy geared to the patient's current overall functional status, psychosocial situation, interpersonal and family relationships, cognitive capacities, and emotional needs is a very important element in the treatment of any patient with a brain tumor. The devastating psychological stress of initially being diagnosed with a brain tumor and then having to undergo various invasive, painful, and potentially debilitating treatments for it can trigger both recurrences of preexisting primary psychiatric disorders as well as the de novo appearance in the patient of reactive psychiatric symptoms resulting from having to cope with the multiple stressors associated with the illness and its treatment. Likewise, the diagnosis and treatment of a brain tumor in a loved one is enormously stressful for families. Under any clinical scenario, supportive psychotherapy for patients and supportive psychoeducation for their families are likely to be well received and very helpful for both and should play a major role in overall clinical management.

Supportive psychotherapy ideally should involve both the patient and the family or significant others and should generally focus on concrete, reality-based, cognitive, and psychoeducational issues relating to diagnosis, treatment, and prognosis. Psychotherapeutic interactions with patients should be geared to the patient's cognitive capacities, which may be diminished by the tumor itself or by one or more of the therapeutic interventions. Over time, the focus of psychotherapy may often shift to the impact of the illness on the patient's emotional and functional status, its effect on the family, the real and imagined challenges of coping with actual or anticipated functional disabilities, and the difficult processes of dealing with anticipatory grief related to potential losses and eventual death. Not surprisingly, patients with brain tumors worry a great deal about anticipated or additional decrements in their cognitive and intellectual functioning, physical disability and incapacity, and ultimately, death. Patients vary widely in their capacity to adjust to and cope with the potentially devastating consequences of brain tumors, and the success of their adjustment and adaptation greatly depends on the flexibility of their premorbid coping abilities. Some patients may appear to be little affected, whereas others may experience severe and even overwhelming symptoms of anxiety and depression. These latter patients may experience greater difficulty continuing to function optimally in their usual work and family roles and need more aggressive psychotherapeutic and psychopharmacologic interventions.

Coping through the use of the defense mechanism of denial is common and may often be adaptive and effective in helping patients to cope with their fears and anxieties, especially in the early stages of a life-threatening illness such as a brain tumor. On the other hand, maladaptive denial may result in the failure of patients and their families to comply with optimal treatment measures or deal appropriately and in a timely fashion with important legal, personal, family, and other reality-based issues and obligations that need to be addressed while the patient is still able. When denial is producing such maladaptive effects, the clinician may, in a sensitive and supportive manner, need to directly confront and encourage the patient and family to begin to address painful yet inevitable issues such as increasing disability, growing incapacity, and even impending death and how to best deal with them.

Although there are no clear-cut, generally accepted guidelines for the optimal nature and timing of discussions of prognosis with brain tumor patients, most clinicians believe that patients and families should be given realistic prognostic information in a time frame that will allow them the opportunity to make timely and well-considered decisions and appropriate plans. Such prognostic information should, of course, be conveyed by the physician in as sensitive and supportive a fashion as possible, with ample opportunity provided for questions from and discussion with the patient and family. This is another juncture where the involvement of the consulting psychiatrist may be important in helping the patient and family to process such information in a helpful and constructive way.

Some patients who have been completely cured of a brain tumor may still manifest significant psychiatric symptoms, including anxiety, fear, and depression. They, like other patients with brain tumors, may also benefit from psychiatric treatment. Unless the psychiatric symptoms are causing functional disability, are severe and distressing, persist over extended periods of time, or evolve into an autonomous psychiatric syndrome, psychotherapy rather than pharmacotherapy is generally the preferred treatment approach for such patients. Short-term, symptomatically targeted pharmacotherapy can, at times, be a useful adjunct in certain cases, even if the major ongoing treatment emphasis is on psychotherapy.

It should be kept in mind that psychodynamically focused, insight-oriented psychotherapy, which is used with certain primary psychiatric syndromes and which generally requires intact higher-level cognitive and abstracting capacities, may be relatively contraindicated in psychiatrically ill patients with brain tumors. This is because such patients may often have some degree of neurocognitive impairment in addition to their psychiatric and behavioral symptoms as a result of the effects of the tumor or of the various neurosurgical, chemotherapeutic, or radiotherapeutic interventions he or she may have undergone. When such cognitive impairment is present, not only will psychodynamically oriented thera-

pies be unlikely to be beneficial, they may also cause substantial frustration and acute psychic distress as patients are confronted with psychological tasks and cognitive demands that they are unable to meet. In general, and in contradistinction to the more traditional, relatively passive role of the psychiatrist in insight-oriented psychotherapy, more concretely focused, "here-and-now" psychotherapeutic approaches based on a cognitive-behavioral orientation with the psychiatrist assuming an active, supportive, and educational role in verbal interactions with the patient are likely to be most beneficial.

## Somatic Treatment of Mental Disorders Due to Brain Tumors

The psychopharmacologic treatment of organic mental symptoms and syndromes caused by cerebral tumors, whether characterized by psychotic, affective, anxiety, or neurocognitive disturbances, follows the same general principles as the drug treatment of phenomenologically similar symptoms due to primary psychiatric illnesses. In treating secondary psychiatric symptoms in patients with brain tumors, some important caveats must be borne in mind. Patients with psychiatric symptoms that are a direct consequence of a brain tumor, like other patients with identifiable brain pathology, frequently respond favorably to and will only tolerate significantly lower doses of psychotropic medications. Thus, side-effect profiles of psychotropic drugs being considered for the treatment of such patients need to be very carefully evaluated, especially with regard to sedative, extrapyramidal, deliriogenic, and epileptogenic effects, as well as the potential for drug interactions. The latter four are especially important for the clinician to keep in mind because they can result in substantial, and largely avoidable, additional clinical morbidity.

## Drug Treatment of Psychotic Disorders Due to Brain Tumors

Standard antipsychotic medications may be beneficial in treating the hallucinations, delusions, and thought content and process disturbances that may accompany tumor-associated psychotic syndromes. High-potency antipsychotics, which have fewer non-neurologic side effects than do the low-potency antipsychotics, are generally preferable if one of the standard neuroleptics is to be used. The former more often cause extrapyramidal symptoms, which may be more severe and persistent in patients with brain tumors. In patients with "organic" psychotic disorders, the therapeutically effective dose of an antipsychotic is often lower than that required for the treatment of primary "functional" psychoses. Thus, as little as 1–5 mg, rather than 10–20 mg, of haloperidol per day (or equivalent doses with other antipsychotics) may be effective. Although there is currently a paucity of controlled research on the efficacy of the newer atypical antipsychotics in the treatment of psychotic symptoms in brain tumor patients, given that they have been anecdotally reported to be effective in other psychotic syndromes associated with neurologic disorders and have, in view of their low side-effect profile, generally been well tolerated, they may well turn out to be the treatment of choice in brain tumor patients with psychotic symptoms. As per the general rule with the use of other psychotropics in patients with brain tumors, when initiating treatment with antipsychotics one should "start low and go slow." This is especially true in elderly patients, in whom effective antipsychotic doses may be lower than they are in younger patients because of aging-related pharmacokinetic and pharmacodynamic factors.

Antiparkinsonian agents, such as benztropine, trihexyphenidyl, and orphenadrine, are effective in the treatment of extrapyramidal side effects resulting from the use of neuroleptics in patients with brain tumors. However, in such patients these agents have a greater likelihood of causing or contributing to the occurrence of anticholinergic delirium when they are used in conjunction with low-potency neuroleptics and/or tertiary amine TCAs. Thus, their use should generally be avoided unless there is a clear-cut clinical indication, and the dose should be minimized when they are used. Diphenhydramine or amantadine for dystonic and parkinsonian symptoms and benzodiazepines for akathisia are effective alternatives and have less potential for causing delirium.

## Treatment of Mood Disorders Due to Brain Tumors

Antidepressant medications are often effective in the treatment of mood disorders with depressive features in patients with brain tumors. Standard TCAs are useful, although currently the SSRIs, newer-generation heterocyclic antidepressants, or secondary amine TCAs are often used preferentially because of their lower anticholinergic activity and sedating effects and greater patient acceptance, which results in improved treatment compliance. The SSRIs are therapeutically effective and do not cause delirium, have a favorable side-effect profile, and, despite their relatively high cost, are often effective in such patients. In recent years, methylphenidate has been shown to be effective (Masand et al. 1991) and to have a more rapid onset of action (Woods et al. 1986) in patients with secondary depression related to medical

and neurologic disorders, including brain tumors. Because it is generally well tolerated and does not lower the seizure threshold, its use as an antidepressant in brain tumor patients is increasing. Methylphenidate may also have other important therapeutic effects and may be a highly beneficial adjuvant to brain tumor therapy in some patients. In 30 patients with malignant gliomas with progressive neurobehavioral deficits resulting from their tumors and the radiation therapy and chemotherapy they had received for them, Meyers et al. (1998) showed that methylphenidate in as low a dosage as 10 mg twice a day had multiple significant beneficial effects. These included significant improvement in cognitive function, improved gait, increased stamina and motivation, and, in one case, improved bladder control, all of which occurred despite evidence of progressive neurologic changes on MRI during the time of treatment. Untoward effects reported were minimal; there was no increase in seizure frequency, and many patients who were taking glucocorticoids were able to have their doses reduced.

Monoamine oxidase inhibitors may be effective when other antidepressants are not. They do not ordinarily pose an undue risk in patients with brain tumors, but, of course, the clinician must bear in mind that the cognitive impairment that often occurs in such patients may interfere with their ability to maintain a tyramine-free diet, thereby increasing the risk associated with the use of these drugs.

If single antidepressant medication regimens are ineffective, various combinations may work. When pharmacologic treatments have failed, electroconvulsive therapy should be given serious consideration. Previously, brain tumors were thought to be an absolute contraindication to electroconvulsive therapy, especially when the tumor was associated with increased intracranial pressure. Recent studies (Starkstein and Migliorelli 1993; Zwil et al. 1990), however, have reported a number of cases of refractory depression associated with brain tumors without associated evidence of increased intracranial pressure that have been treated successfully and safely with electroconvulsive therapy.

Mood disorders with manic features due to brain tumors, though relatively rare, generally respond to lithium in the usual therapeutic range of 0.8–1.4 mEq/L. For patients in whom seizures have been a part of the clinical picture, however, carbamazepine, valproate, lorazepam, clonazepam, gabapentin, or—in cases where drug therapy has been ineffective—electroconvulsive therapy are preferable alternatives, because they do not have the epileptogenic potential of lithium and have anticonvulsant properties of their own.

Newer, still largely experimental and unapproved

treatment approaches, including vagal nerve stimulation and transcranial magnetic stimulation, have shown promise in early clinical trials with a variety of affective disorders, including depression that has been refractory to other treatments, mania (Berman et al. 2000; Grisaru et al. 1998; Rush et al. 2000), and psychotic symptoms (Hoffman et al. 1999). Clarification of their future role in the treatment of brain tumor patients with depression and other neuropsychiatric syndromes awaits further research.

## Treatment of Anxiety Disorders Due to Brain Tumors

Anxiety symptoms caused either directly or indirectly by brain tumors should not be treated with neuroleptics unless psychotic features are present, for reasons noted previously as well as the fact that neuroleptics are generally not effective in patients with such symptoms and often result in dysphoria in nonpsychotic patients. The benzodiazepines, on the other hand, are often effective and have the added benefit of possessing anticonvulsant properties. Thus, they are frequently used. However, benzodiazepines, particularly the long-acting varieties, may induce delirium in patients with organic brain disease, including brain tumors, when used in high doses and in older age groups. This argues for the preferential use of short-acting agents in lower doses, especially in older patients. Other disadvantages of benzodiazepines include their abuse potential and the occasional propensity (especially with the varieties that have long half-lives) to cause seemingly paradoxical reactions, characterized by increased arousal and agitation. Buspirone, which is free of these potentially negative effects, should be considered an alternative to the benzodiazepines. Its main drawbacks are its delayed onset and only modest degree of anxiolytic action. Hydroxyzine, SSRIs, or low doses of tertiary amine TCAs, such as doxepin or amitriptyline, may also have beneficial anxiolytic effects in some patients. Finally, panic attacks associated with temporal lobe tumors may respond to carbamazepine, valproate, or primidone, as well as to the usual antidepressant and anti-anxiety drugs.

## Treatment of Delirium

Delirium in patients with brain tumors may be associated with a wide variety of psychiatric and behavioral symptoms in addition to the characteristic cognitive impairments. Hallucinations, especially visual, and delusions are common in these patients and often respond to symptomatic treatment with low doses of haloperidol, other high-potency neuroleptics, or one of the new atypical antipsychotics while the underlying cause(s) of the delirium are being sought and treated.

## Treatment of Personality Changes Due to Brain Tumors

Mood lability may be a manifestation of a personality change due to a brain tumor and may respond to lithium or carbamazepine. Some patients with frontal lobe syndromes associated with tumors may respond to carbamazepine, as do some patients with temporal lobe tumors who may present with associated interictal aggression and violent behavior. Patients with brain tumors who have impulse dyscontrol and rageful, explosive episodes, like patients with intermittent explosive disorders due to other medical and neurologic conditions, may respond to empirical therapeutic trials of anticonvulsants, such as carbamazepine, valproic acid, or phenytoin; psychotropics, including lithium; high-potency neuroleptics; and/or stimulants or β-blockers.

## Cognitive Rehabilitation

In addition to psychopharmacologic and psychotherapeutic treatments, cognitive, occupational, and vocational rehabilitative interventions can be very helpful for patients whose tumors, or the treatments they have received for them, have produced behavioral, cognitive, or functional sequelae. Such sequelae can be identified and quantified by comparing preoperative with postoperative test results using the Halstead-Reitan Neuropsychological Test Battery (Reitan 1979) or other comprehensive neuropsychological test batteries and various functional assessment tools. Serial testing at intervals during the patient's postoperative rehabilitation allows for objective documentation of neuropsychological and functional deficits and allows for objective monitoring of their improvement or deterioration over time. Thus, in general, neuropsychological and functional assessments should be a standard part of the pretreatment evaluation and posttreatment follow-up for patients with brain tumors.

Cognitive, occupational, and vocational rehabilitative strategies can be developed that will seek to address deficits in intellectual, language, visuospatial, memory, and neurocognitive functioning, as well as vocational functioning and ability to carry out activities of daily living resulting from a brain tumor. In addition, behavioral techniques have been successfully applied to problematic behaviors resulting from insults to the brain. Such interventions may be used alone or in conjunction with other therapies. For a more detailed discussion of these various approaches, see Chapter 37 of this book.

## Neuropsychiatric Consequences of Treatments of Brain Tumors

A number of psychiatric and behavioral symptoms, as well as neurocognitive deficits, may result from surgical, pharmacologic, and radiation treatments of brain tumors and their complications. Unavoidable intraoperative injury to normal brain tissue in the vicinity of a brain tumor during the course of resection or debulking may result in the postoperative appearance of new or exacerbated behavioral or neurocognitive symptoms, depending on the location and connectivity of the tissues involved. The same is true of other perioperative and postoperative complications, such as infections and bleeding. Chemotherapy of brain tumors may cause transient delirium and neurocognitive dysfunction as well as other neurologic complications, and the administration of steroids for secondary phenomena such as cerebral edema and/or increased intracranial pressure may result in the appearance of psychotic symptoms or manic, depressive, or mixed manic and depressive affective syndromes. Radiation therapy directed at brain tumors may result in immediate or delayed neurocognitive and behavioral sequelae due to radiation-induced damage to white matter. These sequelae may be either transient (Hylton et al. 1987) or permanent (Al-Mefty et al. 1990; Burger et al. 1979) and vary considerably in severity from completely reversible changes, presumably related to edema, to widespread, permanent changes due to parenchymal necrosis. In the most severe cases, which are fortunately quite rare, progressive dementia and eventual coma and death may occur.

## Conclusions

Brain tumors are often associated and frequently present with a broad range of psychiatric, behavioral, and/or neurocognitive symptoms. The differential diagnosis of any patient who displays acute or progressive changes in behavior, personality, or cognitive function should include a brain tumor, especially if there are any associated focal neurologic signs and symptoms. In addition to assessment of psychiatric and behavioral symptoms, a full neuropsychiatric evaluation should include physical, neu-

rologic, and mental status examinations; appropriate brain imaging and other neurodiagnostic studies; and formal neuropsychological testing, particularly when there is any question of neurocognitive dysfunction on bedside testing with the MMSE.

The nature, frequency, and severity of psychiatric symptoms observed in patients with brain tumors depend on the combined effects of a number of clinical factors, including the type, location, size, rate of growth, and malignancy of the tumor. In general, behavioral symptoms associated with smaller, slower-growing, less aggressive tumors are most likely to be misdiagnosed as psychiatric in origin, particularly when they occur in "silent" regions of the brain, which do not give rise to focal neurologic signs or symptoms.

Although tumors of the frontal lobe, temporal lobe, and diencephalon appear to be most commonly associated with psychiatric and behavioral symptoms, the variation in symptoms that may occur with each of these types of tumors is exceedingly broad. In general, the relationship between particular neuropsychiatric symptoms and specific anatomic locations of the brain tumors that are causing them is not very robust.

Optimal treatment of tumor-associated psychiatric, neuropsychiatric, and neuropsychological dysfunctions should be multifaceted and is dependent on the coordinated interventions of a multidisciplinary treatment team. The psychopharmacologic treatment of psychiatric and behavioral syndromes should follow the same general principles as that of corresponding primary psychiatric disorders. However, the choice of drugs and/or dosages may require modification, because many of the psychotropic agents induce seizures or delirium, and patients with brain tumors are more vulnerable to these and other side effects.

Adjunctive, supportive psychotherapy for both the patient and the family is very important, as are psychosocial and psychoeducational interventions tailored to their specific needs. Such psychotherapeutic and psychosocial interventions must be carefully integrated with psychopharmacologic; neurocognitive, physical, occupational, and vocational rehabilitative; and behavioral treatment approaches as clinically indicated. In turn, all of these must be coordinated with the neurosurgeon's ongoing treatment interventions to optimize the patient's overall medical management. With well-planned integration and coordination of these multiple complementary therapeutic approaches, both the quantity and quality of the patient's life may be substantially enhanced.

# References

Albert MS, Feldman RG, Willis A: The "subcortical dementia" syndrome of progressive supranuclear palsy. J Neurol Neurosurg Psychiatry 37:121–130, 1974

Alexander GE, Crutcher MD: Functional architecture of basal ganglia circuits: neural substrates of parallel processing. Trends Neurosci 13:266–271, 1990

Allen IM: A clinical study of tumors involving the occipital lobe. Brain 53:196–243, 1930

Al-Mefty O, Kersh JE, Routh A, et al: The long-term side effects of radiation therapy for benign brain tumors in adults. J Neurosurg 73:502–512, 1990

Alpers BJ: Relation of the hypothalamus to disorders of personality. Archives of Neurology and Psychiatry 38:291–303, 1937

American Psychiatric Association: Diagnostic and Statistical Manual of Mental Disorders, 4th Edition. Washington, DC, American Psychiatric Association, 1994

Avery TL: A case of acromegaly and gigantism with depression. Br J Psychiatry 122:599–600, 1973

Bauer RM, Tobias B, Valenstein E: Amnesic disorders, in Clinical Neuropsychology, 3rd Edition. Edited by Heilman KM, Valenstein E. New York, Oxford University Press, 1993, pp 523–578

Bear DM, Fedio P: Quantitative analysis of interictal behavior in temporal lobe epilepsy. Arch Neurol 34:454–467, 1977

Belyi BI: Mental impairment in unilateral frontal tumors: role of the laterality of the lesion. Int J Neurosci 32:799–810, 1987

Benson DF: Aphasia, Alexia, and Agraphia. New York, Churchill Livingstone, 1979

Berman RM, Narasimhan M, Sanacora G, et al: A randomized clinical trial of repetitive transcranial magnetic stimulation in the treatment of major depression. Biol Psychiatry 47:332–337, 2000

Bhatia MS: Cotard's syndrome in parietal lobe tumor. Indian Pediatrics 30:1019–1021, 1993

Bigler ED: Diagnostic Clinical Neuropsychology. Austin, TX, University of Texas Press, 1984

Blackman M, Wheler GH: A case of mistaken identity: a fourth ventricular tumor presenting as school phobia in a 12 year old boy. Can J Psychiatry 32:584–587, 1987

Burger PC, Mahaley MS, Dudka L, et al: The morphologic effects of radiation administered therapeutically for intracranial gliomas. Cancer 44:1256–1272, 1979

Burger PC, Scheithauer BW, Vogel FS: Surgical Pathology of the Nervous System and Its Coverings, 3rd Edition. New York, Churchill Livingstone, 1991

Burkle FM, Lipowski ZJ: Colloid cyst of the third ventricle presenting as psychiatric disorder. Am J Psychiatry 135:373–374, 1978

Butters N, Milotis P: Amnestic disorders, in Clinical Neuropsychology. Edited by Heilman KM, Valenstein E. New York, Oxford University Press, 1979, pp 403–439

Cairns H: Mental disorders with tumors of the pons. Folia Psychiatrica Neurologica Neurochirurgica 53:193–203, 1950

Cairns H, Mosberg WH: Colloid cysts of the third ventricle. Surgery, Gynecology, and Obstetrics 92:545–570, 1951

Cairns H, Oldfield RC, Pennybacker JB, et al: Akinetic mutism with an epidermoid cyst of the 3rd ventricle. Brain 64:273–290, 1941

Chipkevitch E: Brain tumors and anorexia nervosa syndrome. Brain Dev 16:175–179, 1994

Coffey RJ: Hypothalamic and basal forebrain germinoma presenting with amnesia and hyperphagia. Surg Neurol 31:228–233, 1989

Critchley M: The problem of visual agnosia. J Neurol Sci 1:274–290, 1964a

Critchley M: Psychiatric symptoms and parietal disease: differential diagnosis. Proceedings of the Royal Society of Medicine 57:422–428, 1964b

Cummings JL: Subcortical Dementia. New York, Oxford University Press, 1990

Cummings JL: Frontal-subcortical circuits and human behavior. Arch Neurol 50:873–880, 1993

Cummings JL, Mendez MF: Secondary mania with focal cerebrovascular lesions. Am J Psychiatry 141:1084–1087, 1984

Davison K, Bagley CR: Schizophrenia-like psychoses associated with organic disorders of the central nervous system: a review of the literature, in Current Problems in Neuropsychiatry: Schizophrenia, Epilepsy, the Temporal Lobe (British Journal of Psychiatry Special Publication No 4). Edited by Harrington RN. London, Headley Brothers, 1969, pp 126–130

Direkze M, Bayliss SG, Cutting JC: Primary tumors of the frontal lobe. British Journal of Clinical Practice 25:207–213, 1971

Drubach DA, Kelly MP: Panic disorder associated with a right paralimbic lesion. Neuropsychiatry Neuropsychol Behav Neurol 2:282–289, 1989

Dubovsky SL: Psychopharmacological treatment in neuropsychiatry, in The American Psychiatric Press Textbook of Neuropsychiatry. Edited by Yudofsky SC, Hales RE. Washington, DC, American Psychiatric Press, 1992, pp 663–701

Dunn DW, Weisberg LA: Peduncular hallucinations caused by brainstem compression. Neurology 33:1360–1361, 1983

Edwards JG, Long SK, Sedgwick EM: Antidepressants and convulsive seizures: clinical, electroencephalographic, and pharmacologic aspects. Clin Neuropharmacol 9:329–360, 1986

Filley CM, Kleinschmidt-DeMasters BK: Neurobehavioral presentations of brain neoplasms. West J Med 163:19–25, 1995

Folstein MF, Folstein SE, McHugh PR: Mini-Mental State: a practical method for grading the cognitive state of patients for the clinician. J Psychiatr Res 12:189–198, 1975

Fox S: Use of a quality of life instrument to improve assessment of brain tumor patients in an outpatient setting. J Neurosci Nurs 30:322–325, 1998

Frazier CH: Tumor involving the frontal lobe alone: a symptomatic survey of 105 verified cases. Archives of Neurology and Psychiatry 35:525–571, 1935

Galasko D, Kwo-On-Yuen PF, Thal L: Intracranial mass lesions associated with late-onset psychosis and depression. Psychiatr Clin North Am 11:151–166, 1988

Gautier-Smith P: Parasagittal and Falx Meningiomas. London, Butterworth, 1970

Ghadirian AM, Gauthier S, Bertrand S: Anxiety attacks in a patient with a right temporal lobe meningioma. J Clin Psychiatry 47:270–271, 1986

Goldberg E: Varieties of perseverations: comparison of two taxonomies. J Clin Exp Neuropsychol 6:710–726, 1986

Greenberg DB, Brown GL: Mania resulting from brain stem tumor: single case study. J Nerv Ment Dis 173:434–436, 1985

Grisaru N, Chudakov B, Yaroslavsky Y, et al: Transcranial magnetic stimulation in mania: a controlled study. Am J Psychiatry 155:1608–1610, 1998

Gutmann DH, Grossman RI, Mollman JE: Personality changes associated with thalamic infiltration. J Neurooncol 8:263–267, 1990

Heaton RK: Wisconsin Card Sorting Test. Odessa, FL, Psychological Assessment Resources, 1985

Hobbs GE: Brain tumors simulating psychiatric disorder. Canadian Medical Association Journal 88:186–188, 1963

Hoffman RE, Boutros NN, Berman RM, et al: Transcranial magnetic stimulation of left temporoparietal cortex in three patients reporting hallucinated "voices." Biol Psychiatry 46:130–132, 1999

Hollister LE, Boutros N: Clinical use of CT and MR scans in psychiatric patients. J Psychiatry Neurosci 16:194–198, 1991

Hylton PD, Reichman OH, Palutsis R: Monitoring of transient central nervous system postirradiation effects by 133-xenon inhalation regional cerebral blood flow measurements. Neurosurgery 21:843–848, 1987

Jamieson RC, Wells CE: Manic psychosis in a patient with multiple metastatic brain tumors. J Clin Psychiatry 40:280–283, 1979

Jones JB, Barklage NE: Conversion disorder: camouflage for brain lesions in two cases. Arch Intern Med 150:1343–1345, 1990

Kalayam B, Young RC, Tsuboyama GK: Mood disorders associated with acoustic neuromas. Int J Psychiatry Med 24:31–43, 1994

Kaplan CP, Miner ME: Anxiety and depression in elderly patients receiving treatment for cerebral tumours. Brain Inj 11:129–135, 1997

Keschner M, Bender MB, Strauss I: Mental symptoms in cases of tumor of the temporal lobe. Archives of Neurology and Psychiatry 35:572–596, 1936

Keschner M, Bender MB, Strauss I: Mental symptoms associated with brain tumor: a study of 530 verified cases. JAMA 110:714–718, 1938

Khouzam HR, Emery PE, Reaves B: Secondary mania in late life. J Am Geriatr Soc 42:85–87, 1994

Klotz M: Incidence of brain tumors in patients hospitalized for chronic mental disorders. Psychiatr Q 31:669–680, 1957

Ko SM, Kok LP: Cerebral tumours presenting with psychiatric symptoms. Singapore Med J 30:282–284, 1989

Kocher R, Linder M, Stula D: Primary brain tumors in psychiatry. Schweizer Archiv fur Neurologie, Neurochirurgie und Psychiatrie 135:217–227, 1984

Lampl Y, Barak Y, Achiron A, et al: Intracranial meningiomas: correlation of peritumoral edema and psychiatric disturbances. Psychiatry Res 58:177–180, 1995

Lezak MD: Neuropsychological Assessment, 3rd Edition. New York, Oxford University Press, 1995

Lishman WA: Organic Psychiatry: The Psychological Consequences of Cerebral Disorder. New York, Oxford University Press, 1987

Lohr JB, Cadet JL: Neuropsychiatric aspects of brain tumors, in The American Psychiatric Press Textbook of Neuropsychiatry. Edited by Talbott JA, Hales RE, Yudofsky SC. Washington, DC, American Psychiatric Press, 1987, pp 351–364

Luria AR: The Working Brain: An Introduction to Neuropsychology. New York, Basic Books, 1973

Luria AR: Higher Cortical Functions in Man. New York, Basic Books, 1980

Malamud N: Psychiatric disorder with intracranial tumors of limbic system. Arch Neurol 17:113–123, 1967

Masand P, Murray GB, Pickett P: Psychostimulants in poststroke depression. J Neuropsychiatry Clin Neurosci 3:23–27, 1991

Massey EW, Folger WN: Seizures activated by therapeutic levels of lithium carbonate. South Med J 77:1173–1175, 1984

McAllister TW, Price TRP: Aspects of the behavior of psychiatric inpatients with frontal lobe damage: some implications for diagnosis and treatment. Compr Psychiatry 28:14–21, 1987

McIntyre HD, McIntyre AP: The problem of brain tumor in psychiatric diagnosis. Am J Psychiatry 98:720–726, 1942

Meadows JC: The anatomical basis of prosopagnosia. J Neurol Neurosurg Psychiatry 37:489–501, 1974

Mendez MF, Cummings JL, Benson DF: Epilepsy: psychiatric aspects and use of psychotropics. Psychosomatics 25:883–894, 1984

Meyers CA, Weitzner MA, Valentine AD, et al: Methylphenidate therapy improves cognition, mood, and function of brain tumor patients. J Clin Oncol 16:2522–2527, 1998

Minski L: The mental symptoms associated with 58 cases of cerebral tumor. Journal of Neurology and Psychopathology 13:330–343, 1933

Mulder DW, Daly D: Psychiatric symptoms associated with lesions of temporal lobe. JAMA 150:173–176, 1952

Mungas D: Interictal behavior abnormality in temporal lobe epilepsy: a specific syndrome or non-specific psychopathology? Arch Gen Psychiatry 39:108–111, 1982

Nadvi SS, van Dellen JR: Transient peduncular hallucinations secondary to brain stem compression by a medulloblastoma. Surg Neurol 41:250–252, 1994

Nasrallah HA, McChesney CM: Psychopathology of corpus callosum tumors. Biol Psychiatry 16:663–669, 1981

Neuman E, Rancurel G, Lecrubier Y, et al: Schizophreniform catatonia in 6 cases secondary to hydrocephalus with subthalamic mesencephalic tumor associated with hypodopaminergia. Neuropsychobiology 34:76–81, 1996

Oliver AP, Luchins DJ, Wyatt RJ: Neuroleptic-induced seizures: an in vitro technique for assessing relative risk. Arch Gen Psychiatry 39:206–209, 1982

Olney JW, Farber NB, Spitznagel E, et al: Increasing brain tumor rates: is there a link to aspartame? J Neuropathol Exp Neurol 55:1115–1123, 1996

Patton RB, Sheppard JA: Intracranial tumors found at autopsy in mental patients. Am J Psychiatry 113:319–324, 1956

Percy AK, Elveback LR, Okazaki H, et al: Neoplasms of the central nervous system: epidemiologic considerations. Neurology 22:40–48, 1972

Pincus JH, Tucker GJ: Behavioral Neurology, 2nd Edition. New York, Oxford University Press, 1978

Pollack L, Klein C, Rabey JM, et al: Posterior fossa lesions associated with neuropsychiatric symptomatology. Int J Neurosci 87:119–126, 1996

Pringle AM, Taylor R, Whittle IR: Anxiety and depression in patients with an intracranial neoplasm before and after tumor surgery. Br J Neurosurg 13:46–51, 1999

Radhakrishnan K, Bohnen NI, Kurland LT: Epidemiology of brain tumors, in Brain Tumors: A Comprehensive Text. Edited by Morantz RA, Walsh JW. New York, Marcel Dekker, 1994, pp 1–18

Reiman EM, Raichle ME, Robins E, et al: The application of positron-emission tomography to the study of panic disorder. Am J Psychiatry 143:469–477, 1986

Reitan RM: An investigation of the validity of Halstead's measures of biological intelligence. Archives of Neurology and Psychiatry 73:28–35, 1979

Reitan RM, Wolfson D: Neuroanatomy and Neuropathology for Neuropsychologists. Tucson, AZ, Neuropsychology Press, 1985, pp 167–192

Remington FB, Robert SL: Why patients with brain tumors come to a psychiatric hospital: a thirty-year survey. Am J Psychiatry 119:256–257, 1962

Roberts GW, Done DJ, Bruton C, et al: A "mock up" of schizophrenia: temporal lobe epilepsy and schizophrenia-like psychosis. Biol Psychiatry 28:127–143, 1990

Roberts JKA, Lishman WA: The use of CAT head scanner in clinical psychiatry. Br J Psychiatry 145:152–158, 1984

Robinson RG, Kubos KL, Starr LB, et al: Mood disorders in stroke patients: importance of location of lesion. Brain 107:81–93, 1984

Rodin E, Schmaltz S: The Bear-Fedio personality inventory and temporal lobe epilepsy. Neurology 34:591–596, 1984

Ross E: Prosody and brain lateralization: fact vs. fancy or is it all just semantics? Arch Neurol 45:338–339, 1988

Ruiz A, Ganz WI, Donovan Post J, et al: Use of thallium-201 brain SPECT to differentiate cerebral lymphoma from toxoplasma encephalitis in AIDS patients. AJNR Am J Neuroradiol 15:1885–1894, 1994

Rush AJ, George MS, Sackheim HA, et al: Vagus nerve stimulation (VNS) for refractory depressions: a multicenter study. Biol Psychiatry 47:276–286, 2000

Russell RW, Pennybacker JB: Craniopharyngioma in the elderly. J Neurol Neurosurg Psychiatry 24:1–13, 1961

Salazar-Calderon Perriggo VH, Oommen KJ, Sobonya RE: Silent solitary right parietal chondroma resulting in secondary mania. Clin Neuropathol 12:325–329, 1993

Scheibel RS, Meyers CA, Levin VA: Cognitive dysfunction following surgery for intracerebral glioma: influence of histopathology, lesion location, and treatment. J Neurooncol 30:61–67, 1996

Schirmer M, Bock WJ: The primary symptoms of intracranial metastases, in Advances in Neurosurgery, Vol 12. Edited by Piotrowski W, Brock M, Klinger M. Berlin, Springer Verlag, 1984, pp 25–29

Schlesinger B: Mental changes in intracranial tumors and related problems. Confinia Neurologica 10:225–263, 1950

Selecki BR: Cerebral mid-line tumours involving the corpus callosum among mental hospital patients. Med J Aust 2:954–960, 1964

Selecki BR: Intracranial space-occupying lesions among patients admitted to mental hospitals. Med J Aust 1:383–390, 1965

Sperry RW: Lateral specialization in the surgically separated hemispheres, in The Neurosciences: 3rd Study Program. Edited by Worden FG. Cambridge, MA, MIT Press, 1974, pp 5–19

Spreen O, Benton A, Fincham R: Auditory agnosia without aphasia. Arch Neurol 13:84–92, 1965

Starkstein SE, Migliorelli R: ECT in a patient with a frontal craniotomy and residual meningioma. J Neuropsychiatry Clin Neurosci 5:428–430, 1993

Starkstein SE, Boston JD, Robinson RG: Mechanisms of mania after brain injury: 12 case reports and review of the literature. J Nerv Ment Dis 176:87–100, 1988

Stoudemire A, Fogel BS, Gulley LR, et al: Psychopharmacology in the medical patient, in Psychiatric Care of the Medical Patient. Edited by Stoudemire A, Fogel BS. New York, Oxford University Press, 1993, pp 155–206

Strauss I, Keschner M: Mental symptoms in cases of tumor of the frontal lobe. Archives of Neurology and Psychiatry 33:986–1005, 1935

Strobos RRJ: Tumors of the temporal lobe. Neurology 3:752–760, 1953

Tanaghow A, Lewis J, Jones GH: Anterior tumour of the corpus callosum with atypical depression. Br J Psychiatry 155:854–856, 1989

Teuber HL: Unity and diversity of frontal lobe functions. Acta Neurobiol Exp 32:615–656, 1972

Tucker GJ, Price TRP, Johnson VB, et al: Phenomenology of temporal lobe dysfunction: a link to atypical psychosis: a series of cases. J Nerv Ment Dis 174:348–356, 1986

von Monakow C: Die Lokalisation im Grossheim und der Abbav der Funktion durch Kortikale Herde. Weisbaden, JF Bergmann, 1914

Warrington EK, Rabin P: Perceptual matching in patients with cerebral lesions. Neuropsychologia 8:475–487, 1970

Weitzner MA: Psychosocial and neuropsychiatric aspects of patients with primary brain tumors. Cancer Invest 17:285–291, 1999

White J, Cobb S: Psychological changes associated with giant pituitary neoplasms. Archives of Neurology and Psychiatry 74:383–396, 1955

Wilson G, Rupp C: Mental symptoms associated with extramedullary posterior fossa tumors. Transactions of the American Neurological Association 71:104–107, 1946

Woods SW, Tesar GE, Murray GB, et al: Psychostimulant treatment of depressive disorders secondary to medical illness. J Clin Psychiatry 47:12–15, 1986

Zwil AS, Bowring MA, Price TRP, et al: ECT in the presence of a brain tumor: case reports and a review of the literature. Convulsive Therapy 6:299–307, 1990

# Neuropsychiatric Aspects of Human Immunodeficiency Virus Infection of the Central Nervous System

Francisco Fernandez, M.D.

George M. Ringholz, M.D., Ph.D.

Joel K. Levy, Ph.D.

Human immunodeficiency virus (HIV) infection has become a major health and social issue of this era. It contributed to the first known decrease in average life expectancy in the United States (Kranczer 1995). Because of its complex nature, HIV may well continue to defy complete cure for some time to come. HIV not only devastates an individual's constitutional health but also attacks the central and peripheral nervous systems and causes a range of neurological syndromes and organic mental disorders with sometimes insidious courses. Our aim is to outline the neuropathology and neurobehavioral symptomatology associated with HIV infection and delineate the challenging and perplexing range of possible neuropsychiatric complications that clinicians may encounter. We discuss treatment of the various neuropsychiatric entities in relation to the special characteristics and needs of this medically ill population.

## HIV: Medical Factors

Since initial reports of the acquired immunodeficiency syndrome (AIDS) (Gottlieb et al. 1981) and the discovery that the syndrome and related illnesses were associated with a specific virus—HIV (Barre-Sinoussi et al. 1983; Gallo et al. 1983; J.A. Levy et al. 1984)—researchers have noted that infections can result from several high-risk situations. These risk factors include a venereal mode of transmission in which the virus borne on body fluids enters the bloodstream through breaks in mucous membranes; intravenous drug use with shared needles; and administration of blood transfusions, blood products, or blood factor concentrates infected with the virus; infants are infected perinatally and through infected breast milk during lactation. Current terminology designates transmission patterns into two types: 1) the "horizontal" pattern, which includes body fluid contact through sexual activity, intravenous drug administration, and administration of blood products; and 2) the "vertical" pattern, by which infants are infected as just described.

Efforts to control this viral infection by pharmacological treatments have advanced remarkably since the outset of the pandemic. Unfortunately, there is no cure at this time, and attempts to develop vaccines for this organism have met with a confounding complexity of genetic features. HIV, a lentivirus and a retrovirus, possesses the capacity for amazing diversity and mutation. During the process of transcription of the double-stranded ribonucleic acid genome into deoxyribonucleic acid (DNA), two basic types of this highly genetically diverse virus have been identified: HIV-1 and HIV-2, both of which are thought to have originated in Africa (Clavel et al. 1986; Markovitz 1993; Miyazaki 1995; Rolfe 1994). There is increasing information that the main virus was zoonotic, with early infections arising from contact with chimpanzees. HIV-1 is more associated with the AIDS epidemic in central and East Africa (Clavel et al. 1986), whereas HIV-2 is epidemic in West Africa but rare outside of that continent (Clavel et al. 1986; Markovitz 1993; Marlink et al. 1994; Miyazaki 1995; Rolfe 1994). Through advances in genomic sequencing, several subtypes (referred to as *clades*) of HIV-1 (10, specified as A through J) and HIV-2 (5, indicated by A through E), and an atypical form of HIV-1, termed "O" for "outlier," have been identified. Moreover, each clade has several strains. Epidemiologically, the subtypes of HIV-1 were found to have rather specific geographic distributions (Brodine et al. 1997; Louwagie et al. 1993). HIV-1 clades A, C, and D are the most prevalent in Africa, whereas clade E is the modal virus in Southeast Asia, and clade C occurs most frequently in India and China (Brodine et al. 1997). Clade B is the predominant virus in North and South America and Europe (Brodine et al. 1997). It is not yet known if there are types that have a special affinity for the central nervous system (CNS), but it is known that there are mutations in a particular sequence of the viral envelope protein that more readily enter the brain. This virus possesses an amazing capacity for further diversity in that one individual, once infected, can produce myriad subspecies (Diaz et al. 1997). This is partially because during the reverse transcription process, the DNA genome that has just been produced is not proofread. This can result in a thousand-fold higher rate of nucleotide substitutions that may occur with herpesvirus DNA genomes (Brodine et al. 1997).

Both transmission modes apply to both HIV types (Miyazaki 1995), but there is evidence that HIV-2 has a wider range of pathogenicity (Gao et al. 1994; Marlink et al. 1994). However, neurotropism is considered to be equivalent (Rolfe 1994). HIV-1 has been most investigated in research and clinical reports with regard to the pathology of AIDS and is the focus of this chapter wherever HIV is referenced.

As of June 2000, the reported cumulative number of cases of fully developed AIDS in the United States was in excess of 753,907 (Centers for Disease Control and Prevention 2000), since the first cases were reported in the late 1970s and early 1980s. Current research estimates that 650,000–900,000 persons in the United States, or about 1 in 300, were infected with HIV (for the index year 1992)

but may be asymptomatic. Of these cases, epidemiological studies provide estimates that up to 30% may be expected to develop HIV-1-associated dementia (HAD; Heaton et al. 1995; Janssen et al. 1991, 1992), the most severe phase of HIV-1-associated cognitive/motor complex (HACMC; Janssen et al. 1991), during the course of the infection. In the very young (younger than 15 years) and in the elderly (75 years or older), 13% and 19%, respectively, may have encephalopathy (Janssen et al. 1992; Mitsuyasu 1989). The appearance of this complication is ominous; the median survival duration after this diagnosis is about 6 months (McArthur et al. 1993).

The virus may have a long period of asymptomatic activity or dormancy, intracellularly, before symptoms of immune, neuromuscular, and CNS decline manifest (Bernad 1991; Brew et al. 1988; Hollander 1991; Koralnik et al. 1990; J.A. Levy 1993; Mitsuyasu 1989; Rowen and Carne 1991). This latency may be longer than 5–7 years until severe constitutional symptoms appear; however, cases of cognitive and psychiatric manifestations have been reported to occur even before the onset of AIDS case–defining criteria such as opportunistic infections, characteristic malignancies, or neurological syndromes (Beckett et al. 1987; Maccario and Scharre 1987; Navia and Price 1987).

## CNS Pathology Resulting Directly From HIV

AIDS is the term denoting the ultimate stage of systemic infection with HIV. However, before the realization that the disease was caused by a virus, clinicians noted that patients complained of cognitive and mood disorders. After researchers proposed a viral etiology of AIDS and AIDS-related disorders, investigations revealed that HIV may be not only the agent of immune compromise but also neurotropic and neuropathogenic. The most common CNS complication is cognitive impairment of sufficient severity to warrant the diagnosis of a dementia. According to the Centers for Disease Control and Prevention (CDCP) of the United States (1987), this dementia status is independently a diagnostic, case-defining criterion for the status of fully developed AIDS.

Cognitive disorders were originally believed to affect only a small proportion of HIV-infected individuals. Studies have now reported that the prevalence and severity of cognitive impairment increases as the disease progresses (Heaton et al. 1995).

At the outset of the HIV epidemic, severe cognitive decline was thought to be a part of the end stage of HIV infection, associated only with AIDS. At that point, patients had opportunistic infections in addition to the effects of HIV brain infection; this combination could cause gross impairment. This severe cognitive disorder was often found to be composed of a combination of disturbances in cognitive functioning, motor behavior, and affective functioning, and this triad was termed *AIDS dementia complex* by Price and colleagues (Brew et al. 1988). Investigators also found that HIV itself produced an encephalitis or encephalopathy, which was variously termed *subacute encephalitis*, *HIV encephalopathy*, or *AIDS encephalopathy*. More recently, a behaviorally based set of criteria to distinguish levels of neurological and neurobehavioral impairment has been proposed by the American Academy of Neurology (AAN; see the section "Neurobehavioral Assessment of HIV Infection of the CNS," later in this chapter), which has termed these conditions HACMC (Janssen et al. 1991). These criteria mainly distinguish motor impairments from mild cognitive deficits (HIV-1-associated minor cognitive/motor disorder; HA) from the actual dementia (HAD), which is a profound state of disability.

Direct brain infection by HIV, therefore, is now widely believed to be the likely cause of related cognitive and other neurobehavioral disorders (Janssen et al. 1991). The evidence for this theory includes detection of HIV-1 in CNS 14 days after initial infection (Davis et al. 1992), presence of viral nucleic acid in the brains of some patients with this disorder, direct HIV isolation from the brain and cerebrospinal fluid (CSF) (Chiodi et al. 1992), electron microscopic findings of viral particles within infiltrating macrophages (Schindelmeiser and Gullotta 1991), and detection of viral antigens within the brains of infected individuals (Pumarola-Sune et al. 1987). The studies that showed direct brain infection by HIV provide a clear rationale for attempting to treat HIV-related cognitive disorder with an antiviral drug (see the section, "Treatment of HIV Infection of the CNS," later in this chapter). In addition, because the CNS in HIV infection can be regarded as a possible reservoir or sanctuary for the virus, antiviral drugs that can penetrate the blood-brain barrier and the blood-CSF barrier are clearly necessary.

With respect to how HIV gains entry to the CNS, Gyorkey and colleagues (1987), after reviewing autopsy material, postulated early in the history of the epidemic that this virus may enter the brain substance by passing through endothelial gaps in brain capillaries. A non-CD4+-dependent HIV infection of brain capillary endothelial cells has also been identified (Moses et al. 1993). Investigators have also proposed that the virus gains entry to the brain parenchyma via infiltration of infected macrophage leukocytes, the so-called Trojan Horse effect (Dickson et al. 1991; Schindelmeiser and Gullotta 1991; Vazeux 1991). Regardless of the mode of entry, the virus attaches via its coat glycoprotein gp120 to binding sites (most notably, CD4+ receptors) on brain microglial cells (J.A. Levy 1993; S.A. Lipton and Gendleman 1995). Hill and colleagues (1987) have detailed numerous brain sites where the virus seems to have an affinity. These areas are rich with CD4+ receptors and include basal ganglia and temporolimbic structures. This localization of receptors may relate to the typical neurobehavioral symptoms associated with HAD (Hill et al. 1987; Ruscetti et al. 1988).

Much of the knowledge of central neuropathology associated with HIV infection has come from the pioneering work of Price and colleagues (Brew et al. 1988; Navia et al. 1986a, 1986b) and Wiley and colleagues (Masliah et al. 1992, 1995; Wiley et al. 1991), who have extensively reviewed autopsy material of patients with fully developed AIDS, and from subsequent histological examinations that have further delineated regional involvement. Gross examination of the brain indicates that the white matter, subcortical structures, and vacuolar myelopathy of the spinal cord are commonly involved (Brew et al. 1988). Also, at this stage, extensive atrophy, most notably reflected in increased ventricular size (as opposed to widened sulcal spaces), is found. Although neurons are thought not to be the direct target of the virus (yet some investigators have found regional neuronal loss in HIV-1 brain infection [Ketzler et al. 1990; Weis et al. 1993]), they sustain neurotoxic effects. Frequently involved subcortical gray-matter structures include basal ganglia, thalamus, and temporolimbic structures. The cerebral cortex is often spared; however, some investigators have noted extensive cortical changes (Ciardi et al. 1990; Everall et al. 1991; Ketzler et al. 1990; Masliah et al. 1992; Navia et al. 1986a; Wiley et al. 1991). Wiley and colleagues applied sensitive quantitative methods to the histological analysis of cerebral cortex and found up to a 40% loss of cortical dendritic area (Masliah et al. 1992). In this analysis, the severity of cortical damage was found to be correlated with level of HIV gp41 immunoreactivity (Masliah et al. 1992).

This CNS neuropathology often results in cognitive changes from mild memory decline and cognitive slowing to a profound dementia (Everall et al. 1993; Grafe et al. 1990). In addition, Price and colleagues noted in their series of findings that HIV-1 could be recovered mainly from brains of patients with the most severe form of dementia in which multinucleated giant cell creation has occurred (Brew et al. 1988). However, dementia has also developed in individuals in whom the virus could not be recovered from the CNS, either directly or by hybridization methods.

Once the virus has entered the CNS, a complex cascade of events can occur to cause neural injury, which is thought to result in the various neurobehavioral syndromes (S.A. Lipton and Gendleman 1995). S.A. Lipton and Gendleman (1995) have detailed what is currently known about these events. First, in the process of binding to a CD4+ receptor–containing cell, HIV gp120 irreversibly binds to a calcium channel and increases intracellular free calcium (Giulian et al. 1990; Stefano et al. 1993). HIV gp120 also induces the cell to increase neurotoxin production (S.A. Lipton and Gendleman 1995) and may alter brain glucose metabolism, which could lead to brain dysfunction (Kaiser et al. 1990; S.A. Lipton and Gendleman 1995). Second, after the virus enters the cell and incorporates its genome into the host's genome, it can induce the infected macrophage to release more injurious compounds in the presence of other stimulators, such as other CNS infectious by-products and cytokines produced in response to infections by other immunologically active cells. S.A. Lipton and Gendleman (1995) describe these compounds to include glutamate-like substances such as quinolic acid; free radicals such as superoxide anions; other cytokines such as tumor necrosis factor-$\alpha$, interleukin-1-$\beta$, and interferon-$\gamma$; and eicosanoids such as arachidonic acid. Additionally, gp120 and certain fragment peptides are powerful activators of $N$-methyl-D-aspartate (NMDA) receptors of the CNS, the mechanism associated with neuroexcitotoxicity (Gemignani et al. 2000). These are all thought to cause neurocellular injury by several mechanisms, including increased intracellular calcium and increased concentrations of the toxic inorganic compound nitric oxide.

Another process—apoptosis, or programmed cell destruction—was proposed as an additional factor in the destruction of CD4+ cells in HIV disease, for both lymphocytes and neural tissues. Apoptosis is the genetically determined cell death (Bellamy et al. 1995; Silvestris et al. 1995; Steller 1995) that is thought to maintain homeostasis in the body by eliminating excess and worn-out cells. One protein thought to participate in this process is FAS (Lynch et al. 1995; Silvestris et al. 1995), and this genetically driven action has been shown to culminate in disruption of the cell's nucleus by activation of endonucleases (Silvestris et al. 1995). The process of homeostasis is thought to go awry in cancer, AIDS, and neurodegenerative diseases (Bellamy et al. 1995; Steller 1995; Thompson 1995). Certain immune factors can trigger apoptosis, such as tumor necrosis factor-$\alpha$ (Talley et al. 1995).

In the case of HIV infection, a number of virus-related proteins can trigger apoptosis. Gp120 also has

been reported to induce apoptosis (Maccarrone et al. 2000). Tumor necrosis factor-$\alpha$ can be produced by HIV-related gp120 binding to macrophages, which may lead to this process (Sekigawa et al. 1995). Apoptosis has also been shown to be induced peripherally by the HIV-related Tat protein (Li et al. 1995). This cell-destroying mechanism can be inhibited, and knowledge of how to effect this inhibition can be applied to clinical AIDS treatment. Certain immunosuppressive compounds such as FK506 (Sekigawa et al. 1995) and glucocorticoids (Lu et al. 1995) have inhibited apoptosis, as have growth factors (Li et al. 1995), soluble CD4 (Maldarelli et al. 1995), $N$-acetylcysteine (Talley et al. 1995), and didanosine (preinfection only) (Corbeil and Richman 1995), but not zidovudine (Maldarelli et al. 1995). However, inhibiting apoptosis can present further difficulties because it has been shown that it can enhance viral production and lead to high levels of persistent viral infection (B.A. Antoni et al. 1995).

HIV-related apoptosis apparently also can affect the CNS in HIV encephalitis (Petito and Roberts 1995; Talley et al. 1995). Apoptosis was considered to be operational in the demise of neurons and astrocytes as determined by characteristic morphology and immunohistochemical labeling of cell fragments. The stimulatory mechanism for this CNS apoptosis was thought to be a viral product or component or tumor necrosis factor, the latter supported by an in vitro study in which tumor necrosis factor-$\alpha$ caused apoptosis in neuroblastoma cell culture (Talley et al. 1995). Thus, this naturally regulated process may be dysregulated by the complex actions of viral infection and its by-products, which may become a major contributor to the various ways that the CNS is impaired in HIV infection.

Investigators who have searched for a biochemical marker that would correlate with or predict the level of the neurobehavioral disturbance in HAD have found that levels of $\beta_2$-microglobulin, eicosanoids, prostaglandin $E_2$, and neopterin are promising assays at this time (Brew et al. 1992; Elovaara et al. 1989; Griffin et al. 1994; Harrison and Skidmore 1990; Karlsen et al. 1991). These levels correlated highly with degree of dementia.

Additional work on the neuropathology of excitotoxins (Cotton 1990; Guillian et al. 1990; Heyes et al. 1991, 1992; Kieburtz et al. 1991a; S.A. Lipton 1992; S.A. Lipton and Gendleman 1995; Sardar et al. 1995; Schwarcz et al. 1983; Walker et al. 1989), the role of NMDA receptor physiology and dysregulation (Kieburtz et al. 1991a; S.A. Lipton 1992; S.A. Lipton and Gendleman 1995), and the specific neurotoxicity of quinolic acid, a metabolite of tryptophan (Kieburtz et al. 1991a; S.A. Lipton and Gendleman 1995; Schwarcz et al. 1983), is also contributing to the explanation of how neuronal tissue is injured by remote metabolic effects of HIV infection. Quinolic acid levels have been found to be highly correlated with levels of $\beta_2$-microglobulin and neopterin (Heyes et al. 1992; Kieburtz et al. 1991a) and with cognitive impairment (Heyes et al. 1991).

# CNS Neuropathology Due to Opportunistic Infections and Neoplasia

As mentioned earlier in this chapter, when severe neurological disease, opportunistic infections, or malignancies such as Kaposi's sarcoma and HIV-related lymphomas arise, the patient's condition meets criteria for full-blown AIDS. This may occur at any time, although immune compromise is usually reflected by the clinical and laboratory markers; namely, fewer than 200 CD4+ cells/mm$^3$. Additionally, syphilis and tuberculosis are increasingly found as coinfections in patients with AIDS. These disorders must be considered in the differential diagnosis of CNS infection. These opportunistic infections and malignancies may contribute to severe neurological disorders or overwhelming dementia (Bedri et al. 1983; Belman et al. 1986; Brew et al. 1988; Budka 1989; Filley et al. 1988; Gonzales and David 1988; Gray et al. 1988; Ho et al. 1987; Lantos et al. 1989; Petito 1988). Thus, it is important to investigate and treat aggressively the cause of the neurological problem in order to postpone mortality and to seek to restore normal neurobehavioral function. Bredesen and colleagues (1988) have reviewed common CNS infections, as well as neoplasia and other infection- or treatment-induced complications. This range of CNS involvement is listed in Table 23–1 (Bredesen et al. 1988).

*Toxoplasma gondii* is perhaps the most common opportunistic infection in AIDS and may present as a focal or diffuse cognitive or affective disturbance. Clinically, toxoplasmosis symptoms include malaise, confusion, lethargy, headache, fever, and focal deficits. The authors have seen a case of cerebral toxoplasmosis (Figure 23–1), which initially presented as a presumed postpartum depression. This affective disorder was refractory to antidepressant treatment. Later, the patient developed hemiballismus. A neurodiagnostic evaluation, including computed tomographic imaging, subsequently revealed CNS toxoplasmosis.

The results of serologic testing are of limited diagnostic value. Neuroimaging may be normal, but a typical presentation of toxoplasmal involvement is a ring-

**TABLE 23–1.** CNS conditions associated with AIDS and HIV infection

**HIV-associated disorders**
 HIV-1-associated cognitive/motor complex (HACMC)
  HIV-1-associated dementia (HAD)
  HIV-1-associated minor cognitive/motor disorder (HAMCMD)
 HIV-1-associated myelopathy

**Opportunistic viral infections**
 Cytomegalovirus
 Herpes simplex virus, types I and II
 Herpes varicella zoster virus
 Papovavirus (progressive multifocal leukoencephalopathy)
 Adenovirus type 2

**Other opportunistic infections of the CNS**
 *Toxoplasma gondii*
 *Cryptococcus neoformans*
 *Candida albicans*
 *Aspergillus fumigatus*
 *Coccidioides immitis*
 Mucormycosis
 *Rhizopus* species
 *Acremonium alabamensis*
 *Histoplasma capsulatum*
 *Mycobacterium tuberculosis*
 *Mycobacterium avium-intracellulare*
 *Listeria monocytogenes*
 *Nocardia asteroides*

**Neoplasms**
 Primary CNS lymphoma
 Metastatic lymphoma
 Metastatic Kaposi's sarcoma

**Cerebrovascular**
 Infarction
 Hemorrhage
 Vasculitis

**Adverse effects of treatments for HIV and AIDS-related disorders**

*Note.* AIDS = acquired immunodeficiency syndrome; CNS = central nervous system; HIV = human immunodeficiency virus.
*Source.* Adapted from Bredesen et al. 1988.

enhancing lesion near the subcortical gray-matter structures (Jarvik et al. 1988; Kelly and Brant-Zawadzki 1983; Whelan et al. 1983). Multiple lesions are common on magnetic resonance imaging (MRI), with toxoplasmal foci on T2 scans represented as areas of heightened signal intensity (Bredesen et al. 1988). Thallium-201 SPECT can be helpful in distinguishing cerebral toxoplasmosis (negative uptake) from lymphoma (increased uptake). Definitive diagnosis for toxoplasmosis is determined by biopsy.

*Cryptococcus neoformans*, the other common AIDS-related intracranial infection, presents principally as a

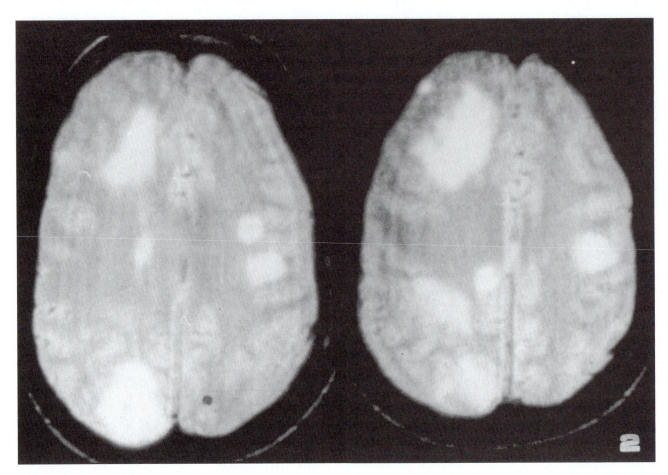

**FIGURE 23–1.** Magnetic resonance imaging scan of a 35-year-old female presenting with severe postpartum depression and history of long-term intravenous drug use. The patient was refractory to antidepressant pharmacotherapy and was being evaluated for electroconvulsive therapy. Multiple foci of cerebral toxoplasmosis, confirmed by cerebrospinal fluid titer, are seen as bright patches with the largest in the left frontal and occipital areas.

meningitis, with headache (R.B. Lipton et al. 1991), altered mental status, nuchal rigidity, fever, and nausea and vomiting. Definitive diagnosis is based on analysis of CSF.

Other viral infections producing personality and behavioral changes and cognitive impairment, with and without sensorimotor impairments, that have been frequently reported in the CNS include progressive multifocal leukoencephalopathy (PML; Bedri et al. 1983; Berger et al. 1987; Fong and Toma 1995; J.K. Miller et al. 1982; Portegies et al. 1991) due to a papovavirus (JC); cytomegalovirus (CMV); herpes simplex virus (HSV); and herpes zoster virus (HZV). The prognosis for PML remains grave; however, combination treatment with cytarabine and zidovudine appears promising for not only extending life but also producing remission (Portegies et al. 1991). New treatments aimed at inhibiting JC virus replication are expected to improve patient survival (Berger and Concha 1995; Kerr et al. 1993).

CMV is commonly seen in the CNS of AIDS patients and may produce encephalitis, retinitis, and peripheral neuropathies and demyelination (Bredesen et al. 1988; Masdeu et al. 1988). Treatment of CMV infection is currently limited to chronic administration of ganciclovir (dihydroxypropoxymethyl guanine; DHPG), foscarnet (Reddy et al. 1992; SOCA 1994), or, more problematically, cidofovir (Akler et al. 1998; Lalezari et al. 1998). It has also been recently found the protease inhibitors and HAART, used systemically for general HIV treatment, also help control the retinitis (Macdonald et al. 1998; Reed et al. 1997). HSV infections may manifest in temporal-lobe encephalitis or encephalomyelitis in immune-deficient patients. The severity of the infection seems to correlate with the level of immune dysfunction (Bredesen et al. 1988). Progression to a chronic mental disorder due to a general medical condition with amnestic features is a danger. The usual emergency treatment for suspected HSV encephalitis—intravenous acyclovir—would apply in these cases. HZV can reactivate in AIDS patients, causing a range of peripheral and cranial nerve inflammatory responses, encephalitis, myelitis, and inflammations of brain vasculature (Beilke 1989; Bredesen et al. 1988; Scaravilli et al. 1989; Vinters et al. 1988). Diagnosis of HZV in the CNS is associated with elevated HZV antibody titers in the CSF (Bredesen et al. 1988). HZV is treated with intravenous acyclovir or vidarabine.

Mycobacterial (especially tuberculosis) and fungal infections also occur in the brain (Table 23–1). Diagnosis is aided through biopsy. Tuberculous meningitis is the most frequent extrapulmonary manifestation in HIV-1 infection. Aggressive treatment for longer periods is required to avoid relapses.

Syphilis occurs as a concurrent CNS infection, and its diagnosis is problematic. It can be asymptomatic, and other causes of meningitis can obscure the picture. Cases with a negative CSF Venereal Disease Research Laboratory result have been reported (Musher et al. 1990), and the fluorescent treponemal antibody absorption test (FTA-ABS) also has not been conclusive. Other newer techniques such as polymerase chain reaction for the nucleic material of the treponema may lead to better differentiation (DeBiasi and Tyler 1999). Treatment of syphilis is with intravenous aqueous crystalline penicillin G, followed by intramuscular penicillin G benzathine.

Non-Hodgkin's lymphoma is commonly seen as a primary CNS tumor in AIDS patients (Bredesen et al. 1988). Patients with lymphoma usually present with altered mental status, hemiparesis, aphasia, seizures, or other focal symptoms. One patient in our emergency room presented with a manic episode. He had no history of affective disorder. At first, he was given a diagnosis of toxoplasmosis, but he ultimately received an accurate diagnosis of CNS lymphoma (Figure 23–2). A diagnostic investigation, including computed tomographic imaging, revealed a right frontal ring-enhancing lesion in this patient. Diagnosis of lymphoma is confirmed with the aid of neuroimaging, biopsy, and/or recovery of malignant cells from the CSF. The prognosis for survival ranges from less than 6 months to 1 year or more.

Cerebrovascular problems (Beilke 1989; Bredesen et al. 1988; Engstrom et al. 1989; Frank et al. 1989; Scaravilli et al. 1989; Snider et al. 1983; Vinters et al. 1988) commonly occur in AIDS patients. These problems may result from viral (e.g., VZV; Frank et al. 1989) or bacterial/treponemal vasculitis (Brightbill et al. 1995). Also, cerebral infarcts may result from emboli secondary to nonbacterial thrombotic endocarditis (Bredesen et al. 1988). Other causes of cerebrovascular problems include vasculotoxic responses to treatment of systemic infections and malignancies. Behaviorally, a multi-infarct state may be reflected as a stepwise decline in cognitive func-

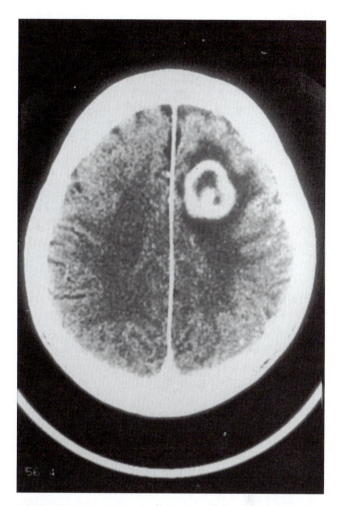

**FIGURE 23–2.** Computed tomography scan of a 21-year-old male presenting in an emergency room with a first episode of mania.

tioning and must be differentiated from the more protracted progressive viral encephalopathic process.

Thus, clinicians must rapidly assess patients presenting with focal neurocognitive findings, which may be the result of potentially treatable infections, to forestall more serious global mental status decline or death.

## Direct Assessment of CNS Injury in HIV Disease

### Neuroimaging Findings

Imaging, by both computed tomography (CT) and MRI, has proved helpful in demonstrating injury by the virus and other pathological processes in the brain (Bishburg et al. 1989; Dooneief et al. 1992; Flowers et al. 1990; Freund-Levi et al. 1989; Jarvik et al. 1988; Kelly and Brant-Zawadzki 1983; Levin et al. 1990; Post et al. 1991; Whelan et al. 1983). Aside from either method being able to show atrophy, as reflected by increased ventricular size and sulcal size, both can help to define pathological entities such as ring-enhancing lesions and some aspects of white-matter involvement. MRI is superior to CT in showing areas of focal high-signal intensities in subcortical white and gray matter by the $T_2$-weighted signal (Dooneief et al. 1992). $T_1$ relaxation times have been examined and have not indicated structural differences between aged HIV-infected patients and control subjects or temporal changes in these aged patients as their disease progressed (Freund-Levi et al. 1989). MRI also has not proven useful in depicting structural correlates of neurologically asymptomatic HIV infection (Post et al. 1991). MRI, however, has disclosed neurostructural changes in medically symptomatic but neurologically asymptomatic HIV-positive patients. Jernigan et al. (1993) found volumetric reductions in cerebral gray and white matter in these patients. Most recently, MRI using diffusion tensor imaging (DTI) to study white-matter abnormalities such as white-matter pallor has been found useful in distinguishing between HIV-1-infected patients and normal control subjects (Pomara et al. 2001).

Imaging reflecting functioning of the nervous system, such as positron emission tomography (PET) (Brunetti et al. 1989; Hinkin et al. 1995), single photon emission computed tomography (SPECT) (Kuni et al. 1991; Masdeu et al. 1991; Sacktor et al. 1995a), magnetic resonance spectroscopy (MRS) (Deicken et al. 1991; Jarvik et al. 1993; Menon et al. 1990), functional magnetic resonance imaging (fMRI) (Navia and Gonzalez 1997), and regional cerebral blood flow (rCBF) (Schielke et al. 1990), have shown regional functional abnormalities in HIV. These imaging modalities have established themselves as sensitive to different aspects of functioning: PET reflects metabolism, SPECT and fMRI and rCBF reflect brain perfusion, and MRS reflects biochemical function and dysfunction.

In one study (Brunetti et al. 1989), PET-detected subcortical hypermetabolism in basal ganglia and thalamus was seen early in the course of CNS disease, followed by regional and then general hypometabolism as the disease progressed. PET scanning has also proved to be helpful in ascertaining the therapeutic effects of antiviral treatment. PET scanning noted reversal of focal cortical abnormalities of glucose metabolism after the AIDS dementia complex was treated with zidovudine (Brunetti et al. 1989). In other patients without abnormalities at baseline, glucose metabolism increased after zidovudine treatment. Improved brain glucose utilization was correlated with neurological functional improvement. As mentioned earlier in this chapter, CNS glucose utilization was found to be, in part, dysregulated by a glycoprotein asso-

ciated with the HIV viral coat (Kaiser et al. 1990); thus, reduction in viral activity could be associated with this increased glucose metabolism.

SPECT scanning was improved recently to provide more qualitative and quantitative reflection of brain cortical and subcortical perfusion. One study (Sacktor et al. 1995b), however, was not able to correlate focal perfusion deficits with neuropsychological deficits; only motor function impairment correlated with global perfusion deficits.

Proton MRS presented functional evidence of neuronal loss in HIV-infected patients who had normal structure on MRI (Menon et al. 1990) and identified decreased brain adenosine triphosphate and phosphocreatine concentrations in the white matter of HIV-positive neuropsychiatric patients (Deicken et al. 1991). MRS using a quantitation of choline-to-creatine signals ratio has been suggested to characterize neuronal dysfunction. This ratio was determined to increase with cellular membrane turnover (Chong et al. 1993). The N-acetyl aspartate–to–creatine ratio (Barker et al. 1995; Chong et al. 1993; Tracey et al. 1996) and phosphocreatine (Deicken et al. 1991) concentration also were found to decrease in relation to neuronal dysfunction. Proton MRS may be a useful way to follow patients from the neurologically asymptomatic stage through HAMCMD and HAD (Cecil and Lenkinski 1998). It may provide an early marker of neuronal dysfunction before irreversible damage to the CNS occurs.

## CSF Findings

The CSF of HIV-infected patients with altered mental status or with complaints about mental functioning should be evaluated quickly for signs of opportunistic infection such as toxoplasmosis, cryptococcal infection, HSV, VZV, and CMV so that appropriate anti-infective treatment can be initiated before CNS damage occurs (Buffet et al. 1991). Specific signs of HIV infection that are reflected in CSF values include HIV virions, immunoglobulin G (IgG; in abnormally large quantities), HIV-specific antibody, mononuclear cells, neopterin, $\beta_2$-microglobulin, and oligoclonal bands (Brew et al. 1992; Buffet et al. 1991; Carrieri et al. 1992; Chiodi et al. 1992; Heyes et al. 1991; Larsson et al. 1991; Lolli et al. 1990; Marshall et al. 1988, 1991; McArthur et al. 1992; Portegies et al. 1989; Reboul et al. 1989; Shaskan et al. 1992; Tartaglione et al. 1991). The amount of intrathecal virus and antibody, however, has not been found to correlate with severity of neurological or cognitive symptomatology (Reboul et al. 1989). IgG production was found to increase throughout duration of infection

(1-year sampling), regardless of CD4+ cell count, in neurologically healthy patients (Marshall et al. 1991). The concentration of CSF $\beta_2$-microglobulin is highly correlated with both dementia severity (Brew et al. 1992; McArthur et al. 1992) and level of systemic disease (asymptomatic seropositivity to fully developed AIDS). CSF $\beta_2$-microglobulin has shown some specificity in differentiating HAD from multiple sclerosis and other CNS disorders (Carrieri et al. 1992) with regard to absolute levels and CSF-to-serum ratios. Additionally, it can reflect positive symptomatic zidovudine therapy (Brew et al. 1992) (although the amount of virus in the CSF may not be reduced with treatment [Tartaglione et al. 1991]).

Merrill (1992) has suggested that the presence of cytokines, namely interleukin-1, tumor necrosis factor-$\alpha$, interleukin-6, and transforming growth factor-$\beta$, may be associated with both pro- and anti-inflammatory events in the CNS. He compared differences in myelin damage in multiple sclerosis and HIV infection of the CNS; in multiple sclerosis, effector cell–mediated lesion production, destruction of oligodendrocytes, and demyelination occur; in HIV, virus-induced toxin production via macrophages and microglia, which can produce myelin pallor, occurs. This syndrome may cause neural dysfunction throughout the brain without frank destruction of myelin, which would be reflected in an increase in CSF levels of myelin basic protein (Marshall et al. 1988, 1991). Others have reported that demyelination occurs in HIV disease (e.g., Greenberg 1995). HIV has been associated with a demyelinating chronic inflammatory peripheral polyneuropathy that presents as Guillain-Barré syndrome (Cornblath et al. 1987; Dalakas and Pezeshkpour 1988), but debate continues as to whether it also may be centrally demyelinating (Gray and Lescs 1993; Merrill 1987; Power et al. 1993; Vago et al. 1993).

Analysis of neurotransmitter metabolites in CSF, specifically those of noradrenaline and dopamine, failed to detect significantly different levels of 3-methoxy-4-hydroxyphenylglycol (MHPG) between HIV-infected patients and noninfected, healthy volunteers (Larsson et al. 1991). However, CSF levels of homovanillic acid (HVA) were lower by almost half in HIV-infected patients than in noninfected volunteers and lowest in patients with AIDS; no direct relation was found between HVA levels and severity of dementia. The level of quinolinic acid, an excitotoxin and an NMDA receptor agonist (see earlier discussion in the section, "CNS Pathology Resulting Directly From HIV"), is related to severity of dementia/clinical status (Heyes et al. 1991). In patients with early-stage disease, quinolinic acid levels were twice those of non-HIV-infected subjects, and more than 20 times normal levels were detected in

patients with severe dementia or CNS AIDS involvement (opportunistic infection or CNS neoplasms) (Heyes et al. 1991). More recently, CSF quinolinic acid levels were found to correlate with regional brain atrophy as quantified by MRI, whereas CSF $\beta_2$-microglobulin levels were not (Heyes et al. 2001). The significance of these levels of an excitotoxin in the CNS continues to be investigated with regard to pathogenesis and pathophysiology of cognitive disorders.

A relationship between endorsed depressive or anxious symptoms and CSF immune function markers has been found in HIV-positive United States Air Force personnel (Praus et al. 1990). These investigators found significant correlations between CSF nucleated cell counts or protein levels and Hamilton Rating Scale for Depression scores greater than 10 and between CSF nucleated cell counts or absolute CD4a cell counts and Hamilton Anxiety Rating Scale scores greater than 10.

## Electrophysiological Findings

Electrophysiological examination of HIV-infected patients with cognitive and neurological complaints is helpful in establishing an organic basis for these conditions and has detected neural dysfunction before other behavioral markers could (Goodin et al. 1990; Goodwin et al. 1990; Ollo et al. 1990, 1991; Tinuper et al. 1990). Both electroencephalogram (EEG) and specific evoked potentials have been used in this regard. HIV infection may cause a convulsive disorder (Parisi et al. 1991), but most studies have shown that, groupwise, the percentage of patients with abnormal EEG findings increases as the systemic disease progresses and that slowing of dominant frequencies is unusual. In CDC group II (asymptomatic) patients, 25% were found to have abnormal EEG results, with frontotemporal theta slowing as the predominant finding (Elovaara et al. 1991; Parisi et al. 1989). In CDC group III (persistent generalized lymphadenopathy) patients, 30% had a variety of abnormalities somewhat evenly divided among frontotemporal theta slowing, diffuse theta slowing, and frontotemporal delta slowing (Parisi et al. 1989). Thus, these significant electrophysiological disturbances occurred in pre-AIDS groups. Others (Gabuzda et al. 1988) have found even higher percentages of abnormalities in more physically symptomatic patients. Thirty-five percent of patients with pre-AIDS had mildly to severely abnormal findings, whereas 65% of patients with AIDS had mildly to severely abnormal EEG activity. Across both of these diagnostic groups, intermittent or continuous symmetric theta or delta slowing was characteristic.

Sleep-related EEG findings have also reflected

effects of HIV on the CNS. Sleep is often disturbed in patients with HIV disease (Darko et al. 1995), and polysomnography has been used to investigate patients' complaints of dyssomnia. These studies have uncovered gross disturbances in sleep architecture (Itil et al. 1990; Norman et al. 1990; Wiegand et al. 1991a, 1991b). The viral infection may play a central role in these disorders, and medication effects such as those of zidovudine must also be included in the analysis of sleep disturbances due to HIV disease.

Evoked potential studies were able to detect abnormalities in neurologically and physically asymptomatic HIV-seropositive patients (Goodin et al. 1990; Goodwin et al. 1990; Smith et al. 1988). Brain-stem auditory and somatosensory evoked potentials from tibial nerve stimulation and oculomotor activity recordings showed significant delays in latencies of response compared with those of control subjects. These authors concluded that evoked potentials may represent an early direct indication of neurological involvement in HIV disease, before overt symptomatology occurs.

## Neurobehavioral Assessment of HIV Infection of the CNS

Dementia is generally regarded as an acquired intellectual impairment characterized by persistent deficits in multiple areas, including memory, language, cognition, visuospatial skills, personality, and emotional functioning (Cummings and Benson 1983). HAD has been portrayed as a subcortical type of dementia affecting subcortical and frontostriatal brain processes (Brew et al. 1988). However, because other CNS cortical areas have been identified as being affected (Ciardi et al. 1990; Everall et al. 1991; Grant et al. 1987; Ketzler et al. 1990; Masliah et al. 1992; Navia et al. 1986a; Wiley et al. 1991), a strict definition of HIV-related cognitive impairment as a subcortical disorder has been questioned (Poutiainen et al. 1991). Dementia's persistent cognitive impairment differentiates it from another common HIV-related mental disorder due to a general medical condition—delirium. The symptoms most frequently described and most closely associated with subcortical disorders such as Parkinson's disease and progressive supranuclear palsy, as well as multiple sclerosis, are found in HIV infection of the CNS. The description of HAD as a subcortical process suggests that neuropsychological tests that reflect memory registration, storage, and retrieval, psychomotor speed, information processing rate, and fine motor function are important in a neuropsychological battery for

assessment of HIV-related cognitive impairment (Butters et al. 1990). Other traditionally cortical syndromes, such as aphasia, agnosia, apraxia, and other sensory-perceptual functions, can also be present but usually not until later in the course of the disease and perhaps as a result of some focal opportunistic infection or neoplastic invasion of the CNS.

The earliest level of cognitive impairment is a subclinical cognitive inefficiency that can range in severity from a decrement in previous level of functioning in attention, speed of information processing, memory, abstraction, and fine motor skills to formal test-defined deficits in some of these domains. Disturbances in these functions may have no observable effects on activities of daily living or functional performance. These changes occur in more than 20% of asymptomatic HIV-1 infected individuals (Wilkie et al. 1990a), but the proportion of patients having these problems doubles with advanced disease (Heaton et al. 1995). More severe impairment interfering minimally with functional status is now defined by the AAN as HAMCMD (Table 23–2). Prevalence of HAMCMD is unknown, but estimates suggest that 20%–30% of asymptomatic HIV-1 infected individuals may meet formal AAN criteria for this disorder (Goodkin 2001). Indications of early HAMCMD may be mild and, as such, are frequently attributed to the systemic illness or a psychosocial reaction to HIV infection. However, even under the influence of an early organic process that affects cognition, many patients will be cognizant of their own mental and physical sluggishness and personality changes, and affective symptoms may occur concomitantly.

Fully developed HAD is commonly associated with significant declines in functional status. Table 23–3 shows signs and symptoms of both cognitive and psychiatric disturbances commonly encountered early in the course of HAD (Brew et al. 1988), and Table 23–4 shows signs and symptoms of cognitive and psychiatric difficulties encountered late in the course of HAD (Brew et al. 1988). The course of HAD can steadily worsen with the development of moderate to severe cognitive deficits, confusion, psychomotor slowing, and seizures. Patients may appear mute and catatonic. Socially inappropriate behavior, psychosis, mania, marked motor abnormalities such as ataxia, spasticity, and hyperreflexia, and incontinence of bladder and bowel can occur.

Clinicians must seriously evaluate patients' complaints, such as memory problems, mental slowing, and difficulty with attention and concentration, however, at any stage of the disease. Dysphoria due to the seriousness of the illness or induced by medications or affective disturbances could theoretically cause cognitive difficulties

**TABLE 23–2.** HIV-1-associated minor cognitive/motor disorder: American Academy of Neurology criteria

The patient must have all of the following:

A. Cognitive/motor/behavioral dysfunctions:
   At least 2 of the following (acquired and present for at least 1 month):
   • Impaired attention/concentration
   • Mental slowing
   • Impaired memory
   • Slowed movements
   • Incoordination
   • Personality change, irritability, or emotional lability
   These cognitive/motor dysfunctions must be documented by neurological examination or neuropsychological testing.

B. The dysfunction in cognitive/motor/behavioral abilities must cause mild impairment of work-related activities or activities of daily living.

C. The level of disturbance does not meet the criteria for HIV-1-associated dementia complex or HIV-1-associated myelopathy.

D. There must be no evidence of another etiology, such as CNS opportunistic infection or malignancy or severe systemic illness (documented by history, physical examination, and laboratory and radiological investigations), or effects related to alcohol/substance use, acute or chronic substance withdrawal, adjustment disorder, or other psychiatric disorders.

*Note.* CNS = central nervous system; HIV = human immunodeficiency virus.

*Source.* Adapted from Janssen et al. 1991.

(e.g., pseudodementia of depression) (Cummings and Benson 1983), but several studies (Kovner et al. 1989; Pace et al. 1992; Syndulko et al. 1990) have reported that cognitive dysfunction is not correlated with mood disorder, and the level of cognitive impairment surpasses that expected by distraction from affective causes. Because of the possibility of early cognitive involvement, efforts have been devoted to construction of a neuropsychological battery of tests that would be sensitive to the earliest signs of HIV effects on cognition (Butters et al. 1990; Franzblau et al. 1991; Gibbs et al. 1990; Hart et al. 1990; Heaton et al. 1995; Jacobs et al. 1992; Klusman et al. 1991; Lunn et al. 1991; Marotta and Perry 1989; E.N. Miller et al. 1991; Perry et al. 1989; Van Gorp et al. 1989a; Wilkie et al. 1990a).

The cardinal signs of HIV-related cognitive impairment remain consistent by many reports (Butters et al. 1990; Collier et al. 1992; Dunlop et al. 1992; Fernandez et al. 1989a; Franzblau et al. 1991; Gibbs et al. 1990; Hart et al. 1990; Jacobs et al. 1992; Janssen et al. 1988; Kaemingk and Kasizniak 1989; Karlsen et al. 1992; Klus-

**TABLE 23–3.** Early signs and symptoms of HIV-related neurobehavioral impairment

| Cognitive | Affective/behavioral |
|---|---|
| Memory impairment (especially with verbal, rote, or episodic) | Apathy |
| Concentration/attention disturbance | Depressed mood |
| Language comprehension problems | Anxiety |
| Conceptualization difficulties | Mild agitation |
| Problem-solving difficulties | Mild disinhibition |
| Visuospatial constructional deficits | Hallucinations or misperceptions |
| Motor slowing or impairment in coordination | |
| Mental tracking difficulties | |
| Mild frontal-lobe-type symptoms | |
| Handwriting and fine motor control difficulties | |

*Note.* HIV = human immunodeficiency virus.

*Source.* Adapted from Brew et al. 1988.

**TABLE 23–4.** Late signs and symptoms of HIV-related neurobehavioral impairment

| Cognitive | Affective/behavioral |
|---|---|
| Severe dementia affecting multiple cognitive areas | Severe behavioral disinhibition |
| Aphasia and/or mutism | Manic symptoms |
| Severe frontal-lobe symptoms | Delusions |
| Severe psychomotor slowing | Severe hallucinations |
| Intense distractibility | Severe agitation |
| Disorientation | Paranoid ideation |
| | Severe depression with or without suicidality |

*Note.* HIV = human immunodeficiency virus.

*Source.* Adapted from Brew et al. 1988.

man et al. 1991; Krikorian and Wrobel 1991; Lunn et al. 1991; Marotta and Perry 1989; Martin et al. 1992; E.N. Miller et al. 1991; Morgan et al. 1988; Nance et al. 1990; Pajeau and Roman 1991; Perry 1990; Perry et al. 1989; Riedel et al. 1992; Rubinow et al. 1988; Ryan et al. 1992; Skoraszewski et al. 1991; Y. Stern et al. 1991; Tross et al. 1988; Van Gorp et al. 1989a, 1989b, 1991; Wilkie et al. 1990a, 1990b) and include problems with verbal memory, difficulties with attention and concentration, slowing of information processing, slowed psychomotor speed, and impairment of cognitive flexibility; in some cases, the nonverbal abilities of problem solving, visuospatial integration and construction, and nonverbal memory are impaired (Butters et al. 1990). Studies have shown that psychomotor tasks, such as the Digit Symbol and Block Design tests of the Wechsler Adult Intelligence Scale and the Trail Making Test Part B from the Halstead-Reitan Battery, and memory tasks, such as the delayed Visual Reproduction subtest from the Wechsler Memory Scale and the delayed recall of the Rey-Osterreith Complex Figure were most affected in the early stages of cognitive impairment associated with HIV (Van Gorp et al. 1989a). We and others have found that tasks detecting psychomotor and neuromotor disturbances in HIV-related neural dysfunction such as visuomotor reaction time (Dunlop et al. 1992; Karlsen et al. 1992; Nance et al. 1990) and fine motor dexterity as measured by pegboard activities are also sensitive measures for the early detection of impairment. Such motor speed tasks may be more vulnerable to the effects of HIV than central processing speed. One investigation (Martin et al. 1992) implied that graphomotor and manual slowing may be a major component of impairment on psychomotor tasks. When a memory search/reaction time paradigm was used, speed of memory search in HIV-positive patients did not differ significantly from that in control subjects. This task did not test speed of movement but rather a cognitive reaction latency.

Other areas of cognitive function usually assessed by neuropsychological batteries include aphasia, apraxia, and other complex language-associated functioning; verbal abstract reasoning and problem solving; and perceptual functioning of the different sensory modalities. These assessments, however, have not been universally sensitive for the early detection of HIV-related CNS dysfunction. Any impairment found in these areas of intellectual functioning may be associated with a more focal attack on the nervous system, such as an HIV-related opportunistic infection that forms a focal abscess or an HIV-related tumor. However, neuropsychological evaluations encompassing a broad range of cognitive areas (Butters et al. 1990), as are effectively implemented with other clinical entities such as head trauma or other dementias, would seem to yield adequate information about focality of involvement in the later stages of HIV disease. These cognitive areas should be considered in research, as well as clinical investigations, so as to span all functions that might be attacked by the disease's neurotropism and not incur the chance of a false-negative finding (Kovner et al. 1989; Van Gorp et al. 1991). If the patient's lack of stamina or other situation precludes an extensive battery, a comprehensive but briefer battery employing the tests listed in Table 23–5 (Selnes et al. 1991), or tests that address similar functions (Butters et al. 1990), can assess the critical areas of cognitive functioning to detect HIV involvement at an early stage.

**TABLE 23–5.** HIV neuropsychological screening battery

**Attention and memory**
 Wechsler Adult Intelligence Scale—Revised, Digit Span subtest
 Rey Auditory-Verbal Learning Test
**Language/speech and speed of cognitive production**
 Controlled Oral Word Association Test (from Benton Multilingual Aphasia Examination)
**Executive/psychomotor**
 Symbol Digit Modalities Test
 Trail Making Test, Parts A and B
 Grooved Pegboard

*Note.* HIV = human immunodeficiency virus.

*Source.* Adapted from Selnes et al. 1991.

The ability of HIV-related cognitive dysfunction to disrupt the capacity to work and perform activities of daily living was formerly thought to occur only at the end of the infection's cycle during fully developed AIDS. However, because early cognitive impairment may occur before the diagnosis of AIDS, a means of measuring cognitive functioning was needed to define cognitive disabilities at earlier stages of infection. Early in the epidemic, an attempt was made to characterize functional impairment using a scale validated for Alzheimer's disease. This instrument, the Global Deterioration Scale of Reisberg and colleagues (1982), has been criticized as not linearly characterizing the cognitive and functional decline of Alzheimer's disease (Eisdorfer et al. 1991), but it appears to be useful as a clinical tool for rating cognitive impairment as it affects everyday functioning in HIV-infected individuals before neuropsychological quantification of specific deficits. This scale can be used for investigational purposes to compare the cognitive impairment associated with HIV with that of other dementias (Fernandez and Levy 1990). It is also useful for rating functional level as required (but no scale has been specifically mandated) by the American Academy of Neurology's nomenclature for degree of impairment to determine HAD.

Another scale that has been proposed to discriminate patients with HIV infection and dementia from patients with HIV infection but not dementia is the HIV-Dementia Scale (HDS) (Power et al. 1995). It appears to be more sensitive than the Mini-Mental Status Examination to the HIV-related subcortical effects of CNS infection. The HDS has been criticized because portions of the scale are difficult to administer by nonneurologically trained individuals. For example, it requires saccadic eye movement examination, for which there is no standardized scoring. However, even if this component is deleted, the HDS retains the ability to grossly discriminate among mild-moderate and moderate-severe dementia (Skolasky et al. 1998).

## Treatment of HIV Infection of the CNS

### Primary Therapy: Antivirals

Studies have found that zidovudine is a potent inhibitor of human retrovirus replication in vitro and is effective in reducing morbidity by decreasing the number of serious complications in patients with AIDS as well as in asymptomatic patients (Fischl et al. 1987; Groopman 1991a, 1991b; Merigan 1991; Moore et al. 1991). Preliminary observations from several studies also suggest that zidovudine therapy can attenuate the symptomatic course of the dementia and neurological disease in some patients (Arendt et al. 1991; Hollweg et al. 1991; Riccio et al. 1990; Schmitt et al. 1988; Yarchoan et al. 1987). Experimental data show that the compound penetrates the brain at a level at which one-half can be recovered from CSF (Wong et al. 1992). Therefore, findings such as those of Sidtis and colleagues (1993) that report improved cognitive functioning in patients who receive high levels of zidovudine—up to 2,000 mg/day—are consistent with this brain parenchymal bioavailability characteristic. Additionally, doses may need to be high to maintain therapeutic levels of zidovudine in the CNS, because investigators have found that zidovudine is cleared from the brain through an active transport process (Stahle et al. 1993; Wang and Sawchuk 1995; Wong et al. 1993). Clinicians should keep this finding in mind when calculating the maintenance dose of zidovudine in the patient with subjective complaints consistent with HAMCMD or HAD.

Human data regarding the pharmacology and toxicology of zidovudine indicate that, with careful clinical monitoring and appropriate dose modification, it is a safe drug to use in neurologically impaired patients (Yarchoan et al. 1987). The principal toxicity of zidovudine is hematological, with decrease in the red blood cell, neutrophil, and, less commonly, platelet counts. Of these, neutrophil depression has proved to be the major limiting toxicity because anemia can be treated with transfusion. Most hematological side effects of zidovudine usually emerge after 6 weeks or more of therapy and, in many cases, require dose reduction or discontinuation. Typically, resuming treatment with zidovudine at a lower dose can be effective once hematopoietic toxicity has resolved. Furthermore, some studies suggest that a reduced or low-normal vitamin $B_{12}$ level may be associated with a greater risk for neutrophil depression (Richman et al. 1987). Other minor side effects of zidovudine include myalgias, headache, insomnia, nausea, and depersonalization and derealization. Mania has been reported (Maxwell et al. 1988; Wright et al. 1989), and delirium has also been reported (Fernandez 1988). Macrocytosis is the only consistent laboratory index, excluding the previously described hematological changes. The only significant drug-drug interaction reported occurs with acetaminophen. Concurrent treatment with acetaminophen may result in an increased frequency of neutropenia. Theoretically, drugs that are hepatically cleared and disturb the process of glucuronidation also have the potential to cause neutropenia. Thus, zidovudine should be used cautiously, with regular hematological monitoring. A single report exists of a patient who developed severe neurotoxicity and died (Hagler and Frame 1986); however, confirmatory studies of mortality risk from zidovudine are lacking.

Newer antivirals such as zalcitabine (ddC) (Dickover et al. 1991; Neuzil 1994), didanosine (ddI) (Connolly et al. 1991; Neuzil 1994), lamivudine (3TC) (van Leeuwen et al. 1995), and stavudine (d4T) (Murray et al. 1995; Neuzil 1994) are now being used in the control of HIV replication and, as such, may play a role in reducing the viral load available to the CNS via circulatory spread. These drugs, however, do not penetrate the blood-brain barrier as well as zidovudine does. Additionally, a new class of antivirals—the protease inhibitors—that prevents maturation of HIV particles (Neuzil 1994) is showing promise alone and in proposed combination therapy with the reverse transcriptase agents (Highly Active Anti-Retroviral Therapy [HAART]) (Greenlee et al. 2000). Significant improvement in both cognitive (Tozzi et al. 1999) and motor (Sacktor et al. 2001) abilities on neuropsychological testing has been reported. Thus, antiviral therapy currently provides an important direct intervention for cognitive and emotional effects of HIV infection of the CNS.

### Adjunctive Therapy: Additional Biological/ Pharmacological Interventions

Peptide T (Bridge et al. 1991; Buzy et al. 1992; Julander et al. 1990; Rosen et al. 1992) has been the subject of controversy in the treatment of HIV infection of the CNS. It differs from the other antivirals in that, instead of inhibiting reverse transcriptase activity, it blocks the binding of gp120 to CD4+ receptors, which, as mentioned earlier in this chapter, appears to be the incipient pathophysiological mechanism for neurovirulence.

Therefore, peptide T may serve as a primary intervention for HIV systemic and CNS proliferation. It appears to be less toxic than other antivirals, and one study (Rosen et al. 1992) reported reversal of neurobehavioral impairment.

Because of the observation that gp120 may be associated with neuronal cell injury by altering cellular calcium flux (S.A. Lipton 1991; S.A. Lipton and Gendleman 1995; Stefano et al. 1993), a remedy was suggested to counteract this calcium-induced injury. S.A. Lipton (1991) suggested that certain calcium channel blockers (e.g., flunarizine) were protective against gp120 toxicity in vitro. Nimodipine (30–60 mg orally 4–6 times daily) was also found to be protective and is being used to regulate neuron-injuring intracellular calcium increments (Dreyer et al. 1990). One calcium channel blocker cannot be readily substituted for another; verapamil and diltiazem were not as effective as nimodipine or did not help. In fact, in another study, verapamil enhanced HIV-1 replication in lymphoid cells (Harbison et al. 1991).

In addition, new agents are being tested that provide a rational approach to the treatment of the elements of neuronal injury outlined above—cytokines, NMDA, and calcium flux. Pentoxifylline (400 mg orally three times a day) is being tested to counter tumor necrosis factor-$\alpha$, although troublesome side effects such as hallucinations have been reported (Dezube et al. 1993). NMDA receptor blockers are being evaluated to block the excitotoxin quinolinic acid from instituting the damage of increased intracellular calcium (American Psychiatric Association 1994). Memantine (10–30 mg/day orally; usual dose, 20 mg/day), an antiparkinsonian drug, binds to the NMDA receptor and also blocks gp120 toxicity (Kornhuber et al. 1991). Vitamin E (typically 1,600 IU/day orally; may require up to 3,000 IU/day) and $N$-acetylcysteine (9,600 mg/day orally) (Dröge 1993), well-known antioxidants, are apparently directed toward free radicals. Vitamin B$_6$ (25–50 mg/day orally for nonclinical deficiency; 50–200 mg/day orally for clinical deficiency, but observe for toxicity, manifesting as a neuropathic syndrome, at doses from 50 to 2,000 mg/day) is a cofactor in the metabolism of tryptophan into serotonin. Vitamin B$_6$ has been used to enhance the production of serotonin in preference to an alternative production of quinolinic acid (Shor-Posner et al. 1994). Vitamin B$_{12}$ deficiency has been reported in a proportion of HIV-infected patients and can lead to "excess" cognitive disability; vitamin supplementation has been shown to improve cognition (Beach et al. 1992). Dosages for treatment of a clinical deficiency begin with 100 mg/day intramuscularly for a week, then twice a week for 1–2 months (6 months if neurological symptoms are present), and then 1,000 mg intramuscularly

every month indefinitely (American Psychiatric Association 1994).

## Adjuvant Therapy: Psychopharmacological Enhancement of Function

Adjuvant therapy in the form of psychostimulant treatment (see also the section, "Depression in HIV Disease," later in this chapter) can help improve functioning in cognitive domains. Early data indicated that methylphenidate, used to treat affective disorders in HIV-infected patients, significantly improved verbal rote memory and rate of cognitive tracking and mental set shifting (Fernandez et al. 1988a, 1988c). On average, this amounted to elevating associated scores on neuropsychological instruments into the normal range. Subsequent investigations (Angrist et al. 1991; White et al. 1992) have confirmed this effect. Possible support for the efficacy of psychostimulants may come from their enhancement of dopaminergic functioning in neural populations that subtend attention/concentration, memory retrieval, and speed of cognitive processing (Fernandez and Levy 1990).

## Behavioral Methods in the Treatment of Cognitive Disorder

Adaptive functioning can be improved with behavioral methods of cognitive rehabilitation currently used in patients with brain trauma, stroke, and Alzheimer's disease (Boccellari 1990; Boccellari and Zeifert 1994; J.K. Levy and Fernandez 1993, 1995). Memory compensation techniques, such as keeping notebooks and using cueing signs and timer signals, and home environmental manipulation, such as labeling contents of cabinets and making daily activity checklists, can optimize day-to-day functioning (J.K. Levy and Fernandez 1993, 1995). These techniques provide a structure to cognitive functioning that allows many patients to retain some control over their daily activities and extend active participation in their medical regimens.

## Manifestations of Specific HIV-Related Neuropsychiatric Disorders and Their Treatment

The range of HIV-related neuropsychiatric disorders includes most of the major mental disorders listed in DSM-IV-TR (American Psychiatric Association 2000), including major depressive disorder, manic episode, psychotic disorder, delusional disorder, paranoid personality disorder, and anxiety disorder (Atkinson et al. 1988; Perry 1990; Perry and Marotta 1987). The most common psychiatric effects in HIV disease, in DSM-IV-TR terminology, are those "due to general medical conditions," such as delirium and psychosis (Fernandez and Levy 1993; Fernandez et al. 1989b; Harris et al. 1991; Jones et al. 1987; Maccario and Scharre 1987; Wolcott et al. 1985); dementia; affective disorder, including depression (Fernandez et al. 1995b; Hintz et al. 1990; Markowitz et al. 1994) and mania (Kieburtz et al. 1991b; McGowan et al. 1991); and stress/distress syndromes such as anxiety disorders (Fernandez 1989). Personality disorder and delusional disorder may also be seen, depending on specific focal effects of the infection.

## Delirium and Psychosis in HIV Disease

Of all the mental disorders due to a medical condition, delirium is the most prevalent and most frequently undiagnosed; as many as 30% of hospitalized medical-surgical patients have an undetected delirium (Guze and Daengsurisri 1967; Knights and Folstein 1977). The prompt detection of delirium is crucial because of potential reversibility and, thus, diminished morbidity and mortality.

Although delirium reflects diffuse cerebral cellular metabolic dysfunction (Lipowski 1987), there is often a prodromal phase in which patients complain of difficulty in thinking, restlessness, irritability, or insomnia interrupted with short periods of sleep containing vivid nightmares. The clinician must be alert to these symptoms and search for the causes of the delirious process. A brief mental status examination during the prodromal phase should focus on arousal, attention, short-term memory, and orientation. Diurnal variations (i.e., symptoms that are worse at night than during the day) are common. Along with cognitive deficits, abnormal involuntary movements such as tremor, picking at clothing, multifocal myoclonus, and asterixis are seen in delirium.

Timely pharmacological intervention may help to suppress the delirium symptoms; however, in our study, complete reversal of delirium occurred in only 37% of patients with AIDS (Fernandez et al. 1989b). The use of high-potency neuroleptics to control delirium has found increasing acceptance (Adams 1988; Adams et al. 1986; Ayd 1978; Fernandez and Levy 1991; Fernandez et al. 1989a, 1989b; Tesar et al. 1985). Oral or intramuscular haloperidol has been an effective treatment of delirium without any serious adverse effects.

Breitbart and colleagues (1996a) performed a double-blind prospective trial comparing haloperidol, chlorpromazine, and lorazepam in the treatment of patients with AIDS and delirium. A mean dose as low as 2.8 mg of haloperidol or 50 mg of chlorpromazine was shown to effect improvement in delirious symptoms within the first 24 hours of treatment, with minimal extrapyramidal side effects. Lorazepam alone was not shown to be effective in this study; however, in combination with an intravenous neuroleptic, it has been shown to be of benefit (see next paragraph).

The safety and efficacy of intravenous haloperidol treatment for delirium, either alone or in combination with lorazepam or additionally with hydromorphone for agitated patients with delirium, have been observed (Adams et al. 1986; Fernandez et al. 1989a; Tesar et al. 1985). Investigators have even reported that a continuous intravenous infusion of haloperidol can be used to achieve full control in refractory cases of delirium associated with agitation (Fernandez et al. 1988b). Although the administration of intravenous haloperidol is still considered investigational and not approved by the U.S. Food and Drug Administration (FDA), the relative rarity of treatment-related adverse effects (Huyse and Van Schijndel 1988; Konikoff et al. 1984) must be weighed against the dangers of delirium. Neuroleptic malignant syndrome is perhaps the most ominous potential adverse effect (Breitbart et al. 1988); however, in our experience, this syndrome is rare in this population. The rarity of this complication may stem from the intravenous route of administration. The possible protective influence of lorazepam, when coadministered with haloperidol, against the extrapyramidal side effects of haloperidol must be delineated with further controlled trials. Intravenous haloperidol can be approved for compassionate use if the clinician obtains permission through an institutional review process.

The ideal dose of any therapeutic medication is the smallest dose that achieves the desired clinical effects. We have found that HIV-positive patients are often more sensitive to neuroleptics and may require lower doses than do other medically ill patients with delirium (Fernandez et al. 1989b). Doses of intravenous medications, however, may need to be increased to high levels, provided that careful observation is maintained, to achieve effective and immediate control of severe agitation, which is essential to the individual's continued well-being as well as that of other patients and staff. Adverse effects of haloperidol in HIV-infected patients are mainly extrapyramidal and are significantly more frequent if the patient has another coexisting mental disorder due to a general medical condition (Fernandez et al. 1989b). However, we found that this therapy did not aggravate concurrent seizure disorders or cause adverse cardiovascular effects in patients who are not hypovolemic, hypokalemic, or hypomagnesmic.

New onset of psychosis in HIV-infected patients has also been reported (Edelstein and Knight 1987; Harris et al. 1991; Jones et al. 1987; Maccario and Scharre 1987). In one patient, schizophreniform conditions occurred before HIV seropositivity was identified (Maccario and Scharre 1987). In another study, dopamine supplementation in a patient with a parkinsonian syndrome ascribed to the effects of HIV induced psychosis that was reversible at the cost of relapse of the movement disorder (Edelstein and Knight 1987). Treatment with neuroleptics with the above-mentioned cautions has been beneficial.

In patients with delirium or psychosis who cannot tolerate other neuroleptics because of extrapyramidal side effects, molindone may be tried for control of delirious or psychotic symptoms. We have noted that significant treatment-emergent side effects typically experienced with neuroleptic treatment were absent when using molindone (Fernandez and Levy 1993). Richelson (1984) reported that this agent has little affinity for the $D_1$ or $D_2$ receptors centrally and is surpassed only by clozapine in this regard. It also has minimal affinity for other relevant central receptors such as the $H_1$, muscarinic, and $\alpha_1$-adrenergic receptors (Richelson 1984). In our experience, molindone is particularly useful in the management of delirious or psychotic symptoms associated with HIV disease. In patients who are able to comply with an oral regimen, molindone is tolerated better than other neuroleptics and is equally effective in control of neuropsychiatric symptomatology. Thus, molindone is an alternative agent that the clinician should consider when reinstituting pharmacotherapy with a neuroleptic for patients with a history of extrapyramidal reactions and neuroleptic malignant syndrome (Fernandez and Levy 1993).

Newer agents are entering the armamentarium to treat delirium as well as psychotic disorders. Risperidone (Keltner 1995) and remoxipride (Eriksson 1994) are being used with success to target these symptoms specifically. Olanzapine may also be used, but its affinity for the cytochrome P450 3A4 isoenzyme system may be problematic for patients on specific protease inhibitors. Quetiapine, which can be less sedating, may also be tried, but there is little experience to date with this agent.

## Depression in HIV Disease

Disturbances of mood, primarily depressive (Atkinson et al. 1988; Fernandez et al. 1989a, 1995b; Grant 1990; Hintz et al. 1990; Levine et al. 1990; Maj et al. 1991; Rabkin and Harrison 1990; Rabkin et al. 1991) but also manic and hypomanic episodes (Holmes and Fricchone

1989; Kieburtz et al. 1991b; McGowan et al. 1991), are found in HIV disease. The diagnosis of HIV-related mood disturbances is complex and requires that the clinician consider the interaction of organic and nonorganic factors. This consideration may produce the most timely and effective intervention. From the outset of this discussion, we emphasize that depression in HIV has heterogeneous etiologies; depression should not be considered a *normal* phenomenon of HIV infection.

The prevalence of mood disorders in HIV-infected patients, especially during the asymptomatic stage, has been an issue of investigation since the first patients presented with these affective symptoms. Atkinson and colleagues (1988) found a high lifetime prevalence of depression in HIV-infected homosexual men (30.3%), but the patients often had a mood disorder diagnosis before the development of HIV infection. Perkins and colleagues (1994), however, found that HIV-infected and non-HIV-infected homosexual men had similar high lifetime and current diagnoses of depression (29% versus 45%, and 8% versus 3%, respectively). These rates were higher than those in the general population but were not related to stage of infection because the HIV-positive and HIV-negative subjects had similar proportions. Additionally, current depression was not related to neuropsychological test performance. The major risk factor for current depression in both groups was a history of depression.

The most malignant aspect of depression, of course, is suicide. Suicidal ideation may present throughout the course of the spectrum of illnesses, even from the apprehension regarding antibody testing (Perry et al. 1990). The physician's role is to assess the process accurately, particularly in cases of severe depression (Frierson and Lippthann 1988; Hall and Stevens 1988; Marzuk et al. 1988; Perry et al. 1990). The natural instinct of self-preservation, even that found with the diagnosis of HIV infection, vies with the serious consideration of the concept of rational suicide (Brown et al. 1986; Siegel 1986). The relative risk of suicide is very high. Marzuk and colleagues (1988) found that the relative risk of suicide in men with AIDS living in New York City was 36.3 times that for men without an AIDS diagnosis and 66.2 times that of the general population. Research has indicated that terminally ill patients who complete suicide had evidence of stress-impaired decision making or had been clinically depressed before the suicide (Brown et al. 1986). Breitbart and colleagues (1996b), in a survey of 370 ambulatory HIV-infected patients, found that 55% considered physician-assisted suicide for themselves; however, this wish was strongly related to high scores on instruments assessing psychological distress, such as with depression, hopelessness, and general psychological distress. The investigators reported that interest in physician-assisted suicide was not related to severity of pain, functional impairment associated with pain, other physical symptomatology, or extent of HIV disease. Therefore, because HIV-infected persons may also have this stress/distress-related impairment of judgment, in addition to any judgment difficulties associated with cognitive impairment, the therapist must react assertively to any evidence of suicidal ideation. This reaction would include an accurate diagnostic assessment and a treatment plan that includes constant observation by someone who can provide interpersonal support until the condition can be stabilized. Although pharmacotherapy provides the most rapid intervention for symptom remission, specific guidelines for drug selection are conspicuously absent.

Anecdotal and clinical research observations (Fernandez et al. 1989b) have attested that the CNS of HIV-infected patients is susceptible to increased sensitivity to and intensity of medication side effects (Brown et al. 1986; Holmes and Fricchone 1989). The low-anticholinergic tricyclic antidepressants may be useful for treating depression in HIV-infected patients because these drugs have less risk than the highly anticholinergic tricyclics of exacerbating cognitive deficits or causing a delirious process and also are not as apt as the highly anticholinergic tricyclics to excessively dry the mucous membranes (an important consideration in this population because of their susceptibility to candidiasis). The choice of a particular tricyclic antidepressant should be guided by its specific action and side effects (Richelson 1988) in relation to the patient's depressive symptoms and concomitant medical condition (Fernandez and Levy 1991). The therapeutic dose of a tricyclic antidepressant may be much lower (10–75 mg) for an HIV-infected patient with neuropsychiatric impairment than for a noninfected person.

Other antidepressants such as fluoxetine (Judd et al. 1995; Levine et al. 1990) and bupropion (Golden et al. 1988a, 1988b), monoamine oxidase inhibitors (Fernandez and Levy 1991), trazodone (Roccatagliata et al. 1977), clomipramine (Feravelli et al. 1983; Pollock et al. 1985), maprotiline (Drago et al. 1984), paroxetine (Elliott et al. 1998), sertraline (Ferrando et al. 1997) and psychostimulants such as methylphenidate and dextroamphetamine (Fernandez et al. 1988a, 1988c, 1995b; Holmes et al. 1989; Walling and Pfefferbaum 1991; White et al. 1992) also may be useful in the management of depression in HIV-infected patients. The psychostimulants seem to be especially effective in HIV-infected patients who have cognitive impairment or depression

and dementia (Fernandez and Levy 1991; Fernandez et al. 1988a, 1988c; Holmes et al. 1989). In HIV-infected patients without cognitive impairment, treatment with methylphenidate was associated with a remission of depressive symptoms that was statistically indistinguishable from that achieved with the tricyclic desipramine (Fernandez et al. 1995b). In this study, scores on depression inventories were not significantly different between patients taking the two medications, and the time frame to reduction of symptoms was overlapping. The usual dosage for methylphenidate is 5–20 mg taken on awakening in the morning, at midmorning, and again in early afternoon to avoid disturbing nighttime sleep (Fernandez et al. 1989a).

Two recent additions to the antidepressant armamentarium are nefazodone (Feighner et al. 1989; Fernandez et al. 1995a; Fontaine et al. 1994) and venlafaxine (Fernandez et al. 1995a; Hollister 1994). Nefazodone is a serotonin receptor antagonist and serotonin reuptake inhibitor that works at the $5\text{-}HT_2$ site and is similar to trazodone in structure. It also is a minor noradrenergic reuptake inhibitor. Along with nefazodone's effectiveness in significant depressive illness, it appears not to potentiate the depressant effects of alcohol (Frewer and Lader 1993). Venlafaxine is a newer reuptake inhibitor that works against both serotonin and norepinephrine (Hollister 1994). In addition to its effectiveness as an antidepressive agent, we have noticed a qualitative energizing or stimulant-like effect. Indeed, this agent is receiving attention as an alternative to psychostimulants in adult attention-deficit disorder. Although there are no known clinical data available on the use of citalopram in HIV-related depression, anecdotal reports suggest it is equally effective and well tolerated. Likewise, mirtazapine is particularly useful in patients with HIV-1 infection and severe dyssomnia associated with weight loss.

In general, all nontricyclic antidepressant agents are effective and lack significant anticholinergic, histaminergic, adrenergic, and cardiac side effects. However, most do inhibit the biochemical activity of drugs that metabolize the isoenzyme cytochrome P450 2D6 or 3A4. Thus, antidepressant choices should be made after careful review of their pharmacology. It is worth noting that citalopram, nefazodone, venlafaxine, and mirtazapine are the weakest 2D6 isoenzyme inhibitors (Greenblatt et al. 1998). Citalopram, venlafaxine, and mirtazapine are the weakest 3A isoenzyme inhibitors (Greenblatt et al. 1998). Clinicians may use these agents with low affinity for the 3A isoenzyme system in HIV-related depression while carefully monitoring the coadministration of both prescribed and over-the-counter medications.

Depressed HIV-infected patients with psychotic

symptoms or an organic mood disturbance, or for whom pharmacological treatment has failed, may benefit from electroconvulsive therapy. This modality may be tried after very careful review of its use in patients with complex medical illness (Weiner 1983); however, ECT may increase confusion in some encephalopathic HIV-infected patients (Schaerf et al. 1989).

## Mania in HIV Disease

Acute mania has been reported in patients with HIV disease and may be the result of premorbid bipolar disorder; brain lesions from HIV, opportunistic infections, or AIDS-related neoplasms; or medications (Kieburtz et al. 1991b; Maxwell et al. 1988; McGowan et al. 1991; O'Dowd and McKegney 1988; Wright et al. 1989). Mania is not as common as depression in this population, but it presents as a sign more suspicious of organic involvement. It may also be the behavioral manifestation of a right frontal lobe tumor or focus of infection. Zidovudine has been reported to induce mania in susceptible individuals (Hagler and Frame 1986; Kieburtz et al. 1991b; Maxwell et al. 1988; O'Dowd and McKegney 1988).

Treatment of manic disorder in HIV-infected patients is similar to that in non-HIV-infected patients: cautious rapid tranquilization by neuroleptics (being on guard for the potential for seizure induction) followed by lithium treatment. Lithium has been found useful in the treatment of secondary mania due to zidovudine (O'Dowd and McKegney 1988). Close monitoring of levels as well as blood chemistry is essential for avoidance of toxicity in debilitated patients or those with the wasting syndrome. It is especially critical when infectious complications occur, such as with cryptosporidial infection or other causes of severe diarrhea, or with other severe fluid losses. Even when doses are used to maintain therapeutic serum concentrations of 0.5–1.0 mEq/L, patients with advanced disease cannot tolerate treatment with lithium. The anticonvulsant valproate has also been approved as a treatment for mania (McElroy et al. 1992). It may be tried cautiously in patients whose renal or electrolyte status makes lithium problematic. The efficacy of valproate provides support to the theory that, in some cases, manic symptomatology may be the reflection of complex partial seizures or temporal-lobe dysrhythmias (Gillig et al. 1988). Halman and colleagues (1993) found that valproate worked better against manic symptoms when an MRI showed structural abnormalities in the brain, which corroborates the hypothesis that structural abnormalities may be related to the bases of these dysrhythmias. Electrodiagnostic evaluation of de novo presentations of mania in HIV-infected patients may also be helpful in clarifying this etiology. One should note that there is a single report of valproic acid decreasing intracellular concentration of glutathione and stimulating HIV (Melton et al. 1997). We have retrospectively evaluated our valproate treated patients' medical records and have not found any increases in viral load to suggest that this is a clinically relevant concern. However, psychiatrists must be prepared to deal with the fear associated with this report in both their patients and their colleagues. At this time, there are no clinical reports on the efficacy of newer antiepileptic agents such as gabapentin, lamotrigine, or topiramate in HIV-related mania.

## Anxiety in HIV Disease

The stresses associated with antibody testing, diagnosis, and treatment of HIV infection obviously elicit symptoms of anxiety (Fernandez 1989; Forstein 1984; Holland and Tross 1985; Nichols 1983, 1985; Perry et al. 1992; Sonnex et al. 1987), especially for those individuals predisposed to anxiety disorders. An initial intervention of supportive care may be offered through reassurance from friends, family, and medical support staff (Perry et al. 1992). In addition to this support, the use of anxiolytic agents may help the patient to function better in all aspects of daily living, including participation in the medical treatment he or she is receiving.

The systemic effects of HIV-spectrum illnesses may trigger an anxiety disorder. For example, anxiety may arise in conjunction with prophylactic treatment by sulfamethoxazole and trimethoprim for *Pneumocystis carinii* pneumonia. Pulmonary insufficiency during pneumonia, leading to hypoxemia, may also trigger highly anxious states. CNS infections and neoplastic lesions may elicit anxiety states. Again, comprehensive neurodiagnostic investigation helps in the differential diagnosis.

Anxiolytic medication is selected on the basis of the nature and severity of the situation. Neuroleptics are often effective for the treatment of debilitating anxiety, which may approach irrational, overwhelming panic. However, the appearance of extrapyramidal side effects should be monitored closely, especially with patients in the advanced stages of HIV disease (Breitbart et al. 1988; Fernandez et al. 1989b). The automatic use of benzodiazepines as anxiolytics is risky in cases of severe anxiety or restlessness because these compounds may further compromise the patient's coping capacity and may have a disinhibiting effect.

On the other hand, the anxiety and insomnia (ranging from mild to severe) that may result from treatment with zidovudine or steroids, or be secondary to the effects of HIV on the CNS, may be helped with brief periods of pharmacotherapy with short- to intermediate-acting benzodiazepines such as lorazepam, alprazolam, and oxazepam (Fernandez 1988). However, chronic use may be warranted in some patients. If so, we advocate use of alprazolam and/or clonazepam. If tolerance develops in these patients, 50–200 mg of trazodone at bedtime may be combined with or substituted for the benzodiazepine. Although the β-blocker propranolol is often useful for healthy individuals who are anxious or phobic, its propensity to result in hypotensive episodes, particularly in patients who may have undiagnosed HIV-related dysautonomia (Lin-Greenberger and Taneja-Uppal 1987), makes it undesirable for general use in persons with HIV disease. Antihistamines, such as hydroxyzine, have low efficacy for anxiolysis unless the anxiety is accompanied by specific respiratory problems.

Early studies of the effectiveness of the nonbenzodiazepine anxiolytic buspirone (Kastenholz and Crismon 1984) in HIV-infected patients indicate its value when the immediate attenuation of acute or situational anxiety or phobias is not essential. Buspirone's anxiolytic effects are not accompanied by excessive sedation or potential for dependence; however, several weeks of regular administration are often required to achieve optimal results. Batki (1990) found that buspirone can be effective in treating anxiety disorders in substance-abusing patients who are at risk for misuse or excess sedation from benzodiazepines. Buspirone should be prescribed with caution for HIV-infected patients with CNS impairment, and its use should be monitored closely, because buspirone-related dyskinesias (Strauss 1988) and myoclonus may be more easily elicited in neurologically compromised HIV-infected patients than in noninfected, neurologically intact patients with anxiety. Cases of possible buspirone-related mania have been reported (McDaniel et al. 1990; Price and Bielefeld 1989), and use of this agent in an HIV-positive patient was reported to induce confusion and psychosis with delusions (Nazzareno and Yeragani 1988).

## Conclusions

The neuropsychiatric complications of HIV infection and AIDS are a perplexing assortment of neurological, neurocognitive, and affective/behavioral effects that may arise at any time during the course of the illness. As such, all neuropsychiatrists should maintain a high index of suspicion of even the most subtle of behavioral symptoms in previously asymptomatic persons, because a number of means of investigation (e.g., electrophysiological, neuro-

psychological) have disclosed that neurological involvement may occur early in the course of the disease. As the AIDS epidemic continues, these symptoms may arise in individuals other than those in the initial high-risk categories, and a careful history of possible exposure must be included in any workup of unusual cognitive, neurological, or neuropsychiatric symptoms fitting the pattern described in this chapter. If the etiology is found to be HIV related, prompt aggressive treatment of the conditions, perhaps using innovative measures, is warranted, to maintain as optimal a quality of life as can be promoted, for as long as possible.

## References

Adams F: Emergency intravenous sedation of the delirious medically ill patient. J Clin Psychiatry 49 (suppl):22–26, 1988

Adams F, Fernandez F, Andersson BS: Emergency pharmacotherapy and delirium in the critically ill cancer patient: intravenous combination drug approach. Psychosomatics 27 (suppl 1):33–37, 1986

Akler ME, Johnson DW, Burman WJ, et al: Anterior uveitis and hypotony after intravenous cidofovir for the treatment of cytomegalovirus retinitis. Ophthalmology 105:651–657, 1998

American Psychiatric Association: AIDS Training Curriculum: HIV-Related Neuropsychiatric Complications and Treatments. Washington, DC, American Psychiatric Association, 1994

American Psychiatric Association: Diagnostic and Statistical Manual of Mental Disorders, 4th Edition, Text Revision. Washington, DC, American Psychiatric Association, 2000

Angrist B, D'Hollosy M, Sanfilipo M, et al: Central nervous system stimulants as symptomatic treatments for AIDS-related neuropsychiatric impairment. J Clin Psychopharmacol 12:268–272, 1991

Antoni BA, Sabbatini P, Rabson AB, et al: Inhibition of apoptosis in human immunodeficiency virus–infected cells enhances virus production and facilitates persistent infection. J Virol 69:2384–2392, 1995

Arendt G, Hefter H, Buesher L, et al: Improvement of motor performance of HIV-positive patients under AZT therapy. Neurology 42:891–895, 1991

Atkinson JH, Grant I, Kennedy CJ, et al: Prevalence of psychiatric disorders among men infected with human immunodeficiency virus: a controlled study. Arch Gen Psychiatry 45:859–864, 1988

Ayd FF Jr: Haloperidol: twenty years' clinical experience. J Clin Psychiatry 39:807–814, 1978

Barker PB, Lee RR, McArthur JC: AIDS dementia complex: evaluation with proton MR spectroscopic imaging. Radiology 195:58–64, 1995

Barre-Sinoussi F, Chermann JC, Rey F, et al: Isolation of a T-lymphotropic retrovirus from a patient at risk for acquired immune deficiency syndrome (AIDS). Science 220:868–871, 1983

Batki SA: Buspirone in drug users with AIDS or AIDS related complex. J Clin Psychopharmacol 10 (suppl):1115–1155, 1990

Beach RS, Morgan R, Wilkie F, et al: Plasma vitamin $B_{12}$ level as a potential cofactor in studies of human immunodeficiency virus type 1–related cognitive changes. Arch Neurol 49:501–506, 1992

Beckett A, Summergrad P, Manschreck T, et al: Symptomatic HIV infection of the CNS in a patient without clinical evidence of immune deficiency. Am J Psychiatry 144:1342–1344, 1987

Bedri J, Weinstein W, DeGregoria P, et al: Progressive multifocal leukoencephalopathy in acquired immunodeficiency syndrome. N Engl J Med 309:492–493, 1983

Beilke MA: Vascular endothelium in immunology and infectious disease. Rev Infect Dis 11:273–283, 1989

Bellamy CO, Malcomson RD, Harrison DJ, et al: Cell death in health and disease: the biology and regulation of apoptosis. Semin Cancer Biol 6:3–16, 1995

Belman AL, Lantos G, Horoupian D, et al: AIDS: calcification of the basal ganglia in infants and children. Neurology 36:1192–1199, 1986

Berger JR, Concha M: Progressive multifocal leukoencephalopathy: the evolution of a disease once considered rare. J Neurovirol 1(1):5–18, 1995

Berger JR, Kaszovitz B, Post MJ, et al: Progressive multifocal leukoencephalopathy associated with human immunodeficiency virus infection: a review of the literature with a report of sixteen cases. Ann Intern Med 107:78–87, 1987

Bernad PG: The neurological and electroencephalographic changes in AIDS. Clin Electroencephalogr 22:65–70, 1991

Bishburg E, Eng RHK, Slim J, et al: Brain lesions in patients with acquired immunodeficiency syndrome. Arch Intern Med 149:941–943, 1989

Boccellari A: Living with and caring for the individual with AIDS dementia complex, in Caregiver Education Series on AIDS Dementia Complex Training Manual. San Francisco, CA, Family Survival Project, 1990

Boccellari A, Zeifert P: Management of neurobehavioral impairment in HIV-1 infection. Psychiatr Clin North Am 17: 183–203, 1994

Bredesen DE, Levy RM, Rosenblum ML: The neurology of human immunodeficiency virus infection. QJM 68:665–677, 1988

Breitbart W, Marotta RF, Call P: AIDS and neuroleptic malignant syndrome. Lancet 2:1488–1489, 1988

Breitbart W, Marotta RF, Platt MM, et al: A double-blind trial of haloperidol, chlorpromazine, and lorazepam in the treatment of delirium in hospitalized AIDS patients. Am J Psychiatry 153:231–237, 1996a

Breitbart W, Rosenfeld BD, Passik SD: Interest in physician-assisted suicide among ambulatory HIV-infected patients. Am J Psychiatry 153:238–242, 1996b

Brew BJ, Sidtis JJ, Petito CK, et al: The neurologic complications of AIDS and human immunodeficiency virus infection, in Advances in Contemporary Neurology. Edited by Plum F. Philadelphia, PA, FA Davis, 1988, pp 1–49

Brew BJ, Bhalla RB, Paul M, et al: Cerebrospinal fluid β2 microglobulin in patients infected with AIDS dementia complex: an expanded series including response to zidovudine treatment. AIDS 6:461–465, 1992

Bridge TP, Heseltine PN, Parker ES, et al: Results of extended peptide T administration in AIDS and ARC patients. Psychopharmacol Bull 27:237–245, 1991

Brightbill TC, Ihmeidan IH, Post MJD, et al: Neurosyphilis in HIV-positive and HIV-negative patients: neuroimaging findings. American Journal of Neuroradiology 16:703–711, 1995

Brodine SK, Mascola JR, McCutchan FE: Genotypic variation and molecular epidemiology of HIV. Infections in Medicine 14:739–748, 1997

Brown JH, Henteleff P, Barakat S, et al: Is it normal for terminally ill patients to desire death? Am J Psychiatry 143:208–211, 1986

Brunetti A, Berg G, DiChiro G, et al: Reversal of brain metabolic abnormalities following treatment of AIDS dementia complex with 3′-azido-2′,3′-dideoxythymidine (AZT, zidovudine): a PET-FDG study. J Nucl Med 30:581–590, 1989

Budka H: Human immunodeficiency virus (HIV)-induced disease of the central nervous system: pathology and implications for pathogenesis. Acta Neuropathol 77:225–236, 1989

Buffet R, Agut H, Chieze F, et al: Virological markers in the cerebrospinal fluid from HIV-1 infected individuals. AIDS 5:1419–1424, 1991

Butters N, Grant I, Haxby J, et al: Assessment of AIDS-related cognitive changes: recommendations of the NIMH workshop on neuropsychological assessment approaches. J Clin Exp Neuropsychol 12:963–978, 1990

Buzy J, Brenneman DE, Pert CB, et al: Potent gp120-like neurotoxic activity in the cerebrospinal fluid of HIV-infected individuals is blocked by peptide T. Brain Res 598:10–18, 1992

Carrieri PB, Indaco A, Maiorino A, et al: Cerebrospinal fluid beta-2-microglobulin in multiple sclerosis and AIDS dementia complex. Neurol Res 14:282–283, 1992

Cecil KM, Lenkinski RE. Proton MR spectroscopy in inflammatory and infectious brain disorders. Neuroimaging Clin North Am 8(4):863–880, 1998

Centers for Disease Control: Revision of the CDC surveillance case definition for acquired immunodeficiency syndrome. MMWR Morb Mortal Wkly Rep 36 (suppl 1S):3S–15S, 1987

Centers for Disease Control and Prevention: HIV/AIDS Surveillance Report. Atlanta, GA, Centers for Disease Control and Prevention, April 25, 1995

Chiodi F, Keys B, Albert J, et al: Human immunodeficiency virus type 1 is present in the cerebrospinal fluid of a majority of infected individuals. J Clin Microbiol 30:1768–1771, 1992

Chong WK, Sweeney B, Wilkinson ID, et al: Proton spectroscopy of the brain in HIV infection: correlation with clinical, immunologic, and MR imaging findings. Neuroradiology 188:119–124, 1993

Ciardi A, Sindair E, Scaravilli F, et al: The involvement of the cerebral cortex in human immunodeficiency virus encephalopathy: a morphological and immunohistochemical study. Acta Neuropathol 81:51–59, 1990

Clavel F, Guyader M, Guetard D, et al: Molecular cloning and polymorphism of the human immune deficiency virus type 2. Nature 324(6098):691–695, 1986

Collier AC, Marra C, Coombs RW, et al: Central nervous system manifestations in human immunodeficiency virus infection without AIDS. J Acquir Immune Defic Syndr 5:229–241, 1992

Connolly KJ, Allan JD, Fitch H, et al: Phase I study of 2'-3'-dideoxyinosine administered orally twice daily to patients with AIDS or AIDS-related complex and hematologic intolerance to zidovudine. Am J Med 91:471–478, 1991

Corbeil J, Richman DD: Productive infection and subsequent interaction of CD4-gp120 at the cellular membrane is required for HIV-induced apoptosis of CD4+ T cells. J Gen Virol 76 (pt 3): 681–690, 1995

Cornblath DR, McArthur JC, Kennedy PG, et al: Inflammatory demyelinating peripheral neuropathies associated with human T-cell lymphotropic virus type III infection. Ann Neurol 21:32–40, 1987

Cotton P: AIDS dementia may be linked to metabolite of tryptophan. JAMA 264:305–306, 1990

Cummings JL, Benson DF: Dementia: A Clinical Approach. Boston, MA, Butterworths, 1983

Dalakas MC, Pezeshkpour GH: Neuromuscular diseases associated with human immunodeficiency virus infection. Ann Neurol 23 (suppl):S38–S48, 1988

Darko DF, Miller JC, Gallen C, et al: Sleep encephalogram delta-frequency amplitude, night plasma levels of tumor necrosis factor α and human immunodeficiency virus infection. Proc Natl Acad Sci U S A 92:12080–12084, 1995

Davis LE, Hjelle BL, Miller VE, et al: Early viral brain invasion in iatrogenic human immunodeficiency virus infection. Neurology 42(9):1736–1739, 1992

DeBiasi R, Tyler KL: Polymerase chain reaction in the diagnosis and management of central nervous system infections. Arch Neurol 56:1215–1219, 1999

Deicken RF, Hubesch B, Jensen PC, et al: Alterations in brain phosphate metabolite concentrations in patients with human immunodeficiency virus infection. Arch Neurol 48:203–209, 1991

Dezube BJ, Pardee AB, Chapman B, et al: Pentoxifylline decreases tumor necrosis factor expression and serum triglycerides in people with AIDS. J Acquir Immune Defic Syndr 6:787–794, 1993

Diaz RS, de Oliveira CF, Mayer A, et al: Evidence of enhanced v3 region diversity and recombination in a dually infected transfusion recipient (abstract), in Program and abstracts of the 4th Conference on Retroviruses and Opportunistic Infections, Washington, DC, January 22–26, 1997

Dickover RE, Donovan RM, Goldstein E, et al: Decreases in unintegrated HIV DNA are associated with antiretroviral therapy in AIDS patients. J Acquir Immune Defic Syndr 5:31–36, 1991

Dickson DW, Mattiace LA, Kure K, et al: Biology of disease: microglia in human disease, with an emphasis on acquired immune deficiency syndrome. Lab Invest 64:135–156, 1991

Dooneief G, Bello J, Todak G, et al: A prospective controlled study of magnetic resonance imaging of the brain in gay men and parenteral drug users with human immunodeficiency virus infection. Arch Neurol 49:38–43, 1992

Drago F, Motta A, Grossi E: Intravenous maprotiline in severe and resistant primary depression: a double blind comparison with clomipramine. Journal of International Medical Research 11:78–84, 1984

Dreyer EB, Kaiser PK, Offermann JT, et al: HIV-1 coat protein neurotoxicity prevented by calcium channel antagonists. Science 248:364–367, 1990

Dröge W: Cysteine and glutathione deficiency in AIDS patients: a rationale for the treatment with N-acetyl-cysteine. Pharmacology 46:61–65, 1993

Dunlop O, Bjørklund RA, Abedelnoor M, et al: Five different tests of reaction time evaluated in HIV seropositive men. Acta Neurol Scand 8:260–266, 1992

Edelstein H, Knight RT: Severe parkinsonism in two AIDS patients taking a prochlorperazine (letter). Lancet 2:314–342, 1987

Eisdorfer C, Cohen D, Paveza GJ, et al: An empirical evaluation of the Global Deterioration Scale for staging Alzheimer's disease. Am J Psychiatry 149:190–194, 1991

Elliott AJ, Uldall KK, Bergam K, et al: Randomized placebo-controlled trial of paroxetine versus imipramine on depressed HIV-positive outpatients. Am J Psychiatry 155:367–372, 1998

Elovaara I, Iivanianen M, Portiainer E, et al: CSF and serum β2-microglobulin in HIV infection related to neurological dysfunction. Acta Neurol Scand 79:81–87, 1989

Elovaara I, Saar P, Valle S-L, et al: EEG in early HIV-1 infection is characterized by anterior dysrhythmicity of low maximal amplitude. Clin Electroencephalogr 22:131–140, 1991

Engstrom JW, Lowenstein DH, Bredesen DE: Cerebral infarctions and transient neurologic deficits associated with acquired immunodeficiency syndrome. Am J Med 86:528–532, 1989

Eriksson L: Remoxipride in the treatment of psychoses. Prog Neuropsychopharmacol Biol Psychiatry 18:619–623, 1994

Everall I, Luthert PJ, Lantos PL: Neuronal loss in the frontal cortex in HIV infection. Lancet 337:1119–1121, 1991

Everall I, Luthert PJ, Lantos PL: A review of neuronal damage in human immunodeficiency virus infection: its assessment, possible mechanism and relationship to dementia. J Neuropathol Exp Neurol 52:561–566, 1993

Feighner JP, Pambakian R, Fowler RC, et al: A comparison of nefazodone, imipramine, and placebo in patients with moderate to severe depression. Psychopharmacol Bull 25:219–221, 1989

Feravelli C, Broadhurst AD, Ambonetti A, et al: Double blind trial with oral versus intravenous clomipramine in primary depression. Biol Psychiatry 18:695–706, 1983

Fernandez F: Psychiatric complications in HIV-related illnesses, in American Psychiatric Association AIDS Primer. Washington, DC, American Psychiatric Press, 1988

Fernandez F: Anxiety and the neuropsychiatry of AIDS. J Clin Psychiatry 50 (suppl):9–14, 1989

Fernandez F, Levy JK: Adjuvant treatment of HIV dementia with psychostimulants, in Behavioral Aspects of AIDS and Other Sexually Transmitted Diseases. Edited by Ostrow D. New York, Plenum, 1990, pp 279–286

Fernandez F, Levy JK: Psychopharmacotherapy of psychiatric syndromes in asymptomatic and symptomatic HIV infection. Psychiatr Med 9:377–393, 1991

Fernandez F, Levy JK: The use of molindone in the treatment of psychotic patients infected with the human immunodeficiency virus: case reports. Gen Hosp Psychiatry 15:31–35, 1993

Fernandez F, Adams F, Levy JK, et al: Cognitive impairment due to AIDS-related complex and its response to psychostimulants. Psychosomatics 29:38–46, 1988a

Fernandez F, Holmes VF, Adams F, et al: Treatment of severe, refractory agitation with a haloperidol drip. J Clin Psychiatry 49:239–241, 1988b

Fernandez F, Levy JK, Galizzi H: Response of HIV-related depression to psychostimulants: case reports. Hosp Community Psychiatry 39:628–631, 1988c

Fernandez F, Holmes VF, Levy JK, et al: Consultation-liaison psychiatry and HIV-related disorders. Hosp Community Psychiatry 40:146–153, 1989a

Fernandez F, Levy JK, Mansell PWA: Management of delirium in terminally ill AIDS patients. Int J Psychiatry Med 19:165–172, 1989b

Fernandez F, Levy JK, Lachar BL, et al: The management of depression and anxiety in the elderly. J Clin Psychiatry 56 (suppl 2):20–29, 1995a

Fernandez F, Levy JK, Sampley HR, et al: Effects of methylphenidate in HIV-related depression: a comparative trial with desipramine. Int J Psychiatry Med 25:53–67, 1995b

Ferrando SJ, Goldman JD, Charness WE: Selective serotonin reuptake inhibitor treatment of depression in symptomatic HIV infection and AIDS: improvements in affective and somatic symptoms. Gen Hosp Psychiatry 19:89–97, 1997

Filley CM, Franklin GM, Heaton RK, et al: White matter dementia: clinical disorders and implications. Neuropsychiatry, Neuropsychology, and Behavioral Neurology 1:239–254, 1988

Fischl MA, Richman DD, Grieco MH, et al: The efficacy of azidothymidine (AZT) in the treatment of patients with AIDS and AIDS-related complex: a double-blind, placebo-controlled study. N Engl J Med 317:185–191, 1987

Flowers CH, Mafee MF, Crowell R, et al: Encephalopathy in AIDS patients: evaluation with MR imaging. American Journal of Neuroradiology 11:1235–1245, 1990

Fong IW, Toma E: The natural history of progressive multifocal leukoencephalopathy in patients with AIDS. Clin Infect Dis 20:1305–1310, 1995

Fontaine R, Ontiveros A, Elie R, et al: A double-blind comparison of nefazodone, imipramine, and placebo in major depression. J Clin Psychiatry 55:234–241, 1994

Forstein M: The psychosocial impact of the acquired immunodeficiency syndrome. Semin Oncol 11:77–82, 1984

Frank Y, Lin W, Kahn E, et al: Multiple ischemic infarcts in a child with AIDS, varicella zoster infection, and cerebral vasculitis. Pediatr Neurol 5:64–67, 1989

Franzblau A, Letz R, Hershman D, et al: Quantitative neurologic and neurobehavioral testing of persons infected with human immunodeficiency virus type 1. Arch Neurol 48:263–268, 1991

Freund-Levi Y, Saaf J, Wahlund L-O, et al: Ultra low field brain MRI in HIV transfusion infected patients. Magn Reson Imaging 7:225–230, 1989

Frewer LJ, Lader M: The effects of nefazodone, imipramine, and placebo, alone and combined with alcohol, in normal subjects. Int Clin Psychopharmacol 8:13–20, 1993

Frierson RL, Lippthann SB: Suicide and AIDS. Psychosomatics 29:226–231, 1988

Gabuzda DA, Levy SR, Chiappa KH: Electroencephalography in AIDS and AIDS-related complex. Clin Electroencephalogr 19:1–6, 1988

Gallo RC, Sarin PS, Gelmann EP, et al: Isolation of human T-cell leukemia virus in acquired immune deficiency syndrome. Science 220:865–867, 1983

Gao F, Yue L, Robertson DL, et al: Genetic diversity of human immunodeficiency virus type 2: evidence for distinct sequence subtypes with differences in virus biology. J Virol 68:743–747, 1994

Gemignani A, Paudice P, Pittaluga A, et al: The HIV-1 coat protein gp120 and some of its fragments potently activate native cerebral NMDA receptors mediating neuropeptide release. Eur J Neurosci 12:2839–2846, 2000

Gibbs A, Andrewes DG, Szmukler G, et al: Early HIV-related neuropsychological impairment: relationship to stage of viral infection. J Clin Exp Neuropsychol 12:766–780, 1990

Gillig P, Sackellares JC, Greenberg HS: Right hemisphere partial complex seizures: mania, hallucinations, and speech disturbances during ictal events. Epilepsia 29:26–29, 1988

Giulian D, Vaca K, Noonan CA: Secretion of neurotoxins by mononuclear phagocytes infected with HIV-1. Science 250:1593–1595, 1990

Golden RN, De Vane CL, Laizure SC, et al: Bupropion in depression, II: the role of metabolites in clinical outcome. Arch Gen Psychiatry 45:145–149, 1988a

Golden RN, Rudorfer MV, Sherer MA, et al: Bupropion in depression, I: biochemical effects and clinical responses. Arch Gen Psychiatry 45:139–143, 1988b

Gonzales MF, David RL: Neuropathology of acquired immunodeficiency syndrome. Neuropathol Appl Neurobiol 14:345–363, 1988

Goodin DS, Aminoff MJ, Chernoff DN, et al: Long latency event-related potentials in patients infected with human immunodeficiency virus. Ann Neurol 27:414–419, 1990

Goodwin GM, Chiswick A, Egan V, et al: The Edinburgh cohort of HIV-positive drug users: auditory event-related potentials show progressive slowing in patients with Centers for Disease Control stage IV disease. AIDS 4:1243–1250, 1990

Gottlieb MS, Schroff R, Schanker RM, et al: Pneumocystis carinii pneumonia and mucosal candidiasis in previously healthy homosexual men: evidence of a new acquired cellular immunodeficiency. N Engl J Med 305:1425–1431, 1981

Grafe MR, Press GA, Berthoty DP, et al: Abnormalities of the brain in AIDS patients: correlation of postmortem MR findings with neuropathology. American Journal of Neuroradiology 11:905–913, 1990

Grant I: The neuropsychiatry of human immunodeficiency virus. Semin Neurol 10:267–275, 1990

Grant I, Atkinson JH, Hesselink JR, et al: Evidence for early central nervous system involvement in the immunodeficiency syndrome (AIDS) and other human immunodeficiency virus (HIV) infections: studied with neuropsychological testing and magnetic resonance imaging. Ann Intern Med 107:828–836, 1987

Gray F, Lescs MC: HIV-related demyelinating diseases. European Journal of Medicine 2:89–96, 1993

Gray F, Gherard R, Keohane C, et al: Pathology of the central nervous system in 40 cases of acquired immune deficiency syndrome (AIDS). Neuropathol Appl Neurobiol 14:365–380, 1988

Greenberg SJ: Human retroviruses and demyelinating diseases. Neurologic Clinics 13:75–97, 1995

Greenblatt DJ, VonMolke LL, Harmatz JS, et al: Drug interactions with newer antidepressants: role of human cytochromes P450. J Clin Psychiatry 59 (suppl 15):19–27, 1998

Greenlee JE, Rose JW: Controversies in neurological infectious diseases. Semin Neurol 20:375–386, 2000

Griffin DE, Wesselingh SL, McArthur JC: Elevated central nervous system prostaglandins in human immunodeficiency virus–associated dementia. Ann Neurol 35:592–597, 1994

Groopman JE: Antiretroviral therapy and immunomodulators in patients with AIDS. Am J Med 90 (suppl 4A):18S–21S, 1991a

Groopman JE: Treatment of AIDS with combinations of antiretroviral agents. Am J Med 90 (suppl 4A):27S–30S, 1991b

Guze SB, Daengsurisri S: Organic brain syndromes' prognostic significance in general medical patients. Arch Gen Psychiatry 17:365–366, 1967

Gyorkey F, Melnick JL, Gyorkey P: Human immunodeficiency virus in brain biopsies of patients with AIDS and progressive encephalopathy. J Infect Dis 155:870–876, 1987

Hagler DN, Frame PT: Azidothymidine neurotoxicity. Lancet 2:1392–1393, 1986

Hall JM, Stevens PE: AIDS: a guide to suicide assessment. Arch Psychiatr Nurs 1:115–120, 1988

Halman MH, Worth JL, Sanders KM, et al: Anticonvulsant use in the treatment of manic syndromes in patients with HIV-1 infection. J Neuropsychiatry Clin Neurosci 5:430–434, 1993

Harbison MA, Kim S, Gillis JM, et al: Effect of the calcium channel blocker verapamil on human immunodeficiency virus type 1 replication in lymphoid cells. J Infect Dis 164:43–60, 1991

Harris MJ, Jeste DV, Gleghorn A, et al: New-onset psychosis in HIV-infected patients. J Clin Psychiatry 52:369–376, 1991

Harrison NA, Skidmore SJ: Neopterin and beta-2 microglobulin levels in asymptomatic HIV infection: the predictive value of combining markers. J Med Virol 32:128–133, 1990

Hart RP, Wade JB, Klinger RL, et al: Slowed information processing as an early cognitive change associated with AIDS and ARC (abstract). J Clin Exp Neuropsychol 12:72, 1990

Heaton RK, Grant I, Butters N, et al: The HNRC 500—neuropsychology of HIV infection at different disease stages. Journal of the International Neuropsychological Society 1:231–251, 1995

Heyes MP, Brew BJ, Martin A, et al: Quinolinic acid in cerebrospinal fluid and serum in HIV-1 infection: relationship to clinical neurological status. Ann Neurol 29:202–209, 1991

Heyes MP, Brew BJ, Saito K, et al: Inter-relationships between quinolinic acid, neuroactive kynurenines, neopterin and β2-microglobulin in cerebrospinal fluid and HIV-1-infected patients. J Neuroimmunol 40:71–80, 1992

Heyes MP, Ellis RJ, Ryan L, et al: Elevated cerebrospinal fluid quinolinic acid levels are associated with region-specific cerebral volume loss in HIV infection. Brain 124 (pt 5):1033–1042, 2001

Hill JM, Farrar WL, Pert CB: Autoradiographic localization of T4 antigen, the HIV receptor, in human brain. Int J Neurosci 32:687–693, 1987

Hinkin CH, van Gorp WG, Mandelkern MA, et al: Cerebral metabolic change in patients with AIDS: report of a six-month follow-up using positron-emission tomography. J Neuropsychiatry Clin Neurosci 7:1880–1887, 1995

Hintz S, Kuck J, Peterkin JJ, et al: Depression in the context of human immunodeficiency virus infection: implications for treatment. J Clin Psychiatry 51:497–501, 1990

Ho DD, Pomerantz RJ, Kaplan JC: Pathogenesis of infection with human immunodeficiency virus. N Engl J Med 317:278–286, 1987

Holland JC, Tross S: The psychosocial and neuropsychiatric sequelae of the acquired immunodeficiency syndrome. Ann Intern Med 103:760–764, 1985

Hollander H: Neurologic and psychiatric manifestations of HIV disease. J Gen Intern Med 6 (Jan/Feb suppl):S24–S31, 1991

Hollister LE: New psychotherapeutic drugs. J Clin Psychopharmacol 14:50–63, 1994

Hollweg M, Riedel R-R, Goebel F-D, et al: Remarkable improvement of neuropsychiatric symptoms in HIV-infected patients after AZT therapy. Klinische Wochenschrift 69:409–412, 1991

Holmes VF, Fricchone GL: Hypomania in an AIDS patient receiving amitriptyline for neuropathic pain (clinical/scientific note). Neurology 39:305, 1989

Holmes VF, Fernandez F, Levy JK: Psychostimulant response in AIDS-related complex patients. J Clin Psychiatry 50:5–8, 1989

Huyse F, Van Schijndel RS: Haloperidol and cardiac arrest. Lancet 2:568–569, 1988

Itil TM, Ferracuti S, Freedman AM, et al: Computer-analyzed EEG (CEEG) and dynamic brain mapping in AIDS and HIV related syndrome: a pilot study. Clin Electroencephalogr 21:140–144, 1990

Jacobs D, Peavy G, Velin R, et al: Verbal memory in asymptomatic HIV-infection: evidence of subcortical dysfunction in a subgroup of patients (abstract). J Clin Exp Neuropsychol 14:101, 1992

Janssen RS, Saykin AJ, Kaplan JE, et al: Neurological complications of human immunodeficiency virus infection in patients with lymphadenopathy syndrome. Ann Neurol 23:49–55, 1988

Janssen RS, Cornblath DR, Epstein LG, and the Working Group of the American Academy of Neurology AIDS Task Force: Nomenclature and research case definitions for neurologic manifestations of human immunodeficiency virus-type 1 (HIV-1) infection. Neurology 41:778–785, 1991

Janssen RS, Nwanyanwu OC, Selik PM, et al: Epidemiology of human immunodeficiency virus encephalopathy in the United States. Neurology 42:1472–1476, 1992

Jarvik JG, Hesselink JR, Kennedy C, et al: Acquired immunodeficiency syndrome: magnetic resonance patterns of brain involvement with pathologic correlation. Arch Neurol 45:731–736, 1988

Jarvik JG, Lenkinski RE, Grossman RI, et al: Proton MR spectroscopy of HIV-infected patients: characterization of abnormalities with imaging and clinical correlation. Radiology 186:739–744, 1993

Jernigan TL, Archibald S, Hesselink JR, et al: Magnetic resonance imaging morphometric analysis of cerebral volume loss in human immunodeficiency virus: the HNRC group. Arch Neurol 50:250–255, 1993

Jones GH, Kelly CL, Davies JA: HIV and onset of schizophrenia (letter). Lancet 1:982, 1987

Judd FK, Mijch AM, Cockram A: Fluoxetine treatment of depressed patients with HIV-infection. Aust N Z J Psychiatry 29:433–436, 1995

Julander I, Alexius B, Britton S, et al: Treatment of HIV-1 infected patients with peptide T. Antiviral Chemistry and Chemotherapy 1:349–354, 1990

Kaemingk KL, Kaszniak AW: Neuropsychological aspects of human immunodeficiency virus infection. The Clinical Neuropsychologist 3:309–326, 1989

Kaiser PK, Offerman JT, Lipton SA: Neuronal injury due to HIV-1 envelope protein is blocked by anti-gp120 antibodies but not by anti-CD4 antibodies. Neurology 40:1757–1761, 1990

Karlsen NR, Reinvang I, Frøland SS: Serum level of neopterin, CD8+ cell count, and neuropsychological function in HIV-infected patients (abstract). J Clin Exp Neuropsychol 14:101, 1991

Karlsen NR, Reinvang I, Fruland SS: Slowed reaction time in asymptomatic HIV-positive patients. Acta Neurol Scand 86:242–246, 1992

Kastenholz KV, Crismon ML: Buspirone, a novel nonbenzodiazepine anxiolytic. Clin Pharmacol Ther 3:600–607, 1984

Kelly WM, Brant-Zawadzki M: Acquired immunodeficiency syndrome: neuroradiologic findings. Radiology 149:485–491, 1983

Keltner NL: Risperidone: the search for a better antipsychotic. Perspectives in Psychiatric Care 31:30–33, 1995

Kerr DA, Chang CF, Gordon J, et al: Inhibition of human neurotropic virus (JCV) DNA replication in glial cells by camptothecin. Virology 196(2):612–618, 1993

Ketzler S, Weis S, Haug H, et al: Loss of neurons in the frontal cortex in AIDS patients. Acta Neuropathol (Berl) 80:92–94, 1990

Kieburtz KD, Epstein LG, Gelbard HA, et al: Excitotoxicity and dopaminergic dysfunction in the acquired immunodeficiency syndrome dementia complex: therapeutic implications. Arch Neurol 48:1281–1284, 1991a

Kieburtz K, Zettelmaier AE, Ketonen L, et al: Manic syndrome in AIDS. Am J Psychiatry 148:1068–1070, 1991b

Klusman LE, Moulton JM, Hornbostel LK, et al: Neuropsychological abnormalities in asymptomatic HIV seropositive military personnel. J Neuropsychiatry Clin Neurosci 3:422–428, 1991

Knights EB, Folstein MF: Unsuspected emotional and cognitive disturbance in medical patients. Ann Intern Med 87:723–724, 1977

Konikoff F, Kuritzky A, Jerushalmi Y, et al: Neuroleptic malignant syndrome induced by a single injection of haloperidol. BMJ 289:1228–1229, 1984

Koralnik IJ, Beaumanoir A, Hausler R, et al: A controlled study of early neurologic abnormalities in men with asymptomatic human immunodeficiency virus infection. N Engl J Med 323:864–870, 1990

Kornhuber J, Bormann J, Hubers M, et al: Effects of 1-amino-adamantanes at the MK-801-binding site of the NMDA-receptor-gated ion channel: a human postmortem brain study. Eur J Pharmacol 206:297–300, 1991

Kovner R, Perecman E, Lazar W, et al: Relation of personality and attentional factors to cognitive deficits in human immunodeficiency virus–infected subjects. Arch Neurol 46:274–277, 1989

Kranczer S: U.S. longevity unchanged. Stat Bull Metrop Insur Co 76:12–20, 1995

Krikorian R, Wrobel AJ: Cognitive impairment in HIV infection. AIDS 5:1501–1507, 1991

Kuni CC, Phame FS, Meier MJ, et al: Quantitative I-123-IMP brain SPECT and neuropsychological testing in AIDS dementia. Clin Nucl Med 16:174–177, 1991

Lalezari JP, Holland GN, Kramer F, et al: Randomized, controlled study of the safety and efficacy of intravenous cidofovir for the treatment of relapsing cytomegalovirus retinitis in patients with AIDS. J Acquir Immune Defic Syndr Hum Retrovirol 17:339–344, 1998

Lantos PL, McLaughlin JE, Scholtz CL, et al: Neuropathology of the brain in HIV infection. Lancet 1:309–311, 1989

Larsson M, Hagbreg L, Forsman A, et al: Cerebrospinal fluid catecholamine metabolites in HIV-infected patients. J Neurosci Res 28:406–409, 1991

Levin HS, Williams DH, Borucki MJ, et al: Magnetic resonance imaging and neuropsychological findings in human immunodeficiency virus infection. J Acquir Immune Defic Syndr 3:757–762, 1990

Levine S, Anderson D, Bystritsky A, et al: A report of eight HIV-seropositive patients with major depression responding to fluoxetine. J Acquir Immune Defic Syndr 3:1074–1077, 1990

Levy JA: Pathogenesis of human immunodeficiency virus infection. Microbiological Rev 57:183–289, 1993

Levy JA, Hoffman AD, Kramer SM, et al: Isolation of lymphocytopathic retroviruses from San Francisco patients with AIDS. Science 225:840–842, 1984

Levy JK, Fernandez F: Memory rehabilitation in HIV encephalopathy. Clin Neuropathol 12 (suppl 1):S27–S28, 1993

Levy JK, Fernandez F: Effects of methylphenidate on HIV-related memory impairment (NR404). Paper presented at the 148th annual meeting of the American Psychiatric Association, Miami, FL, May 20–25, 1995, p 164

Li CJ, Friedman DJ, Wang C, et al: Induction of apoptosis in uninfected lymphocytes by HIV-1 Tat protein. Science 268:429–431, 1995

Lin-Greenberger A, Taneja-Uppal N: Dysautonomia and infection with the human immunodeficiency virus (letter). Ann Intern Med 106:167, 1987

Lipowski ZJ: Delirium (acute confusional states). JAMA 258:1789–1792, 1987

Lipton RB, Ferairu ER, Weiss G, et al: Headache in HIV-1-related disorders. Headache 31:518–522, 1991

Lipton SA: Calcium channel antagonists and human immunodeficiency virus coat protein-mediated neuronal injury. Ann Neurol 30:110–114, 1991

Lipton SA: Models of neuronal injury in AIDS: another role for the NMDA receptor. Trends Neurosci 15:75–79, 1992

Lipton SA, Gendleman HE: Dementia associated with the acquired immunodeficiency syndrome. N Engl J Med 332:934–940, 1995

Lolli F, Colao MG, De Maio E, et al: Intrathecal synthesis of anti-HIV antibodies in AIDS patients. J Neurol Sci 99:281–289, 1990

Louwagie J, McCutchan FE, Peeters M, et al: Phylogenetic analysis of gag genes from 70 international HIV-1 isolates provides evidence for multiple genotypes. AIDS. 7(6):769–780, 1993

Lu W, Salerno-Goncalves R, Yuan J, et al: Glucocorticoids rescue CD4+ T lymphocytes from activation-induced apoptosis triggered by HIV-1: implications for pathogenesis and therapy. AIDS 9:35–42, 1995

Lunn S, Skydzbjerg M, Schulsinger H, et al: A preliminary report on the neuropsychologic sequelae of human immunodeficiency virus. Arch Gen Psychiatry 48:139–142, 1991

Lynch DH, Ramsdell F, Alderson MR: Fas and FasL in the homeostatic regulation of immune responses. Immunol Today 16:569–574, 1995

Maccario M, Scharre DW: HIV and acute onset of psychosis (letter). Lancet 2:342, 1987

Maccarrone M, Bari M, Corasaniti MT, et al: HIV-1 coat glycoprotein gp 120 induces apoptosis in rat brain neocortex by deranging the arachidonate cascade in favor of prostanoids. J Neurochem 75:196–203, 2000

Macdonald JC, Torriani FJ, Morse LS, et al: Lack of reactivation of cytomegalovirus (CMV) retinitis after stopping CMV maintenance therapy in AIDS patients with sustained elevations in CD4 T cells in response to highly active antiretroviral therapy. J Infect Dis 177:1182–1187, 1998

Maj M, Janssen R, Satz P, et al: The World Health Organization's cross-cultural study on neuropsychiatric aspects of infection with the human immunodeficiency virus 1 (HIV-1): preparation and pilot phase. Br J Psychiatry 159:351–356, 1991

Maldarelli F, Sato H, Berthold E, et al: Rapid induction of apoptosis by cell-to-cell transmission of human immunodeficiency virus type 1. J Virol 69:6457–6465, 1995

Markovitz DM: Infection with the human immunodeficiency virus type 2 (review). Ann Intern Med 118:211–218, 1993

Markowitz JC, Rabkin JG, Perry SW: Treating depression in HIV-positive patients. AIDS 8:403–412, 1994

Marlink R, Kanki P, Thior I, et al: Reduced rate of disease development after HIV-2 infection as compared to HIV-1. Science 265:1587–1590, 1994

Marotta R, Perry S: Early neuropsychological dysfunction caused by human immunodeficiency virus. J Neuropsychiatry Clin Neurosci 1:225–235, 1989

Marshall DW, Brey RL, Cahill WT, et al: Spectrum of cerebrospinal fluid findings in various stages of human immunodeficiency virus infection. Arch Neurol 45:954–958, 1988

Marshall DW, Brey RL, Butzin CA, et al: CSF changes in a longitudinal study of 124 neurologically normal HIV-1-infected U.S. Air Force personnel. J Acquir Immune Defic Syndr 4:777–781, 1991

Martin EM, Robertson LC, Sorensen DJ, et al: Speed of memory scanning is not affected in early HIV-1 infection (abstract). J Clin Exp Neuropsychol 14:102, 1992

Marzuk PM, Tierney H, Tardiff K, et al: Increased risk of suicide in persons with AIDS. JAMA 259:1333–1337, 1988

Masdeu JC, Small CB, Weiss L, et al: Multifocal cytomegalovirus encephalitis in AIDS. Ann Neurol 23:97–99, 1988

Masdeu JC, Yudd A, Van Herrtum RL, et al: Single-photon-emission computed tomography in human immunodeficiency virus encephalopathy: a preliminary report. J Nucl Med 32:1471–1475, 1991

Masliah E, Achim CL, Ge N, et al: Spectrum of human immunodeficiency virus–associated neocortical damage. Ann Neurol 32:321–329, 1992

Masliah E, Ge N, Achim CL, et al: Differential vulnerability of calbindin-immunoreactive neurons in HIV encephalitis. J Neuropathol Exp Neurol 54:350–357, 1995

Maxwell S, Scheftner WA, Kessler HA, et al: Manic syndrome associated with zidovudine treatment. JAMA 259:3406–3407, 1988

McArthur JC, Nance-Sproson TE, Griffin DE, et al: The diagnostic utility of elevation in cerebral spinal fluid β2-microglobulin in HIV-1 dementia. Neurology 42:1707–1712, 1992

McArthur JC, Hoover DR, Bacellar H, et al: Dementia in AIDS patients: incidence and risk factors. Neurology 43:2245–2253, 1993

McDaniel SJ, Niran PT, Magnuson JV: Possible induction of mania by buspirone. Am J Psychiatry 147:125–126, 1990

McElroy SL, Keck PE, Pope HG, et al: Valproate in the treatment of bipolar disorder: literature review and clinical guidelines. J Clin Psychopharmacol 12 (suppl 1):42S–52S, 1992

McGowan I, Potter M, George RJD, et al: HIV encephalopathy presenting as hypomania. Genitourin Med 67:420–424, 1991

Melton ST, Kirkwood CK, Ghanemi SN: Pharmacotherapy of HIV dementia. Ann Pharmacother 31:457–473, 1997

Menon DK, Baudouin CJ, Tomlinson D, et al: Proton MR spectroscopy and imaging of the brain in AIDS: evidence of neuronal loss in regions that appear normal with imaging. J Comput Assist Tomogr 14:882–885, 1990

Merigan TC: Treatment of AIDS with combinations of antiretroviral agents. Am J Med 90 (suppl 4A):8S–17S, 1991

Merrill JE: Macroglia: neural cells responsive to lymphokines and growth factors. Immunol Today 8:146–150, 1987

Merrill JE: Proinflammatory and antiinflammatory cytokines in multiple sclerosis and central nervous system acquired immunodeficiency syndrome. J Immunother Emphasis Tumor Immunol 12:167–170, 1992

Miller EN, Satz P, Visscher B: Computerized and conventional neuropsychological assessment of HIV-1-infected homosexual men. Neurology 41:1608–1616, 1991

Miller JK, Barrett RE, Britton CB, et al: Progressive multifocal leukoencephalopathy in a male homosexual with T-cell immune deficiency. N Engl J Med 307:1436–1438, 1982

Mitsuyasu RT: Medical aspects of HIV spectrum disease. Psychiatr Med 7:5–22, 1989

Miyazaki M: Epidemiological characteristics of human immunodeficiency virus type–2 infection in Africa (editorial and review). Int J STD AIDS 6:75–80, 1995

Moore RD, Hidalgo J, Sugland BW, et al: Zidovudine and the natural history of the acquired immunodeficiency syndrome. N Engl J Med 324:1412–1416, 1991

Morgan MK, Clark ME, Hartman WL: AIDS-related dementias: a case report of rapid cognitive decline. J Clin Psychol 44:1024–1028, 1988

Moses A, Bloom FE, Pauza CD, et al: Human immunodeficiency virus infection of human brain capillary endothelial cells occurs via a CD4/galactosylceramide-independent mechanism. Proc Natl Acad Sci U S A 90:10474–10478, 1993

Murray HW, Squires KE, Weiss W, et al: Stavudine in patients with AIDS and AIDS-related complex: AIDS Clinical Trials Group 089. J Infect Dis 171 (suppl 2):S123–S130, 1995

Musher DM, Hamill RJ, Baughn RE: Effects of human immunodeficiency virus (HIV) infection on the course of syphilis and on the response to treatment. Ann Intern Med 113:872–881, 1990

Nance M, Pirozzolo FJ, Levy JK, et al: Simple and choice reaction time in HIV-seronegative, HIV-seropositive and AIDS patients. Abstracts of the 6th International Conference on AIDS, Vol 2. San Francisco, CA, June 22, 1990, p 173

Navia BA, Gonzalez RG: Functional imaging of the AIDS dementia complex and the metabolic pathology of the HIV-1-infected brain. Neuroimaging Clin North Am 7(3):431–445, 1997

Navia BA, Price RW: The acquired immunodeficiency syndrome dementia complex as the presenting or sole manifestation of human immunodeficiency virus infection. Arch Neurol 44:65–69, 1987

Navia BA, Cho E-S, Petito CK, et al: The AIDS dementia complex, II: neuropathology. Ann Neurol 19:525–535, 1986a

Navia BA, Jordan BD, Price RW: The AIDS dementia complex, I: clinical features. Ann Neurol 19:517–524, 1986b

Nazzareno EL, Yeragani VK: Buspirone induced hypomania: a case report (letter). J Clin Psychopharmacol 8:226, 1988

Neuzil KM: Pharmacologic therapy for human immunodeficiency virus infection: a review. Am J Med Sci 307:368–373, 1994

Nichols SE: Psychiatric aspects of AIDS. Psychosomatics 24:1083–1089, 1983

Nichols SE: Psychosocial reactions of persons with the acquired immunodeficiency syndrome. Ann Intern Med 103:765–767, 1985

Norman SE, Chediak AD, Kiel M, et al: Sleep disturbances in HIV-infected homosexual men. AIDS 4:175–178, 1990

O'Dowd MA, McKegney FP: Manic syndrome associated with zidovudine. JAMA 260:3587–3588, 1988

Ollo C, Litman R, Rubinow D, et al: Neuropsychological correlates of smooth pursuit eye movements in HIV disease (abstract). J Clin Neuropsychol 12:73, 1990

Ollo C, Johnson R Jr, Grafman J: Signs of cognitive change in HIV disease: an event-related brain potential study. Neurology 41:209–215, 1991

Pace PL, Fama R, Bornstein RA: Depression and neuropsychological performance in asymptomatic HIV infection (abstract). J Clin Exp Neuropsychol 14:101, 1992

Pajeau AK, Roman GC: HIV encephalopathy and dementia. Psychiatr Clin North Am 15:455–466, 1991

Parisi A, Strosselli M, DiPerri G, et al: Electroencephalography in the early diagnosis of HIV-related subacute encephalitis: analysis of 185 patients. Clin Electroencephogr 20:1–5, 1989

Parisi A, Strosselli M, Pan A, et al: HIV-related encephalitis presenting as convulsant disease. Clin Electroencephalogr 22:1–4, 1991

Perkins DO, Stern RA, Golden RN, et al: Mood disorders in HIV infection: prevalence and risk factors in a nonepicenter of the AIDS epidemic. Am J Psychiatry 151:233–236, 1994

Perry SW: Organic mental disorders caused by HIV: update on early diagnosis and treatment. Am J Psychiatry 147:696–710, 1990

Perry S, Marotta RF: AIDS dementia: a review of the literature. Alzheimer Dis Assoc Disord 1:221–235, 1987

Perry S, Belsky-Barr D, Barr WB, et al: Neuropsychological function in physically asymptomatic, HIV-seropositive men. J Neuropsychiatry Clin Neurosci 3:296–302, 1989

Perry S, Jacobsberg L, Fishman B: Suicidal ideation of HIV testing. JAMA 263:679–682, 1990

Perry S, Fishman B, Jacobsberg L, et al: Relationships over 1 year between lymphocyte subsets and psychosocial variables among adults with infection by human immunodeficiency virus. Arch Gen Psychiatry 49:396–401, 1992

Petito CK: Review of central nervous system pathology in human immunodeficiency virus infection. Ann Neurol 23 (suppl):S54–S57, 1988

Petito CK, Roberts B: Evidence of apoptotic cell death in HIV encephalitis. Am J Pathol 146:1121–1130, 1995

Pollock GB, Perel JM, Shostak M: Rapid achievement of antidepressant effect with intravenous clomipramine (letter). N Engl J Med 312:1130, 1985

Portegies P, Epstein LG, Hung STA, et al: Human immunodeficiency virus type 1 antigen in cerebrospinal fluid: correlation with clinical neurologic status. Arch Neurol 46:261–264, 1989

Portegies P, Algra PR, Hollak CEM, et al: Response to cytarabine in progressive multifocal leucoencephalopathy in AIDS (letter). Lancet 337:680–681, 1991

Post MJD, Berger JR, Quencer RM: Asymptomatic and neurologically symptomatic HIV-seropositive individuals: prospective evaluation with cranial MR imaging. Radiology 178:131–139, 1991

Poutiainen E, Haltia M, Elovaara I, et al: Dementia associated with human immunodeficiency virus: subcortical or cortical? Acta Psychiatr Scand 83:297–301, 1991

Power C, Kong PA, Crawford TO, et al: Cerebral white matter changes in acquired immunodeficiency syndrome dementia: alterations of the blood-brain barrier. Ann Neurol 34:339–350, 1993

Power C, Selnes OA, Grim JA: HIV-dementia scale: a rapid screening test. Journal of Acquired Immune Deficiency Syndrome and Human Retrovirology 8:273–278, 1995

Praus DJ, Brown GR, Rundell JR, et al: Associations between cerebrospinal fluid parameters and high degrees of anxiety or depression in United States Air Force personnel infected with human immunodeficiency virus. J Nerv Ment Dis 178:392–395, 1990

Price WA, Bielefeld M: Buspirone induced mania. J Clin Psychopharmacol 9:150–151, 1989

Pumarola-Sune T, Navia BA, Cordon-Cardo C, et al: HIV antigen in the brains of patients with the AIDS dementia complex. Ann Neurol 21:490–496, 1987

Rabkin JG, Harrison WM: Effect of imipramine on depression and immune status in a sample of men with HIV infection. Am J Psychiatry 147:495–497, 1990

Rabkin JG, Williams JBW, Remien RH, et al: Depression, distress, lymphocyte subsets, and human immunodeficiency virus symptoms on two occasions in HIV-positive homosexual men. Arch Gen Psychiatry 48:111–119, 1991

Reboul J, Schuller E, Pialoux G, et al: Immunoglobulins and complement components in 37 patients infected by HIV-1 virus: comparison of general (systemic) and intrathecal immunity. J Neurol Sci 89:243–252, 1989

Reddy MM, Grieco MH, McKinley GF, et al: Effect of foscarnet therapy on human immunodeficiency virus p24 antigen levels in AIDS patients with cytomegalovirus retinitis. J Infect Dis 166:607–610, 1992

Reed JB, Schwab IR, Gordon J, et al: Regression of cytomegalovirus retinitis associated with protease inhibitor treatment in patients with AIDS. Am J Ophthalmol 124:199–205, 1997

Reisberg B, Ferris SH, de Leon MJ, et al: The Global Deterioration Scale (GDS): an instrument for the assessment of primary degenerative dementia (PDD). Am J Psychiatry 139:1136–1139, 1982

Riccio M, Burgess A, Hawkins D, et al: Neuropsychological and psychiatric changes following treatment of ARC patients with zidovudine. Int J STD AIDS 1:435–437, 1990

Richelson E: Neurodiagnostic affinities for human brain receptors and their use in predicting adverse effects. J Clin Psychiatry 45:331–336, 1984

Richelson E: Synaptic pharmacology of antidepressants: an update. McLean Hospital Journal 13:67–88, 1988

Richman DD, Fischl MA, Grieco MH, et al: The toxicity of azidothymidine (AZT) in the treatment of patients with AIDS and AIDS-related complex: a double-blind, placebo-controlled trial. N Engl J Med 317:192–197, 1987

Riedel R-R, Helmstaedter C, Bulau P, et al: Early signs of cognitive deficits among human immunodeficiency virus–positive hemophiliacs. Acta Psychiatr Scand 85:321–326, 1992

Roccatagliata G, Abbruzzese G, Albano C, et al: Trazodone by intravenous infusion in depressions secondary to organic disease. International Pharmacopsychiatry 12:72–79, 1977

Rolfe M: HIV-2 and its neurological manifestations (review). S Afr Med J 84:503–505, 1994

Rosen MI, Bridge TP, O'Malley SS, et al: Peptide T treatment of cognitive impairment in HIV-positive intravenous drug users. American Journal on Addictions 1:332–338, 1992

Rowen D, Carne CA: Neurological manifestation of HIV infection. Int J STD AIDS 2:79–90, 1991

Rubinow DR, Berrettini CH, Brouwers P, et al: Neuropsychiatric consequences of AIDS. Ann Neurol 23 (suppl):S24–S26, 1988

Ruscetti F, Farrar WL, Hill JM, et al: Visualization of human helper T lymphocyte differentiation antigen in primate brain. Peptides 9 (suppl 1):97–104, 1988

Ryan JJ, Paolo AM, Skrade M: Rey auditory verbal learning test performance of a federal corrections sample with acquired immunodeficiency syndrome. Int J Neurosci 64:177–181, 1992

Sacktor N, Prohovnik I, Van Heertum RL, et al: Cerebral single-photon emission computed tomography abnormalities in human immunodeficiency virus type 1–infected gay men without cognitive impairment. Arch Neurol 52:607–611, 1995a

Sacktor N, Van Heertum RL, Dooneief G, et al: A comparison of cerebral SPECT abnormalities in HIV-positive homosexual men with and without cognitive impairment. Arch Neurol 52:1170–1173, 1995b

Sacktor N, Tarwater PM, Skolasky RL, et al: CSF antiretroviral drug penetrance and the treatment of HIV-associated psychomotor slowing. Neurology 57(3):542–544, 2001

Sardar AM, Bell JE, Reynolds GP: Increased concentrations of the neurotoxin 3-hydroxykynurenine in the frontal cortex of HIV-1-positive patients. J Neurochem 64:932–935, 1995

Scaravilli F, Daniel SE, Harcourt-Webster N, et al: Chronic basal meningitis and vasculitis in acquired immunodeficiency syndrome: a possible role for human immunodeficiency virus. Arch Pathol Lab Med 113:192–195, 1989

Schaerf FW, Miller RS, Lipsey JR, et al: ECT for major depression in four patients infected with human immunodeficiency virus. Am J Psychiatry 146:782–784, 1989

Schielke E, Tatsch K, Pfister HW, et al: Reduced cerebral blood flow in early stages of human immunodeficiency virus infection. Arch Neurol 47:1342–1345, 1990

Schindelmeiser J, Gullotta F: HIV-p24-antigen-bearing macrophages are only present in brains of HIV-seropositive patients with AIDS-encephalopathy. Clin Neuropathol 10:109–111, 1991

Schmitt FA, Bigley JW, McKinnis R, et al: Neuropsychological outcome of zidovudine (AZT) treatment of patients with AIDS and AIDS-related complex. N Engl J Med 319:1573–1578, 1988

Schwarcz R, Whetsell WO, Mangano RM: Quinolinic acid: an endogenous metabolite that produces axon-sparing lesions in the rat brain. Science 219:316–318, 1983

Sekigawa I, Koshino K, Hishikawa T, et al: Inhibitory effect of the immunosuppressant FK506 on apoptotic cell death induced by HIV-1-gp120. J Clin Immunol 15:312–317, 1995

Selnes O, Jacobson L, Machado AM, et al: Normative data for a brief neuropsychological screening battery. Percept Mot Skills 73:539–550, 1991

Shaskan EG, Brew BJ, Rosenblum M, et al: Increased neopterin levels in brains of patients with human immunodeficiency virus type 1 infection. J Neurochem 59:1541–1546, 1992

Shor-Posner G, Feaster D, Blaney NT, et al: Impact of vitamin B6 status on psychological distress in a longitudinal study of HIV-1 infection. Int J Psychiatry Med 24:209–222, 1994

Sidtis JJ, Gatsonis C, Price RW, et al: Zidovudine treatment of the AIDS dementia complex: results of a placebo-controlled trial: AIDS Clinical Trials Group. Ann Neurol 33:343–349, 1993

Siegel K: Psychosocial aspects of rational suicide. Am J Psychother 40:405–417, 1986

Silvestris F, Ribatti D, Nico B, et al: Apoptosi, o morte cellulare programmata: meccanismi regolatori e fisiopatologia [Apoptosis or programmed cell death: regulatory and pathophysiological mechanisms]. Ann Ital Med Int 10:7–13, 1995

Skolasky RL, Eposito DR, Selnes OA, et al: Modified HIV dementia scale: accurate staging of HIV-associated dementia: neuroscience of HIV Infection. J Neurovirol 4 (suppl):366, 1998

Skoraszewski MJ, Ball JD, Mikulka P: Neuropsychological functioning of HIV-infected males. J Clin Exp Neuropsychol 13:278–290, 1991

Smith T, Jakobsen J, Gaub J, et al: Clinical and electrophysiological studies of human immunodeficiency virus–seropositive men without AIDS. Ann Neurol 23:295–297, 1988

Snider ND, Simpson DM, Nielsen S, et al: Neurological complications of acquired immune deficiency syndrome: analysis of 50 patients. Ann Neurol 14:403–418, 1983

Sonnex C, Petherick A, Adler MW, et al: HIV infection increase in public awareness and anxiety. BMJ 295:193–195, 1987

Stahle L, Guzenda E, Ljungdahl-Stahle E: Pharmacokinetics and extracellular distribution to blood, brain, and muscle of alovudine (3′-fluorothymidine) and zidovudine in the rat studied by microdialysis. J Acquir Immune Defic Syndr 6:435–439, 1993

Stefano GB, Smith EM, Cadet P, et al: HIV gp120 alteration of DAMA and IL-1 alpha induced chemotaxic responses in human and invertebrate immunocytes. J Neuroimmunol 43:177–184, 1993

Steller H: Mechanisms and genes of cellular suicide. Science 267:1445–1449, 1995

Stern Y, Marder K, Bell K, et al: Multidisciplinary baseline assessment of homosexual men with and without human immunodeficiency virus infection, III: neurologic and neuropsychologic findings. Arch Gen Psychiatry 48:131–138, 1991

Strauss A: Oral dyskinesia associated with buspirone use in an elderly woman. J Clin Psychiatry 49:322–323, 1988

Studies of the Ocular Complications of AIDS Research Group (SOCA), in collaboration with the AIDS Clinical Trials Group. Foscarnet-ganciclovir cytomegalovirus retinitis trial 4: visual outcomes. Ophthalmology 101:1250–1261, 1994

Syndulko K, Singer E, Fahychandon B, et al: Relationship of self-rated depression and neuropsychological changes in HIV-1 neurological dysfunction (abstract). J Clin Exp Neuropsychol 12:72, 1990

Talley AK, Dewhurst S, Perry SW, et al: Tumor necrosis factor alpha-induced apoptosis in human neuronal cells: protection by the antioxidant N-acetylcysteine and the genes bcl-2 and crmA. Mol Cell Biol 15:2359–2366, 1995

Tartaglione TA, Collier AC, Coombs RW, et al: Acquired immunodeficiency syndrome, cerebrospinal fluid findings in patients before and during long-term oral zidovudine therapy. Arch Neurol 48:695–699, 1991

Tesar GE, Murray GB, Cassem NH: Use of high-dose intravenous haloperidol in the treatment of agitated cardiac patients. J Clin Psychopharmacol 5:344–347, 1985

Thompson CB: Apoptosis in the pathogenesis and treatment of disease. Science 267:1456–1462, 1995

Tinuper P, de Carolis P, Galeotti M, et al: Electroencephalogram and HIV infection: a prospective study in 100 patients. Clin Electroencephalogr 21:145–150, 1990

Tozzi V, Balestra P, Galgani S, et al: Positive and sustained effects of highly active antiretroviral therapy on HIV-1-associated neurocognitive impairment. AIDS 13(14):1889–1897, 1999

Tracey I, Carr CA, Guimares AR, et al: Brain choline-containing compounds are elevated in HIV-positive patients before the onset of AIDS dementia complex: a proton magnetic resonance spectroscopic study. Neurology 46:783–788, 1996

Tross S, Price RW, Navia B, et al: Neuropsychological characterization of the AIDS dementia complex: a preliminary report. AIDS 2:81–88, 1988

Vago L, Castagna A, Lazzarin A, et al: Reduced frequency of HIV-induced brain lesions in AIDS patients treated with zidovudine. J Acquir Immune Defic Syndr 6:42–45, 1993

Van Gorp WG, Miller E, Satz P, et al: Neuropsychological performance in HIV-1 immunocompromised patients (abstract). J Clin Exp Neuropsychol 11:35, 1989a

Van Gorp WG, Mitrushina M, Cummings JL, et al: Normal aging and the subcortical encephalopathy of AIDS: a neuropsychological comparison. Neuropsychiatry, Neuropsychology, and Behavioral Neurology 2:5–20, 1989b

Van Gorp WG, Satz P, Hinkin C, et al: Metacognition in HIV-1 seropositive asymptomatic individuals: self-ratings versus objective neuropsychological performance. J Clin Exp Neuropsychol 13:812–819, 1991

van Leeuwen R, Katlama C, Kitchen V, et al: Evaluation of safety and efficacy of 3TC (Lamivudine) in patients with asymptomatic or mildly symptomatic human immunodeficiency virus infection: a phase I/II study. J Infect Dis 171:1166–1171, 1995

Vazeux R: AIDS encephalopathy and tropism of HIV for brain monocytes/macrophages and microglial cells. Pathobiology 59:214–218, 1991

Vinters HV, Guerra WG, Eppolito L, et al: Necrotizing vasculitis of the nervous system in a patient with AIDS-related complex. Neuropathol Appl Neurobiol 14:417–424, 1988

Walker DG, Itagaki J, Berry K, et al: Examination of brains of AIDS cases for human immunodeficiency virus and human cytomegalovirus nucleic acids. J Neurol Neurosurg Psychiatry 52:583–590, 1989

Walling VR, Pfefferbaum B: Methylphenidate: its use in a depressed adolescent with AIDS. AIDS Patient Care 5:4–5, 1991

Wang Y, Sawchuk RJ: Zidovudine transport in the rabbit brain during intravenous and intracerebroventricular infusion. J Pharm Sci 84:871–876, 1995

Weiner RD: ECT in the physically ill. Journal of Psychiatric Treatment Evaluation 5:457–462, 1983

Weis S, Haug H, Budka H: Neuronal damage in the cerebral cortex of AIDS brains: a morphometric study. Acta Neuropathol (Berl) 85:185–189, 1993

Whelan MA, Kricheff II, Handler M, et al: Acquired immunodeficiency syndrome: cerebral computed tomographic manifestations. Radiology 149:477–484, 1983

White JC, Christensen JF, Singer CM: Methylphenidate as a treatment for depression in acquired immunodeficiency syndrome: An n-of-1 trial. J Clin Psychiatry 53:153–156, 1992

Wiegand M, Möller AA, Schreiber W, et al: Alterations of nocturnal sleep in patients with HIV infection. Acta Neurol Scand 83:141–142, 1991a

Wiegand M, Möller AA, Schreiber W, et al: Nocturnal sleep EEG in patients with HIV infection. Eur Arch Psychiatry Clin Neurosci 240:153–158, 1991b

Wiley CA, Masliah E, Morey M, et al: Neocortical damage during HIV infection. Ann Neurol 29:651–657, 1991

Wilkie FL, Eisdorfer C, Morgan R, et al: Cognition in early human immunodeficiency virus infection. Arch Neurol 47:433–440, 1990a

Wilkie F, Guterman A, Morgan R, et al: Cognition and electrophysiologic measures in early HIV infection (abstract). J Clin Exp Neuropsychol 12:48, 1990b

Wolcott DL, Fawzy FI, Pasnau RO: Acquired immune deficiency syndrome (AIDS) and consultation-liaison psychiatry. Gen Hosp Psychiatry 7:280–293, 1985

Wong SL, Wang Y, Sawchuk RJ: Analysis of zidovudine distribution to specific regions in rabbit brain using microdialysis. Pharm Res 9:332–338, 1992

Wong SL, Van Bell K, Sawchuk RJ: Distributional transport kinetics of zidovudine between plasma and brain extracellular fluid/cerebrospinal fluid in the rabbit: investigation of the inhibitory effect of probenecid utilizing microdialysis. J Pharmacol Exp Ther 264:899–909, 1993

Wright JM, Sachdev PS, Perkins RJ, et al: Zidovudine related mania. Med J Aust 150:339–341, 1989

Yarchoan R, Berg G, Brouwers P, et al: Response of human immunodeficiency virus associated neurological disease to 3'-azido-3'-deoxythymidine. Lancet 1:132–135, 1987

# CHAPTER 24

# Neuropsychiatric Aspects of Rheumatic Disease

Fred Ovsiew, M.D.

Tammy Utset, M.D., M.P.H.

In this chapter, we review organic cerebral derangements in the rheumatic diseases. The most space is devoted to the discussion of systemic lupus erythematosus. There follows a survey of rheumatic syndromes and their neuropsychiatric expressions. Nervous system manifestations outside the mental sphere are given brief mention. Throughout, the emphasis is on mechanisms of pathogenesis and tools for diagnosis. Ancillary topics such as the production of autoimmune phenomena by psychotropic drugs, the evidence of autoimmunity in functional psychiatric syndromes, and the controversial hypothesis of a link between autoimmunity and learning disabilities are briefly reviewed.

## Approach to the Patient With Rheumatic Disease

In patients with known rheumatic disease, interpretation of psychiatric symptoms can be facilitated by knowledge of the neuropsychiatric manifestations of their disease as described in this chapter. In patients presenting with neuropsychiatric disease that may be due to occult systemic disorders, it is helpful to remember that most patients with rheumatic disease will have signs or symptoms that indicate their underlying autoimmune process.

Because systemic lupus is one of the most common autoimmune diseases with cerebral involvement, review of systems should emphasize symptoms of lupus such as hair loss, joint pain, oral or nasal ulcerations, rashes, fevers, seizures, strokes, pleurisy, blood disorders, and kidney disease. Sjögren's syndrome, also a relatively common autoimmune cause of neuropsychiatric disorders, may manifest as dryness in the eyes, mouth, and vagina; new problems with dental caries due to loss of the protective effects of adequate saliva on dentition; or swelling and discomfort in the parotid glands. The presence of asthma should lead to consideration of sarcoidosis or Churg-Strauss vasculitis in appropriate patients. A history of inflammatory eye disease raises the possibility of Behçet's disease, sarcoidosis, Cogan's syndrome, systemic vasculitis, and occasionally lupus or rheumatoid arthritis. Diarrhea may suggest Behçet's disease, Whipple's disease, or celiac disease. Recurrent thrombophlebitis or recurrent miscarriages is typical of antiphospholipid antibody syndrome or systemic lupus erythematosus, whereas superficial thrombophlebitis or large venous thrombosis such as Budd-Chiari syndrome is characteristic of Behçet's disease. Thus likely disorders can be identified by the complex of symptoms and medical history and the diagnostic evaluation appropriately pursued.

The family history of organ-specific or systemic autoimmunity may also be helpful in directing the evaluation of patients with neuropsychiatric disorders. Such positive family history is common in patients with the classic connective tissue diseases (e.g., systemic lupus erythematosus or Sjögren's syndrome) and should raise the level of suspicion for an autoimmune syndrome.

A family history of thyroiditis, pernicious anemia, type I diabetes mellitus, multiple sclerosis, myasthenia gravis, lupus, scleroderma, or rheumatoid arthritis should be specifically sought.

Finally, physical signs can often be found to suggest rheumatic disease even in the unconscious or delirious patient. Alopecia, malar, discoid, or vasculitic rashes, and periungual inflammation may suggest systemic lupus. The malar rash in lupus is usually slightly palpable and may be mildly itchy or tender. It crosses the bridge of the nose and extends on to the cheeks to a varying extent while sparing the nasolabial folds. Discoid rashes are highly scarring, and thus stigmata remain long after the active lesions resolve. They are more common in lupus patients of African ethnicity, and most often involve the face, scalp, pinnae, and extensor surfaces of the arms. When active, these lesions are hyperkeratotic plaques with areas of atrophy, follicular plugging, and loss of pigment. When inactive, scars are characterized by atrophy, destruction of skin appendages such as hair follicles, and marked pigmentary changes. Vasculitic rashes are typically purpuric and may be palpable or macular in quality. Periungual findings in lupus most often consist of rosy pink inflammation at the cuticles. Inflammatory arthritis may be differentiated from the very common noninflammatory disorders of osteoarthritis or soft-tissue syndromes by findings of swelling, warmth, erythema, and pain or limitation in the range of motion of involved joints. Distribution is also helpful. The base of the thumb, distal interphalangeal joints, and spine are extremely common sites of simple osteoarthritis, whereas wrist, ankle, and metacarpophalangeal joint involvement is common in rheumatic disease. Knee and proximal interphalangeal joint disease can occur in both osteoarthritis and connective tissue disorders. Inflammatory arthritis, livedo reticularis, vasculitic rashes, fever, and mucosal ulcers are significant findings, but they do not differentiate among various rheumatic disorders. Uveitis—inflammation of the anterior portion of the eye—is likewise a feature of several rheumatic diseases, and ophthalmologic consultation with slit-lamp examination in suspected cases may identify an autoimmune process.

Basic laboratory testing in patients suspected to have rheumatic disorders will vary with the suspected disorder. If lupus is suspected, an antinuclear antibody (ANA) titer, complete blood count, creatinine, and urinalysis are reasonable first steps. If the ANAs are elevated, or if cytopenias, proteinuria, or hematuria is present, then further serological evaluation and rheumatologic consultation are needed. Relevant laboratory testing for other rheumatic disorders is described in the appropriate sections of this chapter.

**TABLE 24–1.** American College of Rheumatology criteria for systemic lupus erythematosus

Malar rash

Discoid rash

Photosensitivity

Oral ulcers

Arthritis

Serositis (pleuritis or pericarditis)

Renal disorder (proteinuria or cellular casts)

Neurological disorder (seizures or psychosis)

Hematological disorder (hemolytic anemia, leukopenia, lymphopenia, thrombocytopenia)

Immunological disorder (anti-DNA, anti-Smith, or anti-phospholipid antibody)

*Source.* Adapted from Hochberg 1997 and Tan 1982.

## Systemic Lupus Erythematosus

The prototypical autoimmune disease, systemic lupus erythematosus (SLE), has protean manifestations leading to inflammation or organ dysfunction throughout the body. The formal diagnosis of SLE for research purposes (see Table 24–1) is dependent on the presence of characteristic types of organ involvement, usually supported by abnormal serological tests (Hochberg 1997; Tan et al. 1982). In practice, the sensitivity of the American College of Rheumatology (ACR) criteria may be as low as 72% in identifying patients with clinically defined lupus (Gilboe and Husby 1999), so the diagnosis of SLE for clinical purposes can be made without fulfilling the ACR criteria.

Although the neuropsychiatric manifestations listed in the ACR criteria for the diagnosis of SLE are limited to seizures and psychosis, the protean clinical features of neuropsychiatric lupus include many other symptoms (see Table 24–2) (Ad Hoc Committee on Neuropsychiatric Lupus Nomenclature 1999) (see also http://www.rheumatology.org/ar/ar.html). The pathophysiology and phenomenology of psychosis, mood disturbance, and cognitive impairment will be discussed in greater detail later in this chapter. But the clinician first must be warned that commonly used terms such as *lupus cerebritis* and *lupus vasculitis* are inaccurate simplifications of the complex cerebral disease found in SLE patients.

### Pathogenesis

In understanding cerebral dysfunction in lupus, it is important to remember that SLE is a systemic disease; SLE patients are often quite medically sick. Cerebral dysfunction can result directly from involvement of the brain but also indirectly from lupus involvement of other organ systems, for example, uremia due to renal disease or emboli from a cardiac vegetation related to lupus. SLE patients often have other chronic medical diseases such as diabetes and severe hypertension, and these too can affect CNS function. Medicines used to treat SLE patients, including high-dose corticosteroids, analgesics, anticonvulsants, and antiemetics, can also cause neuropsychiatric symptoms. Depression is common in the setting of chronic illness and can result in symptoms that may be hard to differentiate from neuropsychiatric lupus. Thus a broad perspective on patient health is necessary in assessing neuropsychiatric symptoms in suspected or known cases of SLE.

**TABLE 24–2.** Manifestations of cerebral involvement in systemic lupus erythematosus

Aseptic meningitis
Stroke
Demyelination
Migraine
Benign intracranial hypertension
Chorea or other movement disorder
Seizure
Delirium
Anxiety or mood disorder
Psychosis
Cognitive impairment

*Source.* Modified from Ad Hoc Committee 1999.

Cliniconeuropathological studies cast some light on the mechanisms of cerebral lupus. Johnson and Richardson (1968) found cerebral involvement in 18 of 24 (75%) autopsied patients. The major pathological finding was microinfarction associated with fibrinoid necrosis of small vessels. In only three cases were inflammatory cells found within vessel walls (true vasculitis). The authors doubted that a vascular mechanism of cerebral dysfunction could account for all the clinical phenomena seen. Ellis and Verity (1979) reviewed 57 pathological cases of central nervous system (CNS) lupus. In four (7%), vasculitis was seen; in the others, hyaline change, endothelial proliferation, and perivascular inflammation were the characteristic vascular pathology. Infarctions (both large and small), infection, and hemorrhage were other findings. Budka (1981) compared autopsy data from 15 lupus patients with findings in other rheumatic diseases. Fibrinoid necrosis, endothelial proliferation, meningeal and perivascular inflammatory cells, and infarction were again prominent in lupus brains. The finding of immune complex deposition in vessel walls and other evidence of

direct immune attack on CNS tissue were stressed as providing a "previously missing link" (p. 370) in the pathogenesis of cerebral dysfunction. Cerebrovascular events were shown pathologically by Tsokos and colleagues (1986) to be of multiple origins; emboli, vasculitis, and coagulopathy all were thought to play a role, with no cause identified even after autopsy in some patients. Devinsky and colleagues (1988) found neuropsychiatric disturbances in 37 of 50 (74%) autopsied patients with lupus. The clinical and neuropathological data disclosed embolism (sometimes from Libman-Sacks endocarditis), infection, and thrombotic thrombocytopenic purpura (TTP) as common causes of brain lesions. Acute vasculitis was not seen, although two patients had arterial lesions suggestive of old, healed vasculitis. Futrell and colleagues (1992) reviewed 91 lupus patients, of whom 63 (69%) had evidence of CNS disease; autopsy data were available in 5. The authors stressed the importance of infection, with pathological examination sometimes disclosing unsuspected brain infection when death would otherwise have been attributed to "CNS lupus." Hanly and colleagues (1992b) reviewed 10 autopsied lupus patients, of whom 7 had had clinical neuropsychiatric manifestations. Focal and segmental fibrinoid necrosis of small vessels with associated microinfarction was found in four cases, and a healed larger-artery vasculitis in one. Although the fibrinoid necrosis was thought similar to the familiar immune complex–mediated renal lesions of lupus, significant deposition of complement and immunoglobulin G (IgG) was seen only in the patient with other evidence of vasculitis. Findings suggestive of emboli or of TTP were absent. A Japanese group reported several cases of perivenous necrosis, without evidence of inflammation (Matsumoto et al. 1997, 1998; Shintaku and Matsumoto 1998). These autopsy findings of vascular damage (with only rare vasculitis), thrombosis, microinfarctions, and a paucity of gross neuronal damage support several mechanisms of cerebral dysfunction for further discussion: medium-vessel vasculitis, small-vessel vasculopathy, antineuronal antibodies, and cytokines.

As is clear from the autopsy studies just reviewed, medium- or large-vessel cerebral vasculitis is rare in SLE (Weiner and Allen 1991); its clinical correlate is stroke. Stroke in lupus patients is generally due to other mechanisms, including thrombosis, cardiogenic embolism, and infection (Mitsias and Levine 1994; Tsokos et al. 1986). Medium- or large-vessel vasculitis is also relatively uncommon in other organs of lupus patients. Outside the CNS, small-vessel vasculitis is felt to result from immune complex deposition in vessel walls, with secondary "bystander" injury to the vessel by activated complement causing true vasculitis. However, the blood-brain barrier minimizes immune complex deposition in the CNS. Most likely this is why true vasculitis is uncommon in the CNS of lupus patients. Rather, microinfarction in the CNS of SLE patients may occur because of thrombosis or leukothrombosis. Leukothrombosis occurs when ambient immune complexes activate complement intravascularly. This intravascular activation of complement (along with an inflammatory cytokine milieu) leads to upregulation of adhesion molecules on both vascular endothelium and leukocytes. As vessel diameter narrows, the interaction of adhesion molecules results in a thrombus of platelets, leukocytes, and neutrophils in CNS vessels with secondary microinfarction of brain tissue (Belmont et al. 1996; Hess 1997; Hopkins et al. 1988).

Noninflammatory vasculopathy may develop from repeated brief attacks of focal vasculitis (Ellison et al. 1993; Smith et al. 1994), or the initial injury itself may be noninflammatory. Antiphospholipid antibodies (aPL) are associated with noninflammatory vasculopathy, probably via direct endothelial injury, followed by connective tissue proliferation. Vessel occlusion is the result (Alarcón-Segovia et al. 1989; Hughson et al. 1993; Westerman et al. 1992). Thrombotic microangiopathy may be seen pathologically in both the aPL syndrome and in TTP, an occasional complication of SLE that causes thrombocytopenia, renal dysfunction, and encephalopathy (Devinsky et al. 1988; Jain et al. 1994; Nesher et al. 1994).

In a disorder characterized by the elaboration of autoantibodies, the possibility of cerebral dysfunction due to antibodies against brain constituents must be considered. Several studies have identified antibodies present in serum and cerebrospinal fluid (CSF) that react with brain tissues (Bruyn 1995) and may obtain access to the CNS by disruption of the blood-brain barrier or by intrathecal synthesis (Mevorach et al. 1994). The clinical correlate is often assumed to be "nonfocal" cerebral lupus, characterized by cognitive impairment, psychosis, and other psychopathology. However, designating psychosis and cognitive impairment as nonfocal or diffuse manifestations of cerebral disease may be erroneous; they may be due to multifocal damage or to focal damage at an unidentified locus.

Antineuronal antibodies have not been impressively associated with cerebral lupus. Kelly and Denburg (1987) found antineuronal antibodies in CSF of only 4 of 24 (17%) patients with neuropsychiatric lupus, and Hanly and colleagues (1993) were unable to find an association between cognitive impairment and serum titers of any putative brain-reactive autoantibodies. In many patients with antineuronal antibodies, the titers vary with

systemic disease activity and are not helpful in diagnosing CNS disease (Hanly et al. 1989; Hay and Isenberg 1993).

Antibodies to ribosomal P protein, which are highly specific for SLE, may be related to "diffuse" neuropsychiatric lupus. Early reports of this association (Bonfa et al. 1987; Nojima et al. 1992; Schneebaum et al. 1991) were followed by some negative studies (Derksen et al. 1990; Kozora et al. 1996; Press et al. 1996; Teh and Isenberg 1994; Teh et al. 1992; van Dam et al. 1991). Although most recent data support the association (Georgescu et al. 1997; Isshi and Hirohata 1996, 1998; Tzioufas et al. 2000; Watanabe et al. 1996), a recent expert panel considered testing for antiribosomal P still "investigational" (Ad Hoc Committee on Neuropsychiatric Lupus Nomenclature 1999, p. 603).

Many methodological problems, both of immunological technique and of description and classification of neuropsychiatric phenomena, make the definition of the role of brain-reactive antibodies in the mechanism of disease controversial. Although unsatisfying, this lack of organ-specific antibodies parallels autoimmunity in non-CNS locations. Lupus arthritis or nephritis is not associated with antibodies specific for joint or renal antigens. The antigenic targets that typify the classic lupus autoantibodies are common to all nucleated cells, such as DNA/histone complexes and the nuclear contents expressed on apoptotic blebs. Perhaps the immune process occurring in cerebral lupus is passive bystander injury as is seen in other body tissues. However, in a murine model of autoimmune disease, brain-reactive antibodies appear to be associated with altered emotionality (Sakic et al. 1993a, 1993b). Much research remains to be done in this very provocative area.

An appreciation of the relevance of aPL to CNS disease is growing. These data will be summarized later in this chapter, in the discussion of the primary aPL syndrome.

Cytokines clearly can produce neuropsychiatric dysfunction, as shown by the mood and cognitive abnormalities evoked by therapeutic administration of interferon-α, interferon-γ, and IL-2 (Bernard et al. 1990; Bonaccorso et al. 2000; Caraceni et al. 1992; Denicoff et al. 1987; Ovsiew 1995; Smith et al. 1988). These reports highlight the importance of findings of elevated IL-6, IL-8, soluble IL-2 receptor, and interferon-α in CSF of patients with lupus psychosis (Gilad et al. 1997; Hirohata et al. 1985; Isshi et al. 1994; Jara et al. 1998; Lebon et al. 1983; Shiozawa et al. 1992; Trysberg et al. 2000; Winfield et al. 1983). Quinolinic acid, a putative excitotoxin, is a product of tryptophan metabolism induced by immune activation, specifically by interferon-γ and tumor necrosis factor-α. Elevated quinolinic acid in the

CSF of patients with neuropsychiatric manifestations of lupus is plausibly related to the clinical phenomena (Vogelsang et al. 1996). Conversely, diversion of tryptophan to production of quinolinic acid and kynurenine by immune activation of indoleamine 2,3-dioxygenase may lead to tryptophan depletion, a state well known to have psychiatric consequences, especially depression (Widner et al. 1999).

## Clinical Features

The reported prevalence of CNS involvement and of various neuropsychiatric features varies widely. We stress data from prospective studies using contemporary diagnostic methods. An epidemiologically sound but retrospective prevalence figure of 18% for CNS events represents a conservative estimate (Sibley et al. 1992). Many other investigators would give a figure of 50% or more (Khamashta et al. 1991). CNS events most often occur early in the course of the disease, but they may occur at any time and are not strongly associated with systemic disease activity (Sibley et al. 1992; Ward and Studenski 1991). Uncommonly, lupus can present with neuropsychiatric features (Tola et al. 1992). Presentations with catatonia (Lanham et al. 1985; Mac and Pardo 1983) and de novo presentations in the elderly (Dennis et al. 1992; Mavrikakis et al. 1992) may be particularly difficult to diagnose.

Most of the variation in the prevalence estimates relates to neuropsychiatric manifestations such as psychosis and cognitive impairment, and the large discrepancies may indicate selection bias in reported populations, varying definitions of psychopathology, difficulty in assigning psychopathology to CNS lupus, and varying methods and quality of assessment (Iverson 1993). Hay and colleagues (1992) found a point prevalence of psychiatric disorder of 20.5% (15 of 73) and a lifetime prevalence of 42% (31 of 73) in a population drawn from a specialty clinic at an English teaching hospital. Hugo and colleagues (1996) found a point prevalence of 18.2% (16 of 88) and a lifetime prevalence of 30.7% (27 of 88) for psychiatric disorder in a consecutive series from a South African teaching hospital using standard psychiatric evaluation methods. A prospective assessment of 91 Icelandic lupus patients disclosed a rate of lifetime psychiatric diagnosis of 49%, which did not significantly differ from the rate for population-based control subjects (Lindal et al. 1995). No attempt was made to distinguish clinically which disorders were of organic origin, but anxiety disorders (including agoraphobia and simple and social phobia) and alcohol abuse were more common in the study than the control population; psychotic and mood disorders were not. Other studies likewise found few differences in psychopathology between lupus patients and control subjects (Wekking 1993). Of 20 consecutive patients with active lupus studied by Segui and colleagues (2000), 8 (40%) had psychiatric disorders, all anxiety states. When reevaluated a year later, when the disease was inactive, only 2 cases were found. No cognitive difference between active and inactive patients was found. The researchers presumed that the anxiety states, which they considered "mild," were mediated by the psychological stress of acute illness. In contrast, Purandare and colleagues (1999) studied 30 patients, of whom 15 (50%) had psychiatric diagnoses, 11 of which were either major depression or an organic syndrome.

Psychotic states in lupus, although long included in the diagnostic criteria for SLE, have not been well characterized. Until recently, few investigators distinguished between psychotic states in clear consciousness and psychotic symptoms, such as hallucinations and delusions, occurring in the context of delirium. In recent studies using modern standardized assessments and diagnostic criteria, psychosis is unusual. For example, Lim and colleagues (1988), working in a London teaching hospital, found that 25 (62.5%) of 40 lupus patients had psychiatric illness at any time after onset of lupus; 5 of the 40 patients (12.5%) had psychosis. In 2 of the patients with psychosis, transient disorientation and alteration in conscious level were seen, although a DSM-III (American Psychiatric Association 1980) diagnosis of atypical psychosis was made in all 5. At the time of evaluation, two (5%) lupus patients—but also one control patient—were psychotic. Rimon and colleagues (1988) found one patient with a "functional psychosis" in a group of 67 consecutive patients in a lupus research program in Finland; in one other patient, psychotic features occurred in the context of disorientation. Magner (1990) found no psychotic patients in a study of 25 South African lupus patients attending a teaching hospital outpatient clinic. In the series of Hay and colleagues (1992), only one patient with psychosis, diagnosed with "paranoid psychosis," was found. Miguel and colleagues (1994) studied 43 patients for lupus manifestations at the time of their admission to a Brazilian teaching hospital. Twenty-seven (63%) met DSM-III-R (American Psychiatric Association 1987) criteria for psychiatric diagnoses; 3 of 46 (6.5%) had delirium, but only 1 (2%) had organic hallucinosis. In addition, 3 patients had depression with mood-incongruent psychotic features. In the series of Hugo and colleagues (1996), 3 of 88 patients (3.4%) had current delirium, none had current schizophrenia or other psychotic diagnoses, and past diagnoses of schizophrenia were questionable. Thus, psychotic states certainly occur in lupus, but they are neither typical nor the only major psychiatric manifestation of the disease; in many instances, psychotic manifestations signal a delirious state.

There is no doubt that depression is common in lupus patients, as it is in people with other chronic diseases. For example, Lim and colleagues (1988) made "lifetime" (i.e., since onset of lupus) diagnoses of major depression in 16 of 40 (40%) patients and found anxiety disorders in an additional 4 of 40 (10%). Miguel and colleagues (1994) diagnosed organic mood disorder, in all cases depressive, in 19 of 43 (44%) patients. The origin of such symptoms is what causes debate. Miguel and colleagues (1994) made organic diagnoses of the depressive symptoms and argued that the timing, association with neurological and neuroimaging findings, and phenomenology of the psychiatric features proved an organic cause. Similarly, Utset and colleagues (1994) found an association of depression (defined as "symptoms severe enough to require recommendation of antidepressant therapy or referral to psychiatry," p. 2040) not only with neuropsychiatric lupus but also with the presence of secondary Sjögren's syndrome. The occurrence of suicide in lupus patients was found to be associated with active disease and a diffusely slow electroencephalogram (EEG) (Matsukawa et al. 1994). Other investigators, however, stressed the association of mood symptoms with social stress and the lack of a clear excess of mood disorders in patients with lupus as compared with appropriate control subjects; these findings support the argument for psychosocial factors in the pathogenesis of depressive states (Hay 1994; Lim et al. 1988). For example, Shortall and colleagues (1995) found that mood disturbance and anxiety correlated with psychosocial factors such as problems with fatigue and pain and alteration of appearance. By contrast, no relation was found with disease activity. Similarly, Hugo and colleagues (1996) found only one case of major depression and one case of organic mood disorder among their 88 carefully assessed patients; by contrast, 10 (11%) had adjustment disorders, with depressive symptoms often prominent and a trend toward higher scores on ratings of stressful life events.

Although more data from methodologically sound inquiries will help resolve the uncertainties, some tentative conclusions are possible. Psychosis appears to have been overemphasized and anxiety states underemphasized as a psychiatric concomitant of lupus. The pathogenesis of nonpsychotic disorders remains obscure, but psychosocial factors are of great importance. Possibly a few patients develop mood or anxiety disorders due to primarily or solely organic reasons, most primarily in response to the social stress of a chronic illness, with others in response to social stress acting on an impaired brain.

The understanding of cognitive impairment in lupus has benefited from a number of recent neuropsychologically sophisticated studies, although the data are still confounded by selection biases, differences in neuropsychological methods, and varying criteria for impairment or neuropsychological "caseness." For example, Carbotte and colleagues (1986) found that 81% of patients with present and 87% with prior neuropsychiatric lupus had cognitive impairment, compared with 42% of those who never had such involvement, yielding an overall prevalence figure of 66%. Notably, healthy subjects and control subjects with rheumatoid arthritis had cognitive impairment at rates of 14% and 17%, respectively, in this study. A subsequent study by this group indicated that a third of patients with lupus but no history of cerebral involvement showed cognitive impairment (Denburg et al. 1992). Hanly and colleagues (1992a), who believed that they were studying an epidemiologically representative population, found that 15 of 70 (21%) lupus patients were cognitively impaired; 11 of 55 (20%) of those who had never experienced cerebral involvement were cognitively impaired. Similarly, Hay and colleagues (1992) found that 26% of lupus patients at a tertiary center had impairment on more than one cognitive test. Kozora and colleagues (1996) found that 29% of a group of lupus patients with no history of cerebral involvement showed cognitive impairment. Although the impairment might have been due to subclinical cerebral disease, the fact that 31% of patients with rheumatoid arthritis also showed impairment suggested that the disturbance was either a concomitant of reactive psychological distress or due to systemic inflammatory activity. Gladman and colleagues (2000; Glanz et al. 1997) found that 25 of 58 (43%) patients with inactive lupus had cognitive impairment, as did 9 of 47 (19%) healthy control subjects. Carlomagno and colleagues (2000) found 10 of 51 (20%) SLE patients to have cognitive impairment at initial examination. At repeat examination, 9 of 10 SLE patients had persistent stable deficits and one improved, but 4 of 41 SLE patients with previously normal cognitive testing had developed cognitive dysfunction.

An issue of particular interest is the prevalence of cognitive impairment in SLE patients without previously recognized CNS involvement. As noted already, several studies suggested that such patients have a high rate of abnormality. Kozora and colleagues (1998) found neuropsychological deficits in 7 of 20 (35%) SLE patients without previous CNS disease. A similar number had magnetic resonance imaging (MRI) evidence of white-matter abnormalities, but there was no correlation between the two findings. Sabbadini and colleagues (1999) found nearly equal rates of impairment in SLE patients with (24 of 56, 43%) and without (45 of 101, 45%) previous CNS involvement. Gladman and colleagues (2000) and Carlomagno and colleagues (2000) found only a nonsignificant trend for greater cognitive impairment in SLE patients with a history of CNS disease. The correlation between known CNS SLE and cognitive impairment seems to be surprisingly weak.

In general, studies also fail to demonstrate correlation between cognitive impairment and disease activity, organ system involvement, or serological status (Carbotte et al. 1995; Gladman et al. 2000; Hay 1994; Kozora et al. 1996). The exception is aPL. Several studies demonstrated correlation between cognitive impairment and the presence of these antibodies. Denburg and colleagues (1997) had data only on lupus anticoagulant (LA). Patients who had never had known neuropsychiatric lupus were nearly three times more likely to have cognitive impairment if they were LA positive; patients with previous known neuropsychiatric lupus were nearly twice as likely. Hanly and colleagues (1999) studied a group of lupus patients longitudinally over a mean period of over 5 years. Those who were persistently positive for IgG or immunoglobulin A (IgA) antibodies to cardiolipin (aCL) showed cognitive decline. Similarly, Menon and colleagues (1999) studied a group of patients with lupus on two occasions 12 to 18 months apart. Persistent elevation of IgG aCL was associated with cognitive decline. Whitelaw and colleagues (1999) compared patients with and without the aPL syndrome. Despite their being otherwise well matched, the group with aPL syndrome showed a correlation between six neuropsychological measures and duration of disease, whereas in the aPL-negative patients only one test showed a correlation with duration of disease. Strikingly, the abnormal findings across studies consistently showed a pattern of psychomotor slowing and impaired executive functions suggestive of subcortical dysfunction.

Whether cognitive impairment is associated with psychiatric disorder is controversial. Carbotte and colleagues (1986), Gladman and colleagues (2000), and Carlomagno (2000) found that it is not. Kozora and colleagues (1996) found a significant association between a measure of psychological distress and the presence of cognitive impairment. Hay and colleagues (1992) found that cognitive dysfunction usually did not persist over time—a finding confirmed by Hanly and colleagues (1994)—and that it fluctuated in relation to psychiatric symptoms. Whereas Hay and colleagues (1992) believed that this indicated that the psychiatric disorder "explained" cognitive dysfunction, one might equally hypothesize that cognitive dysfunction leads to reactive distress or that both psychiatric symptoms and cognitive impairment arise from the same reversible organic state. Again, the data raise the possibility of multiple origins of cognitive impairment, including both reversible effects of systemic or cerebral inflammation and irreversible structural cerebral injury.

## Diagnosis

The diagnosis of cerebral involvement in lupus is a difficult enterprise; at present, there is no unequivocal diagnostic test. Most serum autoantibody titers bear no relationship to CNS disease activity, as discussed above (Toubi et al. 1995).

EEG is an insensitive and nonspecific tool for identifying CNS disease. Abnormalities may be seen in as few as 17% (Ritchlin et al. 1992) to 32% (Sibley et al. 1992) of cases. The rate of abnormalities in depression and psychosis, a particularly important issue, is uncertain, but Hugo and colleagues (1996) found no association between EEG abnormalities and psychiatric status. A claim for the sensitivity and specificity of quantitative EEG is weakened by the lack of a control group of lupus patients with nonorganic psychiatric disorders and is unreplicated (Ritchlin et al. 1992). Because seizures may cause psychotic episodes, EEG evaluation should be obtained in SLE patients manifesting psychosis.

MRI often discloses abnormalities in patients with lupus, usually either cerebral atrophy or T2 hyperintensities in gray or white matter. In lupus, the white-matter lesions are prominently subcortical rather than periventricular as compared with those in multiple sclerosis (MS), although the appearances can be identical. The lesions in lupus patients can be enhanced with gadolinium, sometimes more extensively than those in MS patients (Miller et al. 1992). Focal abnormalities are associated with focal cerebral syndromes and with the presence of aPL (Baum et al. 1993; Bell et al. 1991; Stimmler et al. 1993; Toubi et al. 1995). However, MRI abnormalities are commonly seen in lupus patients with no history of cerebral involvement (Gonzalez-Crespo et al. 1995). Stimmler and colleagues (1993) found that episodes of suspected brain dysfunction in lupus patients were as frequently accompanied by MRI abnormalities when due to cerebral lupus as when not. Davie and colleagues (1995), Hugo and colleagues (1996), and Kozora and colleagues (1998) found no correlation between MRI findings and either cognitive or psychiatric status. Thus, as a tool for assigning mental syndromes to cerebral lupus, MRI leaves much to be desired. However, advances in imaging techniques may promise new revelations (Bosma et al. 2000; Rovaris et al. 2000).

Functional neuroimaging with single photon emission computed tomography (SPECT), positron emission tomography (PET), and magnetic resonance spectroscopy (MRS) has promise for recognizing the cerebral involvement of lupus. Early studies suggested reduced cerebral blood flow and metabolism associated with encephalopathy or psychosis and multifocal abnormalities varying with clinical state (Kushner et al. 1990; Pinching et al. 1978). Kodama and colleagues (1995) found a strong correlation between bilateral frontal blood flow deficits by SPECT and active psychosis, with the SPECT abnormality disappearing upon clinical remission; two (of three) control patients who showed this pattern developed an encephalopathy shortly afterward. This pattern of perfusion deficit may result from systemic cytokine elevations (Meyers et al. 1994). However, a high rate of SPECT abnormalities is consistently found without correlation to clinical evidence of cerebral disease (Colamussi et al. 1995; Emmi et al. 1993; Kao et al. 1999; Maeshima et al. 1992; Nossent et al. 1991; Postiglione et al. 1998; Rubbert et al. 1993; Totta et al. 1996). Whether such findings represent otherwise undetected cerebral SLE or false positives is unknown. Conceivably an endothelial alteration related to disease, though not necessarily pathogenic itself, produces a change in handling of the SPECT tracer. In any event, at the present time SPECT data are an uncertain basis for clinical decision making (Sibbitt et al. 1999).

PET discloses a similar high rate of abnormal metabolism (Sibbitt et al. 1999), again without clear concurrence with clinical, structural imaging, or serological findings (Sailer et al. 1997). Although some data suggest a potential role for PET (Weiner et al. 2000), the nonspecific nature of PET data and the expense and restricted availability of the technique limit its present clinical utility. MRS showed abnormalities related to disease activity, with biochemical indices suggesting neuronal loss, in several studies (Davie et al. 1995; Sibbitt and Sibbitt 1993). Even brain regions appearing normal by MRI may show neurochemical abnormalities (Brooks et al. 1997; Sabet et al. 1998). The available data are insufficient to gauge the role of these technologies for diagnostic purposes.

CSF in patients with active cerebral involvement shows pleocytosis in a minority of patients; there were only two cases of pleocytosis in 51 episodes of CNS disease in one series (Gibson and Myers 1976). Considering all patients with cerebral lupus together, about a quarter have an abnormal blood-brain barrier, and a quarter or more have intrathecal oligoclonal IgG synthesis (McLean et al. 1995; Winfield et al. 1983). The rate of these abnormalities may be much higher in patients with diffuse dysfunction (Hirohata et al. 1985; Weiss et al. 1970). In contrast with pleocytosis and elevated protein, the specificity of which are low in this setting, an elevated IgG index[1] marks intrathecal IgG synthesis. When immunoglobulins leak into the CSF from the serum, this figure is normal, but Q albumin,[2] a measure of blood-brain barrier function, is elevated. The presence of oligoclonal bands may be useful in identifying diffuse cerebral involvement (West et al. 1995). However, demyelinating disease, infection, carcinomatous meningitis, and paraneoplastic syndromes can show similar patterns (Winfield et al. 1983). The infrequent finding of CSF antineuronal antibodies may be relatively specific for CNS lupus (West et al. 1995).

In summary, currently no simple means can assign neuropsychiatric disorders to brain physiology disturbed by cerebral lupus. Knowledgeable and experienced clinicians must interpret multiple laboratory measures of inflammatory activity and physiological or anatomical disruption in the context of the clinical findings. Infection and the consequences of systemic dysfunction (such as uremia and hypertension) always must be considered in the differential diagnosis. However, in the near future, there may be greater understanding of the pathogenesis of cerebral lupus, particularly regarding cytokines, and thus new diagnostic technologies.

## Treatment

The treatment of cerebral lupus is untested by controlled trials (Bruyn 1995; Trevisani et al. 2001). High-dose corticosteroids are the mainstay of management. Anticoagulants may be indicated for symptoms related to aPL. Cyclophosphamide, usually as intravenous (IV) pulse therapy, may be useful in severe cases (Neuwelt et al. 1995). Symptomatic treatment of mental symptoms, with antidepressants, antipsychotics, and electroconvulsive therapy, proceeds along standard lines (Fricchione et al. 1990).

## Antiphospholipid Antibody Syndrome (Hughes Syndrome)

The early recognition of the biological false-positive test for syphilis in lupus was a forerunner of the identification of aPL as a feature of connective tissue disease. Current

---

[1]IgG index = (CSF IgG/serum albumin)/(serum IgG/CSF albumin). The upper limit of normal is 0.76.

[2]Q albumin = (CSF albumin × 103)/serum albumin. The upper limit of normal is 9.0 (Hirohata et al. 1985).

practice requires evaluation for the presence of a lupus anticoagulant (which despite its name is prothrombotic), aCL, and antibodies to $\beta_2$-glycoprotein-1 (anti-$\beta_2$GP1). Both IgG and immunoglobulin M (IgM) aCL are relevant, and (especially in African Americans) IgG, IgM, and IgA anti-$\beta_2$GP1 should be sought as well (Carreras et al. 2000; Diri et al. 1999; Greco et al. 2000). Brey and colleagues (1993) noted that of patients with aPL and neurological syndromes, only 10%–14% met criteria for a diagnosis of lupus; perhaps half had a lupus-like syndrome without meeting the standard criteria. The remaining cases made up a primary aPL syndrome. Of the latter, Asherson and colleagues (1989) found 46% to be ANA-positive, although lacking other clinical or serological features of SLE. aPL may also occur as a consequence of neoplasia (Asherson 2000). The key systemic clinical features of aPL syndrome, whether primary or part of SLE, are arterial and venous thrombosis, thrombocytopenia, and recurrent spontaneous fetal loss.

Stroke is the most important neurological correlate of aPL (Chancellor et al. 1991; Levine et al. 1990); pathological data suggest that fibrin thrombi in small- to medium-sized vessels lead to infarction (Briley et al. 1989). Given the high prevalence of cardiac valvular abnormalities in patients with aPL, embolic events must be considered as well. Vasculitis is not seen, except when it is a separate consequence of an underlying disease such as lupus (Cervera et al. 1995). Multi-infarct dementia is a well-described consequence of stroke (Coull et al. 1987), but progressive dementia without recognized stroke also may occur (Asherson et al. 1987; Fukui et al. 2000; Harlé et al. 1992; Inzelberg et al. 1992; Van Horn et al. 1996). A subacute encephalopathy featuring confusion or obtundation, quadriparesis, and seizures may occur (Briley et al. 1989; Levine et al. 1990; Sunseri et al. 1990). Chorea occurs in the primary aPL syndrome, and in lupus it is undoubtedly associated with the presence of aPL (Bouchez et al. 1985; Cervera et al. 1997; Omdal and Roalsø 1992). However, it does not appear to be the result of cerebral infarction, as metabolism is increased and imaging sequelae of stroke are rarely found (Galanaud et al. 2000; Sundén-Cullberg et al. 1998). Binding of aPL to basal ganglia neurons was proposed (Asherson and Hughes 1988), and recent data suggest that aPL may have direct neuronal effects as well as causing damage by vascular thrombosis (Chapman et al. 1999).

aPL may be a risk factor for infarction in migraine (Cuadrado et al. 2000b; Silvestrini et al. 1994), but contrary to early speculation, migraine itself does not appear to be associated with aPL whether in or outside the setting of SLE (Markus and Hopkinson 1992; Montalbán et al. 1992; Sfikakis et al. 1998; Tsakiris et al. 1993). The presence of aPL in patients with epilepsy is of uncertain significance (Peltola et al. 2000; Verrot et al. 1997). A single report of the frequent presence of aCL in never-medicated psychotic patients (all asymptomatic for aPL syndrome) is also of uncertain significance (Schwartz et al. 1998).

A controversial issue is whether, or how often, aPL can produce a picture leading to a diagnosis of MS. The possibility of confusion between MS and connective tissue disease was recognized early under the rubric of "lupoid sclerosis" (Fulford et al. 1972). Subsequent investigations of the frequency of indicators of systemic autoimmunity in MS populations have been inconsistent. Some investigators concluded that aPL syndrome can closely mimic MS (Cuadrado et al. 2000a; IJdo et al. 1999); others feel that when aPL are present they are likely to be unrelated to the disease process (Cordoliani et al. 1998; Tourbah et al. 1998). Some patients with an MS-like illness and aPL appear to respond to anticoagulants (Ruiz-Irastorza and Khamashta 2000).

Other neurobehavioral presentations of primary aPL syndrome have been reported. Brey and colleagues (1993) noted anecdotally that episodic forgetfulness and confusion are common, and a case of transient global amnesia was reported (Montalbán et al. 1989). Gorman and Cummings (1993) described a patient with memory impairment and derealization and another with visual illusions and psychosis requiring psychiatric hospitalization. Aharon-Peretz and colleagues (1996) found cognitive impairment even in aPL cases without known neurological involvement; 3 of 20 (15%) patients had schizophreniform disorder, and 3 had a mood disorder. Jacobson and colleagues (1999) found neuropsychological impairment across a range of cognitive domains in asymptomatic middle-aged subjects who were aPL-positive. Nearly a third of the subjects showed impairment in seven or more tests of a nature and degree thought to be clinically significant. The pattern of impairment pointed to frontosubcortical dysfunction, but imaging data were not available in this study. A different investigation showed that aPL-positive subjects had cerebral atrophy and an increased prevalence of subcortical hyperintensities on MRI as compared with healthy control subjects (Hachulla et al. 1998). These cognitive findings correspond to the data cited above regarding the association of cognitive impairment in lupus with the presence of aPL.

Tests for aPL are indicated for young stroke patients as well as others with unexplained cerebrovascular disease, unexplained confusional states or dementia, chorea, or migrainous infarction. The finding of an unexplained false-positive reagin test for syphilis or elevated partial thromboplastin time (PTT) also should prompt aPL testing. Treatment is of uncertain efficacy, but low-dose aspirin and, for those with major clinical manifestations, long-term anticoagulation with warfarin are indicated (Greaves et al. 2000).

## Sjögren's Syndrome

Sjögren's syndrome (SS), or autoimmune exocrinopathy, is the sicca syndrome of dry mouth and dry eyes, often with the airways, vagina, and extraglandular viscera subclinically or symptomatically affected. Constitutional symptoms are common, and some patients with chronic fatigue syndrome have SS (Barendregt et al. 1998; Nishikai et al. 1996). The syndrome can accompany other rheumatic disease (secondary SS) or stand alone (primary SS). Salivary, lacrimal, and other exocrine glands are progressively infiltrated and destroyed by lymphocytes and plasma cells. Patients are at substantially increased risk of developing lymphoma. Clinical identification of sicca symptoms should be confirmed by a Schirmer test or rose bengal staining to assess dry eyes and by biopsy of minor salivary glands. Primary SS is a very common disease of older women; 1%–2% of older adults are thought to have definite SS and 12% possible SS, with the prevalence possibly even higher (Jacobsson et al. 1992). About one-half of SS patients have antibodies to Ro (SS-A) by gel double immunodiffusion, and one-third have antibodies to La (SS-B). Anti-La (SS-B) is almost never seen in the absence of anti-Ro (SS-A). Thus, about half of SS patients are seronegative for both anti-Ro (SS-A) and anti-La (SS-B). Anti-Ro (SS-A)-positive patients often have other autoantibodies, such as ANA and rheumatoid factor (Alexander 1992).

A peripheral neuropathy is common in SS, seen in perhaps one-quarter of patients (Gemignani et al. 1994; Mauch et al. 1994). The frequency of CNS involvement is controversial. Its prominence was initially stressed by Alexander and colleagues (Alexander 1993) in a highly select population of SS patients. Although some subsequent authors indicated that CNS disease in SS was rare (Binder et al. 1988; Ioannidis and Moutsopoulos 1999), reports from several other centers have now confirmed that important cerebral manifestations do occur, although the epidemiology of CNS disease remains to be fully clarified.

Dementia, in most cases with a subcortical pattern, was described by several groups (Caselli et al. 1999; Créange et al. 1992; Govoni et al. 1999; Kawashima et al. 1993; Montane de la Roque et al. 1990; Olsen et al. 1989). Selnes and colleagues (1985) examined 26 SS

patients in a tertiary care setting who were referred for neuropsychological assessment because of cognitive complaints. Twelve (46%) showed impaired attention and concentration or other disturbances. Cortical features, such as language impairment or an amnestic syndrome, were not found. Mauch and colleagues (1994) found mental slowing on a trail making test in 11 of 16 (69%) patients with primary SS and diminished visual memory in 4 of 16 (25%). Belin and colleagues (1999) found slowing, executive dysfunction, and memory impairment—a subcortical dementia—in all of 14 SS patients, only 4 of whom had a relevant history. Brain MRI showed subcortical hyperintensities in half the patients; SPECT showed periventricular and subcortical perfusion defects in all. Other studies also showed a high rate of SPECT abnormality (Kao et al. 1998; Lass et al. 2000). The consistency of results across methods and settings commands attention.

Psychiatric symptoms or personality disturbances have been reported, but methodological problems limit confidence in the conclusions. Drosos and colleagues (1989) found elevations in scores for hostility, "intropunitiveness," somatization, anxiety, depression, and obsessive-compulsiveness in patients with primary SS. None of the patients had evidence of CNS disease, and the disorders were attributed to a reaction to chronic illness. However, neuroimaging and clinical psychiatric evaluation were not performed. Malinow and colleagues (1985) used chart review and the Minnesota Multiphasic Personality Inventory (MMPI) to assess psychiatric status; depression was defined so as to include patients with depressed mood or depressive ideation with or without other features of a depressive syndrome. They found 25 of 40 (62.5%) SS patients had psychiatric disturbance and 19 had depression. Other mood and anxiety disturbances also were seen. Abnormalities on MMPI were common, with 23 of 30 (77%) showing at least one abnormal scale, most frequently hypochondriasis, depression, or hysteria. The lack of psychiatric evaluation, the absence of a control group, and the idiosyncratic definition of depression require these results to be considered preliminary. Hietaharju and colleagues (1990) also found MMPI elevations on at least one scale in 33 of 43 (77%) SS patients; again, the three scales most frequently abnormal were hypochondriasis, depression, and hysteria. No control group was studied, and the prevalence of clinical depressive illness was not assessed. Mauch and colleagues (1994) found elevations in "nervosity"—irritability, fatigability, and other psychosomatic disturbances—on a German personality inventory, but again clinical psychiatric data were not provided, and no control group was available. Belin and colleagues (1999) found "depression" in 4 of 12 patients and "emotional withdrawal" in 5 of 12, but these terms were undefined. Valtysdottir and colleagues (2000) administered a questionnaire rating anxiety and depression to 67 patients with primary SS. They scored significantly higher than a rheumatoid arthritis control group, with about a half showing anxiety scores and a third depression scores in the range suggestive of clinical disturbance. Quality of life was found to be substantially impaired, but no further clinical analyses were performed. In summary, abnormalities of psychiatric states and traits have an uncertain relation to the pathophysiology of the illness, and no distinctive profile has emerged as characteristic of SS. The roles of depressive illness, cognitive decline, subcortical disease, and chronic somatic illness in the abnormal findings are yet to be clarified.

Several other CNS disorders due to SS have been reported. Parkinsonism stands out as distinctive for SS among the rheumatic disorders (Walker et al. 1999), as does meningeal inflammation (Caselli et al. 1993, 1999; de la Monte et al. 1983; Gerraty et al. 1993; Li et al. 1999). Stroke (Bragoni et al. 1994; Olsen et al. 1989), dystonia (van den Berg et al. 1999), venous sinus thrombosis (Urban et al. 1994), cerebral vasculitis (Giordano et al. 1995; Sato et al. 1987), parenchymal inflammation comparable to that seen in paraneoplastic syndromes (Bakchine et al. 1991; Terao et al. 1994), and a relapsing-remitting multifocal disorder with clinical, imaging, and CSF features akin to MS (Berman et al. 1990; Lafforgue et al. 1993; Ménage et al. 1993; Ohtsuka et al. 1995; Tesar et al. 1992) are all reported.

The pathogenesis of many of these CNS disorders is likely to be an immune-mediated small-vessel vasculopathy. MRI showing multiple small white- and gray-matter T2 hyperintensities, even in asymptomatic patients, is consistent with this hypothesis (Coates et al. 1999; Manthorpe et al. 1992; Pierot et al. 1993). Intrathecal immunoglobulin synthesis is commonly seen, again even in patients without clinical CNS involvement, and suggests a cerebral inflammatory process; pleocytosis is less common (Vrethem et al. 1990). Whether antineuronal antibodies are related to CNS disease is uncertain. Moll and colleagues (1993) found that serum antineuronal antibodies were significantly more common in SS patients with "major neurological complications," such as seizures, focal signs, altered level of consciousness, psychosis, and severe depression, than in those without such findings. Spezialetti and colleagues (1993), however, did not confirm this result. In the latter large but highly select series, neither antiribosomal P nor antineuronal antibodies were associated with CNS involvement. However, anti-Ro (SS-A)-positive SS patients may have more frequent and more severe CNS disease (Alexander et al. 1994). Limited neuropathological data show a small-vessel vasculopathy, always including venules, accompanied by mononuclear cell infiltrates in the meninges and choroid plexus (Alexander 1993). The inflammation surrounds the blood vessels and in some cases invades the vessel wall; white matter is preferentially involved.

Treatment of cerebral SS has not been subjected to controlled clinical trials, but steroids and pulse IV cyclophosphamide have been used.

## Vasculitides

The manifestations and classification of the vasculitides can be bewildering to the nonspecialist. The systemic vasculitides and their CNS presentations are rare problems in neuropsychiatric practice, and only a brief description is provided. Vasculitis primarily involving the CNS is discussed at greater length. Schmidley (2000) recently comprehensively reviewed the topic of central nervous system vasculitis.

*Polyarteritis nodosa* (PAN) and microscopic polyangiitis involve small- and medium-sized arteries of visceral organs, muscle, skin, and testes. Current proposals distinguish necrotizing vasculitis involving only medium-sized arteries (classic PAN) from that in which small vessels with or without medium-sized vessels are affected (microscopic polyangiitis) (Jennette et al. 1994). According to this nomenclature, glomerulonephritis is characteristic of microscopic polyangiitis and is absent in PAN. The distinction is of pathophysiological importance because microscopic polyangiitis is typically accompanied by antineutrophil cytoplasmic antibody (ANCA), whereas ANCA is seen in only about 20% of patients with PAN (Jennette and Falk 1995; Kallenberg et al. 1994). The literature addressing cerebral complications of PAN largely predates this diagnostic distinction, although cerebral dysfunction may be common in microscopic polyangiitis as well (Savage et al. 1985).

Classic PAN is most common in middle-aged men. Fever, weight loss, fatigue; new hypertension; purpura, ulcers, livedo reticularis; abdominal pain, hematemesis, melena; and myocardial ischemia or congestive heart failure may be seen. Vasa nervorum of peripheral nerves are commonly affected, with resulting mononeuritis multiplex or polyneuropathy. The erythrocyte sedimentation rate (ESR) is elevated, and a leukocytosis is present. Hepatitis B or C antigen and antibody are frequently present. Mesenteric and renal arteriography, with the distinctive finding of saccular aneurysm, is the gold standard for diagnosis. PAN affects the CNS in substantially fewer than half the cases (Fieschi et al. 1998). CNS disease is rarely present initially and is always accompanied by systemic manifestations; headache is common. A diffuse encephalopathy may present with a confusional state, progressive dementia, or psychotic manifestations. Stroke may occur with consequent focal deficits.

*Takayasu's arteritis* involves the aorta and its branches. Young women are most commonly affected. Constitutional symptoms and features referable to systemic arterial occlusion are characteristic; distal extremity pulses are often absent. Orthostatic symptoms, including syncope, are common. The ESR is elevated in most patients early in the course; angiography confirms the diagnosis; and ANCA is absent. With regard to neuropsychiatric symptoms, headache occurs in about half of the patients. Transient ischemic attack (TIA) or stroke, which occur infrequently, may be due to carotid stenosis, renovascular hypertension with hemorrhage, or subclavian steal (Ferro 1998).

*Giant cell arteritis* is characterized by granulomatous inflammation of medium-sized and large arteries, in particular branches of the external carotid artery. However, different pathological pictures are possible (Moore 1995). The pathogenesis is uncertain but may involve an immune reaction to a (perhaps altered) constituent of the blood vessel associated with elevation of serum IL-6 (Hunder et al. 1993; Roche et al. 1993). ANCA is absent. It is a disease of late life, with a female predominance. Fever and constitutional symptoms, polymyalgia rheumatica (symmetrical proximal myalgia and arthralgia), jaw claudication, scalp and particularly temporal artery pain and tenderness, and headache are clinical hallmarks. Loss of vision from vascular occlusion is a severe but often preventable complication, mandating aggressive evaluation of the older patient who has new headache. The ESR is usually elevated. Temporal artery biopsy—with due regard to the possibility of false negatives—is advisable for tissue confirmation before committing a patient to long-term high-dose steroid treatment. Stroke may occur from cervical vessel occlusion, and stroke from involvement of intracranial vessels occurs rarely (Imakita et al. 1993; Mclean et al. 1993).

Early investigators (Andrews 1966; Paulley and Hughes 1960; Vereker 1952) observed that an encephalopathy, with "madness (confusion, depression, dementia)" (Paulley and Hughes 1960, p. 1562), was common. In a study of 76 patients, 35 (46%) had "mental symptoms prominent" and 12 (16%) "mental symptoms predominant" (Paulley and Hughes 1960). Depression was said to be particularly characteristic in the prodromal period. In view of the rarity of intracranial vascular involvement, an encephalopathy due to systemic inflammatory activity, perhaps elevated IL-6, may explain these observations. Subsequent investigators (Caselli 1990; Caselli et al. 1988) occasionally found an encephalopathy but did not confirm the prominence of mental manifestations, although Berlit (1992) noted a "depressive syndrome" in 9 of 49 patients (18%). Giant cell arteritis should be considered in the differential diagnosis of a confusional state of obscure origin or other psychiatric symptoms with an elevated ESR in a patient older than age 50 years, even in the absence of the classic manifestations such as headache (Johnson et al. 1997; Shenberger et al. 1981).

*Wegener's granulomatosis* (WG) is a necrotizing granulomatous small-vessel vasculitis primarily of the upper and lower respiratory tract; glomerulonephritis is characteristic, and skin and ocular involvement is common. The peak incidence is in late midlife, with upper respiratory tract symptoms such as sinus disease predominating in the presentation. c-ANCA (antiproteinase 3) is present in as many as 90% of cases, and most of the remainder have p-ANCA (antimyeloperoxidase) (Kallenberg et al. 1994). The brain may be involved by direct extension of granulomatous lesions from the upper respiratory tract or by vasculitis. Headache, usually of sinus or ocular origin, and mononeuropathy multiplex (including cranial neuropathies) or polyneuropathy are common (Nishino et al. 1993a). Cerebral disease, however, is rare. MRI most commonly demonstrates diffuse meningeal involvement (Murphy et al. 1999). Stroke and encephalopathy may be due to intracranial arteritis (Bajema et al. 1997; Nordmark et al. 1997; Satoh et al. 1988). Giant cell arteritis rarely may be mimicked by temporal artery involvement by WG (Nishino et al. 1993b; Small and Brisson 1991).

The *Churg-Strauss syndrome* comprises asthma, allergic rhinitis, eosinophilia, and a systemic vasculitis affecting small- or medium-sized vessels. It is a disease primarily of early adult life but can occur at any age. Constitutional symptoms, fever, arthralgias, weakness, skin lesions, and visceral involvement reflect the vasculitic process. p-ANCA is present in most patients (Lhote et al. 1998). Mononeuritis multiplex or polyneuropathy occurs in the majority of patients. Cranial neuropathies, including ischemic optic neuropathy, are reported. An encephalopathy or stroke due to cerebral vasculitis occurs occasionally (Ferro 1998; Fieschi et al. 1998).

*Cogan's syndrome* is the concurrence of interstitial keratitis and vestibuloauditory dysfunction. Other parts of the eye are unaffected, and redness, pain, photophobia, and visual disturbance respond to topical treatment. Vertigo, tinnitus, and ataxia are succeeded by deafness. Features of systemic inflammation, including constitutional symptoms and elevated ESR, are common. CNS involvement, manifested by meningoencephalitis, altered mental states, seizures, and stroke, occurs rarely (Bicknell and Holland 1978; Calopa et al. 1991; Haynes et al. 1980; Karni et al. 1991; Vollertsen et al. 1986).

*Primary*, or *isolated, angiitis of the CNS* (PACNS) is an increasingly recognized disorder. Previously called granulomatous arteritis, the disorder has pathology sufficiently diverse that this designation is inappropriate. Small leptomeningeal and cerebral arteries (and to a lesser extent veins) are involved in a focal and segmental pattern. The vessel lesions involve lymphocytic, plasma cell, and histiocytic infiltration and necrosis, with giant cells often present. Granulomas are not seen in all patients or in all involved areas in every patient (Lie 1992). Onset is usually in midlife and may be gradual or sudden. Headache, a diffuse encephalopathy, and focal neurological features with or without the time course of stroke are characteristic (Schmidley 2000). In patients with biopsy-proven isolated cerebral angiitis, progressive alteration of the mental state due to involvement of cortical and leptomeningeal vessels dominates the clinical picture. Patients with angiographically diagnosed disease differ clinically from patients with pathologically proven disease; in the former group, there are more females, stroke is more common, the CSF shows less inflammation, and the course is more benign (Abu-Shakra et al. 1994; Calabrese et al. 1993; Rhodes et al. 1995). Some cases falling into a category of acute benign cerebral angiopathy may be vasculitic, but others may result from migraine, an abnormal cerebral arterial response to systemic hypertension, or other noninflammatory processes (Berger et al. 1995; Call et al. 1988; Michel et al. 1985).

Routine laboratory studies give no evidence of systemic inflammation, except that the ESR is occasionally elevated (Lie 1992; Vollmer et al. 1993). MRI often shows infarction or nonspecific T2 hyperintensities, usually in white matter. However, the sensitivity of MRI for the disease may be as low as 76% (Alhalabi and Moore 1994; Ehsan et al. 1995), and the MRI findings are entirely nonspecific. Angiographically abnormal territories may show no MRI abnormality (Greenan et al. 1992). Angiography may show segmental arterial narrowings and dilations ("beading") along with small-vessel occlusions and collateral formation. However, the sensitivity of angiography for tissue-proven PACNS may be as low as 36% (Alrawi et al. 1999). Pathologically proven disease may be angiographically invisible because of sole involvement of small vessels. Moreover, the angiographic findings are nonspecific, being seen also in vasospasm (e.g., after subarachnoid hemorrhage or with pheochro-

mocytoma), infectious vasculitis, angiotropic lymphoma (neoplastic angioendotheliosis), and drug-induced angiopathy. Magnetic resonance angiography, in its present technological state, is inadequate for the diagnosis of vasculitis. CSF characteristically shows a mild lymphocytic pleocytosis and elevated protein (Calabrese et al. 1997). An elevated IgG index and oligoclonal bands have been observed (Pou Serradell et al. 1995). In one series of 30 patients, all had abnormal CSF (Duna and Calabrese 1995). Biopsy has limited sensitivity, estimated at only 75% (Calabrese and Duna 1995). Biopsy material should include both leptomeningeal and cortical tissue. Treatment of biopsy-proven disease probably should include corticosteroids and cyclophosphamide (Calabrese et al. 1997). However, some patients with biopsy-proven angiitis may do well without specific treatment (Berger et al. 1995), and other patients, especially those described above as having a more benign process, may require a short course of corticosteroids or antivasospastic therapy but not immunosuppression (Calabrese et al. 1997).

*Drug-induced vasculitis* involving or confined to the brain is uncommon but well characterized. Citron and colleagues (1970) described 14 polysubstance abusers with a systemic necrotizing angiitis; 4 had neurological manifestations. The histopathology in four fatal cases was identical to that of PAN (as then defined); one or two of these cases had cerebral involvement, with encephalopathy and headache. Amphetamine was thought to be the most likely culprit, and later case reports confirmed that stimulant drugs, including both drugs of abuse such as cocaine and over-the-counter agents such as phenylpropanolamine, are most commonly responsible for this disorder (Calabrese and Duna 1996). In one case reported as hallucinogen-induced, abuse of other drugs was likely (Heazlewood et al. 1981).

Many case reports relied only on angiography for diagnosing vasculitis. Because stimulant drugs can cause vasospasm angiographically indistinguishable from vasculitis, a definitive determination of drug-induced cerebral vasculitis should be based on pathological diagnosis (see Table 24–3). Indeed, in some cases where there was clinical suspicion of drug-induced cerebral vasculitis, cerebral biopsy in patients failed to show vasculitis (Forman et al. 1989; Martin et al. 1995). Aggarwal and colleagues (1996) and Nolte and colleagues (1996) found no evidence of vasculitis in a total of 31 autopsied patients with cocaine-associated intracranial hemorrhage.

Even short-term use of drugs may produce vasculitis. Ischemic or hemorrhagic stroke in the drug abuser need not imply vasculitis, but progressive dysfunction, persistent headache, and encephalopathy raise suspicion. Angiography for all drug abusers who have had a stroke

**TABLE 24–3.** Tissue-proven cases of drug-induced cerebral vasculitis

| Reference | Drugs of abuse | ESR/WBC | CSF | Angiogram | Neuropathology |
|---|---|---|---|---|---|
| Citron et al. 1970 | Amphetamines, barbiturates, heroin | ?/16,000 | ? | ? | Necrotizing arteritis |
| Weiss et al. 1970 | Amphetamines | ?/5,800 | ? | No vasculitis | Walls of small vessels infiltrated by lymphocytes |
| Rumbaugh et al. 1971 | Barbiturates | ? | ? | Small-vessel occlusions | Round cells in vessel wall |
| Kessler et al. 1978 | Heroin, cocaine, amphetamines | 13/24,600 | ? | Beading | Leukocytes in vessel walls and necrosis of small arteries |
| Bostwick 1981 | Heroin, cocaine, amphetamines | 25/6,800 | ? | Occlusion or narrowing of internal carotids | Large-artery thrombosis and few infiltrating lymphocytes |
| Glick et al. 1987 | Phenylpropanolamine | 14/N | ? | Segmental narrowing of small, medium, large arteries | Necrotizing vasculitis of small arteries and veins, PMNLs in intima, fragmentation of elastic lamina |
| Krendel et al. 1990 | Cocaine | 85/N | N | Right middle cerebral occlusions, basilar occlusion, no beading | Vasculitis of small cortical vessels, multinucleated cells, no granulomas |
| Krendel et al. 1990 | Cocaine | 108/N | ? | ? | Lymphocytic infiltration of small vessels, no systemic vasculitis |
| Yin 1990 | Ephedrine | ? | ? | Segmental irregularity of small and medium arteries | Necrotizing small-artery vasculitis with PMNLs in intima |
| Fredericks et al. 1991 | Cocaine | N/N | Protein 185, lymphocytes 10 | ? | Lymphocytes in walls of small arteries |
| Morrow and McQuillen 1993 | Cocaine | ?/16,000 | ? | ? | Infiltration of small-vessel walls with lymphocytes and few PMNLs, no systemic vasculitis |
| Merkel et al. 1995 | Cocaine | 32/N | ? | No vasculitis | Nonnecrotizing leukocytoclastic angiitis |
| Merkel et al. 1995 | Cocaine | 20/N | ? | Segmental narrowing in medium-sized branches | PMNLs in walls of small arterioles and veins |
| Bane et al. 1999 | Physeptone | ?/? | ? | ? | Lymphocytic vasculitis at margin of hemorrhage, no evidence of infection |

*Note.* ? = unreported; N = normal; PMNLs = polymorphonuclear leukocytes.

has been recommended (Case Records of the Massachusetts General Hospital 1993). Laboratory tests are often nonspecific or unhelpful. ESR may be normal or elevated, and other studies may be unrevealing. CSF may be normal or may show an inflammatory process. Angiography may show vasculitic changes, but as previously noted, these may be indistinguishable from those of spasm due to stimulant drugs. Biopsy may help determine the necessity for treatment more aggressive than calcium channel blockers and a short course of corticosteroids (Calabrese and Duna 1996; Merkel et al. 1995).

## Sneddon's Syndrome

Sneddon's syndrome, a rare disorder, is the concurrence of cerebrovascular disease with the skin lesion livedo reticularis (or livedo racemosa). The nomenclature of the skin lesion has been confusing, but the phenomenon is agreed upon: a violaceous, reticulated pattern seen predominantly on the trunk and lower extremities, never the extremities only (Francès and Piette 2000). A similar but more benign lesion, called cutis marmorata by some (and called livedo reticularis by those who refer to the more ominous lesion as livedo racemosa), has a more regular shape and unbroken "fishnet" pattern and disappears with warming of the skin. Livedo reticularis is seen with many rheumatic diseases as well as with infection, neoplasia, and hematological disorders (Bruyn 1989). In Sneddon's syndrome, livedo reticularis is accompanied by nonspecific cerebral symptoms, notably headache and vertigo, then recurrent episodes of transient ischemia and stroke (Stockhammer et al. 1993). Deep white-matter changes are common. Vascular dementia often ensues (Ceccaldi et al. 1993; Weissenborn et al. 1989, 1996), even without clinically apparent stroke (Devuyst et al. 1996; R.A. Wright and Kokmen 1999). Cardiac valvular thickening is common (Tourbah et al. 1997b). Acrocyanosis, Raynaud's phenomenon, and seizures are inconstant features (Rebollo et al. 1983). Some data suggest subclinical involvement of other organs such as kidneys and heart (Pellat et al. 1976; Zelger et al. 1993).

The age at onset is usually in the second through the fourth decade; females are more often affected than males (Rebollo et al. 1983; Stockhammer et al. 1993; Weissenborn et al. 1989). Familial, apparently autosomal dominant cases are repeatedly mentioned in the literature (Pettee et al. 1994; Rebollo et al. 1983; Scott and Boyle 1986). Angiography commonly shows medium- and large-vessel occlusive disease, sometimes with evidence of extensive collateralization, including formation of moya-moya vessels (Bruyn 1989; Rebollo et al. 1983). Skin histopathology shows thrombotic vessel occlusions and proliferation of smooth muscle cells; an endothelial inflammatory lesion may be an initial stage of the process (Zelger et al. 1992, 1993). Histopathological data about the cerebral vasculature are limited. In one autopsied case, lesions like those in the skin were seen, including "endothelitis" (Pinol Aguad et al. 1975, cited in Zelger et al. 1993). In another, only "endarteritis obliterans" was seen, without inflammatory features (Rautenberg et al. 1988). In a thoroughly studied case, described without use of the term *Sneddon's syndrome*, cerebral vasculature showed fibrosis of small arteries along with granuloma formation in the most recent lesions (Pellat et al. 1976). In two instances, brain biopsy disclosed normal vessels (D.H. Geschwind et al. 1995; Scott and Boyle 1986). Another brain biopsy showed leptomeningeal granuloma formation (Boortz-Marx et al. 1995).

A role for aPL in pathogenesis was initially suggested

by Jonas and colleagues (1986) and Levine and colleagues (1988). Subsequent reports indicated patients sometimes had and sometimes lacked aPL. Kalashnikova and colleagues (1990) found aPL in 6 of 17 (35%) examined patients; Stockhammer and colleagues (1993), in none of 17 patients; Sitzer and colleagues (1995), in 3 of 13 (23%) patients; and Tourbah and colleagues (1997a) in 11 of 26 (42%). aPL-positive and aPL-negative patients are at most subtly different in clinical presentation (Francès et al. 1999; Tourbah et al. 1997a). Possibly aPL is important in pathogenesis but absent at the time of clinical presentation (Hughes 1993); repeated testing for aPL is necessary as the level may fluctuate (Pettee et al. 1994). However, in some cases even repeated tests failed to disclose aPL (Boortz-Marx et al. 1995; D.H. Geschwind et al. 1995), and other routes to occlusive vasculopathy seem likely in some instances of Sneddon's syndrome.

The treatment of Sneddon's syndrome remains uncertain. Antiplatelet agents, anticoagulation with warfarin, steroids, plasmapheresis, and immunosuppressants have all been tried without definite evidence for efficacy (Rautenberg et al. 1988; Thomas et al. 1993; Zelger et al. 1993).

## Sydenham's Chorea and PANDAS

Chorea is a diagnostic feature of rheumatic fever but usually appears weeks or months after the precipitating streptococcal infection, after other elements of rheumatic fever have abated. Swedo and colleagues (Swedo 1994; Swedo et al. 1993) described how the chorea may be preceded by acute or subacute onset of mental change in children or adolescents, featuring emotional lability, obsessive-compulsive symptoms, inattentiveness, and separation anxiety. At least a mild degree of emotional lability and inattentiveness is very common (Moore 1996). The symptoms generally last for some months and disappear entirely, but brief recurrences in subsequent months and occasional late recurrences years after the childhood illness are recognized (Swedo et al. 1993). The rate of psychopathology, particularly schizophrenia, in adulthood after childhood Sydenham's chorea may be elevated (Wilcox and Nasrallah 1986, 1988), and chorea gravidarum and oral contraceptive–induced chorea may develop on a background of Sydenham's chorea (Nausieda 1986). These disorders may be due to altered striatal dopamine responsiveness (Nausieda et al. 1983). A preponderance of females with Sydenham's chorea is seen in postpubertal children only, suggesting (as do chorea gravidarum and oral contraceptive–induced chorea) a role of estrogens in modulating dopamine responsiveness (Nausieda et al. 1980; Thiebaut 1968).

Throat culture may reveal group A β-hemolytic streptococci (GABHS), and the anti–streptolysin O titer is elevated. The ESR may be elevated, and ANA may be transiently present. Two studies (Kiessling et al. 1993; Swedo et al. 1993) found antineuronal antibodies. Although the presence of antineuronal antibodies significantly distinguished patients from control subjects, up to 50% of control subjects showed antineuronal antibodies; this work requires replication. aCL are absent, an important finding in view of the relation of aPL to chorea in lupus (Cervera et al. 1997). CSF is entirely normal in Sydenham's chorea, with immunoglobulin abnormalities absent (Gledhill and Thompson 1990). EEG is commonly abnormal, usually diffusely slow (Gledhill and Thompson 1990; Swedo et al. 1993; Thiebaut 1968). Quantitative MRI in one study demonstrated increased basal ganglion size, a finding taken to suggest inflammation (Giedd et al. 1995). Functional imaging with PET showed striatal hypermetabolism (as in aPL syndrome, discussed previously) in three patients (Goldman et al. 1993; Weindl et al. 1993). MRS also pointed to basal ganglion disease in a single patient (Lynch and Stack 1996).

Contemporary neuropathological studies of this nonfatal disorder are scanty. Older data showed nonspecific, often vascular abnormalities generally located in the cerebral cortex as well as the striatum (Breutsch 1944; Colony and Malamud 1956; de Gortari et al. 1947; Neuberger 1947; Thiebaut 1968). Lesions in fatal cases may differ from those in the more typical cases, and some of the older reported cases may not be Sydenham's chorea as currently defined (Colony and Malamud 1956). Of greatest importance is the finding of an antibody cross-reactive to GABHS and neurons in the caudate and subthalamic nuclei (Husby et al. 1976). This finding, however, did not rely on pathological material from Sydenham cases and has not been replicated.

The occurrence of obsessive and compulsive symptoms and of tics is of particular interest. Swedo and colleagues (1994) reported the preliminary observations that children with obsessive-compulsive disorder (OCD) often have chorea, show both antineuronal antibodies and throat-culture positivity for GABHS, and respond to penicillin or plasmapheresis. Pursuit of these observations led to the description of pediatric autoimmune neuropsychiatric disorders associated with streptococcal infections, or PANDAS (Swedo et al. 1998). Criteria for this diagnosis include 1) presence of OCD or a tic disorder, 2) onset after age 3 years and before puberty, 3) abrupt onset or dramatic exacerbations, 4) temporal association of exacerbations with GABHS infection, and 5) presence of neurological signs (such as hyperactivity and adventitious movements) during exacerbations. Of children who met these criteria, boys outnumbered girls. Attention-deficit/hyperactivity disorder (ADHD) and mood and anxiety disorders were commonly present. Children with PANDAS carried an HLA marker for vulnerability to rheumatic fever as often as children with Sydenham's chorea and five times more often than the healthy comparison children (Swedo et al. 1997). Basal ganglia were larger than in comparison children (Giedd et al. 2000). Treatment with plasma exchange and intravenous immune globulin was shown to be helpful in a preliminary study (Perlmutter et al. 1999).

However, a number of concerns about this hypothesis remain. Some of the findings attributed to PANDAS may be prevalent in childhood tic or OCD irrespective of the other criteria for the syndrome. For example, the HLA marker for rheumatic fever found in PANDAS also was common in childhood OCD and Tourette's syndrome in general (Murphy et al. 1997). Antibodies to putamen (Singer et al. 1998) and to a neuronlike cell (Singer et al. 1999) were identified in children with Tourette's syndrome, yet the antibodies bore no distinct relation to antistreptococcal antibodies. Although this could mean that the role of streptococcal infection is much broader even than claimed, it could also mean that the findings in PANDAS result from an unrecognized confound. Peterson and colleagues (2000) suggested that the true association of antistreptococcal antibodies and increased basal ganglion volumes in childhood neuropsychiatric disorders was with ADHD, commonly comorbid with Tourette's syndrome and OCD but not specifically controlled for in the analyses of PANDAS. Thus the PANDAS hypothesis, although intriguing and heuristically powerful, remains controversial (Kurlan 1998). Certainly immunomodulatory treatment should be limited at present to controlled trials (Singer 1999).

The chorea of rheumatic fever responds to dopamine blockade, as do other types of chorea. Valproic acid appears to have a beneficial effect (Daoud et al. 1990), and steroids may have a role in treatment (Green 1978).

## Hashimoto's Encephalopathy

Rare patients with autoimmune thyroiditis and high antithyroid antibody titers show a subacutely evolving, relapsing-remitting encephalopathy, often with abrupt strokelike deteriorations. The encephalopathy is characterized by a confusional state or reduced level of consciousness, myoclonus, and seizures (Brain et al. 1966;

Ghika-Schmidt et al. 1996; Kothbauer-Margreiter et al. 1996). The encephalopathy can occur before thyroid disease is recognized or perhaps even present (Peschen-Rosin et al. 1999). Cases in which the mental manifestations were seen as psychotic, depressive, and hysterical were reported (Cohen et al. 1996; Peschen-Rosin et al. 1999). Cerebellar and spinal cord signs are seen rarely (Manto et al. 1996).

EEG shows generalized slowing, at times with frontal intermittent rhythmic delta activity, focal slowing, or triphasic waves (Henchey et al. 1995). CSF protein is often elevated, and intrathecal immunoglobulin synthesis is generally, but not always, absent. Neuroimaging is usually unrevealing, but diffuse or focal hyperintensities on T2-weighted images can be seen (Bohnen et al. 1997; McCabe et al. 2000). A case in which the 14–3–3 protein was found in the CSF is of importance, because the combination of subacute mental deterioration and myoclonus makes Hashimoto's encephalopathy an important differential diagnostic consideration for prion disease (Hernández Echevarría et al. 2000). The patients are generally euthyroid, and thyroid hormone abnormalities themselves cannot explain the encephalopathy. A case in which Graves' disease rather than Hashimoto's thyroiditis was present was reported (Cantón et al. 2000). An autoimmune vasculitis (Nolte et al. 2000) or encephalomyelitis (Henderson et al. 1987) may be the pathogenetic mechanism. The syndrome responds to steroids.

## Susac's Syndrome

This syndrome, initially described in 1979 (Susac et al. 1979) and later reported under several names, predominantly affects young women in the third and fourth decades of life. About one case in seven is in a male. The syndrome comprises encephalopathy, hearing loss, and occlusions of retinal artery branches, which may produce visual impairment (O'Halloran et al. 1998; Papo et al. 1998; Petty et al. 1998). Headache is common at onset. The encephalopathy may be acute and marked by confusion as well as psychosis, but the presentation may also be with subacutely evolving personality change and cognitive impairment. Susac (1994) noted that "these patients are often encountered on the psychiatric floor" (p. 591). Systemic features are characteristically absent, although fever, rash, arthralgia, and myalgia are occasional findings. The course is relapsing-remitting and self-limited, but residual dementia, visual and hearing impairment, and motor disability are common. EEG is slow, and MRI demonstrates multiple small gray- and white-matter hyperintensities on T2-weighted images, which may enhance with gadolinium. CSF protein is usually elevated, and sometimes a mild lymphocytic pleocytosis is present. The IgG index is occasionally elevated, but oligoclonal bands are absent. Angiography and serological testing are unrevealing.

The neuropathological basis of the syndrome is known from brain biopsy in a few cases (Bogousslavsky et al. 1989; Heiskala et al. 1988; Monteiro et al. 1985; Susac et al. 1979; Vila et al. 1995); no autopsy material has been reported. Perivascular inflammation with microinfarctions was found; vasculitis was not seen. Similar pathology can be found in muscle (Petty et al. 1998). The pathogenetic relation between this syndrome and other small-vessel noninflammatory vasculopathies remains uncertain. Treatment with steroids and, if needed, immunosuppressants is recommended (Petty et al. 1998), although some have favored a preliminary trial of aspirin and nimodipine (Papo et al. 1998; Susac 1994; Wildemann et al. 1996).

## Sarcoidosis

Sarcoidosis is a multiorgan disease that predominantly affects the lung; other manifestations include constitutional symptoms, lymphadenopathy, uveitis, skin lesions, parotiditis, and joint involvement. The pathology is noncaseating granulomatous inflammatory lesions containing giant cells. The etiology of the disorder is unknown. The nervous system is involved in a minority of cases, perhaps 5%. However, in patients with neurological manifestations as few as half have systemic involvement (Chapelon et al. 1990; Oksanen 1994; Stern et al. 1985), so that neurosarcoidosis can present a formidable diagnostic challenge.

The most common manifestations of neurosarcoidosis are cranial nerve palsies, notably optic neuropathy or facial nerve palsy, often bilateral (Sharma 1997; Zajicek et al. 1999). Peripheral neuropathy, seizures, hydrocephalus, and acute or chronic meningitis are relatively common features. Skeletal muscle involvement, although usually asymptomatic, may be indicated by abnormal muscle enzymes and electomyography and may provide an accessible site for biopsy proof of the diagnosis. Meningeal disease characteristically involves the basal meninges, so hypothalamic-pituitary dysfunction is common (Bullmann et al. 2000). Mass lesions of sarcoidosis can involve any portion of the neuraxis.

Mental manifestations of sarcoidosis may be more frequent than recognized (Oksanen 1994) and are potentially diagnostically puzzling. Dementia, personality change, and frontal syndromes are reported (Cordingley et al. 1981; Mendez and Zander 1992; Sanson et al. 1996; Schielke et al. 2001). Of interest are several reports of an amnestic syndrome due to localized granulomatous lesions (Hier et al. 1983; Thompson and Checkley 1981; Willigers and Koehler 1993). Several cases of organic psychosis are recorded (John and Ovsiew 1996; O'Brien et al. 1994; Sabaawi et al. 1992; Tate et al. 1993).

Gallium scanning may demonstrate systemic inflammation in a patient with neuropsychiatric symptoms; standard chest radiographs may suffice to demonstrate lung involvement. Brain MRI sensitively detects abnormalities, including nonspecific periventricular white-matter hyperintensities on T2 images (Miller et al. 1988; Zajicek et al. 1999). Gadolinium contrast is crucial and may show dramatic meningeal enhancement in an otherwise normal scan. CSF typically shows a mild lymphocytic pleocytosis with elevated protein and often an increased IgG with oligoclonal bands (McLean et al. 1995; Zajicek et al. 1999). The glucose may be low, simulating infection. Angiotensin-converting enzyme may be elevated in the CSF as it is in the serum. However, the specificity of this finding is uncertain (Scott 1993). Biopsy proof of the diagnosis is often desirable; bronchoscopic lung biopsy and skin or muscle biopsy are approaches that may avoid brain biopsy in appropriate instances.

## Behçet's Disease

Behçet's disease comprises oral and genital aphthous ulcers and uveitis, with a broad range of systemic features, including arthritis, gastrointestinal symptoms, cutaneous vasculitis, and thrombophlebitis. Genital ulcerations primarily involve the scrotum and leave residual scars. The disease affects predominantly young adult males, with a geographic or ethnic predilection for the Mediterranean basin and Japan (Benamour et al. 1990). The brain is involved in a minority of cases, for example, 5% (Benamour et al. 1990) and 16% (Serdaroglu et al. 1989) in two large Middle Eastern series. Rarely, cerebral manifestations are the presenting feature (Akman-Demir et al. 2000; Gille et al. 1990). Meningoencephalitis, focal syndromes especially referable to the brain stem, and cerebral venous thrombosis with elevated intracranial pressure are characteristic (Akman-Demir et al. 2000; Kidd et al. 1999). Headache is common but usually benign.

Organic mental changes are common. In a review by

Kawakita and colleagues (1967), 9 of 42 (21%) patients had dementia, and 20 (48%) patients had "emotional disturbances"; depression was seen in 4 patients and visual hallucinations in 4 patients. One was called "schizophrenia-like." Other Japanese series suggested that up to half (Arai et al. 1994) or more than half (Motomura et al. 1980) of patients with brain involvement have dementia or personality change. Pseudobulbar palsy with pathological affect was particularly noted. In the series of Rougemont and colleagues (1982), 3 of 24 (13%) patients presented predominant mental disturbance, notably confusion and hallucinations. Akman-Demir and colleagues (2000) found that 87 of 200 (44%) patients with neuro-Behçet syndrome had behavioral change, described as apathy in one-third and disinhibition in two-thirds. The cognitive findings are of subcortical damage, with executive dysfunction, personality change, a disorder of memory retrieval, and attentional impairment (Akman-Demir et al. 2000; Öktem-Tanör et al. 1999). Neuropsychological impairment may be seen before MRI-visible cerebral lesions and tends to be chronic and progressive (Öktem-Tanör et al. 1999).

The presentation and relapsing-remitting or chronic course can mimic MS; the clinical key to the differential diagnosis is in the characteristic systemic features of Behçet's disease. In contrast with MS, internuclear ophthalmoplegia is rare in Behçet's disease, as is a cerebellar syndrome without pyramidal signs (Serdaroglu 1998). MRI characteristically shows brain-stem and basal ganglion involvement, often extensive. In chronic cases, brain-stem atrophy is characteristic. In hemispheric white matter, the lesions are equally distributed between periventricular and other areas; in contrast, MS features predominantly periventricular, and lupus predominantly nonperiventricular, involvement (Çoban et al. 1999; Koçer et al. 1999). The CSF shows a moderate neutrophilic or lymphocytic pleocytosis and elevated protein; CSF synthesis of immunoglobulins is common but oligoclonal bands infrequent (Akman-Demir et al. 2000; Kidd et al. 1999; Serdaroglu 1998). Occasionally, CSF glucose is low (Gille et al. 1990; Rougemont et al. 1982; Serdaroglu et al. 1989). Persistent elevation of CSF IL-6 may mark the inflammatory process responsible for progressive disease (Hirohata et al. 1997). Evoked potentials may be abnormal in any modality (Akman-Demir et al. 2000; Kidd et al. 1999). Functional neuroimaging with SPECT may reveal frontal and other abnormalities in patients with mental change, even in the absence of abnormalities on MRI (Markus et al. 1992). An elevated ESR and other indicators of inflammation are present, but collagen-vascular serologies are negative. Neuropathologically, focal areas of gliosis and perivenular infiltration of lymphocytes and plasma cells are seen on a background of mild inflammatory activity throughout the CNS (Serdaroglu 1998). Corticosteroids and immunosuppressants are the mainstays of treatment.

## Celiac Disease

Celiac disease (gluten-sensitive enteropathy) can cause a symmetrical polyarthritis, skin lesions (dermatitis herpetiformis), and constitutional symptoms, as well as the more characteristic intestinal disturbance with malabsorption. Furthermore, bowel symptoms are absent or occult in many gluten-sensitive individuals, perhaps more than half (Marsh 1995). The disease may be immune-mediated, with antigliadin and antiendomysial antibodies seen in more than 90% of untreated symptomatic cases (Michalski and McCombs 1994). Screening with IgA endomysial antibody is sensitive and specific, but bowel biopsy remains the gold standard for diagnosis (Trier 1998).

Several CNS syndromes have been described in association with celiac disease. A syndrome of occipital calcification and epilepsy, usually presenting in childhood before the recognition of celiac disease, is the most distinctive (Dickey 1994; Magaudda et al. 1993). Celiac disease may occur at an elevated rate in epileptic populations even in the absence of this distinctive syndrome (Cronin et al. 1998). Cerebellar degeneration, accompanied by other neurological features, including myoclonus, peripheral neuropathy, and sometimes cognitive impairment, was described (Hadjivassiliou et al. 1998; Kinney et al. 1982). Brain-stem encephalitis and CNS vasculitis also were reported in conjunction with celiac disease (Brücke et al. 1988; Mumford et al. 1996; Rush et al. 1986). Dementia as the presenting feature was reported in a Finnish series and a single American case (Beversdorf et al. 1996; Collin et al. 1991). Depressive symptoms may be disproportionately common in patients with celiac disease (Hallert and Åström 1982; Hallert and Derefeldt 1982).

Whether these disorders are due to malabsorption—of folate, vitamin E or $B_{12}$, monoamine precursors, or other nutrients—or to an immunological mechanism is controversial, but patients with progression of disease despite a gluten-free diet and vitamin replacement were clearly described (Bhatia et al. 1995; Collin et al. 1991). Hadjivassiliou and colleagues (1998) reported autopsy material showing lymphocytic infiltration in cerebellum and peripheral nerves. The diagnosis deserves consideration in unexplained dementia, epilepsy, and other neuropsychiatric syndromes, especially in the presence of weight loss or bowel symptoms, iron deficiency, or low serum folate or $B_{12}$ on routine laboratory testing.

## Rheumatoid Arthritis

Rheumatoid arthritis patients commonly have clinical or subclinical peripheral neuropathy, either a distal symmetric polyneuropathy or mononeuritis multiplex from rheumatoid vasculitis, which usually occurs late in the disease when joint inflammation is burnt out (Lanzillo et al. 1998; Rosenbaum 2001). Organic cerebral complications of rheumatoid arthritis are rare (Bathon et al. 1989; Singleton et al. 1995). Meningeal rheumatoid nodules are usually asymptomatic, but diffuse meningeal inflammation may present clinically with altered mental state, seizures, fever, cranial neuropathy, and an inflammatory pattern in the CSF. Cerebral vasculitis is rare and may occur with or without systemic vasculitis. Active synovitis may not be present at the time of CNS presentation. Cerebral disease also rarely may occur in the course of adult-onset Still's disease (Brücke et al. 1988). Curiously, a negative association between rheumatoid arthritis and idiopathic schizophrenia is well replicated, with a rate of rheumatoid arthritis in schizophrenic patients of only 29% of that expected (Oken and Schulzer 1999).

## Steroid-Induced Neuropsychiatric Disorder

Overt psychiatric syndromes are produced by glucocorticoid treatment in a small proportion of patients, estimated by Lewis and Smith (1983) to be 5.7%. Mood disturbance, either depressive or manic, is common and sometimes accompanied by psychotic features (Naber et al. 1996). Delirium also can occur. Sleep disturbance and sensory "flooding"—a sense of being overwhelmed by perceptual intensity—are characteristic and may presage a syndromal state. Subjective adverse reactions, involving both cognition and mood, are common and often hidden by patients and ignored by doctors (Patten et al. 1995; Reckart and Eisendrath 1990). The psychiatric symptoms characteristically appear early in the course of treatment and disappear rapidly when treatment is discontinued, although psychiatric symptoms may also occur as part of a glucocorticoid withdrawal syndrome (Wolkowitz et al. 1997). Cognitive disturbance is characterized by memory impairment, the pattern of which suggests hippocampal dysfunction (Keenan et al. 1996); defects in executive cognitive function are also found (Young et al.

1999). Rarely, the cognitive impairment is out of proportion to any psychiatric symptoms and may present as a "steroid dementia" (Varney et al. 1984). Apparent cases of irreversible cognitive toxicity were recorded (Wolkowitz et al. 1993). However, steroid treatment does not appear to contribute to observed cognitive abnormalities in patients with lupus (or presumably other rheumatic diseases) (Carbotte et al. 1986; Denburg et al. 1994; Ginsburg et al. 1992; Hay 1994; Kozora et al. 1996).

A dose of prednisone greater than 40 mg/day (or the equivalent) is more likely to be associated with psychiatric disturbance; at doses greater than 80 mg/day, as many as one patient in five shows severe psychiatric symptoms (Boston Collaborative Drug Surveillance Program 1972). Neither prior psychiatric illness nor a history of psychiatric symptoms due to steroids in a previous course of treatment appears to increase risk (Wolkowitz et al. 1993). In a study of asthmatic schizophrenic patients, steroid treatment did not appear to worsen psychotic symptoms (Sonin and Patterson 1984). The EEG in steroid psychosis sometimes shows slowing but may be normal (Wolkowitz et al. 1993).

Patients prescribed glucocorticoids should be warned of psychiatric side effects and asked about them during treatment (Reckart and Eisendrath 1990). Antipsychotic drugs, lithium, and electroconvulsive therapy are useful in appropriate circumstances, and lithium or perhaps other mood stabilizers may serve as prophylaxis; antidepressants may worsen manic or confusional symptoms (Patten and Neutel 2000; Wolkowitz et al. 1997). Alterations by exogenous glucocorticoids of a variety of neurotransmitters and neuropeptides may account for the mental changes (Piazza et al. 1996; Wolkowitz 1994).

## Neuroleptic-Induced Immunopathy

A variety of autoantibodies and a polyclonal increase in IgM are commonly seen in patients treated with chlorpromazine and other psychotropic drugs. Yannitsi and colleagues (1990) found ANA in 39.7% of 307 unselected chronic psychiatric patients; other autoantibodies, such as rheumatoid factor, anti-Ro, anti-La, and aCL, were not significantly more common in psychiatric patients than in healthy control subjects. ANA positivity was associated with an age greater than 55 years, female sex, and a diagnosis of schizophrenia; chlorpromazine was the only drug associated with a positive ANA. Canoso and colleagues (1990) found that the lupus anticoagulant was seen in 45% of chlorpromazine-treated patients and 13% of those treated with other antipsychotic drugs; aCL was seen in 34% and 16%, respectively; ANA was seen in

39% and 9%, respectively; and rheumatoid factor was seen in 50% of those taking chlorpromazine, 41% of those taking other phenothiazines, and 61% of those taking nonphenothiazine neuroleptics. An elevated IgM was seen in 27% of those taking chlorpromazine, 25% of those taking other phenothiazines, and 3% of those taking nonphenothiazine neuroleptics. Among other psychotropics, lithium was found to induce ANA and possibly antiparietal cell antibodies (Presley et al. 1976).

Thrombosis is usually not seen in association with drug-induced aPL in these patients (Canoso and de Oliveira 1988; Lillicrap et al. 1990), although rare instances may occur (Ducloux et al. 1999; El-Mallakh et al. 1988). A clinical drug-induced lupus syndrome is unusual (Canoso et al. 1990; Fabius and Gaulhofer 1971). The progressive increase in IgM may rarely lead to malignant transformation and Waldenström's macroglobulinemia, and discontinuation of chlorpromazine in any patient developing increased IgM was recommended (Zucker et al. 1990).

## Autoimmunity in Idiopathic Psychiatric Syndromes

Immune mechanisms in the idiopathic psychiatric disorders, especially schizophrenia, have come under increasing scrutiny in recent years (Kirch 1993). Features common to idiopathic psychiatric disorder and autoimmune disease, such as adolescent onset and relapsing-remitting course, suggest to some a pathophysiological relationship (Ganguli et al. 1995). Cytokines such as IL-1 and tumor necrosis factor-$\alpha$ play a role in brain development (Merrill 1992). Cytokines also have a role in regulating brain function, including stimulation of dopamine release by IL-2 (Alonso et al. 1993; Zalcman et al. 1994), alteration of neuroendocrine secretion (Goetzl et al. 1988), and evocation of the characteristic manifestations of systemic infection such as anorexia, fever, and fatigue (Faggioni et al. 1995). These discoveries increase the plausibility of a role for immune pathology in disorders such as schizophrenia and depression (Kronfol and Remick 2000).

Ganguli and colleagues (1993) found that schizophrenic patients have an elevated prevalence of autoimmune diseases compared with healthy control subjects; rheumatoid arthritis (Oken and Schulzer 1999) and possibly type I diabetes (Finney 1989) are interesting exceptions. Many investigators, even controlling for neuroleptic treatment, found an elevated prevalence of autoantibodies in schizophrenic or other psychotic patients, including ANA (Yannitsi et al. 1990), anti-DNA (Sirota et al. 1993b), anti-Smith (Sirota et al. 1993a), and aCL (Chengappa et al.

1991; Firer et al. 1994; Schwartz et al. 1998). Not all studies showed positive results, however (de Vries et al. 1994). Antibodies against brain tissue (Yang et al. 1994), nicotinic receptors (Mukherjee et al. 1994), nerve growth factor (Klyushnik et al. 1999), and a heat shock protein (Leykin et al. 1999) were reported; again, not all results are positive (Schott et al. 1998). Spivak and colleagues (1995) examined ANA status in relation to the presence of antihistone antibodies, as a marker of drug-induced autoimmunity, and neuroleptic treatment in a group of schizophrenic patients. Within that group of patients, 21% had a positive ANA, but no antihistone antibodies were found; ANA status was unrelated to neuroleptic treatment status. Villemain and colleagues (1988), however, found that antihistone antibodies in 6 of 51 (12%) schizophrenic patients were associated with low-titer ANA positivity.

P. Wright and colleagues proposed that women with a genetic predisposition produce an antibody response to influenza with the characteristic of crossing the placenta and fetal blood-brain barrier and altering neurodevelopment in a way that increases the risk of schizophrenia. Their research group found that thyrotoxicosis and insulin-dependent diabetes were significantly more common in the mothers of psychotic patients than in the mothers of control subjects (Gilvarry et al. 1996). (Their method could not verify that the diabetes was type I.) In a separate sample, they found that schizophrenic patients with a first-degree relative with schizophrenia were significantly more likely also to have a first-degree relative with an autoimmune disease (P. Wright et al. 1996). Further, there was an excess of insulin-dependent diabetes in the first-degree relatives of patients as compared with healthy control subjects. Thus, they concluded, familial schizophrenia behaves as an autoimmune disease does in respect of cosegregating with other autoimmune diseases within pedigrees.

Chengappa (1995) found a higher prevalence of autoantibodies in schizophrenic patients who had suffered obstetrical complications than in those who had not. Chengappa and colleagues (1992a, 1992b) also found an association between left-handedness and autoantibodies: two-thirds of left-handed but only one-quarter of right-handed, first-episode, neuroleptic-naive patients had autoantibodies. They proposed that early brain injury could lead to immune dysregulation and nonspecific polyclonal B cell activation. Parts of this hypothesis are supported by animal studies of the effects of brain lesions on immune function (Neveu 1992).

Increased circulating interleukin-2 receptor (IL-2R), together with decreased mitogen-stimulated in vitro IL-2 production, suggest in vivo T cell activation in schizophrenic patients (Bessler et al. 1995; Ganguli et al. 1993,

1995; Hornberg et al. 1995; Maes et al. 1994b). Rapaport and Lohr (1994) found that serum IL-2R was increased in neuroleptic-naive schizophrenic patients and that the higher levels of IL-2R were associated with the presence of tardive dyskinesia. Ganguli and colleagues (1995) further found that reduced IL-2 production was associated with earlier age at onset and more negative symptoms. In vitro IL-2 production was lower in schizophrenic patients who had autoantibodies (Ganguli et al. 1992) and was inversely correlated with the titer of antihippocampal antibodies (Yang et al. 1994). Serum IL-6 may be increased in schizophrenic patients (Ganguli et al. 1994; Maes et al. 1994a, 1995a). Schizophrenic patients may show lymphopenia, which correlated with poor outcome of treatment; patients with autoantibodies may show more prominent negative symptoms (Zorilla et al. 1996, 1998). Lymphopenia was proposed to be a trait marker, shared by family members, whereas monocytosis was associated with illness state (Zorilla et al. 1996).

Two studies examined CSF IL-2. Licinio and colleagues (1993) found elevated CSF IL-2 in 10 neuroleptic-free schizophrenic patients. McAllister and colleagues (1995) subsequently found that high CSF IL-2 predicted relapse following haloperidol withdrawal. IL-2 rises during stress, and its effects on dopamine release may mediate the precipitation of psychosis by stress. The pathological finding of activated microglia in schizophrenia further suggests a pathogenetic role for immune activation in psychiatric disorders (Bayer et al. 1999).

Evidence for a pathogenetic role of autoimmunity in depression is not impressive. Maes (1995; Maes et al. 1995b) summarized the substantial evidence, much from his own laboratory, for immune activation in depression. Autoantibodies in depressed patients may represent a nonspecific epiphenomenon of an activated immune system. Early studies suggested frequent ANA positivity in depressed patients (Deberdt et al. 1976; von Brauchitsch 1972). Maes and colleagues (1991) confirmed this finding and noted that aPL also are commonly present in depressed patients. However, despite statistical significance of their association with depression, these autoantibodies are present in a much lower titer in depression than in the classical autoimmune diseases (Maes et al. 1993).

## Geschwind-Behan-Galaburda Hypothesis

Geschwind and Behan (1982) proposed that cerebral lateralization and handedness were associated with immune disease, with the mediating factor being the level of testosterone in fetal life. This startling hypothesis was elaborated by Geschwind and Galaburda (1985a, 1985b, 1985c). The final theory proposed that elevated fetal testosterone alters the growth of the left hemisphere, which produces anomalous cerebral dominance, including left-handedness, and increases the risk of dyslexia and other developmental cognitive abnormalities. At the same time, a testosterone effect on the thymus results in immune derangements, notably an increased incidence of autoimmune diseases.

The theory has provoked much research, some confirmatory, some disconfirmatory, and some consistent with the Geschwind-Behan-Galaburda hypothesis but also with simpler hypotheses about cerebral lateralization and handedness. Only the claim of this theory that an association exists between autoimmune disease and handedness, dyslexia, and other developmental disorders is relevant to the theme of this chapter.

Some of the studies present striking data. For example, Behan and colleagues (1985) found that mothers of dyslexic children had a markedly increased rate of anti-Ro antibody positivity as compared with control mothers, although the study group mothers were not themselves symptomatic. Lahita (1988) found 45% of the male children of 109 SLE patients had developmental cognitive disorder, dyslexia in almost all cases. Anomalous dominance as assessed by handedness was not a prominent correlate. Wood and Cooper (1992) examined men with autoimmune thyroid disease; men with nonimmune thyroid disease constituted the control group. An excessive number of nondextral men was found in the autoimmune group, who also more commonly had histories suggesting dyslexia. However, in a large study based on data from the National Collaborative Perinatal Project, ulcerative colitis or asthma in the mother (the only disorders for which information was available) was not associated with brain disorders in offspring (Flannery and Liederman 1994). Non-right-handedness was associated not with left-hemisphere learning disorders but with disorders suggesting generalized brain injury, such as cerebral palsy and mental retardation (Flannery and Liederman 1995). Galaburda (1990) stressed the similarity of neuropathology in the available dyslexia material and in autoimmune disease affecting the brain, reviewed the evidence that autoimmune attack on the developing fetus could be the mechanism responsible for dyslexia and cognate disorders, and provided an animal model (Rosen et al. 1995).

A meta-analysis of studies addressing these questions led to the following conclusions (Bryden et al. 1994). First, only "marginal" support was found for an association between left-handedness and immune disorders, with the lower limit of the 95% confidence interval for an association being 1.003. Although allergies, asthma, and inflammatory bowel disease showed a significant association with left-handedness, individuals with arthritis and myasthenia gravis had a lower incidence of left-handedness than did healthy control subjects. Second, available evidence supported an association between immune disorders and dyslexia and developmental language disorders. In some studies, the association extended to relatives of patients with immune disorders, a finding suggesting a genetic factor leading to the association. Gilger and colleagues (1998), however, in a study of a large number of families, failed to find an association between immune disorders and dyslexia. The large sample, the twin methodology, and the use of laboratory as well as clinical assessment for immune disorders make this negative study particularly important.

## Conclusions

The goal of this chapter is to bring to the attention of neuropsychiatrists the range of psychopathology seen in autoimmune rheumatic disease. Both organic psychiatric manifestations and psychological reactions to severe and chronic illness are seen. We have stressed the features of the former and the techniques available for making diagnostic assessments of cerebral involvement of the disease process.

## References

Abu-Shakra M, Khraishi M, Grosman H, et al: Primary angiitis of the CNS diagnosed by angiography. Quart J Med 87:351–358, 1994

Ad Hoc Committee on Neuropsychiatric Lupus Nomenclature: The American College of Rheumatology nomenclature and case definitions for neuropsychiatric lupus syndromes. Arthritis Rheum 42:599–608, 1999

Aggarwal SK, Williams V, Levine SR, et al: Cocaine-associated intracranial hemorrhage: absence of vasculitis in 14 cases. Neurology 46:1741–1743, 1996

Aharon-Peretz J, Brenner B, Amyel-Zvi E, et al: Neurocognitive dysfunction in the antiphospholipid antibody syndrome (APS). Neuropsychiatry Neuropsychol Behav Neurol 9:123–126, 1996

Akman-Demir G, Serdaroglu P, Tasçi B, et al: Clinical patterns of neurological involvement in Behçet's disease: evaluation of 200 patients. Brain 122:2171–2181, 2000

Alarcón-Segovia D, Cardiel MH, Reyes E: Antiphospholipid arterial vasculopathy. J Rheumatol 16:762–767, 1989

Alexander EL: Central nervous system disease in Sjögren's syndrome: new insights into immunopathogenesis. Rheum Dis Clin North Am 18:637–672, 1992

Alexander EL: Neurologic disease in Sjögren's syndrome: mononuclear inflammatory vasculopathy affecting central/ peripheral nervous system and muscle: a clinical review and update of immunopathogenesis. Rheum Dis Clin North Am 19:869–908, 1993

Alexander EL, Ranzenbach MR, Kumar AJ, et al: Anti-Ro (SS-A) autoantibodies in central nervous system disease associated with Sjögren's syndrome (CNS-SS): clinical, neuroimaging, and angiographic correlates. Neurology 44:899–908, 1994

Alhalabi M, Moore PM: Serial angiography in isolated angiitis of the central nervous system. Neurology 44:1221–1226, 1994

Alonso R, Chaudieu I, Diorio J, et al: Interleukin-2 modulates evoked release of [3H]dopamine in rat cultured mesencephalic cells. J Neurochem 61:1284–1290, 1993

Alrawi A, Trobe JD, Blaivas M, et al: Brain biopsy in primary angiitis of the central nervous system. Neurology 53:858–860, 1999

American Psychiatric Association: Diagnostic and Statistical Manual of Mental Disorders, 3rd Edition. Washington, DC, American Psychiatric Association, 1980

American Psychiatric Association: Diagnostic and Statistical Manual of Mental Disorders, 3rd Edition, Revised. Washington, DC, American Psychiatric Association, 1987

Andrews JM: Giant-cell ("temporal") arteritis: a disease with variable clinical manifestations. Neurology 16:963–971, 1966

Arai T, Mizukami K, Sasaki M, et al: Clinicopathological study on a case of neuro-Behçet's disease: in special reference to MRI, SPECT and neuropathological findings. Jpn J Psychiatry Neurol 48:77–84, 1994

Asherson RA: Antiphospholipid antibodies, malignancies and paraproteinemias. J Autoimmun 15:117–122, 2000

Asherson RA, Hughes GRV: Antiphospholipid antibodies and chorea. J Rheumatol 15:377–379, 1988

Asherson RA, Mercey D, Phillips G, et al: Recurrent stroke and multi-infarct dementia in systemic lupus erythematosus: association with antiphospholipid antibodies. Ann Rheum Dis 46:605–611, 1987

Asherson RA, Khamashta MA, Ordi-Ros J, et al: The "primary" antiphospholipid syndrome: major clinical and serological features. Medicine 68:366–374, 1989

Bajema IM, Hagen EC, Weverling-Rijnsburger AWE, et al: Cerebral involvement in two patients with Wegener's granulomatosis. Clin Nephrol 47:401–406, 1997

Bakchine S, Duyckaerts C, Hassine L, et al: Lésions neurologiques centrales et périphériques au cours d'un syndrome de Gougerot-Sjögren primitif: étude clinicopathologique d'un cas. Rev Neurol (Paris) 147:368–375, 1991

Bane A, Annessley-Williams D, Sweeny E, et al: Cerebral vasculitis and haemorrhage in a HIV positive intravenous drug abuser (case report). Ir Med J 92:340, 1999

Barendregt PJ, Visser MRM, Smets EMA, et al: Fatigue in primary Sjögren's syndrome. Ann Rheum Dis 57:291–295, 1998

Bathon JM, Moreland LW, DiBartolomeo AG: Inflammatory central nervous system involvement in rheumatoid arthritis. Semin Arthritis Rheum 18:258–266, 1989

Baum KA, Hopf U, Nehrig C, et al: Systemic lupus erythematosus: neuropsychiatric signs and symptoms related to cerebral MRI findings. Clin Neurol Neurosurg 95:29–34, 1993

Bayer TA, Buslei R, Havas L, et al: Evidence for activation of microglia in patients with psychiatric illnesses. Neurosci Lett 271:126–128, 1999

Behan WMH, Behan PO, Geschwind N: Anti-Ro antibody in mothers of dyslexic children. Dev Med Child Neurol 27:538–540, 1985

Belin C, Mroni C, Caillat-Vigneron N, et al: Central nervous system involvement in Sjögren's syndrome: evidence from neuropsychological testing and HMPAO-SPECT. Ann Med Interne (Paris) 150:598–604, 1999

Bell CL, Partington C, Robbins M, et al: Magnetic resonance imaging of central nervous system lesions in patients with lupus erythematosus: correlation with clinical remission and antineurofilament and anticardiolipin antibody titers. Arthritis Rheum 34:432–441, 1991

Belmont HM, Abramson SB, Lie JT: Pathology and pathogenesis of vascular injury in systemic lupus erythematosus: interactions of inflammatory cells and activated endothelium. Arthritis Rheum 39:9–22, 1996

Benamour S, Zeroual B, Bennis R, et al: Maladie de Behçet: 316 cas. Presse Méd 19:1485–1489, 1990

Berger JR, Romano J, Menkin M, et al: Benign focal cerebral vasculitis: case report. Neurology 45:1731–1734, 1995

Berlit P: Clinical and laboratory findings with giant cell arteritis. J Neurol Sci 111:1–12, 1992

Berman JL, Kashii S, Trachtman MS, et al: Optic neuropathy and central nervous system disease secondary to Sjögren's syndrome in a child. Ophthalmology 97:1606–1609, 1990

Bernard JT, Ameriso S, Kempf RA, et al: Transient focal neurologic deficits complicating interleukin-2 therapy. Neurology 40:154–155, 1990

Bessler H, Levental Z, Karp L, et al: Cytokine production in drug-free and neuroleptic-treated schizophrenic patients. Biol Psychiatry 38:297–302, 1995

Beversdorf D, Moses P, Reeves A, et al: A man with weight loss, ataxia, and confusion for 3 months. Lancet 347:446, 1996

Bhatia KP, Brown P, Gregory R, et al: Progressive myoclonic ataxia associated with coeliac disease: the myoclonus is of cortical origin, but the pathology is in the cerebellum. Brain 118:1087–1093, 1995

Bicknell JM, Holland JV: Neurologic manifestations of Cogan syndrome. Neurology 28:278–281, 1978

Binder A, Snaith ML, Isenberg D: Sjögren's syndrome: a study of its neurological complications. Br J Rheumatol 27:275–280, 1988

Bogousslavsky J, Gaio J-M, Caplan LR, et al: Encephalopathy, deafness and blindness in young women: a distinct retinocochleocerebral arteriolopathy? J Neurol Neurosurg Psychiatry 52:43–46, 1989

Bohnen NILJ, Parnell KJ, Harper CM: Reversible MRI findings in a patient with Hashimoto's encephalopathy. Neurology 49:246–247, 1997

Bonaccorso S, Meltzer H, Maes M: Psychological and behavioural effects of interferons. Current Opinion in Psychiatry 13:673–677, 2000

Bonfa E, Golombek SJ, Kaufman LD, et al: Association between lupus psychosis and anti-ribosomal P protein antibodies. N Engl J Med 317:265–271, 1987

Boortz-Marx RL, Clark HB, Taylor S, et al: Sneddon's syndrome with granulomatous leptomeningeal infiltration. Stroke 26:492–495, 1995

Bosma GPT, Rood MJ, Huizinga TWJ, et al: Detection of cerebral involvement in patients with active neuropsychiatric systemic lupus erythematosus by the use of volumetric magnetization transfer imaging. Arthritis Rheum 43:2428–2436, 2000

Boston Collaborative Drug Surveillance Program: Acute adverse reactions to prednisone in relation to dosage. Clin Pharmacol Ther 13:694–698, 1972

Bostwick DG: Amphetamine induced cerebral vasculitis. Hum Pathol 12:1031–1033, 1981

Bouchez B, Arnott G, Hatron PY, et al: Chorée et lupus érythémateux disséminé avec anticoagulant circulant. Trois cas. Rev Neurol (Paris) 141:571–577, 1985

Bragoni M, Di Piero V, Priori R, et al: Sjögren's syndrome presenting as ischemic stroke. Stroke 25:2276–2279, 1994

Brain L, Jellinek EH, Ball K: Hashimoto's disease and encephalopathy. Lancet 2:512–514, 1966

Breutsch WL: Late cerebral sequelae of rheumatic fever. Arch Intern Med 73:472–476, 1944

Brey RL, Gharavi AE, Lockshin MD: Neurologic complications of antiphospholipid antibodies. Rheum Dis Clin North Am 19:833–850, 1993

Briley DP, Coull BM, Goodnight SH: Neurological disease associated with antiphospholipid antibodies. Ann Neurol 25:221–227, 1989

Brooks WM, Sabet A, Sibbitt WL, et al: Neurochemistry of brain lesions determined by spectroscopic imaging in systemic lupus erythematosus. J Rheumatol 24:2323–2329, 1997

Brücke T, Kollegger H, Schmidbauer M, et al: Adult coeliac disease and brainstem encephalitis (letter). J Neurol Neurosurg Psychiatry 51:456–457, 1988

Bruyn GAW: Controversies in lupus: nervous system involvement. Ann Rheum Dis 54:159–167, 1995

Bruyn RPM: Sneddon's syndrome, in Handbook of Clinical Neurology, Vol 11: Vascular Diseases, Part III. Edited by Toole JF. Amsterdam, The Netherlands, Elsevier Science, 1989, pp 401–410

Bryden MP, McManus IC, Bulman-Fleming MB: Evaluating the empirical support for the Geschwind-Behan-Galaburda model of cerebral lateralization. Brain Cogn 26:103–167, 1994

Budka H: Brain pathology in the collagen vascular diseases. Angiology 32:365–372, 1981

Bullmann C, Faust M, Hoffmann A, et al: Five cases with central diabetes insipidus and hypogonadism as first presentations of neurosarcoidosis. Eur J Endocrinol 142:365–372, 2000

Calabrese LH, Duna GF: Evaluation and treatment of central nervous system vasculitis. Curr Opinion Rheumatol 7:37–44, 1995

Calabrese LH, Duna GF: Drug-induced vasculitis. Curr Opinion Rheumatol 8:34–40, 1996

Calabrese LH, Gragg LA, Furlan AJ: Benign angiopathy: a distinct subset of angiographically defined primary angiitis of the central nervous system. J Rheumatol 20:2046–2050, 1993

Calabrese LH, Duna GF, Lie JT: Vasculitis in the central nervous system. Arthritis Rheum 40:1189–1201, 1997

Call GK, Fleming MC, Sealfon S, et al: Reversible cerebral segmental vasoconstriction. Stroke 19:1159–1170, 1988

Calopa M, Marti T, Rubio F, et al: Imagerie par résonance magnétique et syndrome de Cogan. Rev Neurol (Paris) 147:161–163, 1991

Canoso RT, de Oliveira RM: Chlorpromazine-induced anticardiolipin antibodies and lupus anticoagulant: absence of thrombosis. Am J Hematol 27:272–275, 1988

Canoso RT, de Oliveira RM, Nixon RA: Neuroleptic-associated autoantibodies: a prevalence study. Biol Psychiatry 27:863–870, 1990

Cantón A, de Fàbregas O, Tintoré M, et al: Encephalopathy associated to autoimmune thyroid disease: a more appropriate term for an underestimated condition? J Neurol Sci 176:65–69, 2000

Caraceni A, Martini C, Belli F, et al: Neuropsychological and neurophysiological assessment of the central effects of interleukin-2 administration. Eur J Cancer 29A:1266–1269, 1992

Carbotte RM, Denburg SD, Denburg JA: Prevalence of cognitive impairment in systemic lupus erythematosus. J Nerv Ment Dis 174:357–364, 1986

Carbotte RM, Denburg SD, Denburg JA: Cognitive deficit associated with rheumatic diseases: neuropsychological perspectives. Arthritis Rheum 38:1363–1374, 1995

Carlomagno S, Migliaresi S, Ambrosone L, et al: Cognitive impairment in systemic lupus erythematosus: a follow-up study. J Neurol 247:273–279, 2000

Carreras LO, Forastiero RR, Martinuzzo ME: Which are the best biological markers of the antiphospholipid syndrome? J Autoimmun 15:163–172, 2000

Case Records of the Massachusetts General Hospital: Case 27–1993. N Engl J Med 329:117–124, 1993

Caselli RJ: Giant cell (temporal) arteritis: a treatable cause of multi-infarct dementia. Neurology 40:753–755, 1990

Caselli RJ, Hunder GG, Whisnant JP: Neurologic disease in biopsy-proven giant cell (temporal) arteritis. Neurology 38:352–359, 1988

Caselli RJ, Scheithauer BW, O'Duffy JD, et al: Chronic inflammatory meningoencephalitis should not be mistaken for Alzheimer's disease. Mayo Clin Proc 68:846–853, 1993

Caselli RJ, Boeve BF, Scheithauer BW, et al: Nonvasculitic autoimmune inflammatory meningoencephalitis (NAIM): a reversible form of encephalopathy. Neurology 53:1579–1581, 1999

Ceccaldi M, Harlé JR, Sangla I, et al: Encéphalopathie progressive du syndrome des anticorps antiphospholipides. Presse Med 22:1313–1316, 1993

Cervera R, Asherson RA, Lie JT: Clinicopathologic correlations of the antiphospholipid syndrome. Semin Arthritis Rheum 24:262–272, 1995

Cervera R, Asherson RA, Font J, et al: Chorea in the antiphospholipid syndrome: clinical, radiologic, and immunologic characteristics of 50 patients from our clinics and the recent literature. Medicine 76:203–212, 1997

Chancellor AM, Cull RE, Kilpatrick DC, et al: Neurological disease associated with anticardiolipin antibodies in patients without systemic lupus erythematosus: clinical and immunological features. J Neurol 238:401–407, 1991

Chapelon C, Ziza JM, Piette JC, et al: Neurosarcoidosis: signs, course and treatment in 35 confirmed cases. Medicine 69:261–276, 1990

Chapman J, Cohen-Armon M, Shoenfeld Y, et al: Antiphospholipid antibodies permeabilize and depolarize brain synaptoneurosomes. Lupus 8:127–133, 1999

Chengappa KNR: Obstetric complications and autoantibodies in schizophrenia. Acta Psychiatr Scand 92:270–273, 1995

Chengappa KNR, Carpenter AB, Keshavan MS, et al: Elevated IGG and IGM anticardiolipin antibodies in a subgroup of medicated and unmedicated schizophrenic patients. Biol Psychiatry 30:731–735, 1991

Chengappa KNR, Ganguli R, Ulrich R, et al: The prevalence of autoantibodies among right and left handed schizophrenic patients and control subjects. Biol Psychiatry 32:803–811, 1992a

Chengappa KNR, Ganguli R, Yang ZW, et al: Left-handed first-episode, neuroleptic-naive schizophrenic patients have a higher prevalence of autoantibodies. Schizophr Res 8:75–80, 1992b

Citron BP, Halpern M, McCarron M, et al: Necrotizing angiitis associated with drug abuse. N Engl J Med 283:1003–1011, 1970

Coates T, Slavotinek JP, Rischmueller M, et al: Cerebral white matter lesions in primary Sjögren's syndrome: a controlled study. J Rheumatol 26:1301–1305, 1999

Çoban O, Bahar S, Akman-Demir G, et al: Masked assessment of MRI findings: is it possible to differentiate neuro-Behçet's disease from other central nervous system diseases? Neuroradiology 41:255–260, 1999

Cohen L, Mouly S, Tassan P, et al: A woman with a relapsing psychosis who got better with prednisone. Lancet 347:1228, 1996

Colamussi P, Giganti M, Cittanti C, et al: Brain single-photon emission tomography with 99mTc-HMPAO in neuropsychiatric systemic lupus erythematosus: relations with EEG and MRI findings and clinical manifestations. Eur J Nucl Med 22:17–24, 1995

Collin P, Pirttilä T, Nurmikko T, et al: Celiac disease, brain atrophy, and dementia. Neurology 41:372–375, 1991

Colony HS, Malamud N: Sydenham's chorea: a clinicopathologic study. Neurology 6:672–676, 1956

Cordingley G, Navarro C, Brust JCM, et al: Sarcoidosis presenting as senile dementia. Neurology 31:1148–1151, 1981

Cordoliani MA, Michon-Pasturel U, Rerat K, et al: Sclérose en plaques et anticorps antiphospholipides: étude consécutive de 62 patients. Rev Med Interne 19:635–639, 1998

Coull BM, Bourdette DN, Goodnight SH, et al: Multiple cerebral infarctions and dementia associated with anticardiolipin antibodies. Stroke 18:1107–1112, 1987

Créange A, Laplane D, Habib K, et al: Démence révélatrice du syndrome de Gougerot-Sjögren primitif. Rev Neurol (Paris) 148:376–380, 1992

Cronin CC, Jackson LM, Feighery C, et al: Coeliac disease and epilepsy. Quart J Med 91:303–308, 1998

Cuadrado MJ, Khamashta MA, Ballesteros A, et al: Can neurologic manifestations of Hughes (antiphospholipid) syndrome be distinguished from multiple sclerosis? Analysis of 27 patients and a review of the literature. Medicine 79:57–68, 2000a

Cuadrado MJ, Khamashta MA, Hughes GRV: Migraine and stroke in young women. Quart J Med 93:317–319, 2000b

Daoud AS, Zaki M, Shakir, et al: Effectiveness of sodium valproate in the treatment of Sydenham's chorea. Neurology 40:1140–1141, 1990

Davie CA, Feinstein A, Kartsounis LD, et al: Proton magnetic resonance spectroscopy of systemic lupus erythematosus involving the central nervous system. J Neurol 242:522–528, 1995

Deberdt R, van Hooren J, Biesbouck M, et al: Antinuclear fator-positive mental depression: a single disease entity? Biol Psychiatry 11:69–74, 1976 de Gortari A, Pellon R, Costero I: Encephalopathy of the rheumatic patients. Am Heart J 33:717–717, 1947

de la Monte SM, Hutchins GM, Gupta PK: Polymorphous meningitis with atypical mononuclear cells in Sjögren's syndrome. Ann Neurol 14:455–461, 1983

Denburg SD, Carbotte RM, Denburg JA: Cognitive deficit in non-neuropsychiatric SLE (fact or fiction?). Arthritis Rheum 35:S208, 1992

Denburg SD, Carbotte RM, Denburg JA: Corticosteroids and neuropsychological functioning in patients with systemic lupus erythematosus. Arthritis Rheum 37:1311–1320, 1994

Denburg SD, Carbotte RM, Ginsberg JS, et al: The relationship of antiphospholipid antibodies to cognitive function in patients with systemic lupus erythematosus. J Int Neuropsychol Soc 3:377–386, 1997

Denicoff KD, Rubinow DR, Papa MZ, et al: The neuropsychiatric effects of treatment with interleukin-2 and lymphokine-activated killer cells. Ann Intern Med 107:293–300, 1987

Dennis MS, Byrne EJ, Hopkinson N, et al: Neuropsychiatric systemic lupus erythematosus in elderly people: a case series. J Neurol Neurosurg Psychiatry 55:1157–1161, 1992

Derksen RHWM, van Dam AP, Gmelig Meyling FHJ, et al: A prospective study on antiribosomal P proteins in two cases of familial lupus and recurrent psychosis. Ann Rheum Dis 49:770–782, 1990

Devinsky O, Petito CK, Alonso DR: Clinical and neuropathological findings in systemic lupus erythematosus: the role of vasculitis, heart emboli, and thrombotic thrombocytopenic purpura. Ann Neurol 23:380–384, 1988

de Vries E, Schipperijn AJM, Breedveld FC: Antinuclear antibodies in psychiatric patients. Acta Psychiatr Scand 89:289–290, 1994

Devuyst G, Sindic C, Laterre É-C: Neuropathological findings of a Sneddon's syndrome presenting with dementia not preceded by clinical cerebrovascular events (letter). Stroke 27:1008–1009, 1996

Dickey W: Epilepsy, cerebral calcifications, and coeliac disease. Lancet 344:1585–1586, 1994

Diri E, Cucurull E, Gharavi AE, et al: Antiphospholipid (Hughes') syndrome in African-Americans: IgA aCL and aβ2 glycoprotein-1 is the most frequent isotype. Lupus 8:263ñ268, 1999

Drosos AA, Andonopoulos AP, Lagos G, et al: Neuropsychiatric abnormalities in primary Sjögren's syndrome. Clin Exp Rheumatol 7:207–209, 1989

Ducloux D, Florea A, Fournier B, et al: Inferior vena cava thrombosis in a patient with chlorpromazin-induced anticardiolipin antibodies (letter). Nephrol Dial Transplant 14:1335–1336, 1999

Duna GF, Calabrese LH: Limitations of invasive modalities in the diagnosis of primary angiitis of the central nervous system. J Rheumatol 22:662–667, 1995

Ehsan T, Hasan S, Powers JM, et al: Serial magnetic resonance imaging in isolated angiitis of the central nervous system. Neurology 45:1462–1465, 1995

El-Mallakh RS, Donaldson JO, Kranzler HR, et al: Phenothiazine-associated lupus anticoagulant and thrombotic disease. Psychosomatics 29:109–113, 1988

Ellis SG, Verity MA: Central nervous system involvement in systemic lupus erythematosus: a review of neuropathologic findings in 57 cases, 1955–1977. Semin Arthritis Rheum 8:212–221, 1979

Ellison D, Gatter K, Heryet A, et al: Intramural platelet deposition in cerebral vasculopathy of systemic lupus erythematosus. J Clin Pathol 46:37–40, 1993

Emmi L, Bramati M, De Cristofaro MTR, et al: MRI and SPECT investigations of the CNS in SLE patients. Clin Exp Rheumatol 11:13–20, 1993

Fabius AJM, Gaulhofer WK: Systemic lupus erythematosus induced by psychotropic drugs. Acta Rheumatol Scand 17:137–147, 1971

Faggioni R, Benigni F, Ghezzi P: Proinflammatory cytokines as pathogenetic mediators in the central nervous system: brain-periphery connections. Neuroimmunomodulation 2:2–15, 1995

Ferro JM: Vasculitis of the central nervous system. J Neurol 245:766–776, 1998

Fieschi C, Rasura M, Anzini A, et al: Central nervous system vasculitis. J Neurol Sci 153:159–171, 1998

Finney GOH: Juvenile onset diabetes and schizophrenia (letter)? Lancet 2:1214–1215, 1989

Firer M, Sirota P, Schild K, et al: Anticardiolipin antibodies are elevated in drug-free, multiply affected families with schizophrenia. J Clin Immunol 14:73–78, 1994

Flannery KA, Liederman J: A test of the immunoreactive theory for the origin of neurodevelopmental disorders in the offspring of women with immune disorders. Cortex 30:635–646, 1994

Flannery KA, Liederman J: Is there really a syndrome involving the co-occurrence of neurodevelopmental disorder, non-right handedness and immune disorder among children? Cortex 31:503–515, 1995

Forman HP, Levin S, Stewart B, et al: Cerebral vasculitis and hemorrhage in an adolescent taking diet pills containing phenylpropanolamine: case report and review of literature. Pediatrics 83:737–741, 1989

Francès C, Papo T, Wechsler B, et al: Sneddon syndrome with or without antiphospholipid antibodies. Medicine 78:209–219, 1999

Francès C, Piette JC: The mystery of Sneddon syndrome: relationship with antiphospholipid syndrome and systemic lupus erythematosus. J Autoimmun 15:139–143, 2000

Fredericks RK, Lefkowitz DS, Challa VR, et al: Cerebral vasculitis associated with cocaine abuse. Stroke 22:1437–1439, 1991

Fricchione GL, Kaufman LD, Gruber BL, et al: Electroconvulsive therapy and cyclophosphamide in combination for severe neuropsychiatric lupus with catatonia (letter). Am J Med 88:442–443, 1990

Fukui T, Kawamura M, Hasegawa Y, et al: Multiple cognitive impairments associated with systemic lupus erythematosus and antiphospholipid antibody syndrome: a form of progressive vascular dementia? Eur Neurol 43:115–116, 2000

Fulford KWM, Catterall RD, Delhants JJ, et al: Collagen disorder of the nervous system presenting as multiple sclerosis. Brain 95:373–376, 1972

Futrell N, Schultz LR, Millikan C: Central nervous system disease in patients with systemic lupus erythematosus. Neurology 42:1649–1657, 1992

Galaburda AM: The testosterone hypothesis: assessment since Geschwind and Behan, 1982. Annals of Dyslexia 40:18–38, 1990

Galanaud D, Dormont D, Marsault C, et al: Brain MRI in patients with past lupus-associated chorea. Stroke 31:3080–3081, 2000

Ganguli R, Brar JS, Solomon W, et al: Altered interleukin-2 production in schizophrenia: association between clinical state and autoantibody production. Psychiatry Res 44:113–123, 1992

Ganguli R, Brar JS, Chengappa KNR, et al: Autoimmunity in schizophrenia: a review of recent findings. Ann Med 25:489–496, 1993

Ganguli R, Yang Z, Shurin G, et al: Serum interleukin-6 concentration in schizophrenia: elevation associated with duration of illness. Psychiatry Res 51:1–10, 1994

Ganguli R, Brar JS, Chengappa KNR, et al: Mitogen-stimulated interleukin-2 production in never-medicated, first-episode schizophrenic patients: the influence of age at onset and negative symptoms. Arch Gen Psychiatry 52:668–672, 1995

Gemignani F, Marbini A, Pavesi G, et al: Peripheral neuropathy associated with primary Sjögren's syndrome. J Neurol Neurosurg Psychiatry 57:983–986, 1994

Georgescu L, Mevorach D, Arnett FC, et al: Anti-P antibodies and neuropsychiatric lupus erythematosus. Ann N Y Acad Sci 823:263–269, 1997

Gerraty RP, McKelvie PA, Byrne E: Aseptic meningoencephalitis in primary Sjögren's syndrome: response to plasmapheresis and absence of CNS vasculitis at autopsy. Acta Neurol Scand 88:309–311, 1993

Geschwind DH, FitzPatrick M, Mischel PS, et al: Sneddon's syndrome is a thrombotic vasculopathy: neuropathologic and neuroradiologic evidence. Neurology 45:557–560, 1995

Geschwind N, Behan P: Left-handedness: association with immune disease, migraine, and developmental learning disorder. Proc Natl Acad Sci U S A 79:5096–5100, 1982

Geschwind N, Galaburda AM: Cerebral lateralization. Biological mechanisms, associations, and pathology, I: a hypothesis and a program for research. Arch Neurol 42:428–459, 1985a

Geschwind N, Galaburda AM: Cerebral lateralization. Biological mechanisms, associations, and pathology, II: a hypothesis and a program for research. Arch Neurol 42:521–552, 1985b

Geschwind N, Galaburda AM: Cerebral lateralization. Biological mechanisms, associations, and pathology, III: a hypothesis and a program for research. Arch Neurol 42:634–654, 1985c

Ghika-Schmidt F, Ghika J, Regli F, et al: Hashimoto's myoclonic encephalopathy: an underdiagnosed treatable condition? Mov Disord 11:555–562, 1996

Gibson T, Myers AR: Nervous system involvement in systemic lupus erythematosus. Ann Rheum Dis 35:398–406, 1976

Giedd JN, Rapoport JL, Kruesi MJP, et al: Sydenham's chorea: magnetic resonance imaging of the basal ganglia. Neurology 45:2199–2202, 1995

Giedd JN, Rapoport JL, Garvey MA, et al: MRI assessment of children with obsessive-compulsive disorder or tics associated with streptococcal infection. Am J Psychiatry 157:281–283, 2000

Gilad R, Lampl Y, Eshel Y, et al: Cerebrospinal fluid soluble interleukin-2 receptor in cerebral lupus. Br J Rheumatol 36:190–193, 1997

Gilboe IM, Husby G: Application of the 1982 revised criteria for the classification of systemic lupus erythematosus on a cohort of 346 Norwegian patients with connective tissue disease. Scand J Rheumatol 28:81–87, 1999

Gilger JW, Pennington BF, Harbeck RJ, et al: A twin and family study of the association between immune system dysfunction and dyslexia using blood serum immunoassay and survey data. Brain Cogn 36:310–333, 1998

Gille M, Sindic CJM, Laterre PF, et al: Atteinte neurologiques révélatrices d'une maladie de Behçet: quatre observations clinique. Acta Neurol Belg 90:233–247, 1990

Gilvarry CM, Sham PC, Jones PB, et al: Family history of autoimmune diseases in psychosis. Schizophr Res 19:33–40, 1996

Ginsburg KS, Wright EA, Larson MG, et al: A controlled study of the prevalence of cognitive dysfunction in randomly selected patients with systemic lupus erythematosus. Arthritis Rheum 35:776–782, 1992

Giordano MJ, Commins D, Silbergeld DL: Sjögren's cerebritis complicated by subarachnoid hemorrhage and bilateral superior cerebellar artery occlusion: case report. Surg Neurol 43:48–51, 1995

Gladman DD, Urowitz MB, Slonim D, et al: Evaluation of predictive factors for neurocognitive dysfunction in patients with inactive systemic lupus erythematosus. J Rheumatol 27:2367–2371, 2000

Glanz BI, Slonim D, Urowitz MB, et al: Pattern of neuropsychological dysfunction in inactive systemic lupus erythematosus. Neuropsychiatry Neuropsychol Behav Neurol 10:232–238, 1997

Gledhill RF, Thompson PD: Standard neurodiagnostic tests in Sydenham's chorea (letter). J Neurol Neurosurg Psychiatry 53:534–535, 1990

Glick R, Hoying J, Cerullo L, et al: Phenylpropanolamine: an over-the-counter drug causing central nervous system vasculitis and intracerebral hemorrhage: case report and review. Neurosurgery 20:969–974, 1987

Goetzl EJ, Sreedharan SP, Harkonen WS: Pathogenetic roles of neuroimmunologic mediators. Immunology and Allergy Clinics of North America 8:183–200, 1988

Goldman S, Amrom D, Szliwowski HB, et al: Reversible striatal hypermetabolism in a case of Sydenham's chorea. Mov Disord 8:355–358, 1993

Gonzalez-Crespo MR, Blanco FJ, ramos A, et al: Magnetic resonance imaging of the brain in systemic lupus erythematosus. Br J Rheumatol 34:1055–1060, 1995

Gorman DG, Cummings JL: Neurobehavioral presentations of the antiphospholipid antibody syndrome. J Neuropsychiatry Clin Neurosci 5:37–42, 1993

Govoni M, Bajocchi G, Rizzo N, et al: Neurological involvement in primary Sjögren's syndrome: clinical and instrumental evaluation in a cohort of Italian patients. Clin Rheumatol 18:299–303, 1999

Greaves M, Cohen H, MacHin SJ, et al: Guidelines on the investigation and management of the antiphospholipid syndrome. Br J Haematol 109:704–715, 2000

Greco TP, Amos AM, Conti-Kelly AM, et al: Testing for the antiphospholipid syndrome: importance of IgA anti-beta 2-glycoprotein I. Lupus 9:33–41, 2000

Green LN: Corticosteroids in the treatment of Sydenham's chorea. Arch Neurol 35:53–54, 1978

Greenan TJ, Grossman RI, Goldberg HI: Cerebral vasculitis: MR imaging and angiographic correlation. Radiology 182:65–72, 1992

Hachulla E, Michon-Psturel U, Leys D, et al: Cerebral magnetic resonance imaging in patients with or without antiphospholipid antibodies. Lupus 7:124–131, 1998

Hadjivassiliou M, Grünewald RA, Cahttopadhyay AK, et al: Clinical, radiological, neurophysiological, and neuropathological characteristics of gluten ataxia. Lancet 352:1582–1585, 1998

Hallert C, Åström J: Psychic disturbances in adult coeliac disease, II: psychological findings. Scand J Gastroenterol 17:21–24, 1982

Hallert C, Derefeldt T: Psychic disturbances in adult coeliac disease, I: clinical observations. Scand J Gastroenterol 17:17–19, 1982

Hanly JG, Behmann S, Denburg SD, et al: The association between sequential changes in serum antineuronal antibodies and neuropsychiatric systemic lupus erythematosus. Postgrad Med J 65:622–627, 1989

Hanly JG, Fisk JD, Sherwood G, et al: Cognitive impairment in patients with systemic lupus erythematosus. J Rheumatol 19:562–567, 1992a

Hanly JG, Walsh NMG, Sangalang V: Brain pathology in systemic lupus erythematosus. J Rheumatol 19:732–741, 1992b

Hanly JG, Walsh NM, Fisk JD, et al: Cognitive impairment and autoantibodies in systemic lupus erythematosus. Br J Rheumatol 32:291–296, 1993

Hanly JG, Fisk JD, Sherwood G, et al: Clinical course of cognitive dysfunction in systemic lupus erythematosus. J Rheumatol 21:1825–1831, 1994

Hanly JG, Hong C, Smith S, et al: A prospective analysis of cognitive function and anticardiolipid antibodies in systemic lupus erythematosus. Arthritis Rheum 42:728–734, 1999

Harlé JR, Disdier P, Ali Cherif A, et al: Trouble mnésique isolé rélévant un syndrome des anticorps anti-phospholipides. Rev Neurol (Paris) 148:635–637, 1992

Hay EM: Psychiatric disorder and cognitive impairment in SLE. Lupus 3:145–148, 1994

Hay EM, Isenberg DA: Autoantibodies in central nervous system lupus. Br J Rheumatol 32:329–332, 1993

Hay EM, Black D, Huddy A, et al: Psychiatric disorder and cognitive impairment in systemic lupus erythematosus. Arthritis Rheum 35:411–416, 1992

Haynes BF, Kaiser-Kupfer MI, Mason P, et al: Cogan syndrome: studies in thirteen patients, long-term follow-up, and a review of the literature. Medicine 59:426–441, 1980

Heazlewood VJ, Bochner F, Craswell PW: Hallucinogenic drug induced vasculitis. Med J Aust 1:359–360, 1981

Heiskala H, Somer H, Kovanen J, et al: Microangiopathy with encephalopathy, hearing loss and retinal arteriolar occlusions: two new cases. J Neurol Sci 86:239–250, 1988

Henchey R, Cibula J, Helveston W, et al: Electroencephalographic findings in Hashimoto's encephalopathy. Neurology 45:977–981, 1995

Henderson LM, Behan PO, Aarli J, et al: Hashimoto's encephalopathy: a new neuroimmunological syndrome (abstract). Ann Neurol 22:140–141, 1987

Hernández Echevarría LE, Saiz A, Graus F, et al: Detection of 14–3–3 protein in the CSF of a patient with Hashimoto's encephalopathy. Neurology 54:1539–1540, 2000

Hess DC: Cerebral lupus vasculopathy: mechanisms and clinical relevance. Ann N Y Acad Sci 823:154–168, 1997

Hier DB, Thomas C, Shindler AG: A case of subcortical dementia due to sarcoidosis of the hypothalamus and fornices. Brain Cogn 2:189–198, 1983

Hietaharju A, Yli-Kerttula U, Häkkinen V, et al: Nervous system manifestations in Sjögren's syndrome. Acta Neurol Scand 81:144–152, 1990

Hirohata S, Hirose S, Miyamoto T: Cerebrospinal fluid IgM, IgA, and IgG indexes in systemic lupus erythematosus: their use as estimates of central nervous system disease activity. Arch Intern Med 145:1843–1846, 1985

Hirohata S, Isshi K, Oguchi H, et al: Cerebrospinal fluid interleukin-6 in progressive neuro-Behçet's syndrome. Clin Immunol Immunopathol 82:12–17, 1997

Hochberg MC: Updating the American College of Rheumatology Revised Criteria for the Classification of Systemic Lupus Erythematosus (letter). Arthritis Rheum 40:1725, 1997

Hopkins P, Belmont HM, Buyon J, et al: Increased levels of plasma anaphylatoxins in systemic lupus erythematosus predict flares of the disease and may elicit vascular injury in lupus cerebritis. Arthritis Rheum 31:632–641, 1988

Hornberg M, Arolt V, Wilke I, et al: Production of interferons and lymphokines in leukocyte cultures of patients with schizophrenia. Schizophr Res 15:237–242, 1995

Hughes GRV: The antiphospholipid syndrome: ten years on. Lancet 342:341–344, 1993

Hughson MD, McCarty GA, Sholer CM, et al: Thrombotic cerebral arteriopathy in patients with the antiphospholipid syndrome. Mod Pathol 6:644–653, 1993

Hugo FJ, Halland AM, Spangenberg JJ, et al: DSM-III-R classification of psychiatric symptoms in systemic lupus erythematosus. Psychosomatics 37:262–269, 1996

Hunder GG, Lie JT, Goronzy JJ, et al: Pathogenesis of giant cell arteritis. Arthritis Rheum 36:757–761, 1993

Husby G, van de Rijn I, Zabriskie JB, et al: Antibodies reacting with cytoplasm of subthalamic and caudate nuclei neurons in chorea and acute rheumatic fever. J Exp Med 144:1094–1110, 1976

IJdo JW, Conti-Kelly AM, Greco P, et al: Anti-phospholipid antibodies inpatients with multiple sclerosis and MS-like illnesses: MS or APS? Lupus 8:109–115, 1999

Imakita M, Yutani C, Ishibashi-Ueda H: Giant cell arteritis involving the cerebral artery [sic]. Arch Pathol Lab Med 117:729–733, 1993

Inzelberg R, Bornstein NM, Reider I, et al: The lupus anticoagulant and dementia in non-SLE patients. Dementia 3:140–145, 1992

Ioannidis JPA, Moutsopoulos HM: Sjögren's syndrome: too many associations, too limited evidence: the enigmatic example of CNS involvement. Semin Arthritis Rheum 29:1–3, 1999

Isshi K, Hirohata S: Association of anti-ribosomal P protein antibodies with neuropsychiatric systemic lupus erythematosus. Arthritis Rheum 39:1483–1490, 1996

Isshi K, Hirohata S: Differential roles of the anti-ribosomal P antibody and antineuronal antibody in the pathogenesis of central nervous system involvement in systemic lupus erythematosus. Arthritis Rheum 41:1819–1827, 1998

Isshi K, Hirohata S, Hashimoto T, et al: Systemic lupus erythematosus presenting with diffuse low density lesions in the cerebral white matter on computed axial tomography scans: its implication in the pathogenesis of diffuse central nervous system lupus. J Rheumatol 21:1758–1762, 1994

Iverson GL: Psychopathology associated with systemic lupus erythematosus: a methodological review. Semin Arthritis Rheum 22:242–251, 1993

Jacobson MW, Rapport LJ, Keenan PA, et al: Neuropsychological deficits associated with antiphospholipid antibodies. J Clin Exp Neuropsychol 21:251–264, 1999

Jacobsson L, Hansen BU, Manthorpe R, et al: Association of dry eyes and dry mouth with anti-Ro/SS-A and anti-La/SS-B autoantibodies in normal adults. Arthritis Rheum 35:1492–1500, 1992

Jain R, Chartash E, Susin M, et al: Systemic lupus erythematosus complicated by thrombotic microangiopathy. Semin Arthritis Rheum 24:173–182, 1994

Jara LJ, Irigoyen L, Ortiz MJ, et al: Prolactin and interleukin-6 in neuropsychiatric lupus erythematosus. Clin Rheumatol 17:110–114, 1998

Jennette JC, Falk RJ: Clinical and pathological classification of ANCA-associated vasculitis: what are the controversies? Clin Exp Immunol 101 (suppl 1):18–22, 1995

Jennette JC, Falk RJ, Andrassy K, et al: Nomenclature of systemic vasculitides: proposal of an International Consensus Conference. Arthritis Rheum 37:187–192, 1994

John S, Ovsiew F: Schizophrenia vs. neurosarcoidosis in a young male (letter). Psychosomatics 37:166–168, 1996

Johnson H, Bouman W, Pinner G: Psychiatric aspects of temporal arteritis: a case report and review of the literature. J Geriatr Psychiatry Neurol 10:142–145, 1997

Johnson RT, Richardson EP: The neurological manifestations of systemic lupus erythematosus: a clinical-pathological study of 24 cases and review of the literature. Medicine 47:337–369, 1968

Jonas J, Kölble K, Völcker HE, et al: Central retinal artery occlusion in Sneddon's disease associated with antiphospholipid antibodies. Am J Ophthalmol 102:37–40, 1986

Kalashnikova LA, Nasonov EL, Kshekbaeva AE, et al: Anticardiolipin antibodies in Sneddon's syndrome. Neurology 40:464–467, 1990

Kallenberg CGM, Brouwer E, Weening JJ, et al: Anti-neutrophil cytoplasmic antibodies: current diagnostic and pathophysiological potential. Kidney Int 46:1–15, 1994

Kao C-H, Ho Y-J, ChangLai S-P, et al: Regional cerebral blood flow and glucose metabolism in Sjögren's syndrome. J Nucl Med 39:1354–1356, 1998

Kao C-H, Ho Y-J, Lan J-L, et al: Discrepancy between regional cerebral blood flow and glucose metabolism of the brain in systemic lupus erythematosus patients with normal brain magnetic resonance imaging findings. Arthritis Rheum 42:61–68, 1999

Karni A, Sadeh M, Blatt I, et al: Cogan's syndrome complicated by lacunar brain infarcts. J Neurol Neurosurg Psychiatry 54:169–171, 1991

Kawakita H, Nishimura M, Satoh Y, et al: Neurological aspects of Behçet's disease: a case report and clinico-pathological review of the literature in Japan. J Neurol Sci 5:417–439, 1967

Kawashima N, Shindo R, Kohno M: Primary Sjögren's syndrome with subcortical dementia. Intern Med 32:561–564, 1993

Keenan PA, Jacobson MW, Soleymani RM, et al: The effect on memory of chronic prednisone treatment in patients with systemic disease. Neurology 47:1396–1402, 1996

Kelly MC, Denburg JA: Cerebrospinal fluid immunoglobulins and neuronal antibodies in neuropsychiatric systemic lupus erythematosus and related conditions. J Rheumatol 14: 740–744, 1987

Kessler JT, Jortner BS, Adapon BD: Cerebral vasculitis in a drug abuser. J Clin Psychiatry 39:559–564, 1978

Khamashta MA, Cervera R, Hughes GRV: The central nervous system in systemic lupus erythematosus. Rheumatol Int 11:117–119, 1991

Kidd D, Steuer A, Denman AM, et al: Neurological complications in Behçet's syndrome. Brain 122:2183–2194, 1999

Kiessling LS, Marcotte AC, Culpepper L: Antineuronal antibodies in movement disorders. Pediatrics 92:39–43, 1993

Kinney HC, Burger PC, Hurwitz BJ, et al: Degeneration of the central nervous system associated with celiac disease. J Neurol Sci 53:9–22, 1982

Kirch DG: Infection and autoimmunity as etiologic factors in schizophrenia: a review and reappraisal. Schizophr Bull 19:355–370, 1993

Klyushnik TP, Danilovskaya EV, Vatolkina OE, et al: Changes in the serum levels of autoantibody to nerve growth factor in patients with schizophrenia. Neurosci Behav Physiol 29: 355–357, 1999

Koçer N, Islak C, Siva A, et al: CNS involvement in neuro-Behçet syndrome: an MR study. AJNR Am J Neuroradiol 20:1015–1024, 1999

Kodama K, Okada S, Hino T, et al: Single photon emission computed tomography in systemic lupus erythematosus with psychiatric features. J Neurol Neurosurg Psychiatry 58: 307–311, 1995

Kothbauer-Margreiter I, Sturzenegger M, Komor J, et al: Encephalopathy associated with Hashimoto thyroiditis: diagnosis and treatment. J Neurol 243:585–593, 1996

Kozora E, Thompson LL, West SG, et al: Analysis of cognitive and psychological deficits in systemic lupus erythematosus patients without overt central nervous system disease. Arthritis Rheum 39:2035–2045, 1996

Kozora E, West SG, Kotzin BL, et al: Magnetic resonance imaging abnormalities and cognitive deficits in systemic lupus erythematosus patients without overt central nervous system involvement. Arthritis Rheum 41:41–47, 1998

Krendel DA, Ditter SM, Frankel MR, et al: Biopsy-proven cerebral vasculitis associated with cocaine abuse. Neurology 40:1092–1094, 1990

Kronfol Z, Remick DG: Cytokines and the brain: implications for clinical psychiatry. Am J Psychiatry 157:683–694, 2000

Kurlan R: Tourette's syndrome and "PANDAS." Neurology 50:1530–1534, 1998

Kushner MJ, Tobin M, Fazekas F, et al: Cerebral blood flow variations in CNS lupus. Neurology 40:99–102, 1990

Lafforgue P, Toussirot E, Billé F, et al: Astasia-abasia revealing a primary Sjögren's syndrome. Clin Rheumatol 12:261–264, 1993

Lahita RG: Systemic lupus erythematosus: learning disability in the male offspring of female patients and relationship to laterality. Psychoneuroendocrinology 13:385–396, 1988

Lanham JG, Brown MM, Hughes GRV: Cerebral systemic lupus erythematosus presenting with catatonia. Postgrad Med J 61:329–330, 1985

Lanzillo B, Pappone N, Crisci C, et al: Subclinical peripheral nerve involvement in patients with rheumatoid arthritis. Arthritis Rheum 41:1196–1202, 1998

Lass P, Krajka-Lauer J, Homziuk M, et al: Cerebral blood flow in Sjögren's syndrome using 99Tcm-HMPAO brain SPET. Nucl Med Commun 21:31–35, 2000

Lebon P, Lenoir GR, Fischer A, et al: Synthesis of intrathecal interferon in systemic lupus erythematosus with neurological complications. BMJ 287:1165–1167, 1983

Levine SR, Langer SL, Albers JW, et al: Sneddon's syndrome: an antiphospholipid antibody syndrome? Neurology 38:798–800, 1988

Levine SR, Deegan MJ, Futrell N, et al: Cerebrovascular and neurological disease associated with antiphospholipid antibodies: 48 cases. Neurology 40:1181–1189, 1990

Lewis DA, Smith RE: Steroid-induced psychiatric syndromes: a report of 14 cases and a review of the literature. J Affect Disord 5:319–332, 1983

Leykin I, Spivak B, Weizman A, et al: Elevated cellular immune response to human heat-shock protein-60 in schizophrenic patients. Eur Arch Psychiatry Clin Neurosci 249:238–246, 1999

Lhote F, Cohen P, Guillevin L: Polyarteritis nodosa, microscopic polyangiitis and Churg-Strauss syndrome. Lupus 7:238–258, 1998

Li J-Y, Lai P-H, Lam H-C, et al: Hypertrophic cranial pachymeningitis and lymphocytic hypophysitis in Sjögren's syndrome. Neurology 52:420–423, 1999

Licinio J, Seibyl JP, Altemus M, et al: Elevated CSF levels of interleukin-2 in neuroleptic-free schizophrenic patients. Am J Psychiatry 150:1408–1410, 1993

Lie JT: Primary (granulomatous) angiitis of the central nervous system: a clinicopathologic analysis of 15 new cases and a review of the literature. Hum Pathol 23:164–171, 1992

Lillicrap DP, Pinto M, Benford K, et al: Heterogeneity of laboratory test results for antiphospholipid antibodies in patients treated with chlorpromazine and other phenothiazines. Am J Clin Pathol 93:771–775, 1990

Lim L, Ron MA, Ormerod IEC, et al: Psychiatric and neurological manifestations in systemic lupus erythematosus. Quart J Med 66:27–38, 1988

Lindal E, Shorlacius S, Steinsson K, et al: Psychiatric disorders among subjects with systemic lupus erythematosus in an unselected population. Scand J Rheumatol 24:346–351, 1995

Lynch J, Stack C: Magnetic resonance spectroscopy abnormalities in Syndenham's [sic] chorea. Neurology 46:A146, 1996

Mac DS, Pardo MP: Systemic lupus erythematosus and catatonia: a case report. J Clin Psychiatry 44:155–156, 1983

Maes M: Evidence for an immune response in major depression: a review and hypothesis. Prog Neuropsychopharmacol Biol Psychiatry 19:11–38, 1995

Maes M, Bosmans E, Suy E, et al: Antiphospholipid, antinuclear, Epstein-Barr and cytomegalovirus antibodies, and soluble interleukin-2 receptors in depressive patients. J Affect Disord 21:133–140, 1991

Maes M, Meltzer H, Jacobs J, et al: Autoimmunity in depression: increased antiphospholipid autoantibodies. Acta Psychiatr Scand 87:160–166, 1993

Maes M, Meltzer HY, Bosmans E: Immune-inflammatory markers in schizophrenia: comparison to normal controls and effects of clozapine. Acta Psychiatr Scand 89:346–351, 1994a

Maes M, Scharpé S, Meltzer HY, et al: Increased neopterin and interferon-gamma secretion and lower availability of L-tryptophan in major depression: further evidence for an immune response. Psychiatry Res 54:143–160, 1994b

Maes M, Boosmans E, Calabrese J, et al: Interleukin-2 and interleukin-6 in schizophrenia and mania: effects of neuroleptics and mood stabilizers. J Psychiatr Res 29:141–152, 1995a

Maes M, Smith R, Scharpé S: The monocyte-T-lymphocyte hypothesis of major depression. Psychoneuroendocrinology 20:111–116, 1995b

Maeshima E, Yamada Y, Yukawa S, et al: Higher cortical dysfunction, antiphospholipid antibodies and neuroradiological examinations in systemic lupus erythematosus. Internal Medicine 31:1169–1174, 1992

Magaudda A, Dalla Bernardina B, De Marco P, et al: Bilateral occipital calcification, epilepsy and coeliac disease: clinical and neuroimaging features of a new syndrome. J Neurol Neurosurg Psychiatry 56:885–889, 1993

Magner MB: Psychiatric morbidity in outpatients with systemic lupus erythematosus. S Afr Med J 80:291–293, 1990

Malinow KL, Molina R, Gordon B, et al: Neuropsychiatric dysfunction in primary Sjögren's syndrome. Ann Intern Med 103:344–349, 1985

Manthorpe R, Manthorpe T, Sjöberg S: Magnetic resonance imaging of the brain in patients with primary Sjögren's syndrome. Scand J Rheumatol 21:148–149, 1992

Manto M, Goldman S, Bodur H: Syndrome cérébelleux associé à une encéphalopathie d'Hashimoto. Rev Neurol (Paris) 152:202–204, 1996

Markus HS, Bunker CR, Kouris K, et al: rCBF abnormalities detected, and sequentially followed, by SPECT in neuro-Behçet's syndrome with normal CT and MRI imaging. J Neurol 239:363–366, 1992

Markus HS, Hopkinson N: Migraine and headache in systemic lupus erythematosus and their relationship with antibodies against phospholipids. J Neurol 239:39–42, 1992

Marsh MN: The natural history of gluten sensitivity: defining, refining, and re-defining. Quart J Med 88:9–13, 1995

Martin K, Rogers T, Kavanaugh A: Central nervous system angiopathy associated with cocaine abuse. J Rheumatol 22:780–782, 1995

Matsukawa Y, Sawada S, Hayama T, et al: Suicide in patients with systemic lupus erythematosus: a clinical analysis of seven suicidal patients. Lupus 3:31–35, 1994

Matsumoto R, Nakano I, Shiga J, et al: Systemic lupus erythematosus with multiple perivascular spongy changes in the cerebral deep structures, midbrain and cerebellar white matter: a case report. J Neurol Sci 145:147–153, 1997

Matsumoto R, Shintaku M, Suzuki S, et al: Cerebral perivenous calcification in neuropsychiatric lupus erythematosus: a case report. Neuroradiology 40:583–586, 1998

Mauch E, Völk C, Kratzsch G, et al: Neurological and neuropsychiatric dysfunction in primary Sjögren's syndrome. Acta Neurol Scand 89:31–35, 1994

Mavrikakis ME, Antoniades LG, Germanides JB, et al: Organic brain syndrome with psychosis as an initial manifestation of systemic lupus erythematosus in an elderly woman. Ann Rheum Dis 51:117–119, 1992

McAllister CG, van Kammen DP, Rehn TJ, et al: Increases in CSF levels of interleukin-2 in schizophrenia: effects of recurrence of psychosis and medication status. Am J Psychiatry 152:1291–1297, 1995

McCabe DJH, Burke T, Connolly S, et al: Amnesic syndrome with bilateral mesial temporal lobe involvement in Hashimoto's encephalopathy. Neurology 54:737–739, 2000

McLean BN, Miller D, Thompson D: Oligoclonal banding of IgG in CSF, blood-brain barrier function, and MRI findings in patients with sarcoidosis, systemic lupus erythematosus, and Behçet's disease involving the nervous system. J Neurol Neurosurg Psychiatry 58:548–554, 1995

Mclean CA, Gonzales MF, Dowling JP: Systemic giant cell arteritis and cerebellar infarction. Stroke 24:899–902, 1993

Ménage P, de Toffol B, Degenne D, et al: Syndrome de Gougerot-Sjögren primitif. Atteinte neurologique centrale évoluant par poussées. Rev Neurol (Paris) 149:554–556, 1993

Mendez MF, Zander B: Frontal lobe dysfunction from meningeal sarcoidosis. Psychosomatics 33:215–217, 1992

Menon S, Jameson-Shortall E, Newman SP, et al: A longitudinal study of anticardiolipin antibody levels and cognitive functioning in systemic lupus erythematosus. Arthritis Rheum 42:735–741, 1999

Merkel PA, Koroshetz WJ, Irizarry MC, et al: Cocaine-associated cerebral vasculitis. Semin Arthritis Rheum 25:172–183, 1995

Merrill J: Tumor necrosis factor alpha, interleukin 1 and related cytokines in brain development: normal and pathological. Dev Neurosci 14:1–10, 1992

Mevorach D, Raz E, Steiner I: Evidence for intrathecal synthesis of autoantibodies in systemic lupus erythematosus with neurological involvement. Lupus 3:117–121, 1994

Meyers CA, Valentine AD, Wong FCL, et al: Reversible neurotoxicity of interleukin-2 and tumor necrosis factor: correlation of SPECT with neuropsychological testing. J Neuropsychiatry Clin Neurosci 6:285–288, 1994

Michalski JP, McCombs CC: Celiac disease: clinical features and pathogenesis. Am J Med Sci 307:204–211, 1994

Michel D, Vial C, Antoine JC, et al: Angiopathie cérébrale aiguë bénigne: quatre cas. Rev Neurol (Paris) 141:786–792, 1985

Miguel EC, Rodrigues Pereira RM, de Bragança Pereira CA, et al: Psychiatric manifestations of systemic lupus erythematosus: clinical features, symptoms, and signs of central nervous system activity in 43 patients. Medicine 73:224–232, 1994

Miller DH, Kendall BE, Barter S, et al: Magnetic resonance imaging in central nervous system sarcoidosis. Neurology 38:378–383, 1988

Miller DH, Buchanan N, Barker G, et al: Gadolinium-enhanced magnetic resonance imaging of the central nervous system in systemic lupus erythematosus. J Neurol 239:460–464, 1992

Mitsias P, Levine SR: Large cerebral vessel occlusive disease in systemic lupus erythematosus. Neurology 44:385–393, 1994

Moll JWB, Markusse HM, Pijnenburg JJJM, et al: Antineuronal antibodies in patients with neurologic complications of primary Sjögren's syndrome. Neurology 43:2574–2581, 1993

Montalbán J, Arboix A, Staub H, et al: Transient global amnesia and antiphospholipid antibodies. Clin Exp Rheumatol 7:85–87, 1989

Montalbán J, Cervera R, Font J, et al: Lack of association between anticardiolipin antibodies and migraine in systemic lupus erythematosus. Neurology 42:681–682, 1992

Montane de la Roque P, Arlet P, Berry I, et al: Manifestations neuro-psychiatriques du syndrome de Gougerot-Sjögren primitif. Intérêt de l'IRM cerebral: a propos de deu cas. Revue de la littérature. Sem Hôp Paris 66:1577–1582, 1990

Monteiro MLR, Swanson RA, Coppeto JR, et al: A microangiopathic syndrome of encephalopathy, hearing loss, and retinal arteriolar occlusions. Neurology 35:1113–1121, 1985

Moore DP: Neuropsychiatric aspects of Sydenham's chorea: a comprehensive review. J Clin Psychiatry 57:407–414, 1996

Moore PM: Neurological manifestation of vasculitis: update on immunopathogenic mechanisms and clinical features. Ann Neurol 37 (suppl 1):S131–S141, 1995

Morrow PL, McQuillen JB: Cerebral vasculitis associated with cocaine abuse. J Forensic Sci 38:732–738, 1993

Motomura S, Tabira T, Kuroiwa Y: A clinical comparative study of multiple sclerosis and neuro-Behçet's syndrome. J Neurol Neurosurg Psychiatry 43:210–213, 1980

Mukherjee S, Mahadik SP, Korenovsky A, et al: Serum antibodies to nicotinic acetylcholine receptors in schizophrenic patients. Schizophr Res 12:131–136, 1994

Mumford CJ, Fletcher NA, Ironside JW, et al: Progressive ataxia, focal seizures, and malabsorption syndrome in a 41 year old woman. J Neurol Neurosurg Psychiatry 60:225–230, 1996

Murphy JM, Gomez-Anson B, Gillard JH, et al: Wegener granulomatosis: MR imaging findings in brain and meninges. Radiology 213:794–799, 1999

Murphy TK, Goodman WK, Fudge MW, et al: B lymphocyte antigen D8/17: a peripheral marker for childhood-onset obsessive-compulsive disorder and Tourette's syndrome? Am J Psychiatry 154:402–407, 1997

Naber D, Sand P, Heigl B: Psychopathological and neuropsychological effects of 8-days' corticosteroid treatment: a prospective study. Psychoneuroendocrinology 21:25–31, 1996

Nausieda PA: Sydenham's chorea, chorea gravidarum and contraceptive-induced chorea, in Handbook of Clinical Neurology, Vol 5: Extrapyramidal Disorders. Edited by Vinken PJ, Bruyn GW, Klawans HL. Amsterdam, The Netherlands, Elsevier Science, 1986, 359–367

Nausieda PA, Bieliauskas LA, Bacon LD, et al: Chronic dopaminergic sensitivity after Sydenham's chorea. Neurology 33:750–754, 1983

Nausieda PA, Grossman BJ, Koller WC, et al: Sydenham chorea: an update. Neurology 30:331–334, 1980

Nesher G, Hanna VE, Moore TL, et al: Thrombotic microangiopathic hemolytic anemia in systemic lupus erythematosus. Semin Arthritis Rheum 24:165–172, 1994

Neubuerger KT: The brain in rheumatic fever. Diseases of the Nervous System 8:259–262, 1947

Neuwelt CM, Lacks S, Kaye BR, et al: Role of intravenous cyclophosphamide in the treatment of severe neuropsychiatric systemic lupus erythematosus. Am J Med 98:32–41, 1995

Neveu PJ: Asymmetrical brain modulation of the immune response. Brain Res Rev 17:101–107, 1992

Nishikai M, Akiya K, Tojo T, et al: "Seronegative" Sjögren's syndrome manifested as a subset of chronic fatigue syndrome. Br J Rheumatol 35:471–474, 1996

Nishino H, Rubino FA, DeRemee RA, et al: Neurological involvement in Wegener's granulomatosis: an analysis of 324 consecutive patients at the Mayo Clinic. Ann Neurol 33:4–9, 1993a

Nishino H, DeRemee RA, Rubino RA, et al: Wegener's granulomatosis associated with vasculitis of the temporal artery: report of five cases. Mayo Clin Proc 68:115–121, 1993b

Nojima Y, Sinota S, Yamada A, et al: Correlation of antibodies to ribosomal P protein with psychosis in patients with systemic lupus erythematosus. Ann Rheum Dis 51:1053–1055, 1992

Nolte KB, Brass LM, Fletterick CF: Intracranial hemorrhage associated with cocaine abuse: a prospective autopsy study. Neurology 46:1291–1296, 1996

Nolte KW, Unbehaun A, Sieker H, et al: Hashimoto encephalopathy: a brainstem vasculitis? Neurology 54:769–770, 2000

Nordmark G, Boquist L, Rönnblom L: Limited Wegener's granulomatosis with central nervous system involvement and fatal outcome. J Int Med 242:433–436, 1997

Nossent JC, Hovestadt A, Schönfeld DHW, et al: Single-photon-emission computed tomography of the brain in the evaluation of cerebral lupus. Arthritis Rheum 34:1397–1403, 1991

O'Brien GM, Baughman RP, Broderick JP, et al: Paranoid psychosis due to neurosarcoidosis. Sarcoidosis 11:34–36, 1994

O'Halloran HS, Pearson PA, Lee WB, et al: Microangiopathy of the brain, retina, and cochlea (Susac syndrome). Ophthalmology 105:1038–1044, 1998

Ohtsuka T, Saito Y, Hasgawa M, et al: Central nervous system disease in a child with primary Sjögren syndrome. J Pediatr 127:961–963, 1995

Oken RJ, Schulzer M: At issue: schizophrenia and rheumatoid arthritis: the negative association revisited. Schizophr Bull 25:625–638, 1999

Oksanen V: Neurosarcoidosis. Sarcoidosis 11:76–79, 1994

Öktem-Tanör Ö, Baykan-Kurt B, Hakan Gürvit I, et al: Neuropsychological follow-up of 12 patients with neuro-Behçet disease. J Neurol 246:113–119, 1999

Olsen ML, Arnett FC, Rosenbaum D, et al: Sjögren's syndrome and other rheumatic disorders presenting to a neurology service. J Autoimmun 2:477–483, 1989

Omdal R, Roalsø S: Chorea gravidarum and chorea associated with oral contraceptives: diseases due to antiphospholipid antibodies? Acta Neurol Scand 86:219–220, 1992

Ovsiew F: Neuropathogenesis of delirium (letter). Psychosomatics 36:156, 1995

Papo T, Biousse V, Lehoang P, et al: Susac syndrome. Medicine 77:3–11, 1998

Patten SB, Neutel CI: Corticosteroid-induced adverse psychiatric effects: incidence, diagnosis and management. Drug Saf 22:111–122, 2000

Patten SB, Williams JVA, Love EJ: Self-reported depressive symptoms in association with medication exposures among medical inpatients: a cross-sectional study. Can J Psychiatry 40:264–269, 1995

Paulley JW, Hughes JP: Giant-cell arteritis, or arteritis of the aged. BMJ 2:1562–1567, 1960

Pellat J, Perret J, Pasquier B, et al: Étude anatomoclinique et angiographique d'une observation de thromboangiose disséminée à manifestations cérébrales prédominantes. Rev Neurol (Paris) 132:517–535, 1976

Peltola JT, Haapala A-M, Isojärvi JI, et al: Antiphospholipid and antinuclear antibodies in patients with epilepsy or new-onset seizure disorders. Am J Med 109:712–717, 2000

Perlmutter SJ, Leitman SF, Hamburger S, et al: Therapeutic plasma exchange and intravenous immunoglobulin for obsessive-compulsive disorder and tic disorders in childhood. Lancet 354:1153–1158, 1999

Peschen-Rosin R, Schabet M, Dichgans J: Manifestation of Hashimoto's encephalopathy years before onset of thyroid disease. Eur Neurol 41:79–84, 1999

Peterson BS, Leckman JF, Tucker D, et al: Preliminary findings of antistreptococcal antibody titers and basal ganglia volumes in tic, obsessive-compulsive, and attention-deficit/hyperactivity disorders. Arch Gen Psychiatry 57:364–372, 2000

Pettee AD, Wasserman BA, Adams NL, et al: Familial Sneddon's syndrome: clinical, hematologic, and radiographic findings in two brothers. Neurology 44:399–405, 1994

Petty GW, Engel AG, Younge BR, et al: Retinocochleocerebral vasculopathy. Medicine 77:12–40, 1998

Piazza PV, Rougé-Pont F, Deroche V, et al: Glucocorticoids have state-dependent stimulant effects on the mesencephalic dopaminergic transmission. Proc Natl Acad Sci U S A 93:8716–8720, 1996

Pierot L, Sauve C, Leger J-M, et al: Asymptomatic cerebral involvement in Sjögren's syndrome: MRI findings of 15 cases. Neuroradiology 35:378–380, 1993

Pinching AJ, Travers RL, Hughes GRV, et al: Oxygen-15 brain scanning for detection of cerebral involvement in systemic lupus erythematosus. Lancet 1:898–900, 1978

Postiglione A, De Chiara S, Soricelli A, et al: Alterations of cerebral blood flow and antiphospholipid antibodies in patients with systemic lupus erythematosus. Int J Clin Lab Res 28:34–38, 1998

Pou Serradell A, Masó E, Roquer J, et al: Angéite isolée du système nerveux central. Étude clinique et neuropathologique de deux cas. Rev Neurol (Paris) 151:258–266, 1995

Presley AP, Kahn A, Williamson N: Antinuclear antibodies in patients on lithium carbonate. BMJ 2:280–281, 1976

Press J, Palayew K, Laxer RM, et al: Antiribosomal P antibodies in pediatric patients with systemic lupus erythematosus and psychosis. Arthritis Rheum 39:671–676, 1996

Purandare KN, Wagle AC, Parker SR: Psychiatric morbidity in patients with systemic lupus erythematosus. Quart J Med 92:283–286, 1999

Rapaport MH, Lohr JB: Serum-soluble interleukin-2 receptors in neuroleptic-naive schizophrenic subjects and in medicated schizophrenic subjects with and without tardive dyskinesia. Acta Psychiatr Scand 90:311–315, 1994

Rautenberg W, Hennerici M, Aulich A, et al: Immunosuppressive therapy and Sneddon's syndrome (letter). Lancet 2:629–630, 1988

Rebollo M, Val JF, Garijo F, et al: Livedo reticularis and cerebrovascular lesions (Sneddon's syndrome): clinical, radiological and pathological features in eight cases. Brain 106:965–979, 1983

Reckart MD, Eisendrath SJ: Exogenous corticosteroid effects on mood and cognition: case presentations. Int J Psychosom 37:57–61, 1990

Rhodes RH, Madelaire NC, Petrelli M, et al: Primary angiitis and angiopathy of the central nervous system and their relationship to systemic giant cell arteritis. Arch Pathol Lab Med 119:334–349, 1995

Rimon R, Kronqvist K, Helve T: Overt psychopathology in systemic lupus erythematosus. Scand J Rheumatol 17:143–146, 1988

Ritchlin CT, Chabot RJ, Alper K, et al: Quantitative electroencephalography: a new approach to the diagnosis of cerebral dysfunction in systemic lupus erythematosus. Arthritis Rheum 35:1330–1342, 1992

Roche NE, Fulbright JW, Wagner AD, et al: Correlation of interleukin-6 production and disease activity in polymyalgia rheumatica and giant cell arteritis. Arthritis Rheum 36:1286–1294, 1993

Rosen GD, Waters NS, Galaburda AM, et al: Behavioral consequences of neonatal injury of the cortex. Brain Res 681:177–189, 1995

Rosenbaum R: Neuromuscular complications of connective tissue disease. Muscle Nerve 24:154–169, 2001

Rougemont D, Bousser MG, Wechsler B, et al: Manifestations neurologique de la maladie de Behçet: vingt-quatre observations. Rev Neurol (Paris) 138:493–505, 1982

Rovaris M, Viti B, Ciboddo G, et al: Brain involvement in systemic immune mediated diseases: magnetic resonance and magnetisation transfer imaging study. J Neurol Neurosurg Psychiatry 68:170–177, 2000

Rubbert A, Marienhagen J, Pirner K, et al: Single-photon-emission computed tomography of cerebral blood flow in the evaluation of central nervous system involvement in patients with systemic lupus erythematosus. Arthritis Rheum 36:1253–1262, 1993

Ruiz-Irastorza G, Khamashta MA: Warfarin for multiple sclerosis (editorial)? Quart J Med 93:497–499, 2000

Rumbaugh CL, Bergeron RT, Fang HCH, et al: Cerebral angiographic changes in the drug abuse patient. Radiology 101:335–344, 1971

Rush PJ, Inman R, Bernstein M, et al: Isolated vasculitis of the central nervous system in a patient with celiac disease. Am J Med 81:1092–1094, 1986

Sabaawi M, Gutierrez-Nunez J, Fragala MR: Neurosarcoidosis presenting as schizophreniform disorder. Int J Psychiatry Med 22:269–274, 1992

Sabbadini MG, Manfredi AA, Bozzolo E, et al: Central nervous system involvement in systemic lupus erythematosus patients without overt neuropsychiatric manifestations. Lupus 8:11–19, 1999

Sabet A, Sibbitt WL, Stidley CA, et al: Neurometabolite markers of cerebral injury in the antiphospholipid antibody syndrome of systemic lupus erythematosus. Stroke 29:2254–2260, 1998

Sailer M, Burchert W, Ehrenheim C, et al: Positron emission tomography and magnetic resonance imaging for cerebral involvement in patients with systemic lupus erythematosus. J Neurol 244:186–193, 1997

Sakic B, Szechtman H, Denburg S, et al: Brain-reactive antibodies and behavior of autoimmune MRL-lpr mice. Physiol Behav 54:1025–1029, 1993a

Sakic B, Szechtman H, Denburg S, et al: Spatial learning during the course of autoimmune disease in MRL mice. Behav Brain Res 54:57–66, 1993b

Sanson M, Duyckaerts C, Thibault J-L, et al: Sarcoidosis presenting as late-onset dementia. J Neurol 243:484–487, 1996

Sato K, Miyasaka N, Nishioka K, et al: Primary Sjögren's syndrome associated with systemic necrotizing vasculitis: a fatal case (letter). Arthritis Rheum 30:717–718, 1987

Satoh J, Miyasaka N, Yamada T, et al: Extensive cerebral infarction due to involvement of both anterior cerebral arteries by Wegener's granulomatosis. Ann Rheum Dis 47:606–611, 1988

Savage COS, Winearls CG, Evans DJ, et al: Microscopic polyarteritis: presentation, pathology and prognosis. Quart J Med 56:467–483, 1985

Schielke E, Nolte C, Müller W, et al: Sarcoidosis presenting as rapidly progressive dementia: clinical and neuropathological evaluation. J Neurol 248:522–524, 2001

Schmidley JW: Central Nervous System Angiitis. Boston, MA, Butterworth Heinemann, 2000

Schneebaum AB, Singleton JD, West SG, et al: Association of psychiatric manifestations with antibodies to ribosomal P proteins in systemic lupus erythematosus. Am J Med 90:54–62, 1991

Schott K, Batra A, Richartz E, et al: Antibrain antibodies in mental disorder: no evidence for antibodies against synaptic membranes. J Neural Transm 105:517–524, 1998

Schwartz M, Rochas M, Weller B, et al: High association of anticardiolipin antibodies with psychosis. J Clin Psychiatry 59:20–23, 1998

Scott IA, Boyle RS: Sneddon's syndrome. Aust N Z J Med 16:799–802, 1986

Scott TF: Neurosarcoidosis: progress and clinical aspects. Neurology 43:8–12, 1993

Segui J, Ramos-Casals M, de Flores T, et al: Psychiatric and psychosocial disorders in patients with systemic lupus erythematosus: a longitudinal study of active and inactive stages of the disease. Lupus 9:584–588, 2000

Selnes OA, Gordon B, Malinow KL, et al: Cognitive dysfunction in primary Sjögren's syndrome (abstract). Neurology 35:S179, 1985

Serdaroglu P: Behçet's disease and the nervous system. J Neurol 245:197–205, 1998

Serdaroglu P, Yazici H, Özdemir C, et al: Neurologic involvement in Behçet's syndrome: a prospective study. Arch Neurol 46:265–269, 1989

Sfikakis PP, Mitsikostas DD, Manoussakis MN, et al: Headache in systemic lupus erythematosus: a controlled study. Br J Rheumatol 37:300–303, 1998

Sharma OP: Neurosarcoidosis: a personal perspective based on the study of 37 patients. Chest 112:220–228, 1997

Shenberger KN, Meharg JG, Lane CD: Temporal arteritis presenting as ataxia and dementia. Postgrad Med 69:246–249, 1981

Shintaku M, Matsumoto R: Disseminated perivenous necrotizing encephalomyelitis in systemic lupus erythematosus: report of an autopsy case. Acta Neuropathologica 95:313–317, 1998

Shiozawa S, Kuroki Y, Kim M, et al: Interferon-alpha in lupus psychosis. Arthritis Rheum 35:417–422, 1992

Shortall E, Isenberg D, Newman SP: Factors associated with mood and mood disorders in SLE. Lupus 4:272–279, 1995

Sibbitt WL, Sibbitt RR: Magnetic resonance spectroscopy and positron emission tomography scanning in neuropsychiatric systemic lupus erythematosus. Rheum Dis Clin North Am 19:851–868, 1993

Sibbitt WL, Sibbitt RR, Brooks WM: Neuroimaging in neuropsychiatric systemic lupus erythematosus. Arthritis Rheum 42:2026–2038, 1999

Sibley JT, Olszynski WP, DeCoteau WE, et al: The incidence and prognosis of central nervous system disease in systemic lupus erythematosus. J Rheumatol 19:47–52, 1992

Silvestrini M, Matteis M, Troisi E, et al: Migrainous stroke and the antiphospholipid antibodies. Eur Neurol 34:316–319, 1994

Singer HS: PANDAS and immunomodulatory therapy (editorial). Lancet 354:1137–1138, 1999

Singer HS, Giuliano JD, Hansen BH, et al: Antibodies against human putamen in children with Tourette syndrome. Neurology 50:1618–1624, 1998

Singer HS, Giuliano JD, Hansen BH, et al: Antibodies against a neuron-like (HTB-10 neuroblastoma) cell in children with Tourette syndrome. Biol Psychiatry 46:775–780, 1999

Singleton JD, West SG, Reddy VVB, et al: Cerebral vasculitis complicating rheumatoid arthritis. South Med J 88:470–474, 1995

Sirota P, Firer M, Schild K, et al: Increased anti-Sm antibodies in schizophrenic patients and their families. Prog Neuropsychopharmacol Biol Psychiatry 17:793–900, 1993a

Sirota P, Firer MA, Schild K, et al: Autoantibodies to DNA in multicase families with schizophrenia. Biol Psychiatry 33:450–455, 1993b

Sitzer M, Söhngen D, Siebler M, et al: Cerebral microembolism in patients with Sneddon's syndrome. Arch Neurol 52:271–275, 1995

Small P, Brisson M-L: Wegener's granulomatosis presenting as temporal arteritis. Arthritis Rheum 34:220–223, 1991

Smith A, Tyrrell D, Coyle K, et al: Effects of interferon alpha on performance in man: a preliminary report. Psychopharmacology (Berl) 96:414–416, 1988

Smith RW, Ellison DW, Jenkins EA, et al: Cerebellum and brainstem vasculopathy in systemic lupus erythematosus: two clinico-pathological cases. Ann Rheum Dis 53:327–330, 1994

Sonin L, Patterson R: Corticosteroid-dependent asthma and schizophrenia. Arch Intern Med 144:554–556, 1984

Spezialetti R, Bluestein HG, Peter JB, et al: Neuropsychiatric disease in Sjögren's syndrome: anti-ribosomal P and anti-neuronal antibodies. Am J Med 95:153–160, 1993

Spivak B, Radwan M, Bartur P, et al: Antinuclear autoantibodies in chronic schizophrenia. Acta Psychiatr Scand 92:266–269, 1995

Stern BJ, Krumholz A, Johns C, et al: Sarcoidosis and its neurological manifestations. Arch Neurol 42:909–917, 1985

Stimmler MM, Coletti PM, Quismorio FP: Magnetic resonance imaging of the brain in neuropsychiatric systemic lupus erythematosus. Semin Arthritis Rheum 22:335–349, 1993

Stockhammer G, Felber SR, Zelger B, et al: Sneddon's syndrome: diagnosis by skin biopsy and MRI in 17 patients. Stroke 24:685–690, 1993

Sundén-Cullberg J, Tedroff J, Aquilonius S-M: Reversible chorea in primary antiphospholipid syndrome. Mov Disord 13:147–149, 1998

Sunseri M, Murphy FM, Kattah J, et al: Subacute encephalopathy associated with lupus anticoagulant. Neurology 40 (suppl 1):354, 1990

Susac JO: Susac's syndrome: the triad of microangiopathy of the brain and retina with hearing loss in young women. Neurology 44:591–593, 1994

Susac JO, Hardman JM, Selhorst JB: Microangiopathy of the brain and retina. Neurology 29:313–316, 1979

Swedo SE: Sydenham's chorea: a model for childhood autoimmune neuropsychiatric disorders. JAMA 272:1788–1791, 1994

Swedo SE, Leonard HL, Schapiro MB, et al: Sydenham's chorea: physical and psychological symptoms of St Vitus dance. Pediatrics 91:706–713, 1993

Swedo SE, Leonard HL, Kiessling LS: Speculations on antineuronal antibody-mediated neuropsychiatric disorders of childhood. Pediatrics 93:323–326, 1994

Swedo SE, Leonard HL, Mittleman BB, et al: Identification of children with pediatric autoimmune neuropsychiatric disorders associated with streptococcal infections by a marker associated with rheumatic fever. Am J Psychiatry 154:110–112, 1997

Swedo SE, Leonard HL, Garvey M, et al: Pediatric Autoimmune Neuropsychiatric Disorders Associated with Streptococcal Infections: clinical description of the first 50 cases. Am J Psychiatry 155:264–271, 1998

Tan EM, Cohen AS, Fries JF, et al: The 1982 revised criteria for the classification of systemic lupus erythematosus. Arthritis Rheum 25:1271–1277, 1982

Tate C, Salloway S, Rogg J: Case conference: behavior change, hallucinations, and memory loss in a 25-year-old man. J Neuropsychiatry Clin Neurosci 5:435–441, 1993

Teh LS, Isenberg DA: Antiribosomal P protein antibodies in systemic lupus erythematosus: a reappraisal. Arthritis Rheum 37:307–315, 1994

Teh LS, Bedwell AE, Isenberg DA, et al: Antibodies to protein P in systemic lupus erythematosus. Ann Rheum Dis 51:489–494, 1992

Terao Y, Sakai K, Kato S, et al: Antineuronal antibody in Sjögren's syndrome masquerading as paraneoplastic cerebellar degeneration (letter). Lancet 343:790, 1994

Tesar JT, McMillan V, Molina R, et al: Optic neuropathy and central nervous system disease associated with primary Sjögren's syndrome. Am J Med 92:686–692, 1992

Thiebaut F: Sydenham's chorea, in Handbook of Clinical Neurology, Vol 6. Edited by Vinken PJ, Bruyn GW. Amsterdam, The Netherlands, Elsevier, 1968, pp 409–434

Thomas P, Lebrun C, Mahagne MH, et al: Encéphalopathie ischémique au cours d'un syndrome primaire des anticorps antiphospholipides. Rev Neurol (Paris) 149:336–339, 1993

Thompson C, Checkley S: Short term memory deficit in a patient with cerebral sarcoidosis. Brit J Psychiatry 139:160–161, 1981

Tola MR, Granieri E, Caniatti L, et al: Systemic lupus erythematosus presenting with neurological disorders. J Neurol 239:61–64, 1992

Totta F, Colamussi P, Bajocchi G: Single photon emission computed tomography in neuropsychiatrtic systemic lupus erythematosus (letter). J Rheumatol 23:1310, 1996

Toubi E, Khamashta MA, Panarra A, et al: Association of antiphospholipid antibodies with central nervous system disease in systemic lupus erythematosus. Am J Med 99:397–401, 1995

Tourbah A, Piette J-C, Benoît N, et al: Aspects clinicques, biologiques et neuroradiologiques du syndrome de Sneddon: 26 observations. Rev Neurol (Paris) 153:652–658, 1997a

Tourbah A, Piette JC, Iba-Zizen MT, et al: The natural course of cerebral lesions in Sneddon syndrome. Arch Neurol 54:53–60, 1997b

Tourbah A, Clapin A, Gout O, et al: Systemic autoimmune features and multiple sclerosis: a 5-year follow-up study. Arch Neurol 55:517–521, 1998

Trevisani VFM, Castro AA, Neves Neto JF, et al: Cyclophosphamide versus methylprednisolone for treating neuropsychiatric involvement in systemic lupus erythematosus (Cochrane Review), in The Cochrane Library, Issue 4. Oxford, UK, Update Software Ltd, 2001

Trier JS: Diagnosis of celiac sprue. Gastroenterology 115:211–216, 1998

Trysberg E, Carlsten H, Tarkowski A: Intrathecal cytokines in systemic lupus erythematosus with central nervous system involvement. Lupus 9:498–503, 2000

Tsakiris DA, Kappos L, Reber G, et al: Lack of association between antiphospholipid antibodies and migraine. Thromb Haemost 69:415–417, 1993

Tsokos GC, Tsokos M, le Riche NGH, et al: A clinical and pathological study of cerebrovascular disease in patients with systemic lupus erythematosus. Semin Arthritis Rheum 16:70–78, 1986

Tzioufas AG, Tzortzakis NG, Panou-Pomonis E, et al: The clinical relevance of antibodies to ribosomal-P common epitope in two targeted systemic lupus erythematosus populations: a large cohort of consecutive patients and patients with active central nervous system disease. Ann Rheum Dis 59:99–104, 2000

Urban E, Jabbari B, Robles H: Concurrent cerebral venous sinus thrombosis and myeloradiculopathy in Sjögren's syndrome. Neurology 44:554–556, 1994

Utset TO, Golden M, Siberry G, et al: Depressive symptoms in patients with systemic lupus erythematosus: association with central nervous system lupus and Sjögren's syndrome. J Rheumatol 21:2039–2045, 1994

Valtysdottir ST, Gudbjörnsson G, Lindqvist U, et al: Anxiety and depression in patients with primary Sjögren's syndrome. J Rheumatol 27:165–169, 2000

van Dam A, Nossent H, de Jong J, et al: Diagnostic value of antibodies against ribosomal phosphoproteins. A cross sectional and longitudinal study. J Rheumatol 18:1026–1034, 1991

van den Berg JSP, Horstink MWIM, van den Hoogen FHJ, et al: Dystonia; a central nervous system presentation of Sjogren's syndrome. Mov Disord 14:374–375, 1999

Van Horn G, Arnett FC, Dimachkie MM: Reversible dementia and chorea in a young woman with the lupus anticoagulant. Neurology 46:1599–1603, 1996

Varney NR, Alexander B, MacIndoe JH: Reversible steroid dementia in patients without steroid psychosis. Am J Psychiatry 141:369–372, 1984

Vereker R: The psychiatric aspects of temporal arteritis. J Ment Sci 98:280–286, 1952

Verrot D, San-Marco M, Dravet C, et al: Prevalence and signification of antinuclear and anticardiolipin antibodies in patients with epilepsy. Am J Med 103:33–37, 1997

Vila N, Graus F, Blesa R, et al: Microangiopathy of the brain and retina (Susac's syndrome): two patients with atypical features. Neurology 45:1225–1226, 1995

Villemain F, Magnin M, Feuillet-Fieux M-N, et al: Anti-histone antibodies in schizophrenia and affective disorders. Psychiatry Res 24:53–60, 1988

Vogelsang SA, Heyes MP, West SG, et al: Quinolinic acid in patients with systemic lupus erythematosus and neuropsychiatric manifestations. J Rheumatol 23:850–855, 1996

Vollertsen RS, McDonald TJ, Banks PM, et al: Cogan's syndrome: 18 cases and a review of the literature. Mayo Clin Proc 61:344–361, 1986

Vollmer TL, Guarnaccia J, Harrington W, et al: Idiopathic granulomatous angiitis of the central nervous system: diagnostic challenges. Arch Neurol 50:925–930, 1993

von Brauchitsch H: Antinuclear factors in psychiatric disorders. Am J Psychiatry 128:1552–1554, 1972

Vrethem M, Ernerudh J, Lindström F, et al: Immunoglobulins within the central nervous system in primary Sjögren's syndrome. J Neurol Sci 100:186–192, 1990

Walker RH, Spiera H, Brin MF, et al: Parkinsonism associated with Sjögren's syndrome: three cases and a review of the literature. Mov Disord 14:262–268, 1999

Ward MM, Studenski S: The time course of acute psychiatric episodes in systemic lupus erythematosus. J Rheumatol 18:535–539, 1991

Watanabe T, Sato T, Uchiumi T, et al: Neuropsychiatric manifestations in patients with systemic lupus erythematosus: diagnostic and predictive value of longitudinal examination of anti-ribosomal P antibody. Lupus 5:178–183, 1996

Weindl A, Kuwert T, Leenders KL, et al: Increased striatal glucose consumption in Sydenham's chorea. Mov Disord 8:437–444, 1993

Weiner DK, Allen NB: Large vessel vasculitis of the central nervous system in systemic lupus erythematosus: report and review of the literature. J Rheumatol 18:748–751, 1991

Weiner SM, Otte A, Schumacher M, et al: Diagnosis and monitoring of central nervous system involvement in systemic lupus erythematosus: value of F-18 fluorodeoxyglucose PET. Ann Rheum Dis 59:377–385, 2000

Weiss SR, Raskind R, Morganstern NL, et al: Intracerebral and subarachnoid hemorrhage following use of methamphetamine ("speed"). Surg Int 53:123–127, 1970

Weissenborn K, Lubach D, Schwabe C, et al: Sneddon's syndrome: clinical course and outcome. J Neurol 236:34–37, 1989

Weissenborn K, Rückert N, Ehrenheim C, et al: Neuropsychological deficits in patients with Sneddon's syndrome. J Neurol 243:357–363, 1996

Wekking EM: Psychiatric symptoms in systemic lupus erythematosus: an update. Psychosom Med 55:219–228, 1993

West SG, Emlen W, Wener MH, et al: Neuropsychiatric lupus erythematosus: a 10-year prospective study on the value of diagnostic tests. Am J Med 99:153–163, 1995

Westerman EM, Miles JM, Backonja M, et al: Neuropathologic findings in multi-infarct dementia associated with anticardiolipin antibody: evidence for endothelial injury as the primary event. Arthritis Rheum 35:1038–1041, 1992

Whitelaw DA, Spangenberg JJ, Rickman R, et al: The association between the antiphospholipid antibody syndrome and neuropsychological impairment in SLE. Lupus 8:444–448, 1999

Widner B, Sepp N, Kowald E, et al: Degradation of tryptophan in patients with systemic lupus erythematosus, in Tryptophan, Serotonin, and Melatonin: Basic Aspects and Applications. Edited by Huether G, Kochen W, Simat TJ, et al. New York, Plenum, 1999, pp 571–577

Wilcox JA, Nasrallah HA: Sydenham's chorea and psychosis. Neuropsychobiology 15:13–14, 1986

Wilcox JA, Nasrallah H: Sydenham's chorea and psychopathology. Neuropsychobiology 19:6–8, 1988

Wildemann B, Schülin C, Storch-Hagenlocher B, et al: Susac's syndrome: improvement with combined antiplatelet and calcium antagonist therapy. Stroke 27:149–151, 1996

Willigers H, Koehler PJ: Amnesic syndrome caused by neurosarcoidosis. Clin Neurol Neurosurg 95:131–135, 1993

Winfield JB, Shaw M, Silverman LM, et al: Intrathecal IgG synthesis and blood-brain barrier impairment in patients with systemic lupus erythematosus and central nervous system dysfunction. Am J Med 74:837–844, 1983

Wolkowitz OM: Prospective controlled studies of the behavioral and biological effects of exogenous corticosteroids. Psychoneuroendocrinology 19:233–255, 1994

Wolkowitz OM, Coppola R, Breier A, et al: Quantitative electroencephalographic correlates of steroid administration in man. Neuropsychobiology 27:224–230, 1993

Wolkowitz O, Reus VI, Canick J, et al: Glucocorticoid medication, memory and steroid psychosis in medical illness. Ann NY Acad Sci 823:81–96, 1997

Wood LC, Cooper DS: Autoimmune thyroid disease, left-handedness, and developmental dyslexia. Psychoneuroendocrinology 17:95–99, 1992

Wright P, Sham PC, Gilvarry CM, et al: Autoimmune diseases in the pedigrees of schizophrenic and control subjects. Schizophr Res 20:261–267, 1996

Wright RA, Kokmen E: Gradually progressive dementia without discrete cerebrovascular events in a patient with Sneddon's syndrome. Mayo Clin Proc 74:57–61, 1999

Yang ZW, Chengappa KNR, Shurin G, et al: An association between anti-hippocampal antibody concentration and lymphocyte production of IL-2 in patients with schizophrenia. Psychol Med 24:449–455, 1994

Yannitsi SG, Manoussakis MN, Mavridis AK, et al: Factors related to the presence of autoantibodies in patients with chronic mental disorders. Biol Psychiatry 27:747–756, 1990

Yin P-A: Ephedrine-induced intracerebral hemorrhage and central nervous system vasculitis (letter). Stroke 21:1641, 1990

Young AH, Sahakian BJ, Robbins TW, et al: The effects of chronic administration of hydrocortisone on cognitive function in normal male volunteers. Psychopharmacology 145:260–266, 1999

Zajicek JP, Scolding NJ, Foster O, et al: Central nervous system sarcoidosis—diagnosis and management. Quart J Med 92:103–117, 1999

Zalcman S, Green-Johnson JM, Murray L, et al: Cytokine-specific central monoamine alterations induced by interleukin-1, -2 and -6. Brain Res 643:40–49, 1994

Zelger B, Sepp N, Schmid KW, et al: Life history of cutaneous vascular lesions in Sneddon's syndrome. Hum Pathol 23:668–675, 1992

Zelger B, Sepp N, Stockhammer G, et al: Sneddon's syndrome: a long-term follow-up of 21 patients. Arch Dermatol 129:437–447, 1993

Zorilla EP, Cannon TD, Gur RE, et al: Leukocytes and organ-nonspecific autoantibodies in schizophrenics and their siblings: markers of vulnerability or disease? Biol Psychiatry 40:825–833, 1996

Zorilla EP, Cannon TD, Kessler J, et al: Leukocyte differentials predict short-term clinical outcome following antipsychotic treatment in schizophrenia. Biol Psychiatry 43:887–896, 1998

Zucker S, Zarrabi HM, Schubach WH, et al: Chlorpromazine-induced immunopathy: progressive increase in serum IgM. Medicine 69:92–100, 1990

# CHAPTER 25

# Neuropsychiatric Aspects of Endocrine Disorders

Elizabeth B. Boswell, M.D.

Theodore J. Anfinson, M.D.

Charles B. Nemeroff, M.D., Ph.D.

The relationship between endocrine disturbances and psychiatric symptomatology has been recognized for centuries. Indeed, it was the recognition of these phenomena that in part spawned the field of psychoneuroendocrinology. The epidemiology and phenomenology of psychiatric disorders is reviewed as they occur in diabetes mellitus and thyroid, adrenal, and parathyroid disorders, as well as in hyperprolactinemia. Pathophysiology is discussed when appropriate and available data permit. The cardinal signs and symptoms of each disorder are presented together with the psychiatric findings to assist clinicians in reviewing the context in which the psychiatric symptoms present.

The case literature was reviewed with scrutiny, with particular emphasis on determination of the qualitative nature of the psychiatric symptoms in a given case, the temporal relationship between onset of psychiatric symptoms and underlying endocrine disturbance, and the response to treatment. The methodology is similar to that utilized by Whybrow and Hurwitz (1976) in their classic review of the subject. Studies characterized by prospective design and structured interview techniques are emphasized.

## Diabetes Mellitus

### Cardinal Features of the Disorder

The presenting symptoms of type I or insulin-dependent diabetes mellitus (IDDM) are usually hunger, fatigue, weight loss, polyuria, and polydipsia. The majority of patients present by age 30 and are generally quite thin. Demonstration of an unequivocally high random glucose level (>200 mg/dL), an elevated fasting glucose level (>140 mg/dL) on more than one occasion, or sustained elevation of serum glucose level following a 75-g oral glucose loading dose is required to confirm the diagnosis. These patients are insulin deficient and require insulin to prevent weight loss, ketoacidosis, or death.

Type II or non-insulin-dependent diabetes mellitus (NIDDM) is often asymptomatic, being detected only through blood screening. The age at onset of NIDDM is typically after age 40 years, though presentations may occur earlier in obese patients or in Native Americans, African Americans, or persons of Mexican descent (Sherwin 1996). Presenting symptoms commonly include

Supported by the National Institute of Mental Health Conte Center for the Psychobiology of Major Mood Disorders.

polydipsia, polyuria, polyphagia, weight loss or gain, pruritus, dry mouth, visual disturbance, fatigue, and candidal vaginitis or balanitis. Diagnosis is made on demonstration of hyperglycemia. Hyperosmolar hyperglycemic nonketonic coma is the most serious acute metabolic complication of NIDDM.

## Psychiatric Symptoms in Diabetes Mellitus

Two community studies have evaluated the prevalence of psychiatric disorders in patients with diabetes mellitus. In the first study, a sample of 2,554 subjects revealed that the presence of psychiatric disorders was not higher among patients with diabetes than in those without medical illness (Wells et al. 1988). In contrast, Weyerer et al. (1989) used the Diagnostic Interview Schedule (DIS) in their community study of 1,536 subjects and revealed that the prevalence of psychiatric disorders was higher in patients with diabetes (43.1%) and other chronic medical conditions (50.7%) compared with control subjects (26.2%). Depressive disorders accounted for the significant difference noted between diabetic patients and control subjects.

### Cognitive Disorders

Numerous studies have revealed significant cognitive deficits occurring in patients with diabetes mellitus. Several mechanisms may account for impaired cognitive performance in patients with diabetes mellitus, including metabolic dyscontrol, such as ketoacidosis, hyperosmolar states, chronic hyperglycemia, recurrent mild hypoglycemia, hypoglycemic seizures, and the high prevalence of cerebrovascular disease (Richardson 1990).

Among patients with IDDM, several factors consistently emerge as important variables in the development of cognitive impairment, including age at onset, absenteeism from school, poor metabolic control, and episodes of hypoglycemia (Ryan 1988). Children with the onset of IDDM before age 4 years were compared with children with later-onset IDDM and sibling control subjects. Children with early-onset IDDM scored lower on visuospatial tasks and had more hypoglycemic seizures than did the other diabetic patients and sibling control subjects (Rovet et al. 1987). In a larger study of adolescents, patients with IDDM developing before age 5 years learned new information less efficiently and remembered less of that information over a 30-minute retention interval. More errors also were noted on visuospatial tasks, in addition to slower motor performance and lower scores of general intelligence. Moreover, 24% of early-onset IDDM

patients were judged to be clinically significantly impaired, compared with 6% of either the later-onset IDDM patients or nondiabetic control subjects (Ryan et al. 1985).

It is important to note that mild, superficially "asymptomatic" hypoglycemia is associated with deficits in neuropsychological performance as well. In a study of 23 children with IDDM, abstract and visual reasoning was more impaired among patients with frequent asymptomatic hypoglycemia (>40 mg/dL) than among those in whom asymptomatic hypoglycemia was an infrequent event (Golden et al. 1989).

In a study of 16 male subjects with IDDM (mean age: 28 years) who were exposed to a controlled reduction in blood glucose level via insulin infusion and recovery with intravenous glucose, subjective symptoms were recorded in addition to performance on a variety of neuropsychological tests (serial 7s, categorization, trail making, digit span, story recall, finger tapping). No patients showed symptoms at a blood glucose level of 52.3 mg/dL, and 25% of patients showed no symptoms at a blood glucose level of 32.4 mg/dL. In contrast, neuropsychological test results showed a decremental decline correlating with subnormal serum glucose levels and improvement with recovery (Pramming et al. 1986).

Howorka et al. (2000) compared the electroencephalographic patterns of 13 type I diabetes patients with a history of recurrent hypoglycemia with those of 14 type I diabetes patients without a history of recurrent hypoglycemia. The patients with a history of recurrent hypoglycemia showed decreased brain vigilance by electroencephalographic mapping compared with the patients without the hypoglycemia history.

These findings are important because of the recent emphasis on tighter metabolic control resulting from the Diabetes Control and Complications Trial (Diabetes Control and Complications Trial Research Group 1993). With tighter metabolic control, the risk of hypoglycemia increases, and clinicians must be aware of the neurobehavioral risks of even mild hypoglycemia.

Early studies finding a relationship between poor metabolic control and impaired neuropsychological performance relied on end-organ complications of diabetes as a marker for poor control (Rennick et al. 1968; Skenazy and Bigler 1984). Subsequent studies have utilized measurement of glycosylated hemoglobin (HgA1c) as a more precise determinant of longitudinal metabolic control.

Two separate investigations of older NIDDM patients revealed an association between poor metabolic control and neuropsychological impairment. In the first study (Perlmuter et al. 1984), 140 NIDDM patients (ages 55–74 years) were compared with 38 nondiabetic control subjects by using a serial learning task. Diabetic patients learned and recalled fewer words and required more study trials than did control subjects. These deficits correlated with elevations in HgA1c concentration and the severity of peripheral neuropathy (Perlmuter et al. 1984). In a later study (Reaven et al. 1990), 29 elderly patients with NIDDM (mean age: 69.8 years) exhibited more impairment on measures of verbal learning, abstract reasoning, and complex psychomotor functioning compared with 30 nondiabetic control subjects. In addition, the degree of neuropsychological impairment correlated with the degree of metabolic dyscontrol as measured by HgA1c determination (Reaven et al. 1990).

Furthermore, structural and functional central nervous system (CNS) abnormalities may result from long-term poor metabolic control and may contribute to the progression of cognitive deficits. In a study comparing 12 drug-treated NIDDM patients with 13 diet-treated NIDDM patients and 59 nondiabetic control subjects, greater temporal lobe atrophy was noted in the drug-treated groups (Soininen et al. 1992). This atrophy was negatively correlated with the level of fasting serum glucose. In two separate investigations, electroencephalographic abnormalities were noted to occur more frequently in children with IDDM who had recurrent severe hypoglycemia (Halonen et al. 1983; Haumont et al. 1979).

## Mood Disorders

As noted previously, depressive disorders accounted for the increased prevalence of psychiatric diagnoses in a community sample comparing diabetic patients with community members who did not have a medical illness (Weyerer et al. 1989). In a review of 20 studies of the prevalence of depression in patients with diabetes mellitus, Gavard et al. (1993) noted that prevalence rates of major depression varied from 8.5% to 27.3% in 9 controlled studies and varied from 11.0% to 19.9% in 11 uncontrolled investigations. Studies utilizing symptom subscales revealed depressive symptom rates ranging from 21.8% to 60.0% in controlled studies and from 10.0% to 28.0% in uncontrolled studies. In the excellent review by Gavard et al. (1993), numerous methodological problems are cited that account for the wide variance in prevalence rates. Carney's (1998) review of studies of prevalence of depression in diabetes emphasized that depression in diabetes is no more prevalent than depression in other chronic disease states. However, in a study of native Hawaiians with type II diabetes, Grandinetti et al. (2000) found a significant association between depressive symptoms and elevated HgA1c that remained after adjusting for age, body mass index, education, and gender and after excluding participants who reported a history of diabetes. Grandinetti suggests that the relationship of depression to type II diabetes may be more pathophysiological in nature rather than a psychological reaction to the disease. Despite differences in methodology, the literature generally supports the notion that depressive symptoms are common in diabetes and that careful clinical assessment is indicated.

Phenomenologically, depression associated with diabetes is very similar to primary major depressive disorder. In a study by Lustman et al. (1992a), the Beck Depression Inventory was administered to a sample of 41 diabetic patients who fulfilled DSM-III-R (American Psychiatric Association 1987) criteria for depression, 68 depressed patients without medical illness, and 58 nondepressed diabetic patients; the prevalence and severity of symptoms were similar between diabetic depressed patients and patients with primary major depressive disorder.

One of the problems in assessing depression in diabetic patients concerns the validity of current depression diagnostic criteria in the setting of medical illness. Lustman et al. (1986) evaluated the prevalence of depression in a sample of 114 patients with diabetes mellitus and compared the prevalence rates with and without inclusion of symptoms that may be attributable to the underlying diabetes. They noted that when the symptoms of weight loss, fatigue, hypersomnia, psychomotor retardation, and decreased libido were excluded, due to their association with diabetes, the rate of depression changed from 36% to 32.5% (Lustman et al. 1986). Other authors have also noted a modest change in prevalence rates when an inclusive versus an etiological approach is used for diagnosis of depression and have advocated an inclusive approach in the clinical care of patients (Cohen-Cole et al. 1993).

Other aspects of depression associated with diabetes also resemble primary major depressive disorder, including a female predominance (Lustman et al. 1986; Robinson et al. 1988) and a higher likelihood of a positive family history of depression when comparing depressed diabetic patients with nondepressed diabetic patients (Lustman et al. 1987). Lustman et al. (1997) noted that the Beck Depression Inventory is an effective screening test for major depression in diabetic patients.

Depression comorbid with IDDM differs from depression comorbid with NIDDM in two respects: 1) the mean age at onset of depression is 22.1 years in IDDM patients and 28.6 years in NIDDM patients; and 2) in patients with NIDDM, the depressive symptoms appear to precede the development of diabetes, whereas in patients with IDDM, the diabetic presentation precedes that of the depressive phenomenology (Lustman et al. 1988).

The presence of major depression has a negative impact on participation in diabetes treatment as measured by attendance at a weight-loss program for obese patients with NIDDM (Marcus et al. 1992). In addition, the presence of depression correlates with the worsened glycemic control in patients with IDDM (de Groot et al. 1999; Lustman et al. 1992b; Sachs et al. 1991). Winokur et al. (1988) administered a 5-hour oral glucose tolerance test (GTT) to 28 patients with depression and 21 nondepressed volunteers and found that depressed patients demonstrated significantly higher basal glucose levels and higher cumulative glucose responses after the GTT and showed larger cumulative insulin responses after the GTT than control subjects. These findings indicated the presence of a functional state of insulin resistance during major depressive illness in some patients. Poor glycemic control is well documented to be associated with complications of diabetes (Klein et al. 1988); therefore, the depressed diabetic patient may be at risk for later diabetic complications. Higher Beck Depression Inventory scores were found in patients with diabetic complications compared with those without complications or nondiabetic control subjects (Leedom et al. 1991; Tun et al. 1990). In a 10-year prospective study, depression was found to be one of three factors independently associated with the onset of diabetic retinopathy in 24 children with IDDM (Kovacs et al. 1997). Likewise, S.T. Cohen et al. (1997) studied 49 patients with type I diabetes mellitus and found that patients with a history of psychiatric illness had significantly worse retinopathy than did patients without psychiatric illness. Other studies, however, failed to show a relationship between complications of diabetes and psychiatric illness (Lustman et al. 1988; Popkin et al. 1988).

The psychopharmacologic treatment of depression in diabetic patients requires some discussion because of the different effects of various classes of antidepressants on appetite, weight, glucose control, cognition, cholinergic antagonism, and sexual function and because of their propensity to exacerbate autonomic neuropathy–mediated orthostatic hypotension (Goodnick et al. 1995; Lustman et al. 1992b). In addition to psychopharmacologic treatment of depression, Lustman et al. (1998) demonstrated that cognitive behavioral therapy and supportive diabetes education is an efficacious treatment for major depression in patients with type II diabetes.

Regarding the issues of appetite, weight, and glucose control, monoamine oxidase inhibitors (MAOIs) tend to exacerbate hypoglycemia and are associated with significant weight gain. The tricyclic antidepressants (TCAs) are associated with marked increases in appetite, body weight, and blood glucose. The selective serotonin reuptake inhibitors (SSRIs) are associated with modest reductions in serum glucose and body weight and have little effect on appetite (Goodnick et al. 1995).

Cognitive interactions between the underlying illness and the selected medication need to be considered as well. Medications with high anticholinergic or sedating properties are associated with more cognitive impairment and can interfere with the daily management of diabetes (Lustman et al. 1992b). Furthermore, the impaired cognition often seen in diabetic patients may render compliance with an MAOI diet unattainable (Goodnick et al. 1995). In addition to the adverse effects on cognition associated with anticholinergic medications, the decrease in bowel motility caused by such agents may worsen underlying diabetes-related gastroparesis or constipation (Lustman et al. 1992b).

Because of the combined effects of improved glucose control, modest weight loss, and minimal cognitive and anticholinergic effects, Goodnick et al. (1995) advocate using SSRIs as the first-line antidepressant of choice in treating the diabetic patient. Jimenez and Goodnick (1999) further advocate for sertraline as the first-line treatment of depression in diabetes, given its modest effect on the cytochrome P450 system and its apparent positive impact on cognition.

Table 25–1 summarizes the effects of antidepressants used in treating the diabetic patient.

Mania is a distinctly uncommon finding in diabetic patients. Wells et al. (1988) noted that the prevalence of mania in medically ill patients was no higher than in members of the general population, whereas the tertiary referral population evaluated by Lustman et al. (1986) revealed three cases of mania in 114 patients.

## Hypoglycemia

Because of the importance of insulin-induced hypoglycemia as a risk factor for the development of cognitive impairment in diabetes, a brief discussion of the phenomenology of hypoglycemia is warranted.

Traditionally, the signs and symptoms of hypoglycemia are divided into autonomic and neuroglycopenic groups. The autonomic signs and symptoms include diaphoresis, palpitations, tremor, and hunger, whereas the neuroglycopenic symptoms include confusion, lethargy, speech and behavioral changes, and incoordination. Recently, some authors have prospectively validated this

**TABLE 25–1.** Effects of antidepressant medications in diabetes mellitus

| | |
|---|---|
| **Monoamine oxidase inhibitors** | Associated with acute hypoglycemic episodes. Associated with long-term weight gain. May cause cognitive disturbances. Dietary restrictions may complicate the diabetic diet. |
| **Tricyclic antidepressants** | Increased noradrenergic (and dopaminergic) tone may block insulin release and result in higher blood glucose. Long-term use leads to weight gain, carbohydrate craving, and increased insulin requirements. May cause impaired memory and concentration. May help with chronic pain associated with diabetic neuropathy. |
| **Selective serotonin reuptake inhibitors** | Shown to decrease insulin requirements in some studies. May decrease body weight. Has fewer anticholinergic, orthostatic, hypotensive, and cardiovascular side effects. Paroxetine, sertraline, and citalopram have been found helpful in neuropathic pain. |
| **Bupropion, mirtazapine, venlafaxine, nefazodone** | Little known. Bupropion, venlafaxine, and nefazodone may be helpful in diabetic neuropathic pain. |

*Source.* Adapted from Carney 1998; Goodnick et al. 1995; Jimenez and Goodnick 1999.

construct with the inclusion of nausea and headache into a separately validated "malaise" category (Deary et al. 1993).

In a study of 125 prospective emergency room visits for symptomatic hypoglycemia, 65 patients had obtundation, stupor, or coma; 38 had confusional or bizarre behavior; 10 were dizzy or tremulous; 9 had seizures; and 3 had sudden hemiparesis (Malouf and Brust 1985). The most common underlying medical conditions were diabetes, alcoholism, or sepsis, alone or in combination. Other associated conditions included fasting, cancer, gastroenteritis, insulin abuse, and hypothyroidism. The overall mortality rate was 11%, and focal neurologic sequelae were present in 4 patients (Malouf and Brust 1985). In a retrospective study of 51 patients admitted to the emergency room for acute hypoglycemia (Hart and Frier 1998), 80% were diabetic patients being treated with insulin. The other patients had hypoglycemia induced by excessive consumption of alcohol or deliberate self-poisoning with insulin. Hart noticed increased incidences of psychiatric illness and chronic alcoholism in the population studied.

Reactive hypoglycemia is a relatively rare meal-induced hypoglycemic disorder occurring in patients with diabetes mellitus, gastrointestinal disease, and hormonal deficiency states, such as adrenal insufficiency or hypothyroidism. In these states, hyperinsulinemia is responsible for the hypoglycemia. Idiopathic postprandial hypoglycemia is a controversial entity with uncertain validity. It should be emphasized that the vast majority of patients who have adrenergic symptoms have diagnoses other than hypoglycemia to account for their symptoms, with panic, conversion, and somatization disorders accounting for many of the psychiatric cases (Hofeldt 1989).

Factitious hypoglycemia due to exogenous insulin administration is relatively uncommon but is suggested by the presence of elevated insulin antibodies, hypoglycemia, and low C-peptide levels (Horwitz 1989; Scarlett et al. 1977). C peptide is secreted as a portion of endogenous proinsulin and is not a part of commercially prepared insulin.

## Hypothyroidism

## Cardinal Features of the Disorder

The classic symptoms of hypothyroidism include weight gain, lethargy, cold intolerance, slow and hoarse speech, constipation, cognitive slowing, depression, and decreased energy and libido. Signs of hypothyroidism include weight gain, hypothermia, bradycardia, thickening of the nails and hair, dryness of the skin, thickening of the tongue and facial skin, and a delayed relaxation phase of deep tendon reflexes. Detectable changes in thyroid size vary depending on the etiology of the syndrome. Diagnosis depends on the demonstration of decreased circulating thyroid hormone. Because more than 90% of patients with hypothyroidism have primary hypothyroidism as the underlying cause, measurement of thyroid-stimulating hormone (TSH) level is considered the most useful screening test (Klee and Hay 1986); patients with primary hypothyroidism will have an elevated TSH concentration.

## Psychiatric Symptoms in Hypothyroidism

Patients with hypothyroidism frequently exhibit cognitive, affective, psychotic, and anxiety symptoms. Early reports emphasized the psychotic and cognitive manifestations of hypothyroidism, whereas subsequent research has attempted to enhance our understanding of the phe-

**TABLE 25–2.** Psychiatric symptoms in hypothyroidism

| Study | N | Type of psychiatric disturbance | | | | |
|---|---|---|---|---|---|---|
| | | Cognitive | Psychosis | Depression | Mania | Anxiety |
| **Selected hypothyroid cases** | | | | | | |
| Asher 1949 | 14 | 12 | 9 | 5 | | |
| Miller 1952 | 2 | | | | | |
| Wiesel 1952 | 1 | | 1 | 1 | | |
| Jonas 1952 | 1 | | | 1 | | |
| Pitts and Guze 1961 | 3 | 3 | 2 | 3 | | 1 |
| Logothetis 1963 | 4 | 4 | 3 | 2 | | |
| Tonks 1964 | 18 | 5 | 7 | 6 | | |
| Libow and Durell 1965 | 1 | | 1 | 1 | | |
| Pomeranze and King 1966 | 1 | | | 1 | | |
| Ward and Rastall 1967 | 1 | 1 | | | | |
| Treadway et al. 1967 | 1 | 1 | 1 | 1 | | |
| Hall et al. 1982 | 4 | | 1 | 3 | 1 | 1 |
| **Unselected hypothyroid populations** | | | | | | |
| Crown 1949 | 4 | 4 | | | | |
| Reitan 1953 | 15 | 15 | | | | |
| Schon et al. 1962 | 24 | 24 | | | | |
| Jellinek 1962 | 56 | 6 | Noted | Noted | Noted | Noted |
| Easson 1966 | 19 | 1 | 11 | 2 | | |
| Whybrow et al. 1969 | 7 | 6 | 1 | 5 | | 1 |
| Jain 1972 | 30 | 8 | 3 | 13 | | 10 |

*Note.* Numbers in columns reflect numbers of patients exhibiting specific symptom or syndrome.

nomenology of psychiatric symptoms in hypothyroidism through the use of more sophisticated assessment tools. Psychiatric symptoms are often the first manifestation of thyroid disturbance (Logothetis 1963; Pitts and Guze 1961; Pomeranze and King 1966). This literature is summarized in Table 25–2. Figure 25–1 shows the relative prevalence of psychiatric symptoms in patients with hypothyroidism, both in the case literature and in unselected case series.

## Cognitive Disorders

Disturbances in cognition are the most commonly reported psychiatric symptom in hypothyroidism, occurring in 46.3% of unselected cases and 48.2% of psychiatrically ill hypothyroid patients (see Figure 25–1). The severity of the disturbance varies from mild subjective cognitive slowing to severe delirious and encephalopathic states. In the classic monograph on "myxoedema madness," Asher (1949) noted that 12 of 14 patients had evidence of cognitive impairment. This finding has been replicated repeatedly both in hypothyroid patients and in those with psychiatric symptoms (see Table 25–2). In one of the first studies to objectively measure the severity of cognitive disturbance, Whybrow et al. (1969) noted that hypothyroid patients had significantly

impaired performance on the Trail Making and Porteus Maze tests compared with hyperthyroid patients. Significant improvement was noted with treatment. Delirium is the most severe manifestation of hypothyroidism. In a study of 56 patients with hypothyroidism and neurologic symptoms, Jellinek (1962) noted that 6 of these patients had severe disturbances in their level of consciousness, being either stuporous or comatose, whereas 10 patients had clinical evidence of seizure disorders. The pathophysiology of delirium in hypothyroidism is probably multifactorial, with hypoxia, hypercarbia, hyponatremia, panhypopituitarism, seizures, and autoimmune mechanisms (i.e., antithyroid antibodies) having been described (Jellinek 1962; Royce 1971; Shaw et al. 1991). Bunevicius et al. (1999) compared the effects of treatment with thyroxine ($T_4$) alone with those of $T_4$ plus triiodothyronine ($T_3$) in 33 patients with hypothyroidism, measuring biochemical, physiologic, and psychological parameters. The researchers found that partial substitution of $T_3$ for $T_4$ resulted in lower Beck Depression Inventory scores and higher scores on neuropsychological tasks than in patients with $T_4$-only supplementation for hypothyroidism. This study suggests a specific effect of $T_3$ (which is normally secreted by the thyroid gland) on mood and cognition.

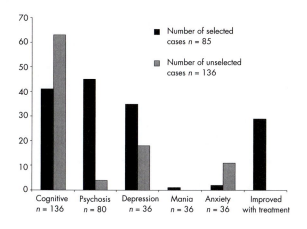

**FIGURE 25–1.** Psychiatric symptoms in hypothyroidism. Numbers under bars indicating unselected cases reflect the number of patients in whom the symptom was sought.
*Source.* Adapted from the case literature in Table 25–2.

It has been suspected that the severity of psychiatric symptoms often correlates with the severity of hypothyroidism. In one of the few studies to provide data in support of this hypothesis, Jain (1972) prospectively evaluated 30 hypothyroid patients; 8 were noted to have cognitive difficulties, and the prevalence of cognitive dysfunction increased with the severity of hypothyroidism. Prinz et al. (1999) found a positive relationship between total $T_4$ and overall cognition in healthy, euthyroid older men (mean age: 72 years).

## Mood Disorders

Depression is the second most frequent psychiatric syndrome to occur in unselected hypothyroid patients. Although the overwhelming majority of psychiatrically ill hypothyroid patients have depressive symptoms, about 50% of unselected hypothyroid patients have depressive syndromes (see Figure 25–1). Mania and hypomania are quite uncommon, occurring in only two cases in the literature (Hall et al. 1982; Mahendran 1999).

Table 25–2 summarizes the literature concerning prevalence of depression in hypothyroidism; however, some studies deserve specific mention. Whybrow et al. (1969) noted that five of seven hypothyroid patients appeared clinically depressed, one with psychotic depression. Compared with hyperthyroid patients, the hypothyroid group had higher depressive scores as measured by the Minnesota Multiphasic Personality Inventory (MMPI), the Clyde Mood Scale, and the Brief Psychiatric Rating Scale (BPRS). In contrast to the data regarding cognitive dysfunction, Jain (1972) could find no relationship between the severity of depression as

measured by Hamilton and Beck depression severity scores and the severity of hypothyroidism.

## Anxiety

Anxiety occurs in approximately 30% of unselected hypothyroid patients. No correlation between the severity of anxiety as measured by the Hamilton Anxiety Scale and the severity of hypothyroidism was noted in a sample of 30 hypothyroid patients (Jain 1972). Our understanding of the phenomenology of anxiety in hypothyroidism is limited by a paucity of data. Clinical experience suggests that it is often accompanied by significant depressive symptoms and is more generalized.

## Psychosis

Although psychosis is the most common symptom in the case literature on hypothyroidism (52.9%), it represents only 5% of the psychiatric morbidity in unselected samples. This disparity likely reflects a reporting bias because of the dramatic nature of psychotic symptoms. The psychotic symptoms may occur comorbidly with depression or independent of a significant affective disturbance. Paranoid delusions and auditory and visual hallucinations have been described as well. No careful assessment of thought disorders in hypothyroidism exists in the literature.

# Grades of Hypothyroidism and the Concept of Subclinical Hypothyroidism

Because our ability to measure thyroid function has become more sophisticated, a continuum of disturbance in thyroid function has now been identified. Grade I (overt) or classic primary hypothyroidism is defined by low levels of circulating thyroid hormones and an elevated TSH concentration accompanied by clinical symptoms. Grade II hypothyroidism is defined by elevated TSH levels with normal levels of thyroid hormones. An exaggerated TSH response to thyrotropin-releasing hormone (TRH) is seen in both grade I and grade II hypothyroidism, presumably due to a lack of thyroid hormone feedback. The term *subclinical hypothyroidism* generally refers to grade II hypothyroidism. Grade III hypothyroidism is characterized by an exaggerated TSH response to TRH in the setting of normal basal TSH, $T_3$, and $T_4$ levels. Grade IV, or symptomless autoimmune thyroiditis (SAT), is characterized by the presence of antithyroid antibodies in the serum but with normal circulating basal

TSH and T$_4$ levels and a normal TRH stimulation test.

Several interesting associations between affective illness and subclinical hypothyroidism have been identified; however, the clinical significance of these associations remains unclear. There appears to be an increased prevalence of grade II hypothyroidism in patients with major depression (Gold et al. 1981; Haggerty et al. 1993). Furthermore, subclinical hypothyroidism may be a risk factor for the development of major depression. Haggerty et al. (1993) compared the lifetime history of major depression in 16 depressed patients with grade II hypothyroidism with 15 depressed patients with normal thyroid function. The lifetime history of major depression was 56% in the patients with grade II hypothyroidism and 20% in control subjects. Hamilton Depression Rating Scale scores did not differ between the groups (Haggerty et al. 1993).

Several studies have suggested that depressed patients with grade II hypothyroidism respond poorly to antidepressant treatment (Joffe and Levitt 1992; Prange et al. 1988; Targum et al. 1984). In a study of 139 patients with major depression, patients who had subclinical hypothyroidism responded less favorably to treatment with tricyclic antidepressants than the euthyroid group (Joffe and Levitt 1992). There are reports that grade II hypothyroidism is associated with rapid cycling among patients with affective illness, though there are discrepant reports also (Bauer and Whybrow 1988; Cowdry et al. 1983; Joffe et al. 1988; Wehr et al. 1988). Pop et al. (1998) found that an elevated level of thyroid peroxidase antibodies, a measure of SAT, was significantly associated with later development of depression in perimenopausal women.

Controversy exists as to whether or not hormone replacement therapy is indicated in subclinical (grade II) hypothyroidism. In a study of 33 patients with grade II hypothyroidism, 8 of 14 patients (57%) receiving levothyroxine and 3 of 12 patients (25%) receiving placebo reported symptomatic improvement, and improvement in left ventricular performance was noted in a subset of the patients treated with levothyroxine (Cooper et al. 1984). In a discussion of 2 patients with psychiatric symptoms and grade II hypothyroidism, clinical improvement in mood and psychotic symptoms was noted after treatment with levothyroxine, antidepressants, and antipsychotics, but no improvement in cognitive symptoms was seen (Haggerty et al. 1986). However, Baldini et al. (1997) evaluated affective and cognitive dysfunction in patients with euthyroidism and subclinical hypothyroidism and found that a significant decrease in logical memory was present in the subclinical hypothyroid group but not the euthyroid group. Treatment with levothyroxine

significantly improved memory performance in the subclinical hypothyroid group. In a recent review, Smallridge (2000) noted that thyroid replacement therapy is recommended for patients with a TSH level of 10 mIU/L or higher and that replacement therapy is generally helpful for psychiatric symptoms associated with subclinical hypothyroidism.

# Hyperthyroidism

## Cardinal Features of the Disorder

The cardinal symptoms of hyperthyroidism vary, but the most common manifestations include diaphoresis, heat intolerance, fatigue, dyspnea, palpitations, weakness (especially in proximal muscles), anxiety, weight loss despite an increased appetite, hyperdefecation, and visual complaints. Signs of hyperthyroidism include noticeable anxiety and increased psychomotor activity; tachycardia, often with atrial fibrillation; bounding peripheral pulses; moist and warm skin; thinning of the individual hair shafts, as well as alopecia; tremor and hyperreflexia; and eye findings ranging from simple retraction of the upper lid with lid lag to overt exophthalmos with impairment of extraocular movement. The thyroid gland is usually enlarged, with the most notable exceptions in the elderly and in those with substernal thyroid tissue.

## Psychiatric Symptoms in Hyperthyroidism

Although many authors have emphasized the ubiquitous presence of psychiatric symptoms in patients with hyperthyroidism, scrutiny of the literature suggests that serious psychopathology occurs in only a minority of patients. Most commonly, depression, anxiety, and cognitive changes are seen, and manic and psychotic manifestations are encountered less frequently. Table 25–3 summarizes the case literature and studies involving unselected hyperthyroid patients, and Figure 25–2 compares the prevalence of psychiatric symptoms in these two groups.

### Cognitive Disorders

Cognitive changes associated with thyrotoxicosis range from subtle defects in attention and concentration to overt delirium. The prevalence of cognitive disturbance in thyrotoxicosis is 7.4%, considerably less than that observed in hypothyroidism. Robbins and Vinson (1960) noted frequent errors in simple conceptual tasks and an

**TABLE 25–3.** Psychiatric symptoms in hyperthyroidism

| Study | N | Type of psychiatric disturbance | | | | |
|---|---|---|---|---|---|---|
| | | Cognitive | Psychosis | Depression | Mania | Anxiety |
| **Selected hyperthyroid cases** | | | | | | |
| Bursten 1961 | 10 | 3 | 10 | 1 | 1 | |
| Taylor 1975 | 1 | | 1 | 1 | | |
| Katerndahl and Vande Creek 1983 | 1 | | | 1 | | 1 |
| **Unselected hyperthyroid populations** | | | | | | |
| Lidz and Whitehorn 1949 | 15 | | | 9 | | |
| Mandelbrote and Wittkower 1955 | 25 | | | Noted | | Noted |
| Kleinschmidt et al. 1956 | 17 | | 2 | Noted | | Noted |
| Robbins and Vinson 1960 | 10 | 1 | 1 | | | 1 |
| Wilson et al. 1962 | 26 | 14 | | 15 | 2 | 6 |
| Artunkal and Togrol 1964 | 20 | | | | | |
| Hermann and Quarton 1965 | 24 | Noted | 1 | | | Noted |
| Whybrow et al. 1969 | 10 | 4 | 2 | 2 | | 2 |
| F.B. Thomas et al. 1970 | 9 | | | 6 | | |
| MacCrimmon et al. 1979 | 19 | | | | | |
| Rockey and Griep 1980 | 14 | | | 1 | | 11 |
| Kathol and Delahunt 1986 | 33 | | | 10 | | 20 |
| Trzepacz et al. 1988 | 13 | | | 9 | 3 | 8 |

*Note.* Numbers in columns reflect numbers of patients exhibiting specific symptom or syndrome.

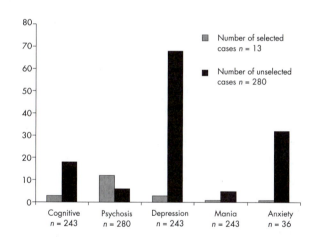

**FIGURE 25–2.** Psychiatric symptoms in hyperthyroidism. Numbers under bars indicating unselected cases reflect the number of patients in whom the symptom was sought.
*Source.* Adapted from the case literature in Table 25–3.

increased time for problem solving in patients with hyperthyroidism. Trzepacz et al. (1988) noted mild deficits in complex attention, immediate memory, and higher-level problem solving.

The data are mixed as to whether the severity of cognitive impairment correlates with the severity of hyperthyroidism. Alvarez et al. (1983) noted significant impairment in concentration and attention as measured by the Tolouse-Pierson Concentration Attention test in 27 patients with untreated Graves' disease compared with healthy control subjects. These deficits in attention and concentration did not correlate with the severity of hyperthyroidism. In contrast, MacCrimmon et al. (1979) noted that the severity of hyperthyroidism correlated with the severity of concentration and memory impairment. In addition, successful treatment of hyperthyroidism resulted in test scores that were indistinguishable from those of healthy control subjects.

## Mood Disorders

Major depression is the most common psychiatric manifestation of hyperthyroidism, occurring in approximately 28% of unselected patients (see Figure 25–2). Furthermore, the mood symptoms may precede the development of physical signs and symptoms in some patients. In the largest sample in the literature, Sonino et al. (1993) noted that major depression occurred in 23% of 70 patients with Graves' disease. They also noted that depression occurred in the prodromal phase in 14% of these patients. In another study, Wilson et al. (1962) reported that 24 of 26 patients (92%) with hyperthyroidism noted mood changes and neurovegetative symptoms involving sleep, appetite, libido, and psychomotor activity before the physical signs and symptoms of hyperthyroidism occurred. None of these patients required psychiatric treatment after euthyroidism was achieved.

In the first study to use modern operational criteria

for psychiatric disorders in hyperthyroid patients, Kathol and Delahunt (1986) noted that 10 of 32 patients (31%) with untreated hyperthyroidism fulfilled DSM-III (American Psychiatric Association 1980) criteria for major depression. The severity of hyperthyroidism did not appear to predict the prevalence of depression. Trzepacz et al. (1988) noted that 9 of 13 (69%) untreated Graves' disease patients fulfilled criteria for major depression using Research Diagnostic Criteria (RDC) and the Schedule for Affective Disorders and Schizophrenia (SADS). The finding of weight loss in the presence of a voracious appetite represented a striking phenomenological difference from patients with typical major depression.

Apathetic thyrotoxicosis also has been reported and is usually seen in elderly patients with a longer duration of symptoms and more dramatic weight loss. Typically, elderly patients have apathy, depression, an increased prevalence of cardiovascular events, and a decreased prevalence of ocular manifestations. F.B. Thomas et al. (1970) found that 6 of 9 patients (67%) with apathetic thyrotoxicosis had features of mental depression; however, specific depression criteria were not described.

Mania or hypomania secondary to hyperthyroidism is distinctly uncommon, occurring in only 2.1% of unselected cases. Wilson et al. (1962) noted that 2 patients described elation as the predominant mood, and 1 patient was considered manic. Trzepacz et al. (1988) noted that 3 of 13 untreated Graves' disease patients were hypomanic. One patient with mania has been described following initiation of thyroid hormone replacement, but review of the longitudinal course of the patient's disorder suggests that the patient likely had preexisting bipolar disorder (Josephson and MacKenzie 1979).

## Anxiety

Despite the fact that anxiety is cited as one of the cardinal features of hyperthyroidism, it appears in only 13% of unselected patients in whom anxiety symptoms were sought (see Figure 25–2). Anxiety due to hyperthyroidism generally has an insidious onset, often preceding overt physical signs of the disorder (Dietch 1981). Others have noted that the anxiety associated with thyrotoxicosis was indistinguishable from that observed in primary anxiety disorders (Greer et al. 1973). MacCrimmon et al. (1979) noted that more than one-half of 19 patients with untreated hyperthyroidism and psychiatric symptoms reported nervousness, jumpiness, restlessness, tension, irritability, and anxiety.

Two studies have applied operational anxiety criteria to untreated Graves' disease patients. Using RDC, Trzepacz et al. (1988) revealed that 8 of 13 patients (62%) had generalized anxiety disorder, 4 of 13 (31%) met criteria for panic disorder, and 1 (8%) had agoraphobia. Kathol and Delahunt (1986) noted that 15 of 32 patients (47%) with untreated Graves' disease fulfilled DSM-III criteria for generalized anxiety disorder. Both groups noted that the severity of anxiety correlated with the severity of hyperthyroidism, and that most patients with anxiety had concurrent major depression.

## Psychosis

Psychosis is an uncommon manifestation of thyrotoxicosis, occurring in 2.1% of unselected patients. Earlier estimates of prevalence ranged from 15% to 25% (Clower et al. 1969). However, review of the symptoms reported in these patients indicates that many of them would be classified as having affective disorders. Clower et al. (1969) described only 3 patients with comorbid thyrotoxicosis and psychosis in a series of 228 patients with elevated protein-bound iodine (PBI) determinations; the number of patients with elevated PBI who actually had hyperthyroidism was not noted. Bursten (1961) described 10 psychotic patients with thyrotoxicosis and noted paranoid, delusional, and hallucinatory phenomena similar to those seen in schizophreniform illnesses. Two case reports noted findings of mania with psychotic features (Irwin et al. 1997) and psychosis (Bewsher et al. 1971) following the rapid normalization of thyroid function in patients with severe, prolonged, untreated Graves' disease.

A recent study by Fahrenfort et al. (2000) noted that many patients with hyperthyroidism continued to have psychiatric symptoms, including depression, anxiety, fatigue, and functional impairment even after 12 months of normalization of the thyroid. The researchers advocated longer-term psychiatric follow-up of psychiatrically symptomatic hyperthyroid patients.

# Hashimoto's Encephalitis

Hashimoto's encephalitis is an unusual clinical syndrome that warrants separate discussion. Since 1974, several cases have been reported of a severe encephalopathic state associated with the presence of high titers of antithyroid antibodies. Most importantly, in the literature, only 3 of 13 patients (23%) were overtly hypothyroid. Ten patients (77%) were considered biochemically euthyroid when the neuropsychiatric syndrome developed (Shaw et al. 1991; Shein et al. 1986; Thrush and Boddie 1974). It is unclear whether circulating antithyroid antibodies are directly responsible for the neuropsychiatric symptoms or whether they represent a nonspecific phenomenon of immune activation. Some patients may improve by treatment with corticosteroids (van Oostrom et al. 1999).

## Hypothalamic-Pituitary-Thyroid Axis and Depression

Affective symptoms have long been identified in thyroid disease, leading many investigators to search for the role of thyroid-axis abnormalities in affective disorders. Thyroid hormone supplementation has been found to increase the rapidity of action of TCA agents (Prange et al. 1969) and was equally effective as lithium in producing a response in depressed patients who did not respond to TCAs (Joffe et al. 1993). However, the precise relationship between the hypothalamic-pituitary-thyroid (HPT) axis and affective disorders remains unclear. The complexities involved in this relationship are 1) symptoms of depression occur in both hypothyroidism and hyperthyroidism; 2) most depressed patients have thyroid functions within the normal range (Esposito et al. 1997; Joffe and Sokolov 1994); 3) elevated levels of TRH have been reported in cerebrospinal fluid of patients with major depression (Banki et al. 1988; Kirkegaard et al. 1979); 4) 25% of patients with major depressive disorder exhibit a blunted TSH response to exogenously administered TRH (Prange et al. 1972), whereas 15% of depressed patients show an exaggerated response (Extein et al. 1981); 5) there is a higher prevalence rate of SAT in depressed patients (Gold et al. 1982; Nemeroff et al. 1985); and 6) functioning of the HPT axis can be influenced by a variety of states such as systemic or chronic illness, chronic physiologic stress, nutritional status, circadian rhythms, and cognitive processes (Esposito et al. 1997). These findings preclude a simple understanding of HPT axis dysfunction in depression and emphasize the fact that considerably more research is needed.

## Cushing's Syndrome and Disease

### Cardinal Features of the Disorder

The most common signs and symptoms of Cushing's syndrome are centripetal obesity, hirsutism, menstrual irregularities, decreased libido, impotence, hypertension, proximal weakness, red to purple striae, acne, and easy bruisability. Osteopenia and glucose intolerance also may occur. Cushing's syndrome is classified as either adreno-

corticotropic hormone (ACTH) dependent or ACTH independent. Most cases of Cushing's syndrome are due to high-dose corticosteroid administration, with adrenal carcinoma and ectopic ACTH production occurring less frequently. The term *Cushing's disease* is reserved for cases of hypercortisolism due to ACTH production from a pituitary adenoma. Laboratory diagnosis of Cushing's syndrome depends on demonstration of either elevated urinary cortisol concentration or an abnormal dexamethasone suppression test (DST). Adrenal carcinoma, ectopic ACTH production, and Cushing's disease can be further differentiated by measuring plasma ACTH concentration, administering a high-dose DST, and performing computed tomography (CT) or magnetic resonance imaging (MRI) of the abdomen and head.

## Psychiatric Symptoms in Cushing's Syndrome

Psychiatric symptoms occurring in Cushing's syndrome have been well documented in the literature (Spillane 1951; Whybrow and Hurwitz 1976; Zeiger et al. 1993). In 1913, Harvey Cushing noted psychiatric disturbance, particularly depression, in his first description of the illness that bears his name (Cushing 1932).

### Mood and Anxiety Disorders

Mood disorders, especially unipolar depression, are by far the most frequently reported psychiatric manifestations of Cushing's syndrome. Before 1980, depression was frequently noted in Cushing's syndrome, but most studies were retrospective and did not use diagnostic criteria. Whybrow and Hurwitz (1976) reviewed the literature and found that 35.0% of patients with Cushing's syndrome reported depressive symptoms, compared with 3.7% who reported mania. Delirium was noted in 16.2% and psychosis in 9.3% of patients. In addition, suicide attempts (Gotch 1994; Haskett 1985; Starkman et al. 1981) and completed suicides (Jeffcoate et al. 1979; Zeiger et al. 1993) have been reported during the course of Cushing's syndrome. Several investigators have used structured interviews and diagnostic criteria to scrutinize affective illness in this population. Haskett (1985) applied RDC to 30 patients with Cushing's syndrome and noted that 16 (53%) fulfilled criteria for unipolar depression and 9 (30%) met criteria for bipolar disorder. Other studies have suggested prevalence rates of depressive symptoms in Cushing's syndrome as high as 62%–94% (Mazet et al. 1981; Kelly et al. 1996; Starkman et al. 1981).

Recent evidence suggests that mixed anxiety and

depressive symptoms may be the most common psychiatric manifestation of Cushing's syndrome (Loosen et al. 1992; Mazet et al. 1981). Starkman et al. (1981) noted anxiety symptoms in 63% of 35 patients with Cushing's syndrome. Using the Structured Clinical Interview for DSM-III-R (SCID), Loosen et al. (1992) compared 20 patients with Cushing's disease with 20 patients with major depressive disorder and noted that generalized anxiety disorder was the most common psychiatric diagnosis (79%) in Cushing's disease patients. Major depression was present in 68% and panic disorder in 53%. Only one Cushing's disease patient with major depression had no syndromal comorbid anxiety diagnosis. Other investigators also have noted prominent irritability and emotional lability in depressed patients with Cushing's syndrome (Haskett 1985; Starkman et al. 1981). It is likely that reporting and investigator bias has resulted in an underappreciation of the presence of mixed anxiety and depressed states in Cushing's syndrome. Figure 25–3 illustrates the effect of reporting bias on the relative prevalence of psychiatric symptoms in Cushing's syndrome. Depression associated with Cushing's disease also may differ from primary major depression in that symptoms are often more intermittent in the former (Haskett 1985; Loosen et al. 1992; Starkman et al. 1981).

Several authors have noted that depressive symptoms occur early in the disorder. Sonino et al. (1993) noted that prodromal depressive symptoms occurred in 27% of 66 patients with Cushing's syndrome. Some evidence suggests that patients with antecedent psychiatric symptoms have a less favorable psychiatric outcome after treatment of the endocrinopathy (Jeffcoate et al. 1979).

Treating Cushing's syndrome, whether with metyrapone, adrenalectomy, or pituitary irradiation or resection, has been shown to improve the mood disorder in most patients. Sonino et al. (1993) noted that 70% of depressed Cushing's syndrome patients improved with reduced serum cortisol. In a series of 34 patients with Cushing's syndrome, 8 of 9 depressed patients with hypercortisolism (89%) responded to bilateral adrenalectomy with improvement in their depressive symptoms (Zeiger et al. 1993). Kelly et al. (1983) reported a reduction in Hamilton Depression Rating Scale scores in 26 patients with Cushing's syndrome after successful treatment. Furthermore, improvement may be related to the severity of the symptoms. In a study of 38 patients with Cushing's syndrome, 8 of 9 moderately to severely depressed patients (89%) responded to reduced plasma cortisol with an improvement in depressive symptoms compared with 6 of 13 mildly depressed patients (46%) (Jeffcoate et al. 1979). The most compelling data have arguably been provided by Starkman et al. (1986), who

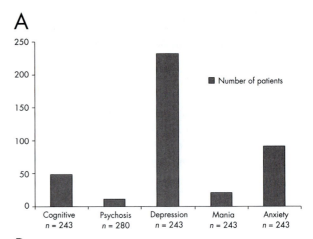

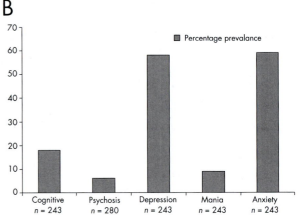

**FIGURE 25–3.** Psychiatric symptoms in Cushing's syndrome: the influence of publication bias on relative prevalence phenomenology. *Panel A.* All cases of psychiatric disturbances in Cushing's syndrome. *Panel B.* Relative prevalence of major psychiatric symptoms in cases of Cushing's syndrome using broad clinical or structured interview.

noted that improvement in symptoms correlated with reduced circulating cortisol level.

Secondary mania and hypomania are relatively infrequent findings in Cushing's syndrome. Hypomania was noted in 3 (9%) and mania in 1 (3%) of 35 patients by Starkman et al. (1981). Mazet et al. (1981) noted manic symptoms in 7 of 50 patients with Cushing's syndrome (14%). Haskett (1985) used the Schedule for Affective Disorders and Schizophrenia—Lifetime Version (SADS-L) and reported the highest prevalence rate (30%) in the literature of bipolar illness in Cushing's syndrome.

## Psychosis and Cognitive Disorders

Psychosis and overt delirium are rarely reported in the Cushing's disease literature. Psychotic symptoms in Cushing's syndrome are usually associated with affective syndromes (S.I. Cohen 1980; Haskett 1985). Recently, a case of delirium secondary to a mixed adrenal tumor secreting estrogen and cortisol in a 14-year-old boy was reported (Ghazi et al. 1994).

Cognitive impairment in Cushing's syndrome has been relatively infrequently reported, and when documented it has been mild. In a questionnaire study of 62 patients with Cushing's syndrome, subjective complaints of concentration and memory impairment were reported in 20 of the 41 patients (49%) who returned the questionnaire (Gotch 1994). Whelan et al. (1980) administered the Michigan Neuropsychological Test Battery to 35 patients with Cushing's syndrome. They divided the patients into four groups: group 1 (13 patients) had normal or equivocal neuropsychological findings, group 2 (10 patients) had mild or infrequent deficits, group 3 (8 patients) had moderate or frequent deficits, and group 4 (4 patients) had marked and frequent deficits in neuropsychological testing. Deficits in nonverbal visual ideation and spatial-construction abilities were more common than problems with language and verbal reasoning. In addition, impaired manual dexterity as measured by the Purdue Pegboard was noted in 46% of patients.

Disturbances in verbal memory in Cushing's syndrome appear to be related to loss of hippocampal volume as measured by MRI. Twelve patients with Cushing's syndrome underwent neuropsychological testing with the Wechsler Memory Scale (WMS), the Wechsler Adult Intelligence Scale—Revised (WAIS-R), and the Trails A and B tests. Volumetric measurements of the hippocampal formations were performed, and serum cortisol was measured. Verbal memory and verbal recall were associated with hippocampal volume, whereas age, educational level, and performance on the Trails A and B tests and full-scale IQ tests were not significantly correlated with hippocampal volume. Furthermore, the loss of hippocampal volume correlated with the serum cortisol concentrations (Starkman et al. 1992). Brunetti et al. (1998) analyzed positron-emission tomographic scans in 13 patients with Cushing's disease and compared them with 13 age-matched healthy control subjects. Patients with Cushing's disease had significant reduction in cerebral glucose metabolism, which the investigators theorized might contribute to the cognitive and psychiatric symptoms in patients with Cushing's disease.

## Exogenous Corticosteroid Administration

Psychiatric complications of corticosteroids were recognized shortly after they were introduced into clinical prac-

tice in the 1950s (Clark et al. 1953). Nearly all corticosteroid preparations have been implicated, including ACTH (which stimulates cortisol release), cortisone, prednisone, prednisolone, methylprednisolone, and inhaled beclomethasone (Hayreh and Watson 1970; Ling et al. 1981; Perry et al. 1984; Rosenberg et al. 1976). Psychiatric symptoms are predominantly affective, although psychosis, delirium, and anxiety also have been reported (Campbell 1987; D'Orban 1989; Hall et al. 1979; Ling et al. 1981; Perry et al. 1984; Silva and Tolstunov 1995). In addition, Newcomer et al. (1994) demonstrated that 4 days of dexamethasone administration results in impaired verbal declarative memory performance. It has been hypothesized that this effect may be mediated by site-specific glucocorticoid effects on hippocampal neurons (Bardgett et al. 1994).

Clinical experience suggests a correlation between severity of symptoms and corticosteroid dose, but controlled data are lacking. However, the prevalence of psychiatric disturbances associated with corticosteroid administration appears to be a dose-related phenomenon. In a prospective study of 718 hospitalized patients receiving prednisone, 1.3% had psychiatric reactions at a dosage less than or equal to 40 mg/day. This rate increased to 4.6% at dosages ranging from 41 mg/day to 80 mg/day and to 18.4% at dosages of 80 mg/day or more (Boston Collaborative Drug Surveillance Program 1972) (Figure 25–4). In a prospective evaluation of 32 asthmatic children, high-dose prednisone (mean dosage: 61.4 mg/day) was associated with more depression and anxiety symptoms and decreased verbal memory compared with low-dose prednisone (7 mg/day) (Bender et al. 1991).

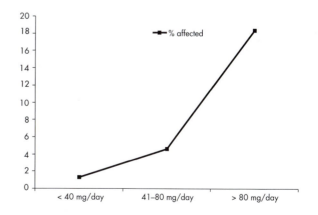

**FIGURE 25–4.** Prevalence of corticosteroid-related psychiatric disturbances: relationship to dosage.
*Source.* Adapted from Boston Collaborative Drug Surveillance Program 1972.

A variety of strategies have been employed to prevent steroid-induced psychiatric disturbances, including administering divided doses, enteric-coated preparations (Glynne-Jones and Vernon 1986), lithium (Falk et al. 1979; Siegal 1978), and valproic acid (Abbas and Styra 1994). Although antipsychotics appear to be well tolerated and effective, 3 of 14 patients (21%) had an exacerbation of symptoms when treated with TCAs (Hall et al. 1979) (Figure 25–5).

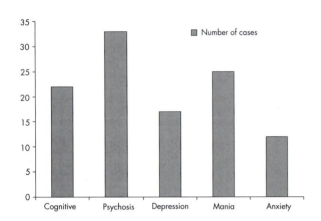

**FIGURE 25–5.** Psychiatric symptoms with corticosteroid administration: findings from the case literature.
*Source.* Adapted from Hall et al. 1979 and Perry et al. 1984.

## Addison's Disease (Adrenal Insufficiency)

### Cardinal Features of the Disorder

The symptoms of adrenal insufficiency are best understood in terms of acute and chronic symptoms. Chronic adrenal insufficiency is manifested by fatigue, malaise, weakness, weight loss, anorexia, hyperpigmentation, hypotension, nausea, and vomiting. Hyponatremia, hyperkalemia, metabolic acidosis, anemia, and eosinophilia are often present on laboratory testing. Acute adrenal insufficiency is manifested by more profound gastrointestinal symptoms, including pain—which may mimic acute abdomen—fever, and shock.

### Psychiatric Symptoms in Adrenal Insufficiency

In contrast to many of the endocrinopathies discussed in this chapter, psychiatric symptoms are relatively uncommon in adrenal insufficiency. Addison's (1868) initial description of the disorder noted evidence of impaired cognition. In a review of 25 cases of Addison's disease, 16 patients (64%) were noted to have disturbances in cognition (Engel and Margolin 1941). A review of these cases revealed 2 patients (13%) with delirium, 1 (6%) with psychotic symptoms, and 5 (31%) with depressive symptoms (Whybrow and Hurwitz 1976). Three other cases are present in the literature, with anxiety and depressive symptoms dominating the clinical picture (Thompson 1973; Varadaraj and Cooper 1986).

An unusual case of ACTH deficiency accompanied by delirium has been described. Mineralocorticoid functioning in the patient was normal, although he manifested severe orthostatic hypotension. The delirium resolved after administration of replacement doses of cortisone acetate (Fang and Jaspan 1989).

## Hypothalamic-Pituitary-Adrenal Axis and Depression

Hypercortisolemia has been widely documented in patients with major depression (Rosenbaum et al. 1983). In 1965, Bunney and Fawcett measured 24-hour urine 17-hydroxycorticosteroid levels in 143 depressed patients. Patients who later had severe or completed suicide attempts had the highest levels. Elevated cortisol levels return to normal after recovery from depression (Sachar et al. 1970). Hypercortisolemia appears to represent a state as opposed to a trait marker for depression (Musselman and Nemeroff 1996). Kiraly et al. (1997) theorized that hypercortisolemia is a treatable factor in a subset of affective and psychotic disorders and that the geriatric population may be more vulnerable to the neurotoxic effects of cortisol. Murphy et al. (1991) studied 10 patients with treatment-resistant depression and found that treatment with a steroid-suppressive agent resulted in significant improvement in 6 patients.

There is a growing body of literature relating stressful life events to activation of the hypothalamic-pituitary-adrenal (HPA) axis. Using Paykel's Interview for Recent Life Events, Sonino et al. (1988) investigated the presence of stressful life events in 30 consecutive patients with Cushing's syndrome and 30 control subjects. Patients with Cushing's syndrome had significantly more stressful life events. In a larger study in 1993, Sonino et al. noted that patients with the pituitary-dependent form of the disease had a higher number of total negative life events before onset of the disease compared with patients with pituitary-independent Cushing's syndrome. Heim et al. (2000) investigated whether early life stress resulted in a sensitization of the HPA axis later in life in a study involving women without histories of childhood abuse and women with histories of childhood abuse. Women with a history of childhood abuse exhibited increased pituitary-adrenal and autonomic responses to stress compared with the control group of women who experienced no childhood abuse. Heim proposed that HPA axis and autonomic nervous system hyperreactivity, presumably due to hypersecretion of corticotropin-releasing factor (CRF), may be a persistent consequence of childhood abuse and contribute to the vulnerability to psychopathological conditions in adulthood.

Carroll et al. (1968) reported nonsuppression of plasma hydroxycorticosteroid levels after administration of dexamethasone in depressed patients. DST nonsuppression has been highly correlated with more severe forms of depression, such as psychotic depression (Evans and Nemeroff 1983). Persistent DST nonsuppression may be associated with early relapse or a poorer prognosis (Arana et al. 1985).

Increased levels of CRF have been repeatedly found in cerebrospinal fluid in depressed patients (Arato et al. 1986; Nemeroff et al. 1984; Risch et al. 1992). In addition, pituitary gland enlargement (Krishnan et al. 1991) and adrenal gland enlargement (Amsterdam et al. 1987; Nemeroff et al. 1992) have been reported in depressed patients. Murphy (1991) provides an excellent review of the glucocorticosteroids and depression.

## Pheochromocytoma

### Cardinal Features of the Disorder

Common signs in pheochromocytoma include sustained or paroxysmal hypertension, orthostatic hypotension, hyperhidrosis, hypertensive retinopathy, pallor (very rarely flushing), Raynaud's phenomenon, and livedo reticularis. Prominent symptoms include headache, diaphoresis, palpitations, tremulousness, abdominal or chest pain, nausea, vomiting, and weakness (Manger et al. 1985). In a study of 2,585 hypertensive patients, the symptom triad of headache, palpitations, and diaphoresis was predictive of a diagnosis of pheochromocytoma, with a sensitivity of 93.8%, a specificity of 90.9%, and an exclusion value of 99.9%. The absence of this triad of symptoms reduced the likelihood of pheochromocytoma to less than 1 in 1,000 (Plouin et al. 1981). Diagnosis depends on demonstration of elevated circulating catecholamines, after which localization of the tumor is undertaken (Manger et al. 1985).

### Psychiatric Symptoms in Pheochromocytoma

Anxiety is the most frequent psychiatric symptom in pheochromocytoma, having been described in 22%–44%

of patients with this tumor (Modlin et al. 1979; J.E. Thomas et al. 1966). When other symptoms such as diaphoresis and palpitations are included in this evaluation, the prevalence increases to 86% (Modlin et al. 1979). Although anxiety symptoms are frequently encountered in patients with pheochromocytoma, full syndromal states resembling panic disorder or generalized anxiety disorder are relatively uncommon. In a study of 17 patients with pheochromocytoma, only 1 patient fulfilled criteria for possible panic disorder, 2 for generalized anxiety disorder, and 2 for major depressive episode. None of the patients experienced the apprehension and fear characteristic of panic attacks, and none had agoraphobia (Starkman et al. 1985). Given the relative rarity of the syndrome even in hypertensive populations, evaluation for pheochromocytoma should probably be reserved for those patients whose anxiety symptoms are accompanied by headache, palpitations, significant blood pressure abnormalities, and diaphoresis.

## Hyperprolactinemia

### Cardinal Features of the Disorder

The primary consequence of hyperprolactinemia is the presence of gonadal dysfunction. Amenorrhea and galactorrhea are the primary manifestations in females, whereas impotence is the primary symptom in males, though gynecomastia and galactorrhea can occur. Diagnosis requires demonstration of an elevated serum prolactin level (>25 ng/mL). Drug-induced causes of hyperprolactinemia need to be considered in the differential diagnosis, along with hyperprolactinemia due to other endocrinopathies or due to liver or renal disease. Idiopathic hyperprolactinemia and pituitary adenomas constitute the remainder of cases. MRI of the sella is the preferred modality for pituitary imaging. Treatment involves administration of dopamine agonists or surgical resection.

### Psychiatric Symptoms in Hyperprolactinemia

Compared with other endocrinopathies, the association of psychiatric symptoms and hyperprolactinemia has received relatively little attention. To date, no standardized psychiatric diagnostic assessment of hyperprolactinemic patients has been performed.

Most of the literature regarding psychiatric manifestations of hyperprolactinemia concerns the phenomena of aggression and hostility. Data on animals reveal high levels of aggression in lactating mammals in association with high prolactin levels (Erskine et al. 1978). In humans, the first studies suggesting a relationship between prolactin levels and hostility involved patients with premenstrual syndrome (Steiner et al. 1984). In another investigation, Kellner et al. (1984) used the Kellner Symptom Questionnaire (SQ) to compare hyperprolactinemic patients with family practice patient control subjects, psychiatric patient control subjects, and nonpatient employees. The SQ is a 92-item self-report scale concerning emotional symptoms and statements of well-being. Four scales are contained within the questionnaire concerning depression, anxiety, somatization, and anger-hostility. Hyperprolactinemic patients differed from family practice control subjects and nonpatient employees in the anger-hostility domain of the SQ (Kellner et al. 1984). In another study (Mastrogiacomo et al. 1983), 10 postpartum patients were compared with 10 hyperprolactinemic patients and 10 employee control subjects. Hostility scores were higher in the postpartum group than in either the control subjects or patients with hyperprolactinemia. Depression scores were higher in the hyperprolactinemic patients than in both the postpartum and control subjects (Mastrogiacomo et al. 1983). Hostility and anger are nonspecific symptoms, occurring as a manifestation of normal behavior and noted in increased frequency in a variety of disease states. Although an attempt was made to correlate hostility and depression scales of the SQ, no attempt was made in these studies to evaluate the relationship between hostility and psychiatric diagnostic entities as currently defined.

Bromocriptine, a dopamine agonist used in treating hyperprolactinemia, has been demonstrated to reduce depression, anxiety, and anger-hostility, based on the SQ scales; this improvement in symptoms correlated with a reduced serum prolactin level (Buckman and Kellner 1982). In a double-blind crossover study, six patients with hyperprolactinemia were given bromocriptine, and significant reductions in Hamilton Depression Rating Scale scores were noted (Koppelman et al. 1987). Furthermore, bromocriptine has been demonstrated to have antidepressant properties in primary affectively ill patients (Theohar et al. 1982). All of these data suggest that hyperprolactinemia may have a significant effect on affective symptoms, although the relationship between hyperprolactinemia and specific diagnostic syndromes remains to be defined. In a case report, Soygur et al. (1997) described a patient with organic delusional syndrome induced by hyperprolactinemia. The patient's case was notable for the worsening of psychiatric symptoms under bromocriptine therapy and a worsening of her prolactin levels with conventional neuroleptic therapy. The atypical neuroleptic melperone successfully

treated her psychotic symptoms without affecting the prolactin levels.

## Hyperparathyroidism

### Cardinal Features of the Disorder

The ability to diagnose primary hyperparathyroidism has changed dramatically over the last several decades, primarily because of automated screening laboratory panels (Heath 1991). Most patients today are either asymptomatic or have vague, nonspecific complaints. Fatigue, malaise, weakness, and cognitive complaints are common. Other manifestations include nephrolithiasis, proximal weakness of the lower extremities, chondrocalcinosis, and band keratopathy. Subperiosteal bone resorption and osteitis fibrosa cystica are rarely seen today. Most cases are caused by a solitary adenoma, with hyperplasia of multiple glands being the second most common etiology, usually in the setting of one of the multiple endocrine neoplasia syndromes. Diagnosis depends on demonstration of elevated circulating parathyroid hormone.

### Psychiatric Symptoms in Hyperparathyroidism

A variety of psychiatric disturbances have been associated with hyperparathyroidism, including mood, anxiety, psychotic, and cognitive disorders. Most of the literature consists of case reports and small case series; prospective studies have been undertaken more recently. Okamoto et al. (1997) provided a comprehensive review of the literature on the relationship of primary hyperparathyroidism with mild hypercalcemia and psychiatric disturbances. Table 25–4 summarizes the case literature. Alarcon and Franceschini (1984) reviewed the early literature and noted that affective and cognitive changes were the predominant symptoms and that most of the patients were elderly women.

In a retrospective series of 33 patients with primary hyperparathyroidism, Karpati and Frame (1964) noted that 14 patients had only psychiatric symptoms, with anxiety symptoms being most common, whereas 4 patients had both depression and cognitive symptoms. Petersen (1968) prospectively evaluated 54 patients with hyperparathyroidism and noted that more than 50% had psychiatric symptoms. Furthermore, he noted that the severity of psychiatric symptoms correlated with the degree of elevated serum calcium.

Review of the case literature reveals that most patients improve with correction of serum calcium. In a

**TABLE 25–4.** Psychiatric symptoms in hyperparathyroidism: case reports

| Reference | Age/sex | Symptoms | Serum Ca²⁺ (mg/dL) | Improved with treatment |
|-----------|---------|----------|---------------------|-------------------------|
| Fitz and Hallman 1952 | 55/M | Psychosis | 14 | Yes |
| | 52/M | Delirium | 19 | Yes |
| Nielsen 1955 | 47/F | Mood symptoms | 13 | Yes |
| Bogdonoff 1956 | 58/F | Depression/anxiety | 15.4 | |
| W.C. Thomas 1958 | 69/F | Delirium | 18.3 | |
| Lehrer and Levitt 1960 | 62/F | Delirium | 13.3 | No (died) |
| Reinfrank 1961 | 38/M | Depression | 11.1 | Yes |
| Agras and Oliveau 1964 | 64/F | Psychotic depression | 15 | Yes |
| Karpati and Frame 1964 | 40/F | Depression | 12.8 | Yes |
| | 64/F | Depression/anxiety | 11.6 | Yes |
| | ?/F | Delirium | 12.2 | Yes |
| | 43/F | Anxiety/obsessive-compulsive symptoms | 11.6 | Yes |
| Reilly and Wilson 1965 | 34/M | Psychosis | 11.6 | Yes |
| | 62/F | Delirium | 12.2 | Yes |
| | 67/F | Anxiety/depression | 13.8 | Yes |
| Jacobs and Merritt 1966 | 63/F | Delirium | 21.2 | Yes |
| Noble 1974 | 53/F | Depression | 14.2 | No |
| Gatewood et al. 1975 | 63/M | Delirium | 11.9 | Yes |
| Rosenblatt and Faillace 1977 | 30/M | Psychosis | 12.9 | Yes |
| Alarcon and Franceschini 1984 | 53/F | Psychosis | 13 | Yes |
| Kleinfeld et al. 1984 | 67/F | Psychosis | 13.2 | Yes |
| Borer and Bhanot 1985 | 45/F | Depression/delirium | 12.3 | Yes |
| Oztunc et al. 1986 | 45/M | Delirium | 12.4 | No (suicide 4 months later) |
| G.G. Brown et al. 1987 | 49/F | Depression/anxiety | 11.4 | No |
| | 60/F | Depression/anxiety | 11.2 | No |
| | 73/F | Anxiety | 10.9 | No |
| | 59/F | Psychosis/cognitive changes | 12.5 | No |
| R.S. Brown et al. 1987 | 68/M | Psychosis | 12.3 | Yes |
| Hayabara et al. 1987 | 68/F | Psychosis | 11 | Yes |
| | 60/F | Delirium | 15 | Yes |
| Thurling 1987 | 52/F | Psychosis | 14.8 | Yes |

prospective study of 18 patients scheduled for hyperparathyroidectomy, Solomon et al. (1994) noted that preoperative symptoms of psychological distress as measured by the Symptom Checklist–90—Revised (SCL-90-R) improved within 1 month after removal of the parathyroid adenoma. In another prospective series of 34 patients with hyperparathyroidism, a detailed neurobehavioral assessment was performed in addition to a psychiatric interview (G.G. Brown et al. 1987). Only 29% of patients with hyperparathyroidism were neurobehaviorally asymptomatic; 32% had signs of affective disorder; and 39% had evidence of cognitive impairment. In addition, the serum calcium increased with progression

from the asymptomatic (mean: 10.9 mg/dL) to the affectively ill (11.3 mg/dL) and cognitively impaired groups (12.2 mg/dL). Despite the correlation between psychiatric syndromes and serum calcium, no improvement occurred with correction of the serum calcium in the series by G.G. Brown et al. (1987). However, Joborn et al. (1988) described a case-control study measuring psychiatric symptom severity before and after parathyroidectomy and found a significant reduction in the Comprehensive Psychopathological Rating Scale 1–1.5 years after surgery. Figure 25–6 illustrates the relationship between serum calcium and the nature of the psychiatric disturbance.

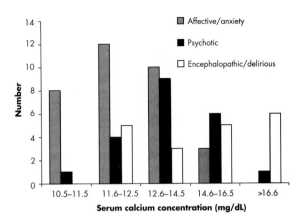

**FIGURE 25-6.** Psychiatric symptoms in hyperparathyroidism: phenomenologic association with changes in serum calcium.

*Source.* Adapted from Peterson et al. 1968, updated to include case data from Table 25-4.

## Hypoparathyroidism

### Cardinal Features of the Disorder

Hypoparathyroidism most commonly occurs as an idiopathic variant and in surgical patients after thyroidectomy. The most prominent feature of hypoparathyroidism is evidence of neuromuscular irritability, ranging from paresthesias to muscle cramps, carpopedal spasm, laryngospasm, and seizures. However, deep tendon reflexes are often decreased or absent. Ocular findings include cataracts and, more rarely, papilledema. Skin changes include alopecia; transverse nail growth; dry, scaling, pigmented skin; and a propensity to develop candidal infections (Juan 1979).

### Psychiatric Symptoms in Hypoparathyroidism

#### Phenomenology

Numerous psychiatric symptoms have been reported in hypoparathyroidism, including irritability and affective, anxiety, psychotic, and cognitive disorders. Cognitive disorders are the most frequently encountered syndromes. Researchers have emphasized the importance of recognizing anxiety features of hypoparathyroidism (Carlson 1986; Lawlor 1988).

The literature on psychiatric manifestations of hypoparathyroidism continues to be dominated by the exhaustive study by Denko and Kaelbling (1962). They reviewed 268 cases of hypoparathyroidism selected for psychiatric symptoms and compared them with 58 cases

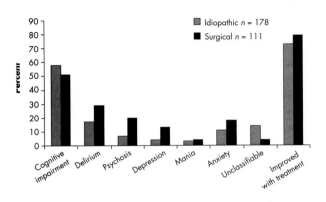

**FIGURE 25-7.** Psychiatric symptoms in hypoparathyroidism.

*Source.* Adapted from Denko and Kaelbling 1962.

of pseudohypoparathyroidism and 11 cases of pseudopseudohypoparathyroidism. Among patients with hypoparathyroidism, these investigators noted severe intellectual impairment in 56 patients, organic brain syndromes in 47, psychotic symptoms in 29, and neurotic symptoms in 32. Fifty-seven patients were considered to have undiagnosable psychiatric illness, yet scrutiny of the data reveals that several of these patients had affective and anxiety symptoms.

Several differences emerged between patients with surgical hypoparathyroidism and those with the idiopathic form. Although the overall prevalence of cognitive dysfunction was approximately 50% in both groups, isolated intellectual dysfunction was more uncommon in patients with surgical hypoparathyroidism (3.7% versus 19.0%), and delirium was much more prevalent in the surgical patients (29.2% versus 17.2%). Depressive, psychotic, and anxiety symptoms were more common in the surgical group than in the patients with idiopathic hypoparathyroidism. Depressive symptoms were present in 13.2% of surgical patients, compared with 4.9% of the idiopathic group. Psychotic symptoms were present in 19.8% of surgical patients, compared with 6.2% of the patients with idiopathic hypoparathyroidism. Anxiety symptoms were noted in 17.9% of surgical cases, whereas 11.7% of idiopathic cases were characterized by anxiety. Interestingly, manic symptoms were equally represented in both groups, being present in 4.3% of idiopathic hypoparathyroid patients and 4.7% of surgical patients. These results are summarized in Figure 25-7.

#### Improvement With Treatment

The overwhelming majority of the patients in the Denko and Kaelbling (1962) series improved in their psychiatric symptoms with treatment of the underlying hypoparathyroidism. Seventy-four percent of the idiopathic hypoparathyroidism patients improved, compared with 79% of the surgical patients. Residual symptoms were noted in many patients. Other investigators have noted improved symptoms with correction of serum calcium concentration (Carlson 1986; Gertner et al. 1976; Hossain 1970; Lawlor 1988).

# Conclusions

The foregoing review represents a clinically oriented discussion of the prevalence and phenomenology of psychiatric symptoms in endocrine disease. It remains unknown whether the associated psychiatric disturbances are directly the result of primary metabolic derangement in each endocrine disorder or due to some heretofore unknown factors. The pathophysiologic mechanisms involved in the development of psychiatric symptoms in endocrine disturbances undoubtedly vary with the particular endocrine disorder. Therefore, an understanding of the phenomenology of these relationships is also critical to developing hypotheses concerning the precise mechanisms by which endocrine disorders can produce psychiatric symptoms.

It appears that the severity of the endocrine disturbance is often correlated with the prevalence or severity of psychiatric symptoms, although this is not always the case. In addition, it is important to note that serious psychiatric syndromes are often present in only a minority of patients. Potential risk factors (i.e., genetic predisposition) for the development of psychiatric symptoms in endocrine disease need to be identified as well. Continued neuroendocrine studies with these patients will be important to enhance our understanding of the pathophysiology of their psychiatric symptoms.

# References

Abbas A, Styra R: Valproate prophylaxis against steroid-induced psychosis. Can J Psychiatry 39:188–189, 1994

Addison T: Disease of the supra-renal capsules, in Collection of the Published Writings of the Late Thomas Addison. London, New Sydenham Society, 1868, pp 209–239

Agras S, Oliveau DC: Primary hyperparathyroidism and psychosis. Canadian Medical Association Journal 91:1366–1367, 1964

Alarcon RD, Franceschini JA: Hyperparathyroidism and paranoid psychosis: case report and review of the literature. Br J Psychiatry 145:477–486, 1984

Alvarez MA, Gomez A, Alvarez E, et al: Short communication attention disturbance in Graves' disease. Psychoneuroendocrinology 8:451–454, 1983

American Psychiatric Association: Diagnostic and Statistical Manual of Mental Disorders, 3rd Edition. Washington, DC, American Psychiatric Association, 1980

American Psychiatric Association: Diagnostic and Statistical Manual of Mental Disorders, 3rd Edition, Revised. Washington, DC, American Psychiatric Association, 1987

Amsterdam JD, Marinelli DL, Arger P, et al: Assessment of adrenal gland volume by computed tomography in depressed patients and healthy volunteers. Psychiatry Res 21:189–197, 1987

Arana GW, Baldessarini RJ, Ornsteen M: The dexamethasone suppression test for diagnosis and prognosis in psychiatry. Arch Gen Psychiatry 42:1193–1204, 1985

Arato M, Banki CM, Nemeroff CB: Hypothalamic-pituitary-adrenal axis and suicide. Ann N Y Acad Sci 487:263–270, 1986

Artunkal S, Togrol B: Psychological studies in hyperthyroidism. Brain Thyroid Relationships 92–114, 1964

Asher R: Myxoedematous madness. BMJ 2:555–562, 1949

Baldini IM, Vita A, Mauri MC, et al.: Psychopathological and cognitive features in subclinical hypothyroidism. Prog Neuropsychopharmacol Biol Psychiatry 21:925–935, 1997

Banki CM, Bissette G, Arato M, et al: Elevation of immunoreactive CSF TRH in depressed patients. Am J Psychiatry 145:1526–1531, 1988

Bardgett ME, Taylor GT, Csernansky JG, et al: Chronic corticosterone treatment impairs spontaneous alternation behavior in rats. Behavioral and Neural Biology 61:186–190, 1994

Bauer MS, Whybrow PC: Thyroid hormones and the central nervous system in affective illness: interactions that may have clinical significance. Integrative Psychiatry 6:75–100, 1988

Bender BG, Lerner JA, Poland JE: Association between corticosteroids and psychologic change in hospitalized asthmatic children. Annals of Allergy 66:414–419, 1991

Bewsher PD, Gardiner AQ, Hedley AJ, et al: Psychosis after acute alteration of thyroid status. Psychol Med 1:260–262, 1971

Bogdonoff MD: Hyperparathyroidism. Am J Med 21:583–595, 1956

Borer MS, Bhanot VK: Hyperparathyroidism: neuropsychiatric manifestations. Psychosomatics 26:597–601, 1985

Boston Collaborative Drug Surveillance Program: Acute adverse reactions to prednisone in relation to dosage. Clin Pharmacol Ther 13:694–698, 1972

Brown GG, Preisman RC, Kleerkoper M: Neurobehavioral symptoms in mild primary hyperparathyroidism: related to hypercalcemia but not improved by parathyroidectomy. Henry Ford Hospital Medical Journal 35:211–215, 1987

Brown RS, Fischman A, Showalter CR: Primary hyperparathyroidism, hypercalcemia, paranoid delusions, homicide and attempted murder. J Forensic Sci 32:1460–1463, 1987

Brunetti A, Fulham MJ, Aloj L, et al: Decreased brain glucose utilization in patients with Cushing's disease. J Nucl Med 39:786–790, 1998

Buckman MT, Kellner R: Reduction of distress in hyperprolactinemia with bromocriptine. Am J Psychiatry 142:242–244, 1982

Bunevicius R, Kazanavicius G, Zalinkevicius R, et al: Effects of thyroxine as compared with thyroxine plus triiodothyronine in patients with hypothyroidism. N Engl J Med 340:424–429, 1999

Bunney WE, Fawcett SA: Possibility of a biochemical test for suicide potential. Arch Gen Psychiatry 13:232–239, 1965

Bursten B: Psychosis associated with thyrotoxicosis. Arch Gen Psychiatry 4:267–273, 1961

Campbell IA: Aggressive psychosis in AIDS patient on high-dose steroids. Lancet 2:750–751, 1987

Carlson RJ: Longitudinal observations of two cases of organic anxiety syndrome. Psychosomatics 27:529–531, 1986

Carney C: Diabetes mellitus and major depressive disorder: an overview of prevalence, complications, and treatment. Depression and Anxiety 7:149–157, 1998

Carroll BJ, Martin FI, Davis B: Pituitary-adrenal function in depression. Lancet 556:1373–1374, 1968

Clark LD, Quarton GC, Cobb S, et al: Further observations on mental disturbances associated with cortisone and ACTH therapy. N Engl J Med 249:178–183, 1953

Clower CG, Young AJ, Kepas D: Psychotic states resulting from disorders of thyroid function. Johns Hopkins Medical Journal 124:305–310, 1969

Cohen SI: Cushing's syndrome: a psychiatric study of 29 patients. Br J Psychiatry 136:120–124, 1980

Cohen ST, Welch G, Jacobson AM, et al.: The association of lifetime psychiatric illness and increased retinopathy in patients with type I diabetes mellitus. Psychosomatics 38:98–108, 1997

Cohen-Cole S, Brown FW, McDaniel JS: Assessment of depression and grief reactions in the medically ill, in Psychiatric Care of the Medical Patient. Edited by Stoudemire A, Fogel BS. New York, Oxford University Press, 1993, pp 53–70

Cooper DS, Halpern R, Wood LC, et al: L-Thyroxine therapy in subclinical hypothyroidism: a double-blind placebo controlled trial. Ann Intern Med 101:18–24, 1984

Cowdry RW, Wehr TA, Ziz AP, et al: Thyroid abnormalities associated with rapid-cycling bipolar illness. Arch Gen Psychiatry 40:414–420, 1983

Crown S: Notes on an experimental study of intellectual deterioration. BMJ 2:684–685, 1949

Cushing H: The basophil adenomas of the pituitary body and their clinical manifestations (pituitary basophilism). Bulletin of the Johns Hopkins Hospital 50:137–195, 1932

Deary IJ, Hepburn DA, MacLeod KM, et al: Partitioning the symptoms of hypoglycemia using multi-sample confirmatory factor analysis. Diabetologia 36:771–777, 1993

de Groot M, Jacobson AM, Samson JA, et al: Glycemic control and major depression in patients with type 1 and type 2 diabetes mellitus. J Psychosom Res 46:425–435, 1999

Denko J, Kaelbling R: The psychiatric aspects of hypoparathyroidism. Acta Psychiatr Scand Suppl 164:1–70, 1962

Diabetes Control and Complications Trial Research Group: The effect of intensive treatment of diabetes on the development and progression of long term complications in insulin-dependent diabetes mellitus. N Engl J Med 329:977–986, 1993

Dietch JT: Diagnosis of organic anxiety disorders. Psychosomatics 22:661–669, 1981

D'Orban PT: Steroid-induced psychosis (letter). Lancet 2:684, 1989

Easson WM: Myxedema with psychosis. Arch Gen Psychiatry 14:277–283, 1966

Engel GL, Margolin SG: Neuropsychiatric disturbances in Addison's disease and the role of impaired carbohydrate metabolism in production of abnormal cerebral function. Archives of Neurology and Psychiatry 45:881–884, 1941

Erskine MS, Barfield JR, Goldman BD: Intraspecific fighting during late pregnancy and lactation in rats and effects of litter removal. Behavioral and Neural Biology 23:206–213, 1978

Esposito S, Prange AJ, Golden RN: The thyroid axis and mood disorders: overview and future prospects. Psychopharmacology Bulletin 33:205–217, 1997

Evans D, Nemeroff CB: Use of dexamethasone suppression test using DSM-III criteria on an inpatient psychiatric unit. Biol Psychiatry 18:505–511, 1983

Extein I, Pottash ALC, Gold MS: The thyrotropin-releasing hormone test in the diagnosis of unipolar depression. Psychiatry Res 5:311–316, 1981

Fahrenfort JJ, Wilterdink AM, van der Veen EA: long-term residual complaints and psychosocial sequelae after remission of hyperthyroidism. Psychoneuroendocrinology 25:201–211, 2000

Falk WE, Mahnke MW, Pozkanzer DC: Lithium prophylaxis of corticotropin-induced psychosis. JAMA 241:1011–1012, 1979

Fang VS, Jaspan JB: Delirium and neuromuscular symptoms in an elderly man with isolated corticotroph-deficiency syndrome completely reversed with glucocorticoid replacement. J Clin Endocrinol Metab 69:1073–1077, 1989

Fitz TE, Hallman BL: Mental changes associated with hyperparathyroidism. Arch Intern Med 89:547–551, 1952

Gatewood JW, Organ CH, Mead BT: Mental changes associated with hyperparathyroidism. Am J Psychiatry 132:129–132, 1975

Gavard JA, Lustman PJ, Clouse RE: Prevalence of depression in adults with diabetes: an epidemiological evaluation. Diabetes Care 16:1167–1178, 1993

Gertner JM, Hodsman AB, Neuberger JN: 1-Alpha-hydroxycalciferol in the treatment of hypocalcaemic psychosis. Clin Endocrinol (Oxf) 5:539–543, 1976

Ghazi AAM, Mofid D, Rahimi F, et al: Oestrogen and cortisol producing adrenal tumor. Arch Dis Child 71:358–359, 1994

Glynne-Jones R, Vernon CC: Is steroid psychosis preventable by divided doses? (letter). Lancet 2:1404, 1986

Gold MS, Pottash ALC, Extein I: Hypothyroidism and depression: evidence from complete thyroid function evaluation. JAMA 245:1919–1922, 1981

Gold MS, Pottash ALC, Extein I: "Symptomless" autoimmune thyroiditis in depression. Psychiatry Res 6:261–269, 1982

Golden MP, Ingersoll GM, Brack CJ, et al: Longitudinal relationship of asymptomatic hypoglycemia to cognitive function in IDDM. Diabetes Care 12:89–93, 1989

Goodnick PJ, Henry JH, Buki VMV: Treatment of depression in patients with diabetes. J Clin Psychiatry 56:128–136, 1995

Gotch PM: Cushing's syndrome from the patient's perspective. Endocrinol Metab Clin North Am 23:607–617, 1994

Grandinetti A, Kaholokula JK, Crabbe KM, et al: Relationship between depressive symptoms and diabetes among native Hawaiians. Psychoneuroendocrinology 25:239–246, 2000

Greer S, Ramsay I, Bagley C: Neurotoxic and thyrotoxic anxiety: clinical, psychological and physiological measurements. Br J Psychiatry 122:549–554, 1973

Haggerty JJ, Evans DL, Prange AJ: Organic brain syndrome associated with marginal hypothyroidism. Am J Psychiatry 143:785–786, 1986

Haggerty JJ, Stern RA, Mason GA, et al: Subclinical hypothyroidism: a modifiable risk factor for depression? Am J Psychiatry 150:508–510, 1993

Hall RCW, Popkin MK, Stickney SK, et al: Presentation of the steroid psychosis. J Nerv Ment Dis 167:229–236, 1979

Hall RCW, Popkin MK, DeVaul R, et al: Psychiatric manifestations of Hashimoto's thyroiditis. Psychosomatics 23:337–342, 1982

Halonen H, Hiekkala H, Huupponen T, et al: A follow-up EEG study in diabetic children. Annals of Clinical Research 15:167–172, 1983

Hart SP, Frier BM: Causes, management and morbidity of acute hypoglycaemia in adults requiring hospital admission. QJM 91:505–510, 1998

Haskett RF: Diagnostic categorization of psychiatric disturbance in Cushing's syndrome. Am J Psychiatry 142:911–916, 1985

Haumont D, Dorchy H, Pelc S: EEG abnormalities in diabetic children: influence of hypoglycemia and vascular complications. Clin Pediatr (Phila) 18:750–753, 1979

Hayabara T, Hashimoto K, Izumi H, et al: Neuropsychiatric disorders in primary hyperparathyroidism. Japanese Journal of Psychiatry and Neurology 41:33–40, 1987

Hayreh SS, Watson PG: Prednisolone-21-stearoylglycolate in scleritis. Br J Ophthalmol 54:394–398, 1970

Heath H III: Clinical spectrum of primary hyperparathyroidism: evolution with changes in medical practice and technology. J Bone Miner Res 6 (suppl 2):S63–S70, 1991

Heim C, Newport D, Heit S, et al: Pituitary-adrenal and autonomic responses to stress in women after sexual and physical abuse in childhood. JAMA 284:592–597, 2000

Hermann HT, Quarton GC: Psychological changes and psychogenesis in thyroid hormone disorders. J Clin Endocrinol Metab 25:327–338, 1965

Hofeldt FD: Reactive hypoglycemia. Endocrinol Metab Clin North Am 18:185–201, 1989

Horwitz DL: Factitious and artifactual hypoglycemia. Endocrinol Metab Clin North Am 18:203–210, 1989

Hossain M: Neurologic and psychiatric manifestations in idiopathic hypoparathyroidism: response to treatment. J Neurol Neurosurg Psychiatry 33:153–156, 1970

Howorka K, Pumprla J, Saletu B, et al: Decrease of vigilance assessed by EEG-mapping in type I diabetic patients with history of recurrent severe hypoglycaemia. Psychoneuroendocrinology 25:85–105, 2000

Irwin R, Ellis PM, Delahunt J: Psychosis following acute alteration of thyroid status. Aust N Z J Psychiatry 31:762–764, 1997

Jacobs JK, Merritt CR: Magnesium deficiency in hyperparathyroidism: case report of toxic psychosis. Ann Surg 162:260–262, 1966

Jain VK: A psychiatric study of hypothyroidism. Psychiatrica Clinica 5:121–130, 1972

Jeffcoate WJ, Silverstone JT, Edwards CRW, et al: Psychiatric manifestations of Cushing's syndrome: response to lowering of plasma cortisol. QJM 191:465–472, 1979

Jellinek EH: Fits, faints, coma, and dementia in myxoedema. Lancet 2:1010–1012, 1962

Jimenez IM, Goodnick P: Depression in patients with diabetes mellitus. Directions in Psychiatry 19:231–248, 1999

Joborn C, Hetta J, Rastad J, et al: Psychiatric symptoms and cerebrospinal fluid monoamine metabolites in primary hyperparathyroidism. Biol Psychiatry 23:149–158, 1988

Joffe RT, Levitt AJ: Major depression and subclinical hypothyroidism. Psychoneuroendocrinology 17:215–221, 1992

Joffe RT, Sokolov STH: Thyroid hormones, the brain, and affective disorders. Crit Rev Neurobiol 8:45–63, 1994

Joffe RT, Kutcher S, MacDonald C: Thyroid function and bipolar affective disorder. Psychiatry Res 25:117–121, 1988

Joffe RT, Singer W, Levitt AJ, et al: A placebo-controlled comparison of lithium and triiodothyronine augmentation of tricyclic antidepressants in unipolar refractory depression. Arch Gen Psychiatry 50:387–394, 1993

Jonas AD: Hypothyroidism and neurotic depression. American Practitioner 3:103–105, 1952

Josephson AM, MacKenzie TB: Appearance of manic psychosis following rapid normalization of thyroid status. Am J Psychiatry 136:846–847, 1979

Juan D: Hypocalcemia: differential diagnosis and mechanisms. Arch Intern Med 139:1166–1171, 1979

Karpati G, Frame B: Neuropsychiatric disorders in primary hyperparathyroidism. Arch Neurol 10:387–397, 1964

Katerndahl DA, Vande Creek L: Hyperthyroidism and panic attacks. Psychosomatics 24:491–496, 1983

Kathol RG, Delahunt JW: The relationship of anxiety and depression to symptoms of hyperthyroidism using operational criteria. Gen Hosp Psychiatry 8:23–28, 1986

Kellner R, Buckman MT, Fava M, et al: Prolactin, aggression, and hostility: a discussion of recent studies. Psychiatric Developments 2:131–138, 1984

Kelly WF, Checkley SA, Bender DA, et al: Cushing's syndrome and depression: a prospective study of 26 patients. Br J Psychiatry 142:16–19, 1983

Kelly WF, Kelly MJ, Faragher B: A prospective study of psychiatric and psychological aspects of Cushing's syndrome. Clin Endocrinol (Oxf) 45:715–720, 1996

Kiraly SF, Ancill RJ, Dimitrova G: The relationship of endogenous cortisol to psychiatric disorder: a review. Can J Psychiatry 42:415–420, 1997

Kirkegaard CJ, Faber J, Hummer L, et al: Increased levels of TRH in cerebrospinal fluid from patients with endogenous depression. Psychoneuroendocrinology 4:227–235, 1979

Klee GC, Hay ID: Assessment of sensitive thyrotropin assays for an expanded role in thyroid function testing: proposed criteria for analytic performance and clinical utility. J Clin Endocrinol Metab 64:461–471, 1986

Klein R, Klein BE, Moss SE, et al: Glycosylated hemoglobin predicts the incidence and progression of diabetic retinopathy. JAMA 260:2864–2871, 1988

Kleinfeld M, Peter S, Gilbert GM: Delirium as the predominant manifestation of hyperparathyroidism: reversal after parathyroidectomy. J Am Geriatr Soc 32:689–690, 1984

Kleinschmidt HJ, Waxenberg SE, Cuker R: Psychophysiology and psychiatric management of thyrotoxicosis: a two year follow-up study. Journal of the Mount Sinai Hospital 23:131–153, 1956

Koppelman MCS, Parry BL, Hamilton JA, et al: Effect of bromocriptine on affect and libido in hyperprolactinemia. Am J Psychiatry 144:1037–1041, 1987

Kovacs M, Obrosky DS, Goldstone D, et al: Major depressive disorder in youth with IDDM. A controlled prospective study of course and outcome. Diabetes Care 20:45–51, 1997

Krishnan KRR, Doraiswamy PM, Lurie SN, et al: Pituitary size in depression. J Clin Endocrinol Metab 72:256–259, 1991

Lawlor BA: Hypocalcemia, hypoparathyroidism, and organic anxiety syndrome. J Clin Psychiatry 49:317–318, 1988

Leedom L, Meehan WP, Procci W, et al: Symptoms of depression in patients with type II diabetes mellitus. Psychosomatics 32:280–286, 1991

Lehrer G, Levitt M: Neuropsychiatric presentation of hypercalcemia. Journal of the Mount Sinai Hospital 27:10–18, 1960

Libow LS, Durell J: Clinical studies on the relationship between psychosis and the regulation of thyroid gland activity. Psychosom Med 27:369–376, 1965

Lidz T, Whitehorn JC: Psychiatric problems in a thyroid clinic. JAMA 139:698–701, 1949

Ling MH, Perry PJ, Tsuang MT: Side effects of corticosteroid therapy: psychiatric aspects. Arch Gen Psychiatry 38:741–747, 1981

Logothetis J: Psychotic behavior as the initial indicator of adult myxedema. J Nerv Ment Dis 136:561–568, 1963

Loosen PT, Chambliss R, DeBold CR, et al: Psychiatric phenomenology in Cushing's disease. Pharmacopsychiatry 25:192–198, 1992

Lustman PJ, Harper GW, Griffith LS, et al: Use of the Diagnostic Interview Schedule in patients with diabetes mellitus. J Nerv Ment Dis 174:743–746, 1986

Lustman PJ, Clouse RE, Carney RM, et al: Characteristics of depression in adults with diabetes, in Proceedings of the National Institute of Mental Health Conference on Mental Disorders in the General Health Care Setting, Vol 1. Seattle, WA, 1987, pp 127–129

Lustman PJ, Griffith LS, Clouse RE: Depression in adults with diabetes: results of a 5-year follow-up study. Diabetes Care 11:605–612, 1988

Lustman PJ, Freedland KE, Carney RM, et al: Similarity of depression in diabetic and psychiatric patients. Psychosom Med 54:602–611, 1992a

Lustman PJ, Griffith LS, Gavard JA, et al: Depression in adults with diabetes. Diabetes Care 15:1631–1639, 1992b

Lustman PJ, Clouse RE, Griffith LS, et al: Screening for depression in diabetes using the Beck Depression Inventory. Psychosom Med 59:24–31, 1997

Lustman PJ, Griffith LS, Freedland KE, et al: Cognitive behavior therapy for depression in type 2 diabetes mellitus. A randomized, controlled trial. Ann Intern Med 129(8):613–621, 1998

MacCrimmon DJ, Wallace JE, Goldberg WM, et al: Emotional disturbance and cognitive deficits in hyperthyroidism. Psychosom Med 41:331–340, 1979

Mahendran R: Hypomania in a patient with congenital familial hypothyroidism and mild mental retardation. Singapore Med J 40:425–427, 1999

Malouf R, Brust JCM: Hypoglycemia: causes, neurological manifestations, and outcome. Ann Neurol 17:421–430, 1985

Mandelbrote BM, Wittkower ED: Emotional factors in Graves' disease. Psychosom Med 17:109–123, 1955

Manger WM, Gifford RW Jr, Hoffman BB: Pheochromocytoma: a clinical and experimental overview. Curr Probl Cancer 9(5):1–85, 1985

Marcus MD, Winey RR, Guare J, et al: Lifetime prevalence of major depression and its effect on treatment outcome in obese type II diabetic patients. Diabetes Care 15:253–255, 1992

Mastrogiacomo I, Fava M, Fava G, et al: Postpartum hostility and prolactin. Int J Psychiatry Med 12:289–294, 1983

Mazet P, Simon D, Luton J-P, et al: Syndrome de Cushing: symptomatologie psychique et personnalite de 50 malades. Nouvelle Presse Medicale 10:2565–2570, 1981

Miller R: Mental symptoms from myxedema. J Lab Clin Med 40:267–270, 1952

Modlin IM, Farndon JR, Shepherd A, et al: Phaeochromocytomas in 72 patients: clinical and diagnostic features, treatment and long-term results. Br J Surg 66:456–465, 1979

Murphy BEP: Steroids and depression. J Steroid Biochem Mol Biol 38:537–559, 1991

Murphy BEP, Dhar V, Ghadirian AM, et al: Response to steroid suppression in major depression resistant to antidepressant therapy. J Clin Psychopharmacol 11:121–126, 1991

Musselman DL, Nemeroff CB: Depression and endocrine disorders: focus on the thyroid and adrenal system. Br J Psychiatry Suppl (30):123–128, 1996

Nemeroff CB, Widerlov E, Bissette G, et al: Elevated concentrations of CSF corticotropin-releasing factor–like immunoreactivity in depressed patients. Science 226:1342–1344, 1984

Nemeroff CB, Simon JS, Haggerty JJ, et al: Antithyroid antibodies in depressed patients. Am J Psychiatry 142:840–843, 1985

Nemeroff CB, Krishnan KKR, Reed D, et al: Adrenal gland enlargement in major depression: a computed tomographic study. Arch Gen Psychiatry 49:384–387, 1992

Newcomer JW, Craft S, Hershey T, et al: Glucocorticoid-induced impairment in declarative memory performance in adult humans. J Neurosci 14:2047–2053, 1994

Nielsen H: Familial occurrence, gastro-intestinal symptoms and mental disturbances in hyperparathyroidism. Acta Medica Scandinavica 15:359–366, 1955

Noble P: Depressive illness and hyperparathyroidism. Proceedings of the Royal Society of Medicine 67:1066–1067, 1974

Okamoto T, Gerstein HC, Obara T: Psychiatric symptoms, bone density and non-specific symptoms in patients with mild hypercalcemia due to primary hyperparathyroidism: a systematic overview of the literature. Endocr J 44:367–374, 1997

Oztunc A, Guscott RG, Soni J, et al: Psychosis resulting in suicide in a patient with primary hyperparathyroidism. Can J Psychiatry 31:342–343, 1986

Perlmuter LC, Hakami MK, Hodgson-Harrington C, et al: Decreased cognitive function in aging non–insulin-dependent patients. Am J Med 77:1043–1048, 1984

Perry PJ, Tsuang MT, Hwang MH: Prednisolone psychosis: clinical observations. Drug Intelligence and Clinical Pharmacology 18:603–609, 1984

Petersen P: Psychiatric disorders in primary hyperparathyroidism. J Clin Endocrinol Metab 28:1491–1495, 1968

Pitts FN, Guze SB: Psychiatric disorders and myxedema. Am J Psychiatry 118:142–147, 1961

Plouin PF, Degoulet P, Tugaye A, et al: Le depistage du pheochromocytome: chez quels hypertendus? etude semiologique chez 2585 hypertendus dont 11 ayant un pheochromocytome. Nouvelle Presse Medicale 10:869–872, 1981

Pomeranze J, King E: Psychosis as first sign of thyroid dysfunction. Geriatrics 21:211–212, 1966

Pop VJ, Maartens LH, Leusink G, et al: Are autoimmune thyroid dysfunction and depression related? J Clin Endocrinol Metab 83:3194–3197, 1998

Popkin MK, Callies AL, Lentz RD, et al: Prevalence of major depression, simple phobia, and other psychiatric disorders in patients with longstanding type I diabetes mellitus. Arch Gen Psychiatry 45:64–68, 1988

Pramming S, Thorsteinsson B, Theilgaard A, et al: Cognitive function during hypoglycemia in type I diabetes mellitus. BMJ 292:647–650, 1986

Prange AJ, Wilson IC, Rabon AM, et al: Enhancement of imipramine antidepressant activity by thyroid hormone. Am J Psychiatry 126:457–469, 1969

Prange AJ, Lara PP, Wilson IC, et al: Effects of thyrotropin-releasing hormone in depression. Lancet 2:999–1002, 1972

Prange AJ, Haggerty JJ, Rice J, et al: Marginal hypothyroidism in mental illness: preliminary assessments of prevalence and significance. Proceedings of the 16th Congress of International Neuropharmacology Conference, Munich, West Germany, August 1988

Prinz PN, Vitaliano PP, Moe KE, et al: Thyroid hormones: positive relationships with cognition in healthy, euthyroid older men. Journals of Gerontology Series A, Biological Sciences and Medical Sciences 54:M111–116, 1999

Reaven GM, Thompson LW, Nahum D, et al: Relationship between hyperglycemia and cognitive function in older NIDDM patients. Diabetes Care 13:16–21, 1990

Reilly EL, Wilson WP: Mental symptoms in hyperparathyroidism: a report of three cases. Diseases of the Nervous System 26:361–363, 1965

Reinfrank RF: Primary hyperparathyroidism with depression. Arch Intern Med 108:162–166, 1961

Reitan RM: Intellectual functions in myxedema. Archives of Neurology and Psychiatry 69:436–449, 1953

Rennick PM, Wilder RM, Sargent J, et al: Retinopathy as an indicator of cognitive-perceptual-motor impairment in diabetic adults (summary), in Proceedings of the 76th Annual Convention of the American Psychological Association, San Francisco, CA, August 1968, pp 473–474

Richardson JT: Cognitive function in diabetes mellitus. Neurosci Biobehav Rev 14:385–388, 1990

Risch SC, Lewine RJ, Kalin NH, et al: Limbic-hypothalamic-pituitary-adrenal axis activity and ventricular-to-brain ratio studies in affective illness and schizophrenia. Neuropsychopharmacology 6:95–100, 1992

Robbins LR, Vinson DB: Objective psychological assessment of the thyrotoxic patient and the response to treatment: preliminary report. Journal of Clinical Endocrinology 20:120–129, 1960

Robinson N, Fuller JH, Edmeades SP: Depression and diabetes. Diabet Med 5:268–274, 1988

Rockey PH, Griep RJ: Behavioral dysfunction in hyperthyroidism. Arch Intern Med 140:1194–1197, 1980

Rosenbaum AH, Maruta T, Schatzberg AF, et al: Toward a biochemical classification of depressive disorders, VII: urinary free cortisol and urinary MHPG in depression. Am J Psychiatry 140:314–317, 1983

Rosenberg FR, Sander S, Nelson CT: Pemphigus: a 20-year review of 107 patients treated with corticosteroids. Arch Dermatol 112:962–970, 1976

Rosenblatt S, Faillace LA: Psychiatric manifestations of hyperparathyroidism. Tex Med 73:59–60, 1977

Rovet JF, Ehrlich RM, Hoppe M: Intellectual deficits associated with early onset of insulin-dependent diabetes mellitus in children. Diabetes Care 10:510–515, 1987

Royce PC: Severely impaired consciousness in myxedema: a review. Am J Med Sci 261:46–50, 1971

Ryan CM: Neurobehavioral complications of type-I diabetes: examination of possible risk factors. Diabetes Care 11:86–93, 1988

Ryan CM, Vega A, Drash A: Cognitive deficits in adolescents who developed diabetes early in life. Pediatrics 75:921–927, 1985

Sachar E, Hellman L, Fukushima D, et al: Cortisol production in depressive illness. Arch Gen Psychiatry 23:289–298, 1970

Sachs G, Spiess K, Moser G, et al: Glycosylated hemoglobin and diabetes—self-monitoring (compliance) in depressed and non-depressed type I diabetes patients. Psychother Psychosom Med Psychol 41:306–312, 1991

Scarlett JA, Mako ME, Rubenstein AH, et al: Factitious hypoglycemia: diagnosis by measurement of serum C-peptide immunoreactivity and insulin-binding antibodies. N Engl J Med 297:1029–1032, 1977

Schon M, Sutherland AM, Rawson RW: Hormones and neuroses: the psychological effects of thyroid deficiency, in Proceedings of the 3rd World Congress of Psychiatry. Toronto, University of Toronto Press, 1962, pp 835–839

Shaw PJ, Walls TJ, Newman PK, et al: Hashimoto's encephalopathy: a steroid-responsive disorder associated with high anti-thyroid antibody titers: report of 5 cases. Neurology 41:228–233, 1991

Shein M, Apter A, Dickerman Z, et al: Encephalopathy in compensated Hashimoto thyroiditis: a clinical expression of autoimmune cerebral vasculitis. Brain Dev 8:60–64, 1986

Sherwin RS: Diabetes mellitus, in Cecil Textbook of Medicine, 20th Edition. Edited by Bennett JC, Plum F. Philadelphia, PA, WB Saunders, 1996, pp 1258–1277

Siegal FP: Lithium for steroid-induced psychosis. N Engl J Med 299:155–156, 1978

Silva RG, Tolstunov L: Steroid-induced psychosis: report of a case. J Oral Maxillofac Surg 53:183–186, 1995

Skenazy JA, Bigler ED: Neuropsychological findings in diabetes mellitus. J Clin Psychol 40:246–258, 1984

Smallridge RC: Disclosing subclinical thyroid disease. Postgrad Med 107:143–152, 2000

Soininen H, Puranen M, Helkala E-L, et al: Diabetes mellitus and brain atrophy: a computerized tomography study in an elderly population. Neurobiol Aging 13:717–721, 1992

Solomon BL, Schaaf M, Smallridge RC: Psychologic symptoms before and after parathyroid surgery. Am J Med 96:101–106, 1994

Sonino N, Fava GA, Boscaro M: A role for life events in the pathogenesis of Cushing's disease. Clin Endocrinol (Oxf) 38:261–264, 1988

Sonino N, Fava G, Belluardo P, et al: Course of depression in Cushing's syndrome: response to treatment and comparison with Graves' disease. Horm Res 39:202–206, 1993

Soygur H, Palaoglu O, Altinors N, et al: Melperone treatment in an organic delusional syndrome induced by hyperprolactinemia: a case report. European Neuropsychopharmacology 7:161–163, 1997

Spillane JD: Nervous and mental disorders in Cushing's syndrome. Brain 74:72–94, 1951

Starkman MN, Schteingart DE, Schork MA: Depressed mood and other psychiatric manifestations of Cushing's syndrome: relationship to hormone levels. Psychosom Med 43:3–18, 1981

Starkman MN, Zelnick TC, Nesse RM, et al: Anxiety in patients with pheochromocytomas. Arch Intern Med 145:248–252, 1985

Starkman MN, Schteingart DE, Schork MA: Cushing's syndrome after treatment. Psychiatry Res 19:177–188, 1986

Starkman MN, Gebarski SS, Berent S, et al: Hippocampal formation volume, memory dysfunction, and cortisol levels in patient's with Cushing's syndrome. Biol Psychiatry 32:756–765, 1992

Steiner M, Haskett RF, Carroll BJ, et al: Plasma prolactin and severe premenstrual tension. Psychoneuroendocrinology 9:29–35, 1984

Targum SD, Greenberg RD, Harmon RL, et al: Thyroid hormone and the TRH stimulation test in refractory depression. J Clin Psychiatry 45:345–346, 1984

Taylor JW: Depression in thyrotoxicosis. Am J Psychiatry 132:552–553, 1975

Theohar C, Fischer-Cornellssen K, Brosch H, et al: A comparative, multi-center trial between bromocriptine and amitriptyline in the treatment of endogenous depression. Arzneimittelforschung 32:783–787, 1982

Thomas FB, Mazzaferri EL, Skillman TG: Apathetic thyrotoxicosis: a distinctive clinical and laboratory entity. Ann Intern Med 72:679–685, 1970

Thomas JE, Rooke ED, Kuale WF: The neurologist's experience with pheochromocytoma: a review of 100 cases. JAMA 197:754–758, 1966

Thomas WC: Hypercalcemic crisis due to hyperparathyroidism. Am J Med 24:229–239, 1958

Thompson WF: Psychiatric aspects of Addison's disease: report of a case. Medical Annals of the District of Columbia 42:62–64, 1973

Thrush DC, Boddie HG: Episodic encephalopathy associated with thyroid disorders. J Neurol Neurosurg Psychiatry 37:696–700, 1974

Thurling ML: Primary hyperparathyroidism in a schizophrenic woman. Can J Psychiatry 32:785–787, 1987

Tonks CM: Mental illness in hypothyroid patients. Br J Psychiatry 110:706–710, 1964

Treadway CR, Prange AJ, Doehne EF, et al: Myxedema psychosis: clinical and biochemical changes during recovery. J Psychiatr Res 5:289–296, 1967

Trzepacz P, McCue M, Klein I, et al: A psychiatric and neuropsychological study of patients with untreated Graves' disease. Gen Hosp Psychiatry 10:49–55, 1988

Tun PA, Nathan DM, Pulmuter LC: Cognitive and affective disorders in elderly diabetics. Clin Geriatr Med 6:731–746, 1990

van Oostrom JC, Schaafsma A, Haaxma R: Variable manifestations of Hashimoto's encephalopathy. Ned Tijdschr Geneeskd 143:25, 1319–1322, 1999

Varadaraj R, Cooper AJ: Addison's disease presenting with psychiatric symptoms (letter). Am J Psychiatry 143:553–554, 1986

Ward DJ, Rastall ML: Prognosis in "myxoedematous madness." Br J Psychiatry 113:149–151, 1967

Wehr T, Sack D, Rosenthal N, et al: Rapid cycling affective disorder: contributing factors in treatment response in 51 patients. Am J Psychiatry 145:179–184, 1988

Wells KB, Golding JM, Burnam MA: Psychiatric disorder in a sample of the general population with and without chronic medical conditions. Am J Psychiatry 145:976–981, 1988

Weyerer S, Hewer W, Pfeifer-Kurda M, et al: Psychiatric disorders and diabetes: results from a community study. J Psychosom Res 33:633–640, 1989

Whelan TB, Schteingart DE, Starkman MN, et al: Neuropsychological deficits in Cushing's syndrome. J Nerv Ment Dis 168:753–757, 1980

Whybrow PC, Hurwitz T: Psychological disturbances associated with endocrine disease and hormone therapy, in Hormones, Behavior, and Psychopathology. Edited by Sachar EJ. New York, Raven, 1976, pp 125–143

Whybrow PC, Prange AJ, Treadway CR: Mental changes accompanying thyroid gland dysfunction. Arch Gen Psychiatry 20:48–63, 1969

Wiesel C: Psychosis with myxedema. J Ky Med Assoc 50:395–397, 1952

Wilson WP, Johnson JE, Smith RB: Affective change in thyrotoxicosis and experimental hypermetabolism. Recent Advances in Biological Psychiatry 4:234–243, 1962

Winokur A, Maislin G, Phillips J, et al: Insulin resistance after oral glucose tolerance testing in patients with major depression. Am J Psychiatry 145:325–330, 1988

Zeiger MA, Fraker DL, Pass HI, et al: Effective reversibility of the signs and symptoms of hypercortisolism by bilateral adrenalectomy. Surgery 114:1138–1143, 1993

# Neuropsychiatric Aspects of Poisons and Toxins

Shreenath V. Doctor, M.D., Ph.D.

All substances are poisons; there is none which is not a poison. The right dose differentiates a poison and a remedy.

—*Paracelsus, sixteenth century*

A poison is defined in this chapter as a material or chemical that is capable of producing a deleterious response in a biological system, seriously injuring function or producing death. Toxins are further categorized as poisons produced by various animal, plant, and microbial species to which humans are either unintentionally or intentionally exposed. Neurotoxic agents, or neurotoxins, are poisons that produce an adverse change in the structure and/or function of the nervous system. Several different classes of neurotoxic agents are shown in Table 26–1. Short-term or long-term exposure to neurotoxic agents can result in various neuropsychiatric manifestations, such as those shown in Tables 26–2 through 26–5.

In our industrialized society, exposure to neurotoxins can occur from the air, water, food, environmental surfaces, soil, microbes, plants, and animals or by envenomation via bites and stings. The number of new chemicals produced every year, each with the potential for neuropsychiatric sequelae, is estimated to be in the thousands. Included are biocides, chemicals that are deliberately placed in our environment to selectively injure or kill plant, animal, or microbial life.

The variety of potential adverse effects of the numerous diverse inorganic and organic chemicals present in our environment make the subject of this chapter a broad topic area. In the following pages, I discuss poisons and toxins that have prominent neuropsychiatric sequelae in humans, along with information, if available, on their exposure, absorption, mechanisms of action, diagnosis, and on the treatment of their effects. Intoxications due to medications are not covered here.

## Metals

### Aluminum

Constituting 5% of the earth's crust, aluminum is mined and refined for use in electrical wiring, thermal insulation, paint, bricks, mufflers, and household and industrial utensils. Sources of exposure include processed food such as pickles, aluminum-containing deodorants, oral antidiarrheal and antacid agents, and phosphate-binding gels. Other medical sources of aluminum exposure

**TABLE 26–1.** Selected poisons producing neuropsychiatric sequelae

| Gases | Metals | Organic solvents | Pesticides |
|---|---|---|---|
| Carbon monoxide | Alkyltins | Acetone | Carbamates |
| Ethylene oxide | Aluminum | Carbon disulfide | Organochlorines |
| | Arsenic | Ethylbenzene | Organophosphates |
| | Lead | Methanol | Pyrethroids |
| | Manganese | Methyl-*n*-butyl ketone | |
| | Mercury | Methyl chloride | |
| | Thallium | Styrene | |
| | | Toluene | |
| | | Trichloroethylene | |
| | | Xylene | |

*Source.* Adapted from Bleecker 1994.

include aluminum-contaminated dialysis solutions, total parenteral nutrition solutions, and human serum albumin used in plasmapheresis.

Aluminum is poorly absorbed through the gastrointestinal tract; however, depending on the intraluminal speciation, quantity, competing or complexing substances, and intraluminal pH (Van der Voet 1992a, 1992b), absorption can range from approximately 0.0005% to 24% in humans (Wilhelm et al. 1990). Transport in the blood occurs in association with high-molecular-weight transferrin as well as low-molecular-weight phosphate, citrate, and hydroxide (Harris 1992). Transport across the blood-brain barrier is also variable, similar to intestinal absorption.

## Neuropsychiatric Manifestations

Neurotoxicity from aluminum occurs almost exclusively in persons who are unable to excrete dietary aluminum. Patients with chronic renal failure on long-term dialysis develop a disease known as dialysis encephalopathy (Alfrey and Froment 1990; D.N.S. Kerr et al. 1992), which is characterized by gradual development of personality changes and visual and auditory hallucinations leading to paranoid and suicidal behavior. A combination of dysarthria, dyspraxia, and dysphasia—considered to be the early-onset symptoms of the disease—can occur both during and immediately after dialysis. Myoclonic jerks, usually occurring in the facial region and upper limbs, are often present with speech disturbances. Focal motor and generalized tonic-clonic seizures can also occur with a high incidence. Dementia, the most consistent feature of dialysis encephalopathy, manifests gradually as disturbances of concentration, attention, orientation, and memory. In later stages, confusion and gross signs of dementia are noted. Electroencephalographic abnormali-

ties, such as paroxysms of high-voltage delta activity with spike and wave discharges, may precede the clinical symptoms by many months.

After focal accumulations of the metal were observed in the central cores of senile plaques and in neurons bearing neurofibrillary tangles, it was suggested that aluminum may have a role in the etiology of Alzheimer's disease (D.P. Perl and Brody 1980). Neurofibrillary tangles, senile plaques, and granulovacuolar degeneration are the diagnostic hallmarks of Alzheimer's disease. However, no causal relationship between aluminum and this neurologic disorder has yet been elucidated.

As in Alzheimer's disease, focal accumulations of aluminum have been detected in patients with endemic amyotrophic lateral sclerosis and parkinsonian dementia, which has a high incidence of occurrence among the Chamorro population of Guam and nearby islands in the South Pacific (Garruto 1991). Epidemiologic evidence suggests a link between these endemic illnesses in the Guamanian population and the prevalence of high aluminum and low calcium levels in the soil of the area.

## Mechanism of Action

The hallmarks of neurotoxicity of aluminum in experimental animal models are aberrations of cytoskeletal proteins (Bugiani and Ghetti 1990). Neurofilaments and neurofibrillary tangles form in these experimental encephalopathies; however, the symptomatology and pathology are different from those seen in subjects with Alzheimer's disease, dialysis encephalopathy, or the parkinsonian dementia/amyotrophic lateral sclerosis complex of Guam. The molecular mechanisms of these cytoskeletal derangements are unclear. Binding of aluminum to nuclear and cytosolic phosphates and the resultant derangement of nuclear and second-messenger processes

**TABLE 26–2.** Neuropsychiatric sequelae associated with metal exposure

| Metal | Neuropsychiatric symptoms |
|---|---|
| Alkyltin (trimethyltin) | Depression, rage, loss of libido and motivation, sleep disturbance, forgetfulness, personality deterioration |
| Aluminum | Personality change, fatigue, impaired memory and attention and executive motor functions |
| Arsenic | Impaired verbal memory, agitation, drowsiness, confusion, emotional lability, stupor, delirium, psychosis resembling paranoid schizophrenia |
| Bismuth | Depression, anxiety, irritability, tremulousness, confusion, dysarthria |
| Copper | Schizophrenia-like symptoms; personality changes; irritability; dysarthria; impaired cognition, memory, and abstract reasoning |
| Gold | Depression, hallucinations |
| Lead | |
| *Inorganic* | |
| Children | Lethargy; hyperactivity; impaired intellect, reaction time, perceptual motor performance, memory, reading, spelling, auditory processing, and attention |
| Adults | Depression; apathy; confusion; fatigue; tension; restlessness; anger; decreases in visual intelligence, general intelligence, memory, psychomotor speed, rate of learning, attention, and visuoconstruction |
| *Organic* | Euphoria; psychosis; hallucinations; restlessness; nightmares; delirium; impaired concentration, memory, and abstract reasoning |
| Manganese | Somnolence, asthenia, anorexia, impaired speech, insomnia, hallucinations, excitement, aggression, mania, dementia, frontal lobe dysfunction, emotional lability, Parkinson-like symptoms, impaired judgment and memory |
| Mercury | |
| *Inorganic* | Irritability; avoidance; shyness; depression; lassitude; fatigue; agitation; decreases in visual memory, reaction time, motor speech, and learning |
| *Organic (methylmercury)* | Incoordination, mood lability, dementia |
| Thallium | Emotional lability, anxiety and hysteriform behavior, dyssomnia, headache, tremor, ataxia, polyneuritis, peripheral sensory and motor neuropathy |
| Zinc | Irritability |

*Source.* Adapted from Bleecker 1994 and Bolla and Roca 1994.

**TABLE 26–3.** Neuropsychiatric sequelae associated with solvent exposure

| Solvent | Neuropsychiatric symptoms |
|---|---|
| Carbon disulfide | Psychosis; depression; personality change; insomnia; retarded speech; impaired hand-eye coordination, motor speed, energy level, psychomotor performance, reaction time, vigilance, visuomotor functions, and construction |
| Carbon tetrachloride | Lethargy, confusion |
| Ethylbenzene | Headache, irritability, fatigue |
| Ethylene glycol | Fatigue, personality change, depression |
| Methanol | Visual toxicity with diminution of pupillary light reflex, loss of visual acuity and papilledema, parkinsonian syndrome with reduced emotions, hypophonia, masked facies, tremor, rigidity, bradykinesia |
| Methyl chloride | Somnolence; confusion; euphoria; personality change; depression; emotional lability; impaired psychomotor speed, vigilance, reaction time, and hand-eye coordination |
| Methyl-*n*-butyl ketone | Peripheral neuropathy |
| Styrene | Depression; fatigue; dizziness; impaired memory, concentration, vigilance, reaction time, psychomotor speed, and visual construction |
| Toluene | |
| Short-term exposure | Initial excitation with depression at higher concentrations, fatigue, confusion, anxiety, increased reaction time, and impaired concentration |
| Long-term exposure | Exhilaration; euphoria; disinhibition; impaired performance IQ, memory, motor control, and attention; flattened affect; apathy; dementia |
| Trichloroethylene | Headaches; dizziness; fatigue; diplopia; anxiety; lability; insomnia; impaired concentration, manual dexterity, reaction time, memory, and visuospatial accuracy |
| Xylene | Confusion; impaired reaction time, attention, and concentration |

*Source.* Adapted from Bleecker 1994 and Bolla and Roca 1994.

**TABLE 26–4.** Neuropsychiatric sequelae associated with gas exposure

| Gas | Neuropsychiatric symptoms |
|---|---|
| Carbon monoxide | Impaired cognitive efficiency and flexibility and verbal and visual memory, disorientation, irritability, distractibility, masklike facies, dementia, amnesia |
| Ethylene oxide | Polyneuropathy, diminished intelligence, impaired verbal and visual memory and auditory and visual attention |
| Formaldehyde | Lightheadedness, dizziness, impaired concentration and memory, mood alteration |
| Hydrogen sulfide | Headaches; dizziness; lightheadedness; nervousness; fatigue; sleep disturbances; extremity weakness; spasms; convulsions; delirium; impaired cognition, memory, and psychomotor and perceptual abilities |
| Nitrous oxide | Polyneuropathy, confusion, visual hallucinations and delusions, episodic crying and agitation, sexual misbehavior, mild ataxia, impaired attention |

*Source.* Adapted from Bleecker 1994 and Bolla and Roca 1994.

**TABLE 26–5.** Neuropsychiatric sequelae associated with pesticide exposure

| Pesticide | Neuropsychiatric symptoms |
|---|---|
| **Cholinesterase inhibitors (e.g., carbaril)** | |
| Carbamates | Headache, nausea, giddiness, blurred vision, weakness, increased sweating, vomiting, miosis, delayed neuropathy |
| **Organophosphates (e.g., chlorpyrifos)** | |
| Mild | Weakness, headache, dizziness, nausea, salivation, lacrimation, miosis, moderate bronchial spasm |
| Moderate | Abrupt weakness, visual disturbances, excessive salivation, sweating, vomiting, diarrhea, bradycardia, hypertonia, tremor of hands and head, impaired gait, miosis, chest pain, cyanosis of mucous membranes |
| Severe | Abrupt tremor, generalized convulsions, psychiatric disturbance, intense cyanosis, death from respiratory or cardiac failure |
| **Organochlorines (e.g., kepone)** | Nervousness, tremor, ataxia, weight loss, headache, disorientation, confusion, auditory and visual hallucinations, irritability, memory loss |

*Source.* Adapted from Bleecker 1994 and Bolla and Roca 1994.

have been hypothesized in a cascade model (Lukiw and McLachlan 1993).

## Diagnosis

After oral or parenteral exposure, the diagnosis of aluminum neurotoxicity is established by characteristic electroencephalographic changes, clinical abnormalities, and concentration in plasma or serum (Alfrey and Froment 1990). The electroencephalogram (EEG) is distinct from that of other metabolic encephalopathies by the fairly normal background frequency and characteristic mild slowing of the dominant rhythm, including bursts of predominantly anterior high-voltage delta waves with intermittent spike activity. Clinical abnormalities include intermittent speech disturbances, mutism, asterixis, myoclonic jerks, seizures, personality changes, and dementia. In healthy control subjects, the normal concentration of aluminum is less than 10 mg/L of plasma or serum. Table 26–6 lists plasma or serum aluminum levels and their correlation with clinical effects.

## Treatment

Preventive measures are more effective than treatment of aluminum exposure and are carried out by

**TABLE 26–6.** Serum aluminum concentrations associated with neurotoxicity

| Plasma aluminum concentration ($\mu$g/L) | Effect |
|---|---|
| <10 | None |
| 10–60 | Increased body burden |
| 61–100 | Potential toxicity |
| 101–200 | Toxicity noted |
| >200 | Overt toxic symptoms |

*Source.* Reprinted from Ellenhorn MJ: *Ellenhorn's Medical Toxicology.* Baltimore, MD, Williams & Wilkins 1997. Used with permission.

preventing accumulation of a "body burden," or exchangeable pool of aluminum. Levels of aluminum in the dialysis medium need to be kept at a minimum (<10 mg/L) because aluminum readily crosses the dialyzing membrane. Oral aluminum compounds should be administered in quantities as low as possible, and plasma aluminum should be checked on a regular basis to confirm the absence of any accumulation (De Wolff and Van der Voet 1986). The progressive and fatal course of aluminum encephalopathy can be treated and reversed by chelation and removal using deferox-amine, with repeated administration over a period of several months (Alfrey and Froment 1990).

# Arsenic

Industry continues to be the major source of arsenic compounds. Arsenic trioxide is obtained mainly from copper smelting (Stokinger 1981), a process that continues to be a source of arsenic exposure. Arsenic is also used in the manufacture of agricultural agents, such as insecticides and rodenticides, and is applied in wood preservatives. Other applications of arsenic include marine paints and pigments, glassware, and food additives to promote growth in farm animals. Arsine gas ($AsH_3$) is being used in the production of microchips in the semiconductor industry (Ellenhorn 1997).

Inorganic arsenic has been used in the past as a constituent in pharmaceutical preparations for the treatment of anemia, rheumatism, psoriasis, and syphilis. Arsenic has also been used as a poison. Even today, arsenic is a constituent of a number of preparations such as Korean herbal remedies (Mitchell-Heggs et al. 1990). It is also used in a number of homeopathic preparations (H.D. Kerr and Saryan 1986).

The biodistribution of arsenic is dependent on the duration of exposure and the chemical species. After absorption, rapid localization in erythrocytes and leukocytes is noted. Arsenic is also detected in the liver, kidney, heart, and lung and is retained in bone and teeth. Smaller amounts are found in nerve and muscle tissue. Although there is minimal penetration of the blood-brain barrier, arsenic readily crosses the placenta and may produce fetal damage (Klaassen 1990a).

## Neuropsychiatric Manifestations

Neuropsychiatric symptoms of acute arsenic poisoning include spasms, muscular twitching, and seizures. Long-term exposure may result in peripheral neuropathies (Hall and Robertson 1990); cardiac irregularities; and visual disturbances, photophobia, conjunctivitis, and other ocular effects. In addition to neuropsychiatric sequelae, ingestion of high doses of inorganic arsenic compounds leads to dramatic gastrointestinal manifestations. Intense nausea and vomiting precede diarrhea. The stool may be watery and may contain blood. A burning sensation in the throat and esophagus may occur, and a garliclike odor may be noted from the breath. Arsenic also causes damage to blood vessel and vascular linings, resulting in fluid leakage into interstitial spaces. This may lead to depletion of intravascular volume and shock.

## Mechanism of Action

Arsenate, the pentavalent form of arsenic, is considerably less toxic than the trivalent arsenite and is commonly found in nature. However, for the most part arsenate is reduced by cellular reduction and methylation to arsenite. In the tissues, arsenite exerts toxic effects by two mechanisms. First, it may interact with biological micromolecules by combining with sulfhydryl groups. Enzyme systems such as the pyruvate and succinate pathways are especially sensitive to arsenite. Second, a loss of high-energy phosphate bonds may occur as arsenic anions substitute for phosphate and disrupt oxidative phosphorylation. Thus, arsenic is able to exert cytotoxicity by inhibiting oxidative phosphorylation by two separate mechanisms (Winship 1984).

## Diagnosis

Diagnosis of arsenic poisoning requires laboratory support because no signs of acute or chronic arsenic poisoning are specific. When symptoms lead to a differential diagnosis that includes arsenic poisoning, a request for arsenic analysis should be made to a laboratory specializing in the analysis of trace elements. The most sensitive and expensive method is neutron activation analysis (Lauwerys et al. 1979). The human sample of choice for arsenic analysis is urine for establishing recent exposure and hair for establishing information on long-term exposure.

## Treatment

At present, the antidote of choice in the treatment of arsenic poisoning is meso-2,3,-dimercaptosuccinic acid (DMSA) or 2,3,-dimercapto-1-propanesulfonic acid (DMPS). Both drugs have been shown to be more effective in the treatment of experimental arsenic poisoning than British anti-Lewisite (BAL or dimercaprol) (Aposhian et al. 1984), the classic antidote for arsenic poisoning. BAL should no longer be used because it has been shown to increase arsenic content in the brain, probably by forming a lipophilic complex that readily passes the blood-brain barrier (Aposhian et al. 1984; Kreppel et al. 1990).

# Lead

Lead is the sixth most ubiquitous metal on our planet, and its use by humans was extensive in early recorded history. Plumbism, or lead poisoning, was probably the first disease recognized as an occupational hazard, by Nikander around 150 B.C. (Major 1945). Even now, after its removal from gasoline and paints, it is used in a multitude of industries (Table 26–7). Although lead can be absorbed through the lungs, skin, and digestive tract, the main route of exposure is oral. Adults usually absorb about 15%–20% of intake; children usually absorb about 45%.

## Neuropsychiatric Manifestations

Clinical symptoms of lead poisoning in adults appear when blood levels reach approximately 400 mg/L and consist of fatigue, anorexia, nervousness, dyssomnia, loss of libido, and myalgia (Ellenhorn 1997). Pallor may also be present. As blood levels increase, headaches and tremor may follow, as well as attacks of abdominal pain alternating with diarrhea. Persistent headaches, vomiting, ataxia, and generalized or focal seizures that are refractory to medication characterize acute lead encephalopathy. Heralding symptoms are fatigue, bradyphrenia, memory impairment, dyssomnia, and anxiety. The patient is obtunded and confused, with episodes of stupor and intermittent lucid intervals. If the condition remains unrecognized, death may ensue (Bruyn and De Wolf 1994). In children, clinical symptoms begin at lower blood levels than in adults (Ellenhorn 1997).

## Mechanism of Action

Lead is a heavy metal affecting a number of biochemical processes, which may explain the diverse symptoms of lead poisoning. Lead interferes with the function of erythrocytes, kidneys, the peripheral and central nervous system, and the intestinal tract. Lead produces diffuse effects as it complexes ligands, particularly sulfhydryl groups, at active sites of enzyme systems throughout the body (Ellenhorn 1997).

**TABLE 26–7.** Major industries associated with risk of lead exposure

| | |
|---|---|
| Battery production | Metal refining |
| Brass works | Paint production |
| Bronze works | Pigment production |
| Cable making/splicing | Pipe cutting |
| Chemical operations | Pottery manufacturing |
| Glassworks | Printing |
| Ammunition production | Soldering |
| Jewelry production | Stained-glass manufacturing |
| Lead smelting | Welding |
| Metal casting | |

*Source.* Modified from Ellenhorn MJ: *Ellenhorn's Medical Toxicology.* Baltimore, MD, Williams & Wilkins, 1997.

## Diagnosis

To diagnose lead poisoning, a history of exposure should be obtained and urine and blood samples evaluated. Magnetic resonance imaging (MRI) scans reveal widespread calcification, particularly in the cerebellar hemispheres, basal ganglia, and thalamus, and increased signal intensity of T2-weighted images of the periventricular white matter, basal ganglia, hypothalamus, and pons (Petsas et al. 1992).

## Treatment

The only detoxification method available for lead poisoning is chelation therapy. At present, the least toxic of the chelating agents are DMSA and DMPS (Aposhian and Aposhian 1990). Recommended dosages of these compounds are 30 mg/kg three times a day for 5 days. Elimination of lead in urine should be monitored before, during, and after treatment to evaluate the effectiveness of treatment.

# Manganese

Manganese is an essential trace element that is widely distributed in the earth's crust primarily as pyrolusite, a mineral form of manganese dioxide. Manganese is used in the production of dry-cell batteries, metal alloys, fungicides, germicides, antiseptics, glass, matches, fireworks, fertilizers, animal feeds, paints, varnish, welding rods, and antiknock gasoline additives. Manganese is also used in textile bleaching and leather tanning. Exposure is usually by inhalation or the oral route. Intestinal absorption is estimated at 3% (Mena 1980).

After its absorption through the intestinal wall, manganese is carried through the blood stream bound to a $\beta_1$-globulin in plasma. Manganese crosses the blood-brain barrier with iron (Aschner and Aschner 1990). Murphy et al. (1991) demonstrated that entry into the brain is through a saturable transport mechanism, primarily across the cerebral capillary-glial network.

## Neuropsychiatric Manifestations

The early stages of manganese intoxication are characterized by mood changes, emotional lability, auditory and visual hallucinations, and neuropsychological impairment referred to as manganese psychosis. Continuing long-term exposure may cause progression to a second stage, a parkinsonian disorder that includes gait disturbance, speech disorder, slowing and clumsiness of movements, and postural imbalance. In the third stage, signs of dystonia may appear, including an awkward, high-stepping gait, tremor, and chorea (Feldman 1994).

Individual susceptibility and progression to further stages of intoxication are probably related to preexisting states of deficiency of other divalent cations, such as calcium and iron, and preexisting illnesses, such as hepatic cirrhosis, alcoholism, and chronic infections (Mena 1980). The presence of other metallotoxins may also contribute to the severity of toxicity by a given exposure (Shukla and Singhal 1984).

## Mechanism of Action

Manganese can form the powerfully oxidizing species $Mn^{3+}$, which can oxidize catecholamines by transfer of one electron to semiquinones and orthoquinones, generating superoxide and hydroxyl radicals as well as hydrogen peroxide (Graham 1984). Oxidative stress on the cell increases with the depletion of protective enzymes—such as superoxide dismutase, catalase, and glutathione peroxidase—and substrates, such as reduced glutathione. Oxidative stress on the cell in dopamine-containing neurons increases with the formation of neurotoxins such as 6-hydroxydopamine (Garner and Nachtman 1989). Cell death occurs when continued oxidative stress damages the hydroxy radicals of critical neuronal membrane sites and results in the peroxidation of cell membrane lipids (Segura-Aguilar and Lind 1989). Manganese poisoning results in damage to neuromelanin cells in the substantia nigra and locus coeruleus as well as loss of cells in the caudate nucleus, pallidum, putamen, and thalamus.

## Diagnosis

Correlations between blood manganese and intoxication are rather poor (Chandra et al. 1974). Similarly, urinary manganese concentration does not correlate with changes in clinical neurologic status; however, urinary manganese does indicate recent exposure (Cook et al. 1974; Roels et al. 1987). The most promising techniques for differentiation of Parkinson's disease from parkinsonism secondary to a neurotoxin are MRI and positron emission tomography (PET) (Wolters et al. 1989), in addition to a good clinical history. In patients with Parkinson's disease, MRI and PET reveal selective abnormalities and decreased dopamine binding sites, respectively, in the area of the substantia nigra. The clinical history should include the symptoms, age at onset, identification and proof of exposure, and nature of response to levodopa therapy. The presence of Lewy bodies indicates Parkinson's disease. Also, more selective and severe degeneration of the substantia nigra on postmortem would indicate primary Parkinson's disease.

## Treatment

Preventive measures that decrease body burden are most effective in the treatment of manganese exposure. Chelation therapy with calcium disodium ethylenediaminetetraacetic acid (EDTA) may be used to hasten elimination (Cook et al. 1974) but has limited success when given in the presence of existing neurologic damage (Wynter 1962).

A lack of response to levodopa therapy in relieving the persistent extrapyramidal effects of manganese poisoning suggests more widespread damage. Moreover, the use of levodopa therapy may actually add to the neurotoxicity by increasing the production of free radicals (Parenti et al. 1988).

# Mercury

Currently, poisoning from mercury occurs during the mining of mercury; the milling of cinnabar (HgS); the production of lye, chlorine, mercury batteries, thermometers, carbon brushes, paints, and paper pulps; the making of jewelry; the recovery of lead from batteries and dental amalgam; and playing with mercury (Wide 1986). Mercury in elemental form is a liquid and vaporizes easily. It is well absorbed by inhalation, has a predilection for the central nervous system, and is poorly absorbed through the gastrointestinal tract. Organic mercury, particularly alkyl mercury, is lipid soluble, is well absorbed through the gastrointestinal tract, and has substantial neurotoxic effects.

## Neuropsychiatric Manifestations

Exposure to inhaled elemental mercury vapor is associated with symptoms such as insomnia; nervousness; mild tremor; headache; emotional lability; fatigue; decreased sexual drive; depression; and impaired cognition, judgment, and coordination (Louria 1988). Chronic low-level toxicity from inhalation of mercury vapor includes a syndrome known as erythrism, consisting of irritability; pathologic shyness; and impairment of memory, attention span, and intellect (Landrigan 1982). Ngim et al. (1995) reported that dentists who were occupationally exposed to elemental mercury vapor had significant deficits in motor speed, visual scanning, concentration, memory, and coordination.

Methylmercury, the most toxic of the short-chain alkylmercury compounds, produces early symptoms such as paresthesia, followed by motor incoordination, ataxic gait and loss of position sense, dysarthria, constriction of visual fields, hearing defects, and muscle rigidity or spasticity with hyperreflexia. Neuropsychiatric symptoms reported include headache, sleep disturbances, dizziness, irritability, emotional instability, mania, and depression (Elhassani 1983).

## Mechanism of Action

Mercury has a high affinity for sulfhydryl groups, leading to inhibition of various enzymes such as choline acetyltransferase. Mercury also binds to membrane proteins, causing disruption of transport processes (Elhassani 1983).

## Diagnosis

Physical examination; history of exposure; and determination of blood, urine, hair, and food levels of mercury will help confirm the diagnosis of mercury poisoning. The normal concentration of mercury in the blood is less than 3–4 mg/L (Klaassen 1990a).

## Treatment

After acute ingestion of inorganic and organic mercury, treatment consists of inducing emesis or performing gastric lavage, in addition to administering activated charcoal. The use of BAL and its derivatives, as well as penicillamine, has been shown to be helpful in the treatment of poisoning with elemental and inorganic mercury. However, these agents have minimal effect in patients with organic mercury intoxication. BAL is actually contraindicated in the treatment of methylmercury poisoning, as it has been shown to increase methylmercury levels in laboratory animals (Klaassen 1990a). Polymeric vinyl resins may be more effective than penicillamine in removing the organic mercury compounds from the body (Klaassen 1990a). In patients with renal impairment secondary to acute inorganic mercury poisoning, hemodialysis may be very helpful. Conventional hemodialysis in the treatment of organic mercury intoxication is of little value; however, the use of L-cysteine has been effective in complexing methylmercury into a form that is more dialyzable (Klaassen 1990a). Mercury is sequestered in lysosomal dense bodies in neurons and is known to persist in the brain for long periods (Cavanagh 1988). In the central and peripheral nervous system, the damage caused by mercury poisoning appears to be permanent. Elhassani (1983) reported that the administration of neostigmine improved motor strength in patients with methylmercury intoxication.

## Organotins

Organotin compounds are a group of biologically active organometallics that are increasingly being used as bio-

cides, preservatives, catalysts, and polymer stabilizers (Van der Kerk 1976). The trimethyltin and triethyltin compounds (Figure 26–1) are absorbed via the gastrointestinal tract and skin and are the most neurotoxic of the organotin compounds.

## Neuropsychiatric Manifestations

Trimethyltin has been implicated in cases of occupational poisoning in the chemical industry (Ross et al. 1981). After exposure due to spillage, 22 chemical plant workers were noted to develop symptoms of depression, including forgetfulness, fatigue and weakness, loss of libido, headaches, sleep disturbance, and loss of motivation. In another case, six chemical factory workers (Ross et al. 1981) who had been exposed for multiple short periods over a 3-day period developed headache, tinnitus, deafness, impaired memory, disorientation, aggressiveness, psychosis, syncope, and loss of consciousness. The severity of symptoms correlated with urinary tin concentrations. Electroencephalographic findings included right-sided frontal temporal delta waves, and in one case focal spikes in the temporal region. Fortemps et al. (1978) had previously described memory dysfunction, anorexia, insomnia, headache, disorientation that progressed to acute mental confusion and seizures. In the early 1950s, a preparation with diethyltin iodide (Stalinon), containing the contaminant triethyltin, was responsible for the poisoning of several hundred people (Rouzaud and Lutier 1954). Increased intracranial pressure and seizures, common clinical findings in subjects exposed to trimethyltin, were present in the individuals poisoned with the contaminated diethyltin iodide.

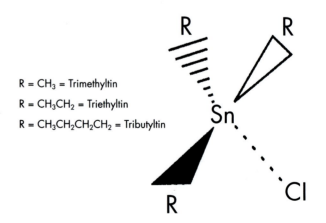

R = CH₃ = Trimethyltin

R = CH₃CH₂ = Triethyltin

R = CH₃CH₂CH₂CH₂ = Tributyltin

**FIGURE 26–1.** Chemical structure of trialkyltin compounds.

## Mechanism of Action

Neuropathologic examination of mice treated with trimethyltin reveals damage to the hippocampus, primarily a loss of pyramidal cells in the CA1 and CA3 regions (Dyer et al. 1982), as well as some alteration in the pyriform cortex, amygdala, and neocortex (Brown et al. 1979). Triethyltin appears to have a different neuronal target than trimethyltin in rats. White-matter edema of the brain and spinal cord, intramyelinic vacuolation, and myelin splitting are found in subjects poisoned with triethyltin (Magee et al. 1957).

Although the exact mechanism of neurotoxicity is unclear, organotins are reported to inhibit oxidative phosphorylation in vitro and in vivo (Aldridge and Street 1971), as well as adenosine triphosphatases (Selwyn 1976; Wassenar and Kroon 1973). It has been shown that trimethyltin can inhibit the uptake of neurotransmitters into mouse forebrain synaptosomes in vitro and in vivo (Doctor et al. 1982), as well as protein synthesis in the cortex and hippocampus of treated mice (Costa and Sulaiman 1986).

## Diagnosis and Treatment

Diagnosis of organotin poisoning is based on a history of exposure together with clinical symptoms. Supportive care is the mainstay of treatment.

# Gases

# Carbon Monoxide

Carbon monoxide (CO) poisoning continues to be a significant cause of death throughout the world. In the United States, approximately 3,500 deaths occur each year as a result of carbon monoxide intoxication. It occurs less frequently in developed countries today, owing to changes in combustion systems and heating fuels. The most common source of carbon monoxide poisoning is the incomplete combustion of carbon-based fuels and inadequate ventilation during the operation of machinery using internal combustion engines. Space heaters, oil or gas burners, tobacco smoke, blast furnaces, and building fires are other sources of the gas (Bleecker 1994).

## Neuropsychiatric Manifestations

Very low concentrations (0.01%) of carbon monoxide in the air can cause a slight headache. At concentrations of 0.05%, 0.1%, and 0.2%, carbon monoxide can cause severe headaches, dizziness, tachycardia, tachypnea, and coma (Ellenhorn 1997). Inhalation of 1% carbon monox-

ide is usually fatal within 30–45 minutes. Very low concentrations of carboxyhemoglobin can produce impairment of visual, auditory, and temporal discriminations (Beard and Grandstaff 1970). Headache, nausea, and vomiting, as well as dizziness and disorientation to time, place, and person follow acute intoxication. The patient may also experience arousal, lethargy, and, at times, coma. Generalized muscular hypertonia and spasticity may occur. Seizures may also be a presenting feature.

Neurologic examination of a carbon monoxide–intoxicated patient reveals a "lead-pipe" rigidity (i.e., an even resistance) without cogwheeling (i.e., a rhythmically interrupted or ratchetlike resistance). Parkinsonism, generalized dystonia, tremor, tics, and chorea have also been reported. Patients may also exhibit a delayed clinical picture of neuropsychiatric symptoms (Ellenhorn 1997). Patients may recover from a short-term exposure after several days, during which initial neuropsychiatric symptoms may have already disappeared. After a period averaging 2–4 weeks, a sudden deterioration may develop consisting of amnestic disturbances, disorientation, signs of dementia, hypokinesia, bizarre and occasionally psychotic behavior, urinary incontinence, personality changes, apathy, emotional instability, anxiety, and autonomic dysregulation (Min 1986). Table 26–8 lists the delayed neuropsychiatric sequelae after carbon monoxide intoxication. Patients may also experience diarrhea, vomiting, periodic nausea, fever, and palpitations.

## Mechanism of Action

Carbon monoxide combines with hemoglobin in the blood to form carboxyhemoglobin. Hemoglobin in its carboxyhemoglobin form cannot bind with oxygen and cannot oxygenate the tissues. The affinity of hemoglobin for carbon monoxide is 200 times greater than that for oxygen. It is this intrinsic affinity for carbon monoxide that accounts for the potency and lethality of carboxyhemoglobin.

Factors involved in determining the toxicity of carbon monoxide include the concentration of the gas in the air, duration of exposure, respiratory minute volume, cardiac output, hematocrit, oxygen demand of tissues, and preexisting cerebrovascular disease. Children are inherently more sensitive than adults to the effects of carbon monoxide because of increased metabolic activity (Klaassen 1990b).

Carbon monoxide poisoning results in increased intracranial pressure due to transudation across capillaries. Pathologic changes in the brain observed in postmortem examination include congestion, edema, petechiae, hemorrhagic focal necrosis, and perivascular infarcts. The characteristic pathology of carbon monoxide toxicity is

**TABLE 26–8.** Neuropsychiatric symptoms in delayed syndrome associated with carbon monoxide intoxication

| Symptom | Number (%) of patients (N=86) |
|---|---|
| **Psychiatric** | |
| Apathy | 86 (100) |
| Disorientation | 86 (100) |
| Amnesia | 86 (100) |
| Hypokinesia | 82 (95) |
| Mutism | 82 (95) |
| Irritability, distractibility | 78 (91) |
| Apraxia | 65 (76) |
| Bizarre behaviors | 60 (70) |
| Stereotyped behavior | 35 (41) |
| Confabulation | 26 (30) |
| Insomnia | 16 (19) |
| Depressed mood | 13 (15) |
| Delusions | 10 (12) |
| Echolalia | 2 (2) |
| Elated mood | 2 (2) |
| **Neurologic** | |
| Urinary and fecal incontinence | 80 (93) |
| Gait disturbance | 78 (91) |
| Glabella sign | 78 (91) |
| Grasp reflex | 75 (87) |
| Increased muscle tone | 74 (86) |
| Retropulsion | 62 (72) |
| Increased deep tendon reflexes | 19 (22) |
| Flaccid paralysis | 16 (19) |
| Tremor | 12 (14) |
| Dysarthria | 8 (9) |

*Source.* Reprinted from Ellenhorn MJ: *Ellenhorn's Medical Toxicology.* Baltimore, MD, Williams & Wilkins, 1997; and Min SK: "A Brain Syndrome Associated With Delayed Neuropsychiatric Sequelae Following Acute Carbon Monoxide Intoxication." *Acta Psychiatrica Scandinavica* 73:80–86, 1986. Used with permission.

bilateral necrosis of the globus pallidus. The hippocampus, cerebral cortex, cerebellum, and substantia nigra are also vulnerable to carbon monoxide toxicity (Ginsberg 1985).

## Diagnosis

The clinical features of carbon monoxide poisoning roughly correlate with carboxyhemoglobin levels. Laboratory tests are usually not helpful in establishing the diagnosis. Abnormal electroencephalographic findings such as low-voltage waves and diffuse slowing are common and can reflect the progression of hypoxic encephalopathy. However, EEGs are not thought to have much predictive value because patients with markedly abnormal EEGs may show complete recovery (Ellenhorn 1997). Horowitz et al. (1987), reporting MRI findings in two patients, described areas of high signal intensity in the globus pallidus.

## Treatment

Control of airway, support of breathing, a high oxygen concentration, and cardiac monitoring should be initiated in a patient with carbon monoxide toxicity. Supplemental oxygen is usually continued until the carboxyhemoglobin level is significantly reduced (Ellenhorn 1997).

# Ethylene Oxide

Ethylene oxide is an intermediary agent used in the production of antifreeze, polyester fibers and bottles, photographic films, glycol ethers, and nonionic surface-active agents. Health care workers are exposed through its use as a sterilant for heat-sensitive materials in central supply units.

## Neuropsychiatric Manifestations

High levels of exposure to ethylene oxide result in acute encephalopathy and peripheral neuropathy (Gross 1979). Ethylene oxide has been reported to produce persistent neurologic and neuropsychological impairment after long-term low-level exposure (Crystal et al. 1988). Impairments in visual and verbal memory and auditory and visual attention decrements were noted in individuals after exposure. Central processing of visual and verbal information was also slowed.

## Mechanism of Action

Ethylene oxide is a highly reactive gas that produces a primary axonal neuropathy and mild Schwann cell changes. It also affects myelinated fibers (Kuzuhara et al. 1983).

## Diagnosis

A history of exposure to ethylene oxide is of prime importance in establishing the diagnosis. Tests found to be helpful are the P300 evoked potential amplitude and psychomotor speed tests. Workers exposed to ethylene oxide had lower P300 amplitude, hypoactive reflexes, and poor performance on tests measuring psychomotor speed (Metter and Bleecker 1994).

## Treatment

At present, no treatment is known for ethylene oxide poisoning. Symptoms improve when an exposed individual is removed from the environment containing the gas, and long-term improvement is noticeably present when ethylene oxide exposure ceases altogether (Gross 1979).

## Solvents

Hydrocarbon solvents have been used for many years as therapeutic agents for anesthesia, in the chemical industry to dissolve chemicals, as refrigerant agents, as typewriter correction fluid, and as cleaning agents. Workers are exposed primarily through inhalation and dermal exposure. Abuse of solvents occurs commonly through sniffing of glue or paint.

### Neuropsychiatric Manifestations

Long-term exposure to solvents often results in subjective complaints of headache, dizziness, fatigue, malaise, weakness, memory impairment, and anxiety. Table 26–3 lists some of the neuropsychiatric manifestations of solvent exposure. Exposed individuals may also have emotional lability, irritability, sexual dysfunction, difficulties in concentration and problem solving, and general intellectual slowing, as well as sensory and motor neuropathies after long-term exposure (Bleecker 1994). Solvent toxicity may also cause cardiac effects such as dysrhythmias, which are caused by the abuse of freons and other fluorinated hydrocarbons as well as industrial exposure in the manufacture of aliphatic and aromatic solvents.

Trichloroethylene is well known for causing peripheral neuropathy, particularly of the trigeminal nerve, an effect known as tic douloureux. Chlorinated hydrocarbon solvents are likely to cause hepatocellular damage, and periodic measurements of enzymes may be a useful technique to detect overexposure (Ellenhorn 1997).

n-Hexane is an industrial solvent that is also known to cause peripheral neuropathy, which is a major manifestation of its toxicity. Although used primarily as a glue and adhesive solvent, it may also be found in gasoline. n-Hexane neuropathy has been described, and its metabolite methyl-n-butylketone-2-5-hexanedione is known to be a reactive intermediate agent that inhibits the glycolytic pathway of metabolism, resulting in peripheral neuropathy. Although most of the solvents produce fairly consistent neuropsychiatric sequelae with short-term exposure, certain solvents, such as n-hexane, produce peripheral neuropathies due to metabolites produced by the liver and structural differences of the original solvent (Ellenhorn 1997).

## Diagnosis and Treatment

A history of exposure, cognitive impairment as shown on a neuropsychological test battery, and the presence of clinical symptoms are helpful in establishing the diagnosis of solvent toxicity. At present, few treatments exist for solvent-induced neurotoxicity. Improvement is noted as symptoms decrease when the patient is removed from the offending agent. Treatment primarily involves minimizing future exposure. Monitoring of levels in the workplace is helpful.

## Pesticides

Pesticides are unique among environmental chemicals in that they are placed deliberately into the environment to injure or kill animal, plant, or microbial life. The well-known classes of pesticides are the organochlorines, organophosphates, carbamates, and pyrethroids. Figure 26–2 shows the chemical structures of several organophosphate pesticides that are of neuropsychiatric interest. More than 50,000 organophosphates have been synthesized, and more than 40 are currently in commercial use. Particularly potent organophosphates have also been used for chemical warfare or as nerve agents or gases (Figure 26–3).

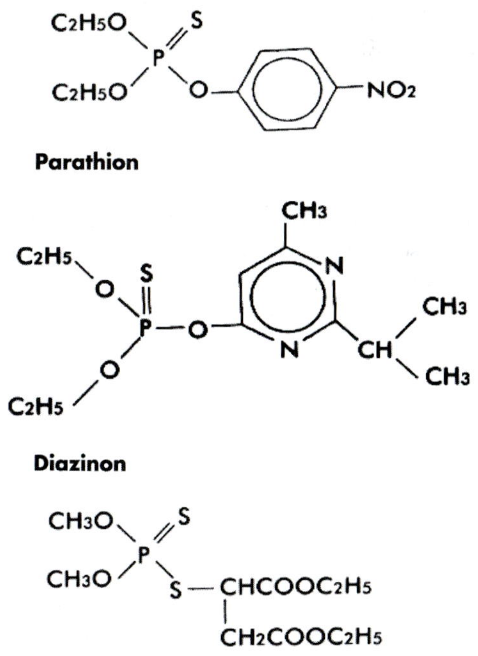

**FIGURE 26–2.** Chemical structures of organophosphate pesticides Parathion, Diazinon, and Malathion.

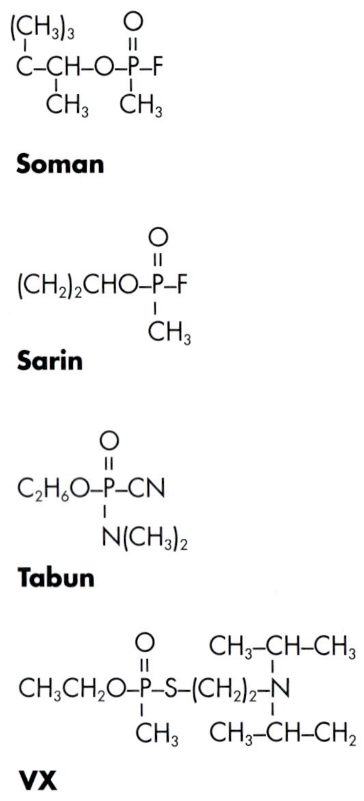

$$(CH_3)_3$$
$$C-CH-O-P-F$$
$$CH_3 \quad CH_3$$

**Soman**

$$(CH_2)_2CHO-P-F$$
$$CH_3$$

**Sarin**

$$C_2H_6O-P-CN$$
$$N(CH_3)_2$$

**Tabun**

$$CH_3CH_2O-P-S-(CH_2)_2-N$$

**VX**

**FIGURE 26–3.** Chemical structures of nerve agents soman (GD), sarin (GB), tabun (GA), and VX.

## Organochlorine

The organochlorine insecticides, such as chlordane and chlordecone (Kepone), are no longer used because they are not biodegradable and appear to accumulate in the environment. Chlordane, an organochlorine, is toxic through ingestion, and its primary use in the past was for termite control. Its delivery, sale, and use in the United States have been prohibited by the Environmental Protection Agency because the National Cancer Institute has found that it causes hepatocellular carcinoma in mice (Bleecker 1994).

The neuropsychiatric sequelae of long-term exposure to chlordane include early symptoms of fatigue, nausea, anorexia, and circumoral numbness. After a delay of 1 month, myoclonic jerks have been observed. After a longer period of time, cramps, seizures, and tremors occur. Cramps have been noted to be severe enough to produce vertebral fractures (Aldrich and Holmes 1969; Curley and Gerrettson 1969; Stranger and Kerridge 1968).

Chlordecone, an organochlorine pesticide, was used in the past for the extermination of ants and roaches. In August 1974, its sale and use were prohibited by the Environmental Protection Agency. The main route of chlordecone poisoning is by dermal or oral exposure due

to careless use. Neuropsychiatric manifestations include nervousness, tremor, ataxia, weight loss, opsoclonus, and headaches. Changes in mental status, in addition to startle myoclonus, disorientation, confusion, and auditory and visual hallucinations, occur in many poisoned individuals (Taylor et al. 1978).

Chlorophenoxy compounds (Figure 26–4), such as 2,4-dichlorophenoxyacetic acid (2,4-D) and 2,4,5-trichlorophenoxyacetic acid (2,4,5-T) are herbicides that have received considerable attention due to their content of 2,3,7,8-tetrachlorodibenzo-*p*-dioxin (TCDD or dioxin), a contaminant in Agent Orange, the toxicity of which is now being intensively studied. Agent Orange is a herbicide that was used as a defoliant in the Vietnam War (Roberts 1991a, 1991b). The neuropsychiatric sequelae of acute intoxication with 2,4-D include paresthesia, pain in the extremities, decreased vibration sense, reversible flaccid paralysis, and peripheral neuropathy (Food and Agriculture Organization/World Health Organization 1975). Acute intoxication with 2,4,5-T produces weakness in the muscles of mastication and swallowing, lethargy, anorexia, weakness in the lower extremities, and fatigue (Food and Agriculture Organization/World Health Organization 1975).

## Pyrethroids

Pyrethroids are recently developed, economical synthetic pesticides that have greater selective toxicity against insects than do carbamates or organophosphates. These synthetic insecticides are derived from an older class of botanical insecticides known as pyrethrins, a mixture of six insecticidal esters derived from desiccated chrysanthemum or pyrethrum flowers. Despite their selectivity, pyrethroids are neurotoxic; exposed workers have reported tingling and burning of the face on skin contact (Le Quesne et al. 1980). In addition to paresthesia, cotton growers experienced severe headaches, dizziness, fatigue, nausea, and anorexia after exposure to pyrethroids from several sprayings. Transient alterations in EEGs were also observed. In more severe cases, subjects developed tremors, convulsions accompanied by fasciculations, and repetitive discharges on electromyograms (EMGs) (He et al. 1984).

Pyrethroids act on the membrane level, particularly on sodium channels, resulting in a period of increased neuronal excitability followed by reduced excitability on submaximal stimulus (Le Quesne 1980). Vitamin E, a biologic antioxidant that may stabilize membranes, is recommended for preventing dysesthesias secondary to dermal exposure (Flannigan et al. 1984). Mephenesin is also an effective compound that provides some protection against pyrethroid neurotoxicity (Bradbury et al. 1983).

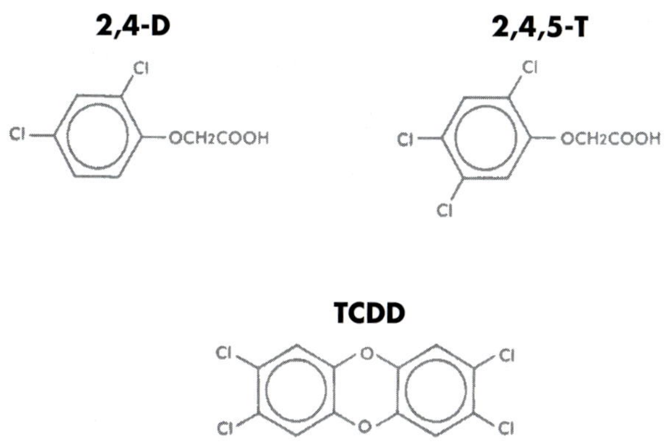

**2,4-D**

**2,4,5-T**

**TCDD**

**FIGURE 26–4.** Structures of 2,4-dichlorophenoxyacetic acid (2,4-D), 2,4,5-trichlorophenoxyacetic acid (2,4,5-T), and 2,3,7,8-tetrachlorodibenzo-*p*-dioxin (TCDD).

# Organophosphate Compounds

In contrast to the organochlorine pesticides, which tend to accumulate in the environment, the organophosphate pesticides (which constitute the largest group of pesticides) are degraded fairly rapidly. The organophosphate pesticides include approximately 60–100 individual compounds that are used throughout the world, more than 40 of which are currently in commercial use in the United States.

In searching for organophosphorus pesticides, German chemists developed several anticholinesterase nerve agents with extremely lethal potency. In 1937, Germany developed sarin and tabun and followed with soman in 1944. Great Britain developed VX in 1952. Research on nerve agents ceased in Britain and the United States in 1959 and in 1969, respectively. During and following the Cold War, the United States stockpiled tens of thousands of tons of sarin and VX loaded in weapons. The former Soviet Union held reserves of tabun and soman. In 1981, the United States began to produce components for binary weapons in which precursors of nerve agents are stored in separate chambers of the artillery shells or warheads and mixed on firing to form the lethal nerve agents.

Recently, there has been a renewed interest in organophosphate compounds due to production and deployment of nerve agents by hostile military forces in the past few years. An increase in terrorism and concern that these lethal agents would be used on civilian populations in the United States has led to civil disaster preparations that included the training of physicians and other medical personnel to identify and treat organophosphate nerve agent exposure and toxicity. Tabun was used offensively by Iraq during the Iran-Iraq war in the 1980s. In late January and February 1991, coalition forces (including those of the United States) conducted aerial bombing that

damaged two chemical munitions facilities in the central part of Iraq in which approximately 3 metric tons of sarin and 17 metric tons of cyclosarin were stored. The large release of sarin and cyclosarin and prevailing winds resulted in likely low-level exposure to coalition troops; however, no acute illness is known to have been reported. In June 1994 and March 1995, terrorists deployed a nerve agent thought to be sarin against civilian populations in the Japanese cities of Matsumoto and Tokyo, respectively, which resulted in acute symptoms. In 1990, the U.S. Army began destroying the decades-old stockpiles of weapons containing sarin, soman and VX, a process that is expected to continue into the new millennium. Accidental exposures of workers and civilians during stockpile destruction have been cited by the U.S. Centers for Disease Control and Prevention as being associated with delayed peripheral neuropathy and electroencephalographic changes as well as birth defects.

## Neuropsychiatric Manifestations

Neuropsychiatric effects of exposure to organophosphates include anxiety, restlessness, apprehension, tension, labile mood, insomnia, and headache (Table 26–5). Increasing levels of exposure may result in tremors, nightmares, increased dreaming, apathy, withdrawal, and depression. On further exposure, drowsiness, confusion, slurred speech, ataxia, generalized weakness, and coma predominate.

The onset of action of organophosphates is dependent on the type of organophosphate and the route of exposure. The onset may be quite sudden after massive ingestion or can be delayed by as long as 12–48 hours. Organophosphates, which are highly lipophilic, produce mild initial symptoms that are followed by severe cholinergic symptoms 48 hours later (Ellenhorn 1997).

The organophosphates produce chronic and delayed effects, including polyneuropathies and neurobehavioral alterations. Sensorimotor peripheral neuropathies may occur 8–14 days after exposure and do not necessarily follow acute cholinergic symptoms (Barret and Oehme 1985). Neuropsychiatric symptoms of drowsiness, lability, depression, fatigue, anxiety, and irritability may be long lasting and may persist for as long as a year. Memory and concentration deficits may cause a decline in work performance (Lerman et al. 1984).

The peripheral neuropathy associated with long-term exposure to organophosphates (known as organophosphate-induced delayed neurotoxicity) may begin with cramping in the calves and numbness and tingling in the feet, followed by progressive weakness in the lower extremities. Eventually, bilateral foot drop and equilibrium are also disturbed. In addition to triorthocresyl phosphate, mipafox and leptophos have also been known to cause organophosphate-induced delayed neurotoxicity, from which recovery is poor.

## Mechanisms of Action

Organophosphate and carbamate compounds inhibit the enzyme acetylcholinesterase by binding with the serine hydroxyl group in the active site of the enzyme (Figure 26–5). A resultant increase in acetylcholine concentration, particularly in the central nervous system, is responsible for many of the symptoms produced by exposure to organophosphates.

Concern that many of the other organophosphates also cause delayed neurotoxicity has resulted in intensive study of the mechanisms by which these agents produce this condition. The neuropathy is not affected by treatment with atropine and apparently is related to the inhibition of a target enzyme known as neurotoxic esterase (Bertoncin et al. 1985; Bidstrup et al. 1953; Morgan and Penovich 1978).

## Diagnosis

The diagnosis of organophosphate toxicity is primarily made by a history of exposure to pesticides. Organophosphates usually have a garliclike odor, which may emanate either from the patient or from the container from which the poison was dispensed and may help to confirm the diagnosis. Red blood cell cholinesterase is the preferred marker for organophosphate toxicity because it is the same enzyme found in nervous tissue. Decreased acetylcholinesterase activity, in conjunction with a history of exposure, usually confirms the diagnosis. Short-term exposure may decrease acetylcholinesterase activity to 50% of baseline. There may be a return to normal activity after several weeks (Ellenhorn 1997).

## Treatment

After exposure to organophosphates, the primary concern is stabilization of vital signs, followed by decontamination. Decontamination procedures include removing all contaminated clothing and thoroughly washing all exposed skin surfaces. Atropine is usually administered because it noncompetitively antagonizes both muscarinic and nicotinic receptors, thereby blocking the effect of excess acetylcholine (Ellenhorn 1997). Pralidoxime may be used in addition to atropine to provide for reactivation of acetylcholinesterase. The side effects of pralidoxime usually occur in only a small group of patients and include excitement, confusion, tachycardia, headache, and blurred vision possibly due to central anticholinergic toxicity (Goetz 1985).

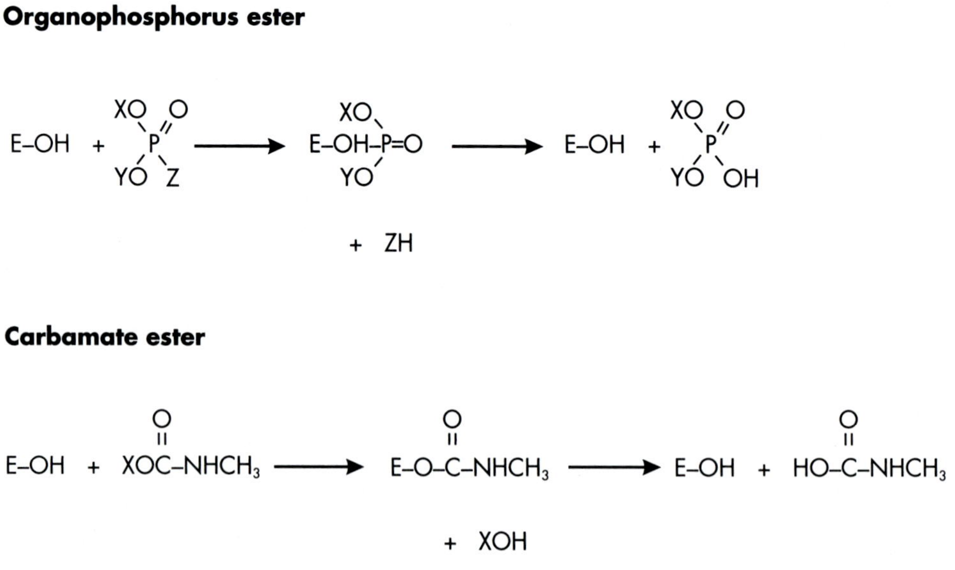

**FIGURE 26–5.** Interaction between an organophosphate or carbamate ester with the serine hydroxyl group in the active site of the enzyme acetylcholinesterase (E-OH). The dephosphorylation or decarbamoylation of the inhibited enzyme is the rate-limiting step to forming free enzyme.
*Source.* Adapted from Ecobichon 1991.

# Toxins

Naturally occurring neurotoxins from marine, microbial, plant, and animal species have led to many episodes of poisoning in humans. Clinical observations of these episodes of poisoning and their resulting sequelae have led to the study of these toxic compounds in model systems. Some of these naturally occurring neurotoxins have become significant tools in studying the pathogenesis of neurodegeneration within the central nervous system as well as the etiology of resultant neuropsychiatric manifestations. Because the neuropsychiatric sequelae of neurotoxins are currently a matter of interest, the subject can be only partially covered in this chapter. Rather, I focus on a few selective compounds with mechanisms and neuropsychiatric sequelae that seem to be of major relevance. For a complete review of the general toxicology of marine, microbial, plant, and animal toxins, the interested reader is referred to the work of Ellenhorn (1997).

## Marine Toxins

### Domoic Acid

Domoic acid is a heat-stable, potent, excitatory tricarboxylic amino acid found in high concentrations in cultured blue mussels (*Mytilus edulis*). It is formed by *Nitzchia pungens*, a phytoplanktonic diatom that is bioconcentrated in the blue mussel. In November 1987, at least 145 people in Canada had acute symptoms of intoxication after consuming cultured blue mussels.

The neuropsychiatric consequences of domoic acid intoxication include altered states of arousal, including coma, abdominal paralysis, limbic seizures, and myoclonus (T.M. Perl et al. 1990; Teitelbaum et al. 1990). Chronic impairment of memory, as well as atrophy of distal musculature and motor weakness, were also noted. These symptoms were usually not accompanied by sensory deficits (Teitelbaum et al. 1990). Elderly persons appeared to be more affected than younger patients.

PET studies carried out in four subjects 2–3 months after intoxication revealed decreased glucose metabolism in the mesial temporal lobe, which correlated well with the patients' memory scores. Neuropathologic studies in four patients also demonstrated a marked loss of neurons in the hippocampus and amygdaloid nucleus, as well as lesions in the septal area, secondary olfactory area, claustrum, dorsal medial nucleus of the thalamus, and insular and subfrontal cortex. The pattern of neurotoxic injury, particularly hippocampal damage, seems to be similar to the abnormalities induced experimentally by the excitotoxin kainate in the same structures of rodents (Teitelbaum et al. 1990). In monkeys, excitatory damage from domoic acid administration is predominantly observed in the hypothalamus, hippocampus, and area postrema (Tryphonas et al. 1990), a pattern similar to that of neuronal degeneration produced by kainate. It seems that domoic acid, a naturally occurring excitatory amino acid, appears to induce a pattern of acute neuropsychiatric change and permanent neurologic deficits that resemble changes induced experimentally by kainate.

### Tetrodotoxin

Puffer fish poisoning or tetrodotoxin intoxication due to improper preparation of the fish causes gastroenteritis and severe neurologic manifestations. One of the most toxic of the natural toxins, tetrodotoxin prevents the flow of sodium ions by blocking the channel through which sodium ions flow, producing neuronal conduction abnormalities in both motor and sensory nerves. Neuropsychiatric manifestations of tetrodotoxin after oral ingestion include weakness, ataxia, paresthesia in the face spreading to the extremities, nausea, diarrhea, pallor, and sweating. Intoxication may begin with oral paresthesia, sometimes with gastroenteric symptoms, that progresses to generalized paresthesia and motor paralysis of the extremities. Hypoactive reflexes, gross muscular incoordination, aphonia, dysphagia, and respiratory distress in severe cases may follow this. However, consciousness is retained. The last stages of the illness are characterized by mental impairment and respiratory paralysis. Rapid onset of symptoms and greater severity are associated with poorer prognosis (Ellenhorn 1997).

## Microbial Toxins

### Botulinum Toxin

Botulinum toxin is produced by *Clostridium botulinum* and is the most potent natural poison known. Of the seven immunologically distinct types of botulinum toxin, types A, B, and E are the causes of most human cases of poisoning. Epidemiological analysis of cases of botulism has shown that 60% of cases are caused by type A toxin, 30% by type B, and 10% by type E, usually associated with ingestion of contaminated seafood. The bacterial spores may be found during the home canning process and tend to be resistant to heat. They may survive at temperatures greater than 120°C. The exotoxin is heat labile and can be inactivated at 85°C, in contrast to the heat-resistant spores (Dunbar 1990).

Neuropsychiatric manifestations of botulinum toxin appear within 12–36 hours after ingestion of contaminated food. The patient initially develops bulbar symptoms, including diplopia, ptosis, dysarthria, and dysphagia. These symptoms are followed by a descending pattern of weakness affecting first the upper and then the lower limbs (Cherington 1974, 1990). In severe cases, respiratory paralysis occurs, requiring assisted ventilation. Mild forms of botulism may be characterized by bulbar findings and subtle weakness of muscles of the limbs that may mimic myasthenia gravis. A striking response to intravenous anticholinesterase agents is noted (Ryan and Cherington 1971). The pattern of descending weakness is a clinical hallmark of botulism and distinguishes it from the classic form of Guillain-Barré syndrome, which usually presents with an ascending pattern of weakness.

## Tetanus Toxin

Tetanospasmin, or tetanus toxin, is a soluble-protein exotoxin produced by the bacterium *Clostridium tetani*. Tetanus is a syndrome of autonomic dysfunction, neuromuscular junction blockade, muscle stiffness, and spasms caused by tetanospasmin. Although tetanus is rare in countries with immunization programs, an estimated 800,000 newborns die from neonatal tetanus every year. At present, tetanus is the second leading cause of death from diseases included in the expanded immunization program of the World Health Organization (WHO) (Traverso et al. 1991; World Health Organization 1988).

In most cases, the incubation period for tetanus after the introduction of organisms into a wound is 3–14 days, with an average of 7 days (Habermann 1978). Neuropsychiatric manifestations include backache, stiff neck, leg pains, spasms, dysphagia, abdominal cramps, vertigo, and facial weakness resembling Bell's palsy. The most common presentation is trismus due to the spasm of masseter muscles. The initial symptoms are followed by generalized rigidity as well as spasms with painful tonic contractions of both agonist and antagonist muscles. Superimposed on the baseline rigidity are proximal spasms that can be so severe that they resemble a generalized seizure or intense decorticate posturing, referred to as tetanic seizures (Weinstein 1973). Patients often remain conscious during these episodes (Bleck 1991). Treatment of tetanus involves wound care, antitoxin therapy and immunization, management of rigidity and spasms, and treatment of the autonomic derangements.

## Plant Toxins

Exposure to poisonous plants is a common occurrence. Fortunately, most commonly encountered plants produce either no toxicity or mild to moderate toxicity consisting of gastroenteritis. A few plants produce serious neuropsychiatric effects. These include oleander and foxglove, which cause digitalis-type toxicity; jequirity pea and castor beans, which contain the neurotoxic polypeptides abrin and ricin, respectively; water hemlock herbal remedies that have convulsant properties; and mushrooms with hallucinogenic properties.

Diagnosis of plant toxicity involves identification of the plant, which is often difficult. Because individual susceptibility varies, prediction of toxicity is also difficult. Further complicating management is the lack of antidotes to most plant toxins (Ellenhorn 1997). Table 26–9 lists psychoactive substances with neuropsychiatric effects found in herbal preparations, and Table 26–10 lists the major hallucinogenic plants and their active ingredients. Mushrooms are discussed here because they are used in religious rites, are consumed recreationally, and may be ingested accidentally by children (Ellenhorn 1997).

Mushrooms fall into two classes: those with delayed toxic response after ingestion and those with an immediate effect. Mushrooms producing a delayed response seldom affect the nervous system. Fungi that predominantly affect the central nervous system generally produce an immediate response, such as hallucinations. Mushrooms in the genus *Psilocybe* contain the indolealkylamine hallucinogen psilocybin and its dephosphorylated congener psilocin (Figure 26–6). Psilocin is about 1.5 times more potent than psilocybin.

Neuropsychiatric manifestations of mushroom toxins may be observed 20–30 minutes after ingestion. Visual hypersensitivity usually leads to illusions and hallucinations. Dysphoria, hyperreflexia, drowsiness, and euphoria may also occur. The individual may experience flushing of the face, tachycardia, hyperthermia, and hypertension. Dangerous complications may be suicidality and trauma secondary to reckless behavior under the influence of the substance, and psychiatric symptoms may persist long after immediate effects have abated (Benjamin 1979).

There is no specific therapy for psilocybin intoxication. Anxiety may be treated with benzodiazepines (Ellenhorn 1997), and anticholinergic effects may be reversed with physostigmine (Van Poorten et al. 1982).

## Animal Toxins

Animals capable of secreting a poison by biting or stinging are termed venomous. Animals referred to as poisonous are organisms whose tissues, in part or in entirety, are toxic.

Venoms are complex mixtures of enzymes and proteins (Table 26–11) with various compositions that can

**TABLE 26–9.** Psychoactive substances found in herbal preparations

| Labeled ingredient | Botanical source | Pharmacologic agent | Use | Effects |
|---|---|---|---|---|
| African yohimbine bark, yohimbe | *Corynanthe yohimbe* | Yohimbine | Smoke or tea as stimulant | Mild hallucinogen |
| Broom, Scotch broom | *Cytisus* species | Sparteine | Smoke for relaxation | Questionable sedative-hypnotic |
| California poppy | *Eschscholtzia californica* | Coptisine, sanguinarine | Smoke as marijuana substitute | Probably none |
| Catnip | *Nepeta cataria* | Nepetalactone | Smoke or tea as marijuana substitute | Mild hallucinogen |
| Cinnamon | *Cinnamomum camphora* | ? | Smoke with marijuana | Mild stimulant |
| Damiana | *Turnera diffusa* | ? | Smoke as marijuana substitute | Mild stimulant |
| Hops | *Humulus lupulus* | Lupulina | Smoke or tea as sedative and marijuana substitute | None |
| Hydrangea | *Hydrangea paniculata* | Cyanogenic glycosides | Smoke as marijuana substitute | Cyanide toxicity |
| Juniper | *Juniperus macropoda* | ? | Smoke | Strong hallucinogen |
| Kava kava | *Piper methysticum* | Yangonin, pyrones | Smoke or tea as marijuana substitute | Mild hallucinogen |
| Khat | *Catha edulis* | Cathine, cathinone | Tea, chew | Strong stimulant |
| Kola nut, gotu kola | *Cola* species | Caffeine, theobromine, kolanin | Smoke, tea, or capsules | Stimulant |
| Lobelia | *Lobelia inflata* | Lobeline | Smoke or tea as marijuana substitute | Mild euphoriant |
| Mandrake | *Mandragora officinalis* | Scopolamine, hyoscyamine | Tea as hallucinogen | Anticholinergic toxicity |
| Maté | *Ilex paraguariensis* | Caffeine | Tea | Stimulant |
| Mormon tea | *Ephedra nevadensis* | Ephedrine | Tea | Stimulant |
| Nutmeg | *Myristica fragrans* | Myristicin | Tea | Hallucinogen |
| Passion flower | *Passiflora incarnata* | Harmine alkaloids | Smoke, tea, or capsules as marijuana substitute | Mild stimulant, convulsions, tremors in excess |
| Periwinkle | *Catharanthus roseus* | Indole alkaloids | Smoke or tea as euphoriant | Hallucinogen |
| Prickly poppy | *Argemone mexicana* | Protopine, berberine isoquinolines | Smoke as euphoriant | Narcotic-analgesic |
| Snakeroot | *Rauwolfia serpentina* | Reserpine | Smoke or tea as tobacco substitute | Tranquilizer |
| Thorn-apple | *Datura stramonium* | Atropine, scopolamine | Smoke or tea as tobacco substitute or hallucinogen | Anticholinergic toxicity |
| Tobacco | *Nicotiana* species | Nicotine | Smoke | Strong stimulant |
| Valerian | *Valeriana officinalis* | Chatinine, velerine alkaloids | Tea or capsules | Tranquilizer |
| Wild lettuce | *Lactuca sativa* | Lactucarine | Smoke as opium substitute | Questionable narcotic-analgesic |
| Wormwood | *Artemisia absinthium* | Absinthine | Smoke or tea as relaxant | Narcotic-analgesic |

*Source.* Reprinted from Ellenhorn MJ: *Ellenhorn's Medical Toxicology.* Baltimore, MD, Williams & Wilkins, 1997; Siegel RK: "Herbal Intoxication." *JAMA* 236:474, 1976. Used with permission.

**TABLE 26–10.**  Major hallucinogenic plants and their active ingredients

| Plant | Family | Active ingredient |
|---|---|---|
| *Cannabis sativa* | Cannabinaceae | $\Delta^9$-Tetrahydrocannabinol |
| *Lophophora williamsii* | Cactaceae | Mescaline |
| *Piptadenia* species | Leguminosae | Substituted tryptamines |
| *Mimosa* species | Leguminosae | Substituted tryptamines |
| *Virola* species | Myristicaceae | Substituted tryptamines |
| *Banistereopsis* species | Malpighiaceae | Harmaline, harmine |
| *Peganum harmala* | Zygophyllaceae | Harmaline, harmine |
| *Tabernanthe iboga* | Apocynaceae | Ibogaine |
| *Ipomoea violacea* | Convolvulaceae | *d*-Lysergic acid amide |
|  |  | *d*-Isolysergic acid amide |
| *Turbina corymbosa* | Convolvulaceae | *d*-Lysergic acid amide |
|  |  | *d*-Isolysergic acid amide |
| *Datura* species | Solanaceae | Scopolamine |
| *Methysticodendron amesianum* | Solanaceae | Scopolamine |
| *Amanita muscaria* | Agaricaceae | Pantherine, ibotenic acid |
| *Psilocybe mexicana* | Agaricaceae | Psilocybin |

*Source.*  Reprinted from Ellenhorn MJ: *Ellenhorn's Medical Toxicology.* Baltimore, MD, Williams & Wilkins, 1997; Farnsworth NR: "Hallucinogenic Plants." *Science* 162:1090, 1986. Used with permission.

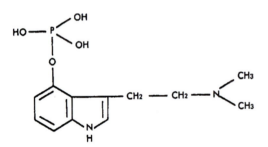

**Psilocybin**

**Psilocin**

**FIGURE 26–6.**  Structure of psilocybin and psilocin.

result in neuropsychiatric effects in addition to syndromes of bleeding, coagulopathy, myonecrosis, shock, and renal failure (Nelson 1989). Venomous snakes cause more than 30,000 deaths worldwide each year. Most deaths caused by snakebites in the United States are due

to rattlesnake bites. Of the five families of venomous snakes, only Hydrophiidae (sea snakes) and Elapidae (cobras, mambas, kraits, death adders) produce neuropsychiatric symptoms. Effects of bites from these snakes include ptosis, impaired vision, dysarthria, dysphagia, hypersalivation, paresthesia, muscle weakness, respiratory paralysis, and death (Ellenhorn 1997; Nelson 1989).

Treatment of venomous snake bites consists of local wound care, supportive measures, administration of antibiotics, tetanus prophylaxis and, if possible, administration of antivenin (Ellenhorn 1997). Cholinergic agents may be helpful for reversing the paralysis of Elapidae bites, and hemodialysis may be useful in cases of Hydrophiidae envenomization.

## Assessment of Toxic Exposure

In cases of suspected toxic exposure, a thorough history and clinical evaluation, including physical and laboratory studies, are indicated. Laboratory studies should include a complete blood count and differential. In addition, electrolytes, liver function tests, thyroid function tests, urine drug screens, and qualitative and quantitative analysis of blood and urine for heavy metals and organics are recommended to correlate and evaluate manifestations of toxic exposure. The Poison Severity Score is a useful guide for communicating the severity of neurotoxic

**TABLE 26–11.** Composition of snake venoms

| | |
|---|---|
| Proteolytic enzymes | Phosphomonoesterase |
| Arginine ester hydrolase | Phosphodiesterase |
| Thrombinlike enzyme | Acetylcholinesterase |
| Collagenase | RNase |
| Hyaluronidase | DNase |
| Phospholipase $A_2$ (A) | 5'-Nucleotidase |
| Phospholipase B | Nicotinamide adenine dinucleotide |
| Phospholipase C | (NAD)-nucleotidase |
| Lactate dehydrogenase | L-Amino acid oxidase |

*Source.* Reprinted from Ellenhorn MJ: *Ellenhorn's Medical Toxicology.* Baltimore, MD, Williams & Wilkins, 1997; Russell FE: *Snake Venom Poisoning.* Great Neck, NY, Scholiom International, 1983. Used with permission.

symptoms to poison control centers (Ellenhorn 1997).

Neuropsychological assessment may also be helpful. A number of tests are available to assess the level of neuropsychological impairment (Hartman 1988). Because various neurotoxins affect various brain areas, differing batteries of neuropsychological testing are indicated for the various solvents, pesticides, metals, drugs, and other neurotoxins.

History should include general effects such as common symptoms, as well as length, level, and, if possible, route of exposure. Ideally, workers in the chemical industry have had preexposure neuropsychological testing as part of the preemployment physical examination.

Electroencephalography may be invaluable in certain cases in determining encephalopathic states induced by toxins. The use of computed tomography, and particularly MRI, is helpful in identifying and localizing structural abnormalities secondary to toxin exposure (Prockop 1995). The use of single photon emission computed tomography (SPECT) might be helpful in studying metabolic derangements secondary to neurotoxin exposure. The use of PET scanning is promising as a tool to quantitate neurologic effects occurring as a result of neurotoxin exposure (Prockop 1995).

## Developmental Influences

The neuropsychiatric manifestations of toxin exposure discussed in this chapter are primarily those reported for adults. In experimental animals, the degrees of neurologic damage from neurotoxins such as metals are also influenced by the age of the exposed animal, and the highest risks occur during the fetal and perinatal periods. In general, young children are reported to be at greater risk than adults for the development of neurotoxicity. At present, there continues to be little known about the various neuropsychiatric sequelae of exposure to neurotoxins at different stages in human development. Moreover, in older adults, the process of neuronal aging, cell death, and loss of "plasticity" and compensatory mechanisms may result in greater susceptibility of the aging nervous system to neurotoxins. The study of neurotoxins and their use as research tools continues to be important in that they may aid in the understanding of the pathophysiology of both psychiatric and neurologic illness.

## References

Aldrich F, Holmes J: Acute chlordane intoxication in a child. Case report with toxicological data. Arch Environ Health 19:129–132, 1969

Aldridge WN, Street BW: The relationship between the specific binding of trimethyltin and triethyltin to mitochondria and their effects on various mitochondrial functions. Biochem J 124:221–234, 1971

Alfrey AC, Froment DC: Dialysis encephalopathy, in Aluminum and Renal Failure. Edited by DeBroe ME, Coburn JW. Dordrecht, Netherlands, Kluwer, 1990, pp 249–257

Aposhian HV, Aposhian MM: meso-2,3-Dimercaptosuccinic acid: chemical, pharmacological and toxicological properties of an orally effective metal chelating agent. Annu Rev Pharmacol Toxicol 30:279–306, 1990

Aposhian HV, Carter DE, Hoover TD, et al: DMSA, DMPS, and DMPA: as arsenic antidotes. Fundamental and Applied Toxicology 4:58–70, 1984

Aschner M, Aschner JL: Manganese transport across the blood-brain barrier: relationship to iron homeostasis. Brain Res Bull 24:857–860, 1990

Barret DS, Oehme FW: A review of organophosphate ester induced delayed neurotoxicity. Vet Hum Toxicol 27:22–37, 1985

Beard RR, Grandstaff N: Carbon monoxide exposure and cerebral function. Ann N Y Acad Sci 174:385–395, 1970

Benjamin C: Persistent psychiatric symptoms after eating psilocybin mushrooms. BMJ 1:1319–1320, 1979

Bertoncin D, Russolo A, Caroldi S, et al: Neuropathy target esterase in human lymphocytes. Arch Environ Health 40:139–144, 1985

Bidstrup PL, Bonnell JA, Beckett AG: Paralysis following poisoning by a new organic phosphorus insecticide (mipafox): report on two cases. BMJ 1:1068–1072, 1953

Bleck TP: Tetanus: pathophysiology, management, and prophylaxis. Disease-a-Month 37(9):547–603, 1991

Bleecker M: Clinical presentation of selected neurotoxic compounds, in Occupational Neurology and Clinical Neurotoxicology. Edited by Bleecker ML, Hansen J. Baltimore, MD, Williams & Wilkins, 1994, pp 207–233

Bolla KI, Roca R: Neuropsychiatric sequelae of occupational exposure to neurotoxins, in Occupational Neurology and Clinical Neurotoxicology. Edited by Bleecker ML, Hansen JA. Baltimore, MD, Williams & Wilkins, 1994, pp 133–159

Bradbury JE, Forshaw PJ, Gray AJ, et al: The action of mephenesin and other agents on the effects produced by two neurotoxic pyrethroids in the intact and spinal rat. Neuropharmacology 22:907–914, 1983

Brown AW, Aldridge WN, Street BW, et al: Behavioral and neuropathological sequela of intoxication by trimethyltin compounds in the rat. Am J Pathol 97:59–82, 1979

Bruyn GW, De Wolff FA: Plumbism, in Handbook of Clinical Neurology: Intoxications of the Nervous System. Edited by De Wolff FA. New York, Elsevier, 1994, pp 431–442

Bugiani O, Ghetti B: Aluminum encephalopathy: experimental vs human, in Aluminum and Renal Failure. Edited by De Broe ME, Coburn JW. Dordrecht, Netherlands, Kluwer, 1990, pp 109–125

Cavanagh JB: Long term persistence of mercury in the brain. British Journal of Industrial Medicine 45:649–651, 1988

Chandra SV, Seth PK, Mankeshwar JK: Manganese poisoning: clinical and biochemical observations. Environ Res 7:374–380, 1974

Cherington M: Botulism: ten year experience. Arch Neurol 30:432–437, 1974

Cherington M: Botulism. Semin Neurol 10:27–31, 1990

Cook DG, Fahn S, Brait KA: Chronic manganese intoxication. Arch Neurol 30:59–64, 1974

Costa LG, Sulaiman R: Inhibition of protein synthesis by trimethyltin. Toxicol Appl Pharmacol 86:189–196, 1986

Crystal HA, Schaumburg HH, Grober E, et al: Cognitive impairment and sensory loss associated with chronic low level ethylene oxide exposure. Neurology 29:978–983, 1988

Curley A, Gerrettson L: Acute chlordane poisoning. Arch Environ Health 18:211–215, 1969

De Wolff FA, Van der Voet GB: Biological monitoring of aluminum in renal patients. Clin Chim Acta 160:183–188, 1986

Doctor SV, Costa LG, Kendall DA, et al: Trimethyltin inhibits the uptake of neurotransmitters into mouse forebrain synaptosomes. Toxicol Appl Pharmacol 25:213–221, 1982

Dunbar EM: Botulism. J Infect 20:1–3, 1990

Dyer RS, Walsh TJ, Wonderlin WF, et al: The trimethyltin syndrome in rats. Neurobehavioral Toxicology and Teratology 4:127–133, 1982

Ecobichon DJ: Toxic effects of pesticides, in Toxicology: the Basic Science of Poisons, 4th Edition. Edited by Amdur MO, Doull J, Klassen CD. New York, Pergamon, 1991, pp 565–614

Elhassani SB: The many faces of methylmercury poisoning. J Toxicol Clin Toxicol 19:875–906, 1983

Ellenhorn MJ: Ellenhorn's Medical Toxicology: Diagnosis and Treatment of Human Poisoning. Baltimore, MD, Williams & Wilkins, 1997

Farnsworth NR: Hallucinogenic plants. Science 162:1086–1092, 1986

Feldman RG: Manganese, in Handbook of Clinical Neurology: Intoxications of the Nervous System. Edited by De Wolff FA. New York, Elsevier, 1994, pp 303–322

Flannigan SA, Tucker SB, Key MM: Prophylaxis of synthetic pyrethroid exposure. Journal of Social and Occupational Medicine 34:24–26, 1984

Food and Agriculture Organization/World Health Organization: 2,4,5-T Data Sheet on Pesticides. WHO/FAO Bulletin. Geneva, Switzerland, World Health Organization, 1975

Fortemps E, Anand G, Bomboir A, et al: Trimethyltin poisoning: a report of two cases. International Archives of Occupational Health 41:1–6, 1978

Garner CD, Nachtman JP: Manganese catalyzed auto-oxidation of dopamine to 6-hydroxydopamine in vitro. Chem Biol Interact 69:345–351, 1989

Garruto RM: Pacific paradigms of environmentally induced neurological disorders: clinical, epidemiological and molecular perspectives. Neurotoxicology 12:347–378, 1991

Ginsberg MD: Carbon monoxide intoxication: clinical features, neuropathology and mechanisms of injury. Clinical Toxicology 23:281–288, 1985

Goetz CG: Neurotoxins in clinical practice. Jamaica, NY, Spectrum, 1985

Graham DG: Catecholamine toxicity: a proposal for the molecular pathogenesis of manganese neurotoxicity and Parkinson's disease. Neurotoxicology 5:83–96, 1984

Gross JA: Ethylene oxide toxicity. Neurology 29:978–983, 1979

Habermann E: Tetanus, in Handbook of Clinical Neurology. Edited by Vinker PJ, Bruyn GW. Amsterdam, The Netherlands, Elsevier/North-Holland, 1978, pp 491–547

Hall AH, Robertson WO: Arsenic and other heavy metals, in Clinical Management of Poisoning and Drug Overdose. Edited by Haddad LM, Winchester JF. Philadelphia, PA, WB Saunders, 1990, pp 1024–1028

Harris WR: Equilibrium model for speciation of aluminum in serum. Clin Chem 38:1809–1882, 1992

Hartman DE: Neuropsychological Toxicology: Identification and Assessment of Human Neurotoxic Syndromes. New York, Pergamon, 1988

He F, Wang X, Zhow X, et al: Clinical observations on two patients of acute deltamethrin poisoning (abstract), in Proceedings of the 21st International Congress on Occupational Health, Dublin, Ireland, September 9–14, 1984, p 354

Horowitz AL, Kaplan R, Sarpel G: Carbon monoxide toxicity: MRI imaging in the brain. Radiology 62:787–788, 1987

Kerr DNS, Ward MK, Ellis W, et al: Aluminum intoxication in renal disease, in Aluminum in Biology and Medicine. Edited by Chadwick PJ, Whelan J. Chichester, England, Wiley, 1992, pp 123–141

Kerr HD, Saryan LA: Arsenic content of homeopathic medicines. Clin Toxicol 24:451–459, 1986

Klaassen CD: Heavy metals and heavy-metal antagonists, in Goodman and Gilman's The Pharmacological Basis of Therapeutics, 8th Edition. Edited by Goodman-Gilman A, Rall TA, Nies AS, et al. New York, Pergamon, 1990a, pp 1592–1614

Klaassen CD: Nonmetallic environmental toxicants, air pollutants, solvents, vapors, and pesticides, in Goodman and Gilman's The Pharmacological Basis of Therapeutics, 8th Edition. Edited by Goodman-Gilman A, Rall TA, Nies AS, et al. New York, Pergamon, 1990b, pp 1615–1639

Kreppel H, Reichl FX, Szinicz L, et al: Efficacy of various dithiol compounds in acute As$_2$O$_3$ poisoning in mice. Arch Toxicol 64:387–392, 1990

Kuzuhara S, Kanazawa S, Nakanishi T, et al: Ethylene oxide polyneuropathy. Neurology 33:377–380, 1983

Landrigan PJ: Occupational and community exposures to toxic metals: lead, cadmium, mercury and arsenic. West J Med 137:531–539, 1982

Lauwerys RR, Buchet JP, Roels H: The determination of trace levels of arsenic in human biological materials. Arch Toxicol 41:239–247, 1979

Le Quesne PM, Maxwell IC, Butterworth STG: Transient facial sensory symptoms following exposure to synthetic pyrethroids: a clinical and electrophysiological assessment. Neurotoxicology 2:1–11, 1980

Lerman Y, Hirshberg A, Shteger Z: Organophosphate and carbamate pesticide poisoning: the usefulness of a computerized clinical information system. Am J Ind Med 6:17–26, 1984

Louria DB: Trace metal poisoning, in Cecil Textbook of Medicine. Edited by Wyngaarden JB, Smith LHJ. Philadelphia, PA, WB Saunders, 1988, pp 2385–2393

Lukiw WJ, McLachlan DRC: Aluminum neurotoxicity, in Handbook of Neurotoxicology: Effects and Mechanisms. Edited by Chang LW, Dyer RS. New York, Marcel Dekker, 1993, pp 105–142

Magee PN, Stoner HB, Barnes JM: The experimental production of oedema in the central nervous system of rats by triethyltin compounds. Journal of Pathology and Bacteriology 73:107–124, 1957

Major RH: Classic Descriptions of Disease. Springfield, IL, Charles C Thomas, 1945, pp 311–312

Mena I: Manganese, in Metals in the Environment. Edited by Waldron H. New York, Academic Press, 1980, pp 199–220

Metter JE, Bleecker ML: Quantitative neurological examination, in Occupational Neurology and Clinical Neurotoxicology. Edited by Bleecker ML, Hansen J. Baltimore, MD, Williams & Wilkins, 1994, pp 207–233

Min SK: A brain syndrome associated with delayed neuropsychiatric sequelae following acute carbon monoxide intoxication. Acta Psychiatr Scand 73:80–86, 1986

Mitchell-Heggs CAW, Conway M, Cassar J: Herbal medicine as a cause of combined lead and arsenic poisoning. Hum Exp Toxicol 9:195–196, 1990

Morgan JP, Penovich P: Jamaica ginger paralysis. Arch Neurol 35:530–532, 1978

Murphy VA, Wadhwani KC, Smith QR, et al: Saturable transport of manganese (II) across the rat blood brain barrier. J Neurochem 57:948–954, 1991

Nelson BK: Snake envenomation: incidence, clinical presentation and management. Medical Toxicology and Adverse Drug Experience 4:17–31, 1989

Ngim CH, Foo SC, Boey KW, et al: Chronic neurobehavioral effects of elemental mercury in dentists. Br J Psychiatry 167:95–98, 1995

Parenti M, Rusconi L, Cappabianca V, et al: Role of dopamine in manganese neurotoxicity. Brain Res 473:236–240, 1988

Perl DP, Brody AR: Alzheimer's disease: x-ray spectrometric evidence of aluminum accumulation in neurofibrillary tangle bearing neurons. Science 208:297–299, 1980

Perl TM, Bedard L, Kosatsky T, et al: An outbreak of toxic encephalopathy caused by eating mussels contaminated with domoic acid. N Engl J Med 322:1775–1780, 1990

Petsas T, Fezoulidis I, Ziogas D: Gehirn Verkalkung bei chronischer Bleivergiftung. Rofo Fortschr Geb Rontgenstr Neuen Bildgeb Verfahr 157:192–193, 1992

Prockop LD: Neuroimaging in neurotoxicology, in Neurotoxicology: Approaches and Methods. Edited by Chang LW, Slikker W. New York, Academic Press, 1995, pp 753–763

Roberts L: EPA moves to reassess the risk of dioxin. Science 252:911, 1991a

Roberts L: More pieces in the dioxin puzzle. Science 254:377, 1991b

Roels H, Lauwerys R, Genet P, et al: Relationship between external and internal parameters of exposure to manganese in workers from a manganese oxide and salt producing plant. Am J Ind Med 11:297–305, 1987

Ross WD, Emmett EA, Steiner J, et al: Neurotoxic effects of occupational exposure to organotins. Am J Psychiatry 138:1092–1095, 1981

Rouzaud M, Lutier J: Oedeme subaigu cerebromeninge du a une intoxication d'actualite. Presse Med 62:1075–1079, 1954

Russell FE: Snake Venom Poisoning. Great Neck, NY, Scholiom International, 1983

Ryan DW, Cherington M: Human type A botulism. JAMA 216:513–514, 1971

Segura-Aguilar J, Lind C: On the mechanism of the Mn$^{3+}$-induced neurotoxicity of dopamine: prevention of quinone-derived oxygen toxicity by DT diaphorase and superoxide dismutase. Chem Biol Interact 72:309–324, 1989

Selwyn MJ: Triorganotin compounds as ionophores and inhibitors of ion translocating ATPases, in Organotin Compounds: New Chemistry and Applications. Edited by

Zuckerman J. Washington, DC, American Chemical Society, 1976, pp 204–226

Shukla GS, Singhal RL: The present status of biological effects of toxic metals in the environment: lead, cadmium and manganese. Can J Physiol Pharmacol 62:1015–1031, 1984

Siegel RK: Herbal intoxication. JAMA 236:474–476, 1976

Stokinger HE: Arsenic, in Patty's Industrial Hygiene and Toxicology. Edited by Clayton GD, Clayton FE. New York, Wiley, 1981, pp 1517–1531

Stranger J, Kerridge G: Multiple fractures of the dorsal part of the spine following chlordane poisoning. Med J Aust 1:267–268, 1968

Taylor JR, Selhorst JB, Houff SA, et al: Chlordecone intoxication in man, I: clinical observations. Neurology 28:626–630, 1978

Teitelbaum JS, Zatorre RJ, Carpenter S, et al: Neurological sequela of domoic acid intoxication due to the ingestion of contaminated mussels. N Engl J Med 322:1781–1787, 1990

Traverso HP, Kamil S, Rahim H, et al: A reassessment of risk factors for neonatal tetanus. Bull World Health Organ 69:573–579, 1991

Tryphonas L, Truelove J, Nera E, et al: Acute neurotoxicity of domoic acid in the rat. Toxicol Pathol 18:1–9, 1990

Van der Kerk GJM: Organotin chemistry: past, present and future, in Organotin Compounds: New Chemistry and Applications. Edited by Zuckerman J. Washington, DC, American Chemical Society, 1976, pp 1–25

Van der Voet GB: Intestinal absorption of aluminum, in Aluminum in Biology and Medicine (Ciba Foundation Symposium No 169). Edited by Chadwick DJ, Whelan J. Chichester, England, Wiley, 1992a, pp 109–122

Van der Voet GB: Intestinal absorption of aluminum: relation to neurotoxicity, in The Vulnerable Brain and Environmental Risks: Toxins in Food. Edited by Isaacson RL, Jensen KF. New York, Plenum, 1992b, pp 35–47

Van Poorten JF, Stienstra R, Dworacek B, et al: Physostigmine reversal of psilocybin intoxication (letter). Anesthesiology 56:313, 1982

Wassenar JS, Kroon AM: Effects of triethyltin on different ATPases, 5'-nucleotidase, and phosphodiesterases in grey and white matter of rabbit brain and their relation to brain edema. Eur Neurol 10:349–370, 1973

Weinstein L: Current concepts: tetanus. N Engl J Med 289:1293–1296, 1973

Wide C: Mercury hazards arising from the repair of sphygmomanometers. BMJ 293:1409–1410, 1986

Wilhelm JM, Jager DE, Ohnesorge FK: Aluminum toxicokinetics. Pharmacol Toxicol 66:4–9, 1990

Winship KA: Toxicity of inorganic arsenic salts. Adverse Drug Reactions and Acute Poisoning Reviews 3:129–160, 1984

Wolters E, Huang CC, Clark C, et al: Positron emission tomography in manganese intoxication. Ann Neurol 26:647–651, 1989

World Health Organization: Expanded Program on Immunization. Geneva, World Health Organization, 1988

Wynter JE: The preventions of manganese poisoning. Industrial Medicine and Surgery 31:308–310, 1962

# CHAPTER 27

# Neuropsychiatric Aspects of Ethanol and Other Chemical Dependencies

Eric J. Nestler, M.D., Ph.D.

David W. Self, Ph.D.

Drug addiction continues to exact enormous human and financial costs on society, at a time when available treatments remain inadequately effective for most people. Given that advances in treating other medical disorders have resulted directly from research of the molecular and cellular pathophysiology of the disease process, an improved understanding of the basic neurobiology of addiction should likewise translate into more efficacious treatments.

Our knowledge of the basic neurobiology of drug addiction is leading psychiatric neuroscience in establishing the biological basis of a complex and clinically important behavioral abnormality. This is because many features of drug addiction in people can be reproduced in laboratory animals, where findings are directly referable back to the clinical situation. Earlier work on drug reinforcement mechanisms, and more recently developed animal models that target the addiction process and drug craving, have made it possible to identify regions of the brain that play important roles in distinct behavioral features of addiction. These neural substrates are now the focus of extensive research on the molecular and cellular alterations that underlie these behavioral changes.

This chapter provides an overview of recent progress made in our understanding of the neurobiological basis of drug addiction. After providing brief definitions of commonly used terminology, we summarize the anatomic and neurochemical substrates that mediate the reinforcing effects of short-term drug exposure. We then describe how repeated drug exposure can induce gradually developing, progressive alterations in molecular and cellular signaling pathways, and how these neuroadaptive changes may ultimately contribute to addictive behavior.

## Definition of Terms

From a pharmacologic perspective, drug addiction can be defined by processes such as tolerance, sensitization, dependence, and withdrawal. *Tolerance* refers to a progressive weakening of a given drug effect after repeated exposure, which may contribute to an escalation of drug intake as the addiction process proceeds. *Sensitization*, or *reverse tolerance*, refers to the opposite circumstance, whereby repeated administration of the same drug dose elicits an even stronger effect; sensitization to certain "incentive motivational" effects of drugs is believed to contribute to high relapse rates seen in addicted individuals. Thus, both tolerance and sensitization to different aspects of drug action can occur simultaneously. *Dependence* is defined as the need for continued drug exposure to avoid a withdrawal syndrome, which is characterized by physical or motivational disturbances when the drug is withdrawn. Presumably, the processes of tolerance, sen-

This work was supported by grants from the National Institute on Drug Abuse.

sitization, dependence, and withdrawal are each caused by molecular and cellular adaptations in specific brain regions in response to repeated drug exposure. It is important to emphasize that these phenomena are not associated uniquely with drugs of abuse, as many clinically used medications that are not addicting (e.g., clonidine, propranolol, tricyclic antidepressants) can also produce similar phenomena. Rather, the manifestation of tolerance, sensitization, dependence, and withdrawal specifically in brain regions that regulate motivation is believed to underlie addiction-related changes in behavior.

Drugs of abuse are unique in terms of their reinforcing properties. A drug is defined as a reinforcer if the probability of a drug-seeking response is increased and maintained by pairing drug exposure with the response. Initially, most abused drugs function as positive reinforcers, presumably because they produce a positive affective state (e.g., euphoria). Such rapid and powerful associations between a drug reinforcer and a drug-seeking response probably reflect the drug's ability to usurp preexisting brain reinforcement mechanisms, which normally mediate the reinforcing effects of natural reinforcers such as food, sex, and social interaction.

Long-term exposure to reinforcing drugs can lead to drug addiction, which is characterized by an escalation in both the frequency and the amount of drug use and by intense drug craving during withdrawal despite grave adverse consequences. In the context of long-term drug use, a drug may serve not only as a positive reinforcer but also as a negative reinforcer by alleviating the negative consequences of drug withdrawal. The persistence of drug craving and drug seeking (relapse) despite prolonged periods of abstinence suggests that long-lasting adaptations have occurred in the neural substrates that mediate acute drug reinforcement.

Addictive disorders are often defined clinically as a state of "psychological dependence," for example, in DSM-IV-TR (American Psychiatric Association 2000). However, it is important to emphasize that in more precise pharmacologic terms, we do not yet know the relative contributions of neurobiological changes that underlie tolerance, sensitization, or dependence to the compulsive drug-seeking behavior that is the clinical hallmark of an addictive disorder. It is possible that drug craving and relapse involve dependence-related dysphoria associated with drug withdrawal. Such factors are likely to be important during the relatively early phases of abstinence. However, a major question remains the types of adaptations that underlie particularly long-lived aspects of addiction, for example, the increased risk of relapse that many addicts show even after years of absti-

nence. As stated above, such persistent drug craving may involve adaptations that underlie sensitization to the incentive motivational properties of drugs, drug-associated (conditioned) stimuli, and stressful events. In other words, sensitization to these various stimuli would increase their ability to "reinstate"—or "prime"—drug seeking despite prolonged abstinence. Identification of long-lasting adaptations that underlie these persisting behavioral changes is paramount to the ultimate development of truly effective treatments.

## The Synapse as the Immediate Target of Drugs of Abuse

The initial actions of drugs of abuse on the brain can be understood at the level of synaptic transmission. Figure 27–1 depicts a classic view of a synapse, in which a presynaptic nerve terminal, in response to a nerve impulse along its axon, releases a neurotransmitter that acts on a postsynaptic receptor to elicit changes in neuronal excitability of the postsynaptic neuron. The activity of the neurotransmitter is then turned off by its reuptake into the nerve terminal, or by enzymatic degradation (for review, see Nestler et al. 2001).

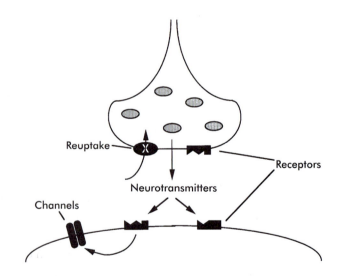

**FIGURE 27–1.** A classic working model of synaptic transmission. In classic terms, synaptic transmission was conceived as the release of neurotransmitter from a nerve terminal, the binding of the neurotransmitter to specific receptor sites on target neurons, and the resulting alterations in the conductances of specific ion channels. The action of the neurotransmitter is then terminated by its reuptake into the nerve terminal or by enzymatic degradation (not shown).

All drugs of abuse initially affect the brain by influencing the amount of a neurotransmitter present at the synapse or by interacting with specific neurotransmitter receptors. Table 27–1 lists examples of such acute pharmacologic actions of some commonly used drugs of abuse. The fact that drugs of abuse initially influence different neurotransmitter and receptor systems in the brain explains the very different actions produced by these drugs acutely. For example, the presence of very high levels of opioid receptors in the brain stem and spinal cord explains why opiates can exert such profound effects on respiration, level of consciousness, and nociception. In contrast, the importance of noradrenergic mechanisms in the regulation of cardiac function explains why cocaine can exert such profound cardiotoxic effects.

In contrast to the many disparate acute actions of drugs of abuse, the drugs do appear to exert some common behavioral effects: as discussed above, they are all positively reinforcing after short-term exposure. This suggests that there are certain regions of the brain where the distinct acute pharmacologic actions of these drugs converge at the level of a common reinforcement substrate. That is, in certain regions of the brain, which are discussed below, activation of opioid receptors (by opiates), inhibition of monoamine reuptake (by cocaine), or facilitation of GABAergic and inhibition of $N$-methyl-D-aspartate (NMDA) glutamatergic neurotransmission (by ethanol) would appear to elicit some common neurobiological response(s) that mediates their reinforcing properties.

## Molecular and Cellular Adaptations as the Long-Term Consequences of Drugs of Abuse

The acute pharmacologic actions of a drug of abuse per se do not explain the long-term effects of repeated drug exposure. To understand such long-term effects, it is necessary to move beyond the classic view of a synapse to a more sophisticated, complete view, such as that shown in Figure 27–2. Thus, we now know that neurotransmitter-receptor activation does more to influence a target neuron than simply regulate its ion channels and immediate electrical properties: virtually every process in a neuron can be affected by neurotransmitter-receptor activation (Nestler et al. 2001). Such effects are mediated by modulating the functional activity of proteins that are already present in the neuron or by regulating the actual amount of the proteins. Neurotransmitter-receptor activation produces these diverse effects through biochemical cas-

**TABLE 27–1.** Examples of acute pharmacologic actions of drugs of abuse

| Drug | Action |
|---|---|
| Opiates | Agonist at $\mu$, $\delta$, and $\kappa$ opioid receptors[a] |
| Cocaine | Inhibits monoamine reuptake transporters |
| Amphetamine | Stimulates monoamine release |
| Ethanol | Facilitates GABA$_A$ receptor function and inhibits NMDA glutamate receptor function[b] |
| Nicotine | Agonist at nicotinic acetylcholine receptors |
| Cannabinoids | Agonist at CB$_1$ cannabinoid receptors[c] |
| Hallucinogens | Partial agonist at 5-HT$_2$ serotonin receptors |
| Phencyclidine (PCP) | Antagonist at NMDA glutamate receptors |

*Note.* GABA$_A$ = $\gamma$-aminobutyric acid type A; NMDA = $N$-methyl-D-aspartate; 5-HT$_2$ = 5-hydroxytryptamine (serotonin) type 2.
[a]Activity at $\mu$ and $\delta$ receptors is thought to mediate the reinforcing actions of opiates.
[b]The mechanism by which ethanol produces these effects has not been established.
[c]The endogenous ligand(s) for this receptor has not yet been definitively identified; one candidate is anandamide.
*Source.* See Nestler et al. 2001 for references.

cades of intracellular messengers, which involve G proteins (guanosine triphosphate–binding membrane proteins that couple extracellular receptors to intracellular effector proteins), and the subsequent regulation of second messengers (such as cyclic adenosine monophosphate [cAMP], calcium, phosphatidylinositol, or nitric oxide) and protein phosphorylation (see Nestler et al. 2001). Protein phosphorylation is a process whereby phosphate groups are added to proteins by protein kinases or are removed from proteins by protein phosphatases. The addition or removal of phosphate groups dramatically alters protein function and leads to the myriad biological responses in question.

Neurotransmitter receptors function presynaptically to regulate the synthesis and storage of neurotransmitter via phosphorylation of synthetic enzymes and transporter proteins. In addition, altered phosphorylation of synaptic vesicle–associated proteins can modulate the release of neurotransmitters from presynaptic nerve terminals. Postsynaptically, altered phosphorylation of receptors and ion channels can modify the ability of neurotransmitters to regulate the physiologic responses to the same or different neurotransmitter stimuli. Neurotransmitter-mediated phosphorylation of cytoskeletal proteins can produce structural and morphologic changes in target neurons. Finally, altered phosphorylation of nuclear or ribosomal proteins can alter gene transcription and protein synthesis and hence the total amounts of these various types of proteins in the target neurons. Given the

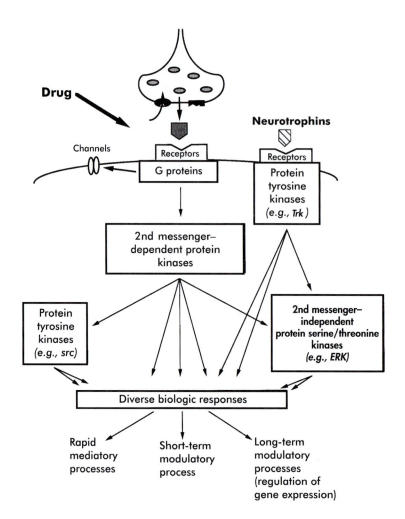

**FIGURE 27–2.** A working model of synaptic transmission. Studies in basic neuroscience have provided a much more complex view of synaptic transmission than that shown in Figure 27–1. These studies focused on the involvement of intracellular messenger systems involving coupling factors (termed G proteins), second messengers (e.g., cyclic adenosine monophosphate [cAMP], calcium, nitric oxide, and the metabolites of phosphatidylinositol), and protein phosphorylation (involving the phosphorylation of phosphoproteins by protein kinases and their dephosphorylation by protein phosphatases) in mediating multiple actions of neurotransmitters on their target neurons. Second messenger–dependent protein kinases (e.g., those activated by cAMP or calcium) are classified as protein serine/threonine kinases, because they phosphorylate substrate proteins on serine or threonine residues. Each second messenger–dependent protein kinase phosphorylates a specific array of substrate proteins (which can be considered third messengers) and thereby leads to multiple biological responses of the neurotransmitter. Brain also contains many important intracellular regulatory pathways in addition to those regulated directly by G proteins and second messengers. This includes numerous protein serine/ threonine kinases (e.g., the extracellular signal–regulated kinases [ERKs] or mitogen-activated protein [MAP] kinases), as well as numerous protein tyrosine kinases (which phosphorylate substrate proteins on tyrosine residues), some of which reside in the receptors for neurotrophins and most other growth factors (e.g., the trk proteins), and others that are not associated with growth factor receptors (e.g., src kinase). Each of these various protein kinases are highly regulated by extracellular stimuli. The second messenger–dependent protein kinases are regulated by receptor–G protein–second messenger pathways as mentioned above. The receptor-associated protein tyrosine kinases are activated on growth factor binding to the receptor. The second messenger–independent protein serine/threonine kinases and the protein tyrosine kinases that are not receptor associated seem to be regulated indirectly via the second messenger–dependent and growth factor–dependent pathways as depicted in the figure. The brain also contains numerous types of protein serine/threonine and protein tyrosine phosphatases, not shown in the figure, which are also subject to regulation by extracellular and intracellular stimuli. Thus, the binding of neurotransmitter to its receptor extracellularly results in numerous short-term and long-term biological responses through the complex regulation of multiple intracellular regulatory pathways and the phosphorylation or dephosphorylation of numerous substrate proteins.

gradual development of drug addiction in most people and the persistence of drug craving for long periods after cessation of drug exposure, it is likely that repeated drug exposure causes altered patterns of gene expression and protein synthesis that underlie some of these long-term actions of drugs of abuse on the nervous system (Nestler 1992; Nestler et al. 1993).

Neurotransmitter regulation of G proteins and second messenger–dependent protein phosphorylation is a small part of a neuron's intracellular regulatory machinery (Figure 27–2) (Nestler et al. 2001). Neurons also express high levels of protein tyrosine kinases (e.g., Trk proteins) that mediate the actions of neurotrophins and other growth factors. Growth factors play an important role in neuronal development, but more recently they have been shown to exert powerful effects on fully differentiated adult neurons. This implies that the traditional distinction between neurotransmitters and growth factors is becoming increasingly arbitrary. In addition, neurons contain high levels of protein kinases that are not regulated directly by extracellular signals but are influenced by those signals indirectly via "crosstalk" among various intracellular pathways. Thus, each neurotransmitter-receptor system can interact with others via secondary, tertiary, etc., effects on various intracellular signaling pathways, all of which will contribute to the myriad effects of the original neurotransmitter stimulus.

This means that, despite the initial actions of a drug of abuse on the activity of a neurotransmitter or receptor system, the many actions of drugs of abuse on brain function are achieved ultimately through the complex network of intracellular messenger pathways that mediate physiologic responses to neurotransmitter-receptor interactions. Moreover, repeated exposure to drugs of abuse would be expected to produce molecular and cellular adaptations as a result of repeated perturbation of these intracellular pathways. These adaptations may be responsible for tolerance, sensitization, dependence, withdrawal, and, ultimately, the addiction process.

We will begin our discussion of specific molecular and cellular adaptations that result from long-term drug exposure by considering the locus coeruleus, where adaptations in the cAMP second messenger and protein phosphorylation systems have been implicated in the molecular, cellular, and behavioral changes associated with physical signs of opiate dependence and withdrawal. Because similar molecular adaptations to long-term drug exposure are seen in brain regions associated with drug reinforcement and craving, the locus coeruleus has served as a model system to guide investigations into the molecular mechanisms underlying motivational dependence. These studies suggest that both physical and moti-vational changes associated with drug addiction are caused by some similar molecular adaptations, but in distinct neural substrates that regulate these behaviors.

## Role of the Locus Coeruleus in Opiate Physical Dependence

The locus coeruleus is located on the floor of the fourth ventricle in the anterior pons (Figure 27–3). It contains the major noradrenergic nucleus in the brain with widespread projections to both the brain and spinal cord. This diffuse innervation allows the locus coeruleus to regulate the animal's general state of arousal, attention, and autonomic tone. An important role for the locus coeruleus in opiate physical dependence and withdrawal has been established at both the behavioral and electrophysiological levels: overactivation of locus coeruleus neurons is both necessary and sufficient for producing many behavioral signs of opiate withdrawal (see Aghajanian 1978; Koob et al. 1992; Maldonado and Koob 1993; Nestler 1992; Nestler and Aghajanian 1997; Rasmussen et al. 1990). Indeed, it was this knowledge of the role of the locus coeruleus in physical dependence to opiates that led to the introduction of clonidine—an $\alpha_2$-adrenergic agonist that produces effects similar to those of morphine on neurons of the locus coeruleus (Aghajanian 1978)—as the first nonopiate treatment for opiate withdrawal in humans (Gold et al. 1978). Overactivation of locus coeruleus neurons during withdrawal arises from both extrinsic and intrinsic sources. The extrinsic source involves a hyperactive, excitatory glutamatergic input to the locus coeruleus from the nucleus paragigantocellularis (PGi). The intrinsic source involves intracellular adaptations in opioid receptor–coupled signal transduction pathways in locus coeruleus neurons.

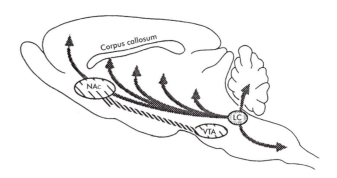

**FIGURE 27–3.**  Locations of the locus coeruleus (LC), ventral tegmental area (VTA), and nucleus accumbens (NAc) in rat brain.

## Mechanisms Intrinsic to the Locus Coeruleus

Acutely, opiates inhibit locus coeruleus neurons via activation of an inward-rectifying $K^+$ channel and inhibition of an inward $Na^+$ current (e.g., Alreja and Aghajanian 1991, 1993; North et al. 1987). Both actions are mediated via pertussis toxin–sensitive G proteins (i.e., Gi and Go). Opiates directly activate the $K^+$ channel via Gi and Go. In contrast, inhibition of the $Na^+$ current appears to be indirect, through Gi-mediated inhibition of cAMP formation and reduced activation of cAMP-dependent protein kinase (protein kinase A). Biochemical studies confirm that opiates acutely inhibit adenylyl cyclase activity and cAMP-dependent protein phosphorylation in the locus coeruleus (Figure 27–4, top) (Nestler 1992).

With long-term exposure, locus coeruleus neurons develop tolerance to these acute inhibitory actions, as neuronal activity recovers toward preexposure levels (Aghajanian 1978; Christie et al. 1987). Administration of an opioid receptor antagonist causes a rebound increase in neuronal firing rates above preexposure levels both in vivo and in isolated slice preparations (Aghajanian 1978; Kogan et al. 1992; Rasmussen et al. 1990). These electrophysiological correlates of tolerance, dependence, and withdrawal are mediated in part via upregulation of the cAMP pathway as a compensatory, or homeostatic, adaptation to long-term exposure to opiates. Long-term opiate exposure increases locus coeruleus levels of Gi and Go, adenylyl cyclase types I and VIII, catalytic and regulatory protein kinase A, and several phosphoprotein substrates for the kinase (see Lane-Ladd et al. 1997; Nestler 1992; Nestler and Aghajanian 1997). One of these substrates, tyrosine hydroxylase, is the rate-limiting enzyme in the biosynthesis of norepinephrine (and other catecholamines), which suggests that norepinephrine synthesis is increased after long-term opiate administration. Upregulation of the cAMP pathway occurs in the absence of alterations in several other intracellular signaling pathways in this brain region.

The mechanisms by which long-term opiate exposure upregulates the cAMP pathway are complex. Some of the adaptations, including induction of adenylyl cyclase type VIII and tyrosine hydroxylase, occur via increased gene expression that involves the transcription factor cAMP response element binding protein (CREB) (Boundy et al. 1998b; Lane-Ladd et al. 1997). CREB is activated when it is phosphorylated by protein kinase A or other protein kinases, and it is itself upregulated in the locus coeruleus after long-term morphine administration. A role for CREB-regulated genes in opiate physical dependence is consistent with the observation that mice lacking CREB show reduced opiate withdrawal symptoms (Maldonado et al. 1996). Other aspects of the upregulated cAMP pathway—for example, induction of protein kinase A subunits—appear to occur at a posttranscriptional level, apparently independent of gene transcription (Boundy et al. 1998a).

The upregulated cAMP pathway is thought to contribute to the reduced ability of opiates to inhibit the activity of locus coeruleus neurons and thus accounts, at least in part, for opiate tolerance. In addition, these compensatory adaptations appear to contribute to the intrinsic hyperexcitability of locus coeruleus neurons seen during withdrawal (Kogan et al. 1992; Nestler 1992; Nestler et al. 1993) (Figure 27–4, bottom). This scheme is similar to one proposed earlier based on studies of neuroblastoma x glioma cells (Sharma et al. 1975). Although other mechanisms of opiate dependence in the locus coeruleus and elsewhere likely exist, manifestations of opiate dependence can be attributed directly to molecular and cellular adaptations in the cAMP pathway in specific neurons (Nestler and Aghajanian 1997). Related work suggests that similar types of adaptations underlie the long-term actions of opiates in other regions of the central nervous system (see, for example, Bonci and Williams 1997; Jolas et al. 2000; Terwilliger et al.1991; Tjon et al. 1994; Unterwald et al. 1993).

Alterations in the ability of opioid receptors to couple to G proteins also could contribute to opiate tolerance (Figure 27–5). For example, an upregulated cAMP system could enhance the degree of opioid receptor desensitization through phosphorylation of the receptor. By promoting desensitization, the upregulated cAMP system in the tolerant state could lead to a reduced ability of opiates to acutely activate G proteins, the $K^+$ channel, and the $Na^+$ current. Chronic opiate-induced alterations in β-adrenergic receptor kinases (βARKs)—more generally referred to as G protein–coupled receptor kinases (GRKs)—or other protein components of this system (e.g., the arrestins) could also be involved in tolerance. This possibility is based on the role of GRKs and arrestins in mediating ligand-induced desensitizations of opioid and other G protein–coupled receptors, which occurs independently of second messengers such as cAMP (see Lefkowitz 1998; Whistler et al. 1999). GRK-mediated desensitization is believed to occur via the following scheme: ligand binding to the receptor facilitates GRK phosphorylation of the receptor, which then triggers its binding to arrestin, thereby attenuating coupling of the receptor to its G protein. This process also probably stimulates receptor internalization via endocytosis. Still another potential mechanism of opioid receptor desensitization involves drug-induced adaptations in G proteins

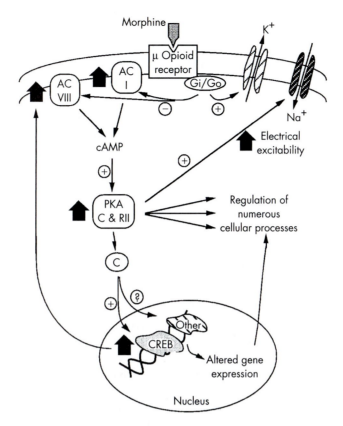

**FIGURE 27–4.** Schematic illustration of opiate actions in the locus coeruleus (LC). Opiates acutely inhibit LC neurons by increasing the conductance of an inwardly rectifying $K^+$ channel (*light crosshatch*) via coupling with subtypes of Gi and Go and by decreasing an $Na^+$-dependent inward current (*dark crosshatch*) via coupling with Gi and Go and the consequent inhibition of adenylyl cyclase. Reduced levels of cyclic adenosine monophosphate (cAMP) decrease protein kinase A (PKA) activity and the phosphorylation of the responsible channel or pump. Inhibition of the cAMP pathway also decreases phosphorylation of numerous other proteins and thereby affects many additional processes in the neuron. For example, it reduces the phosphorylation state of cAMP response element binding protein (CREB), which may initiate some of the longer-term changes in locus coeruleus function. Upward bold arrows summarize effects of long-term morphine use in the locus coeruleus. Long-term morphine use increases levels of types I and VIII adenylyl cyclase (AC), PKA catalytic (C) and regulatory type II (RII) subunits, and several phosphoproteins, including CREB. These changes contribute to the altered phenotype of the drug-addicted state. For example, the intrinsic excitability of LC neurons is increased via enhanced activity of the cAMP pathway and $Na^+$-dependent inward current, which contributes to the tolerance, dependence, and withdrawal exhibited by these neurons. Upregulation of type VIII adenylyl cyclase is mediated via CREB, whereas upregulation of type I adenylyl cyclase of the PKA subunits appears to occur via a CREB-independent mechanism not yet identified.
*Source.* Reprinted from Nestler EJ, Aghajanian GK: "Molecular and Cellular Basis of Addiction." Science 278:58–63, 1997. Used with permission.

themselves or in proteins that modulate the function of G proteins, such as the recently discovered family of regulators of G protein signaling (RGS) proteins (Potenza et al. 1999). Each of these mechanisms has been shown to operate in vitro, but the extent to which each contributes to opiate tolerance and dependence at the electrophysiological and behavioral levels is not yet known.

## Mechanisms Extrinsic to the Locus Coeruleus

In addition to the intrinsic factors discussed above, it is known that extrinsic factors also contribute to the dra-matic activation of locus coeruleus neurons that occurs during opiate withdrawal. The PGi, a region in the rostral medulla, provides a major excitatory input to the locus coeruleus (Ennis and Aston-Jones 1988), and lesions of this region partially attenuate withdrawal-induced activation of locus coeruleus neurons seen in vivo (Rasmussen and Aghajanian 1989). Administration of glutamate receptor antagonists into the cerebral ventricles or the locus coeruleus produces a similar effect (Akaoka and Aston-Jones 1991; Rasmussen and Aghajanian 1989), consistent with the view that the PGi input to the locus coeruleus is involved in driving locus coeruleus hyperactivity during withdrawal. Thus, it would appear that both

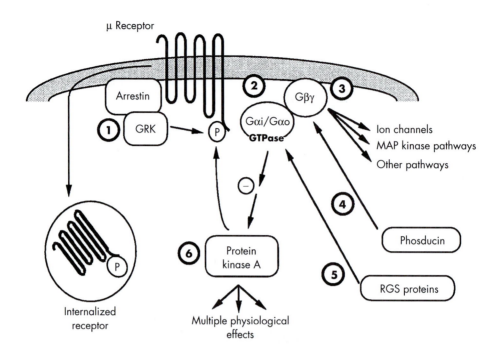

**FIGURE 27–5.** Schematic illustration of possible mechanisms of drug-induced changes in opioid receptor sensitivity. Drug-induced adaptations in the efficacy of receptor-Gi/Go coupling could contribute to aspects of drug tolerance or sensitization. One possible mechanism is adaptations in processes that mediate acute desensitization of receptor function, such as receptor phosphorylation by G protein–coupled receptor kinases (GRKs) (1). Other possible mechanisms include alterations in levels of G protein α (2) or βγ (3) subunits or of other proteins [for example, phosducin (4); regulators of G protein signaling (RGS) proteins (5)] that modulate G protein function. Phosphorylation of the receptor by protein kinase A could not mediate acute receptor desensitization (since receptor activation leads to inhibition of the kinase); however, upregulation of the kinase (6) after long-term drug administration (see Figure 27–2) could phosphorylate and regulate receptor function during withdrawal states. Also shown in the figure is agonist-induced receptor internalization, which may be mediated via receptor phosphorylation. MAP=mitogen-activated protein.

*Source.*   Reprinted from Nestler EJ, Aghajanian GK: "Molecular and Cellular Basis of Addiction." Science 278:58–63, 1997. Used with permission.

intrinsic and extrinsic factors contribute to the overall withdrawal activation of locus coeruleus neurons observed in vivo.

Of course, this leaves unanswered the resulting question, namely, the location and nature of the opiate-induced adaptations that underlie increased PGi activity in withdrawal. Such changes conceivably could occur in nerve terminals within the locus coeruleus that are derived from the PGi, in PGi cell bodies, or in any afferents that innervate the PGi (e.g., spinal regions). Chronic opiate-induced upregulation of the cAMP system, similar to that observed in the locus coeruleus, has been observed in dorsal root ganglion–spinal cord cultures and, in preliminary studies, in the PGi itself (see Nestler 1992). These findings raise the possibility that an upregulated cAMP system may contribute to opiate dependence in several neuronal cell types, which—through extrinsic inputs and intrinsic adaptations—add to the greatly increased firing rates of locus coeruleus neurons.

## Role of the Mesolimbic Dopamine System in Drug Reinforcement

A substantial body of literature has established the mesolimbic dopamine system as a major neural substrate for the reinforcing effects of opiates, psychostimulants, ethanol, nicotine, and cannabinoids in animals (see Dworkin and Smith 1993; Koob 1992; Kuhar et al. 1991; Olds 1982; Wise 1998). This system consists of dopaminergic neurons in the ventral tegmental area (VTA) of the midbrain and their target neurons in forebrain regions such as the nucleus accumbens (Figure 27–3). For example, rats will self-administer dopamine, amphetamine (which releases dopamine), and cocaine and nomifensine (which elevate dopamine levels by blocking reuptake) directly into the nucleus accumbens, suggesting that dopamine receptors in the nucleus accumbens mediate reinforcing stimuli. In contrast, opiates are self-administered directly into the dopamine cell body region of the VTA, where they activate dopamine neurons via disinhibitory mechanisms (see Johnson and North 1992) and thereby stimulate dopamine release in the nucleus accumbens. Other drugs of abuse, such as ethanol, nicotine, and cannabinoids, also cause increased dopamine release in the nucleus accumbens (Chen et al. 1990; Di Chiara and Imperato 1988), possibly through similar disinhibition of VTA dopamine neurons (Tanda et al. 1997). These findings have led some investigators to suggest that dopamine release in the nucleus accumbens is a final common mechanism in the acute reinforcing effects of opiates, psychostimulants, and other abused drugs.

However, there is evidence that opiates such as heroin and morphine can produce reinforcement independently of the dopamine system, by acting directly on opioid receptors in the nucleus accumbens and other brain regions (for review, see Bardo 1998). Dopamine antagonists and lesions of mesolimbic dopamine neurons, for example, fail to affect intravenous heroin self-administration. Animals also will self-administer opiates directly into the nucleus accumbens, where opioid receptors on nucleus accumbens neurons in essence bypass dopamine inputs. These data indicate that opiates can utilize both dopaminergic and nondopaminergic mechanisms in the nucleus accumbens to produce reinforcement of drug self-administration. Importantly, lesions of nucleus accumbens neurons attenuate both cocaine and heroin self-administration, suggesting that the nucleus accumbens is a critical neural substrate for both psychostimulant and opiate reinforcement.

## Neurobiological Mechanisms of Relapse

Whereas drug self-administration is thought to provide a measure of the acute reinforcing properties of a drug, it is quite different from drug craving and drug seeking, which are the core behavioral abnormalities that define a state of addiction. Drug craving and drug seeking are cognitive states that are measured by subjective reports in humans and cannot be directly measured in laboratory animals. However, relapse is an operational event that can be measured directly when a laboratory animal reinitiates lever-press responding after abstaining from drug self-administration. To measure relapse in an experimental setting, investigators first introduce extinction conditions to animals with drug self-administration experience, thereby attenuating reinforcement of further lever-press responding. As animals learn that the drug is no longer available, their efforts to self-administer the drug quickly diminish. After a given period of abstinence, the animals are presented with specific stimuli that induce responding at the lever that previously delivered drug injections. This reinitiation of responding is interpreted as relapse to drug-seeking behavior. The level of drug-seeking behavior is measured by the amount of effort (lever-pressing) exerted by the animals to self-administer the drug. Because these efforts are no longer reinforced by drug infusions, this behavior is also referred to as non-reinforced responding. In essence, this behavioral paradigm separates the incentive motivational component of drug reinforcement (drug seeking) from the consummatory component (drug taking) and is believed to measure changes in the motivational state of the animal in the absence of drug reinforcement.

Only three types of stimuli have been shown to induce relapse to drug-seeking behavior in animals. These stimuli consist of low doses of the drug that was previously self-administered (for a review, see Self and Nestler 1998; Shaham et al. 2000), drug-associated (conditioned) cues, and stress. Because all three of these stimuli also trigger drug craving in human drug abusers, relapse to drug-seeking behavior in animals may represent a valid model of drug craving. Moreover, given that measures of drug craving can be confounded by the subjective nature of self-reports in humans (Tiffany et al. 1993), animal models of relapse may offer a more direct and objective measure of relapse to drug seeking than human reports of drug craving.

## Drug-Induced Relapse to Drug-Seeking Behavior

A powerful trigger of relapse in animal models is a low "priming" injection with the drug that was self-administered by the animal on previous occasions (see Self and Nestler 1998; Shaham et al. 2000). This priming effect has been demonstrated for both opiates and psychostimulants. Interestingly, opiates such as morphine can trigger relapse to cocaine-seeking behavior (De Wit and Stewart 1981; Slikker et al. 1984), and vice versa (De Wit and Stewart 1983). Such "cross-priming" may reflect activation of a common neural substrate, perhaps the common ability of these drugs to activate the mesolimbic dopamine system.

Indeed, considerable evidence suggests that relapse triggered by priming injections of opiates and psychostimulants is mediated by the mesolimbic dopamine system. For example, microinfusion of amphetamine directly into the nucleus accumbens, where it causes local dopamine release, effectively induces relapse to heroin-seeking behavior (Stewart and Vezina 1988). Conversely, microinfusion of morphine into the VTA, which indirectly activates dopamine neurons and consequently increases dopamine release in the nucleus accumbens, induces relapse to heroin- and cocaine-seeking behavior (Stewart et al. 1984). In contrast, microinfusion of morphine into other brain regions rich in opioid receptors is ineffective at inducing relapse to drug-seeking behavior. Dopaminergic involvement in drug-induced relapse is bolstered by the fact that several directly acting dopaminergic agonists are powerful inducers of relapse to both cocaine- and heroin-seeking behavior (De Wit and Stewart 1983; Self et al. 1996; Wise et al. 1990), whereas dopamine antagonists can block the priming effects of heroin, amphetamine, and cocaine (Ettenberg 1990; Shaham and Stewart 1996; Weissenborn et al. 1996). Taken together, these studies suggest that dopamine release in the nucleus accumbens is both necessary and sufficient for inducing relapse to opiate- and psychostimulant-seeking behavior that is elicited by priming injections of the drugs (Figure 27–6).

## Cue-Induced Relapse to Drug-Seeking Behavior

Cue-induced relapse to drug-seeking behavior involves the process of classical conditioning, whereby environmental stimuli, through repeated and specific association with drug exposure, acquire the ability to trigger relapse when presented in the absence of the drug (e.g., Ehrman et al. 1992; O'Brien et al. 1992; Robinson and Berridge 1993). The fact that these drug-associated cues can trigger appetitive or approach behavior has led investigators to hypothesize that these stimuli also activate the mesolimbic dopamine system (Robinson and Berridge 1993; Stewart et al. 1984; Wise 1998). At present, this hypothesis remains equivocal because the conditioned behavioral effects of drugs such as cocaine are not necessarily associated with an increase in dopamine release in the nucleus accumbens (Brown and Fibiger 1992). However, at least two studies have reported enhanced dopamine release in the nucleus accumbens following presentation of drug-associated cues (Di Ciano et al. 1998; Fontana et al. 1993). In addition, others have found that presentation of cues associated with food rewards do in fact activate dopamine neurons in the VTA and elicit food-seeking behavior (Mirenowicz and Schultz 1996). Although elusive, the question of dopamine involvement in conditioned drug effects is crucial to our understanding of how drug-associated cues gain access to appetitive motivational systems in the brain to trigger relapse.

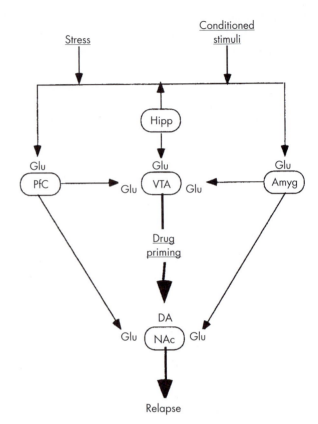

**FIGURE 27–6.** Schematic representation of the primary pathways through which stress, drugs of abuse, and drug-associated conditioned stimuli are hypothesized to trigger drug craving and relapse to drug seeking. Stress and conditioned stimuli can activate excitatory glutamatergic projections (Glu) to the ventral tegmental area (VTA) from the prefrontal cortex (PfC), amygdala (Amyg), and hippocampus (Hipp), whereas priming injections of drugs directly stimulate dopamine (DA) release in the nucleus accumbens (NAc). In this sense, dopamine release in the nucleus accumbens may be a final common trigger of drug craving by all three stimuli. At the level of nucleus accumbens neurons, dopamine from the VTA modulates direct excitatory signals from the prefrontal cortex, amygdala, and hippocampus, where complex spatiotemporal integration of relapse-related information occurs. Studies showing involvement of these brain regions in relapse to drug seeking suggest that long-term changes in gene expression in these regions would alter the functionality of this circuitry and could produce profound changes in reactivity to stimuli that trigger drug craving and relapse to drug seeking.

Growing evidence implicates the amygdala as a critical substrate for cue-induced relapse to drug-seeking behavior. For example, lesions of the amygdala attenuate the ability of drug-associated cues to induce relapse (Meil and See 1997). Cue-induced relapse is attenuated even when the lesions are produced after learned associations between cues and drugs have already formed, which suggests that conditioned cues utilize the amygdala to access and activate appetitive motivational systems. In this regard, projections from the amygdala are known to activate VTA dopamine neurons through both monosynaptic and polysynaptic pathways, presumably leading to increased dopaminergic transmission in the nucleus accumbens. Figure 27–6 illustrates this pathway whereby drug-associated cues can activate the mesolimbic dopamine system via known excitatory (glutamatergic) inputs from the amygdala. Also illustrated is an amygdala projection to the prefrontal cortex, which could form a secondary pathway whereby drug-associated cues activate VTA dopamine neurons.

## Stress-Induced Relapse to Drug-Seeking Behavior

Psychological stress can also trigger drug craving in humans and relapse to drug seeking in animals. In animals, stress-induced relapse is triggered after a brief period of mild intermittent footshock. Presentation of this stress effectively induces relapse to both cocaine- and heroin-seeking behavior (Ahmed and Koob 1997; Erb et al. 1996; Shaham and Stewart 1995). Interestingly, stress-induced relapse to heroin-seeking behavior is equally effective whether animals are physically dependent on heroin or not (Shaham et al. 1996). Similar to drug- and cue-induced relapse, stress-induced relapse also may involve activation of the mesolimbic dopamine system. This idea is supported by the finding that stress-induced dopamine release in the nucleus accumbens correlates temporally with relapse to heroin-seeking behavior (Shaham and Stewart 1995). Moreover, stress-induced relapse is partially attenuated by pretreatment with dopamine antagonists (Shaham and Stewart 1996). A primary neural pathway through which stress can stimulate dopamine release in the nucleus accumbens may involve stress-induced activation of the prefrontal cortex (Karreman and Moghaddam 1996; Moghaddam 1993; Taber et al. 1995) and, consequently, activation of an excitatory projection from the prefrontal cortex to dopamine neurons in the VTA (Figure 27–6).

Another pathway by which stress can activate the mesolimbic dopamine system involves the ability of stress to stimulate release of the neuropeptide corticotropin-releasing factor (CRF). Infusion of CRF into the cerebral ventricles mimics the effects of stress in inducing relapse to heroin-seeking behavior, and similar infusions of a CRF antagonist reduce stress-induced relapse (Shaham et al. 1997). Because CRF can activate central dopamine systems (e.g., via the hypothalamic-pituitary-adrenal axis and corticosterone secretion [Overton et al.

1996; Piazza et al. 1996]), CRF-induced relapse may also involve activation of the mesolimbic dopamine system. Indeed, systemic injections of corticosterone can induce relapse to cocaine-seeking behavior (Deroche et al. 1997). However, because stress can trigger relapse in adrenalectomized animals (Shaham et al. 1997), and stress-induced relapse is associated with relatively small increases in dopamine release in the nucleus accumbens (Shaham et al. 1996), stress-induced relapse likely involves corticosterone- and dopamine-independent mechanisms as well.

Clearly, the effects of stress, cues, and drugs themselves on the mesolimbic dopamine system resemble druglike, or proponent, processes. In contrast, drug opposite or withdrawal-like processes fail to induce relapse to drug-seeking behavior in animal models. For example, precipitation of opiate withdrawal with naltrexone fails to induce relapse in animals with heroin self-administration experience, even when the animals are markedly physically dependent on the opiate (Shaham et al. 1996). Similarly, blockade of dopamine receptors with dopamine antagonists fails to induce heroin- or cocaine-seeking behavior (Shaham and Stewart 1996; Weissenborn et al. 1996), despite their ability to produce aversive consequences. Although these data contrast sharply with human studies in which drug craving is associated with negative emotionality during opiate and ethanol withdrawal, they agree with reports of druglike, and even mood-elevating, symptoms of craving in cocaine addicts (Childress et al. 1988; Robbins et al. 1997).

Even though naltrexone-precipitated withdrawal fails to trigger relapse to heroin-seeking behavior in animals, spontaneous withdrawal from heroin has been associated with relapse in the same models (Shaham et al. 1996). This finding may be relevant to factors involved in maintaining daily drug use in active drug abusers. In this sense, dependence and withdrawal may play a more prominent role in drug craving during active drug use, whereas druglike processes (e.g., sensitization) may be more important in triggering drug craving and relapse after prolonged periods of abstinence, when withdrawal symptoms are no longer apparent.

Although it has not been clearly resolved, cue- and stress-induced reinstatement of drug-seeking behavior also may involve dopamine-independent neural substrates (reviewed in Self 1998). Thus, the basolateral and central nuclei of the amygdala, as well as the prefrontal cortex and hippocampus, send direct excitatory projections to the nucleus accumbens in addition to the VTA. Excitatory inputs from these regions converge with VTA dopamine inputs at the level of nucleus accumbens neurons, where excitatory transmission in the nucleus accumbens has been implicated in relapse to cocaine-seeking behavior (Cornish and Kalivas 2000). Together, these brain regions all form a complex circuit with primary sites of convergence in both the VTA and the nucleus accumbens of the mesolimbic dopamine system, as depicted in Figure 27–6. Given the central role of the nucleus accumbens in the output of these circuits, regulation of nucleus accumbens neuronal activity, whether by dopamine or glutamate, may be a critical event in triggering drug craving.

## Mechanisms of Dopamine-Induced Relapse

The studies described in the preceding sections suggest that relapse to drug seeking can be triggered by activation of dopamine receptors on nucleus accumbens neurons. Dopamine receptors are divided into two general classes that are distinguishable by their structural properties and opposite modulation of adenylyl cyclase. The $D_1$-like receptors ($D_1$ and $D_5$) are positively coupled to adenylyl cyclase activity, whereas the $D_2$-like receptors ($D_2$, $D_3$, and $D_4$) are either negatively coupled or have no detectable effect on the enzyme. The two receptor classes also exert opposite effects on phosphatidylinositol turnover. Neurons intrinsic to the nucleus accumbens express both $D_1$-like and $D_2$-like dopamine receptors, but in somewhat different neuronal populations (Curran and Watson 1995; Meador-Woodruff et al. 1991). In most cases, these receptors produce similar, even synergistic, responses at the physiologic and behavioral levels (Waddington and Daly 1993, Hu and White 1994).

In contrast to these cooperative actions, activation of $D_2$-like, but not of $D_1$-like, dopamine receptors induces a profound and prolonged relapse to cocaine-seeking behavior in rats (De Vries et al. 1999; Self et al. 1996). These findings suggest that $D_2$-like receptors are primarily involved in inducing drug-seeking behavior by priming stimuli that release dopamine in the nucleus accumbens. Although selective activation of $D_1$-like receptors fails to markedly induce cocaine-seeking behavior, $D_1$ receptors may have a permissive role in the priming effects mediated by $D_2$ receptors, as both $D_1$ and $D_2$ receptor antagonists can block the priming effects of cocaine and heroin (Shaham and Stewart 1996; Weissenborn et al. 1996). Thus, transmission of $D_2$-mediated priming signals may require some minimal level of $D_1$ receptor activation. Interestingly, however, $D_1$-like receptor activation completely abolishes the ability of cocaine to induce relapse (Self et al. 1996). The opposing influence of $D_1$-like and $D_2$-like dopamine receptor activation on relapse to cocaine-seeking behavior is intriguing, because both $D_1$ and $D_2$ receptor agonists have reinforcing properties, have similar abilities to mimic the subjective effects of cocaine, and stimulate locomotor activity. One possible explanation for these findings is that $D_2$-like receptors mediate the incentive to seek further drug reinforcement, whereas $D_1$-like receptors could mediate some aspect of drug reward related to gratification, drive reduction, or satiety.

Opposite modulation of drug-seeking behavior by $D_1$ and $D_2$ dopamine receptors could involve their opposite effects on cAMP formation. In this regard, microinfusion of a selective inhibitor of protein kinase A into the nucleus accumbens triggers relapse to cocaine-seeking behavior and potentiates cocaine-induced relapse to cocaine-seeking behavior in rats (Self et al. 1998). The effect of the protein kinase inhibitor resembles the effect of $D_2$ receptor stimulation, suggesting that dopamine triggers relapse by stimulating $D_2$ receptors that function via inhibition of protein kinase A activity. In any event, these findings suggest that protein kinase A activity in certain nucleus accumbens neurons could play a pivotal role in regulating incentive motivation during drug craving and relapse.

## Adaptations in the Mesolimbic Dopamine System After Long-Term Drug Exposure

Although symptoms of physical withdrawal from opiates and other drugs typically persist for short periods of time after cessation of long-term drug exposure, drug addicts report intense drug craving long after these physical symptoms have subsided. This suggests that different brain regions mediate physical and motivational symptoms of drug dependence, a view supported by direct experimental evidence (e.g., Koob et al. 1992). The motivational symptoms, which include an escalation of drug intake (tolerance), increased drug craving (sensitization), and withdrawal-induced dysphoria (dependence), could result from drug-induced adaptations in the normal functioning of reinforcement-related brain regions, such as the VTA and nucleus accumbens. Recent studies have found that long-term drug exposure produces adaptations at the molecular and cellular levels in VTA dopamine neurons, and in their target neurons in the nucleus accumbens, that may underlie motivational aspects of tolerance, sensitization, and dependence associated with drug addiction (e.g., see Nestler and Aghajanian 1997; Self 1998; Self and Nestler 1998; White and Kalivas 1998; M.E. Wolf 1998). The results from these studies provide the basis for specific hypotheses that now guide future investigations to test, more directly, the role of specific adaptations in mediating drug craving in addicted subjects.

The ability of various drugs of abuse to produce similar types of changes in drug-taking and drug-seeking behavior after repeated administration raises the possibility that these drugs also produce similar types of molecular and cellular adaptations in specific brain regions. Support for this possibility comes from behavioral data, in which long-term exposure to stimulants, opiates, or ethanol can cross-sensitize the animal to the effects of the other drugs (e.g., Cunningham and Kelley 1992; Fahlke et al. 1994; Vezina and Stewart 1990). As demonstrated below, there is also now considerable biochemical evidence that different drugs of abuse can produce similar molecular adaptations in the VTA–nucleus accumbens pathway after long-term administration. These adaptations may be part of a common general mechanism of drug addiction and craving (Figure 27–7).

## Regulation of Dopamine in the Ventral Tegmental Area–Nucleus Accumbens Pathway

A widely held view is that repeated exposure to a drug of abuse may produce some of its behavioral effects, for example drug craving or locomotor sensitization, by facilitating drug-induced dopamine release in the nucleus accumbens. This possibility is best established for stimulants and opiates, which can result in augmented synaptic levels of dopamine as measured by in vivo microdialysis, under some experimental conditions. However, the large body of literature on this subject is inconsistent and confusing overall, given that these drugs have been reported to both increase and decrease synaptic levels of dopamine depending on the drug-treatment regimen employed and the time of withdrawal studied (for references, see Kalivas and Nakamura 1999; Robinson and Berridge 1993; Self and Nestler 1995; Spanagel and Weiss 1999; White and Kalivas 1998; M.E. Wolf 1998). Although altered regulation of dopamine release in the nucleus accumbens or other brain regions is one likely mechanism underlying aspects of long-term drug exposure, its precise role remains uncertain.

It also has been difficult to identify the precise molecular targets of drugs of abuse that mediate the altered synaptic levels of dopamine observed. Long-term exposure to cocaine upregulates dopamine reuptake transporter proteins specifically in the mesolimbic dopamine system during late phases of withdrawal from the

drug (Pilotte 1997). By increasing dopamine reuptake at the synapse, this molecular change would be expected to reduce synaptic levels of dopamine in the VTA–nucleus accumbens pathway. Long-term exposure to opiates, cocaine, amphetamine, or ethanol has been shown to increase levels of tyrosine hydroxylase in the VTA but to reduce the total amount and phosphorylation state (and hence the enzymatic activity) of the enzyme in the nucleus accumbens during early phases of withdrawal (Nestler 1992; Ortiz et al. 1995; Schmidt et al. 2001). Decreases in tyrosine hydroxylase activity in the nucleus accumbens and increases in presynaptic dopamine reuptake could contribute to the reductions in basal extracellular dopamine levels and anhedonia seen during withdrawal (see Koob and Le Moal 1997).

## Regulation of Opioid and Dopamine Receptors in the Ventral Tegmental Area and Nucleus Accumbens

It also has been proposed that altered levels of various opioid, dopamine, or other neurotransmitter receptors in the mesolimbic dopamine system could mediate some of the long-term effects of drugs of abuse on this neural pathway. The literature on this subject, although vast, is unsatisfying. In general it has been difficult to establish altered levels of opioid receptors in the VTA and nucleus accumbens or any other brain regions in response to long-term opiate treatment, although $\mu$ and $\kappa$ receptors are reported to be upregulated by long-term cocaine treatment (Unterwald et al. 1994). There have also been numerous reports of stimulant regulation of dopamine receptors in specific brain regions. Although conflicting data exist, most studies have found reductions in $D_1$ and $D_2$ receptors in the nucleus accumbens in early withdrawal from self-administration or binge-like administration of cocaine. An in vivo positron emission tomographic study in rats found reductions in $D_1$ receptor binding that were mainly attributable to a reduced receptor affinity (Tsukada et al. 1996). In contrast, long-term self-administration or binge-like administration of cocaine is reportedly associated with a reduction in $D_1$ and $D_2$ receptor numbers in the nucleus accumbens and with a reduction in maximal $D_1$-stimulated adenylyl cyclase activity (De Montis et al. 1998; Maggos et al. 1998; Moore et al. 1998), consistent with receptor downregulation. These findings in laboratory animals are consistent with observations in human cocaine addicts, in whom decreases in $D_2$ receptor binding have been documented by brain imaging (Volkow et al. 1999).

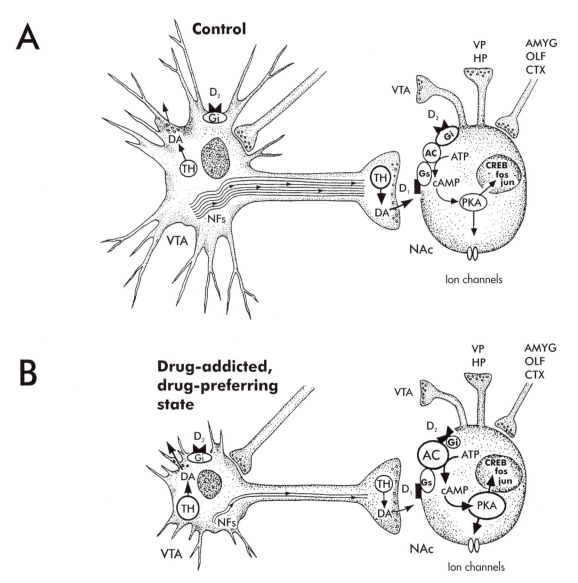

**FIGURE 27–7.** Schematic summary of similar biochemical manifestations hypothesized to be associated with the drug-addicted state. *Panel A.* A normal ventral tegmental area (VTA) neuron projecting to a nucleus accumbens (NAc) neuron. Shown in the VTA neuron are tyrosine hydroxylase (TH), dopamine (DA), presynaptic dopamine receptors ($D_2$) coupled to G proteins (Gi), and neurofilaments (NFs). Shown in the nucleus accumbens neuron are dopamine receptors ($D_1$ and $D_2$), G proteins (Gi and Gs), components of the intracellular cyclic adenosine monophosphate (cAMP) system (adenylyl cyclase [AC], cAMP-dependent protein kinase A [PKA], and possible substrates for the kinase-ion channels and the nuclear transcription factors CREB, fos, and jun), as well as major inputs and outputs of this region (ventral pallidum [VP], hippocampus [HP], amygdala [AMYG], olfactory cortex [OLF], other cortical regions [CTX]). *Panel B.* A VTA neuron projecting to the nucleus accumbens after long-term morphine, cocaine, or alcohol treatment. In the drug-addicted animal, TH levels are increased in the VTA and decreased in the nucleus accumbens, and neurofilament levels are decreased in the VTA. This decrease in neurofilaments may be associated with alterations in neuronal structure, decreases in axonal caliber, and/ or decreases in axonal transport in these cells. Such changes, which have been demonstrated in the case of morphine, may account for the lack of correspondingly increased levels of TH in dopaminergic terminals in the nucleus accumbens. Decreased TH levels may imply decreased dopamine synthesis and may result in reduced dopaminergic transmission to the nucleus accumbens. In the nucleus accumbens of the drug-addicted animal, Gi is decreased and adenylyl cyclase and protein kinase A activities are increased, changes that could account for $D_1$-receptor supersensitivity observed electrophysiologically. A similar pattern of biochemical differences in the VTA and nucleus accumbens is seen in some inbred rodent strains that appear to show increased inherent preference for drugs of abuse (see Nestler 1992).

*Source.*   Reprinted from Beitner-Johnson D, Guitart X, Nestler EJ: "Common Intracellular Actions of Chronic Morphine and Chronic Cocaine in Dopaminergic Brain Reward Regions. *Annals of the New York Academy of Sciences* 654:70–87, 1992a. Used with permission.

The various changes seen at the receptor level cannot, however, explain consistent effects of stimulants on dopamine receptor function, which have been well documented in recent years. Electrophysiological studies have shown that long-term exposure to cocaine or other stimulants causes transient subsensitivity of $D_2$-like autoreceptors in the VTA as well as longer-lasting supersensitivity to the effects of $D_1$-like receptor activation in the nucleus accumbens at later withdrawal times (see White and Kalivas 1998; M.E. Wolf 1998). These changes in dopamine receptor function in both the VTA and the nucleus accumbens are not accompanied by corresponding changes in dopamine receptor levels, which suggests that they are mediated via adaptations in postreceptor, intracellular signaling pathways.

## Role of Glutamatergic Systems in Long-Term Drug Action

Adaptations in glutamatergic systems have gained significant attention because of their prominent interactions with central dopamine function and their reported role in locomotor sensitization (see Kalivas and Nakamura 1999; White and Kalivas 1998; M.E. Wolf 1998). Specifically, glutamate receptor antagonists can block the development of locomotor sensitization to stimulants and opiates as well as the electrophysiological perturbations in mesolimbic dopamine function that accompany repeated stimulant exposure. Repeated stimulant exposure has been shown to increase the electrophysiological responsiveness of VTA dopamine neurons to glutamate and to decrease the responsiveness of nucleus accumbens neurons to glutamate (White et al. 1995). Supersensitivity of VTA dopamine neurons to glutamate could be mediated via upregulation of specific glutamate receptor subunits in this region, specifically GluR1, which has been seen after long-term administration of cocaine, opiates, or ethanol (Carlezon et al. 1997; Fitzgerald et al. 1996). Altered levels of glutamate receptor subunits in the nucleus accumbens are more variable, with both increases in late withdrawal (Churchill et al. 1999) and decreases in early withdrawal (Lu and Wolf 1999) reported.

## Regulation of G Proteins and the cAMP Pathway in the Ventral Tegmental Area and Nucleus Accumbens

Repeated cocaine treatment produces transient decreases in the level of inhibitory G protein subunits, Gi and Go, that couple to $D_2$ autoreceptors in the VTA (Nestler 1992; Striplin and Kalivas 1992). The level of these G proteins in the VTA is negatively correlated with the initial level of locomotor activation produced by cocaine (Striplin and Kalivas 1992). In addition, pertussis toxin injected directly into the VTA, which functionally inactivate these G proteins, increases the locomotor activating effects of cocaine and thereby mimics locomotor sensitization. Together, these findings support the possibility that reduced levels of Gi and Go could account for the $D_2$ receptor subsensitivity observed electrophysiologically after long-term cocaine exposure and may play a role in some of the long-term effects of cocaine on mesolimbic dopamine function.

Repeated cocaine treatment also decreases levels of Gi and Go in the nucleus accumbens (Nestler 1992; Striplin and Kalivas 1993) and increases levels of adenylyl cyclase and of cAMP-dependent protein kinase in this brain region (Terwilliger et al. 1991). Together, these changes would be expected to result in a concerted upregulation in the functional activity of the cAMP pathway. Because $D_1$ receptors are generally thought to produce their effects via activation of the cAMP pathway, these molecular adaptations could account for $D_1$ receptor supersensitivity observed during later withdrawal times. Long-term exposure to morphine, cocaine, heroin, or ethanol—but not to several drugs without reinforcing properties—produces similar changes in G proteins and the cAMP pathway (Ortiz et al. 1995; Self et al. 1995; Terwilliger et al. 1991). Although the long-term effects of morphine and ethanol on the electrophysiological state of nucleus accumbens neurons have not yet been investigated, the biochemical findings suggest that an upregulated cAMP pathway may be part of a common mechanism of altered nucleus accumbens function associated with the drug-treated state (see Figure 27–7). A critical question regarding these neuroadaptations is whether they contribute to changes in drug self-administration habits and to drug craving and relapse during abstinence.

We tested the former possibility by artificially upregulating the cAMP pathway in the nucleus accumbens of animals during drug self-administration tests (Self et al. 1994, 1998). In these studies, escalation of drug self-administration is produced by inactivation of inhibitory G proteins with pertussis toxin or by sustained protein kinase A activity after microinfusion of a membrane-permeable cAMP analog into the nucleus accumbens. Artificially mimicking the drug-induced neuroadaptations by sustained downregulation of inhibitory G proteins or by sustained increases in protein kinase A activity produces increases in drug-self-administration. This effect is usually interpreted as a reduction in drug reward, with animals compensating by increasing their drug intake. These findings suggest that neuroadaptations in the nucleus accumbens–cAMP pathway caused by repeated drug use may represent an intracellular mechanism of tolerance to the rewarding effects of drugs, which leads to escalating drug intake during drug self-administration. One possible mechanism for such tolerance may involve protein kinase A–mediated phosphorylation, desensitization, and down-regulation of $D_1$ receptors (see Sibley et al. 1998). On the other hand, activation of the cAMP pathway in the nucleus accumbens was shown to produce an enhancement of conditioned reinforcement produced by cues associated with food reward (Kelley and Holahan 1997). This suggests that upregulation of the cAMP pathway in the nucleus accumbens may potentiate the incentive motivational effects of reward-associated cues, and possibly their ability to elicit craving. Further work is needed to study this latter hypothesis.

## Evidence for Structural Changes in the Ventral Tegmental Area–Nucleus Accumbens Pathway

Although changes in levels of signal transduction proteins could mediate some of the long-term actions of drugs of abuse, they are unlikely to be responsible for the extremely long-lived adaptations that characterize an addicted state. One hypothesis is that adaptations in signaling pathways may cause longer-lasting structural changes in neurons. Several examples of such changes have been documented in recent years.

Long-term administration of morphine, for example, has been shown to decrease the size of VTA dopamine neurons as well as the caliber of their proximal processes (Sklair-Tavron et al. 1996). This is depicted in Figure 27–7. Morphine also causes a reduction in axoplasmic transport from the VTA to the nucleus accumbens (see Nestler 1992). These findings may be related to the observation that long-term morphine use decreases levels of neurofilament proteins in this brain region, an effect also seen after long-term cocaine or ethanol exposure (Beitner-Johnson et al. 1992b; Nestler 1992; Ortiz et al. 1995). The observed decrease in axonal transport rates could decrease the amount of tyrosine hydroxylase transported from dopamine cell bodies in the VTA to nerve terminals in the nucleus accumbens. At a constant rate of tyrosine hydroxylase synthesis, this would tend to lead to the buildup of tyrosine hydroxylase observed in the VTA (see above) and to decreased levels of enzyme in the nucleus accumbens. Such decreased levels of tyrosine hydroxylase, along with its reduced phosphorylation,

have been reported (Nestler 1992; Schmidt et al. 2001; Self et al. 1995). Decreases in tyrosine hydroxylase in the nucleus accumbens could explain the short-term reductions in levels of basal and stimulated dopamine release during early phases of drug withdrawal (see above).

Long-term morphine, cocaine, or ethanol treatment also increases levels of glial fibrillary acidic protein (GFAP), specifically in the VTA (Beitner-Johnson et al. 1993; Ortiz et al. 1995). Drug-induced decreases in neurofilament proteins and increases in glial filament proteins in the VTA are reminiscent of neural insult or injury (see Figure 27–7). Such findings raised the possibility that perturbations in neurotrophic factor signaling are involved in long-term drug action. Indeed, direct infusion of any of several neurotrophic factors into the VTA has been shown to oppose the ability of long-term drug exposure to produce some of its characteristic biochemical and morphologic changes in the VTA (Berhow et al. 1995; Messer et al. 2000; Sklair-Tavron et al. 1996). Such infusions of neurotrophic factors also potently modify behavioral responses to drug exposure (Horger et al. 1999; Pierce et al. 1999). Of particular interest are the abnormal biochemical and behavioral responses to drugs of abuse in mice lacking brain-derived neurotrophic factor (BDNF) or glial cell line–derived neurotrophic factor (GDNF) and the alterations in certain neurotrophic factor signaling proteins after long-term drug exposure (Horger et al. 1999; Messer et al. 2000; D.H. Wolf et al. 1999). Together, these results indicate not only that exogenous neurotrophic factors can modify responses to drugs of abuse, but also that endogenous neurotrophic factor pathways are involved in mediating some of the long-term effects of drug exposure on the brain.

Drugs of abuse also cause structural changes in the medium spiny neurons of the nucleus accumbens. Long-term administration of cocaine or amphetamine increases the dendritic arborizations of these neurons as well as the density of their terminal dendritic spines (Robinson and Kolb 1997). Similar changes have been found for pyramidal neurons in the prefrontal cortex. In contrast, long-term morphine administration causes the opposite changes in dendritic structure in the nucleus accumbens (Robinson and Kolb 1999). Because alterations in dendritic spines are implicated in controlling the efficacy of synaptic transmission in other regions of brain, the observed drug-induced changes in the nucleus accumbens represent an attractive mechanism by which long-term drug exposure might produce very long-lived changes in nucleus accumbens function and, hence, motivational processes.

## Molecular Mechanisms Underlying Drug-Induced Adaptations in the Nucleus Accumbens

The precise mechanisms by which long-term drug treatment alters levels of specific proteins in the VTA–nucleus accumbens pathway are still unknown, but there are now many studies that show that gene expression can be regulated by drug exposure (see Nestler 1992; Nestler et al. 1993). Such studies have focused on the role played by two families of transcription factors (shown in Figure 27–8): CREB and CREB-like proteins and the products of certain immediate early genes (IEGs), such as the Fos and Jun family proteins (see Nestler 2001). Fos and Jun proteins form heterodimeric complexes that bind to specific DNA sequences referred to as activator protein 1 (AP-1) sites to regulate transcription of a target gene. Most genes likely contain numerous response elements for these and many other transcription factors, suggesting that complex interactions and multiple mechanisms control the expression of a given gene.

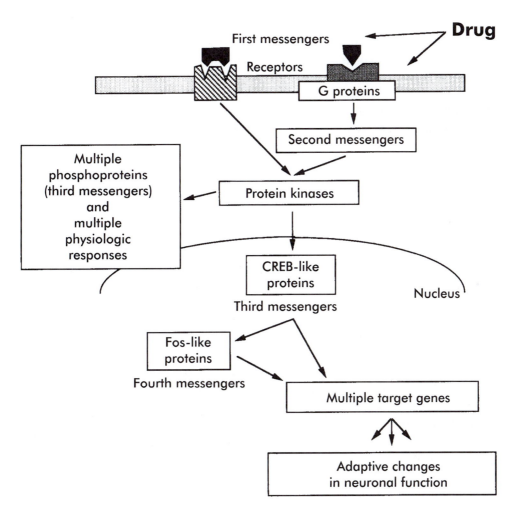

**FIGURE 27–8.** Schematic illustration of the hypothetical role played by gene expression in drug addiction. According to this scheme, an initial extracellular effect of a drug of abuse would trigger changes in multiple intracellular messenger pathways in target neurons. Changes in the intracellular messengers would result in numerous physiologic responses to the drug (as shown in Figure 27–2), including alterations in gene expression. The latter types of alterations would occur through the regulation of many classes of nuclear, DNA-binding proteins termed transcription factors, such as CREB and Fos. CREB exemplifies a transcription factor that is regulated by extracellular agents primarily through changes in its degree of phosphorylation. Fos exemplifies a transcription factor that is expressed at very low levels under basal conditions and is regulated by extracellular agents primarily through induction of its expression (in some cases via CREB). Both types of transcription factors would then result in altered levels of expression of specific target proteins that underlie the adaptive changes in brain function associated with addiction.

Short-term administration of cocaine or amphetamine increases the expression of several Fos and Jun family members and increases AP-1 binding activity in the nucleus accumbens and striatum (for references, see Nestler et al. 1993). One possible mechanism of cocaine action is that the drug induces c-Fos via dopamine activation of $D_1$ receptors and the subsequent activation of the cAMP pathway. These drugs also induce Egr1 (also known as Zif268) in these brain regions. Egr1 is a transcription factor that binds to a distinct response element but is regulated as an IEG product in a fashion similar to Fos- and Jun-like proteins (O'Donovan et al. 1999). Other drugs of abuse also induce these various IEGs in the nucleus accumbens and striatum.

The ability to induce c-Fos and the other IEG products in the nucleus accumbens is attenuated on repeated cocaine treatment, whereas the increased AP-1 binding activity persists for weeks after drug treatment ceases (Daunais and McGinty 1994; Hope et al. 1992). We now know that this persistent AP-1 binding activity is caused by the long-lived expression of biochemically modified isoforms of ΔFosB, a member of the Fos family of transcription factors. ΔFosB persists in the brain for a long time due to its extraordinary stability, and it could represent a type of sustained molecular switch that contributes to prolonged aspects of cocaine addiction (Figure 27–9). Similar induction of ΔFosB is seen after long-term (but not after short-term) administration of opiates, nicotine, and phencyclidine (Atkins et al. 1999; Nye and Nestler 1996; Pich et al. 1997). Recent studies of transgenic mice in which ΔFosB can be induced in adult animals selectively within the nucleus accumbens and striatum (Kelz et al. 1999) demonstrated that ΔFosB expression increases an animal's sensitivity to the rewarding and locomotor-activating effects of cocaine. These behavioral changes appear to be mediated, at least in part, via ΔFosB-induced increases in levels of the α-amino-3-hydroxy-5-methyl-4-isoxalone propionic acid (AMPA) glutamate receptor subunit GluR2 within nucleus accumbens neurons. This study provides a causal link between long-term induction of ΔFosB and sensitization to repeated drug treatment.

Because long-term cocaine and morphine treatments upregulate the cAMP pathway in the nucleus accumbens, the CREB family of transcription factors are also likely influenced by these drugs. Indeed, long-term drug treatments regulate CREB phosphorylation or immunoreactivity in this brain region (Cole et al. 1995; Widnell et al. 1996). By use of viral-mediated gene transfer, it has been shown that increases in CREB levels in the nucleus accumbens decrease an animal's sensitivity to the rewarding effects of cocaine, whereas inactivation of

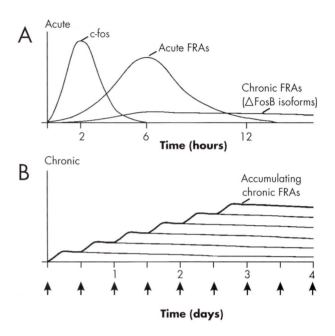

**FIGURE 27–9.** Scheme for the gradual accumulation of ΔFosB (also called chronic Fos-related antigens [FRAs]) versus the rapid and transient induction of acute FRAs in the brain. *Panel A.* Several waves of FRAs are induced in neurons by many acute stimuli. c-Fos is induced rapidly and degrades within several hours of the acute stimulus, whereas other "acute FRAs" (e.g., FosB, FRA-1, and FRA-2) are induced somewhat later and persist somewhat longer than c-Fos. The chronic FRAs are biochemically modified forms of ΔFosB; they, too, are induced (although at low levels) after a single acute stimulus but persist in the brain for long periods (with a half-life longer than 1 week). In a complex with Jun-like proteins, these waves of FRAs form activator protein 1 (AP-1)–binding complexes with shifting composition over time. *Panel B.* With repeated (e.g., twice daily) stimulation, each acute stimulus induces a low level of ΔFosB. This is indicated by the lower set of overlapping lines, which indicate ΔFosB induced by each acute stimulus. The result is a gradual increase in the total levels of ΔFosB with repeated stimuli during a course of long-term treatment. This is indicated by the increasing stepped line in the graph. The increasing levels of ΔFosB with repeated stimulation would result in the gradual induction of significant levels of a long-lasting AP-1 complex, which could underlie persisting forms of neural plasticity in the brain.
*Source.* Adapted from Hope et al. 1994.

CREB has the opposite effect (Carlezon et al. 1998). The effects of CREB are mediated in part by the opioid peptide dynorphin, which is increased by CREB and decreased on inactivation of CREB. Dynorphin acts on κ opioid receptors within the nucleus accumbens and VTA to produce aversive effects. Thus, activation of CREB, and the resulting induction of dynorphin, in response to long-term drug exposure would appear to represent a mechanism of tolerance to drug reward as well as dysphoria during drug withdrawal (dependence).

Current research is focused on identifying additional target genes for CREB and for ΔFosB and on identifying additional transcriptional control mechanisms that mediate the long-term actions of drugs of abuse on the mesolimbic dopamine system.

## Conclusions

The availability of animal models that accurately reproduce important features of drug addiction in humans has made it possible to identify specific regions in the brain that play an important role in addictive disorders. Whereas the locus coeruleus plays an important role in physical dependence on opiates, it is the mesolimbic dopamine system as well as regions of the prefrontal cortex and amygdala that appear to be integrally involved in drug-seeking behavior, the essential clinical feature of drug addiction. Basic neurobiological investigations are now providing an increasingly complete understanding of the adaptations at the molecular and cellular levels that occur in these various brain regions and are responsible for behavioral features of drug addiction. Work to date has focused on adaptations in intracellular messenger pathways, particularly G proteins and the cAMP pathway, although many other types of adaptations will also prove to be involved. As the pathophysiological mechanisms underlying drug addiction become increasingly understood, it will be possible to develop more efficacious pharmacotherapies for the treatment of addictive disorders. Parallel studies, not covered in this chapter, of different inbred animal strains and of individual differences among large outbred populations promise to yield information concerning the specific proteins that underlie inherent differences in an individual's responsiveness to drugs of abuse. This work will lead eventually to the identification of specific genes and environmental factors that control individual variations in the susceptibility to drug addiction. Ultimately, this work could lead to the development of specific interventions that prevent drug addiction in particularly vulnerable individuals.

## References

Aghajanian GK: Tolerance of locus coeruleus neurons to morphine and suppression of withdrawal response by clonidine. Nature 276:186–188, 1978

Ahmed SH, Koob GF: Cocaine- but not food-seeking behavior is reinstated by stress after prolonged extinction. Psychopharmacology (Berl) 132:289–295, 1997

Akaoka A, Aston-Jones G: Opiate withdrawal-induced hyperactivity of locus coeruleus neurons is substantially mediated by augmented excitatory amino acid input. J Neurosci 11:3830–3839, 1991

Alreja M, Aghajanian GK: Pacemaker activity of locus coeruleus neurons: whole-cell recordings in brain slices show dependence on cAMP and protein kinase A. Brain Res 556:339–343, 1991

Alreja M, Aghajanian GK: Opiates suppress a resting sodium-dependent inward current in addition to activating an outward potassium current in locus coeruleus neurons. J Neurosci 13:3525–3532, 1993

American Psychiatric Association: Diagnostic and Statistical Manual of Mental Disorders, 4th Edition, Text Revision. Washington, DC, American Psychiatric Association, 2000

Atkins J, Carlezon WA, Chlan J, et al: Region-specific induction of deltaFosB by repeated administration of typical versus atypical antipsychotic drugs. Synapse 33:118–128, 1999

Bardo MT: Neuropharmacological mechanisms of drug reward: beyond dopamine in the nucleus accumbens. Crit Rev Neurobiol 12:37–67, 1998

Beitner-Johnson D, Guitart X, Nestler EJ: Common intracellular actions of chronic morphine and chronic cocaine in dopaminergic brain reward regions. Ann N Y Acad Sci 654:70–87, 1992a

Beitner-Johnson D, Guitart X, Nestler EJ: Neurofilament proteins and the mesolimbic dopamine system: common regulation by chronic morphine and chronic cocaine in the rat ventral tegmental area. J Neurosci 12:2165–2176, 1992b

Beitner-Johnson D, Guitart X, Nestler EJ: Glial fibrillary acidic protein and the mesolimbic dopamine system: regulation by chronic morphine and Lewis-Fischer strain differences in the rat ventral tegmental area. J Neurochem 61:1766–1773, 1993

Berhow MT, Russell DS, Terwilliger RZ, et al: Influence of neurotrophic factors on morphine- and cocaine-induced biochemical changes in the mesolimbic dopamine system. Neuroscience 68:969–979, 1995

Bonci A, Williams JT: Increased probability of GABA release during withdrawal from morphine. J Neurosci 17:796–803, 1997

Boundy VA, Chen JS, Nestler EJ: Regulation of cAMP-dependent protein kinase subunit expression in CATH.a and SH-SY5Y cells. J Pharmacol Exp Ther 286:1058–1065, 1998a

Boundy VA, Gold SJ, Messer CJ, et al: Regulation of tyrosine hydroxylase promoter activity by chronic morphine in TH9.0-LacZ transgenic mice. J Neurosci 18:9989–9995, 1998b

Brown EE, Fibiger HC: Cocaine-induced conditioned locomotion: absence of associated increases in dopamine release. Neuroscience 48:621–629, 1992

Carlezon WA Jr, Boundy VA, Haile CN, et al: Sensitization to morphine induced by viral-mediated gene transfer. Science 277:812–814, 1997

Carlezon WA Jr, Thome J, Olson VG, et al: Regulation of cocaine reward by CREB. Science 282:2272–2275, 1998

Chen J, Paredes W, Li J, et al: Delta 9-tetrahydrocannabinol produces naloxone blockable enhancement of presynaptic dopamine efflux in nucleus accumbens of conscious, freely moving rats as measured by intracerebral microdialysis. Psychopharmacology (Berl) 102:156–162, 1990

Childress AR, McLellan AT, O'Brien CP: Extinguishing conditioned responses in drug dependent persons, in Learning Factors in Drug Dependence: NIDA Research Monograph. Edited by Ray B. Washington, DC, U.S. Government Printing Office, 1988, pp 137–144

Christie MJ, Williams JT, North RA: Cellular mechanisms of opioid tolerance: studies in single brain neurons. Mol Pharmacol 32:633–638, 1987

Churchill L, Swanson CJ, Urbina M, et al: Repeated cocaine alters glutamate receptor subunit levels in the nucleus accumbens and ventral tegmental area of rats that develop behavioral sensitization. J Neurochem 72:2397–2403, 1999

Cole RL, Konradi C, Douglass J, et al: Neuronal adaptation to amphetamine and dopamine: molecular mechanisms of prodynorphin gene regulation in rat striatum. Neuron 14:813–823, 1995

Cornish JL, Kalivas PW: Glutamate transmission in the nucleus accumbens mediates relapse in cocaine addiction. J Neurosci 20(15):RC89, 2000

Cunningham ST, Kelley AE: Evidence for opiate-dopamine cross-sensitization in nucleus accumbens: studies of conditioned reward. Brain Res Bull 29:675–680, 1992

Curran EJ, Watson SJ: Dopamine receptor mRNA expression patterns by opioid peptide cells in the nucleus accumbens of the rat: a double in situ hybridization study. J Comp Neurol 361:57–76, 1995

Daunais JB, McGinty JF: Acute and chronic cocaine administration differentially alters striatal opioid and nuclear transcription factor mRNAs. Synapse 18:35–46, 1994

De Montis MG, Co C, Dworking SI, et al: Modifications of dopamine D1 receptor complex in rats self-administering cocaine. Eur J Pharmacol 362:9–15, 1998

Deroche V, Marinelli M, Le Moal M, et al: Glucocorticoids and behavioral effects of psychostimulants, II: cocaine intravenous self-administration and reinstatement depend on glucocorticoid levels. J Pharmacol Exp Ther 281:1401–1407, 1997

De Vries TJ, Schoffelmeer ANM, Binnekade R, et al: Dopaminergic mechanisms mediating the incentive to seek cocaine and heroin following long-term withdrawal of IV drug self-administration. Psychopharmacology (Berl) 143:254–260, 1999

De Wit H, Stewart J: Reinstatement of cocaine-reinforced responding in the rat. Psychopharmacology (Berl) 75:134–143, 1981

De Wit H, Stewart J: Drug reinstatement of heroin-reinforced responding in the rat. Psychopharmacology (Berl) 79:29–31, 1983

Di Chiara G, Imperato A: Drugs abused by humans preferentially increase synaptic dopamine concentrations in the mesolimbic system of freely moving rats. Proc Natl Acad Sci U S A 85:5274–5278, 1988

Di Ciano P, Blaha CD, Phillips AG: Conditioned changes in dopamine oxidation currents in the nucleus accumbens of rats by stimuli paired with self-administration or yoked-administration of d-amphetamine. Eur J Neurosci 10:1121–1127, 1998

Dworkin SI, Smith JE: Opiates/opioids and reinforcement, in Biological Basis of Substance Abuse. Edited by Korenman SG, Barchas JD. New York, Oxford University Press, 1993, pp 327–338

Ehrman RN, Robbins SJ, Childress AR, et al: Conditioned responses to cocaine-related stimuli in cocaine abuse patients. Psychopharmacology (Berl) 107:523–529, 1992

Ennis M, Aston-Jones G: Activation of locus coeruleus from nucleus paraginto-cellularis: a new excitatory amino acid pathway in brain. J Neurosci 8:3644–3657, 1988

Erb S, Shaham Y, Stewart J: Stress reinstates cocaine-seeking behavior after prolonged extinction and a drug-free period. Psychopharmacology (Berl) 128:408–412, 1996

Ettenberg A: Haloperidol prevents the reinstatement of amphetamine-rewarded runway responding in rats. Pharmacol Biochem Behav 36:635–638, 1990

Fahlke C, Hansen S, Engel JA, et al: Effects of ventral striatal 6-OHDA lesions or amphetamine sensitization on ethanol consumption in the rat. Pharmacol Biochem Behav 47:345–349, 1994

Fitzgerald LW, Ortiz J, Hamedani AG, et al: Regulation of glutamate receptor subunit expression by drugs of abuse and stress: common adaptations among cross-sensitizing agents. J Neurosci 16:274–282, 1996

Fontana DJ, Post RM, Pert A: Conditioned increases in mesolimbic dopamine overflow by stimuli associated with cocaine. Brain Res 629:31–39, 1993

Gold MS, Redmond DE, Kleber HD: Clonidine in opiate withdrawal. Lancet 11:599–602, 1978

Hope BT, Nye HE, Kelz MB, et al: Induction of a long-lasting AP-1 complex composed of altered Fos-like proteins in brain by chronic cocaine and other chronic treatments. Neuron 13:1235–1244, 1994

Horger BA, Iyasere CA, Berhow MT, et al: Enhancement of locomotor activity and conditioned reward to cocaine by brain-derived neurotrophic factor. J Neurosci 19:4110–4122, 1999

Hu XT, White FJ: Loss of D1/D2 dopamine receptor synergisms following repeated administration of D1 or D2 receptor selective antagonists: electrophysiological and behavioral studies. Synapse 17(1):43–61, 1994

Johnson SW, North RA: Opioids excite dopamine neurons by hyperpolarization of local interneurons. J Neurosci 12:483–488, 1992

Jolas T, Nestler EJ, Aghajanian GK: Chronic morphine increases GABA tone on serotonergic neurons of the dorsal raphe nucleus: association with an upregulation of the cyclic AMP pathway. Neuroscience 95:433–443, 2000

Kalivas PW, Nakamura M: Neural systems for behavioral activation and reward. Curr Opin Neurobiol 9:223–227, 1999

Karreman M, Moghaddam B: The prefrontal cortex regulates the basal release of dopamine in the limbic striatum: an effect mediated by ventral tegmental area. J Neurochem 66:589–598, 1996

Kelley AE, Holahan MR: Enhanced reward-related responding following cholera toxin infusion into the nucleus accumbens. Synapse 26:46–54, 1997

Kelz MB, Chen JS, Carlezon WA, et al: Expression of the transcription factor deltaFosB in the brain controls sensitivity to cocaine. Nature 401:272–276, 1999

Kogan JH, Nestler EJ, Aghajanian GK: Elevated basal firing rates and enhanced responses to 8-Br-cAMP in locus coeruleus neurons in brain slices from opiate-dependent rats. Eur J Pharmacol 211:47–53, 1992

Koob GF: Drugs of abuse: anatomy, pharmacology and function of reward pathways. Trends Pharmacol Sci 13:177–184, 1992

Koob GF, Le Moal M: Drug abuse: hedonic homeostatic dysregulation. Science 278:52–58, 1997

Koob GF, Maldonado R, Stinus L: Neural substrates of opiate withdrawal. Trends Neurosci 15:186–191, 1992

Kuhar MJ, Ritz MC, Boja JW: The dopamine hypothesis of the reinforcing properties of cocaine. Trends Neurosci 14:299–302, 1991

Lane-Ladd SB, Pineda J, Boundy V, et al: CREB in the locus coeruleus: biochemical, physiological, and behavioral evidence for a role in opiate dependence. J Neurosci 17:7890–7901, 1997

Lefkowitz RJ: G protein–coupled receptors, III: new roles for receptor kinases and arrestins in receptor signaling and desensitization. J Biol Chem 273:18677–18680, 1998

Lu W, Wolf ME: Repeated amphetamine administration alters AMPA receptor subunit expression in rat nucleus accumbens and medial prefrontal cortex. Synapse 32:119–131, 1999

Maggos CE, Tsukada H, Kakiuchi T, et al: Sustained withdrawal allows normalization of in vivo [11C]N-methylspiperone dopamine D2 receptor binding after chronic binge cocaine: a positron emission tomography study in rats. Neuropsychopharmacology 19:146–153, 1998

Maldonado R, Koob GF: Destruction of the locus coeruleus decreases physical signs of opiate withdrawal. Brain Res 605:128–138, 1993

Maldonado R, Blendy JA, Tzavara E, et al: Reduction of morphine abstinence in mice with a mutation in the gene encoding CREB. Science 273:657–659, 1996

Meador-Woodruff JH, Mansour A, Healy DJ, et al: Comparison of the distribution of D1 and D2 dopamine receptor mRNAs in rat brain. Neuropsychopharmacology 5:231–242, 1991

Meil WM, See RE: Lesions of the basolateral amygdala abolish the ability of drug associated cues to reinstate responding during withdrawal from self-administered cocaine. Behav Brain Res 87:139–148, 1997

Messer CJ, Eisch AJ, Carlezon WA Jr, et al: Role of GDNF in biochemical and behavioral adaptations to drugs of abuse. Neuron 26:247–257, 2000

Mirenowicz J, Schultz W: Preferential activation of midbrain dopamine neurons by appetitive rather than aversive stimuli. Nature 379:449–451, 1996

Moghaddam B: Stress preferentially increases extraneuronal levels of excitatory amino acids in the prefrontal cortex: comparison to hippocampus and basal ganglia. J Neurochem 60:1650–1657, 1993

Moore RJ, Vinsant SL, Nader MA, et al: Effect of cocaine self-administration on striatal dopamine D1 receptors in rhesus monkeys. Synapse 28:1–9, 1998

Nestler EJ: Molecular mechanisms of drug addiction. J Neurosci 12:2439–2450, 1992

Nestler EJ: Molecular basis of long-term plasticity underlying addiction. Nat Rev Neurosci 2(2):119–128, 2001

Nestler EJ, Aghajanian GK: Molecular and cellular basis of addiction. Science 278:58–63, 1997

Nestler EJ, Hope BT, Widnell KL: Drug addiction: a model for the molecular basis of neural plasticity. Neuron 11:995–1006, 1993

Nestler EJ, Hyman SE, Malenka RC: Molecular Neuropharmacology: A Foundation for Clinical Neuroscience. New York, McGraw-Hill, 2001

North RA, Williams JT, Suprenant A, et al: Mu and delta receptors belong to a family of receptors that are coupled to potassium channels. Proc Natl Acad Sci U S A 84:5487–5491, 1987

Nye HE, Nestler EJ: Induction of chronic Fras (Fos-related antigens) in rat brain by chronic morphine administration. Mol Pharmacol 49:636–645, 1996

O'Brien C, Childress A, McLellan A, et al: A learning model of addiction, in Addictive States. Edited by O'Brien CP, Jaffe JH. New York, Raven, 1992, pp 157–177

O'Donovan KJ, Tourtellotte WG, Millbrandt J, et al: The EGR family of transcription-regulatory factors: progress at the interface of molecular and systems neuroscience. Trends Neurosci 22:167–173, 1999

Olds ME: Reinforcing effects of morphine in the nucleus accumbens. Brain Res 237:429–440, 1982

Ortiz J, Fitzgerald LW, Charlton M, et al: Biochemical actions of chronic ethanol exposure in the mesolimbic dopamine system. Synapse 21:289–298, 1995

Overton PG, Tong ZY, Brain PF, et al: Preferential occupation of mineralocorticoid receptors by corticosterone enhances glutamate-induced burst firing in rat midbrain dopaminergic neurons. Brain Res 737:146–154, 1996

Piazza PV, Rouge-Pont F, Deroche V, et al: Glucocorticoids have state-dependent stimulant effects on the mesencephalic dopamine transmission. Proc Natl Acad Sci U S A 93: 8716–8720, 1996

Pich EM, Pagliusi SR, Tessari M, et al: Common neural substrates for the addictive properties of nicotine and cocaine. Science 275:83–86, 1997

Pierce RC, Pierce-Bancroft AF, Prasad BM: Neurotrophin-3 contributes to the initiation of behavioral sensitization to cocaine by activating the Ras/mitogen-activated protein kinase signal transduction cascade. J Neurosci 19:8685–8695, 1999

Pilotte NS: Neurochemistry of cocaine withdrawal. Curr Opin Neurol 10:534–538, 1997

Potenza MN, Nestler EJ: Effects of G protein–signaling proteins on the functional response of the mu opioid receptor in a melanophore-based assay. J Pharmacol Exp Ther 291:482–491, 1999

Rasmussen K, Aghajanian GK: Withdrawal-induced activation of locus coeruleus neurons in opiate-dependent rats: attenuation by lesions of the nucleus paragigantocellularis. Brain Res 505:346–350, 1989

Rasmussen K, Beitner-Johnson D, Krystal JH, et al: Opiate withdrawal and the rat locus coeruleus: behavioral, electrophysiological, and biochemical correlates. J Neurosci 10:2308–2317, 1990

Robbins SJ, Ehrman RN, Childress AR, et al: Relationships among physiological and self-report responses produced by cocaine-related cues. Addict Behav 22:157–167, 1997

Robinson TE, Berridge KC: The neural basis of drug craving: an incentive-sensitization theory of addiction. Brain Res Rev 18:247–291, 1993

Robinson TE, Kolb B: Persistent structural modifications in nucleus accumbens and prefrontal neurons produced by previous experience with amphetamine. J Neurosci 17:8491–8497, 1997

Robinson TE, Kolb B: Morphine alters the structure of neurons in the nucleus accumbens and neocortex of rats. Synapse 33:160–162, 1999

Schmidt EF, Sutton MA, Schad CA, et al: Extinction training regulates tyrosine hydroxylase during withdrawal from cocaine self-administration. J Neurosci 21:RC137, 2001

Self DW: Neural substrates of drug craving and relapse in drug addiction. Ann Med 30:379–389, 1998

Self DW, Nestler EJ: Molecular mechanisms of drug reinforcement and addiction. Annu Rev Neurosci 18:463–495, 1995

Self DW, Nestler EJ: Relapse to drug seeking: neural and molecular mechanisms. Drug Alcohol Depend 51:49–60, 1998

Self DW, Terwilliger RZ, Nestler EJ, et al: Inactivation of Gi and Go proteins in nucleus accumbens reduces both cocaine and heroin reinforcement. J Neurosci 14:6239–6247, 1994

Self DW, McClenahan AW, Beitner-Johnson D, et al: Biochemical adaptations in the mesolimbic dopamine system in response to heroin self-administration. Synapse 21:312–318, 1995

Self DW, Barnhart WJ, Lehman DA, et al: Opposite modulation of cocaine-seeking behavior by D1-like and D2-like dopamine receptor agonists. Science 271:1586–1589, 1996

Self DW, Genova LM, Hope BT, et al: Involvement of cAMP-dependent protein kinase in the nucleus accumbens in cocaine self-administration and relapse of cocaine-seeking behavior. J Neurosci 18:1848–1859, 1998

Shaham Y, Stewart J: Stress reinstates heroin-seeking in drug-free animals: an effect mimicking heroin, not withdrawal. Psychopharmacology (Berl) 119:334–341, 1995

Shaham Y, Stewart J: Effects of opioid and dopamine receptor antagonists on relapse induced by stress and re-exposure to heroin in rats. Psychopharmacology (Berl) 125:385–391, 1996

Shaham Y, Rajabi H, Stewart J: Relapse to heroin-seeking in rats under opioid maintenance: the effects of stress, heroin priming, and withdrawal. J Neurosci 16:1957–1963, 1996

Shaham Y, Funk D, Erb S, et al: Corticotropin-releasing factor in stress-induced relapse to heroin-seeking in rats. J Neurosci 17:2605–2614, 1997

Shaham Y, Erb S, Stewart J: Stress-induced relapse to heroin and cocaine seeking in rats: a review. Brain Res Brain Res Rev 33:13–33, 2000

Sharma SK, Klee WA, Nirenberg M: Dual regulation of adenylate cyclase accounts for narcotic dependence and tolerance. Proc Natl Acad Sci U S A 72:3092–3096, 1975

Sibley DR, Ventura AL, Jiang D, et al: Regulation of the D1 receptor through cAMP-mediated pathways. Adv Pharmacol 42:447–450, 1998

Sklair-Tavron L, Shi W-X, Lane SB, et al: Chronic morphine induces visible changes in the morphology of mesolimbic dopamine neurons. Proc Natl Acad Sci U S A 93:11202–11207, 1996

Slikker WJ, Brocco MJ, Killam KFJ: Reinstatement of responding maintained by cocaine or thiamylal. J Pharmacol Exp Ther 228:43–52, 1984

Spanagel R, Weiss F: The dopamine hypothesis of reward: past and current status. Trends Neurosci 22:521–527, 1999

Stewart J, Vezina P: A comparison of the effects of intra-accumbens injections of amphetamine and morphine on reinstatement of heroin intravenous self-administration behavior. Brain Res 457:287–294, 1988

Stewart J, De Wit H, Eikelboom R: Role of unconditioned and conditioned drug effects in the self-administration of opiates and stimulants. Psychol Rev 91:251–268, 1984

Striplin CD, Kalivas PW: Correlation between behavioral sensitization to cocaine and G protein ADP-ribosylation in the ventral tegmental area. Brain Res 579:181–186, 1992

Striplin CD, Kalivas PW: Robustness of G protein changes in cocaine sensitization shown with immunoblotting. Synapse 14:10–15, 1993

Taber MT, Das S, Fibiger HC: Cortical regulation of subcortical dopamine release: mediation via the ventral tegmental area. J Neurochem 65:1407–1410, 1995

Tanda G, Pontieri FE, Di Chiara G: Cannabinoid and heroin activation of mesolimbic dopamine transmission by a common mu1 opioid receptor mechanism. Science 276:2048–2050, 1997

Terwilliger RZ, Beitner-Johnson D, Sevarino KA, et al: A general roll for adaptations in G-proteins and the cyclic AMP system in mediating the chronic actions of morphine and cocaine on neuronal function. Brain Res 548:100–110, 1991

Tiffany ST, Singleton E, Haertzen CA, et al: The development of a cocaine craving questionnaire. Drug Alcohol Depend 34:19–28, 1993

Tjon GH, De Vries TJ, Ronken E, et al: Repeated and chronic morphine administration causes differential long-lasting changes in dopaminergic neurotransmission in rat striatum without changing its delta- and kappa-opioid receptor regulation. Eur J Pharmacol 252:205–212, 1994

Tsukada H, Kreuter J, Maggos CE, et al: Effects of binge pattern cocaine administration on dopamine D1 and D2 receptors in the rat brain: an in vivo study using positron emission tomography. J Neurosci 16:7670–7677, 1996

Unterwald EM, Cox BM, Creek MJ, et al: Chronic repeated cocaine administration alters basal and opioid-regulated adenylyl cyclase activity. Synapse 15:33–38, 1993

Unterwald EM, Rubenfeld JM, Kreek MJ: Repeated cocaine administration up-regulates kappa and mu, but not delta, opioids. Neuroreport 5:1613–1616, 1994

Vezina P, Stewart J: Amphetamine administered to the ventral tegmental area but not to the nucleus accumbens sensitizes rats to systemic morphine: lack of conditioned effects. Brain Res 516:99–106, 1990

Volkow ND, Fowler JS, Wang GJ: Imaging studies on the role of dopamine in cocaine reinforcement and addiction in humans. J Psychopharmacol 13:337–345, 1999

Waddington JL, Daly SA: Regulation of unconditioned motor behaviour by D1:D2 interaction, in D-1:D-2 Dopamine Receptor Interactions. Edited by Waddington JL. London, Academic Press, 1993, pp 203–233

Weissenborn R, Deroche V, Koob G, et al: Effects of dopamine agonists and antagonists on cocaine-induced operant responding for a cocaine-associated stimulus. Psychopharmacology (Berl) 126:311–322, 1996

Whistler JL, Chuang HH, Chu P, et al: Functional dissociation of mu opioid receptor signaling and endocytosis: implications for the biology of opiate tolerance and addiction. Neuron 23:737–746, 1999

White FJ, Kalivas PW: Neuroadaptations involved in amphetamine and cocaine addiction. Drug Alcohol Depend 51:141–153, 1998

White FJ, Hu X-T, Zhang X-F, et al: Repeated administration of cocaine or amphetamine alters neuronal responses to glutamate in the mesoaccumbens dopamine system. J Pharmacol Exp Ther 273:445–454, 1995

Widnell KL, Self DW, Lane SB, et al: Regulation of CREB expression: in vivo evidence for a functional role in morphine action in the nucleus accumbens. J Pharmacol Exp Ther 276:306–315, 1996

Wise RA: Drug-activation of brain reward pathways. Drug Alcohol Depend 51:13–22, 1998

Wise RA, Murray A, Bozarth MA: Bromocriptine self-administration and bromocriptine-reinstatement of cocaine-trained and heroin-trained lever pressing in rats. Psychopharmacology (Berl) 100:355–360, 1990

Wolf DH, Numan S, Nestler EJ, et al: Regulation of phospholipase Cgamma in the mesolimbic dopamine system by chronic morphine administration. J Neurochem 73:1520–1528, 1999

Wolf ME: The role of excitatory amino acids in behavioral sensitization to psychomotor stimulants. Prog Neurobiol 54:679–720, 1998

# CHAPTER 28

# Neuropsychiatric Aspects of Dementias Associated With Motor Dysfunction

Alan J. Lerner, M.D.

Peter J. Whitehouse, M.D., Ph.D.

The degenerative dementias that are associated with motor system dysfunction are a diverse group of disorders that present a particular challenge to the clinician. Depending on where the primary pathology occurs in the motor system (basal ganglia, cerebellum, or motor neuron), the motor symptoms can include abnormal movements, incoordination, or weakness. In this chapter, we review Huntington's disease (HD), Parkinson's disease (PD), progressive supranuclear palsy (PSP), and other rarer conditions that are characterized by dementia and movement or motor disorders (Table 28–1). In contrast, in primary degenerative dementias such as Alzheimer's disease (AD) and Pick's disease, motor signs are rare, usually occurring only in the later stages of the disease.

As degenerative disorders, the dementias included in this chapter are characterized by gradual loss of function due to progressive loss of neurons in specific regions of the brain associated with pathologic hallmarks that are characteristic of the individual diseases. The specific etiologies of these diseases are often unknown, and clinical features frequently overlap among different conditions, making a clear nosology difficult.

The genetic basis of these overlapping conditions is being elucidated at a rapid pace, allowing a firm basis for deciphering the variability in clinical and neuropsychiatric symptoms. When the genetic basis of a condition is known, it is briefly reviewed here. However, despite these impressive, concerted advances in knowledge, specific biological interventions are limited in effectiveness (Table 28–2).

These conditions are particularly stressful for patients, family members, and professional caregivers because they cause significant impairment in quality of life due to a combination of motor, cognitive, and behavioral abnormalities. Although in some conditions, drugs are available to treat the motor symptoms, these drugs frequently contribute to the cognitive and behavioral dysfunction. The motor impairments themselves create special difficulties in neuropsychiatric and neuropsychological testing of the cognitive and psychiatric dysfunction.

The classification of the dementias included in this chapter and their nosologic relationships to those considered in Chapter 29 are controversial. Ideally, classification depends on proper understanding of essential clinical and biological features. Our understanding of the relationships between brain changes and behavioral alterations in these disorders, however, is limited. Many attempts have been made to define subtypes of dementia; for example, age at onset has been used to characterize different forms of AD, HD, and PD. One attempt to develop a classification of dementia based on an understanding of biology is the development of the concept of cortical and subcortical dementia (Albert et al. 1974; McHugh and Folstein 1975). AD and Pick's disease are thought to represent cortical dementias in which the predominant pathology is neocortical and the clinical symptoms—such as aphasia, apraxia, and agnosia—supposedly reflect cortical pathology. The clinical picture of the

**TABLE 28–1.** Degenerative dementias associated with motor system impairment

**Extrapyramidal diseases**
  Parkinson's disease
  Huntington's disease
  Diffuse Lewy body disease
  Progressive supranuclear palsy
  Cortical–Basal Ganglionic degeneration
  Multiple system atrophy
  Thalamic dementias
  Wilson's disease
  Hallervorden-Spatz disease
  Fahr's disease
  Frontotemporal dementia
**Cerebellar diseases**
  Olivopontocerebellar atrophy
  Friedreich's ataxia
  Spinocerebellar degenerations
**Motor neuron diseases**
  Motor neuron disease with dementia
  Amyotrophic lateral sclerosis/parkinsonism dementia
    complex
**Other**
  Normal pressure hydrocephalus
  Creutzfeldt-Jakob disease

dementias considered in this chapter is claimed to be due to primary pathology in subcortical structures and includes dysfunction in affect, speed of processing, and memory (Cummings 1990). This attempt to categorize dementias into these two superordinate categories has stimulated research and debate concerning nosology. Many authors have come to the conclusion that all dementias cannot be easily classified into these two large categories, and, for example, that the dementias of HD and PD are as clinically different from one another as they are from AD (R.E. Brown and Marsden 1988; Cummings 1990; Mayeux et al. 1983; Whitehouse 1986).

## Huntington's Disease

Huntington's disease (HD) is a genetically transmitted, progressive neuropsychiatric disorder that can appear at any time in life. The peak period of onset is in the fourth and fifth decades. Because of their clinical prominence and central place in Huntington's (1872) description, dyskinesias, particularly chorea—defined as a random, nonstereotyped, purposeless movement—is usually considered the first sign of the disease. However, clinical presentation is quite variable in early stages of HD, and cognitive and psychiatric symptoms are often evident

well before the movement disorder (S.E. Folstein 1989). Depression, irritability, and impulsive or erratic behavior are the most common psychiatric symptoms. Memory and concentration difficulties are cognitive symptoms that appear early (S.E. Folstein 1989; Martin and Gusella 1986).

## Epidemiology

HD is an autosomal dominant disorder with variable age at onset. Presentation differs between juvenile-onset and adult-onset cases. Chorea is the cardinal motor symptom in adult-onset HD. In the 3%–9% of cases in which onset occurs before adolescence, rigidity, myoclonus, or dystonic movements are characteristic. Early onset is typically associated with paternal transmission and has a more rapid course (S.E. Folstein 1989; Martin and Gusella 1986). In adult-onset cases, death usually occurs after 16–20 years (S.E. Folstein 1989). The rate of decline may be slower in patients with onset after the fifth decade of life (Martin and Gusella 1986). The age at onset has been associated with the number of CAG repeats present in the HD gene, located on chromosome 4. Some cases of so-called senile chorea have now been recognized to be very late-onset HD.

Estimates of the prevalence of HD vary widely. S.E. Folstein (1989) concluded that the best estimate of point prevalence among Caucasians is 5–7 cases per 100,000. In general, the prevalence of HD in European populations is relatively uniform, although there are pockets of isolated populations in which the rates are much higher, as well as areas in Europe where they are much lower (e.g., Spain, Finland) (S.E. Folstein 1989; Harper 1992). Variability in rates may be artifacts of the instability of estimates based on small samples, but in the case of high prevalence they may be also the consequence of reproductive isolation. These isolated populations are invaluable for genetic studies, as illustrated in Gusella and associates' (1983) location of the chromosome carrying the HD gene using a Venezuelan population with a very high prevalence of the disease. The study of this population ultimately led to the discovery of the gene itself 10 years later (Huntington's Disease Collaborative Research Group 1993).

## Etiology

George Huntington was fortunate to practice medicine in the same location as his father, giving him ample opportunity to observe the familial transmission of this disease (Huntington 1872). He correctly concluded that the familial transmission was hereditary and, although

**TABLE 28–2.**    Genes associated with degenerative disorders with motor involvement

| Disease entity | Inheritance | Gene locus | Gene product |
| --- | --- | --- | --- |
| Huntington's disease | AD | 4q16.3 | Huntingtin |
| Parkinson's disease | AD | 4q21 | α-Synuclein |
| | AR | 6q25.2–q27 | Parkin |
| Friedreich's ataxia | AD | 9q13 | Frataxin |
| Frontotemporal dementia | AD | 17q21.1 | Tau |
| Progressive supranuclear palsy | AD | 17q21.1 | Tau |
| Corticobasal degeneration | AD | 17q21.1 | Tau |
| Wilson's disease | AR | 13q14.1–q21.1 | ATPase |
| Hallervorden-Spatz disease | | 20p13–p12.3 | |
| Fahr's disease | | 14q | |
| Spinocerebellar degenerations | | | |
| SCA-1 | AD | 6p23 | Ataxin 1 |
| SCA-2 | AD | 12q23–q24.1 | Ataxin 2 |
| SCA-3 (Machado-Joseph disease) | AD | 14q21 | Ataxin 3 |
| SCA-4 | AD | 16q24-ter | |
| SCA-5 | AD | 11p11–q11 | |
| SCA-6 | AD | 19p13 | Alpha-1A calcium channel subunit |
| SCA-7 (OPCA with retinal degeneration) | AD | 3p21.1–p12 | |
| SCA-8 (infantile-onset SCA) | AR | 10q23.3–q24.1 | |
| SCA-10 | AD | 22q13 | |
| SCA-11 | AD | 15q14–21.3 | |
| SCA-12 | AD | 5q31–q33 | |

*Note.* AD = autosomal dominant; AR = autosomal recessive; SCA = spinocerebellar atrophy; OPCA = olivopontocerebellar atrophy.

the concepts were not yet developed, appreciated that it was a dominant, fully penetrant, autosomal condition (S.E. Folstein 1989).

In 1983, genetic linkage analysis identified the HD gene locus at the distal end of the short arm of chromosome 4 (Gusella et al. 1983), and after intensive research the gene itself was identified (Huntington's Disease Collaborative Research Group 1993). The gene is an unstable CAG trinucleotide repeat sequence that is longer than the repeat sequence of the normal gene. Normal alleles have a range of 9–30 CAG repeats, whereas the repeats in HD patients range from 40 to at least 121 (Albin and Tagle 1995; Huntington's Disease Collaborative Research Group 1993; Monckton and Caskey 1995).

The isolation of the gene has permitted some accounting for the apparent allelic heterogeneity of the disease, with family, race, and gender variation in age at onset (Farrer and Conneally 1985; S.E. Folstein et al. 1987). Longer CAG repeats tend to be associated with earlier age at onset and male transmission, with the largest repeats seen in patients with juvenile onset. However, the CAG repeat is very unstable, and the length of repeat does not have strong clinical correlates. Unaffected first-degree relatives of HD patients have repeat lengths above the typical normal limit but shorter than those of HD patients (Gusella et al. 1983).

Huntington's disease appears to be one of several diseases characterized by trinucleotide repeats, which include myotonic dystrophy, fragile X syndrome, spinobulbar muscular atrophy, and several of the spinocerebellar atrophies (SCAs) (especially SCA type 1) (Monckton and Caskey 1995). The gene product of the HD gene is a protein termed Huntingtin. In unaffected individuals it is a cytosolic protein, but in HD it is transported to the cell nucleus (Reddy et al. 1999). The mechanism by which its abnormal transport and deposition in intraneuronal inclusions relates to molecular pathophysiology is a current area of research.

## Diagnosis and Clinical Features

In her monograph, S.E. Folstein (1989) notes, "In principle, the diagnosis of HD is straightforward: it is a clinical-pathological entity defined by involuntary movements and abnormalities of voluntary motor control. Most patients also suffer from non-aphasic dementia and emotional symptoms, particularly irritability and depression.... There is almost always a history of an affected parent." (p. 125)

Cross-sectional assessment of patients may result in diagnostic inaccuracy because many conditions may present with chorea, and also because there is substantial variability in presentation early in the disease. Nearly half of HD patients initially present with emotional or cognitive symptoms. These symptoms can be very diverse and include depression, irritability, hallucinations, and apathy. Motor symptoms, if present, may be mild rigidity, restlessness, or ticlike jerks that are easily attributable to another disorder (S.E. Folstein 1989). Other conditions such as Parkinson's disease, Sydenham's chorea, ataxias, cerebrovascular disease, systemic lupus erythematosus, schizophrenia, affective disorder, thyroid disease, acanthocytosis, drug-induced chorea, or alcoholism are other considerations in the differential diagnosis (see Table 28–1). However, when there is a positive family history consistent with autosomal dominant transmission, HD is a very likely explanation of these symptoms. S.E. Folstein (1989) suggests that a second reason for failing to diagnose HD is failure to take an adequate family history. Direct genetic testing produces unequivocal diagnosis in these uncertain cases. Neuroimaging studies, especially positron emission tomography (PET) demonstrating glucose hypometabolism in the caudate nucleus, can be quite sensitive diagnostic aids (Furtado and Suchowersky 1995).

The clinical and ethical issues involved in preclinical testing for HD—first considered when linkage studies became available (Brandt et al. 1989; Martin and Gusella 1986)—have become even more salient and critical because of the availability of the DNA test (Codori and Brandt 1994; Codori et al. 1994; Hayden et al. 1995; Hersch et al. 1994). These issues must be explored on an individual basis and may be aided by employing an experienced genetic counselor.

## Neurobiology

The most obvious gross pathology in HD occurs in the basal ganglia. The striatum is consistently affected, with degeneration beginning in the medial caudate nucleus and proceeding laterally to the putamen and occasionally to the globus pallidus (S.E. Folstein 1989). γ-Aminobutyric acid (GABA), the most abundant neurotransmitter of the spiny output neurons, and acetylcholine, the principal neurotransmitter of type I aspiny interneurons, are especially affected (S.E. Folstein 1989; Martin and Gusella 1986). Other neurotransmitter changes in HD include increased concentrations of somatostatin (Albin and Tagle 1995; Pearson and Reynolds 1994; Reynolds and Pearson 1993). In the caudate nucleus, for example, somatostatin levels increase because of the selective survival of type II spiny interneurons (S.E. Folstein 1989). In an animal model, injection of somatostatin into the caudate nucleus increases dopamine turnover, offering a possible explanation of the utility of neuroleptics in the control of chorea in HD (Martin and Gusella 1986). The alterations in absolute neurotransmitter concentrations and relative balance among different systems may account for some of the symptoms of HD (S.E. Folstein 1989). Hope that a selective neurotransmitter deficit would lead to corrective therapies has not yet been realized (Martin and Gusella 1986).

The actual mechanisms of cell destruction in the caudate nucleus are not known. Two models have been proposed. One focuses on abnormal posttranslation cleavage products that disturb cellular metabolism and function (Albin and Tagle 1995). A second model proposes a excitotoxic basis for HD involving the glutamate/$N$-methyl-$D$-aspartate (NDMA) receptor (Reynolds and Pearson 1993). This model rests heavily on the finding of abnormal 3-hydroxykynurenine levels in the brains of individuals with HD, which may indicate a excitotoxic basis for cell death. This model may be a valuable heuristic for pharmacotherapeutic developments.

Developing knowledge of basic neuroanatomy and neurochemistry have done much to elucidate the mechanisms of symptoms and symptom patterns in HD. There are rich interconnections between the striatum and the prefrontal and parietal cortices (S.E. Folstein 1989; S.E. Folstein et al. 1990). Alexander et al. (1986) summarized evidence that there are five distinct parallel corticostriatal circuits subserving distinct neurobehavioral functions, including eye movements, motor behavior, emotion, and cognitive functions. Except for the motor circuit involving the putamen, the others are caudate nucleus–frontal circuits. Interestingly, lesions at any of the segments of the circuit produce similar functional consequences.

In addition, major sources of input to the basal ganglia (caudate nucleus and putamen) include limbic structures, the primary motor cortex, and motor association areas. The helps to account for the co-occurrence of movement abnormalities and behavioral symptoms and for the often-noted influence of emotional states on the severity of motor symptoms. There is substantial overlap in the neurotransmitter systems implicated in HD and those involved in extrapyramidal and psychiatric disorders, and the psychiatric syndromes of HD are substantially the result of brain changes. Caudate nucleus pathology and disruptions in caudate nucleus–prefrontal connections are associated with the mood disorders of HD (Mendez 1994).

The degree of atrophy of the caudate nucleus (Figure 28–1) correlates with cognitive dysfunction, including intelligence, memory, and visuospatial deficits (Bamford et al. 1989; Sax et al. 1983). Atrophy of the caudate

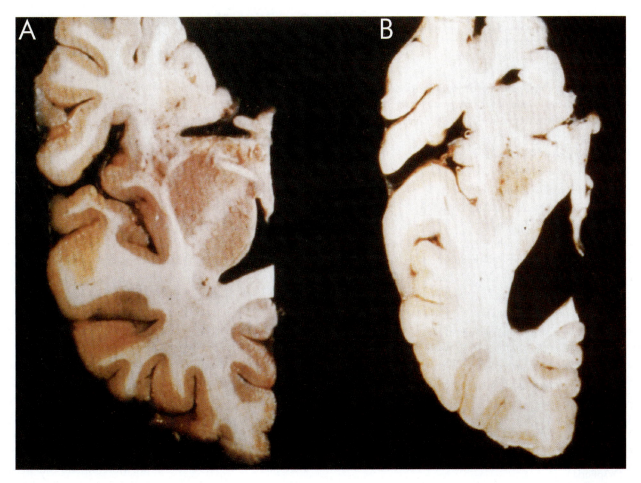

**FIGURE 28–1.** Atrophy of the caudate nucleus in Huntington's disease (coronal section). *Panel A.* A healthy control subject. *Panel B.* A patient with Huntington's disease.

nucleus is generally more robustly correlated than measures of frontal atrophy, with executive functions typically considered to be evidence of prefrontal cortical pathology (Bamford et al. 1989; Starkstein et al. 1988). Similar associations between functional impairments and caudate nucleus pathology have been reported with PET (Bamford et al. 1989). The deterioration in neuropsychological functions in HD appears to derive principally from disruptions in neural circuits due to basal ganglia pathology (Bamford et al. 1989; S.E. Folstein et al. 1989; M. Morris 1995).

## Motor Abnormalities

Both involuntary movements and abnormal voluntary movements occur in HD (S.E. Folstein 1989; S.E. Folstein et al. 1983b; Leigh et al. 1983) (Table 28–3). The earlier name of the disease in the United States, Huntington's chorea, emphasized the prominence of sudden, jerky movements of the limbs, face, or trunk. These are less abrupt and of longer duration and involve more mus-

cle groups than those seen in Sydenham's chorea. Unlike tics, choreic movements are not repetitive or periodic. They can occur while the individual is at rest or in the course of planned movement (e.g., walking, reaching), although they are absent during sleep. Stress, such as that experienced during cognitive challenges (serial 7s, mental calculation), can increase chorea. Patients can generally suppress chorea for only short periods of time. Motor restlessness may occur before chorea, and dystonia, in the absence of chorea, is frequent in juvenile-onset (Westphal variant) cases (S.E. Folstein 1989).

Motor abnormalities change over the course of the disease. Early there are brief, irregular, jerky movements along with slower, writhing movements, which often occur in conjunction with the initiation of action. Flexion-extension of fingers ("piano playing") and ulnar deviation of the hands while walking are also common. Later, movements become almost constant, with severe grimacing, nodding, head bobbing, and a "dancing" gait. Choreoathetosis decreases and dystonia and an akinetic-rigid syndrome supervenes (Feigin et al. 1995; Furtado and Suchowersky 1995).

**TABLE 28–3.** Clinical features of Huntington's disease

**Motor symptoms**

*Involuntary movement abnormalities*

Chorea, consisting of nonrepetitive, nonperiodic, jerky movements of limbs, face, or trunk; exacerbated by stress; absent during sleep; may be consciously suppressed only for short periods

*Voluntary movement abnormalities*

Initiation and inhibition of eye movements

Coordination of limb movements

Articulation problems and dysphagia

**Neuropsychological symptoms**

Declarative memory problems, with greater impairment in information retrieval than recognition memory

Procedural memory deficits

Verbal fluency deficits

Impaired visuospatial skills

Problems with sustained concentration

Impaired executive functions (i.e., mental planning, organization of sequential actions, mental flexibility)

Language functions relatively preserved

**Psychiatric features**

*Common symptoms*

Apathy

Irritability

Dysphoria

Anxiety

*Common syndromes*

Mood disorders (especially symptomatic major depression and bipolar disorder)

Intermittent explosive disorder

Schizophreniform disorder

Atypical psychosis

It is possible to misdiagnosis choreoathetosis as nervousness, mannerisms, or intentional movements early in the course of the disease. Abnormalities in voluntary movements are helpful in the diagnosis, because they are present in HD even in the absence of chorea. As summarized by S.E. Folstein (1989) and others (Furtado and Suchowersky 1995; Mendez 1994), there are abnormalities in initiation and inhibition of eye movements (saccades, fixation, and smooth pursuit), coordination of limb movements, and articulation. Although they are nonspecific features of the illness, these abnormalities are important to assess because they have a more robust relationship with intellectual impairment, memory disorder, and capacity for activities of daily living than does the severity of chorea (Brandt et al. 1984; S.E. Folstein 1989).

## Cognitive Abnormalities

Cognitive deficits appear early in the course of HD and are progressive (M. Morris 1995) (see Table 28–3). If they are sufficiently severe they can be detected and coarsely evaluated in brief, formal mental status testing, such as with the Mini-Mental State Exam (MMSE) (M.F. Folstein et al. 1975). Very early in the disease, intelligence may be normal, but deficits in memory and verbal fluency can be detected on neuropsychological testing (Butters et al. 1978). Intellectual impairment is a major contributor to disability even early in the illness (Mayeux et al. 1986a).

Detailed neuropsychological evaluation of patients with HD is often useful because of the range of deficits encountered and the variability in the course of this dementia. Although cognitive deficits occur very early in the disease, it is questionable whether neuropsychological deficits appear before other clinical signs of the disease (Diamond et al. 1992; Giordani et al. 1995; Jason et al. 1988; Strauss and Brandt 1990).

Dementia of similar severity (e.g., as assessed by the MMSE) may be due to different disabilities in different illnesses. At any given level of dementia, the pattern of failure for specific items is different in HD and AD (Mendez 1994). At mild levels of dementia (MMSE score of 20–24), HD patients are more impaired than AD patients in the serial subtraction of 7 from 100, whereas AD patients are less likely to recall three items learned earlier in the examination. Object naming is relatively preserved even in advanced HD (Brandt et al. 1988). Naming and other language functions appear to be relatively preserved in HD (Butters et al. 1978; Cummings and Benson 1988), but not invariably.

The cognitive deficits of HD include, in addition to those of memory and verbal fluency, difficulties in tasks requiring sustained concentration (e.g., mental arithmetic) and visuospatial skills. The deficits in visuospatial tasks are most easily seen in tests measuring constructional ability (e.g., the Wechsler Adult Intelligence Scale Block Design and Object Assembly tests) but can also be detected with tasks that do not require coordinated motor activity (Fedio et al. 1979). Patients with HD also have difficulty identifying or using their position in space relative to some fixed point (S.E. Folstein et al. 1990). This difficulty in personal space contrasts with AD, in which the deficit is mainly in the perception of extrapersonal space.

Planning, organizing, and mental flexibility—the executive functions that are typically impaired in patients with frontal-subcortical pathology—are also affected early in HD (Brandt and Butters 1986; Caine et al. 1978). These cognitive deficits of HD patients are most prominent in tasks that require keeping track of several things at once, discovering rules, or frequently changing mental sets (Bylsma et al. 1990; Fedio et al. 1979; Starkstein et al. 1988; Wexler 1979). Deficits in discriminating facial identity and affect may be seen (Jacobs et al. 1995). Awareness of deficits is present in HD, but judgment is poor.

The memory deficits of HD are the best-characterized neuropsychological feature of the disease. HD patients are often compared with AD and Korsakoff's disease patients. Early studies of learning and memory in HD (Brandt and Butters 1986; Butters et al. 1976) suggested that the disease was characterized by major deficits in the encoding or storage of new information. However, deficits in retrieval of memories and the acquisition of procedural memory appear to be even more pronounced (S.E. Folstein et al. 1990).

Unlike individuals with AD or Korsakoff's disease, HD patients are better able to recognize than recall information to which they have recently been exposed and are able to make use of verbal mediators to improve their memory performance (Butters et al. 1983; Martone et al. 1984; see S.E. Folstein 1989). The relative sparing of recognition memory may be limited to verbal material and reflect the relatively intact language abilities of HD patients (Josiassen et al. 1982). Moss et al. (1986) found that recognition memory for designs, colors, or the positions of objects on a board were as impaired in HD patients as in those with AD or Korsakoff's disease. HD patients do not benefit from increased encoding opportunities and do not show a gradient of retrograde amnesia, such that more recent memories are more difficult to retrieve than more distant events.

Language, with the exception of verbal fluency and prosody, is relatively preserved in HD (Furtado and Suchowersky 1995; Mendez 1994; M. Morris 1995). Patients tend to answer questions with single words or short phrases, punctuated by pauses and silences. There is some deficit in the ability to understand prosodic elements of speech, which may contribute to the impairments in interpersonal relations that can occur in HD. Not surprisingly, writing by persons with HD is slow and effortful and is characterized by sudden stops, omissions, and perseveration.

## Psychiatric Abnormalities

Psychiatric symptoms are common in HD and are often the first signs of the disorder. "Insanity with a tendency to suicide" was one of the three cardinal features of the disease noted by Huntington (1872). Estimates of the proportion of patients who first present with psychiatric symptoms range from 24% to 79%, and the prevalence of psychiatric disorders in HD patients ranges from 35% to 73% (Cummings 1995; Mendez 1994). These wide ranges reflect methodological differences among studies in sampling, diagnostic criteria, and assessment methods.

Several studies have attempted to correlate genetic information with psychiatric symptoms. Shiwach and Norbury (1994) studied psychiatric symptoms in asymptomatic, at-risk HD heterozygotes and compared them with their non-gene-carrying siblings. They found no increase in schizophrenia, depression, psychiatric episodes, or behavioral disorders; however, HD family members had more psychopathology than did partner control subjects. The number of CAG repeats has not correlated with psychiatric symptoms or onset symptoms in two studies in which this variable was included (Claes et al. 1995; Zappacosta et al. 1996).

Although mood disorders had been emphasized by some early workers (McHugh and Folstein 1975), a schizophrenia-like syndrome was thought to be the most common psychiatric manifestation of HD until recently (Garron 1973). Schizophrenia syndromes may be more common in more advanced cases of HD (S.E. Folstein 1989; S.E. Folstein et al. 1983a). The early emphasis on this syndrome may have been related to ascertainment bias from reporting mental hospitals.

More recent literature—especially studies using explicit diagnostic criteria and standardized assessments—suggests that intermittent explosive disorders and affective disorders are the most prevalent psychiatric conditions in HD (S.E. Folstein 1989; S.E. Folstein et al. 1990). Although unipolar depression is more common, mania can be seen in conjunction with HD. There is a markedly elevated risk of suicide in persons with HD. The period of greatest risk is in the 50s and 60s (Cummings 1995; Mendez 1994).

These dysphoric states might be seen as an understandable reaction to the degenerative neurologic disorder (Caine and Shoulson 1983). However, clinical evidence suggests an intrinsic association between HD and affective disorder. S.E. Folstein et al. (1983a) found familial aggregation for affective disorder and HD in families identified by a proband with both disorders. The rate of affective disorder in families of probands with HD but no affective disorder was much lower. Affective disorder preceded the onset of HD by nearly a decade in this series. Earlier onset of psychiatric than motor or cognitive symptoms had been found in an earlier series as well (S.E. Folstein et al. 1979).

Irritability, often precipitated by the kinds of events that previously had not provoked such reactions, and anxiety are also common. These symptoms are rarely reported by the patient, but the caregiver must inquire about them. They are more common in patients with such traits earlier in life (S.E. Folstein 1989). Approximately 30% of patients are reported to exhibit altered sexual behavior, including sexual aggression, promiscuity, exhibitionism, voyeurism, and pedophilia (Cummings 1995; Mendez 1994). Some reports have indicated that alcoholism is frequent among HD patients, but S.E. Folstein et al. (1983a, 1987) did not find an increased rate.

Although psychiatric symptoms are generally independent of progressive cognitive impairment, there appear to be changes in psychiatric manifestations over the course of the disease. In general, early HD may be accompanied by irritability, anxiety, aggression, and antisocial behavior, and the middle stages often contain depression, psychosis, or mania. Later on in the disease, apathy and abulia are common psychiatric manifestations.

Personality changes—especially irritable, hostile, or angry mood—can be important harbingers of the onset of HD in at-risk individuals. Conduct disorder is not uncommon in the offspring of HD patients, even in those not carrying the genetic mutation. Although both of these disorders might be taken as results of limbic–basal ganglia–cortex disruptions, environmental factors associated with rearing by an affected parent may contribute to the personality disorders seen in the children of HD patients (Cummings 1995; S.E. Folstein 1989; Mendez 1994).

## Treatment

HD is preventable but, as yet, incurable. There are no effective treatments for influencing the course of the disease (S.E. Folstein 1989; Martin and Gusella 1986). A number of medical treatments have been used palliatively to manage concurrent psychiatric disorder and chorea. A combination of medical therapy and psychosocial intervention for patient and family can be beneficial in the management of the disease. Efforts to pharmacologically affect the deterioration in functional capacity that occurs in HD have proved to be of no marked benefit (Gram and Bentsen 1985; Martin and Gusella 1986; Mendez 1994; Nutt 1983).

Early in the course of the disease, chorea can be treated with low-dose neuroleptic pharmacotherapy. S.E. Folstein (1989) recommends withholding treatment until involuntary movements become disabling because of the dysphoria and feeling of cognitive dulling that neuroleptics can induce. Fluphenazine is less likely to produce dysphoria than is haloperidol. Later in the disease

course, larger doses may be helpful, as may a combination of presynaptic (tetrabenazine or reserpine) and postsynaptic dopamine blockers (S.E. Folstein 1989). Treatment is not always effective, and use of dopamine blockade brings with it risk of tardive dyskinesia, worsening depression, and cognitive effects (S.E. Folstein 1989; Mendez 1994). The differential effectiveness of various neuroleptics has not been established (Girotti et al. 1984). Atypical neuroleptics may help to some degree in suppressing involuntary movements but are less potent than haloperidol in this regard. Their attractiveness in this setting is decreased risk of developing dyskinesias, albeit at a cost of some reduced efficacy. For akinetic patients, antiparkinsonian drugs may be tried. There are no adequate controlled trials of the treatment of involuntary movements in HD, and neuroleptics are ineffective for the voluntary movement symptoms.

Psychotic symptoms, especially hallucinations, are often responsive to neuroleptic therapy (Caine and Shoulson 1983; S.E. Folstein 1989). Atypical neuroleptics appear to be effective in this setting without the complication of inducing motor symptoms.

Treatment of the emotional symptoms of HD can be more successful at times. Tricyclic antidepressants or lithium is often effective in the treatment of depressive symptoms (Caine and Shoulson 1983; S.E. Folstein 1989; Mendez 1994). Improvement may be greater for the somatic-vegetative aspects of the syndrome than for the subjective elements of depression (Caine and Shoulson 1983). The lessened responsivity of helplessness-hopeless to pharmacotherapy is understandable. Although they are rarely needed, monoamine oxidase inhibitors were reported to be useful by Ford (1986) and S.E. Folstein (1989), as has electroconvulsive therapy (Ranen et al. 1994). Manic symptoms may respond to neuroleptics (S.E. Folstein et al. 1979; McHugh and Folstein 1975) as well as to carbamazepine, more so than to lithium (Mendez 1994).

Irritability and aggressive outbursts respond to both environmental and pharmacologic management. Irritability can be decreased by reduction in environmental complexity and the institution of unchanging routines. Neuroleptics can also be effective in reducing irritability (S.E. Folstein 1989). Successful treatment with β-adrenergic blockers has been reported in three patients who had aggressive outbursts but limited response to neuroleptics (Stewart et al. 1987). A paradoxical response in HD to pindolol has been reported (von Hafften and Jensen 1989). Reliable, effective pharmacologic treatment of episodic dyscontrol in HD awaits development.

Environmental management is important in the care of HD patients, particularly to minimize incontinence and the risk of dehydration (S.E. Folstein 1989). Social support along with case management can be very important in the adaptation of the family to the diagnosis of HD and the management of the illness within the family (Shoulson 1982). Referral to the Huntington's Disease Society is helpful to provide educational materials and needed psychological support.

## Parkinson's Disease

In 1817, James Parkinson described a new disorder he referred to as *paralysis agitans*, now referred to as idiopathic Parkinson's disease (PD). The cardinal neurologic features include tremor, muscle rigidity, bradykinesia, and postural instability. When these features occur in another identified entity, the term *parkinsonism* or *secondary parkinsonism* is used. Neuropsychiatric symptoms, particularly dementia and depression, are frequently associated with PD or parkinsonism.

### Epidemiology

PD affects perhaps 1 million individuals in North America and shows dramatic age-related increases in incidence and prevalence. The prevalence of PD is approximately 150 per 100,000, increasing after age 65 to nearly 1,100 per 100,000 (Kessler 1972). In addition to age, some studies (Martilla and Rinne 1980) have reported a protective effect of smoking, although sampling artifacts may explain this association. The prevalence of PD is higher in industrialized societies, and epidemiologic associations have been made with rural living and consumption of well water. These associations may reflect exposure to environmental toxins such as pesticides with homologies to the known toxin MPTP (Hammerstad and Carter 1995; Langston et al. 1983). Cases of familial PD have been reported (Mjones 1949; Pollock and Hornabrook 1966), but a low concordance rate in identical twins does not support a strong role for genetics in the majority of PD cases (Ward et al. 1983). Recent studies have focused on families with autosomal dominant mutations in the α-synuclein gene located on chromosome 4q21–q23. α-Synuclein is the major component of classic Lewy bodies, which are the pathologic hallmark of PD and dementia with Lewy bodies (DLB; also called diffuse Lewy body disease). Mutations associated with PD also occur in the ubiquitin carboxy-terminal hydrolase L1 gene and the *Parkin* gene (Lucking et al. 2000).

Prevalence studies estimate that dementia occurs in 10%–30% of patients with PD. Sample differences probably explain most of this variability, with early studies demonstrating the highest estimates (Ebmeier et al. 1990; Lieberman et al. 1979; Martilla and Rinne 1976; Rajput et al. 1984; Sutcliffe 1985). Mayeaux (1990) found that the cumulative incidence of dementia in PD may be as high as 60% by age 88. In addition to age, family history for dementia, depression, and severe motor disability is a risk factor for developing dementia in PD (Aarsland et al. 1996; Hofman et al. 1989; Marder et al. 1990, 1995). In PD, depression occurs in 15%–30% of patients (Mayeux et al. 1986b).

### Etiology

Because its cause is unknown, PD fits into the category of degenerative diseases because of the progressive clinical course of the disease in association with neuronal loss. The association between PD and arteriosclerosis has been controversial (Celesia and Wanamaker 1972; Martilla and Rinne 1976; Pollock and Hornabrook 1966), although most authors agree that infarcts can cause parkinsonism. Postencephalitic parkinsonism, characterized by symmetric rigidity and oculogyric crises, was common early in the twentieth century but is now rare. The second most common cause of parkinsonism now is administration of phenothiazines or related dopamine receptor blocking agents for the treatment of psychiatric symptoms. This extrapyramidal effect may be less common since the introduction of atypical neuroleptic agents with much less dopamine receptor blocking potential.

The description of parkinsonism in drug abusers by the intravenous use of MPTP (Langston et al. 1983) led to speculations that the idiopathic disease may result from subclinical exposure to toxic agents (Calne et al. 1986; Hammerstad and Carter 1995). Epidemiologic studies have indicated that rural living and obtaining drinking water from underground wells may be a risk factor for PD. The presumed mechanism of this relates to groundwater contamination with undetermined compounds, such as pesticides, some of which may act like MPTP analogs. No consistent pattern in cytochrome P450 genotypes has been found, following initial studies indicating that a large percentage of PD patients were slow metabolizers of debrisoquine. Manganese intoxication has also been associated with parkinsonism.

### Neurobiology

In several brain regions, the neuronal loss in PD is accompanied by the formation of Lewy bodies—hyaline inclusion bodies that were first described in the pigmented cells of the dorsal vagus nucleus and the substantia nominata or nucleus basalis of Meynert. Lewy bodies can also be seen in the brain-stem nuclei, particularly the locus coeruleus and substantia nigra (Jellinger 1986). Lewy bodies are composed mainly of the protein α-synuclein, mutations of which are associated with familial PD.

In recent years, attention on Lewy bodies occurring in the neocortex has led to the recognition of DLB. The nosology of this subject is discussed below, because many patients with Lewy body disease develop dementia and may have concomitant AD histopathology. Hurtig et al. (2000) found that cortical Lewy bodies are both sensitive and specific for dementia in PD in a prospectively studied cohort of patients with clinical PD.

The loss of dopaminergic cells in the substantia nigra is thought to relate most directly to the motor abnormalities—particularly the bradykinesia and rigidity—and can be partially compensated for by the administration of levodopa or dopamine agonists. Neuronal loss in the nucleus basalis of Meynert occurs to a small degree in all patients with idiopathic PD but not postencephalitic PD (Arendt et al. 1983; Tagliavini et al. 1984; Whitehouse et al. 1983). Cortical cell loss also occurs, and abnormalities have been reported in two neurotransmitters present in cortical interneurons, somatostatin (Epelbaum et al. 1983) and corticotropin-releasing factor (Whitehouse et al. 1987).

In addition to neurotransmitter changes, alterations also occur in neurotransmitter receptors. Ruberg et al. (1982) reported increases in muscarinic cholinergic receptors in PD with dementia, whereas most studies show few changes in AD with the exception of a possible increase in presynaptic muscarinic receptors (reviewed in Whitehouse et al. 1988). Nicotinic cholinergic receptors are reduced in both AD and PD (E.K. Perry et al. 1987; Whitehouse et al. 1988). Some types of serotonin receptors are also affected in both disorders (E.K. Perry et al. 1984). PET studies of dopaminergic function in PD using the catecholamine reuptake blocker [$^{11}$C]nomifensine have demonstrated reduced dopamine reuptake sites in the putamen contralateral to the most-involved extremity (Tedroff et al. 1988). Reduced [$^{18}$F]6-fluoro-L-dopa uptake in the contralateral putamen has also been observed (Brooks et al. 1990; Leenders et al. 1986; Nahmias et al. 1985). Depression in PD has been linked to bilateral decreases in regional cerebral blood flow in anteromedial frontal and cingulate cortex, overlapping with areas shown to be affected in primary depression (Ring et al. 1994).

The relationships among this cellular and neurochemical pathology and the neuropsychiatric symptoms are unclear. Some but not all dementia patients with PD develop senile plaques and neurofibrillary tangles (NFTs) identical to those found in AD (Boller et al. 1980; Chui

et al. 1986; Hakim and Mathieson 1979). The strongest correlation between neuronal loss and cognitive symptoms has been between loss of cortical cholinergic markers and dementia (R.H. Perry et al. 1983; Ruberg et al. 1982). Neuronal loss occurs in cholinergic basal forebrain to a greater extent in patients with dementia than in those with no dementia. Neuronal loss in the dopaminergic cells of the midbrain—particularly the ventral tegmental area—may also relate to cognitive impairment (Javoy-Agid and Agid 1980; Rinne et al. 1989; Uhl et al. 1985). Other researchers have proposed that alterations in the locus coeruleus may contribute to the cognitive disabilities, particularly bradyphrenia (Mayeux et al. 1988). Mayeux et al. (1984) associated raphe pathology with depression by providing evidence of loss of serotoninergic markers in cerebrospinal fluid (CSF), which correlates with the presence of affective symptoms. It is also possible that alterations in noradrenaline and corticotropin-releasing factor may relate to psychiatric symptoms as well.

## Motor Symptoms

The most disabling motor features of PD are bradykinesia and rigidity (Table 28–4). The patient has difficulty initiating movements, and when movement is started, it occurs slowly. Poverty of automatic movements (such as movement of the arms when walking) are characteristic. Lack of facial expression reflects hypokinesia of facial musculature. Rigidity can affect all muscle groups—proximal and distal, agonist and antagonist—and in idiopathic PD can occur asymmetrically. Tremor is the presenting feature in most cases and is slow (5–10 Hz), often occurs distally, and occurs most often at rest. It can be brought out with distraction and may be prominent when walking. Postural instability, associated with a characteristic flexion at the trunk and neck, occurs (frequently as a late symptom in idiopathic PD) and can lead to serious falls. Early occurrence of postural instability or orthostatic hypotension should raise suspicion of a parkinsonian syndrome such as progressive supranuclear palsy, Shy-Drager syndrome, or another akinetic-rigid syndrome. Treatment may improve all symptoms, with tremor responding best and postural instability and dementia least well.

## Cognition

Many patients with PD show cognitive impairment; in some patients the impairment may not be severe enough to warrant the label of dementia (see Table 28–4). In one study, 93% of patients with PD showed some form of

**TABLE 28–4.** Clinical features of Parkinson's disease

**Motor symptoms**
  Bradykinesia
  Tremor
  Rigidity
  Postural instability
**Neuropsychological deficits**
  Bradykinesia and bradyphrenia
  Verbal and visual memory deficits
  Impaired visuospatial skills
  Executive dysfunction (e.g., sequencing, switching set)
  Language difficulties (e.g., naming)
**Psychiatric features**
  Possible premorbid personality characteristics
  Affective disorder
  Psychosis—often medication induced

cognitive impairment (Pirozzolo et al. 1982). Rare patients have been reported in which dementia was the first sign of autopsy-proven idiopathic PD (Hedera et al. 1994).

A large body of literature exists describing problems in visuospatial impairment, including spatial capacities, facial recognition, body schema, pursuit tracking, spatial attention, visual analysis, and judgments concerning position in space (Boller et al. 1984; Growdon and Corkin 1986; Levin 1990). Visuospatial function is composed of many separate abilities that are difficult to isolate and test separately (R.E. Brown and Marsden 1986). Visual analysis is impaired in PD (Levin et al. 1989; Pirozzolo 1982; Villardita et al. 1982). Similarly, operating on objects in physical space (i.e., constructional praxis) is affected in PD, perhaps partly due to problems with spatial attention (Levin 1990). Abnormalities in memory involving verbal and nonverbal tasks with stimuli presented in different modalities occur.

The communication difficulties of PD are mostly due to speech abnormalities, including hypophonia and dysarthria. However, language impairments can also occur and include reduced verbal fluency and naming difficulties (Matison et al. 1982). Abnormalities in syntax have been reported in PD (Cummings et al. 1988), although most studies have focused on semantics, comprehension, and naming (Bayles 1990). Few studies of phonology or pragmatics have been undertaken.

Executive and attentional abnormalities have also been reported that are similar to deficits attributed to frontal lobe dysfunction (Freedman 1990). These deficits include sequencing voluntary motor activities, difficulties in maintaining and switching set, and abnormalities in selective attention. These abnormalities may also be seen in the setting of surgical treatments for PD, including pallidotomy and deep brain stimulation (see below).

The relationships between the cognitive impairments in PD and the motor symptoms are complex. Poor performance on cognitive tests is not purely related to motor abnormalities. For example, visuospatial deficits continue to be detectable using tasks with limited roles for eye movements (e.g., tachistoscopy). However, the presence of akinetic-rigid motor deficit makes comparisons with dementias such as AD or HD difficult to interpret.

# Psychiatric Abnormalities in Parkinson's Disease

## Premorbid Personality

In the 1940s, patients who appeared to suppress anger and be quite perfectionistic were claimed to be more at risk for developing PD (Booth 1948; Sands 1942). Sands described the so-called masked personality, in which the patient's outward appearance of calm belied the inner state of turmoil. Later studies did not show such strong relationships between premorbid personality and PD (Diller and Riklan 1956; Lishman 1978; Pollock and Hornabrook 1966). Although they are difficult to undertake, new and better-designed studies with more modern personality inventories may help elucidate the relationships between premorbid psychological characteristics and psychiatric sequelae of neurodegenerative disease.

## Affective Disorder

Affective disorder is the most common psychiatric disturbance associated with PD, with estimates of its occurrence ranging from 20% to 90% (Mayeux et al. 1986b). Mayeux et al. found that major depression and dysthymic disorder were the most frequent types. Early in PD, some instances of depression are believed to be reactive. However, this model may be too simplistic, and in PD, as in other chronic illnesses, the relationship of disease severity to depression is nonlinear (Starkstein et al. 1989). Relatively few associations between depression and disease factors such as duration of disease, degree of disability, and response to medications have been established (Troster et al. 1995). A higher frequency of depression has been found in early-onset cases in which depression correlated with cognitive impairment and duration of disease (Kostic et al. 1994). Mayeux et al. (1981) also found an association between depression and dementia. Based on their CSF studies mentioned earlier, Mayeux et al. (1988) used the precursor of serotonin, 5-

hydroxytryptophan, to alleviate depression with some success. Menza and Mark (1994) found that depression did not correlate with novelty seeking, a personality trait related to dopaminergic systems. However, they found that harm avoidance, related to serotoninergic systems, correlated with and explained 31% of the variance in depression scores in PD. A symptom complex suggesting guilt and body image change may be more common in PD than in other chronic illnesses.

Atypical depressive disorders can also occur. Schiffer and colleagues (1988) described a condition in which predominant anxiety occurs. Patients frequently develop phobias, such as the fear of falling, which often have some basis in reality. Berrios et al. (1995) found that anxiety and depression in some PD patients was due to a "behavioral phenocopy" caused by autonomic failure. Sleep is frequently affected in PD, but this disturbance is frequently multifactorial, with medications, motor symptoms, and age playing as large a role as depression and anxiety (Menza and Rosen 1995).

## Psychosis

Psychosis of a schizophrenic nature has been reported in PD in the absence of medication effects (Mjones 1949). However, most authors believe that medications are the most common cause of psychosis in PD. Celesia and Wanamaker (1972) observed psychotic episodes in 12% of their 153 patients. Most were due to drugs and occurred in patients who were cognitively impaired. Anticholinergic drugs, such as trihexyphenidyl, may be particularly likely to produce delirium with psychotic features, although they are also effective in suppressing the tremor (and are frequently used in tremor-predominant early PD). All of the antiparkinsonian medications have been implicated in the occurrence of hallucinations in PD.

## Treatment

Great strides have been made in treating the motor dysfunction in PD. Alone or in combination, levodopa, dopamine agonists, and anticholinergic agents can effectively treat rigidity, bradykinesia, and tremor. Postural instability is resistant to the beneficial effects of drugs. Complicated motor phenomena can occur (especially later in therapy), such as on/off fluctuations and freezing episodes (Yahr 1986), which can be very stressful to patients and caregivers. Selegiline, newer dopamine agonists, and catechol-O-methyl transferase inhibitors may help alleviate motor fluctuations in some patients.

Common side effects with anti-PD medications include dyskinesias, nausea, and postural hypotension. Selegiline combined with a selective serotonin reuptake inhibitor may produce a hypertensive crisis related to nonspecific inhibition of monoamine oxidase by selegiline. Other neuropsychiatric complications reported with PD medications include excessive somnolence associated with pramipexole and a neuroleptic-malignant syndrome occurring on rapid discontinuation of medications.

Treatment of the neuropsychiatric symptoms involves both behavioral and biological approaches. Behavioral treatment must begin with a careful assessment, which includes not only the medical aspects of the illness but also the effects of the illness on the patient's life (for example, functional disability as measured by ability to perform activities of daily living) and on the patient's family. Nursing and social work assessments can therefore play an important role in providing a baseline for following the course of the illness. Education about the disease process and course is important. Frequent reassessments followed by modifications of care plans are necessary.

A variety of interventions are available for the individual patient, including individual psychotherapy, particularly to deal with depression early in the illness. For patients with dementia, some authors (Gilmore et al. 1989) suggest that certain forms of cognitive training or rehabilitation may be helpful. Particularly in the dementias associated with motor problems, physical and occupational therapy may be very helpful. Since these disorders potentially affect the whole family, marriage therapy and family counseling may be appropriate in some circumstances. Careful attention should be paid to environmental modifications. For example, a safety check at home—including the appropriate use of handrails, avoiding stairs if possible, and stowing away loose objects such as rugs and electrical cords—is the most important intervention to prevent falls. As the illness progresses, particularly if there are associated neuropsychiatric symptoms, home care, day care, and eventually institutional care may be necessary. Early planning, both financial and legal, is helpful to minimize the difficulty of getting access to and financing for appropriate long-term-care services. Discussions with the individual and family members early in the disease when the patient can participate in decision making and prepare advance directives such as a living will are probably desirable.

### Biological Treatment

The most important role for the physician in caring for patients with dementia is to avoid so-called excess disability. Intercurrent illnesses and psychological stress can increase the intensity of neuropsychiatric symptoms and need to be prevented as best as possible. Iatrogenic disease, usually due to overuse of medication, needs to be monitored carefully, particularly if more than one physician is involved in care. The most effective biological interventions are probably those for the treatment of affective disorders and include the use of antidepressant medications, and, if necessary, electroconvulsive therapy (ECT). ECT can be transiently helpful in the treatment of psychosis associated with excess dopaminergic states and may improve motor function as well (Abrams 1989; G.I. Brown 1975). However, post-ECT delirium may occur, and ECT may worsen memory function in demented PD patients. Antidepressants or other medications with profound anticholinergic side effects should be avoided in patients with dementia or autonomic failure, although they carry some potential benefit for motor function and tremor control. Donepezil has the potential to worsen the motor symptoms in PD, but this is generally not a limiting side effect of its usage in this population.

Treatment of psychosis in these disorders is difficult, because the medications used to treat the hallucinations and delusions can exacerbate some of the symptoms. The first step should be to identify drugs or other stresses that are contributing to the psychosis and eliminate those factors (Saint-Cyr et al. 1993). If necessary, major tranquilizers can be employed if they are monitored carefully for the side effects on motor (especially worsening parkinsonism) and cognitive symptoms. Atypical neuroleptics such as clozapine, olanzapine, or quetiapine cause little or no extrapyramidal side effects and have a role in treating psychosis in these disorders without worsening motor function (Friedman and Factor 2000; Parsa and Bastani 1998). However, all of these medications have significant anticholinergic effects that may induce early side effects of lethargy and may conceivably affect cognition. Sleep disturbances are common with these disorders, and primary focus should be placed on sleep hygiene (i.e., increased daytime activity, a regular pattern of sleep preparation behavior, and avoidance of stimulants).

## Surgical Treatment

Surgical lesions of both the thalamus and the globus pallidus are associated with improvement of motor dysfunction in PD. More consistent outcomes for tremor reduction, reduced levodopa-induced dyskinesias, and greater reduction in bradykinesia result from pallidotomy, most commonly involving lesions of the internal portion of the globus pallidus (Fine et al. 2000; Lang et al. 1997). Side effects include those related to the procedure, including hemorrhage and infarction, with location determining symptoms.

Although the initial studies on pallidotomy emphasized the functional motor outcomes, neuropsychological side effects occur with pallidotomy. Stebbins et al. (2000) found symptoms of frontostriatal deficits in psychomotor processing speed, executive functioning, and reasoning after unilateral posteroventral pallidotomy. Decreases in verbal fluency have been reported, particularly after left-sided pallidotomy (Kubu et al. 2000). Bilateral pallidotomy may be complicated by abulia, postoperative depression, and eyelid apraxia, which may limit the practicality of this approach. However, many of the reported series have been small, and not all series report consistent effects on cognition (Schmand et al. 2000). There is evidence for anatomic segregation of motor and cognitive functional circuitry in the globus pallidus (Lombardi et al. 2000). With recent improvements in the ability to localize lesions, it is hoped that neuropsychiatric complications can be minimized in this population consisting primarily of patients with advanced PD.

Implantation of deep brain stimulating electrodes has similar effects on contralateral motor function. The most consistent improvements occur with tremor reduction and increase in "on" time, and corresponding decreases in "off" period contralateral bradykinesia. Deep brain stimulation has been associated with similar cognitive risks as pallidotomy. A decrease in verbal fluency, particularly with left subthalamic nucleus stimulation, has been reported. Changes in personality and acute depression have also been reported (Hugdahl and Wester 2000; R. Kumar et al. 1999; Starr et al. 1998). In one well-documented case in which reproducible acute depression was associated with left substantia nigra stimulation, increases in left orbitofrontal and right parietal blood flow were demonstrated on PET scanning, but the neural circuitry involved in this interesting phenomenon are not fully understood (Bejjani et al. 1999).

## Dementia With Lewy Body Disease

Dementia with Lewy bodies (DLB) is an increasingly recognized and studied form of dementia, accounting in some series for as many of 20% of cases. There is a complex relationship with AD being seen in a relatively pure form of Lewy body dementia and in combination with AD as the so-called Lewy body variant (LBV) of AD.

## Clinical Diagnosis

Clinical criteria for DLB have been proposed based on the presence of features such as hallucinations, extrapyramidal signs, daily fluctuations in cognition, and different responses to drugs, most notably a tendency not to respond to antiparkinsonian medications. A number of longitudinal studies, followed by autopsy, have examined the reliability and validity of these clinical criteria. Hohl et al. (2000) demonstrated that the clinical diagnostic accuracy of DLB was poor. These researchers believe that extrapyramidal signs are overemphasized and that the distinction between DLB and other dementias is better made with a greater emphasis on early hallucinations in DLB. Most studies now do not identify that there are differences in age at onset, age at death, or duration of disease in cohorts of DLB patients compared with AD (Z. Walker et al. 2000). Verghese et al. (1999) conclude that the new consortium on DLB criteria have high negative predictive value and exclude patients without DLB. These authors believe that a positive predictive value of 75% could be obtained. Litvan et al. (1998b) also examined sensitivity, specificity, and positive and negative predictive value of clinical criteria. They also determined that interrater reliability for diagnosis of DLB was not particularly good and varied across different visits as the disease evolved. These authors emphasized that postural imbalance is not particularly helpful in differentiating DLB from PD (Table 28–5).

Louis et al. (1997) compared the clinical features of DLB with those of PD. They found that rest tremor was more common in PD, whereas myoclonus was more common in DLB. The frequency of rigidity, bradykinesia, dystonia, or gaze palsies did not differ in their studies. In the earlier literature, response to levodopa may have been better in PD than in DLB.

One of the interesting clinical features of DLB is fluctuating consciousness. M.P. Walker et al. (2000) used a variety of techniques, including reaction time and electroencephalography, to measure episodes of fluctuating consciousness. Their methods demonstrated that these phenomena were more common in DLB, although they also occurred in vascular dementia more than in AD. Periodicity of fluctuating consciousness varies in the different conditions.

**TABLE 28–5.** Clinical characteristics of diffuse Lewy body disease

Dementia
Attentional impairment
Visuospatial difficulties
Fluctuations in cognitive functioning
Persistent, well-formed visual hallucinations
Parkinsonism

Much recent attention has also been paid to LBV. LBV is diagnosed by the presence of a large enough number of neuritic plaques to meet diagnostic criteria for AD and neurofibrillary pathologies usually intermediate between AD and DLB. Hansen et al. (1998) believe that ApoE-4 is overrepresented in LBV as in AD, but not in DLB. Thus, it remains controversial as how to distinguish AD, DLB, and LBV, although claims have been made that their respective biologies are significantly different enough to allow differentiation (McKeith et al. 1998). Although other authors (Papka et al. 1998) claim that one cannot reliably differentiate these entities clinically, a previously underemphasized feature, depression, is more common in DLB. Mori et al. (2000) demonstrated a considerable amount of visual perceptual disturbances in DLB based on tests of size and form discrimination.

## Neurobiology

Genetic forms of DLB exist, including autosomal dominant forms. Ishikawa presented five cases with familial autosomal dominant DLB. These patients surprisingly responded well to levodopa therapy. As mentioned above, overlap occurs in clinical and pathological features of DLB, AD, and PD. The articles on clinical features suggest that clinical diagnosis is not yet adequate. DLB also overlaps with other degenerative syndromes, such as multiple system atrophy (Dickson et al. 1999). These authors claim that multiple system atrophy and DLB are both α-synucleinopathies that may fall in different parts of the spectrum of this disease. Autopsy studies have shown that DLB has similar numbers of neuritic plaques to AD, but fewer NFTs (Samuel et al. 1997a). Attempts have been made to correlate pathologic features with clinical findings. Samuel et al. (1997b) found that neocortical neuritic plaque burden and NFT counts in entorhinal cortex and loss of choline acetyltransferase were correlated with the severity of dementia. However, neocortical NFTs and antisynaptophysin were not correlated with dementia. The marked level of variability was reported in neuronal counts in entorhinal cortex in DLB—an area consistently and severely affected in AD. Sabbagh et al. (1999) also found that reductions in synaptophysin and choline acetyltransferase did not correlate as well, in DLB as in AD.

Galvin et al. (1999) studied different forms of synuclein in PD and DLB. Antibodies to both α-synuclein and γ-synuclein detect aggregation of these products in dystrophic neurites. These researchers suggest that their findings support a role for all three synucleins—α, β, and γ—in the pathology of both PD and DLB. Arima et al. (1999) studied the colocalization of tau, which is associated with NFTs, and α-synuclein. NFTs or tau is rarely found in neurons in DLB; however, tau can be found in some Lewy bodies in a variety of different patterns, which raises the issue of whether it is related to aggregation and hyperphosphorylation. Mori et al. (2000) demonstrated a considerable amount of visual perceptual disturbances in DLB, based on tests of size and form discrimination.

## Neuroimaging

Standard structural imaging with computed tomography (CT) or magnetic resonance imaging (MRI) is not particularly helpful in differentiating AD from DLB. One may see more frontal lobe atrophy in DLB, but not sufficient difference to be helpful in clinical differentiation. Attempts are being made to use other forms of neuroimaging to differentiate these conditions. Using CT scanning, medial temporal lobe volumes were measured, and although differences were found between depressed subjects in dementia, no differences were found in the groups that were diagnosed as having vascular dementia, AD, or DLB (O'Brien et al. 2000). Talbot et al. (1998) studied standard single photon emission tomography measuring blood flow in DLB. Some differences could be found between vascular dementia and frontal temporal dementia and AD, but DLB could not be well differentiated from AD.

## Treatment

In addition to responsiveness to levodopa, patients with DLB need to be watched carefully when neuroleptics are employed because they may develop complex and life-threatening neuroleptic malignant syndrome and related phenomena. On the other hand, DLB patients may respond as well or better to cholinesterase inhibitors than AD patients (Fergusson and Howard 2000).

## Other Degenerative Dementias Associated With Motor Abnormalities

## Progressive Supranuclear Palsy

Progressive supranuclear palsy (PSP) (also known as Steele-Richardson-Olszewski syndrome) is a chronic, progressive disorder associated with eye movement abnormalities, parkinsonism, and dementia. It may have onset with deficient downward gaze, which causes trouble walking down stairs. The prevalence of PSP has been estimated at 1.4 per 100,000 (Golbe et al. 1988). Median age at onset of symptoms is approximately 63 years, with a median survival of 6–10 years (Golbe et al. 1988). Men are somewhat more likely to develop PSP. Postulated risk factors include previous history of hypertension, but there is no evidence that smoking cigarettes lowers PSP risk (Vanacore et al. 2000). Familial cases have been described, and the disease may be more common, relative to PD, in Indians and Afro-Caribbeans (Chaudhuri et al. 2000).

## Diagnosis

The diagnosis of PSP is suggested by the presence of dementia with parkinsonism and eye movement abnormalities. The earliest eye movement abnormalities include loss of vertical saccade velocity as distinct from deficits in smooth pursuit velocity. This can be tested for by verbal request (e.g., "Look up, look down"). With disease progression, pursuit eye movements (e.g., following a moving object) are also slowed. When testing reflex eye movements with oculocephalic maneuvers (head turning), there is relative integrity in vertical eye movements. This has led to the distinction of the eye movement abnormality in PSP as being supranuclear, because the oculocephalic reflexes demonstrate the integrity of the lower motor neuron pathways for up and down gaze. Litvan et al. (1999) found that patients lacking vertical eye movement abnormalities presented a major source of error in correct antemortem diagnosis of PSP. Ultimately, it is the constellation of clinical findings—that is, bilateral parkinsonism without tremor dominance, unstable gait with postural instability, and vertical eye movement abnormality without alien limb movements—that best distinguish PSP from PD, multiple system atrophy, corticobasal degeneration, and Pick's disease (Litvan et al. 1997).

Not all patients with PSP have noticeable dementia (Maher et al. 1985), and dementia is often not severe early in the course of PSP. It may be characterized by forgetfulness, slowing of thought processes, emotional or personality changes, and impaired ability to manipulate knowledge in the relative absence of aphasia, apraxia, or agnosia (Albert et al. 1974). PSP patients are particularly impaired on tests of frontal lobe function. PSP patients may also have deficits in visual scanning and search as well as verbal fluency, digit span, verbal memory, and logical memory.

There is usually extensive rigidity of the neck and spasticity of the face and extremities with bradykinesia and a parkinsonian gait. Unlike PD or corticobasal degeneration, parkinsonism in PSP is almost always symmetrical in severity. Other signs include axial dystonia, bradyphrenia, perseveration, forced grasping, and utilization behaviors. Pseudobulbar palsy and pathological laughing and crying may be observed in the later stages. The gait disturbance is associated with postural instability and a tendency toward retropulsion. Many patients with PSP are misdiagnosed as having PD, AD, hydrocephalus, or psychotic illness.

## Neuropsychiatric Manifestations

PSP patients often have disturbances of sleep and depression, occasionally with schizophreniform psychoses (Aldrich et al. 1989). Also seen are memory loss, slowness of thought processes, changes in personality with apathy or depression, irritability, and forced inappropriate crying or laughing with outbursts of rage. Episodes of irritability may be seen. PSP may also be associated with compulsive behaviors of the obsessive type (Destee et al. 1990).

Apathy is particularly prominent in many cases and should be differentiated from concomitant depression. In a study using the Neuropsychiatric Inventory, Levy et al. (1998) found that apathy correlated with lower cognitive function but not with depression subscale scores. Patients with PSP are particularly impaired in tasks requiring sequential movements, shifting of concepts, monitoring the frequency of stimuli, or rapid retrieval of verbal information (Grafman et al. 1990). These symptoms, particularly the lack of motivation, are thought to be a reflection of frontal lobe impairment due to pathology in orbitofrontal-cortical circuits.

## Diagnostic Imaging

X-ray CT and MRI studies show early involvement of midbrain structures with later atrophy of the pons and frontotemporal regions. PET scanning has shown reduced spiperone binding in the basal ganglia. Fluorodeoxyglucose PET studies show marked frontal and temporal hypometabolism (D'Antona et al. 1985; Cambier et al. 1985; Maher et al. 1985). There is also decreased fluorodopa uptake in the striatum reflective of decreased striatal dopamine formation and storage (Leenders et al. 1988). The loss of striatal dopamine receptors, as demonstrated by PET scanning, during life may explain the poor therapeutic efficacy of dopamine agonist therapy in PSP.

## Neurobiology

Neuropathologic findings include neuronal loss associated with gliosis and NFTs, most marked in the substantia nigra, basal forebrain, subthalamic nucleus, pallidum, and superior colliculus. The tangles in PSP are straight filaments, not twisted as in AD (Takahashi et al. 1989). There is extensive disruption in fibrillar proteins in subcortical neurons, with antigenic similarities in neurofibrillary pathology between PSP and AD (Galloway 1988; Probst et al. 1988). Additional areas involved to a lesser extent include the locus coeruleus, striatum, and a variety of upper brain stem and midbrain structures (Agid et al. 1986). The neurochemistry of PSP is characterized by massive dopamine depletion in the striatum and reduced density of dopamine $D_2$ receptors in the caudate nucleus and putamen (Pierot et al. 1988); widespread reduction in choline acetyltransferase levels in frontal cortex, basal forebrain, and basal ganglia (Whitehouse et al. 1988); diminished nicotinic receptors in the basal forebrain; diminished serotonin receptors in the temporal lobe (Maloteaux et al. 1988); and a variable reduction in GABAergic neurotransmitter systems in certain subcortical regions (Ruberg 1985). Available evidence concerning cortical and subcortical as well as multiple neurotransmitter system abnormalities demonstrates that PSP is not a pure subcortical or dopaminergic dementia). Standardized criteria for the neuropathologic diagnosis of PSP have been proposed and should widen our understanding of the clinical spectrum of PSP (Litvan et al. 1996) (Table 28–6).

With the discovery that mutations in the tau gene on chromosome 17 are responsible for the majority of clinical cases of PSP, similarities to other tauopathies such as frontotemporal dementia and corticobasal degeneration have emerged. In PSP, only the four-repeat-tau isoform aggregating into straight filaments is found. The relationship of these neuronal pathologies to clinical phenotypes is unknown at present.

**TABLE 28–6.** Clinical characteristics of progressive supranuclear palsy

Gait instability with falls
Axial rigidity
Bradykinesia
Supranuclear gaze abnormalities
Dysarthria
Dementia

## Treatment

No treatment has been found to be effective in relieving the motor or cognitive deficiencies in PSP. Levodopa treatment is generally not successful, correlating with the loss of postsynaptic striatal dopamine receptors. Poor responses with frequent dose-limiting side effects also occur with dopamine agonists. A report of effective treatment of violent behavior in a PSP patient with trazodone has been published and may be explained by the serotoninergic effects of the drug (Schneider et al. 1989). Studies using cholinesterase inhibitors are under way, but this would be considered an experimental therapy at this time.

## Cortical–Basal Ganglionic Degeneration

Cortical–basal ganglionic degeneration (CBGD) presents with asymmetric rigidity, cortical sensory loss, and an "alien hand syndrome" (Riley et al. 1990). This latter sign is seen with parietal, medial frontal, and corpus callosum pathology. Dementia is a variable part of this syndrome but has been the presenting symptom in numerous case reports. The neuropsychological profile is similar to that seen in PSP, with prominent executive dysfunction and explicit learning deficits without retention difficulties. However, asymmetric apraxias are frequent (Pillon et al. 1995). Arima et al. (1994) described a case of CBGD presenting with primary progressive aphasia. Insofar as CBGD appears etiologically related to the Pick's complex, some cases of primary progressive aphasia that have atypical Pick's disease pathology may fall within the CBGD spectrum (Kertesz et al. 1994). Depression is common, and other neuropsychiatric abnormalities include apathy/disinhibition, aberrant motor behaviors, and delusions (Litvan et al. 1998a). Oculomotor involvement similar to PSP may occur, particularly in advanced cases. Survival ranges from 2.5 to 12 years, with a median of about 8 years (Table 28–7).

Mutations in the tau gene appear to form the genetic basis of CBGD, PSP, Pick's disease, and frontotemporal dementia. The tau gene is located on chromosome 17, and several distinct mutations have been associated with these syndromes (Di Maria et al. 2000). Classic CBGD pathology shows abundant ballooned, achromatic neurons and focal cortical atrophy. There are also astrocytic plaques in CBGD cortex. The achromatic ballooned neurons are not found in increased numbers in other tauopathies. CBGD neuronal tau pathology shows wispy, fine threaded tau inclusions, in comparison with the dense, compacted inclusions of PSP; the distribution of pathology falls mainly in basal ganglia and brain stem in PSP, whereas CBGD shows widespread cerebral involvement as well (Dickson 1999). Differences in which tau isoforms accumulate in patients' brains may relate to different clinical phenotypes.

MRI may show asymmetric atrophy in the frontal

**TABLE 28–7.** Clinical characteristics of cortical–basal ganglionic degeneration

Parkinsonism, often asymmetric
Limb dystonia
Postural or action tremor
Focal reflex myoclonus
Apraxia
Cortical sensory loss
Alien limb phenomena
Choreiform dyskinesias
Dementia
Dysarthria
Hyperreflexia

and parietal lobes contralateral to the dominantly affected limbs (Soliveri et al. 1999). Cerebral blood flow studies show asymmetric decreased glucose utilization throughout the frontal cortex, superior parietal cortex, and contralateral caudate nucleus and thalamus to areas involved clinically, and cognitive impairment (Hirono et al. 2000; Laureys et al. 1999; Yamauchi et al. 1998). Single photon emission computed tomographic studies also show decreased blood flow in the basal ganglia and widespread areas of frontal, temporal, and parietal cortex; however, PSP patients show only frontal hypoperfusion (Okuda et al. 2000). Dopamine binding is also reduced asymmetrically in CBGD, as studied by both fluorodopa uptake and iodobenzamide single photon emission CT (Frisoni et al. 1995; Sawle et al. 1991). CSF tau levels are higher in patients with CBGD than in patients with PSP or healthy control subjects, but the specificity of these findings are unclear.

Treatment of CBGD is limited, with only a minority of patients responding to levodopa preparations given for parkinsonism. Myoclonus may respond to benzodiazepines, particularly clonazepam. No specific treatment for the dementia is available. Depression is common in CBGD, but little data exist on response to antidepressants (Kampoliti et al. 1998; Litvan et al. 1998a).

## Frontotemporal Dementia

The frontotemporal dementias (FTDs) constitute a heterogeneous group of conditions, often with prominent early behavioral disinhibitory symptoms. The clinical phenotypes now classified as FTD include Pick's disease, semantic aphasia, hereditary dysphasic dementia (J.C. Morris et al. 1984), and PSP and CBGD. This familial syndrome may present with symptoms of Klüver-Bucy syndrome, or social withdrawal, depression, and a schizophrenia-like picture in middle adulthood. Patients then develop parkinsonism and occasionally amyotrophy. Thus, not all of these patients have prominent motor disorders, often making diagnosis from primary psychiatric conditions difficult.

The FTDs have been linked to mutations in the tau protein gene as described previously in the sections on PSP and CBGD. Although consensus diagnostic criteria have been proposed, the incidence of these conditions has varied widely in different regions, possibly because of differences in case identification.

## Dementia With Degenerative Disorders of the Cerebellum

Clinical classification of the diseases of the cerebellum associated with cognitive impairment is difficult, but tremendous progress in deciphering the genetic basis of these disorders has begun to shed light on the complicated relationships of genotype to phenotype. Disorders of the cerebellum may involve pure cerebellar dysfunction or combinations of abnormalities in the cerebellum and brain stem; cerebellum and basal ganglia; or cerebellum, spinal cord, and brain stem. Involvement of the optic nerves (optic atrophy) or retina (retinitis pigmentosa) or peripheral neuropathy may also be found. Cases are frequently sporadic, and variable phenotypes are common within families (Rosenberg 1995a, 1995b).

## Olivopontocerebellar Atrophies

The olivopontocerebellar atrophies (OPCAs) are a heterogeneous group of disorders presenting with progressive ataxia and associated with cerebellar degeneration. Dementia may be found in types III and V, using the classification of Konigsmark and Winer (1970). The occurrence of dementia in type III OPCA is controversial. In type V OPCA, there is ataxia with parkinsonism, ophthalmoplegia, and dementia. OPCA may be associated with progressive autonomic failure and parkinsonism with striatonigral degeneration. In dominantly inherited OPCA of the Schut type, frontal lobe deficits may occur, as measured by delayed alternation tasks. How these test-specific cognitive abnormalities relate to the presence of any more global and pervasive syndrome of dementia remains to be determined. Two small studies of OPCA patients found visuospatial deficits in addition to slow visual and auditory reaction times, and deficits in classical conditioning responses; these changes may be due to the role of the cerebellum in the timing of conditioned responses (Botez-Marquard and Botez 1993; Topka et al. 1993). Frontal lobe deficits in hand sequencing, verbal reasoning, and proverb interpretation, and

parietal-type deficits in figure copying and visuospatial memory have been reported more recently (Arroyo-Anllo and Botez-Marquard 1998). Underlying these deficits may be the phenomenon of "reverse diaschisis," wherein bilateral cerebellar deficits contribute to both basal ganglionic and frontal-type dysfunction (Botez-Marquard and Botez 1997).

Kish et al. (1989) reported reduction in brain choline acetyltransferase (ChAT) activity in dominantly inherited OPCA. Mean ChAT activities in OPCA were reduced by 39%–72% in the cortex, thalamus, caudate nucleus, globus pallidus, basal forebrain, and medial olfactory area. Atrophy of the cerebellum, pons, and middle cerebellar peduncles with areas of abnormal signal intensity is seen on MRI imaging (Savoirardo et al. 1989). Diminished glucose metabolism in the cerebellar vermis and hemispheres and brain stem is found in OPCA PET studies. Treatment is mainly supportive.

## Friedreich's Ataxia

Friedreich's ataxia (FA) presents with a slowly progressive ataxia and may be associated with dementia. Its mode of inheritance is autosomal recessive, with the genetic defect in the gene termed Frataxin mapping to chromosome 9. With the availability of direct genetic testing, some atypical cases of spinocerebellar degeneration have been shown to be FA variants.

Mental function changes are often seen but have not been well characterized; they are present in about a quarter of cases. In some instances, a syndrome of "generalized intellectual deterioration" has been noted. In others, specific nonverbal intellectual impairments have been identified. In other cases, a variety of psychiatric disorders, including schizophrenia-like psychoses and depression, have been believed to be the primary cognitive behavioral abnormality. These psychotic states often feature paranoia, agitated behavior, and nocturnal hallucinations. Changes in performance IQ, conceptual ability, and visual constructive tasks, as well as in tasks of three-dimensional spatial functions, have been found to be abnormal in FA. Personality abnormalities may be marked and are associated with juvenile delinquency and irritability. There may be excessive religiosity or mysticism.

## Other Spinocerebellar Degenerations

The other cerebellar ataxias may be either hereditary or sporadic. Abortive forms are common and intrafamily variability is extremely common, with individuals sometimes showing little more than pes cavus or kyphoscoliosis. These disorders may present in childhood, early adulthood, or late adulthood and are usually slowly progressive. Associated findings of ataxic gait, intention tremor, decreased rapid alternating movements, past pointing, loss of the ability to check rebound, and dysarthria are common. The ataxic disorders may not be accompanied by intellectual changes until late in the illness. In a study reported by Skre (1974), dementia was found in 36% of patients with autosomal dominant spinocerebellar degeneration, 58% of patients with autosomal recessive cerebellar disease, and 82% of patients with autosomal recessive spinocerebellar degeneration. Memory and attentional deficits are found with apathy and psychomotor retardation, and occasionally with depression or schizophrenia-like psychosis.

## Motor Neuron Disease With Dementia

Loss of strength with diminished muscle mass (amyotrophy) and dementia may be seen in motor neuron disease, or amyotrophic lateral sclerosis (ALS) (Mitsuyama et al. 1985). Familial motor neuron disease may be associated with other neurodegenerative conditions, including Huntington's disease, Pick's disease, frontotemporal dementia, parkinsonism, and spinocerebellar degeneration (Rosenberg 1982). Approximately 5% of ALS patients demonstrate dementia or parkinsonism (Tyler 1982). Whether nondemented patients with sporadic ALS demonstrate a specific pattern of neuropsychological abnormalities (Gallassi et al. 1985; Montgomery and Erickson 1987) remains to be elucidated. Personality changes and hallucinations may occur in patients with ALS, as well as impairments in judgment, memory, abstract thinking, calculations, and anomia in individual patients.

The occurrence of dementia with ALS has been called classic ALS with dementia (Wikstrom et al. 1982), dementia of motor neuron disease (Horoupian et al. 1984), progressive dementia with motor disease (Mitsuyama et al. 1985), and amyotrophy dementia complex (Morita et al. 1987). The disease may begin with personality changes or with motor system degeneration. There may be early personality changes in association with frontotemporal atrophy on CT and a normal electroencephalogram. Spongy changes are found in 90% of patients with gliosis. NFTs, Lewy bodies, and Pick bodies are not found. Extensive neuronal loss with gliosis is found in the substantia nigra in some cases (Horoupian et al. 1984). There is a loss of neurons (particularly over 90 square microns) in layers 2 and 3 of the cortical mantle, particularly in the frontal and temporal regions. The syndrome of dementia with amyotrophy may also be found in Creutzfeldt-Jakob disease. However, in cases of Creutz-feldt-Jakob disease there is usually rapid onset with an interval from onset to death less than 1 year.

In western New Guinea, the Kii peninsula of Japan, and the island of Guam, a high incidence of ALS occurs, often associated with parkinsonism and dementia. On Guam, 10% of adult deaths in the native Chomorro population result from ALS, and 7% are attributed to the Parkinson-dementia complex. In addition to bradykinesia and rigidity, mental slowing, apathy, and depression occur in the relative absence of aphasia, apraxia, or agnosia. Gross frontotemporal cortical atrophy is found at autopsy. NFTs are present in great abundance, with a relative absence of neuritic plaques in affected cortical regions, as well as in hippocampus, amygdala, and substantia nigra. Severe neuronal loss with depigmentation of the substantia nigra without Lewy body formation is seen. Pathologic changes in the spinal cord include loss of anterior horn cells and neurofibrillary changes. Although various toxins have been implicated in its etiology, the exact cause of this symptom complex is unknown.

## Thalamic Degeneration

Thalamic degeneration may be found rarely in isolation or in association with multisystem atrophy. Abnormal movements of the limb and trunk are seen with tremor, choreoathetosis, and occasionally myoclonus. Alterations in sleep may be observed, such as in the prion-related disorder of fatal familial insomnia (FFI) (Gambetti et al. 1995; Reder et al. 1995). Ataxia, paraparesis, blindness, spasticity, optic atrophy, nystagmus, and dysarthria may also be present. Aphasia, agnosia, or apraxia are usually absent. Depression may be prominent, and patients may be apathetic with personality changes and hypersomnolence. Memory and calculations are poor, and there is occasionally incomprehensible spontaneous verbal output; judgment and calculations are impaired relatively early. Insight into the disease is limited. There is severe gliosis and neuronal loss in the thalamus; gliosis and neuronal loss are also found in limbic projection nuclei.

Fatal familial insomnia is associated with a missense mutation at codon 178 and methionine homozygosity at codon 129 of the prion protein gene. In subjects who are heterozygotes at codon 129, expressing valine in the nonmutated allele, the disease has onset at a later age and slower progression. These latter individuals tend to have widespread cortical lesions along with ataxia and dysarthria. FFI preferentially involves limbic thalamocortical circuits, correlating with the prominent sleep and autonomic disturbance, sympathetic hyperactivity, and flattening of circadian rhythms (Cortelli et al. 1999).

## Wilson's Disease

In Wilson's disease, also called hepatolenticular degeneration, the basal ganglia degenerate in association with abnormalities in liver function. It has autosomal recessive inheritance due to a mutation on chromosome 13 and is caused by a defect in copper metabolism, caused by a defective P-type ATPase (Cuthbert 1995; Petrukhin and Gilliam 1994). This leads to excessive copper deposition in the liver, corneas, and basal ganglia. Onset is usually in the second or third decade and is heralded by tremor, poor coordination, dystonia, rigidity, or changes in gait. There may also be dysarthria, dysphagia, hypophonia, or seizures. Chronic hepatitis or hemolytic anemia may be detected. Kayser-Fleischer rings are seen in nearly all patients and consist of brown or green discolorations near the limbus of the cornea. Ventricular enlargement and cortical atrophy may be seen on x-ray computed tomographic scanning, and MRI reveals abnormal signal in the lenticular nuclei, caudate nuclei, thalamus, dentate nuclei, and brain stem. The diagnosis may be made on slit-lamp examination of the cornea and laboratory studies demonstrating a serum ceruloplasmin level less than 20 mg/dL, a 24-hour copper excretion of more than 100 mg, or liver biopsy demonstrating increased hepatic copper concentration. Although the diagnosis may be relatively easy, Wilson's disease needs to be suspected in children and younger adults presenting with unknown hepatic or central nervous system syndromes.

Affective and behavioral changes are common in Wilson's disease and may include schizophrenia-like changes with depression or manic depressive states. Sexual preoccupation and reduced sexual inhibitions are common. Aggressive and self-destructive or antisocial acts may be noted, and schizoid hysterical or sociopathic personality traits have been reported. Intellectual deterioration in Wilson's disease is relatively mild in the early symptomatic stages (Akil and Brewer 1995). Pathologically, there is atrophy of the brain stem, dentate nucleus, and cerebellum with cavitary necrosis of the putamen.

Treatment of Wilson's disease consists of maintaining a negative copper balance. Maintaining a copper-deficient diet and preventing absorption with zinc may do this. Several copper chelating agents, including D-penicillamine, are available for symptomatic patients (Brewer 1995). Advanced patients may require liver transplantation. Neurologic symptoms, including the dementia syndrome, improve with long-term therapy. Levodopa may be of some benefit in reversing neurologic symptoms not improved by D-penicillamine.

## Fahr's Disease

Fahr's disease (idiopathic basal ganglia calcification) is a rare inherited (autosomal dominant) disorder with idiopathic calcification of the basal ganglia. There are extrapyramidal movement abnormalities together with dementia and neuropsychiatric disturbances. Computed tomographic scans demonstrate extensive calcification of the basal ganglia and periventricular white matter. Patients may present in early adulthood with a schizophrenia-like psychosis or mood disorder, or may present later in life with an extrapyramidal syndrome, dementia, and mood changes. Psychosis in Fahr's disease may respond to lithium. Parkinsonism, choreoathetosis, cerebellar ataxia, dystonia, and paroxysmal chorea may also be seen. Apathy, poor judgment, and memory are usually prominent, and language function is often spared. Cerebral blood flow to the calcified regions is markedly decreased and appears to correlate with the patient's condition (Uygur et al. 1995). Despite diffuse striatal calcifications, Manyam et al. (1992) found normal [$^{18}$F]6-fluoro-L-dopa uptake in one family with Fahr's disease.

Fahr's disease has been associated with hypoparathyroidism, and there are case reports of association with astrocytomas. It must be differentiated from other disorders in which brain calcifications are present, such as pediatric acquired immune deficiency syndrome, Aicardi-Goutières syndrome (D. Kumar et al. 1998), Down syndrome, Kearns-Sayre syndrome, and tumors or vascular lesions with dystrophic calcification. Familial cases have been reported, and linkage to chromosome 14 has been reported in one family (Geschwind et al. 1999).

## Hallervorden-Spatz Disease

Hallervorden-Spatz disease (HSD) is a rare progressive autosomal recessive disease of childhood and adolescence characterized by stiffness of gait, distal wasting, dysarthria, and occasionally dementia. The nosology of this disease now distinguishes between the rare pediatric degenerative syndrome known as HSD and Hallervorden-Spatz syndrome (HSS), a group of nonspecific disorders encompassing the triad of pallidal iron deposition, axonal spheroids, and gliosis. This latter group has variable clinical findings and an age at onset from adolescence through middle age. HSD is part of the group of infantile neuraxonal dystrophies, of which it mat be an allelic variant. Some authors refer to HSS as neurodegeneration with brain iron accumulation type 1 (Arawaka et al. 1998). One reason for preferring this new syndromic name is the documentation of Hallervorden's association with euthanasia programs in Nazi Germany (Shevell 1992).

Pathologically, there is olive or golden brown discoloration of the medial segment of the globus pallidus. Some cases of both HSD and HSS show widespread α-synuclein–positive Lewy bodies and axonal swellings. There are reports of cases with and without lipid abnormalities, acanthocytosis, and pigmentary retinal degeneration (Arawaka et al. 1998; Halliday 1995; Newell et al. 1999). Neurochemical analysis in a single case of a 68-year-old man revealed widespread dopamine deficiency in substantia nigra and striatum, but relatively preserved limbic system dopamine concentrations (Jankovic et al. 1985).

X-ray CT shows mild atrophy with flattening of the caudate nucleus. MRI scans may show the so-called eye of the tiger, due to bilateral hyperintensity of the rostral globus pallidus. There may be loss of T2-weighted signal in the substantia nigra pars reticularis, red nucleus, pulvinar, and globus pallidus due to iron accumulation (Lechner et al. 1999; Porter-Grenn et al. 1993; Tuite et al. 1996).

Granules of an iron-containing pigment similar to neuromelanin occur within and outside of neurons and hyperplastic astrocytes. Increased amounts of iron and other metals (zinc, copper, and calcium) are found in the affected tissue. Familial cases with autosomal recessive inheritance have been reported, and a gene localized to chromosome 20p12.3–13 has been identified (Taylor et al. 1996).

Limited data on treatment of HSS has been reported. Dystonia may respond to pallidotomy or thalamotomy, and dopa-responsive parkinsonism has been described (Justesen et al. 1999; Seibel et al. 1993; Tsukamoto et al. 1992; Tuite et al. 1996). No specific treatment for the dementia is available.

## Normal-Pressure Hydrocephalus

Normal-pressure hydrocephalus (NPH) is a syndrome composed of dementia, gait disturbance, and urinary incontinence. It may be associated with a history of meningitis, intracranial bleeding, or head injury (Friedland 1989). Idiopathic cases are also seen. A wide base with slow steps, and difficulty initiating locomotion characterizes gait. No changes occur in motor strength or tone. It is thought that this disturbance results from an obstruction to the flow of cerebrospinal fluid around the convexities in the basal cisterns.

Diagnosis of NPH is difficult but is based on recognition of the symptoms and correlative neuroimaging showing an enlarged ventricular system without corresponding cerebral atrophy. MRI scanning may also show transependymal fluid flux. The difficulties in diagnosis arise in determining whether atrophy is merely age related, although enlargement of the temporal horns may be indicative of a true hydrocephalic picture. Conversely, it may be difficult to effectively determine that dementia in suspected NPH is not due to concomitant primary degenerative dementia. In series in which shunted patients also underwent brain biopsy, the prevalence of AD ranged from 31% to 50% (Savolainen et al. 1999). The width of the perihippocampal fissures as determined by quantitative brain volume analysis may help differentiate AD from NPH (Holodny et al. 1998).

Dynamic testing including CSF pressure measurement and analysis is frequently employed, although the sensitivity and specificity of these techniques are unclear. Transient improvement in standardized neuropsychological and functional gait and motor testing after large-volume lumbar puncture (20 to 40 mL) may help predict individuals who will respond to surgical treatment. Radioisotope scanning after intrathecal injection of radioactive indium may also help in determining which patients have evidence of NPH. In NPH there is isotope reflux into the enlarged ventricular system after 24 to 72 hours. Pathophysiologically, this may represent failure of CSF absorption at the level of the superior sagittal sinus.

The dementia of NPH presents primarily with attentional difficulties in the early stages. Anterograde memory deficits are usually absent in early NPH, although up to 50% of patients have some memory dysfunction (Fisher 1977). Language is typically spared early in the course, although late-stage patients may manifest as an akinetic-mutism syndrome. "Frontal dysfunction," including apathy, lethargy, mental slowing, and perseveration is extremely common in NPH. Occasional patients may present with psychosis as an initial symptom. The motor deficits of hydrocephalic patients may be similar to those seen in PD or other basal ganglia disorders. This may be due to the proximity of nigrostriatal pathways to the enlarged ventricles causing mass effect or ischemia (Curran and Lang 1994).

Improvement may follow a cerebrospinal fluid shunting procedure, but it is difficult to predict which individuals will respond to surgery. The best results occur in cases where the cognitive disturbances are relatively mild with early onset of urinary incontinence and gait disturbance. Patients who respond to high-volume lumbar puncture are also more likely to show improvement after surgical CSF shunting. Iddon and colleagues (1999) found that memory improved more than frontostriatal dysfunction after shunting. The presence of AD on concomitant brain biopsy does not preclude a successful outcome as measured by gait, restoration of urinary control, or psychometric study (Golomb et al. 2000). Occult shunt failure after shunting, primarily due to obstruction of peritoneal catheters, has been reported (Williams et al. 1998). The use of programmable pressure valves may reduce the complication rate of post-shunting hematomas while ensuring optimal shunting in a given patient.

# References

Aarsland D, Tandberg E, Larson JP, et al: Frequency of dementia in Parkinson's disease. Arch Neurol 53:538–542, 1996

Abrams R: ECT for Parkinson's disease. Am J Psychiatry 146: 1391–1393, 1989

Agid Y, Javoy-Agid F, Ruberg M, et al: Progressive supranuclear palsy: anatomoclinical and biochemical considerations, in Advances in Neurology Series, Vol 45: Parkinson's Disease. Edited by Yahr MD, Bergmann KJ. New York, Raven, 1986, pp 191–206

Akil M, Brewer GJ: Psychiatric and Behavioral Abnormalities in Wilson's Disease (Advances in Neurology Series, Vol 65), in Behavioral Neurology of Movement Disorders. Edited by Weiner WS, Lang AE. New York, Raven, 1995, pp 171–178

Albert ML, Feldman RG, Willis AL: The "subcortical dementia" of progressive supranuclear palsy. J Neurol Neurosurg Psychiatry 37:121–130, 1974

Albin RL, Tagle DA: Genetics and molecular biology of Huntington's disease. Trends Neurosci 18:11–14, 1995

Aldrich MS, Foster NL, White RF, et al: Sleep abnormalities in progressive supranuclear palsy. Ann Neurol 25(6):577–581, 1989

Alexander GE, DeLong MR, Strick PL: Parallel organization of functionally segregated circuits linking basal ganglia and cortex. Annu Rev Neurosci 9:357–381, 1986

Arawaka S, Saito Y, Murayama S, et al: Lewy body in neurodegeneration with brain iron accumulation type 1 is immunoreactive for alpha-synuclein. Neurology 51(3):887–889, 1998

Arendt T, Bigl V, Arendt A, et al: Loss of neurons in the nucleus basalis of Meynert in Alzheimer's disease, paralysis agitans, and Korsakoff's disease. Acta Neuropathol (Berl) 61:101–108, 1983

Arima K, Uesigi H, Fujita I, et al: Corticonigral degeneration with neural achromasia presenting with primary progressive aphasia: ultrastructural and immunocytochemical studies. J Neurol Sci 20:186–197, 1994

Arima K, Hirai S, Sunohara N, et al: Cellular co-localization of phosphorylated tau- and NACP/alpha-synuclein-epitopes in Lewy bodies in sporadic Parkinson's disease and in dementia with Lewy bodies. Brain Res 843:53–61, 1999

Arroyo-Anllo EM, Botez-Marquard T: Neurobehavioral dimensions of olivopontocerebellar atrophy. J Clin Exp Neuropsychol 20:52–59, 1998

Bamford K, Caine E, Kido D, et al: Clinical-pathologic correlation in Huntington's disease: a neuropsychological and computed tomography study. Neurology 39:796–801, 1989

Bayles KA: Language and Parkinson disease. Alzheimer Dis Assoc Disord 4(3):171–180, 1990

Bejjani B-P, Damier P, Arnulf A-M, et al: Transient acute depression induced by high-frequency deep-brain stimulation. N Engl J Med 340:1476–1480, 1999

Berrios GE, Campbell C, Politynska BE: Autonomic failure, depression and anxiety in Parkinson's disease. Br J Psychiatry 166(6):789–792, 1995

Boller F, Mizutani R, Roessmann U, et al: Parkinson's disease, dementia, and Alzheimer's disease: clinicopathologic correlations. Ann Neurol 7:329–335, 1980

Boller F, Passafiume D, Keefe NC, et al: Visuospatial impairment in Parkinson's disease. Arch Neurol 41:485–490, 1984

Booth G: Psychodynamics in parkinsonism. Psychosom Med 10:1–14, 1948

Botez-Marquard T, Botez MI: Cognitive behavior in heredodegenerative ataxias. Eur Neurol 33:351–357, 1993

Botez-Marquard T, Botez MI: Olivopontocerebellar atrophy and Friedreich's ataxia: neuropsychological consequences of bilateral versus unilateral cerebellar lesions. Int Rev Neurobiol 47:387–410, 1997

Brandt J, Butters N: The neuropsychology of Huntington's disease. Trends Neurosci 9:118–120, 1986

Brandt J, Strauss ME, Larus J, et al: Clinical correlates of dementia and disability in Huntington's disease. Journal of Clinical Neuropsychology 6:401–412, 1984

Brandt J, Folstein SE, Folstein MF: Differential cognitive impairment in Alzheimer's disease and Huntington's disease. Ann Neurol 23:555–561, 1988

Brandt J, Quaid SE, Folstein SE, et al: Presymptomatic diagnosis of delayed onset disease with linked DNA markers: the experience with Huntington's disease. JAMA 216:3108–3114, 1989

Brewer GJ: Practical recommendations and new therapies for Wilson's disease. Drugs 50:240–249, 1995

Brooks DJ, Ibanez V, Sawle GV, et al: Differing patterns of striatal 18F-dopa uptake in Parkinson's disease, multiple system atrophy, and progressive supranuclear palsy. Ann Neurol 28:547–555, 1990

Brown RE, Marsden CD: Visuospatial function in Parkinson's disease. Brain 109:987–1002, 1986

Brown RE, Marsden CD: "Subcortical dementia": the neuropsychological evidence. Neuroscience 25:363–387, 1988

Butters N, Tarlow S, Cermak LS, et al: A comparison of the information processing deficits of patients with Huntington's disease and Korsakoff's syndrome. Cortex 12:134–144, 1976

Butters N, Sax D, Montgomery K, et al: Comparison of the neuropsychological deficits associated with early and advanced Huntington's disease. Arch Neurol 35:585–589, 1978

Butters N, Albert MS, Sax DS, et al: The effect of verbal mediators on the pictorial memory of brain-damaged patients. Neuropsychologia 21:307–323, 1983

Bylsma FW, Brandt J, Strauss ME: Aspects of procedural memory are differentially impaired in Huntington's disease. Archives of Clinical Neuropsychology 5:287–297, 1990

Caine ED, Shoulson I: Psychiatric symptoms in Huntington's disease. Am J Psychiatry 140(6):728–733, 1983

Caine ED, Hunt RD, Weingartner H, et al: Huntington's dementia: clinical and neuropsychological features. Arch Gen Psychiatry 35:377–384, 1978

Calne DB, Eisen A, McGeer E, et al: Alzheimer's disease, Parkinson's disease, and mononeurone disease: abiotrophic interaction between aging and environment? Lancet 2:1067–1070, 1986

Cambier J, Masson M, Viader F, et al: Le syndrome frontal de la maladie de Steele-Richardson-Olszewski. Rev Neurol (Paris) 141:528–536, 1985

Celesia GG, Wanamaker WM: Psychiatric disturbances in Parkinson's disease. Diseases of the Nervous System 33:577–583, 1972

Chaudhuri KR, Hu MT, Brooks DJ: Atypical parkinsonism in Afro-Caribbean and Indian origin immigrants to the UK. Mov Disord 15:18–23, 2000

Chui HC, Mortimer JA, Slager U, et al: Pathologic correlates of dementia in Parkinson's disease. Arch Neurol 43:991–995, 1986

Claes S, Van Zand K, Legius K, et al: Correlations between triplet repeat expansion and clinical features in Huntington's disease. Arch Neurol 52:749–753, 1995

Codori AM, Brandt J: Psychological costs and benefits of predictive testing for Huntington's disease. Am J Med Genet 54:174–184, 1994

Codori AM, Hanson R, Brandt J: Self-selection in predictive testing for Huntington's disease. Am J Med Genet 54:167–173, 1994

Cortelli P, Gambetti P, Montagna P, et al: Fatal familial insomnia: clinical features and molecular genetics. J Sleep Res 8 (suppl 1):23–29, 1999

Cummings JL (ed): Subcortical Dementia. New York, Oxford University Press, 1990

Cummings JL: Behavioral and psychiatric symptoms associated with huntington's disease (Advances in Neurology Series, Vol 65), in Behavioral Neurology of Movement Disorders. Edited by Weiner WJ, Lang AE.. New York, Raven, 1995, pp 179–186

Cummings JL, Benson DF: Psychological dysfunction accompanying subcortical dementias. Annu Rev Med 39:53–61, 1988

Cummings JL, Darkins A, Mendez M, et al: Alzheimer's disease and Parkinson's disease: comparison of speech and language alterations. Neurology 38:680–684, 1988

Curran T, Lang AE: Parkinsonian syndromes associated with hydrocephalus: case reports, a review of the literature, and pathophysiological hypotheses. Mov Disord 9:508–520, 1994

Cuthbert JA: Wilson's disease: a new gene and an animal model for an old disease. J Investig Med 43:323–326, 1995

D'Antona R, Baron JC, Samson Y, et al: Subcortical dementia: frontal cortex hypometabolism detected by positron tomography in patients with progressive supranuclear palsy. Brain 108:785–799, 1985

Destee A, Gray F, Parent M, et al: Obsessive-compulsive behavior and progressive supranuclear palsy. Rev Neurol 146 (1):12–18, 1990

Diamond R, White RF, Myers RH, et al: Evidence of presymptomatic cognitive decline in Huntington's disease. J Clin Exp Neuropsychol 14:961–975, 1992

Dickson DW: Neuropathologic differentiation of progressive supranuclear palsy and corticobasal degeneration. J Neurol 246 (suppl 2):6–15, 1999

Dickson DW, Lin W, Liu WK, et al: Multiple system atrophy: a sporadic synucleinopathy. Brain Pathol 9:721–732, 1999

Diller L, Riklan M: Psychosocial factors in Parkinson's disease. J Am Geriatr Soc 4:1291–1300, 1956

Di Maria E, Tabaton M, Vigo T, et al: Corticobasal degeneration shares a common genetic background with progressive supranuclear palsy. Ann Neurol 47:374–377, 2000

Ebmeier KP, Calder SA, Craford JR, et al: Clinical features predicting dementia in idiopathic Parkinson's disease: a follow-up study. Neurology 40:1222–1224, 1990

Epelbaum J, Ruberg M, Moyse E, et al: Somatostatin and dementia in Parkinson's disease. Brain Res 278:376–379, 1983

Farrer LA, Conneally PM: A genetic model for age at onset in Huntington's disease. Am J Hum Genet 37:350–357, 1985

Fedio P, Cox CS, Neophytides A, et al: Neuropsychological Profiles in Huntington's Disease: Patients and Those at Risk (Advances in Neurology Series, Vol 23: Huntington's Disease. Edited by Chase TN, Wexler NS, Barbeau A). New York, Raven, 1979, pp 239–255

Feigin A, Kieburtz K, Bordwell K, et al: Functional decline in Huntington's disease. Mov Disord 10:211–214, 1995

Fergusson E, Howard R: Donepezil for the treatment of psychosis in dementia with Lewy bodies. Int J Geriatr Psychiatry 15:280–281, 2000

Fine J, Duff J, Chen R, et al: Long-term follow-up of unilateral pallidotomy in advanced Parkinson's disease. N Engl J Med 342:1708–1714, 2000

Fisher CM: The clinical picture of normal pressure hydrocephalus. Clin Neurosurg 24:270–284, 1977

Folstein MF, Folstein SE, McHugh PR: Mini-Mental State: a practical method for grading the cognitive state of patients for the clinician. J Psychiatr Res 12:189–198, 1975

Folstein SE: Huntington's Disease: A Disorder of Families. Baltimore, MD, Johns Hopkins University Press, 1989

Folstein SE, Folstein MF, McHugh PR: Psychiatric Syndromes in Huntington's Disease (Advances in Neurology Series, Vol 23: Huntington's Disease. Edited by Chase TN, Wexler NS, Barbeau A). New York, Raven, 1979, pp 281–289

Folstein SE, Abbott MH, Chase GA, et al: The association of affective disorder with Huntington's disease in a case series and in families. Psychol Med 13:537–542, 1983a

Folstein SE, Jensen B, Leigh RJ, et al: The measurement of abnormal movement: methods developed for Huntington's disease. Neurobehavioral Toxicology and Teratology 5:605–609, 1983b

Folstein SE, Chase GA, Wahl WE, et al: Huntington's disease in Maryland: clinical aspects of racial variation. Am J Hum Genet 41:168–179, 1987

Folstein SE, Brandt J, Folstein MF: Huntington's disease, in Subcortical Dementia. Edited by Cummings JL. New York, Oxford University Press, 1990, pp 87–107

Ford MF: Treatment of depression in Huntington's disease with monoamine oxidase inhibitors. Br J Psychiatry 149:654–656, 1986

Freedman M: Parkinson's disease, in Subcortical Dementia. Edited by Cummings JL. New York, Oxford University Press, 1990, pp 108–122

Friedland RP: "Normal"-pressure hydrocephalus and the saga of the treatable dementias. JAMA 262:2577–2581, 1989

Friedman JH, Factor SA: Atypical antipsychotics in the treatment of drug-induced psychosis in Parkinson's disease. Mov Disord 15:201–211, 2000

Frisoni GB, Pizzolato G, Zanetti O, et al: Corticobasal degeneration: neuropsychological assessment and dopamine D2 receptor SPECT analysis. Eur Neurol 35:50–54, 1995

Furtado S, Suchowersky O: Huntington's disease: recent advances in diagnosis and management. Can J Neurol Sci 22(1):5–12, 1995

Gallassi P, Montagna P, Ciardulli C, et al: Cognitive impairment in motor neuron disease. Acta Neurol Scand 71:480–484, 1985

Galloway PG: Antigenic characteristics of neurofibrillary tangles in progressive supranuclear palsy. Neurosci Lett 91(2):148–153, 1988

Galvin JE, Uryu K, Lee VM, et al: Axon pathology in Parkinson's disease and Lewy body dementia hippocampus contains alpha-, beta-, and gamma-synuclein. Proc Natl Acad Sci U S A 96:13450–13455, 1999

Gambetti P, Parchi P, Petersen RB, et al: Fatal familial insomnia and familial Creutzfeldt-Jakob disease: clinical, pathological and molecular features. Brain Pathol 5:43–51, 1995

Garron DC: Huntington's chorea and schizophrenia (Advances in Neurology Series, Vol 1), in Huntington's Chorea: 1872–1972. Edited by Barbeau A. New York, Raven, 1973, pp 729–734

Geschwind DH, Loginov M, Stern JM: Identification of a locus on chromosome 14Q for idiopathic basal ganglia calcification (Fahr disease). Am J Hum Genet 65(3):764–772, 1999

Gilmore GC, Wykle M, Whitehouse PJ: Memory, Aging, and Dementia: Theory, Testing, and Treatment. New York, Springer-Verlag, 1989

Giordani B, Berent S, Boivin MJ, et al: Longitudinal neuropsychological and genetic linkage analysis of persons at risk for Huntington's disease. Arch Neurol 52:59–64, 1995

Girotti F, Carella F, Scigliano G, et al: Effect of neuroleptic treatment on involuntary movements and motor performances in Huntington's disease. J Neurol Neurosurg Psychiatry 47:848–852, 1984

Golbe LI, Davis PH, Schoenberg BS, et al: Prevalence and natural history of progressive supranuclear palsy. Neurology 38:1031–1034, 1988

Golomb J, Wisoff J, Miller DC, et al: Alzheimer's disease comorbidity in normal pressure hydrocephalus: prevalence and shunt response. J Neurol Neurosurg Psychiatry 68(6):778–781, 2000

Grafman J, Litvan I, Gomez C, et al: Frontal lobe function in progressive supranuclear palsy. Arch Neurol 47(5):553–558, 1990

Gram L, Bentsen KD: Valproate: an updated review. Acta Neurol Scand 72:129–139, 1985

Growdon JH, Corkin S: Cognitive Impairments in Parkinson's Disease (Advances in Neurology Series, Vol 45: Parkinson's Disease. Edited by Yahr MD, Bergmann KJ). New York, Raven, 1986, pp 383–392

Gusella J, Wexler NS, Conneally PM, et al: A polymorphic DNA marker genetically linked to Huntington's disease. Nature 306:234–238, 1983

Hakim AM, Mathieson G: Dementia in Parkinson disease: a neuropathologic study. Neurology 29:1209–1214, 1979

Halliday W: The nosology of Hallervorden-Spatz disease. J Neurol Sci 134 (suppl):84–91, 1995

Hammerstad JP, Carter JH: Movement Disorders in Occupational and Environmental Neurology. Edited by Rosenberg N. Newton, MA, Butterworth-Heinemann, 1995, pp 139–174

Hansen LA, Daniel SE, Wilcock GK, et al: Frontal cortical synaptophysin in Lewy body diseases: relation to Alzheimer's disease and dementia. J Neurol Neurosurg Psychiatry 64:653–656, 1998

Harper PS: The epidemiology of Huntington's disease. Hum Genet 89:365–376, 1992

Hayden MR, Bloch M, Wiggins S: Psychological effects of predictive testing for Huntington's disease (Advances in Neurology Series, Vol 65), in Behavioral Neurology of Movement Disorders. Edited by Weiner WS, Lang AE. New York, Raven, 1995, pp 201–210

Hedera P, Cohen ML, Lerner AJ, et al: Dementia preceding motor symptoms in Parkinson's disease: a case study. Neuropsychiatry Neuropsychol Behav Neurol 7:67–72, 1994

Hersch S, Jones R, Koroshetz W, et al: The neurogenetics genie: testing for the Huntington's disease mutation. Neurology 44:1369–1373, 1994

Hirono N, Ishii K, Sasaki M, et al: Features of regional cerebral glucose metabolism abnormality in corticobasal degeneration. Dement Geriatr Cogn Disord 11(3):139–146, 2000

Hofman A, Schulte W, Tanja TA, et al: History of dementia and Parkinson's disease in 1st-degree relatives of patients with Alzheimer's disease. Neurology 39:1589–1592, 1989

Hohl U, Tiraboschi P, Hansen LA, et al: Diagnostic accuracy of dementia with Lewy bodies. Arch Neurol 57:347–351, 2000

Holodny AI, Waxman R, George AE, et al: MR differential diagnosis of normal-pressure hydrocephalus and Alzheimer disease: significance of perihippocampal fissures. AJNR Am J Neuroradiol 19(5):813–819, 1998

Horoupian DL, Thal L, Katzman R, et al: Dementia and motor neuron disease: morphometric, biochemical, and Golgi studies. Ann Neurol 16:305–313, 1984

Hugdahl K, Wester K: Neurocognitive correlates of stereotactic thalamotomy and thalamic stimulation in Parkinsonian patients. Brain Cogn 42:231–252, 2000

Huntington G: On chorea (Advances in Neurology Series, Vol 1), in Huntington's Chorea: 1872–1972. Edited by Barbeau A. New York, Raven, 1973, pp 33–35

Huntington's Disease Collaborative Research Group: A novel gene containing a trinucleotide repeat that is expanded and unstable on Huntington's disease chromosomes. Cell 72:971–983, 1993

Hurtig HI, Trojanowski JQ, Galvin J, et al: Alpha-synuclein cortical Lewy bodies correlate with dementia in Parkinson's disease. Neurology 54:1916–1921, 2000

Iddon JL, Pickard JD, Cross JJ, et al: Specific patterns of cognitive impairment in patients with idiopathic normal pressure hydrocephalus and Alzheimer's disease: a pilot study. J Neurol Neurosurg Psychiatry 67(6):723–732, 1999

Jacobs DH, Shuren J, Heilman K: Impaired perception of facial identity and facial affect in Huntington's disease. Neurology 45:1217–1218, 1995

Jankovic J, Kirkpatrick JB, Blomquist KA, et al: Late-onset Hallervorden-Spatz disease presenting as familial parkinsonism. Neurology 35(2):227–234, 1985

Jason GW, Pajurkova EM, Suchowersky O, et al: Presymptomatic neuropsychological impairment in Huntington's disease. Arch Neurol 45:769–773, 1988

Javoy-Agid F, Agid Y: Is the mesocortical dopaminergic system involved in Parkinson's disease? Neurology 30:1326–1330, 1980

Jellinger K: Overview of Morphological Changes in Parkinson's Disease (Advances in Neurology Series, Vol 45: Parkinson's Disease. Edited by Yahr MD, Bergmann KJ). New York, Raven, 1986, pp 1–18

Josiassen RC, Curry L, Roemer RA, et al: Patterns of intellectual deficit in Huntington's disease. Journal of Clinical Neuropsychology 4:173–183, 1982

Justesen CR, Penn RD, Kroin JS, et al: Stereotactic pallidotomy in a child with Hallervorden-Spatz disease. Case report. J Neurosurg 90(3):551–554, 1999

Kampoliti K, Goetz CG, Boeve BF, et al: Clinical presentation and pharmacological therapy in corticobasal degeneration. Arch Neurol 55(7):957–961, 1998

Kertesz A, Hudson L, Mackenzie IR, et al: The pathology and nosology of primary progressive aphasia. Neurology 44:2065–2072, 1994

Kessler H: Epidemiological studies of Parkinson's disease, III: a community based study. Am J Epidemiol 96:242–254, 1972

Kish SJ, Robitaille Y, el-Awar M, et al: Non–Alzheimer-type pattern of brain cholineacetyltransferase reduction in dominantly inherited olivopontocerebellar atrophy. Ann Neurol 26(3):362–367, 1989

Konigsmark BW, Weiner LP: The olivopontocerebellar atrophies: a review. Medicine (Baltimore) 49:227–241, 1970

Kostic VS, Filipovic SR, Lecic D, et al: Effect of age at onset on frequency of depression in Parkinson's disease. J Neurol Neurosurg Psychiatry 57(10):1265–1267, 1994

Kubu CS, Grace GM, Parrent AG: Cognitive outcome following pallidotomy: the influence of side of surgery and age of patient at disease onset. J Neurosurg 92:384–389, 2000

Kumar D, Rittey C, Cameron AH, et al: Recognizable inherited syndrome of progressive central nervous system degeneration and generalized intracranial calcification with overlapping phenotype of the syndrome of Aicardi and Goutieres. Am J Med Genet 75(5):508–515, 1998

Kumar R, Lozano AM, Sime E, et al: Comparative effects of unilateral and bilateral subthalamic nucleus deep brain stimulation. Neurology 53:561–566, 1999

Lang AE, Lozano AM, Montgomery E, et al: Posteroventral medial pallidotomy in advanced Parkinson's disease. N Engl J Med 337:1036–1042, 1997

Langston JW, Ballard P, Tetrud JW, et al: Chronic parkinsonism in humans due to a product of meperidine-analog synthesis. Science 219:979–980, 1983

Laureys S, Salmon E, Garraux G, et al: Fluorodopa uptake and glucose metabolism in early stages of corticobasal degeneration. J Neurol 246(12):1151–1158, 1999

Lechner C, Meisenzahl EM, Uhlemann H, et al: [Hallervorden-Spatz syndrome. Differential diagnosis of early onset dementia.] Nervenarzt 70:471–475, 1999

Leenders KL, Palmer AJ, Quinn N, et al: Brain dopamine metabolism in patients with Parkinson's disease measured with positron emission tomography. J Neurol Neurosurg Psychiatry 49:853–860, 1986

Leenders KL, Frackowiak RS, Lees AJ: Steele-Richardson-Olszewski syndrome: brain energy metabolism, blood flow and fluorodopa uptake measured by positron emission tomography. Brain 111:615–630, 1988

Leigh RJ, Newman SA, Folstein SE, et al: Abnormal ocular motor control in Huntington's disease. Neurology 33:1268–1275, 1983

Levin BE: Spatial cognition in Parkinson's disease. Alzheimer Dis Assoc Disord 4(3):161–170, 1990

Levin BE, Llabre MM, Weiner WJ: Cognitive impairments associated with early Parkinson's disease. Neurology 39:557–561, 1989

Levy ML, Cummings JL, Fairbanks LA, et al: Apathy is not depression. J Neuropsychiatry Clin Neurosci 10:314–319, 1998

Lieberman A, Dziatolowski M, Coopersmith M, et al: Dementia in Parkinson's disease. Ann Neurol 6:355–359, 1979

Lishman WA: Organic Psychiatry: The Psychological Consequences of Cerebral Disorder. Oxford, Blackwell Scientific, 1978

Litvan I, Hauw JJ, Bartko JJ, et al: Validity and reliability of the preliminary NINDS neuropathologic criteria for progressive supranuclear palsy and related disorders. J Neuropathol Exp Neurol 55:97–105, 1996

Litvan I, Campbell G, Mangone CA, et al: Which clinical features differentiate progressive supranuclear palsy (Steele-Richardson-Olszewski syndrome) from related disorders? A clinicopathological study. Brain 120:65–74, 1997

Litvan I, Cummings JL, Mega M: Neuropsychiatric features of corticobasal degeneration. J Neurol Neurosurg Psychiatry 65(5):717–721, 1998a

Litvan I, MacIntyre A, Goetz CG, et al: Accuracy of the clinical diagnoses of Lewy body disease, Parkinson disease, and dementia with Lewy bodies: a clinicopathologic study. Arch Neurol 55:969–978, 1998b

Litvan I, Grimes DA, Lang AE, et al: Clinical features differentiating patients with postmortem confirmed progressive supranuclear palsy and corticobasal degeneration. J Neurol 246 (suppl 2): 1–5, 1999

Lombardi WJ, Gross RE, Trepanier LL, et al: Relationship of lesion location to cognitive outcome following microelectrode-guided pallidotomy for Parkinson's disease: support for the existence of cognitive circuits in the human pallidum. Brain 123:746–758, 2000

Louis ED, Klatka LA, Liu Y, et al: Comparison of extrapyramidal features in 31 pathologically confirmed cases of diffuse Lewy body disease and 34 pathologically confirmed cases of Parkinson's disease. Neurology 48:376–380, 1997

Lucking CB, Durr A, Bonifati V, et al: Association between early onset Parkinson's disease and mutations in the Parkin gene. N Engl J Med 342:1560–1567, 2000

Maher ER, Smith EM, Lees AJ, et al: Cognitive deficits in the Steele-Richardson-Olszewski syndrome (progressive supranuclear palsy). J Neurol Neurosurg Psychiatry 48:1234–1239, 1985

Maloteaux JM, Vanisberg MA, Laterre C, et al: [3H]GBR 12935 binding to dopamine uptake sites: subcellular localization and reduction in Parkinson's disease and progressive supranuclear palsy. Eur J Pharmacol 156(3):331–340, 1988

Manyam BV, Bhatt MH, Moore WD, et al: Bilateral striopallidodentate calcinosis: cerebrospinal fluid, imaging and electrophysiological studies. Ann Neurol 31(4):379–384, 1992

Marder K, Flood P, Cote, L, et al: A pilot study of risk factors for dementia in Parkinson's disease. Mov Disord 5:156–161, 1990

Marder K, Tang MX, Cote L, et al: The frequency and associated risk factors for dementia in patients with Parkinson's disease. Arch Neurol 52:695–701, 1995

Martilla RJ, Rinne UK: Dementia in Parkinson's disease. Acta Neurol Scand 54:431–441, 1976

Martilla RJ, Rinne UK: Smoking and Parkinson's disease. Acta Neurol Scand 62:322–325, 1980

Martin JB, Gusella JF: Huntington's disease: pathogenesis and management. N Engl J Med 20:1267–1276, 1986

Martone M, Butters N, Payne M, et al: Dissociations between skill learning and verbal recognition in amnesia and dementia. Arch Neurol 41:965–970, 1984

Matison R, Mayeux R, Rosen J, et al: "Tip-of-the-tongue" phenomenon in Parkinson's disease. Neurology 32:567–570, 1982

Mayeux R: Dementia in extrapyramidal disorders. Current Opinion in Neurology and Neurosurgery 3:98–102, 1990

Mayeux R, Stern Y, Rosen J, et al: Depression, intellectual impairment and Parkinson's disease. Neurology 31:645–650, 1981

Mayeux R, Stern Y, Rosen J, et al: Is "subcortical dementia" a recognizable clinical entity? Ann Neurol 14:278–283, 1983

Mayeux R, Stern Y, Cote L, et al: Altered serotonin metabolism in depressed patients with Parkinson's disease. Neurology 34:642–646, 1984

Mayeux R, Stern Y, Herman A, et al: Correlates of early disability in Huntington's disease. Ann Neurol 20:727–731, 1986a

Mayeux R, Stern Y, Williams JBW, et al: Clinical and biochemical features of depression in Parkinson's disease. Am J Psychiatry 143:756–759, 1986b

Mayeux R, Stern Y, Sano M, et al: The relationship of serotonin to depression in Parkinson's disease. Mov Dis 3:236–244, 1988

McHugh PR, Folstein ME: Psychiatric syndromes in Huntington's disease: a clinical and phenomenologic study, in Psychiatric Aspects of Neurologic Disease. Edited by Benson DF, Blumer D. New York, Grune & Stratton, 1975, pp 267–285

McKeith IG, Ince P, Jaros EB, et al: What are the relations between Lewy body disease and AD? J Neural Transm Suppl 54:107–116, 1998

Mendez MF: Huntington's disease: update and review of neuropsychiatric aspects. Int J Psychiatry Med 24(3):189–208, 1994

Menza MA, Mark MH: Parkinson's disease: the relationship to disability and personality. J Neuropsychiatry Clin Neurosci 6(2):165–169, 1994

Menza MA, Rosen RC: Sleep in Parkinson's disease. The role of depression and anxiety. Psychosomatics 36(3):262–266, 1995

Mitsuyama Y, Kogoh H, Ata K, et al: Progressive dementia with motor neuron disease: an additional case report and neuropathological review of 20 cases in Japan. European Archives of Psychiatry and Neurological Sciences 235:1–8, 1985

Mjones H: Paralysis agitans, a clinical and genetic study. Acta Psychiatr Scand 54:1–195, 1949

Monckton DG, Caskey CT: Unstable triplet repeat diseases. Circulation 91:513–520, 1995

Montgomery GK, Erickson LM: Neuropsychological perspectives in amyotrophic lateral sclerosis. Neurol Clin 5:61–81, 1987

Mori E, Shimomura T, Fujimori M, et al: Visuoperceptual impairment in dementia with Lewy bodies. Arch Neurol 57:489–493, 2000

Morita K, Kaiya H, Ikeda T, et al: Presenile dementia combined with amyotrophy: a review of 34 Japanese cases. Archives of Gerontology and Geriatrics 6:263–277, 1987

Morris JC, Cole M, Banker BQ, et al: Hereditary dysphasic dementia and the Pick-Alzheimer spectrum. Ann Neurol 16:455–466, 1984

Morris M: Dementia and Cognitive Changes in Huntington's Disease (Advances in Neurology Series, Vol 65), in Behavioral Neurology of Movement Disorders. Edited by Weiner WS, Lang AE. New York, Raven, 1995, pp 187–200

Moss MB, Albert MS, Butters N, et al: Differential patterns of memory loss among patients with Alzheimer's disease, Huntington's disease, and alcoholic Korsakoff's syndrome. Arch Neurol 43:239–246, 1986

Nahmias C, Garnett ES, Firnau G, et al: Striatal dopamine distribution in parkinsonian patients during life. J Neurol Sci 69:223–230, 1985

Newell KL, Boyer P, Gomez-Tortosa E, et al: Alpha-synuclein immunoreactivity is present in axonal swellings in neuroaxonal dystrophy and acute traumatic brain injury. J Neuropathol Exp Neurol 58:1263–1268, 1999

Nutt JG: Effects of cholinergic agents in Huntington's disease: a reappraisal. Neurology 33:932–935, 1983

O'Brien JT, Metcalfe S, Swann A, et al: Medial temporal lobe width on CT scanning in Alzheimer's disease: comparison with vascular dementia, depression and dementia with Lewy bodies. Dement Geriatr Cogn Disord 11:114–118, 2000

Okuda B, Tachibana H, Kawabata K, et al: Cerebral blood flow in corticobasal degeneration and progressive supranuclear palsy. Alzheimer Dis Assoc Disord 1491:46–52, 2000

Papka M, Rubio A, Schiffer RB: Lewy body disease: can we diagnose it? J Neuropsychiatry Clin Neurosci 10:405–412, 1998

Parsa MA, Bastani B: Quetiapine (Seroquel) in the treatment of psychosis in patients with Parkinson's disease. J Neuropsychiatry Clin Neurosci 10:216–219, 1998

Pearson SJ, Reynolds GP: Neocortical neurotransmitter markers in Huntington's disease. J Neural Transm Gen Sect 98:197–207, 1994

Perry EK, Perry RH, Candy JM, et al: Cortical serotonin-S2 receptor binding abnormalities in patients with Alzheimer's disease: comparisons with Parkinson's disease. Neurosci Lett 51:353–357, 1984

Perry EK, Perry RH, Smith CJ, et al: Nicotinic receptor abnormalities in Alzheimer's and Parkinson's disease. J Neurol Neurosurg Psychiatry 50:806–809, 1987

Perry RH, Tomlinson BE, Candy JM, et al: Cortical cholinergic deficit in mentally impaired parkinsonian patients. Lancet 2:789–790, 1983

Petrukhin K, Gilliam TC: Genetic disorders of copper metabolism. Curr Opin Pediatr 6:698–701, 1994

Pierot L, Desnos C, Blin J, et al: D1 and D2-type dopamine receptors in patients with Parkinson's disease and progressive supranuclear palsy. J Neurol Sci 86(2–3):291–306, 1988

Pillon B, Blin J, Vidailhet M, et al: The neuropsychological pattern of corticobasal degeneration: comparison with progressive supranuclear palsy and Alzheimer's disease. Neurology 45:1477–1483, 1995

Pirozzolo FJ, Hansch EC, Mortimer JA, et al: Dementia in Parkinson disease: a neuropsychological analysis. Brain Cogn 1:71–83, 1982

Pollock M, Hornabrook RW: The prevalence, natural history and dementia of Parkinson's disease. Brain 89:429–448, 1966

Porter-Grenn L, Silbergleit R, Mehta BA: Hallervorden-Spatz disease with bilateral involvement of globus pallidus and substantia nigra: MR demonstration. J Comput Assist Tomogr 17(6):961–963, 1993

Probst A, Langui D, Lautenschlager C, et al: Progressive supranuclear palsy: extensive neuropil threads in addition to neurofibrillary tangles. Very similar antigenicity of subcortical neuronal pathology in progressive supranuclear palsy and Alzheimer's disease. Acta Neuropathol 77(1):61–68, 1988

Rajput AH, Offord KP, Beard CM, et al: Epidemiology of parkinsonism: incidence, classification and mortality. Ann Neurol 16:278–282, 1984

Ranen NG, Peyser CE, Folstein SE: ECT as a treatment for depression in Huntington's disease. J Neuropsychiatry Clin Neurosci 6:154–159, 1994

Reder AT, Mednick AS, Brown P, et al: Clinical and genetic features of fatal familial insomnia. Neurology 45:1068–1075, 1995

Reynolds GP, Pearson SJ: Neurochemical-clinical correlates in Huntington's disease—applications of brain banking techniques. J Neural Transm Suppl 39:207–214,1993

Riley DE, Lang AE, Lewis A, et al: Cortical-basal ganglionic degeneration. Neurology 40:1203–1212, 1990

Ring HA, Bench CJ, Trimble MR, et al: Depression in Parkinson's disease: a positron emission study. Br J Psychiatry 165(3):333–339, 1994

Rinne JO, Rummukainen J, Paljarvi L, et al: Dementia in Parkinson's disease is related to neuronal loss in the medial substantia nigra. Ann Neurol 26:47–50, 1989

Rosenberg RN: Amyotrophy in multisystem genetic diseases, in Human Motor Neuron Diseases. Edited by Rowland LP. New York, Raven, 1982, pp 149–157

Rosenberg RN: The genetic basis of ataxia. Clin Neurosci 3:1–4, 1995a

Rosenberg RN: Spinocerebellar ataxia and ataxins. N Engl J Med 333:1351–1353, 1995b

Ruberg M, Ploska A, Javoy-Agid F, et al: Muscarinic binding and choline acetyltransferase activity in parkinsonian subjects with reference to dementia. Brain Res 232:129–139, 1982

Ruberg M, Javoy-Agid F, Hirsch E, et al: Dopaminergic and cholinergic lesions in progressive supranuclear palsy. Ann Neurol 18:523–529, 1985

Sabbagh MN, Corey-Bloom J, Tiraboschi P, et al: Neurochemical markers do not correlate with cognitive decline in the Lewy body variant of Alzheimer disease. Arch Neurol 45:1458–1461, 1999

Saint-Cyr JA, Taylor AE, Lang AE: Neuropsychological and psychiatric side effects in the treatment of Parkinson's disease. Neurology 43 (suppl 6):S47–S52, 1993

Samuel W, Alford M, Hofstetter CR, et al: Dementia with Lewy bodies versus pure Alzheimer disease: differences in cognition, neuropathology, cholinergic dysfunction, and synapse density. J Neuropathol Exp Neurol 56:499–508, 1997a

Samuel W, Crowder R, Hofstetter CR, et al: Neuritic plaques in the Lewy body variant of Alzheimer disease lack paired helical filaments. Neurosci Lett 223:73–76, 1997b

Sands IR: The type of personality susceptible to Parkinson disease. Journal of the Mount Sinai Hospital 9:792–794, 1942

Savoiardo M, Strada L, Girotti F, et al: MR imaging in progressive supranuclear palsy and Shy-Drager syndrome. J Comput Assist Tomogr 13(4):555–560, 1989

Savolainen S, Paljarvi L, Vapalahti M: Prevalence of Alzheimer's disease in patients investigated for presumed normal pressure hydrocephalus: a clinical and neuropathological study. Acta Neurochir (Wien) 141(8):849–853, 1999

Sawle GV, Brooks DJ, Marsden CD, et al: Corticobasal degeneration. A unique pattern of regional cortical oxygen hypometabolism and striatal fluorodopa uptake demonstrated by positron emission tomography. Brain 114(Pt 1B):541–556, 1991

Sax DS, O'Donnell B, Butters N, et al: Computer tomographic, neurologic, and neuropsychological correlates of Huntington's disease. Int J Neurosci 18:21–36, 1983

Schiffer R, Kurlan R, Rubin AJ, et al: Evidence for atypical depression in Parkinson's disease. Am J Psychiatry 145:1020–1022, 1988

Schmand B, de Bie RM, Koning-Haanstra M, et al: Unilateral pallidotomy in PD: a controlled study of cognitive and behavioral effects. The Netherlands Pallidotomy Study (NEPAS) group. Neurology 54:1058–1064, 2000

Schneider LS, Gleason RP, Chui HC: Progressive supranuclear palsy with agitation: response to trazodone but not to thiothixene or carbamazepine. J Geriatr Psychiatry Neurol 2(2):109–112, 1989

Seibel MO, Date ES, Zeiner H, et al: Rehabilitation of patients with Hallervorden-Spatz syndrome. Arch Phys Med Rehabil 74(3):328–329, 1993

Shevell M: Racial hygiene, active euthanasia, and Julius Hallervorden. Neurology 42:2214–2219, 1992

Shiwach RS, Norbury CG: A controlled psychiatric study of individuals at risk for Huntington's disease. Br J Psychiatry 165:500–505, 1994

Shoulson I: Care of patients and families with Huntington's disease, in Movement Disorders. Edited by Marsden CD, Fahn S. London, Butterworths International Medical Reviews, 1982, pp 277–290

Skre H: Spino-cerebellar ataxia in Western Norway. Clin Genet 6:265–288, 1974

Soliveri P, Monza D, Paridi D, et al: Cognitive and magnetic resonance imaging aspects of corticobasal degeneration and progressive supranuclear palsy. Neurology 53:502–507, 1999

Starkstein SE, Brandt J, Folstein S, et al: Neuropsychologic and neuropathologic correlates in Huntington's disease. J Neurol Neurosurg Psychiatry 51:1259–1263, 1988

Starkstein SE, Berthier ML, Bolduc PL, et al: Depression in patients with early versus late onset of Parkinson's disease. Neurology 39:1441–1445, 1989

Starr PA, Vitek JL, Bakay RAE: Ablative surgery and deep brain stimulation for Parkinson's disease. Neurosurgery 43:989–1015, 1998

Stebbins GT, Gabrieli JD, Shannon KM, et al: Impaired frontostriatal cognitive functioning following posteroventral pallidotomy in advanced Parkinson's disease. Brain Cogn 42:348–363, 2000

Stewart JT, Mounts ML, Clark RL: Aggressive behavior in Huntington's disease: treatment with propranolol. J Clin Psychiatry 48(3):106–108, 1987

Strauss ME, Brandt J: Are there neuropsychologic manifestations of the gene for Huntington's disease in asymptomatic, at-risk individuals? Arch Neurol 47:905–908, 1990

Sutcliffe RLG: Parkinson's disease in the district of Northampton Health Authority, United Kingdom—a study of prevalence and disability. Acta Neurol Scand 72:363–379, 1985

Tagliavini F, Pilleri G, Bouras C, et al: The basal nucleus of Meynert in idiopathic Parkinson's disease. Acta Neurol Scand 69:20–28, 1984

Takahashi H, Oyanagi K, Takeda S, et al: Occurrence of 15-nm-wide straight tubules in neocortical neurons in progressive supranuclear palsy. Acta Neuropathol (Berl) 79 (3):233–239, 1989

Talbot PR, Lloyd JJ, Snowden JS, et al: A clinical role for 99mTc-HMPAO SPECT in the investigation of dementia? J Neurol Neurosurg Psychiatry 64:306–313, 1998

Taylor ND, Litt M, Kramer P, et al: Homozygosity mapping of Hallervorden-Spatz syndrome to chromosome 20p12.3-p13. Nat Genet 16(1):479–481, 1996

Tedroff J, Aquilonious S-M, Hartvig P, et al: Monoamine re-uptake sites in the human brain evaluated in vivo by means of 11C-nomifensine and positron emission tomography: the effects of age and Parkinson's disease. Acta Neurol Scand 77:192–201, 1988

Topka H, Valls-Sole J, Massaquoi SG, et al: Deficit in classical conditioning in patients with cerebellar degeneration. Brain 116:961–969, 1993

Troster AI, Stalp LD, Paolo AM, et al: Neuropsychological impairment in Parkinson's disease with and without depression. Arch Neurol 52:1164–1169, 1995

Tsukamoto H, Inui K, Taniike M, et al: A case of Hallervorden-Spatz disease: progressive intractable dystonia controlled by bilateral thalamotomy. Brain Dev 14(4):269–272, 1992

Tuite PJ, Provias JP, Lang AE: Atypical dopa responsive parkinsonism in a patient with megalencephaly, midbrain Lewy body disease, and some pathological features of Hallervorden-Spatz disease. J Neurol Neurosurg Psychiatry 61:523–527, 1996

Tyler HR: Nonfamilial amyotrophy with dementia or multisystem degeneration and other neurological disorders, in Human Motor Neuron Diseases. Edited by Rowland LP. New York, Raven, 1982, pp 173–179

Uhl GR, Hedreen JC, Price DL: Parkinson's disease: loss of neurons from the ventral tegmental area contralateral to therapeutic surgical lesions. Neurology 35:1215–1218, 1985

Uygur GA, Liu Y, Hellman RS, et al: Evaluation of regional cerebral blood flow in massive intracranial calcification. J Nucl Med 36(4):610–612, 1995

Vanacore N, Bonifati V, Fabbrini G, et al: Smoking habits in multiple system atrophy and progressive nuclear palsy. European Study Group on Atypical Parkinsonisms. Neurology 54:114–119, 2000

Verghese J, Crystal HA, Dickson DW, et al: Validity of clinical criteria for the diagnosis of dementia with Lewy bodies. Neurology 53:1974–1982, 1999

Villardita C, Smirni P, Le Pira F, et al: Mental deterioration, visuoperceptive disabilities and constructional apraxia in Parkinson's disease. Acta Neurol Scand 66:112–120, 1982

von Hafften AH, Jensen CF: Paradoxical response to pindolol treatment for aggression in a patient with Huntington's disease. J Clin Psychiatry 50(6):230–231, 1989

Walker MP, Ayre GA, Cummings JL, et al: Quantifying fluctuation in dementia with Lewy bodies, Alzheimer's disease, and vascular dementia. Neurology 54:1616–1625, 2000

Walker Z, Allen RL, Shergill S, et al: Three years survival in patients with a clinical diagnosis of dementia with Lewy bodies. Int J Geriatr Psychiatry 15:267–273, 2000

Ward CD, Duvoisin RC, Ince SE, et al: Parkinson's disease in 65 pairs of twins and in a set of quadruplets. Neurology 33:815–824, 1983

Wexler NS: Perceptual-Motor, Cognitive, and Emotional Characteristics of Persons at Risk for Huntington's Disease (Advances in Neurology Series, Vol 23: Huntington's Disease. Edited by Chase TN, Wexler NS, Barbeau A). New York, Raven, 1979, pp 257–271

Whitehouse PJ: The concept of subcortical and cortical dementia: another look. Ann Neurol 19:1–6, 1986

Whitehouse PJ, Hedreen JC, White CL, et al: Basal forebrain neurons in the dementia of Parkinson's disease. Ann Neurol 13:243–248, 1983

Whitehouse PJ, Vale WW, Zweig RM, et al: Reductions in corticotropin releasing factor–like immunoreactivity in cerebral cortex in Alzheimer's disease, Parkinson's disease, and progressive supranuclear palsy. Neurology 37:905–909, 1987

Whitehouse PJ, Martino AM, Marcus KA, et al: Reductions in acetylcholine and nicotine binding in several degenerative diseases. Arch Neurol 45:722–724, 1988

Wikstrom J, Patenu A, Palo J, et al: Classic amyotrophic lateral sclerosis with dementia. Arch Neurol 39:681–683, 1982

Wilder J, Brown GL, Lebensohn ZM: Parkinsonism, depression and ECT. Am J Psychiatry 132:1083–1084, 1975

Williams MA, Razumovsky AY, Hanley DF: Evaluation of shunt function in patients who are never better, or better than worse after shunt surgery for NPH. Acta Neurochir (Wien) 71:368–370, 1998

Yahr MD: Introduction, in Clinical Neuropharmacology. New York, Raven, 1986, p S1

Yamauchi H, Fukuyama H, Nagahama Y, et al: Atrophy of the corpus callosum, cortical hypometabolism, and cognitive impairment in corticobasal degeneration. Arch Neurol 55:609–614, 1998

Zappacosta B, Monza D, Meoni C, et al: Psychiatric symptoms do not correlate with cognitive decline, motor symptoms, or CAG repeat length in Huntington's disease. Arch Neurol 53:493–497, 1996

# CHAPTER 29

# Neuropsychiatric Aspects of Alzheimer's Disease and Other Dementing Illnesses

Sylvia Askin-Edgar, M.D., Ph.D.

Katherine E. White, M.D.

Jeffrey L. Cummings, M.D.

Dementia is a common disorder in the later stages of life that is assuming increasing prominence with the demographic shift toward an ever-increasing aging population. Dementia is a generic term for a syndrome that has a variety of etiologies. The most common etiology is Alzheimer's disease (AD), which accounts for approximately 60%–70% of cases of late-onset dementia. In this chapter, we review the neuropsychiatric aspects of AD; dementia with Lewy bodies (DLB); frontotemporal dementia (FTD); dementia syndromes of the lenticulostriatal system—Huntington's disease (HD), Parkinson's disease (PD), Wilson's disease (WD), Fahr's disease or idiopathic basal ganglia calcification, Hallervorden-Spatz (HS) disease, corticobasal degeneration (CBD), multisystem atrophy (MSA), and progressive supranuclear palsy (PSP)—as well as vascular dementia (VaD), hydrocephalic dementia, and Creutzfeldt-Jakob disease (CJD). The evaluation and treatment of dementia syndromes and their neuropsychiatric manifestations are discussed. Dementias associated with other brain diseases are described in the relevant chapters of this volume addressing head injury (Chapter 18), cerebral tumors (Chapter 22), acquired immunodeficiency syndrome (AIDS) and other infectious and inflammatory disorders (Chapter 23), metabolic disorders (Chapter 25), toxic disorders (Chapter 26), and alcoholism and substance use disorders (Chapter 27).

## Demography and Definitions

DSM-IV-TR (American Psychiatric Association 2000) defines dementia as a syndrome with impairment of memory and at least one other cognitive ability and is disabling, represents a decline from a previous higher level of intellectual functioning, and is not present exclusively during a delirium. The requirement that the syndrome be acquired distinguishes dementia from mental retardation. The presence of a minimum of two cognitive disturbances (memory impairment plus a disturbance in one other cognitive domain) differentiates dementia from amnesia, a syndrome limited to memory loss. Abnormalities are typically present in language, constructional skills and visuospatial perception, calculation, and problem solving. Dementia is distinguished from acute confusional states (delirium) by intact arousal, more preserved

Jeffrey L. Cummings is supported by National Institute on Aging Alzheimer's Disease Research Center Grant AG16570, an Alzheimer's Disease Research Center of California grant, and the Sidell-Kagan Foundation.

attention, less fluctuation, and persistence of intellectual changes. The course of dementia is usually progressive, although 10%–15% of cases may be reversible (e.g., hypothyroid dementia) or treatable without reversing existing intellectual deficits (e.g., prevention of further ischemic injury in patients with VaD). Treatments of AD include those that are disease-modifying (e.g., vitamin E) or are intended to improve cognitive symptoms (e.g., cholinesterase inhibitors). Dementing diseases are often accompanied by neuropsychiatric syndromes, including personality alterations, mood changes, and psychosis. Behavioral disorders are often the principal determinants of residential placement of patients with dementia.

Most dementia syndromes are age-related, and the greatest risk for developing dementia is advancing age. One percent of the population between ages 60 and 65 years suffers from dementia, and the frequency doubles every 5 years. It is estimated that by age 80, 30%–50% of the population will suffer from the condition. With greater longevity and an increase in the number of elderly individuals in society, the population of intellectually impaired patients is expanding rapidly and dementia may become the major public health challenge of the twenty-first century (Ineichman 1987). There are currently 4 million patients with AD in the United States and given the demographic trends this number will grow to at least 14 million by the year 2050. The current combined estimated direct and indirect cost of caring for these patients exceeds 100 billion dollars per year (Ernst and Hay 1994).

## Alzheimer's Disease

AD is the single most common dementing illness of the elderly and is a progressive degenerative disorder that affects primarily the neurons of the cerebral cortex. Neuropathological and neurotransmitter changes are two pathophysiological components of the disease process. AD is a disease that starts in the mesial temporal lobe, in the entorhinal cortex. Limbic, paralimbic, and heteromodal association cortex are maximally affected, whereas primary sensory and motor areas, thalamus, basal ganglia, and cerebellum are comparatively spared (Cummings and Benson 1992). Pathologic changes include neurofibrillary tangles (NFTs), neuritic plaques (NPs), and synaptic and neuronal loss. The accumulation of amyloid in the brain leads to formation of plaques and nerve cell death. Loss of cells in the transmitter-related nuclei in turn leads to transmitter deficits, especially the loss of acetylcholine (ACh), which contribute to the cognitive deficit and the behavioral changes of AD. Drug

treatment of AD with cholinesterase inhibitors (ChE-Is) blocks acetylcholinesterase (AChE), the enzyme that catabolizes ACh, thereby increasing ACh in the synapse.

AD usually begins after age 55, its greatest risk factor being increasing age. Women are at slightly increased risk of developing AD compared with men (1.2 to 1). Genetic factors also contribute to the risk for AD (having one close relative triples the risk for developing the disease). Siblings of patients have twice the expected lifetime risk of developing the disease, and concordance of AD between monozygotic twins is significantly greater than for dizygotic twins (Cummings and Benson 1992).

Mutations in three genes, the amyloid precursor protein (APP) gene on chromosome 21, presenilin 1 (PS1) gene on chromosome 14, and presenilin 2 (PS2) gene on chromosome 1, produce the autosomal dominant form of AD, which can manifest as early as the third decade of life. The mutations, which are rare (2%–3% of all cases of AD), are highly penetrant and essentially all carriers develop AD. Nearly all patients with Down syndrome, a condition resulting from trisomy of chromosome 21, develop neuropathologic evidence of AD by the time of death if they survive into middle age, and Down syndrome is found in excess in the families of AD patients (Heyman et al. 1984; Schupf et al. 1994).

A polymorphism of the apolipoprotein-E (APOE) gene on chromosome 19 has been identified as a susceptibility marker for AD (Kamboh 1995). APOE has three allelic forms, 2, 3, and 4. Absence of the E4 allele correlates with a risk of late-onset AD of approximately 15%; this risk increases to 30%–50% with one copy and up to 60%–90% with two copies of the E4 allele (Kamboh 1995). In some families with late-onset AD, each APOE-4 allele lowers the age at onset (Corder et al. 1993). The presence of APOE-4 is neither necessary nor sufficient for the development of AD. Despite the increased frequency of APOE-4 in patients with AD, not all patients with the E4 allele develop AD, nor do all patients with AD carry the E4 allele. Routine testing for this gene in asymptomatic individuals is not of value.

A history of head injury, especially one associated with loss of consciousness of 1 hour or more, also increases the risk for AD. The presence of the E4 variant of APOE combined with head trauma increases risk for AD eightfold (Nemetz et al. 1999).

A number of factors that are seemingly protective against developing AD have been identified. The number of years of education and associated professional achievement appear to have profound influence on the frequency of the disease (Stern et al. 1994). Higher educational levels are associated with lower rates of AD. Use of anti-inflammatory agents seems to confer protection

(W.F. Stewart et al. 1997). Estrogen in postmenopausal women may decrease the risk for developing AD (Baldereschi et al. 1998; Henderson et al. 1994; Kawas et al. 1997; Paganini-Hill and Henderson 1994; Tang et al. 1996).

## Clinical Diagnosis

The diagnosis of AD is stratified as definite, probable, or possible according to the certainty of the available information (McKhann et al. 1984) (Table 29–1). A diagnosis of definite AD requires that the patient exhibit 1) a characteristic clinical syndrome meeting criteria for probable AD and 2) histologic evidence of AD pathology obtained from biopsy or autopsy. The diagnosis of probable AD requires that 1) the patient meets criteria for dementia based on a clinical examination, structured mental status questionnaire, and neuropsychological testing; 2) the patient has deficits in at least two areas of intellectual function—memory impairment and abnormalities in at least one other domain; 3) memory and other intellectual functions progressively worsen; 4) consciousness is not disturbed; 5) the disease begins between age 40 and 90; and 6) no systemic or other brain disorder could account for the deficits observed. Thus, accurate diagnosis depends on a combination of inclusionary clinical features as well as excluding other possible causes of dementia. AD should not be regarded as purely an exclusionary diagnosis. Neuropathologic studies demonstrate that 65%–90% of patients identified as having probable AD will have the diagnosis confirmed at autopsy (Risse et al. 1990; Tierney et al. 1988).

Possible AD is diagnosed when 1) deviations from the classic pattern of AD in the onset, presentation, or course of a dementing illness are present with no alternative explanation; 2) a systemic illness or brain disease is present that is not considered to be the cause of the dementia syndrome; or 3) there is a single gradually progressive cognitive deficit in the absence of any other brain disorder. Focal neurologic signs, sudden onset, the early occurrence of a gait disorder, or seizures make the diagnosis of AD unlikely.

The classic dementia syndrome of AD includes impairment of learning new information; poor recall of remote material; impaired naming and auditory comprehension; deterioration in constructional and visuospatial abilities; and poor calculation, abstraction, and judgment (Cummings and Benson 1992). Usually the patient lacks insight and shows little or no concern regarding the failing cognitive abilities. Apraxia (the inability to perform on command an act that can be performed spontaneously) may be an early feature, whereas agnosia (impaired rec-

**TABLE 29–1.** Criteria for definite, probable, and possible Alzheimer's disease (AD)

**Definite AD**
- Clinical criteria for probable AD
- Histopathologic evidence of AD (autopsy or biopsy)

**Probable AD**
- Dementia established by clinical examination and documented by mental status questionnaire
- Dementia confirmed by neuropsychological testing
- Deficits in two or more areas of cognition
- Progressive worsening of memory and other cognitive functions
- No disturbance of consciousness
- Onset between ages 40 and 90
- Absence of systematic disorders or other brain diseases capable of producing a dementia syndrome

**Possible AD**
- Presence of a systemic disorder or other brain disease capable of producing dementia but not thought to be the cause of the dementia
- Gradually progressive decline in a single intellectual function in the absence of any other identifiable cause (e.g., memory loss or aphasia)

**Unlikely AD**
- Sudden onset
- Focal neurologic signs
- Seizures or gait disturbance early in the course of the illness

*Source.* Adapted from McKhann et al. 1984.

ognition of objects, familiar faces, or well-known places) is associated with the later stages of the disease. Fluency of verbal output, repetition skills, and the ability to read aloud are retained until late in the disease. Motor and sensory functions are spared throughout most of the course. In the final phases of the disease there is near total abolition of intellectual function, as well as progressive loss of ambulation and coordination, dysphagia, and incontinence. Aspiration pneumonia, urinary tract infection, sepsis associated with infected decubitus ulceration, or an independent age-related disease (e.g., heart disease, cancer) typically account for the patient's death. The course is inexorably progressive, and patients generally survive a decade from diagnosis to death (Katzman et al. 1988).

## Neuropsychiatric Aspects

Neuropsychiatric symptoms are ubiquitous in AD, affecting nearly all patients during the course of illness, and they are the primary cause of caregiver burden and nursing home placement.

Personality alterations, apathy, mood changes, anxiety, irritability, disinhibition, disturbances of psychomotor activity, delusions, hallucinations, and a variety of miscellaneous behavioral changes, including disturbances of sleep and appetite, altered sexual behavior, and Klüver-Bucy syndrome can be associated with AD (Cummings and Victoroff 1990; Mega et al. 1996).

The most common personality change is passivity or disengagement: patients exhibit diminished emotional responsiveness, decreased initiative, loss of enthusiasm, diminished energy, and decreased emotion (Petry et al. 1988; Rubin et al. 1987). Self-centered, resistive, and disinhibited behaviors also may occur. Patients may be emotionally coarse, labile, insensitive, rash, excitable, or unreasonable (Petry et al. 1988). Personality changes affect essentially all patients with AD; they often occur early in the course of the disease and can predate intellectual abnormalities (Petry et al. 1989).

Delusions are common in patients with AD, affecting 30%–50% of patients (Cummings et al. 1987; Wragg and Jeste 1989). The most frequent delusions involve false beliefs of theft, infidelity of the spouse, abandonment, persecution, a phantom boarder, or Capgras' syndrome (Reisberg et al. 1987). No specific delusional content distinguishes the psychosis of AD from that of organic or idiopathic disorders. Delusions are most common in the middle phases of the illness, but they can occur early in the clinical course and they sometimes persist until late in the disease. Delusions are more common in patients with greater cognitive impairment; correlations between specific cognitive deficits and delusions are limited (Drevets and Rubin 1989). Delusional patients are more behaviorally disturbed and difficult to manage than those without delusions (Flynn et al. 1991), and AD patients with delusions exhibit more rapid intellectual decline than those without (Drevets and Rubin 1989).

Hallucinations are not a common manifestation of AD; 9%–27% of patients have hallucinatory experiences. Visual hallucinations are most common, followed by auditory or combined auditory and visual hallucinations. Typical visual hallucinations include visions of persons from the past (e.g., deceased parents), intruders, animals, complex scenes, or inanimate objects (Mendez et al. 1990). Auditory hallucinations are often persecutory and usually accompany delusions. Visual hallucinations may be indicative of a co-occurring delirium (Cummings et al. 1987).

A variety of mood changes, including depressive symptoms, elation, and lability, have been observed in patients with AD. Few patients meet the criteria for major depressive episodes, but elements of a depressive syndrome are frequent, occurring in 20%–40% of patients with AD (Cummings et al. 1987; Mendez et al.

1990). Tearfulness may be prominent, and thoughts of being a burden and of worthlessness may be expressed. Suicide is rare in patients with AD. Patients experiencing depression in the course of AD often have family histories of depressive disorders (Pearlson et al. 1990). Angry outbursts are seen in 50% of patients, and elation is reported in up to 20% of patients (Cummings and Victoroff 1990; Swearer et al. 1988; Teri et al. 1988). Anxiety has been reported in approximately 40% of patients with AD. The most common manifestation is excessive anticipatory concern regarding upcoming events (Mendez et al. 1990).

Disturbances in psychomotor activity and troublesome behaviors are common in patients with AD and become increasingly evident as the disease progresses. Wandering and pacing are pervasive behaviors in the middle and later stages of the illness; providing safe, contained spaces for wandering is a major challenge for residential facilities (Morishita 1990). Restlessness is reported in up to 60% of patients, and assaultive behavior is observed in 20% of patients (Swearer et al. 1988; Teri et al. 1988).

In a recent study (Mega et al. 1996) 50 patients with AD and 40 age-matched control subjects were evaluated for behavioral disturbances occurring over a 1-month period. Information was obtained from the subjects' caregivers and spouses on the frequency and severity of 10 abnormal behaviors. Most (88%) of the AD patients demonstrated behavioral symptoms during the month of the investigation, and scores on all of the behavioral measures employed were significantly higher in AD patients than in control subjects. Apathy was reported in 72% of AD patients, followed by agitation (60%), anxiety (48%), and irritability (42%). During the month they were evaluated, 38% of AD patients demonstrated dysphoria (tearfulness, low spirits, self-deprecation) or aberrant motor behavior (e.g., pacing, fidgeting, rummaging through drawers or closets); 36% exhibited disinhibited behavior; and 22% and 10% experienced delusions and hallucinations, respectively. Frequency and severity of apathy, agitation, dysphoria, and aberrant motor behavior were found to correlate significantly with the degree of cognitive impairment.

Various other behavioral changes have also been described in patients with AD. Most patients exhibit diminished sexual interest, but a few have transient periods of moderately to markedly increased sexual activity (Shapira and Cummings 1989). Eating also changes in the course of AD; most patients show less interest in food and experience weight loss as the illness progresses (C.H. Morris et al. 1989). Sleep disturbances with frequent interruptions of nocturnal sleep are common, occurring

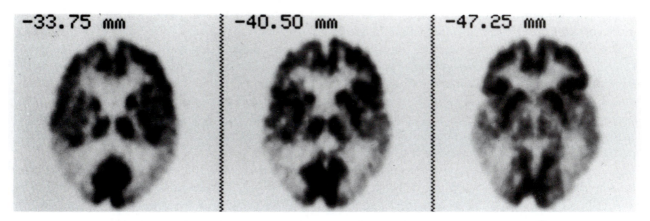

**FIGURE 29–1.** Transaxial positron emission tomography (PET) revealing decreased glucose metabolism bilaterally in the parietal lobes characteristic of Alzheimer's disease.

in 45%–70% of patients (Merriam et al. 1988; Rabins et al. 1982; Swearer et al. 1988). Klüver-Bucy syndrome is a complex behavioral disorder consisting of hyperorality, hypermetamorphosis, emotional placidity, agnosia, and altered sexual behavior. It may occur in fragmentary form in the late stages of AD (Lilly et al. 1983).

Computed tomography (CT) and magnetic resonance imaging (MRI) provide structural information; positron emission tomography (PET) and single photon emission computed tomography (SPECT) reflect cerebral metabolism and blood flow. MRI demonstrates atrophy of the hippocampus and related structures early in the disease (de Leon et al. 1997; Jack et al. 1992, 1999). Positron-emission tomography with fluorodeoxyglucose (FDG-PET) reveals a characteristic pattern of hypometabolism (Figure 29–1). Early in the disease, when memory is only mildly impaired and other cognitive functions are intact, glucose utilization is diminished in the parietal lobes; the frontal lobes are affected as the disease progresses. Subcortical structures and primary motor and sensory cortices are spared (Fazekas et al. 1989; Foster et al. 1983; Haxby et al. 1986; Jagust et al. 1988).

SPECT measures cerebral blood flow. Brain perfusion is determined by local cerebral metabolic activity, and the pattern of reduced blood flow revealed by SPECT in AD patients closely resembles the topography of cerebral glucose metabolism demonstrated by FDG-PET. SPECT reveals diminished cerebral perfusion in the parietal and posterior temporal lobes of both hemispheres in most AD patients (Figure 29–2) (Johnson et al. 1987; Miller et al. 1990). Frontal lobe perfusion declines as the disease progresses.

Electroencephalography (EEG) usually reveals theta and delta slowing as the disease advances, and computerized EEG studies with brain mapping demonstrate maximal abnormalities in the parietal regions of both hemi-

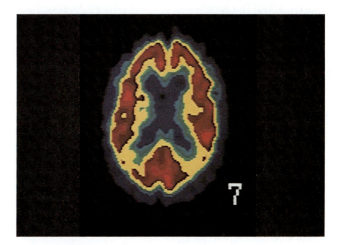

**FIGURE 29–2.** Transaxial single photon emission computed tomography of a patient with Alzheimer's disease revealing diminished cerebral perfusion in the temporoparietal regions bilaterally. Red areas indicate normal blood flow, and yellow regions indicate diminished perfusion.
*Source.* Image courtesy of Dr. Ismael Mena.

spheres (Jordan et al. 1989).

Neuropsychological testing can help distinguish dementia from normal aging and provides details regarding the pattern of cognitive impairment. Lumbar puncture is an optional procedure and should be considered if one suspects central nervous system (CNS) infection, neoplasm, inflammation, or demyelination. Cerebrospinal fluid (CSF) tau, amyloid, and other components of the pathophysiological process are currently being investigated as biological markers of AD (Galasko et al. 1998; Van Nostrand et al. 1992; Wahlund 1996).

## Neuropathology

The major pathologic alterations of AD include neuronal loss, cortical gliosis, intraneuronal cytoplasmic NFTs, NPs, granulovacuolar degeneration, and amyloid angiopathy of the cerebral vessels (Cummings and Benson 1992; Katzman 1986). NFTs are composed of the altered microtubule associated protein (MAP) tau. Tau is hyperphosphorylated, producing a highly insoluble protein comprising paired helical filaments (PHF) (Ohtsubo et al. 1990). NPs are the other main structural change in AD. Amyloid beta protein is deposited in the center of these plaques. The APP is a large transmembrane protein from which the beta peptide is derived. Beta- and gamma-secretases are responsible for generating the beta amyloid fragment from APP (Haass and Selkoe 1993; Sinha et al. 1999; Vassar et al. 1999; Yan et al. 1999). The pathologic burden of the disease is greatest in the medial temporal, posterior cingulate, and temporoparietal junction regions. The frontal cortex is moderately involved, and the primary motor and sensory cortices have fewer pathologic abnormalities (Brun and Gustafson 1976). Neurotransmitter alterations include marked reductions of choline acetyltransferase and somatostatin as well as more modest and variable losses of serotonin, γ-aminobutyric acid (GABA), and norepinephrine (Cummings and Benson 1992; Procter et al. 1988).

Although much remains to be determined about the pathophysiology of AD, increased amyloid deposition appears to be central to the illness. Amyloid aggregation leads to the formation of NP and neuronal death. NFT may be related to the amyloid toxicity or may represent a distinct pathologic lesion. Aggregation of amyloid in the brain may be facilitated by APOE-4.

The pathologic basis of the neuropsychiatric symptoms of AD is not fully understood. Changes in the temporal and parietal lobes can contribute to patients' indifference, and pathology of the frontal lobe and paralimbic cortex can account for symptoms of disinhibition, lability, agitation, and depression. Delusions can reflect temporoparietal alterations and the cholinergic deficit of AD (Cummings and Victoroff 1990).

## Treatment

Agents approved in the United States for the treatment of cognitive decline in AD include tacrine, donepezil, rivastigmine, and galantamine. Tacrine (Cognex) was the first of these agents to be approved but, as a result of requirements for multiple daily dosing and adverse side effects, this agent has limited use. Donepezil (Aricept) is a reversible ChE-I that is well tolerated, is not associated with liver toxicity, and has a long half-life allowing once daily dosing. Nausea and diarrhea may occur. Galantamine (Reminyl) has similar efficacy and tolerability. It is initiated at 4 mg twice daily and increased to 8–12 mg twice daily. Rivastigmine (Exelon), a pseudoirreversible

ChE-I, requires twice daily dosing and is gradually increased from 1.5 mg twice daily to 6 mg twice daily. Nausea, vomiting, and weight loss are common side effects. These agents produce a modest and temporary effect on cognitive function. They may improve behavior, delay loss of function, and defer nursing home placement. The ChE-Is are not disease-modifying agents and no effect is sustained once the drug is discontinued (Giacobini 2000).

Vitamin E and selegiline are antioxidant compounds that have been shown to delay development of severe cognitive impairment, decline in activities of daily living, death, and nursing home placement (Sano et al. 1997). Both agents were superior to placebo, and combined administration was not more efficacious than treatment with either agent alone. Vitamin E (2,000 IU daily) or selegiline (10 mg daily) is standard therapy for AD in combination with a ChE-I.

Management of the neuropsychiatric disturbance of AD and other dementias is discussed at the end of this chapter.

## Dementia With Lewy Bodies

DLB should be suspected in the presence of a dementia syndrome with the triad of fluctuating cognitive impairment, extrapyramidal symptoms, and visual hallucinations (McKeith and O'Brien 1999; McKeith et al. 1996). The extrapyramidal symptoms in DLB are preceded by dementia or can occur simultaneously with it. MRI reveals relative preservation of the temporal lobes and SPECT demonstrates loss of presynaptic and postsynaptic dopaminergic markers. The key neuropathologic feature is the Lewy body, a spherical intraneuronal cytoplasmic inclusion that had formerly been noted in brain-stem nuclei in PD. In DLB, Lewy bodies are scattered throughout the subcortical nuclei, the substantia nigra, and the cortex, particularly in the paralimbic regions. Consensus guidelines for the clinical and pathologic diagnosis of DLB were established in 1996 (McKeith et al. 1996) (Table 29–2).

---

**TABLE 29–2.** Criteria for dementia with Lewy bodies

Dementia syndrome
Two of the following three:
    Fluctuating cognitive impairment
    Visual and/or auditory hallucinations
    Parkinsonism

*Source.* Adapted from McKeith et al. 1996.

Accurate diagnosis is of importance because patients with DLB are exquisitely sensitive to neuroleptics, which should be avoided. First-line therapy for DLB should be ChE-Is, which in addition to potentially improving memory and cognition may have psychotropic effects, obviating the need for antipsychotic medication (Cummings 2000; McKeith et al. 2000).

# Frontotemporal Dementias

FTDs are a group of disorders with lobar atrophy of frontal and temporal lobes. Mutations on chromosome 17 account for 20%–40% of cases of the familial form of FTD (Clark et al. 1998; Hutton et al. 1998; McKeith et al. 1992; Poorkaj et al. 1998). Familial FTD is inherited as an autosomal dominant condition (Chow et al. 1999). The mutations have been found to effect the gene responsible for coding tau protein (van Swieten et al. 1999).

The hallmark of FTD is personality alteration with disinhibition, emotional coarsening, loss of ability for empathy, apathy, inability to interpret social cues, lack of insight and judgment, and poor planning (Neary et al. 1998). The disease typically begins between ages 40 and 65 years. Memory and visuospatial skills are relatively preserved; language disturbances can be prominent. Three FTD syndromes are recognized: 1) a disinhibition syndrome, 2) primary progressive aphasia with nonfluent aphasia and early mutism, and 3) semantic dementia with loss of word meaning and face and object recognition. The Lund-Manchester consensus (Lund and Manchester Groups 1994) established guidelines for the diagnosis of FTD (Table 29–3).

## Clinical and Neuropsychiatric Features

The clinical criteria for FTD are presented in Table 29–3. Neuropsychiatric features dominate the presentation of FTD. Personality alterations are often florid, and depression or psychosis can be prominent. Patients can be apathetic or disinhibited (Miller et al. 1991). Apathetic individuals exhibit social and occupational withdrawal, loss of motivation, and diminished interpersonal engagement. Disinhibited patients are often boisterous and prone to make vulgar or socially inappropriate remarks, exhibit undue familiarity with strangers, and have poor judgment; they may be unusually irritable. Depression may occur early in the clinical course and is usually transient. Elation occurs in approximately one-third of patients. Delusions are evident in 10%–25% of patients (Gustafson 1987; Miller et al. 1991). Klüver-Bucy syndrome, or fragments of the condition, may be evident in the initial phases of the disease, and often patients gain weight

as their eating habits become less discriminating (Cummings and Duchen 1981). Restless motor activity and roaming behavior are common (Mendez et al. 1993), and stereotyped behaviors with compulsive rituals and complex repetitive acts might also be observed in the course of FTD (Gustafson 1987).

Neuropsychologic deficits are less marked in patients with FTD than in those with AD. Memory, visuospatial skills, and mathematical abilities are relatively spared in the early and middle stages of the disease (Cummings and Benson 1992; Knopman et al. 1989). Patients have deficits in executive functioning, including difficulty with set-shifting tasks (e.g., card sorting), word list generation (e.g., number of animals named in 1 minute), divided attention, and response inhibition (Miller et al. 1991). Language may be affected relatively early in the disease. Naming deficits, impairment of auditory comprehension, and increasingly sparse verbal output are common. Speech stereotypies, echolalia, and mutism also may occur (Cummings and Benson 1992; Graff-Radford et al. 1990; Gustafson 1987).

# Laboratory Investigations and Neuroimaging

Routine studies of serum, urine, and CSF are normal in patients with FTD. In cases of FTD associated with amyotrophic lateral sclerosis, electromyography reveals findings consistent with motor neuron disease. Frontal atrophy and enlargement of the Sylvian fissures are evident on CT and MRI; frontotemporal deficits are observed on SPECT and PET (Duara et al. 1999) (Figure 29–3).

# Neuropathology

Three pathologic variants of FTD are recognized: 1) Pick's disease, 2) frontal and temporal lobar degeneration without distinctive histopathologic changes, and 3) FTD with motor neuron disease (Lund and Manchester Groups 1994). The macroscopic pathology of Pick's disease includes marked atrophy of the frontal lobe anterior to the precentral sulcus and of the anterior temporal lobe (Cummings and Benson 1992). Neurons are atrophic, and there is intense astrocytic gliosis involving all cortical layers in affected regions (Brun et al. 1994). Some of the remaining neurons contain intracytoplasmic argyrophilic Pick bodies, and examination of the dendrites reveals almost total absence of dendritic spines (Wechsler et al. 1982). Enlarged neurons with uniformly argyrophilic cytoplasm, known as ballooned cells, can occur in affected regions. Ultrastructurally, the Pick bodies are composed of straight filaments (Murayama et al. 1990).

FTD patients without Pick's-type pathology have

**TABLE 29–3.** Clinical criteria for frontotemporal dementia

**Core diagnostic features**

*Behavioral disturbance*

 Insidious onset and slow progression

 Early loss of personal and social awareness: poor personal hygiene, lack of social tact

 Early signs of disinhibition: excessive jocularity, inappropriate sexuality, aggression

 Mental rigidity and inflexibility

 Hyperorality: oral exploration of objects, dietary changes, excessive tobacco/alcohol use

 Stereotyped and perseverative behavior: wandering, ritualistic preoccupation

 Utilization behavior: unrestrained exploration of objects in the environment

 Distractibility, impulsivity, impersistence

 Early loss of insight into altered behavioral condition

*Affective disturbance*

 Depression: excessive sentimentality, delusions, anxiety, or suicidal ideation

 Hypochondriasis: bizarre somatic preoccupation

 Emotional indifference and apathy

 Inertia and aspontaneity

*Speech disturbance*

 Progressive reduction of verbal output

 Stereotypy of speech: repetition of limited-repertoire words, phrases, or themes

 Echolalia and perseveration

 Late mutism

*Preserved spatial orientation and praxis: intact abilities to negotiate the environment*

 Physical signs

 Early primitive reflexes

 Early incontinence

 Late akinesis, rigidity, tremor

 Low and labile blood pressure

*Laboratory investigations*

 EEG: normal

 MRI/CT: predominant frontal and/or anterior temporal atrophy

 SPECT/PET: predominant frontal and/or anterior temporal abnormality

 Neuropsychological testing: prominent executive dysfunction

**Supportive diagnostic features**

 Onset before age 65

 Positive family history of similar disorder

 Symptoms consistent with motor neuron disease

**Diagnostic exclusion features**

 Abrupt onset with ictal events

 Head trauma related to onset

 Early severe amnesia, apraxia, or spatial disorientation

 Myoclonus, cortical bulbar and spinal deficits, cerebellar ataxia, or choreoathetosis

 Early, severe, pathologic electroencephalographic changes

 Neuroimaging with predominant postcentral deficit or multifocal lesions

 Laboratory tests consistent with infectious or inflammatory disorder

**Relative diagnostic exclusion features: history of chronic alcoholism, sustained hypertension, or vascular disease**

*Note.* EEG = electroencephalogram; MRI = magnetic resonance imaging; CT = computed tomography; SPECT = single photon emission computed tomography; PET = positron emission tomography.

*Source.* Adapted from Brun et al. 1994.

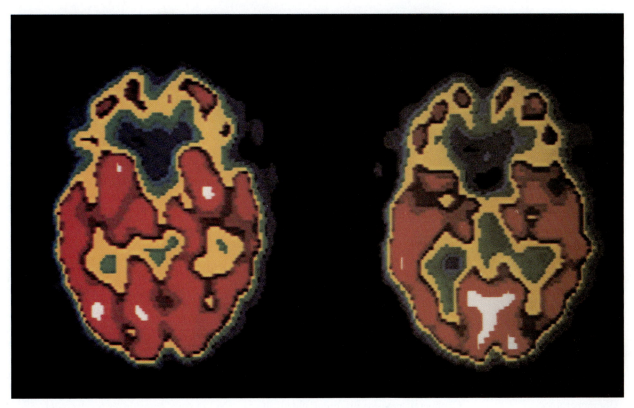

**FIGURE 29–3.** Transaxial single photon emission computed tomography of a patient with frontal lobe degeneration demonstrating decreased cerebral blood flow in the frontal lobes. *Red* areas indicate normal blood flow, and *yellow* regions indicate diminished perfusion.

nonspecific neuronal loss and astrocytic gliosis in a similar lobar distribution. The gliosis is less severe and more circumscribed than that observed in patients with Pick's disease, involving primarily the outer (I–III) cortical layers. Spongiform change (microvacuolation) is observed in affected regions, and Pick bodies and ballooned cells are absent. As many as 15% of patients with amyotrophic lateral sclerosis develop clinical symptoms consistent with FTD (Miller et al. 1994). These patients demonstrate combined frontotemporal and motor neuron degeneration at autopsy, and their disease represents a third category of FTD, the motor neuron disease type.

Neurochemical investigations also have been carried out in patients with FTD. Cortical choline acetyltransferase, L-glutamic acid decarboxylase, and dopamine are preserved (Yates et al. 1980), whereas cortical serotonin levels are decreased. In the basal ganglia, levels of dopamine, GABA, and substance P are reduced, and those of choline acetyltransferase are variably diminished (Kanazawa et al. 1988).

## Differential Diagnosis

FTD can usually be distinguished from AD on the basis of contrasting clinical characteristics (Table 29–4).

Although both are cortical diseases with gradually progressive courses and prominent language abnormalities, they differ in a number of other features. In patients with AD, memory impairment, constructional disturbances, and acalculia appear early in the clinical course, whereas these deficits are delayed until the middle or late phases of FTD. Conspicuous personality changes and executive deficits herald the onset of FTD and are more modest and delayed in patients with AD. CT and MRI reveal generalized atrophy in patients with AD and frontal or temporal lobar atrophy in those with FTD. FDG-PET and SPECT demonstrate diminished posterior temporal and parietal function in AD and decreased frontotemporal function in FTD (Cummings and Benson 1992; Miller et al. 1991).

A number of diseases in addition to FTD can affect frontal lobe function. Diseases of the extrapyramidal system (discussed in the next section) may produce dementia syndromes with features like those of frontal lobe dysfunction. A rare degenerative disorder, progressive subcortical gliosis, also affects the frontal and temporal lobes. It is characterized by variable cortical involvement and marked subcortical and white-matter gliosis (Verity and Wechsler 1987). Nondegenerative diseases also can produce frontal lobe syndromes with dementia (Cum-

**TABLE 29–4.** Features that distinguish Alzheimer's disease and frontotemporal dementia

| Feature | Alzheimer's disease | Frontotemporal dementia |
|---|---|---|
| **Clinical** | | |
| Personality changes | Disengagement | Disinhibition or apathy |
| Social skills | Late deterioration | Early deterioration |
| Klüver-Bucy syndrome | Late onset | Early onset |
| Memory deficits | Early onset | Late onset |
| Executive function | Spared early | Prominent early |
| Speech-language disturbances | Fluent aphasia | Stereotyped speech; terminal mutism |
| Anomia | Lexical anomia | Semantic anomia |
| Visuospatial disturbances | Early onset | Late onset |
| Acalculia | Prominent early | Spared early |
| **Neuroimaging studies** | | |
| CT and MRI | Generalized atrophy | Generalized atrophy, more prominent in frontotemporal regions |
| SPECT | Posterior temporal and parietal hypoperfusion | Anterior frontal and temporal hypoperfusion |
| PET | Parietal hypometabolism | Frontal hypometabolism |
| **Pathology** | | |
| Gross pathology | Posterior hemispheric atrophy | Anterior hemispheric atrophy |
| Histopathology | Granulovacuolar degeneration, amyloid angiopathy, neuritic plaques, neurofibrillary tangles | Non-Pick type: spongiform change, astrocytic gliosis in outer cortical areas<br>Pick type: Pick bodies, ballooned cells, severe astrocytic gliosis |
| Chemopathology | Cholinergic neurons preferentially involved | No selective transmitter involvement |

*Note.* MRI = magnetic resonance imaging; CT = computed tomography; SPECT = single photon emission computed tomography; PET = positron emission tomography.

mings 1985). Infarctions in the territories of the anterior cerebral arteries produce a syndrome of apathy and lack of initiative that can be accompanied by weakness and sensory loss in both lower extremities. Syphilitic brain infections preferentially affect the frontal lobes and may produce the grandiose hypomanic dementia syndrome of general paresis. White-matter diseases that can disproportionately affect the frontal lobes include multiple sclerosis and Marchiafava-Bignami disease. Hydrocephalus (discussed later in this chapter) may present with a frontal lobe syndrome. Depression is associated with reduced metabolism and perfusion of the frontal cortex, and the dementia syndrome of depression is characterized by frontal lobe–type neuropsychological deficits (Baxter et al. 1989; Cummings and Benson 1992). Patients with schizophrenia have impaired frontal activity as measured by PET when performing executive tasks.

## Dementias of the Lenticulostriatal Diseases

Diseases of the lenticulostriatal system are often associated with cognitive and neuropsychiatric disturbances.

The major illnesses in this category include HD, PSP, and PD. WD, Fahr's disease (idiopathic basal ganglia calcification), HS disease, CBD, and the MSAs represent rarer forms of extrapyramidal disorders associated with dementia syndromes. These illnesses affect predominately subcortical structures such as the basal ganglia, thalamus, and rostral brain-stem nuclei, as well as the frontal lobe projection regions of these nuclei. The principal neuropsychiatric and cognitive features of these illnesses include bradyphrenia, impairment of executive function, memory retrieval deficits, visuospatial abnormalities, and mood and motivational disturbances. Psychosis is a feature of some disorders. This contrasts with the cortical dementias previously discussed, wherein language disturbances, combined recall and recognition deficits, and indifference predominate. The extrapyramidal disorders are further characterized by prominent movement disorders that, depending on the specific disorder, can be hyperkinetic, hypokinetic, or ataxic in nature.

The basal ganglia lenticulostriatal system is connected to the frontal cortex through five circuits implicated in motor, cognitive, and psychiatric manifestations of basal ganglia diseases. The dorsal prefrontal, orbitofrontal, and anterior cingulate circuits are implicated in psychiatric illnesses such as depression, obsessive-compulsive disorder, and schizophrenia (Alexander et al. 1986; Cummings 1993). Neurologic diseases involving these circuits have a predominance of neuropsychiatric and behavioral disorders.

## Huntington's Disease

HD is a genetically transmitted, progressive, neurodegenerative disorder affecting primarily the striatum. It is a paradigmatic neuropsychiatric disorder exhibiting the triadic syndrome of dyskinesia, dementia, and behavioral abnormalities. An array of psychiatric disturbances such as depression, mania, psychosis, obsessive-compulsive disorders, aggression, irritability, apathy, and sexual disorders occur in HD (Rosenblatt and Leroi 2000).

HD is inherited in an autosomal dominant fashion with complete penetrance. The HD gene has been localized to the short arm of chromosome 4 (specifically at the IT15 gene locus); the mutation consists of an expanded and unstable CAG trinucleotide repeat (Huntington's Disease Collaborative Research Group 1993).

The mutation can be detected in asymptomatic individuals; CAG repeat lengths of greater than 38–40 are considered diagnostic of the disorder (Gusella et al. 1993). Because HD remains a chronic and disabling disorder with no known cure, psychological counseling is of extreme importance and should be a requisite component of any diagnostic testing program.

HD prevalence is 4.1–7.5 per 100,000 and has been reported in all ethnic groups and all regions of the world, but occurs less in people of African or Japanese descent (Folstein 1989). HD typically has its onset between ages 35 and 50, and average life expectancy after onset is 15 years (Cummings and Benson 1992; Folstein 1989). Although the peak period of onset is in the fourth and fifth decades of life, juvenile and late-onset forms also occur. Men and women are equally likely to have the disease. Death often occurs secondary to pneumonia, trauma, or suicide.

The most striking neurologic features of HD are abnormal involuntary choreiform movements, dysarthria, dystonia, and rigidity. These involuntary movements are a defining feature of HD and are characterized by irregular, arrhythmic, and purposeless movements of the face, limbs, and trunk that occur at rest or in concert with purposeful activity such as walking or eating. These movements tend to increase with emotional stress and mental concentration and are generally absent during sleep. Choreic movements in patients with HD are slower, more athetoid, and more proximally distributed than those observed in Sydenham's chorea (Cummings and

Benson 1992) and lack the stereotypy associated with motor tics. Impairment of voluntary movement, such as impaired control of oculomotor function, faulty articulation of speech, and poor limb coordination, are common and can exist in the absence of chorea in patients with juvenile-onset disease. Parkinsonian features also are common in patients with juvenile-onset HD (Folstein et al. 1990). The movement disorder can be followed by use of the Quantified Neurologic Examination and the Unified Huntington's Disease Rating Scale (Huntington Study Group 1996).

## Cognitive and Neuropsychiatric Aspects

Dementia is a uniform part of HD and can be the initial manifestation in some patients (Cummings and Benson 1992). All HD patients develop progressive subcortical dementia with initial impairment in cognitive speed, mental flexibility, concentration, new verbal learning, executive dysfunction, and memory deficits (Cummings and Benson 1992). Neuropsychological testing reveals deficits in recent and remote memory, visuospatial function, set shifting, strategy, and planning. Language skills, including naming, comprehension, and repetition, are typically spared until late in the disease. Deficits in sustained attention are apparent early in the course of HD (Folstein et al. 1990), and impaired memory retrieval, characterized by poor spontaneous recall with preserved recognition of acquired information, is typical. Retrieval of both new and old information is affected, and patients demonstrate equal impairment in their recollection of events across all periods of time (M.S. Albert et al. 1981). This impairment differs qualitatively from the memory disturbances seen in the early stages of AD, in which deficits in encoding and a clear temporal gradient (i.e., relative preservation of old versus new memories) predominate (Cummings and Benson 1992). Procedural memory, involving the ability to acquire new skills, also is impaired in patients with HD (Martone et al. 1984), and visuospatial skills, including constructional abilities and spatial orientation, deteriorate as the disease progresses. The ability to synthesize information and produce flexible strategies for problem solving is markedly impaired in patients with HD, and patients consistently demonstrate deficits in the organization, planning, and sequencing of material necessary to perform complex tasks (Caine et al. 1978).

Psychiatric symptoms are ubiquitous and present in up to 80% of patients; they may herald the onset of the disorder. Personality changes occur before the onset of chorea in many cases, and depression, when present, antedates the movement disorder in approximately two-thirds of patients (Cummings 1995). Personality changes can occur early or even prodromally in the disease and are almost universal with its progression (Cummings 1995). Apathy and aggression are more prominent in HD than in AD (Burns et al. 1990). Diminished self-control can manifest in emotional outbursts, aggressive behavior, substance abuse, or sexual promiscuity (Cummings 1995; Mendez 1994). Violence can be expressed in assault, arson, and homicide (Dewhurst et al. 1970). Personality characteristics associated with poor impulse control, aggression, intermittent explosive behavior, and antisocial traits have been described in patients with HD (Folstein 1989), as has abnormal sexual behavior with disinhibition, hypersexuality, and paraphilias (Dewhurst et al. 1970). With disease progression, hyposexuality and impotence develop (Folstein 1989).

Approximately one-third of patients with HD meet the criteria for major depression or dysthymic disorder, and many more exhibit intermittent dysphoria (Cummings 1995). Depression is more common in the families of some HD patients than in others, occurs more frequently among African Americans than whites, and is more often associated with late-onset disease (Folstein 1989). When present, depression frequently antedates the onset of both chorea and dementia by several years (Mendez 1994). In addition, approximately 10% of patients with HD experience episodes of mania or hypomania characterized by mood elevation with concurrent symptoms of undue optimism, pressured speech, increased energy, grandiose ideation, or disturbed sleep. These episodes are of variable duration, but are generally short lived (Folstein 1989).

The prevalence of affective disturbance among patients with HD is evidenced in the high frequency of suicide in this population. Suicide accounts for 5.7% of deaths in patients with HD, and up to 25% of HD patients attempt suicide at least once (Farrer 1986). The mood disturbances associated with HD typically respond to pharmacotherapy with conventional agents (e.g., antidepressants, carbamazepine, valproic acid). Electroconvulsive therapy also has proven effective in the treatment of depression in patients with HD (Cummings 1995) and might be more expedient in life-threatening affective disorder.

Anxiety disorders are present in 10%–15% of HD patients, and anxiety may be a prodromal psychiatric symptom (Dewhurst et al. 1969). Obsessive-compulsive disorder may also be observed (Cummings and Cunningham 1992). In addition to affective disturbances and anxiety disorders, a schizophrenia-like psychosis characterized by auditory hallucinations and persecutory delusions can occur in patients with HD. Psychoses occur in approximately 10% of HD patients and correlate with medial caudate pathology and reduced anterior hemispheric metabolism (Beckson and Cummings 1992; Cummings 1995). Specific delusional beliefs (e.g., delusional jealousy or delusional infestation) in the absence of other psychotic symptoms also have been described (Morris 1991). Treatment with conventional antipsychotic agents has been shown to reduce delusions in some but not all HD patients (Caine and Shoulson 1983), and preliminary reports indicate that clozapine, an atypical dibenzodiazepine antipsychotic, has modest efficacy in the treatment of refractory psychosis in these patients. Olanzapine, risperidone, quetiapine, and other atypical antipsychotics can be beneficial. Recent SPECT imaging studies before and after administration of olanzapine could show improved perfusion in the basal ganglia region of a HD patient (Etchebehere et al. 1999).

## Laboratory Investigations and Neuroimaging

Results of routine serum, urine, and CSF studies are unremarkable in patients with HD. The EEG reveals low voltage and poorly developed or absent alpha activity in symptomatic patients (Cummings and Benson 1992). Structural neuroimaging (CT or MRI) demonstrates atrophy of the caudate and putamen, most readily appreciated as enlargement of the frontal horns of the lateral ventricles (Figure 29–4). PET shows reduction in caudate glucose metabolism; SPECT demonstrates decreased caudate blood flow even before clear evidence of structural changes. SPECT and PET demonstrate increasing abnormalities as the disease advances.

## Neuropathology

The most striking pathology in patients with HD occurs in the basal ganglia. On gross inspection, atrophy of the caudate nucleus and, less dramatically, the putamen is visible. The globus pallidus may be affected (Folstein 1989). Microscopically, these structures reveal degenerative changes, with preferential loss of the small spiny neurons of the striatum accompanied by gliosis. Neurochemical alterations are numerous in patients with HD, but GABA and its synthesizing enzyme, glutamic acid decarboxylase, are markedly reduced in striatal regions. Acetylcholine transferase, cysteic acid decarboxylase, dopamine, and several neurokinins are reduced to a lesser extent (Cummings and Benson 1992).

The pathophysiology of mood disorders and psychosis in patients with HD is linked to striatal pathology. The caudate nuclei, which make up the portion of the stria-

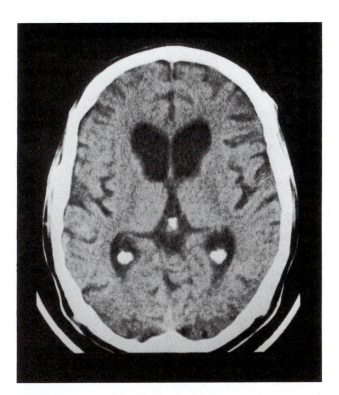

**FIGURE 29–4.** Computed tomography of a patient with Huntington's disease demonstrating marked atrophy of the caudate nucleus and putamen, evidenced by enlargement of the frontal horns of the lateral ventricles.

tum most severely and consistently affected in patients with HD, play a critical role in several major neuroanatomic pathways involved in mediating behavior, including the descending prefrontal-subcortical circuits and the limbic system. Caudate lesions may result in both depression and mania (Mendez et al. 1989), and caudate involvement is associated with elevated rates of psychosis in other extrapyramidal disorders (Cummings 1995). PET studies demonstrate hypometabolism in both the caudate nuclei and orbitofrontal/inferior prefrontal cortex in depressed HD patients (Mayberg et al. 1992), and reduced anterior metabolism in relation to posterior metabolism has been reported in psychotic HD patients (Kuwert et al. 1989). Disruption of frontal-subcortical pathways as a result of caudate pathology can thus be critical to the genesis of neuropsychiatric disturbances in patients with HD.

## Treatment

Pharmacologically the choreiform movements of HD are treated with antipsychotic medication, which reduces their severity. Conventional antipsychotics such as haloperidol or fluphenazine carry the risk of tardive dyskinesia with long-term treatment. No specific treatments exist for the cognitive disorders of HD. Sertraline and

propranolol may curb aggression (Ranen et al. 1996; J.T. Stewart 1993). Major depression responds to serotonergic or tricyclic antidepressants. Carbamazepine is the preferred agent for the treatment of mania in patients with HD (Cummings 1995); lithium, valproic acid, and clonazepam can also be effective.

## Parkinson's Disease

PD is a degenerative disorder of unknown etiology that affects mainly the pigmented brain-stem nuclei and basal ganglia and produces a characteristic triad of bradykinesia, rigidity, and resting tremor. The prevalence of the disease is approximately 1 per 1,000. Onset generally occurs between the ages of 50 and 70 years, and the disease reaches its highest prevalence in the eighth decade (Martilla 1987). The etiology is still unclear, and genetic as well as environmental factors are implicated. Although familial occurrence has been reported, it is usually a sporadic disorder whose prevalence rates are uniform throughout the world (Freedman 1990). Two rare causative mutations in the α-synuclein gene have been described, A53T in many families of Greek origin (Polymeropoulos et al. 1997) and A30P in a family of German origin (Krüger et al. 1998). The disease is more common among men than it is among women. The mean duration of the illness is 12.8 years, and a range of 2–30 years has been described (Hughes et al. 1992). Death results from a variety of causes, including aspiration pneumonia, urinary tract infection, and unrelated medical conditions.

## Clinical Features

Bradykinesia, expressed as slowness in initiation and execution of movement, is a primary symptom of PD and accounts for many of its clinical manifestations. Decreased facial expression, prolonged response latencies, slowed gait with diminished arm swing, sialorrhea, hypophonic speech, and micrographia are all common bradykinetic features of PD. Rigidity is present in the trunk and limb musculature, and superimposed tremor gives rise to cogwheel rigidity. The typical tremor of PD consists of alternating flexion and extension movements of the fingers and wrists that occur when the patient is alert but resting; the tremor disappears with action. Rigidity and tremor are often unilateral at the onset of the disease and can show asymmetry throughout its course. Other typical characteristics include postural instability and autonomic dysfunction (e.g., hypotension, constipation, and impotence). The clinical diagnostic criteria for PD are presented in Table 29–5.

**TABLE 29–5.** Clinical diagnostic criteria for Parkinson's disease

**Step 1: Diagnosis of parkinsonian syndrome**
Bradykinesia and at least one of the following:
Muscular rigidity
4–6 Hz rest tremor
Postural instability not caused by primary visual, vestibular, cerebellar, or proprioceptive dysfunction

**Step 2: Exclusion criteria for Parkinson's disease**
History of repeated strokes with stepwise progression of parkinsonian features
History of repeated head injury
History of definite encephalitis
Oculogyric crisis
Neuroleptic treatment at onset of symptoms
More than one affected relative
Sustained remission
Strictly unilateral features after 3 years
Supranuclear gaze palsy
Cerebellar signs
Early severe autonomic involvement
Early severe dementia with disturbances
Babinski's sign
Presence of cerebral tumor or communicating hydrocephalus on neuroimaging
Negative responses to large doses of levodopa
1-Methyl-4-phenyl-1,2,3,6-tetrahydropyridine (MPTP) exposure

**Step 3: Supportive prospective criteria for Parkinson's disease**[a]
Unilateral onset
Resting tremor present
Progressive disorder
Persistent asymmetry affecting side of onset most
Excellent response (70%–100%) to levodopa
Severe levodopa-induced chorea
Levodopa response for 5 years or more
Clinical course of 10 years or more

[a]Three or more of these criteria are required for the diagnosis of definite Parkinson's disease.
*Source.* Adapted from Hughes et al. 1992.

## Cognitive and Neuropsychiatric Aspects

Approximately 40% of patients with PD demonstrate overt dementia, and most exhibit more subtle neuropsychological deficits (Cummings and Benson 1992; Pirozzolo et al. 1982). The subcortical dementia of PD is characterized by memory impairment, visuospatial disturbances, executive dysfunction, and bradyphrenia. Spontaneous recall and skill acquisition (procedural memory) are impaired, whereas recognition memory is largely spared (Cummings and Benson 1992). Visuospatial deficits are apparent on both motor-dependent and motor-free tasks (Boller et al. 1984; Vil-

lardita et al. 1982), and disturbances of executive function, including poor concept formation, strategy formulation, and difficulties with set shifting, are consistently observed (Cummings 1988a). In some cases, patients with PD have dementia syndromes with cortical features. These patients may have concomitant AD, nucleus basalis atrophy with cortical cholinergic depletion, or cortical Lewy bodies.

Neuropsychiatric manifestations are common in patients with PD and can arise as an integral feature of the disorder or in association with antiparkinsonian treatment. Depression occurs in 40%–60% of PD patients (Cummings and Benson 1992), and several lines of evidence suggest that it is intrinsic to the disorder. Mayeux and colleagues (1981) found that 43% of PD patients exhibited depressive symptomatology before the onset of motor symptoms, suggesting that their mood disorder was not simply a reaction to motor dysfunction. In addition, depression is significantly more common among patients with PD than among other disabled patients matched for extent of functional impairment (Ehmann et al. 1990), and the severity of depression in PD patients does not correlate well with the degree of functional disability experienced (Cummings and Benson 1992). Finally, the frequency of depression is similar among untreated patients and patients responsive to antiparkinsonian agents (Cummings 1991).

Approximately 10%–20% of patients with PD meet the criteria for major depressive episodes; an additional 30%–40% have milder symptoms consistent with dysthymia (Cummings 1992). On the Beck Depression Inventory (Beck 1978), patients with PD evidence elevated scores in areas of dysphoria, pessimism about the future, sadness, irritability, and suicidal ideation, and only limited endorsement of guilt, self-blame, or feelings of failure (R.G. Brown et al. 1988). This pattern of dysphoria without guilt or self-reproach has been confirmed in several studies (Huber et al. 1990; Levin et al. 1988; Taylor et al. 1986). Other distinctive features of the depression seen in PD patients include high rates of associated anxiety, a low incidence of psychotic symptomatology, and low rates of completed suicide despite frequent suicidal ideation (Cummings 1992). Manic behavior is rare among patients with PD but has been reported in conjunction with levodopa therapy (see "Drug-Associated Psychiatric States").

The depression associated with PD responds to pharmacotherapy with conventional antidepressant agents. Imipramine, nortriptyline, and desipramine have all been shown to be efficacious in controlled studies (Cummings 1992). PD patients may be exquisitely sensitive to the anticholinergic, orthostatic, and sedating properties of these medications, and careful monitoring is required.

Bupropion, an antidepressant with indirect dopaminergic properties, improved depressive symptoms in 42% of patients in one study, and 30% also showed improved motor function (Goetz et al. 1984). Fluoxetine, a selective serotonin reuptake inhibitor (SSRI) with known dopamine-antagonistic properties, has been used effectively in some PD patients (Caley and Friedman 1992) but occasionally it increases parkinsonian symptoms (Steur 1993). SSRIs are the agents of choice to treat depression in PD. Antidepressants should not be used concomitantly with selegiline, a monoamine oxidase type B inhibitor often used in the treatment of PD (see the "Treatment" section that follows). Electroconvulsive therapy improves both depression and motor symptoms in patients with PD (Cummings 1992) and can be of particular utility when antidepressants are ineffective or when side effects preclude their use.

Anxiety disorders also occur in patients with PD. Stein et al. (Stein et al. 1990) reported generalized anxiety disorders in 38% of PD patients studied. The presence of anxiety did not correlate with either degree of motor disability or treatment with levodopa. Because anxiety is a common manifestation of depression in PD patients, an underlying mood disturbance must always be sought. Panic disorder, obsessive-compulsive disorder, and discrete phobias also have been observed in patients with PD. Anxiety is generally responsive to treatment with benzodiazepines, and panic disorder has been effectively treated with a variety of agents, including imipramine, desipramine, nortriptyline, and fluoxetine (Koller and Megaffin 1994).

## Drug-Associated Psychiatric Disorders

A variety of neuropharmacologic agents, including anticholinergic drugs, amantadine, levodopa, selegiline, and dopamine receptor agonists, are used in the treatment of PD. These drugs directly affect central neurotransmitter function, and their administration can precipitate adverse behavioral side effects. Behavioral complications of antiparkinsonian therapy include hallucinations, delusions, attentional impairment, mood disorders, anxiety, and alterations in sexual behavior. These effects can be of sufficient magnitude to limit the use of antiparkinsonian medications.

### Hallucinations

Visual hallucinations are the most common neuropsychiatric side effects associated with PD treatment. Approximately 30% of treated patients experience visual hallucinations, whereas other types of hallucinations (auditory or tactile) are comparatively rare (Cummings 1991).

Visual hallucinations can be induced by any antiparkinsonian agent and typically occur at night, may be preceded by sleep disturbances, and usually consist of fully formed visions of human or animal figures (Moskovitz et al. 1978; Shaw et al. 1980). Dementia, older age, a history of multiple drug therapy, longer duration of treatment, and the use of anticholinergic medications have all been found to be risk factors for visual hallucinosis (Tanner et al. 1983). In contrast to those associated with dopaminergic toxicity, hallucinations associated with anticholinergic toxicity tend to be more threatening, less well formed, combine auditory and tactile components, and can be accompanied by delirium (Goetz et al. 1982). Effective management of visual hallucinations can usually be achieved through reduction of the causative agent(s) or use of atypical antipsychotic agents.

### Delusions

Delusions are notably rare in patients with untreated PD and usually indicate an adverse response to treatment. Like hallucinations, delusions can occur with all types of antiparkinsonian therapy. The frequency of delusions is 3%–17% (Cummings 1991). Delusions can be antedated by vivid dreams or visual hallucinations, are typically persecutory in content (Cummings 1991), and can occur in conjunction with either a clear or a clouded sensorium (Moskovitz et al. 1978). Older patients and those with preexisting dementia syndromes are at increased risk for the development of delusions.

Management of delusions should begin with discontinuation of anticholinergic agents, selegiline, and amantadine. This should be followed by reductions in levodopa and other dopaminergic agents. Persistent delusional syndromes can require the administration of antipsychotic agents. Clozapine, an atypical antipsychotic that produces few extrapyramidal side effects, has been shown to be effective in the treatment of delusions in PD patients (Friedman and Lannon 1989; Roberts et al. 1989) and appears to be well tolerated in low doses (12.5–75 mg) (Factor et al. 1994). Clozapine may cause bone marrow suppression, and weekly hematologic monitoring is required. Other antipsychotic agents do not require hematologic monitoring, cause variable exacerbation of parkinsonism, and control psychotic symptoms in many cases.

### Delirium

Acute confusional states with fluctuating arousal, impaired attention, or incoherent verbal output can occur in patients receiving antiparkinsonian medications. The reported frequency of this syndrome is 5%–25%, and confusion is particularly likely to occur in PD patients with overt dementia and in those receiving anticholinergic medications. Among dopaminergic compounds, the higher-potency receptor agonists (e.g., bromocriptine and pergolide) are most often implicated (Cummings 1991). Management involves elimination of the offending agent(s).

## Alterations in Mood

Dopaminergic agents have been associated with mood elevation in some patients. Behavioral manifestations range from a feeling of unusual well-being to fully developed manic episodes with elation, grandiosity, pressured speech, diminished need for sleep, and increased libido (Celesia and Barr 1970). These symptoms typically subside with dose reduction. Depression occurs at approximately the same frequency in both treated and untreated PD patients and does not appear to be a consequence of antiparkinsonian therapy (Cummings 1991).

## Anxiety

Levodopa therapy can initiate the onset of anxiety in patients not previously predisposed to this disorder. Symptoms include apprehension, irritability, nervousness, palpitations, hyperventilation, and insomnia (Celesia and Barr 1970). In addition, levodopa can exacerbate anxiety in PD patients with a history of prior symptomatology. These symptoms usually improve with dose adjustments, although anxiolytic agents might be required in some cases.

## Altered Sexual Behavior

PD patients may experience a renewal of sexual interest and potency in conjunction with antiparkinsonian therapy. This leads to the return of normal sexual activity in many individuals. In rare cases, however, increased libido reaches pathologic proportions with hypersexuality. Reported hypersexual responses include increased masturbation, marked increases in marital intercourse, and the active pursuit of extramarital affairs for sexual gratification. Hypersexuality is reported more often in men than in women, and levodopa is the most common causative agent (Cummings 1991; Koller and Megaffin 1994). Paraphilic behavior has occasionally been reported in conjunction with dopaminergic therapy. Treatment involves reduction of drug dose.

## Laboratory Investigations and Neuroimaging

PD is a clinical diagnosis, and routine laboratory studies are uninformative. Results of routine blood, urine, and CSF assays are normal. EEG reveals no abnormality in most patients but can show nonspecific slowing in some

(Neufeld et al. 1988). CT scans are normal or show findings consistent with cortical atrophy, and MRI has demonstrated reductions in the size of the substantia nigra in advanced cases of PD (Duguid et al. 1986). FDG-PET investigations reveal posteriorly predominant reductions in cerebral glucose metabolism (Cummings and Benson 1992), and PET studies with fluorodopa reveal markedly diminished uptake in the striatum (Leenders et al. 1986).

## Neuropathology

Loss of pigmented cells in the substantia nigra and other pigmented nuclei (locus coeruleus, dorsal motor nucleus of the vagus) is the most consistently observed finding in patients with PD. Prominent depigmentation of the substantia nigra is grossly apparent, and microscopic inspection reveals reactive gliosis in the areas of cell loss (Cummings and Benson 1992). The remaining neurons of the involved nuclei contain distinctive eosinophilic cytoplasmic inclusions called Lewy bodies. On microscopic examination, Lewy bodies appear as round intracellular hyaline bodies with a pale peripheral halo. They may be single or multiple and occur in the cell cytoplasm and have been observed in the nucleus basalis of Meynert and in the hypothalamus of patients with PD as well as in the substantia nigra (Cummings and Benson 1992; Whitehouse et al. 1983). Lewy body formation is common in cortical regions in patients manifesting dementia syndromes.

Subcortical nuclei are major sources of neurotransmitters, and their pathologic involvement leads to neurochemical depletion in patients with PD. Neurochemical analysis of the basal ganglia reveals that the dopamine content of this region is markedly diminished. Norepinephrine, GABA, and serotonin and its metabolite 5-hydroxyindoleacetic acid also are decreased in PD patients, although these reductions are less severe (Cummings and Benson 1992). Atrophy of the nucleus basalis and concomitant reduction in cortical choline acetyltransferase is present in some patients with PD, particularly those with dementia (Whitehouse et al. 1983; Wikkelso et al. 1982).

## Treatment

The movement disorder of PD responds to levodopa in most patients (Cummings and Benson 1992). Unfortunately, the benefits of levodopa therapy last only 5–10 years, and disabling symptoms (progressive rigidity, tremor, and bradykinesia) eventually reemerge (Dogali et al. 1995). Selegiline can slow the progression of the disorder and thus can defer the need for dopaminergic therapy (Cummings and Benson 1992). Anticholinergic agents, amantadine, and dopamine receptor agonists (bromocriptine, pergolide, pramipexole, ropinirole) are useful adjuncts in the therapy of PD and form the mainstay of treatment in patients who are unable to tolerate levodopa. The affinity of pramipexole and ropinirole for the $D_3$ receptor subtype can allow those agents to treat motor as well as psychiatric symptoms, particularly depression (Bennet and Piercey 1999; Hall et al. 1996; Parkinson's Study Group 1997). In patients whose condition is refractory to medical therapy, surgical procedures such as stereotactic ventral pallidotomy or deep brain stimulation can significantly reduce parkinsonian symptoms (Dogali et al. 1995).

## Progressive Supranuclear Palsy

PSP is an idiopathic neurodegenerative disorder that affects the brain stem and basal ganglia and is characterized by supranuclear gaze paresis, pseudobulbar palsy, axial rigidity, and dementia. Onset usually occurs in the sixth or seventh decade, and the average course from onset to death is 5–10 years. The disease is sporadic and affects men more commonly than women (Steele 1972; Steele et al. 1964). Its prevalence is estimated to be 1.4 per 100,000 population but is likely underestimated because of frequent misdiagnosis as PD (Golbe 1994; Hughes et al. 1992). PSP occasionally occurs in families and some families with chromosome 17 mutations have PSP-like phenotypes. Of the two alleles of tau occurring in the general population, H1 and H2, PSP is associated with homozygosity for the H1 allele (Baker et al. 1999; Conrad et al. 1997). This needs to be seen in the context of the fact that approximately 50% of Caucasians are H1 homozygotes and 95% of PSP patients are Caucasian (Higgins et al. 2000).

### Movement Disorder

The characteristic motor features of PSP include bradykinesia, axial rigidity, pseudobulbar palsy, and supranuclear gaze paresis. During the course of the disease, patients with PSP develop a profound bradykinesia that is similar to that seen in patients with PD. Rigidity affects truncal and neck tone more than limb tone, resulting in axial dystonia with nuchal rigidity as the disease progresses. The posture is typically one of extension (contrasting with the flexed posture of PD). Pseudobulbar palsy is manifested by dysphagia, sialorrhea, and dysarthria. Supranuclear ophthalmoplegia is the hallmark of the disorder and presents with marked restrictions in

volitional gaze that are more prominent in the vertical than the horizontal plane. Loss of downward gaze, coupled with disturbances of gait and stability, results in frequent falls in PSP patients. Unlike those of PD, the motor disturbances associated with PSP are often refractory to therapy. The clinical criteria for PSP are presented in Table 29–6.

## Cognitive and Neuropsychiatric Features

The cognitive alterations in patients with PSP are similar to those seen in patients with other extrapyramidal syndromes and include slowing of thought processes, difficulties with set shifting and abstraction, memory retrieval disturbances, and personality alterations. Disorders reflecting primary cortical involvement, such as agnosia, apraxia, and aphasia, are typically absent in patients with PSP (M. L. Albert et al. 1974). PSP patients are impaired on tasks measuring frontal lobe function and, in comparison with PD and HD patients, demonstrate a greater frequency of abnormal behaviors (e.g., imitation and utilization behavior) associated with frontal lobe dysfunction (Pillon et al. 1986). Slowed central processing, with deficits in verbal memory, calculating ability, and the synthesis of complex information, are characteristic (M. L. Albert et al. 1974). Initial cognitive deficits can be mild, and dementia might not be apparent until late in the course of the disease, when a dysexecutive syndrome with decreased verbal fluency, concrete thinking, lack of insight, impaired reasoning, slowed information processing, poor information retrieval, impaired control over attention or execution of sequential actions, and problems with set-shifting is observable (Cummings and Benson 1992; Litvan et al. 1996).

Personality and mood disturbances occur in patients with PSP. The most commonly reported disturbances are apathy, emotional indifference, and depression. Irritability, inappropriate crying or laughing, and episodic outbursts of rage can emerge (M. L. Albert et al. 1974). PSP has been associated with obsessive-compulsive behaviors (Destee et al. 1990) and, rarely, with schizophreniform psychoses.

## Laboratory Investigations and Neuroimaging

Results of blood, serum, urine, and CSF studies are all within normal limits in patients with PSP. EEGs may be normal or can show nonspecific findings, including generalized background slowing or diffuse theta activity (Cummings and Benson 1992). CT and MRI reveal diminished

**TABLE 29–6.** Clinical diagnostic criteria for progressive supranuclear palsy (PSP)

**Essential for diagnosis**
> Onset after age 40
> Progressive course
> Bilateral supranuclear disorder of ocular motility
> Rigidity with axial predominance
> Bradykinesia

**Confirmatory manifestations**
> Poor or absent response to levodopa therapy
> Severe bradyphrenia with frontal lobe features (e.g., grasping, perseveration, utilization behavior)
> Axial dystonia with cervical hyperextension
> Onset with gait impairment, frequent falls, and postural instability
> Dysarthria with dysphasia
> Ocular fixation instability
> Apraxia of eyelid opening and/or closing; infrequency of eye blink
> Echolalia, palilalia

**Manifestations consistent with, but not diagnostic of, PSP**
> Tremor: postural, action, or resting
> Pyramidal tract signs
> Focal or segmental dystonia
> Amyotrophy
> Sleep disorders
> Depression or schizophreniform psychosis

**Features inconsistent with diagnosis of PSP**
> Early or prominent cerebellar signs
> Unexplained polyneuropathy
> Aphasia or agnosia
> Sensory deficits
> Seizures

*Source.* Adapted from Duvoisin 1992.

midbrain size; cortical atrophy involving the frontotemporal regions also may be seen (Lees 1990). PET studies of glucose metabolism reveal marked metabolic reductions in the frontal lobes (Foster et al. 1988), and SPECT reveals bilateral frontal lobe hypoperfusion (Lees 1990). Fluorodopa PET demonstrates diminished striatal dopamine formation and storage (Leenders et al. 1988).

## Neuropathology

Postmortem examinations of patients with PSP disclose cell loss, gliosis, and NFTs involving primarily the structures of the mesencephalic-diencephalic junction. The NFTs in patients with PSP are composed of straight filaments, unlike the twisted filaments seen in AD patients (Cummings and Benson 1992). Tau protein is observable in the NFTs (H.R. Morris et al. 1999). The structures maximally affected are the subthalamic nucleus, globus pallidus, red nucleus, substantia nigra, superior colliculi, dentate nuclei, and the nuclei of cranial nerves IV, VI, and VIII. The thalamus and hypothalamus are minimally affected, and the cerebral cortex is relatively spared (Steele 1972). Neurochemical alterations include marked nigrostriatal dopamine deficiency with less pronounced cholinergic system impairment. Cortical nicotinic cholinergic receptors and subcortical dopamine, subtype 2 ($D_2$), receptors are reduced (Cummings and Benson 1992).

## Treatment

PSP has no cure; supportive therapy is critical in this relentlessly progressive disease. Contact with patient and family support groups should be recommended. In the early course of the illness, physiotherapy for mobilization, balance, and fall prevention as well as occupational therapy are important. Identification of problems in swallowing and referral to speech therapy and swallowing assessment are important to avoid aspiration. Dopaminergic medication is generally not useful as a result of the widespread damage to the basal ganglia, although a few patients respond at least transiently. Tricyclic antidepressants may be of some benefit in improving depressive symptoms in patients with PSP (Kvale 1982; Newman 1985), and violent outbursts have been treated effectively with serotonergic agents (Schneider et al. 1989).

## Fahr's Disease

Fahr's disease, or idiopathic basal ganglia calcification, is a rare genetic disorder that is characterized by abnormal involuntary movements, neuropsychiatric disturbances, and extensive calcification of the basal ganglia. Serum calcium and phosphorus levels are normal and the etiology of calcium deposition is unknown. Parkinsonism is the most common movement disturbance, but choreoathetosis, dystonia, and ataxia have been described (Hier and Cummings 1990). Dementia occurs in most patients with Fahr's disease and is characterized by concentration deficits, memory disturbances, and impaired abstraction with relative preservation of language skills (Cummings and Benson 1992; Hier and Cummings 1990). A schizophrenia-like psychosis can antedate the onset of both cognitive and neurologic symptoms (Cummings and Benson 1992), and mood disorders of either depressed or manic type are common (Trautner et al. 1988).

Structural neuroimaging (CT or MRI) demonstrates dense mineral deposition in the basal ganglia, periventricular white matter, and dentate nuclei of the cerebellum of patients with Fahr's disease (Hier and Cummings 1990). Ferrocalcific deposition in the affected regions is confirmed on postmortem examination (Trautner et al. 1988).

No effective treatment exists for Fahr's disease, although some improvement in psychotic and mood disturbances can occur with psychotropic medications (Trautner et al. 1988).

## Hallervorden-Spatz Disease

Hallervorden-Spatz (HS) disease is an extremely rare neurodegenerative disorder. It is an inherited autosomal recessive condition with onset usually in childhood or adolescence. Recently its causative mutation has been identified to chromosome 20. Pathologically, HS disease displays the triad of iron deposition, axonal spheroids, and gliosis (Halliday 1995). The disease is characterized by mixed extrapyramidal and pyramidal motor disturbances, marked intellectual deterioration, and a variety of personality disturbances that include depression, impulsivity, and aggression (Cummings and Benson 1992; Nardocci et al. 1994). CT demonstrates various degrees of atrophy and loss of basal ganglia bulk (Cummings and Benson 1992), and MRI reveals a characteristic "eye of the tiger" change in the basal ganglia. Postmortem studies reveal accumulation of iron-containing pigment in the globus pallidus, substantia nigra, and red nucleus (Adams and Victor 1993). Iron-chelating agents have proven unsuccessful in the treatment of HS disease, and death usually occurs in young adulthood. A rare adult variant of the disease presenting in midlife and associated with parkinsonism has been described (Cummings and Benson 1992).

## Wilson's Disease (Hepatolenticular Degeneration)

WD, also called hepatolenticular degeneration, is an autosomal recessive disorder of copper metabolism leading to abnormal deposition of copper, primarily in the basal ganglia of the brain, liver, and cornea. WD was first described by Westphal in 1883 and later by Wilson in 1912. The gene for WD has been localized to chromosome 13, and the disorder occurs with an estimated frequency of 1 in 40,000 births (Akil and Brewer 1995). The worldwide incidence of WD approximates 12–30 per million with higher prevalences reported in Japan. Age at onset ranges from 5 to 35, with mean age 17; onset and initial manifestations vary among families. Males and

females are affected with equal frequency. Neurological and psychiatric symptoms are the most prominent features of WD, however, liver disease can be the presenting manifestation. The manifestations of WD can be divided approximately into thirds, with one-third each presenting predominantly with hepatic, neurologic, or psychiatric symptomatology.

Impaired hepatic protein binding of copper results in toxic accumulations of the metal primarily in the liver, cornea, and basal ganglia. Deficiency of the copper-carrying protein ceruloplasmin is a characteristic feature of the disorder (Hier and Cummings 1990). Presymptomatic molecular genetic testing using DNA linkage analysis can be considered in asymptomatic siblings (Maier-Dobersberger et al. 1995).

## Clinical Features

The neurologic manifestations of WD include tremor, rigidity, dystonia, poor coordination, and abnormalities of gait and posture. Dysarthria, dysphagia, and hypophonia may be present. Chronic hepatitis and hemolytic anemia may be detected on laboratory assessment, and slit-lamp examination reveals the presence of corneal copper deposits (Kayser-Fleischer rings) in most patients with neurologic disturbances (Akil and Brewer 1995). CT reveals ventricular enlargement, and MRI demonstrates increased signal on T2-weighted images as a result of copper deposition in the lenticular, caudate, thalamic, and dentate nuclei (Hier and Cummings 1990). The diagnosis of WD is confirmed by decreased blood ceruloplasmin level (<20 mg/dL), increased 24-hour urine copper excretion (>100 mg), or the presence of excessive hepatic copper in needle biopsy tissue (Akil and Brewer 1995). Reduced glucose metabolism can be seen on PET in the cerebellum, striatum, cerebral cortex, and thalamus (Kuwert et al. 1989). Reduced striatal glucose metabolism is correlated with neurological sign severity and improves in response to chelation therapy (Schlaug et al. 1996).

Patients with WD demonstrate mild impairment in memory retrieval and executive functions (abstraction and set shifting) that is consistent with the deficits observed in other extrapyramidal syndromes (Hier and Cummings 1990). Psychiatric disturbances can be prominent and precede other manifestations of the disorder in 20% of patients (Akil and Brewer 1995). Common personality alterations include increased irritability, impulsivity, and lability. Aggressive, reckless, disinhibited, and criminal behavior may be observed (Dening and Berrios 1989). Depression is reported in 20%–30% of patients, and other mood disorders, such as hypomania or overt mania, can occur. Rarely, a schizophrenia-like psychosis can occur (Akil and Brewer 1995), but whether this exceeds the rate of psychosis observed in the general population has been challenged. Psychiatric manifestations to correlate with the presence of neurologic symptoms (dystonic and bulbar disorders) rather than with hepatic dysfunction (Dening and Berrios 1989). Of key importance is to consider WD in the differential diagnosis of psychiatric illness in young patients because many individuals with WD initially are misdiagnosed as having a primary psychiatric disorder. Treatment and clinical improvement are most successful with early recognition and intervention (Akil and Brewer 1995).

## Neuropathology

The major pathologic finding in patients with WD is cavitary necrosis of the putamen. Atrophy of the brain stem and dentate nuclei of the cerebellum also may be marked. Histologic findings include neuronal loss, liquefaction, reactive gliosis, and the presence of Opalski cells (large oval cells with a finely granular cytoplasm) in affected regions (Cummings and Benson 1992).

## Treatment

Early treatment with penicillamine, which is a copper-chelating agent, and maintenance of a copper-deficient diet can lead to significant improvement in both the neurologic and neuropsychiatric manifestations of WD (Akil and Brewer 1995; Hier and Cummings 1990). However penicillamine therapy can lead to further neurological disability, seizures, movement disorders, and psychosis in some cases. These reactions can be irreversible and can occur in previously asymptomatic patients (Glass et al. 1990; McDonald and Lake 1995).

Tetrathiomolybdate has received support for the initial treatment of WD and has been suggested as first-line treatment; exacerbations generally did not occur but more data are needed (Brewer and Cummings 1995). Dramatic improvements as evidenced by neurologic examination and near complete T2 signal resolution in putamen, thalamus, and brain stem were demonstrated in patients undergoing zinc treatment, though neurologic exacerbations are possible with this agent (Heckmann et al. 1994; Lang et al. 1993).

## Corticobasal Degeneration

CBD is a rare neurodegenerative disorder characterized by parkinsonism, supranuclear gaze palsy, "alien hand"

phenomenon, myoclonus, and dementia. Aphasia, apraxia, and marked visuospatial deficits are common in patients with this condition. Impaired recall, acalculia, right-left disorientation, attentional deficits, and personality alterations have also been reported (Cohen and Freedman 1995). Neuropsychiatric syndromes include depression, frontal lobe–type behavioral abnormalities, and obsessive-compulsive behaviors (Cummings and Litvan 2000). Pathologically, neuronal loss and gliosis are seen in the substantia nigra, and round, faintly fibrillar, inclusion bodies are apparent in the remaining pigmented cells. Focal cortical degeneration is seen in the frontal and parietal lobes bilaterally and can be associated with sparse Pick cell formation. Subcortical white-matter gliosis exists in proportion to the degree of overlying cortical cell loss (Gibb 1992). Table 29–7 summarizes the diagnostic criteria for CBD.

**TABLE 29–7.** Diagnostic criteria for corticobasal degeneration (CBD)

**Inclusion criteria**

  Rigidity plus one cortical sign (apraxia, cortical sensory loss, or alien limb phenomenon); or

  Asymmetric rigidity, dystonia, and focal reflex myoclonus

**Qualifications of clinical features**

  Rigidity: easily detectable without reinforcement

  Apraxia: more than simple use of limb as object; clear absence of cognitive or motor deficit sufficient to explain disturbance

  Cortical sensory loss: preserved primary sensation; asymmetrical

  Alien limb phenomenon: more than simple levitation

  Dystonia: focal in limb; present at rest at onset

  Myoclonus: reflex myoclonus spreads beyond stimulated digits

**Exclusion criteria**

  Early dementia (this will exclude some patients who have CBD but whose illness cannot be clinically distinguished from other primary dementing diseases)

  Early vertical gaze palsy

  Rest tremor

  Severe autonomic disturbances

  Sustained responsiveness to levodopa

  Lesions on imaging studies indicating another pathologic process is responsible

## Multiple System Atrophies

The MSAs are a diverse group of disorders with pathology that demonstrates various degrees of combined striatonigral and olivopontocerebellar degeneration. The four domains of clinical features are autonomic failure/urinary dysfunction, parkinsonism, cerebellar ataxia, and corticospinal dysfunction. The diagnosis of possible MSA requires one criterion plus features from two other domains (Table 29–8). The diagnosis of probable MSA requires the criterion for autonomic failure/urinary dysfunction plus poorly levodopa responsive parkinsonism and cerebellar ataxia. The diagnosis of definite MSA is a postmortem diagnosis (Table 29–8) (Gilman et al. 1999). The disease affects both genders, usually starting in middle age with a median survival of 9.3 years from time of first symptoms (Wenning et al. 1994). A recent consensus group recommended the designation MSA-P if parkinsonian features predominate or MSA-C if cerebellar features predominate; this nomenclature is to replace the terms of olivopontocerebellar atrophies and striatonigral degeneration. These disorders can present with a wide array of neurologic disturbances, including ataxia, limb incoordination, parkinsonism, dysautonomia, choreoathetosis, and hyperreflexia (Adams and Victor 1993). Dementia with prominent frontal deficits occurs in some but not all cases of MSA (Cohen and Freedman 1995), and neuropsychiatric manifestations, including mood lability, depression, and a schizophrenia-like psychosis have been reported (Cohen and Freedman 1995; Cummings and Benson 1992). The parkinsonian features usually respond poorly to levodopa, but therapy should be tried because up to 30% of patients improve at least transiently (Hughes et al. 1992).

## Vascular Dementia

VaD is a dementing condition produced by ischemic or hemorrhagic brain injury. In its classic form, it is characterized by an abrupt onset, stepwise deterioration, a patchy pattern of intellectual deficits, focal neurologic symptoms (transient ischemic attacks), focal neurologic signs, a history of hypertension, and evidence of associated cardiovascular disease (American Psychiatric Association 2000; Hachinski et al. 1975). Most cases of VaD are produced by hypertensive cerebrovascular disease and thrombo-occlusive disease, but the condition can also occur with multiple cerebral emboli, systemic hypotension, intracerebral hemorrhage, and inflammatory and infectious vascular disease (Cummings and Benson 1992; Meyer et al. 1988; Sulkava and Erkinjuntti 1987). Symptoms generally appear when a certain volume of infarcted tissue is present or if small strokes are strategically placed. The significance of other vascular or circulatory defects including leukoaraiosis, a form of deep white-matter demyelination, multiple cortical infarcts, and

**TABLE 29–8.** Diagnostic categories of multisystem atrophy (MSA)

**Possible MSA**

One criterion plus two factors (one each) from two other domains. When the criterion is parkinsonism, a poor levodopa response qualifies as one feature (one additional feature required).

Criterion for autonomic features of urinary dysfunction: orthostatic fall in blood pressure (by 30 mm Hg systolic or 15 mm Hg diastolic) or urinary incontinence.

Criterion for parkinsonism: bradykinesia plus one of rigidity, postural instability, tremor.

Criterion for cerebellar dysfunction: gait ataxia plus one of ataxia dysarthria, limb ataxia, sustained gaze-evoked nystagmus.

**Probable MSA**

Criterion for autonomic failure/urinary dysfunction plus poor levodopa responsive parkinsonism or cerebellar dysfunction.

**Definite MSA**

Pathologically confirmed by the presence of a high density of glial cytoplasmic inclusions in association with a combination of degenerative changes in the nigrostriatal and olivopontocerebellar pathways.

cerebral hypoperfusion is less well delineated (Petersen et al. 2000). Combined VaD and AD is common and underrecognized.

VaD is most common after the age of 50 and affects men more often than it affects women. Patients commonly survive for 6–8 years after onset, and death usually results from cardiovascular disease or stroke.

## Clinical Diagnosis

The diagnosis of VaD is difficult and several diagnostic approaches have evolved. A diagnosis of VaD can be based on one of several different clinical definitions, including the Hachinski Ischemic Score (HIS), the Alzheimer Disease Diagnostic and Treatment Centers (ADDTC), the National Institute for Neurologic Disorders and Stroke–Association Internationale pour la Recherche et l'Enseignement en Neurosciences (NINDS-AIREN) criteria, and DSM-IV-TR. Reported prevalence rates vary depending on which diagnostic approach is used.

The NINDS-AIREN criteria for the diagnosis of definite, probable, and possible VaD are presented in Table 29–9 (Roman et al. 1993). The diagnosis of *definite VaD* requires that the patient meet the clinical criteria for probable VaD and that there be histologic confirmation of ischemic brain injury obtained at autopsy.

**TABLE 29–9.** Diagnostic criteria for definite, probable, and possible vascular dementia (VaD)

**Definite VaD**

Clinical criteria for probable VaD

Autopsy demonstration of appropriate ischemic brain injury and no other cause of dementia

**Probable VaD**

Dementia

Decline from a previous higher level of cognitive functioning

Impairment of two or more cognitive domains

Deficits severe enough to interfere with activities of daily living and not due to physical effects of stroke alone

Absence of delirium; absence of psychosis, aphasia, or sensorimotor impairment that precludes neuropsychological testing; and absence of any other disorder capable of producing a dementia syndrome

Cerebrovascular disease

Focal neurologic signs consistent with stroke

Neuroimaging evidence of extensive vascular lesions

Relationship between dementia and cerebrovascular disease, as evidenced by one or more of the following:

Onset of dementia within 3 months of a recognized stroke

Abrupt deterioration or fluctuating or stepwise progression of the cognitive deficit

**Supporting features**

Subtle onset and variable course of cognitive deficits

Early presence of gait disturbance

History of unsteadiness, frequent and unprovoked falls

Early urinary frequency, urgency, and other urinary symptoms not explained by urologic disease

Pseudobulbar palsy

Personality and mood changes, abulia, depression, emotional incontinence, and subcortical deficits, including psychomotor retardation and abnormal executive function

**Possible VaD**

Dementia with focal neurologic signs but without neuroimaging confirmation of definite cerebrovascular disease

Dementia with focal signs but without a clear temporal relationship between dementia and stroke

Dementia and focal signs but with subtle onset and variable course of cognitive deficits

*Source.* Adapted from Roman et al. 1993.

The diagnosis of *probable VaD* requires the presence of dementia, evidence of cerebrovascular disease, and a relationship between the onset or course of the dementia and the cerebrovascular disease. Dementia, defined as a decline in two or more cognitive domains, is established by clinical examination and confirmed by neuropsychological testing. Deficits must be of sufficient severity to interfere with activities of daily living and should exceed those imposed by the physical effects of stroke alone. Cerebrovascular disease is established by focal neurologic signs consistent with stroke (e.g., hemiparesis, sensory deficit, Babinski's sign) and neuroimaging (CT or MRI) evidence of vascular lesions. A relationship between dementia and cerebrovascular disease must be demonstrated by at least one of the following: 1) onset of dementia within 3 months after a known stroke, 2) abrupt deterioration in cognitive ability, or 3) fluctuation in or stepwise progression of cognitive impairment. Exclusionary criteria include the presence of delirium, psychosis, aphasia, or sensorimotor deficits that preclude neuropsychological testing. Finally, the diagnosis of probable VaD requires the absence of any other disorder capable of producing a dementia syndrome.

*Possible VaD* is diagnosed in the presence of dementia and neurologic signs when neuroimaging confirmation of cerebrovascular disease is lacking; when the temporal relationship between dementia and stroke is unclear; or when there are variations in the onset, course, or presentation of cognitive deficits despite evidence of relevant cerebrovascular disease. The diagnosis of VaD cannot be made with certainty in the absence of focal neurologic signs or neuroimaging confirmation of cerebrovascular disease.

On examination, patients with VaD exhibit a combination of motor abnormalities, neuropsychological deficits, and neuropsychiatric symptoms. Motor findings may include weakness, spasticity, hyperreflexia, extensor plantar responses, bradykinesia, parkinsonism, and pseudobulbar palsy (Ishii et al. 1986). Gait abnormalities are common and can appear early in the course of the disorder.

The pattern of neuropsychological abnormalities in patients with VaD is characterized by "patchiness," with preservation of some abilities and mild to severe compromise of others. Thus, the profile of deficits varies among patients. In most cases, IQ testing and memory evaluations reveal diminished cognitive and memory abilities (Ladurner et al. 1982; Perez et al. 1975), and visuospatial abnormalities are demonstrable in most patients (Reichman et al. 1991). Speech and language assessments reveal dysarthria with relative preservation of language functions (Hier et al. 1985; Powell et al. 1988). Slowing of cognitive function and impairment of executive function are common elements of the dementia syndrome.

## Neuropsychiatric Aspects

Neuropsychiatric abnormalities are common in patients with VaD: personality changes, depression, lability of mood, and delusions occur regularly. Personality changes are the most common neuropsychiatric alterations in patients with VaD. Apathy, abulia, and aspontaneity dominate the clinical syndrome; interpersonal relatedness and affect, however, are more preserved in patients with VaD than in those with AD (Dian et al. 1990; Ishii et al. 1986).

Major depressive disorders occur in 25%–50% of patients with VaD, and up to 60% show symptoms of a depressive syndrome (Cummings 1988b; Cummings et al. 1987; Erkinjuntti 1987). Sadness, anxiety, psychomotor retardation, and somatic complaints are the most commonly reported depressive symptoms. Little relationship exists between the severity of depression and the degree of dementia (Cummings et al. 1987). Lability of mood and affect are common in patients with VaD.

Psychosis with delusional ideation occurs in approximately 50% of VaD patients. The delusional content is similar to that of AD patients and can include persecutory beliefs, fears of infidelity, phantom boarder syndrome, and Capgras' syndrome (Cummings et al. 1987; Flynn et al. 1991). Delusions are most common in patients with lesions involving the temporoparietal structures of either hemisphere.

## Laboratory Investigations

Serum studies of VaD patients should routinely include complete blood count, erythrocyte sedimentation rate, and serum cholesterol and triglyceride levels. In young patients or those without risk factors for stroke, the potential etiologic contribution of inflammatory vasculitis should be investigated. These circumstances require more extensive laboratory studies, including antinuclear antibodies, antiphospholipid antibodies, and lupus anticoagulant levels (Briley et al. 1989; Cummings and Benson 1992; Young et al. 1989).

Neuroimaging studies provide support for the clinical diagnosis of VaD. CT can reveal cortical infarctions or evidence of periventricular ischemic changes (Aharon-Peretz et al. 1988; Erkinjuntti 1987; Loeb and Gandolfo 1983). MRI is more revealing than is CT and demonstrates small subcortical infarctions and ischemic white-matter changes that are invisible on CT (J.J. Brown et al. 1988; Hershey et al. 1987). MRI is the technique of choice for the identification of structural changes in VaD (Figure 29–5). It is of note, however, that the role of imaging in VaD is controversial because white-matter changes are nonspecific and must be extensive to support diagnosis of VaD. FDG-PET and SPECT show multiple irregular areas of hypometabolism or hypoperfusion that are consistent with focal regions of tissue infarction (Benson et al. 1983; Gemmell et al. 1987).

## Classification and Neuropathology

Several subtypes of VaD, based on the mechanism of cerebrovascular injury and size of the affected vessel, have been described (Roman et al. 1993) (Table 29–10). Multi-infarct dementia results from the cumulative effect of multiple large- and small-vessel occlusions. Both cortical and subcortical regions can be affected, and infarction can result from atherosclerotic or arteriosclerotic disease or cardiac embolization. The resulting clinical picture is variable but often includes memory impairment in addition to patchy deficits across several domains of cognitive function. Neurologic signs and symptoms (e.g., hemiparesis, hemisensory loss, visual field disturbances, or reflex asymmetries) are consistent with the region(s) affected.

Strategic single-infarct dementia occurs with infarction to a focal cortical or subcortical area that is critical to cognitive function. Strategically placed, solitary infarcts can result in well-defined dementia syndromes (Roman et al. 1993). For example, small lesions involving the left angular gyrus or medial thalamic nuclei can disrupt multiple cognitive faculties and result in the abrupt onset of dementia. These lesions can be a product of atherosclerotic disease, cardiac embolization, or sustained hypertension with hyaline necrosis of arterioles.

Subcortical small-vessel disease can result in dementia. Sustained hypertension leads to fibrinoid necrosis of small arteries and arterioles. These vessels supply the deep gray-matter nuclei, including the striatum and thalamus, as well as the hemispheric white matter. Multiple small lacunar infarctions of the basal ganglia and thalamus produce the syndrome of lacunar state. Binswanger's disease is a syndrome characterized by extensive ischemic injury of white matter. Small-vessel disease is often associated with memory loss, personality and behavioral changes, pseudobulbar palsy, psychomotor slowing, and parkinsonism. In most cases, lacunar state and Binswanger's disease coexist (Roman 1987).

Reduced cerebral perfusion as a result of cardiac arrest, loss of blood volume, or profound hypotension can lead to border zone infarction. Border zone regions (or "watershed areas") lie between the territories served by the three principal intracranial vessels and are thus particularly vulnerable to ischemic insult. Associated cognitive deficits include transcortical aphasia, apraxia, and

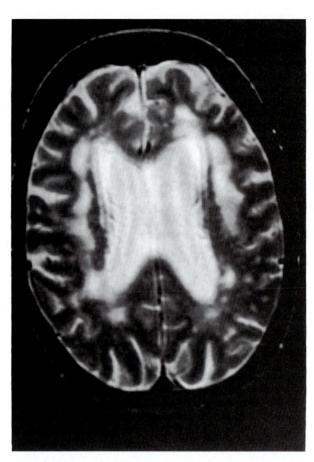

**FIGURE 29–5.** T2-weighted magnetic resonance imaging scan of a patient with vascular dementia revealing irregular periventricular lesions and confluent high signal areas in the hemispheric white matter, consistent with ischemic cerebral injury.

memory disturbances. Hemorrhagic dementia can result from intracerebral hemorrhage or ruptured cerebral aneurysm or as the sequela of subarachnoid hemorrhage. The etiology and clinical manifestations of hemorrhagic stroke are discussed in Chapter 21.

Mixed AD and cerebrovascular disease is commonly found at autopsy in VaD patients.

## Treatment

Treatment of VaD consists of control of blood pressure in the upper normal range and administration of aspirin or other platelet antiaggregants (Meyer et al. 1986; 1988). Nonaspirin antiaggregants are appropriate alternatives in patients who are resistant to or intolerant of aspirin's effects. In rare circumstances, the use of anticoagulants or steroids might be warranted. Administration of baclofen can assist with spasticity in the poststroke patient. Supportive measures such as gait retraining, prophylaxis against limb contractures, and speech therapy are indi-

cated in selected patients. Pseudobulbar affect has been successfully treated with nortriptyline and selective serotonin reuptake inhibitors, and patients with depression or psychosis typically respond to antidepressant or antipsychotic therapy (Starkstein and Robinson 1994).

## Hydrocephalic Dementia

Hydrocephalus refers to enlargement of the cerebral ventricles with an increased amount of intraventricular CSF. Ventricular enlargement can be on an *ex vacuo* basis (from loss of cerebral tissue) or as a result of interruption of CSF flow (obstructive hydrocephalus). Hydrocephalus ex vacuo occurs in patients with AD, VaD, and other dementing illnesses and is not discussed further here.

The two types of obstructive hydrocephalus are noncommunicating and communicating. Noncommunicating hydrocephalus arises from obstruction of CSF flow within the ventricular system or between the ventricles and the subarachnoid space. Communicating hydrocephalus occurs with obstruction of CSF flow within the subarachnoid space, preventing absorption of the CSF into the superior sagittal sinus. Noncommunicating hydrocephalus is usually an acute process accompanied by headache, confusion, and ophthalmoplegia; intracranial pressure is typically elevated. Communicating hydrocephalus presents as a dementia syndrome with normal intracranial pressure, hence the alternate name "normal-pressure hydrocephalus" (NPH). NPH accounts for approximately 2%–5% of dementia syndromes in adults (Cummings and Benson 1992).

## Clinical and Neuropsychiatric Features

The classic syndrome of NPH consists of dementia, gait disturbance, and incontinence. The dementia of NPH has prominent features of frontal-subcortical dysfunction, including impaired attention and mental control, poor learning, visuospatial disturbances, and impaired abstraction and judgment (Cummings and Benson 1992; Gustafson and Hagberg 1978; Thomsen et al. 1986). Aphasia, apraxia, and agnosia are absent or mild. The gait abnormalities of NPH are variable but commonly include shortened stride, diminished step height, and slow speed (Sudarsky and Simon 1987). Urinary incontinence is more common than loss of bowel control.

A variety of neuropsychiatric syndromes have been described in patients with NPH, including personality alterations, anxiety, mood changes, and rarely psychosis. Apathy, inertia, and indifference are the typical personality alterations; aggressive outbursts have also been

**TABLE 29–10.** Subtypes of vascular dementia

| Syndrome | Specific vessels | Common etiologies | Anatomic region of involvement |
|---|---|---|---|
| Multi-infarct | Large and small arteries | Atherosclerosis, hypertension | Cortical and subcortical regions |
| Strategic single infarct | Major intracranial arteries and branches, arterioles of the thalamus and caudate | Atherosclerosis, cardiac emboli, hypertension | Small, localized ischemic damage in functionally important regions (e.g., angular gyrus, caudate, medial nuclei of the thalamus) |
| Small-vessel disease (lacunar state and Binswanger's disease) | Arterioles of the deep gray nuclei, arterioles of white matter | Hypertension | Basal ganglia, periventricular white matter |
| Hypoperfusion (border zone infarction) | Distal segments of the major intracranial arteries | Cardiac arrest, hypotension, loss of blood volume | Border zone ischemia involving frontal and/or parietal regions, including periventricular white matter |
| Hemorrhagic | Bridging veins, major intracranial arteries and branches, arterioles | Trauma, ruptured saccular aneurysms or arteriovenous malformations, hypertension, hemorrhagic disorders | Subdural and subarachnoid spaces, cerebral hemorrhage involving subcortical white matter, basal ganglia, thalamus, pons |

reported (Crowell et al. 1973; Gustafson and Hagberg 1978). A wide range of mood disturbances have been described in patients with NPH. Patients may manifest euphoria, mania, or depression (Gustafson and Hagberg 1978; Kwentus and Hart 1987).

## Etiologies

NPH results from obstruction of CSF flow over the cerebral convexities and impaired absorption of fluid into the superior sagittal sinus (Cummings and Benson 1992). Classic NPH follows subarachnoid hemorrhage, head trauma, encephalitis, or meningitis. Less common causes include carcinomatous meningitis and partial aqueductal stenosis. Many cases have no identified etiology.

## Diagnosis

Although the syndrome's classic triad of ataxia, dementia, and urinary incontinence is a hallmark of NPH, the diagnosis remains a challenge. Many patients with gait disorder, bladder dysfunction, and mental deterioration have other diseases; many have subcortical arteriosclerotic encephalopathy or VaD (Gallassi et al. 1991). Likewise, a combination of spondylotic cervical myelopathy, prostatism, and mild cognitive decline can simulate the classic NPH triad (Vanneste 2000). Many patients do not display the classic symptoms and MRI is often equivocal.

The diagnosis of NPH depends on a combination of neuroimaging, CSF flow, and CSF pressure observations.

CT studies reveal markedly enlarged ventricles and periventricular lucencies. Ventriculomegaly is most evident anteriorly, with enlarged frontal and temporal horns. MRI demonstrates the same pattern of ventricular enlargement, increased periventricular signal on T2-weighted images, and an aqueductal flow void (Cummings and Benson 1992). Routine lumbar puncture reveals normal CSF pressure, and 24-hour pressure monitoring demonstrates increased B waves (Graff-Radford et al. 1989). Cisternography provides a means of assessing the pattern of CSF flow. After injection of radionuclide tracer into the lumbar subarachnoid space, there is reflux into the enlarged ventricular system and an absence of expected flow over the convexities to the superior sagittal sinus. Isotope cisternography has limited utility in predicting shunt responsiveness (Larsson et al. 1994).

## Treatment

NPH is treated with ventriculoperitoneal shunting and diversion of CSF from the ventricles into the peritoneum. Lumboperitoneal shunts, diverting CSF from the lumbar subarachnoid space into the peritoneum, also can be employed. Not all patients meeting the diagnostic criteria for NPH improve after shunting. Increased B waves, shorter duration of dementia preceding surgery, known cause of the hydrocephalus, visible periventricular changes on CT or MRI, and onset of gait changes before dementia all predict a more favorable response to shunting (Graff-Radford et al.

1989; Thomsen et al. 1986). Patients who temporarily improve after removal of 50 mL of CSF are likely to recover intellectual function after shunt placement (Wikkelso et al. 1982). The mean rate of improvement is 30%–50% in idiopathic and 50%–70% in secondary NPH. The rate of perisurgical and postsurgical complications ranges between 20% and 40%, with serious complications not exceeding 5%–8% (Vanneste 2000). Even with successful shunting, the threat of shunt dysfunction remains. This may be seen in all types of shunts, usually as a result of delayed outflow or obstruction of the peritoneal catheter (Williams et al. 1998).

Neuropsychiatric disturbances improve in concert with the cognitive impairment when shunting is successful. Before recommending a patient for a shunt procedure, the risk-benefit ratio should be discussed with patient and family.

## Subacute Spongiform Encephalopathies

The human subacute spongiform encephalopathies (SSEs) are divided into sporadic CJD, acquired SSE (kuru, iatrogenic CJD, new variant CJD [nvCJD]), and familial SSEs. Most cases of SSE are sporadic, but about 10% have an inherited mode of transmission of the autosomal dominant type. These are familial CJD, Gerstmann-Straussler-Scheinker disease (GSS), and fatal familial insomnia (FFI) with mutations of the human gene that encodes prion protein (PrP) (Weihl and Roos 1999). The term *prion* was coined in 1982 by Prusiner and colleagues, who believed that the cause of scrapie was not a virus but a novel proteinaceous infectious agent (Prusiner 1982). The hallmark of all prion diseases is the aberrant metabolism of the PrP. Animal SSE has been observed in sheep and goats and is known as scrapie, because the animals obsessively scrape themselves to the point of excoriation and tearing of their flesh. It occurs in mink, elk, deer, felines, and captive ungulates (kudu, nyala, eland) (Weihl and Roos 1999). The human prion diseases mainly present as rapidly progressive dementias, whereas the animal diseases manifest primarily as ataxic illnesses.

### Creutzfeldt-Jakob Disease

CJD is the most common SSE in humans, with an incidence of 1 per million worldwide. Usually the affected persons are 50–70 years of age, although cases in teenagers and in those older than 80 years have been reported (Ironside 1996).

Often there is a prodrome with nonspecific complaints of asthenia, anxiety, sleep disturbance, decreased appetite, and weight loss. Cognitive or other neurologic dysfunction such as cerebellar ataxia, pyramidal or extrapyramidal signs, and visual impairment are common, as are behavioral abnormalities. Most patients develop myoclonic jerks, occurring spontaneously or precipitated by noise or tactile stimulation. The EEG typically shows periodic or pseudoperiodic paroxysms of sharp waves or spikes against background slowing. Neuroimaging, CT or T2-weighted MRI, is useful primarily to exclude other disorders. Spinal fluid is normal except for mild protein and neuron-specific enolase elevation caused by neuronal loss. Protein 14–3–3, if present, supports the diagnosis (Hsich et al. 1996). The average duration of illness is limited to 4–5 months (Weihl and Roos 1999). On autopsy the brain contains numerous amyloid plaques as well as spongiform changes (Josephson 1998).

nvCJD represents the communication to humans of bovine spongiform encephalopathy (BSE) in the United Kingdom and some other European countries. Dementia is common to all forms of CJD, but nvCJD differs by much younger age at onset with average onset being 29 and ranging from 16 to 48 years of age. Illness is of longer duration (9–38 months), and behavioral changes are prominent, often prompting psychiatric consultation. Ataxia follows psychiatric changes and, unlike CJD, typical EEG abnormalities are often absent. MRI can show increased signal in the pulvinar on T2-weighted images (Will et al. 2000). Cases of nvCJD have a distinctive neuropathological profile. Findings include large PrP immunoreactive amyloid plaques with eosinophilic cores and a pale periphery surrounded by spongiform change, known as florid plaques. These features were present in addition to the typical spongiform changes, astrogliosis, and neuronal loss in the basal ganglia and thalamus, typical of classic CJD (Will et al. 1996, 2000).

### Treatment

SSEs are fatal diseases for which there is no current treatment. CJD patients can be treated symptomatically by addressing target symptoms such as extrapyramidal signs and epileptiform discharges.

## Evaluation of Neuropsychiatric Alterations in Patients With Dementia

Evaluation of the patient with dementia should include a careful history, mental-status testing, and general physical and neurologic examination. An assessment of past and current neuropsychiatric alterations (e.g., personality changes, anxiety, depression, mania, psychosis, and hallucinations) should be included (Cummings et al. 1994).

## Laboratory Investigations

Five to fifteen percent of all dementias have potentially reversible causes when treated early enough (Clarfield 1988; Larson et al. 1986). Routine tests include a complete blood count, electrolytes, serum glucose, blood urea nitrogen, vitamin $B_{12}$, and thyroid-stimulating hormone. Tests for human immunodeficiency virus, Lyme disease, heavy metal intoxication, urinary tract infection, and syphilis are optional (Knopman et al. 2001).

Rarely, inherited metabolic disorders can present as dementia in midlife. Most of these disorders represent recessively inherited biochemical derangements recognized in adolescence or young adulthood, and many are associated with specific enzyme deficiencies. Diagnosis rests on unique clinical features, a family history of the disorder, and enzyme assays in appropriate tissues (Coker 1991). Metabolic disorders with secondary dementias can result from enzyme deficiencies in $\beta$-galactosidase ($GM_1$ gangliosidosis); hexosaminidase A ($GM_2$ gangliosidosis); $\beta$-glucocerebrosidase (Gaucher's disease type I); sphingomyelinase (Niemann-Pick disease type II-C); $\alpha$-N-acetylglucosaminidase (mucopolysaccharidosis type III-B); arylsulfatase A (metachromatic leukodystrophy); $\alpha$-galactosidase (Fabry's disease); and galactocerebroside $\beta$-galactosidase (Krabbe's disease).

Neuroimaging procedures are an important part of the evaluation of the patient with dementia (Knopman et al. 2001; Martin et al. 1987). CT is adequate for identifying intracranial tumors, hydrocephalus, larger strokes, abscesses, or subdural hematomas. Contrast enhancement can increase the detection of acute ischemic and demyelinating lesions. MRI is more sensitive to detection of ischemic injury and demyelination and is capable of revealing more intracranial pathology than CT can reveal (J.J. Brown et al. 1988; Erkinjuntti 1987). When available, MRI is the imaging procedure of choice in the evaluation of patients with dementia. Although low yield, a dementia workup should be considered incomplete without at least one imaging study to exclude potentially reversible etiologies (Fleming et al. 1995).

PET and SPECT, which allow imaging of cerebral metabolism and perfusion, add another important dimension to the evaluation of dementia. In the degenerative disorders, where structural imaging techniques such as CT and MRI reveal only nonspecific atrophy, these tests may reveal characteristic topographies of brain dys-

function that can be helpful in differential diagnosis (Benson et al. 1983; Cummings and Benson 1992; Gemmell et al. 1987). Electrophysiologic studies, cisternography, CSF pressure monitoring, angiography, and other neurologic investigations are used as indicated to explicate the diagnosis.

## Management

The treatment of dementia involves halting the progression of disease (when possible) and minimizing disability. AD has no curative therapy, but ChE-Is can improve or temporarily stabilize cognitive deficits in some patients. Vitamin E delays the progression of AD. Novel agents that can be used to intervene in the cascade of events leading to cell death in patients with AD are currently under development and promise increased therapeutic alternatives for AD patients in the future. Pharmacologic intervention in patients with FTD is limited to the behavioral manifestations of the disorder; no agent ameliorates the progressive cognitive deterioration associated with the disease. Dopaminergic agents improve motor performance in selected patients with extrapyramidal disorders, but these agents have little effect on cognition. Hydrocephalic patients have ventriculoperitoneal shunts placed (with the caveats as outlined above), and VaD patients are currently managed with control of hypertension and administration of platelet antiaggregants (Meyer et al. 1986, 1988).

Late medical complications of dementia include seizures, pneumonia, urinary tract infections, and pressure ulcers. Patients with AD and VaD can develop seizures; management involves treatment with phenytoin or other anticonvulsants. Appropriate preventive measures (position rotation, ambulation) can reduce pressure ulcer formation; respiratory and urinary tract infections require antibiotic therapy. Early recognition and management of the medical complications of dementia lead to improved quality of life in these patients.

Most treatment of patients with dementia is directed at control of associated behavioral disturbances rather than the underlying dementing illness. Table 29–11 lists neuropsychiatric disorders that occur in dementia syndromes and the pharmacologic agents most commonly used in their treatment. In general, the drugs used in patients with dementia are the same as those used for similar behaviors in nondemented patients, but dosages should be adjusted to reflect that most dementias occur in older individuals (Montamat et al. 1989). Conventional neuroleptics traditionally have been the agents of choice for the control of delusions and agitation in

**TABLE 29–11.** Neuropsychiatric alterations of dementia syndromes and the pharmacologic agents commonly used in their treatment

| Symptom | Available agents | Usual daily oral dose (range) |
|---|---|---|
| Psychosis | Olanzapine | 5 mg (5–10 mg) |
| | Quetiapine | 100 mg (25–300 mg) |
| | Clozapine | 25 mg (12.5–75.0 mg) |
| | Risperidone | 1 mg (0.5–2.0 mg) |
| | Haloperidol | 1 mg (0.5–3.0 mg) |
| Agitation | Antipsychotic agents | |
| | Olanzapine | 5 mg (5–10 mg) |
| | Quetiapine | 100 mg (25–300 mg) |
| | Risperidone | 1 mg (0.5–2.0 mg) |
| | Haloperidol | 1 mg (0.5–3.0 mg) |
| | Nonantipsychotic agents | |
| | Trazodone | 100 mg (100–300 mg) |
| | Carbamazepine | 600 mg (200–1,200 mg) |
| | Buspirone | 15 mg (15–30 mg) |
| | Divalproex | 1,000 mg (250–2,000 mg) |
| | Lorazepam | 1 mg (0.5–6.0 mg) |
| | Propranolol | 120 mg (80–240 mg) |
| Depression | Nortriptyline | 50 mg (50–100 mg) |
| | Desipramine | 50 mg (50–150 mg) |
| | Citalopram | 20 mg (10–30 mg) |
| | Sertraline | 100 mg (50–150 mg) |
| | Paroxetine | 20 mg (20–40 mg) |
| | Fluoxetine | 20 mg (10–40 mg) |
| | Bupropion | 300 mg (200–450 mg) |
| | Venlafaxine | 150 mg (75–350 mg) |
| | Nefazodone | 300 mg (300–600 mg) |
| Mania | Carbamazepine | 600 mg (200–1,200 mg) |
| | Divalproex | 1,000 mg (250–2,000 mg) |
| | Clonazepam | 4 mg (0.5–15.0 mg) |
| | Lithium | 300 mg (150–1,200 mg) |
| Anxiety | Buspirone | 15 mg (15–30 mg) |
| | Oxazepam | 30 mg (20–60 mg) |
| | Lorazepam | 1 mg (0.5–6.0 mg) |
| | Propranolol | 120 mg (80–240 mg) |
| Insomnia | Temazepam | 15 mg (15–30 mg) |
| | Nortriptyline | 25 mg (20–75 mg) |
| | Trazodone | 50 mg (25–150 mg) |
| | Zolpidem | 5 mg (5–10 mg) |
| | Zaleplon | 5 mg (5–10 mg) |
| Sexual aggression (males) | Medroxyprogesterone | 300 mg/week intramuscularly |
| | Leuprolide | 7.5 mg/month intramuscularly |

patients with dementia (Devanand et al. 1988; Helms 1985; Raskind and Risse 1986), but novel antipsychotic agents such as olanzapine, risperidone, quetiapine, and clozapine have proven antipsychotic and antiagitation efficacy and the advantage of fewer adverse extrapyrami-

dal effects (De Deyn et al. 1999; Street et al. 2000). The potential for agranulocytosis and the need for weekly hematologic monitoring can preclude the use of clozapine in some patients. Agitated patients who are unresponsive or unable to tolerate antipsychotic drugs might respond to treatment with trazodone, carbamazepine, valproate, buspirone, lorazepam, fluoxetine, or propranolol (Risse and Barnes 1986). Depression is treated with nortriptyline, desipramine, trazodone, nefazodone, sertraline, paroxetine, fluoxetine, bupropion, or venlafaxine (Cummings and Benson 1992). Agents used in the treatment of mania include carbamazepine, valproic acid, clonazepam, and lithium; anxiety can be managed with buspirone, oxazepam, lorazepam, or propranolol. Temazepam, lorazepam, nortriptyline, trazodone, zaleplon, and zolpidem can afford relief of insomnia. Men with sexually aggressive behavior can improve with administration of medroxyprogesterone or leuprolide (Cooper 1987; Rich and Ovsiew 1994).

Medication should be directed toward target symptoms. Elderly patients generally need lower dosages of psychotropics than do younger individuals. Benzodiazepines should be avoided and, if used at all, then only sparingly; lorazepam is better metabolized by the elderly than is diazepam. Anticholinergic medications should be avoided, as many of these patients already have a cholinergic deficit. Pain medications can accentuate the cognitive deficit, add confusion, and precipitate delirium; they should be used cautiously in this population.

A variety of nonpharmacologic interventions can be employed in patients with dementia in different phases of their illness. These include cognitive therapy, family therapy, supportive therapy, reminiscent therapy, and behavioral modification (Maletta 1988). Other valuable adjuncts are memory training, physical activity, and nutrition. Memory training can be helpful in the earlier stages of dementias.

Care of dementia patients is delivered primarily by family members, and the educational, psychological, social, and legal needs of caregivers must be addressed. Education regarding the diagnosis, nature, and prognosis of the particular dementia syndrome is essential to the caregiver's understanding and care of the patient with dementia. Reading materials such as *The 36-Hour Day* (Mace and Rabins 1991) can complement physician instruction. Symptoms of depression and psychological distress are common among caregiving relatives (Pruchno and Potashnik 1989), and individual or group therapy might be indicated. Support groups in which caregivers can exchange information and share their emotional hardships are beneficial. Families should be educated regarding social service resources such as home health aides, in-home respite, day care programs, institutional respite care, and nursing home care. Legal consultation regarding durable power of attorney for health care and estate management is warranted. The Alzheimer's Association, a lay organization devoted to helping patients and families of patients with dementia, can provide significant support and is an excellent source of information regarding available community resources.

# References

Adams RD, Victor M: Principles of Neurology. New York, McGraw-Hill, 1993

Aharon-Peretz J, Cummings JL, Hill MA: Vascular dementia and dementia of the Alzheimer type: cognition, ventricular size, and leuko-araiosis. Arch Neurol 45:719–721, 1988

Akil M, Brewer GJ: Psychiatric and behavioral abnormalities in Wilson's disease, in Behavioral Neurology of Movement Disorders (Advances in Neurology, Vol 65). Edited by Weiner WJ, Lang AE. New York, Raven, 1995, pp 171–178

Albert ML, Feldman RG, Willis AL: The "subcortical dementia" of progressive supranuclear palsy. J Neurol Neurosurg Psychiatry 37:121–130, 1974

Albert MS, Butters N, Brandt J, et al: Patterns of remote memory in amnestic and demented patients. Arch Neurol 38:495–500, 1981

Alexander GE, DeLong MR, Strick PL: Parallel organization of functionally segregated circuits linking basal ganglia and cortex. Annu Rev Neurosci 9:357–381, 1986

American Psychiatric Association: Diagnostic and Statistical Manual of Mental Disorders, 4th Edition, Text Revision. Washington, DC, American Psychiatric Association, 2000

Baker M, Litvan I, Houlden H, et al: Association of an extended haplotype in the tau gene with progressive supranuclear palsy. Hum Mol Genet 8(4):711–715, 1999

Baldereschi M, Di Carlo A, Lepore V, et al: Estrogen-replacement therapy and Alzheimer's disease in the Italian Longitudinal Study on Aging. Neurology 50(4):996–1002, 1998

Baxter LR, Schwartz JM, Phelps ME, et al: Reduction of prefrontal cortex glucose metabolism common to three types of depression. Arch Gen Psychiatry 46:243–250, 1989

Beck AT: Depression Inventory. Philadelphia, PA, Philadelphia Center for Cognitive Therapy, 1978

Beckson M, Cummings JL: Psychosis in basal ganglia disorders. Neuropsychiatry Neuropsychol Behav Neurol 5(2):126–131, 1992

Bennet JP, Piercey MF: Pramipexole—a new dopamine agonist for the treatment of Parkinson's disease. J Neurol Sci 63(1):25–31, 1999

Benson DF, Kuhl DE, Hawkins RA, et al: The fluorodeoxyglucose 18F scan in Alzheimer's disease and multi-infarct dementia. Arch Neurol 40:711–714, 1983

Boller F, Passafiume D, Keefe NC, et al: Visuospatial impairment in Parkinson's disease. Role of perceptual and motor factors. Arch Neurol 41:485–490, 1984

Brewer M, Cummings JL: Interactions of zinc and molybdenum with copper in therapy of Wilson's disease. Nutrition 11 (suppl 1):114–116, 1995

Briley DP, Coull BM, Goodnight SH Jr: Neurological disease associated with antiphospholipid antibodies. Ann Neurol 25:221–227, 1989

Brown JJ, Hesselink JR, Rothrock JF: MR and CT of lacunar infarcts. American Journal of Radiology 151:367–372, 1988

Brown RG, MacCarthy B, Gotham AM, et al: Depression and disability in Parkinson's disease: a follow-up study of 132 cases. Psychol Med 18:49–55, 1988

Brun A, Gustafson L: Distribution of cerebral degeneration in Alzheimer's disease. Archiv fur Psychiatrie und Nervenkrankheiten 223:15–33, 1976

Brun A, Englund B, Gustafson L, et al: Clinical and neuropathological criteria for frontotemporal dementia. J Neurol Neurosurg Psychiatry 57:416–418, 1994

Burns A, Folstein S, Brandt J, et al: Clinical assessment of irritability, aggression, and apathy in Huntington and Alzheimer disease. J Nerv Ment Dis 178(1):20–26, 1990

Caine ED, Shoulson I: Psychiatric syndromes in Huntington's disease. Am J Psychiatry 140:728–733, 1983

Caine ED, Hunt RD, Weingartner H, et al: Huntington's dementia. Arch Gen Psychiatry 35:377–384, 1978

Caley CF, Friedman JH: Does fluoxetine exacerbate Parkinson's disease? J Clin Psychiatry 53:278–282, 1992

Celesia GG, Barr AN: Psychosis and other psychiatric manifestations of levodopa therapy, in Huntington's Disease (Advances in Neurology Series, Vol 23). Edited by Chase TN, Wexler NS, Barbeau A. New York, Raven, 1970, pp 193–200

Chow TW, Miller BL, Hayashi VN, et al: Inheritance of frontotemporal dementia. Arch Neurol 56(7):817–822, 1999

Clarfield AM: The reversible dementias: do they reverse? Ann Intern Med 109(6):476–486, 1988

Clark LN, Poorkaj P, Wszolek Z, et al: Pathogenic implications of mutations in the tau gene in pallido-ponto-nigral degeneration and related neurodegenerative disorders linked to chromosome 17. Proc Natl Acad Sci U S A 95(22):13103–13107, 1998

Cohen S, Freedman M: Cognitive and behavioral changes in the Parkinson-plus syndromes, in Behavioral Neurology of Movement Disorders (Advances in Neurology, Vol 65). Edited by Weiner WJ, Lang AE. New York, Raven, 1995, pp 139–157

Coker SB: The diagnosis of childhood neurodegenerative disorders presenting as dementia in adults. Neurology 41:794–798, 1991

Conrad C, Andreadis A, Trojanowski JQ, et al: Genetic evidence for the involvement of tau in progressive supranuclear palsy. Ann Neurol 41(2):277–281, 1997

Cooper AJ: Medroxyprogesterone acetate (MPA) treatment of sexual acting out in men suffering from dementia. J Clin Psychiatry 48:368–370, 1987

Corder EH, Saunders AM, Strittmatter WJ, et al: Gene dose of apolipoprotein E type 4 allele and the risk of Alzheimer's disease in late onset families. Science 261:921–923, 1993

Crowell RM, Tew JM Jr, Mark VH: Aggressive dementia associated with normal pressure hydrocephalus. Neurology 23:461–464, 1973

Cummings JL: Clinical Neuropsychiatry. New York, Grune & Stratton, 1985

Cummings JL: The dementias of Parkinson's disease: prevalence, characteristics, neurobiology, and comparison with dementia of the Alzheimer type. Eur Neurol 28 (suppl 1):15–23, 1988a

Cummings JL: Depression in vascular dementia. Hillside Journal of Clinical Psychiatry 10:209–231, 1988b

Cummings JL: Behavioral complications of drug treatment of Parkinson's disease. J Am Geriatr Soc 39:708–716, 1991

Cummings JL: Depression and Parkinson's disease: a review. Am J Psychiatry 149:443–454, 1992

Cummings JL: Frontal-subcortical circuits and human behavior. Arch Neurol 50:873–880, 1993

Cummings JL: Behavioral and psychiatric symptoms associated with Huntington's disease, in Behavioral Neurology of Movement Disorders (Advances in Neurology, Vol 65). Edited by Weiner WJ, Lang AE. New York, Raven, 1995, pp 179–186

Cummings JL: Cholinesterase inhibitors: a new class of psychotropic compounds. Am J Psychiatry 157:4–15, 2000

Cummings JL, Benson DF: Dementia: A Clinical Approach. Boston, MA, Butterworth, 1992

Cummings JL, Cunningham K: Obsessive-compulsive disorder in Huntington's disease. Biol Psychiatry 31(3):263–270, 1992

Cummings JL, Duchen LW: Klüver-Bucy syndrome in Pick disease: clinical and pathologic correlations. Neurology 31:1415–1422, 1981

Cummings JL, Litvan I: Neuropsychiatric aspects of corticobasal degeneration. Adv Neurol 82:147–152, 2000

Cummings JL, Victoroff JI: Noncognitive neuropsychiatric syndromes in Alzheimer's disease. Neuropsychiatry Neuropsychol Behav Neurol 3(2):140–158, 1990

Cummings JL, Miller B, Hill MA, et al: Neuropsychiatric aspects of multi-infarct dementia and dementia of the Alzheimer type. Arch Neurol 44(4):389–393, 1987

Cummings JL, Mega M, Gray K, et al: The Neuropsychiatric Inventory: comprehensive assessment of psychopathology in dementia. Neurology 44:2308–2314, 1994

De Deyn PP, Rabheru K, Rasmussen A, et al: A randomized trial of risperidone, placebo, and haloperidol for behavioral symptoms of dementia. Neurology 53:946–955, 1999

de Leon MJ, George AE, Golomb J, et al: Frequency of hippocampal formation atrophy in normal aging and Alzheimer's disease. Neurobiol Aging 18(1):1–11, 1997

Dening TR, Berrios GE: Wilson's disease: psychiatric symptoms in 195 cases. Arch Gen Psychiatry 46:1126–1134, 1989

Destee A, Gray F, Parent M, et al: Obsessive-compulsive behavior and progressive supranuclear palsy. Rev Neurol 146:12–18, 1990

Devanand DP, Sackeim HA, Mayeux R: Psychosis, behavioral disturbance, and the use of neuroleptics in dementia. Compr Psychiatry 29:387–401, 1988

Dewhurst K, Oliver J, Trick KL, et al: Neuro-psychiatric aspects of Huntington's disease. Confinia Neurologica 31(4):258–268, 1969

Dewhurst K, Oliver JE, McKnight AL, et al: Socio-psychiatric consequences of Huntington's disease. Br J Psychiatry 116(532):255–258, 1970

Dian L, Cummings JL, Petry S, et al: Personality alterations in vascular dementia. Psychosomatics 31:415–419, 1990

Dogali M, Fazzini DO, Kolodny E, et al: Stereotactic ventral pallidotomy for Parkinson's disease. Neurology 45:753–761, 1995

Drevets WC, Rubin EH: Psychotic symptoms and the longitudinal course of senile dementia of the Alzheimer type. Biol Psychiatry 25(1):39–48, 1989

Duara R, Barker W, Luis CA, et al: Frontotemporal dementia and Alzheimer's disease: differential diagnosis. Dement Geriatr Cogn Disord 10 (suppl 1):37–42, 1999

Duguid JR, De La Paz R, DeGroot J: Magnetic resonance imaging of the midbrain in Parkinson's disease. Ann Neurol 20:744–747, 1986

Duvoisin RC: Clinical diagnosis, in Progressive Supranuclear Palsy: Clinical and Research Approaches. Edited by Litvan I, Agid Y. New York, Oxford University Press, 1992, pp 17–33

Ehmann TS, Beninger RJ, Gawel MJ, et al: Depressive symptoms in Parkinson's disease: a comparison with disabled control subjects. J Geriatr Psychiatry Neurol 2:3–9, 1990

Erkinjuntti T: Types of multi-infarct dementia. Acta Neurol Scand 75:391–399, 1987

Ernst RL, Hay JW: The U.S. economic and social costs of Alzheimer's disease revisited. Am J Public Health 84:1261–1264, 1994

Etchebehere EC, Lima MC, Passos W, et al: Brain SPECT imaging in Huntington's disease before and after therapy with olanzapine. Case report. Arq Neuropsiquiatr 57(3B):863–866, 1999

Factor SA, Brown D, Molho ES, et al: Clozapine: a two year open trial in Parkinson's disease patients with psychosis. Neurology 44:544–546, 1994

Farrer LA: Suicide and attempted suicide in Huntington's disease: implications for preclinical testing of persons at risk. Am J Med Genet 24:305–311, 1986

Fazekas F, Alavi A, Chawluk JB, et al: Comparison of CT, MR, and PET in Alzheimer's dementia and normal aging. J Nucl Med 30(10):1607–1615, 1989

Fleming KC, Adams AC, Petersen RC: Dementia: diagnosis and evaluation. Mayo Clin Proc 70(11):1093–1107, 1995

Flynn FG, Cummings JL, Gornbein J, et al: Delusions in dementia syndromes: behavioral and neuropsychological correlates. J Neuropsychiatry Clin Neurosci 3:364–370, 1991

Folstein SE: Huntington's Disease: A Disorder of Families. Baltimore, MD, Johns Hopkins University Press, 1989

Folstein SE, Brandt J, Folstein MF: Huntington's disease, in Subcortical Dementia. Edited by Cummings JL. New York, Oxford University Press, 1990, pp 87–107

Foster NL, Chase TN, Fedio P, et al: Alzheimer's disease: focal cortical changes shown by positron emission tomography. Neurology 33:961–965, 1983

Foster NL, Gilman S, Berent S, et al: Cerebral hypometabolism in progressive supranuclear palsy studied with positron emission tomography. Ann Neurol 24:399–406, 1988

Freedman M: Parkinson's disease, in Subcortical Dementia. Edited by Cummings JL. New York, Oxford University Press, 1990, pp 108–122

Friedman JH, Lannon MC: Clozapine in the treatment of psychosis in Parkinson's disease. Neurology 39:1219–1221, 1989

Galasko DL, Chang L, Motter R, et al: High cerebrospinal fluid tau and low amyloid B42 levels in the clinical diagnosis of Alzheimer disease and relation to apolipoprotein E genotype. Arch Neurol 55:937–945, 1998

Gallassi R, Morreale A, Montagna P, et al: Binswanger's disease and normal-pressure hydrocephalus: clinical and neuropsychological comparison. Arch Neurol 48(11):1156–1159, 1991

Gemmell HG, Sharp PF, Besson JAO, et al: Differential diagnosis in dementia using the cerebral blood flow agent 99mTc HM-PAO: a SPECT study. J Comput Assist Tomogr 11:398–402, 1987

Giacobini E: Cholinesterase inhibitors: from the calabar bean to Alzheimer therapy, in Cholinesterases and Cholinesterase Inhibitors. Edited by Giacobini E. London, Martin Dunitz, 2000, pp 181–226

Gibb WRG: Neuropathology of Parkinson's disease and related syndromes. Neurol Clin 10:361–376, 1992

Gilman S, Low PA, Quinn N, et al: Consensus statement on the diagnosis of multiple system atrophy. J Neurol Sci 163(1):94–98, 1999

Glass JD, Reich SG, De Long MR: Wilson's disease. Development of neurological disease after beginning penicillamine therapy. Arch Neurol 47(5):595–596, 1990

Goetz CG, Tanner CM, Klawans HL: Pharmacology of hallucinations induced by long-term drug therapy. Am J Psychiatry 139:494–497, 1982

Goetz CG, Tanner CM, Klawans HL: Bupropion in Parkinson's disease. Neurology 34:1092–1094, 1984

Golbe LI: The epidemiology of PSP. J Neural Transm Suppl 42:263–273, 1994

Graff-Radford NR, Godersky JC, Jones MP: Variables predicting surgical outcome in symptomatic hydrocephalus in the elderly. Neurology 36:1601–1604, 1989

Graff-Radford NR, Damasio AR, Hyman BT, et al: Progressive aphasia in a patient with Pick's disease: a neuropsychological, radiologic, and anatomic study. Neurology 40:620–626, 1990

Gusella JF, MacDonald ME, Ambrose CM, et al: Molecular genetics of Huntington's disease. Arch Neurol 50:1157–1163, 1993

Gustafson L: Frontal lobe degeneration of non-Alzheimer type, II: clinical picture and differential diagnosis. Archives of Gerontology and Geriatrics 6:209–233, 1987

Gustafson L, Hagberg B: Recovery of hydrocephalic dementia after shunt operation. J Neurol Neurosurg Psychiatry 41:940–947, 1978

Haass C, Selkoe DJ: Cellular processing of beta-amyloid precursor protein and the genesis of amyloid beta-peptide. Cell 75:1039–1042, 1993

Hachinski VC, Iliff LD, Zilhka E, et al: Cerebral blood flow in dementia. Arch Neurol 32:632–637, 1975

Hall PK, Andrus JA, Oostveen JA, et al: Neuroprotective effects of the dopamine D2/D3 agonist pramipexole against postischemic or methamphetamine-induced degeneration of nigrostriatal neurons. Brain Res 742:80–88, 1996

Halliday W: The nosology of Hallervorden-Spatz disease. J Neurol Sci 134 (suppl):84–91, 1995

Haxby JV, Grady CL, Duara R, et al: Neocortical metabolic abnormalities precede nonmemory cognitive defects in early Alzheimer's-type dementia. Arch Neurol 43:882–885, 1986

Heckmann JM, Eastman RW, De Villiers JC, et al: Wilson's disease: neurological and magnetic resonance imaging improvement on zinc treatment. J Neurol Neurosurg Psychiatry 57(10):1273–1274, 1994

Helms PM: Efficacy of antipsychotics in the treatment of behavioral complications of dementia: a review of the literature. J Am Geriatr Soc 33:206–209, 1985

Henderson VW, Paganini-Hill A, Emanuel CK, et al: Estrogen replacement therapy in older women: comparisons between Alzheimer's disease cases and nondemented control subjects. Arch Neurol 51(9):896–900, 1994

Hershey LA, Modic MT, Greenough G, et al: Magnetic resonance imaging in vascular dementia. Neurology 37:29–36, 1987

Heyman A, Wilkinson WE, Stafford JA, et al: Alzheimer's disease: a study of epidemiological aspects. Ann Neurol 15:335–341, 1984

Hier DB, Cummings JL: Rare acquired and degenerative dementias, in Subcortical Dementia. Edited by Cummings JL. New York, Oxford University Press, 1990, pp 199–217

Hier DB, Hagenlocker K, Shindler AD: Language disintegration in dementia: effects of etiology and severity. Brain Lang 25:117–133, 1985

Higgins JJ, Golbe LI, De Biase A, et al: An extended 5'-tau susceptibility haplotype in progressive supranuclear palsy. Neurology 55:1364–1367, 2000

Holland AL, McBurney DH, Moossey J, et al: The dissolution of language in Pick's disease with neurofibrillary tangles: a case study. Brain Lang 24:36–58, 1985

Hsich G, Kenney K, Gibbs CJ, et al: The 14–3–3 brain protein in cerebrospinal fluid as a marker for transmissible spongiform encephalopathies. N Engl J Med 335:924–930, 1996

Huber SJ, Freidenberg DL, Paulson GW, et al: The pattern of progressive symptoms varies with progression of Parkinson's disease. J Neurol Neurosurg Psychiatry 53:275–278, 1990

Hughes AJ, Daniel SE, Kilford L, et al: Accuracy of clinical diagnosis of idiopathic Parkinson's disease: a clinico-pathological study of 100 cases. J Neurol Neurosurg Psychiatry 55:181–184, 1992

Huntington Study Group: Unified Huntington's Disease Rating Scale: reliability and consistency. Mov Disord 11:136–142, 1996

Huntington's Disease Collaborative Research Group: A novel gene containing a trinucleotide repeat that is expanded and unstable on Huntington's disease chromosomes. Cell 72:971–983, 1993

Hutton M, Lendon CL, Rizzu P, et al: Association of missense and 5´-splice-site mutations in tau with the inherited dementia FTDP-17. Nature 393:702–705, 1998

Ineichman B: Measuring the rising tide: how many dementia cases will there be in 2001? Br J Psychiatry 150:193–200, 1987

Ironside JW: Review: Creutzfeldt-Jakob disease. Brain Pathol 6:527–530, 1996

Ishii N, Nishihara Y, Imamura T: Why do frontal lobe symptoms predominate in vascular dementia with lacunes? Neurology 36:340–345, 1986

Jack CR Jr, Petersen RC, O'Brien PC, et al: MR-based hippocampal volumetry in the diagnosis of Alzheimer's disease. Neurology 42(1):183–188, 1992

Jack CR Jr, Petersen RC, Xu YC, et al: Prediction of AD with MRI-based hippocampal volume in mild cognitive impairment. Neurology 52(7):1397–1403, 1999

Jagust WJ, Friedland RP, Budinger TF, et al: Longitudinal studies of regional cerebral metabolism in Alzheimer's disease. Neurology 38(6):909–912, 1988

Johnson KA, Mueller ST, Walsh TM, et al: Cerebral perfusion imaging in Alzheimer's disease. Arch Neurol 44:165–168, 1987

Jordan SE, Nowacki R, Nuwer M: Computerized electroencephalography in the evaluation of early dementia. Brain Topogr 1:271–274, 1989

Josephson J: Focus: cows for fear. Environ Health Perspect 106:A137–A138, 1998

Kamboh MI: Apolipoprotein E polymorphism and susceptibility to Alzheimer's disease. Hum Biol 67:195–215, 1995

Kanazawa I, Kwak S, Sasaki H, et al: Studies on neurotransmitter markers of the basal ganglia in Pick's disease, with special reference to dopamine reduction. J Neurol Sci 83(1): 63–74, 1988

Katzman R: Alzheimer's disease. N Engl J Med 314:964–973, 1986

Katzman R, Brown T, Thal LJ, et al: Comparison of rate of annual change of mental status score in four independent studies of patients with Alzheimer's disease. Ann Neurol 24:384–389, 1988

Kawas C, Resnick S, Morrison A, et al: A prospective study of estrogen replacement therapy and the risk of developing Alzheimer's disease: the Baltimore Longitudinal Study of Aging. Neurology 48:1517–1521, 1997

Knopman DS, Christensen KJ, Schut LJ, et al: The spectrum of imaging and neuropsychological findings in Pick's disease. Neurology 39:362–368, 1989

Knopman DS, DeKosky ST, Cummings JL, et al: Practice parameter: diagnosis of dementia (an evidence-based review). Report of the Quality Standards Subcommittee of the American Academy of Neurology. Neurology 56:1143–1153, 2001

Koller WC, Megaffin BB: Parkinson's disease and parkinsonism, in Textbook of Geriatric Neuropsychiatry. Edited by Coffey CE, Cummings JL. Washington, DC, American Psychiatric Press, 1994, pp 434–456

Krüger R, Kuhn W, Muller T, et al: Ala30Pro mutation in the gene encoding alpha-synuclein in Parkinson's disease. Nat Genet 18:106–108, 1998

Kuwert T, Lange HW, Langen KJ, et al: Cerebral glucose consumption measured by PET in patients with and without psychiatric symptoms of Huntington's disease. Psychiatry Res 29:361–362, 1989

Kvale JN: Amitriptyline in the management of progressive supranuclear palsy. Arch Neurol 39:387–388, 1982

Kwentus JA, Hart RP: Normal pressure hydrocephalus presenting as mania. J Nerv Ment Dis 175:500–502, 1987

Ladurner G, Iliff LD, Lechner H: Clinical factors associated with dementia in ischaemic stroke. J Neurol Neurosurg Psychiatry 45:97–101, 1982

Lang CJ, Rabas-Kolominsky P, Engelhardt A, et al: Fatal deterioration of Wilson's disease after institution of oral zinc therapy. Arch Neurol 50(10):1007–1008, 1993

Larson EB, Reifler BV, Sumi SM, et al: Diagnostic tests in the evaluation of dementia. A prospective study of 200 elderly outpatients. Arch Intern Med 146(10):1917–1922, 1986

Larsson A, Arlig A, Bergh AC, et al: Quantitative SPECT cisternography in normal pressure hydrocephalus. Acta Neurol Scand 90(3):190–196, 1994

Leenders KL, Palmer AJ, Quinn N, et al: Brain dopamine metabolism in patients with Parkinson's disease measured with positron emission tomography. J Neurol Neurosurg Psychiatry 49:853–860, 1986

Leenders KL, Frackowiak RSJ, Lees AJ: Steele-Richardson-Olszewski syndrome: brain energy metabolism, blood flow, and fluorodopa uptake measured by positron emission tomography. Brain 111:615–630, 1988

Lees AJ: Progressive supranuclear palsy (Steele-Richardson-Olszewski syndrome), in Subcortical Dementia. Edited by Cummings JL. New York, Oxford University Press, 1990, pp 121–131

Levin BE, Llabre MM, Weiner WJ: Parkinson's disease and depression: psychometric properties of the Beck Depression Inventory. J Neurol Neurosurg Psychiatry 51:1401–1404, 1988

Lilly R, Cummings JL, Benson DF, et al: The human Klüver-Bucy syndrome. Neurology 33(9):1141–1145, 1983

Litvan I, Mega MS, Cummings JL, et al: Neuropsychiatric aspects of progressive supranuclear palsy. Neurology 47(5):1184–1189, 1996

Loeb C, Gandolfo C: Diagnostic evaluation of degenerative and vascular dementia. Stroke 14:390–401, 1983

Lund and Manchester Groups: Consensus statement: clinical and neuropathological criteria for frontotemporal dementia. J Neurol Neurosurg Psychiatry 57:416–418, 1994

Mace N, Rabins P: The 36-Hour Day: A Family Guide to Caring for Persons with Alzheimer's Disease, Related Dementing Illnesses, and Memory Loss Later in Life. Baltimore, MD, Johns Hopkins University Press, 1991

Maier-Dobersberger T, Mannhalter C, Rack S, et al: Diagnosis of Wilson's disease in an asymptomatic sibling by DNA linkage analysis. Gastroenterology 109(6):2015–2018, 1995

Maletta GJ: Management of behavior problems in elderly patients with Alzheimer's disease and other dementias. Clin Geriatr Med 4:719–747, 1988

Martilla RJ: Epidemiology, in Handbook of Parkinson's Disease. Edited by Koller WC. New York, Marcel Dekker, 1987, pp 35–50

Martin DC, Miller J, Kapoor W, et al: Clinical prediction rules for computed tomographic scanning in senile dementia. Arch Intern Med 147:77–80, 1987

Martone M, Butters N, Payne M, et al: Dissociations between skill learning and verbal recognition in amnesia and dementia. Arch Neurol 41:965–970, 1984

Mayberg HS, Starkstein SE, Peyser CE, et al: Paralimbic frontal lobe hypometabolism in depression associated with Huntington's disease. Neurology 42:1791–1797, 1992

Mayeux R, Stern Y, Rosen J, et al: Depression, intellectual impairment and Parkinson's disease. Neurology 31:645–650, 1981

McDonald LV, Lake CR: Psychosis in an adolescent patient with Wilson's disease: effects of chelation therapy. Psychosom Med 57(2):202–204, 1995

McKeith I, O'Brien J: Dementia with Lewy bodies. Aust N Z J Psychiatry 33(6):800–808, 1999

McKeith IG, Perry RH, Fairbairn SJ, et al: Operational criteria for senile dementia of Lewy body type (SDLT). Psychol Med 22:911–922, 1992

McKeith IG, Galasko D, Kosaka K, et al: Consensus guidelines for the clinical and pathologic diagnosis of dementia with

Lewy bodies (DLB): report of the consortium on DLB international workshop. Neurology 47:1113–1124, 1996

McKeith I, Del Ser T, Spano P, et al: Efficacy of rivastigmine in dementia with Lewy bodies: a randomised, double-blind, placebo-controlled international study. Lancet 356:2031–2036, 2000

McKhann G, Drachman D, Folstein M, et al: Clinical diagnosis of Alzheimer's disease: report of the NINCDS-ADRDA Work Group under the auspices of Department of Health and Human Services Task Force on Alzheimer's Disease. Neurology 34(7):939–944, 1984

Mega MS, Cummings JL, Fiorello T, et al: The spectrum of behavioral changes in Alzheimer's disease. Neurology 46(1):130–135, 1996

Mendez MF: Huntington's disease: update and review of neuropsychiatric aspects. Int J Psychiatry Med 24:189–208, 1994

Mendez MF, Adams NL, Skoog-Lewandowski KM: Neurobehavioral changes associated with caudate lesions. Neurology 39:349–354, 1989

Mendez MF, Martin RJ, Smyth KA, et al: Psychiatric symptoms associated with Alzheimer's disease. J Neuropsychiatry Clin Neurosci 2:28–33, 1990

Mendez MF, Selwood A, Mastri AR, et al: Pick's disease versus Alzheimer's disease: a comparison of clinical characteristics. Neurology 43:289–292, 1993

Merriam AE, Aronson MK, Gaston P, et al: The psychiatric symptoms of Alzheimer's disease. J Am Geriatr Soc 36:7–12, 1988

Meyer JS, Judd BW, Tawakina T, et al: Improved cognition after control of risk factors for multi-infarct dementia. JAMA 256:2203–2209, 1986

Meyer JS, McClintic KL, Rogers RL, et al: Aetiological considerations and risk factors for multi-infarct dementia. J Neurol Neurosurg Psychiatry 51:1489–1497, 1988

Miller BL, Mena I, Daly J, et al: Temporal-parietal hypoperfusion with single-photon emission computerized tomography in conditions other than Alzheimer's disease. Dementia 1:41–45, 1990

Miller BL, Cummings JL, Villanueva-Mayer J, et al: Frontal lobe degeneration: clinical, neuropsychological, and SPECT characteristics. Neurology 41(9):1374–1382, 1991

Miller BL, Chang L, Oropilla G, et al: Alzheimer's disease and frontal lobe dementias, in Textbook of Geriatric Neuropsychiatry. Edited by Coffey CE Cummings JL. Washington, DC, American Psychiatric Press, 1994, pp 390–404

Montamat SC, Cusack BJ, Vestal RE: Management of drug therapy in the elderly. N Engl J Med 321:303–309, 1989

Morishita L: Wandering behavior, in Alzheimer's Disease: Treatment and Long-term Management. Edited by Cummings JL, Miller BL. New York, Marcel Dekker, 1990 pp 157–176

Morris CH, Hope RA, Fairburn CG: Eating habits in dementia: a descriptive study. Br J Psychiatry 154:801–806, 1989

Morris HR, Perez-Tur J, Janssen JC, et al: Mutation in the tau exon 10 splice site region in familial frontotemporal dementia. Ann Neurol 45(2):270–271, 1999

Morris M: Psychiatric aspects of Huntington's disease, in Huntington's Disease. Edited by Harper PS. Philadelphia, PA, WB Saunders, 1991, pp 81–126

Moskovitz C, Moses H III, Klawans HL: Levodopa induced psychosis: a kindling phenomenon. Am J Psychiatry 135:669–675, 1978

Murayama S, Mori H, Ihara Y, et al: Immunocytochemical and ultrastructural studies of Pick's disease. Ann Neurol 27:394–405, 1990

Nardocci N, Rumi V, Combi ML, et al: Complex tics, stereotypies, and compulsive behavior as clinical presentation of a juvenile progressive dystonia suggestive of Hallervorden-Spatz disease. Mov Disord 9:369–371, 1994

Neary D, Snowden JS, Gustafson L, et al: Frontotemporal lobar degeneration: a consensus on clinical diagnostic criteria. Neurology 51(6):1546–1554, 1998

Nemetz PN, Leibson C, Naessens JM, et al: Traumatic brain injury and time to onset of Alzheimer's disease: a population-based study. Am J Epidemiol 149(1):32–40, 1999

Neufeld R, Inzelberg R, Korczyn AD: EEG in demented and non-demented parkinsonian patients. Acta Neurol Scand 78:1–5, 1988

Newman GC: Treatment of progressive supranuclear palsy with tricyclic antidepressants. Neurology 35:1189–1193, 1985

Ohtsubo K, Isumiyama N, Shimada H, et al: Three-dimensional structure of Alzheimer's neurofibrillary tangles of the aged human brain revealed by the quick-freeze, deep-etch and replica method. Acta Neuropathol (Berl) 79:480–485, 1990

Paganini-Hill A, Henderson VW: Estrogen deficiency and risk of Alzheimer's disease in women. Am J Epidemiol 140:256–261, 1994

Parkinson's Study Group: Safety and efficacy of pramipexole in early Parkinson disease: a randomized dose-ranging study. JAMA 278:125–130, 1997

Pearlson GD, Ross CA, Lohr WD, et al: Association between family history of affective disorder and the depressive syndrome of Alzheimer's disease. Am J Psychiatry 147:452–456, 1990

Perez FI, Rivera VM, Meyer JS, et al: Analysis of intellectual and cognitive performance in patients with multi-infarct dementia, vertebrobasilar insufficiency with dementia, and Alzheimer's disease. J Neurol Neurosurg Psychiatry 38:533–540, 1975

Petersen RC, Jack CR Jr, Xu YC, et al: Memory and MRI-based hippocampal volumes in aging and AD. Neurology 54(3):581–587, 2000

Petry S, Cummings JL, Hill MA, et al: Personality alterations in dementia of the Alzheimer type. Arch Neurol 45(11):1187–1190, 1988

Petry S, Cummings JL, Hill MA, et al: Personality alterations in dementia of the Alzheimer type: a three-year follow-up study. J Geriatr Psychiatry Neurol 2(4):203–207, 1989

Pillon B, Dubois B, L'Hermitte F, et al: Heterogeneity of intellectual impairment in progressive supranuclear palsy, Parkinson's disease and Alzheimer's disease. Neurology 36: 1179–1185, 1986

Pirozzolo FJ, Hansch EC, Mortimer JA, et al: Dementia in Parkinson's disease: a neuropsychological analysis. Brain Cogn 1:71–83, 1982

Polymeropoulos MH, Lavedan C, Leroy E, et al: Mutation in the alpha-synuclein gene identified in families with Parkinson's disease. Science 276:2045–2047, 1997

Poorkaj P, Bird TD, Wijsman E, et al: Tau is a candidate gene for chromosome 17 frontotemporal dementia. Ann Neurol 43:815–825, 1998

Powell AL, Cummings JL, Hill MA, et al: Speech and language alterations in multi-infarct dementia. Neurology 38:717–719, 1988

Procter A, Lowe SL, Palmer AM, et al: Topographical distribution of neurochemical changes in Alzheimer's disease. J Neurol Sci 84:125–140, 1988

Pruchno RA, Potashnik SL: Caregiving spouses. J Am Geriatr Soc 37:697–705, 1989

Prusiner SB: Novel proteinaceous infectious particles cause scrapie. Science 216:136–144, 1982

Rabins PV, Mace NL, Lucas MJ: The impact of dementia on the family. JAMA 248:333–335, 1982

Ranen NG, Lipsey JR, Treisman G, et al: Sertraline in the treatment of severe aggressiveness in Huntington's disease. J Neuropsychiatry Clin Neurosci 8(3):338–340, 1996

Raskind MA, Risse SC: Antipsychotic drugs and the elderly. J Clin Psychiatry 45:17–22, 1986

Reichman WR, Cummings JL, McDaniel KD, et al: Visuoconstructional impairment in dementia syndromes. Behavioral Neurology 4:153–162, 1991

Reisberg B, Borenstein J, Salob SP, et al: Behavioral symptoms in Alzheimer's disease: phenomenology and treatment. J Clin Psychiatry 48 (5 suppl):9–15, 1987

Reynolds CF III, Hoch CC, Stack J, et al: The nature and management of sleep/wake disturbance in Alzheimer's dementia. Psychopharmacology Bulletin 24:43–48, 1988

Rich SS, Ovsiew F: Leuprolide acetate for exhibitionism in Huntington's disease. Mov Disord 9:353–357, 1994

Risse SC, Barnes R: Pharmacologic treatment of agitation associated with dementia. J Am Geriatr Soc 34:368–376, 1986

Risse SC, Raskind MA, Nochlin D, et al: Neuropathological findings in patients with clinical diagnoses of probable Alzheimer's disease. Am J Psychiatry 147(2):168–172, 1990

Roberts HE, Dean RC, Stoudemire A: Clozapine treatment of psychosis in Parkinson's disease. J Neuropsychiatry Clin Neurosci 1:190–192, 1989

Roman GC: Senile dementia of the Binswanger type. JAMA 258:1782–1788, 1987

Roman GC, Tatemichi TK, Erkinjuntti T, et al: Vascular dementia: diagnostic criteria for research studies. Report of the NINDA-AIREN International Workshop. Neurology 43: 250–260, 1993

Rosenblatt A, Leroi I: Neuropsychiatry of Huntington's disease and other basal ganglia disorders. Psychosomatics 41(1): 24–30, 2000

Rubin EH, Morris JC, Storandt M, et al: Behavioral changes in patients with mild senile dementia of the Alzheimer's type. Psychiatry Res 21:55–62, 1987

Sano M, Ernesto C, Thomas RG, et al: A controlled trial of selegiline, alpha-tocopherol, or both as treatment for Alzheimer's disease. The Alzheimer's Disease Cooperative Study. N Engl J Med 336:1216–1222, 1997

Schlaug G, Hefter H, Engelbrecht V, et al: Neurological impairment and recovery in Wilson's disease: evidence from PET and MRI. J Neurol Sci 136(1–2):129–139, 1996

Schneider LS, Gleason RP, Chui HC: Progressive supranuclear palsy with agitation: response to trazodone but not to thiothixene or carbamazepine. J Geriatr Psychiatry Neurol 2:109–112, 1989

Schupf N, Kapell D, Lee JH, et al: Alzheimer's disease in mothers of adults with Down's syndrome. Lancet 344:353–356, 1994

Shapira J, Cummings JL: Alzheimer's disease: changes in sexual behavior. Medical Aspects of Human Sexuality 23:32–35, 1989

Shaw KM, Lees AJ, Stern GM: The impact of treatment with levodopa on Parkinson's disease. QJM 49:283–293, 1980

Sinha S, Anderson JP, Barbour R, et al: Purification and cloning of amyloid precursor protein beta-secretase from human brain. Nature 402:537–540, 1999

Starkstein SE, Robinson RG: Neuropsychiatric aspects of stroke, in Textbook of Geriatric Neuropsychiatry. Edited by Coffey CE, Cummings JL. Washington, DC, American Psychiatric Press, 1994, pp 457–475

Steele JC: Progressive supranuclear palsy. Brain 95:693–704, 1972

Steele JC, Richardson JC, Olszewski J: Progressive supranuclear palsy. Arch Neurol 10:333–359, 1964

Stein MB, Heuser IJ, Juncos JL, et al: Anxiety disorders in patients with Parkinson's disease. Am J Psychiatry 147:217–220, 1990

Stern Y, Gurland B, Tatemichi TK, et al: Influence of education and occupation on the incidence of Alzheimer's disease. JAMA 271(13):1004–1010, 1994

Steur EN: Increase of Parkinson disability after fluoxetine medication. Neurology 43:211–213, 1993

Stewart JT: Huntington's disease and propranolol. Am J Psychiatry 150(1):166–167, 1993

Stewart WF, Kawas C, Corrada M, et al: Risk of Alzheimer's disease and duration of NSAID use. Neurology 48:626–632, 1997

Street JS, Clark WS, Gannon KS, et al: Olanzapine treatment of psychotic and behavioral symptoms in patients with Alzheimer disease in nursing care facilities: a double-blind, randomized, placebo-controlled trial. The HGEU Study Group. Arch Gen Psychiatry 57:968–976, 2000

Sudarsky L, Simon S: Gait disturbances in late-life hydrocephalus. Arch Neurol 44:263–267, 1987

Sulkava R, Erkinjuntti T: Vascular dementia due to cardiac arrhythmias and systemic hypotension. Acta Neurol Scand 76:123–128, 1987

Swearer JM, Drachman DA, O'Donnell BF, et al: Troublesome and disruptive behaviors in dementia. J Am Geriatr Soc 36:784–790, 1988

Tang MX, Jacobs D, Stern Y, et al: Effect of estrogen during menopause on risk and age at onset of Alzheimer's disease. Lancet 348:429–432, 1996

Tanner CM, Vogel C, Goetz CG, et al: Hallucinations in Parkinson's disease: a population study (abstract). Ann Neurol 14:136, 1983

Taylor AE, Saint-Cyr JA, Lang AE, et al: Parkinson's disease and depression: a critical re-evaluation. Brain 109:279–292, 1986

Teri L, Larson EB, Reifler BV: Behavioral disturbance in dementia of the Alzheimer's type. J Am Geriatr Soc 36:1–6, 1988

Thomsen AM, Borgesen SE, Bruhn P, et al: Prognosis of dementia in normal-pressure hydrocephalus after a shunt operation. Ann Neurol 20:304–310, 1986

Tierney MC, Fisher RH, Lewis AJ, et al: The NINCDS-ADRDA Work Group criteria for the clinical diagnosis of probable Alzheimer's disease: a clinicopathologic study of 57 cases. Neurology 38(3):359–364, 1988

Trautner RJ, Cummings JL, Read SL, et al: Idiopathic basal ganglia calcification and organic mood disorder. Am J Psychiatry 145:350–353, 1988

Vanneste JA: Diagnosis and management of normal-pressure hydrocephalus. Neurology 247(1):5–14, 2000

Van Nostrand WE, Wagner SL, Shankle WR, et al: Decreased levels of soluble amyloid beta-protein precursor in cerebrospinal fluid of live Alzheimer disease patients. Proc Natl Acad Sci U S A 89:2551–2555, 1992

van Swieten JC, Stevens M, Rosso SM, et al: Phenotypic variation in hereditary frontotemporal dementia with tau mutations. Ann Neurol 46:617–626, 1999

Vassar R, Bennett BD, Babu-Kahn S, et al: Beta-secretase cleavage of Alzheimer's amyloid precursor protein by the transmembrane aspartic protease BACE. Science 286:735–741, 1999

Verity MA, Wechsler AF: Progressive subcortical gliosis of Neumann: A clinicopathologic study of two cases with review. Archives of Gerontology and Geriatrics 6(3):245–261, 1987

Villardita C, Smirni P, Le Pira F, et al: Mental deterioration, visuoperceptive disabilities, and constructional apraxia in Parkinson's disease. Acta Neurol Scand 66:112–120, 1982

Wahlund LO: Biological markers and diagnostic investigations in Alzheimer's disease. Acta Neurol Scand Suppl 165:85–91, 1996

Wechsler AF, Verity A, Rosenschein S, et al: Pick's disease: a clinical, computed tomographic, and histologic study with Golgi impregnation observations. Arch Neurol 39:287–290, 1982

Weihl CC, Roos RP: Creutzfeldt-Jakob disease, new variant Creutzfeldt-Jakob disease, and bovine spongiform encephalopathy. Neurol Clin 17:835–855, 1999

Wenning GK, Ben Shlomo Y, Magalhaes M, et al: Clinical features and natural history of multiple system atrophy. An analysis of 100 cases. Brain 117(4):835–845, 1994

Westphal KFO: Über eine dem Bilde der cerebrospinalen grauen Degeneration ähnliche Erkrankung des centralen Nervensystems ohne anatomischen Befund, nebst einigen Bemerkungen über paradoxe Contraktion. Archiv für Psychiatrie und Nervenkrankheiten 14:87–134, 767–769, 1883

Whitehouse PJ, Hedreen JC, White CL III, et al: Basal forebrain neurons in the dementia of Parkinson's disease. Ann Neurol 1:243–248, 1983

Wikkelso C, Andersson H, Blomstrand C, et al: The clinical effect of lumbar puncture in normal pressure hydrocephalus. J Neurol Neurosurg Psychiatry 45:64–69, 1982

Will RG, Ironside JW, Zeidler M, et al: A new variant of Creutzfeldt-Jakob disease in the UK. Lancet 347:921–925, 1996

Will RG, Zeidler M, Stewart GE, et al: Diagnosis of new variant Creutzfeldt-Jakob disease. Ann Neurol 47:575–582, 2000

Williams MA, Razumovsky AY, Hanley DF, et al: Evaluation of shunt function in patients who are never better, or better than worse after shunt surgery for NPH. Acta Neurochir (Wien) 71:368–370, 1998

Wilson SAK: Progressive lenticular degeneration. A familial nervous disease associated with cirrhosis of the liver. Brain 34:295–507, 1912

Wragg RE, Jeste DV: Overview of depression and psychosis in Alzheimer's disease. Am J Psychiatry 146(5):577–587, 1989

Yan R, Bienkowski JM, Shuck ME, et al: Membrane-anchored aspartyl protease with Alzheimer's disease beta-secretase activity. Nature 402:533–537, 1999

Yates CM, Simpson J, Maloney AFJ, et al: Neurochemical observations in a case of Pick's disease. J Neurol Sci 48(2):257–263, 1980

Young SM, Fisher M, Sigsbee A, et al: Cardiogenic brain embolism and lupus anticoagulant. Ann Neurol 26:390–392, 1989

# CHAPTER 30

# Neuropsychiatric Aspects of Schizophrenia

Carol A. Tamminga, M.D.

Gunvant K. Thaker, M.D.

Deborah R. Medoff, Ph.D.

Despite centuries of curiosity and study focused on schizophrenia, its pathophysiology remains unknown. There are few medical illnesses for which the etiologies and mechanisms are so completely obscure. Although our eventual knowledge of this process is certain, the exact explanation has escaped current understanding. We know that schizophrenia is a psychiatric illness with well-established diagnostic criteria, clear signs and symptoms, and variably effective symptomatic treatments (Andreasen 1995; Carpenter and Buchanan 1994). However, not enough of the pieces of this puzzle have yet been manifested to arrange with any certainty the areas of sure knowledge into a complete disease picture. Having acknowledged this limitation, it is always a challenging exercise to lay out the current pieces of knowledge about schizophrenia, to examine all parts for level of certainty, then to fit these ideas together into testable hypotheses of mechanism. Soon, relevant information will expand, both in quantity and in quality, because of the increased sensitivity of newer human research techniques—from rating precision to diagnostic specificity to functional imaging resolution—and because of the exponential increase in basic neuroscience knowledge, and now the completed human genome. In this chapter we examine the pieces of knowledge we possess today that define the biology of schizophrenia and the ways we can view these pieces to rationally increase our understanding of the illness.

## Clinical Characteristics of Schizophrenia

Historically, schizophrenia-like conditions have been known for millennia. The Greeks clearly described the mental symptoms and personality deterioration of schizophrenia in the first and second centuries A.D. The Middle Ages brought a regression in any preexisting scientific approach to the illness and often completely misidentified the condition as willful or evil. Not until the eighteenth century did schizophrenia reappear as a disease construct; and it was not until the nineteenth century that psychotic disorders were viewed as entities, then called insanity or madness. Toward the end of the nineteenth century, moral treatment was practiced whereby patients were treated with compassion and

Support for this chapter was generated by an NIMH grant for dopaminergic treatments (MH49667), GABAergic treatments for tardive dyskinesia (MH37073), and ketamine and cerebral blood flow (DA-94–03), as well as an NIMH CRC Center Grant (MH40279). Several scientific collaborators contributed data, advice, and critique: X.-M. Gao, H.H. Holcomb, A.C. Lahti, R.C. Lahti, and R. Roberts. Patients and staff of the Maryland Psychiatric Research Center Residential Treatment Unit invested their time and energy to many of these scientific projects.

kindness in lieu of any other effective treatment. Not until the mid–twentieth century were broadly effective pharmacologic treatments available and modern disease formulations applied to the condition.

## Diagnosis

Throughout history, the identification of psychosis has always been straightforward because of its distinctive cognitive symptoms. Adequately distinguishing schizophrenia from other psychotic disorders was problematic but became clearer as etiologies and treatments of some of the organically based psychotic disorders were developed. For example, it was discovered that niacin was an effective treatment for pellagra, and penicillin for central nervous system (CNS) syphilis—both of which are diseases that can manifest themselves with psychotic conditions. Between the 1920s and the 1950s, the carving off of psychotic affective illness on the one hand, and schizotypal personality disorders on the other hand, created yet clearer and more specific diagnostic criteria for schizophrenia (Carpenter and Buchanan 1995). DSM-IV-TR (American Psychiatric Association 2000) details clear diagnostic criteria accepted throughout North America and the scientific community worldwide; its criteria are based on extensive research, study, and review. The use of these criteria has led to the consistent and reliable diagnosis of schizophrenia. The DSM-IV-TR criteria and the tenth revision of the International Classification of Diseases and Related Health Problems (ICD-10) (World Health Organization 1992) are the world's two major diagnostic systems for schizophrenia, and with the current editions have reconciled their major differences. Such structured diagnostic criteria have led to the examination and identification of schizophrenia around the world and to the observation that incidence and the symptomatic expression are similar between countries and across cultures (Sartorius 1974).

Although the schizophrenia phenotype has been traditionally defined by chronic psychosis and functional deterioration, the boundary of the phenotype is now often viewed as broader than the schizophrenia diagnosis itself. Schizophrenia may well be the tip of an iceberg of schizophrenia-related diagnoses, augmented by the related personality disorders (Tsuang et al. 2000). Schizophrenia-related personality disorders evidence subtle symptoms and signs similar to schizophrenia, especially in some nonpsychotic first-degree relatives (Faraone et al. 2000). Moreover, antipsychotic treatment may improve functioning in persons with certain personality disorders (Tsuang et al. 1999).

## Symptoms

In the International Pilot Study of Schizophrenia conducted by the World Health Organization (WHO) (Sartorius 1974), symptoms were rated in schizophrenic persons in seven different countries. The symptoms were noted to be similar around the world. The list of the most frequently reported symptoms (Table 30–1) is descriptive of the disease we see today.

**TABLE 30–1.** Frequency of psychotic symptoms in schizophrenia (as reported by the International Pilot Study of Schizophrenia)

| Symptom | Frequency |
|---|---|
| Lack of insight | 97% |
| Auditory hallucinations | 74% |
| Verbal hallucinations | 70% |
| Ideas of reference | 70% |
| Suspiciousness | 65% |
| Flatness of affect | 65% |
| Voices speaking | 65% |
| Paranoid state | 64% |
| Thought alienation | 52% |
| Thoughts spoken aloud | 50% |

*Source.* Reprinted from Sartorius N: "The International Pilot Study of Schizophrenia." *Schizophrenia Bulletin* (Winter):21–34, 1974. Used with permission.

Although the use of DSM-IV-TR clearly identifies a syndrome, investigators remain unsure that schizophrenia is a unitary illness with a single etiology and pathophysiology as opposed to a group of syndromes or a collection of interrelated conditions (Carpenter and Buchanan 1994). Therefore, various attempts have been made to delineate testable subtypes of the illness on the basis of clinical characteristics, which then can be evaluated for distinguishing brain characteristics (Carpenter et al. 1993). In several investigations of large schizophrenic patient populations, the symptom presentations have been analyzed for the clustering of symptoms into symptomatic subgroups. These analyses have consistently revealed three distinct symptom domains in schizophrenia: 1) hallucinations, delusions, and paranoia; 2) thought disorder and bizarre behavior; and 3) negative symptoms of anhedonia, social withdrawal, and thought poverty (Andreasen et al. 1995; Arndt et al. 1991; T.R. Barnes and Liddle 1990; Carpenter and Buchanan 1989; Kay and Sevy 1990; Lenzenweger et al. 1991; Liddle 1987). Although these symptom clusters characteristically occur together, and one cluster may predominate in some patients, one domain is not exclusive of another. It is not yet understood whether these symptom domains are meaningful as the multiple manifestations of a single disease pathophysiology or whether each is a partially independent disease construct of its own with distinct etiologies and partially independent pathophysiologies. One importance of this distinction lies in its therapeutic implications. Is there one treatment for schizophrenia? Or are there several treatments for symptom-specific domains of the illness? This question still remains open, and its answer is being aggressively pursued in ongoing research.

## Course

The diagnosis of schizophrenia usually implies a lifelong course of psychotic illness. Occasionally, the illness is of fast onset and episodic, with symptoms first occurring in late teen and early adult years, and showing satisfactory recovery between episodes. However, more often other patterns of illness occur characterized by an insidious onset, partial recovery, or a remarkable lack of recovery between episodes (Bleuler 1978; Ciompi and Müller 1976). In most schizophrenic patients, a profound deterioration in mental and social functioning occurs within the first few years of the illness. After the initial deteriorating years, the further course of illness settles at a low, but flat, plateau. Surprisingly, symptoms often improve in later life after age 50. Whereas schizophrenia used to be described with an inevitably deteriorating long-term course, the Vermont study found considerable heterogeneity in outcome in later life among schizophrenic patients, including some frank late improvers; moreover, the Vermont study included chronic, poorly responsive patients who are most likely to have poor outcomes (Harding et al. 1987a, 1987b). Specifically, in this study of 269 patients (with a 97% follow-up rate), more than half of the individuals had no psychotic symptoms after 10 years of study (after approximately 15–20 years of illness), and most had a "good" level of functioning in their later life. These data are consistent with several other outcome studies conducted in Europe and the United States, which report frequent good outcome in later years for individuals with schizophrenia (Bleuler 1978; Ciompi and Müller 1976; Huber et al. 1979; Tsuang et al. 1979). Whether elder years are merely less demanding periods for mental performance or whether the normal aging process is therapeutic in the illness is not known. That the disease course is generally flat in its middle years distinguishes schizophrenia from traditional neurodegenerative disorders in which the course is progressively downhill (such as Parkinson's disease or Alzheimer's dementia) and from traditional neurodevelopmental disorders (such as mental retardation) in which the course is steady and low from the beginning of life.

## Risk Factors in Schizophrenia

Although the etiology of schizophrenia is not known, certain factors have been associated with a propensity toward the illness. Genetic predisposition is clear. Prenatal maternal illness and birth complications appear to be involved, at least as predisposing factors. In addition, winter birth of the proband is associated with a definite, although small, proportion of those with the diagnosis. Each risk factor alone confers a small risk, yet when they occur together these risks may be multiplicative (Barr et al. 1990; Kendell and Kemp 1989; Mednick and Cannon 1991; O'Callaghan et al. 1991). Moreover, these risk factors suggest the importance of very early life events in the onset of an illness whose florid symptoms appear much later in life.

## Genetics

The evidence is currently clear and consistent across many methodologically sound studies that schizophrenia aggregates in families. First-degree relatives of schizophrenic individuals have a lifetime risk of 3%–7% of manifesting schizophrenia compared with a 0.5%–1% lifetime risk of relatives of control subjects (Kendler and Diehl 1995). Twin studies have been pivotal in identifying the familial factor as a genetic rather than an environmental risk (Gottesman and Shields 1982; Kety 1987). The monozygotic twin of a person with schizophrenia has a 31%–78% chance of contracting the illness, compared with a 0%–28% chance for a dizygotic twin. Although schizophrenia is firmly believed to be genetic, the genetic mechanism of transmission has not been defined despite significant efforts in both association and linkage studies (Kendler and Diehl 1993).

## Perinatal Factors

The proposal that pregnancy and birth complications are associated with schizophrenia has been extensively studied and is generally accepted despite some controversy (S. W. Lewis and Murray 1987). Most studies show an association between perinatal accidents and schizophrenia; a few studies have failed to confirm this. The overall effect when calculated is small, increasing risk of disease by only 1% or so. The markers used to indicate these perinatal insults include low birth weight, prematurity, preeclampsia, prolonged labor, hypoxia, and fetal distress (McGrath and Murray 1995). That some abnormality such as one of these could occur at birth to "cause" or "facilitate" schizophrenia is an attractive idea, implying a causal connection between perinatal accidents and the illness. This is especially compelling because hippocampal pyramidal neurons (often directly implicated in schizophrenia pathology) are exquisitely sensitive to hypoxia. However, any evidence of causality is lacking in these studies; the only available evidence is for an association between the two. As such, these pregnancy and birth complications, even if actually more frequent in schizophrenia than in the general population, could be an epiphenomena of the schizophrenia genotype without any causal relationship to the illness. Of course, most schizophrenic persons do not have a positive history for these early birth events; nor do most persons who experience such early birth trauma develop schizophrenia.

## Winter Birth

A consistently found epidemiologic characteristic of schizophrenia is the excess of winter births over spring births among schizophrenic individuals (Bradbury and Miller 1985). The effect is small but highly replicable. Despite the strength of the finding, the reason for the association remains obscure. Seasonal variations in birth complications, temperature, lifestyle, diet, and rates of infections are the possibilities that have been most discussed. It is tempting to suggest that a warm-weather infective organism is causally involved in predisposing the young summer fetus (which will ultimately become the winter-born person) to the illness. Although this remains a possibility, direct evidence to support any causal association is lacking. Until such a causal association is found, the excessive occurrence of schizophrenia among those born in winter is a firm observation in search of a proper explanation.

## Anatomic Features of Schizophrenia

## In Vivo Brain Structure Using Magnetic Resonance Imaging

The application of magnetic resonance imaging (MRI) to the study of brain structure in schizophrenia, using adequate patient numbers and the sufficient image resolution of modern cameras, has resulted in clear findings that have contributed greatly to our knowledge of the illness (R.E. Gur and Pearlson 1993). MRI studies

have benefited from meticulous clinical technique and attention to the many possible sources of imaging artifacts. The first MRI studies revealed a reduction in overall brain size, an increase in ventricular size, and variable cortical wasting in schizophrenia (Shelton and Weinberger 1987). The studies confirmed and extended older literature describing the examination of schizophrenic patients with computed axial tomography (CAT), which demonstrated the ventricular enlargement with the cruder (CAT) technique (Johnstone et al. 1976). More recently, MRI studies have frequently revealed a volume decrease in the medial temporal cortical structures, hippocampus, amygdala, and parahippocampal gyrus with some consistency, especially in the studies with dense sampling (Barta et al. 1990; Bogerts et al. 1990; Breier et al. 1992; Suddath et al. 1990). New analytic techniques allowing shape analysis of the hippocampus have revealed striking regional shape differences of the hippocampus in schizophrenia (Csernansky et al. 1998). Not only has the volume of the superior temporal gyrus been reported to be reduced in schizophrenia, but the magnitude of the reduction has been correlated with the presence of hallucinations (Menon et al. 1995; Shenton et al. 1992) and with electrophysiologic changes in the patients (McCarley et al. 1993). Other than volume reductions in these temporal and limbic regions, reports of other structural changes assessed by MRI have been less consistent but not uninteresting. Some investigators have found increases in sulcal size, decreases in gray-matter volume, and altered gyral patterns (Pearlson and Marsh 1995). Even changes (increases) in white-matter volume have been reported (Breier et al. 1992). Neocortical volume reduction may be present in only some symptomatic subgroups of schizophrenic subjects, for example middle frontal cortex volume reduction in negative-symptom schizophrenia (Andreasen et al. 1992). The thalamus may have a reduced volume in schizophrenia, particularly the posterior portion (Andreasen et al. 1994); this is an observation that should direct future interest to this structure.

The extent to which the overall volume of a brain structure reflects any internal pathology, especially if the pathology is subtle, is necessarily limited. Although positive MRI data can identify a brain area for further study, negative results do not rule out areas as pathologic; moreover, MRI as a technique does not provide critical knowledge to differentiate functional relevance. Thus it is important to follow up the identification of structural abnormalities with functional, pharmacologic, or electrophysiologic techniques.

## Microscopic Analysis of Postmortem CNS Tissue

The question of importance to be answered by the microscopic study of tissue from schizophrenic persons is whether a systematic neuropathologic lesion can be identified, by type or location in the illness, that could provide a clue to pathophysiology. Here structure is able to more precisely indicate pathology than with in vivo imaging techniques because of the cellular resolution of this approach. It is widely accepted that no obvious, currently identifiable neuropathologic lesion is present in schizophrenia as occurs in Parkinson's disease or Alzheimer's dementia. Certainly a more subtle pathology must be the expectation. Since the time when schizophrenia was called the "graveyard of neuropathology," a considerable resurgence of interest in the neuropathologic characteristics of the schizophrenic brain has taken place, particularly within the last 10 years. Of universal caution in reviewing any schizophrenia neuropathologic studies are careful attention to the possible confounds of tissue artifacts, long-term neuroleptic treatment, lifelong altered mental state, and relevant demographic factors.

A significant number of modern postmortem studies of pathology in tissue of schizophrenic persons have now been published (Bogerts 1993; Harrison 1999). The technical range of measures performed on CNS tissue represents a great breadth of anatomic expertise. However, the application of these multiple techniques in the face of incomplete guiding hypotheses has left the postmortem literature of schizophrenia very broad and sometimes fragmented. The changes that have most consistently been found suggest a common localization for a neural defect in the illness (that is, in limbic cortex) but not necessarily a common neuropathologic feature. The primary limbic structures in brain (namely, hippocampus, cingulate cortex, anterior thalamus, and mammillary bodies) and their intimately associated cortical areas (entorhinal cortex) have been found to regularly display pathologic abnormalities. These are abnormalities of cell size (Jeste and Lohr 1989), cell number (Falkai and Bogerts 1986), area (Suddath et al. 1989), neuronal organization (Scheibel and Kovelman 1981), and gross structure (Colter et al. 1987). Moreover, the entorhinal cortex has been observed to show abnormalities of cellular organization in layer 2 neurons (Arnold et al. 1991a). It is interesting to recall that both structural changes on MRI (Suddath et al. 1989) and (as will be described shortly) functional changes in positron emission tomography (PET) (Tamminga et al. 1992b) have targeted these same areas for interest in schizophrenia pathophysiology. The consistency of this localizing pathology, despite the variety of concrete findings, is striking across technically different studies. As increasingly sophisticated and diverse neuropathologic techniques are applied to this analysis, important findings may emerge.

Even though they are consistently altered, limbic structures are not the only ones affected in the postmortem schizophrenic brain. The neocortex (especially frontal cortex) has been more recently studied, with varying reports of cell or tissue loss: one study reported volume reductions in gray matter (Pakkenberg 1987), two did not (Heckers et al. 1991; Rosenthal and Bigelow 1972), and one reported increased neuronal packing in frontal cortex (Goldman-Rakic 1995). The thalamus, because of its pivotal position in relationship to afferent sensory information and as a station in the cortical-subcortical circuits, has been the occasional object of study with inconsistent but not negative results. Several studies report cell loss and reduced tissue volume in thalamus (Pakkenberg 1990; Treff and Hempel 1958), whereas another study reports none of this (Lesch and Bogerts 1984). Additional study in both frontal cortex and thalamus must be done before firm conclusions can be made. Moreover, it is possible that variability might be reduced (and the answer made clearer) by seeking neuropathologic changes within symptom domains.

The interesting neuropathologic finding of basal ganglia enlargement in schizophrenia (in both caudate nucleus and putamen) (Heckers et al. 1991) was subsequently confirmed using in vivo MRI techniques (Breier 1992; Chakos et al. 1994). These studies showed a small but clear increase in the size of both caudate nucleus and putamen in schizophrenic patients treated with neuroleptics. That this volume increase occurs only after long-term neuroleptic treatment but not before (Chakos et al. 1994) suggests that it is an effect of long-term treatment with neuroleptics. It has also been observed that long-term neuroleptic treatment in laboratory rats increases striatal mitochondrial size (Roberts et al. 1995), increases the size of some axon terminals, and causes a trend toward an increase in the size of dendrites; these findings are consistent with a striatal volume increase with neuroleptic treatment in schizophrenic patients. This finding is a good example of a postmortem finding in schizophrenia that is associated not with the illness but probably with its treatment (Figure 30–1).

## Anatomic Markers of Brain Development

Findings from several kinds of postmortem investigations using CNS tissue of schizophrenic persons have suggested abnormal cerebral development in the illness

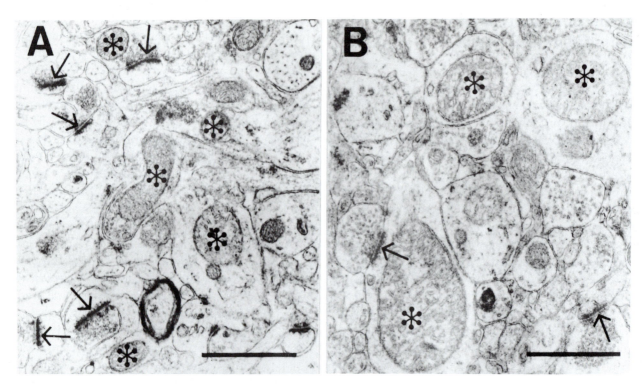

**FIGURE 30–1.** Electron micrographs of striatal neurophil in control (*Panel A*) and high-VCM (*Panel B*) groups. Note the decreased synaptic density and hypertrophied mitochondria in the high-VCM group compared with the control group. Arrows indicate synapses; asterisks indicate mitochondrial profiles. Scale bars=1 μm. VCM=vacuous chewing movements.
*Source.* Micrograph contributed by Dr. Rosalinda Roberts.

(Benes 1989; Benes et al. 1992; Goldman-Rakic et al. 1983; Weinberger 1987). Some studies have focused on the position in cortical layers (along an axis perpendicular to the brain surface) of particular neurons in schizophrenic brain, with an abnormally inferior position signaling abnormal development. During the second trimester of human fetal development as the cortex is forming, neurons migrate upward from the ventricular wall to their target cortical layer and form functional contacts. Regional studies of postmortem cortical tissue from schizophrenic individuals have generated several persuasive observations consistent with the idea that developmental mistakes in migratory pattern may be associated with schizophrenia. This evidence consists of cortical neurons appearing incorrectly in cortical layers lower (more inferior) than expected. Akbarian et al. (1993) reported a reduction in nicotinamide adenine dinucleotide phosphate (NADPH)–diaphorase staining neurons in the higher cortical layers of the schizophrenic dorsolateral prefrontal cortex and an increase ("trailing") in these neurons in underlying white-matter layers. The researchers interpreted these findings as being consistent with an impairment of neuronal migration of these particular cells into upper layers of frontal cortex during their critical developmental period (second trimester) in schizo-

phrenia. Earlier studies reported alterations in superficial cellular organization (for example, in layer 2) in entorhinal cortex, with layer 2 cell "trailing" in the lower cortical layers, again consistent with a neuronal migratory failure in this area of cortex (Altshuler et al. 1987; Arnold et al. 1991a; Jakob and Beckman 1986). Another study found cingulate and middle frontal cortices to have more neurons present in lower rather than in superficial layers, again consistent with a concept of migratory failure (Benes 1993). Other kinds of developmental studies have focused on changes in structural and/or growth-related elements in the neurons themselves that would disturb normal development. The early observations of hippocampal neuronal disarray in schizophrenia are consistent with the recently reported selective loss of two microtubule-associated proteins (MAP2 and MAP5) in schizophrenic postmortem hippocampal tissue (Arnold et al. 1991b). Another study found that the protein GAP-43 is increased in frontal and lingual gyral tissue of schizophrenic persons (Sower et al. 1995). GAP-43, a synaptic marker associated with the establishment and remodeling of synaptic connections, is normally enriched in associational cortex and hippocampus. This finding suggests the possibility of unusual synaptic remodeling in frontal and lingual cortices in schizophrenia and is consistent with altered neuronal activity in these areas, possibly secondary to failed or incomplete neuronal projection systems to or within these regions.

Akbarian and colleagues (1995) and Volk et al. (2000) reported decreased expression of glutamic acid decarboxylase (GAD) mRNA in prefrontal cortex of schizophrenic persons without significant cell loss. It is thought that only one of the multiple types of γ-aminobutyric acid (GABA)–containing cortical neurons may be reduced in schizophrenia, the chandelier cell (D.A. Lewis 2000). These alterations in GABA system activity may be the basis of the already observed frontal hypometabolism repeatedly reported in functional imaging studies of the illness. In the excitatory glutamatergic system, alteration in the composition of the N-methyl-D-aspartate (NMDA)–sensitive glutamate receptor in hippocampus has been reported (Gao et al. 2000), possibly reflecting disruption of limbic system function.

Although these postmortem findings are highly provocative and interesting, replication and extension studies are critical to confirm the initial results obtained and reported with low subject number and specialized technical procedures. Although it is necessary to report early on these findings to inform the field, further replication is certainly necessary. These kinds of postmortem results are compelling in schizophrenia because their presence is theoretically consistent with the cognitive changes of the illness.

## Biochemical Studies in Schizophrenia

The compelling impetus to study biochemical measures in schizophrenia derived from the early pharmacologic observation that blockade of dopamine receptors in the brain reduces psychotic symptoms in schizophrenia (A. Carlsson and Lindquist 1963). The obvious idea that dysfunction of the CNS dopaminergic system either in whole or in part accounted for psychosis in schizophrenia was explored in all body fluids and in various conditions of rest and stimulation (Elkashef et al. 1995). Other transmitter systems have more recently drawn interest as well, including serotonergic (Reynolds 1983; van Praag 1983), peptidergic (Nemeroff et al. 1983; Widerlöv et al. 1982), and most recently glutamatergic systems (reviewed in Tamminga 1998). Because of its ubiquitous location in the CNS and because the antiglutamatergic drugs phencyclidine (PCP) and ketamine cause a schizophrenia-like reaction in humans, the glutamate system has become a focus of study. Earlier studies of the biochemistry of schizophrenia were technically limited by access to relevant body fluid or tissue. Although peripheral body fluids such as urine and plasma have been widely used to provide information about the brain (Bowers et al. 1984), such methods are obviously highly indirect and are becoming less necessary. Because cerebrospinal fluid (CSF) bathes the brain itself, studies of transmitters, metabolites, and enzymes in lumbar CSF should provide information more directly reflective of cerebral activity (van Kammen et al. 1986; Widerlöv 1988). On the other hand, the regional characteristics of brain biochemistry, often the most interesting and pivotal to questions of functional pathology, may be obscured because the contribution from a target area of interest is diluted by biochemical markers from all other areas (Elsworth et al. 1987). Currently, the use of postmortem tissue, carefully collected and clinically well characterized, has become increasingly useful in studies of schizophrenia biochemistry (Jaskew and Kleinman 1989).

## Dopamine

Concentrations of dopamine in the CNS were originally identified in the 1950s, and its function was defined as a neurotransmitter in the CNS. Dopamine neuronal cell bodies in the brain have a highly localized distribution in the mesencephalon, limited here to the substantia nigra pars compacta (SNC) and to the ventral tegmental area (VTA); projection fibers from the SNC travel predominantly to the caudate nucleus and putamen, and less dense fibers from the VTA largely project to frontal and cingulate cortices. Release of dopamine into the synapse is characteristically phasic, not tonic, although recent studies tend to suggest that both may occur (Grace 1991). Considerable basic pharmacology about the dopamine system has been described in the last three decades. This has provided a rich opportunity for study in schizophrenia and in other related diseases of the brain.

In schizophrenia studies, measurement of the dopamine metabolite homovanillic acid (HVA) in plasma has provided interesting results in its correlation with good treatment outcome (Bowers et al. 1984; Davidson and Davis 1988; Pickar et al. 1986). Although it is tempting to take this peripheral metabolite measure as an indicator of brain dopamine metabolism, both common sense and data tend to discourage this (Elsworth et al. 1987). Activation and stress have been proposed as potentially critical primary factors in altering plasma HVA in schizophrenia. The use of plasma HVA as a marker of a disease characteristic rather than a measure of regional brain biochemistry is still being pursued with positive results.

The measurement of transmitters and metabolites in lumbar CSF as a reflection of neurotransmitter activity in the brain has not critically contributed to our understanding of schizophrenia pathophysiology even though the CSF is in direct contact with brain tissue; moreover, its sampling and analysis are beset with potential confounds. Significant influences on study outcome include subject size, diet, seasonal and circadian variability, and sample dilution by CSF from nontarget areas. HVA is the CSF metabolite most studied (Bowers et al. 1969). Not surprisingly, results of these CSF studies of HVA are conflicting, with most studies reporting no change (reviewed in Issa et al. 1994a, 1994b) but with two studies reporting an HVA decrease in schizophrenia (Bjerkenstedt et al. 1985; Lindström et al. 1985). Correlational studies relating schizophrenia features to CSF HVA levels have been done but have not resulted in any strong findings. Postmortem tissue has provided the most valuable specimen source for biochemical studies. Several investigators have found regional increases in dopamine and/or its major metabolite HVA in schizophrenic brain in postmortem studies of tissue from schizophrenic individuals (Bacopoulos et al. 1979; Mackay et al. 1982; Owen et al. 1978; Reynolds 1983; Toru et al. 1988). These results can be expected to be regularly confounded by the ubiquitous use of neuroleptic medication in life in these patients, even when the analytic techniques are adequate and tissue collection is consistent. However, in at least one case a regional change in HVA was reported that is not likely to have been caused by neuroleptic treatment due to its localized nature (Reynolds 1983). Likewise, in the measurement of dopamine receptor density, studies have regularly reported increased dopamine type 2 ($D_2$)–family receptor density in caudate nucleus and putamen of schizophrenic individuals (Cross et al. 1981; Mackay et al. 1982; Reynolds and Mason 1995; Seeman et al. 1984). This latter change is almost always taken to be a consequence of long-term neuroleptic treatment and can be similarly demonstrated in rats (Clow et al. 1980; Shirakawa et al. 1994), monkeys (Lidow and Goldman-Rakic 1994), and neuroleptic-treated nonschizophrenic humans. Recent interest in $D_2$-family receptor density in schizophrenia has been heightened by the report of increased $D_4$ density in the caudate nucleus and putamen of schizophrenic individuals (Seeman et al. 1993). However, because $D_4$ density is also known to increase with long-term neuroleptic treatment, further study of tissue from untreated schizophrenic individuals is needed to draw final conclusions. The work comparing individual $D_2$-family receptors ($D_2$, $D_3$, and $D_4$) in tissue from neuroleptic-free schizophrenic persons with caudate nucleus or putamen tissue from healthy control subjects is currently being done in several laboratories and so far shows no differences in density of the $D_2$-family subtypes in

striatum (R.A. Lahti et al. 1995a; Reynolds and Mason 1995) (Figure 30–2). However, work is still in progress in this area, and new findings may emerge. $D_1$-family receptors may be increased in striatum of schizophrenic persons (Karlsson et al. 1993; Memo et al. 1983); this is a small but replicated finding, the significance of which is currently unknown.

Human brain imaging studies performed in vivo have been carried out with dopamine receptor ligands to look for dopamine receptor defects in schizophrenia. Although an initial study reported increases in $D_2$-family receptors in neuroleptic-naive and neuroleptic-free schizophrenic patients (Wong et al. 1986) and a later report suggested similar increases in psychotic nonschizophrenic individuals (Pearlson et al. 1995), subsequent studies using various other $D_2$ ligands and replications with the initial ligand have been unable to replicate this finding (Farde et al. 1990; Hietala et al. 1991; Martinot et al. 1990, 1991). Subsequent studies have suggested that an alteration in $D_2$ density may be characteristic of a subgroup of schizophrenic patients, perhaps those with a long duration of illness or other special clinical characteristics (Hietala et al. 1994). Surely all schizophrenic individuals do not have increased $D_2$-family receptors in the caudate nucleus and putamen. The question remains whether $D_2$-family receptors may be elevated in a subgroup of schizophrenic patients. It could be that the initial report included the confound of neuroleptic treatment.

Laruelle et al. (1996) studied schizophrenia using single photon emission computed tomography (SPECT) or PET imaging of low-affinity dopamine receptor ligands to measure the quantity of dopamine released into the synapse under certain circumstances. These researchers reported that persons with schizophrenia, during the acute phases of their illness, have an increased release of dopamine into the synapse in response to amphetamine challenge relative to healthy control subjects (Abi-Dargham et al. 1998). This increased release does not appear to be secondary to chronic antipsychotic treatment, as augmented release also occurs in first-episode patients (Laruelle et al. 1999). Persons with other psychiatric illnesses do not show increased release. This is one of the first replicated findings of dopaminergic dysfunction in schizophrenia.

In summary, the pharmacologic evidence is strong and consistent that blocking dopamine-mediated neurotransmission improves symptoms in schizophrenia; some early evidence has now emerged that a defect exists in the release of dopamine in the disease. This finding still requires broader confirmation. Moreover, new aspects of dopaminergic function will be studied in

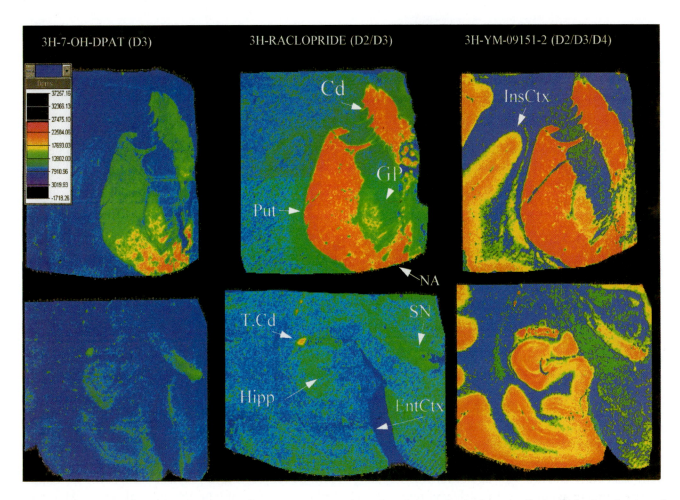

**FIGURE 30–2.** Binding of three different dopamine receptor ligands in human brain tissue to illustrate the localization of the dopamine type 2 ($D_2$) family receptors. The top row includes three contiguous slices taken from a midstriatal coronal brain section; the bottom row includes three contiguous slices taken from an inferior midhippocampal coronal brain section. The left column shows binding of [$^3$H]7-OH DPAT, a ligand that labels dopamine type 3 ($D_3$) receptors, in both of these areas. $D_3$ receptors are localized chiefly in the inferior striatum nucleus accumbens (NA) and substantia nigra pars compacta (SN). The middle column shows binding of $^3$H-raclopride, a ligand labeling $D_2$ and $D_3$ receptors. $D_2$ receptors are densely represented in the caudate nucleus (Cd) and putamen (Put) and are even apparent in the tail of the caudate nucleus (T.Cd); $D_2$ and $D_3$ receptors are intermingled in the nucleus accumbens and substantia nigra. The right column shows binding of [$^3$H]YM-09151-2, a ligand labeling $D_2$, $D_3$, and dopamine type 4 ($D_4$) receptors, in the two regions. A "mental" subtraction of the middle from the right autoradiograph suggests the $D_4$ localization to be predominantly in neocortex (InsCtx), hippocampus (Hipp), and entorhinal cortex (EntCtx). This illustration suggests that the $D_2$ receptor is predominantly localized in the caudate nucleus and putamen; the $D_2$ and $D_3$ receptors are localized in the nucleus accumbens and substantia nigra; and the $D_4$ receptor is predominant in the neocortex and in the hippocampal and parahippocampal cortices.

*Source.* Autoradiograph contributed by Dr. Robert Lahti.

schizophrenia as they are discovered to exhaust this still-rational direction.

## Other Monoamines

Norepinephrine levels have consistently been found to be elevated in several studies of CSF in schizophrenia (Beckmann et al. 1983; Lake et al. 1980), even if only to a slight degree. Complementary studies looking for changes in noradrenergic receptors have been predominantly negative. Moreover, noradrenergic antagonist drugs do not reduce psychotic symptoms in schizophrenia. It has been suggested that the norepinephrine increases in CSF in schizophrenic individuals may be related to stress (van Kammen et al. 1990), but the increases have not been linked with psychosis.

Serotonin has recently been revisited for its potential role in schizophrenia because of the strong antiserotonergic action of clozapine. The unique antipsychotic clozapine is a potent 5-hydroxytryptamine type 2 (5-HT$_2$) receptor antagonist, suggesting a possible positive role (even if not primary) of this neurotransmitter system in psychosis response. The inconsistency of changes in serotonin levels in CSF or brain tissue or in its metabolite levels, or even in serotonin receptor binding in vivo, is apparent in this literature, discouraging a formulation of serotonin pathology as primary in schizophrenia. Also, the potential confound of long-term neuroleptic treatment in schizophrenia altering this measure in CSF or in postmortem brain tissue must again be recognized (Elkashef et al. 1995). However, the possibility that modifying serotonin transmission may be important to an optimal antipsychotic response in schizophrenia is interesting.

On the rather timely assumption that neurotransmitter interactions may be important in schizophrenia, a recent study compared the levels of 17 neurotransmitters and their related metabolites in the CSF of untreated schizophrenic patients with those in healthy control subjects. While the levels of metabolites of dopamine, serotonin, or norepinephrine were found not to discriminate groups, a multivariate analysis of the entire data set found that the combination of tryptophan, tryptophol, and epinephrine discriminated the schizophrenic group from the control group. Although they do not identify anything specific about biochemistry in schizophrenia, these results—along with reports of kynurenic acid abnormalities in postmortem cortex from schizophrenic individuals (Schwarcz et al. 2001)—focus attention on the potential importance of the kynurenine pathway of tryptophan metabolism in schizophrenia (Issa et al. 1994a, 1994b). The identification of this association does not imply causality, especially knowing that it is reasonable to consider changes in excitatory neural transmission as a consequence, as well as a possible cause, of schizophrenia. Biochemical evidence of monoamine involvement in schizophrenia mechanisms is not strong, but the potential involvement of these systems in therapeutics remains an active possibility.

## Glutamate

More than a decade ago, the report of reduced glutamate levels in CSF of schizophrenic patients was interpreted to suggest neuronal hypoglutamatergic function in the illness (Kim et al. 1980). This report was not consistently replicated (Gattaz et al. 1985; Korpi et al. 1987; Macciardi et al. 1990). Because the fraction of CSF glutamate considered to come from the transmitter pool is so small (<5%), this CSF method was not considered sensitive

enough to uncover potential changes. However, Kornhuber's idea (Kim et al. 1980) of reduced glutamatergic transmission in schizophrenia has continued to capture the interest of the field. This has been the case in part because of the demonstration of the antiglutamatergic action of PCP (Anis et al. 1983), a drug with psychotomimetic (perhaps schizophrenia-like) properties at the NMDA receptor (Domino and Luby 1981). This demonstration allowed the hypothesis that PCP has its psychotomimetic properties secondary to its antiglutamatergic actions and that perhaps this is the mechanism of endogenous psychosis (Deutsch et al. 1989; Olney and Farber 1995). This hypothesis continues to be actively explored.

Meanwhile, using receptor binding assays, the density of the glutamate receptors in human postmortem brain tissue was assessed in schizophrenia. Nishikawa et al. (1983) reported an increase in [$^3$H]kainate binding in the prefrontal cortex but not in the putamen in the disorder. Toru et al. (1988) extended these data in schizophrenia by finding an inverse correlation between the increased kainate receptors in prefrontal cortex and glutamic acid concentrations in other brain areas. Deakin et al. (1989) noted an increase in kainate and aspartate binding in schizophrenic orbitofrontal cortex and simultaneously a decrease in aspartate binding (putatively a marker for presynaptic reuptake sites) in the left temporal cortex tissue of schizophrenic individuals. Moreover, these researchers also reported an increase in *N*-[1-(2-thienyl)cyclohexyl]-piperidine (TCP) binding (presumably to PCP receptors) in cortex. Harrison et al. (1991) reported decreased message for the combination of all non-NMDA receptors in hippocampal CA3; consistent with this, Kerwin et al. (1990) reported a reduction in kainate receptors in the hippocampus, without a change in NMDA sites. Kornhuber et al. (1989) has reported increased MK801 binding in several brain regions of schizophrenic individuals, including hippocampus and entorhinal cortex, but this has not been replicated in later study. Ulas and Cotman (1993) looked carefully at NMDA, α-amino-3-hydroxy-5-methyl-4-isoxalone propionic acid (AMPA), and kainate receptors in schizophrenic hippocampus, albeit in a limited number of patients ($N = 4$), without identifying definite group changes. These researchers commented on striking individual changes, however, leading to their suggestion of deafferentation of the hippocampus in some schizophrenic subjects. More recent studies of NMDA-sensitive receptor subunits suggest the possibility of a change in NMDA receptor composition in schizophrenia, which could alter glutamatergic transmission (Gao et al. 2000).

Overall, the literature on the involvement of glutamate in schizophrenia is suggestive, but the findings have not been entirely consistent in pointing out a particular defect (Tamminga 1998). It is important to note that many assessments for the glutamate system in mammalian brain are early and lack sensitivity and selectivity. Moreover, our understanding of the processes involved in glutamatergic transmission is yet incomplete. Techniques and strategies to assess glutamatergic system function in schizophrenia are clearly improving. Thus, technical and conceptual issues may be relevant to the failure to replicate findings. Perhaps the variety of disparate hippocampal glutamatergic findings themselves may be important, as suggested by Ulas and Cotman (1993), leading to a final common blockade or inhibition of hippocampal efferent pathway activity in schizophrenia.

# Functional Processing in Schizophrenia: Psychological and Electrophysiological

Psychological assessment of brain activity in schizophrenia might be expected to provide the most relevant clues to abnormalities in the illness, because the core symptoms of schizophrenia are of a cognitive variety. Even though it is difficult to distinguish the brain of a schizophrenic person from the brain of a healthy person by traditional anatomical or biochemical features, several psychological and physiologic measures are clearly able to provide distinguishing features between the two groups. Any ability to account for these differences with a compelling biological explanation would certainly enable advances in our concepts of mechanisms in the illness.

## Psychological Characteristics of Schizophrenia

Schizophrenic patients as a group perform poorly on most neuropsychological tests compared with healthy subjects. This poor performance is likely partly due to symptoms of schizophrenia (e.g., poor motivation or distraction from psychotic symptoms), and the negative effects of early onset of the illness and long-term institutionalization lead to the generalized deficits in these patients (Chapman and Chapman 1973). One approach to identify the specific neurocognitive deficits associated with schizophrenia is to examine the differential deficits associated with the illness (Chapman and Chapman 1973). A generalized neurocognitive impairment equally affects a person's performance in all tests, as long as these tests are approximately equal with respect to difficulty.

Measures that show selective impairment in testing when applied in schizophrenia are more likely to be associated with the pathophysiology of schizophrenia. Abnormalities in abstraction, problem solving, and other executive functions have been particularly noted in individuals with schizophrenia (Goldberg et al. 1987).

Specific neuropsychological deficits in schizophrenia are broad; they include memory, executive function, and motor performance (Braff et al. 1991; Gold et al. 1992; Goldberg et al. 1990; Gruzelier et al. 1988; R.C. Gur et al. 1991; Liddle and Morris 1991). No cognitive domains are entirely spared, and deficits in performance are highly intercorrelated within persons (Sullivan et al. 1994). Schizophrenic subjects in many of the studies show a pattern of deficits, ruling out a complete lack of motivation as a factor in performance. In schizophrenic persons, memory deficits occur (as shown, for example, in the recurring digit span test) that are consistent with temporohippocampal dysfunction (Gruzelier et al. 1988). Tests of frontal cortical function are also abnormal (for example, verbal fluency, spatial performance, pattern recognition), and long-term memory deficits have been documented (Gruzelier et al. 1988). The study of identical twins discordant for schizophrenia has been a highly productive technique in providing a genetically matched control group, circumventing critical comparison confounds. In such a study, Goldberg and colleagues found that almost all schizophrenic twins performed more poorly than their unaffected identical co-twin on all performance measures. Specifically, the schizophrenic twin performed significantly worse on assessments of intelligence, memory, attention, verbal fluency, and pattern recognition than their identical twin control subject. The performance of nonschizophrenic twins did not differ from that of unrelated healthy control subjects except for reduced performance in "logical memory" (Wechsler Adult Intelligence Scale [WAIS]) and in Trails A; in both of these cognitive areas, performance was still considerably different between the schizophrenic and nonschizophrenic twins (Goldberg et al. 1990).

Similarly, persons with schizophrenia consistently perform poorly on tasks that require sustained attention or vigilance (Nuechterlein et al. 1992). Other studies document deficits in memory, including explicit memory and verbal memory (Gold et al. 1994; Saykin et al. 1991). Working memory, which permits task-relevant information to be kept active for brief periods, has received much attention in the schizophrenia literature. Individuals with schizophrenia have difficulties maintaining working memory (Goldman-Rakic 1994; Park and Holzman 1992). Deficits in working memory may explain serious disorganization and functional deterioration observed in the schizophrenia spectrum. This is because the ability to hold information "online" is critical for organizing future thoughts and actions in the context of the recent past (Goldman-Rakic 1994).

The question of whether the cognitive deficits observed in schizophrenia are primary or secondary to the symptoms and related factors can be addressed more fully by studying nonpsychotic relatives of schizophrenic patients. Several studies have observed that the first-degree relatives of schizophrenic probands demonstrate many of the cognitive deficits observed in schizophrenia, even though these individuals do not experience overt psychosis (Asarnow et al. 1991; Balogh and Merritt 1985; Braff 1981; Cornblatt et al. 1989; Green et al. 1997; Nuechterlein 1983; Park et al. 1995). These deficits include impairments in different dimensions of attention, language comprehension, verbal fluency, verbal memory, and spatial working memory. This pattern of findings has recently been documented by two of the most comprehensive studies of relatives of schizophrenic patients (Cannon et al. 1994; Faraone et al. 1995). These studies show that even after adjusting for IQ, measures of auditory attention, abstraction, and verbal memory differentiated relatives of patients with schizophrenia from the comparison groups. It is unclear whether the observed neurocognitive impairments in relatives are associated with schizophrenia-spectrum personality symptoms. Some studies show that relatives meeting criteria for definite or probable schizotypal personality disorder have the most pronounced impairment, although not all cognitively impaired relatives met the diagnostic criteria for the probable or definite schizotypal personality disorder (Condray et al. 1992, 1996). It is possible that a lower threshold for schizotypal diagnosis and/or inclusion of relatives with negative and paranoid symptoms would capture the remaining cognitively impaired subjects. Other investigators (Keefe et al. 1997; Pogue-Geile et al. 1991; Roxborough et al. 1993), using various instruments (Wisconsin Card Sorting Test, Trail Making, verbal fluency, Symbol Digit, and/or WAIS variables), noted abnormalities among relatives of schizophrenic probands independent of schizotypal diagnosis.

Cohen and Serven-Schreiber (1992) suggested that these widespread disturbances in attention and language processing are caused by "a disturbance in the internal representation of contextual information," potentially arising from frontal cortical dysfunction and associated with dopamine deficiency. Cognitive psychologists have suggested that a defect in the connections between "cognitive modules" occurs in the illness, rather than an abnormality within the individual module itself (Frith 1995). However, the concrete nature of that defect has

been elusive. These data on neuropsychological function in schizophrenia are consistent with an overall brain disturbance in cognitive ability. To complicate these considerations further are the observations that the cognitive defects are not present in every person at all times and that the pattern of defects can change over time within an individual. This makes it hard to propose permanent changes in connectivity in the illness and forces a concept of flexible or reversible functional changes.

## Neurophysiological Deficits in Schizophrenia

Abnormalities in smooth-pursuit and saccadic eye movements have been extensively reported in schizophrenia (Holzman et al. 1984). Smooth pursuit is the use of slow eye movement to track a small moving object. Normally, humans capture the image of the moving object onto the fovea, the most sensitive region of the retina, and approximately maintain the moving image on the fovea by generating smooth and slow predictive eye movements that match the velocity of the target (G.R. Barnes and Asselman 1991). To carry out this function, the ocular motor system processes the motion of the target image on the retina and then generates a combination of fast (i.e., saccadic) and slow (i.e., smooth pursuit) eye movements to quickly capture the image on the fovea (Lisberger et al. 1987). This is called the initiation phase of the smooth-pursuit eye movements and is subserved by neuronal network of several brain regions, including mediotemporal cortex and brain-stem ocular motor regions. Subsequently, the smooth-pursuit function becomes more complex during the so-called maintenance phase. The eye tracks the target mostly by predictive smooth-pursuit eye movements combined with some predictive saccades and occasional increases in smooth eye velocity or saccades to catch up with the target. Normally, the brain integrates these complex ocular motor processes to execute a coordinated output, which results in the most efficient tracking (i.e., the image remains on the fovea for the maximum duration). This complex function is supported by a widely distributed neuronal network. This includes posterior parietal and mediosuperior temporal cortical regions, which hold an internal representation of the velocity information of the target and eye (Assad and Maunsell 1995; Newsome et al. 1988); mediotemporal cortex and cerebellum, which encode the difference in velocity between eye and target; and frontal cortical and brain stem regions, which generate predictive responses.

From the beginning of the twentieth century, studies have suggested an abnormality in the smooth-pursuit eye movements in schizophrenia (Clementz and Sweeney

1990; Holzman 1987). Extensive work carried out by Holzman and others in schizophrenic patients has shown that the measure is stable, and the findings in schizophrenia cannot be explained by disease-related factors or overt psychotic symptoms (Clementz and Sweeney 1990; Holzman 1987). Many of the nonpsychotic family members of schizophrenic patients also show poor pursuit as measured globally (Keefe et al. 1997; Thaker et al. 1996, 1998), by pursuit gain (Clementz et al. 1990), or by other measures (Clementz and Sweeney 1990; Whicker et al. 1985). Most studies note that abnormalities in smooth-pursuit eye movements occur mostly in relatives with schizophrenia-spectrum personality symptoms (Arolt et al. 1996a; Clementz et al. 1990; Thaker et al. 1996); one study did not find such an association (Keefe et al. 1997). Studies that examined eye movements in individuals with schizophrenia-spectrum personality with and without a known family history of schizophrenia noted smooth-pursuit deficits only in subjects who had a positive family history of schizophrenia (Thaker et al. 1996, 1998). A preliminary report found linkage of the smooth-pursuit eye movement abnormality to chromosome 6p21 in relatives of patients with schizophrenia (Arolt et al. 1996b). Based on psychophysical motion perception experiments, some investigators have argued that there is a deficit in motion processing in schizophrenia, thus explaining the smooth-pursuit eye movement abnormality (Chen et al. 1999). Based on the findings of normal saccadic eye movements to a moving target, others have argued that the underlying deficit occurs subsequent to the motion processing, during either the integration of the motion signal into a smooth-pursuit response (Sweeney et al. 1994) or the holding of the motion signal "online" for the smooth-pursuit maintenance (Thaker et al. 1998, 1999). The latter hypothesis would implicate lesions in posterior parietal and/or frontal cortical ocular motor regions associated with the smooth-pursuit abnormality in schizophrenia. This assertion is supported by the findings from two functional imaging studies in schizophrenia-spectrum disorders (O'Driscoll et al. 1999; Ross et al. 1995).

In addition to the smooth-pursuit abnormality, recent studies note subtle abnormalities in saccadic measures in schizophrenic patients (Crawford et al. 1998; Fukushima et al. 1988; Thaker et al. 1996). These studies examined performance in an antisaccade task in which subjects were instructed to look in the opposite direction of a target jump. Patients with schizophrenia made more errors (i.e., made saccades to the target rather than away from the target) than the comparison groups. Nonpsychotic relatives, akin to the findings in schizophrenia, also show an inability to inhibit an inappropriate saccade

toward the target (Clementz et al. 1994; Crawford et al. 1998; Katsanis et al. 1997; McDowell et al. 1999; Thaker et al. 1996, 2000). This deficit is modestly correlated with the smooth-pursuit abnormality in the relatives of schizophrenic patients (Thaker et al. 2000). The saccadic findings also implicate frontal cortical regions in schizophrenia (Berman et al. 1999).

## Evoked Potentials and Sensory Gating in Schizophrenia

In contrast to the neuropsychological and eye-movement studies, neurophysiological studies have identified abnormalities in information processing that can often be elicited in the absence of a behavioral response. Many studies have used signal averaging of electroencephalographic changes that are time-locked to sensory or cognitive events. Such event-related potentials have several time-bound segments that facilitate the examination of distinct aspects of information processing. P300 evoked potential response is a reliable positive change in potential occurring about 300 msec after a task-relevant stimulus or an unexpected stimulus. P300 has increased latency and decreased amplitude in persons with schizophrenia. Although these electroencephalographic measures may vary with changes in symptoms, the P300 amplitude is consistently small in schizophrenia even during relative remission of psychotic symptoms (Blackwood et al. 1991; Pfefferbaum et al. 1984). Other components of evoked potential are observed to be abnormal in schizophrenia. Mismatched negativity response that occurs earlier than P300 is observed to have smaller amplitude in schizophrenia, which suggests an abnormality in the early response to stimulus novelty (Javitt et al. 1995).

Although several studies report significant correlations between abnormalities in information processing and clinical symptoms, it is unclear what, if any, role the information processing deficits play in the development of clinical symptoms of the schizophrenia phenotype. Neurophysiological paradigms that examine sensory gating provide a theoretical framework for understanding the development of the core symptoms of schizophrenia. Measures of sensory gating are obtained by examining a process called prepulse inhibition. In this test, a person's ability to inhibit a startle response to a strong sensory stimulus in the presence of a preceding weak "prepulse" stimulus is evaluated. In contrast to a healthy comparison group, persons with schizophrenia show poor prepulse inhibition. Braff and others have proposed that schizophrenia is associated with an inability to gate sensory information, leading to sensory overload (Braff 1993).

According to this hypothesis, positive symptoms develop due to misinterpretation or misidentification of unfiltered sensory information. Negative symptoms may occur due to the withdrawal from the sensory overload.

Sensory gating is also evaluated by using positive change in the evoked potentials 50 msec (P50) after each of two auditory stimuli presented about 500 msec apart (Freedman et al. 1987). Normally, subjects show a much muted evoked potential response to the second stimulus compared with the first stimulus. In contrast, the P50 evoked potential response in schizophrenia is of similar amplitude as the response to the preceding stimulus. The ratio of amplitude of P50 response to the second (test) stimulus to the amplitude of the first (conditioning) stimulus is generally used as a measure of gating. Using a ratio of 0.4 or lower as normal and 0.5 or higher as abnormal gating, a segregation analysis in the families of patients with schizophrenia suggested that P50 gating deficit is a result of an autosomal dominant effect of a single gene. Subsequent linkage analysis showed evidence for linkage of the gating deficit in families of schizophrenic patients with markers of location in the chromosome 15q14 region (Freedman et al. 1997). This region has been shown to be the locus of the α-7 nicotinic cholinergic receptor subunit gene, although no molecular abnormality has yet been found in this region of linkage (Freedman et al. 1999).

## Functional Studies in Schizophrenia Using In Vivo Imaging Techniques

## Positron Emission Tomography With Fluorodeoxyglucose

PET with fluorodeoxyglucose (FDG) was the first high-resolution functional imaging modality used in schizophrenia. This technique relies on quantifying with PET the retention of $^{18}$F-labeled glucose in CNS tissue regionally, a measure that is proportional to the neuronal activity of that tissue (Reivich et al. 1979; Sokoloff et al. 1977). This FDG signal is integrated over 45 minutes, thereby magnifying small, steady signals but minimizing short-lived or small intermittent signals. Local uptake of FDG correlates with synaptic neuronal activity under physiologic conditions (Kadekaro 1987). FDG PET used as a survey technique is designed to localize regional neuronal metabolic changes that accompany brain perturbations or disease. However, the technique is quite likely to be sensitive to environmental conditions during scanning, as well as to disease state, symptoms, cognitive and emotional processes, and psychoactive drug use. Detecting

evidence of disease requires careful control of test conditions and a robust primary effect.

Initial studies with the early lower-resolution PET cameras produced long-sought pictures of the living schizophrenic brain "at work." These studies reported several different cortical and subcortical findings in the illness. First, studies reported relative hypometabolism in frontal cortex, a finding consistent with earlier blood-flow studies (Buchsbaum et al. 1982; Ingvar and Franzen 1971). Subsequent FDG PET studies in schizophrenia produced inconsistent detection of frontal cortex hypometabolism, with some studies continuing to find it (Buchsbaum et al. 1984), others reporting no change in the measure (Tamminga et al. 1992b), and still others finding frontal hypermetabolism (Cleghorn et al. 1989). These controversies now can be partially explained by two potential confounds: a neuroleptic effect and a skewed target population effect. Neuroleptics reduce cerebral metabolism in frontal cortex (Holcomb et al. 1996a), thus likely producing a confound in those early studies that compared neuroleptic-treated schizophrenic persons with healthy control subjects. We also know that frontal cortical dysfunction is associated with deficit (negative)–type schizophrenia, seemingly selectively. The composition of a patient group with neuroleptic-treated, deficit-type schizophrenic persons (who are often available for study) will skew the results. Other results at first associated with the disease (for example, increased metabolism in the caudate nucleus and putamen) are now known to be a neuroleptic effect (Holcomb et al. 1996a; Szechtman et al. 1988).

Our own studies with FDG PET were conducted in young, drug-free, floridly psychotic schizophrenic individuals (Tamminga et al. 1992b). We detected metabolic differences in schizophrenia in limbic structures (anterior cingulate and hippocampal cortices) with both areas showing reduced metabolism (Figure 30–3). No other differences developed between the schizophrenic individuals and healthy volunteers. However, within the schizophrenic group, primary negative-symptom patients showed the additional abnormalities of reduced metabolism in frontal and parietal cortices and thalamus compared with the non-negative-symptom group. Both of these findings (limbic changes overall in schizophrenia, and frontal cortex reductions in negative symptoms) are consistent with considerable other literature in their regional localization (Andreasen et al. 1992; Tamminga et al. 1992b). Reflecting the pathology found in postmortem tissue studies of schizophrenia, these results are consistent with limbic cortical dysfunction associated with the illness, particularly with its positive symptoms.

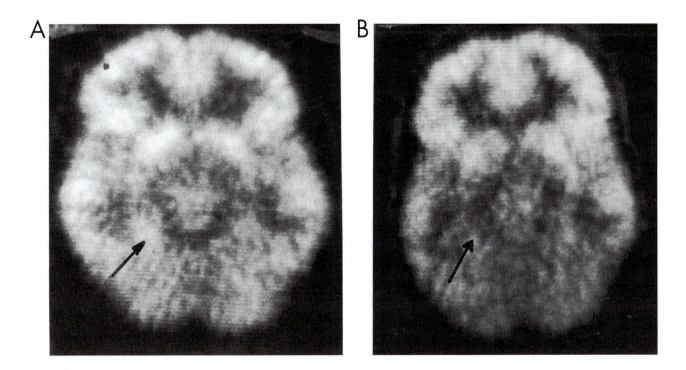

**FIGURE 30–3.** Positron emission tomographic images with fluorodeoxyglucose. Both images are at the same axial level and show, among other areas, the medial temporal structures. *Panel A* is an image from a healthy control subject; the general area of parahippocampal gyrus/hippocampus is indicated by the arrow. In the schizophrenic individual (*Panel B*) there is a remarkable reduction in glucose metabolism in the medial temporal structures (*arrow*). This reduction in parahippocampal gyrus metabolism is representative of differences in the entire schizophrenic group.

## Regional Cerebral Blood Flow Studies

Regional cerebral blood flow (rCBF) studies were originally done using xenon 133 with individual cortical detectors. Although these data were of relatively low spatial resolution, their temporal resolution was much higher than that of FDG PET. Spatial resolution improved with the use of $^{15}$O-labeled water with PET to study rCBF. Early $^{133}$Xe studies originally identified (Ingvar and Franzen 1971) and then extended (Weinberger et al. 1986) the observation of frontal cortex blood flow abnormalities, especially associated with impaired task performance. Schizophrenic subjects did not activate frontal cortex areas when performing a task known to involve frontal cortex activity (for example, the Wisconsin Card Sorting Test) in association with their inability to perform the task (reviewed in Holcomb et al. 1989).

More recently, blood flow studies using contemporary scanning and analytic techniques to examine normal and schizophrenic persons during performance of hierarchical tasks within a single task modality (Raichle 1994) have begun to reveal fascinating aspects of CNS function. Because schizophrenic patients characteristically (even

though variably) perform many tasks more poorly than nonschizophrenic persons, imaging assessment with a nongraded task will include a performance confound in its interpretation. The use of a variable error-rate task with all subjects fixed to the same performance level has been an innovation in this area, allowing comparisons without a prominent performance confound (Holcomb et al. 1996b, 2000). We have generated an rCBF comparison between schizophrenic patients and matched nonschizophrenic control subjects, conducted while both groups are performing a practiced auditory recognition task at a similar performance level (for example, with task difficulty set to an 80% error level). The task involves discriminating between two auditory tones; the difference in tone frequency is varied to shape performance to 80% accuracy. The sensorimotor control (SMC) task involves repetitive tone and motor stimulations; there is also a rest-condition task. Image analysis resulted in two subtracted group images for each group: SMC minus rest (the control condition) and auditory recognition minus SMC (the decision condition) after group normalization. Using the Statistical Parametric Mapping (SPM) software of Karl Friston and colleagues

(1991), localized areas of activation associated with sensorimotor performance and decision were identified during the control condition and during the decision condition. Consistent with a priori predictions, the nonschizophrenic individuals activated a small area in the posterior superior temporal auditory cortex (right > left) and a spot in the left motor cortex in the control task. For the decision task, control subjects activated the anterior cingulate cortex, right insula, and right middle frontal cortex. The schizophrenic subjects had considerably more activation in extent and magnitude of response in the control task, showing activation not only in the superior temporal auditory cortex (left > right) but also in the left premotor cortex, left parietal cortex, right insula, and cingulate cortex. In the decision task (in which control subjects demonstrated considerable activation in these regions) the schizophrenic subjects showed very little incremental increase in activation except for a mild flow increase in right frontal cortex (Figure 30–4). Overall, in comparing the "decision minus rest" subtraction between groups, the schizophrenic patients show activation of approximately the same areas as control subjects. Significantly more of this activation (which accompanied the decision task in nonschizophrenic subjects) was recruited for the relatively easy control (sensorimotor) task in the schizophrenic subjects. Moreover, when the patients increased their performance in the decision task (demonstrated by reduced accuracy and slower response times), no additional flow changes were apparent. Patients were performing this task at a similar accuracy level as nonschizophrenic subjects.

However, the mental mechanism (perhaps attention) that recruits brain areas into action for a task had activated all pertinent areas for performance of a relatively simple task and altered flow to a diminished extent when difficulty increased. One might speculate that schizophrenic persons need "full effort" to perform the easiest of tasks. One could expect a good deal of mental inefficiency with this abnormality. However, these data are concretely consistent with the psychological and symptomatic abnormalities of the illness.

Other scientists have used this method to understand the localization and type of functional defects in schizophrenia as well. Liddle and colleagues (1992) studied the correlation between well-delineated symptom clusters in schizophrenia (negative symptoms, hallucinations/delusions, and disorganization) and rCBF. Most interesting was the demonstration in this study, as well as elsewhere, that in vivo functional manifestations associated with schizophrenia are diverse. In overview, Liddle reported that negative symptoms were negatively associated with rCBF in left frontal cortex and left parietal

areas. Hallucinations and delusions were positively associated with flow in the left parahippocampal gyrus and the left ventral striatum. Disorganization was associated with flow in anterior cingulate cortex and mediodorsal thalamus. This study shows that different brain areas are differently involved in symptom manifestations in schizophrenia, perhaps either as a cause or an effect of the disorder. Recently, a $H_2^{15}O$ PET study of hallucinating schizophrenic persons revealed several CNS regions that activated in the subjects in association with hallucinations; these were the left and right thalamus, right putamen, left and right parahippocampal areas, and right anterior cingulate cortex. Cortical activations were present, but their cortical localizations were highly variable between the subjects and not significant in group analysis (Silbersweig et al. 1995). Further work from this group has shown that apomorphine (which is antipsychotic in schizophrenia, despite being a dopamine agonist) improves (that is, "normalizes") the anterior cingulate cortical blood flow of schizophrenic persons during verbal fluency task performance (Dolan et al. 1995).

Recently, other studies have also found evidence for limbic abnormalities in schizophrenia both at rest (Taylor et al. 1999) and with cognitive challenge (Artiges et al. 2000; Heckers et al. 1998; Spence et al. 1997). Heckers et al. (1998) found reduced hippocampal activation in schizophrenic subjects during a memory-retrieval task of previously studied words. These findings complement other postmortem and structural imaging studies of abnormalities in medial temporal lobe structures of schizophrenic individuals (Gao et al. 2000). Spence et al. (1997) studied schizophrenic subjects performing a complex motor task during an acute exacerbation of their illness and 4–6 weeks later, after their symptoms had improved. Although the subjects were acutely ill, they showed signs of prefrontal hypometabolism. When the schizophrenic volunteers' symptoms improved, the prefrontal regions were normal. However, when the schizophrenics were less symptomatic, rCBF in the anterior cingulate and bilateral parietal regions was still found to be decreased. These limbic region abnormalities are probably the result of a dysfunctional network of regions and not a series of separate lesions.

Abnormal functional connections between brain regions has been suggested as the cause of abnormal rCBF patterns seen in schizophrenia (Frith et al. 1995; Weinberger et al. 1992). In studies of verbal fluency (Spence et al. 2000) and semantic processing (Jennings et al. 1998), a network analysis revealed a functional disconnection between the anterior cingulate and prefrontal regions of schizophrenic subjects. Frontal-lobe functional connectivity was abnormal in the schizophrenic subjects,

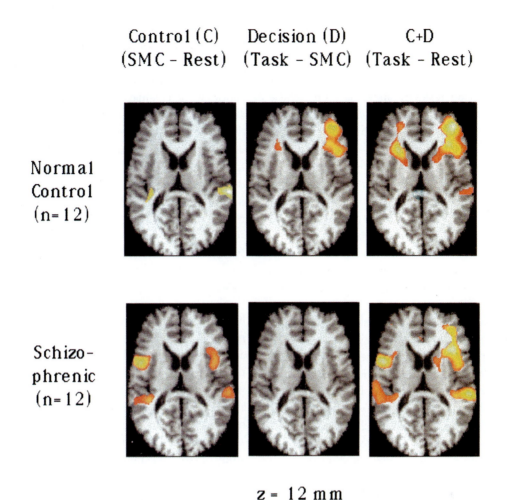

Control (C)     Decision (D)        C+D
(SMC – Rest)    (Task – SMC)   (Task – Rest)

Normal
Control
(n=12)

Schizo-
phrenic
(n=12)

z = 12 mm

**FIGURE 30–4.** Regional cerebral blood flow elevations seen at an axial level 12 mm above the anterior commissure–posterior commissure (ACPC) line in healthy control (*top row*) and schizophrenic (*bottom row*) subjects, each in a sensorimotor control (SMC) (*left column*) and a decision performance (*middle column*) condition. Control subjects merely activate the auditory cortex bilaterally (*upper left scan*) and the left motor cortex (data not shown) in the sensorimotor task, whereas the schizophrenic subjects activate those more and in more areas than control subjects (*bottom left scan*). During the decision task, the control subjects activate middle and inferior frontal cortex (*upper middle scan*) and anterior cingulate gyrus (data not shown); however the schizophrenic subjects do not recruit any additional areas or increase flow at all in their decision condition (*lower middle scan*). Overall, the schizophrenic subjects resemble the control subjects in the "task minus rest" analysis (*upper and lower right scans*), even though that activation occurred primarily in the control, not the decision, scan.
*Source.* Images contributed by Dr. Henry Holcomb and Dr. Adrienne Lahti.

even though they had significantly activated the regions and their behavior on the tasks was not impaired. These findings suggest that the abnormalities seen in the frontal lobes of schizophrenic persons may be a problem of integration across regions and not a specific regional abnormality.

## Functional Magnetic Resonance Imaging Studies

The magnetic properties of deoxygenated and oxygenated blood provide the rCBF signal that can be detected

with functional magnetic resonance imaging (fMRI). The blood oxygen level dependent (BOLD) signal results from the spin dephasing that occurs in response to field inhomogeneities created by the changing concentrations of deoxyhemoglobin that occur with brain activity (Ogawa et al. 1990, 1992). As a method for assessing regional brain activity, fMRI offers several advantages over other imaging modalities. fMRI does not require the injection of radioactive tracers and provides increased spatial and temporal resolution compared with PET.

Several fMRI studies have explored whether rCBF changes in response to simple motor tasks are normal in schizophrenic volunteers. Braus et al. (1999) found no rCBF differences between first-episode, never-medicated schizophrenic volunteers and nonschizophrenic volunteers while they were performing a sequential finger-thumb opposition task. In the same study, these researchers found a decrease in the BOLD response in the sensorimotor cortices of schizophrenic volunteers medicated with traditional neuroleptics. Other studies of this task found no differences (Buckley et al. 1997), increased rCBF in the sensorimotor cortices of the schizophrenic subjects (Mattay et al. 1997), and decreases in those regions (Schroder et al. 1999). In these studies, the schizophrenic volunteers were medicated with a mixture of traditional and atypical neuroleptics. These results suggest that previous exposure to neuroleptics can have an interactive effect with task performance.

In more cognitively demanding tasks, such as working memory tasks, the fMRI results are also inconsistent. Manoach et al. (1999, 2000) used the Sternberg Item Recognition working memory paradigm, which required the subjects to remember either two or five digits. Unlike in many PET studies of working memory, these researchers found an increase instead of a decrease in prefrontal rCBF in the schizophrenic volunteers compared with the nonschizophrenic control subjects. Callicott et al. (1998), using the N-back task, and Stevens et al. (1998), using the Word and Tone serial position task, found decreases in rCBF in inferior frontal regions of schizophrenic subjects. The task performance of the schizophrenic subjects was significantly worse on the N-back and word serial position tasks but was matched on the tone task. Research has shown that although rCBF increases in prefrontal regions with greater working memory demands, if working memory capacity is exceeded, the activation decreases (Callicott et al. 1999). Manoach suggests that the discrepant findings in schizophrenia may be explained by an overload of working memory in schizophrenic subjects for some tasks.

These kinds of rCBF studies provide us with information now about brain mechanisms and schizophrenia, and they indicate the extent to which in vivo imaging techniques can teach us about schizophrenia brain mechanisms.

## Clinical Therapeutics in Schizophrenia

The clinical therapeutics of psychotic illness have episodically but progressively advanced in the second half of the twentieth century. However, these advances have all been empirical, not theoretical, and rarely rational. Chlorpromazine was first tested in schizophrenic patients because of its known sedative properties as a preanesthetic agent (Delnay and Deniker 1952). Its selective antipsychotic activity was immediately noted and quickly demonstrated. This became the springboard for hypotheses of altered dopaminergic transmission in schizophrenia. In addition to this observation generating decades of research in therapeutics, it has been highly pivotal as well in promoting pharmacologic approaches to the exploration of schizophrenia pathophysiology.

## Neuroleptic Pharmacology

Drug development in the area of schizophrenia therapeutics has focused on dopamine receptor blockade and has been highly productive, even though empirical. Many potent, broadly active, and selective dopamine receptor antagonists were developed during the first 15 years after the discovery of chlorpromazine; these have become widely available for clinical use and have been universally applied. The drugs are all similar in their primary actions but distinctive in side-effect profile (reviewed in Klein and Davis 1969). Not until the recent U.S. controlled study of clozapine in the late 1980s was it clearly demonstrated that any single neuroleptic had a unique antipsychotic action in the illness and that potential therapeutic gains could be expected from new pharmacologic approaches. Clozapine has a unique antipsychotic action in neuroleptic nonresponding schizophrenics compared with chlorpromazine (Kane et al. 1988). Also, clozapine produces few if any motor side effects (despite its other serious side effects), thus increasing patient comfort, social adjustment, and medication compliance. Since the clinical actions of clozapine have been clarified, several clozapine-like new neuroleptic compounds with fewer side effects have been developed and are becoming available. All have reduced motor side effects, but their advantage in treating psychosis better than typical neuroleptics, if any, has not yet been demonstrated. The pharmacologic characteristics speculatively identified as important in these new antipsychotic drugs include 1) a restricted action on dopamine neurons, as reflected in a limited expression of depolarization inactivation in A10 but not A9 dopamine cell body areas; 2) multiple monoamine receptor blockade; 3) lower dopamine receptor affinity; and/or 4) selective $D_4$ or $D_3$ receptor affinity (R.A. Lahti et al. 1995b). It is important to note that, to date, only dopamine receptor antagonists in the $D_2$ family show broad and potent antipsychotic efficacy in schizophrenia.

We have studied the localization of haloperidol action in the brain in schizophrenia using PET with FDG (Holcomb et al. 1996a). Previous reports documented an increase in glucose metabolism in the caudate nucleus and putamen with typical neuroleptics (R.E. Gur et al. 1987; Szechtman et al. 1988). Our study confirms that finding. In addition, we found hypermetabolism in the anterior thalamus and decreased metabolism in the frontal cortex (middle and inferior gyri) and anterior cingulate areas (Figure 30–5). Based on the known anatomic connections and their primary transmitters between basal ganglia structures and neocortex, we have hypothesized a primary drug action of haloperidol in the basal ganglia (caudate nucleus and putamen) with secondary and tertiary effects being propagated to other related brain areas over the parallel distributed neuronal circuits. This interpretation of haloperidol action would suggest that the drug acts primarily in the caudate nucleus and putamen, with that action distributed out to other related brain areas through the parallel segmented cortical-subcortical motor circuit that is well described in the literature (M. Carlsson and Carlsson 1990; DeLong 1990; Graybiel 1990). This theory of antipsychotic drug mechanisms needs further expansion and testing. In addition, we might anticipate being able to show reduced metabolic changes in the putamen with newer antipsychotics with low motor side effects (studies in progress).

## Other Dopamine System Pharmacology

Not only is dopamine receptor blockade antipsychotic, but other mechanisms known to diminish dopamine-mediated neurotransmission have been shown to be antipsychotic as well, although they do not seem as potent or as consistently effective as the $D_2$-family receptor antagonists. An effect was initially demonstrated with tetrabenazine, a dopamine synthesis inhibitor, which decreased the dose requirement for thioridazine during schizophrenia treatment in a case-controlled study (Walinder et al. 1976). Also reserpine, which functions to deplete dopamine stores from nerve terminals, shows antipsychotic activity in schizophrenia as well as other psychoses. This action of reserpine was known even before the discovery of neuroleptics and was often used to treat acute psychosis early in the twentieth century. More recently, the evaluation of full and partial dopamine agonists has been tested theoretically in schizophrenia. Dopamine agonists reduce dopamine synthesis and release by their action at the dopamine autoreceptor. The antipsychotic actions (even though mild) of drugs like apomorphine and preclamol in schizophrenia may be based on this mechanism—that is, a stimulation of dopamine autoreceptors to diminish dopamine release and thereby diminish dopamine-mediated neurotransmission (Tamminga et al. 1978, 1992a). These strategies for therapeutics have not yet been demonstrated to be potent and practical, but at this time they are of great theoretical importance.

Based on the recent discoveries of multiple structurally distinct dopamine receptors with their own distinctive distributions and pharmacologies (R.A. Lahti et al. 1995a), the question about the importance of one or a combination of the distinct $D_2$-family receptors in treating schizophrenia has emerged. The $D_2$-family ($D_2$, $D_3$, and $D_4$) receptors mediate the antipsychotic actions of neuroleptics, with most neuroleptics having a measurable affinity at all three sites (with several exceptions). Whether one or another of these three sites is pivotal to schizophrenia therapeutics remains to be tested. There are new selective ligands emerging that will be tested soon. The $D_4$ receptor is potentially interesting for a primary role in mediating neuroleptic action because of the high affinity of clozapine at $D_4$ receptor sites and because of the several, although controversial, reports of $D_4$ upregulation in schizophrenia (R.A. Lahti et al. 1995b; Reynolds and Mason 1995). The $D_3$ receptor is interesting to consider for schizophrenia therapeutics because of its striking restricted localization to the ventral pallidum (R.A. Lahti et al. 1995b). New clinical trials information remains to be gathered and reported to answer therapeutic questions. Overall, the breadth of new dopaminergic agents—the new neuroleptics, experimental antidopaminergics, and novel antipsychotics—shows current interest and future strength.

## Glutamate System Pharmacology

Although there is no current evidence that glutamatergic drugs are therapeutic in schizophrenia, there are several reasons to be interested in the pharmacology of this system. First, the excitatory amino acid (EAA) system, the chief transmitter of which is glutamate, is ubiquitous in the brain; nearly every CNS cell bears EAA-sensitive receptors, indicating the extent of this system's influence. It is a complex system that has at least two major transmitters (glutamate and aspartate) and probably several minor ones; it has at least four families of receptors, three ionotropic (NMDA-sensitive, AMPA, and kainate) and one metabotropic family, with each individual receptor having its own unique distribution, pharmacology, and probably distinctive functions. EAAs are the chief excitatory transmitters in the brain. They mediate not only everyday information transmission functions but are also thought to be involved in other kinds of brain activity,

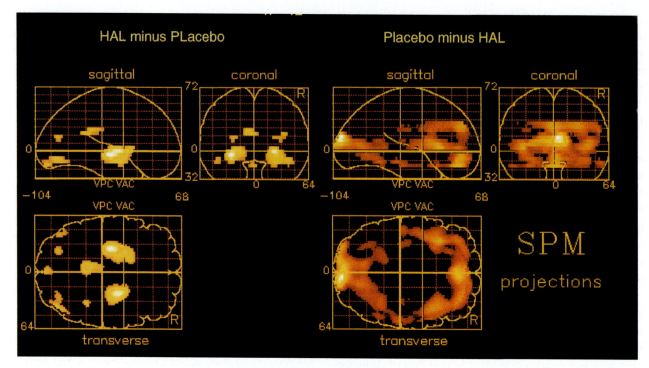

**FIGURE 30–5.** Projection images showing significant areas of haloperidol (HAL)–induced increases (*left*) and decreases (*right*) in regional cerebral metabolic rate for glucose (rCMRglu) from group subtraction Statistical Parametric Mapping (SPM) analyses, in within-subject comparisons. On the left, rCMRglu increases are apparent in the caudate nucleus, putamen, and anterior thalamus; on the right, rCMRglu decreases are apparent in anterior cingulate gyrus, occipital area, and frontal cortex (middle and inferior gyri). VAC=vertical anterior commissure line; VPC=vertical posterior commissure line.

*Source.* Images contributed by Dr. Henry Holcomb.

such as developmental pruning, learning and memory, and neuronal plasticity. Certainly the EAAs must mediate some aspects of psychosis due to their ubiquitous involvement in the CNS. Whether they are involved in schizophrenia in a more primary way is an interesting speculation.

The reason to suspect a connection between one part of the glutamate system, the NMDA-sensitive glutamate receptor system, and schizophrenia is based on the actions of PCP and its congener ketamine on human cognition. PCP produces a complex array of behaviors in humans. It can induce a psychotic state in nonschizophrenic persons (without delirium) that is characterized by many of the signs and symptoms often found in schizophrenia. Moreover, PCP (Luby et al. 1959) and ketamine (A.C. Lahti et al. 1995b) can both selectively exacerbate a patient's psychotic symptoms in schizophrenia, suggesting an action on (or near) the site of schizophrenia pathophysiology. Associated with the NMDA-sensitive glutamate receptor is a PCP recognition site located inside of the NMDA-gated ion channel; the PCP site antagonizes ionic flow through the channel. This is a complex receptor site where NMDA, glycine, and poly-

amines positively gate ion flow into the cell and PCP, $Zn^{2+}$, and $Mg^{2+}$ inhibit flow. It is presumed, based on a number of different observations, that PCP and ketamine both exert several of their important behavior actions through effects at the NMDA receptor (Javitt and Zukin 1991; A.C. Lahti et al. 1995b).

Not only does ketamine cause psychosis-like experiences in nonschizophrenic persons and exacerbate psychosis in schizophrenia, it also functionally affects rCBF directly in the brain areas in which postmortem tissue and in vivo imaging studies indicate dysfunction in schizophrenic persons—specifically, in hippocampal and anterior cingulate cortices. Behaviorally, ketamine increases psychosis at subanesthetic doses in both neuroleptic-treated and neuroleptic-free schizophrenic patients to the same degree. Ketamine stimulates positive, not negative, symptoms in schizophrenia, and its action is not blocked by dopamine receptor antagonism (A.C. Lahti et al. 1995b). Symptoms that are stimulated by ketamine are that person's characteristic set of schizophrenic hallucinations, delusions, and/or thought disorder. This is unlike other psychotomimetics (for example, amphetamine or muscimol), which stimulate psychotomimetic symptoms typical of the drug. This action of ketamine would be most parsimoniously explained by assuming that the drug stimulates a brain system that is already active in mediating (possibly even in originating) the psychosis.

We studied the localization and time course of ketamine action in brain using $H_2^{15}O$ and PET, measuring rCBF (Figure 30–6). Schizophrenic subjects, at a dose of ketamine active in exacerbating psychosis (0.3 mg/kg), showed increased rCBF in the anterior cingulate gyrus and decreased rCBF in hippocampus and lingual gyrus (A.C. Lahti et al. 1995a). The brain areas that showed a change had different time course patterns of rCBF over the 60 minutes after ketamine administration. This suggests that each area of brain has its own sensitivity to ketamine (which might be predicted on the basis of receptor localization and anatomic connections) and its own unique time course of response. Because other drugs have not been studied this way in humans, it is impossible to know whether this phenomenon is common, unusual, or unique. It does mean that ketamine at a behaviorally active (not anesthetic) dose produces rCBF actions in specific brain regions (more restricted than its receptor distribution would predict) and that the response of various cerebral regions appears independent. Questions of how this ketamine-induced psychosis stimulation might be related to schizophrenia still need to be answered.

## Integrative Basic Brain Mechanisms Important to Understanding Cerebral Function

Advances in basic knowledge about the mammalian brain relevant to function have been not only fascinating but pivotal to modern concepts of brain mechanisms. Decades ago, lesion studies contributed one kind of information to function localization in CNS. Currently, more subtle, yet functionally critical, principles are emerging, which include evidence of complex neuronal pathways, strategies for connectivity between brain areas, neuronal plasticity, and cognitive strategies. Because of its complexity, there remains much to learn about the principles of brain structure as they subserve function. The following sections describe only two (nonrepresentative) examples of emerging concepts in neuroscience that should someday be relevant to studies of schizophrenia.

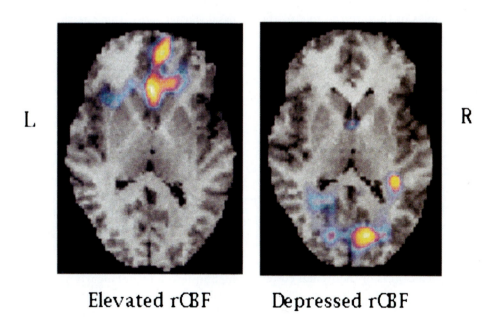

**FIGURE 30–6.** Regional cerebral blood flow (rCBF) localization of ketamine action in schizophrenic brain. rCBF increases occurred in anterior cingulate gyrus, extending to medial frontal areas (*left scan*); rCBF decreases are apparent in hippocampus and in the lingual gyrus (*right scan*). The colored areas indicating significant flow change are plotted onto a magnetic resonance imaging template for ease of localization. SPM=Statistical Parametric Mapping.

*Source.* Images contributed by Dr. Henry Holcomb and Dr. Adrienne Lahti.

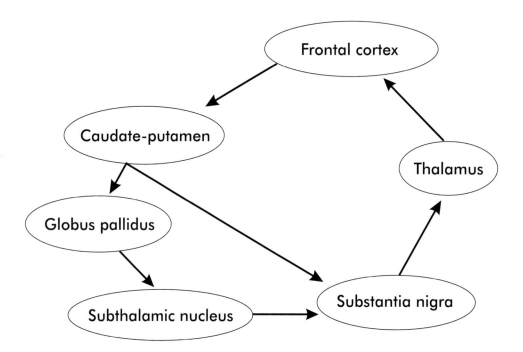

**FIGURE 30–7.** A schematized illustration of one of the parallel, segregated neural pathways that connect the cortex with the basal ganglia. These kinds of pathways serve to disperse influences on and to modulate voluntary motor behavior and probably cognitive behavior as well.

## Cortical-Subcortical Circuits

It is generally understood that local areas in brain perform delimited tasks, that is, they have a functional concentration. Clear examples of this are the role of the occipital cortex in visual perception and visually related memory; the superior temporal cortex in sound perception and auditory association functions; and the frontal cortex in integrative functions such as working memory, attention, and motor control. To coordinate these functions effectively, the brain must use a variety of communication systems to connect specialized areas with each other. One example of the way the brain has arranged such a system is the series of cortical-subcortical circuits described most recently by Alexander and DeLong (Alexander and Crutcher 1990; Alexander et al. 1986) and applied by them to a new treatment approach in Parkinson's disease (DeLong 1990). These investigators have found evidence for multiple parallel segregated neural circuits that connect specific areas of the frontal cortex reciprocally with specific regions of the basal ganglia and thalamus. Additional investigators of relatively recent (M. Carlsson and Carlsson 1990; Graybiel 1990) and more distant eras (Nauta 1989) have also speculated about such a system, usually with respect to motor functions and output because of their easy definition and quantitative convenience. Parallel, segregated neuronal

tracts project from specific areas in the frontal cortex to homologous target areas of basal ganglia, organized somatotopically and by functional system (for example, motor, oculomotor, limbic, prefrontal); both within the basal ganglia and within the thalamus the somatotopic organization is preserved. Within the basal ganglia (between striatum and substantia nigra pars reticulata) two legs of the pathway are connected in parallel, each having functionally opposite actions, presumably to subserve additional modulation. Efferents from the basal ganglia circuits project to their targets in thalamus. These thalamic areas project back to the originating frontal area, completing the feedback circuit (Figure 30–7). The neurochemical transmitters and firing characteristics of many of these pathways are known, thus providing possible sites and techniques for pharmacologic intervention (M. Carlsson and Carlsson 1990; Graybiel 1990). Although our understanding of the contributions of basal ganglia and thalamus to cognitive activity is remarkably incomplete and not nearly as well studied as their involvement in motor function, these pathways must certainly set the tone for various cognitive activities just as they have more clearly been demonstrated to do for motor functions. Concretely, one might imagine that the frontal cortex seeks to cue and to receive feedback from the basal ganglia and thalamus through these circuits, to set in motion other cerebral processing needed to accompany the cortically generated behavior, and for sensitivity settings on planned behavior. The potency of the influence of basal ganglia–thalamic feedback on frontal cortical activity is obvious in a neurologic disorder like Parkinson's disease, in which substantial motor feedback inhibition occurs (from the putamen) because of extreme deficiency there of nigral dopamine; this same feedback pathway may also function to mediate the antipsychotic action (and motor side effects) of neuroleptics in psychosis (Holcomb et al. 1996a). Alexander and DeLong (1986) have extrapolated from the importance of this feedback system in motor control that this same mechanism should also be operative in other frontal functions (memory, attention, and other aspects of cognition). They suggest that an area in the frontal cortex actually originates a voluntary cerebral (frontal) function but that the eventual expression of that function is powerfully modulated by the basal ganglia and thalamus through parallel segregated neuronal circuits. Schizophrenia, by extrapolation, could hypothetically result from abnormal basal ganglia or thalamic regulation of some aspect of frontal cortex cognitive function (actually not an uncommon idea now). There is only speculation to support this idea at present, but the known neuroanatomy would support such a formulation.

## Neural Plasticity

The brain remains a plastic organ throughout its life, even though neural plasticity is greatest in the developing brain. Developmental directives serve to first form the brain into its basic structure, with activity-dependent and activity-independent influences (Aoki and Siekevitz 1988); then these same mechanisms and probably others remain operative in shaping the mature brain to conform to its task directives. These fascinating but incompletely understood processes influence the localization, extent, connectivity, and electrophysiologic characteristics of specific cortical functions in the brain. Alterations in the spatial extent or the magnitude (over time) of sensory stimulation alter the somatosensory receptive field (in the groups of responsive neurons) in the cortex. That is, the functionally relevant neuronal field in the brain for a particular kind of sensory input depends on the characteristics of that input. Extensive research suggests some generalizations about plasticity in the neocortex: 1) that the excitatory activity of neocortical neurons can change with use and is mediated by a dynamic cortical mechanism; 2) that the coincidence of inputs can strongly influence their shaping potency; and 3) that coincidence-based input selection may account, at least in part, for the creation and continuity of local representational organization in the cortex (Merzenich et al. 1988). Learning a task, even in adults, results in neuronal activity changes in relevant brain regions with respect to the local extent of neuronal activation and in the magnitude of its activity. Moreover, the performance of a novel task recruits additional areas of CNS for task performance in comparison with when that task is practiced and learned (Raichle 1994). This process dramatically emphasizes the important role of practice and everyday mental activity in the functional organization of the CNS. What the brain commonly does will have a concrete impact on its observed functional characteristics. In chronic psychotic diseases, in which usual mental activity is bizarre, illogical, and not connected to reality, anatomic findings may be secondary to, not causal of, the illness.

## Synthesis

## Clinical Observations About Schizophrenia Important for Formulating Pathophysiology

Several characteristics of schizophrenic illness are strikingly consistent across clinics, laboratories, and cultures, such that any theory of the illness must take them into account. These include but are not limited to the following: schizophrenic symptoms are clear and their clustering is common although not exclusive; symptoms fluctuate during the course of illness and may disappear entirely between episodes but then reappear; the illness is most often lifelong, with the most flagrant symptoms and psychosocial deterioration appearing early in the illness, showing a plateau during middle years, and frequently ending with some degree of symptom resolution in later years. The illness has a genetic component but is by no means fully genetically determined. Although no traditional anatomic or biochemical change has come to be pathognomonic of the illness, the limbic system (especially hippocampus and entorhinal and cingulate cortices) is the cerebral location where anatomic and functional changes are highly concentrated, albeit changes of a varied pathologic nature. Pharmacologically, only the antagonism of dopamine-mediated transmission with neuroleptics has been therapeutic. Other pharmacologic approaches have so far resulted in negative outcomes. On the other hand, several pharmacologic strategies are psychotomimetic, including such drugs as amphetamine, lysergic acid diethylamide (LSD), mescaline, muscimol, and PCP/ketamine. Of these, PCP/ketamine is the drug class that most faithfully mimics schizophrenia in normal persons and most potently and validly exacerbates schizophrenia symptoms in affected patients even while inducing minimal primary drug symptoms. In addition, ketamine alters rCBF in cingulate cortex, hippocampus, and lingual gyrus, the first two areas being those previously related to schizophrenia using other functional imaging techniques. People with schizophrenia have pervasive, patterned, but interrelated cognitive dysfunction, suggesting a failure of an interactive connective function. Schizophrenic subjects, even when they are performing a task equivalent to healthy control subjects, utilize similar brain areas but activate them prematurely and not in relationship to difficulty, as is the case in nonschizophrenic individuals. The anterior cingulate cortex especially demonstrates these differences. Moreover, whereas limbic areas might be broadly affected in all or most schizophrenic subjects, the frontal cortex and other neocortical areas seem to be associated with other discrete manifestations of illness, such as negative symptoms or deficit syndrome. Evidence of consistent, highly replicable biochemical change in the brain in schizophrenia has yet evaded the study of this illness. This does not mean that these parameters should not be studied, but it might suggest that only a composite biochemical change will give a clue (see, for example, Issa et al. 1994a and 1994b) or that an entirely new (perhaps functional) approach is needed.

## Pitfalls and Confounds in Schizophrenia Studies

Schizophrenia is a difficult disease to study biologically for methodological as well as theoretical reasons. The brain is a highly protected organ whose tissue or integrated function cannot easily be sampled in vivo, even in illness. Schizophrenic individuals themselves often have compromised cognitive ability, and they may not be able to collaborate fully with a demanding research study. The long-term use of neuroleptic drugs is almost ubiquitous in schizophrenia and regularly confounds biological study. This long-term treatment alters much of the brain neurochemistry, as well as aspects of its structure, portions of its function, and probably more. Neuroleptic withdrawal for biological study is difficult, because it frequently results in symptom reemergence. Symptom diversity is a hallmark of the illness, as is symptom fluctuation over time and within single individuals. Moreover, this diversity and fluctuation is most often masked by neuroleptic treatment in what we would have to assume is a complex manner.

Although they are difficult to manage for experimental designs, these issues can be worked with through careful clinical, pharmacologic, and imaging assessment. Certainly these areas are always important parameters to assess in evaluating study results.

## Toward a Pathophysiology of Schizophrenia

Studies of schizophrenia proceed on many fronts. Investigators use information from patients, family members, birth records, life histories, in vivo imaging, postmortem tissue, and phenomenologic presentation to formulate hypotheses. Research techniques with high sensitivity and resolution are now becoming available. Moreover, the techniques are broad, utilizing molecular and functional probes as well as traditional measures. Therapeutics is expanding, and new information in this area may inform our ideas of pathophysiology and/or etiology. So although the exact nature of schizophrenia is now unknown, it is not likely to remain unknown for much longer.

## References

Abi-Dargham A, Gil R, Krystal J, et al: Increased striatal dopamine transmission in schizophrenia: confirmation in a second cohort. Am J Psychiatry 155:761–767, 1998

Akbarian S, Bunney WE, Potkin SG, et al: Altered distribution of nicotinamide-adenine dinucleotide phosphate-diaphorase cells in frontal lobe of schizophrenics implies disturbances of cortical development. Arch Gen Psychiatry 50:169–177, 1993

Akbarian S, Kim JJ, Potkin SG, et al: Gene expression for glutamic acid decarboxylase is reduced without loss of neurons in prefrontal cortex of schizophrenics. Arch Gen Psychiatry 52:258–266, 1995

Alexander GE, Crutcher MD: Functional architecture of basal ganglia circuits: neural substrates of parallel processing. Trends Neurosci 13(7):266–271, 1990

Alexander GE, DeLong MR, Strick PL: Parallel organization of functionally segregated circuits linking basal ganglia and cortex. Annu Rev Neurosci 9:357–381, 1986

Altshuler LL, Conrad A, Kovelman JA, et al: Hippocampal pyramidal cell orientation in schizophrenia. Arch Gen Psychiatry 44:1094–1098, 1987

American Psychiatric Association: Diagnostic and Statistical Manual of Mental Disorders, 4th Edition, Text Revision. Washington, DC, American Psychiatric Association, 2000

Andreasen NC: Symptoms, signs, and diagnosis of schizophrenia. Lancet 346:477–481, 1995

Andreasen NC, Rezai K, Alliger R, et al: Hypofrontality in neuroleptic-naive patients and in patients with chronic schizophrenia. Arch Gen Psychiatry 49:943–958, 1992

Andreasen NC, Arndt S, Swayze V II, et al: Thalamic abnormalities in schizophrenia visualized through magnetic resonance image averaging. Science 266:294–298, 1994

Andreasen NC, Arndt S, Alliger R, et al: Symptoms of schizophrenia. Methods, meanings, and mechanisms. Arch Gen Psychiatry 52:341–351, 1995

Anis NA, Berry SC, Burton NR, et al: The dissociative anesthetics ketamine and phencyclidine selectively reduce excitation of central mammalian neurons by N-methyl-aspartate. Br J Pharmacol 79:5654–5675, 1983

Aoki C, Siekevitz P: Plasticity in brain development. Sci Am 259(6):56–64, 1988

Arndt S, Alliger RJ, Andreasen NC: The distinction of positive and negative symptoms: the failure of a two-dimensional model. Br J Psychiatry 158:317–322, 1991

Arnold SE, Hyman BT, Van Hoesen GW, et al: Some cytoarchitectural abnormalities of the entorhinal cortex in schizophrenia. Arch Gen Psychiatry 48:625–632, 1991a

Arnold SE, Lee VM-Y, Gur RE, et al: Abnormal expression of two microtubule-associated proteins (MAP2 and MAP5) in specific subfields of the hippocampal formation in schizophrenia. Proc Natl Acad Sci U S A 88:10850–10854, 1991b

Arolt V, Lencer R, Nolte A, et al: Eye tracking dysfunction in families with multiple cases of schizophrenia. Eur Arch Psychiatry Clin Neurosci 246(4):175–181, 1996a

Arolt V, Lencer R, Nolte A, et al: Eye tracking dysfunction is a putative phenotypic susceptibility marker of schizophrenia and maps to a locus on chromosome 6p in families with multiple occurrence of the disease. Am J Med Genet 67(6):564–579, 1996b

Artiges E, Salame P, Recasens C, et al: Working memory control in patients with schizophrenia: a PET study during a random number generation task. Am J Psychiatry 157:1517–1519, 2000

Asarnow RF, Granholm E, Sherman T: Span of Apprehension in schizophrenia, in Handbook of Schizophrenia, Vol 5: Neuropsychology, Psychophysiology and Information Processing. Edited by Steinhauer SR, Gruzelier JH, Zubin J. Amsterdam, Elsevier, 1991, pp 335–370

Assad JA, Maunsell JH: Neuronal correlates of inferred motion in primate posterior parietal cortex. Nature 373:518–521, 1995

Bacopoulos NG, Spokes EG, Bird ED, et al: Antipsychotic drug action in schizophrenic patients: effect on cortical dopamine metabolism after long-term treatment. Science 205:1405–1407, 1979

Balogh DW, Merritt RD: Susceptibility to type A backward pattern masking among hypothetically psychosis-prone college students. J Abnorm Psychol 94(3):377–383, 1985

Barnes GR, Asselman PT: The mechanism of prediction in human smooth pursuit eye movements. J Physiol (Lond) 439:439–461, 1991

Barnes TR, Liddle PF: Evidence for the validity of negative symptoms. Mod Probl Pharmacopsychiatry 24:43–72, 1990

Barr CE, Mednick SA, Munk-Jorgensen P: Exposure to influenza during gestation and adult schizophrenia. Arch Gen Psychiatry 47:869–874, 1990

Barta PE, Pearlson GD, Powers RE, et al: Auditory hallucinations and smaller superior temporal gyral volume in schizophrenia. Am J Psychiatry 146:1457–1462, 1990

Beckmann H, Waldmeier P, Lauber J, et al: Phenylethylamine and monoamine metabolites in CSF of schizophrenics: effects of neuroleptic treatment. J Neural Transm 57:103–110, 1983

Benes FM: Myelination of cortical-hippocampal relays during late adolescence. Schizophr Bull 15(4):585–593, 1989

Benes FM: Neurobiological investigations in cingulate cortex of schizophrenic brain. Schizophr Bull 19(3):537–549, 1993

Benes FM, Vincent SL, Alsterberg G, et al: Increased GABA$_A$-receptor binding in superficial layers of cingulate cortex in schizophrenics. J Neurosci 12:924–929, 1992

Berman RA, Colby CL, Genovese CR, et al: Cortical networks subserving pursuit and saccadic eye movements in humans: an fMRI study. Hum Brain Mapp 8:209–225, 1999

Bjerkenstedt I, Edman G, Hagenfeldt I, et al: Plasma amino acids in relation to cerebrospinal fluid monoamine metabolites in schizophrenic patients and healthy controls. Br J Psychiatry 147:276–282, 1985

Blackwood DH, St Clair DM, Muir WJ, et al: Auditory P300 and eye tracking dysfunction in schizophrenic pedigrees. Arch Gen Psychiatry 48(10):899–909, 1991

Bleuler M: The Schizophrenic Disorders: Long-Term Patient and Family Studies. Translated by Clemens SM. New Haven, CT, Yale University Press, 1978

Bogerts B: Recent advances in the neuropathology of schizophrenia. Schizophr Bull 19(2):431–445, 1993

Bogerts B, Ashtari M, Degreef G, et al: Reduced temporal limbic structure volumes on magnetic resonance images in first episode schizophrenia. Psychiatry Res 35:1–13, 1990

Bowers MB Jr, Heninger GR, Gerbode FA: Cerebrospinal fluid, 5-hydroxyindoleacetic acid and homovanillic acid in psychiatric patients. International Journal of Neuropharmacology 8:255–262, 1969

Bowers MB Jr, Swigar ME, Jatlow PI, et al: Plasma catecholamine metabolites and early response to haloperidol. J Clin Psychiatry 45:248–251, 1984

Bradbury TN, Miller GA: Season of birth in schizophrenia: a review of evidence, methodology, and etiology. Psychological Bulletin 98:569–594, 1985

Braff DL: Impaired speed of information processing in nonmedicated schizotypal patients. Schizophr Bull 7(3):499–508, 1981

Braff DL: Information processing and attention dysfunctions in schizophrenia. Schizophr Bull 19(2):233–259, 1993

Braff DL, Heaton R, Kuck J, et al: The generalized pattern of neuropsychological deficits in outpatients with chronic schizophrenia with heterogeneous Wisconsin Card Sorting Test results. Arch Gen Psychiatry 48:891–898, 1991

Braus DF, Ende G, Weber-Fahr W, et al: Antipsychotic drug effects on motor activation measured by functional magnetic resonance imaging in schizophrenic patients. Schizophr Res 39:19–29, 1999

Breier A, Buchanan RW, Elkashef A, et al: Brain morphology and schizophrenia: a magnetic resonance imaging study of limbic, prefrontal cortex, and caudate structures. Arch Gen Psychiatry 49:921–926, 1992

Buchsbaum MS, Ingvar DH, Kessler R, et al: Cerebral glucography with positron tomography. Arch Gen Psychiatry 39:251–259, 1982

Buchsbaum MS, DeLisi LE, Holcomb HH, et al: Anteroposterior gradients in cerebral glucose use in schizophrenia and affective disorders. Arch Gen Psychiatry 41:1159–1166, 1984

Buckley PF, Friedman L, Wu D, et al: Functional magnetic resonance imaging in schizophrenia: initial methodology and evaluation of the motor cortex. Psychiatry Res 74:13–23, 1997

Callicott JH, Ramsey NF, Tallent K, et al: Functional magnetic resonance imaging brain mapping in psychiatry: methodological issues illustrated in a study of working memory in schizophrenia. Neuropsychopharmacology 18:186–196, 1998

Callicott JH, Mattay VS, Bertolino A, et al: Physiological characteristics of capacity constraints in working memory as revealed by functional MRI. Cereb Cortex 9:20–26, 1999

Cannon TD, Mednick SA, Parnas J, et al: Developmental brain abnormalities in the offspring of schizophrenic mothers, II: structural brain characteristics of schizophrenia and schizotypal personality disorder. Arch Gen Psychiatry 51(12): 955–962, 1994

Carlsson A, Lindquist M: Effect of chlorpromazine and haloperidol on formation of 3-methoxytyramine and normetanephrine in mouse brain. Acta Pharmacol Toxicol 20:140–144, 1963

Carlsson M, Carlsson A: Interactions between glutamatergic and monoaminergic systems within the basal ganglia—implications for schizophrenia and Parkinson's disease. Trends Neurosci 13(7):272–276, 1990

Carpenter WT Jr, Buchanan RW: Domains of psychopathology relevant to the study of etiology and treatment in schizophrenia, in Schizophrenia: Scientific Progress. Edited by Schulz SC, Tamminga CA. New York, Oxford University Press, 1989, pp. 13–22

Carpenter WT Jr, Buchanan RW: Schizophrenia. N Engl J Med 330:681–690, 1994

Carpenter WT Jr, Buchanan RW: Schizophrenia: introduction and overview, in Comprehensive Textbook of Psychiatry/VI. Edited by Kaplan HI, Sadock BJ. Baltimore, MD, Williams & Wilkins, 1995, pp 889–942

Carpenter WT Jr, Buchanan RW, Kirkpatrick B, et al: Strong inference, theory testing and the neuroanatomy of schizophrenia. Arch Gen Psychiatry 50:825–831, 1993

Chakos MH, Lieberman JA, Bilder RM, et al: Increase in caudate nuclei volumes of first-episode schizophrenic patients taking antipsychotic drugs. Am J Psychiatry 151:1430–1436, 1994

Chapman LJ, Chapman JP: Problems in the measurement of cognitive deficit. Psychol Bull 79(6):380–385, 1973

Chen Y, Nakayama K, Levy DL, et al: Psychophysical isolation of a motion-processing deficit in schizophrenics and their relatives and its association with impaired smooth pursuit. Proc Natl Acad Sci U S A 96(8):4724–4729, 1999

Ciompi L, Müller C: Lebensweg und alter der schizophrenen. Eine katamnestische lonzeitstudies bis ins senium. Berlin, Springer-Verlag, 1976

Cleghorn JM, Kaplan RD, Nahmias C, et al: Inferior parietal region implicated in neurocognitive impairment in schizophrenia. Arch Gen Psychiatry 46:758–760, 1989

Clementz BA, Sweeney JA: Is eye movement dysfunction a biological marker for schizophrenia? A methodological review. Psychological Bulletin 108(1):77–92, 1990

Clementz BA, Sweeney JA, Hirt M, et al: Pursuit gain and saccadic intrusions in first-degree relatives of probands with schizophrenia. J Abnorm Psychol 99(4):327–335, 1990

Clementz BA, McDowell JE, Zisook S: Saccadic system functioning among schizophrenia patients and their first-degree biological relatives. J Abnorm Psychol 103(2):277–287, 1994

Clow A, Theodorou A, Jenner P, et al: Changes in cerebral dopamine function induced by a year's administration of trifluoperazine or thioridazine and their subsequent withdrawal. Advances in Biochemical Psychopharmacology 24:335–340, 1980

Cohen JD, Servan-Schreiber D: Context, cortex, and dopamine: a connectionist approach to behavior and biology in schizophrenia. Psychol Rev 99(1):45–77, 1992

Colter N, Battal S, Crow TJ: White matter reduction in the parahippocampal gyrus of patients with schizophrenia. Arch Gen Psychiatry 44:1023–1026, 1987

Condray R, Steinhauer SR, Goldstein G: Language comprehension in schizophrenics and their brothers. Biol Psychiatry 32:790–802, 1992

Condray R, Steinhauer SR, van Kammen DP, et al: Working memory capacity predicts language comprehension in schizophrenic patients. Schizophr Res 20:1–13, 1996

Cornblatt BA, Winters L, Erlenmeyer-Kimling L: Attentional markers of schizophrenia: evidence from the New York high-risk study, in Schizophrenia: Scientific Progress. Edited by Schulz S, Tamminga C. New York, Oxford University Press, 1989, pp 83–92

Crawford TJ, Sharma T, Puri BK, et al: Saccadic eye movements in families multiply affected with schizophrenia: the Maudsley Family Study. Am J Psychiatry 155(12):1703–1710, 1998

Cross AJ, Crow TJ, Owen F: 3H-Flupenthixol binding in post-mortem brains of schizophrenics: evidence for a selective increase in dopamine D2 receptors. Psychopharmacology 74:122–124, 1981

Csernansky JG, Joshi S, Wang L, et al: Hippocampal morphometry in schizophrenia by high dimensional brain mapping. Proc Natl Acad Sci U S A 95(19):11406–11411, 1998

Davidson M, Davis KL: A comparison of plasma homovanillic acid concentrations in schizophrenics and normal controls. Arch Gen Psychiatry 45:561–563, 1988

Deakin JF, Slater P, Simpson M, et al: Frontal cortical and left temporal glutamatergic dysfunction in schizophrenia. J Neurochem 52:1781–1786, 1989

Delnay J, Deniker P: Le traitement des psychoses par une méthode neurolytique dérivée de l'hibernotherapie, in Congrès des Médecins Aliénistes et Neurologistes de France. Luxembourg, 1952, pp 497–502

DeLong MR: Primate models of movement disorders of basal ganglia origin. Trends Neurosci 13(7):281–285, 1990

Deutsch SI, Mastropaolo J, Schwartz B, et al: A "glutamatergic hypothesis" of schizophrenia. Rationale for pharmacotherapy with glycine. Clin Neuropharmacol 12:1–13, 1989

Dolan RJ, Fletcher P, Frith CD, et al: Dopaminergic modulation of impaired cognitive activation in the anterior cingulate cortex in schizophrenia. Nature 378:180–182, 1995

Domino EF, Luby E: Abnormal mental states induced by phencyclidine as a model of schizophrenia, in PCP (Phencyclidine): Historical and Current Perspectives. Edited by Domino EF. Ann Arbor, MI, NPP Books, 1981, pp 123–128

Elkashef AM, Issa F, Wyatt RJ: The biochemical basis of schizophrenia, in Contemporary Issues in the Treatment of Schizophrenia. Edited by Shriqui CL, Nasrallah HA. Washington, DC, American Psychiatric Press, 1995, pp 3–41

Elsworth JD, Leahy DJ, Roth RH, et al: Homovanillic acid concentrations in brain, CSF and plasma as indicators of central dopamine function in primates. J Neural Transm 68:51–62, 1987

Falkai P, Bogerts B: Cell loss in the hippocampus of schizophrenics. European Archives of Psychiatry and Neurological Sciences 236:154–161, 1986

Faraone SV, Seidman LJ, Kremen WS, et al: Neuropsychological functioning among the nonpsychotic relatives of schizophrenic patients: a diagnostic efficiency analysis. J Abnorm Psychol 104:286–304, 1995

Faraone SV, Seidman LJ, Kremen WS, et al: Neuropsychologic functioning among the nonpsychotic relatives of schizophrenic patients: the effect of genetic loading. Biol Psychiatry 48(2):120–126, 2000

Farde L, Wiesel F-A, Hall H, et al: D2 dopamine receptors in neuroleptic-naive schizophrenic patients: a positron emission tomography study with [11C]raclopride. Arch Gen Psychiatry 47:213–219, 1990

Freedman R, Adler LE, Gerhardt GA, et al: Neurobiological studies of sensory gating in schizophrenia. Schizophr Bull 13(4):669–678, 1987

Freedman R, Coon H, Myles-Worsley M, et al: Linkage of a neurophysiological deficit in schizophrenia to a chromosome 15 locus. Proc Natl Acad Sci U S A 94(2):587–592, 1997

Freedman R, Adler LE, Leonard S: Alternative phenotypes for the complex genetics of schizophrenia. Biol Psychiatry 45:551–558, 1999

Friston KJ, Frith CD, Liddle PF, et al: Comparing functional (PET) images: the assessment of significant change. J Cereb Blood Flow Metab 11(4):690–699, 1991

Frith C: Functional imaging and cognitive abnormalities. Lancet 346:615–620, 1995

Frith CD, Friston KJ, Herold S, et al: Regional brain activity in chronic schizophrenic patients during the performance of a verbal fluency task. Br J Psychiatry 167:343–349, 1995

Fukushima J, Fukushima K., Chiba T, et al: Disturbances of voluntary control of saccadic eye movements in schizophrenic patients. Biol Psychiatry 23(7):670–677, 1988

Gao X-M, Sakai K, Roberts RC, et al: Ionotropic glutamate receptors and expression of N-methyl-D-aspartate receptor subunits in subregions of human hippocampus: effects of schizophrenia. Am J Psychiatry 157:1141–1149, 2000

Gattaz WF, Gasser T, Beckmann H: Multidimensional analysis of the concentrations of 17 substances in the CSF of schizophrenics and controls. Biol Psychiatry 20:360–366, 1985

Gold J, Goldberg T, Weinberger D: Prefrontal function and schizophrenic symptoms. Neuropsychiatry Neuropsychol Behav Neurol 5:253–261, 1992

Gold JM, Hermann BP, Randolph C, et al: Schizophrenia and temporal lobe epilepsy. A neuropsychological analysis. Arch Gen Psychiatry 51:265–272, 1994

Goldberg TE, Weinberger DR, Berman KF, et al: Further evidence for dementia of the prefrontal type in schizophrenia? A controlled study of teaching the Wisconsin Card Sorting Test. Arch Gen Psychiatry 44:1008–1014, 1987

Goldberg TE, Ragland D, Torrey EF, et al: Neuropsychological assessment of monozygotic twins discordant for schizophrenia. Arch Gen Psychiatry 47:1066–1072, 1990

Goldman-Rakic PS: Working memory dysfunction in schizophrenia. J Neuropsychiatry Clin Neurosci 6:348–357, 1994

Goldman-Rakic PS: Psychopathology and neuropathology of prefrontal cortex in schizophrenia, in Schizophrenia: An Integrated View. Alfred Benzon Symposium 38. Edited by Fog R, Gerlach J, Hemmingsen R. Copenhagen, Denmark, Munksgaard, 1995, pp 126–138

Goldman-Rakic PS, Isseroff A, Schwartz ML, et al: The neurobiology of cognitive development, in Handbook of Child Psychology: Biology and Infancy Development. Edited by Mussen P. New York, Wiley, 1983, pp 281–344

Gottesman II, Shields J: Schizophrenia: The Epigenetic Puzzle. New York, Cambridge University Press, 1982

Grace AA: Phasic versus tonic dopamine release and the modulation of dopamine system responsivity: a hypothesis for the etiology of schizophrenia. Neuroscience 41(1):1–24, 1991

Graybiel AM: Neurotransmitters and neuromodulators in the basal ganglia. Trends Neurosci 13(7):244–254, 1990

Green MF, Nuechterlein KH, Breitmeyer B: Backward masking performance in unaffected siblings of schizophrenic patients. Evidence for a vulnerability indicator. Arch Gen Psychiatry 54:465–472, 1997

Gruzelier J, Seymour K, Wilson L: Impairments on neuropsychotic tests of temporohippocampal and frontohippocampal functions and word fluency in remitting schizophrenia and affective disorders. Arch Gen Psychiatry 45:623–629, 1988

Gur RC, Saykin AJ, Gur RE: Neuropsychological study of schizophrenia. Schizophr Res 1:153–162, 1991

Gur RE, Pearlson GD: Neuroimaging in schizophrenia research. Schizophr Bull 19(2):337–353, 1993

Gur RE, Resnick SM, Alavi A, et al: Regional brain function in schizophrenia. Arch Gen Psychiatry 44:119–125, 1987

Harding CM, Brooks GW, Takamaru A, et al: The Vermont longitudinal study of persons with severe mental illness, I: methodology, study sample, and overall status 32 years later. Am J Psychiatry 144:718–726, 1987a

Harding CM, Brooks GW, Takamaru A, et al: The Vermont longitudinal study of persons with severe mental illness, II: long-term outcome of subjects who retrospectively met DSM-III criteria for schizophrenia. Am J Psychiatry 144 (6):727–735, 1987b

Harrison PJ: The neuropathology of schizophrenia. A critical review of the data and their interpretation. Brain 122:593–624, 1999

Harrison PJ, McLaughlin D, Kerwin RW: Decreased hippocampal expression of a glutamate receptor gene in schizophrenia. Lancet 337:450–452, 1991

Heckers S, Heinsen H, Heinsen YC, et al: Cortex, white matter, and basal ganglia in schizophrenia: a volumetric postmortem study. Biol Psychiatry 29:556–566, 1991

Heckers S, Rauch SL, Goff D, et al: Impaired recruitment of the hippocampus during conscious recollection in schizophrenia. Nat Neurosci 1:318–323, 1998

Hietala J, Syvälahti E, Vuorio K: Striatal dopamine D2 receptor density in neuroleptic-naive schizophrenics studied with positron emission tomography, in Biological Psychiatry, Vol 2. Edited by Racagni G, Brunello N, Fukuda T. Amsterdam, The Netherlands, Excerpta Medica, 1991, pp 386–387

Hietala J, Syvälahti E, Vuorio K, et al: Striatal D2 dopamine receptor characteristics in neuroleptic-naive schizophrenic patients studied with positron emission tomography. Arch Gen Psychiatry 51:116–123, 1994

Holcomb HH, Links J, Smith C, et al: Positron emission tomography: measuring the metabolic and neurochemical characteristics of the living human nervous system, in Brain Imaging Applications in Psychiatry. Edited by Andreasen NC.

Washington, DC, American Psychiatric Press, 1989, pp 235–370

Holcomb HH, Cascella NG, Thaker GK, et al: Functional sites of neuroleptic drug action in human brain: PET/FDG studies with and without haloperidol. Am J Psychiatry 153:41–49, 1996a

Holcomb HH, Gordon B, Loats HL, et al: Brain metabolism patterns are sensitive to attentional effort associated with a tone recognition task. Biol Psychiatry 39:1013–1022, 1996b

Holcomb HH, Lahti AC, Medoff DR, et al: Brain activation patterns in schizophrenic and comparison volunteers during a matched-performance auditory recognition task. Am J Psychiatry 157:1634–1645, 2000

Holzman PS: Recent studies of psychophysiology in schizophrenia. Schizophr Bull 13:49–75, 1987

Holzman PS, Solomon CM, Levin S, et al: Pursuit eye movement dysfunctions in schizophrenia. Family evidence for specificity. Arch Gen Psychiatry 41:136–139, 1984

Huber G, Gross G, Schüttler R: Schizophrenie: Verlaufs und socialpsychiatrische langzeit unter suchungen an den 1945 bis 1959 in Bonn hospitalisierten schizophrenen Kranken: Monographien aus dem Gesamtgebiete der Psychiatrie, Bd 21. Berlin, Springer-Verlag, 1979

Ingvar DH, Franzen G: Abnormalities of cerebral blood flow distribution in patients with chronic schizophrenia. Acta Psychiatr Scand 50:425–462, 1971

Issa F, Gerhardt GA, Bartko JJ, et al: A multidimensional approach to analysis of cerebrospinal fluid biogenic amines in schizophrenia, I: comparisons with healthy control subjects and neuroleptic-treated/unmedicated pairs analyses. Psychiatry Res 52:237–249, 1994a

Issa F, Kirch DG, Gerhardt GA, et al: A multidimensional approach to analysis of cerebrospinal fluid biogenic amines in schizophrenia, II: correlations with psychopathology. Psychiatry Res 52:251–258, 1994b

Jakob H, Beckmann H: Prenatal development disturbances in the limbic allocortex in schizophrenics. J Neural Transm 65:303–326, 1986

Jaskew G, Kleinman J: Postmortem neurochemistry studies in schizophrenia, in Schizophrenia: Scientific Progress. Edited by Schulz SC, Tamminga CA. New York, Oxford University Press, 1989, pp 264–273

Javitt DC, Zukin SR: Recent advances in the phencyclidine model of schizophrenia. Am J Psychiatry 148 (10):1301–1308, 1991

Javitt DC, Doneshka P, Grochowski S, et al: Impaired mismatch negativity generation reflects widespread dysfunction of working memory in schizophrenia. Arch Gen Psychiatry 52(7):550–558, 1995

Jennings JM, McIntosh AR, Kapur S, et al: Functional network differences in schizophrenia: a rCBF study of semantic processing. Neuroreport 9:1697–1700, 1998

Jeste DV, Lohr JB: Hippocampal pathologic findings in schizophrenia. Arch Gen Psychiatry 46:1019–1026, 1989

Johnstone EC, Crow TJ, Frith DC, et al: Cerebral ventricular size and cognitive impairment in schizophrenia. Lancet 2:924–926, 1976

Kadekaro M, Vance WH, Terrell ML, et al: Effects of antidromic stimulation of the ventral root on glucose utilization in the ventral horn of the spinal cord in the rat. Proc Natl Acad Sci U S A 84:5492–5495, 1987

Kane JM, Honigfeld G, Singer J, et al, and the Clozapine Study Group: Clozapine for the treatment-resistant schizophrenic: a double-blind comparison with chlorpromazine. Arch Gen Psychiatry 45:789–796, 1988

Karlsson P, Farde L, Halldin C, et al: D1 dopamine receptor binding in drug naive schizophrenic patients measured by PET (abstract). J Cereb Blood Flow Metab 13 (suppl 1): S556, 1993

Katsanis J, Kortenkamp S, Iacono WG, et al: Antisaccade performance in patients with schizophrenia and affective disorder. J Abnorm Psychol 106(3):468–472, 1997

Kay SR, Sevy S: Pyramidical model of schizophrenia. Schizophr Bull 16:537–545, 1990

Keefe RS, Silverman JM, Mohs RC, et al: Eye tracking, attention, and schizotypal symptoms in nonpsychotic relatives of patients with schizophrenia. Arch Gen Psychiatry 54(2):169–176, 1997

Kendell RE, Kemp IW: Maternal influence in the etiology of schizophrenia. Arch Gen Psychiatry 46:878–882, 1989

Kendler KS, Diehl SR: The genetics of schizophrenia: a current genetic-epidemiologic perspective. Schizophr Bull 192: 261–279, 1993

Kendler KS, Diehl SR: Schizophrenia: genetics, in Comprehensive Textbook of Psychiatry/VI. Edited by Kaplan HI, Sadock BJ. Baltimore, MD, Williams & Wilkins, 1995, pp 942–957

Kerwin R, Patel S, Meldrum B: Quantitative autoradiographic analysis of glutamate binding sites in the hippocampal formation in normal and schizophrenic brain post mortem. Neuroscience 39:25–32, 1990

Kety SS: The significance of genetic factors in the etiology of schizophrenia: results from the national study of adoptees in Denmark. J Psychiatr Res 21:423–429, 1987

Kim JS, Kornhuber HH, Schmid-Burgk W, et al: Low cerebrospinal fluid glutamate in schizophrenic patients and a new hypothesis on schizophrenia. Neurosci Lett 20:379–382, 1980

Klein DF, Davis JM: Diagnosis and Drug Treatment of Psychiatric Disorders. Baltimore, MD, Williams & Wilkins, 1969

Kornhuber J, Mack-Burkhardt F, Riederer P, et al: [3H]MK-801 binding sites in postmortem brain regions of schizophrenic patients. J Neural Transm 77:231–236, 1989

Korpi ER, Kaufmann CA, Marnela KM, et al: Cerebrospinal fluid amino acid concentrations in chronic schizophrenia. Psychiatry Res 20:337–345, 1987

Lahti AC, Holcomb HH, Medoff DR, et al: Ketamine activates psychosis and alters limbic blood flow in schizophrenia. Neuroreport 6(6):869–872, 1995a

Lahti AC, Koffel B, LaPorte D, et al: Subanesthetic doses of ketamine stimulate psychosis in schizophrenia. Neuropsychopharmacology 13:9–19, 1995b

Lahti RA, Lahti AC, Tamminga CA: D2-family receptors in schizophrenia: distribution and implications for treatment. Clin Neuropharmacol 18(1):S110–S120, 1995a

Lahti RA, Roberts RC, Tamminga CA: D2-family receptor distribution in human postmortem tissue: an autoradiographic study. Neuroreport 6:2505–2512, 1995b

Lake CR, Sternberg DE, van Kammen DP, et al: Schizophrenia: elevated cerebrospinal fluid norepinephrine. Science 207:331–333, 1980

Laruelle M, Abi-Dargham A, van Dyck CH, et al: Single photon emission computerized tomography imaging of amphetamine-induced dopamine release in drug-free schizophrenic subjects. Proc Natl Acad Sci U S A 93:9235–9240, 1996

Laruelle M, Abi-Dargham A, Gil R, et al: Increased dopamine transmission in schizophrenia: relationship to illness phases. Biol Psychiatry 46:56–72, 1999

Lenzenweger MF, Dworkin RH, Wethington E: Examining the underlying structure of schizophrenic phenomenology: evidence for a three-process model. Schizophr Bull 17:515–524, 1991

Lesch A, Bogerts B: The diencephalon in schizophrenia: evidence for reduced thickness of the periventricular grey matter. European Archives of Psychiatry and Neurological Sciences 234:212–219, 1984

Lewis DA: GABAergic local circuit neurons and prefrontal cortical dysfunction in schizophrenia. Brain Res 31:270–276, 2000

Lewis SW, Murray RM: Obstetrical complications, neurodevelopmental deviance, and risk of schizophrenia. J Psychiatr Res 21:413–421, 1987

Liddle PF: The symptoms of chronic schizophrenia: a re-examination of the positive-negative dichotomy. Br J Psychiatry 151:145–151, 1987

Liddle PF, Morris DL: Schizophrenic syndromes and frontal lobe performance. Br J Psychiatry 158:340–345, 1991

Liddle PF, Friston KJ, Frith CD, et al: Patterns of cerebral blood flow in schizophrenia. Br J Psychiatry 160:179–186, 1992

Lidow MS, Goldman-Rakic PS: A common action of clozapine, haloperidol and remoxipride on D1- and D2-dopaminergic receptors in the primate cerebral cortex. Proc Natl Acad Sci U S A 91:4353–4356, 1994

Lindström LH: Low HVA and normal 5-HIAA CSF levels in drug-free schizophrenic patients compared to healthy volunteers: correlations to symptomatology and family history. Psychiatry Res 14:265–273, 1985

Lisberger SG, Morris EJ, Tychsen L: Visual motion processing and sensory-motor integration for smooth pursuit eye movements. Annu Rev Neurosci 10:97–129, 1987

Luby ED, Cohen BD, Rosenbaum G, et al: Study of a new schizophrenomimetic drug—Sernyl. Arch Gen Psychiatry 81:363–369, 1959

Macciardi F, Lucca A, Catalano M, et al: Amino acid patterns in schizophrenia: some new findings. Psychiatry Res 32:63–70, 1990

Mackay AVP, Iversen LL, Rossor M, et al: Increased brain dopamine and dopamine receptors in schizophrenia. Arch Gen Psychiatry 39:991–997, 1982

Manoach DS, Press DZ, Thangaraj V, et al: Schizophrenic subjects activate dorsolateral prefrontal cortex during a working memory task, as measured by fMRI. Biol Psychiatry 45:1128–1137, 1999

Manoach DS, Gollub RL, Benson ES, et al: Schizophrenic subjects show aberrant fMRI activation of dorsolateral prefrontal cortex and basal ganglia during working memory performance. Biol Psychiatry 48:99–109, 2000

Martinot JL, Peron-Magnan P, Huret JD, et al: Striatal D2 dopaminergic receptors assessed with positron emission tomography and [76Br]bromospiperone in untreated schizophrenic patients. Am J Psychiatry 147:44–50, 1990

Martinot JL, Paillère-Martinot ML, Loch C, et al: The estimated density of D2 striatal receptors in schizophrenia: a study with positron emission tomography and 76Br-bromolisuride. Br J Psychiatry 158:346–350, 1991

Mattay VS, Callicott JH, Bertolino A, et al: Abnormal functional lateralization of the sensorimotor cortex in patients with schizophrenia. Neuroreport 8:2977–2984, 1997

McCarley RW, Shenton ME, O'Donnell, et al: Auditory P300 abnormalities and left posterior superior temporal gyrus volume reduction in schizophrenia. Arch Gen Psychiatry 50:190–197, 1993

McDowell JE, Myles-Worsley M, Coon H, et al: Measuring liability for schizophrenia using optimized antisaccade stimulus parameters. Psychophysiology 36(1):138–141, 1999

McGrath J, Murray RM: Risk factors for schizophrenia: from conception to birth, in Schizophrenia. Edited by Hirsch SR, Weinberger DR. Oxford, UK, Blackwell Science, 1995, pp 187–205

Mednick SA, Cannon TD: Fetal development, birth and the syndromes of adult schizophrenia, in Fetal Neural Development and Adult Schizophrenia. Edited by Mednick SA, Cannon TD, Barr CE, et al. New York, Cambridge University Press, 1991, pp 29–33

Memo M, Kleinman JE, Hanbauer I: Coupling of dopamine D1 recognition sites with adenylate cyclase in nuclei accumbens and caudatus of schizophrenics. Science 221:1304–1307, 1983

Menon RR, Barta PE, Aylward EH, et al: Posterior superior temporal gyrus in schizophrenia: grey matter changes and clinical correlates. Schizophr Res 16:127–135, 1995

Merzenich MM, Recanzone G, Jenkins WM, et al: Cortical representational plasticity, in Neurobiology of Neocortex. Edited by Rakic P, Winger W. New York, Wiley, 1988, pp 41–67

Nauta WJH: Reciprocal links of the corpus striatum with the cerebral cortex and limbic system: a common substrate for movement and thought?, in Neurology and Psychiatry: A Meeting of Minds. Edited by Mueller J. Basel, Karger, 1989, pp 43–63

Nemeroff CB, Youngblood W, Manberg PJ, et al: Regional brain concentrations of neuropeptides in Huntington's chorea and schizophrenia. Science 221:972–975, 1983

Newsome WT, Wurtz RH, Komatsu H: Relation of cortical areas MT and MST to pursuit eye movements, II: differentiation of retinal from extraretinal inputs. J Neurophysiol 60:604–620, 1988

Nishikawa T, Takashima M, Toru M: Increased [3H]kainic acid binding in the prefrontal cortex in schizophrenia. Neurosci Lett 40:245–250, 1983

Nuechterlein KH, Dawson ME, Gitlin M, et al: Developmental processes in schizophrenic disorders: longitudinal studies of vulnerability and stress. Schizophr Bull 18:387–425, 1992

O'Callaghan E, Sham P, Takei N, et al: Schizophrenia after prenatal exposure to 1957 A2 influenza epidemic. Lancet 337:1248–1250, 1991

O'Driscoll GA, Benkelfat C, Florencio PS, et al: Neural correlates of eye tracking deficits in first-degree relatives of schizophrenic patients: a positron emission tomography study. Arch Gen Psychiatry 56:1127–1134, 1999

Ogawa S, Lee TM, Kay AR, et al: Brain magnetic resonance imaging with contrast dependent on blood oxygenation. Proc Natl Acad Sci U S A 87:9868–9872, 1990

Ogawa S, Tank DW, Menon R, et al: Intrinsic signal changes accompanying sensory stimulation: functional brain mapping with magnetic resonance imaging. Proc Natl Acad Sci U S A 89:5951–5955, 1992

Olney JW, Farber NB: Glutamate receptor dysfunction in schizophrenia. Arch Gen Psychiatry 52:998–1007, 1995

Owen F, Cross AJ, Crow TJ: Increased dopamine-receptor sensitivity in schizophrenia. Lancet 2:223–226, 1978

Pakkenberg B: Postmortem study of chronic schizophrenic brains. Br J Psychiatry 151:744–752, 1987

Pakkenberg B: Pronounced reduction of total neuron number in mediodorsal thalamic nucleus and nucleus accumbens in schizophrenics. Arch Gen Psychiatry 47:1023–1028, 1990

Park S, Holzman PS: Schizophrenics show spatial working memory deficits. Arch Gen Psychiatry 49:975–982, 1992

Park S, Holzman PS, Goldman-Rakic PS: Spatial working memory deficits in the relatives of schizophrenic patients. Arch Gen Psychiatry 52:821–828, 1995

Pearlson GD, Marsh L: MRI in psychiatry, in American Psychiatric Press Review of Psychiatry, Vol 12. Edited by Oldham JM, Riba MB, Tasman A. Washington, DC, American Psychiatric Association, 1995

Pearlson GD, Wong DF, Tune LE, et al: In vivo D2 dopamine receptor density in psychotic and nonpsychotic patients with bipolar disorder. Arch Gen Psychiatry 52(6):471–477, 1995

Pfefferbaum A, Wenegrat BG, Ford JM, et al: Clinical application of the P3 component of event-related potentials, II:

dementia, depression and schizophrenia. Electroencephalogr Clin Neurophysiol 59(2):104–124, 1984

Pickar D, Labarca R, Doran AR: Longitudinal measurement of plasma homovanillic acid levels in schizophrenic patients. Arch Gen Psychiatry 43:669–676, 1986

Pogue-Geile MF, Garrett AH, Brunke JJ, et al: Neuropsychological impairments are increased in siblings of schizophrenic patients. Schizophr Res 4:390–395, 1991

Raichle ME: Images of the mind: studies with modern imaging techniques. Annu Rev Psychol 45:333–356, 1994

Reivich M, Kuhl D, Wolf A, et al: The [18F]fluorodeoxyglucose method for the measurement of local cerebral glucose utilization in man. Circ Res 44:127–137, 1979

Reynolds GP: Increased concentrations and lateral asymmetry of amygdala dopamine in schizophrenia. Nature 305:527–529, 1983

Reynolds GP, Mason SL: Absence of detectable striatal dopamine D4 receptors in drug-treated schizophrenia. Eur J Pharmacol 281:R5–R6, 1995

Roberts RC, Gaither LA, Gao X-M, et al: Ultrastructural correlates of haloperidol-induced oral dyskinesias in rat striatum. Synapse 20:234–243, 1995

Rosenthal R, Bigelow LB: Quantitative brain measurements in chronic schizophrenia. Br J Psychiatry 121:259–264, 1972

Ross DE, Thaker GK, Holcomb HH, et al: Abnormal smooth pursuit eye movements in schizophrenic patients are associated with cerebral glucose metabolism in oculomotor regions. Psychiatry Res 58:53–67, 1995

Roxborough H, Muir WJ, Blackwood DH, et al: Neuropsychological and P300 abnormalities in schizophrenics and their relatives. Psychol Med 23:305–314, 1993

Sartorius N: The International Pilot Study of Schizophrenia. Schizophr Bull (Winter):21–34, 1974

Saykin AJ, Gur RC, Gur RE, et al: Neuropsychological function in schizophrenia. Selective impairment in memory and learning. Arch Gen Psychiatry 48:618–624, 1991

Scheibel AB, Kovelman JA: Disorientation of the hippocampal pyramidal cell and its processes in schizophrenia patients. Biol Psychiatry 16:101–102, 1981

Schroder J, Essig M, Baudendistel K, et al: Motor dysfunction and sensorimotor cortex activation changes in schizophrenia: a study with functional magnetic resonance imaging. Neuroimage 9:81–87, 1999

Schwarcz R, Rassoulpour A, Wu H, et al: Increased cortical kynurenate content in schizophrenia. Biol Psychiatry 50:521–530, 2001

Seeman P, Ulpian C, Bergeron C, et al: Bimodal distribution of dopamine receptor densities in brains of schizophrenics. Science 225:728–731, 1984

Seeman P, Guan H-C, Van Tol HHM: Dopamine D4 receptors are elevated in schizophrenia. Nature 365:441–445, 1993

Shelton RC, Weinberger DR: Brain morphology in schizophrenia, in Psychopharmacology: The Third Generation of Progress. Edited by Meltzer HY. New York, Raven, 1987, pp 773–781

Shenton ME, Kikinis R, Jolesz FA, et al: Abnormalities of the left temporal lobe and thought disorder in schizophrenia: a quantitative magnetic resonance imaging study. N Engl J Med 327:604–612, 1992

Shirakawa O, Tamminga CA: Basal ganglia $GABA_A$ and dopamine D1 binding site correlates of haloperidol-induced oral dyskinesias in rat. Exp Neurol 127:62–69, 1994

Silbersweig DA, Stern E, Frith C, et al: A functional neuroanatomy of hallucinations in schizophrenia. Nature 378:176–179, 1995

Sokoloff L, Reivich M, Kennedy C, et al: The [14C]deoxyglucose method for measurement of local cerebral glucose utilization: theory, procedure, and normal values in the conscious and anesthetized albino rat. J Neurochem 28:897–916, 1977

Sower AC, Bird ED, Perrone-Bizzozero NI: Increased levels of GAP-43 protein in schizophrenic brain tissues demonstrated by a novel immunodetection method. Molecular and Chemical Neuropathology 23:1–30, 1995

Spence SA, Brooks DJ, Hirsch SR, et al: A PET study of voluntary movement in schizophrenic patients experiencing passivity phenomena (delusions of alien control). Brain 120:1997–2011, 1997

Spence SA, Liddle PF, Stefan MD, et al: Functional anatomy of verbal fluency in people with schizophrenia and those at genetic risk. Focal dysfunction and distributed disconnectivity reappraised. Br J Psychiatry 176:52–60, 2000

Stevens AA, Goldman-Rakic PS, Gore JC, et al: Cortical dysfunction in schizophrenia during auditory word and tone working memory demonstrated by functional magnetic resonance imaging. Arch Gen Psychiatry 55:1097–1103, 1998

Suddath RL, Casanova MF, Goldberg TE: Temporal lobe pathology in schizophrenia: a quantitative magnetic resonance imaging study. Am J Psychiatry 146:464–472, 1989

Suddath RL, Christison GW, Torrey EF, et al: Anatomical abnormalities in the brains of monozygotic twins discordant for schizophrenia. N Engl J Med 322(12):789–794, 1990

Sullivan EV, Shear PK, Zipursky RB, et al: A deficit profile of executive, memory, and motor functions in schizophrenia. Biol Psychiatry 36:641–653, 1994

Sweeney JA, Clementz BA, Haas GL, et al: Eye tracking dysfunction in schizophrenia: characterization of component eye movement abnormalities, diagnostic specificity, and the role of attention. J Abnorm Psychol 103(2):222–230, 1994

Szechtman H, Nahmias C, Garnett S, et al: Effect of neuroleptics on altered cerebral glucose metabolism in schizophrenia. Arch Gen Psychiatry 145:251–253, 1988

Tamminga CA: Schizophrenia and glutamatergic transmission. Crit Rev Neurobiol 12:21–36, 1998

Tamminga CA, Schaffer MH, Smith RC, et al: Schizophrenic symptoms improve with apomorphine. Science 200:567–568, 1978

Tamminga CA, Cascella NG, Lahti RA, et al: Pharmacologic properties of (-)-3PPP (preclamol) in man. J Neural Transm 88:165–175, 1992a

Tamminga CA, Thaker GK, Buchanan R, et al: Limbic system abnormalities identified in schizophrenia using positron emission tomography with fluorodeoxyglucose and neocortical alterations with deficit syndrome. Arch Gen Psychiatry 49:522–530, 1992b

Taylor SF, Tandon R, Koeppe RA: Global cerebral blood flow increase reveals focal hypoperfusion in schizophrenia. Neuropsychopharmacology 21:368–371, 1999

Thaker GK, Cassady S, Adami H, et al: Eye movements in spectrum personality disorders: comparison of community subjects and relatives of schizophrenic patients. Am J Psychiatry 153(3):362–368, 1996

Thaker GK, Ross DE, Cassady SL, et al: Smooth pursuit eye movements to extraretinal motion signals: deficits in relatives of patients with schizophrenia. Arch Gen Psychiatry 55(9):830–836, 1998

Thaker GK, Ross DE, Buchanan RW, et al: Smooth pursuit eye movements to extraretinal motion signals: deficits in patients with schizophrenia. Psychiatry Res 88:209–219, 1999

Thaker GK, Ross DE, Cassady SL, et al: Saccadic eye movement abnormalities in relatives of patients with schizophrenia. Schizophr Res 45:235–244, 2000

Toru M, Watanabe S, Shibuya H, et al: Neurotransmitters, receptors and neuropeptides in post-mortem brains of chronic schizophrenic patients. Acta Psychiatr Scand 78: 121–137, 1988

Treff WM, Hempel KJ: Die Zelidichte bei Schizophrenen und klinisch Gesunden. J Hirnforsch 4:314–369, 1958

Tsuang MT, Woolson RD, Fleming JA: Long-term outcome of major psychoses, I: schizophrenia and affective disorders compared with psychiatrically symptom-free surgical conditions. Arch Gen Psychiatry 36:1295–1301, 1979

Tsuang MT, Stone WS, Seidman LJ, et al: Treatment of nonpsychotic relatives of patients with schizophrenia: four case studies. Biol Psychiatry 1(45):1412–1418, 1999

Tsuang MT, Stone WS, Faraone SV: Toward reformulating the diagnosis of schizophrenia. Am J Psychiatry 157:1041–1050, 2000

Ulas J, Cotman CW: Excitatory amino acid receptors in schizophrenia. Schizophr Bull 19:105–117, 1993

van Kammen DP, Peters J, van Kammen WB: Cerebrospinal fluid studies of monoamine metabolism in schizophrenia. Psychiatr Clin North Am 9:81–97, 1986

van Kammen DP, Peters J, Yao J, et al: Norepinephrine and relapse in chronic schizophrenia: negative symptoms revisited. Arch Gen Psychiatry 47:161–168, 1990

van Praag HM: CSF 5-HIAA and suicide in non-depressed schizophrenics. Lancet 2:977–978, 1983

Volk DW, Austin MC, Pierri JN, et al: Decreased glutamic acid decarboxylase67 messenger RNA expression in a subset of prefrontal cortical gamma-aminobutyric acid neurons in subjects with schizophrenia. Arch Gen Psychiatry 57:237–245, 2000

Walinder J, Skott A, Carlsson A, et al: Potentiation by metyrosine of thioridazine effects in chronic schizophrenics. Arch Gen Psychiatry 33:501–505, 1976

Weinberger DR: Implications of normal brain development for the pathogenesis of schizophrenia. Arch Gen Psychiatry 44:660–669, 1987

Weinberger DR, Berman KF, Zee RF: Physiologic dysfunction of dorso-lateral prefrontal cortex in schizophrenia, I: regional cerebral blood flow evidence. Arch Gen Psychiatry 43:114–124, 1986

Weinberger DR, Berman KF, Suddath R, et al: Evidence of dysfunction of a prefrontal-limbic network in schizophrenia: a magnetic resonance imaging and regional cerebral blood flow study of discordant monozygotic twins. Am J Psychiatry 149:890–897, 1992

Whicker L, Abel LA, Dell'Osso LF: Smooth pursuit eye movements in the parents of schizophrenics. Neuroophthalmology 5:1–8, 1985

Widerlöv E: A critical appraisal of CSF monoamine metabolite studies in schizophrenia. Ann N Y Acad Sci 537:309–323, 1988

Widerlöv E, Lindstrom LH, Bissette G, et al: Subnormal CSF levels of neurotensin in a subgroup of schizophrenic patients: normalization after neuroleptic treatment. Am J Psychiatry 139:1122–1126, 1982

Wong D, Wagner HN Jr, Tune LE, et al: Positron emission tomography reveals elevated D2 dopamine receptors in drug-naive schizophrenics. Science 234:1558–1563, 1986

World Health Organization: International Statistical Classification of Diseases and Related Health Problems, 10th Revision. Geneva, World Health Organization, 1992

# CHAPTER 31

# Neuropsychiatric Aspects of Mood and Affective Disorders

Helen S. Mayberg, M.D.

Michelle Keightley, M.A.

Roderick K. Mahurin, Ph.D.

Stephen K. Brannan, M.D.

Disturbances of mood and affect are among the most prevalent of all behavioral disorders. Depression is especially common and is a prominent feature of many neurological conditions. Diagnosis is generally straightforward, and a wide range of treatments are available that alleviate symptoms in most patients. Although definitive mechanisms for depression have yet to be identified, theories implicating specific neurochemical and neuropeptide systems, focal lesions in specific brain regions, and selective dysfunction of known neural pathways have been proposed, supported by a growing number of clinical and basic studies demonstrating anatomic, neurochemical, genetic, endocrine, sleep, and cognitive abnormalities in depressed patients. In this chapter, we review the clinical, biochemical, neuropsychological, and imaging markers of depression. Changes in these parameters are discussed in the context of a neurobiological model of depression and mood regulation.

## Clinical Features

### Diagnostic Criteria

The diagnosis of primary major depression is based on the presence of a persistent negative mood state in association with disturbances in attention, motivation, motor and mental speed, sleep, appetite, and libido, as well as anhedonia, anxiety, excessive or inappropriate guilt, recurrent thoughts of death with suicidal ideations, and, in some cases, suicide attempts (Table 31–1) (Spitzer et al. 1988). This diversity of clinical symptoms argues against an etiology associated with a single brain location, lesion type, or neurochemical system. Rather, the associated impairment of cognitive, motor, somatic, and circadian functions in patients with dysphoria suggests that depression is a composite disorder affecting discrete but

Research described in this chapter was supported by National Institute of Mental Health Grant MH49553, the National Alliance for Research on Schizophrenia and Depression, the Charles A. Dana Foundation, the Theodore and Vada Stanley Foundation, and Eli Lilly.

functionally interconnected limbic, paralimbic, and neo-cortical circuits (Mayberg 1994, 1997).

## Demographics and Epidemiology

The average lifetime prevalence of depression is about 15% and is twofold greater in women than in men (Blazer et al. 1994; Fava and Kendler 2000). That depression has a biologic etiology is suggested by family, adoption, and twin studies in which a high degree of heritability is reported (Golden and Gershon 1988; Kendler et al. 1995, 1999). Major depressive disorder generally begins after age 20 and before age 50. A later age at onset is associated with a higher incidence of structural brain lesions, including strokes and subcortical and periventricular white-matter changes (reviewed in Sheline 2000; Soares and Mann 1997). Biologic mechanisms for the increased vulnerability of women or the relative constancy of age at onset are unknown.

The influence of environmental factors in the etiology of depression is equally complex (Kessler 1997). No correlations between depression and socioeconomic status, education, or specific lifestyle have been demonstrated. Although stress is often seen as a precipitant (Kendler et al. 1995; Robins et al. 1984), the causal relationship between stress and vulnerability to, or precipitation of, a depressive disorder is far from clear. Recent studies provide new evidence that early life trauma and stress may contribute to an increased vulnerability to develop various types of affective disorders (Heim et al. 2000; Kaufman et al. 2000; Lopez et al. 1999; Lyons et al. 2000; McEwen 2000; Meany et al. 1988; Shively et al. 1997).

The association of stress-provoking events with the onset of a major depressive episode appears to be stronger for the first episode than for subsequent episodes (Kessler 1997). Although not everyone who has a single episode of depression has another episode, recurrent episodes are more the rule than the exception. Furthermore, the natural course of major depressive disorder, although punctuated by periods of normality, appears to follow a recurrent pattern, and episodes occur more frequently and with greater intensity in the absence of successful intervention (Frank and Thase 1999; Keller et al. 1983).

## Treatment Considerations

An untreated major depressive episode generally lasts 6–13 months, although treatment can significantly reduce this period. Options for the treatment of major depression include pharmacologic as well as nonpharmacologic strategies (American Psychiatric Association 2000; Elkin et al. 1989). For patients with mild to moderate depres-

**TABLE 31–1.** Clinical features of depression

| Symptom domain | Specific symptom |
| --- | --- |
| Mood | Dysphoria |
| | Anhedonia |
| | Pessimism and hopelessness |
| | Excessive or inappropriate guilt |
| | Low self-esteem |
| | Crying spells |
| | Suicidality |
| | Anxiety |
| Motor | Motor slowing |
| | Restlessness, agitation |
| Somatic | Sleep disturbance |
| | Abnormal appetite |
| | Weight change |
| | Decreased libido |
| | Easy fatigability, low energy |
| | Apathy, decreased drive |
| Cognitive | Impaired attention and short-term memory |
| | Poor executive functioning |
| | Psychomotor retardation |
| | Poor motivation |
| | Ruminations |

sion, medication and cognitive therapies have been shown to be equal in their efficacy to treat depressive symptoms (DeRubeis et al. 1999; Hickie et al. 1999; Hollon et al. 1992). Empirically, it is well recognized that patients with a poor or incomplete response to one form of treatment often respond well to another. Others will respond to treatment augmentation or combination strategies using drugs with complementary pharmacological actions, combined drug and cognitive-behavioral therapy, or, in medication-resistant patients, electroconvulsive therapy (Bourgon and Kellner 2000; Nemeroff 1996–1997; Nurnberg et al. 1999; Schatzberg 1998; Thase and Rush 1995). Such resistance to treatment is reported to occur in 20%–40% of cases (Keller et al. 1983; Thase and Rush 1995). Newer strategies for patients with more severe depression now also include repetitive transcranial magnetic stimulation (rTMS) and vagal nerve stimulation (VNS) (George et al. 1999; Rush et al. 2000). More rarely, patients with refractory depression are treated surgically with subcaudate tractotomy, anterior capsulotomy, or cingulotomy (Cosgrove and Rauch 1995; Malizia 1997; Ovsiew and Frim 1997). Patient subtyping for the purpose of treatment selection has been attempted, but at present, few reliable clinical algorithms exist to guide treatment selection at any stage of illness. Neither are there clinical, neurochemical, or imaging markers that can identify which patients will have a protracted disease course (Coryell et al. 1990; Frank and Thase 1999; Keller et al. 1983; Maj et al. 1992).

## Differential Diagnosis

Depression may accompany a variety of neurological, psychiatric, and medical illnesses, and recognition of these comorbid conditions can influence the approach to treatment as well as affect outcome (Table 31–2). Depressive symptoms accompanying grief and bereavement; dysthymia; anxiety; schizoaffective disorder; bipolar illness; and obsessive-compulsive, panic, and certain personality disorders often require alternative treatment strategies for full remission of clinical symptoms.

In evaluating a patient who may have an affective disorder, drug-induced mood changes, comorbid general medical illnesses, and substance abuse should always be considered, particularly in patients whose symptoms are atypical or of uncharacteristic onset. In some patients the diagnosis of depression can be obscured by other neurological or psychiatric conditions, delaying appropriate treatment (Starkstein and Robinson 1993; Starkstein et al. 1990d). Certain neurological findings, such as pseudobulbar palsy (Langworthy and Hesser 1940), apathy (Marin 1990), or bradyphrenia (Rogers et al. 1987), in the absence of a true mood disturbance can superficially mimic depressive illness, potentially delaying more appropriate diagnostic or treatment interventions.

## Biological Markers

## Neurochemical Abnormalities

No single neurotransmitter abnormality has been identified that fully explains the pathophysiology of the depressive disorders or the associated constellation of mood, motor, cognitive, and somatic manifestations (Bauer and Frazer 1994). Changes in norepinephrine, serotonin, dopamine, acetylcholine, opiates, and γ-aminobutyric acid (GABA) (Arango et al. 1997; Caldecott-Hazzard et al. 1991; Klimek et al. 1997; Stancer and Cooke 1988) have all been reported (Table 31–3) with new studies additionally focused on dysregulation of second messenger systems, gene transcription and neurotrophic factors, and cell turnover (Duman et al. 2000; Jacobs et al. 2000; Manji et al. 2000; Reiach et al. 1999).

Postulated disturbances in serotonergic (5-HT) and noradrenergic mechanisms have dominated the neurochemical literature on depression for more than 30 years,

**TABLE 31–2.** Disorders associated with depression

| | |
|---|---|
| **Neurologic disorders** | *Substance abuse* |
| *Focal lesions* | Alcohol and sedatives/ |
| Stroke (frontal, basal | hypnotics |
| ganglia) | Cocaine, amphetamines, |
| Tumor | and other stimu- |
| Surgical ablation | lants |
| Epilepsy (temporal, frontal, | *Miscellaneous disorders* |
| cingulate) | Grief and bereavement |
| *Regional degenerative diseases* | Somatoform disorders |
| Parkinson's disease | Adjustment disorder |
| Huntington's disease | with depressed |
| Pick's disease | mood |
| Fahr's disease | Personality disorders |
| Progressive supranuclear | **Systemic disorders** |
| palsy | *Endocrine disorders* |
| Carbon monoxide exposure | Hypothyroidism and |
| Wilson's disease | hyperthyroidism |
| *Diffuse degenerative diseases* | Adrenal diseases (Cush- |
| Alzheimer's disease | ing's disease, Addi- |
| AIDS dementia | son's disease) |
| Multiple sclerosis | Parathyroid disorders |
| *Miscellaneous disorders* | *Inflammatory/infectious* |
| Migraine | *diseases* |
| Paraneoplastic syndromes | Systemic lupus erythe- |
| (limbic encephalitis) | matosus |
| **Psychiatric disorders** | Neurosyphilis |
| *Mood disorders* | AIDS |
| Major depressive disorder | Tuberculosis |
| Bipolar disorder | Mononucleosis |
| Schizoaffective disorder | Sjögren's syndrome |
| Dysthymia | Chronic fatigue syn- |
| Cyclothymia | drome |
| *Anxiety disorders* | *Metabolic disorders* |
| Panic disorder | Uremia |
| Obsessive-compulsive | Porphyria |
| disorder | Eating disorders |
| Posttraumatic stress | Anorexia nervosa |
| disorder | Bulimia nervosa |
| Generalized anxiety | Vitamin deficiencies |
| disorder | *Miscellaneous disorders* |
| *Eating disorders* | Medication side effects |
| Anorexia nervosa | Chronic pain syndromes |
| Bulimia nervosa | Sleep apnea |
| | Cancer |

based in large part on the consistent observations that most antidepressant drugs affect synaptic concentrations of these two transmitters (Bunney and Davis 1965; Charney 1998; Ressler and Nemeroff 1999; Schildkraut 1965; Vetulani and Sulser 1975). Serotonergic and noradrenergic metabolite abnormalities have been identified in spinal fluid, blood, and urine in subsets of depressed patients (Roy et al. 1988), but the relationship of these

**TABLE 31–3.** Neurotransmitter abnormalities associated with depression

**Noradrenergic abnormalities**

*In depressed patients*
Blunted growth hormone response to clonidine[a]
↓ Urinary[a] and plasma MHPG
↑ Platelet $\alpha_2$ binding
↓ Leukocyte $\beta_2$ response (cAMP)
↑ Plasma NE
↓ Hippocampal $\alpha_2$ and $\beta_2$ binding in postmortem brains
*Acute antidepressant effects*
↓ Firing rate of the locus coeruleus[a]
↓ Neuronal norepinephrine uptake[a]
↓ Norepinephrine turnover
*Chronic antidepressant effects*
Desensitization of NE stimulated adenylate cyclase activity[a]
Downregulation of cortical $\beta_1$[a] and $\alpha_2$ receptors
Upregulation of cortical $\alpha_1$ receptors
↓ Tyrosine hydroxylase activity

**Serotonergic abnormalities**

*In depressed patients*
Blunted prolactin response to serotonergic challenge[a]
↓ Platelet imipramine binding[a]
↓ CSF[a] and urinary 5-HIAA
↓ CSF 5-HT
↓ Plasma tryptophan
↓ Platelet 5-HT uptake
↓ Plasma 5-HT
↓ Imipramine binding in postmortem brains
↑ $5\text{-HT}_2$ receptor binding in brains of suicide victims
*Acute antidepressant effects*
↓ Neuronal serotonin uptake[a]
↓ Serotonin turnover[a]
Chronic antidepressant effects
Downregulation of $5\text{-HT}_2$ receptors[a]
↑ 5-HT neuronal responsiveness to 5-HT

**Other neurotransmitter abnormalities**

*Dopamine*
↓ CSF HVA
↓ Sensitivity of somatodendritic dopamine receptors
*Opiates*
↑ μ receptors in frontal cortex, hippocampus
↑ Plasma endorphins
↑ Brain enkephalins
*GABA*
↓ CSF and plasma GABA
Antidepressant-induced upregulation of $GABA_B$ receptors
*Acetylcholine*
↑ Depression acutely with cholinomimetics
↑ Muscarinic receptors in cultured fibroblasts and in brains of suicide victims
↓ REM latency with cholinomimetics

*Note.* MHPG = 3-methoxy-4-hydroxyphenylglycol; cAMP = cyclic adenosine monophosphate; NE = norepinephrine; CSF = cerebrospinal fluid; 5-HIAA = 5-hydroxyindoleacetic acid; 5-HT = 5-hydroxytryptamine; HVA = homovanillic acid; GABA = γ-aminobutyric acid; REM = rapid eye movement.

[a]Most conclusive findings.

peripheral measures to changes in brain-stem nuclei or their cortical projections is unknown (Langer and Schoemaker 1988; Maas et al. 1984). Consistent with these findings, decreased serotonin transporter binding has been demonstrated in unipolar depressed patients using the single photon emission computed tomography (SPECT) ligand [$^{123}$I]2β-carbomethoxy-3β-(4-iodophenyl)tropane, an important observation directly implicating brain-stem serotonergic dysfunction (Malison et al. 1998). $5\text{-HT}_{1A}$ and $5\text{-HT}_{2A}$ receptor densities have also been examined using imaging, but with inconsistent findings in the drug-free state (D'haenen et al. 1992; Drevets et al. 1999; Meltzer et al. 1999; Meyer et al. 1999; Sargent et al. 2000). Postmortem brain studies of depressed people who committed suicide report changes in a number of additional serotonin markers including regional transmitter and metabolite levels, transporter and postsynaptic receptor density, and second messenger and transcription proteins (Arango et al. 1995, 1997; Mann et al. 2000). Involved regions include brain stem, hypothalamus, hippocampus, and frontal cortex, but with considerable variability. Recent work examining the serotonin transporter in depressed patients, some of whom committed suicide, has focused on brain regions identified in imaging studies, with selective attention to variability in various parts of the frontal cortex and anterior cingulate (Arango et al. 1999). Ligands to image the noradrenergic system are not yet available.

In support of a biogenic amine etiology, dietary restriction of tryptophan, resulting in an acute decrease in brain serotonin (the tryptophan depletion challenge), and catecholamines (the α-methyl-para-tyrosine challenge) are selectively associated with an abrupt transient relapse in patients whose depression was in remission (Delgado et al.1990; Leyton et al. 2000). Changes in regional glucose metabolism associated with the tryptophan depletion test have also been reported and are reminiscent of patterns seen in pretreatment resting-state studies (see summary later in this chapter), suggesting a critical role for serotonergic tone in maintaining the remitted state (Bremner et al. 1997; K.A. Smith et al. 1999).

Although a primary dopaminergic mechanism for depression is generally considered unlikely, a role for dopamine in some aspects of the depressive syndrome is supported by several experimental observations (Cantello et al. 1989; Fibiger 1984; Kestler et al. 2000; Rogers et al. 1987; Zacharko and Anisman 1991). The mood-enhancing properties and clinical utility of methylphenidate in treating some depressed patients are well documented (Martin et al. 1971), although dopaminergic stimulation alone does not generally alleviate all depressive symptoms. Dopaminergic projections from the ventral tegmental area show regional specificity for the orbital/ventral prefrontal cortex, striatum, and anterior cingulate—areas repeatedly identified in functional imaging studies of primary and secondary depression (Grabiel 1990; Simon et al. 1979). Degeneration of neurons or their projections from the ventral tegmental area, however, has not been demonstrated in patients with primary unipolar depression.

Opioid, cholinergic, GABA, and corticotropin-releasing factor (CRF) changes have also been reported but have been investigated less (see Table 31–3) (Caldecott-Hazzard et al. 1991; Gross-Isseroff et al. 1990). Functional imaging ligands for many of the systems of interest either have not been tested (Janowsky et al. 1988; Petty et al. 1992) or are not yet developed (Duncan et al. 1996; Nemeroff et al. 1984; Nibuya et al. 1996; Trullas and Skolnick 1990; Vaidya et al. 1997).

## Endocrine Changes

Studies of endocrine function in patients with depression have identified dysregulation of the hypothalamic-pituitary-adrenal (HPA) axis (Table 31–4). The most reproducible finding is a disturbance in the normal pattern of cortisol secretion (Carroll et al. 1976; Nemeroff et al. 1984). The dexamethasone suppression test, previously considered a specific marker of depressive illness, is abnormal in subsets of depressed patients and additionally may identify patients with a more selective abnormality of the HPA axis (Arana et al. 1987; Carroll et al. 1981; Posener et al. 2000). Recent reports of alterations in cortisol regulation associated with transient stress in patients with a history of early life trauma or abuse further suggest that HPA axis dysregulation may be an important marker of vulnerability to various types of affective disorders in later life (Heim et al. 2000; Kaufman et al. 2000; Lopez et al. 1999). More recent studies further emphasize the role of CRF in modulating serotonergic and noradrenergic activity (Isogawa et al. 2000).

Thyroid markers also have been examined in patients with affective disorder. Even with normal levels of circulating thyroid hormone, elevated levels of thyroid antibodies have been demonstrated in patients with depression but without overt thyroid dysfunction (Nemeroff et al. 1985). A blunted response of thyroid-stimulating hormone to exogenous thyroid-releasing hormone (thyroid stimulation test) also has been described (Loosen 1985).

## Sleep Disturbance

Abnormal sleep is a core symptom of major depressive disorder (Table 31–5). Symptoms include difficulty fall-

**TABLE 31–4.** Endocrine abnormalities

| Hormone | Effect |
| --- | --- |
| Cortisol | Blunted ACTH response to exogenous CRH |
| | Failure of dexamethasone to suppress cortisol secretion |
| | Blunting of diurnal cortisol secretion variation |
| | ↑ CRH in spinal fluid |
| | ↑ Urinary and plasma cortisol |
| | ↓ CRF binding in frontal cortex of suicide victims |
| Thyroid | ↑ Thyroid antibodies |
| | ↓ Blunted TSH response to exogenous TRH |
| Melatonin | ↓ Nocturnal secretion of melatonin |

*Note.* ACTH = adrenocorticotropic hormone; CRH = corticotropin-releasing hormone; CRF = corticotropin-releasing factor; TSH = thyroid-stimulating hormone; TRH = thyroid-releasing hormone.

ing asleep (initial insomnia) or staying asleep (middle insomnia), early morning awakening (terminal insomnia), or, more rarely, hypersomnia. Electroencephalography abnormalities in depressed patients include prolonged sleep latency, decreased slow-wave sleep, and reduced rapid eye movement (REM) latency with disturbances in the relative time spent in both REM and non-REM sleep (Benca et al. 1992).

Reduced REM latency probably is the best studied and most reproducible sleep-related electroencephalography finding in depressed patients, and this abnormality is reversed by most antidepressants (Sharpley and Cowen 1995). Sleep deprivation, particularly if instituted in the second half of the night, has an effect similar to medication, although the rapid, dramatic improvement in depressive symptoms is short-lived (Wu and Bunney 1990). Changes in nocturnal body temperature and attenuation of the normal fluctuations in core body temperature during sleep further suggest a more generalized dysregulation of normal circadian rhythms in patients with depression (Benca 1994). To date, however, none of these markers have proven to be specific to depression.

The physiology of sleep disturbances in patients with mania and bipolar depression is less well characterized. Clinically, it has long been observed that sleep deprivation is a common precipitant of manic episodes, again suggesting an important biologic link between sleep and affective symptoms. Patients with bipolar depression who are hypersomnic, however, do not show a consistent reduction in REM latency (Nofzinger et al. 1991).

**TABLE 31–5.** Sleep abnormalities associated with depression

| Sleep domain | Effect |
|---|---|
| Disturbed sleep continuity | Prolonged sleep latency |
| | ↑ Wake time during sleep (sleep fragmentation) |
| | ↓ Sleep efficiency (with either ↓ or ↑ total sleep time) |
| Slow-wave sleep (SWS) | ↓ SWS (especially in the first non-REM period) |
| | ↓ SWS percentage of total sleep |
| REM abnormalities | ↓ REM latency |
| | ↑ REM percentage of total sleep |
| | Prolonged first REM period |

*Note.* REM = rapid eye movement.

Marked changes in sleep continuity and other REM measures comparable to those seen in patients with major depressive disorder also have been described (Benca 1994).

## Behavioral and Performance Deficits

### Motor Performance

Motor and psychomotor deficits in depression involve a range of behaviors including changes in motility, mental activity, and speech (Caligiuri and Ellwanger 2000; Dantchev and Widlocher 1998; Flint et al. 1993; Sobin and Sackeim 1997). Depressed patients often perceive these signs as motor slowness, difficulty translating thought to action, lack of interest, or fatigue. Motor signs appear to be well correlated with both the severity of depression and treatment outcome (Lemke et al. 1999). Spontaneous motor activity is significantly lower when patients are depressed compared with when they are in the euthymic state in which a progressive increase in activity levels is seen (Dantchev and Widlocher 1998; Royant-Parola et al. 1986). Also, evidence suggests that significantly long speech-pause times in acutely depressed patients are shortened after successful antidepressant treatment (Szabadi et al. 1976).

### Cognitive Dysfunction

Cognitive deficits are a common and potentially debilitating feature of major depression. Impairment is most often encountered in the cognitive domains of attention, memory, and psychomotor speed. In contrast to deficits associated with many structural neurological disorders, specific impairments in language, perception, and spatial abilities usually are not seen except as a secondary consequence of poor attention, motivation, or organizational abilities (Blaney 1986; Brown et al. 1994; Calev et al. 1986; Elliott 1998; Weingartner et al. 1981). Cognitive deficits usually are of moderate intensity but can become severe in prolonged or intractable depression, adding to everyday functional disability. Clinically significant anxiety, which further impairs cognitive efficiency, occurs in many patients with depression (Nutt 1999; Rathus and Reber 1994).

### Postulated Mechanisms

Several authors have proposed a model of depression-related cognitive deficits based on reduced cognitive capacity or impaired ability to efficiently allocate cognitive resources to meet specific task demands (Ellis and Ashbrook 1991; Hasher and Zacks 1979). These theories posit the presence of a diffuse "energetic" impairment, rather than domain-specific cognitive deficits, in patients with depression. This generalized impairment involves either an inability to increase the "gain" of the system sufficiently to handle complex cognitive material or an inability to sustain cognitive effort across memory and learning (visual and verbal, short-term and long-term) tasks (Cohen et al. 1982), as well as tests of executive function (e.g., Tower of London and Wisconsin Card Sort) (Elliott et al. 1997a).

Support for this hypothesis comes from studies showing a differential impairment in effortful versus automatic cognitive tasks in depressed patients, as well as from findings of disproportionate cognitive impairment in depressed versus nondepressed subjects when presented with concurrent tasks competing for limited attentional resources (Hertel and Milan 1994; Roy-Byrne et al. 1986). When compared with nondepressed subjects, depressed subjects perform disproportionately worse on recall of unstructured verbal material than on structured material, the former presumably requiring more effortful cognitive processing (Watts et al. 1990; Wolfe et al. 1987). In addition, depression-related cognitive dysfunction has been found to increase in accord with increased complexity and degree of encoding required by task material (Weingartner 1981). Other explanations for nonspecific impairment in patients with depression include decreased task motivation, intrusion of depressive thought content, and secondary effects of fatigue or restlessness (M.H. Johnson and Magaro 1987).

An alternative model for cognitive impairment in patients with depression involves the assumption of correlations between specific deficits and localizable neuroanatomic structures. The pattern of memory deficits seen in patients with major depression has been found to be statistically similar to that in those with prefrontal-subcortical disorders (Parkinson's disease and Huntington's disease), in contrast to a "cortical" pattern of memory performance seen in patients with Alzheimer's disease (Massman et al. 1992). Other studies comparing patients with primary depression with those with neurological depression (such as Parkinson's disease) have also demonstrated similarities in patterns of cognitive impairment, including deficits in concentration, working memory, and psychomotor speed, planning, strategic searching, and flexibility of goal-directed mental activity (Flint et al. 1993; Rogers et al. 1987). More recently, studies have focused on the specific motivation deficit of response to performance feedback (e.g., Elliott et al. 1997b, 1997c). In particular, depressed patients fail to use negative feedback as a motivational stimulus to improve subsequent performance, an observation that implicates orbitofrontal and ventral-striatal pathways (Elliott et al. 1997b, 1997c). State-trait factors contributing to these findings are not yet defined; however, studies of cognitive bias suggest persistent deficits even in patients whose depression was in remission (Segal et al. 1999; Teasdale 1983, 1999). The relationships between deficits in verbal memory, cortisol dysregulation, and hippocampal atrophy are another area of active research (Lyons et al. 2000; McEwen 2000; Sapolsky 2000; Sheline 2000).

## Impact of Medications

Medication use can be an additional and significant determinant of performance on neuropsychological tests. Traditional tricyclic antidepressants (TCAs) have well-recognized negative effects on both psychomotor speed and memory (Deptula and Pomara 1990; Lamping et al. 1984). Selective serotonin reuptake inhibitors (SSRIs), now the most commonly prescribed antidepressants, have minimal negative, and often positive, effects on cognitive efficiency (Fudge et al. 1990; Hindmarch et al. 1990). Studies directly comparing TCAs with SSRIs such as fluoxetine and sertraline have revealed improvements in memory for patients taking SSRIs but either no improvement or a worsening of cognition for those taking TCAs (Keegan et al. 1991; Spring et al. 1992). Clinical trials additionally report that noradrenergic reuptake inhibitors (NRIs) such as reboxetine significantly improve social functioning compared with improvement with fluoxetine, suggesting that noradrenergic and serotonergic modulation preferentially affects different cognitive dimensions (Dubini et al. 1997; Healy and Healy

1998). Electroconvulsive therapy, used to treat otherwise refractory major depression, has only minor adverse long-term effects on cognition in most patients (Price and McAllister 1989; Stoudemire et al. 1993). Although both anterograde and retrograde amnesias are common side effects, these memory difficulties generally resolve within about 6 months and can be minimized (but not ameliorated) by judicious placement of electrodes and adjustment of stimulation parameters (Lawson et al. 1990; Weiner et al. 1986). Nevertheless, memory loss for a period of hours to several days before and after the procedure is often permanent and appears to be related to the anticholinergic effects of electroconvulsive therapy (Mann and Kapur 1994; Squire 1986). Older patients are at significantly greater risk for both physical complications and long-term cognitive impairment (Lipman et al. 1993; Sackeim et al. 1986), suggesting that caution should be used with electroconvulsive therapy in elderly patients.

## The Dementia of Depression

Age in general is an influential factor with respect to cognitive deficits of depression (Lyness et al. 1994). Patients older than 40 generally demonstrate more focal deficits in tests of attention, information-processing speed, and executive function, whereas those over 50 often show more widespread abnormalities in memory and executive function (Elliott 1998; Lockwood et al. 2000). First onset of depression after age 70 is associated with an increased risk of subsequent dementia (King et al. 1995; Raskin 1986; van Reekum et al. 1999).

Depressive dementia, also referred to as pseudodementia, is encountered in a subset of depressed patients, especially in the elderly (Emery and Oxman 1992; Stoudemire et al. 1989). Estimates of the occurrence of depressive dementia range up to 15% in this clinical population (Bulbena and Berrios 1986; Reifler et al. 1982). The differentiation of depression from dementia usually is not difficult. Most elderly patients with depression perform better overall on neuropsychological tests than do age-matched subjects with primary dementia. Elderly depressed patients also show a pattern of cognitive deficits (e.g., poor memory and attention but intact language and visuospatial abilities) that is different from that seen in subjects with dementia, as well as a number of clinical features that are specific to depression (e.g., sadness, poor self-esteem, somatic symptoms) (Jones et al. 1992; LaRue 1982). Nevertheless, occasionally a clinician may encounter a depressed patient with cognitive decline that is difficult to distinguish from early dementia. In these cases, a trial of antidepressant medication is often warranted. The general finding is a return to normal levels of cognitive function in patients with depression, but not those with dementia, after an adequate course of treatment (Abas et al. 1990; Stoudemire et al. 1991). However, more recent studies more strongly suggest that comorbid depression and cognitive impairment can be an early sign of Alzheimer's disease (van Reekum et al. 1999).

## Trait Markers of Depression

Psychological studies have shown that depressed patients are cognitively biased toward the processing of negative emotional stimuli. Depressed patients, for example, show better recall for negative words when presented with a list of words varying in emotional tone (Bradley and Mogg 1994; Murphy et al. 1999; Norman et al. 1987) and are faster than nondepressed individuals at identifying negative adjectives as self-descriptive (Alloy et al. 1999). Depressed patients also produce higher probability estimates for future negative events (MacLeod and Byrne 1996) and make more pessimistic predictions for themselves and others (Alloy and Ahrens 1987).

Sensitivity to mood-congruent stimuli can in fact be present in some patients before they experience their first major depressive episode. Individual differences in the propensity to experience negative emotional states and the use of strategies to directly change, maintain, or eliminate these emotional states might increase vulnerability to a major depressive episode (Beck et al. 1979; Henriques et al. 1994; Segal et al. 1999; Teasdale 1987). Additionally, mood states such as depression and anxiety can interact with individual differences in emotionally relevant personality traits to influence the cognitive processing of emotional stimuli. The broad trait of negative affectivity, also known as neuroticism, refers to temperamental hypersensitivity to negative stimuli or the tendency to experience exaggerated negative mood states in situations of emotional instability or dissonance (Santor et al. 1997).

Scores of neuroticism as measured by the NEO Personality Inventory (NEO-PI; Costa and McCrae 1997) are strongly correlated with measures of depression (e.g., Hamilton Rating Scale for Depression) during initial consultation, and reduction in the severity of depression after treatment is accompanied by a decrease in scores. However, neuroticism is more than a measure of depressed mood because scores in remitted patients continue to be significantly higher than the norm and scores remain relatively stable over time, suggesting an interaction between trait disposition and mood state (Santor et al. 1997). As observed in depressed patients, individuals scoring high on neuroticism also respond faster to, and recall more, negative cue words (Bradley and Mogg 1994), make more pessimistic predictions for self and others (Alloy and Ahrens 1987), and demonstrate a susceptibility to retrieving more negative personal memories. Although little is known about the neural correlates of neuroticism, positron emission tomography (PET) studies examining the relationships between regional cerebral blood flow and dopamine receptor markers and personality domains provide some support for biological differences among personality traits (D.L. Johnson et al. 1999; Kestler et al. 2000).

## Brain Imaging Studies

Modern theories regarding the neurolocalization of depressive illness have evolved from several complementary sources. The early observations of Kleist (1937) on mood and emotional sensations after direct stimulation of the ventral frontal lobes (Brodmann's areas 47 and 11) focused attention on paralimbic brain regions. Studies by Broca (1878) and, later, Papez (1937) and Maclean (1990) elaborated many of the anatomic details of these cytoarchitecturally primitive regions of the cortex, as well as adjacent limbic structures, including the cingulate gyrus, amygdala, and hippocampus. These studies were among the first to suggest a role for these regions in reward, motivation, and affective behaviors. Additional clinical observations in depressed patients have similarly identified a prominent role for the frontal and temporal lobes and the striatum in the expression and modulation of mood and affect (Bear 1983; Damasio and Van Hoesen 1983; Mesulam 1985; Robinson 1998; Stuss and Benson 1986).

## Depression in Neurologic Disease

### Anatomic Studies

Neurological diseases associated with depression can be categorized into three main groups: 1) focal lesions, 2) degenerative diseases with diffuse or random pathology, and 3) degenerative disorders with regionally confined pathology (see Table 31–2). Computed tomography and magnetic resonance imaging (MRI) studies in stroke patients with and without mood disorders have demonstrated a high association of mood changes with infarctions of the frontal lobe and basal ganglia, particularly those occurring in close proximity to the frontal pole or involving the caudate nucleus (Robinson et al. 1984; Starkstein et al. 1987). Studies of patients with head trauma or brain tumors or who have undergone neurosurgery (Damasio and Van Hoesen 1983; Grafman et al. 1986; Stuss and Benson 1986) further suggest that dorsolateral rather than ventral-frontal lesions are more commonly associated with depression and depressive-like symptoms such as apathy and psychomotor slowing. As might be expected, more precise localization is hampered by the heterogeneity of these types of lesions.

Studies of systemic disorders, such as lupus erythematosus (Omdal et al. 1988), Sjögren's syndrome (Hietaharju et al. 1990), thyroid and adrenal disease (Nemeroff 1989), acquired immunodeficiency syndrome (AIDS) (Krikorian and Wrobel 1991), and cancer (Meyers and Scheibel 1990), describe mood symptoms in subsets of patients. As with the more diffuse neurodegenerative diseases, such as Alzheimer's disease (Cummings and Victoroff 1990; Reed et al. 1993; Zubenko and Moossy 1988), a classic lesion-deficit approach is generally difficult because consistent focal abnormalities are uncommon. Studies of plaque loci in patients with multiple sclerosis suggest an association of depression with lesions in the temporal lobes, although it is not yet clear whether this effect is lateralized (Honer et al. 1987).

These limitations shifted focus to those diseases in which the neurochemical or neurodegenerative changes are reasonably well localized, as in Parkinson's disease (Mayberg and Solomon 1995), Huntington's disease (Folstein et al. 1983), progressive supranuclear palsy (Albert et al. 1974), Fahr's disease (Seidler 1985), Wilson's disease (Dening and Berrios 1989), and carbon monoxide poisoning (Laplane et al. 1989). In these disorders, consistent evidence shows direct or indirect involvement of the basal ganglia and associated pathways. These observations directly complement the findings described in studies of discrete brain lesions and further support the importance of cortical-striatal pathways in the development of affective disorders (Alexander et al. 1990). A paradox remains in that both depression and mania can occur as part of a given illness. With the exception of stroke, no localizing or regional differences can be offered to explain this phenomenon.

## Lateralization

No consensus has been reached as to whether the left or the right hemisphere is dominant in the expression of depressive symptoms. Reports of patients with traumatic frontal lobe injury indicate a high correlation between affective disturbances and right-hemisphere pathology (Grafman et al. 1986). Secondary mania, although rare, is most consistently seen with right-sided basal frontal-temporal or subcortical damage (Starkstein et al. 1990b). Some studies in patients who have experienced stroke suggest that left-sided lesions of both the frontal cortex and the basal ganglia are more likely to result in depressive symptoms than are right-sided lesions, where displays of euphoria or indifference predominate. Considerable debate continues on this issue (Carson et al. 2000; Gainotti 1972; Robinson et al. 1984; Ross and Rush 1981; Sinyor et al. 1986; Starkstein et al. 1987).

Similar contradictions are seen in studies of patients with temporal lobe epilepsy, in which an association between affective symptoms (both mania and depression) and left, right, and nonlateralized foci has been described (Altshuler et al. 1990; Bear and Fedio 1977; Flor-Henry 1969; Mendez et al. 1986; Robertson et al. 1987). Anatomic studies have yet to define the critical sites within the temporal lobe that are most closely associated with mood changes. Additional evidence supporting lateralization of emotional behaviors is provided in studies of pathologic (pseudobulbar) laughing and crying. Crying is more common with left-hemisphere lesions, whereas laughter is seen in patients with right-hemisphere lesions (Sackeim et al. 1982), consistent with reports of poststroke mood changes.

## Functional Imaging Studies

Despite the many similarities among different neurological conditions, the location of identified lesions by anatomic methods is still considerably variable. This variability is due in part to the technical and theoretical limitations of the anatomic imaging approach, which restricts lesion identification to those brain areas that are structurally damaged. Functional imaging can complement structural imaging in that the consequences of anatomic or chemical lesions on global and regional brain function can also be assessed. These methods provide an alternative strategy to test both how similar mood symptoms occur with anatomically or neurochemically distinct disease states and why comparable lesions do not always result in comparable behavioral phenomena. Using this approach, one can examine disease-specific control subjects, such as nondepressed patients with matched demographic and neurological characteristics. Parallel studies of patients with primary affective disorder and patients with neurological depressions provide complementary perspectives (Figure 31–1).

Mayberg and colleagues, in a series of studies (Bromfield et al. 1992; Mayberg et al. 1990, 1991, 1992, 1994; Starkstein 1990b), focused on neurological diseases

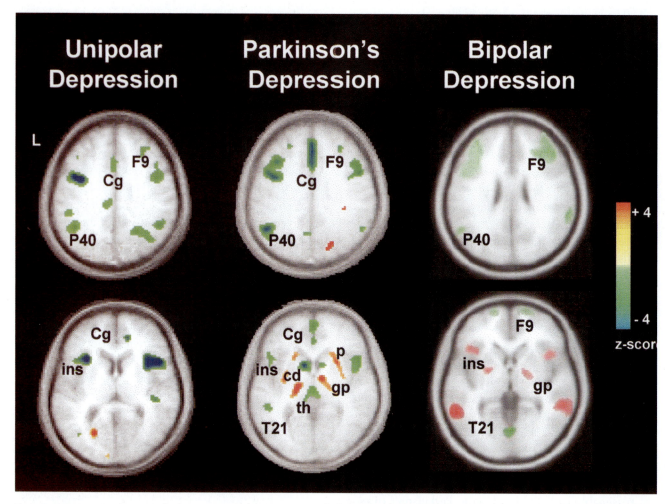

**FIGURE 31–1.** Positron emission tomographic imaging with fluorodeoxyglucose showing the metabolic changes common to unipolar depression, bipolar depression, and depression with Parkinson's disease (PD). Symmetrical dorsal and ventral prefrontal (F9), inferior parietal (P40), and anterior cingulate gyrus (Cg) hypometabolism (negative z values, shown in green) characterizes the depressive syndrome, independent of underlying disease etiology. Additional disease-specific changes are seen in insula and the striatum. Striatal hypermetabolism (positive z values, shown in red) is seen in those with bipolar disorder and PD but not in unipolar patients. Insula hypometabolism is seen in unipolar and PD patients in contrast to the hypermetabolism seen in bipolar patients. Insula activity may reflect pretreatment compensatory changes, as further reductions in this region are seen with antidepressant treatment. Resting hyperactivity in bipolar patients may reflect an altered threshold for switches in mood state—a defining feature of bipolar disorder. Of note, increases in insular activity are seen with normal shifts in mood state in both patients and healthy control subjects (see Figure 31–2 and Lane et al. 1997; Liotti et al. 2000b). Striatal hypermetabolism, common to bipolar disorder and PD, may contribute to mood lability, characteristic of bipolar disorder but also seen in many PD patients. F=frontal; cd=caudate nucleus; gp=globus pallidus; th=thalamus; ins=anterior insula; T=temporal; P=parietal; Cg=anterior cingulate gyrus. Numbers are Brodmann designations.

*Source.* Data from Mayberg et al. 1996, 1997, and Krueger et al. 2000.

where functional abnormalities would not be confounded by gross cortical lesions. This approach allowed functional confirmation of lesion-deficit observations, as well as characterization of functional changes remote from the site of primary injury or degeneration (Baron 1989). As such, studies were restricted to those disorders with known or identifiable neurochemical, neurodegenerative, or focal changes, and where the primary pathology spared frontal cortex (the region repeatedly implicated in the lesion-deficit literature). Parkinson's disease, Huntington's disease, and lacunar strokes of the basal ganglia best fit these criteria. Not only did clinical signs and symptoms in these depressed patients mirror those seen in patients with idiopathic depression, but several plausible biochemical mechanisms for mood symptoms had already been postulated (Mayeux et al. 1988; Peyser and

Folstein 1993; Robinson 1998). The additional observation that motor and cognitive features present in these patients often obscured recognition of mood symptoms further suggested testable anatomic hypotheses. These clinical findings in combination with published animal and human studies of regional connectivity (Alexander et al. 1990; Goldman-Rakic and Selemon 1984) provided additional foundation to postulate that regional dysfunction of specific frontal-subcortical pathways would discriminate depressed from nondepressed patients, independent of the underlying neurological disorder (Mayberg 1994).

## Parkinson's Disease

Depression in patients with Parkinson's disease is common (Cummings 1992; Starkstein et al. 1990a, 1990c), and several neurochemical mechanisms have been proposed to explain mood symptoms (Mayberg and Solomon 1995). A serotonergic etiology is supported by reduced serotonin and serotonin metabolites in the spinal fluid of depressed, but not nondepressed, patients with Parkinson's disease (Mayeux et al. 1988). A dopaminergic etiology, with differential involvement of the mesolimbic and mesocortical dopamine system, has also been proposed (Cantello et al. 1989; Fibiger 1984). This hypothesis is supported by identification of selective cell loss in the ventral tegmental area of patients with Parkinson's disease who have prominent mood and cognitive features (Torack and Morris 1988). These findings suggest that patients with Parkinson's disease who have preferential degeneration of neurons of the ventral tegmental area may be more likely to develop depression than are those without involvement of this area.

Functional imaging studies using PET with fluorodeoxyglucose provide support for both hypotheses. As a group, patients with Parkinson's disease without dementia or depression show relatively normal cortical metabolism. A comparison of depressed and nondepressed patients, however, shows that depressed patients have selective hypometabolism involving the caudate nucleus and prefrontal and orbitofrontal cortices (Jagust et al. 1992; Mayberg et al. 1990; Ring et al. 1994), areas with specific dopaminergic and serotonergic innervations. As described in patients with primary depression, prefrontal metabolism inversely correlates with depressive symptom severity. Although frontal changes distinguish depressed from nondepressed patients, mood and cognitive performance are not easily dissociated, suggesting a more complicated relationship between regional hypometabolic changes, depression, and cognitive-behavioral deficits in patients with Parkinson's disease (see Figure 31–1, center).

## Huntington's Disease

Depression is the most prevalent mood disorder seen in patients with Huntington's disease, affecting about half of all patients (Peyser and Folstein 1993). Mania also occurs in these patients, and impulsivity and suicide are common. Depression in these patients is not merely a reaction to a terminal disease diagnosis. Rather, as in patients with Parkinson's disease, the mood disorder often precedes the motor abnormalities, even in people who may not recognize that they are genetically at risk. Pathologically, there is degeneration of the basal ganglia. Although the gene for Huntington's disease is now known, it is still unclear how this defect translates into progressive loss of cells in the caudate nucleus and putamen, with the eventual development of chorea, depression, and dementia. Neurochemical mechanisms are more obscure (Peyser and Folstein 1993).

Functional imaging studies readily identify basal ganglia dysfunction—hypometabolism and hypoperfusion of the caudate nucleus and putamen—in both symptomatic patients and genetically at-risk subjects before the emergence of symptoms (Grafton et al. 1990). Analogous to the regional abnormalities identified in depressed Parkinson's patients, depressed patients with Huntington's disease show similar decreases in paralimbic orbitofrontal and inferior prefrontal cortices. The relationship between this paralimbic frontal hypometabolism and degeneration of the basal ganglia is unclear, although disruption of the frontolimbic–basal ganglia–thalamic pathways has been proposed (Mayberg et al. 1992).

## Strokes Involving the Basal Ganglia

Clinical signs and symptoms seen with strokes generally correlate with the site of direct brain injury. However, anatomically uninjured brain regions that are functionally connected but anatomically removed from the stroke lesion may also be affected (Baron 1989). This phenomenon, termed remote diaschisis, likely explains the occurrence of frontal lobe deficits in patients with subcortical strokes, for example. Therefore, to best localize both the anatomic and physiologic "lesions" that occur with strokes, structural and functional imaging methods are best used in combination. With this approach, one can determine what pattern of cortical or subcortical dysfunction is common in patients with similar clinical findings and different brain lesions, or, alternatively, what is different about patients with seemingly similar lesions but with discordant clinical symptoms.

This strategy has been used to identify the pattern of cortical hypometabolism specific to patients with secondary mood changes after unilateral lacunar subcortical strokes (Grasso et al. 1994; Mayberg 1994; Mayberg et al. 1991; Starkstein et al. 1990b). Although precise localization of the anatomic lesion in these studies was limited by the resolution of the available computed tomography images, the pattern of cortical metabolic changes nonetheless differentiated depressed from euthymic patients. Temporal- rather than frontal-lobe changes distinguished the two groups, with bilateral hypometabolism characterizing the depressed patients. In contrast to the findings in Parkinson's disease and Huntington's disease, frontal metabolism did not identify the patients with mood changes because both depressed and nondepressed stroke patients showed bilateral frontal decreases (Mayberg 1994; Mayberg et al. 1991). These remote effects in orbitoinferior frontal cortex may be lesion specific, disrupting orbitofrontal–striatal–thalamic circuits in all patient subgroups, including a group of patients with similar lesions and secondary mania (Starkstein et al. 1990b). Temporal-lobe changes, however, appear to be mood-state specific, implicating selective disruption of basotemporal limbic pathways in the patients with mood changes (Fulton 1951; Nauta 1971, 1986).

## Common Findings Across Studies

In summary, lesion-deficit and functional imaging studies of depressed neurological patients have consistently identified involvement of frontal and temporal cortices and the striatum. These common abnormalities have been interpreted as evidence of disease-specific disruption of known neurochemical pathways involving frontal-striatal-thalamic and basotemporal limbic circuits (Alexander et al. 1990; Mesulam 1985; Nauta 1971). This theory is consistent with known neurochemical and degenerative abnormalities previously characterized in patients with these disorders, as well as with known anatomic projections described in human and primate studies (Goldman-Rakic and Selemon 1984; Maclean 1990; Nauta 1971, 1986). The role of limbic regions such as the amygdala, hippocampus, and hypothalamus is less clear, despite evidence that these structures are fundamentally involved in critical aspects of motivational, affective, and emotional behaviors (Damasio 1994; Kleist 1937; LeDoux 1996; MacLean 1990; Mesulam 1985; Papez 1937; Rolls 1985, 2000) and appear to be important targets of various antidepressant treatments (Blier and Montigny 1999; Duman et al. 1999; Hyman and Nestler 1996). Systematic comparisons of frontosubcortical and corticolimbic patterns in neurological patients to those identified in patients with primary affective disorders are needed to fully characterize common functional markers of the depressive syndrome. Divergent patterns may

additionally provide explanations for subtle and not-so-subtle clinical differences across different depressed patient groups (see Figure 31–1).

# Primary Affective Disorder

## Anatomic Studies

Anatomic studies of patients with primary affective disorders have been less consistent than those of depressed patients with neurological disorders (reviewed in Soares and Mann 1997). Brain anatomy is grossly normal, and focal neocortical abnormalities have not been identified using imaging. Focal volume loss in subgenual medial frontal cortex has been described using both MRI and postmortem anatomic measurements (Drevets et al. 1997; Ongur et al. 1998; Rajkowska 2000). Reduced hippocampal and amygdala volumes have also been reported in patients with recurrent major depression (Sheline 2000; Sheline et al. 1996, 1998), with a postulated mechanism of glucocorticoid neurotoxicity, consistent with both animal models (Sapolsky 1994, 2000) and studies of patients with posttraumatic stress disorder (Bremner et al. 1995). Nonspecific changes in ventricular size, and T2-weighted MRI changes in subcortical gray and periventricular white matter, have also been reported in some patient subgroups, most notably elderly depressed patients (Coffey et al. 1993; Dupont et al. 1995; Greenwald et al. 1996; Hickie et al. 1997; Steffens et al. 1998; Zubenko et al. 1990). The parallels, if any, of these observations to the regional abnormalities described in neurological patients with depression are unclear. Studies of patients with new onset of depression or preclinical-at-risk subjects are needed to clarify whether these changes reflect disease pathophysiology or are the consequence of chronic illness or treatment.

## Clues From Surgical Ablation Therapy

Observations of patients undergoing ablative surgery to alleviate refractory melancholia and unremitting emotional ruminations provide complementary evidence for regional localization of mood and affective behaviors (Cosgrove and Rausch 1995; Fulton 1951). The mechanisms by which these destructive lesions improve mood are unknown, as is the precise lesion site necessary for amelioration of depressive symptoms. Improved mood, however, is seen in many severely ill patients after anterior leukotomy or subcallosal or superior cingulotomy (Malizia 1997; Ovsiew and Frim 1997). These seemingly paradoxical effects suggest a more complicated interaction among limbic, paralimbic, and neocortical pathways in both normal and abnormal emotional processing than the lesion-deficit literature would intimate.

## Functional Imaging Studies

Resting-state PET and SPECT studies in patients with primary depression also report frontal and cingulate abnormalities, in general agreement with the pattern seen in neurological depressions. Across studies, the most robust and consistent finding is decreased frontal lobe function (Baxter et al. 1989; Bench et al. 1992; Buchsbaum et al. 1986; Drevets et al. 1997; Ebert and Ebmeier 1996; George et al. 1994c; Ketter et al. 1996; Lesser et al. 1994; Mayberg et al. 1994, 1997). The anatomic localization of frontal changes involves both dorsolateral prefrontal cortex (Brodmann areas 9, 10, 46) and ventral prefrontal and orbitofrontal cortices (Brodmann areas 10, 11, 47). Findings are generally bilateral, although asymmetries have been reported. Other limbic-paralimbic (amygdala anterior temporal, insula) and subcortical (basal ganglia, thalamus) abnormalities have also been identified, but the findings are more variable (Bonne et al. 1996; Buchsbaum et al. 1986; Drevets et al. 1992; Hornig et al. 1997; Mayberg et al. 1994, 1997; Post et al. 1987). Differences among patient subgroups (familial, bipolar, unipolar), as well as heterogeneous expression of clinical symptoms, are thought to contribute to this variance, but a consensus has not yet been reached. Use of different analytic strategies (voxelwise versus region-of-interest) likely also accounts for some of these apparent inconsistencies.

Several neurochemical markers have also been examined in depressed patients using imaging, but findings are quite variable. Decreases in serotonin transporter binding has been reported in brain stem (Malison et al. 1998), but not in any of the other regions identified in postmortem studies of depressed people who committed suicide, for example, ventral prefrontal cortex or anterior cingulate (Arango et al. 1997, 1999). 5-HT$_{1A}$ and 5-HT$_{2A}$ receptor densities have also been examined, but with inconsistent findings in the drug-free state, as previously described (Drevets et al. 1999; Mayberg et al. 1988; Meyer et al. 1999; Sargent et al. 2000). Parallel studies of other markers of interest are limited by available imaging ligands. Relationships between receptor and transporter markers or between neurochemical and regional metabolic changes have not been explored.

### Clinical Correlates

Despite the general consensus as to the regional localization of functional change patterns, some variability exists

(by example, Baxter 1989; Drevets et al. 1992; Mayberg et al. 1997). A critical unresolved question is how these different patterns might reflect specific symptoms, such as apathy, anxiety, psychomotor slowing, and executive cognitive dysfunction, present in varying combinations with dysphoric mood in individual depressed patients (Bench et al. 1993; Dolan et al. 1992; Mayberg et al. 1994; Osuch et al. 2000).

Many studies have demonstrated an inverse relationship between prefrontal activity and depression severity (reviewed by Ketter et al. 1996). Significant correlations have also been shown for psychomotor speed (negative correlation with prefrontal and angular gyrus, Bench et al. 1993; negative correlation with ventral frontal, Mayberg et al. 1994), anxiety (positive correlation with inferior parietal lobule, Bench et al. 1993; and with parahippocampal gyrus, Osuch et al. 2000), and cognitive performance (positive correlation with medial frontal/cingulate, Bench et al. 1993; Dolan et al. 1992).

Direct mapping of these behaviors is an alternative approach, allowing head-to-head comparisons of patients and nondepressed control subjects (Dolan et al. 1993; George et al. 1994a, 1994b, 1997). With this type of design, one can quantify the neural correlates of the performance decrement as well as identify potential disease-specific sites of task reorganization. These types of studies can be performed with any of the available functional methods, including PET, functional magnetic resonance imaging (fMRI), and event-related potentials (ERPs) (Liotti et al. 1997, 2000a, 2000b; Whalen et al. 1998).

Using this strategy, George et al. (1994a, 1997) demonstrated blunting of an expected left anterior cingulate increase during performance of a Stroop task. A shift to the left dorsolateral prefrontal cortex, a region not normally recruited for this task in healthy subjects, was also observed. Elliott et al. (1997a), using the Tower of London test, described similar attenuation of an expected increase in dorsolateral prefrontal cortex and failure to activate anterior cingulate and caudate—regions recruited in control subjects. These researchers, in an additional set of experiments (Elliot et al. 1997b, 1997c), further demonstrated that, unlike healthy subjects, depressed patients also failed to activate the caudate in response to positive or negative feedback given while they performed this same task (e.g., "You were right" vs. "You were wrong"). That feedback valence influenced cognitive performance in nondepressed subjects and more dramatically in depressed individuals illustrates the highly interactive nature of mood and cognitive systems.

Provocation of transient sadness has also been used

to identify putative pathways mediating sustained dysphoria in depressed patients. Pardo et al. (1993) first described blood flow increases using PET in superior and inferior prefrontal cortex during spontaneous recollection of previous sad events. Subsequent studies by George et al. (1995), Schneider et al. (1995), Lane et al. (1997), Gemar et al. (1996), Mayberg et al. (1999), Liotti et al. (2000a), and Damasio et al. (2000), using a variety of provocation methods, identified additional changes involving varying combinations of regions including insula, hypothalamus, cerebellum, and amygdala. Across studies, increases in regional activity were most prominent. Frontal decreases reminiscent of resting-state findings in clinically depressed patients were also seen, but not consistently (Damasio et al. 2000; Gemar et al. 1996; Liotti et al. 2000b; Mayberg et al. 1999) (Figure 31–2, left). Timing of scans and the specific instructions appear to have a critical impact on both patterns and direction of regional changes. For example, while cingulate increases are quite consistent across studies, the direction of frontal changes appears to be affected by whether scanning is performed during active recollection of the sad memory (increases as seen in George et al. 1995; Pardo et al. 1993) or only once the mood state has been provoked and sustained (decreases seen in Mayberg et al. 1999 and in Liotti et al. 2000b). Interestingly, frontal decreases overlap areas shown to activate with sustained attentional tasks in the absence of mood manipulations (Corbetta et al. 1993; Pardo et al. 1991)—behaviors commonly disturbed in depressed patients (Cohen et al. 1982; Roy-Byrne et al. 1986; Weingartner et al. 1981).

The critical importance of limbic and paralimbic regions in the mediation of negative emotions is further supported by a recent case of transient depression during deep-brain stimulation for treatment of intractable Parkinson's disease (Bejjani et al. 1999). Selective high-frequency stimulation to the left substantia nigra (2 mm below the subthalamic site that alleviated parkinsonian symptoms) provoked a reproducible and reversible depressive syndrome in a woman with no previous psychiatry history. Stimulation-induced mood changes were associated with focal blood flow increases in left orbitofrontal cortex, amygdala, globus pallidus, anterior thalamus, and right parietal cortex. This pattern of regional activation is similar to changes seen with memory-induced sadness in healthy volunteers, although there are clear differences requiring additional further studies. Nonetheless, this remarkable case provides important additional clues regarding regional circuits mediating normal and abnormal mood states and suggests a novel strategy for future research.

## Baseline Predictors of Treatment Response

Pretreatment rostral (pregenual) cingulate metabolism has been reported to predict response to pharmacotherapy (Brannan et al. 2000; Mayberg et al. 1997). Hypermetabolism was seen in eventual treatment responders; hypometabolism, in nonresponders. A similar hypermetabolic pattern in a nearby region of the dorsal anterior cingulate has also been shown to predict good response to one night of sleep deprivation (Wu et al. 1990, 1999). A related observation has been made in patients with obsessive-compulsive disorder, where ventral frontal hypermetabolism and hypometabolism preferentially respond to behavioral therapy or medication (Brody et al. 1998; Saxena et al. 1999). In depression, differential patterns predictive of response to one treatment over another have not yet been characterized. Nonetheless, these data suggest physiological differences among patient subgroups that can be critical to understanding brain plasticity and adaptation to illness, including propensity to respond to treatment. Evidence of persistent hypermetabolism in patients in full remission on maintenance SSRI treatment for more than a year further suggests a critical compensatory or adaptive role for rostral cingulate in facilitating and maintaining clinical response (Mayberg et al. 1998).

## Brain Changes With Antidepressant Treatments

Functional changes in cortical (dorsal/ventral prefrontal, parietal), limbic-paralimbic (cingulate, insula), and subcortical (caudate, thalamus) regions have been described after various types of treatments (medication, sleep deprivation, electroconvulsive therapy [ECT], rTMS, ablative surgery). Normalization of frontal hypometabolism is the best replicated finding, seen mainly with medication (tricyclics, monoamine oxidase inhibitors, various SSRIs), suggesting that frontal abnormalities may be state markers of the illness (Baxter et al. 1989; Bench et al. 1995; Buchsbaum et al. 1997; Ebert and Ebmeier 1996; Goodwin et al. 1993; Martinot et al. 1990; Mayberg et al. 1999, 2000). Changes in associated limbic, paralimbic, and subcortical regions are more variable (Bonne and Krausz 1997; Brody et al. 1999; Malizia 1997; Mayberg et al. 2000; G. S. Smith et al. 1999; Teneback et al. 1999). Few drug-treatment studies report regional decreases; although both limbic and cortical decreases are seen in studies of ECT (Nobler et al. 1994). No studies have directly compared changes common to antidepressants with different modes of action, although some literature exists on regional differences associated with response to different medications in patients with bipolar disorder (Little et al. 1996). Although certain change patterns (prefrontal, anterior cingulate increases;

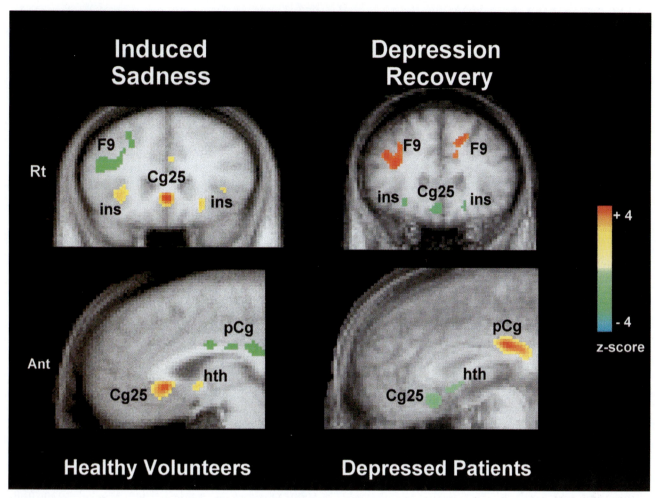

**FIGURE 31–2.** Common reciprocal changes in cortical and paralimbic function with shifts in mood state as measured with two different positron emission tomographic imaging techniques. Recovery from major depression (fluoxetine- and placebo-treated responders combined, *left images*) is associated with increases in dorsal cortical (positive z scores in *red-yellow*) and decreases in ventral paralimbic regional metabolism (negative z score in *green*). The reverse is seen with provocation of intense sadness in healthy volunteers, in whom dorsal decreases and ventral increases in blood flow accompany the acute changes in mood state (*right images*). F=frontal; ins=anterior insula; Cg25=subgenual cingulate gyrus; hth=hypothalamus; pCg=posterior cingulate gyrus. Numbers are Brodmann designations.
*Source.* Adapted from Mayberg et al. 1999.

ventral medial frontal decreases) appear to occur more often than others, a consistent and reliable pattern has not been demonstrated.

Treatment-induced changes in neurochemical markers have also been reported. 5-HT$_{2A}$ receptor downregulation has been demonstrated with SSRI and TCA treatment, consistent with studies in animals (Attar-Levy et al. 1999; Meyer et al. 2001; Yatham et al. 1999). Reported changes have been global rather than focal, with little to no regional selectivity. Similar global changes have been reported for 5-HT$_{1A}$ binding (Sargent et al. 2000). To date, no direct comparisons have been made of drugs with different primary targets of action (SSRIs, NRIs, monoamine oxidase inhibitors, bupropion) to define common changes in serotonergic or other

receptor subtypes with treatment. Correlations between metabolic and biochemical changes have not been examined. Although D$_2$ dopamine changes have been reported (Ebert et al. 1996; Klimke et al. 1999), other systems of interest such as glucocorticoid, norepinephrine, and glutamate have not been studied because imaging ligands for these sites have not yet been developed.

## Relation to Clinical Response

A critical issue in better understanding the reported variability in location and direction of regional changes with treatment is to consider that drug-induced effects may be different in patients who respond compared to those who do not, as suggested by the pretreatment resting-state studies described above. In support of this hypothesis, Mayberg and colleagues (2000) examined regional metabolic changes associated with 6 weeks of fluoxetine treatment in patients with major depression. Distinct patterns of change were seen at 1 and 6 weeks of treatment, with the time course of metabolic changes reflecting the temporal delay in clinical response. Clinical improvement was associated with limbic-paralimbic and striatal decreases (subgenual cingulate, hippocampus, pallidum, insula) and brain-stem and dorsal cortical increases (prefrontal, parietal, anterior/posterior cingulate). Failed response to fluoxetine was associated with a persistent 1-week pattern (hippocampal increases; pallidal, posterior cingulate decreases) and absence of either subgenual cingulate or prefrontal changes (Figure 31–3). These findings suggest not only an interaction between limbic-paralimbic and neocortical pathways in depression but also differences among patients in adaptation of specific target regions to chronic serotonergic modulation. Failure to induce the requisite adaptive changes might be seen as a contributing cause of treatment nonresponse. Although specific neurochemical mechanisms for these limbic, paralimbic, and neocortical metabolic changes remain speculative, preclinical studies implicated a series of receptor second messenger and molecular events (Blier and Montigny 1999; Duman et al. 2000; Hyman and Nestler 1996; Vaidya et al. 1997). As placebo responders show comparable changes in neocortex and subgenual cingulate (but not brain stem or hippocampus) to those seen with active drug, it is further hypothesized that clinical response, regardless of treatment mode, requires specific changes in critical target brain regions and pathways (Mayberg et al. 1999, 2000) (see Figure 31–2, right). This hypothesis is the focus of ongoing research.

## A Working Depression Model: Emphasis on Functional Neurocircuitry

Data presented in this chapter strongly support a critical role for frontal-subcortical circuits, and more specifically frontal-limbic pathways, in the mediation of clinical symptoms in patients with primary and secondary depression. The overall pattern of cortical, subcortical, and limbic changes suggests the involvement of several well-characterized pathways, schematically organized as an interactive network (Mayberg 1997; Mayberg et al. 2000) (Figure 31–4).

Brain regions with known anatomic interconnections that also show consistent and synchronized changes using PET in various behavioral states—transient sadness, baseline depressed, and pretreatment and posttreatment (as described in previous sections of this chapter)—have been grouped into three general compartments: dorsal, ventral, and subcortical. The dorsal-ventral segregation additionally defines those brain regions in which an inverse relationship is seen across experiments.

The dorsal compartment (Figure 31–4, attention-cognition) includes both neocortical and superior limbic elements and is postulated to mediate cognitive aspects of negative emotion such as apathy, psychomotor slowing, and impaired attention and executive function, based on complementary structural and functional lesion-deficit correlational studies (Bench et al. 1992; Devinsky et al. 1995; Dolan et al. 1993; Mayberg et al. 1994; Stuss and Benson 1986), symptom-specific treatment effects in depressed patients (Bench et al. 1993; Buchsbaum et al. 1997; Mayberg et al. 2000), activation studies designed to explicitly map these behaviors in healthy volunteers (George et al. 1995; Pardo et al. 1991), and connectivity patterns in primates (Morecraft et al. 1993; Petrides and Pandya 1984).

The ventral compartment (Figure 31–4, somatic-circadian) is composed predominantly of limbic and paralimbic regions known to mediate circadian, somatic, and vegetative aspects of depression, including sleep, appetite, libidinal, and endocrine disturbances, based on clinical and related animal studies (Augustine 1996; Maclean 1990; Mesulam and Mufson 1992; Neafsey 1990; Rolls 2000).

The rostral cingulate (Figure 31–4, rCg24a) is isolated from both the ventral and dorsal compartments based on its cytoarchitectural characteristics and reciprocal connections to both dorsal and ventral anterior cingulate (Vogt and Pandya 1987; Vogt et al. 1995). Contributing to this position in the model are the observations that metabolism in this region uniquely predicts antidepressant response in acutely depressed patients (Mayberg et al. 1997) and is also the principal site of aberrant response during mood induction in patients whose depression is in remission (Mayberg et al. 1998). These anatomic and clinical distinctions suggest that the rostral anterior cingulate may serve an important regulatory role in the overall network by facilitating the interactions between the dorsal and ventral compartments (Crino et al. 1993; Pandya and Yeterian 1996; Petrides and Pandya 1984). As such, dysfunction in this area could have significant impact on remote brain regions regulating a variety of behaviors, including the interaction between mood and cognitive, somatic, and circadian responses that characterize an emotional state.

Strategic modulation of specific subcortical (brain

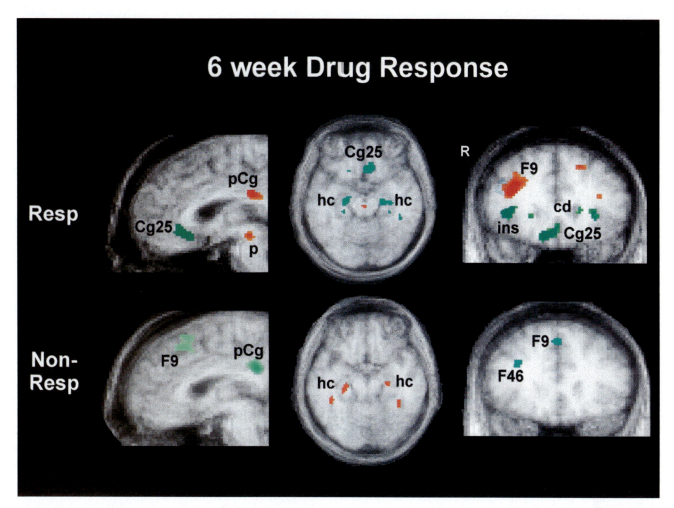

**FIGURE 31–3.** Changes in regional glucose metabolism in treatment responders (Resp; *top*) and nonresponders (Non-Resp; *bottom*) after 6 weeks of fluoxetine. Sagittal (*left*), axial (*middle*), and coronal (*right*) views. Improvement in clinical symptoms is uniquely associated with specific regional limbic-paralimbic decreases (shown in *green*) and cortical increases (shown in *red*). Nonresponse at 6 weeks is associated with a pattern identical to that seen in all patients at 1 week of treatment, specifically increases in metabolism in hippocampus and decreases in posterior cingulate gyrus and prefrontal cortex. F=prefrontal; ins=anterior insula; Cg=subgenual cingulate gyrus; pCg=posterior cingulate gyrus; hc=hippocampus. Numbers are Brodmann designations.
*Source.* Adapted from Mayberg et al. 2000.

stem, hypothalamus, hippocampus, posterior cingulate, striatal) "nodes" is seen as a primary mechanism for the observed widespread, reciprocal effects in ventral and dorsal cortical-limbic regions seen with antidepressant drug treatment (Mayberg et al. 1999, 2000). Although additional experimental studies are clearly needed, it is postulated that illness remission, whether facilitated by medication, psychotherapy, electroconvulsive therapy, or surgery, requires the reconfiguration of these reciprocally interactive pathways initiated through either top-down (cortical-limbic) or bottom-up (limbic-cortical) interventional strategies. If one assumes that both of these approaches are equally efficacious, the question shifts away from whether suppression of ventral limbic regions allows the normalization of dorsal cortical hypometabo-

lism or whether normalization of cortical activity causes a decrease in ventral limbic regions to a focus on patterns and mechanisms underlying successful and failed responses to different forms of treatment. This will be an important area of research in coming years.

## Conclusions

Although cognitive, endocrine, neurochemical, and sleep markers have been identified, a comprehensive neurobiological model for the syndrome of depression has yet to be elucidated. To this end, functional imaging studies have demonstrated critical biologic similarities between neurologically depressed patients and those with primary

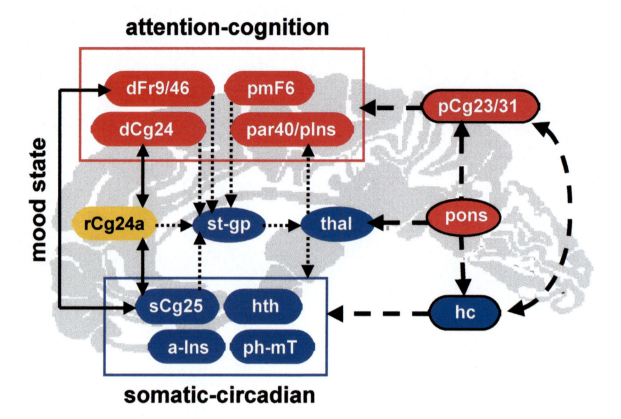

**FIGURE 31–4.** Depression model. Regions with known anatomic interconnections that also show synchronized changes using positron emission tomography (PET) in three behavioral states––normal transient sadness (control subjects), baseline depression (patients), and posttreatment state (patients)––are grouped into three main compartments: dorsal (*red box*), ventral (*blue box*), and subcortical. The dorsal-ventral segregation additionally identifies the brain regions where an inverse relationship is seen across the different PET paradigms. Sadness and depressive illness are both associated with decreases in dorsal limbic and neocortical regions (*red areas*) and relative increases in ventral paralimbic areas (*blue areas*). The model, in turn, proposes that illness remission occurs when there is inhibition of the overactive ventral regions and activation of the previously hypofunctioning dorsal areas, an effect facilitated by antidepressant action in the brain stem, hippocampus, and posterior cingulate gyrus (*black dashed arrows*). Normal or abnormal functioning of the rostral cingulate gyrus (Cg24 in *yellow*) with its bidirectional connections to both dorsal anterior cingulate gyrus (dCg24) and subgenual cingulate gyrus (Cg25) is postulated to facilitate interactions between dorsal cortical and more ventral paralimbic systems and to strategically influence pharmacologically mediated changes across the network. *Solid black arrows* identify known reciprocal corticolimbic, limbic-paralimbic, and cingulate-cingulate connections. *Dotted small black arrows* indicate known cortical-striatal-thalamic pathways. dFr=dorsolateral prefrontal; pmF=premotor; dCg=dorsal anterior cingulate; par=parietal; pIns=posterior insula; pCg=posterior cingulate; rCg24a=rostral anterior cingulate; st-gp=striatum-globus pallidus; thal=thalamus; sCg=subgenual cingulate; hth=hypothalamus; hc=hippocampus; a-Ins=anterior insula; ph-mT=parahippocampus-medial temporal. Numbers are Brodmann designations.
*Source.* Adapted from Mayberg 1997 and Mayberg et al. 2000.

affective disorders, focusing further attention on specific brain regions and associated chemical systems. In the future, the combined use of these research tools will prove useful in reassessing patients in whom standard therapy fails, in identifying depression in patients whose clinical presentation is atypical, and in recognizing depression that is confounded by the presence of concurrent neurological or other psychiatric diagnoses.

## References

Abas MA, Sahakian BJ, Levy R: Neuropsychological deficits and CT scan changes in elderly depressives. Psychol Med 20:507–520, 1990

Albert ML, Feldman RG, Willis AL: The subcortical dementia of progressive supranuclear palsy. J Neurol Neurosurg Psychiatry 37:121–130, 1974

Alexander GE, Crutcher MD, De Long MR: Basal ganglia-thalamocortical circuits: parallel substrates for motor, oculomotor, "prefrontal" and "limbic" functions. Prog Brain Res 85:119–146, 1990

Alloy LB, Ahrens AH: Depression and pessimism for the future: biased use of statistically relevant information in predictions for self versus others. J Pers Soc Psychol 52:366–378, 1987

Alloy LB, Abramson LY, Whitehouse WG, et al: Depressogenic cognitive styles: predictive validity, information processing and personality characteristics, and developmental origins. Behav Res Ther 37(6):503–531, 1999

Altshuler LL, Devinsky O, Post RM, et al: Depression, anxiety, and temporal lobe epilepsy: laterality of focus and symptoms. Arch Neurol 47:284–288, 1990

American Psychiatric Association: Practice Guideline for the Treatment of Patients With Major Depressive Disorder (revision). Am J Psychiatry 157:1–45, 2000

Arana GW, Baldessarini RJ, Brown WA, et al: The dexamethasone suppression test: an overview of its current status in psychiatry. Task Force Report for the American Psychiatric Association. Washington, DC, American Psychiatric Association, 1987

Arango V, Underwood MD, Gubbi AV, et al: Localized alterations in pre- and postsynaptic serotonin binding sites in the ventrolateral prefrontal cortex of suicide victims. Brain Res 688(1–2):121–133, 1995

Arango V, Underwood MD, Mann JJ: Postmortem findings in suicide victims. Implications for in vivo imaging studies. Ann N Y Acad Sci 836:269–287, 1997

Arango V, Underwood MD, Kassir SA, et al: Reduction in SERT binding in prefrontal cortex in depression and suicide. Abstract and poster presentation, 38th Annual Meeting of the American College of Neuropsychopharmacology, Acapulco, Mexico, December 12–16, 1999, p 158

Attar-Levy D, Martinot JL, Blin J, et al: The cortical serotonin2 receptors studied with positron-emission tomography and [18F]-setoperone during depressive illness and antidepressant treatment with clomipramine. Biol Psychiatry 45(2):180–186, 1999

Augustine JR: Circuitry and functional aspects of the insular lobe in primates including humans. Brain Res Brain Res Rev 22:229–244, 1996

Baron JC: Depression of energy metabolism in distant brain structures: studies with positron emission tomography in stroke patients. Semin Neurol 9:281–285, 1989

Bauer M, Frazer A: Mood disorders, in Biological Bases of Brain Function and Disease, 2nd Edition. Edited by Frazer A, Molinoff P, Winokur A. New York, Raven, 1994, pp 303–323

Baxter LR, Schwartz JM, Phelps ME, et al: Reduction of prefrontal cortex glucose metabolism common to three types of depression. Arch Gen Psychiatry 46:243–250, 1989

Bear DM: Hemispheric specialization and the neurology of emotion. Arch Neurol 40:195–202, 1983

Bear DM, Fedio P: Quantitative analysis of interictal behavior in temporal lobe epilepsy. Arch Neurol 34:454–467, 1977

Beck AT, Rush AJ, Shaw BF, et al: Cognitive Therapy of Depression. New York, Guilford, 1979

Bejjani BP, Damier P, Arnulf I, et al: Transient acute depression induced by high-frequency deep-brain stimulation. New Engl J Med 340:1476–1480, 1999

Benca RM: Mood disorders, in Principles and Practice of Sleep Medicine. Edited by Kryger MH, Roth T, Dement WC. Philadelphia, WB Saunders, 1994, pp 899–913

Benca RM, Obermeyer WH, Thisted RA, et al: Sleep and psychiatric disorders: a meta-analysis. Arch Gen Psychiatry 49:651–668, 1992

Bench CJ, Friston KJ, Brown RG, et al: The anatomy of melancholia—focal abnormalities of cerebral blood flow in major depression. Psychol Med 22:607–615, 1992

Bench CJ, Friston KJ, Brown RG, et al: Regional cerebral blood flow in depression measured by positron emission tomography: the relationship with clinical dimensions. Psychol Med 23:579–590, 1993

Bench CJ, Frackowiak RSJ, Dolan RJ: Changes in regional cerebral blood flow on recovery from depression. Psychol Med 25:247–251, 1995

Blaney PH: Affect and memory: a review. Psychol Bull 99:229–246, 1986

Blazer DG, Kessler RC, McGonagle KA, et al: The Prevalence and Distribution of Major Depression in a National Community Sample: The National Comorbidity Survey. Am J Psychiatry 151:979–986, 1994

Blier P, de Montigny C: Serotonin and drug-induced therapeutic responses in major depression, obsessive compulsive and panic disorders. Neuropsychopharmacology 21:170–178, 1999

Bonne O, Krausz Y: Pathophysiological significance of cerebral perfusion abnormalities in major depression: trait or state marker? Eur Neuropsychopharmacol 7:225–233, 1997

Bonne O, Krausz Y, Gorfine M, et al: Cerebral hypoperfusion in medication resistant, depressed patients assessed by Tc99m-HMPAO SPECT. J Affect Disord 41:163–171, 1996

Bourgon LN, Kellner CH: Relapse of depression after ECT: a review. J ECT 16:19–31, 2000

Bradley BP, Mogg K: Mood and personality in recall of positive and negative information. Behav Res Ther 32(1):137–141, 1994

Brannan SK, Mayberg HS, McGinnis S, et al: Cingulate metabolism predicts treatment response: a replication (abstract). Biol Psychiatry 47(107S):355, 2000

Bremner JD, Randall P, Scott TM, et al: MRI-based measurement of hippocampal volume in post-traumatic stress disorder. Am J Psychiatry 152:973–981, 1995

Bremner JD, Innis RB, Salomon RM, et al: Positron emission tomography measurement of cerebral metabolic correlates of tryptophan depletion-induced depressive relapse. Arch Gen Psychiatry 54(4):364–374, 1997

Broca P: Anatomie comparée des circonvolutions cérébrales. le grant lobe limbique et la scissure limbique dans la série des mammiféres. Revue Anthropologie 1:385–498, 1878

Brody AL, Saxena S, Schwartz JM, et al: FDG PET predictors of response to behavioral therapy and pharmacotherapy in OCD. Psychiatry Res 84:1–6, 1998

Brody AL, Saxena S, Silverman DH, et al: Brain metabolic changes in major depressive disorder from pre- to post-treatment with paroxetine. Psychiatry Res 91:127–139, 1999

Bromfield EB, Altshuler L, Leiderman DB, et al: Cerebral metabolism and depression in patients with complex partial seizures. Arch Neurol 49:617–623, 1992

Brown RG, Scott LC, Bench CJ, et al: Cognitive function in depression: its relationship to the presence and severity of intellectual decline. Psychol Med 24:829–847, 1994

Buchsbaum MS, Wu J, DeLisi LE, et al: Frontal cortex and basal ganglia metabolic rates assessed by positron emission tomography with 18F-2-deoxyglucose in affective illness. J Affect Disord 10:137–152, 1986

Buchsbaum MS, Wu J, Siegel BV, et al: Effect of sertraline on regional metabolic rate in patients with affective disorder. Biol Psychiatry 41:15–22, 1997

Bulbena A, Berrios G: Pseudodementia: facts and figures. Br J Psychiatry 148:87–94, 1986

Bunney WEJ, Davis JM: Norepinephrine in depressive reactions. Arch Gen Psychiatry 13:438–493, 1965

Caldecott-Hazzard S, Morgan DG, Delison-Jones F, et al: Clinical and biochemical aspects of depressive disorders, II: transmitter/receptor theories. Synapse 9:251–301, 1991

Calev A, Korin Y, Shapira B, et al: Verbal and non-verbal recall by depressed and euthymic affective patients. Psychol Med 16:789–794, 1986

Caligiuri MP, Ellwanger J: Motor and cognitive aspects of motor retardation in depression. J Affect Disord 57(1–3):83–93, 2000

Cantello R, Aguaggia M, Gilli M, et al: Major depression in Parkinson's disease and the mood response to intravenous methylphenidate: possible role of the "hedonic" dopamine synapse. J Neurol Neurosurg Psychiatry 52:724–731, 1989

Carroll BJ, Curtis GC, Mendels J: Neuroendocrine regulation in depression. Arch Gen Psychiatry 33:1039–1044, 1976

Carroll BJ, Feinberg M, Greden J: The dexamethasone suppression test, a specific laboratory test for the diagnosis of melancholia: standardization, validation and clinical utility. Arch Gen Psychiatry 38:15–22, 1981

Carson AJ, MacHale S, Allen K, et al: Depression after stroke and lesion location: a systematic review. Lancet 356 (9224):122–126, 2000

Charney DS: Monoamine dysfunction and the pathophysiology and treatment of depression. J Clin Psychiatry 59 (suppl 14):11–14, 1998

Coffey CE, Wilkinson WE, Weiner RD, et al: Quantitative cerebral anatomy in depression: a controlled magnetic resonance imaging study. Arch Gen Psychiatry 50:7–16, 1993

Cohen RM, Weingartner H, Smallberg SA, et al: Effort and cognition in depression. Arch Gen Psychiatry 39:593–597, 1982

Corbetta M, Miezin FM, Shulman GL, et al: A PET study of visuospatial attention. J Neurosci 13:1202–1226, 1993

Coryell W, Endicott J, Keller MB: Outcome of patients with chronic affective disorders: a five year follow-up. Am J Psychiatry 147:1627–1633, 1990

Cosgrove GR, Rauch SL: Psychosurgery. Neurosurg Clin N Am 6:167–176, 1995

Costa PT Jr, McCrae RR: Stability and change in personality assessment: the revised NEO Personality Inventory in the year 2000. J Pers Assess 68:86–94, 1997

Crino PB, Morrison JH, Hof PR: Monoamine innervation of cingulate cortex, in The Neurobiology of Cingulate Cortex and Limbic Thalamus: A Comprehensive Handbook. Edited by Vogt BA, Gabriel M. Boston MA, Birkhauser, 1993, pp 285–310

Cummings JL: Depression and Parkinson's disease: a review. Am J Psychiatry 149:443–454, 1992

Cummings JL, Victoroff JI: Noncognitive neuropsychiatric syndromes in Alzheimer's disease. Neuropsychiatry Neuropsychol Behav Neurol 2:140–158, 1990

Damasio AR: Descartes' Error. New York, GP Putnam's Sons, 1994

Damasio AR, Van Hoesen GW: Emotional disturbances associated with focal lesions of the limbic frontal lobe, in Neuropsychology of Human Emotion. Edited by Heilman KM, Satz P. New York, Guilford, 1983, pp 85–110

Damasio AR, Grabowsky TJ, Bechara A, et al: Subcortical and cortical brain activity during the felling of self-generated emotions. Nat Neurosci 3:1049–1056, 2000

Dantchev N, Widlocher DJ: The measurement of retardation in depression. J Clin Psychiatry 59 (suppl 14):19–25, 1998

Delgado PL, Charney DS, Price LH, et al: Serotonin function and the mechanism of antidepressant action: reversal of antidepressant-induced remission by rapid depletion of plasma tryptophan. Arch Gen Psychiatry 47:411–418, 1990

Dening TR, Berrios GE: Wilson's disease: psychiatric symptoms in 195 patients. Arch Gen Psychiatry 46:1126–1134, 1989

Deptula D, Pomara N: Effects of antidepressants on human performance: a review. J Clin Psychopharmacol 10:105–111, 1990

DeRubeis RJ, Gelfand LA, Tang TZ, et al: Medications versus cognitive behavioral therapy for severely depressed outpatients: mega-analysis of four randomized comparisons. Am J Psychiatry 156:1007–1013, 1999

Devinsky O, Morrell MJ, Vogt BA: Contributions of anterior cingulate cortex to behavior. Brain 118:279–306, 1995

D'haenen HA, Bossuyt A, Mertens J, et al: SPECT imaging of serotonin-2 receptors in depression. Psychiatry Res 45:227–237, 1992

Dolan RJ, Bench CJ, Brown RG, et al: Regional cerebral blood flow abnormalities in depressed patients with cognitive impairment. J Neurol Neurosurg Psychiatry 55:768–773, 1992

Dolan RJ, Bench CJ, Liddle PF, et al: Dorsolateral prefrontal cortex dysfunction in the major psychoses: symptom or disease specificity? J Neurol Neurosurg Psychiatry 56:1290–1294, 1993

Drevets WC, Videen TO, Price JL, et al: A functional anatomical study of unipolar depression. J Neurosci 12:3628–3641, 1992

Drevets WC, Price JL, Simpson JR Jr, et al: Subgenual prefrontal cortex abnormalities in mood disorders. Nature 386:824–827, 1997

Drevets WC, Frank E, Price JC, et al: PET imaging of serotonin 1A receptor binding in depression. Biol Psychiatry 46:1375–1387, 1999

Dubini A, Bosc M, Polin V: Noradrenaline-selective versus serotonin-selective antidepressant therapy: differential effects on social functioning. J Psychopharmacol 11 (suppl 4):S17–23, 1997

Duman RS, Malberg J, Thome J: Neural plasticity to stress and antidepressant treatment. Biol Psychiatry 46:1181–1191, 1999

Duman RS, Malberg J, Nakagawa S, et al: Neuronal plasticity and survival in mood disorders. Biol Psychiatry 48:732–739, 2000

Duncan GE, Knapp DJ, Johnson KB, et al: Functional classification of antidepressants based on antagonism of swim stress-induced fos-like immunoreactivity. J Pharmacol Exp Ther 277:1076–1089, 1996

Dupont RM, Jernigan TL, Heindel W, et al: Magnetic resonance imaging and mood disorders. Localization of white matter and other subcortical abnormalities. Arch Gen Psychiatry 52:747–755, 1995

Ebert D, Ebmeier K: Role of the cingulate gyrus in depression: from functional anatomy to depression. Biol Psychiatry 39:1044–1050, 1996

Ebert D, Feistel H, Loew T, et al: Dopamine and depression—striatal dopamine D2 receptor SPECT before and after antidepressant therapy. Psychopharmacology (Berl) 126(1):91–94, 1996

Elkin I, Shea MT, Watkins JT, et al: NIMH Treatment of Depression Collaborative Research Program. General effectiveness of treatments. Arch Gen Psychiatry 46:971–982, 1989

Elliott R: The neuropsychological profile in unipolar depression. Trends in Cognitive Sciences 2:449–454, 1998

Elliott R, Baker SC, Rogers RD, et al: Prefrontal dysfunction in depressed patients performing a complex planning task: a study using positron emission tomography. Psychol Med 27(4):931–942, 1997a

Elliott R, Frith CD, Dolan RJ: Differential neural response to positive and negative feedback in planning and guessing tasks. Neuropsychologia 35:1395–1404, 1997b

Elliott R, Sahakian BJ, Herrod JJ: Abnormal response to negative feedback in unipolar depression: evidence for a diagnosis specific impairment. J Neurol Neurosurg Psychiatry 63(1):74–82, 1997c

Ellis HC, Ashbrook PW: The "state" of mood and memory research, in Mood and Memory: Theory, Research, and Applications. Edited by Kuiken D. Newbury Park, CA, Sage, 1991, pp 1–21

Emery VO, Oxman TE: Update on the dementia spectrum of depression. Am J Psychiatry 149:305–317, 1992

Fava M, Kendler KS: Major depressive disorder. Neuron 28:335–341, 2000

Fibiger HC: The neurobiological substrates of depression in Parkinson's disease: a hypothesis. Can J Neurol Sci 11:105–107, 1984

Flint AJ, Black SE, Campbell-Taylor I, et al: Abnormal speech articulation, psychomotor retardation, and subcortical dysfunction in major depression. J Psychiatr Res 27:285–287, 1993

Flor-Henry P: Psychosis and temporal lobe epilepsy. Epilepsia 10:363–395, 1969

Folstein SE, Abbott MH, Chase GA, et al: The association of affective disorder with Huntington's disease in a case series and in families. Psychol Med 13:537–542, 1983

Frank E, Thase ME: Natural history and preventative treatment of recurrent mood disorders. Annu Rev Med 50:453–468, 1999

Fudge JL, Perry PJ, Garvey MJ: A comparison of the effect of fluoxetine and trazodone on the cognitive functioning of depressed outpatients. J Affect Disord 18:275–280, 1990

Fulton JF: Frontal Lobotomy and Affective Behavior: A Neurophysiological Analysis. London, Chapman & Hall, 1951

Gainotti G: Emotional behavior and hemispheric side of the lesion. Cortex 8:41–55, 1972

Gemar MC, Kapur S, Segal ZV, et al: Effects of self-generated sad mood on regional cerebral activity: a PET study in normal subjects. Depression 4:81–88, 1996

George MS, Ketter TA, Parekh PI, et al: Regional brain activity when selecting a response despite interference: an H215O PET study of the Stroop and an emotional Stroop. Hum Brain Mapp 1:194–209, 1994a

George MS, Ketter TA, Parekh PI, et al: Spatial ability in affective illness: differences in regional brain activation during a spatial matching task (H215O PET). Neuropsychiatry Neuropsychol Behav Neurol 7:143–153, 1994b

George MS, Ketter TA, Post RM: Prefrontal cortex dysfunction in clinical depression. Depression 2:59–72, 1994c

George MS, Ketter TA, Parekh PI, et al: Brain activity during transient sadness and happiness in healthy women. Am J Psychiatry 152:341–351, 1995

George MS, Ketter TA, Parekh PI, et al: Blunted left cingulate activation in mood disorder subjects during a response interference task (the Stroop). J Neuropsychiatry Clin Neurosci 9:55–63, 1997

George MS, Lisanby SH, Sackeim HA: Transcranial magnetic stimulation: applications in neuropsychiatry. Arch Gen Psychiatry 56(4):300–311, 1999

Golden LR, Gershon ES: The genetic epidemiology of major depressive illness, in Review of Psychiatry, Vol 7. Edited by Frances AJ, Hales RE. Washington, DC, American Psychiatric Press, 1988, pp 148–168

Goldman-Rakic PS, Selemon LD: Topography of corticostriatal projections in nonhuman primates and implications for functional parcellation of the neostriatum, in Cerebral Cortex. Edited by Jones EG, Peters A. New York, Plenum, 1984, pp 447–466

Goodwin GM, Austin MP, Dougall N, et al: State changes in brain activity shown by the uptake of 99mTc-exametazime with single photon emission tomography in major depression before and after treatment. J Affect Disord 29:243–253, 1993

Grabiel AM: Neurotransmitters and neuromodulators in the basal ganglia. Trends Neurosci 13:244–254, 1990

Grafman J, Vance SC, Weingartner H, et al: The effects of lateralized frontal lesions on mood regulation. Brain 109:1127–1148, 1986

Grafton ST, Mazziotta JC, Pahl JJ, et al: A comparison of neurological, metabolic, structural and genetic evaluations in persons at risk for Huntington's disease. Ann Neurol 28:614–621, 1990

Grasso MG, Pantano P, Ricci M, et al: Mesial temporal cortex hypoperfusion is associated with depression in subcortical stroke. Stroke 25:980–985, 1994

Greenwald BS, Kramer-Ginsberg E, Krishnan RR: MRI signal hyperintensities in geriatric depression. Am J Psychiatry 153:1212–1215, 1996

Gross-Isseroff R, Dollon KA, Israeli M, et al: Regionally selective increases in mu opioid receptor density in the brains of suicide victims. Brain Res 530:312–316, 1990

Hasher L, Zacks RT: Automatic and effortful processes in memory. J Exp Psychol Gen 108:356–388, 1979

Healy D, Healy H: The clinical pharmacologic profile of reboxetine: does it involve the putative neurobiological substrates of well-being? J Affect Disord 51:313–322, 1998

Heim C, Newport DJ, Miller AH, et al: Long-term neuroendocrine effects of childhood maltreatment (letter). JAMA 284(18):2321, 2000

Henriques JB, Glowacki JM, Davidson RJ: Reward fails to alter response bias in depression. J Abnorm Psychol 103(3):460–466, 1994

Hertel PT, Milan S: Depressive deficits in recognition: dissociation of recollection and familiarity. J Abnorm Psychol 103:736–742, 1994

Hickie I, Scott E, Wilhelm K, et al: Subcortical hyperintensities on magnetic resonance imaging in patients with severe depression—a longitudinal evaluation. Biol Psychiatry 42(5):367–374, 1997

Hickie IB, Scott EM, Davenport TA: Are antidepressant all the same? surveying the opinions of Australian psychiatrists. Aust N Z J Psychiatry 33:642–649, 1999

Hietaharju A, Yli-Kerttula U, Hakkinen V, et al: Nervous system manifestations in Sjogren's syndrome. Acta Neurol Scand 81:144–152, 1990

Hindmarch I, Shillingford J, Shillingford C: The effects of sertraline on psychomotor performance in elderly volunteers. J Clin Psychiatry 5:34–36, 1990

Hollon SD, DeRubeis RJ, Evans MD, et al: Cognitive therapy and pharmacotherapy for depression. Singly and in combination. Arch Gen Psychiatry 49:774–781, 1992

Honer WG, Hurwitz T, Li DKB, et al: Temporal lobe involvement in multiple sclerosis patients with psychiatric disorders. Arch Neurol 44:187–190, 1987

Hornig M, Mozley PD, Amsterdam JD: HMPAO SPECT brain imaging in treatment-resistant depression. Prog Neuropsychopharmacol Biol Psychiatry 21:1097–1114, 1997

Hyman SE, Nestler EJ: Initiation and adaptation: a paradigm for understanding psychotropic drug action. Am J Psychiatry 153:151–162, 1996

Isogawa K, Akiyoshi J, Hikichi T, et al: Effect of corticotropin releasing factor receptor 1 antagonist on extracellular norepinephrine, dopamine and serotonin in hippocampus and prefrontal cortex of rats in vivo. Neuropeptides 34:234–239, 2000

Jacobs BL, vanPraag H, Gage FH: Depression and the birth and death of cells. American Scientist 88:340–345, 2000

Jagust WJ, Reed BR, Martin EM, et al: Cognitive function and regional cerebral blood flow in Parkinson's disease. Brain 115:521–537, 1992

Janowsky DS, Risch SC, Gillin JC: Cholinergic involvement in affective illness, in Receptors and Ligands in Psychiatry. Edited by Sen AK, Lee T. New York, Cambridge University Press, 1988, pp 228–244

Johnson DL, Wiebe JS, Gold SM, et al: Cerebral blood flow and personality: a positron emission tomography study. Am J Psychiatry 156(2):252–257, 1999

Johnson MH, Magaro PA: Effects of mood and severity on memory processes in depression and mania. Psychol Bull 101:28–40, 1987

Jones RD, Tranel D, Benton A, et al: Differentiating dementia from "pseudodementia" early in the clinical course: utility of neuropsychological tests. Neuropsychology 6:13–21, 1992

Kaufman J, Plotsky P, Nemeroff CB, et al: Effects of early adverse experiences on brain structure and function: clinical implications. Biol Psychiatry 48:778–790, 2000

Keegan D, Bowen RC, Blackshaw S, et al: A comparison of fluoxetine and amitriptyline in the treatment of major depression. Int Clin Psychopharmacol 6:117–124, 1991

Keller MB, Lavori PW, Klerman GL: Predictors of relapse in major depressive disorder. JAMA 250:3299–3304, 1983

Kendler KS, Kessler RC, Walters EE, et al: Stressful life events, genetic liability, and onset of an episode of major depression in women. Am J Psychiatry 152:833–842, 1995

Kendler KS, Gardner CO, Prescott CA: Clinical characteristics of major depression that predict risk of depression in relatives. Arch Gen Psychiatry 56:322–327, 1999

Kessler RC: The effects of stressful life events on depression. Annu Rev Psychol 48:191–214, 1997

Kestler LP, Malhotra AK, Finch C, et al: The relation between dopamine D2 receptor density and personality: preliminary evidence from the NEO personality inventory–revised. Neuropsychiatry Neuropsychol Behav Neurol 13(1):48–52, 2000

Ketter TA, George MS, Kimbrell TA, et al: Functional brain imaging, limbic function, and affective disorders. The Neuroscientist 2:55–65, 1996

King DA, Cox C, Lyness JM, et al: Neuropsychological effects of depression and age in an elderly sample: a confirmatory study. Neuropsychology 9:399–408, 1995

Kleist K: Bericht über die Gehirnpathologie in ihrer Bedeutung für Neurologie und Psychiatrie. Zeitschrift fur des Gesamte Neurologie und Psychiatrie 158:159–193, 1937

Klimek V, Stockmeier C, Overholser J, et al: Reduced levels of NE transporters in the LC in major depression. J Neurosci 17:8451–8458, 1997

Klimke A, Larisch R, Janz A, et al: Dopamine D2 receptor binding before and after treatment of major depression measured by [123I]IBZM SPECT. Psychiatry Res 90(2):91–101, 1999

Krikorian R, Wrobel AJ: Cognitive impairment in HIV infection. AIDS 5:1501–1507, 1991

Krueger S, Goldapple K, Liotti M, et al: Regional changes in cerebral blood flow following transient sadness in bipolar affective disorder. Society for Neuroscience Abstracts 26:866.2, 2000

Lamping DL, Spring B, Gelenberg AJ: Effects of two antidepressants on memory performance in depressed outpatients: a double-blind study. Psychopharmacology (Berl) 84:254–261, 1984

Lane RD, Reiman EM, Ahern GL, et al: Neuroanatomical correlates of happiness, sadness and disgust. Am J Psychiatry 154:926–933, 1997

Langer SZ, Schoemaker H: Platelet imipramine binding in depression, in Receptors and Ligands in Psychiatry. Edited by Sen AK, Lee T. New York, Cambridge University Press, 1988, pp 327–346

Langworthy OR, Hesser FH: Syndrome of pseudobulbar palsy: an anatomic and physiologic analysis. Arch Intern Med 65:106–121, 1940

Laplane D, Levasseur M, Pillon B, et al: Obsessive-compulsive and other behavioural changes with bilateral basal ganglia lesions: a neuropsychological, magnetic resonance imaging and positron tomography study. Brain 12:699–725, 1989

LaRue A: Memory loss and aging: distinguishing dementia from benign senescent forgetfulness and depressive pseudodementia. Psychiatr Clin North Am 5:89–103, 1982

Lawson JS, Inglis J, Delva NJ, et al: Electrode placement in ECT: cognitive effects. Psychol Med 20:335–344, 1990

LeDoux J: The Emotional Brain. New York, Simon & Schuster, 1996

Lemke MR, Puhl P, Koethe N, et al: Psychomotor retardation and anhedonia in depression. Acta Psychiatr Scand 99:252–256, 1999

Lesser I, Mena I, Boone KB, et al: Reduction of cerebral blood flow in older depressed patients. Arch Gen Psychiatry 51:677–686, 1994

Leyton M, Young SN, Pihl RO, et al: Effects on mood of acute phenylalanine/tyrosine depletion in healthy women. Neuropsychopharmacology 22(1):52–63, 2000

Liotti M, Mayberg HS, Ryder K, et al: An ERP study of mood provocation in remitted depression. Society for Neuroscience Abstracts 23(2):1657, 1997

Liotti M, Mayberg HS, Brannan SK, et al: Differential neural correlates of sadness and fear in healthy subjects: implications for affective disorders. Biol Psychiatry 48(1):30–42, 2000a

Liotti M, Woldorff MG, Perez R, et al: An ERP study of the temporal course of the Stroop color-word interference effect. Neuropsychologia 38(5):706–716, 2000b

Lipman RS, Brown EA, Silbert GA, et al: Cognitive performance as modified by age and ECT history. Prog Neuropsychopharmacol Biol Psychiatry 17:581–594, 1993

Little JT, Ketter TA, Kimbrell TA, et al. Venlafaxine or bupropion responders but not nonresponders show baseline prefrontal and paralimbic hypometabolism compared with controls. Psychopharmacology Bulletin 32:629–635, 1996

Lockwood KA, Alexopoulos GS, Kakuma T, et al: Subtypes of cognitive impairment in depressed older adults. Am J Geriatr Psychiatry 8(3):201–208, 2000

Loosen PT: The TRH-induced TSH response in psychiatric patients: a possible neuroendocrine marker. Psychoneuroendocrinology 10:237–260, 1985

Lopez JF, Akil H, Watson SJ: Neural circuits mediating stress. Biol Psychiatry 46:1461–1471, 1999

Lyness SA, Eaton EM, Schneider LS: Cognitive performance in older and middle-aged depressed outpatients and controls. J Gerontol 49(3):P129–P136, 1994

Lyons DM, Yang C, Mobley BW, et al: Early environmental regulation of glucocorticoid feedback sensitivity in young adult monkeys. J Neuroendocrinol 12(8):723–728, 2000

Maas JW, Koslow SH, Katz MM, et al: Pretreatment neurotransmitter metabolite levels and response to tricyclic antidepressant drugs. Am J Psychiatry 141:1159–1171, 1984

Maclean PD: The Triune Brain in Evolution: Role in Paleocerebral Function. New York, Plenum, 1990

MacLeod AK, Byrne A: Anxiety, depression, and the anticipation of future positive and negative experiences. J Abnorm Psychol 105:286–289, 1996

Maj M, Veltro F, Pirozzi R, et al: Patterns of recurrence of illness after recovery from an episode of major depression: a prospective study. Am J Psychiatry 149:795–800, 1992

Malison RT, Price LH, Berman RM, et al: Reduced midbrain serotonin transporter availability in major depression as measured by [$^{123}$I]-2beta-carbomethoxy-3beta-(4-iodophenyl)tropane and single photon emission computed tomography. Biol Psychiatry 44:1090–1098, 1998

Malizia AL: The frontal lobes and neurosurgery for psychiatric disorders. J Psychopharmacol 11(2):179–187, 1997

Manji HK, Moore GJ, Chen G: Clinical and preclinical evidence for the neurotrophic effects of mood stabilizers: implications for the pathophysiology and treatment of manic-depressive illness. Biol Psychiatry 48:740–754, 2000

Mann JJ, Kapur S: Elucidation of biochemical basis of the antidepressant action of electroconvulsive therapy by human studies. Psychopharmacology Bulletin 30:445–453, 1994

Mann JJ, Huang Y, Underwood MD, et al: A serotonin transporter gene promoter polymorphism (5-HTTLPR) and prefrontal cortical binding in major depression and suicide. Arch Gen Psychiatry 57:729–738, 2000

Marin RS: Differential diagnosis and classification of apathy. Am J Psychiatry 147:22–30, 1990

Martin WR, Sloan JW, Sapira JD, et al: Physiologic, subjective, and behavioural effects of amphetamine, methamphetamine, ephedrine, phenmetrazine, and methylphenidate in man. Clin Pharmacol Ther 32:632–637, 1971

Martinot JL, Hardy P, Feline A, et al: Left prefrontal glucose hypometabolism in the depressed state: a confirmation. Am J Psychiatry 147:1313–1317, 1990

Massman PJ, Delis DC, Butters N, et al: The subcortical dysfunction hypothesis of memory deficits in depression: neuropsychological validation in a subgroup of patients. J Clin Exp Neuropsychol 14:687–706, 1992

Mayberg HS: Frontal lobe dysfunction in secondary depression. J Neuropsychiatry Clin Neurosci 6:428–442, 1994

Mayberg HS: Limbic-cortical dysregulation: a proposed model of depression. J Neuropsychiatry Clin Neurosci 9:471–481, 1997

Mayberg HS, Solomon DH: Depression in PD: a biochemical and organic viewpoint, in Behavioral Neurology of Movement Disorders: Advances in Neurology Series, Vol 65. Edited by Weiner WJ, Lang AE. New York, Raven, 1995, pp 49–60

Mayberg HS, Robinson RG, Wong DF, et al: PET imaging of cortical S2-serotonin receptors after stroke: lateralized changes and relationship to depression. Am J Psychiatry 145:937–943, 1988

Mayberg HS, Starkstein SE, Sadzot B, et al: Selective hypometabolism in the inferior frontal lobe in depressed patients with Parkinson's disease. Ann Neurol 28:57–64, 1990

Mayberg HS, Starkstein SE, Morris PL, et al: Remote cortical hypometabolism following focal basal ganglia injury: relationship to secondary changes in mood (abstract). Neurology 41 (suppl):266, 1991

Mayberg HS, Starkstein SE, Peyser CE, et al: Paralimbic frontal lobe hypometabolism in depression associated with Huntington's disease. Neurology 42:1791–1797, 1992

Mayberg HS, Lewis PJ, Regenold W, et al: Paralimbic hypoperfusion in unipolar depression. J Nucl Med 35:929–934, 1994

Mayberg HS, Brannan SK, Mahurin RK, et al: Anterior cingulate function and mood: evidence from FDG PET studies of primary and secondary depression (abstract). Neurology 46:A327, 1996

Mayberg HS, Brannan SK, Mahurin RK, et al: Cingulate function in depression: a potential predictor of treatment response. Neuroreport 8:1057–1061, 1997

Mayberg HS, Liotti M, Brannan SK, et al: Disease and state-specific effects of mood challenge on rCBF (abstract). Neuroimage 7(4):S901, 1998

Mayberg HS, Liotti M, Brannan SK, et al: Reciprocal limbic-cortical function and negative mood: converging PET findings in depression and normal sadness. Am J Psychiatry 156(5):675–682, 1999

Mayberg HS, Brannan SK, Mahurin RK, et al: Regional metabolic effects of fluoxetine in major depression: serial changes and relationship to clinical response. Biol Psychiatry 48:830–843, 2000

Mayeux R, Stern Y, Sano M, et al: The relationship of serotonin to depression in Parkinson's disease. Mov Disord 3:237–244, 1988

McEwen BS: Effects of adverse experiences for brain structure and function. Biol Psychiatry 48:721–731, 2000

Meany M, Aitken D, Berkel H, et al: Effects of neonatal handling of age-related impairments associated with the hippocampus. Science 239:766–768, 1998

Meltzer CC, Price JC, Mathis CA, et al: PET imaging of serotonin type 2A receptors in late-life neuropsychiatric disorders. Am J Psychiatry 156(12):1871–1878, 1999

Mendez MF, Cummings UL, Benson DF: Depression in epilepsy. Arch Neurol 43:766–770, 1986

Mesulam MM: Patterns in behavioral neuroanatomy: association areas, the limbic system, and hemispheric specialization, in Principles of Behavioral Neurology. Edited by Mesulam MM. Philadelphia, PA, FA Davis, 1985, pp 1–70

Mesulam MM, Mufson EJ: Insula of the old world monkey I, II, III. J Comp Neurol 212:1–52, 1992

Meyer JH, Kapur S, Houle S, et al: Prefrontal cortex 5-HT2 receptors in depression: a [18F]setoperone PET imaging study. Am J Psychiatry 156:1029–1034, 1999

Meyer JH, Kapur S, Eisfeld B, et al: The effect of paroxetine on 5-Ht(2a) receptors in depression: an [18F]setoperone PET imaging study. Am J Psychiatry 158(1):78–85, 2001

Meyers CA, Scheibel RS: Early detection and diagnosis of neurobehavioral disorders associated with cancer and its treatment. Oncology (Huntingt) 4:115–130, 1990

Morecraft RJ, Geula C, Mesulam MM: Architecture of connectivity within a cingulo-fronto-parietal neurocognitive network for directed attention. Arch Neurol 50:279–284, 1993

Murphy FC, Sahakina BJ, Rubinsztein JS, et al: Emotional bias and inhibitory control processes in mania and depression. Psychol Med 29:1307–1321, 1999

Nauta WJH: The problem of the frontal lobe: a reinterpretation. Journal of Psychology Research 8:167–187, 1971

Nauta WJH: Circuitous connections linking cerebral cortex, limbic system, and corpus striatum, in The Limbic System: Functional Organization and Clinical Disorders. Edited by Doane BK, Livingston KE. New York, Raven, 1986, pp 43–54

Neafsey EJ: Prefrontal cortical control of the autonomic nervous system: anatomical and physiological observations. Prog Brain Res 85:147–166, 1990

Nemeroff CB: Augmentation strategies in patients with refractory depression. Depress Anxiety 4:169–181, 1996–1997

Nemeroff CB: Clinical significance of psychoneuroendocrinology in psychiatry: focus on the thyroid and adrenal. J Clin Psychiatry 50 (suppl):13–22, 1989

Nemeroff CB, Widerlov E, Bissette G, et al: Elevated concentrations of CSF corticotropin-releasing factor–like immunoreactivity in depressed patients. Science 226:1342–1343, 1984

Nemeroff CB, Simon JS, Haggerty JJ, et al: Antithyroid antibodies in depressed patients. Am J Psychiatry 142:840–843, 1985

Nibuya M, Nestler EJ, Duman RS: Chronic antidepressant administration increases the expression of cAMP response element binding protein (CREB) in rat hippocampus. J Neurosci 16:2365–2372, 1996

Nobler MS, Sackeim HA, Prohovnik I, et al: Regional cerebral blood flow in mood disorders, III: treatment and clinical response. Arch Gen Psychiatry 51:884–897, 1994

Nofzinger EA, Thase ME, Reynolds CF, et al: Hypersomnia in bipolar depression: a comparison with narcolepsy using the multiple sleep latency test. Am J Psychiatry 148:1177–1181, 1991

Norman WH, Miller IW, Keitner GI: Relationship between dysfunctional cognitions and depressive subtypes. Can J Psychiatry 32(3):194–198, 1987

Nurnberg HG, Thompson PM, Hensley PL: Antidepressant medication change in a clinical treatment setting: a comparison of the effectiveness of SSRI. J Clin Psychiatry 60:574–579, 1999

Nutt DJ: Care of depressed patients with anxiety symptoms. J Clin Psychiatry 60 (suppl 17):23–27, 1999

Omdal R, Mellgren SI, Husby G: Clinical neuropsychiatric and neuromuscular manifestations in systemic lupus erythematosus. Scand J Rheumatol 17:113–117, 1988

Ongur D, Drevets WC, Price JL: Glial reduction in the subgenual prefrontal cortex in mood disorders. Proc Natl Acad Sci U S A 95:13290–13295, 1998

Osuch EA, Ketter TA, Kimbrell TA, et al: Regional cerebral metabolism associated with anxiety symptoms in affective disorder patients. Biol Psychiatry 48(10):1020–1023, 2000

Ovsiew F, Frim DM: Neurosurgery for psychiatric disorders. J Neurol Neurosurg Psychiatry 63(6):701–705, 1997

Pandya DN, Yeterian EH: Comparison of prefrontal architecture and connections. Philos Trans R Soc Lond B Biol Sci 351:1423–1432, 1996

Papez JW: A proposed mechanism of emotion. Archives of Neurology and Psychiatry 38:725–743, 1937

Pardo JV, Raichle ME, Fox PT: Localization of a human system for sustained attention by positron emission tomography. Nature 349:61–63, 1991

Pardo JV, Pardo PJ, Raichel ME: Neural correlates of self-induced dysphoria. Am J Psychiatry 150:713–719, 1993

Petrides M, Pandya DN: Projections to the frontal cortex from the posterior parietal region in the rhesus monkey. J Comp Neurol 228:105–116, 1984

Petty F, Kramer GL, Gullion CM, et al: Low plasma gamma-aminobutyric acid levels in male patients with depression. Biol Psychiatry 32:354–363, 1992

Peyser CE, Folstein SE: Depression in Huntington's disease, in Depression in Neurologic Diseases. Edited by Starkstein SE, Robinson RG. Baltimore, MD, Johns Hopkins University Press, 1993, pp 117–138

Posener JA, DeBattista C, Williams GH, et al: 24-Hour monitoring of cortisol and corticotropin secretion in psychotic and nonpsychotic major depression Arch Gen Psychiatry 57(8):755–760, 2000

Post RM, DeLisi LE, Holcomb HH, et al: Glucose utilization in the temporal cortex of affectively ill patients: positron emission tomography. Biol Psychiatry 22:545–553, 1987

Price TP, McAllister TW: Safety and efficacy of ECT in depressed patients with dementia: a review of clinical experience. Convulsive Therapy 5:61–74, 1989

Rajkowska G: Postmortem studies in mood disorders indicate altered numbers of neurons and glial cells. Biol Psychiatry 48:766–777, 2000

Raskin A: Partialing out the effects of depression and age on cognitive functions: experimental data and methodological issues, in Handbook for Clinical Memory Assessment of Older Adults. Edited by Poon LW. Washington, DC, American Psychological Association, 1986, pp 244–256

Rathus JH, Reber AS: Implicit and explicit learning: differential effects of affective states. Percept Mot Skills 79:163–184, 1994

Reed BR, Jagust WJ, Coulter L: Anosognosia in Alzheimer's disease: relationships to depression, cognitive function and cerebral perfusion. J Clin Exp Neuropsychol 15:231–244, 1993

Reiach JS, Li PP, Warsh JJ, et al: Reduced adenyl cyclase immunolabeling and activity in post-mortem temporal cortex of depressed suicide victims. J Affect Disord 56:141–151, 1999

Reifler BV, Larson E, Hanley R: Coexistence of cognitive impairment and depression in geriatric outpatients. Am J Psychiatry 139:623–626, 1982

Ressler KJ, Nemeroff CB: Role of norepinephrine in the pathophysiology and treatment of mood disorders. Biol Psychiatry 46:1219–1233, 1999

Ring HA, Bench CJ, Trimble MR, et al: Depression in Parkinson's disease: a positron emission study. Br J Psychiatry 165:333–339, 1994

Robertson MM, Trimble MR, Townsend HRA: Phenomenology of depression in epilepsy. Epilepsia 28:364–368, 1987

Robins LN, Helzer JE, Weissman MM, et al: Lifetime prevalence of specific psychiatric disorders in three sites. Arch Gen Psychiatry 41:949–958, 1984

Robinson RG: The Clinical Neuropsychiatry of Stroke. Cambridge, UK, Cambridge University Press, 1998

Robinson RG, Kubos KL, Starr LB, et al: Mood disorders in stroke patients: importance of location of lesion. Brain 107:81–93, 1984

Rogers D, Lees AJ, Smith E, et al: Bradyphrenia in Parkinson's disease and psychomotor retardation in depressive illness: an experimental study. Brain 110:761–776, 1987

Rolls E: Connections, functions and dysfunctions of limbic structures, the prefrontal cortex and hypothalamus, in The Scientific Basis of Clinical Neurology. Edited by Swash M, Kennard C. London, Churchill Livingstone, 1985, pp 201–213

Rolls ET: The orbitofrontal cortex and reward. Cereb Cortex 10:284–294, 2000

Ross ED, Rush AJ: Diagnosis and neuroanatomical correlates of depression in brain-damaged patients. Arch Gen Psychiatry 39:1344–1354, 1981

Roy A, Pickar D, De Jong J, et al: Norepinephrine and its metabolites in cerebrospinal fluid, plasma, and urine. Arch Gen Psychiatry 45:849–857, 1988

Royant-Parola S, Borbely AA, Tobler I, et al: Monitoring of long-term motor activity in depressed patients. Br J Psychiatry 149:288–293, 1986

Roy-Byrne PP, Weingartner H, Bierer LM, et al: Effortful and automatic cognitive processes in depression. Arch Gen Psychiatry 43:265–267, 1986

Rush AJ, George MS, Sackeim HA, et al: Vagus nerve stimulation (VNS) for treatment-resistant depressions: a multicenter study. Biol Psychiatry 47:276–286, 2000

Sackeim HA, Greenberg MS, Weiman AL, et al: Hemispheric asymmetry in the expression of positive and negative emotions. Arch Neurol 39:210–218, 1982

Sackeim HA, Portnoy S, Neeley P, et al: Cognitive consequences of low-dosage electroconvulsive therapy. Ann N Y Acad Sci 462:326–340, 1986

Santor DA, Bagby RM, Joffe RT: Evaluating stability and change in personality and depression. J Pers Soc Psychol 73:1354–1362, 1997

Sapolsky RM: The physiological relevance of glucocorticoid endangerment of the hippocampus. Ann N Y Acad Sci 746:294–304, 1994

Sapolsky RM: The possibility of neurotoxicity in the hippocampus in major depression: a primer on neuron death. Biol Psychiatry 48:755–765, 2000

Sargent PA, Kjaer KH, Bench CJ, et al: Brain serotonin-1A receptor binding measured by PET with 11C-Way-100635. Arch Gen Psychiatry 57:174–180, 2000

Saxena S, Brody AL, Maidment KM, et al: Localized orbitofrontal and subcortical metabolic changes and predictors of response to paroxetine treatment in obsessive-compulsive disorder. Neuropsychopharmacology 21:683–694, 1999

Schatzberg AF: NE vs 5-HT antidepressants: predictors of treatment response. J Clin Psychiatry 59 (suppl 14):15–18, 1998

Schildkraut JJ: The catecholamine hypothesis of affective disorders: a review of supporting evidence. Am J Psychiatry 122:509–522, 1965

Schneider F, Gur RE, Mozley LH, et al: Mood effects on limbic blood flow correlate with emotional self-rating: a PET study with O-15 labeled water. Psychiatry Res 61:265–283, 1995

Segal ZV, Gemar M, Williams S: Differential cognitive response to a mood challenge following successful cognitive therapy or pharmacotherapy for unipolar depression. J Abnorm Psychol 108(1):3–10, 1999

Seidler GH: Psychiatrisch-psychologische Aspekte des Fahr-Syndroms. Psychiatr Prax 12:203–205, 1985

Sharpley AL, Cowen PJ: Effect of pharmacologic treatments on the sleep of depressed patients. Biol Psychiatry 37:85–98, 1995

Sheline YI: 3D MRI studies of neuroanatomic changes in unipolar major depression: the role of stress and medical comorbidity. Biol Psychiatry 48:791–800, 2000

Sheline YI, Wang PW, Gado MH, et al: Hippocampal atrophy in recurrent major depression. Proc Natl Acad Sci U S A 93:3908–3913, 1996

Sheline YI, Gado MH, Price JL: Amygdala core nuclei volumes are decreased in recurrent major depression. Neuroreport 22:2023–2028, 1998

Shively CA, Laber-Laird K, Anton RF: Behavior and physiology of social stress and depression in female cynomolgus monkeys. Biol Psychiatry 41:871–882, 1997

Simon H, LeMoal M, Calas A: Efferents and afferents of the ventral tegmental-A10 region studied after local injection of [3H]-leucine and horseradish peroxidase. Brain Res 178:17–40, 1979

Sinyor D, Jacques P, Kaloupek DG, et al: Post stroke depression and lesion location: an attempted replication. Brain 109:537–546, 1986

Smith GS, Reynolds CF, Pollock B, et al: Cerebral glucose metabolic response to combined total sleep deprivation and antidepressant Rx in geriatric depression. Am J Psychiatry 156:683–689, 1999

Smith KA, Morris JS, Friston KJ, et al: Brain mechanisms associated with depressive relapse and associated cognitive impairment following acute tryptophan depletion. Br J Psychiatry 174:525–529, 1999

Soares JC, Mann JJ: The anatomy of mood disorders—review of structural neuroimaging studies. Biol Psychiatry 41:86–106, 1997

Sobin C, Sackeim HA: Psychomotor symptoms of depression. Am J Psychiatry 154:4–17, 1997

Spitzer RL, Williams JBW, Gibbon M, et al: Manual for the Structured Clinical Interview for DSMIIIR (SCID). New York, NY State Psychiatric Institute, Biometrics Research, 1988

Spring B, Gelenberg AJ, Garvin R, et al: Amitriptyline, clovoxamine and cognitive function: a placebo controlled comparison in depressed outpatients. Psychopharmacology (Berl) 108:327–332, 1992

Squire LR: Memory functions as affected by electroconvulsive therapy. Ann N Y Acad Sci 462:307–314, 1986

Stancer HC, Cooke RG: Receptors in affective illness, in Receptors and Ligands in Psychiatry. Edited by Sen AK, Lee T. New York, Cambridge University Press, 1988, pp 303–326

Starkstein SE, Robinson RG (eds): Depression in Neurologic Diseases. Baltimore, MD, Johns Hopkins University Press, 1993

Starkstein SE, Robinson RG, Price TR: Comparison of cortical and subcortical lesions in the production of post-stroke mood disorders. Brain 110:1045–1059, 1987

Starkstein SE, Bolduc PL, Mayberg HS, et al: Cognitive impairments and depression in Parkinson's disease: a follow-up study. J Neurol Neurosurg Psychiatry 53:597–602, 1990a

Starkstein SE, Mayberg HS, Berthier ML, et al: Mania after brain injury: neuroradiological and metabolic findings. Ann Neurol 27:652–659, 1990b

Starkstein SE, Preziosi TJ, Bolduc PL, et al: Depression in Parkinson's disease. J Nerv Ment Dis 178:27–31, 1990c

Starkstein SE, Preziosi TJ, Forrester AW, et al: Specificity of affective and autonomic symptoms of depression in Parkinson's disease. J Neurol Neurosurg Psychiatry 53:869–873, 1990d

Steffens DC, Tupler LA, Ranga K, et al: Magnetic resonance imaging signal hypointensity and iron content of putamen nuclei in elderly depressed patients. Psychiatry Res 83:95–103, 1998

Stoudemire A, Hill CD, Gulley LR: Neuropsychological and biomedical assessment of depression-dementia syndromes. J Neuropsychiatry Clin Neurosci 1:347–361, 1989

Stoudemire A, Hill CD, Morris R, et al: Cognitive outcome following tricyclic and electroconvulsive treatment of major depression in the elderly. Am J Psychiatry 148:1336–1340, 1991

Stoudemire A, Hill CD, Morris R, et al: Long-term affective and cognitive outcome in depressed older adults. Am J Psychiatry 150:896–900, 1993

Stuss DT, Benson DF: The Frontal Lobes. New York, Raven, 1986

Szabadi E, Bradshaw CM, Besson JA: Elongation of pause-time in speech: a simple, objective measure of motor retardation in depression. Br J Psychiatry 129:592–597, 1976

Teasdale JD: Emotional processing, three modes of mind and the prevention of relapse in depression. Behav Res Ther 37:S53–S77, 1999

Teasdale JD, Dent J: Cognitive vulnerability to depression: an investigation of two hypotheses. Br J Clin Psychol 26 (Pt 2):113–126, 1987

Teneback CC, Nahas Z, Speer AM, et al: Changes in prefrontal cortex and paralimbic activity in depression following two weeks of daily left prefrontal TMS. J Neuropsychiatry Clin Neurosci 11(4):426–435, 1999

Thase ME, Rush AJ: Treatment-Resistant Depression: Psychopharmacology: The Fourth Generation of Progress. Edited by Bloom FE, Kupfer DJ. New York, Raven, 1995, pp 1081–1097

Torack RM, Morris JC: The association of ventral tegmental area histopathology with adult dementia. Arch Neurol 45:211–218, 1988

Trullas R., Skolnick P: Functional antagonists at the NMDA receptor complex exhibit antidepressant actions. Eur J Pharmacol 185(1):1–10, 1990

Vaidya VA, Marek GJ, Aghajanian GK, et al: 5-HT2A receptor-mediated regulation of brain-derived neurotrophic factor mRNA in the hippocampus and the neocortex. J Neurosci 17:2785–2795, 1997

van Reekum R, Simard M, Clarke D, et al: Late-life depression as a possible predictor of dementia: cross-sectional and short-term follow-up results. Am J Geriatr Psychiatry 7(2):151–159, 1999

Vetulani J, Sulser F: Actions of various antidepressant treatments reduces reactivity of noradrenergic cyclic AMP-generating system in limbic forebrain. Nature 257:455–456, 1975

Vogt BA, Pandya DN: Cingulate cortex of the rhesus monkey: II, cortical afferents. J Comp Neurol 262:271–289, 1987

Vogt BA, Nimchinsky EA, Vogt LJ, et al: Human cingulate cortex: surface features, flat maps, and cytoarchitecture. J Comp Neurol 359:490–506, 1995

Watts FN, Dalgleish T, Bourke P, et al: Memory deficit in clinical depression: processing resources and the structure of materials. Psychol Med 20:345–349, 1990

Weiner RD, Rogers HJ, Davison JR, et al: Effects of stimulus parameters on cognitive side effects. Ann N Y Acad Sci 462:315–325, 1986

Weingartner H, Cohen RM, Murphy DL, et al: Cognitive processes in depression. Arch Gen Psychiatry 38:42–47, 1981

Whalen PJ, Bush G, McNally RJ, et al: The emotional counting Stroop paradigm: a functional magnetic resonance imaging probe of the anterior cingulate affective division Biol Psychiatry 44(12):1219–1228, 1998

Wolfe J, Granholm E, Butters N, et al: Verbal memory deficits associated with major affective disorders: a comparison of unipolar and bipolar patients. J Affect Disord 13:83–91, 1987

Wu JC, Bunney WE: The biological basis of an antidepressant response to sleep deprivation and relapse: review and hypothesis. Am J Psychiatry 147:14–21, 1990

Wu J, Buchsbaum MS, Gillin JC, et al: Prediction of antidepressant effects of sleep deprivation on metabolic rates in the ventral anterior cingulate and medial prefrontal cortex. Am J Psychiatry 156:1149–1158, 1999

Yatham LN, Liddle PF, Dennis J, et al: Decrease in brain serotonin 2 receptor binding in patients with major depression following desipramine treatment. Arch Gen Psychiatry 56:705–711, 1999

Zacharko RM, Anisman H: Stressor-induced anhedonia in the mesocorticolimbic system. Neurosci Biobehav Rev 15:391–405, 1991

Zubenko GS, Moossy J: Major depression in primary dementia. Arch Neurol 45:1182–1186, 1988

Zubenko GS, Sullivan P, Nelson JP, et al: Brain imaging abnormalities in mental disorders of late life. Arch Neurol 47:1107–1111, 1990

# Neuropsychiatric Aspects of Anxiety Disorders

Dan J. Stein, M.D., Ph.D.

Frans J. Hugo, M.B.Ch.B., M.Med.(Psych.)

Although anxiety has long held a central place in theories of psychopathology (Freud 1926/1959), it has only recently been appreciated that the anxiety disorders are among the most prevalent of the psychiatric disorders (Kessler et al. 1994) and that they account for perhaps a third of all costs of mental illness (Dupont et al. 1996). Furthermore, although it has long been recognized that specific neurological lesions may lead to anxiety symptoms (von Economo 1931), only in the past several years have advances in research allowed particular neuroanatomic hypotheses to be put forward about each of the different anxiety disorders. In this chapter, we review these developments in the understanding of the anxiety disorders from the perspective of neuropsychiatry. We begin by reviewing neurological disorders that may present with anxiety symptoms and then outline neuroanatomic models of each of the main anxiety disorders.

DSM-III (American Psychiatric Association 1980) provided significant impetus to research on the anxiety disorders by replacing the category of "anxiety neurosis" with several different conditions and by providing each with operational diagnostic criteria. DSM-IV-TR (American Psychiatric Association 2000) anxiety disorders include panic disorder with and without agoraphobia, social phobia (social anxiety disorder), posttraumatic stress disorder (PTSD), generalized anxiety disorder

(GAD), obsessive-compulsive disorder (OCD), substance-induced anxiety disorder, and anxiety disorder due to a general medical condition. Although the inclusion of OCD in the category of anxiety disorders remains somewhat controversial (Montgomery 1993), for the purposes of this volume, we use the current DSM classification.

In each of the anxiety disorders, it is perhaps possible to discern a component comprising anxiety symptoms and a component comprising avoidance symptoms. In panic disorder, the anxiety symptoms are those of the panic attack—a discrete period of anxiety that develops rapidly, often spontaneously. The person also may develop agoraphobia symptoms, or avoidance of those stimuli that appear to promote panic attacks. In social phobia, panic attacks develop only in the context of social or performance situations in which the person fears embarrassment or humiliation. As a result of these fears, the person may avoid these situations. In PTSD, in the aftermath of a traumatic event, the person has reexperiencing and hyperarousal symptoms, as well as a range of avoidance and numbing symptoms.

OCD is similarly characterized by both obsessions—intrusive thoughts or images that increase anxiety—and compulsions—repetitive behaviors or mental acts undertaken in response to obsessions or performed according

The authors are supported by the Medical Research Council of South Africa.

to particular rules, which reduce anxiety. Several disorders have overlapping phenomenological and neurobiological features with OCD; these putative OCD spectrum disorders may include body dysmorphic disorder (characterized by intrusive thoughts of imagined ugliness), Tourette's disorder (in which OCD symptoms are often comorbid), and trichotillomania (characterized by repetitive hair pulling). Further brief notes on symptomatology are provided in the relevant sections below.

# Neurological Disorders With Anxiety Symptoms

Neurological conditions that affect a range of different neuroanatomic structures may be associated with anxiety symptoms or disorders (Wise and Rundell 1999). Given that temporolimbic regions, striatum, and prefrontal cortex all likely play an important role in the pathogenesis of certain anxiety disorders, we begin by reviewing the association between lesions in these areas and subsequent anxiety symptoms before moving to disorders with more widespread pathology. This literature not only is clinically relevant but also raises valuable questions for further research.

Various lesions of the temporolimbic regions have been associated with the subsequent development of panic disorder. Temporal lobe seizures (Cavenar and Harris 1979; Young et al. 1995), tumors (Ghadirian et al. 1986; Kellner et al. 1996), arteriovenous malformation (Wall et al. 1985), lobectomy (Wall et al. 1986), and parahippocampal infarction (Maricle et al. 1991) all have been reported to present with panic attacks. The association seems particularly strong with right-sided lesions. (Conversely, removal of the amygdala results in placidity toward previously feared objects [Downer 1961; Klüver and Bucy 1939] and in deficits in fear conditioning [Bechara et al. 1995].)

This literature, taken together with clinical observations that panic disorder may be accompanied by dissociation and depersonalization (Toni et al. 1996) and possibly by electroencephalographic abnormalities (Bystritsky et al. 1999) and temporal disturbances (see the section on Panic Disorder), as well as preliminary data that panic disorder may respond to anticonvulsants, raises the question of whether partially overlapping mechanisms may be at work in both temporal lobe seizure disorder and panic disorder (Weilburg et al. 1987). Certainly, it has been suggested that electroencephalogram (EEG) and anticonvulsant trials may be appropriate in panic disorder patients refractory to conventional treatment (McNamara and Fogel 1990).

Lesions of the basal ganglia have been associated with obsessions and compulsions, a finding that has been crucial to the development of a "cortico-striatal-thalamic-cortical" (CSTC) hypothesis of OCD. An early "striatal topography" hypothesis was that caudate lesions in particular are associated with OCD, whereas putamen lesions result in tics (Rauch and Baxter 1998). However, evidence also indicates that OCD is mediated by a range of CSTC circuits (Rosenberg and Keshavan 1998), and particular projection fields or cell types may be associated with specific kinds of symptoms.

The 1915–1926 pandemic of viral encephalitis lethargica provided early evidence of a specific neurological basis for OCD. The outbreak was followed by the presentation of numerous patients with a somnolent-like state and parkinsonian features. Various focal brain lesions, including involvement of the basal ganglia, were documented in these cases, and patients also were observed to have obsessive-compulsive symptoms and tics (von Economo 1931). A series of authors confirmed these associations (Cheyette and Cummings 1995).

OCD symptoms also have been reported in a range of other basal ganglia lesions of various etiologies. Thus, OCD may be seen in Huntington's disease (Cummings and Cunningham 1992), Parkinson's disease (Hardie et al. 1984), spasmodic torticollis (Bihari et al. 1992), and basal ganglia lesions of a range of etiologies, including calcification, infarction, intoxication, and trauma (Cummings and Cunningham 1992). In this context, it is noteworthy that the basal ganglia may be particularly sensitive to prenatal and perinatal hypoxic-ischemic injury (in twins with Tourette's disorder, for example, an association exists between lower birthweight and increased severity of Tourette's disorder [Hyde and Weinberger 1995]).

Furthermore, early studies suggested a link between Sydenham's chorea and OCD symptoms (Grimshaw 1964), and a study by Swedo et al. (1989) reported that rheumatic fever patients with Sydenham's chorea had significantly more OCD symptoms than did those without chorea. This work has had exciting implications, insofar as it has formed the basis for an autoimmune theory of at least some cases of OCD. Swedo and colleagues (1998) coined the term *PANDAS*, or pediatric autoimmune neuropsychiatric disorders associated with streptococcal infections, to describe patients who present with acute obsessive-compulsive or tic symptoms, hypothetically after developing antistriatal antibodies in response to infection.

Some of the most promising research on the association between OCD and a movement disorder focused on the relation of OCD to Tourette's disorder. Gilles de la

Tourette's (1885) initial description of the disorder included a patient with tics, vocalizations, and perhaps obsessions. Increasing evidence suggests that a subgroup of patients with Tourette's disorder also has OCD (Hollander et al. 1989). Conversely, a subgroup of OCD patients has tics (Goodman et al. 1990). Furthermore, family studies have shown a high rate of OCD and/or tics in relatives of Tourette's disorder patients and a high rate of Tourette's disorder and/or tics in relatives of OCD patients (Pauls et al. 1986).

Anxiety symptoms other than OCD may, however, also be seen in striatal disorders (Lauterbach et al. 1998). In Huntington's disease, for example, anxiety has been reported as the most common prodromal symptom, with later development of GAD, panic disorder, mixed anxiety and depression, or OCD. In their review, Richard et al. (1996) found that anxiety disorders, particularly GAD, panic disorder, and social phobia, occur in up to 40% of the patients with Parkinson's disease. Most patients experience increased anxiety during the "off" phase of motor fluctuations, and the anxiety frequently coexists with depression. Such findings arguably indicate that further attention should be paid to the role of the dopaminergic system in anxiety disorders (M.B. Stein et al. 1990), although dopamine deficiency in Parkinson's disease also may result in the alteration of noradrenergic and other systems involved in mediating anxiety symptoms.

Lesions of the frontal cortex may be associated with a range of perseverative symptoms. In the classic case of Phineas Gage, in addition to impairment in executive functions, the patient also had perseverative symptoms and hoarding behaviors (Damasio et al. 1994). Similarly, more recent cases of OCD after frontal lobe involvement have been documented. Ames et al. (1994) reviewed the literature on frontal lobe degeneration and subsequent obsessive-compulsive symptoms and noted descriptions of a range of repetitive behaviors from motor stereotypies to OCD.

Anxiety symptoms and disorders, of course, can be seen in a range of neurological disorders that affect multiple brain regions, including frontal cortex. In multiple sclerosis (MS), for example, anxiety symptoms may be found in up to 37% of subjects (Diaz-Olavarrieta et al. 1999), and anxiety disorders are also not uncommon (Joffe et al. 1987). Although simple association does not indicate a causal relation, in a retrospective analysis, Minden et al. (1987) reported anxiety disorders in only 8% of subjects before onset of MS but in 24% after onset. Such symptoms may reflect the deposition of demyelinating plaques, and their treatment should not be ignored (Riether 1999).

Similarly, anxiety symptoms have been noted to be common in Alzheimer's disease, particularly in moderate Alzheimer's disease (Mini-Mental State Exam score = 11–20); these symptoms were reported in 65% of subjects (Mega et al. 1996). The relation between regional pathology and anxiety symptoms in Alzheimer's disease deserves further attention. Although anxiety symptoms are also present in frontotemporal dementias (Levy et al. 1996), they appear less common in patients with supranuclear palsy (Litvan et al. 1996), suggesting that there is some specificity to their pathogenesis.

Although the prevalence of depression after stroke has been well studied, less research has focused on anxiety after stroke. In one study, however, of 309 admissions to a stroke unit, DSM-III-R (American Psychiatric Association 1987) GAD was present in 27% of the patients (Castillo et al. 1993). The authors reported that anxiety plus depression was associated with left cortical lesions, whereas anxiety alone was associated with right-hemisphere lesions. Also, worry was associated with anterior and GAD with right posterior lesions. A longitudinal study found a prevalence of 28% for GAD after stroke, with 19% continuing to have GAD at 3 years (Astrom 1996). Again, anxiety plus depression was associated with left-hemisphere lesions, and anxiety alone was associated with right-hemisphere lesions. Finally, it has been reported that agoraphobia was even more common than GAD after stroke (Burvill et al. 1995).

Anxiety disorders also have been reported in the aftermath of traumatic brain injury. In one study, prevalence rates were 19% for PTSD, 15% for OCD, 14% for panic disorder, 10% for phobias, and 9% for GAD (Hibbard et al. 1998). Of particular interest is the finding that PTSD can develop even when the patient has neurogenic amnesia for the traumatic event; this finding suggests that implicit memories of trauma may be sufficient for later PTSD to emerge, although subsequent appraisal processes also may be relevant (Joseph and Masterson 1999). In either event, PTSD in such patients may be unusual insofar as reexperiencing symptoms are absent (Warden et al. 1997).

## Neuroanatomy of Anxiety Disorders

In the following sections, we consider the neuropsychiatry of each of the major anxiety disorders. Each section begins by sketching a simplistic neuroanatomic model of the relevant anxiety disorder. This sketch is then used as a framework for attempting a more complex integration of animal data, clinical biological research (e.g., pharmacological probe studies), and brain imaging studies.

Although much remains to be learned about the neurobiology of the anxiety disorders, there is a growing consolidation of different avenues of information, with increasingly specific models now existing for each of the major anxiety disorders.

## Generalized Anxiety Disorder

The term *GAD* was first introduced in DSM-III, where it represented a refinement of the earlier concept of anxiety neurosis. In DSM-III, GAD was viewed as a residual diagnosis, to be made in the absence of other disorders. More recent editions of DSM have, however, increasingly emphasized the cognitive symptoms of GAD and have also emphasized that GAD is an independent entity that may be found alone or comorbidly with other anxiety and mood conditions. GAD is the least common anxiety disorder in specialty anxiety clinics but the most common anxiety disorder in primary care practice (Sherbourne et al. 1996).

Neuroanatomic models of GAD have not been well delineated to date. However, it may be speculated that GAD involves 1) a general "limbic circuit," including paralimbic cortex (e.g., anterior temporal cortex, posterior medial orbitofrontal cortex) and related subcortical structures (e.g., nucleus accumbens), which may be activated across a range of different anxiety disorders; and perhaps 2) some degree of prefrontal hyperactivity, which may represent an attempt across the anxiety disorders to suppress subcortically mediated anxiety or which may arguably reflect more specific GAD symptoms of excessive worrying and planning (Figure 32–1). In reviewing research relevant to this speculative model, we consider first neurochemical studies and then neuroanatomic findings.

### Neurochemical Studies

Serotonergic mediation of GAD is supported by several findings. First, reduced cerebrospinal fluid levels of serotonin and reduced platelet paroxetine binding have been observed in this disorder (Iny et al. 1994). Second, administration of the pharmacological probe *m*-chlorophenylpiperazine (m-CPP), a serotonergic agonist, results in increased anxiety and hostility (Germine et al. 1992). Third, serotonergic compounds appear effective in the pharmacotherapy for GAD; buspirone, a serotonin type 1A (5-HT$_{1A}$) receptor partial agonist is effective in some studies, and growing evidence now shows the efficacy of the selective serotonin reuptake inhibitors (SSRIs) in this disorder (Sussman 1998). Serotonergic neurons branch widely throughout the brain, affecting each of the main regions postulated to mediate anxiety

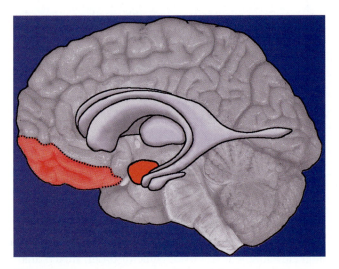

**FIGURE 32–1.** Neuroanatomic model of generalized anxiety disorder. Note the increased activity in temporolimbic (Tiihonen et al. 1997b; Wu et al. 1991) and paralimbic areas (Rauch et al. 1997b) as well as in prefrontal areas (Rauch et al. 1997b; Wu et al. 1991).

*Source.* Reprinted from Stein DJ: *False Alarm!: How to Conquer the Anxiety Disorders.* Cape Town, South Africa, University of Stellenbosch, 2000. Used with permission.

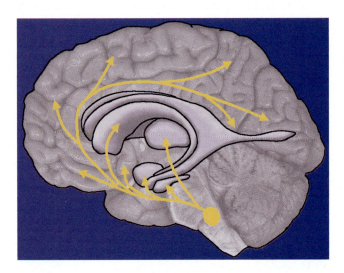

**FIGURE 32–2.** Serotonergic circuits project to key regions (prefrontal cortex, orbitofrontal cortex, anterior cingulate, amygdala, hippocampus, basal ganglia, thalamus) involved in the mediation of anxiety disorders.

*Source.* Reprinted from Stein DJ: *False Alarm!: How to Conquer the Anxiety Disorders.* Cape Town, South Africa, University of Stellenbosch, 2000. Used with permission.

symptoms (Figure 32–2); although there is little work on pre- and post-SSRI imaging studies in GAD, it might be hypothesized that SSRI treatment results in a normalization of limbic, paralimbic, and frontal hyperactivity in GAD.

Animal work has long demonstrated the involvement of the locus coeruleus–norepinephrine–sympathetic nervous system in fear and arousal (S.J. Grant and Redmond 1981). In clinical studies of GAD, increased plasma norepinephrine and 3-methoxy-4-hydroxyphenylglycol (MHPG) (Sevy et al. 1989) and reduced platelet $\alpha_2$-adrenergic peripheral receptor binding sites have been reported (Cameron et al. 1990; Sevy et al. 1989), although not all studies of static noradrenergic measures have produced consistent positive findings. Administration of more dynamic adrenergic probes has, however, indicated reduced adrenergic receptor sensitivity in GAD, perhaps an adaptation to high circulating catecholamines. The locus coeruleus system may well play a regulatory role in GAD, even if it is not the sole dysfunctional neurochemical system in the disorder. Indeed, dual serotonin and noradrenergic reuptake inhibitors have been shown effective in GAD. The locus coeruleus system projects to the amygdala and to other structures involved in anxiety responses, so that noradrenergic involvement is not inconsistent with the neuroanatomic model outlined above.

Involvement of the γ-aminobutyric acid (GABA)–benzodiazepine receptor complex in GAD is supported by several studies, including the responsiveness of this disorder to benzodiazepine treatment. Thus, anxious subjects (Weizman et al. 1987) and GAD patients (Rocca et al. 1991) have reduced benzodiazepine binding capacity, with normalization of findings after benzodiazepine treatment. GABA is the brain's predominant inhibitory neurotransmitter, and GABAergic pathways are widely distributed; nevertheless, the distribution of GABA/benzodiazepine receptors is particularly dense in limbic and paralimbic areas.

## Neuroanatomic Studies

Neuroimaging research on GAD is at a relatively preliminary stage. Nevertheless, findings are arguably consistent with involvement of limbic, paralimbic, and prefrontal regions. An early topographic EEG study indicated differences between patients with GAD and nonanxious control subjects in temporal and occipital regions (Buchsbaum et al. 1985). Later work by this group with positron emission tomography (PET) found that GAD patients had increased relative metabolic rates in the right posterior temporal lobe, right precentral frontal gyrus, and left inferior area 17 in the occipital lobe but reduced absolute basal ganglia metabolic rates (Wu et al. 1991). Furthermore, benzodiazepine treatment resulted in decreases in absolute metabolic rates for limbic system and cortical surface (Wu et al. 1991). Analyses of changes in basal ganglia metabolic rate during benzodiazepine treatment were inconsistent (Buchsbaum et al. 1987; Wu et al. 1991).

Imaging studies that have pooled or compared findings across different anxiety disorders may also shed light on the underlying neuroanatomy of anxiety symptoms that are not disorder specific. An analysis of pooled PET symptom provocation data from patients with OCD, PTSD, and specific phobia, for example, reported activation of paralimbic structures (right posterior medial orbitofrontal cortex, bilateral insular cortex), right inferior frontal cortex, bilateral lenticulate nuclei, and bilateral brain-stem foci (Rauch et al. 1997b). This finding would arguably provide indirect support for a role for the paralimbic system, which serves as a conduit from sensory, motor, and association cortex to the limbic system itself, as well as for inferior frontal regions, in GAD.

Preliminary imaging data on receptor binding in GAD are also available. In a study of female GAD patients, for example, left temporal pole benzodiazepine receptor binding was significantly reduced (Tiihonen et al. 1997b). This work provides persuasive support for a role for temporolimbic regions, and the GABA/benzodiazepine receptor complex, in mediating GAD symptoms.

Another interesting set of research at the intersection of neurochemistry and neuroanatomy has combined administration of the pharmacological probe procaine with PET imaging. Procaine activates limbic structures in animals, and in humans, acute administration results in a range of emotional and psychosensory experiences, including anxiety. PET studies after procaine infusion in healthy control subjects have shown increased regional cerebral blood flow (rCBF) in amygdala and anterior paralimbic regions (Ketter et al. 1996; Servan-Schreiber et al. 1998), and, indeed, fear ratings correlated positively with left amygdala cerebral blood flow changes (Ketter et al. 1996). Such findings suggest that environmentally induced and pharmacologically induced fear are both mediated by a similar functional neuroanatomy, with amygdala and paralimbic regions key.

## Obsessive-Compulsive Disorder

The characteristic obsessions and compulsions of OCD have a strikingly similar form and content across different patients and different contexts, an observation that perhaps immediately raises the question of a specific neuropsychiatric basis for this condition. In addition, OCD has a lifetime prevalence of 2%–3% in most countries in which data are available (Weissman et al. 1994), again supporting a biomedical model. Also remarkable is the recent finding that OCD is the tenth most disabling of all medical conditions worldwide (Murray and Lopez 1996). Certainly the cost to the world economy of OCD is likely to run into the billions of dollars annually (Stein 2000b).

Current neuroanatomic models of OCD emphasize the role of CSTC circuits (Figure 32–3). There is growing realization of the importance of various CSTC loops in a range of behavior disorders (Cummings 1993); ventral cognitive circuits, involving anterior and lateral orbitofrontal cortex, ventromedial caudate, and dorsomedial nuclei of the thalamus appear to play a role in response inhibition, particularly in relation to certain kinds of cognitive affective cues, and appear most relevant to OCD. This kind of model of OCD was first suggested by early findings of an association between neurological lesions of the striatum and OCD (see the earlier section, Neurological Disorders With Anxiety Symptoms) and has been supported by a range of subsequent additional studies.

Similar CSTC circuits also have been hypothesized to be involved in various putative OCD spectrum disorders (such as Tourette's disorder). An early "striatal topography" model of OCD spectrum disorders suggested that, whereas the ventral cognitive system mediated OCD symptoms, the sensorimotor cortex and putamen would instead be involved in Tourette's disorder and perhaps trichotillomania (Rauch and Baxter 1998). The data have not, however, fully supported such a model (Rosenberg and Keshavan 1998), and it is possible rather that particular striatal projection fields or cell types are involved in specific kinds of symptoms. We review findings relevant to the CSTC model in the following sections on neurochemical and neuroanatomic studies in OCD.

## Neurochemical Studies

Interest in the neurochemical substrate of OCD received significant impetus from the early finding that the disorder responded to clomipramine, a serotonin reuptake inhibitor. Subsequent studies confirmed that clomipramine is more robust than desipramine, a noradrenergic reuptake inhibitor, in OCD (Zohar and Insel 1987). Furthermore, each of the SSRIs studied to date has been effective for the treatment of OCD (D.J. Stein et al. 1995). During effective treatment with a serotonin reuptake inhibitor, cerebrospinal fluid 5-hydroxyindoleacetic acid decreases (Thoren et al. 1980), and exacerbation of obsessive-compulsive symptoms by m-CPP is no longer seen after treatment with an SSRI (Zohar et al. 1988).

The serotonergic system innervates not only the basal ganglia but also the orbitofrontal cortex. Serotonergic abnormalities in OCD may be region specific; for

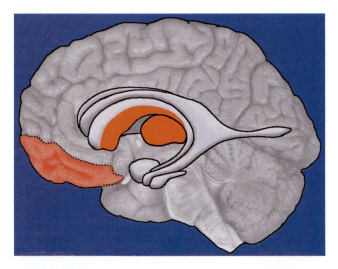

**FIGURE 32–3.** Neuroanatomic model of obsessive-compulsive disorder. Note the increased activity in the ventromedial cortico-striatal-thalamic-cortical circuit (Rauch and Baxter 1998).

*Source.* Reprinted from Stein DJ: *False Alarm!: How to Conquer the Anxiety Disorders.* Cape Town, South Africa, University of Stellenbosch, 2000. Used with permission.

example, in some studies, after administration of m-CPP, exacerbation of OCD symptoms (perhaps mediated by orbitofrontal cortex) but also a blunted neuroendocrine response (presumably mediated by hypothalamus) occur (Hollander et al. 1992). Of particular interest is recent animal work showing that downregulation of serotonin terminal autoreceptors in orbitofrontal cortex occurs only after relatively long periods and with relatively high doses of medication and does not occur after electroconvulsive therapy (El Mansari et al. 1995). This provides an elegant parallel with clinical findings that OCD pharmacotherapy differs from that used for depression.

Nevertheless, it is notable that only about 50%–60% of OCD patients respond to serotonin reuptake inhibitors and that not all patients show abnormal responses to m-CPP, suggesting that other neurochemical systems also are important. Of particular interest, administration of dopamine agonists results in stereotypic behavior in animals and in tics in humans, and conversely, dopamine blockers are effective for the treatment of tics (Goodman et al. 1990). Furthermore, it turns out that OCD patients with comorbid tics are less likely to respond to serotonin reuptake inhibitors but more likely to respond to augmentation of serotonin reuptake inhibitors with typical neuroleptics (McDougle et al. 1994).

Given the dopaminergic innervation of the striatum and the interaction between the serotonin and the dopaminergic systems (Kapur and Remington 1996), these findings are consistent with the CSTC model. Indeed, infusion of dopamine into the caudate results in stereotyped orofacial behaviors (grooming, gnawing) in animals (Fog and Pakkenberg 1971). Conversely, infusion of dopamine blockers into the same areas reduces amphetamine-induced stereotypy (Costall et al. 1972). Dopaminergic striatal circuits are presumably likely to be particularly important in OCD patients with tics and in patients with OCD spectrum disorders, such as Tourette's disorder, that are characterized by involuntary movements.

Other neurochemical systems, including glutamate and GABA, also play an important role in CSTC circuits (Moore et al. 1998). In the future, manipulation of such systems may turn out to be useful for the pharmacotherapy of OCD (Cora-Locatelli et al. 1998).

## Neuroanatomic Studies

A range of evidence indicates that cortico-striatal circuits are important in mediating stereotypic behavior (Ridley 1994). Isolation of primates during development, for example, results in basal ganglia cytoarchitectural abnormalities and stereotypic behavior (Martin et al. 1991). MacClean (1978) noted that lesions of the striatum resulted in stereotypic behavior and suggested that this was a repository for fixed action patterns or inherited motor sequences (e.g., grooming, nest-building). Indeed, the animal literature on stereotypies and disorders of grooming parallels not only the phenomenology of OCD but also its psychopharmacology (Rapoport et al. 1992).

There is, however, a growing appreciation of the role of the striatum in cognition and learning. In particular, striatal function has increasingly been associated with the development, maintenance, and selection of motoric and cognitive procedural strategies. Different terms given to allude to this group of functions include *habit system* (Mishkin and Petri 1984), *response set* (Robbins and Brown 1990), and *procedural mobilization* (Saint-Cyr et al. 1995). Basal ganglia may play a particularly important role in the implicit learning of procedural strategies and their subsequent automatic execution. Certainly, neurological soft sign abnormalities and neuropsychological dysfunction in patients with OCD are consistent with dysfunction in CSTC circuits (Savage et al. 1999; D.J. Stein et al. 1994).

Structural imaging studies also are consistent with a role for CSTC circuits in OCD. An early study found reduced caudate volume in OCD patients (Luxenberg et al. 1988), but not all subsequent research has replicated this finding. The finding that patients with PANDAS have increased basal ganglia volume (Giedd et al. 2000) may partly explain this inconsistency; in some OCD patients, basal ganglia volume initially may be increased, with subsequent reduction over time. Structural studies also have shown neuronal abnormalities or volume loss in orbitofrontal cortex, cingulate, amygdala, and thalamus in OCD (Ebert et al. 1997; Fitzgerald et al. 2000; Grachev et al. 1998; Rosenberg and Keshavan 1998; Szeszko et al. 1999). Also, putamen volume may be reduced in certain putative OCD spectrum disorders such as Tourette's disorder (Hyde and Weinberger 1995; Peterson et al. 1993) and trichotillomania (O'Sullivan et al. 1997).

Functional imaging studies, however, provide some of the most persuasive evidence of the role of CSTC circuits in OCD. OCD patients at rest, and especially when exposed to feared stimuli, have increased activity in the orbitofrontal cortex, anterior cingulate, and basal ganglia (Rauch and Baxter 1998). A range of functional abnormalities has also been found in Tourette's disorder; one study, for example, found increased metabolism in the orbitofrontal cortex and putamen that correlated with complex behavioral and cognitive features (Braun et al. 1995). Interestingly, a recent single photon emission computed tomography (SPECT) study of patients with obsessive-compulsive symptoms found that rCBF differed depending on whether a family history of Tourette's disorder was present, with patterns similar to those seen in Tourette's disorder in patients from Tourette's disorder families (Moriarty et al. 1997).

Functional imaging findings may have particular explanatory power when they also integrate cognitive neuroscience constructs and findings. Rauch and colleagues (1997a), for example, showed that during brain imaging of an implicit sequence learning task, control subjects without OCD showed striatal activation, but patients with OCD instead appeared to recruit medial temporal regions. These latter regions are typically involved in conscious cognitive-affective processing. Control subjects can process procedural strategies outside of awareness, but in OCD, intrusion of these into consciousness occurs.

An additional important set of findings that relate to the CSTC hypothesis of OCD emerges from work on neurosurgical treatments for OCD. Several different procedures have been used, but the general effect of these interventions is to interrupt CSTC circuits (Martuza et al. 1990). Some preliminary evidence suggests that right-sided neurosurgical lesions are most effective, a finding that raises interesting issues for future research on the laterality of OCD (Lippitz et al. 1999).

The "standard" neuroanatomic model of OCD may, however, be insufficiently complex to account for all cases. There is, for example, a literature on temporal lobe involvement in OCD. In some cases of OCD, temporal EEG abnormalities are seen (Jenike and Brotman 1984), and anticonvulsants may on occasion be useful (Khanna 1988). Similarly, in a study of OCD secondary to neurological abnormalities, SPECT scanning detected alterations not only in frontal areas but also in temporal regions (Hugo et al. 1999). A recent report described temporal lobe abnormalities in functional imaging of OCD patients with musical obsessions (Zungu-Dirwayi et al. 1999). Certainly, although OCD is in many ways a homogeneous entity, further research is necessary to delineate different neurobiological mechanisms in subtypes of the disorder.

Several studies have successfully integrated neurochemical and neuroimaging data. An early study reported that m-CPP exacerbation of OCD symptoms was associated with increased frontal rCBF (Hollander et al. 1995). A later SPECT study that used the 5-HT$_{1D}$ probe sumatriptan also confirmed correlations between symptom changes and prefrontal rCBF, supporting a role for the terminal autoreceptor in OCD (D.J. Stein et al. 1999). In OCD, there is now preliminary evidence of altered serotonin synthesis in frontostriatal circuitry (Rosenberg and Keshavan 1998). In contrast, in Tourette's disorder, striatal dopamine transport densities were increased (Malison et al. 1995), and in monozygotic twins with Tourette's disorder, increased caudate dopamine D$_2$ receptor binding was associated with increased tic severity (Wolf et al. 1996). Finally, a seminal publication reported that patients with OCD treated with either serotonin reuptake inhibitors or behavior therapy had normalization of activity in CSTC circuits (Baxter et al. 1992); effective interventions appear to work via a final common pathway of specific brain structures.

Nevertheless, several important questions remain unresolved about the CSTC model of OCD. It is unclear, for example, how presumptive lesions to the CSTC circuit occur. Despite the documentation of cases of PANDAS, the extent to which autoimmune processes contribute to OCD in general is not known. Also, there may be differential pathogenic mechanisms across different OCD spectrum disorders; for example, Tourette's disorder has been associated with autoantibodies against putamen but not caudate or globus pallidus (Singer et al. 1998). Finally, genetic variability may play some role; for example, some studies have found differences in dopamine system polymorphisms in OCD patients with and without tics.

Additionally, questions remain about the precise nature of CSTC dysfunction in OCD and its normalization by effective treatment. It is interesting, for example, that decreased orbitofrontal activity in OCD predicts positive response to pharmacotherapy, whereas higher orbitofrontal activity predicts positive response to behavior therapy (Brody et al. 1998). If orbitofrontal cortex is analogous to rodent medial frontal cortex and plays a role in extinguishing conditioned fear (LeDoux 1998), then perhaps patients who already show such activity are those for whom behavior therapy is possible. However, such hyperactivity may demand maximal serotonergic activation, and in patients who already have this, further SSRI-induced autoreceptor desensitization may be ineffective. Further work to consolidate fully a neuroanatomic model of both pharmacological and behavioral interventions in OCD is necessary.

## Panic Disorder

Panic disorder is a highly prevalent disorder, with rates fairly similar across different social and cultural settings. It is now well recognized that panic disorder may be associated with significant morbidity (mood, anxiety, and substance use disorders) as well as with severe impairments in occupational and social functioning. Indeed, a growing pharmacoeconomic literature has emphasized the personal and financial costs of panic disorder; this is a serious disorder that has substantial negative effect on quality of life.

Over the past decade or two, models of panic disorder have become increasingly sophisticated (Coplan and Lydiard 1998; Goddard and Charney 1997; Gorman et al. 1989, 2000). Current neuroanatomic models of panic (Figure 32–4) emphasize 1) afferents from viscerosensory pathways to thalamus to lateral nucleus of the amygdala, as well as from thalamus to cortical association areas to the lateral nucleus of the amygdala; 2) the extended amygdala, which is thought to play a central role in conditioned fear (LeDoux 1998) and anxiety (Davis and Shi 1999); 3) the hippocampus, which is thought crucial for conditioning to the context of the fear (and so perhaps for phobic avoidance); and 4) efferent tracts from the amygdala to the hypothalamus and brain-stem structures, which mediate many of the symptoms of panic. Thus, efferents of the central nucleus of the amygdala include the lateral nucleus (autonomic arousal and sympathetic discharge) and paraventricular nucleus (increased adrenocorticoid release) of the hypothalamus, and the locus coeruleus (increased norepinephrine release), parabrachial nucleus (increased respiratory rate), and periaqueductal gray (defensive behaviors and postural freezing) in the brain stem. This kind of general outline can be used as a starting framework for considering the range of data relevant to the neurobiology of panic disorder.

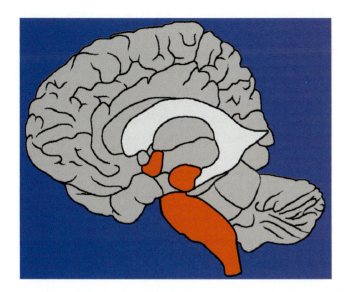

**FIGURE 32–4.** Neuroanatomic model of panic disorder. Note the activation of the amygdala, which has efferents to hypothalamus and brain-stem sites (Gorman et al. 2000). *Source.* Reprinted from Stein DJ: *False Alarm!: How to Conquer the Anxiety Disorders.* Cape Town, South Africa, University of Stellenbosch, 2000. Used with permission.

## Neurochemical Studies

Early animal studies found that the locus coeruleus plays a key role in fear and anxiety (S.J. Grant and Redmond 1981), with both electrical and pharmacological stimulation resulting in fear responses. The locus coeruleus contains the highest concentration of noradrenergic-producing neurons in the brain. Viscerosensory input reaches the locus coeruleus via the nucleus tractus solitarius and the medullary nucleus paragigantocellularis, and the locus coeruleus sends efferents to a range of important structures, including the amygdala, hypothalamus, and brain stem periaqueductal gray (Coplan and Lydiard 1998).

Several clinical studies of panic disorder provide support for the role of the locus coeruleus; administration of yohimbine, for example, resulted in greater increases in MHPG in panic disorder patients than in control subjects without panic disorder. However, not all studies have replicated such findings, and studies of noradrenergic function in lactate-induced panic also have been inconsistent (Gorman et al. 1989), suggesting that additional neurochemical factors are important in the mediation of panic attacks.

Certainly, increasing evidence indicates that the serotonergic system plays a crucial role in panic disorder. A range of studies provides evidence for this; for example, several studies have found that m-CPP administration leads to an acute exacerbation of panic symptoms in panic disorder patients. Particularly compelling, however, is growing evidence of the effectiveness of the SSRIs in panic disorder, with some indications that they may in fact be more effective than earlier classes of agents (Boyer 1995).

The serotonergic system interacts at several points with neuroanatomic structures thought important in panic disorder (Coplan and Lydiard 1998). First, serotonergic projections from the dorsal raphe nucleus generally inhibit the locus coeruleus, whereas projections from the locus coeruleus stimulate dorsal raphe nucleus serotonergic neurons and inhibit median raphe nucleus neurons. Furthermore, the dorsal raphe nucleus sends projections to prefrontal cortex, amygdala, hypothalamus, and periaqueductal gray among other structures. Thus, modulation of the serotonin system has the potential to influence the major regions of the panic disorder circuit, resulting in decreased noradrenergic activity, diminished release of corticotropin-releasing factor, and modification of defense/escape behaviors.

Indeed, clinical research confirms important interactions between the serotonin and the noradrenaline system in panic disorder. In one study of fluoxetine treatment in panic disorder, degree of clinical global improvement correlated with the magnitude of plasma MHPG (a primary noradrenergic metabolite) decline, and significant elevations in plasma MHPG volatility during clonidine challenge in untreated panic disorder patients were normalized by SSRI treatment. The authors concluded that fluoxetine exerted a stabilizing influence on a dysregulated noradrenergic system (Coplan et al. 1997).

Peripheral benzodiazepine receptor binding is decreased in panic disorder (Marazziti et al. 1994), and benzodiazepines are effective in treating this condition (Lydiard et al. 1996). In animal models, direct administration of a benzodiazepine agonist into the amygdala produces anxiolytic effects, which are weakened by pretreatment with a benzodiazepine receptor antagonist (Coplan and Lydiard 1998). The GABA/benzodiazepine receptor is widely distributed in the brain, but the basolateral and lateral amygdala nucleus and the hippocampus, as well as frontal and occipital cortex, have high densities (see also the imaging studies in the following subsection).

A consideration of the various afferents to the locus coeruleus and amygdala is relevant to considering the extensive literature on panicogenic stimuli. It has been argued that respiratory panicogens (e.g., carbon dioxide, lactate), baroceptor stimulation (β-agonists), and circulating peptides (cholecystokinin) promote panic via a limbic visceroreceptor pathway. In contrast, panic attacks that are conditioned by visuospatial, auditory, or cognitive cues may be mediated by pathways from cortical association areas to the amygdala (Coplan and Lydiard 1998). Ultimately, it may be possible to determine particular genetic loci that are involved in contextual fear conditioning, allowing for an integration of the neurochemical, genetic, and environmental data on panic disorder (Gorman et al. 2000).

## Neuroanatomic Studies

Preliminary evidence from brain imaging shows the importance of the amygdala and paralimbic structures in panic disorder. Preliminary studies in nonanxious control subjects reported activation of amygdala and periamygdaloid cortical areas during conditioned fear acquisition and extinction (Gorman et al. 2000). Furthermore, an early magnetic resonance imaging study reported focal abnormalities in the temporal lobe, particularly on the right side, in patients with panic disorder (Fontaine et al. 1990). Finally, PET scanning during anxious anticipation in control subjects (Reiman et al. 1989a) and lactate-induced panic attacks in panic disorder patients (Reiman et al. 1989b) both identified increased activity in paralimbic regions (temporal poles).

An early study suggested that only panic patients susceptible to lactate-induced panic had abnormal asymmetry of a parahippocampal region at rest (Reiman et al. 1986). Subsequent functional imaging studies have confirmed dysfunctions of hippocampus or parahippocampal regions in panic disorder, although the precise abnormalities documented have not always been consistent (Bisaglo et al. 1998; De Cristofaro et al. 1993; Nordahl et al. 1990). Hypocapnia-induced vasoconstriction has made the results of certain imaging studies in panic disorder difficult to interpret (Gorman et al. 2000).

Additional abnormalities have been documented in some imaging studies of panic disorder. These include a computed tomography study suggesting prefrontal abnormalities (Wurthmann et al. 1998), a SPECT study showing asymmetry of inferior frontal cortical perfusion (De Cristofaro et al. 1993), and a PET study showing increased activity in medial orbitofrontal regions (Nordahl et al. 1990). In contrast, the basal ganglia have not commonly been implicated in panic disorder; for example, a study comparing SPECT in OCD, panic disorder, and healthy control subjects found that caudate abnormalities were present in OCD patients but not in panic disorder patients (Lucey et al. 1997). Although it has been hypothesized that cognitive-behavioral treatments exert effects in panic disorder by behavioral desensitization of hippocampal-mediated contextual conditioning,

or by cognitive techniques that strengthen medial prefrontal cortex inhibition of amygdala (Gorman et al. 2000; LeDoux 1998), the relevant empirical studies have not yet been undertaken.

Advances in brain imaging methods have, however, begun to tackle the integration of neuroanatomic and neurochemical data. Some groups, for example, have reported decreased benzodiazepine binding in left temporal regions (Kaschka et al. 1995); right orbitofrontal cortex and right insula (Malizia et al. 1998); and frontal, temporal, and occipital cortex (Schlegel et al. 1994). However, not all studies have been consistent; some groups have reported increased benzodiazepine receptor binding in right middle and inferior frontal gyri (Kuikka et al. 1995) and in right supraorbital cortex and perhaps right temporal cortex (Brandt et al. 1998). A subgroup of panic disorder patients may have upregulation of benzodiazepine receptors.

## Posttraumatic Stress Disorder

PTSD begins, by definition, in the aftermath of exposure to a trauma; in men, common traumas include combat exposure, and in women, the most common traumas include rape and sexual molestation (Kessler et al. 1994). Three sets of subsequent symptoms characterize PTSD: reexperiencing phenomena (such as visual flashbacks), avoidant and numbing symptoms, and hyperarousal. It should be emphasized that the prevalence of exposure to trauma is significantly higher than the prevalence of PTSD, indicating that most trauma does not lead to this disorder.

Indeed, an important development in the PTSD literature is a growing emphasis that this is not a "normal" reaction to an abnormal event (Yehuda and McFarlane 1995). Rather, PTSD is increasingly viewed as a serious disorder that is associated with significant morbidity and mediated by neurobiological and psychological dysfunctions.

Features of current neuroanatomic models of PTSD (Figure 32–5) include the following: 1) amygdalothalamic pathways are involved in the rapid, automatic (implicit) processing of incoming information; 2) the amygdala, which sends afferents to other regions involved in the anxiety response (hypothalamus, brainstem nuclei) is hyperactivated; 3) the hippocampus is involved in (explicitly) remembering the context of traumatic memories; and 4) activity is decreased in certain frontal-cortical areas, such as Broca's area, consistent with the decreased verbalization during the processing of trauma and with the inability to override automatic amygdala processing.

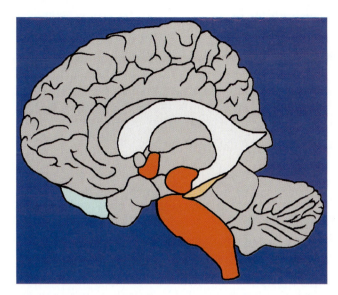

**FIGURE 32–5.** Neuroanatomic model of posttraumatic stress disorder. Note the increased activity in the amygdala and its efferents (Rauch et al. 1996), decreased activity in Broca's area (Shin et al. 1997a), and decreased volume of the hippocampus (Brenner et al. 1997b; M.B. Stein et al. 1997).

*Source.* Reprinted from Stein DJ: *False Alarm!: How to Conquer the Anxiety Disorders.* Cape Town, South Africa, University of Stellenbosch, 2000. Used with permission.

## Neurochemical Studies

A range of neurochemical findings in PTSD are consistent with sensitization of various neurotransmitter systems (Charney et al. 1993). In particular, there is evidence of hyperactive noradrenergic function and dopaminergic sensitization. Such sensitization is also consistent with the role of environmental traumas in PTSD; it turns out that dopamine agonists and environmental traumas act as cross-sensitizers of each other. Evidence indicates that the amygdala and related limbic regions may play a particularly important role in the final common pathway of such hyperactivation (Charney et al. 1993).

Also, growing evidence suggests the importance of the serotonin system in mediating PTSD symptoms (Connor and Davidson 1998). Clinical studies of abnormal paroxetine binding and exacerbations of symptoms in response to administration of m-CPP are certainly consistent with a role for serotonin in PTSD (Southwick et al. 1997). Furthermore, evidence is increasing for the efficacy of serotonin reuptake inhibitors in PTSD, with preliminary indications that these agents may be more effective than other classes of medication (Dow and Kline 1997; Penava et al. 1996). These agents may act on amygdala circuits, helping to inhibit efferents to structures such as hypothalamus and brain-stem nuclei, which mediate fear.

A third set of neurochemical findings in PTSD has focused on the hypothalamic-pituitary-adrenal system. PTSD is characterized by decreased plasma levels of cortisol, as well as increased glucocorticoid receptor responsiveness, suggesting that negative feedback inhibition may play an important role in the pathogenesis of the disorder. Such findings differ from those found in other anxiety disorders and in depression (Yehuda and McFarlane 1995; Yehuda et al. 1993). Notably, cortisol-releasing factor receptors are also prominent in the amygdala, particularly in the central nucleus.

One important implication of the hypothalamic-pituitary-adrenal findings is the possibility that dysfunction in this system results in neuronal damage, particularly to the hippocampus. Animal studies have documented hippocampal damage after exposure to either glucocorticoids or naturalistic psychosocial stressors (Magarinos et al. 1996). Parallel neurotoxicity in human PTSD could account for some of the cognitive impairments that are characteristic of this disorder.

## Neuroanatomic Studies

A range of structural imaging studies are in fact consistent with the possibility of hippocampal dysfunction occurring in PTSD. In an early magnetic resonance imaging study, combat veterans with PTSD had smaller right hippocampal volumes than did healthy control subjects, and in PTSD patients, hippocampal volume reduction correlated with deficits in short-term verbal memory (Bremner et al. 1995). A different group of investigators reported consistent findings; both right and left hippocampal volumes were significantly reduced in combat veterans with PTSD compared with both combat control subjects and healthy subjects (Gurvits et al. 1996). Furthermore, hippocampal volume was directly correlated with combat exposure (Gurvits et al. 1996). Findings with magnetic resonance spectroscopy may be even more robust (Schuff et al. 1997).

A similar set of findings has been reported in adult patients with PTSD secondary to childhood abuse. Two studies both found smaller left hippocampal volume in such subjects compared with healthy control subjects (Bremner et al. 1997b; M.B. Stein et al. 1997). Furthermore, left-sided hippocampal volume reduction was associated with increased dissociative symptoms (M.B. Stein et al. 1997). PTSD patients have increased neurological soft signs (Gurvits et al. 2000) and neurodevelopmental abnormalities (Myslobodsky et al. 1995), and it is theoretically possible that diminished hippocampal size is a risk factor for the development of psychiatric complications following trauma exposure rather than a consequence of trauma. Nevertheless, these preliminary findings are consistent in pointing to a role for the hippocampus in PTSD.

Functional imaging studies have provided additional information to help build a neuroanatomic model of PTSD. First, several studies in control subjects without PTSD have provided evidence for subcortical processing of masked emotional stimuli by the amygdala. Furthermore, in an early study, PTSD patients exposed to audiotaped traumatic and neutral scripts during PET had increases in normalized blood flow in right-sided limbic, paralimbic, and visual areas and decreases in blood flow in left inferior frontal and middle temporal cortex (Rauch et al. 1996). The authors concluded that emotions associated with the PTSD symptomatic state were mediated by the limbic and paralimbic systems within the right hemisphere, with activation of visual cortex perhaps corresponding to visual reexperiencing.

Not dissimilarly, bank officials shown a videotape of a previously experienced bank robbery while undergoing PET scanning had increased rCBF in the posterior cingulate, the left orbitofrontal cortex, and the primary and secondary visual cortex, with decreased rCBF in Broca's area, the left angular gyrus, the left operculum, and the secondary somatosensory cortex (Fischer et al. 1996). It has been suggested that decreased activity in Broca's area during exposure to trauma in PTSD is consistent with patients' inability to verbally process traumatic memories (Rauch et al. 1998).

Subsequent studies have replicated many of the initial findings. Thus, when combat veterans generated mental images of combat-related trauma, subjects with PTSD had increased rCBF in right amygdala and ventral anterior cingulate, and when combat veterans viewed combat-related pictures, these subjects had decreased rCBF in Broca's area (Shin et al. 1997a). Again, in women with histories of childhood abuse, during script-driven exposure to trauma, rCBF was increased in anterior paralimbic regions (orbitofrontal cortex and temporal poles) (Shin et al. 1997b). However, the PTSD group had greater increases in anterior temporal pole and orbitofrontal cortex and greater decreases in bilateral anterior frontal regions and left inferior frontal gyrus, whereas the comparison group had greater increases in anterior cingulate gyrus (Shin et al. 1997a). These authors suggested that anterior cingulate may be the human equivalent of rodent medial frontal cortex (LeDoux 1998), with insufficient recruitment of these circuits perhaps contributing to PTSD.

Although involvement of the basal ganglia typically has not been found in functional imaging studies of PTSD, Lucey et al. (1997) reported that SPECT scans in patients with PTSD and OCD had similarities in comparison to scans in patients with panic disorder and healthy control subjects. They suggested that this might reflect the existence of repetitive intrusive symptoms in both PTSD and OCD. The possibility of certain phenomenological and psychopharmacological similarities between PTSD and OCD certainly bears further thought. Also, interactions between the amygdala and the corticostriatal systems may be important in mediating the transition from emotional reaction to emotional action (LeDoux 1998).

Are there differences in functional imaging during symptom provocation and processing of cognitive tasks in PTSD? During a continuous performance task and verb-generation condition, PTSD patients showed greater rCBF in the orbitofrontal cortex and reduced left-to-right ratio of rCBF within the hippocampus (Semple et al. 1993). However, in a second study by this group, in which an attentional task was used again, parietal blood flow was decreased in the right parietal cortex in PTSD subjects (Semple et al. 1996).

Once again, modern techniques have recently allowed for the integration of neurochemical and neuroanatomic data. PET was undertaken in combat veterans with PTSD and healthy control subjects after administration of yohimbine (Bremner et al. 1997a). Yohimbine resulted in a significant increase in anxiety in the patients with PTSD, and this group of subjects also had a decrease in several areas, including prefrontal, temporal, parietal, and orbitofrontal cortex. This is perhaps consistent with previous literature suggesting that during intense anxiety states, rCBF decreases (Gur et al. 1987).

## Social Phobia (Social Anxiety Disorder)

Social phobia (social anxiety disorder) is characterized by a fear of social situations in which the individual may be exposed to the scrutiny of others. These fears may be divided into those that concern social interaction situations (e.g., dating, meetings) and performance fears (e.g., of talking, eating, or writing in public). These fears result in avoidance of social situations or endurance of these situations with considerable distress. Growing evidence indicates that social phobia is a chronic disorder, with substantial comorbidity (particularly of mood and substance use disorders) and significant morbidity. Patients with social phobia are more likely to be unmarried, to have weaker social networks, to fail to complete high school and college, and to be unemployed (Ballenger et al. 1998).

Detailed neuroanatomic models of social phobia remain to be delineated. Nevertheless, it may be hypothesized again that temporolimbic circuitry is important in mediating the fear responses that characterize this disorder. Furthermore, serotonin and dopamine neurocircuitry, presumably involving prefrontal and basal ganglia regions, also may play a crucial role. We review some of the neurotransmitter and neuroimaging data that support such a model (Figure 32–6).

## Neurochemical Studies

A range of evidence supports the role of serotonergic circuits in social phobia. A pharmacological probe study was performed with agents that affect the serotonergic (fenfluramine), dopaminergic (levodopa), and noradrenergic (clonidine) systems; the only positive finding was an augmented cortisol response to fenfluramine administration in patients with social phobia (Tancer et al. 1994). The authors concluded that patients with social phobia may have selective supersensitivity of serotonergic systems.

Also, a range of evidence indicates involvement of the dopaminergic system in social phobia. Timid mice have decreased cerebrospinal fluid dopamine levels, and introverted depressed patients also may have decreased cerebrospinal fluid dopamine levels (Nutt et al. 1998). Social status in monkeys may be reflected in differences in dopamine $D_2$ striatal density (K.A. Grant et al. 1998). More persuasively, social phobia may be associated with Parkinson's disease or may appear after the administration of neuroleptics (M.B. Stein 1998).

Evidence that the hypothalamic-pituitary-adrenal axis may be dysfunctional in social phobia is inconsistent to date. Socially subordinate baboons have been reported to have elevated basal cortisol and to be less responsive to dexamethasone inhibition (Sapolsky et al. 1997). Also, children with a high frequency of wary behavior during peer play and "behavioral inhibition" had relatively high morning salivary cortisol levels (Schmidt et al. 1997). Social phobia patients, however, have normal levels of urinary and plasma cortisol and normal dexamethasone suppression test results (M.B. Stein 1998), although some evidence shows an association between social phobia and hypothalamic growth hormone dysfunction (Uhde 1994).

## Neuroanatomic Studies

An early brain SPECT study of social phobia did not show any evidence of focal abnormalities in CBF (M.B. Stein and Leslie 1996). Although studies are preliminary,

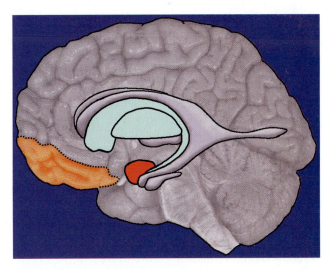

**FIGURE 32–6.** Neuroanatomic model of social phobia. Note the increased temporolimbic activity (van der Linden et al. 2000), decreased basal ganglia dopaminergic activity (Tiihonen et al. 1997a), and perhaps some increased prefrontal activity (Rauch et al. 1997b; van der Linden et al. 2000).

*Source.* Reprinted from Stein DJ: *False Alarm!: How to Conquer the Anxiety Disorders.* Cape Town, South Africa, University of Stellenbosch, 2000. Used with permission.

some evidence does suggest that patients with social phobia have selective activation of the amygdala when exposed to potentially fear-relevant stimuli (Birbaumer et al. 1998; Tillfors et al. 2001).

Furthermore, after treatment with an SSRI, patients with social phobia had significantly reduced activity in the anterior and lateral part of the left temporal cortex; the left cingulum; and the anterior, lateral, and posterior part of the left midfrontal cortex (van der Linden et al. 2000). Speculatively, patients with social phobia may use verbal-linear processing (left frontal hemisphere processes) in social situations to overcome subcortically mediated fear responses (temporolimbic areas). With SSRI treatment, however, circuitry appears to normalize.

Furthermore, some imaging studies suggest that the striatum also may play a role in social phobia (Davidson et al. 1993; Potts et al. 1994). Indeed, a recent study of the density of dopamine reuptake sites found that striatal dopamine reuptake site densities were markedly lower in patients than in nonphobic control subjects (Tiihonen et al. 1997a). Moreover, striatal $D_2$ receptor binding was lower in social phobia patients than in control subjects (Schneier et al. 2000). These findings support the hypothesis that social phobia may be associated with a dysfunction of the striatal dopaminergic system.

## Conclusions

Several lessons emerge from a review of the neuropsychiatry of anxiety disorders. First, the anxiety disorders are common and disabling disorders not only in general clinical settings but also in patients with neurological illnesses such as Alzheimer's disease, stroke, and traumatic brain injury. Although the link between depression and neuropsychiatric disorders is increasingly recognized, the importance of anxiety disorders in this context has perhaps been relatively overlooked, paralleling the underdiagnosis and undertreatment of anxiety disorders in primary care settings. The anxiety disorders deserve to be carefully diagnosed and rigorously treated.

Second, both animal and clinical studies increasingly indicate that the amygdala and paralimbic structures play an important role in conditioned fear and in anxiety disorders. Amygdala lesions are classically associated with decreased fear responses, and conversely, hyperactivation of the limbic system is characteristic of several different anxiety disorders. Paralimbic regions, such as the anterior cingulate, appear to play a key role at the interface of cognition and emotion. The apparent centrality of such systems to different anxiety disorders may account in part for their high comorbidity. Additional features of limbic involvement may, however, be specific to particular disorders (e.g., hippocampal shrinkage in PTSD or parahippocampal asymmetry in panic disorder). Serotonin reuptake inhibitors are increasingly viewed as first-line treatments for anxiety disorders, and innervation of amygdala and paralimbic structures by serotonergic neurons may be crucial in explaining their efficacy.

Finally, CSTC pathways also may be important in anxiety disorders, particularly in OCD and certain putative OCD spectrum disorders, such as Tourette's disorder. There is growing consolidation of imaging, immunologic, genetic, and treatment data around this model. It is particularly remarkable that CSTC pathways can be normalized by pharmacotherapy, by psychotherapy, and by neurosurgery. In some ways, it can be argued that although OCD was once viewed as the key to a psychodynamic understanding of the mind, OCD and some OCD spectrum disorders such as Tourette's disorder are now the neuropsychiatric disorders par excellence. Certainly, such disorders provide a key paradigm and challenge for those who are interested in integrating "brain" and "mind" approaches to psychiatric disorders.

## References

American Psychiatric Association: Diagnostic and Statistical Manual of Mental Disorders, 3rd Edition. Washington, DC, American Psychiatric Association, 1980

American Psychiatric Association: Diagnostic and Statistical Manual of Mental Disorders, 3rd Edition, Revised. Washington, DC, American Psychiatric Association, 1987

American Psychiatric Association: Diagnostic and Statistical Manual of Mental Disorders, 4th Edition, Text Revision. Washington, DC, American Psychiatric Association, 2000

Ames D, Cummings JL, Wirshing WC, et al: Repetitive and compulsive behavior in frontal lobe degenerations. J Neuropsychiatry Clin Neurosci 6:100–113, 1994

Astrom M: Generalized anxiety disorder in stroke patients: a 3-year longitudinal study. Stroke 27:270–275, 1996

Ballenger JC, Davidson JR, Lecrubier Y, et al: Consensus statement on social anxiety disorder from the International Consensus Group on Depression and Anxiety. J Clin Psychiatry 59 (suppl 17):54–60, 1998

Baxter LR, Schwartz JM, Bergman KS: Caudate glucose metabolic rate changes with both drug and behavior therapy for OCD. Arch Gen Psychiatry 49:681–689, 1992

Bechara A, Tranel D, Damasio H, et al: Double dissociation of conditioning and declarative knowledge relative to the amygdala and hippocampus in humans. Science 269:1115–1118, 1995

Bihari K, Hill JL, Murphy DL: Obsessive-compulsive characteristics in patients with idiopathic spasmodic torticollis. Psychiatry Res 42:267–272, 1992

Birbaumer N, Grodd W, Diedrich O, et al: FMRI reveals amygdala activation to human faces in social phobics. Neuroreport 9:1223–1226, 1998

Bisaglo A, Katz JL, Antonini A, et al: Cerebral glucose metabolism in women with panic disorder. Am J Psychiatry 155:1178–1183, 1998

Boyer W: Serotonin uptake inhibitors are superior to imipramine and alprazolam in alleviating panic attacks: a meta-analysis. Int Clin Psychopharmacol 10:45–49, 1995

Brandt CA, Meller J, Keweloh L, et al: Increased benzodiazepine receptor density in the prefrontal cortex in patients with panic disorder. J Neural Transm 105:1325–1333, 1998

Braun AR, Randolph C, Stoetter B, et al: The functional neuroanatomy of Tourette's syndrome: an FDG-PET study, II: relationships between regional cerebral metabolism and associated behavioral and cognitive features of the illness. Neuropsychopharmacology 13:151–168, 1995

Bremner JD, Randall P, Scott TM, et al: MRI-based measurement of hippocampal volume in patients with combat-related posttraumatic stress disorder [see comments]. Am J Psychiatry 152:973–981, 1995

Bremner JD, Innis RB, Ng CK, et al: Positron emission tomography measurement of cerebral metabolic correlates of yohimbine administration in combat-related posttraumatic stress disorder. Arch Gen Psychiatry 54:246–254, 1997a

Bremner JD, Randall P, Vermetten E, et al: Magnetic resonance imaging-based measurement of hippocampal volume in posttraumatic stress disorder related to childhood physical and sexual abuse—a preliminary report. Biol Psychiatry 41:23–32, 1997b

Brody AL, Saxena S, Schwartz JM: FDG-PET predictors of response to behavioral therapy and pharmacotherapy in obsessive compulsive disorder. Psychiatry Res 84:1–6, 1998

Buchsbaum MS, Hazlett E, Sicotte N, et al: Topographic EEG changes with benzodiazepine administration in generalized anxiety disorder. Biol Psychiatry 20:832–842, 1985

Buchsbaum MS, Wu J, Haier R, et al: Positron emission tomography assessment of effects of benzodiazepines on regional glucose metabolic rate in patients with anxiety disorder. Life Sci 40:2393–2400, 1987

Burvill PW, Johnson GA, Jamrozik KD, et al: Anxiety disorders after stroke: results from the Perth Community Stroke Study. Br J Psychiatry 166:328–332, 1995

Bystritsky A, Leuchter AF, Vapnik T: EEG abnormalities in nonmedicated panic disorder. J Nerv Ment Dis 187:113–114, 1999

Cameron OG, Smith CB, Lee MA, et al: Adrenergic status in anxiety disorders: platelet alpha two-adrenergic receptor binding, blood pressure, pulse, and plasma catecholamines in panic and generalized anxiety disorder. Biol Psychiatry 28:3–20, 1990

Castillo CS, Starkstein SE, Fedoroff JP, et al: Generalized anxiety disorder after stroke. J Nerv Ment Dis 181:100–106, 1993

Cavenar JO, Harris MA: Temporal lobe seizures simulating anxiety attacks. US Navy Medicine 70:22–23, 1979

Charney DS, Deutch AY, Krystal JH, et al: Psychobiologic mechanisms of posttraumatic stress disorder. Arch Gen Psychiatry 50:295–305, 1993

Cheyette SR, Cummings JL: Encephalitis lethargica: lessons for contemporary neuropsychiatry. J Neuropsychiatry Clin Neurosci 7:125–134, 1995

Connor KM, Davidson JRT: The role of serotonin in posttraumatic stress disorder: neurobiology and pharmacotherapy. CNS Spectrums 3:43–51, 1998

Coplan JD, Lydiard RB: Brain circuits in panic disorder. Biol Psychiatry 44:1264–1276, 1998

Coplan JD, Papp LA, Pine D, et al: Clinical improvement with fluoxetine therapy and noradrenergic function in patients with panic disorder. Arch Gen Psychiatry 54:643–648, 1997

Cora-Locatelli G, Greenberg BD, Martin J, et al: Gabapentin augmentation for fluoxetine-treated patients with obsessive-compulsive disorder (letter). J Clin Psychiatry 59:480–481, 1998

Costall B, Naylor RJ, Olley JE: Stereotypic and anticataleptic activities of amphetamine after intracerebral injections. Eur J Pharmacol 18(1):83–94, 1972

Cummings JL: Frontal-subcortical circuits and human behavior. Arch Neurol 50:873–880, 1993

Cummings JL, Cunningham K: Obsessive-compulsive disorder in Huntington's disease. Biol Psychiatry 31:263–270, 1992

Damasio H, Grabowski T, Frank R, et al: The return of Phineas Gage: clues about the brain from the skull of a famous patient. Science 264:1102–1105, 1994

Davidson JR, Krishnan KR, Charles HC, et al: Magnetic resonance spectroscopy in social phobia: preliminary findings. J Clin Psychiatry 54 (suppl):19–25, 1993

Davis M, Shi C: The extended amygdala: are the central nucleus of the amygdala and the bed nucleus of the stria terminalis differentially involved in fear versus anxiety? Ann N Y Acad Sci 877:281–291, 1999

De Cristofaro MT, Sessarego A, Pupi A, et al: Brain perfusion abnormalities in drug-naive, lactate-sensitive panic patients: a SPECT study. Biol Psychiatry 33:505–512, 1993

de la Tourette G: Etude sur une affection nerveuse caraterisee par de l'incoordination motrice accompagnee d'echolalie et de coprolie. Arch Neurol 9:19–42, 1885

Diaz-Olavarrieta C, Cummings JL, Velazquez J, et al: Neuropsychiatric manifestations of multiple sclerosis. J Neuropsychiatry Clin Neurosci 11:51–57, 1999

Dow B, Kline N: Antidepressant treatment of posttraumatic stress disorder and major depression in veterans. Ann Clin Psychiatry 9:1–5, 1997

Downer JL: Changes in visual gnostic functions and emotional behavior following unilateral temporal pole damage in the "split-brain" monkey. Nature 191:50–51, 1961

Dupont RL, Rice DP, Miller LS, et al: Economic costs of anxiety disorders. Anxiety 2:167–172, 1996

Ebert D, Speck O, Konig A: 1H-magnetic resonance spectroscopy in obsessive-compulsive disorder: evidence for neuronal loss in the cingulate gyrus and the right striatum. Psychiatry Res 74:173–176, 1997

El Mansari M, Bouchard C, Blier P: Alteration of serotonin release in the guinea pig orbito-frontal cortex by selective serotonin reuptake inhibitors. Neuropsychopharmacology 13:117–127, 1995

Fischer H, Wik G, Fredrikson M: Functional neuroanatomy of robbery re-experience: affective memories studied with PET. Neuroreport 7:2081–2086, 1996

Fitzgerald KD, Moore GJ, Paulson LA: Proton spectroscopic imaging of the thalamus in treatment-naive pediatric obsessive-compulsive disorder. Biol Psychiatry 47:174–182, 2000

Fog R, Pakkenberg H: Behavioral effects of dopamine and p-hydroxyamphetamine injected into corpus striatum of rats. Exp Neurol 31:75–86, 1971

Fontaine R, Breton G, Dery R, et al: Temporal lobe abnormalities in panic disorder: an MRI study. Biol Psychiatry 27:304–310, 1990

Freud S: Inhibitions, symptoms, and anxiety (1926), in Standard Edition of the Complete Psychological Works of Sigmund Freud, Vol 20. Translated and edited by Strachey J. London, Hogarth Press, 1959, pp 75–175

Germine M, Goddard AW, Woods SW, et al: Anger and anxiety responses to m-chlorophenylpiperazine in generalized anxiety disorder. Biol Psychiatry 32:457–467, 1992

Ghadirian AM, Gauthier S, Bertrand S: Anxiety attacks in a patient with a right temporal lobe meningioma. J Clin Psychiatry 47:270–271, 1986

Giedd JN, Rapoport JL, Garvey MA, et al: MRI assessment of children with obsessive-compulsive disorder or tics associated with streptococcal infection. Am J Psychiatry 157:281–283, 2000

Goddard AW, Charney DS: Toward an integrated neurobiology of panic disorder. J Clin Psychiatry 58 (suppl 2):4–11, 1997

Goodman WK, McDougle CJ, Lawrence HP: Beyond the serotonin hypothesis: a role for dopamine in some forms of obsessive-compulsive disorder. J Clin Psychiatry 51 (suppl 8):36–43, 1990

Gorman JM, Liebowitz MR, Fyer AJ, et al: A neuroanatomical hypothesis for panic disorder [see comments]. Am J Psychiatry 146:148–161, 1989

Gorman JM, Kent JM, Sullivan GM, et al: Neuroanatomical hypothesis of panic disorder, revised. Am J Psychiatry 157:493–505, 2000

Grachev ID, Breiter HC, Rauch SL, et al: Structural abnormalities of frontal neocortex in obsessive-compulsive disorder. Arch Gen Psychiatry 55:181–182, 1998

Grant KA, Shively CA, Nader MA, et al: Effect of social status on striatal dopamine D2 receptor binding characteristics in cynomolgus monkeys assessed with positron emission tomography. Synapse 29:80–83, 1998

Grant SJ, Redmond DE Jr: The neuroanatomy and pharmacology of the nucleus locus coeruleus. Prog Clin Biol Res 71:5–27, 1981

Grimshaw L: Obsessional disorder and neurological illness. J Neurol Neurosurg Psychiatry 27:229–231, 1964

Gur RC, Gur RE, Resnick SM, et al: The effect of anxiety on cortical cerebral blood flow and metabolism. J Cereb Blood Flow Metab 7:173–177, 1987

Gurvits TV, Gilbertson MW, Lasko NB, et al: Neurologic soft signs in chronic posttraumatic stress disorder. Arch Gen Psychiatry 57:181–186, 2000

Gurvits TV, Shenton ME, Hokama H, et al: Magnetic resonance imaging study of hippocampal volume in chronic, combat-related posttraumatic stress disorder. Biol Psychiatry 40:1091–1099, 1996

Hardie RJ, Lees AJ, Stern GM: On-off fluctuations in Parkinson's disease. Brain 107:487–506, 1984

Hibbard MR, Uysal S, Kepler K, et al: Axis I psychopathology in individuals with traumatic brain injury. J Head Trauma Rehabil 13:24–39, 1998

Hollander E, Liebowitz MR, DeCaria C: Conceptual and methodological issues in studies of obsessive-compulsive and Tourette's disorders. Psychiatric Developments 4:267–296, 1989

Hollander E, DeCaria C, Nitescu A: Serotonergic function in obsessive compulsive disorder: behavioral and neuroendocrine responses to oral m-CPP and fenfluramine in patients and healthy volunteers. Arch Gen Psychiatry 49:21–28, 1992

Hollander E, Prohovnik I, Stein DJ: Increased cerebral blood flow during m-CPP exacerbation of obsessive-compulsive disorder. J Neuropsychiatry Clin Neurosci 7:485–490, 1995

Hugo FJ, Van Heerden B, Zungu-Dirwayi N, et al: Functional brain imaging in obsessive-compulsive disorder secondary to neurological lesions. Depress Anxiety 10:129–136, 1999

Hyde TM, Weinberger DR: Tourette's syndrome: a model neuropsychiatric disorder. JAMA 273:498–501, 1995

Iny LJ, Pecknold J, Suranyi-Cadotte BE, et al: Studies of a neurochemical link between depression, anxiety, and stress from [3H] imipramine and [3H] paroxetine binding on human platelets. Biol Psychiatry 36:281–291, 1994

Jenike MA, Brotman AW: The EEG in obsessive-compulsive disorder. J Clin Psychiatry 45:122–124, 1984

Joffe RT, Lippert GP, Gray TA, et al: Mood disorder and multiple sclerosis. Arch Neurol 44:376–378, 1987

Joseph S, Masterson J: Posttraumatic stress disorder and traumatic brain injury: are they mutually exclusive? J Trauma Stress 12:437–453, 1999

Kapur S, Remington G: Serotonin-dopamine interaction and its relevance to schizophrenia. Am J Psychiatry 153:466–476, 1996

Kaschka W, Feistel H, Ebert D: Reduced benzodiazepine receptor binding in panic disorders measured by iomazenil SPECT. J Psychiatr Res 29:427–434, 1995

Kellner M, Hirschmann M, Wiedemann K: Panic attacks caused by temporal tumors: an exemplary new case and a review. Depress Anxiety 4:243–245, 1996

Kessler RC, McGonagle KA, Zhao S, et al: Lifetime and 12-month prevalence of DSM-III-R psychiatric disorders in the United States: results from the National Comorbidity Survey. Arch Gen Psychiatry 51:8–19, 1994

Ketter TA, Andreason PJ, George MS, et al: Anterior paralimbic mediation of procaine-induced emotional and psychosensory experiences [see comments]. Arch Gen Psychiatry 53:59–69, 1996

Khanna S: Carbamazepine in obsessive-compulsive disorder. Clin Neuropharmacol 11:478–481, 1988

Klüver H, Bucy PC: Preliminary analysis of functions of the temporal lobes in monkeys. AMA Archives of Neurology and Psychiatry 42:979–1000, 1939

Kuikka JT, Pitkanen A, Lepola U, et al: Abnormal regional benzodiazepine receptor uptake in the prefrontal cortex in patients with panic disorder. Nucl Med Commun 16:273–280, 1995

Lauterbach EC, Cummings JL, Duffy J, et al: Neuropsychiatric correlates and treatment of lenticulostriatal diseases: a review of literature and overview of research opportunities in Huntington's, Wilson's, and Fahr's diseases. J Neuropsychiatry Clin Neurosci 10:249–266, 1998

LeDoux J: Fear and the brain: where have we been, and where are we going? Biol Psychiatry 44:1229–1238, 1998

Levy LL, Miller BL, Cummings JL, et al: Alzheimer disease and frontotemporal dementias: behavioral distinctions. Arch Neurol 53:687–690, 1996

Lippitz BE, Mindus P, Meyerson BA, et al: Lesion topography and outcome after thermocapsulotomy or gamma knife capsulotomy for obsessive-compulsive disorder: relevance of the right hemisphere. Neurosurgery 44:452–458, 1999

Litvan I, Mega MS, Cummings JL, et al: Neuropsychiatric aspects of progressive supranuclear palsy. Neurology 47:1184–1189, 1996

Lucey JV, Costa DC, Adshead G, et al: Brain blood flow in anxiety disorders: OCD, panic disorder with agoraphobia, and post-traumatic stress disorder on 99mTcHMPAO single photon emission tomography (SPET). Br J Psychiatry 171:346–350, 1997

Luxenberg J, Swedo S, Flament M, et al: Neuroanatomical abnormalities in obsessive-compulsive disorder detected with quantitative X-ray computed tomography. Am J Psychiatry 145:1089–1093, 1988

Lydiard RB, Brawman-Mintzer O, Ballenger JC: Recent developments in the psychopharmacology of anxiety disorders. J Consult Clin Psychol 64:660–668, 1996

MacClean PD: Effects of lesions of globus pallidus on species-typical display behavior of squirrel monkeys. Brain Res 149:175–196, 1978

Magarinos AM, McEwen BS, Flugge G, et al: Chronic psychosocial stress causes apical dendritic atrophy of hippocampal CA3 pyramidal neurons in subordinate tree shrews. J Neurosci 16:3534–3540, 1996

Malison RT, McDougle CJ, van Dyck CH, et al: [123I]beta-CIT SPECT imaging of striatal dopamine transporter binding in Tourette's disorder. Am J Psychiatry 152:1359–1361, 1995

Malizia AL, Cunningham VJ, Bell CJ, et al: Decreased brain GABA(A)-benzodiazepine receptor binding in panic disorder: preliminary results from a quantitative PET study. Arch Gen Psychiatry 55:715–720, 1998

Marazziti D, Rotondo A, Martini C, et al: Changes in peripheral benzodiazepine receptors in patients with panic disorder and obsessive-compulsive disorder. Neuropsychobiology 29:8–11, 1994

Maricle RA, Sennhauser S, Burry M: Panic disorder associated with right parahippocampal infarction. J Nerv Ment Dis 179:374–375, 1991

Martin LJ, Spicer DM, Lewis MH: Social deprivation of infant monkeys alters the chemoarchitecture of the brain, I: subcortical regions. J Neurosci 11:3344–3358, 1991

Martuza RL, Chiocca EA, Jenike MA, et al: Stereotactic radiofrequency thermal cingulotomy for obsessive compulsive disorder [see comments]. J Neuropsychiatry Clin Neurosci 2:331–336, 1990

McDougle CJ, Goodman WK, Leckman JF: Haloperidol addition in fluvoxamine-refractory obsessive-compulsive disorder: a double-blind placebo-controlled study in patients with and without tics. Arch Gen Psychiatry 51:302–308, 1994

McNamara ME, Fogel BS: Anticonvulsant-responsive panic attacks with temporal lobe EEG abnormalities. J Neuropsychiatry Clin Neurosci 2:193–196, 1990

Mega MS, Cummings JL, Fiorello T, et al: The spectrum of behavioral changes in Alzheimer's disease. Neurology 46:130–135, 1996

Minden SL, Orav J, Reich P: Depression in multiple sclerosis. Gen Hosp Psychiatry 9:426–434, 1987

Mishkin M, Petri H: Memories and habits: some implications for the analysis of learning and retentions, in Neuropsychology of Memory. Edited by Squire LR, Butters N. New York, Guilford, 1984, pp 287–296

Montgomery SA: Obsessive compulsive disorder is not an anxiety disorder. Int Clin Psychopharmacol 8 (suppl 1):57–62, 1993

Moore GJ, MacMaster FP, Stewart C, et al: Case study: caudate glutamatergic changes with paroxetine therapy for pediatric obsessive-compulsive disorder. J Am Acad Child Adolesc Psychiatry 37:663–667, 1998

Moriarty J, Eapen V, Costa DC, et al: HAMPAO SPET does not distinguish obsessive-compulsive and tic syndromes in families multiply affected with Gilles de la Tourette's syndrome. Psychol Med 27:737–740, 1997

Murray CJL, Lopez AD: Global Burden of Disease: A Comprehensive Assessment of Mortality and Morbidity From Diseases, Injuries and Risk Factors in 1990 and Projected to 2020, Vol I: Harvard. Geneva, Switzerland, World Health Organization, 1996

Myslobodsky MS, Glicksohn J, Singer J, et al: Changes of brain anatomy in patients with posttraumatic stress disorder: a pilot magnetic resonance imaging study. Psychiatry Res 58:259–264, 1995

Nordahl TE, Semple WE, Gross M, et al: Cerebral glucose metabolic differences in patients with panic disorder. Neuropsychopharmacology 3:261–272, 1990

Nutt DJ, Bell CJ, Malizia AL: Brain mechanisms of social anxiety disorder. J Clin Psychiatry 59 (suppl 17):4–11, 1998

O'Sullivan RL, Rauch SL, Breiter HC, et al: Reduced basal ganglia volumes in trichotillomania measured via morphometric magnetic resonance imaging. Biol Psychiatry 42:39–45, 1997

Pauls DL, Towbin KE, Leckman JF: Gilles de la Tourette's syndrome and obsessive compulsive disorder: evidence supporting a genetic relationship. Arch Gen Psychiatry 43:1180–1182, 1986

Penava SJ, Otto MW, Pollack MH, et al: Current status of pharmacotherapy for PTSD: an effect size analysis of controlled studies. Depress Anxiety 4:240–242, 1996

Peterson B, Riddle MA, Cohen DJ: Reduced basal ganglia volumes in Tourette's syndrome using three-dimensional reconstruction techniques from magnetic resonance images. Neurology 43:941–949, 1993

Potts NL, Davidson JR, Krishnan KR, et al: Magnetic resonance imaging in social phobia. Psychiatry Res 52:35–42, 1994

Rapoport JL, Ryland DH, Kriete M: Drug treatment of canine acral lick. Arch Gen Psychiatry 48:517–521, 1992

Rauch SL, Baxter LR: Neuroimaging in obsessive-compulsive and related disorders, in Obsessive-Compulsive Disorders: Practical Management, 3rd Edition. Edited by Jenike MA, Baer L, Minichiello WE. St. Louis, MO, Mosby, 1998, pp 289–316

Rauch SL, van der Kolk BA, Fisler RE, et al: A symptom provocation study of posttraumatic stress disorder using positron emission tomography and script-driven imagery. Arch Gen Psychiatry 53:380–387, 1996

Rauch SL, Savage CR, Alpert NM, et al: Probing striatal function in obsessive-compulsive disorder: a PET study of implicit sequence learning. J Neuropsychiatry Clin Neurosci 9:568–573, 1997a

Rauch SL, Savage CR, Alpert NM, et al: The functional neuroanatomy of anxiety: a study of three disorders using positron emission tomography and symptom provocation. Biol Psychiatry 42:446–452, 1997b

Rauch SL, Shin LM, Whalen PJ, et al: Neuroimaging and the neuroanatomy of posttraumatic stress disorder. CNS Spectrums 3:31–41, 1998

Reiman EM, Raichle ME, Robins E, et al: The application of positron emission tomography to the study of panic disorder. Am J Psychiatry 143:469–477, 1986

Reiman EM, Fusselman MJ, Fox PT, et al: Neuroanatomical correlates of anticipatory anxiety. Science 243:1071–1074, 1989a

Reiman EM, Raichle ME, Robins E, et al: Neuroanatomical correlates of a lactate-induced anxiety attack. Arch Gen Psychiatry 46:493–500, 1989b

Richard IH, Schiffer RB, Kurlan R: Anxiety and Parkinson's disease. J Neuropsychiatry Clin Neurosci 8:383–392, 1996

Ridley RM: The psychology of perseverative and stereotyped behavior. Prog Neurobiol 44:221–231, 1994

Riether AM: Anxiety in patients with multiple sclerosis. Semin Clin Neuropsychiatry 4:103–113, 1999

Robbins TW, Brown VJ: The role of the striatum in the mental chronometry of action: a theoretical review. Rev Neurosci 2:181–213, 1990

Rocca P, Ferrero P, Gualerzi A, et al: Peripheral-type benzodiazepine receptors in anxiety disorders. Acta Psychiatr Scand 84:537–544, 1991

Rosenberg DR, Keshavan MS: A.E. Bennett Research Award: toward a neurodevelopmental model of obsessive-compulsive disorder. Biol Psychiatry 43:623–640, 1998

Saint-Cyr JA, Taylor AE, Nicholson K: Behavior and the basal ganglia, in Behavioral Neurology of Movement Disorders. Edited by Weiner WJ, Lang AE. New York, Raven, 1995, pp 1–28

Sapolsky RM, Alberts SC, Altmann J: Hypercortisolism associated with social subordinance or social isolation among wild baboons. Arch Gen Psychiatry 54:1137–1143, 1997

Savage CR, Baer L, Keuthen NJ: Organizational strategies mediate nonverbal memory impairment in obsessive-compulsive disorder. Biol Psychiatry 45:905–916, 1999

Schlegel S, Steinert H, Bockisch A, et al: Decreased benzodiazepine receptor binding in panic disorder measured by IOMAZENIL-SPECT: a preliminary report. Eur Arch Psychiatry Clin Neurosci 244:49–51, 1994

Schmidt LA, Fox NA, Rubin KH, et al: Behavioral and neuroendocrine responses in shy children. Dev Psychobiol 30:127–140, 1997

Schneier FR, Liebowitz MR, Abi-Dargham A, et al: Low dopamine D(2) receptor binding potential in social phobia. Am J Psychiatry 157(3):457–459, 2000

Schuff N, Marmar CR, Weiss DS, et al: Reduced hippocampal volume and n-acetyl aspartate in posttraumatic stress disorder. Ann N Y Acad Sci 821:516–520, 1997

Semple WE, Goyer P, McCormick R, et al: Preliminary report: brain blood flow using PET in patients with posttraumatic stress disorder and substance-abuse histories. Biol Psychiatry 34:115–118, 1993

Semple WE, Goyer PF, McCormick R, et al: Attention and regional cerebral blood flow in posttraumatic stress disorder patients with substance abuse histories. Psychiatry Res 67:17–28, 1996

Servan-Schreiber D, Perlstein WM, Cohen JD, et al: Selective pharmacological activation of limbic structures in human volunteers: a positron emission tomography study. J Neuropsychiatry Clin Neurosci 10:148–159, 1998

Sevy S, Papadimitriou GN, Surmont DW, et al: Noradrenergic function in generalized anxiety disorder, major depressive disorder, and healthy subjects. Biol Psychiatry 25:141–152, 1989

Sherbourne CD, Jackson CA, Meredith LS, et al: Prevalence of comorbid anxiety disorders in primary care outpatients. Arch Fam Med 5:27–34, 1996

Shin LM, Kosslyn SM, McNally RJ, et al: Visual imagery and perception in posttraumatic stress disorder: a positron emission tomographic investigation. Arch Gen Psychiatry 54:233–241, 1997a

Shin LM, McNally RJ, Kosslyn SM, et al: A positron emission tomographic study of symptom provocation in PTSD. Ann N Y Acad Sci 821:521–523, 1997b

Singer HS, Giuliano JD, Hansen BH: Antibodies against human putamen in children with Tourette syndrome. Neurology 50:1618–1624, 1998

Southwick SM, Krystal JH, Bremner JD, et al: Noradrenergic and serotonergic function in posttraumatic stress disorder. Arch Gen Psychiatry 54:749–758, 1997

Stein DJ: False Alarm!: How to Conquer the Anxiety Disorders. Cape Town, South Africa, University of Stellenbosch, 2000a

Stein DJ: Neurobiology of the obsessive-compulsive spectrum disorders [in process citation]. Biol Psychiatry 47:296–304, 2000b

Stein DJ, Hollander E, Cohen L: Neuropsychiatry of obsessive-compulsive disorder, in Current Insights in Obsessive-Compulsive Disorder. Edited by Hollander E, Zohar J, Marazziti D, et al. Chichester, England, Wiley, 1994, pp 167–182

Stein DJ, Spadaccini E, Hollander E: Meta-analysis of pharmacotherapy trials for obsessive compulsive disorder. Int Clin Psychopharmacol 10:11–18, 1995

Stein DJ, Van HB, Wessels CJ, et al: Single photon emission computed tomography of the brain with Tc-99m HMPAO during sumatriptan challenge in obsessive-compulsive disorder: investigating the functional role of the serotonin auto-receptor. Prog Neuropsychopharmacol Biol Psychiatry 23:1079–1099, 1999

Stein MB: Neurobiological perspectives on social phobia: from affiliation to zoology. Biol Psychiatry 44:1277–1285, 1998

Stein MB, Leslie WD: A brain single photon-emission computed tomography (SPECT) study of generalized social phobia. Biol Psychiatry 39:825–828, 1996

Stein MB, Heuser IJ, Juncos JL, et al: Anxiety disorders in patients with Parkinson's disease [see comments]. Am J Psychiatry 147:217–220, 1990

Stein MB, Koverola C, Hanna C, et al: Hippocampal volume in women victimized by childhood sexual abuse. Psychol Med 27:951–959, 1997

Sussman N: Anxiolytic antidepressant augmentation. J Clin Psychiatry 59 (suppl 5):42–48, 1998

Swedo SE, Rapoport JL, Cheslow DL, et al: High prevalence of obsessive-compulsive symptoms in patients with Sydenham's chorea. Am J Psychiatry 146:246–249, 1989

Swedo SE, Leonard HL, Garvey M: Pediatric autoimmune neuropsychiatric disorders associated with streptococcal infections: clinical description of the first 50 cases. Am J Psychiatry 155:264–271, 1998

Szeszko PR, Robinson D, Alvir JMJ: Orbital frontal and amygdala volume reductions in obsessive-compulsive disorder. Arch Gen Psychiatry 56:913–919, 1999

Tancer ME, Mailman RB, Stein MB, et al: Neuroendocrine responsivity to monoaminergic system probes in generalized social phobia. Anxiety 1:216–223, 1994

Thoren P, Asberg M, Bertilsson L: Clomipramine treatment of obsessive-compulsive disorder, II: biochemical aspects. Arch Gen Psychiatry 37:1289–1294, 1980

Tiihonen J, Kuikka J, Bergstrom K, et al: Dopamine reuptake site densities in patients with social phobia. Am J Psychiatry 154:239–242, 1997a

Tiihonen JF, Kuikka J, Rasanen P, et al: Cerebral benzodiazepine receptor binding and distribution in generalized anxiety disorder: a fractal analysis. Mol Psychiatry 2:463–471, 1997b

Tillfors M, Furmark T, Marteinsdottir I, et al: Cerebral blood flow in subjects with social phobia during stressful speaking tasks: a PET study. Am J Psychiatry 158(8):1220–1226, 2001

Toni C, Cassano GB, Perugi G, et al: Psychosensorial and related phenomena in panic disorder and in temporal lobe epilepsy. Compr Psychiatry 37:125–133, 1996

Uhde TW: Anxiety and growth disturbance: is there a connection? A review of biological studies in social phobia. J Clin Psychiatry 55 (suppl):17–22, 1994

van der Linden G, van Heerden B, Warwick J, et al: Functional brain imaging and pharmacotherapy in social phobia: single photon emission tomography before and after treatment with the selective serotonin reuptake inhibitor citalopram. Prog Neuropsychopharmacol Biol Psychiatry 24:419–438, 2000

von Economo C: Encephalitis Lethargica: Its Sequelae and Treatment. London, England, Oxford University Press, 1931

Wall M, Tuchman M, Mielke D: Panic attacks and temporal lobe seizures associated with a right temporal lobe arteriovenous malformation: case report. J Clin Psychiatry 46:143–145, 1985

Wall M, Mielke D, Luther JS: Panic attacks and psychomotor seizures following right temple lobectomy (letter). J Clin Psychiatry 47:219, 1986

Warden DL, Labbate LA, Salazar AM, et al: Posttraumatic stress disorder in patients with traumatic brain injury and amnesia for the event? J Neuropsychiatry Clin Neurosci 9:18–22, 1997

Weilburg JB, Bear DM, Sachs G: Three patients with concomitant panic attacks and seizure disorder: possible clues to the neurology of anxiety. Am J Psychiatry 144:1053–1056, 1987

Weissman MM, Bland RC, Canino GJ, et al: The cross national epidemiology of obsessive compulsive disorder. J Clin Psychiatry 55S:5–10, 1994

Weizman R, Tanne Z, Granek M, et al: Peripheral benzodiazepine binding sites on platelet membranes are increased during diazepam treatment of anxious patients. Eur J Pharmacol 138:289–292, 1987

Wise MG, Rundell JR: Anxiety and neurological disorders. Seminars in Clinical Neuropsychiatry 4:98–102, 1999

Wolf SS, Jones DW, Knable MB, et al: Tourette syndrome: prediction of phenotypic variation in monozygotic twins by caudate nucleus D2 receptor binding. Science 273:1225–1227, 1996

Wu JC, Buchsbaum MS, Hershey TG, et al: PET in generalized anxiety disorder. Biol Psychiatry 29:1181–1199, 1991

Wurthmann C, Grego J, Baumann B, et al: [Qualitative evaluation of brain structure in panic disorders]. Nervenarzt 69:763–768, 1998

Yehuda R, McFarlane AC: Conflict between current knowledge about posttraumatic stress disorder and its original conceptual basis. Am J Psychiatry 152:1705–1713, 1995

Yehuda R, Southwick SM, Krystal JH, et al: Enhanced suppression of cortisol following dexamethasone administration in posttraumatic stress disorder. Am J Psychiatry 150:83–86, 1993

Young GB, Chandarana PC, Blume WT, et al: Mesial temporal lobe seizures presenting as anxiety disorders. J Neuropsychiatry Clin Neurosci 7:352–357, 1995

Zohar J, Insel TR: Obsessive-compulsive disorder: psychobiological approaches to diagnosis, treatment, and pathophysiology. Biol Psychiatry 22:667–687, 1987

Zohar J, Insel TR, Zohar-Kadouch RC: Serotonergic responsivity in obsessive-compulsive disorder: effects of chronic clomipramine treatment. Arch Gen Psychiatry 45:167–172, 1988

Zungu-Dirwayi N, Hugo FJ, Van Heerden B, et al: Are musical obsessions a temporal lobe phenomenon? J Neuropsychiatry Clin Neurosci 11:398–400, 1999

# Neuropsychiatric Disorders of Childhood and Adolescence

Martin H. Teicher, M.D., Ph.D.

Susan L. Andersen, Ph.D.

Carryl P. Navalta, Ph.D.

Ann Polcari, Ph.D., R.N.

Dennis Kim, M.D.

In this chapter, we emphasize brain-based psychiatric disorders that invariably emerge during childhood and adolescence. Virtually all neuropsychiatric disorders can appear in pediatric patients; however, certain disorders such as attention-deficit/hyperactivity disorder (ADHD), mental retardation, and Tourette's syndrome (TS) must present before adulthood for diagnosis. These disorders are the focus of this chapter.

## Brain Development

The human brain is an enormously complex organ consisting, at the simplest level, of billions of neurons and trillions of synaptic interconnections. Genetic information from 60% of our 100,000 genes provides the basic architecture, but the final form and function is sculpted by experience. Such an intrinsically complex process is inherently vulnerable to numerous errors, which set the stage for the emergence of childhood and adolescent neuropsychiatric disorders.

The brain develops through a series of overlapping stages, which are illustrated in Figure 33–1. The first stage is mitosis, in which neural progenitor cells multiply and divide in the neural tube in the area destined to become the ventricular surface. Eventually, during a specific delineated period of embryogenesis, the germinal cells undergo their final mitotic division to form immature nerve cells that can no longer reproduce. These neuroblasts are laid down inside out, with larger cells generally appearing at an earlier stage than smaller cells. During this period the brain produces two to three times the full adult complement of neurons. Neuronal mitosis is a critical process, and mitotic inhibitors can exert devastating effects on brain development. Although neurogenesis ceases in most brain regions at birth, stem cells continue to generate neurons within the subventricular zone and hippocampal dentate gyrus throughout life (Gage 2000).

The second stage involves the migration of neurons to their final destination. This is a complex process in which immature neurons follow chemical, spatial, and mechanical gradients to reach their destination and establish connections with appropriate targets (Landis 1983; Purves 1980). In many regions, glial cells provide elongated processes that serve as guide wires to facilitate migration (Rakic 1994). Learning disorders and some forms of mental retardation can arise from abnormal

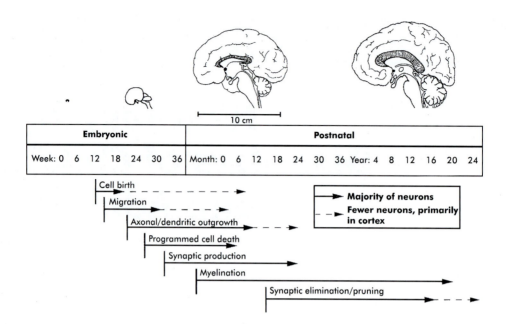

**FIGURE 33–1.**   Major overlapping stages of human brain development and approximate temporal sequence.

migration. Once neurons reach their final destination at about the sixteenth fetal week, they branch in an attempt to establish appropriate connections (Sidman and Rakic 1973). In a striking turn of events, more than 50% of these neurons are eliminated before birth in a process known as *cell death* or *apoptosis* (Landmesser 1980). Cell survival depends on the level of activity the neuron receives and the presence of trophic factors that stabilize its growth (Cowan et al. 1984).

Synaptic development is also characterized by distinct waves of overproduction and elimination. Synaptic density in the human brain increases dramatically during the early postnatal period. Formation of synapses in the cerebellum peaks during the first 2–4 months, whereas synaptic density of the cortex continues to increase throughout early childhood (Huttenlocher 1979). From birth to age 5, the brain triples in mass from 350 g to a near-adult weight of 1.2 kg. Part of this increase is a result of the marked arborization and enhanced connection of neurons. Much of the gain stems from the vigorous myelination of fiber tracts. Myelination markedly increases the speed of information exchange and is at least partially responsible for the emergence of our rich behavioral repertoire. Delayed myelination of frontocortical connections during the second and third decade may be associated with enhanced behavioral regulation and impulse control that emerges after adolescence.

During the transition from childhood to adulthood, a second dramatic elimination phase occurs in which synaptic contacts and neurotransmitter receptors overproduced during childhood are pruned back to final adult

configuration. Between ages 7 and 15 years, synaptic density in the frontal cortex decreases by approximately 40% (Huttenlocher 1979). Similar changes occur in the density of dopamine (Seeman et al. 1987) (Figure 33–2), glutamate (Barks et al. 1988), and neurotensin (Mailleux et al. 1990) receptors. Overly extensive or insufficient pruning has been associated with some forms of mental retardation (Huttenlocher 1979) and has been hypothesized to play a key role in the emergence of schizophrenia (Feinberg 1982–1983; Keshaven et al. 1994). Teicher and Andersen (Andersen et al. 2000; Teicher et al. 1995) found that dopamine receptors prune very rapidly after the onset of puberty in the nigrostriatal system of rats, prune in early adulthood in the prefrontal cortex, but do not prune in the limbic connections to the nucleus accumbens. It is conceivable that pruning of striatal dopamine receptors is associated with the attenuation of hyperactivity and motor tics during adolescence. Delayed pruning in the prefrontal cortex possibly unmasks an early lesion that may be associated with the emergence of schizophrenia. Synaptic pruning may represent an important developmental stage in which high synaptic density, facilitating acquisition of new knowledge and skills at considerable metabolic cost, is partially traded for a lower density, facilitating rapid analysis and performance through established patterns (Teicher et al. 1995). In concert with this transition, there is a reduction in synaptic plasticity, attenuating capacity to recover from injury. Synaptic pruning may also be responsible for the plateau in the growth of intellectual capacity (*mental age*) that occurs at about 16 years (Walker 1994).

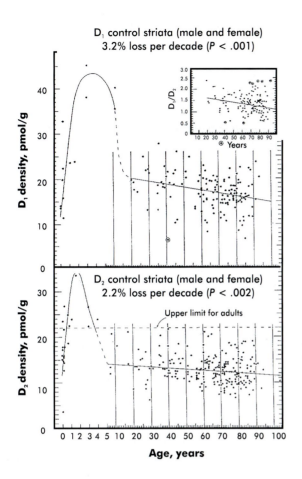

**D₁ control striata (male and female)**
**3.2% loss per decade (P < .001)**

**D₂ control striata (male and female)**
**2.2% loss per decade (P < .002)**

Upper limit for adults

**Age, years**

**Figure 33–2.** Overproduction and pruning of dopamine D₁ and D₂ receptors in human corpus striatum during childhood and adolescence.

*Source.* Reprinted from Seeman P, Bzowej N, Guan H, et al.: "Human Brain Receptors in Children and Aging Adults." *Synapse* 1:399–404, 1987. Used with permission.

## Development of Lateralization and Hemispheric Asymmetry

The human brain is anatomically, neurochemically, and functionally asymmetric. Lateralization is largely established before age 5 years (Krashen 1973) and emerges through a multistage process that begins in utero (Chi et al. 1972; Molfese et al. 1975; Wada et al. 1975). Delayed myelination of the corpus callosum enables the two hemispheres to develop relatively independently. During the first few months, the right hemisphere develops more rapidly than the left, with more advanced dendritic outgrowth in Broca's area and motor cortex (Galaburda 1984; Simonds and Scheibel 1989). However, by age 5–6 months, dendritic growth in the left hemisphere surpasses that in the right and continues at a rapid pace for the next 2 years. Between ages 3 and 6 years, the right hemisphere accelerates in its development and helps pro-

vide the prosodic components of language that flower between ages 5 and 6 years. The left hemisphere, however, remains more differentiated. Early experience can exert marked effect on lateralization in laboratory animals (Bulman-Fleming et al. 1992; Camp et al. 1984; Denenberg and Yutzey 1985). This may also be true for humans and may be an important factor in the genesis of psychiatric disorders (Teicher et al. 1994, 1996a).

## Disorders of Excessive Motor Activity, Movement, Impulse, and Thought

One of the most prevalent and treatable clusters of childhood neuropsychiatric disorders includes ADHD, TS, and obsessive-compulsive disorder (OCD). These conditions often co-occur or run in families (Knell and Comings 1993; Pauls 1991; Pauls and Leckman 1986). They likely occur as a consequence of different but interrelated defects in corticolimbic–basal ganglia circuits (Lou et al. 1990; Luxenberg et al. 1988; Peterson et al. 1993; Singer et al. 1993; Zametkin et al. 1990). TS and ADHD are discussed together to emphasize their communality. OCD is discussed elsewhere in this book.

## Attention-Deficit/ Hyperactivity Disorder

ADHD is one of the most common neuropsychiatric disorders of childhood, estimated to affect 3%–9% of school-age children (J.C. Anderson et al. 1987; Bird et al. 1988; Szatmari et al. 1989). This is a serious disorder that persists beyond childhood in about 40% of affected individuals (Klein and Mannuzza 1991). It is associated with a dramatically increased incidence of antisocial personality, drug abuse, delinquency, and criminality (Gittelman et al. 1985; Klein and Mannuzza 1991; Mannuzza et al. 1989; Satterfield et al. 1982; G. Weiss et al. 1985).

ADHD was first identified as a medical disorder after the 1917 pandemic of von Economo's encephalitis. Affected adults who survived developed *encephalitis lethargica*, a severe form of Parkinson's disease, poignantly described in the film *Awakenings* (Sacks 1973). Affected children, in contrast, developed diametrically opposite symptoms of hyperactivity and impulsivity (Wender 1971). Subsequently, children presenting with problems of hyperactivity were given the diagnosis *minimal brain damage*, but, in the absence of direct evidence for brain damage, this term was changed to *minimal brain dysfunction*. DSM-III (American Psychiatric Association 1980) brought forth a new stage in our understanding of this condition when it renamed the syndrome attention-deficit disorder and revised it to *attention-deficit/hyperactivity disorder* in DSM-III-R (American Psychiatric Association 1987).

## Characteristic Features

ADHD is characterized by a triad of symptoms involving age-inappropriate problems with attention, impulse control, and hyperactivity (Barkley 1990; Tryon 1993). Currently, DSM-IV (American Psychiatric Association 1994) divides the symptom triad into two factors: inattention and hyperactivity-impulsivity. To meet criteria for the disorder, children need to have, during the previous 6 months, at least six symptoms of inattention or six symptoms of hyperactivity-impulsivity. If they meet criteria for both inattention and hyperactivity-impulsivity, they are diagnosed with ADHD combined type, which is the most prevalent form. Otherwise, they are diagnosed as either ADHD predominantly inattentive type or ADHD predominantly hyperactive-impulsive type. In addition to meeting symptom criteria, accurate diagnosis requires that some of these symptoms emerge before age 7 years and be of sufficient severity to cause impairment. Symptoms must also be present in at least two different settings, must produce significant impairment in social or school endeavors, and not be better accounted for by another mental disorder or occur exclusively during the course of a pervasive developmental disorder or psychotic disorder.

Although many sources state that ADHD is predominantly a disorder of males, substantial disparity exists in reported gender ratios (J.C. Anderson et al. 1987; Bird et al. 1988; Safer and Krager 1988). McGee et al. (1987) argued that gender differences were purely an artifact of the higher overall baseline rate of behavioral disturbance in boys. The Ontario Child Health Study (Szatmari et al. 1989) provides an interesting epidemiological perspective. According to parents' reports, boys had only a slightly greater prevalence of inattention, impulsivity, and hyperactivity. Even more striking was the observation that adolescent girls report that they had the same prevalence of symptoms as adolescent boys. This was not an artifact of boys being unaware of their difficulties; they endorsed significantly more symptoms than their parents perceived. Only teachers found these symptoms to be significantly more prevalent in boys. In short, it is conceivable that gender differences may be relatively minor.

Although ADHD is defined by potentially measurable behavioral signs, it remains a controversial disorder, and its validity and prevalence have been disputed (Prior and Sanson 1986). Critics often point to the disparity in

ADHD prevalence rates between the United States and England. This disparity is largely a result of differing diagnostic criteria. In England, children are required to be pervasively hyperactive in all situations, whereas in the United States (until DSM-IV) presenting symptoms could be more situationally specific. However, this distinction may not matter clinically (Rapoport et al. 1986). Further, the comorbid occurrence of ADHD and conduct disorder would be diagnosed as conduct disorder in England and as ADHD with associated conduct disorder in the United States (Popper and Steingard 1995).

Studies using objective tests have documented the presence of hyperactivity (see Teicher 1995 for review) and have verified that this is not merely a subjective problem (Henker and Whalen 1989). Using a precise infrared motion analysis system to track body movement patterns during a computerized attention task, Teicher et al. (1996b) found that children with ADHD spent 66% less time immobile than normal, moved their head 3.4 times as far, and covered a 3.8 times greater area. Hyperactivity is most apparent when children with ADHD are required to sit still, and it is also present while they are asleep (Porrino et al. 1983). However, they are no more active than normal when allowed to play (Porrino et al. 1983). Hence, their motor problem appears to stem from a diminished ability to inhibit activity to low levels (Teicher 1995). Deficient inhibition may also explain symptoms of inattention and impulsivity. Inattention usually manifests as failure to sustain interest in tasks that are boring or challenging and in distraction by irrelevant stimuli. These difficulties may arise from failure to inhibit initiation of competing actions. Impulsivity in ADHD largely manifests as impatience and social intrusion, which can be explained by a failure to inhibit immature behaviors through social learning. Conceptualizing ADHD as a primary defect in inhibitory capacity provides the foundation for specific pathophysiological models. This conceptualization is in accord with Robins (1992) and Korkman and Pesonen (1994), who found that impaired self-regulation and capacity to inhibit impulses, rather than inattention, were the factors that distinguished children with ADHD from children with learning disorders.

ADHD commonly occurs in conjunction with several other psychiatric disorders. Conduct disorder occurs in 40%–70% of subjects with ADHD. This is a serious behavioral problem in which patients violate major societal rules and fail to respect individual rights. Conduct disorder appears to arise specifically in children who show signs of excessive aggressiveness (August et al. 1983). Learning disorders are also prevalent in children with ADHD (Semrud-Clikeman et al. 1992), as are mood disorders. Children abused early in life who develop symptoms of posttraumatic stress disorder (PTSD) also frequently meet criteria for ADHD. McLeer et al. (1994) found that 23% of children with PTSD met criteria for ADHD. More recently, Glod and Teicher (1996) found that 38% of hospitalized abused children with PTSD met criteria for ADHD and that on average the entire group of children with PTSD were more active than normal children or abused children without PTSD. It is, however, unclear whether this is true ADHD or a look-alike state (phenocopy). There is also a high incidence of ADHD among boys with TS (Comings and Comings 1987). Generalized resistance to thyroid hormone has also been associated with a high incidence of ADHD (P. Hauser et al. 1993), but it is a rare disorder almost never found in children diagnosed with ADHD (R. E. Weiss et al. 1993). ADHD-like symptoms may also emerge as an indicator of genetic risk in children with a family history of schizophrenia (Marcus et al. 1985).

## Clinical Course

Mothers often indicate that children with ADHD were extremely active in utero and that they started running and climbing as soon as they learned to walk. However, it is hard to diagnose ADHD before age 4 or 5, and most cases remain undiagnosed until school. Using older criteria it has been estimated that remission occurs in 30% by adolescence and in 50%–70% by adulthood (Barkley 1990; Gittelman et al. 1985). In persisting cases it is often stated that the hyperactivity abates but problems with inattention continue. Objective measures of activity in adults with ADHD indicate that many continue to have difficulty inhibiting activity to low levels (Teicher 1995).

## Etiology and Pathophysiology

ADHD should be regarded as a syndrome in which the clinical phenotype can arise from multiple etiologies, probably through a number of different pathways. Worldwide, the leading cause of ADHD may be severe early malnutrition during the first year of life (Galler et al. 1983). In the United States, low birth weight, fetal alcohol exposure, and prenatal or postnatal lead exposure can be more common etiological factors. Genetic factors also play a major role. ADHD runs in families, particularly in the male relatives of ADHD children (Pauls 1991). Girls with ADHD have a stronger family history than do boys, suggesting even greater genetic loading but lower penetrance. Twin studies indicate that heritability may be as high as 0.91 (Levy et al. 1997).

Efforts to identify a selective neurochemical imbalance in blood, urine, or cerebrospinal fluid (CSF) have been disappointing. Zametkin and Rapoport (1987) concluded that no reliable differences were found between control subjects without ADHD and boys with ADHD on measures of dopamine or norepinephrine metabolites. However, molecular studies of polymorphism of dopamine transporter and receptor genes have produced some exciting initial findings. Cook et al. (1995) first suggested that there was a highly significant association between polymorphism of the dopamine transporter (reuptake) gene locus (DAT1) and ADHD, and this observation has been replicated in other studies (Comings et al. 1996; Daly et al. 1999; Gill et al. 1997; Waldman et al. 1998, but see Palmer et al. 1999). This finding suggests that a mutation in DAT1 may be associated with hereditary risk for ADHD. The dopamine transporter is the primary target of stimulant medications used to treat ADHD. Complete deletion (knockout) of the dopamine transporter gene produces incessant hyperactivity in mice (Giros et al. 1996). Winsberg and Comings (1999) found that homozygosity of the 10-repeat allele was associated with nonresponse to methylphenidate (reviewed by Swanson et al. 2000).

Other molecular studies have failed to find an association with the DAT1 gene, but have found an association with the dopamine $D_4$ receptor gene (e.g., LaHoste et al. 1996). The $D_4$ receptor has been associated with novelty seeking (Benjamin et al. 1996; Ebstein et al. 1996), and individuals with high levels of this trait are impulsive, excitable, and quick-tempered as are patients with ADHD. The $D_4$ receptor is an interesting candidate gene in that it is preferentially located in frontal and prefrontal cortical regions in the brain (Sunahara et al. 1993) that are involved in executive control and regulation of attention. This gene has a 48–base pair variable repeat in the third cytoplasmic loop that is associated with functional differences in response to dopamine (Asghari et al. 1995). In particular, the 7-repeat allelic variant that has been linked to ADHD is hyporesponsive to dopamine. LaHoste et al. (1996) found that 49% of the subjects with ADHD had at least one 7-repeat allele in comparison with only 21% of ethnically matched case control subjects. These researchers replicated this observation in a refined sample that met both DSM-IV and ICD-10 (World Health Organization 1992) diagnostic criteria for ADHD and confirmed the significance of the genetic association using more stringent haplotype relative risk analysis (Swanson et al. 1998). This association has been replicated in some studies (Barr et al. 2000, Comings et al. 1999b, Faraone et al. 1999; Tahir et al. 2000), but not others (Castellanos et al. 1998, Eisenberg et al. 2000).

Comings et al. (2000) viewed ADHD as a complex disorder that emerged from the interaction of multiple genes. They examined the relationship between 20 genes for dopamine, serotonin, and noradrenergic metabolism and quantitative score for ADHD in 336 unrelated subjects. Multivariate linear regression indicated that three dopamine genes, three serotonin genes, and six adrenergic genes contributed 2.3%, 3%, and 6.9%, respectively, to the variance. Altogether, 12 genes contributed 11.6% to the total variance, which, though highly significant, also means that the amassed genetic knowledge of ADHD is still vastly incomplete. The Comings et al. (1999a, 2000) research also suggests that noradrenergic genes may contribute substantially to ADHD, particularly to patients with both ADHD and learning disabilities.

Imaging studies have helped to delineate and define a network of brain regions involved in ADHD. Morphometric magnetic resonance imaging (MRI) studies have identified abnormalities in the size or symmetry of the frontal cortex, caudate nucleus, corpus callosum, and cerebellar vermis. Castellanos et al. (1996) performed volumetric analysis of the cerebrum, caudate nucleus, putamen, globus pallidus, amygdala, hippocampus, temporal lobe, cerebellum, and prefrontal cortex in 57 boys with ADHD and 55 control subjects. Children with ADHD had a 4.7% smaller cerebral volume, a significant loss of normal right-greater-than-left caudate asymmetry, smaller right globus pallidus, smaller right anterior frontal region, smaller cerebellum, and reversal of normal lateral ventricular asymmetry. For boys without ADHD, caudate volume decreased substantially with age, whereas in boys with ADHD, caudate volume showed no age-related change. Semrud-Clikeman et al. (2000) found that reversed caudate asymmetry was associated with poorer performance on measures of inhibition. Casey et al. (1997) found that impaired performance on three tests of response inhibition was associated with abnormalities in the prefrontal cortex, caudate, and globus pallidus, but not in the putamen. Results suggested a role of the right prefrontal cortex in suppressing responses to salient but otherwise irrelevant events, whereas the basal ganglia appeared to be involved in executing these behavioral responses (Casey et al. 1997).

Further evidence for the involvement of the basal ganglia emerged from studies of children who developed secondary ADHD. Herskovits et al. (1999) examined, 3 months after closed-head injury, 76 children without a history of ADHD. Fifteen of these children developed secondary ADHD, and they had more lesions in their right putamen than did children who did not develop ADHD. ADHD has also been associated with titers of two distinct antistreptococcal antibodies, antistreptoly-sin O and antideoxyribonuclease B. Higher antibody titers in patients with ADHD or OCD were associated with larger volumes of the putamen and globus pallidus (Peterson et al. 2000).

Early studies also found that the anterior portion of the corpus callosum, which relays information between the left and right frontal cortex, was decreased in size in boys with ADHD (Giedd et al. 1994; Hynd et al. 1991). A significant inverse correlation was found between size of the anterior corpus callosum and indices of impulsivity/hyperactivity on the Conner's Rating Scale (Giedd et al. 1994). Other reports have documented a decrease in size of the posterior corpus callosum, which may be related to certain aspects of attention (Hynd et al. 1991; Semrud-Clikeman et al. 1994). However, Castellanos et al. (1996) in the most comprehensive study with the largest sample sizes failed to find a difference in any region of the corpus callosum. Overmeyer et al. (2000) also found no differences in the corpus callosum between a subgroup of children with a refined subtype of ADHD and control subjects without ADHD who had siblings with ADHD.

Animal and human studies have expanded our understanding of cerebellar processes and indicated that the cerebellum plays a role in executive function normally attributed to the prefrontal cortex (Thach et al. 1992). As a consequence, this region has come under scrutiny in ADHD. Mostofsky et al. (1998) measured the cerebellar vermis in 12 males with ADHD and 23 male control subjects matched for age and IQ. The researchers found a significant reduction in the size of the inferior posterior lobe (lobules VIII–X). Berquin et al. (1998) also reported a significant reduction in the size of the inferior posterior lobe in 46 right-handed boys with ADHD versus 47 matched control subjects without ADHD. These findings suggest that a cerebello-striatal-prefrontal circuit dysfunction may underlie the motor control, inhibition, and executive function deficits encountered in ADHD.

Functional imaging studies have confirmed and expanded the anatomical studies. First, a number of studies documented basal state differences in metabolism and regional blood flow in the prefrontal cortex and striatum (caudate nucleus and putamen). Lou et al. (1990) found that 11 of 11 children with ADHD had hypoperfusion of the frontal lobes, and 7 of 11 had hypoperfusion of the striatum. Stimulant drugs increased blood flow in the striatum and decreased blood flow in primary sensory and motor cortex. Using positron emission tomography (PET), Zametkin et al. (1990) found that adults with a history of childhood ADHD had an overall 8% reduction in cerebral glucose metabolism, with a significant reduction in 30 of 60 cortical regions. The largest decreases were in the premotor and superior prefrontal cortex. Ernst et al. (1994) found a reduction in global cerebral blood flow in adolescent girls with ADHD compared with that in female control subjects without ADHD. However, a comparable effect was not observed in adolescent boys. Sieg et al. (1995) used [$^{123}$I]-iodoamphetamine (IMP) single photon emission computed tomography (SPECT) to assess regional distribution of blood flow and metabolism in 10 children or adolescents with ADHD and 6 control subjects without ADHD. ADHD patients had a greater cortical asymmetry characterized by diminished left frontal and left parietal activity. More recently, Teicher et al. (2000b) developed a novel functional magnetic resonance imaging (fMRI) procedure called T$_2$ relaxometry that provides a noninvasive indirect assessment of steady-state regional cerebral blood volume. Using this technique, we compared 11 boys with ADHD to 6 control subjects without ADHD. We found significant elevations of T$_2$ relaxation time (T$_2$RT) in the putamen, suggestive of diminished blood flow and neuronal activity. A robust relationship was found between T$_2$RT in the putamen and objective measures of hyperactivity (incapacity to sit still) and attention using infrared motion analysis. Additional correlates with hyperactivity and attention emerged in left dorsolateral prefrontal cortex (Teicher et al. 1996b) and cerebellar vermis (C.M. Anderson et al. 1999). Chronic treatment with methylphenidate altered T$_2$RT in each region, though the direction and magnitude of the effect was strongly dependent on the basal level of hyperactivity (Teicher et al. 2000b). In those children with ADHD who were objectively hyperactive, methylphenidate reduced T$_2$RT in putamen and increased T$_2$RT in the cerebellar vermis. T$_2$RT changed in the opposite manner in ADHD children who had a more normal capacity to sit still. Similarly, methylphenidate markedly reduced seated activity in the objectively hyperactive children but either increased or exerted no effect on activity of nonhyperactive children with ADHD.

Functional imaging studies have also revealed corticostriatal defects during performance of cognitive tasks, particularly those that measure aspects of inhibitory control or working memory. Schweitzer et al. (2000) found, using [$^{15}$O]H$_2$O PET, that a working memory task enhanced regional cerebral blood flow in the prefrontal and temporal cortex of six men without ADHD. The same task produced more diffuse and predominantly occipital activation in six men with ADHD. These findings suggested that adults with ADHD used compensatory mental and neural strategies, particularly internalized speech, to guide behavior. Similar results emerged in

a blood oxygen level–dependent (BOLD) fMRI study of eight adults with ADHD and eight adults without ADHD during performance of the Counting Stroop. Both groups showed an interference effect, and a prominent activation of the cognitive division of their anterior cingulate was demonstrated in control subjects but not in patients with ADHD (Bush et al. 1999). Rubia et al. (1999) found hypofunction of the right mesial prefrontal cortex during motor inhibition and motor timing tasks and hypofunction of the right inferior prefrontal cortex and left caudate during motor inhibition using BOLD fMRI. Vaidya et al. (1998) found that ADHD children had greater BOLD fMRI activation in frontal cortex on one attention task and reduced striatal activation on another. Methylphenidate increased frontal activation to an equal extent in both groups. However, it increased striatal activation in children with ADHD but reduced striatal activation in control subjects.

Most recently, imaging studies have been used to measure neurochemistry. Dougherty et al. (1999) assessed dopamine transporter density in six adults with ADHD and found a 70% increase in age-corrected transporter density relative to control subjects without ADHD. Similarly, Krause et al. (2000) assessed binding to the dopamine transporter using Tc-99m tropane dopamine transporter (TRODAT)–1 SPECT. Ten previously untreated adults with ADHD had a highly significant increase in specific binding of the ligand to the transporter. Specific binding to the transporter was markedly reduced after 4 weeks of treatment with methylphenidate. Ernst et al. (1998, 1999b) assessed 3,4-dihydroxyphenylalanine (DOPA) decarboxylase activity (a measure of dopamine innervation) with [$^{18}$F]DOPA PET. They found that DOPA decarboxylase activity was reduced by approximately 50% in the prefrontal cortex (Ernst et al. 1998) of adults with ADHD and suggested that a prefrontal dopamine dysfunction mediated ADHD symptoms. They also found a significantly higher accumulation of DOPA in the midbrain of 10 children with ADHD. This region contains the substantia nigra and ventral tegmental area, and higher DOPA accumulation is consistent with a secondary increase in dopamine turnover in this region.

Animal studies indicate that many forms of early brain injury produce hyperactivity. Of particular interest is the neonatal dopamine depletion model (B.A. Shaywitz et al. 1976a, 1976b), which is based on the von Economo's encephalitis paradox (i.e., that affected adults become parkinsonian, whereas affected children develop hyperactivity). Chemical ablation of dopamine nerve fibers produces a profound parkinsonian state in adult rats (Stricker and Zigmond 1976) but causes neonates to become hyperactive (B.A. Shaywitz et al. 1976b). These hyperactive rats perform poorly on a range of learning tasks, and stimulant drugs partially ameliorate these deficits (B.A. Shaywitz et al. 1976a). The hyperactivity often abates after puberty (B.A. Shaywitz et al. 1976b) unless the depletion is extremely profound (F.E. Miller et al. 1981). Curiously, the rats' hyperactivity is situationally specific (Teicher et al. 1981), and the degree and time course of the impairments are influenced by the rats' early experience (Pearson et al. 1980). Heffner et al. (1983) found that the critical feature of this model was depletion of dopamine within the frontal cortex. Early postnatal depletions of dopamine produced a concomitant increase in $D_4$ receptor binding in rats (Zhang et al. 2000). Shaywitz et al. (Raskin et al. 1983; B.A. Shaywitz et al. 1984) also found that relatively selective neonatal norepinephrine depletions produced impaired learning performance without hyperactivity. Thus, neonatal norepinephrine depletion may provide a model for the inattentive form of ADHD.

## Pathophysiological Models of ADHD

A detailed pathophysiological model of ADHD needs to incorporate several factors. First, ADHD has a discrete time course. Symptoms emerge early in childhood (generally before age 7) and often abate or wane by adulthood. Second, many more boys than girls are diagnosed and treated for ADHD. However, ADHD symptoms are less likely to abate with age in girls. Third, pharmacological studies demonstrate that the most highly effective drugs for ADHD target either dopamine or norepinephrine. Fourth, imaging studies provide converging evidence for a disturbance in corticostriatal loops. Fifth, reverse asymmetries are found in brain structure and function in patients with ADHD. Malone et al. (1994) have argued that an imbalance exists between a left hemisphere (or anterior) attention system that provides focused sustained attention on a task (Jutai 1984) and a right (or posterior) attention system that regulates overall arousal and rapidly shifts attention to peripheral stimuli for processing novel information (Goldberg and Costa 1981; Heilman and Van Den Abell 1980). Finally, emerging evidence suggests that the cerebellar vermis is affected in ADHD and may play a pivotal role in symptomatology.

We believe that the waxing and waning of symptoms with age, gender differences in prevalence, and greater persistence of ADHD symptoms in girls are all a consequence of the normal process of synaptic overproduction and pruning (Andersen and Teicher 2000). As illustrated in Figure 33–2, a marked overproduction of dopamine receptors in the striatum during childhood is pruned by adulthood. Furthermore, we have shown that this pro-

cess occurs in male rats but is hardly apparent in female rats (Andersen et al. 1997). Gender differences in overproduction of dopamine receptors and other neural elements may account for the apparent shrinkage that occurs in the caudate nucleus of boys without ADHD but not girls with age (Castellanos et al. 1996). Our hypothesis is that at least one class of overexpressed receptors is a permissive factor in the clinical manifestation of ADHD. Overexpression in boys leads to greater clinical prevalence during the period of overproduction, but may explain why fewer girls develop ADHD because this permissive factor is not expressed. Greater abatement of symptoms in boys occurs with pruning; however, girls with ADHD who remain symptomatic do so because the permissive factor is not pruned. By adulthood, striatal $D_2$ density becomes equal (Teicher et al. 1995), and gender differences in prevalence largely disappear (Biederman et al. 1994). Further, it appears that the caudate nucleus does not shrink with age in boys who meet diagnostic criteria for ADHD (Castellanos et al. 1996). We would hypothesize that it shrinks in boys with ADHD who are no longer symptomatic. Andersen et al. (2000) also found that pruning of dopamine receptors in the prefrontal cortex occurs later in adulthood than pruning in the striatum. This may help explain why symptoms of motor hyperactivity remit or diminish at an earlier age than attentional symptoms.

It is possible that the permissive factor may be a member of the dopamine $D_2$ receptor family ($D_2$, $D_3$, or $D_4$). $D_2$ family receptor density is a permissive factor in the expression of TS. Wolf et al. (1996) has shown that differences in Tourette's symptomatology between identical twins is completely explained by their differences in striatal $D_2$ receptor binding. However, this is an open question in ADHD because other neural elements are also overproduced and pruned in the striatum during the same period.

Figure 33–3 provides a schematic that integrates findings regarding drug response, hemispheric asymmetries in attention, and the role of corticostriatal circuits and the cerebellar vermis. As reviewed below, drugs that effectively treat ADHD act on catecholamine systems. Stimulant drugs bind to the dopamine transporter attenuating dopamine reuptake and stimulating dopamine release (Breese et al. 1975; Gatley et al. 1996). This effect is attenuated and checked by the action of released dopamine on autoreceptors that control pulsatile release rates (Grace 1995; Seeman and Madras 1998). Stimulants also affect other monoamine systems and increase serotonin neurotransmission to variable degrees (Hernandez et al. 1987; Kuczenski et al. 1987). Methylphenidate appears to augment noradrenergic neurotransmission in

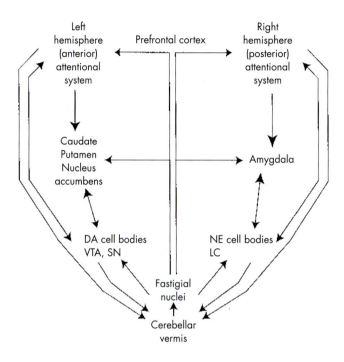

**Figure 33–3.** Simplified neural circuit diagram indicating the interconnections between brain regions and neurotransmitter systems involved in the regulation of activity and attention. Dysfunction in any component could induce symptoms of ADHD.

humans, whereas dextroamphetamine decreases noradrenergic tone (Zametkin et al. 1985). This occurs because the primary amphetamine metabolite, *p*-hydroxyamphetamine, is taken up in noradrenergic neuron, where it is converted into *p*-hydroxynorephedrine, a false neurotransmitter that displaces some of the active transmitter (Lewander 1971a, 1971b; Rangno et al. 1973). Hence, treatment with methylphenidate increases levels of the norepinephrine metabolite 3-methoxy-4-hydroxyphenyl glycol (MHPG), whereas amphetamine causes MHPG levels to fall (Zametkin et al. 1985). ADHD symptoms are also attenuated by clonidine, which is an $\alpha_2$-adrenoreceptor agonist (Hunt 1987; Hunt et al. 1985). Clonidine generally acts on noradrenergic autoreceptors within the locus coeruleus to attenuate noradrenergic neurotransmission. However, clonidine also acts as a partial agonist at postsynaptic $\alpha_2$ receptors and can preserve or augment transmission through a component of the noradrenergic signal pathway, enhancing prefrontal cortex function (Arnsten et al. 1996). Selective norepinephrine reuptake inhibitors such as desipramine and nortriptyline have been shown to be effective in ADHD when administered in high doses (Popper 1997). Although these agents are highly selective in their

action on the norepinephrine transporter, microdialysis studies show that they markedly increase levels of dopamine in the prefrontal cortex (Gresch et al. 1995).

Dopamine and norepinephrine play pivotal roles in our two attentional systems. Dopamine is primarily involved in the left/anterior attention system that is predominantly a motor control system. This system modulates sustained focused attention within the foveal field of vision, facilitates visually guided motor behavior, and suppresses unnecessary movement in order to focus and attend (Malone et al. 1994). In contrast, norepinephrine is primarily involved in the right/posterior attention system that is primarily a sensory alerting system (Aston-Jones and Bloom 1981; Foote et al. 1980). This system modulates rapid phasic shifts in our attention, particularly to events in our peripheral field of vision. This is a rapid system that can grab our attention and enhance arousal when salient or dangerous events are about to occur. The central amygdala, a key component of the fear and anxiety system (LaBar et al. 1998; LeDoux et al. 1988), connects to the locus coeruleus through corticotropin-releasing factor terminals that enhance noradrenergic activity (Van Bockstaele et al. 1998). Hence, the noradrenergically mediated right/posterior attentional system is coupled to fight-or-flight and startle responses.

The primary components of the left/anterior attention system are the corticostriatal pathways (prefrontal cortex, cingulate cortex, caudate, putamen, globus pallidus, and ventrolateral thalamus) along with dopamine projections from the substantia nigra and ventral tegmental area. Major components of the right/posterior attention system are temporal and parietal cortex, locus coeruleus, amygdala, hippocampus, and thalamus. In general, patients with ADHD have a deficiency in the left/anterior attention system that leads to impaired focused attention, diminished capacity to suppress motor activity, and increased impulsivity (Malone et al. 1994). Some patients with ADHD may have (or also have) an overactive right/posterior system that can produce high distractibility and rapid intense shifts in attention and affect. It is also possible that some children with ADHD have an underactive right/posterior system, which can lead to left-hemisphere-driven hyperfocus coupled with diminished awareness of the environment or external events. This may occur in some inattentive ADHD patients who are "spacey" and hypoactive.

Stimulants through their strong effects on the dopamine system augment the left/anterior attention system and enhance focused attention and motor suppression. Clonidine through its effects on norepinephrine would likely suppress the right/posterior system and decrease distractibility and hyperarousal. Noradrenergic reuptake inhibitors should facilitate right/posterior function in situations in which it is diminished and bring an overactive noradrenergic system into better homeostasis, as it appears to do in panic disorder or PTSD (Goddard and Charney 1997). High doses of noradrenergic reuptake inhibitors can also produce an indirect increase in prefrontal dopamine levels facilitating the left/anterior attention system.

Coordinated interplay and balance between these attentional systems is crucial for safety and success. The cerebellar vermis is in a key position to coordinate balance between these systems. First, the vermis receives multimodal sensory information (Brons et al. 1990; Donaldson and Hawthorne 1979; Huang and Liu 1990) and is intimately involved in the control of eye movements (Suzuki and Keller 1988). The vermis also receives vestibular (Denoth et al. 1979) and proprioceptive (Eccles et al. 1971) information to rapidly guide or adjust body position through its motor pathways. The vermis receives projections from prefrontal cortex (Schmahmann and Pandya 1995) along with noradrenergic and dopaminergic projections from the midbrain (Ariano et al. 1997; Dennett and Hubbard 1988; Melchitzky and Lewis 2000). The vermis outputs through the deep cerebellar fastigial nuclei. These nuclei exert robust effects on global cerebral blood flow and metabolism (Doba and Reis 1972; Goadsby and Lambert 1989). They also modulate the turnover of dopamine and norepinephrine (Dempsey and Richardson 1987). Hence, the vermis is ideally wired to affect cortical arousal and catecholamine neurotransmission in response to input from the prefrontal cortex and multimodal sensory systems. These observations underscore the tight association emerging between cerebellar vermis and prefrontal cortex in normal function and psychiatric disorders (Andreasen et al. 1996; Ciesielski et al. 1997; Diamond 2000; Sweeney et al. 1998).

We suspect that ADHD can arise in a number of possible ways from defects or imbalances in the activity and regulation of these attentional systems. The defect may be located specifically within an attentional system or may be vermal in origin, leading to an impaired capacity to balance and coordinate the systems. A variety of defects can produce similar syndromic manifestations and benefit from one or more drugs that enhance catecholamine neurotransmission. We suspect that, in the near future, use of objective behavioral measures, newer imaging technologies, and molecular studies will identify a number of specific etiologies that comprise the ADHD behavioral syndrome.

## Treatment

Comprehensive treatment of ADHD includes both pharmacological and nonpharmacological interventions. Primary medication options include psychostimulants, antidepressants, and antihypertensives. Stimulants, the use of which continues to be clouded by unfounded concerns, remain the mainstay of treatment. In numerous studies, stimulants have been shown to attenuate hyperactivity, improve attention, and diminish impulsivity (Wilens and Biederman 1992). Methylphenidate, in daily doses of 10–60 mg, and dextroamphetamine, given in daily doses of 5–40 mg, are the major agents of choice. Unfortunately, both have a brief duration of action (as short as 3 hours). Effective treatment usually requires multiple daily doses, and children typically receive their first dose in the morning shortly before school and a second dose at lunch time. Many children also benefit from a smaller dose after school. Older longer acting preparations of methylphenidate and dextroamphetamine often fail to significantly extend therapeutic duration (G.L. Brown et al. 1980; Pelham et al. 1987, 1990). Adderall, a mixture of amphetamine and dextroamphetamine, has gained popularity as a single-dose preparation. It is a mixture of four amphetamine salts that provide a more gradual onset and longer duration. Pliszka et al. (2000) found that Adderall was at least as effective as regular methylphenidate, and 70% of their sample responded well to Adderall taken as a single dose. Average daily Adderall dose was 25 mg for preadolescents. Concerta has recently been developed as a new delivery system for methylphenidate. Briefly, an osmotic minipump delivers methylphenidate in a manner that produces escalating blood levels throughout the day. The pump is surrounded by a shell of methylphenidate that provides an initial bolus. Studies suggest that once-daily Concerta is as effective as regular methylphenidate delivered in three equal doses throughout the day. Methamphetamine, a much less frequently prescribed stimulant, is available in a sustained release form (Desoxyn Gradumet) that seems to work reasonably well (Wender 1993). Pemoline is another effective stimulant with a longer duration of action and reduced potential for abuse. However, a relatively high (1%–3%) incidence of adverse hepatic effects has markedly restricted its use. High initial doses (37.5–112.5 mg) have been found to produce rapid and sustained beneficial effects (Pelham et al. 1995). An average effective dose of pemoline for a child would be approximately 56 mg (Pelham et al. 1990).

Common side effects of stimulants include anorexia, stomachaches, insomnia, and mood changes (irritability, mood lability, dysphoria). Tics and stereotypic movements occur less commonly (discussion follows). Concerns about diminishing growth and stature from using stimulants is unfounded. If stimulants attenuate final height, the consequence is less than an inch (Popper and

Steingard 1995). Spencer et al. (1996) provide data that suggest that ADHD, as a disorder, is associated with delayed growth during early childhood with compensatory growth by late adolescents. They found that stimulants played no role in the process. Risk for stimulant abuse in the ADHD population appears small. Stimulants exert dysphoric, rather than euphoriant, effects on children (Rapoport et al. 1980), and compliance can be a significant problem. Individuals with ADHD do not generally like how the medication makes them feel, though many appreciate how the medication enhances performance and leads to greater acceptance by peers, teachers, or supervisors. Biederman et al. (1999), in an important study, found that stimulant treatment of ADHD in childhood actually diminished risk for substance abuse in adulthood. Overall, psychostimulants are effective in the treatment of the core features of ADHD. Consistent and appropriate use can lead to enhanced self-esteem and improved quality of life.

The second major class of medications with demonstrated effectiveness in ADHD is the antidepressants, most notably the selective noradrenergic tricyclics desipramine and nortriptyline (Popper 1997). Studies also indicated that bupropion (Wellbutrin, 0.7 mg/kg/day) can be as effective as methylphenidate in improving attention and reducing conduct problems (Barrickman et al. 1995). Although monoamine oxidase inhibitors are also effective, dietary restrictions preclude their use in pediatric populations. Tricyclic antidepressants have the advantage of sustained effect and can be well suited for children with comorbid mood disorders. Reports of sudden death in prepubertal children receiving desipramine have raised serious concerns about this agent and other tricyclics (Abromowicz 1990; Popper and Zimnitzky 1995; Riddle et al. 1991, 1993). The most common cardiac effects of tricyclics in pediatric patients include sinus tachycardia, intraventricular conduction delay of the right bundle branch block type (QRS > 100 msec), and increased QTc intervals (Biederman et al. 1989; Leonard et al. 1995). As a consequence, maximum desipramine doses should be 5 mg/kg/day, cardiac status and family cardiac history need to be carefully evaluated, and electrocardiogram and plasma levels need to be closely monitored. Although no direct causal relationship has been established between desipramine use and sudden death, cardiovascular toxicity remains a potential risk, and parents need to be informed of this possibility. Selective noradrenergic reuptake inhibitors have been developed that appear to be free of the adverse cardiac affects of tricyclics. Studies suggest that they are effective in ADHD and await U.S. Food and Drug Administration approval. The new antidepressant venlafaxine (Effexor)

exerts strong effects on both noradrenergic and serotonergic reuptake and should theoretically be beneficial for ADHD with a much more benign cardiac profile than that of tricyclics. However, data are only beginning to emerge about its utility (Olvera et al. 1996; Pleak and Gormly 1995; Wilens et al. 1995). The more selective serotonin reuptake inhibitors (SSRIs), such as fluoxetine, have been reported to be useful in an open trial (Barrickman et al. 1991) and await further testing. The general clinical consensus is that SSRIs provide little effect on core symptoms of ADHD, can be helpful with comorbid mood and anxiety symptoms, but can also worsen symptoms (Popper 1997).

Emerging evidence suggests that the $\alpha_2$-adrenergic agonists clonidine and guanfacine are potentially effective treatments. Hunt et al. (1985; Hunt 1987) reported in a small sample that clonidine may be comparable in efficacy to methylphenidate in reducing hyperactivity and impulsivity. Oral doses are generally initiated at 0.025–0.05 mg and increased to a maximum of 3–10 $\mu$g/kg. Transdermal patches can provide more consistent drug effects and decreased propensity for allergic reactions. Common side effects include sedation, rash, and increased appetite and weight gain, whereas less common reactions include headaches, rebound insomnia, cardiovascular effects, and mood lability. Rebound hypertension can occur upon abrupt cessation. In an open trial, guanfacine has also been reported to be efficacious in children with ADHD (Hunt et al. 1995) and those with comorbid TS (Chappell et al. 1995). Guanfacine may produce less sedation and hypotension. Common initial doses are 0.25–0.5 mg, which can be titrated to up to 4 mg/day (Hunt et al. 1995).

Selection of a particular pharmacological agent depends on clinical presentation, comorbidity, duration of effect, and abuse potential by other family members. We find it useful to fully inform family members about potential risks and benefits of treatment and to have them decide which option they prefer. Effectiveness should be based on reports from the child, parents, and teachers. Standardized rating scales have been well validated and are often indispensable. Dosage adjustments are needed to optimize treatment and to compensate for growth and development. Some children and families tolerate reemergence of symptoms with medication discontinuation during weekends and summers. Most children require long-term treatment continuing into adolescence and possibly adulthood.

Despite the benefits of pharmacotherapy, additional treatment and support is often required. Environmental manipulation, such as reducing stimuli and distractions, may help modulate symptoms, and education tailored to the student's learning style may be necessary to improve academic performance. A variety of behavioral management programs have been created for parents (Barkley 1987; Robin and Foster 1989). Barkley et al. (1992) compared three different programs and found that they were all helpful, although clinically significant change was evident in only 5%–30% of subjects (Barkley et al. 1992). In a detailed and elaborate study, the Multimodal Treatment Group evaluated the effects of behavioral therapy versus medication management. Altogether, 579 children with ADHD combined type, ages 7 to 9.9 years, were assigned to 14 months of medication management (titration followed by monthly visits); intensive behavioral treatment (parent, school, and child components); the two combined; or standard community care. Children in the combined treatment and medication management groups showed significantly greater improvement than those given intensive behavioral treatment or community care. No significant differences were seen on any measure between combined treatment and medication management. Combined treatment may have advantages in more complex cases. Medication management was superior to community treatment, in part, because average methylphenidate dose was twice as high in the study, suggesting that subjects in the community did not receive an optimal dose. Methylphenidate was usually administered three times a day in the study versus twice daily in the community. No studies support the effectiveness of psychotherapy alone, sugar toxicity or withdrawal, or restriction of salicylates or food dyes, although omitting food dyes may be helpful in a small minority. Electroencephalograph (EEG) biofeedback has been touted as an alternative to medications that can exert sustained beneficial effects (J.F. Lubar et al. 1995; J.O. Lubar and Lubar 1984; Nash 2000). Despite the availability of instruments and practitioners providing this service, controlled efficacy studies are absent.

## Tourette's Syndrome and Other Tic Disorders

TS is an intriguing neuropsychiatric disorder, presumably arising from deep within the basal ganglia, that illustrates the prominent associations between hyperactivity, impulsivity, tics, obsessions, and compulsions. Tics are stereotyped, brief, repetitive, purposeless, nonrhythmic motor and vocal responses. Although temporarily suppressible, tics are not under full voluntary control, and the individual often experiences increasing internal tension that is only relieved when the tic is released.

Clinically, tic disorders are divided into four catego-

ries: transient tic disorder, chronic tic disorder, TS, and tic disorder not otherwise specified. Transient tic disorder is diagnosed when an individual experiences either single or multiple motor and/or vocal tics many times a day on a near daily basis for at least 4 consecutive weeks, but for no more than 12 months (American Psychiatric Association 1994). The tics must be distressing or cause significant impairment. Onset must occur before 18 years, and tics may not be due to the direct effect of a drug or a more generalized neurological disorder such as Huntington's disease or postviral encephalitis. Transient tic disorder can be a single episode or can reoccur after a period of remission. Chronic tic disorder is diagnosed when an individual has motor tics or vocal tics (but not both) for more than a year with no more than a 3-month consecutive hiatus. Onset must be before 18 years, and the same exclusionary criteria apply as in transient tic disorder. TS is diagnosed when an individual meets criteria for a chronic tic disorder involving the presence of both motor and vocal tics. Tic disorder not otherwise specified is used for cases that fail to fall into one of these three primary categories.

### Characteristic Features

Tics can be simple or complex. Simple motor tics include jerking movements, shrugging, and eye blinking. Simple vocal tics include grunting, sniffing, and throat clearing. More complex motor tics involve grimacing, banging, or temper tantrums, whereas complex vocal tics include echolalia and coprolalia. Tics wax and wane over time, and the primary muscle groups affected gradually change as well.

TS is a chronic condition in which both motor and vocal tics are observable. The tics are often presaged by premonitory sensory urges that build in tension until the tic is released (Leckman et al. 1993). Many patients feel more troubled by the pre-tic tension than by the tics themselves (Leckman et al. 1993), and some patients can successfully control their tics in public and unleash them when they are alone. Tics are markedly attenuated by sleep (Fish et al. 1991; Hashimoto et al. 1981). TS waxes and wanes over time and can vary enormously in severity from mild and undiagnosed to disabling. Anxiety and stress can increase symptoms. The modal age at onset is 6–7 years but can range from 2 to 17 years (Leckman et al. 1995b). Tic symptoms are generally most severe during the period preceding puberty (average $10 \pm 2.4$ years of age) and gradually improve thereafter, except in the most severe cases (Leckman et al. 1998). For this reason, it is important to note that tic severity during childhood is not a predictor of tic severity at 18 years of age (Leckman et al. 1998). In half of patients, symptoms start as a single tic involving eyes, face, or head and progress in a rostrocaudal manner. Before the first appearance of tics, 25%–50% of TS patients have a history of hyperactivity, inattention, and impulsivity consistent with ADHD (Comings and Comings 1987). Phonic and vocal tics generally emerge at about 11 years of age, often starting with a single syllable and then progressing to longer exclamations. Coprolalia occurs in about 60% of patients and emerges in early adolescence. Complex motor tics may be purposeless or camouflaged by a sequence of intentional actions and can be self destructive or violent. In a pilot study, Budman et al. (1998) concluded that rage attacks are not related to tic severity, but rather reflect an underlying pathophysiology with other comorbid conditions. Obsessive-compulsive symptoms appear in 60% of cases (Leckman et al. 1995b), and OCD is observed in 7%–10%. Obsessive-compulsive symptoms usually emerge 5–10 years after the first appearance of simple tics (Bruun 1988). Tic-related OCD may differ from the classic OCD with an earlier age of onset; more prominent symptoms of ritualized touching, tapping, and rubbing; less satisfactory response to SSRIs and an enhanced response to neuroleptic augmentation (Leckman et al. 1995b). TS is not an uncommon condition of childhood and is believed to affect between one and six boys per thousand. The disorder is three- to fourfold more prevalent in boys than in girls. As TS often wanes after puberty, prevalence rates drop by about an order of magnitude (Leckman et al. 1995b).

## Etiology and Pathophysiology

Tic disorders have a substantial genetic basis, but additional factors play a key role. A large study of affected sib-pair families found that first-degree relatives had a tenfold increased risk (Tourette Syndrome Association International Consortium for Genetics 1999). Tics are present in about two-thirds of relatives of TS patients, and linkage studies suggest that TS is transmitted in a Mendelian fashion. Monozygotic twins have about a 53% concordance rate versus an 8% concordance rate for dizygotic twins (Leckman et al. 1995b). However, the relevant environmental risk factors have yet to be identified. Possible candidate genes on chromosome 4q (a recessive gene) and on 8p (a dominant gene) show linkage to TS. Mathematical models suggest that TS and OCD may be transmitted by a single autosomal dominant gene with variable penetrance (Curtis et al. 1992; Eapen et al. 1993; Pauls and Leckman 1986). Gender differences can be explained by a substantially higher penetrance in males than females (Eapen et al. 1993). Although the TS gene is transmitted equally well by mothers and fathers,

differences in clinical presentation can occur. Lichter et al. (1995) reported that maternal transmission was characterized by greater motor tic complexity and more frequent noninterfering rituals, whereas paternal transmission was associated with increased vocal tic frequency, earlier onset of vocal tics relative to motor tics, and more prominent ADHD behaviors. This mode of transmission is an example of genomic imprinting, in which certain genes may be differentially altered based on maternal or paternal lineage. Approximately 10% of individuals with TS have a nonfamilial version, which in all other ways is similar to the familial form.

Epigenetic factors play a role in the expression of TS. Examination of monozygotic twins discordant for TS indicates that the affected twin had a lower birth weight, suggesting involvement of perinatal factors. Other potential factors include exposure to high levels of gonadal androgens and stress hormones during early central nervous system (CNS) development or recurrent stress, anabolic steroids, cocaine, or other stimulants during postnatal development (Leckman and Scahill 1990; Leckman et al. 1990). Emerging evidence suggests that Group A, β-hemolytic streptococcal infection can result in some forms of TS and OCD (Swedo 1994). Sydenham's chorea is a well-known neurological manifestation of rheumatic fever. Studies suggest that antibodies produced in response to streptococcal infection target neurons within the basal ganglia, causing inflammation resulting in chorea, muscle weakness, and fatigue. This autoimmune mechanism has been proposed as an etiology for some cases of TS, and the acronym PANDAS (pediatric autoimmune neuropsychiatric disorders associated with streptococcal infection) encompasses this diagnostic classification. Antineuronal antibodies have been isolated from sera of TS patients (Singer et al. 1998), and an 83-kilodalton protein (β-lymphocyte antigen D8/17) has been identified with a high frequency in TS patients (Murphy et al. 1997; Singer et al. 1998). Injection of sera from TS patients into the striatum of rats produces stereotypies and episodic utterances (Hallett et al. 2000). In a preliminary study, plasmapheresis to remove circulating antibodies produces both short- and long-term clinical improvement in tics and OCD symptoms (Perlmutter et al. 1999). However, Singer et al. (1999) found that the association with streptococcal antibodies was true only for a limited subgroup. Hence, TS patients differed from control subjects in median, but not mean, antibody titers. No phenotypic differences were seen between TS patients with high and low titers (Singer et al. 1999).

Although the definite pathophysiology of TS is not known, consensus has been reached that the basal ganglia and related thalamocortical circuitry is involved. Evidence derives from several sources, including the ameliorative effects of thalamic lesions and surgical disconnection of the prefrontal cortex (Leckman et al. 1991b). MRI studies have revealed abnormalities in lateralization of basal ganglia structures, corpus callosum morphology, and insular and frontocortical paramagnetic properties (Peterson et al. 1993, 1994; Riddle et al. 1992; Singer et al. 1993). When monozygotic twins discordant for degree of TS severity were compared, Hyde et al. (1995) found that the more severely affected twin had a smaller right anterior caudate and smaller left lateral ventricle. Girls with TS alone had smaller lateral ventricles than did girls with TS and ADHD or than did control subjects (Zimmerman et al. 2000).

Functional imaging studies confirm the presence of altered striatal metabolism but also reveal more widespread involvement affecting frontal, cingulate, and insular cortex. George et al. (1992) found that TS subjects had significantly elevated right frontal cortex activity. Braun et al. (1993) found that regional glucose utilization was decreased in left hemispheric regions of the paralimbic and ventral prefrontal cortices (particularly orbitofrontal, inferior insular, and parahippocampal regions) and in subcortical regions including the nucleus accumbens and ventromedial caudate. Concomitant bilateral increases in regional glucose utilization in the supplementary motor, lateral premotor, and Rolandic cortices was also observed. In a more definitive study, Peterson et al. (1998) found that TS patients endeavoring to suppress their tics had increased neuronal activity in the right midfrontal cortex, bilateral superior and temporal gyrus, and right anterior cingulate and decreased neuronal activity in the ventral globus pallidus, putamen, midthalamus, right posterior cingulate, and left sensory motor cortex. When TS patients could freely express their tics, neuronal activity increased in the head of the caudate, primarily on the right side (Peterson et al. 1998). Neuroimaging findings significantly overlap among TS, ADHD, and OCD. OCD appears to involve metabolic changes in orbitofrontal cortex and caudate (Baxter et al. 1992; Nordahl et al. 1989), whereas ADHD can involve prefrontal, cingulate superior sensorimotor, and premotor cortex, along with the caudate, putamen, and cerebellar vermis (as discussed above).

A variety of neurotransmitter abnormalities have been postulated to explain the pathophysiology of TS. A leading hypothesis describes an abnormality in striatal dopamine function, stemming from either greater presynaptic innervation or release or excessive postsynaptic receptor sensitivity (Leckman et al. 1995b). Compelling support comes indirectly from pharmacological studies that show that drugs that either antagonize dopamine $D_2$ family receptors (haloperidol, pimozide) or diminish dopamine synthesis suppress tics, whereas agents that increase dopamine activity (e.g., L-dopa, cocaine) increase tics (Leckman et al. 1995b). Actual measures of dopaminergic function have produced mixed results. CSF and tissue levels of the dopamine metabolite homovanillic acid (HVA) are reduced in TS (Leckman et al. 1995a). Reduced levels of HVA can arise from diminished dopamine turnover, which could result from postsynaptic supersensitivity. However, autopsy studies (Singer et al. 1991) and preliminary PET and SPECT studies (George et al. 1994; Turjanski et al. 1994) have not found an elevation in dopamine $D_1$ or $D_2$ receptor density indicative of supersensitivity. Linkage studies have excluded dopamine $D_1$ and $D_2$ family receptors and the enzymes dopamine β-hydroxylase, tyrosinase, and tyrosine hydroxylase from being closely linked with TS (Brett et al. 1995a; Gelernter et al. 1990, 1993). Thus, a mutation in a dopamine receptor gene or biosynthetic enzyme does not appear to be responsible for the genetic transmission of TS. Singer et al. (1991) found that TS patients at autopsy had a 37% greater density of dopamine transporter (reuptake) sites in caudate than did control subjects and 50% greater density in putamen. Malison et al. (1995) confirmed this finding with SPECT. Increased transporter density may explain the diminished HVA findings, as released dopamine recaptured by transport is predominantly converted into dihydroxyphenylacetic acid rather than HVA (Keller et al. 1973). TS patients also have greater accumulation of fluorodopa in the left caudate (a 25% increase) and right midbrain (53% increase) that do control subjects, suggesting an increase in DOPA decarboxylase enzyme activity (Ernst et al. 1999a). These findings are consistent with a greater degree of dopamine terminal innervation. Wolf et al. (1996) observed in monozygotic twins discordant for Tourette's severity that the more affected twin had a greater density of dopamine $D_2$ receptors in the caudate but not the putamen. Furthermore, within each twin pair a precise match was found between the degree of differences in $D_2$ binding in the head of the caudate and the degree of difference in severity. Thus, it appears that dopamine receptor density may be a modifying factor that explains the high degree of phenotypic variation in this disorder.

Noradrenergic theories about TS have also emerged based on the efficacy of clonidine, an $\alpha_2$-agonist, which is believed to directly diminish firing rates of noradrenergic neurons and to indirectly modulate the activity of dopamine neurons (Leckman et al. 1995a; Scahill et al. 2000). Adults with TS had elevated levels of CSF norepinephrine (Leckman et al. 1995a), a blunted growth hormone response to clonidine (Muller et al. 1994), and abnormally high secretion of urinary norepinephrine in response to stress (Chappell et al. 1994). However, studies of the norepinephrine metabolite MHPG have been inconclusive (Leckman et al. 1995a).

Preliminary postmortem brain studies have shown that 5-hydroxytryptamine (5-HT) and its major metabolite 5-hydroxyindoleacetic acid (5-HIAA) may be globally decreased in the basal ganglia and other brain regions (G.M. Anderson et al. 1992). CSF studies have sometimes reported diminished levels of 5-HIAA (Leckman et al. 1995a, 1995b), and blood levels of 5-HT and tryptophan are also reduced (Comings 1990). Despite the well-known association between OCD and 5-HT, SSRIs have little efficacy against tics (Kurlan et al. 1993). Genetic studies exclude variation in the 5-HT$_{1A}$ and 5-HT$_7$ receptor genes and the tryptophan oxygenase gene from the etiology of TS (Brett et al. 1995b; Gelernter et al. 1995).

Cholinergic interneurons play a critical role in modulating and balancing the effects of dopamine in the extrapyramidal system. Nicotine potentiates the therapeutic effects of neuroleptics (McConville et al. 1991), and muscarinic receptor binding is reduced in TS lymphocytes (Rabey et al. 1992). Clinical trials of choline, lecithin, and deanol have not been particularly efficacious (Leckman et al. 1995a). Treatment with a nicotine patch, which is believed to inactivate nicotinic receptors during chronic exposure, and mecamylamine, a nicotinic antagonist, have been effective in ameliorating TS symptoms (Sanberg et al. 1997, 1998).

Leckman et al. (1991b) postulated that TS arises from a failure to habituate one or more components of the corticostriatal-thalamocortical circuit (Figure 33–3). Oral facial tics may arise from insufficient habituation or excess excitation in circuits located within the ventromedian areas of the caudate and putamen that receive topographic projections from the orofacial regions of the primary motor and premotor cortex. It is also noteworthy that the amygdala projects to widespread areas of the nucleus accumbens and ventral portions of the caudate and putamen. Electrical stimulation of the amygdala produces motor and vocal responses resembling tics (Jadresic 1992). Based on the age at onset and proclivity for these conditions to attenuate or remit during puberty, we propose that they emerge during the period of synaptic overproduction and hyperinnervation that takes place during childhood (Figure 33–2). Receptor overproduction may alter the balance between excitation and inhibition in circumscribed regions that control specific motor programs. Waning of symptoms after puberty may be related to the pruning of overproduced receptors and dopamine terminals.

## Treatment

TS is a complicated and multifaceted condition in which there is enormous variability between patients. In some patients, ADHD is the major problem and tic symptoms may be relatively mild. For these individuals the risk of exacerbating tics with stimulant treatment may be a significant concern, but treatment can often be accomplished safely. Other patients are beset by tics that are disfiguring and result in social ostracism or unemployment. Still other patients have serious problems with premonitory sensory urges, obsession, and compulsions, but in public have no discernible tics.

In general, neuroleptic drugs are effective in attenuating or suppressing tics in 60%–80% of patients (Popper and Steingard 1995). Traditionally, haloperidol (0.5–5 mg/day) and pimozide (1–3 mg/day) have been the drugs of choice (see Teicher and Glod 1990 for review of neuroleptic use in childhood). Both are high-potency dopamine D$_2$ receptor antagonists and are relatively nonsedating. Neuroleptic drugs will also attenuate symptoms of hyperactivity and impulsivity that emerge from comorbid ADHD. However, neuroleptics fail to facilitate attention and can cause substantial cognitive blunting. Pimozide may produce less cognitive blunting than haloperidol and can even have a beneficial cognitive effect in children with comorbid ADHD (Sallee et al. 1994). Pimozide is usually reserved for cases in which haloperidol has not proven entirely satisfactory because pimozide can produce cardiac arrhythmias and requires more extensive monitoring. Case studies suggest that risperidone can also effectively attenuate tics (Lombroso et al. 1995). This is a significant development because risperidone may be associated with a lower incidence of extrapyramidal side effects than are conventional neuroleptics. Localized injections of botulinum toxin into the site of the most problematic tics has been highly effective. This treatment also attenuated premonitory sensations in 21 of 25 patients tested (Kwak et al. 2000).

The most serious side effect of neuroleptic treatment is the emergence of neuroleptic malignant syndrome, a potentially lethal state of muscle tension, hyperpyrexia, and autonomic nervous system lability. Reviews indicate that children are vulnerable to the emergence of neuroleptic malignant syndrome; however, there appear to be no reported cases in children treated with neuroleptics for TS (Steingard et al. 1992). An unusual but significant side effect of neuroleptic treatment is the development of phobic anxiety, which can result in school avoidance and social phobias (Linet 1985; Mikkelsen et al. 1981).

Clonidine is often prescribed as an alternative that may be useful in approximately 50% of cases (Leckman et al. 1991a). It attenuates hyperactivity and impulsivity and may be valuable in children with comorbid ADHD and behavioral problems (Steingard et al. 1993). Clonidine, however, is sedating and can blunt cognitive performance. In a double-blind placebo-controlled study, Singer et al. (1995) found that clonidine was less efficacious than desipramine for children with combined ADHD and TS. Efficacy of clonidine may increase over the course of 2–3 months, and dosage needs to be slowly titrated; blood pressure requires frequent monitoring, even after attaining stable dose. Guanfacine has been discussed as an alternative $\alpha_2$-adrenoreceptor agonist. It produces less sedation and hypotension but it remains to be determined if it is as efficacious.

Studies have produced a marked revision in our understanding of the use of stimulants to treat ADHD in children with TS. Initially, tics were viewed as a serious contraindication, as stimulants can worsen tics or bring tics forth in an otherwise asymptomatic individual (Denckla et al. 1976). However, studies by Sverd et al. (1989) and Gadow et al. (1992) have shown that children with stable TS can respond to stimulants without worsening of tics. As a general guideline, stimulants should not be used in a child in whom stimulants have previously brought forth or worsened tics. Stimulants can be cautiously administered to patients with stable TS. Patients should be carefully monitored for tic frequency or impairment, and in the absence of symptom exacerbation, treatment can continue and be adjusted for optimal efficacy. Evidence indicates that noradrenergic tricyclic antidepressants such as desipramine and nortriptyline are beneficial in patients with comorbid ADHD and chronic tic disorders (Spencer et al. 1993a, 1993c). Desipramine was more effective than clonidine in controlling comorbid symptoms of ADHD and exerted greater effects on tic symptoms, although neither drug in this study was very effective against tics (Singer et al. 1995). In contrast, bupropion, which affects both dopamine and norepinephrine, is more prone to exacerbate tics (Spencer et al. 1993b). Case reports have suggested that lithium can also attenuate tics (Erickson et al. 1977; Kerbeshian and Burd 1988).

TS with associated OCD can be relatively refractory to treatment with SSRIs and may require augmentation with a neuroleptic (McDougle et al. 1994). Although TS is clearly a brain-based disorder, it can be exacerbated by stress and anxiety and can be a severely stigmatizing illness with grievous psychosocial consequences. Psychotherapy can be useful to help reduce anxiety that can exacerbate symptoms, and it can promote the develop-

ment of interpersonal comfort and social skills that may be crucial for successful employment and personal relationships (Popper and Steingard 1995).

## Mental Retardation

An enormous number of genetic, biochemical, and environmental factors can adversely affect brain development, leading to low general intelligence and limited adaptive capacity. Mental retardation is diagnosed when an individual presents, before 18 years of age, with an intelligence score of approximately 70 or below and concurrent deficits in adaptive functioning (American Psychiatric Association 2000). Mental retardation is a common syndrome, with an estimated prevalence of 1%–3% of the adult population. Clinically, mental retardation is divided by severity. The most prevalent form is mild mental retardation, in which intelligence scores range from 50 to 70. Nearly 90% of the mentally retarded fall within this range. These individuals can learn many skills and generally achieve the equivalent of a sixth-grade education. They can live in the community, manage a job, and, with effort or assistance, handle financial matters, although they require support from families and communities to maintain this level of integration. Historically, mild mental retardation was thought to represent the lower end of the normal distribution of intelligence scores, and psychological factors were believed to play an important role. Studies continue to identifying an increasing percentage of chromosomal abnormalities in patients who are mildly retarded (currently 4%–19%). Mild mental retardation is a heterogeneous set of disorders that sometimes arise from chromosomal abnormalities, environmental effects, or complex multifactorial polygenic inheritance (Thapar et al. 1994).

The next most prevalent cluster is moderate mental retardation, in which intelligence scores range from a low of 35–40 to a high of 50–55. Approximately 7% of the mentally retarded fall within this range. These individuals can often learn to manage some aspects of daily living, such as making small change. They usually live in supervised residences and attain the equivalent of a second-grade education. They communicate at the level of a preschool or early grade school child. About 3% of the mentally retarded fall into the severe range, with intelligence scores ranging from 20–25 up to 35–40. These individuals typically learn few adaptive skills and live in highly structured and closely supervised settings. They have an increased prevalence of neurological complications such as seizures and spasticity, and often there is a discernible etiology, such as Down syndrome or fragile X syndrome.

Only about 1% of the mentally retarded fall within the profound range, with IQ scores below 20–25. These individuals typically die within their 20s and have a host of severe neurological and medical problems. They need to live in highly structured and supervised settings, and are completely dependent on others. Self-injurious behavior can occur in half of these patients.

Historically, it made sense to differentiate forms of mental retardation by severity because most cases arose from unknown etiologies. With the emergence of new molecular tools and the steady advance in behavioral phenotyping (State et al. 1997), this reliance on identification by severity alone is changing. Instead of attempting to distill the generic features of hundreds of different responsible disorders, it seems more reasonable to review some of the major known disorders that present with mental retardation.

## Down Syndrome

Down syndrome is the most common chromosomal abnormality that produces mental retardation. The incidence varies greatly with maternal age. In all newborns, the incidence is 1 per 1,000. However, if the mother is 45 years of age or older, the incidence approaches 1 in 50. Down syndrome may be lethal, resulting in fetal death or still birth. Clinical presentation varies considerably. Characteristic features include microcephaly with large anterior fontanel, depressed nasal bridge, bilateral epicanthic folds, upward slanting (mongoloid) palpebral fissure, low set and misformed ears with hypoplastic tragus and narrow auditory meatus, and lingual protrusion with small mouth (Gold 1992). Other observable features include short stature, hands with a single transverse (simian) crease, brachyclinodactyly of the fifth finger, and wide separation between the large and second toe (Gold 1992). Neurologically, developmental delays and intellectual deficits are significant. Motor milestones are delayed as a result of generalized hypotonia, and expressive and receptive language is usually delayed and impaired. Hearing is also frequently affected as a result of middle ear disease or sensorineural hearing loss (Gold 1992). Seizures occur in less than 10% of cases, but can emerge at any age. Quadriplegia can result at any time from cervical subluxation of the atlantoaxial process. Life expectancy is approximately 50 years, with about 40% developing Alzheimer's disease by this point (Holland et al. 1998). Factors that influence longevity include coexisting congenital heart disease and gastrointestinal anomalies (Gold 1992). Leukemia occurs with increased frequency, and neural changes characteristic of Alzheimer's disease begins to emerge in all who survive beyond 30 years. Behaviorally, patients with Down syndrome tend to have greater relative social skills and less psychopathology than patients with other forms of mental retardation (State et al. 1997).

### Etiology and Pathophysiology

Down syndrome is a prototypic chromosomal disorder involving extra replication of all or part of the 21 chromosome. The classic cause is nondisjunction during meiosis leading to trisomy 21, which is a noninherited genetic anomaly. The syndrome can also arise from inheritance of a translocation of part of the 21 chromosome (most often to chromosomes 14 or 22) from asymptomatic mothers. It appears that extra replication of a 3,000-kilobase fragment of DNA in the 21q22 region is sufficient to produce many of the features of Down syndrome, including mental retardation (Park et al. 1987). Down syndrome arising from either nondisjunction or translocation can be diagnosed prenatally through chorionic villi sampling or amniocentesis. Although it is unclear how this extra genetic material leads to mental retardation, research has identified remarkable similarities between Down syndrome and Alzheimer's disease (Rumble et al. 1989). Patients with Down syndrome undergo progressive neuropathological changes leading to formation of neurofibrillary tangles and neuritic plaques at a relatively young adult age (Wisniewski et al. 1985). They also have other Alzheimer's-like neurochemical abnormalities, including a major loss of acetylcholine neurons in the nucleus basalis, somatostatin neurons in the cerebral cortex, and reduced levels of norepinephrine and 5-HT (Godridge et al. 1987). Chromosome 21 contains the precursor gene for $\beta$-amyloid, which is the protein that accumulates in neuritic plaques. Additional biochemical abnormalities include elevated levels of CuZn, superoxide dismutase, and protein S100$\beta$ (Huret et al. 1987; Lejeune 1990). Superoxide dismutase is an important housekeeping enzyme that prevents intracellular damage from free radicals; a mutation in the encoding gene is associated with the familial form of amyotrophic lateral sclerosis. Studies using model systems overexpressing this enzyme have impaired monoamine neurotransmitter uptake and storage (Groner et al. 1994). The S100$\beta$ protein appears to target and activate astrocytes and specific neurons to stimulate neurite growth. Elevated levels of S100$\beta$ may lead to nonsensical growth of imperfect neurites, an early step in the formation of neuritic plaques (Sheng et al. 1994).

# Fragile X Syndrome

Fragile X is the most common known inherited cause of mental retardation, with an estimated prevalence rate of 1 in 1,250 males and 1 in 2,000 females (Thapar et al. 1994). Fragile X accounts for approximately 7% of moderate and 4% of mild mental retardation in males and 2.5% of moderate and 3% of mild retardation in females (Thapar et al. 1994). The name derives from the observation that the X chromosome shows a "fragile" site, specifically a bent or broken appearing segment, when grown in the appropriate culture medium. The polymerase chain reaction provides a reliable and economic means for detecting this disorder (Thapar et al. 1994). The phenotypic presentation of this disorder is varied and more prominent in males. Infants present with relative macrocrania and facial edema, whereas older children and adults have a long face and a prominent chin. Large, floppy, seashell-shaped ears are characteristic at any age. Males entering adolescence have characteristic macroorchidism (enlarged testes) and a normal-size penis (Gold 1992). Affected individuals have an increased rate of psychiatric difficulties with abnormal speech and language, impaired social relations, and ADHD (Turk 1992). Many affected individuals show autistic features such as gaze avoidance, hand flapping, tactile defensiveness, and perseveration (Hagerman and Sobesky 1989), though social withdrawal and reduced attachment to caregivers are not characteristic (State et al. 1997). Seventy percent of female carriers are not mentally retarded, but they have an increased prevalence of schizotypal features, depression, and below-average intelligence (Freund et al. 1992), and their level of symptomatology correlates with the degree of cytogenetically evident fragility (Chudley et al. 1983; Thapar et al. 1994).

## Etiology and Pathophysiology

Fragile X has an unusual and important mode of inheritance that also appears in myotonic dystrophy and Huntington's chorea. In all of these disorders the severity of the syndrome increases in successive generations. Other features of fragile X include the observation that phenotypically and cytogenetically normal males (normal transmitting males) can transmit the defect to apparently normal females who can then produce affected male offsprings. These clinical observations have now been explained at the molecular level and stem from a process known as *anticipation*. The gene directly responsible for fragile X syndrome, *FMR1*, is located on the X chromosome at Xq27.3 (Verkerk et al. 1991). The 5′ untranslated region of the *FMR1* gene contains a polymorphic

CGG trinucleotide repeat (6–60 repeats in normal subjects), which can be amplified to hundreds or thousands of repeats producing the disorder (Verkerk et al. 1991). Fragile X usually results from expansion of the CGG repeats leading to hypermethylation of the CpG island adjacent to *FMR1*, loss of transcription of the *FMR1* gene, and lack of FMR1 protein (Siomi et al. 1995). *FMR1* mRNA and protein are expressed in many tissues, but particularly high levels are found in brain and testes (Siomi et al. 1995). The role of FMR1 protein is incompletely understood but is known to serve as an RNA-binding protein (Siomi et al. 1995). Fragile X carriers, including normal transmitting males, have this elongated sequence of repeats, which increase in size, particularly when transmitted by females. If the permutation is transmitted by a normal transmitting male, the sequence is not elongated in the offspring (Thapar et al. 1994).

# Prader-Willi Syndrome and Angelman's Syndrome

Prader-Willi syndrome and Angelman's syndrome are two distinct genetic forms of mental retardation that usually arise from de novo deletion of a segment of chromosome 15. Prader-Willi syndrome is characterized by obesity associated with hyperphagia, hypogenitalism, short stature, small hands and feet, almond-shaped eyes, and strabismus (Thapar et al. 1994). Although about 40% show mental retardation, most affected individuals are of normal or borderline IQ, but some may have associated behavior problems such as temper tantrums, stubbornness, foraging for food (Akefeldt and Gillberg 1999; Thapar et al. 1994), and OCD symptomatology (State et al. 1999). The estimated incidence is approximately 1 in 25,000. Most cases are sporadic with a recurrence risk of less than 1 in 1,000 (Thapar et al. 1994). Angelman's syndrome is characterized by severe mental retardation; stiff, jerky movements; ataxia; seizures; and unprovoked laughter. The estimated incidence is approximately 1 in 20,000, and most cases are sporadic (Thapar et al. 1994).

## Etiology and Pathophysiology

Prader-Willi and Angelman's syndromes illustrate an important genetic principle, known as *genomic imprinting*. The majority of individuals with both disorders have remarkably similar deletions of a segment of chromosome 15, particularly surrounding 15q12 (Thapar et al. 1994). It has now been discovered that the difference between Prader-Willi and Angelman's syndromes stems from the gender of the parent from whom the defective 15 chromosome is inherited. Prader-Willi syndrome emerges most frequently from the 15q12 deletion of paternal origin. It can also occur in uniparental disomy where both chromosomes 15 are inherited from the mother (Nicholls et al. 1989) and is usually milder (Cassidy et al. 1997; Dykens et al. 1999; Roof et al. 2000). In contrast, Angelman's syndrome most often emerges from deletion in maternally derived chromosome 15 (15q11–13) or from uniparental disomy when both 15 chromosomes are inherited from the father (Malcolm et al. 1991; Thapar et al. 1994).

Neurochemical studies have found elevated levels of oxytocin (Martin et al. 1998), dopamine, and serotonin (Akefeldt et al. 1998) in the cerebrospinal fluid of Prader-Willi patients. Administration of growth hormone has been reported to be helpful for somatic features of this disorder (Lindgren and Ritzen 1999; Ritzen et al. 1999); however, this treatment may not improve the behavioral symptoms (Akefeldt and Gillberg 1999).

# Autism and Pervasive Developmental Disorders

Autism is a rare but serious neuropsychiatric syndrome affecting 4–5 children per 10,000 births (Fombonne et al. 1997). Boys are affected three- to fourfold more often than girls are affected (Wing and Gould 1979). Kanner (1943) introduced the term *early infantile autism* to describe a group of 11 such children. DSM-IV-TR (American Psychiatric Association 2000) distinguishes autistic disorder from other pervasive developmental disorders, including Rett's disorder, childhood disintegrative disorder, Asperger's disorder, and pervasive developmental disorder not otherwise specified. These disorders share a common set of severe disturbances in social recognition and interaction, impaired communication, and a restricted stereotypic behavioral repertoire and range of interests.

## Characteristic Features

Children with autism often seem indifferent to others. Their lack of interest may be manifested by minimal eye contact, delayed or absent facial signals, and impaired imitation of appropriate social behaviors. Autistic children have few if any friends; they may not engage in comfort seeking when distressed and often exhibit a preference for solitary play. Extreme cases find all physical contact aversive. Children with autism are frequently nonverbal when first diagnosed. If speech is present, it is often highly deviant and of limited communicative func-

tion. Abnormal speech patterns include echolalia, pronoun reversal, metaphorical language, poor grammatical structure, atonality, and arrhythmia. Autistic children also have deficient nonverbal communication skills.

Stereotypies are common in autism and can involve the flicking, twirling, or spinning of objects, or hand flapping, whirling, and posturing. Autistic children are often fascinated by spinning tops and other devices. Many autistic children resist change in their environment by ordering and arranging objects in precise ways to ensure sameness. Later in development, insistence on sameness can be observed in rigidified, ritualistic behavior patterns and routines.

Mental retardation is present in 75%–80% of children with autism and appears to be stable over time (Freeman et al. 1985, 1991). Children with autism may be underresponsive or overresponsive to sensory stimuli (Ornitz 1974; Ornitz and Ritvo 1968). Abnormal mood states can also be present and are often characterized by temper tantrums, aggression, self-injury, or unexplainable giggling. Deviant motility, such as toe walking, can also be observed. Research suggests that the social problems of autistic children may stem, in part, from the inability to establish joint attention, such as pointing or showing objects (Baron-Cohen 1989), and this may render them incapable of sharing mutual interests. Autistic children may also lack the ability to infer another person's state of mind, an inability that may be a core feature of the disorder (Leslie and Frith 1988; Perner et al. 1989; Rutter and Bailey 1993).

## Etiology and Pathophysiology

Autism appears to stem from both genetic and nongenetic factors that affect brain development (Cirianello and Cirianello 1995). The concordance rate in monozygotic twins is 60%, but no concordance has been found between dizygotic twins (Bailey et al. 1995). Cognitive and social abnormalities are nearly ubiquitous in monozygotic twins of affected probands. Dizygotic twins and siblings have a significant but much lower incidence of cognitive disturbance (August et al. 1981; Bailey et al. 1995). Although many etiological factors have been proposed, no single cause has been elucidated. Minshew (1991) argued that less than 5% of individuals with autism have an identifiable etiology. Potential causal factors include tuberous sclerosis, cytomegalovirus, encephalitis, meningitis, and fragile X. Immune abnormalities have also been proposed (Warren et al. 1995). Conservative sources estimate that fragile X may be present in 7% of males and 4% of females with autism (Bolton and Rutter 1990). A number of recent reports has documented deletions and duplications of chromosome 15, especially in the 15q11–13 region (Cook 2001); however, no candidate genes have been identified (Tanguay 2000). The International Molecular Genetic Study of Autism Consortium obtained the highest linkage scores for regions on chromosomes 7q and 16p, with lesser scores on chromosomes 4, 10, 19, and 22 in a two-stage genome search for susceptibility loci in 87 affected sib pairs and 12 nonsib affected relatives (International Molecular Genetic Study of Autism Consortium 1998). A follow-up study from this group found no chromosome 22q11 deletions (Ogilvie et al. 2000).

Neuroanatomic studies have suggested that autism arises from premature cessation of development in the cerebellum, cerebrum, and limbic system. Postmortem studies have identified regions of cellular loss unaccompanied by gliosis. These findings suggest that the lesion occurred in fetal life or was the result of misdirected development (Bauman 1991). Courchesne et al. (1991) reported a 25% reduction in the size of cerebellar vermal lobes VI and VII in 14 of 18 subjects with autism. This reduction could result in faulty cortical projections. Differences in vermal size, however, correlated with low IQ rather than autism per se (Holttum et al. 1992; Levitt et al. 1999). Damage to the cerebellum may manifest as damage to the frontal lobes and affect attention, memory, and language (Riva and Giorgi 2000). Children with vermal lesions (as a consequence of CNS radiation or chemotherapy) can develop symptoms suggesting autism. Some theories suggest that autism results from coordinated developmental anomalies affecting the posterior-superior vermis and frontal, temporal, and parietal lobes. Kemper and Bauman (1993) observed progressive developmental changes in neurons in the cerebellum, inferior olive, and diagonal band of Broca. In brains of young adults with autism, neurons in these regions were large and fetal in appearance. Brains of older adults with autism showed a marked decline in neuronal number, size, and extent of dendrites. Kemper and Bauman theorized that deficient Purkinje cell production resulted in a failure to form appropriate corticocerebellar synaptic connections and that these circuits regressed with age. This process may also explain the high density of small neurons observed in the hippocampus and amygdala (Bauman and Kemper 1985). Bailey et al. (1998) found abnormal neuronal migration patterns in the brain stem and cerebellum, and reduced numbers of Purkinje cells in adult cases. A striking inverse correlation was found between Purkinje cell number and cortical thickness. Carper and Courchesne (2000) also found a significant inverse correlation between the size of vermal lobules VI–VII and volume of frontal gray matter in patients with autism, but not in control subjects. Deficient development of corticocerebellar connections may have impaired the normal process of cortical development and attenuated the pruning process because this depends on the establishment of strong appropriate connections. Lack of pruning is consistent with the elevated rates of glucose metabolism (Horwitz et al. 1988) and adenosine triphosphate utilization observed in the frontal and parietal lobes of patients with autism. Gyral malformations have also been found in the cortex, including pachygyria, polymicrogyria, heterotopia, and schizencephaly (Piven et al. 1990).

The deficits in cognitive functioning characteristic of autism have not been linked to specific anatomical defects. Individuals with autism perform normally on tasks that assess perception, attention, and classification of stimuli and appear to have intact sensory and basic memory functions (Courchesne 1991). However, in children with autism slowed orienting to visual cues correlates with degree of cerebellar hypoplasia (Harris et al. 1999). Abnormalities have been observed in certain evoked potential responses (e.g., auditory P300) that are probably indicative of deficient auditory processing (Novic et al. 1980). A reversal in hemispheric asymmetry has been proposed (Ornitz and Ritvo 1968) and supported by MRI studies (Hashimoto et al. 1988). Glucose utilization is not as strongly correlated between the two hemispheres as it is in control subjects without autism (Horwitz et al. 1988). In 43% of subjects with autism studied, thinning of the corpus callosum has been found (Egaas et al. 1995), especially the anterior subregions (Hardan et al. 2000), and is consonant with diminished hemispheric communication. This decrease in callosal size is more a consequence of diminished axon numbers than decreased myelination (Belmonte et al. 1995).

Social deficits in autism have been examined with fMRI using facial perception tests. Patients with autism had attenuated responses in mesolimbic and temporal lobe cortical regions and in left amygdala and left cerebellum during facial processing (Critchley et al. 2000). Schultz and colleagues (2000) found that individuals with autism relied on feature-based strategies for facial recognition and had greater activation in the inferior temporal gyri.

Neurochemically, the most noted observation has been a significant increase in whole-blood 5-HT levels in 30% of autistic individuals (Young et al. 1985). High levels of 5-HT have also been found in most first-degree relatives (Piven et al. 1991). McBride et al. (2000) found that whole-blood 5-HT levels vary by race and pubertal status. They found, after correcting for race, a significant elevation in whole-blood 5-HT levels in about 25% of prepubertal but not postpubertal children with autism. Chugani and colleagues (1997, 1999) found decreased 5-HT synthesis and uptake in frontal cortex and thalamus, especially in boys. Mixed findings have emerged regarding a possible linkage of the 5-HT transporter gene and autism (Cook et al. 1997; Klauck et al. 1997). Elevated levels of endogenous opioids have also been noted in patients with autism. This observation emerged from the apparently high pain threshold of autistic individuals with self-abusive behaviors. Research suggests that levels of β-endorphin and endorphin fraction II may be elevated in the CSF (Ross et al. 1987).

## Treatment

Pharmacotherapy for autism has had mixed results. However, many autistic children have appropriate target symptoms (e.g., hyperactivity, temper tantrums, irritability, stereotypies, self-injury, depression, and obsessive-compulsive behaviors) that warrant a therapeutic trial (Campbell et al. 1996). Fenfluramine, which stimulates 5-HT release, has been used in numerous trials. Although initial reports were promising (e.g., Ritvo et al. 1983, 1986), later studies have been disappointing (e.g., Leventhal et al. 1993). There may, however, have been a subgroup that responds favorably. Fenfluramine has been withdrawn as a result of emergence of adverse effects on the heart. Opiate antagonists such as naltrexone have been used to enhance cognitive processing (Lensing et al. 1995) and reduce self-injury and hyperactivity (Campbell et al. 1993; Gillberg 1995), with equivocal results. Neuroleptics, particularly haloperidol, have been extensively evaluated in double-blind, placebo-controlled protocols (Campbell et al. 1996). Haloperidol reduces symptoms of anger, uncooperativeness, and hyperactivity, and also exerts some effects on core features of autistic behavior and deviant speech (Campbell et al. 1996). Clomipramine has also been found to be effective in controlled studies in attenuating stereotypies, compulsions, ritualized behaviors, and aggression (Campbell et al. 1996). The few published reports indicate that SSRIs are modestly effective in decreasing hyperactivity, restlessness, agitation, obsessive thoughts, and preoccupations (McDougle et al. 1998; Posey et al. 1999). Although anecdotal reports indicated that secretin, a gastrointestinal hormone, had therapeutic benefits, initial controlled studies have been negative (Chez et al. 2000; Sandler et al. 1999). Further research needs to be conducted on SSRIs, lithium, and atypical antipsychotics (McDougle et al. 2000).

Long-term interventions focus on community-based special educational programs and subsequent residential services for those who cannot be cared for at home. An initial study by Lovaas (1987) and a follow-up study (McEachin et al. 1993) suggest that as many as half of preschool-age children with autism can attain normal educational and intellectual function with extremely intensive early behavioral treatment. The interventions were designed to increase skills in the areas of attention, emotionality, language, toy play, peer interaction, and self-help while reducing tantrums, aggression, and self-stimulation (Lovaas and Smith 1989). Although Lovaas's findings are encouraging, long-term care continues to be the norm for children with autism over the course of their lifetime (Nordin and Gillberg 1998).

## Rett's Disorder

Rett's disorder is an X-linked dominant progressive degenerative disorder found exclusively in females, as it is lethal in males. Development often appears to be normal until about 18 months of age, but is followed by the emergence of autistic symptoms, often leading to a diagnosis of autism. Development of distinctive hand stereotypies (i.e., twisting or wringing), deceleration in normal head growth leading to microcephaly, and progressive neurological deterioration help establish the correct diagnosis. Children develop gait ataxia between 1 and 4 years of age and may lose ambulation completely as they mature.

Monozygotic twins show complete concordance, whereas dizygotic twins are not concordant (Lotspeich 1995). Progressive clinical deterioration is mirrored by progressive cortical atrophy and neuronal loss (Zoghbi et al. 1985). There is a marked attenuation in levels of the noradrenergic metabolite MHPG and the dopamine metabolite HVA in the CSF (Zoghbi et al. 1985). Children with Rett's disorder show some of the motor problems observed in Parkinson's disease and suffer from reduced dopaminergic activity in the basal ganglia, substantia nigra, and cortex (Rett 1966, 1977; Wenk et al. 1991). Mutations in a gene called *MeCP2* is responsible for about one-third of cases (Amir et al. 1999).

Imaging and postmortem studies indicate that children with Rett's disorder have curtailed development, characterized by reduced cerebral volume (Jellinger et al. 1988; Reiss et al. 1993), cortical dysplasia with limited gliosis, decreased cell size, increased packing density (Bauman et al. 1995), global reductions in gray- and white-matter volumes (Subramaniam et al. 1997), and greater loss of gray matter versus white matter (Reiss et al. 1993), particularly in the prefrontal, posterior-frontal, and anterior-temporal regions (Subramaniam et al. 1997). Abnormalities in amino acid receptors have been demonstrated in basal ganglia (Blue et al. 1999a) and superior frontal gyrus (Blue et al. 1999b). N-methyl-D-aspartate (NMDA) receptor density in the superior frontal gyrus changes dramatically with age. NMDA receptor density is higher in brains of younger patients with Rett's disorder than it is in the brains of control subjects, and it is lower in the brains of older patients with Rett's disorder than it is in the brains of control subjects (Blue et al. 1999b). Dendritic arborization is reduced in many cortical regions (Armstrong et al. 1998).

PET scans demonstrate reduced frontal blood flow, and reveal an immature blood flow and metabolism pattern comparable to that observed in early infancy (Nielsen et al. 1990). Magnetic resonance spectroscopy (MRS) imaging reveals a significant reduction of N-acetyl aspartate concentration and increased choline concentration in frontal, parietal, insular, and hippocampal regions. These findings are consistent with reduced neuronal arborization and gliosis in these regions (Horska et al. 2000).

## Asperger's Disorder

Asperger's disorder is characterized by social dysfunction, pedantic speech, and idiosyncratic interests. Children with Asperger's disorder are distinguished from autistic children by better social function, normal intelligence, undelayed language development, and greater clumsiness. Although Asperger's disorder is, at present, nosologically distinct from autism, many argue that the disorder is merely a milder form of autism and should be categorized as such. For example, J.N. Miller and Ozonoff (2000) found no significant differences in motor, visuospatial, or executive functions between high-functioning patients with autism and subjects with Asperger's disorder, after controlling for the superior intellectual abilities of the group with Asperger's disorder.

## Specific Disorders of Learning

Learning disorders are specific delineated deficits in the acquisition and performance of reading, writing, or arithmetic skills in the presence of normal intelligence and aptitude. These disorders often come to attention in grammar school and are estimated to affect up to 10% of school-age children, though many cases go undiagnosed. Learning disorders frequently persist into adulthood (American Academy of Child and Adolescent Psychiatry 1998; American Psychiatric Association 1994). Learning disorders are thought to be a consequence of neurocortical impairment, yet their expression is affected by paren-

tal support, educational resources, and the individual's personality, initiative, and motivation. Although learning disorders can be comorbid with many other psychiatric conditions, it is important to distinguish learning disorders from mental retardation, sensory impairments, and other psychiatric or neurological conditions that can affect attention, motivation, and behavior.

The evaluation of a learning disorder consists of intelligence tests, specific achievement tests, and a description of the child's classroom behavior. Because learning disabilities often entitle children to special services, most states have adopted specific guidelines for their diagnosis based on standardized tests (Frankenberger and Fronzaglio 1991). Typically, the learning-disabled child demonstrates a significant discrepancy between nonverbal (performance) IQ and verbal IQ, with a history of delayed or impaired speech, language, or reading skills (American Academy of Child and Adolescent Psychiatry 1998; Tallal et al. 1991). Overlooked or left untreated, learning disorders can lead to underachievement in a number of domains, along with diminished self-esteem, disinterest in school, truancy, and conduct and substance abuse disorders (Benasich et al. 1993; Karacostas and Fisher 1993; Naylor et al. 1994; Rowe and Rowe 1992). Approximately 40% of children with learning disorders eventually drop out of school (Popper and Steingard 1995). Delinquent behaviors have been associated with learning disabilities; however, current data suggest that, although reading disorders can worsen preexisting aggressive behavior, evidence is insufficient to presume that reading disability causes aggression (Cornwall and Bawden 1992).

## Characteristic Features

At present, three identifiable learning disorders are recognized: reading disorder, mathematics disorder, and disorders of written expression. *Reading disorder* is characterized by slow acquisition of reading skills despite normal intelligence, education, motivation, and emotional control. Prominent characteristics include letter and word reversals, word omissions and distortions, spelling errors, and substitution of words (American Psychiatric Association 1994). Left-right orientation, sound and phoneme discrimination, rapid visual and auditory sensory processing, and perceptual-motor skills are also impaired. Approximately 4% of school-age children are affected by reading disorder, and boys are affected three to four times more frequently than girls (C. Lewis et al. 1994).

*Mathematics disorder* is characterized by difficulty with counting, mathematical reasoning, calculations, and object conceptualization (American Psychiatric Association 1994). Impairment in spatial skills and in right-left, up-down, and east-west differentiation is evident. Children with mathematics disorder often have difficulty copying shapes, memorizing numbers, and sequencing tasks. Mathematics disorder affects about 1% of the school-age population, whereas 2% of children are affected by both arithmetic and reading difficulties (C. Lewis et al. 1994). Boys and girls appear to be equally affected (C. Lewis et al. 1994).

Compared with reading and mathematics disorders, the *disorders of written expression* are not well characterized, and prevalence rates are unknown. Children have impairments in spelling, grammar, punctuation, sentence and paragraph formation, and organizational structure. Characteristic features include slow ability to write or produce writing assignments, illegibility, letter reversals, word-finding and syntax errors, and punctuation and spelling problems (American Psychiatric Association 1994).

## Etiology and Pathophysiology

Learning disorders have both a genetic and environmental basis. Environmental factors include prenatal ethanol exposure, perinatal complications, postnatal lead exposure, diminished parental and environmental stimulation, and head trauma (Ewing-Cobbs et al. 1998; Pennington and Smith 1983). Evidence also suggests that there are heritable forms of learning disorders (Cardon et al. 1994, 1995; Pennington and Smith 1983). However, critical questions about the nature of learning disorders color any discussion of etiology and pathophysiology. One major view is that learning disorders are relatively discrete neuropsychiatric syndromes affecting a specific set of higher cognitive functions without affecting general intelligence. Thus, learning disorders are identified by a clear discrepancy between aptitude and actual ability. The contrasting view is that learning disorders are not discrete neurological syndromes and that they merely represent the tail end of a normal distribution of aptitudes and abilities (B.A. Shaywitz et al. 1995; S.E. Shaywitz et al. 1992). In this view no discrete cutoff exists between a learning disorder and normal ability, and the diagnosis is inherently unstable, with different individuals meeting criteria in different years (S.E. Shaywitz et al. 1992). Evidence supporting the latter view derives mostly from the realm of psychological testing, in which an important study showed that reading ability scores were normally distributed without an expected bimodal hump in the lower range, indicative of a second population with lower mean value (S.E. Shaywitz et al. 1992; but see Rutter and Yule

1975). This argues that there is not a discrete population of patients with reading disorders and that such individuals are merely the lower range of a normal population. This does not preclude the possibility that a small subset of patients may have discrete neurological disorders affecting reading ability, but that any such subset would be relatively small and would not account for the preponderance of patients with reading disability (S.E. Shaywitz et al. 1992). Psychological tests indicate that discrepancy scores used to diagnose learning disorders are unstable, identifying different individuals in different years, and are of questionable validity for establishing which individuals need special assistance (Cole et al. 1992; Haddad et al. 1994; S.E. Shaywitz et al. 1992).

In contrast to this view, burgeoning literature suggests that some children with learning disorders have identifiable neurological abnormalities and that some learning disorders follow simple genetic models. Numerous studies have shown that learning disorders are highly hereditable. Concordance for dyslexia may be as high as 91% in monozygotic twin pairs versus 31% for dizygotic twins (Pennington and Smith 1983). Reading, mathematical, and spelling ability are all inherited traits with heritability indices of 0.78 (Gillis et al. 1992), 0.51 (Gillis et al. 1992), and 0.53 (Stevenson et al. 1987), respectively. Cardon et al. (1994, 1995) identified a quantitative trait locus on chromosome 6 (region 6p21.3) for reading disability in two carefully selected, independent groups of sibling pairs. This region is found in the human leukocyte antigen encoding region, supporting the suspected association between autoimmune disorders and dyslexia (Geschwind and Behan 1982; Schacter and Galaburda 1986). In short, it appears that progress is being made in delineating a specific gene that may be responsible for many inherited cases of reading disorder.

Patterns of family inheritance have also helped to unravel the association between learning disorders and ADHD. Conservative estimates suggest that 8% of children with ADHD have a learning disorder, but actual estimates range from 0% to 92% (Semrud-Clikeman et al. 1992). Most studies show that ADHD and learning disorders are transmitted independently (Faraone et al. 1993; Gilger et al. 1992) and suggest that comorbidity between ADHD and learning disorder may be a consequence of nonrandom mating between individuals with family histories of ADHD and learning disability (Faraone et al. 1993).

Autopsy findings in learning disorders include arteriovenous malformations, atypical gyral patterns in parietal lobes, thin corpus callosum in the region connecting the parietal lobes, and premature cessation of neuronal migration to the cortex, revealed by an excess number of neurons in white matter (Drake 1968; Geschwind and Galaburda 1985). Also, Galaburda et al. (1985, 1994) observed anomalies in medial geniculate and the lateral posterior thalamic nuclei. Perhaps the most interesting anomalies involve the cortex, particularly the left peri-sylvian region. These include neuronal ectopias in layer I, which are often nodular in appearance (brain warts) and associated with dysplasia of the underlying cortex (Galaburda et al. 1994). Micropolygyria has also been observed in some patients and in animals with autoimmune disorders that have deficient learning performance (Schrott et al. 1992).

Visual information from the retina is transmitted to the cerebral cortex by way of the lateral geniculate nucleus (LGN) in the thalamus. In primates, most of the retinal ganglion cells that project to the LGN belong to one of two classes, P and M, whose axons terminate in the parvocellular or magnocellular subdivisions of the LGN, respectively. These cell classes give rise to two channels that have been distinguished anatomically, physiologically, and behaviorally (Deyoe and Van Essen 1988). The magnocellular pathway has fast conduction velocities, large receptive fields, and operates in a transient manner. In contrast, the parvocellular pathway is slow with much finer receptive fields (Fitch et al. 1997; J. Stein and Walsh 1997). The visual cortex also can be subdivided into two pathways, one specialized for motion processing and the other for color and form information. Responses in the motion pathway in the cortex depend primarily on magnocellular LGN, whereas visual responses in the color/form pathway depend on both P and M input (Ferrera et al. 1992). Based on electrophysiological studies and autopsy analysis of the LGN from five subjects, Livingstone et al. (1991) proposed that dyslexic subjects have a specific defect in the magnocellular pathway. They further suggested that dyslexic subjects perform poorly on auditory and somatosensory tests that require rapid discrimination and proposed an underlying defect in the fast subdivision of multiple cortical sensory systems. Evidence in support of this theory has been mixed. Studies using motion-based tests of the magnocellular pathway have been more supportive than tests using low-contrast stimuli (Demb et al. 1998; Greatrex and Drasdo 1995; Johannes et al. 1996; Kubova et al. 1996; Skottun 2000). J. Stein and Walsh (1997) emphasized the importance of the magnocellular pathway in guiding visual attention and suggested that dyslexia in some patients may result from impaired temporal processing in phonological, visual, and motor domains. Steinman et al. (1998) and Facoetti et al. (2000) have also reiterated the association between magnocellular defects and impaired visuospatial attention in dyslexia.

Imaging studies reveal evidence for abnormalities in cerebral lateralization, in which normal asymmetries associated with brain specialization for language function have been reduced. The planum temporale is often abnormally symmetric in children with reading disorders; that is, subjects have an underdeveloped Broca's area relative to the homologous cortical area in the right hemisphere (Dalby et al. 1998; Haslam et al. 1981; Jernigan et al. 1991). Similarly, children with reading disorders have reduced blood flow in the left hemisphere (left temporoparietal cortex) under challenge conditions (Georgiewa et al. 1999; Lou et al. 1990; Rumsey et al. 1992; Simos et al. 2000) and may have reduced size of the left dorsolateral prefrontal cortex (Jernigan et al. 1991). Similarly, the cerebral blood flow pattern in the left angular gyrus of men with developmental dyslexia is not commensurate with blood flow in the extrastriate occipital and temporal lobes during single-word reading, suggesting a disconnection of the left angular gyrus in dyslexia (Horwitz et al. 1998).

Left hemisphere EEG activity is diminished relative to right-sided activity in children with reading disorders (Ackerman et al. 1998; Mattson et al. 1992), whereas right hemisphere activity is reduced in children with arithmetic disabilities (Mattson et al. 1992). Differences in the size of the perisylvian region may reflect a familial genetic factor (Plante 1991). Reduced lateralization of language centers is consistent with results from dichotic listening tasks (Morton 1994), which suggest either less efficient callosal transfer or right hemispheric processing of information. The size of the corpus callosum does not vary directly with the severity of learning disorders for all subjects. The corpus callosum is thicker in children with familial history of dysphasia/dyslexia, probably indicative of reduced cerebral dominance in this subgroup (Njiokiktjien et al. 1994). In contrast, children who have suffered from perinatal adverse events that could impair cognitive skills have a corpus callosum that is reduced in comparison with that of family members without learning impairment. Several mechanisms have been proposed to explain reductions in cerebral asymmetry, including reduced neuronal migration into the perisylvian region (Galaburda et al. 1985). At present these mechanisms require additional empirical support.

It is tempting to speculate that learning disorders affecting reading and spelling ability may stem from left-hemisphere abnormalities, whereas disorders of arithmetic ability and social-emotional competence may arise from right-hemisphere defects (Mattson et al. 1992; Semrud-Clikeman and Hynd 1990). Although this may be true in many instances, it is not necessarily so. Sandson et al. (1994) described two patients with social-emotional processing disorder, a developmental syndrome usually ascribed to right-hemisphere dysfunction. In these two patients, neurological examinations, EEG, and neuroimaging studies all revealed left-hemisphere dysfunction. Both patients were left-handed and had findings suggestive of anomalous language dominance. Sandson et al. (1994) proposed that early injury to the left hemisphere can result in functional reorganization of the right hemisphere, sparing language and motor skills at the expense of functions that the right hemisphere normally subserves.

Nongenetic environmental factors clearly influence the appearance of learning disabilities. Fall conception significantly increases the risk of developing reading and arithmetic disabilities as well as mental retardation, presumably as a result of increased risk of viral infections during early stages of brain development (Liederman and Flannery 1994). Early exposure to environmental toxins can also manifest as learning disorders (Pihl and Parkes 1977). Prenatal and postnatal exposure to low-level lead is significantly associated with learning deficits in girls but not in boys (Leviton et al. 1993). Alcohol is another powerful factor that can produce learning disabilities in the presence of normal intelligence (Streissguth et al. 1990). Geschwind and Galaburda (1985) have proposed that increased fetal testosterone modifies neuronal, immune, and neural crest development. Testosterone can also inhibit neuronal migration by altering the ability of the CNS to identify trophic markers (Schacter and Galaburda 1986). The Geschwind-Behan-Galaburda theory has been used to explain the relative superiority of males over females in spatial skills, the greater preponderance of learning disorders in males, the association between learning disorder and immune disorder, and giftedness of left-handed individuals in other non-language-based skills (Geschwind and Behan 1982; Geschwind and Galaburda 1985). More recent studies have found that this influential theory is only partially supported by empirical evidence and is not consistent with current data on the development of the neural crest (Bryden et al. 1994).

## Treatment

No systematic study supports any one educational intervention for the treatment of learning disorders. Primarily, mandated special education, provided in the least restrictive environment, is the major treatment for children with learning disorders. Special education is characterized by an individual educational plan and can include services provided as part of the usual classroom instruction or removal from the classroom part-time to designated "resource rooms." Specialized full-time class-

rooms, programs, or residential schools are usually reserved for those with severe learning disorders or concomitant psychiatric disorders. Alternative writing formats, skill building, and use of word processors can aid in the treatment of learning disorders, particularly disorders of written expression. Homework assignments for children with learning disabilities should emphasize simple, short tasks; careful monitoring and reinforcement by teachers; and parental involvement (Cooper and Nye 1994). Practical parent-based programs have become available (Jenson et al. 1994). In addition, efforts to increase the child's self-esteem are essential for successful treatment. Treatment should also include parental guidance to adjust expectations and to provide support and encouragement. No evidence supports the efficacy of medications, diet restrictions, or vitamin therapy. Similarly, sensory integration therapy has little empirical support as a beneficial intervention (Hoehn and Baumeister 1994; Humphries et al. 1992; Kaplan et al. 1993).

Two remediative treatments have demonstrated some promise. Possibly through improving binocular stability, monocular occlusion for 6 months while reading and writing improved reading ability in approximately half of dyslexic children whose primary problem involved gaze control (J. Stein and Fowler 1985). Through intensive exposure and training using acoustically modified speech, Tallal et al. (1996) demonstrated rapid gains in auditory comprehension in children with combined language-learning disorders. Tallal's group designed a computer program that altered recorded speech by prolonging the duration of the speech signal and enhancing fast speech elements in order to facilitate comprehension of speech elements that involve rapid frequency discrimination. Intensive training over a 4-week period with acoustically modified speech resulted in improved ability of children with language-learning impairment. Further studies of the remediative efficacy of these and other treatments are required.

## Seizure Disorders

Epilepsy is a recurrent paroxysmal disorder involving excessive neural firing. It is a relatively common disorder with an incidence of 0.5%. Onset most often occurs before adulthood. Epilepsy is estimated to affect 0.15% of preschoolers and 0.5% of school-age children and adolescents. Seizures are more prevalent in boys than in girls, and the incidence is higher in nonwhites (W.A. Hauser and Hesdorffer 1990). Seizure disorders can present at birth and can be associated with chromosomal or structural abnormalities or in utero infections. Epilepsy can develop as a consequence of meningitis, encephalitis, head trauma, exposure to environmental toxins such as lead, inborn errors of metabolism, arteriovenous malformations, abnormalities in brain development, and a host of idiopathic causes. Differential diagnosis is crucial. Many children suspected of having epilepsy have pseudoseizures of other paroxysmal nonepileptiform events (Andriola and Ettinger 1999; Rothner 1992). These include mitral valve prolapse, cardiac arrhythmias, sleep disorders (pavor nocturnus, cataplexy, somnambulism), migraine headaches, movement disorders (e.g., Tourette's syndrome, paroxysmal choreoathetosis), episodic dyscontrol, and panic disorder.

## Classification and Features

Epilepsies are broadly classified by the location of the seizure focus. Primarily, generalized seizures involve the simultaneous emergence of seizure activity in both hemispheres presumably from a subcortical focus. Partial seizures, in contrast, begin with discharge arising in a focal cortical area, though seizure activity can then spread (Dreifuss 1989). The major forms of generalized seizures are tonic-clonic seizures, absence seizures, myoclonic seizures, and infantile spasms. The major forms of partial seizures include simple seizures, complex partial seizures, and partial seizures secondarily generalized.

### Generalized Seizures

*Tonic-clonic seizures* are also known as *grand mal seizures*. Both hemispheres are simultaneously involved at the outset, producing immediate loss of consciousness, tonic extension, muscular stiffness, and inhibition of respiration. During the clonic phase of the attack, symmetrical jerking of all extremities occurs and is usually accompanied by oral and fecal incontinence (Rothner 1992). Typically tonic-clonic seizures last 2–5 minutes and are followed by somnolence and confusion. Severe headaches and muscle aches are also common in the postictal period.

*Absence seizures* are also known as *petit mal seizures*. They are characterized by abrupt onset of impaired consciousness that generally lasts for 10–20 seconds. During this period, children typically stare straight ahead and may flutter their eyelids, but there is usually an absence of movement. Posture is maintained and incontinence does not occur. Immediately after the seizure, consciousness is regained without postictal confusion. However, petit mal seizures can occur frequently, up to 20–30 times per day, taking a serious toll on attention, and can be brought on by stress and exercise. EEG reveals a highly characteristic 3-Hz spike-and-wave pattern (Rothner 1992). In some children, absence seizures remit during adolescence; in others, they may be replaced by tonic-clonic seizures.

*Infantile spasms* are relatively uncommon. They occur in association with mental retardation in children from ages 3 months to 1 year. The spasms involve a brief jackknife-like flexion or extension of arms and legs. The spasms occur in clusters, particularly around sleep-wake transitions. They are associated with characteristic hypsarrhythmic EEG, with a chaotic mixture of irregular high-voltage spike-and-wave discharge, multifocal sharp waves, and burst suppression. Most children with infantile spasms demonstrate moderate to profound mental retardation and will suffer from lifelong intractable seizures (Pellock 1998; Rothner 1992).

*Myoclonic seizures*, including atonic, akinetic, and tonic forms, usually emerge during the first 10 years of life and affect 0.1% of children. The combination of mental retardation, myoclonic seizures, and other seizure types is called *Lennox-Gastaut syndrome*. The myoclonic seizures are brief but occur frequently, and they are largely refractory to treatment. Ketogenic diet and corpus callostomy can be of benefit for some children (Pellock 1998; Rothner 1992).

*Juvenile myoclonic epilepsy* often emerges in adolescence and is a more benign and treatment-responsive condition. The seizures most frequently occur in the morning and take the form of myoclonic jerks or tonic-clonic convulsions. The EEG reveals characteristic generalized polyspikes. Children who develop this disorder were often healthy and free of neurological disturbance until the onset of the seizures. This condition persists throughout life but usually responds well to treatment with sodium valproate (Pellock 1998; Rothner 1992).

### Partial Seizures

*Simple partial seizures* may be motor or sensory. A simple partial motor seizure consists of recurrent clonic movements of one part of the body without loss of consciousness. Sometimes motor activity can spread ipsilaterally (jacksonian march) or even spread to the contralateral hemisphere, resulting in a secondarily generalized tonic-clonic seizure. Partial sensory seizures consist of paresthesias or pain referred to a single part of the body. They also can spread. In general, partial seizures last 1–2 minutes and are not associated with loss of consciousness unless secondarily generalized (Rothner 1992).

*Rolandic epilepsy* is a benign, inherited focal epileptic disorder of childhood that is the most common form of focal seizure seen in children less than 15 years old

(Rothner 1992). These seizures are characterized by emergence of sharp waves in the central temporal region and may or may not be accompanied by either seizure or neurological deficits. Children often report an aura around the mouth preceding the seizure, which is followed by the jerking of the mouth and face before spreading to the rest of the body. Children retain consciousness and do not have postictal confusion. The seizure lasts between 30 seconds and 3 minutes and usually occurs during sleep. Prognosis for spontaneous remission is excellent, and treatment is rarely required (Rothner 1992).

*Complex partial seizures*, also known as psychomotor or temporal lobe seizures, are distinguished from other partial seizures by alterations in consciousness. Auras such as unpleasant odors, tastes, or sensations frequently precede the seizure. The seizure may be characterized by staring, altered consciousness, and eye-blinking with maintenance of balance. Approximately 80% of patients with complex partial seizures engage in simple, repetitive, and purposeless automatism, which can include swallowing, kissing, lip-smacking, fumbling, scratching, or rubbing movements. Rarely, special sensory phenomenon can occur that can include visual distortions or hallucinations, auditory hallucinations, dreamlike or dissociative states, and abnormal body sensations (Kaufman 1985). The seizures last about 2 minutes and are often followed by confusion, drowsiness, and amnesia for the events. The EEG often shows sharp waves or spikes from the temporal region (Rothner 1992). Partial complex seizure attacks occur far less frequently than absence spells.

## Psychiatric Consequences of Epilepsy

Bear and Fedio (1977) proposed that patients with temporal lobe epilepsy had distinctive personality aberrations. Many were hyposexual, humorless, circumstantial, overly metaphysical, hyperreligious, hypergraphic, and interpersonally viscous. It was also proposed that right-sided foci predisposed a patient to anger, sadness, and elation, whereas left-sided foci led to ruminative and intellectual tendencies. More recent studies, however, have cast doubt on these theories (Kaufman 1985; Rodin and Schmalz 1984).

An association exists between childhood epilepsy and behavioral, academic, and cognitive problems (Dunn and Austin 1999; Metz-Lutz et al. 1999). Children with epilepsy demonstrate more behavioral problems and psychiatric dysfunction than those in the general population and have more physical deformities or other chronic illness such as diabetes mellitus or asthma. In addition, several cognitive difficulties have been associated with epi-

lepsy, including academic underachievement and greater academic difficulties than would be expected from IQ test scores (Dunn and Austin 1999). One prospective study (Metz-Lutz et al. 1999) suggests that, in addition to cognitive deficits, children with benign focal epilepsy demonstrate abnormalities in a attention, response organization, and fine motor skills.

Old literature suggests that psychosis can emerge in patients with temporal lobe epilepsy. The seizure disorder most often emerges in childhood (5–10 years of age), whereas the psychosis is generally delayed in onset until about age 30. Left-handed patients with left-sided seizure foci were believed to be the most susceptible to psychosis (Kaufman 1985; Perez and Trimble 1980). Interestingly, we have found that childhood abuse was associated with an increased incidence of left-hemisphere EEG abnormalities (Ito et al. 1993) and abnormal left but not right EEG coherence, suggesting decreased left cortical differentiation (Teicher et al. 1997). Davies (1979) previously reported that childhood incest was associated with a high incidence of abnormal EEGs and seizure disorder in 36% of survivors. It is plausible that the stress of childhood trauma can affect aspects of brain development, thereby increasing the risk for emergence of seizure. Moreover, this particular etiology can be associated with development of serious psychopathology, including dissociation and perception of internal voices that can be mistaken for psychosis.

An association is well established between epilepsy and high incidence of criminality. Incarcerated men have a fourfold increased incidence of epilepsy compared with the general population (Kaufman 1985). It is likely that both epilepsy and criminality result from common causes such as head trauma and low socioeconomic status. As suggested above, a common association may exist among childhood abuse, EEG abnormalities, and criminal behavior. In a study of 14 juvenile murderers condemned to death, 12 had a history of brutal physical abuse and 5 had been sodomized by relatives (D.O. Lewis et al. 1988). EEG abnormalities and seizure disorders were common in this group (D.O. Lewis et al. 1988). Sexual trauma has often been identified in the life histories of sex offenders (Groth 1979; Seghorn et al. 1987). Thus, early abuse can lead to a vicious cycle of intergenerational transmission and perpetuation associated with neuropsychiatric sequelae.

Finally, there is a prominent association between epilepsy, suicidality, and self-destructive behavior. One of the earliest pioneering studies on the physiological determinants of suicide reported a strong positive association between paroxysmal EEG disturbances and suicidal ideation, attempts, and assaultive-destructive behavior

(Struve et al. 1972). It has also been reported that the risk of completed suicide is four to five times greater in individuals with epilepsy than among patients without epilepsy and that this risk may be 25-fold greater in patients with temporal lobe epilepsy (Barraclough 1981; Mathews and Barabas 1981). As many as one-third of all patients with epilepsy have attempted suicide at some point in their life (Delay et al. 1957; Jensen 1975). This risk is far greater for patients with epilepsy than for patients with other medical disorders producing comparable degrees of handicap or disability (Mendez et al. 1986). Mendez et al. (1989) provided data suggesting that this risk can be related to interictal psychopathological changes, particularly the high prevalence of borderline personality disorder. We have found that children with early abuse and abnormal EEGs have a marked increase in self-destructive behavior (Teicher et al. 1996a) and that abused children's ratings of suicidal ideation and interictal seizure symptomatology correlate very strongly (Teicher et al., unpublished observations, September 1996). Brent et al. (1987) examined 15 children with epilepsy treated with phenobarbital and 24 children with epilepsy treated with carbamazepine. The groups were similar across a wide range of demographic, seizure-related, familial, and environmental factors. Patients treated with phenobarbital had a much higher prevalence of major depression (40% versus 4%, $P = 0.02$) and a much greater prevalence of suicidal ideation (47% versus 4%, $P = 0.005$). It is unclear whether phenobarbital produced these psychiatric disturbances or failed to alleviate them. However, the implications for treatment are clear.

## Treatment

Tonic-clonic seizures are often responsive to valproic acid, phenytoin, carbamazepine, and phenobarbital. Phenobarbital, and its associated congener primidone, are associated with hyperactivity, fussiness, lethargy, disturbed sleep, irritability, depression, and cognitive disturbance in children (Rothner 1992). They should not be used as drugs of first choice in the pediatric population. Chronic administration of phenytoin can lead to gingival hyperplasia and hirsutism. Phenytoin causes behavioral problems less frequently than phenobarbital but can impair attention and coordination and produce dizziness, ataxia, and diplopia. Carbamazepine is structurally similar to tricyclic antidepressants but lacks prominent effects on monoamine reuptake. Common side effects include diplopia, dizziness, drowsiness, and transient leukopenia. Carbamazepine can also impair neuropsychological performance but is usually less problematic than

phenobarbital or phenytoin (Rothner 1992). Rarely, aplastic anemia and hepatotoxicity can occur. Sodium valproate is often the most tolerated anticonvulsant for children and adolescents. Common side effects include gastrointestinal distress and thinning of the hair. Rare cases of fetal hepatotoxicity have occurred, though these cases are almost entirely limited to infants and young children, and the majority have followed combination chemotherapy with other drugs that induce hepatic microsomal enzymes, which can foster buildup of a toxic valproate metabolite. Pancreatitis is another rare complication. Occasionally drowsiness may arise, which can be related to elevated ammonia levels.

Absence seizures are treated with ethosuximide or valproic acid. Although ethosuximide is useful in the treatment of absence seizures, it has no effect against possible coexisting major motor seizures. Major side effects include nausea, vomiting, and anorexia. Cognitive and behavioral side effects are uncommon.

Infantile spasms and myoclonic seizures of childhood are often treatment refractory. Potentially useful medications include adrenocorticotropic hormone, valproic acid, and benzodiazepines. Juvenile myoclonic epilepsy often responds favorably to valproic acid. Uncomplicated partial seizures are treated with carbamazepine, phenytoin, or phenobarbital. Neurosurgery to remove an underlying lesion may be the treatment of choice depending on the region affected (Wyllie et al. 1989). Partial complex seizures are also treated with carbamazepine, phenytoin, or phenobarbital. Acetazolamide can also have efficacy with seizures that occur premenstrually. Many cases of partial complex seizure fail to fully respond to monotherapy and may require combination treatment.

Newer anticonvulsants include felbamate, gabapentin, and lamotrigine (Ben-Menachem 2000). Felbamate is not a first-line anticonvulsant, and it is used only in those patients who have not responded to more conventional drugs and whose seizures are so severe as to warrant treatment with a drug that has a markedly elevated risk of aplastic anemia and hepatic failure. In children, the main indication are multiple seizures of Lennox-Gestaut syndrome (Schmidt and Bourgeois 2000). Gabapentin and lamotrigine are indicated for adjunctive therapy of partial seizures with and without generalization. This represents a new approach to seizure management. The old rule was to pursue monopharmacy even to extreme doses to avoid polypharmacy, with the belief that multiple anticonvulsants would produce supra-additive toxicity. Controlled trials of gabapentin and lamotrigine indicate that they can potentiate anticonvulsant efficacy with little increase in side effects. The most common side effects of gabapentin include somnolence ataxia, fatigue, and nausea. Lamotrigine is sometimes associated with development of a rash that can presage serious dermatological consequences. Common side effects include dizziness, ataxia, diplopia, blurred vision, and nausea.

Duration of treatment needs to be individualized. After a child has been free of seizures for 2–5 years, it may be possible to discontinue seizure medications. Discontinuation is less likely to succeed if the child has had a persistently abnormal EEG; known structural lesion; mental retardation; focal, complex partial seizures; or multiple seizure types. Medications should be withdrawn slowly, generally one medication at a time (Rothner 1992).

## Trauma, Infections, and Stress

The developing brain is highly susceptible to adverse environmental factors. In the final section, we summarize recent research on the neuropsychiatric consequences of traumatic brain injury, congenital human immunodeficiency virus (HIV) infection, and physical and sexual abuse during childhood. These are widespread and largely preventable environmental insults that can produce severe neuropsychiatric sequelae.

### Traumatic Brain Injury

The leading cause of disability in children between birth and 19 years of age is injury. Data from the National Pediatric Trauma Registry (1993) indicate that more than 25% of children injured and admitted for hospital care receive a diagnosis of head injury. Traumatic brain injury is generally classified as penetrating or closed. After discharge from the hospital, a significant number of children continue to present with potentially detrimental psychiatric sequelae (Russo and Navalta 1995). Outcome is most strongly related to the severity of brain injury, although posttraumatic amnesia, length of coma, presence of brain-stem injury, seizures, and increased intracranial pressure also affect prognosis (Beers 1992; Lieh-Lai et al. 1992). Intelligence, fine motor skills, sensorimotor function, problem-solving ability, memory, adaptive function, attention, and language processing can all be affected (for a review, see Fletcher and Levin 1988). In addition, the presence of posttraumatic behavioral disorders compounds these problems (Michaud et al. 1993). Aggression, poor anger control, hyperactivity, and deficient social skills are typical behavioral symptoms (Asarnow et al. 1991). The emergence of these symptoms depends on the severity (G. Brown et al. 1981) and location of the injury (Sollee and Kindlon 1987). The symp-

toms are exacerbated by premorbid factors, including substance abuse, psychiatric disability, and dysfunctional family relations (Rivara et al. 1993).

The remarkable capacity of the developing brain to adapt to certain congenital anomalies and injuries has led many to believe that children will invariably show greater recovery than adults to traumatic brain injury (Rosner 1974). Others have hypothesized that children can be more vulnerable than adults. The relationship between age of injury and extent of disability is complex. Before puberty a high density of synaptic connections allows for considerable adaptive plasticity, which is most evident in the capacity to develop language after severe left-hemisphere injury. However, there are also sensitive and critical periods for establishment of connections and synaptic relations, and if these opportunities are lost, enduring consequences can result. A striking example of a critical period in neural development is the formation of ocular dominance columns. Eye muscle dysfunction that would produce only double vision in adulthood causes amblyopia anopsia in childhood, in which vision is suppressed and permanently lost in the weaker eye. Hence, losses during childhood can affect important maturational events and can have more severe consequences. Children with brain injury can also require rehabilitation and special education services as well as neurological and psychiatric treatment.

Max and colleagues (Max and Dunisch 1997; Max et al. 1997a, 1997b, 1997c, 1998a, 1998b, 1998c, 1998d) have published extensively on the psychiatric consequences of head trauma. A retrospective analysis revealed that 5.6% of 1,333 consecutive patients presenting to a child psychiatry outpatient clinic had a definite history of traumatic brain injury and that children with such a history were clinically indistinguishable from children without such a history (Max and Dunisch 1997). In a large prospective study, 50 subjects were evaluated upon hospitalization for traumatic brain injury and reassessed upon follow-up at 3, 6, 12, and 24 months (Max et al. 1997a, 1997b, 1997c). The most consistently significant factors associated with the development of subsequent psychiatric disorders were increased severity of injury, family psychiatric history, and family dysfunction. Posttraumatic psychiatric disorders included organic personality syndrome, major depression, attention-deficit/hyperactivity disorder, oppositional defiant disorder, PTSD, simple phobia, separation anxiety disorder, OCD, adjustment disorder, mania, hypomania, and marijuana dependence. Some psychiatric sequelae were clinically apparent by 3 months after injury.

Further analysis of individual disorders revealed mixed results. The change in attention-deficit/hyperactivity symptomatology after brain injury was directly and proportionally related to the severity of brain injury, suggesting a "dose-response" relationship (Max et al. 1998a). Development of oppositional symptomatology in the first year after injury was strongly associated with psychosocial factors, whereas its persistence in the second year was more significantly related to severity of brain injury (Max et al. 1998b). Sixty-eight percent of subjects experienced at least one PTSD symptom in the first 3 months, decreasing to 12% at 2 years. Only 4% of subjects met criteria for PTSD at any point in the study (Max et al. 1998c). Overall, severe traumatic brain injury is significantly associated with a greater incidence of psychiatric disorders (63%) compared to mild injury (21%) and orthopedic injury (4%) (Max et al. 1998d). Psychosocial intervention and family support may contribute to the care of brain-injured patients throughout the first 2 years after injury (Kinsella et al. 1999; Max et al. 1997c), although their therapeutic efficacy remains to be established.

## Neuropsychiatric Features of HIV-1 Infection in Children and Young Adults

Approximately 1.5 million individuals in the United States are infected with HIV-1, and 20%–30% can eventually develop dementia. The incidence in parts of Asia and Africa is substantially higher. In the United States and in Europe, the incidence of childhood HIV infection has reportedly plateaued after a period of growth (Dal Maso et al. 1999). According to data published in 1995 by the Centers for Disease Control and Prevention (CDC), 14,920 HIV-infected infants were born in the United States between 1978 and 1993. In 1999, 2,026 new cases of pediatric HIV were reported to the CDC (Centers for Disease Control and Prevention 1999), although this statistic is an underestimate because cases were obtained only from states that report HIV infections. HIV-1 has become the most frequent cause of dementia in young people (Janssen et al. 1992). HIV-1 infection also results in encephalopathy that can affect between 30% and 60% of children with acquired immunodeficiency syndrome (AIDS) (Simpson 1999). Infants are more susceptible to encephalopathy compared with children and adults with AIDS (Tardieu et al. 2000). Infants with perinatally acquired AIDS have a 4% risk of developing encephalopathy by 12 months of age, making HIV encephalopathy a common condition in this population (Lobato et al. 1995).

The American Academy of Neurology has defined the clinical features of HIV-1 dementia, or AIDS dementia complex (ADC), as cognitive impairment, motor skill impairment, and behavioral changes (Janssen et al. 1991). ADC presents as a subcortical dementia in which primary language abnormalities and seizures are uncommon (Navia et al. 1986). People with ADC usually have rapid progression of symptoms, with a mean survival time of approximately 6 months (McArthur 1987). Progressive neurological deficits do not occur during the latent phases of HIV-1 infection but rather occur after the onset of severe immunodeficiency (McArthur 1987; McArthur et al. 1989). McArthur et al. (1993) estimated that 20%–30% of all individuals with AIDS will eventually develop dementia, though this may change with new treatments.

HIV-1 infection of the CNS results in neurological abnormalities in 40%–90% of children and can be associated with neurological complications such as stroke, seizure, vasculitis, vasculopathy, or myelopathy (Mintz 1996; Pontrelli et al. 1999). A bimodal distribution appears to exist in children with congenital HIV-1 infection: children who present with HIV-1 symptoms by 4 months of age and children who present with symptoms by 6 years of age (Auger et al. 1988). Three types of clinical presentations are found in children with HIV-1 infection: children with encephalopathy, children with neuropsychological dysfunction, and children without evidence of neuropsychological impairment (Working Group of the American Academy of Neurology AIDS Task Force 1991). Children with encephalopathy have clinical findings that include microcephaly, spastic diparesis or quadriparesis, extrapyramidal signs, and ataxia. Children with encephalopathy can have a clinical course characterized by a progressive subacute loss of previously acquired motor and language milestones. Other children with encephalopathy have neurological plateaus during which they neither acquire nor lose motor or cognitive milestones. In contrast, children with neuropsychological deficits, but without encephalopathy, can exhibit diminished speech production and difficulties with articulation (Epstein et al. 1985; Ultmann et al. 1987). Receptive language skills are typically less affected (Wolters et al. 1995). Cognitive deficits can manifest in older children as attention deficits (Cohen et al. 1991). Interestingly, adults with HIV-1–associated dementia appear to benefit from methylphenidate treatment (Fernandez et al. 1988). No large-scale study has established whether children show similar benefits. Another important neuropsychological consequence of HIV-1 is impaired social interactions (Ultmann et al. 1987). Children often become withdrawn and apathetic. Those with progressive encephalopathy can have features similar to autism, including flat affect, mutism, and minimal interest in their environment. The association of

AIDS with poverty, poor social support, and limited resources compounds the problem (Starace et al. 1998; Zierler et al. 2000).

In contrast to those in adults, the neurological abnormalities seen in children are largely a result of a primary HIV-1 encephalopathy. In one series, only 5% of children had opportunistic infections of their CNS. The pathological hallmarks of HIV-1 encephalopathy include HIV-1–infected macrophages and multinucleated giant cells, astrogliosis, microglial activation, and myelin pallor. Neuronal loss in discrete areas of the retina, neocortex, and subcortical brain (Scarmato et al. 1996), as well as loss of synaptic density and vacuolation of dendritic spines (Everall et al. 1991; Ketzler et al. 1990; Sharer 1992; Sharer et al. 1986; Tenhula et al. 1992; Wiley et al. 1986) takes place.

This disease complex is most striking in infected children (Sharer 1992). A direct relationship between the stage of HIV-1 infection, neuroimaging abnormalities, and neurobehavioral measures in HIV-infected children has been reported (Brouwers et al. 1995). MRS reveals reduced $N$-acetyl aspartate/creatine ratios in childhood AIDS encephalopathy and includes the basal ganglia (Lu et al. 1996; Pavlakis et al. 1995, 1998; Salvan et al. 1998). HIV-1 RNA has been found to be elevated in the CSF independently of plasma RNA levels in AIDS subjects with cognitive impairment (Brew et al. 1997; Ellis et al. 1997). Neurons do not appear to be productively affected by HIV-1 (Epstein and Gendelman 1993; Sharer et al. 1996), even though substantial loss of large neurons occurs through apoptosis (Fischer et al. 1999; Gelbard et al. 1995). Preclinical studies demonstrate that infected brain macrophages and microglia produce HIV-1 gene products and soluble neurotoxins (Epstein and Gendelman 1993) and that apoptotic neurons cluster in close proximity to these HIV-1–infected cells (Gelbard et al. 1995). These findings suggest that neurological dysfunction can result from the production of HIV-1–associated neurotoxins by macrophages or microglia that activate pathways for neuronal apoptosis (Dewhurst et al. 1996; Epstein and Gelbard 1999; Gelbard and Epstein 1995; James et al. 1999).

The cascade of events leading from HIV-1–infected macrophages and microglia to neuronal apoptosis and neurological dysfunction remains unclear. Recent studies suggest the involvement of the HIV-1 regulatory protein Tat as a neurotoxic activator of apoptosis (Bonwetsch et al. 1999; Maggirwar et al. 1999; New et al. 1997, 1998). Alternatively, HIV-1 gene products such as *Tat* can induced secretion of human tumor necrosis factor-$\alpha$ and other inflammatory products (New et al. 1998) that cause apoptosis (Perry et al. 1998; Talley et al. 1995).

Numerous additional theories have also been proposed. Human herpesvirus-6 has become a focus of attention. Previously, human herpesvirus-6 was considered to be a benign commensal organism. It has now been found to be neuroinvasive, associated with progressive multifocal leukoencephalopathy and multiple sclerosis and is potentially involved in the pathogenesis of HIV encephalopathy (Blumberg et al. 2000; Saito et al. 1995). Novel treatment strategies may emerge from the elucidation of the mechanism of HIV-1 apoptosis (Gelbard et al. 1997).

Therapeutic advances have extended the survival of HIV-infected children past 5 years of age for more than 65% of cases (L. K. Brown et al. 2000). Prevention of vertical transmission has the most potential in reducing the neuropsychiatric sequelae of HIV, given the greater vulnerability of the developing brain before birth. Antiretroviral treatment of HIV-infected women during pregnancy and labor may decrease vertical transmission by 50% (Giaquinto et al. 1998). Zidovudine has been the most thoroughly investigated antiretroviral therapy for children with HIV encephalopathy (Bakashi et al. 1997; Brady et al. 1996; Sei et al. 1996). Administration of zidovudine has been associated with improved neuropsychological functioning (Simpson 1999) and reductions in the typically elevated levels of HIV-1 RNA in CSF (Sei et al. 1996). Also, antiretroviral therapies have been associated with reversal of reduced $N$-acetyl aspartate/creatine ratios on MRS, suggesting some recovery in neuronal arborization (Pavlakis et al. 1998). Ritonavir has also produced neurodevelopmental recovery (Tepper et al. 1998). The addition of zalcitabine to zidovudine in stable pediatric patients can be helpful (Bakashi et al. 1997).

## Neuropsychiatric Consequences of Childhood Abuse

Physical or sexual traumatization during childhood can contribute to the development of a spectrum of psychiatric disorders. Early traumatization can be a risk factor in dissociative identity disorder (Wilbur 1984), refractory psychosis (Beck and van der Kolk 1987), borderline personality disorder (Herman et al. 1989; Stone 1981), somatoform disorder (Krystal 1978), and panic disorder (Faravelli et al. 1985). Childhood physical abuse can also sensitize patients to the development of PTSD (Bremner et al. 1993). Animal studies clearly suggest that early deprivation or stress can result in neurobiological abnormalities (Hofer 1975; Hubel 1978; Teicher 1989). However, little evidence for this has been shown in humans (van der Kolk and Greenberg 1987). Green et al. (1981; Green 1983) found that many abused children had evidence of neurological damage and nonspecific EEG abnormalities, even in the absence of apparent or reported head injury. Childhood incest has been associated with reports of abnormal EEG activity. Davies (1979) found in a sample of 22 patients involved as a child or as the younger member of an incestuous relationship that 77% had abnormal EEGs, and 36% had clinical seizures. Davies suggested that these children were more at risk for being sexually abused by family members because of their neurological handicap. Teicher and colleagues (Ito et al. 1993, 1998; Schiffer et al. 1995; Teicher 1989; Teicher et al. 1993, 1994, 1997) hypothesized that early traumatic experience, in the form of childhood abuse, could affect the development of the cerebral cortex and limbic system. Using a scale to evaluate the frequency of symptoms suggestive of temporal lobe epilepsy, they found prominent effects of early abuse (Teicher et al. 1993). Physical abuse was associated with a 38% increase, sexual abuse with a 49% increase, and combined abuse with a 113% increase in symptom scores. Physical or sexual abuse alone were associated with elevated scores only if the abuse occurred before age 18. A blind chart review examined the association between abuse history and neurological abnormalities in 115 consecutive patients admitted to a child and adolescent psychiatric inpatient unit (Ito et al. 1993). Abused children had a greater incidence of electrophysiological abnormalities compared with that in nonabused patients (54.4% versus 26.9%). Interestingly, abused and nonabused patients differed only in the prevalence of left-hemisphere abnormalities. Neuropsychological testing also indicated that left hemisphere deficits were 6.7-fold more prevalent than right-hemisphere deficits in the abused group, whereas this ratio was three-fold less in nonabused patients.

Schiffer et al. (1995) used probe auditory–evoked potentials as an indirect measure of auditory cortex activity. They compared 10 unmedicated adults, with no currently active psychopathology, who grew up in psychologically abusive families, to 10 control subjects from nonabusive families. Probe-evoked potentials were measured while subjects focused on a neutral work-related memory or a distressing childhood memory. In comparison to control subjects, adults from psychologically abusive families had highly lateralized evoked potential patterns. During the neutral memory task, evoked potentials were strongly suppressed over the left cortex in the abused group (indicative of enhanced left cortex cognitive activity), and this pattern switched to right cortical suppression during recall of the distressing memory. Control subjects showed no significant degree of laterality or switch between these two tasks, even though they had equally strong emotional reactions. These findings sug-

gest that the two hemispheres may function more autonomously in patients with childhood abuse.

To more precisely evaluate the effects of abuse on EEG asymmetry and cortical development, a quantitative EEG study was conducted (Ito et al. 1998; Teicher et al. 1997). Fifteen child and adolescent inpatients with a history of documented intense abuse were recruited, as were 15 control subjects. Artifact-free awake EEGs were analyzed to compare the power of paired right- and left-hemisphere leads in the alpha frequency band and to calculate global hemispheric and regional EEG coherence. (Coherence is a measure of cortical interconnectivity and displays a prominent developmental sequence that parallels cortical maturation.) Abused children had higher overall levels of left-hemisphere coherence and a reversed hemispheric asymmetry. Further, left-hemisphere coherence decayed more slowly across electrode distance in abused children. These findings strongly suggest that increased left-hemisphere coherence in abused patients is a consequence of deficient left-cortical differentiation and development.

Evidence for left hemisphere disturbance was also found in MRI studies. M. B. Stein et al. (1997) and Bremner et al. (1997) found evidence for reduced left hippocampal volume in adults with a history of childhood abuse and current symptoms of PTSD. Bremner et al. (1997) compared MRI scans of 17 adults with physical or sexual abuse and PTSD with scans of 17 matched subjects with no abuse history or PTSD. The left hippocampus was 12% smaller in the abused group than that in the nonabused adults. M. B. Stein et al. (1997) measured hippocampal volume in 21 women with childhood sexual abuse. Fifteen patients had current PTSD and 15 had dissociative disorder. There was a significant reduction in left hippocampal size, which also correlated inversely with dissociative symptoms.

Because childhood abuse appeared to be associated with altered left hemisphere development and diminished right/left hippocampal development, we examined the corpus callosum as the major fiber tract connecting the hemispheres. MRI scans were obtained from 51 child psychiatric patients and 97 carefully screened control subjects from the National Institute of Mental Health. We found that there was a major reduction in the middle portions of the corpus callosum in hospitalized boys with a history of abuse or neglect. No differences emerged between psychiatrically healthy control subjects and hospitalized boys with psychiatric illness but no history of maltreatment (Teicher et al. 1997). Stepwise regression analysis showed that childhood neglect was the determining factor for corpus callosum shrinkage in boys (Teicher et al. 2000a). The corpus callosum of girls was less affected, and in these subjects sexual abuse appeared to be the major decisive factor. De Billis (1999) has also measured the corpus callosum in children with a history of abuse and PTSD. They also found that the midportion of the corpus callosum was markedly diminished in size, and they found that boys were more affected than girls. Sanchez et al. (1998) also reported that differential rearing experiences affected the development of the corpus callosum and cognitive function of male Rhesus monkeys, emphasizing the importance of the environment.

More recently we used fMRI with $T_2$ relaxometry as an indirect measure of blood flow into the cerebellar vermis. The vermis is an interesting target for stress-mediated effects because it has a protracted ontogeny and high density of glucocorticoid receptors. Previous work by Harlow on the effects of isolation rearing in primates showed that the adverse effects were partially ameliorated by rocking and swinging, which provides robust sensory stimulation of the vermis. We found that $T_2$ relaxation time was strongly affected by degree of irritability on the limbic system checklist in both adults with a history of abuse and in control subjects without an abuse history. However, control subjects had lower adjusted $T_2$ relaxation time measures, suggesting hypoperfusion of the vermis in abused subjects (C.M. Anderson et al. 1999).

It should be noted that these studies are correlational and do not prove causation. They are, however, consistent with animal studies that indicate that early experience and stress affect brain development including laterality and neurotransmitter levels (Denenberg and Yutzey 1985; Plotsky and Meaney 1993). These studies do suggest that early experience can be a powerful chisel that shapes the developing brain in enduring ways and can be associated with the emergence of neuropsychiatric consequences (Teicher 2000).

## Conclusions

As noted at the outset of this chapter, brain development is a plastic process programmed by genes and sculpted by experience. Anomalous experience can exert persisting deleterious effects. In contrast, research in autism (Lovaas 1987; McEachin et al. 1993) and in communicative disorders (Merzenich et al. 1996) suggests that early directed interventions can have the capacity to correct developmental disabilities. Increased understanding of the processes regulating brain development may eventually lead to new strategies that not only treat but also prevent these disorders.

## References

Abromowicz M (ed): Sudden death in children treated with a tricyclic antidepressant. Med Lett Drugs Ther 32(819):53, 1990

Ackerman PT, McPherson WB, Oglesby DM, et al: EEG power spectra of adolescent poor readers. J Learn Disabil 31:83–90, 1998

Akefeldt A, Ekman R, Gillberg C, et al: Cerebrospinal fluid monoamines in Prader-Willi syndrome. Biol Psychiatry 44 (12):1321–1328, 1998

Akefeldt A, Gillberg C: Behavior and personality characteristics of children and young adults with Prader-Willi syndrome: a controlled study. J Am Acad Child Adolesc Psychiatry 38:761–769, 1999

American Academy of Child and Adolescent Psychiatry: Practice parameters for the assessment and treatment of children and adolescents with language and learning disorders. J Am Acad Child Adolesc Psychiatry 37 (10 suppl):46S–62S, 1998

American Psychiatric Association: Diagnostic and Statistical Manual of Mental Disorders, 3rd Edition. Washington, DC, American Psychiatric Association, 1980

American Psychiatric Association: Diagnostic and Statistical Manual of Mental Disorders, 3rd Edition, Revised. Washington, DC, American Psychiatric Association, 1987

American Psychiatric Association: Diagnostic and Statistical Manual of Mental Disorders, 4th Edition. Washington, DC, American Psychiatric Association, 1994

American Psychiatric Association: Diagnostic and Statistical Manual of Mental Disorders, 4th Edition, Text Revision. Washington, DC, American Psychiatric Association, 2000

Amir RE, Van den Veyver IB, Wan M, et al: Rett syndrome is caused by mutations in X-linked MECP2, encoding methyl-CpG-binding protein 2. Nat Genet 23:185–189, 1999

Andersen SL, Teicher MH: Sex differences in dopamine receptors and their relevance to ADHD. Neurosci Biobehav Rev 24:137–141, 2000

Andersen SL, Rutstein M, Benzo J, et al: Sex differences in brain development: dopamine receptor overproduction and elimination. Neuroreport 8:1495–1498, 1997

Andersen SL, Thomphson AP, Rutstein M, et al: Dopamine receptor pruning in prefrontal cortex during the periadolescent period in rats. Synapse 37:167–169, 2000

Anderson CM, Polcari AM, McGreenery CE, et al: Childhood abuse: Limbic System Checklist–33 and cerebellar vermis blood flow (NR384), in 1999 New Research Program and Abstracts, American Psychiatric Association 152nd Annual Meeting, Washington, DC, May 15–20, 1999. Washington, DC, American Psychiatric Association, 1999, p 171

Anderson GM, Pollak ES, Chatterjee D, et al: Postmortem analyses of brain monoamine and amino acids in Tourette's syndrome: a preliminary study of subcortical regions. Arch Gen Psychiatry 49:584–586, 1992

Anderson JC, Williams S, McGee R, et al: DSM-III disorders in preadolescent children: prevalence in a large sample from the general population. Arch Gen Psychiatry 44:69–76, 1987

Andreasen NC, O'Leary DS, Cizadlo T, et al: Schizophrenia and cognitive dysmetria: a positron-emission tomography study of dysfunctional prefrontal-thalamic-cerebellar circuitry. Proc Natl Acad Sci U S A 93:9985–9990, 1996

Andriola MR, Ettinger AB: Pseudoseizures and other nonepileptic paroxysmal disorders in children and adolescents. Neurology 53 (5 suppl 2):S89–95, 1999

Ariano MA, Wang J, Noblett KL, et al: Cellular distribution of the rat D4 dopamine receptor protein in the CNS using anti-receptor antisera. Brain Res 752:26–34, 1997

Armstrong DD, Dunn K, Antalffy B: Decreased dendritic branching in frontal, motor and limbic cortex in Rett syndrome compared with trisomy 21. J Neuropathol Exp Neurol 57:1013–1017, 1998

Arnsten AFT, Steere JC, Hunt RD: The contribution of noradrenergic mechanisms to prefrontal cortex cognitive function: potential significance for attention-deficit hyperactivity disorder. Arch Gen Psychiatry 53:448–455, 1996

Asarnow RF, Saltz P, Light R, et al: Behavioral problems and adaptive functioning in children with mild and severe closed head injury. J Pediatr Psychol 16:543–555, 1991

Asghari V, Sanyal S, Vuchwaldt S, et al: Modulation of intracellular cyclic AMP levels by different human D4 receptor variants. J Neurochem 65:1157–1165, 1995

Aston-Jones G, Bloom FE: Norepinephrine-containing locus coeruleus neurons in behaving rats exhibit pronounced responses to non-noxious environmental stimuli. J Neurosci 1:887–900, 1981

Auger I, Thomas P, De Gruttola V, et al: Incubation periods for paediatric AIDS patients. Nature 336:575–577, 1988

August GJ, Stewart MA, Tsai L: The incidence of cognitive disabilities in the siblings of autistic children. Br J Psychiatry 138:416–422, 1981

August GJ, Stewart MA, Holmes CS: A four-year follow-up of hyperactive boys with and without conduct disorder. Br J Psychiatry 143:192–198, 1983

Bailey A, Le Couteur A, Gottesman I, et al: Autism as a strongly genetic disorder: evidence from a British twin study. Psychol Med 25:63–77, 1995

Bailey A, Luthert P, Dean A, et al: A clinicopathological study of autism. Brain 121:889–905, 1998

Bakashi SS, Britto P, Capparelli E, et al: Evaluation of pharmacokinetics, safety, tolerance, and activity of combination of zalcitabine and zidovudine in stable, zidovudine-treated pediatric patients with human immunodeficiency virus infection. J Infect Dis 175:1039–1050, 1997

Barkley RA: Defiant Children: A Clinician's Manual for Parent Training. New York, Guilford, 1987

Barkley RA: A critique of current diagnostic criteria for attention deficit hyperactivity disorder: clinical and research implications. J Dev Behav Pediatr 11:343–352, 1990

Barkley RA, Guevremont DC, Anastopoulos AD, et al: A comparison of three family therapy programs for treating family conflicts in adolescents with attention-deficit hyperactivity disorder. J Consult Clin Psychol 60:450–462, 1992

Barks JD, Silverstein FS, Sims K, et al: Glutamate recognition sites in human fetal brain. Neurosci Lett 84:131–136, 1988

Baron-Cohen S: Perceptual role-taking and protodeclarative pointing in autism. British Journal of Developmental Psychology 7:113–127, 1989

Barr CL, Wigg KG, Bloom S, et al: Further evidence from haplotype analysis for linkage of the dopamine D4 receptor gene and attention-deficit hyperactivity disorder. Am J Med Genet 96:262–267, 2000

Barraclough B: Suicide and epilepsy, in Epilepsy and Psychiatry. Edited by Reynolds E, Trimble MR. New York, Churchill Livingstone, 1981, pp 72–76

Barrickman L, Noyes R, Kuperman S, et al: Treatment of ADHD with fluoxetine: a preliminary trial. J Am Acad Child Adolesc Psychiatry 30:762–767, 1991

Barrickman LL, Perry PJ, Allen AJ, et al: Bupropion versus methylphenidate in the treatment of attention-deficit hyperactivity disorder. J Am Acad Child Adolesc Psychiatry 34:649–657, 1995

Bauman ML: Microscopic neuroanatomic abnormalities in autism. Pediatrics 87:791–795, 1991

Bauman ML, Kemper TL: Histoanatomic observations of the brain in early infantile autism. Neurology 35:866–874, 1985

Bauman ML, Kemper TL, Arin DM: Pervasive neuroanatomic abnormalities of the brain in three cases of Rett's syndrome. Neurology 45:1581–1586, 1995

Baxter LR Jr, Schwartz JA, Bergman KS, et al: Caudate glucose metabolic rate changes with both drug and behavior therapy for obsessive-compulsive disorder. Arch Gen Psychiatry 49:681–689, 1992

Bear DM, Fedio P: Quantitative analysis of interictal behavior in temporal lobe epilepsy. Arch Neurol 34:454–467, 1977

Beck JC, van der Kolk B: Reports of childhood incest and current behavior of chronically hospitalized psychotic women. Am J Psychiatry 144:1474–1476, 1987

Beers SR: Cognitive effects of mild head injury in children and adolescents. Neuropsychol Rev 3:281–320, 1992

Belmonte M, Egaas B, Townsend J, et al: NMR intensity of corpus callosum differs with age but not with diagnosis of autism. Neuroreport 6:1253–1256, 1995

Benasich AA, Curtiss S, Tallal P: Language, learning, and behavioral disturbances in childhood: a longitudinal perspective. J Am Acad Child Adolesc Psychiatry 32:585–594, 1993

Benjamin J, Li L, Patterson C, et al: Population and familial association between the D4 dopamine receptor gene and measures of novelty seeking. Nat Genet 12:81–84, 1996

Ben-Menachem E: New antiepileptic drugs and non-pharmacological treatments. Curr Opin Neurol 13:165–170, 2000

Berquin PC, Giedd JN, Jacobsen LK, et al: Cerebellum in attention-deficit hyperactivity disorder: a morphometric MRI study. Neurology 50:1098–1093, 1998

Biederman J, Baldessarini RJ, Wright V, et al: A double-blind placebo-controlled study of desipramine in the treatment of ADD, II: serum drugs levels and cardiovascular findings. J Am Acad Child Adolesc Psychiatry 28:903–911, 1989

Biederman J, Faraone SV, Spencer T, et al: Gender differences in a sample of adults with attention deficit hyperactivity disorder. Psychiatry Res 53:13–29, 1994

Biederman J, Wilens T, Mick E, et al: Pharmacotherapy of attention-deficit/hyperactivity disorder reduces risk for substance use disorder (electronic article). Pediatrics 104(2): e20, 1999

Bird HR, Canino G, Rubio-Stipec M, et al: Estimates of the prevalence of childhood maladjustment in a community survey in Puerto Rico. Arch Gen Psychiatry 45:1120–1126, 1988

Blue ME, Naidu S, Johnston MV: Altered development of glutamate and GABA receptors in the basal ganglia of girls with Rett syndrome. Exp Neurol 156:345–352, 1999a

Blue ME, Naidu S, Johnston MV: Development of amino acid receptors in frontal cortex from girls with Rett syndrome. Ann Neurol 45:541–545, 1999b

Blumberg BM, Mock DJ, Powers JM, et al: The HHV6 paradox: ubiquitous commensal or insidious pathogen? A two-step in situ PCR approach. J Clin Virol 16:159–178, 2000

Bolton P, Rutter M: Genetic influences in autism. International Review of Psychiatry 2:67–80, 1990

Bonwetsch R, Croul S, Richardson MW, et al: Role of HIV-1 Tat and CC chemokine MIP-1alpha in the pathogenesis of HIV associated central nervous system disorders. J Neurovirol 5:685–694, 1999

Brady MT, McGrath N, Brouwers P, et al: Randomized study of the tolerance and efficacy of high- versus low-dose zidovudine in human immunodeficiency virus-infected children with mild to moderate symptoms (AIDS Clinical Trials Group 128). Pediatric AIDS Clinical Trials Group. J Infect Dis 173(5):1097–1106, 1996

Braun AR, Stoetter B, Randolph C, et al: The functional neuroanatomy of Tourette's syndrome: an FDG-PET study, I: regional changes in cerebral glucose metabolism differentiating patients and controls. Neuropsychopharmacology 9:277–291, 1993

Breese GR, Cooper BR, Hollister AS: Involvement of brain monoamines in the stimulant and paradoxical inhibitory effects of methylphenidate. Psychopharmacologia 44(1):5–10, 1975

Bremner JD, Southwick SM, Johnson DR, et al: Childhood physical abuse and combat-related posttraumatic stress disorder in Vietnam veterans. Am J Psychiatry 150:235–239, 1993

Bremner JD, Randall P, Vermetten E, et al: Magnetic resonance imaging–based measurement of hippocampal volume in posttraumatic stress disorder related to childhood physical and sexual abuse—a preliminary report. Biol Psychiatry 41:23–32, 1997

Brent DA, Crumrine PK, Varma RR, et al: Phenobarbital treatment and major depressive disorder in children with epilepsy. Pediatrics 80:909–917, 1987

Brett PM, Curtis D, Robertson MM, et al: The genetic susceptibility to Gilles de la Tourette syndrome in a large multiple affected British kindred: linkage analysis excludes a role for the genes coding for dopamine D1, D2, D3, D4, D5 receptors, dopamine beta hydroxylase, tyrosinase, and tyrosine hydroxylase. Biol Psychiatry 37:533–540, 1995a

Brett PM, Curtis D, Robertson MM, et al: Exclusion of the 5-HTIA serotonin neuroreceptor and tryptophan oxygenase genes in a large British kindred multiply affected with Tourette's syndrome, chronic motor tics, and obsessive-compulsive behavior. Am J Psychiatry 152:437–440, 1995b

Brew BJ, Pemberton L, Cunningham P, et al: Levels of human immunodeficiency virus type 1 RNA in cerebrospinal fluid correlate with AIDS dementia stage. J Infect Dis 175(4): 963–966, 1997

Brons J, Robertson LT, Tong G: Somatosensory climbing fiber responses in the caudal posterior vermis of the cat cerebellum. Brain Res 519:243–248, 1990

Brouwers P, Tudor-Williams G, DeCarli C, et al: Relation between stage of disease and neurobehavioral measures in children with symptomatic HIV disease. AIDS 9:713–720, 1995

Brown GL, Ebert MH, Mikkelsen EJ, et al: Behavior and motor activity response in hyperactive children and plasma amphetamine levels following a sustained release preparation. J Am Acad Child Adolesc Psychiatry 19:225–239, 1980

Brown G, Chadwick O, Shaffer D, et al: A prospective study of children with head injuries, III: psychiatric sequelae. Psychol Med 11:63–78, 1981

Brown LK, Lourie KJ, Pao M: Children and adolescents living with HIV and AIDS: a review. J Child Psychol Psychiatry 41:81–96, 2000

Bruun RD: Subtle and underrecognized side effects of neuroleptic treatment in children with Tourette's disorder. Am J Psychiatry 145:621–624, 1988

Bryden MP, McManus IC, Bulman-Fleming MB: Evaluating the empirical support for the Geschwind-Behan-Galaburda model of cerebral lateralization. Brain Cogn 26:103–167, 1994

Budman CL, Bruun RD, Parks KS, et al: Rage attacks in children and adolescents with Tourette's disorder: a pilot study. J Clin Psychiatry 59:576–580, 1998

Bulman-Fleming B, Wainwright PE, Collins RL: The effects of early experience on callosal development and functional lateralization in pigmented BALB/c mice. Behav Brain Res 50:31–42, 1992

Bush G, Frazier JA, Rauch SL, et al: Anterior cingulate cortex dysfunction in attention deficit/hyperactivity disorder revealed by fMRI and the Counting Stroop. Biol Psychiatry 45:1542–1552, 1999

Camp DM, Robinson TE, Becker JB: Sex differences in the effects of early experience on the development of behavioral and brain asymmetries in rats. Physiol Behav 33:433–439, 1984

Campbell M, Anderson LT, Small AM, et al: Naltrexone in autistic children: behavioral symptoms and attentional learning. J Am Acad Child Adolesc Psychiatry 32:1283–1291, 1993

Campbell M, Schopler E, Cueva JE, et al: Treatment of autistic disorder. J Am Acad Child Adolesc Psychiatry 35:134–143, 1996

Cardon LR, Smith SD, Fulker DW, et al: Quantitative trait locus for reading disability on chromosome 6. Science 266:276–279, 1994

Cardon LR, Smith SD, Fulker DW, et al: Quantitative trait locus for reading disability: correction (letter). Science 268:1553, 1995

Carper RA, Courchesne E: Inverse correlation between frontal lobe and cerebellum sizes in children with autism. Brain 123 (pt 4):836–844, 2000

Casey BJ, Castellanos FX, Giedd JN, et al: Implication of right frontostriatal circuitry in response inhibition and attention-deficit/hyperactivity disorder. J Am Acad Child Adolesc Psychiatry 36:374–383, 1997

Cassidy SB, Forsythe M, Heeger S, et al: Comparison of phenotype between patients with Prader-Willi syndrome due to deletion 15q and uniparental disomy 15. Am J Med Genet 68:433–440, 1997

Castellanos FX, Giedd JN, Marsh WL, et al: Quantitative brain magnetic resonance imaging in attention-deficit hyperactivity disorder. Arch Gen Psychiatry 53:607–616, 1996

Castellanos FX, Lau E, Tayebi N, et al: Lack of an association between a dopamine-4 receptor polymorphism and attention-deficit/hyperactivity disorder: genetic and brain morphometric analyses. Mol Psychiatry 3:431–434, 1998

Chappell P, Riddle M, Anderson G, et al: Enhanced stress responsivity of Tourette syndrome patients undergoing lumbar puncture. Biol Psychiatry 36:35–43, 1994

Chappell PB, Riddle MA, Scahill L, et al: Guanfacine treatment of comorbid attention-deficit hyperactivity disorder and Tourette's syndrome: preliminary clinical experience. J Am Acad Child Adolesc Psychiatry 34:1140–1146, 1995

Chez MG, Buchanan CP, Bagan BT, et al: Secretin and autism: a two-part investigation. J Autism Dev Disord 30:87–94, 2000

Chi J, Dooling E, Giles F: Left-right asymmetries of the temporal speech areas of the human fetus. Arch Neurol 34:346–348, 1972

Chudley AE, Knoll J, Gerrard JW, et al: Fragile (X) X-linked mental retardation, I: relationship between age and intelligence and the frequency of expression of fragile (X) (q28). Am J Med Genet 14:699–712, 1983

Chugani DC, Muzik O, Rothermel R, et al: Altered serotonin synthesis in the dentatothalamocortical pathway in autistic boys. Ann Neurol 42:666–669, 1997

Chugani DC, Muzik O, Behen M, et al: Developmental changes in brain serotonin synthesis capacity in autistic and nonautistic children. Ann Neurol 45:287–295, 1999

Ciesielski KT, Harris RJ, Hart BL, et al: Cerebellar hypoplasia and frontal lobe cognitive deficits in disorders of early childhood. Neuropsychologia 35:643–655, 1997

Cirianello RD, Cirianello SD: The neurobiology of infantile autism. Annu Rev Neurosci 18:1010–1028, 1995

Cohen SE, Mundy T, Karassik B, et al: Neuropsychological functioning in human immunodeficiency virus type 1 seropositive children infected through neonatal blood transfusion. Pediatrics 88:58–68, 1991

Cole KN, Dale PS, Mills PE: Stability of the intelligence quotient–language quotient relation: is discrepancy modeling based on a myth? Am J Ment Retard 97:131–143, 1992

Comings DE: Blood serotonin and tryptophan in Tourette syndrome. Am J Med Genet 36:418–430, 1990

Comings DE, Comings BG: A controlled study of Tourette syndrome; I: attention-deficit disorder, learning disorders, and school problems. Am J Hum Genet 41:701–741, 1987

Comings DE, Wu H, Ring RH, et al: Polygenetic inheritance of Tourette syndrome, stuttering, ADHD, conduct disorder and oppositional defiant disorder: the additive and subtractive effect of the three dopamine genes—DRD2, DBH and DAT1. Am J Med Genet 67:264–288, 1996

Comings DE, Gade-Andavolu R, Gonzalez N, et al: Additive effect of three noradrenergic genes (ADRA2a, ADRA2C, DBH) on attention-deficit hyperactivity disorder and learning disabilities in Tourette syndrome subjects. Clin Genet 55:160–172, 1999a

Comings DE, Gonzalez N, Wu S, et al: Studies of the 48 bp repeat polymorphism of the DRD4 gene in impulsive, compulsive, addictive behaviors: Tourette syndrome, ADHD, pathological gambling, and substance abuse. Am J Med Genet 88:358–368, 1999b

Comings DE, Gade-Andavolu R, Gonzalez N, et al: Comparison of the role of dopamine, serotonin, and noradrenaline genes in ADHD, ODD and conduct disorder: multivariate regression analysis of 20 genes. Clin Genet 57:178–196, 2000

Cook EH Jr: Genetics of autism. Child Adolesc Psychiatr Clin N Am 10(2):333–359, 2001

Cook EH Jr, Stein MA, Krasowski MD, et al: Association of attention-deficit disorder and the dopamine transporter gene. Am J Hum Genet 56:993–998, 1995

Cook EH Jr, Courchesne R, Lord C, et al: Evidence of linkage between the serotonin transporter and autistic disorder. Mol Psychiatry 2:247–250, 1997

Cooper H, Nye B: Homework for students with learning disabilities: the implications of research for policy and practice. Journal of Learning Disabilities 27:470–479, 1994

Cornwall A, Bawden HN: Reading disabilities and aggression: a critical review. Journal of Learning Disabilities 25:281–288, 1992

Courchesne E: Neuroanatomic imaging in autism. Pediatrics 87:781–790, 1991

Cowan WM, Fawcett JW, O'Leary DDM, et al: Regressive events in neurogenesis. Science 225:1258–1265, 1984

Critchley HD, Daly EM, Bullmore ET, et al: The functional neuroanatomy of social behaviour: changes in cerebral blood flow when people with autistic disorder process facial expressions. Brain 123:2203–2212, 2000

Curtis D, Robertson MM, Gurling HM: Autosomal dominant gene transmission in a large kindred with Gilles de la Tourette syndrome. Br J Psychiatry 160:845–849, 1992

Dal Maso L, Parazzini F, Lo Re A, et al: Paediatric AIDS incidence in Europe and the USA, 1985–96. J Epidemiol Biostat 4:75–81, 1999

Dalby MA, Elbro C, Stodkilde-Jorgensen H: Temporal lobe asymmetry and dyslexia: an in vivo study using MRI. Brain Lang 62:51–69, 1998

Daly G, Hawi Z, Fitzgerald M, et al: Mapping susceptibility loci in attention deficit hyperactivity disorder: preferential transmission of parental alleles at DAT1, DBH and DRD5 to affected children. Mol Psychiatry 4:192–196, 1999

Davies RK: Incest: some neuropsychiatric findings. Int J Psychiatry Med 9:117–121, 1979

De Bellis MD, Keshavan MS, Clark DB, et al: A.E. Bennett Research Award. Developmental traumatology, part II: brain development. Biol Psychiatry 45(10):1271–1284, 1999

Delay J, Deniker P, Barande R: Le suicide des epileptique. Encephale 46:401–436, 1957

Demb JB, Boynton GM, Best M, et al: Psychophysical evidence for a magnocellular pathway deficit in dyslexia. Vision Res 38:1555–1559, 1998

Dempsey CW, Richardson DE: Paleocerebellar stimulation induces in vivo release of endogenously synthesized [3H]dopamine and [3H]norepinephrine from rat caudal dorsomedial nucleus accumbens. Neuroscience 21:565–571, 1987

Denckla MB, Bemporad JR, MacKay MC: Tics following methylphenidate administration: a report of 20 cases. JAMA 235:1349–1351, 1976

Denenberg VH, Yutzey DA: Hemispheric laterality, behavioral asymmetry, and the effects of early experience in rats, in Cerebral Lateralization in Nonhuman Species. Edited by Glick SD. Orlando, FL, Academic Press, 1985, pp 109–133

Dennett ER, Hubbard JI: Noradrenaline excites neurons in the guinea pig cerebellar vermis in vitro. Brain Res Bull 21:245–249, 1988

Denoth F, Magherini PC, Pompeiano O, et al: Responses of Purkinje cells of the cerebellar vermis to neck and macular vestibular inputs. Pflugers Arch 381:87–98, 1979

Dewhurst S, Gelbard HA, Fine SM: Neuropathogenesis of AIDS. Mol Med Today 2:16–23, 1996

DeYoe EA, Van Essen DC: Concurrent processing streams in monkey visual cortex. Trends Neurosci 11(5):219–226, 1988

Diamond A: Close interrelation of motor development and cognitive development and of the cerebellum and prefrontal cortex. Child Dev 71:44–56, 2000

Doba N, Reis DJ: Changes in regional blood flow and cardiodynamics evoked by electrical stimulation of the fastigial nucleus in the cat and their similarity to orthostatic reflexes. J Physiol (Lond) 227:729–747, 1972

Donaldson IM, Hawthorne ME: Coding of visual information by units in the cat cerebellar vermis. Exp Brain Res 34:27–48, 1979

Dougherty DD, Bonab AA, Spencer TJ, et al: Dopamine transporter density in patients with attention deficit hyperactivity disorder (letter). Lancet 354:2132–2133, 1999

Drake W: Clinical and pathological findings in a child with a developmental learning disability. Journal of Learning Disabilities 1:468–475, 1968

Dreifuss FE: Classification of epileptic seizures and the epilepsies. Pediatr Clin North Am 36:265–279, 1989

Dunn DW, Austin JK: Behavioral issues in pediatric epilepsy. Neurology 53:S96–100, 1999

Dykens EM, Cassidy SB, King BH: Maladaptive behavior differences in Prader-Willi syndrome due to paternal deletion versus maternal uniparental disomy. Am J Ment Retard 104:67–77, 1999

Eapen V, Pusls D, Robertson MM: Evidence for autosomal dominant transmission in Tourette's syndrome. United Kingdom cohort study. Br J Psychiatry 162:593–596, 1993

Ebstein RP, Novick O, Umansky R, et al: Dopamine D4 (D4DR) exon III polymorphism associated with the human personality trait of novelty seeking. Nat Genet 12:78–80, 1996

Eccles JC, Sabah NH, Schmidt RF, et al: Cerebellar Purkyne cell responses to cutaneous mechanoreceptors. Brain Res 30:419–424, 1971

Egaas B, Courchesne C, Saitoh O: Reduced size of corpus callosum in autism. Arch Neurol 52:794–801, 1995

Eisenberg J, Zohar A, Mei-Tal G, et al: A haplotype relative risk study of the dopamine D4 receptor (DRD4) exon III repeat polymorphism and attention deficit hyperactivity disorder (ADHD). Am J Med Genet 96:258–261, 2000

Ellis RJ, Hsia K, Spector SA, et al; Cerebrospinal fluid human immunodeficiency virus type 1 RNA levels are elevated in neurocognitively impaired individuals with acquired immunodeficiency syndrome. HIV Neurobehavioral Research Center Group. Ann Neurol 42(5):679–688, 1997

Epstein LG, Gelbard HA: HIV-1–induced neuronal injury in the developing brain. J Leukoc Biol 65:453–457, 1999

Epstein LG, Gendelman HE: Human immunodeficiency virus type I infection of the nervous system: pathogenetic mechanisms. Ann Neurol 33:429–436, 1993

Epstein LG, Sharer LR, Joshi VV, et al: Progressive encephalopathy in children with acquired immune deficiency syndrome. Ann Neurol 17:488–496, 1985

Erickson HM Jr, Goggin JE, Messiha FS: Comparison of lithium and haloperidol therapy in Gilles de la Tourette syndrome. Adv Exp Med Biol 90:197–205, 1977

Ernst M, Liebenauer LL, King C, et al: Reduced brain metabolism in hyperactive girls. J Am Acad Child Adolesc Psychiatry 33:858–868, 1994

Ernst M, Zametkin AJ, Matochik JA, et al: DOPA decarboxylase activity in attention deficit hyperactivity disorder adults. A [fluorine-18]fluorodopa positron emission tomographic study. J Neurosci 18:5901–5907, 1998

Ernst M, Zametkin AJ, Jons PH, et al: High presynaptic dopaminergic activity in children with Tourette's disorder. J Am Acad Child Adolesc Psychiatry 38:86–94, 1999a

Ernst M, Zametkin AJ, Matochik JA, et al: High midbrain [18F]DOPA accumulation in children with attention deficit hyperactivity disorder. Am J Psychiatry 156:1209–1215, 1999b

Everall IP, Luthbert PJ, Lantos PL: Neuronal loss in the frontal cortex in HIV infection. Lancet 337:1119–1121, 1991

Ewing-Cobbs L, Fletcher JM, Levin HS, et al: Academic achievement and academic placement following traumatic brain injury in children and adolescents: a two-year longitudinal study. J Clin Exp Neuropsychol 20:769–781, 1998

Facoetti A, Paganoni P, Lorusso ML: The spatial distribution of visual attention in developmental dyslexia. Exp Brain Res 132:531–538, 2000

Faraone SV, Biederman J, Lehman BK, et al: Evidence for the independent familial transmission of attention deficit hyperactivity disorder and learning disabilities: results from a family genetic study. Am J Psychiatry 150:891–895, 1993

Faraone SV, Biederman J, Weiffenbach B, et al: Dopamine D4 gene 7-repeat allele and attention deficit hyperactivity disorder. Am J Psychiatry 156:768–770, 1999

Faravelli C, Webb T, Ambonetti A: Prevalence of traumatic early life events in 31 agoraphobic patients with panic attacks. Am J Psychiatry 142:1493–1494, 1985

Feinberg I: Schizophrenia: caused by a fault in programmed synaptic elimination during adolescence? J Psychiatr Res 17:319–334, 1982–1983

Fernandez F, Adams F, Levy JK, et al: Cognitive impairment due to AIDS-related complex and its response to psychostimulants. Psychosomatics 29:38–46, 1988

Ferrera VP, Nealey TA, Maunsell JH: Mixed parvocellular and magnocellular geniculate signals in visual area V4. Nature 358:756–761, 1992

Fischer CP, Jorgen G, Gundersen H, et al: Preferential loss of large neocortical neurons during HIV infection: a study of the size distribution of neocortical neurons in the human brain. Brain Res 828:119–126, 1999

Fish DR, Sawyers D, Allen PJ: The effect of sleep on the dyskinetic movements of Parkinson's disease, Gilles de la Tourette syndrome, Huntington's disease and torsion dystonia. Arch Neurol 48:210–214, 1991

Fitch RH, Miller S, Tallal P: Neurobiology of speech perception. Annu Rev Neurosci 20:331–353, 1997

Fletcher JM, Levin HS: Neurobehavioral effects of brain injury in children, in Handbook of Pediatric Psychology. Edited by Routh DK. New York, Guilford, 1988, pp 258–296

Fombonne E, Du MC, Cans C, et al: Autism and associated medical disorders in a French epidemiological survey. J Am Acad Child Adolesc Psychiatry 36:1561–1569, 1997

Foote S, Aston-Jones G, Bloom FE: Impulse activity of locus coeruleus neurons in awake rats and squirrel monkeys is a function of sensory stimulation and arousal. Proc Natl Acad Sci U S A 77:3033–3037, 1980

Frankenberger W, Fronzaglio K: A review of states' criteria and procedures for identifying children with learning disabilities. Journal of Learning Disabilities 24:495–500, 1991

Freeman BJ, Ritvo ER, Needleman R, et al: The stability of cognitive and linguistic parameters in autism: a 5 year study. Journal of the American Academy of Child Psychiatry 24:290–311, 1985

Freeman BJ, Rahbar B, Ritvo ER, et al: The stability of cognitive and behavioral parameters in autism: a twelve-year prospective study. J Am Acad Child Adolesc Psychiatry 30:479–482, 1991

Freund LS, Reiss AL, Hagerman R, et al: Chromosome fragility and psychopathology in obligate female carriers of the fragile X chromosome. Arch Gen Psychiatry 49:54–60, 1992

Gadow KD, Nolan EE, Sverd J: Methylphenidate in hyperactive boys with comorbid tic disorder; II: short-term behavioral effects in school settings. J Am Acad Child Adolesc Psychiatry 31:462–471, 1992

Gage FH: Mammalian neural stem cells. Science 287:1433–1438, 2000

Galaburda AM: Anatomical asymmetries, in Cerebral Dominance: The Biological Foundations. Edited by Geschwind N, Galaburda AM. Cambridge, MA, Harvard University Press, 1984, pp 11–25

Galaburda AM, Sherman GF, Rosen GD, et al: Developmental dyslexia: four consecutive patients with cortical anomalies. Ann Neurol 18:222–233, 1985

Galaburda AM, Menard MT, Rosen GD: Evidence for aberrant auditory anatomy in developmental dyslexia. Proc Natl Acad Sci U S A 91:8010–8013, 1994

Galler JR, Ramsey F, Solimano G, et al: The influence of early malnutrition on subsequent behavioral development; II: classroom behavior. Journal of the American Academy of Child Psychiatry 22:16–22, 1983

Gatley SJ, Pan D, Chen R, et al: Affinities of methylphenidate derivatives for dopamine, norepinephrine and serotonin transporters. Life Sci 58:231–239, 1996

Gelbard HA, Epstein LG: HIV-1 encephalopathy in children. Curr Opin Pediatr 7:655–662, 1995

Gelbard HA, James H, Sharer L, et al: Apoptotic neurons in brains of pediatric patients with HIV-1 encephalitis and progressive encephalopathy. Neuropathol Appl Neurobiol 21:208–217, 1995

Gelbard HA, Boustany RM, Schor NF: Apoptosis in development and disease of the nervous system, II: apoptosis in childhood neurologic disease. Pediatr Neurol 16:93–97, 1997

Gelernter J, Pakstis AJ, Pauls DL, et al: Gilles de la Tourette syndrome is not linked to D2-dopamine receptor. Arch Gen Psychiatry 47:1073–1077, 1990

Gelernter J, Kennedy JL, Grandy DK, et al: Exclusion of close linkage of Tourette's syndrome to D1 dopamine receptor. Am J Psychiatry 150:449–453, 1993

Gelernter J, Rao PA, Pauls DL, et al: Assignment of the 5HT7 receptor gene (HTR7) to chromosome 10q and exclusion of genetic linkage with Tourette syndrome. Genomics 26:207–209, 1995

George MS, Trimble MR, Costa DC, et al: Elevated frontal cerebral blood flow in Gilles de la Tourette syndrome: a 99Tcm-HMPAO SPECT study. Psychiatry Res 45:143–151, 1992

George MS, Robertson MM, Costa DC, et al: Dopamine receptor availability in Tourette's syndrome. Psychiatry Res 55:193–203, 1994

Georgiewa P, Rzanny R, Hopf JM, et al: fMRI during word processing in dyslexic and normal reading children. Neuroreport 10:3459–3465, 1999

Geschwind N, Behan P: Left-handedness: association with immune disease, migraine, and developmental learning disorder. Proc Natl Acad Sci U S A 79:5097–5100, 1982

Geschwind N, Galaburda AM: Cerebral Lateralization. Cambridge, MA, MIT Press, 1985

Giaquinto C, Ruga E, Giacomet V, et al: HIV: mother to child transmission, current knowledge and on-going studies. Int J Gynaecol Obstet 63 (suppl 1):S161–165, 1998

Giedd JN, Castellanos FX, Casey BJ, et al: Quantitative morphology of the corpus callosum in attention deficit hyperactivity disorder. Am J Psychiatry 151:665–669, 1994

Gilger JW, Pennington BF, DeFries JC: A twin study of the etiology of comorbidity: attention-deficit hyperactivity disorder and dyslexia. J Am Acad Child Adolesc Psychiatry 31:343–348, 1992

Gill M, Daly G, Heron S, et al: Confirmation of association between attention deficit disorder and a dopamine transporter polymorphism. Mol Psychiatry 2:311–313, 1997

Gillberg C: Endogenous opioids and opiate antagonists in autism: brief review of empirical findings and implications for clinicians. Dev Med Child Neurol 37:239–245, 1995

Gillis JJ, DeFries JC, Fulker DW: Confirmatory factor analysis of reading and mathematics performance: a twin study. Acta Genet Med Gemellol (Roma) 41:287–300, 1992

Giros M, Jaber M, Jones SR, et al: Hyperlocomotion and indifference to cocaine and amphetamine in mice lacking the dopamine transporter. Nature 379:606–612, 1996

Gittelman R, Mannuzza S, Shenker R, et al: Hyperactive boys almost grown up; I: psychiatric status. Arch Gen Psychiatry 42:937–947, 1985

Glod CA, Teicher MH: Relationship between early abuse, posttraumatic stress disorder, and activity levels in prepubertal children. J Am Acad Child Adolesc Psychiatry 35:1384–1393, 1996

Goadsby PJ, Lambert GA: Electrical stimulation of the fastigial nucleus increases total cerebral blood flow in the monkey. Neurosci Lett 107:141–144, 1989

Goddard AW, Charney DS: Toward an integrated neurobiology of panic disorder. J Clin Psychiatry 58 (suppl 2):4–11, 1997

Godridge H, Reynolds GP, Czudek C, et al: Alzheimer-like neurotransmitter deficits in adult Down's syndrome. J Neurol Neurosurg Psychiatry 50:775–778, 1987

Gold AP: Evaluation and diagnosis by inspection, in Child and Adolescent Neurology for Psychiatrists. Edited by Kaufman DM, Solomon GE, Pfeffer CR. Baltimore, MD, Williams & Wilkins, 1992, pp 1–12

Goldberg E, Costa LD: Hemisphere differences in the acquisition and use of descriptive systems. Brain Lang 14(1):144–173, 1981

Grace AA: The tonic/phasic model of dopamine system regulation: its relevance for understanding how stimulant abuse can alter basal ganglia function. Drug Alcohol Depend 37(2):111–129, 1995

Greatrex JC, Drasdo N: The magnocellular deficit hypothesis in dyslexia: a review of reported evidence. Ophthalmic Physiol Opt 15:501–506, 1995

Green AH: Dimensions of psychological trauma in abused children. Journal of the American Academy of Child Psychiatry 22:231–237, 1983

Green A, Voeller K, Gaines R, et al: Neurological impairment in maltreated children. Child Abuse Negl 5:129–134, 1981

Gresch PJ, Sved AF, Zigmond MJ, et al: Local influence of endogenous norepinephrine on extracellular dopamine in rat medial prefrontal cortex. J Neurochem 65:111–116, 1995

Groner Y, Elroy Stein O, Avaraham KB, et al: Cell damage by excess CuZnSOD and Down's syndrome. Biomed Pharmacother 48:231–240, 1994

Groth AN: Sexual trauma in the life histories of sex offenders. Victimology 4:6–10, 1979

Haddad FA, Juliano JM, Vaughan D: Long-term stability of individual WISC-R IQs of learning disabled children. Psychol Rep 74:15–18, 1994

Hagerman RJ, Sobesky WE: Psychopathology in fragile X syndrome. Am J Orthopsychiatry 59:142–152, 1989

Hallett JJ, Harling-Berg CJ, Knopf PM, et al: Anti-striatal antibodies in Tourette syndrome cause neuronal dysfunction. J Neuroimmunol 111(1-2):195–202, 2000

Hardan AY, Minshew NJ, Keshavan MS: Corpus callosum size in autism. Neurology 55:1033–1036, 2000

Harris NS, Courchesne E, Townsend J, et al: Neuroanatomic contributions to slowed orienting of attention in children with autism. Brain Res Cogn Brain Res 8:61–71, 1999

Hashimoto T, Endo S, Fukuda K, et al: Increased body movements during sleep in Gilles de la Tourette syndrome. Brain Dev 3:31–35, 1981

Hashitmoto T, Tayama M, Mori K, et al: Magnetic resonance imaging in autism: preliminary report. Neuropediatrics 20:142–146, 1988

Haslam RH, Dalby JT, Johns RD, et al: Cerebral asymmetry in developmental dyslexia. Arch Neurol 38:679–682, 1981

Hauser P, Zametkin AJ, Martinez P, et al: Attention deficit–hyperactivity disorder in people with generalized resistance to thyroid hormone. N Engl J Med 328:997–1001, 1993

Hauser WA, Hesdorffer DC (eds): Facts About Epilepsy. New York, Demos Publications, 1990

Heffner TG, Heller A, Miller FE, et al: Locomotor hyperactivity in neonatal rats following electrolytic lesions of mesocortical dopamine neurons. Brain Res 285:29–37, 1983

Heilman K, Van Den Abell T: Right hemisphere dominance for attention: the mechanism underling hemispheric asymmetry of inattention. Neurology 30:327–330, 1980

Henker B, Whalen CK: Hyperactivity and attention deficits. Am Psychol 44:216–223, 1989

Herman JL, Perry JC, van der Kolk BA: Childhood trauma in borderline personality disorder. Am J Psychiatry 146:490–495, 1989

Hernandez L, Lee F, Hoebel BG: Simultaneous microdialysis and amphetamine infusion in the nucleus accumbens and striatum of freely moving rats: increase in extracellular dopamine and serotonin. Brain Res Bull 19:623–628, 1987

Herskovits EH, Megalooikonomou V, Davatzikos C, et al: Is the spatial distribution of brain lesions associated with closed-head injury predictive of subsequent development of attention-deficit/hyperactivity disorder? analysis with brain-image database. Radiology 213:389–394, 1999

Hoehn TP, Baumeister AA: A critique of the application of sensory integration therapy to children with learning disabilities. Journal of Learning Disabilities 27:338–350, 1994

Hofer MA: Studies on how early maternal deprivation produces behavioral change in young rats. Psychosom Med 37:245–264, 1975

Holland AJ, Hon J, Huppert FA, et al: Population-based study of the prevalence and presentation of dementia in adults with Down's syndrome. Br J Psychiatry 172:493–498, 1998

Holttum JR, Minshew NJ, Sanders RS, et al: Magnetic resonance imaging of the posterior fossa in autism. Biol Psychiatry 32:1091–1101, 1992

Horska A, Naidu S, Hershovits EH, et al: Quantitative ¹H MR spectroscopic imaging in early Rett syndrome. Neurology 54:715–722, 2000

Horwitz B, Rumsey J, Grady C, et al: The cerebral metabolic landscape in autism: intercorrelations of regional glucose utilization. Ann Neurol 22:749–755, 1988

Horwitz B, Rumsey JM, Donohue BC: Functional connectivity of the angular gyrus in normal reading and dyslexia. Proc Natl Acad Sci U S A 95:8939–8944, 1998

Huang C, Liu G: Organization of the auditory area in the posterior cerebellar vermis of the cat. Exp Brain Res 81:377–383, 1990

Hubel DH: Effects of deprivation on the visual cortex of cat and monkey. Harvey Lect 72:1–51, 1978

Humphries T, Wright M, Snider L, et al: A comparison of the effectiveness of sensory integrative therapy and perceptual-motor training in treating children with learning disabilities. J Dev Behav Pediatr 13:31–40, 1992

Hunt RD: Treatment effects of oral and transdermal clonidine in relation to methylphenidate: an open pilot study in ADHD. Psychopharmacology Bulletin 23:111–114, 1987

Hunt RD, Minderaa RB, Cohen DJ: Clonidine benefits children with attention deficit disorder and hyperactivity: report of a double-blind placebo-crossover therapeutic trial. J Am Acad Child Adolesc Psychiatry 24:617–629, 1985

Hunt RD, Arnsten AFT, Asbell MD: An open trial of guanfacine in the treatment of attention-deficit hyperactivity disorder. J Am Acad Child Adolesc Psychiatry 34:50–54, 1995

Huret JL, Delabar JM, Marlhens F, et al: Down syndrome with duplication of a region of chromosome 21 containing the CuZn superoxide dismutase gene without detectable karyotypic abnormality. Hum Genet 75:251–257, 1987

Huttenlocher PR: Synaptic density in human frontal cortex—developmental changes and effects of aging. Brain Res 163:195–205, 1979

Hyde TM, Stacey ME, Coppola R: Cerebral morphometric abnormalities in Tourette's syndrome: a quantitative MRI study of monozygotic twins. Neurology 45:1176–1182, 1995

Hynd GW, Semrud-Clikeman M, Lorys AR, et al: Corpus callosum morphology in attention deficit hyperactivity disorder: morphometric analysis of MRI. Journal of Learning Disabilities 24:141–146, 1991

International Molecular Genetic Study of Autism Consortium: A full genome screen with evidence for linkage to a region on chromosome 7q. Hum Mol Genet 7:571–578, 1998

Ito Y, Teicher MH, Glod CA, et al: Increased prevalence of electrophysiological abnormalities in children with psychological, physical, and sexual abuse. J Neuropsychiatry Clin Neurosci 5:401–408, 1993

Ito Y, Teicher MH, Glod CA, et al: Preliminary evidence for aberrant cortical development in abused children: a quantitative EEG study. J Neuropsychiatry Clin Neurosci 10:298–307, 1998

Jadresic D: The role of the amygdaloid complex in Gilles de la Tourette's syndrome. Br J Psychiatry 16:532–534, 1992

James HJ, Sharer LR, Zhang Q, et al: Expression of caspase-3 in brains from paediatric patients with HIV-1 encephalitis. Neuropathol Appl Neurobiol 25:380–386, 1999

Janssen RS, Cornblath DR, Epstein LG, et al: Nomenclature and research case definitions for neurological manifestations of human immunodeficiency virus type-1 (HIV-1) infection: report of a working group of the American Academy of Neurology AIDS Task Force. Neurology 41:778–785, 1991

Janssen RS, Nwanyanwu OC, Selik RM, et al: Epidemiology of human immunodeficiency virus encephalopathy in the United States. Neurology 42:1472–1476, 1992

Jellinger K, Armstrong D, Zoghbi HY, et al: Neuropathology of Rett syndrome. Acta Neuropathol (Berl) 76:142–158, 1988

Jensen I: Temporal lobe epilepsy: late morality in patients treated with unilateral temporal lobe resections. Acta Neurol Scand 52:374–380, 1975

Jenson WR, Sheridan SM, Olympia D, et al: Homework and students with learning disabilities and behavior disorders: a practical, parent-based approach. Journal of Learning Disabilities 27:538–548, 1994

Jernigan TL, Hesselink JR, Sowell E, et al: Cerebral structure on magnetic resonance imaging in language- and learning-impaired children. Arch Neurol 48:539–545, 1991

Johannes S, Kussmaul CL, Munte TF, et al: Developmental dyslexia: passive visual stimulation provides no evidence for a magnocellular processing defect. Neuropsychologia 34:1123–1127, 1996

Jutai JW: Cerebral asymmetry and the psychophysiology of attention. Int J Psychophysiol 1:219–225, 1984

Kanner L: Autistic disturbances of affective contact. Nervous Child 2:217–250, 1943

Kaplan BJ, Polatajko HJ, Wilson BN, et al: Reexamination of sensory integration treatment: a combination of two efficacy studies. Journal of Learning Disabilities 26:342–347, 1993

Karacostas DD, Fisher GL: Chemical dependency in students with and without learning disabilities. Journal of Learning Disabilities 26:491–495, 1993

Kaufman DM: Clinical Neurology for Psychiatrists, 2nd Edition. Orlando, FL, Grune & Stratton, 1985, pp 172–197

Keller HH, Bartholini G, Pletscher A: Spontaneous and drug-induced changes of cerebral dopamine turnover during postnatal development of rats. Brain Res 64:371–378, 1973

Kemper TL, Bauman ML: The contribution of neuropathologic studies to the understanding of autism. Neurol Clin 11:175–187, 1993

Kerbeshian J, Burd L: Differential responsiveness to lithium in patients with Tourette disorder. Neurosci Biobehav Rev 12:247–250, 1988

Keshaven M, Anderson S, Pettegrew JW: Is schizophrenia due to excessive synaptic pruning in the prefrontal cortex? The Feinberg hypothesis revisited. J Psychiatr Res 28:239–264, 1994

Ketzler S, Weis S, Haug H, et al: Loss of neurons in the frontal cortex in AIDS brains. Acta Neuropathol (Berl) 80:92–94, 1990

Kinsella G, Ong B, Murtagh D, et al: The role of the family for behavioral outcome in children and adolescents following traumatic brain injury. J Consult Clin Psychol 67:116–123, 1999

Klauck SM, Poustka F, Benner A, et al: Serotonin transporter (5-HTT) gene variants associated with autism? Hum Mol Genet 6:2233–2238, 1997

Klein RG, Mannuzza S: Long-term outcome of hyperactive children: a review. J Am Acad Child Adolesc Psychiatry 30:383–387, 1991

Knell ER, Comings DE: Tourette's syndrome and attention-deficit hyperactivity disorder: evidence for a genetic relationship. J Clin Psychiatry 54:331–337, 1993

Korkman M, Pesonen AE: A comparison of neuropsychological test profiles of children with attention deficit–hyperactivity disorder and/or learning disorder. Journal of Learning Disabilities 27:383–392, 1994

Krashen S: Lateralization, language learning, and the critical period: some new evidence. Language Learning 23:63–74, 1973

Krause KH, Dresel SH, Krause J, et al: Increased striatal dopamine transporter in adult patients with attention deficit hyperactivity disorder: effects of methylphenidate as measured by single photon emission computed tomography. Neurosci Lett 285:107–110, 2000

Krystal H: Trauma and affects. Psychoanal Study Child 33:81–116, 1978

Kubova Z, Kuba M, Peregrin J, et al: Visual evoked potential evidence for magnocellular system deficit in dyslexia. Physiol Res 45:87–89, 1996

Kuczenski R, Segal DS, Leith NJ, et al: Effects of amphetamine, methylphenidate, and apomorphine on regional brain serotonin and 5-hydroxyindole acetic acid. Psychopharmacology (Berl) 93(3):329–335, 1987

Kurlan R, Corno PG, Deeley C, et al: A pilot controlled study of fluoxetine for obsessive-compulsive symptoms in children with Tourette's syndrome. Clin Neuropharmacol 16:167–172, 1993

Kwak CH, Hanna PA, Jankovic J: Botulinum toxin in the treatment of tics. Arch Neurol 57:1190–1193, 2000

LaBar KS, Gatenby JC, Gore JC, et al: Human amygdala activation during conditioned fear acquisition and extinction: a mixed-trial fMRI study. Neuron 20:937–945, 1998

LaHoste GJ, Swanson JM, Wigal SB, et al: Dopamine D4 receptor gene polymorphism is associated with attention deficit hyperactivity disorder. Mol Psychiatry 1:121–124, 1996

Landis SC: Neuronal growth cones. Annu Rev Physiol 45:567–580, 1983

Landmesser LT: The generation of neuromuscular specificity. Annu Rev Neurosci 3:279–302, 1980

Leckman JF, Scahill L: Possible exacerbation of tics by androgenic steroids (letter). N Engl J Med 322:1674, 1990

Leckman JF, Dolnansky ES, Hardin MT, et al: Perinatal factors in the expression of Tourette's syndrome: an exploratory study. J Am Acad Child Adolesc Psychiatry 29:220–226, 1990

Leckman JF, Hardin MT, Riddle MA, et al: Clonidine treatment of Gilles de la Tourette's syndrome. Arch Gen Psychiatry 48:324–328, 1991a

Leckman JF, Knorr AM, Rasmussen AM, et al: Basal ganglia research and Tourette's syndrome (letter). Trends Neurosci 14:94, 1991b

Leckman JF, Walker DE, Cohen DJ: Premonitory urges in Tourette's syndrome. Am J Psychiatry 150:98–102, 1993

Leckman JF, Goodman WK, Anderson GM, et al: Cerebrospinal fluid biogenic amines in obsessive compulsive disorder, Tourette's syndrome, and healthy controls. Neuropsychopharmacology 12:73–86, 1995a

Leckman JF, Pauls DL, Cohen DJ: Tic disorders, in Psychopharmacology: The Fourth Generation of Progress. Edited by Bloom FE, Kupfer DJ. New York, Raven, 1995b, pp 1665–1674

Leckman JF, Zhang H, Vitale A, et al: Course of tic severity in Tourette syndrome: the first two decades. Pediatrics 102:14–19, 1998

LeDoux JE, Iwata J, Cicchetti P, et al: Different projections of the central amygdaloid nucleus mediate autonomic and behavioral correlates of conditioned fear. J Neurosci 8:2517–2529, 1988

Lejeune J: Pathogenesis of mental deficiency in trisomy 21. Am J Med Genet Suppl 7:20–30, 1990

Lensing P, Schimke H, Klimesch W, et al: Clinical case report: opiate antagonist and event-related desynchronization in 2 autistic boys. Neuropsychobiology 31:16–23, 1995

Leonard HL, Meyer MC, Swedo SE, et al: Electrocardiographic changes during desipramine and clomipramine treatment in children and adolescents. J Am Acad Child Adolesc Psychiatry 34:1460–1468, 1995

Leslie AM, Frith U: Autistic children's understanding of seeing, knowing and believing. British Journal of Developmental Psychology 6:315–324, 1988

Leventhal BL, Cook EH Jr, Morford M, et al: Clinical and neurochemical effects of fenfluramine in children with autism. J Neuropsychiatry Clin Neurosci 5:307–315, 1993

Leviton A, Bellinger D, Allred EN, et al: Pre- and postnatal low-level lead exposure and children's dysfunction in school. Environ Res 60:30–43, 1993

Levitt JG, Blanton R, Capetillo-Cunliffe L, et al: Cerebellar vermis lobules VIII-X in autism. Prog Neuropsychopharmacol Biol Psychiatry 23:625–633, 1999

Levy F, Hay DA, McStephen M, et al: Attention-deficit hyperactivity disorder: a category or a continuum? genetic analysis of a large-scale twin study. J Am Acad Child Adolesc Psychiatry 36:737–744, 1997

Lewander T: Displacement of brain and heart noradrenaline by p-hydroxynorephedrine after administration of p-hydroxyamphetamine. Acta Pharmacologica et Toxicologica 29:20–32, 1971a

Lewander T: On the presence of p-hydroxynorephedrine in the rat brain and heart in relation to changes in catecholamine levels after administration of amphetamine. Acta Pharmacologica et Toxicologica 29:3–8, 1971b

Lewis C, Hitch GJ, Walker P: The prevalence of specific arithmetic difficulties and specific reading difficulties in 9- to 10-year-old boys and girls. J Child Psychol Psychiatry 35:283–292, 1994

Lewis DO, Pincus JH, Bard B, et al: Neuropsychiatric, psychoeducational, and family characteristics of 14 juveniles condemned to death in the United States. Am J Psychiatry 145:584–589, 1988

Lichter DG, Jackson LA, Schachter M: Clinical evidence for genomic imprinting in Tourette's syndrome. Neurology 45:924–928, 1995

Liederman J, Flannery KA: Fall conception increases the risk of neurodevelopmental disorder in offspring. J Clin Exp Neuropsychol 16:754–768, 1994

Lieh-Lai MW, Theodorou AA, Sarnaik AP, et al: Limitations of the Glasgow Coma Scale in predicting outcome in children with traumatic brain injury. J Pediatr 120:195–199, 1992

Lindgren AC, Ritzen EM: Five years of growth hormone treatment in children with Prader-Willi syndrome. Acta Paediatr Suppl 88:109–111, 1999

Linet LS: Tourette syndrome, pimozide, and school phobia: the neuroleptic separation anxiety syndrome. Am J Psychiatry 142:613–615, 1985

Livingstone MS, Rosen GD, Drislane FW, et al: Physiological and anatomical evidence for a magnocellular defect in developmental dyslexia. Proc Natl Acad Sci U S A 88:7943–7947, 1991

Lobato MN, Caldwell MB, Ng P, et al: Encephalopathy in children with perinatally acquired human immunodeficiency virus infection. Pediatric Spectrum of Disease Clinical Consortium. J Pediatr 126(5 pt 1):710–715, 1995

Lombroso PJ, Scahill L, King RA, et al: Risperidone treatment of children and adolescents with chronic tic disorders: a preliminary report. J Am Acad Child Adolesc Psychiatry 34:1147–1152, 1995

Lotspeich LJ: Autism and pervasive developmental disorders, in Psychopharmacology: The Fourth Generation of Progress. Edited by Bloom FE, Kupfer DJ. New York, Raven, 1995, pp 1653–1663

Lou HC, Henriksen L, Bruhn P, et al: Striatal dysfunction in attention deficit and hyperkinetic disorder. Arch Neurol 46:48–52, 1990

Lovaas OI: Behavioral treatment and normal educational and intellectual functioning in young autistic children. J Consult Clin Psychol 55:3–9, 1987

Lovaas OI, Smith T: A comprehensive behavioral theory of autistic children: paradigm for research and treatment. J Behav Ther Exp Psychiatry 20:17–29, 1989

Lu D, Pavlakis SG, Frank Y, et al: Proton MR spectroscopy of the basal ganglia in healthy children and children with AIDS. Radiology 199:423–428, 1996

Lubar JO, Lubar JF: Electroencephalographic biofeedback of SMR and beta for treatment of attention deficit disorders in a clinical setting. Biofeedback and Self-Regulation 9:1–23, 1984

Lubar JF, Swartwood MO, Swartwood JN, et al: Evaluation of the effectiveness of EEG neurofeedback training for ADHD in a clinical setting as measured by changes in T.O.V.A. scores, behavioral ratings, and WISC-R performance. Biofeedback Self Regul 20:83–99, 1995

Luxenberg JS, Swedo SE, Flament MF, et al: Neuroanatomical abnormalities in obsessive-compulsive disorder detected with quantitative X-ray computed tomography. Am J Psychiatry 145:1089–1093, 1988

Maggirwar SB, Tong N, Ramirez S, et al: HIV-1 Tat-mediated activation of glycogen synthase kinase-3beta contributes to Tat-mediated neurotoxicity. J Neurochem 73:578–586, 1999

Mailleux P, Pelaprat D, Vanderhaeghen JJ: Transient neurotensin high-affinity binding sites in the human inferior olive during development. Brain Res 508:345–348, 1990

Malcolm S, Clayton-Smith J, Nichols M, et al: Uniparental disomy in Angelman's syndrome. Lancet 337:694–697, 1991

Malison RT, McDougle CJ, van Dyck CH, et al: [123]beta-CIT SPECT imaging of striatal dopamine transporter binding in Tourette's disorder. Am J Psychiatry 152:1359–1361, 1995

Malone MA, Kershner JR, Swanson JM: Hemispheric processing and methylphenidate effects in attention-deficit hyperactivity disorder. J Child Neurol 9:181–189, 1994

Mannuzza S, Klein RG, Konig PH, et al: Hyperactive boys almost grown up, IV: criminality and its relationship to psychiatric status. Arch Gen Psychiatry 46:1073–1079, 1989

Marcus J, Hans SL, Mednick SA, et al: Neurological dysfunctioning in offspring of schizophrenics in Israel and Denmark: a replication analysis. Arch Gen Psychiatry 42:753–761, 1985

Martin A, State M, Anderson GM, et al: Cerebrospinal fluid levels of oxytocin in Prader-Willi syndrome: a preliminary report. Biol Psychiatry 44:1349–1352, 1998

Mathews WS, Barabas G: Suicide and epilepsy: a review of the literature. Psychosomatics 22:515–524, 1981

Mattson AJ, Sheer DE, Fletcher JM: Electrophysiological evidence of lateralized disturbances in children with learning disabilities. J Clin Exp Neuropsychol 14:707–716, 1992

Max JE, Dunisch DL: Traumatic brain injury in a child psychiatry outpatient clinic: a controlled study. J Am Acad Child Adolesc Psychiatry 35:404–411, 1997

Max JE, Lindgren SD, Robin DA, et al: Traumatic brain injury in children and adolescents: psychiatric disorders in the second three months. J Nerv Ment Dis 185:394–401, 1997a

Max JE, Robin DA, Lindgren SD, et al: Traumatic brain injury in children and adolescents: psychiatric disorders at two years. J Am Acad Child Adolesc Psychiatry 36:1278–1285, 1997b

Max JE, Smith WL, Sato Y, et al: Traumatic brain injury in children and adolescents: psychiatric disorders in the first three months. J Am Acad Child Adolesc Psychiatry 36:94–102, 1997c

Max JE, Arndt S, Castillo CS, et al: Attention-deficit hyperactivity symptomatology after traumatic brain injury: a prospective study. J Am Acad Child Adolesc Psychiatry 37:841–847, 1998a

Max JE, Castillo CS, Bokura H, et al: Oppositional defiant disorder symptomatology after traumatic brain injury: a prospective study. J Nerv Ment Dis 186:325–332, 1998b

Max JE, Castillo CS, Robin DA, et al: Posttraumatic stress symptomatology after childhood traumatic brain injury. J Nerv Ment Dis 186(10):589–596, 1998c

Max JE, Koele SL, Smith WL, et al: Psychiatric disorders in children and adolescents after severe traumatic brain injury: a controlled study. J Am Acad Child Adolesc Psychiatry 37:832–840, 1998d

McArthur JC: Neurologic manifestations of AIDS. Medicine (Baltimore) 66:407–437, 1987

McArthur JC, Cohen BA, Selnes OA, et al: Low prevalence of neurological and neuropsychological abnormalities in otherwise healthy HIV-1–infected individuals: results from the multicenter AIDS Cohort Study. Ann Neurol 26:601–611, 1989

McArthur JC, Hoover DR, Bacellar H, et al: Dementia in AIDS patients: incidence and risk factors. Neurology 43:2245–2252, 1993

McBride PA, Anderson GM, Hertzig ME, et al: Effects of diagnosis, race, and puberty on platelet serotonin levels in autism and mental retardation. J Am Acad Child Adolesc Psychiatry 37:767–776, 2000

McConville BJ, Fogelson MH, Norman AB, et al: Nicotine potentiation of haloperidol in reducing tic frequency in Tourette's disorder. Am J Psychiatry 148:793–794, 1991

McDougle CJ, Goddman WK, Price LH: Dopamine antagonists in tic-related and psychotic spectrum obsessive compulsive disorder. J Clin Psychiatry 55 (suppl):24–31, 1994

McDougle CJ, Brodkin ES, Naylor ST, et al: Sertraline in adults with pervasive developmental disorders: a prospective open-label investigation. J Clin Psychopharmacol 18:62–66, 1998

McDougle CJ, Scahill L, McCracken JT, et al: Research Units on Pediatric Psychopharmacology (RUPP) Autism Network. Background and rationale for an initial controlled study of risperidone. Child Adolesc Psychiatr Clin N Am 9:201–224, 2000

McEachin JJ, Smith T, Lovaas OI: Long-term outcome for children with autism who received early intensive behavioral treatment. Am J Ment Retard 97:359–372, 1993

McGee R, Williams S, Silva OA: A comparison of girls and boys with teacher-identified problems of attention. J Am Acad Child Adolesc Psychiatry 26:711–717, 1987

McLeer SV, Callaghan M, Henry D, et al: Psychiatric disorders in sexually abused children. J Am Acad Child Adolesc Psychiatry 33:313–319, 1994

Melchitzky DS, Lewis DA: Tyrosine hydroxylase- and dopamine transporter–immunoreactive axons in the primate cerebellum. Evidence for a lobular- and laminar-specific dopamine innervation. Neuropsychopharmacology 22:466–472, 2000

Mendez MF, Cummings JL, Benson DF: Depression in epilepsy: significance and phenomenology. Arch Neurol 43:766–770, 1986

Mendez MF, Lanska DJ, Manon-Espaillat R, et al: Causative factors for suicide attempts by overdose in epileptics. Arch Neurol 46:1065–1068, 1989

Merzenich MM, Jenkins WM, Johnston P, et al: Temporal processing deficits of language-learning impaired children ameliorated by training. Science 271:77–81, 1996

Metz-Lutz MN, Kleitz C, de Saint Martin A, et al: Cognitive development in benign focal epilepsies of childhood. Dev Neurosci 21:182–190, 1999

Michaud LJ, Rivara FP, Jafle KM, et al: Traumatic brain injury as a risk factor for behavioral disorders in children. Arch Phys Med Rehabil 74:368–375, 1993

Mikkelsen EJ, Detlor J, Cohen DJ: School avoidance and social phobia triggered by haloperidol in patients with Tourette's disorder. Am J Psychiatry 138:1572–1576, 1981

Miller FE, Heffner TG, Kotake C, et al: Magnitude and duration of hyperactivity following neonatal 6-hydroxydopamine is related to the extent of brain dopamine depletion. Brain Res 229:123–132, 1981

Miller JN, Ozonoff S: The external validity of Asperger disorder: lack of evidence from the domain of neuropsychology. J Abnorm Psychol 109:227–238, 2000

Minshew NJ: Indices of neural function in autism: clinical and biologic implications. Pediatrics 87:774–780, 1991

Mintz M: Neurological and developmental problems in pediatric HIV infection. J Nutr 126 (10 suppl):2663S–2673S, 1996

Molfese DL, Freeman RB Jr, Palermo DS: The ontogeny of brain lateralization for speech and nonspeech stimuli. Brain Lang 2:356–368, 1975

Morton LL: Interhemispheric balance patterns detected by selective phonemic dichotic laterality measures in four clinical subtypes or reading disabled children. J Clin Exp Neuropsychol 16:556–567, 1994

Mostofsky SH, Mazzocco MM, Aakalu G, et al: Decreased cerebellar posterior vermis size in fragile X syndrome: correlation with neurocognitive performance. Neurology 50:121–130, 1998

Muller N, Putz A, Klages U, et al: Blunted growth hormone response to clonidine in Gilles de la Tourette syndrome. Psychoneuroendocrinology 19:335–341, 1994

Murphy TK, Goodman WK, Fudge MW, et al: B lymphocyte antigen D8/17: a peripheral marker for childhood-onset obsessive compulsive disorder and Tourette's syndrome? Am J Psychiatry 153:402–407, 1997

Nash JK: Treatment of attention deficit hyperactivity disorder with neurotherapy. Clin Electroencephalogr 31(1):30–37, 2000

National Pediatric Trauma Registry: Facts From the National Pediatric Trauma Registry—Fact Sheet 1. Boston, MA, Research and Training Center in Rehabilitation and Childhood Trauma, 1993

Navia BA, Jordan BD, Price RW: The AIDS dementia complex, I: clinical features. Ann Neurol 19:517–524, 1986

Naylor MW, Staskowski M, Kenney MC, et al: Language disorders and learning disabilities in school-refusing adolescents. J Am Acad Child Adolesc Psychiatry 33:1331–1337, 1994

New DR, Ma M, Epstein LG, et al: Human immunodeficiency virus type 1 Tat protein induces death by apoptosis in primary human neuron cultures. J Neurobiol 3:168–173, 1997

New DR, Maggirwar SB, Epstein LG, et al: HIV-1 Tat induced neuronal death via tumor necrosis factor–alpha and activation of non-N-methyl-D-aspartate receptors by the NfkappaB-independent mechanism. J Biol Chem 273:17852–17858, 1998

Nicholls RD, Knoll JH, Butler MG, et al: Genetic imprinting suggested by maternal heterodisomy in nondeletion Prader-Willi syndrome. Nature 342:281–285, 1989

Nielsen J, Friberg L, Lou H, et al: Immature patterns of brain activity in Rett syndrome. Arch Neurol 47:982–986, 1990

Njiokiktjien C, de Sonneville L, Vaal J: Callosal size in children with learning disabilities. Behav Brain Res 64:213–218, 1994

Nordahl TE, Benkelfat C, Semple WE, et al: Cerebral glucose metabolic rates in obsessive compulsive disorder. Neuropsychopharmacology 2:23–28, 1989

Nordin V, Gillberg C: The long-term course of autistic disorders: update on follow-up studies. Acta Psychiatr Scand 97:99–108, 1998

Novic B, Vaugham HG Jr, Kurtzberg D, et al: An electrophysiologic indication of auditory processing defects in autism. Psychiatry Res 3:107–114, 1980

Ogilvie CM, Moore J, Daker M, et al: Chromosome 22q11 deletions are not found in autistic patients identified using strict diagnostic criteria. IMGSAC. International Molecular Genetic Study of Autism Consortium. Am J Med Genet 96:15–17, 2000

Olvera RL, Pliszka SR, Luh J, et al: An open trial of venlafaxine in the treatment of attention-deficit/hyperactivity disorder in children and adolescents. J Child Adolesc Psychopharmacol 6(4):241–250, 1996

Ornitz EM: The modulation of sensory input and motor output in autistic children. Journal of Autism and Childhood Schizophrenia 4:197–215, 1974

Ornitz EM, Ritvo ER: Perceptual inconstancy in early infantile autism. Arch Gen Psychiatry 18:76–98, 1968

Overmeyer S, Simmons A, Santosh J, et al: Corpus callosum may be similar in children with ADHD and siblings of children with ADHD. Dev Med Child Neurol 42:8–13, 2000

Palmer CG, Bailey JN, Ramsey C, et al: No evidence of linkage or linkage disequilibrium between DAT1 and attention deficit hyperactivity disorder in a large sample. Psychiatr Genet 9(3):157–160, 1999

Park JP, Wurster-Hill DH, Andrews PA, et al: Free proximal trisomy 21 without the Down's syndrome. Clin Genet 32:342–348, 1987

Pauls DL: Genetic factors in the expression of attention-deficit hyperactivity disorder. J Child Adolesc Psychopharmacol 1:353–360, 1991

Pauls DL, Leckman JF: The inheritance of Gilles de la Tourette's syndrome and associated behaviors. N Engl J Med 315:993–997, 1986

Pavlakis SG, Lu D, Frank Y, et al: Magnetic resonance spectroscopy in childhood AIDS encephalopathy. Pediatr Neurol 12:277–282, 1995

Pavlakis SG, Lu D, Frank Y, et al: Brain lactate and N-acetylaspartate in pediatric AIDS encephalopathy. AJNR Am J Neuroradiol 19:383–385, 1998

Pearson DE, Teicher MH, Shaywitz BA, et al: Environmental influences on body weight and behavior in developing rats after neonatal 6-hydroxydopamine. Science 209:715–717, 1980

Pelham WE, Sturges J, Hoza J, et al: Sustained release and standard methylphenidate effects on cognitive and social behavior in children with attention deficit disorder. Pediatrics 80:491–501, 1987

Pelham WE, Greenslade KE, Vodde-Hamilton MA, et al: Relative efficacy of long-acting CNS stimulants on children with attention deficit–hyperactivity disorder: a comparison of standard methylphenidate, sustained-release methylphenidate, sustained-release dextroamphetamine, and pemoline. Pediatrics 86:226–237, 1990

Pelham WE, Swanson JM, Furman MB, et al: Pemoline effects on children with ADHD: a time-response by dose-response analysis on classroom measures. J Am Acad Child Adolesc Psychiatry 34:1504–1513, 1995

Pellock JM: Treatment of seizures and epilepsy in children and adolescents. Neurology 51:S8–14, 1998

Pennington BF, Smith SD: Genetic influences on learning disabilities and speech and language disorders. Child Dev 54:369–387, 1983

Perez MM, Trimble MR: Epileptic psychosis-diagnostic comparison with process schizophrenia. Br J Psychiatry 137:245–249, 1980

Perlmutter SJ, Leitman SF, Garvey MA, et al: Therapeutic plasma exchange and intravenous immunoglobulin for obsessive-compulsive disorder and tic disorders in childhood. Lancet 354:1153–1158, 1999

Perner J, Frith U, Leslie AM, et al: Exploration of the autistic child's theory of mind: Knowledge, belief, and communication. Child Dev 60:689–700, 1989

Perry SW, Hamilton JA, Tjoelker LW, et al: Platelet-activating factor receptor activation. An initiator step in HIV-1 neuropathogenesis. J Biol Chem 273:17660–17664, 1998

Peterson BS, Riddle MA, Cohen DJ, et al: Reduced basal ganglia volumes in Tourette's syndrome using 3-dimensional reconstruction techniques from magnetic resonance images. Neurology 43:941–949, 1993

Peterson BS, Gore JC, Riddle MA, et al: Abnormal magnetic resonance imaging T2 relaxation time asymmetries in Tourette's syndrome. Psychiatry Res 55:205–221, 1994

Peterson BS, Skudlarski P, Anderson AW, et al: A functional magnetic resonance imaging study of tic suppression in Tourette syndrome. Arch Gen Psychiatry 55:326–333, 1998

Peterson BS, Leckman JF, Tucker D, et al: Preliminary findings of antistreptococcal antibody titers and basal ganglia volumes in tic, obsessive-compulsive, and attention deficit/hyperactivity disorders. Arch Gen Psychiatry 57:364–372, 2000

Pihl RO, Parkes M: Hair element content in learning disabled children. Science 198:204–206, 1977

Piven J, Berthier ML, Starkstein SE, et al: Magnetic resonance imaging evidence for a defect of cerebral cortical development in autism. Am J Psychiatry 147:731–739, 1990

Piven J, Tsai G, Nehme E, et al: Platelet serotonin, a possible marker for familial autism. J Autism Dev Disord 21:51–59, 1991

Plante E: MRI findings in the parents and siblings of specifically language-impaired boys. Brain Lang 41:67–80, 1991

Pleak RR, Gormly LJ: Effects of venlafaxine treatment for ADHD in a child (letter). Am J Psychiatry 152:1099, 1995

Pliszka SR, Browne RG, Olvera RL, et al: A double-blind, placebo-controlled study of Adderall and methylphenidate in the treatment of attention-deficit/hyperactivity disorder. J Am Acad Child Adolesc Psychiatry 39(5):619–626, 2000

Plotsky PM, Meaney JM: Early postnatal experience alters hypothalamic corticotropin-releasing factor (CRF) mRNA, median eminence CRF content and stress-induced release in rats. Molecular Brain Research 18:195–200, 1993

Pontrelli L, Pavlakis S, Krilov LR: Neurobehavioral manifestations and sequelae of HIV and other infections. Child Adolesc Psychiatr Clin N Am 8:869–878, 1999

Popper CW: Antidepressants in the treatment of attention-deficit/hyperactivity disorder. J Clin Psychiatry 58 (suppl 14):14–29; discussion 30-31, 1997

Popper CW, Steingard RJ: Disorders usually first diagnosed in infancy, childhood, or adolescence, in American Psychiatric Press Textbook of Psychiatry, 2nd Edition. Edited by Hales RE, Yudofsky SC, Talbott JA. Washington, DC, American Psychiatric Press, 1995, pp 729–832

Popper CW, Zimnitzky B: Sudden death putatively related to desipramine treatment in youth: a fifth case and a review of speculative mechanisms. J Child Adolesc Psychopharmacol 5:283–300, 1995

Porrino LJ, Rapoport JL, Behar D: A naturalistic assessment of the motor activity of hyperactive boys, I: comparison with normal controls. Arch Gen Psychiatry 40:681–687, 1983

Posey DJ, Litwiller M, Koburn A, et al: Paroxetine in autism. J Am Acad Child Adolesc Psychiatry 38:111–112, 1999

Prior M, Sanson A: Attention deficit disorder with hyperactivity: a critique. J Child Psychol Psychiatry 27:307–319, 1986

Purves D: Neural Activity and the Growth of the Brain. Cambridge, England, Cambridge University Press, 1980

Rabey JM, Lewis A, Graff E, et al: Decreased (3H) quinuclidinyl benzilate binding to lymphocytes in Gilles de la Tourette syndrome. Biol Psychiatry 31:889–895, 1992

Rakic P: Development of the primate cerebral cortex, in Child and Adolescent Psychiatry. Edited by Lewis M. Baltimore, MD, Williams & Wilkins, 1994, pp 11–28

Rangno RE, Kaufmann JS, Cavanaugh JH, et al: Effects of a false neurotransmitter, p-hydroxynorephedrine, on the function of adrenergic neurons in hypertensive patients. J Clin Invest 52:952–960, 1973

Rapoport JL, Buchsbaum MS, Weingartner H, et al: Dextroamphetamine. Its cognitive and behavioral effects in normal and hyperactive boys and normal men. Arch Gen Psychiatry 37:933–943, 1980

Rapoport JL, Donnelly M, Zametkin A, et al: "Situational hyperactivity" in a U.S. clinical setting. J Child Psychol Psychiatry 27:639–646, 1986

Raskin LA, Shaywitz BA, Anderson GM, et al: Differential effects of selective dopamine, norepinephrine or catecholamine depletion on activity and learning in the developing rat. Pharmacol Biochem Behav 19:743–749, 1983

Reiss AL, Faruque F, Naidu S, et al: Neuroanatomy of Rett syndrome: a volumetric imaging study. Ann Neurol 34:227–234, 1993

Rett A: Uber Ein Zerebral-Atrophisches Syndrom Bei Hyperammonamie. Wein, Bruder Hollinek, 1966, pp 1–68

Rett A: Soziale Praventivmassnahmen bei entwicklungsgestorten Kindern. Ther Umsch 34:49–51, 1977

Riddle MA, Nelson JC, Kleinman CS, et al: Case study: sudden death in children receiving Norpramin: a review of three reported cases and commentary. J Am Acad Child Adolesc Psychiatry 30:104–108, 1991

Riddle MA, Rasmussen AM, Woods SW, et al: SPECT imaging of cerebral blood flow in Tourette syndrome, in Tourette Syndrome: Genetics, Neurobiology, and Treatment, Advances in Neurology, Vol 58. Edited by Chase TN, Friedhoff AJ, Cohen DJ. New York, Raven, 1992, pp 207–211

Riddle MA, Geller B, Ryan ND: Case study: another sudden death in a child treated with desipramine. J Am Acad Child Adolesc Psychiatry 32:792–797, 1993

Ritvo ER, Freeman BJ, Geller E, et al: Effects of fenfluramine on 14 outpatients with the syndrome of autism. Journal of the American Academy of Child Psychiatry 22:549–558, 1983

Ritvo ER, Freeman BJ, Yuwiler A, et al: Fenfluramine treatment of autism: UCLA collaborative study of 81 patients at nine medical centers. Psychopharmacology Bulletin 22:133–140, 1986

Ritzen EM, Lindgren AC, Hagenas L, et al: Growth hormone treatment of patients with Prader-Willi syndrome. J Pediatr Endocrinol Metab 12 (suppl 1):345–349, 1999

Riva D, Giorgi C: The cerebellum contributes to higher functions during development: evidence from a series of children surgically treated for posterior fossa tumours. Brain 123 (pt 5):1051–1061, 2000

Rivara JB, Jaffe KM, Fay GC, et al: Family functioning and injury severity as predictors of child functioning one year following traumatic brain injury. Arch Phys Med Rehabil 74:1047–1055, 1993

Robin AL, Foster S: Negotiating Parent-Adolescent Conflict. New York, Guilford, 1989

Robins PM: A comparison of behavioral and attentional functioning in children diagnosed as hyperactive or learning-disabled. J Abnorm Child Psychol 20:65–82, 1992

Rodin E, Schmalz S: The Bear-Fedio personality inventory and temporal lobe epilepsy. Neurology 34:591–596, 1984

Roof E, Stone W, MacLean W, et al: Intellectual characteristics of Prader-Willi syndrome: comparison of genetic subtypes. J Intellect Disabil Res 44:25–30, 2000

Rosner BS: Recovery of function and localization of function in historical perspective, in Plasticity and Recovery of Function in the Central Nervous System. Edited by Stein DG, Rosen JJ, Butters N. New York, Academic Press, 1974, pp 1–29

Ross DL, Klykylo WM, Hitzemann R: Reduction of elevated CSF beta-endorphin by fenfluramine in infantile autism. Am J Psychiatry 3:83–86, 1987

Rothner AD: Epilepsy, in Child and Adolescent Neurology for Psychiatrists. Edited by Kaufman DM, Solomon GE, Pfeffer CR. Baltimore, MD, Williams & Wilkins, 1992, pp 96–113

Rowe KJ, Rowe KS: The relationship between inattentiveness in the classroom and reading achievement. J Am Acad Child Adolesc Psychiatry 31:357–368, 1992

Rubia K, Overmeyer S, Taylor E, et al: Hypofrontality in attention deficit hyperactivity disorder during higher-order motor control: a study with functional MRI. Am J Psychiatry 156:891–896, 1999

Rumble B, Retallack R, Hilbich C, et al: Amyloid A4 protein and its precursor in Down's syndrome and Alzheimer's disease. N Engl J Med 320:1446–1452, 1989

Rumsey JM, Andreason P, Zametkin AJ, et al: Failure to activate the left temporoparietal cortex in dyslexia: an oxygen 15 positron emission tomographic study. Arch Neurol 49:527–534, 1992

Russo DC, Navalta CP: Some new dimensions of behavioral analysis and therapy, in Behavioral Approaches for Children and Adolescents: Challenges for the Next Century. Edited by Van Bilsen HPJG, Kendall PC, Slavenberg JH. New York, Plenum, 1995, pp 19–39

Rutter M, Bailey A: Thinking and relationships: mind and brain (some reflections on theory of mind and autism), in Understanding Other Minds: Perspectives From Autism. Edited by Baron-Cohen S, Tager-Flusberg H, Cohen D. New York, Oxford University Press, 1993, pp 481–504

Rutter M, Yule W: The concept of specific reading retardation. J Child Psychol Psychiatry 16:181–197, 1975

Sacks O: Awakenings. New York, Harper Perennial, 1973

Safer DJ, Krager JM: A survey of medication treatment for hyperactive/inattentive students. JAMA 260:2256–2258, 1988

Saito Y, Sharer LR, Dewhurst S, et al: Cellular localization of human herpes virus–6 in the brains of children with AIDS encephalopathy. J Neurovirol 1:30–39, 1995

Sallee FR, Sethuraman G, Rock CM: Effects of pimozide on cognition in children with Tourette syndrome: interaction with comorbid attention deficit hyperactivity disorder. Acta Psychiatr Scand 90:4–9, 1994

Salvan AM, Lamoureux S, Michel G, et al: Localized proton magnetic resonance spectroscopy of the brain in children infected with human immunodeficiency virus with and without encephalopathy. Pediatr Res 44:755–762, 1998

Sanberg PR, Silver AA, Shytle RD, et al: Nicotine for the treatment of Tourette's syndrome. Pharmacol Ther 74:21–25, 1997

Sanberg PR, Shytle RD, Silver AA: Treatment of Tourette's syndrome with mecamylamine. Lancet 352:705–706, 1998

Sanchez MM, Hearn EF, Do D, et al: Differential rearing affects corpus callosum size and cognitive function of rhesus monkeys. Brain Res 812:38–49, 1998

Sandler AD, Sutton KA, DeWeese J, et al: Lack of benefit of a single dose of synthetic human secretin in the treatment of autism and pervasive developmental disorder. N Engl J Med 341:1801–1806, 1999

Sandson TA, Manoach DS, Price BH, et al: Right hemisphere learning disability associated with left hemisphere dysfunction: anomalous dominance and development. J Neurol Neurosurg Psychiatry 57:1129–1132, 1994

Satterfield JH, Hoppe CM, Schell AM: A prospective study of delinquency in 110 adolescent boys with attention deficit disorder and 88 normal adolescent boys. Am J Psychiatry 139:795–798, 1982

Scahill L, Chappell PB, King RA, et al: Pharmacologic treatment of tic disorders. Child Adolesc Psychiatr Clin N Am 9(1):99–117, 2000

Scarmato V, Frank Y, Rozenstein A, et al: Central brain atrophy in childhood AIDS encephalopathy. AIDS 10:1227–1231, 1996

Schacter SC, Galaburda AM: Development and biological associations of cerebral dominance: review and possible mechanisms. Journal of the American Academy of Child Psychiatry 25:7411–7450, 1986

Schiffer F, Teicher MH, Papanicolaou AC: Evoked potential evidence for right brain activity during recall of traumatic memories. J Neuropsychiatry Clin Neurosci 7:169–175, 1995

Schmahmann JD, Pandya DN: Prefrontal cortex projections to the basilar pons in rhesus monkey: implications for the cerebellar contribution to higher function. Neurosci Lett 199:175–178, 1995

Schmidt D, Bourgeois B: A risk-benefit assessment of therapies for Lennox-Gastaut syndrome. Drug Saf 22:467–477, 2000

Schrott LM, Denenberg VH, Sherman GF, et al: Environmental enrichment, neocortical ectopias, and behavior in the autoimmune NZB mouse. Developmental Brain Research 67:85–93, 1992

Schultz RT, Gauthier I, Klin A, et al: Abnormal ventral temporal cortical activity during face discrimination among individuals with autism and Asperger syndrome. Arch Gen Psychiatry 57:331–340, 2000

Schweitzer JB, Faber TL, Grafton ST, et al: Alterations in the functional anatomy of working memory in adult attention deficit hyperactivity disorder. Am J Psychiatry 157:278–280, 2000

Seeman P, Madras BK: Anti-hyperactivity medication: methylphenidate and amphetamine (comments). Mol Psychiatry 3:386–396, 1998

Seeman P, Bzowej N, Guan H, et al: Human brain receptors in children and aging adults. Synapse 1:399–404, 1987

Seghorn TK, Boucher RJ, Prentky RA: Childhood sexual abuse in the lives of sexually aggressive offenders. J Am Acad Child Adolesc Psychiatry 26:262–267, 1987

Sei S, Stewart SK, Farley M, et al: Evaluation of human immunodeficiency virus (HIV) type 1 RNA levels in cerebrospinal fluid and viral resistance to zidovudine in children with HIV-encephalopathy. J Infect Dis 174(6):1200–1206, 1996

Semrud-Clikeman M, Hynd GW: Right hemispheric dysfunction in nonverbal learning disabilities: social, academic and adaptive functioning in adults and children. Psychol Bull 107:196–209, 1990

Semrud-Clikeman M, Biederman J, Sprich-Buckminster S, et al: Comorbidity between ADHD and learning disability: a review and report in a clinically referred sample. J Am Acad Child Adolesc Psychiatry 31:439–448, 1992

Semrud-Clikeman M, Filipek PA, Biederman J, et al: Attention-deficit hyperactivity disorder: magnetic resonance imaging morphometric analysis of the corpus callosum. J Am Acad Child Adolesc Psychiatry 33:875–881, 1994

Semrud-Clikeman M, Steingard RJ, Filipek P, et al: Using MRI to examine brain-behavior relationships in males with attention deficit disorder with hyperactivity. J Am Acad Child Adolesc Psychiatry 39:477–484, 2000

Sharer LR: Pathology of HIV-1 infection of the central nervous system. A review. J Neuropathol Exp Neurol 51:3–11, 1992

Sharer LR, Epstein LG, Cho E-S, et al: Pathologic features of AIDS encephalopathy in children: Evidence for LAV/HTLV-III infection of brain. Hum Pathol 17:271–284, 1986

Sharer LR, Saito Y, Da Cunha A, et al: In situ amplification and detection of HIV-1 DNA in fixed pediatric AIDS brain tissue. Hum Pathol 27:614–617, 1996

Shaywitz BA, Klopper JH, Yager RD, et al: Paradoxical response to amphetamine in developing rats treated with 6-hydroxydopamine. Nature 261:153–155, 1976a

Shaywitz BA, Yager RD, Klopper JH: Selective brain dopamine depletion in developing rats: an experimental model of minimal brain dysfunction. Science 191:305–308, 1976b

Shaywitz BA, Teicher MH, Cohen DJ, et al: Dopaminergic but not noradrenergic mediation of hyperactivity and performance deficits in the developing rat pup. Psychopharmacology (Berl) 82:73–77, 1984

Shaywitz BA, Fletcher JM, Shaywitz SE: Defining and classifying learning disabilities and attention-deficit/hyperactivity disorder. J Child Neurol 10 (suppl):S50–S57, 1995

Shaywitz SE, Escobar MD, Shaywitz BA, et al: Evidence that dyslexia may represent the lower tail of a normal distribution of reading ability. N Engl J Med 326:145–150, 1992

Sheng JG, Mrak RE, Griffin WS: S100 beta protein expression in Alzheimer disease: potential role in the pathogenesis of neuritic plaques. J Neurosci Res 39:398–404, 1994

Sidman RL, Rakic P: Neuronal migration with special reference to developing human brain: a review. Brain Res 62:1–35, 1973

Sieg KG, Gaffney GR, Preston DF, et al: SPECT brain imaging abnormalities in attention deficit hyperactivity disorder. Clin Nucl Med 20:55–60, 1995

Simonds RJ, Scheibel AB: The postnatal development of the motor speech area: a preliminary study. Brain Lang 37:42–58, 1989

Simos PG, Breier JI, Fletcher JM, et al: Brain activation profiles in dyslexic children during non-word reading: a magnetic source imaging study. Neurosci Lett 290:61–65, 2000

Simpson DM: Human immunodeficiency virus–associated dementia: review of pathogenesis, prophylaxis, and treatment studies of zidovudine therapy. Clin Infect Dis 29:19–34, 1999

Singer HS, Hahn IH, Moran TH: Tourette's syndrome: abnormal dopamine uptake sites in postmortem striatum from patients with Tourette's syndrome. Ann Neurol 30:558–562, 1991

Singer HS, Reiss AL, Brown JE, et al: Volumetric MRI changes in the basal ganglia of children with Tourette's syndrome. Neurology 43:950–956, 1993

Singer HS, Brown J, Quaskey S, et al: The treatment of attention-deficit hyperactivity disorder in Tourette's syndrome: a double-blind placebo-controlled study with clonidine and desipramine. Pediatrics 95:74–81, 1995

Singer HS, Giuliano JD, Hansen BH, et al: Antibodies against human putamen in children with Tourette syndrome. Neurology 50:1618–1624, 1998

Singer HS, Guulian JD, Hansen BH, et al: Antibodies against a neuron-like (HTB-10 neuroblastoma) cell in children with Tourette syndrome. Biol Psychiatry 15:775–780, 1999

Siomi MC, Siomi H, Sauer WH, et al: FXR1, an autosomal homolog of the fragile X mental retardation gene. EMBO J 14:2401–2408, 1995

Skottun BC: The magnocellular deficit theory of dyslexia: the evidence from contrast sensitivity. Vision Res 40:111–127, 2000

Sollee ND, Kindlon DJ: Lateralized brain injury and behavior problems in children. J Abnorm Child Psychol 15:479–491, 1987

Spencer T, Biederman J, Kerman K, et al: Desipramine treatment of children with attention-deficit hyperactivity disorder and tic disorder or Tourette's syndrome. J Am Acad Child Adolesc Psychiatry 32:354–360, 1993a

Spencer T, Biederman J, Steingard R, et al: Bupropion exacerbates tics in children with attention-deficit hyperactivity disorder and Tourette's syndrome. J Am Acad Child Adolesc Psychiatry 32:211–214, 1993b

Spencer T, Biederman J, Wilens T, et al: Nortriptyline treatment of children with attention-deficit hyperactivity disorder and tic disorder or Tourette's syndrome. J Am Acad Child Adolesc Psychiatry 32:205–210, 1993c

Spencer TJ, Biederman J, Harding M, et al: Growth deficits in ADHD children revisited: evidence for disorder-associated growth delays? J Am Acad Child Adolesc Psychiatry 35(11):1460–1469, 1996

Starace F, Dijkgraaf M, Houweling H, et al: HIV-associated dementia: clinical, epidemiological and resource utilization issues. AIDS Care 10 (suppl 2):S113–S121, 1998

State MW, King BH, Dykens E: Mental retardation: a review of the past 10 years. Part II. J Am Acad Child Adolesc Psychiatry 36(12):1664–1671, 1997

State MW, Dykens EM, Rosner B, et al: Obsessive-compulsive symptoms in Prader-Willi and "Prader-Willi–like" patients. J Am Acad Child Adolesc Psychiatry 38:329–334, 1999

Stein J, Fowler S: Effect of monocular occlusion on visuomotor perception and reading in dyslexic children. Lancet 2:69–73, 1985

Stein J, Walsh V: To see but not to read: the magnocellular theory of dyslexia. Trends Neurosci 20:147–152, 1997

Stein MB, Koverola C, Hanna C, et al: Hippocampal volume in women victimized by childhood sexual abuse. Psychol Med 27:951–959, 1997

Steingard R, Khan A, Gonzalez A, et al: Neuroleptic malignant syndrome: review of experience with children and adolescents. J Child Adolesc Psychopharmacol 2:183–198, 1992

Steingard R, Biederman J, Spencer T, et al: Comparison of clonidine response in the treatment of attention-deficit hyperactivity disorder with and without comorbid tic disorders. J Am Acad Child Adolesc Psychiatry 32:350–353, 1993

Steinman SB, Steinman BA, Garzia RP: Vision and attention, II: is visual attention a mechanism through which a deficient magnocellular pathway might cause reading disability? Optom Vis Sci 75:674–681, 1998

Stevenson J, Graham P, Fredman G, et al: A twin study of genetic influences on reading and spelling ability and disability. J Child Psychol Psychiatry 28:229–247, 1987

Stone MH: Borderline syndromes: a consideration of subtypes and an overview, directions for research. Psychiatr Clin North Am 4:3–13, 1981

Streissguth AP, Barr HM, Sampson PD: Moderate prenatal alcohol exposure: effects on child IQ and learning problems at age 7-1/2 years. Alcohol Clin Exp Res 14:662–669, 1990

Stricker EM, Zigmond MJ: Recovery of function following damage to central catecholamine-containing neurons: a neurochemical model for the lateral hypothalamic syndrome, in Progress in Psychobiology, Physiology, and Psychology, Vol 6. New York, Academic Press, 1976, pp 121–188

Struve FA, Klein DF, Saraf KR: Electroencephalographic correlates of suicide ideation and attempts. Arch Gen Psychiatry 27:363–365, 1972

Subramaniam B, Naidu S, Reiss AL: Neuroanatomy in Rett syndrome: cerebral cortex and posterior fossa. Neurology 48:399–407, 1997

Sunahara RK, Seeman P, Van Tol HH, et al: Dopamine receptors and antipsychotic drug response. Br J Psychiatry Suppl (22):31–38, 1993

Suzuki DA, Keller EL: The role of the posterior vermis of monkey cerebellum in smooth-pursuit eye movement control, II: target velocity-related Purkinje cell activity. J Neurophysiol 59:19–40, 1988

Sverd J, Gadow KD, Paolicelli LM: Methylphenidate treatment of attention-deficit hyperactivity disorder in boys with Tourette's syndrome. J Am Acad Child Adolesc Psychiatry 28:574–579, 1989

Swanson JM, Sunohara GA, Kennedy JL, et al: Association of the dopamine receptor D4 (DRD4) gene with a refined phenotype of attention deficit hyperactivity disorder (ADHD): a family based approach. Mol Psychiatry 3:38–41, 1998

Swanson J, Oosterlaan J, Murias M, et al: Attention deficit/hyperactivity disorder children with a 7-repeat allele of the dopamine receptor D4 gene have extreme behavior but normal performance on critical neuropsychological tests of attention. Proc Natl Acad Sci U S A 97(9):4754–4759, 2000

Swedo SE: Sydenham's chorea: a model for childhood autoimmune neuropsychiatric disorders. JAMA 272:1788–1791, 1994

Sweeney JA, Strojwas MH, Mann JJ, et al: Prefrontal and cerebellar abnormalities in major depression: evidence from oculomotor studies. Biol Psychiatry 43:584–594, 1998

Szatmari P, Offord DR, Boyle MH: Ontario Child Health Study: prevalence of attention deficit disorder with hyperactivity. J Child Psychol Psychiatry 30:219–230, 1989

Tahir E, Yazgan Y, Cirakoglu B, et al: Association and linkage of DRD4 and DRD5 with attention deficit hyperactivity disorder (ADHD) in a sample of Turkish children. Mol Psychiatry 5:396–404, 2000

Tallal P, Townsend J, Curtiss S, et al: Phenotypic profiles of language-impaired children based on genetic/family history. Brain Lang 41:81–95, 1991

Tallal P, Miller SL, Bedi G, et al: Language comprehension in language-learning impaired children improved with acoustically modified speech. Science 271:81–84, 1996

Talley A, Dewhurst S, Perry S, et al: Tumor necrosis factor alpha induces apoptosis in human neuronal cells: protection by the antioxidant N-acetylcysteine and the genes bcl-2 and crmA. Mol Cell Biol 15:2359–2366, 1995

Tanguay PE: Pervasive developmental disorders: a 10-year review. J Am Acad Child Adolesc Psychiatry 39:1079–1095, 2000

Tardieu M, Le Chenadec J, Persoz A, et al: HIV-1–related encephalopathy in infants compared with children and adults. French Pediatric HIV Infection Study and the SEROCO Group. Neurology 54:1089–1095, 2000

Teicher MH: Psychological factors in neurological development, in Neurobiological Development, Vol 12. Edited by Evrard P, Minkowski A. New York, Nestle Nutrition Workshop Series, Raven, 1989, pp 243–258

Teicher MH: Actigraphy and motion analysis: new tools for psychiatry. Harvard Review of Psychiatry 3:18–35, 1995

Teicher MH: Wounds that time won't heal: the neurobiology of child abuse. Cerebrum 2:50–67, 2000

Teicher MH, Glod CA: Neuroleptic drugs: indications and guidelines for their rational use in children and adolescents. J Child Adolesc Psychopharmacol 1:33–56, 1990

Teicher MH, Shaywitz BA, Kootz HL, et al: Differential effects of maternal and sibling presence on the hyperactivity of 6-hydroxydopamine treated developing rats. Journal of Comparative Physiological Psychology 95:134–135, 1981

Teicher MH, Glod CA, Surrey J, et al: Early childhood abuse and limbic system ratings in adult psychiatric outpatients. J Neuropsychiatry Clin Neurosci 5:301–306, 1993

Teicher MH, Ito Y, Glod CA, et al: Early abuse, limbic system dysfunction, and borderline personality disorder, in Biological and Neurobehavioral Studies of Borderline Personality Disorder. Edited by Silk K. Washington, DC, American Psychiatric Press, 1994, pp 177–207

Teicher MH, Andersen SL, Hostetter JC Jr: Evidence for dopamine receptor pruning between adolescence and adulthood in striatum but not nucleus accumbens. Brain Res Dev Brain Res 89:167–172, 1995

Teicher MH, Ito Y, Glod CA, et al: Neurophysiological mechanisms of stress response in children, in Severe Stress and Mental Disturbance in Children. Edited by Pfeffer C. Washington, DC, American Psychiatric Press, 1996a, pp 59–84

Teicher MH, Ito Y, Glod CA, et al: Objective measurement of hyperactivity and attentional problems in ADHD. J Am Acad Child Adolesc Psychiatry 35:334–342, 1996b

Teicher MH, Polcari A, Anderson CH, et al: Dose dependent effects of methylphenidate on activity, attention, and magnetic resonance measures in children with ADHD. Society for Neuroscience Abstracts 22:1191, 1996c

Teicher MH, Ito Y, Glod CA, et al: Preliminary evidence for abnormal cortical development in physically and sexually abused children using EEG coherence and MRI. Ann N Y Acad Sci 821:160–175, 1997

Teicher MH, Andersen SL, Dumont NL, et al: Childhood neglect attenuates development of the corpus callosum. Society for Neuroscience Abstracts 26:549, 2000a

Teicher MH, Anderson CM, Polcari A, et al: Functional deficits in basal ganglia of children with attention-deficit/hyperactivity disorder shown with functional magnetic imaging relaxometry. Nat Med 6:470–473, 2000b

Tenhula WN, Xu SZ, Madigan MC, et al: Morphometric comparisons of optic nerve axon loss in acquired immunodeficiency syndrome. Am J Ophthalmol 15:14–20, 1992

Tepper BJ, Farley JJ, Rothman MI, et al: Neurodevelopmental/neuroradiologic recovery of a child infected with HIV after treatment with combination antiretroviral therapy using the HIV-specific protease inhibitor ritonavir (case report). Pediatrics 101:E7, 1998

Thach WT, Goodkin HP, Keating JG: The cerebellum and the adaptive coordination of movement. Annu Rev Neurosci 15:403–442, 1992

Thapar A, Gottesman, Owen MJ, et al: The genetics of mental retardation. Br J Psychiatry 164:747–758, 1994

Tourette Syndrome Association International Consortium for Genetics: A complete genome screen in sib pairs affected by Gilles de la Tourette syndrome. Am J Hum Genet 65:1428–1436, 1999

Tryon WW: The role of motor excess and instrumented activity measurement in attention deficit hyperactivity disorder. Behav Modif 17:371–406, 1993

Turjanski N, Sawle GV, Playford ED, et al: PET studies of the presynaptic and postsynaptic dopaminergic system in Tourette's syndrome. J Neurol Neurosurg Psychiatry 57:688–692, 1994

Turk J: The fragile-X syndrome: on the way to a behavioural phenotype. Br J Psychiatry 160:24–35, 1992

Ultmann MH, Belman AL, Ruff HA, et al: Developmental abnormalities in children with acquired immune deficiency syndrome (AIDS): a follow up study. Int J Neurosci 32:661–667, 1987

Vaidya CJ, Austin G, Kirkorian G, et al: Selective effects of methylphenidate in attention deficit hyperactivity disorder: a functional magnetic resonance study. Proc Natl Acad Sci U S A 95:14494–14499, 1998

Van Bockstaele EJ, Colago EE, Valentino RJ: Amygdaloid corticotropin-releasing factor targets locus coeruleus dendrites: substrate for the co-ordination of emotional and cognitive limbs of the stress response. J Neuroendocrinol 10:743–757, 1998

van der Kolk B, Greenberg MS: The psychobiology of the trauma response: hyperarousal, constriction, and addiction to traumatic reexposure, in Psychological Trauma. Edited by van der Kolk B. Washington, DC, American Psychiatric Press, 1987, pp 63–87

Verkerk AJ, Pieretti M, Sutcliffe JS, et al: Identification of a gene (FMR1) containing a CGG repeat coincident with a breakage point cluster region exhibiting length variation in fragile X syndrome. Cell 65:905–914, 1991

Wada JA, Clarke R, Hamm A: Cerebral hemispheric asymmetry in humans. Arch Neurol 32:239–246, 1975

Waldman ID, Rowe A, Abramowitz S, et al: Association and linkage of the dopamine transporter gene and attention deficit hyperactivity disorder in children: heterogeneity owing to diagnostic subtype and severity. Am J Hum Genet 63:1767–1776, 1998

Walker EF: Developmentally moderated expressions of the neuropathology underlying schizophrenia. Schizophr Bull 20:453–480, 1994

Warren RP, Yonk J, Burger RW, et al: DR-positive T cells in autism: association with decreased plasma levels of the complement C4B protein. Neuropsychobiology 31:53–57, 1995

Weiss G, Milroy T, Perlman T: Psychiatric status of hyperactives as adults: a controlled prospective 15-year follow-up of 63 hyperactive children. Journal of the American Academy of Child Psychiatry 24:211–220, 1985

Weiss RE, Stein MA, Trommer B, et al: Attention-deficit hyperactivity disorder and thyroid function. J Pediatr 123:539–545, 1993

Wender PH: Minimal Brain Dysfunction in Children. New York, Wiley-Interscience, 1971, p 37

Wender PH: Methamphetamine in child psychiatry. J Child Adolesc Psychopharmacol 3:iv–vi, 1993

Wenk GL, Naidu S, Casanova MG, et al: Altered neurochemicals markers in Rett's syndrome. Neurology 41:1753–1756, 1991

Wilbur CB: Multiple personality and child abuse. An overview. Psychiatr Clin North Am 7:3–7, 1984

Wilens TE, Biederman J: The stimulants. Psychiatr Clin North Am 41:191–222, 1992

Wilens TE, Biederman J, Spencer TJ: Venlafaxine for adult ADHD (letter). Am J Psychiatry 152:1099–1100, 1995

Wiley CA, Schrier RD, Nelson JA, et al: Cellular localization of human immunodeficiency virus infection within the brains of acquired immune deficiency syndrome patients. Proc Natl Acad Sci U S A 83:7089–7093, 1986

Wing L, Gould J: Severe impairments of social interaction and associated abnormalities in children: epidemiology and classification. Journal of Autism and Childhood Schizophrenia 9:11–29, 1979

Winsberg B, Comings DE: Association of the dopamine transporter gene (DAT1) with poor methylphenidate response. J Am Acad Child Adolesc Psychiatry 38:1474–1477, 1999

Wisniewski KE, Wisniewski HM, Wen GY: Occurrence of neuropathological changes and dementia of Alzheimer's disease in Down's syndrome. Ann Neurol 17:278–282, 1985

Wolf SS, Jones DW, Knable MB, et al: Tourette's syndrome: prediction of phenotypic variation in monozygotic twins by caudate nucleus D2 receptor binding. Science 273:1225–1227, 1996

Wolters PL, Brouwers P, Moss HA, et al: Differential receptive and expressive language functioning of children with symptomatic HIV disease and relation to CT scan brain abnormalities. Pediatrics 95:112–119, 1995

Working Group of the American Academy of Neurology AIDS Task Force: Nomenclature and research case definitions for neurologic manifestations of human immunodeficiency virus type 1 infection. Neurology 41:778–785, 1991

World Health Organization: International Statistical Classification of Diseases and Related Health Problems, 10th Revision. Geneva, Switzerland, World Health Organization, 1992

Wyllie E, Rothner AD, Luders H: Partial seizures in children: clinical features, medical treatment, and surgical considerations. Pediatr Clin North Am 36:343–364, 1989

Young JG, Leven LI, Newcorn JH, et al: Genetic and neurobiological approaches to the pathophysiology of autism and the pervasive developmental disorders, in Psychopharmacology: The Third Generation of Progress. Edited by Meltzer HY. New York, Raven, 1985, pp 825–836

Zametkin AJ, Rapoport JL: Neurobiology of attention deficit disorder with hyperactivity: where have we come in 50 years? J Am Acad Child Adolesc Psychiatry 26:676–686, 1987

Zametkin AJ, Karoum F, Linnoila M, et al: Stimulants, urinary catecholamines, and indoleamines in hyperactivity. A comparison of methylphenidate and dextroamphetamine. Arch Gen Psychiatry 42:251–255, 1985

Zametkin AJ, Nordahl TE, Gross M, et al: Cerebral glucose metabolism in adults with hyperactivity of childhood onset. N Engl J Med 323:1361–1366, 1990

Zhang K, Tarazi FT, Baldessarini RJ: Regulation of dopamine D1- and D2-like receptors in transient hyperactivity following neonatal 6-hydroxydopamine lesions. Society for Neuroscience Abstracts 26:841, 2000

Zierler S, Krieger N, Tang Y, et al: Economic deprivation and AIDS incidence in Massachusetts. Am J Public Health 90:1064–1073, 2000

Zimmerman AM, Abrams MT, Giuliano JD, et al: Subcortical volumes in girls with Tourette syndrome: support for a gender effect. Neurology 54:2224–2229, 2000

Zoghbi HY, Percy AK, Glaze DG, et al: Reduction of biogenic amine levels in the Rett syndrome. N Engl J Med 313:921–941, 1985

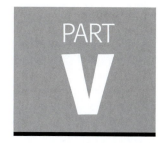

# Neuropsychiatric Treatments

# Intracellular and Intercellular Principles of Pharmacotherapy for Neuropsychiatric Disorders

W. Dale Horst, Ph.D.

Michael J. Burke, M.D., Ph.D.

The technical advances for identifying the genes responsible for specific protein components of the neurotransmission process is revolutionizing psychopharmacology. These molecular biologic methods are changing the manner in which new drugs are being discovered, providing more specific knowledge of the biologic nature of mental illness, and redefining basic concepts of psychopharmacologic therapy and even the lexicon of psychopharmacology.

For example, psychotherapeutic drugs have traditionally been referred to by the disorders that they treat, such as *antidepressants, anxiolytics,* and *antipsychotics.* This nomenclature is understandable in the case of drugs such as the tricyclic antidepressants, which have multiple sites of actions and complex pharmacodynamics, but it is inadequate in terms of newer, more specific therapeutic agents. Thus, it has become more common to speak of *benzodiazepine receptor agonists, antagonists, inverse agonists,* or *serotonin specific reuptake inhibitors* (SSRIs), terms that not only define the site of action but also characterize the type of activity of the agent.

New advances always bring new questions and new problems. The ability to develop agents with ever-increasing specificity may give rise to the question of whether this is a desirable goal. Is it reasonable to assume that disorders such as major depression or schizophrenia are the result of one specific lesion in the neurotransmis-

sion process? Are several concurrent lesions necessary to express the disorder or can any one of several different lesions be responsible for similar symptoms and the same diagnosis?

The answers to such basic questions not only will influence the development of new therapeutic agents but also will have a major impact on how physicians diagnose disorders in their patients and how they arrive at an effective course of therapy. In this chapter, we summarize our understanding of the basic elements of neurotransmission and how this knowledge is influencing drug development and treatment strategies.

## Historical Perspectives

For centuries humankind has been taking drugs and concoctions to relieve the symptoms of abnormal behavior. As far back as the third century B.C. cathartic herbs were used to cure melancholy (Burton 1621). Despite that these treatments could not have been effective, the traditions surrounding their use lasted for centuries. Not until early in the twentieth century were attempts made to scientifically evaluate the effectiveness of drugs in mental illness (Wright 1926).

Modern psychopharmacology began rather dramatically in the 1950s when a series of serendipitous observations revealed the therapeutic properties of several psychotherapeutic agents. Not only did these new agents prove useful in therapy, but they served as important research tools for the discovery of new frontiers of neurochemistry and neurophysiology. This process encouraged the development of theories based on the organic nature of brain function and mental dysfunction (Wooley 1962). The development of these frontiers has, in turn, lead to the development of better drugs for the treatment of mental illnesses.

The therapeutic effect of chlorpromazine in psychotic patients was demonstrated in 1952. Chlorpromazine was under development as a drug to reduce fluid loss in surgery. At about the same time, the tranquilizing properties of a *Rauwolfia* extract, reserpine, were being observed in psychotic patients (for a review of these developments see Cole 1959). Iproniazid, a drug used in the treatment of tuberculosis, was observed to have antidepressant effects in 1952 and became available to practicing physicians in 1957. In 1954 meprobamate was identified as a specific anxiolytic and was used in the treatment of neuroses (Caldwell 1978).

The discovery of drugs that appeared to be effective in alleviating the symptoms of specific mental illnesses such as depression, psychosis, and neurosis led to an intensive search for additional drugs of this type. Because chlorpromazine was a tricyclic compound, many drugs with this basic structure were tested for antipsychotic activity. This research eventually led to the discovery of the antidepressant class of tricyclics, for many years the drugs of choice in treating depression. Similarly, the search for new chemical structures with antipsychotic activity led to the discovery of the benzodiazepines as specific anxiolytics (Sternbach and Horst 1982).

The rapid and dramatic developments in psychopharmacology during the 1950s had an equally dramatic influence on psychiatry and how the human brain was viewed by society ("Pills for the Mind" 1955). Over the years, our ability to treat mental illness with drugs promoted the chemical nature of the brain and deemphasized Freudian concepts (Wallis and Willwerth 1992). This change in view was further enhanced by our knowledge of such mind-altering drugs as lysergic acid diethylamide (LSD). Although LSD did not achieve therapeutic status, its influences on mental functions were well known (Rosenfeld 1966) by the lay public as well as by psychopharmacologists.

The development of modern neuropsychopharmacology not only provided tools with which neurophysiologists and neurochemists could learn more about brain function, but more importantly, this era stimulated great interest in the neurosciences with the result that our increase in basic knowledge of brain function has enhanced the discovery of newer, better therapeutic agents for the treatment of mental illness.

# Neurobiology

During the past several decades, tremendous strides have been made in understanding the basic mechanisms of brain function. Progress has been aided by advances in neuropsychopharmacology and the availability of technologies such as receptor binding techniques, patch clamp techniques, and, more recently, molecular genetic procedures. The advances in our understanding of the basic process of brain function permits a better understanding of the brain in dysfunction, which in turn assists in the development of specifically targeted therapeutic agents.

The brain consists of approximately 100 million neurons, which account for one half of the brain's volume, the other half being made up of glial cells. Glial cells guide the synaptic formation of neurons during brain development (Bacci et al. 1999), influence the extracellular environment of the neurons (Zahs 1998), synthesize neurotransmitter precursors (Martin 1992), and respond to, or in some cases can cause, brain damage (Aschner et al. 1999; McGeer and McGeer 1998; Raivich et al. 1999). In turn, neurons are known to produce factors influencing the development and function of glia (Melcangi et al. 1999; Vardimon et al. 1999).

## Glia

For many years glia were thought to have a somewhat limited or passive role in brain function, but more recent revelations indicate that glia have receptors, uptake mechanisms, and enzymes for several neurotransmitters, suggesting that the functions of these cells are closely integrated with neuronal functions (Attwell 1994; Inagaki and Wada 1994; Martin 1992; Otero and Merrill 1994; Ransom and Sontheimer 1992) (Table 34–1).

An important example of this type of interaction is described shown in Figure 34–1. Glutamate and γ-aminobutyric acid (GABA) are ubiquitous neurotransmitters in the brain, serving as primary excitatory and inhibitory neurotransmitters. Glial cells (astrocytes) play a prominent role in recycling and conserving both glutamate and GABA by recapturing them from the synapse, converting them to glutamine, and then returning glutamine to the presynaptic neurons for conversion back to the appropriate neurotransmitter (Shank et al. 1989). In addition to the conservation of neurotransmitter, glia protect neu-

**TABLE 34–1.** Membrane elements of mammalian glia

| Receptors[a] | Response mode |
|---|---|
| Noradrenergic (α and β) | G protein |
| Adenosine | G protein |
| Acetylcholine (muscarinic) | G protein |
| Neuropeptides (substance P) | G protein |
| Glutamate (quisqualate, kainate) | Ion gating |
| γ-Aminobutyric acid (GABA$_A$) | Ion gating |

**Ion channels (voltage sensitive)**
   Potassium (inwardly rectifying,
      outwardly rectifying, and
      transient A-type)
   Sodium—tetrodotoxin sensitive
      ("neuronal") and tetrodotoxin
      resistant ("glial")
   Calcium (L- and T-type)
   Chloride

**Transporters (uptake sites)**
   GABA
   Glutamate
   Glycine

[a]Although nearly all neuronal-type neuroreceptors have been shown to occur on glial membranes, only those which have been shown to produce a response have been included here.
*Source.* Adapted from Krantz et al. 1999; Ransom and Sontheimer 1992; Sontheimer 1994.

rons by limiting synaptic levels of glutamate (Bacci et al. 1999; Vardimon et al. 1999). Prominent among glutamate's several cellular influences is the opening of specific calcium channels that allow the influx of calcium ions into neurons. The overstimulation of neurons via this mechanism has been associated with neurotoxicity and neuronal death. Thus, it is of considerable importance that extraneuronal concentrations of glutamate be controlled and that mechanisms exist to limit the synaptic activity of this neurotransmitter. Glial cells have been shown to possess membrane transporters or uptake sites for glutamate; it has also been demonstrated that glutamate uptake into glial cells is the primary route for clearing synaptic glutamate. Once inside the glial cell, the glutamate is metabolized to glutamine, a neuronally inactive substance. The conversion of glutamate to glutamine occurs primarily in glial cells via the enzyme glutamine synthetase. Thus, glial cells play a critical roll in limiting the synaptic concentrations of glutamate and conserving the neurotransmitter for reuse. An important element in the above functions is the maintenance of appropriate levels of glutamine synthetase activity in glial cells. Significant factors in the regulation of glutamine synthetase activity are glucocorticoid stimulation of gene expression and the absolute requirement for the astrocyte and neu-

ron to be in juxtaposition. The critical neuronal factor required for gene expression of glutamine synthetase has not been identified (Vardimon et al. 1999).

Further evidence of the role astrocytes play in limiting synaptic levels of glutamate is demonstrated by the influence that neuronal factors play in the regulation of glutamate transporter expression in glial membranes (Schlag et al. 1998; Swanson et al. 1997). A soluble, diffusible substance secreted by neurons has been shown to increase the expression of glutamate transporter molecules in astrocytes. Thus, it would appear that the level of neuronal activity plays a role in regulating the rate at which glutamate is transported into the glia for inactivation as described above. Although the substance has not been identified, the above effects can be mimicked by cyclic AMP analogs (Schlag et al. 1998; Swanson et al. 1997).

Neuron-dependent expression of two types of calcium channels has also been shown in astrocytes (Corvalan et al. 1990). The agent responsible for this intercellular communication has not been identified but may be cyclic AMP or a related substance (Corvalan et al. 1990).

Recent investigations have revealed a metabolic coupling between glia and neurons (Bacci et al. 1999; Poitry-Yamate et al. 1995; Tsacopoulos and Magistretti 1996). Considerable energy is consumed in the various processes of synaptic transmission. The preferred energy source for brain function is glucose. Astrocytes are capable of transporting glucose across the cell membrane via an active, carrier-assisted mechanism. Because astrocytes are well known to be in intimate contact with the brain's vascular system, it is assumed that glucose is transported directly into the glia from the circulation. Inside the glia, glycolysis transforms the glucose to lactose and in the process provides energy for the transport of neurotransmitters and ions across the glial membrane. Lactose is then transferred out of the glia and accumulated by neurons, where it is the preferred substrate for oxidative metabolism. This energy transfer process is stimulated by the uptake of neurotransmitters such as glutamate and GABA. Neurotransmitter uptake by glia is accompanied by the influx of sodium ions. The accumulation of sodium ions stimulates a sodium/potassium adenosine triphosphatase ($Na^+/K^+$-ATPase) pump, which consumes adenosine triphosphate (ATP) and exchanges intracellular sodium ions for extracellular potassium ions. The activity of the ATPase stimulates the metabolism of glucose, resulting in increased lactose production. Thus, the production of metabolic precursor keeps pace with the overall synaptic activity.

In some cases astrocytes have been shown to possess functional ion channels controlled by neurotransmitter

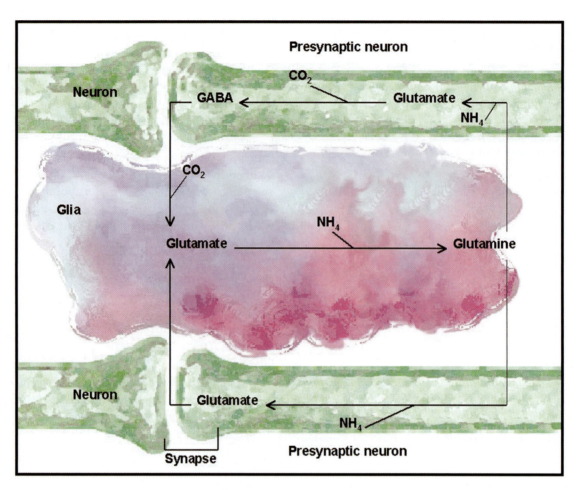

**FIGURE 34–1.** The role of glia (astrocytes) in accumulating, metabolizing, and conserving synaptic γ-aminobutyric acid (GABA) and glutamate. Specific membrane transporters move GABA and glutamate into glia cells, where GABA is carboxylated (combined with $CO_2$) to form glutamate; glutamate is in turn aminated (combined with $NH_4$) to create glutamine. Glutamine is then transported out of the glia and is available to GABAergic and glutamatergic presynaptic neurons for conversion to their respective neurotransmitters. Through these mechanisms, glia play an important role in maintaining synaptic concentrations below neurotoxic levels and salvage two ubiquitous and important neurotransmitters.

receptors. In this way glia have been associated with long-distance signal transmission in brain via gap junctions across glial membranes (Cornell-Bell and Finkbeiner 1991; Cornell-Bell et al. 1990; Robinson et al. 1993). The observation that glial gap junctions are in part controlled by components of second-messenger systems (Enkvist and McCarthy 1992) supports the active role of glia cells in brain function. Glial dysfunction has been suggested to play a role in epilepsy and the degenerative diseases, Parkinson's and Huntington's (Ransom and Sontheimer 1992). Although several psychopharmacological agents interact with glial elements, as well as those same elements found on neurons, the contributions of these glial interactions to the agents' overall pharmacodynamics remain the subject of intensive investigation.

One exciting, potential, therapeutic lead is represented by research with glial cell line–derived neuro-trophic factor (GDNF). GDNF was isolated from a culture of glial cells and found to stimulate the growth of embryonic dopamine neurons (Bohn 1999). Since this observation on dopaminergic neurons, GDNF has been found to elicit a trophic response on several other brain neuron types including motor neurons and noradrenergic, cholinergic, and serotonergic neurons (Bohn 1999). In addition, other neurotrophic factors have been identified with activity similar to that of GDNF (Saarma and Sariola 1999); these factors include neurturin, persephin, and artemin. GDNF, a chain of 134 peptides synthesized from a larger propeptide, exerts its biological activity through a series of complex receptor interactions, requiring cofactors, and a tyrosine kinase receptor (Grondin and Gash 1998; Saarma and Sariola 1999). Although the exact role of GDNF in brain development and maintenance is not known, it has been shown to be active in a variety of animal models for Parkinson's disease (Bohn 1999; Grondin and Gash 1998; Lapchak 1998) and has been proposed as a potential therapeutic agent for the treatment of Parkinson's disease, amyotrophic lateral sclerosis, and other neurodegenerative diseases. Although the activity of GDNF is promising in that it demonstrates efficacy in a variety of midbrain, dopamine-deficient models, many hurdles must be cleared before GDNF represents a therapeutic reality. For example, what are the effects of long-term GDNF administration? (Dopamine enhancement may result in psychotic symptoms.) How will the substance be administered? (It is a long-chain peptide and will not cross the blood-brain barrier.) Are there subpopulations of patients who will not respond to GDNF? (They may be deficient of receptors or essential components of the messenger system.) A small sampling of patients with Parkinson's disease did not reveal genetic abnormality in the GDNF gene (Wartiovaara et al. 1998).

# Neurons

The basic function of neurons is to convey electrical signals in a highly organized and integrated way, each neuron receiving input from many other neurons and in turn providing input to many other neurons. This function is the product of complex chemical processes transmitting signals across neuronal synapses—a symphony of intraneuronal and interneuronal events, layers of feedback and control mechanisms ensuring the correct or appropriate response. Although chemical transmission is a complex, multistepped system, it provides for maximum flexibility and unidirectional flow of neuronal signals.

Resting neurons maintain an electrical polarization between the inside and outside of the cellular membrane. This polarization is negative on the inside and positive on the outside of the neuron. Key elements in maintaining the polarized state include the presence of large (nondiffusible), intracellular, negatively charged proteins and specific ion pumps, located in the neuronal membrane, which use cellular energy to pump ions against concentration gradients. Changes in the state of transmembranal polarization are effected by a system of specific ion channels activated by neurotransmitter substances or by the degree of transmembrane (voltage-sensitive) depolarization. Ions move through the channels because of concentration (from high to low concentrations) or electrogenic (opposite charges attract) gradients. Activation of neurotransmitter-controlled ion channels reduces the level of polarization to a critical level at which voltage-sensitive channels open and permit the rapid influx of cations (e.g., $Na^+$). This influx completely depolarizes the neuron and even reverses the polarization for a brief period. Membrane ion channels adjacent to the area of depolarization open, thus extending the depolarization along the neuron and causing the formation of an action potential. In this way electrical signals are carried from one end of the neuron to the other. Repolarization occurs by the opening of voltage-sensitive $K^+$ channels. Because $K^+$ concentrations are high inside the neuron and low outside, $K^+$ carries positive charges to the outside of the membrane, making the inside more negative. The restoration of conditions in the resting state is completed by the exchange of intracellular $Na^+$ ions for extracellular $K^+$ ions. The ion exchange is accomplished by an energy-dependent pump. (Excellent reviews of the electrical nature of neurons may be found in Levitan and Kaczmarek 1997 and Shepherd 1994.)

## The Synapse

The synapse is defined as the juncture of two neurons. The neuron from which the signal is coming is known as the presynaptic neuron whereas the receiving neuron is called the postsynaptic neuron. Signals are passed across the synapse by either of two mechanisms. The first is by direct connection of the presynaptic and postsynaptic neurons via gap junctions (similar to the connection of astrocytes described above). The physiological significance of this type of connection is that transmission is rapid, can occur in two directions, and can synchronize the activity of many neurons. Electrogenic coupling of neurons occurs in only a few populations of neurons located primarily in the brain stem (Baker and Llinas 1971; Korn et al. 1973; Llinas et al. 1974). Cortical precursor cells are also known to communicate via gap junctions (LoTurco and Kriegstein 1991), although this function is lost as the cells develop into mature functioning neurons. Other neurons in the suprachiasmatic nucleus are also known to transmit signals via gap junctions, which are at least partially influenced by the neurotransmitter GABA (Shinohara et al. 2000). These gap junctions can be unique in that they are electrogenic in nature but are influenced by a neurotransmitter. Thus, they may exhibit the advantages of both modes of interneuronal communication.

## Chemical Transmission

By far the dominant means of neuron-to-neuron communication or transmission occurs by means of specific chemicals or neurotransmitters. Chemical transmission requires the presence of several elements to operate effectively (Table 34–2). These elements consist of specific proteins in the form of enzymes, storage binding proteins, uptake/membrane transport structures, receptors, and response systems (ion channels/second-messenger systems). Each element represents an opportunity for malfunction (disease state) and/or a point for modulation of transmission through pharmacological intervention. In fact, the manipulation of these elements serves as the basis of modern psychopharmacology. The functional relationship of the elements of neurotransmission is illustrated in Figures 34–2 and 34–3.

**Neurotransmitter synthesis.** The final enzymatic steps in synthesizing a neurotransmitter generally occur in or near the storage site. This ensures maximum efficiency in the neurotransmitter molecules getting to the storage sites. Neuropeptides are a notable exception to this role because their synthesis involves gene activation followed by DNA transcription and RNA translation to form large polypeptides. The polypeptides are then broken down into the component neuropeptides. All of this occurs within the neuronal soma so that the neuropeptides must be transported along the axon to the nerve terminal for storage. In several cases, neurotransmitter-synthesizing enzymes are shared by more than one neurotransmitter system. For example, the neurotransmitters norepinephrine and dopamine share the enzymes tyrosine hydroxylase and L-3,4-dihydroxyphenylalanine decarboxylase, whereas several peptides share common peptidases. Although many drugs are known to inhibit specific neurotransmitter-synthesizing enzymes, these drugs have not proven useful as therapeutic agents, either because the neurotransmitters they influence are ubiquitous and important to many life processes or because the enzymes influence multiple neurotransmitters and thus produce broad, nonspecific effects.

---

**TABLE 34–2.** Elements required for chemical transmission

**Presynaptic**
    Enzymes for neurotransmitter synthesis
    Mechanism for neurotransmitter storage
    Mechanism for appropriate neurotransmitter release
    Neurotransmitter receptors for feedback modification of
        neurotransmitter release
**Synaptic**
    Mechanism for terminating neurotransmitter action
**Postsynaptic**
    Neurotransmitter receptors to initiate response
    Coupler proteins
    Mechanism for response (ion channels/second-messenger
        systems)

---

**Neurotransmitter storage and release.** Many neurotransmitters are stored in organelles known as synaptic vesicles (Thiel 1995). These structures, constructed in the soma and transported along the axons with their full complement of neurotransmitter, concentrate near the nerve terminal. The vesicular membranes contain many specific protein structures involved in the multiple functions of the storage vesicles (Kelly 1999; Krantz et al. 1999; Rahamimoff et al. 1999). Vesicular functions include neurotransmitter synthesis, neurotransmitter transport across the vesicular membrane, neurotransmitter binding inside the vesicle, docking proteins for attaching to the neuronal plasma membrane, calcium-binding proteins for membrane fusion and neurotransmitter release, and special coating proteins for vesicular endocytosis and recycling processes.

Calcium ions are an essential element for the release of neurotransmitters. A major mechanism for calcium entry results from the activation of voltage-gated ion channels located in the plasma membrane (Rahamimoff et al. 1999; Zhang and Ramaswami 1999). The activation of the voltage-gated ion channels depends on many factors such as the activity of numerous other membrane ion channels (Rahamimoff et al. 1999) and a variety of presynaptic ligand-gated ion channels (MacDermott et al. 1999) as well as autoreceptors (MacDermott et al. 1999). Given the absolute requirement for $Ca^{2+}$ in the neurotransmitter release process, it is perhaps not surprising that the proteins that compose the voltage-gated calcium channel are intimately bound to specific proteins associated with storage vesicle docking and fusion processes (Catterall 1999). This would ensure that neurotransmitter release is occurring in a microenvironment containing an appropriate concentration of calcium.

Proteins involved in the storage and release mechanisms of neurotransmitters are well conserved in many different neurotransmitter systems so that drugs that interfere with storage and release tend to have broad nonspecific effects. Reserpine is a well-known example of such a drug. Reserpine destroys the ability of presynaptic storage vesicles to transport and store all biogenic amines, including norepinephrine, dopamine, serotonin, and histamine (Krantz et al. 1999). Because this effect is not reversible, recovery from the effects of reserpine requires the synthesis and transport of new storage vesicles to the nerve terminals, a process that requires several days. For these reasons reserpine has had a short-lived and limited use in psychiatry.

The pharmacology surrounding the control of neurotransmitter release via heterosynaptic, ligand-gated mechanisms presents some clinically significant examples. Neurotransmitters for the presynaptic, ligand-gated

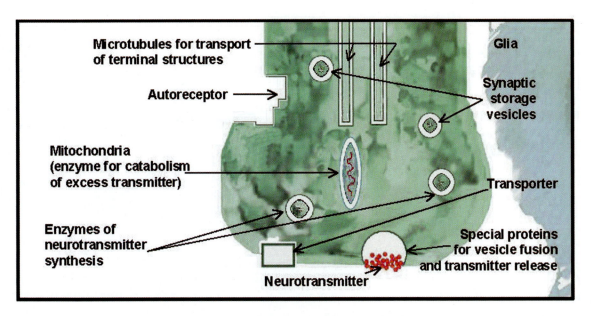

**FIGURE 34–2.** Typical presynaptic neuron with key structures relevant to neurotransmission. Microtubules transport storage vesicles, enzymes, and a variety of proteins from the neuronal soma, where they are synthesized, to the nerve ending, where they are required for carrying out their physiological functions. Storage vesicles maintain stores of neurotransmitter molecules for eventual release into the synaptic cleft. Mitochondria contain enzymes vital to providing energy to the neuron; in many cases (such as the biogenic amines) they contain enzymes, such as monoamine oxidase, which help to regulate neurotransmitter levels in the nerve ending. Calcium and a variety of special fusion proteins fuse the storage vesicle membranes with the neuronal membrane to release the neurotransmitter into the synaptic cleft. Transporter pumps are proteins incorporated into the neuronal membrane that transport the neurotransmitter from the synapse into the neuron, where it can be reincorporated back into the storage vesicle. Autoreceptors respond to neurotransmitter released from the nerve ending to provide feedback regulation of presynaptic depolarization.

channels include GABA, glutamate, acetylcholine, serotonin, and ATP (MacDermott et al. 1999).

Presynaptic GABA receptors are of the $GABA_A$ type and thus relevant to the inhibitory actions of the benzodiazepines (Tallman et al. 1999). The presynaptic $GABA_A$ receptors are channels for chloride ions, and their activation hyperpolarizes the presynaptic neuron, resulting in inhibition of presynaptic release of neurotransmitters. Presynaptic cholinergic receptors are of the nicotinic type, and when activated tend to depolarize the neuron by admitting sodium and calcium ions. The activation of these presynaptic receptors by nicotine is the source of tobacco's central pharmacological and addictive properties (Grady et al. 1992; MacDermott et al. 1999; Watkins et al. 1999; Wonnacott 1997; Yeomans and Baptista 1997). Presynaptic serotonin receptors such as the 5-hydroxytryptamine type 3 ($5\text{-}HT_3$), when activated, admit calcium into the neuron, thus promoting depolarization and neurotransmitter release (Ronde and Nichols 1998). As with all other serotonergic receptors, the activity of the $5\text{-}HT_3$ receptors is enhanced by drugs that block the reuptake of serotonin (MacDermott et al. 1999).

In addition, ethanol has been demonstrated to influence several of these presynaptic receptors such as $GABA_A$; glutamate; and nicotinic, cholinergic, and $5\text{-}HT_3$ serotonergic types (Lovinger 1997; Narahashi et al. 1999). The relevance of ethanol's influence on these structures to its pharmacological actions is the subject of continued investigations.

**Neurotransmitter inactivation.** Once liberated into the synapse, neurotransmitters are available to transmit their signals until they are removed or inactivated in some manner. Thus, neurotransmitter inactivation is an important element in controlling synaptic transmission. Rapid inactivation would attenuate transmission, whereas slow inactivation would accentuate signal transmission. Three major routes for neurotransmitter inactivation are known. First, neurotransmitters may be removed by washout or turnover of the extraneuronal fluid. This occurs at a relatively slow rate in brain and would appear to be inadequate for rapid control of neurotransmitter activity.

A second mode of neurotransmitter inactivation is by enzymatic degradation of the neurotransmitter. A nota-

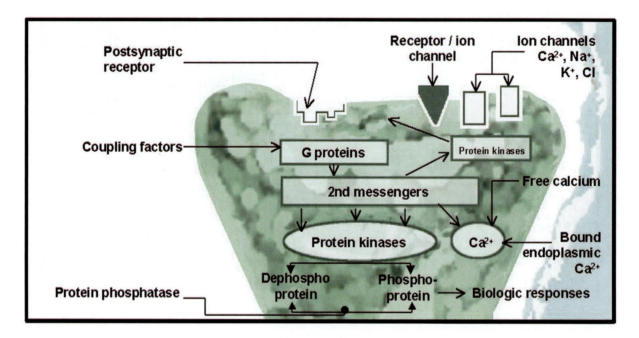

**FIGURE 34–3.** Typical postsynaptic neuron with key structures relevant to neurotransmission. Neurotransmitter substances bind to postsynaptic receptors that may be one of two major types, G protein or ion channel coupled. Other ion channels are regulated by intraneuronal ions such as calcium or potassium, as well as by transmembrane voltages. G proteins couple receptors with second-messenger systems that in turn regulate a variety of protein kinases that are responsible for initiating biological responses. Second messengers also directly regulate intraneuronal calcium levels. The various elements in the illustration are shown in their functional sequence, not in their anatomical domains. Postsynaptic receptors, G proteins, and second messengers are in fact are neuronal membrane–associated elements.

ble example of this mode is with acetylcholine, a major excitatory neurotransmitter in brain, in which the time span in the synapse is vital for proper function. Acetylcholine is rapidly metabolized in the synapse by acetylcholinesterase, a process that splits the neurotransmitter into two parts, acetate and choline. These two components are then transported back into the presynaptic neuron where another enzyme, choline acetyltransferase, rejoins them to form acetylcholine. Thus, these two enzymes and the transport of the precursors across the membrane form an effective and efficient means of rapidly terminating the synaptic activity of the neurotransmitter while protecting the availability of the precursors required for neurotransmitter synthesis.

A third mechanism for neurotransmitter inactivation is a variation of the second. In this case, rather than transporting the individual components of the neurotransmitter, the intact neurotransmitter is transported across the presynaptic neuronal membrane and into the cytoplasm, where it is eventually accumulated by storage vesicles and available for release once again. This transport, or reuptake, is accomplished by special transmembrane proteins that serve as carriers. Because the concentrations of neurotransmitter are generally greater in the presynaptic

terminal than in the synaptic fluid, cellular energy in the form of ATP is expended in the reuptake process. Many major neurotransmitters are primarily inactivated by this reuptake process. These include the biogenic amines norepinephrine, dopamine, and serotonin, and the amino acids GABA, glycine, and glutamine. The transporter proteins for the majority of neurotransmitters have similar properties (Krantz et al. 1999; Nelson 1998) such as a requirement for sodium and chloride ions. The transporters characteristically have 12 transmembrane sections, with a large extracellular loop between the third and fourth sections. This third loop contains a site or sites for glycosylation (Blakely et al. 1997; Gegelashvili and Schousboe 1997; Krantz et al. 1999; Nelson 1998). Inhibition of glycosylation at these sites appears to diminish the function or efficiency of the transporter but does not influence substrate affinity (Melikian et al. 1996).

A second set of transporters, similar to, but genetically distinct from, those found in the neuronal membrane, is located within the membranes of the neurotransmitter storage vesicles. These transporters move the neurotransmitters from the neuronal cytoplasm to the interior of the vesicles, where they are ready for release once again (Krantz et al. 1999).

The serotonin transporter has been the subject of intensive investigation because it is the site of action for the SSRIs, the drugs of choice in the treatment of major depression. A transporter protein structure approximating the serotonin transporter is shown in Figure 34–4. In common with other neurotransmitter transporters, the serotonergic transporter has 12 transmembrane sections with both the amino and carboxyl terminals within the neuron (Blakely et al. 1997; Nelson 1998). The serotonin transporter molecule includes intraneuronal sites for phosphorylation that are critical for the regulation of transporter activity (Blakely et al. 1997, 1998). These sites appear to be primarily phosphorylated by kinase C and dephosphorylated via the action of phosphatase 2A (Blakely et al. 1998). Phosporylation inactivates the transporter molecules and therefore slows the clearing of serotonin from the synaptic cleft. This phosphorylation process is likely to serve as a kind of feedback control because kinase C activity is regulated via neurotransmitter interaction with neuroreceptors (see the section "Second messengers" and Figure 34–7, later in this chapter).

Recognition, or binding sites, for serotonin to the transporter are located at extraneuronal loops of the molecule. A precondition for substrate binding is the binding of one each of sodium and chloride ions to the transporter (Krantz et al. 1999; Nelson 1998). Presumably the binding of these ions places the tertiary configuration of the transporter in the best position for substrate binding. The exact location of the site of attachment of inhibitory drugs, such as many of the antidepressant compounds, is not known for all drugs but is most likely to occur at a variety of external sites. The tricyclic antidepressants are known to bind to the central loops (Blakely et al. 1991; Nelson 1998) in the transport domain for serotonin.

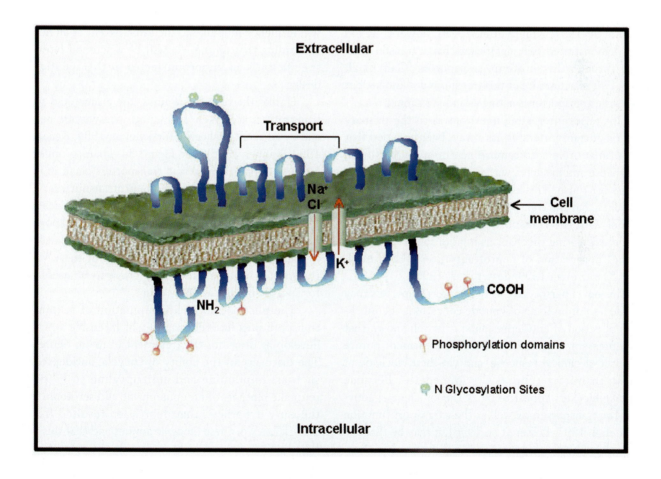

**FIGURE 34–4.** A typical neurotransmitter transporter protein. Although neurotransmitter transporters exhibit specificity for the neurotransmitter transported, they have many structural features in common. Each has 12 transmembrane sections, a large extraneuronal loop between the third and fourth transmembrane sections, intraneuronal sites for phosphorylation, and a requirement for ion binding. The figure approximates a serotonin transporter.

The transporters for several types of neurotransmitters, including those for the amino acids GABA and glutamate, the catecholamines dopamine and norepinephrine, and the biogenic amine serotonin, have long been known to have a requirement for the presence of sodium and chloride ions in order to function. In general, binding of these monovalent ions appears to be required for the neurotransmitter to bind to the transporter. Recent information suggests that transporters for the neurotransmitters may actually serve a significant role as ion channels and thus play a part in neuronal function and regulation of neuronal activity (Galli et al. 1997; Krantz et al. 1999; Lester et al. 1996; Nelson 1998). Although the ion requirements can vary, depending on which transporter is involved, the basic mechanisms appear to be similar for the entire family of transporters.

As an example, the serotonin transporter appears to function with neutral stoichiometry. Thus, $Na^+/Cl^-/$serotonin$^+$ are transported into the neuron while $K^+$ is transported out, resulting in no net transfer of charge (Galli et al. 1997; Krantz et al. 1999); however, it has been demonstrated that significant charge transfer does occur through the serotonin transporter (Galli et al. 1997). The exact nature of this transfer is not known, but clearly the transporter is acting as an ion channel.

This raises interesting questions as to the primary function of transporters. It has always been assumed that their primary role is to remove neurotransmitters from the synapse and in such a way as to conserve neurotransmitters for reuse. This recent information presents the possibility that the transporters' primary role is as an ion channel with the transport of neurotransmitters as a channel-regulating mechanism in addition to providing for the conservation of neurotransmitters (Galli et al. 1997; Krantz et al. 1999; Lester et al. 1996).

This novel perspective of the neurotransporters may provide a solution to an old puzzle concerning the mechanism of action of antidepressants. It is well known that antidepressants require a few weeks treatment before the onset of clinical response, and yet their blockade of neurotransmitter reuptake is immediate. Because reuptake blockers appear to block the ion channel activity of the transporters as well as their transport function (Galli et al. 1997; Lester et al. 1996), it may be that the reuptake inhibitor antidepressants' significant pharmacological action relates more to the presynaptic, intraneuronal, ionic milieu than to increased synaptic neurotransmitter concentrations.

Whether transporter or ion channel, these structures are important for proper brain function. Approximately 4% of the human population has been found to have a genetic defect that reduces the transcription process for the serotonin gene, resulting in individuals with reduced transporter function (Lesch et al. 1996). Such individuals have been found to demonstrate relatively high anxiety–related traits (Lesch et al. 1996). In addition, this defect has been suggested as having a possible link to neurodevelopment and neurodegenerative disorders (Lesch and Mossner 1998).

In the case of the biogenic amines, although reuptake is the major means of limiting their synaptic activity, significant contributions to inactivation are made via the enzymes catechol-O-methyl transferase (Guldberg and Mardsen 1975; Mannisto et al. 1992) and monoamine oxidase (Singer and Ramsay 1995). Inactivation by these enzymes does not result in any known reusable or physiologically active products. The reuptake sites for the biogenic amines exhibit some specificity for each amine, but the sites for each amine appear to be identical on all neurons and in all brain regions containing that amine. Thus, it is possible to design a drug that will specifically block the reuptake of a specific biogenic amine, but that drug will influence reuptake to the same extent at all neurons containing that amine. As will be discussed later, this specificity is an important factor in therapeutic drug design.

Unlike the biogenic amines, the amino acid neurotransmitters are taken up by both presynaptic neurons and by adjacent glial cells (Jursky et al. 1994; Kanai et al. 1994; Kanner 1995) (see Figure 34–1). Also unlike the biogenic amines, amino acid transporters occur in multiple variations for each of the neurotransmitters. Thus, three variations of the glutamate transporter (Kanai et al. 1994) have been identified, whereas four are known for GABA and three for glycine (Jursky et al. 1994). As more is learned about the physiological role of these various transporter subtypes, they may prove to be useful sites for specific modification by drugs.

The pharmacological manipulation of reuptake or transport sites has been an area of intensive activity in developing drugs for the treatment of major depression. The discovery of the ability of tricyclic antidepressants such as imipramine and amitriptyline to be potent reuptake blockers of norepinephrine and serotonin led to the early hypothesis that depression resulted from an insufficiency of these biogenic amines and that this insufficiency was corrected by reducing the rate at which these neurotransmitters were removed from the synapse. This hypothesis was supported by other pharmacological and biological observations. More recent clinical success with a new class of antidepressants, the SSRIs, underscores the importance of amine reuptake as an appropriate mechanism of action for antidepressant activity, although it is now apparent that reuptake inhibition alone may not be directly responsible for the antidepressant activity. Rather, reuptake inhibition initiates changes or adjustments in receptors, ion fluxes, and intracellular messenger systems, which alter neurotransmission in key pathways (Galli et al. 1997; Kilts 1994; I.A. Paul et al. 1994).

**Receptors.** Neuroreceptors are specific, membrane-bound proteins that bind neurotransmitter molecules and translate that molecular attachment into a physiological response. The amino acid sequence of each receptor type imparts a specificity for the particular neurotransmitter that will bind to it. Of particular importance in defining a receptor is that a physiological response results when the receptor is activated. Many proteins are capable of binding neurotransmitter substances but are not capable of eliciting a response. Such binding proteins are better referred to as acceptors.

Neuroreceptors can be placed into four broad cate-gories, depending on the mode of action of their physio-logical response (J.R. Cooper et al. 1996). The most prevalent of these are those receptors that connect to a second-messenger system through one of a family of pro-teins referred to as G proteins. This receptor type is char-acterized by having seven transmembrane sections of the protein with extracellular and intracellular loops that serve as neurotransmitter binding sites and sites for receptor regulation (Figure 34–5).

A second class of receptors consists of those recep-tors that form membrane ion channels or ionophores. Stimulation of receptors in this class opens ion channels specific for sodium, potassium, calcium, and chloride ions. The receptor/ion channel consists of five individual proteins, each with four transmembrane sections. The receptors are made up of a combination of protein sub-types; each subtype can exist in several variations. Thus, receptor/ion channels for a specific neurotransmitter can exist in several variations.

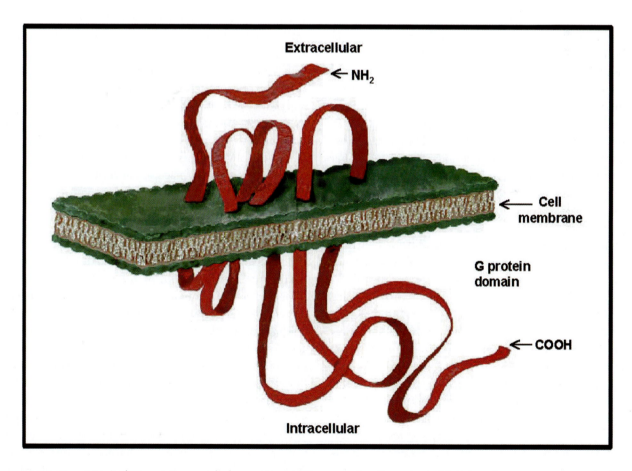

**FIGURE 34–5.** A typical G protein–coupled neurotransmitter receptor. Receptors of this type have seven transmembrane sections, with the carboxyl terminal on the inside of the neuron. The figure approximates a serotonin type 1A receptor. Receptors of this type vary with regard to their amino acid composition and the lengths of the extracellular and intracellular segments.

The third receptor class consists of receptors that attach to allosteric sites on other neuroreceptors regulating receptor ligand affinities. Examples of receptors that act at allosteric sites include the benzodiazepine and associated receptors that modify GABA receptor activity, as well as the glycine B receptor, associated with the *N*-methyl-D-aspartate (NMDA) subtype of glutamate receptor. The presence of glycine on the glycine B receptor is one of the requirements for glutamate activation of the NMDA receptor.

The fourth receptor class is made up of intraneuronal receptors best characterized by steroid transcription factor binding and the synthesis of various components of synaptic transmission, such as enzymes, receptors, and second-messenger systems (Joels and de Kloet 1994). As might be expected, the effects mediated by these receptors have a slow onset and last over an extended period of time.

Neuroreceptors generally exhibit specificity for neurotransmitters and are usually identified by the neurotransmitter that binds to them and to which they elicit a response. The existence of subtypes of receptors for specific neurotransmitters has been known for several decades. For example, acetylcholine receptors were traditionally thought of as being either nicotinic or muscarinic, based on their pharmacological response. It is now known that they not only exhibit different pharmacological characteristics but that they are entirely different in their functions and mode of responses. The nicotinic acetylcholine receptor is a five-protein, sodium ion channel that is opened in the presence of acetylcholine, whereas the muscarinic receptor is a single-protein unit coupled to a second-messenger system (inositol phosphate) by a G protein.

Historically, receptor subtypes have been identified by pharmacological studies in which specific drugs are used to stimulate or block receptor activity. Such techniques are limited in that they do not differentiate between receptor subtypes as either two different proteins or one protein in different membrane configurations. Pharmacological techniques are also limited in the number of subtypes that can be identified, particularly as the pharmacological differences become more subtle or if specific pharmacological agents are not available.

In recent years biomolecular techniques have been used to identify and characterize many new receptor subtypes. Specific genes have been identified that express neuroreceptor subtypes for many of the neurotransmitters. Through these techniques, populations of "pure" receptor types have been produced, which may then be used for identifying specific ligands for the receptors. Specific ligands are in turn useful for determining the location and density of specific receptors. Methods also exist by which transcription paths are altered to prevent the expression of specific receptors (Lucas and Hen 1995), thus providing animal models that are lacking specific receptors. Such studies provide important clues as to the physiological function of specific receptors (Furth et al. 1994; Lai et al. 1994; Saudou et al. 1994; Silvia et al. 1994; Standifer et al. 1994; Tecott et al. 1995; Thomas and Capecchi 1990; Wahlestedt et al. 1993; Zhou et al. 1994).

As seen in Table 34–3, receptors for various neurotransmitters come in a variety of subtypes. For example, 14 subtypes have been identified for serotonin, with the possibility of more to be discovered (Lucas and Hen 1995). Nearly all receptors for the various neurotransmitters come in several subtypes. This fact is important from a pharmacological perspective because it means that it is possible to identify compounds for a specific receptor subtype, thus limiting the pharmacological effects.

Neuroreceptors are important sites for pharmacological intervention in psychiatric disorders. For example, all antipsychotic medications are known to have antagonist activity at dopamine receptors. Antidepressant drugs are well known to influence receptors either directly as antagonists or indirectly by up- or downregulation of receptor populations (Kilts 1994). Many antidepressants, the tricyclic antidepressants in particular, are known to interact with receptors of several neurotransmitter systems. Anxiolytic agents, the benzodiazepines and buspirone, exert their pharmacological actions through interaction with benzodiazepine and serotonin type 1A (5-$HT_{1A}$) receptors, respectively.

Drugs can interact with receptors in one of several ways. They can bind to the receptor and cause a physiological response similar to that of a natural neurotransmitter; such a drug would be referred to as an agonist. Other drugs can also bind to the receptor and not elicit a physiological response, but instead prevent agonists from binding to the receptor; this would describe antagonist activity. A third type of ligand-receptor interaction is one referred to as inverse agonism. An inverse agonist is a drug that binds to a receptor but produces an effect opposite that of agonist activity. This type of action has been described in studies of the benzodiazepine receptor (Stephens et al. 1986); a single receptor mediates agonist, antagonist, and inverse agonist activities. Pharmaceutical agents appear to exhibit mixtures of these basic reactions, for example, mixed antagonist/agonist actions that produce partial or limited agonist activities, but when in the presence of full agonists may behave as antagonists.

**TABLE 34–3.** Some major types of neurotransmitters

| Neurotransmitter | Mode of response | Messenger system | Receptor subtypes | |
|---|---|---|---|---|
| **Amines** | | | | |
| Acetylcholine | Ionophore | $Na^+/K^+/Ca^{2+}$ channels | Nicotinic | Multiple subunit variations |
| | G protein | cAMP IP$_3$ | Muscarinic | 5 |
| Norepinephrine | Ionophore and G protein | $Ca^{2+}$ channels and cAMP | Alpha | 6 |
| | G protein | cAMP | Beta | 3 |
| Dopamine | G protein | cAMP | | 5 |
| Serotonin | G protein | cAMP | 5-HT$_{1A-F}$ 5-HT$_{2A-C}$ 5-HT$_{4-7}$ | 13 |
| | Ionophore | Cation channel | 5-HT$_3$ | 1 |
| **Amino acids** | | | | |
| Glutamate (ionotropic) | Ionophore | $Na^+/K^+$ | Kainate, quisqualate | 2 |
| Glutamate | Ionophore | $Ca^{2+}$ | NMDA | 1 |
| Glutamate (metabotropic) | G protein | cAMP, IP$_3$ | mGlu$_{1-7}$ | 7 |
| Glycine | Ionophore | Cl$^-$ | | Multiple subunit variations |
| | Allosteric site on glutamate receptor | Required for glutamate (NMDA) receptor activation | | |
| GABA | Ionophore | Cl$^-$ | GABA$_A$ | 1 |
| | G protein | cAMP | GABA$_B$ | 1 |
| Benzodiazepine | Allosteric site | Occupation of this site increases efficacy of GABA receptor | | |
| **Purines** | | | | |
| Adenosine | G protein | | A$_1$ A$_{2a-b}$ A$_3$ | 4 |
| ATP/ADP/VDP | Ionophore | | | 4 |
| | G protein | | | |
| **Peptides** | | | | |
| Opioid (enkephalins/ endorphins) | G protein | cAMP | Mu, sigma, kappa | 3 |
| Angiotensin | G protein | cGMP | AT$_1$ and AT$_2$ | 2 |
| Cholecystokinin | G protein | | CCK$_A$ and CCK$_B$ | 2 |
| Vasopressin/oxytocin | G protein | | V$_{1A}$, V$_{1B}$, V$_2$; OT | 3; 1 |
| Somatostatin | G protein | | SST$_{1-5}$ | 5 |
| Neurotensin | G protein | | | 1 |
| **Steroids** | | | | |
| Corticosterone/cortisol | Gene transcription | Modification of neurotransmission elements | Mr$_s$ Gr$_s$ | 2 |

*Note.* A=adenosine; ADP=adenosine diphosphate; AT=angiotensin; ATP=adenosine triphosphate; cAMP=cyclic adenosine monophosphate; CCK=cholecystokinin; cGMP=cyclic guanosine monophosphate; GABA=γ-aminobutyric acid; Gr=glucocorticoid; IP$_3$=inositol-1,4,5-triphosphate; 5-HT=5-hydroxytryptamine; mGlu=metabotropic glutamate; Mr=mineralocorticoid; NMDA=$N$-methyl-D-aspartate; OT=oxytocin; SST=somatostatin; V=vasopressin.

Another distinctive interaction between psychotropic drugs and receptors is well known to occur with long-term antidepressant treatment. Multiple but not single doses of many antidepressant compounds are known to down-regulate β-adrenergic receptors (Wolfe et al. 1978) and NMDA receptors in brain tissue (I.A. Paul et al. 1994); that is, they reduce the actual number of receptor sites. Because many of these drugs do not interact with these receptor populations directly, the induced changes may be the result of some second-messenger system activity, although the precise mechanisms for these effects are not known. Because the slow onset of the receptor adaptations is similar to the timing of the onset of the clinical antidepressant effect (Oswald et al. 1972), it has been suggested that one or the other of these changes may be related to the antidepressant effect itself (Caldecott-Hazard et al. 1991; I.A. Paul et al. 1994).

**G proteins.** Serving as linking proteins between extracellular receptors and intracellular effector mechanisms (second messengers), the G proteins (regulatory guanosine triphosphate [GTP]-binding proteins) constitute a large family of related structures vital to the transmission of interneuronal signals. G proteins are actually heterotrimeric structures composed of one each of three protein subunits termed α, β, and γ (Rens-Domiao and Hamm 1995). To date, 18 specific α subunits, 5 β subunits, and 7 γ subunits have been identified. The various subunits are not all interchangeable and some combinations of the subunits are not compatible.

The α subunits play a key role in the transduction process. The α unit binds the guanine nucleotide and exhibits intrinsic GTPase activity. It is also the α subunit that interacts with the neuroreceptor to initiate the transduction process. Frequently it is the α subunit that interacts with the effector proteins, although this function has been attributed to the β/γ subunit in some instances (Clapham and Neer 1993; Haga and Haga 1992; Pitcher et al. 1992). Although the α subunit disengages from the other two subunits at certain stages of transduction, the β and γ subunits remain bound to each other at all times.

The sequence of events of the G protein transduction cycle are illustrated in Figure 34–6. The binding of an agonist to a neuroreceptor causes the release of guanine diphosphate (GDP) from the α subunit with the subsequent binding of GTP. The binding of GTP releases the α subunit from the β/γ subunit complex and at the same time binds the α subunit to the effector protein. After the interaction with the effector, the α subunit converts GTP to GDP (intrinsically) and recombines with the β/γ subunits to begin the cycle over again.

All of the neuroreceptors known at this time to stimulate G protein regulatory units are of the seven-transmembrane, helical type. G proteins are known to interact with a variety of effectors, which include adenyl cyclase, phosphodiesterase (phosphatidylinositol turnover), calcium and potassium channels, and receptor-coupled kinases. Through these effectors, G proteins are involved in both excitatory and inhibitory roles. Through the stimulation of receptor-coupled kinases and the phosphorylation of specific intracellular domains of the receptor proteins, G proteins provide feedback control of receptor sensitivity (Hausdorff et al. 1990).

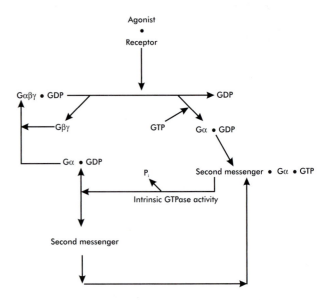

**FIGURE 34–6.** Regulatory cycle of G protein signal coupling. G protein exists as a triprotein with α, β, and γ subunits. Binding of an agonist to a receptor induces the release of the α subunit from the β/γ subunits and guanine diphosphate (GDP) from the α subunit. Guanosine triphosphate (GTP) binds to the α subunit; this complex then binds to a second messenger (adenylate cyclase or phospholipase C). The intrinsic GTPase converts GTP to GDP, which results in the uncoupling of the α subunit from the second messenger. The second messenger is then available for recoupling to an α/GTP complex. The α/GDP complex then binds to a β/γ subunit complex, and the cycle is ready to begin again.

Relatively little is known about drug influences on G protein functions. Lithium is known to inhibit G protein function in the adrenergic stimulation of adenylate cyclase (Belmaker et al. 1990); however, the role of this effect in the therapeutics of lithium is not known. G proteins are only recently being considered as sites for drug actions (see the section, "Novel Mechanisms of Action"). No psychiatric disorders have been identified that result from defects in the G protein regulatory systems. As more is learned about this vital link in neuronal transmission, opportunities for pharmacological manipulation may become increasingly evident.

**Second messengers.** As stated above, many types of neuroreceptors are connected via a family of G proteins to one of two classes of second-messenger systems, the cyclic adenosine monophosphate (cAMP)/protein phosphorylation system or the inositol triphosphate/diacylglycerol system. Each of these two systems is regulated by the action of G proteins, and the effectors for each system include protein kinases, which catalyze the transfer of the terminal phosphate group of ATP to a wide variety of substrate proteins (Table 34–4). In addition to activating protein kinases, the inositol triphosphate pathway is directly involved in the regulation of intraneuronal calcium concentrations. Unlike the localized effects of changes in ions, second-messenger actions are known to spread over long distances in neurons, thus influencing many types of neuronal functions (Kasai and Petersen 1994).

Neuroreceptors, through specific G proteins, either stimulate or inhibit the enzyme adenylate cyclase, which catalyzes the formation of cAMP (Gilman 1989) (Figure 34–6). cAMP in turn binds to protein kinases, which activate specific effector proteins through the process of phosphorylation (Figure 34–7 and Table 34–4). A key element in this pathway is the intraneuronal concentration of cAMP. The rate of synthesis of cAMP is the ratio of stimulatory to inhibitory receptor input, whereas the rate of metabolic degradation of cAMP is determined by the activity of the enzyme phosphodiesterase. Multiple genetic forms of adenylate cyclase (D.M. Cooper et al. 1995) and phosphodiesterase (McKnight 1991) have been identified. More than 300 specific forms of protein kinase are known (Walsh and Van Patten 1994) and they result in diverse activities.

---

**TABLE 34–4.** Classes of proteins that are targets for phosphorylation by protein kinases

G proteins
Microtubule-associated proteins or neurofilaments
Synaptic vesicle proteins
Neurotransmitter-synthesizing enzymes
Neurotransmitter receptors
Ion channel proteins
Neurotransmitter transporters

---

In the case of the inositol/diacylglycerol system, extraneuronal signals are transmitted via a neurotransmitter receptor through a G protein to a phosphodiesterase, phospholipase C, which in turn hydrolyzes phosphatidylinositol-4,5-bisphosphate ($PIP_2$), an inter-membrane-bound phospholipid (Figure 34–8). The products of this hydrolyzation are inositol 1,4,5-triphosphate ($IP_3$) and diacylglycerol, both of which serve second-messenger roles (Hokin and Dixon 1993). $IP_3$ diffuses to the endoplasmic reticulum and stimulates a specific $IP_3$ receptor to release sequestered $Ca^{2+}$. The $IP_3$ receptor is now known to exist in multiple subtypes (Danoff and Ross 1994; Marshall and Taylor 1993). The activity of $IP_3$ receptors is regulated by several allosteric sites for $Ca^{2+}$, adenine nucleotides, and protein kinases. $IP_3$ is inactivated by the removal of phosphate through a series of

phosphatase enzymes, and the inositol moiety is recycled back to phosphatidylinositol.

The diacylglycerol formed by the action of phospholipase C activates a widely distributed kinase, kinase C. Kinase C phosphorylates several proteins associated with a variety of neuronal membranes, such as those of synaptic vesicles, microtubules, receptor proteins (Nalepa 1994; Premont et al. 1995), and transporters (Blakely et al. 1998). The action of diacylglycerol is quite short, and it is rapidly recycled into phosphatidylinositol or metabolized to enter prostaglandin synthetic pathways.

The activity level of a protein that is activated by phosphorylation is determined by the relative rates of phosphorylation versus dephosphorylation. Calcineurin has been identified as a major factor in the dephosphorylation of a wide variety of proteins with key roles in synaptic transmission (Yakel 1997). These processes include ion channels (receptor and voltage gated), neuroreceptors, and neurotransmitter release (Table 34–5). Calcineurin is approximately 50% bound to the neuronal membrane and thus influences many membrane-bound processes.

Calcineurin is composed of two subunits, designated A and B. The A subunit binds $Ca^{2+}$ and calmodulin; $Ca^{2+}$ binding is required for the binding of calmodulin. The B unit also binds $Ca^{2+}$, and full phosphatase activity is not realized unless all of these components are in place (Yakel 1997).

Calcineurin has been demonstrated to regulate receptor-gated ion channels such as those gated by glutamate (NMDA), GABA, serotonin ($5-HT_3$) and acetylcholine (nicotinic type). Calcineurin appears to have a major influence on voltage-gated $Ca^{2+}$ channels. Calcineurin is also implicated in the processes of synaptic release of neurotransmitters and the recycling of the synaptic structures themselves. Nitric oxide synthetase is a substrate for calcineurin, the dephosphorylation of nitric oxide synthetase increasing its activity and enhancing the production of nitric oxide. This latter process may be involved in certain neurotoxicity mechanisms. Finally, calcineurin regulates gene transcription and synaptic plasticity in learning and memory-related processes through influences on cAMP response element binding protein (CREB) (Yakel 1997) (see Table 34–5).

Although no psychotherapeutic agents are known to influence calcineurin, immunosuppressant drugs such as cyclosporine A and FK506 are known to be potent inhibitors of calcineurin (Yakel 1997). The clinical significance of these immunosuppressant drugs with respect to their inhibition of calcineurin is not known; however, these drugs are known to cause neurotoxicity and sympathetic hypertension in in vivo animal studies (Hughes 1990;

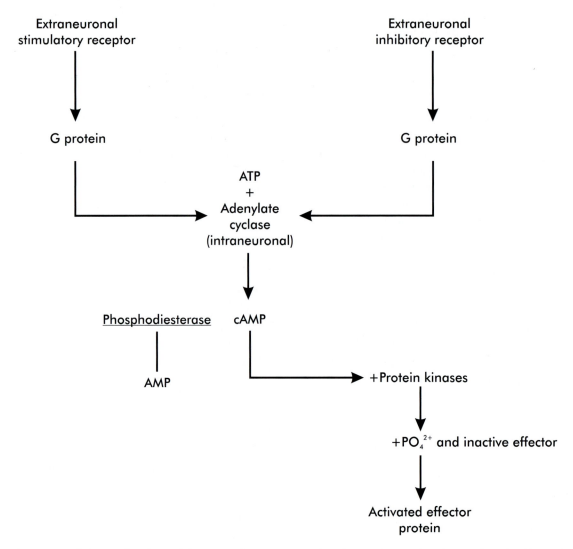

**FIGURE 34–7.** Regulation and actions of the second messenger adenylate cyclase. Adenylate cyclase is either stimulated or inhibited in its production of cyclic adenosine monophosphate (cAMP) by specific receptors and G proteins. cAMP stimulates a variety of protein kinases, which in turn phosphorylate (combine with $PO_4^{2+}$) an effector that activates it and produces biological responses. cAMP is inactivated by the enzyme phosphodiesterase, which converts cAMP to AMP.

Lyson et al. 1993; Yakel 1997).

Traditionally, the components of second-messenger systems have not been the primary targets of psychopharmacological agents. This is because second messengers are few in number and therefore not specific or selective compared with neurotransmitter receptors or reuptake sites. For example, a drug that influences the intracellular levels of cAMP would be expected to have the same influence in many types of synapses simultaneously, or, for that matter, in many kinds of tissues, because second messengers exist in many types of cells outside the nervous system (Nishizuka 1995). Now that subtypes of such elements as phospholipase, phosphodiesterase, adenylate cyclase, and $IP_3$ receptors are known, the identification of more selective agents may be possible.

At this time only one psychotherapeutic agent is known that likely has its mechanism of action in a second-messenger system. Lithium, as an agent for treating mania, is well known to block inositol monophosphatase, a critical enzyme in the synthesis of phosphatidylinositol and the subsequent production of $IP_3$ (Hokin and Dixon 1993; Parthasarathy et al. 1994). This is a suggested mechanism of lithium's antimanic action because the influences on $IP_3$ occur at therapeutic doses (Baraban et al. 1989; Belmaker et al. 1990). Other pharmacological observations support this hypothesis (Kofman and Belmaker 1993). It is becoming more evident that a great deal of interaction takes place among the various components of the second-messenger systems and that some drug effects may be accounted for in this way. For example, the antidepressants are known to influence cAMP levels through their influences on adrenergic receptors;

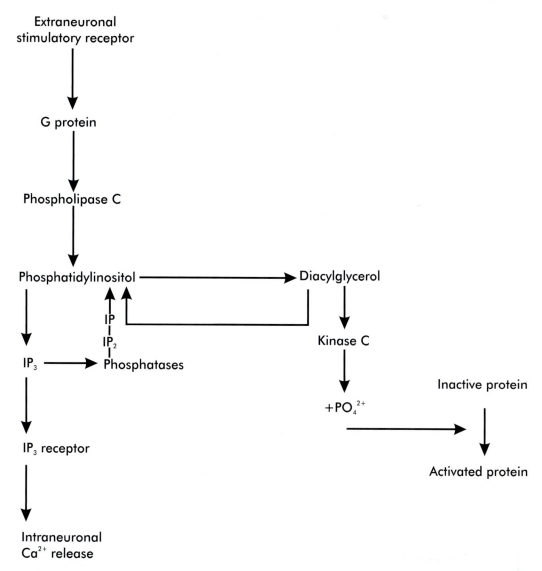

**FIGURE 34–8.** Intraneuronal actions of phospholipase C activity. Phospholipase C is activated via a receptor-stimulated G protein. Phospholipase C splits phosphatidylinositol into inositol triphosphate (IP₃) and diacylglycerol moieties. The diacylglycerol stimulates kinase C, which activates effector proteins through phosphorylation. The inositol triphosphate binds to a receptor on the endoplasmic reticulum. Stimulation of this receptor releases bound calcium into the cytoplasm. Inositol triphosphate is inactivated by a series of phosphatases. Inositol is reincorporated into phosphatidylinositol. The antimanic drug lithium is a potent inhibitor of phosphatase and blocks the reincorporation of inositol back into phosphatidylinositol.

however, they also influence the inositol/diacylglycerol system by modifying the action of kinase C (Nalepa 1994). Thus, antidepressant effects may be produced through more than one neurotransmitter system.

The ultimate influence that an agonist exerts on a neuronal system depends on a complex series of interactions between the agonist and the receptor, the receptor and the G protein, and the G protein and the second-messenger system (Kenakin 1995a, 1995b). Although it has not yet been demonstrated, different agonists may influence receptors in ways that alter the interaction of the receptors with a variety of G proteins. It is known that receptors may activate more than one kind of G protein, thus providing qualitatively differing biological responses. It has also been demonstrated that the relative concentrations of receptors to G proteins may be an important determinant in the qualitative response to agonist activity. High concentrations of receptors relative to G proteins result in interactions with multiple types of G proteins providing multiple effects. The role that these factors play in disease states or drug mechanisms of action are not known at this time, but certainly psycho-

**TABLE 34–5.** Synaptic structures that are substrates for calcineurin regulation

**Receptors**
   Serotonin (5-HT$_3$)
   GABA$_A$
   Glutamate (NMDA)
   Acetylcholine
**Ion channels (voltage gated)**
   Calcium
   Sodium
   Potassium (M-current)
**Other proteins**
   Nitric oxide synthase
   Dynamin I (vesicle recycling)
   DARPP-32 (regulator of protein phosphatase 1)
   CREB (synaptic plasticity)
   Inhibitor-1 (regulator of protein kinase A)

*Note.*   CREB = cyclic adenosine monophosphate (cAMP) response element binding protein; DARPP = dopamine- and cAMP-regulated phosphoprotein; GABA = γ-aminobutyric acid; NMDA = *N*-methyl-D-aspartate; 5-HT = 5-hydroxytryptamine.
*Source.*   Reprinted from Yakel JL: Calcineurin regulation of synaptic function: from ion channels to transmitter release and gene transcription. Trends Pharmacol Sci 18:124–134, 1997. Used with permission.

tropic agents such as antidepressants and antipsychotics are well known for their influences on receptor populations and some of their pharmacological actions may result from changes in the interaction of these crucial elements in neurotransmission.

## Psychotropic Drug Development

In the last century, efforts to refine psychiatric diagnoses and uncover the biological bases of psychiatric disorders have typically followed advances in neuroscience in general and neuropharmacology in particular. Historically, identification of the sites of action of clinically effective psychotropic drugs led to hypotheses of disease pathophysiology, many of which have now been held for decades with only slight modification. A case in point is the *dopamine excess* hypothesis of psychosis, supported by the discovery of the dopamine antagonist properties of chlorpromazine (Snyder et al. 1974). This hypothesis provided the framework for subsequent research and development of other dopamine antagonist drugs over the last 50 years.

In the latter half of the twentieth century, the psychotropic drug development process was based on the use of animal tests that modeled the responses to the index drug, which had often been discovered serendipitously (e.g., chlorpromazine, amitriptyline). Because the animal models were selected on the basis of drug response rather than disease pathophysiology, the new drugs tended to have pharmacological profiles similar to those drugs employed to establish the research models. Hence, successive generations of psychotropic drugs were developed, with some improvements relating to side-effect profiles and pharmacokinetic features, but no major advances.

## Advances in Molecular Pharmacology

Twenty years ago, it would have been difficult to imagine that an alternative strategy to animal models of psychiatric disorders could be used to rationally develop psychotropic drugs. Even more difficult to imagine at that time is a debate of the wisdom of choosing to develop one new drug over another based on its relative potency for specific biological targets in the central nervous system (CNS). Only in recent times has a new approach become a possibility, and now rational or targeted drug development includes psychopharmacology.

The transition in the psychotropic drug development process is a result of powerful technical advances in molecular biology and genetics, which are revolutionizing molecular pharmacology. These new laboratory techniques make it possible to reliably identify, isolate, and then produce the protein components of synaptic transmission. In this process, once identified, a new protein can be cloned, and then functionally assessed for effects on cell metabolism and protein synthesis. For new receptor proteins, specific ligands are synthesized and radiolabeled to examine their location, density, and function in the CNS. Together these techniques are helping us understand how heretofore undiscovered components of neurotransmission may be at fault in psychiatric disorders and then provide a means to correct the function of the errant component.

## Neuroreceptor Pharmacology

The benefits of the technical advances in molecular biology are nowhere more apparent in psychiatry than in the area of receptor pharmacology. In little over a decade numerous new receptors have been identified and cloned (see Table 34–3). These receptors are characterized as to second-messenger systems, cellular locations, and regional distribution in the CNS. At last count there are 14 serotonin receptor subtypes, of which 13 have been successfully cloned (Sanders-Bush and Canton 1995). This is a dramatic advance considering that less than 20 years ago only two serotonin receptor subtypes were known to exist. During this same period, five dopamine receptor subtypes and five muscarinic acetylcholine receptor subtypes have been isolated. As quickly as new receptor subtypes are identified, agonist and antagonists have been developed to explore their clinical significance. The result has been a cascade of new research, some of which has already proved successful (e.g., the 5-HT$_{1A}$ agonist buspirone, the 5-HT$_{1D}$ agonist sumatriptan, the 5-HT$_3$ antagonist alosetron).

As new neuroreceptor subtypes are identified, a number of phenomena now occur in a relatively efficient manner: exploration of receptor action on cellular function, evaluation of established therapeutic agents for binding affinity at the newly identified sites, generation of new theories of disease pathophysiology, and subsequent clinical evaluation of selective receptor ligands. This dynamic process has been recently illustrated in the area of antipsychotic drug development.

## Antipsychotic Pharmacodynamics

For several decades it has been recognized that all effective antipsychotic drugs inhibit dopamine receptors in the brain (Spano et al. 1978). It was widely believed that two types of dopamine receptors existed and that antipsychotic activity was related to inhibition of one of these, the D$_2$ dopamine receptor (Stoof and Kebabian 1984). With the successful identification of at least five functional dopamine receptors came the consideration that perhaps a subtype other than the D$_2$ might be a more effective target for antipsychotic drugs (Meador-Woodruff 1994).

After its identification in brain tissue, the dopamine D$_4$ receptor subtype attracted particular attention as a target for antipsychotic drug therapy for a number of reasons. This particular dopamine receptor was identified to be present in relatively high concentrations in the mesocortical areas of the brain but in relatively low concentrations in nigrostriatal regions (Todd and O'Malley 1993). Because blockade of dopamine receptors in the nigrostriatal regions is thought to be responsible for the unwanted movement disorders associated with antipsychotic drugs, the distribution of D$_4$ receptors suggested a means of selectively blocking dopamine transmission with respect to brain regions. With the recognition that clozapine had relatively high affinity for D$_4$ receptors, the theory was proposed that this biological activity might be responsible for the unique clinical features of clozapine (e.g., minimal extrapyramidal effects, efficacy in treating negative signs and symptoms of schizophrenia) (Seeman and Van Tol, 1993; Van Tol et al. 1991).

The D$_4$ hypothesis provided the basis for broad investigation, including receptor binding studies, assay of D$_4$ mRNA in the brains of patients with schizophrenia, and a clinical trial of a D$_4$ antagonist (Kramer et al. 1997; Mulcrone and Kerwin 1996; Seeman et al. 1995). The D$_4$ antagonist did not demonstrate efficacy for treating acute psychosis, and taken together the basic science studies did not identify an abnormality in this receptor associated with schizophrenia. Although the enthusiasm about a particular role of the D$_4$ receptor subtype in the pathophysiology of schizophrenia or as a preferred target of antipsychotic therapy has been dampened, the "D$_4$ story" is still an achievement (Kerwin and Owen 1999). It illustrates our current capabilities and the efficiency of the process from rational hypothesis to molecular research to clinical analysis.

Recent data continue to support the consensus that the D$_2$ binding affinity of antipsychotic drugs predicts their clinical efficacy (Kapur et al. 2000). However, as new, nondopamine neuroreceptors are identified, it has been recognized that many antipsychotic drugs bind with relatively high affinity to these sites. As such, nondopamine receptors are being considered as sites of action for antipsychotic drugs, which may mitigate some of the adverse effects or enhance the efficacy of D$_2$ (Richelson 1999).

The atypical antipsychotic drugs appear to have a higher binding affinity for serotonin 2A receptors (5-HT$_{2A}$) over dopamine D$_2$ receptors (Bymaster et al. 1996; Seeman and Van Tol 1993) (Table 34–6). With the clinical success of the atypical agents, the combination of 5-HT$_{2A}$ and D$_2$ receptor binding properties has become a prototype for selecting compounds to develop as antipsychotic agents (Remington and Kapur 1999; Richelson 1999). How these two mechanisms interact to mediate the clinically desirable effects of atypical antipsychotics is not yet clear. Studies in rats suggest that 5-HT$_{2A}$ antagonism increases serotonin and dopamine levels in the rat brain (Devaud et al. 1992). Based on this observation, it has been advanced that 5-HT$_{2A}$ antagonism could have effects on the negative symptoms of schizophrenia by increasing prefrontal dopamine transmission and mitigate the extrapyramidal symptoms (EPS) of D$_2$ blockade through an increased dopamine synaptic tone (Richelson 1999).

Another area of investigation into the nondopamine pharmacodynamics of antipsychotic drugs follows the observation that a number of antipsychotic agents bind with relatively high affinity to the serotonin receptor subtypes 5-HT$_6$ and 5-HT$_7$ (Glatt et al. 1995; Roth et al. 1994) (see Table 34–6). These findings have drawn attention to the possible psychoactive properties of 5-HT$_6$ and 5-HT$_7$ receptors. Whether these new serotonin receptor subtypes will turn out to be incidental or pivotal to anti-

**TABLE 34–6.** Receptor binding affinity for selected antipsychotic drugs

| Drug | $D_2$ | $D_4$ | 5-HT$_{2A}$ | 5-HT$_6$ | 5-HT$_7$ | 5-HT$_{2A}$/D$_2$ |
|---|---|---|---|---|---|---|
| Clozapine | 125 | 21 | 12 | 4 | 63 | 0.1 |
| Olanzapine | 11 | 27 | 4 | 2.5 | 104 | 0.4 |
| Risperidone | 3 | 7 | 0.6 | 425 | 1.4 | 0.2 |
| Haloperidol | 1 | 5 | 78 | >5,000 | 263 | 78 |

*Note.* The affinity constants (Ki values in nanomolar) were determined in vitro using both rat and human brain tissue. A lower numerical value of Ki indicates greater receptor binding affinity. $D_2$, $D_4$ = dopamine receptor subtypes; 5-HT$_{2A}$, 5-HT$_6$, 5-HT$_7$ = serotonin receptor subtypes; 5-HT$_{2A}$/ $D_2$ = ratio of binding affinities for the serotonin and dopamine receptor subtypes.
*Source.* Data adapted from Bymaster et al. 1996; Roth et al. 1994; Seeman and Van Tol 1993.

psychotic drug efficacy can at this time only be the subject of speculation. It is clear, however, that we have entered a new era of molecular pharmacology in which the means are available to generate and address these provocative questions.

## Merits of Psychotropic Drug Selectivity

The first successful drugs for treating depression and psychosis were characterized by having complicated pharmacodynamic profiles with multiple biological activities at clinically relevant doses. Over time, it was realized that for drugs such as imipramine and chlorpromazine certain biological actions (e.g., α-adrenergic receptor blockade) contributed little to the therapeutic effect of the drugs but were responsible for a variety of adverse effects. At best, these adverse effects were a nuisance for the patient and compromised treatment compliance; at worst, they narrowed the therapeutic index with resultant safety concerns.

The further disadvantage of a drug with multiple mechanisms of action is that the ratio of potency of the various components is fixed, which limits the ability to adjust treatment with dosing (e.g., poor tolerability of one mechanism prevents advancing the drug dose to increase another action). In this sense, when treating a condition for which multiple drug actions are necessary, it would be preferable to have an armamentarium of highly selective agents that would permit each action in a therapeutic regimen to be adjusted independently. Hence, the concept of selectivity arose as a desirable feature for psychotropic agents. The concept became a reality with the advent of the SSRIs.

The SSRIs represented the first generation of psychotropic drugs to be rationally designed to target a selected site in the CNS with minimal biological effects at other sites. The selected target for SSRIs is the presynaptic transmembrane protein that transports serotonin from the synapse back into the cell, hence "reuptake."

The logic held true and this class of antidepressant went on to become the current cornerstone of antidepressant pharmacotherapy. A key feature in the success of the SSRIs has been that, by virtue of their selectivity, drug tolerability and safety was greatly improved over their antidepressant predecessors.

As we depart down the path of synthesizing highly selective ligands for newly identified sites in the CNS, one wonders if the time has come when a psychotropic drug may be made selective to the point that its utility can no longer be detected by conventional clinical investigation. Particularly for psychiatric disorders, which are syndromal in nature, and for a lack of biological markers, one is likely to have a heterogeneous clinical population. In such a population, with the potential for diverse pathophysiology, the effects of a drug with a highly specific mechanism of action may improve too few subjects to be detected reliably. Hence, agents that are particularly beneficial for some but not all patients could fail to be identified. Continued achievement in drug development for psychiatric disorders necessitates that efforts in molecular pharmacology proceed hand in hand with efforts to identify genotypes or physiological measures that characterize subpopulations of patients with similar pathophysiology.

Despite the clinical benefits of drug selectivity, within the context of our current capabilities in molecular pharmacology, how selective can a new drug be and still be practical to develop and useful in therapy? Is a highly selective, single-mechanism drug an end in and of itself? Are psychiatric disorders such as depression and schizophrenia likely to be the result of a single malfunctioning component in the chain of events of neurotransmission and hence treatable by selecting a singular target? The ancient advice of Burton (1621) may still apply:

Mixed diseases must have mixed remedies, and such simples are commonly mixed as have reference to the part affected, some to qualify, the rest to comfort, some one part, some another.

Several examples of post-SSRI-era psychotropic agents are nonselective with multiple biological activities. Many of these agents have proven clinically useful (e.g., mirtazapine, a $5\text{-HT}_{2A}$, $5\text{-HT}_{2C}$, and $5\text{-HT}_3$ antagonist). In some cases these agents have even become prototypes for developing new therapies (e.g., clozapine, a $5\text{-HT}_{2A}$ and $D_2$ antagonist). If the focus in drug development had been selectivity at all cost, these agents, and the provocative research directions they have provided, may not have been identified. For major advances in drug development, the novelty of the pharmacological profile is of principal importance. Drug selectivity, albeit a feature of importance, represents a refinement that enhances clinical effectiveness. Although the SSRIs revolutionized antidepressant pharmacotherapy, they did so with the same basic mechanism of action as the earliest antidepressants.

## Novel Mechanisms of Action

The development of new drugs with novel mechanisms of action to treat psychiatric disorders has been constrained by our limited understanding of disease pathophysiology and the mechanisms that mediate the therapeutic effects of established treatments. Newer psychotropic drugs provide many therapeutic advantages, but they essentially recapitulate the mechanisms of action of their earliest predecessors. Antidepressant therapy is a case in point. Although the antidepressant drug armamentarium has expanded at an unprecedented rate over the last decade, the new agents remain focused on biogenic amine neurotransmitters and extracellular neuronal membranes.

Clearly the expanded antidepressant armamentarium has advanced the clinical treatment of depression. The skillful clinician can now select from among these agents with regard to the specific neurotransmitter target(s) and mechanism of action (Table 34–7). However, despite this increase in antidepressant options and a rationale for treatment selection, drug therapy is still ineffective in many patients, is often associated with distressing adverse effects, and may take a prolonged period to be effective. The same drawbacks exist for antipsychotic drug therapy. Hence, there is a need to continue the search for improved psychotropic drugs. With our new skill in studying and manipulating the components of neurotransmission, there is enthusiasm that novel molecular targets will be identified for drug therapy. Developing psychotropic agents with completely novel mechanisms of action is of considerable interest, not only among clinicians (Stahl 1999a, 1999b; Triggle 1999) and the pharmaceutical industry (Nutt 1998; Wahlestedt

1998) but also in the financial world (Langreth 1998, 1999).

In psychotropic drug development, numerous possibilities are open to explore in the search for novel mechanisms of action. In large part, research efforts have been focused on the "first messenger" in neurotransmission, namely, the neurotransmitter and its membrane-binding site. This remains an exciting and potentially profitable level of exploration. New receptors are being identified at an unprecedented rate and each represents a possible therapeutic target. At the same time, nonclassical neurotransmitters, such as the neurokinins, are being studied for their psychoactive properties (Stahl 1999b).

Substance P is the most abundant of several neurokinins in the CNS (J.R. Cooper et al. 1996). Several properties and characteristics of substance P have suggested that it may be a reasonable target for novel antidepressant therapy. This evidence has been recently summarized (Kramer et al. 1998). The observation that administration of substance P induces an anxiogenic behavioral profile led to the development of a substance P antagonist, MK-869. In preliminary clinical trials, MK-869 was well tolerated and produced significant reductions in both depression and anxiety rating scale scores (Kramer et al. 1998). This report has stimulated much activity, and currently a number of substance P receptor antagonists are under development.

Intense interest is focused on looking for therapeutic targets distal to the neurotransmitter receptor along the signal transduction pathway (S. Paul 1999). The family of G proteins and the second-messenger systems that act to regulate intracellular effector systems are considered attractive potential targets for antidepressant drugs. Already there are data demonstrating that long-term administration of a wide variety of established antidepressant drugs regulate G protein $\alpha$ subunit expression (Lesch and Manji 1992). This finding suggests that G protein alteration may be an integral part of the neuroadaptive mechanisms that underlie therapeutic response (Rasenick et al. 1996). Additionally, considerable evidence suggests that antidepressant drug therapies affect second-messenger systems such as the cyclic adenosine monophosphate (cAMP) pathway and in this way modulate gene expression in the CNS to bring about their therapeutic affects (Chen et al. 1999; Nibuya et al. 1996).

With the recent advances in molecular genetics, the third messenger systems in neurotransmission can now be investigated for novel therapeutic targets. At this level of signal transduction, protein kinase–mediated phosphoproteins regulate gene expression. This area of research is particularly provocative, focusing attention away from the acute biochemical response to pharmacological inter-

**TABLE 34–7.** Antidepressant agents organized by target neurotransmitter and presumed mechanism of action/efficacy

| Target neurotransmitter | Mechanism | Antidepressant |
|---|---|---|
| Serotonin | Selective reuptake inhibitor | Fluoxetine |
| | | Paroxetine |
| | | Sertraline |
| | | Fluvoxamine |
| | | Citalopram |
| | | Clomipramine |
| | $5\text{-HT}_{2A}$ antagonist | Nefazodone |
| | | Trazodone |
| | $5\text{-HT}_{1A}$ agonist | Buspirone |
| Serotonin and norepinephrine | Selective reuptake inhibitor | Venlafaxine |
| | Nonselective reuptake inhibitor | Amitriptyline |
| | | Imipramine |
| | | Doxepin |
| | $5\text{-HT}_{2A}$, $5\text{-HT}_3$, and $\alpha_2$-adrenergic antagonist | Mirtazapine |
| Norepinephrine | Nonselective reuptake inhibitor | Desipramine |
| Norepinephrine and dopamine | Selective reuptake inhibitor | Bupropion |
| Norepinephrine, dopamine, and serotonin | MAO-A and MAO-B inhibitor | Phenelzine |
| | Selective MAO-B inhibitor | Tranylcypromine |
| | Selective MAO-A inhibitor | Selegiline |
| | | Moclobemide |

*Note.* "Selective" designates agents that are most potent for the desired biological activity presumed to mediate antidepressant efficacy. "Nonselective" is used to designate agents that have greater or equal potency for biological sites other than those presumed to mediate antidepressant efficacy (e.g., mirtazapine is designated nonselective because its most potent action is histamine-1 receptor antagonism). Drug selectivity is often dose dependent, with additional biological activities becoming more prominent as drug dose/concentration is increased. 5-HT = 5-hydroxytryptamine (serotonin); MAOI = monoamine oxidase.

ventions to the long-term neuroadaptive mechanisms that more likely mediate therapeutic response. As these neuroadaptive mechanisms are elucidated, the possibilities for novel therapies increase dramatically, from drugs that alter the protein phosphorylation cascade to agents that directly modify encoding of specific genes.

A number of research teams have already identified changes in neuronal gene expression and protein synthesis that occur in response to diverse antidepressant therapies and are commensurate with the 2- to 3-week lag time to onset of therapeutic effect. Tricyclic antidepressants, SSRIs, and even electroconvulsive therapy, but not selected nonantidepressant drugs, have been found to increase transcription of CREB and the mitochondrial protein cytochrome *b* in brain tissue (Huang et al. 1997; Nibuya et al. 1996). More recently, tricyclic antidepressants and the SSRI paroxetine have been found to increase glucocorticoid receptor gene expression in rodent and human tissue (Barden 1999; Okugawa et al. 1999; Vedder et al. 1999). The significance of these particular proteins to antidepressant efficacy is still obscure. But in the search for new treatments, these proteins or the genes that encode them may be targets for more effective antidepressant pharmacotherapy.

With the advances in molecular biology and genetics, the discipline of neuropharmacology is poised to identify novel therapeutic targets for psychiatric disorders. At this time the possible sites for pharmacological intervention in the neurotransmission process seem endless. As research efforts progress, it is likely that many of the novel sites of action that are explored will not become preferred targets for psychotropic pharmacotherapy. However, the ultimate achievement is that each attempt to develop a novel psychotropic agent brings us closer to understanding the complex process of neurotransmission and the pathophysiology of psychiatric disorders.

## Conclusions

Considering the relative lack of effective treatments for mental illness during the first half of this century, the discovery of effective drugs in the 1950s was a milestone. The availability of these agents not only provided relief of symptoms to millions of patients but opened the door to our understanding of basic brain physiology and chemistry. Increased knowledge of brain diseases and psychopharmacology have lead to the reality of rational drug design and targeted drug discovery. As knowledge increases, the targets get smaller and the drug effects more specific.

The ability to target drug action has totally changed the preclinical processes of drug development. The process is faster and more efficient and depends more on logic and knowledge than luck. The clinical elements of drug development in psychiatry, on the other hand, have not kept pace. Clinical trials still require large-scale multisite studies of patients with vaguely defined psychiatric syndromes that may consist of multiple disorders as defined by pathophysiology. The approach is one of sheer numbers to determine drug efficacy. Many useful drugs may actually be determined to be ineffective through this methodology because they may improve only a small subset of the study population.

The clinical phase of drug development therefore should be upgraded coincident with the advances being made in preclinical development. Such an upgrade would include a return to open label studies either in late phase I or early phase II. These studies would represent advanced behavioral pharmacology studies to better characterize the drugs and effects seen at particular doses. Such studies would include both behavioral observations as well as surrogate markers to measure clinical response when possible. When possible and appropriate, studies would be done in both psychiatrically healthy volunteers and patients with the target illness. The goals of such studies would be to define 1) the dose response and time curves, 2) the measures that would be most suited for larger studies needed to document efficacy, and 3) the types of patients that should be enrolled in those later pivotal studies.

# References

Aschner M, Allen JW, Kimelberg HK, et al: Glial cells in neurotoxicity development. Annu Rev Pharmacol Toxicol 39:151–173, 1999

Attwell D: Neurobiology: glia and neurons in dialogue. Nature 369:707–708, 1994

Bacci A, Verderio C, Pravettoni E, et al: The role of glial cells in synaptic function. Philos Trans R Soc Lond B Biol Sci 354:403–409, 1999

Baker R, Llinas R: Electronic coupling between neurons in the rat mesencephalic nucleus. J Physiol (Lond) 212:45–63, 1971

Baraban JM, Worley PF, Snyder SH: Second messenger systems and psychoactive drug action: focus on the phosphoinositide system and lithium. Am J Psychiatry 146(10):1251–1259, 1989

Barden N: Regulation of corticosteroid receptor gene expression in depression and antidepressant action. J Psychiatry Neurosci 24:25–39, 1999

Belmaker RH, Livne A, Agam G, et al: Role of inositol-1-phosphatase inhibition in the mechanism of action of lithium. Pharmacol Toxicol 66 (suppl 3):76–83, 1990

Blakely RD, Berson HE, Fremeau RT Jr, et al: Cloning and expression of a functional serotonin transporter from rat brain. Nature 354:66–70, 1991

Blakely RD, Ramamoorthy S, Qian Y, et al: Regulation of antidepressant-sensitive serotonin transporters, in Neurotransmitter Transporters: Structure, Function, and Regulation. Edited by Reith MEA. Totowa, NJ, Humana, 1997, pp 29–72

Blakely RD, Ramamoorthy S, Schroeter S, et al: Regulated phosphorylation and trafficking of antidepressant-sensitive serotonin transporter proteins. Biol Psychiatry 44:169–178, 1998

Bohn MC: A commentary on glial cell line-derived neurotrophic factor (GDNF). From a glial secreted molecule to gene therapy. Biochem Pharmacol 57:135–142, 1999

Burton R: The Anatomy of Melancholy, 1st Edition. Oxford, Henry Cripps, 1621

Bymaster FP, Hemrick-Luecke SK, Perry KW, et al: Neurochemical evidence for antagonism by olanzapine of dopamine, serotonin, alpha 1–adrenergic and muscarinic receptors in vivo in rats. Psychopharmacology (Berl) 124:87–94, 1996

Caldecott-Hazard S, Morgan DG, DeLeon-Jones F, et al: Clinical and biochemical aspects of depressive disorders, II: transmitter/receptor theories. Synapse 9:251–301, 1991

Caldwell AE: History of psychopharmacology, in Principles of Psychopharmacology, 2nd Edition. Edited by Clark WG, Delgiudice J. New York, Academic Press, 1978, pp 9–40

Catterall WA: Interactions of presynaptic $Ca^{2+}$ channels and snare proteins in neurotransmitter release, in Molecular and Functional Diversity of Ion Channels and Receptors. Edited by Rudy B, Seeburg P. New York, New York Academy of Sciences, 1999, pp 144–159

Chen G, Hasanat K, Bebchuk JM, et al: Regulation of signal transduction pathways and gene expression by mood stabilizers and antidepressants. Psychosom Med 61:599–617, 1999

Clapham DE, Neer EJ: New roles for G-protein beta gamma-dimers in transmembrane signaling. Nature 365:403–406, 1993

Cole JO: Psychopharmacology: problems in evolution, in National Research Council Information. Edited by Cole JO, Gerard RW. Washington, DC, National Academy of Sciences, 1959, pp 92–107

Cooper DM, Mons N, Karpen JW: Adenylyl cyclases and the interaction between calcium and cAMP signalling. Nature 374(6521):421–424, 1995

Cooper JR, Bloom FE, Roth RH: The Biochemical Basis of Neuropharmacology, 7th Edition. New York, Oxford University Press, 1996, pp 3–510

Cornell-Bell AH, Finkbeiner SM: Ca$^{2+}$ waves in astrocytes. Cell Calcium 12:185–204, 1991

Cornell-Bell AH, Finkbeiner SM, Cooper MS, et al: Glutamate induces calcium waves in cultured astrocytes: long-range glial signaling. Science 247:470–473, 1990

Corvalan V, Cole R, de Vellis J, et al: Neuronal modulation of calcium channel activity in cultured rat astrocytes. Proc Natl Acad Sci U S A 87:4345–4348, 1990

Danoff SK, Ross CA: The inositol trisphosphate receptor gene family: implications for normal and abnormal brain function. Prog Neuropsychopharmacol Biol Psychiatry 18(1):1–16, 1994

Devaud LL, Hollingsworth EB, Cooper BR: Alterations in extracellular and tissue levels of biogenic amines in rat brain induced by the serotonin(2) receptor antagonist, ritanserin. J Neurochem 59:1459–1466, 1992

Enkvist MOK, McCarthy KD: Activation of protein kinase C blocks astroglial gap junction communication and inhibits the spread of calcium waves. J Neurochem 59:519–526, 1992

Furth PA, St Onge L, Boger H, et al: Temporal control of gene expression in transgenic mice by a tetracycline-responsive promoter. Proc Natl Acad Sci U S A 91(20):9302–9306, 1994

Galli A, Petersen CI, deBlaquiere M, et al: Drosophila serotonin transporters have voltage-dependent uptake coupled to a serotonin-gated ion channel. J Neurosci 17:3401–3411, 1997

Gegelashvili G, Schousboe A: High affinity glutamate transporters: regulation of expression and activity. Mol Pharmacol 52:6–15, 1997

Gilman AG: G proteins and regulation of adenylyl cyclase. JAMA 262(13):1819–1825, 1989

Glatt CE, Snowman AM, Sibley DR, et al: Clozapine: selective labeling of sites resembling 5HT6 serotonin receptors may reflect psychoactive profile. Mol Med 1:398–406, 1995

Grady S, Marks MJ, Wonnacott S, et al: Characterization of nicotinic receptor-mediated [3H]dopamine release from synaptosomes prepared from mouse striatum. J Neurochem 59:848–856, 1992

Grondin R, Gash DM: Glial cell line–derived neurotrophic factor (GDNF): a drug candidate for the treatment of Parkinson's disease. J Neurol 245:35–42, 1998

Guldberg HC, Mardsen CA: Catechol-O-methyl transferase: pharmacological aspects and physiological role. Pharmacol Rev 27:135–206, 1975

Haga K, Haga T: Activation by G protein beta gamma subunits of agonist- or light-dependent phosphorylation of muscarinic acetylcholine receptors and rhodopsin. J Biol Chem 267:2222–2227, 1992

Hausdorff WP, Caron MG, Lefkowitz RJ: Turning off the signal: desensitization of beta-adrenergic receptor function. FASEB J 4:2881–2889, 1990

Hokin LE, Dixon JF: The phosphoinositide signalling system, I: historical background. II: effects of lithium on the accumulation of second messenger inositol 1,4,5-trisphosphate in brain cortex slices. Prog Brain Res 98:309–315, 1993

Huang N, Strakhova M, Layer RT, et al: Chronic antidepressant treatments increase cytochrome b mRNA levels in mouse cerebral cortex. J Mol Neurosci 9:167–176, 1997

Hughes RL: Cyclosporine-related central nervous system toxicity in cardiac transplantation (letter). N Engl J Med 323:420–421, 1990

Inagaki N, Wada H: Histamine and prostanoid receptors on glial cells. Glia 11:102–109, 1994

Joels M, de Kloet ER: Mineralocorticoid and glucocorticoid receptors in the brain. Implications for ion permeability and transmitter systems. Progress in Neurobiology 43:1–36, 1994

Jursky F, Tamura S, Tamura A, et al: Structure, function and brain localization of neurotransmitter transporters. J Exp Biol 196:283–295, 1994

Kanai Y, Smith CP, Hediger MA: A new family of neurotransmitter transporters: the high-affinity glutamate transporters. FASEB J 8(15):1450–1459, 1994

Kanner BI: Sodium-coupled neurotransmitter transport: structure, function and regulation. J Exp Biol 196:237–249, 1995

Kapur S, Zipursky R, Jones C, et al: Relationship between dopamine D2 occupancy, clinical response, and side effects: a double blind PET study of first-episode schizophrenia. Am J Psychiatry 157:514–520, 2000

Kasai H, Petersen OH: Spatial dynamics of second messengers: IP3 and cAMP as long-range and associative messengers. Trends Neurosci 17(3):95–101, 1994

Kelly RB: An introduction to the nerve terminal, in Neurotransmitter Release. Edited by Bellen HJ. Oxford, Oxford University Press, 1999, pp 1–33

Kenakin T: Agonist-receptor efficacy, I: mechanisms of efficacy and receptor promiscuity. Trends Pharmacol Sci 16(6):188–192, 1995a

Kenakin T: Agonist-receptor efficacy, II: agonist trafficking of receptor signals. Trends Pharmacol Sci 16(7):232–238, 1995b

Kerwin R, Owen M: Genetics of novel therapeutic targets in schizophrenia. Br J Psychiatry 174:1–4, 1999

Kilts CD: Recent pharmacologic advances in antidepressant therapy. Am J Med 97 (suppl 6A):3S–12S, 1994

Kofman O, Belmaker RH: Ziskind-Somerfeld Research Award 1993. Biochemical, behavioral, and clinical studies of the role of inositol in lithium treatment and depression. Biol Psychiatry 34(12):839–852, 1993

Korn H, Sotelo C, Crepel F: Electronic coupling between neurons in rat lateral vestibular nucleus. Exp Brain Res 16:255–275, 1973

Kramer MS, Last B, Getson A, et al: The effects of a selective D4 dopamine receptor antagonist (L-745,870) in acutely psychotic inpatients with schizophrenia. Arch Gen Psychiatry 54:567–572, 1997

Kramer MS, Cutler N, Feighner J, et al: Distinct mechanism for antidepressant activity by blockade of central substance P receptors (comments). Science 281:1640–1645, 1998

Krantz DE, Chaudhry FA, Edwards RH: Neurotransmitter transporters, in Neurotransmitter Release. Edited by Bellen HJ. Oxford, UK, Oxford University Press, 1999, pp 145–207

Lai J, Bilsky EJ, Rothman RB, et al: Treatment with antisense oligodeoxynucleotide to the opioid delta receptor selectively inhibits delta 2–agonist antinociception. Neuroreport 5(9):1049–1052, 1994

Langreth R: Merck reports positive test results for new type of antidepressant drug. Wall Street Journal, September 11, 1998

Langreth R: Merck and Co. hits a stumbling block in testing experimental antidepressant. Wall Street Journal, January 23, 1999

Lapchak PA: A preclinical development strategy designed to optimize the use of glial cell line–derived neurotrophic factor in the treatment of Parkinson's disease. Mov Disord 13 (suppl 1):49–54, 1998

Lesch K, Manji H: Signal-transducing G proteins and antidepressant drugs: evidence for modulation of alpha subunit gene expression in rat brain. Biol Psychiatry 32:549–579, 1992

Lesch KP, Mossner R: Genetically driven variation in serotonin uptake: is there a link to affective spectrum, neurodevelopmental, and neurodegenerative disorders? Biol Psychiatry 44:179–192, 1998

Lesch KP, Bengel D, Heils A, et al: Association of anxiety-related traits with a polymorphism in the serotonin transporter gene regulatory region (comments). Science 274:1527–1531, 1996

Lester HA, Cao Y, Mager S: Listening to neurotransmitter transporters. Neuron 17:807–810, 1996

Levitan IB, Kaczmarek LK: The Neuron: Cell and Molecular Biology, 2nd Edition. New York, Oxford University Press, 1997

Llinas R, Baker R, Sotelo C: Electronic coupling between neurons in the cat inferior olive. J Neurophysiol 37:560–571, 1974

LoTurco JJ, Kriegstein AR: Clusters of coupled neuroblasts in embryonic neocortex. Science 252:563–566, 1991

Lovinger DM: Alcohols and neurotransmitter gated ion channels: past, present and future. Naunyn Schmiedebergs Arch Pharmacol 356:267–282, 1997

Lucas JJ, Hen R: New players in the 5-HT receptor field: genes and knockouts. Trends Pharmacol Sci 16(7):246–252, 1995

Lyson T, Ermel LD, Belshaw PJ, et al: Cyclosporine- and FK506-induced sympathetic activation correlates with calcineurin-mediated inhibition of T-cell signaling. Circ Res 73:596–602, 1993

MacDermott AB, Role LW, Siegelbaum SA: Presynaptic ionotropic receptors and the control of transmitter release. Annu Rev Neurosci 22:443–485, 1999

Mannisto PT, Ulmanen I, Lundstrom K, et al: Characteristics of catechol O-methyl-transferase (COMT) and properties of selective COMT inhibitors. Prog Drug Res 39:291–350, 1992

Marshall IC, Taylor CW: Regulation of inositol 1,4,5-trisphosphate receptors. J Exp Biol 184:161–182, 1993

Martin DL: Synthesis and release of neuroactive substances by glial cells. Glia 5:81–94, 1992

McGeer PL, McGeer EG: Glial cell reactions in neurodegenerative diseases: pathophysiology and therapeutic interventions. Alzheimer Dis Assoc Disord 12 (suppl 2):S1–S6, 1998

McKnight GS: Cyclic AMP second messenger systems. Curr Opin Cell Biol 3(2):213–217, 1991

Meador-Woodruff JH: Update on dopamine receptors. Ann Clin Psychiatry 6(2):79–90, 1994

Melcangi RC, Magnaghi V, Martini L: Steroid metabolism and effects in central and peripheral glial cells. J Neurobiol 40:471–483, 1999

Melikian HE, Ramamoorthy S, Tate CG, et al: Inability to N-glycosylate the human norepinephrine transporter reduces protein stability, surface trafficking, and transport activity but not ligand recognition. Mol Pharmacol 50:266–276, 1996

Mulcrone J, Kerwin RW: No difference in the expression of the D4 gene in post-mortem frontal cortex from controls and schizophrenics. Neurosci Lett 219:163–166, 1996

Nalepa I: The effect of psychotropic drugs on the interaction of protein kinase C with second messenger systems in the rat cerebral cortex. Pol J Pharmacol 46(1–2):1–14, 1994

Narahashi T, Aistrup GL, Marszalec W, et al: Neuronal nicotinic acetylcholine receptors: a new target site of ethanol. Neurochem Int 35:131–141, 1999

Nelson N: The family of Na⁺/Cl⁻ neurotransmitter transporters. J Neurochem 71:1785–1803, 1998

Nibuya M, Nestler E, Duman R: Chronic antidepressant administration increases the expression of cAMP response element binding protein (CREB) in rat hippocampus. J Neurosci 316:2365–2372, 1996

Nishizuka Y: Protein kinase C and lipid signaling for sustained cellular responses. FASEB J 9(7):484–496, 1995

Nutt D: Substance-P antagonists: a new treatment for depression? Lancet 352:1644–1646, 1998

Okugawa G, Omori K, Suzukawa J, et al: Long-term treatment with antidepressants increases glucocorticoid receptor binding and gene expression in cultured rat hippocampal neurons. J Neuroendocrinol 11:887–895, 1999

Oswald I, Brezinova V, Dunleavy DLF: On the slowness of action of tricyclic antidepressant drugs. Br J Psychiatry 120:673–677, 1972

Otero GC, Merrill JE: Cytokine receptors on glial cells. Glia 11:117–128, 1994

Parthasarathy L, Vadnal RE, Parthasarathy R, et al: Biochemical and molecular properties of lithium-sensitive myo-inositol monophosphatase. Life Sci 54(16):1127–1142, 1994

Paul IA, Nowak G, Layer RT, et al: Adaptation of the N-methyl-D-aspartate receptor complex following chronic antidepressant treatments. J Pharmacol Exp Ther 269(1):95–102, 1994

Paul S: CNS drug discovery in the 21st century. From genomics to combinatorial chemistry and back. Br J Psychiatry 174:23–25, 1999

Pills for the mind: new era in psychiatry. Time, 65(10):63–69, March 7, 1955

Pitcher JA, Inglese J, Higgins JB, et al: Role of beta gamma subunits of G proteins in targeting the beta-adrenergic receptor kinase to membrane-bound receptors. Science 257:1264–1267, 1992

Poitry-Yamate CL, Poitry S, Tsacopoulos M: Lactate released by Muller glial cells is metabolized by photoreceptors from mammalian retina. J Neurosci 15:5179–5191, 1995

Premont RT, Inglese J, Lefkowitz RJ: Protein kinases that phosphorylate activated G protein–coupled receptors. FASEB J 9:175–182, 1995

Rahamimoff R, Butkevich A, Duridanova D, et al: Multitude of ion channels in the regulation of transmitter release. Philos Trans R Soc Lond B Biol Sci 354:281–288, 1999

Raivich G, Jones LL, Werner A, et al: Molecular signals for glial activation: pro- and anti-inflammatory cytokines in the injured brain. Acta Neurochir Suppl (Wien) 73:21–30, 1999

Ransom BR, Sontheimer H: The neurophysiology of glial cells. J Clin Neurophysiol 9(2):224–251, 1992

Rasenick M, Chaney K, Chen J: G protein–mediated signal transduction as a target of antidepressant and antibipolar drug action: evidence from model systems. J Clin Psychiatry 57:49–55, 1996

Remington G, Kapur S: D2 and 5-HT-2 receptor effects of antipsychotics: bridging basic and clinical findings using PET. J Clin Psychiatry 60:15–19, 1999

Rens-Domiao S, Hamm HE: Structural and functional relationships of heterotrimeric G-proteins. FASEB J 9:1059–1066, 1995

Richelson E: Receptor pharmacology of neuroleptics: relation to clinical effects. J Clin Psychiatry 60:5–14, 1999

Robinson SR, Hampson E, Munro MN, et al: Unidirectional coupling of gap junctions between neuroglia. Science 262:1072–1074, 1993

Ronde P, Nichols RA: High calcium permeability of serotonin 5-HT3 receptors on presynaptic nerve terminals from rat striatum. J Neurochem 70:1094–1103, 1998

Rosenfeld A: The vital facts about the drug and its affects. Life 60(12):30–31, March 25, 1966

Roth BL, Craigo SC, Choudhary MS, et al: Binding of typical and atypical antipsychotic agents to 5-hydroxytryptamine-6 and 5-hydroxytryptamine-7 receptors. J Pharmacol Exp Ther 268:1403–1410, 1994

Saarma M, Sariola H: Other neurotrophic factors: glial cell line–derived neurotrophic factor (GDNF). Microsc Res Tech 45:292–302, 1999

Sanders-Bush E, Canton H: Serotonin receptors: signal transduction pathways, in Psychopharmacology: The Fourth Generation of Progress. Edited by Bloom FE, Kupfer DJ. New York, Raven, 1995, pp 431–441

Saudou F, Amara DA, Dierich A, et al: Enhanced aggressive behavior in mice lacking 5-HT1B receptor. Science 265(5180):1875–1878, 1994

Schlag BD, Vondrasek JR, Munir M, et al: Regulation of the glial Na+-dependent glutamate transporters by cyclic AMP analogs and neurons. Mol Pharmacol 53:355–369, 1998

Seeman P, Van Tol HH: Dopamine receptor pharmacology. Current Opinions in Neurology and Neurosurgery 6(4):602–608, 1993

Seeman P, Guan HC, Van Tol HH: Schizophrenia: elevation of dopamine D4–like sites using 3H-nemonapride and 125I-epidepride. Eur J Pharmacol 286:R3–R5, 1995

Shank RP, William JB, Charles WA: Glutamine and 2-oxoglutarate as metabolic precursors of the transmitter pools of glutamate and GABA: correlation of regional uptake by rat brain synaptosomes. Neurochem Res 16:29–34, 1989

Shepherd GM: Neurobiology, 2nd Edition. New York, Oxford University Press, 1994

Shinohara K, Hiruma H, Funabashi T, et al: GABAergic modulation of gap junction communication in slice cultures of the rat suprachiasmatic nucleus. Neuroscience 96:591–596, 2000

Silvia CP, King GR, Lee TH, et al: Intranigral administration of D2 dopamine receptor antisense oligodeoxynucleotides establishes a role for nigrostriatal D2 autoreceptors in the motor actions of cocaine. Mol Pharmacol 46(1):51–57, 1994

Singer TP, Ramsay RR: Monoamine oxidases: old friends hold many surprises. FASEB J 9:605–610, 1995

Snyder SH, Banerjee SP, Yamamura HI, et al: Drugs, neurotransmitters, and schizophrenia. Science 184:1243–1253, 1974

Sontheimer H: Voltage-dependent ion channels in glial cells. Glia 2:202–210, 1994

Spano PF, Govoni S, Trabucchi M: Studies on the pharmacological properties of dopamine receptors in various areas of the central nervous system. Advances in Biochemical Psychopharmacology 19:155–165, 1978

Stahl SM: Peptides and psychiatry, Part 3: substance P and serendipity: novel psychotropics are a possibility. J Clin Psychiatry 60:140–141, 1999a

Stahl SM: Substance P and the neurokinins: novel peptide neurotransmitters in psychopharmacology. J Clin Psychiatry 60:77–78, 1999b

Standifer KM, Chien CC, Wahlestedt C, et al: Selective loss of delta opioid analgesia and binding by antisense oligodeoxynucleotides to a delta opioid receptor. Neuron 12(4):805–810, 1994

Stephens DN, Kehr W, Duka T: Anxiolytic and anxiogenic beta-carbolines: tools for the study of anxiety mechanisms, in GABAergic Transmission and Anxiety. Edited by Biggio G, Costa E. New York, Raven, 1986, pp 91–106

Sternbach LH, Horst WD: Psychopharmacological agents, in Kirk-Othmer: Encyclopedia of Chemical Technology, 3rd Edition. New York, Wiley, 1982, pp 342–379

Stoof JC, Kebabian JW: Two dopamine receptors: biochemistry, physiology and pharmacology. Life Sci 35:2281–2296, 1984

Swanson RA, Liu J, Miller JW, et al: Neuronal regulation of glutamate transporter subtype expression in astrocytes. J Neurosci 17:932–940, 1997

Tallman JF, Cassela JV, White G, et al: GABA$_A$ receptors: diversity and its implications for CNS disease. The Neuroscientist 5:351–361, 1999

Tecott LH, Sun LM, Acana SF, et al: Eating disorder and epilepsy in mice lacking 5-HT2c serotonin receptors. Nature 374:542–546, 1995

Thiel G: Recent breakthroughs in neurotransmitter release: paradigm for regulated exocytosis? News in Physiological Science 10:42–46, 1995

Thomas KR, Capecchi MR: Targeted disruption of the murine int-1 proto-oncogene resulting in severe abnormalities in midbrain and cerebellar development. Nature 346(6287): 847–850, 1990

Todd RD, O'Malley KL: Family ties: dopamine D2 like receptors. Neurotransmissions 9:1–4, 1993

Triggle DJ: The pharmacology of ion channels: with particular reference to voltage-gated $Ca^{2+}$ channels. Eur J Pharmacol 375:311–325, 1999

Tsacopoulos M, Magistretti PJ: Metabolic coupling between glia and neurons. J Neurosci 16:877–885, 1996

Van Tol HH, Bunzow JR, Guan HC, et al: Cloning of the gene for a human dopamine D4 receptor with high affinity for the antipsychotic clozapine. Nature 350(6319):610–614, 1991

Vardimon L, Ben-Dror I, Avisar N, et al: Glucocorticoid control of glial gene expression. J Neurobiol 40:513–527, 1999

Vedder H, Bening-Abu-Shach U, Lanquillon S, et al: Regulation of glucocorticoid receptor mRNA in human blood cells by amitriptyline and dexamethasone. J Psychiatr Res 33:303–308, 1999

Wahlestedt C: Reward for persistence in substance P research (comment). Science 281:1624–1625, 1998

Wahlestedt C, Pich EM, Koob GF, et al: Modulation of anxiety and neuropeptide Y-Y1 receptors by antisense oligodeoxynucleotides. Science 259(5094):528–531, 1993

Wallis C, Willwerth J: Schizophrenia: a new drug brings patients back to life. Time 140(1):52–58, July 6, 1992

Walsh DA, Van Patten SM: Multiple pathway signal transduction by the cAMP-dependent protein kinase. FASEB J 8(15):1227–1236, 1994

Wartiovaara K, Hytonen M, Vuori M, et al: Mutation analysis of the glial cell line–derived neurotrophic factor gene in Parkinson's disease. Exp Neurol 152:307–309, 1998

Watkins SS, Epping-Jordan MP, Koob GF, et al: Blockade of nicotine self-administration with nicotinic antagonists in rats. Pharmacol Biochem Behav 62:743–751, 1999

Wolfe BB, Harden TK, Sporn JR, et al: Presynaptic modulation of beta adrenergic receptors in rat cerebral cortex after treatment with antidepressants. J Pharmacol Exp Ther 207:446–457, 1978

Wonnacott S: Presynaptic nicotinic ACh receptors. Trends Neurosci 20:92–98, 1997

Wooley DW: The Biochemical Bases of Psychoses: Serotonin Hypothesis about Mental Diseases. New York, Wiley, 1962, pp 1–331

Wright WW: Results obtained by the intensive use of bromides in functional psychoses. Am J Psychiatry 82:365–389, 1926

Yakel JL: Calcineurin regulation of synaptic function: from ion channels to transmitter release and gene transcription. Trends Pharmacol Sci 18:124–134, 1997

Yeomans J, Baptista M: Both nicotinic and muscarinic receptors in ventral tegmental area contribute to brain-stimulation reward. Pharmacol Biochem Behav 57:915–921, 1997

Zahs KR: Heterotypic coupling between glial cells of the mammalian central nervous system. Glia 24:85–96, 1998

Zhang B, Ramaswami M: Synaptic vesicle endocytosis and recycling, in Neurotransmitter Release. Edited by Bellen HJ. Oxford, UK, Oxford University Press, 1999, pp 389–431

Zhou LW, Zhang SP, Qin ZH, et al: In vivo administration of an oligodeoxynucleotide antisense to the D2 dopamine receptor messenger RNA inhibits D2 dopamine receptor–mediated behavior and the expression of D2 dopamine receptors in mouse striatum. J Pharmacol Exp Ther 268(2): 1015–1023, 1994

# Psychopharmacologic Treatments for Patients With Neuropsychiatric Disorders

Peter P. Roy-Byrne, M.D.

Mahendra Upadhyaya, M.D.

Modern neuropsychiatry is concerned with the understanding and treatment of cognitive, emotional, and behavioral syndromes in patients with known neurologic illness or central nervous system (CNS) dysfunction. Although some syndromes (e.g., major depression) in patients with neurologic disease (e.g., cerebrovascular accident [CVA], head trauma) are clinically similar to those seen in well patients experiencing the syndrome de novo, treatment response may be quite different. Furthermore, the neuropsychiatric sequelae of a number of neurologic disorders frequently seem an amalgam of several syndromes and often do not fit neatly into DSM-IV (American Psychiatric Association 1994) syndromal definitions. Does the combative, irritable, agitated, brain-injured patient have dysphoric mania, agitated depression, or posttraumatic stress disorder (PTSD)? Does the apathetic, withdrawn, poststroke patient really have major depression? Although DSM-IV may be a useful starting point, departing from it is a frequent necessity.

Despite likely dissimilarities in the clinical presentation and treatment response of neuropsychiatric and psychiatric syndromes, the treatment of patients with neuropsychiatric illness has largely been modeled on known treatments of whatever syndrome (e.g., depression, psychosis) seems to be present. Unfortunately, the paucity of double-blind, placebo-controlled treatment studies in neuropsychiatric patients and the scarcity of even large

case series make treatment at this point more art than science. In addition, the selection and execution of pharmacologic treatment in this population are as important as attention to altered side-effect sensitivity and pertinent interactions with commonly used neurologic drugs.

For this reason, this chapter does not duplicate material commonly found in numerous textbooks of psychopharmacology and psychiatric treatment. The neuropsychiatrist needs information on the psychopharmacologic treatment of neuropsychiatric patients and their syndromes rather than drug treatment of psychiatric illness in general. The reader is referred to other standard textbooks for this latter information (Schatzberg and Nemeroff 1998). The chapter is not organized by medication but rather by syndrome so that the interested physician and trainee can more easily locate information relevant to a specific patient with a specific array of cognitive, emotional, and behavioral abnormalities. Side effects, drug interactions, and pharmacokinetic considerations are included only as they are pertinent to the neuropsychiatric context.

This chapter focuses on five major syndromes commonly seen by the treating neuropsychiatrist: depression, including apathetic, "deficit" states; psychosis; states of agitation, including anxiety and mania; aggression, impulsivity, and behavioral dyscontrol; and cognitive disturbance (amnesia, dementia). These syndromes are seen more often in combination than in isolation, and the presence of one often increases the chance of another (e.g., cognitive impairment increases risk of depression in both Parkinson's disease [Tandberg et al. 1997] and Alzheimer's disease [Payne et al. 1998]). Throughout the chapter a common organization is employed. Each syndrome is defined in enough detail to appreciate how it borders on and overlaps with the others. The most common etiologies and possible neuroanatomic-neurochemical substrates of these syndromes are reviewed. Following this, studies, case series, and isolated case reports are reviewed. Issues of dosage, treatment duration, and response course are considered. Finally, side effects, pharmacokinetic considerations, and drug interactions are highlighted.

## Approach to the Neuropsychiatric Patient

The psychiatrist who is asked to assess a neuropsychiatric patient for pharmacologic treatment must first become familiar with the nature and course of the underlying neurologic illness. This includes an understanding of the disorder's neuroanatomy and neurochemistry, because apparently distinct neurologic and psychiatric symptoms often arise from similar mechanisms intrinsic to the neurologic disorder (e.g., psychosis in CNS neoplasms). Conversely, similar symptoms can be caused by distinct neurologic and psychiatric disorders as well as by the side effects of both neurologic and psychotropic medications (e.g., both Parkinson's bradykinesia and phenytoin-induced lethargy may be mistaken for signs of depression). Furthermore, many psychiatric medications can worsen the neurologic illness (e.g., neuroleptics administered for Parkinson's psychosis; antidepressants administered for multiple sclerosis mood lability), whereas neurologic medications can precipitate psychiatric syndromes (e.g., levodopa psychosis and anxiety in Parkinson's disease; steroid-induced mania in CNS lupus). Therefore, treatment must first consider the primary neurologic disorder and its medications.

Consideration of other medical conditions and treatments, recent surgeries, and health habits is also helpful. Pallidotomy for Parkinson's disease can produce cognitive or other psychiatric effects (Kubu et al. 2000). Herbal medicines can produce neuropsychiatric symptoms and interact with medications (La France et al. 2000). History of alcohol and drug use must also be explored, since substance abuse can itself lead to psychiatric symptoms (e.g., depression, impulsivity, and cognitive impairment) that may be inappropriately attributed

to the neurologic illness (Rosse et al. 1997).

The manner of initial patient contact often determines the amount of useful information that is obtained as well as the likelihood of patient adherence to treatment recommendations. Many patients have no prior experience with the mental health system and may feel surprised and even threatened that a psychiatrist has been called. The fear of further loss of control in a situation that already feels out of control may be quite profound. Usually, however, once the patient's psychological and behavioral symptoms are explained as those that are frequently encountered as part of the symptom complex of the neurologic disorder—and can potentially be treated—the patient will be placed at ease and relieved. Initially explaining the patient's symptoms and treatment in the context of a medical model is the most effective approach, because the patient is often already overwhelmed by his or her symptoms and functional impairment, as well as by the array of medical opinions and treatments presented to him or her, and may not be either emotionally or cognitively ready for sophisticated psychotherapeutic explanations or interventions. Presenting the pharmacologic intervention as a way to assist recovery during a period of intense stress and adaptation will help the patient feel more hopeful and maintain an internal locus of control. Realistic expectations, including the possibility of incomplete remission of symptoms, must be conveyed from the outset so that the patient who is already frustrated with an often slow and arduous rehabilitation process does not become even more hopeless if some symptoms persist. All of the psychiatric symptoms may not be alleviated, but treatment may significantly benefit the rehabilitation process.

The neuropsychiatrist must also be aware of the strong impact of not only the patient's and family's urgent wish to have the patient's psychiatric symptoms treated but also the clinician's intense desire to help. There is often an urge to "do something, anything" that must be resisted. Some symptoms may be long-standing and unlikely to resolve quickly, whereas others may result from an adjustment disorder that may dissipate without pharmacologic treatment.

When assessing a neurologic patient for psychopathology, the clinician must look beyond DSM-IV diagnoses when a patient does not meet the DSM criteria and carefully explore the nature of the patient's complaints to identify symptoms that may be treatable. This flexibility and persistence allow the clinician to better treat the individual needs of the patient.

The next step in evaluating a neurologic patient's appropriateness for psychotropic medication involves obtaining a careful history of premorbid psychiatric problems, personality traits, and coping styles. Multiple informants often will minimize informational bias (Strauss et al. 1997). The psychiatric symptoms may have predated the onset of neurologic symptoms and will provide clues regarding diagnosis and subsequent treatment. Because CNS, particularly frontal lobe, insults frequently amplify underlying character traits (Prigatano 1992), it may be unrealistic to attempt to completely attenuate certain behaviors and traits that appear to be a direct result of the neurologic insult. Optimal treatment must take into account whether the psychiatric symptoms preexisted the neurologic disorder, arose as a neurologically or psychologically mediated result of the neurologic insult, or surfaced as a reaction to the resulting disability and loss. Certain premorbid traits, such as IQ, may have implications for course of illness (Palsson et al. 1999).

While interviewing the patient, the clinician must remember that the neurologic disorder may dampen the patient's ability to express emotions and affect, particularly in older patients. Thus, the clinician must rely equally on the patient's subjective and somatic complaints and the reports of friends, family members, and caregivers for clues to emotional and behavioral problems. A patient often reports cognitive difficulties as being more severe, whereas family members may view the patient's emotional changes as more disabling (Hendryx 1989). Documentation of symptoms will help in tracking what is often slow improvement that appears subjectively inapparent to the patient and caregivers but may be real improvement in functioning. Although it may be impractical to completely document all symptoms, specific target symptoms and functional goals should be measured and documented in as great detail as possible. Neuropsychiatrists must join the movement toward documenting outcomes, an endeavor in which they have unfortunately lagged (Coffey et al. 1995). Caregivers, significant others, and, in certain cases, patients can be asked to use simple, anchored 0–10 scales to rate the severity of symptoms and functional impairment over time. When appropriate, a directed physical examination should be performed before initiating treatment to document symptoms that may either improve or worsen with treatment, such as rigidity in the psychotic patient with Parkinson's disease. Figure 35–1 depicts one simple example of such a scale, which allows the clinician to fill in items tailored to the particular patient's symptoms and problems.

A basic tenet of treating psychiatric symptoms in patients with neurologic disorders is to treat as many signs and symptoms with as few medications as possible. Patients with CNS pathology are more susceptible to CNS medication side effects, such as sedative, anticho-

linergic, extrapyramidal, and epileptogenic effects. Therefore, a patient with a severe head injury who may be having complex partial seizures and is exhibiting labile affect and impulsivity should be considered for treatment with carbamazepine or valproate, which may treat both the patient's seizure disorder and his or her affective and behavioral symptoms, rather than combining phenytoin and lithium. Similarly, a patient with both depression and aggression after a stroke may improve with monotherapy with a selective serotonin reuptake inhibitor (SSRI) because of its proven efficacy in treating poststroke depression and its suggested efficacy in attenuating aggression. Potential "neuroprotective" effects of psychotropic medications should be considered in stroke or head-injury patients (Alexopoulos et al. 1997), as should the rare possibility that the effects of medications could worsen the underlying illness.

Detailed knowledge of the patient's stage in rehabilitation as well as the patient's current social, occupational, and interpersonal status is required to tailor the pharmacologic regimen to specific practical needs and limitations. For example, starting a potentially sedating medication at a time when a rigorous physical therapy regimen is being initiated or during a long-awaited reentry into the workplace would be ill-advised. Social and interpersonal status can affect access to treatment (Ferrando et al. 1999), ability of caregivers to participate in treatment (Donaldson et al. 1997), vulnerability of patients to domestic violence (Díaz-Olavarrieta et al. 1999), and psychiatric outcome (Max et al. 1998).

Before administering psychotropic medications, pertinent laboratory tests must be obtained. Because of the patient's susceptibility to medication side effects, the clinician should start at a lower dose of medication and titrate more slowly, although the patient may ultimately require the same dose of medication as the nonneurologic patient (i.e., "Start low and go slow, but go"). Side effects should be well documented, using standardized measures, whenever possible. Because these patients may have cognitive deficits as a result of their neurologic problems, the anticipated benefit of the medication, the dosing regimen, and any potential side effects must be thoroughly explained to the patient and caregiver and should be communicated to other physicians caring for the patient. For example, a patient who is receiving meperidine for pain from his neurologist and is also receiving an SSRI for depressive symptoms from his psychiatrist may be at risk for developing a life-threatening central serotonin syndrome. Also, a patient who has experienced a stroke may be susceptible to low blood pressure and should be prescribed drugs with anticholinergic and β-blocking properties only with great caution.

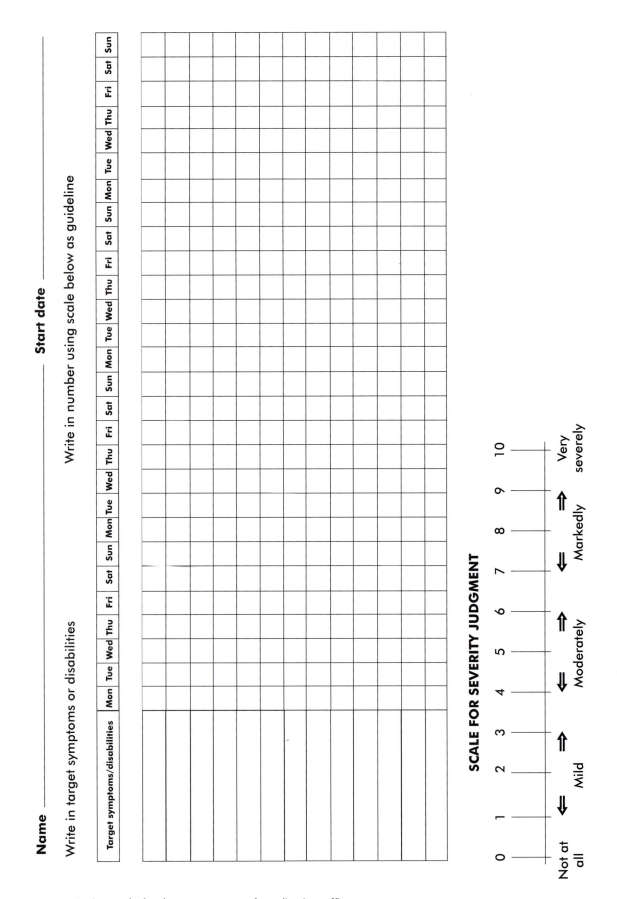

**FIGURE 35–1.** Rating scale for the assessment of medication efficacy.

Treatment of symptoms secondary to the primary neurologic disorder, such as pain and sleep disturbance, may decrease psychiatric symptoms sufficiently to allow avoidance of further psychopharmacotherapy. For example, analgesia has been shown to alleviate agitation, irritability, and anger in both patients and caregivers (Perry et al. 1991). Similarly, appropriately treating a psychiatric symptom early in its presentation before it can exacerbate the neurologic disorder may significantly improve the patient's overall functioning. For example, emotional distress has been shown to worsen, and even precipitate, exacerbations of multiple sclerosis (Grant et al. 1989).

Once medication has been initiated, all available tools to subjectively follow pharmacokinetics and pharmacologic efficacy must be considered. For example, medication blood levels, physiologic response (such as vital signs), laboratory monitoring (such as electroencephalography), and neuropsychological testing can all be helpful. Medication blood levels do not necessarily correlate with medication efficacy but may give information about compliance and drug metabolism. Further monitoring is of particular importance in neuropsychiatric patients, as they may be less likely to report side effects due to impaired cognition and the myriad of other symptoms that they may be experiencing. Figure 35–2 sums up many of the points in this section.

## Depression, Apathy, and "Deficit" States

Major depression and dysthymia are among the most common psychiatric disorders. Although decades of clinical observation and research have clearly delineated retarded and agitated subtypes of depression, few consistent clinical or biological differences between the two have emerged (Goodwin and Jamison 1990), and even the clinical maxim of avoiding the use of "activating" antidepressants in anxious depressed individuals has been disproved (Tollefson et al. 1994). In contrast, this distinction is more important in the assessment and treatment of neuropsychiatric patients. In these patients, the overlap of agitated states with behavioral dyscontrol, delirium, and occasionally psychosis, along with the greater prevalence of states of apathy—in which cognitive and behavioral slowing occur in the absence of mood disturbance (M. L. Levy et al. 1998)—argues for separate consideration of retarded depression, in conjunction with apathetic and other deficit-like states. However, admixtures of subjective anxiety, nervousness, and worry, without significant (i.e., clinically predominant) agitation, is also considered in this section.

## Common Etiologies

Depression and apathy are extremely common following CVA or traumatic brain injury (TBI); with Parkinson's disease or Huntington's disease; with multiple sclerosis or epilepsy; in association with diencephalic, frontal, and temporal lobe tumors; and during the course of Alzheimer's and multi-infarct dementias. Depression, when it occurs in patients with human immunodeficiency virus (HIV) infection—although not more prevalent than in matched control subjects (Williams et al. 1991)—is often associated with marked apathy and subtle deficits in neurocognitive function (Castellon et al. 1998) that can progress in later stages to dementia. Most studies, except those in HIV infection, have demonstrated a prevalence of depression greater than that in comparably disabling physical illness not involving the CNS and have failed to find a consistent association of severity of depression with progression of neurologic illness or subsequent disability. This argues that depression is not simply a reaction to neurologic illness or subsequent disability but, when it occurs, is a core feature of these illnesses, with partially overlapping pathophysiology (Lyketsos et al. 1998). Nonetheless, psychological reaction either to the causative event (i.e., a posttraumatic stress reaction—see Bryant et al. 2000) or to the subsequent neurologic disability (i.e., a grief reaction), and discomfort related to the underlying illness (e.g., pain, insomnia), will often be important factors in the individual patient and must be considered and vigorously addressed before initiating pharmacotherapy. The possibility that currently prescribed medications might be contributing to depression also needs to be carefully considered. These include anticonvulsants, sedative-hypnotics, β-blockers, corticosteroids, metoclopramide, histamine type 2 receptor ($H_2$) blockers, calcium channel blockers, and angiotensin-converting enzyme inhibitors. However, most studies have failed to show group mean differences between treated and untreated patients for many drugs, suggesting that these effects are likely confined to a small subgroup of treated patients. Patients with prior histories of depression may be more likely to develop depression side effects from some drugs (e.g., depression following interferon treatment of multiple sclerosis [Mohr et al. 1999]). Withdrawal from some agents, including anticonvulsants, benzodiazepines, and stimulants, may also be associated with depression.

### Anatomy and Neurochemistry

The range of neuroanatomic and neurochemical substrates that have been associated with depressive and

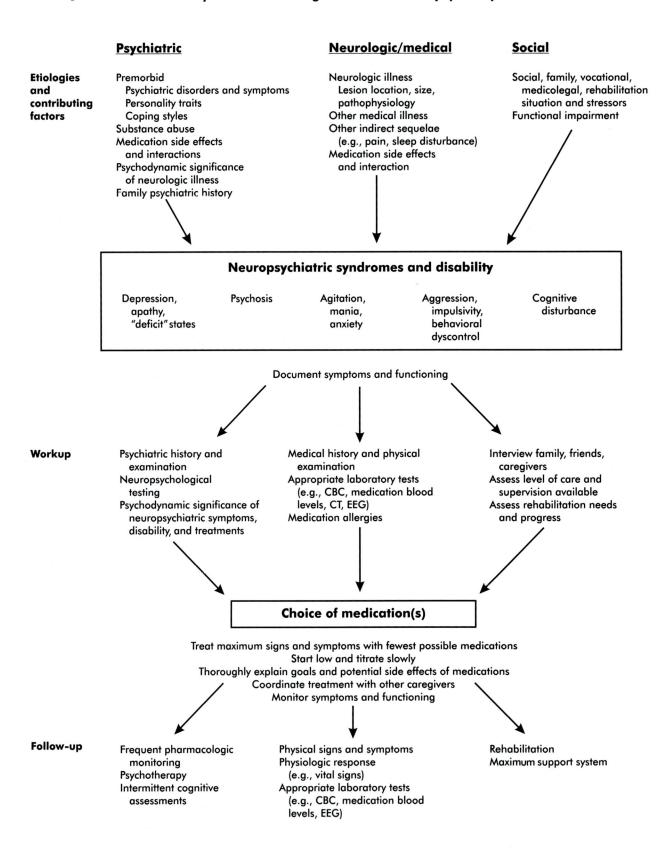

**FIGURE 35–2.**  Algorithm for the psychopharmacologic evaluation and treatment of neuropsychiatric patients.

*Note.*   CBC = complete blood cell count; CT = computed tomography; EEG = electroencephalogram.

apathetic states in neurologically ill patients is extremely wide. However, the most common pathophysiologic substrates have involved disruption of frontal lobe–basal ganglia circuits and possible perturbation of ascending monoaminergic pathways that rise from their brain-stem nuclei to fan out anteriorly over these areas. This is supported by the greater incidence of depression with left frontal CVAs (Morris et al. 1996b) and left frontal and basal ganglia TBI; the predominance of depression/apathy versus other psychiatric disturbances in basal ganglia disease (Lauterbach et al. 1997); greater involvement revealed by positron emission tomography (PET) and greater frontostriatal involvement discovered on postmortem examination in depressed Alzheimer's disease patients (Zubenko and Moossy 1988); and actual neuroimaging studies comparing anatomic and neurochemical profiles in depression with and without neurologic illness. Depressed patients with CVA, TBI, or Parkinson's disease all show decreased glucose metabolism in orbital-inferior frontal and anterior temporal cortex, the latter presumably due to disruption of paralimbic pathways linking frontal cortex, temporal cortex, and striatum (Mayberg 1997). Patients with temporal lobe epilepsy and depression also show similar inferior frontal hypometabolism on PET scan, presumably mediated via paralimbic pathways (Bromfield et al. 1992), and more than 50% of those with depression have no further depressive episodes after temporal lobe surgery (Altshuler et al. 1999). Multiple sclerosis patients with depression show disturbed blood flow only in limbic cortex (Sabatini et al. 1996), consistent with notions that dysregulation of paralimbic areas such as the cingulate cortex can disconnect intact frontal cortical and subcortical areas, producing depression in the absence of frontostriatal damage (Ebert and Ebmeier 1996). Right-hemisphere lesions also produce a state in which patients lose the capacity for normal emotional expression (aprosodias), which may be confused with depression.

Human postmortem pathologic (C.P. Chen et al. 1994, 1996; Raisman et al. 1986; Zubenko and Moossy 1988), cerebrospinal fluid (CSF) (Mayeux et al. 1988), imaging (Mayberg et al. 1991), and neuroendocrine (Kostic et al. 1996) evidence supports a role for serotonin (5-hydroxytryptamine; 5-HT) in the depression of Parkinson's disease, of CVA, and of Alzheimer's dementias. Frontal lobe damage from TBI is also selectively associated with reduced brain 5-HT function (Van Woerkom et al. 1977), and even depressed patients with mild TBI have altered 5-HT function on neuroendocrine testing compared with nondepressed mild TBI patients (Mobayed and Dinan 1990). Depressed Alzheimer's disease patients have greater locus coeruleus neuronal loss than those without depression (Forstl et al. 1992), implicating central noradrenergic activity. Finally, although it is less consistent, there is some evidence for a role for dopamine (Torack and Morris 1988), especially for states of cognitive and behavioral slowing (e.g., apathy associated with Parkinson's disease and frontal lobe CVA). Reduced prefrontal lobe dopaminergic function has also been implicated in negative deficit–state symptoms associated with schizophrenia (Davis et al. 1991).

Although these abnormalities are particularly relevant because currently available antidepressants affect these transmitter systems, it should be emphasized that monoamine neurotransmitter hypotheses of depression have given way over the last decade to considerably more sophisticated models that emphasize alterations in multiple receptor subtypes and associated signal transduction mechanisms, as well as changes in other transmitter (e.g., glutamate, γ-aminobutyric acid [GABA]) and neuropeptide systems. Therefore, these findings are largely presented for heuristic purposes, since most antidepressants still target monoaminergic systems. Similarly, evidence is mounting that less specific damage and dysfunction in multiple neuroanatomic areas are associated with the specific neuropsychiatric syndromes discussed in this chapter (see especially the case of TBI [Gross et al. 1996 and also Morris et al. 1996a]), so hypotheses of regional specificity are also presented solely for heuristic purposes.

## Treatment

In contrast to the plethora of double-blind, placebo-controlled trials of various antidepressants in major depression, there are relatively few such studies in depressed patients with neurologic illness. This is extremely unfortunate, because depression has been associated with both increased mortality (Morris et al. 1993b) and disability (Ramasubbu et al. 1998) rates in this population. Furthermore, the well-known undertreatment of psychiatric illness in the general medical setting is likely to be even more severe in the neuropsychiatric setting, where access to expert pharmacotherapists is more limited.

Placebo-controlled studies have examined the efficacy of nortriptyline (Lipsey et al. 1984), trazodone (Reding et al. 1986), and citalopram (G. Andersen et al. 1994) in depressed CVA patients; of imipramine (Strang 1965), nortriptyline (J. Andersen et al. 1980), desipramine (Laitinen 1969), and bupropion (Goetz et al. 1984) in depressed Parkinson's disease patients; of desipramine in depressed multiple sclerosis patients (Schiffer and Wineman 1990); of imipramine (Reifler et al. 1989), clomipramine (Petracca et al. 1996), moclobemide

(M. Roth et al. 1996), maprotiline (Fuchs et al.1993), citalopram (Nyth et al. 1992), and sertraline (Magai et al. 2000) in depressed Alzheimer's disease patients; of desipramine in depressed TBI patients (Wroblewski et al. 1996); and of fluoxetine in depressed patients with Huntington's disease (Como et al. 1997). Although studies have documented SSRI (Elliott et al. 1998; Zisook et al. 1998) and imipramine (Elliott et al. 1998; Rabkin et al. 1994) efficacy in depressed patients with HIV disease, most patients in these studies were not in the late stages of HIV illness and likely had major depression relatively little affected by CNS viral involvement. Several studies of the monoamine oxidase B (MAO-B) inhibitor selegiline in Parkinson's disease patients measured effects on depression as a secondary phenomenon (Klaassen et al. 1995).

All but four of the studies cited above report a greater efficacy of the active drug compared with placebo in the course of trial durations between 4 and 8 weeks. Type of illness (Huntington's disease, Como et al. 1997) and patient (advanced Alzheimer's disease, Magai et al. 2000) may have affected response in these negative studies. The group of Parkinson's disease studies reported response rates somewhat lower (i.e., 60%) than in non–medically ill depressed patients. Many studies have purposely employed lower (e.g., trazodone 200 mg [Reding et al. 1986]) doses, as would be used in elderly patients, and earlier studies using normal doses of tricyclics have sometimes shown a high frequency of side effects (e.g., 18% rate of delirium in CVA patients [Lipsey et al. 1984]) and an inability to reach therapeutic blood levels in multiple sclerosis due to side effects [Schiffer and Wineman 1990]).

A provocative 12-week comparison study (Robinson et al. 2000) showed that nortriptyline was superior to fluoxetine in depressed CVA patients, although a similar comparison of amitriptyline and fluoxetine in depressed patients with Alzheimer's disease (Taragano et al. 1997) showed equal efficacy, and a study of nondepressed CVA patients with hemiplegia showed that fluoxetine was superior to both maprotiline and placebo in facilitating rehabilitation therapy, supporting a distinct functional effect in the absence of depression (Dam et al. 1996). This finding, effects of SSRIs on "emotional incontinence" (i.e., pathologic crying in the absence of depression) (Nahas et al. 1998; Seliger et al. 1992), and the broader spectrum of action of SSRIs in general probably make them advantageous in many situations, despite the findings of Robinson et al. (2000).

Uncontrolled reports of antidepressant treatment are mixed, with two early reports showing little effect of amitriptyline and phenelzine in moderately injured TBI patients (Dinan and Mobayed 1992; Saran 1985), whereas a more recent trial in mild TBI patients showed good effect with sertraline (Fann et al. 2000). Although other patient groups with depression have not been formally studied, numerous case reports in epilepsy, brain tumors, and other dementias have documented patient response to various antidepressants.

Except for the possibility that anticholinergic activity could be a theoretical advantage in Parkinson's disease, the sedation, postural hypotension, modest hypertensive, and seizure threshold lowering effects of tricyclic antidepressants (TCAs) limit their usefulness in most neuropsychiatric patients. In one study of 68 brain-injured patients (Wroblewski et al. 1990), 20% of them developed seizures, largely due to TCAs they were taking. In HIV disease patients, imipramine was much less tolerable than paroxetine (Elliott et al. 1998), and in multiple sclerosis patients TCAs produced twice the side-effect rate of SSRIs (Scott et al. 1996). With the substantial experience with SSRIs during the last decade, there is good reason to believe their lower side-effect profile and once-daily dosing would make them preferable agents in neurologically compromised depressed patients. Among isolated reports noting CNS side effects with SSRIs, extrapyramidal side effects (EPS) are most common (Leo 1996), although large case series suggest these effects are not typical for more obviously vulnerable patients with either Parkinson's disease (Caley and Friedman 1992) or multiple sclerosis (Flax et al. 1991).

There would seem to be little reason to use nonselective monoamine oxidase inhibitors (MAOIs). Selegiline, a selective MAO-B inhibitor, would seem to be a good choice for Parkinson's disease patients because it has primary effects on the underlying illness. However, the lower doses used to treat Parkinson's disease symptoms have not usually been effective in studies of primary major depression, which usually requires higher doses that also inhibit MAO-A. Finally, bupropion was found to be effective in fewer than half of Parkinson's disease patients in one study (Goetz et al. 1984). Although its potential to lower seizure threshold is a particular liability in a neurologically ill population, the dose dependence of this side effect may make lower doses more acceptable. Few reports have examined the use of other antidepressants in neuropsychiatric patients.

Although strategies using dopaminergic agents have been particularly recommended for states of apathy often seen in Parkinson's disease patients, sometimes without accompanying depression (Marin et al. 1995), Parkinson's disease patients do not experience euphoria in response to methylphenidate, possibly reflecting degeneration of dopaminergic neurons with decreased dopamine availability (Cantello et al. 1989). However, more direct-acting agonists such as bromocriptine and amantadine have been found to be effective in these groups of patients (Jouvent et al. 1983) as well as in individual patients with TBI-associated apathy (Van Reekum et al. 1995). Stimulants such as methylphenidate have been extremely effective in Alzheimer's dementia and vascular dementia (Galynker et al. 1997) and in CVA patients (Grade et al. 1998); can work within 2 days (Masand et al. 1991); and promote improved participation in rehabilitation and enhanced functioning (Crisostomo et al. 1988). One retrospective case series documented efficacy in depressed CVA patients comparable to that of nortriptyline, with a more rapid onset of effect and a similar side-effect profile (Lazarus et al. 1994). A tendency for stimulants to reduce seizure frequency (Wroblewski et al. 1992) or to enhance neuronal recovery (Feeney et al. 1982) in brain injury patients may be other advantages. Methylphenidate has also been effective in improving impairments in psychomotor speech and arousal in three apathetic patients with brain tumors (Weitzner et al. 1995). A documented effect of pemoline compared with placebo on fatigue in 50% of multiple sclerosis patients is noteworthy (Weinshenker et al. 1992), although the drug was not very well tolerated because of anorexia, irritability, and insomnia. Patients with HIV-related apathetic depression have done particularly well with methylphenidate in case reports (White et al. 1992). However, other reports have claimed that dopaminergic agents, while improving affect and cognitive function, may be less effective on core symptoms of apathy such as lack of initiative (Salloway 1994), and they could provoke psychosis in Parkinson's disease and other vulnerable patients.

Finally, electroconvulsive therapy (ECT) is an effective treatment in Parkinson's disease patients that also transiently improves core motor symptoms (Kellner 1994). Five of six patients with Huntington's disease also improved with ECT, although one patient developed delirium and another developed a worsening of the movement disorder (Ranen et al. 1994). ECT has been used to treat depression in a patient with frontal craniotomy and residual meningioma (Starkstein and Migliorelli 1993). Reports of a high rate of ECT-induced delirium in Parkinson's disease patients, alone (Oh et al. 1992) and in comparison with CVA patients (Fiegel 1992), have been interpreted as being due to denervation supersensitivity of dopamine receptors, and reduction of dopaminergic drugs before ECT has been advised (Rudorfer et al. 1992). In general, patients with more severe depression often accompanied by psychosis may be the best candidates for ECT. States of catatonia are extreme examples of deficit states and are known to be most strongly related to affective illness rather than psychosis. Although ECT is certainly effective in these conditions as well, parenteral benzodiazepines are also highly effective (Gaind et al. 1994) and can result in reversal of the catatonic state, usually within hours to days.

In summary, SSRIs may be the treatment of choice in neuropsychiatrically ill patients with depression, especially if there is more anxiety or at least a relative absence of apathy. The question of whether tricyclics really are superior to SSRIs in CVA patients requires further study. SSRIs with relatively shorter half-lives (paroxetine, fluvoxamine) or absence of inhibition of select microsomal enzyme systems (citalopram, sertraline, paroxetine, fluvoxamine) may be advantageous in some cases. Because of the potentially activating properties of the SSRIs, they should be started at about half the usual starting dose and titrated up to standard antidepressant doses in the first 1–3 weeks. Brain-injured patients may also be at an increased risk for sedation with the SSRIs (Cassidy 1989). Venlafaxine at lower doses is less likely to cause hypertension but also acts more like a pure SSRI, with noradrenergic properties requiring higher ($\geq$225 mg) doses. Nefazodone, a serotonin type 2 (5-HT$_2$) receptor blocker with mild reuptake blocking effects, may also have a place in treating patients with anxiety (Balon 1998) or HIV depression (Elliott et al. 1999). Mirtazapine's effect in increasing appetite could be advantageous in HIV (Elliott and Roy-Byrne 2000) or Alzheimer's (Raji and Brady 2001) patients with wasting, although sedative side effects may limit its use in some patients. More apathetic states could be treated with dopaminergic strategies, including bupropion, bromocriptine, amantadine, and stimulants. TCAs, if used, should probably be limited to desipramine (lowest anticholinergic effects) and nortriptyline (lowest hypotensive effects, low anticholinergic effects, and good blood level data for interpretation). If an MAOI is to be used, tranylcypromine should probably be avoided because of occasional spontaneous hypertensive crises, even when an MAOI diet is followed (Keck et al. 1989). Table 35–1 lists characteristic antidepressants recommended in this section, dose ranges, side effects, and relevant drug interactions.

## Psychosis

Psychotic states (hallucinations, delusions, and formal thought disorder) principally occur in schizophrenia and less commonly in mania and depression. Psychosis occurs less frequently overall in neurologic patients than does depression, agitation, or cognitive impairment and often

**TABLE 35–1.** Antidepressants

| Drug | Starting daily dose (mg) | Target daily dose (mg) | Neuropsychiatric side effects | Neuropsychiatric drug interactions | Comments |
|---|---|---|---|---|---|
| **Tricyclic antidepressants (TCAs)** | | | | | |
| Nortriptyline | 10 | 30–100 | Dizziness, fatigue, drowsiness, tremor, nervousness, confusion (esp. w/nortriptyline), insomnia (esp. w/desipramine), headache, seizures, anticholinergic effects. Other: orthostatic hypotension, ECG alterations, cardiac conduction delay, tachycardia, sexual dysfunction, weight gain | ↑ Blood level w/SSRIs, methylphenidate, neuroleptics, valproate, opioids; ↓ Blood level w/CBZ, phenytoin, barbiturates; ↑ Blood level of neuroleptics, CBZ, opioids; ↓ Blood level of levodopa; Additive anticholinergic effects w/neuroleptics, antiparkinsonians, antihistamines | Low, but present, anticholinergic and hypotensive potential; Blood level monitoring available; Antiarrhythmic properties; Analgesic effects, including for neuropathic pain |
| Desipramine | 25 | 75–200 | | | |
| **Selective serotonin reuptake inhibitors (SSRIs)** | | | | | |
| Fluoxetine | 5 | 10–80 | Drowsiness (esp. w/paroxetine, fluvoxamine), nervousness (esp. w/fluoxetine), fatigue (esp. w/paroxetine), insomnia, tremor, dizziness, headache, confusion, paresthesia. Other: nausea, sexual dysfunction, weight loss | Sedation w/antihistamines, chloral hydrate; Lethargy, impaired consciousness w/metoprolol, propranolol; Excitation and hallucinations w/narcotics; EPS w/neuroleptics; Neurotoxicity w/lithium; Serotonergic effects w/lithium, buspirone, sumatriptan; Serotonin syndrome w/other serotonergic drugs (e.g., MAOIs, opioids); Contraindicated w/MAOIs; ↑ Blood level w/valproate; ↓ Blood level w/CBZ; ↑ Blood level of TCAs, neuroleptics, BZDs, CBZ, valproate, phenytoin, propranolol (esp. w/fluoxetine, paroxetine) | *Fluoxetine:* May have "therapeutic window"; May require up to 8 weeks to reach steady state; Most inhibition of hepatic cytochrome P450 2D6 enzymes of the SSRIs; also inhibits 2C and $3A_4$; Potential use in cataplexy; Antimyoclonic adjunct w/oxitriptan; *Sertraline:* ↑ Plasma level w/food; Most likely to cause diarrhea; Least inhibition of cytochrome P450 2D6 but does inhibit 2C and $3A_4$; *Paroxetine:* More sedating, less stimulating, and shorter half-life than sertraline and fluoxetine; withdrawal syndrome more likely; Inhibition of cytochrome P450 2D6 but not 2C and $3A_4$; can inhibit trazodone metabolism; withdrawal syndrome more likely |
| Sertraline | 25 | 50–200 | | | |
| Paroxetine | 10 | 20–60 | | | |
| Fluvoxamine | 25 | 50–300 | | | |
| Citalopram | 10 | 20–60 | | | |

**TABLE 35–1.** Antidepressants (*continued*)

| Drug | Starting daily dose (mg) | Target daily dose (mg) | Neuropsychiatric side effects | Neuropsychiatric drug interactions | Comments |
|---|---|---|---|---|---|
| | | | | | *Fluvoxamine:*<br>Twice-daily administration<br>Most sedating and shortest half-life of SSRIs; withdrawal syndrome most likely<br>Least bound to plasma proteins and no inhibition of hepatic cytochrome P450 2D6 enzymes; does inhibit 1A2, 2C, and 3A$_4$ enzymes<br>Least ejaculatory delay of SSRIs<br>*Citalopram:*<br>Minimal to no cytochrome inhibition<br>Most purely serotonergic in vitro |
| **Atypical antidepressants** | | | | | |
| Bupropion | 75–100 | 200–450 | Nervousness, tremor, dizziness, insomnia, headache, confusion, paresthesia, drowsiness, seizures | Contraindicated w/MAOIs<br>Caution w/levodopa<br>↑Blood level w/CBZ | ↑Risk of seizures, esp. w/doses >450 mg/day, >150 mg/dose<br>Contraindicated in seizure disorders, bulimia, anorexia nervosa<br>Fewer drug interactions than SSRIs |
| Trazodone | 50–100 | 150–400 | Drowsiness, dizziness, confusion, fatigue, nervousness, incoordination, headache, tremor, paresthesia<br>Other: hypotension, priapism | Additive CNS depressant effects w/other CNS depressants<br>Serotonin syndrome w/other serotonergic drugs<br>↑Blood level w/paroxetine, phenytoin<br>↑Blood level of phenytoin<br>Inhibits antihypertensive effects of clonidine | Risk of hypotension<br>Occasionally enhances sex drive<br>Two to three divided doses<br>May be useful in drug-induced dyskinesia<br>Priapism very rare but serious |
| Venlafaxine | 18.75–50.0 | 75–225 | Drowsiness, nervousness, dizziness, anorexia, insomnia, fatigue, tremor, headache, confusion, paresthesia<br>Other: sexual dysfunction, hypertension | Contraindicated w/MAOIs | Risk of hypertension, esp. w/doses >200 mg<br>No known cytochrome P450 effects |

**TABLE 35–1.** Antidepressants (continued)

| Drug | Starting daily dose (mg) | Target daily dose (mg) | Neuropsychiatric side effects | Neuropsychiatric drug interactions | Comments |
|---|---|---|---|---|---|
| Nefazodone | 50–100 | 200–500 | Dizziness, drowsiness, confusion, fatigue, headache, insomnia, paresthesia, tremor | Potential interaction w/MAOIs ↑Blood levels of triazolam, alprazolam Potential ↑ of nefazodone and other drugs that are highly protein bound | Risk of hypotension Two divided doses Potent inhibitor of P450 3A₄ |
| Mirtazapine | 15 | 30–45 | Sedation (less with higher doses); weight gain, agranulocytosis (very rare) | Contraindicated w/MAOIs | No in vitro cytochrome enzyme inhibition Minimal controlled data in conditions other than depression |
| **Psychostimulants** | | | | | |
| Methylphenidate | 5–30 | 10–90 | Nervousness, insomnia, dizziness, headache, dyskinesia, drowsiness, confusion, delusions, rebound depression, hallucinations, Tourette's, tics Other: anorexia, palpitations, blood pressure and pulse changes, cardiac arrhythmia, weight loss | Hypertension w/MAOIs ↑Blood levels of TCAs, phenytoin, phenobarbital, primidone Antagonistic effect by neuroleptics, phenobarbital | Contraindicated in marked anxiety, tension, agitation Fast onset of action Give early in day, divided doses (methylphenidate three times daily, dextroamphetamine twice daily) Dependence rare in medically ill May precipitate or worsen Tourette's or dyskinesia |
| Dextroamphetamine | 2.5–20 | 5–60 | | | |

*Note.* BZDs = benzodiazepines; CBZ = carbamazepine; CNS = central nervous system; ECG = electrocardiogram; MAOIs = monoamine oxidase inhibitors; OCD = obsessive-compulsive disorder; SSRIs = selective serotonin reuptake inhibitors; TCAs = tricyclic antidepressants.

may be associated with and a result of cognitive impairment, as in the paranoid delusions of Alzheimer's disease patients. When it occurs, psychosis can have a serious impact on patient care, causing noncompliance with needed medical interventions, behavior that may lead to self-harm or injury, and caregiver withdrawal from the patient. In these circumstances, rapid and definitive treatment of psychosis is always indicated whether it occurs in isolation or, more commonly, in combination with states of agitation, cognitive impairment, and occasionally aggression.

## Common Etiologies

Unlike depression and agitation, psychosis is relatively uncommon in stroke and multiple sclerosis and is less common in TBI and early and middle-phase Parkinson's disease. It is more commonly seen in association with complex partial epilepsy, Huntington's disease and late-state Parkinson's disease, HIV infection, limbic encephalitis (e.g., herpes simplex), multi-infarct (i.e., subcortical) and Alzheimer's dementias, and tumors involving the temporal lobe and diencephalon (Feinstein and Ron 1998). In these latter conditions, all of which involve characteristic temporal lobe subcortical-limbic anatomic regions, the rate of occurrence is also greater than in the general population (Bredkjaer et al. 1998). Psychosis in HIV infection is often associated with greater neurocognitive impairment (i.e., dementia) but is also associated with prior substance abuse, suggesting that extraneurologic factors may often be relevant (Sewell et al. 1994a). In contrast to HIV infection, in Alzheimer's dementia, psychosis is associated with more severe dementia and rapid disease progression. Psychosis in Parkinson's disease is often a complication of antiparkinsonian treatment and ranges from benign hallucinations in a clear sensorium to delusions with or without delirium. More advanced disease and cognitive impairment seem to increase the risk (Aarsland et al. 1999a). Psychosis is an uncommon initial presentation of all of these conditions but must be particularly considered as a disguised presentation of HIV infection, mass lesions, limbic encephalitis, and temporal lobe epilepsy. Metachromatic leukodystrophy often presents with psychosis as the first symptom. Psychosis in epilepsy can occur in three forms: a more common chronic interictal psychosis, a much rarer alternating psychosis that remits with seizure activity (forced normalization) (Sachdev 1998), and, more rarely, periictal or postictal psychotic behavior. A host of toxic-metabolic etiologies can cause psychosis, mostly in combination with a delirious picture. Antiparkinsonian drugs are a common cause of psychosis in Parkinson's disease

patients. Antidepressants, especially bupropion, buspirone (Trachman 1992), and corticosteroids, can also cause psychosis in vulnerable individuals. Digitalis, propranolol, anticonvulsants, $H_2$ blockers, and nonsteroidal anti-inflammatory drugs (NSAIDs), usually in high doses, also can rarely cause psychotic symptoms. Thus, careful assessment of the patient's metabolic status, medications, and history of exposure to various toxins and chemicals is crucial.

## Anatomy and Neurochemistry

Anatomic and neurochemical correlates of psychotic symptoms in schizophrenia and of the overall illness have been better delineated than those of almost any other behavioral syndrome. Studies have suggested that schizophrenia is a neurodevelopmental illness that begins with in utero defects in the medial temporal lobe and midline periventricular (i.e., brain stem) structures (Shapiro 1993). The former results in disturbed development, both cytoarchitecturally and neurochemically, of multiple components of a neural limbic loop (one of several parallel cortico-striato-thalamo-cortical circuits) including ventral striatum and cingulate, entorhinal, and temporal cortices, whereas the latter may give rise to subfrontal and striatal circuit disturbances thought to underlie the negative (cognitive and affective) schizophrenic symptoms. "Neural connectivity" is disturbed in both prefrontal and temporal areas (Benes 1999; Kegeles et al. 1998; Selemon and Goldman-Rakik 1999), and abnormalities are lateralized for both neuroanatomic (Levitan et al. 1999) and neurochemical (Laakso et al. 2000) findings. Metabolic changes in superior temporal gyrus (Suzuki et al. 1993), cingulum, and striatum (Cleghorn et al. 1992) have been associated specifically with hallucinations. Frontal lobe dysfunction also plays a role in nonschizophrenic psychotic symptoms (S. Simpson et al. 1999) and in schizophrenia may play a role in "releasing" subcortical dopamine activity (Bertolino et al. 1999).

All three major monoamine neurotransmitters play a role in the limbic loop (Joyce 1993). Dopamine type 2 ($D_2$) receptors in ventral striatum, temporal cortex, perirhinal cortex, and hippocampus, along with ventral striatal glutamate and $5-HT_2$ receptors in ventral striatum and temporal cortex, are well positioned to modulate activity in the loop.

Anatomic and neurochemical findings in psychosis in neurologic patients are surprisingly consistent with these abnormalities. Epileptic patients with psychosis more often have lesions that originated prenatally or perinatally and that affect medial temporal lobe neurons on the left

(Roberts et al. 1990; Sachdev 1998); have reductions in left medial temporal lobe blood flow on single photon emission computed tomography (SPECT) (Marshall et al. 1993); have higher magnetic resonance imaging (MRI) $T_1$ values in the left temporal lobe (Conlon et al. 1990); and have increased striatal dopamine metabolism (Reith et al. 1994). Patients with metachromatic leukodystrophy and psychosis have demyelinating lesions of subfrontal white matter disconnecting frontotemporal and frontal striatal circuits (Hyde et al. 1992). The rare occurrence of psychosis in multiple sclerosis is associated with MRI lesions in temporoparietal areas (Feinstein et al. 1992; Ron and Logsdail 1989). In contrast, psychosis in Alzheimer's disease patients is less specific, being associated with damage and defects in the parietal lobe (Kotrla et al. 1995; Mentis et al. 1995—delusions), occipital lobe (Hirono et al. 1998), basal ganglia (Caliguri and Peavy 2000), temporoparietal areas (Lopez et al. 1991), and frontal lobe (Kotrla et al. 1995—hallucinations) and with reduced levels of 5-HT in multiple areas (Zubenko et al. 1991). In Parkinson's disease, intraventricular infusions of dopamine produce psychosis (Kulkarni et al. 1992), as do dopaminergic medications used to treat the illness. Despite loss of nigrostriatal dopamine neurons in Parkinson's disease, supersensitive dopamine receptors in other areas (e.g., the limbic loop) are likely responsible for the psychotic effects. "Release" of subcortical dopamine in frontotemporal dementia may occur secondary to cortical damage (Nitrini and Rosenberg 1998), as it does in schizophrenia (Bertolino et al. 1999).

## Treatment

Neuroleptic (antipsychotic) medications remain the mainstay in pharmacologic treatment of psychosis. There is little evidence that other agents sometimes used as effective adjuncts to neuroleptics (e.g., anticonvulsants, benzodiazepines) have primary antipsychotic effects of their own. Although typical neuroleptics vary in side-effect profile and hence tolerability, there is also little evidence of any difference in efficacy between these drugs. In rare cases, a patient who does not respond to a trial of one class may respond to the other. The recent introduction of the atypical neuroleptics risperidone, olanzapine, and quetiapine offers for the first time both a chance of expanded efficacy and diminished side effects. These advantages are even more prominent in neuropsychiatric patients, who are more prone to neurologic side effects. For example, patients with HIV psychosis have a several-fold higher rate of side effects even at daily doses as low as 100–250 mg in chlorpromazine equivalents (Sewell et al. 1994b) and even when com-

pared with medically ill control subjects (Ramachandran et al. 1997).

Typical neuroleptics have been most often studied in the mixed psychosis and agitation of dementia patients. Although an early placebo-controlled study showing superiority of both haloperidol (mean dose, 4.6 mg) and loxapine (mean dose, 22 mg) (Petrie et al. 1982) reported that only one-third of patients showed significant improvement, a more recent study (Devanand et al. 1998) showed a response rate of 55%–60% with 2–3 mg haloperidol, superior to the 30% rate with 0.5 mg and consistent with the surprisingly high correlations obtained between blood levels of haloperidol and change on the psychosis factor of the Brief Psychiatric Rating Scale (BPRS) in the earlier study by the same researchers (Devanand et al. 1992). In contrast, correlations between blood level and hostility/agitation were much lower. Unfortunately, studies still suggest that patients with dementia are overtreated with neuroleptics, with 20 of 22 nursing-home patients able to successfully discontinue these drugs in a recent study (Bridges-Parlet et al. 1997).

Despite a long history of use of typical neuroleptics in epilepsy-related psychosis, the treatment of psychosis in epilepsy has not been subjected to controlled study, and even uncontrolled reports are scarce. The often-cited phenomenon of forced normalization (i.e., worsening psychosis with better seizure control) is actually quite rare. However, if psychosis can be documented to worsen with better seizure control, a slight increase in seizure frequency in someone with nondangerous complex partial seizures could improve psychosis. More likely, chronic interictal psychosis should be treated with neuroleptics, with careful attention to effects on seizure frequency. In one report (Onuma et al. 1991), 11 of 21 patients (52%) showed aggravation of symptoms with decrease or discontinuation of neuroleptics. This suggests that patients should be carefully monitored to determine if ongoing neuroleptics are truly required.

Much of the recent literature on atypical neuroleptics has focused on Parkinson's disease patients, who, because of their unique sensitivity to EPS, provide the most sensitive test for neuroleptic side effects. The only medication with confirmed antipsychotic benefit without worsening Parkinson's disease is clozapine, based on a recent double-blind, placebo-controlled trial (Parkinson Study Group 1999) with a mean dose of 25 mg. This is consistent with a recent review (Musser and Akil 1996) citing 16 reports in 167 patients documenting antipsychotic efficacy, often with several days' onset and usually at very low doses. Long-term treatment (1–2 years) continued to be effective in many patients. Improvements in tremor at 12.5 mg (Jansen 1994), increased "on" time with less dyskinesia at 75–200 mg (Bennett et al. 1994), greater motor effects in the "off" period at 25 mg (Arevalo and Gershanik 1993), improvement in nocturnal akathisia (Linazasoro et al. 1993), reduction in dyskinesia (Pierelli et al. 1998), and minimal to no neutropenia (1 of 60 patients in the recent controlled trial) are additional reported advantages. In many patients, doses of levodopa can be increased without motor or psychotic decompensation. Experts recommend starting with very low doses (e.g., 6.25 mg), because sedation is a major problem.

Clozapine significantly lowers the seizure threshold and produces electroencephalographic abnormalities in most non–neurologically ill patients at some time during treatment (Malow et al. 1994; Welch et al. 1994). In schizophrenic patients, seizures are dose dependent (Haller and Binder 1990), and both slow titration and lower ceiling doses (below 600 mg) may reduce the likelihood of seizures. In the neuropsychiatric population, doses far lower than these are likely to provoke seizures. Both seizures and myoclonus due to clozapine may respond to valproate (Meltzer and Ranjan 1994). Reports in neuropsychiatric groups suggest that preexisting electroencephalographic abnormalities predict liability to develop delirium (Duffy and Kant 1996).

Although risperidone, olanzapine, and quetiapine have all been shown to produce minimal extrapyramidal side effects in schizophrenic patients, the emerging data in Parkinson's disease patients suggest that, although they are a vast improvement over typical neuroleptics, clozapine is probably superior to them (Gimenez-Roldan et al. 2001), and they may still produce EPS to varying degrees. Hence, in Parkinson's disease, reports show that olanzapine and risperidone can either worsen (Ford et al. 1994; Graham et al. 1998) or have no effect (Aarsland et al. 1999b; Wolters et al. 1996; Workman et al. 1997) on underlying Parkinson's disease. The less widely used drug quetiapine has mostly been reported to work without worsening underlying disease (Dewey and O'Suillebhain 2000; Fernandez et al. 1999; Parsa and Bastani 1998; Targum and Abbott 2000), consistent with a recent study suggesting that it produces fewer EPS in a heterogeneous group of psychotic elderly patients compared with risperidone (Yeung et al. 1999). However, switching patients from olanzapine to quetiapine is only variably successful (Fernandez et al. 1999), and in one report quetiapine was only useful for visual hallucinations and had poor efficacy against delusions. Nonetheless, one recent review suggests that quetiapine probably produces less worsening of motor features of Parkinson's disease than

does olanzapine, which may cause fewer EPS compared with risperidone (J.H. Friedman and Factor 2000), although its limited use and distribution compared with the others may compromise this interpretation. This review also emphasized more fine-tuning of antiparkinsonian medications, with lowering doses of both anticholinergics and dopaminergics before initiation of neuroleptics. Although many patients may be unable to switch from clozapine to olanzapine (J.H. Friedman et al. 1998) or quetiapine (Fernandez et al. 1999), the side-effect burden of clozapine suggests that other agents may be preferable first-line medications in Parkinson's disease.

There is a growing number of recent reports on the efficacy of atypical neuroleptics in dementia-related psychoses. A 12-week double-blind, placebo-controlled study in 625 patients with severe dementia and significant psychosis tested three daily doses of risperidone and found 1 and 2 mg, but not 0.5 mg, to be effective. Only the 1-mg dose gave a frequency of EPS not different from placebo (Katz et al. 1999). In open studies in dementia using mean doses closer to 2 mg, the rate of EPS was 32% (Irizarry et al. 1999) and 50% (Herrmann et al. 1998), supporting a narrow dose window for this drug. A 6-week double-blind, placebo-controlled study of 206 nursing home patients with Alzheimer's disease showed antipsychotic effects with 5 mg and 10 mg, but not 20 mg, of olanzapine (Street et al. 2000). Reports in the more severe Lewy body dementia suggest marked side effects of confusion with clozapine (Burke et al. 1998) and intolerance in 3 of 8 patients with olanzapine (Walker et al. 1999), although other reports (Allen et al. 1995 with risperidone; Chacko et al. 1993 with clozapine) indicate efficacy with good tolerability.

Results are mixed in other patient groups. Singh et al. (1997) report substantial efficacy without EPS for risperidone in 20 of 21 psychotic HIV patients, and Lera and Zirulnik (1999) report good efficacy for clozapine in psychotic HIV patients who experienced EPS with typical neuroleptics, although other reports indicate both EPS with risperidone and akathisia with olanzapine (Meyer et al. 1998). Use of atypicals in movement disorders such as Huntington's disease indicate benefits on chorea as well as psychosis only when higher doses of 6 mg of risperidone are used (Dallocchio et al. 1999; Parsa et al. 1997); studies also show problems with Huntington's disease patients tolerating the high doses of clozapine needed to be effective, with marked disability in most of these patients with doses of 150 mg (van Vugt et al. 1997). Risperidone has been effective in 5 of 6 patients with TBI without EPS (Duffy and Kant 1996) and, in other reports, was superior to conventional neuroleptics in improving TBI psychosis, sleep and daytime alertness (Schreiber et al. 1998), and psychosis following ischemic brain damage (Zimnitzky et al. 1996). Finally, risperidone has been effective for psychosis associated with neurosarcoidosis (Popli 1997). Doses between 3 and 6 mg were used in these studies.

Few novel antipsychotic treatments are available. One report noted good antipsychotic efficacy without worsening of motor symptoms in 15 of 16 Parkinson's disease patients given the 5-HT$_3$ antagonist antiemetic ondansetron at doses of 12–24 mg/day (Zoldan et al. 1995). This drug has not been found to be effective in schizophrenia (Newcomer et al. 1992), suggesting some divergence of mechanism in Parkinson's disease psychosis and schizophrenia. In contrast, glutamatergic medications offer a potential avenue for antipsychotic effects in Parkinson's disease patients based on pathophysiologic theories of schizophrenia (see above), the psychotomimetic potential of N-methyl-D-aspartate (NMDA) antagonists (Knable and Rickler 1995), their possible beneficial effects in Parkinson's disease (Lange and Riederer 1994), and the utility in schizophrenia of D-cycloserine, an NMDA receptor–complex agonist at the glycine site (Goff et al. 1999).

In summary, neuroleptic medications appear to be the mainstay treatments for psychosis although they still have side effects in some patients. Clozapine is least likely to have motor side effects, although seizure threshold–lowering effects are more problematic in neurologically compromised patients. It may be preferred in unusually EPS-sensitive patients with Parkinson's disease, Huntington's disease, and other conditions with basal ganglia involvement. The use of very low doses may mitigate this effect. In most neurologic disorders, patients will show exaggerated sensitivity to motor side effects, making atypical neuroleptics the treatment of choice. Studies of discontinuation of neuroleptics have also shown that long-term treatment in Alzheimer's disease patients is often unnecessary (Risse et al. 1987). Table 35–2 lists characteristic antipsychotics recommended in this section, dose ranges, side effects, and relevant drug interactions.

## Agitated States, Including Anxiety and Mania

Syndromes of agitation span the entire spectrum of psychiatric illness, occurring in mood, anxiety, psychotic, dementing, and impulse dyscontrol disorders. In the absence of frank psychosis, dementia, or delirium, the differential diagnosis of prominent agitation is still extremely difficult, as states of agitated depression, mixed bipolar affective state/dysphoric mania, and severe panic anxiety merge with frequently ambiguous boundaries. This section highlights this symptom complex, principally as it presents in states of anxiety, mania, and severe agitated depression. We use this syndrome to discuss two major classes of drugs: the anxiolytics (e.g., benzodiazepines and azapirones) and the thymoleptics (e.g., lithium, valproic acid, and carbamazepine). Effects of antidepressants and neuroleptics on agitation are also highlighted.

## Common Etiologies

CVA is commonly associated with generalized anxiety at a rate comparable to depression; it is more rarely associated with mania. In contrast, there is a much greater incidence of mania in TBI than in the general population. Patients with multiple sclerosis are more likely to have mania than both general and psychiatric inpatient populations. Temporal lobe epilepsy is among the most common causes of secondary mania seen in the general medical setting. In CVA, patients with both anxiety and depression are more likely to have cortical lesions (and to have a poorer prognosis [Shimoda and Robinson 1998]), whereas patients with depression alone are more likely to have subcortical lesions (Starkstein et al. 1990), suggesting that an intact subcortex may be required for the expression of anxiety. The same exclusively cortical pattern has been found for pure mania versus mixed bipolar states (Starkstein et al. 1991). Similarly, the high incidence of agitation in Alzheimer's dementia (its most common behavioral disturbance [Devanand et al. 1997]), but not in multi-infarct dementias, highlights the importance of cortical damage and subcortical preservation. However, the high rate of anxiety disorders and symptoms in patients with Parkinson's disease, the occurrence of mania with brain-stem lesions (Drake et al. 1990), elevated rates of mania in the HIV-infected population eight times normal (Lyketsos 1994), and findings that poststroke bipolar disorder is strongly associated with right-hemisphere lesions that involve subcortical and midline structures (Berthier et al. 1996) suggest that subcortical involvement alone is capable of producing states of agitation, although more likely with manic appearance.

The majority of studies show that these conditions occur for the most part at rates greater than in the general population, are not necessarily associated with a greater rate of familial psychiatric illness, and have characteristic lesion location (discussion follows), suggesting that they are not merely a reaction to illness. Treatment of the underlying illness may sometimes affect these syndromes

**TABLE 35–2.** Antipsychotics

| Drug | Starting daily dose (mg) | Target daily dose (mg) | Neuropsychiatric side effects | Neuropsychiatric drug interactions | Comments |
|---|---|---|---|---|---|
| Haloperidol | 1–5 | 2–20 | Parkinsonism, dystonia, akathisia, perioral (rabbit) tremor, anticholinergic effects, sedation, confusion, impaired psychomotor performance, TD, NMS, orthostatic hypotension, ejaculatory inhibition, priapism, dysphagia, urinary incontinence, temperature dysregulation, sudden death | Additive CNS depressant effects w/ other CNS depressants | Haloperidol: Most EPS potential, esp. w/low calcium, akathisia w/low iron Intravenous route provides rapid onset of action w/potentially lower risk of EPS Available in decanoate form Useful in Huntington's, Tourette's |
| Perphenazine | 4–16 | 8–40 | | Additive anticholinergic effects w/ other anticholinergic drugs ↑ EPS w/SSRIs, lithium, buspirone Neurotoxicity w/lithium | |
| Thioridazine | 10–200 | 100–800 | Other: slowed cardiac conduction (esp. w/thioridazine), photosensitivity, hyperthermia, hyperprolactinemia, weight gain | ↑Blood level w/TCAs, SSRIs, MAOIs, alprazolam, buspirone, β-adrenergic blockers ↓ Blood level w/lithium, CBZ, phenytoin, phenobarbital, antiparkinsonians ↓ Blood level of TCAs, valproate, phenytoin, β-adrenergic blockers | Thioridazine: Most anticholinergic, sedating, and risk for hypotension at doses >800 mg Has been used for symptomatic management of agitation, anxiety, depressed mood, sleep disturbances, and fears in geriatric patients |
| Risperidone | 1–2 | 2–10 | Insomnia, agitation, EPS, headache, anxiety, dizziness, somnolence, aggressive reaction, NMS, risk of TD not yet determined | May antagonize effects of levodopa and dopamine agonists ↑Blood level w/clozapine, inhibitors of cytochrome P450 2D6 ↓ Blood level w/CBZ | Maximum efficacy for most patients at 4–6 mg/day Less EPS potential than haloperidol at doses <8 mg/day Two divided doses |
| Clozapine | 15–50 | 200–600 | Drowsiness, dizziness, headache, tremor, syncope, insomnia, restlessness, hypokinesia/akinesia, agitation, seizures, rigidity, akathisia, confusion, fatigue, hyperkinesia, weakness, lethargy, ataxia, slurred speech, depression, abnormal movements, anxiety, EPS, NMS, obsessive-compulsive symptoms Other: salivation, agranulocytosis | Additive CNS depressant effects w/ other CNS depressants Occasional collapse (hypotension, respiratory depression, loss of consciousness) w/BZDs ↑ Risk of bone marrow suppression w/ CBZ, possibly lithium ↑ Risk of NMS w/other antipsychotics, lithium, CBZ ↓ Blood level w/CBZ, phenytoin | Monitor WBC weekly More effective for negative schizophrenic symptoms, lower risk of EPS, TD, NMS, and higher risk of lowering seizure threshold (dose related) than standard neuroleptics May improve motor function in Tourette's, Huntington's, drug-induced persistent dyskinesia, spasmodic torticollis, Parkinson's, essential tremor |

**TABLE 35–2.** Antipsychotics (*continued*)

| Drug | Starting daily dose (mg) | Target daily dose (mg) | Neuropsychiatric side effects | Neuropsychiatric drug interactions | Comments |
|---|---|---|---|---|---|
| Olanzapine | 5 | 10–20 | Somnolence, dry mouth, weight gain with increased lipid abnormalities and possible diabetes risk, nausea, dizziness, constipation, headache, transient elevation transaminase | ↓ Blood level w/smoking and CBZ ↑ Blood level w/fluoxetine | Once-daily dosing Antimanic effect |
| Quetiapine | 25 | 300–450 | Sedation, moderate weight gain, EPS, dizziness, agitation, postural hypotension, dry mouth, elevated transaminase | — | ? Lower EPS risk, no prolactin elevation, twice-daily dosing, less experience than w/other atypicals |

*Note.*   BZDs = benzodiazepines; CBZ = carbamazepine; CNS = central nervous system; EPS = extrapyramidal side effects; MAOIs = monoamine oxidase inhibitors; NMS = neuroleptic malignant syndrome; SSRIs = selective serotonin reuptake inhibitors; TCAs = tricyclic antidepressants; TD = tardive dyskinesia; WBC = white blood count.

(e.g., reduced mania in zidovudine [AZT]-treated HIV illness [Mijch et al. 1999]). However, the important role of agitation in the intrusive, repetitive, reexperiencing aspect of PTSD suggests that PTSD needs to be considered as an important component of a possible pathologic reaction to illness requiring psychotherapeutic intervention. Medications of an entirely different spectrum— including corticosteroids, psychostimulants, anti-obesity agents, cocaine, caffeine, other dopaminergic agents (levodopa, bromocriptine), felbamate, dextromethorphan, interferon alfa, and angiotensin-converting enzyme inhibitors—are more commonly associated with agitation, anxiety, and mania. Withdrawal states from alcohol, sedative-hypnotics, and opiate drugs also produce significant agitation. Finally, withdrawal from SSRIs may produce agitation, along with dizziness, malaise, headache, and nausea.

## Anatomy and Neurochemistry

As with depression, a variety of neuroanatomic and neurochemical substrates have been associated with agitated states. However, there is a surprising convergence of neuroanatomic data associated with both anxious and manic states, implicating the right anterior inferior temporal lobe and its connections to orbital frontal and related limbic (amygdala, hippocampus, and parahippocampus) circuits. This is supported by data on lesion location in post-CVA mania (Robinson and Starkstein 1989) and anxiety (Castillo et al. 1993) and TBI mania (Jorge et al. 1993). It is also consistent with SPECT findings in primary mania (lower perfusion in right temporal basal cortex [Migliorelli et al. 1993]), medial temporal lobe hypoplasia in bipolar patients (Olson et al. 1990), PET findings in induced anxiety in healthy control subjects (decreases in right posterotemporal and right medial frontal cortex [Kimbrell et al. 1999]), improvement in mania with right frontal repetitive transcranial magnetic stimulation (rTMS) (Grisaru et al. 1998), and right temporal lobe MRI (Ontiveros et al. 1989) and electroencephalographic (Weilburg et al. 1995) abnormalities in panic disorder patients. In fact, this convergence of findings may compromise the differential diagnostic utility of MRI for patients with mood lability suspected of having multiple sclerosis (McDonald et al. 1999; Young et al. 1997). Nonetheless, agitated states occur less reliably after right posterior cortical lesions than do depressed states after left anterior cortical lesions, so that additional factors (e.g., vulnerability based on personal or family psychiatric history) are likely to be important determinants of their occurrence.

The only data examining neurochemical perturbations as they might relate to agitated states in neuropsychiatry relate to Alzheimer's dementia. Although one study failed to show a relation between agitation and postmortem indices of dopaminergic function (Bierer et al. 1993), greater disturbance of dopaminergic metabolism with cognitive decline (Itoh et al. 1994), loss of dopamine transporter sites in the nucleus accumbens (Murray et al. 1995), and the efficacy of low-dose neuroleptics all suggest that disturbed dopaminergic function may be involved. Increased central noradrenergic function may also be implicated, because damaged neurons in certain brain areas seem to result in compensatory increased norepinephrine release from remaining noradrenergic neurons and actual increases in brain noradrenergic functional activity (Elrod et al. 1997; Raskind et al. 1999). This enhanced activity is likely augmented by an increase in cortical β-adrenergic receptors (Kalaria et al. 1989). Heterocyclic antidepressants, by stabilizing and increasing the efficiency of this system, could potentially be of benefit, as could β-blockers (Weiler et al. 1988). Although there is consistent evidence of serotonergic deficiencies in Alzheimer's disease patients (Raskind and Peskind 1994), these deficiencies have been inconsistently related to agitation (Mintzer et al. 1998).

Finally, the sensitivity of medial temporal lobe and related limbic structures to electrophysiologic dysregulation following damage (along with the previously mentioned association between lesions in this area and secondary states of anxiety) is consistent with the utility of both anticonvulsants and benzodiazepines in the treatment of agitation. Both types of agents have been found useful in control of acute mania as well as drug withdrawal–related anxiety and even panic attacks. Medial temporal and limbic areas are rich in both benzodiazepine and 5-HT$_{1A}$ receptors, the latter presumably important in the mechanism of action of the novel anxiolytic buspirone.

## Treatment

Despite the high prevalence of agitated states in various neuropsychiatric conditions, there are far fewer double-blind, placebo-controlled studies than for depressed states. Much of our information continues to come from case series that often combine elements of anxiety, aggression, confusion, and dysphoria. Although virtually every psychotropic agent has been, and will continue to be, used for agitation, there is emerging evidence that the anticonvulsants may have particular utility in managing secondary mania, withdrawal-related anxiety states, panic anxiety associated with electroencephalographic abnormalities, and the agitation seen in some dementias.

However, there is still only scattered scientific validation of the following treatment suggestions.

In the management of manic states, anticonvulsants have been recommended for some time in cases in which "neurologic" factors, including substance abuse, have been present (Pope et al. 1988). Scattered reports have suggested efficacy for carbamazepine in elderly neurologic manic patients intolerant to lithium (McFarland et al. 1990); in mentally retarded manic patients (Glue 1989); in patients with HIV-related mania resistant to lithium (Halman et al. 1993); in TBI patients with agitation (Azouvi et al. 1999); and in patients with Alzheimer's-related agitation resistant to neuroleptics (Gleason and Schneider 1990; Lemke 1995). Valproate has reportedly been effective in mentally retarded manic patients (Sovner 1989); in agitated patients with dementia (8 of 10, Lott et al. 1995; 7 of 15, Narayan and Nelson 1997; 6 of 13, Porsteinsson et al. 1997; but see also only 1 of 15, Herrmann 1998); and in agitated patients with brain injury (Horne and Lindley 1995). Blood levels have varied widely (14–107 µg/mL), although all reports showed some responders at levels below 50 µg/mL. These uncontrolled reports have now been validated for both drugs in placebo-controlled trials. For carbamazepine, a placebo-controlled trial in 51 patients showed such superior efficacy (71% vs. 21% response; mean level, 5.3 µg/mL) that the trial was prematurely terminated (Tariot et al. 1998b). More recently, Porsteinsson et al. (2001) documented efficacy for valproate, with a much higher rate of "marked improvement" (about 40%) compared with the only carbamazepine study (about 5%) (Tariot et al. 1998a). It is of interest that one survey noted that valproate is preferred by clinicians to carbamazepine (Alexopoulos et al. 2000), perhaps because of its greater use in bipolar illness, despite the unavailability of a controlled study at that time. Both carbamazepine and valproate have been effective in alcohol withdrawal (Myrick et al. 2000; Stuppaeck et al. 1992), and valproate has some efficacy in panic (Roy-Byrne and Cowley 1998). Because of carbamazepine's potential for bone marrow suppression and valproate's potential for hepatotoxicity, complete blood cell count and liver function tests should be monitored, and the patient and caregiver should be advised to watch for signs of acute infection that may signal a drop in white blood cell count. Carbamazepine and valproate blood levels do not necessarily correlate with clinical response but should be used to monitor compliance and drug metabolism. Preliminary evidence of efficacy of gabapentin for agitation is mixed (3 of 4, Roane et al. 2000; but only 2 of 12, Herrmann et al. 2000). Because gabapentin also has anxiolytic properties, nonhepatic clearance, and better tolerance, it could be a safer, easier-to-use alternative in the future.

Lithium is considerably less useful in secondary mania in neuropsychiatric patients. In addition to the previously cited reports in which carbamazepine was preferable, two reports have shown that lithium at low levels lost its previous efficacy and produced severe side effects after head trauma (Hornstein and Seliger 1989) and CVA (Moskowitz and Altshuler 1991). Lithium has also been shown to be inadequate without clozapine augmentation in Parkinson's disease (E. Kim et al. 1994) and to be less effective in mental retardation (Glue 1989). The elderly are well known to be more sensitive to lithium neurotoxicity, which can occur at low-normal lithium levels (Bell et al. 1993) and can persist for some period of time after lithium discontinuation (Saxena and Mallikarjuna 1988). Except for a possibly unique effect on steroid-induced mania and agitation (Falk et al. 1979), and utility in treating the "on-off" phenomenon of Parkinson's disease (Coffey et al. 1982), lithium would appear not to be a first-line choice for many neuropsychiatric patients. Its proconvulsant effect (Moore 1981; Parmelee and O'Shannick 1988; Sacristan et al. 1991) and ability to cause or aggravate EPS (Lecamwasam et al. 1994) are other shortcomings. In dementia, most reports show that it has minimal effect (Holton and George 1985; Kunik et al. 1994), although it may be useful in certain HIV-related manic syndromes (Halman et al. 1993). Lithium has no known effects in primary anxiety disorders.

Benzodiazepines are potent inhibitors of both primary mania and anxiety. However, in agitated states secondary to neurologic illness, these agents have many drawbacks. Although their overall effect in reducing arousal and akathisia are well known, they can cause confusion, cognitive impairment, psychomotor slowing, and disinhibition presenting as a paradoxical reaction. They are rarely considered for agitated patients with Alzheimer's dementia and are not even mentioned in some reviews (Raskind 1993). Earlier controlled studies in Alzheimer's disease patients showed that superiority over placebo for oxazepam is lost at 8 weeks due to tolerance (J.F. Sanders 1965) and that diazepam is worse than thiothixene (Kirven and Montero 1973). There are few reports attesting to their positive effects in neuropsychiatric patients. One study suggested that oxazepam was inferior to haloperidol and diphenhydramine in elderly institutionalized patients (Coccaro et al. 1990). Another single-case design report (Herz et al. 1992) also suggested that oxazepam was inferior to thiothixene. A double-blind study in hospitalized acquired immune deficiency syndrome (AIDS) patients with delirium showed that lorazepam was markedly inferior to both haloperidol and chlorpromazine and was associated with such severe, treatment-limiting adverse effects that this arm of the study was prematurely terminated (Breitbart et al. 1996). A drug discontinuation study showed that dementia patients tapered from long-term use of benzodiazepines had improved memory without worsening of anxiety (Salzman et al. 1992). All this is consistent with the fact that less than 10% of benzodiazepine use in the elderly is for dementia (Kirby et al. 1999). Nonetheless, judicious use of these agents, often in combination with other medications such as neuroleptics (which may allow lower doses to be used) and antidepressants (which can reverse activating side effects), can be extremely beneficial. Extremely low doses and careful titration are necessary. Agents with short half-lives and without active metabolites (e.g., lorazepam, oxazepam) are the benzodiazepines of choice. Clonazepam, because of its potent anticonvulsant effect, and alprazolam, because it has some mild antidepressant properties, may be useful in certain cases.

The nonbenzodiazepine anxiolytic buspirone has shown some efficacy in agitated states associated with dementia (Colenda 1988; Sakauye et al. 1993) and TBI (Levine 1988), especially when no severe motor or cognitive deficits were present (Gualtieri 1991). In Huntington's disease, one study reported improvement in both agitation and choreoathetoid movements with 120 mg/day (Hamner et al. 1996). In developmentally delayed patients, 16 of 22 had a good response to 15–45 mg/day (Buitelaar et al. 1998). Although a recent study (Cantillon et al. 1996) showed that low-dose buspirone was superior to haloperidol in agitated dementia, the effects were extremely modest. Unfortunately, placebo-controlled trials in agitated patients are still unavailable. Antiaggression effects are discussed in the next section.

Neuroleptics are frequently used as a nonspecific treatment to calm agitated patients, even when they are not obviously psychotic, with reasonably good effect (Salzman 1987). The use of the parenteral route, including intravenous injection, is not uncommon (Tesar et al. 1985), especially with medically ill patients in cardiac and intensive care units (K.M. Sanders et al. 1991). The neuroleptic pimozide, because of unique effects on reducing intracellular calcium influx, has been found especially helpful in agitated delirium associated with hypercalcemia (Mark et al. 1993). A recent study documented significant improvement in symptoms in hospitalized AIDS patients using either haloperidol or chlorpromazine (Breitbart et al. 1996). However, major EPS, sedation, and hypotension limit the use of neuroleptics, and there are questions about how specific their effect is beyond a generally powerful sedating and motor-inhibiting one. In patients with dementia, several placebo-controlled studies have shown these drugs to be only marginally more effective in the absence of more classic psychotic symptoms (Raskind 1993). Because neurologic patients appear to be at increased risk for developing tardive dyskinesia and akathisia (Rifkin et al. 1975) and because animal studies have implicated typical neuroleptics in being deleterious to cortical recovery (Feeney et al. 1982), the potential utility of atypical neuroleptics for agitation or delirium is of special interest. Unfortunately, only risperidone has been studied, and it was effective at low dose in the controlled study by Katz et al. (1999). However, Herrmann et al. (1998) report a 58% rate of EPS with similar low doses. Effects on agitation also take longer than effects on psychosis (7 vs. 3 weeks, Lavretsky and Sulzer 1998). Other reports have noted efficacy for both risperidone (Sipahimalani and Masand 1997a, 1997b) and olanzapine (K.S. Kim et al. 2001; Passik and Cooper 1999; Sipahimalani and Masand 1998) in agitated delirium at low doses. Evidence that neuroleptics interfere with compensatory serotonergic changes in Alzheimer's disease patients provides one possible reason for this (C.P. Chen et al. 1996). Periodic trials of neuroleptic discontinuation in agitated patients with dementia may show these drugs to be unnecessary (Bridges-Parlet et al. 1997).

Antidepressants have also been shown, not surprisingly, to have some efficacy. The SSRI citalopram was effective for anxiety, fear, and panic in 65 Alzheimer's dementia patients but not in 24 patients with vascular dementia (Nyth and Gottfries 1990); fluoxetine reduced anxiety, fear-panic, and irritability (but not depressed mood) in 10 Alzheimer's disease patients (Lebert et al. 1994), although in a small ($N = 15$) study it was no more effective than placebo (Auchus and Bissey-Black 1997). Although SSRIs are known to cause agitation as a side effect in primary depression, they work equally well in patients with agitated and retarded primary depression (Tollefson et al. 1994). Other reports have noted the utility of TCAs in brain injury–related agitation (Mysiw et al. 1988), in states of pathologic emotional lability in stroke (Robinson et al. 1993), and in multiple sclerosis (Schiffer et al. 1985). Fluoxetine has also reportedly been effective for emotional lability in stroke, multiple sclerosis, brain injury, amyotrophic lateral sclerosis, and encephalitis (Iannaccone and Ferini-Strambi 1996; Sloan et al. 1992; W.C. Tsai et al. 1998) and, remarkably, works in 2–6 days. Sertraline is also effective (Burns et al. 1999; Peterson et al. 1995). One crossover study (Lawlor et al. 1994) showed trazodone (150 mg) to be superior to both buspirone (30 mg) and placebo in agitated Alzheimer's disease patients, and a parallel group study showed efficacy equal to that of haloperidol in patients who were not psychotic (Sultzer et al. 1997).

Finally, there is preliminary evidence that calcium channel blockers, such as verapamil, have utility in both primary mania (Dubovsky et al. 1986) and panic disorder (Klein and Uhde 1988). Although no reports exist regarding the use of calcium channel blockers in neuropsychiatric patients with agitation, reports that HIV-related mania may be associated with direct increases in intracellular calcium triggered by the HIV coat protein gp 120 (Dreyer et al. 1990) provide a rationale for their use in these patients. Evidence is also emerging that cholinergic medications, discussed in detail in the final section of this chapter, also have antiagitation effects (Lanctot and Herrmann 2000; Mega et al. 1999; Rösler et al. 1998).

In summary, anticonvulsants are emerging as an extremely useful strategy for agitated neuropsychiatric patients with mania, dementia, or anxiety. When significant dysphoria is present, suggesting an element of depression, antidepressants may be indicated as an adjunct. Low-dose neuroleptics, long a mainstay in the treatment of agitation with dementia, may exacerbate dysphoria and depression in some patients, lower seizure threshold, impair cortical recovery, and have major motor side effects; they should be avoided if psychosis is absent. Newer antipsychotic agents such as risperidone and olanzapine, although imperfect, are likely an improvement, and they usually reduce agitation along with psychosis (see previous section). Of the primary anxiolytics, the azapirones are more effective and have fewer side effects than benzodiazepines. These latter agents should probably be reserved as an adjunct to be used with other agents. Tables 35–3 and 35–4 list characteristic anxiolytics and mood stabilizers recommended in this section, with dose ranges, side effects, and relevant drug interactions.

## Aggression, Impulsivity, and Behavioral Dyscontrol

Behavioral dyscontrol is often associated with psychotic (Chemerinski et al. 1998), agitated, or manic states; depression (Lyketsos et al. 1999); and cognitive impairment (Paradiso et al. 1996). It also may be part of acute delirium or chronic severe brain dysfunction. Less often, dyscontrol (e.g., aggression, hypersexuality) may emerge from more specific neurologic lesions (Mendez et al. 2000). The severity of symptoms can range from mild irritability to marked physical violence. Aggressive behav-

ior may occur in 10%–40% of brain-injured individuals. As more severely compromised neurologic patients survive due to improved medical care, the neuropsychiatrist will increasingly confront this problem. Although behavioral management remains a core treatment of impulsivity and aggression (Wong et al. 1988), psychopharmacologic interventions have become increasingly important.

Behavioral dyscontrol is extremely varied in nature and includes aggressive acts, paraphilias, compulsions, rituals, self-mutilation, and socially inappropriate behaviors. It may often occur in association with other maladaptive behaviors (Collacott et al. 1998). Such admixtures of symptoms require thorough exploration of potential neurologic and psychiatric etiologies and clarification of the temporal relationships among symptoms, both longitudinally and acutely. It is important to document the behavioral dysfunction and its potential response to treatment with observer ratings, because self-rating scales can be unreliable. The Overt Aggression Scale (Yudofsky et al. 1986) is one reliable and valid method. The Aberrant Behavior Checklist, measuring irritability, social withdrawal, stereotyping, hyperactivity, and excessive speech in mentally retarded populations, is another (Aman et al. 1985).

## Common Etiologies

Aggression and impulsivity have been described as sequelae of a diverse variety of brain disorders. They have most frequently been observed in disorders marked by more diffuse and global neurologic dysfunction such as TBI, mental retardation, delirium, and dementia. However, more focal disease of the orbitofrontal and basal ganglia regions (Huntington's disease and Parkinson's disease) and temporal lobes (epilepsy and Klüver-Bucy syndrome) are also associated with aggression, impulsivity, and, more rarely, hypersexuality. The much greater frequency of dyscontrol in frontotemporal versus Alzheimer's dementia is proof of this point (Miller et al. 1997).

The psychodynamic significance of a chronically debilitating neurologic illness can play a role in further exacerbating any premorbid maladaptive characterological traits and coping strategies. Furthermore, an inability to carry out adaptive planning, problem solving, and other executive functions, caused by CNS damage, can lead to frustration, anxiety, and nonproductive, impulsive acts when a patient is confronted with external stressors. Hence, it is useful to try to understand dyscontrol as a failed attempt to deal with a stressful environment or event (S. Halliday and Mackrell 1998).

Many neurologic medications can potentially cause behavioral problems by agitating or activating a patient.

**TABLE 35–3.** Mood stabilizers

| Drug | Starting daily dose (mg) | Target daily dose (mg) | Neuropsychiatric side effects | Neuropsychiatric drug interactions | Comments |
|------|--------------------------|------------------------|-------------------------------|------------------------------------|----------|
| Lithium | 300–900 | 600–2,400 | Lethargy, fatigue, muscle weakness, tremor, headache, confusion, dulled senses, ataxia, dysarthria, aphasia, muscle hyperirritability, hyperactive deep tendon reflexes, hypertonia, choreoathetoid movements, cogwheel rigidity, dizziness, drowsiness, disturbed accommodation, dystonia, seizures, EPS<br><br>Other: nausea, diarrhea, polyuria, nephrogenic diabetes insipidus, hypothyroidism, hyperparathyroidism, T-wave depression, acne, leukocytosis | EPS and NMS w/neuroleptics<br>Neurotoxicity w/SSRIs, neuroleptics, CBZ, valproate, phenytoin, calcium channel blockers<br>↑ Blood level w/SSRIs<br>↑ or ↓ Blood level of neuroleptics | Lowers seizure threshold<br>Predominantly renally excreted<br>Once-daily dosing more tolerable w/less renal toxicity<br>Blood levels correlate w/therapeutic response<br>Used in Huntington's, cluster headaches, torticollis, Tourette's, SIADH, leukopenia |
| Carbamazepine | 200–600 | 400–2,000 | Dizziness, drowsiness, incoordination, confusion, headache, fatigue, blurred vision, hallucinations, diplopia, oculomotor disturbance, nystagmus, speech disturbance, abnormal involuntary movement, peripheral neuritis, paresthesia, depression, agitation, talkativeness, tinnitus, hyperacusis<br><br>Other: nausea, bone marrow suppression, hepatotoxicity, SIADH | Additive CNS depressant effects w/other CNS depressants<br>Contraindicated w/MAOIs<br>Neurotoxicity w/lithium, neuroleptics<br>Bone marrow suppression w/clozapine<br>↑ Blood level w/SSRIs, verapamil<br>↓ Blood level w/TCAs, haloperidol, valproate, phenytoin, phenobarbital<br>↓ Blood level of TCAs, BZDs, neuroleptics, valproate, phenytoin, phenobarbital, methadone, propranolol | Induces own hepatic metabolism (2–5 weeks)<br>Monitor CBC, LFTs, electrolytes<br>Blood level of approx. 4–12 μg/mL<br>Useful in trigeminal neuralgia, neuropathic pain, sedative/hypnotic withdrawal |
| Valproate | 250–750 | 500–3,000 | Sedation, tremor, paresthesia, headache, lethargy, dizziness, diplopia, confusion, incoordination, ataxia, dysarthria, psychosis, nystagmus, asterixis, "spots before eyes"<br><br>Other: nausea, hair loss, thrombocytopenia, impaired platelet aggregation, elevated liver transaminases, hepatotoxicity, pancreatitis | Additive CNS depressant effects w/other CNS depressants<br>↑ Blood level w/chlorpromazine<br>↓ Blood level w/SSRIs, CBZ, phenytoin, phenobarbital<br>↑ Blood level of TCAs, chlorpromazine, CBZ, phenytoin, phenobarbital, primidone, benzodiazepines | Monitor CBC w/platelets, LFTs<br>Blood level of approx. 50–150 μg/mL<br>Useful in neuropathic pain |
| Neurontin | 100–300 | 600–1,800 | Somnolence, fatigue, ataxia, dizziness, GI upset | Exclusively renal clearance, not bound to plasma protein, pharmacodynamic interactions possible but unknown | 6-Hour half-life, dose dependent<br>↓ Bioavailability, need three-times-daily schedule w/larger doses, otherwise twice daily may suffice |

*Note.*  BZDs = benzodiazepines; CBC = complete blood count; CBZ = carbamazepine; CNS = central nervous system; EPS = extrapyramidal side effects; GI = gastrointestinal; LFTs = liver function tests; MAOIs = monoamine oxidase inhibitors; NMS = neuroleptic malignant syndrome; SIADH = syndrome of inappropriate antidiuretic hormone; SSRIs = selective serotonin reuptake inhibitors; TCAs = tricyclic antidepressants.

**TABLE 35–4.** Anxiolytics and sedative/hypnotics

| Drug | Starting daily dose (mg) | Target daily dose (mg) | Neuropsychiatric side effects | Neuropsychiatric drug interactions | Comments |
|---|---|---|---|---|---|
| **Benzodiazepines** | | | Drowsiness, incoordination, confusion, dysarthria, fatigue, agitation, dizziness, akathisia, anterograde amnesia (esp. alprazolam, lorazepam) Other: sexual dysfunction | Augments respiratory depression w/opioids; Neurotoxicity and sexual dysfunction w/lithium; Additive CNS depressant effects w/other CNS depressants; ↑ Blood level w/SSRIs, phenytoin; ↓ Blood level w/CBZ; ↓ Blood level of levodopa, phenytoin | May develop tolerance to psychotropic and anticonvulsant effects; Do not induce own metabolism; Addictive potential; May cause withdrawal syndrome; Alprazolam has antidepressant properties; May cause EEG changes; May worsen delirium and dementia; Useful in treating akathisia; Clonazepam: May accumulate in bloodstream; May have utility in pain syndromes, movement disorders |
| Alprazolam | 0.25–0.50 | 0.75–6.00 | | | |
| Lorazepam | 0.5–1.0 | 1.5–12.0 | | | |
| Clonazepam | 0.25–0.5 | 1–5 | | | |
| Buspirone | 10–15 | 15–60 | Nervousness, headache, confusion, weakness, numbness, drowsiness, paresthesia, incoordination, tremor | EPS w/neuroleptics; Hypertension w/MAOIs; ↑ ALT w/trazodone; ↑ Blood level of BZDs, haloperidol | Has antidepressant effects but may produce dysphoria at higher doses; Slow onset of action; Nonaddictive; Usually does not impair psychomotor performance |
| Diphenhydramine | 25–50 | 25–200 | Drowsiness, dizziness, anticholinergic effects, incoordination, fatigue, confusion, nervousness, tremor, insomnia, euphoria, paresthesia | Additive CNS depressant effects w/other CNS depressants; ↑ Anticholinergic effects w/MAOIs, TCAs | Minimal effects on EEG; Anticholinergic effects may decrease EPS but may exacerbate delirium; May help with insomnia; tolerance may develop; Unpredictable antianxiety properties |
| Zolpidem | 5–10 | 5–10 | Drowsiness, dizziness, lethargy, depression, abnormal dreams, anterograde amnesia, sleep disorder | Additive CNS depressant effects w/other CNS depressants | Used for short-term treatment of insomnia; No significant anxiolytic or anticonvulsant effects; Abuse and withdrawal reported |

*Note.* ALT = alanine aminotransferase; BZDs = benzodiazepines; CBZ = carbamazepine; CNS = central nervous system; EEG = electroencephalogram; EPS = extrapyramidal side effects; MAOIs = monoamine oxidase inhibitors; SSRIs = selective serotonin reuptake inhibitors; TCAs = tricyclic antidepressants.

Such medications include levodopa, corticosteroids, amantadine, bromocriptine, interferon, selegiline, and AZT. Sedative-hypnotics (such as barbiturates and benzodiazepines), analgesics (opiates and other narcotics), anabolic steroids, antidepressants, psychostimulants, antipsychotics, and anticholinergic drugs have also been associated with aggression. Stimulants, dopaminergic agents, and testosterone-containing agents may increase sexual drive. Alcohol and drugs of abuse, such as cocaine, amphetamines, barbiturates, and phencyclidine, can cause or exacerbate behavioral dyscontrol (Swanson et al. 1990) and adversely interact with medications.

## Anatomy and Neurochemistry

Damage to the frontal and basotemporal lobes has been shown to be associated with impulsivity, aggression, and violence, although data in neuropsychiatric patients are limited (Fornazzari et al. 1992; Starkstein et al. 1994; Tonkonogy 1991). A lateral orbitofrontal circuit involving orbitofrontal cortex, striatum, subthalamic nucleus, substantia nigra, and thalamus is thought to regulate empathic and socially appropriate behavior (Mega and Cummings 1994). Damage may lead to irritability, tactlessness, impulsivity, environmental dependency, and mood lability. On the other hand, obsessive-compulsive spectrum disorders, which involve increased behavioral control and concern for social behavioral appropriateness, have been shown to be associated with increased metabolic activity in the orbitofrontal cortex and caudate nucleus (Baxter et al. 1987; Braun et al. 1995). Damage to the dorsolateral prefrontal cortex, causing executive cognitive dysfunction, may also lead to aggressive behavior by impairing the patient's problem-solving ability, resulting in frustration over his or her inability to rely on previously familiar coping strategies. More subtle dysfunction in this area may be associated with reduction in autonomic activity that could impede the fear conditioning needed to have a "conscience" and inhibit antisocial behavior (Raine et al. 2000). Damage to basotemporal lobe and related areas (amygdala, septum, hippocampus) that project to orbitofrontal cortex may also disrupt behavioral programs and result in disinhibition (Starkstein and Robinson 1997). The beneficial effect of stereotactic amygdalotomy for intractable aggression is instructive in this regard (Lee et al. 1998). More diffuse white matter injury, such as in multiple sclerosis, HIV encephalopathy, and diffuse axonal injury from TBI, can also produce behavioral dyscontrol, possibly by damaging these previously mentioned areas.

Animal and human studies show that norepinephrine enhances aggressive behavior (Brown et al. 1979; Higley et al. 1992), consistent with findings of MAO dysfunction in violent kindreds (Brunner et al. 1993) and aggression in MAO "knockout" mice (Cases et al. 1995). Low 5-HT levels in the prefrontal regions have been associated with impulsivity, aggression, and completed suicide (Linnoila and Virkkunen 1992; Owens et al. 1986), consistent with impairment in ability of serotonergic drug stimulation to increase frontal lobe activity in impulsive (Soloff et al. 2000) and autoaggressive (T. Rinne et al. 2000) borderline patients. Animal models suggest that an increase in dopamine may lead to aggression (J.J. Mann 1995), and preservation of neurons in substantia nigra pars compacta is associated with aggression in Alzheimer's disease patients (possibly by providing normal dopamine input to degenerate supersensitive target neurons [Victoroff et al. 1996]). Aggression in Alzheimer's disease is also associated with genetic variation in genes for $D_1$ and $D_3$ receptors (Sweet et al. 1998). GABA may play an indirect modulatory role, as increasing GABA levels in animals has been shown to reduce aggressive behavior, whereas acetylcholine has been reported to increase aggressive behaviors (J.J. Mann 1995). The endogenous opioid system has also been implicated in the development of self-injurious, stereotypic, and deviant social behavior, but treatment studies with opioid antagonists have yielded equivocal results (discussion follows), calling this hypothesis into question. Finally, aggression has been associated with elevated levels of arginine vasopressin in CSF (Coccaro et al. 1998) in personality disorder patients and with elevated levels of testosterone in elderly men with dementia (Orengo et al. 1997).

## Treatment

There are no U.S. Food and Drug Administration (FDA)–approved medications for the treatment of aggression and impulsivity, few standardized classification and assessment tools, and few randomized controlled trials. Treatment often targets the clinical syndromes associated with the maladaptive behavior. Thus, the irritable, depressed patient should first be given an antidepressant; the agitated, paranoid patient should receive a trial of a neuroleptic; and the hyperaroused, angry patient may benefit from an anticonvulsant. However, common side effects of medications used to treat anger and aggression can themselves exacerbate the symptoms (e.g., akathisia from neuroleptics; benzodiazepine-induced disinhibition; overactivation from antidepressants), and anticholinergic agents can aggravate cognitive deficits, lower seizure threshold, and promote delirium, particularly when combined with other delirium-promoting agents.

β-Adrenergic receptor blockers—such as propranolol, pindolol, and nadolol—have been studied in both open (Alpert et al. 1990; Connor et al. 1997; Greendyke and Kanter 1986; Greendyke et al. 1986; Ratey et al. 1992b) and double-blind, placebo-controlled trials (Allan et al. 1996; Ratey et al. 1992b) and have been found to be effective in reducing anger and aggression in a wide range of neuropsychiatric disorders. However, more recent studies using placebo-control (Allan et al. 1996) and placebo-discontinuation (Silver et al. 1999) designs show only modest changes and low rates (30%) of response, respectively. Investigation is plagued by heterogeneous diagnosis, and it is possible that patients with more clear-cut brain damage, as in developmental disability (Connor et al. 1997), may do better. Many of these patients did not respond to other medications, such as neuroleptics, anxiolytics, anticonvulsants, and lithium. Response may take up to 8 weeks, and both central and peripheral effects may contribute to therapeutic action (Ruedrich 1996). Pindolol is less likely to cause bradycardia, and nadolol and long-acting propranolol allow once-daily dosing, which may be necessary in the noncompliant or cognitively impaired patient. Secondary depression due to β-blockers appears to be a rare occurrence, but these medications are contraindicated in patients with asthma, chronic obstructive pulmonary disease, insulin-dependent diabetes, congestive heart failure, persistent angina, significant peripheral vascular disease, and hyperthyroidism (Yudofsky et al. 1987). Yudofsky et al. (1987) propose titrating the dose of propranolol as high as 12 mg/kg or up to 800 mg and maintaining maximum tolerable dosages for up to 8 weeks to achieve the desired clinical response, although doses in the range of 160–320 mg/day have been effective.

Parenteral benzodiazepines are often used to manage both acute aggression and behavioral dyscontrol and can be as effective as neuroleptics (Dorevitch et al. 1999). However, they can also produce disinhibition, which worsens agitation and arousal (Yudofsky et al. 1987). Benzodiazepines with rapid onset of action and relatively short half-lives that can be given intramuscularly or intravenously, such as lorazepam, are most useful in the acute situation. Diazepam and chlordiazepoxide are less reliably and rapidly absorbed intramuscularly (Garza-Trevino et al. 1989). Although longer-acting benzodiazepines, such as clonazepam (Feinbar and Alvarez 1986), can be useful in patients with more chronic agitation and aggression, particularly when symptoms of anxiety coexist, their use in treating or preventing more chronic aggression is not supported (Salzman 1988). Impairment of cognitive functioning by benzodiazepines could potentially aggravate aggression by increasing confusion.

Buspirone can reduce anxiety-associated agitation and has a benign side-effect profile. It has been reported to be effective in treating aggression in patients with head injury (Gualtieri 1991), developmental disability (Ratey et al. 1991a; Verhoeven and Tuinier 1996), dementia (M.A. Levy 1994; Tiller 1989), and Huntington's disease (Byrne et al. 1994). Although the effect of buspirone on anxiety can reduce agitation, its effect on aggression is probably independent of anxiolysis. Although doses between 30 and 60 mg are usually employed (Verhoeven and Tuinier 1996), lower doses (5–15 mg) have been useful in some reports (Ratey et al. 1991a, 1991b, 1992a).

Serotonergic antidepressants have also been effective in the treatment of aggression and behavioral dyscontrol. In open trials, this includes fluoxetine in depressed (Fava et al. 1983), brain-injured (Sobin et al. 1989), and mentally retarded (King 1991; Markowitz 1992) patients; sertraline in mentally retarded (Hellings et al. 1996), Huntington's disease (Ranen et al. 1996), developmentally disabled (J.J. Campbell and Duffy 1995), and intermittent explosive disorder (Feder 1999) patients; paroxetine in mentally retarded patients (although the effect wore off after 1 month) (Davanzo et al. 1998) and in patients with dementia (J.R. Swartz et al. 1997); and citalopram in patients with dementia (Pollock et al. 1997). Standard dose ranges were used. Two controlled studies show effects superior to those of placebo for fluoxetine in patients with personality disorder (Coccaro and Kavoussi 1997) and fluvoxamine in adult autistic patients (McDougle et al. 1996). Two case reports show fluoxetine to be effective in treating obsessive-compulsive disorder in HIV-infected persons (McDaniel and Johnson 1995). SSRIs are the treatment of choice over clomipramine for obsessive-compulsive syndromes, as they are significantly less sedating and anticholinergic. The efficacy of the same drug in conditions with dramatically opposite frontostriatal circuit pathophysiology is noteworthy and points out the limitations of simplistic "serotonergic" hypotheses. Trazodone is also effective in reducing aggression secondary to organic mental disorders and dementia (Greenwald et al. 1986; Mashiko et al. 1996; Pinner and Rich 1988; D.M. Simpson and Foster 1986; Zubieta and Alessi 1992). Concomitant use of tryptophan in some of these reports confounds interpretation of efficacy, however. Because of its potential for causing orthostatic hypotension, use of trazodone should be monitored closely, particularly in elderly and motorically compromised patients. Although sedation can be a problem initially, it often goes away in a few days.

Although anticonvulsants are particularly effective in treating mood lability, impulsivity, and aggression in patients with known seizure disorders, lack of electroencephalographic abnormalities does not preclude potential benefit from anticonvulsants (Mattes 1990). Carbamazepine has been effective in managing aggression and irritability in a variety of patients with CNS impairment, including dementia, developmental disorders, schizophrenia, seizures, and TBI (Chatham-Showalter 1996; Evans and Gualtieri 1985; Luchins 1984; Mattes 1990; McAllister 1985; Yatham and McHale 1988). However, a placebo-controlled trial in children with conduct disorder showed no benefit (Cueva et al. 1996). Valproate has also been found to be effective for aggression in patients with mental retardation (Ruedrich et al. 1999), TBI (Wroblewski et al. 1997), dementia (Haas et al. 1997), and personality disorder (Kavoussi and Coccaro 1998) and may be better tolerated than carbamazepine. Blood levels below 50 µg/mL have been effective in some reports (Mazure et al. 1992). A recent review of 17 reports showed a 77% response rate with normal blood level range (Lindenmayer and Kotsaftis 2000). Phenytoin has been effective for impulsive aggression in inmates using placebo crossover (Barratt et al. 1997), whereas lamotrigine (Beran and Gibson 1998) and gabapentin (Tallian et al. 1996) have worsened aggression in epileptic patients, perhaps because of "forced normalization" (see earlier comments).

Lithium was effective in treating aggressive behavior and affective instability in brain-injured patients (Glenn et al. 1989) and in a double-blind, placebo-controlled trial with 42 adult mentally retarded patients (M. Craft et al. 1987). Open trials in aggressive children with mental retardation and patients chronically hospitalized for severe aggression (Bellus et al. 1996) also support its use (M. Campbell et al. 1995). Although higher plasma levels are more likely to result in clinical improvement, the potential neurotoxic side effects of lithium at lower levels than in psychiatric patients may limit its use in the neurologically compromised patient.

Neuroleptics are effective in treating aggression in neuropsychiatric patients (Rao et al. 1985). They should be reserved, however, for patients who exhibit psychotic symptoms or who require rapid behavioral control. Although neuroleptics may decrease arousal and agitation in the acute setting, the extrapyramidal and anticholinergic properties of these medications can further increase agitation, particularly when combined with other drugs with anticholinergic properties (Tune et al. 1992). Akathisia can be confused with worsening aggression, thus prompting a detrimental rise in neuroleptic dosage. Neuroleptics can also, in some cases, impair executive cognitive functioning (Medalia et al. 1988). Despite these risks, a very effective means of rapid tranquilization

in the agitated patient is the combination of haloperidol (2–5 mg) with lorazepam (1–2 mg), either orally, intramuscularly, or intravenously. In the chronically aggressive psychotic patient, clozapine at doses of 300–500 mg may be the most effective antipsychotic (Cohen and Underwood 1994; Michals et al. 1993). Risperidone is certainly better tolerated, but placebo-controlled evidence that it is more effective for aggression than typical neuroleptics is conflicting, with two studies (Czobor et al. 1995; De Deyn et al. 1999) showing superior effects to haloperidol in schizophrenia and dementia, whereas another study (Beck et al. 1997) found no difference in a small but select group of forensic schizophrenic subjects. Open studies show good effects in autistic (Horrigan and Barnhill 1997) and mentally retarded (Cohen et al. 1998) patients. However, recent reviews emphasize that atypicals should not be used for acute management (Buckley 1999). No data have been published for quetiapine or olanzapine.

Methylphenidate and dextroamphetamine can be useful in patients with distractibility, impaired attention, impulsivity, and irritability (Mooney and Haas 1993), symptoms also seen in attention-deficit/hyperactivity disorder. These stimulants are generally well tolerated in the neurologic patient (Kaufman et al. 1984), do not appear to lower the seizure threshold at therapeutic doses (Wroblewski et al. 1992), and may even enhance cortical recovery (Feeney et al. 1982). However, they should be used with caution due to their potential to aggravate irritability and delusional thought content.

Although an emerging body of literature on the treatment of the developmentally disabled suggests that opiate antagonists such as naltrexone (up to 2 mg/kg) decrease self-injury behavior by 30%–50% (Buzan et al. 1995), the only double-blind, placebo-controlled study (in autistic, mentally retarded adults) did not show an effect (Willemsen-Swinkels et al. 1995). However, a small crossover study showed good effects of 50-mg doses of naltrexone in females with self-mutilation behavior and bipolar disorder (Sonne et al. 1996), and open studies with the same population showed similar effects (A. S. Roth et al. 1996). A retrospective study showed good response in 50% of 56 children with self-injurious behavior (Casner et al. 1996), and an open report showed effects in patients with impulse control disorders (S. W. Kim 1998). Nonetheless, use of naltrexone for this indication should not at present be routine.

Other medications, such as amantadine, a dopamine agonist, and clonidine, an α-adrenergic agonist, have been used to treat aggression. Gualtieri et al. (1989) used amantadine successfully in doses of 50–400 mg/day in agitated patients recovering from coma. Clonidine at 0.6

mg/day reduced violent outbursts in an autistic adult (Koshes and Rock 1994), but its depressogenic and hypotensive risks may be problematic in the neurologic patient. Although a novel class of 5-HT$_{1B}$ receptor agonists called serenics are prompting excitement (Olivier et al. 1994), they currently are not available in the United States and require more testing. Finally, a recent randomized, placebo-controlled study showed an antiaggressive effect of estrogen in both men and women with dementia that was rapid and sustained (Kyomen et al. 1999)

Because of the heterogeneity of symptoms and pathophysiology in this population, and the ethical issues involved in carrying out placebo-controlled studies in aggressive neuropsychiatric patients, animal studies must continue to be used, and the adoption of single-subject research designs may prove to be the most practical approach in studying this population (Eichelman 1992). Table 35–5 lists characteristic antihypertensives recommended in this section, dose ranges, side effects, and relevant drug interactions.

## Cognitive Disturbance

Unlike depression, anxiety, mania, and psychosis, all of which can occur as "primary" disorders independent of gross neurologic disease, cognitive disturbance is almost always a result of etiologically identifiable brain dysfunction and has previously served to largely define disorders known as organic brain syndromes. Moreover, cognitive impairment is often associated with other mood and behavioral features (e.g., agitation and depression predict greater cognitive disturbance in Alzheimer's disease and Parkinson's disease, respectively [S. T. Chen et al. 1998; Kuzis et al. 1997]), as well as with functional status and survival time (e.g., in HIV illness [Wilkie et al. 1998]). However, difficulties with concentration, memory, and more complicated executive cognitive functions occur not just as primary components of neurologic disease and CNS dysfunction but also as epiphenomena in the course of major mood disturbance (i.e., pseudodementia) and as a core feature of schizophrenia (Lancon et al. 2000) and chronic bipolar disorder (Ferrier et al. 1999), as a measurable but more subtle aspect of PTSD and obsessive-compulsive disorder, and secondary to many medications used to treat neurologic and other medical illnesses. Most importantly, even minor improvements in cognition can produce substantial health care cost savings (Ernst et al. 1997). Although the increasing sophistication of modern neuropsychologic testing has allowed extensive batteries to dissect cognitive dysfunction into multiple, partially overlapping components, thereby serving to better define

the deficits of individual patients, these multiple components have, for the most part, not yet been related to distinct neuropathologic or neurochemical processes, nor have they been used in aggregate to evaluate the effects of novel treatments that seek to retard or arrest cognitive dysfunction in the dementias or promote and enhance cognitive function in normal healthy subjects.

## Common Etiologies

The list of neuropsychiatric conditions characterized by cognitive disturbance is so widespread as to conceivably include virtually every neuropsychiatric disorder. These include the primary dementias (Alzheimer's and vascular), later-occurring dementias associated with subcortical degenerative diseases (Parkinson's disease and Huntington's disease), TBI, chronic alcoholism (Korsakoff's syndrome), a host of rarer degenerative dementias, and CNS infectious disease, the most commonly seen now being HIV infection with its late-occurring subcortical dementia. The neuropathologic processes associated with all these conditions are thought to be irreversible, although there is hope that their speed of progression could be retarded. For example, AZT has been shown to have an effect in slowing cognitive deterioration in HIV-dementia patients (Portegies et al. 1989), and cholinergic medications are thought to act similarly in patients with Alzheimer's dementia.

Other etiologies of cognitive impairment might be thought of as potentially reversible processes depending on whether their severity and duration are sufficient to produce more permanent neurologic damage. These include CNS inflammatory disease (e.g., lupus); exposure to heavy metals, organophosphates, and organic solvents; endocrinopathies; and other toxic or infectious processes. Additional CNS inflammatory processes may contribute to the cognitive impairment seen in both HIV infection (Glass et al. 1993; Tyor et al. 1992) and Alzheimer's dementia (Aisen and Davis 1994) and provide another target for treatment intervention. Finally, the list of medications able to impair cognitive functions is widespread and includes commonly used neurologic medications (anticonvulsants, barbiturates, steroids, β-blockers), cardiac medications (digoxin, procainamide, calcium channel blockers), chemotherapeutic agents (especially biologic response modifiers such as interleukin-2) and H$_2$ blockers.

## Anatomy and Neurochemistry

The range of disorders associated with cognitive impairment produces neuropathologic deficits covering the

**TABLE 35–5.** Antihypertensives

| Drug | Starting daily dose (mg) | Target daily dose (mg) | Neuropsychiatric side effects | Neuropsychiatric drug interactions | Comments |
|------|------|------|------|------|------|
| Propranolol | 20–80 | 40–800 | Light-headedness, insomnia, lassitude, weakness, fatigue, catatonia, visual disturbance, hallucinations, vivid dreams, confusion, emotional lability, clouded sensorium, impaired psychomotor | Hypotension w/MAOIs<br>↑ Blood level of both propranolol and chlorpromazine when taken together<br>↓ Blood level w/CBZ, phenytoin, phenobarbital performance | Discontinue if heart rate <50 bpm, SBP <90 mm Hg<br>Clinical response may take 4–8 weeks<br>Useful for migraine, essential tremor, akathisia, performance anxiety, lithium tremor, aggression, mania, social phobia |
| Verapamil | 80–240 | 160–480 | Confusion, equilibrium disorders, insomnia, muscle cramps, paresthesia, psychosis, akathisia, somnolence, headache, CVA | Hypotension w/MAOIs<br>↑ Neurotoxicity w/lithium, CBZ<br>↑ Parkinsonism w/neuroleptics<br>↓ Blood level w/TCAs, phenobarbital<br>↑ Blood level of CBZ<br>↑ or ↓ Blood level of lithium | Useful in mania, migraine, TD, Tourette's, panic disorder |
| Clonidine | 0.05–0.20 | 0.15–0.80 | Nervousness, agitation, mental depression, headache, insomnia, vivid dreams or nightmares, behavioral changes, restlessness, anxiety, hallucinations, delirium, sedation, weakness, fatigue | Additive CNS depressant effects w/other CNS depressants<br>Impaired BP control w/ neuroleptics<br>↓ Blood level w/TCAs | Useful in opiate withdrawal, Tourette's, and possibly mania, anxiety, akathisia, ADHD, aggression<br>Available in transdermal form |

*Note.* ADHD = attention-deficit/hyperactivity disorder; BP = blood pressure; bpm = beats per minute; CBZ = carbamazepine; CNS = central nervous system; CVA = cerebrovascular accident; MAOIs = monoamine oxidase inhibitors; SBP = systolic blood pressure; TCAs = tricyclic antidepressants; TD = tardive dyskinesia.

entire spectrum of cortical and subcortical areas. Thus, it is hard to implicate damage to one structure or set of structures. The important role of the hippocampus and adjacent inferior temporal neocortical and limbic areas in mediating memory is well known (Squire and Zola-Morgan 1991), and these areas are commonly affected in Alzheimer's dementia, dementias of other etiology, and TBI. The frontal lobe and related striatal circuits also play a key role in organizational and retrieval strategies and in working memory (Petrides et al. 1993; B.E. Swartz et al. 1996). These areas are obviously affected in Huntington's disease, Parkinson's disease, and HIV and Korsakoff's dementia and have been implicated in the executive dysfunction of multiple sclerosis (Foong et al. 1999) and the cognitive impairment of neurosyphilis (Russouw

et al. 1997). However, imaging studies clearly show that abnormal activation patterns in patients with memory disturbance extend far beyond morphologic deficits detected by computed tomography or MRI scanning (Heiss et al. 1992). For example, subcortical CVA produces cortical hypometabolism that correlates with degree of cognitive impairment (Kwan et al. 1999).

Many biochemical processes influence memory and cognition, among them acetylcholine, the monoamine neurotransmitters, intracellular signaling enzymes, cyclic nucleotides and other second and third messengers, and hormones such as vasopressin and oxytocin. Alzheimer's disease patients have loss of cerebral choline acetyltransferase—the biosynthetic enzyme for acetylcholine that correlates with decreasing cognitive function (Baskin et al. 1999)—once the disease has progressed beyond the early phases. In contrast, changes in the locus coeruleus of these patients (D.M. Mann et al. 1984) and decreases in 5-HT (Zubenko et al. 1990) seem more related to depression than to dementia severity. However, in stroke patients, cognitive function was positively correlated with right frontal cortical 5-HT receptor binding in one PET scan study (Morris et al. 1993a), suggesting differing neurochemical substrates for cognitive impairments of different etiology. Korsakoff's disease patients have lowered levels of CSF 3-methoxy-4-hydroxyphenylglycol (MHPG), homovanillic acid (HVA), and, in some patients, 5-hydroxyindoleacetic acid (5-HIAA) (G. Halliday et al. 1993), along with a small change in cholinergic neurons (McEntee and Mair 1990). Alzheimer's disease patients have increased levels of plasma MHPG that directly correlate with increasing cognitive impairment (Lawlor et al. 1995). In Parkinson's disease patients, there is also a loss of cortical cholinergic markers (Perry et al. 1991), and Parkinson's disease patients with dementia, compared with those without dementia, have a greater loss of midbrain dopaminergic neurons (J.O. Rinne 1989). Disturbances of calcium homeostasis are thought to play some role in Alzheimer's and vascular (Fischhof 1993) as well as HIV (Lipton 1991) dementias. High levels of corticosteroids are thought to be capable of damaging hippocampal neurons and may contribute to the cognitive impairment in both Korsakoff's (Emsley et al. 1994) and Alzheimer's (Sunderland et al. 1989) dementias. Glutamate and NMDA receptors and subsequent calcium-dependent biochemical processes may play a key role in linking physiology to structural change (both the cellular damage that results from ischemic and traumatic brain injury and the laying down of longer-term memory traces via long-term potentiation). Neuropeptide systems are also differentially affected by neurodegeneration, with decreases in corticotropin-releasing hormone, β-endorphin, and somatostatin being prominent in Alzheimer's and vascular dementias (Heilig et al. 1995), and corticotropin-releasing hormone decreases occurring in the earliest stage of Alzheimer's dementia when cholinergic markers are still preserved (Davis et al. 1999). Finally, genotyping may inform clinical practice in the future. The E4 allele of ApoE marker has been associated with greater cognitive impairment in Alzheimer's disease patients (Rasmusson et al. 1996) and with greater sensitivity to drug-induced cognitive impairment in elderly patients (Pomara et al. 1998), and the number of trinucleotide repeats in Huntington's disease is related to cognitive decline in early stages of the disease (Jason et al. 1997).

## Treatment

The majority of treatment studies continue to focus on Alzheimer's dementia, the most prevalent cause of cognitive impairment in the U.S. population. During the past 5 years, a growing number of studies have documented the palliative efficacy of reversible cholinesterase inhibitors in these patients. Tacrine hydrochloride, the first FDA-approved agent for this indication, clearly has a beneficial, though small, effect on cognition (0.62 points on Mini-Mental State Exam score) compared with placebo declines of about a point (Qizilbash et al. 1998) over 3 months. The effect may delay the need for nursing home placement (Knopman et al. 1996), although it does not appear to alter the long-term trajectory of the illness. Because of gastrointestinal side effects and liver transaminase elevations, tolerability is poor, with more than 75% of patients in a representative clinic population declining open treatment in a recent report (Lyketsos et al. 1996). Beneficial effects may be dose dependent (Knapp et al. 1994), and variability in study results may be due to variable CNS penetration of the drug (Grothe et al. 1998) and differences in disease severity (Kaufer et al. 1998).

Donepezil, also now FDA approved and similar to tacrine except for less peripheral activity and the absence of liver transaminase effects, is better tolerated with comparable efficacy for both short-term (24 weeks) and longer term (5 years) treatment (Greenberg et al. 2000; S.L. Rogers et al. 1998, 2000). Evidence also suggests beneficial psychotropic effects in patients with problematic depression, psychosis, agitation, and disinhibition, although other patients without obvious behavioral problems may experience behavioral worsening (Mega et al. 1999). It may also have efficacy in vascular dementia (Mendez et al. 1999) and for psychotropic-induced memory loss in patients without dementia (Jacobsen and Comas-Díaz 1999).

Other cholinesterase inhibitors, including rivastigmine (Farlow et al. 2000; McKeith et al. 2000; Rösler et al. 1999), galantamine (Wilcock et al. 2000; Wilkinson and Murray 2001), and metrifonate (Cummings et al. 1998), have shown efficacy and tolerability comparable to donepezil. Effect sizes of metrifonate are similar to those of the three marketed agents (improvements of 3–5 points on the Alzheimer's Disease Assessment Scale [ADAS-cog] over 6 months compared with placebo). Demonstration that metrifonate also lowers caregiver burden (Shikiar et al. 2000) provides another more novel measure of beneficial outcome. Extended-release physostigmine also is effective, but, because tolerability is poorer and efficacy perhaps a bit less (Thal et al. 1996; van Dyck et al. 2000), it is unlikely to be used except in patients nonresponsive to other agents. Unfortunately, because all these studies are short in duration and focus on patients without the usual medical and other comorbidities seen in practice, they are poorly generalizable.

Although muscarinic agonists have not been practical to employ due to requirements for either frequent intravenous (arecoline) or intracerebroventricular (bethanechol) administration and because of high rates of nausea and other side effects, studies have documented the efficacy of arecoline (Raffaele et al. 1991) and bethanechol (Penn et al. 1988), suggesting that newer muscarinic agonists, now under development, may prove to be more practically effective. Nicotine agonists may also prove useful in both Alzheimer's (Potter et al. 1999) and Parkinson's (Newhouse et al. 1997) dementias. Although galantamine has nicotinic effects in addition to its cholinesterase inhibition (Maelicke et al. 2001), no advantage over other marketed inhibitors has been identified.

Selegiline, an MAO-B inhibitor commonly used in Parkinson's disease, was initially shown at an open daily dose of 20 mg to improve cognitive performance of 14 Alzheimer's dementia patients (Schneider et al. 1991). Subsequently, double-blind studies at low 10-mg doses likely to act principally by increasing CNS dopamine showed superiority to placebo (Finali et al. 1991), to phosphatidylserine (Monteverde et al. 1990), and to oxiracetam (Falsaperla et al. 1990) on a variety of cognitive tests. However, as summarized in a recent negative crossover study (Tariot et al. 1998b), positive effects of this drug on agitation and depression in some patients make it hard to separate mood state–dependent effects on cognition from a primary cognitive effect. The two most recent studies show no effect (Freedman et al. 1998) and a modest effect on delaying functional impairment (Sano et al. 1997). Because the former study was one of the few longer-term evaluations, the utility of the agent requires further study.

A number of naturalistic case-control studies have shown that anti-inflammatory drugs may help Alzheimer's dementia patients. In one study, patients taking daily NSAIDs or aspirin had shorter duration of illness and better cognitive performance (Rich et al. 1995). In another study, the onset of Alzheimer's dementia in monozygotic twin pairs was inversely proportional to prior use of steroids or adrenocorticotropic hormone (ACTH) (Breitner et al. 1994). Finally, a third naturalistic study (Prince et al. 1998) showed that NSAID use was associated with less cognitive decline, particularly in younger subjects. One placebo-controlled study of 44 patients actually supported an effect for indomethacin (J. Rogers et al. 1993), and NSAIDs are associated with histopathologic evidence of slowed progression of Alzhei-

mer's dementia (Alafuzoff et al. 2000). However, another study failed to show an effect for diclofenac/misoprostol (Scharf et al. 1999), and a study of prednisone was also negative (Aisen et al. 2000), although the dose was quite low and adverse effects on hippocampal cells could have counteracted anti-inflammatory effects. Although no reports have examined effects of therapy aimed at the cytokine-related inflammatory pathways in HIV disease patients, this strategy also holds some promise.

Before the approval of tacrine, donepezil, and rivastigmine, the only approved cognitive drugs were ergoloid mesylates (Hydergine). Their cognitive benefits have always been said to be modest at best and hard to distinguish from nonspecific activating properties. A review (Schneider and Olin 1994) confirms this, showing effect sizes of 0.56 for clinical ratings but only 0.27 for neuropsychological measures. Furthermore, patients with vascular dementia did better than Alzheimer's dementia patients. A previous study in 80 Alzheimer's dementia patients that failed to show an effect (Thompson et al. 1990) may have been compromised by its 3-mg/day dose, because there is a strong dose-response relationship with this drug, and some authors believe higher doses (e.g., 8 mg) might be better (Schneider and Olin 1994). One study showed increases in glucose metabolism on PET scan in both cortical and basal ganglia areas with the drug (Nagasawa et al. 1990).

Two recent studies support very modest effects of antioxidants. Le Bars et al. (1997) showed that Ginkgo biloba was superior to placebo by 1.4 ADAS-cog points in a mixed Alzheimer's and vascular dementia group. These results are inferior to those seen with tacrine or donepezil, and the predominance of mild cases makes the generalizability of results unclear. A recent meta-analysis of studies with this agent (Oken et al. 1998) shows that few reports were well designed with clearly described patient groups, although these few also show similar modest effects. An increase in bleeding risk, especially for patients taking anticoagulants, warrants caution, however. A second study (Sano et al. 1997) showed that 2,000 IU of $\alpha$-tocopherol slowed functional decline in Alzheimer's disease patients, with a delay of roughly a half year over a 2-year period. However, no cognitive improvements were noted, despite these functional benefits.

Initial studies showing that fewer Alzheimer's and vascular dementia patients take replacement estrogen than do matched control subjects (Mortel and Meyer 1995) and that those who do have better cognitive function than those who do not (Henderson et al. 1994) have been replicated in several other uncontrolled naturalistic designs showing that estrogen use is associated with reduced incidence of Alzheimer's disease (Slooter et al. 1999). These associations were convergent with preclinical studies showing genomic and receptor-mediated effects of estrogen on learning, memory, and neuronal growth and connections (Shaywitz and Shaywitz 2000). Unfortunately, a recent well-designed study (Mulnard et al. 2000) failed to show a beneficial effect of estrogen supplements for mild to moderate elderly (75 years) women with Alzheimer's disease, although beneficial effects in postmenopausal women without dementia (Kampen and Sherwin 1994) suggest that preventive effects might be possible.

Based on the possibility that calcium blockade will slow mechanisms of neuronal death that depend on increased free intracellular calcium in Alzheimer's disease, studies of 90 mg/day nimodipine in these patients have shown some promise. Ban et al. (1990) showed 12 weeks of nimodipine to be more effective than placebo on the Mini-Mental State Exam and the Wechsler Memory Scale. Improvement continued between 60 and 90 days. Tollefson (1990) also showed that the same dose improved recall on the Buschke test, although 180 mg proved worse than placebo. However, one naturalistic study (Maxwell et al. 1999) showed that elderly patients taking calcium channel blockers are more likely to develop dementia. Unique calcium channel effects of nimodipine could explain some of these differences.

A variety of other agents have been either tested briefly or reported on. Stimulants (methylphenidate or dextroamphetamine) have been found in one open trial to improve scores on several neuropsychological tests in HIV disease patients (Angrist et al. 1992) and have been found in a placebo-controlled crossover trial to improve cognition in cognitively impaired HIV disease patients (van Dyck et al. 1997). Opiate antagonists have helped improve TBI-associated memory impairment in one case series (Tennant and Wild 1987). The 5-HT antidepressant fluvoxamine has improved memory impairment in Korsakoff's dementia in two studies (Martin et al. 1989, 1995). Clonidine variably improved memory in Korsakoff's dementia, and this was correlated with increased cingulate gyrus and thalamic blood flow (Moffoot et al. 1994). Both clonidine and another $\alpha_2$ agonist, guanfacine, improve various aspects of cognition in healthy humans (Jäkälä et al. 1999a, 1999b, 1999c). Phosphatidylserine, a lipid membrane processor, improved several cognitive measures in Alzheimer's dementia patients (Crook et al. 1992). Citicoline, a metabolic intermediate that enhances the formation of neural membranes and promotes acetylcholine biosynthesis, improved verbal memory in older individuals with "inefficient" memories

who did not have dementia (Spiers et al. 1996). Milacemide, a prodrug for glycine (Dysken et al. 1992), did not work in Alzheimer's dementia patients despite the plausibility of NMDA-glutamate theories of cognition (Ingram et al. 1994) and increased word retrieval in young and old subjects without dementia treated with it (Schwartz et al. 1991). However, cycloserine improved cognition relative to placebo in 17 Alzheimer's disease patients, suggesting that NMDA strategies need to be pursued further (G.E. Tsai et al. 1999). Finally, preliminary studies show a beneficial effect for both insulin and somatostatin acutely administered to Alzheimer's disease patients (S. Craft et al. 1999), whereas peptide T may be associated with improved performance in more cognitively impaired HIV disease patients with relatively preserved immunologic status (Heseltine et al. 1998).

In conclusion, few approved treatments for cognitive impairment, principally in Alzheimer's dementia, are available. Tacrine is perhaps a bit more effective than ergoloid mesylates but with more side-effect morbidity. Donepezil is a much more tolerable alternative, although its efficacy is also only modest. NSAIDs could be employed more readily if there are no medical contraindications. Patients with hypertension might take nimodipine to address both blood pressure and dementia. Selegiline is an option, as are psychostimulants, although activating effects may obscure true cognitive effects. Antioxidants may have some utility, and estrogens deserve further exploration in at-risk patients. Emerging strategies are now emphasizing the use of combinations of agents, especially because effect sizes for all agents are quite modest (Knopman et al. 1998). Studies have already shown effects for both estrogen (Schneider et al. 1997) and selegiline (Schneider et al. 1993) when added to cholinesterase inhibitors. This strategy is consistent with differential effects of these agents on separable cognitive processes (Riekkinen and Riekkinen 1999) and the unique prominence of different individual transmitter abnormalities in different diseases associated with cognitive impairment (J.I. Friedman et al. 1999).

# References

Aarsland D, Larsen JP, Cummings JL, et al: Prevalence and clinical correlates of psychotic symptoms in Parkinson disease: a community-based study. Arch Neurol 56:595–601, 1999a

Aarsland D, Larsen JP, Lim NG, et al: Olanzapine for psychosis in patients with Parkinson's disease with and without dementia. J Neuropsychiatry Clin Neurosci 11:392–394, 1999b

Aisen PS, Davis KL: Inflammatory mechanisms in Alzheimer's disease: implications for therapy. Am J Psychiatry 151: 1105–1113, 1994

Aisen PS, Davis KL, Berg JD, et al: A randomized controlled trial of prednisone in Alzheimer's disease. Neurology 54:588–593, 2000

Alafuzoff P: Lower counts of astroglia and activated microglia in patients with Alzheimer's disease with regular use of NSAIDs. Journal of Alzheimers Disease 2:37–46, 2000

Alexopoulos GS, Meyers BS, Young RC, et al: "Vascular depression" hypothesis. Arch Gen Psychiatry 54:915–922, 1997

Alexopoulos GS, Silver JM, Kahn DA, et al: Treatment of agitation in older persons with dementia. A special report. Postgrad Med April:1–88, 2000

Allan ER, Alpert M, Sison CE, et al: Adjunctive nadolol in the treatment of acutely aggressive schizophrenic patients. J Clin Psychiatry 57:455–459, 1996

Allen RL, Walker Z, D'Ath PJ, et al: Risperidone for psychotic and behavioural symptoms in Lewy body dementia (letter). Lancet 346:185, 1995

Alpert M, Allan ER, Citrome L, et al: A double-blind, placebo-controlled study of adjunctive nadolol in the management of violent psychiatric patients. Psychopharmacology Bulletin 28:367–371, 1990

Altshuler L, Rausch R, Delrahim S, et al: Temporal lobe epilepsy, temporal lobectomy, and major depression. J Neuropsychiatry Clin Neurosci 11:436–443, 1999

Aman MG, Singh NN, Stewart AW, et al: The Aberrant Behavior Checklist: a behavior rating scale for the assessment of treatment effects. American Journal of Mental Deficiency 89:485–491, 1985

American Psychiatric Association: Diagnostic and Statistical Manual of Mental Disorders, 4th Edition. Washington, DC, American Psychiatric Association, 1994

Andersen G, Vestergaard K, Lauritzen L: Effective treatment of poststroke depression with the selective serotonin reuptake inhibitor citalopram. Stroke 25:1099–1104, 1994

Andersen J, Aabro E, Gulmann N, et al: Anti-depressive treatment in Parkinson's disease: a controlled trial of the effect of nortriptyline in patients with Parkinson's disease treated with L-dopa. Acta Neurol Scand 62:210–219, 1980

Angrist B, d'Hollosy M, Sanfilipo M, et al: Central nervous system stimulants as symptomatic treatments for AIDS-related neuropsychiatric impairment. J Clin Psychopharmacol 12:268–272, 1992

Arevalo GJ, Gershanik OS: Modulatory effect of clozapine on levodopa response in Parkinson's disease: a preliminary study. Mov Disord 8:349–354, 1993

Auchus AP, Bissey-Black C: Pilot study of haloperidol, fluoxetine, and placebo for agitation in Alzheimer's disease. J Neuropsychiatry Clin Neurosci 9:591–593, 1997

Azouvi P, Jokic C, Attal N, et al: Carbamazepine in agitation and aggressive behaviour following severe closed-head injury: results of an open trial. Brain Inj 13:797–804, 1999

Balon R: Nefazodone for mood disorder associated with epilepsy (letter). J Clin Psychiatry 59:690, 1998

Ban TA, Morey L, Aguglia E, et al: Nimodipine in the treatment of old age dementias. Prog Neuropsychopharmacol Biol Psychiatry 14:525–551, 1990

Barratt ES, Stanford MS, Felthous AR, et al: The effects of phenytoin on impulsive and premeditated aggression: a controlled study. J Clin Psychopharmacol 17:341–349, 1997

Baskin DS, Browning JL, Pirozzolo FJ, et al: Brain choline acetyltransferase and mental function in Alzheimer disease. Arch Neurol 56:1121–1123, 1999

Baxter LR, Phelps ME, Mazziotta JC, et al: Local cerebral glucose metabolic rates in obsessive-compulsive disorder. Arch Gen Psychiatry 44:211–218, 1987

Beck NC, Greenfield SR, Gotham H, et al: Risperidone in the management of violent, treatment-resistant schizophrenics hospitalized in a maximum security forensic facility. J Am Acad Psychiatry Law 25:461–468, 1997

Bell AJ, Cole A, Eccleston D, et al: Lithium neurotoxicity at normal therapeutic levels. Br J Psychiatry 162:689–692, 1993

Bellus SB, Stewart D, Vergo JG, et al: The use of lithium in the treatment of aggressive behaviours with two brain-injured individuals in a state psychiatric hospital. Brain Inj 10:849–860, 1996

Benes FM: Evidence for altered trisynaptic circuitry in schizophrenic hippocampus. Biol Psychiatry 46:589–599, 1999

Bennett JP, Landow ER, Dietrich S, et al: Suppression of dyskinesias in advanced Parkinson's disease: moderate daily clozapine doses provide long-term dyskinesia reduction. Mov Disord 9:409–414, 1994

Beran RG, Gibson RJ: Aggressive behaviour in intellectually challenged patients with epilepsy treated with lamotrigine. Epilepsia 39:280–282, 1998

Berthier ML, Kulisevsky J, Gironell A, et al: Poststroke bipolar affective disorder: clinical subtypes, concurrent movement disorders, and anatomical correlates. J Neuropsychiatry Clin Neurosci 8:160–167, 1996

Bertolino A, Knable MB, Saunders RC, et al: The relationship between dorsolateral prefrontal N-acetylaspartate measures and striatal dopamine activity in schizophrenia. Biol Psychiatry 45:660–667, 1999

Bierer LM, Knott PJ, Schmeidler JM, et al: Post-mortem examination of dopaminergic parameters in Alzheimer's disease: relationship to noncognitive symptoms. Psychiatry Res 49:211–217, 1993

Braun AR, Randolph C, Stoetter B, et al: The functional neuroanatomy of Tourette's syndrome: an FDG-PET study, II: relationships between regional cerebral metabolism and associated behavioral and cognitive features of the illness. Neuropsychopharmacology 13:151–168, 1995

Bredkjaer SR, Mortensen PB, Parnas J: Epilepsy and non-organic non-affective psychosis: national epidemiologic study. Br J Psychiatry 172:235–238, 1998

Breitbart W, Marotta R, Platt MM, et al: A double-blind trial of haloperidol, chlorpromazine, and lorazepam in the treatment of delirium in hospitalized AIDS patients. Am J Psychiatry 153:231–237, 1996

Breitner JC, Gau BA, Welsh KA, et al: Inverse association of anti-inflammatory treatments and Alzheimer's disease: initial results of a co-twin control study. Neurology 44:227–232, 1994

Bridges-Parlet S, Knopman D, Steffes S: Withdrawal of neuroleptic medications from institutionalized dementia patients: results of a double-blind, baseline-treatment-controlled pilot study. J Geriatr Psychiatry Neurol 10:119–126, 1997

Bromfield EB, Altshuler L, Leiderman DB, et al: Cerebral metabolism and depression in patients with complex partial seizures. Arch Neurol 49:617–623, 1992

Brown GL, Goodwin FK, Ballenger JC, et al: Aggression in humans correlates with cerebrospinal fluid amine metabolites. Psychiatry Res 1:131–139, 1979

Brunner HG, Nelen M, Breakefield XO, et al: Abnormal behavior associated with a point mutation in the structural gene for monoamine oxidase A. Science 262:578–580, 1993

Bryant RA, Marosszeky JE, Crooks J, et al: Posttraumatic stress disorder after severe traumatic brain injury. Am J Psychiatry 157:629–631, 2000

Buckley PF: The role of typical and atypical antipsychotic medications in the management of agitation and aggression. J Clin Psychiatry 10:52–60, 1999

Buitelaar JK, van der Gaag RJ, van der Hoeven J: Buspirone in the management of anxiety and irritability in children with pervasive developmental disorders: results of an open-label study. J Clin Psychiatry 59:56–59, 1998

Burke WJ, Pfeiffer RF, McComb RD: Neuroleptic sensitivity to clozapine in dementia with Lewy bodies. J Neuropsychiatry Clin Neurosci 10:227–229, 1998

Burns A, Russell E, Stratton-Powell H, et al: Sertraline in stroke-associated lability of mood. Int J Geriatr Psychiatry 14:681–685, 1999

Buzan RD, Thomas M, Dubovsky SL: The use of opiate antagonists for recurrent self-injurious behavior. J Neuropsychiatry Clin Neurosci 7:437–444, 1995

Byrne A, Martin W, Hnatko G: Beneficial effects of buspirone therapy in Huntington's disease (letter). Am J Psychiatry 151:1097, 1994

Caley CF, Friedman JH: Does fluoxetine exacerbate Parkinson's disease? J Clin Psychiatry 53:278–282, 1992

Caliguri MP, Peavy G: An instrumental study of the relationship between extrapyramidal signs and psychosis in Alzheimer's disease. J Neuropsychiatry Clin Neurosci 12:34–39, 2000

Campbell JJ III, Duffy JD: Sertraline treatment of aggression in a developmentally disabled patient (letter). J Clin Psychiatry 56:123–124, 1995

Campbell M, Kafanteris V, Cueva JE: An update on the use of lithium carbonate in aggressive children and adolescents with conduct disorder. Psychopharmacology Bulletin 31:93–102, 1995

Cantello R, Aquaggia M, Gilli M, et al: Major depression in Parkinson's disease and the mood response to intravenous methylphenidate: possible role of the hedonic dopamine synapse. J Neurol Neurosurg Psychiatry 52:724–731, 1989

Cantillon M, Brunswick R, Molina D, et al: Buspirone vs haloperidol: a double-blind trial for agitation in a nursing home population with Alzheimer's disease. Am J Geriatr Psychiatry 4:263–267, 1996

Cases O, Seif I, Grimsby J, et al: Aggressive behavior and altered amounts of brain serotonin and norepinephrine in mice lacking MAOA. Science 268:1763–1766, 1995

Casner JA, Weinheimer B, Gualtieri CT: Naltrexone and self-injurious behavior: a retrospective population study. J Clin Psychopharmacol 16:389–394, 1996

Cassidy JW: Fluoxetine: a new serotonergically active antidepressant. J Head Trauma Rehabil 4:67–69, 1989

Castellon SA, Hinkin CH, Wood S, et al: Apathy, depression, and cognitive performance in HIV-1 infection. J Neuropsychiatry Clin Neurosci 10:320–329, 1998

Castillo CS, Starkstein SE, Fedoroff JP, et al: Generalized anxiety disorder after stroke. J Nerv Ment Dis 181:100–106, 1993

Chacko RC, Hurley RA, Jankovic J: Clozapine use in diffuse Lewy body disease. J Neuropsychiatry Clin Neurosci 5:206–208, 1993

Chatham-Showalter PE: Carbamazepine for combativeness in acute traumatic brain injury. J Neuropsychiatry Clin Neurosci 8:96–99, 1996

Chemerinski E, Petracca G, Tesón A, et al: Prevalence and correlates of aggressive behavior in Alzheimer's disease. J Neuropsychiatry Clin Neurosci 10:421–425, 1998

Chen CPL-H, Hope RA, Alder JT, et al: Loss of 5HT2A receptors in Alzheimer's disease neocortex is associated with cognitive decline while preservation of 5HT2A receptors is associated with anxiety. Ann Neurol 36:308–309, 1994

Chen CPL-H, Alder JT, Bowen DM, et al: Presynaptic serotonergic markers in community-acquired cases of Alzheimer's disease: correlations with depression and neuroleptic medication. J Neurochem 66:1592–1598, 1996

Chen ST, Sultzer DL, Hinkin CH, et al: Executive dysfunction in Alzheimer's disease: association with neuropsychiatric symptoms and functional impairment. J Neuropsychiatry Clin Neurosci 10:426–432, 1998

Cleghorn JM, Franco S, Szechtman B, et al: Toward a brain map of auditory hallucinations. Am J Psychiatry 149:1062–1069, 1992

Coccaro EF, Kavoussi RJ: Fluoxetine and impulsive aggressive behavior in personality-disordered subjects. Arch Gen Psychiatry 54:1081–1088, 1997

Coccaro EF, Zemishlany Z, Thorne A: Pharmacologic treatment of noncognitive behavioral disturbance in elderly demented patients. Am J Psychiatry 147:1640–1645, 1990

Coccaro EF, Kavoussi RJ, Hauger RL, et al: Cerebrospinal fluid vasopressin levels: correlates with aggression and serotonin function in personality-disordered subjects. Arch Gen Psychiatry 55:708–714, 1998

Coffey CE, Ross DR, Ferren EL, et al: Treatment of the "on-off" phenomenon in parkinsonism with lithium carbonate. Ann Neurol 12:375–379, 1982

Coffey CE, Cummings JL, Duffy JD, et al: Assessment of treatment outcomes in neuropsychiatry: a report from the Committee on Research of the American Neuropsychiatric Association. J Neuropsychiatry Clin Neurosci 7:287–289, 1995

Cohen SA, Underwood MT: The use of clozapine in a mentally retarded and aggressive population. J Clin Psychiatry 55:440–444, 1994

Cohen SA, Ihrig K, Lott RS, et al: Risperidone for aggression and self-injurious behavior in adults with mental retardation. J Autism Dev Disord 28:229–233, 1998

Colenda CC: Buspirone in treatment of agitated demented patients (letter). Lancet 1:1169, 1988

Collacott RA, Cooper S-A, Branford D, et al: Epidemiology of self-injurious behaviour in adults with learning disabilities. Br J Psychiatry 173:428–432, 1998

Como PG, Rubin AJ, O'Brien CF, et al: A controlled trial of fluoxetine in nondepressed patients with Huntington's disease. Mov Disord 12:397–401, 1997

Conlon P, Trimble MR, Rogers D: A study of epileptic psychosis using magnetic resonance imaging. Br J Psychiatry 156:231–235, 1990

Connor DF, Ozbayrak KR, Benjamin S, et al: A pilot study of nadolol for overt aggression in developmentally delayed individuals. J Am Acad Child Adolesc Psychiatry 36:826–834, 1997

Craft M, Ismail A, Krishnamurti D, et al: Lithium in the treatment of aggression in mentally handicapped patients. Br J Psychiatry 150:685–689, 1987

Craft S, Asthana S, Newcomer JW, et al: Enhancement of memory in Alzheimer disease with insulin and somatostatin, but not glucose. Arch Gen Psychiatry 56:1135–1140, 1999

Crisostomo EA, Duncan PW, Propst M, et al: Evidence that amphetamine with physical therapy promotes recovery of motor function in stroke patients. Ann Neurol 23:94–97, 1988

Crook T, Petrie W, Wells C, et al: Effects of phosphatidylserine in Alzheimer's disease. Psychopharmacology Bulletin 28:61–66, 1992

Cueva JE, Overall JE, Small AM, et al: Carbamazepine in aggressive children with conduct disorder: a double-blind and placebo-controlled study. J Am Acad Child Adolesc Psychiatry 35:480–490, 1996

Cummings JL, Cyrus PA, Bieber F, et al: Metrifonate treatment of the cognitive deficits of Alzheimer's disease. Neurology 50:1214–1221, 1998

Czobor P, Volavka J, Meibach RC: Effect of risperidone on hostility in schizophrenia. J Clin Psychopharmacol 15:243–249, 1995

Dallocchio C, Buffa C, Tinelli C, et al: Effectiveness of risperidone in Huntington chorea patients (letter). J Clin Psychopharmacol 19:101–103, 1999

Dam M, Tonin P, De Boni A, et al: Effects of fluoxetine and maprotiline on functional recovery in poststroke hemiplegic patients undergoing rehabilitation therapy. Stroke 27:1211–1214, 1996

Davanzo PA, Belin TR, Widawski MH, et al: Paroxetine treatment of aggression and self-injury in persons with mental retardation. Am J Ment Retard 102:427–437, 1998

Davis KL, Kahn RS, Ko G, et al: Dopamine in schizophrenia: a review and reconceptualization. Am J Psychiatry 148:1474–1486, 1991

Davis KL, Mohs RC, Marin DB, et al: Neuropeptide abnormalities in patients with early Alzheimer disease. Arch Gen Psychiatry 56:981–987, 1999

De Deyn PP, Rabheru K, Rasmussen A, et al: A randomized trial of risperidone, placebo, and haloperidol for behavioral symptoms of dementia (comments). Neurology 53:946–955, 1999

Devanand DP, Cooper T, Sackeim HA, et al: Low dose oral haloperidol and blood levels in Alzheimer's disease: a preliminary study. Psychopharmacology Bulletin 28:169–173, 1992

Devanand DP, Jacobs DM, Tang M-X, et al: The course of psychopathologic features in mild to moderate Alzheimer disease. Arch Gen Psychiatry 54:257–263, 1997

Devanand DP, Marder K, Michaels KS, et al: A randomized, placebo-controlled dose-comparison trial of haloperidol for psychosis and disruptive behaviors in Alzheimer's disease. Am J Psychiatry 155:1512–1520, 1998

Dewey RB Jr, O'Suilleabhain PE: Treatment of drug-induced psychosis with quetiapine and clozapine in Parkinson's disease Neurology 55(11):1753–1754, 2000

Díaz-Olavarrieta C, Campbell J, Garcia de la Cadena C, et al: Domestic violence against patients with chronic neurologic disorders. Arch Neurol 56:681–685, 1999

Dinan TG, Mobayed M: Treatment resistance of depression after head injury: a preliminary study of amitriptyline response. Acta Psychiatr Scand 85:292–294, 1992

Donaldson C, Tarrier N, Burns A: The impact of the symptoms of dementia on caregivers. Br J Psychiatry 170:62–68, 1997

Dorevitch A, Katz N, Zemishlany Z, et al: Intramuscular flunitrazepam versus intramuscular haloperidol in the emergency treatment of aggressive psychotic behavior. Am J Psychiatry 156:142–144, 1999

Drake ME, Pakalnis A, Phillips B: Secondary mania after ventral pontine infarction. J Neuropsychiatry Clin Neurosci 2:322–325, 1990

Dreyer EB, Kaiser PK, Offermann JT, et al: HIV-1 coat protein neurotoxicity prevented by calcium channel antagonists. Science 248:364–367, 1990

Dubovsky SL, Franks RD, Allen S, et al: Calcium antagonists in mania. Psychiatry Res 18:309–320, 1986

Duffy JD, Kant R: Clinical utility of clozapine in 16 patients with neurological disease. J Neuropsychiatry Clin Neurosci 8:92–95, 1996

Dysken MW, Mendels J, Lewitt P, et al: Milacemide: a placebo-controlled study in senile dementia of the Alzheimer type. J Am Geriatr Soc 40:503–506, 1992

Ebert D, Ebmeier KP: The role of the cingulate gyrus in depression: from functional anatomy to neurochemistry. Biol Psychiatry 39:1044–1050, 1996

Eichelman B: Aggressive behavior: from laboratory to clinic. Arch Gen Psychiatry 49:488–492, 1992

Elliott AJ, Roy-Byrne PP: Mirtazapine for depression in patients with human immunodeficiency virus. J Clin Psychopharmacol 20:265–267, 2000

Elliott AJ, Uldall KK, Bergam K, et al: Randomized, placebo-controlled trial of paroxetine versus imipramine in depressed HIV-positive outpatients. Am J Psychiatry 155:367–372, 1998

Elliott AJ, Russo J, Bergam K, et al: Antidepressant efficacy in HIV-seropositive outpatients with major depressive disorder: an open trial of nefazodone. J Clin Psychiatry 60:226–231, 1999

Elrod R, Peskind ER, DiGiacomo L, et al: Effects of Alzheimer's disease severity on cerebrospinal fluid norepinephrine concentration. Am J Psychiatry 154:25–30, 1997

Emsley RA, Roberts MC, Aalbers C, et al: Endocrine function in alcoholic Korsakoff's syndrome. Alcohol Alcohol 29:187–191, 1994

Ernst RL, Hay JW, Fenn C, et al: Cognitive function and the costs of Alzheimer disease: an exploratory study. Arch Neurol 54:687–693, 1997

Evans RW, Gualtieri CT: Carbamazepine: a neuropsychological and psychiatric profile. Clin Neuropharmacol 8:221–241, 1985

Falk WE, Mahnke MW, Poskanzer DC: Lithium prophylaxis of corticotropin-induced psychosis. JAMA 241:1011–1012, 1979

Falsaperla A, Monici-Preti PA, Oliani C: Selegiline versus oxiracetam in patients with Alzheimer-type dementia. Clin Ther 12:376–384, 1990

Fann JR, Uomoto JM, Katon WJ: Sertraline in the treatment of major depression following mild traumatic brain injury. J Neuropsychiatry Clin Neurosci 12(2):226–232, 2000

Farlow M, Anand R, Messina J Jr, et al: A 52-week study of the efficacy of rivastigmine in patients with mild to moderately severe Alzheimer's disease. Eur Neurol 44(4):236–241, 2000

Fava M, Rosenbaum JF, Pava JA: Anger attacks in unipolar depression, I: clinical correlates and response to fluoxetine treatment. Am J Psychiatry 150:1158–1163, 1983

Feder R: Treatment of intermittent explosive disorder with sertraline in 3 patients. J Clin Psychiatry 60:195–196, 1999

Feeney D, Gonzales A, Law W: Amphetamine, haloperidol and experience interact to affect rate of recovery after motor cortex injury. Science 217:855–857, 1982

Feinbar JP, Alvarez WA: Clonazepam treatment of organic brain syndromes in three elderly patients. J Clin Psychiatry 47:525–526, 1986

Feinstein A, Ron M: A longitudinal study of psychosis due to a general medical (neurological) condition: establishing predictive and construct validity. J Neuropsychiatry Clin Neurosci 10:448–452, 1998

Feinstein A, du Boulay G, Ron MA: Psychotic illness in multiple sclerosis: a clinical and magnetic resonance imaging study. Br J Psychiatry 161:680–685, 1992

Fernandez HH, Friedman JH, Jacques C, et al: Quetiapine for the treatment of drug-induced psychosis in Parkinson's disease. Mov Disord 14:484–487, 1999

Ferrando SJ, Rabkin JG, Moore GM, et al: Antidepressant treatment of depression in HIV-seropositive women. J Clin Psychiatry 60:741–746, 1999

Ferrier IN, Stanton BR, Kelly TP, et al: Neuropsychological function in euthymic patients with bipolar disorder. Br J Psychiatry 175:246–251, 1999

Fiegel GS: ECT and delirium in Parkinson's disease (letter). Am J Psychiatry 149:1759, 1992

Finali G, Piccirilli M, Oliani C, et al: L-Deprenyl therapy improves verbal memory in amnesic Alzheimer patients. Clin Neuropharmacol 14:523–536, 1991

Fischhof PK: Divergent neuroprotective effects of nimodipine in PDD and MID provide indirect evidence of disturbances in Ca2+ homeostasis in dementia. Methods Find Exp Clin Pharmacol 15:549–555, 1993

Flax JW, Gray J, Herbert J: Effect of fluoxetine on patients with multiple sclerosis (letter). Am J Psychiatry 148:1603, 1991

Foong J, Rozewicz L, Davie CA, et al: Correlates of executive function in multiple sclerosis: the use of magnetic resonance spectroscopy as an index of focal pathology. J Neuropsychiatry Clin Neurosci 11:45–50, 1999

Ford B, Lynch T, Greene P: Risperidone in Parkinson's disease (letter). Lancet 344:681, 1994

Fornazzari L, Farenik K, Smith I, et al: Violent visual hallucinations and aggression in frontal lobe dysfunction: clinical manifestations of deep orbitofrontal foci. J Neuropsychiatry Clin Neurosci 4:42–44, 1992

Forstl H, Burns A, Luthert P, et al: Clinical and neuropathological correlates of depression in Alzheimer's disease. Psychol Med 22:877–884, 1992

Freedman M, Rewilak D, Xerri T, et al: L-Deprenyl in Alzheimer's disease: cognitive and behavioral effects. Neurology 50:660–668, 1998

Friedman JH, Factor SA: Atypical antipsychotics in the treatment of drug-induced psychosis in Parkinson's disease. Mov Disord 15:201–211, 2000

Friedman JH, Goldstein S, Jacques C: Substituting clozapine for olanzapine in psychiatrically stable Parkinson's disease patients: results of an open label pilot study. Clin Neuropharmacol 21:285–288, 1998

Friedman JI, Adler DN, Davis KL: The role of norepinephrine in the pathophysiology of cognitive disorders: potential applications to the treatment of cognitive dysfunction in schizophrenia and Alzheimer's disease. Biol Psychiatry 46:1243–1252, 1999

Fuchs A, Hehnke U, Erhart C, et al: Video rating analyses of effect of maprotiline in patients with dementia and depression. Pharmacopsychiatry 26:37–41, 1993

Gaind GS, Rosebush PI, Mazurek MF: Lorazepam treatment of acute and chronic catatonia in two mentally retarded brothers. J Clin Psychiatry 55:20–30, 1994

Galynker I, Ieronimo C, Miner C, et al: Methylphenidate treatment of negative symptoms in patients with dementia. J Neuropsychiatry Clin Neurosci 9:231–239, 1997

Garza-Trevino ES, Hollister LE, Overall JE, et al: Efficacy of combinations of intramuscular antipsychotics and sedative-hypnotics for control of psychotic agitation. Am J Psychiatry 146:1598–1601, 1989

Gimenez-Roldan S, Mateo D, Navarro E, et al: Efficacy and safety of clozapine and olanzapine: an open-label study comparing two groups of Parkinson's disease patients with dopaminergic-induced psychosis. Parkinsonism Relat Disord 7(2):121–127, 2001

Glass JD, Wesselingh SL, Selnes OA, et al: Clinical-neuropathologic correlation in HIV-associated dementia. Neurology 43:2230–2237, 1993

Gleason RP, Schneider LS: Carbamazepine treatment of agitation in Alzheimer's outpatients refractory to neuroleptics. J Clin Psychiatry 51:115–118, 1990

Glenn MB, Wroblewski B, Parziale J: Lithium carbonate for aggressive behavior or affective instability in ten brain injured patients. Am J Phys Med Rehabil 68:221–226, 1989

Glue P: Rapid cycling affective disorders in the mentally retarded. Biol Psychiatry 26:250–256, 1989

Goetz GG, Tanner CM, Klawans HL: Bupropion in Parkinson's disease. Neurology 34:1092–1094, 1984

Goff DC, Tsai E, Levitt J, et al: A placebo-controlled trial of D-cycloserine added to conventional neuroleptics in patients with schizophrenia. Arch Gen Psychiatry 56:21–27, 1999

Goodwin FK, Jamison KR: Manic Depressive Illness. New York, Oxford University Press, 1990

Grade C, Redford B, Chrostowski J, et al: Methylphenidate in early poststroke recovery: a double-blind, placebo-controlled study. Arch Phys Med Rehabil 79:1047–1050, 1998

Graham JM, Sussman JD, Ford KS, et al: Olanzapine in the treatment of hallucinosis in idiopathic Parkinson's disease: a cautionary note. J Neurol Neurosurg Psychiatry 65:774–777, 1998

Grant I, Brown GW, Harris T, et al: Severely threatening events and marked life difficulties preceding onset or exacerbation of multiple sclerosis. J Neurol Neurosurg Psychiatry 52:8–13, 1989

Greenberg SM, Tennis MK, Brown LB, et al: Donepezil therapy in clinical practice. Arch Neurol 57:94–99, 2000

Greendyke RM, Kanter DR: Therapeutic effects of pindolol on behavioral disturbances associated with organic brain disease. J Clin Psychiatry 47:423–426, 1986

Greendyke RM, Kanter DR, Schuster DB, et al: Propranolol in the treatment of assaultive patients with organic brain disease. J Nerv Ment Dis 174:290–294, 1986

Greenwald BS, Marin DB, Silvermans M: Serotonergic treatment of screaming and banging in dementia. Lancet 2:1464–1465, 1986

Grisaru N, Chudakov B, Yaroslavsky Y, et al: Transcranial magnetic stimulation in mania: a controlled study. Am J Psychiatry 155:1608–1610, 1998

Gross H, Kling A, Henry G, et al: Local cerebral glucose metabolism in patients with long-term behavioral and cognitive deficits following mild traumatic brain injury. J Neuropsychiatry Clin Neurosci 8:324–334, 1996

Grothe DR, Piscitelli SC, Dukoff R: Penetration of tacrine into cerebrospinal fluid in patients with Alzheimer's disease. J Clin Psychopharmacol 18:78–81, 1998

Gualtieri CT: Buspirone for the behavior problems of patients with organic brain disorders. J Clin Psychopharmacol 11:280–281, 1991

Gualtieri CT, Chandler M, Coons TB, et al: Amantadine: a new clinical profile for traumatic brain injury. Clin Neuropharmacol 12:258–270, 1989

Haas S, Vincent K, Holt J, et al: Divalproex: a possible treatment alternative for demented, elderly aggressive patients. Ann Clin Psychiatry 9:145–147, 1997

Haller E, Binder RL: Clozapine and seizures. Am J Psychiatry 147:1069–1071, 1990

Halliday G, Ellis J, Heard R, et al: Brainstem serotonergic neurons in chronic alcoholics with and without the memory impairment of Korsakoff's psychosis. J Neuropathol Exp Neurol 52:567–579, 1993

Halliday S, Mackrell K: Psychological interventions in self-injurious behaviour: working with people with a learning disability. Br J Psychiatry 172:395–400, 1998

Halman MH, Worth JL, Sanders KM, et al: Anticonvulsant use in the treatment of manic syndromes in patients with HIV-1 infection. J Neuropsychiatry Clin Neurosci 5:430–434, 1993

Hamner M, Huber M, Gardner VT: Patient with progressive dementia and choreoathetoid movements treated with buspirone. J Clin Psychopharmacol 16:261–262, 1996

Heilig M, Sjogren M, Blennow K, et al: Cerebrospinal fluid neuropeptides in Alzheimer's disease and vascular dementia. Biol Psychiatry 38:210–216, 1995

Heiss WD, Pawlik G, Holthoff V, et al: PET correlates of normal and impaired memory functions. Cerebrovascular and Brain Metabolism Reviews 4:1–27, 1992

Hellings JA, Kelley LA, Gabrielli WF, et al: Sertraline response in adults with mental retardation and autistic disorder. J Clin Psychiatry 57:333–336, 1996

Henderson VW, Paganini-Hill A, Emanuel CK, et al: Estrogen replacement therapy in older women: comparisons between Alzheimer's disease cases and nondemented control subjects. Arch Neurol 51:896–900, 1994

Hendryx PM: Psychosocial changes perceived by closed-head–injured adults and their families. Arch Phys Med Rehabil 70:526–530, 1989

Herrmann N: Valproic acid treatment of agitation in dementia. Can J Psychiatry 43:69–72, 1998

Herrmann N, Rivard M-F, Flynn M, et al: Risperidone for the treatment of behavioral disturbances in dementia: a case series. J Neuropsychiatry Clin Neurosci 10:220–223, 1998

Herrmann N, Lanctot K, Myszak M: Effectiveness of gabapentin for the treatment of behavioral disorders in dementia. J Clin Psychopharmacol 20:90–93, 2000

Herz LR, Volicer L, Rheume Y: Pharmacotherapy of agitation in dementia. Am J Psychiatry 149:1757–1758, 1992

Heseltine PNR, Goodkin K, Atkinson JH, et al: Randomized double-blind placebo-controlled trial of peptide T for HIV-associated cognitive impairment. Arch Neurol 55:41–51, 1998

Higley JD, Mehlman PT, Taum DM, et al: Cerebrospinal fluid monoamine and adrenal correlates of aggression in free-ranging rhesus monkeys. Arch Gen Psychiatry 49:436–441, 1992

Hirono N, Mori E, Ishii K, et al: Alteration of regional cerebral glucose utilization with delusions in Alzheimer's disease. J Neuropsychiatry Clin Neurosci 10:433–439, 1998

Holton A, George K: The use of lithium in severely demented patients with behavioral disturbance. Br J Psychiatry 146:99–100, 1985

Horne M, Lindley SE: Divalproex sodium in the treatment of aggressive behavior and dysphoria in patients with organic brain syndromes. J Clin Psychiatry 56:430–431, 1995

Hornstein A, Seliger G: Cognitive side effects of lithium in closed head injury. J Neuropsychiatry Clin Neurosci 1:446–447, 1989

Horrigan JP, Barnhill LJ: Risperidone and explosive aggressive autism. J Autism Dev Disord 27:313–323, 1997

Hyde TM, Ziegler JC, Weinberger DR: Psychiatric disturbances in metachromatic leukodystrophy: insights into the neurobiology of psychosis. Arch Neurol 49:401–406, 1992

Iannaccone S, Ferini-Strambi L: Pharmacologic treatment of emotional lability. Clin Neuropharmacol 19:532–535, 1996

Ingram DK, Spangler EL, Iijima S, et al: New pharmacological strategies for cognitive enhancement using a rat model of age-related memory impairment. Ann N Y Acad Sci 717:16–32, 1994

Irizarry MC, Ghaemi SN, Lee-Cherry ER, et al: Risperidone treatment of behavioral disturbances in outpatients with dementia. J Neuropsychiatry Clin Neurosci 11:336–342, 1999

Itoh M, Meguro K, Fujiwara T, et al: Assessment of dopamine metabolism in brain of patients with dementia by means of 18F-fluorodopa and PET. Ann Nucl Med 8:245–251, 1994

Jacobsen FM, Comas-Díaz L: Donepezil for psychotropic-induced memory loss. J Clin Psychiatry 60:698–704, 1999

Jäkälä P, Riekkinen M, Sirviö J, et al: Clonidine, but not guanfacine, impairs choice reaction time performance in young healthy volunteers. Neuropsychopharmacology 21:495–502, 1999a

Jäkälä P, Riekkinen M, Sirviö J, et al: Guanfacine, but not clonidine, improves planning and working memory performance in humans. Neuropsychopharmacology 20:460–470, 1999b

Jäkälä P, Sirviö J, Riekkinen M, et al: Guanfacine and clonidine, alpha2-agonists, improve paired associates learning, but not delayed matching to sample, in humans. Neuropsychopharmacology 20:119–130, 1999c

Jansen EN: Clozapine in the treatment of tremor in Parkinson's disease. Acta Neurol Scand 89:262–265, 1994

Jason GW, Suchowersky O, Pajurkova EM, et al: Cognitive manifestations of Huntington disease in relation to genetic structure and clinical onset. Arch Neurol 54:1081–1088, 1997

Jorge RE, Robinson RG, Starkstein SE, et al: Secondary mania following traumatic brain injury. Am J Psychiatry 150:916–921, 1993

Jouvent R, Absensour P, Bonnet AM, et al: Antiparkinsonian and antidepressant effects of high doses of bromocriptine: an independent comparison. J Affect Disord 5:141–145, 1983

Joyce JN: The dopamine hypothesis of schizophrenia: limbic interactions with serotonin and norepinephrine. Psychopharmacology (Berl) 112:S16–S34, 1993

Kalaria RN, Andorn AC, Tabaton M, et al: Adrenergic receptors in aging and Alzheimer's disease: increased receptors in prefrontal cortex and hippocampus. J Neurochem 53:1772–1781, 1989

Kampen DL, Sherwin BB: Estrogen use and verbal memory in healthy postmenopausal women. Obstet Gynecol 83:979–983, 1994

Katz IR, Jeste DV, Mintzer JE, et al: Comparison of risperidone and placebo for psychosis and behavioral disturbances associated with dementia: a randomized, double-blind trial. J Clin Psychiatry 60:107–115, 1999

Kaufer D, Cummings JL, Christine D: Differential neuropsychiatric symptom responses to tacrine in Alzheimer's disease: relationship to dementia severity. J Neuropsychiatry Clin Neurosci 10:55–63, 1998

Kaufman M, Cassem N, Murray G, et al: Use of psychostimulants in medically ill patients with neurologic disease and major depression. Can J Psychiatry 29:46–49, 1984

Kavoussi RJ, Coccaro EF: Divalproex sodium for impulsive aggressive behavior in patients with personality disorder. J Clin Psychiatry 59:676–680, 1998

Keck PE Jr, Pope HG Jr, Nierenberg AA: Autoinduction of hypertensive reactions by tranylcypromine? J Clin Psychopharmacol 9:48–51, 1989

Kegeles LS, Humaran TJ, Mann JJ: In vivo neurochemistry of the brain in schizophrenia as revealed by magnetic resonance spectroscopy. Biol Psychiatry 44:382–398, 1998

Kellner CH, Beale MD, Pritchett JT, et al: Electroconvulsive therapy and Parkinson's disease: the case for further study. Psychopharmacology Bulletin 30:495–500, 1994

Kim E, Zwil AS, McAllister TW, et al: Treatment of organic bipolar mood disorders in Parkinson's disease. J Neuropsychiatry Clin Neurosci 6:181–184, 1994

Kim KS, Pae CU, Chae JH, et al: An open pilot trial of olanzapine for delirium in the Korean population. Psychiatry Clin Neurosci 55(5):515–519, 2001

Kim SW: Opioid antagonists in the treatment of impulse-control disorders. J Clin Psychiatry 59:159–164, 1998

Kimbrell TA, George MS, Parekh PI, et al: Regional brain activity during transient self-induced anxiety and anger in healthy adults. Biol Psychiatry 46:454–465, 1999

King BH: Fluoxetine reduced self-injurious behavior in an adolescent with mental retardation. J Child Adolesc Psychopharmacol 1:321–329, 1991

Kirby M, Denihan A, Bruce I, et al: Benzodiazepine use among the elderly in the community. Int J Geriatr Psychiatry 14:280–284, 1999

Kirven LE, Montero EF: Comparison of thioridazine and diazepam in the control of nonpsychotic symptoms associated with senility: double-blind study. J Am Geriatr Soc 21:546–551, 1973

Klaassen T, Verhey FRJ, Sneijders GHJM, et al: Treatment of depression in Parkinson's disease: a meta-analysis. J Neuropsychiatry Clin Neurosci 7:281–286, 1995

Klein E, Uhde TW: Controlled study of verapamil for treatment of panic disorder. Am J Psychiatry 145:431–434, 1988

Knable MB, Rickler K: Psychosis associated with felbamate treatment. J Clin Psychopharmacol 15:292–293, 1995

Knapp MJ, Knopman DS, Solomon PR, et al: A 30-week randomized controlled trial of high dose tacrine in patients with Alzheimer's disease. JAMA 271:985–991, 1994

Knopman D, Schneider L, Davis K, et al: Long-term tacrine (Cognex) treatment: effects on nursing home placement and mortality. Neurology 47:166–177, 1996

Knopman D, Kahn J, Miles S: Clinical research designs for emerging treatments for Alzheimer disease. Arch Neurol 55:1425–1429, 1998

Koshes RJ, Rock NL: Use of clonidine for behavioral control in an adult patient with autism (letter). Am J Psychiatry 151:11, 1994

Kostic VS, Lecic D, Doder M, et al: Prolactin and cortisol responses to fenfluramine in Parkinson's disease. Biol Psychiatry 40:769–775, 1996

Kotrla KJ, Chacko RC, Harper RG, et al: SPECT findings on psychosis in Alzheimer's disease. Am J Psychiatry 152:1470–1475, 1995

Kubu CS, Grace GM, Parent AG: Cognitive outcome following pallidotomy: the influence of side of surgery and age of patient at disease outset. J Neurosurg 92:384–389, 2000

Kulkarni J, Horne M, Butler E, et al: Psychotic symptoms resulting from intraventricular infusion of dopamine in Parkinson's disease. Biol Psychiatry 31:1225–1227, 1992

Kunik ME, Yudofsky SC, Silver JM, et al: Pharmacologic approach to management of agitation associated with dementia. J Clin Psychiatry 55 (suppl):13–17, 1994

Kuzis G, Sabe L, Tiberti C, et al: Cognitive functions in major depression and Parkinson's disease. Arch Neurol 54:982–986, 1997

Kwan LT, Reed BR, Eberling JL, et al: Effects of subcortical cerebral infarction on cortical glucose metabolism and cognitive function. Arch Neurol 56:809–814, 1999

Kyomen HH, Satlin A, Hennen J, et al: Estrogen therapy and aggressive behavior in elderly patients with moderate-to-severe dementia: results from a short-term, randomized, double-blind trial. Am J Geriatr Psychiatry 7:339–348, 1999

La France WC, Lauterbach EC, Coffey CE, et al: The use of herbal alternative medicines in neuropsychiatry. J Neuropsychiatry Clin Neurosci 12:177–192, 2000

Laakso A, Vilkman H, Alakare B, et al: Striatal dopamine transporter binding in neuroleptic-naive patients with schizophrenia studied with positron emission tomography. Am J Psychiatry 157:269–271, 2000

Laitinen L: Desipramine in treatment of Parkinson's disease. Acta Neurol Scand 45:109–113, 1969

Lancon C, Auquier P, Nayt G, et al: Stability of the five-factor structure of the positive and negative syndrome scale. Schizophr Res 42:231–239, 2000

Lanctot KL, Herrmann N: Donepezil for behavioural disorders associated with Lewy bodies: a case series. Int J Geriatr Psychiatry 15:338–345, 2000

Lange KW, Riederer P: Glutamatergic drugs in Parkinson's disease. Life Sci 55:2067–2075, 1994

Lauterbach EC, Jackson JG, Price ST, et al: Clinical, motor, and biological correlates of depressive disorders after focal subcortical lesions. J Neuropsychiatry Clin Neurosci 9:259–266, 1997

Lavretsky H, Sultzer D: A structured trial of risperidone for the treatment of agitation in dementia. Am J Geriatr Psychiatry 6:127–135, 1998

Lawlor BA, Radcliffe H, Molchan SE, et al: A pilot placebo-controlled study of trazodone and buspirone in Alzheimer's disease. Int J Geriatr Psychiatry 9:55–59, 1994

Lawlor BA, Bierer LM, Ryan TM, et al: Plasma 3-methoxy-4-hydroxyphenylglycol (MHPG) and clinical symptoms in Alzheimer's disease. Biol Psychiatry 38:185–188, 1995

Lazarus LW, Moberg PJ, Langsley PR, et al: Methylphenidate and nortriptyline in the treatment of poststroke depression: a retrospective comparison. Arch Phys Med Rehabil 75:403–406, 1994

Le Bars PL, Katz MM, Berman N, et al: A placebo-controlled, double-blind, randomized trial of an extract of Ginkgo biloba for dementia. JAMA 278:1327–1332, 1997

Lebert F, Pasquier F, Petit H: Behavioral effects of fluoxetine in dementia of the Alzheimer type. International Journal of the Geriatric Society 9:590–591, 1994

Lecamwasam D, Synek B, Moyles K, et al: Chronic lithium neurotoxicity presenting as Parkinson's disease. Int Clin Psychopharmacol 9:127–129, 1994

Lee GP, Bechara A, Adolphs R, et al: Clinical and physiological effects of stereotaxic bilateral amygdalotomy for intractable aggression. J Neuropsychiatry Clin Neurosci 10:413–420, 1998

Lemke MR: Effect of carbamazepine on agitation in Alzheimer's inpatients refractory to neuroleptics. J Clin Psychiatry 56: 354–357, 1995

Leo RJ: Movement disorders associated with the serotonin selective reuptake inhibitors. J Clin Psychiatry 57:449–454, 1996

Lera G, Zirulnik J: Pilot study with clozapine in patients with HIV-associated psychosis and drug-induced parkinsonism. Mov Disord 14:128–131, 1999

Levine AM: Buspirone and agitation in head injury. Brain Inj 2:165–187, 1988

Levitan C, Ward PB, Catts SV: Superior temporal gyral volumes and laterality correlates of auditory hallucinations in schizophrenia. Biol Psychiatry 46:955–962, 1999

Levy MA: A trial of buspirone for the control of disruptive behaviors in community-dwelling patients with dementia. Int J Geriatr Psychiatry 9:841–848, 1994

Levy ML, Cummings JL, Fairbanks LA, et al: Apathy is not depression. J Neuropsychiatry Clin Neurosci 10:314–319, 1998

Linazasoro G, Martí-Massó JF, Suárez JA: Nocturnal akathisia in Parkinson's disease: treatment with clozapine. Mov Disord 8:171–174, 1993

Lindenmayer J-P, Kotsaftis A: Use of sodium valproate in violent and aggressive behaviors: a critical review. J Clin Psychiatry 61:123–128, 2000

Linnoila VMI, Virkkunen M: Aggression, suicidality, and serotonin. J Clin Psychiatry 53 (suppl 10):46–51, 1992

Lipsey JR, Robinson RG, Pearlson GD, et al: Nortriptyline treatment of post-stroke depression: a double-blind study. Lancet 8372:297–300, 1984

Lipton SA: Calcium channel antagonists and human immunodeficiency virus coat protein-mediated neuronal injury. Ann Neurol 30:110–114, 1991

Lopez OL, Becker JT, Brenner RP, et al: Alzheimer's disease with delusions and hallucinations: neuropsychological and electroencephalographic correlates. Neurology 41:906–912, 1991

Lott AD, McElroy SL, Keys MA: Valproate in the treatment of behavioral agitation in elderly patients with dementia. J Neuropsychiatry Clin Neurosci 7:314–319, 1995

Luchins DI: Carbamazepine in psychiatric syndromes: clinical and neuropharmacological perspectives. Psychopharmacology Bulletin 20:269–271, 1984

Lyketsos C: Assessment and management of mania in the HIV infected patient (abstract). Neuropsychopharmacology 10:401S, 1994

Lyketsos CG, Corazzini K, Steele CD, et al: Guidelines for the use of tacrine in Alzheimer's disease: clinical application and effectiveness. J Neuropsychiatry Clin Neurosci 8:67–73, 1996

Lyketsos CG, Treisman GJ, Lipsey JR, et al: Does stroke cause depression? J Neuropsychiatry Clin Neurosci 10:103–106, 1998

Lyketsos CG, Steele C, Galik E, et al: Physical aggression in dementia patients and its relationship to depression. Am J Psychiatry 156:66–71, 1999

Maelicke A, Samochocki M, Jostock R, et al: Allosteric sensitization of nicotinic receptors by galantamine, a new treatment strategy for Alzheimer's disease. Biol Psychiatry 49(3):279–288, 2001

Magai C, Kennedy G, Cohen CI, et al: A controlled clinical trial of sertraline in the treatment of depression in nursing home patients with late-stage Alzheimer's disease. Am J Geriatr Psychiatry 8:66–74, 2000

Malow BA, Reese KB, Sato S, et al: Spectrum of EEG abnormalities during clozapine treatment. Electroencephalogr Clin Neurophysiol 91:205–211, 1994

Mann DMA, Yates PO, Marcyniuk B: A comparison of changes in the nucleus basalis and locus ceruleus in Alzheimer's disease. J Neurol Neurosurg Psychiatry 47:201–203, 1984

Mann JJ: Violence and aggression, in Psychopharmacology: The Fourth Generation of Progress. Edited by Bloom FE, Kupfer DJ. New York, Raven, 1995, pp 1919–1928

Marin RS, Fogel BS, Hawkins J, et al: Apathy: a treatable syndrome. J Neuropsychiatry Clin Neurosci 7:23–30, 1995

Mark BZ, Kunkel EJS, Fabi MB, et al: Pimozide is effective in delirium secondary to hypercalcemia when other neuroleptics fail. Psychosomatics 34:446–449, 1993

Markowitz P: Effect of fluoxetine on self-injurious behavior in the developmentally disabled: a preliminary study. J Clin Pharmacol 12:27–31, 1992

Marshall EJ, Syed GM, Fenwick PB, et al: A pilot study of schizophrenia-like psychosis in epilepsy using single-photon emission computerised tomography. Br J Psychiatry 163:32–36, 1993

Martin PR, Adinoff B, Eckardt MJ, et al: Effective pharmaco-therapy of alcoholic amnestic disorder with fluvoxamine. Arch Gen Psychiatry 46:617–621, 1989

Martin PR, Adinoff B, Lane E, et al: Fluvoxamine treatment of alcoholic amnestic disorder. Eur Neuropsychopharmacol 5:27–33, 1995

Masand P, Murray GB, Pickett P: Psychostimulants in post-stroke depression. J Neuropsychiatry Clin Neurosci 3:23–27, 1991

Mashiko H, Yokoyama H, Matsumoto H, et al: Trazodone for aggression in an adolescent with hydrocephalus. J Neuropsychiatry Clin Neurosci 50:133–136, 1996

Mattes JA: Comparative effectiveness of carbamazepine and propranolol for rage outbursts. J Neuropsychiatry Clin Neurosci 2:159–164, 1990

Max JE, Robin DA, Lindgren SD, et al: Traumatic brain injury in children and adolescents: psychiatric disorders at one year. J Neuropsychiatry Clin Neurosci 10:290–297, 1998

Maxwell CJ, Hogan DB, Ebly EM: Calcium-channel blockers and cognitive function in elderly people: results from the Canadian Study of Health and Aging. Can Med Assoc J 161:501–506, 1999

Mayberg HS: Limbic-cortical dysregulation: a proposed model of depression. J Neuropsychiatry Clin Neurosci 9:471–481, 1997

Mayberg HS, Parikh RM, Morris PLP, et al: Spontaneous remission of post-stroke depression and temporal changes in cortical S2-serotonin receptors. J Neuropsychiatry Clin Neurosci 3:80–83, 1991

Mayeux R, Stern Y, Sano M, et al: The relationship of serotonin to depression in Parkinson's disease. Mov Disord 3:237–244, 1988

Mazure CM, Druss BG, Cellar JS: Valproate treatment of older psychotic patients with organic mental syndromes and behavioral dyscontrol. J Am Geriatr Soc 40:914–916, 1992

McAllister TW: Carbamazepine in mixed frontal lobe and psychiatric disorders. J Clin Psychiatry 46:393–394, 1985

McDaniel JS, Johnson KM: Obsessive-compulsive disorder in HIV disease: response to fluoxetine. Psychosomatics 36:147–150, 1995

McDonald WM, Tupler LA, Marsteller FA, et al: Hyperintense lesions on magnetic resonance images in bipolar disorder. Biol Psychiatry 45:965–971, 1999

McDougle CJ, Naylor ST, Cohen DJ, et al: A double-blind, placebo-controlled study of fluvoxamine in adults with autistic disorder. Arch Gen Psychiatry 53:1001–1008, 1996

McEntee WJ, Mair RG: The Korsakoff syndrome: a neurochemical perspective. Trends Neurosci 13:340–344, 1990

McFarland BH, Miller MR, Straumfjord AA: Valproate use in the older manic patients. J Clin Psychiatry 51:479–481, 1990

McKeith I, Del Ser T, Spano P, et al: Efficacy of rivastigmine in dementia with Lewy bodies: a randomised, double-blind, placebo-controlled international study. Lancet 356(9247): 2031–2036, 2000

Medalia A, Gold J, Merriam A: The effects of neuroleptics on neuropsychological test results of schizophrenics. Archives of Clinical Neuropsychology 3:249–271, 1988

Mega MS, Cummings JL: Frontal-subcortical circuits and neuropsychiatric disorders. J Neuropsychiatry Clin Neurosci 6:358–370, 1994

Mega MS, Masterman DM, O'Connor SM, et al: The spectrum of behavioral responses to cholinesterase inhibitor therapy in Alzheimer disease. Arch Neurol 56:1388–1393, 1999

Meltzer HY, Ranjan R: Valproic acid treatment of clozapine induced myoclonus. Am J Psychiatry 151:1246–1247, 1994

Mendez MF, Younesi FL, Perryman KM: Use of donepezil for vascular dementia: preliminary clinical experience. J Neuropsychiatry Clin Neurosci 11:268–270, 1999

Mendez MF, Chow T, Ringman J, et al: Pedophilia and temporal lobe disturbances. J Neuropsychiatry Clin Neurosci 12:71–76, 2000

Mentis MJ, Weinstein EA, Horwitz B, et al: Abnormal brain glucose metabolism in the delusional misidentification syndromes: a positron emission tomography study in Alzheimer disease. Biol Psychiatry 38:438–449, 1995

Meyer JM, Marsh J, Simpson G: Differential sensitivities to risperidone and olanzapine in a human immunodeficiency virus patient. Biol Psychiatry 44:791–794, 1998

Michals ML, Crismon ML, Roberts S, et al: Clozapine response and adverse effects in nine brain-injured patients. J Clin Psychopharmacol 13:198–203, 1993

Migliorelli R, Starkstein SE, Teson A, et al: SPECT findings in patients with primary mania. J Neuropsychiatry Clin Neurosci 5:379–383, 1993

Mijch AM, Judd FK, Lyketsos CG, et al: Secondary mania in patients with HIV infection: are antiretrovirals protective? J Neuropsychiatry Clin Neurosci 11:475–480, 1999

Miller BL, Darby A, Benson DF, et al: Aggressive, socially disruptive and antisocial behaviour associated with fronto-temporal dementia. Br J Psychiatry 170:150–155, 1997

Mintzer J, Brawman-Mintzer O, Mirski DF, et al: Fenfluramine challenge test as a marker of serotonin activity in patients with Alzheimer's dementia and agitation. Biol Psychiatry 44:918–921, 1998

Mobayed M, Dinan T: Buspirone/prolactin response in post head injury depression. J Affect Disord 19:237–241, 1990

Moffoot A, O'Carroll RE, Murray C, et al: Clonidine infusion increases uptake of 99mTc-exametazime in anterior cingulate cortex in Korsakoff's psychosis. Psychol Med 24:53–61, 1994

Mohr DC, Likosky W, Dwyer P, et al: Course of depression during the initiation of interferon beta-1a treatment for multiple sclerosis. Arch Neurol 56:1263–1265, 1999

Monteverde A, Gnemmi P, Rossi F, et al: Selegiline in the treatment of mild to moderate Alzheimer-type dementia. Clin Ther 12:315–322, 1990

Mooney GF, Haas LJ: Effect of methylphenidate on brain-related anger. Arch Phys Med Rehabil 74:153–160, 1993

Moore DP: A case of petit mal epilepsy aggravated by lithium. Am J Psychiatry 138:690–691, 1981

Morris PLP, Mayberg HS, Bolla K, et al: A preliminary study of cortical S2 serotonin receptors and cognitive performance following stroke. J Neuropsychiatry Clin Neurosci 5:395–400, 1993a

Morris PLP, Robinson RG, Andrzejewski P, et al: Association of depression with 10-year poststroke mortality. Am J Psychiatry 150:124–129, 1993b

Morris PL, Robinson RG, de Carvalho ML, et al: Lesion characteristics and depressed mood in the stroke data bank study. J Neuropsychiatry Clin Neurosci 8:153–159, 1996a

Morris PLP, Robinson RG, Raphael B, et al: Lesion location and poststroke depression. J Neuropsychiatry Clin Neurosci 8:399–403, 1996b

Mortel KF, Meyer JS: Lack of postmenopausal estrogen replacement therapy and the risk of dementia. J Neuropsychiatry Clin Neurosci 7:334–337, 1995

Moskowitz AS, Altshuler L: Increased sensitivity to lithium-induced neurotoxicity after stroke: a case report. J Clin Psychopharmacol 11:272–273, 1991

Mulnard RA, Cotman CW, Kawas C, et al: Estrogen replacement therapy for treatment of mild to moderate Alzheimer disease: a randomized controlled trial. JAMA 283:1007–1015, 2000

Murray AM, Weihmueller FB, Marshall JF, et al: Damage to dopamine systems differs between Parkinson's disease and Alzheimer's disease with parkinsonism. Ann Neurol 37:300–312, 1995

Musser WS, Akil M: Clozapine as a treatment for psychosis in Parkinson's disease: a review. J Neuropsychiatry Clin Neurosci 8:1–9, 1996

Myrick H, Brady KT, Malcolm R: Divalproex in the treatment of alcohol withdrawal. Am J Drug Alcohol Abuse 26:155–160, 2000

Mysiw WJ, Jackson RD, Corrigan JD: Amitriptyline for posttraumatic agitation. Am J Phys Med Rehabil 67:29–33, 1988

Nagasawa H, Kogure K, Kawashima K, et al: Effects of co-dergocrine mesylate (Hydergine) in multi-infarct dementia as evaluated by positron emission tomography. Tohoku J Exp Med 162:225–233, 1990

Nahas Z, Arlinghaus KA, Kotrla KJ, et al: Rapid response of emotional incontinence to selective serotonin reuptake inhibitors. J Neuropsychiatry Clin Neurosci 10:453–455, 1998

Narayan M, Nelson JC: Treatment of dementia with behavioral disturbance using divalproex or a combination of divalproex and a neuroleptic. J Clin Psychiatry 58:351–354, 1997

Newcomer JW, Faustman WO, Zipursky RB, et al: Zacopride in schizophrenia: a single-blind serotonin type 3 antagonist trial. Arch Gen Psychiatry 49:751–752, 1992

Newhouse PA, Porter A, Corwin J, et al: The potential for nicotinic modulation of cognitive and motor functioning in Parkinson's disease. Paper presented at the 4th Symposium on Neurodegenerative Disorders, Ocho Rios, Jamaica, February 23–28, 1997

Nitrini R, Rosemberg S: Psychotic symptoms in dementia associated with motor neuron disease: a pathophysiological hypothesis. J Neuropsychiatry Clin Neurosci 10:456–458, 1998

Nyth AL, Gottfries CG: The clinical efficacy of citalopram in treatment of emotional disturbances in dementia disorders: a Nordic multicentre study. Br J Psychiatry 157:894–901, 1990

Nyth AL, Gottfries CE, Lyby K, et al: A controlled multicenter clinical study of citalopram and placebo in elderly depressed patients with and without concomitant dementia. Acta Psychiatr Scand 86:138–145, 1992

Oh JJ, Rummans TA, O'Connor MK, et al: Cognitive impairment after ECT in patients with Parkinson's disease and psychiatric illness (letter). Am J Psychiatry 149:271, 1992

Oken BS, Storzbach DM, Kaye JA: The efficacy of Ginkgo biloba on cognitive function in Alzheimer disease. Arch Neurol 55:1409–1415, 1998

Olivier B, Mos J, Raghoebar M, et al: Serenics. Prog Drug Res 42:167–308, 1994

Olson SC, Bogerts B, Coffman JA: Medical temporal and ventricular abnormalities by MRI: comparing major psychoses. Biol Psychiatry 27:59A–60A, 1990

Ontiveros A, Fontaine R, Breton G, et al: Correlation of severity of panic disorder and neuroanatomical changes on magnetic resonance imaging. J Neuropsychiatry Clin Neurosci 1:404–408, 1989

Onuma T, Adachi N, Hisano T, et al: 10-year follow-up study of epilepsy with psychosis. Jpn J Psychiatry Neurol 45:360–361, 1991

Orengo CA, Kunik ME, Ghusn H, et al: Correlation of testosterone with aggression in demented elderly men. J Nerv Ment Dis 185:349–351, 1997

Owens F, Chambers D, Cooper S: Serotonergic mechanisms in the brains of suicide victims. Brain Res 362:185–188, 1986

Palsson S, Aevarsson O, Skoog I: Depression, cerebral atrophy, cognitive performance and incidence of dementia: population study of 85-year-olds. Br J Psychiatry 174:249–253, 1999

Paradiso S, Robinson RG, Arndt S: Self-reported aggressive behavior in patients with stroke. J Nerv Ment Dis 184:746–753, 1996

Parkinson Study Group: Low-dose clozapine for the treatment of drug-induced psychosis in Parkinson's disease. N Engl J Med 340:757–763, 1999

Parmelee DX, O'Shannick GH: Carbamazepine-lithium toxicity in brain damaged adolescents. Brain Inj 2:305–308, 1988

Parsa MA, Bastani B: Quetiapine (Seroquel) in the treatment of psychosis in patients with Parkinson's disease. J Neuropsychiatry Clin Neurosci 10:216–219, 1998

Parsa MA, Szigethy E, Voci JM, et al: Risperidone in treatment of choreoathetosis of Huntington's disease (letter). J Clin Psychopharmacol 17:134–135, 1997

Passik SD, Cooper M: Complicated delirium in a cancer patient successfully treated with olanzapine. J Pain Symptom Manage 17:219–223, 1999

Payne JL, Lyketsos CG, Steele C, et al: Relationship of cognitive and functional impairment to depressive features in Alzheimer's disease and other dementias. J Neuropsychiatry Clin Neurosci 10:440–447, 1998

Penn RD, Martin EM, Wilson RS, et al: Intraventricular bethanechol infusion for Alzheimer's disease: results of double-blind and escalating dose trials. Neurology 39:219–222, 1988

Perry EK, McKeith I, Thompson P, et al: Topography, extent, and clinical relevance of neurochemical deficits in dementia of Lewy body type, Parkinson's disease, and Alzheimer's disease. Ann N Y Acad Sci 640:197–202, 1991

Peterson K, Armstrong S, Moseley J: Pathologic crying responsive to treatment with sertraline (letter). Am J Psychiatry 152:953–954, 1995

Petracca G, Teson A, Chemerinski E, et al: A double-blind placebo-controlled study of clomipramine in depressed patients with Alzheimer's disease. J Neuropsychiatry Clin Neurosci 8:270–275, 1996

Petrides M, Alivisatos B, Meyer E, et al: Functional activation of the human frontal cortex during the performance of verbal working memory tasks. Proc Natl Acad Sci U S A 90:878–882, 1993

Petrie WM, Ban TA, Berney S, et al: Loxapine in psychogeriatrics: a placebo and standard controlled clinical investigation. J Clin Psychopharmacol 2:122–126, 1982

Pierelli F, Adipietro A, Soldati G, et al: Low dosage clozapine effects on L-dopa induced dyskinesias in parkinsonian patients. Acta Neurol Scand 97:295–299, 1998

Pinner AE, Rich C: Effects of trazodone on aggressive behavior in seven patients with organic mental disorders. Am J Psychiatry 145:1295–1296, 1988

Pollock BG, Mulsant BH, Sweet R, et al: An open pilot study of citalopram for behavioral disturbances of dementia: plasma levels and real-time observations. Am J Geriatr Psychiatry 5:70–78, 1997

Pomara N, Tun H, Deptula D, et al: ApoE-epsilon4 allele and susceptibility to drug-induced memory impairment in the elderly (letter). J Clin Psychopharmacol 18:179–181, 1998

Pope HG, McElroy SL, Satlin A, et al: Head injury, bipolar disorder, and response to valproate. Compr Psychiatry 29:34–38, 1988

Popli AP: Risperidone for the treatment of psychosis associated with neurosarcoidosis (letter). J Clin Psychopharmacol 17:132–133, 1997

Porsteinsson A, Tariot PN, Erb R, et al: An open trial of valproate for agitation in geriatric neuropsychiatric disorders. Am J Geriatr Psychiatry 5:344–351, 1997

Porsteinsson AP, Tariot PN, Erb R, et al: Placebo-controlled study of divalproex sodium for agitation in dementia. Am J Geriatr Psychiatry 9(1):58–66, 2001

Portegies P, de Gans J, Lange JM, et al: Declining incidence of AIDS dementia complex after introduction of zidovudine treatment. BMJ 299:819–821, 1989

Potter A, Corwin J, Lang J, et al: Acute effects of the selective nicotine agonist ABT-418 in Alzheimer's disease. Psychopharmacology (Berl) 142:334–342, 1999

Prigatano G: Personality disturbances associated with traumatic brain injury. J Consult Clin Psychol 60:360–368, 1992

Prince M, Rabe-Hesketh S, Brennan P: Do antiarthritic drugs decrease the risk for cognitive decline? An analysis based on data from the MRC Treatment Trial of Hypertension in Older Adults. Neurology 50:374–379, 1998

Qizilbash N, Whitehead A, Higgins J, et al: Cholinesterase inhibition for Alzheimer disease: a meta-analysis of the tacrine trials. JAMA 280:1777–1782, 1998

Rabkin JG, Rabkin R, Harrison W, et al: Effect of imipramine on mood and enumerative measures of immune status in depressed patients with HIV illness. Am J Psychiatry 151:516–523, 1994

Raffaele KC, Berardi A, Asthana S, et al: Effects of long-term continuous infusion of the muscarinic cholinergic agonist arecoline on verbal memory in dementia of the Alzheimer type. Psychopharmacology Bulletin 27:315–320, 1991

Raine A, Lencz T, Bihrle S, et al: Reduced prefrontal gray matter volume and reduced autonomic activity in antisocial personality disorder. Arch Gen Psychiatry 57:119–127, 2000

Raisman R, Cash R, Agid Y: Parkinson's disease: decreased density of 3H-imipramine and 3H-paroxetine binding sites in putamen. Neurology 36:556–560, 1986

Raji MA, Brady SR: Mirtazapine for treatment of depression and comorbidities in Alzheimer disease. Ann Pharmacother 35(9):1024–1027, 2001

Ramachandran G, Glickman L, Levenson J, et al: Incidence of extrapyramidal syndromes in AIDS patients and a comparison group of medically ill inpatients. J Neuropsychiatry Clin Neurosci 9:579–583, 1997

Ramasubbu R, Robinson RG, Flint AJ, et al: Functional impairment associated with acute poststroke depression: the Stroke Data Bank Study. J Neuropsychiatry Clin Neurosci 10:26–33, 1998

Ranen NG, Peyser CE, Folstein SE: ECT as a treatment for depression in Huntington's disease. J Neuropsychiatry Clin Neurosci 6:154–159, 1994

Ranen NG, Lipsey J, Treisman G, et al: Sertraline in the treatment of severe aggressiveness in Huntington's disease. J Neuropsychiatry Clin Neurosci 8:338–339, 1996

Rao N, Jellinek HM, Woolston DC: Agitation in closed head injury: haloperidol effects on rehabilitation outcome. Arch Phys Med Rehabil 66:30–34, 1985

Raskind MA: Geriatric psychopharmacology: management of late-life depression and the noncognitive behavioral disturbances of Alzheimer's disease. Psychopharmacology (Berl) 16:815–827, 1993

Raskind MA, Peskind ER: Neurobiologic bases of noncognitive behavioral problems in Alzheimer disease. Alzheimer Dis Assoc Disord 8 (suppl 3):54–60, 1994

Raskind MA, Peskind ER, Holmes C, et al: Patterns of cerebrospinal fluid catechols support increased central noradrenergic responsiveness in aging and Alzheimer's disease. Biol Psychiatry 46:756–765, 1999

Rasmusson DX, Dal Forno G, Brandt J, et al: Apo-E genotype and verbal deficits in Alzheimer's disease. J Neuropsychiatry Clin Neurosci 8:335–337, 1996

Ratey JJ, Sovner R, Parks A, et al: Buspirone treatment of aggression and anxiety in mentally retarded patients: a multiple-baseline, placebo lead in study. J Clin Psychiatry 52:159–162, 1991a

Ratey JJ, Sovner R, Parks A, et al: The use of buspirone in the treatment of aggression and anxiety in mentally retarded patients. J Clin Psychiatry 52:159–162, 1991b

Ratey JJ, Leveroni CL, Miller AC, et al: Low-dose buspirone to treat agitation and maladaptive behavior in brain-injured patients: two case reports. J Clin Psychopharmacol 12:362–364, 1992a

Ratey JJ, Sorgi P, O'Driscoll GA, et al: Nadolol to treat aggression and psychiatric symptomatology in chronic psychiatric inpatients: a double-blind, placebo-controlled study. J Clin Psychiatry 53:41–46, 1992b

Reding MJ, Orto LA, Winter SW, et al: Antidepressant therapy after stroke: a double-blind trial. Arch Neurol 43:763–765, 1986

Reifler BV, Teri L, Raskind M, et al: Double blind trial of imipramine in Alzheimer's disease patients with and without depression. Am J Psychiatry 146:45–49, 1989

Reith J, Benkelfat C, Sherwin A, et al: Elevated dopa decarboxylase activity in living brain of patients with psychosis. Proc Natl Acad Sci U S A 91:11651–11654, 1994

Rich JB, Rasmusson DX, Folstein MF, et al: Nonsteroidal anti-inflammatory drugs in Alzheimer's disease. Neurology 45:51–55, 1995

Riekkinen P Jr, Riekkinen M: THA improves word priming and clonidine enhances fluency and working memory in Alzheimer's disease. Neuropsychopharmacology 20:357–364, 1999

Rifkin A, Quitkin F, Klein D: Akinesia: a poorly recognized drug-induced extrapyramidal behavioral disorder. Arch Gen Psychiatry 32:672–674, 1975

Rinne JO: Neuronal loss in the substantia nigra in patients with Alzheimer's disease and Parkinson's disease in relation to extrapyramidal symptoms and dementia. Prog Clin Biol Res 317:325–332, 1989

Rinne T, Westenberg HGM, den Boer JA, et al: Serotonergic blunting to meta-chlorophenylpiperazine (m-CPP) highly correlates with sustained childhood abuse in impulsive and autoaggressive female borderline patients. Biol Psychiatry 47:548–556, 2000

Risse SC, Cubberly Z, Lawpe JH, et al: Acute effects of neuroleptic withdrawal in elderly dementia patients. Journal of Geriatric Drug Therapy 2:65–67, 1987

Roane DM, Feinberg TE, Meckler L, et al: Treatment of dementia-associated agitation with gabapentin. J Neuropsychiatry Clin Neurosci 12:40–43, 2000

Roberts GW, Done DJ, Bruton C, et al: A "mock up" of schizophrenia: temporal lobe epilepsy and schizophrenia-like psychosis. Biol Psychiatry 28:127–143, 1990

Robinson RG, Starkstein SE: Mood disorders following stroke: new findings and future directions. J Geriatr Psychiatry 22:1–15, 1989

Robinson RG, Parikh RM, Lipsey JR, et al: Pathological laughing and crying following stroke: validation of a measurement scale and a double-blind treatment study. Am J Psychiatry 150:290–291, 1993

Robinson RG, Schultz SK, Castillo C, et al: Nortriptyline versus fluoxetine in the treatment of depression and in short-term recovery after stroke: a placebo-controlled, double-blind study. Am J Psychiatry 157:351–359, 2000

Rogers J, Kirby LC, Hempelman SR, et al: Clinical trial of indomethacin in Alzheimer's disease. Neurology 43:1609–1611, 1993

Rogers SL, Farlow MR, Doody RS, et al: A 24-week, double-blind, placebo-controlled trial of donepezil in patients with Alzheimer's disease. Donepezil Study Group. Neurology 50(1):136–145, 1998

Rogers SL, Doody RS, Pratt RD, et al: Long-term efficacy and safety of donepezil in the treatment of Alzheimer's disease: final analysis of a US multicentre open-label study. Eur Neuropsychopharmacol 10(3):195–203, 2000

Ron MA, Logsdail SJ: Psychiatric morbidity in multiple sclerosis: a clinical and MRI study. Psychol Med 19:887–895, 1989

Rösler M, Retz W, Retz-Junginger P, et al: Effects of two-year treatment with the cholinesterase inhibitor rivastigmine on behavioural symptoms in Alzheimer's disease. Behav Neurol 11(4):211–216, 1998

Rösler M, Anand R, Cicin-Sain A, et al: Efficacy and safety of rivastigmine in patients with Alzheimer's disease: international randomised controlled trial. BMJ 318:633–640, 1999

Rosse RB, Riggs RL, Dietrich AM, et al: Frontal cortical atrophy and negative symptoms in patients with chronic alcohol dependence. J Neuropsychiatry Clin Neurosci 9:280–282, 1997

Roth AS, Ostroff RB, Hoffman RE: Naltrexone as a treatment for repetitive self-injurious behavior: an open-label trial. J Clin Psychiatry 57:233–237, 1996

Roth M, Mountjoy CQ, Amrein R, et al: Moclobemide in elderly patients with cognitive decline and depression: an international double-blind, placebo-controlled trial. Br J Psychiatry 168:149–157, 1996

Roy-Byrne P, Cowley DS: Clinical approach to treatment-resistant panic disorder, in Panic Disorder and Its Treatment. Edited by Rosenbaum JF, Pollack MH. New York: Marcel Dekker, 1998, pp 207–227

Rudorfer MU, Manji HK, Potter WZ: ECT and delirium in Parkinson's disease. Am J Psychiatry 149:1758–1759, 1992

Ruedrich SL: Beta adrenergic blocking medications for treatment of rage outbursts in mentally retarded persons. Semin Clin Neuropsychiatry 1:115–121, 1996

Ruedrich S, Swales TP, Fossaceca C, et al: Effect of divalproex sodium on aggression and self-injurious behaviour in adults with intellectual disability: a retrospective review. J Intellect Disabil Res 43:105–111, 1999

Russouw HG, Roberts MC, Emsley RA, et al: Psychiatric manifestations and magnetic resonance imaging in HIV-negative neurosyphilis. Biol Psychiatry 47:467–473, 1997

Sabatini U, Pozzilli C, Pantano P, et al: Involvement of the limbic system in multiple sclerosis patients with depressive disorders. Biol Psychiatry 39:970–975, 1996

Sachdev P: Schizophrenia-like psychosis and epilepsy: the status of the association. Am J Psychiatry 155:325–336, 1998

Sacristan JA, Iglesias C, Arellano F, et al: Absence seizures induced by lithium: possible interaction with fluoxetine. Am J Psychiatry 148:146–147, 1991

Sakauye KM, Camp CJ, Ford PA: Effects of buspirone on agitation associated with dementia. Am J Geriatr Psychiatry 1:82–84, 1993

Salloway SP: Diagnosis and treatment of patients with "frontal lobe" syndromes. J Neuropsychiatry Clin Neurosci 6:388–398, 1994

Salzman C: Treatment of the elderly agitated patient. J Clin Psychiatry 48 (suppl 5):19–21, 1987

Salzman C: Use of benzodiazepines to control disruptive behavior in inpatients. J Clin Psychiatry 49 (suppl 12):13–15, 1988

Salzman C, Fisher J, Nobel K, et al: Cognitive improvement following benzodiazepine discontinuation in elderly nursing home residents. Int J Geriatr Psychiatry 7:89–93, 1992

Sanders JF: Evaluation of oxazepam and placebo in emotionally disturbed aged patients. Geriatrics 20:739–746, 1965

Sanders KM, Murray GB, Cassem NH: High-dose intravenous haloperidol for agitated delirium in a cardiac patient on intra-aortic balloon pump. J Clin Psychopharmacol 11:146–147, 1991

Sano M, Ernesto C, Thomas RG, et al: A controlled trial of selegiline, alpha-tocopherol, or both as treatment for Alzheimer's disease. N Engl J Med 336:1216–1222, 1997

Saran AS: Depression after minor closed head injury: role of dexamethasone suppression test and antidepressants. J Clin Psychiatry 46:335–338, 1985

Saxena S, Mallikarjuna P: Severe memory impairment with acute overdose lithium toxicity: a case report. Br J Psychiatry 152: 853–854, 1988

Scharf S, Mander A, Ugoni A, et al: A double-blind, placebo-controlled trial of diclofenac/misoprostol in Alzheimer's disease. Neurology 53:197–201, 1999

Schatzberg AE, Nemeroff CB: The American Psychiatric Press Textbook of Psychopharmacology, 2nd Edition. Washington, DC, American Psychiatric Press, 1998

Schiffer RB, Wineman NM: Antidepressant pharmacotherapy of depression associated with multiple sclerosis. Am J Psychiatry 147:1493–1497, 1990

Schiffer RB, Herndon RM, Rudick RA: Treatment of pathologic laughing and weeping with amitriptyline. N Engl J Med 312:1480–1482, 1985

Schneider LS, Olin JT: Overview of clinical trials of hydergine in dementia. Arch Neurol 51:787–798, 1994

Schneider LS, Pollock VE, Zemansky MF, et al: A pilot study of low dose L-deprenyl in Alzheimer's disease. J Geriatr Psychiatry Neurol 4:143–148, 1991

Schneider LS, Olin JT, Pawluczyk S: A double-blind crossover pilot study of L-deprenyl (selegiline) combined with cholinesterase inhibitor in Alzheimer's disease. Am J Psychiatry 150:321–323, 1993

Schneider LS, Farlow MR, Pogoda JM: Potential role for estrogen replacement in the treatment of Alzheimer's dementia. Am J Med 103:46S–50S, 1997

Schreiber S, Klag E, Gross Y, et al: Beneficial effect of risperidone on sleep disturbance and psychosis following traumatic brain injury. Int Clin Psychopharmacol 13:273–275, 1998

Schwartz BL, Hashtroudi S, Herting RL, et al: Glycine prodrug facilitates memory retrieval in humans. Neurology 41: 341–1343, 1991

Scott TF, Allen D, Price TRP, et al: Characterization of major depression symptoms in multiple sclerosis patients. J Neuropsychiatry Clin Neurosci 8:318–323, 1996

Selemon LD, Goldman-Rakic PS: The reduced neuropil hypothesis: a circuit based model of schizophrenia. Biol Psychiatry 45:17–25, 1999

Seliger GM, Hornstein A, Flax J, et al: Fluoxetine improves emotional incontinence. Brain Inj 6:267–270, 1992

Sewell DD, Jeste DV, Atkinson JH, et al: HIV-associated psychosis: a study of 20 cases. Am J Psychiatry 151:237–242, 1994a

Sewell DD, Jeste DV, McAdams LA, et al: Neuroleptic treatment of HIV-associated psychosis. Neuropsychopharmacology 10:223–229, 1994b

Shapiro RM: Regional neuropathology in schizophrenia: where are we? where are we going? Schizophr Res 10:187–239, 1993

Shaywitz BA, Shaywitz SE: Estrogen and Alzheimer disease: plausible theory, negative clinical trial. JAMA 283:1055–1056, 2000

Shikiar R, Shakespeare A, Sagnier P-P, et al: The impact of metrifonate therapy on caregivers of patients with Alzheimer's disease: results from the MALT clinical trial. J Am Geriatr Soc 48:268–274, 2000

Shimoda K, Robinson RG: Effect of anxiety disorder on impairment and recovery from stroke. J Neuropsychiatry Clin Neurosci 10:34–40, 1998

Silver JM, Yudofsky SC, Slater JA, et al: Propranolol treatment of chronically hospitalized aggressive patients. J Neuropsychiatry Clin Neurosci 11:328–335, 1999

Simpson DM, Foster D: Improvement in organically disturbed behavior with trazodone treatment. J Clin Psychiatry 47:191–193, 1986

Simpson S, Baldwin RC, Jackson A, et al: The differentiation of DSM-III-R psychotic depression in later life from nonpsychotic depression: comparisons of brain changes measured by multispectral analysis of magnetic resonance brain images, neuropsychological findings, and clinical features. Biol Psychiatry 45:193–204, 1999

Singh AN, Golledge H, Catalan J: Treatment of HIV-related psychotic disorders with risperidone: a series of 21 cases. J Psychosom Res 42:489–493, 1997

Sipahimalani A, Masand PS: Treatment of delirium with risperidone. International Journal of Geriatric Psychopharmacology 1:24–26, 1997a

Sipahimalani A, Masand PS: Use of risperidone in delirium: case reports. Ann Clin Psychiatry 9:105–107, 1997b

Sipahimalani A, Masand PS: Olanzapine in the treatment of delirium. Psychosomatics 39:422–430, 1998

Sloan RL, Brown KW, Pentland B: Fluoxetine as a treatment for emotional lability after brain injury. Brain Inj 6:315–319, 1992

Slooter AJ, Bronzova J, Witteman JC, et al: Estrogen use and early onset Alzheimer's disease: a population-based study. J Neurol Neurosurg Psychiatry 67:779–781, 1999

Sobin P, Schneider L, McDermott H: Fluoxetine in the treatment of agitated dementia (letter). Am J Psychiatry 146:1636, 1989

Soloff PH, Meltzer CC, Greer PJ, et al: A fenfluramine-activated FDG-PET study of borderline personality disorder. Biol Psychiatry 47:540–547, 2000

Sonne S, Rubey R, Brady K, et al: Naltrexone treatment of self-injurious thoughts and behaviors. J Nerv Ment Dis 184:192–195, 1996

Sovner R: The use of valproate in the treatment of mentally retarded persons with typical and atypical bipolar disorders. J Clin Psychiatry 50 (suppl):40–43, 1989

Spiers P, Myers D, Hochanadel G, et al: Citicoline improves verbal memory in aging. Arch Neurol 53:441–448, 1996

Squire LR, Zola-Morgan S: The medial temporal lobe memory system. Science 253:1380–1386, 1991

Starkstein SE, Migliorelli R: ECT in a patient with frontal craniotomy and residual meningioma. J Neuropsychiatry Clin Neurosci 5:428–430, 1993

Starkstein SE, Robinson RG: Mechanism of disinhibition after brain lesions. J Nerv Ment Dis 185:108–114, 1997

Starkstein SE, Cohen BS, Federoff P, et al: Relationship between anxiety disorders and depressive disorders in patients with cerebrovascular injury. Arch Gen Psychiatry 47:246–251, 1990

Starkstein SE, Fedoroff JP, Berthier ML, et al: Manic-depressive and pure manic states after brain lesions. Br J Psychiatry 29:149–158, 1991

Starkstein SE, Migliorelli R, Tesón A, et al: The specificity of cerebral blood flow changes in patients with frontal lobe dementia. J Neurol Neurosurg Psychiatry 57:790–796, 1994

Strang RR: Imipramine in treatment of parkinsonism: a double-blind placebo study. BMJ 2:33–34, 1965

Strauss ME, Lee MM, DiFilippo JM: Premorbid personality and behavioral symptoms in Alzheimer's disease: some cautions. Arch Neurol 54:257–259, 1997

Street JS, Clark WS, Gannon KS, et al: Olanzapine treatment of psychotic and behavioral symptoms in patients with Alzheimer disease in nursing care facilities: a double-blind, randomized, placebo-controlled trial. The HGEU Study Group. Arch Gen Psychiatry 57(10):968–976, 2000

Stuppaeck CH, Pycha R, Miller C, et al: Carbamazepine versus oxazepam in the treatment of alcohol withdrawal: a double-blind study. Alcohol Alcohol 27:153–158, 1992

Sultzer DL, Gray KF, Gunay I, et al: A double-blind comparison of trazodone and haloperidol for treatment of agitation in patients with dementia. Am J Geriatr Psychiatry 5:60–69, 1997

Sunderland T, Merril CR, Harrington MG, et al: Reduced plasma dehydroepiandrosterone concentrations in Alzheimer's disease (letter). Lancet 2:570, 1989

Suzuki M, Yuasa S, Minabe Y, et al: Left superior temporal blood flow increases in schizophrenic and schizophreniform patients with auditory hallucination: a longitudinal case study using 123I-IMP SPECT. Eur Arch Psychiatry Clin Neurosci 242:257–261, 1993

Swanson JW, Holzer CE, Ganju VK, et al: Violence and psychiatric disorder in the community: evidence from the Epidemiologic Catchment Area surveys. Hospital and Community Psychiatry 41:761–770, 1990

Swartz BE, Halgren E, Simpkins F, et al: Primary or working memory in frontal lobe epilepsy: an 18FDG-PET study of dysfunctional zones. Neurology 46:737–747, 1996

Swartz JR, Miller BL, Lesser IM, et al: Frontotemporal dementia: treatment response to serotonin selective reuptake inhibitors. J Clin Psychiatry 58:212–216, 1997

Sweet RA, Nimgaonkar VL, Kamboh MI, et al: Dopamine receptor genetic variation, psychosis, and aggression in Alzheimer disease. Arch Neurol 55:1335–1340, 1998

Tallian KB, Nahata MC, Lo W, et al: Gabapentin associated with aggressive behavior in pediatric patients with seizures. Epilepsia 37:501–502, 1996

Tandberg E, Larson JP, Aarsland D, et al: Risk factors for depression in Parkinson disease. Arch Neurol 54:625–630, 1997

Taragano FE, Lyketsos CG, Mangone CA, et al: A double-blind, randomized, fixed-dose trial of fluoxetine vs amitriptyline in the treatment of major depression complicating Alzheimer's disease. Psychosomatics 38:246–252, 1997

Targum SD, Abbott JL: Efficacy of quetiapine in Parkinson's patients with psychosis. J Clin Psychopharmacol 20:54–60, 2000

Tariot PN, Erb R, Podgorski CA, et al: Efficacy and tolerability of carbamazepine for agitation and aggression in dementia. Am J Psychiatry 155:54–61, 1998a

Tariot PN, Goldstein B, Podgorski CA, et al: Short-term administration of selegiline for mild-to-moderate dementia of the Alzheimer's type. Am J Geriatr Psychiatry 6:145–154, 1998b

Tennant FS, Wild J: Naltrexone treatment for postconcussional syndrome. Am J Psychiatry 144:813–814, 1987

Tesar GE, Murray GB, Cassem NH: Use of high-dose intravenous haloperidol in the treatment of agitated cardiac patients. J Clin Psychopharmacol 5:344–347, 1985

Thal LJ, Schwartz G, Sano M, et al: A multicenter double-blind study of controlled-release physostigmine for the treatment of symptoms secondary to Alzheimer's disease. Neurology 47:1389–1395, 1996

Thompson TL, Filley CM, Mitchell WD, et al: Lack of efficacy of hydergine in patients with Alzheimer's disease. N Engl J Med 323:445–448, 1990

Tiller JG: Short-term buspirone treatment in disinhibition with dementia (letter). Lancet 1:1169, 1989

Tollefson GD: Short-term effects of the calcium channel blocker nimodipine (bay-e 9736) in the management of primary degenerative dementia. Biol Psychiatry 27:1133–1142, 1990

Tollefson GD, Greist JH, Jefferson JW, et al: Is baseline agitation a relative contraindication for a selective serotonin reuptake inhibitor: a comparative trial of fluoxetine versus imipramine. J Clin Psychopharmacol 14:385–391, 1994

Tonkonogy JM: Violence and temporal lobe lesion: head CT and MRI data. J Neuropsychiatry Clin Neurosci 3:189–196, 1991

Torack RM, Morris JC: The association of ventral tegmental area histopathology with adult dementia. Arch Neurol 45:211–218, 1988

Trachman SB: Buspirone-induced psychosis in a human immunodeficiency virus–infected man. Psychosomatics 33:332–335, 1992

Tsai GE, Falk WE, Gunther J, et al: Improved cognition in Alzheimer's disease with short-term D-cycloserine treatment. Am J Psychiatry 156:470–473, 1999

Tsai WC, Lai JS, Wang TG: Treatment of emotionalism with fluoxetine during rehabilitation. Scand J Rehabil Med 30:145–149, 1998

Tune L, Carr S, Hoag E, et al: Anticholinergic effects of drugs commonly prescribed for the elderly: potential means for assessing risk of delirium. Am J Psychiatry 149:1393–1394, 1992

Tyor WR, Glass JD, Griffin JW, et al: Cytokine expression in the brain during the acquired immunodeficiency syndrome. Ann Neurol 31:349–360, 1992

van Dyck CH, McMahon TJ, Rosen MI, et al: Sustained-release methylphenidate for cognitive impairment in HIV-1–infected drug abusers: a pilot study. J Neuropsychiatry Clin Neurosci 9:29–36, 1997

van Dyck CH, Newhouse P, Falk WE, et al: Extended-release physostigmine in Alzheimer disease: a multicenter, double-blind, 12-week study with dose enrichment. Arch Gen Psychiatry 57:157–164, 2000

Van Reekum R, Bayley M, Garner S, et al: N of 1 study: amantadine for the amotivation syndrome in patient with traumatic brain injury. Brain Inj 9:49–53, 1995

van Vugt JP, Siesling S, Vergeer M, et al: Clozapine versus placebo in Huntington's disease: a double blind randomised comparative study. J Neurol Neurosurg Psychiatry 63:35–39, 1997

Van Woerkom TC, Teelken AW, Minderhous JM: Difference in neurotransmitter metabolism in frontotemporal lobe contusion and diffuse cerebral contusion. Lancet 1:812–813, 1977

Verhoeven WM, Tuinier S: The effect of buspirone on challenging behaviour in mentally retarded patients: an open prospective multiple-case study. J Intellect Disabil Res 40:502–508, 1996

Victoroff J, Zarow C, Mack W, et al: Physical aggression is associated with preservation of substantia nigra pars compacta in Alzheimer's disease. Arch Neurol 53:428–434, 1996

Walker Z, Grace J, Overshot R, et al: Olanzapine in dementia with Lewy bodies: a clinical study. Int J Geriatr Psychiatry 14:459–466, 1999

Weilburg JB, Schachter S, Worth J, et al: EEG abnormalities in patients with atypical panic attacks. J Clin Psychiatry 56:358–362, 1995

Weiler PG, Mungas D, Bernick C: Propranolol for the control of disruptive behavior in senile dementia. J Geriatr Psychiatry Neurol 1:226–30, 1988

Weinshenker BG, Penman M, Bass B, et al: A double-blind, randomized, crossover trial of pemoline in fatigue associated with multiple sclerosis. Neurology 42:1468–1471, 1992

Weitzner MA, Meyers CA, Valentine AD: Methylphenidate in the treatment of neurobehavioral slowing associated with cancer and cancer treatment. J Neuropsychiatry Clin Neurosci 7:347–350, 1995

Welch J, Manschreck T, Redmond D: Clozapine-induced seizures and EEG changes. J Neuropsychiatry Clin Neurosci 6:250–256, 1994

White JC, Christensen JF, Singer CM: Methylphenidate as a treatment for depression in acquired immunodeficiency syndrome: an n-of-1 trial. J Clin Psychiatry 53:153–156, 1992

Wilcock GK, Lilienfeld S, Gaens E: Efficacy and safety of galantamine in patients with mild to moderate Alzheimer's disease: multicentre randomised controlled trial. Galantamine International-1 Study Group. BMJ 321(7274): 1445–1449, 2000

Wilkie FL, Goodkin K, Eisdorfer C, et al: Mild cognitive impairment and risk of mortality in HIV-1 infection. J Neuropsychiatry Clin Neurosci 10:125–132, 1998

Wilkinson D, Murray J: Galantamine: a randomized, double-blind, dose comparison in patients with Alzheimer's disease. Int J Geriatr Psychiatry 16(9):852–857, 2001

Willemsen-Swinkels S, Buitelaar JK, Nijof GJ, et al: Failure of naltrexone hydrochloride to reduce self-injurious and autistic behavior in mentally retarded. Arch Gen Psychiatry 52:766–773, 1995

Williams JB, Rabkin JG, Remieu RH, et al: Multidisciplinary baseline assessment of homosexual men with and without HIV infection: standardized clinical assessment of current and lifetime psychopathology. Arch Gen Psychiatry 48: 124–130, 1991

Wolters EC, Jansen EN, Tuynman-Qua HG, et al: Olanzapine in the treatment of dopaminomimetic psychosis in patients with Parkinson's disease. Neurology 47:1085–1087, 1996

Wong SE, Woolsey JE, Innocent AJ, et al: Behavioral treatment of violent psychiatric patients. Psychiatr Clin North Am 11:569–580, 1988

Workman RH Jr, Orengo CA, Bakey AA, et al: The use of risperidone for psychosis and agitation in demented patients with Parkinson's disease. J Neuropsychiatry Clin Neurosci 9:594–597, 1997

Wroblewski BA, McColgan K, Smith K, et al: The incidence of seizures during tricyclic antidepressant drug treatment in a brain-injured population. J Clin Psychopharmacol 10:124–125, 1990

Wroblewski BA, Leary JM, Phelan AM, et al: Methylphenidate and seizure frequency in brain injured patients with seizure disorders. J Clin Psychiatry 53:86–89, 1992

Wroblewski BA, Joseph AB, Cornblatt RR: Antidepressant pharmacotherapy and the treatment of depression in patients with severe traumatic brain injury: a controlled, prospective study. J Clin Psychiatry 57:582–587, 1996

Wroblewski BA, Joseph AB, Kupfer J, et al: Effectiveness of valproic acid on destructive and aggressive behaviours in patients with acquired brain injury. Brain Inj 11:37–47, 1997

Yatham LN, McHale PA: Carbamazepine in the treatment of aggression: a case report and a review of the literature. Acta Psychiatr Scand 78:188–190, 1988

Yeung PP, Mintzer JE, Mullen JA, et al: Extrapyramidal symptoms in elderly outpatients treated with either quetiapine or risperidone. Paper presented at Annual Meeting of the American College of Neuropsychopharmacology, Acapulco, Mexico, December 12–16, 1999

Young CR, Weiss EL, Bowers MB Jr, et al: The differential diagnosis of multiple sclerosis and bipolar disorder (letter). J Clin Psychiatry 58:3, 1997

Yudofsky SC, Silver JM, Jackson W, et al: The Overt Aggression Scale for the objective rating of verbal and physical aggression. Am J Psychiatry 143:35–39, 1986

Yudofsky SC, Silver JM, Schneider SE: Pharmacologic treatment of aggression. Psychiatric Annals 17:397–407, 1987

Zimnitzky BM, DeMaso DR, Steingard RJ: Use of risperidone in psychotic disorder following ischemic brain damage. J Child Adolesc Psychopharmacol 6:75–78, 1996

Zisook S, Peterkin J, Goggin KJ, et al: Treatment of major depression in HIV-seropositive men. J Clin Psychiatry 59: 217–224, 1998

Zoldan J, Friedberg G, Livneh M, et al: Psychosis in advanced Parkinson's disease. Neurology 45:1305–1308, 1995

Zubenko GS, Moossy J: Major depression in primary dementia. Arch Neurol 45:1182–1186, 1988

Zubenko GS, Moossy J, Kopp U: Neurochemical correlates of major depression in primary dementia. Arch Neurol 47:209–214, 1990

Zubenko GS, Moossy J, Martinez AJ, et al: Neuropathologic and neurochemical correlates of psychosis in primary dementia. Arch Neurol 48:619–624, 1991

Zubieta JK, Alessi NE: Acute and chronic administration of trazodone in the treatment of disruptive behavior disorders in children. J Clin Psychopharmacol 12:346–351, 1992

# CHAPTER 36

# Psychotherapy for Patients With Neuropsychiatric Disorders

David V. Forrest, M.D.

John Nemiah (1973, p. 4) stated that "to see into the mind of another, we must repeatedly immerse ourselves in the flood of his associations and feelings; we must be ourselves the instrument that sounds him." Nadelson (1996, p. 7), citing Nemiah, noted that "evolution and civilization mutually enfold the human ability to resonate to the anguish of others…a species altruism directed toward repair of human problems is coupled with the skills of affectively linked 'deep thinking.' There is a continuing marginalization of such efforts, which now need to be cared for deeply." Compromised medical care organizations currently not only marginalize and limit empathic care but also tend to deprive patients of their first and foremost asset in responding to the challenge of illness: the sense of control of their own care. While this aggravates morale in all illnesses, neuropsychiatric patients are especially threatened by losses of control because, as this chapter shows, their conditions so typically and devastatingly impair control.

As crucial as empathy is, or an awareness of the intersubjective relatedness of the minds of physician and patient, in neuropsychiatry these must be expertly informed by the knowledge of the natural and pathologic processes of the brain. Just as contact with patients with gross neurologic impairment helps us assess neurologic abnormalities in psychiatric patients, so, too, can familiarity with the needs of more impaired psychiatric patients—especially those with schizophrenia, organic mental disorders, and substance use disorders—help us frame a psychotherapeutic approach that is tailored to the cognitive and affective needs of patients with neurologic disorders.

Many of the same mechanisms overlap in neurologic and psychiatric conditions. Woods and Short (1985) found that 50% of 270 newly admitted patients with major psychiatric disorders had neurologic abnormalities, and Schiffer (1983) established psychiatric diagnoses in 41.9% of 241 neurology patients. Thus, in formulating an approach to neuropsychiatry, empathic medical psychotherapy techniques must be adapted to the specific neurologic features of the patient.

## Psychodynamic Aspects of the Mental Examination

Structured examinations and formal neuropsychologic testing do not bring out the information necessary to formulate a comprehensive treatment plan and only hint at the difficulties that will be encountered as the psychiatrist adjusts the treatment to an individual's treatment course. At some point, the checklist is set aside, and a shift is made to a psychodynamically oriented interview with ample open-ended questions that will enable the psychiatrist to appreciate each patient's unique personality and affective qualities. Such an interview should provide an understanding of the hereditary, constitutional, developmental, experiential, and interpersonal contributions to the formation of personality structure and the major traumata and conflicts the patient has encountered along the way. The effect of the illness is assessed similarly and placed in the context of the person's longitudinal history. The psychiatrist goes beyond assessing the elements of function, as in physical medicine, and is interested in the operational aspects of how the patient will fare while at home and/or at work, as in rehabilitation medicine.

The administration of any structured mental examination marks a shift away from a psychotherapeutic relatedness to the patient toward an evaluative mode that always has a distancing effect and sometimes is experienced as threatening by the patient. The analogy to the physical examination is not complete because the patient's very ability to make sense of the proceedings is being questioned. This is a time for warmth and reassurance on the part of the examiner, which pays the scientific dividend of eliciting the patient's best performance. The patient may experience emotions as strong as self-loathing and humiliation, depending on the deficits involved and the degree of investment in the integrity of those functions.

The examining psychiatrist must ensure that a methodical approach is not mistaken by the patient for scorn and must avoid a smug supplying of the correct answers, which could be taken for an air of superiority. Seemingly "playing to the crowd" at the patient's expense, whether before assembled family or in front of residents and medical students, is to be scrupulously avoided. Sympathetic recognition of all deficits should be directed first to the patient. Even complex concepts such as the operationally crucial faculty of constructional ability can be evaluated empathetically. For example, the psychiatrist may ask, "Has it been difficult lately to plan your day or to grasp the overall picture in complicated situations? Have you noticed difficulty in getting things together to do something?"

## Contact in Neuropsychiatric Patients

On entering the patient's room, the psychiatrist should be aware that impairments in the patient's hierarchy of capacities are likely to impede any beneficial encounter between patient and physician in specific ways that require adaptations and compensations in psychotherapeutic technique. In general, each capacity in Table 36–1 is dependent on the integrity of those that precede it.

## Defenses: The Neuropsychodynamic Continuum

The psychiatrist who is well trained in psychodynamic psychotherapy brings to the study of defense mechanisms in neuropsychiatry a relevant but incomplete description. Defenses are psychodynamic mechanisms used by a person interacting with the surprises and dangers of the world and with drives and emotions from within. Traditionally, defenses have been classified on a dimension from the most mature to the most immature (Forrest 1980). The most mature defenses (such as sublimation, suppression, and laughter) are viewed as the healthiest ones. Less mature defenses (such as reaction formation, rationalization, displacement, and isolation) are thought to be characteristic of a neurotic level of function. The most immature defenses (such as denial, splitting, merging, projection, and projective identification) are considered the most unhealthy, typifying psychotic functioning. Although psychodynamic theory originally recognized a somatic contribution to the mental defenses, it did not specify which mental defenses are associated with organic impairment or how the defenses are related to organic processes.

In approaching defenses in neuropsychiatry, parallels may be sought between the mental mechanisms of defense and defensive brain (or cortical) reactions. At the very least, patient and family can be helped to see which defensive reactions are exacerbations of characterologic armor (under varying degrees of voluntary control and amenable to interpretation) and which are more primitive, automatic defenses of an injured brain that may be compensated for by tolerant understanding and environmental manipulation. Between these two extremes lie defensive formations that are rooted in both psyche and brain. Finally, one must not assume that a learning process is absent in cortical defenses, so that improvement occurs only with spontaneous recovery, or that the mental defenses always have a plasticity that is completely reeducable by psychotherapy.

Comparisons on the basis of operational principles may be made among cortical defenses, mental defenses, and a bridging area of what might be termed *neuropsychic defenses*. In Table 36–2, parallels are drawn among defensive structures of similar shape that are 1) mental defenses of the psyche, 2) somatopsychic or neuromental defenses clearly influenced by the neurologic state, and 3) cortical neurologic reactions. Potential continua among these three types of defensive structures are implied. For example, the neuromental domain, which I have designated *impaired view of others*, includes prosopagnosia, a brain disorder in which one cannot recognize faces; the mental phenomena of transference; and in between, the neuromental misidentification syndromes. Signer (1987) described eight variant forms of misidentification (see Figure 36–2):

1. In Capgras' delusions, the "Body Snatchers" type, people are being replaced by identical doubles.

**TABLE 36–1.** Hierarchy of capacities for psychotherapeutic contact that may be impaired in neuropsychiatric patients

| Capacity | Adaptations in psychiatric technique |
|---|---|
| Consciousness | Adopt a reassuring manner. Avoid agitation by avoiding overstimulation. Limit time of visit. Assess changing tolerance for interventions. Keep affect positive even if patient is apparently unconscious or not fully conscious. |
| Attention | Eliminate distractions. Keep contacts one on one. Speak clearly and simplify language. Use brief syntax. Make sure your presence is registered. Note perceptual impairments such as field cuts or hearing deficits and position self helpfully. |
| Retention | Repeat from time to time. Simplify. Break down communications into simple steps. Reinforce with other channels and modalities (e.g., writing and diagrams). Practice mnemonics with patient. Identify yourself at each visit, and keep your appearance constant. |
| Orientation | Remind patient (as needed) of time, place, and person. Keep calendar and clock in view. Visit at the same time daily. |
| Recognition | Tailor approach to compensate for specific impairments of any of the many parallel brain processors, from trouble with simple geometric perceptions through facial recognition to more complex perceptual components of relationship. Adapt communication to assist and circumvent dysphasic channels (e.g., reassure with affects when verbal reception is poor). |
| Construction | Assist in putting together cause and effect, as well as spatial and temporal connection. Help to see how necessary activities or outing will fit into time slots of the day. Offer structures. |
| Emotion | Assess underlying drives of anxiety, aggressiveness, and sexuality. Do not stress patient's having difficulty with control. Identify and read out to the patient degrees of joy, fear, anger, shame, guilt, or sadness being felt by the patient. Name more specific emotions under these main headings to reduce resistance and increase the feeling of being understood. |
| Conation | Help patient build on fragile will and find his or her own direction in confusion. Do not be overbearing, as your very presence may be commanding to the point of causing automatic obedience or opposition, echopraxia, echolalia, or cataplexy. Respect elements of prosocial intentionality in actions. |
| Motivation | Facilitate positive incentives by behavioral manipulation and removal of negative influences. Help patient identify latent longings for improved adaptation. Guard against helplessness. |
| Proposition | Accept that the first stage of proposition during recovery is usually opposition, as with a child in the "terrible twos." Respect the inherent positive energy, but set limits. Encourage half-baked initiatives and help structure only after they get going. Do not discourage the patient or complicate things. |
| Delineation | Help patient see origins of affects in self or from others and help him or her work on impairment in self, not project it onto world. Use projections onto the psychiatrist or onto paralyzed body parts as clues to self-concepts. Excessive blame-taking often may best be handled as a failure of delineation from family anger or disappointment about the patient's not being sufficiently restored to normal (see Figure 36–1). |
| Relation | Note quality of and changes in relationships with significant others. The patient's caring about the needs of others is an extremely good sign that social function will recover and psychotherapy will be helpful. Balance looking out for the patient's needs against validating reasonable perceptions and needs of spouse and family, on whom the patient is dependent. |

2. In subjective doubles, the Capgras' type, unseen doubles, phantom boarders, or deceased persons are felt to be present.

3. In the Frégoli type, named for the great Italian actor who was a master of disguised identities, a familiar person has assumed another bodily form.

4. In intermetamorphosis, both minds and bodies of people are interchanging.

5. In subjective doubles, the autoscopic type, a person's own double is projected onto another person in the positive form, and in the negative form, the person cannot see himself or herself, even in a mirror.

6. In reverse subjective doubles, the autoscopic type, the person feels either like an imposter or as if in the process of being replaced.

7. In the reverse Frégoli type, the person believes that other people are misidentifying him or her as if *they* have Frégoli delusions of misidentification.

As I have noted elsewhere (Forrest, in press), the Frégoli type is closest to the normal mechanisms of transference that have become excessive. It is often associated with pathologically reduced frontal brain function. The misidentification syndromes, which are clearly related to

**FIGURE 36–1.** Tracing of a drawing titled "the goose that layed [sic] (the golden egg)" by a 17-year-old male patient with early-onset schizophrenia and delineation disorder. Delineation disorder, which occurs in schizophrenic, borderline, and numerous neuropsychiatric conditions, is characterized by difficulties in determining interpersonal boundaries and self- versus others' ownership of intentionality.

brain disorders and which often can be localized anatomically, appear to dissect Freudian object relations and may help explain the self-concept in neuromental terms.

## Techniques From Psychotherapy for Schizophrenia

Schizophrenia is a neuromental symptom formation that is more complex than its neurologic deficit, but its treatment may serve as a model for psychiatric work with less familiar neurologic conditions. All of the dysfunctional features previously catalogued for schizophrenia (Forrest 1983c) may be variably present in the neurologic patient with a brain injury (especially those with mesolimbic involvement) and require sensitive adjustments of technique by the neuropsychiatrist similar to those described for schizophrenia (Forrest 1983c).

The mechanisms that occur both in patients with

schizophrenia and in neurologic patients with disordered brain function include undifferentiated "catastrophic" reactions to stresses when the patient becomes overwhelmed; involuntary concreteness or metonymy (taking a part of a concept for the entire concept); incapability of moving among levels of abstraction, especially regarding affective interpersonal relationships; fear of novel situations; segmentalization and deautomatization of previously automatic sequences of emotional response; slow habituation and extinction of reactions to stimuli; and probabilistic incapacity (poor ability to evaluate likely outcome) (Forrest 1983b, 1983c).

Frequently, patients with impaired brain function have an additional feature of language disturbance not present in patients with schizophrenia. Although the schizophrenic person almost always has an impairment of language in a larger sense, other patients with impaired brain function usually have some difficulty *accessing* language. This problem is typically absent in schizophrenia (Benson 1975), and verbally facile schizophrenic patients may even engage in poiesis, or wish-fulfilling verbal constructions (Forrest 1999). The crucial practical difference for psychotherapy is that emotions in most neurologic patients are recruited to overcome cognitive and linguistic problems and to make interpersonal sense, whereas in schizophrenia, cognitive and linguistic elements—often exaggerated and fanciful—are recruited to compensate for poor command of affects, and the result often frustrates interpersonal sense. The abnormally small thalamus visualized by Andreasen et al. (1994) through magnetic resonance imaging (MRI) averaging is in keeping with the basic schizophrenic difficulty with attaching affective valuations to, and thereby organizing, thoughts, sensations, and perceptions (Forrest 1983a, 1983d).

The neuropsychiatrist must be crucially attuned to nuances of a patient's affect. One's own perception of affect can be calibrated against the highly reliable means of affect scoring of short videotaped interview segments by professional audiences (Forrest 1982). The six affects—joy, fear, anger, shame, guilt, and sadness—can each be rated on a scale of 0 to 4+, like any other medical measurement. Under these general affect rubrics, cognitive shadings of emotions can be specified. The most common error in treating patients with impaired brain function is not adjusting one's own projection of emotional tone to the patient's needs (Forrest 1983b). For example, patients with hyperemotionalism may require neuropsychiatrists to throttle down their emotions. The challenge for most neuropsychiatrists is to increase the benevolent emotion they project toward certain patients who for various reasons are receiving signals poorly. Psy-

**TABLE 36–2.** Neuropsychiatric defense continuum

| Continuum | Mental defenses | Neuromental defenses | Cortical reactions |
|---|---|---|---|
| Nonrecognition | Denial of damage, avoidance, disavowal; or conscious caring for paralyzed limb | Neglect of body part or side, with preservation of the concept of a damaged limb | Hemi-inattention because of diminished cortical representation |
| Misdirection | Circumstantiality, tangentiality | Overinclusion, ellipsis | Inattention, distractibility |
| Nondenotation | Metaphor, metonymy, symptom and symbol formation, circumlocution, poetic language and logic | Rhyming, clang associations, neologism, substitution | Aphasic paraphasias, jargon, dysnomia |
| Nonrecall (or nongrasp) | Obsessive ordering, hysterical evasion, paranoid reductiveness, schizoid invention, sociopathic approximate answers (Ganser's syndrome) | Confabulation, structure by constant talking, compensatory grandiloquence (poststroke, to prove smart), ignore what one cannot structure, repeating and quoting self | Amnestic or state-dependent lapses, failure of processing with information overload |
| Referential loss | Delusions of reference and influence and of dementia in depression (pseudodementia) | Delusions of loss or impoverishment; metaphorical substitution of time, feces, money, or other measurable things for unacceptable and incomprehensible loss of brain function | Diminished capacity for construction, proposition, and planning |
| Affect application | Helplessness, hopelessness; compensation; or plaintive self-denigration with realization of deficit; schizophrenic substitutions of (sociopolitical or religiophilosophical) abstractions for interpersonal focus on emotions | Beneficence toward or degradation of self or object world without realization or recognition of deficit; parapathic substitutions of schizophrenic language for affects | Apathy, emotionalism, organic mania; flat affect in schizophrenia |
| Regression | Ontogenic regression to less mature states of mind, with diminished object constancy, tantrums, or catastrophic reactions to stress (Goldstein 1942) | Stereotypy and other complex innate primitive patterns such as mechanical repetition in stimulant abuse, touching the face in Huntington's disease, and regression to silly humor or puns (*Witzelsucht*) | Phylogenetic regression to neural reactions characteristic of lower mammalian and vertebrate predecessors (e.g., grasp and snout) |
| Kindling or temporolimbic hyperconnection (interictal) | Hypermoralism, intensified religiosity, and proselytizing; sense of urgency and mission; anger and remorse; and graphomania | Viscosity, emotional deepening, sensations of immanence, transcendence, and divine presence; thought insertion | Organic sensations of otherness or bodily intrusion; hyposexuality |
| Impaired world view | "My relationship to the world has changed." | "The world is bigger, harder to deal with, more confusing," or (in schizophrenia) more aesthetically awesome | "The world has been changed, reduplicated, substituted" in patients with brain injury |
| Impaired view of others | Transference reactions: "It's I who have changed, my perceptions differ because I'm injured"; degrees of insight; interpersonal shallowness and manipulativeness | Misidentification: "People have changed, are different, are to blame, have been replaced by impostors"; splitting and projective identification; "underlying defect" in borderline syndrome of failure of delineation | Prosopagnosia: state-dependent change in cognition of people or their relation to self |
| Sex object shift | Avoidance of parental object to preserve ties to family | Failure to integrate affects and sexuality | Failure to differentiate sexual object (Klüver-Bucy syndrome of bilateral hippocampal damage) or own gender |

**TABLE 36–2.**  Neuropsychiatric defense continuum *(continued)*

| Continuum | Mental defenses | Neuromental defenses | Cortical reactions |
|---|---|---|---|
| Impaired ego boundary | Creativity and regression in the service of the ego | Disturbing nightmares, other vulnerability to internal and external processes, and schizophrenia | Diminished stimulus barrier |
| Impairment of conation or will | Identification with the aggressor, and introjection and incorporation in health, neurosis, and depression | Made cognition, made volition, and command hallucinations in schizophrenia | Echolalia, echopraxia, and involuntary reflex activity in brain injury |
| Impaired movement or spatial play | Disorientation, agoraphobia, diminished sense of mastery and mobility and of bodily feedback and control, and lowered confidence in actions | Vestibular defensiveness, fear of moving, fear of falling or of whirling (twirling a soft sign in children), incoordination, and clumsiness | Vertigo, motor or proprioceptive impairment, incoordination, poor eye tracking, ataxia, and tremor |

chotherapy in neuropsychiatry should be eclectic, adapting elements that are helpful from various modalities (Table 36–3).

# Traumatic Brain Injury

Traumatic brain injury results principally from vehicular accidents, falls, acts of violence, and sports injuries and is more than twice as likely to occur in men as in women. The highest incidence is among persons age 15–24 years and 75 years or older, with a less striking peak in children age 5 years or younger (National Institutes of Health Consensus Development Panel 1999). Thus, these patients may not be very mature, resilient, or resourceful.

Childs (1985) stated that the most difficult sequelae of head injury to treat are the psychosocial disabilities; impaired cognition is next in degree of difficulty, and impaired physical abilities are the least difficult. Also, perhaps contrary to common assumption, the patient's family suffers most severely from the disruption of emotions and object relations, next most from the intellectual impairments, and least from the physical impairments (Oddy et al. 1978). This is why psychotherapy can play a crucial role in individual and family recovery after head injury.

The emotional climate is worsened by the typical emergence of bad temper in the patient 3 or more months after the injury. The family's optimism that full recovery will occur, based on successes in physical rehabilitation, turns to disappointment when the patient's impulse control worsens. The doctors often bear the transferred brunt of family anger. Interventions should aim at legitimizing family disappointment and avoiding comments that abet the splitting. Unconscious or unacknowledged family anger at the patient for being injured

contributes to the patient's internalized anger within the family system and must be addressed to head off severe self-loathing or suicidal trends as the protection of denial wears off.

Regression in the patient's mental processes may parallel neurologic regression, and both mental and neuromental defenses parallel pathologic brain reactions. Often, borderline or other organic personality disorders result that comprise an array roughly paralleling functional personality syndromes (Childs 1985). It is important to interview family and friends to determine the premorbid personality of the patient in calculating effects of injury, which may be easier to change.

Psychotherapeutic interventions optimally begin soon after the patient is hospitalized, and management of the emotional climate is crucial to recovery. Childs (1985) recommended placing a priority on the reestablishment of object constancy in cognitively impaired patients by staff members who are carefully selected for their lack of personal tension or anger and work one-on-one all day with each patient. This familiar and consistent other person enacts an early stage in cognitive retraining of a regressively lost relational skill. This is accomplished with a soothing voice and touch, with limitation of talk to familiar subjects and to the patient only, and the restriction of stimulation to a single channel. Later, active exercises include practice in following directions requiring progressively more sequential steps (Luria 1973), problem solving, and movement from the concrete to the abstract, retracing developmental steps and hoping for generalization of learning. Martelli et al. (1999) reported that posttraumatic headache, estimated to persist for 6 months in up to 44% of patients, exerts a significant negative effect on postconcussive adaptation and therefore should be managed. Other measures the psychiatrist should consider are summarized in Table 36–4.

Capgras'

Subjective doubles, Capgras' type

Frégoli

Intermetamorphosis

Subjective doubles, autoscopic type, postive form

Subjective doubles, autoscopic type, negative form

Reverse subjective doubles

Reverse Frégoli

D.V. Forrest, M.D. '00

**FIGURE 36–2.** Eight variant forms of misidentification (see Table 36–2 for description). Misidentification is commonly found in neuromental conditions when specifically asked about.

# Language and Other Psychotherapeutic Correlates

Verbal impairment to some degree is found in all patients with closed head injuries who have been referred to a rehabilitation medicine center. Sarno (1980) found that 32% of the patients with brain injury had classic aphasia, 38% had motor dysarthria, and 30% had no discernible aphasic deficit in spontaneous speech but clear evidence of verbal deficit on testing. Dysarthric patients, without

**TABLE 36–3.** Modalities of psychotherapy in neuropsychiatry

**Helpful aspects of the psychoanalytic approach for neuropsychiatry**

1. Respect for the patient's autonomy and self-determination
2. Theoretic concept of defense organization
3. Most sufficient map of mental, cognitive, and emotional function
4. Model based on conflict among mental structures
5. Emphasis on shared meaning, attunement, affirmative empathy, intersubjective awareness, and emotions in general (Anshin 1995)

**Inappropriate aspects of the psychoanalytic approach for neuropsychiatry**

1. Too passive a receptiveness rather than making affective contact
2. Too much reliance on free association and dreams
3. Searching for remote causes and relationships
4. Attribution of treatment events to abstract forces and entities in talking to patients
5. Overemphasis on transference versus reality issues
6. Intentional lack of frames and structures
7. Interpersonal relations considered as inner object relations
8. Avoidance of direct answers or being a "blank screen" rather than being a beacon to security

**Other modalities of psychotherapy in neuropsychiatry**

1. Behaviorist approaches to the patient's learning system as a black box may be helpful in structuring relearning, but they are "brainless" in their theoretic avoidance of capacities, defenses, conflicts, recruitment of affect to aid cognition, and other neuromental dynamics that are helpful in explanation.
2. Interpersonal and family approaches are surprisingly helpful communication systems despite the clear nidus of difficulty in a neuropathologically "designated patient" because of the effect on relatives and their involvement in the care of the disabilities. As there is both direct influence and imitation and a hereditary factor in neurotic, characterologic, and major psychiatric disorders, the families of patients with acquired neuropsychiatric disorders may themselves be less disordered and more of a help in the treatment.
3. Cognitive approaches help in an educative way to spell out the "baby steps" that need to be accomplished to achieve complex goals, but to work better, they require attention to intersubjective emotions, conflicts, and goals.

**TABLE 36–4.** Measures to assist recovery of patients with brain injury

1. Relate interventions to family grieving stage (denial, anger, grief resolution).
2. Structure daily events to assist patient's internalizing of routine and reestablishing circadian rhythms.
3. Establish positive rewards to reinforce responsible behavior; individualize rewards to what patient likes.
4. Approach disabilities with expectancy they will be overcome cheerfully, never as excuse for misbehavior.
5. Individualize treatment goals to patient's specific problems; for example, reward withdrawn frontal patients for conversation and aggressive patients for not reacting.
6. Break maladaptive habits by vigilance and restraint, because motivation to become involved in positive change follows elimination of irresponsible behavior.
7. Orient family extensively to structure needed before discharge to home so gains are maintained.

*Source.* Adapted from Berry 1984.

The task of psychotherapy for the patient with brain damage is to assess his or her capability for each step in the cognitive sequence of defenses against threat, to help break down difficult steps into subroutines, and to assist in bridging gaps with the psychiatrist's own analytic functions. Hamburg (1985) outlined a sequence of cognitive defenses, which includes 11 elements:

1. Regulate the timing and dosage of the threat.
2. Deal with stresses one at a time.
3. Seek information from multiple sources.
4. Formulate expectations.
5. Delineate manageable goals.
6. Rehearse coping strategies and practice in safe situations.
7. Test coping strategies in situations of moderate risk.
8. Appraise feedback from those situations.
9. Try more than one approach, keeping several options open.
10. Commit to one approach.
11. Develop buffers against disappointment and develop contingency plans.

The psychiatrist should consider how the person stressed with brain damage is deprived of each and all of these optimal mental and psychosocial mechanisms of mastery. The stress arises from within and cannot be eliminated by avoidance or flight. The organic disease cannot be viewed at a distance from the self because it is in the very organ of self-perception. On the other hand, the cognitively distorted perceptions of a paralyzed limb involve highly metaphoric removals from the self and

exception, showed subclinical linguistic effects. Because psychotherapy depends on the use of language with an emotional dimension, the psychiatrist should be alert to subtle evidence of dysarthria, identify any linguistic problems, and consciously adapt the psychotherapeutic technique to the deficit in the particular patient.

illustrate the difficulty one has in grasping an illness of one's own brain. The virtual impossibility of clearly grasping the disease of the perceiving organ itself renders the regulation of the timing, dosage, and sequence of multiple threats as formidable problems for psychotherapy. Formulation of expectations and delineation of goals are frequently impossible when the requisite cognitive skills are absent. "Safe" and "moderate-risk" situations are lacking for the patient haunted by a global sense of impairment that intrudes into every pleasurable aspect of life. Finally, the choice of multiple options, the use of feedback from situations, and the possibility of contingency plans are all techniques that may be quite unreachable for the patient with brain damage.

In one study by Andersson et al. (1999), the two-thirds of the traumatic brain injury patients classified as more apathetic had a poorer response to the rehabilitation process. Associated factors during the therapy were decreased autonomic reactivity in cardiovascular and electrodermal monitoring, less perceived emotional discomfort, and reduced self-awareness and insight, with disengagement and lack of concern about their situation. An implication is that psychotherapy should be aimed at improving self-awareness in apathetic patients.

Mateer (1999) recommended that frontal lobe disorders of executive function impairing initiation, sequencing impulse control, attention, prospective memory, and self-awareness, leading to disorganized and maladaptive behaviors, can be approached through environmental manipulations, training in compensatory strategies, and techniques to improve underlying skills, including attention and prospective memory. The goal is movement from dependent external to independent external self-regulation of behavior. Environmental manipulations, behavioral strategies, and external cuing are used early and with those who have little initiative and response to internal cues; later, and with patients with more self-direction and awareness, cognitive training, compensatory devices such as memory books, and self-instructional and metacognitive strategies are more appropriate. Metacognitive strategies regulate behavior by replacing lost implicit and unconscious inner speech controls with explicit and conscious control though self-talk, covert internalized self-monitoring, and behavioral schemata for specified situations. Practice on attentional tasks is supplemented with proactive practice in identifying potentially difficult situations. Prospective memory, or remembering to remember (e.g., to take medications or call in), is more correlated with functional independence than is cued recall, is trained by practice carrying out actions with more and more intervening distractions and tasks. Problem-solving training involves brainstorming alterna-

tives, comparing information from multiple sources (e.g., several clothing catalogues), and drawing inferences (e.g., perusing short detective stories for clues). Although growth in self-awareness of deficits may initiate emotional problems, improved awareness of internal and external emotional cues that signal or trigger emotions may lead to better self-management. Other behavioral and emotional residua noted by Delmonico et al. (1998) include substance abuse, depression, anxiety, chronic suicidal or homicidal ideation, poor impulse control, and degrees of frustration and anger. These are all approachable in group psychotherapy.

Grosswasser and Stern (1998) proposed a psychodynamic model of the neurobehavioral manifestations, which are viewed as a default means of emotional expression by the patients and therefore not entirely abnormal in the patients' interpersonal contexts. Anderson and Silver (1998), citing Yudofsky et al. (1990), noted the characteristic inappropriate features of aggression in patients with brain injury. Aggression is reactive, triggered by trivial stimuli; nonreflective and unpremeditated; nonpurposeful, serving no long-term goals; explosive, not gradual in buildup; periodic, occurring in brief outbursts punctuating long periods of calm; and ego-dystonic, followed by embarrassment and regret rather than blaming others or justifying it. All these features can and should be approached by the behavioral techniques previously mentioned in addition to pharmacotherapy.

Flashman et al. (1998) suggested an approach to a lack of awareness that begins with ascertaining whether the patient has a lack of knowledge of the deficit, an inappropriate response to it, or an inability to appreciate its consequences on daily living. The therapeutic relationship is primary to helping the patient approach the likely combination of neurologic and psychologic denial along the neuromental spectrum. Treatment judiciously validates the self and world view without fostering unrealistic expectations or forcing complete awareness all at once. Some deficits such as anosognosia with hemiplegia usually resolve in weeks, but other deficits, especially in social behavior and anger management, may persist and may include resistance to the need for help. Relying on an established relationship, explorations identify the discrepancies between the patients' own views of their strengths and abilities and feedback from others. Education and supportive therapy for significant others, and modeling for them a process of gentle teaching, play a vital role in appreciating the issues regarding awareness in their loved one. Awareness alone does not ensure application to real-life situations. A common cuing system uses simple, affectively neutral, nonthreatening cues the patient finds easy to detect to alert the patient to target behaviors that are occurring. Group therapy and other feedback may also be helpful.

Bellus et al. (1998) pointed out that despite early success with the cognitive symptoms of schizophrenia, little effort at cognitive remediation is directed to long-term psychiatric patients, including those who have brain injury; however, in the brain injury rehabilitation community, there is strong support for cognitive remediation despite mixed results in the literature. A single case study illustrated improved verbal and nonverbal cognitive functioning on IQ testing over 20 years. Treatment included "low-tech" small group interventions within intensive behavioral rehabilitation programs.

## Sexual Disturbances After Brain Injury

Sexual disturbances may follow brain injury, especially damage to the limbic system. According to Weinstein (1974), "Changes in sexual behavior observed in brain-damaged patients are often abnormal by reason of the [inappropriate] circumstances in which they occur, rather than their intrinsic nature" (p. 16) or by their being different from the person's habitual conduct. It is often helpful to make it clear to the family that the patient with a brain injury has not become oversexed and that the patient is just enacting a normal sexuality in the wrong context because of a more general disorder of judgment.

Sexual behavior in individuals with brain damage usually is marked by a loss of specificity as to objects or forms of excitation rather than a new focus. Although specific behavior such as fetishism has been linked to temporal lobe seizure activity (as well as hyper- and hyposexuality), intermediary personality factors and learning are more probably the cause than postulated so-called sexual centers, as has been suggested for heterosexual pursuit.

Verbal seductiveness frequently occurs in a situation of stress, such as when a patient is asked about his or her illness or is being tested, and thus may have a defensive, avoidant quality. Another stress-related phenomenon is ludic play, which appears as punning or joking about illness, caricaturing disabilities, or imitating or mimicking the examiner's behavior. Often patients classify their disabilities in sexual terms, or sex enters into the content of their confabulations and delusions in the acute state, which Weinstein (1974) declared are useful signs that sexual behavior will be acted out later in a real-life situation. Some patients seek relatedness through physical contact that may "put off" visitors or staff, all the more so when the dementia is secondary to a contagious disease.

A study of the psychosexual consequences of brain injury by Kreutzer and Zasler (1989) showed that most patients reported a lessening of sexual drive, erectile function, and frequency of intercourse; reduced self-esteem and self-perceived sex appeal; and no relation between the level of affect and sexual behavior. Despite the changes, the quality of the patients' marital relationships appeared preserved.

To some, patients with traumatic brain injury may seem remote from the usual psychodynamic practice, which lacks patients with dementia pugilistica or of the status in which being knocked out is a regular occurrence. However, automobile accidents are common; sports as diverse as football, soccer, and competitive diving include head trauma (from the water alone in the high dive, apart from hitting the board); and many elderly and alcoholic patients have had falls with blows to the head. Thus, traumatic components may enter into many psychiatric disorders. Pollack (1994) provided a comprehensive approach to the psychotherapeutic processes and goals in more significant traumatic brain injury. Particularly valuable, and often ignored, are the affective and countertransferential aspects of work with these patients.

Chief among the affects encountered is sadness arising in loneliness from the social isolation that results. A loss of morale afflicts both patient and family and requires the psychiatrist to instill hope without making insubstantial predictions of a successful outcome, especially in the face of the usual uncertainty of the recovery process.

Countertransference is complicated by the limits of the patient's self-awareness and self-monitoring. Frequent problems are the wishful underestimation of the severity of the disabilities, returning the patient too soon to challenging situations with resulting catastrophic reactions, and a lack of patience with the patient's problems with memory, comprehension, or executive inflexibility. Lack of recovery, inactivity, and behavior problems may be misinterpreted as a lack of motivation or sabotage.

Frustration and anger may lead to a wish to abandon the patient, who reacts with hurt feelings and even hate. Sometimes the patients are stimulus-seeking adolescent males who view seeking even necessary help as compromising their proud independence.

Maintaining good boundaries in the treatment process can moderate the intensity of the countertransference.

## Family Approach to Traumatic Brain Injury

In a very real psychiatric sense, the locus of traumatic brain injury is not within a single cranium but in a family. As Solomon and Scherzer (1991), suggesting a more "ecologic" approach, have reported, there is a severe increase in the level of stress within the family....Wives and mothers of the TBI [traumatic brain-injured] victim experience increases in anxiety, social dysfunction and perceived burden as a function of the severity of the injury, and these symptoms persist at least 1–2 years post-trauma....The cognitive and affective changes rather than the physical deficits are the most troublesome for the family....Whereas the family plays out their own dynamics in the hospital room, the hospital staff is often guilty of both condescension and wrongly attributing pathology to the family in order to explain conflicts with the hospital staff. The consequences of such conflict include the alienation of the family, who often represent the last resource of the patient, and the loss of potential allies in the rehabilitation process....We have interviewed over 100 families ...these interviews reveal that the father is least likely to be able to tolerate the stress. He may abandon the family either physically or psychologically....When the father leaves, the mother is left with full parental responsibility for looking after the traumatically brain-injured member and feels overwhelmed....When the offspring is discharged from the hospital, it is usually the mother who takes on the role of case manager (p. 255).

The mother as caregiver must deal with the patient's depressed, apathetic, or abusive emotions and obscene language. The male patient may be sexually harassing, the female lewd and aggressive. The mother is confused by the strange behavior, but with partial recovery the patient, still not ready to be independent, no longer listens to her. The effects on the mothers parallel those on the wives of brain-injured patients, who have a deterioration in social and marital adjustment during the first year. Children find that they have to compete for attention, cannot express anger, and are often assigned responsibilities that are not age-appropriate.

Ideally, the family should be integrated into the treatment process from the beginning. Solomon and Scherzer (1991) proposed detailed guidelines for the therapist, who should be highly directive, informed, and informing; an advocate for brain-injured patients; a guardian against exploitation; and a model for both patient and family while showing the family that they are also models for the patient. The therapist should monitor comprehension, assist generalization of learning from one situation to another, and help the family to avoid being manipulated and to be free to protect themselves and to refuse to tolerate unacceptable behavior.

## Stroke

According to a study of stroke survivors by Kotila et al. (1984), clear improvement can be expected after stroke from the acute stage to 3 months, continuing to a lesser degree to 12 months. At 12 months, 78% of the patients who had survived strokes were living at home, and 58% were independent in activities of daily living. Of those patients who were gainfully employed before having a stroke, 55% had returned to work after 12 months. The authors emphasized that emotional reactions as well as neurologic deficits influence outcome and should be considered in assessing prognosis.

A stroke is unwelcome at any age, but Goodstein (1983) noted that for the older patient, a stroke activates preexisting fears of losing control or sanity, dying, and becoming disfigured or impaired physically or sexually. The elderly also are more insecure about sudden recurrences, long stays away from home, and running out of retirement funds.

The useful British term *emotionalism* has been defined by House et al. (1989, p. 991) as "an increase in frequency of crying or laughing, where the crying or laughing comes with little or no warning, and emotional expression is outside normal control, so that the subject cries or laughs in social situations where he or she would not previously have done so" and affects 20%–25% of stroke survivors in the first 6 months. Also referred to as *emotional lability* or *pseudobulbar affect*, it is not limited to bilateral brain damage and not predicted by unilateral lesion location. Calvert et al. (1998) compared emotionalism with posttraumatic stress disorder; in both, the patient experiences irritability and recurring, uncontrollable, emotionally charged mental events. Calvert et al. noted that emotionalism is not a meaningless accompaniment of brain injury; patients consider the precipitating thoughts and memories meaningful, and just as in posttraumatic stress disorder, the patient relives meaningful experiences. Ideas of reference were present in about a third of the stroke patients with emotionalism as compared with a tenth of those without, and this may be a product of embarrassment and social unease. Although antidepressive agents may aid these pathologic affects, psychotherapeutic attention should be directed to the patient's experience of meaningful content.

Lorig et al. (1999) reported that a self-management program for chronic disease, including stroke, improved self-reported health; decreased distress, fatigue, disability, and social role activities limitations; and led to fewer hospitalizations and hospital days. No differences were found in pain or psychologic well-being. Suhr and Anderson (1998) treated medication-resistant hallucinations in a 52-year-old patient with a right middle cerebral artery stroke with cognitive restructuring that included education of the patient and his family and training in compensatory strategies for the effect of symptoms on daily activities. Similarly, Goldenberg and Hagman (1998) trained patients with aphasia and right-sided hemiplegia after left-hemisphere stroke, whose apraxia prevented activities of daily living, and found that no generalization occurred from trained to nontrained activities and that success was preserved at 6 months only in those who had practiced the specific activities in their daily routines at home.

## Postdischarge Planning

Several studies have underscored the importance of social support in the patient's adjustment to physical deficits from a stroke. Evans and Northwood (1983) related the wide variation in individual differences in adjustment to expressed interpersonal needs for social support. Labi et al. (1980) studied long-term survivors of stroke and found that a significant proportion manifested social disability, despite complete physical restoration. The parameters of social function in the study were socialization inside and outside the home, hobbies, and interests; much of the subjects' disability could not be accounted for by age, physical impairment, or specific neurologic deficits. The distribution of documented functional disabilities suggested that, in addition to organic deficits, psychosocial factors were major determinants.

The psychiatrist should be aware, as Wilson and Smith (1983) determined, that poststroke patients often will attempt to drive. However, these patients may have special difficulty handling all aspects of driving. Many of these difficulties are predictable from the clinical examination, and the patient should be warned. In addition to these deficits, problems with diminished vision, personality change, the prominence of denial and projection as mental defenses, and alcoholism are likely to increase the risks of driving for these patients. I have noted, in an era of availability of oversize vehicles, that feelings of vulnerability from subconsciously perceived mental deficits sometimes lead a patient to purchase a larger vehicle for self-protection, when switching to a slower-moving, 3-wheeled motorized cart would be more appropriate to the patient's skills.

## Defenses and Object Relations in Hemiplegia

A discussion by Critchley (1979) of patients' reactions to hemiplegia contains observations of a variety of defensive maneuvers that epitomize the "neurologizing" of the dynamic defenses of psychiatry. In the loss of the sensation and control of parts of the body, remarkable changes occur in relation to those parts that Critchley calls "personification of the paralyzed limbs" (p. 117). This devel-

ops after an initial period of anosognosia and may be an overcompensation. The patient becomes a detached onlooker and the limb a foreign body outside the self. A patient may refer to the paralyzed limb as if it were an object such as a pet, a plaything, or a person of another sex, often with attributed personality traits. Splitting and lateralization into good and bad sides of the body, which ordinarily require a psychotic personality to be manifested in the absence of neurologic disease, become accessible, readily used defenses against the changed representation of the impaired body part, in brain and mind. Patients may insult or scream abuse at the limb. Beneath the level of denotative meaning and concrete representation that neurology comprehends, metaphors appear that speak to psychiatrists in fuller connotations about the state of the personality in relation to the diseased limb.

## Approach to Patients Who Are Unstable on Their Feet

The fearful, usually elderly patient who feels unstable on his or her feet is a common neuropsychiatric problem. An educational therapeutic approach is often helpful and may serve as a model of that approach within the context of an ongoing therapeutic relationship. The patient is taught that there are at least six components of balance, any and all of which, once improved, will contribute to them all. This immediately begins to dispel the sense of helplessness and maps a multipronged offensive effort that the patient can marshal.

Treatment of gait can target 1) muscular conditioning, 2) footing and dorsal-column feedback from legs, 3) vestibular and circulatory dizziness, 4) visual input to balance, 5) basal gangliar function, and 6) phobic and other neuromental content. The neuromental dimension is often the most important. The patient may express the feeling of a lack of support in symbolic somatic language of unsteadiness and a fear of falling. Often, the patient has become isolated through the deaths of relatives and friends, and therapy must deal with a resistance to affiliate that usually expresses the sentiment that the loved ones cannot be replaced. This sentiment must be given its due because it is a form of loving memorial. But progress is rapid once the patient sees associating with others as compatible with loving memories. Even the acquisition of a pet that stays in the home can improve the sense of security. Physical immobility diminishes the patient's sense of participation in life. While not working on the gait in the ways described above, patients are encouraged to correspond with distant friends, authors whose books and articles they have enjoyed, and new contacts through clubs and interests that encourage correspondence via letter and e-mail.

## Spinal Cord Injury

A quarter of a million Americans live permanently paralyzed from spinal cord injuries, and 10,000 new cases occur each year (most often young persons), with devastating impacts on career and emotional costs for the patients and their families (National Advisory Neurological Disorders and Stroke Council 1990). These patients, insofar as they are brain intact, may have emotional reactions that are similar to those mourning the death of a loved one or other situations of severe loss (Bracken and Shepard 1980). Consequently, premorbid personality and the influence of significant others play a central role in coping with injury. These devastating injuries attract the greatest sympathy when they are sustained by famous figures in sports or entertainment, and the leadership of those who have adapted well to the most severe limitations, as in high cervical lesions, can provide role models for patient identification. An overly sympathetic "kindness mode" or "kid glove treatment" based on countertransference reactions to the devastating disability can be less helpful to patients with spinal cord injuries and may contribute to denial when they are also substance abusers (Perez and Pilsecker 1994).

Manifest depression is not an inevitable psychologic sequel to spinal cord injury. Howell et al. (1981) found diagnosable depression in only 5 of 22 patients with spinal cord injuries of less than 6 months' duration. Bodenhamer et al. (1983) found that patients with spinal cord injuries reported less depression and more anxiety and optimism than their caregivers predicted. Bodenhamer et al. (1983) also pointed out that traditional stage theories of what is said to be a mourning-like adjustment must be individualized.

One of the most sophisticated accounts of the experiential dimension of spinal cord injury has been contributed by the noted anthropologist Robert Murphy (1987), who some 18 years before his death developed a spinal cord tumor that eventually separated him from the sense of his body. The *social* estrangement that resulted, which he compared to turning into a bug in Kafka's *Metamorphosis* (p. 108), despite his continued abilities to work, is discussed sensitively and professionally. He felt that he was "undergoing a savage parody of life itself" (Murphy 1987, p. 221) and that "the most important aspect of human behavior is that it derives its organization and content in the interaction of our biological drives with culture" (p. 225). He found that

the four most far-reaching changes in consciousness of the disabled are: lowered self-esteem; the invasion of thought by physical deficits; a strong undercurrent of anger; and the acquisition of a new, total, and undesirable identity. I can only liken the situation to a curious kind of "invasion of the body snatchers," in which the alien intruder and the old occupant coexist in mutual hostility in the same body. (Murphy 1987, p. 108)

In correspondence (R.F. Murphy, personal communication, May 1987), Murphy responded to my inquiry about his dreams, reporting that they were only about his condition and often denied its reality. They began with his walking and then remembering that he was paralyzed and also could not drive a car, so he could not get home. There was no resolution of the dilemma, and eventually the dreams began only with his being able to pull himself up into a walker and take a few steps, also long impossible. His book has helped others in the same situation; reading this first-person account in a professional voice also can help the treating psychiatrist develop empathic understanding of the patient with spinal cord injury.

The best predictor of future self-care by these patients is past self-care behavior, augmented by knowledge of personality tendencies. Green et al. (1984), studying persons who had had spinal cord injuries at least 4 years previously, administered the Tennessee Self-Concept Scale (Fitts 1965) and found, in comparison with scale norms, that the respondents had significantly *higher* personal self, moral-ethical self, and social self scores, although they had significantly lower physical self scores. The higher-than-normal self-concept scores were related to perceived independence, provision of one's own transportation, assistance needed, and living arrangements. These findings suggest the possibility of *enhanced* self-concepts through mastery of handicaps and that the psychiatrist often need not settle for limitations in the patient's mental health.

Craig et al. (1999) found that persons who initially perceived life as externally controlled and who received structured cognitive-behavioral therapy in specialized groups during the rehabilitation phase were more likely than control subjects to feel in control of themselves 2 years postinjury and had fewer readmissions, used fewer drugs, and reported higher levels of adjustment. An external locus of control was associated with depressive mood 2 years after admission. Not everyone with spinal cord injury needs cognitive-behavioral therapy during their hospitalized phase, but those who reported high levels of depressive mood benefited greatly.

The psychotherapeutic approach to the chronic pain that is a persistent problem for 50% of the patients with spinal cord injuries also emphasizes the development of patient self-management, as reviewed by Umlauf (1992). The patient's responsibility is to himself or herself, not the physician. Coping abilities already demonstrated with the injury are reinforced and applied to the problem of pain, which is never minimized or generalized in conversations with the patient. For this reason, a period of stability in postinjury adaptation should be established before beginning the intervention of a self-management program, which can otherwise seem intimidating and disheartening. Increased physical activity and decreased sedentary or prone time are often combined with increased supervised aerobic and strength exercise, with the involvement of the personal care attendant in therapy. The goals of pain management include an increase in positive affects, improved sleep despite care demands such as a midnight turning schedule for skin care, learning to self-monitor emotions and situations that promote pain, and improvement in self-appraisal in coping with severe pain episodes. A useful question suggested by Umlauf (1992) is, "If we took away your pain, what activities would you be able to do that you are not able to do now?" (p. 114). Thus, an attempt is made to separate the patient's perspective on achievement from his or her pain problems. Clear distinctions are taught between the levels of nocioception (a reflex nerve arc), pain perception (e.g., "a hot poker shoved up my spine"), suffering (including dysphoric emotions, anger, insomnia), and pain behavior (rubbing, verbalizing, grimacing) to instruct that the intervention is aimed at the latter two levels. Muscle relaxation techniques and self-hypnosis depend on and are attuned to patient ability. Peer support groups and role models are helpful here. Stress reduction focuses on situations that contribute to both pain and spasticity, and cognitive interventions emphasize rational thinking, attention distraction, and pain reinterpretation (e.g., "It's not killing me").

The social level demands analysis of pain as a communication. The patient can learn that when he or she is silent because of pain, others may interpret this as negativity. Integration of pain management strategies into workplace adaptation is much needed in view of low percentages of return to work by patients with spinal cord injuries. Social skills training and videotapes may be useful. Demographically, these patients are young men who are activity oriented rather than passive and introspective and may resist group or individual therapy that is not action oriented and peer involving. Appropriate use of pain medications; dealing with anger at the situation, oneself, and one's doctors; developing purposes for the rest of one's life; and avoiding compensation neuroses are major therapy themes.

In a longitudinal study, Rosenstiel and Roth (1981)

found that their best adjusted patients with spinal cord injuries predominantly used the defenses of rationalization and denial, in keeping with the notion that the psychiatrist ought to respect the so-called more primitive defenses, if they work. Other traits that favored adjustment were avoidance of catastrophizing and of worrying what their lives would be like, thinking about goals to be achieved after leaving the rehabilitation center, and use of internal forms of mental rehearsal in anticipation of going home. DeJong et al. (1984) found that the best predictors of independent living outcome were marital status, education, transportation barriers, economic disincentives, and severity of disability. Table 36–5 summarizes management issues for patients who have spinal cord injuries.

---

**TABLE 36–5.** Managing patients with spinal injury

1. Recognize injured patients are not generally greater risk-takers.
2. Expect mourning reactions to loss of use of body.
3. Evaluate premorbid personality to understand coping techniques.
4. Consider anxiety and optimism as well as depression.
5. Individualize traditional stage theories of mourning.
6. Avoid giving priority to medication over psychotherapy.
7. Gauge self-care ability based on past self-care.
8. Expect enhanced self-concepts with experience of mastery.
9. Avoid learned helplessness with early rehabilitation.
10. Treat interfering affective reactions before discharge.
11. Respect "primitive" rationalization and denial if they work.
12. Help avoid catastrophizing and worrying.
13. Encourage mental rehearsal for goals after discharge.
14. Consider spouse and socioeconomic and educational level in plans.

---

## Sexual Therapy for Patients With Spinal Cord Injuries

Sexual therapy for the patient with a spinal cord injury, like sexual counseling for other patients, requires that the psychiatrist be comfortable and specially trained in such work. Schuler (1982) culled the techniques from five programs. The myth that patients with spinal cord injuries are asexual should be dispelled, and these patients should be helped to derive satisfaction from their sexual relations. The psychiatrist should emphasize resolving the high rate of marital discord. This includes not provoking guilt in the spouses with homilies about mutual responsibility, but instead giving close attention to the spouse's role in the vital area of sexuality. Ovulation still occurs in women with spinal cord injuries, and testicular atrophy is avoided in many men who receive excellent care. Pregnancy is possible with artificial insemination. Attitudes toward sexuality may be changed with the exploration of neglected erogenous zones in each partner, and sexuality should be redefined as any activity that is mutually stimulating.

A person with spinal cord injury can be taught to prepare a new partner by explaining the physical condition and improving communication. New techniques that use mechanical devices for stimulation and the expanded use of fantasy may be introduced. The psychiatrist should be sensitive to a patient's embarrassment and should be willing to spend sufficient time to discuss the topics. A psychosexual history may be used to obtain information that initially may be controversial (e.g., prosthetic devices, oral sex, and masturbation). Disabled male patients and their spouses must be helped to avoid rigid sex-role stereotypes of male domination and female passivity.

## The Family Model in Spinal Cord Injury

Whereas family attitudes about the injured person's entitlements are pervasive, all members of the family are affected differently according to their roles. Children must be specially prepared for their first confrontation with their parent's disability (Romano 1976), especially in dealing with fantasies of divine punishment. Children and other family members who construe human relationships in overly corporeal terms may also fear that with paralysis, the disabled parent has lost all effectiveness as an authority to admire or control them. Questions about the meaning of suffering almost always arise in persons with strong religious beliefs; often persons whose religiousness is less than mature have fantasies that they or their entire families are being punished for their intrinsic "badness." Steinglass et al. (1982) considered the suddenness of the effect of spinal cord injury on families and how an overemphasis on short-term stability of family life may lead patients to sacrifice family needs for growth and development. Family involvement with the rehabilitation process decreases feelings of anxiety, helplessness, and isolation.

## Epilepsy

Twenty million Americans will have at least one seizure during their lives, and 2 million will have spontaneously recurrent seizures. Although seizures generally can be controlled and patients remain relatively well adjusted, in one study of patients with epilepsy, Roberts and Guberman (1989) found that 33% had been treated for mental disorder.

Kardiner (1932) emphasized the regressive nature of seizure states, in which elements of early infancy are reexperienced, and Cregeen (1993), reviewing such psychoanalytic formulations, presented a case in which wishes for fusion with mother were combined with fantasies of Mr. Spock's Vulcan Mind Meld from the television series *Star Trek*. All seizures engender fantasies that must be explored.

In formulating psychotherapy, the neuropsychiatrist may consider the functional context in which epilepsy occurs (Sands 1982). Differing age-related needs and tasks may be delayed or arrested at each stage of life by seizures, which usually have a regressive, exhibitionistic, and shame-producing effect. In preschool-aged children, it is important to consider the effect on the affective climate of the family and whether the family reaction manifests enlightenment or neurotic enmeshment. In the school-aged child, the psychiatrist should consider the effects of peer acceptance or scapegoating on the patient's compliance with medication regimens. In the adolescent, issues related to epilepsy and driving, dating, sexuality, employability, and substance abuse should be explored. It is also important to determine whether there is any linkage of seizure occurrence to menstruation and, if so, what the teenage girl's ideas about this relationship may be. The visibility of medication side effects may be mortifying for an adolescent. For a young adult, the psychiatrist should help the patient consider the degree of autonomy as opposed to inhibition of independence. Travel becomes relevant for such a patient, as well as issues regarding the pursuit of a career and the acceptance of seizures by employers, prospective mates, or the patient's own family. In the older adult, the psychiatrist needs to help the patient accept any necessary limitations on living alone or to face issues such as forced retirement or placement in a nursing home.

## Management of Interictal Behavior and Personality Changes

From Blumer (1982), we may adapt hints for the management of the behavior and personality changes that he associated with the interictal states of temporal lobe epilepsy (complex partial seizure state) and that may occur in other seizure states:

1. Viscosity, or stickiness, to a subject in conversation (or to the interviewer) by a laborious, detailed, and emphatic conversation and delay at the door on the way out may be worked with if the psychiatrist is neither rejecting nor overly passive. Self-critical patients with left temporal foci accept this issue better than

do patients with right temporal foci, who tend to deny it.

2. Deepened emotionality is associated with conflict around a hyperreligious overpreoccupation with righteousness and a Dostoevskian concern with crime and punishment. In these patients, cheerful hypermoralism alternates with briefer episodes of explosive verbalized anger and threatened violence, followed by remorse or denial. A patient may benefit from the psychiatrist's explaining how others learn to avoid the patient because of this deepened emotionality. These patients also may be coached to drop the proselytizing mode and remove themselves physically from entanglements.

3. Hyposexuality is seldom complained of but further isolates patients with temporal lobe epilepsy, especially males. Although the hyposexuality may be drug responsive, the psychiatrist should address the isolation and the needs of the spouse and encourage closeness.

4. Mood swings, especially those that build up over several days to a seizure, may be difficult for relatives, who try to avoid outbursts.

5. Schizophrenia-like psychosis may occur after many years in the presence of a personality more like that of the patient with temporal lobe epilepsy than that of the schizoid patient. The psychiatrist should adapt the treatment approach to specific features, as with patients who are schizophrenic. Psychosis may diminish when anticonvulsants are discontinued for a few days.

6. Memory disorders, which are related in severity to seizure severity and bitemporality, occur retrograde and anterograde during postictal confusion. Having the patient write memos at the first sign of an aura may help. Psychomotor automatisms also are a postictal phenomenon to be identified and explained.

## Alzheimer's Disease

Cummings and Jeste (1999) stated that demographic projections to the year 2010 indicate a 25% increase in Alzheimer's disease and other dementias and call for advocacy and education of those involved in managed care organizations.

The neuropsychiatrist should approach the effect of Alzheimer's disease on the patient and his or her family in a way that is comprehensive yet sensitive to the stage of the disease. The following suggestions are adapted and amplified from Aronson (1984), Jenicke (1985), and Rabins et al. (1982).

Because attention and memory are impaired in patients with Alzheimer's disease, a dyadic psychotherapeutic learning process is usually impossible. In speaking with the patient and the family together, however, the psychiatrist should convey by affects directed toward the patient that the patient is valued by the psychiatrist. This provides for attitudinal modeling by the family and helps prevent retaliatory behavior by the patient against the family. It may be difficult for physicians and other professionals to have genuine feelings of appreciation of the Alzheimer's patient because professionals are selected and trained to value intellect and memory in themselves over personality, sensation, or pleasure.

The single overriding principle for treatment of the family of the Alzheimer's patient is the maintenance of family homeostasis and equilibrium despite the great changes in roles that result. Both patient and family benefit most if the family life can preserve its function as a holding environment for all its members and a social entity in which the members can feel loved and be loving.

Sleep is the first consideration in home care. The family cannot care for the patient and will resent the patient more if family members have sleep deficits caused by the patient's reversed sleep cycle. A strict diurnal schedule is prescribed, as with any insomnia, with sufficient daily activity and exercise so that the characteristically physically vigorous patient does not have an unusual amount of leftover energy during the night.

Quality-of-life considerations for the family should be immediately addressed by the psychiatrist. Discussions should counter the family's irrational feelings of guilt, family shame, punitive self-denial, and taking responsibility for the disease, all of which may lead to resentment and the potential for abuse of the patient. The physician must *prescribe* family fun with and without the patient. Small et al. (1997) reported that psychotherapeutic intervention with family members is often indicated because nearly half of all caregivers become depressed. Teri et al. (1997), in a controlled study of two nine-session behavioral treatments for depression in dementia, one emphasizing patient-pleasant events and one emphasizing caregiver problem solving, showed that both yielded significant patient and caregiver improvement in depressive symptoms lasting to 6-month follow-up, as compared with control subjects receiving typical care or wait list. In the pleasant-events therapy (lacking behavioral strategies), after an introductory session, four sessions were devoted to identifying, planning, and increasing pleasant events for the patient; following this, caregiver problems and pleasant-event planning for themselves were addressed. In the problem-solving therapy, the focus was on patient depressive behaviors of specific concern to caregivers. It is significant that the caregivers, many of whom were significantly depressed, also had improved depression scores, even though they were not seeking treatment for themselves and treatment was not targeted to them but rather trained them to aid the patient.

Financial planning based on clinical reality should be addressed as soon as possible after diagnosis. Early consultation with a social worker to access available care resources and legal advice about the shifting of financial responsibility can help avoid bankrupting the family. The psychiatrist should neither shun relevant financial concerns nor take sides in financial disputes. Aspects of the patient's clinical condition may enter into court proceedings, and the psychiatrist should keep clinical notes grounded in specific observations, quotes, and evaluations.

Care of the patient, a new dependent, requires help from the whole family, but children and other immature family members may find it especially taxing and may be less than helpful because of their own unanswered needs for support and inability to tolerate a situation that does not conform with ideal expectations. The psychiatrist should assist the family in avoiding situations that are stressful to the patient's diminished processing ability. Just as a person with cardiac failure should not be physically overtaxed, a person with brain failure should not be pressed to evaluate multiple inputs or to negotiate complex interpersonal situations, to compensate for changes in plans or schedules that were attuned to bodily cycles, or to weather a physical illness without special help.

The family can prevent the patient from making errors and straying by eliminating dangerous choices. Weapons, dangerous tools, or substances that could be erroneously ingested by the patient must be locked away, and outside door locks that cannot be opened at night should be installed. Keys to the car can be made unavailable, knobs can be removed from stoves, and matches should be hidden. The patient should not be left alone with minors who would be vulnerable to molestation. Secondary systems of memory enhancement may be used, such as posted signs, arrows, daily schedules, and identifying labels on objects or clothes. Simple syntax should be used in all conversations so that the patient's memory and attention are not taxed.

Frank fear in the patient should be investigated as a possible index of victimization by the family. The psychiatrist should employ knowledge of the 15 predictable functional assessment stages in the progression of both normal aging and Alzheimer's disease, as described by Reisberg (1985), to weigh the presence of other, treatable factors. For example, incontinence should only occur late in Alzheimer's disease; if the patient experiences this problem sooner, there may be a treatable infection. Loss of the ability to dress properly never precedes loss of the ability to choose clothing properly and could mean the patient is misbehaving. However, skills that the patient had yesterday may be gone today, and the family should be helped to accept the deterioration. As the sad saying goes, first it's forgetting names, then forgetting to zip up, then forgetting to zip down.

Katz (1998), noting that depression with reversible cognitive impairment may be a prodrome for dementia, concluded that recent research supports the reliability of assessment of typical depressive symptoms, even in patients with mild to moderate cognitive impairment, by self-rating with the Geriatric Depression Scale, which remains valid in patients with a Mini-Mental State Exam (Folstein et al. 1975) score of 15 or more. Potential difficulties with assessment include families' tendencies to report greater depression in patients than clinicians do and the ambiguity of apathy and related symptoms that can result from both depression and Alzheimer's disease.

Chen et al. (1991) found that in the early stages of Alzheimer's disease, extrapyramidal signs and psychosis were more likely to develop than myoclonus but that as the disease progressed, the risk of developing myoclonus equaled that of the other two signs. They concluded that all three signs are developmental features marking the progression of the disease rather than disease subtypes. Although it may reflect their negative stereotyping of psychiatric illness, families frequently prefer to view psychosis as secondary to the progression of Alzheimer's disease rather than as a primary disease. When the symptoms or brain imagery suggest elements of vascular dementia, the family may prefer to emphasize that their loved one is having "a series of little strokes," even though the impeded ambulation in patients with subcortical multiinfarct dementia is among the most trying of symptoms for caregivers. Although the psychiatrist stands for medical reality, clinical tact dictates forbearance in not hammering insistently at diagnostic classification. Relatives may see themselves as future patients. Mayeux et al. (1991) found a 50% chance of dementia by age 91 years in the first-degree relatives of patients with Alzheimer's disease but almost the same percentage in relatives of patients with other dementias and cognitive disorders in Parkinson's disease, a sixfold higher incidence than in the relatives of healthy elderly subjects.

It is an emotional reality that families may "premourn" the loss of the personality of Alzheimer's patients before the death of these patients and may thereby devalue what is left of the person. Often the patient is protected by the disease from awareness of this emotional abandonment, but at times when sensibility lingers, the caring physician remains the last real representative of "other people." Table 36–6 summarizes management issues for patients with Alzheimer's disease.

---

**TABLE 36–6.** Management issues for patients with Alzheimer's disease

1. Convey valuation of patient for attitudinal modeling.
2. Maintain equilibrium of family when roles must shift.
3. Prescribe sleep and exercise schedule so patient sleeps at night.
4. Discuss family guilt and shame about affected member.
5. Prescribe family fun with and without patient.
6. Refer to social worker to access care resources.
7. Suggest legal help with financial responsibility.
8. Avoid taking sides in family financial disputes.
9. Encourage log of incapacities in advanced patient.
10. Note effect of newly dependent patient on dependent family members.
11. Attend to age-specific needs of children, teenagers.
12. Encourage substitute role models for children.
13. Discuss wounded pride about loss of ideal family image.
14. Assist family in avoiding situations that tax brain failure.
15. Coach family in avoiding changes in plans and schedules.
16. Give added help at times of stress, such as during physical illness.
17. Capitalize on poor memory to distract patient from stress.
18. Lock up weapons, poisons, money, and car keys.
19. Remove matches, lighters, and knobs from stove.
20. Do not leave patient alone with minors vulnerable to molesting.
21. Set timers for comforting radio and television programs in patient's room.
22. Post signs, labels, and arrows as memory reinforcers.
23. Avoid household clutter and distracting background sounds.
24. Speak in short clauses and simple syntax to patient.
25. Investigate frank fear in patient for possible abuse.
26. Check emerging problems against known stages to see if avoidable.
27. Help patient find appropriate substitute activities with friends.
28. Attend closely to mental health needs of spouse.
29. Note overconcern about care, concealing feeling of family that patient would be "better off dead."
30. Note that patient gait impediments are among the most frustrating for caregivers.
31. Recognize family may premourn physical death of patient.

## Other Suggestions for Psychotherapy With Memory-Impaired Patients

Clinicians should facilitate trust by establishing a therapeutic relationship with the memory-impaired patient, as much as possible, that has a higher priority than that with relatives and caregivers. Hushed-voice discussions with family should be particularly avoided. The memory impaired are *not* hard of hearing and may piece together overheard fragments into planning that excludes their interests and wishes. The psychiatrist should avoid causing iatrogenic paranoia. His or her respect for the patient serves as a model for imitation by family and caregivers.

More than most patients, memory-impaired patients track affects. They pay particular attention not so much to what is said but to the expressiveness with which it is said. Memory of affective experiences with the psychiatrist persists when cognitive recall of what was said does not. The psychiatrist must tune his or her own affect projections up or down as dictated by the patient's condition.

It is helpful to get the patient on a platform of familiarity to optimize mnemonic function. An example is asking the patient to say something in a language learned as a youth. One patient, remembering early French studies, enjoyed recalling and repronouncing the historical name *Vercingetorix*.

Sessions should be scheduled at the same time of day to capitalize on continuity of state-dependent memory based on circadian rhythms. Registration can be facilitated by not overloading the patient with too much information or gratuitous elaboration. The patient's attention can be maintained by projection of affect and sympathetic interest. Distractions, especially ambient noise, but also clutter and unessential comments, should be eliminated.

The patient should not be expected to converse while walking into the consulting room; the psychiatrist should wait to talk until the patient is settled in a chair and should not speak while the patient is speaking or engaged in an action, such as signing a Medicare form. The psychiatrist must be tolerant of perseveration at session's end; it is usually a sign that the therapeutic relationship is beneficial.

The patient should always be allowed to complete a thought, even if it is repetitive, stereotyped, or perseverative. For the patient, it may have the power of repeating reassuring prayers or imprecations to ward off chaos. An example is one patient who would recite the names of his former caregivers in reverse whenever the current one was brought up. Another patient described the frail memory structures that would reemerge as she spoke animatedly about a topic as "a house of cards" that would collapse when she would be interrupted by a person intent on another mission, however trivial, such as arranging a pillow behind her.

Repeating and, if possible, restating in a briefer and more pithy way what patients say helps them remember and feel welcome.

Patients should be taught to use notes to keep track and helped to construct hierarchies. A labeled photograph album of familiar persons can be shared with the psychiatrist.

Interpretations, communications, or instructions should be broken down into simpler steps in sequence. Statements should be to the point and not overly drawn out or complex in syntax. I use the term *sound bytes* in instructing families and spouses not to string together chained associations. If ideas require multiple sentences, topic sentences and summaries should be used.

The patient's ability to abstract and generalize should be reevaluated periodically. If the patient generalizes poorly, he or she should be allowed to approach and master each situation as separate and distinct.

Patients should be affectively rewarded with varying facial expressions and tones to praise achievements of insight. Therapeutic reactions and interventions should be expressed by the psychiatrist without delay to underscore emphases and facilitate recall. For example, one gentleman with preserved fastidiousness about hanging up his clothing and preserving the creases saved his family cleaning and pressing expenses and effort.

An incessant or haranguing style that might overtire the patient should be avoided. Chronic brain failure, like heart failure, requires rests. Things that were automatic before require effort at every step.

The more general premise that life is worth living may be more tenuously held by aging patients who are losing their memory and feel like they are losing their personality with it. A useful interpretation is that the patient's presence, which everyone but the patient is aware of, is more important to his or her family and friends than is his or her memory. The family may be enlisted to reinforce this. In one case of vascular dementia, the patient's daughter, unprompted, told her memory-impaired mother that her dignity in the face of her impairment had been a model for her and her siblings and reminded her how much her grandson had looked forward to introducing his fiancée to her. Prior to this, the mother had reported lying in bed each night praying that God would take her away and said "to live without a memory is to live without a consciousness of yourself." Now she said, "you all have to stay close to me and preserve what's left of me to matter to you all."

Matteson et al. (1997) helpfully approached treating the regressive aspects of Alzheimer's disease and related disorders within a Piagetian framework. Patients with normal forgetfulness maintain formal operations (age 12 and older), those with borderline or mild disease use concrete operations (ages 7–12) and benefit by set routines, those with moderate disease use preoperational thinking (ages 2–7) and benefit by instructions one at a time and aid with bathing and dressing, and those with moderately severe and late-stage disease use sensorimotor cognition (ages 0–2) and benefit by assistance in daily and basic activities, such as hygiene, toileting, and eating.

## Care for the Caregiver

Maintenance of the caregiver is of prime importance. The defense mechanism I have termed *heterostasis*, the reliance on another to maintain one's cognitive and emotional integrity, commonly appears in the memory-impaired person reliant on a spouse or other caregiver. The patient's separation anxiety, although more understandable, is also more imprisoning for the caregiver, who may need to run errands and write checks as well as have time to herself or himself. Some suggestions for the caregiver include ways of taking leave of the patient.

When leaving, the caregiver should break cleanly and move out smartly. The analogous situation is the mother of a kindergartner, but one for whom every day seems like the first day. The child fusses until the mother is gone, then begins to relate to whomever he or she is left with. The presence of the spouse may be extended in various ways:

- *The visual souvenir*—a smiling portrait of the spouse is produced and placed prominently, with the time of return noted.
- *The auditory fetish*—the sound of the caregiver's voice is reassuring. For example, a spouse who had experience reading for the blind was encouraged to produce a reassuring script recalling pleasant times together that can be played in her absence on a tape recorder.
- *The videocassette surrogate*—with the help of other family members, a videotaped interview with the spouse, on whom the patient relies for heterostasis, is prepared. This runs from 2 to 6 hours and allows the spouse sufficient time away. The camera is kept largely on the full face. With poor enough memory, it remains fresh.
- *The cellular telephone umbilical link*—cellular telephones are ideal for the caregiver to take with him or her, when the memory-impaired patient is able to answer the telephone or be directed to it. Usually

finding the ringing phone is no problem. After suddenly or surreptitiously leaving, the caregiver immediately dials the home number from the hallway. When the patient answers the telephone, he or she is told the caregiver is completing an errand and will be home soon. The timing of the next call is based on experience with the latency of the patient's reaccumulating separation anxiety. The psychiatrist can help determine this by asking the patient to wait alone in the waiting room while consulting with the spouse. Usually, after a time the patient will knock on the door, if he or she still remembers the caregiver is behind it. Alternatively, the caregiver can be asked to leave and the patient's discomfort observed.

In the happy situation of other patients who have an abundance of family or staff at hand to help, a great deal of heterostasis is adaptive, compensates greatly for the memory impairment, and may be praised as an accomplishment ("You have been very successful in using others for your memory"). But even here, tensions arise, and the patient may be ready for help with some more independent techniques, such as a memory book as described by Burke et al. (1994). As in all other matters, the patient can be helped to be as normal as possible by using a standard daily appointment reminder book with added sections on orientation, memory log, calendar, things to do, transportation, feelings log, names, and today's tasks. Reviewing of the memory book should be scheduled several times during the day and sometimes prompted by a wristwatch alarm. Practice sessions are essential, with shopping, outings, therapy assignments, and so forth. The physician adopts a coaching style, and the patient writes entries into the book.

## Treating the Working Memory

Research by Goldman-Rakic (1992, 1994) and others has described a component of memory that is short term, accessed to be used or applied, and driven by attentional processes. It functions like random access memory (RAM) computer chips, which hold data temporarily for processing that has been stored in long-term components (the hard drive or CD-ROM in the computer analogy). Goldman-Rakic showed that the working memory, located in the prefrontal cortex, is connected to sensory memories and can be inactivated in specific segments, much like visual field cuts. Working memory lasts for 10–15 seconds of mental focus and has a span that includes the sentence before and after the one that is being spoken. It also differs in the right and left prefrontal cortices, similarly to differences in right and left cortices generally,

in that the right side pictures the memory (of a face, for example) and the left side encodes information about it.

The working memory, especially the keeping of a train of thought, is hypothesized to be impaired in schizophrenia. Weinberger et al. (1986) has shown in positron emission tomography studies a diminished prefrontal cortical response to challenge by the Wisconsin Card Sorting Test (Heaton 1985), which constantly changes the rules of a classification task. But schizophrenia brings other problems, especially with attention itself, and other conditions with prefrontal damage (and damage to other areas of the brain where working memory may be distributed) can create problems with the working memory.

The spatiality of this memory (and in this humans are like other mammals, such as rats) offers clues as to how to approach its impairment therapeutically. The patient can be encouraged to approach memory tasks spatially. Any of us who has moved our office and all of its books (especially in middle age) can appreciate how much of our functioning memory is pegged to the location of our printed sources. Visualizing a familiar room with objects positioned in familiar places may be helpful. Some computer programs have used this principle to become more user friendly. Anything that gets the patients to move, such as sports or dancing, is helpful, even if they do not recall the scores or the steps. Many patients recall essential contacts or resources in a maplike way, and this should be encouraged. Drawings, cartoons, and maps can be produced by the patient, sometimes with help, and kept for reference. Geography games are good, but work with maps should emphasize neighborhood and floor plans (e.g., the way to the psychiatrist's office) as well as countries and continents. In all of this, we count on some brain plasticity, which may lead to improvement with practice. Memory is only one component of general intelligence, and intellectual activity can help stave off its deterioration.

## Contribution of the Somatic Memory

The somatic, motoric, procedural, or action type of memory has been recognized as distinct from the explicit or declarative memory, and it may be preserved or impaired with some independence and also some plasticity. Performing a neurologic examination is valuable in evaluating the intactness or impairment of the motor and action system, which I have classified functionally (Forrest 1994). People with motor impairment may have difficulty remembering or conceptualizing spatial relationships. This is one reason to prescribe exercise for patients with a variety of disorders from depression to Parkinson's disease. In aging and senile dementia of the Alzheimer's type, the declarative memory may be quite disturbed with more preservation of the somatic procedural memory. If possible, the physician should try to link this with cortical spatiality by prescribing the maintenance of physical mobility through exercise and sports and encouraging visual and pictorial activities such as the mapmaking and diagramming of familiar spaces mentioned above. Such exercises have more applicability and generalizability than do abstract cognitive remediation exercises. The rebuilding of habits capitalizes on the automatic activities being separately represented (and, rarely, vulnerable to loss in isolation—as of automatic speech such as prayer). Ordinarily, musical activities may be more easily recalled or performed. For example, Matteson et al. (1997) recommended the consistent use of certain songs to announce patient meetings.

## Approach to Agitation in the Profoundly Demented

Cohen-Mansfield and Deutsch (1996) analyzed the catchall term *agitation* as meaningful communication and suggested therapeutic responses that are adapted to the patients' capabilities. Even though neurologic impairment sets the stage, there is some indication that verbal agitation such as screams and abusive language, although usually undirected, occurs more on awakening, suggesting toilet needs, or preceding staff manipulation, perhaps to avoid painful handling. These behaviors also occurred when the patient was alone at night or fearful. Determining when a confused person is too cold or in pain requires careful attention. Individualized treatment included reinforcing desirable behavior and ignoring inappropriate behavior.

For physically aggressive persons, staff handling should be monitored. Physically nonaggressive behaviors often may be adaptive and can be accommodated in a protected manner (e.g., allowing the patient to pace in a sheltered garden or making meal and bath times flexible). Often, agitation signals nonphysical, existential needs, such as for human contact, meaningful activities, stimulation, and reassurance about fears and losses. Activities can be provided to harness the patients' energy that are tailored to the patients' sense of identity, former work role, and preferences; their sensory abilities (which may need to be augmented with eyeglasses or hearing aids); and their current needs, such as for contact, stimulation, exercise, or a specific activity such as being helpful or useful. Intact sensory modalities can be used. For example, visual capacity permits gazing at mirrors, windows, videotapes of family, and old movies. The patient can lis-

ten to audiotapes, telephone contacts, music, and religious services. Mobility permits social visits, rocking chairs, walks, and tasks. Intact touch can be occupied with massage, jacuzzi, pillows or stuffed animals, exploring materials, and pet care.

Patients can be helped to value the strengths and purposes of their minds at every stage. As the curve for raw memory retention falls, the curve for wisdom often rises, at least for a time. Capacities for loving and caring should be treasured. Later, the capability of mere sensual pleasure and comfort may be the best one can expect.

## Parkinson's Disease

In describing the "shaking palsy" as a purely motor rather than mental degeneration, Parkinson (1817) referred to depression and terminal delirium, and it was once taught that the mind is not affected in patients with Parkinson's disease. Reflecting the more recent recognition of concomitant mental involvement, Mayeux and Stern (1983) described some of the specific mental processes that are impaired. Building on such observations, the psychiatrist may make a more educated psychotherapeutic approach to the patient with this syndrome.

## Treatment Considerations in Early Parkinson's Disease

Although the cognitive impairments of late Parkinson's disease may be underestimated under the surmise that it is a purely motor disorder, this is largely true at the onset of the disease when there is a prospect of many years of good function. Early cases should be exposed as little as possible to the most advanced cases in support groups or waiting areas. The patient's significant other should not be addressed as the *caregiver* because this conjures up for many people the specter of a complete dependent on their hands in the near future. The term *partner* is preferable, emphasizing that the couple are partners in living. As soon as possible after diagnosis, the couple should be urged to take a vacation, even a brief one, to stake out pleasure goals, which should be renewed on a continuing basis. Concealment of the diagnosis may be of the highest priority early in the disorder, depending on the patient's occupation, and demands for secrecy are realistic, not paranoid. Whatever the pharmacologic therapy, the couple can benefit from psychotherapy to counter stresses that amplify the tremor and bradykinesia. The couple should be encouraged to compensate for the parkinsonian facies by practice in remembering to animate the affect, enunciate clearly and loudly enough, and restore normal gestural fluency as much as possible. If aging ballerinas and actors can play young persons, Parkinson's patients can often imitate nonparkinsonian mannerisms. Just as inattention to or distraction from the affected parts can amplify symptoms, attention and volition can diminish them. The parkinsonian facies is a default position in the early stages, and interpersonal and videotaped feedback can teach the patient to be more facially expressive, to smile when encountering others, to move the eyes, and to avoid the fixed, astonished, expressionless mask that occurs in face-to-face listening.

Psychotherapeutic support of patient and partner is indicated. Waters (1999), following Golbe and Sage (1995), suggested a timetable for illness-related discussions:

- At diagnosis, the clinician should generalize about the disease and its treatability.
- At 1–2 months, the clinician should explain the typical prognosis (progression over two decades), tell of the promise of research, and recommend lay literature and *national* support societies.
- At 8 months, the clinician should educate about treatment complications if L-dopa has been started.
- At 2 years, the clinician should recommend a *local* support group and regular exercise if sedentary.

Although tremor, rigidity, and bradykinesia cannot be eliminated by nonpharmacologic approaches, their functional effect can be modified by physical and occupational therapy. Waters (1999) illustrated helpful exercises and recommended walking a mile a day, swimming to aid symmetrical use of muscles, and favorite activities, such as ballroom dancing. Environmental measures include removing doorsills, scatter rugs, obstructing furniture, and difficult faucets or handles. Cathy Curtis, P.T. (personal communication, May 2000), recommended smooth, nonslippery flooring that does not have dazzling reflections.

In a controlled study of behavioral strategies in Parkinson's disease patients over a 10-week period in which their medication was held constant, Müller et al. (1997) used an optoelectronic two-camera motion analysis system to show improvement in postural control and the initiation of movement. As the authors noted, parkinsonian patients were able to improve their shuffling and small-stepped gait voluntarily as long as they concentrated. Difficulty initiating and maintaining stepping also can be influenced by external visual cues, such as a striped floor; auditory cues, such as a marching song; or internal cues, such as silently speaking a command to move oneself.

Emotional or psychosocial stress also strongly influences gait posture and other motor performance. Behavioral interventions are aimed at standing straighter, balancing better, starting more quickly to walk, and stepping more rhythmically with normal arm swing. Special strategies taught include using external cues (visual, acoustic, or tactile) when walking or during motor freezing episodes and practice in getting up from a chair, turning in bed, and handwriting. Dividing complex movements into several simpler movements (chaining) is positively reinforced with the handwriting or longer distance walking. When training the gait, videotaped feedback and rehearsals are used, and progressive muscle relaxation is taught to control movements, especially when stressed. Social skills training helps to apply the new learning to problematic situations. Forward bending (a stooped posture) appeared to be very sensitive to behavioral changes and may be clinically useful in quantifying disease progression.

Dementia is estimated to affect 20% of the patients with Parkinson's disease (Waters 1999), more among older- than younger-onset disease, and usually is a subcortical dementia, with memory loss associated with poor concentration and initiative and slow responses (bradyphrenia) rather than with the aphasia, apraxia, and agnosia of cortical dementias such as Alzheimer's. Hallucinosis occurs in 30% of the L-dopa-treated patients, but the hallucinations are nonthreatening and can be managed without neuroleptics in most patients, some of whom even appear amused by them.

Because the degree of intellectual impairment tends to increase as the severity of motoric symptoms increases (Mayeux and Stern 1983), the psychiatrist should also assume that the patient will have greater impairment in the ability to make therapeutic contact if motor ability is more impaired. Furthermore, the psychiatrist should not conclude that all psychopathology is reactive to impairment or that the constriction of the patient's life is due solely to motoric limitations. Beatty et al. (1989) found the Mini-Mental State Exam useful in assessing the cognitive impairments of Parkinson's disease, and they also found that tests of frontal lobe function, such as the Wisconsin Card Sorting Test, did not indicate that the cognitive impairments experienced by these patients arose principally from typical frontal lobe dysfunction. Instead, such tests suggested that cerebral dysfunction extended beyond subcortical-frontal circuits.

Mayeux and Stern (1983) found that bradykinesia and rigidity, but not tremor, gait disturbance, or posture, predicted overall intellectual performance for a patient taking the Mini-Mental State Exam. The neuropsychiatrist should not hesitate to examine the patient neurologically to gauge potential areas of mental difficulty. Although this would appear to be a roundabout approach compared with doing a mental status examination, it is often less threatening and efficiently yields a preliminary clinical impression. The types of motor impairments tell us much about the patient's quality of thought, insight, and ability to relate to the therapist. Mayeux and Stern (1983) and Hallet (1979) noted that the activities that are impaired require directed attention to the task, sequencing of cognitive processes, and often additional motor interaction. In more psychiatric terms, these activities involve an inherent motoric or spatial mental action.

Other disturbances characteristic of patients with Parkinson's disease are impaired perceptual motor or visuospatial functions, especially the inability to perform sequential or predictive voluntary movements (Stern et al. 1984). This results in impaired internal spatial representation (from which may arise the initiation of independent thought and mental action) and articulatory difficulty without impaired language reception or production. In fact, Parkinson's disease is distinct from other neuropsychiatric disorders because of the paucity of language impairment, a significant boon to the psychiatrist trying to do psychotherapeutic work.

Memory in these patients is often slowed without being impaired. Trouble with word finding, which worsens with increased motoric symptoms in some parkinsonian patients, was considered a form of the "tip of the tongue" phenomenon similar to anomia in aphasic patients with frontal lobe lesions. Mayeux (1984) summarized a review of the literature on Parkinson's disease and Huntington's disease by stating that "nearly every patient with a movement disorder has some type of behavioral dysfunction, whether it is personality change or intellectual impairment" (p. 537). The close linkage of motor and mental action may be turned to advantage by using a number of behavioral techniques.

For example, patients should be encouraged to keep fit by regular moderate exercise, especially if their occupations are sedentary. Fitness does not stop the progression of Parkinson's disease, but it does help patients cope with symptoms. Free-moving calisthenics and sports such as swimming are best, but safety, especially with patients who freeze motorically, must be considered.

It is important to employ sensory, rhythmic, and other cues and reminders to keep the bradykinetic patient moving. A patient can put taplike nails in the shoes to provide an auditory cue to keep the rhythm of walking constant and prevent festination. A small piece of raw carrot in the mouth may remind the patient to swallow and prevent drooling. Many techniques helpful to movement and mental state seem mechanical: wearing slippery rather than rubber soles to permit shuffling without falling, dispensing with canes and walkers when there is retropulsion, raising the back legs of chairs and toilet seats 2 inches to facilitate rising, and removing doorsills to prevent a patient from freezing in a doorway. An L-shaped extension at the tip of a cane can be stepped over so that the patient can keep moving. A simple device to quantify tremor (Forrest 1990) reassures patients of preserved control of intentional movements (see Figure 36–3) and can be used to monitor other patients whose hands shake from a variety of causes, including familial tremor and medication, and who are sensitive about this, usually in social contexts where they may be mistaken for alcoholic persons.

Motor blocks are among the most disabling and therapeutically frustrating problems in the management of Parkinson's disease. Sudden transient freezing and related phenomena are associated with narrow spaces such as doorways in 25% of patients, with turning in 45% of patients, and with starting to walk in 86% of patients, according to a large database review by Giladi et al. (1992), and occur more often in patients whose symptoms began in the gait or trunk than in the upper body. Involving "the abnormal retrieval or execution of complex motor tasks" (Giladi et al. 1992, p. 333), whether from the disease itself or a side effect of L-dopa, motor blocks also are influenced by emotional factors and visual perceptual input. Hesitation at constricted points may be an atavistic feature resembling liminal cautiousness in other animals, such as felines. The patients may be encouraged to focus on pattern continuities that may bring them past constricted points (see Figure 36–4), a feature that has been capitalized on in the experimental use of virtual-reality helmets that superimpose repetitive apparent perceptual stepping stones on the visual field.

## Nonmotor Experiences in Parkinsonism and Related Conditions

The somatosensory discomforts of parkinsonism, tardive conditions, and other movement disorders may be underestimated by the physician unfamiliar with them. Feelings of cold or burning; back, neck, and other pain; and peculiar dysphoric sensations are particularly troublesome at night, when external sensations are diminished and the rest tremor may be more noticeable, disturbing sleep. There is often a thoracospinal (axial) vibration (internal tremor) as well. Position shifting is difficult, and stiffness and cramps are troublesome. Autonomic and myoclonic complications may be present in patients with multiple system atrophy and olivopontocerebellar atrophy, respectively, and impediments of information pro-

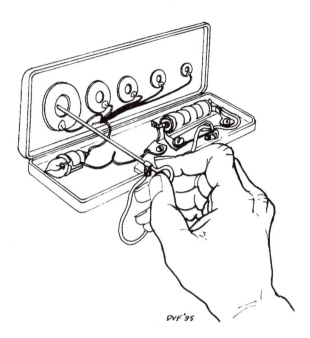

**FIGURE 36–3.** The tremometer is a simple device that closes a circuit and lights a bulb when the patient is unable to hold the probe in progressively smaller holes without touching the washers. The suggested sizes for the inside diameters of the washers are 9/16″, 3/8″, 5/16″, 1/4″, and 3/16″. Although the device quantitates tremor, it is most useful for reassuring patients that they are able to accomplish the task despite their shaky hands. Full instructions for the tremometer, suggestions for use, and clinical examples are presented in Forrest D: "The Tremometer: A Convenient Device to Measure Postural Tremor From Lithium and Other Causes." *Journal of Neuropsychiatry and Clinical Neurosciences* 2:391–394, 1990.

**FIGURE 36–4.** Patients with parkinsonism may have difficulty with motor blocks, which often occur in narrowed spaces such as doorways. This behavior has an atavistic quality and resembles the liminal wariness of animals. Concentration on visual continuities may help to counter this problem.

cessing also result. Ford et al. (1994) described painful oral and genital sensations in 11 patients with tardive akathisia, tardive dyskinesia, or tardive dystonia. Patients should be helped to learn to distract themselves from focusing on these internal symptoms. Pleasant music or reading at bedtime until sleepiness comes may be helpful, as in the psychotherapeutic approaches to insomnia generally.

Constipation is such a common feature that it has been called "the number one movement disorder" and requires constant attention to exercise, hydration, stool bulking, and balancing constipating anticholinergics against the need to reduce tremor. Patients often discontinue medications on their own and have difficulty distinguishing among the effects of polypharmacy, which is frequent. When relief from medication is only partial, especially when striatonigral degeneration is present, the psychotherapeutic role of the psychiatrist may be greater in exploring fears and mental resources. Of patients with

Parkinson's disease, 70% have impaired voice and speech, and 41% have impaired chewing and swallowing (Hartelius 1994). Speech therapy and behavioral approaches to swallowing can be helpful, but the psychiatrist's listening style also must be adapted considerably to the decreased quantity and forcefulness of the patients' speech.

Parkinson's disease is a disorder of knife-edge tolerances and balances. The response to L-dopa is so dramatic that the patient and family are exquisitely conscious of the central role of drug effects. Patient and family, building on this medication response, may try to convey the idea that the psychiatrist is dealing with a cumbersome apparatus—a thing rather than a person. The psychiatrist should avoid becoming so totally immersed in the intricacies of compelling medicomotor phenomena such as on-off reactions and sudden transient freezing that the emotional issues are neglected.

A previous strategy of being reluctant to make the diagnosis or treat it in the earliest stages may be changing, as selegiline and antioxidant therapy now may be used to slow the course and keep the patient employed (National Advisory Neurological Disorders and Stroke Council 1990). The patient whose Parkinson's disease is in an early stage should be watched closely for symptoms of depression. The psychiatrist should seriously consider the increased risk of suicide, especially in males who overvalue physical mobility and power and are extremely anxious about their continued performance in competitive and exacting sports such as tennis and golf. Activities less aggravating for the patient with mild Parkinson's disease may be chosen. More confusion than meets the eye (because of the preservation of language) contributes to the consternation felt by these patients over adaptation to the new challenge of disability. Furthermore, early pharmacotherapy for the disorder often involves anticholinergic agents, which have an additional potential for confusion.

## Treatment Considerations in Late Parkinson's Disease

Often, antiparkinsonian drugs lose their efficacy with time. This can result in severe disillusionment to patients and their families. Increasing the doses can aggravate side effects. Emotional sequelae of L-dopa treatment may include domineering behavior, increased libido, manic hyperactivity or depression, confused irrational behavior, and activation of latent psychosis, vivid nightmares that may disturb sleep, and visual hallucinations. Psychiatrists may be called on to help with these effects. Attention to the requirements for a patient's orientation (e.g., nightlights and familiar schedules), decreasing the stimulus level to diminish irritability, encouraging the beleaguered spouse to set limits, informing the spouse that the libidinal changes seldom persist, and, most of all, ensuring compliance with the times of dosing all may be helpful.

Doonief et al. (1992), in a survey of 336 patients with Parkinson's disease from 1984 to 1989, found that depression had a prevalence of 47% and an incidence rate of 1.86% per year compared with an incidence rate of 0.17% for individuals older than 40 in the general population.

Starkstein et al. (1990) studied patients with Parkinson's disease and found that 40% had major or minor depression and that depression was associated with left-hemisphere involvement in patients with unilateral symptoms. Thus, depression in the early stages of Parkinson's disease may be generally related to left-hemisphere dysfunction, although some studies have not found a lateral bias. Another peak of depression late in the course of the disease correlated with impairment of activities of daily living and of cognitive function.

The psychiatrist should explore the patient's image of the disease process. Parkinson's disease is common enough to be a vivid caricature in the minds of patients, who fear they will become an exaggeration of the motor tendencies of the aged that are assumed by stage actors and comics who portray shuffling old duffers. Fear of humiliation because of such an image may be allayed by emphasizing the medical manageability of the condition, its usual slow progression, and intense research efforts, including transplantation and brain stimulation, that are based on knowledge of the pathophysiology of the disease. Later symptoms of emotional flattening, apathy, and impoverishment of the ability to relate to loved ones can be especially painful for the spouse.

If the capability for empathic, loving relatedness is lost, as it frequently is late in a variety of organic and degenerative brain states such as Parkinson's disease, the patient may not be able to invest an inner representation of the spouse with emotion. The tragic result late in the course of the disease may be a lack of appreciation of the spouse's loving care. A patient in an advanced stage of the disease may not even miss the caregiving spouse on his or her death if the patient's practical needs are satisfied. This attitude, or lack of attitude, can alienate or demoralize the most important caregiver. Often the psychiatrist must sensitively weigh the couple's unequal relationship, including the need of the spouse who is not the patient to recognize the discouraging lack of emotional mutuality. Lucien Cote, M.D., a neurologist with extensive experience in Parkinson's disease, noted (personal communication, February 2000) that in this primarily motoric disorder, the patients particularly fail to appreciate and come to take for granted the motor assistance that is given to them. Because they are so dependent on it, the caregiver's help becomes part of their physical self-concept, which is extraordinarily malleable in all of us, as Ramachandran (1998) elegantly demonstrated experimentally. An analogy would be the fighter pilot who begins to feel that his or her body is coextensive with the airplane and its control surfaces.

## Dopamine and Personality in Parkinson's Disease

Personality is not only a learned and habitual phenomenon simply to be unlearned in the psychotherapeutic analysis of character defenses. Evidence is growing that neurotransmitters have specific influences on personality. Dopamine has been associated with novelty seeking (analogous to exploratory behavior in animals), serotonin with harm avoidance, and norepinephrine with reward dependence. Menza et al. (1990), viewing Parkinson's disease with its low dopamine levels as a natural experiment, showed by rating scales completed by patients and their families that there was significantly less novelty-seeking behavior in patients with Parkinson's disease, both currently and premorbidly, than in control subjects with rheumatologic and orthopedic diseases, and there were no differences in serotonin- and norepinephrine-mediated behaviors. The psychotherapeutic approach to the "reflective, rigid, stoic, slow-tempered, frugal, and orderly behaviors," as Menza et al. (1990, p. 286) characterized them, can include admiration of these traits as virtues. Table 36–7 summarizes management issues for patients with Parkinson's disease.

## Huntington's Disease

In a large kindred of Huntington's disease families from Venezuela, in whom the G8 DNA marker was localized to chromosome 4, all descendants were said to "inherit" the disease, but only those who were affected by it were said to "have" it (Gusella et al. 1983). Wexler (1985) pointed out that, although this distorts genetic truth, it expresses the experience of being at risk as a distinct state of mind. Because this state is stressful and conflict ridden, the psychiatrist may be consulted on various issues.

Ambiguity about whether one will be affected, as with any late-onset autosomal dominant disease, may dominate the mental life of people at risk for Huntington's disease. Administration of the genetic test for persons at risk requires much sensitivity to the emotional dimensions of determining whether an individual has the gene, and the test should always be administered as part of a personal physician-patient relationship. Only a tiny percentage of those at risk have taken the test, for a variety of reasons, including cost and fears of discrimination, especially by insurers (Mechcatie 1990). Leroi and Michalon (1998) recommended that minors usually not be tested, and a counseling program with preestablished guidelines should accompany testing of adults.

**TABLE 36–7.** Management issues for patients with Parkinson's disease

1. Estimate problems of therapeutic contact by motor impairment.
2. Estimate cognitive impairment by bradykinesia and rigidity.
3. Employ neurologic examination readily because less threatening than cognitive examination.
4. Capitalize on language preservation without underestimating impairment of spatial planning.
5. Coordinate psychotherapy with occupational and physical therapy sessions.
6. Encourage exercise and fitness to help cope with symptoms.
7. Employ sensory, mechanical, and cognitive aids to movement.
8. Anticipate symbiotic relationship with pharmacotherapy process.
9. Avoid neglecting emotional issues amidst dosing schedule.
10. Observe early in course for depression and suicide risk.
11. Choose activities and sports appropriate to abilities.
12. Distinguish early neuropsychiatric depression from later reaction to impairment.
13. Explore patient's embarrassment about image of appearance.
14. Emphasize manageability and slow progression of illness.
15. Anticipate disillusionment as drugs lose efficacy in time.
16. Anticipate side effects of L-dopa treatment.
17. Aid orientation with night-lights and schedules.
18. Decrease stimulus level to decrease irritability.
19. Anticipate spouse's pain confronted by affective flattening.
20. Praise reflective, stoic, frugal, and orderly premorbid personality.

The overlap of the initial symptoms of Huntington's disease and everyday experience, such as incidences of clumsiness, irritability, nocturnal myoclonus, emotional instability, or infrequent lapses of memory or judgment, can lead to hypochondriacal worries. The psychiatrist may help the patient by taking over the responsibility of the symptom search, distinguishing between those symptoms that overlap with normality and the disease, or by teaching the patient to delegate this function to the neurologist.

## Management of Affected Patients

van Vugt and Roos (1999) remarked that despite the recent discovery of the gene defect (an expanded trinucleotide repeat) and its product huntingtin, no curative therapy is available, and psychosocial support remains the hallmark in the care of patients and relatives confronted with genetically determined inevitable functional decline.

Knowing that one has Huntington's disease and knowing which parent is affected often leads to an unreasonable conscious or unconscious blaming of the gene-donating parent. This can disrupt vital processes of internalization of character from that parent during development. Psychotherapy can help patients deal with their longings for a healthy parental model and control primitive, envious rage against unaffected siblings. Positive aspects of the affected parent as a model should be sought. Psychotherapy can help with fantasies that the disease is a punishment, that anyone is to blame, and that alternative behaviors could have prevented it, while recognizing that such thoughts are defenses against helplessness and lack of control. In some instances, knowledge of the risk of the disorder has been denied by persons at risk, and even their professional caregivers, with the result of needless transmission of the gene to another generation (Table 36–8).

Leroi and Michalon (1998) reviewed the sparse treatment literature noting that the presence of major affective disorder in the patients (33%) is strongly correlated with that in their offspring and is associated with a positive diagnosis in the offspring. Small doses of nonsedating and nonanticholinergic antidepressants can spare remaining cognitive reserve and aid response to psychotherapy. Huntington's patients have more trouble with aggression than do Alzheimer's patients, and it may constitute the main need for hospitalization; however, a careful search should be made to determine whether provocations such as pain, thirst, hunger, frustration at changing capabilities, or imposed changes in routine are present. Irritability and social withdrawal may respond to support and structuring, and situational apathy (withdrawal, poorer hygiene, decreased initiative and motivation) may respond to structured and stimulating settings.

The disease itself adds the further incapacitation of a movement disorder to a progressive, unremitting dementia affecting higher intellectual skills and judgment. Frequently, speech is impaired, and intelligibility of communication with loved ones may be better maintained through referral to speech therapy for help with the dysarthria; speech augmentation devices may become necessary. Patients with Huntington's disease remain oriented to their surroundings, are able to recognize family and caregivers, and are able to convey their likes and dislikes somewhat better than patients with Alzheimer's disease and other dementias. In keeping with this, they have more depression and less psychosis. Choreic movements eventually may increase a patient's caloric needs to 6,000 calories per day, while the coordination required to eat and swallow the food is impaired.

Ambivalence on the part of family and staff may arise

**TABLE 36–8.** Management issues for patients with Huntington's disease

1. Interpret blaming of gene-donating parent.
2. Help patient internalize healthy heritage from affected parent.
3. Ventilate wishes for healthy parental model.
4. Work with envy and rage against unaffected siblings.
5. Discuss fantasies that disease is a punishment.
6. Recognize that ideas of blame and prevention are strategies for control.
7. Do not participate in denial of transmissibility.
8. Recognize that movement disorder adds disability to dementia.
9. Note that preservation of recognition may lead to depression.
10. Ensure that family has aid of physiatrists and nutritionists.
11. Improvise mechanical assistance to movement function.
12. Discuss family ambivalence about preserving life in downhill course.
13. Help family take pride in giving nutrition and learning Heimlich maneuver for choking.
14. Encourage caregivers to pace themselves and take recreation.

around the sad irony of the daily struggle to keep the patient adequately nourished, in view of the disease's progressive downhill course and the likelihood that the patient will one day die of choking. However, there is comfort for the family and staff in treating the patient properly, managing nutrition efficiently, and knowing the Heimlich maneuver. Care of patients with Huntington's disease is a great burden, and those who do it need to monitor and pace themselves to avoid undue discouragement while deriving the satisfaction of being compassionate and useful.

## Infections and Inflammations of the Central Nervous System

Fallon and Nields (1994), writing about the complications of Lyme disease, cautioned that previously in the history of many neuropsychiatrically significant infections—whether caused by other bacteria (neurosyphilis, tuberculosis), parasites (neurocysticercosis, toxoplasmosis), fungi (coccidiomycosis, cryptococcosis), or viruses (herpes simplex virus, human immunodeficiency virus [HIV])—as well as of inflammations of the central nervous system (CNS), such as lupus and multiple sclerosis, the associated psychiatric symptoms were thought to be functional or hysterical. Physiologically based cognitive and mood changes were erroneously attributed exclusively to emotional reactions to the illness.

This is not to say that there is no functional dimension of these conditions. Fallon et al. (1992) discussed the complex secondary reactions, on an emotional basis, to Lyme disease, with its peculiar constellation of a fluctuating course of bizarre symptoms, cognitive disability, chronic pain, and uncertainties of diagnosis and treatment.

But the physiologically based symptoms of Lyme disease include some that are among those frequently chosen for histrionic conversion. Shadick et al. (1994) found that physiologically significant late symptoms include, at $P = 0.0001$, arthralgias; at $P \leq 0.05$, extremity numbness, tingling or burning, unusual fatigue, poor concentration and/or memory loss, emotional lability, and difficulty sleeping. Not significant were myalgias, seizures, and depression.

Clearly, the psychotherapeutic approach demands a high index of suspicion to credit a physiologic basis. This is often a preferred strategy anyway in building a therapeutic alliance that will encourage the emergence of conflicts and secondary gain. Generally, the patient is reassured, but not encouraged to act more ill. In the case of HIV infection, the appearance of the first noticeable neuropsychiatric symptoms may have a grave effect on the patient, so that it is good to consider other explanations. Substantial neurologic involvement with the tickborne Lyme spirochete indicates a more aggressive treatment with intravenous antibiotics to diminish, but not necessarily eliminate, late complications. Some cases that result in residua will require neuropsychiatrically informed psychotherapy.

## Multiple Sclerosis

Whitlock (1984) reviewed the variety of affective conditions in patients with multiple sclerosis (MS) and concluded that it is difficult to separate the reactive from the organic (frontal and limbic) sources. The influential view of Cottrell and Wilson (1926) that 63% of the patients were unusually euphoric has been supplanted by numerous studies, beginning with that of Braceland and Giffin (1950), which showed more depression among these patients.

Minden and Schiffer (1990), in reviewing affective disorders in patients with MS, stated that the euphoria is usually described as a mental serenity, a cheerful feeling of physical well-being found more frequently later in the course of the disease, an affect dissociated from the cognitive awareness of the disability. This is not a fluctuating, reversible affect but a persistent change of personality.

Although a positive affect is unlikely to stir a clamor for psychotherapy, it is advisable to have a close look to address the patient's possible pain beneath the euphoria in view of the frequent depressive symptoms that do respond to psychotherapy. Minden and Schiffer (1990) noted a higher rate of bipolar disorder in MS patients. Minden (1992), plumbing more deeply into apparent euphoria in MS patients, did not view it as an unmitigated blessing, particularly when it is an outward affective display disconnected from subjectively experienced depressive feelings that become apparent on "patient and empathic inquiry" (p. 201). Emotional instability of a labile nature responds so well to antidepressants that psychotherapy alone should not be considered.

Ron and Logsdail (1989) found no evidence that psychiatric symptoms in isolation were the first manifestation of MS and that, whereas elation correlated with widespread MRI abnormalities, flattening of affect, delusions, and thought disorder correlated with temporoparietal pathology on MRI. Grant et al. (1989) found that 77% of new MS patients, compared with only 35% of control subjects, experienced marked life stress in the year before the onset of symptoms, perhaps explaining the timing of symptom exacerbation for some patients by a psychosomatic process of further destabilizing an already unstable neuroimmunologic system.

Psychiatrists should help the patient focus on the lack of certainty in prognosis in a positive sense rather than on the myriad of possible symptoms. It is important to point out that the absence of sure knowledge reflects the general uncertainty of life, including variability of the disease over time. The psychiatrist should emphasize the presence of medical support and treatment rather than the lack of cure and should be aware that the mysterious nature of the disease encourages magical theories of self-blame and of interpreting the illness as an ominous metaphor (Simons 1984).

The psychiatrist should not reinforce the sick role for these patients; rather, he or she must reiterate the concept that although the MS patient has a disease, he or she is not ill in the traditional sense. Thus, encouraging the realistic, but temporary and selective, omission of activities that are onerous for the patient becomes important. However, family fun needs to be preserved as well. Psychiatrists should recognize differences in patients' expectations about self-reliance and involvement in their own care, compared with passivity toward medical authority, in this illness, which has a great capacity to stimulate dependence on physicians. Most patients with MS are unemployed (LaRocca et al. 1985), compounding the financial strain of medical expenses and prospects of nursing home care at an unacceptably early age. If direct questioning indicates that the MS patient has sexual difficulties, the psychiatrist should distinguish between degrees of organic and psychogenic sexual dysfunction in males by nocturnal penile tumescence monitoring. Many people have erectile difficulties and anorgasmia unrelated to MS. A spouse's resistance to the labeling of a partner as "disabled" may indicate a lesser likelihood of marital breakdown than with immediate acceptance.

In assessing the potential of MS for creating disappointment with the self, the psychiatrist needs to recognize that MS is a disease of young adults that occurs in the prime of their lives, when they may have the highest performance expectations of themselves. Because extensive frontal lobe involvement of MS greatly impairs analytic ability, planning and organizing, flexibility, and emotional lability and limits the value of psychotherapy, it is important not to reach beyond reasonable therapeutic goals or to attempt sweeping revision of defenses when neuropsychiatric assessment suggests such involvement of the frontal lobe. Psychiatrists should help these patients to manage fatigue and other limitations by assisting them in selecting and planning participation in activities rather than seeing the patients withdraw or regress as a result of frustration at attempting too much. It is imperative to focus on what the patient is able to do, not what he or she is unable to do. This means that the psychiatrist should advise the patient to avoid undue stress, which temporarily worsens symptoms, and should reassure the patient that these flare-ups do not permanently advance the disease.

In a discussion that could serve as a model approach to psychotherapy for a specific neuropsychiatric condition, with implications for any infectious or inflammatory condition with a remitting and recurrent course, Minden (1992) offered suggestions for treating MS that begin with the diagnostic difficulties and phenomenologic variability and proceed from elemental principles of psychotherapy to issues of the therapeutic relationship, transference, and countertransference.

Of general interest for neuropsychiatry is Minden's advice to apply a spectrum of strategies, from insight-oriented to supportive, in a flexible way over time, as determined by the patient's needs in dealing with a fluctuating disorder and one that varies unpredictably in severity in individuals from little disability (20% of MS patients have benign disease) and moderate disability (20%–30% have relapsing-remitting MS) to severe disability (50%–60% have chronic progressive MS). In summary, Minden (1992) offered "a simple principle: when external reality is overwhelming, it must be addressed before internal reality can be explored" (p. 207). Compounding the anxiety and dread of unpredictability, not only of the course

but also of each acute episode, is the effect on the physician-patient relationship of the diagnostic difficulty: physicians are seen as evasive and insensitive and patients as demanding, annoying, or attention seeking. Fatigue, present in 90% of MS patients and incapacitating for nearly 70%, together with altered sensation and visual blurring, are subjective symptoms that often fail to elicit sympathy from professionals and family.

Minden (1992) pointed out that when there are "few objective findings, unmistakable secondary gain, and perhaps hysterical personality traits or intense preoccupation with symptoms, it is not difficult to see why a person with MS may be thought to have conversion disorder, somatization disorder or hypochondriasis" (p. 200). Somatoform disorders or emotional elaboration may coexist with MS, especially in view of the reality of the frequent disruptions of the course of life originating in the body. Minden asks us to consider whether bodily expression of emotions may be not only understandable but also healthy to some degree in patients with MS and, correspondingly, is concerned that physicians not discourage frank and frequent discussion of the symptoms that so trouble these patients.

The cognitive deficits of MS, as in other subcortical dementias, affect retrieval more than encoding and storage of information (Rao 1990, cited in Minden 1992) and are variable in degree but also in effect according to the demands of the patient's lifestyle for mental acuity. Although speech slurring is common, communication by language is less affected, and most difficulties with the larger aspects of mental planning require compensatory reevaluation and frank work with the patient.

Common themes that may be anticipated in psychotherapy for MS patients arise at characteristic points in the illness course: when function deteriorates, when the patient must use crutches or a wheelchair, when employment ends, and when nursing home placement looms. Minden (1992) noted that the wheelchair is more threatening as a symbol of humiliating loss of control early in the disease than when it is helpful and needed. She found that wives fear abandonment by spouses more than husbands do (and twice as many women develop MS). Visible impairments such as the dragging of a foot or the use of a cane cause shame, and conflicts arise over unaccustomed wishes to be cared for. Because patients attribute personal meanings to the illness, such as its being a punishment for something they were responsible for doing, Minden inferred that this may be easier to contemplate than their real powerlessness in the face of the disease. Defenses must be respected as positive attempts of the personality to cope and are not necessarily to be analyzed away unless they can be replaced with something better.

For example, much as the psychiatrist may object on a scientific or moral basis to the implication that MS patients have been bad persons, assumed guilt permits confession, expiation, and forgiveness by others or in structured religious resources.

Minden (1992) suggested that the actual course of therapy should be tailored to the condition, beginning with reservations about loss of control in being sent to a psychiatrist. The therapeutic alliance is easier to build when the initial session resembles the familiar structure of medical consultations in which the doctor actively questions the patient, replies directly to the patient's questions, and "asks about cognitive changes as easily as a neurologist asks about changes in walking" (Minden 1992, p. 204). The patient's defense of focusing on symptoms over feelings is not challenged, and there is no assumption that the patient will enter formal psychotherapy. Even if they do, patients should be encouraged to come and go in therapy according to the vicissitudes of the illness. Leaving may be more healthy than staying. Fixed rules about missed appointments are less appropriate with MS patients, in whom function is so medically context–dependent. Self-help groups such as those offered by the National Multiple Sclerosis Society should be encouraged, but fears of seeing others with advanced cases of the disease should be respected. Minden cited the work of Schiffer (1987), concluding that patients whose depression failed to improve and who were more concerned with losing their dependent gratifications had psychiatric problems that predated the MS and would be more effectively given psychiatric help.

Neuropsychologic assessments can be useful in patients who are unaware of or are denying their deficits. Before ordering the tests for this purpose, however, the neuropsychologic tester should be made aware of this intention so that the patient can be handled with tact and care.

Transference issues also were noted by Minden (1992), including the perception of the psychiatrist as "a source of stability in an otherwise unpredictable life" (p. 210). As elsewhere, idealization may lead to devaluation and disappointment. Other patients may be suspicious and anxious. Transference is always noted but not usually explored or analyzed. Countertransference problems include discomfort with chronic debilitation; embarrassment at unfamiliarity with the latest research; hesitation at necessary exploration in detail of daily dressing, bathing, and toilet function; feelings of defeat and hopelessness; impatience with scanning speech and dysarthria; guilt at being healthy and enjoying life when the patient is not; pain at watching intellectual impairment; and aggravation at failure to follow therapeutic

plans because of frontal lobe involvement. Valleroy and Kraft (1984) found that one-half to three-quarters of the persons with MS say that they have sexual impairment, which also requires special attention to transferential envy and countertransferential guilt, as in the case of other spinal cord disorders (see section "Spinal Cord Injury" earlier in this chapter).

Reflecting the murky waters of MS therapy, a meta-analysis by Mohr and Goodkin (1999) indicated that efficacy between psychotherapy and antidepressants was not significantly different for depression in MS, that improving coping skills was better than increasing insight, and that all treatments were more effective than none. Jean et al. (1999) found that neuropsychologic variables chosen for their sensitivity to MS did not predict coping styles or their effectiveness but that higher levels of distress were associated with emotion-focused coping strategies, indicating psychotherapeutic interventions aimed at improving ways of coping. Brassington and Marsh (1998) designated MS as a subcortical dementia and considered that cognitively heterogeneous patient groups may disguise more specific focal neuropsychologic impairment; they called for more evaluation of psychologic and rehabilitation interventions. Shnek et al. (1997) found that MS patients have greater levels of depression and helplessness and lower levels of self-efficacy than do spinal cord injury patients, perhaps because of the unpredictable course and possibility of being affected in many different ways. Helplessness and lower self-efficacy predicted depression, but cognitive distortions had no independent effect.

Minden (1992) also noted that what MS patients want "is simply a compassionate, understanding person with whom to share their worries and sadness" (p. 211). Table 36–9 summarizes management issues for MS patients.

## Psychogenic Movement Disorders

Tremor and dystonia are most frequently imitated. Tremor is seldom mistaken and easily tested. The posturing of dystonia is another matter; before 1978, 44% of the real dystonia cases had been previously misdiagnosed as emotional in origin (Williams and Fahn 1988). Peculiarities of the disorder may mislead. A sensory trick, such as the patient touching his or her cheek, may correct cervical dystonia (Naumann et al. 2000); patients may be able to walk backward but not forward; and symptoms may vary with emotions. In an overcorrection, by 1975, for a time no case of proven psychogenic dystonia was acknowledged. According to Williams and Fahn (1988),

**TABLE 36–9.** Management issues for patients with multiple sclerosis

1. Expect more depression than euphoria, especially early.
2. Look past euphoria for coexistent depressive symptoms.
3. Consider possible bipolar disease or steroid effects during psychotherapy.
4. Avoid relying on psychotherapy alone for treatment of emotional instability.
5. Avoid unnecessarily medicating euphoria.
6. Note likely presence of life stress before episode.
7. Suggest psychotherapy, especially after diagnosis.
8. Disclose diagnosis to significant others, not to all.
9. Assist those who are dating with disclosure after rapport with partner.
10. Help patient see uncertainty of prognosis in a positive sense of possibility.
11. Plan for the possibility of disability, as in choosing a new home, but hope for the best.
12. Anticipate magical theories of self-blame in view of mysterious nature of the disease's etiology and fluctuations.
13. Avoid reinforcing sick or disabled role.
14. Select activities to substitute for those posing difficulties.
15. Accept differences in patients' relying on selves versus doctors.
16. Inquire directly about sexual difficulties.
17. Approach sexual area cautiously and involve spouse eventually.
18. Consider urologic treatment options for male patients.
19. Adapt therapeutic goals and discourse in impaired planning ability.
20. Help to manage fatigue by selection and planning.
21. Focus on capacities, not disabilities.
22. Advise avoidance of stresses that worsen symptoms.
23. Reassure that flare-ups do not permanently advance the disease.
24. Keep newly diagnosed patients from support groups for wheelchair-bound, blind, or incontinent patients.

*Source.* Items 7–9 and 11 were adapted from Scheinberg 1983.

about 3%–5% of the cases are now estimated to be psychogenic, more likely so if the dystonia begins in the foot and at rest rather than in action, is paroxysmal rather than continual, and is accompanied by other psychogenic features such as false weakness or sensory findings, self-inflicted injuries, or multiple somatizations.

## General Suggestions for the Management of Psychogenic Dystonia

Williams and Fahn (1988) strongly suggested that patients with psychogenic dystonia be admitted to the hospital, not so much for the necessary diagnostic studies (such as a sleep study) as for the support during the explanation that their symptoms are emotional in origin, and for effective behavior therapy, employing rewards for progress. They have insisted that a neurologist be involved in the diagnosis. Placebo ruses may aid diagnosis but are not a lasting treatment, and the patient must be told immediately to avoid a sense of betrayal. The patient is told "firmly that he/she has dystonia and that it is caused by unconscious conflicts which cause real physical symptoms. Pent-up emotions need to be expressed, and when there has been some blockage of this process, they do so by producing these abnormal movements" (p. 453). Patronizing, condescending, or morally judgmental attitudes sabotage prospects for engagement.

Constricting reimbursement for care now makes hospitalization less often possible, yet an intervention is called for on an outpatient basis. The following are suggestions from our experience at the Movement Disorder Clinic at The Neurological Institute of New York.

## Studies in Hysteria Revisited: Multidisciplinary Approach to Conversion Disorder in an Outpatient Movement Disorder Clinic

There are few such dramatic demonstrations of the dynamic unconscious as those patients whose conflicts are expressed in psychogenic movement disorders that are not conscious malingering. Yet, a delving, uncovering approach may be especially unsuited to these patients' needs, at least initially, for several reasons. These cases also strain the diagnostic acumen of both psychiatrists and neurologists. It is possible to adopt a helpful psychotherapeutic stance that bridges the organic-functional dilemma before diagnostic certainty.

As in psychiatry generally, our cases are context dependent, and our procedures are not rigid. But general guidelines are emerging from our experience. These apply to unconsciously or mostly unconsciously maintained symptoms rather than primarily malingering or compensation neuroses.

- *Use proximity, immediacy, and expectancy.* These three cardinal principles from military psychiatry denote the availability of psychiatric consultation at the site and at the time of the neurologic consultation, together with a positively maintained expectancy of symptomatic improvement. The psychiatric function should appear to the patient to be naturally and seamlessly integrated into the consultation, rather than at a remove, suggesting banishment.
- *Capitalize on the patient's wish to change.* The patient may be fed up with the inconvenience of the symptom and secretly disgusted with himself or herself. This

may be more likely late in the chain of referral, when frustration has mounted.

- *Employ the cachet of the specialty clinic.* Prestige of place coupled with acceptance by the elite specialists, when these can be offered, provide a narcissistic booster.
- *Provide multidisciplinary attention.* Being presented before at least half a dozen clinic specialists fulfills a wish for attention and signals that a definitive opinion will be given. The presence of an overwhelming number of staff is sometimes also used in emergency room and military care stations to calm the obstreperous or violent patient. Here, the effect of group pressure applied with admiring and caring attentiveness has greater clout than an individual professional could muster.
- *Sort out the components of the patient's dilemma.* How can he or she extricate himself or herself from the limiting trap of the symptom formation, and what are the perpetuating rewards? Ideally, a psychodynamic formulation should be arrived at, but for numerous reasons, such as the press of time in a neurologic clinic and the lower likelihood that the patient or relatives have insight or can provide in-depth information, a greater degree of inference may be needed.
- *Assess the interpersonal world of the patient.* At the very least, the significant human connections should be inquired about to gauge the patient's main support system, particularly if the symptoms would be relinquished. Possible gain factors should be identified, with calculation as to how they might be diminished.
- *Limit disability rewards.* Psychogenic movement disorders on an unconscious conversion or factitious basis (as opposed to conscious malingering) confer genuine disability on the patient, but an attempt should be made to limit or wean from disability payments with positive expectancy and the reassurance that the muscles will learn to move more normally.
- *Read the patient's body language.* These physically, not mentally, oriented patients do not speak meaningfully in words about their conflicts. What could he or she be saying nonverbally? What do the movements say, considered as an expressive dance or pantomime? What is the emotion they express (joy, fear, anger, shame, guilt, sadness)? The term *alexithymia* describes having a lack of words for feelings, but these patients do not lack gestural language. Moreover, these patients are performers, albeit unconscious ones, putting on a show. They appreciate an audience, especially a large one of specialists intent on observing every last motion.
- *Deconstruct the objective correlative.* The term comes from drama criticism (T.S. Eliot) and refers to the concrete bit of stage business that conveys the significant emotional action or vector of the moment. For example, Lear's helplessness is shown when he cannot undo a button. Some of the patient's gestural language is more pertinent than the rest.
- *Speak the patient's language.* If these patients wanted verbal psychotherapy, they would have asked for it. Just as they are not expressive in words, they do not comprehend very well the words that might be spoken by therapists about their conflicts. Instead, they may be acutely sensitive to facial expressions, tone of voice, and the speed with which a professional might whirl on his or her heel and leave the room. The patient's language is action and gesture, and the main brunt of the therapeutic intervention must be carried out nonverbally. The way in which the patient is touched, examined, and spoken to by the neurologist begins the treatment. Therapeutic actions include participation of nursing staff and social workers to assess situational factors. Specially prescribed maneuvers by physical therapy and rehabilitation medicine establish a graded timetable for progress. The psychiatrist assesses emotional expression and suggests medication for mood disorders.
- *Guard the patient's secret.* The patient's behavior conceals yet often betrays secrets that are strongly defended against. Early in the psychoanalytic movement, the simple goal was to make the unconscious conscious, but this did not do justice to the analysis of defenses that is usually necessary in psychodynamic treatment. Based on the limits of contact with these patients, usually the secret must be left unspoken and implicit, even if symptoms are relinquished. If the patient was sexually abused, for example, the patient still may repress or not have verbal access to the recollection. It may take months or years for a history of incest to emerge in the therapeutic process. Leading the witness can result in false memory syndrome. Aggressive "lancing of the boil" of the unconscious conflict is contraindicated. Setbacks have occurred when psychiatrists, flushed with joy about their patient's cooperative improvement and equating it with verbal comprehension, have said something overly interpretive or shown him or her something in writing about conversion symptoms that jarred the patient.
- *Medicate implicit mood disorders.* The patient may have entered this symptomatic detour from living well because of a depressive lack of confidence about succeeding in more usual ways. Antidepressant medication may help supply the mental energy to engage in psychotherapy and find the way back to the competi-

tive real world. As an active placebo, it may provide a face-saving excuse to relinquish the symptom. Medication, like the physical examination, also reassures the patient of the physician's interest. Medication other than antidepressants may be helpful; for example, analgesics may ease the painful spasm from holding postures.

The following case illustrates psychogenic dystonia.

A 58-year-old Hispanic man, formerly a machinist, worked as a cook until 1 year ago, when he felt a pain in his right leg that developed into psychogenic dystonia, with a stiffly extended right leg while sitting or walking and back pain from the maintained posture. For 8 months, he had been walking with a cane. He had been given gabapentin, baclofen, and carisoprodol.

He did not want to see a psychiatrist but agreed to the psychiatrist's presence. The psychiatrist advised the neurologist in English, who spoke to the patient in Spanish. On psychiatric examination, the patient had a forlorn affect, which he attributed to a divorce and his subsequent loneliness. The neurologist was encouraged to take an admiring stance and to tell the patient that he was a handsome man, looked young for his age, and should be attractive to women.

Further inquiry suggested by the symbolism of his symptom revealed that he had sexual dysfunction secondary to diabetes. The physical therapist suggested relaxation and strengthening exercises for his leg, and her demonstration was done in the presence of several of our female staff, who paid close attention. The neurologist, at the psychiatrist's suggestion, said that there was hope that his sexual dysfunction could be improved. A medicine with some of that effect, bupropion, would be begun. He also suggested that the patient obtain a job where he could work sitting down.

When the patient returned to the clinic in 6 weeks, he had returned to work part-time (3 hours a day) at a restaurant preparing food. He also noted that he had a little more sexual desire. He elaborated on the sensations he was feeling in his right leg. Not only did it stiffen up, but he saw the foot and leg get longer, and his right leg would swell and enlarge. These symptoms further pointed to the symbolic content of compensating for his acquired impotency by enacting an erect and tumescent leg. The patient was praised liberally by the assembled group for his progress in obtaining part-time work. The physical therapist gave him more exercises, and—with considerable attention and praise—got him to do modified deep knee bends. The group all paid attention to this and, in fact, actually applauded. The patient himself smiled in pride for the first time. He was told that we were impressed with his progress and that as his leg became less stiff and his back loosened up, we would consider further medication to aid his sexual recovery.

## Brain Tumor

The brain tumors most likely to produce behavioral difficulties in patients for which a psychiatrist might be consulted are those of the temporal lobe, and the tumors do so by becoming an irritative focus for temporal lobe epilepsy. Blumer and Benson (1975) noted the difficulties for psychotherapy that are caused by the viscous type of verbal expression in patients with temporal lobe epilepsy, including a deepening of emotional response that is not reversed by anticonvulsant therapy as are the changes in sexuality and episodic aggressivity. These authors argued in favor of nondrug psychiatric management of temporal lobe emotional features.

Blumer and Benson (1975) stated that the "pseudodepressed" change in personality caused by lesions of the convexity of the frontal lobes warrants early and ongoing rehabilitative efforts and mobilization; that is, patients should not be allowed to sit around. Patients with the "pseudopsychopathic" alteration of personality, more attributed to lesions of the orbital surface, have misbehavior that tries the patience of family members, who may benefit with psychiatric support. In patients with recurrent or intractable CNS tumors, more diffuse signs of increased intracranial pressure sometimes supplant the specific personality changes already mentioned.

J. Jaffe (personal communication, August 1990) found that psychiatric consultation in several hundred patients with neurosurgical brain tumor and arteriovenous malformation led to an appreciation of how much warm understanding and explanation by a consistent figure can minimize the distress before and after surgery. Certain communications are often useful. For example, the CNS anatomic basis of puzzling peripheral symptoms can be explained, because patients are not so familiar with brain symptoms as they are with cardiac symptoms. In patients who face a terminal course, reassurance may be given to these patients about competency, with assistance in arranging for their wishes to be respected. The patient who fears a painful and frightening death can be told that death will likely come after lapsing into a coma and (with the exception of certain headache patients) will bring little, or controllable, pain. Table 36–10 summarizes management issues for patients with brain tumors.

## Conclusions

Neuropsychiatry has been thought to involve poor prognoses, but when the statistics are in the patient's favor,

**TABLE 36–10.** Management issues for patients with brain tumors

1. Correlate observations of specific impairments with tumor location, as in the case of temporal lobe involvement.
2. Expect diffuse difficulties and trouble with novel situations.
3. Mobilize patients with frontal "pseudodepressed" changes.
4. Watch for communication of fears, sometimes nonverbally.
5. Provide warmth, understanding, and explanation as a consistent figure before and after surgery.
6. Explain puzzling anatomic symptoms, such as contralateral effects.
7. Discuss permissibility of exertion and sex in arteriovenous malformations.
8. Distinguish between growth and malignancy of tumor.
9. Explain that malignancy may differ in degree and is not black and white.
10. Invite reporting of psychotic symptoms on high-dose steroids.
11. Reassure about competency and arrange for wishes to be respected in terminal patients.
12. Reassure that death will come after a coma, and there will be little or controllable pain.

they may aid the psychiatrist's supportive role. For example, in a study by Thorngren et al. (1990) of stroke patients discharged from the hospital to independent living, 1 year later, 90% were still in their own homes, 99% could walk independently, 92%–95% could climb a staircase, and 90% could manage their daily hygiene. Six percent had died, and 25% had been rehospitalized.

When the statistics are not so favorable, the psychiatrist's objective and relativistic viewpoint may be tested. Psychiatrists and other physicians often have such high demands for their own performance that they must guard against identifying too easily with suicidal impulses in impaired patients who might later be grateful for aggressive intervention against depression and suicide. Lessons that can be learned from this include the need for a relativistic viewpoint that can adopt the patients' differing standards for acceptable living. It is also imperative to recognize that emotional exhaustion and burnout sometimes may affect young professionals with high standards more than most people, who have more relaxed standards of performance and may be better able to contemplate enduring life with prolonged morbidity and a chronic downhill course. In general, patients with neurologic deficits that affect their performance may be better able to accept them than are some of their physicians, and it is up to physicians to help them make the most of living.

# References

Anderson K, Silver JM: Modulation of anger and aggression. Seminars in Clinical Neuropsychiatry 3:232–241, 1998

Andersson S, Gundersen OM, Finset A: Emotional activation during therapeutic interaction in traumatic brain injury: effect of apathy, self-awareness and implications for rehabilitation. Brain Inj 13:393–404, 1999

Andreasen NC, Arndt S, Swayze V, et al: Thalamic abnormalities in schizophrenia visualized through magnetic resonance imaging. Science 266:294–298, 1994

Anshin RN: Intersubjectivity, creative uncertainty, and systems theory: an approach to the therapeutic use of empathy. J Am Acad Psychoanal 23:369–378, 1995

Aronson MK: Alzheimer's and Other Dementias. Carrier Letter No 102. Belle Meade, NJ, Carrier Foundation, November 1984

Beatty WW, Staton RD, Weir WS, et al: Cognitive disturbances in Parkinson's disease. J Geriatr Psychiatry Neurol 2:22–33, 1989

Bellus SB, Kost PP, Vergo JG, et al: Improvements in cognitive functioning following intensive behavioral rehabilitation. Brain Inj 12:139–145, 1998

Benson DF: Disorders of verbal expression, in Psychiatric Aspects of Neurological Disease. Edited by Benson DF, Blumer D. New York, Grune & Stratton, 1975, pp 121–135

Berry V: Partners/Families and Professionals Together: A Model of Posttraumatic Rehabilitation. Austin, TX, Ranch Treatment Center, 1984

Blumer D: Specific psychiatric complications in certain forms of epilepsy and their treatment, in Epilepsy: A Handbook for the Mental Health Professional. Edited by Sands H. New York, Brunner/Mazel, 1982, pp 97–111

Blumer D, Benson DF: Personality changes with frontal and temporal lobe lesions, in Psychiatric Aspects of Neurologic Disease, Vol 1. Edited by Benson DF, Blumer D. New York, Grune & Stratton, 1975, pp 151–170

Bodenhamer E, Achterberg-Lawlis J, Kevorkian G, et al: Staff and patient perceptions of the psychosocial concerns of spinal cord injured persons. American Journal of Physical Medicine 62:182–193, 1983

Braceland FJ, Giffin ME: The mental changes associated with MS: an interim report. Association for Research in Nervous and Mental Disease 28:450–455, 1950

Bracken MB, Shepard MJ: Coping and adaptation following acute spinal cord injury: a theoretical analysis. Paraplegia 18:74–85, 1980

Brassington JC, Marsh NV: Neuropsychological aspects of multiple sclerosis. Neuropsychol Rev 8(2):42–77, 1998

Burke JM, Danick JA, Bemis B, et al: A process approach to memory book training for neurological patients. Brain Inj 8:71–81, 1994

Calvert T, Knapp P, House A: Psychological associations with emotionalism after stroke. J Neurol Neurosurg Psychiatry 65:928–929, 1998

Chen JY, Stern Y, Sano M, et al: Cumulative risks of developing extrapyramidal signs, psychosis, or myoclonus in the course of Alzheimer's disease. Arch Neurol 48:1141–1143, 1991

Childs AH: Brain injury: "Now what shall we do?" Problems in treating brain injuries. Psychiatric Times, April 1985, pp 15–17

Cohen-Mansfield J, Deutsch LH: Agitation: subtypes and their mechanisms. Semin Clin Neuropsychiatry 1(4):325–339, 1996

Cottrell SS, Wilson SAK: The affective symptomatology of disseminated sclerosis. Journal of Neurology and Psychopathology 7:1, 1926

Craig A, Hancock K, Dickson H: Improving the long term adjustment of spinal cord injured persons. Spinal Cord 37:345–350, 1999

Cregeen S: Epileptic seizures and infantile states: some thoughts from psychodynamic therapy. Seizure 2:291–294, 1993

Critchley M: The Divine Banquet of the Brain and Other Essays. New York, Raven, 1979

Cummings JL, Jeste DV: Alzheimer's disease and its management in the year 2010. Psychiatr Serv 50:1173–1177, 1999

DeJong G, Branch LG, Corcoran PJ: Independent living outcomes in spinal cord injury: multivariate analyses. Arch Phys Med Rehabil 65:66–73, 1984

Delmonico RL, Hanley-Peterson P, Englander J: Group psychotherapy for persons with traumatic brain injury: management of frustration and substance abuse. J Head Trauma Rehabil 13:10–22, 1998

Doonief G, Mirabello E, Bell K, et al: An estimate of the incidence of depression in idiopathic Parkinson's disease. Arch Neurol 49:305–307, 1992

Evans RL, Northwood LK: Social support needs in adjustment to stroke. Arch Phys Med Rehabil 64:61–64, 1983

Fallon BA, Nields JA: Lyme disease: a neuropsychiatric illness. Am J Psychiatry 151:1571–1582, 1994

Fallon BA, Nields JA, Burrascano JJ, et al: The neuropsychiatric manifestations of Lyme borreliosis. Psychiatr Q 63:95–115, 1992

Fitts WH: Manual for Tennessee Self-Concept Scale. Nashville, TN, Counselor Recordings & Tests, 1965

Flashman LA, Amador A, McAllister TW: Lack of awareness of deficits in traumatic brain injury. Seminars in Clinical Neuropsychiatry 3:201–210, 1998

Folstein MF, Folstein SE, McHugh PR: "Mini-Mental State": a practical method of grading the cognitive state of patients for the clinician. J Psychiatr Res 12:189–198, 1975

Ford B, Greene P, Fahn S: Oral and genital tardive pain syndromes. Neurology 44:2115–2119, 1994

Forrest DV: E. E. Cummings and the thoughts that lie too deep for tears: of defenses in poetry. Psychiatry 43:13–42, 1980

Forrest DV: Selected American Expressions for the Foreign-Born Psychiatrist and Other Professionals. New York, Educational Research, 1982

Forrest DV: Schizophrenic language: vantages from neurology, in Treating Schizophrenic Patients. Edited by Stone MH, Albert HD, Forrest DV, et al. New York, McGraw-Hill, 1983a, pp 325–335

Forrest DV: Therapeutic adaptations to the affective features of schizophrenia, in Treating Schizophrenic Patients. Edited by Stone MH, Albert HD, Forrest DV, et al. New York, McGraw-Hill, 1983b, pp 217–226

Forrest DV: Therapeutic adaptations to the cognitive features of schizophrenia, in Treating Schizophrenic Patients. Edited by Stone MH, Albert HD, Forrest DV, et al. New York, McGraw-Hill, 1983c, pp 165–182

Forrest DV: With two heads you can think twice: relations in the language of madness. J Am Acad Psychoanal 11:113–132, 1983d

Forrest DV: The tremometer: a convenient device to measure postural tremor from lithium and other causes. J Neuropsychiatry Clin Neurosci 2:391–394, 1990

Forrest DV: Mind, brain and machine: action and creation. J Am Acad Psychoanal 22:29–56, 1994

Forrest DV: Language and psychosis: seeking the poetry of malfunction in the spirit of Silvano Arieti. J Am Acad Psychoanal 27(4):563–574, 1999

Forrest DV: Freud's neuromental model: analytical structures and local habitations, in Whose Freud? The Place of Psychoanalysis in Contemporary Culture. Edited by Brooks P, Woloch A. New Haven, CT, Yale University Press (in press)

Giladi N, McMahon D, Przborski S, et al: Motor blocks in Parkinson's disease. Neurology 42:333–339, 1992

Golbe LI, Sage JI: Medical treatment of Parkinson's disease, in Treatment of Movement Disorders. Edited by Kurlan R. Philadelphia, PA, JB Lippincott, 1995, pp 1–56

Goldenberg G, Hagman S: Therapy of activities of daily living in patients with apraxia. Neuropsychological Rehabilitation 8:123–141, 1998

Goldman-Rakic PS: Working memory and the mind. Sci Am 267:110–117, 1992

Goldman-Rakic PS: Working memory dysfunction in schizophrenia. J Neuropsychiatry Clin Neurosci 6:348–357, 1994

Goldstein K: Aftereffects of Brain Injuries in War. New York, Grune & Stratton, 1942

Goodstein RK: Overview: cerebrovascular accident and the hospitalized elderly: a multidimensional clinical problem. Am J Psychiatry 140:141–147, 1983

Grant I, Brown GW, Harris T, et al: Severely threatening events and marked life difficulties preceding onset or exacerbation of multiple sclerosis. J Neurol Neurosurg Psychiatry 52:8–13, 1989

Green BC, Pratt CC, Grigsby TE: Self-concept among persons with long-term spinal cord injury. Arch Phys Med Rehabil 65:751–754, 1984

Grosswasser Z, Stern MJ: A psychodynamic model of behavior after acute central nervous system damage. J Head Trauma Rehabil 13:69–79, 1998

Gusella JF, Wexler NS, Coneally PM, et al: A polymorphic DNA marker genetically linked to Huntington's disease. Nature 306:234–238, 1983

Hallet M: Physiology and pathophysiology of voluntary movement. Current Neurology 2:351–376, 1979

Hamburg D: Brain, behavior and health. VanGieson Award Address presented at the New York State Psychiatric Institute, New York, November 1985

Hartelius L: Speech and swallowing in Parkinson's disease. Folia Phoniatr Logop 46:9–17, 1994

Heaton R: Wisconsin Card Sorting Test. Odessa, TX, Psychological Assessment Resources, 1985

House A, Dennis M, Molyneux A, et al: Emotionalism after stroke. BMJ 298:991–994, 1989

Howell T, Fullerton DT, Harvey RF, et al: Depression in spinal cord injured patients. Paraplegia 19:284–288, 1981

Jean VM, Paul RH, Beatty WW: Psychological and neuropsychological predictors of coping patterns by patients with multiple sclerosis. J Clin Psychol 55:21–26, 1999

Jenicke MA: Alzheimer's Disease: Diagnosis, Treatment and Management. Philadelphia, PA, Clinical Perspectives on Aging, Wyeth Laboratories Division American Home Products Corporation, 1985

Kardiner A: The bioanalysis of the epileptic reaction. Psychoanal Q 1:420–430, 1932

Katz IR: Diagnosis and treatment of depression in patients with Alzheimer's disease and other dementias. J Clin Psychiatry 59 (suppl 9):38–44, 1998

Kotila M, Waltimo O, Niemi ML, et al: The profile of recovery from stroke and factors influencing outcome. Stroke 15:1039–1044, 1984

Kreutzer JS, Zasler ND: Psychosexual consequences of traumatic brain injury: methodology and preliminary findings. Brain Inj 3:177–186, 1989

Labi MJ, Phillips TF, Greshman GE: Psychosocial disability in physically restored long-term stroke survivors. Arch Phys Med Rehabil 61:561–565, 1980

LaRocca N, Kalb R, Scheinberg L, et al: Factors associated with unemployment of patients with multiple sclerosis. Journal of Chronic Diseases 38:203–210, 1985

Leroi I, Michalon M: Treatment of the psychiatric manifestations of Huntington's disease: a review of the literature. Canadian Journal of Psychiatry 43:933–940, 1998

Lorig KR, Sobel DS, Stewart AL, et al: Evidence suggesting that a chronic disease self-management program can improve health status while reducing hospitalization. Med Care 37:5–14, 1999

Luria AR: The Working Brain: An Introduction to Neuropsychology. New York, Basic Books, 1973

Martelli MF, Grayson RL, Zasler ND: Posttraumatic headache: neuropsychological and psychological effects and treatment implications. J Head Trauma Rehabil 14:49–69, 1999

Mateer CA: Executive function disorders: rehabilitation challenges and strategies. Seminars in Clinical Neuropsychiatry 4:50–59, 1999

Matteson MA, Linton AD, Cleary BL, et al: Management of problematic behavioral symptoms associated with dementia: a cognitive developmental approach. Aging (Milano) 9:342–355, 1997

Mayeux R: Behavior manifestations of movement disorders: Parkinson's and Huntington's disease. Neurol Clin 2:527–540, 1984

Mayeux R, Stern Y: Intellectual dysfunction and dementia in Parkinson disease, in The Dementias. Edited by Mayeux R, Rosen WG. New York, Raven, 1983, pp 211–227

Mayeux R, Sano M, Chen J, et al: Risk of dementia in first degree relatives of patients with Alzheimer's disease and related disorders. Arch Neurol 48:269–273, 1991

Mechcatie E: Guidelines for Huntington's genetic testing, follow up. Clinical Psychiatry News 18:2, 22, 1990

Menza MA, Forman NE, Goldstein HS, et al: Parkinson's disease, personality and dopamine. J Neuropsychiatry Clin Neurosci 2:282–287, 1990

Minden SL: Psychotherapy for people with multiple sclerosis. J Neuropsychiatry Clin Neurosci 4:198–213, 1992

Minden SL, Schiffer RB: Affective disorders in multiple sclerosis: review and recommendations for clinical research. Arch Neurol 47:98–104, 1990

Mohr DC, Goodkin DE: Treatment of depression in multiple sclerosis: review and meta-analysis. Clinical Psychology—Science and Practice 6(1):1–9, 1999

Müller V, Mohr B, Rosin R, et al: Short-term effects of behavioral treatment on movement initiation and postural control in Parkinson's disease: a controlled clinical study. Mov Disord 12:306–314, 1997

Murphy RF: The Body Silent. New York, Holt, 1987

Nadelson T: Psychotherapy, revelation, science, and deep thinking. Am J Psychiatry 153 (Festshrift Supplement):7–10, 1996

National Advisory Neurological Disorders and Stroke Council: Implementation Plan: Decade of the Brain. Washington, DC, National Institute of Neurological Disorders and Stroke, 1990

National Institutes of Health Consensus Development Panel: Consensus conference: rehabilitation of persons with traumatic brain injury. NIH Consensus Development Panel on Rehabilitation of Persons With Traumatic Brain Injury. JAMA 282:974–983, 1999

Naumann M, Magyar-Lehmann S, Reiners K, et al: Sensory tricks in cervical dystonia: perceptual dysbalance of parietal cortex modulates frontal motor programming, Ann Neurol 47:322–328, 2000

Nemiah JC: Foundations of Psychopathology. New York, Jason Aronson, 1973

Oddy M, Humphrey M, Uttley D: Subjective impairment and social recovery after closed head injury. J Neurol Neurosurg Psychiatry 41:611–616, 1978

Parkinson J: An Essay on the Shaking Palsy. London, England, Sherwood, Neely & Jones, 1817

Perez M, Pilsecker C: Group therapy with spinal cord injured substance abusers. Paraplegia 32:188–192, 1994

Pollack IW: Individual psychotherapy, in Neuropsychiatry of Traumatic Brain Injury. Edited by Silver JM, Yudofsky SC, Hales RE. Washington, DC, American Psychiatric Press, 1994, pp 671–702

Rabins PV, Mace NL, Lucas MJ: The impact of dementia on the family. JAMA 248:333–335, 1982

Ramachandran VS: Phantoms in the Brain: Exploring the Mysteries of the Human Mind. New York, William Morrow, 1998, pp 59–62

Rao SM (ed): Neurobehavioral Aspects of Multiple Sclerosis. New York, Oxford University Press, 1990

Reisberg B: Alzheimer's disease update. Psychiatric Annals 15:319–322, 1985

Roberts JK, Guberman A: Religion and epilepsy. Psychiatric Journal of the University of Ottawa 14:282–286, 1989

Romano MD: Preparing children for parental disability. Soc Work Health Care 1:309–315, 1976

Ron MA, Logsdail SJ: Psychiatric morbidity in multiple sclerosis: a clinical and MRI study. Psychol Med 19:887–895, 1989

Rosenstiel AK, Roth S: Relationship between cognitive activity and adjustment in four spinal cord-injured individuals: a longitudinal investigation. Journal of Human Stress 7:35–43, 1981

Sands H: Psychodynamic management of epilepsy, in Epilepsy: A Handbook for the Mental Health Professional. Edited by Sands H. New York, Brunner/Mazel, 1982, pp 135–157

Sarno MT: The nature of verbal impairment after closed head injury. J Nerv Ment Dis 168:685–692, 1980

Scheinberg LC: Multiple Sclerosis: A Guide for Patients and Their Families. New York, Raven, 1983

Schiffer RB: Psychiatric aspects of clinical neurology. Am J Psychiatry 140:205–211, 1983

Schiffer RB: The spectrum of depression in multiple sclerosis: an approach for clinical management. Arch Neurol 44:596–599, 1987

Schuler M: Sexual counseling for the spinal cord injured: a review of 5 programs. J Sex Marital Ther 8:241–252, 1982

Shadick NA, Phillips CB, Logigian EL, et al: The long-term clinical outcomes of Lyme disease. Ann Intern Med 121:560–567, 1994

Shnek ZM, Foley FW, LaRocca NG, et al: Helplessness, self-efficacy, cognitive distortions, and depression in multiple sclerosis and spinal cord injury. Ann Behav Med 19:287–294, 1997

Signer SF: Capgras syndrome: the delusion of substitution. J Clin Psychiatry 481:47–50, 1987

Simons AF: Problems of providing support for people with MS and their families, in Multiple Sclerosis: Psychological and Social Aspects. Edited by Simons AF. London, England, Heinemann Medical Books, 1984, pp 1–20

Small GW, Rabins PV, Barry PP, et al: Diagnosis and treatment of Alzheimer disease and related disorders: consensus statement of the American Association of Geriatric Psychiatry, the Alzheimer's Association, and the American Geriatrics Society. JAMA 278:1363–1371, 1997

Solomon CR, Scherzer BP: Some guidelines for family therapists working with the traumatically brain injured and their families. Brain Inj 5:253–266, 1991

Starkstein SE, Preziosi TJ, Bolduc PL, et al: Depression in Parkinson's disease. J Nerv Ment Dis 178:27–31, 1990

Steinglass P, Temple S, Lisman SA, et al: Coping with spinal cord injury: the family perspective. Gen Hosp Psychiatry 4:259–264, 1982

Stern Y, Mayeux R, Rosen J: Contribution of perceptual motor dysfunction to construction and tracing disturbances in Parkinson's disease. J Neurol Neurosurg Psychiatry 47:987–989, 1984

Suhr JA, Anderson SW: Behavioral management of chronic hallucinations and delusions following right middle cerebral artery stroke. Psychotherapy 35:464–471, 1998

Teri LA, Logsdon RG, Uomoto J, et al: Behavioral treatment of depression in dementia patients: a controlled clinical trial. J Gerontol B Psychol Sci Soc Sci 52:P159–P166, 1997

Thorngren M, Westling B, Norrving B: Outcome after stroke in patients discharged to independent living. Stroke 21:236–240, 1990

Umlauf RL: Psychological interventions for chronic pain following spinal cord injury. Clin J Pain 8:111–118, 1992

Valleroy ML, Kraft GH: Sexual dysfunction in multiple sclerosis. Arch Phys Med Rehabil 65:125–128, 1984

van Vugt JPP, Roos RAC: Huntington's disease: options for controlling symptoms. CNS Drugs 11:105–123, 1999

Waters CH: Diagnosis and Treatment of Parkinson's Disease. Caddo, OK, Professional Communications, 1999

Weinberger DR, Berman KF, Zec RF: Physiological dysfunction of dorsolateral prefrontal cortex in schizophrenia, I: regional cerebral blood flow (CBF) evidence. Arch Gen Psychiatry 43:114–125, 1986

Weinstein EA: Sexual disturbances after brain injury. Medical Aspects of Human Sexuality 8:10–31, 1974

Wexler NS: Genetic jeopardy and the new clairvoyance, in Progress in Medical Genetics, Vol 6. Edited by Beam A, Child B, Motulsky A. New York, Praeger, 1985, pp 277–304

Whitlock A: Emotional disorder in multiple sclerosis, in Multiple Sclerosis: Psychological and Social Aspects. Edited by Simons AF. London, England, Heinemann Medical Books, 1984, pp 72–81

Williams DT, Fahn S: Psychogenic dystonia, in Advances in Neurology, Vol 50: Dystonia 2. Edited by Fahn S, Marsden CD, Calne DB. New York, Raven, 1988, pp 431–455

Wilson T, Smith T: Driving after stroke. International Rehabilitation Medicine 5:170–177, 1983

Woods BT, Short MP: Neurological dimensions of psychiatry. Biol Psychiatry 20:192–198, 1985

Yudofsky SC, Silver JM, Hales RE: Pharmacologic management of aggression in the elderly. J Clin Psychiatry 51 (suppl): 22–28; discussion 29–32, 1990

# Cognitive Rehabilitation and Behavior Therapy for Patients With Neuropsychiatric Disorders

Michael D. Franzen, Ph.D.

Mark R. Lovell, Ph.D.

Increasing evidence and awareness indicate that treatment of central nervous system (CNS) disorders is a viable and productive endeavor. For example, although traumatic brain injury has been typically conceptualized as permanently devastating, some agreement exists that certain treatments can have positive effects (NIH Consensus Statement 1998). Psychiatry plays a central role in the assessment and treatment of individuals with neurologic impairment. There is an increasing need for a broad-based understanding of methods of promoting recovery from brain injury and disease. The role of the psychiatrist in the diagnosis and treatment of the sequelae of CNS dysfunction has become a crucial one and promises to become even more central with the continued development of sophisticated neuropharmacologic treatments for both the cognitive and the psychosocial components of brain impairment (Gualtieri 1988).

In particular, the recent application of selective serotonin reuptake inhibitors with brain-injured patients appears to hold some promise. In addition to these exciting new developments, an understanding of nonpharmacologic, behavioral methods of assessment and treatment can greatly enhance the patient's recovery from cognitive deficits as well as provide a useful adjunct treatment for behavioral deficits and excesses that are commonly associated with CNS dysfunction. In this chapter, we review the role of psychologic treatments for the neuropsycho-logic (cognitive) and behavioral consequences of CNS dysfunction.

In response to the increase in the number of patients requiring treatment for CNS dysfunction, there has been a proliferation of treatment agencies structured to provide rehabilitation services, as well as an accompanying increase in research efforts designed to assess the efficacy of these treatment programs. There has been a particularly intense focus over the last few years on the development of rehabilitation programs designed specifically to treat the neuropsychologic and psychosocial sequelae of neuropsychiatric disorders. Before turning to a discussion of specific treatment modalities that may be useful with neuropsychiatric patients, we briefly review neuroanatomic influences on the recovery process.

## Neuroanatomic and Neurophysiologic Determinants of Recovery

Recovery from brain injury or disease can be conceptualized as involving a number of separate but interacting processes. Although a complete discussion of existing research concerning neuroanatomic and neurophysiologic aspects of the recovery process is beyond the scope of this chapter, we provide here a brief review. (For a more complete review of current theories of recovery from brain injury, see Gouvier et al. 1986.)

After an acute brain injury, such as a stroke or head injury, some degree of improvement is likely because of a lessening of the temporary or treatable consequences of the injury. Factors such as degree of cerebral edema and extent of increased intracranial pressure are well known to temporarily affect brain function after a closed head injury or stroke (Lezak 1995). Extracellular changes after injury to the cell also have been shown to affect neural functioning. In addition, the regrowth of neural tissue to compensate for an injured area has been shown to occur to some minimal extent in animal studies on both anatomic (Kolata 1983) and physiologic (Wall and Egger 1971) levels and may have some limited relevance for humans. With many acute brain injuries, functioning improves as these temporary effects subside. However, with degenerative illnesses, such as Alzheimer's disease and Huntington's disease, the condition actually worsens over time.

The differences in prognosis among various neurologic disorders obviously affect the structuring of the rehabilitation program. For example, the expectations and goals of a rehabilitation program that is structured to improve memory function in patients with head injury are likely to be much different from those of a program for patients with Alzheimer's disease. Similarly, the goals will vary as a function of the severity of memory impairment in patients with closed head injury. A program designed for patients with head injury and consequent moderate memory impairment is likely to focus on teaching alternative strategies for remembering new information. In contrast, a program designed for a patient with Alzheimer's disease would probably focus on improving the patient's functioning with regard to activities of daily living. Previously, the amount of time since the injury also was seen as a determining variable in the design of rehabilitation efforts, with treatment aimed at improving the skill or substituting other cognitive mechanisms used in the early stages of recovery and treatment aimed at compensatory behaviors in the late stages of recovery. However, some intriguing data suggest that at least for stroke, brain reorganization for motor skills may be possible even a decade past the time of the stroke (Liepert et al. 2000).

## Cognitive Rehabilitation of Patients With Neuropsychiatric Disorders

The terms *cognitive rehabilitation* and *cognitive retraining* have been variously used to describe treatments designed to maximize recovery of the individual's abilities in the areas of intellectual functioning, visual processing, language, and particularly, memory. It is important to note that the techniques used to improve cognitive functioning after a neurologic event represent an extremely heterogeneous group of procedures that vary widely in their focus according to the nature of the patient's cognitive difficulties, the specific skills and training of the staff members, and the medium through which information is presented (i.e., computer vs. individual therapy vs. group therapy). Ideally, a cognitive rehabilitation program should be tailored to each patient's particular needs and should be based on a thorough, individualized neuropsychologic assessment of the patient's psychometric deficits, as well as an estimation of how these deficits are likely to affect the patient in his or her daily life.

Because patients with different neurologic or neuropsychiatric syndromes often have different cognitive deficits, the focus of the treatment is likely to vary greatly. For example, a treatment program designed primarily to treat patients with head injury is likely to focus on the amelioration of attentional and memory deficits, whereas a rehabilitation program designed for stroke patients is likely to focus on a more specific deficit, such as language disorders or other disorders that tend to occur after lateralized brain damage, and to have less emphasis on co-occurring attentional and memory deficits.

Attention to psychiatric problems in patients with neurologic impairment is an increasingly important component of rehabilitation efforts (e.g., Robinson 1997). The use of pharmacologic agents in the treatment of affective and behavior changes following traumatic brain injury has been reported in case studies (Khouzam and Donnelly 1998; Mendez et al. 1999). Carbamazepine has been used in the treatment of behavioral agitation following severe traumatic brain injury (Azouvi et al. 1999).

The systematic research concerning the effectiveness of cognitive and behavioral treatment strategies in this group is increasing. However, this area is still a developing endeavor. Some work has been reported in the area of treating social skills deficits and anger control. Medd and Tate (2000) reported the effects of anger management training in individuals with traumatic brain injury. In addition to psychologically based methods, pharmacologic methods have been used to treat the physical and emotional symptoms (Holzer 1998; McIntosh 1997; Wroblewski et al. 1997). Although amantadine was at first promising, it has not provided robust effects in improving cognitive and behavioral functioning in brain-injured subjects (Schneider et al. 1999). The treatment of frontal lobe injury with dopaminergic agents may beneficially affect other rehabilitation efforts (Kraus and

Maki 1997). Furthermore, the use of psychostimulants in facilitating treatment effects has been reported for pediatric subjects with traumatic brain injury (Williams et al. 1998) as well as for adults (Glen 1998). Most of our information comes from experience with patients in rehabilitation settings. Following is a brief review of cognitive rehabilitation strategies designed to treat specific cognitive deficits that may be associated with neuropsychiatric disorders.

The results of psychologic treatment methods for the cognitive deficits associated with traumatic brain injury generally show larger effects for skills as measured by standardized tests than as measured by ecologically relevant behaviors (Ho and Bennett 1997). This is a vexing problem because the ultimate goal of the treatment is to provide some socially relevant and valid effect. Future research is needed to investigate the variables that govern generalizability and ecologic validity.

There has been some interest in the cognitive rehabilitation of individuals with schizophrenia. Although schizophrenia is not an acquired disorder of cognitive impairment, it does have similarities to other neuropsychiatric disorders that have received attention in the clinical neuropsychologic literature. Flesher (1990) presented an intriguing discussion of an approach to using this type of intervention with schizophrenic patients; however, there have been limited reports of applications, an exception being Benedict et al. (1994), who reported on the use of information-processing rehabilitation. In that study, computer vigilance training was used to treat the attentional deficits shown by a group of schizophrenic patients. Although it may be too early to critically evaluate the efficacy of this approach (Bellak and Mueser 1993), it certainly bears watching. In contrast, the use of behavioral methods for training in social skills in schizophrenic patients is well documented.

## Attentional Processes

Disorders of attention are common sequelae of several neurologic disorders, particularly traumatic brain injury. Recognition and treatment of attentional disorders are extremely important because an inability to focus and sustain attention may directly limit the patient's ability to actively participate in the rehabilitation program and may therefore affect progress in other areas of cognitive functioning. It must be stressed that attention is not a unitary process. A number of components of attention have been identified, including alertness and the ability to selectively attend to incoming information, as well as the capacity to focus and maintain attention or vigilance (Posner and Rafal 1987).

Rehabilitation programs designed to improve attention usually attempt to address all of these processes. One such program is the Orientation Remedial module developed by Ben-Yishay and associates (Ben-Yishay and Diller 1981) at New York University. The Orientation Remedial program consists of five separate tasks that are presented by microcomputer and vary in degree of difficulty; they involve training in the following areas:

1. Attending and reacting to environmental signals
2. Timing responses in relation to changing environmental cues
3. Being actively vigilant
4. Estimating time
5. Synchronizing of response with complex rhythms

Progress on these tasks is a prerequisite for further training on higher-level tasks.

## Memory

Within the field of cognitive rehabilitation, much emphasis has been placed on the development of treatment approaches to improve memory. This is not surprising, given the importance of memory functions in everyday life and the pervasiveness of memory disorders in many different neurologically impaired populations. In reviewing the empirical literature, Franzen and Haut (1991) divided the strategies into three basic categories: 1) the use of spared skills in the form of mnemonic devices or alternative functional systems, 2) direct retraining with the use of repetitive practice and drills, and 3) the use of behavioral prosthetics or external devices or strategies to improve memory.

### Use of Spared Skills

Because memory is not a unitary construct, impairment in one form of memory is often coupled with a spared skill in another form of memory. Mnemonic strategies are approaches to memory rehabilitation that are specifically designed to promote the encoding and remembering of a specific type of information, depending on the patient's particular memory impairment, by capitalizing on the spared skills. Currently, several different types of mnemonic strategies may be of use in neuropsychiatric settings. Visual imagery is one of the most well-known and commonly used mnemonic strategies (Glisky and Schacter 1986) and involves the use of visual images to assist in the learning and retention of verbal information. Probably the oldest and best-known visual imagery strategy is the method of loci, which involves the association of verbal information to be remembered with locations that are familiar to the patient (e.g., the room in a house or the location on a street). When recall of the information is required, the patient visualizes each room and the item(s) that are to be remembered in each location (Moffat 1984). Initial research suggested that this method may be particularly useful for elderly patients (Robertson-Tchabo et al. 1976).

A related method of learning and remembering new information, generally referred to as *peg mnemonics*, requires the patient to learn a list of peg words and to associate these words with a given visual image, such as "one bun," "two shoe," and so on. After the learned association of the numbers with the visual image, sequential information can be remembered in order by association with the visual image (Gouvier et al. 1986). This strategy has been widely used by professional mnemonists and showed some early promise in patients with brain injuries (Patten 1972). More recent research, however, suggested that this approach may not be highly effective because patients with brain injuries are unable to generate visual images (Crovitz et al. 1979) and have difficulty maintaining this information over time.

Another type of visual-imagery procedure that has been widely used in clinical settings and has been studied extensively is face-name association. As the name implies, this procedure has been used by patients with brain injuries to promote the remembering of peoples' names based on visual cues. The technique involves associating the components of the name with a distinctive visual image. For example, the name "Angela Harper" might be encoded by the patient by visualizing an angel playing a harp. Obviously, the ease with which this method can be used by patients with brain injuries depends on their ability to form internal visual images, as well as the ease with which the name can be transferred into a distinct visual image. Whereas it may be relatively easy to find visual associations for a name such as "Angela Harper," a name such as "Jane Johnson" may be much more difficult to encode in this manner.

Overall, visual-imagery strategies may be useful for specific groups of patients (e.g., those with impairments in verbal memory who need to use nonverbal cues to assist them in recall) and in patients whose impairments are mild enough to allow them to recall the series of steps necessary to spontaneously use these strategies once they return to their natural environments. A series of single-subject experiments reported by Wilson (1987) indicated that the strategy of visual imagery to learn peoples' names may be differentially effective for different individuals, even when the etiology of memory impairment is similar.

In addition to the extensive use of visual-imagery strategies for improving memory in patients with brain injuries, the use of verbally based mnemonic strategies also has become quite popular, particularly with patients who have difficulty using visual imagery. One such procedure, semantic elaboration, involves constructing a story out of new information to be remembered. This type of procedure may be particularly useful in patients who are unable to use imagery strategies because of a reduced ability to generate internal visual images.

Rhyming strategies involve remembering verbal information by incorporating the information into a rhyme. This procedure was originally demonstrated by Gardner (1977) with a globally amnesic patient who was able to recall pertinent personal information by the learning and subsequent singing of the following rhyme:

Henry's my name/Memory's my game/I'm in the V.A. in Jamaica Plain
My bed's on 7D/The year is '73/Every day I make a little gain.

For patients who have difficulty learning and remembering written information, Glasgow et al. (1977) used a structured procedure called *PQRST*. This strategy involves application of the following five steps:

1. **P**review the information.
2. Form **Q**uestions about the information.
3. **R**ead the information.
4. **S**tate the questions.
5. **T**est for retention by answering the questions after the material has been read.

## Repetitive Practice

Cognitive rehabilitation strategies that emphasize repetitive practice of the information to be remembered have become extremely popular in rehabilitation settings despite little experimental evidence that these procedures produce lasting improvement in memory. Repetitive-practice strategies rely heavily on the use of drills and appear to be based on a mental muscle conceptualization of memory (Harris and Sunderland 1981), in which it is assumed that memory can be improved merely by repeated exposure to the information to be learned. Although it is generally accepted that patients with brain injuries can learn specific pieces of information through repeated exposure, studies designed to show generalization of this training to new settings or tasks have not been encouraging. (For a review, see Schacter and Glisky 1986.)

In view of the lack of evidence that repetitive-practice strategies are effective in producing improvement in memory in patients with brain damage, Glisky and Schacter (1986) suggested that attempts to remedy memory disorders should be focused on the acquisition of domain-specific knowledge that is likely to be specifically relevant to the patient's ability to function in everyday life. This approach differs from the use of traditional cognitive remediation strategies in that 1) the goal of this treatment is not to improve memory functioning in general but rather to deal with specific problems associated with memory impairment, 2) the information acquired through this treatment has practical value to the individual, and 3) the information learned through training exercises is chosen on the basis of having some practical value in the patient's natural environment. Initial research has established that even patients with severe brain injuries are indeed capable of acquiring discrete pieces of information that are important to their ability to function on a daily basis (Glasgow et al. 1977; Wilson 1982).

## External Memory Aids

External aids to memory can take various forms, but generally they fall into the two categories of memory storage devices and memory-cuing strategies (Harris 1984). Probably the most basic memory storage devices are in the form of written lists and memory books. Lists and memory books are widely used by patients with brain injuries to record information that is vital to his or her daily function (e.g., the daily schedule of activities and chores to be performed) and that is then consulted at a given time. These strategies are not designed to provide a general improvement in the patient's ability to learn and retain new information but are used as memory support devices. A study reported by Schmitter-Edgecombe et al. (1995) supported the efficacy of memory notebook training to improve memory for everyday activities, although there was no difference in laboratory-based memory tasks, and the gains were not maintained as well at a 6-month follow-up evaluation.

With recent advances in the field of microelectronics, hand-held electronic storage devices have become increasingly popular in rehabilitation settings. Although these devices allow for the storage of large amounts of information, their often complicated operation requirements may obviate their use in all but the mildest cases of brain injury or disease. Another problem inherent in the use of external storage devices is that the device must be consulted at the appropriate time in order to be useful. This may be a difficult task for the patient with brain injury and often requires the use of cuing strategies that remind the patient to engage in a behavior at a given time.

The application of cuing involves the use of prompts designed to remind the patient to engage in a specific behavioral sequence at a given time. To be maximally effective, the cue should be given as close as possible to the time that the behavior is required, must be active (e.g., such as use of an alarm clock) rather than passive, and should provide a reminder of the specific behavior that is desired (Harris 1984). One particularly useful cuing device currently in use is the alarm wristwatch. This device can be set to sound an alarm at a given time. Although this technique does not provide specific information about the desired response, it can provide a useful cue to prompt the patient to check a list or other storage device for further instructions. Thus, a patient with brain injury can be cued to engage in some behavior on a regular basis.

## Visual-Perceptual Disorders

In addition to memory impairment, individuals with brain injuries may have difficulties with visual perception. Deficits in visual perception are most common in patients who have undergone right-hemisphere cerebrovascular accidents (Gouvier et al. 1986). Given the importance of visual-perceptual processing to many occupational tasks and to the safe operation of an automobile (Sivak et al. 1985), the rehabilitation of deficits in this area could have important implications for the recovery of neuropsychiatric patients.

A deficit that is particularly common in stroke patients is hemispatial neglect syndrome. This deficit is characterized by an inability to recognize stimuli in the contralateral visual field. One strategy that has been used extensively to treat hemispatial neglect is visual scanning training. This procedure, which has been designed to promote scanning to the neglected hemifield, has been extensively used at the Rusk Institute of Rehabilitation of the New York Medical Center (Diller and Weinberg 1977), as well as by others (Gianutsos et al. 1983). The New York Medical Center program uses a light board with 20 colored lights and a target that can be moved around the board at different speeds. With this device, the patient can be systematically trained to attend to the neglected visual field. This procedure, with the addition of other tasks (e.g., a size estimation and body awareness task) was found to improve visual-perceptual functioning in a group of patients with brain injuries in comparison with a group of similar patients who received standard occupational therapy (Gordon et al. 1985). Other researchers have produced similar therapeutic gains in scanning and other aspects of visual-perceptual functioning through rehabilitation strategies. (For a more complete review of this area, see Gianutsos and Matheson 1987 and Gordon et al. 1985.)

# Problem Solving and Executive Functions

Patients who have sustained brain injuries often experience a breakdown in their ability to reason, to form concepts, to solve problems, to execute and terminate behavioral sequences, and to engage in other complex cognitive activities (F.C. Goldstein and Levin 1987). Deficits in these areas are among the most debilitating to the neuropsychiatric patient because they often underlie changes in the basic abilities to function interpersonally, socially, and vocationally. Despite a general recognition of the effect on the individual of disorders of intellectual and executive processes, relatively little effort has been dedicated to the systematic development of rehabilitation programs to ameliorate these disorders. This may be due, at least in part, to the complex and multifaceted nature of intellectual and executive functions.

Intellectual and executive functioning cannot be conceptualized as unitary constructs but rather involve numerous processes that include motivation, abstract thinking, and concept formation, as well as the ability to plan, reason, and execute and terminate behaviors. Therefore, breakdowns in intellectual and executive functioning can occur for various reasons depending on the underlying core deficit(s) and can vary based on the area of the brain that is injured. For example, injury to the parieto-occipital area is likely to result in a problem-solving deficit secondary to difficulty with comprehension of logical-grammatical structure, whereas a frontal lobe injury may impede problem solving by disrupting the individual's ability to plan and to carry out the series of steps necessary to process the grammatical material (Luria and Tsvetkova 1990).

An apparent breakdown in the patient's ability to function intellectually also can occur secondary to deficits in other related areas of neuropsychologic functioning, such as attention, memory, and language. The type of rehabilitation strategy best suited for such a patient depends on the underlying core deficit that needs to be addressed. The goal of rehabilitation for a patient with a left parieto-occipital lesion might be to help the patient develop the skill to correctly analyze the grammatical structure of the problem. Rehabilitation efforts for a patient with frontal lobe injury might emphasize impulse control and execution of the appropriate behavioral sequence to solve the problem.

Because of the multitude of factors that can result in difficulties in intellectual and executive functioning in patients with brain injuries, programs designed to rehabilitate these patients have necessarily involved attempts to address these deficits in a hierarchical manner, as originally proposed by Luria (1963). One such program was developed at New York University by Ben-Yishay and associates (Ben-Yishay and Diller 1983). They developed a two-tiered approach that defines five basic deficit areas—1) arousal and attention, 2) memory, 3) impairment in underlying skill structure, 4) language and thought, and 5) feeling tone—and two domains of higher-level problem solving. This model proposes that deficits in the higher-level skills are often produced by core deficits and that the patient's behavior is likely to depend on an interaction between the two domains (F.C. Goldstein and Levin 1987).

# Speech and Language

Disorders of speech and language are common sequelae of neurologic damage, particularly when the dominant (usually left) hemisphere is injured. Because the ability to communicate is often central to the patient's personal, social, and vocational readjustment after brain injury or disease, rehabilitation efforts in this area are extremely important. In most rehabilitation settings, speech and language therapies have traditionally been the province of speech pathologists. Therapy has often involved a wide variety of treatments depending on the training, interest, and theoretic orientation of the therapist. The goal of therapy has variously been the improvement of comprehension (receptive language) and expression (expressive language), and it has been shown that patients who receive speech therapy after a stroke improve more than patients who do not (Basso et al. 1979).

In treating speech and language impairment, it is important to consider the reason for the observed speech deficit in designing the treatment; that is, it is not sufficient simply to identify the behavioral deficit and attempt to increase the rate of production (Franzen 1991). For example, Giles et al. (1988) increased appropriate verbalizations in a patient with head injury by providing cuing to keep verbalization short and to pause in planning his speech. Here the remediation attempted to affect the mediating behavior rather than to decrease unwanted behavior through extinction.

# Molar Behaviors

The final test of rehabilitation efforts is frequently the change in ecologically relevant molar behaviors—that is, in behaviors that would be used in the open environment. Examples of such molar behaviors include driving, the completion of occupational work tasks, successful social interaction, and, at a simpler level, activities of daily living. The results of standardized testing may account for most of the variance reported for molar behaviors such as driving skill (Galski et al. 1997). However, the improvement in these molar behaviors also may depend on treatment aimed directly at the production of the behaviors, even when the component cognitive skills have been optimized. Giles et al. (1997) used behavioral techniques to improve washing and dressing skills in a series of individuals with severe brain injury.

## Use of Computers in Cognitive Rehabilitation

The use of microcomputers in cognitive rehabilitation, as in many other facets of everyday life, has increased dramatically over the last decade. The microcomputer has great potential for use in rehabilitation settings and may offer several advantages over more conventional, therapist-based treatments (Grimm and Bleiberg 1986). Microcomputers may have the advantage of being potentially self-instructional and self-paced, of requiring less direct staff time, and of accurately providing direct feedback to the patient about performance. Microcomputers also facilitate research by accurately and consistently recording the large amounts of potentially useful data that are generated during the rehabilitation process.

Notwithstanding these advantages, several cautions must be mentioned concerning the use of microcomputers in the rehabilitation process. First, it must be emphasized that the microcomputer is merely a tool (albeit a highly sophisticated one), and its usefulness is limited by the availability of software that meets the needs of the individual patient and the skill of the therapist in implementing the program(s). As noted by Harris (1984), the danger is that cognitive rehabilitation will become centered around the software that is available through a given treatment program rather than being based on the individual needs of the patient. Second, microcomputers are not capable of simulating human social interaction and should not be used in lieu of human therapeutic contact.

## Behavioral Dysfunction After Brain Injury

Understanding of the full range of behavioral dysfunction in individuals with brain injury or disease is far from complete. Unfortunately, relatively few follow-up studies to date have systematically investigated the efficacy of neu-

ropsychiatric treatment programs. In addition, as is the case with the literature on cognitive rehabilitation, much of what is known comes from studies conducted in rehabilitation settings rather than in hospitals specifically designed to treat patients with neuropsychiatric disorders. Most of the recent studies in this area have focused on patients with traumatic brain injuries.

Behavioral dysfunction associated with other neurologic disorders, such as cerebrovascular accidents and progressive dementing disorders, also has received considerable attention but has not been the subject of a great deal of research to evaluate treatment procedures that are likely to be effective. Despite the relatively sparse amount of literature on treatment outcome in this area, the studies that have been reported have been useful in guiding the development of practical strategies for dealing with the behavioral-psychiatric consequences of brain injury. In particular, behaviorally based treatments have been heavily used. Behavioral dysfunction after brain injury can have a marked effect on the recovery process itself, as well as on the more general aspects of psychosocial adjustment. It is indeed ironic and unfortunate that the patients most needing cognitive rehabilitation services are often kept out of many treatment facilities because of their disruptive behavior. In fact, research studies (Levin et al. 1982; Lishman 1978; Weddell et al. 1980) have shown that behavioral dysfunction is often associated with reduced abilities to comply with rehabilitation programs, to return to work, to engage in recreational and leisure activities, and to sustain positive interpersonal relationships.

Levin and Grossman (1978) reported behavior problems that were present 1 month after traumatic brain injury and that occurred in areas such as emotional withdrawal, conceptual disorganization, motor slowing, unusual thought content, blunt affect, excitement, and disorientation. At 6 months after injury, those patients who had poor social and occupational recovery continued to manifest significant cognitive and behavioral disruption. Complaints of tangential thinking, fragmented speech, slowness of thought and action, depressed mood, increased anxiety, and marital and/or family conflict also were frequently noted (Levin et al. 1979). Other behavioral changes reported to have the potential to cause psychosocial disruption include increased irritability (Rosenthal 1983), social inappropriateness (Lewis et al. 1988), aggression (Mungas 1988), and expansiveness, helplessness, suspiciousness, and anxiety (Grant and Alves 1987).

Behavioral dysfunction is not limited to individuals with traumatic brain injuries. Patients with lesions in specific brain regions secondary to other pathologic conditions also can have characteristic patterns of dysfunctional behavior. For example, frontal lobe dysfunction secondary to stroke, tumor, or other disease processes is often associated with a cluster of symptoms, including social disinhibition, reduced attention, distractibility, impaired judgment, affective lability, and more pervasive mood disorder (Bond 1984; Stuss and Benson 1984). In contrast, Prigatano (1987) noted that individuals with temporal lobe dysfunction can show heightened interpersonal sensitivity, which can evolve into frank paranoid ideation.

In addition to differences between patients with different types of brain injury or disease, the variability in the severity and extent of behavioral disruption after injury within each patient group is remarkable. Eames and Wood (1985), for example, vividly described the variability in severity of impairment in a group of patients who received treatment on a special unit for patients with behavior disorders and head injuries. Verbal and physical aggression, inappropriate social and sexual behavior, self-injury, irritability, and markedly altered levels of drive and motivation represent the kinds of behaviors shown by their patients. The magnitude of their dysfunction precluded many of the patients from participating in traditional rehabilitation programs. They could not be managed at home, in extended-care facilities, or even in general inpatient psychiatric settings. Perhaps not too surprisingly, individuals with mild head injuries are less prone to debilitating behavioral changes but still can experience physical, cognitive, and affective changes of sufficient magnitude to affect their ability to return to preaccident activities (Dikmen et al. 1986; Levin et al. 1987).

It seems clear that adjustment (and failure to adjust) after brain injury appears to be related to a multitude of neurologic and nonneurologic factors, each of which requires consideration in the choice of an appropriate course of intervention for any observed behavioral dysfunction. In addition to the extent and severity of the neurologic injury itself, some of the other factors that can contribute to the presence and type of behavioral dysfunction include the amount of time elapsed since the injury, premorbid psychiatric and psychosocial adjustment, financial resources, social supports, and personal awareness of (and reaction to) acquired deficits (Eames 1988; G. Goldstein and Ruthven 1983; Gross and Schutz 1986; Meier et al. 1987).

Given the large number of factors that influence recovery from brain injury, a multidimensional approach to the behavioral treatment of patients with brain injury is likely to result in an optimal recovery. This approach should take into consideration the patient's premorbid level of functioning (in terms of both psychologic adjustment and neuropsychologic functioning), as well as his or her current psychologic and neuropsychologic resources. Individuals with more severe cognitive impairments are more likely to profit from highly structured behavioral programs. Those whose neuropsychologic functioning is more intact, in contrast, may profit from interventions with a more active cognitive component that requires them to use abstract thought as well as self-evaluative and self-corrective processes. Not surprisingly, therapeutic approaches that fall under the general heading of behavior therapy represent an approach that is gaining increasing interest as a component of the overall treatment plan for patients with neuropsychiatric impairment.

## Behavior Therapy for Patients With Brain Impairment

The domain of behavior therapy has expanded considerably in the past 20 years. Although it is not the primary purpose of this chapter to review the history of behaviorally based therapies, it is useful to keep in mind that behavioral assessment and treatment have extended far beyond their early roots in classical and operant conditioning and have been adapted for use with numerous special populations, most recently including persons with brain injuries. (For more comprehensive and critical presentations of the recent status and direction of behavior therapies, see Haynes 1984, Hersen and Bellack 1985, and Kazdin 1979; for excellent compendia describing both assessment and treatment approaches in clinically useful terms, see Bellack and Hersen 1985b and Hersen and Bellack 1988.)

Despite a broadening scope that has included the treatment of patients with neurologic impairment, behavioral approaches remain committed to the original principles derived from experimental and social psychology. They also emphasize the empirical and objective implementation and evaluation of treatment (Bellack and Hersen 1985a).

The general assumptions about the nature of behavior disorders that form the basis of behavioral approaches include the following (Haynes 1984):

- Disordered behavior can be expressed through overt actions, thoughts, verbalizations, and physiologic reactions.

- These reactions do not necessarily vary in the same way for different individuals or for different behavior disorders.

- Changing one specific behavior may result in changes in other related behaviors.
- Environmental conditions play an important role in the initiation, maintenance, and alteration of behavior.

These assumptions have led to approaches emphasizing the objective evaluation of observable aspects of the individual and his or her interaction with the environment. The range of observable events is limited only by the clinician's ability to establish a reliable, valid quantification of the target behavior or environmental condition. As previously noted, this could range from a specific physiologic reaction, such as heart rate, to a self-report of the number of obsessive thoughts occurring during a 24-hour period.

Intervention focuses on the active interaction between the individual and the environment. The goal of treatment is to alter those aspects of the environment that have become associated with the initiation or maintenance of maladaptive behaviors or to alter the patient's response to those aspects of the environment in some way.

The application of a behavioral intervention with a neuropsychiatric patient requires careful consideration of both the neuropsychologic and the environmental aspects of the presenting problem. Although this may seem obvious, the attempted synthesis of these two separate disciplines is still in the early stages of development. Few clinicians have the training, time, or energy to become and remain equally competent in both neuropsychology and behavioral psychology. There is, however, a growing effort to explore areas of commonality between these two specialties. Professional-interest groups among behavioral psychologists are attempting to define more precisely the domain of behavioral neuropsychology (Horton and Barrett 1988).

At present, the accumulated body of evidence remains limited regarding the specific types of behavioral interventions that are most effective in treating the various dysfunctional behaviors observed in individuals with different kinds of brain injuries. Despite this limitation, there is optimism, based on the current literature, that behavior therapy can be effective for patients with brain injuries (Horton and Miller 1985). Indeed, an increasing number of books, primarily on the rehabilitation of patients with brain injuries, describe the potential applications of behavioral approaches for persons with neurologic impairment (Edelstein and Couture 1984; G. Goldstein and Ruthven 1983; Seron 1987; Wood 1984). Such sources provide an excellent introduction to the basic models, methods, and limitations of behavioral treatments of patients with brain injuries.

Behavioral approaches can be broadly classified into at least three general models (Calhoun and Turner 1981): 1) a traditional behavioral approach, 2) a social learning approach, and 3) a cognitive-behavioral approach. The degree to which the client or patient is required to participate actively in the identification and alteration of the environmental conditions assumed to be supporting the maladaptive behavior varies across these models.

## Traditional Behavioral Approach

The traditional behavioral approach emphasizes the effects of environmental events that occur after (consequences), as well as before (antecedents), a particular behavior of interest. We address these two aspects of environmental influence separately.

### Interventions Aimed at the Consequences of Behavior

A consequence that increases the probability of a specific behavior occurring again under similar circumstances is termed a *reinforcer*. Consequences can either increase or decrease the likelihood of a particular behavior occurring again.

A behavior followed by an environmental consequence that increases the likelihood that the behavior will occur again is called a *positive reinforcer*. A behavior followed by the removal of a negative or aversive environmental condition is called a *negative reinforcer*. A behavior followed by an aversive environmental event is termed a *punishment*. The effect of punishment is to reduce the probability that the behavior will occur under similar conditions. There has often been confusion concerning the difference between negative reinforcers and punishments. It is useful to remember that reinforcers (positive or negative) always increase the likelihood of the behavior occurring again, whereas punishments decrease the likelihood of a behavior occurring again. When the reliable relation between a specific behavior and an environmental consequence is removed, the behavioral effect is to reduce the target behavior to a near-zero level of occurrence. This process is called *extinction*. Self-management skills (relaxation training, biofeedback) have been used in the treatment of ataxia (Guercio et al. 1997).

### Interventions Aimed at the Antecedents of Behavior

Behavior is controlled or affected not only by the consequences that follow it but also by events that precede it. These events are called *antecedents*. For example, an aggressive patient may have outbursts only in the presence of the nursing staff and never in the presence of the physician. In this case, a failure to search for potential antecedents (e.g., female sex or physical size) that may be eliciting the behavior may leave half of the behavioral assessment undone and may result in difficulty decreasing the aggressive behavior. This type of approach may be particularly useful in patients for whom the behavior is disruptive enough that approaches aimed at manipulation of consequences hold some danger for staff and family (e.g., in the case of a patient with explosive or violent outbursts). In this situation, treatment is structured to decrease the likelihood of an outburst by restructuring the events that lead to the violent behavior. Some patients are able to learn to anticipate these antecedents themselves, whereas for others, it becomes the task of the treatment staff to identify and modify the antecedents that lead to unwanted behavior. For example, if the stress of verbal communication leads to aggressive behavior in an aphasic patient, the patient may be initially trained to use an alternative form of communication, such as writing or sign language (Franzen and Lovell 1987).

## Other Behavioral Approaches

Yet another class of approaches involves the use of differential reinforcement of other behaviors. In this approach, the problem behavior is not consequated—that is, the effect of the problem behavior is not addressed. Instead, another behavior that is inconsistent with the problem target behavior is reinforced. As the other behavior increases in frequency, the problem behavior decreases. Hegel and Ferguson (2000) reported the successful use of this approach in reducing aggressive behavior in a subject with brain injury. Differential reinforcement of low rates of responding also may be used to reduce undesired behaviors (Alderman and Knight 1997). Finally, noncontingent reinforcement in the form of increased attention to a subject resulted in a decrease in aggression toward others and a decrease in self-injurious behaviors (Persel et al. 1997).

## Social Learning Approach

With the social learning approach, cognitive processes that mediate between environmental conditions and behavioral responses are included in explanations of the learning process. Social learning approaches take advantage of learning through modeling—by systematically arranging opportunities for patients to observe socially adaptive examples of social interaction. Emphasis is also placed on practicing the components of social skills in role-playing situations, where the patient can receive corrective feedback. Intervention that focuses on social skills training is one example of a treatment that is often useful for patients with brain injuries who have lost the ability to effectively monitor their behavior and to respond appropriately in a given situation.

Socially skilled behavior is generally divided into three components: 1) social perception, 2) social problem solving, and 3) social expression. Training can occur at any one of these levels. For the patient who has lost the ability to interact appropriately with conversational skills, this behavior may be modeled by staff members. (For a comprehensive review, see Bandura 1977.)

## Cognitive-Behavioral Approach

The term *cognitive-behavioral approach* refers to a heterogeneous group of procedures that emphasize the individual's cognitive mediation (self-messages) in explaining behavioral responses within environmental contexts. The thoughts, beliefs, and predictions about one's own actions and their potential environmental consequences are emphasized. Treatment focuses on changing maladaptive beliefs and increasing an individual's self-control within the current social environment by changing maladaptive thoughts or beliefs. This approach is particularly useful with patients who have relatively intact language and self-evaluative abilities.

Cognitive-behavioral treatments originally were designed to treat affective disorders and symptoms. However, the use of the approach has widened to include anxiety, personality disorders, and skills deficits. For example, Suzman et al. (1997) used cognitive-behavioral methods to improve the problem-solving skills of children with cognitive deficits following traumatic brain injury.

## Assessment of Treatment Effects

In addition to providing a set of methodologies to affect the disordered behavior produced by cognitive deficits, the literature on behavior therapy has provided a conceptual scheme for evaluating the effects of intervention. One of the most influential products of the tradition of behavior therapy has been the development of single-subject designs to evaluate the effect of interventions. Although originally conceived as a method of evaluating the effect of environmental interventions, the single-subject design has been successfully applied in the evaluation of pharmacologic interventions as well. Because each patient is an individual and treatment of cognitive dysfunction is still a relatively nascent endeavor, interventions often need to be specifically tailored to the individual patient. Interventions

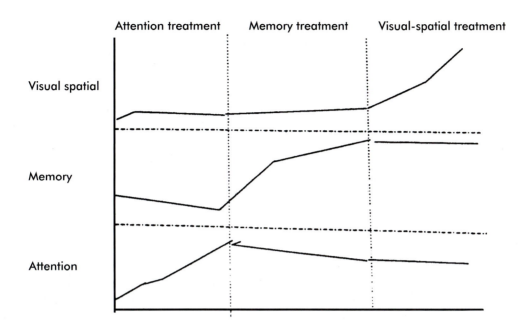

**FIGURE 37–1.** Multiple baseline design for the treatment of a patient with brain injury and deficits in attention, memory, and visual-spatial processing. Attention, memory, and visual-spatial skills are each treated in sequence; improvement is seen in one area before beginning the next phase of treatment, and performance in untreated skill areas is used as a comparison for the treated areas. The vertical axis represents level of performance in each skill area (visual spatial, memory, and attention). The passage of time is represented on the horizontal axis. The dotted vertical lines are those times at which treatment was switched from the previous focus to the current focus, such as from attention training to memory training.

often must be applied before the period of spontaneous recovery has ended, and a method to distinguish the effects of intervention from the effects of recovery of acute physiologic disturbance is needed. The multiple-baseline design is a single-subject design that addresses these issues (Franzen and Iverson 1990).

The design of multiple baselines across behaviors involves the evaluation of more than one behavior taking place at the same time. However, only one of the behaviors is targeted for intervention at a time. In this way, the nontargeted behaviors are used as control comparisons for the targeted behaviors. For example, behavior A is targeted for intervention first, and monitors on behaviors B and C are used as control comparisons. After completion of the treatment phase for behavior A, an intervention is implemented for behavior B, and monitors on behaviors A and C are used as control comparisons.

Figure 37–1 presents an example of a multiple-baseline design in the treatment of an individual with brain injury and deficits in memory, attention, and visual-spatial processing. The attention skills receive treatment in the first phase, with a concomitant improvement in skill level. At the second phase, memory skills are treated, with a concomitant improvement. Finally, visual-spatial skills are treated at the third phase, and improvement is

seen there. At each phase, performance in the other untreated skill areas is used as a control comparison for the treated skill areas.

In an application of the multiple-baseline design to the treatment of a patient with brain injury, Franzen and Harris (1993) reported a case in which a patient had deficits in attention-based memory and in abstraction and planning as the result of a closed head injury. This patient was first seen 23 days after the closed head injury occurred. He was seen for a series of weekly appointments. At these appointments, the emotional adjustment was discussed and support was provided. Additionally, the patient received psychotherapy in the form of anger-control training and social reinforcement for increasing his daily level of activity and self-initiated social interactions, two areas identified as problems during the evaluation. Finally, cognitive retraining exercises were implemented and taught to the patient and his family so that home practice could take place on a daily basis. The family was instructed in the methods used to record the scores from the exercises, which were then entered into a daily log.

The cognitive retraining was conducted according to a design in which multiple baselines across behaviors were used. Cognitive-retraining treatment was first aimed at improving attention and memory with a set of four exercises implemented both during outpatient appointments and at home. An assessment conducted on both of the targeted treatment areas of memory and abstraction and planning skills indicated improvement in the memory realm but not in the abstraction and planning realm. During the second phase, treatment was aimed at improving abstraction and planning skills with a set of exercises that were again implemented during outpatient appointments and at home. Evaluations during this phase indicated improvement in abstraction and planning skills but no further improvement in memory skills. A complete neuropsychologic battery of tests was administered at the first contact and again after the termination of treatment. Additionally, short tests of relevant neuropsychologic function were administered before the initiation of treatment, at each phase change, and at the termination of treatment. The results of the standardized neuropsychologic tests were consistent with the behavioral monitoring conducted on the skill exercises, namely, improvement in attention and memory as a result of the treatment in the first phase and improvement in abstraction and planning skills as a result of the treatment in the second phase.

## Case Examples of Behavioral Intervention

In this section, we present two case examples of how behavioral interventions can be applied within the context of the comprehensive care provided in an acute neuropsychiatric inpatient setting. Although the focus of the cases is on behavioral treatment, patients are monitored by an interdisciplinary treatment team representing neuropsychiatry, neuropsychology, psychiatric nursing, occupational therapy, recreational therapy, speech-language pathology, and physical therapy. The emphasis here is on the application of behavioral procedures, not on the attribution of outcome. The cases selected represent typical behavior complaints within this type of setting. In this chapter, we have discussed the application of behavioral technology to the remediation of cognitive deficits. A more common use of behavioral methods is in the treatment of problematic behavior that might otherwise interfere with the rehabilitation process.

### Case Example 1: Inappropriate Sexual and Aggressive Language and Behavior

Mr. A, a 27-year-old single man, had received a closed head injury as the result of a suicide attempt at age 19.

He had been significantly involved with drug abuse and had attempted suicide while intoxicated after discharge from a substance treatment center to which he had been sent by his parents. Before his suicide attempt, he had been involved in a motorcycle accident while intoxicated, and the accident had left him unable to ambulate without the use of a wheelchair. The suicide attempt involved taking an overdose of sleeping pills with alcohol and firing a pistol into his right temple. He was discovered by his mother after the shot was fired. He had a significant and noticeable cranial depression as the result of his injury.

Mr. A had received inpatient acute rehabilitation services and had been placed in various personal-care facilities. Each time, he was discharged because of disruptive behavior, including sexually inappropriate language, touching staff and female residents, and aggressive language, with occasional escalation to aggressive behavior. Although, at first, he expressed relief at being sent to a rehabilitation hospital, where "at least the staff know what they're doing," he soon became involved in conflicts with the staff and began showing the inappropriate behavior that had been the cause of his referral to the rehabilitation hospital. He made sexual comments directed at female staff and would attempt to fondle them. He would place his wheelchair in the hallway such that it was difficult for people to walk past him without his grabbing them. On his third night at the hospital, he was found behind the closed door of a confused female patient's room. Mr. A was found with his hands beneath her bedclothes, although he was fully clothed and still in his wheelchair. Mr. A also was seen lighting his cigarettes in his bedroom instead of in the smoking area outside of the hospital. There were circumscribed times for smoking, but Mr. A insisted on smoking throughout the day. He would use threats of physical violence or legal action against any staff who would attempt to control his behavior. In fact, he had obtained the services of a pro-bono lawyer to file suit against a previous placement because of what he termed "abuse by the staff." The suit was dismissed by a judge, but the reputation he acquired from this behavior made it difficult to find another personal-care facility to house him afterward.

The neuropsychologic evaluation indicated an average IQ, with a value of 107 for the Full-Scale IQ. His Wechsler Memory Scale—Revised (WMS-R; Wechsler 1987) General Memory Index was 96, and his Delayed Recall Index was somewhat lower, at 87. His performance on the Halstead Category Test (Reitan and Wolfson 1985) indicated only mild problems with abstract problem solving. Verbal generativity and naming were intact. Motor speed was slowed, especially on the right side. Visual-perceptual performance was adequate. There were no signs of significant cognitive impairment otherwise. Performance on the Trail Making Test (Reitan and Wolfson 1985) and on the Stroop Color-Word Test (Golden 1978) was adequate. There were no signs of an organic basis for impulsivity or perseveration.

Although his free behavior might be construed as being a manifestation of impulsivity, Mr. A did not show signs of that problem on standardized tests. He also showed reasonable problem-solving and planning skills, both on standardized tests and on the basis of his history (e.g., hiring the lawyer to press suit against the personal-care facility). However, the fact that he engaged the attorney while still a resident in the facility in question indicated a tendency to let his negative feelings override his better judgment. His memory test performance indicated that he should be able to remember a contingency system if it were described to him in simple terms and on multiple occasions.

On the basis of the evaluation, a behavior management program was designed in which Mr. A received full information about the contingencies and the reasons for implementing them, namely, to help him control his behavior and to learn more appropriate and, ultimately, more effective ways of pursuing his wants. The underlying principles involved were to minimize punishment because he used aggression to escape punishing situations and to increase social reinforcement and social control over his behavior so that the treatment gains could be maintained in a nonhospital setting.

A functional analysis of the aggressive behavior indicated that Mr. A used aggressive language when it appeared that limits would be placed on his behaviors. For example, if a staff member attempted to enforce the rules regarding smoking or keeping perishable food in his room, Mr. A would threaten to physically attack the staff member or would engage in verbal vituperation and vulgarity. Especially because of his history, the staff members would typically back down and leave Mr. A to his own desires. This appeared to be a pattern at several care facilities, especially after the unsuccessful lawsuit.

A functional analysis of the sexual behavior indicated that Mr. A initiated sexual behavior against individuals who could not retaliate. For example, he would fondle confused patients, or female staff members would be constrained in their responses to him. He did not approach the nonprofessional staff, who would presumably be more inclined to provide a negative consequence to his behavior.

Mr. A was able to escape or avoid undesirable circumstances (e.g., frustration of his desire to smoke or to engage in desired behaviors contrary to hospital policy or schedule) by engaging in aggressive behavior. The contingency management program included informing Mr. A that aggressive behavior would not result in being allowed to have his way. Instead, Mr. A would be reminded of the rules regarding the issue in question. If he continued to threaten aggression, he would be escorted to his room. If he threatened to sue the hospital, he would be advised to discuss all such matters with the hospital counsel, who had been briefed on the situation. Mr. A also was informed of the usual grievance procedure already implemented in the hospital and was introduced to the patient representative.

Mr. A was hypothesized to be seeking sexual contact with individuals who could not refuse him because of his concerns about rejection. Therefore, the contingency management system used to treat this problem behavior included a verbal indication that such behavior would not be tolerated. If Mr. A initiated fondling or sexual language with a patient, his access to that patient would be severely limited. If he initiated it with a staff member, that staff member would immediately leave the room and be replaced by a male staff member. Additionally, Mr. A received individual counseling regarding sexuality in disabled individuals. He was given the opportunity to attend social mixers with the local paraplegic and head injury survivor groups, where he could meet young people with similar concerns.

The result of the treatment intervention was a dramatic reduction in aggressive behavior in a short time. The inappropriate sexual behavior decreased, although the inappropriate sexual verbalizations remained. An interview with Mr. A's mother indicated that vulgar and, at times, explicit sexual talk was a premorbid behavior pattern for Mr. A. It was not thought that treatment would be effective in totally changing that aspect.

## Case Example 2: Depression With Failure to Use Ambulatory Assistance

Ms. B, a 68-year-old, right-handed woman with a high-school education, had a history of diabetes and moderate hypertension, both of which were of recent onset. She lived alone and one evening had a stroke that left her with ambulatory difficulties, significant memory deficits, and depression. She was receiving inpatient rehabilitation, including physical therapy, memory retraining, and psychotherapy. She tended to try to ambulate without her walker, which was a concern to the staff because of the potential for falls and injury.

The neuropsychologic evaluation indicated generally intact language skills. Her motor functions were slow in comparison with age-appropriate norms, and her left side showed relatively more slowing. Motor strength was attenuated on the left side, and balance and gait problems were noted. Attention was moderately impaired; she had the ability to repeat up to six digits, but only inconsistently. She showed difficulty on tasks requiring concentration and mental manipulation of information. Her Visual Memory Index on the WMS-R was 82, her Verbal Memory Index was 91, and her Delayed Memory Index was 71. Her performance on abstract problem-solving tasks was adequate but somewhat lower than average.

Ms. B often would attempt to walk without the use of her walker. She would attempt to rise from a chair or from her bed without calling for assistance or using the walker to steady herself. In physical therapy sessions, she willingly used the walker or the assistance of the physical therapist. Individual psychotherapy with Ms. B centered on the themes of change and aging. She had been relatively healthy until approximately 4 years earlier and had been living independently until the time of her stroke. She had been driving and had been a resource for her children by babysitting and running errands for them. The conceptualization of her failure to use the walker involved her memory deficits, whereby she would forget that the use of a walker was necessary. A secondary reason involved her difficulty in accepting the changes in her situation.

The individual psychotherapist addressed the issues of accepting her current situation. Ms. B was helped to focus on her abilities rather than on her disabilities. The importance of realistically evaluating her needs was emphasized. Other staff members were instructed to remind Ms. B of her strengths whenever she became focused on her difficulties. Staff members, including housekeeping and transportation workers, were encouraged not to minimize her difficulties while not focusing extensively on them.

As intervention for her memory difficulties, Ms. B was given overlearning procedures involving getting out of bed and rising from a chair. Each day, Ms. B would practice (with supervision and feedback) getting out of bed and reaching for her walker for 30 minutes. In the afternoon, she would receive 15 minutes of practice in rising from a chair and reaching for her walker. It was believed that overlearning with dense practice would help make the use of the walker second nature. Ms. B was taught to repeat the phrase "Before I stand, I need my walker" multiple times and to use that phrase each time she wanted to stand. Each staff member also repeated that phrase each time they helped Ms. B get out of bed or up from a chair.

A small can was attached to the frame of her walker. Staff members were given tokens and instructed to randomly provide social reinforcement and to place a token in the can when they saw Ms. B using the walker. Twenty tokens could be exchanged for an extra time period in the crafts room. This procedure was chosen to develop a positive valence toward the use of the walker, as well as to increase use of the walker. Staff members also randomly quizzed Ms. B on the procedures needed to arise from bed and arise from a chair. The dependent measures used were the number of times that Ms. B needed to be reminded to use the walker, the number of tokens collected in the can attached to the walker, and the number of correct answers to the quiz questions.

Ms. B showed appropriate changes in behavior in response to the contingencies. The staff felt that the treatment was successful when, on awakening and not finding her walker, Ms. B called for a nurse rather than attempting to stand on her own.

## Conclusions

Neuropsychologic and behavioral dysfunction associated with brain injury can be varied and complex. Effective intervention requires an integrated interdisciplinary approach that focuses on the individual patient and his or her specific needs. Behaviorally based formulations can provide a valuable framework from which to understand the interaction between an individual with compromised physical, neuropsychologic, and emotional functioning, as well as the psychosocial environment in which he or she is trying to adjust.

Much work remains to define the most effective cognitive and behaviorally based treatments for various neuropsychiatric disorders. The evidence to date suggests that this area is indeed an area worthy of continued pursuit.

## References

Alderman N, Knight C: The effectiveness of DRL in the management of severe behaviour disorders following brain injury. Brain Inj 11:79–101, 1997

Azouvi P, Jokic C, Attal N, et al: Carbamazepine in agitation and aggressive behaviour following severe closed-head injury. Brain Inj 13:797–804, 1999

Bandura A: Social Learning Theory. Englewood Cliffs, NJ, Prentice-Hall, 1977

Basso A, Capotani E, Vignolo L: Influence of rehabilitation on language skills in aphasic patients. Arch Neurol 36:190–196, 1979

Bellack AS, Hersen M: General considerations, in Handbook of Clinical Behavior Therapy With Adults. Edited by Hersen M, Bellack AS. New York, Plenum, 1985a, pp 3–19

Bellack AS, Hersen M: Dictionary of Behavior Therapy Techniques. New York, Pergamon, 1985b

Bellack AS, Mueser KT: Psychosocial treatment for schizophrenia. Schizophr Bull 19:317–336, 1993

Ben-Yishay Y, Diller L: Rehabilitation of cognitive and perceptual deficits in people with traumatic brain damage. Int J Rehabil Res 4:208–210, 1981

Ben-Yishay Y, Diller L: Cognitive deficits, in Rehabilitation of the Head-Injured Adult. Edited by Griffith EA, Bond M, Miller J. Philadelphia, PA, FA Davis, 1983, pp 167–183

Benedict RH, Harris AE, Markow T, et al: Effects of attention training on information processing in schizophrenia. Schizophr Bull 20:537–546, 1994

Bond M: The psychiatry of closed head injury, in Closed Head Injury: Psychosocial, Social and Family Consequences. Edited by Brooks PN. Oxford, England, Oxford University Press, 1984, pp 148–178

Calhoun KS, Turner SM: Historical perspectives and current issues in behavior therapy, in Handbook of Clinical Behavior Therapy. Edited by Turner SM, Calhoun KS, Adams HE. New York, Wiley, 1981, pp 1–11

Crovitz H, Harvey M, Horn R: Problems in the acquisition of imagery mnemonics: three brain damaged cases. Cortex 15:225–234, 1979

Dikmen S, McLean A, Temkin N: Neuropsychological and psychosocial consequences of minor head injury. J Neurol Neurosurg Psychiatry 49:1227–1232, 1986

Diller L, Weinberg J: Hemi-inattention in rehabilitation: the evolution of a rational remediation program. Adv Neurol 18:63–82, 1977

Eames P: Behavior disorders after severe head injury: their nature, causes and strategies for management. J Head Trauma Rehabil 3:1–6, 1988

Eames P, Wood R: Rehabilitation after severe brain injury: a follow-up study of a behavior modification approach. J Neurol Neurosurg Psychiatry 48:613–619, 1985

Edelstein BA, Couture ET: Behavioral Assessment and Rehabilitation of the Traumatically Brain-Damaged. New York, Plenum, 1984

Flesher S: Cognitive habilitation in schizophrenia: a theoretical review and model of treatment. Neuropsychol Rev 1:223–246, 1990

Franzen MD: Behavioral assessment and treatment of brain-impaired individuals, in Progress in Behavior Modification. Edited by Hersen M, Eisler RM. Newbury Park, CA, Sage, 1991, pp 56–85

Franzen MD, Harris CV: Neuropsychological rehabilitation: application of a modified multiple baseline design. Brain Inj 7:525–534, 1993

Franzen MD, Haut MW: The psychological treatment of memory impairment: a review of empirical studies. Neuropsychol Rev 2:29–63, 1991

Franzen MD, Iverson GL: Applications of single subject design to cognitive rehabilitation, in Neuropsychology Across the Lifespan. Edited by Horton AM. New York, Springer, 1990, pp 155–174

Franzen MD, Lovell MR: Behavioral treatments of aggressive sequelae of brain injury. Psychiatric Annals 17:389–396, 1987

Galski T, Ehle HT, Williams JB: Off-road driving evaluations for persons with cerebral injury: a factor analytic study of pre-driver and simulator testing. Am J Occup Ther 51:352–359, 1997

Gardner H: The Shattered Mind: The Person After Brain Damage. London, England, Routledge & Kegan Paul, 1977

Gianutsos R, Matheson P: The rehabilitation of visual perceptual disorders attributable to brain injury, in Neuropsychological Rehabilitation. Edited by Meier MJ, Benton AL, Diller L. New York, Guilford, 1987, pp 202–241

Gianutsos R, Glosser D, Elbaum J, et al: Visual imperception in brain injured adults: multifaceted measures. Arch Phys Med Rehabil 64:456–461, 1983

Giles GM, Pussey I, Burgess P: The behavioral treatment of verbal interaction skills following severe head injury: a single case study. Brain Inj 2:75–79, 1988

Giles GM, Ridley JE, Dill A, et al: A consecutive series of adults with brain injury treated with a washing and dressing retraining program. Am J Occup Ther 51:256–266, 1997

Glasgow RE, Zeiss RA, Barrera M, et al: Case studies on remediating memory deficits in brain damaged individuals. J Clin Psychol 33:1049–1054, 1977

Glen MB: Methylphenidate for cognitive and behavioral dysfunction after traumatic brain injury. J Head Trauma Rehabil 13:87–90, 1998

Glisky EL, Schacter DL: Remediation of organic memory disorders: current status and future prospects. J Head Trauma Rehabil 4:54–63, 1986

Golden CJ: The Stroop Color-Word Test: Clinical and Experimental Manual. Chicago, IL, Stoelting, 1978

Goldstein FC, Levin HS: Disorders of reasoning and problem solving ability, in Neuropsychological Rehabilitation. Edited by Meier MJ, Benton AL, Diller L. New York, Guilford, 1987, pp 327–354

Goldstein G, Ruthven L: Rehabilitation of the Brain-Damaged Adult. New York, Plenum, 1983

Gordon W, Hibbard M, Egelko S, et al: Perceptual remediation in patients with right brain damage: a comprehensive program. Arch Phys Med Rehabil 66:353–359, 1985

Gouvier WD, Webster JS, Blanton PD: Cognitive retraining with brain damaged patients, in The Neuropsychology Handbook: Behavioral and Clinical Perspectives. Edited by Wedding D, Horton AM, Webster J. New York, Springer, 1986, pp 278–324

Grant I, Alves W: Psychiatric and psychosocial disturbances in head injury, in Neurobehavioral Recovery From Head Injury. Edited by Levin HS, Grafman J, Eisenberg HM. New York, Oxford University Press, 1987, pp 222–246

Grimm BH, Bleiberg J: Psychological rehabilitation in traumatic brain injury, in Handbook of Clinical Neuropsychology, Vol 2. Edited by Filskov SB, Boll TJ. New York, Wiley, 1986, pp 495–560

Gross Y, Schutz LF: Intervention models in neuropsychology, in Clinical Neuropsychology of Intervention. Edited by Uzzell BP, Gross Y. Boston, MA, Martinus Highoff, 1986, pp 179–204

Gualtieri CT: Pharmacotherapy and the neurobehavioral sequelae of traumatic brain injury. Brain Inj 2:101–109, 1988

Guercio J, Chittum R, McMorrow M: Self-management in the treatment of ataxia: a case study in reducing ataxic tremor through relaxation and biofeedback. Brain Inj 11:353–362, 1997

Harris JE: Methods of improving memory, in Clinical Management of Memory Problems. Edited by Wilson BA, Moffat N. Rockville, MD, Aspen, 1984, pp 46–62

Harris JE, Sunderland A: A brief survey of the management of memory disorders in rehabilitation units in Britain. International Rehabilitation Medicine 3:206–209, 1981

Haynes SN: Behavioral assessment of adults, in Handbook of Psychological Assessment. Edited by Goldstein G, Hersen M. New York, Pergamon, 1984, pp 369–401

Hegel MT, Ferguson RJ: Differential reinforcement of other behavior (DRO) to reduce aggressive behavior following traumatic brain injury. Behav Modif 24:94–101, 2000

Hersen M, Bellack AS: Handbook of Clinical Behavior Therapy With Adults. New York, Plenum, 1985

Hersen M, Bellack AS: Dictionary of Behavioral Assessment Techniques. New York, Pergamon, 1988

Ho MR, Bennett TL: Efficacy of neuropsychological rehabilitation of mild-moderate traumatic brain injury. Archives of Clinical Neuropsychology 12:1–11, 1997

Holzer JC: Buspirone and brain injury (letter). J Neuropsychiatry Clin Neurosci 10:113, 1998

Horton AM, Barrett D: Neuropsychological assessment and behavior therapy: new directions in head trauma rehabilitation. J Head Trauma Rehabil 3:57–64, 1988

Horton AM, Miller WA: Neuropsychology and behavior therapy, in Progress in Behavior Modifications. Edited by Hersen M, Eisler R, Miller PM. New York, Academic Press, 1985, pp 1–55

Kazdin AE: Fictions, factions, and functions of behavior therapy. Behavior Therapy 10:629–654, 1979

Khouzam HR, Donnelly NJ: Remission of traumatic brain injury-induced compulsions during venlafaxine treatment. Gen Hosp Psychiatry 20:62–63, 1998

Kolata G: Brain-grafting work shows promise (letter). Science 221:1277, 1983

Kraus MF, Maki M: Effect of amantadine hydrochloride on symptoms of frontal lobe dysfunction in brain injury: case studies and review. J Neuropsychiatry Clin Neurosci 9:222–230, 1997

Levin HS, Grossman RG: Behavioral sequelae of closed head injury: a quantitative study. Arch Neurol 35:720–727, 1978

Levin HS, Grossman RG, Ross JE, et al: Long-term neuropsychological outcome of closed head injury. J Neurosurg 50:412–422, 1979

Levin HS, Benton AL, Grossman RG: Neurobehavioral Consequences of Closed Head Injury. New York, Oxford University Press, 1982

Levin HS, Mattis S, Ruff R, et al: Neurobehavioral outcome following minor head injury: a three center study. J Neurosurg 66:234–243, 1987

Lewis FD, Nelson J, Nelson C, et al: Effects of three feedback contingencies on the socially inappropriate talk of a brain-injured adult. Behavior Therapy 19:203–211, 1988

Lezak MD: Neuropsychological Assessment, 3rd Edition. New York, Oxford University Press, 1995

Liepert J, Bauder H, Miltner WHR, et al: Treatment-induced cortical reorganization after stroke in humans. Stroke 31(6):1210–1216, 2000

Lishman WA: Organic Psychiatry. St. Louis, MO, Blackwell Scientific, 1978

Luria AR: Restoration of Function After Brain Injury. New York, Macmillan, 1963

Luria AR, Tsvetkova LS: The Neuropsychological Analysis of Problem Solving. Orlando, FL, Paul Deutsch, 1990

McIntosh GC: Medical management of noncognitive sequelae of minor traumatic brain injury. Applied Neuropsychology 4:62–68, 1997

Medd J, Tate RL: Evaluation of anger management therapy programme following acquired brain injury: a preliminary study. Neuropsychological Rehabilitation 10:185–201, 2000

Meier MJ, Strauman S, Thompson WG: Individual differences in neuropsychological recovery: an overview, in Neuropsychological Rehabilitation. Edited by Meier MJ, Benton AL, Diller L. New York, Guilford, 1987, pp 71–110

Mendez MF, Nakawatase TV, Brown CV: Involuntary laughter and inappropriate hilarity. J Neuropsychiatry Clin Neurosci 11:253–258, 1999

Moffat N: Strategies of memory therapy, in Clinical Management of Memory Problems. Edited by Wilson BA, Moffat N. Rockville, MD, Aspen, 1984, pp 63–88

Mungas D: Psychometric correlates of episodic violent behavior: a multidimensional neuropsychological approach. Br J Psychiatry 152:180–187, 1988

NIH Consensus Statement: Rehabilitation of Persons With Traumatic Brain Injury. Vol 16, No 1. October 26–28, 1998

Rehabilitation of Persons With Traumatic Brain Injury. NIH Consensus Statement Online 16(1):1–41, October 26–28, 1998. Available at http://odp.od.nih.gov/consensus/cons/109/109_statement.htm

Patten BM: The ancient art of memory. Arch Neurol 26:25–31, 1972

Persel CS, Persel CH, Ashley MJ, et al: The use of noncontingent reinforcement and contingent restrain to reduce physical aggression and self-injurious behaviour in a traumatically brain injured adult. Brain Inj 11:751–760, 1997

Posner HI, Rafal RD: Cognitive theories of attention and the rehabilitation of attentional deficits, in Neuropsychological Rehabilitation. Edited by Meier MJ, Benton AL, Diller L. New York, Guilford, 1987, pp 182–201

Prigatano GP: Personality and psychosocial consequences after brain injury, in Neuropsychological Rehabilitation. Edited by Meier MJ, Benton AL, Diller L. New York, Guilford, 1987, pp 355–378

Reitan RM, Wolfson D: The Halstead-Reitan Neuropsychological Test Battery: Theory and Clinical Interpretation. Tucson, AZ, Neuropsychology Press, 1985

Robertson-Tchabo EA, Hausman CP, Arenberg D: A classical mnemonic for older learners: a trip that works. Educational Gerontologist 1:215–216, 1976

Robinson RG: Neuropsychiatric consequences of stroke. Annu Rev Med 48:217–229, 1997

Rosenthal M: Behavioral sequelae, in Rehabilitation of the Head Injured Adult. Edited by Rosenthal M, Griffith ER, Bond MR, et al. Philadelphia, PA, FA Davis, 1983, pp 297–308

Schacter DL, Glisky EL: Memory rehabilitation: restoration, alleviation, and the acquisition of domain specific knowledge, in Clinical Neuropsychology of Intervention. Edited by Uzzell B, Gross Y. Boston, MA, Martinus Nijhof, 1986, pp 257–287

Schmitter-Edgecombe M, Fahy JF, Whelan JP, et al: Memory remediation after severe closed head injury: notebook training versus supportive therapy. J Consult Clin Psychol 63:484–489, 1995

Schneider WN, Drew-Cates J, Wong TM, et al: Cognitive and behavioural efficacy of amantadine in acute traumatic brain injury: an initial double-blind placebo-controlled study. Brain Inj 13:863–872, 1999

Seron X: Operant procedures and neuropsychological rehabilitation, in Neuropsychological Rehabilitation. Edited by Meier MJ, Benton AL, Diller L. New York, Guilford, 1987, pp 132–161

Sivak M, Hill C, Henson D, et al: Improved driving performance following perceptual training of persons with brain damage. Arch Phys Med Rehabil 65:163–167, 1985

Stuss DT, Benson DF: Neuropsychological studies of the frontal lobes. Psychol Bull 95:3–28, 1984

Suzman KB, Morris RD, Morris MK, et al: Cognitive remediation of problem solving deficits in children with acquired brain injury. J Behav Ther Exp Psychiatry 28:203–212, 1997

Wall P, Egger M: Mechanisms of plasticity of new connection following brain damage in adult mammalian nervous systems, in Recovery of Function: Theoretical Considerations for Brain Injury Rehabilitation. Edited by Bach-y-Rita P. Baltimore, MD, Park, 1971, pp 117–129

Wechsler D: Wechsler Memory Scale—Revised. San Antonio, TX, Psychological Corporation, 1987

Weddell R, Oddy M, Jenkins D: Social adjustment after rehabilitation: a two year follow up of patients with severe head injury. Psychol Med 10:257–263, 1980

Williams SE, Ris DM, Ayyangar R, et al: Recovery in pediatric brain injury: is psychostimulant medication beneficial? J Head Trauma Rehabil 13:73–81, 1998

Wilson B: Success and failure in memory training following a cerebral vascular accident. Cortex 18:581–594, 1982

Wilson B: Identification and remediation of everyday problems in memory-impaired patients, in Neuropsychology of Alcoholism: Implications for Diagnosis and Treatment. Edited by Parsons GA, Butters N, Nathan PE. New York, Guilford, 1987, pp 322–338

Wood RL: Behavior disorders following severe brain injury: their presentation and psychological management, in Closed Head Injury: Psychological, Social and Family Consequences. Edited by Brooks N. New York, Oxford University Press, 1984, pp 195–219

Wroblewski BA, Joseph AB, Kupfer J, et al: Effectiveness of valproic acid on destructive and aggressive behaviours in patients with acquired brain injury. Brain Inj 11: 37–47, 1997.

PART

VI

# Special Topics

# CHAPTER 38

# Ethical and Legal Issues in Neuropsychiatry

Robert I. Simon, M.D.

The practice of psychiatry today requires a working knowledge of neurobiological principles, treatments, and research. Most clinicians do not regard patients as having "pure" psychological disorders. Few psychiatrists use only psychological therapies. Even patients with so-called problems in living frequently require psychotropic medications. Under the salutary influence of the medical model, mind and body are again merging together in psychiatric practice. The term *neuropsychiatrist* refers to psychiatrists who diagnose and treat organic and other mental disorders by a combination of somatic and psychological therapies.

The body of law applied to the practice of psychiatry does not distinguish between the treatment of functional and organic mental disorders. The diagnosis, treatment, and management of organic mental disorders present not only unique clinical and ethical concerns but also legal considerations. For example, an assessment of competency may be required to determine a psychiatric patient's capacity to make health care decisions, to manage business or personal affairs, or to continue in a work situation that involves the public good. This is especially true for patients with Alzheimer's disease, acquired immunodeficiency syndrome (AIDS)–related dementia, or alcohol and/or drug dependence. Ethical and legal issues such as informed consent, the right to refuse treatment, alternative care providers, and advance directives are likely to be confronted in treating psychiatric patients.

Persons who have been criminally charged must be legally competent to stand trial. Criminal defendants

with neuropsychiatric impairments may not meet the competency standard. Pretrial evaluations of their mental capacity to understand the charges against them and their ability to assist counsel in their defense will be required. Moreover, a criminal defendant with a mental disorder may seek acquittal or have the charges reduced based on the argument that he or she was legally insane at the time the offense occurred.

The risk of psychiatric malpractice may be heightened in certain areas of neuropsychiatric practice. For example, the use of various somatic therapies, the assessment and prediction of violence, involuntary hospitalization, and the discharge of potentially dangerous patients are all areas of potential liability.

Last, personal injury litigation involving head injuries has increased annually. Because of the complexities often associated with establishing the extent and cause of a plaintiff's damages, forensic expertise in neuropsychiatry frequently is needed in providing testimony about the common psychiatric sequelae that may be caused by head injuries.

In this chapter, I provide a brief review of some of the salient clinical, ethical, and legal issues that link neuropsychiatry to criminal law and personal injury litigation. Readers interested in a more comprehensive discussion of the medical and psychiatric-legal aspects of general psychiatry, which incorporates neuropsychiatry, are referred to a number of contemporary texts (Alexander and Scheflin 1998; Appelbaum and Gutheil 2000; Melton et al. 1997; Perlin 1989a, 1989b, 1989c; Reisner and Slobogin 1990; Rosner 1994; Shuman 1986; Simon

1992a, 1992c; Simon and Sadoff 1992; Slovenko 1995b; B.A. Weiner and Wettstein 1993).

## Ethical Considerations

During the first half of the twentieth century, the principle of patient autonomy was clearly recognized in the medical malpractice case *Schloendorff v. Society of New York Hospital* (1914). Justice Cardozo enunciated the principle of patient self-determination by stating that "every human being of adult years and sound mind has a right to determine what shall be done with his own body, and a surgeon who performs an operation without his patient's consent commits an assault, for which he is liable in damages."

Since the late 1950s and early 1960s, the medical profession has moved away from an authoritarian, physician-oriented stance toward a more collaborative relationship with patients concerning their health care decisions. This greater sense of collaboration is reflected in contemporary ethical principles (American Psychiatric Association 1998, Section 5, p. 7). Ethical psychiatrists encourage competent patients to exercise their legal right of autonomy in determining their medical care. Apart from any legal compulsion, most psychiatrists disclose truthful and pertinent medical information to their patients in a way that enhances the therapeutic alliance (Simon 1992a, p. 124).

The ethical principles of beneficence, nonmaleficence, and the respect for the dignity and autonomy of the patient provide the moral-ethical foundation for the doctor-patient relationship. Accordingly, patients with dementia or other brain disorders that significantly interfere with their decision-making capacity require active intervention by the psychiatrist. For example, the psychiatrist has a legal and ethical duty to obtain consent from substitute decision makers when a patient is incapable of making an informed decision. The rights of all patients are the same; only how these rights are exercised differ (J.W. Parry and Beck 1990).

The ethics of social justice call for the fair allocation of medical resources in accordance with medical need (Ruchs 1984). Although seemingly a new development, the ethical concerns about equitable health care distribution are found in the Hippocratic oath and in the tradition of medicine and psychiatry (Dyer 1988, p. 34). Thus, psychiatric patients are ethically entitled to the same medical resources available to other patients.

Ethical issues arise daily for psychiatrists who provide consultation for critical care patients. Medical decision making, informed consent, resuscitation, "brain death," organ transplantation, the withholding and withdrawing of life support, and the allocation of medical resources all give rise to complex ethical and legal problems (Luce 1990). Moreover, what is considered ethical in clinical practice today may become a legal requirement tomorrow.

## Medical-Legal Issues

### Competency: The Basic Concept

#### Case Example 1

Mr. A, a 78-year-old man, has progressive impairment of recent and past memory, concentration, orientation, and social and self-care functioning. These symptoms greatly limit his ability to effectively manage his real estate business. He is hospitalized on a general medical service for evaluation of vague complaints of pain and "disorientation." Depression, however, is a prominent symptom. A psychiatric consultant makes a presumptive clinical diagnosis of dementia of the Alzheimer's type, with late onset, with depressed mood. The psychiatrist determines that Mr. A is unable to manage his business affairs. Because the patient's competency to make health care decisions also is questionable (i.e., to give a competent consent to start antidepressant medication), the treating physician obtains permission from the family to start drug therapy. Meanwhile, the family seeks an adjudication of incompetency. The court, after reviewing the psychiatrist's evaluation, declares Mr. A incompetent for managing his finances but not for health care decisions. A limited guardianship is created.

*Competency* is defined as "having sufficient capacity, ability…[or] possessing the requisite physical, mental, natural, or legal qualifications" (Black 1990, p. 284). This definition is deliberately vague and ambiguous because competency is a broad concept that encompasses many different legal issues and contexts. Its definition, requirements, and application can vary widely, depending on the circumstances in which it is being measured (e.g., making health care decisions, executing a will, standing trial or confessing to a crime).

Competency refers to some *minimal* mental, cognitive, or behavioral ability, trait, or capability required to perform a specific, legally recognized act or to assume some legal role. The term *capacity*, which is often interchanged with the term *competency*, refers to an individual's actual ability to understand or to form an intention with regard to some act. For patients whose mental capacity is in doubt, a court would be most interested initially in the patient's perception of reality and memory functions because these abilities would have the most bearing on the *reliability* of his or her responses or testimony. With patients with traumatic brain injuries, fluctuations in mental capacity are common, especially in the days or months immediately following injury. Considerable change in mental functioning can occur from hour to hour and from day to day.

The legal designation *incompetent* is applied to individuals who fail one of the tests of mental capacity. These individuals are considered by law not to be mentally capable of performing a particular act or of assuming a particular role. The adjudication of incompetence is subject or issue specific. The fact that a psychiatric patient is adjudicated incompetent to execute a will does not automatically render that patient incompetent to do other things, such as consenting to treatment, testifying as a witness, marrying, driving, or entering into a legally binding contract. In case example 1 earlier in this section, to preserve as much individual autonomy as possible, the court created a limited guardianship for financial matters only.

Generally, the law will recognize only those decisions or choices that have been made by a competent individual. The law seeks to protect incompetent individuals from the harmful effects of their acts. Persons older than the age of majority, which is now 18 (U.S. Department of Health and Human Services 1981, p. 41), are presumed by our legal system to be competent (*Meek v. City of Loveland* 1929). This presumption of competence is rebuttable by evidence of an individual's incapacity (*Scaria v. St. Paul Fire & Marine Ins. Co.* 1975). Mental functions such as perception, short- and long-term memory, judgment, language comprehension, verbal fluency, and reality orientation are the most likely areas of cerebral functioning to be implicated when questions regarding impairment of *competency* of a patient are raised.

Competency, whether in a civil or a criminal context, is commonly raised as an issue in two situations: when the person is either a minor or mentally disabled. In some situations, minors are not considered to be legally competent. Therefore, decisions involving a minor require the consent of a parent or designated guardian. There are exceptions to this general rule, however, such as minors who are considered emancipated (Smith 1986), mature (*Gulf S I R Co. v. Sullivan* 1928), or competent to consent in some cases of medical need (*Planned Parenthood v. Danforth* 1976; ILL ANN STAT 1990) or emergency (*Jehovah's Witnesses v. King County Hospital* 1967).

Mentally disabled individuals present a more complex problem in evaluating competency. With very few exceptions, competent patients retain the right to refuse treatment. Lack of capacity or competency *cannot* be presumed either from treatment for mental illness (*Wilson v. Lehman* 1964) or from institutionalization (*Rennie v. Klein* 1978). Mental disability or illness does *not* necessarily render a person incompetent in all areas of functioning. Idiosyncratic or foolish decisions, by themselves, do not denote mental incompetence. Foolish decisions are an inevitable consequence of our human condition. Psychiatric evaluation may be necessary to determine whether the patient has specific functional incapacities that render him or her incapable of making a particular kind of decision or of performing a particular type of task.

Respect for individual autonomy demands that persons, even if seriously mentally ill, developmentally arrested, or organically impaired, be allowed to make decisions of which they are capable. As a rule, a patient with a neuropsychiatric disorder that produces mental incapacity generally must be declared incompetent judicially before his or her legal rights can be abridged. The person's current or past history of physical and mental illness is but one factor to be weighed in determining whether a particular test of competency is met.

## Health Care Decision Making

### Case Example 2

Ms. B, an agitated, homeless, confused 74-year-old woman, is admitted to the psychiatric ward of a general hospital. After a complete physical and psychiatric examination, preliminary diagnoses of Parkinson's disease and vascular dementia are made. She is severely agitated and confused. The physician, doubtful that the patient has the mental capacity to provide informed consent for treatment, seeks a substituted judgment from the court on Ms. B's behalf as required by law. Pursuant to this procedure, consent is granted by the court. Ms. B is given haloperidol 0.5 mg, four times a day. Within a few days, the extreme agitation and confusion abate considerably.

The difficulty associated with obtaining a valid informed consent to proposed diagnostic procedures and treatments can be both challenging in psychiatric patients and frustrating in patients with impaired mental functioning. One study that used three assessment instruments of competency for treatment decisions found that the study's schizophrenia and depression groups had poorer understanding of treatment disclosures, poorer reasoning in decision making regarding treatment, and a greater likelihood of failing to appreciate their illnesses or the potential treatment benefits compared with medically ill and nonill groups (Grisso and Appelbaum 1995b). Nonetheless, most of the schizophrenic patients did not perform worse than other patients and nonpatients. As case example 2 illustrates, the legal requirement to obtain competent informed consent is not negated simply because it "appears" that the patient is in need of medical intervention or would likely benefit from such intervention. Instead, clinicians must be sure that the patient or an appropriate substitute decision maker has given a competent consent before proceeding with treatment. Some states require a judicial determination of incompetence and the court's consent before the administration of neuroleptic medications to a nonconsenting patient deemed to lack the mental capacity to make health care decisions.

The term *informed consent* is a legal principle in medical jurisprudence that holds that a physician must disclose to a patient sufficient information in order for the patient to make an "informed" decision about a proposed treatment or procedure. For a patient's consent to be considered informed, it must adequately address three essential elements: competency, information, and voluntariness. Each of these elements must be satisfied or the consent given may not be considered informed and legally valid (Table 38–1). Thus, a *competent* patient must be given enough *information* to make a truly knowledgeable decision, and that decision (consent) must be given *voluntarily.* "Gag rules" imposed on psychiatrists and other physicians by some managed care organizations to prevent fully informing patients about their treatment options obviously are inimical to obtaining a valid informed consent.

The law recognizes several exceptions to the requirement of informed consent (Rozovsky 1984). The most notable is the "emergency exception," which states that consent is implied in circumstances in which the patient is unable to give consent (e.g., unconsciousness) and is experiencing an acute, life-threatening crisis that requires immediate medical attention. The definition of a medical emergency is open to debate. Generally, two situations constitute a medical emergency. First, the patient must be incapacitated and lack the mental capacity to make an informed choice. Second, the injury or disease must be life threatening and require immediate treatment. State statutes and courts have defined medical emergency in both narrow and expansive terms (Swartz 1987). Clinicians who see acutely ill patients should know the legal definition of a medical emergency in their jurisdiction. At the time of an emergency, the provision of good clinical care to the patient is of primary concern.

Only a *competent* person is legally recognized as being able to give informed consent. This principle is particularly important for health care providers working with patients who sometimes are of questionable competence

**TABLE 38–1.** Informed consent: reasonable information to be disclosed

Although there exists no consistently accepted standard for information disclosure for any given medical or psychiatric situation, as a rule of thumb, five areas of information are generally provided:

1. Diagnosis—description of the condition or problem
2. Treatment—nature and purpose of proposed treatment
3. Consequences—risks and benefits of the proposed treatment
4. Alternatives—viable alternatives to the proposed treatment including risks and benefits
5. Prognosis—projected outcome with and without treatment

*Source.* Reprinted from Simon RI: *Clinical Psychiatry and the Law,* 2nd Edition. Washington, DC, American Psychiatric Press, 1992. Copyright 1992, Robert I. Simon. Used with permission.

because of mental illness, narcotic abuse, or alcoholism. When physicians treat patients with neuropsychiatric deficits, the responsibility to obtain a valid informed consent can be clinically daunting because of the vacillating and unpredictable mental states associated with many central nervous system disorders.

Competency is legally defined narrowly as *cognitive capacity.* There are no established or set criteria for determining a patient's competence. A minimal level of decision making must exist. The patient should be able to comprehend and perform at least all of the following:

1. Understand the particular treatment being offered.
2. Make a discernible decision, one way or another, regarding the treatment that has been offered.
3. Communicate, verbally or nonverbally, his or her decision.

A fundamental problem with this minimal standard of decision-making capacity is that a decision made at such a level constitutes a *simple* consent. The patient does not give an *informed* consent because alternative treatment choices are not provided.

A review of the case law and scholarly literature reveals, in general, four standards for determining incompetency in decision making (Appelbaum et al. 1987, p. 84). In order of levels of mental capacity required, these standards are

1. Communication of choice
2. Understanding of information provided
3. Appreciation of one's situation and of the risks and benefits of options available
4. Rational decision making

Psychiatrists generally feel most comfortable with a rational decision-making standard in determining whether an individual lacks mental capacity in decision making. Most courts prefer the first two standards above. Rational decision making takes place when a patient's consent reflects his or her autonomy, personal needs, and values applied to the risks and benefits of appropriate treatment options. When the patient seems competent, a decision that appears irrational or foolish is not, by itself, a basis for a determination of incompetence (Benesch 1989). Spectacular follies have been committed by perfectly competent people. Legal advice may be needed if the competency issue cannot be resolved by additional medical and psychiatric consultation.

Grisso and Appelbaum (1995a) pointed out that the choice of standards for determining competence will affect the type and proportion of patients classified as "impaired." When compound standards were used, the proportion of patients identified as "impaired" increased. The authors counsel that clinicians should be aware of the applicable standards in their jurisdictions.

The psychiatrist who treats a patient suspected of having mental capacity deficits should conduct a thorough assessment of cognitive functioning. The sole objective of such an evaluation should be the determination of the patient's ability to meet the minimum requirements for consent. At the very least, a mental status assessment of the patient's language, memory, judgment, insight, mood, orientation, concentration, and attention span should be performed (Folstein et al. 1975). Certain neuropsychiatric patients may be cognitively intact but manifest such severe mood lability that they are rendered affectively incompetent.

Except in an emergency, the patient lacking health care decision-making capacity will require an authorized representative or guardian appointed to make health care decisions on his or her behalf (*Aponte v. United States* 1984; *Frasier v. Department of Health and Human Resources* 1986). A number of consent options may be available, depending on the jurisdiction (Table 38–2).

## Right to Die

Legal decisions addressing the issue of a patient's "right to die" fall into one of two categories: those dealing with individuals incompetent at the time that removal of life-support systems is sought (*In re Conroy* 1985; *In re Quinlin* 1976) and those dealing with competent patients.

**Incompetent patients.** In what was hoped to be the "final word" on this very difficult and personal question of patient autonomy, the U.S. Supreme Court ruled in

**TABLE 38–2.** Common consent and review options for patients lacking the mental capacity for health care decisions

Proxy consent of next of kin[a]
Adjudication of incompetence, appointment of a guardian
Institutional administrators or committees
Treatment review panels
Substituted consent of the court
Advance directives (living will, durable power of attorney, or, in some cases, health care proxy)
Statutory surrogates (spouse or court-appointed guardian)[a,b]

[a]May be excluded for treatment of mental disorders.
[b]Medical statutory surrogate laws (when treatment wishes of patient are unstated).

*Source.* Reprinted and adapted from Simon RI: *Clinical Psychiatry and the Law,* 2nd Edition. Washington, DC, American Psychiatric Press, 1992, p. 109. Copyright 1992, Robert I. Simon. Used with permission.

*Cruzan v. Director, Missouri Department of Health* (1990a, 1990b, 1990c) that the state of Missouri may refuse to remove a feeding tube surgically implanted in the stomach of Nancy Cruzan without clear and convincing evidence of her wishes. She had been in a persistent vegetative state for 7 years. Without clear and convincing evidence of a patient's decision to have life-sustaining measures withheld in a particular circumstance, the state has the right to maintain that individual's life, even to the exclusion of the family's wishes.

Although this decision appears to leave unanswered more questions than it answers, the Court's decision does buttress the position of "right to refuse" treatment advocates in three significant ways:

1. The Court seemed to give constitutional status to a competent person's right to refuse treatment.
2. The Court did not distinguish between artificially administered food and water and other life-sustaining measures, such as respirators. This distinction had been a hotly contested sticking point in some prior lower-court decisions.
3. An incompetent person who makes his or her wishes known in advance while competent, such as through a living will, may have a constitutional right to halt life-sustaining intervention, depending on the proof of those wishes.

The importance of the *Cruzan* decision for physicians treating severely or terminally impaired patients is that they must seek clear and competent instructions regarding foreseeable treatment decisions. For example, physicians treating patients with progressive degenerative diseases should discover the patient's wishes regarding the use of life-sustaining measures *while that patient can still competently articulate those wishes*. This information is best provided in the form of a living will or durable power of attorney agreement. Any written manifestation that clearly and convincingly documents the patient's wishes also would serve the same purpose. Although physicians fear civil or criminal liability for stopping life-sustaining treatment, liability may now arise from overtreating critically or terminally ill patients (Weir and Gostin 1990).

**Competent patients.** A small but growing body of cases has emerged involving *competent* patients—usually suffering from excruciating pain and terminal diseases—who seek the termination of further medical treatment. The single most significant influence in the development of this body of law is the doctrine of informed consent. Beginning with the fundamental tenet that "no right is held more sacred…than the right of every individual to the possession and control of his own person" (*Schloendorff v. Society of New York Hospital* 1914; *Union Pacific Railway Co. v. Botsford* 1891), courts have fashioned the present-day "informed consent" doctrine and applied it to "right to die" cases.

Notwithstanding these principles, the right to decline life-sustaining medical intervention, even for a competent person, is not absolute. As noted in *In re Conroy* (1985), four countervailing state interests generally exist that may limit the exercise of that right: preservation of life, prevention of suicide, safeguarding of the integrity of the medical profession, and protection of innocent third parties. In each of these situations, and depending on the surrounding circumstances, the trend has been to support a competent patient's right to have artificial life-support systems discontinued (*Bartling v. Superior Court* 1984; *Bouvia v. Superior Court* 1986; *In re Farrell* 1987; *In re Jobes* 1987; *In re Peter* 1987; *Tune v. Walter Reed Army Medical Hospital* 1985).

As a result of the *Cruzan* decision, courts will focus primarily on the reliability of the evidence proffered in establishing the patient's competence and, specifically, the clarity and certainty with which a decision is made to withhold medical treatment. Assuming that a terminally ill patient has chosen to forgo any further medical intervention *and* the patient is competent at the time this decision is made, courts will be reluctant to overrule or subvert the patient's right to privacy and autonomy.

### Physician-Assisted Suicide

With increasing legal recognition of physician-assisted suicide, psychiatrists are likely to be called on to become gatekeepers. Such a role would be a radical departure from the physician's code of ethics, which prohibits participation by an ethical doctor in any intervention that hastens death. Every proposal for physician-assisted suicide requires a psychiatric screening or consultation to determine the person's competency to commit suicide. The presence of psychiatric disorders associated with suicide, particularly depression, will have to be ruled out as the driving factor behind the patient's decision to undertake physician-assisted suicide. Much controversy rages over the ethics of this gatekeeping function (American Medical Association 1994).

### Do-Not-Resuscitate Orders

## Case Example 3

Mr. C, a 47-year-old man with terminal brain cancer and moderate depression, has a cardiac arrest and is resuscitated. A psychiatric consultant determines that Mr. C retains sufficient mental capacity to make health care decisions. The patient instructs his physician not to resuscitate him if another cardiac arrest occurs. The family disagrees. They want the patient to be resuscitated because they feel that the do-not-resuscitate (DNR) decision is based on a treatable depression. Nevertheless, the primary physician determines that Mr. C is competent when he makes the request. She writes the DNR order.

Cardiopulmonary resuscitation (CPR) is a medical lifesaving technology. To be effective, it must be applied immediately, leaving no time to think about the consequences of reviving a patient. Usually, patients requiring CPR have not thought about or expressed a preference for or against its use.

With chronic degenerative brain diseases, terminal brain tumors, or end-stage traumatic head injury, the psychiatrist and the substitute medical decision maker have time to consider whether CPR should be offered based on the patient's earlier expressed wishes. The ethical principle of patient autonomy justifies the position that the patient or substitute decision maker should make the final decision regarding the use of CPR. Patients and families who are not offered the option of CPR may feel helpless and abandoned. Psychiatrists must remain mindful of this reaction in order to properly assist the patient and family.

Malpractice liability for not offering or providing futile care is unlikely, whereas the clinician is exposed to greater liability if such care is provided (Marsh and Staver 1991). The American Medical Association has taken the position that when CPR is perceived as futile, the physician may unilaterally withhold the procedure, as in case example 3. However, the patient or substitute decision maker must be notified, reasons must be given for the DNR decision, and an opportunity must be provided for a second opinion or change of physicians (American Medical Association 1991). In case example 3, a psychiatric consultation would have addressed the family's concern about the patient having a treatable depression.

Schwartz (1987) noted that two key principles have emerged concerning DNR decisions:

1. In accordance with the ethical principle of autonomy and with the legal doctrine of informed consent, DNR decisions should be reached consensually by the attending physician and the patient or substitute decision maker.
2. DNR orders should be written, and the reasoning behind the DNR order should be documented in the chart.

Hospital CPR policies make DNR decisions discretionary (Luce 1990). Physicians should be familiar with the specific hospital policy whenever a DNR order is written. Medicolegal and ethical principles have been promulgated concerning CPR and emergency cardiac care ("Standards for Cardiopulmonary Resuscitation and Emergency Cardiac Care" 1986).

## Advance Directives

The use of advance directives such as a living will, health care proxy, or durable medical power of attorney is recommended to avoid ethical and legal complications associated with requests to withhold life-sustaining treatment measures (Simon 1992c; Solnick 1985). The Patient Self-Determination Act that took effect on December 1, 1991, requires hospitals, nursing homes, hospices, managed care organizations, and home health care agencies to advise patients or family members of their right to accept or refuse medical care and to execute an advance directive (LaPuma et al. 1991). These advance directives provide a method for individuals, while competent, to choose proxy health care decision makers in the event of future incompetency. A living will can be a subsection of the durable power of attorney agreement. In the ordinary power of attorney created for the management of business and financial matters, the power of attorney generally becomes null and void if the person creating it becomes incompetent.

Federal law does not specify the right to formulate advance directives. Therefore, state law applies. Recently, state legislators have recognized that individuals may want to indicate who should make important health care decisions in case they become incapacitated

and unable to act in their own behalf. All 50 states and the District of Columbia permit individuals to create a *durable* power of attorney—that is, one that endures even if the competence of the creator does not (*Cruzan v. Director, Missouri Department of Health* 1990c). Several states, as well as the District of Columbia, do have durable power of attorney statutes that expressly authorize the appointment of proxies for making health care decisions (*Cruzan v. Director, Missouri Department of Health* 1990b). Such a document is much broader and more flexible than a living will, which covers just the period of a diagnosed terminal illness, specifying only that no "extraordinary treatments" be used that would prolong the act of dying (Mishkin 1985).

To rectify the sometimes uncertain status of the durable power of attorney as applied to health care decisions, a number of states have passed health care proxy laws. The *health care proxy* is a legal instrument akin to the durable power of attorney but specifically created for health care decision making. Despite the growing use of advance directives, there is increasing evidence that physician values, rather than patient values, are more decisive in end-of-life decisions (Orentlicher 1992).

In a durable power of attorney or health care proxy, general or specific directions are set forth about how future health care decisions should be made in the event one becomes unable to make these decisions. The determination of a patient's competence, however, is not specified in most durable power of attorney and health care proxy statutes. Usually, the examination by two physicians concerning the patient's ability to understand the nature and consequences of the proposed treatment or procedure, to make a choice, and to communicate that choice is minimally sufficient. This information, like all significant medical observations, should be clearly documented in the patient's record.

Because of the frequent absence of advance directives, statutory surrogate laws have been enacted in some states. These laws authorize certain persons, such as a spouse or court-appointed guardian, to make health care decisions when the patient has not stated his or her wishes in writing.

The application of advance directives to psychiatric patients presents difficulties. The classic example arises when the bipolar (manic-depressive) patient who is currently asymptomatic draws up a durable power of attorney directing that "If I become manic again, administer lithium even if I strenuously object or resist." Gutheil (personal communication, October 1985) described this as the "Ulysses contract." In Greek mythology, Ulysses was bound to the mast of his ship so he could hear the irresistibly beautiful, although lethal, sirens' song rather than have to cover his ears. When he heard the sirens sing, Ulysses struggled to free himself. When this failed, he demanded to be untied. Similarly, when mania recurs, the bipolar patient may strenuously object to lithium treatment.

Because durable power of attorney agreements can be easily revoked, the treating physician or institution has little choice but to honor the patient's refusal, even if reasonable evidence indicates that the patient is incompetent. If the patient is grossly disordered and is in immediate danger to self and/or others, the physician or hospital is on firmer medical-legal grounds to temporarily override the patient's treatment refusal. Otherwise, it is better to seek a court order for treatment than to risk legal entanglement with the patient over an advance directive. Unless there are compelling medical reasons to do otherwise, courts generally will honor the patient's original treatment directions given while competent.

## Guardianship

Guardianship is a method of substitute decision making for individuals who have been judicially determined to be unable to act for themselves (Brakel et al. 1985, p. 370). Historically, the state or sovereign had the power and authority to safeguard the estate of incompetent persons (Regan 1972). This traditional role still reflects the purpose of guardianship today. In some states, there are separate provisions for the appointment of a "guardian of one's person" (e.g., substitute health care decision maker) and for a "guardian of one's estate" (e.g., someone authorized to make contracts to sell one's property) (Sale et al. 1982, p. 461). The latter guardian is frequently referred to as a *conservator*, although this designation is not uniformly used throughout the United States. Further distinctions also found in some jurisdictions are *general* (plenary) and *specific* guardianships (Sale et al. 1982, p. 462). As the name implies, the latter guardian is restricted to exercising decisions about a particular area. For example, the specific guardian may be authorized to make decisions about major or emergency medical procedures, while the disabled person retains the freedom to make decisions about all other medical matters. General guardians, in contrast, have total control over the disabled individual's person, estate, or both (Sale et al. 1982, pp. 461–462).

Guardianship arrangements are increasingly used with patients who have dementia, particularly AIDS-related dementia and dementia of the Alzheimer's type (Overman and Stoudemire 1988). Under the Anglo-American system of law, an individual is presumed to be competent unless adjudicated incompetent. Thus,

incompetence is a legal determination made by a court of law, based on evidence provided by health care providers and others, that the individual's functional mental capacity is significantly impaired. The Uniform Guardianship and Protective Proceeding Act (UGPPA) or the Uniform Probate Code (UPC) is used as a basis for laws governing competency in many states (Mishkin 1989). Drafted by legal scholars and practicing attorneys, the Uniform Acts (UGPPA and UPC) serve as models for the enactment of future laws whose purpose is to achieve uniformity among the state laws.

The threshold requirement of incompetency, as defined by the UGPPA (5-101), is impairment "by reason of mental illness, mental deficiency, physical illness or disability, advanced age, chronic use of drugs, chronic intoxication, or other cause (except minority) to the extent of lacking sufficient understanding or capacity to make or communicate reasonable decisions."

A significant number of patients with psychiatric disorders have impairment that meets the above definition. The standard of proof required for a judicial determination of incompetency is *clear and convincing evidence*. Although the law does not assign percentages to proof, clear and convincing evidence is in the range of 75% certainty (Simon 1992a). This is a much higher standard of proof than a *preponderance of evidence* (i.e., more likely than not) used in many civil suits, reflecting the importance our society places on individual freedoms and an individual's right to privacy.

States vary concerning the extent of their reliance on psychiatric assessments. Nonmedical personnel such as social workers, psychologists, family members, friends, colleagues, and even the individual who is the subject of the proceeding may testify.

## Substituted Judgment

Psychiatrists often find that the time and effort required to obtain an adjudication of incompetence is unduly burdensome. Adjudications can be disruptive to providing quality treatment in a timely manner. Moreover, families are often reluctant to face formal court proceedings necessary to declare their family member incompetent, particularly when sensitive family matters may be disclosed. A common solution to both of these problems is to seek the legally authorized consent of a spouse or relative acting as guardian when the patient who refuses treatment is believed to be incompetent. Such proxy consent, however, is not available in every state or is only available for medical-surgical conditions.

Several states permit proxy decision making by statute (Solnick 1985). Some statutes specify that another person may authorize consent on behalf of the incompetent patient. Others mention specific relatives.

Unless proxy consent by a relative is provided by statute or by case law, it is not recommended that good-faith consents by next of kin be relied on by the psychiatrist in treating a patient believed to be incompetent (Macbeth et al. 1994). The legally appropriate procedure is to seek judicial recognition of the family member as the substitute or proxy decision maker.

Perr (1984) noted the advantages associated with having the family serve as decision makers. First, use of responsible family members as surrogate decision makers maintains the integrity of the family unit and relies on the sources that are most likely to know the patient's wishes. Second, it is more efficient and less costly. There are some disadvantages, however. Ambivalent feelings, conflicts within the family and with the patient, and conflicting economic interests may make certain family members suspect as guardians (Gutheil and Appelbaum 1980). Moreover, family members who could serve as surrogate decision makers also may lack sufficient mental capacity for this task. Furthermore, relatives may not be available or may not want to get involved.

The President's Commission for the Study of Ethical Problems in Medicine and Biomedical and Behavioral Research (1982) recommended that the relatives of incompetent patients be selected as proxy decision makers for three reasons:

1. The family is generally most concerned about the good of the patient.
2. The family usually will be most knowledgeable about the patient's goals, preferences, and values.
3. The family deserves recognition as an important social unit to be treated, within limits, as a single decision maker in matters that intimately affect its members.

Some patients who are treated in an emergency situation may be expected to recover competency within a few days. As soon as the patient is able to competently consent to further treatment, consent should be obtained directly from the patient. An increasing number of states provide administrative procedures authorized by statute that permit involuntary treatment of the incompetent and treatment-refusing mentally ill patient who does not meet current standards for involuntary civil commitment (Hassenfeld and Grumet 1984; Zito et al. 1984). In most jurisdictions, a durable power of attorney agreement permits the next of kin to consent through durable power of attorney statutes (Solnick 1985). However, in some instances, this procedure may not meet judicial challenge.

# Criminal Proceedings

## Case Example 4

Mr. D, a 43-year-old man, is charged with first-degree murder of his mother. The defendant has a long history of paranoid schizophrenia with frequent psychiatric hospitalizations. As a child, he was struck on the head with a baseball bat. He remained comatose for 1 month. After he emerged from the coma, his personality changed. He became hyperactive, emotionally labile, impulsive, and episodically violent.

Immediately after the murder, Mr. D is found to be grossly psychotic. He describes command hallucinations directing him to kill his mother. He is hospitalized on a forensic psychiatric unit. A computed tomography scan shows bilateral moderate atrophy of the frontal lobes.

Two months after the murder, Mr. D is brought before the court for a competency-to-stand-trial hearing. The defendant is taking haloperidol 5 mg, four times a day. No auditory hallucinations are present. The court finds that Mr. D is competent to stand trial. His lawyers pursue an insanity defense at trial.

As case example 4 illustrates, individuals charged with committing crimes frequently have significant psychiatric and neurologic impairment. A history of severe head injury may be present. The possibility of a neuropsychiatric disorder must be thoroughly investigated (Simon 1992d). For example, Lewis et al. (1986) examined 15 death-row inmates who were chosen for examination because of imminent execution rather than evidence of neuropathology. In each case, evidence of severe head injury and neurologic impairment was found.

The causal connection between brain damage and violence remains opaque. Violent behavior spans a wide spectrum, from normal responses to a threatening situation to violence emanating directly from an organic brain disorder such as Klüver-Bucy syndrome, hypothalamic tumors, or temporal lobe epilepsy (Strub and Black 1988). Moreover, violent behavior is often the result of the interaction between the individual and a specific situation. Brain damage and mental illness may or may not play a significant role in this equation. In fact, in the National Institute of Mental Health Epidemiologic Catchment Area study (Swanson et al. 1990), it was estimated that 90% of the persons with current mental illnesses are not violent within 1 year. If a person is not having a psychotic episode or if psychotic symptoms are not part of the psychiatric problem, the individual is no more likely to be involved in violent behavior than is the average person. When psychotic symptoms are present, there is only a modest increase in violence above the norm. The most dangerous persons are young males of lower socioeconomic status who are substance abusers. Psychiatrists must acknowledge limitations in their expertise concerning the possible connection between brain damage and violence.

# Criminal Intent (*Mens Rea*)

Under common law, the constituent elements of a crime are 1) the mental state or level of intent to commit the act (known as *mens rea*, or guilty mind), 2) the act itself or conduct associated with committing the crime (known as *actus reus*, or guilty act), and 3) a concurrence in time between the guilty act and the guilty mental state (*Bethea v. United States* 1977). To convict a person of a particular crime, the state must prove beyond a reasonable doubt that the defendant committed the criminal act with the requisite intent. All three elements are necessary to satisfy the threshold requirements for the imposition of criminal sanctions.

Persons with certain mental handicaps or impairments represent a challenge for prosecutors, defense counsel, and judges in determining what, if any, retribution is justifiable. Mental impairment often raises serious questions about the intent to commit a crime and the appreciation of its consequences.

The question of intent is a particularly vexing problem for the courts. For example, everyone would agree that killing another person is deplorable conduct. But should a person's reckless driving leading to the death of a child in a car accident, a husband's shooting his wife's lover in the heat of passion, and an individual's murdering a bank teller in "cold blood" during a robbery all be punished the same? The determination of the defendant's intent, or *mens rea*, at the time of the offense is the law's "equalizer" and trigger mechanism for deciding criminal culpability and the appropriate division of retribution. For instance, a person who deliberately plans to commit a crime is more culpable than one who accidentally commits one.

Two classes of intent are used to categorize *mens rea*: specific and general. *Specific intent* refers to the *mens rea* in those crimes in which a *further intention* exists beyond that which is identified with the physical act associated with committing a criminal offense. For instance, the courts will frequently state that the intent necessary for first-degree murder includes a "specific intent to kill," or a person charged with assault with intent to rape must clearly be shown to have had "the intent to rape" (Melton et al. 1997, p. 204). Unlike general criminal intent, spe-

cific criminal intent cannot be presumed from the unlawful criminal act but must be proved independently. General criminal intent may be presumed from commission of the criminal act. Quite simply, it is the intent to do that which the law prohibits. It is not necessary for the state to prove that the defendant intended the specific harm or result that occurred (Black 1990, p. 810). *General intent* is used by the law to explain criminal liability when a defendant was merely conscious or should have been conscious of one's physical actions at the time of the offense (*Dusky v. United States* 1960). To deal with the vagueness of these two standards, many states have enacted their own definitions of intent.

The American Law Institute's (ALI's) Model Penal Code (§2.02) simplifies *mens rea* by designating four different mental state categories:

1. *Purpose*—the criminal conduct is the offender's conscious object.
2. *Knowledge*—the offender does not intend criminal conduct but is aware of the circumstances that make the conduct criminal.
3. *Recklessness*—the offender acts in conscious disregard that a substantial and unjustifiable risk exists that the conduct will produce a given result.
4. *Negligence*—the offender, although not actually aware of such a risk, nevertheless should have been aware of the risk.

Specific intent most closely corresponds with *purpose* and *knowledge*, whereas general intent coincides with *recklessness* and *negligence* (Melton et al. 1997, p. 205).

In addition to *mens rea*, a person's mental status and reality testing can play a deciding role in whether the defendant will 1) be ordered to stand trial to face criminal charges (*Dusky v. United States* 1960), 2) be acquitted of the alleged crime (*M'Naghten's Case* 1843; *United States v. Brawner* 1972), 3) be sent to prison or be hospitalized (*Commonwealth v. Robinson* 1981; "Mental Aberration and Post Conviction Sanctions" 1981; *State v. Hehman* 1974), or 4) be sentenced, in some extreme cases, to death (*Ford v. Wainwright* 1986; "Note, The Eighth Amendment and the Execution of the Presently Incompetent" 1980). Before any defendant can be criminally prosecuted, the court must be satisfied that the accused is competent to stand trial (i.e., can understand the charges brought against her or him and has sufficient rational mental capacity to assist counsel with the defense).

## Competency to Stand Trial

As discussed earlier in this chapter, in every situation in which competency is an issue, the law seeks to reiterate a common theme: only the acts of a rational individual are to be given recognition by society (*Neely v. United States* 1945). In doing so, the law attempts to reaffirm the integrity of the individual and of society in general.

The legal standard for assessing pretrial competency was established by the U.S. Supreme Court in *Dusky v. United States* (1960). Throughout involvement with the trial process, the defendant must have "sufficient present ability to consult with his lawyer with a reasonable degree of rational understanding [and have] a rational as well as factual understanding of the proceedings against him." In *Pate v. Robinson* (1966), the U.S. Supreme Court held that a conviction of an accused person while he or she is legally incompetent deprives him or her of his or her liberty without due process of law.

Typically, the impairment that raises the question of the defendant's competence will be associated with a mental disorder or defect. However, a person may be held to be incompetent to stand trial even if he or she does not have a mental disease or defect as defined by the American Psychiatric Association (2000). Although most impairments implicated in competency examinations are functional rather than organic (Reich and Wels 1985), various forms of neuropsychiatric impairments will typically raise questions about a defendant's competency to stand trial. For example, in *Wilson v. United States* (1968) (see Reich and Wels 1985), the defendant had no memory regarding the time of the alleged robbery because he had permanent retrograde amnesia. This impairment was caused by injuries resulting from an automobile accident that occurred as he was being pursued by the police following the offense. Of the various criteria that the court established in determining the defendant's competence to stand trial, the following are directly relevant to the issue of neuropsychiatric impairment:

(1) The extent to which the amnesia affected the defendant's ability to consult with and assist his lawyer, and
(2) The extent to which the amnesia affected the defendant's ability to testify in his own behalf.
(*Wilson v. United States* (1968), pp. 463–464

Any psychiatric disorder or condition that significantly impairs a defendant's cognitive and communicative abilities is likely to have an effect on a defendant's competency. However, the actual *functional* capability to meet the minimal standard of trial competency, not the severity of the deficits, will determine whether an individual is cognitively capable to be tried. For example, Slovenko (1995a) questioned whether psychiatric diagnosis is really relevant to triability. The presence or absence of a mental illness is irrelevant if the defendant is capable of meeting competency requirements. Legal criteria, not medical or psychiatric diagnosis, govern competency. Diagnosis is relevant only to the question of restoring the defendant's competency to stand trial with treatment.

Checklists and structured interviews have been developed to assess specific psychological factors applicable to the competency standards established in *Dusky*. The Interdisciplinary Fitness Interview (Schreiber et al. 1987) is designed for use by lawyers and mental health professionals. It provides for a detailed examination of psychopathology and legal knowledge, with explicit scales for rating each response to the competency evaluation. The text by Thomas Grisso (1986), *Evaluating Competencies: Forensic Assessments and Instruments*, is a standard reference in the field.

The degree of a defendant's impairment in one particular function does not automatically render the accused incompetent. For example, the fact that the defendant is manifesting constructional deficits on the mental status examination because of damage to the parietal lobe does not necessarily mean that the defendant lacks the requisite cognitive ability to aid in one's own defense at trial (Taylor et al. 1987). The ultimate determination of incompetency is solely for the court to decide (*United States v. David* 1975). Moreover, the impairment must be considered in the context of the particular case or proceeding. Mental impairment may render an individual incompetent to stand trial in a complicated tax fraud case but competent for a misdemeanor trial. To be of assistance to the court, psychiatrists must be able to apply their clinical findings to the legal standards enunciated in *Dusky* when assessing competency to stand trial.

## Insanity Defense

In American jurisprudence, one of the most controversial issues is the insanity defense. Defendants with mental disabilities who are found competent to stand trial may seek acquittal on the basis that because of insanity, they were not criminally responsible for their actions at the time the offense was committed.

Criminals commit crimes for a variety of reasons, but the law presumes that all of them do so rationally and with their own free will. As a result, the law concludes that they are deserving of some form of punishment. Some offenders, however, are so mentally disturbed or illogical in their thinking and behavior that they are thought to be incapable of acting rationally. Under these circumstances, civilized societies have deemed it unjust to punish a "crazy" or an "insane" person (Blackstone 1769; Coke 1680). This view is in part based on fundamental principles of fairness and morality. Additionally, the punishment of persons who cannot rationally appreciate the consequences of their actions thwarts the two major tenets of punishment: retribution and deterrence.

It is estimated that, nationally, the insanity defense is successful in only one out of the four times it is attempted (Melton et al. 1997, p. 188). Many cases are initially diverted into the mental health system. More than 70% of the insanity acquittals result from plea bargains. From recent data collected in five state jurisdictions, the annual average of not guilty by reason of insanity verdicts was well below 1% of all felony arrests (Melton et al. 1997, p. 188).

More than one insanity defense standard exists in the United States, depending on which state or jurisdiction has control over the defendant raising the defense. For example, in the Superior Court of the District of Columbia, the standard states that

> [a] person is not responsible for [his] criminal conduct at the time of such conduct as a result of a mental disease or defect (*McDonald v. United States* 1962) if he lacked substantial capacity either to recognize the wrongfulness of his conduct or to conform his conduct to the requirements of the law. (*Bethea v. United States* 1976; *United States v. Shorter* 1975)

By contrast, defendants tried in a federal court are governed by the standard enunciated in the Comprehensive Crime Control Act (CCCA) of 1984. The CCCA was passed following public outrage over the acquittal of John Hinckley by reason of insanity for attempting to assassinate President Ronald Reagan. The CCCA provides that it is an affirmative defense to all federal crimes that, at the time of the offense, "the defendant, as a result of a severe mental disease or defect, was unable to appreciate the nature and quality or the wrongfulness of his acts. Mental disease or defect does not otherwise constitute a defense" (18 U.S.C. 20(a)). This codification eliminates the volitional or irresistible impulse prong of the insanity defense. That is, it does not allow an insanity defense based on a defendant's inability to conform his or her conduct to the requirements of the law. The defense is now limited to only those defendants who are unable to appreciate the wrongfulness of their acts (i.e., the *cog-*

*nitive prong* of the defense). In several jurisdictions, as well as in federal law (CCCA), the burden of proof has been shifted from the prosecution to the defense (Miller 1994).

From 1978 to 1985, approximately 75% of all states made some substantive changes in their insanity defense (Perlin 1989c, p. 404). However, some states continued to adhere to the ALI insanity defense standard or a version of it. The ALI test provides that

> a person is not responsible for criminal conduct if at the time of such conduct as a result of mental disease or defect he lacks substantial capacity either to appreciate the criminality (wrongfulness) of his conduct or to conform his conduct to the requirements of law. As used in the Article, the terms "mental disease or defect" do not include an abnormality manifested only by repeated criminal or otherwise antisocial conduct. (Model Penal Code § 4.01 [1962]; 10 ULA 490-91 [1974])

The ALI standard contains both a cognitive and a volitional prong. The cognitive prong originates from the 1843 *M'Naghten* rule exculpating the defendant who does not know the nature and quality of the alleged act or does not know that the act was wrong. The volitional prong is a vestige of the irresistible impulse rule. It states that the defendant who is overcome by an irresistible impulse that causes an alleged act is not responsible for that act. Experts disagree most about the volitional prong in individual cases.

Montana, Idaho, Utah, and Kansas have abolished the special plea of insanity. In these states, the defendant's mental state at the time of the offense is admissible to negate *mens rea* as an element of the offense.

The threshold issue in making an insanity determination is not the existence of a mental disease or defect per se, but the lack of substantial capacity because of it. Therefore, lack of capacity due to causes other than mental illness may be sufficient. For example, mental retardation may represent an adequate basis for an insanity defense under certain circumstances. Less commonly considered disorders or conditions that may be related to central nervous system dysfunction could *potentially* render a defendant legally incapable of conforming his or her behavior to the dictates of the law. These conditions include metabolic conditions (e.g., functional hypoglycemia), premenstrual dysphoric states, and episodic dyscontrol syndrome.

Depending on the severity of the condition and its actual effect on an offender's cognitive and affective processes, a defense of insanity might be warranted. At the very least, however, these conditions should be investigated as potential *mitigating* factors that may have caused the offender to have *diminished capacity.*

## Diminished Capacity

A person may have the required *mens rea* but still be declared legally insane. For instance, a defendant's actions may be considered so "crazy" as to convince a jury that he or she was criminally insane and therefore not legally responsible. Yet the defendant's knowledge of what he or she was doing (e.g., committing a murder) was relatively intact. From this distinction, the law recognized that there are "shades" of mental impairment that obviously can affect *mens rea* but not necessarily to the extent of completely nullifying it. In recognition of this fact, the concept of *diminished capacity* was developed (Melton et al. 1997).

Diminished capacity permits the accused to introduce medical and psychological evidence that relates directly to the *mens rea* for the crime charged without having to assert a defense of insanity (Melton et al. 1997). For example, in the crime of assault with the intent to kill, psychiatric testimony could address whether the offender acted with the purpose of committing homicide at the time of the assault. When a defendant's *mens rea* for the crime charged is nullified by clinical evidence, the defendant is acquitted only of that charge. Persons with neuropsychiatric disorders who commit criminal acts may be eligible for a diminished capacity defense. The defense does not lead to total exculpation of criminal responsibility or to automatic commitment to a mental institution (Slovenko 1995b).

## Exculpatory and Mitigating Disorders

Several other defenses, although lesser known and statistically limited in success, bear mentioning because of their potential connection to neuropsychiatric conditions or causes.

### Automatisms

For conviction of a crime, there must be not only a criminal state of mind (*mens rea*) but also the commission of a prohibited act (*actus reus*). The physical movement necessary to satisfy the actus reus requirement must be conscious and volitional. In addition to statutory and common law in many jurisdictions, Section 2.01(2) of the Model Penal Code (1962) specifically excludes from the *actus reus* the following: "(a) a reflex or convulsion; (b) a bodily movement during unconsciousness or sleep; (c) conduct during hypnosis or resulting from hypnotic suggestion; [and] (d) a bodily movement that otherwise is not the product of the effort or determination of the actor."

The *automatism* (or unconscious) defense recognizes that some criminal acts may be committed involuntarily. Automatism is defined as "having performed in a state of mental unconsciousness or dissociation without full awareness" and is applied to actions or conduct occurring "without will, purpose, or reasoned intention" (Black 1990, p. 134).

The classic, although rare, example is the person who commits an offense while sleepwalking. Courts have held that such an individual does not have conscious control of his or her physical actions and therefore acts involuntarily (*Fain v. Commonwealth* 1879; *H.M. Advocate v. Fraser* 1878). This defense might apply when a crime is committed during a state of unconsciousness caused by a concussion following a head injury, involuntary ingestion of drugs or alcohol, hypoxia or hypoglycemia, or epileptic seizures (Low et al. 1982, pp. 152–154).

There are, however, limitations to the automatism defense. Most notably, some courts hold that if the person asserting the automatism defense was aware of the condition before the offense and failed to take reasonable steps to prevent the criminal occurrence, then the defense is not available. For example, if a defendant with a known history of uncontrolled epileptic seizures loses control of a car during a seizure and kills someone, that defendant will not be permitted to assert the defense of automatism.

## Intoxication

Ordinarily, *intoxication* is not a defense to a criminal charge. Because intoxication, unlike mental illness, mental retardation, and most neuropsychiatric conditions, is usually the product of a person's own actions, the law is naturally cautious about viewing it as a complete defense or a mitigating factor. Most states consider voluntary alcoholism as relevant to the issue of whether the defendant possessed the *mens rea* necessary to commit a specific intent crime or whether the defendant premeditated a crime of murder. However, the mere fact that the defendant was voluntarily intoxicated will not justify a finding of automatism or insanity. A distinct difference does arise when, because of chronic, heavy use of alcohol, the defendant has an alcohol-induced organic mental disorder, such as alcohol hallucinosis, withdrawal delirium, amnestic disorder, or dementia associated with alcoholism. If credible clinical evidence is presented that an alcohol-related neuropsychiatric disorder caused significant cognitive or volitional impairment, a defense of insanity or diminished capacity might be sustainable.

## Temporal Lobe Seizures

Another "mental state" defense occasionally raised by defendants regarding violent crimes is that the assaultive behavior was involuntarily precipitated by a seizure disorder. This condition is frequently diagnosed as temporal lobe epilepsy (Devinsky and Bear 1984). Studies have hypothesized that there are "centers of aggression" in the temporal lobe or limbic system—primarily the amygdala. This hypothesis states that sustained aggressive behavior by persons with temporal lobe seizure disorders may be primarily the product of an uncontrollable, randomly occurring abnormal brain dysrhythmia. Hence, the legal argument is raised that these individuals should not be held accountable for their actions. Despite the simplicity and occasional success of this argument in the courts, few empirically significant data support this theory (Blumer 1984).

## Metabolic Disorders

Defenses based on *metabolic disorders* also have been tried. The novel "Twinkie defense" was used as part of a successful strategy to defend Dan White, who was charged with two counts of murder in the shooting of San Francisco Mayor George Moscone and Supervisor Harvey Milk. The jury returned a verdict of voluntary manslaughter. This defense was based on the theory that the ingestion of large amounts of sugar contributed to a state of temporary insanity (*People v. White* 1981). The forensic psychiatric report stated that the defendant had been "drinking copious quantities of soda pop and eating high sugar cupcakes and candy bars" (Blinder 1981–1982). After specifying several factors, including depression, that contributed to the murders, the forensic expert concluded his report with the following opinion concerning Dan White's ingestion of certain foods:

> Finally, there is much evidence to suggest recently recognized physiological aberrations consequent to consumption of noxious edibles by susceptibles. There are cases in the literature challenged with large quantities of refined sugar. Furthermore, there are studies of cerebral allergic reactions to the chemicals in highly processed foods; some studies have documented a marked reduction in violent and antisocial behavior in "career criminals" upon the elimination of these substances from their diet, as well as the production of rage reactions in susceptible individuals when challenged by the offending food substances. For these reasons, I would suggest a repeat electroencephalogram preceded by a glucose-tolerance test, as well as a clinical challenge of Mr. White's mental functions with known food antigens, in a controlled setting. (Blinder 1981–1982)

Public outrage over the verdict in the Dan White case led to the repeal of the diminished capacity defense by the California Legislature in 1981 (Slovenko 1995b). After his release from prison, Dan White committed suicide.

Hypoglycemic states also may be associated with significant psychiatric impairment (Rubin and King 1995). When a substantial decrease in blood glucose occurs, a wide variety of responses may occur, including episodic and repetitive dyscontrol, temporary amnesia, depression, and hostility, with spontaneous recovery following the consumption of appropriate nutrients. The degree of mental abnormality associated with hypoglycemic states varies from mild to severe according to blood glucose level. It is the degree of disturbance, not the mere presence of an etiologic metabolic disorder or condition, that is determinative in a mental state defense. This principle also applies to mental dysfunctions produced by other metabolic disorders.

## Posttraumatic Stress Disorder

In criminal law, defendants have pleaded not guilty by reason of insanity secondary to posttraumatic stress disorder (PTSD) (Sparr and Boehnlein 1990). The diagnosis of PTSD has been alleged in criminal proceedings by prosecutors to bolster the credibility of the victim or by experts who attempt to argue backward from PTSD symptoms to establish the occurrence of a traumatic stressor (syndrome evidence). Victims of criminal acts who develop PTSD or other psychiatric disorders may sue under criminal injuries compensation acts. PTSD has bolstered advocacy of "victim rights," which pose a threat to the constitutional rights of defendants (Stone 1993). An insanity defense based on PTSD is more likely to succeed if it can be shown that the individual committed a crime while experiencing a dissociative behavioral reenactment of a prior traumatic event. Guidelines for the assessment of PTSD in litigation have been proposed (Simon 1995).

## Guilty but Mentally Ill

In some states, an alternative verdict of *guilty but mentally ill* has been established. Under guilty but mentally ill statutes, if the defendant pleads not guilty by reason of insanity, this alternative verdict is available to the jury (Slovenko 1982). Under an insanity plea, the verdict may be one of the following:

- Not guilty
- Not guilty by reason of insanity
- Guilty but mentally ill
- Guilty

The problem with guilty but mentally ill is that it is an alternative verdict without a difference from finding the defendant just plain guilty. The court must still impose a sentence on the convicted person. Although the convicted person will receive psychiatric treatment if necessary, this treatment provision is also available to any other prisoner. Moreover, the frequent unavailability of appropriate psychiatric treatment for prisoners adds an additional element of spuriousness to the guilty but mentally ill verdict. Guilty but mentally ill has as much relevance as, for example, pleading guilty but having lumbago.

## Psychiatric Malpractice

Psychiatric malpractice is medical malpractice. *Malpractice* is the provision of substandard professional care that causes a compensable injury to a person with whom a professional relationship existed. Although this concept may seem relatively clear and simple, it has its share of conditions and caveats. For example, the essential issue is *not* the existence of substandard care per se, but whether there is actual compensable liability. For a physician to be found *liable* to a patient for malpractice, several fundamental concepts must be established.

Medical malpractice is a tort or civil wrong—that is, a noncriminal or non-contract-related wrong—committed as a result of negligence by physicians or other health care professionals that causes injury to a patient in their care. *Negligence*, the fundamental concept underlying a malpractice lawsuit, is simply described as doing something that a person with a duty of care (to the patient) should not have done or failing to do something that a person with a duty of care should have done. The fact that a psychiatrist commits an act of negligence does not automatically create malpractice liability. Liability for malpractice is based on the plaintiff's (e.g., patient's) establishing by a preponderance of the evidence that 1) there was a duty of care owed by the defendant (duty), 2) the duty of care was breached (deviation), 3) the plaintiff endured actual damages (damages), and 4) the deviation was the direct cause of the damages (direct causation). These elements are sometimes referred to as the *four Ds of malpractice* (Simon 1992a, p. 542).

Each of these elements must be met or else there can be no finding of liability, regardless of any finding of negligence. In other words, negligence by itself is not sufficient to sustain a malpractice claim. For example, if the plaintiff experienced no real injuries because of the negligence, or if an injury occurred but it was not directly caused by the doctor's negligence, no malpractice exists.

Critical to the establishment of a claim of professional negligence is the requirement that the defendant's conduct was substandard or was a deviation in the standard of care owed to the plaintiff. The law presumes and holds all physicians (psychiatrists) to a standard of *ordinary care*, which is measured by its *reasonableness* according to the clinical circumstances in which it is provided.

## Confidentiality and Testimonial Privilege

*Confidentiality* refers to the right of a patient to have communications spoken or written in confidence to the physician not disclosed to outside parties without implied or expressed authorization. *Privilege*, or more accurately testimonial privilege, can be viewed as a derivation of the right of confidentiality. *Testimonial privilege* is a statutorily created rule of evidence that permits the holder of the privilege (e.g., the patient) to exercise the right to prevent the person to whom confidential information was given (e.g., the psychiatrist) from disclosing it in a judicial proceeding.

### Confidentiality

#### Clinical-Legal Foundation

The basis for recognizing and safeguarding patient confidences is derived from four general sources. First, all 50 states and the District of Columbia have acknowledged this right of protection by including some form of confidentiality provisions in either professional licensure laws or confidentiality and privilege statutes. Second, and probably the most traditional source, the various mental health professions have ethical codes regarding confidentiality. Third, the common law recognizes an attorney-client privilege, but developing case law also has carved out this source of protection for physicians and psychotherapists. In 1996, the U.S. Supreme Court ruled that communications between psychotherapist and patient are confidential and need not be disclosed in federal trials (*Jaffee v. Redmond* 1996). Fourth, the right of confidentiality may be subsumed under the right of privacy.

## Breach of Confidentiality

Once the doctor-patient relationship has been created, the clinician assumes an automatic duty to safeguard a patient's disclosures. This duty is not absolute, and in some circumstances, breaching confidentiality is both ethical and legal.

Patients waive confidentiality in a variety of situations. Medical records are regularly sent to potential employers or to insurance companies and to managed care organizations to obtain benefits. A limited waiver of confidentiality ordinarily exits when a patient participates in group therapy. Legally, whether one group member can be compelled in court to disclose information shared by another group member during group therapy is still unsettled. Many state confidentiality statutes provide statutory exceptions to confidentiality between the psychiatrist and the patient in one or more situations (Slovenko 1998) (Table 38–3).

Patients' access to their own records is normally controlled by state statutes. These statutory provisions are found under the heading of "medical records" or the much broader term *privilege*.

## Testimonial Privilege

The patient—not the psychiatrist—is the holder of testimonial privilege that controls the release of confidential information. Because this privilege applies only to the judicial setting, it is called "testimonial privilege." Privilege statutes represent the most common recognition by the state of the importance of protecting information provided by a patient to a psychotherapist. This recognition moves away from the essential purpose of the American system of justice (e.g., "truth finding") by insulating certain information from disclosure in court. This protection is justified on the basis that the special need for privacy in the doctor-patient relationship outweighs the unbridled quest for an accurate outcome in court.

Privilege statutes usually are drafted in one of four ways, depending on the type of practitioner:

**TABLE 38–3.** Common statutory exceptions to confidentiality between psychiatrist and patient

Child abuse
Competency proceedings
Court-ordered examination
Dangerousness to self or others
Patient-litigant exception
Intent to commit a crime or harmful act
Civil commitment proceedings
Communication with other treatment providers

- Physician-patient (general)
- Psychiatrist-patient
- Psychologist-patient
- Psychotherapist-patient

Cases have been successfully litigated in which the broader physician-patient category has applied to the psychotherapist when an applicable statute did not exist.

## Exceptions to Testimonial Privilege

Privilege statutes also specify exceptions to testimonial privilege. Although exceptions vary, the most common include the following:

- Child abuse reporting
- Civil commitment proceedings
- Court-ordered evaluations
- Cases in which a patient's mental state is in question as part of litigation

This last exception, known as the *patient-litigant exception*, commonly occurs in will contests, workers' compensation cases, child custody disputes, personal injury litigation, and malpractice actions in which the therapist is sued by the patient.

## Liability

An unauthorized or unwarranted breach of confidentiality can cause a patient considerable emotional harm. As a result, a psychiatrist typically can be held liable for such a breach based on at least four theories:

1. Malpractice (breach of confidentiality)
2. Breach of statutory duty
3. Invasion of privacy
4. Breach of (implied) contract

## Somatic Therapies

Generally speaking, psychiatric intervention with patients who have serious affective, delusional, or aggressive disorders involves drug therapy and electroconvulsive therapy (ECT). A brief review of the standard of care of these treatments is instructive in understanding the basis for lawsuits involving neuropsychiatric treatment procedures.

The therapeutic use of a somatic therapy, including ECT, is evaluated no differently from use of any other medical or psychiatric procedure regarding potential liability. The same general standard of *ordinary* and *reasonable* care will, therefore, govern the assessment of whether a psychiatrist's use of or failure to use a somatic intervention is actionable (Annotation 1979, 1985).

It is generally acknowledged within the psychiatric profession that there is no *absolute standard* protocol for the administration of psychotropic medication or ECT. Nevertheless, the existence of practice guidelines, procedures, and clinical resources regularly accepted or used by a significant percentage of psychiatrists should alert clinicians to consider them. For example, the American Psychiatric Association (1990, 1992) published comprehensive findings in the form of task force reports on ECT and tardive dyskinesia. The task force report on ECT should be considered a leading resource with regard to ECT.

These or any other publications do not per se establish the standard of care by which a court might evaluate a psychiatrist's treatment. They do represent, however, credible sources of information that a reasonable psychiatrist should at least be familiar with and have considered (*Stone v. Proctor* 1963). In addition to expert testimony, courts consider the current psychiatric literature in determining the standard of care in specific cases.

Some evidence indicates that less professional autonomy and flexibility are associated with the use of ECT. Normally, the "reasonable care" standard that is applied to psychiatric treatment is construed in a fairly broad manner because psychiatry is currently considered an inexact medical discipline. However, some psychiatric treatments, such as ECT, appear more rigidly regulated than others. For instance, the Joint Commission on Accreditation of Healthcare Organizations (JCAHO; 2000) considers ECT a *special treatment* procedure, requiring hospitals to have written policies concerning its use. JCAHO standards, coupled with specific regulations promulgated by a facility regarding ECT, can serve as establishing the basis for liability, if violated. Nevertheless, no official guidelines should be interpreted as a substitute for sound clinical judgment.

The "standard" for judging the use and administration of medication, however, appears to be consistent with the more flexible and general "reasonable care" requirement. The third reference source that bears highlighting is the use of the *Physicians' Desk Reference* (PDR) to establish or dispute a psychiatrist's pharmacotherapy procedures. The PDR is a commercially distributed, privately published reference regarding medication products used in the United States. The Food and Drug Administration (FDA) requires that drug manufacturers have their official package inserts reported in the PDR (Simon and Sadoff 1992). Accordingly, to stay abreast of new medication treatments and to provide patients with current and accurate medication information, psychiatrists periodically consult publications like the PDR.

Although numerous courts have cited the PDR as a credible source of medication-related information in the medical profession (*Gowan v. United States* 1985; *Witherell v. Weimer* 1986), it does not by itself establish *the* standard of care. Instead, the PDR may be used as one piece of evidence to establish the standard of care in a particular situation (*Callan v. Norland* 1983; *Doerr v. Hurley Medical Center* 1984). Courts generally follow the ruling in *Ramon v. Farr* (1989), which held that drug inserts alone do not set the standard of care, but are only one factor to be considered among other pertinent factors, such as previous personal experience, the scientific literature, approvals in other countries, and expert testimony. The PDR or any other reference cannot serve as a substitute for the practitioner's clinical judgment. Similarly, in managed care settings, psychiatrists should vigorously resist any attempt to restrict their choice of drugs according to a predetermined, limited formulary. The prescribing of a specific drug should be determined only by the psychiatrist based on the clinical needs of the patient.

Fortunately, courts recognize the importance of professional judgment and will give psychiatrists and other medical specialists latitude in explaining any special diagnostic or treatment considerations that guided their decision making. For instance, the research data on pharmacologic treatment of aggression in patients indicate that there are a variety of potentially useful drug therapies, some of which are considered experimental or cutting edge. However, no drug has been approved by the FDA specifically for the treatment of aggression (Yudofsky et al. 1998).

Accordingly, the courts will consider the fact that rarely does only one treatment of choice exist and that treatment applications are still being developed. Moreover, evidence that a treatment procedure is accepted by at least a respectable minority of professionals in the field could establish that the modality is a reasonable professional practice (Simon 1993). Practice guidelines recommend a variety of treatment approaches but defer to the clinical judgment of the practitioner for the ultimate treatment decision.

The standard of care associated with the use of a somatic therapy to treat a psychiatric patient, *at a minimum*, should include some variation of the following recommendations:

## Pretreatment

- Complete clinical history (e.g., medical, psychological)
- Current physical examination (when indicated, performed by the patient's physician or the psychiatrist)
- Administration of necessary laboratory tests and review of all test results
- Disclosure of sufficient information to obtain informed consent, including information about the consequences of *not* receiving treatment
- Thorough documentation of clinical decisions, informed consent information, patient responses, and other relevant treatment data

## Treatment

- Careful monitoring of the patient's response to treatment, including frequent patient evaluations and appropriate laboratory testing
- Prompt adjustments in treatment, as needed
- Obtaining a renewed informed consent when appreciably altering treatment or initiating new treatment

The final word on evaluation and treatment depends on the clinician's judgment and the clinical needs of the patient, not the law.

## Theories of Liability in Psychiatry

The term *psychiatric malpractice* is a misnomer because the same basic legal principles will be applied to any lawsuit in which a patient alleges malpractice by a physician, regardless of medical subspecialty. Prefixes such as "psychiatric" or "neuropsychiatric" reflect the general recognition that the theories of liability to be discussed represent the most common areas of malpractice associated with that subspecialty. The following is a brief review of the most common litigation areas in treating neuropsychiatric patients.

**TABLE 38–4.** Frequency of primary allegations for claims filed between 1984 and 1999

| Reason for claim | Frequency (%) |
| --- | --- |
| Incorrect treatment | 24.3 |
| Suicide | 12.3 |
| Incorrect diagnosis | 14.7 |
| Improper supervision | 4.8 |
| Drug reaction | 7.4 |
| Breach of confidentiality | 2.2 |
| Unnecessary commitment | 4.2 |
| Undue familiarity | 3.3 |
| Other (e.g., abandonment, electroconvulsive therapy, third-party injury, libel, and slander) | 26.7 |

*Source.* Adapted from Program Participants' Report, 1998–1999. The APA-Sponsored Professional Liability Insurance Program, Arlington, VA, 1999.

## Medication

The potential for negligence by psychiatrists appears to be high in clinical situations involving the use of psychotropic medication. The approximate frequencies of alleged claims (by reason for claim as a percentage of total claims), based on the recent malpractice claims experience of the Psychiatrists' Purchasing Group, the liability insurer of members of the American Psychiatric Association, are presented in Table 38–4. The alleged medication mismanagement likely overlaps with the categories of incorrect treatment, suicide, and improper supervision as well.

A review of the relevant case law indicates that a variety of mistakes, omissions, and poor pharmacologic treatment practices may result in malpractice actions brought against psychiatrists or other physicians. The following list, although not exhaustive, identifies areas of potential legal liability associated with medication treatment.

1. *Failure to properly evaluate:* Sound clinical practice requires that before any form of somatic treatment is initiated, the patient should be properly evaluated. The examination is largely dictated by the patient's clinical condition and type of treatment being contemplated. A current physical examination (when indicated), a complete clinical history, and a mental status examination should be conducted. A recent medical examination or continuing medical follow-up may suffice, or the patient may be referred for a medical evaluation, when necessary. A few lawsuits have resulted from the failure to properly evaluate a patient before administering psychotropic medication (*Blanchard v. Levine* 1985; *Shaughnessy v. Spray*

1981). As a result of this omission, a patient's condition may be misdiagnosed and remain untreated. Additionally, the patient may be exposed to unnecessary side effects and risks.

2. *Failure to monitor or supervise:* Probably the most common act of negligence associated with pharmacotherapy is the failure to supervise the patient's progress on the medication, including monitoring the patient for adverse side effects.

    Once psychotropic medication is prescribed, the psychiatrist must monitor or supervise the patient. Monitoring may require the use of laboratory testing, physical examination, and medical referral, if necessary. Serum drug levels are obtainable for several psychotropic medications. The primary indications for laboratory tests include assessing therapeutic and toxic levels of medication and patient compliance with treatment (Nelson 1992). The use of carbamazepine, valproic acid, and clozapine requires close monitoring of the hematopoietic system and the liver. A failure to properly supervise patients taking psychotropic medication can unnecessarily subject them to harmful side effects or may delay a change to more effective treatment. If a patient is harmed from these omissions, a malpractice action could result (*Chaires v. St. John's Episcopal Hospital* 1984; *Clifford v. United States* 1985; *Kilgore v. County of Santa Clara* 1982).

    Fragmented care, in which the psychiatrist functions as only a prescriber of medication while remaining uninformed about the patient's overall clinical status, constitutes substandard treatment. In managed care or other settings, the mere prescribing of medication, in the absence of a therapeutic alliance with the patient, is a prime example of fragmented care. Such a practice will diminish the efficacy of the drug treatment itself or may even lead to the patient's failure to take the prescribed medication.

    Split treatment situations require that the psychiatrist stay fully informed of the patient's clinical status as well as of the nature and quality of treatment the patient is receiving from the nonmedical therapist. In a collaborative relationship, responsibility for the patient's care is shared according to the qualifications and limitations of each discipline. The responsibilities of each discipline do not diminish those of the other disciplines. Patients should be informed of the separate responsibilities of each discipline. Regular communication between the psychiatrist and the nonmedical therapist regarding the patient's clinical condition and needs is necessary. On termination of the collaborative relationship, the patient should be informed either separately or jointly. In split treat-

ments, if negligence is claimed on the part of the nonmedical therapist, the collaborating psychiatrist likely will be sued, and vice versa (Meyer and Simon 1999a, 1999b).

Psychiatrists who prescribe medications in a split treatment arrangement should be able to hospitalize the patient, if that becomes necessary. If the psychiatrist does not have admitting privileges, then prearrangements should exist with other psychiatrists who can hospitalize patients if emergencies arise. Split treatment, a practice favored by managed care companies, is a potential malpractice minefield.

3. *Negligent prescription practices:* The selection of a medication, initial dosage, form of administration, and other related procedures are all decisions left to the sound discretion of the treating psychiatrist. The law recognizes that the physician is in the best position to "know the patient" and to determine what course of treatment is best under the circumstances. Accordingly, the standard by which a psychiatrist's prescription practices will be evaluated is whether they are *reasonable*. In administering psychotropic medication, psychiatrists need only conform their procedures and decision making to those that are *ordinarily* practiced by other psychiatrists under similar circumstances.

    Negligent prescription procedures usually involve serious deviations from generally accepted treatment practice. These practices may include exceeding recommended dosages that cause toxicity and then failing to adjust the medication level to therapeutic levels, mixing drugs unreasonably, prescribing medication for unapproved uses without proper indications and justification, inappropriately prescribing "unapproved" medications, and failing to obtain informed consent. When prescribing medications for unapproved uses, informed consent requirements are correspondingly heightened.

    Obtaining competent informed consent may be complicated by the fact that a significant number of psychiatric patients have diminished cognitive capacity because of mental illness and chronic brain impairment. Each time a medication is changed and a new drug is introduced, informed consent should be obtained. Failure to properly inform a patient of the risks and consequences of taking a medication may be grounds for a malpractice action, if the patient is injured as a result (*Karasik v. Bird* 1984; *Moran v. Botsford General Hospital* 1984; *Wright v. State* 1986).

4. *Other:* Lawsuits alleging negligence involving medication also include failure to treat side effects once they

were recognized or should have been recognized, failure to monitor a patient's compliance with prescription limits, failure to prescribe medication or appropriate levels of medication according to the treatment needs of the patient, prescription of addicting drugs to a vulnerable patient, failure to refer a patient for consultation or treatment by a specialist when necessary, and negligent withdrawal from medication.

In managed care settings, psychiatrists may be required to prescribe medications from a closed formulary. For example, selective serotonin reuptake inhibitors (SSRIs) are currently considered first-line treatment for depression. However, some managed care companies may allow only the prescribing of tricyclic antidepressants (TCAs). TCAs are more lethal than SSRIs in patients who overdose. Psychiatrists, in their professional discretion, should determine which medications will be prescribed according to the special clinical needs of the patient.

## Tardive Dyskinesia

The following case example illustrates the potential for legal liability when a patient receiving treatment with neuroleptics is not monitored carefully.

## Case Example 5

Ms. E, a 58-year-old woman with a history of mild mental retardation and schizophrenia, is seen for medication appointments every 6–9 months. She has been taking major tranquilizers for nearly 30 years. The patient lives in a distant rural area, making it difficult for the psychiatrist to see her more often. After a 9-month interval between appointments, she develops oral-lingual dyskinesia. On discontinuation of the neuroleptic, her dyskinetic symptoms spread to her trunk and become more severe. The patient is unable to continue work as a dishwasher and maintain herself independently. The family brings a lawsuit against the psychiatrist for negligence in failing to monitor the patient and her medications.

The development of neuroleptic medications in the mid-1950s created considerable excitement and hope for the treatment and management of schizophrenia. Shortly after the introduction of neuroleptic medications as therapeutic agents, researchers and clinicians observed unusual muscle movements in some patients, later referred to as *tardive dyskinesia* (TD). Numerically, the number of psychiatric patients being treated with neuroleptics is quite high (H.J. Parry et al. 1973). It is estimated that *at least* 10%–20% of patients and perhaps as many as 50% of patients exposed to neuroleptic drugs for more than 1 year show some degree of probable TD

(Gardos and Cole 1980). These projections are even higher for elderly patients (Kane et al. 1982; Klawans and Barr 1982). Given these data, the potential for *TD litigation* appears obvious. Nevertheless, relatively few psychiatrists have been sued under this cause of action. In addition, patients who develop TD may not have the physical and psychological staying power required to pursue litigation.

Allegations of negligence following a patient's developing TD are based on the same legal elements as in any other malpractice action. Moreover, the bases for negligence mirror those that have been previously identified with general medication cases. These areas include, but are not limited to, failure to properly evaluate a patient, failure to obtain informed consent, negligent diagnosis of a patient's condition, and failure to monitor.

In *Clites v. State* (1982), a landmark TD case, the plaintiff was a mentally retarded man who had been institutionalized since age 11 and treated with major tranquilizers from age 18 to 23. TD was diagnosed at age 23. The plaintiff's family subsequently sued. The family claimed that the defendants had negligently prescribed medication, had not informed the patient of the possibility of developing TD, and had failed to monitor and subsequently treat the patient's resulting side effects. The jury returned a verdict for the plaintiff and awarded damages in the amount of $760,165. This award was affirmed on appeal.

In *Hyde v. University of Michigan Board of Regents* (1986), a woman was awarded $1 million from a medical center that misdiagnosed her condition as Huntington's chorea instead of TD. This verdict was later reversed on the basis of a subsequent case that expanded the state's sovereign immunity coverage (*Faigenbaum v. Oakland Medical Center* 1985).

In *Dovido v. Vasquez* (1986), $700,000 was awarded to a 42-year-old plaintiff who had TD as a result of the defendant psychiatrist's negligent prescription of extremely high doses of fluphenazine. The court ruled that the defendants were negligent because they deviated from the standards of the "industry." Specifically, the court cited various omissions in common psychiatric practice that reasonable psychiatrists would have provided. Among the "deviations" they noted were failure to conduct regular physical examinations and laboratory tests, failure to intervene at the first sign of TD, inappropriate use of multiple medications at the same time, use of drugs for convenience (e.g., "behavior management") rather than therapy, and failure to obtain the plaintiff's informed consent.

As case example 5 illustrates, patients receiving neuroleptic medication need to be monitored frequently. No stock answer can be given to the question of how frequently the psychiatrist should see the patient. Generally, psychiatrists should schedule return visits with a frequency that accords with the patient's clinical need. The longer the time between visits, however, the greater the risk of adverse drug reactions and untoward developments in the patient's condition. Generally, the interval between visits should not be longer than 6 months.

The defenses and preventive measures applicable to TD-related malpractice claims are consistent with those used in most cases alleging negligent drug treatment. In general, the application of sound clinical practice that is appropriately communicated to the patient and documented in the treatment chart should serve as an effective foil to allegations of negligence if TD develops (*Frasier v. Department of Health and Human Resources* 1986; *Radank v. Heyl* 1986).

The use of the newer atypical antipsychotic medications as first-line treatment for schizophrenia and other psychotic conditions in many patients is now common practice (Kaye and Reed 1999). The extrapyramidal side-effect profile is much more benign than that of the typical neuroleptics. Clinical trials of the atypical antipsychotic drugs suggest that these medications have a lower potential for causing TD (Glazer 1997). Whether the incidence and severity of TD will be any less with the atypical agents in the long run remains to be seen. Negative symptoms of schizophrenia such as flat affect, social withdrawal, and poverty of speech respond to the atypical drugs. Atypical antipsychotic drugs have shown superior efficacy for treatment-resistant schizophrenia. Enhanced patient compliance is another advantage. Psychiatrists still must be guided by their clinical judgments and the individual clinical needs of patients.

The use of antipsychotic medication to treat chronic aggression involves a substantial risk of TD. The prevalence of TD among patients receiving long-term neuroleptic treatment is about 25%. Yudofsky et al. (1987) recommended a conservative approach:

> While antipsychotic agents are the treatment of choice for aggression due to psychosis and also may be helpful in the acute short-term management of violence through sedative action, we do *not* recommend their use in the long-term management of aggression, especially that which is secondary to organic brain syndrome.

## Electroconvulsive Therapy

Although a significant proportion of psychiatrists believe that ECT is a viable treatment for certain mental disorders (O'Connell 1982), it has been estimated that only 3%–5% of all psychiatric inpatients in the United States receive this form of treatment (R.D. Weiner 1979). As can be expected from these figures, the potential number of legal actions alleging negligence associated with ECT is low (Perr 1980). Nevertheless, lawsuits involving ECT are occasionally brought. Cases of ECT-related injuries represent a variety of circumstances in which alleged negligence has occurred. These cases can be categorized into three areas: pretreatment, treatment, and posttreatment.

### Pretreatment

Although there is some variation in pre-ECT evaluations, generally the following procedures recommended by the American Psychiatric Association Task Force on ECT (American Psychiatric Association 1990) should be observed:

1. A psychiatric history and examination to evaluate the indications for ECT
2. A medical examination to determine risk factors
3. An anesthesia evaluation
4. Written informed consent
5. An evaluation by a physician privileged to administer ECT

Although the American Psychiatric Association Task Force on ECT recommendations do not define in any absolute sense the standard of care for ECT, they may be proffered as evidence of the standard of care by attorneys in malpractice suits involving ECT. Official treatment guidelines should not be considered a substitute for the psychiatrist's sound clinical judgment. Nevertheless, failure to adequately conduct one of these procedures could endanger the welfare of the patient and secondarily result in a lawsuit.

### Treatment

It is well established in the law that a physician will not be held liable for a mere mistake in judgment; also, he or she will not be held to a standard of 100% accuracy or perfect performance (*Holton v. Pfingst* 1976; *Smith* 1986). Therefore, a *bad result* does not automatically establish a claim for malpractice (*Howe v. Citizens Memorial Hospital* 1968). Instead, a patient must prove, by a preponderance of the evidence (i.e., more likely than not), that the physician deviated from the standard of care and that deviation proximately caused the patient some injury or damage.

The procedure for evaluating the care and treatment afforded a patient when ECT is used is no different. Cases involving ECT-related injuries in which the negligence has occurred during the actual *treatment process* include 1) failure to use a muscle relaxant to reduce the chance of a bone fracture, 2) negligent administration of the procedure, and 3) failure to conduct an evaluation of the patient, including the use of X rays, before initiating or continuing treatment.

## Posttreatment

After the administration of ECT, patients may experience common side effects, such as temporary confusion, disorientation, and memory loss (O'Connell 1982). Because these side effects may be temporarily debilitating to the patient, sound clinical practice requires that psychiatrists provide reasonable posttreatment care and safeguards. Courts have held that the failure to properly attend to a patient for a period of time following the administration of ECT can result in malpractice liability. Posttreatment circumstances in which negligence may be alleged include 1) failure to evaluate complaints of pain or discomfort following treatment, 2) failure to evaluate a patient's condition before resuming ECT treatments, 3) failure to properly monitor a patient in order to prevent falls, and 4) failure to properly supervise a patient who had been injured as a result of ECT.

As a source of *civil liability*, ECT-related lawsuits today are quite rare and are not likely to represent a significant problem area for psychiatrists. But, as Perlin (1989c) cautioned, "recent developments in right-to-refuse treatment law and statutory regulation of intrusive therapy are likely to insure that any future ECT litigation will still be considered carefully" (pp. 47–48).

## The Violent Patient

Patients can turn violence against themselves, others, or both. Suicide and violence may occur following brain injury that is complicated by poor impulse control and depression. The following case example illustrates the legal liability associated with the treatment and management of the violent patient.

### Case Example 6

Mr. F, an 18-year-old man, is found to have extensive frontal lobe damage after an automobile accident. The patient's symptoms include poor frustration tolerance, impulsiveness, and violent outbursts. He threatens to kill a student at his high school who has been teasing him. Mr. F is consistently noncompliant with treatment. He threatens to overdose with his medications. His psychiatrist persuades him to enter a psychiatric hospital. A new regimen of medication is rec-

ommended by a psychiatric consultant. In addition, the psychiatrist and other staff employ behavior modification and biofeedback techniques.

One month after admission, Mr. F is assessed to be "psychiatrically stable" and is released. Five days after his discharge, he fatally shoots a high school student who was tormenting him. The parents of the deceased file suit against the hospital, the treating psychiatrist, and the consulting psychiatrist for negligent treatment and negligent discharge of the patient. They also allege that the treating psychiatrist failed to warn them and their son of the threats made by Mr. F.

The proposition that psychiatric patients are no more violent than the general public can no longer be sustained. Evidence indicates that acute psychotic disorders may be a consistent, although modest, risk factor for the occurrence of violence (Monahan 1992). The National Institute of Mental Health Epidemiologic Catchment Area study estimated that 90% of the persons with current mental illnesses are not violent (Swanson et al. 1990). If a person was not having an acute psychotic episode or if psychotic symptoms were not part of the psychiatric problems, the individual was no more likely to be involved in violent behavior than was the average person. Even when psychotic symptoms were present, there was only a modest increase in risk of violence above the norm. The persons with the highest risk of violence were young, substance-using males from lower socioeconomic classes. Seriously mentally ill patients with schizophrenia, major depression, mania, or bipolar disorder had an incidence of violence 5 times higher than that of persons with no diagnosed mental illness. The incidence of violence was 12–15 times higher among persons who were alcohol and substance abusers.

When psychiatrists treat violent or potentially violent patients, an increased risk of legal liability exists alleging *failure to control aggressive outpatients* and the *discharge of violent inpatients*.

In the landmark case *Tarasoff v. Regents of the University of California* (1976), the California Supreme Court held that mental health professionals had a duty to protect identifiable, endangered third parties from imminent threats of serious harm made by patients in their care. If a patient threatens harm to a third party, most states require that the psychiatrist perform *some* intervention that might prevent the harm from occurring. In states with duty-to-warn statutes, the responses available to psychiatrists and psychotherapists are defined by law. An increasing number of states provide immunity from liability when the psychiatrist fulfills statutorily defined duties to warn and protect endangered third parties. In states offering no such guidance, health care providers are required to use the clinical judgment that will accomplish the objective of protecting the object of the patient's threat. For example, various options are clinically and legally available, such as voluntary hospitalization, involuntary hospitalization (if civil commitment requirements are met), warning the intended victim of the threat, notifying the police, adjusting medication, and seeing the patient more frequently (Simon and Sadoff 1992, pp. 211–214).

The following case example illustrates discharge and release considerations in working with violent or potentially violent inpatients.

## Case Example 7

Ms. G, a 47-year-old epileptic woman, is discharged from a psychiatric hospital after treatment for alcohol intoxication and random violence toward persons and property. Ms. G has had numerous similar psychiatric hospital admissions in the past. Violent acts occur only when alcohol intoxication is combined with the discontinuance of her anticonvulsant medication. The psychiatrist works closely with Ms. G to ensure follow-up treatment within the first week of discharge. The patient seems motivated to stop drinking, promising to continue attending Alcoholics Anonymous meetings begun in the hospital. As an extra precaution, the psychiatrist calls the patient's outpatient therapist to verify that the first appointment a week after discharge is kept. Ms. G does not keep her outpatient appointment. The psychiatrist calls Ms. G, who admits that she has resumed drinking. She agrees to return to the hospital for detoxification and further treatment.

Violent or potentially violent patients in an inpatient setting represent a unique and challenging situation for treating psychiatrists. In a hospital, there is more control over the patient than is available in an outpatient setting. Courts scrutinize closely decisions made by psychiatrists treating inpatients that might adversely affect the patient or a third party.

The psychiatric-legal issues surrounding seclusion and restraint of violent inpatients are complicated and are discussed fully elsewhere (Simon 1992a, pp. 371–382). Seclusion and restraint as clinical management modalities have both indications and contraindications (Tables 38–5 and 38–6). The legal regulation of seclusion and restraint has become increasingly more stringent in recent years (Appelbaum 1999).

Cases involving the injury or death of individuals because of the negligent release or discharge of a violent patient far exceed in number those cases involving outpatient *Tarasoff* cases (Simon and Sadoff 1992, p. 327). Negligent release cases are likely to increase under managed care pressures for rapid discharge of psychiatric

**TABLE 38–5.** Indications for seclusion and restraint

1. To prevent clear, imminent harm to the patient or others
2. To prevent significant disruption to treatment program or physical surroundings
3. To assist in treatment as part of ongoing behavior therapy
4. To decrease sensory overstimulation[a]
5. To comply with patient's voluntary reasonable request[b]

[a]Seclusion only.

[b]First seclusion; then, if necessary, restraints.

*Source.* Reprinted from Simon RI: *Concise Guide to Psychiatry and the Law for Clinicians,* 2nd Edition. Washington, DC, American Psychiatric Press, 1998, p. 112. Copyright 1998, American Psychiatric Press. Used with permission.

**TABLE 38–6.** Contraindications to seclusion and restraint

1. Extremely unstable medical and psychiatric conditions[a]
2. Delirious or demented patients unable to tolerate decreased stimulation[a]
3. Overtly suicidal patients[a]
4. Patients with severe drug reactions or with overdoses, or requiring close monitoring of drug dosages[a]
5. Punishment or convenience of staff

[a]Unless close supervision and direct observation are provided.

*Source.* Reprinted from Simon RI: *Concise Guide to Psychiatry and the Law for Clinicians,* 2nd Edition. Washington, DC, American Psychiatric Press, 1998, p. 114. Copyright 1998, American Psychiatric Press. Used with permission.

inpatients (Simon 1998b). Case example 7 illustrates the importance of carefully following up the discharge of the potentially violent patient. Psychiatrists should not discharge patients without adequate aftercare planning (Simon 1997). The patient's willingness to cooperate with the psychiatrist is critical to maintaining follow-up treatment. The psychiatrist should structure the follow-up visits in such a fashion as to encourage compliance. A study of Veterans Administration (VA) outpatient referrals showed that of 24% of the total sample of inpatients referred to the VA mental health clinic, approximately 50% failed to keep their first appointments (Zeldow and Taub 1981). Nonetheless, limitations do exist on the extent of the psychiatrist's ability to ensure follow-up care. Most discharged patients retain the right to refuse further treatment. This must be acknowledged by both the psychiatric and the legal communities (Simon and Sadoff 1992, pp. 233–248).

In either the outpatient or the inpatient situation, psychiatrists must reasonably assess a patient's *potential risk* for violence toward self or others, which then directs the clinical interventions chosen (Simon 1998a). Professional standards do exist for the assessment of the risk factors for suicide or violence toward others (Simon 1992b, 1992c, pp. 131–136; see also Blumenthal and Kupfer 1990). No standard of care exists, however, for the *prediction* of violent behavior. Violence risk assessment is a continuing process. The risk of violence should be assessed frequently, updating the assessment at significant clinical junctures (e.g., ward changes, off-ward privileges, passes, discharge). A risk-benefit assessment that considers both continued hospitalization and discharge should be conducted and recorded before issuing a pass or discharge. Assessments of the risk of violence are here-and-now determinations. Probability assessments of the risk of violence become progressively less accurate beyond the immediate short term (e.g., 24–48 hours).

## Involuntary Hospitalization

The following case example illustrates a common clinical indication for initiating a medical certification for involuntary hospitalization:

### Case Example 8

Mr. H, a 78-year-old man living by himself, is unable to function independently because of a progressive dementia. He refuses to allow anyone into his home. At night, he is heard screaming and cursing. Police are called, forcibly enter the home, and take the man to an emergency room. Mr. H is confused, disoriented, and dehydrated. The emergency room physician signs medical certification papers indicating that Mr. H is gravely disabled by severe dementia and is a danger to himself. Mr. H is detained on a 7-day hold for psychiatric examination before the commitment hearing. At the hearing, the judge hears psychiatric evidence that Mr. H is severely demented and a danger to himself. The court orders involuntary hospitalization for a period of 30 days.

A person may be involuntarily hospitalized only if certain statutorily mandated criteria are met. Three main substantive criteria serve as the foundation for all statutory commitment requirements: that the individual be 1) mentally ill, 2) dangerous to self or others, and 3) unable to provide for one's basic needs (gravely disabled). Generally, each state defines which criteria are required and what each means. Terms such as *mentally ill* often are loosely described, thus shifting the responsibility for proper definition onto the clinical judgment of the petitioner.

In addition to individuals with mental illness, certain states have enacted legislation that permits the involuntary hospitalization of three other distinct groups: developmentally disabled (mentally retarded) persons, per-

sons with substance addiction (alcohol, drugs), and mentally disabled minors. Special commitment provisions may exist governing requirements for the admission and discharge of mentally disabled minors as well as numerous due-process rights afforded these individuals.

Involuntary hospitalization of psychiatric patients usually arises when violent behavior threatens to erupt and/or when patients become unable to care for themselves. These patients frequently manifest mental disorders and conditions that readily meet the substantive criteria for involuntary hospitalization. In case example 8, the patient had severe dementia and was unable to care for himself. Thus, he clearly met the substantive criteria of mentally ill and gravely disabled (i.e., inability to provide for his basic needs). Threatened or actual violence in the absence of a diagnosable psychiatric disorder is a matter for the law enforcement authorities.

Clinicians should remember that *they* do not commit patients. Civil commitment is under the sole jurisdiction of courts or other quasi-judicial bodies. The psychiatrist initiates medical certification that brings the patient before the court, usually after a brief period of evaluation. The psychiatrist must be guided by the treatment needs of the patient in seeking medical certification. For example, involuntarily hospitalizing a patient merely because a managed care organization will no longer provide insurance coverage is wrong and potentially legally actionable.

The most common type of lawsuit involving involuntary hospitalization relates to a physician's or psychiatrist's failure to act in good faith and to adhere to statutory requirements, resulting in a wrongful commitment. Often, these lawsuits are brought under the theory of false imprisonment. Other areas of liability that may arise from wrongful commitment include assault and battery, malicious prosecution, abuse of authority, and intentional infliction of emotional distress.

In many states, psychiatrists are granted immunity from liability as long as they use reasonable professional judgment and act in good faith when petitioning for commitment (Mishkin 1989). Performing a careful examination of the patient, abiding by the requirements of the law, and ensuring that sound reasoning motivates the certification of the patient constitute good clinical practice and, only secondarily, good risk management. Evidence of willful, blatant, or gross failure to adhere to statutorily defined commitment procedures may expose a psychiatrist to a lawsuit.

When a patient is involuntarily hospitalized, the hospitalization does not negate a presumption of competence. In most states, patients involuntarily hospitalized who refuse medication require a separate court hearing for an adjudication of incompetence and the provision of substituted consent by the court. Recently, persons hospitalized under criminal commitment have been accorded the right to refuse treatment. The courts have found that a patient's constitutional right to due process is adequately protected by the exercise of professional judgment within the medical peer review process of the institution (*United States v. Charters* 1988).

Hospitalized patients have other rights. Patients possess the right of visitation, although this right can be temporarily suspended for proper cause relating to the patient's care and treatment. Free communications of hospitalized patients through mail, telephone, or visitors are considered a right, unless protection of the patient or others requires supervision of communications. The right to privacy includes allowing patients to have secure locker space, private toilet and shower facilities, and minimum square footage of floor space. Protection of confidentiality is also included. Economic rights include the right to have and spend money and to handle one's own financial affairs responsibly. In most jurisdictions, involuntarily hospitalized patients do not lose their civil rights, such as the right to manage their own money. Hospitalized patients must be paid for their work in certain jurisdictions unless it is truly therapeutic labor (i.e., work not connected with maintenance of the hospital). "Patient rights" are not absolute and often must be tempered by the clinical judgment of the mental health professional. Inevitably, disputes arise over perceived or real violations of patients' rights. In some jurisdictions, a civil rights officer or ombudsman is mandated by statute to mediate these disputes.

## National Practitioner Data Bank

On September 1, 1990, the National Practitioner Data Bank, established by the Health Care Quality Improvement Act of 1986 (42 U.S.C. 11101 [Supp. V 1987]), went into effect. The data bank tracks disciplinary actions, malpractice judgments, and settlements against physicians, dentists, and other health care professionals (Johnson 1991).

Hospitals, health maintenance organizations (HMOs), professional societies, state medical boards, and other health care organizations are required to report any disciplinary action taken against providers lasting more than 30 days. Disciplinary actions include limitation, suspension, or revocation of privileges or professional society membership. Under the act, immunity from liability is granted for health care entities and providers making peer review reports in good faith (Walzer 1990).

Managed care organizations do not report physicians to the data bank merely because they do not follow treatment protocols. "Deselection without cause" by the managed care organization is not a reportable offense. However, the managed care organization must report the physician when she or he is deselected for a quality of care issue. The physician is permitted by law to appeal ("National Practitioners Data Bank and MCOs" 1999).

Hospitals are required to request information from the data bank concerning all physicians who apply for staff privileges. Every 2 years, a query of the data bank will be required concerning each physician or other practitioner on the hospital staff. Hospitals that do not comply face loss of immunity for professional peer review activities.

## Personal Injury Litigation

This final case example illustrates the double agent role assumed by a therapist who becomes an expert witness for his or her patient:

### Case Example 9

Ms. I, a 53-year-old woman, has been treated by insight psychotherapy for moderate anxiety and depression for 3 years. She experiences a moderate concussion when her car is struck from behind by a truck while waiting at a traffic light. Severe symptoms of a postconcussion syndrome persist for 10 months after the accident. The treating psychiatrist agrees to act as Ms. I's expert witness. At the trial, he is closely questioned about psychiatric problems that preexisted the accident. Highly personal, embarrassing details about Ms. I's life are brought out by opposing counsel on cross-examination of the psychiatrist. The jury awards the patient nominal monetary damages. The patient does not return to therapy.

## Head Injuries

Traumatic head injury is an enormous medical, social, and economic problem. The annual incidence of traumatic brain injury is estimated at 200 per 100,000 population (Kraus and Sorenson 1994). It is reported that 1,975,000 head injuries occur per year (Collins 1990).

Patients with compromised brain function may manifest difficulties in judgment, mood regulation, memory, orientation, insight, impulse control, and the maintenance of a clear sensorium. In addition, they are likely to have a plethora of psychiatric symptoms. The claimant's organic and psychiatric injuries are likely to produce large economic losses as a result of permanent unemployability. In combination with current and future medical expenses, it is easy to see that compensable damages from head trauma can be substantial.

Expert testimony will be required to establish in court the nature and extent of any psychiatric and neurologic problems as well as to determine their relation to the event causing the head trauma. One of the most important experts in this type of litigation is the psychiatrist.

## Psychiatric Expert

The ensuing civil litigation in head injury cases generally requires the evaluation and testimony of psychiatrists as well as neurologists, neuropsychologists, and other mental health professionals. These professionals can become involved in litigation as witnesses in two ways: as *treaters* or as *expert witnesses.*

Psychiatrists who venture into the legal arena must be aware of the fundamentally different roles that exist between a treating psychiatrist and the forensic psychiatric expert. For the treating psychiatrist, treatment and expert roles do not mix. Unlike the orthopedist, who has objective, concrete information such as the X ray of a broken limb to show orthopedic damages in court, the treating psychiatrist must rely heavily on the subjective reporting of the patient. In a clinical context, psychiatrists are interested primarily in the patient's perception of difficulties (narrative truth), not necessarily objective reality (historical truth) (Simon 1996). As a consequence, many psychiatrists do not speak to third parties or other sources in order to gain information about a patient or to corroborate the patient's statements. The law, however, is only interested in what can reasonably be established as fact. Uncorroborated, subjective patient data are frequently attacked in court as being speculative, self-serving, and unreliable. The treating psychiatrist usually is not well equipped to counter these charges.

Credibility issues also abound. The treating psychiatrist is, and should be, a total ally of the patient. This patient bias is a proper treatment stance that fosters a working therapeutic alliance. Furthermore, the patient must be "liked" by the psychiatrist. No psychiatrist can effectively treat a patient for very long if he or she dislikes the patient. Moreover, the psychiatrist's attention is directed toward the diagnosis and treatment of mental disorders. This again is an appropriate focus for the treating psychiatrist.

In court, credibility is a critical asset to possess when testifying. Opposing counsel will take every opportunity to portray the treating psychiatrist as a subjective mouthpiece for the plaintiff—which may or may not be true. Also, as case example 9 illustrates, court testimony by the treating psychiatrist may compel the disclosure of information that may not be *legally* privileged but that nonetheless is perceived as private and confidential by the patient. This disclosure by the formerly trusted therapist is bound to cause serious harm to the therapeutic relationship (Strasburger 1987). In addition, psychiatrists must be careful to inform patients about the consequences of releasing treatment information, particularly in legal matters. Section 4, Annotation 2 of the *Principles of Medical Ethics With Annotations Especially Applicable to Psychiatry* (American Psychiatric Association 1998, p. 6) states the following:

> The continuing duty of the psychiatrist to protect the patient includes fully apprising him/her of the connotations of waiving the privilege of privacy. This may become an issue when the patient is being investigated by a government agency, is applying for a position, or is involved in legal action.

Finally, when the treating psychiatrist testifies concerning the need for further treatment, an economic conflict of interest is readily apparent. In making such treatment prognostications, the therapist stands to benefit monetarily from further treatment. Although this may not be the intention of the psychiatrist whatsoever, opposing counsel is sure to point out that the psychiatrist has a financial interest in the case.

Although opposing counsel may attempt to depict the forensic expert as a "hired gun," she or he is free of the treater's conflicting roles. No doctor-patient relationship is created during forensic evaluation with its treatment biases toward the patient. The expert can review a variety of records and speak to numerous people who know the litigant. Furthermore, the forensic expert is not as easily distracted from considering exaggeration or malingering because of a clear appreciation of the litigation context and the absence of treatment bias. Finally, the forensic psychiatrist is not placed in a conflict of interest position of recommending additional treatment from which the treating psychiatrist would appear to personally benefit.

The treating psychiatrist should attempt to remain solely in a treatment role (Strasburger et al. 1997). If it becomes necessary to testify on behalf of the patient, the psychiatrist should testify as a fact witness rather than as an expert witness. As a fact witness, the psychiatrist will be asked to describe the number and length of visits, diagnosis, and treatment. No opinion evidence will be requested about causation of the injury or extent of damages. Nonetheless, in some jurisdictions, the court may convert a fact witness into an expert witness at the time of trial.

In litigation, both the treating psychiatrist and the expert psychiatric witness for the patient will need to coordinate their efforts with other medical and nonmedical professionals. After appropriate authorizations have been secured, obtaining additional information from others who also are assisting the patient enhances the credibility of testimony. Psychiatrists must remain ever mindful of the many double agent roles that can develop when mixing psychiatry and litigation (Simon 1987).

## Conclusions

The psychiatrist today must remain informed about the legal regulation of psychiatric practice. Without a working knowledge of the law, the psychiatrist's ability to provide good clinical care will be significantly impaired by fear and uncertainty. Psychiatrists who are forensically knowledgeable are in a much better position to practice relatively unencumbered within the requirements of the law, while also minimizing the potential adverse clinical effects of burgeoning legal regulation on patient care.

## References

Alexander GJ, Scheflin AW: Law and Mental Disorder. Durham, NC, Carolina Academic Press, 1998

American Medical Association, Council on Ethical and Judicial Affairs: Guidelines for the appropriate use of do-not-resuscitate orders. JAMA 265:1868–1871, 1991

American Medical Association: Physician-Assisted Suicide. Code of Medical Ethics Reports, Vol V, No 2. Chicago, IL, American Medical Association, July 1994, pp 269–275

American Psychiatric Association: The Practice of Electroconvulsive Therapy: Recommendations for Treatment, Training, and Privileging. A Task Force Report of the American Psychiatric Association. Washington, DC, American Psychiatric Association, 1990

American Psychiatric Association: Tardive Dyskinesia: A Task Force Report of the American Psychiatric Association. Washington, DC, American Psychiatric Association, 1992

American Psychiatric Association: The Principles of Medical Ethics With Annotations Especially Applicable to Psychiatry. Section 5. Washington, DC, American Psychiatric Association, 1998

American Psychiatric Association: Diagnostic and Statistical Manual of Mental Disorders, 4th Edition, Text Revision. Washington, DC, American Psychiatric Association, 2000

Annotation, Malpractice in connection with electroshock treatment, 94 ALR 3rd 317 (1979)

Annotation, Physician's liability to third person for prescribing drug to known drug addict, 42 ALR 4th 586 (1985)

Aponte v United States, 582 F Supp 555, 566–69 (D PR 1984)

Appelbaum PS: Seclusion and restraint: Congress reacts to reports of abuse. Psychiatr Serv 50:881–882, 1999

Appelbaum PS, Gutheil TG: Clinical Handbook of Psychiatry and the Law, 3rd Edition. Baltimore, MD, Williams & Wilkins, 2000

Appelbaum PS, Lidz CW, Meisel A: Informed Consent: Legal Theory and Clinical Practice. New York, Oxford University Press, 1987

Bartling v Superior Court, 163 Cal App3d 186, 209 Cal Rptr 220 (1984)

Benesch K: Legal issues in determining competence to make treatment decisions, in Legal Implications of Hospital Policies and Practices. Edited by Miller RD. San Francisco, CA, Jossey-Bass, 1989, pp 97–105

Bethea v United States, 365 A2d 64 (DC 1976), cert denied, 433 U.S. 911 (1977)

Black HC: Black's Law Dictionary, 6th Edition. St. Paul, MN, West Publishing, 1990

Blackstone W: Commentaries, Vol 4, 24–25 (1769)

Blanchard v Levine, No D 014550 Fulton Cty Sup Ct (Ga 1985)

Blinder M: My examination of Dan White. American Journal of Forensic Psychiatry II:12–22, 1981–1982

Blumenthal SJ, Kupfer DJ: Suicide Over the Life Cycle: Risk Factors, Assessment, and Treatment of Suicidal Patients. Washington, DC, American Psychiatric Press, 1990

Blumer D (ed): Psychiatric Aspects of Epilepsy. Washington, DC, American Psychiatric Press, 1984

Bouvia v Superior Court, 179 Cal App3d 1127, 225 Cal Rptr 297 (1986)

Brakel SJ, Parry J, Weiner BA: The Mentally Disabled and the Law, 3rd Edition. Chicago, IL, American Bar Foundation, 1985

Callan v Norland, 114 Ill App3d 196, 448 NE2d 651 (1983)

Chaires v St John's Episcopal Hosp, No 20808/75 NY Cty Sup Ct (NY Feb 21, 1984)

Clifford v United States, No 82-5002 USDC (SD 1985)

Clites v State, 322 NW2d 917 (Iowa Ct App 1982)

Coke E: Third Institute 6 (6th ed 1680)

Collins JG: Types of Injuries by Selected Characteristics: United States, 1985–1987 (Vital and Health Statistics, Series 10: Data From the National Health Survey, No 175) (DHHS Publ No [PHS]91-1503). Hyattsville, MD, U.S. Department of Health and Human Services, 1990

Commonwealth v Robinson, 494 Pa 372, 431 A2d 901 (1981)

Cruzan v Director, Missouri Department of Health, 497 U.S. 261 (1990a)

Cruzan v Director, Missouri Department of Health, 110 S Ct 2841, 2857 n 2 (1990b)

Cruzan v Director, Missouri Department of Health, 110 S Ct 2841, 2857 n 3 (1990c)

Devinsky P, Bear DM: Varieties of aggressive behavior in patients with temporal lobe epilepsy. Am J Psychiatry 141:651–655, 1984

Doerr v Hurley Medical Center, No 82-674-39 NM (Mich Aug 1984)

Dovido v Vasquez, No 84-674 CA(L)(H) 15th Jud Dist Cir Ct, Palm Beach Cty (Fl Apr 4, 1986)

Dusky v United States, 362 U.S. 402 (1960)

Dyer AR: Ethics and Psychiatry: Toward Professional Definition. Washington, DC, American Psychiatric Press, 1988

Faigenbaum v Oakland Medical Center, 143 Mich App 303, 373 NW2d 161 (Mich Ct App 1985, aff'd)

Fain v Commonwealth, 78 Ky 183 (1879)

Folstein MF, Folstein SW, McHugh PR: "Mini-Mental State": a practical method of grading the cognitive state of patients for the clinician. J Psychiatr Res 12:189–198, 1975

Ford v Wainwright, 477 U.S. 399 (1986)

Frasier v Department of Health and Human Resources, 500 So2d 858, 864 (La Ct App 1986)

Gardos G, Cole JO: Overview: public health issues in tardive dyskinesia. Am J Psychiatry 137:776–781, 1980

Glazer WM: Clinical outcomes of pharmacotherapy for schizophrenia and implications for health economics (monograph). J Clin Psychiatry 15(2):30–33, 1997

Gowan v United States, 601 F Supp 1297 (D Or 1985)

Grisso T: Evaluating Competencies: Forensic Assessments and Instruments. New York, Plenum, 1986

Grisso T, Appelbaum PS: Comparison of standards for assessing patients' capacities to make treatment decisions. Am J Psychiatry 152:1033–1037, 1995a

Grisso T, Appelbaum PS: The MacArthur Treatment Competence Study, III: abilities of patients to consent to psychiatric and medical treatments. Law Hum Behav 19:149–174, 1995b

Gulf S I R Co v Sullivan, 155 Miss 1, 119 So 501 (1928)

Gutheil TG, Appelbaum PS: Substituted judgment and the physician's ethical dilemma: with special reference to the problem of the psychiatric patient. J Clin Psychiatry 41:303–305, 1980

Hassenfeld IN, Grumet B: A study of the right to refuse treatment. Bull Am Acad Psychiatry Law 12:65–74, 1984

H.M. Advocate v Fraser, 4 Couper 70 (1878)

Holton v Pfingst, 534 SW2d 786, 789 (Ky 1976)

Howe v Citizens Memorial Hosp, 426 SW2d 882 (Tex Civ App 1968), rev'd, 436 SW2d 115 (Tex 1968)

Hyde v University of Michigan Board of Regents, 426 Mich 223, 393 NW2d 847 (1986)

ILL ANN STAT ch 91 1/2, para 3-501(a) (Smith-Hurd Supp 1990)

In re Conroy, 98 NJ 321, 486 A2d 1209, 1222–23 (1985)

In re Farrell, 108 NJ 335, 529 A2d 404 (1987)

In re Jobes, 108 NJ 365, 529 A2d 434 (1987)

In re Peter, 108 NJ 365, 529 A2d 419 (1987)

In re Quinlin, 70 NJ 10, 355 A2d 647, cert denied, 429 U.S. 922 (1976)

Jaffee v Redmond, U.S. Lexis 3879 (1996)

Jehovah's Witnesses v King County Hospital, 278 F Supp 488 (WD Wash 1967), aff'd, 390 U.S. 598 (1968)

Johnson ID: Reports to the National Practitioner Data Bank. JAMA 265:407–411, 1991

Joint Commission on Accreditation of Healthcare Organizations: 2000 Comprehensive Accreditation Manual for Hospitals: The Official Handbook. Oakbrook Terrace, IL, Joint Commission on Accreditation of Healthcare Organizations, 2000

Kane JM, Weinhold P, Kinon B, et al: Prevalence of abnormal involuntary movements ("spontaneous dyskinesia") in the normal elderly. Psychopharmacology (Berl) 77:105–108, 1982

Karasik v Bird, 98 AD2d 359, 470 NYS2d 605 (1984)

Kaye NS, Reed TJ: Tardive dyskinesia: tremors in law and medicine. J Am Acad Psychiatry Law 27:315–333, 1999

Kilgore v County of Santa Clara, No 397–525 Santa Clara Cty Super Ct (Cal 1982)

Klawans HL, Barr A: Prevalence of spontaneous lingual-facial-buccal dyskinesia in the elderly. Neurology 32:558–559, 1982

Kraus JF, Sorenson SB: Epidemiology, in Neuropsychiatry of Traumatic Brain Injury. Edited by Silver J, Yudofsky S, Hales R. Washington, DC, American Psychiatric Press, 1994, pp 3–42

LaPuma J, Orentlicher D, Moss RJ: Advance directives on admission: clinical implications and analysis of the Patient Self-Determination Act of 1990. JAMA 266:402–405, 1991

Lewis DO, Pincus JH, Feldman M, et al: Psychiatric, neurological, and psychoeducational characteristics of 15 death row inmates in the United States. Am J Psychiatry 143:838–845, 1986

Low P, Jeffries J, Bonnie R: Criminal Law: Cases and Materials. Mineola, NY, Foundation Press, 1982

Luce JM: Ethical principles in critical care. JAMA 263:696–700, 1990

Macbeth JE, Wheeler AM, Sither JW, et al: Legal and Risk Management Issues in the Practice of Psychiatry. Washington, DC, Psychiatrists' Purchasing Group, 1994

Marsh FH, Staver A: Physician authority for unilateral DNR orders. J Leg Med 12:115–165, 1991

McDonald v United States, 312 F2d 847, 851 (DC 1962)

Meek v City of Loveland, 85 Colo 346, 276 P 30 (1929)

Melton GB, Petrilla J, Poythress NG, et al: Psychological Evaluations for the Courts, 2nd Edition. New York, Guilford, 1997

Mental aberration and post conviction sanctions. Suffolk University Law Review 15:1219, 1981

Meyer D, Simon RI: Split treatment: clarity between psychiatrists and psychotherapists, part I. Psychiatric Annals 29:241–245, 1999a

Meyer D, Simon RI: Split treatment: clarity between psychiatrists and psychotherapists, part II. Psychiatric Annals. 29:327–332, 1999b

Miller RD: Criminal responsibility, in Principles and Practice of Forensic Psychiatry. Edited by Rosner R. New York, Chapman & Hall, 1994, pp 198–215

Mishkin B: Decisions in Hospice. Arlington, VA, National Hospice Organization, 1985

Mishkin B: Determining the capacity for making health care decisions. Adv Psychosom Med 19:151–166, 1989

M'Naghten's Case, 10 Cl F 200, 8 Eng Rep 718 (HL 1843)

Monahan J: Mental disorder and violent behavior: perceptions and evidence. Am Psychol 47:511–521, 1992

Moran v Botsford General Hospital, No 81-225-533 Wayne Cty Cir Ct (Mich Oct 1, 1984)

National Practitioners Data Bank and MCOs. Psychiatric Practice and Managed Care, Vol 5, September/October 1999, pp 1, 9–10

Neely v United States, 150 F2d 977 (DC Cir), cert denied, 326 U.S. 768 (1945)

Nelson JC: Blood level monitoring of antidepressant and antipsychotic drugs: how is it useful? Psychiatric Times, October 1992, pp 20–26

Note, The Eighth Amendment and the Execution of the Presently Incompetent. Stanford Law Review 32:765, 1980

O'Connell RA: A review of the use of electroconvulsive therapy. Hospital and Community Psychiatry 33:469–473, 1982

Orentlicher D: The illusion of patient choice in end-of-life decisions. JAMA 267:2101–2104, 1992

Overman W, Stoudemire A: Guidelines for legal and financial counseling of Alzheimer's disease patients and their families. Am J Psychiatry 145:1495–1500, 1988

Parry HJ, Balter MB, Mellinger GD, et al: National patterns of psychotherapeutic drug usage. Arch Gen Psychiatry 28:769–783, 1973

Parry JW, Beck JC: Revisiting the civil commitment/involuntary treatment stalemate using limited guardianship, substituted judgment and different due process considerations: a work in progress. Medical and Physical Disability Law Reporter 14:102–114, 1990

Pate v Robinson, 383 U.S. 375, 378 (1966)

People v White, 117 Cal App3d 270, 172 Cal Rptr 612 (1981)

Perlin ML: Mental Disability Law: Civil and Criminal, Vol I. Charlottesville, VA, Michie, 1989a

Perlin ML: Mental Disability Law: Civil and Criminal, Vol II. Charlottesville, VA, Michie, 1989b

Perlin ML: Mental Disability Law: Civil and Criminal, Vol III. Charlottesville, VA, Michie, 1989c

Perr IN: Liability and electroshock therapy. J Forensic Sci 25:508–513, 1980

Perr IN: The clinical considerations of medication refusal. Legal Aspects of Psychiatric Practice 1:5–8, 1984

Planned Parenthood v Danforth, 428 U.S. 52, 74 (1976)

President's Commission for the Study of Ethical Problems in Medicine and Biomedical and Behavioral Research: Making Health Care Decisions, Vol 1: A Report on the Ethical and Legal Implications of Informed Consent in the Patient-Practitioner Relationship. Washington, DC, Superintendent of Documents, October 1982

Radank v Heyl, No F4-2316 Wisc Comp Bd (1986)

Ramon v Farr, 770 P2d 131 (Utah 1989)

Regan M: Protective services for the elderly: commitment, guardianship, and alternatives. William and Mary Law Review 13:569, 570–573, 1972

Reich J, Wels J: Psychiatric diagnosis and competency to stand trial. Compr Psychiatry 26:421–432, 1985

Reisner R, Slobogin C: Law and the Mental Health System: Civil and Criminal Aspects, 2nd Edition. St. Paul, MN, West Publishing, 1990

Rennie v Klein, 462 F Supp 1131 (DNJ 1978), modified, 653 F2d 836 (3d Cir 1981), vacated, 458 U.S. 1119 (1982), on remand, 720 F2d 266 (3d Cir 1983)

Rosner R (ed): Principles and Practice of Forensic Psychiatry. New York, Chapman, 1994

Rozovsky FA: Consent to Treatment: A Practical Guide. Boston, MA, Little, Brown, 1984, pp 87–122

Rubin RT, King BH: Endocrine and metabolic disorders, in Comprehensive Textbook of Psychiatry/VI, 6th Edition, Vol 2. Edited by Kaplan HI, Saddock BJ. Baltimore, MD, Williams & Wilkins, 1995, pp 1514–1528

Ruchs VR: The "rationing" of medical care. N Engl J Med 311:1572–1573, 1984

Sale B, Powell DM, Van Duizend R: Disabled Persons and the Law: State Legislative Issues 1982

Scaria v St Paul Fire & Marine Ins Co, 68 Wis2d 1, 227 NW2d 647 (1975)

Schloendorff v Society of New York Hospital, 211 NY 125, 126, 105 NE 92, 93 (1914)

Schreiber J, Roesch R, Golding S: An evaluation of procedures for assessing competency to stand trial. Bull Am Acad Psychiatry Law 155:187–203, 1987

Schwartz HR: Do not resuscitate orders: the impact of guidelines on clinical practice, in Geriatric Psychiatry and the Law. Edited by Rosner R, Schwartz HR. New York, Plenum, 1987, pp 91–100

Shaughnessy v Spray, 55 Ore App 42, 637 P2d 182 (1981)

Shuman DW: Psychiatric and Psychological Evidence. Colorado Springs, CO, Shephard's/McGraw-Hill, 1986

Simon RI: The psychiatrist as a fiduciary: avoiding the double agent role. Psychiatric Annals 17:622–626, 1987

Simon RI: Clinical Psychiatry and the Law, 2nd Edition. Washington, DC, American Psychiatric Press, 1992a

Simon RI: Clinical risk management of suicidal patients: assessing the unpredictable, in American Psychiatric Press Review of Clinical Psychiatry and the Law, Vol 3. Edited by Simon RI. Washington, DC, American Psychiatric Press, 1992b, pp 3–63

Simon RI: Concise Guide to Psychiatry and Law for Clinicians. Washington, DC, American Psychiatric Press, 1992c

Simon RI: The evaluation of criminal responsibility: a psychobiological approach. Psychiatric Annals 22:544–546, 1992d

Simon RI: Innovative psychiatric therapies and legal uncertainty: a survival guide for clinicians. Psychiatric Annals 23:473–479, 1993

Simon RI: Toward the development of guidelines in the forensic psychiatric examination of posttraumatic stress disorder claimants, in Posttraumatic Stress Disorder in Litigation: Guidelines for Forensic Assessment. Edited by Simon RI. Washington, DC, American Psychiatric Press, 1995, pp 31–84

Simon RI: Bad Men Do What Good Men Dream: A Forensic Psychiatrist Illuminates the Darker Side of Human Behavior. Washington, DC, American Psychiatric Press, 1996

Simon RI: Discharging sicker, potentially violent psychiatric inpatients in the managed care era: standard of care and risk management. Psychiatric Annals 27:726–733, 1997

Simon RI: Psychiatrists awake! Suicide risk assessments are all about a good night's sleep. Psychiatric Annals 28:479–485, 1998a

Simon RI: Psychiatrists' duties in discharging sicker and potentially violent inpatients in the managed care era. Psychiatr Serv 49:62–67, 1998b

Simon RI, Sadoff RL: Psychiatric Malpractice: Cases and Comments for Clinicians. Washington, DC, American Psychiatric Press, 1992

Slovenko R: Commentaries on psychiatry and law: "guilty but mentally ill." Journal of Psychiatry and Law 10:541–555, 1982

Slovenko R: Assessing competency to stand trial. Psychiatric Annals 26:392–393, 397, 1995a

Slovenko R: Psychiatry and Criminal Culpability. New York, Wiley, 1995b, pp 151–153

Slovenko R: Psychotherapy and Confidentiality. Springfield, MA, Charles C Thomas, 1998

Smith JT: Medical Malpractice: Psychiatric Care. Colorado Springs, CO, Shephard's/McGraw-Hill, 1986, pp 178–179

Solnick PB: Proxy consent for incompetent nonterminally ill adult patients. J Leg Med 6:1–49, 1985

Sparr LF, Boehnlein JK: Posttraumatic stress disorder in tort actions: forensic minefield. Bull Am Acad Psychiatry Law 18:283–302, 1990

Standards for cardiopulmonary resuscitation and emergency cardiac care, part VIII: medicolegal considerations and recommendations. JAMA 255:2979–2984, 1986

State v Hehman, 110 Ariz 459, 520 P2d 507 (1974)

Stone AA: Post-traumatic stress disorder and the law: critical review of the new frontier. Bull Am Acad Psychiatry Law 21:23–36, 1993

Stone v Proctor, 259 NC 633, 131 SE2d 297 (1963)

Strasburger LH: "Crudely, without any finesse": the defendant hears his psychiatric evaluation. Bull Am Acad Psychiatry Law 15:229–233, 1987

Strasburger LH, Gutheil TG, Brodsky A: On wearing two hats: role conflict in serving as both psychotherapist and expert witness. Am J Psychiatry 154:448–456, 1997

Strub RL, Black FW: The Mental Status Examination in Neurology, 2nd Edition. Philadelphia, PA, FA Davis, 1988

Swanson JW, Holzer CE, Ganju UK, et al: Violence and psychiatric disorder in the community: evidence from the Epidemiologic Catchment Area surveys. Hosp Community Psychiatry 41:761–770, 1990

Swartz MS: What constitutes a psychiatric emergency: legal dimensions. Bull Am Acad Psychiatry Law 15:57–68, 1987

Tarasoff v Regents of the University of California, 17 Cal3d 425, 131 Cal Rptr 14, 551 P2d 334 (1976)

Taylor MA, Sierles FS, Abrams R: The neuropsychiatric evaluation, in The American Psychiatric Press Textbook of Neuropsychiatry. Edited by Hales RE, Yudofsky SC. Washington, DC, American Psychiatric Press, 1987, pp 3–16

Tune v Walter Reed Army Medical Hosp, 602 F Supp 1452 (DDC 1985)

Union Pacific Railway Co v Botsford, 141 U.S. 250, 251 (1891)

U.S. Department of Health and Human Services: The Legal Status of Adolescents 1980. Washington, DC, U.S. Department of Health and Human Services, 1981, p 41

United States v Brawner, 471 F2d 969 (DC Cir 1972), superseded by statute, see Shannon v United States, 512 U.S. 573 (1994)

United States v Charters, 863 F2d 302 (4th Cir 1988) (en banc), cert denied, Charters v United States, 110 S Ct 1317 (1990)

United States v David, 511 F2d 355 (DC Cir 1975)

United States v Shorter, 343 A2d 569 (DC 1975)

Walzer RS: Impaired physicians: an overview and update of legal issues. J Leg Med 11:131–198, 1990

Weiner BA, Wettstein RM: Legal Issues in Mental Health Care. New York, Plenum, 1993

Weiner RD: The psychiatric use of electrically induced seizures. Am J Psychiatry 136:1507–1517, 1979

Weir RF, Gostin L: Decisions to abate life-sustaining treatment for nonautonomous patients: ethical standards and legal liability for physicians after Cruzan. JAMA 264:1846–1853, 1990

Wilson v Lehman, 379 SW2d 478, 479 (Ky 1964)

Wilson v United States, 391 F2d 460, 463 (DC Cir 1968)

Witherell v Weimer, 148 Ill App3d 32, 499 NE2d 46 (1986), rev'd on other grounds, 118 Ill2d 515 NE2d 68 (1987)

Wright v State, No 83-5035 Orleans Parish Civ Dist Ct (La April 1986)

Yudofsky SC, Silver JM, Schneider SE: Pharmacologic treatment of aggression. Psychiatric Annals 17:397, 400, 1987

Yudofsky SC, Silver JM, Hales RE: Treatment of agitation and aggression, in The American Psychiatric Press Textbook of Psychopharmacology, 2nd Edition. Edited by Schatzberg AF, Nemeroff CB. Washington, DC, American Psychiatric Press, 1998, pp 881–900

Zeldow PB, Taub HA: Evaluating psychiatric discharge and aftercare in a VA medical center. Hospital and Community Psychiatry 32:57–58, 1981

Zito JM, Lentz SL, Routt WW, et al: The treatment review panel: a solution to treatment refusal? Bull Am Acad Psychiatry Law 12:349–358, 1984

# CHAPTER 39

# Educational and Certification Issues in Neuropsychiatry

Sheldon Benjamin, M.D.

Linda Mah, M.D.

The reemergence of neuropsychiatry as a clinical field within psychiatry and neurology has raised several educational issues pertaining to the training of both neuropsychiatric specialists and general psychiatrists. Although there are an increasing number of neuropsychiatric textbooks and journals, numerous specialty training programs, and a national professional organization (the American Neuropsychiatric Association) that has enjoyed remarkable growth since its founding in 1988, work toward a nationally recognized accreditation process for neuropsychiatric training and a nationally recognized certification process for neuropsychiatrists has just begun. Coincident with the increased interest in neuropsychiatry have come increased marketplace pressures on general psychiatrists to treat more medically and neurologically complex patients. In the early twentieth century, the term *neuropsychiatry* was used to describe more medically oriented psychiatry as distinguished from psychoanalysis. However, a tradition dating back to Greisinger in the mid-nineteenth century held that the underlying pathophysiology of major mental illness would gradually be discovered as psychiatry evolved the tools to study the brain basis of these conditions. In Stanley Cobb's *Foundations of Neuropsychiatry*, the illustration in Figure 39–1 was included to show that the basic neurosciences would become the foundation for psychiatric therapies as the tools to elucidate their connection were developed (Cobb 1944). In this chapter, we review the current state of neuropsychiatric education of general psychiatrists and neuropsychiatric specialists.

## Neurologic Education of Psychiatrists in the United States

### Accreditation Council on Graduate Medical Education Requirements

Since 1987, the Accreditation Council on Graduate Medical Education (ACGME), the body that accredits medical training programs in the United States, has required that general psychiatry residency training include a minimum of 2 months of neurology experience. From 1939 to 1987, a minimum number of months of neurology training was not specified, but the ACGME required that training be provided in basic neurologic sciences, as outlined in Table 39–1. Through the late 1960s, it was not uncommon for psychiatry trainees to have up to 1 year of neurology training, even though it was not required by the ACGME.

### American Board of Psychiatry and Neurology Examinations

When the first 31 candidates for certification by the American Board of Psychiatry and Neurology (ABPN)

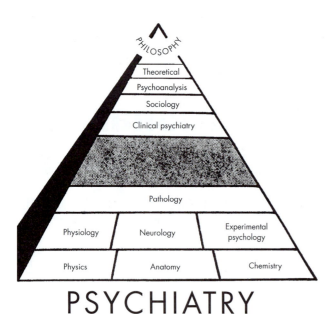

**FIGURE 39–1.** Psychiatry represented as a pyramid with its apex philosophy, its base consisting of the basic sciences, and its center awaiting the research necessary to complete the connection.

*Source.* From Cobb S: *Foundations of Neuropsychiatry*, 3rd Edition. Baltimore, MD, Williams & Wilkins, 1944.

were tested at Philadelphia General Hospital in 1935, psychiatry and neurology candidates took the same examination. The examination consisted of 2 hours of questions on neuroanatomy, neuropathology (including interpretation of gross and microscopic specimens), neuroradiology, psychobiology, and psychopathology, followed by examination of two neurology and two psychiatry patients for 1 hour each. Greater proficiency in either psychiatry or neurology was expected of candidates depending on the field in which they were seeking certification.

In 1946, separate 6-hour examinations were instituted for psychiatrists and neurologists, and the content was changed from 50% in each specialty to 67% in the "major" specialty and 33% in the "minor" specialty. Candidates seeking certification in both fields or additional certification in either specialty after having been certified in the other specialty were required to undergo 2 additional years of training to be eligible for the examination.

The idea of replacing the basic science part of the oral examination with a written examination that included basic neurology for psychiatrists and basic psychiatry for neurologists was piloted in 1966. The following year, the written examination was increased to 3 hours, the oral and written examinations were separated, and passage of the part I written examination became a prerequisite for taking the part II oral examination. In 1972, the part I examination format

was changed to include 1 hour of basic psychiatry and 1 hour of basic neurology for all candidates, followed by 2 hours of questions in the candidate's specialty. With the shift of testing knowledge in the basic sciences to the written examination, the part II examination became entirely clinical in nature. The part II examination was decreased that year to 3 hours for psychiatrists and 4 hours for neurologists (the neurology examination included 1 hour of child neurology), with 1 of the hours devoted to clinical examination in the complementary field for candidates in each specialty. In 1975, the previously shared basic neurology and psychiatry sections of the written examination were replaced by separate examinations for candidates in each field.

The live neurology patient examination for psychiatrists was supplanted in 1977 by a series of videotaped vignettes with multiple-choice questions because of the increasing difficulty in finding sufficient numbers of patients for the examination and the increasing reluctance of neurology examiners to spend more time testing psychiatrists than they did neurologists. Finally, in 1982, the neurology section was eliminated from the part II psychiatry examination, and the psychiatry section was deleted from the part II neurology examination. In the end, it was not philosophical differences but the enormous numbers of psychiatry candidates in the 1970s that finally led to the elimination of the neurologic component of the part II psychiatry examination (Hollender 1991).

## Comparison of Neuropsychiatric Education in the United States With That in Other Countries

Although United States psychiatrists are now required to have a minimum of 2 months of neurology training, this standard is by no means internationally accepted. As can be seen in Table 39–2, a great deal of variation exists as to neurologic requirements of psychiatry trainees, with five European countries requiring a full year of neurology training and with most countries from whom information is available having no neurology requirement.

## Content of Neuropsychiatric Training of General Psychiatrists in the United States

The neurologic education of psychiatric residents in the United States is driven in part by the content of the ABPN part I written examination. The neurology section

**TABLE 39–1.** History of neurology requirements for psychiatry training

| Year | Neurology requirements |
| --- | --- |
| Council on Medical Education and Hospitals 1939 | ACGME: "A program of graduate studies should run concurrently with clinical instruction, covering the fundamentals of neuroanatomy, neuropathology, neurophysiology, psychobiology, and psychopathology" (Council on Medical Education and Hospitals of the American Medical Association 1939).<br>ABPN: Required subjects: neuroanatomy, neuropathology, neurophysiology, clinical neurology, psychobiology, psychopathology, neuroroentgenology, clinical psychiatry. |
| Council on Medical Education and Hospitals 1947 | ABPN: "A basic knowledge of the form, function, and pertinent pathology of the nervous system"; "sufficient training in neurology to recognize and to evaluate the evidences of organic neurological disease" (Council on Medical Education and Hospitals of the American Medical Association 1947). |
| Nunemaker 1960 | ACGME: "Approved training in either specialty must include instruction in the basic and clinical sciences as applied to both specialties and clinical experience in both specialties." "Organized instruction in medical neurology sufficient to gain competence in neurological history-taking, neurological examination, and the differential diagnosis and treatment of the more common affections of the nervous system. This requirement is particularly important because of the natural and frequent blend of the manifest psychiatric processes with the underlying, yet not always immediately obvious, neurological disorders."<br>ABPN: No change (Nunemaker et al. 1960). |
| 1977 | Internship year requirement (eleminated in 1970) reinstituted (Hollender 1991). |
| American Medical Association 1980 | ACGME: "Adequate and systematic instruction in such basic sciences relevant to psychiatry and neurology, and neuroanatomy, neurophysiology, neuropathology, neurochemistry" (American Medical Association 1980).<br>ABPN: Up to 1 year of training in neurology may constitute a portion of the training program in psychiatry. |
| American Medical Association 1987 | ACGME and ABPN: Minimum 2 months of neurology experience (American Medical Association 1987). |

*Note.* ACGME = Accreditation Council on Graduate Medical Education; ABPN = American Board of Psychiatry and Neurology.

of the examination is not oriented as much toward the neurobiology of mental illness (covered in the psychiatry section) as it is toward general neurology questions thought relevant to psychiatric practice. Table 39–3 contains a list of topics covered in this examination.

Another major driving force for psychiatric education is the ACGME Essentials for Training in General Psychiatry. Psychiatry training programs must comply with these requirements to maintain their accreditation. The January 2001 revision lists the following neuropsychiatry-related training requirements for general psychiatry residencies:

- The didactic curriculum should include comprehension of the diagnosis and treatment of neurologic disorders commonly encountered in psychiatric practice, such as neoplasms, dementia, headaches, traumatic brain injury, infectious diseases, movement disorders, multiple sclerosis, Parkinson's disease, seizure disorders, stroke, intractable pain, and other related disorders, and information on the use, reliability, and validity of generally accepted diagnostic techniques, including neurophysiologic and neuropsychologic testing.
- Clinical training should provide sufficient experience in neurologic and mental status examination and indications for and limitations of the more common neuropsychologic tests.

- Adequate clinical experience should be provided in the diagnosis and management of the medical and neurologic disorders encountered in psychiatric practice.
- Training must include 2 months (or equivalent) of supervised clinical experience in the diagnosis and treatment of neurologic disorders or conditions.
- Training must include supervised experience with the more common psychologic test procedures, including neuropsychologic assessment, in a sufficient number of patients to give the resident an understanding of the clinical usefulness of these procedures and of the correlation of psychologic test findings with clinical data.
- The curriculum must include a significant number of interdisciplinary clinical conferences and didactic seminars for residents in which psychiatric faculty members collaborate with neurologists, internists, and colleagues from other medical specialties and mental health disciplines.
- The curriculum must include adequate and systematic instruction in neurobiology.
- Experiences should be provided in integrative case formulation that includes neurobiologic, phenomenologic, psychologic, and sociocultural issues involved in the diagnosis and management of cases presented.
- The resident must be able to record an adequate history and perform mental status, physical, and neurologic examinations.

**TABLE 39–2.** Neurology training requirements of psychiatry residents in various countries

| Country | Total residency (years) | Neurology requirement (months) |
|---|---|---|
| Australia | 6 | 0 |
| Austria | 5 | 12 |
| Belgium | 4 | 12 |
| Canada | 5 | 0 |
| China | 5 | 6 |
| Denmark | 4.5 | 12 |
| Finland | 6 | 0 |
| France | 4 | 0 |
| Germany | 4 | 12 |
| Greece | 5 | 12 |
| Hungary | 4 | 3 |
| Israel | 4 | 6 (or 3 + 3 internal medicine) |
| Italy | 4 | 0 |
| Netherlands | 4.5 | 0 |
| Norway | 5 | 0 |
| Portugal | 4 | 0 |
| Slovenia | 4 | 3 |
| South Africa | 5 | 0 |
| Spain | 4 | 0 |
| Sweden | 4 | 6 |
| Switzerland | 6 | 0 |
| United Kingdom | 4 | 0 (Central Approval Panel Court of Electors 1994) |
| United States | 4 | 2 |

*Source.* Adapted from S. Benjamin, personal communications, 2000; Hohagen and Lindhardt 1997.

The ACGME training essentials are rather broad and vague. A more specific consensus statement on neuropsychiatry training objectives for general psychiatry residents was developed by the American Neuropsychiatric Association Education Committee in the early 1990s (American Neuropsychiatric Association 1994). The preamble states that

> Graduates of psychiatry training programs should be able to conduct a sufficient neuropsychiatric evaluation to enable them to form a hypothesis as to what may be causing their patients' symptoms. They should be able to specify exactly why they are ordering neurodiagnostic tests or neurological consultations and be able to utilize the information gained for treatment planning. Modern psychiatrists must have at least a rudimentary understanding of the major categories of brain dysfunction that produce psychiatric symptoms.

The American Neuropsychiatric Association Training Objectives are reproduced in Table 39–4, modified for

**TABLE 39–3.** Neurology content areas of the ABPN part I written examination

I. **Basic science aspects of neurologic disorders**
    A. Cellular and molecular neurobiology
    B. Neuroanatomy
    C. Neuropathology
    D. Neurophysiology (e.g., neuroimmunology, neuroendocrinology)

II. **Incidence/risk of neurologic disorders**
    A. Neuroepidemiology
    B. Neurogenetics (e.g., mitochondrial, genetic testing)

III. **Diagnostic procedures related to neurologic disorders**
    A. History, neurologic examination, and interpretation
    B. Neurochemistry (e.g., blood, cerebrospinal fluid)
    C. Neuroelectrophysiology (e.g., electroencephalogram, evoked potentials)
    D. Neuroradiology (e.g., computed tomography, magnetic resonance imaging, positron emission tomography)
    E. Neuropsychologic testing (basic sciences aspects)

IV. **Clinical evaluation of neurologic disorders and syndromes**
    A. Infections of the nervous system
    B. Vascular diseases
    C. Disorders of cerebrospinal and brain fluids
    D. Tumors
    E. Traumas
    F. Birth injuries and developmental abnormalities
    G. Genetic diseases of recognized biochemical abnormality
    H. Cerebral degenerations of childhood
    I. Neurocutaneous disorders
    J. Cranial nerve disorders
    K. Peripheral neuropathies
    L. Ataxias
    M. Dementias
    N. Movement disorders
    O. Spinal cord diseases
    P. Neuromuscular junction disorders
    Q. Myopathy
    R. Demyelinating diseases
    S. Autonomic nervous system conditions
    T. Intermittent or paroxysmal disorders
    U. Systemic diseases
    V. Environmental disorders
    W. Other disorders/conditions (e.g., dizziness, pain syndromes)

V. **Management and treatment of neurologic disorders**
    A. Neuropharmacotherapy (indications and side effects)
    B. Neuropharmacologic mechanisms of action and drug interactions
    C. Cognitive, behavioral, and psychosocial/rehabilitative interventions
    D. Genetic counseling
    E. Neurosurgical procedures
    F. Ethical and legal issues or considerations

*Note.* ABPN = American Board of Psychiatry and Neurology.

current practice with suggested references for each area added.

## Opinions of Psychiatry Educators on Neuropsychiatry Education

Of the psychiatry training directors who responded to a national survey (46% of 190 directors responding) by Duffy and Camlin (1995), 40% indicated that specific training in neuropsychiatry was provided in their training programs, with 50% having identified neuropsychiatric faculty. One-third of the respondents' programs offered a clinical rotation in neuropsychiatry, with only 10% making this a required rotation. Regarding specific skills, fewer than half of the respondents believed that the ability to interpret neuroimaging studies, including computed tomography (CT), magnetic resonance imaging (MRI), and single photon emission computed tomography (SPECT), was a required skill of graduating psychiatry residents. Fewer than one-quarter thought that residents should be able to interpret electroencephalograms (EEGs). Most (75%) believed that residents should be able to interpret neuropsychologic testing reports. Nearly half of the respondents indicated that lumber puncture was a necessary skill for graduating psychiatry residents. Of those who thought that any of the aforementioned skills were important, fewer than 25% believed that graduating residents were competent in any of these skills. A core didactic curriculum in neuropsychologic assessment, mental status examination, and neurologic examination was reported to be available in more than 70% of the programs, but training in neuroimaging and EEG interpretation was provided in only 50% and 20%, respectively. Regarding clinical neuropsychiatric competencies, the majority of program directors (more than 50% overall) believed that graduating residents were able to evaluate and treat behavior disorders associated with epilepsy, head injury, multiple sclerosis, mental retardation, cerebrovascular disease, Parkinson's disease, Huntington's disease, and other dementing illnesses.

---

**TABLE 39–4.** Neuropsychiatry training objectives for general psychiatry residents

By completion of residency training, the general psychiatrist should possess the following neuropsychiatric skills:

I. **Neuropsychiatric evaluation, theory, and technique**

  A. *Conducting and recording the neurologic examination* (Benjamin 1997; Kaufman 2001; Kowall and Berman 1999; Munetz and Benjamin 1988; Woods 1999; see also Chapter 5 in this volume).

    1. Be able to perform a complete neurologic examination.

    2. Be able to conduct a partial neurologic assessment by observation in the case of uncooperative patients.

    3. Be able to obtain a thorough neurodevelopmental history.

    4. Be able to recognize subtle neurologic signs, including
- Neurodevelopmental signs ("soft signs")
- Release signs
- Overflow movements
- Asymmetry of involuntary (spontaneous) smile
- Pseudobulbar palsy
- Gait-evoked dystonic posturing

    5. Be able to perform the Abnormal Involuntary Movement Scale examination for assessment of tardive dyskinesia.

    6. Be familiar with the neurologic examination findings in the major hypokinetic and hyperkinetic movement disorders.

    7. Be familiar with the neurologic examination in dementia.

  B. *Conducting and recording the formal mental status examination* (Mueller and Fogel 1996; Trzepacz and Baker 1993; see also Chapter 5 in this volume).

    1. Be familiar with the tests used in detailed formal mental status examination and the reasons for doing each.

    2. Be able to accurately describe a patient's behavior in objective, nonjudgmental language and in neurologically relevant terms.

    3. Be able to apply a flexible approach to mental and cognitive status evaluation to complement the routine basic mental status examination with specific tests linked to diagnostic hypotheses; this requires familiarity with several methods of evaluating attention, memory, language, visuospatial, and higher intellectual functions.

    4. Be able to present the mental status examination results orally and in writing in a concise, organized fashion.

  C. *Use of mental status rating scales* (Blacker 2000)

    1. Be familiar with the administration and interpretation of the most widely used clinical rating scales for depressed mood, psychosis, cognitive function, and general psychopathology.

**TABLE 39–4.** Neuropsychiatry training objectives for general psychiatry residents *(continued)*

D. *Use of neuropsychologic testing* (Kaplan 1990; Keefe 1995; Prigatano and Redner 1993; see also Chapter 7 in this volume)
  1. Be familiar with the common major neuropsychologic tests and the purposes they serve.
  2. Know when and how to appropriately order neuropsychologic testing.
  3. Understand how the IQ is determined.
  4. Understand the significance of a verbal/performance split.
  5. Be able to appreciate
    • Sensitivity/specificity issues
    • Influence of educational and social background on test performance
    • Influence of substance use or medications on test performance
    • Influence of primary psychiatric disorders on test performance
  6. Know how to incorporate the results of neuropsychologic testing into a patient's evaluation and treatment planning.

E. *Use of structural neuroimaging* (Garber et al. 1988; Weinberger 1984; see also Chapter 8 in this volume)
  1. Be able to state what abnormality is suspected when requesting neuroimaging.
  2. Be able to locate the major anatomic landmarks of the brain on computed tomography and magnetic resonance imaging scans.
  3. Know the indications for contrast-enhanced computed tomography and magnetic resonance imaging scanning.
  4. Be able to choose an appropriate imaging technique in a minimally cooperative patient.
  5. Be familiar with indications for magnetic resonance imaging versus computed tomography scanning.
  6. Be able to recognize bleeding, edema, hydrocephalus, signs of atrophy, and major focal lesions.
  7. Be able to recognize common computed tomography and magnetic resonance imaging artifacts.

F. *Use of electroencephalogram, evoked potentials, and brain mapping* (Boutros 1992; Drake 1990; Hughes 1995, 1996; Kaufman 2001; see also Chapter 6 in this volume)
  1. Know when to order an electroencephalogram, what leads or special techniques to specify, how to prepare the patient, and how to use the results in diagnosis and patient follow-up.
  2. Be familiar with the major types of epileptiform abnormalities and the diagnostic implications of negative or positive studies.
  3. Be familiar with the effects of psychoactive agents on the electroencephalogram.
  4. Be familiar with the use of the electroencephalogram in dementia, delirium, and other encephalopathies.
  5. Know the major indications for visual, brain stem auditory, and somatosensory evoked potential testing.
  6. Know generally what long-latency evoked potentials are.
  7. Know generally what information may be gained through spectral analysis and brain mapping techniques.

G. *Interpretation of cerebrospinal fluid findings* (Kaufman 2001)
  1. Know when the examination of cerebrospinal fluid is indicated in the evaluation of psychiatric patients, what constitutes a complete examination, and how the cerebrospinal fluid examination should be followed up.
  2. Be aware of the basic cerebrospinal fluid findings of infection, hemorrhage, and demyelinating disease.

H. *Awareness of functional brain imaging* (Bench et al. 1990; Guze 1991; Holman and Devous 1992; Levin et al. 1995; Silbersweig and Stern 1997; Trzepacz et al. 1992; Van Heertum et al. 1993; see also Chapter 9 in this volume)
  1. Be able to explain generally how positron emission tomography and single photon emission computed tomography images are obtained, what some of the problems with the technology are, and in what conditions functional imaging may be useful.
  2. Be aware of the positron emission tomography and single photon emission computed tomography findings described in Alzheimer's disease, Huntington's disease, and schizophrenia. Be able to describe the potential pathophysiologic information to be gained and the ethical considerations inherent in these procedures.
  3. Be aware of the major types of functional magnetic resonance imaging, including BOLD, diffusion/perfusion, and magnetic resonance spectroscopy, and know generally how they are used in research.

I. *Awareness of neuroanatomic sites of psychiatric significance* (Marino and Cosgrove 1997; Strub and Black 1988; see also Chapter 3 in this volume)
  1. Know the major structures of the limbic system and basal ganglia.
  2. Know the nuclei of origin and target regions of the major neurotransmitter systems.
  3. Know the anatomic sites associated with major neurobehavioral syndromes.
  4. Be aware of the sites of neurosurgical intervention for refractory obsessive-compulsive disorder.

J. *Conducting forensic evaluations*

      1. Be familiar with the principles of determining testamentary capacity, specific competencies, criminal responsibility, and degree of disability in patients with brain dysfunction.

**II. Neuropsychiatric symptoms, syndromes, and therapeutics**

  A. *Neuropsychiatric aspects of psychopharmacologic treatment* (George et al. 1999; Kaufman 2001; Krystal and Coffey 1997; Meador 1998; Munetz and Benjamin 1988)

    1. Be familiar with the following common neurologic side effects of psychoactive drug treatment and be able to develop treatment strategies for them:
- Lithium tremor
- Lithium encephalopathy
- Neuroleptic-induced cognitive impairment
- Drug-induced delirium
- Neuroleptic malignant syndrome
- Suprasensitivity psychosis
- Pseudoparkinsonism
- Rabbit syndrome
- Dystonia
- Akathisia
- Tardive dyskinesia and its variants

    2. Be able to perform the Abnormal Involuntary Movement Scale examination.

    3. Know which medications in general use are commonly associated with mental status abnormalities.

    4. Be familiar with the pharmacologic management of psychiatric conditions in patients with underlying neurologic disorders such as dementia, epilepsy, multiple sclerosis, traumatic brain injury, and Parkinson's disease.

    5. Be familiar with alternative drugs to neuroleptics for aggression/agitation of various types.

    6. Be aware of the psychiatric indications for anticonvulsant treatment and know how to appropriately manage anticonvulsant treatment.

    7. Know the relative indications for and contraindications to electroconvulsive therapy.

    8. Be aware of the theory and uses of regional transcranial magnetic stimulation.

    9. Be familiar with the common and the dangerous interactions among psychoactive agents of different classes.

    10. Be aware of the cognitive side effects of commonly used psychotropic agents.

  B. *Diagnosis of major psychiatric symptoms* (Benjamin 1999; Coker 1991; Davison and Bagley 1969; Frumin et al. 1998; Gualtieri 1991; Kaufman 2001; Krumholz 1999; Massion and Benjamin 1989; Rogers 1991; Ross and Rush 1981; Siegel et al. 1998; Skuster et al. 1992)

    1. Know the most common medical, neurologic, and primary psychiatric etiologies of
- Delirium
- Dementia
- Violent episodes
- Self-injurious behavior
- Catatonia
- Visual hallucinations
- Nonepileptic episodic behaviors
- Mutism
- Personality change due to medical condition
- Mood disorder due to medical condition, manic and depressed types
- Psychotic disorder due to medical condition: with delusions, with hallucinations
- Anxiety disorder due to medical condition
- Atypical psychosis presenting in young adulthood, middle age, and old age
- Major involuntary movement disorders (including tremor, choreoathetoid movements, tics, parkinsonism)
- Compulsive water drinking
- Behaviors in retarded or autistic individuals such as stereotypy, aggression, self-injurious behavior, pica

    2. Recognize the common features of acquired (nonhereditary) subtypes of major psychiatric syndromes

  C. *Diagnosis of delirium* (Lipowski 1992; see also Chapter 14 in this volume)

    1. Be able to recognize delirium.

    2. Be familiar with the mental status findings common in delirium.

**TABLE 39–4.**  Neuropsychiatry training objectives for general psychiatry residents *(continued)*

    3. Be able to apply a methodical approach to the differential diagnosis of delirium.

    4. Know the common toxic and metabolic causes of delirium.

    5. Be familiar with the electroencephalogram changes that are common in delirium.

    6. Be able to suggest appropriate nursing and medication interventions in the management of delirium.

  D. *Diagnosis of dementia* (Cummings 1986; Cummings and Victoroff 1990; McLoughlin and Levy 1996; Neary et al. 1998; see also Chapters 28 and 29 in this volume)

    1. Be able to apply a methodical approach to the differential diagnosis of dementia including relevant diagnostic tests.

    2. Differentiate among the major categories of dementia (e.g., dementia of the Alzheimer's type, vascular).

    3. Recognize the stages of Alzheimer's disease.

    4. Be familiar with the principal neurologic and mental status examination findings in dementia.

    5. Understand the interaction of depression and dementia.

    6. Be familiar with the interaction of delirium and dementia.

    7. Be familiar with the psychiatric and behavioral complications of dementia.

    8. Be familiar with the concept of primarily subcortical dementia.

    9. Be familiar with the differential diagnosis of rapidly progressive dementia.

   10. Be aware of some of the major issues that arise in psychotherapy for patients with early dementia.

   11. Be aware of the resources available in one's own community for patients with Alzheimer's disease and their families.

  E. *Diagnosis of epilepsy* (Alper 1994; Bear 1979; Bear and Fedio 1977; Cascino 1992; Clifford et al. 1985; Devinsky and Pacia 1993; Devinsky and Thacker 1995; Engel 1993; Gross et al. 2000; International League Against Epilepsy 1985; Krumholz 1999; Lambert and Robertson 1999; Morrell 1993; Oliver et al. 1982; Pellock and Willmore 1991; Pisani et al. 1999; Schmitz 1999; Tisher et al. 1993; Torta and Keller 1999; Tucker 1998; Waxman and Geschwind 1975; see also Chapter 19 in this volume)

    1. Be familiar with the international classification of epileptic seizures and be able to describe seizures with those terms.

    2. Be able to perform a reasonable differential diagnosis for possible seizures. Be familiar with the phenomenology of simple and complex partial seizures and of complex partial status epilepticus.

    3. Know which tests to order, how to order them, and how to use the results when epilepsy is suspected.

    4. Know how to manage psychiatric disturbances occurring ictally, postictally, and interictally.

    5. Know how to manage anticonvulsant treatment.

    6. Be familiar with the cognitive effects of anticonvulsants.

    7. Be familiar with the effects of various psychotropic agents on seizure threshold.

    8. Be aware of the use of temporal lobectomy for treatment of individuals with refractory seizures or inability to tolerate medication.

    9. Be familiar with the psychosocial effects of having epilepsy.

   10. Be familiar with the theories about interictal personality characteristics associated with epilepsy.

   11. Be familiar with the kindling hypothesis.

   12. Be familiar with the differentiation of psychogenic from epileptic seizures, and be aware of some techniques for management of psychogenic seizures.

   13. Be familiar with the evaluation and management of seizures in patients taking psychotropic medication.

   14. Be aware of the resources available in one's own community for individuals with epilepsy.

   15. Be aware of some of the common issues encountered in psychotherapy for patients with epilepsy.

  F. *Diagnosis and management of neuropsychiatric sequelae of traumatic brain injury (TBI)* (Benjamin 1999; McAllister 1992; see also Chapter 18 in this volume)

    1. Be aware of the association between substance abuse and TBI.

    2. Be able to gather the appropriate historical data to help formulate the organic component in the diagnosis of patients with major psychiatric disorders and a history of TBI.

    3. Know the salient points to elicit in taking the history of a TBI that would help establish the severity and behavioral prognosis.

    4. Know the signs and symptoms of postconcussional syndrome.

    5. Know how to appropriately advise a patient who has had a mild brain injury or concussion to minimize chances of avoidable problems on the job, with family, and in interpersonal relationships.

    6. Be able to identify and manage the following common sequelae of TBI:

      • Diminished attention

      • Mood disorder due to medical condition

**TABLE 39–4.** Neuropsychiatry training objectives for general psychiatry residents *(continued)*

- • Psychotic disorder due to medical condition, with delusions
- • Personality change due to medical condition, including frontal syndromes, interictal behavior syndromes
- • Aggressive behavior
- • Alterations of sleep, appetite, sexual behavior
7. Be able to evaluate for the presence of posttraumatic seizures.
8. Be able to help supervise the rehabilitation of patients with neuropsychiatric sequelae of TBI if specialized head injury rehabilitation facilities are not available. Be able to work with occupational therapists, speech pathologists, neuropsychologists, and neurologists in the rehabilitation of head injury patients when such services are available. Be able to use results of neurodiagnostic and neuropsychologic testing in planning for the rehabilitation of and assessing the progress of patients with TBI.
9. Be familiar with some of the major issues that arise in psychotherapy for patients recovering from TBI.
10. Be aware of the resources available in one's own community for patients with TBI and their families.

G. *Diagnosis and management of neuropsychiatric sequelae of stroke* (Graff-Radford and Biller 1992; Kaufman 2001; Robinson 1997; Robinson et al. 1984; Ross and Rush 1981; see also Chapter 21 in this volume)
1. Be aware of the major stroke syndromes and the focal neuropsychiatric syndromes with which they are typically associated.
2. Be able to approximate lesion localization, formulate a basic differential diagnosis as to stroke etiology, and estimate severity of deficit and urgency of further evaluation.
3. Be able to diagnose and treat mood disorders as well as adjustment disorders in patients with stroke.
4. Be aware of the neuropsychiatric causes for failure to progress in stroke rehabilitation.
5. Know how to diagnose and treat pseudobulbar palsy.
6. Know how to explain neuropsychiatric deficits to a patient's family or caregiving facility to prevent predictable behavior problems.

H. *Diagnosis of basal ganglia/movement disorders* (Akil and Brewer 1995; Caine and Shoulson 1983; Kaufman 2001; Leckman et al. 1997; Marsh 2000; Oder et al. 1991; Rosenblatt and Leroi 2000)
1. Be familiar with the association between movement disorders and psychiatric or cognitive deficits.
2. Be able to conduct appropriate evaluations for Parkinson's disease, Huntington's disease, Wilson's disease, and Gilles de la Tourette syndrome.
3. Be familiar with the differential diagnosis and treatment of catatonia.
4. Be able to diagnose and treat the psychiatric disorders commonly associated with basal ganglia disorders.
5. Be familiar with the concept of primarily subcortical dementia.
6. Be aware of the association among tic disorders and obsessive-compulsive disorder and know how to elicit an appropriate history that takes this association into account.
7. Be familiar with the standard treatment approaches for Gilles de la Tourette syndrome.
8. Be aware of the resources available in one's own community for patients with Parkinson's disease, Huntington's disease, and Gilles de la Tourette syndrome.

I. *Diagnosis of major focal neurobehavioral syndromes* (Alexander 1997; DeRenzi 1997; Farah and Feinberg 1997; Lilly et al. 1983)
1. Be aware of the following major focal neurobehavioral syndromes and their differential diagnosis:
- • Broca's aphasia
- • Wernicke's aphasia
- • Right-hemisphere syndromes
- • Prosopagnosia
- • Visual agnosia
- • Klüver-Bucy syndrome
- • Frontal syndromes (with predominantly orbitofrontal, dorsolateral, or medial frontal characteristics)
- • Korsakoff's psychosis

J. *Diagnosis of autoimmune and demyelinating disease* (Beatty 1993; Brown et al. 1999; Calabrese and Stern 1995; Kaufman 2001; White 1990)
1. Know the salient features in the history and neurologic examination consistent with multiple sclerosis and systemic lupus erythematosus (SLE).
2. Know how to establish the diagnosis of multiple sclerosis and SLE.

**TABLE 39–4.** Neuropsychiatry training objectives for general psychiatry residents *(continued)*

  3. Be familiar with the psychiatric complications of multiple sclerosis and SLE, including mood disturbances, personality change due to neurologic condition, dementia, and pseudobulbar palsy.
  4. Be familiar with the psychiatric complications of steroid therapy.

K. *Diagnosis and management of attention-deficit/hyperactivity disorder and learning disabilities* (Price et al. 1990; Weintraub and Mesulam 1983; see also Chapter 32 in this volume)
  1. Know how to elicit a history of learning disorder.
  2. Be familiar with the syndrome of dyslexia.
  3. Be aware of the concept of focal learning disorders.
  4. Be able to diagnose attention-deficit disorders in children and adults.
  5. Be aware of the differential diagnosis of disorders of attention.
  6. Be aware of the Axis I and Axis II disorders frequently associated with disorders of attention.
  7. Be able to appropriately select patients for treatment with psychostimulants or alternative medication approaches.
  8. Know how to manage patients taking psychostimulant medications.

L. *Diagnosis and management of sleep disorders* (Culebras 1992; Obermeyer and Benca 1996; Reite 1998; see also Chapter 20 in this volume)
  1. Be familiar with the *Diagnostic and Statistical Manual of Mental Disorders*, Fourth Edition, Text Revision (DSM-IV-TR; American Psychiatric Association 2000) classification of sleep disorders.
  2. Be familiar with the following common sleep disorders:
     - Narcolepsy
     - Sleep apnea
     - Psychophysiologic insomnia
     - Parasomnias
     - Circadian rhythm sleep disorder
     - Restless legs syndrome
  3. Be aware of the existence of rapid eye movement sleep behavior disorder.
  4. Know how to take a sleep history.
  5. Know when and how to order polysomnography and multiple sleep latency testing and how to use the results in treatment planning.
  6. Be familiar with the sleep disorders associated with major psychiatric disorders, with use of major categories of psychoactive drugs, and with substance abuse.
  7. Be able to instruct patients in proper sleep hygiene.
  8. Be able to prescribe treatment for common sleep disorders and know when to refer patients to sleep disorder specialists.

M. *Diagnosis and management of behavior disorders in mental retardation, autism, and other developmental disabilities* (Benjamin 1999; Gualtieri 1991; Nordin and Gillberg 1998)
  1. Be familiar with the diagnosis and natural history of autism and the major mental retardation syndromes (Down syndrome, fragile X syndrome).
  2. Be familiar with the common behavior disorders that occur in developmentally disabled individuals.
  3. Be familiar with the basic principles of behavior therapy as they apply to the management of behavior disorders in developmentally disabled individuals.
  4. Be able to evaluate for and treat major psychiatric syndromes that occur in developmentally disabled patients.
  5. Be aware of the psychopharmacologic strategies that have been used for behavior disorders in developmentally disabled individuals.
  6. Be able to work with staff of group homes or institutions to gather appropriate behavioral data to facilitate treatment of behavior disorders.

N. *Differential diagnosis of new-onset psychosis* (Kaufman 2001)
  1. Develop a methodical approach to the evaluation and differential diagnosis of first psychotic breaks in adolescents, young adults, and middle-aged and elderly individuals.
  2. Be familiar with the more common neurodegenerative disorders that may present with psychiatric disturbances (e.g., metachromatic leukodystrophy, Wilson's disease, Huntington's disease)

O. *Diagnosis and management of mood disorder due to medical condition* (Hutto 1998; Massion and Benjamin 1989)
  1. Know the major toxic, metabolic, and neurologic etiologies of mood syndromes due to medical or neurologic condition of the depressed and manic types.

**TABLE 39–4.** Neuropsychiatry training objectives for general psychiatry residents *(continued)*

      2. Be able to conduct a diagnostic evaluation for depression or manic behavior in the face of cognitive deficits or neurologic impairment of affective expression.

      3. Be able to select appropriate drug treatments for depression or mania that take into account a patient's cognitive deficits and differential sensitivities to drug side effects.

P. *Diagnosis of amnestic syndromes* (see also Chapter 17 in this volume)

      1. Be familiar with the diagnosis and course of Korsakoff's syndrome, and be aware of the anatomic lesions associated with it.

      2. Be aware of other possible etiologies of amnestic syndromes.

Q. *Diagnosis of substance-related syndromes* (Parsons and Nixon 1993; Rubino 1992; Yudofsky and Hales 2002; see also Chapter 27 in this volume)

      1. Be familiar with the neuropsychiatric sequelae of chronic alcohol abuse and chronic cocaine abuse.

      2. Be aware of the presentation of the other major categories of substance abuse disorders.

      3. Be able to diagnose and manage acute intoxication with or withdrawal from the major categories of abused substances.

R. *Diagnosis of conversion disorder* (Boffeli and Guze 1992; Silver 1996)

      1. Be familiar with features commonly elicited in the history of a patient with conversion disorder.

      2. Be aware of some of the diagnostic maneuvers used in the diagnosis of conversion.

      3. Be aware of some of the techniques used in the treatment of conversion disorders.

S. *Diagnosis and management of headache* (Marks and Rapoport 1997; Newman and Lipton 1998; Saper 1999; see also Chapter 12 in this volume)

      1. Be familiar with the common types of headache.

      2. Be able to recognize the danger signs in acute headache.

      3. Be able to manage common headache types that occur in psychiatric patients.

      4. Know when to refer patients for further neurologic evaluation.

T. *Diagnosis and management of chronic pain syndromes* (Fishbain 1999; Galer 1995; McQuay 1999; Rowbotham 1995; see also Chapter 11 in this volume)

      1. Be familiar with the salient features to elicit in obtaining the history from a patient with a chronic pain syndrome.

      2. Be able to recognize common patterns of neuropathic pain (e.g., causalgia).

      3. Be aware of the interactions between pain syndromes and psychiatric syndromes such as affective disorders, anxiety disorders, somatization disorder, or personality disorders.

      4. Be familiar with the commonly used analgesics and know how to use adjunctive medications or alternative medications in the management of pain.

      5. Know how and when to refer to other specialists such as neurologists, anesthesiologists, physiatrists, orthopedists, and behavioral psychologists.

U. *Diagnosis of neuropsychiatric manifestations of human immunodeficiency virus (HIV) and other central nervous system infections* (Atkinson and Grant 1994; Lishman 1998; Roos 1992; Zegans et al. 1994; see also Chapter 23 in this volume)

      1. Be familiar with the neuropsychiatric manifestations of HIV, neurosyphilis, and herpes encephalitis.

      2. Be familiar with the differential diagnosis of depression in patients with HIV infection.

      3. Be aware of the resources available in one's own community for individuals with acquired immunodeficiency syndrome (AIDS).

      4. Be aware of some of the major issues that may arise in psychotherapy for patients with AIDS.

V. *Diagnosis of occupational exposure-related syndromes* (see also Chapter 26 in this volume)

      1. Be aware of some of the major industrial toxins that are associated with neuropsychiatric syndromes, with special attention to those encountered in one's own community.

      2. Know how to take a relevant exposure history.

*Source.* American Neuropsychiatric Association Education Committee: Benjamin S, Duffy J, Fogel B, Faber R, Greene R, Streeter C; modified and referenced by Benjamin S and Mah L.

Yager (1994) surveyed core psychiatry and neurology faculty in the University of California–Los Angeles Psychiatry Program to determine what level of competency in 23 neuropsychiatric conditions should be expected from general psychiatrists compared with specialists in geriatric psychiatry, consultation-liaison psychiatry, and neuropsychiatry. Suggested competencies were rated as ability to screen, monitor, diagnose definitively, and treat definitively or have the expertise to interpret relevant neurodiagnostic tests. Twenty-five general psychiatrists, 15 psychiatric subspecialists, and 7 neurologists, or about 70% of those surveyed, responded. General psychiatrists and psychiatric subspecialists tended to agree on the expected competencies for general psychiatrists. Neurologists tended to expect a higher degree of neuropsychiatric competence in general psychiatrists than did psychiatrists. The modal response for general psychiatrist competencies in most of the neuropsychiatric syndromes was the ability to monitor the conditions, with somewhat higher expectations of psychiatric subspecialists. Expectations were higher for competency in neuropsychiatric syndromes more commonly seen by psychiatrists, such as tardive dyskinesia, neuroleptic side effects, Alzheimer's disease, and mood disorders in brain-damaged individuals.

A decade earlier, a survey of neurologic competencies in practicing psychiatrists was conducted in South Africa (Gledhill 1983). Of the 65% who responded, the majority (two-thirds or greater) believed that graduating psychiatry residents should be able to elicit a neurologic history; perform a neurologic examination; interpret abnormal physical signs; evaluate cortical functions, including apraxia, agnosia, aphasia, and memory deficits; and differentiate physical disability from simulation. Most believed that graduating psychiatrists should be able to evaluate and manage loss of consciousness, headache and other pain syndromes, dizziness and vertigo, and involuntary movements. Most psychiatrists thought that graduates should have specific knowledge in disorders involving the central nervous system, including trauma, epilepsy, dementia, cerebrovascular disorders, parkinsonism, multiple sclerosis, infections, metabolic encephalopathies, and sleep disorders. Approximately one-third overall thought that residents should be able to recognize presentations of various neuromuscular disorders. Regarding specific competencies, more than 50% believed that graduating psychiatrists should be able to interpret skull X rays and recognize features of a normal EEG. Three-quarters believed that psychiatry residents should know the indications for and contraindications to lumbar puncture, whereas fewer than one-third of the respondents believed that graduates should be able to recognize features of a normal CT scan. Although half of the respondents reported that the following skills were desirable, most did not agree that psychiatry residents should be required to know the indications for ordering electromyography, caloric responses, and visual and auditory evoked potentials.

## Neuropsychiatry Textbooks and Journals

The last 10 years have seen a tremendous increase in the number of textbooks and journals available in the closely allied fields of neuropsychiatry and behavioral neurology. When *The American Psychiatric Press Textbook of Neuropsychiatry* first appeared, there were fewer than 25 texts in the field. Now, more than 70 are available. Neuropsychiatry and behavioral neurology textbooks and journals are listed in Tables 39–5 and 39–6, respectively.

## Educational Techniques in Neuropsychiatry

Hospitals with combined programs or neuropsychiatry fellowships in which faculty are ABPN-certified in neurology sometimes offer clinical neuropsychiatry rotations that may be used to fulfill one or both of the required months of neurology training. Most psychiatry training programs in the United States are based at institutions that do not offer advanced training in neuropsychiatry and that may not have neuropsychiatrists on faculty. To ensure that neuropsychiatric aspects of general psychiatry training are not overlooked, neurologists and neuropsychologists should be included in the psychiatry faculty and invited both to participate in didactic seminars and to serve as the attending at case conferences. General psychiatry faculty should be encouraged to model a neuropsychiatric formulation in the assessment of all patients discussed in case conferences. Residents should be encouraged to review all neurodiagnostic tests done on their patients with a faculty member or with the consultant interpreting the test.

A didactic curriculum can be structured in many ways to meet the neuropsychiatric objectives for general psychiatry training. A list of learning objectives for medical students on neurology clerkships promulgated by the Education Committee of the American Academy of Neurology can be adapted for use by psychiatry trainees (Scherokman et al. 1994). At Dartmouth University, the psychiatry curriculum includes in-depth neuroanatomy teaching based on 13 brain cutting sessions (Green et al. 1999). The University of Massachusetts Psychiatry Program uses the following curriculum:

- Postgraduate Year I: Three 4-week blocks of neurology, including one block of adult neurology wards (pediatric neurology substituted for trainees entering child psychiatry), one block of adult neurology consultation, and one block of neuropsychiatry. The neuropsychiatry rotation includes neurology consultation clinics in general and state hospital psychiatric units; an outpatient neuropsychiatry consultation clinic; a neurodevelopmental disabilities clinic; neuroradiology,

**TABLE 39–5.** Neuropsychiatry textbooks

Benson DF: *Aphasia, Alexia, and Agraphia.* New York, Churchill Livingstone, 1979

Benson DF: *The Neurology of Thinking.* New York, Oxford University Press, 1994

Benson DF, Blumer D: *Psychiatric Aspects of Neurologic Disease.* New York, Grune & Stratton, 1975

Benson DF, Blumer D: *Psychiatric Aspects of Neurologic Disease,* Vol II. New York, Grune & Stratton, 1982

Berman J: *Study Guide to the American Psychiatric Press Textbook of Neuropsychiatry.* Washington, DC, American Psychiatric Press, 1997

Bogousslavsky J, Cummings JL: *Behavior and Mood Disorders in Focal Brain Lesions.* New York, Cambridge University Press, 2000

Coffey CE, Brumback RA: *Textbook of Pediatric Neuropsychiatry.* Washington, DC, American Psychiatric Press, 1998

Coffey CE, Cummings JL: *Textbook of Geriatric Neuropsychiatry,* 2nd Edition. Washington, DC, American Psychiatric Press, 2000

Cummings JL: *Clinical Neuropsychiatry.* New York, Grune & Stratton, 1985

Cummings JL: *Subcortical Dementia.* New York, Oxford University Press, 1990

Cummings JL, Benson DF: *Dementia: A Clinical Approach,* 2nd Edition. Boston, MA, Butterworth-Heinemann, 1992

Cummings JL, Trimble MR: *Concise Guide to Neuropsychiatry and Behavioral Neurology.* Washington, DC, American Psychiatric Press, 1995

Cutting J: *The Right Cerebral Hemisphere and Psychiatric Disorders.* New York, Oxford University Press, 1990

Devinsky O: *Behavioral Neurology: 100 Maxims.* St. Louis, MO, Mosby Year Book, 1992

Devinsky O, Theodore WH: *Epilepsy and Behavior.* New York, Wiley-Liss, 1991

Doane BK, Livingston KF: *The Limbic System: Functional Organization and Clinical Disorders.* New York, Raven, 1986

Feinberg TE, Farah MJ: *Behavioral Neurology and Neuropsychology.* New York, McGraw-Hill, 1997

Feinstein A: *Neuropsychiatry of Multiple Sclerosis.* Cambridge, MA, Cambridge University Press, 1999

Fogel BS, Schiffer RB, Rao SM: *Neuropsychiatry.* Baltimore, MD, Williams & Wilkins, 1996

Fogel BS, Schiffer RB, Rao SM: *Synopsis of Neuropsychiatry.* Philadelphia, PA, Lippincott Williams & Wilkins, 2000

Gainotti G, Caltagirone C: *Emotions and the Dual Brain.* New York, Springer-Verlag, 1989

Giannini AJ, Gilliland RL: *The Neurologic, Neurogenic and Neuropsychiatric Disorders Handbook.* Garden City, NY, Medical Examination Publishing, 1982

Gillberg C: *Clinical Child Neuropsychiatry.* Cambridge, MA, Cambridge University Press, 1995

Gualtieri CT: *Neuropsychiatry and Behavioral Pharmacology.* New York, Springer-Verlag, 1991

Harris JC: *Developmental Neuropsychiatry.* New York, Oxford University Press, 1995

Heilman KM, Satz P: *Neuropsychology of Human Emotion.* New York, Guilford, 1983

Heilman KM, Valenstein E: *Clinical Neuropsychology,* 3rd Edition. New York, Oxford University Press, 1993

Hier DB, Gorelick PB, Shindler AG: *Topics in Behavioral Neurology and Neuropsychology.* Boston, MA, Butterworths, 1987

Huber SJ, Cummings JL: *Parkinson's Disease: Neurobehavioral Aspects.* New York, Oxford University Press, 1992

Jeste DV, Wyatt RJ: *Neuropsychiatric Movement Disorders.* Washington, DC, American Psychiatric Press, 1984

Jobe T, Gaviria M, Kovilparambil A: *Clinical Neuropsychiatry.* Malden, MA, Blackwell Scientific, 1997

Joseph AB, Young RR: *Movement Disorders in Neurology and Neuropsychiatry,* 2nd Edition. Boston, MA, Blackwell Scientific, 1999

Joseph R: *Clinical Neuroscience, Neuropsychology, and Neuropsychiatry: Development, Sexuality, Emotion, Evolution, Language, Cognition, Memory, and Abnormal Behavior,* 3rd Edition. San Diego, CA, Academic Press, 2000

Kalivas PW, Barns CD: *Limbic Motor Circuits and Neuropsychiatry.* Boca Raton, FL, CRC Press, 1993

Kirshner HS: *Behavioral Neurology: A Practical Approach.* New York, Churchill Livingstone, 1986

Lauterbach EC: *Psychiatric Management in Neurological Disease.* Washington, DC, American Psychiatric Press, 2000

Lautin A: *The Limbic Brain.* New York, Plenum, 2000

Lishman WA: *Organic Psychiatry: The Psychological Consequences of Cerebral Disorder,* 3rd Edition. London, England, Blackwell Scientific, 1998

Lohr JB, Wisniewski AA: *Movements Disorders: A Neuropsychiatric Approach.* New York, Guilford, 1987

Merikangas JR: *Brain-Behavior Relationships.* Lexington, MA, Lexington Books, 1981

Mesulam M-M: *Principles of Behavioral and Cognitive Neurology,* 2nd Edition. New York, Oxford University Press, 2000

Miller BL, Cummings JL: *The Human Frontal Lobes: Functions and Disorders.* New York, Guilford, 1999

Mueller J, Yingling CD, Zegans LS: *Neurology and Psychiatry: A Meeting of Minds.* New York, Karger, 1989

**TABLE 39–5.** Neuropsychiatry textbooks *(continued)*

Myslobodsky MS: *Hemisyndromes: Psychobiology, Neurology, and Psychiatry.* New York, Academic Press, 1983

Njiokiktjien C: *Pediatric Behavioural Neurology: Clinical Principles.* Amsterdam, The Netherlands, Suyi Publicaties, 1988

Ovsiew F: *Neuropsychiatry and Mental Health Services.* Washington, DC, American Psychiatric Press, 1999

Pincus HA, Pardes H: *The Integration of Neuroscience and Psychiatry.* Washington, DC, American Psychiatric Press, 1985

Pincus JH, Tucker GJ: *Behavioral Neurology,* 3rd Edition. New York, Oxford University Press, 1985

Rao SM: *Neurobehavioral Aspects of Multiple Sclerosis.* New York, Oxford University Press, 1990

Ratey JJ: *Neuropsychiatry of Personality Disorders.* Cambridge, MA, Blackwell Scientific, 1995

Reynolds EH, Trimble MR: *The Bridge Between Neurology and Psychiatry.* New York, Churchill Livingstone, 1989

Roberts GW, Leigh PN, Weinberger DR: *Neuropsychiatric Disorders.* St. Louis, MO, Mosby Europe Limited, 1993

Roberts JKA: *Differential Diagnosis in Neuropsychiatry.* New York, Wiley, 1984

Rogers D: *Motor Disorder in Psychiatry: Towards a Neurological Psychiatry.* New York, Wiley, 1992

Ron MA, David AS: *Disorders of Brain and Mind.* Cambridge, MA, Cambridge University Press, 1999

Rutter M: *Developmental Neuropsychiatry.* New York, Guilford, 1983

Salloway S, Malloy P, Cummings JL: *The Neuropsychiatry of Limbic and Subcortical Disorders.* Washington, DC, American Psychiatric Press, 1998

Satz P, Heilman KM: *Neuropsychology of Human Emotion.* New York, Guilford, 1983

Schachter SC, Devinsky O: *Behavioral Neurology and the Legacy of Norman Geschwind.* Philadelphia, PA, Lippincott-Raven, 1997

Silver JM, Yudofsky SC, Hales RE: *Neuropsychiatry of Traumatic Brain Injury.* Washington, DC, American Psychiatric Press, 1994

Starkstein SE, Robinson RG: *Depression in Neurologic Disease.* Baltimore, MD, Johns Hopkins University Press, 1993

Stirling JD: *Cortical Functions.* New York, Routledge, 1999

Strub RL, Black FW: *Neurobehavioral Disorders: A Clinical Approach,* 2nd Edition, Philadelphia, PA, FA Davis, 1988

Strub RL, Black FW: *The Mental Status Examination in Neurology,* 4th Edition. Philadelphia, PA, FA Davis, 2000

Stuss DT, Benson DF: *The Frontal Lobes.* New York, Raven, 1986

Taylor MA: *The Neuropsychiatric Mental Status Examination,* 2nd Edition. New York, PMA Publishing, 1988

Taylor MA: *The Neuropsychiatric Guide to Modern Everyday Psychiatry.* New York, Free Press, 1993

Taylor MA: *The Fundamentals of Clinical Neuropsychiatry.* New York, Oxford University Press, 1999

Trimble MR: *Neuropsychiatry.* New York, Wiley, 1981

Trimble MR: *The Interface Between Neurology and Psychiatry.* New York, Karger, 1985

Trimble MR: *Psychiatric Syndromes Associated With Neurologic Disease.* New York, Thieme Medical Publishers, 1990

Trimble MR: *Biological Psychiatry,* 2nd Edition. New York, Wiley, 1996

Trimble MR, Cummings JL: *Contemporary Behavioral Neurology.* Boston, MA, Butterworth-Heinemann, 1997

Vinken PJ, Frederiks JAM: *Neurobehavioural Disorders.* New York, Elsevier Science Publishers, 1985

Wood RL: *Neurobehavioral Sequelae of Traumatic Brain Injury.* New York, Taylor & Francis, 1990

Yudofsky SC, Hales RE: *Synopsis of Neuropsychiatry.* Washington, DC, American Psychiatric Press, 1994

Yudofsky SC, Hales RE: *The American Psychiatric Press Textbook of Neuropsychiatry,* 4th Edition. Washington, DC, American Psychiatric Press, 2002

EEG, and brain SPECT reading rounds; and a neuropsychiatry journal club.

- Postgraduate Year II: Portions of the inpatient and consultation case conferences throughout the year are designated as neuropsychiatry case conferences. The didactic curriculum includes 35 hours of the following topics: the neurologic examination (2 hours), the mental status examination (6 hours), neurologic emergencies, the Abnormal Involuntary Movement Scale (AIMS) examination, recognition of common movement disorders, neuroanatomy for psychiatrists (brain cutting laboratory, 3 hours), history of neuropsychiatry, diagnosis of seizures, EEG fundamentals, epilepsy and behavior, neuropsychiatry of aggression, neuropsychologic assessment (4 hours), CT and MRI reading (2 hours), brain SPECT and functional MRI reading, neuropsychiatry of affective disorders (2 hours), neuropsychiatric aspects of schizophrenia (2 hours), sleep disorders (2 hours), and neurodevelopmental disabilities (3 hours).

- Postgraduate Year III: A portion of the outpatient case conferences are designated for neuropsychiatric case discussions. The Biological Psychiatry Seminar, required for postgraduate year III and postgraduate year IV trainees, is organized around a series of psychopathology topics of 1 or 2 months' duration, each including a case conference, and phenomenology, psychopharmacology, and neuroscience journal clubs, related to the topic of that month. Traumatic brain injury, dementia, neurodevelopmental disorders, and

**TABLE 39–6.** Neuropsychiatry-related journals

*Behavioral Neurology*
*Behavioral Neuropsychiatry*
*Behavioral Neuroscience*
*Brain*
*Brain and Behavior*
*Bulletin of Clinical Neurosciences*
*Cortex*
*Epilepsy and Behavior*
*European Archives of Psychiatry and Clinical Neuroscience*
*European Archives of Psychiatry and Neurological Sciences*
*European Neuropsychopharmacology*
*International Journal of Neuropsychiatry*
*Journal of Cognitive Neuroscience*
*Journal of Geriatric Psychiatry and Neurology*
*Journal of Neurology, Neurosurgery, and Psychiatry*
*Journal of Neuropsychiatry and Clinical Neuroscience (Official Journal of the American Neuropsychiatric Association)*
*Journal of Psychiatry and Neuroscience*
*Neuropsychiatry, Neuropsychology, and Behavioral Neurology (Official Journal of the Behavioral Neurology Society)*
*Progress in Neurology and Psychiatry*
*Progress in Neuro-Psychopharmacology and Biological Psychiatry*
*Psychiatry and Clinical Neurosciences*
*Seminars in Clinical Neuropsychiatry*

movement disorders are included, in addition to the usual psychopathology areas. The child psychiatry seminar includes approximately 8 hours on pediatric neuropsychiatry.

- Postgraduate Year IV: Residents may elect to participate in the university's outpatient neuropsychiatry clinic, performing neuropsychiatric evaluations and follow-up visits 1 half-day per week for the entire year. They also may elect to spend up to half time working in the neuropsychiatry services and participating in a research project.

Examples of neuropsychiatry case conferences held in the past several years at the University of Massachusetts are listed in Table 39–7.

## Neuropsychiatry Careers

Several training pathways can serve as the foundation for a career in neuropsychiatry (Benjamin et al. 1995). Some psychiatrists refer to themselves as neuropsychiatrists because of the diagnoses they prefer to treat. After standard residency training in general adult psychiatry, they develop clinical or research interests in neuropsychiatry.

Combined training in neurology and psychiatry leading to fulfillment of the ACGME requirements in both fields may be undertaken, enabling the trainee to become eligible for both the neurology and the psychiatry board certification examinations. Combined training requires a minimum of 6 years, including an internship containing at least 8 months of medicine experience, and 2.5 years spent in each field. If one is planning to practice both psychiatry and neurology, dual board certification is important for inclusion on managed care panels and may be a prerequisite for dual hospital privileges. Alternatively, trainees may undergo fellowship training in neuropsychiatry or behavioral neurology (Green et al. 1995) following residency in either psychiatry or neurology. Generally, clinical fellowships are 1 year in length, and research fellowships require 2–3 years. This pathway will not lead to board eligibility in the complementary field, but it will give the trainee the necessary expertise to practice in the field.

As of 1999, there were 16 combined neurology and psychiatry residencies (9 of which were accredited), 13 fellowship programs in neuropsychiatry, and 16 programs in behavioral neurology that responded to a survey by the American Neuropsychiatric Association Education Committee. A formal accreditation process for these fellowship programs does not yet exist, although the American Neuropsychiatric Association Education Committee has taken the first steps toward a voluntary accreditation process. Programs without specific accreditation for combined training in neurology and psychiatry may establish a combined training track for a given resident with approval of the ABPN, providing both host programs are ACGME accredited. Table 39–8 lists combined neuropsychiatry training and fellowship programs at the time of publication.

## Neuropsychiatry Certification Issues

Given the variation in training of clinicians describing themselves as neuropsychiatric specialists, a set of minimum competency standards for neuropsychiatry training would assure patients, hospitals, and third-party payers that they are getting the expertise they seek when they consult a neuropsychiatrist. These standards could take several forms: examination-based certification, completion of an accredited training program in which accreditation is based on compliance with a set of minimum acceptable training standards, or continuing education–based certification. Absent the establishment of formal certification (under the aegis of the ABPN) or accreditation standards by the appropriate national bodies, infor-

**TABLE 39–7.** Examples of neuropsychiatry case conferences at the University of Massachusetts Medical School

| | |
|---|---|
| A Neurodevelopmental Syndrome With Severe Press of Speech and Manic Behavior | Affective and Behavioral Changes Following Right-Hemisphere Stroke |
| An Unusual Case of Hypersexuality, Hyperphagia, and Aggression | An Unusual Nondominant Developmental Syndrome |
| Asperger's or Abuse? A Diagnostic Challenge From the Adolescent Program | Three Cases of Tardive Dystonia |
| Childhood Hyperactivity Grown Up | Childhood Hyperlexia and Adult Social Incompetence: Asperger's Syndrome or Right-Hemisphere Disorder? |
| Communicating With Autistic Individuals Using New Technologies: A Critical Appraisal | Dementia, Abnormal Involuntary Movements, and Gait Disorder |
| Disinhibition, Depression, and Dysmnesia Following Minor Head Injury: A Neuropsychologic Detective Story | Down Syndrome and Refractory Catatonia: The Story of an Awakening |
| Effects of Early Physical and Sexual Abuse on Brain Development | Follow-Up of Temporal Lobectomy for Refractory Partial Epilepsy |
| Frontal Dementia, Compulsive Behavior, and the Need to Move | Frontal Lobe Epilepsy and Mania: Coincidence or Cause? |
| Frontal Lobe Epilepsy and Manic Behavior | Issues in the Assessment of Adult Attention-Deficit Disorder |
| Life After Anoxic Encephalopathy: A Self-Made Man Struggles to Adapt | Management of Compulsive Self-Injury in an Adolescent With Gilles de la Tourette Syndrome: A Clinical Balancing Act |
| Mania in a Patient With Right Orbitofrontal AVM: Primary or Secondary? | Memory Loss of Unknown Etiology in a Cyclothymic Female |
| Movement, Hypermetamorphosis, and Mutism: 5 Year Follow-Up of a Craftsman With Frontal Dementia | Neuropsychiatric Applications of Brain SPECT Imaging |
| | Neurosyphilis With Psychosis and Progressive Dysarthria |
| Neuropsychiatric Sequelae of Closed Head Injury: The Influence of Personality | Personality Disorder, Psychosis, and Dreamy State With Ongoing Temporoparietal Epileptiform Activity |
| Paranoid Delusions Following Head Injury | Postinfectious Leukoencephalitis With Refractory Psychosis: Successful Treatment With Clozapine |
| Pharmacologic Treatment of Adult ADHD | Psychiatric Presentation of Neurodegenerative Illness: Niemann-Pick Type C Disease |
| Prosody, Marriage, and the Frontal Lobe | Psychosis, Steroids, and the Pugilist |
| Psychiatric Symptoms Following Infectious Illness: Seizures or Anxiety? | Seizure-Induced Aphasia in Childhood: A Case of Landau-Kleffner Syndrome |
| Schizophrenia and Head Injury: The Split Personality of Descriptive Diagnosis | Sixty-One-Year-Old Male With Memory Loss: Alzheimer's Disease or Korsakoff's? |
| Frontal Dementia, Vertical Gaze Palsy, and Alien Hand in a Physician With Mood Disorder | The Interaction of Mild Head Injury and Character Pathology |

*Note.*  AVM = arteriovenous malformation; ADHD = attention-deficit/hyperactivity disorder; SPECT = single photon emission computed tomography.

mal voluntary certification and accreditation supervised by specialty organizations would be an alternative mechanism. In 1994, the American Neuropsychiatric Association joined with the Behavioral Neurology Society to propose a common core curriculum for behavioral neurology and neuropsychiatry fellowship programs. Together, they initiated an attempt to establish a certificate of added qualifications in neuropsychiatry and behavioral neurology and an accreditation process for fellowship programs based on this common core curriculum. Although the attempt proved unsuccessful, work continues on alternative mechanisms for recognition of neuropsychiatric expertise. The American Neuropsychiatric Association Education Committee currently recommends the areas of core competence shown in Table 39–9 as the basis for clinical neuropsychiatric fellowship training. For updated

information about neuropsychiatry training programs and core competencies in neuropsychiatric education, see the American Neuropsychiatric Association Training web page at http://www.neuropsychiatry.com/ANPA.

## Limitations on the Training of Neuropsychiatrists

Despite the growing popularity of neuropsychiatry among trainees, practical limitations have tended to retard growth in the number of practicing neuropsychiatrists. The bulk of graduate medical training in the United States is funded by Medicare Part A dollars provided to hospitals expressly for training. This funding is available only to ACGME-accredited residencies and fel-

**TABLE 39–8.** Training programs in neuropsychiatry and behavioral neurology

**Combined psychiatry and neurology residency programs**[a]

Brown University[b]
Duke University
Indiana University[b]
Long Island Jewish Medical Center[b]
Medical College of Wisconsin
New York University[b]
Tulane University[b]
University of Arizona[b]
University of Colorado
University of Florida
University of Massachusetts[b]
University of Miami[b]
University of Minnesota
University of Rochester
University of Vermont
West Virginia University[b]

**Behavioral neurology fellowships**

Barrow Neurological Institute
Beth Israel Deaconess Medical Center
Brown University
Emory University
Indiana University
Massachusetts General Hospital
Northwestern University
Oregon Health Sciences University
University of Alabama
University of Arizona
University of California at Los Angeles
University of Florida
University of Oklahoma
University of Rochester
University of Texas, Southwestern
University of Toronto

**Neuropsychiatry fellowships**

Beth Israel Medical Center
Brown University
Dartmouth-Hitchcock Medical Center
Duke University
Finch/Chicago Medical School
Johns Hopkins University
Loyola University
Massachusetts General Hospital/McLean
Northwestern University
Texas Tech University
University of Illinois at Chicago
University of Massachusetts
University of Rochester

[a]*Source.* American Medical Association FRIEDA database and survey by American Neuropsychiatric Association Education Committee 1999.
[b]American Board of Psychiatry and Neurology accreditation.

**TABLE 39–9.** American Neuropsychiatric Association–recommended core content of neuropsychiatry fellowship training

Functional neuroanatomy
Behavioral and cognitive assessment
Evaluation and biopsychosocial treatment of neuropsychiatric syndromes
Neuroimaging
Basic electrophysiology
Neuropsychologic testing
Neuropathology
Neurologic examination

Additional expertise encouraged in at least two of the following areas:
Polysomnography
Geriatric psychiatry
Child psychiatry
Neurorehabilitation
Genetics
Teaching

lowship programs. In the absence of a formal ACGME accreditation process for neuropsychiatry and behavioral neurology fellowship programs, funding is limited to grant support and collections for clinical service provided. For candidates in 6-year combined training programs in neurology and psychiatry, there are also funding issues. The portion of Medicare Part A dollars available for resident salaries decreases by half when a trainee achieves board eligibility in a single field. Hospitals offering 6-year combined neuropsychiatry programs must therefore underwrite the part of the training not covered by Medicare Part A. For this reason, some hospitals have been putting pressure on combined training programs to close in recent years. Ironically, at the same time that advances in neuroscience have contributed to tremendous growth in the field of neuropsychiatry, economic forces have made training increasingly difficult to fund. The promotion of neuropsychiatric education remains one of the principle goals of the American Neuropsychiatric Association and its sister organization, the Behavioral Neurology Society.

# References

Akil M, Brewer GJ: Psychiatric and behavioral abnormalities in Wilson's disease. Adv Neurol 65:171–178, 1995

Alper K: Nonepileptic seizures. Neurol Clin 12(1):153–173, 1994

Alexander MP: Aphasia: Clinical and anatomic aspects, in Behavioral Neurology and Neuropsychology. Edited by Feinberg TE, Farah MJ. New York, McGraw-Hill, 1997, pp 133–149

American Medical Association: 1980–1981 Directory of Residency Training Programs. Chicago, IL, American Medical Association, 1980

American Medical Association: 1987–1988 Directory of Graduate Medical Education Programs. Chicago, IL, American Medical Association, 1987

American Neuropsychiatric Association Education Committee: Neuropsychiatry Training Objectives for General Psychiatry Residents. Columbus, OH, American Neuropsychiatric Association, 1994

American Psychiatric Association: Diagnostic and Statistical Manual of Mental Disorders, Fourth Edition, Text Revision (DSM-IV-TR). Washington, DC, American Psychiatric Association, 2000

Atkinson JH, Grant I: Natural history of neuropsychiatric manifestations of HIV disease. Psychiatr Clin North Am 17:17–33, 1994

Bear DM: Temporal lobe epilepsy—a syndrome of sensory-limbic hyperconnection. Cortex 15:357–384, 1979

Bear DM, Fedio P: Quantitative analysis of interictal behavior in temporal lobe epilepsy. Arch Neurol 34:454–467, 1977

Beatty WW: Cognitive and emotional disturbances in multiple sclerosis. Neurol Clin 11(1):189–204, 1993

Bench CJ, Dolan RJ, Friston KJ, et al: Positron emission tomography in the study of brain metabolism in psychiatric and neuropsychiatric disorders. Br J Psychiatry 157 (suppl 9):82–95, 1990

Benjamin S: Neuropsychiatry, in Psychiatry for Medical Students, 3rd Edition. Edited by Waldinger R. Washington, DC, American Psychiatric Press, 1997, pp 335–377

Benjamin S: A neuropsychiatric approach to aggressive behavior, in Neuropsychiatry and Mental Health Services. Edited by Ovsiew F. Washington, DC, American Psychiatric Press, 1999, pp 149–196

Benjamin S, Cummings JL, Duffy J, et al: Pathways to neuropsychiatry. J Neuropsychiatry Clin Neurosci 7:96–101, 1995

Blacker D: Psychiatric rating scales, in Comprehensive Textbook of Psychiatry, 7th Edition. Edited by Kaplan BJ, Sadock VA. Philadelphia, PA, Lippincott, Williams & Wilkins, 2000, pp 755–783

Boffeli TJ, Guze SB: The simulation of neurologic disease. Psychiatr Clin North Am 15(2):301–310, 1992

Boutros NN: A review of indications for routine EEG in clinical psychiatry. Hospital and Community Psychiatry 43:716–719, 1992

Brown ES, Khan DA, Nejtek VA: The psychiatric side effects of corticosteroids. Ann Allergy Asthma Immunol 83(6 pt 1):495–503; quiz 503-504, 1999

Caine ED, Shoulson I: Psychiatric syndromes in Huntington's disease. Am J Psychiatry 140(6):728–733, 1983

Calabrese LV, Stern TA: Neuropsychiatric manifestations of systemic lupus erythematosus. Psychosomatics 36(4): 344–359, 1995

Cascino GD: Complex partial seizures. Clinical features and differential diagnosis. Psychiatr Clin North Am 15(2): 373–382, 1992

Central Approval Panel Court of Electors: Statement of training schemes for general professional training for the MRCPsych. Psychiatric Bulletin 18:514–524, 1994

Clifford DB, Rutherford JL, Hicks FG, et al: Acute effects of antidepressants on hippocampal seizures. Ann Neurol 18:692–697, 1985

Cobb S: Foundations of Neuropsychiatry, 3rd Edition. Baltimore, MD, Williams & Wilkins, 1944

Coker SB: The diagnosis of childhood neurodegenerative disorders presenting as dementia in adults. Neurology 41:794–798, 1991

Council on Medical Education and Hospitals of the American Medical Association: Medical education in the United States and Canada. JAMA 113:797–798, 1939

Council on Medical Education and Hospitals of the American Medical Association: Medical education in the United States and Canada. JAMA 134:1417–1418, 1947

Culebras A: Update on disorders of sleep and the sleep-wake cycle. Psychiatr Clin North Am 15:467–489, 1992

Cummings JL: Subcortical dementia. Neuropsychology, neuropsychiatry, and pathophysiology. Br J Psychiatry 149:682–697, 1986

Cummings JL, Victoroff JI: Neurocognitive neuropsychiatric syndromes in Alzheimer's disease. Neuropsychiatry, Neuropsychology, and Behavioral Neurology 3(2):140–158, 1990

Davison K, Bagley CR: Schizophrenia-like psychoses associated with organic disorders of the central nervous system: a review of the literature, in Current Problems in Neuropsychiatry (Br J Psychiatry Special Publ No. 4). Edited by Herrington RN. Ashford, Kent, England, Headley Brothers, 1969, pp 113–184

DeRenzi E: Prosopagnosia, in Behavioral Neurology and Neuropsychology. Edited by Feinberg TE, Farah MJ. New York, McGraw-Hill, 1997, pp 245–255

Devinsky O, Pacia S: Epilepsy surgery. Neurol Clin 11(4):951–971, 1993

Devinsky O, Thacker K: Nonepileptic seizures. Neurol Clin 13(2):299–319, 1995

Drake ME Jr: Clinical utility of event-related potentials in neurology and psychiatry. Semin Neurol 10(2):196–203, 1990

Duffy JD, Camlin H: Neuropsychiatry training in American psychiatry residency training programs. J Neuropsychiatry Clin Neurosci 7:290–294, 1995

Engel J: Update on surgical treatment of the epilepsies: summary of the Second International Palm Desert Conference on the Surgical Treatment of the Epilepsies (1992). Neurology 43:1612–1617, 1993

Farah MJ, Feinberg TE: Visual object agnosia, in Behavioral Neurology and Neuropsychology. Edited by Feinberg TE, Farah MJ. New York, McGraw-Hill, 1997, pp 239–244

Fishbain DA: Approaches to treatment decisions for psychiatric comorbidity in the management of the chronic pain patient. Med Clin North Am 83:737–760, 1999

Frumin M, Chisholm T, Dickey CC, et al: Psychiatric and behavioral problems. Neurologic Clinics of North America 16:521–544, 1998

Galer BS: Neuropathic pain of peripheral origin: advances in pharmacologic treatment. Neurology 45 (suppl 9):S17–S25, 1995

Garber HJ, Weilburg JB, Buonanno FS, et al: Use of magnetic resonance imaging in psychiatry. Am J Psychiatry 145:164–171, 1988

George MS, Lisanby SH, Sackeim HA: Transcranial magnetic stimulation: applications in neuropsychiatry. Arch Gen Psychiatry 56(4):300–311, 1999

Gledhill RF: Neurological competencies in the graduating psychiatrist (letter). J Neurol Neurosurg Psychiatry 46:871, 1983

Graff-Radford NR, Biller J: Behavioral neurology and stroke. Psychiatr Clin North Am 15(2):415–425, 1992

Green RC, Benjamin S, Cummings JL: Fellowship programs in behavioral neurology. Neurology 45:412–415, 1995

Green R, Clark A, Hickey W, et al: Braincutting for psychiatrists: the time is ripe. J Neuropsychiatry Clin Neurosci 11(3):301–306, 1999

Gross A, Devinsky O, Westbrook LE, et al: Psychotropic medication use in patients with epilepsy: effect on seizure frequency. J Neuropsychiatry Clin Neurosci 12(4):458–464, 2000

Gualtieri CT: Neuropsychiatry and Behavioral Pharmacology. New York, Springer-Verlag, 1991

Guze BH: Magnetic resonance spectroscopy. Arch Gen Psychiatry 48:572–574, 1991

Hohagen F, Lindhardt A: Training in psychiatry: a European perspective. Eur Arch Psychiatry Clin Neurosci 247(6 suppl 1):S1–S2, 1997

Hollender MH (ed): The American Board of Psychiatry: The First Fifty Years. Deerfield, IL, American Board of Psychiatry and Neurology, 1991

Holman BL, Devous MD: Functional brain SPECT: the emergence of a powerful clinical method. J Nucl Med 33:1888–1904, 1992

Hughes JR: The EEG in psychiatry: an outline with summarized points and references. Clin Electroencephalogr 26:92–101, 1995

Hughes JR: A review of the usefulness of the standard EEG in psychiatry. Clin Electroencephalogr 27:35–39, 1996

Hutto B: Subtle psychiatric presentations of endocrine diseases. Psychiatr Clin North Am 21(4):905–916, 1998

International League Against Epilepsy: Proposal for a classification of the epilepsies and epileptic syndromes. Epilepsia 26:268–278, 1985

Kaplan E: The process approach to neuropsychological assessment of psychiatric patients. J Neuropsychiatry Clin Neurosci 2:72–87, 1990

Kaufman DM: Clinical Neurology for Psychiatrists, 5th Edition. Philadelphia, PA, WB Saunders, 2001

Keefe RSE: The contribution of neuropsychology to psychiatry. Am J Psychiatry 152:6–15, 1995

Kowall NW, Berman SA: Primitive reflexes in psychiatry and neurology, in Disorders of Movement in Psychiatry and Neurology, 2nd Edition. Edited by Joseph AB, Young R. London, England, Blackwell Scientific, 1999, pp 650–655

Krumholz A: Nonepileptic seizures: diagnosis and management. Neurology 53(5 suppl 2):S76–S83, 1999

Krystal AD, Coffey CE: Neuropsychiatric considerations in the use of electroconvulsive therapy. J Neuropsychiatry Clin Neurosci 9(2):283–292, 1997

Lambert MV, Robertson MM: Depression in epilepsy: etiology, phenomenology, and treatment. Epilepsia 40 (suppl 10):S21–S47, 1999

Leckman JF, Peterson BS, Pauls DL, et al: Tic disorders. Psychiatr Clin North Am 20(4):839–861, 1997

Levin JM, Ross MH, Renshaw PF: Clinical applications of functional MRI in neuropsychiatry. J Neuropsychiatry Clin Neurosci 7(4):511–522, 1995

Lilly R, Cummings JL, Benson DF, et al: The human Klüver-Bucy syndrome. Neurology 33:1141–1145, 1983

Lipowski ZJ: Update on delirium. Psychiatr Clin North Am 15:335–346, 1992

Lishman WA: Organic Psychiatry: The Psychological Consequences of Cerebral Disorder, 3rd Edition. London, England, Blackwell Scientific, 1998

Marino Junior R, Cosgrove GR: Neurosurgical treatment of neuropsychiatric illness. Psychiatr Clin North Am 20(4): 933–943, 1997

Marks DR, Rapoport AM: Practical evaluation and diagnosis of headache. Semin Neurol 17:307–312, 1997

Marsh L: Neuropsychiatric aspects of Parkinson's disease. Psychosomatics 41(1):15–23, 2000

Massion A, Benjamin S: Manic behavior, in Outpatient Psychiatry. Edited by Lazare A. Baltimore, MD, Williams & Wilkins, 1989, pp 256–266

McAllister TW: Neuropsychiatric sequelae of head injuries. Psychiatr Clin North Am 15:395–413, 1992

McLoughlin DM, Levy R: The differential diagnosis of dementia. Acta Neurol Scand Suppl 165:92–100, 1996

McQuay H: Opioids in pain management. Lancet 353:2229–2232, 1999

Meador KJ: Cognitive side effects of medications. Neurol Clin 16(1):141–155, 1998

Morrell MJ: Differential diagnosis of seizures. Neurol Clin 11(4):737–754, 1993

Mueller J, Fogel BS: Neuropsychiatric examination, in Neuropsychiatry. Edited by Fogel BS, Schiffer RB, Rao SM. Baltimore, MD, Williams & Wilkins, 1996, pp 11–28

Munetz M, Benjamin S: How to examine patients using the Abnormal Involuntary Movement Scale. Hospital and Community Psychiatry 39:1172–1177, 1988

Neary D, Snowden JS, Gustafson L, et al: Frontotemporal lobar degeneration: a consensus on clinical diagnostic criteria. Neurology 51:1546–1554, 1998

Newman LC, Lipton RB: Emergency evaluation of headache. Neurologic Clinics of North America 16:285–303, 1998

Nordin V, Gillberg C: The long-term course of autistic disorders: update on follow-up studies. Acta Psychiatr Scand 97:99–108, 1998

Nunemaker J, Hinman J, Thompson W, et al: Graduate medical education in the United States. JAMA 174:376–380, 413–416, 1960

Obermeyer WH, Benca RM: Effects of drugs on sleep. Neurol Clin 14(4):827–840, 1996

Oder W, Grimm G, Kollegger H, et al: Neurological and neuropsychiatric spectrum of Wilson's disease: a prospective study of 45 cases. J Neurol 238(5):281–287, 1991

Oliver AP, Luchins DJ, Wyatt RJ: Neuroleptic-induced seizures. Arch Gen Psychiatry 39:206–209, 1982

Parsons OA, Nixon SJ: Neurobehavioral sequelae of alcoholism. Neurol Clin 11(1):205–218, 1993

Pellock JM, Willmore LJ: A rational guide to routine blood monitoring in patients receiving antiepileptic drugs. Neurology 41:961–964, 1991

Pisani F, Spina E, Oteri G: Antidepressant drugs and seizure susceptibility: from in vitro data to clinical practice. Epilepsia 40 (suppl 10):S48–S56, 1999

Price BH, Daffner KR, Stowe RM, et al: The comportmental learning disabilities of early frontal lobe damage. Brain 113:1383–1393, 1990

Prigatano GP, Redner JE: Uses and abuses of neuropsychological testing in behavioral neurology. Neurol Clin 11(1):219–231, 1993

Reite M: Sleep disorders presenting as psychiatric disorders. Psychiatr Clin North Am 21(3):591–607, 1998

Robinson RG: Neuropsychiatric consequences of stroke. Annu Rev Med 48:217–229, 1997

Robinson RG, Kubos KL, Starr LB, et al: Mood disorders in stroke patients. Importance of location of lesion. Brain 107(pt 1):81–93, 1984

Rogers D: Catatonia: a contemporary approach. J Neuropsychiatry Clin Neurosci 3(3):334–340, 1991

Roos KL: Neurosyphilis. Semin Neurol 12:209–212, 1992

Rosenblatt A, Leroi I: Neuropsychiatry of Huntington's disease and other basal ganglia disorders. Psychosomatics 41(1):24–30, 2000

Ross E, Rush A: Diagnosis and neuroanatomical correlates of depression in brain-damaged patients: implications for a neurology of depression. Arch Gen Psychiatry 38:1344–1354, 1981

Rowbotham MC: Chronic pain: from theory to practical management. Neurology 45 (suppl 9):S5–S10, 1995

Rubino FA: Neurologic complications of alcoholism. Psychiatr Clin North Am 15(2):359–372, 1992

Saper JR: Headache disorders. Med Clin North Am 83:663–690, 1999

Scherokman B, Cannard K, Miller JQ: What should a graduating medical student know about neurology? The American Academy of Neurology Undergraduate Education Subcommittee. Neurology 44(6):1170–1176, 1994

Schmitz B: Psychiatric syndromes related to antiepileptic drugs. Epilepsia 40 (suppl 10):S65–S70, 1999

Siegel AJ, Baldessarini RJ, Klepser MB, et al: Primary and drug-induced disorders of water homeostasis in psychiatric patients: principles of diagnosis and management. Harv Rev Psychiatry 6(4):190–200, 1998

Silbersweig DA, Stern E: Symptom localization in neuropsychiatry. A functional neuroimaging approach. Ann N Y Acad Sci 835:410–420, 1997

Silver FW: Management of conversion disorder. Am J Phys Med Rehabil 75(2):134–140, 1996

Skuster DZ, Digre KB, Corbett JJ: Neurologic conditions presenting as psychiatric disorders. Psychiatr Clin North Am 15:311–333, 1992

Strub RL, Black FW: Neurobehavioral Disorders: A Clinical Approach, 2nd Edition. Philadelphia, PA, FA Davis, 1988

Tisher PW, Holzer JC, Greenberg M, et al: Psychiatric presentations of epilepsy. Harv Rev Psychiatry 1:219–228, 1993

Torta R, Keller R: Behavioral, psychotic, and anxiety disorders in epilepsy: etiology, clinical features, and therapeutic implications. Epilepsia 40 (suppl 10):S2–S20, 1999

Trzepacz PT, Baker RW: The Psychiatric Mental Status Examination. New York, Oxford University Press, 1993

Trzepacz PT, Hertweck PA, Starratt C, et al: The relationship of SPECT scans to behavioral dysfunction in neuropsychiatric patients. Psychosomatics 33:62–71, 1992

Tucker GJ: Seizure disorders presenting with psychiatric symptomatology. Psychiatr Clin North Am 21(3):625–635, 1998

Van Heertum RL, Miller SH, Mosesson RE: SPECT brain imaging in neurologic disease. Radiol Clin North Am 31:881–907, 1993

Waxman SG, Geschwind N: The interictal behavior syndrome of temporal lobe epilepsy. Arch Gen Psychiatry 32:1580–1586, 1975

Weinberger DR: Brain disease and psychiatric illness: when should a psychiatrist order a CAT scan? Am J Psychiatry 141:1521–1527, 1984

Weintraub S, Mesulam M-M: Developmental learning disabilities and the right hemisphere: emotional, interpersonal, and cognitive components. Arch Neurol 40:463–468, 1983

White RF: Emotional and cognitive correlates of multiple sclerosis. J Neuropsychiatry Clin Neurosci 2(4):422–428, 1990

Woods BT: Neurologic soft signs in psychiatric disorders, in Disorders of Movement in Psychiatry and Neurology, 2nd Edition. Edited by Joseph AB, Young R. London, England, Blackwell Scientific, 1999, pp 404–413

Yager J: Neurological proficiencies for psychiatrists: a pilot survey. Academic Psychiatry 18:129–135, 1994

Zegans LS, Gerhard AL, Coates TJ: Psychotherapies for the person with HIV disease. Psychiatr Clin North Am 17:149–163, 1994

# Index

*Page numbers printed in **boldface** type refer to tables or figures.*

Aberrant Behavior Checklist, 1172
ABPN (American Board of Psychiatry and Neurology), 1289–1290, **1291**
Absence seizures, 675, 1094
Abulia, 177
Academic skill deficits, **220**
  attention-deficit/hyperactivity disorder and, 513, 514
    recommendations for, **515**, 517, 1080
  learning disorders, 1090–1093
  traumatic brain injury and, 635
Acalculia, **91**, 92, 762
Accreditation Council on Graduate Medical Education (ACGME), 1289, **1291**, 1291–1292, 1303
Acetaminophen, for migraine, **474**, 475
Acetazolamide, 1096
*N*-Acetyl aspartate (NAA), 290, 298, 311, **312**, 608, 631
Acetylcholine (ACh), 9, 14
  Alzheimer's disease and, 352, 553, 954, 1179–1180
  delirium and, 544, 548, 552–553
  depression and, **1024**
  Down syndrome and, 1085
  enzymatic degradation of, 1130
  Huntington's disease and, 926
  receptors for, 1134 (*See* Cholinergic receptors)
  REM sleep and, 49, 57–58, **58**
  Tourette's syndrome and, 1083
  traumatic brain injury and, 627
Acetylcholinesterase, 10, 1130
*N*-Acetylcysteine, 796
α–*N*-Acetylglucosaminidase deficiency, 979
ACGME (Accreditation Council on Graduate Medical Education), 1289, **1291**, 1291–1292, 1303
ACh. *See* Acetylcholine
Achromatopsia, acquired, **83**, 87, 173

Acoustic neuromas, **754**, 764
Acquired immune deficiency syndrome. *See* Human immunodeficiency virus infection/acquired immune deficiency syndrome
Acquired immunity, 116, **118**, 118–121, **120**
Acrocyanosis, 827
ACTH. *See* Adrenocorticotropic hormone
Actigraphy, **209**, 209–210
Actin, 4
Action initiation and organization, 176–179
  abulia, 177
  anarchic hand, 179
  disinhibition, 178
  environment-driven responses, 179
  ideational apraxia, 178–179
  impersistence, 179
  perseveration, 177–178, **178**
Action potentials, 5–6, 1127
  all-or-none property of, 6
  conduction of, 6, **7**
  generation of, 5–6, **6**
Activities of daily living (ADL) deficits
  poststroke, 734, 738, 746
  rehabilitation for, 1242–1243
Activity monitoring, **209**, 209–210
*Actus reus*, 1269
Acupuncture, 444
Acute brain failure, 526
Acute intermittent porphyria, **325**
Acute organic brain syndrome, 526
Acute phase proteins, 116–118
  in schizophrenia, 131–132
  stress and, 123
AD. *See* Alzheimer's disease
ADAS (Alzheimer's Disease Assessment Scale), 1180
Adderall, 1078
Addison's disease, 864

cardinal features of, 864
  psychiatric symptoms in, 864
Adenoma, pituitary, **754**, 764
Adenosine
  receptors for, **1135**
  in sleep-wakefulness, 53–55, **54**
Adenosine diphosphate (ADP), **1135**
Adenosine triphosphatase (ATPase), **925**
Adenosine triphosphate (ATP), 6, 334, 337, 1125, 1130, **1135**
Adenylyl cyclase, **16**, 33, 1136, 1137, **1138**
ADHD. *See* Attention-deficit/hyperactivity disorder
Adhesion molecules, 27
ADL deficits. *See* Activities of daily living deficits
Adolescents. *See* Children and adolescents
Adoption studies, 325
  of attention-deficit/hyperactivity disorder, 367
  of autism, 344
  of bipolar disorder, 369
  of obsessive-compulsive disorder, 378
  of panic disorder, 374
  of schizophrenia, 382
ADP (adenosine diphosphate), **1135**
Adrenal insufficiency, 864
  cardinal features of, 864
  psychiatric symptoms in, 864
α₂-Adrenergic agonists
  for attention-deficit/hyperactivity disorder, 1077, 1079
  for cognitive impairment, 1182
β-Adrenergic receptor, 133
β-Adrenergic receptor kinases, 904
Adrenocorticotropic hormone (ACTH), 861, 863
  for childhood seizures, 1096

Adrenocorticotropic hormone (ACTH)
(continued)
deficiency of, 864
Advance directives, 1263–1264
Affect application, **1203**
Affected sib pair strategy, 328
Affective disorders. See Mood disorders
Age/aging
brain tumors and, 753
delirium and, 528–529
dementia and, 954
in depression, 1027
electroencephalography and, **202,**
206
memory and, 611
sleep patterns and, 700, **701**
stroke and, 723, **724**
Agent Orange, 888
Aggression, 579–592, 1172
association between criminality and
brain damage, 1265–1266
conditions associated with, 579,
1172
antisocial personality disorder,
589–590
borderline personality disorder,
588–589
epilepsy, 687
Huntington's disease, 929, 930,
964
hyperprolactinemia, 586, 865–
866
impulse control disorders, 590
posterior aphasia behavioral
syndrome, 574
traumatic brain injury, 643, 651–
654
definition of, 579
drug-induced, 1175
epidemiology of, 580
factors contributing to, 579, **580**
history taking for, 156
impulsive, 579 (See also Impulsivity)
legal issues relating to violent
patients, 1278–1280
assessing risk for violence, 1279–
1280
case examples of, 1278, 1279
discharge and release
considerations, 1279
duty-to-warn statutes, 1278
seclusion and restraint guidelines,
1279, **1279**
measurement of, 580–581
direct laboratory assessments,
581

interview assessments, 581
self-report assessments, 581
morbidity and mortality from, 579,
580
neurobiology of, 584–588, **585,** 1175
decreased serotonin function,
**584,** 584–586
endocrine studies, 588
genetic studies, 587–588
pharmacologic challenge studies,
586–587
role of 5-HT$_{1B}$ receptor, 588
neurologic structures involved in,
582–583, 1175
amygdala, 582–583
hypothalamus, 582
prefrontal cortex, 583
neuropsychiatric/neuropsychological
studies of, 588–590
physical, 580
social stigmatization of, 580
treatment of, 590–592, 651–654,
**654**
acute aggression, 651–652
chronic aggression, 652–654
in developmental disabled
persons, 592
in patients with traumatic brain
injury, 651–654
pharmacotherapy, 1175–1178,
**1179**
verbal, 580
Agitated Behavior Scale, **629,** 630
Agitation, 163, 1166–1172. See also
Anxiety; Mania
Alzheimer's disease and, 1169
anatomy and neurochemistry of,
1169
definition of, 163
differential diagnosis of, 1166
drug-induced, 1169
etiologies of, 1166, 1169
during neuroimaging procedures, 247
posttraumatic stress disorder and,
1169
traumatic brain injury and, 643, **654**
treatment of
in patients with dementia, **980,**
1219
pharmacotherapy, 651–654, **654,**
1169–1172, **1173–1174**
acute agitation, 651–652
chronic agitation, 652–654
Agnosia
aphasia and, 573
apperceptive, 87–89, 573

associative, 81, 573
auditory, 92
color, 87
definition of, 573
evaluation for, 231
for faces, 81–82, **83**
finger, 573, 762
tactile object, **91,** 94
visual, 81, **83,** 173–174
Agonists, 1134, 1139
Agoraphobia, 1049
Agranulocytosis, clozapine-induced, 550
Agraphesthesia, 762
Agraphia, 172, 573
Aicardi-Goutières syndrome, 942
AIDS. See Human immunodeficiency
virus infection/acquired immune
deficiency syndrome
AIDS dementia complex, 785
Akathisia, 163
Akinesia, 162–163
pure psychic, 177
Akinetic mutism, 95–97, **97, 100,** 506
Alcohol withdrawal
anticonvulsants for, 1170
benzodiazepines for, 546
delirium due to, 554
Alcoholism
bipolar disorder and, 369
criminal liability and, 1269–1270
history taking for, 155
insomnia and, 706, **707**
intoxication and traumatic brain
injury, 633, 658
pharmacologic actions of ethanol,
**901**
Wernicke-Korsakoff syndrome and,
603
Alexia, 172, 573
acquired (pure), **83,** 89
Alkyltin poisoning, **879**
Allelic association method, 329
Allergic diseases, 121, 122
Allergic reactions to radiologic contrast
agents
for computed tomography, 252, 254
for magnetic resonance imaging, 262
Allesthesia, 507
Allokinesia, 507
Alpha rhythm, 45, 697, 698
Almotriptan, **474,** 476, 477
Alosetron, 1141
Alpha rhythm, 45, 697, 698
Alprazolam, **1174**
for patients with HIV/AIDS, 801
ALS. See Amyotrophic lateral sclerosis
Aluminum poisoning, 877–881

Alzheimer's disease and, 353
diagnosis of, 880, **880**
mechanism of action of, 878–880
neuropsychiatric symptoms of, 878, **879**
sources of exposure, 877–878
treatment of, 880–881
Alzheimer's Association, 981
Alzheimer's disease (AD), 351–357, 954–958
age at onset of, 351, 352, 954
agitation in, 1169
amnesia in, 510–511, 605, 1179
animal model of, **330**
anxiety in, 1051
aphasia in, 565, 573
apoptosis in, 22
attentional disturbances in, 510–511
Balint's syndrome and, 86
delirium in, 527, 553
depression in, 956
treatment of, 1158
diagnosis of, 351, 352, 955, **955**
differentiation from frontotemporal dementias, 961, **962**
Down syndrome and, 954, 1085
electroencephalography in, 206, 957
epidemiologic studies of, 352–354
genetic studies of, 354–357, 954
family studies, 354, 954
high-risk studies, 355
mode of inheritance, 355
molecular approaches, 355–357
relative risk, **325**
twin studies, 355, 954
guardianship for persons with, 1264
Lewy body variant of, 935, 936
neurochemistry of, 1180
neuroimaging in, 957, **962**
neuropathology of, 4, 34, 78, 351–352, 954, 957–958, **962**, 1164
neuropsychiatric symptoms of, 351, 923, 955–957, **962**
neuropsychological evaluation in, 219, 235, 957
testing word generation, 177
Parkinson's disease in relatives of probands with, 338
protective factors against development of, 954–955, 1181–1182
risk factors for, 954
stress and immunity in caregivers of patients with, 124
traumatic brain injury and, 954
treatment of

family support, 1214–1215
pharmacotherapy, 958, 1180–1182
psychotherapeutic approach, 1214–1216, **1216**
wandering in, 163
Alzheimer's Disease Assessment Scale (ADAS), 1180
Amantadine, 1238
for aggression, 1177
mechanism of action of, 648
for Parkinson's disease, 969, 1159
for patients with traumatic brain injury, 649
use in patients with brain tumors, 775
Ambien. *See* Zolpidem
Amelodia, 572
American Academy of Neurology, 1300
American Board of Psychiatry and Neurology (ABPN), 1289–1290, **1291**
American Migraine Study, 463–464
American Neuropsychiatric Association, 1289
recommended core content training, 1304, **1305**
Training Objectives of, 1292–1293, **1293–1299**
American Psychiatric Association, practice guidelines for treatment of delirium, 546
American Sign Language, 73
α-Amino-3-hydroxy-5-methylisoxazole-4-propionic acid (AMPA) receptors, 14, 17, 18
in excitotoxicity, 33
in impulsive aggression, 585
in long-term potentiation, 19, 21
in schizophrenia, 998
in synapse formation, 27–29
γ-Aminobutyric acid (GABA), 9, 1124
in aggression, 1175
in delirium, 554
in depression, **1024**
in frontotemporal dementias, 961
in generalized anxiety disorder, 1053
in Huntington's disease, 926, 964
in impulsive aggression, 585, **585**
in obsessive-compulsive disorder, 1055
in REM sleep, 61–62, **62**
reuptake of, 1130
role of glia in regulation of, 1124, **1126**

in signal transmission via gap junctions, 1127
transporter for, 1132
in traumatic brain injury, 627, 655
γ-Aminobutyric acid (GABA) receptors, 14–15, 1129
binding of central nervous system depressants to, 15
classes of, 14–15, **1135**
ethanol effects on, **901**
neurogenesis and, 24
presynaptic GABA$_A$ receptors, 1129
Amitriptyline
dosage of, **436**
effects on sleep, 711
indications for
aggression, 653
migraine prophylaxis, **474**
pain, **437**
pathological laughing and crying, 647
patients with traumatic brain injury, 646, 653, 1158
mechanism of action of, **1144**
seizures induced by, 686
terminal half-life of, **436**
Amnesia, 602–611. *See also* Memory
aging and, 611
anterograde, **77, 97,** 103, **103,** 104, 602
brain lesions associated with, 1179
basal forebrain lesion, 97, **97, 101**
diencephalic tumors, 763
dorsolateral prefrontal region lesions, 101–102
frontal lobe lesions, 603–605
hypothalamic lesions, 277–278, 280
mamillary body lesions, 280–281
mesial temporal lobe lesions, 77, 602–603
thalamic lesions, 104–105, 281
classic, 601
cognitive rehabilitation for, 1239–1241
external memory aids, 1241
repetitive practice, 1240–1241
use of spared skills, 1239–1240
confabulation and, 602
definition of, 602
diagnostic criteria for amnestic disorder, **602**
diencephalic, 104–105
dissociative, 609–611, **610**

Amnesia *(continued)*
  electroconvulsive therapy-induced,
      601, 602, 614–615, 1027
    subjective evaluation of, 612, **612**
  evaluation of, 229–230
    testing for validity of memory
        complaints, 234
  intellectual function and, 602
  posttraumatic, 525
  psychotherapy for patients with,
      1216–1219
    care for caregiver, 1217–1218
    contribution of somatic memory,
        1218–1219
    treating the working memory,
        1218
  retrograde, 79, **97, 103, 104,** 601,
      602
  in specific disorders, 230
    Alzheimer's disease, 510–511,
        605, 1179
    delirium, 541, **541**
    depression, 219, 511, 1026
    epilepsy, 1214
    Huntington's disease, 230, 928–
        929, 963
    mood disorders, 605–607
    multiple sclerosis, 509
    schizophrenia, 607–609, 999
    Wernicke-Korsakoff syndrome,
        603
Amotivation, 506
AMPA receptors. *See* α-Amino-3-
    hydroxy-5-methylisoxazole-4-
    propionic acid receptors
Amphetamine. *See also*
    Dextroamphetamine
  as coanalgesic, 438
  mechanism of action of, 10
  for narcolepsy, 715
  pharmacologic actions of, **901**
  stereotypies in intoxication with, 166
  vasculitis induced by, **826**
Amusia, **91**
Amygdala, 74, 75
  in aggression, 582–583, 1175
  anatomy of, **271, 278,** 280
  in anxiety, 1062
    panic disorder, 1056–1058, **1057**
    posttraumatic stress disorder,
        1058, **1059**
  in cue-induced relapse to drug-
      seeking behavior, 908–909
  deficits associated with lesions of,
      280
  in memory, 79

  in secondary mania, 742
  in Tourette's syndrome, 1083
Amygdalotomy, 1175
Amyloid precursor protein (APP), 355,
    357, 958
Amyotrophic lateral sclerosis (ALS),
    941
  apoptosis in, 22, 30
  with dementia, 941, 959, 961
  Guam amyotrophic lateral sclerosis/
      parkinsonism-dementia
      complex, 33, 941
Analgesics. *See also* Pain management
  adjuvants for, 436–438, **437**
  antidepressants, 435–436, **436**
  cyclooxygenase inhibitors, 430, 434
  delirium induced by, **547**
  for headache, 455
    migraine, 473–478, **474**
    overuse of, 453–454, 457
  nonsteroidal anti-inflammatory
      drugs, 434–435, **435**
  opioids, 432–433, **433, 434,** 438–
      444, **440, 441, 443**
  prevalence of use of, 419
Analytic epidemiologic studies, 324
Anaphylactoid reaction to contrast
    agent, 252
Anarchic hand, 179
ANAs (antinuclear antibodies), 814
Androgen insensitivity syndrome, 588
Androgenital syndrome, 588
Androsterone, 15
Aneurysms, cerebral, 727
Angelman's syndrome, 1086–1087
  clinical features of, 1086
  etiology and pathophysiology of,
      1086–1087
  incidence of, 1086
Angiitis of central nervous system,
    primary, 825
Angiography, cerebral, 217, 770, 825,
    979
Angiotensin, **1135**
Angular gyrus, 89, 92
Animal testing of drugs, 1140
Animal toxins, 892–894, **895**
Anomic aphasia, 172, 228, **568,** 572
Anorexia nervosa, 156
  diencephalic tumors and, 763
  pituitary tumors and, 764
Anosmia, 157
Anosodiaphoria, **91,** 93–94
Anosognosia, **91,** 92–94, 508
  parietal lobe tumors and, 762
  poststroke, **729**

Antagonists, 1134
Antecedents of behavior, 1245–1246
Anterior aphasia behavioral syndrome,
    574
Anterior capsulotomy, 1022
Anterior cingulate syndrome, 759
Antiandrogens, 588
Antibiotics
  delirium induced by, **547**
  for syphilis, 789
Antibodies, 118, **120**
Anticholinergic drugs
  delirium induced by, **547,** 548, 553
  effects on memory, 613
  for Parkinson's disease, 969
Anticipation, genetic, 329
  in bipolar disorder, 372
Anticonvulsants, 689–690. *See also*
    specific drugs
  adverse effects of, 436, 1096–1097,
      **1173**
    cognitive and emotional effects,
        639
    delirium, **547**
    depression, 686
  dosage of, **1173**
  drug interactions with, 689, **689,**
      **1173**
  indications for
    aggression, 591, 652–653, 1176–
        1177
    agitation and mania, 1170, 1172
    alcohol withdrawal, 1170
    epilepsy, 689–690, 1096–1097
    migraine prophylaxis, 473, **474,**
        478
    mood disorders in patients with
        epilepsy, 686
    obsessive-compulsive disorder,
        1056
    pain, 436, **437**
    patients with traumatic brain
        injury, 639–640, 647, 652–
        653
    psychosis in epileptic patients,
        684
    secondary mania, 647, 743
  new drugs, 690
    adverse effects of, **691**
    mechanisms of action of, 690
  use in patients with brain tumors,
      772, 773
Antideoxyribonuclease B, 1074
Antidepressants, 1157–1159, **1160–
    1162.** *See also* specific drugs and
    classes

adverse effects of, 1142, **1160–1162**
    aggravation of delirium, 528
    seizures, 647, 686, 773
brain changes after treatment with, 1034–1035
dosage of, **1160–1162**
drug interactions with, **1160–1162**
effects on cognitive deficits in depression, 1027
effects on memory, 613–614
effects on sleep, 703, 711
epileptiform
    electroencephalographic activity in patients receiving, 206
immunologic effects of, 141–142
indications for, 1157–1159
    aggression, 653
    agitation, 1171
    aphasic patients, 577
    attention-deficit/hyperactivity disorder, 1079
    headache, 455, 457
    migraine prophylaxis, 473, **474,** 478
    pain, 435–436, **436, 437**
    patients with brain tumors, 772, 773, 775–776
    patients with dementia, **980,** 981
    patients with diabetes mellitus, 854, **855**
    patients with epilepsy, 686–687
    patients with HIV/AIDS, 799
    patients with Huntington's disease, 965
    patients with Parkinson's disease, 935, 967
    patients with traumatic brain injury, 646–647, 653
    poststroke depression, **740,** 740–741, **741**
    poststroke pathological emotions, 747–748, **748**
mechanisms of action of, 10, 1142–1144, **1144**
    interactions with neuroreceptors, 1134–1136
    manipulation of neurotransmitter reuptake, 1132–1133
    merits of drug selectivity, 1142–1143
    novel mechanisms, 1143–1144
Antidepressants, tricyclic (TCAs), **1160**
absorption of, 435
adverse effects of, 435, **1160**
    cardiac effects in children, 1079
dosage of, **1160**

drug interactions with, **1160**
effects on cognitive deficits in depression, 1027
effects on sleep, 703, 711
immunologic effects of, 141–142
indications for, 1158, 1159
    agitation, 1171
    attention-deficit/hyperactivity disorder, 1079
    Huntington's disease, 930
    impulsive aggression, 591
    narcolepsy, 715
    patients with diabetes mellitus, 854, **855**
    patients with HIV/AIDS, 799
    patients with traumatic brain injury, 649, 1158, 1171
    sleep-disordered breathing, 714
mechanism of action of, 10, 1144, **1144**
    effects at neuroreceptors, 1134
    serotonin binding, 1131
use in patients with brain tumors, 772, 773, 776
Antiemetics, for migraine, 475, 477
Antigens, 116, 118, **120**
Antihypertensive agents, **1179**
Antineuronal antibodies, 816
Antinuclear antibodies (ANAs), 814
Antioxidants
    for Alzheimer's disease, 1181
    for HIV/AIDS, 796
    for Parkinson's disease, 341, 1223
Antiparkinsonian drugs, 934–935
adverse effects of, 934, 967–968
    altered sexual behavior, 968
    anxiety, 968
    delirium, **547,** 554, 967–968
    delusions, 967
    hallucinations, 967
    mood alterations, 968
use in patients with brain tumors, 772, 775
Antiphospholipid antibody (aPL) syndrome, 820–822
    clinical features of, 813
    cognitive impairment in, 821
    dementia and, 821
    differentiation from multiple sclerosis, 821
    stroke and, 821
    tests for, 821–822
Antiproteases, 117
Antipsychotics, 1164–1166, **1167–1168**. *See also* specific drugs

adverse effects of, 1142, 1164–1165, 1177
    neuroleptic-induced immunopathy, 832
    neuroleptic malignant syndrome, 1083
    seizures, 773
atypical, 1164–1166, **1167–1168**
    for agitation or delirium, 549–550, 1171
    for aphasic patients, 577
    effects on memory, 614
    for patients with Parkinson's disease, 1165
efficacy of, 1164
epileptiform
    electroencephalographic activity in patients receiving, 206
immunologic effects of, 142
indications for, 1164–1166
    aggression, 591, 651, 652, 1177
    agitation or delirium, 548–550, 1171, 1172
    autism, 1089
    borderline personality disorder, 587
    pain, 437, **437**
    patients with brain tumors, 772–776
    patients with dementia, 980, **980,** 1166
    patients with HIV/AIDS, 797–798
    patients with Huntington's disease, 930, 964, 965
    patients with Parkinson's disease, 935, 1164–1166
    patients with traumatic brain injury, 650–652
    Tourette's syndrome, 1083
mechanism of action of
    effects at neuroreceptors, 1134, 1141
    merits of drug selectivity, 1142
pharmacodynamics of, 1141–1142, **1142**
pharmacology in schizophrenia, 1006–1007, **1008**
Antiretroviral therapy, 795
    for children, 1099
Antiribosomal P antibodies, 816
Antisocial personality disorder (ASPD), 589–590
    conduct disorder and, 589–590
    criminality and, 589

Antisocial personality disorder (ASPD) (continued)
  impulsivity and aggression in, 589–590
  substance abuse and, 590
Antistreptolysin O, 1074
α₁-Antitrypsin, 123
Antituberculosis drugs, **547**
Anton's syndrome, 179
Anxiety, 1049–1062. See also specific anxiety disorders
  Alzheimer's disease and, 1051
  depression and, 1026
  DSM classification of anxiety disorders, 1049
  due to general medical condition, 1049
  effect on sleep patterns, 703
  endocrine disorders and
    Cushing's syndrome, 861–862, **862**
    hyperthyroidism, **859,** 860
    hypothyroidism, **856,** 857, **857**
    pheochromocytoma, 865
  functional neuroimaging in, 299–301
  headache and, 454–455
  HIV/AIDS and, 800–801
  migraine and, 466
  neurobiology of, 1051–1052
    generalized anxiety disorder, 1052–1053
    obsessive-compulsive disorder, 1053–1056
    panic disorder, 1056–1058
    posttraumatic stress disorder, 1058–1060
    social phobia, 1060–1061
  neurological disorders and, 1050–1051, 1166
    brain tumors, 761, 776
    epilepsy, 684–685, **685**
    Huntington's disease, 964, 1051
    multiple sclerosis, 1051
    Parkinson's disease, 336, 934, 1051
    drug-induced, 968
    stroke, **729, 744,** 744–745, 749, 1051
    traumatic brain injury, 636, 640–641, 1051
  pain and, 421
  substance-induced, 1049
  treatment of, 1170–1171, **1174**
    in patients with brain tumors, 776
    in patients with dementia, **980,** 981

  in patients with epilepsy, 685
Anxiolytics, 1170–1171, **1174.** See also Benzodiazepines; Sedative-hypnotics
  for aggression, 651–652, 1176
  for dementia, **980**
  mechanism of action of, 1134
  for patients with brain tumors, 776
  for patients with HIV/AIDS, 800–801
APACHE II, 530
Apathy, 176
  abulia and, 177
  Alzheimer's disease and, 956
  anatomy and neurochemistry of, 1155–1157
  definition of, 746
  etiologies of, 1155
  Huntington's disease and, 963
  pharmacotherapy for, 1157–1159
  poststroke, **729,** 746, 749
  progressive supranuclear palsy and, 938
Aphasia, 565–577, **568**
  anomic, 172, 228, **568,** 572
  assessment for, 172, 228, 576
    language examination, 567–568
    test selection for, 228
  atypical, 103, **103**
  background on, 565–567
  Broca's, 95, **97, 98,** 568, **568, 569,** 574
    frontal lobe tumors and, 760
    neuropathology of, 568, **569**
  classification of, 567, **568**
  conditions associated with, 565, 575
    dementia, 573
    frontal operculum lesions, 95, **99**
    stroke, 565, 575
    traumatic brain injury, 565, 1205
  conduction, **91,** 92, **93,** 172, 228, **568,** 570
  definition of, 565
  expressive, 228
  global (total), **568,** 570
  jargon, 568
  neuropsychiatric aspects of, 573–576
    anterior aphasia behavioral syndrome, 574
    cognitive aspects, 574–575
    posterior aphasia behavioral syndrome, 574
    psychosocial aspects, 575–576
  primary progressive, 565, 573
  prognosis for, 576
  receptive, 228

  semantic, 573, 939, 959
  subcortical, 572
  thalamic, **103**
  transcortical, **568,** 570–572
  treatment of, 576–577
  Wernicke-Geschwind model of, 566, **567**
  Wernicke's, 89–90, **91,** 568, **568, 571,** 574
    compared with delirium, schizophrenia, and mania, **570**
    neuropathology of, 568, **571**
    temporal lobe tumors and, 762
Aphasia Screening Test, 235
Aphemia, 573
aPL syndrome. See Antiphospholipid antibody syndrome
Aplysia, 3, 18–19, **19**
Apnea, in sleep-disordered breathing, **707,** 708, 713–714
Apolipoprotein E4
  Alzheimer's disease and, 355–357, 954, 1180
  traumatic brain injury prognosis and, 633
Apoptosis, 22, 29–30, 1070
  in Alzheimer's disease, 22
  in amyotrophic lateral sclerosis, 22, 30
  in epilepsy, 22
  in HIV/AIDS, 786, 1099
  in Huntington's disease, 22, 333–334
APP (amyloid precursor protein), 355, 357, 958
APP gene, 355–357
Appearance of patient, 157
  asymmetry, 157
  minor physical anomalies, 157, **157**
Apperceptive agnosia, 87–89, 573
Appetitive functions, 155–156, **220**
Approximate answers, 174–175
Apraxia
  conditions associated with, 231
  constructional, **539**
  definition of, 172, 573
  evaluation for, 231
  examination for, 573
  of eyelid opening, 159
  gaze, 85, 159
  ideational, 178–179
  ideomotor, 172–173
  language disturbances and, 568, 573
  ocular, 85, 159, 174
  oral, 172–173

Aprosody, **103,** 160–161, 572
    definition of, 748
        frontal lobe tumors and, 760
        poststroke, **729,** 748
Arachidonic acid, **16,** 17, 434
ARAS (ascending reticular activating system), 49
Arecoline, 703, 1181
Arginine vasopressin
        aggression and, 1175
        for persistent coldness after brain injury, 643–645
Argyll Robertson pupils, 158
Aricept. *See* Donepezil
Arrhythmias, tricyclic antidepressant-induced, 1079
Arsenic poisoning, 881
        diagnosis of, 881
        mechanism of action of, 881
        neuropsychiatric manifestations of, **879,** 881
        sources of exposure, 881
        treatment of, 881
Arsine gas, 881
Arterial spin tagging (AST), 285–286, 291
Arteriovenous malformations (AVMs), 727
Arteritis. *See also* Vasculitis
        giant cell, 728, 824
        granulomatous, 825
        polyarteritis nodosa, 823–824
        Takayasu's, 824
Arthritis
        osteoarthritis, 814
        rheumatoid, 831
            pain management in, 434
            stress, depression, and immunity in, 128
Arylsulfatase A deficiency, 347–349, 979
Arylsulfatase A pseudodeficiency, 347
Ascending reticular activating system (ARAS), 49
Ascending sensory pathways, 426, **428, 429**
ASPD. *See* Antisocial personality disorder
Asperger's disorder, 173, 1090
Aspirin, 430, **435**
        for migraine, **474**
Assessment, neuropsychiatric
        at bedside, 153–181
        clinical imaging, 245–281
        electrodiagnostic techniques, 199–210

functional neuroimaging, 285–311
        neuropsychological evaluation, 217–236
Association studies, 328–329
        in schizophrenia, 383–384
Associative agnosia, 81, 573
AST (arterial spin tagging), 285–286, 291
Astereognosis, 762
Asterixis, 165
Astrocytes, 4, 1124–1125. *See also* Glial cells
Astrocytomas, **754,** 765
Ataxia
        episodic, 5
        Friedreich's, **925,** 940
        optic, 85–86, 174
Ataxin, **925**
Atherosclerosis, 726. *See also* Cerebrovascular disease
        Parkinson's disease and, 931
Ativan. *See* Lorazepam
ATP (adenosine triphosphate), 6, 334, 337, 1125, 1130, **1135**
*ATP7B* gene, 342–343
ATPase (adenosine triphosphatase), **925**
Atropine, for organophosphate exposure, 890
Attention, 489–506
        assessment of, 498–506
            behavioral observation, 498–499
            clinical interview and medical history, 498
            neuropsychological tests, 228–229, **229, 499,** 499–505
                attentional capacity and focus, 500–501, **501, 502**
                response selection and executive control, 503–504, **504**
                sensory selective attention, 501–503, **502**
                steps in decision making for, 504–505
                sustained attention and vigilance, 504
                trends in use of, 505
            psychophysiological methods, 505–506
            functional neuroimaging, 292–293, 496, **497,** 506
            rating inventories, 498
        capacity for, 490
        controlled-effortful, 491
        definition of, 489
        divided, 491

elements of, 490, **490**
        facilitative function of, 492, 499
        fluctuation of, 498
        focused, 490–492
        functional neuroimaging of, 292–293, 496, **497,** 506
            in schizophrenia, 309
        habituation and, 492
        importance in neuropsychiatry, 489–490
        models of, 493–498, **494, 495**
        neurochemistry of, 496–498, 1077
        to pain, 420
        physiology of, 491–492
        relation to consciousness, 489–490
        response selection and executive control in, 492–493
        selective, 492
        sustained, 493
Attention-deficit/hyperactivity disorder (ADHD), 489, 512–517, 1071–1080
        in adults, 513–515, 1073
        characteristic features of, 513, 1072–1073
        clinical course of, 1073, 1076
        comorbidity with, 513, 514, 1071–1073
            abused children with posttraumatic stress disorder, 1073
            conduct disorder, 1072
            learning disorders, 513, 1072, 1091
            mood disorders, 1073
            myotonic dystrophy, 365
            Tourette's syndrome, 1073, 1081, 1084
            traumatic brain injury, 1097–1098
        diagnosis of, 513–515
            age at, 1073
            criteria for, 513, **513**
            inventories for, 498
            office evaluation, **516**
        etiology and pathophysiology of, 1073–1076
            pathophysiological models, 1076–1078, **1077**
        functional neuroimaging in, 299, **300,** 513–514, 1074–1075
        gender distribution of, 1072, 1076
        genetic studies of, 366–368, 513, 1073–1074
            adoption studies, 367
            family studies, 366–367, 513
            high-risk studies, 367

Attention-deficit/hyperactivity disorder (ADHD) *(continued)*
  genetic studies of *(continued)*
    linkage analysis, 367
    mode of inheritance, 367
    molecular approaches, 367–368
    twin studies, 367, 1073
  historical terminology for, 1071–1072
  neuroanatomy of, 1074, 1076
  neurochemistry of, 1073
    dopamine, 299, 367–368, 513–514, 1073, 1075–1077
  prevalence of, 366, 1071, 1072
  treatment of, 516–517, 1078–1080
    academic programs, **515,** 517, 1080
    α₂-adrenergic agonists, 1077, 1079
    antidepressants, 1079
    behavioral treatments, 517, 1080
    in patients with Tourette's syndrome, 1084
    planning for, 516
    stimulants, 516–517, 1078–1080
Attentional disturbances, 170, 506–517
  adaptations in psychiatric technique for, **1201**
  Alzheimer's disease and, 510–511
  attention-deficit/hyperactivity disorder, 512–517, 1071–1080
  closed head injury and, 509–510
  cognitive rehabilitation for, 1239
  delirium and, 536, 541, **541**
  diagnosis of, 498
  epilepsy and, 510
  frontal lobe tumors and, 760
  hypermetamorphosis, 171
  levels of consciousness and, 506–507
  metabolic encephalopathy and, 507
  mild cognitive impairment and, 155
  mood disorders and, 511–512, 605–607
  multiple sclerosis and, 508–509, **509**
  neglect syndrome, 170–171
    poststroke, 507–508
  schizophrenia and, 512, 999
Auditory agnosia, 92
Auditory comprehension, 567
Autism, 343–347, 1087–1089
  age at onset of, 343
  apoptosis and, 22
  characteristic features of, 1087
  etiologic subgroups of, 344
  etiology and pathophysiology of, 1087–1089

functional neuroimaging in, 296–298, 1088
gender differences in, 343
genetic studies of, 343–347, 1087–1088
  adoption studies, 344
  family studies, 343–344
  high-risk studies, 344
  linkage analysis, 345–346
  mode of inheritance, 344–345
  molecular approaches, 346–347
  twin studies, 344, 1087
mental retardation and, 344, 1087
neuroanatomy of, 1088
neurochemistry of, 1088–1089
prevalence of, 343, 1087
treatment of, 1089
  for impulsivity and aggression, 592
Autoimmune diseases, 121, 122, 813–814
  antiphospholipid antibody syndrome, 820–822
  family history of, 813–814
  gender distribution of, 138
  in idiopathic psychiatric syndromes, 832–833
  neuroleptic-induced immunopathy, 832
  schizophrenia and, 832–833
  Sjögren's syndrome, 822–823
  stress, depression, and immunity in, 127–129
  systemic lupus erythematosus, 814–820
Automatism defense, 1269
Autonomic nervous system
  immunologic effects of sympathetic nervous system, 135–136
  innervation of immune tissues by, 132–133, **133**
  measuring responses during attentional tasks, 505
  regulation of sleep by, 700–702, **702**
Autonomy of patient, 1258, 1259. *See also* Legal issues
  advance directives, 1263–1264
  competency, 1258–1259
  do-not-resuscitate orders, 1262–1263
  guardianship, 1264
  health care decision making, 1259–1261
  involuntary hospitalization, 1280–1281
  right to die, 1261–1262

AVMs (arteriovenous malformations), 727
Avoidance reflex, **167,** 168
Awareness of deficit, 179, 221
  in patients with traumatic brain injury, 1207
Axon hillock, 5, **5**
Axons, 4, **5**
  in conduction of action potentials, 6, **7**
  connections with, 8
  diffuse axonal injury, 626
  growth cones of, **26,** 26–27
  presynaptic, 8

B cells, 116, 118, **120**
Babinski's sign, 974
BAC (blood alcohol concentration), 658
Backwards Spelling test, 500
Baclofen, 433, 438, 443
  for vascular dementia, 976
BADS (Behavioral Assessment of the Dysexecutive Syndrome), 235
BAL (British anti-Lewisite), 881, 884
Balint's syndrome, **83,** 85–86, **86,** 159, 174
Ballistic movements, 164
BAM (Buss "Aggression Machine"), 581
Barbiturates
  abuse potential of, 706
  binding to GABA receptors, 15
  electroencephalogram in intoxication with, **202**
  for insomnia, 711
  vasculitis induced by, **826**
Basal forebrain, 97–98
Basal ganglia
  anatomy of, 266, 269, **271–275, 277, 278,** 279
  in attention-deficit/hyperactivity disorder, 1074
  cortical-basal ganglionic degeneration, 939
  in delirium, 552
  in depression, 1028–1029
  epidemiologic and genetic studies of diseases of, 331–343
  functional neuroanatomy of, 103–104, **104,** 266
  functional neuroimaging of strokes involving, 1031–1032
  in Huntington's disease, 926–927, **927,** 964–965
  idiopathic calcification of, 942, 970–971
  lenticulostriatal system of, 962–963

neurotransmitters in, 269
in obsessive-compulsive disorder, 300, 1050, 1055
in posttraumatic stress disorder, 1060
in schizophrenia, 992
in social phobia, 1061, **1061**
in Tourette's syndrome, 1081–1082
in Wilson's disease, 942, 971–972
Basic fibroblast growth factor, 24, 30
Basic rest activity cycle (BRAC), 698
Basophils, 116
BBB. *See* Blood-brain barrier
*Bcl-2* gene, 30
BDAE (Boston Diagnostic Aphasia Examination), 172, 174, 228, 576
BDHI (Buss-Durkee Hostility Inventory), 581, 585
BEAM (brain electrical activity mapping), **629,** 632, 770
Beck Depression Inventory, 455, 631, 637, 641, 853, 856, 857, 966
Bedside Evaluation Screening Test (BEST-2), 228
Bedside neuropsychiatric assessment, 153–181
    for delirium, 536–537
    examination of patient, 157–179
        asymmetry and minor physical anomalies, 157, **157**
        attention, 170–171
        awareness of deficit, 179
        blinking, 158
        content of thought, 175–176
        emotion, 176
        eye movements, 158–159
        eyes, 158
        facial movement, 159
        form of thought, 174–175
        initiation and organization of action, 176–179
        language and praxis, 172–173
        memory, 171–172
        movement abnormalities, 162–167
        olfaction, 157–158
        orientation, 170
        primitive reflexes, **167,** 167–168
        signs of callosal disconnection, 168–169
        soft signs, 168, **169**
        speech, 160–162
        visual fields, 158
        visuospatial function, 173–174
    history taking, 154–156

presence of family members during, 180
psychological management in, 179–180
screening batteries and rating scales, 180–181
    Behavioral Dyscontrol Scale, 180, **181,** 235
    Executive Interview, 180, 235
    Frontal Assessment Battery, 180–181, **182**
    for HIV-related dementia, 180
    Mini-Mental State Exam, 180
    Neurobehavioral Rating Scale, 181, **183,** 234
    Neuropsychiatric Inventory, 181
    Trail Mental Alternation Test, 180
Behavior therapy, 1244–1250
    assessing effects of, 1246–1248, **1247**
    case examples of, 1248–1250
        depression with failure to use ambulatory assistance, 1249–1250
        inappropriate sexual and aggressive language and behavior, 1248–1249
    cognitive-behavioral approach for, 1246
    goal of, 1245
    models for, 1245
    social learning approach for, 1246
    for specific conditions
        attention-deficit/hyperactivity disorder, 517, 1080
        autism, 1089
        insomnia, 708–711
        Parkinson's disease, 934
        patients with HIV/AIDS, 796
        traumatic brain injury, 656
    traditional behavioral approach for, 1245–1246
        differential reinforcement, 1246
        interventions aimed at antecedents of behavior, 1245–1246
        interventions aimed at consequences of behavior, 1245
        noncontingent reinforcement, 1246
    underlying assumptions for, 1244–1245
Behavioral Assessment of the Dysexecutive Syndrome (BADS), 235

Behavioral Dyscontrol Scale, 180, **181,** 235
Behavioral dysfunction, **220,** 1172–1178, 1243–1244. *See also* Aggression; Agitation; Impulsivity; Personality changes; Sexual behavior changes
    Alzheimer's disease and, 956
    anatomy and neurochemistry of, 1175
    behavior therapy for, 1244–1250
    brain tumors and, 756–757
        corpus callosum tumors, 763–764
        diencephalic tumors, 763
        frontal lobe tumors, 759–760
            acquired sociopathy, **97,** 98–101
        occipital lobe tumors, 762–763
        parietal lobe tumors, 762
        pituitary tumors, 764
        posterior fossa tumors, 764
        temporal lobe tumors, 760–761
    drug-induced, 1175
    epilepsy and, 673, 687, 1095
    frontotemporal dementias and, 959, **960**
    schizophrenia and, 990
    traumatic brain injury and, 98–99, 634, 1243
    variability in severity of, 1244
Behavioral immobilization theory of non-REM sleep, 67
Behavioral Neurology Society, 1304
Behçet's disease, 830–831
    clinical features of, 813, 830
    diagnosis of, 830–831
    differentiation from multiple sclerosis, 830
    treatment of, 831
Bender-Gestalt test, 173, 233
Beneficence, 1258
Benzodiazepine receptor, 15, 1134, **1135**
    agonist, antagonist, and inverse agonist actions at, 1123
    functional imaging of, **288**
    in generalized anxiety disorder, 1053
    in panic disorder, 1057
    in schizophrenia, 308
Benzodiazepines
    abuse potential of, 706
    adverse effects of, 651–652, **1174**
        disinhibition, 1176
        rebound insomnia, 706
    dosage of, **1174**
    drug interactions with, **1174**

Benzodiazepines *(continued)*
  effects on memory, 613
  electroencephalographic effects of
      intoxication with, **202**
  electroencephalographic effects of
      long-term use of, 706
  indications for
      aggression, 1176
      agitation, 651–652, 1170–1171
      alcohol or sedative-hypnotic
          withdrawal, 546
      anxiety in Parkinson's disease,
          967
      aphasic patients, 577
      cortical-basal ganglionic
          degeneration, 939
      delirium, 546–548
      generalized anxiety disorder,
          1053
      insomnia, 711–712
      pain, **437**
      patients with Alzheimer's disease,
          1170
      patients with HIV/AIDS,
          800–801, 1170–1171
      patients with traumatic brain
          injury, 651–652
      periodic limb movement disorder
          and restless legs syndrome,
          **710**
  intramuscular, 1176
  mechanism of action of, 1134
  pharmacokinetics of, **712**
  use in elderly patients, 1171
  use in patients with brain tumors,
      772, 775, 776
Benztropine, 775
*Bereitschaftspotential,* 166
BEST-2 (Bedside Evaluation Screening
    Test), 228
Bethanechol, 1181
BGA (Brown-Goodwin Assessment) for
    Life History of Aggression, 581,
    585
Bilevel positive airway pressure, 714
Binswanger's disease, 975, **977**
Biofeedback, for attention-deficit/
    hyperactivity disorder, 1080
Bipolar disorder
  attentional disturbances in, 511
  bipolar II disorder, 368
  catecholamine hypothesis of, 372
  clinical features of, 368
  epidemiologic studies of, 368
  functional neuroimaging in, 303–305,
      **304**

genetic studies of, 368–372
    adoption studies, 369
    anticipation, 329, 372
    candidate genes, 372
    family studies, 368–369
    high-risk studies, 369–370
    linkage analysis, 370–371
    mode of inheritance, 370
    molecular approaches, 372
    relative risk, **325**
    twin studies, 369
  headache and, 454, 455
  Huntington's disease and, 331
  immune function and, 132
  migraine and, 466
  "permissive hypothesis" of serotonin
      activity in, 372
  poststroke, **729,** 743–744, 749
  psychiatric symptoms in children of
      patients with, 369–370
Birth-cohort studies, 325–326
  prospective vs. retrospective, 324
Bismuth poisoning, **879**
Blepharospasm, 159, 164
Blinking, 158
Block Design Test, 228, 231, 794
β-Blockers
  adverse effects of, 653–654
      nightmares, 718
  for aggression, 653–654, 1176
      in developmentally disabled
          persons, 592
  contraindications to, 1176
  for migraine prophylaxis, 473, **474,**
      478
Blood alcohol concentration (BAC), 658
Blood-brain barrier (BBB), 4
  delirium and increased permeability
      of, 534
  diffusion of radiologic contrast agents
      through, 247
"Blurting," 161
Body dysmorphic disorder, 1050
Bone marrow, 116
Bone marrow transplantation, for
    metachromatic leukodystrophy,
    347–349, **348**
Borderline personality disorder (BPD),
    588–589
  arson and, 590
  electroencephalography in, 589
  impulsivity and aggression in, 588–
      589
  neurological soft signs in, 589
  P300 potential in, 203
  pharmacotherapy for, 586, 587, 591

platelet monoamine oxidase in,
    585–586
  positron emission tomography in,
    583
  serotonin in, 585
Boston Diagnostic Aphasia Examination
    (BDAE), 172, 174, 228, 576
Botulinum toxin, 891–892
  for Tourette's syndrome, 1083
Bovine spongiform encephalopathy
    (BSE), 358–361
BPD. *See* Borderline personality
    disorder
BPRS (Brief Psychiatric Rating Scale),
    181, 857, 1164
BRAC (basic rest activity cycle), 698
Bradykinesia, 335
Brain, 264–281, **270–279.** *See also*
    Cerebellum; Cerebral cortex;
    Hemispheric lateralization;
    Neurons
  cellular composition of, 4, 1124
  determinants of recovery from injury
      or disease of, 1237–1238
  development of, 3, 22–35, 1069–
      1071, **1070, 1071**
  functional neuroanatomy of, 71–105
  HIV infection of, 785
  imaging of (*See also* Neuroimaging)
      functional, 72, 245, **246,** 285–
          312
      normal anatomy, 264–281, **270–**
          **279**
      structural, 71–72, 245–281, **246**
  integrative basic brain mechanisms
      important to understanding
      cerebral function, 1009–1011
      cortical-subcortical circuits, **1010,**
          1010–1011
      neural plasticity, 22, 33–34, 1011
      intrinsic repair mechanisms in, 34–
          35
  language-processing area of, 71, 565,
      **566**
  lateral specialization of, 72–73, **73,**
      **74**
  longitudinal specialization of, 73–74,
      **75**
  opioid receptors in, 432–433
  pathways of brain to immune
      signaling, 134–138, **135**
      biochemical pathways, 138
      corticotropin-releasing hormone,
          136, **137**
      hypothalamic-pituitary-adrenal
          axis, 134–135

other factors, 137–138

sympathetic nervous system, 135–136

pathways of immune to brain signaling, 138–141, **139, 141**

clinical effects of cytokines, 140–141, **142**

subcortical structures in relationship to cortex and skull, **269**

Brain-behavior relationships, 72–74

lateral specialization, 72–73, **73, 74**

longitudinal specialization, 73–74, **75**

Brain-derived neurotrophic factor, 29

in Parkinson's disease, 34

Brain electrical activity mapping (BEAM), **629,** 632, 770

Brain injury, traumatic (TBI), 625–659

age and gender distribution of, 625, 1204

alcohol intoxication and, 633, 658

Alzheimer's disease and, 954

animal models of, 627, 655, 656

causes of, 625, 628, 1204

in children, 625, 634, 635, 1097–1098

attention-deficit/hyperactivity disorder and, 1097–1098

capacity for recovery from, 1097

due to child abuse, 659

posttraumatic stress disorder and, 1098

prevention of, 658–659

psychiatric consequences of, 1097–1098

clinical features of, 633–645

affective changes, 636–638

aggression, 643, **644**

anxiety disorders, 640–641, 1051

attentional disturbances, 509–510

behavioral dysfunction, 98–99, 634, 1243

delirium, 553, 638, **638**

intellectual changes, 634–636, **635**

language disturbances, 565, 1205–1206

memory impairment, 230

mild traumatic brain injury and postconcussion syndrome, **641,** 641–643

personality changes, 634, **635**

physical problems, 643–645

coldness, 643–645

other somatic problems, 645

posttraumatic epilepsy, 639–640

problems with processing multiple stimuli, 649

psychiatric disorders, 636

psychotic disorders, 638–639

sleep disorders, 641

contusions, 509, 626

deficits in reaction time in, 500

dreaming in patients with, 156

economic cost of, 625–626

in elderly persons, 633

epidemiology of, 625–626, 1204

excitotoxicity and, 33, 627, 656

history taking for, 155

incidence of, 625

loss of consciousness due to, 626–629

mild, 155

definition of, 628–629, **630**

postconcussion syndrome and, **641,** 641–643

mortality from, 625

neuroanatomy of, 626

coup and contrecoup injuries, 626

diffuse axonal injury, 626

neurochemistry of, 627

neuropsychiatric assessment of, 628–632

documentation and rating of symptoms, 628–630, **629–631**

electrophysiological techniques, 632

functional neuroimaging, 630–632

history taking, 628

neuropsychological testing, 632, **632**

structural neuroimaging, 630

pathophysiology of, **626,** 626–627

personal injury litigation related to, 1281–1283

prevention of, 657–659

in children, 658–659

motor vehicle accidents, 657–658

prognosis for recovery from, 633, **633,** 655, 1097, 1237–1238

recurrence of, 657

as risk factor for Alzheimer's disease, 353

sports-related, 625, 659

subdural hematoma due to, 626, 727

treatment of, 645–657

behavioral and cognitive treatments, 656, 1238–1243

case example of, 1248–1249

family support, 657, 1208–1209

pharmacologic, 645–656

for aggression and agitation, 651–654, **654**

cholinesterase inhibitors, 650

for cognitive function and arousal problems, 648–649

concerns about, 654–655

for depression, 646–647, 1158

effect on recovery, 655

for fatigue, 649–650

for lability of mood and affect, 647–648

to limit extent of brain damage, 655–656

for mania, 647

principles of, 645

for psychosis, 650

for sleep disorders, 650–651

psychological and social interventions, 656–657, 1204–1209, **1206**

Brain Injury Screening Questionnaire, 629, **629**

Brain tumors, 753–777

age and, 753

aphasia and, 565

classification of, 753

clinical manifestations related to laterality of, 764–765

of corpus callosum, 763–764

diagnosis of, 765–770

cerebral angiography, 770

cisternography, 767

computed tomography, 766–767, **768**

electroencephalography, 770

functional neuroimaging, 770, **771**

general clinical characteristics, 765

lumbar puncture, 770

magnetic resonance imaging, 767, **767–769**

magnetoencephalography, 770

neuropsychological testing, 757–759, 770

physical and neurological examinations, 766

skull films, 770

when to suspect in psychiatric patient, 765–766

diencephalic, 763

neuropsychiatric and behavioral manifestations of, 763

Brain tumors *(continued)*
diencephalic *(continued)*
neuropsychological manifestations
of, 763
electroencephalogram in patients
with, **202**
frequency of neuropsychiatric
symptoms in patients with,
754–755
of frontal lobe, 759–760
neuropsychiatric and behavioral
manifestations of, 756, 759–
760
neuropsychological manifestations
of, 760
histologic types of, 753, **754**
incidence of, 753
localization of, 765, 766, **766**
on magnetic resonance imaging, **265**
metastatic, 753, **754**, 756, **767**
mortality from, 753
neuropsychiatric consequences of
treatments for, 777
neuropsychiatric considerations in
patients with, 755–757, **758**
neuropsychological considerations in
patients with, 757–759
of occipital lobe, 762–763, **771**
neuropsychiatric and behavioral
manifestations of, 762–763
neuropsychological manifestations
of, 763
of parietal lobe, 762
neuropsychiatric and behavioral
manifestations of, 762
neuropsychological manifestations
of, 762
pituitary, 764
of posterior fossa, 764
primary, 753
providing prognostic information to
patients with, 774
"silent," 765–766
of temporal lobe, 760–762
neuropsychiatric and behavioral
manifestations of, 756, 757,
**758**, 760–762
neuropsychological manifestations
of, 762
topographic distribution of, 753,
**754, 755**
treating psychiatric and behavioral
symptoms of, 770–777
anxiety disorders, 776
cognitive rehabilitation, 776–777
delirium, 776

general considerations, 770–772
mood disorders, 772–773, 775–
776
personality changes, 776
pharmacotherapy, 772–773
psychotherapy, 773–774, 1231,
**1232**
psychotic disorders, 774–775
somatic treatment, 774
Brainstem
encephalitis of, 166
neural machinery of REM sleep
rhythm in, 55–57, **56**
in pain processing, 426–427, **428,
429**
Breach of confidentiality, 1272
Breast cancer, 126
Breathing, sleep-disordered, **707**, 708,
713–714
causes of, 713
clinical features of, 713
comorbid conditions with, 714
position-dependent, 714
predisposing factors for, 713–714
treatment of, 714
bilevel and self-adjusting positive
airway pressure, 714
continuous positive airway
pressure, 714
oral appliances, 714
other treatments, 714
surgery, 714
Brief Psychiatric Rating Scale (BPRS),
181, 857, 1164
Bright light therapy, for insomnia,
711
British anti-Lewisite (BAL), 881, 884
Broca, Paul, 71, 72, 565
Broca's aphasia, 95, **97, 98**, 568, **568**,
574
frontal lobe tumors and, 760
neuropathology of, 568, **569**
Broca's area, **73**, 74, 95, **566**
in posttraumatic stress disorder,
1058, **1059**, 1060
Bromocriptine
for aphasia, 576
for hyperprolactinemia, 866
mechanism of action of, 648
for Parkinson's disease, 969, 1159
for patients with traumatic brain
injury, 648–649
for periodic limb movement disorder
and restless legs syndrome,
**710**
Brompton's cocktail, 438

Brown-Goodwin Assessment (BGA) for
Life History of Aggression, 581,
585
Bruxism during sleep, **707**, 719
BSE (bovine spongiform
encephalopathy), 358–361
Budd-Chiari syndrome, 813
Bulimia nervosa, 585
Buprenorphine, 439, **441**
Bupropion
adverse effects of, **1161**
seizures, 647, 686, 773
dosage of, **1161**
drug interactions with, **1161**
effects on sleep, 703, 711
indications for, 1157
aphasia, 576
attention-deficit/hyperactivity
disorder, 1079
patients with dementia, **980**, 981
patients with diabetes mellitus,
**855**
patients with HIV/AIDS, 799
patients with Parkinson's disease,
967, 1158
mechanism of action of, **1144**
use in patients with traumatic brain
injury, 646, 647
Burst firing of neurons, 6, **8**
Buspirone
adverse effects of, **1174**
dosage of, **1174**
drug interactions with, **1174**
indications for
aggression, 591, 1176
in developmentally disabled
persons, 592
in patients with traumatic
brain injury, 652
agitation, 1171
generalized anxiety disorder,
1052
patients with dementia, **980**, 981
patients with HIV/AIDS, 801
mechanism of action of, 1134, 1141,
**1144**
use in patients with brain tumors,
776
Buss "Aggression Machine" (BAM), 581
Buss-Durkee Hostility Inventory
(BDHI), 581, 585
Butalbital, for migraine, **474**
Butorphanol, **441**

*c-fos* gene, 29, 65
C-reactive protein, 117, 123

Caffeine
as coanalgesic, **437**, 438
for migraine, **474**
Cajal-Retzius cells, 24
Calcineurin, 1137, **1140**
Calcium, 901
interaction of G proteins with, 15,
**16**
in long-term potentiation, 21
in regulation of growth cone
progress, 33, 34
Calcium channel blockers
for Alzheimer's disease, 1182
for HIV/AIDS, 796
for mania, 1172
for migraine prophylaxis, 473, **474,**
475
Calcium disodium
ethylenediaminetetraacetic acid
(EDTA), 883
Calcium ion channels, **1125**
calcineurin regulation of, 1137
in generation of action potential, 5–6,
**6**
role in neurotransmitter release
process, 1128
role of glutamate in opening of, 1125
in synaptic transmission, 10, **11**
voltage-gated, 1128
California Verbal Learning Test, 230
Callosal disconnection syndrome, 168–
169
Calmodulin, **16,** 21
CAM (Confusion Assessment Method),
526, 530, 537, **538**
Cambridge Neurological Inventory
(CNI), **169**
cAMP. *See* Cyclic adenosine
monophosphate
cAMP response element binding protein
(CREB), 904, 915–917, 1137
antidepressant effects on, 1144
Cancer
brain tumors, 753–777
breast, 126
colorectal, 125
delirium due to, **545**
group psychotherapy for patients
with, 126
in HIV/AIDS, 122, 787, **787**
managing pain of, 434, 438, 441, 442
stress, depression, and immunity in,
125–126
Cancer chemotherapy
for brain tumors, neuropsychiatric
consequences of, 777

delirium induced by, **547**
Candidate gene studies, 329. *See also*
Molecular genetic studies
in Alzheimer's disease, 357
in autism, 346–347
in bipolar disorder, 372
in epilepsy, 364
in panic disorder, 376
in Parkinson's disease, 340
in schizophrenia, 384–385
Cannabinoids, **901**
Capgras' syndrome, 175, 956, 975,
1200–1201, **1205**
Capsaicin, 430
Carbamate pesticide exposure, **880**
Carbamazepine, 690
adverse effects of, 647, 690, 1096,
**1173**
dosage of, **1173**
drug interactions with, **689**, 690,
**1173**
indications for
aggression, 652, 1177
in developmentally disabled
persons, 592
agitation, 1170
borderline personality disorder,
587
epilepsy, 1096
Lesch-Nyhan syndrome, 334
mood disorders in patients with
epilepsy, 686
neuropathic pain, 436, **437**
patients with brain tumors, 772,
775, 776
patients with dementia, **980,** 981
patients with traumatic brain
injury, 639, 647, 652
periodic limb movement disorder
and restless legs syndrome,
**710**
secondary mania, 743, 1170
in Huntington's disease, 965
in patients with traumatic
brain injury, 647
Carbon dioxide-induced panic attacks,
374–375
Carbon disulfide exposure, **879**
Carbon monoxide (CO), 17, 21
poisoning with, 885–886
diagnosis of, 886
mechanism of action of, 885–886
neuropsychiatric manifestations
of, **880**, 885, **886**
sources of exposure, 885
treatment of, 886

Carbon tetrachloride exposure, **879**
Cardiac drug-induced delirium, **547**
Cardiac effects of tricyclic
antidepressants, 1079
Cardiopulmonary resuscitation (CPR),
1262–1263
Careers in neuropsychiatry, 1303
Caregivers. *See* Family/caregivers
Carisoprodol, 438
Case-control studies, 324
Caspases, 30
in Huntington's disease, 334
Catalepsy, 167
Cataplexy, 62–64, 715
Catastrophic reaction
definition of, 746
poststroke, 724, 725, **729,** 731–732,
746–747, 749
schizophrenia and, 1202
Catastrophic Reaction Scale, 746
Catatonia, 166–167
Catechol-O-methyltransferase
(COMT), 1132
in bipolar disorder, 372
in obsessive-compulsive disorder,
380
in Parkinson's disease, 341
Category Test, 231–233, 235, 609
Caudate nucleus, 103, 266
anatomy of, 269, **274, 275, 277**
in attention-deficit/hyperactivity
disorder, 1074
deficits associated with lesions of,
269
in depression, 1029
in Huntington's disease, 926–927,
**927,** 964–965
in obsessive-compulsive disorder,
1055
Causalgia, 430
CBF studies. *See* Cerebral blood flow
studies
CBGD (cortical-basal ganglionic
degeneration), **925,** 939, **939**
CCCA (Comprehensive Crime Control
Act), 1268
CD4+ (helper) T cells, 119–121
in depression, 130
in HIV infection, 122, 126
Th1 and Th2, 121
CD8+ (cytotoxic) T cells, **120,** 121
CDH. *See* Chronic daily headache
Celebrex. *See* Celecoxib
Celecoxib, 434
Celiac disease, 831
Cell-mediated immunity, 118–121, **120**

Central anticholinergic syndrome, 548

Central canal, 426

Central executive, 600

Central nervous system (CNS). *See also* Brain

    long-term potentiation in, 19–22, **20**

    neurons of, 3–22, 1127–1140 (*See also* Neurons)

    primary angiitis of, 825

    primary lymphoma of, in HIV infection, 122

    psychotherapeutic approach to patients with infections and inflammations of, 1225–1226

Cerebellum

    in attention-deficit/hyperactivity disorder, 1074

    in autism, 1088

    diseases of, 940–941

        Friedreich's ataxia, 940

        olivopontocerebellar atrophies, 940

        other spinocerebellar degenerations, 940–941

Cerebral aneurysms, 727

Cerebral angiography, 217, 770, 825, 979

Cerebral blood flow (CBF) studies, 285–286. *See also* Neuroimaging, functional

    arterial spin labeling, 291

    correlation with emotions, 295

    positron emission tomography, 287

    single photon emission computed tomography, 289

    in specific conditions

        Alzheimer's disease, 957, **957**

        attention-deficit/hyperactivity disorder, 1074–1075

        child abuse, 1101

        cortical-basal ganglionic degeneration, 939

        Fahr's disease, 942

        generalized anxiety disorder, 1053

        HIV/AIDS, 790

        posttraumatic stress disorder, 1060

        schizophrenia, 1003–1005, **1005**

        social phobia, 1061

        traumatic brain injury, 626–627, **629**

Cerebral contusions, 509, 626. *See also* Brain injury, traumatic

Cerebral cortex

    anatomy of, 266, **275, 276, 278, 279**

    in attention, **494,** 494–496, **495,** 506

    in attention-deficit/hyperactivity disorder, 1074

    development of, 24–26, **25**

    HIV infection of, 785

    integrative basic brain mechanisms important to understanding cerebral function, 1009–1011

        cortical-subcortical circuits, **1010,** 1010–1011

        neural plasticity, 22, 33–34, 1011

    in pain perception, 419–420, 429

    role of prefrontal cortex in aggression, 583

    in schizophrenia, 993–994

    subcortical structures in relationship to skull and, **269**

Cerebral embolism, 726–727

Cerebroside sulfate, 347

Cerebrospinal fluid (CSF)

    findings in specific conditions

        Behçet's disease, 830

        Hashimoto's encephalopathy, 829

        HIV/AIDS, 790–791

        5-hydroxyindoleacetic acid levels in impulsive aggression, **584,** 584–585

        3-methoxy-4-hydroxy-phenylglycol levels and aggression, 587

        normal-pressure hydrocephalus, 943

        primary angiitis of central nervous system, 825

        sarcoidosis, 830

        systemic lupus erythematosus, 820

    measures of cytokines or acute phase proteins in, 121

    shunting for normal-pressure hydrocephalus, 943–944, 977–978

Cerebrovascular disease, 723–749

    age-specific incidence of, 723, **724**

    apoptosis and, 22

    case example of behavior therapy for, 1249–1250

    classification of, 725–728, **726**

        aneurysms and arteriovenous malformations, 727

        atherosclerotic thrombosis, 726

        cerebral embolism, 726–727

        fibromuscular dysplasia, 728

        inflammatory diseases, 728

        intracerebral hemorrhage, 727

        lacunae, 727

        other types, 728

        subdural and epidural hematomas, 727–728

    definition of stroke, 723

    electroencephalogram in patients with, **202**

    excitotoxicity and, 33

    historical perspective on, 723–725

    in HIV/AIDS, 789

    neuropsychiatric syndromes associated with, 723, 728–748, **729**

        antiphospholipid antibody syndrome, 821

        apathy, 746

        aphasia, 565, 575

        aprosody, 748

        attentional disturbances, 507–508

        auditory agnosia, 92

        catastrophic reaction, 724, 725, 731–732, 746–747

        delirium, **545, 551,** 552, 553

        depression, 725

        lesion location and, **729**

        neglect syndrome, 171

        pathologic emotions, 724–725, 747–748, 1209

        poststroke anxiety disorder, 744–745, 1051

        poststroke bipolar disorder, 743–744

        poststroke depression, 725, 728–741, 1031–1032

        poststroke mania, 741–743

        poststroke psychosis, 745–746

        prevalence of, **729**

        Sneddon's syndrome, 826–827

        vascular dementia, 973–976

    primitive reflexes in, 167

    psychotherapy for patients with, 1209–1210

        defenses and object relations in hemiplegia, 1210

        postdischarge planning, 1210

    silent stroke, 219

Certification in neuropsychiatry, 1303–1304

Ceruloplasmin deficiency, 971

cGMP (cyclic guanosine 3',5'-monophosphate), 17, 27, **1135**

Chandelier cell, in schizophrenia, 995

Channelopathies, 361

Charcot-Marie-Tooth disease, 9

Charles Bonnet syndrome, 175

ChAT. *See* Choline acetyltransferase

Chelation therapy

for arsenic poisoning, 881
for Hallervorden-Spatz disease, 971
for lead poisoning, 882
for manganese poisoning, 883
for mercury poisoning, 884
for Wilson's disease, 341, 942, 972
Chemical warfare agents, 887–888, **888**
Chemoattraction/chemorepulsion, **26,**
26–27
Chemokines, 116
Chemotoxic reaction to contrast agent,
252
Cherek Point Subtraction Aggressin
Paradigm (PSAP), 581
Chest radiography, 770
Child safety seats, 658–659
Children and adolescents, 1069–1101
autism and pervasive developmental
disorders in, 343–347, 1087–
1090
Asperger's disorder, 173, 1090
Rett's disorder, 1089–1090
brain development in, 1069–1071,
**1070, 1071**
lateralization and hemispheric
asymmetry, 1071
delirium in, 525, 540
haloperidol for, 549
disorders of excessive motor activity,
movement, impulse, and
thought in, 1071–1084
attention-deficit/hyperactivity
disorder, 512–517, 1071–
1080
Tourette's syndrome and other tic
disorders, 1080–1084
emancipated minors, 1259
HIV infection in, 1098–1099
learning disorders in, 1090–1093
mental retardation in, 1084–1087
Angelman's syndrome, 1086–
1087
Down syndrome, 1085
fragile X syndrome, 1086
Prader-Willi syndrome, 1086–
1087
neuropsychiatric consequences of
abuse of, 1099–1101
of patients with bipolar disorder,
369–370
pediatric autoimmune
neuropsychiatric disorder
associated with streptococcal
infections in, 129, 378–379,
828, 1050, 1055, 1056, 1081
seizure disorders in, 1093–1097

absence epilepsy, 363, 510
traumatic brain injury in, 625, 634,
635, 1097–1098
prevention of, 658–659
Chloral hydrate
for insomnia, 711
for patients with traumatic brain
injury, 652
Chlordane exposure, 888
Chlordecone exposure, 888
Chlordiazepoxide, 1176
Chloride ion channels, 6, **1125**
Chlorisondamine, 136
Chlorophenoxy compounds, 888, **889**
m-Chlorophenylpiperazine (m-CPP),
473, 1052, 1054, 1056, 1057,
1059
2-Chloroprocaine, 437, **437**
Chlorpromazine, 1124
for AIDS-associated delirium, 797,
1171
for anticholinergic delirium, 549
dopamine antagonist properties of,
1140
seizures induced by, 773
Cholecystokinin, **1135**
Choline acetyltransferase (ChAT), 1130
in Alzheimer's disease, 357
in frontotemporal dementias, 961
in olivopontocerebellar atrophies,
940
Cholinergic receptors, 1134
binding activity after traumatic brain
injury, 627
functional imaging of, **288**
muscarinic, 1134, 1141
nicotinic, 15, 1134
in myasthenia gravis, 5
nicotine effects at, **901**
presynaptic, 1129
subtypes of, 1134, **1135,** 1141
in Tourette's syndrome, 1083
Cholinesterase inhibitors, 1180
for agitation, 1172
for Alzheimer's disease, 954, 958,
979, 1180
for dementia with Lewy bodies, 937,
959
for patients with traumatic brain
injury, 650
Chomsky, Noam, 566
Chorea, 164–165
in antiphospholipid antibody
syndrome, 821
in Huntington's disease, 165, 331,
924, 927–928

treatment of, 930
Sydenham's, 378–379, 827–828,
927
obsessive-compulsive disorder
and, 378, 828, 1050
Chromosomal abnormalities, 329. *See
also* Genetic studies; Linkage
analysis
aggression and, 587
autism and, 346
Down syndrome and, 1085
Chronic daily headache (CDH), 452–
457
classification of, 453
definition of, 453
epidemiology of, 454
medication overuse and, 453, 457
psychopathology and, 454–455
treatment of, 455–457
Churg-Strauss syndrome, 813, 824
Ciliary neurotrophic factor, 30
Cingulate gyrus, 266, **280**
in attention, 496, 506
Cingulotomy, 1022
Circadian rhythm dyssomnias, 708
Circadian rhythms
attention and, 494–495
orexin release and, 65
sleep-wakefulness and, 47, **48,** 702–
703
Cisternography, 767, 977, 979
Citalopram, **1160–1161**
adverse effects of, **1160**
dosage of, **1160**
drug interactions with, **1160**
indications for, 1157–1158
agitation, 1171
patients with dementia, **980,**
1176
patients with HIV/AIDS, 799
poststroke depression, 740, 741
poststroke pathological emotions,
747–748, **748**
mechanism of action of, **1144**
use in patients with traumatic brain
injury, 646
Citicoline, 1182
CJD. *See* Creutzfeldt-Jakob disease
Clasp-knife phenomenon, 163
Classical conditioning, 599
cue-induced relapse to drug-seeking
behavior, 908–909
Claustrum, 266
Clinical Global Impression scale, 550
Clinical trials, 1145
Clock face drawing test, 173, 537, **539**

Clomipramine
  dosage of, **436**
  effects on sleep, 711
  indications for
    autism, 1089
    impulsive aggression, 591
    obsessive-compulsive disorder,
      1054
    pain, **437**
    pathological gambling, 590
    patients with HIV/AIDS, 799
  mechanism of action of, **1144**
  seizures induced by, 686
  terminal half-life of, **436**
Clonazepam, **1174**
  for aggression, 1176
    in patients with traumatic brain
      injury, 652
  for delirium, 546–548
  for Huntington's disease, 965
  for neuropathic pain, **437**
  for patients with brain tumors, 772,
    775
  for patients with dementia,
    **980**
  for patients with HIV/AIDS, 801
  for periodic limb movement disorder
    and restless legs syndrome,
    **710**
  pharmacokinetics of, **712**
Clonidine, 433
  adverse effects of, 1079, **1179**
  dosage of, **1179**
  drug interactions with, **1179**
  indications for
    aggression, 1177–1178
    attention-deficit/hyperactivity
      disorder, 1077, 1079
    Korsakoff's dementia, 1182
    secondary mania, 743
    Tourette's syndrome, 1084
  mechanism of action of, 1077
  transdermal, 1079
Clorazepate, **712**
Closed head injury. *See* Brain injury,
  traumatic
*Clostridium botulinum*, 891
*Clostridium tetani*, 892
Clozapine
  adverse effects of, 550, 1006, 1165,
    1166, **1167**
    delirium, 550
    seizures, 650, 773, 1165
  dosage of, **1167**
  drug interactions with, **1167**
  effects on memory, 614

epileptiform
  electroencephalographic activity
    in patients receiving, 206
  indications for
    aggression, 652, 1177
    patients with dementia, 980, **980**
    patients with Huntington's
      disease, 964
    patients with Parkinson's disease,
      935, 1165, 1166
    patients with traumatic brain
      injury, 650, 652
    psychosis in Parkinson's disease,
      336
  pharmacology of, 1006
  receptor binding affinity of, **1142,**
    1143
Cluster headache, 478–481
  comorbidity with, 479
  diagnostic criteria for, 479, **479**
  epidemiology of, 479
  pathophysiology of, 479–480
  treatment of, 480–481
    acute, 480
    preventive, 480–481
Cluttering, 160
Clyde Mood Scale, 857
CMV (cytomegalovirus) infection,
  788
CNI (Cambridge Neurological
  Inventory), **169**
CNS. *See* Central nervous system
CNV (contingent negative variation),
  204
CO. *See* Carbon monoxide
Coanalgesics, 436–438, **437**. *See also*
  Pain management
Cocaine. *See also* Substance abuse
  as coanalgesic, **437**, 438
  history taking for use of, 155
  mechanism of action of, 10–11
  pharmacologic actions of, **901**
  stereotypy and, 166
  vasculitis induced by, **826**
Codeine, **440**
  for periodic limb movement disorder
    and restless legs syndrome, **710**
Cogan's syndrome, 813, 824–825
Cognex. *See* Tacrine
Cognitive Competency Test, 235
Cognitive disturbance, 1178–1182
  anatomy and neurochemistry of,
    1178–1180
  antiphospholipid antibody syndrome
    and, 821
  aphasia and, 574–575

assessment for (*See* Bedside
  neuropsychiatric assessment)
autism and, 1087, 1088
borderline personality disorder and,
  589
brain tumors and, 758–759
  cognitive rehabilitation for, 776–
    777
  diencephalic tumors, 763
  frontal lobe tumors, 760
  occipital lobe tumors, 762
  parietal lobe tumors, 762
  temporal lobe tumors, 762
delirium, 525–555
dementia, 953–981
  Alzheimer's disease, 351–357,
    510–511, 954–958
  frontotemporal dementias, 959–
    962
  HIV-associated, 784–787
depression and, 219, 511, 1026–
  1028
  dementia of depression, 962,
    1027–1028
  impact of medications on, 1027
  poststroke, 738–739, **740**
  postulated mechanisms of, 1026–
    1027
electroconvulsive therapy-induced,
  601, 602, 614–615
electroencephalography in diagnosis
  of, **202**, 206
emotionalism and, 176
endocrine disorders and
  Cushing's syndrome, **862**, 862–
    863
  diabetes mellitus, 852–853
  hyperthyroidism, 858–859,
    **859**
  hypothyroidism, **856**, 856–857,
    **857**
epilepsy and, 510
etiologies of, 1178
history taking for mild cognitive
  impairment, 155
HIV/AIDS and, 784–787
  neurobehavioral assessment of,
    792–795, **793, 794**
Huntington's disease and, **928**, 928–
  929
mental retardation, 1084–1087
multiple sclerosis and, 509
neuropsychological evaluation of,
  217–236
obsessive-compulsive disorder and,
  220

Parkinson's disease and, 336, 932–933, 966, 1220
pharmacotherapy for, 1180–1182
schizophrenia and, 220, 306–307, 999–1000
Sjögren's syndrome and, 822
systemic lupus erythematosus and, 817–819
traumatic brain injury and, 509–510, 634–636, **635**
treatment of, 648–649
Cognitive rehabilitation, 776–777, 1208, 1238–1243
for attentional disturbances, 1239
definition of, 1238
effectiveness of, 1238–1239
individualization of, 1238
for memory impairment, 1239–1241
for molar behaviors, 1242–1243
for problem-solving and executive function deficits, 1242
in schizophrenia, 1239
for speech and language disorders, 1242
use of computers in, 1243
for visual-perceptual disorders, 1241
Cognitive Test for Delirium (CTD), 527, 536–537
Cognitive therapy, 1246. *See also* Behavior therapy
for cancer patients, 126
for patients with spinal cord injury, 1211
for patients with traumatic brain injury, 656
for poststroke depression, 741
Cogwheeling, 163
Cohort studies, 325–326
prospective vs. retrospective, 324
Coldness, after traumatic brain injury, 643–644
Colony-stimulating factors, 116, **117**
Color agnosia, 87
Color anomia, 89
Color blindness, 87
Color perception defect, 87, 173
Colorectal cancer, 125
Coma, 506, **526**
Communicative Abilities of Daily Living, 576
Competency, 1258–1259
adjudication of incompetence, 1259
of aphasic patients, 575–576
case example related to, 1258
definition of, 1258
to give informed consent, 1260

mental capacity and, 1258–1259
of mentally disabled persons, 1259
of minors, 1259
neuropyschological tests for determination of, 235
presumption of, 1259
right to die and, 1261–1262
to stand trial, 1267
Complement proteins, 118
Comprehension, assessment of, 172
Comprehensive Crime Control Act (CCCA), 1268
Compulsions, 1049. *See also* Obsessive-compulsive disorder
vs. tics, 166
Computed tomography (CT), 71–72, 217, 245, **246**, 248–253
compared with magnetic resonance imaging, 264, **264, 266–268**
contraindications to, **264**
contrast agents for, 247, 251–253
allergic reactions to, 252
extravasation of, 252
metformin interaction with, 253
indications for, 264, **264**
patient preparation for, 247
practical considerations for, 247
principles of, 246
in specific conditions
achromatopsia, **88**
acute hemorrhage, **266**
Alzheimer's disease, 957, 961
Balint's syndrome, **86**
brain tumor, 766–767, **768**
Broca's aphasia, 95, **97, 98**
Creutzfeldt-Jakob disease, 978
dementia, 979
dementia with Lewy bodies, 937
epilepsy, 677
Fahr's disease, 970–971
frontotemporal dementias, 959, 961
Hallervorden-Spatz disease, 943, 971
HIV/AIDS, 789–790
Huntington's disease, 964, **965**
normal-pressure hydrocephalus, 977
orbitofrontal meningioma, **102**
panic disorder, 1058
Parkinson's disease, 968
progressive supranuclear palsy, 938, 969–970
schizophrenia, 992
toxin exposure, 895
traumatic brain injury, **629**, 630

vascular dementia, 975
Wernicke's aphasia, **91**
Wilson's disease, 942, 971
standard two-dimensional, 249, **249, 250**
gray-scale values for tissues visible on, 249, **249**
slice thickness for, 249
technological evolution of, 248, **248**
three-dimensional helical (spiral), 249–250, **250, 251**
training for interpretation of, 1293, 1302
xenon-enhanced, 245, 248, 251, **252**
Computers in cognitive rehabilitation, 1243
COMT. *See* Catechol-O-methyltransferase
Conation impairment, **1201, 1204**
Concept formation tests, 231–233
Concurrent production tasks, 501
Concussion, 626. *See also* Brain injury, traumatic
Conduct disorder
antisocial personality disorder and, 589–590
attention-deficit/hyperactivity disorder and, 1072
substance abuse and, 590
Conduction aphasia, **91**, 92, **93**, 172, 228, **568**, 570
Confabulation, 174
amnesia and, 602
basal forebrain lesions and, **97**, 97–98
Korsakoff's syndrome and, 104
neglect syndrome and, 508
Confidentiality, 1271–1272
breach of, 1272
liability for, 1272
clinical-legal foundation for, 1271–1272
definition of, 1271
statutory exceptions to, 1272, **1272**
testimonial privilege and, 1271, 1272
Confusion Assessment Method (CAM), 526, 530, 537, **538**
Confusional State Evaluation, 537
Confusional states, 507
delirium, 525–555
posttraumatic, 638
Conner's Rating Scale, 1074
Connexin, 9

Consciousness
　alterations of, 489
　　adaptations in psychiatric
　　　technique for, **1201**
　　in delirium, 525, **526**, 536, 541,
　　　**541**
　　　due to subdural or epidural
　　　　hematoma, 727
　　definition of, 489
　　fluctuating, in dementia with Lewy
　　　bodies, 936
　　levels of, 506–507
　　loss of
　　　due to traumatic brain injury,
　　　　626–629
　　　during epileptic seizure, 674–675
　　relation to attention, 489–490
Consonant Trigrams Test, **499**, 500
Constructional ability, 231, **232, 539**
　adaptations in psychiatric technique
　　relative to, **1201**
Constructional apraxia, **539**
Contact attraction/repulsion, **26,** 26–27
Contingent negative variation (CNV),
　204
Continuous Performance Test (CPT),
　382, **499,** 504, 514
Continuous positive airway pressure
　(CPAP), 714
Continuous Visual Memory Test, 230
Contrast agents, 247
　for computed tomography,
　　251–253
　　allergic reactions to, 252
　　extravasation of, 252
　　metformin interaction with, 253
　diffusion through blood-brain barrier,
　　247, 262
　for magnetic resonance imaging,
　　262, **265**
　　allergic reactions to, 262
　　development of, 262
　　gadolinium-based, 262
Controlled Word Association Test, 503
Contusions, cerebral, 509, 626. *See also*
　Brain injury, traumatic
Convergence zones, 100
Conversion disorder, 1229–1231
Copper poisoning, **879**
Copper transport
　in Menkes' syndrome, 342
　in Wilson's disease, 341, 971
Coprolalia, 1081
Corgard. *See* Nadolol
Corpus callosum
　in abused children, 1100–1101

in attention-deficit/hyperactivity
　disorder, 1074
　in autism, 1088
　delayed myelination of, 1071
　in learning disorders, 1092
　tumors of, 763–764
Corpus striatum, 266
Corsi Blocks Test, **499,** 500
Cortical-basal ganglionic degeneration
　(CBGD), **925,** 939, **939,** 972, **972**
Cortico-striatal-thalamic-cortical circuit
　in obsessive-compulsive disorder,
　　1050, **1054,** 1054–1056, 1062
　in schizophrenia, 1163
　in Tourette's syndrome, 1083
Corticosteroids
　Alzheimer's disease risk and, 354
　indications for
　　appetite stimulation, 436
　　Behçet's disease, 831
　　cluster headache prophylaxis, 480
　　pain, 436, **437**
　　Sjögren's syndrome, 823
　　systemic lupus erythematosus,
　　　820
　neuropsychiatric disorder induced
　　by, 831–832, **863,** 863–864,
　　**864**
　receptors for, **1135**
Corticotropin-releasing factor (CRF),
　865
　in depression, 1025
　immunologic effects of, 136, **137,**
　　140
　in startle response, 210
　in stress-induced relapse to drug-
　　seeking behavior, 909
　stress-induced release of, 909
Cortisol
　in depression, 1025
　in posttraumatic stress disorder,
　　1059
　in social phobia, 1061
Counting Stroop task, 299, 1075
CPAP (continuous positive airway
　pressure), 714
m-CPP (*m*-chlorophenylpiperazine),
　473, 1052, 1054, 1056, 1057,
　1059
CPR (cardiopulmonary resuscitation),
　1262–1263
CPT (Continuous Performance Test),
　382, **499,** 504, 514
Craniopharyngiomas, 764
CREB. *See* cAMP response element
　binding protein

Crepuscular hallucinations, 176
Creutzfeldt-Jakob disease (CJD), 357–
　358
　clinical features of, 358, 978
　dementia with amyotrophy in,
　　941
　electroencephalogram in, **202,** 358,
　　978
　epidemiology of, 358, 978
　familial, 978
　iatrogenic, 358, 359
　incubation period for, 358
　mode of inheritance of, 360
　molecular approaches to, 361
　myoclonus in, 166
　neuropathology of, 358, **359**
　new variant, 358–360, **359,**
　　978
　sporadic form of, 358, 359
　treatment of, 978
CRF. *See* Corticotropin-releasing factor
Criminal proceedings, 1265–1271
　case example related to, 1265
　competency to stand trial, 1267
　criminal intent, 1266
　diminished capacity, 1269
　exculpatory and mitigating disorders,
　　1269–1270
　　automatisms, 1269
　　intoxication, 1269–1270
　　metabolic disorders, 1270
　　posttraumatic stress disorder,
　　　1270
　　temporal lobe seizures,
　　　1270
　guilty but mentally ill, 1271
　insanity defense, 1267–1269
Criminality
　antisocial personality disorder and,
　　589
　epilepsy and, 1095
Cross-fostering studies, 325
Crying, pathological, 176, 724–725
　amitriptyline for, 647
　poststroke, **729,** 747–749, **748**
　in progressive supranuclear palsy,
　　938, 969
Crying seizures, 176
Cryptococcosis, 787–788
CSF. *See* Cerebrospinal fluid
CT. *See* Computed tomography
CTD (Cognitive Test for Delirium),
　527, 536–537
Cushing's disease, 861
Cushing's syndrome, 861–863
　cardinal features of, 861

psychiatric symptoms in, 861–863,
   **862**
    mood and anxiety disorders, 861–
      862, 864
    psychosis and cognitive disorders,
      862–863
   treatment of, 862
Cutis marmorata, 827
Cutoff scores for neuropsychological
   tests, 224–225
Cyclic adenosine monophosphate
   (cAMP), **16,** 17, 27, 33, 901, 1125,
   **1135,** 1136–1138, **1138**
   opiate upregulation of, 904, **905**
   rate of synthesis of, 1137
   regulation in VTA and NAc in
      response to long-term drug
      exposure, 913–914
Cyclic guanosine 3',5'-monophosphate
   (cGMP), 17, 27, **1135**
Cyclobenzaprine, 438
Cyclooxygenase inhibitors, 430, 434
Cyclophosphamide
   for Sjögren's syndrome, 823
   for systemic lupus erythematosus,
      820
Cyclosarin, 889
Cycloserine, 1166, 1182
Cyclosporin A, 1137
Cytochrome *b*, 1144
Cytokines, 115–116, **117**. *See also*
   specific cytokines
   antidepressant effects on, 142
   antipsychotic effects on, 142
   behavioral effects of, 140
   in bipolar disorder, 132
   corticotropin-releasing hormone–
      induced release of, 136
   in delirium, 555
   in depression, **130,** 130–131, 140
   euthyroid sick syndrome induced by,
      140
   functions of, 116, 832
   in HIV/AIDS, 786, 791
   in immune to brain signaling, 138–
      140, **139**
   proinflammatory, 116
   in schizophrenia, **131,** 131–132
   "sickness behavior" induced by, 140,
      141, **141**
   stress and, 123
   in systemic lupus erythematosus,
      816
   therapeutic uses of, 140–141, **142**
    adverse effects of, 140–141
Cytomegalovirus (CMV) infection, 788

Cytotoxic (CD8+) T cells, **120,** 121

2,4-D (2,4-dichlorophenoxyacetic acid),
   888, **889**
d4T (stavudine), 795
Dacrystic seizures, 176
Dalmane. *See* Flurazepam
Darier's disease, 371
*DAT1* gene, 367, 1073
DCS (dorsal column stimulation), 433,
   444
ddC (zalcitabine), 795
ddI (didanosine), 795
Deep brain stimulation, for Parkinson's
   disease, 935, 969
Defense mechanisms, 1200–1202,
   **1203–1204**
Delayed-type hypersensitivity (DTH)
   reaction, 121
   to radiologic contrast agent
      for computed tomography, 252
      for magnetic resonance imaging,
        262
   stress and, 123
Delineation disorder, **1201,** 1202
*Délire spatial,* 175
Delirium, 507, 525–555
   categories of, 535–536, 544–546
   in children, 525, 540, 549
   cholinergic deficiency hypothesis of,
      544, 548, 552–553
   cognitive assessment for, 536–538
    instruments for, 526, 527, 537–
      538, **538**
   conditions associated with, 544–546,
      **545**
    Cushing's syndrome, 862–863
    HIV/AIDS, 549, 797–798
    hypoalbuminemia, 535
    hypothyroidism, 856
    traumatic brain injury, 638, **638**
   definition of, 525
   diagnosis of, 535–536, **536**
   differential diagnosis of, 526–528,
      **528**
    dementia, 526–528, 953–954
    depression, 528
    mania, 528
    schizophrenia, 528
    Wernicke's aphasia, **570**
   drug-induced, 534, **535, 545,** 546,
      **547,** 772
    antiparkinsonism agents, **547,**
      554, 967–968
   duration of, 532
   effect on hospital length of stay, 530

   in elderly persons, 528–529
   electroencephalography in, **202,** 206,
      527–528, 538–540, **539,** 550
   epidemiology of, 528–529, **530**
   evoked potentials in, 202, 540
   among hospitalized patients, 529,
      **530,** 532
   level of consciousness and, 525, **526,**
      536
   morbidity and mortality from, 529–
      531, **531**
   motoric subtypes of, 525, 526, 528,
      542–544, **543**
   neuropathophysiology of, 550–555
    final common neural pathway,
      541, **542,** 550–552
    neurotransmission, 552–555
    structural neuroimaging of brain
      lesions, **551,** 551–552
   not otherwise specified, 546
   among nursing home patients, 529
   persistent cognitive impairment after
      episode of, 531, 532
   postoperative, 534–535, 553
   reversibility of, 531–532
   risk factors for, 532–535, **533, 534**
   signs and symptoms of, 525, **527,**
      540–542
    attentional disturbances, 536,
      541
    core symptoms, 541, 551
    fluctuation of severity of, 525,
      541
    frequencies of, 541, **541**
   stress-vulnerability models for, 532–
      533, **533**
   subclinical, 525
   temporal course of, 525, **527,** 536
   terms used for, 525–526, **527**
   treatment of, 546–550
    orienting techniques, 546
    in patients with brain tumors,
      776
    pharmacologic, 546–550
   underdetection of, 526, 544
Delirium Assessment Scale, 537
Delirium Rating Scale (DRS), 527,
   537–538, **538**
Delirium Rating Scale–Revised-98
   (DRS-R-98), 537, 538, **538**
Delusions, 175, **1203**. *See also* Psychosis
   in Alzheimer's disease, 956, 958
   antiparkinsonism drug-induced, 967
   Capgras', 1200
   in delirium, 525, **527,** 528, 536, **541,**
      541–542

Delirium *(continued)*
in patients with brain tumors
frontal lobe tumors, 760
pharmacotherapy for, 774–776
pituitary tumors, 764
posterior fossa tumors, 764
temporal lobe tumors, 761
persecutory, 175
poststroke, 745–746
in schizophrenia, 990, **990**
spatial, 175
in vascular dementia, 975
Dementia, 953–981
age-specific prevalence of, 954
Alzheimer's disease, 351–357, 954–958
aphasia and, 565, 573
associated with motor dysfunction, 923–944, **924**
cerebellar diseases, 940–941
Friedreich's ataxia, 940
olivopontocerebellar atrophies, 940
other spinocerebellar degenerations, 940–941
cortical-basal ganglionic degeneration, 939, 972
dementia with Lewy bodies, 176, 553, 935–937, 958–959
Fahr's disease, 942, 970–971
frontotemporal dementia, 939–940, 959–962
genetic basis of, 923, **925**
Hallervorden-Spatz disease, 942–943, 971
Huntington's disease, 331–334, 924–931, 963–965
motor neuron disease, 941
normal-pressure hydrocephalus, 943–944, 976–978
Parkinson's disease, 335–341, 931–935, 965–969, 1220
progressive supranuclear palsy, 937–939, 969–970
thalamic degeneration, 941
Wilson's disease, 165, 341–343, 942, 971–972
classification of, 923–924
cortical, 923
definition of, 953
depressive, 962, 1027–1028
differential diagnosis of, 953–954
delirium, 526–528, **528**, 953–954
economic cost of, 954
electroencephalography in, **202**, 206, 527–528

etiologies of, 953
evaluating neuropsychiatric alterations in patients with, 978–979
laboratory investigations, 979
guardianship for persons with, 1264
hemorrhagic, 976, **977**
hereditary dysphasic, 939
HIV-associated (HAD), 784–787
biochemical markers for, 786–787
neurobehavioral assessment of, 792–795, **793, 794**
neuropathology of, 785
P300 potential in, 203
pathogenesis of, 786
signs and symptoms of, 792–794, **793**
testing for, 180
treatment of, 795–796
hypoperfusion, 975–976, **977**
late medical complications of, 979
of lenticulostriatal diseases, 962–963
management of, 979–981
approach to agitation, 1219
family/caregiver support, 981
nonpharmacologic, 981
pharmacotherapy, 979–981, **980**, 1159, 1171
multi-infarct, 975, **977**
in multiple system atrophies, 972–973
neuropsychological testing in, **226**
reversible, 954
strategic single-infarct, 975, **977**
stress and immunity in caregivers of patients with, 124
in subacute spongiform encephalopathies, 978
subcortical, 792, 924
in multiple sclerosis, 509
in subcortical small-vessel disease, 975, **977**
vascular, 973–976
Dementia praecox, 166
Dementia Rating Scale, 235
Dendrites, 4, **5**
connections with, 8–9
hemispheric lateralization and growth of, 1071
postsynaptic, 5, **5**, 8
Denial, 1200
among patients with brain tumors, 773–774
Depersonalization, 640
Depolarization, 5–6, 14, 1127, 1129
Depression, 1021–1038

Alzheimer's disease and, 956
aphasia and, 574, 576–577
attentional disturbances and, 511–512
biogenic amine hypothesis of, 1132
biological markers for, 1023–1026
endocrine changes, 1025, **1025**
hypothalamic-pituitary-adrenal axis, 864–865, 1025
hypothalamic-pituitary-thyroid axis, 861
neurotransmitters, 1023–1025, **1024**, 1132
sleep disturbance, 1025–1026, **1026**
cholinergic-aminergic imbalance theory of, 703
cognitive deficits and, 219, 511, 1026–1028
age and, 1027
dementia of depression, 962, 1027–1028
impact of medications on, 1027
poststroke, 738–739, **740**
postulated mechanisms of, 1026–1027
conditions associated with, 222, **1023**, 1155
diagnostic criteria for, 1021–1022, **1022**
differential diagnosis of, 1023
delirium, 528, **528**
drug-induced, 1155
duration of untreated episode of, 1022
effects on memory, 605–607
subjective evaluation of, 612, **612**
endocrine abnormalities and, 1025, **1025**
Cushing's syndrome, 861–862, **862**
diabetes mellitus, 853–854
hyperprolactinemia, 866
hyperthyroidism, **859**, 859–860
hypothyroidism, **856**, 857, **857**
environmental factors and, 1022
epidemiology of, 1022
etiologies of, 1155
functional neuroimaging in, **297**, 301–303, **303**, 1029–1032
patients with neurological disease, 1029–1032, **1030**
common findings across studies, 1032
Huntington's disease, 1031

Parkinson's disease, **1030,** 1031

strokes involving basal ganglia, 1031–1032

patients with primary affective disorder, 1033–1036

antidepressant-associated brain changes, 1034–1035

baseline predictors of treatment response, 1034

clinical correlates, 1033–1034, **1035**

relation to clinical response, 1035–1036, **1037**

headache and, 454–455

migraine, 466, 467, **467**

HIV/AIDS and, 798–800, 1155

immune function and, 129–131, **130,** 140

learning and, 606

motor performance deficits in, 1026

neuroanatomical findings in, 1028–1029, 1032, 1155–1157

functional neurocircuitry model, 1036–1037, **1038**

neurochemistry of, 1023–1025, **1024,** 1155–1157

neurologic disorders and, **1023,** 1028–1032, 1155

anatomic studies, 1028–1029

cerebrovascular disease, 725, 728–741, 748, 1031–1032

cortical-basal ganglionic degeneration, 939

epilepsy, 685–687, 1096

functional imaging studies, 1029–1032

Huntington's disease, 222, 331, 929, 964, 1031

lateralization, 1029

Parkinson's disease, 222, 336, 933–934, 966–967, **1030,** 1031

spinal cord injury, 1211

traumatic brain injury, 636–638, 646–647

pain and, 421

poststroke, 725, 728–741, 748, 1031–1032

diagnosis of, 728–731, **730**

duration of, 732–734, **734**

functional neuroimaging of strokes involving basal ganglia, 1031–1032

mechanism of, 739–740

neuroanatomy and neurochemistry of, 1157

phenomenology of, **729, 731,** 731–732

premorbid risk factors for, 737–738

prevalence of, **729,** 732, **733**

psychosocial adjustment and, 741

relationship to cognitive impairment, 738–739, **740**

relationship to lesion variables, **729,** 734–737, **736, 737**

relationship to physical impairment, 738

treatment of, 740–741, **741,** 1157–1159

prevalence of, 1022

primary, 1032–1036

anatomic studies of, 1032

clues from surgical ablation therapy for, 1032–1033

functional imaging in, 1033–1036, **1035, 1037**

refractory, 1022

retarded and agitated subtypes of, 1155

Sjögren's syndrome and, 822–823

sleep disturbances and, 155, 703, 1025–1026, **1026**

stress, immunity and, 125–129

in AIDS, 126

in autoimmune diseases, 127–129

in cancer, 125–126

in other viral infections, 126–127

stress-induced, 1022

systemic lupus erythematosus and, 815, 818

trait markers of, 1028

treatment of, 1022–1023 (*See also* Antidepressants)

options for, 1022

patient subtyping for, 1022

in patients with brain tumors, 772, 773, 775–776

in patients with dementia, **980,** 981

in patients with diabetes mellitus, 854, **855**

in patients with epilepsy, 686–687

in patients with HIV/AIDS, 799

in patients with traumatic brain injury, 646–647, 653

pharmacotherapy, 1155–1159, **1160–1162** (*See also* Antidepressants)

resistance to, 1022

vascular dementia and, 975

Wilson's disease and, 341, 971–972

Depressive pseudodementia, 528

Descending sensory pathways, **428,** 429–430

Descriptive epidemiologic studies, 324

Design fluency task, 503

Desipramine

adverse effects of, **1160**

dosage of, **436,** 1160

drug interactions with, **1160**

indications for, 1157–1158

anxiety in Parkinson's disease, 967

attention-deficit/hyperactivity disorder, 517, 1079

impulsive aggression, 591

patients with dementia, **980,** 981

patients with traumatic brain injury, 646, 649

mechanism of action of, **1144**

terminal half-life of, **436**

Developmental history, 154

Dexamethasone. *See also* Corticosteroids

psychiatric complications of, 863

for spinal cord compression, 436, **437**

Dexamethasone suppression test (DST)

in Cushing's syndrome, 861

in depression, 865, 1025

in social phobia, 1061

Dexedrine. *See* Dextroamphetamine

Dextroamphetamine. *See also* Amphetamine

adverse effects of, 649, **1162**

as coanalgesic, **437,** 438

dosage of, 1078, **1162**

drug interactions with, **1162**

indications for

attention-deficit/hyperactivity disorder, 517, 1078

behavioral disturbances, 1177

HIV-associated dementia, 1182

patients with HIV/AIDS, 799

patients with traumatic brain injury, 648, 649

mechanism of action of, 648, 1077

Dextromoramide, **440**

Dextrorphan, 656

DHE. *See* Dihydroergotamine

Diabetes mellitus, 851–854

cardinal features of, 851–852

Diabetes mellitus *(continued)*
    psychiatric symptoms in, 852–854
        cognitive disorders, 852–853
        mood disorders, 853–854
        prevalence of, 852
        types I and II, 851–852
Diacylglycerol, 1136, 1137, **1139**
Diagnostic Interview Schedule (DIS),
    852
Diagonal band of Broca, 97
Dialysis encephalopathy, 878
Diamorphine, **440**
Diazepam, **712**
    effects on memory, 613
    intramuscular, 1176
Diazinon, **887**
Dichloralphenazone, 475
2,4-Dichlorophenoxyacetic acid (2,4-
    D), 888, **889**
Dichotic listening tests, **499,** 502
Diclofenac, 430, **435**
    for Alzheimer's disease, 1181
Didanosine (ddI), 795
Diencephalic amnesia, 104–105
Diencephalic tumors, 763
Diet
    Alzheimer's disease and, 353
    Parkinson's disease and, 338
Differential reinforcement of behavior,
    1246
Differentiation, neuronal, **26,** 26–27
Diffuse axonal injury, 626. *See also*
    Brain injury, traumatic
Diffusion-weighted imaging, 262, 285
Diflunisal, **435**
Digit Span test, 101, 170, 228, 229,
    499, **499,** 500, 510, 511, 514, 537
Digit Symbol test, 229, 501, 504, 510,
    511, 514, 794
Dignity of patient, 1258
Dihydroergotamine (DHE)
    for cluster headache, 480, 481
    for migraine, 473, **474,** 476
L-3,4-Dihydroxyphenylalanine (DOPA)
    decarboxylase, 1128
    in attention-deficit/hyperactivity
        disorder, 1075
Diltiazem, 796
2,3-Dimercapto-1-propanesulfonic acid
    (DMPS)
    for arsenic poisoning, 881
    for lead poisoning, 882
meso-2,3-Dimercaptosuccinic acid
    (DMSA)
    for arsenic poisoning, 881
    for lead poisoning, 882

Diminished capacity, 1269. *See also*
    Incompetent patient
Dioxin exposure, 888, **889**
Diphenhydramine, **1174**
    for patients with traumatic brain
        injury, 652
    use in patients with brain tumors,
        775
Dipoles, 44, **44**
DIS (Diagnostic Interview Schedule),
    852
Disinhibition, 178. *See also* Behavioral
    dysfunction
    benzodiazepine-induced, 1176
    in frontotemporal dementias, 959
Disorientation, 170
    to date, 170
    delirious, 170, 541, **541**
    delusional, 170
    to place, 170
Displacement, 1200
Dissociated facial paresis, 159
Dissociative amnesia, 609–611
    age and gender distribution of, 609–
        610
    definition of, 609
    diagnosis of, 609, **610**
    differential diagnosis of, 610–611
    hypnotherapy for, 611
    vs. malingering, 611
    transient nature of, 610
Dissociative identity disorder, 640
Distractibility, 155. *See also* Attentional
    disturbances
    in attention-deficit/hyperactivity
        disorder, 514
Divalproex prophylaxis. *See also*
    Valproate
    for cluster headache, 480
    for migraine, **474,** 478
DLB. *See* Lewy bodies, dementia with
*DMPK* gene, 365
DMPS. *See* 2,3-Dimercapto-1-
    propanesulfonic acid
DMSA. *See* meso-2,3-
    Dimercaptosuccinic acid
DNA polymorphisms, 326–328
Do-not-resuscitate (DNR) orders,
    1262–1263
Doctor-patient relationship, 1258
Domoic acid intoxication, 891
Donepezil
    adverse effects of, 650
    for Alzheimer's disease, 958,
        1180
    for delirium, 548, 553

for patients with traumatic brain
    injury, 649, 650
L-Dopa. *See* Levodopa
DOPA decarboxylase. *See* L-3,4-
    Dihydroxyphenylalanine
    decarboxylase
Dopamine, 9
    drug addiction and, 906–914
        adaptations in mesolimbic
            dopamine system after long-
            term drug exposure, 910–
            914, **912**
        mechanisms of dopamine-induced
            relapse, 910
        role of mesolimbic dopamine
            system in drug
            reinforcement, 906–907
    in regulation of growth cone
        progress, 33
    reuptake of, 1130
    in specific conditions
        aggression, 1175
        agitation, 1169
        attention-deficit/hyperactivity
            disorder, 299, 367–368,
            513–514, 1073, 1075–1077
        delirium, 552, 554
        depression, **1024,** 1024–1025
            treatment-induced changes in,
                1035
        frontotemporal dementias, 961
        Hallervorden-Spatz disease, 943
        hepatic encephalopathy, 554
        impulsive aggression, 585, **585**
        Lesch-Nyhan syndrome, 335
        obsessive-compulsive disorder,
            380, 1054–1055
        Parkinson's disease, 335, 498,
            932, 968
        posttraumatic stress disorder,
            1059
        progressive supranuclear palsy,
            938, 970
        psychosis, 1140, 1163–1164
        Rett's disorder, 1089
        schizophrenia, 305–306, **306,**
            995–997, **997,** 1006–1007
        social phobia, 1061
        Tourette's syndrome, 1082
        traumatic brain injury, 627
    synthesis of, 1128
    transporter for, 1132
Dopamine blockers
    for Huntington's disease, 930
    for obsessive-compulsive disorder
        with tics, 1054–1055

for schizophrenia, 1006, 1007
Dopamine receptors, 15
   in aggression, 1175
   antipsychotic drug effects at, 1134,
      1141, **1142**
   D₄
      in attention-deficit/hyperactivity
         disorder, 1073
      novelty-seeking behavior and, 498
      as target for antipsychotic drug
         action, 1141
   in delirium, 554
   mediation of light adaptation by, 17
   modulation of drug-seeking behavior
      by, 910
   neuroleptic affinity for, 1006
   overproduction of
      attention-deficit/hyperactivity
         disorder and, 1076
      developmental pruning and,
         1070, **1071,** 1076
      gender differences in, 1076
      Tourette's syndrome and, 1083
   positron emission tomography of,
      **288**
   regulation in VTA and NAc in
      response to long-term drug
      exposure, 911–913
   in schizophrenia, 996, **997**
   subtypes of, **1135,** 1140–1141
Dopaminergic drugs
   delirium induced by, **547,** 554
   for Parkinson's disease, 341, 1158–
      1159
   for periodic limb movement disorder
      and restless legs syndrome, **710**
Doral. *See* Quazepam
Dorsal column stimulation (DCS), 433,
   444
Dorsal roots, 425
Dorsolateral prefrontal syndrome, 759
Dothiepin, **436**
Down syndrome, 942, 1085
   Alzheimer's disease and, 954, 1085
   clinical features of, 1085
   etiology and pathophysiology of,
      1085
   maternal age and incidence of, 1085
Doxepin
   dosage of, **436**
   effects on sleep, 711
   mechanism of action of, **1144**
   for pain, **437**
   terminal half-life of, **436**
   use in patients with brain tumors,
      776

use in patients with traumatic brain
      injury, 646
*DRD2* gene, 368, 371, 380
*DRD3* gene, 380, 384
*DRD4* gene, 367–368, 380
Dreaming, 65–66, 208, 708. *See also*
      Sleep-wakefulness, REM (dream)
      sleep
   activation-synthesis hypothesis of,
      66, 698
   in brain-injured patients, 156
   Freud's studies of, 65, 698, 718
   nightmares, **707,** 718
   REM sleep and, 65–66, 698
Droperidol, 549
DRS (Delirium Rating Scale), 527,
   537–538, **538**
DRS-R-98 (Delirium Rating Scale–
      Revised-98), 537, 538, **538**
Drug addiction. *See* Substance abuse
Drug development, 1140–1144
   advances in molecular pharmacology,
      1140
   animal testing, 1140
   antipsychotic pharmacodynamics,
      1141–1142, **1142**
   clinical trials, 1145
   merits of drug selectivity, 1142–1143
   neuroreceptor pharmacology, 1140–
      1141
   novel mechanisms of action, 1143–
      1144, **1144**
Drug-induced disorders
   aggression, 1175
   agitation, 1169
   delirium, 534, **535, 545,** 546, **547,**
      553, 554
   depression, 1155
   psychosis, 1163
   vasculitis, 825–826, **826**
Drug interactions
   with antidepressants, **1160–1162**
   with antihypertensive agents, **1179**
   with antipsychotics, **1167–1168**
   with mood stabilizers, **1173**
Drug therapy. *See* Pharmacotherapy
DTH reaction. *See* Delayed-type
      hypersensitivity reaction
Durable medical power of attorney,
   1263–1264
Duty-to-warn statutes, 1278
Dysarthria, 103, **103,** 160
Dyschiria, 170
Dysgraphia, 762
Dyskinesia
   edentulous, 165

tardive, 1171
   vs. chorea, 164–165, **165**
   malpractice claims related to,
      1276–1277
Dyslexia, 349–351, 1090
   clinical features of, 349
   epidemiologic studies of, 350
   genetic studies of, 350–351
      family studies, 350
      linkage analysis, 351
      mode of inheritance, 350–351
      twin studies, 350
   pathophysiology of, 349–350
   relative risk for, **325**
   treatment of, 1093
Dysprosody, 160
Dyssomnias, 703, **704**
   circadian rhythm, 708
   hypersomnia, 713–716
   insomnia, 705–713
Dysthymia, 636
Dystonia, 164
   psychogenic, psychotherapeutic
      approach to patients with,
      1228–1231
   tardive, 165

Eating behavior abnormalities, 156
   brain tumors and, 763, 764
   Huntington's disease and, 964
ECA (Epidemiologic Catchment Area)
      study, 377, 580, 636, 639, 684
ECD ([⁹⁹ᵐTc]ethyl cysteinate dimer),
   289
Echolalia, 161, 172
Educational level, Alzheimer's disease
      risk and, 353–354
EEG. *See* Electroencephalography
Effexor. *See* Venlafaxine
Ego boundary impairment, **1204**
Eicosanoids, 434
   in HIV-associated dementia, 786
Electrical stimulation
   deep brain, for Parkinson's disease,
      935, 969
   for pain, 433–434, 444
Electro-oculography (EOG) during
      sleep, 45, 697–698, **699**
Electroconvulsive therapy (ECT)
   indications for, 1159
      patients with brain tumors, 775
      patients with HIV/AIDS, 800
      patients with Huntington's
         disease, 930, 1159
      patients with Parkinson's disease,
         935, 967, 1159

Electroconvulsive therapy (ECT)
(continued)
indications for (continued)
patients with traumatic brain
injury, 646
poststroke depression, 741
malpractice claims related to, 1273,
1277–1278
memory impairment induced by,
601, 602, 614–615, 1027
subjective evaluation of, 612, **612**
Electrodermal activity, 210
Electrodiagnostic techniques
activity monitoring, **209,** 209–210
electroencephalography, 43–45, 199–
201, **200–202,** 205–208
electromyography, 210
evoked potentials, 43–44, **44,** 201–
204, **203, 204**
magnetoencephalography, 204–205
to measure attention, 505–506
to measure electrodermal activity,
210
polysomnography, **208,** 208–209
Electroencephalography (EEG), 43–45,
199–201
aging and, 206
analysis of, 201
clinical, 200–201, **201**
clinical applications of, 44
conditions associated with
abnormalities on, 201, **202**
Alzheimer's disease, 206, 957
borderline personality disorder,
589
brain tumor, 770
child abuse, 1099–1100
Creutzfeldt-Jakob disease, **202,**
358, 978
delirium, 206, 527–528, 538–
540, **539,** 550
dementia, 206, 527–528
epilepsy, 205–206, 363, 673,
678–679, 1094–1095
generalized anxiety disorder,
1053
Hashimoto's encephalopathy, 829
HIV/AIDS, 791–792
Huntington's disease, 964
long-term benzodiazepine use,
706
obsessive-compulsive disorder,
1056
panic disorder, 1050
Parkinson's disease, 968
schizophrenia, 206

Susac's syndrome, 829
Sydenham's chorea, 828
systemic lupus erythematosus,
819
traumatic brain injury, **629,** 632
epilepsy and epileptiform activity on,
205–206
frequency bands on, 44, **44,** 200, **200**
history with respect to
neuropsychiatry, 199, **200**
magnetoencephalography compared
with, 204–205
to measure attention, 506
patterns in sleep and wakefulness,
44–45, **45,** 49–52, 200, 697–
698, **699**
alpha rhythm, 45, 697, 698
"burst mode" of thalamic relay
cell discharge, 51, **52**
delta activity, 44, 45, 47, 50–51,
**51**
EEG synchronization and
desynchronization, 49
gamma activity, 44, 49, **50**
sleep spindles, 49–50
quantitative, 207–208, 540
screening, 206–207
theoretical overview of EEG activity,
206–207
training for interpretation of, 1293,
1302
Electromyography (EMG) during sleep,
45, 210, 698, **699**
Eletriptan, 476–477
Eltoprazine, 592
Emancipated minors, 1259
Embedded Figures Task, 298
Embolism, cerebral, 726–727
Emergency situations
health care decision making in, 1261
informed consent in, 1260
EMG (electromyography) during sleep,
45, 210, 698, **699**
Emotional incontinence, 747
Emotional lability
antidepressants for, 1171
delirium and, 525, **527**
epilepsy and, 1214
poststroke, 724–725, **729,** 747–749,
**748,** 1209
posttraumatic, 634
treatment of, 647–648, 653
Emotions, **220**
adaptations in psychiatric technique
relative to, **1201**
bedside assessment of, 176

cerebrovascular disease and, 724–
725
emotionalism, 176
functional neuroimaging of, 295
role of limbic system in, 279, 295
tests of emotional status, 234
Empathy, 1199
Empty sella syndrome, 770
Encephalitis
brainstem, 166
electroencephalogram in,
**202**
herpes simplex, **78**
in HIV/AIDS, 788–789
lethargica, 951, 1050, 1071
limbic, 79
subacute sclerosing panencephalitis,
**202**
von Economo's, 1071
Encephalopathy
in antiphospholipid antibody
syndrome, 821
dialysis, 878
Hashimoto's, 828–829, 860–861
hepatic, **202,** 525, 554
HIV/AIDS, 784, 785
metabolic, attentional disturbances
in, 507
post-anoxic, 166
spongiform (See Prion diseases)
uremic, **202**
Endocrine disorders, 851–869
Addison's disease, 864
aggression and, 588
Cushing's syndrome and disease,
861–863
delirium due to, **545**
diabetes mellitus, 851–854
Hashimoto's encephalitis, 860–861
hyperparathyroidism, 866–868
hyperprolactinemia, 865–866
hyperthyroidism, 858–860
hypoglycemia, 854–855
hypoparathyroidism, 868–869
hypothalamic-pituitary-adrenal axis
and depression, 864–865
hypothalamic-pituitary-thyroid axis
and depression, 861
hypothyroidism, 855–858
mood disorders and, 1025, **1025**
pheochromocytoma, 865
pituitary tumors and, 764
psychiatric complications of
exogenous corticosteroid
administration, 831–832, **863,**
863–864, **864**

Endorphins, 9, 432, **434**
  in autism, 1089
  in depression, **1024**
  effects of stress on, 124
Enkephalins, 9, 432, **434**
  in depression, **1024**
Entorhinal cortex, 74, 75, 77
  in schizophrenia, 993
Enuresis, 717–718
Environment-driven responses, 179
Environmental factors, 386
  Alzheimer's disease and, 353
  attention-deficit/hyperactivity
    disorder and, 1079
  Huntington's disease and, 930–931
  joint effects with genes on illness
    risk, 329–331
    additive model, 330
    effect mediation, 331
    effect modification, 330–331
    multiplicative model, 331
  learning disorders and, 1091, 1093
  Parkinson's disease and, 337–338,
    340, 934
  poisons and toxins, 219, 877–895
  schizophrenia and, 380–381
EOG (electro-oculography) during
  sleep, 45, 697–698, **699**
Eosinophils, 116
Ephedrine, **826**
Ephrins, 27
Epidemiologic Catchment Area (ECA)
  study, 377, 580, 636, 639, 684
Epidemiologic studies, 323–324
  analytic, 324
  descriptive, 324
  genetic, **324,** 324–329 (*See also*
    Genetic studies)
  measures of disease frequency, 323–
    324
  questions addressed by, 323
  of specific conditions
    aggression, 580
    Alzheimer's disease, 352–354
    bipolar disorder, 368
    dyslexia, 350
    epilepsy, 362, 676
    Huntington's disease, 331–332,
      924
    Lesch-Nyhan syndrome, 335
    metachromatic leukodystrophy,
      348
    myotonic dystrophy, 365
    narcolepsy, 385
    obsessive-compulsive disorder,
      376–377

panic disorder, 373
    Parkinson's disease, 336–338,
      931, 965
    prion diseases, 359–360
    schizophrenia, 380–381
    traumatic brain injury, 625–626
    Wilson's disease, 341, 971
Epidural analgesia, 442–443, **443**
Epidural hematoma, 727–728
Epilepsy, 361–364, 673–691. *See also*
  Seizures
  age at onset of, 1093
  aggression and, 687
  apoptosis in, 22
  attentional disturbances in, 510
  autosomal dominant nocturnal
    frontal lobe, 363
  celiac disease and, 831
  channelopathies, 361
  in children, 1093–1097
    absence seizures, 363, 510
    classification and features of,
      1094–1095
    differential diagnosis of, 1094
    psychiatric consequences of,
      1095–1096
    treatment of, 1096–1097
  classification of, 361, **674,** 674–675,
    1094–1095
  cryptogenic, 361
  diagnosis of, 677–679
    electroencephalogram, **202,** 205–
      206, 363, 678–679, 1094–
      1095
    history taking, 677
    laboratory findings, 677
    neuroimaging, 677, 1164
  differential diagnosis of behavioral
    symptoms associated with, **679,**
    679–680
  epidemiology of, 362, 676, 1093
  etiologies of, 1093–1094
  frontal lobe, 680
  genetic studies of, 361–364
    family studies, 362
    linkage analysis, 363–364, **364**
    mode of inheritance, 363
    molecular approaches, 364
    relative risk, **325**
    twin studies, 362–363
  glial cell dysfunction and, 1126
  hyposexuality in, 156
  idiopathic, 361
  juvenile myoclonic, 1094
  migraine and, 362, 465
  posttraumatic, 639–640

prevalence of, 206, 361, 362, 676,
    1093, 1213
  prodromal phases of, 155
  psychiatric consequences of, 681–
    688, 1095–1096
    anxiety disorders, 684–685, **685**
    behavioral and personality
      disturbances, 673, 687,
      1095, 1213–1214
    in children, 1095–1096
    mood disorders, 685–687
    psychosis, 682–684, **684,** 1095,
      1163, 1164
    suicidality, 1095–1096
    treatment guidelines for, 687–
      688, **688**
  psychosocial aspects of, 676–677
  rolandic, 1094–1095
  secondary, 361
  startle response in, 166
  syndromes, 675–676
  temporal lobe, 674, 675
    behavioral symptoms of, 675, **676**
    criminal liability and, 1270
    diagnosis of, 679, **679**
    emotional facial weakness in, 159
    personality traits associated with,
      156
    psychopathology and, 681
    temporal lobectomy for, 602
    visual field defects in, 158
  treatment of, 689–690, **691,** 1096–
    1097
    for psychiatric symptoms, 687–
      688, **688**
    psychotherapy, 686, 1213–1214
Epileptiform activity, 206
Epinephrine, 9, 124
Epistasis, 326
EPQ (Eysenck Personality
  Questionnaire), **468,** 468–469
EPS. *See* Extrapyramidal symptoms
EPs. *See* Evoked potentials
Ergoloid mesylates, 1181
Ergotamine
  for cluster headache prophylaxis,
    480
  for migraine, **474,** 476
ERPs (event-related potentials), 201–
  202, 505–506
Estazolam, **712**
Estrogen
  for aggression, 588, 1178
  Alzheimer's disease risk and, 354,
    955, 1181–1182
  immunologic effects of, 138

Ethical issues, 1257–1258. *See also*
    Legal issues
    patient rights, 1258
    preclinical testing for Huntington's
        disease, 926
    social justice, 1258
Ethosuximide, 1096
[$^{99m}$Tc]Ethyl cysteinate dimer (ECD),
    289
Ethylbenzene exposure, **879**
Ethylene glycol exposure, **879**
Ethylene oxide poisoning, 886–887
    diagnosis of, 886
    mechanism of action of, 886
    neuropsychiatric manifestations of,
        **880**, 886–887
    sources of exposure, 886
    treatment of, 886–887
Euphoria, 176
    frontal lobe tumors and, 760
Euthyroid sick syndrome, cytokine-
    induced, 140
Event-related potentials (ERPs), 201–
    202, 505–506
Evoked potentials (EPs), 43–44, **44,**
    **201–204, 203, 204**
    constraints to localizing source of, 44
    contingent negative variation, 204
    definition of, 43
    late, 202, 204
    to measure attention, 505–506
    middle, 202, 204
    P50, 202, **203**
    P300, 203–204, **204**
    signal averaging technique for, 44,
        201
    in specific conditions
        autism, 1088
        child abuse, 1100
        delirium, 202, 540
        HIV/AIDS, 791, 792
        multiple sclerosis, 202
        posttraumatic stress disorder,
            202–204, **203**
        schizophrenia, 202, 203, **204,**
            **205,** 1001–1002
Examination of patient. *See* Bedside
    neuropsychiatric assessment
Excitotoxicity, 33, 34, 1007–1008
    glutamate-induced, 17, 33, 1007,
        1125
    Huntington's disease and, 33, 34,
        334, 926
    traumatic brain injury and, 33, 627,
        656
Exclusion map, 328

Executive functions
    assessment of, 153, 176–179, 233,
        503–504
    attention and, 493
    deficits of, 1242 (*See also* Cognitive
        disturbance)
        cognitive rehabilitation for, 1242
        in delirium, 536
        due to dorsolateral prefrontal
            region lesions, 102
        due to frontal lobe tumors, 760
        due to thalamic lesions, **103**
        in Huntington's disease, 928–929
        in Parkinson's disease, 933
        after traumatic brain injury, 509–
            510, 635, **635**
            psychotherapy for, 1207
    functional imaging in schizophrenia,
        310–311
Executive Interview (EXIT), 180, 235
Exelon. *See* Rivastigmine
EXIT (Executive Interview), 180, 235
Exocytosis, 10
Expert testimony, 1282
Expressive aphasia, 228
Extinction process, 1245
Extrapyramidal symptoms (EPS),
    1164–1165
    treatment in patients with brain
        tumors, 775
Eye examination, 158–159
    blinking, 158
    eye movements, 158–159
        in Huntington's disease, 159,
            928
        in progressive supranuclear palsy,
            159, 937
        in schizophrenia, 159, 1000–1001
    in rheumatic disease, 813
    visual fields, 158
Eysenck Personality Questionnaire
    (EPQ), **468,** 468–469

FA (Friedreich's ataxia), **925,** 940
Fabry's disease, 424, 979
Face-Hand Test, 230
Face-name association, 1240
Facial movements, 159
Factitious hypoglycemia, 855
Fahr's disease, 165, **925,** 942, 970–971
Family/caregivers
    of patient with Alzheimer's disease,
        1214–1215
    of patient with brain tumor, 773
    of patient with dementia, 124, 981,
        1214–1215

of patient with Huntington's disease,
    1225
of patient with memory impairment,
    1217–1218
of patient with Parkinson's disease,
    1223
of patient with poststroke
    depression, 741
of patient with spinal cord injury,
    1213
of patient with traumatic brain
    injury, 657, 1208–1209
presence during patient examination,
    180
Family history, 156
Family studies, 325, **325**
    of Alzheimer's disease, 354, 954
    of attention-deficit/hyperactivity
        disorder, 366–367, 513
    of autism, 343–344
    of bipolar disorder, 368–369
    of dyslexia, 350
    of epilepsy, 362
    of Huntington's disease, 332
    of metachromatic leukodystrophy,
        348
    of narcolepsy, 385
    of obsessive-compulsive disorder,
        377–378
    of panic disorder, 373
    of Parkinson's disease, 338
    of schizophrenia, 381
    of Wilson's disease, 341
Farnsworth-Munsell 100-Hue Test, 87
Fatal familial insomnia (FFI), 358–359,
    941, 978
    age at onset of, 358
    clinical features of, 358
    genetics of, 360, 941
    incidence of, 360
    mode of inheritance of, 358
    neuropathology of, 359
Fatigue
    multiple sclerosis and, 509
    traumatic brain injury and, 649–650
Febrile seizures, 362, 364, 676
Feed-forward inhibition, **9**
Felbamate, 690, **691,** 1096
Fenfluramine
    for autism, 1089
    impulsive aggression and low
        prolactin response to, 586
Fenoprofen, **435**
Fentanyl, 439
Fever
    cytokine-induced, 116

non-REM sleep and, 52
FFI. *See* Fatal familial insomnia
Fibrinogen, 117
Fibromuscular dysplasia, 728
Filamin gene, 26
Finger agnosia, 573, 762
Finger Tapping Test, 235, 511
Fire setting, 587, 590
FK506, 1137
FLAIR (fluid-attenuated inversion
    recovery) imaging, 255, **258, 259,**
    **265,** 266, **629**
Flexeril. *See* Cyclobenzaprine
Fludrocortisone, **437**
Fluency evaluation, 567
Flufenamic acid, **435**
Fluid-attenuated inversion recovery
    (FLAIR) imaging, 255, **258, 259,**
    **265,** 266, **629**
Flumazenil, 554
Flunarizine, 796
Fluoxetine
    adverse effects of, **1160**
    dosage of, **1160**
    drug interactions with, **1160**
    effects on cognitive deficits in
        depression, 1027
    indications for
        aggression, 591, 653, 1176
            in developmentally disabled
                persons, 592
        attention-deficit/hyperactivity
            disorder, 1079
        depression in patients with
            epilepsy, 686
        emotional lability, 648
        panic disorder, 1057
        patients with Alzheimer's disease,
            1171
        patients with dementia, **980,** 981
        patients with HIV/AIDS, 799,
            1176
        patients with Parkinson's disease,
            967
        patients with traumatic brain
            injury, 646–648, 653
        poststroke depression, 740–741
    mechanism of action of, **1144**
Fluphenazine
    for Huntington's disease, 930
    for patients with traumatic brain
        injury, 650
Flurazepam, **712**
Fluvoxamine
    adverse effects of, **1160**
    dosage of, **1160**

drug interactions with, **1160**
for Korsakoff's dementia, 1182
mechanism of action of, **1144**
for pathological gambling, 590, 591
seizures induced by, 686
use in patients with traumatic brain
    injury, 646
*FMR1* gene, 1086
fMRI. *See* Magnetic resonance imaging,
    functional
Foix-Chavany-Marie syndrome, 159
Foreign accent syndrome, 160
Form vision defect, 86–87
Formaldehyde poisoning, **880**
Fornix, 280, **280**
*c-fos* gene, 29, 65
Fragile X syndrome, 1086
    clinical features of, 1086
    etiology and pathophysiology of,
        1086
    genetics of, 329, 925, 1086
    prevalence of, 1086
Frataxin, 925
Frégoli's syndrome, 175, 1201, **1205**
Freiburg Personality Inventory, **468**
Freud's dream studies, 65, 698, 718
Friedreich's ataxia (FA), **925,** 940
Frontal Assessment Battery, 180–181,
    **182**
Frontal lobes
    acquired sociopathy due to lesions of,
        **97,** 98–101
    in aggression and behavioral
        dyscontrol, 583, 1175
    amnesia due to lesions of, 101–102,
        603–605
    in anxiety, 1051
    in attention-deficit/hyperactivity
        disorder, 1074
    autosomal dominant nocturnal
        frontal lobe epilepsy, 363
    in cognitive impairment, 1179
    in depression, 1028–1029, 1157
    functional neuroanatomy of, 94–103,
        **96, 97**
        basal forebrain, 97–98
        dorsolateral prefrontal region,
            101–103
        frontal operculum, 95, **99**
        superior mesial region, 95–97
        ventromedial region, 98–101
    in schizophrenia, 962
    syphilitic infection of, 962
    traumatic injury of, 626
        behavioral syndromes related to,
            634

tumors of, 759–760
    neuropsychiatric and behavioral
        manifestations of, 756, 759–
        760
    neuropsychological manifestations
        of, 760
    white-matter diseases affecting, 962
Frontotemporal dementias (FTDs),
    **925,** 939–940, 959–962
    clinical and neuropsychiatric features
        of, 959, **960**
    differential diagnosis of, 961–962
        Alzheimer's disease, 961, **962**
        progressive subcortical gliosis,
            961
    genetics of, 959
    laboratory evaluation of, 959
    management of, 979
    neuroimaging in, 959, 961, **961**
    neuropathology of, 959–961
Frovatriptan, 476, 477
FTDs. *See* Frontotemporal dementias
Funding for neuropsychiatric education,
    1304–1305
Fusiform gyrus, 86–87

G protein–coupled receptor kinases
    (GRKs), 904, **906**
G proteins, **902, 1125,** 1133, **1133,**
    **1135,** 1136
    drug effects on, 1136, 1139
    effect of chronic exposure to drugs
        of abuse on, 901
        regulation in VTA and NAc, 913–
            914
    interaction with calcium, 15, **16**
    in neurotransmission, **1130,** 1136,
        **1136**
    neurotransmitter regulation of, 903
    opiate effects on, 904–905, **906**
    receptors for, 15–17, **16**
    second messengers and, 1139
    structure of, 1136
    as target for antidepressant therapy,
        1143
G6PD (glucose-6-phosphate
    dehydrogenase) deficiency, 371
GABA. *See* γ-Aminobutyric acid
Gabapentin, 690, **691**
    adverse effects of, 1096–1097, **1173**
    dosage of, **1173**
    drug interactions with, **1173**
    indications for
        agitation, 653, 1170
        migraine prophylaxis, 478
        pain, 436–437

Gabapentin *(continued)*
  indications for *(continued)*
    patients with brain tumors, 775
    periodic limb movement disorder
      and restless legs syndrome,
      **710**
    seizures, 690, 1096
*GABRB1* gene, 371
*GABRB3* gene, 346
GAD. *See* Generalized anxiety disorder
Gadolinium-based contrast agents, 262
"Gag rules" imposed on physicians,
  1260
Gait disturbances, 162
  psychotherapeutic approach to
    patients with, 1210–1211
Galactocerebroside β-galactosidase
  deficiency, 979
α-Galactosidase deficiency, 979
Galantamine, 958, 1180, 1181
Galveston Orientation and Amnesia
  Test (GOAT), 628, **629, 631**
Gambling, pathological, 587, 590
Gangliogliomas, 761
Gangliosidoses, 979
Ganser state, 174–175
GAP-43, 994
Gap junctions, 9, 1126, 1127
Gas exposure, **878,** 885–887
  carbon monoxide, 885–886, **886**
  ethylene oxide, 886–887
  neuropsychiatric sequelae of, **880**
  organophosphate nerve gases, **888,**
    889
Gaucher's disease, 979
Gaze apraxia, 85, 159
Gaze paralysis, psychic, 85, 159
GCS (Glasgow Coma Scale), 628, **629**
GDNF. *See* Glia cell line–derived
  neurotrophic factor
GDP (guanine diphosphate), 1136,
  **1136**
*Gegenhalten,* 163
Gelastic seizures, 176
General Health Questionnaire, 468
Generalized anxiety disorder (GAD),
  1049, 1052–1053
  electroencephalography in, 1053
  Huntington's disease and, 1051
  migraine and, 466
  neuroanatomy of, 1052, **1052,** 1053
  neurochemistry of, **1052,** 1052–
    1053
  Parkinson's disease and, 967, 1051
  poststroke, **729, 744,** 744–745, 749,
    1051

  traumatic brain injury and, 640,
    1051
Genes. *See also* specific genes
  candidate, 329 (*See also* Candidate
    gene studies)
  homeobox, 23
  immediate early response, 29, 65
  involved in apoptosis, 29–30
  involved in neuronal migration, 24–
    26
  involved in sleep-wakefulness, 65
  joint effects with environmental
    exposures on illness risk, 329–
    331
    additive model, 330
    effect mediation, 331
    effect modification, 330–331
    multiplicative model, 331
Genetic studies, **324,** 324–329, 386
  adoption studies, 325
  anticipation, imprinting, and
    mitochondrial inheritance, 329
  birth-cohort studies, 325–326
  of complex disorders, 326
  family studies, 325
  high-risk studies, 325
  identifying mode of inheritance, 326
  linkage analysis, 326–328, **327**
  molecular approaches, 329
  nonparametric, 328–329
  questions addressed by, 324, **324**
  of specific disorders
    Alzheimer's disease, 354–357,
      954
    Angelman's syndrome, 1086–
      1087
    attention-deficit/hyperactivity
      disorder, 366–368, 513,
      1073–1074
    autism, 343–347, 1087–1088
    bipolar disorder, 368–372
    dementia with Lewy bodies, 936
    dementias associated with motor
      dysfunction, **925**
    Down syndrome, 1085
    dyslexia, 350–351
    epilepsy, 362–364, **364**
    fragile X syndrome, 329, 925,
      1086
    Huntington's disease, 331–334,
      924–925, **925,** 1224
    impulsive aggression, 587–588
    learning disorders, 1091
    Lesch-Nyhan syndrome, 335
    metachromatic leukodystrophy,
      348–349

  myotonic dystrophy, 365–366
  narcolepsy, 385
  obsessive-compulsive disorder,
    377–380
  panic disorder, 373–376
  Parkinson's disease, 338–340,
    **925,** 931, 965
  Prader-Will syndrome, 1086–
    1087
  prion diseases, 360–361
  progressive supranuclear palsy,
    **925,** 937, 938, 969
  schizophrenia, 381–385
  Tourette's syndrome, 156, 1081
  Wilson's disease, 341–343, **925,**
    942, 971
  twin studies, 325
  using genetically modified animals,
    329, **330**
Genomic imprinting, 329, 1086
Gerstmann-Sträussler-Sheinker (GSS)
  syndrome, 358, 978
  age at onset of, 358
  aphasia and, 573
  clinical features of, 358
  mode of inheritance of, 360
  molecular approaches to, 360–361
  neuropathology of, 358
    parietal lobe tumors, 762
  prevalence of, 360
  relative risk of, **325**
Geschwind-Behan-Galaburda
  hypothesis, 833–834, 1093
Giant cell arteritis, 728, 824
Gilles de la Tourette syndrome. *See*
  Tourette's syndrome
Ginkgo biloba, 1181
Glasgow Coma Scale (GCS), 628, **629**
Glia cell line–derived neurotrophic
  factor (GDNF), 30, 1126–1127
  in Parkinson's disease, 34, 1127
  therapeutic uses of, 1127
Glial cells, 4, 1124–1127
  development of, 22
  disorders associated with dysfunction
    of, 1126
  functions of, 1124–1127
    gap junctions and, 9, 1126
    neurotransmitter uptake, 1125
    regulation of glutamate and γ-
      aminobutyric acid levels,
      1125, 1126
  membrane elements of, **1125**
  relationship with neurons, 1125
Glioblastomas, **754,** 758, **771**
Gliomas, 753, **754,** 756–757, **768**

Global Deterioration Scale, 794
Globus pallidus, 266
    anatomy of, 269, **274, 277**
    deficits associated with lesions of,
        279
β-Glucocerebrosidase deficiency, 979
Glucocorticoid receptor expression on
    immune cells, 133
Glucocorticoids, immunologic effects
    of, 134–135
Glucose, 1125
Glucose-6-phosphate dehydrogenase
    (G6PD) deficiency, 371
Glucose tolerance test (GTT), 854
Glutamate, 9, **13**, 1124
    activation of NMDA receptor by,
        1134
    in delirium, 555
    developmental pruning of, 1070
    excitotoxicity induced by, 17, 33,
        1007, 1125
    in obsessive-compulsive disorder,
        1055
    in pain modulation, 433
    receptors for, 14, **1135**
        neurogenesis and, 24
    in regulation of growth cone
        progress, 33
    role of glia in regulation of, 1125,
        **1126**
    in schizophrenia, 995, 998–999,
        1007–1009
    transporter for, 1132
    in traumatic brain injury, 627,
        656
Glutamate dehydrogenase deficiency,
    33
Glutamine, 1124, 1125
    reuptake of, 1130
Glutamine synthetase, 1125
Gluten-sensitive enteropathy, 831
Glycine, 9, 433
    reuptake of, 1130
Glycine receptors, 1134, **1135**
GM-CSF (granulocyte-macrophage
    colony-stimulating factor), **117,
    142**
Go/no-go paradigm, 503
GOAT (Galveston Orientation and
    Amnesia Test), 628, **629, 631**
Gold poisoning, **879**
Gonadal steroids. See also Estrogen;
    Testosterone
    binding to GABA receptors, 15
    immunologic effects of, 137–138
Grand mal seizures, 673–674

Granulocyte-macrophage colony-
    stimulating factor (GM-CSF), **117,
    142**
Granulocytes, 116
Granulomatous arteritis, 825
Grasp reflex, 167, **167**, 168
Graves' disease. See Hyperthyroidism
GRKs (G protein–coupled receptor
    kinases), 904, **906**
Grooved Pegboard Test, 233, 503
Group therapy
    for cancer patients, 126
    for poststroke depression, 741
Growth cones, neuronal, **26**, 26–27, 33
Growth effects of stimulants, 1078–
    1079
Growth factors, 24, 29–30, 903
Growth hormone, for Prader-Willi
    syndrome, 1087
Growth-promoting activity, 30
GSS. See Gerstmann-Sträussler-
    Sheinker
GTP (guanosine triphosphate), 15
GTT (glucose tolerance test), 854
Guam amyotrophic lateral sclerosis/
    parkinsonism-dementia complex,
    33, 941
Guanfacine
    for attention-deficit/hyperactivity
        disorder, 1079
    for cognitive impairment, 1182
Guanine diphosphate (GDP), 1136,
    **1136**
Guanosine triphosphate (GTP), 15
Guanylyl cyclase, 21
Guardianship, 1264
Guillain-Barré syndrome, 791
Guilty but mentally ill, 1271

HAART (highly active antiretroviral
    therapy), 795
Habit system, 1055
Habituation, 492
Hachinski Ischemic Score (HIS), 973
HACMC (HIV-1–associated cognitive/
    motor complex), 784, 785
HAD. See Dementia, HIV-associated
Halcion. See Triazolam
Haldol. See Haloperidol
Hallervorden-Spatz disease (HSD),
    **925**, 942–943, 971
Hallervorden-Spatz syndrome (HSS),
    942
Hallucinations, 175–176. See also
    Psychosis
    Alzheimer's disease and, 956

    auditory, 176
    brain tumors and
        frontal lobe tumors, 760
        occipital lobe tumors, 763
        pharmacotherapy for, 774–776
        pituitary tumors, 764
        posterior fossa tumors, 764
        temporal lobe tumors, 761
    crepuscular, 176
    delirium and, 528, 536, **541**, 541–
        542
    dementia with Lewy bodies and,
        935–936
    hypnagogic, 176, 385, 715
    musical, 176
    olfactory, 176
    Parkinson's disease and, 336
        drug-induced, 967
    peduncular, 176
    poststroke, 745–746
    schizophrenia and, 175, 990,
        **990**
    visual, 175–176
Hallucinogens, 892, **894, 901**
Haloperidol
    adverse effects of, **1167**
        cardiac, 548–549
    as coanalgesic, **437**, 438
    dopamine receptor activity of, 554
    dosage of, **1167**
        for children, 549
    drug interactions with, **1167**
    efficacy studies of, 1164
    indications for
        aggression, 651
        autism, 1089
        delirium, 548–549
            in children, 549
            in HIV/AIDS, 797, 1171
        patients with brain tumors, 775,
            776
        patients with dementia, **980**
        patients with traumatic brain
            injury, 651, 655
        rapid tranquilization, 1177
        Tourette's syndrome, 1083
    intravenous, 797
    pharmacology in schizophrenia,
        1007, **1008**
    receptor binding affinity of, **1142**
Halstead-Reitan Neuropsychological
    Test Battery, 234–235, 590, 609,
    776, 794
HAMCMD (HIV-associated minor
    cognitive/motor disorder), 785,
    792, **793**

Hamilton Anxiety Rating Scale (Ham-A), **744,** 745, 791
Hamilton Rating Scale for Depression (Ham-D), 455, **629,** 637, 646, 736, 740, 745, 791, 857, 862, 866, 1026
Handedness, 72, 154
   Geschwind-Behan-Galaburda hypothesis and, 833–834, 1093
Haplotypes, 329
Haptoglobin, 123
Hashimoto's encephalopathy, 828–829, 860–861
HD. *See* Huntington's disease
HDHQ (Hostility and Direction of Hostility Questionnaire), 581
HDS (HIV-Dementia Scale), 794–795
Head banging, 718–719
Head circumference, 157
Head injury. *See* Brain injury, traumatic
Headache, 451–481
   brain tumor and, 765
   classification of, 451, **452**
   cluster, 478–481
      comorbidity with, 479
      diagnostic criteria for, 479, **479**
      epidemiology of, 479
      pathophysiology of, 479–480
      treatment of, 480–481
   diagnosis of, 451
   migraine, 451–452, 457–478 (*See also* Migraine)
   primary vs. secondary, 451
   tension-type headache and chronic daily headache, 452–457
      definition of, 452
      diagnostic criteria for, **452**
      epidemiology of, 454
      episodic vs. chronic, 452, 453, **453**
      mechanisms of, 455
      medication overuse and, 453–454
         treatment of, 457
      psychopathology and, 454–455
      relation to migraine, 452–453
      treatment of, 455–457
Health care decision making, 1259–1261
   advance directives, 1263–1264
   case example related to, 1259
   competency for, 1258–1259
   in emergency situations, 1261
   for incompetent patients, 1260–1261, **1261**
   informed consent, 1259–1260, **1260**
   refusal of treatment, 1259

substituted judgment, 1264–1265
Health care proxy, 1263
Health Care Quality Improvement Act, 1281
Heavy metals. *See* Metal poisoning
Helper (CD4+) T cells, 119–121
   in depression, 130
   in HIV infection, 122, 126
   Th1 and Th2, 121
Hematoma
   epidural, 727–728
   subdural, 626, 727–728
Hemiachromatopsia, **83,** 87, 173
Hemianopsia, 85, 89, 92, 158
   homonymous, 158, 763
Hemineglect, 92, **94,** 170–171, 230, 507–508. *See also* Neglect syndrome
Hemiplegia, 1210. *See also* Cerebrovascular disease
Hemispheric lateralization, 72–73, **73, 74**
   clinical manifestations of brain tumors related to, 764–765
   depression and, 1029
   development of, 1071
   Geschwind-Behan-Galaburda hypothesis and, 833–834, 1093
   learning disorders and, 1092–1093
Hemorrhage, intracerebral, 626, 726, 727
   dementia due to, 976, **977**
Hepatic encephalopathy, 525
   dopamine excess in, 554
   electroencephalogram in, **202**
   flumazenil for, 554
   glutamine levels in, 554
Hepatolenticular degeneration. *See* Wilson's disease
Herbal preparations, **893,** 1123
Heroin-induced vasculitis, **826**
Herpes simplex virus (HSV) infection
   amnesia after, **78**
   HIV/AIDS and, 788–789
   stress, depression, and immunity in, 126–127
Heterostasis, 1217–1218
Heterotopia, X-linked periventricular, 26
[$^{99m}$Tc]Hexamethylpropylene amine oxime (HMPAO), 289
*n*-Hexane exposure, 887
Hexosaminidase A deficiency, 166, 979
HGP (Human Genome Project), 326
5-HIAA. *See* 5-Hydroxyindoleacetic acid

High-risk studies, 325
   of Alzheimer's disease, 355
   of attention-deficit/hyperactivity disorder, 367
   of autism, 344
   of bipolar disorder, 369–370
   of Huntington's disease, 332
   of obsessive-compulsive disorder, 378–379
   of panic disorder, 374–375
   of schizophrenia, 382
   of Wilson's disease, 342
Highly active antiretroviral therapy (HAART), 795
Hippocampal complex, 75–79
   in Alzheimer's disease, 78
   amnesia associated with lesions of, 77–78, 280
   components of, 75
   functions of, 76–77
   interconnections with, 75–76
   in right and left hemispheres, 77
Hippocampus, 74, 75
   anatomy of, **271, 278,** 279–280, **280**
   long-term depression in, 21–22
   long-term potentiation in, 19–22, **20**
   in panic disorder, 1056, 1058
   in posttraumatic stress disorder, 3, 1058–1060
   role in memory, 77–79, 279–280, 598, 1179
   traumatic injury of, 627
HIS (Hachinski Ischemic Score), 973
Hiscock and Hiscock Digit Memory Test, 234
Histamine, 9
   in delirium, 554–555
   sensitization of nociceptors by, 423
History taking, 154–156
   aggression, 156
   alcohol/drug abuse, 155
   appetitive functions, 155–156
   birth, 154
   development, 154
   family history, 156
   handedness, 154
   head injury, 155
   ictal events, 154–155
   mild cognitive impairment, 155
   occupation, 156
   personality change, 156
   seizures, 677
   traumatic brain injury, 628
HIV-1-associated cognitive/motor complex (HACMC), 784, 785

HIV-associated dementia (HAD). *See* Dementia, HIV-associated

HIV-associated minor cognitive/motor disorder (HAMCMD), 785, 792, **793**

HIV-Dementia Scale (HDS), 794–795

HIV infection. *See* Human immunodeficiency virus infection/ acquired immune deficiency syndrome

HLA (human leukocyte antigens), 127, 129

HMPAO ([$^{99m}$Tc]hexamethylpropylene amine oxime), 289

Homeobox (Hox) genes, 23

Homicide, 580

Homonymous hemianopsia, 158, 763

Homovanillic acid (HVA)
    HIV/AIDS and, 791
    Korsakoff's syndrome and, 1180
    Rett's disorder and, 1089
    schizophrenia and, 995–996
    Tourette's syndrome and, 1082
    traumatic brain injury and, 627

Hooper Visual Organization Test, 230

Hormone receptor expression on immune cells, **134**

Hospitalization, involuntary, 1280–1281

Hostility and Direction of Hostility Questionnaire (HDHQ), 581

Hox (homeobox) genes, 23

HPA axis. *See* Hypothalamic-pituitary-adrenal axis

*HPRT* gene
    in bipolar disorder, 371
    in Lesch-Nyhan syndrome, 335

HSD (Hallervorden-Spatz disease), **925**, 942–943, 971

HSS (Hallervorden-Spatz syndrome), 942

HSV. *See* Herpes simplex virus infection

5-HT (5-hydroxytryptamine). *See* Serotonin

*HTR2A* gene, 347

*HTR7* gene, 347

Hughes syndrome. *See* Antiphospholipid antibody syndrome

Human Genome Project (HGP), 326

Human immunodeficiency virus infection/acquired immune deficiency syndrome (HIV/AIDS), 121, 783–801
    antipsychotic therapy in, 1164
    anxiety in, 800–801
    apoptosis in, 786, 1099

CD4+ cell count in, 122, 126

central nervous system pathology due to HIV, 784–787
    in children, 1099

central nervous system pathology due to opportunistic infections and neoplasia in, 122, 785, 787–789, **787–789**
    cerebrovascular disease, 789
    cryptococcosis, 787–788
    lymphoma, 122, 787, 789, **789**
    syphilis, 789
    toxoplasmosis, 787, **788**
    tuberculosis, 787, 789
    viral infections, 788–789

in children, 1098–1099

delirium and psychosis in, 549, 797–798

depression in, 798–800, 1155
    treatment of, 1158

direct assessment of central nervous system injury in, 789–792
    cerebrospinal fluid evaluation, 790–791
    electrophysiological evaluation, 791–792
    neuroimaging, 789–790

encephalopathy of, 784
    in children, 1098–1099

epidemiology of, 784

HIV-1-associated cognitive/motor complex (HACMC), 784, 785

HIV-associated dementia (HAD), 784–787
    biochemical markers for, 786–787
    in children, 1098
    neurobehavioral assessment of, 792–795
    neuropathology of, 785
    P300 potential in, 203
    pathogenesis of, 786
    signs and symptoms of, 792, **793**
    testing for, 180

HIV-associated minor cognitive/ motor disorder (HAMCMD), 785, 792, **793**

incidence of, 784, 1098

latency period in, 784

mania in, 800

medical aspects of, 783–784

neurobehavioral assessment in, 792–795, **793, 794**

neuropsychological evaluation in, 219, 794, **794**

risk factors for, 783

stress, depression, and immunity in, 126

suicidality in, 798–799

transmission of, 783, 784
    prevention of vertical transmission, 1099

treatment of, 783, 795–796
    antiviral therapy, 795
    behavioral methods, 796
    in children, 1099
    other biological/pharmacological interventions, 795–796
    psychopharmacological enhancement of function, 796

vaccine development for, 783

viral cause of, 783–784
    HIV-1 and HIV-2, 784
    neurotropism of, 784

Human leukocyte antigens (HLA), 127, 129

Humoral immunity, 118, **120**

Huntingtin, 333–334, **334**, 925, **925**, 1224

Huntington's disease (HD), 222, 331–334, 924–931, 963–965
    age at onset of, 331–333, **333**, 924, 925
    clinical features of, 165, 331, 925–930, **928**, 963–964
        cognitive abnormalities, 230, 928–929, 963
        eye movement abnormalities, 159, 928
        motor abnormalities, 927–928
        psychiatric abnormalities, 331, 924, 926, 929–930, 963–964
            anxiety, 964, 1051
            mood disorders, 222, 331, 929, 964, 1031, 1158
            obsessive-compulsive disorder, 964, 1050
        prevalence of, 929
    diagnostic evaluation of, 925–926
        electroencephalography, 964
        laboratory evaluation, 964
        preclinical testing, 926
    differential diagnosis of, 926
        tardive dyskinesia, **165**
    epidemiologic studies of, 331–332, 924
    etiology of, 924–925
    genetic studies of, 156, 332–334, 924–925, **925**, 1224
        anticipation, 329

Huntington's disease (HD) *(continued)*
  clinical features of *(continued)*
    correlation with psychiatric
      symptoms, 929
    family studies, 332
    high-risk studies, 332
    mode of inheritance, 332
    molecular approaches, 332–334,
      **333, 334**
    relative risk, **325**
  mortality from, 331, 924
  neurobiology of, 926–927, **927**, 964–
    965
    apoptosis, 22, 333–334
    excitotoxicity, 33, 34, 334, 926
    glial cell dysfunction, 1126
  neuroimaging in, 964, **965**
  prevalence of, 331, 924
  treatment of, 334, 930–931, 965
    antidepressant therapy, 1158
    electroconvulsive therapy, 930,
      1159
    psychotherapy, 1224–1225, **1225**
  Westphal variant (juvenile-onset),
    331
HVA. *See* Homovanillic acid
Hydrocephalus
  communicating vs.
    noncommunicating, 976
  ex vacuo, 976
  normal-pressure (NPH), 943–944,
    976–978
    cerebrospinal fluid shunting for,
      943–944, 977–978
    clinical and neuropsychiatric
      features of, 976–977
    dementia of, 943
    diagnosis of, 943, 977
    etiologies of, 943, 977
Hydrocodone, **710**
Hydrogen sulfide poisoning, **880**
Hydromorphone, **440**
  for AIDS-associated delirium, 797
  for migraine, 475
5-Hydroxyindoleacetic acid (5-HIAA)
  impulsive aggression and, **584,** 584–
    585
  Korsakoff's syndrome and, 1180
  suicidality and, 585
  Tourette's syndrome and, 1083
  traumatic brain injury and, 627
3-Hydroxykynurenine, 926
5-Hydroxytryptamine (5-HT). *See*
  Serotonin
Hydroxyzine
  as coanalgesic, **437,** 438

for patients with HIV/AIDS, 801
use in patients with brain tumors,
  776
Hyperactivity, 163. *See also* Agitation
  animal studies of early brain injury
    producing, 1075–1076
  attention-deficit/hyperactivity
    disorder, 512–517, 1071–1080
  behavioral observation of, 499
  in delirium, 525, 542–544, **543**
Hypercalcemia, 1171
Hypercortisolemia. *See* Cushing's
  syndrome
Hyperglycemia. *See* Diabetes mellitus
Hyperkalemic periodic paralysis, 5
Hypermetamorphosis, 171
Hyperparathyroidism, 866–868
  cardinal features of, 866
  psychiatric symptoms in, 866–868,
    **867, 868**
Hyperphagia, 156
  diencephalic tumors and, 763
Hyperpolarization, 14
Hyperprolactinemia, 865–866
  cardinal features of, 865
  impulsive aggression and, 586, 865–
    866
  psychiatric symptoms in, 865–866
  seizures and, 677
  treatment of, 865
Hypersensitivity reaction, delayed-type
  (DTH), 121
  to radiologic contrast agent
    for computed tomography, 252
    for magnetic resonance imaging,
      262
  stress and, 123
Hypersomnia, 697, 703, 713–716
  causes of, 713
  classification of, **704**
  clinical significance of, 713
  common types of, **707**
  idiopathic, 715–716
  narcolepsy, 715
  sleep-disordered breathing, 713–714
  traumatic brain injury and, 641, 650
Hyperthermia
  cytokine-induced, 116
  non-REM sleep and, 52
Hyperthyroidism, 858–860
  cardinal features of, 858
  psychiatric symptoms in, 858–860,
    **859**
    anxiety, 860
    cognitive disorders, 858–859
    mood disorders, 859–860

psychosis, 860
  stress, depression, and immunity in,
    129
Hypertonus, 163–164
Hypnagogic hallucinations, 176, 385,
  715
Hypnic jerk, 165
Hypnosis
  for dissociative amnesia, 611
  for pain, 445–446
  self-administered, 445
Hypoactivity, in delirium, 525, 526,
  528, 542–544, **543**
Hypoalbuminemia, 535
Hypocretin. *See* Orexin
Hypoglycemia, 854–855
  clinical features of, 854–855
  criminal liability and, 1270
  excitotoxicity and, 33
  factitious, 855
  insulin-induced, 854
  reactive, 855
Hypomania, sleep patterns in, 703
Hypoparathyroidism, 868–869
  clinical features of, 868
  psychiatric symptoms in, **868,** 868–
    869
Hypopnea, 713
Hyposmia, 157
Hypothalamic-pituitary-adrenal (HPA)
  axis, 134–135
  in depression, 864–865, 1025
  in posttraumatic stress disorder,
    1059
  in social phobia, 1061
Hypothalamic-pituitary-thyroid axis, in
  depression, 861
Hypothalamus
  in aggression, 582
  anatomy of, **272, 277,** 281
  deficits associated with lesions of,
    281
  in panic disorder, 1056, **1057**
  tumors of, 756, 763
Hypothesis-testing approach, 222
Hypothyroidism, 855–858
  clinical features of, 855
  grades of, 857–858
  psychiatric symptoms in, 855–857,
    **856**
    anxiety, 857
    cognitive disorders, 856–857
    frequency of, **857**
    mood disorders, 857
    psychosis, 857
  subclinical, 857–858

Hypoxanthine guanine phosphoribosyltransferase
bipolar disorder and, 371
Lesch-Nyhan syndrome and, 334–335
"Hysterical neurosis," 609
Hysteroepilepsy, 679

Ibuprofen, 430, **435**
ICE (interleukin-1β converting enzyme), 30
ICH (intracerebral hemorrhage), 626, 726, 727
Ideational apraxia, 178–179
Ideomotor apraxia, 172–173
IDO (indolamine 2,3-dioxygenase), 140
IEGs (immediate early response genes), 29, 65
IFN. *See* Interferon
Ig. *See* Immunoglobulins
IL. *See* Interleukin
Imaging studies. *See* Neuroimaging
Imipramine
dosage of, **436**
indications for, 1157
anxiety in Parkinson's disease, 967
narcolepsy, 715
pain, **437**
mechanism of action of, **1144**
terminal half-life of, **436**
use in patients with traumatic brain injury, 646
Immediate early response genes (IEGs), 29, 65
Immune deficiency disorders, 121–122
Immune system, 115–143
acquired (specific) immunity, 116, **118**, 118–121, **120**
B cells, 118
T cells, 118–121
components of, 115
dysfunction of, 121–122
functions of, 115
mechanisms of brain-immune interactions, 132–141
immune cell receptors for neurally derived molecules, 133–134, **134**
neural innervation of immune tissues, 132–133, **133**
pathways of brain to immune signaling, 134–138, **135, 137**
pathways of immune to brain signaling, 138–141, **139, 141**

natural (innate) immunity, 116–118, **118, 119**
primary and secondary immune tissues, 116
psychiatric illness and immune function, 129–132
bipolar disorder, 132
depression, 129–131, **130**
schizophrenia, **131,** 131–132
psychotropic drug effects on, 141–142
antidepressants, 141–142
antipsychotics, 142
regulation of, 116
stress, depression, and immunity, 125–129
in AIDS, 126
in autoimmune diseases, 127–129
in cancer, 125–126
in other viral infections, 126–127
stress and immunity, 122–125
tests of immunity, 121
Immunoglobulins (Ig), 118
classes of, 118
IgE and allergies, 122
Impaired conation, **1201, 1204**
Impaired ego boundary, **1204**
Impaired view of others, **1203**
Impaired world view, **1203**
Impersistence, 179
Imprinting, genomic, 329, 1086
Impulsivity, 579–592
aggression and, 579
anatomy and neurochemistry of, 1175
in attention-deficit/hyperactivity disorder, 514, 1072
conditions associated with, 579, 1172
definition of, 579
factors contributing to, 579, **580**
measurement of, 580–581
neurobiology of, 584–588, **585**
decreased serotonin function, **584,** 584–586
endocrine studies, 588
genetic studies, 587–588
pharmacologic challenge studies, 586–587
role of 5-HT$_{1B}$ receptor, 588
neuropsychiatric/neuropsychological studies of, 588–590
antisocial personality disorder, 589–590
borderline personality disorder, 588–589

impulse control disorders, 590
in posterior aphasia behavioral syndrome, 574
treatment of, 590–592, 1177
in developmental disabled persons, 592
Incidence of disease, 323–324
Incompetent patients, 1259. *See also* Competency; Legal issues
guardianship for, 1264
health care decision making for, 1260–1261, **1261**
right to die, 1261–1262
substituted judgment for, 1264–1265
Incubus, **707,** 717
Inderal. *See* Propranolol
Indifference reaction, 724, 725
Indolamine 2,3-dioxygenase (IDO), 140
Indomethacin, 430, **435**
for Alzheimer's disease, 1181
for cluster headache prophylaxis, 480
for migraine, 475
Infantile spasms, 1094, 1096
Infections
cytokines and, 116
delirium due to, **545**
HIV/AIDS, 783–801
immune response to, 115–122, **119, 120** (*See also* Immune system)
pediatric autoimmune neuropsychiatric disorder associated with streptococcal infections, 129, 378–379, 828, 1050, 1055, 1056, 1081
stress, depression, and immunity in, 126–127
Information processing
automatic vs. effortful, 606
P300 potential and, 203–204
speed of, 491
attentional capacity and, 491
deficits in
brain damage and, 500
epilepsy and, 510
multiple sclerosis and, 509
effect of dopamine on, 498
for information in working memory, 491
Informed consent, 1259–1260. *See also* Legal issues
case example related to, 1259
competency to give, 1260
effect of "gag rules" imposed on physicians, 1260

Informed consent (*continued*)
  in emergency situations, 1260
  exceptions to requirement for, 1260
  for incompetent patients, 1260–
    1261, **1261**
  information to be disclosed for,
    1260, **1260**
Inheritance modes, 326
  for Alzheimer's disease, 355
  for attention-deficit/hyperactivity
    disorder, 367
  for autism, 344–345
  for bipolar disorder, 370
  for dyslexia, 350–351
  for epilepsy, 363
  for Huntington's disease, 332
  for metachromatic leukodystrophy,
    348
  for myotonic dystrophy, 365
  for narcolepsy, 385
  for obsessive-compulsive disorder,
    379
  for panic disorder, 375
  for Parkinson's disease, 339
  for schizophrenia, 382–383
  for Wilson's disease, 342
Innate immunity, 116–118, **118, 119**
Inositol 1,4,5-triphosphate (IP$_3$), 1137,
    1138, **1139**
Inositol triphosphate/diacylglycerol
    system, **16**, 1136–1139, **1139**
Insanity defense, 1267–1269
Insecticides. *See* Pesticide exposure
Insomnia, 697, 703, 705–713
  causes of, 705
  circadian rhythm dyssomnias, 708
  classification of, **704,** 705
  common types of, 705, **707**
  depression and, 703, 1025
  due to drug and alcohol dependence,
    706
  fatal familial, 358–359
  "fear of sleeping," 718
  idiopathic, 708
  periodic limb movement disorder
    and restless legs syndrome, 707
  drug treatment of, **710**
  precipitating factors for, 705
  prevalence of, 705
  psychophysiological, 705–706
  self-medication for, 705
  sleep-disordered breathing, 708
  sleep-state misperception and, 707–
    708
  Spielman's dynamic model of, 705,
    **706**

after traumatic brain injury, 650
treatment of, 708–713
  bright light therapy, 711
  for chronic insomnia, 712
  in patients with dementia, **980,**
    981
  recommendations for, 712–713
  relaxation training, 709
  sedative-hypnotic drugs, **711,**
    711–713, **712**
  sleep restriction therapy, 710–711
  stimulus control therapy, 709–
    710
  universal sleep hygiene, 709, **709**
Insufficient sleep syndrome, 713
Intellectual functioning. *See also*
    Cognitive disturbance
  amnesia and, 602
  aphasia and, 575
  mental retardation, 1084–1087
  reaction time and, 491
  tests of, 227–228
  after traumatic brain injury, 509–
    510, 634–636, **636**
Intentionality, assessing impairments of,
    503
Interferon-α (IFN-α), 116, 117
  for systemic lupus erythematosus,
    816
  therapeutic uses of, 140, **142**
Interferon-β (IFN-β), 116, 117
  therapeutic uses of, **142**
Interferon-γ (IFN-γ), 116, 117, **120,** 121
  for systemic lupus erythematosus,
    816
  therapeutic uses of, 140, **142**
Interleukin-1 (IL-1), 116, **117**
  in HIV/AIDS, 791
  in hypersomnia, 52
  stress and, 123
Interleukin-1β converting enzyme
    (ICE), 30
Interleukin-2 (IL-2), **117, 120,** 121
  in schizophrenia, 131, 132, 833
  for systemic lupus erythematosus,
    816
  therapeutic uses of, 140, **142**
Interleukin-4 (IL-4), **117, 120,** 121
Interleukin-5 (IL-5), **117**
Interleukin-6 (IL-6), 116, **117,** 121
  in Behçet's disease, 830
  in HIV/AIDS, 791
  stress and, 123
  in systemic lupus erythematosus,
    816
Interleukin-8 (IL-8), **117**

in systemic lupus erythematosus,
    816
Interleukin-10 (IL-10), 116, **117, 120,**
    121
Interleukin-12 (IL-12), 116, **117, 120**
Interleukin-13 (IL-13), **120**
Intermetamorphosis, 1201, **1205**
Intermittent explosive disorder, 579,
    587, 590
International training in
    neuropsychiatry, 1290, **1292**
Interneurons, 8
Intracerebral hematoma, 626
Intracerebral hemorrhage (ICH), 626,
    726, 727
Inverse agonists, 1134
Involuntary hospitalization, 1280–1281
Ion channels, 4–5
  action potentials and, 5–6, **6, 7**
  calcineurin regulation of, 1137,
    **1140**
  diseases related to defects in, 5
  epilepsy and mutations in genes for,
    361, 364
  formed by neuroreceptors, 1133
  ionotropic receptors linked to, 14
    GABA receptors, 14–15
    glutamate receptors, 14
  ligand-gated, 5, 14, 1128–1129
  in neurotransmission, 1128–1129,
    **1130**
  neurotransmitter transporters as,
    1132
  in opiate physical dependence, 904
  in pacemaker and burst firing, 6, **8**
  voltage-gated, 5, **1125**
    activation of, 1128
IP$_3$ (inositol 1,4,5-triphosphate), 1137,
    1138, **1139**
Iproniazid, 1124
Iris pigmentation, 158
Irritability
  in Huntington's disease, 929–930
  in progressive supranuclear palsy,
    938, 969
Ishihara Color Plate Test, 87
Isolation, 1200
Isometheptene, **474,** 475
*IT15* gene, 332

Jargon aphasia, 568
JC virus, 788
Journals in neuropsychiatry, 1300,
    **1303**
"Jumping Frenchmen of Maine," 166
Juvenile myoclonic epilepsy, 1094

Kainate receptors, 14, **1135**
    in schizophrenia, 998
Kandel, Eric, 18
Kaposi's sarcoma, 122, 787
Kayser-Fleischer rings, 158, 341, 942, 971
Kearns-Sayre syndrome, 942
Kellner Symptom Questionnaire, 866
Kepone. *See* Chlordecone
Ketamine, 1008–1009, **1009**
Ketoprofen, **435**
Ketorolac, 430, **435**
    for migraine, 475
Kindling, 681, **1203**
Kleine-Levin syndrome, 156
Kleptomania, 587, 590
Klippel-Feil syndrome, 167
Klonopin. *See* Clonazepam
Klüver-Bucy syndrome, 156, 171, 1172, 1265
    in Alzheimer's disease, 956, 957
    in frontotemporal dementias, 939, 959
Korsakoff's syndrome, 104, 230, 1180, 1182
Krabbe's disease, 979
Kuru, 360, 978
Kyphoscoliosis, 940–941

LA (lupus anticoagulant), 819, 821
*La belle indifférence*, 234
Lactose, 1125
Lacunae, 727
Lafora's disease, **364**
Lamivudine (3TC), 795
Lamotrigine, 690, **691**, 1096, 1097
Language
    definition of, 565
    examination of, 567–568
    functional neuroimaging of, 294–295, 566–567
        in schizophrenia, 310
    lateralization to left hemisphere, 71, 73–74, **74**, 565, **566**
    lexical retrieval, 77, 80, **81**
Language disturbances, **220**. *See also* Speech disorders
    alexia, 573
    amelodia/aprosodia, 160–161, 572
        poststroke, **729**, 748
    aphasia, 172, 565–577
    aphemia, 573
    apraxia and, 568, 573
    in delirium, 525, **527**, 541, **541**
    due to thalamic lesions, 104
    ideomotor apraxia and, 172–173

pure word deafness, 573
    rehabilitation for, 1242
    schizophrenia and, 1202
    tests for, 228
    traumatic brain injury and, 1205–1206
    verbal dysdecorum, 572–573
Latah, 166
Lateral geniculate nucleus (LGN), 1092
Lathyrism, 33
Laughter
    as defense mechanism, 1200
    laughing seizures, 176
    pathological, 176, 724–725
        amitriptyline for, 647
        poststroke, **729**, 747–749, **748**
        in progressive supranuclear palsy, 938, 969
Law of independent assortment, 326
LC. *See* Locus coeruleus
*Le fou rire prodromique*, 176
*Le geste antagoniste*, 164
Lead poisoning, 881–882
    diagnosis of, 882
    learning disorders and, 1093
    mechanism of action of, 882
    neuropsychiatric manifestations of, **879**, 882
    sources of exposure, 881–882, **882**
    treatment of, 882
Learning. *See also* Memory
    depression and, 606
    functional neuroimaging of, 3, 293
    incidental, 606
    simple associative, 599
    synaptic modulation in memory and, 17–22, **19**, **20**
Learning disorders, 1090–1093
    in adults, 1090
    attention-deficit/hyperactivity disorder and, 513, 1072, 1091
    characteristic features of, 1090–1091
    definition of, 1090
    delinquency and, 1090
    differential diagnosis of, 1090
    disorders of written expression, 1091
    etiology and pathophysiology of, 1091–1093
    evaluation of, 1090
    genetic studies of, 1091
    hemispheric lateralization and, 1092–1093
    mathematics disorder, 1090–1091
    neuroanatomy of, 1091–1092
    reading disorder, 349–351, 1090
    treatment of, 1093

Legal issues, 1257–1283
    advance directives, 1263–1264
    competency, 1258–1259
        adjudication of incompetence, 1259
        of aphasic patients, 575–576
        case example related to, 1258
        definition of, 1258
        mental capacity and, 1258–1259
        of mentally disabled persons, 1259
        of minors, 1259
        neuropsychological tests for determination of, 235
        presumption of, 1259
    criminal proceedings, 1265–1271
        case example related to, 1265
        competency to stand trial, 1267
        criminal intent, 1266
        diminished capacity, 1269
        exculpatory and mitigating disorders, 1269–1270
            automatisms, 1269
            intoxication, 1269–1270
            metabolic disorders, 1270
            posttraumatic stress disorder, 1270
            temporal lobe seizures, 1270
        guilty but mentally ill, 1271
        insanity defense, 1267–1269
    do-not-resuscitate orders, 1262–1263
    guardianship, 1264
    health care decision making, 1259–1261
        case example related to, 1259
        in emergency situations, 1261
        for incompetent patients, 1260–1261, **1261**
        informed consent, 1259–1260, **1260**
        refusal of treatment, 1259
    involuntary hospitalization, 1280–1281
    malpractice claims, 1257, 1271–1278
        definition of, 1271
        four Ds of, 1271
        negligence and, 1271
        related to breach of confidentiality and testimonial privilege, 1271–1272, **1272**

Legal issues (continued)
malpractice claims (continued)
related to somatic therapies, 1273–1278
electroconvulsive therapy, 1277–1278
medication, 1274–1277
standard of care and, 1271
theories of liability, 1274
management of violent patient, 1278–1280
assessing risk for violence, 1279–1280
case examples of, 1278, 1279
discharge and release considerations, 1279
duty-to-warn statutes, 1278
seclusion and restraint guidelines, 1279, **1279**
National Practitioner Data Bank, 1281
personal injury litigation, 1257, 1281–1283
case example of, 1281
expert testimony, 1282–1283
head injuries, 1281–1283
physician-assisted suicide, 1262
right to die, 1261–1262
competent patients, 1262
incompetent patients, 1261–1262
substituted judgment, 1264–1265
Lennox-Gastaut syndrome, 1094
Lenticulostriatal diseases, dementias of, 962–963
Lentiform nucleus, 266
Leonine-mouse syndrome, 479
Lesch-Nyhan syndrome (LNS), 334–335, 587
clinical features of, 334
enzyme deficiency in, 334, 335
epidemiologic studies of, 335
gene therapy for, 335
molecular approaches to, 335
neuroimaging in, 335
relative risk of, **325**
Lethargy, 507
Leukemia inhibitory factor, 30
Leukoaraiosis, 973
Leukotrienes, 434
Leuprolide, **980**
Levodopa
for cortical-basal ganglionic degeneration, 939
nightmares induced by, 718
for Parkinson's disease, 968, 1222–1223

for progressive supranuclear palsy, 938
stereotypies induced by, 166
for Wilson's disease, 942
Levodopa-carbidopa
for Parkinson's disease, 341
for patients with traumatic brain injury, 648
for periodic limb movement disorder and restless legs syndrome, **710**
Levomepromazine, **437**, 438
Levorphanol, **440**
Lewy bodies
in Alzheimer's disease, 935, 936
dementia with (DLB), 932, 935–937, 958–959
delirium in, 553
diagnosis of, 935–936, **936, 958,** 958–959
hallucinations in, 176
neurobiology of, 936–937
neuroimaging in, 937, 958
treatment of, 937, 959
in Hallervorden-Spatz disease, 943
in Parkinson's disease, 337, **337, 339,** 931–932, 968
Lexical retrieval, **77,** 80, **81**
LGN (lateral geniculate nucleus), 1092
Lidocaine
intranasal, for cluster headache, 480
for neuropathic pain, 437, **437**
Light therapy, for insomnia, 711
Limbic encephalitis, 79
Limbic system
in aggression, 582–583
anatomy of, 279, **280**
in anxiety, 1052, **1052,** 1053, 1062
in attention, 494, **495,** 496
in depression, 1036–1037
in dreaming, 66
in emotions and memory, 279
neuropsychiatric symptoms of tumors involving, 756
in schizophrenia, 992
Line Bisection Test, 230
Lingual gyrus, 86–87
Linkage analysis, 326–328, **327**
in Alzheimer's disease, 355–357
in attention-deficit/hyperactivity disorder, 367
in autism, 345–346
in bipolar disorder, 370–371
in dyslexia, 351
in epilepsy, 363–364, **364**
in narcolepsy, 385

in obsessive-compulsive disorder, 379
in panic disorder, 375–376
in schizophrenia, 383–384
in Wilson's disease, 342
Linkage disequilibrium, 329
Lissencephaly, 26
Lithium
adverse effects of, 1170, **1173**
dosage of, **1173**
drug interactions with, **1173**
indications for
aggression, 1177
borderline personality disorder, 586
cluster headache prophylaxis, 480
Huntington's disease, 930, 965
impulsive aggression, 591
in developmentally disabled persons, 592
mania, 647
pathological gambling, 590
patients with dementia, **980**
patients with HIV/AIDS, 800
patients with traumatic brain injury, 647, 653
secondary mania, 743, 1170
mechanism of action of, 1136, 1138
use in elderly patients, 1170
use in patients with brain tumors, 772, 775, 776
Livedo reticularis, 826–827
Liver transplantation, for Wilson's disease, 341, 942
Living will, 1261, 1263
LNS. See Lesch-Nyhan syndrome
Locked-in syndrome, 506
Locus coeruleus (LC)
in cognitive impairment, 1180
in depression, 1157
in generalized anxiety disorder, 1053
location of, 903, **903**
norepinephrine-containing neurons in, 58
in opiate physical dependence, 903–906, **905, 906**
in panic disorder, 1057
Logoclonia, 573
Long-term depression (LTD), 21–22, 34
in ocular dominance column formation, 31
Long-term potentiation (LTP), 19–22, **20,** 29, 34
cellular mechanisms for, 21
early and late phases of, 21

in ocular dominance column formation, 31
postsynaptic locus for, 21
Lorazepam, **1174**
effects on memory, 613
indications for
aggression and agitation, 1176
in patients with traumatic brain injury, 652
delirium, 546–548
during neuroimaging procedures, 247
patients with brain tumors, 772, 775
patients with dementia, **980**, 981
patients with HIV/AIDS, 797, 801, 1170–1171
rapid tranquilization, 1177
intravenous, 652
pharmacokinetics of, **712**
Loxapine, 1164
LSD (lysergic acid diethylamide), 1124
LTD. *See* Long-term depression
LTP. *See* Long-term potentiation
Lumbar puncture, 770, 977
Lupus anticoagulant (LA), 819, 821
Lupus cerebritis/vasculitis, 814. *See also* Systemic lupus erythematosus
Luria-Nebraska Neuropsychological Battery, 235
Lyme disease, 1225–1226
Lymphoid cells, 116
Lymphomas, HIV-related, 122, 787, 789, **789**
Lysergic acid diethylamide (LSD), 1124

Machado-Joseph disease, **925**
Macroglobulin, 117
Macrophages, 116
Magnetic resonance imaging (MRI), 72, 217, 245, **246**, 253–263
brain lesions on
basal ganglia lesion, **104**
inferior parietal lobe lesion, **94**
left frontal lesion, **259**
left temporal tumor, **265**
occipitotemporal lesion, **83**
temporal lobe lesion, **78**
compared with computed tomography, 264, **264**, **266–268**
contraindications to, 263, **264**
contrast agents for, 247, 262, **265**
allergic reactions to, 262
development of, 262
gadolinium-based, 262

gray scale values for tissues visible on, **255**
header information on scans, **263**
indications for, 264, **264**
normal brain on, **256–258, 261, 270–279**
patient preparation for, 247
physical principles of, 253–262
physiologic monitoring during, 263
practical considerations for, 247
in pregnancy, 263
pulse sequences for, 254–262
acquisition parameter ranges for, **255**
diffusion-weighted image, 262, 285
fluid-attenuated inversion recovery image, 255, **258, 259, 265,** 266
gradient echo, 255, **260, 261,** 262
magnetization transfer image, 262
new, 262
spin density weighted image, 255, **270–279**
spin echo, 254–255
susceptibility weighted images, 255
T1 and T2 weighted images, 255, **255–257, 259**
reconstructing an image on, **253,** 253–254, **254**
safety of, 262–263
in specific conditions
acute disseminated encephalomyelitis, **268**
Alzheimer's disease, 957, 961
attention-deficit/hyperactivity disorder, 1074
Behçet's disease, 830
brain tumor, 767, **767–769**
Broca's aphasia, **569**
child abuse, 1100
chronic toluene abuse, **268**
cortical-basal ganglionic degeneration, 939
Creutzfeldt-Jakob disease, 978
dementia, 979
dementia with Lewy bodies, 958
epilepsy, 677, 1164
Fahr's disease, 970–971
frontotemporal dementias, 959, 961
Hallervorden-Spatz disease, 943, 971
Hashimoto's encephalopathy, 829
HIV/AIDS, 789–790

Huntington's disease, 964
hyperprolactinemia, 865
Lesch-Nyhan syndrome, 335
mesial temporal sclerosis, **268**
multiple sclerosis, **268, 509**
normal-pressure hydrocephalus, 977
olivopontocerebellar atrophies, 940
panic disorder, 1058
Parkinson's disease, 883, 968
posttraumatic stress disorder, 1059
primary angiitis of central nervous system, 825
progressive supranuclear palsy, 938, 969–970
sarcoidosis, 830
schizophrenia, 992
Sjögren's syndrome, 823
Susac's syndrome, 829
Sydenham's chorea, 828
systemic lupus erythematosus, 818, 819
Tourette's syndrome, 1082
toxin exposure, 895
toxoplasmosis, 787, **788**
traumatic brain injury, **629,** 630
vascular dementia, 975, **976**
Wernicke's aphasia, **571**
Wilson's disease, 942, 971
training for interpretation of, 1293, 1302
Magnetic resonance imaging, functional (fMRI), 72, 245, **246,** 285–286, 290
advantages and limitations of, 290
of memory, 597
of movement, 292, **292**
in specific conditions
attention-deficit/hyperactivity disorder, 299, **300,** 1075
autism, 298, 1088
child abuse, 1101
HIV/AIDS, 790
migraine, 475
obsessive-compulsive disorder, 301
schizophrenia, 310, 1005–1006
traumatic brain injury, **629,** 630–632
theory of, 290
training for interpretation of, 1302

Magnetic resonance spectroscopy
(MRS), 245, 285, 290–291
advantages and limitations of, 290–
291
in specific conditions
autism, 298
HIV/AIDS, 790, 1099
panic disorder, 299
Rett's disorder, 1090
schizophrenia, 311, **312**
systemic lupus erythematosus,
820
traumatic brain injury, **629,** 631
theory of, 290
Magnetic seizure therapy (MST), 615
Magnetoencephalography (MEG), 72,
204–205, 245, **246,** 285, 770
Major histocompatibility complex
(MHC), 119–121
Malathion, **887**
Malingering, vs. dissociative amnesia,
611
Malpractice claims, 1257, 1271–1278
definition of, 1271
four Ds of, 1271
frequency of primary allegations for,
**1274**
negligence and, 1271
related to breach of confidentiality
and testimonial privilege, 1271–
1272, **1272**
related to somatic therapies, 1273–
1278
electroconvulsive therapy, 1277–
1278
medication, 1274–1277
standard of care and, 1271
theories of liability, 1274
Mamillary body
anatomy of, **272, 277,** 280
deficits associated with lesions of,
280–281
Mamillothalamic tract, 105, 280
Manganese poisoning, 882–883
diagnosis of, 883
mechanism of action of, 883
neuropsychiatric manifestations of,
**879,** 882–883
sources of exposure, 882
treatment of, 883
Mania
anatomy and neurochemistry of,
1169
Bell's, 528, 551
brain tumors and, 756, 772, 775
conditions associated with, 1166

differential diagnosis of
delirium, 528
Wernicke's aphasia, **570**
endocrine disorders and
Cushing's syndrome, 862, **862**
diabetes mellitus, 854
hyperthyroidism, **859,** 860
hypothyroidism, **856, 857, 857**
HIV/AIDS and, 800
Huntington's disease and, 965
memory and, 605–607
migraine and, 466
poststroke, **729,** 741–743, 748–749
lesion location and, 742
mechanism of, 742–743
phenomenology of, 741
risk factors for, 742
sleep patterns in, 703
traumatic brain injury and, 638, 647
treatment of
in patients with brain tumors,
772, 775
in patients with dementia, **980,**
981
in patients with traumatic brain
injury, 647
pharmacotherapy, 1170, **1173**
in poststroke patients, 743
Mannerisms, 166
Maprotiline, 1158
for patients with HIV/AIDS, 799
seizures induced by, 647, 686, 773
use in patients with traumatic brain
injury, 646, 647
Marchiafava-Bignami disease, 962
Marginal cells, 24, 425
Marine toxins, 891
Mast cells, 116
Mathematics disorder, **91,** 92, 1090–
1091
Matrix Reasoning test, 231
Maturation, neuronal, 29–30
Maudsley Personality Inventory, 421
Mayo-Portland Adaptability Inventory
(MPAI), 234
MCV (Medical College of Virginia)
Nurses Rating Scale for Delirium,
537
MDAS (Memorial Delirium Assessment
Scale), 538, **538**
Medical College of Virginia (MCV)
Nurses Rating Scale for Delirium,
537
Medical education. *See*
Neuropsychiatric education
Medroxyprogesterone, **980**

Medulloblastomas, **754**
Mefenamic acid, **435**
MEG (magnetoencephalography), 72,
204–205, 245, **246,** 285, 770
Meige syndrome, 164
Melatonin, 481
Memantine, 796
Membrane potential, 5–6
Membrane stabilizers, 437, **437**
Memorial Delirium Assessment Scale
(MDAS), 538, **538**
Memory, 597–602
aging and, 611
anatomy and neurochemistry of,
1179
amygdala, 79
frontal lobes, 603–605
hippocampus, 77–79, 279–280,
598, 1179
anterograde, **77,** 79
bedside assessment of, 171–172
components of, 597, **598**
consolidation of, 600–601
declarative, 79, 597–598, **598**
definition of, 597
episodic memory, 598
reliance on explicit retrieval, 597
semantic memory, 598
emotional, 79
functional neuroimaging of, 293,
**294,** 597
in schizophrenia, 309–3310
impairment of (*See* Amnesia)
long-term, 600–601
memory systems, 597
coordination of, 601–602
mood disorders and, 605–607
nondeclarative, 77–78, 103, **103,**
104, **598,** 598–600
definition of, 597
priming, 599–600
procedural memory, 599
reliance on implicit retrieval, 597,
598
simple conditioning and simple
associative learning, 599
processing during sleep, 67
prospective, 101
psychotropic drug effects on, 613–
614
retrograde, 78, 79
short-term, 600
subjective evaluation of
(metamemory), **612,** 612–613
synaptic modulation in learning and,
17–22

long-term potentiation in
    mammalian CNS, 19–22, **20**
simple learning in *Aplysia*, 18–19,
    **19**
system vs. process concepts of, 601
tests of, 229–230
working, **97**, 101, 597, **598**, 600–601
    components of, 600
    information-processing rate and,
        491
Memory books, 1241
Memory-cuing strategies, 1241
Memory storage devices, 1241
Mendelian inheritance, 326
Meningiomas, 753, **754**, 756–757, 765,
    **769**
Meningitis, 728
Menkes' syndrome, 342
*Mens rea*, 1266
Mental age, 1070
Mental Control test, 499, 510, 511
Mental retardation (MR), 1084–1087
    Angelman's syndrome, 1086–1087
    autism and, 344, 1087
    diagnosis of, 1084
    Down syndrome, 1085
    fragile X syndrome, 1086
    Lesch-Nyhan syndrome, 334
    mild, 1084
    moderate, 1084
    physical anomalies associated with,
        157
    Prader-Willi syndrome, 1086–1087
    prevalence of, 1084
    profound, 1085
    severe, 1084
    synaptic pruning and, 1070
    treatment of impulsivity and
        aggression in, 592
    in tuberous sclerosis, 344
Mental tracking tests, 228–229, **229**
Meperidine, **440**
    intramuscular, 441
    for migraine, 475
    oral bioavailability of, 439
    rectal, 439–441
Mephenesin, 888
Meprobamate, 1124
Mercury poisoning, 883–884
    diagnosis of, 884
    mechanism of action of, 884
    neuropsychiatric manifestations of,
        **879**, 883–884
    sources of exposure, 883
    treatment of, 884
Merging, 1200

Metabolic disorders
    aggression and, 587–588
    attentional disturbances in, 507
    criminal liability and, 1270
    delirium due to, **545**
    dementia and, 979
Metabotropic receptors, 15–17
Metachromatic leukodystrophy (MLD),
    347–349
    adult-onset, 347
    bone marrow transplantation for,
        347–349, **348**
    clinical features of, 347
    enzyme defect in, 347, 979
    epidemiologic studies of, 348
    genetic studies of, 348–349
        family studies, 348
        mode of inheritance, 348
        molecular approaches, 348–349
    infantile, 347
    juvenile-onset, 347
    mortality from, 347
    mouse models of, 349
    neuroanatomy of, 1164
    prenatal diagnosis of, 347
    relative risk for, **325**
    sphingolipid activator protein B-
        deficient, 347
Metal poisoning, 877–885, **878**
    aluminum, 877–881, **880**
    arsenic, 881
    lead, 881–882, **882**
    manganese, 882–883
    mercury, 883–884
    neuropsychiatric sequelae of
        exposure to, **879**
    organotins, **884**, 884–885
Metamemory, **612**, 612–613
Metformin interactions with radiologic
    contrast agents, 253
Methadone, **440**
    oral bioavailability of, 439
    for periodic limb movement disorder
        and restless legs syndrome, **710**
    sublingual, 439
Methamphetamine, 1078
Methanol exposure, **879**
Method of loci, 1239–1240
3-Methoxy-4-hydroxyphenylglycol
    (MHPG)
    aggression and, 587
    Alzheimer's disease and, 1180
    generalized anxiety disorder and,
        1053
    HIV/AIDS and, 791
    Korsakoff's syndrome and, 1180

panic disorder and, 1057
pathological gambling and, 590
pyromania and, 590
Rett's disorder and, 1089
stimulant effects on, 1077
Methoxyprogesterone acetate, 714
1-Methyl-4-phenyl-1,2,3,6-
    tetrahydropyridine (MPTP), 10,
    11, 34, 337, 340, 498, 931
Methyl chloride exposure, **879**
N-Methyl-D-aspartate (NMDA)
    receptor antagonists
    for HIV/AIDS, 796
    for Parkinson's disease psychosis,
        1166
N-Methyl-D-aspartate (NMDA)
    receptors, 14, 17, **18**, 34, 1134,
    **1135**
    in excitotoxicity, 33, 656
    in long-term potentiation, 19–21
    in pain modulation, 433
    phencyclidine effects at, **901**
    in Rett's disorder, 1090
    in schizophrenia, 998
    in synapse formation, 27–29
Methyl-n-butyl ketone exposure, **879**, 887
α-Methyl-para-tyrosine challenge for
    depression, 1024
β-n-Methylamino-l-alanine, 33
Methylphenidate
    adverse effects of, 516, 649
    dosage of, **1162**
    drug holidays from, 517
    drug interactions with, **1162**
    indications for, 1158–1159
        aphasic patients, 577
        attention-deficit/hyperactivity
            disorder, 516, 1078–1080
            case example of, 514–515
            dosage of, 516, 1078
            nonresponse to, 1073
        behavioral disturbances, 1177
        dementia, 1159
        HIV-associated dementia, 1182
        narcolepsy, 715
        patients with brain tumors, 775
        patients with HIV/AIDS, 796,
            799
        patients with Parkinson's disease,
            1158
        patients with traumatic brain
            injury, 648, 649
    mechanism of action of, 648, 1076–
        1077
    once-daily dose of, 516–517, 1078
    sustained-release, 516

Methysergide prophylaxis
    for cluster headache, 480
    for migraine, **474**
Metoclopramide, 475, 477
Metonymy, 1202
Metrifonate, 1180
Mexiletine, 437, **437**
MHC (major histocompatibility
    complex), 119–121
MHPG. *See* 3-Methoxy-4-
    hydroxyphenylglycol
Mianserin
    for delirium, 548
    dosage of, **436**
    for pain, **437**
    terminal half-life of, **436**
Michigan Neuropsychological Test
    Battery, 853
Microbial toxins, 891–892
    botulinum toxin, 891–892
    tetanus toxin, 892
Microglia, 4
β₂-Microglobulin, in HIV/AIDS, 786–
    787, 791
Microtubules, 4
Midbrain tumors, 756
Migraine, 451–452, 457–478
    with aura (classic migraine), 458–
        461
        association cortex auras, 462
        aura without headache, 462–463
        characteristics of visual aura, 459,
            **459**
        diagnostic criteria for, **458**, 461
        illusions and
            pseudohallucinations, 459
        migraine aura status, 460
        somatosensory phenomena, 459
    without aura (common migraine),
        460–461
        diagnostic criteria for, **453**
    basilar (Bickerstaff's), 461
    comorbidity with, 464–465
    complicated, 458
    confusional, 461–462
    epidemiology of, 463–464, **464**
    epilepsy and, 362, 465
    late-life migrainous accompaniments,
        **463**
    mechanisms of visual system in
        subjects with, 469–471
    pathogenesis of, 455, 471–473
    personality and, 467–469, **468, 470–
        471**
    phases of, 457–460
        aura, 458–460

        headache, 460
        postdrome, 460
        premonitory phase, 458
    psychiatric disorders and, 454, 465–
        467, **467**
    relation to tension-type headache,
        452–453
    treatment of, 473–478, **474,** 475
        abortive (acute), 473, **474,** 475–
            477
        for aura, 475
        preventive, 473, **474,** 477–478
        setting priorities for, 478
Migralepsy, 465
Migration, neuronal, 23–25, **24**
Milacemide, 1182
Mineralocorticoid receptor expression
    on immune cells, 133
MINI (Multinational Neuropsychiatric
    Inventory), 629, **629**
Mini-Mental State Exam (MMSE), 180,
    235, 352, 532, 536–537, 636, 738–
    739, **740,** 928, 1180
Minnesota Multiphasic Personality
    Inventory (MMPI), 223, 234, 455,
    468, 469, **470–471,** 822, 857
Mirror movements, 167
Mirtazapine, 1159
    adverse effects of, **1162**
    dosage of, **1162**
    drug interactions with, **1162**
    mechanism of action of, 1143, **1144**
    for patients with diabetes mellitus,
        **855**
    for patients with HIV/AIDS, 799
    use in patients with traumatic brain
        injury, 646
Misdirection, **1203**
Misidentification syndromes, 1200–
    1202, **1205**
Mitochondrial inheritance, 329
MK-801, 656, 998
MK-869, 1143
MMPI (Minnesota Multiphasic
    Personality Inventory), 223, 234,
    455, 468, 469, **470–471,** 822,
    857
MMSE (Mini-Mental State Exam), 180,
    235, 352, 532, 536–537, 636, 738–
    739, **740,** 928, 1180
Mnemonic strategies, 1239–1241
Moclobemide, **1144,** 1157–1158
Modafinil
    for narcolepsy, 715
    for patients with traumatic brain
        injury, 649–650

Modified Mini-Mental State (3MS),
    180
Molar behaviors, 1242–1243
Molecular genetic studies, 329,
    386
    of Alzheimer's disease, 355–357
    of attention-deficit/hyperactivity
        disorder, 367–368
    of autism, 346–347
    of bipolar disorder, 372
    of drug-induced adaptations in
        nucleus accumbens, **915,** 915–
        917, **916**
    of epilepsy, 364
    of Huntington's disease, 332–334,
        **333, 334**
    of Lesch-Nyhan syndrome, 335
    of metachromatic leukodystrophy,
        348–349
    of myotonic dystrophy, 365–366
    of narcolepsy, 385
    of obsessive-compulsive disorder,
        379–380
    of panic disorder, 376
    of Parkinson's disease, **339,**
        339–340
    role in psychotropic drug
        development, 1140
    of schizophrenia, 384
    of Wilson's disease, **342,** 342–343
Molindone
    for AIDS-associated psychosis or
        delirium, 798
    for patients with traumatic brain
        injury, 650
Monoamine oxidase (MAO), 1132
    in borderline personality disorder,
        585–586
    impulsivity and platelet level of, 585
    MAO-A
        bipolar disorder and, 372
        obsessive-compulsive disorder
            and, 380
Monoamine oxidase inhibitors (MAOIs)
    effects on sleep, 703, 711
    indications for, 1158, 1159
        attention-deficit/hyperactivity
            disorder, 1079
        Huntington's disease, 930
        patients with brain tumors, 775
        patients with diabetes mellitus,
            854, **855**
        patients with HIV/AIDS, 799
    mechanism of action of, **1144**
Monocytes, 116
Monogenic disorders, 326

Mood disorders, 1021–1038. *See also*
  Bipolar disorder; Depression;
  Mania
  Alzheimer's disease and, 956
  antiparkinsonism drug-induced, 968
  attention-deficit/hyperactivity
    disorder and, 1073
  attentional disturbances and, 511–
    512, 605–607
  brain tumors and
    corpus callosum tumors, 763–764
    frontal lobe tumors, 760
    occipital lobe tumors, 762
    parietal lobe tumors, 762
    treatment of, 772–773, 775–776
  depression, 1021–1038
  diabetes mellitus and, 853–854
  effects on memory, 605–607
    subjective evaluation of, 612, **612**
  endocrine abnormalities and, 1025,
    **1025**
    Cushing's syndrome, 861–862,
      **862**
    diabetes mellitus, 853–854
    hyperprolactinemia, 866
    hyperthyroidism, **859**, 859–860
    hypothyroidism, **856**, 857, **857**
  epilepsy and, 685–687
  frontotemporal dementias and, **960**
  functional neuroimaging in, **297**,
    301–305, **303, 304**
  HIV/AIDS and, 798–800
  Huntington's disease and, 222, 331,
    929, 964
  migraine and, 466, 467, **467**
  multiple sclerosis and, 1226
  neurochemistry of, 1023–1025,
    **1024**
  pain and, 421
  Parkinson's disease and, 222, 336,
    933–934
  poststroke, 725, 728–744, 748–749
  sleep disturbances and, 155, 703,
    1025–1026, **1026**
  systemic lupus erythematosus and,
    818
  traumatic brain injury and, 636–638
    treatment of, 646–648
Mood stabilizers, **1173**
Morphine, 433, **440**
  epidural, 442–443, **443**
  immunologic effects of, 137
  intramuscular, 441
  for migraine, 475
  oral bioavailability of, 439
  subcutaneous, 441

  sustained-release, 439
Motion activity monitoring, **209**, 209–
  210
Motivation, **1201**
Motor blocks, in Parkinson's disease,
  1221, **1222**
Motor Continuation Task, 504
Motor cortex, 74
Motor function. *See also* Psychomotor
  deficits
  functional neuroimaging of, 291–
    292, **292**
    in schizophrenia, 309
  tests of, 233–234
"Motor helplessness," 162
Motor neuron disease with dementia,
  941
Motor vehicle accidents, 625, 657–658
Mouth-opening/finger-spreading reflex,
  **167**, 168
Movement abnormalities, 162–167,
  **220, 1204**
  agitation, 163
  akathisia, 163
  akinesia, 162–163
  asterixis, 165
  catatonia, 166–167
  chorea, 164–165
  disordered gait, 162
  dystonia, 164
  hypertonus, 163–164
  myoclonus, 165
  in Parkinson's disease, 162–164, 932,
    1220–1221, **1222**
  psychogenic, psychotherapeutic
    approach to patients with,
    1228–1231
  startle, 166
  stereotypy and mannerism, 166
  synkinesia and mirror movements,
    167
  tardive dyskinesia, **165**
  tics and compulsions, 166
  tremor, 164
  weakness, 162
Movement abnormalities associated
  with dementia, 923–944,
  **924**
  cerebellar diseases, 940–941
    Friedreich's ataxia, 940
    olivopontocerebellar atrophies,
      940
    other spinocerebellar
      degenerations, 940–941
  cortical-basal ganglionic
    degeneration, 939, 972

  dementia with Lewy bodies, 176,
    553, 935–937, 958–959
  Fahr's disease, 942, 970–971
  frontotemporal dementia, 939–940,
    959–962
  genetic basis of, 923, **925**
  Hallervorden-Spatz disease, 942–
    943, 971
  Huntington's disease, 331–334, 924–
    931, 963–965
  motor neuron disease, 941
  normal-pressure hydrocephalus,
    943–944, 976–978
  Parkinson's disease, 335–341, 931–
    935, 965–969, 1220
  progressive supranuclear palsy, 937–
    939, 969–970
  thalamic degeneration, 941
  Wilson's disease, 165, 341–343, 942,
    971–972
MPAI (Mayo-Portland Adaptability
  Inventory), 234
MPTP (1-methyl-4-phenyl-1,2,3,6-
  tetrahydropyridine), 10, 11, 34,
  337, 340, 498, 931
MR. *See* Mental retardation
MRI. *See* Magnetic resonance imaging
MRS. *See* Magnetic resonance
  spectroscopy
MS. *See* Multiple sclerosis
MSA (multiple system atrophy), 972–
  973, **973**
MSLT (Multiple Sleep Latency Test),
  385, 641, 715
MST (magnetic seizure therapy), 615
Mucopolysaccharidosis, 979
Multifactorial causation of disease, 329
Multinational Neuropsychiatric
  Inventory (MINI), 629, **629**
Multiple sclerosis (MS), 4
  affective disorders and, 1226
  anxiety and, 1051
  attentional disturbances in, 508–509,
    **509**
  deficits in reaction time in, 500
  differential diagnosis of
    antiphospholipid antibody
      syndrome, 821
    Behçet's disease, 830
  evoked potentials in, 202
  magnetic resonance imaging in, **268,
    509**
  psychiatric management of
    antidepressant therapy, 1157
    psychotherapy, 1226–1228,
      **1229**

Multiple sclerosis (MS) *(continued)*
    stress, depression, and immunity in, 127–128
Multiple Sleep Latency Test (MSLT), 385, 641, 715
Multiple sulfatase deficiency, 347
Multiple system atrophy (MSA), 972–973, **973**
Muramyl peptides, 52
Muscarinic agonists, for Alzheimer's disease, 1181
Muscle relaxants, 438
Muscle weakness, 162
Mushroom poisoning, 892, **894**
Music recognition defect, 91, **91**
Musical hallucinations, 176
Mutism, 162
    akinetic, 95–97, **97, 100,** 506
Myasthenia gravis, 5
Myelin sheath, 4, **5, 7**
Myeloid cells, 116
Myoclonic seizures, 1094
Myoclonus, 165
    in Creutzfeldt-Jakob disease, 166
    nocturnal, 155, 707
    tardive, 165
Myotonic dystrophy, 365–366
    clinical features of, 365
    congenital, 365
    diagnosis of, 366
    epidemiologic studies of, 365
    genetic studies of, 365–366, 925
        anticipation, 329
        mode of inheritance, 365
        molecular approaches, 365–366
        relative risk, **325**
        twin studies, 365
    psychiatric syndromes and, 365
*Mytilus edulis,* 891

Na$^+$/K$^+$-ATPase (sodium/potassium adenosine triphosphatase) pump, 1125
NAA (*N*-acetyl aspartate), 290, 298, 311, **312,** 608, 631
NAc. *See* Nucleus accumbens
NADH (nicotinamide adenine dinucleotide) dehydrogenase, 337
Nadolol, 653, 1176
Nalbuphine, **441**
Naloxone, 432, 434
Naltrexone, 909
    for autism, 1089
    for self-injurious behavior, 1177
Naming, 80, 172, 567–568
Naproxen, **435**

for migraine prophylaxis, **474**
Naratriptan, **474,** 476
Narcolepsy, 385, **707,** 715
    age at onset of, 385
    clinical features of, 385
    diagnosis of, 715
    epidemiologic studies of, 385
    genetic studies of, 385
        family studies, 385
        linkage analysis, 385
        mode of inheritance, 385
        molecular approaches, 385
        relative risk, **325**
    hallucinations in, 176
    history taking for, 155–156
    orexin and, 62–65
    prevalence of, 385
    sleep architecture in, 715
    symptoms of, 62, 715
    treatment of, 715
Narrative process in interview setting, 175
NART (National Adult Reading Test), 227
National Adult Reading Test (NART), 227
National Practitioner Data Bank, 1281
Natural immunity, 116–118, **118, 119**
Natural killer (NK) cells, 116, 121
    effects of stress on, 124–125
NBRS (Neurobehavioral Rating Scale), 181, **183,** 234, 498, 629, **629**
NCSE (Neurobehavioral Cognitive Status Examination), 235
Nefazodone, 1159
    adverse effects of, **1162**
    dosage of, **1162**
    drug interactions with, **1162**
    effects on sleep, 703, 711
    indications for
        patients with dementia, **980,** 981
        patients with diabetes mellitus, **855**
        patients with HIV/AIDS, 799
    mechanism of action of, **1144**
    use in patients with traumatic brain injury, 646
Negative reinforcers of behavior, 1245
Neglect syndrome, 170–171
    assessment for, 230, 501–502
    as attentional disorder, 494, 496, 508
    inferior parietal lesions and, 92, **94**
    neuroanatomic model of, 494, **495**
    perceptual and body schema hypotheses of, 508
    poststroke, 507

somatosensory, 507
    visual scanning training for, 1241
    visual-spatial, 507
Negligence, 1271. *See also* Malpractice claims
NEO Personality Inventory (NEO-PI), 1028
Neopterin, 786–787
Nerve gas agents, **888**
Nerve growth factor (NGF), 29, 34
NES (Neurological Evaluation Scale), **169**
Neural blockade, 431–432, 444
Neural plasticity, 22, 33–34, 1011
Neural plate, 23
Neurilemmomas, **754**
Neuritic plaques (NPs)
    in Alzheimer's disease, 351–352, 954, 957–958
    in dementia with Lewy bodies, 936
    in Parkinson's disease, 932
Neuroanatomy, functional, 71–105
    brain-behavior relationships, 72–74
        lateral specialization, 72–73, **73, 74**
        longitudinal specialization, 73–74, **75**
    of frontal lobes, 94–103, **96, 97**
        dorsolateral prefrontal region, 101–103
        frontal operculum, 95
        inferior mesial region, 97–101
        superior mesial region, 95–97
    of occipital lobes, 82–89, **83, 84**
        dorsal component, 83–86
        ventral component, 86–89
    of parietal lobes, 89–94, **90, 91**
        inferior parietal lobule, 92–93
        temporoparietal junction, 89–92
    of subcortical structures, **103,** 103–105
        basal ganglia, 103–104, **104**
        thalamus, 104–105
    techniques for study of, 71–72
        functional imaging, 72
        lesion method, 71–72
    of temporal lobes, 74–82, **76, 77**
        anterior, lateral, and inferior temporal regions, 79–82
        mesial temporal region, 75–79
Neurobehavioral Cognitive Status Examination (NCSE), 235
Neurobehavioral Rating Scale (NBRS), 181, **183,** 234, 498, 629, **629**
Neurodegenerative diseases, 3. *See also* specific diseases

apoptosis in, 22
excitotoxicity and, 33
glial cell dysfunction and, 1126
Neurodestructive procedures, 445
Neurodevelopmental disorders, 26
Neurofibrillary tangles (NFTs)
in Alzheimer's disease, 4, 351–352, 954, 957–958
in dementia with Lewy bodies, 936
in Gerstmann-Sträussler-Sheinker syndrome, 360
in Parkinson's disease, 932
in progressive supranuclear palsy, 938, 970
Neurofilaments, 4
Neuroimaging, functional, 72, 245, 285–312. *See also* specific imaging modalities
concepts of, 285–286, **286**
limitations of, 295–296
of normal brain functioning, 291–295
attention, 292–293, 496, **497,** 506
emotion, 295
language, 294–295, 566–567
learning and memory, 293, **294,** 597
movement, 291–292, **292**
vision, 291
in specific conditions, 296–311
acquired achromatopsia, 87
Alzheimer's disease, 957, **957**
anxiety, 299
attention-deficit/hyperactivity disorder, 299, **300,** 513–514, 1074–1075
autism, 296–298, 1088
Behçet's disease, 830
bipolar disorder, 303–305, **304**
borderline personality disorder, 583, 589
brain tumor, 770, **771**
child abuse, 1101
delirium, 552
dementia, 979
dementia with Lewy bodies, 937
depression, **297,** 301–303, **303,** 1029–1032, **1030**
domoic acid intoxication, 891
epilepsy, 677, 1164
frontotemporal dementias, 959, **961**
generalized anxiety disorder, 1053
HIV/AIDS, 790

Huntington's disease, 926, 927, 964, 965
Lesch-Nyhan syndrome, 335
limbic encephalitis, 79
obsessive-compulsive disorder, 299–301, 1055, 1056
olivopontocerebellar atrophies, 940
panic disorder, 299, 1058
Parkinson's disease, 883, 935, 968, 1031
posttraumatic stress disorder, 632, 1060
progressive supranuclear palsy, 938, 970
Rett's disorder, 1090
schizophrenia, 305–311, **306, 312, 313,** 1002–1006, **1003, 1006,** 1009, **1009**
social phobia, 1061
strokes involving basal ganglia, 1031–1032
systemic lupus erythematosus, 819–820
Tourette's syndrome, 301, 1055, 1082
toxin exposure, 895
traumatic brain injury, **629,** 630–632
vascular dementia, 975
Wilson's disease, 971
state vs. trait markers in studies of mental disorders, 296, **297**
techniques for, 245, **246,** 287–291
functional magnetic resonance imaging, 290
magnetic resonance spectroscopy, 290–291
positron emission tomography, 287–288
single photon emission computed tomography, 288–290
training for interpretation of, 1293, 1302
Neuroimaging, structural, 71–72, 245–281. *See also* Computed tomography; Magnetic resonance imaging
indications for, 246, **247,** 264
modalities for, 245, **246**
computed tomography, 248–253
computed tomography vs. magnetic resonance imaging, 264, **264, 266–268**
magnetic resonance imaging, 253–263

normal anatomy on, 264–281, **270–279**
amygdala, 280
basal ganglia, 266, 269
caudate nucleus, 269
cerebral cortex, 266, 269
globus pallidus, 269, 279
hippocampal formation and parahippocampal cortex, 279–280
hypothalamus, 281
limbic system, 279, **280**
mamillary body, 280–281
pons, 281
putamen, 269
substantia nigra, 279
thalamus, 281
practical considerations for, 247
contrast-enhanced studies, 247
ordering examination, 247
patient preparation, 247
understanding scan, 247
principles for, 246
training for interpretation of, 1293, 1302
what can be learned from, 245–246
Neuroleptic-induced immunopathy, 832
Neuroleptic malignant syndrome, 797, 1083
Neuroleptics. *See* Antipsychotics
Neuroligins, 17, **18**
Neurological Evaluation Scale (NES), **169**
Neurological soft signs, 168, **169**
aggression and, 582
borderline personality disorder and, 589
obsessive-compulsive disorder and, 1055
posttraumatic stress disorder and, 1059
Neurolysis, 445
Neuromuscular junction, 14
synaptogenesis at, 27–29, **28**
Neurons, 3–35, 1127–1140
in brain, 4, 1124
cellular function of, 3–22, 1127
cytoskeleton of, 4
development of, 3, **22,** 22–33, 1069–1070, **1070**
determination, 23
differentiation, **26,** 26–27
maturation and survival, 29–30, **30**
migration, 24–26, **25,** 1069–1070

Neurons (continued)
  development of (continued)
    neurotransmitter actions and, 32–33
    proliferation, 23–24
    synapse formation, 27–29, **28**
    synaptic refinement, 30–32, **32**
  excitability of, 4–8
    action potentials, 5–6, **6, 7,** 1127
    intrinsic firing patterns, 6–8, **8**
  functional organization of, 4, **5**
  mechanisms of damage in traumatic brain injury, **626,** 626–627
  pacemaker firing of, 6
  in pain perception, 422–430 (See also Nociceptors)
  postsynaptic, 1127, **1130**
  presynaptic, 1127, **1129**
  resting, 1127
  shape of, 4
  signaling between, 3, 8–13, 1127–1140 (See also Synapses)
    chemical synapses, 9–11, **10–13,** 1127–1140 (See also Neurotransmitters)
    electrical synapses, 9, 1127
    G proteins and, 1136, **1136**
    modes of interneural communication, 8, **9**
    rapid postsynaptic responses, 14–17
    second messengers and, 1136–1140, **1138, 1139**
  synchronous vs. asynchronous firing of, 31
  thalamic, 6–8, **8**
  wide dynamic range, 426
Neurontin. See Gabapentin
Neuropeptides, 9
Neuropsychiatric assessment. See Bedside neuropsychiatric assessment
Neuropsychiatric education, 1289–1305
  Accreditation Council on Graduate Medical Education, 1289
  American Board of Psychiatry and Neurology examinations, 1289–1290
  American Neuropsychiatric Association recommended core content for, 1304, **1305**
  certification issues, 1303–1304
  content of training in United States, 1290–1293, **1292**

American Neuropsychiatric Association Training Objectives, 1290–1293, **1292**
  funding for, 1304–1305
  history of, **1291**
  limitations on, 1304–1305
  opinions of psychiatry educators on, 1293, 1299–1300
  techniques and curriculum for, 1300–1303
  textbooks and journals for, 1300, **1301–1303**
  training programs in neuropsychiatry and behavioral neurology, **1305**
  University of Massachusetts Medical School case conferences, **1304**
  in various countries, 1290, **1292**
Neuropsychiatric Inventory (NPI), 181, **629,** 630, 938
Neuropsychiatric Inventory (NPI) Questionnaire, **629,** 630
Neuropsychiatrist, 1257
Neuropsychiatry careers, 1303
Neuropsychic defenses, 1200
Neuropsychological evaluation, 217–236
  approaches to, 222
  categories of tests for, 227–234
    attention and mental tracking, 228–229, **229, 499,** 499–505
    conceptual functions, 231–233
    constructional ability, 231, **232**
    executive functions, 233
    language, 228
    memory, 229–230
    mental ability, 227–228
    motor functions, 233–234
    perception, 230–231
    personality and emotional status, 234
    praxis, 231
  for competency determination, 235
  computer-aided, 223
  difference from psychological testing, 223
  of emotional and social factors, 222–223
  indications for, 217–221, **220**
  information provided by, 217
  interpretation principles and cautions for, 226–227
  interview for, 221–222
  nature of tests for, 223–226

    ability levels based on deviation from mean, 223–224, **224, 225**
    cutoff scores, 224–225
    intraindividual comparisons, 223
    normal distribution curve, 223, **224**
    reliability, 225
    sensitivity and specificity, 225–226, **226**
    test selection, 226
    validity, 225
    $z$ score, 224, **224**
  persons qualified to perform, 236
  process of, 221–223
  role of referring psychiatrist in, 221
  screening tests, 180–181, 235
  in specific patient populations
    Alzheimer's disease, 219, 235, 957
    brain tumor, 757–759, 770, 776
    Cushing's syndrome, 863
    dementia, **226**
    HIV infection, 219, 794, **794**
    Huntington's disease, 963
    schizophrenia, **225,** 999–1000
    traumatic brain injury, 632, **632**
  test batteries for, 222, 234–235
  treatment and planning based on, 235–236
Neuroreceptors, 901, 1133–1136. See also specific receptors
  action at allosteric sites, 1134
  categories of, 1133–1134
  definition of, 1133
  drug interactions with, 1134–1136, 1140–1141
    agonists, antagonists, and inverse agonists, 1134
    drugs of abuse, 901, **901**
    ethanol, 901, 1129
  G protein–coupled, 1133, **1133,** 1136
  on immune cells, **134**
  intraneuronal, 1134
  ion channels formed by, 1133
  overproduction and pruning of, 1070, **1071,** 1076
  positron emission tomography of, **288**
  presynaptic, 1129
  specificity for neurotransmitters, 1134
  subtypes of, 1134, **1135,** 1140–1141
Neurosarcoidosis, 829–830
Neurotensin, 1070, **1135**

Neuroticism, depression and, 1028
Neurotoxins. *See* Poisons; Toxin exposure
Neurotransmitters, 5, 9–11, 901, 1127–1140. *See also* specific neurotransmitters
    acceptors for, 1133
    in attention, 496–498
    in basal ganglia, 269
    effects of drugs of abuse on, 900–903, **901**
    enzymatic degradation of, 10, 1129–1130
    glial cell interactions with, 1124
    inactivation of, 1129–1133
    in long-term potentiation, 21
    neuropeptide, 9, 1128
    neurotrophic and neurotoxic actions of, 32–33
    positron emission tomography of, 287
    postsynaptic receptors activated by, 14–17, **16**
    receptors for (*See* Neuroreceptors)
    reuptake of, 10–11, **13**, 1130
    small molecule, 9
    in specific conditions
        aggression, 584–586, 1175
        attention-deficit/hyperactivity disorder, 513–514, 1073–1077
        autism, 1088–1089
        cognitive impairment, 1179–1180
        delirium, 552–555
        depression, 302–303, 1023–1025, **1024,** 1157
            treatment-induced changes in, 1035
        frontotemporal dementias, 961
        generalized anxiety disorder, 1052–1053
        HIV/AIDS, 791
        Huntington's disease, 926, 964
        impulsivity and aggression, **584,** 584–586, **585**
        obsessive-compulsive disorder, 1054–1055
        panic disorder, 1057–1058
        Parkinson's disease, 335, 498, 932, 968
        posttraumatic stress disorder, 1059
        progressive supranuclear palsy, 938, 970
        psychosis, 1163–1164
        Rett's disorder, 1089

        schizophrenia, 995–999
        social phobia, 1061
        Tourette's syndrome, 1082–1083
        traumatic brain injury, 627
    spinal, **434**
    storage and release of, 1128–1129
    in synaptic transmission, 9–10, **11,** 1127–1140
    synthesis of, 1128
    transporters for, 10–11, **13,** 1130–1132, **1131**
        function as ion channels, 1132
Neurotrophins, 29–30, **30, 902,** 1126–1127
    in long-term potentiation, 21
    in selective synaptic strengthening, 31–32
Neutrophils, 116
NF-κB (nuclear factor kappa B), 30, 55
NFTs. *See* Neurofibrillary tangles
NGF (nerve growth factor), 29, 34
Nicotinamide adenine dinucleotide (NADH) dehydrogenase, 337
Nicotine addiction. *See* Smoking
Nicotine agonists, for Alzheimer's disease, 1181
Niemann-Pick disease, 979
Night terrors, **707,** 717
Nightmares, **707,** 718
Nimodipine
    for Alzheimer's disease, 1182
    for HIV/AIDS, 796
Nitric oxide (NO), 17, 21, 138, 901
Nitric oxide synthetase (NOS), 17, 1137
Nitrous oxide poisoning, **880**
*Nitzchia pungens*, 891
NK (natural killer) cells, 116, 121
NMDA. *See* N-Methyl-D-aspartate
NO (nitric oxide), 17, 21, 138, 901
Nociceptors, 422–425. *See also* Pain
    activation of, 422, **424**
    in cardiac muscle, 423
    joint, 423
    mechanosensory, 422
    mechanothermal, 422
    polymodal C fiber, 422, **422**
    in skeletal muscle, 423
    thermoreceptive, 422
    visceral, 423
Nocturnal seizures, **707,** 717
Nodes of Ranvier, **5, 6, 7**
Nomifensine, **436**
Non-Hodgkin's lymphoma, HIV-related, 122, 787, 789, **789**

Non-REM sleep. *See* Sleep-wakefulness, non-REM (slow-wave) sleep
Nonallelic heterogeneity, 326
Noncontingent reinforcement of behavior, 1246
Nonepileptic seizures, 679–680, **680**
Nonmaleficence, 1258
Nonrecall, **1203**
Nonsteroidal anti-inflammatory drugs (NSAIDs), 434–435, **435**
    adverse effects of, 434–435
        delirium, **547**
        gastric erosion, 434–435, **435**
    indications for, 434
        Alzheimer's disease, 354, 954, 1181
        headache, 455
        migraine, **474,** 475
Noradrenergic reuptake inhibitors (NRIs), 1027, 1077–1078
Norepinephrine, 9
    brain localization of, 58
    inhibition of REM sleep by, 58–59
    receptors for, **1135**
    reuptake of, 1130
    role in attention, 498, 1077
    in specific conditions
        aggression, 1175
        depression, 1023–1024, **1024**
        generalized anxiety disorder, 1053
        impulsive aggression, **585,** 586–587
        panic disorder, 1057
        posttraumatic stress disorder, 1059
        Rett's disorder, 1089
        schizophrenia, 997
        Tourette's syndrome, 1082–1083
        traumatic brain injury, 627
    synthesis of, 1128
    transporter for, 1132
Normal-pressure hydrocephalus (NPH), 943–944, 976–978
    cerebrospinal fluid shunting for, 943–944, 977–978
    clinical and neuropsychiatric features of, 976–977
    dementia of, 943
    diagnosis of, 943, 977
    etiologies of, 943, 977
Nortriptyline
    adverse effects of, 740, **1160**
    contraindications to, 741
    dosage of, **436,** 1160
    drug interactions with, **1160**

Nortriptyline *(continued)*
  indications for, 1157–1158
    anxiety in Parkinson's disease, 967
    attention-deficit/hyperactivity disorder, 1079
    emotional lability, 648
    patients with dementia, **980**, 981
    patients with traumatic brain injury, 646, 649
    poststroke depression, **740**, 740–741, **741**
      with comorbid generalized anxiety disorder, 745
    poststroke pathological emotions, 747–748, **748**
    terminal half-life of, **436**
NOS (nitric oxide synthetase), 17, 1137
Notochord, 23
NPH. *See* Normal-pressure hydrocephalus
NPI (Neuropsychiatric Inventory), 181, **629**, 630, 938
NPs. *See* Neuritic plaques
NRIs (noradrenergic reuptake inhibitors), 1027, 1077–1078
Nuchocephalic reflex, **167**, 168
Nuclear factor kappa B (NF-κB), 30, 55
Nucleus accumbens (NAc), 97
  adaptations in mesolimbic dopamine system after long-term drug exposure, 910–914, **912**
  evidence for structural changes in VTA-NAc pathway, 914
  molecular mechanisms underlying adaptations in NAc, **915**, 915–917, **916**
  regulation of dopamine in VTA-NAc pathway, 911
  regulation of G proteins and cAMP pathway in VTA and NAc, 913–914
  regulation of opioid and dopamine receptors in VTA and NAc, 911–913
  animal self-administration of opiates into, 907
  location of, **903**
Nucleus paragigantocellularis (PGi), 903, 905–906
Nucleus proprius, 426

OAS (Overt Aggression Scale), **629**, 630, 643, **644**, 1172
OASS (Overt Agitation Severity Scale), 630

Object Assembly test, 231
Obsessions, 1049
Obsessive-compulsive disorder (OCD), 376–380, 1049, 1053–1056
  clinical features of, 376, 1049–1050
  cognitive deficits in, 220
  as disorder of excessive vigilance, 496
  economic cost of, 1054
  electroencephalography in, 1056
  epidemiologic studies of, 376–377
  epilepsy and, 685, **685**
  functional neuroimaging in, 299–301, 1055, 1056
  genetic studies of, 377–380
    adoption studies, 378
    family studies, 377–378
    high-risk studies, 378–379
    linkage analysis, 379
    mode of inheritance, 379
    molecular approaches, 379–380
    twin studies, 378
  Huntington's disease and, 964, 1050
  neuroanatomy of, 1055–1056
    basal ganglia lesions, 1050
    cortico-striatal-thalamic-cortical hypothesis, 1050, **1054**, 1054–1056, 1062
  neurochemistry of, 1054–1055
    serotonin, 379–380, 1054, 1056
  neurological conditions associated with, 299–300
  Parkinson's disease and, 967, 1050
  postencephalitic, 1050
  prevalence of, 376–377, 1053
  spasmodic torticollis and, 1050
  Sydenham's chorea and, 378, 828, 1050
  Tourette's syndrome and, 299, 301, 378, 1050–1051, 1081, 1084
  traumatic brain injury and, 640, 1051
  treatment of, 1054, 1176
    dopamine blockers, 1054, 1055
    orbitofrontal activity as predictor of response to, 1056
    selective serotonin reuptake inhibitors, 1054
    surgical, 1055
Obsessive-compulsive spectrum disorders, 1050, 1056, 1175
Obstetric factors, 154
  schizophrenia and, 381, 991–992
  Tourette's syndrome and, 1050
Occipital lobes

functional neuroanatomy of, 82–89, **83**, **84**
  dorsal component, 83–86
  ventral component, 86–89
  tumors of, 762–763, **771**
    neuropsychiatric and behavioral manifestations of, 762–763
    neuropsychological manifestations of, 763
Occipitotemporal junction, 74, **77**, 80
  associative prosopagnosia and lesions of, 82, **83**
Occupational history, 156
Occupational rehabilitation, 776
OCD. *See* Obsessive-compulsive disorder
Ocular apraxia, 85, 159, 174
Ocular dominance columns in visual cortex, 31, **32**
Oculogyric crisis, 164
Olanzapine, 1164
  adverse effects of, **1168**
  dosage of, **1168**
  drug interactions with, **1168**
  indications for
    aggression, 652
    aphasic patients, 577
    borderline personality disorder, 591
    delirium, 550
      in HIV/AIDS, 798
    patients with dementia, 980, **980**
    patients with Huntington's disease, 964
    patients with Parkinson's disease, 935, 1165
    patients with traumatic brain injury, 650, 652
  receptor binding affinity of, **1142**
Olfactory defects, 157–158
Olfactory hallucinations, 176
Oligodendrocytes, 4, **7**
Olivopontocerebellar atrophies (OPCAs), 33, **925**, 940
Ondansetron
  for delirium, 548
  for migraine, 477
  for Parkinson's disease psychosis, 1166
OPCAs (olivopontocerebellar atrophies), 33, **925**, 940
Opiate addiction
  pharmacologic actions of, **901**
  role of locus coeruleus in, **903**, 903–906, **905**, **906**
Opioid analgesics, 432–433, 438–444

adverse effects of, 439
dosage of, 438, **440–441**
immunologic effects of, 137
intramuscular, 441
intrathecal, 432
intravenous, 441–442
for migraine, **474**, 475
minimum effective concentration of,
    438–439, **440–441**, 442
oral, 439
for patient-controlled analgesia, 442
for periodic limb movement disorder
    and restless legs syndrome, **710**
rectal, 439–441
spinal, 442–444, **443**
subcutaneous, 441
sublingual, 439
terminal half-life of, **440–441**
Opioid receptors, 432–433, **434, 1135**
brain, 432–433
functional imaging of, **288**
opiate effects at, **901,** 904
pharmacodynamic effects of opioid
    agonist interaction with
    subtypes of, **433**
regulation in VTA and NAc in
    response to long-term drug
    exposure, 911–913
spinal cord, 433, 442
Opioids, endogenous, 9, 432
in autism, 1089
in depression, **1024**
effects of stress on, 124
Opium, 432
Optic ataxia, 85–86, 174
Oral appliances
for sleep bruxism, 719
for sleep-disordered breathing, 714
Oral apraxia, 172–173
Orbitofrontal complex, 742–743
Orbitofrontal syndrome, 634, 759
Orexin, 62–65
brain distribution of, **63,** 64
in control of REM sleep, 64–65
in control of wakefulness, 64, 65
factors related to release of, 65
receptors for, 64
Organic Brain Syndrome Scale, 537
Organic brain syndromes, 1178
Organochloride pesticide exposure,
    **880, 888, 889**
Organophosphate exposure, 889–890
chemical structures, **887**
diagnosis of, 890
mechanism of action of, 890, **890**
nerve gas agents, **888,** 889

neuropsychiatric manifestations of,
    **880,** 889–890
sources of, 889
treatment of, 890
Organotin poisoning, **884,** 884–885
chemical structure of trialkyltin
    compounds, **884**
diagnosis of, 885
mechanism of action of, 885
neuropsychiatric manifestations of,
    **879,** 884
sources of exposure, 884
treatment of, 885
Orientation, 170
adaptations in psychiatric technique
    relative to, **1201**
Orientation Remedial program, 1239
Orphenadrine, 775
Oseretsky test, 177
Osteoarthritis, 434, 814
Overt Aggression Scale (OAS), **629,**
    630, 643, **644,** 1172
Overt Agitation Severity Scale (OASS),
    630
β-*n*-Oxalylamino-*l*-alanine, 33
Oxazepam
indications for, 1170
    patients with dementia, **980, 981,**
        1170
    patients with HIV/AIDS, 801
pharmacokinetics of, **712**
Oxcarbazepine, 690, **691**
Oxycodone, **440**
for migraine, 475
for periodic limb movement disorder
    and restless legs syndrome, **710**
rectal, 441
Oxygen free radicals, 30
Oxygen therapy
for carbon monoxide poisoning, 886
for cluster headache, 480
Oxymorphone, **440**
Oxytocin, **1135**

P50 wave, 202
in posttraumatic stress disorder, 202,
    **203**
in schizophrenia, 202, 1002
in traumatic brain injury, 649
P300 potential, 203–204
in autism, 1088
illness duration and delayed latency
    of, 203, **205**
mismatch negativity and, 203
in posttraumatic stress disorder,
    203–204

in schizophrenia, 203, **204, 205,**
    1001
subcomponents of, 203
Paced Auditory Serial Addition Task
    (PASAT), 229, **499,** 501, 511
Pacemaker firing of neurons, 6, **8**
PACNS (primary angiitis of central
    nervous system), 825
Pain, 419–430
cognitive factors influencing, 420–
    421
    attention to pain, 420
    meaning of pain, 421
cortical modulation of, 419–420
definition of, 420
gate control theory of, 420
mood disorders and, 421
neurological mechanisms of, 421–
    430
    peripheral sensory receptors, **422,**
        422–423
        cardiac muscle pain, 423
        cutaneous pain sensation, 422
        joint pain, 423
        skeletal muscle pain, 423
        visceral pain, 423, **424**
    primary afferent transmission,
        423–425, **424**
    spinal cord terminals of primary
        afferents, 425–430
        ascending sensory pathways,
            426, **428**
        brainstem processing, 426–
            427
        cerebral cortex, 429
        descending modulation, **428,**
            429–430, **431**
        dorsal and ventral roots, 425
        dorsal horn, 425, **425**
        lamina I, 425–426
        lamina II, 426
        laminae III and IV, 426, **427**
        lamina X (central canal),
            426
        thalamic relays, 427, **429**
prevalence of, 419
"second pain" phenomenon, 422
secondary gain associated with, 446–
    447
Pain management, 430–447
analgesic adjuvants, 436–438, **437**
antidepressants, 435–436, **436**
electrical stimulation, 433–434, 444
hypnosis, 445–446
neural blockade, 431–432, 444
neurodestructive procedures, 445

Pain management (*continued*)
  nonsteroidal anti-inflammatory
    drugs, 434–435, **435**
  opioid analgesics, 432–433, **433,
    434,** 438–444, **440, 441, 443**
  in patients with spinal cord injury,
    1212
  peripheral desensitization, 430, **4432**
  pharmacology of pain, 430
Paired Associated Learning test, 500
Palilalia, 161, 573
Palinacousis, 176
Pallidotomy
  for Hallervorden-Spatz disease, 943
  for Parkinson's disease, 935, 969,
    1152
Palmomental reflex, 167, **167**
PAN (polyarteritis nodosa), 823–824
PANDAS (pediatric autoimmune
    neuropsychiatric disorder
    associated with streptococcal
    infections), 129, 378–379, 828,
    1050, 1055, 1056, 1081
Panic attacks, carbon dioxide-induced,
    374–375
Panic disorder, 372–376, 1049, 1056–
    1058
  anxiety and avoidance symptoms of,
    1049
  brain tumors and, 761
    pharmacotherapy for, 776
  clinical features of, 373
  electroencephalography in, 1050
  epidemiologic studies of, 373
  epilepsy and, 684–685, **685**
  functional neuroimaging in, 299,
    1058
  genetic studies of, 373–376
    adoption studies, 374
    family studies, 373
    high-risk studies, 374–375
    linkage analysis, 375–376
    mode of inheritance, 375
    molecular approaches, 376
    twin studies, 373–374
  Huntington's disease and, 1051
  migraine and, 454, 466
  neuroanatomy of, 1056, **1057,** 1058
  neurochemistry of, 1057–1058
  Parkinson's disease and, 967, 1051
  prevalence of, 373, 1056
  selective serotonin reuptake
    inhibitors for, 1057
  temporal lobe lesions and, 761, 1050
  traumatic brain injury and, 636, 640,
    1051

PANSS (Positive and Negative
    Symptom Scale), 629, **629**
Parahippocampal gyrus, 74, 75
Parahippocampus, **271, 278,** 279–280
Paraldehyde, 652
Paralysis agitans. *See* Parkinson's disease
Paranoia
  in Huntington's disease, 331
  in schizophrenia, 990, **990**
Paraphasias, 90, 92, 95, 172
Parasomnias, 697, 703, 716–720
  classification of, **704,** 716–717
  clinical significance of, 716
  common types of, **707,** 716–717
  nightmares, 718
  primary snoring, 720
  relationship to sleep-wakefulness,
    716, **716**
  REM sleep behavior disorder, 66,
    716, 719–720
  rhythmic movement disorder, 718–
    719
  sleep bruxism, 719
  sleep enuresis, 717–718
  sleep paralysis, 718
  sleep terrors, 717
  sleepwalking, 717
Parathion, **887**
Parathyroid disorders, 866–869
  hyperparathyroidism, 866–868
  hypoparathyroidism, 868–869
Paratonia, 163
Parietal lobes
  delirium associated with lesions of,
    **551,** 551–552
  functional neuroanatomy of, 89–94,
    **90, 91**
    inferior parietal lobule, 92–93
    temporoparietal junction, 89–92
  tumors of, 762
    neuropsychiatric and behavioral
      manifestations of, 762
    neuropsychological manifestations
      of, 762
*PARK3* gene, **339**
Parkin, 339, **339, 925**
Parkinsonism, 931
  Guam amyotrophic lateral sclerosis/
    parkinsonism-dementia
    complex, 33, 941
  neuroleptic-induced, 931
  postencephalitic, 931, 1071
  Sjögren's syndrome and, 823
Parkinson's disease (PD), 335–341,
    931–935, 965–969
  arteriosclerosis and, 931

clinical features and diagnosis of,
    335, 932–934, **933,** 965–967,
    **966**
  blink rate, 158
  cognitive deficits, 336, 932–933,
    966
  constipation, 1222
  deficits in reaction time, 500
  motor symptoms, 162–164, 932,
    1220–1221
  psychiatric symptoms, 336, 966–
    967
    anxiety, 336, 934, 967, 1051
    dementia, 335–341, 931–935,
      965–969, 1220
    depression, 222, 336, 933–
      934, 966–967, 1031
    drug-induced, 967–968
    obsessive-compulsive disorder,
      967, 1050
    personality and, 933, 1224
    psychosis, 336, 934, 1164–
      1165
    social phobia, 1061
    somatosensory discomforts,
      1221–1222
    speech disorders, 933, 1222
  electroconvulsive therapy in, 935,
    967, 1159
  epidemiologic studies of, 336–338,
    931, 965
    diet, 338
    pesticide and toxin exposure,
      337–338, 931
    protective effect of tobacco,
      338
  etiology of, 931, 965
  genetic studies of, 338–340, **925,**
    931, 965
    family studies, 338
    mode of inheritance, 339
    molecular approaches, **339,** 339–
      340
    relative risk, **325**
    twin studies, 338
  hypotheses for pathophysiology of
    sporadic disease, **340,** 340–341
  juvenile-onset, 338, 339
  laboratory evaluation of, 968
  management of, 341, 934–935, 968–
    969
    antidepressant therapy, 1157–
      1159
    antipsychotic therapy, 1164–1166
    behavioral, 934
    biological, 934–935, 968–969

considerations in late-stage disease, 1223–1224
environmental modifications, 934
psychotherapy, 1219–1224, **1222, 1224**
stem cell therapy, 34, 341
surgical treatment, 934–935, 969, 1152
mortality from, 336, 965
MPTP-induced, 11, 337
neurobiology of, 34, 335–336, **336,** 931–932, 968, 1180
dopamine depletion, 335, 498, 932, 968
glial cell dysfunction, 1126
glial cell line–derived neurotrophic factor, 34, 1127
Lewy bodies, 337, **337, 339,** 931–932, 968
neuroimaging in, 968
prevalence of, 335, 336, 931, 965
age-specific, 336
in relatives of probands with Alzheimer's disease, 338
risk factors for, 931
Paroxetine
adverse effects of, **1160**
dosage of, **1160**
drug interactions with, **1160**
indications for
aggression, 1176
aphasic patients, 577
patients with dementia, **980,** 981
patients with HIV/AIDS, 799
mechanism of action of, 1144, **1144**
use in patients with traumatic brain injury, 646
Pars compacta, 279
Pars reticulata, 279
Partial seizures, 674, 1094–1095
PASAT (Paced Auditory Serial Addition Task), 229, **499,** 501, 511
Pathologic Laughter and Crying Scale (PLACS), 747
Pathological laughter or crying, 176, 724–725
amitriptyline for, 647
poststroke, **729,** 747–749, **748**
in progressive supranuclear palsy, 938, 969
Patient-controlled analgesia (PCA), 441, 442
Patient rights, 1258
Pavor nocturnus, **707,** 717

PCA (patient-controlled analgesia), 441, 442
PCP (phencyclidine), **901,** 1008
PD. *See* Parkinson's disease
PDDs. *See* Pervasive developmental disorders
Pediatric autoimmune neuropsychiatric disorder associated with streptococcal infections (PANDAS), 129, 378–379, 828, 1050, 1055, 1056, 1081
Pedigree analysis, 326
Peduncular hallucinations, 176
Peg mnemonics, 1240
Pemoline
dosage of, 1078
hepatotoxicity of, 1078
indications for
attention-deficit/hyperactivity disorder, 517, 1078
narcolepsy, 715
patients with multiple sclerosis, 1159
D-Penicillamine
for mercury poisoning, 884
for Wilson's disease, 341, 942, 972
Pentoxifylline, 796
Peptide receptor expression on immune cells, **134**
Peptide T, 795–796
Perception
vs. attention, 493
brain region dedicated to, 74
disturbances of, **220**
in delirium, 525, **527, 541,** 541–542
in neglect syndrome, 508
of pain, 422–430
tests of, 230–231
Perceptual representation systems (PRSs), 600
Performance IQ, 228
Pergolide
for Parkinson's disease, 969
for periodic limb movement disorder and restless legs syndrome, **710**
Perinatal factors, 154
schizophrenia and, 381, 991–992
Tourette's syndrome and, 1050
Periodic limb movement disorder (PLMD), 707, **707, 710**
Peripheral desensitization, 430, **432**
Perirhinal cortex, 74, 75
Periventricular heterotopia, X-linked, 26
Perphenazine, **1167**
Perseveration, 177–178, **178**

frontal cortex lesions and, 1051
vs. stereotypy, 166
Persistent vegetative state, 506
Personal injury litigation, 1257, 1281–1283
case example of, 1281
expert testimony, 1282–1283
head injuries, 1281–1283
Personality
depression and, 1028
epilepsy and, 687
masked, 933
migraine and, 467–469, **468, 470–471**
Parkinson's disease and, 933, 1224
tests of, 234
Personality changes
Alzheimer's disease and, 956
amyotrophic lateral sclerosis and, 941
brain tumors and
diencephalic tumors, 763
frontal lobe tumors, 760
temporal lobe tumors, 761
treatment of, 776, 1231
epilepsy and, 673, 687, 1095, 1213–1214
Friedreich's ataxia and, 940
frontotemporal dementias and, 959
history taking for, 156
Huntington's disease and, 331, 930, 963–964
Parkinson's disease and, 336
traumatic brain injury and, 634, **635**
Wilson's disease and, 341, 942, 971
Personality disorders
antisocial personality disorder, 589–590
borderline personality disorder, 588–589
schizophrenia-related, 990
sleep patterns in, 703
Pervasive developmental disorders (PDDs), 1087–1090
Asperger's disorder, 173, 1090
autism, 343–347, 1087–1089
in relatives of autistic probands, 343
Rett's disorder, 1089–1090
tuberous sclerosis and, 344
Pes cavus, 940
Pesticide exposure, **878,** 887–890
chemical structures of insecticides, **887–889**
neuropsychiatric sequelae of, **880**
organochlorine compounds, 888

Personality changes (continued)
   organophosphate compounds, 889–890, **890**
   Parkinson's disease and, 337–338, 340
   pyrethroids, 888
PET. See Positron emission tomography
Petit mal seizures, 675, 1094
PGi (nucleus paragigantocellularis), 903, 905–906
Phagocytes, 116
Phagocytosis, 117
Pharmacotherapy, 1151–1182. See also specific drugs and classes
   adverse effects of, 1153
   algorithm for, **1156**
   approach to neuropsychiatric patient, 1152–1155
   drug nomenclature, 1123
   effects on immune system, 141–142
   effects on memory, 613–614
   history of, 1123–1124
   intracellular and intercellular principles of, 1123–1140
   malpractice claims related to, 1273–1277
   patient evaluation before initiation of, 1153
   patient monitoring during, 1155
   prescription practices, 1275
   psychotropic drug development, 1140–1144
      advances in molecular pharmacology, 1140
      animal testing, 1140
      antipsychotic pharmacodynamics, 1141–1142, **1142**
      clinical trials, 1145
      merits of drug selectivity, 1142–1143
      neuroreceptor pharmacology, 1140–1141
      novel mechanisms of action, 1143–1144, **1144**
   for specific disorders
      aggression, impulsivity, and behavioral dyscontrol, 590–592, 651–654, **654,** 1172, 1175–1178, **1179**
      agitation, 590–592, 651–654, **654,** 1165, 1169–1172, **1173–1174**
      aphasia, 576–577
      attention-deficit/hyperactivity disorder, 516–517, 1078–1080

autism, 1089
borderline personality disorder, 586, 587, 591
cognitive disturbance, 1178–1182
delirium, 546–550
dementia, 979–981, **980**
depression, apathy, and "deficit" states, 1155–1159, **1160–1162**
epilepsy, 1096–1097
Huntington's disease, 930
insomnia, 711–712, **712**
pain, 432–438
Parkinson's disease, 341, 934–935
patients with brain tumors, 772–776
patients with traumatic brain injury, 645–656
psychosis, 1159, 1163–1166, **1167–1168**
Tourette's syndrome, 1083–1084
symptom rating scales to assess efficacy of, 1153, **1154**
Phenazocine, **440**
Phencyclidine (PCP), **901,** 1008
Phenelzine, **1144**
   for patients with traumatic brain injury, 1158
Phenobarbital, 689
   adverse effects of, 689
   for epilepsy, 689, 1096
   overdose of, 689
Phenocopies, 326, 329
Phenothiazines, for pain, **437,** 437–438
Phenylketonuria, 587
Phenylpropanolamine-induced vasculitis, **826**
Phenytoin, 689–690
   adverse effects of, 690, 1096
   for epilepsy, 1096
   for neuropathic pain, 436, **437**
   use in patients with traumatic brain injury, 639, 640
Pheochromocytoma, 865
   cardinal features of, 865
   psychiatric symptoms associated with, 865
Phobias
   migraine and, 466
   traumatic brain injury and, 640, 1051
Phonagnosia, 91, **91**
Phosphatidylinositol, 901, 1136, **1139**
Phosphatidylinositol-4,5-bisphosphate (PIP$_2$), 1137
Phosphatidylserine, 1182

Phosphodiesterase, 1136, 1137
Phospholipase C, 1137, **1139**
Phototherapy, for insomnia, 711
Physeptone-induced vasculitis, **826**
Physical anomalies, 157, **157**
Physician-assisted suicide, 1262
Physostigmine
   for Alzheimer's disease, 1180
   for patients with traumatic brain injury, 650
PICA (Porch Index of Communicative Ability), 228
Pick bodies, 959–960
Pick's disease, 923, 939
   aphasia and, 573
   neuropathology of, 959
   relative risk for, **325**
Picture Arrangement test, 231
Picture Completion test, 228, 231
Pimozide
   for delirium in hypercalcemia, 1171
   for Tourette's syndrome, 1083
Pindolol, 1176
Pinealomas, **754**
PIP$_2$ (phosphatidylinositol-4,5-bisphosphate), 1137
Piroxicam, **435**
Pituitary tumors, **754,** 764
PLACS (Pathologic Laughter and Crying Scale), 747
Plant toxins, 892, **893, 894**
Plasticity, neural, 22, 33–34, 1011
PLMD (periodic limb movement disorder), 707, **707, 710**
PML (progressive multifocal leukoencephalopathy), 788
Poison Severity Score, 894
Poisons, 877–890, **878.** See also Toxin exposure
   definition of, 877
   gases, 885–887
      carbon monoxide, 885–886, **886**
      ethylene oxide, 886–887
      neuropsychiatric sequelae of exposure to, **880**
   metals, 877–885
      aluminum, 877–881, **880**
      arsenic, 881
      lead, 881–882, **882**
      manganese, 882–883
      mercury, 883–884
      neuropsychiatric sequelae of exposure to, **879**
      organotins, **884,** 884–885
   pesticides, 887–890
      chemical structures of, 887–889

neuropsychiatric sequelae of
    exposure to, **880**
organochlorine compounds, 888
organophosphate compounds,
    889–890, **890**
pyrethroids, 888
solvents, 887
    neuropsychiatric sequelae of
        exposure to, **879**
Polyarteritis nodosa (PAN), 823–824
Polygenic disorders, 326
Polysomnography, 45, **45, 208,** 208–
    209, 698, **699**
Pons, **270, 277,** 281
Porch Index of Communicative Ability
    (PICA), 228
Porteus Mazes Test, **499,** 503
Positional cloning, 326
Positive and Negative Symptom Scale
    (PANSS), 629, **629**
Positive reinforcers of behavior, 1245
Positron emission tomography (PET),
    72, 245, **246,** 285–288
    advantages and limitations of, 287–
        288
    of cerebral blood flow and
        metabolism, 287
    of hypnotic analgesia, 446
    of lexical retrieval, 80
    of neurotransmitters and receptors,
        287
    of normal brain function, 291–295
        attention, 292–293, 496, **497,**
            506
        emotion, 295
        language, 294–295
        learning and memory, 293, **294,**
            597
        movement, 291
        vision, 291
    radioligands used in, 287, **288**
    in specific conditions
        Alzheimer's disease, 957, **957**
        anxiety disorders, 1053
        attention-deficit/hyperactivity
            disorder, 299, 1074–1075
        autism, 296–298
        bipolar disorder, 303–305
        borderline personality disorder,
            583, 589
        brain tumor, 770
        delirium, 552
        dementia, 979
        depression, **297,** 302, **303, 1030,**
            1033–1034, **1035, 1037**
        domoic acid intoxication, 891

epilepsy, 677
frontotemporal dementias, 959
HIV/AIDS, 790
Huntington's disease, 926, 927,
    964, 965
Lesch-Nyhan syndrome, 335
limbic encephalitis, 79
obsessive-compulsive disorder,
    300–301
olivopontocerebellar atrophies,
    940
panic disorder, 299, 1058
Parkinson's disease, 883, 935,
    968, 1031
posttraumatic stress disorder,
    1060
progressive supranuclear palsy,
    938, 970
Rett's disorder, 1090
schizophrenia, 305, **306,** 307–
    311, 992, 1002, **1003,** 1009,
    **1009**
systemic lupus erythematosus,
    819–820
Tourette's syndrome, 1082
toxin exposure, 895
traumatic brain injury, **629,** 630,
    632
vascular dementia, 975
Wilson's disease, 971
theory of, 287
Postconcussion syndrome, **641,** 641–
    643
Posterior aphasia behavioral syndrome,
    574
Posterior fossa tumors, 764
Postgraduate education. *See*
    Neuropsychiatric education
Poststroke depression (PSD), 725, 728–
    741, 748
    diagnosis of, 728–731, **730**
    duration of, 732–734, **734**
    functional neuroimaging of strokes
        involving basal ganglia, 1031–
        1032
    mechanism of, 739–740
    neuroanatomy and neurochemistry
        of, 1157
    phenomenology of, **729, 731,** 731–
        732
    premorbid risk factors for,
        737–738
    prevalence of, **729,** 732, **733**
    psychosocial adjustment and, 741
    relationship to cognitive impairment,
        738–739, **740**

relationship to lesion variables, **729,**
    734–737, **736, 737**
relationship to physical impairment,
    738
treatment of, 740–741, **741,** 1157–
    1159
Poststroke Depression Rating Scale
    (PSDRS), 731
Postsynaptic potentials (PSPs), 43–44
Postsynaptic receptors, 14–17
    γ-aminobutyric acid, 14–15
    glutamate, 14
    ionotropic, 14
    metabotropic, 15–17
    organization at synapses, 17, **18**
Posttraumatic stress disorder (PTSD),
    1049, 1058–1060
    agitation and, 1169
    anxiety and, 1049, 1051
    attention-deficit/hyperactivity
        disorder and, 1073
    childhood abuse and, 1099–1101
    criminal liability and, 1270
    electrodiagnostic testing in
        electrodermal activity, 210
        P50 wave, 202, **203**
        P300 potential, 203–204
        startle response, 210
    epilepsy and, 685, **685**
    functional neuroimaging in, 632,
        1060
    hypothalamic-pituitary-adrenal axis
        and, 1059
    neuroanatomy of, 3, 1058–1060,
        **1059**
    neurochemistry of, 1059
    selective serotonin reuptake
        inhibitors for, 1059
    startle response in, 166
    symptoms of, 1058
    traumatic brain injury and, 636, 640–
        643, 1098
Postural equilibrium, 162
Potassium ion channels, **1125**
    defect in episodic ataxia, 5
    in generation and conduction of
        action potentials, 6, **6, 7,** 14
    opiate effects on, 904
Prader-Willi syndrome, 587, 1086–1087
    clinical features of, 1086
    etiology and pathophysiology of,
        1086–1087
    growth hormone for, 1087
    incidence of, 1086
    neurochemistry of, 1087
Pralidoxime, 890

Pramipexole
  for Parkinson's disease, 969
  for periodic limb movement disorder
      and restless legs syndrome, **710**
Praxis tests, 231
Prednisolone, **437**
Prednisone
  for Alzheimer's disease, 1181
  for cluster headache prophylaxis,
      480
  neuropsychiatric complications of,
      832, 863
Pregnancy, magnetic resonance imaging
      in, 263
Pregnenolone, 15
Preplate, 24, **25**
Prescription practices, 1275
Presenilins, 355, 356
Presynaptic inhibition, **9**
Prevalence of disease, 323–324
Primary angiitis of central nervous
      system (PACNS), 825
Primary progressive aphasia, 565, 573
Primidone, 776
Priming, 599–600
Primitive reflexes, **167,** 167–168
Prion diseases, 357–361, 978
  Creutzfeldt-Jakob disease, 357–358,
      **359,** 978
  epidemiologic studies of, 359–360
  fatal familial insomnia, 358–359
  Gerstmann-Sträussler-Sheinker
      syndrome, 358
  mode of inheritance of, 360
  molecular approaches to, 360–361
  "virino hypothesis" for, 361
*PRNP* gene, 357, 358, 360
Problem-solving deficits, 1242. *See also*
      Executive functions
Procedural mobilization, 1055
Prognosis for recovery, 1237
  neuroanatomic and neurophysiologic
      determinants of, 1237–1238
  from traumatic brain injury, 633,
      **633,** 655, 1097
Progressive multifocal
      leukoencephalopathy (PML), 788
Progressive subcortical gliosis, 961
Progressive supranuclear palsy (PSP),
      937–939, 969–970
  age at onset of, 937, 969
  clinical features of, 159, 937–938,
      **938,** 969, **970**
  cognitive and neuropsychiatric
      features of, 938, 969
  diagnosis of, 937–938

  genetics of, **925,** 937, 938, 969
  laboratory evaluation in, 969
  mortality from, 969
  neurobiology of, 938, 970
  neuroimaging in, 938, 969–970
  prevalence of, 937, 969
  risk factors for, 937
  treatment of, 938–939, 970
Projection, 1200
Projective identification, 1200
Proliferation, neuronal, 23–24
Promethazine, 477
Proposition, **1201**
Propoxyphene, **440**
  for migraine, 475
  for periodic limb movement disorder
      and restless legs syndrome, **710**
Propranolol
  adverse effects of, **1179**
  dosage of, 1176, **1179**
  drug interactions with, **1179**
  guidelines for clinical use of, **654**
  indications for
      aggression, 592, 653–654, 1176
      developmentally disabled
          persons, 592
      Huntington's disease, 965
      patients with dementia, **980,** 981
      patients with HIV/AIDS, 801
  long-acting, 653
ProSom. *See* Estazolam
Prosopagnosia, **77,** 81–82, **83,** 173,
      1200
  deep, **77,** 82
  developmental, 173
  occipital lobe lesions and, 88, **89,**
      763
  occipitotemporal junction lesions
      and, 82, **83**
Prospective cohort studies, 324
Prostaglandins, 434
  prostaglandin $D_2$ in non-REM sleep,
      52–53
  prostaglandin $E_2$ in HIV-associated
      dementia, 786
  sensitization of nociceptors by, 423,
      **424**
Protease inhibitors, 795
Protein kinase C, **16,** 21, 1131, 1137,
      **1139**
Protein kinases, **1130,** 1137, **1137**
Protein phosphatases, 17
Protein phosphorylation, 15, 17, 901–
      903, 1136–1137, **1137**
Protein tyrosine kinases, **902,** 903
Protriptyline

  dosage of, **436**
  for narcolepsy, 715
  for sleep-disordered breathing, 714
  terminal half-life of, **436**
PRSs (perceptual representation
      systems), 600
PSAP (Cherek Point Subtraction
      Aggressin Paradigm), 581
PSD. *See* Poststroke depression
PSD-95, 17, **18**
PSDRS (Poststroke Depression Rating
      Scale), 731
Pseudobulbar disorder, 724–725, 1209
Pseudodementia, 1027–1028
Pseudoinsomnia, 708
Pseudoseizures, 679, **680**
Psilocin, 892, **894**
Psilocybin, 892, **894**
PSP. *See* Progressive supranuclear palsy
PSPs (postsynaptic potentials),
      43–44
Psychic gaze paralysis, 85, 159
Psychodynamic aspects of mental
      examination, 1199–1202
  capacity for contact in
      neuropsychiatric patients, 1200,
      **1201**
  defense mechanisms, 1200–1202,
      **1203–1204**
Psycholinguistic Assessment of
      Language Processing in Aphasia,
      576
"Psychological overlay," 234
Psychomotor deficits
  in Alzheimer's disease, 956
  benzodiazepine-induced, 613
  in delirium, 525, 526, **527,** 528,
      542–544, **543**
  dementia associated with motor
      dysfunction, 923–944 (*See also*
      Dementia)
  in depression, 1026
  frontal lobe tumors and, 760
Psychosis
  Alzheimer's disease and, 956, 1164
  anatomy and neurochemistry of,
      1163–1164
  atypical, 683
  brain tumors and, 756, 757
      frontal lobe tumors, 760
      occipital lobe tumors, 763
      parietal lobe tumors, 762
      pharmacotherapy for, 774–775
      pituitary tumors, 764
      posterior fossa tumors, 764
      temporal lobe tumors, 761

conditions associated with, 1159, 1163
delirium and, 525, **527**, 536, **541**, 541–542
dopamine excess hypothesis of, 1140
drug-induced, 1163
endocrine disorders and
Cushing's syndrome, **862**, 862–863
hyperthyroidism, **859**, 860
hypothyroidism, **856**, 857, **857**
epilepsy and, 682–684, **684**, 1095, 1163
episodic, 683–684
etiologies of, 1163
HIV/AIDS and, 797–798
Huntington's disease and, 331, 964
intensive care unit, 525
Korsakoff's, 603
Parkinson's disease and, 336, 934, 935, 1164
poststroke, **729**, 745–746, 749
progressive supranuclear palsy and, 938
schizophrenia, 380–385, 989–1012
systemic lupus erythematosus and, 817–818
toxic, 525
traumatic brain injury and, 638–639, 650
treatment of
in patients with dementia, **980,** 980–981
in patients with epilepsy, 684
in patients with Parkinson's disease, 935
in patients with traumatic brain injury, 650
pharmacotherapy, 1159, 1164–1166, **1167–1168** (*See also* Antipsychotics)
vascular dementia and, 975
Wilson's disease and, 341, 972
Psychosocial aspects
of aphasia, 575–576
of epilepsy, 676–677
of poststroke adjustment, 741
of traumatic brain injury, 656–657
Psychotherapy, 1199–1232
for Alzheimer's disease, 1214–1216, **1216**
for aphasic patients, 576
approach to patients who are unstable on their feet, 1210–1211

for Huntington's disease, 1224–1225, **1225**
modalities in neuropsychiatric patients, **1206**
in multiple sclerosis, 1226–1228, **1229**
for Parkinson's disease, 1219–1224, **1224**
for patients with brain tumors, 773–774, 1231, **1232**
for patients with central nervous system infections and inflammations, 1225–1226
for patients with epilepsy, 686, 1213–1214
for patients with memory impairment, 1216–1219
approach to agitation in profoundly demented, 1219
care for caregiver, 1217–1218
contribution of somatic memory, 1218–1219
treating the working memory, 1218
for patients with psychogenic movement disorders, 1228–1231
for patients with spinal cord injury, 1211–1213
for patients with traumatic brain injury, 656–657, 1204–1209, **1206**
for poststroke patients, 741, 1209–1210
psychodynamic aspects of mental examination, 1199–1202
capacity for contact in neuropsychiatric patients, 1200, **1201**
defense mechanisms, 1200–1202, **1203–1204**
for schizophrenia, 1202–1204
Puffer fish poisoning, 891
*Punding*, 166
Punishment, 1245
Pupillary abnormalities, 158
Purdue Pegboard Test, 233
Purkinje cells, autism and, 1088
Putamen, 103, 266
anatomy of, 269, **274, 277, 278**
deficits associated with lesions of, 269
Pyrethroid exposure, 888
Pyromania, 587, 590

QEEG (quantitative electroencephalography), 207–208, 540
$QT_c$ interval prolongation, drug-induced droperidol, 549
haloperidol, 548–549
Quantitative electroencephalography (QEEG), 207–208, 540
Quazepam, **712**
Quetiapine, 1164
adverse effects of, **1168**
dosage of, **1168**
indications for
aphasic patients, 577
delirium, 550
patients with dementia, 980, **980**
patients with Huntington's disease, 964
patients with Parkinson's disease, 935, 1165
patients with traumatic brain injury, 650, 652
Quinolinic acid
in HIV/AIDS, 786–787, 791, 796
in systemic lupus erythematosus, 816–817

RA. *See* Rheumatoid arthritis
Radiation therapy for brain tumors, 777
Radioligands
for positron emission tomography, 287, **288**
for single photon emission computed tomography, **289**
Ramón y Cajal, Santiago, 4
Rancho Los Amigos Cognitive Scale, 628, **630**
Rankin Scale, 741
Rapid tranquilization, 1177
Rate of disease, 324
Rationalization, 1200
Ravens Progressive Matrices (RPM), 310
Raynaud's phenomenon, 827
RDC (Research Diagnostic Criteria), 728, 860
Reaching movement abnormalities, 174
Reaction formation, 1200
Reaction time, 491
disorders associated with deficits of, 500
effect of dopamine on, 498
measurement of, 500–501
Readiness potential, 204

Reading disorder, 1090
    assessment for, 172
    dyslexia, 349–351
    pure alexia, 89
    treatment of, 1093
Reboxetine, 1027
Receptive aphasia, 228
Receptors. *See also* specific types
    adenosine, **1135**
    β-adrenergic, 133
    α-amino-3-hydroxy-5-
        methylisoxazole-4-propionic
        acid (AMPA), 14, 17, 18
    γ-aminobutyric acid (GABA), 14–15,
        1129
    benzodiazepine, 15
    cannabinoid, **901**
    cholinergic, 1134, **1135**, 1141
    G protein-linked, 15–17, **16**
    glutamate, 14
    intraneuronal, 1134
    kainate, 14
    metabotropic, 15–17
    N-methyl-D-aspartate (NMDA), 14,
        17, **18**, 34
    neuroreceptors, 901, 1133–1136
    opioid, 432–433, **434**
    orexin, 64
    postsynaptic, 14–17
    T cell, 119
Recognition impairment, **1201,
    1203**
Recognition Memory Test, 230
Recurrent inhibition, **9**
Referential loss, **1203**
Referral for neuropsychological
    evaluation, 221
Reflexes, primitive, **167**, 167–168
Refusal of treatment, 1259
    advance directives, 1263–1264
    informed consent, 1259–1260
    right to die, 1261–1262
Regression, **1203**
Reinforcers of behavior, 1245
Relational capacity, **1201**
Relative risk for neuropsychiatric
    disorders, 324, **325**
Relaxation training, 709
Reliability of neuropsychological tests,
    225
REM sleep. *See* Sleep-wakefulness,
    REM (dream) sleep
REM sleep behavior disorder, 66, 716,
    719–720
Reminyl. *See* Galantamine
Remoxipride, 550, 798

Repetitive-practice strategies, 1240–
    1241
Repolarization, 6, 1127
Repulsion factors, 27
Research Diagnostic Criteria (RDC),
    728, 860
Reserpine, 1124, 1128
    headache induced by, 473
    for Huntington's disease, 930
Residency programs. *See*
    Neuropsychiatric education
Response set, 1055
Rest theory of non-REM sleep, 67
Restless legs syndrome (RLS), 707, **707,
    710**
Restlessness, 163
    Alzheimer's disease and, 956
    frontotemporal dementias and, 959
    traumatic brain injury and, 634
Restoril. *See* Temazepam
Restraint of patient, 1279, **1279**
Restriction fragment length
    polymorphisms (RFLPs), 326–327
Retention, adaptations in psychiatric
    technique relative to, **1201**
Reticular activating system (RAS), **494,**
    494–496
Retrospective cohort studies, 324
Rett's disorder, 1089–1090
Reverse Frégoli-type misidentification
    syndrome, 1201, **1205**
Reverse subjective doubles, 1201, **1205**
Rey Auditory Verbal Learning Test, 230
Rey-Osterreith Complex Figure test,
    173, 231, **232**, 794
RFLPs (restriction fragment length
    polymorphisms), 326–327
RFs (rheumatoid factors), 128
Rheumatic disease, 813–834
    antiphospholipid antibody syndrome,
        820–822
    approach to patient with, 813–814
    autoimmunity in idiopathic
        psychiatric syndromes, 832–833
    Behçet's disease, 830–831
    celiac disease, 831
    diagnostic evaluation for, 813–814
    Geschwind-Behan-Galaburda
        hypothesis, 833–834, 1093
    Hashimoto's encephalopathy, 828–
        829
    laboratory testing in, 814
    neuroleptic-induced immunopathy,
        832
    rheumatoid arthritis, 831
    sarcoidosis, 829–830

Sjögren's syndrome, 822–823
Sneddon's syndrome, 826–827
steroid-induced neuropsychiatric
    disorder, 831–832, **863**, 863–
    864, **864**
Susac's syndrome, 829
Sydenham's chorea and PANDAS,
    827–828
systemic lupus erythematosus, 814–
    820
vasculitides, 823–826
Rheumatoid arthritis (RA), 831
    pain management in, 434
    stress, depression, and immunity in,
        128
Rheumatoid factors (RFs), 128
Rhyming strategies, 1240
Rhythm Test, 235
Rhythmic movement disorder, **707,**
    718–719
Right to die, 1261–1262
    advance directives, 1263–1264
    competent patients, 1262
    incompetent patients, 1261–1262
    physician-assisted suicide, 1262
    refusal of treatment, 1259
Rigidity, 163
Risk for disease
    definition of, 324
    joint effects of genes and
        environmental exposures on,
        329–331
        additive model, 330
        effect mediation, 331
        effect modification,
            330–331
        multiplicative model, 331
Risperidone, 1164
    adverse effects of, 550, **1167**
    dosage of, **1167**
    drug interactions with, **1167**
    effects on memory, 614
    indications for, 1165–1166
        aggression, 651, 652, 1177
        agitation or delirium, 550, 1171,
            1172
        aphasic patients, 577
        delirium, 550
        patients with dementia, 980, **980,**
            1165
        patients with HIV/AIDS, 798,
            1165
        patients with Huntington's
            disease, 964
        patients with Parkinson's disease,
            1165

patients with traumatic brain
injury, 650–652, 1165–1166
Tourette's syndrome, 1083
receptor binding affinity of, **1142**
Rivastigmine, 958, 1180
Rivermead Postconcussion
Questionnaire, 629, **629**
Rizatriptan, **474,** 476, 477
RLS (restless legs syndrome), 707, **707,**
**710**
Rofecoxib, 434
Rolandic epilepsy, 1094–1095
Rolandic sulcus, 73–74, **75**
Ropinirole
for Parkinson's disease, 969
for periodic limb movement disorder
and restless legs syndrome, **710**
Rorschach test, 581, 589
Rouleaux formation, 117
RPM (Ravens Progressive Matrices),
310
rTMS. *See* Transcranial magnetic
stimulation, repetitive

S100β protein, 1085
SADS (Schedule for Affective
Disorders and Schizophrenia), 860,
862
Salicylate, **435**
Sanfilippo's syndrome, 588
Sarcoidosis, 829–830
Sarin, **888,** 889
Saskatoon Delirium Checklist, 537
SCAs (spinocerebellar atrophies), 925,
**925,** 940–941
Schedule for Affective Disorders and
Schizophrenia (SADS), 860, 862
Schizoaffective disorder, 369
Schizophrenia, 380–385, 989–1012. *See*
*also* Psychosis
affect scoring in, 1202
anatomic features of, 992–995,
1163–1164
anatomic markers of brain
development, 993–995
in vivo MRI studies of brain
structure, 992
microscopic analysis of
postmortem CNS tissue,
993, **994**
neuronal developmental defects,
22, 994
autoimmune diseases and,
832–833
biochemistry of, 995–999, 1163–
1164

dopamine, 305–306, **306,** 995–
997, **997,** 1006–1007
glutamate, 995, 998–999, 1007–
1009
norepinephrine, 997
serotonin, 997–998
blink rate in, 158
clinical course of, 991
clinical therapeutics in, 1006–1009
glutamate system pharmacology,
1007–1009, **1009**
neuroleptic pharmacology, 1006–
1007, **1008**
other dopamine system
pharmacology, 1007
cognitive rehabilitation in, 1239
delineation disorder in, **1202**
diagnosis of, 990
differential diagnosis of
delirium, 528, **528**
epilepsy, 682
temporal lobe tumor, 761
Wernicke's aphasia, **570**
electroencephalography in, 206
epidemiologic studies of, 380–381
evoked potentials and sensory gating
in, 202, 203, **205,** 1001–1002
P50, 202, 1002
P300, 203, **204,** 1001
formulating pathophysiology of,
1011–1012
clinical observations important
for, 1011–1012
limitations of studies, 1012
functional neuroimaging in, 305–311,
1002–1006
cognitive dysmetria, 306–307
diffusion white matter anisotropy,
311, **313**
dopamine hypothesis, 305–306,
**306,** 996
functional magnetic resonance
imaging, 310, 1005–1006
magnetic resonance spectroscopy,
311, **312**
neurodevelopmental hypothesis,
306
positron emission tomography
with fluorodeoxyglucose,
1002, **1003**
regional cerebral blood flow
studies, 1003–1005, **1005**
during resting state, 307
studies during cognitive tasks,
308–311
attention, 309

executive function, 310–311
language, 310
memory, 309–310
motor, 309
vision, 308–309
studies linking symptoms with
brain function, 307–308
disorganization, 308
negative symptoms, 307–308
psychoticism, 308
tests of benzodiazepine function,
308
genetic studies of, 381–385, 991
adoption studies, 382
anticipation, 329
candidate genes, 384–385
family studies, 381
high-risk studies, 382
joint effects of genes and
environmental exposures on
illness risk, 330
linkage and association studies,
383–384
mode of inheritance, 382–383
relative risk, **325**
twin studies, 310, 382, 999
historical perspectives on, 989–990
immune function and, **131,** 131–132
impaired frontal lobe activity in, 962
integrative basic brain mechanisms
important to understanding
cerebral function, 1009–1011
cortical-subcortical circuits, **1010,**
1010–1011
neural plasticity, 22, 33–34, 1011
neurodevelopmental hypothesis of,
306
physical anomalies associated with,
157
psychological characteristics of, **225,**
999–1000
attentional disturbances, 512
cognitive deficits, 220, 306–307
confabulation, 174
memory deficits, 607–609, 999
psychotherapy for, 1202–1204
risk factors for, 991–992
genetic predisposition, 991
perinatal factors, 381, 991–992
winter birth, 992
symptoms of, 174, 175, 990–991
clusters of, 990–991
eye movement abnormalities,
159, 1000–1001
frequency of, **990**
hemineglect, 171

Schizophrenia *(continued)*
  symptoms of *(continued)*
    linking with brain function, 307–308
    neurological soft signs, 168
    sleep disturbances, 703
  synaptic pruning and, 1070
Schizotypal personality disorder, 1000
School issues, **220**
  attention-deficit/hyperactivity disorder and, 513, 514
    recommendations for, **515,** 517, 1080
  educational level and Alzheimer's disease risk, 353–354
  learning disorders, 1090–1093
  traumatic brain injury and, 635
Schwann cells, 9
SCID (Structured Clinical Interview for DSM-IV Diagnoses), 455, 629, **629**
SCL-90-R (Symptom Check List–90–Revised), 234, 455
Scopolamine, 703
Scrapie, 360, 978
Scrapie prion protein, 358
Screening batteries and rating scales, 180–181
  Behavioral Dyscontrol Scale, 180, **181,** 235
  Executive Interview, 180, 235
  Frontal Assessment Battery, 180–181, **182**
  for HIV-related dementia, 180
  Mini-Mental State Exam, 180
  Neurobehavioral Rating Scale, 181, **183,** 234
  Neuropsychiatric Inventory, 181
  neuropsychological tests, 234–235
  Trail Mental Alternation Test, 180
Screening electroencephalography, 206–207
SDH (subdural hematoma), 727–728
SDMT (Symbol Digit Modality Test), 501, **501**
Seat belt use, 657–659
Seclusion and restraint guidelines, 1279, **1279**
Second messengers, 6, 9, 15–17, **16,** 21, 901, **902, 1130, 1135,** 1136–1140, 1333
  as target for antidepressant therapy, 1143
Secondary gain, pain and, 446–447
Secretin, 1089

Sedation for neuroimaging procedures, 247
Sedative-hypnotics, **1174.** *See also* Benzodiazepines
  abuse potential of, 706
  cautions for use of, 713
  delirium induced by, **547**
  for insomnia, 711–712
  for patients with traumatic brain injury, 651–652
  pharmacokinetics of, **712**
  profile of ideal hypnotic, **711**
  withdrawal from
    benzodiazepines for, 546
    epileptiform electroencephalographic activity during, 206
Segregation analysis, 326
  in schizophrenia, 382
Seizures, 673–691. *See also* Epilepsy
  absence (petit mal), 675, 1094
  anticonvulsants for, 689–690, **691**
  brain tumor and, 765
  in children, 1093–1097
  classification and features of, 361, **674,** 674–675, 1094–1095
  dacrystic (crying), 176
  drug-induced
    in patients with brain tumors, 773
    in patients with traumatic brain injury
      antidepressants, 647
      antipsychotics, 650
      stimulants, 649
  epidemiology of, 676
  etiological links to psychopathology, 680–681
  family history of, 156
  febrile, 362, 364, 676
  gelastic (laughing), 176
  generalized, 674, 1094
  grand mal, 673–674
  history taking for, 154–155
  infantile spasms, 1094, 1096
  kindling and, 681
  myoclonic, 1094
  nocturnal, **707,** 717
  nonepileptic, 679–680, **680**
  partial (focal), 674, 1094–1095
    complex, 1095
    simple, 1094
  posttraumatic, 639–640
  vs. pseudoseizures, 679, **680**
  in Sneddon's syndrome, 827
  status epilepticus, 675
  tonic-clonic, 674–675, 1094

  treatment of, 689–690, 1096–1097
    for psychiatric symptoms, 687–688, **688**
    psychotherapy, 686, 1213–1214
Selective serotonin reuptake inhibitors (SSRIs), 1123, **1160,** 1237
  adverse effects of, 435, 1158, **1160**
  dosage of, 1159, **1160**
  drug interactions with, **1160**
  effects on cognitive deficits in depression, 1027
  effects on memory, 613–614
  effects on sleep, 703, 711
  immunologic effects of, 142
  indications for, 1158, 1159
    aggression, 591, 653, 1176
    agitation, 1171
    aphasic patients, 577
    attention-deficit/hyperactivity disorder, 517, 1079
    autism, 1089
    emotional lability, 648
    generalized anxiety disorder, 1052
    impulsive aggression, 591
    narcolepsy, 715
    obsessive-compulsive disorder, 1054
    pain, 435–436
    panic disorder, 1057
    patients with brain tumors, 772, 773, 775, 776
    patients with dementia, **980,** 981
    patients with diabetes mellitus, 854, **855**
    patients with HIV/AIDS, 799
    patients with Parkinson's disease, 967
    patients with traumatic brain injury, 646, 647, 653, 1159
    poststroke depression, 740–741
    posttraumatic stress disorder, 1059
    social phobia, 1061
  interaction with selegiline, 934
  mechanism of action of, 10, 1144, **1144**
  merits of drug selectivity, 1142
Selegiline
  for Alzheimer's disease, 958, 1181
  interaction with selective serotonin reuptake inhibitors, 934
  mechanism of action of, **1144**
  for Parkinson's disease, 341, 968, 1158, 1223

for periodic limb movement disorder and restless legs syndrome, **710**
Self-management skills, 1245
Self-mutilation, 590, 591
in Lesch-Nyhan syndrome, 334
naltrexone for, 1177
Self Ordered Pointing Task, 229
Semaphorins, 27
Senile plaques
in Alzheimer's disease, 351–352, 954, 957–958
in dementia with Lewy bodies, 936
in Parkinson's disease, 932
Sensitivity of neuropsychological tests, 225
Sensory gating, 202
in schizophrenia, 1001–1002
Sensory perception abnormalities, brain tumors and, 762, 765
Serax. *See* Oxazepam
Serenics, 1178
Serotonin (5-HT), 9
in attention, 498
brain localization of, 58–59
inhibition of REM sleep by, 58–60, **60**
positron emission tomography studies of, 298, 302–303
reuptake of, 1130
in specific conditions
aggression and behavioral dyscontrol, **584**, 584–586, 652, 1175
attention-deficit/hyperactivity disorder, 513–514
autism, 298, 346, 1088–1089
bipolar disorder, 372
borderline personality disorder, 585
delirium, 554
depression, 302–303, 1023–1024, **1024**, 1157
treatment-induced changes in, 1035
frontotemporal dementias, 961
generalized anxiety disorder, 1052, **1052**
obsessive-compulsive disorder, 379–380, 1054, 1056
panic disorder, 1057
posttraumatic stress disorder, 1059
psychosis in Alzheimer's disease, 1164
schizophrenia, 997–998
social phobia, 1061

suicidality, 585
Tourette's syndrome, 1083
traumatic brain injury, 627
transporter for, 587, 1131–1132
Serotonin (5-HT) receptors, **1135**
antipsychotic effects at, 1141–1142, **1142**
in depression, 1024
hallucinogen effects at 5-HT$_2$ receptors, **901**
positron emission tomography of, **288**
presynaptic 5-HT$_3$ receptors, 1129
role of 5-HT$_{1B}$ receptor in aggression, 588
subtypes of, 1134, **1135**, 1140
Serotonin specific reuptake inhibitors. *See* Selective serotonin reuptake inhibitors
Serotonin syndrome, 1153
Sertraline
adverse effects of, **1160**
dosage of, **1160**
drug interactions with, **1160**
effects on cognitive deficits in depression, 1027
indications for, 1158
aggression, 653, 1176
aphasic patients, 577
emotional lability, 1171
Huntington's disease, 965
patients with dementia, **980**, 981
patients with HIV/AIDS, 799
patients with traumatic brain injury, 646, 653
mechanism of action of, **1144**
Severe combined immunodeficiency, 121
Sex object shift, **1203**
Sexual behavior changes
Alzheimer's disease and, 956
antiparkinsonism drug-induced, 968
epilepsy and, 1214
Huntington's disease and, 930, 964
traumatic brain injury and, 634, 1208
case example of behavior therapy for, 1248–1249
treatment in patients with dementia, **980**, 981
Wilson's disease and, 942
Sexual history, 156
Sexual therapy, for patients with spinal cord injury, 1212–1213
"Shaking palsy." *See* Parkinson's disease
Shared segment mapping, 329

"Sickness behavior," cytokine-induced, 140, 141, **141**
Signal detection tests, 503
Simultanagnosia, 85, 174
Sinemet. *See* Levodopa-carbidopa
Single-nucleotide polymorphisms (SNPs), 327–328
Single photon emission computed tomography (SPECT), 245, **246,** 285–286, 288–290
advantages and limitations of, 289–290
of cerebral blood flow, 289
of neuroreceptors, 289
radioligands used in, **289**
in specific conditions
Alzheimer's disease, 957, **957**
attention-deficit/hyperactivity disorder, 299, 1075
autism, 296–298
Behçet's disease, 830
brain tumor, 770, **771**
cortical-basal ganglionic degeneration, 939
delirium, 552
dementia, 979
dementia with Lewy bodies, 937, 958
depression, 1024, 1033
epilepsy, 677, 1164
frontotemporal dementias, 959, **961**
HIV/AIDS, 790
Huntington's disease, 964
mania, 1169
obsessive-compulsive disorder, 301, 1055, 1056
panic disorder, 1058
posttraumatic stress disorder, 1060
progressive supranuclear palsy, 970
schizophrenia, 308–310, 996
social phobia, 1061
systemic lupus erythematosus, 819–820
Tourette's syndrome, 301, 1082
toxin exposure, 895
toxoplasmosis, 787
traumatic brain injury, **629**, 631, 632
vascular dementia, 975
theory of, 288–289
training for interpretation of, 1293, 1302

Sjögren's syndrome (SS), 822–823
    autoantibodies in, 822, 823
    clinical features of, 813, 822
    cognitive impairment in, 822
    pathogenesis of, 823
    peripheral neuropathy in, 822
    primary vs. secondary, 822
    psychiatric symptoms of, 822–823
    treatment of, 823
Skull radiography, 770
*SLC6A3* gene, 367
*SLC6A4* gene, 346, 379
SLE. *See* Systemic lupus erythematosus
Sleep apnea, 156, 713–714
Sleep bruxism, **707,** 719
Sleep-disordered breathing, **707,** 708,
    713–714
    causes of, 713
    clinical features of, 713
    comorbid conditions with, 714
    position-dependent, 714
    predisposing factors for, 713–714
    treatment of, 714
        bilevel and self-adjusting positive
            airway pressure, 714
        continuous positive airway
            pressure, 714
        oral appliances, 714
        other treatments, 714
        surgery, 714
Sleep disorders, 703–720. *See also*
    Hypersomnia; Insomnia;
    Parasomnias
    classification of, 697, 703–705, **704**
    history taking for, 155–156
    hypersomnia, 713–716
    insomnia, 705–713
    parasomnias, 716–720
    in patients with psychiatric
        conditions, 703
        Alzheimer's disease, 956
        delirium, 525, **527,** 541, **541**
        depression, 155, 703, 1025–
            1026, **1026**
        Parkinson's disease, 934
    polysomnography in, 45, **45, 208,**
        208–209
    after traumatic brain injury, 641
        treatment of, 650–651
Sleep enuresis, 717–718
Sleep hygiene, 709, **709**
Sleep paralysis, **707,** 718
Sleep restriction therapy, 710–711
Sleep spindles, 49–50
Sleep-state misperception, 707–708
Sleep terrors, **707,** 717

Sleep-wakefulness, 45–68, *47,* 697–703
    aging and patterns of, 700, **701**
    circadian rhythm and prior
        wakefulness as factors in
        sleepiness, 47–49, **48**
    electro-oculographic studies of, 45,
        697–698
    electroencephalographic patterns in,
        44–45, **45,** 49–52, 697–698,
        **699**
        alpha rhythm, 45, 697, 698
        "burst mode" of thalamic relay
            cell discharge, 51, **52**
        delta activity, 44, 45, 47, 50–51,
            **51,** 698
        EEG synchronization and
            desynchronization, 49
        gamma activity, 44, 49, **50**
        K complex, 698
        sleep spindles, 49–50
    historical research on, 697–698
    mechanisms regulating sleep, 700–
        703
        autonomic nervous system
            balance, 700–702, **702**
        circadian rhythms, 47, **48,** 702–
            703
        homeostatic sleep drive, 702
    molecular biology of, 65
    motion activity monitoring of, **209,**
        209–210
    non-REM (slow-wave) sleep, 45, 52–
        55, 698–700, **701**
        active non-REM sleep–promoting
            mechanisms, 55
        adenosine in, 53–55, **54**
        functions of, 67
        humoral sleep factors in, 52–53
        physiology of, **700**
    orexin, narcolepsy, and control of,
        62–65, **63**
    physiology of normal sleep, 698–700,
        **700**
    polysomnographic definitions of, 45
    REM (dream) sleep, 45, 47, 55–62,
        697–700, **701**
        without atonia, 66
        cholinergic mechanisms in, 49,
            57–58, **58**
        in depression, 1025–1026, **1026**
        dreaming and, 65–66, 698
        electroencephalographic
            frequencies in, 44
        electromyographic studies of, 45,
            698
        functions of, 67

mathematical and structural
    model of, 60–62, **62**
neural machinery in, 55
orexin and, 64–65
physiology of, **700**
reticular formation neurons in,
    55–57, **56**
suppression by REM-off neurons,
    58–60, **60, 61**
sleep architecture, 45–47, **46,** 698–
    700, **700, 701**
sleep debt, 49, 55, 713
sleep deprivation studies, 702
sleep need, 47
sleep ontogeny and phylogeny, 47
specialty of sleep medicine, 697
Sleepwalking, **707,** 717
Slow and unconventional virus diseases.
    *See* Prion diseases
Slow-wave sleep (SWS). *See* Sleep-
    wakefulness, non-REM (slow-
    wave) sleep
Smoking
    Alzheimer's disease and, 354
    Parkinson's disease and, 338
    pharmacologic actions of nicotine,
        **901**
Snake venoms, 894, **895**
Sneddon's syndrome, 826–827
    age at onset of, 827
    clinical features of, 826–827
    pathogenesis of, 827
    treatment of, 827
Snoring, 720
Snout reflex, 167, **167**
SNPs (single-nucleotide
    polymorphisms), 327–328
Social justice, 1258
Social learning approach, 1246
Social phobia (social anxiety disorder),
    1049, 1060–1061
    hypothalamic-pituitary-adrenal axis
        in, 1061
    migraine and, 466
    morbidity from, 1060
    neuroanatomy of, 1061, **1061**
    neurochemistry of, 1061
    Parkinson's disease and, 1051, 1061
    selective serotonin reuptake
        inhibitors for, 1061
Social withdrawal, in schizophrenia, 990
Sodium ion channels, **1125**
    defect in hyperkalemic periodic
        paralysis, 5
    in generation and conduction of
        action potentials, 6, **6, 7,** 14

opiate effects on, 904
Sodium/potassium adenosine triphosphatase ($Na^+/K^+$-ATPase) pump, 1125
Soft signs, neurological, 168, **169**
  aggression and, 582
  borderline personality disorder and, 589
  obsessive-compulsive disorder and, 1055
  posttraumatic stress disorder and, 1059
Solvent poisoning, **878**, 887
  diagnosis of, 887
  neuropsychiatric manifestations of, **879**, 887
  sources of exposure, 887
  treatment of, 887
Soma. *See* Carisoprodol
Soman, **888**, 889
Somatoform disorders, headache and, 455
Somatosensory cortex, 429
Somatostatin, 9, **1135**
  in Huntington's disease, 926
Sonata. *See* Zaleplon
Spasticity, 163
Spatial summation, 14
Specificity of neuropsychological tests, 225–226, **226**
SPECT. *See* Single photon emission computed tomography
Spectral analysis, 208
Speech
  measurement of discrimination of speech sound, 231
  motor area for, 74
Speech disorders, 160–162, **220**
  aprosodia, 160–161, 572
    poststroke, **729**, 748
  in autism, 1087
  "blurting," 161
  due to thalamic lesions, 104
  dysarthria, 160
  echolalia, 161
  foreign accent syndrome, 160
  in frontotemporal dementias, **960**
  mutism, 162
  palilalia, 161
  in Parkinson's disease, 933, 1222
  rehabilitation for, 1242
  stuttering and cluttering, 160
Speech-language pathologist, 576
Speech Sounds Perception Test, 235
Sperry, Roger, 73

Sphingolipid activator protein B deficiency, 347
Sphingomyelinase deficiency, 979
Spielberger State-Trait Anger Expression Inventory (STAEI), 581
Spinal analgesia, 442–444, **443**
Spinal cord injury, 1211–1213
  adaptation to, 1211–1212
  depression and, 1211
  family model in, 1213
  incidence of, 1211
  pain management in, 1212
  predicting future self-care after, 1211, 1212
  psychotherapeutic approach to patients with, 1211–1212, **1212**
  sexual therapy for patients with, 1212–1213
Spinocerebellar atrophies (SCAs), 925, **925**, 940–941
Spinoreticular tract, 430
Spinothalamic tract, 430
Splitting, 1200
SPM (Statistical Parametric Mapping) software, 1003
Spongiform encephalopathies. *See* Prion diseases
Squire Subjective Memory Questionnaire, 612, **612**
SS. *See* Sjögren's syndrome
SSEs (subacute spongiform encephalopathies). *See* Prion diseases
SSRIs. *See* Selective serotonin reuptake inhibitors
STAEI (Spielberger State-Trait Anger Expression Inventory), 581
Stammering, 160
Standard of care, 1271. *See also* Malpractice claims
  for somatic therapies, 1273–1274
Startle responses, 166, 210
State-Trait Anxiety Inventory-2, 455
Statistical Parametric Mapping (SPM) software, 1003
Status epilepticus, 675. *See also* Epilepsy; Seizures
  excitotoxicity and, 33
  myoclonus and, 165
  nonconvulsive, 165
Status migrainosus, 460
Stavudine (d4T), 795
Steele-Richardson-Olszewski syndrome. *See* Progressive supranuclear palsy
Stem cells, 34

transplantation for Parkinson's disease, 34, 341
Stereotyped movements, 166
  in autism, 1087
  in Rett's disorder, 1089
Sternberg Item Recognition Paradigm, 310
Still's disease, 831
Stimulants
  abuse of, 1079
  adverse effects of, 649, 1078–1079, **1162**
    aggravation of delirium, 548
  as coanalgesics, **437**, 438
  dosage of, **1162**
  drug holidays from, 517, 715
  drug interactions with, **1162**
  indications for
    aphasic patients, 577
    attention-deficit/hyperactivity disorder, 516–517, 1078–1080
    behavioral disturbances, 1177
    HIV-associated dementia, 1182
    narcolepsy, 715
    patients with HIV/AIDS, 796, 799
    patients with traumatic brain injury, 648–650, 1239
    poststroke depression, 741
  mechanism of action of, 10–11, 648, 1076–1077
  use in patients with tic disorders, 1084
Stimulus control therapy, for insomnia, 709–710
Strabismus, 3
Streptococcal infection
  group A β-hemolytic, 129
  pediatric autoimmune neuropsychiatric disorder associated with, 129, 378–379, 828, 1050, 1055, 1056, 1081
Stress
  definition of, 122
  immunity and, 122–125
    in AIDS, 126
    in autoimmune diseases, 127–128
    in cancer, 125–126
    human studies of, **124**, 124–125
      laboratory stressors, 124–125
      naturalistic stressors, 124
    laboratory animal studies of, 122–123, **123**
    in other viral infections, 126–127

Stress *(continued)*
  induction of corticotropin-releasing
    factor release by, 909
  relapse to drug-seeking behavior
    induced by, 909–910
  tension-type headache and, 452, 454
Stroke. *See* Cerebrovascular disease
Stroop Test, 501, **502**, 503, 510, 511
Structured Clinical Interview for DSM-
    IIII-R, 862
Structured Clinical Interview for DSM-
    IV Diagnoses (SCID), 455, 629,
    **629**
Stupor, 506–507, **526**
  vs. severe delirium, 525
Stuttering, 160, 573
Styrene exposure, **879**
Subacute sclerosing panencephalitis,
    **202**
Subacute spongiform encephalopathies
    (SSEs). *See* Prion diseases
Subcaudate tractotomy, 1022
Subcortical aphasia, 572
Subdural hematoma (SDH), 626, 727–
    728
Subjective doubles, 1201, **1205**
Sublimation, 1200
Subplate cells, 24
Substance abuse, 899–917
  acute pharmacologic actions of drugs
    of abuse, 901, **901**
  adaptations in mesolimbic dopamine
    system after long-term drug
    exposure, 910–914, **912**
    evidence for structural changes in
      VTA-NAc pathway, 914
    molecular mechanisms underlying
      adaptations in NAc, **915,**
      915–917, **916**
    regulation of dopamine in VTA-
      NAc pathway, 911
    regulation of G proteins and
      cAMP pathway in VTA and
      NAc, 913–914
    regulation of opioid and dopamine
      receptors in VTA and NAc,
      911–913
    role of glutamatergic systems in
      long-term drug action, 913
  disorders associated with
    antisocial personality disorder,
      590
    attention-deficit/hyperactivity
      disorder, 513, 514
    conduct disorder, 590
    delirium, **545**

drug-induced vasculitis, 825–826,
    **826**
  insomnia, 706, **707**
  migraine, 466
  traumatic brain injury, 636
history taking for, 155
molecular and cellular adaptations as
    long-term consequences of,
    901–903, **902**
neurobiological mechanisms of
    relapse, 907–910, **908**
  cue-induced relapse to drug-
    seeking behavior, 908–909
  drug-induced relapse to drug-
    seeking behavior, 907–908
  mechanisms of dopamine-induced
    relapse, 910
  stress-induced relapse to drug-
    seeking behavior, 909–910
P300 potential in, 203
reinforcing properties of drugs of
    abuse, 900, 901, 906–907
  drug self-administration, 906–907
  role of mesolimbic dopamine
    system, 906–907
role of locus coeruleus in opiate
    physical dependence, **903**, 903–
    906, **905, 906**
  extrinsic mechanisms, 905–906
  intrinsic mechanisms, 904–905
synapse as immediate target of drugs
    of abuse, **900**, 900–901
terminology related to, 899–900
  addiction, 900
  dependence, 899
  drug craving, 900
  reinforcing drugs, 900
  sensitization (reverse tolerance),
    899
  tolerance, 899
  withdrawal, 900
Substance P
  frontotemporal dementias and, 961
  pain perception and, 423, 430
  REM sleep and, 57
  as target for antidepressant therapy,
    1143
Substantia gelatinosa, 426, 433
Substantia innominata, 97
Substantia nigra, 266
  anatomy of, **271, 272,** 279
  deficits associated with lesions of,
    279
  in Parkinson's disease, 968
Substituted judgment, 1264–1265
Subthalamus, 266

Suck reflex, 167, **167**
Suicide
  aphasia and, 577
  bipolar disorder and, 369
  epilepsy and, 1095–1096
  HIV/AIDS and, 798–799
  Huntington's disease and, 331, 964
  physician-assisted, 1262
  serotonin and, 585
  systemic lupus erythematosus and,
    818
  traumatic brain injury and, 637
Sulfamethoxazole-trimethoprim, 800
Sulfite oxidase deficiency, 33
*l*-Sulfocysteine, 33
Sulindac, **435**
Sumatriptan
  for cluster headache, 480
  mechanism of action of, 1141
  for migraine, **474,** 476
Summation, 14
Superior temporal gyrus, 74
Superoxide dismutase, 30
  in Down syndrome, 1085
Suppression, 1200
Suprachiasmatic nucleus, 702, 1127
Supramarginal gyrus, 89, 92
Surgical treatment
  for aggression, 1175
  for Hallervorden-Spatz disease, 943
  for normal-pressure hydrocephalus,
    943
  for obsessive-compulsive disorder,
    1055
  for Parkinson's disease, 34, 341,
    934–935, 969, 1152
  for refractory depression, 1022,
    1032–1033
  for seizures, 1096
  for sleep-disordered breathing, 714
Susac's syndrome, 829
Sustained Motor Tapping Test, 504
SWS (slow-wave sleep). *See* Sleep-
    wakefulness, non-REM (slow-
    wave) sleep
Sydenham's chorea, 378–379, 827–828,
    927
  obsessive-compulsive disorder and,
    378, 828, 1050
Sylvian fissure, 73–74, **75**
Symbol Cancellation task, 501–502,
    **502,** 504
Symbol Digit Modality Test (SDMT),
    501, **501**
Sympathetic nervous system
  immunologic effects of, 135–136

in pain perception, 430
Sympathomimetic agents, **547**
Symptom Check List–90–Revised (SCL-90-R), 234, 455
Symptom Validity Test, 234
Symptomatology
  aphasia and related disorders, 565–577
  attentional disturbances, 489–517
  cerebral localization of, 153
  correlation with real-world performance, 153–154
  delirium, 525–555
  headache, 451–481
  impulsivity and aggression, 579–592
  memory and amnesia, 597–611
  pain, 419–447
Synapses, 3, 4, 8–9, 1127
  chemical, 8–10, **10–12**, 1127–1140 (*See also* Neurotransmitters)
    elements required for transmission across, 1127–1128, **1128**
  developmental pruning of, 1070
  effects of drugs of abuse on, **900**, 900–901, **902**
  electrical, 9, 1127
  experience-dependent refinement of, 30–32, **32**
  formation of, 27–29, **28**, 1070
  modulation in learning and memory, 17–22
    long-term potentiation in mammalian CNS, 19–22, **20**
    simple learning in *Aplysia*, 18–19, **19**
  organization of postsynaptic receptors at, 17, **18**
  silent, 21
  transmission across, 9–11, **10–12**, 901, **902**
Synaptic cleft, 5, 10
Synaptic convergence, **9**
Synaptic divergence, **9**
Synaptic specializations, 4, **5**
Synaptic vesicles, 9–10, **10, 12, 28**, 1128
Synkinesia, 167
α-Synuclein, 337, 339, 339, **925**, 931, 932, 936–937, 965
Syphilis
  affecting frontal lobes, 962
  diagnosis of, 789
  HIV/AIDS and, 787, 789
  stroke and, 728
  treatment of, 789

Systemic lupus erythematosus (SLE), 165, 814–820
  autoantibodies in, 122, 816, 819
  clinical features of, 813, 814, 817–819
  cytokines, 816
  depression in, 815, 818
  diagnosis of, 814, **814**, 819–820
  manifestations of cerebral involvement in, 814, **815**
  neuroimaging in, 818–820
  pathogenesis of, 814–817
  prevalence of central nervous system involvement in, 817
  psychosis in, 817–818
  stress, depression, and immunity in, 128–129
  stroke and, 728
  suicidality in, 818
  treatment of, 820
  vasculitis in, 815–816

2,4,5-T (2,4,5-trichlorophenoxyacetic acid), 888, **889**
T cell receptor, 119
T cells, 116, 118–121
  cytotoxic (CD8+), **120**, 121
  expression of receptors for neurally derived molecules, 133
  helper (CD4+), 119–121, **120**
    in depression, 130
    in HIV infection, 122, 126
    Th1 and Th2, 121
T$_3$ (triiodothyronine), for hypothyroidism, 856
T$_4$ (thyroxine), for hypothyroidism, 856
Tabun, **888**, 889
Tacrine
  for Alzheimer's disease, 958, 1180
  for central anticholinergic syndrome, 548
Tactile object agnosia, **91, 94**
Tactual Performance Test, 235
Takayasu's arteritis, 824
Tardive dyskinesia (TD), 1171
  vs. chorea, 164–165, **165**
  malpractice claims related to, 1276–1277
Tardive dystonia, 165
Tardive myoclonus, 165
TAT (Thematic Apperception Test), 581
Tau gene, 355, **925**, 938–940
Taylor Competitive Reaction Time-Task (TCRTT), 581
TBI. *See* Brain injury, traumatic
TCAs. *See* Antidepressants, tricyclic

TCDD (2,3,7,8-tetrachlorodibenzo-*p*-dioxin), 888, **889**
TCRTT (Taylor Competitive Reaction Time-Task), 581
TD. *See* Tardive dyskinesia
"Telephone test," 177
Temazepam, **712**
  for patients with dementia, **980**, 981
  for periodic limb movement disorder and restless legs syndrome, **710**
Temperature cycle of body, 702–703
Temporal arteritis, 728, 824
Temporal lobe epilepsy, 674, 675
  behavioral symptoms of, 675, **676**
  criminal liability and, 1270
  diagnosis of, 679, **679**
  emotional facial weakness in, 159
  personality traits associated with, 156
  psychopathology and, 681
  temporal lobectomy for, 602
  visual field defects in, 158
Temporal lobes
  in agitation, 1169
  anterior, lateral, and inferior temporal regions, 79–82
  in anxiety disorders, 1050
    obsessive-compulsive disorder, 1055–1056
  contusions of, 626
  functional neuroanatomy of, 74–82, **77**
  in lexical retrieval, 80, **81**
  lobectomy for seizure disorders, 602
  in memory, 77–79, **78**
  mesial temporal region, 75–79
    amnesia due to lesions of, 77, 602–603
  sclerosis of, **268**, 603
  subdivisions of, 74, **76**
  tumors of, 760–762
    magnetic resonance imaging of, **78, 83, 265**
    neuropsychiatric and behavioral manifestations of, 756, 757, **758**, 760–762
    neuropsychological manifestations of, 762
  in visual recognition, 79–82
Temporal pole, 74
Temporoparietal junction, 89–92, **90–91**
Tennessee Self-Concept Scale, 1211
TENS (transcutaneous electrical nerve stimulation), 433, 444

Tension-type headache (TTH), 452–457
  chronic daily headache and, 454–455
  definition of, 452
  diagnostic criteria for, **452**
  epidemiology of, 454
  episodic vs. chronic, 452, 453, **453**
  mechanisms of, 455
  medication overuse and, 453–454
    treatment of, 457
  psychopathology and, 454–455
  relation to migraine, 452–453
  treatment of, 455–457
Test of Memory Malingering (TOMM),
  234
Testimonial privilege, 1272
  definition of, 1271
  exceptions to, 1272
Testosterone
  aggression and, 588
  immunologic effects of, 138
Tetanus toxin, 892
Tetrabenazine, 930
2,3,7,8-Tetrachlorodibenzo-*p*-dioxin
  (TCDD), 888, **889**
Tetrathiomolybdate, 972
Tetrodotoxin intoxication, 891
Textbooks in neuropsychiatry, 1300,
  **1301–1302**
Th1 and Th2 cells, 121
Thalamic aphasia, **103**
Thalamotomy, 943
Thalamus
  anatomy of, **273, 274, 277,** 281
  in attention, 494, **495,** 506
  cortico-striatal-thalamic-cortical
    circuit
    in obsessive-compulsive disorder,
      1050, **1054,** 1054–1056,
      1062
    in schizophrenia, 1163
    in Tourette's syndrome, 1083
  deficits associated with lesions of,
    281
  degeneration of, 941
  delirium associated with lesions of,
    552
  functional neuroanatomy of, 104–
    105
  in pain transmission, 427, **429**
Thallium poisoning, **879**
Thematic Apperception Test (TAT), 581
Theophylline, 714
Thioridazine, **1167**
Third messengers, 1143–1144
Thought disorder, 174, **220**
  in delirium, 525, **527,** 541

in schizophrenia, 174, 990, **990**
Three-shapes test, 173
3MS (Modified Mini-Mental State),
  180
3TC (lamivudine), 795
Thrombophlebitis, 813
Thromboxanes, 434
Thymus, 116
Thyroid disorders, 855–860
  hyperthyroidism, 858–860
  hypothalamic-pituitary-thyroid axis
    and depression, 861
  hypothyroidism, 855–858
Thyroid-stimulating hormone (TSH),
  855, 858, 861
  in depression, 1025
Thyrotoxicosis. *See* Hyperthyroidism
Thyroxine (T$_4$), for hypothyroidism,
  856
Tiagabine, 690, **691**
TIAs (transient ischemic attacks), 725,
  726
Tic disorders, 166
  chronic, 1080
  vs. compulsions, 166
  not otherwise specified, 1080
  simple and complex tics, 1080
  Tourette's syndrome, 1050–1051,
    1080–1084
  transient, 1080
Tinkertoy Test, 233
TNF. *See* Tumor necrosis factor
Tobacco use
  Alzheimer's disease and, 354
  Parkinson's disease and, 338
  pharmacologic actions of nicotine,
    **901**
Tocainide, 437, **437**
Toluene exposure, **879**
TOMM (Test of Memory Malingering),
  234
Tonic-clonic seizures, 674–675, 1094
Topiramate, 690, **691**
  adverse cognitive effects of, 640
  for cluster headache, 481
  for migraine prophylaxis, 478
Torsades de pointes, haloperidol-
  induced, 548–549
Torticollis, 164, 1050
Tourette's syndrome (TS), 1080–1084
  age at onset of, 1080
  attention-deficit/hyperactivity
    disorder and, 1073, 1081,
    1084
  characteristic features of, 1080–1081
  diagnosis of, 1080

etiology and pathophysiology of,
  1081–1083
functional neuroimaging in, 301,
  1055, 1082
gender distribution of, 1081
genetic studies of, 156, 1081
low birthweight and, 1050
neuroanatomy of, 1081–1082
obsessive-compulsive disorder and,
  299, 301, 378, 1050–1051,
  1081, 1084
prevalence of, 1081
relative risk for, **325**
severity of, 1080
startle response in, 166
treatment of, 1083–1084
  clonidine, 1084
  neuroleptics, 1083
  in patients with attention-deficit/
    hyperactivity disorder, 1084
  in patients with obsessive-
    compulsive disorder, 1084
twin studies of, 1081, 1082
Tower of Hanoi test, 233
Tower of London test, 233, 310, 1026
Toxin exposure, 10, 219, 891–895. *See
  also* Poisons
  animal toxins, 892–894, **895**
  assessment of exposure to, 894–895
  definition of, 877
  developmental influences on, 895
  learning disorders and, 1093
  marine toxins, 891
    domoic acid, 891
    tetrodotoxin, 891
  microbial toxins, 891–892
    botulinum toxin, 891–892
    tetanus toxin, 892
  Parkinson's disease and, 337–338,
    340
  plant toxins, 892, **893, 894**
  sources of, 877
Toxoplasmosis, 787, **788**
Trail Making Test, 180, 228, **228,** 235,
  503–504, **504,** 510, 535, 538, 794,
  999
Trail Mental Alternation Test, 180
Training in neuropsychiatry. *See*
  Neuropsychiatric education
Transcortical aphasias, **568,** 570–572
Transcranial magnetic stimulation,
  repetitive (rTMS), 72
  for depression, 1022
  effects on memory, 615
  use in patients with brain tumors,
    776

Transcutaneous electrical nerve stimulation (TENS), 433, 444

Transference, 1200, 1201, **1203**

Transforming growth factor-β, 117, **142** in HIV/AIDS, 791

Transient ischemic attacks (TIAs), 725, 726

Tranxene. *See* Clorazepate

Tranylcypromine, **1144**, 1159

Traumatic brain injury (TBI). *See* Brain injury, traumatic

Trazodone
  adverse effects of, **1161**
  dosage of, **1161**
  drug interactions with, **1161**
  effects on sleep, 711
  indications for, 1157
    aggression, 653
    agitated Alzheimer's disease, 1171–1172
    insomnia, 650
    patients with dementia, **980,** 981
    patients with HIV/AIDS, 799, 801
    in patients with traumatic brain injury, 646, 650, 653
    progressive supranuclear palsy, 939
  mechanism of action of, **1144**

Treatments
  cognitive rehabilitation and behavior therapy, 1237–1250
  pharmacotherapy, 1151–1182
    intracellular and intercellular principles of, 1123–1145
  psychotherapy, 1199–1232

Tremor, 164
  intention, 164
  in Parkinson's disease, 164, 932
  postural, 164
  rest, 164

Triazolam, **712**
  for periodic limb movement disorder and restless legs syndrome, **710**

Trichloroethylene exposure, **879,** 887

2,4,5-Trichlorophenoxyacetic acid (2,4,5-T), 888, **889**

Trichotillomania, 587, 590, 1050

Tridimensional Personality Questionnaire, 376

Trientine, 341

Trihexyphenidyl
  delirium induced by, 934
  use in patients with brain tumors, 775

Triiodothyronine (T$_3$), for hypothyroidism, 856

Trimipramine, 646

Triptans, 476–477
  contraindications to, 476
  for migraine, 473, **474,** 476
  second-generation, 476–477

Trk receptor tyrosine kinases, 29

Tryptophan depletion
  challenge for depression, 1024
  cytokine-induced, 140, **141,** 817

Tryptophan hydroxylase, 587

TS. *See* Tourette's syndrome

*TSC1* and *TSC2* genes, 344

TSH (thyroid-stimulating hormone), 855, 858, 861

TTH. *See* Tension-type headache

Tuberculosis, 787, 789

Tuberous sclerosis, 344

Tubulin, 4

Tumor necrosis factor-α (TNF-α), 116, 117
  in HIV/AIDS, 786, 791
  stress and, 123

Tumor necrosis factor-β (TNF-β), 117

Twenty Questions test, 233

Twin studies, 325
  of aggression, 587
  of Alzheimer's disease, 355, 954
  of attention-deficit/hyperactivity disorder, 367, 1073
  of autism, 344, 1087
  of bipolar disorder, 369
  of dyslexia, 350
  of epilepsy, 362–363
  of learning disorders, 1091
  of myotonic dystrophy, 365
  of obsessive-compulsive disorder, 378
  of panic disorder, 373–374
  of Parkinson's disease, 338
  of Rett's disorder, 1089
  of schizophrenia, 310, 382, 999
  of Tourette's syndrome, 1081, 1082

"Twinkie defense," 1270

Tyrosine hydroxylase, 372, 1128

U-74006F, 656

*UBE3A* gene, 346

Ubiquitin hydrolase, 339

*UCH-L1* gene, 339, **339**

"Ulysses contract," 1263–1264

Uniform Guardianship and Protective Proceeding Act, 1264

Uniform Probate Code, 1264

Universal sleep hygiene, 709, **709**

University of Massachusetts Medical School neuropsychiatry case conferences, **1304**

Uremic encephalopathy, **202**

Urinary tract infection, 526

Uvulopalatopharyngoplasty, 714

VaD. *See* Vascular dementia

Vagal nerve stimulation (VNS)
  for depression, 1022
  effects on memory, 615
  use in patients with brain tumors, 776

Validity of neuropsychological tests, 225

Valium. *See* Diazepam

Valproate, 690
  adverse effects of, 647, 1096, **1173**
  dosage of, **1173**
  drug interactions with, **1173**
  indications for
    aggression, 652–653
      in developmentally disabled persons, 592
    agitation and mania, 1170
    borderline personality disorder, 587, 591–592
    cluster headache prophylaxis, 480
    epilepsy, 1096
    Huntington's disease, 965
    mania in patients with traumatic brain injury, 647
    migraine prophylaxis, **474,** 478
    mood disorders in patients with epilepsy, 686
    neuropathic pain, **437**
    patients with brain tumors, 772, 775, 776
    patients with dementia, **980,** 981
    patients with HIV/AIDS, 800
    patients with traumatic brain injury, 639, 647, 652–653
    secondary mania, 743
  use in children, 690

Variable number tandem repeat sequences, 327

Varicella-zoster virus infection, 127

Vascular dementia (VaD), 973–976
  classification of, 975, **977**
  clinical diagnosis of, 973–974, **974**
  conditions associated with, 973
  laboratory evaluation of, 975
  management of, 979
  neuroimaging in, 975, **976**
  neuropathology of, 975–976
  neuropsychiatric features of, 975

Vasculitis, 823–826
  Churg-Strauss syndrome, 824
  Cogan's syndrome, 824–825
  drug-induced, 825–826, **826**
  giant cell arteritis, 728, 824
  polyarteritis nodosa, 823–824
  primary angiitis of central nervous
    system, 825
  rash in, 814
  in systemic lupus erythematosus,
    815–816
  Takayasu's arteritis, 824
  Wegener's granulomatosis, 824
Vasoactive intestinal peptide, 57–58
Venlafaxine, 1159
  adverse effects of, **1161**
    seizures, 686
  dosage of, **1161**
  drug interactions with, **1161**
  indications for
    attention-deficit/hyperactivity
      disorder, 1079
    patients with dementia, **980,** 981
    patients with diabetes mellitus,
      **855**
    patients with HIV/AIDS, 799
  mechanism of action of, **1144**
  use in patients with traumatic brain
    injury, 646
Venoms, 892–894, **895**
Ventral roots, 425
Ventral tegmental area (VTA)
  adaptations in mesolimbic dopamine
    system after long-term drug
    exposure, 910–914, **912**
    evidence for structural changes in
      VTA-NAc pathway, 914
    regulation of dopamine in VTA-
      NAc pathway, 911
    regulation of G proteins and
      cAMP pathway in VTA and
      NAc, 913–914
    regulation of opioid and dopamine
      receptors in VTA and NAc,
      911–913
    role of glutamatergic systems in
      long-term drug action, 913
  animal self-administration of opiates
    into, 906–907
  location of, **903**
  Parkinson's disease and dopaminergic
    cell loss in, 932
  in relapse to drug-seeking behavior,
    908–910
Ventromedial frontal cortices, 98–101
Verapamil

adverse effects of, **1179**
  for cluster headache prophylaxis,
    480
  dosage of, **1179**
  drug interactions with, **1179**
  in HIV/AIDS, 796
  for migraine prophylaxis, **474**
Verbal dysdecorum, 572
Verbal fluency deficit, 102–103
Verbal IQ, 228
Verbal recall, 171
Vigabatrin, 684, 690, **691**
Vigilance, 493. *See also* Attention
  aggression and, 579
  assessment of, 504
  excessive, in obsessive-compulsive
    disorder, 496
Violent behavior. *See* Aggression
Vioxx. *See* Rofecoxib
Visual agnosia, 81, **83,** 173–174
  apperceptive, 87–89
  associative, 81
  evaluation for, 231
  for faces, 81–82, **83**
  occipital lobe tumors and, 763
Visual cortex, 83–85
  ocular dominance columns in, 31, **32**
Visual disorientation, 85
Visual field defects, 158
Visual hallucinations, 175–176
Visual-imagery procedures, 1239–1240
Visual inattention, 230
Visual processing disorders, 173
  dyslexia, 349
Visual recognition disorders, 80–82, **83**
Visual scanning training, 1241
Visual system
  functional neuroimaging of, 291
    in schizophrenia, 308–309
  in subjects with migraine, 469–471
Visuogestural signals, 73
Visuospatial analysis, 173, **220**
Vitamin E
  for Alzheimer's disease, 958, 979
  for HIV/AIDS, 796
  for Parkinson's disease, 341
  for pyrethroid exposure, 888
Vitamin supplementation, for HIV/
  AIDS, 796
VNS. *See* Vagal nerve stimulation
Vocational rehabilitation, 776
Vogt's syndrome, 588
Voice recognition defect, 91–92
*Vorbeireden (Vorbeigehen),* 174–175
VTA. *See* Ventral tegmental area
VX, 888

WAIS. *See* Wechsler Adult Intelligence
  Scale
Waldrop scale of minor physical
  anomalies, 157, **157**
Wandering
  in Alzheimer's disease, 163, 956
  in frontotemporal dementias, 959
Waxy flexibility, 167
WCST (Wisconsin Card Sorting Test),
  103, 231–233, 310, **499,** 503, 504,
  609, 759, 1026
WD. *See* Wilson's disease
Weakness, 162
Wechsler Adult Intelligence Scale
  (WAIS), 101, 227–228, **499,** 510–
  511, 514, 589, 863, 999
  Arithmetic subtest of, 228, 229, 231,
    500, 514
  Backwards Spelling subtest of, 500
  Block Design subtest of, 228, 231,
    794
  Comprehension subtest of, 231
  constructional tasks of, 231
  Digit Span subtest of, 101–170, 228,
    229, 499, **499,** 500, 510, 511,
    514, 537
  Digit Symbol subtest of, 229, 501,
    504, 514, 794
  Matrix Reasoning subtest of, 231
  Object Assembly subtest of, 231
  Performance scale of, 228
  Picture Arrangement subtest of, 231
  Picture Completion subtest of, 228,
    231
  Similarities subtest of, 231
  Verbal scale of, 228
Wechsler Intelligence Scale for
  Children–III (WISC-III), 228
Wechsler Memory Scale (WMS), **226,**
  230, 499, 509, 863
  Mental Control subtest of, 499, 510,
    511
Wegener's granulomatosis (WG), 824
Wernicke, Karl, 71, 72, 171, 565
Wernicke-Korsakoff syndrome, 603
Wernicke's aphasia, 89–90, **91,** 568,
  **568,** 574
  compared with delirium,
    schizophrenia, and mania, **570**
  neuropathology of, 568, **571**
  temporal lobe tumors and, 762
Wernicke's area, **73,** 74, 89, **566**
WG (Wegener's granulomatosis), 824
Whipple's disease. *See* Celiac disease
Wilson's disease (WD), 165, 341–343,
  942, 971–972

age at onset of, 942
clinical features of, 341, 942, 971–972
    Kayser-Fleischer rings, 158, 341, 942, 971
    psychiatric symptoms, 341, 942, 971–972
copper accumulation in, 341, 971
diagnosis of, 942, 971
epidemiologic studies of, 341, 971
genetic studies of, 341–343, **925**, 942, 971
    family studies, 341
    high-risk studies, 342
    linkage analysis, 342
    mode of inheritance, 342
    molecular approaches, **342**, 342–343
    relative risk, **325**
identification and diagnosis of, 343
mortality from, 341
neuropathology of, 972

pathophysiology of, 343
treatment of, 341, 942, 972
Winter birth, schizophrenia and, 992
WISC-III (Wechsler Intelligence Scale for Children–III), 228
Wisconsin Card Sorting Test (WCST), 103, 231–233, 310, **499**, 503, 504, 609, 759, 1026
*Witzelsucht*, 760
WMS. *See* Wechsler Memory Scale
Word deafness, 573
"Word salad," 568
World view impairment, **1203**
Writer's cramp, 164
Written expression
    assessment of, 172
    disorders of, 1091

X-linked periventricular heterotopia, 26
Xenon-enhanced computed tomography (Xe/CT), 245, 248, 251, **252**
Xylene exposure, **879**

XYY syndrome, 587

Yohimbine, 1057, 1060

z score, 224, **224**
Zalcitabine (ddC), 795, 1099
Zaleplon, 712, **712**
    for patients with dementia, **980**, 981
Ziconotide, 444
Zidovudine, 795, 1099
Zimelidine, **436**
Zinc
    poisoning with, **879**
    for Wilson's disease, 341, 942, 972
Ziprasidone, 550
Zolmitriptan, **474**, 476, 477
Zolpidem, 712, **712**, **1174**
    for patients with dementia, **980**, 981
Zopiclone, 712